THE
ALL ENGLAND
LAW REPORTS

Incorporating the

**LAW TIMES
REPORTS**

**LAW JOURNAL
REPORTS**

1967
VOLUME 2

Consulting Editor for Taxation Cases
CYRIL KING, Q.C.
Bencher of the Middle Temple

Editor
J. T. EDGERLEY
of the Inner Temple and Lincoln's Inn, Barrister-at-Law

LONDON
BUTTERWORTHS

ENGLAND:	BUTTERWORTH & CO. (PUBLISHERS) LTD. LONDON: 88 Kingsway, W.C.2
AUSTRALIA:	BUTTERWORTH & CO. (AUSTRALIA) LTD. SYDNEY: 20 Loftus Street MELBOURNE: 473 Bourke Street BRISBANE: 240 Queen Street
CANADA:	BUTTERWORTH & CO. (CANADA) LTD. TORONTO: 1367 Danforth Avenue, 6
NEW ZEALAND:	BUTTERWORTH & CO. (NEW ZEALAND) LTD. WELLINGTON: 49/51 Ballance Street AUCKLAND: 35 High Street
SOUTH AFRICA:	BUTTERWORTH & CO. (SOUTH AFRICA) LTD. DURBAN: 33/35 Beach Grove

Printed in Great Britain by R. J. Acford, Ltd., Industrial Estate, Chichester, Sussex.

HOUSE OF LORDS

The Lord High Chancellor of Great Britain: The Rt. Hon. Lord Gardiner

Lords of Appeal in Ordinary

The Rt. Hon. Lord Reid
The Rt. Hon. Lord Morris of
Borth-y-Gest
The Rt. Hon. Lord Hodson
The Rt. Hon. Lord Guest

The Rt. Hon. Lord Pearce
The Rt. Hon. Lord Upjohn
The Rt. Hon. Lord Donovan
The Rt. Hon. Lord Wilberforce
The Rt. Hon. Lord Pearson

COURT OF APPEAL

The Lord High Chancellor of Great Britain

Lord Chief Justice of England: The Rt. Hon. Lord Parker

Master of the Rolls: The Rt. Hon. Lord Denning

President of the Probate, Divorce and Admiralty Division:
The Rt. Hon. Sir Jocelyn Simon

The Rt. Hon. Lord Justice Sellers
The Rt. Hon. Lord Justice Willmer
The Rt. Hon. Lord Justice Harman
The Rt. Hon. Lord Justice Danckwerts
The Rt. Hon. Lord Justice Davies
The Rt. Hon. Lord Justice Diplock

The Rt. Hon. Lord Justice Russell
The Rt. Hon. Lord Justice Salmon
The Rt. Hon. Lord Justice Winn
The Rt. Hon. Lord Justice Sachs
The Rt. Hon. Lord Justice Edmund Davies

CHANCERY DIVISION

The Lord High Chancellor of Great Britain

The Hon. Mr. Justice Lloyd-Jacob
The Hon. Mr. Justice Cross
The Hon. Mr. Justice Buckley
The Hon. Mr. Justice Pennycuick

The Hon. Mr. Justice Plowman
The Hon. Mr. Justice Ungoed-Thomas
The Hon. Mr. Justice Stamp
The Hon. Mr. Justice Goff

QUEEN'S BENCH DIVISION

Lord Chief Justice of England: The Rt. Hon. Lord Parker

The Hon. Mr. Justice Stable
The Hon. Mr. Justice Havers
The Hon. Mr. Justice Glyn-Jones
The Hon. Mr. Justice Ashworth
The Hon. Mr. Justice Hinchcliffe
The Hon. Mr. Justice Paull
The Hon. Mr. Justice Melford Stevenson
The Hon. Mr. Justice Thesiger
The Hon. Mr. Justice Phillimore
The Hon. Mr. Justice Fenton Atkinson
The Hon. Mr. Justice Nield
The Hon. Mr' Justice Howard
The Hon. Mr. Justice Veale
The Hon. Mr. Justice Megaw
The Hon. Mr. Justice Lawton
The Hon. Mr. Justice Widgery
The Hon. Mr. Justice MacKenna
The Hon. Mr. Justice Mocatta

The Hon. Mr. Justice Thompson
The Hon. Mr. Justice Brabin
The Hon. Mr. Justice Roskill
The Hon. Mr. Justice Lyell
The Hon. Mr. Justice John Stephenson
The Hon. Mr. Justice Milmo
The Hon. Mr. Justice Cantley
The Hon. Mr. Justice Browne
The Hon. Mr. Justice Waller
The Hon. Mr. Justice James
The Hon. Mr. Justice Blain
The Hon. Mr. Justice Cusack
The Hon. Mr. Justice Chapman
The Hon. Mr. Justice Willis
The Hon. Mr. Justice Swanwick
The Hon. Mr. Justice Donaldson
The Hon. Mr. Justice Geoffrey Lane
The Hon. Mr. Justice O'Connor

The Hon. Mr. Justice Crichton

PROBATE, DIVORCE AND ADMIRALTY DIVISION

President: The Rt. Hon. Sir Jocelyn Simon

The Hon. Mr. Justice Karminski
The Hon. Mr. Justice Wrangham
The Hon. Mr. Justice Lloyd-Jones
The Hon. Mr. Justice Cairns
The Hon. Mr. Justice Baker
The Hon. Mr. Justice Ormrod
The Hon. Mr. Justice Rees
The Hon. Mr. Justice Payne

The Hon. Mr. Justice Faulks
The Hon. Mr. Justice Stirling
The Hon. Mr. Justice Cumming-Bruce
The Hon. Mr. Justice Latey
The Hon. Mr. Justice Park
The Hon. Mrs. Justice Lane
The Hon. Mr. Justice Orr
The Hon. Mr. Justice Brandon

REPORTERS

HOUSE OF LORDS	Kathleen O'Brien	Barrister-at-Law
PRIVY COUNCIL	Kathleen O'Brien	Barrister-at-Law
COURT OF APPEAL [CIVIL DIVISION]	F. Guttman, Esq. F. A. Amies, Esq. Henry Summerfield, Esq.	Barristers-at-Law
COURT OF APPEAL [CRIMINAL DIVISION]	N. P. Metcalfe, Esq.	Barrister-at-Law
COURTS-MARTIAL APPEALS	N. P. Metcalfe, Esq.	Barrister-at-Law
CHANCERY DIVISION	Jenifer Sandell Jacqueline Metcalfe	Barristers-at-Law
QUEEN'S BENCH DIVISION and COURTS OF ASSIZE	M. Denise Chorlton J. M. Collins, Esq. Mary Colton K. B. Edwards, Esq. T. M. Evans, Esq. R. W. Farrin, Esq. S. A. Hatteea, Esq. D. M. Hughes, Esq. Gwynedd Lewis Deirdre McKinney K. Diana Phillips Kaushalya Purie	Barristers-at-Law
RATING CASES	F. A. Amies, Esq.	Barrister-at-Law
REVENUE CASES	F. A. Amies, Esq.	Barrister-at-Law
PROBATE AND DIVORCE	Alice Bloomfield	Barrister-at-Law
ADMIRALTY	N. P. Metcalfe, Esq.	Barrister-at-Law
RESTRICTIVE PRACTICES COURT	Mary Colton	Barrister-at-Law

CITATION

These reports are cited thus:

[1967] 2 All E.R.

REFERENCES

These reports contain references, which follow after the headnotes, to the following major works of legal reference described in the manner indicated below—

HALSBURY'S LAWS OF ENGLAND, SIMONDS EDITION

The reference 2 HALSBURY'S LAWS (3rd Edn.) 20, para. 48, refers to paragraph 48 on page 20 of Volume 2 of the third edition of Halsbury's Laws of England, of which Viscount Simonds is Editor-in-Chief.

HALSBURY'S STATUTES OF ENGLAND, SECOND EDITION

The reference 26 HALSBURY'S STATUTES (2nd Edn.) 138, refers to page 138 of Volume 26 of the second edition of Halsbury's Statutes.

ENGLISH AND EMPIRE DIGEST

References are to the "Blue-Band" volumes of the Digest, and to the Continuation Volumes of the "Blue-Band" or replacement volumes.

The reference 31 DIGEST (Repl.) 244, *3794*, refers to case No. 3794 on page 244 of Digest Replacement Volume 31.

The reference DIGEST (Cont. Vol. B) 287, *7540b*, refers to case No. 7540b on page 287 of Digest Continuation Volume B.

HALSBURY'S STATUTORY INSTRUMENTS

The reference 12 HALSBURY'S STATUTORY INSTRUMENTS 124, refers to page 124 of Volume 12 of Halsbury's Statutory Instruments, first edition.

A reference to a volume as " 1st Re-issue " refers to the first re-issue of the appropriate volume of Halsbury's Statutory Instruments; references to subsequent re-issues are similar.

ENCYCLOPAEDIA OF FORMS AND PRECEDENTS

The reference 15 ENCY. FORMS & PRECEDENTS (3rd Edn.) 938, Form 231, refers to Form 231 on page 938 of Volume 15 of the third edition, and the reference 7 ENCY. FORMS & PRECEDENTS (4th Edn.) 247, Form 12, refers to Form 12 on page 247 of Volume 7 of the fourth edition, of the Encyclopaedia of Forms and Precedents.

CASES REPORTED

IN VOLUME 2

PAGE

A. AND B.C. CHEWING GUM, LTD., DIRECTOR OF PUBLIC PROSECUTIONS v. [Q.B.D. DIVL. CT.] 504
ABLE SECURITIES, LTD., IN LIQUIDATION, FIRST CLAIMANT; SEMPAH (HOLDINGS), LTD., SECOND CLAIMANT. EASTERN HOLDINGS ESTABLISHMENT OF VADUZ v. SINGER & FRIEDLANDER, LTD. [CH.D.] 1192
ABRAHAMS' WILL TRUSTS, Re [CH.D.] 1175
ALLEN v. THORN ELECTRICAL INDUSTRIES, LTD. [C.A.] 1137
ALMOND (VALUATION OFFICER) v. BIRMINGHAM ROYAL INSTITUTION FOR THE BLIND [H.L.] .. 317
ALSOPP (decd.), Re [C.A.] 1056
ANDERSON (W. B.) & SONS, LTD. v. RHODES (LIVERPOOL), LTD. [LIVERPOOL ASSIZES] .. 850
ANISMINIC, LTD. v. FOREIGN COMPENSATION COMMISSION [C.A.] 986
APPAH v. MONSEU [Q.B.D.] 583
AREA COMMITTEE No. 1 (LONDON) LEGAL AID AREA, R. v., Ex parte RONDEL [Q.B.D. DIVL. CT.] 419
ARNOLD v. HARRINGTON (THOMAS), LTD. [Q.B.D. DIVL. CT.] 866
ASHMORE, SOUTH WESTERN MINERAL WATER CO., LTD. v. [CH.D.] 953
ATTORNEY-GENERAL, NISSAN v. [Q.B.D.] .. 200
——, [C.A.] 1238
ATTWOOLL (INSPECTOR OF TAXES), LONDON AND THAMES HAVEN OIL WHARVES, LTD. v. [C.A.] 124
AUSTIN TAYLOR & CO., LTD., SALE CONTINUATION, LTD. v. [Q.B.D.] 1092
BAGSHAW (W. S.) & SONS, BOSTON v. [C.A.] .. 87n.
BAILEY v. PURSER [C.A.] 189
BAILEY v. SPARK [C.A.] 793
BART, DONMAR PRODUCTIONS, LTD. v. (1964) [CH.D.] .. .. 338n.
BATGER & CO., LTD., FITZPATRICK v. [C.A.] .. 657
BAXTER, INGLIS AND, INGLIS v. [DIV.] .. 71
BENABO, OSCROFT v. [C.A.] 548
BENTWORTH FINANCE, LTD. v. LUBERT [C.A.] 810
BERKSHIRE COUNTY COUNCIL, PHILLIPS v. [Q.B.D. DIVL. CT.] 675
BESWICK v. BESWICK [H.L.] 1197
BIGNALL, WARD (R. V.), LTD. v. [C.A.] .. 449
BIRMINGHAM ROYAL INSTITUTION FOR THE BLIND, ALMOND (VALUATION OFFICER) v. [H.L.] 317
BLACKBURN, OAK CO-OPERATIVE BUILDING SOCIETY v. [CH.D.] 340
BLANCH (decd.), Re [CH.D.] 468
BOSTON v. BAGSHAW (W. S.) & SONS [C.A.] .. 87n.
BOULD v. BOULD (BY HER GUARDIAN) [DIV.] .. 1128
BOULTON & PAUL, LTD., DONAGHEY v. [H.L.] .. 1014
BOURNE (INSPECTOR OF TAXES) v. NORWICH CREMATORIUM, LTD. [CH.D.] 576
BOYS v. CHAPLIN [Q.B.D.] 665
BRAVDA (decd.), In the Estate of [PROB.] .. 1233
BRAYHEAD, LTD., HELY-HUTCHINSON v. [Q.B.D.] 14
BRITISH BROADCASTING CORPN., FRISBY v. [CH.D.] 106
BRITISH BROADCASTING CORPN., THORNE v. [C.A.] 1225
BRITISH RAILWAYS BOARD v. LIPTROT [H.L.] .. 1072
BRITISH ROAD SERVICES, LTD. v. CRUTCHLEY (ARTHUR V.) & CO., LTD. (FACTORY GUARDS, LTD., THIRD PARTIES) [LIVERPOOL ASSIZES] 785
——, [C.A.] 792
BRITISH TRANSPORT COMMISSION, CHADWICK v. [Q.B.D.] 945
BRODIE (decd.), Re [CH.D.] 97
BROWN v. CONWAY [C.A.] 793
BUCKLAND v. BUCKLAND [DIV.] 300
BUNGE CORPN., FAURE (H. M. F.) & FAIRCLOUGH, LTD. AND, GARNAC GRAIN CO., INC. v. [H.L.] 353
BUSH v. PROPERTY AND BLOODSTOCK, LTD. [CH.D.] 839

PAGE

CABLE, Ex parte, R. v. INDUSTRIAL INJURIES COMR. [Q.B.D. DIVL. CT.] 119
CAMPBELL (TRUSTEES OF DAVIES'S EDUCATIONAL TRUST) v. INLAND REVENUE COMRS. [C.A.] 625
CHADWICK v. BRITISH TRANSPORT COMMISSION [Q.B.D.] 945
CHALCOTS DEVELOPMENTS, LTD. v. DE GRAY [C.A.] 888
CHAPLIN, BOYS v. [Q.B.D.] 665
CHIEN SING-SHOU, Re [P.C.] 1228
CHUMLEY, CUTTS v. [Q.B.D.] 89
CITYLAND AND PROPERTY (HOLDINGS), LTD. v. DABRAH [CH.D.] 639
CLEARY v. INLAND REVENUE COMRS. [H.L.] .. 48
CLEAVER, PARRY v. [C.A.] 1168
CLORE v. INLAND REVENUE COMRS. [C.A.] .. 238
COLES, LUSH (INSPECTOR OF TAXES) v. [CH.D.] 585
COLLETT (OTHERWISE SAKAZOVA) v. COLLETT [DIV.] 426
COMMERCIAL PROPERTIES, LTD. v. WOOD [C.A.] 916
COMMISSIONER OF ESTATE DUTY, MOLLER v. [P.C.] 1035
COMMISSIONER OF METROPOLITAN POLICE, MOORE v. [C.A.] 827
COMMISSIONER OF MOTOR TRANSPORT, STATE OF NEW SOUTH WALES AND, FREIGHTLINES AND CONSTRUCTION HOLDING, LTD. v. [P.C.] .. 433
CONWAY, BROWN v. [C.A.] 793
CONWAY v. RIMMER [C.A.] 1260
COOPER, MILLS v. [Q.B.D. DIVL. CT.] 100
COPYDEX, LTD., SEAGER v. [C.A.] 415
CORNISH MANURES, LTD., Re [CH.D.] 875
COURTNEY-SOUTHAN v. CRAWLEY URBAN DISTRICT COUNCIL [Q.B.D. DIVL. CT.] 246
COVENTRY, PAPWORTH v. [Q.B.D. DIVL. CT.] .. 41
CRADOCK, S.B.A. PROPERTIES, LTD. v. [CH.D.] 610
CRADOCK, SELANGOR UNITED RUBBER ESTATES, LTD. v. [CH.D.] 1255
CRAWLEY URBAN DISTRICT COUNCIL, COURTNEY-SOUTHAN v. [Q.B.D. DIVL. CT.] 246
CRIMINAL INJURIES COMPENSATION BOARD, R. v. Ex parte LAIN [Q.B.D. DIVL. CT.] 770
CROFTON INVESTMENT TRUST, LTD. v. GREATER LONDON RENT ASSESSMENT COMMITTEE [Q.B.D. DIVL. CT.] 1103
CROYDON DEVELOPMENT PLANS 1954 AND 1959, Re [CH.D.] 589
CRUTCHLEY (ARTHUR V.) & CO., LTD., BRITISH ROAD SERVICES, LTD. v. (FACTORY GUARDS, LTD., THIRD PARTIES) [LIVERPOOL ASSIZES] 785
——, [C.A.].. 792
CURD, DALLOW INDUSTRIAL PROPERTIES, LTD. v. [Q.B.D. DIVL. CT.] 30
CUTLER, HILLINGDON (LONDON BOROUGH) v. [C.A.] 361
CUTLER, LONDON BOROUGH OF HILLINGDON v. [C.A.] 361
CUTTS v. CHUMLEY [Q.B.D.] 89
DABRAH, CITYLAND AND PROPERTY (HOLDINGS), LTD. v. [CH.D.] 639
DALE v. SMITH [Q.B.D. DIVL. CT.] 1133
DALLOW INDUSTRIAL PROPERTIES, LTD. v. CURD [Q.B.D. DIVL. CT.] 30
DALLOW INDUSTRIAL PROPERTIES, LTD. v. ELSE [Q.B.D. DIVL. CT.] 30
DAVEY v. LEE [Q.B.D. DIVL. CT.] 423
DAVIS (P. B. J.) MANUFACTURING CO., LTD. v. FAHN (FAHN CLAIMANT) [C.A.] 1274
DE GRAY, CHALCOTS DEVELOPMENTS, LTD. v. [C.A.] 888
DES SALLES D'EPINOIX v. DES SALLES D'EPINOIX [C.A.] 539
DEVANAYAGAM, UNITED ENGINEERING WORKERS UNION v. [P.C.] 367
DICKSON v. PHARMACEUTICAL SOCIETY OF GREAT BRITAIN [C.A.] 558
DIETZ v. LENNIG CHEMICALS, LTD. [H.L.] .. 282

	PAGE
DIRECTOR OF PUBLIC PROSECUTIONS v. A. AND B.C. CHEWING GUM, LTD. [Q.B.D. DIVL. CT.]	504
DIRECTOR OF PUBLIC PROSECUTIONS v. NASRALLA [P.C.]	161
DONAGHEY v. BOULTON & PAUL, LTD. [H.L.]..	1014
DONMAR PRODUCTIONS, LTD. v. BART (1964) [CH.D.]	338n.
DONNE, Ex parte. R. v. HOVE JUSTICES [Q.B.D. DIVL. CT.]	1253
DOOBAY (R. P.) v. MOHABEER [P.C.]	760
DURAYAPPAH v. FERNANDO [P.C.]	152
DWYER (J. W.), LTD. v. RECEIVER FOR THE METROPOLITAN POLICE DISTRICT [Q.B.D.]..	1051
E. (AN INFANT), Re [C.A.]	881
EASTERN HOLDINGS ESTABLISHMENT OF VADUZ v. SINGER & FRIEDLANDER, LTD. (ABLE SECURITIES, LTD., IN LIQUIDATION, FIRST CLAIMANT; SEMPAH (HOLDINGS), LTD., SECOND CLAIMANT) [CH.D.]	1192
EDUCATIONAL GRANTS ASSOCIATION, LTD., INLAND REVENUE COMRS. v. [C.A.]	893
EDWARDS v. EDWARDS [DIV.]	1032
ELLIS (ALFRED W.) (TRANSPORT), LTD., GARNHAM, HARRIS & ELTON, LTD. v. [Q.B.D.]	940
ELSE, DALLOW INDUSTRIAL PROPERTIES, LTD. v. [Q.B.D. DIVL. CT.]	30
EMERTON, PROPERTY AND BLOODSTOCK, LTD. v. [CH.D.]	839
ENNIS, UNITED DOMINIONS TRUST (COMMERCIAL), LTD. v. [C.A.]	345
EXETER CORPN., JOLLIFFE v. [C.A.]	1099
EYRE, TAPPER (INSPECTOR OF TAXES) v. [CH.D.]	636
FACTORY GUARDS, LTD., THIRD PARTIES. BRITISH ROAD SERVICES, LTD. v. ARTHUR V. CRUTCHLEY & CO., LTD. [LIVERPOOL ASSIZES]	785
——, [C.A.]	792
FAHN, DAVIS (P. B. J.) MANUFACTURING CO., LTD. v. (FAHN CLAIMANT) [C.A.]	1274
FAIRPORT, THE (No. 4) [ADM.]	914
FAURE (H. M. F.) & FAIRCLOUGH, LTD. AND BUNGE CORPN., GARNAC GRAIN CO., INC. v. [H.L.]	353
FERNANDO DURAYAPPAH v. [P.C.]	152
FIELDING v. VARIETY, INC. [C.A.]	497
FITZPATRICK v. BATGER & CO., LTD. [C.A.]	657
FOARD v. FOARD [DIV.]	660
FOREIGN COMPENSATION COMMISSION, ANISMINIC, LTD. v. [C.A.]	986
FOWLEY MARINE (EMSWORTH), LTD. v. GAFFORD [Q.B.D.]	472
FREEDMAN v. FREEDMAN [DIV.]	680
FREEMAN (INSPECTOR OF TAXES), SOMMERFELDS, LTD. v. [CH.D.]	143
FREIGHTLINES AND CONSTRUCTION HOLDINGS, LTD. v. STATE OF NEW SOUTH WALES AND COMMISSIONER OF MOTOR TRANSPORT [P.C.]	433
FRISBY v. BRITISH BROADCASTING CORPN. [CH.D.]	106
FRY, MORGAN v. [Q.B.D.]..	386
FULD (decd.), Re [PROB.]..	649
GAFFORD, FOWLEY MARINE (EMSWORTH), LTD. v. [Q.B.D.]	472
GARNAC GRAIN CO., INC. v. FAURE (H. M. F.) & FAIRCLOUGH, LTD. AND BUNGE CORPN. [H.L.]	353
GARNHAM, HARRIS & ELTON, LTD. v. ELLIS (ALFRED W.) (TRANSPORT), LTD. [Q.B.D.]	940
GARTSIDE v. INLAND REVENUE COMRS. [C.A.]..	173
GERRARD (THOMAS) & SON, LTD., Re [CH.D.]..	525
GLOUCESTER ENGINEERING CO., LTD., LANE v. [C.A.]	293
GNIEZNO, THE [ADM.]	738
GODFREY, HODGSON v. [C.A.]	793
GOSLING v. GOSLING [C.A.]	510
GREATER LONDON RENT ASSESSMENT COMMITTEE, CROFTON INVESTMENT TRUST, LTD. v. [Q.B.D. DIVL. CT.]	1103
GRIFFIN v. RECEIVER FOR THE METROPOLITAN POLICE DISTRICT [C.A.]	1137
HALL (WILLIAM) (CONTRACTORS), LTD., Re [CH.D.]	1150
HALLETT, ROBSON v. [Q.B.D. DIVL. CT.]	407
HARMAN PICTURES, N.V. v. OSBORNE [CH.D.]..	324
HARMSWORTH (decd.), Re [C.A.]..	249
HARRINGTON (THOMAS), LTD., ARNOLD v. [Q.B.D. DIVL. CT.]	866
HARRIS ENGINEERING CO., LTD., MITCHELL v. [C.A.]	682
HARVEY, WORSLEY (BEN), LTD. v. [Q.B.D. DIVL. CT.]	507
HAZELTINE, R. v. [C.A.]	671
HELY-HUTCHINSON v. BRAYHEAD, LTD. [Q.B.D.]	14
HEPWORTH & GRANDAGE, LTD., JAMES v. [C.A.]	829
HILLINGDON (LONDON BOROUGH) v. CUTLER [C.A.]	361

	PAGE
HODGSON v. GODFREY [C.A.]	793
HOVE JUSTICES, R. v., Ex parte DONNE [Q.B.D. DIVL. CT.]	1253
HUBBARD, STANDARD SECURITIES, LTD. v. [CH.D.]	622
IMPERIAL CHEMICAL INDUSTRIES, LTD., MURRAY (INSPECTOR OF TAXES) v. [C.A.]	980
IND COOPE (WEST MIDLANDS), LTD., TROW v. [C.A.]	900
INDUSTRIAL INJURIES COMR., R. v. Ex parte CABLE [Q.B.D. DIVL. CT.]	119
INDYKA v. INDYKA [H.L.]	689
INGLIS v. INGLIS AND BAXTER [DIV.]	71
INLAND REVENUE COMRS., CAMPBELL (TRUSTEES OF DAVIES'S EDUCATIONAL TRUST) v. [C.A.]	625
INLAND REVENUE COMRS., CLEARY v. [H.L.]	48
INLAND REVENUE COMRS., CLORE v. [C.A.]	238
INLAND REVENUE COMRS. v. EDUCATIONAL GRANTS ASSOCIATION, LTD. [C.A.]	893
INLAND REVENUE COMRS., GARTSIDE v. [C.A.]	173
INLAND REVENUE COMRS., PRINCES INVESTMENTS, LTD. v. [C.A.]	238
INNES, MASON (INSPECTOR OF TAXES) v. [C.A.]	926
JAMES v. HEPWORTH & GRANDAGE, LTD. [C.A.]	829
JOLLIFFE v. EXETER CORPN. [C.A.]	1099
JONES (WILLIAM), LTD., PEARSON v. [Q.B.D. DIVL. CT.]	1062
KALINSKI, R. v. [C.A.]	398
KENWARD, PUBLIC TRUSTEE v. [CH.D.]	870
L., Re [DIV.]	1110
L., Re [DIV.]	1126n.
LAIN, Ex parte. R. v. CRIMINAL INJURIES COMPENSATION BOARD [Q.B.D. DIVL. CT.]	770
LAMB, R. v. [C.A.]..	1282
LANE v. GLOUCESTER ENGINEERING CO., LTD. [C.A.]	293
LAWRY v. LAWRY [C.A.]..	1131
LEE, DAVEY v. [Q.B.D. DIVL. CT.]	423
LEEK (decd.), Re [CH.D.]..	1160
LENNIG CHEMICALS, LTD., DIETZ v. [H.L.]	282
LEVY AUTO PARTS OF ENGLAND, LTD., MASON v. [WINCHESTER ASSIZES]	62
LIPTROT, BRITISH RAILWAYS BOARD v. [H.L.]	1072
LITTLE PARK SERVICE STATION, LTD. v. REGENT OIL CO., LTD. [C.A.]	257
LLOYD'S SETTLEMENT, Re [CH.D.]	314
LONDON AND THAMES HAVEN OIL WHARVES, LTD. v. ATTWOOLL (INSPECTOR OF TAXES) [C.A.]	124
LONDON BOROUGH OF HILLINGDON v. CUTLER [C.A.]	361
LUBERT, BENTWORTH FINANCE, LTD. v. [C.A.]..	810
LUCILE BLOOMFIELD, THE [C.A.]	633
LUPTON (INSPECTOR OF TAXES), MACSAGA INVESTMENT CO., LTD. v. [C.A.]	930
LUSH (INSPECTOR OF TAXES) v. COLES [CH.D.]..	585
McCULLOCH (R. H.), LTD. v. MOORE [Q.B.D. DIVL. CT.]	290
McGREGOR, R. v. [C.A.]	267
MACSAGA INVESTMENT CO., LTD. v. LUPTON (INSPECTOR OF TAXES) [C.A.]..	930
MASON (INSPECTOR OF TAXES) v. INNES [C.A.]	926
MASON v. LEVY AUTO PARTS OF ENGLAND, LTD. [WINCHESTER ASSIZES]	62
MIDLETON'S (EARL) WILL TRUSTS, Re [CH.D.]	834
MILLS v. COOPER [Q.B.D. DIVL. CT.]	100
MILLS' WILL TRUSTS, Re [CH.D.]	193
MINISTER OF HOUSING AND LOCAL GOVERNMENT, PAVENHAM (LORD LUKE OF) v. [C.A.]	1066
MINISTER OF HOUSING AND LOCAL GOVERNMENT, WELLS v. [C.A.]	1041
MINISTER OF LABOUR v. MORGAN [Q.B.D. DIVL. CT.]	732
MITCHELL v. HARRIS ENGINEERING CO., LTD. [C.A.]	682
MOHABEER, DOOBAY (R. P.) v. [P.C.]	760
MOHAN v. REGINAM [P.C.]	58
MOLLER v. COMMISSIONER OF ESTATE DUTY [P.C.]	1035
MONACO GARAGE, LTD. v. WATFORD BOROUGH COUNCIL [Q.B.D. DIVL. CT.]	1291
MONSEU, APPAH v. [Q.B.D.]	583
MOORE v. COMMISSIONER OF METROPOLITAN POLICE [C.A.]	827
MOORE, McCULLOCH (R. H.), LTD. v. [Q.B.D. DIVL. CT.]	290
MORGAN v. FRY [Q.B.D.]..	386
MORGAN, MINISTER OF LABOUR v. [Q.B.D. DIVL. CT.]	732
MURPHY, SEMLER v. [C.A.]	185
MURRAY (INSPECTOR OF TAXES) v. IMPERIAL CHEMICAL INDUSTRIES, LTD. [C.A.]..	980
NAIR v. TEIK [P.C.]	34

PAGE

NASRALLA, DIRECTOR OF PUBLIC PROSECUTIONS
v. [P.C.] 161
NATIONAL COAL BOARD, SMITH (FORMERLY
WESTWOOD) v. [H.L.] 593
NAYLOR, YORKSHIRE ELECTRICITY BOARD v.
[H.L.] 1
NISSAN v. ATTORNEY-GENERAL [Q.B.D.] .. 200
——, [C.A.] 1238
NORTHROP v. NORTHROP [C.A.] 961
NORTON-RADSTOCK URBAN DISTRICT COUNCIL,
RADSTOCK CO-OPERATIVE & INDUSTRIAL
SOCIETY, LTD. v. [CH.D.] 812
NORWICH CREMATORIUM, LTD., BOURNE (IN-
SPECTOR OF TAXES) v. [CH.D.].. .. 576
OAK CO-OPERATIVE BUILDING SOCIETY v.
BLACKBURN [CH.D.] 340
OLD WOOD COMMON COMPENSATION FUND, Re
[CH.D.] 1146
O'REILLY, R. v. [C.A.] 766
OSBORNE, HARMAN PICTURES, N.V. v. [CH.D.] 324
OSCROFT v. BENABO [C.A.] 548
OWEN, POOK (INSPECTOR OF TAXES) v. [CH.D.] 579
P. (INFANTS), Re [CH.D.].. 229
PAPWORTH v. COVENTRY [Q.B.D. DIVL. CT.] .. 41
PARRY v. CLEAVER [C.A.].. 1168
PARRY, SANDERS v. [HERTFORD ASSIZES] .. 803
PAVENHAM (LORD LUKE OF) v. MINISTER OF
HOUSING AND LOCAL GOVERNMENT [C.A.].. 1066
PEARSON v. JONES (WILLIAM), LTD. [Q.B.D.
DIVL. CT.] 1062
PHARMACEUTICAL SOCIETY OF GREAT BRITAIN,
DICKSON v. [C.A.] 558
PHILLIPS v. BERKSHIRE COUNTY COUNCIL
[Q.B.D. DIVL. CT.] 675
POOK (INSPECTOR OF TAXES) v. OWEN [CH.D.] 579
PRACTICE DIRECTION (CHANCERY DIVISION:
EVIDENCE: BY STATEMENTS EXHIBITED TO
AFFIDAVITS) [CH.D.] 299
PRACTICE DIRECTION (DIVORCE: ADVERTISE-
MENT) [DIV.] 1196
PRACTICE DIRECTION (DIVORCE: EVIDENCE BY
AFFIDAVIT) [DIV.] 184
PRACTICE DIRECTION (INFANTS: APPEALS FROM
COURTS OF SUMMARY JURISDICTION: TITLE OF
PROCEEDINGS) [CH.D.] 1232
PRINCES INVESTMENTS, LTD. v. INLAND REVENUE
COMRS. [C.A.] 238
PROPERTY AND BLOODSTOCK, LTD., BUSH v.
[CH.D.] 839
PROPERTY AND BLOODSTOCK, LTD. v. EMERTON
[CH.D.] 839
PUBLIC TRUSTEE v. KENWARD [CH.D.].. .. 870
PURSER, BAILEY v. [C.A.] 189
R. v. AREA COMMITTEE NO. 1 (LONDON) LEGAL
AID AREA, Ex parte RONDEL [Q.B.D. DIVL.
CT.] 419
R. v. CRIMINAL INJURIES COMPENSATION BOARD,
Ex parte LAIN [Q.B.D. DIVL. CT.] 770
R. v. HAZELTINE [C.A.] 671
R. v. HOVE JUSTICES, Ex parte DONNE [Q.B.D.
DIVL. CT.] 1253
R. v. INDUSTRIAL INJURIES COMR., Ex parte
CABLE [Q.B.D. DIVL. CT.] 119
R. v. KALINSKI [C.A.] 398
R. v. LAMB [C.A.] 1282
R. v. McGREGOR [C.A.] 267
REGINAM, MOHAN v. [P.C.] 58
R. v. O'REILLY [C.A.] 766
R. v. ROADS [C.A.] 84
R. v. SIMMONDS [C.A.] 399
R. v. TUNDE-OLARINDE [C.A.] 491
R. v. WILSON [C.A.] 1088
RADSTOCK CO-OPERATIVE & INDUSTRIAL SOCIETY,
LTD. v. NORTON-RADSTOCK URBAN DISTRICT
COUNCIL [CH.D.] 812
RECEIVER FOR THE METROPOLITAN POLICE
DISTRICT, DWYER (J. W.), LTD. v. [Q.B.D.].. 1051
RECEIVER FOR THE METROPOLITAN POLICE
DISTRICT, GRIFFIN v. [C.A.] 1137
REED'S TRUSTEE, SKINNER v. [CH.D. .. 1286
REGENT OIL CO., LTD., LITTLE PARK SERVICE
STATION, LTD. v. [C.A.].. 257
RHODES (LIVERPOOL), LTD., ANDERSON (W. B.)
& SONS, LTD. v. [LIVERPOOL ASSIZES] .. 850
RICKETTS, SCOTT (INSPECTOR OF TAXES) v.
[C.A.] 1009
RIMMER, CONWAY v. [C.A.] 1260

PAGE

ROADS, R. v. [C.A.] 84
ROBSON v. HALLETT [Q.B.D. DIVL. CT.] .. 407
RONDEL, Ex parte, R. v. AREA COMMITTEE NO. 1
(LONDON) LEGAL AID AREA [Q.B.D. DIVL.
CT.] 419
S. (decd.), Re [PROB.] 150
S.B.A. PROPERTIES, LTD., Re [CH.D.] 615
S.B.A. PROPERTIES, LTD. v. CRADOCK [CH.D.] 610
SALE CONTINUATION, LTD. v. AUSTIN TAYLOR &
CO., LTD. [Q.B.D.] 1092
SANDERS v. PARRY [HERTFORD ASSIZES] .. 803
SCOTT (INSPECTOR OF TAXES) v. RICKETTS
[C.A.] 1009
SEAFORD (decd.), Re [PROB.] 458
SEAGER v. COPYDEX, LTD. [C.A.] 415
SELANGOR UNITED RUBBER ESTATES, LTD. v.
CRADOCK [CH.D.] 1255
SEMLER v. MURPHY [C.A.] 185
SEMPAH (HOLDINGS), LTD., SECOND CLAIMANT;
ABLE SECURITIES, LTD., IN LIQUIDATION,
FIRST CLAIMANT. EASTERN HOLDINGS ES-
TABLISHMENT OF VADUZ v. SINGER & FRIED-
LANDER, LTD. [CH.D.] 1192
SHULTON (GREAT BRITAIN), LTD. v. SLOUGH
BOROUGH COUNCIL [Q.B.D. DIVL. CT.] .. 137
SIMMONDS, R. v. [C.A.] 399
SINGER & FRIEDLANDER, LTD., EASTERN HOLD-
INGS ESTABLISHMENT OF VADUZ v. (ABLE
SECURITIES, LTD., IN LIQUIDATION, FIRST
CLAIMANT; SEMPAH (HOLDINGS), LTD.,
SECOND CLAIMANT) [CH.D.] 1192
SIOW WONG FATT v. SUSUR ROTAN MINING,
LTD. [P.C.] 492
SKINNER v. TRUSTEE OF THE PROPERTY OF REED
[CH.D.] 1286
SLOUGH BOROUGH COUNCIL, SHULTON (GREAT
BRITAIN), LTD. v. [Q.B.D. DIVL. CT.].. .. 137
SLOUGH BOROUGH COUNCIL, SLOUGH ESTATES,
LTD. v. [CH.D.] 270
SLOUGH ESTATES, LTD. v. SLOUGH BOROUGH
COUNCIL [CH.D.] 270
SMITH, DALE v. [Q.B.D. DIVL. CT.] 1133
SMITH (FORMERLY WESTWOOD) v. NATIONAL
COAL BOARD [H.L.] 593
SNEDDON v. STEVENSON [Q.B.D. DIVL. CT.] .. 1277
SOMMERFELDS, LTD. v. FREEMAN (INSPECTOR OF
TAXES) [CH.D.] 143
SOUTH WESTERN MINERAL WATER CO., LTD. v.
ASHMORE [CH.D.] 953
SPARK, BAILEY v. [C.A.] 793
STANDARD SECURITIES, LTD. v. HUBBARD
[CH.D.] 622
STATE OF NEW SOUTH WALES AND COMMIS-
SIONER OF MOTOR TRANSPORT, FREIGHTLINES
AND CONSTRUCTION HOLDING, LTD. v. [P.C.] 433
STEVENSON, SNEDDON v. [Q.B.D. DIVL. CT.] .. 1277
SUSUR ROTAN MINING, LTD., SIOW WONG FATT
v. [P.C.] 492
TALBOT v. TALBOT [C.A.].. 920
TAPPER (INSPECTOR OF TAXES) v. EYRE [CH.D.] 636
TEIK, NAIR v. [P.C.] 34
THORN ELECTRICAL INDUSTRIES, LTD., ALLEN v.
[C.A.] 1137
THORNE v. BRITISH BROADCASTING CORPN.
[C.A.] 1225
TILLEY'S WILL TRUSTS, Re [CH.D.] 303
TRAVEL & HOLIDAY CLUBS, LTD., Re [CH.D.].. 606
TROW v. IND COOPE (WEST MIDLANDS), LTD.
[C.A.] 900
TUNDE-OLARINDE, R. v. [C.A.] 491
UNITED DOMINIONS TRUST (COMMERCIAL), LTD.
v. ENNIS [C.A.] 345
UNITED ENGINEERING WORKERS UNION v.
DEVANAYAGAM [P.C.] 367
VARIETY, INC., FIELDING v. [C.A.] 497
WARD (R. V.), LTD. v. BIGNALL [C.A.].. .. 449
WATFORD BOROUGH COUNCIL, MONACO GARAGE,
LTD. v. [Q.B.D. DIVL. CT.] 1291
WELLS v. MINISTER OF HOUSING AND LOCAL
GOVERNMENT [C.A.] 1041
WILSON, R. v. [C.A.] 1088
WOOD, COMMERCIAL PROPERTIES, LTD. v. [C.A.] 916
WORSLEY (BEN), LTD. v. HARVEY [Q.B.D.
DIVL. CT.] 507
YORKSHIRE ELECTRICITY BOARD v. NAYLOR
[H.L.] 1

INDEX

PAGE

ACCIDENT
Manslaughter. *See* CRIMINAL LAW (Manslaughter).

ACT OF STATE
See CONSTITUTIONAL LAW.

ACTION
Authority to bring—*Company—Board of Trade bringing action in name of company. See* COMPANY (Investigation by Board of Trade).
Cause of action—*Professional ethics—Restraint of trade also involved. See* TRADE (Restraint of trade—*Corporation—Professional society*).
Want of prosecution. *See* PRACTICE (Want of prosecution).

ADMINISTRATION OF ESTATES
Administration action—*Account—Certificate—Estoppel of party from raising in subsequent action a claim the subject of the account. See* RES JUDICATA (Extent—Issues in action).
Administrator. *See* EXECUTOR AND ADMINISTRATOR (Administrator).
Family provision. *See* FAMILY PROVISION.
Grant of administration—*Generally. See* INTESTACY (Grant of administration).

ADMINISTRATOR
See EXECUTOR AND ADMINISTRATOR.

ADMIRALTY
Practice—*Action in rem—Priorities—Caveat payment entered by second mortgagees—Second mortgagees had issued writ, Folio 117, in April, 1966—Caveat lapsed in May, 1966—Order regarding priorities made in July, 1966, in present action, Folio 62, in absence of second mortgagees—Funds, representing proceeds of sale of vessel, still in court—Whether court would vary its order at the instance of interveners, the second mortgagees, so as to allow adjudication on priority as between them and necessaries men and all other persons interested in the proceeds of sale* [THE FAIRPORT No. 4)] 914
Appearance—Writ in rem not served on defendants—Notice of counterclaim filed by defendants —Writ time-expired when appearance entered—Whether appearance effective—Whether notice of counterclaim effective to raise a counterclaim—R.S.C., Ord. 2, r. 1, Ord. 6, r. 8, Ord. 10, r. 1 (3), Ord. 12, r. 1 [THE GNIEZNO] 738

ADMISSION
Criminal proceedings, in. *See* CRIMINAL LAW (Evidence—*Admission*).
Wife, by—*Whether evidence against co-respondent. See* DIVORCE (Adultery—*Evidence*).

ADVANCEMENT
Estate duty. *See* ESTATE DUTY (Determination of life interest—*Discretionary trust—Accumulation of surplus income*).

ADVERTISEMENT
Divorce—*Notice relating to divorce proceedings. See* DIVORCE (Practice).

AFFIDAVIT
Evidence by affidavit [PRACTICE DIRECTION] 184
Cross-examination of deponent—Locus standi of applicant. See COMPANY (Winding-up—Compulsory winding-up—Board of Trade's application—*Evidence*).
Divorce—Petitioner's evidence at hearing. See DIVORCE (Practice—*Evidence—Affidavit*).
Statement exhibited to—*Infant's case, etc. See* FAMILY PROVISION (Evidence); INFANT (Guardianship of Infants Acts—*Evidence*); WARD OF COURT (Practice—*Evidence*).

AGENT
Authority—*Company—Agent's act binding company where no actual authority. See* COMPANY (Director—*Authority—Ostensible authority*).
Creation of agency—*Agency for entering into contract—Circle of contracts made on same day whereby A. sold goods and subsequently re-bought the goods from another purchaser further down the chain of buyers—Transactions designed by A. for financial reasons—Written contracts enforceable according to their tenor—Whether buyer who re-sold to A. acted in his purchase from a previous buyer as agent for A. as undisclosed principal—Contracts genuine, not shams* [GARNAC GRAIN CO., INC. v. H. M. F. FAURE & FAIRCLOUGH, LTD. AND BUNGE CORPN.] .. 353
Misrepresentation—*Negligent. See* NEGLIGENCE (Duty to take care—*Statement*).

AGENT PROVOCATEUR
Police. *See* POLICE (Conduct).

AGRICULTURAL HOLDING
See AGRICULTURE.

AGRICULTURE
Agricultural holding—*Notice to quit—Consent of tribunal—Greater hardship—Considerations taken into account—Hardship to persons other than the landlord or the tenant—Landlord's death leaving insolvent estate and widow in poverty—Sale of holding sought by son for benefit of estate—Whether greater hardship " caused " by withholding consent—Agricultural Holdings Act, 1948 (c. 63), s. 25 (1) (d) as substituted by Agriculture Act, 1958 (c. 71), s. 3 (2)* [BAILEY v. PURSER] 189

ALLOWANCE
Income tax. *See* INCOME TAX (Allowance).

AMENDMENT
Supreme Court. *See* PRACTICE (Parties).

APPEAL
County court, from. *See* COUNTY COURT.
Estate duty—*Procedure—Condition of appealing from decision of commissioner. See* PRIVY COUNCIL (Hong Kong—*Estate duty*).

APPEAL—*continued*
Guardianship of infants. *See* INFANT (Guardianship of Infants Acts).
Leave to appeal. *See* COURT OF APPEAL (Interlocutory appeal).
Matrimonial cases—*Divisional court, to. See* DIVORCE (Appeal—*Divisional Court*).
New point. *See* COURT OF APPEAL (Ground of appeal).
Person aggrieved, by. *See* HIGHWAY (Street—*Private street works—Appeal to quarter sessions*).

APPEARANCE
Writ in rem, to. *See* ADMIRALTY (Practice—*Appearance*).

APPROPRIATION
Payment—*Appropriation of payment to particular debt. See* MORTGAGE (Sale—*Appropriation of proceeds of sale*).

ARCHITECT
Discipline. *See* PRIVY COUNCIL (Hong Kong).

ARMY
Income tax—*Bounty, etc. See* INCOME TAX (Income—*Bounty*).

ASSAULT
Police officer, on. *See* POLICE (Constable—*Assault on, in execution of duty*).

ASSIZES
Trial—*Crime—Direction by quarter sessions for trial at assizes. See* QUARTER SESSIONS (Direction for trial at assizes).

ATTEMPT
Crime. *See* CRIMINAL LAW.

ATTESTATION
Will. *See* WILL.

ATTORNEY-GENERAL
Injunction—*Contravention of statute—Remedies intended to be under control of Attorney-General. See* INJUNCTION (Statute).

AUCTIONEER
Lien—*Lien on deposit for commission and disbursements—Deposit received as stakeholder—Vendors adjudicated bankrupt before completion—Encumbrances on property sold to which sale not made subject—Purchase money insufficient to discharge encumbrances—Purchaser affirming contract—Whether auctioneer entitled to deduct charges and disbursements from deposit as against purchaser* [SKINNER *v.* TRUSTEE OF THE PROPERTY OF REED] 1286

AUDIT
Company's accounts. *See* COMPANY (Auditors).

AUDITOR
Negligence. *See* COMPANY (Auditors—*Negligence*).

AUSTRALIA
See PRIVY COUNCIL.

AUTHOR
Liability to income tax. *See* INCOME TAX (Profits—*Author*).

AUTREFOIS ACQUIT
See CRIMINAL LAW.

BAILMENT
Negligence—*Independent contractor of bailee vicariously responsible for his employee's negligence—Whether warehouseman (bailee) also responsible. See* INDEPENDENT CONTRACTOR (Negligence).

BANK
Appropriation of proceeds of security to particular indebtedness. *See* MORTGAGE (Sale—*Appropriation of proceeds of sale*).
Documentary credit—*Irrevocable credit—Selling agents opening for their foreign principals, timber exporters, an irrevocable credit with merchant bankers on sale of a shipment of timber to foreign buyers—Application for the credit included an undertaking by selling agents to provide funds to meet drafts on the credit—Draft accepted by merchant bankers—Documents of title to timber shipment delivered by merchant bankers to selling agents to enable them to collect price—Trust receipt given by selling agents—Merchant bankers went into liquidation and ceased to honour acceptances—Selling agents collected purchase price but did not provide funds for merchant bankers—Selling agents bought dishonoured draft from exporters for its face value—Whether liquidator of merchant bankers entitled to recover amount of draft from selling agents* [SALE CONTINUATION, LTD. *v.* AUSTIN TAYLOR & CO., LTD.] 1092

BASTARDY
Legitimation. *See* LEGITIMATION.

BLOOD TESTS
Paternity, to determine. *See* DIVORCE (Custody—*Paternity of child in issue*).

BOARD OF TRADE
Company—*Investigation of affairs—Report. See* COMPANY (Winding-up—*Compulsory winding-up—Board of Trade's application*).

BREACH OF TRUST
See TRUST AND TRUSTEE.

BREAD
Sale. *See* WEIGHTS AND MEASURES.

BUILDING
Building regulations—*Roof—Roof work—Fragile materials covering roof—Fall through hole in roof under repair—Liability of contractors to servant of sub-contractor—Employee of sub-contractors falling through gap whilst re-positioning asbestos sheet—Crawling boards provided but not used—Foreman of contractors and of sub-contractor present but neither ensured that crawling boards used—Building (Safety, Health and Welfare) Regulations, 1948 (S.I. 1948 No. 1145), reg. 4 (ii), reg. 31 (1), (3)* [DONAGHEY *v.* BOULTON & PAUL, LTD.] 1014
Roof work—Sloping surface—Protection against falling down and off roof but not against falling through hole in roof under repair—Liability of contractors to servant of sub-contractor—Crawling boards provided but not used—Building (Safety, Health and Welfare) Regulations, 1948 (S.I. 1948 No. 1145), reg. 31 (1) [DONAGHEY *v.* BOULTON & PAUL, LTD.] 1014

BUILDING—*continued*
Bye-laws—*Consent to building—Deletion of warning against acting on consent until planning approval obtained—Whether determination that such approval not required.* See TOWN AND COUNTRY PLANNING (Development—*Permission for development—Determination whether permission needed*).

BUSINESS
Premises. *See* LANDLORD AND TENANT (New tenancy).

BUSINESS PREMISES
See LANDLORD AND TENANT (Notice to quit).

CAPITAL
Income tax—*Capital or income.* See INCOME TAX (Income).

CARRIAGE BY ROAD
See CARRIERS.

CARRIERS
Contract—*Carriage of goods—Exception clause—Notification of loss out of time allowed by exception clause—Carriage sub-contracted without permission of consignor and without making proper enquiries about sub-contractor—Valuable load of copper wire, untraceable if stolen—Power to sub-contract carriage of such load not conferred by contract—Load lost, probably by theft by sub-contractor—Whether contractor liable in the circumstances for conversion—Road Haulage Association, Ltd.'s Conditions of Carriage, 1961, conditions* 1 (a), 12 (a) [GARNHAM, HARRIS & ELTON, LTD. v. ALFRED W. ELLIS (TRANSPORT), LTD.] 940

CAVEAT
Payment—*Caveat against payment.* See ADMIRALTY (Practice—*Action in rem—Priorities*).

CERTIORARI
Criminal Injuries Compensation Board—*Compensation awarded under prerogative, not under statute—Jurisdiction of High Court to issue certiorari* [R. v. CRIMINAL INJURIES COMPENSATION BOARD, *Ex parte* LAIN] 770
Jurisdiction—*Prerogative acts—Compensation awards.* See Criminal Injuries Compensation Board, *ante.*
Principle—*Statutory tribunal's decision—No certiorari provision in statute—Error going to jurisdiction distinguished from error within jurisdiction—Review of decision for error of law apparent on face of record and within jurisdiction excluded by no certiorari provision—Error going to jurisdiction, however, would render tribunal's decision a nullity notwithstanding no certiorari clause* [ANISMINIC, LTD. v. THE FOREIGN COMPENSATION COMMISSION] 986
Justices—*Witness summons—Witness not able to give relevant and admissible evidence—Jurisdiction of court to set aside witness summonses issued under Magistrate's Courts Act, 1952* (c. 55), s. 77—R.S.C., Ord. 38, r. 19 (1), (5) [R. v. HOVE JUSTICES, *Ex parte* DONNE] .. 1253
Natural justice—*Legal advice to disciplinary board—Whether must be given in presence of parties.* See PRIVY COUNCIL (Hong Kong—*Architect*).
Rule " *audi alteram partem* " *not observed—Who may sue to set aside order made by public authority.* See NATURAL JUSTICE (Public Authority).
Statutory tribunal—*Determination of tribunal to be final—Application to Foreign Compensation Commission—Application of a kind into which the commission had jurisdiction to inquire—Alleged error of commission in construing Order in Council—No power in court to substitute the court's opinion on construction for the commission's—Foreign Compensation (Egypt) (Determination and Registration of Claims) Order, 1962 (S.I. 1962 No. 2187), art. 4 (1) (a), (b), art. 6 (1)—Foreign Compensation Act, 1950 (c. 12), s. 4 (4)* [ANISMINIC, LTD. v. THE FOREIGN COMPENSATION COMMISSION] 986

CHARGE
Contract—*Sale of business—Widow's annuity.* See CONTRACT (Stranger to contract—*Annuitant*).
Legal mortgage. *See* MORTGAGE.

CHARITY
Covenanted payments to charity. *See* INCOME TAX (Annual payment).
Employees—*Education—Preferential treatment.* See INCOME TAX (Charity—*Selection of beneficiaries*).
Income tax. *See* INCOME TAX (Charity).
Rating. *See* RATES (Exemption).

CHILD
Blood test—*Power of court to order.* See DIVORCE (Custody—*Paternity of child in issue*).
Care—*Local authority—Wardship proceedings—Interlocking of court's inherent jurisdiction with local authority's statutory functions in regard to care.* See WARD OF COURT (Jurisdiction—*Previous order of magistrates under Guardianship of Infants Acts, 1886 and 1925, giving custody to father*).
Custody—*Conflict of laws.* See WARD OF COURT (Jurisdiction).
Maintenance. *See* MAGISTRATES (Husband and wife—*Maintenance*).

CHILDREN AND YOUNG PERSONS
Fit person order—*Wardship proceedings brought subsequently—Overlapping jurisdictions.* See WARD OF COURT (Jurisdiction—*Previous order of magistrates under Guardianship of Infants Acts, 1886 and 1925, giving custody to father*).

CIVIL DEFENCE CORPS
Income tax—*Bounty.* See INCOME TAX (Income—*Bounty*).

COLLUSION
See DIVORCE.

COMMONWEALTH
Inter-state trade—*Freedom—Australia.* See PRIVY COUNCIL (Australia—*New South Wales—Transport*).

COMMONS
Rights—*Compensation for requisition—Procedure for ascertaining commoners and common rights.* See PRACTICE (Originating summons—*Continuance of proceedings as if begun by writ*).

COMPANY
Action—*Action brought by Board of Trade in name of company.* See Investigation by Board of Trade, *post.*

COMPANY—*continued*

Auditors—*Negligence—Standard of care and skill required in audit—Stocktaking procedure—Alteration of invoices giving cause for suspicion—Complete examination required, rather than acceptance of managing director's assurance—Companies Act, 1948 (c. 38), s. 162 (1)* [Re THOMAS GERRARD & SON, LTD.] **525**

Contract—*Internal management—Individual contracting with company not concerned with regularity of acts of internal management. See* Director—*Authority—Ostensible authority, post.*

Costs. *See* Winding-up—*Costs, post.*

Director—*Authority—Ostensible authority—Chairman and chief executive of holding company signed letters giving collateral indemnity and guarantee to plaintiff with a view to plaintiff's lending money to a company controlled by the holding company—Plaintiff was director of holding company and chairman of company to which money was to be lent—Plaintiff was not familiar with the articles of association of the holding company and acted in the transaction as an individual—Chairman had ostensible authority to act on behalf of holding company—Articles of association of holding company required disclosure to the board of directors' interests in contracts—Disclosure to board not made—Whether rule in Turquand's case applicable—Whether contracts of indemnity and guarantee were enforceable by plaintiff—Companies Act, 1948 (c. 38), s. 199* [HELY-HUTCHINSON v. BRAYHEAD, LTD.] **14**

Interest—Whether non-disclosure invalidates contract. See Director—*Authority—Ostensible authority, ante.*

Foreign company — *Security — Injunction — Interlocutory — Cross-undertaking — Security for implementing. See* COPYRIGHT (Infringement—*Injunction—Interlocutor relief*).

Interpleader—*Company in liquidation as claimant—Leave. See* COMPANY (Winding-up—*Compulsory winding-up—Stay of proceedings against company*).

Investigation by Board of Trade—*Action begun by Board of Trade in plaintiff company's name consequent on inspector's report—Damages for negligence for breach of duty sought—Payment of balance alleged to be due from bank on current account claimed—Application by defendant bank to stay and strike out proceedings—No allegation of fraud or other such misconduct on the part of the bank—Winding-up petition pending against plaintiff company—Action not authorised by s. 169 (4)—Application adjourned until after hearing of winding-up petition—Companies Act, 1948 (c. 38), s. 169 (4)* [S.B.A. PROPERTIES, LTD. v. CRADOCK] **610**

Security for costs sought by defendant banks—Whether Board of Trade had brought itself within the powers conferred by s. 169 (4)—" Misfeasance " in s. 169 (4) not necessarily connoting moral turpitude—Whether indemnity for costs provided by s. 169 (5) covered costs to be paid by plaintiff company to defendants—Companies Act, 1948 (c. 38), s. 169 (4), (5), s. 447 [SELANGOR UNITED RUBBER ESTATES, LTD. v. CRADOCK] **1255**

Misfeasance—*Whether moral turpitude essential element—Companies Act, 1948 (c. 38), s. 169 (4). See* Investigation of Board of Trade, *ante.*

Shares—*Purchase of shares with financial assistance of company—Debenture to be issued by subsidiary company as security for purchase price of its shares from parent company—Agreement with a view to effecting a purchase by defendant of the business and assets of parent company—Major part of purchase price intended to be paid over a period of years and to be secured by charge—Mode of effecting purchase infringed s. 54—Issue of debenture an integral term of agreement—Rights of parties to agreement in view of effect of s. 54—Companies Act, 1948 (c. 38), s. 54* [SOUTH WESTERN MINERAL WATER CO., LTD. v. ASHMORE] **953**

Investigation by Board of Trade—Subsequent claim. See Investigation by Board of Trade, *ante.*

Want of authority—*Action brought in company's name without authority—Striking out of action adjourned pending hearing of winding-up petition—Possibility of ratification of action* [S.B.A. PROPERTIES, LTD. v. CRADOCK] **610**

Winding-up—*Compulsory winding-up—Board of Trade's application—Evidence—Cross-examination—Affidavit of official of Board of Trade—Application by bank, defendant in action brought by Board of Trade in the name of that company, for an order for cross-examination of official on affidavit—Action previously held to have been brought without authority—Application by defendant bank for stay of proceedings in the action stood over pending hearing of winding-up petition—Whether bank was a contingent creditor of company by reason of possible future order for costs—Whether bank, to which no present debt was owed by company, had locus standi to appear on winding-up petition* [Re S.B.A. PROPERTIES, LTD.] **615**

Board of Trade's application—Just and equitable—Evidence—Inspectors' report—Report admissible—Sufficiency as evidence—Misconduct or fraud—Order made on consideration of report alone when uncontradicted by evidence adduced by company—Companies Act, 1948 (c. 38), s. 169 (3) [Re TRAVEL & HOLIDAY CLUBS, LTD.] **606**

[Re S.B.A. PROPERTIES, LTD.] **615**

Stay of proceedings against company—Interpleader summons, to which company respondent, is within stay—Leave of Companies Court required—Companies Act, 1948 (c. 38), s. 231 [EASTERN HOLDINGS ESTABLISHMENT OF VADUZ v. SINGER & FRIEDLANDER, LTD. (ABLE SECURITIES, LTD., IN LIQUIDATION, FIRST CLAIMANT; SEMPAH (HOLDINGS), LTD., SECOND CLAIMANT)] **1192**

Costs—*Security for costs—Action by Board of Trade in company's name. See* Investigation by Board of Trade, *ante.*

Creditor—*Contingent creditor—Locus standi. See* Winding-up—*Compulsory winding-up—Board of Trade's application—Evidence—Cross-examination, ante.*

Fraudulent preference—*Memoranda of deposit of title deeds to secure indebtedness to bank—Undertaking therein to execute legal mortgage as required by bank—Shortly before company went into creditors' voluntary winding-up bank required company to execute legal charges—Proviso in each of legal charges that bank could determine what part of total liability to bank should be deemed secured by legal charge and what part not so secured—Whether a fraudulent preference—Companies Act, 1948 (c. 38), s. 320* [Re WILLIAM HALL (CONTRACTORS), LTD.] **1150**

Preferential creditor—*Appropriation by secured creditor of proceeds of security to non-preferential claim. See* MORTGAGE (*Sale—Appropriation of proceeds of sale*).

Voluntary winding-up—*Account of winding-up to be made up by liquidator so soon as the affairs of the company are fully wound-up—Sufficient if account made up fully so far as liquidator is aware—Final meeting convened—Subsequent receipt of surtax demand—Sum retained to meet surtax and note of explanation sent with account—Account and return registered—Consequent dissolution of company—More than two years after dissolution application made under s. 352 for declaration that winding-up was void—Registration of account and return effective and dissolution valid—Companies Act, 1948 (c. 38), s. 290 (1), (4)* [Re CORNISH MANURES, LTD.] **875**

COMPENSATION

Act done for another person—*Statutory right to compensation.* See PRIVY COUNCIL (Malaysia—*Compensation—Act done for another person*).

Compulsory acquisition—*Compulsory purchase of land.* See COMPULSORY PURCHASE.

Criminal injuries—*Criminal Injuries Compensation Board—Application to tribunal of three members not an appeal—Scheme for compensation for victims of crimes of violence, para.* 17 [R. v. CRIMINAL INJURIES COMPENSATION BOARD, *Ex parte* LAIN]   770

    Deductions in assessing award—National insurance payments—Police fund payments—Scheme for compensation for victims of crimes of violence, para. 13 [R. v. CRIMINAL INJURIES COMPENSATION BOARD, *Ex parte* LAIN]   770

Income tax. *See* INCOME TAX (Profits).
    Whether capital or income. See INCOME TAX (Income—*Damages*).

Riot (Damages) Act, 1886, under. *See* RIOT (Damage).

Royal prerogative—*Acts done in exercise of. See* CROWN (Prerogative).

War—*Sequestration of property. See CERTIORARI* (Statutory tribunal—*Determination of tribunal to be final*).

COMPROMISE

Infant—*Consent order not perfected. See* FATAL ACCIDENT (Compromise).

COMPULSORY PURCHASE

Compensation—*Assessment—Disputed as to compensation within exclusive jurisdiction of Lands Tribunal—Whether High Court would determine hypothetical question as to basis of assessment* [Re CROYDON DEVELOPMENT PLANS 1954 AND 1959]   589

    Injurious affection—Construction of by-pass—Stopping-up order for existing street made by Minister of Transport, in exercise of statutory powers under which there was not liability for compensation—Street in which claimant owned garage and filling station became cul-de-sac—Whether claimant entitled to compensation for injurious affection—Lands Clauses Consolidation Act, 1845 (c. 18), s. 68—Town and Country Planning Act, 1947 (c. 51), s. 49 (1) [JOLLIFFE v. EXETER CORPN.]   1099

CONDITION

Will, in. *See* WILL.

CONDONATION

See DIVORCE.

CONFIDENTIAL INFORMATION

Breach of confidence. *See* EQUITY (Confidence).

CONFLICT OF LAWS

Children, custody. *See* WARD OF COURT (Jurisdiction).

Divorce. *See* DIVORCE (Foreign decree).

Foreign decree—*Recognition by English court—Comity contemporaneous with commencement of extended jurisdiction of English court. See* DIVORCE (Foreign decree—*Decree granted to wife in Czechoslovakia*).

Tort—*Damages—Remoteness of damage—Accident in Malta between servicemen normally resident in England but stationed in Malta—Action in England—Whether damages to be assessed in accordance with English or Maltese law* [BOYS v. CHAPLIN]   665

CONSENT

Marriage, to. *See* NULLITY (Consent to marriage).

CONSENT ORDER

See JUDGMENT (Order).

CONSORTIUM

See HUSBAND AND WIFE.

CONSPIRACY

Criminal. *See* CRIMINAL LAW.

CONSTABLE

See POLICE.

CONSTITUTIONAL LAW

Act of State—*Emergency—Treaty with foreign independent sovereign power—British subject hotel owner in territory of that power—Occupation of hotel by British troops pursuant to treaty with that power for preservation of internal peace—Claim for compensation and in contract—Defence of act of state* [NISSAN v. ATTORNEY-GENERAL]   1238

Judicial office—*Characteristics of judicial power* [UNITED ENGINEERING WORKERS UNION v. DEVANAYAGAM]   367

CONTRACT

Breach—*Damages—Date at which damages assessed—Sale of goods c.i.f.—Election by buyers to accept sellers' repudiation on Jan.* 24—*Failure of sellers, if contract had continued, to send shipping documents, which would have reached buyers on Feb.* 4—*Damages, difference between value and contract price, assessed at Feb.* 4 [GARNAC GRAIN CO., INC. v. H. M. F. FAURE & FAIRCLOUGH, LTD. AND BUNGE CORPN.]   353

    Measure of damages—Sale of goods—Re-sale by unpaid seller. See SALE OF GOODS (Unpaid seller—*Re-sale—Effect as rescission of contract of sale*).

Carriage of goods. *See* CARRIERS.

Chain of contracts—*Whether genuine transactions. See* AGENT (Creation of agency—*Agency for entering into contract*).

Hire-purchase. *See* HIRE PURCHASE.

Illegality—*Company—Financial assistance for purchase of its own shares—Effect of Companies Act, 1948 (c. 38), s.* 54. *See* COMPANY (Shares—*Purchase of shares with financial assistance of company*).

Implied condition—*Hire-purchase agreement. See* HIRE-PURCHASE (Agreement—*Implied condition*).

Payment—*Action for price—Unpaid seller—Re-sale. See* SALE OF GOODS (Unpaid seller—*Re-sale—Effect as rescission of contract of sale*).

    Appropriation—Proceeds of sale. See MORTGAGE (Sale—*Appropriation of proceeds of sale*).

Repudiation—*Acceptance necessary to terminate contract. See* HIRE-PURCHASE (Termination of agreement).

CONTRACT—Repudiation—*continued*
    Election whether to accept repudiation—Writ issued claiming declaration that contract valid and claiming damages for its breach—Writ not served—Whether election to accept repudiation [GARNAC GRAIN CO., INC. *v.* H.M.F. FAURE & FAIRCLOUGH, LTD. AND BUNGE CORPN.] ..   353
    Rescission—*Re-sale on buyer's default. See* SALE OF GOODS (Unpaid seller—*Re-sale*).
    Sale of land. *See* SALE OF LAND (Lease).
    Statute—*Interference with contract—Construction. See* STATUTE (Contract).
    Stranger to contract—*Annuitant—Widow of deceased owner of business—Sale of business by deceased on terms under which widow was to be paid weekly sum—Charge on business ancillary to other clauses of contract—No trust declared—Widow not party to contract—Death of deceased —Widow obtained letters of administration—Whether widow entitled to maintain action for annuity or specifically to enforce the agreement as regards the annuity—Law of Property Act, 1925 (c. 20), s. 56* (1) [BESWICK *v.* BESWICK]   1197
    Sub-contract—*Power to sub-contract—Carriage of goods—Valuable load, easy to steal—Oral contract including conditions of carriage of Road Haulage Association, Ltd.* [GARNHAM, HARRIS & ELTON, LTD. *v.* ALFRED W. ELLIS (TRANSPORT) LTD.]   940
CONVERSION
    Carriage of goods—*Sub-contracting, by. See* CARRIERS (Contract—*Carriage of goods—Exception clause*).
COPYRIGHT
    Assignment—*Injunction—Interlocutory relief—Principle governing grant of interlocutory injunction—Prima facie right—Preservation of status quo pending trial* [DONMAR PRODUCTIONS, LTD. *v.* BART]   ..   ..   338n.
    Infringement—*Injunction—Interlocutory relief—Preservation of status quo—Screenplay alleged to infringe plaintiffs' film copyright in book—Historical subject—Common sources of material —Plaintiffs' book supplied with others to author of screenplay—Similarities of incidents and situations—Differences in detail—Absence of explanation by author of screenplay of manner and extent of use of plaintiffs' book and of how he worked and for how long—Whether interlocutory injunction should be granted and whether limited in scope* [HARMAN PICTURES, N.V. *v.* OSBORNE]   324
        Interlocutory relief—Security for fulfilment of cross-undertaking—Foreign company as plaintiffs [HARMAN PICTURES, N.V. *v.* OSBORNE]   324
    Licence—*Agreement—Whether licence or partial assignment* [FRISBY *v.* BRITISH BROADCASTING CORPN.]   106
        Dramatic work—Alteration—Licensee has right to make alterations except in so far as licence expressly or impliedly excludes right—B.B.C. licensed by plaintiff member of Screenwriters' Guild, to televise his play—Right of B.B.C. to make alterations not expressly excluded by licence—Agreement by B.B.C. with Screenwriters' Guild not to make structural alterations of script without prior consent of author—B.B.C. claimed right to excise two words from line— Whether agreement applied to licence—Whether proposed alteration structural—Whether interlocutory injunction should be granted [FRISBY *v.* BRITISH BROADCASTING CORPN.] ..   106
CO-RESPONDENT
    See DIVORCE (Adultery—*Evidence; Practice*).
CORROBORATION
    See CRIMINAL LAW (Trial—*Summing-up—Evidence*).
COSTS
    Criminal cases. *See* CRIMINAL LAW (Costs).
    Lien—*Client seeking to withhold solicitors' bill from lodgment for taxation under order to tax on common fund basis. See* Taxation—*Common fund basis, post.*
    Security for costs—*Company in liquidation as plaintiff. See* COMPANY (Investigation by Board of Trade—*Action begun by Board of Trade in plaintiff company's name consequent on inspector's report*).
        Nominal plaintiff—Insolvency of plaintiff—Charge by plaintiff on fruits of the action— Amount secured by charge exceeding amount claimed in action—Whether plaintiff a nominal plaintiff suing for the benefit of some other person, viz., the chargee—R.S.C., Ord. 23, r. 1 (1) *(b)* [SEMLER *v.* MURPHY]   185
        " Plaintiff ordinarily resident out of the jurisdiction "—Action for breach of promise of marriage —Plaintiff a Ghanaian national resident in England since 1956—Plaintiff stated intention to return to Ghana if suitable employment available—Security sought on re-trial of action—Court not satisfied that plaintiff ordinarily resident out of jurisdiction—R.S.C., Ord. 23, r. 1 (1) *(a)* [APPAH *v.* MONSEU]   583
    Taxation—*Common fund basis—Client giving notice to act in person and seeking to vet solicitor's bills of costs before lodgment for taxation—Lien of solicitor for costs—Probate action—Client a defendant in action—Fund held by plaintiffs for defendant client's costs—Form of order— Solicitors Act, 1957 (c. 27), s. 72* [Re FULD (decd.)]   649
COUNTERCLAIM
    Notice of counterclaim—*Admiralty action in rem. See* ADMIRALTY (Practice—*Appearance*).
COUNTY COURT
    Appeal—*Ground of appeal—Point of law not argued in court below—Appeal limited to points raised in court below—Questions of fact not appealable—County Courts Act, 1959 (c. 22), s. 108, s. 109* [OSCROFT *v.* BENABO]   548
COURT
    Judicial office—*Characteristics* [UNITED ENGINEERING WORKERS UNION *v.* DEVANAYAGAM] ..   367
COURT OF APPEAL
    Ground of appeal—*Contention not pressed in court of first instance—Inapplicability of building regulations—All necessary facts found at trial—Whether contention should be allowed to be argued on appeal* [DONAGHEY *v.* BOULTON & PAUL, LTD.]   1014
    Interlocutory appeal—*Leave to appeal—Order refusing leave to bring proceedings in respect of acts done in pursuance of Mental Health Act, 1959—Whether order interlocutory or final— Whether leave to appeal necessary—Supreme Court of Judicature (Consolidation) Act, 1925 (c. 49), s. 31 (1) (i)—Mental Health Act, 1959 (c. 72), s. 141 (2)* [MOORE *v.* COMMISSIONER OF METROPOLITAN POLICE]   827
    Respondent's notice—*Service on third party—Leave not required—R.S.C., Ord. 59, r. 6* (4) [BRITISH ROAD SERVICES, LTD. *v.* ARTHUR V. CRUTCHLEY & CO., LTD. (FACTORY GUARDS, LTD., THIRD PARTIES)]   792

COVENANT
    Seven-year covenant. *See* INCOME TAX (Annual payment).

CREDIT
    Representation—*Negligent. See* MISREPRESENTATION (Credit—*Negligence*).

CREMATORIUM
    Income tax. *See* INCOME TAX (Allowance—*Industrial building or structure*).

CRIME
    Compensation—*Riot. See* RIOT.
    Compensation for victims of crimes of violence. *See* COMPENSATION (Criminal injuries).
    Executor—*Passing over executrix convicted of deceased's manslaughter when granting administra-
    tion to his estate. See* EXECUTOR AND ADMINISTRATOR (Administrator—*Appointment in
    " special circumstances* ").

CRIMINAL LAW
    Aiding and abetting—*Presence at crime—Principals. See* Concerted action, *post.*
    Assault—*Police constable in execution of duty, on. See* POLICE (Constable—*Assault on, in
    execution of duty).*
        Definition of what amounts to an attempt [DAVEY v. LEE]   423
    Autrefois acquit—*General verdict of acquittal sufficient to found plea of autrefois acquit of alterna-
    tive offences—Partial verdict of acquittal good in respect of particular offence* [DIRECTOR OF
    PUBLIC PROSECUTIONS v. NASRALLA]   161
    Concerted action—*Murder—Deceased struck by both appellants in course of quarrel—Uncertainty
    who struck fatal blow—Principals in first or second degree—Proof of pre-arranged plan
    unnecessary. See* PRIVY COUNCIL (Trinidad and Tobago—*Criminal law*).
    Conspiracy—*Continuing single offence—Particulars in terms of a statutory offence, prosecution
    for which was subject to a time limit—Whether time limit applied to charge of common law
    conspiracy so laid—Purchase Tax Act 1963 (c. 9), s. 33 (1), s. 34 (4)* [R. v. SIMMONDS] ..   399
        Practice—*Steps to shorten trial. See* Trial, *post.*
    Costs—*Several accused—Form of order—Joint and several order for payment—Matters to be taken
    into consideration in awarding costs against particular accused—Costs in Criminal Cases
    Act, 1952 (c. 48), s. 2 (1)* [R. v. SIMMONDS]   399
    Evidence—*Admission—Evidence of admission of accused, when giving evidence at first trial,
    admitted on re-trial—Cross-examination of witness as to accused's explanation at first trial—
    Accused not giving evidence at second trial—Whole statement should be left to jury to decide
    as to the truth* [R. v. MCGREGOR]   267
        Identity—*Scientific evidence. See* Trial—*Summing-up—Evidence—Corroboration—Rape, post.*
        Obscene publications. *See* Obscene publication, *post.*
        Witness—*Summons—Setting aside witness summons. See* CERTIORARI (Justices—
        Witness summons*).
    Guilty—*Plea. See* Trial—*Plea, post.*
    Indictment—*Committal to quarter sessions for trial—No indictment preferred before quarter
    sessions—Remitted to assizes for trial—Indictment preferred at assizes containing charge not
    before quarter sessions—Accused lawfully indicted—Administration of Justice (Miscellaneous
    Provisions) Act, 1933 (c. 36), s. 2 (1)* [R. v. WILSON]   1088
    Manslaughter—*Mens rea—Criminal negligence—Accident—Unintentionally causing death by
    pulling trigger of revolver in jest when bullet was not opposite barrel—No knowledge that
    pulling trigger would rotate chamber to bring bullet in line with barrel thus causing it to fire—
    Defence of accident not put to jury—Conviction quashed* [R. v. LAMB]..   1282
    Mens rea—*Manslaughter. See* Manslaughter, *ante.*
    Murder—*Principals in first or second degree. See* Concerted action, *ante.*
    Obscene publications—*Evidence—Expert evidence—Whether admissible to show effect of publica-
    tion on children of various ages—Obscene Publications Act, 1959 (c. 66), s. 4* [DIRECTOR OF
    PUBLIC PROSECUTIONS v. A. AND B.C. CHEWING GUM, LTD.]   504
    Public order—*Incitement to racial hatred—Injunction. See* INJUNCTION (Statute).
    Rape—*Evidence—Corroboration. See* Trial—*Summing-up, post.*
    Soliciting for immoral purposes—*Persistent importuning by male person in public place for
    immoral purposes—Evidence of more than one invitation—Use of word of pleasantry interpreted
    as invitation—Such interpretation permissible as word had been used on previous day coupled
    with undoubted act of importuning—Sexual Offences Act, 1956 (c. 69), s. 32* [DALE v. SMITH]   1133
    Soliciting for the purpose of prostitution—*Soliciting, but to secure evidence against offender. See*
    POLICE (Conduct).
    Trial—*Direction by quarter sessions for trial at assizes. See* Indictment—*Committal to quarter
    sessions for trial, ante.*
        Jury—*Direction to jury—Unanimity in decision—Such direction not normally necessary*
        [R. v. KALINSKI]   398
            Unanimity in verdict [R. v. ROADS]   84
        Length—*Conspiracy to defraud Revenue—Complicated purchase tax evasions—Steps to be
        taken for shortening trials—Severance of counts* [R. v. SIMMONDS]   399
        Plea—*Plea of guilty to a lesser offence—Charge of wounding with intent—Plea of guilty to
        unlawful wounding not accepted by prosecution—Accused tried on charge of wounding with
        intent—Jury returned verdict of not guilty—Accused sentenced for unlawful wounding—Only
        one plea to any one count—Plea was, therefore, not guilty—Conviction quashed—Offences
        against the Person Act, 1861 (c. 100), s. 18, s. 20* [R. v. HAZELTINE]   671
        Severance of counts—*Conspiracy* [R. v. SIMMONDS]   399
        Summing-up—*Evidence—Corroboration—Rape—Identity—Scientific evidence identifying
        accused as assailant—Corroboration not mentioned in summing-up, but jury directed to dis-
        regard evidence of complainant and another and to consider scientific evidence on issue of
        identity—Sufficiency of the direction—Criminal Appeal Act, 1907 (c. 23), s. 4 (1) proviso,
        as amended by Criminal Appeal Act, 1966 (c. 31), s. 4 (1)* [R. v. O'REILLY]   766
    Venue—*Assizes—Direction by quarter sessions for trial at assizes* [R. v. WILSON]   1088
    Verdict—*Types of verdict—General, partial and special. See* PRIVY COUNCIL (Jamaica—
    Criminal Law—Autrefois acquit).
        Unanimity of jury. *See* Trial—*Jury—Direction to jury, ante.*

CROSS-EXAMINATION
Affidavit, on. *See* AFFIDAVIT.

CROWN
Prerogative—*Emergency prerogative—Compensation for loss or damage by exercise of prerogative—Treaty with independent sovereign state—Truce force under British command established to assist sovereign power in preservation of internal peace—Occupation by British troops of hotel on territory of that power—Whether occupation a prerogative act of Crown—Whether an act of state of the Crown—Occupation by British troops later continued as part of the United Nations Force—Whether tenant of hotel, a British subject, entitled to compensation from the Crown—Jurisdiction of the court* [NISSAN v. ATTORNEY-GENERAL] 1238

Privilege. *See* DISCOVERY (Production of documents—*Privilege*).

CUSTODY
Child. *See* DIVORCE; WARD OF COURT.

DAMAGES
Breach of contract. *See* CONTRACT (Breach); SALE OF GOODS (Unpaid seller).

Conflict of laws. *See* CONFLICT OF LAWS (Tort).

Hire-purchase agreement—*Breach. See* PRIVY COUNCIL (Guyana—*Hire-purchase—Warranty*).

Income tax—*Whether capital or income. See* INCOME TAX (Income—*Damages*).

Injunction—*Damages in lieu of injunction. See* INJUNCTION (Damages in lieu of injunction).

Libel. *See* LIBEL.

Measure of damages—*Consortium—Loss of wife's services—Loss of wife's society while in hospital. See* HUSBAND AND WIFE (Consortium—*Damages*).

Loss of earnings—Pension—Compulsory contributory police pension—Whether pension should be taken into account when assessing damages for loss of earnings [PARRY v. CLEAVER] .. 1168

Loss of expectation of life—Matters relevant to assessment—Man aged twenty with real prospects of successful and happy life killed instantaneously—Change in value of money since earlier decisions—Liability of employers for breach of statutory duty—Law Reform (Miscellaneous Provisions) Act, 1934 (c. 41), s. 1 [YORKSHIRE ELECTRICITY BOARD v. NAYLOR] .. 1

Personal injury—*Amount of damages—Brain injury causing grave mental deficiency and personality change—Plaintiff aged twenty-eight, wife and mother of three children, happily married, and a talented commercial artist—Care in private institution necessary throughout rest of her life, probably about twenty-five years—Limited awareness in plaintiff of her deprivation—Element of bodily pain absent* [CUTTS v. CHUMLEY] 89

Loss of expectation of life. See Measure of damages—*Loss of expectation of life, ante.*

Remoteness of damage—*Mental shock—Rescuer helping voluntarily at scene of railway accident with many casualties—Subsequently suffering prolonged and disabling nervous shock—Whether injury too remote* [CHADWICK v. BRITISH TRANSPORT COMMISSION] 945

DEAD BODY
Goods—*Whether. See* INCOME TAX (Allowance—*Industrial building or structure—Crematorium*).

DECLARATION
Jurisdiction—*Hypothetical question—Basis of assessing compensation for compulsory acquisition of land—Whether planning permission might reasonably have been expected to be granted—Question of factual nature, not question of construction—Absence of jurisdiction—Originating summons set aside—Exclusivity of jurisdiction of Lands Tribunal over disputes as to compensation—Land Compensation Act, 1961 (c. 23), s. 16 (3) (b)* [Re CROYDON DEVELOPMENT PLANS 1954 AND 1959] 589

Inferior tribunal—Declaration whether determination of statutory tribunal wrong in law—Action for declaration treated as application for certiorari [ANISMINIC, LTD. v. THE FOREIGN COMPENSATION COMMISSION] 986

Professional society—Rule of conduct. See TRADE (Restraint of trade—*Corporation—Professional society*).

Marriage—*Validity. See* MARRIAGE (Validity).

DELAY
Dismissal of action, for. *See* PRACTICE (Want of prosecution).

DEMOLITION ORDER
See HOUSING.

DEPOSIT
Contract for sale of land. *See* AUCTIONEER (Lien).

DESCRIPTION
Trade. *See* TRADE MARK (False trade description).

DEVELOPMENT
Land. *See* TOWN AND COUNTRY PLANNING.

DIRECTOR
Company, of. *See* COMPANY.

DISABLEMENT BENEFIT
Industrial injury. *See* INDUSTRIAL INJURY.

DISCIPLINE
Architect. *See* PRIVY COUNCIL (Hong Kong).

DISCOVERY
Production of documents—*Privilege—Crown privilege—Disclosure contrary, or injurious, to public interest—Claim in due form conclusive in both contents cases and class cases—Probationary reports on probationer police constable—Report of superintendent of police to chief constable for purpose of obtaining advice of Director of Public Prosecutions—Conclusiveness of certificate of Home Secretary* [CONWAY v. RIMMER] 1260

DISCRETIONARY TRUST
See ESTATE DUTY (Determination of life interest).

DISMISSAL
Want of prosecution—*Action. See* PRACTICE (Want of prosecution).

DISQUALIFICATION
Driving licence. *See* ROAD TRAFFIC (Disqualification for holding licence).

DISSOLUTION
See COMPANY (Winding-up—*Voluntary winding-up—Account of winding-up to be made up by liquidator so soon as the affairs of the company are fully wound-up*).

DIVORCE
Adultery—*Evidence—Evidence against co-respondent—Admission of adultery by wife in her answer supported by affidavit—Memorandum of appearance filed by co-respondent stating intention not to defend by denying adultery—Testimony of wife at hearing showing adultery with co-respondent—Whether evidence of adultery against co-respondent* [INGLIS v. INGLIS AND BAXTER] 71

Advertisement—*Notice of proceedings advertised in newspapers.* See Practice—*Advertisement, post.*

Appeal—*Divisional Court—Appeal from order of magistrates' court—Time for appealing—Extention of time—Factors material to exercise of court's discretion to extend time—Matrimonial Causes Rules,* 1957 (S.I. 1957 No. 619), r. 73 (4) [EDWARDS v. EDWARDS] .. 1032

Collusion—*Agreements and arrangements—Consideration by the court—Test whether likely to lead to decree contrary to the justice of the case—Court should take into consideration what might support respondent's case and counsel's opinion on the merits—Leave to implement agreement, but not approval of an agreement that was collusive—Matrimonial Causes Act* 1965 (c. 72), s. 5 (2) [GOSLING v. GOSLING] 510

Condonation—*Condonation by husband—Adultery by wife—Disclosure—Duty of wife to disclose all material circumstances* [INGLIS v. INGLIS AND BAXTER] 71

Co-respondent. See Adultery—*Evidence, ante;* Practice, *post.*

Custody—*Paternity of child in issue—Custodial jurisdiction—Power of judge in Probate, Divorce and Admiralty Division to order blood test—Power of Official Solicitor as guardian ad litem to refuse consent—R.S.C., Ord.* 80, r. 2 (2) [Re L.] 1110

Decree—*Mutual decrees—Dissolution of marriage and judicial separation—Course not to be commended* [LAWRY v. LAWRY] 1131

Decree absolute—*Judicial act—Application for decree and the filing of the application were one transaction—Decree relating back to beginning of day on which it was made—Matrimonial Causes Rules,* 1957 (S.I. 1957 No. 619), r. 40 (1), (2) [Re SEAFORD (decd.)] 458

Foreign decree—*Decree granted to wife in Czechoslovakia—Residence of wife in territory of foreign court for more than three years preceding application for divorce there—Husband domiciled in England—Avoidance of limping marriages—Public policy—Recognition of foreign decree pronounced before the commencement of s.* 1 of the Law Reform (Miscellaneous Provisions) Act, 1949 (c. 100) [INDYKA v. INDYKA] 689

Recognition by English court—Basis of recognition—Domicil—Nationality—Residence—Relaxation, as regards foreign decrees, of the rule that domicil was the only test of jurisdiction in divorce [INDYKA v. INDYKA] 689

Infant—*Jurisdiction—Powers exercisable by Divorce Division where proceedings properly initiated there in relation to a child—Paternity of child in issue—Blood test* [Re L.] 1110

Injunction—*Molestation.* See INJUNCTION (Husband and wife).

Maintenance of wife—*Secured maintenance—Token order—Substantive order should be based on evidence as to earnings, means, assets and circumstances of parties—Token sum of £10 ordered to be secured to the wife for life—Matrimonial Causes Act* 1965 (c. 72), s. 16 (1) [FOARD v. FOARD] 660

Practice—*Advertisement—Newspaper notice relating to divorce proceedings—Notification by Divorce Registry of any replies to advertisement—If no reply, application for registrar's certificate may be made after period of notice has expired—If publication of notice delayed solicitor will be informed* [PRACTICE DIRECTION] 1196

Co-respondent—Dismissal from suit—Adultery with co-respondent alleged—Discretion of court—No evidence against co-respondent at close of petitioner's case—Matrimonial Causes Act 1965 (c. 72), s. 4 (3) [INGLIS v. INGLIS AND BAXTER] 71

Evidence—Affidavit—Petitioner tendering evidence by affidavit must exhibit petition and depose to truth of its contents [PRACTICE DIRECTION] 184

Service—Substituted service. See Practice—*Advertisement, ante.*

DOCTOR
Income tax—*Expenses.* See INCOME TAX (Deduction in computing profits—*Expenses*).

DOCUMENT
Production of. See DISCOVERY (Production of documents).

DOMICIL
Divorce, in. See DIVORCE.

EDUCATION
Charitable trust for—*Income tax.* See INCOME TAX (Annual payment—*Covenanted payments to charity*).

Income tax—*Children of employees of company.* See INCOME TAX (Charity—*Selection of beneficiaries*).

Proceedings before different tribunals—*Election between.* See PRACTICE (Stay of proceedings—Concurrent proceedings before distinct tribunals).

ELECTIONS
Petition—*Appeal—Interlocutory order—Appeal from.* See PRIVY COUNCIL (Malaysia—*Elections*).

EMPLOYMENT
Duty between employer and employee. See MASTER AND SERVANT (Duty of servant).

Employer and employee. See MASTER AND SERVANT.

Redundancy—*Amount of redundancy payment—Statement of terms of employment referred normal working hours to works rules—Works rules stated normal working hours to be forty hour week—Overtime worked—Whether overtime obligatory under national agreements—Whether over time working to be taken into account in assessing redundancy payment—Redundancy Payments Act* 1965 (c. 62), s. 1, Sch. 1 (5)—*Contracts of Employment Act* 1963 (c. 49), Sch. 2, paras. 1 (1), 3 (1) [PEARSON v. WILLIAM JONES, LTD.] 1062

Dismissal by reason of redundancy—Intention of employers to cease to carry on business in "place" where employee was employed—Notice that there would be no further work in Sussex and offer of employment in other areas—Whether dismissal by reason of redundancy—Redundancy Payments Act 1965 (c. 62), s. 1 (2), s. 3 (1) [R. H. McCULLOCH, LTD. v. MOORE] 290

EMPLOYMENT—Redundancy—*continued*
>*Period of continuous employment—Change of employers consequent on sale of factory premises—Claimants employed for many years by previous employers—Previous employers were manufacturers who sold their factory premises to the present employers who bought the factory to convert it into units for leasing—Claimants dismissed from employment after 101 weeks with present employers—Whether transfer of trade by previous employers to present employers—" Activity "—Whether prior employment could be included in reckoning period of continuous employment—Contracts of Employment Act 1963 (c. 49), Sch. 1, para. 10 (2)—Redundancy Payments Act 1965 (c. 62), s. 8 (1), (2), s. 13 (1), s. 25 (1) [DALLOW INDUSTRIAL PROPERTIES, LTD. v. ELSE. SAME v. CURD]* 30*
>*Work of a particular kind—Fitter operating garage's emergency breakdown service—Fitter occupying flat rent-free in part of business premises connected with another side of employer's business—Sale by employers of that side of the business and of premises which contained flat—Notice given to fitter to terminate employment and vacate flat—Subsequent offer by employers of re-employment as fitter refused—Emergency breakdown service discontinued—Whether fitter entitled to redundancy payment—Redundancy Payments Act 1965 (c. 62), s. 1 (2) [ARNOLD v. THOMAS HARRINGTON, LTD.]* 866*
Tax—*Selective employment tax. See* SELECTIVE EMPLOYMENT TAX.

ENFORCEMENT NOTICE
See TOWN AND COUNTRY PLANNING.

EORUNDEM GENERUM RULE
See PARLIAMENT (Regulation of traffic).

EQUITY
Confidence—*Breach of confidence—Damages—Use of information obtained in confidence—Springboard for activities detrimental to informant—Unpatented device disclosed by inventor as alternative in course of negotiation for marketing his patented device—Patented device already on sale by inventor's firm—Information acquired by defendant company partly private and partly available to public—Application by defendant company for patent, and device sold by them—Damages* [SEAGER v. COPYDEX, LTD.] 415
Money—*Following trust money—Trust money mixed with trustee's own. See* TRUST AND TRUSTEE (Breach of trust).
Redemption. *See* MORTGAGE (Redemption).

ESTATE AGENT
Income tax—*Casual profit—Compensation for withdrawing a claim that had no legal basis. See* INCOME TAX (Profits—*Estate agent—Casual profit*).

ESTATE CONTRACT
Registration as land charge. *See* LAND CHARGE.

ESTATE DUTY
Annuity—*Bequest of annuity conditional on annuitant disposing of capital of hers after her death. See* Exemption and remission—*Purchase, post.*
Appeal—*Procedure—Condition of appealing from the decision of commissioner. See* PRIVY COUNCIL (Hong Kong—*Estate duty*).
Avoidance—*Variation of trusts. See* TRUST AND TRUSTEE (Variation of trusts by the court).
Conditional bequest—*Consequence in regard to estate duty on property bequeathed in fulfilment of condition. See* Exemption and remission, *post.*
Determination of life interest—*Discretionary trust—Accumulation of surplus income—Advancement determining discretionary trust in sums advanced—Whether group of objects of discretionary trust had collectively an " interest in possession "—Whether objects of discretionary trust each had an " interest in possession "—Whether interests in accumulations were to be regarded as separate and independent—Finance Act, 1940 (c. 29), s. 43 (1) as amended by Finance Act, 1950 (c. 15), s. 43 (1)* [GARTSIDE v. INLAND REVENUE COMRS.] 173
Exemption and remission—*Purchase—Property passing by reason of purchase—Annuity bequeathed to wife on condition that she devised one moiety of fund to which she was entitled at time of husband's death to trustees of her will to be held on same trusts as husband's residue—Acceptance of conditional bequest in 1937—Disposition by widow of reversionary interest in moiety fund constituted by such acceptance—Disposition in favour of her relatives—Estate duty exigible as on a gift to them by the disposition—Finance Act, 1894 (c. 30), s. 2 (1) (c), s. 3 (1)—Finance Act, 1940 (c. 29), s. 44 (1) (1A), substituted by Finance Act, 1950 (c. 15), s. 46—Finance Act, 1944 (c. 23), s. 40* [Re HARMSWORTH (*decd.*)] 249
Gift—*Disposition to relative in consideration of annuity. See* Exemption and remission—*Purchase—Property passing by reason of purchase—Annuity bequeathed to wife on condition that she devised one moiety of fund to which she was entitled at time of husband's death to trustees of her will to be held on same trusts as husband's residue, post.*
Passing of property—*Property deemed to pass—Discretionary trust—Determination. See* Determination of life interest—*Discretionary trust, ante.*

ESTOPPEL
Estoppel by record—*Issue estoppel—Whether available in criminal cases. See* HIGHWAY (Obstruction—*Camping by " gipsy " on highway*).
Issues in previous proceedings—Administration action. See RES JUDICATA (Extent—*Issues in action*).
Res judicata. *See* RES JUDICATA

EVIDENCE
Admission. *See* CRIMINAL LAW (Evidence—*Admission*).
Affidavit, by. *See* AFFIDAVIT.
Agent provocateur. *See* POLICE (Conduct).
Criminal proceedings, in. *See* CRIMINAL LAW.
Expert—*Psychiatrist—Effect of publication on children. See* CRIMINAL LAW (Obscene publications).
Fact—*Inferences of fact—Conclusions—Whether themselves facts. See* TOWN AND COUNTRY PLANNING (Development—*Permission for development—Appeal—Appeal to Minister—" Findings of fact "*).
Family provision. *See* FAMILY PROVISION (Evidence).
Guardianship of infants. *See* INFANT (Guardianship of Infants Acts).
Juror—*Evidence as to misapprehension in reaching verdict. See* JURY (Verdict—*Evidence of juror*).

EVIDENCE—*continued*
Wardship case. *See* WARD OF COURT.
Witness—*Summons—Setting aside. See CERTIORARI* (Justices—*Witness summons*).

EXECUTOR AND ADMINISTRATOR
Administrator—*Appointment in " special circumstances "—Executrix convicted of manslaughter of deceased and sentenced to life imprisonment—Supreme Court of Judicature (Consolidation) Act,* 1925 (*c.* 49), *s.* 162 (1), *proviso* (*b*), *as substituted by Administration of Justice Act,* 1928 (*c.* 26), *s.* 9 [Re S. (*decd.*)]   150
Contract—*Action to enforce—Widow, administratrix, a stranger to her deceaesd husband's contract for sale of his business under which she was to be paid annuity. See* CONTRACT (Stranger to contract—*Annuitant*).

EXECUTION
Interpleader. *See* INTERPLEADER.

EXPERT
Witness. *See* CRIMINAL LAW (Obscence publications—*Evidence*).

FACTORY
Building regulations. *See* BUILDING (Building regulations).
Dangerous machinery—*Mobile crane—Failure to fence—Gap between rotating body and wheel— Injury to workman trapped in gap—Crane part of factory equipment containing machinery— Mobility of crane did not exclude it from Factories Act,* 1961 (*c.* 34), *s.* 14 (1) [BRITISH RAILWAYS BOARD *v.* LIPTROT]   1072
Lighting—*Duty of employers to secure and maintain sufficient and suitable lighting—General illumination over areas where persons are regularly employed—General illumination over other interior parts—Workmen tripping over tool lying on floor in shadow of article being constructed in the factory—Shadow reducing otherwise sufficient lighting below required level —Accident occurred before work started or other employees were in factory—Whether employers in breach of statutory duty—Whether accident entirely workman's fault—Factories Act,* 1961 (*c.* 34), *s.* 5 (1)—*Factories (Standards of Lighting) Regulations,* 1941 (*S.R. & O.* 1941 *No.* 94), *reg.* 2 (*a*), (*b*) [LANE *v.* GLOUCESTER ENGINEERING CO., LTD.]..   293

FAMILY PROVISION
Evidence—*By statements exhibited to affidavits* [PRACTICE DIRECTION]   299
Deceased's state of mind admissible—Testamentary capacity not to be investigated—Feebleness of mind did not constitute a reason for deceased's action that was relevant under s. 1 (7)— *Widow not benefiting under deceased's will—Inheritance (Family Provision) Act,* 1938 (*c.* 45), *s.* 1, *as amended by Intestates' Estates Act,* 1952 (*c.* 64), *s.* 7, *Sch.* 3 [Re BLANCH (*decd.*)]   468

FATAL ACCIDENT
Compromise—*Infant not bound until settlement approved by court—Consent order not perfected— Misrepresentation—Defendants consented to order to pay lump sum for widow and infant child not knowing that widow was re-marrying—Widow re-married before order—Order set aside—R.S.C. (Rev.)* 1962, *Ord.* 80, *r.* 11—*R.S.C. (Rev.)* 1965, *Ord.* 80, *r.* 10 [DIETZ *v.* LENNIG CHEMICALS, LTD.]   282

FEAR
Nullity of marriage, ground for. *See* NULLITY (Consent to marriage).

FIRE
Escape of—*Adjoining premises damaged. See* NEGLIGENCE (Escape).

FOLLOWING TRUST PROPERTY
Money—*Mixed with trustee's own money. See* TRUST AND TRUSTEE (Breach of trust—*Mixing trust moneys with trustee's own money*).

FOREIGN COMPANY
See COMPANY.

FOREIGN COMPENSATION COMMISSION
Finality of determination. *See CERTIORARI* (Statutory tribunal).

FOREIGN DECREE
Validity. *See* DIVORCE (Foreign decree).

FOREIGN MARRIAGE
See MARRIAGE.

FORM
Prescribed form—*Inconsistency between note on form and rule of court. See* PRACTICE (Rules of court—*Forms prescribed by rules*).

FRAUDULENT PREFERENCE
See COMPANY (Winding-up).

GARAGE
Compensation—*New road constructed. See* COMPULSORY PURCHASE (Compensation—*Injurious affection*).
Sunday closing. *See* SHOP (Sunday closing).

GIFT
Heir of living person—*Gift to. See* WILL (Gift—*Donee*).
Income tax, on. *See* INCOME TAX (Profits—*Author—Gift of rights in unpublished book to father*).

GUARDIAN
Infants—*Guardianship of Infants Acts. See* INFANT (Guardianship of Infants Acts).

GUARDIAN *AD LITEM*
See DIVORCE (Custody—*Paternity of child in issue*).

GUILTY
Plea. *See* CRIMINAL LAW (Trial—*Plea*).

GUYANA
See PRIVY COUNCIL.

HEIR
Living person—*Gift to. See* WILL (Gift—*Donee*).

HIGHWAY
Construction—*Compensation on compulsory acquisition of land. See* COMPULSORY PURCHASE (Compensation—*Injurious affection*).

HIGHWAY—*continued*
Obstruction—*Camping by " gipsy " on highway—Information alleging offence in December, 1965, dismissed—Magistrates not satisfied that accused a gipsy—Subsequent information charging a like offence in March, 1966—Whether issue estoppel—Whether second information abuse of process of court—Highways Act, 1959 (c. 25), s. 127 (c)* [MILLS v. COOPER].. 100
Street—*Private street works—Appeal to quarter sessions—" Person aggrieved "—Resolution of county council, being both highway authority and street works authority, for making up street—Quashed by order of magistrates' court—Appeal by council to quarter sessions—Whether council a " person aggrieved " within Highways Act, 1959 (c. 25), s. 275 (1)* [PHILLIPS v. BERKSHIRE COUNTY COUNCIL] 675

HIRE-PURCHASE
Agreement—*Implied condition—Log book—Motor car let on hire-purchase but log book not delivered—Hirer consequently did not licence and did not use—Suspensive condition—Contract not enforceable and instalments not recoverable as no log book provided* [BENTWORTH FINANCE, LTD. v. LUBERT].. 810
Indemnity—*Implied condition that log book should be provided on hire-purchase of motor car—Log book not delivered—Contract unenforceable by finance company—Agreement to indemnify finance company against loss or damage arising from hire-purchase agreement being unenforceable inapplicable* [BENTWORTH FINANCE, LTD. v. LUBERT] 810
Termination of agreement—*Option for finance company to terminate agreement for hirer's breach—Option for hirer to terminate agreement—Minimum payment clause applicable on exercise of option—Hirer returning car to dealers and regetting inability to pay instalments—Letter by hirer sent at instance of finance company expressing wish to terminate agreement—Claim by finance company under minimum payment clause—Whether option exercised by finance company or by hirer—Whether repudiation of agreement by hirer—Whether any sum recoverable by finance company under hire-purchase agreement* [UNITED DOMINIONS TRUST (COMMERCIAL), LTD. v. ENNIS] 345
Warranty—*Defective goods—Known defects—Obligation to remedy them assumed by onwer.* See PRIVY COUNCIL (Guyana—*Hire-purchase—Warranty*).

HONG KONG
See PRIVY COUNCIL.

HOUSE OF LORDS
Appeal to—*Legal aid.* See LEGAL AID (Certificate—*Grant*).

HOUSING
Demolition order—*Expenses of demolition—Lump sum price for demolition arranged by local authority with contractor—Price calculated on basis that contractor should retain materials—Whether compliance with statutory requirement to give credit for amount realised by sale of materials—Housing Act, 1957 (c. 56), s. 23 (1), (2)* [LONDON BOROUGH OF HILLINGDON v. CUTLER] 361
Validity—*Duty to make order " forthwith " where no undertaking accepted—Order made eight months after return date on s. 16 notice—No detriment to owner—Validity of order—Whether owner who has not appealed against demolition order can resist claim for expenses on ground that order invalid—Housing Act, 1957 (c. 56), s. 16 (1), s. 17 (1), s. 37 (1)* [LONDON BOROUGH OF HILLINGDON v. CUTLER] 361

HUSBAND AND WIFE
Consortium—*Damages—Wife injured in road accident for which defendant liable—Wife under care in institution for rest of her life, probably about twenty-five years—Total incapacity of wife to render services in the home to husband and children—Husband necessarily employing paid housekeeper to care for three children in his home—Claim for total loss of wife's services* [CUTTS v. CHUMLEY] 89
Injunction. See INJUNCTION (Husband and wife).
Maintenance—*Amount.* See MAGISTRATES.
Divorce suit, in. See DIVORCE (Maintenance of wife).
Injunction—Matrimonial home—Application by respondent husband. See INJUNCTION (Husband and wife—*Matrimonial home*).
Interim order. See MAGISTRATES (Husband and wife—*Maintenance order*).
Marriage. See MARRIAGE.
Matrimonial home—*Injunction.* See INJUNCTION (Husband and wife).
Separation—*Consensual separation—Implication of agreement by husband partly to maintain wife—Maintenance of wife* [NORTHROP v. NORTHROP] 961
Summary matrimonial jurisdiction—*Appeal.* See DIVORCE (Appeal—*Divisional Court*).

IMPORTUNING
Persistent. See CRIMINAL LAW (Soliciting for immoral purposes).

INCOME TAX
Allowance—*Industrial building or structure—Crematorium—Expenditure incurred in construction of furnace chamber and chimney tower of crematorium—Whether furnace chamber and chimney tower industrial building or structure—Whether dead human bodies " goods and materials "—Income Tax Act, 1952 (c. 10), s. 265 (1), s. 266, s. 271 (1) (c)* [BOURNE (INSPECTOR OF TAXES) v. NORWICH CREMATORIUM, LTD.] 576
Investment allowance—Mini van licensed for carriage of goods and used solely for purposes of business of radio engineer—Advertisements relating to business on the sides of the van—Van of a type commonly used as private vehicle and suitable to be so used—No modification made to van—Whether van qualified for an investment allowance—Finance Act, 1954 (c. 44), s. 16 (3) [TAPPER (INSPECTOR OF TAXES) v. EYRE] 636
Machinery or plant—Wear and tear—Sub-lease of building containing heating equipment and lifts—Sub-lessors were property investment company and sub-lessee was a government department—Full repairing covenant by sub-lessee—Machinery likely to require replacement during currency of sub-lease—Whether allowance available only where machinery and plant used for trade—Whether sub-let on terms that burden of wear and tear fell directly on sub-lessor—Income Tax Act, 1952 (c. 10), s. 298 [MACSAGA INVESTMENT CO., LTD. v. LUPTON (INSPECTOR OF TAXES)] 930
Annual payment—*Covenanted payments to charity—Common intention that covenanted payments should be used by charity to buy goodwill of covenantor's educational establishment—Plan to convert tutorial establiishment to educational trust—Covenanted payments not pure bounty and thus not annual payments—Income Tax Act, 1952 (c. 10), s. 169 (1), s. 447 (1) (b)* [CAMPBELL (TRUSTEES OF DAVIES'S EDUCATIONAL TRUST) v. INLAND REVENUE COMRS.] 625

INCOME TAX—*continued*
Avoidance—*Surtax. See* SURTAX.

Capital or income—*Capital receipts. See* Profits—*Computation of profits, post.*

Charity—*Selection of beneficiaries—Preferential application of income for private class—Company established for charitable educational purposes—Main income from another company by way of covenanted payments—Major part of income applied towards education of children associated with covenantor company—Public benefit essential to charitable purpose—Whether income applied to charitable purposes only—Income Tax Act,* 1952 (c. 10), s. 447 (1) (b) [INLAND REVENUE COMRS. *v.* EDUCATIONAL GRANTS ASSOCIATION, LTD.]   893

Damages—*Capital or income. See* Income—*Damages, post.*

Deduction in computing profits—*Expenses—Medical practitioner—General medical practitioner practising at his residence and also holding part-time appointments at hospital fifteen miles away—Hospital work as obstetrician and anaesthetist—Emergency cases—Expenses of travel by car to and from hospital—Whether expenses deductible—Income Tax Act,* 1952 (c. 10), s. 156, *Sch. E, Case* 1, *as substituted by Finance Act,* 1956 (c. 54), s. 10 (1), *and Sch.* 9, r. 7 *to the Act of* 1952 [POOK (INSPECTOR OF TAXES) *v.* OWEN]   579

Exemption—*Charity. See* Charity, *ante.*

Income—*Bounty—Civil Defence Corps—" Public revenue "—Bounty paid to members of Civil Defence Corps out of local authority funds—Local authority being partly reimbursed from central government funds—Whether bounty paid out of public revenue and thus exempted from tax by the Income Tax Act,* 1952 (c. 10), s. 457 (4) [LUSH (INSPECTOR OF TAXES) *v.* COLES]   585

Damages—*Loss of profit from right of pre-emption—Breach of contract to give pre-emption over surplus stocks—Income Tax Act,* 1952 (c. 10), *Sch. D, Case I* [SOMMERFELDS, LTD. *v.* FREEMAN (INSPECTOR OF TAXES)]..   143

Loss of profitable use of asset—*Damage to jetty—Payment by shipowners responsible—Apportionment in negotiations with jetty owner's underwriters—Part attributed to loss of use of jetty—Capital loss or loss of profit—Income Tax Act,* 1952 (c. 10), s. 137 [LONDON AND THAMES HAVEN OIL WHARVES, LTD. *v.* ATTWOOLL (INSPECTOR OF TAXES)]   ..   124

Insurance moneys—*Capital or income. See* Income—*Damages—Loss of capital assets or profit—Damage to jetty, ante.*

Profits—*Author—Gift of rights in unpublished book to father—Whether author taxable on value of rights—Income Tax Act,* 1952 (c. 10), *Sch. D* [MASON (INSPECTOR OF TAXES) *v.* INNES]   926

Computation of profits—*Capital receipts—Licences for manufacture of Terylene in foreign countries—Covenants of licensor not to manufacture or licence manufacture there—Lump sum payments for covenants—Whether capital or income—Income Tax Act,* 1952 (c. 10), *Sch. D, Case* 2 [MURRAY (INSPECTOR OF TAXES) *v.* IMPERIAL CHEMICAL INDUSTRIES, LTD.]   ..   980

Estate agent—*Casual profit—Gratuitous payment for consenting to a deal between a company and a society, the client of the estate agent—Compensation for withdrawal of any claim that the estate agent might have—No legal basis for any claim—Company taking over land under negotiation—Estate agent's intended acquisition of an interest in the land as an investment—Whether compensation taxable as a casual profit—Income Tax Act,* 1952 (c. 10), *Sch. D, Case VI* [SCOTT (INSPECTOR OF TAXES) *v.* RICKETTS]   1009

Surtax. *See* SURTAX.

Tax avoidance—*Variation of trusts. See* TRUST AND TRUSTEE (Variation of trusts by the court).

INDEMNITY
Hire-purchase agreement. *See* HIRE-PURCHASE (Indemnity).

INDEPENDENT CONTRACTOR
Negligence—*Liability of employer for negligence of independent contractor—Warehouseman—Security patrols for guarding warehouse provided by independent contractor—Patrolman negligent—Whether negligence for which independent contractor vicariously responsible attributable also to warehouseman—Whether warehouseman liable as bailee* [BRITISH ROAD SERVICES, LTD. *v.* ARTHUR V. CRUTCHLEY & CO., LTD. (FACTORY GUARDS, LTD., THIRD PARTIES)]   785

INDICTMENT
See CRIMINAL LAW.

INDUSTRIAL INJURY
Disablement benefit—*Assessment of degree of disability—Causation of each disability to be considered—Whether defect of vision in right eye due to disease after accident but before assessment was to be taken into consideration to assess greater disablement than would normally be incurred —National Insurance (Industrial Injuries) Act* 1965 (c. 52), *Sch.* 4, *para.* 1 (b)—*National Insurance (Industrial Injuries) (Benefit) Regulations* 1964 (S.I. 1964 *No.* 504), *reg.* 2 (3) (a) [R. *v.* INDUSTRIAL INJURIES COMR., *Ex parte* CABLE]   119

INFANT
Blood test—*Power of court to order. See* DIVORCE (Custody—*Paternity of child in issue*).

Compromise—*Consent order not perfected. See* FATAL ACCIDENT (Compromise).

Custody—*Conflict of laws. See* WARD OF COURT (Jurisdiction).

Guardianship of Infants Acts—*Appeals from courts of summary jurisdiction—Title of proceedings—Application for leave to adduce further evidence—Guardianship of Infants Acts,* 1886 *and* 1925—*R.S.C., Ord.* 55, r. 3 (1), (2), *Ord.* 91, r. 7 (1), (2) [PRACTICE DIRECTION]   ..   1232

Evidence—*By statements exhibited to affidavits* [PRACTICE DIRECTION]   299

Jurisdiction—*Magistrates' court order—Wardship proceedings. See* WARD OF COURT (Jurisdiction).

INFRINGEMENT
Copyright. *See* COPYRIGHT.

INHERITANCE (FAMILY PROVISION)
See FAMILY PROVISION.

INJUNCTION
Damages in lieu of injunction—*Breach of confidence—Measure of damages. See* EQUITY (Confidence—*Breach of confidence*).

Husband and wife—*Matrimonial home—Husband's application in wife's maintenance proceedings —Husband excluded from matrimonial home—Leasehold premises in joint names—Relief sought by respondent husband not sufficiently related to wife's claim for maintenance—R.S.C., Ord.* 29, r. 1 (1)—*Supreme Court of Judicature (Consolidation) Act,* 1925 (c. 49), s. 45 (1) [DES SALLES D'EPINOIX *v.* DES SALLES D'EPINOIX]   539

Restraining wife from molesting husband—*Wife's petition for judicial separation—Husband's application for injunction to restrain molestation—Husband of sufficient means to live elsewhere than in matrimonial home, but choosing to remain there—Injunction not granted* [FREEDMAN *v.* FREEDMAN]   680

INJUNCTION—*continued*

Interlocutory—*Principle governing grant.* See COPYRIGHT (Assignment—*Injunction*; Infringement—*Injunction*).

Security for implementing cross-undertaking—Foreign plaintiff. See COPYRIGHT (Infringement—*Injunction—Interlocutory relief*).

Statute—*Criminal offence created by statute—No legal right conferred on individual—Enforcement under the control of the Attorney-General—Incitement to racial hatred—Alleged anti-German propaganda by broadcasts and television—No cause of action by individual without consent of Attorney-General—Race Relations Act* 1965 (c. 73), *s.* 3, *s.* 6 [THORNE *v.* BRITISH BROADCASTING CORPN.] 1225

INJURIOUS FALSEHOOD

See MALICIOUS FALSEHOOD.

INSURANCE

Policy moneys—*Trust—Discretionary power under endowment assurance for pension.* See TRUST AND TRUSTEE (Uncertainty—*Discretionary trust—Power of selection, bare power not coupled with duty to select*).

INTERIM MAINTENANCE ORDER

See MAGISTRATES (Husband and wife—*Maintenance order*).

INTERPLEADER

Claimant a company in compulsory liquidation—*Leave of Companies Court required for issue of interpleader summons to which company a respondent—Companies Act*, 1948, (c. 38), *s.* 231 [EASTERN HOLDINGS ESTABLISHMENT OF VADUZ *v.* SINGER & FRIEDLANDER, LTD. (ABLE SECURITIES, LTD., In liquidation, First Claimant; SEMPAH (HOLDINGS), LTD., Second Claimant)] 1192

Sheriff's interpleader—*Claimant the wife of the debtor—Claim to all furniture and goods seized in the matrimonial home—Application by execution creditor for wife to give evidence on oath and be cross-examined—Adjournment refused and wife's claim allowed—Order set aside—Proper practice on such claims—Meaning of words, may " summarily determine the question at issue ", in R.S.C., Ord.* 17, *r.* 5 (2) [P. B. J. DAVIS MANUFACTURING CO., LTD. *v.* FAHN (FAHN CLAIMANT)] 1274

INTESTACY

Grant of administration—*Wife's notice of application for decree nisi to be made absolute received and filed on day deceased husband found dead—Deceased dying during night before application received by registrar—Burden of proof on wife to show marriage subsisting at time of deceased's death* [Re SEAFORD (*decd.*)] 458

INTIMIDATION

See TRADE UNION.

INVENTION

Confidence—*Breach of confidence—Use of information given by inventor in confidence.* See EQUITY (Confidence—*Breach of confidence*).

JUDGMENT

Date—*Relation back.* See DIVORCE (Decree absolute—*Judicial act*).

Order—*Consent order—Setting aside—Order not perfected.* See FATAL ACCIDENT (Compromise).

Interlocutory order. See COURT OF APPEAL (Interlocutory appeal—*Leave to appeal*).

JUDICIAL ACT

Time—*Relation back.* See DIVORCE (Decree absolute).

JUDICIAL POWER

Characteristics. See CONSTITUTIONAL LAW.

JUDICIAL SEPARATION

Generally. See DIVORCE (Decree—*Mutual decrees—Dissolution of marriage and judicial separation*).

JURY

Direction to. See CRIMINAL LAW (Trial).

Verdict—*Evidence of juror—Civil trial—Defamation—Questions put to jury and their answers returned in presence of all jurors—Judgment subsequently given on those answers—Jurors wishing to change answers, as they were dissatisfied with result—Application for new trial—Affidavit by jurors that the answers were given under misapprehension not admissible* [BOSTON *v.* W. S. BAGSHAW & SONS] 87n

Criminal trial—Jury directed that unanimous verdict was necessary—Return of verdict in sight and hearing of all jurors without protest—Evidence of juror that she disagreed with verdict inadmissible [R. *v.* ROADS] 84

LAND CHARGE

Estate contract—*Registration—Name of estate owner should be his proper, formal name—Registration of estate contract in name of "Frank David Blackburn" when true name was "Francis David Blackburn" ineffective to give protection against subsequent mortgage by estate owner—Land Charges Act,* 1925 (c. 22), *s.* 10 (2) [OAK CO-OPERATIVE BUILDING SOCIETY *v.* BLACKBURN] 340

Search—*Official certificate of search—Conclusiveness—Application for search against name of "Francis Davis Blackburn"—True name was "Francis David Blackburn"—Certificate not conclusive—Note on certificate mentioning existence of entries under name "Francis David Blackburn " and a different address—No conclusive effect—Land Charges Act,* 1925 (c. 22), *s.* 17 (3) [OAK CO-OPERATIVE BUILDING SOCIETY *v.* BLACKBURN] 340

LAND REGISTRATION

Charge—*Legal mortgage—Form—Premium.* See MORTGAGE (Collateral advantage—*Premium*).

LANDLORD AND TENANT

Agricultural holding. See AGRICULTURE (Agricultural holding).

Furnished tenancy—*Whether changed to unfurnished tenancy.* See Tenancy—*Grant—Invalid notice to quit to furnished sub-tenant expiring at midnight of Mar.* 25, *post.*

Lease—*Covenant—Covenant against assignment—Sale of leasehold property subject to landlords' consent.* See MORTGAGE (Sale—*Leasehold property*).

Overridden by statutory powers. See NUISANCE (Sewer—*Obstruction to flow of river caused by pipe of sewer constructed by local authority beneath river bed but becoming exposed as river bed washed away*).

PAGE

LANDLORD AND TENANT—*continued*
New tenancy—*Business premises—Opposition by landlord—Intention to demolish and reconstruct premises—Proposed work involving demolition of all buildings and replacement by others—Tenant willing to allow access for work to be carried out—Term of existing tenancy that landlord could do such work during tenancy and that tenant should allow access for it—Whether work could reasonably be done without obtaining possession—Landlord and Tenant Act,* 1954 *(c.* 56), *s.* 30 (1) (*f*) [LITTLE PARK SERVICE STATION, LTD. *v.* REGENT OIL CO., LTD.]   257

    Terms of new tenancy—Rent—Controlled sub-tenancy—All circumstances relevant to what rent might be expected to be obtained in open market to be taken into consideration—Landlord and Tenant Act, 1954 *(c.* 56), *s.* 34 [OSCROFT *v.* BENABO]   548

Notice to quit—*Business premises—Date for which statutory notice may be given—Monthly tenancy —Rent payable monthly in advance on first day of each calendar month—Landlord's notice to terminate on eleventh day of month—Effect—Landlord and Tenant Act,* 1954 *(c.* 56), *s.* 25 (1), (2) [COMMERICAL PROPERTIES, LTD. *v.* WOOD]   916

Rent—*Regulated tenancy. See* RENT RESTRICTION (Rent).

Rent restriction. *See* RENT RESTRICTION.

Tenancy—*Grant—Invalid notice to quit to furnished sub-tenant expiring at midnight of Mar.* 25—*Removal of furniture by tenant earlier on Mar.* 25—*Cesser of tenant's interest at midnight on Mar.* 25—*Sub-tenant remaining in occupation—Subsequent valid notice to quit given by landlord to sub-tenant—Claim by sub-tenant that the tenancy had become an unfurnished tenancy* [CHALCOTS DEVELOPMENTS, LTD. *v.* DE GRAY]   888

LANDS TRIBUNAL
Jurisdiction—*Compensation—Disputes—Exclusivity of jurisdiction over disputes as to compensation. See* DECLARATION (Jurisdiction—*Hypothetical question*).

LAPSE
Will—*Gift—Lapse. See* WILL (Lapse).

LEGAL AID
Certificate—*Grant—Certiorari and mandamus. See* Certificate—*Grant—Matters to be taken into consideration by legal aid committee in determining whether to grant or refuse certificate, post.*

    Matters to be taken into consideration by legal aid committee in determining whether to grant or refuse certificate—View taken by committee on merits conclusive in absence of fresh evidence—"Proceedings"—Appeal to House of Lords—Certiorari and mandamus against refusal of certificate not granted—Legal Aid (General) Regulations, 1962 *(S.I.* 1962 *No.* 148), *reg.* 7 (*f*) [R. *v.* AREA COMMITTEE NO. 1 (LONDON) LEGAL AID AREA, *Ex parte* RONDEL]   419

Costs—*Unassisted persons' costs out of legal aid fund—Wife's appeal in application for leave to implement collusive agreement with a view to divorce—Leave given, but costs not payable out of legal aid fund* [GOSLING *v.* GOSLING]   510

LEGITIMATION
Legitimated child—*Gift to. See* WILL (Lapse—*Statutory exception from lapse*).

LETTER OF CREDIT
See BANK (Documentary credit).

LIBEL
Damages—*Exemplary or punitive damages—No withdrawal of libel or apology—Conduct of defendant taken into account, although exemplary or punitive damages not to be awarded* [FIELDING *v.* VARIETY, INC.]   497

Malicious falsehood. *See* MALICIOUS FALSEHOOD.

Trial—*New trial—Jury under misapprehension—Whether evidence of jurors admissible. See* JURY (Verdict—*Evidence of juror—Civil trial—Defamation*).

LICENCE
Copyright. *See* COPYRIGHT.

Entry—*Licence to enter premises—Police officers approaching front door of house through unlocked garden gate—Revocation of oral licence to enter house—Reasonable time to leave* [ROBSON *v.* HALLETT]   407

LIEN
Auctioneer. *See* AUCTIONEER (Lien).

Vendor's lien—*Sale of goods—Document of title to goods sent by unpaid vendors to merchant bankers. See* BANK (Documentary credit—*Irrevocable credit—Selling agents*).

LIFE
Loss of expectation of life—*Measure of damages. See* DAMAGES (Measure of damages).

LIGHTING
Factory, in. *See* FACTORY.

LIMITATION OF ACTION
Amendment—*Writ—Defendant substituted. See* PRACTICE (Parties).

Land—*Adverse possession—Sea-bed—Whether possession sufficiently exclusive—Limitation Act,* 1939 *(c.* 21), *s.* 4 (1), *proviso* [FOWLEY MARINE (EMSWORTH), LTD. *v.* GAFFORD]   472

LOCAL AUTHORITY
Supersession—*Minister's order of supersession for incompetence. See* PRIVY COUNCIL (Ceylon—*Public authority*).

LOCAL GOVERNMENT
Highway—*Compulsory acquisition of land. See* COMPULSORY PURCHASE (Compensation).

LOG BOOK
Motor vehicle. *See* HIRE-PURCHASE (Agreement—*Implied condition*).

MACHINERY
Dangerous. *See* FACTORY.

Income tax. *See* INCOME TAX (Allowance).

MAGISTRATES
Assault—*Police officer, on. See* POLICE (Constable—*Assault on, in execution of duty*).

Guardianship of infants. *See* INFANT (Guardianship of Infants Acts).

Husband and wife—*Appeal—Time for appealing—Extension. See* DIVORCE (Appeal—*Divisional Court—Appeal from order of magistrates' court*).

MAGISTRATES—Husband and Wife—*continued*

Maintenance—Wilful neglect to maintain—Consensual separation—Implication of agreement by husband to support wife as well as child to the extent to which wife precluded by her obligations to child from supporting herself—Maintenance order on ground of husband's neglect to maintain wife, as distinct from child—Matrimonial Proceedings (Magistrates' Courts) Act, 1960 (c. 48), s. 2 (1) (b) [NORTHROP *v.* NORTHROP]   961

Wilful neglect to maintain—Consensual separation—Neglect to maintain child—Court's power to found on that neglect an order for provision for the wife, in addition to maintenance for the child—Provision such as to enable wife to discharge obligations to child impairing her earning power—Matrimonial Proceedings (Magistrates' Courts) Act, 1960 (c. 48), s. 2 (1) (b), (h) [NORTHROP *v.* NORTHROP]   961

Maintenance order—Interim order—Appeal to High Court from order of magistrates— Whether High Court has power to ante-date interim order—Matrimonial Proceedings (Magistrates' Courts) Act, 1960 (c. 48), s. 6 (1) (c) [BOULD *v.* BOULD (by her Guardian) 1128

Juvenile court—*Jurisdiction—Ward of court—Overlapping jurisdictions.* See WARD OF COURT (Jurisdictions—*Previous order of magistrates under Guardianship of Infants Acts, 1886 and 1925, giving custody to father*).

Witness—*Summons—Setting aside witness summons.* See CERTIORARI (Justices—*Witness summons*).

MAINTENANCE

Child. *See* MAGISTRATES (Husband and wife—*Maintenance*).

Wife–*Divorce. See* DIVORCE (Maintenance of wife).

Summary jurisdiction—Appeal to High Court—Interim order. See MAGISTRATES (Husband and wife—*Maintenance order—Interim order*).

MALAYSIA

See PRIVY COUNCIL.

MALICIOUS FALSEHOOD

Damages—*Pecuniary loss—Damages for injured feelings not recoverable—Damages reduced from £10,000 to £100—Defamation Act, 1952 (c. 66), s. 3 (1)* [FIELDING *v.* VARIETY, INC.] ..   497

MALTA

Tort—*Personal injuries—Action in England.* See CONFLICT OF LAWS (Tort—*Damages— Remoteness of damage*).

MANSLAUGHTER

Generally. *See* CRIMINAL LAW.

MARRIAGE

Breach of promise—*Costs—Security for costs.* See COSTS (Security for costs—*Plaintiff ordinarily resident out of the jurisdiction*).

Foreign marriage—*Validity—Essential requirements of valid marriage distinguished from procedural requirements—Foreign Marriage Act, 1892 (c. 23), s. 8* [COLLETT (otherwise SAKAZOVA) *v.* COLLETT]   426

Nullity of. *See* NULLITY.

Validity—*Declaration—British subject domiciled in England—Procedure to obtain declaration— Matrimonial Causes Act 1965 (c. 45), s. 39—Matrimonial Causes Rules, 1947 (S.I. 1957 No. 619,) r. 74* [COLLETT (otherwise SAKAZOVA) *v.* COLLETT]   426

MASTER AND SERVANT

Dismissal—*Redundancy. See* EMPLOYMENT (Redundancy).

Duty of master—*Safe system of working. See* SAFE SYSTEM OF WORKING.

Duty of servant—*Fidelity—Solicitor employing assistant solicitor—Implied term that assistant solicitor would serve solicitor with good faith and fidelity—Assistant solicitor accepting offer from important client of solicitor to take lease of premises owned by client and to do client's legal work—Assistant solicitor leaving solicitor's employment and entering into agreement with client to undertake all legal work for client for seven years—Whether breach of agreement with solicitor* [SANDERS *v.* PARRY]   803

Tax—*Selective employment tax. See* SELECTIVE EMPLOYMENT TAX.

Wages—*Restrictions on pay increases—No increase above " rate of remuneration paid " before relevant date—Restriction to rate contracted to be paid, as distinct from amount actually paid —Prices and Incomes Act 1966 (c. 73,) s. 28 (2), s. 29 (4)—Temporary Restrictions on Pay Increases (20th July 1966 Levels) (No. 1) Order 1966 (S.I. 1966 No. 1365)—Temporary Restrictions on Pay Increases (No. 2) Order 1966 (S.I. 1966 No. 1468)* [ALLEN *v.* THORN ELECTRICAL INDUSTRIES, LTD. GRIFFIN *v.* RECEIVER FOR THE METROPOLITAN POLICE DISTRICT] .. 1137

MATRIMONIAL HOME

Injunction in matrimonial causes. *See* INJUNCTION (Husband and wife).

MEDICAL PRACTITIONER

Income tax—*Expenses. See* INCOME TAX (Deduction in computing profits—*Expenses*).

MENS REA

Generally. *See* CRIMINAL LAW.

MENTAL HEALTH

Action—*Leave to bring—Refusal of leave to bring action for acts done in pursuance of Mental Health Act, 1959—Appeal—Whether leave required.* See COURT OF APPEAL (Interlocutory appeal—*Leave to appeal*).

MERCHANDISE MARKS ACTS

See TRADE MARK.

MINE

Railway above ground—*Bank of spoil placed less than three feet from track—Loose material on route for shunter going in course of duty from one point to another—Route, formerly safe, osbtructed and side of bank sloping steeply towards track—Shunter not warned—Shunter preceding train, slipped on bank, fell between railway wagons and was killed—Whether negligence on part of employers of shunter—Whether shunter "required " in the course of his duty to pass on foot over that material or between it and the line—Whether breach of statutory duty—Whether contributory negligence by shunter—Coal and Other Mines (Sidings) Order, 1956 (S.I. 1956 No. 1773), Sch. reg. 20* [SMITH (formerly WESTWOOD) *v.* NATIONAL COAL BOARD]   593

MISFEASANCE

Company. *See* COMPANY,

MISREPRESENTATION
    Credit—*Negligence—Oral representation—Whether defence of absence of writing maintainable under Statute of Frauds Amendment Act*, 1828 (*c.* 14), *s.* 6 [W. B. ANDERSON & SONS, LTD. *v.* RHODES (LIVERPOOL), LTD.] 850
    Negligent. *See* NEGLIGENCE (Duty to take care—*Statement*).

MOLESTATION
    Injunction. *See* INJUNCTION (Husband and wife).

MONEY
    Following trust money—*Mixing trust money with trustee's own money. See* TRUST AND TRUSTEE (Breach of Trust).

MORTGAGE
    Collateral advantage—*Premium—Charge on mortgagor's house on occasion of expiration of lease and his purchase of freehold from landlords—Loan of £2,900 by landlords—Purchase price £3,500—£600 provided by mortgagor—Sum charged by mortgage £4,553, payable by seventy-two equal monthly instalments—Premium (£1,653) included in the sum charged—On default whole of money lent and premium would become due—Mortgagor in default—Mortgagees sought to enforce mortgage—Whether charge should stand as security for premium as well as for moneys lent—Whether interest should be allowed* [CITYLAND AND PROPERTY (HOLDINGS), LTD. *v.* DABRAH] 639
    Redemption—*Contract of sale by mortgagee—Whether equity of redemption at an end. See* Sale—Leasehold property, *post.*
    Sale—*Appropriation of proceeds of sale—Secured creditor of company in creditors' voluntary winding-up realised security and appropriated proceeds to satisfying non-preferential part of company's indebtedness—Secured creditor, a bank, also creditor for preferential indebtedness in respect of moneys advanced—Whether appropriation valid against liquidators—Companies Act,* 1948 (*c.* 38), *s.* 319 (4) [Re WILLIAM HALL (CONTRACTORS), LTD.] 1150
        Leasehold property—Covenant by lessee in lease not to assign—Contract for sale by lessee's mortgagee—Condition that sale subject to mortgagee's obtaining consent to assignment of lease to purchaser—Date fixed by contract for completion passed—Mortgagee obtained order for possession—Lessee tendered redemption moneys before time for delivering possession under the order arrived—Lessee applied for stay of proceedings for possession, and brought an action to redeem the mortgage—Whether contract for sale put an end to the right of redemption—Law of Property Act, 1925 (*c.* 20), *s.* 101 (1), *s.* 104 (1) [PROPERTY AND BLOODSTOCK, LTD. *v.* EMERTON. BUSH *v.* PROPERTY AND BLOODSTOCK, LTD.] 839
    Search—*Land charge—Name of estate owner. See* LAND CHARGE (Search).

MOTOR VEHICLE
    Driving licence. *See* ROAD TRAFFIC (Disqualification for holding licence).
    Hire-purchase. *See* HIRE-PURCHASE.
    Income tax—*Investment allowance. See* INCOME TAX (Allowance—*Investment allowance*).
    Log Book. *See* HIRE-PURCHASE (Agreement—*Implied condition*).

NATIONAL HEALTH SERVICE
    Medical practitioner—*Income tax. See* INCOME TAX (Deduction in computing profits—*Expenses*).

NATIONALITY
    Divorce—*Jurisdiction based on nationality—Recognition of foreign decree. See* DIVORCE (Foreign decree).

NATURAL JUSTICE
    Public authority—*Quasi-judicial function—Minister's order superseding municipal council for incompetence—" Audi alteram partem "—Inquiry—No opportunity given to council to be heard in defence—Order voidable only in proceedings by or on behalf of council—Municipal Ordinance (cap.* 252) *of Ceylon, s.* 277 (1) [DURAYAPPAH *v.* FERNANDO] 152
    Tribunal—*Deliberations in private—Legal adviser member of disciplinary board. See* PRIVY COUNCIL (Hong Kong—*Architect*).

NEGLIGENCE
    Auditor. *See* COMPANY (Auditors).
    Contributory negligence—*Shunter. See* MINE (Railway above ground).
    Damages—*Personal injury—Measure of damages—Loss of expectation of life—Instantaneous death—Man of twenty years of age. See* DAMAGES (Measure of damages—*Loss of expectation of life*).
        Pension—Whether taken into account. See DAMAGES (Measure of damages—*Loss of earnings*).
        Wife sustaining severe brain injury in motor accident. See DAMAGES (Personal injury—*Amount of damages*).
    Duty to take care—*Statement—Reply to enquiry—Representation of credit-worthiness of purchaser—Wholesaler and commission agent's buyer purchasing in vegetable market for third party—Negligence by manager of wholesaler in not informing buyer about state of account of third party with wholesaler—Whether wholesaler owed duty of care to prospective vendor to the third party* [W. B. ANDERSON & SONS, LTD. *v.* RHODES (LIVERPOOL), LTD.] 850
    Escape—*Fire—Escape to adjoining premises—Liability of occupier as such—Non-natural user of land by occupier—Yard used as store for machinery greased and stacked in wooden cases pending sale—Serious fire risk to adjoining occupiers—Destruction by fire of neighbour's hedge and garden plants—Whether burden of disproving negligence on occupier—Fires Prevention (Metropolis) Act,* 1774 (*c.* 78), *s.* 86 [MASON *v.* LEVY AUTO PARTS OF ENGLAND, LTD.].. 62
    Independent contractor. *See* INDEPENDENT CONTRACTOR.
    Railway. *See* MINE (Railway above ground).
    Rescue—*Railway collision causing many casualties among passengers—Rescuer voluntarily assisting in rescue work—Whether duty of care owed to rescuer—Rescuer subsequently suffering prolonged mental shock* [CHADWICK *v.* BRITISH TRANSPORT COMMISSION] 945

NEW SOUTH WALES
    See PRIVY COUNCIL (Australia).

NEW TENANCY
    See LANDLORD AND TENANT (New tenancy).

NOTICE
  Counterclaim, of—*Admiralty action.* *See* ADMIRALTY (Practice—*Appearance—Writ in rem not served on defendants*).
  Enforcement notice. *See* TOWN AND COUNTRY PLANNING.
  Respondent's. *See* COURT OF APPEAL (Respondent's notice).

NOTICE TO QUIT
  See AGRICULTURE (Agricultural holding); LANDLORD AND TENANT.

NUISANCE
  Sewer—*Obstruction to flow of river caused by pipe of sewer constructed by local authority beneath river bed but becoming exposed as river bed washed away—Damage to plaintiffs' property from eddies caused—Sewer not out of repair—Whether any breach of duty to plaintiffs by statute or common law established—Covenant, in lease demising sewerage rights, that local authority would not interfere with flow of water in river—Benefit of covenant not assigned to plaintiffs subsequently becoming riparian owners—Statutory powers of sewage disposal overriding lease* [RADSTOCK CO-OPERATIVE & INDUSTRIAL SOCIETY, LTD. *v.* NORTON-RADSTOCK URBAN DISTRICT COUNCIL] 812

NULLITY
  Consent to Marriage—*Fear—Fear must be of sufficient degree to vitiate consent, reasonably entertained and arise from some external circumstance for which petitioner not responsible* [BUCKLAND *v.* BUCKLAND].. 300
  Foreign marriage—*Foreign Marriage Act,* 1892 (c. 23). *See* MARRIAGE (Foreign marriage).

OBSCENE PUBLICATIONS
  See CRIMINAL LAW.

OBSTRUCTION
  Highway, on. *See* HIGHWAY.
  Street. *See* PARLIAMENT (Regulation of traffic).

OFFICIAL SOLICITOR
  Guardian ad litem—*Power to refuse consent to blood test in custody proceedings. See* DIVORCE (Custody—*Paternity of child in issue*).

OPTION
  Hire-purchase agreement—*Option to terminate. See* HIRE-PURCHASE (Termination of agreement).
  Purchase—*Will—Creation of option by testamentary gift—Option to purchase land at reasonable valuation. See* WILL (Option).

ORDER
  Interlocutory. *See* COURT OF APPEAL (Interlocutory appeal—*Leave to appeal*).

ORIGINATING SUMMONS
  Action—*Continuance of proceedings as if begun by writ. See* PRACTICE (Originating summons).
  Declaration—*Hypothetical question. See* DECLARATION (Jurisdiction).

PARLIAMENT
  Regulation of traffic—*Prevention of obstruction of streets in neighbourhood of Parliament—Assemblies—Sessional order of Parliament—Directions issued by the Commissioner of Police of the Metropolis—Validity of directions—Metropolitan Police Act,* 1839 (c. 47), *s.* 52 [PAPWORTH *v.* COVENTRY] 41

PARTIES
  Civil action—*Adding or Substituting. See* PRACTICE (Parties).

PATENT
  Disposition of rights—*Income tax. See* INCOME TAX (Profits—*Computation of profits—Capital receipts—Licences for manufacture of Terylene in foreign countries*).
  Invention—*Breach of confidence—Invention unpatented. See* EQUITY (Confidence—*Breach of confidence*).

PAYMENT
  Appropriation. *See* MORTGAGE (Sale—*Appropriation of proceeds of sale*).

PENALTY
  Hire-purchase agreement. *See* HIRE-PURCHASE.

PENSION
  Damages for personal injuries—*Whether pension taken into account. See* DAMAGES (Measure of damages—*Loss of earnings*).
  Pension scheme—*Endowment assurance—Power for company to select beneficiaries after death of employee. See* TRUST AND TRUSTEE (Uncertainty—*Discretionary trust—Power of selection, bare power not coupled with duty to select*).

PERPETUITIES
  Rule against perpetuities—*Power—Discretion to select beneficiaries. See* TRUST AND TRUSTEE (Uncertainty—*Discretionary trust—Power of selection, bare power not coupled with duty to select*).
  Power of advancement—Conferred by 1948 settlement and exercised by 1957 settlement—Special power of appointment contained in 1957 settlement—Read back into will under which 1948 settlement made—Special power to be exercised " without transgressing the rule against perpetuities "—Invalidity of exercise of power of advancement and of 1957 settlement [Re ABRAHAMS' WILL TRUSTS].. 1175

PERSISTENT IMPORTUNING
  Male person, by. *See* CRIMINAL LAW (Soliciting for immoral purposes).

PERSON OF UNSOUND MIND
  See MENTAL HEALTH.

PERSONAL INJURIES
  Damages. *See* DAMAGES (Measure of damages—*Loss of expectation of life*).

PLANT
  Income tax. *See* INCOME TAX (Allowance).

PLEADING
  Restraint of trade—*Defence. See* TRADE (Restraint of trade—*Pleading*).

PLEDGE
  Sale of goods—*Documents of title to goods sent by unpaid vendors to merchant bankers. See* BANK (Documentary credit—*Irrevocable credit—Selling agents*).

POLICE
Conduct—*Agent provocateur*—*Propriety of practice* [SNEDDON v. STEVENSON] 1277
    Commission of offence to secure evidence against offender—Car used by police officer in such a way as to enable prostitute to solicit—Whether officer using car accomplice for purpose of doctrine of corroboration [SNEDDON v. STEVENSON] 1277
Constable—*Assault on, in execution of duty—Police officers entering garden of house and knocking on front door to inquire about alleged offence—Police sergeant invited inside and leaving when requested to do so by tenant of house—Other officers remaining in garden of house—Assault on police sergeant as he was leaving the house—Other officers coming to sergeant's assistance—Assault on sergeant and officer in general mêlée—Whether officers were trespassers—Implied licence to enter garden and approach front door—Whether officers were acting in execution of duty—Police Act 1964 (c. 48), s. 51* (1) [ROBSON v. HALLETT] 407
Pension—*Damages—Whether pension taken into account when assessing police officer's damages for personal injuries. See* DAMAGES (Measure of damages—*Loss of earnings*).

POSSESSION
Adverse. *See* LIMITATION OF ACTION (Land).
Trespass to land—*Exclusive character of possession. See* TRESPASS TO LAND (Possession).

POWER
Discretionary trust—*Power to select beneficiaries—Perpetuity—Uncertainty. See* TRUST AND TRUSTEE (Uncertainty—*Discretionary trust—Power of selection, bare power not coupled with duty to select*).

POWER OF APPOINTMENT
Delegation of power to make will, as. *See* Exercise—*Special power—Power to will trustees to appoint by way of settlement, post.*
Exercise—*Special power—Power to will trustees to appoint by way of settlement for benefit of testator's son G., his wife and children or remoter issue or for benefit of any such objects and with such ulterior or ultimate trusts as trustees should think fit—Meaning of " ulterior or ultimate trusts "—Whether delegation of testator's power to make a will—Validity* [Re ABRAHAMS' WILL TRUSTS] 1175
Perpetuity. *See* PERPETUITIES (Rule against perpetuities).

PRACTICE
Admiralty. *See* ADMIRALTY.
Appeal—*Respondent's notice. See* COURT OF APPEAL (Respondent's notice).
Compromise. *See* FATAL ACCIDENT (Compromise).
Costs—*Generally. See* COSTS.
Divorce. *See* DIVORCE.
Guardianship of infants. *See* INFANT (Guardianship of Infants Acts).
Interpleader. *See* INTERPLEADER.
Leave to appeal. *See* COURT OF APPEAL (Interlocutory appeal).
Legal aid. *See* LEGAL AID.
Originating summons—*Continuance of proceedings as if begun by writ—Plaintiff seeking inquiry what common rights, and who commoners, were, and declarations regarding compensation fund —Plaintiff uncertain of his own legal position—Action to proceed as if begun by writ so that issues might be clarified—R.S.C., Ord. 28, r. 8* [Re OLD WOOD COMMON COMPENSATION FUND] 1146
Parties—*Adding or substituting party as defendant—Amendment of writ to change defendant from H.E. Co. (Leeds), Ltd. to H.E. Co., Ltd.—Limitation period expired—Whether rule of court permitting amendment was ultra vires—Whether leave to amend was just—Supreme Court of Judicature (Consolidation) Act, 1925 (c. 49), s. 99* (1) (a)—*R.S.C., Ord. 20, r. 5* (2) (3) [MITCHELL v. HARRIS ENGINEERING CO., LTD.].. 682
Rules of court—*Forms prescribed by rules—Note on form inconsistent with order—Time for service of writ prescribed by order inconsistent with note on writ—Order prevails—R.S.C., Ord. 6, r. 1, r. 8* (1), *App. A, forms No. 1, No. 2* [TROW v. IND COOPE (WEST MIDLANDS), LTD.].. 900
Service—*Writ—Duration of period of service. See* TIME (Computation—*Duration of specified period*).
Stay of proceedings—*Company—Action in name of company. See* COMPANY (Investigation by Board of Trade).
    Concurrent proceedings before distinct tribunals—Election by plaintiffs held to be the appropriate course—Factors determining exercise of court's discretion—Material time at which to assess position—Appeal to Minister against planning decision—Application to High Court concurrently for declaration on validity of planning permission—Application for stay of High Court proceedings—Withdrawal of appeal to Minister after argument before High Court and before decision on staying proceedings in High Court—Duplicatiom of proceedings in regard to issue raised in appeal to Minister—Whether abuse of process—Whether discretion to grant stay should be exercised—Supreme Court of Judicature (Consolidation) Act, 1925 (c. 49), s. 41 [SLOUGH ESTATES, LTD. v. SLOUGH BOROUGH COUNCIL] 270
Striking out—*Action—Want of authority. See* COMPANY (Want of authority).
Third party procedure—*Notice—Relief connected with the " original subject-matter of the action "—Specific performance of agreement to sell land to vendors sued for specific performance of their subsequent sale of land—Whether third party notice valid—R.S.C., Ord. 16, r. 1* (1) (b) [STANDARD SECURITIES, LTD. v. HUBBARD] 622
Want of prosecution—*Dismissal of action—Inordinate delay without excuse* [FITZPATRICK v. BATGER & CO., LTD.] 657
Ward of court. *See* WARD OF COURT.

PRE-EMPTION
Creation of right—*Will, by. See* WILL (Option—*Purchase*).

PREMIUM
Clog on equity of redemption. *See* MORTGAGE (Collateral advantage).

PREROGATIVE
Royal prerogative. *See* CROWN.

PRESS AND PRINTING
Manuscript—*Alterations—Licensee, by. See* COPYRIGHT (Licence—*Dramatic work—Alteration*).

PRINCIPAL
  Crime, in. *See* PRIVY COUNCIL (Trinidad and Tobago).
PRIVATE STREET WORKS
  See HIGHWAY (Street).
PRIVILEGE
  Discovery. *See* DISCOVERY (Production of documents).
PRIVY COUNCIL
  Australia—*New South Wales—Transport—Freedom of inter-state trade—Road charge—Provision that owners of certain vehicles having more than a specified load capacity shall pay at a rate per ton per mile towards compensation for wear and tear to public highways—Validity of statute—Constitution of the Commonwealth of Australia, 1900 (c. 12), s. 9, s. 92—Road Maintenance (Contribution) Act, 1958-1965 (N.S.W.)* [FREIGHTLINES AND CONSTRUCTION HOLDING, LTD. *v.* STATE OF NEW SOUTH WALES AND COMMISSIONER OF MOTOR TRANSPORT] 433
  Ceylon—*Judicial officer—President of labour tribunal appointed by Public Service Commission—Order of tribunal for re-instatement of dismissed employee—Validity of order—Whether office of president judicial—Industrial Disputes Act (c. 131), No. 43 of 1950, as amended by Industrial Disputes (Amendment) Act (No. 62 of 1957), s. 31B—Ceylon (Constitution) Order in Council, 1946 (c. 379), s. 55* [UNITED ENGINEERING WORKERS UNION *v.* DEVANAHAGAM] 367
  Public Authority—Quasi-judicial functions—Minister's order superseding municipal council for incompetence—Rule of natural justice—" Audi alteram partem "—No opportunity given to council to be heard in defence—Whether order voidable or a nullity—Voidable only at election of council—Municipal Ordinance (cap. 252), s. 277 (1) [DURAYAPPAH *v.* FERNANDO] .. 152
  Guyana—*Hire-purchase—Warranty—Mill, known to be defective, purchased under hire-purchase agreement—Obligation on owner to remedy defects—Failure to remedy defects—Delivery of mill taken by hire-purchasers—Expenses incurred in installing mill—Measure of damages for breach of contract by failing to remedy mill's defects* [R. P. DOOBAY *v.* MOHABEER].. 760
  Hong Kong—*Architect—Disciplinary board—Board consisting of three authorised architects, the building authority and a legal adviser—Legal adviser having conduct of inquiry—Deliberation of board in private on submissions made on behalf of architect—Rulings given by legal adviser in presence of parties after deliberations concluded—Whether any legal advice given to board by legal adviser must be given in presence of parties and so to appear on the record—Whether breach of rules of natural justice—Hong Kong Buildings Ordinance, 1955 (No. 68 of 1955), s. 5B (2)* [Re CHIEN SING-SHOU] .. 1228
  Estate duty—Appeal from commissioner's decision—Gift inter vivos of shares—Claim for estate duty in respect of shares—Donees not executors of donor's will—No account delivered by donees in respect of shares—Whether condition of appealing that duty should be paid or security be given for it—Hong Kong Estate Duty Ordinance, 1932 (c. 3), s. 19 (1) [MOLLER *v.* COMMISSIONER OF ESTATE DUTY].. 1035
  Jamaica—*Criminal law—Autrefois acquit—Murder—Accused found not guilty of murder and jury not agreed on alternative verdict of manslaughter—Rule that jury entitled not to return a partial verdict obsolete—General verdict of acquittal sufficient to found plea for all alternatives offences—Partial verdict of acquittal sufficient only for crimes in respect of which verdict returned—Jury not entitled to disregard judge's direction for a partial verdict and to return only a general verdict—Whether verdict of jury in this instance was a general verdict* [DIRECTOR OF PUBLIC PROSECUTIONS *v.* NASRALLA].. 161
  Malaysia—*Compensation—Act done for another person—Expenditure on making road to mineral lands—Appellant granted prospector's licence—Agreement by appellant with company for sub-lease of mineral lands to company—Assignments of benefit of agreement vesting benefit in first respondents—Road to mineral lands built by respondents when they were prospectively entitled to mining rights and sub-lease by virtue of assigned agreement—Whether respondents entitled to compensation from appellant for building road, they having ceased to be entitled to the benefit of the agreement—Contract Ordinance, s. 71* [SIOW WONG FATT *v.* SUSUR ROTAN MINING, LTD.] 492
  Elections—Petition—Appeal—Interlocutory order to strike out petition for want of service—Competency of appeal court—No address for service left with registrar by candidate—Advertisement of petition outside time prescribed for service—Whether appeal lay from interlocutory order—Whether rule prescribing time limit for service was mandatory—Election Offences Ordinance (No. 906 of 1954), s. 33 (4), s. 36—Courts of Judicature Act 1964, s. 67, s. 74 [NAIR *v.* TEIK] 34
  Trinidad and Tobago—*Criminal law—Concerted action—Murder—Deceased struck by both appellants in course of quarrel—Uncertainty who struck fatal blow—Common purpose—Principals in first or second degree—Proof of pre-arranged plan unnecessary* [MOHAN *v.* REGINAM] 58
PROBATE
  Action—*Costs—Common fund basis—Defendant seeking to withhold solicitors' bill from taxation in whole or part. See* COSTS (Taxation—*Common fund basis*).
  Exclusion of matter—*Signatures of legatees not intending to witness will. See* WILL (Attestation —*Superfluous signature*).
PRODUCTION
  Documents, of. *See* DISCOVERY (Production of documents).
PROFESSION
  Society—*Rule of conduct—Restraint of trade. See* TRADE (Restraint of trade—*Corporation—Professional society*).
PROFESSIONAL SERVICES
  Gift of—*Whether donor taxable on what he might have charged. See* INCOME TAX (Profits—*Author —Gift of rights in unpublished book to father*).
PROPERTY
  Spes successionis—*Not an interest in property. See* WILL (Gift—*Donee—Person who on death of present Earl should succeed to the earldom*).
PROSECUTION
  Action, of—*Want of. See* PRACTICE (Want of prosecution).
PROSTITUTION
  Soliciting, for the purpose of—*Soliciting, but to procure evidence. See* POLICE (Conduct).
PUBLIC HEALTH
  Water—*Works injuriously affecting water rights. See* NUISANCE (Sewer—*Obstruction to flow of river caused by pipe of sewer constructed by local authority beneath river bed but becoming exposed as river bed washed away*).

PUBLICATION
    Obscene. *See* CRIMINAL LAW (Obscene publications).

PURCHASE TAX
    Evasion—*Conspiracy charges—Shortening trial. See* CRIMINAL LAW (Trial).
        Time limit. See CRIMINAL LAW (Conspiracy—*Continuing single offence*).

QUARTER SESSIONS
    Appeal to—*By " person aggrieved "—Highways Act, 1959 (c. 25), s.* 275 (1). *See* HIGHWAY
        (Street—*Private street works—Appeal to quarter sessions*).
    Direction for trial at assizes—*Jurisdiction under commission of the peace—Indictment first
        preferred at assizes—Accused lawfully indicted and tried—Criminal Justice Act,* 1925 (*c.* 86),
        s. 14 (2) [R. *v.* WILSON] 1088

QUASI-JUDICIAL
    Acting in quasi-judicial capacity. *See* NATURAL JUSTICE (Public Authority).

RACE RELATIONS
    Injunction—*Incitement to racial hatred. See* INJUNCTION (Statute).

RAILWAY
    Mine. *See* MINE (Railway above ground).

RAPE
    See CRIMINAL LAW.

RATES
    Exemption—*Structure—Blind persons' home—Principal building or only annexe or adjunct
        thereof—Institution with main two-storey building—Rating and Valuation (Miscellaneous
        Provisions) Act,* 1955 (*c.* 9), *s.* 9 (1) [ALMOND (VALUATION OFFICER) *v.* BIRMINGHAM ROYAL
        INSTITUTION FOR THE BLIND] 317

REDUNDANCY PAYMENT
    See EMPLOYMENT (Redundancy).

RELATION BACK
    Doctrine, of. *See* DIVORCE (Decree absolute—*Judicial act*).

RENT
    Business premises—*New tenancy. See* LANDLORD AND TENANT (New tenancy—*Business
        premises*).
    Regulated. *See* RENT RESTRICTION (Rent).

RENT RESTRICTION
    Possession—*Succession to statutory tenancy—Tenancy protected by Rent Acts,* 1920-1939 *coming to
        an end before commencement of Rent Act of* 1965—*Widow succeeding as statutory tenant—
        Death of widow before commencement of Act of* 1965—*Claim for possession against child
        resident with widow for over six months before her death—Claim heard after commencement
        of Act of* 1965—*Whether child's occupation protected by Act of* 1965—" Tenancy "—" Regu-
        lated tenancy "—Rent Act* 1965 (*c.* 49), *s.* 20 (1) [BROWN *v.* CONWAY, BAILEY *v.* SPARK,
        HODGSON *v.* GODFREY] 793
    Rateable value—*Evidence—Neighbouring premises* [OSCROFT *v.* BENABO]..   548
    Rent—*Regulated tenancy—Fair rent—Scarcity element—Evidence of capital value not conclusive
        basis of fair rent—Whether rent assessment committee entitled to act on their own knowledge
        in regard to scarcity element—Whether committee bound to notify intention to determine fair
        rent eliminating scarcity element so as to give opportunity for evidence on scarcity to be called
        —Rent Act* 1965 (*c.* 75), *s.* 27 (1), (2) [CROFFTON INVESTMENT TRUST, LTD. *v.* GREATER
        LONDON RENT ASSESSMENT COMMITTEE] 1103

REQUISITION
    Compensation—*Common rights—Procedure. See* PRACTICE (Originating summons—*Continuance
        of proceedings as if begun by writ*).

RES JUDICATA
    Extent—*Issue in action—Administration action—Order for account and inquiry as to defendant's
        indebtedness to estate—Certificate by master of amount due from defendant—Fresh action by
        judicial trustee of estate to recover amount—Application for summary judgment—Defendant
        seeking to raise counterclaim in action that certain assets referred to in certificate were partner-
        ship assets in which he was interested—Claim not made by him at time of taking account—
        Defendant debarred from counterclaiming in action on ground of res judicata* [PUBLIC
        TRUSTEE *v.* KENWARD] 870

RESCISSION
    Contract. *See* CONTRACT.
    Contract for sale of goods. *See* SALE OF GOODS (Unpaid seller—*Re-sale*).

RESCUE
    Liability to rescuer injured. *See* NEGLIGENCE.

RESIDENCE
    Ordinarily resident out of the jurisdiction. *See* COSTS (Security for costs).

RESTRAINT OF TRADE
    Resolution of society. *See* TRADE (Restraint of trade—*Corporation*).

RESTRICTIVE COVENANT
    Trade—*Patent licence to manufacture in foreign country—Covenant by licensor not to manufacture
        there, etc.—Income tax. See* INCOME TAX (Profits—*Computation of profits—Capital receipts
        —Licences for manufacture of Terylene in foreign countries*).

REVENUE
    Selective employment tax. *See* SELECTIVE EMPLOYMENT TAX.

RIOT
    Damage—*Compensation—Four robbers entering shop and threatening occupants—Incident not
        attracting the attention of anyone outside the shop—Whether assembly " tumultuous " as well
        as riotous—Whether police authority liable to pay compensation—Riot (Damages) Act,* 1886
        (*c.* 38), *s.* 2 [J. W. DWYER, LTD. *v.* RECEIVER FOR THE METROPOLITAN POLICE DISTRICT].. 1051

ROAD TRAFFIC
    Disqualification for holding licence—*Life disqualification—Whether for certain period—Road
        Traffic Act,* 1962 (*c.* 59), *s.* 5 [R. *v.* TUNDE-OLARINDE] 491
    Regulation of traffic—*Parliament—Neighbourhood of Parliament. See* PARLIAMENT (Regulation
        of traffic).

ROOF
Building regulations. *See* BUILDING (Building regulations—*Roof*).

ROYAL FORCES
Income tax—*Bounty etc. See* INCOME TAX (Income—*Bounty*).
United Nations—*British troops serving with United Nations force. See* UNITED NATIONS.

ROYAL PREROGATIVE
See CROWN.

RYLANDS v. FLETCHER
Principle of. *See* NEGLIGENCE (Escape).

SAFE SYSTEM OF WORKING
Extent of master's duty—*Duty to give information or advice—Availability of protective clothing —Notice advising workmen of availability and advising him to wear it—Workman unable to read, but master unaware of this—Foundry—Injury from molten metal—Probability that protective clothing would not have been used* [JAMES v. HEPWORTH & GRANDAGE, LTD.] .. 829

SALE OF GOODS
Chain of purchases—*Whether circle of contracts genuine transactions. See* AGENT (Creation of agency—*Agency for entering into contract*).
Damages for breach of contract. *See* CONTRACT (Breach—*Damages*).
Lien—*Vendor's lien—Documents of title to goods sent to merchant bankers—Liquidation of merchant bankers. See* BANK (Documentary credit—*Irrevocable credit—Selling agents*).
Payment—*Letter of credit—Generally. See* BANK (Documentary credit).
Trade description. *See* TRADE MARK (False trade description).
Unpaid seller—*Re-sale—Effect as rescission of contract of sale—Re-sale of part of goods sold— Right to retain proceeds of re-sale—Right to sue for damages for non-acceptance, but not for price—Measure of damages—Sale of Goods Act,* 1893 (c. 71), *s.* 48 (3) [R. V. WARD, LTD. v. BIGNALL] 449

SALE OF LAND
Deposit—*Auction—Deposit received by auctioneer as stake-holder—Bankruptcy of vendor— Purchaser's right to have deposit applied in payment of encumbrances. See* AUCTIONEER (Lien).
Lease—*Contract—Condition—Subject to landlords' consent to assignment being obtained by vendor* [PROPERTY AND BLOODSTOCK, LTD. v. EMERTON. BUSH v. PROPERTY AND BLOODSTOCK, LTD.] 839
Option—*Testamentary and contractual option distinguished—Option to acquire land at reasonable valuation. See* WILL (Option).
Search—*Land charge—Name of estate owner. See* LAND CHARGE (Search).

SECURITY
Injunction—*Cross-undertaking, for. See* COPYRIGHT (Infringement—*Injunction—Interlocutory relief*).

SECURITY FOR COSTS
Action—*High Court. See* COSTS.

SELECTIVE EMPLOYMENT TAX
Refund—*Sub-postmaster employing two women wholly in the handling of money and clerical work—Whether employees engaged in non-qualifying activities carried on for office purposes— Offices, Shops and Railway Premises Act* 1963 (c. 41), *s.* 1 (2)—*Selective Employment Payments Act* 1966 (c. 32), *s.* 2 (2), (*b*) (ii), s. 10 (1) [MINISTER OF LABOUR v. MORGAN] 732

SEPARATION AGREEMENT
See HUSBAND AND WIFE (Separation).

SERVANT
Dismissal—*Redundancy. See* EMPLOYMENT (Redundancy).
Duty of master. *See* MASTER AND SERVANT.
See MASTER AND SERVANT.

SERVICE
Contract of. *See* MASTER AND SERVANT.
Divorce. *See* DIVORCE (Practice).
Writ. *See* TIME (Computation—*Duration of specified period*).

SETTLEMENT
Trust—*Discretionary trust—Uncertainty—Perpetuity. See* TRUST AND TRUSTEE (Uncertainty— *Discretionary trust*).
Variation of trusts—*Court's approval sought under Variation of Trusts Act,* 1958, *s.* 1. *See* TRUST AND TRUSTEE (Variation of trusts by the court).

SEWER
Nuisance—*Obstruction by pipe of sewer in river bed. See* NUISANCE (Sewer).

SHAM
Contract—*Circle of contracts. See* AGENT (Creation of agency—*Agency for entering into contract*).

SHARE
Company, in. *See* COMPANY (Shares).

SHERIFF
Interpleader. *See* INTERPLEADER.

SHIPPING
Collision—*Apportionment of liability—Differentiation between vessels involved not possible— Whether appellate court would interfere with decision* [THE LUCILE BLOOMFIELD] 633

SHOCK
Mental shock—*Damages. See* DAMAGES (Remoteness of damage).

SHOP
Sunday closing—*Garage—Lawful opening for sale of motor or cycle supplies or accessories— Information given about motor cars to potential customer—Isolated transaction—Shops Act,* 1950 (c. 28), *s.* 47 [MONACO GARAGE, LTD. v. WATFORD BOROUGH COUNCIL] 1291

SOCIETY
Incorporated—*Resolution in restraint of trade. See* TRADE (Restraint of trade—*Corporation*).

SOLICITING
Soliciting, but to procure evidence against offender. *See* POLICE (Conduct).
See CRIMINAL LAW (Soliciting for immoral purposes).

SOLICITOR
Assistant solicitor—*Agreement for employment by solicitor—Duty to serve solicitor with good faith and fidelity—Breach.* *See* MASTER AND SERVANT (Duty of servant).
Costs—*Client seeking to withhold bill from taxation on common fund basis in whole or part.* *See* COSTS (Taxation—*Common fund basis*).
Lien—*Costs.* *See* COSTS (Taxation—*Common fund basis*).

SPECIFIC PERFORMANCE
Annuity—*Agreement to pay—Contract for sale of business—Annuity to widow of seller—Widow not party to contract—Business transferred—Death of seller—Widow obtained letters of administration—Whether widow entitled to enforce payment of annuity specifically* [BESWICK v. BESWICK] 1197
Third party procedure—*Vendor defendant seeking specific performance of agreement to sell land to him.* *See* PRACTICE (Third party procedure—*Notice*).

SPES SUCCESSIONIS
Property—*Not an interest in property.* *See* WILL (Gift—*Donee—Person who on death of present Earl should succeed to the earldom*).

STATUTE
Ambiguity—*Contractual rights not taken away—Employer not penalised.* See CONTRACT, *post*.
Construction—*Consolidating statute—Definition—"Unless the context otherwise requires"—Exclusion of application of definition which would effect alteration of the law consolidated—Law of Property Act, 1925 (c. 20), s. 205 (1) (xx)* [BESWICK v. BESWICK] 1197
Mandatory or directory provision—Election petition rule—Time for service of notice of presentation of petition. *See* PRIVY COUNCIL (Malaysia—*Elections—Petition*).
Contract—*Contractual rights taken away—Words must not be ambiguous* [ALLEN v. THORN ELECTRICAL INDUSTRIES, LTD. GRIFFIN v. RECEIVER FOR THE METROPOLITAN POLICE DISTRICT] 1137
Definition. *See* Construction—*Consolidating statute, ante*.
No certiorari clause. *See* CERTIORARI (Jurisdiction—*Principle—Statutory tribunal's decision*).
Offence—*Injunction against contravention of statute.* *See* INJUNCTION (Statute).

STATUTORY DUTY
Breach—*Causation—Accident solely plaintiff's fault* [LANE v. GLOUCESTER ENGINEERING CO., LTD.] 293
Plaintiff's sole fault. *See* BUILDING (Building regulations—*Roof—Roof work—Fragile materials covering roof—Fall through hole in roof under repair*).

STATUTORY INSTRUMENT
Form prescribed by rules of court—*Inconsistency between note on form and terms or rule—Which should prevail.* *See* PRACTICE (Rules of court—*Forms prescribed by rules*).
Ultra vires—*Rules of court—Power of Rules Committee—Practice and procedure.* *See* PRACTICE (Parties—*Adding or substituting party as defendant*).

STAY OF PROCEEDINGS
Action—*Want of authority.* *See* COMPANY (Investigation by Board of Trade).
High Court. *See* PRACTICE.
Winding-up of company. *See* COMPANY (Winding-up—*Compulsory winding-up*).

STREET
Generally. *See* HIGHWAY (Street).

SUNDAY CLOSING
Shop. *See* SHOP.

SURTAX
Investment company—*Apportionments and sub-apportionments—Notice of sub-apportionments —Failure to give notice of sub-apportionments to company given surtax direction—Effect—Income Tax Act, 1952 (c. 10), s. 248 (1), (2), (3), s. 254 (3), (4), (5)* [PRINCES INVESTMENTS, LTD. v. INLAND REVENUE COMRS. CLORE v. INLAND REVENUE COMRS.] 238
Tax advantage—*Counteracting—Transaction in connexion with distribution of profits—Phrase including transfer of assets of company—Advantage by receipt of sum as capital instead of dividends—Shareholders' sale of other company's shares to company—Avoidance of surtax—Finance Act, 1960 (c. 44), s. 28 (1), (2) (d), s. 43 (4) (g)* [CLEARY v. INLAND REVENUE COMRS.] 48
Undistributed income—*Direction and apportionment—Apportionment of actual income of relevant year—Actual income meaning income actually received—Sub-apportionment of excess of apportioned sum over "actual income from all sources" of company—Dividend received in relevant year, but appropriated in accounts of prior year to other purposes, not deductible in computing excess—Income Tax Act, 1952 (c. 10), s. 245, s. 254 (1)* [PRINCESS INVESTMENTS, LTD. v. INLAND REVENUE COMRS. CLORE v. INLAND REVENUE COMRS.] 238

SURVIVORSHIP
Survive—*Meaning.* *See* WILL (" Survive ").

TAX ADVANTAGE
See SURTAX.

TELEVISION
Licence to televise copyright play. *See* COPYRIGHT (Licence—*Dramatic work*).

TENANCY
Grant. *See* LANDLORD AND TENANT (Tenancy).
New tenancy under Landlord and Tenant Act, 1954. *See* LANDLORD AND TENANT (New tenancy).
Regulated—*Rent.* *See* RENT RESTRICTION (Rent).

THIRD PARTY PROCEDURE
Appeal—*Respondent's notice—Service on third party.* *See* COURT OF APPEAL (Respondent's notice).
High Court. *See* PRACTICE.

TIME

Appeal, for. *See* DIVORCE (Appeal—*Divisional Court—Appeal from order of magistrates' court—Time for appealing—Extension of time*).

Computation—*Duration of specified period—Period " beginning with the date of . . ."—Writ of summons issued on Sept. 10, 1965, and served on Sept. 10, 1966—Validity of writ for the purpose of service for twelve months beginning with the date of its issue—Whether service out of time—R.S.C., Ord. 6, r. 8* (1) [TROW *v.* IND COOPE (WEST MIDLANDS), LTD.] ..   900

Judicial act—*Relation back. See* DIVORCE (Decree absolute—Judicial act).

TORT

Abroad—*Damages. See* CONFLICT OF LAWS (Tort—*Damages*).

Intimidation—*Unlawful acts—Threat to induce breaches of contracts of service. See* TRADE UNION (Inducement to commit breach of contract).

TOWN AND COUNTRY PLANNING

Appeals. *See* Development—*Permission for development, post.*

Development—*Appeal to Minister—Concurrent High Court proceedings. See* PRACTICE (Stay of proceedings—*Concurrent proceedings before distinct tribunals*). .

Permission for development—*Appeal—Appeal to Minister—" Findings of fact " by inspector accepted by Minister, but not inspector's " conclusions " or recommendation—No opportunity afforded to applicant to make further representations—Appeal dismissed by Minister—Application to quash Minister's decision—Whether inspector's conclusions were also findings of fact—Town and Country Planning Appeals (Inquiries Procedure) Rules 1965 (S.I. 1965 No. 473), r. 12* (2) [LORD LUKE OF PAVENHAM *v.* MINISTER OF HOUSING AND LOCAL GOVERNMENT]   1066

Determination whether permission needed—*Application for determination—Implicit in application for planning permission—Letter of local planning authority that proposed erection of plant could be regarded as permitted development sufficient determination—Bye-law consent granted subsequently for larger plant—Warning against acting on bye-law consent before planning approval deleted from consent form—Whether deletion on bye-law consent amounted to determination that planning permission not required—Town and Country Planning Act, 1962 (c. 38), s. 43* (1) [WELLS *v.* MINISTER OF HOUSING AND LOCAL GOVERNMENT]..   1041

Enforcement notice—*Service—" Owner " of land—Notice served on husband of freeholder—Land used for parking cars—Business of parking cars carried on by husband and wife jointly—Control of business in hands of husband—Husband described himself as owner when applying for planning permission—Whether service on husband sufficient—Whether enforcement notice enforceable—Town and Country Planning Act, 1962 (c. 38), s. 45* (3), *s. 47* (5), *s. 221* [COURTNEY-SOUTHAN *v.* CRAWLEY URBAN DISTRICT COUNCIL]   246

Owner—*Definition of " owner " of land—Town and Country Planning Act, 1962 (c. 38), s. 221* [COURTNEY-SOUTHAN *v.* CRAWLEY URBAN DISTRICT COUNCIL]   246

Permission for development. *See* Development—*Permission for development, ante.*

TRADE

Description—*False trade description. See* TRADE MARK (False trade description).

Restrain of trade—*Corporation—Professional society—Resolution restraining trading activities of members—Need to establish reasonableness—Reasonableness in interests of members and of public—Reasonableness in interests of members and reasonableness in interests of public not established* [DICKSON *v.* THE PHARMACEUTICAL SOCIETY OF GREAT BRITAIN]   558

Pleading—*Justifying circumstances to be pleaded in defence* [DICKSON *v.* THE PHARMACEUTICAL SOCIETY OF GREAT BRITAIN] ..   558

TRADE MARK

False trade description—*Application—Time of application—" Cause " to apply false trade description to goods—Manufacturer sold goods to retailer in August—Goods displayed by retailer in December and sold—Goods then short in volume or weight—Falsity of trade description at time when manufacturer applied it not proved—Whether false trade description applied at time of sale by retailer—Whether manufacturer caused retailer to apply false trade description—Merchandise Marks Act, 1887 (c. 28), s. 2* (1) [SHULTON (GREAT BRITAIN), LTD. *v.* SLOUGH BOROUGH COUNCIL] ..   137

TRADE UNION

Conspiracy—*Motive—Legitimate protection of interests of trade union. Furtherance of trade dispute—Trade Disputes Act, 1906 (c. 47), s. 5* [MORGAN *v.* FRY]   386

Inducement to commit breach of contract—*Unlawful means—Absence of justification—Threats to call strike—No express prohibition of strikes in contract of employment—Threats made to procure dismissal from employment of plaintiff who had resigned from union—Plaintiff dismissed as result of threats—Whether strike notice would lawfully have terminated employment—Whether implied term in contract permitting strikes—Whether union officers liable for conspiracy or intimidation—Trade Disputes Act, 1906 (c. 47), s. 3* [MORGAN *v.* FRY] ..   386

Trade dispute—*Break-away union. See* Conspiracy—*Motive, ante.*

TRESPASS TO GOODS

Conversion. *See* CARRIERS (Contract).

TRESPASS TO LAND

Police—*Entry through unlocked garden gate to visit house and make enquiries—Implied licence. See* POLICE (Constable—*Assault on, in execution of duty*).

Possession—*Sea-bed—Concurrent possession by persons having moorings placed in sea-bed—Whether exclusive possession necessary to sustain action* [FOWLEY MARINE (EMSWORTH), LTD. *v.* GAFFORD] ..   472

TRIBUNAL

Jurisdiction—*Error going to jurisdiction. See* CERTIORARI (Jurisdiction—*Principle—Statutory tribunal's decision*).

TRUST AND TRUSTEE

Breach of trust—*Mixing trust moneys with trustee's own money—Rights of Beneficiaries—Trust moneys forming part of deceased's estate paid into trustee's (his widow's) own bank account—Overdraft facilities accorded by bank to widow for property dealings—Liabilities of deceased's estate met by widow out of her own moneys—Whether beneficiary in deceased's estate entitled to a share of the profit from widow's property dealings* [Re TILLEY'S WILL TRUSTS] ..   303

Creation of trust—*Acceptance of bequest conditional on bequeathing own property on trusts of donor's will—Trust arising on acceptance of condition* [Re HARMSWORTH (decd.)] ..   249

TRUST AND TRUSTEE—*continued*

Powers of trustee—*Advancement—Estate duty. See* ESTATE DUTY (Determination of life interest —*Discretionary trust—Accumulation of surplus income*).

Uncertainty—*Discretionary trust—Power of selection, bare power not coupled with duty to select— Class of beneficiaries including persons considered to have moral claim on deceased—Impracticability of ascertaining beneficiaries—Power exercisable on several occasions and thus possibly beyond perpetuity limit—Whether void for uncertainty or perpetuity—Trust of proceeds of endowment assurance under pension scheme—Whether resulting trust for deceased* [Re LEEK (decd.)] 1160

Variation of trusts by the court—*Settlor's application—Extension of trust for accumulation in view of possibility of settlor's death terminating trust for accumulation—Deletion of power to provide fund which might be available for meeting liability of settlor for surtax—Variation of Trusts Act, 1958 (c. 53), s. 1* [Re LLOYD'S SETTLEMENT] 314

TUMULT

See RIOT (Damage—*Compensation—Theft*).

TURQUAND'S CASE

Rule in. *See* COMPANY (Director—*Authority—Ostensible authority*).

ULTRA VIRES

Rules made under statute. *See* PRACTICE (Parties—*Adding or substituting party as defendant— Amendment of writ, etc.*).

Traffic regulations. *See* PARLIAMENT (Regulation of traffic).

UNCERTAINTY

Condition—*Will. See* WILL (Condition—*Certainty*).

UNITED NATIONS

Peace-keeping force established pursuant to resolution of Security Council—*British contingents of United Nations Force—Whether acting on behalf of Crown* [NISSAN v. ATTORNEY-GENERAL] 1238

VALUATION

Option—*Purchase—Option to purchase land at reasonable valuation. See* WILL (Option—*Purchase*).

VERDICT

Jury, of. *See* JURY.

Types of verdict—*General, partial and special verdicts. See* PRIVY COUNCIL (Jamaica—*Criminal law—Autrefois acquit*).

Unanimity. *See* CRIMINAL LAW (Trial—*Jury—Direction to jury*).

WARD OF COURT

Jurisdiction—*Alien children—Child, a girl of seven subject to custody order of foreign court, removed from jurisdiction of that court and brought to England—Custody of child previously taken from mother by foreign court and given to father—Father killed in motor accident— Child willingly making her home with father's sister in England—Temporary custody of child awarded by foreign court to mother after father's death—Comity—Special circumstances —Whether care and control of child, made a ward of court in England, should be given to father's sister* [Re E. (an infant)] 881

Previous order of magistrates under Guardianship of Infants Acts, 1886 and 1925, giving custody to father—Children then in charge of local authority under fit person order—Originating summons issued by mother to make children wards of court—Exercise by magistrates of their statutory jurisdiction did not fetter prerogative jurisdiction of High Court—Forum conveniens—Magistrates' order should be reconsidered in magistrates' court unless relief was sought which the magistrates were unable to give—On application to High Court under wardship jurisdiction court would enquire whether magistrates were able to give the relief sought [Re P. (infants)] 229

Practice—*Evidence—By statements exhibited to affidavits* [PRACTICE DIRECTION].. 299

WAREHOUSEMAN

Security patrol—*Whether warehouseman liable for negligence of patrolman employed by independent contractor. See* INDEPENDENT CONTRACTOR (Negligence).

WARRANTY

Breach—*Damages—Hire-purchase—Goods with known defects. See* PRIVY COUNCIL (Guyana—*Hire-purchase—Warranty*).

WATER AND WATERCOURSES

Navigation—*Laying and maintenance of permanent moorings—Whether an ordinary incident of navigation—Whether common law right exists to lay such mooring in the land of another person* [FOWLEY MARINE (EMSWORTH), LTD. v. GAFFORD] 472

Nuisance—*Obstruction to flow of water. See* NUISANCE (Sewer).

WEIGHTS AND MEASURES

Bread—*Weight—" Possession for sale "—Loaves in dispatch area of bakery deficient in weight— Stale bread not for sale also in dispatch area—Notice displayed that no bread was for sale till passed by bread dispatch supervisor—Whether bread in dispatch area that had not been so passed was in possession for sale—Weights and Measures Act* 1963 (c. 31), s. 22 (2) (a) [BEN WORSLEY, LTD. v. HARVEY] 507

Mark stating weight—*False. See* TRADE MARK (False trade description).

WIDOW

Annuity—*Sale of Husband's business—Whether enforceable against purchaser of business when widow not party to contract. See* CONTRACT (Stranger to contract—*Annuitant*).

Provision for, under Inheritance (Family Provision) Act, 1938. *See* FAMILY PROVISION.

Statutory tenancy—*Succession to statutory tenancy on death. See* RENT RESTRICTION (Possession —*Succession to statutory tenancy*).

WIFE

Maintenance—*Divorce. See* DIVORCE (Maintenance of wife).

Summary jurisdiction. *See* MAGISTRATES (Husband and wife—*Maintenance*).

Services—*Loss of wife's services—Damages. See* HUSBAND AND WIFE (Consortium—*Damages*).

WILL

Attestation—*Superfluous signature—Intention with which signature affixed—Will signed by four persons below word " witnessed "—Top two signatures those of testator's two daughters who were his sole residuary legatees—Evidence that other two persons signed first as witnesses, and daughters' signed also at testator's request to make will stronger—Probate without daughters' signatures [In the Estate of* BRAVDA *(decd.)]* 1233

Condition—*Certainty—Condition precedent—Power of appointment exercisable by trustees in event of testator's son G. " becoming engaged to be married to a person professing the Jewish faith "—G. married lady whom trustees considered to profess Jewish faith—Exercise of power of appointment so as to settle whole of G.'s share in testator's residuary estate [*RE ABRAHAMS' WILL TRUSTS] 1175

Conditional bequest—Annuitant to bequeath half her own property on trusts of testator's will—Acceptance of conditional annuity—Date when trust of annuitant's own property arose [Re HARMSWORTH *(decd.)]* 249

Forfeiture—Proviso for forfeiture of share of testator's residuary estate if not " member of the Church of England or some Church abroad professing the same tenets "—Proviso not void for uncertainty—Methodist Church of Australia not a church abroad professing same tenets as Church of England [Re MILLS' WILL TRUSTS] 193

Delegation of power to make will—*Whether power to trustees to settle share of residuary estate amounted to such delegation. See* POWER OF APPOINTMENT (Exercise—*Special power—Power to will trustees to appoint by way of settlement*).

Gift—*Donee—Person who on death of present Earl should succeed to the earldom—Heir presumptive had no interest in property so given [Re* EARL OF MIDLETON'S WILL TRUSTS] 834

Heir—*Bequest to. See* Gift—*Donee—Person who on death of present Earl should succeed to the earldom, ante.*

Lapse—*Statutory exception from lapse—Residuary bequest to illegitimate child—Legitimation and death of child leaving issue before death of testatrix—Whether estate of legitimate child entitled to make gift—Wills Act, 1837 (c. 26), s. 33—Legitimacy Act, 1926 (c. 60), s. 3 [Re* BRODIE *(decd.)]* 97

Option—*Purchase—Gift of option to purchase land at reasonable valuation—No express reference in will to trustees fixing what the price should be—Whether option valid—Inquiry to be held to fix reasonable price [*TALBOT v. TALBOT] 920

Pre-emption—*Creation of right. See* Option, *ante.*

" Survive "—*Gift to such of children of granddaughter as shall survive testator—Testator eighty years old at date of will—Granddaughter married for five years at that time—One child born in his lifetime and living after his death, others born after his death [Re* ALSOPP *(decd.)]* .. 1056

Uncertainty—*Option. See* Option, *ante.*

Witness. *See* Attestation, *ante.*

WINDING-UP

Company, of. *See* COMPANY.

WITNESS

Expert—*Psychiatrist—Effect of publication on children. See* CRIMINAL LAW (Obscene publications —*Evidence*).

Summons—*Setting aside witness summons. See* CERTIORARI (Justices—*Witness summons*).

WRIT

Admiralty—*Writ in rem. See* ADMIRALTY (Practice—*Appearance*).

Service. *See* TIME (Computation—*Duration of specified period*).

CASES NOTED

PAGE

A. v. A. and H. ([1962] 2 All E.R. 573; [1962] P. 196; [1962] 3 W.L.R. 212). *Considered in* Inglis
v. Inglis and Baxter 71
A.B.C. Coupler and Engineering Co., Ltd. (No. 2), Re, ([1962] 3 All E.R. 68; [1962] 1 W.L.R. 1236).
Not followed in Re Travel & Holiday Clubs, Ltd. 606
A.-H. (infants), Re ([1962] 3 All E.R. 853; [1963] Ch. 232; [1962] 3 W.L.R. 1430). *Distinguished*
in Re L. 1110
Aberfoyle Plantations, Ltd. v. Cheng ([1959] 3 All E.R. 910; [1960] A.C. 115; [1959] 3 W.L.R.
1011). *Considered and distinguished in* Property and Bloodstock, Ltd. v. Emerton 839
Allen (*decd.*), Re ([1953] 2 All E.R. 898; [1953] Ch. 810; [1953] 3 W.L.R. 637). *Applied in* Re
Abrahams' Will Trusts 1175
—— ([1953] 2 All E.R. 901; [1953] Ch. 817; [1953] 3 W.L.R. 940). *Observations of* SIR RAYMOND
EVERSHED, M.R., *applied in* Re Leek (*decd.*).. 1160
Almond (Valuation Officer) v. Birmingham Royal Institution for the Blind [(1966] 1 All E.R. 602;
[1966] 2 Q.B. 395; [1966] 2 W.L.R. 374). *Affirmed.* H.L... 317
Andrews (infants), Re [(1958) 2 All E.R. 308; [1958] Ch. 665; [1958] 2 W.L.R. 946). *Followed in*
Re P. (infants) 229
——. *Distinguished in* Re L... 1110
Andrews v. Andrews and Sullivan ([1958] 2 All E.R. 305; [1958] P. 217; [1958] 2 W.L.R. 942).
Distinguished in Re L 1110
A.-G. v. De Keyser's Royal Hotel, Ltd. ([1920] All E.R. Rep. 80; [1920] A.C. 508; 89 L.J.Ch. 417;
122 L.T. 691). *Followed in* Nissan v. Attorney-General 1238
Auten v. Rayner ([1958] 3 All E.R. 566; [1958] 1 W.L.R. 1300). *Followed in* Conway v. Rimmer .. 1260
Bailey v. Purser ([1967] 1 All E.R. 188; [1967] 2 W.L.R. 146). *Affirmed.* C.A. 189
Banbury v. Bank of Montreal ([1918-19] All E.R. Rep. 1; [1918] A.C. 626; 87 L.J.K.B. 1158;
119 L.T. 446). *Applied in* W. B. Anderson & Sons, Ltd. v. Rhodes (Liverpool), Ltd. 850
Benham v. Gambling ([1941] 1 All E.R. 7; [1941] A.C. 157; 110 L.J.K.B. 49; 164 L.T. 290).
Followed in Yorkshire Electricity Board v. Naylor 1
Beswick v. Beswick ([1966] 3 All E.R. 1; [1966] Ch. 538, [1966] 3 W.L.R. 396). *Affirmed.* H.L. .. 1197
Boston v. W. S. Bagshaw & Sons, Ltd. ([1967] 2 All E.R. 87; [1966] 1 W.L.R. 1136, 1137). *Dicta*
of LORD DENNING, M.R., *and* HARMAN, L.J., *applied in* R. v. Roads 84
Bradlaugh, *Ex p.* ((1878) 3 Q.B.D. 509; 47 L.J.M.C. 105; 38 L.T. 680). *Considered in* Anisminic,
Ltd. v. The Foreign Compensation Commission.. 986
Braman v. Peek ([1947] 2 All E.R. 572; [1948] 1 K.B. 68; [1948] L.J.R. 405). *Considered in*
Sneddon v. Stevenson 1277
Bridge v. Campbell Discount Co., Ltd. ([1962] 1 All E.R. 385; [1962] A.C. 600; [1962] 2 W.L.R.
439). *Applied in* United Dominions Trusts (Commercial), Ltd. v. Ennis. 345
Browning v. War Office ([1962] 3 All E.R. 1089; [1963] 1 Q.B. 750; [1963] 2 W.L.R. 52). *Applied*
in Parry v. Cleaver 1168
Bulmer, Re, *Ex p.* Johnson ((1853), 22 L.J. Bcy. 65; 21 L.T.O.S. 109). *Followed in* Re William
Hall (Contractors), Ltd... 1150
Burmah Oil Co. (Burma Trading), Ltd. v. Lord Advocate ([1964] 2 All E.R. 348; [1965] A.C. 75;
[1964] 2 W.L.R. 1231). *Considered in* Nissan v. Attorney-General.. 200
——. *Followed in* Nissan v. Attorney-General 1238
Burston v. Inland Revenue Comrs. (No. 2) ([1945] 1 All E.R. 687). *Not followed in* Princes Invest-
ments, Ltd. v. Inland Revenue Comrs... 238
Bush, Beach & Gent, Ltd. v. Road ([1939] 3 All E.R. 302; [1939] 2 K.B. 524; 108 L.J.K.B. 801;
161 L.T. 117). *Applied in* Sommerfelds, Ltd. v. Freeman (Inspector of Taxes) 143
Campbell v. Inland Revenue Comrs. ([1966] 2 All E.R. 736; [1966] Ch. 439; [1966] 2 W.L.R.
1448). *Affirmed.* C.A. 625
Carrington v. John Summers & Sons, Ltd. ([1957] 1 All E.R. 457; [1957] 1 W.L.R. 504). *Approved*
in British Railways Board v. Liptrot 1072
Carter-Fey ([1894] 2 Ch. 541; 63 L.J.Ch. 723; 70 L.T. 786). *Applied in* Des Salles d'Epinoix v.
Des Salles d'Epinoix 539
Chancery Lane Safe Deposit and Offices Co., Ltd. v. Inland Revenue Comrs. ([1966] 1 All E.R. 1;
[1966] A.C. 85; [1966] 2 W.L.R. 251). *Applied in* Princes Investments, Ltd. v. Inland Revenue
Comrs. 238
Charterhouse Credit Co., Ltd. v. Tolly ([1963] 2 All E.R. 432; [1963] 2 Q.B. 683; [1963] 2 W.L.R.
1168). *Applied in* R. P. Doobay v. Mohabeer 760
Cherry v. International Alloys, Ltd. ([1960] 3 All E.R. 264; [1961] 1 Q.B. 136; [1960] 3 W.L.R.
568). *Overruled in* British Railways Board v. Liptrot 1072
Chichester v. Chichester ([1936] 1 All E.R. 273; [1936] P. 133; 105 L.J.P. 41; 154 L.T. 377).
Principle stated by SIR BOYD MERRIMAN, P., *applied in* Foard v. Foard 660
Christiansborg, The ((1885) 10 P.D. 148; 53 L.T. 615). *Dicta of* LORD ESHER, M.R., *applied in*
Slough Estates, Ltd. v. Slough Borough Council 270
Clifford and O'Sullivan, Re ([1921] 2 A.C. 570; 90 L.J.P.C. 244; 126 L.T. 97). *Distinguished in*
R. v. Criminal Injuries Compensation Board, *Ex parte* Lain 770
Cohen v. West Ham Corpn. ([1933] All E.R. Rep. 24; [1933] Ch. 814; 102 L.J.Ch. 305; 149 L.T.
271). *Considered in* London Borough of Hillingdon v. Cutler 361
Cohen's Will Trusts, Re ([1936] 1 All E.R. 103). *Distinguished in* Re Leek (*decd.*) 1160
Connelly v. Director of Public Prosecutions ([1964] 2 All E.R. 412; [1964] A.C. 1305; [1964] 2
W.L.R. 1157). *Dictum of* LORD MORRIS OF BORTH-Y-GEST *considered and explained in* Director
of Public Prosecutions v. Nasralla 161
Cook v. Whellock ((1890) 24 Q.B.D. 658; 59 L.J.Q.B. 329; 62 L.T. 675). *Distinguished in* Semler
v. Murphy 185
Cooper v. Wandsworth Board of Works ((1863), 32 L.J.C.P. 185; 8 L.T. 279). *Applied in* Dura-
yappah v. Fernando 152
Corfe v. Corfe ([1960] 1 All E.R. 593; [1960] 1 W.L.R. 201). *Distinguished in* Inglis v. Inglis
and Baxter 71
Danish Mercantile Co., Ltd. v. Beaumont ([1951] 1 All E.R. 929; [1951] Ch. 686). *Dictum of*
JENKINS, L.J., *considered in* S.B.A. Properties, Ltd. v. Cradock 610
Davies v. Price ([1958] 1 All E.R. 671; [1958] 1 W.L.R. 434). *Applied in* Anisminic, Ltd. v. The
Foreign Compensation Commission 986
Day v. Singleton ([1899] 2 Ch. 320; 68 L.J.Ch. 593; 81 L.T. 306). *Applied in* Property and Blood-
stock, Ltd. v. Emerton 839
Denaby and Cadeby Main Collieries, Ltd. v. Anson ([1911] 1 K.B. 201, 202; 80 L.J.K.B. 334;
103 L.T. 355. *Dicta of* FLETCHER MOULTON, L.J., *followed in* Fowley Marine (Emsworth),
Ltd. v. Gafford 472

PAGE

Deutsche National Bank v. Paul ([1898] 1 Ch. 283; 67 L.J.Ch. 156; 78 L.T. 35). *Considered in*
Eastern Holdings Establishment of Vaduz v. Singer & Friedlander, Ltd... 1192
Dickson v. The Pharmaceutical Society of Great Britain ([1966] 3 All E.R. 404; [1966] 1 W.L.R.
1539). *Affirmed.* C.A. 558
Dietz v. Lennig Chemicals, Ltd. ([1966] 2 All E.R. 962; [1966] 1 W.L.R. 1349). *Affirmed.* H.L. 282
Donaghey v. P. O'Brien & Co. ([1966] 2 All E.R. 822; [1966] 1 W.L.R. 1170). *Reversed.* H.L. 1014
Donmar Productions, Ltd. v. Bart ([1967] 2 All E.R. 338). *Followed in* Harman Pictures, N.V. v.
Osborne 324
Drive Yourself Hire Co. (London), Ltd. v. Strutt ([1953] 2 All E.R. 1475; [1954] 1 Q.B. 250;
[1953] 3 W.L.R. 1111). *Dicta of* LORD DENNING, M.R., *disapproved in* Beswick v. Beswick .. 1197
Dulieu v. White & Sons ([1900-03] All E.R. Rep. 353; [1901] 2 K.B. 669; 70 L.J.K.B. 837; 85
L.T. 126). *Considered in* Chadwick v. British Transport Commission 945
Duncan v. Cammell Laird & Co., Ltd. ([1942] 1 All E.R. 587; [1942] A.C. 624; 111 L.J.K.B. 406;
166 L.T. 366). *Followed in* Conway v. Rimmer 1260
Dunn v. Chapman ([1920] 2 Ch. 474; 89 L.J.Ch. 385; 123 L.T. 415). *Distinguished in* Oak Co-
operative Building Society v. Blackburn 340
E. (an infant), Re ([1967] 1 All E.R. 329; [1967] 2 W.L.R. 445). *Affirmed.* C.A. 881
Elliott v. Joicey ([1935] All E.R. Rep. 582; [1935] A.C. 218; 104 L.J.Ch. 115; sub nom. Re
Joicey, 152 L.T. 400). *Dictum of* LORD RUSSELL OF KILLOWEN *considered in* Re Alsopp (decd.) 1056
Ellis v. Deheer ([1922] All E.R. Rep. 452; [1922] 2 K.B. 118; 91 L.J.K.B. 938; 121 L.T. 432).
Dicta of BANKES, L.J., *applied in* R. v. Roads 84
Ellis v. Rogers ((1885), 29 Ch.D. 661; 53 L.T. 377). *Applied in* Property and Bloodstock, Ltd. v.
Emerton 839
Emden v. Carte ((1881), 19 Ch.D. 318; 51 L.J.Ch. 374; 45 L.T. 330). *Dictum of* SIR GEORGE
JESSEL, M.R., *considered in* Re Fuld (decd.) 649
Engelbach's Estate, Re ([1923] All E.R. Rep. 93; [1924] Ch. 348; 93 L.J.Ch. 616; 130 L.T. 401).
Disapproved in Beswick v. Beswick 1197
Eyre, Re ((1883), 49 L.T. 259). *Followed in* Re Abraham's Will Trusts.. 1175
Fairplay XIV, The ([1939] P. 57; 108 L.J.P. 65). *Considered in* The Gniezno.. 738
Field v. Metropolitan Police Receiver ([1904-07] All E.R. Rep. 435; [1907] 2 K.B. 853; 76 L.J.K.B.
1015; 97 L.T. 639). *Considered in* J. W. Dwyer, Ltd. v. Receiver for the Metropolitan Police
District 1051
Fisher v. Taylors Furnishing Stores, Ltd. ([1956] 2 All E.R. 84; [1956] 2 Q.B. 92; [1956] 2 W.L.R.
994). *Dicta of* PARKER, L.J., *applied in* Little Park Service Station, Ltd. v. Regent Oil Co., Ltd 257
Flint v. Lovell ([1934] All E.R. Rep. 202, 203; [1935] 1 K.B. 360; 104 L.J.K.B. 202; 152 L.T.
233). *Dictum of* GREER, L.J., *applied in* Yorkshire Electricity Board v. Naylor 1
Forster v. Elvet Colliery Co., Ltd. ([1908] 1 K.B. 629). *Applied in* Beswick v. Beswick 1197
Foster, Re ([1938] 3 All E.R. 357; 158 L.T. 279). *Dicta of* CROSSMAN, J., *approved in* Beswick v.
Beswick 1197
Foster, Re, Ex p. Dickin ((1875), L.R. 20 Eq. 767; 44 L.J.Bcy. 113; 33 L.T. 37). *Followed in* Re
William Hall (Contractors), Ltd. 1150
Foster v. Warblington Urban District Council ([1904-07] All E.R. Rep. 366; [1906] 1 K.B. 648;
75 L.J.K.B. 514; 94 L.T. 876). *Followed in* Fowley Marine (Emsworth), Ltd. v. Gafford .. 472
Fox & Jacobs, Re, Ex p. Discount Banking Co. of England and Wales (1894) 1 Q.B. 438; 63 L.J.Q.B.
191; 69 L.T. 657). *Followed in* Re William Hall (Contractors), Ltd. 1150
Freeman & Lockyer v. Buckhurst Park Properties (Mangal), Ltd. ([1964] 1 All E.R. 630; [1964]
2 Q.B. 480; [1964] 2 W.L.R. 618). *Followed in* Hely-Hutchinson v. Brayhead, Ltd. 14
Gallagher v. Shilcock ([1949] 1 All E.R. 921; [1949] 2 K.B. 765; [1949] L.J.R. 1721). *Overruled in*
R. V. Ward, Ltd. v. Bignall 449
Garnac Grain Co., Inc. v. H. M. F. Faure & Fairclough, Ltd. and Bunge Corpn. ([1965] 3 All E.R.
273; [1966] 1 Q.B. 650; [1965] 3 W.L.R. 934). *Affirmed.* H.L. 353
Garthwaite v. Garthwaite ([1964] 2 All E.R. 233; [1964] P. 356; [1964] 2 W.L.R. 1108). *Distin-*
guished in Collett (otherwise Sakazova) v. Collett 426
Gartside v. Inland Revenue Comrs. ([1966] 3 All E.R. 89; [1966] 3 W.L.R. 759). *Reversed.* C.A. 173
Gestetner (decd.), Re ([1953] 1 All E.R. 1150; [1953] Ch. 672; [1953] 2 W.L.R. 1033). *Applied in*
Re Leek (decd.) 1160
Ginty v. Belmont Supplies, Ltd. ([1959] 1 All E.R. 414). *Distinguished in* Donaghey v. Boulton &
Paul, Ltd. 1014
Goldsmith's Co. v. West Metropolitan Ry. Co. ([1900-03] All E.R. Rep. 667; [1904] 1 K.B. 1; 72
L.J.K.B. 931; 89 L.T. 428). *Distinguished in* Trow v. Ind Coope (West Midlands), Ltd. .. 900
Gorris v. Scott ((1874), L.R. 9 Exch. 125; 43 L.J.Ex. 92; 30 L.T. 431). *Distinguished in* Donaghey
v. Boulton & Paul, Ltd... 1014
Greenhalgh v. Mallard ([1947] 2 All E.R. 257). *Dicta of* SOMERVELL, L.J., *applied in* Public Trustee
v. Kenward 870
Grosvenor & West-End Railway Terminus Hotel Co., Ltd., Re, ((1897), 76 L.T. 337). *Distinguished*
in Re S.B.A. Properties, Ltd. 615
Grosvenor Hotel, London (No. 2), Re, ([1964] 3 All E.R. 354; [1965] Ch. 1210; [1964] 3 W.L.R. 992).
Not followed in Conway v. Rimmer 1260
H. (G. J.) (an infant), Re ([1966] 1 All E.R. 952; [1966] 1 W.L.R. 706). *Followed in* Re P. (infants) 229
H. (otherwise D.) v. H. ([1953] 2 All E.R. 1229; [1954] P. 258; [1953] 3 W.L.R. 849). *Followed in*
Buckland v. Buckland 300
Hall v. Hall ([1963] 2 All E.R. 140; [1963] P. 378; [1963] 2 W.L.R. 1054). *Followed in* Re P.
(infants) 229
——. *Distinguished in* Re L. 1110
Hallett's Estate, Re ([1874-80] All E.R. Re. 793; (1880), 13 Ch.D. 696; 49 L.J.Ch. 415; 42 L.T.
421). *Considered in* Re Tilley's Will Trusts 303
Hancock v. Watson ([1900-03] All E.R. Rep. 87; [1902] A.C. 14; 71 L.J.Ch. 149; 85 L.T. 729).
Applied in Re Leek (decd.) 1160
Hare v. Gocher ([1962] 2 All E.R. 763; [1962] 2 Q.B. 641; [1962] 3 W.L.R. 339). *Applied in* Trow
v. Ind Coope (West Midlands), Ltd. 900
Harman v. Park ((1880), 6 Q.B.D. 323; 50 L.J.Q.B. 227; 44 L.T. 81). *Applied in* Nair v. Teik .. 34
Harmsworth (decd.), Re ([1966] 3 All E.R. 309; [1966] 3 W.L.R. 1077). *Affirmed in part, reversed*
in part. C.A. 249
Hart v. Hart ((1881), 18 Ch.D. 670; 50 L.J.Ch. 697; 45 L.T. 13). *Dictum of* KAY, J., *applied in*
Beswick v. Beswick 1197
Harte v. Fampton ([1947] 2 All E.R. 606; [1948] 1 K.B. 79; [1948] L.J.R. 1127). *Dictum of*
ASQUITH, L.J., *applied in* Bailey v. Purser 189
Hay (or Bourhill) v. Young ([1942] 2 All E.R. 396; [1943] A.C. 92; 111 L.J.P.C. 97; 167 L.T.
261). *Principle applied in* Chadwick v. British Transport Commission 945
—— ([1942] 2 All E.R. 405, 406; [1943] A.C. 110; 111 L.J.P.C. 106; 167 L.T. 267). *Dictum of*
LORD WRIGHT *distinguished in* Chadwick v. British Transport Commission 945
Hedley Byrne & Co., Ltd. v. Heller & Partners, Ltd. ([1963] 2 All E.R. 575; [1964] A.C. 465;
[1963] 3 W.L.R. 101). *Applied in* W. B. Anderson & Sons, Ltd. v. Rhodes (Liverpool), Ltd... 850

Henaghan v. Rederiet Forangirene ([1936] 2 All E.R. 1433). *Dictum of* LEWIS, J., *applied in* Smith
  (formerly Westwood) v. National Coal Board 593
Henderson v. Henderson ([1843-60] All E.R. Rep. 381, 382). *Dicta of* WIGRAM, V.-C., *applied in*
  Public Trustee v. Kenward 870
Hivac, Ltd. v. Park Royal Scientific Instruments, Ltd. ([1946] 1 All E.R. 353, 354, 356, 357;
  [1946] Ch. 174, 175, 178, 180; 115 L.J.Ch. 245, 246, 247, 249; 174 L.T. 424, 425, 426). *Dicta*
  of LORD GREENE, M.R., *and of* MORTON, L.J., *applied in* Sanders v. Parry 803
Hohler v. Aston ([1920] 2 Ch. 420; 90 L.J.Ch. 78; 124 L.T. 233). *Applied in* Beswick v. Beswick 1197
Howard v. Patent Ivory Manufacturing Co. ((1888), 38 Ch.D. 156; 57 L.J.Ch. 878; 58 L.T. 395).
  Distinguished in Hely-Hutchinson v. Brayhead, Ltd. 14
Hughes & Vale Proprietary, Ltd. v. State of New South Wales ([1954] 3 All E.R. 607; [1955] A.C.
  241; [1954] 3 W.L.R. 824). *Followed in* Freightlines and Construction Holding, Ltd. v. State
  of New South Wales and The Commissioner of Motor Transport 433
Indyka v. Indyka ([1966] 3 All E.R. 583; [1966] 3 W.L.R. 603). *Affirmed.* H.L. 689
Inland Revenue Comrs. v. British Salmson Aero Engines, Ltd. ([1938] 3 All E.R. 283; [1938] 2
  K.B. 482; 107 L.J.K.B. 648; 159 L.T. 147). *Applied in* Murray (Inspector of Taxes) v.
  Imperial Chemical Industries, Ltd. 980
Inland Revenue Comrs. v. City of London Corpn. ([1953] 1 All E.R. 1075; [1953] 1 W.L.R. 652).
  Applied in Campbell v. Inland Revenue Comrs. 625
Inland Revenue Comrs. v. Cleary ([1966] 2 All E.R. 19; [1966] Ch. 365; [1966] 2 W.L.R. 790).
  Affirmed. H.L. 48
Inland Revenue Comrs. v. Educational Grants Association, Ltd. ([1966] 3 All E.R. 708; [1967]
  Ch. 123; [1966] 3 W.L.R. 724). *Affirmed.* C.A. 893
Inland Revenue Comrs. v. National Book League ([1957] 2 All E.R. 644; [1957] Ch. 488; [1957]
  3 W.L.R. 222). *Applied in* Campbell v. Inland Revenue Comrs. 625
Inland Revenue Comrs. v. Parker ([1966] 1 All E.R. 415; [1966] A.C. 178, 179; [1966] 2 W.L.R.
  509). *Dictum of* LORD WILBERFORCE *followed in* Cleary v. Inland Revenue Comrs. 48
International Pulp and Paper Co., Ltd. *Re* ((1876) 3 Ch.D. 599; 45 L.J.Ch. 448; 35 L.T. 230).
  Dictum of SIR GEORGE JESSEL, M.R. *considered in* Eastern Holdings Establishment of Vaduz
  v. Singer & Friedlander, Ltd. 1192
Jensen v. Jensen and Howard ([1964] 2 All E.R. 231; [1964] 1 W.L.R. 859). *Considered in* Inglis
  v. Inglis and Baxter 71
Jewish Blind Society Trustees v. Henning (Valuation Officer) ([1961] 1 All E.R. 49, 52, 54; [1961]
  1 W.L.R. 29, 34, 36). *Dicta of* LORD EVERSHED, M.R., PEARCE *and* HARMAN, L.JJ., *considered*
  in Almond (Valuation Officer) v. Birmingham Royal Institution for the Blind 317
Johnstone v. Pedlar ([1921] All E.R. Rep. 176; [1921] 2 A.C. 262; 90 L.J.P.C. 181; 125 L.T. 809).
  Distinguished in Nissan v. Attorney-General.. 200
Jolliffe v. Exeter Corpn. ([1967] 1 All E.R. 258; [1967] 1 W.L.R. 350). *Reversed.* C.A. .. 1099
K. (K.J.S.) (an infant), Re ([1966] 3 All E.R. 154; [1966] 1 W.L.R. 1241). *Followed in* Re P.
  (infants) 229
Kassim (otherwise Widmann) v. Kassim (otherwise Hassim) (Carl and Dickson cited) ([1962] 3 All
  E.R. 432, 433; [1962] P. 233, 234; [1962] 3 W.L.R. 873, 874). *Dicta of* ORMROD, J., *followed in*
  Collett (otherwise Sakazova) v. Collett 426
King v. Reginam ([1962] 1 All E.R. 819; [1962] A.C. 207; [1962] 2 W.L.R. 305). *Dictum of* LORD
  MORRIS OF BORTH-Y-GEST *approved in* Mohan v. Reginam 58
Kingston Cotton Mill Co. (No. 2), Re, [1896] 2 Ch. 279; 65 L.J.Ch. 673; 75 L.T. 568). *Principle*
  applied in Re Thomas Gerrard & Son, Ltd. 525
Kinnane v. Kinnane ([1953] 2 All E.R. 1144; [1954] P. 41; [1953] 3 W.L.R. 782). *Applied in*
  Northrop v. Northrop 961
—— ([1953] 2 All E.R. 1146; [1954] P. 43, 44; [1953] 3 W.L.R. 785, 786). *Dicta of* LORD MERRIMAN,
  P., *applied in* Northrop v. Northrop 961
Kitcat v. King ([1930] P. 266; 99 L.J.P. 126; 143 L.T. 408). *Followed in* In the Estate of Bravda
  (*dece.*) 1233
Kreglinger v. New Patagonia Meat and Cold Storage Co., Ltd. ([1911-13] All E.R. Rep. 970; [1914]
  A.C. 25; 83 L.J.Ch. 79; 109 L.T. 802; *Followed in* Cityland and Property (Holdings) Ltd. v.
  Dabrah 639
Kruhlak v. Kruhlak (No. 2) ([1958] 2 All E.R. 294; [1958] 1 W.L.R. 606). *Applied in* Re Seaford
  (*decd.*) 458
Lawrence v. Biddle ([1966] 1 All E.R. 575; [1966] 2 Q.B. 504; [1966] 2 W.L.R. 930). *Followed in*
  Cutts v. Chumley 89
Le Mesurier v. Le Mesurier ([1895-99] All E.R. Rep. 836; [1895] A.C. 517; 64 L.J.P.C. 97; 72
  L.T. 873). *Considered and criticised in* Indyka v. Indyka 689
Liptrot v. British Railways Board ([1966] 2 All E.R. 247; [1966] 2 Q.B. 353; [1966] 2 W.L.R. 841).
  Affirmed. H.L. 1072
Lloyd v. Hathern Station Brick Co., Ltd. ((1901), 85 L.T. 158). *Applied in* Semler v. Murphy .. 185
London and Caledonian Marine Insurance Co., Re ((1879), 11 Ch.D. 140; 40 L.T. 666). *Considered*
  in Re Cornish Manures, Ltd. 875
London and Thames Haven Oil Wharves, Ltd. v. Attwooll (Inspector of Taxes) ([1966] 3 All E.R.
  145; [1966] 3 W.L.R. 325). *Reversed.* C.A. 124
——. *Applied in* Sommerfelds, Ltd. v. Freeman (Inspector of Taxes) 143
Lord Advocate v. Young ((1887), 12 App. Cas. 553). *Dictum of* LORD WATSON *considered in* Fowley
  Marine (Emsworth), Ltd. v. Gafford 472
Lucile Bloomfield, The ([1966] 3 All E.R. 294; [1966] 1 W.L.R. 1525). *Affirmed.* C.A. .. 633
M. v. M. (No. 1) ([1967] 1 All E.R. 870; [1967] 2 W.L.R. 1168). *Considered in* Gosling v. Gosling.. 510
Machado v. Fontes ([1897] 2 Q.B. 231; 66 L.J.Q.B. 542; 76 L.T. 588). *Followed in* Boys v. Chaplin 665
Macsaga Investments Co., Ltd. v. Lupton (Inspector of Taxes) ([1966] 3 All E.R. 375; [1967]
  Ch. 167; [1966] 3 W.L.R. 1184). *Affirmed.* C.A. 930
Maradana Mosque (Board of Trustees) v. Badi-Un-Din Mahmud ([1966] 1 All E.R. 545; [1967]
  A.C. 13; [1966] 2 W.L.R. 921). *Criticised in* Anisminic, Ltd. v. The Foreign Compensation
  Commission 986
Margetson and Jones, Re ([1897] 2 Ch. 314; 66 L.J.Ch. 619; 76 L.T. 805). *Distinguished in* Re
  Fuld (*decd.*) 649
Marshall v. Ulleswater Steam Navigation Co. ((1871), L.R. 7 Q.B. 172; 41 L.J.Q.B. 45; 35 L.T.
  796). *Dicta of* BLACKBURN, J., *followed in* Fowley Marine (Emsworth), Ltd. v. Gafford.. .. 472
Mason (Inspector of Taxes) v. Innes ([1967] 1 All E.R. 760; [1967] 2 W.L.R. 479). *Affirmed.* C.A. 926
Merricks v. Nott-Bower ([1964] 1 All E.R. 717; [1965] 1 Q.B. 57; [1964] 2 W.L.R. 702). *Not followed*
  in Conway v. Rimmer 1260
Miller's Agreement, Re ([1947] 2 All E.R. 78; [1947] Ch. 615; [1948] L.J.R. 567; 177 L.T. 129).
  Applied in Beswick v. Beswick.. 1197
Moffat and Paige, Ltd. v. George Hill & Sons, Ltd. and Marshall ((1902), 86 L.T. 470, 471). *Dicta of*
  SIR RICHARD HENN-COLLINS, M.R., *applied in* Harman Pictures, N.V. v. Osborne 324
Monkswell (Lord) v. Thompson ([1898] 1 Q.B. 353; 67 L.J.Q.B. 243; 77 L.T. 707). *Applied in* Nair
  v. Teik 34

Moore v. Lambeth Waterworks Co. ((1886), 17 Q.B.D. 462; 55 L.J.Q.B. 304; 55 L.T. 309). *Followed in* Radstock Co-operative & Industrial Society, Ltd. v. Norton-Radstock Urban District Council ... 812

Morris v. Kanssen ([1946] 1 All E.R. 586; [1946] A.C. 459; 115 L.J.Ch. 177; 174 L.T. 353). *Distinguished in* Hely-Hutchinson v. Brayhead, Ltd. ... 14

Morris v. C. W. Martin & Sons, Ltd. ([1965] 2 All E.R. 735; [1966] 1 Q.B. 732; [1965] 3 W.L.R. 288). *Dictum of* DIPLOCK, L.J., *considered and applied in* Garnham, Harris & Elton, Ltd. v. Alfred W. Ellis (Transport), Ltd. ... 940

Mulholland & Tedd, Ltd. v. Baker ([1939] 3 All E.R. 255; 161 L.T. 21). *Dictum of* ASQUITH, J., *applied in* Mason v. Levy Auto Parts of England, Ltd. ... 62

Mulready v. J. H. & W. Bell, Ltd. ([1952] 2 All E.R. 663). *Decision of* PEARSON, J., *approved in* Donaghey v. Boulton & Paul, Ltd. ... 1014

—— ([1953] 2 All E.R. 215; [1953] 2 Q.B. 117; [1953] 3 W.L.R. 100). *Ratio decidendi in, disapproved in* Donaghey v. Boulton & Paul, Ltd. ... 1014

Murray (Inspector of Taxes) v. Imperial Chemical Industries, Ltd. ([1967] 1 All E.R. 369; [1967] 1 W.L.R. 304). *Affirmed.* C.A. ... 980

Musgrove v. Pandelis ([1918-19] All E.R. Rep. 589; [1919] 2 K.B. 43; 88 L.J.K.B. 915; 120 L.T. 601). *Followed in* Mason v. Levy Auto Parts of England, Ltd. ... 62

Nash v. Nash ([1965] 1 All E.R. 480; [1965] P. 266; [1965] 2 W.L.R. 317. *Considered and approved in* Gosling v. Gosling ... 510

Naylor v. Yorkshire Electricity Board ([1966] 3 All E.R. 327; [1966] 3 W.L.R. 654). *Reversed.* H.L. ... 1

Nethersole v. Withers (Inspector of Taxes) ([1946] 1 All E.R. 716). *Dicta of* LORD GREENE, M.R. *applied in* Murray (Inspector of Taxes) v. Imperial Chemical Industries, Ltd. ... 980

Nissan v. A.-G. ([1967] 2 All E.R. 200; [1967] 3 W.L.R. 109). *Reversed in part, affirmed in part.* C.A. ... 1238

North Riding Garages, Ltd. v. Butterwick ([1967] 1 All E.R. 647; [1967] 2 W.L.R. 575). *Dictum of* WIDGERY, J., *considered and explained in* Arnold v. Thomas Harrington, Ltd. ... 866

Northrop v. Northrop ([1966] 3 All E.R. 797; [1966] 3 W.L.R. 1193). *Affirmed.* C.A. ... 961

Oatway, Re ([1903] 2 Ch. 356; 72 L.J.Ch. 575; 88 L.T. 622). *Considered in* Re Tilley's Will Trusts ... 303

Oppenheim v. Tobacco Securities Trust Co., Ltd. ([1951] 1 All E.R. 31; [1951] A.C. 297). *Applied in* Inland Revenue Comrs. v. Educational Grants Association, Ltd. ... 893

Orr Ewing v. Colquhoun ((1877), 2 App. Cas. 861, 862). *Dictum of* LORD BLACKBURN *applied in* Radstock Co-operative & Industrial Society, Ltd. v. Norton-Radstock Urban District Council ... 812

Owens v. Liverpool Corpn. ([1938] 4 All E.R. 727; [1939] 1 K.B. 394; 108 L.J.K.B. 155; 160 L.T. 8). *Considered in* Chadwick v. British Transport Commission ... 945

Park, Re ([1931] All E.R. Rep. 633; [1932] 1 Ch. 580; 101 L.J.Ch. 295; 147 L.T. 118). *Considered in* Re Abrahams' Will Trusts ... 1197

Parsons, Re ((1890), 45 Ch.D. 51; 59 L.J.Ch. 668; 62 L.T. 929). *Applied in* Re Earl of Midleton's Will Trusts ... 834

Parsons v. B.N.M. Laboratories, Ltd. ([1963] 2 All E.R. 658; [1964] 1 Q.B. 95; [1963] 2 W.L.R. 1273). *Applied in* Parry v. Cleaver ... 1168

Pavenham (Lord Luke of) v. Minister of Housing and Local Government ([1967] 1 All E.R. 351; [1967] 2 W.L.R. 623). *Reversed.* C.A. ... 1066

Pidduck v. Pidduck and Linbrick ([1961] 3 All E.R. 481; [1961] 1 W.L.R. 1313). *Distinguished in* Inglis v. Inglis and Baxter ... 71

Pike v. Michael Nairn & Co., Ltd. ([1960] 2 All E.R. 186; [1960] Ch. 560; [1960] 2 W.L.R. 901). *Dictum of* CROSS, J., *followed in* The Gniezno ... 738

Pike v. Nicholas ((1869), 5 Ch. App. 251; 39 L.J.Ch. 435). *Distinguished in* Harman Pictures N.V. v. Osborne ... 324

Pilkington v. Inland Revenue Comrs. ([1962] 3 All E.R. 622; [1964] A.C. 612; [1962] 3 W.L.R. 1051). *Distinguished in* Re Abrahams' Will Trusts ... 1175

Pilkington's Will Trusts, Re ([1961] 2 All E.R. 330; [1961] Ch. 466; [1961] 2 W.L.R. 776). *Distinguished in* Re Abrahams' Will Trusts ... 1175

Pinto Silver Mining Co., Re ((1878), 8 Ch.D. 273; 47 L.J.Ch. 591; 38 L.T. 336). *Considered in* Re Cornish Manures, Ltd. ... 875

Practice Direction ([1960] 2 All E.R. 862; [1960] 1 W.L.R. 744). *Superseded by* Practice Direction ... 1232

Princes Investments, Ltd. v. Inland Revenue Comrs. ([1966] 2 All E.R. 832; [1966] 1 W.L.R. 1186). *Affirmed.* C.A. ... 238

R. v. Barron ([1914] 2 K.B. 574; 87 L.J.K.B. 789). *Dictum of* LORD READING, C.J., *considered and explained in* Director of Public Prosecutions v. Nasralla ... 161

R. v. Blamires Transport Services, Ltd. ([1963] 3 All E.R. 170; [1964] 1 Q.B. 278; [1963] 3 W.L.R. 496). *Applied in* R. v. Simmonds ... 399

R. v. Brighton and Area Rent Tribunal, *Ex p.* Marine Parade Estates (1936), Ltd. ([1950] 2 K.B. 420, 421). *Dictum of* LORD GODDARD, C.J., *applied in* Crofton Investment Trusts, Ltd. v. Greater London Rent Assessment Committee ... 1103

R. v. Cole ([1965] 2 All E.R. 29; [1965] 2 Q.B. 388; [1965] 3 W.L.R. 263. *Explained and distinguished in* R. v. Hazeltine ... 671

R. v. Electricity Comrs., *Ex parte* London Electricity Joint Committee Co. ([1923] All E.R. Rep. 161; [1924] 1 K.B. 205; 93 L.J.K.B. 405; 130 L.T. 171). *Dictum of* ATKIN, L.J., *explained in* R. v. Criminal Injuries Compensation Board, *Ex parte* Lain ... 770

R. v. Gyngall ([1893] 2 Q.B. 232; 69 L.T. 481; sub nom. Re Gyngall, 62 L.J.Q.B. 559). *Applied in* Re L. ... 1110

R. v. Holmen [1918] 2 K.B. 864; 88 L.J.K.B. 31; 119 L.T. 683). *Dictum of* AVORY, J., *applied in* R. v. WILSON ... 1088

R. v. London Sessions Appeal Committee, *Ex p.* Westminster City Council ([1951] 1 All E.R. 1032; sub nom. R. v. London Quarter Sessions, *Ex p.* Westminster Corpn., [1951] 2 K.B. 508). *Distinguished in* Phillips v. Berkshire County Council ... 675

R. v. Manchester Legal Aid Committee, *Ex parte* Brand & Co., Ltd. ([1952] 1 All E.R. 480; [1952] 2 Q.B. 413). *Applied in* R. v. Criminal Injuries Compensation Board, *Ex parte* Lain ... 770

R. v. Nottingham Quarter Sessions, *Ex p.* Harlow ([1952] 2 All E.R. 78; [1952] 2 Q.B. 601). *Applied in* Phillips v. Berkshire County Council ... 675

R. v. Shoreditch Assessment Committee, *Ex p.* Morgan ([1908-10] All E.R. Rep. 792; [1910] 2 K.B. 859; 80 L.J.K.B. 185; 103 L.T. 262). *Considered in* Anisminic, Ltd. v. The Foreign Compensation Commission ... 986

R. v. Trigg ([1963] 1 All E.R. 490; [1963] 1 W.L.R. 305). *Considered and distinguished in* R. v. O'Reilly ... 766

Redfern v. Redfern ([1886-90] All E.R. Rep. 524; [1891] P. 139; 60 L.J.P. 9; 64 L.T. 68). *Considered in* Inglis v. Inglis and Baxter ... 71

Remon v. City of London Real Property Co., Ltd. ([1921] 1 K.B. 49; 89 L.J.K.B. 1105; 123 L.T. 617). *Distinguished in* Brown v. Conway ... 793

Richardson Re, *Ex parte* St. Thomas's Hospital (Governors) ([1911] 2 K.B. 711; 80 L.J.K.B. 1237; 105 L.T. 229). *Applied in* Selangor United Rubber Estates, Ltd. v. Cradock ... 1255

Ricketts (Inspector of Taxes) v. Colquhoun ([1926] A.C. 1; 95 L.J.K.B. 82; 134 L.T. 106). *Applied in* Pook (Inspector of Taxes) v. Owen.. ... 579

Ridge *v.* Baldwin ([1963] 2 All E.R. 87, 110; [1964] A.C. 90, 125; [1963] 2 W.L.R. 962, 992). *Dicta of* LORD EVERSHED *and* LORD MORRIS OF BORTH-Y-GEST *applied in* Durayappah *v.* Fernando 152

Roberts *v.* Gwyrfai District Council ([1899] 2 Ch. 608; 68 L.J.Ch. 757; 81 L.T. 465). *Distinguished in* Radstock Co-operative & Industrial Society, Ltd. *v.* Norton-Radstock Urban District Council 812

Rookes *v.* Barnard ([1964] 1 All E.R. 367; [1964] A.C. 1129; [1964] 2 W.L.R. 269). *Followed in* Morgan *v.* Fry 386

—— ([1964] 1 All E.R. 398, 400; [1964] A.C. 1206, 1209; [1964] 2 W.L.R. 311, 314). *Dictum of* LORD DEVLIN *considered in* Morgan *v.* Fry 386

—— ([1964] 1 All E.R. 407; [1964] A.C. 1221; [1964] 2 W.L.R. 324). *Dictum of* LORD DEVLIN *applied in* Fielding *v.* Variety, Inc. 497

Rose *v.* Hurst [1949] 2 All E.R. 24; [1949] 2 K.B. 372; [1949] L.J.R. 1491). *Distinguished in* Oscroft *v.* Benabo 548

Rustomjee *v.* Reginam ((1876), 2 Q.B.D. 69; 46 L.J.Q.B. 238); 36 L.T. 190). *Applied in* Nissan *v.* Attorney-General 200

S. (an infant), Re ([1965] 1 All E.R. 865; [1965] 1 W.L.R. 483). *Distinguished in* Re P. (infants).. 229

S. (an infant), Re ([1967] 1 All E.R. 209; [1967] 1 W.L.R. 407). *Dictum of* CROSS, J., *applied in* Re L. 1110

S.B.A. Properties, Ltd. *v.* Craddock ([1967] 2 All E.R. 610; [1967] 1 W.L.R. 716). *Not followed in* Selangor United Rubber Estates, Ltd. *v.* Cradock 1255

St. Albans' (Duke) Will Trusts, Re ([1962] 2 All E.R. 402; [1963] Ch. 365; [1962] 3 W.L.R. 206). *Not followed in* Re Earl of Midleton's Will Trusts 834

Salaman *v.* Secretary of State for India ([1906] 1 K.B. 613; 75 L.J.K.B. 418; 94 L.T. 858). *Applied in* Nissan *v.* Attorney-General 200

Sandwell Park Colliery Co., Re ([1928] All E.R. Rep. 651; [1929] 1 Ch. 277; 98 L.J.Ch. 229). *Considered and distinguished in* Property and Bloodstock, Ltd. *v.* Emerton .. 839

Saskatchewan Labour Relations Board *v.* John East Iron Works, Ltd. ([1949] A.C. 151; [1949] L.J.R. 72). *Dicta of* LORD SIMMONDS *applied in* United Engineering Workers Union *v.* Devanayagam 367

Saxicava, The ([1924] P. 131; 93 L.J.P. 66; 131 L.T. 342). *Followed in* The Gniezno 738

Scholl Mfg. Co., Ltd. *v.* Clifton (Slim-Line), Ltd. ([1966] 3 All E.R. 16; [1966] 3 W.L.R. 575). *Applied in* Commercial Properties, Ltd. *v.* Wood 916

Scott, Re ([1901] 1 K.B. 228; 70 L.J.Q.B. 66; 83 L.T. 613). *Applied in* Re Brodie (*decd.*).. .. 97

Scott (Inspector of Taxes) *v.* Ricketts ([1966] 3 All E.R. 791; [1967] 1 W.L.R. 90). *Reversed.* C.A. 1009

Selby's Will Trusts, Re ([1965] 3 All E.R. 386; [1966] 1 W.L.R. 43). *Applied in* Re Abrahams' Will Trusts 1175

Sharkey (Inspector of Taxes) *v.* Wernher [1955] 3 All E.R. 493; [1956] A.C. 58; [1955] 3 W.L.R. 671). *Distinguished in* Mason (Inspector of Taxes) *v.* Innes 926

Shave *v.* Rosner [1954] 2 All E.R. 282; [1954] 2 Q.B. 117; [1954] 2 W.L.R. 1061). *Dictum of* DONOVAN, J., *applied in* Shulton (Great Britain), Ltd. *v.* Slough Borough Council .. 137

Sheldon *v.* Brown Bailey's Steel Works, Ltd. ([1953] 2 All E.R. 894; [1953] 2 Q.B. 393; [1953] 2 W.L.R. 542). *Applied in* The Gniezno 738

Shell Co. of Australia, Ltd. *v.* Federal Comr. of Taxation ([1930] All E.R. Rep. 680; [1931] A.C. 297; 100 L.J.P.C. 63; 144 L.T. 427). *Dictum of* LORD SANKEY, L.C., *applied in* United Engineering Workers Union *v.* Devanayagam 367

Sidebotham *v.* Holland ([1891-94] All E.R. Rep. 617; [1895] 1 Q.B. 378; 64 L.J.Q.B. 200; 72 L.T. 62). *Applied in* Trow *v.* Ind Coope (West Midlands), Ltd. 900

Sinclair *v.* Brougham ([1914-15] All E.R. Rep. 643; [1914] A.C. 442; 83 L.J.Ch. 488; 111 L.T. 14). *Dictum of* LORD PARKER OF WADDINGTON *explained in* Re Tilley's Will Trusts .. 303

Smith *v.* Baker & Sons ([1891-94] All E.R. Rep. 69; [1891] A.C. 325; 60 L.J.Q.B. 683; 65 L.T. 467). *Followed in* Oscroft *v.* Benabo 548

Smith *v.* River Douglas Catchment Board ([1949] 2 All E.R. 179). *Dicta of* LORD DENNING, M.R., *disapproved in* Beswick *v.* Beswick 1197

Soya Margareta, The ([1960] 2 All E.R. 756; [1961] 1 W.L.R. 709). *Considered in* Slough Estates, Ltd. *v.* Slough Borough Council 270

Starkie *v.* Starkie (No. 2) ([1953] 2 All E.R. 1522; [1954] 1 W.L.R. 105). *Dicta of* LORD MERRIMAN, P., *applied in* Northrop *v.* Northrop 961

Stevens *v.* Gourley ((1859), 29 L.J.C.P. 7; 1 L.T. 36). *Dictum of* BYLES, J., *not applied in* Almond (Valuation Officer) *v.* Birmingham Royal Institution for the Blind 317

Stratford (J. T.) & Son, Ltd. *v.* Lindley ([1964] 3 All E.R. 114; [1965] A.C. 336; [1964] 3 W.L.R. 557). *Dictum of* LORD PEARCE *applied in* Morgan *v.* Fry 386

Strickland (Lord) *v.* Grima ([1930] A.C. 285; sub nom. Parnis *v.* Agius, 99 L.J.P.C. 81; 142 L.T. 386). *Distinguished in* Nair *v.* Teik 34

Swaine *v.* Wilson ((1889), 24 Q.B.D. 252; 59 L.J.Q.B. 76; 62 L.T. 309). *Applied in* Dickson *v.* The Pharmaceutical Society of Great Britain 558

Talbot *v.* Talbot ([1967] 1 All E.R. 601). *Affirmed.* C.A... 920

Tarn, Re ([1893] 2 Ch. 280; 62 L.J.Ch. 564; 68 L.T. 311). *Applied in* P. B. J. Davis Manufacturing Co., Ltd. *v.* Fahn (Fahn claimant) 1274

Taunton Case, Marshall *v.* James ((1874), L.R. 9 C.P. 712; 43 L.J.C.P. 284; 30 L.T. 561). *Dictum of* LORD COLERIDGE, C.J., *explained in* Re Seaford (*decd.*) 458

Travel & Holiday Clubs, Ltd., Re, ([1967] 2 All E.R. 606). *Followed in* Re S.B.A. Properties, Ltd. 615

Travers *v.* Holley and Holley ([1953] 2 All E.R. 794; [1953] P. 246; [1953] 3 W.L.R. 507). *Approved in* Indyka *v.* Indyka.. 689

Trow *v.* Ind Coope (West Midlands), Ltd. ([1967] 1 All E.R. 19; [1966] 3 W.L.R. 1300). *Affirmed.* C.A. 900

Vaux, Re [1938] 4 All E.R. 297; [1939] Ch. 465; 108 L.J.Ch. 60; 160 L.T. 65). *Distinguished in* Re Abrahams' Will Trusts 1175

W. *v.* W. (No. 4) ([1963] 2 All E.R. 841; sub nom. W. *v.* W. [(1964] P. 67; [1963] 3 W.L.R. 540). *Distinguished in* Re L. 1110

Walker *v.* Baird ([1892] A.C. 491; 61 L.J.P.C. 92; 67 L.T. 513). *Distinguished in* Nissan *v.* Attorney-General 200

Walker (Valuation Officer) *v.* Wood ([1962] 3 All E.R. 188; [1962] 1 W.L.R. 1060). *Considered in* Almond (Valuation Officer) *v.* Birmingham Royal Institution for the Blind 317

Ward *v.* T. E. Hopkins & Son, Ltd. ([1959] 3 All E.R. 225; [1959] 1 W.L.R. 966). *Followed in* Chadwick *v.* British Transport Commission 945

Waring (Lord) *v.* London and Manchester Assurance Co., Ltd. ([1934] All E.R. Rep. 642; [1935] Ch. 310; 104 L.J.Ch. 201; 152 L.T. 390). *Followed in* Property and Bloodstock, Ltd. *v.* Emerton 839

Watts *v.* Battersea Corpn. [(1929] All E.R. Rep. 201; [1929] 2 K.B. 63; 98 L.J.K.B. 273; 140 L.T. 594). *Distinguished in* Courtney-Southan *v.* Crawley Urban District Council .. 246

Wednesbury Corpn. *v.* Ministry of Housing and Local Government ([1965] 1 All E.R. 186; [1965] 1 W.L.R. 261). *Not followed in* Conway *v.* Rimmer.. 1260

Wells *v.* Wells ([1954] 3 All E.R. 491; [1954] 1 W.L.R. 1390). *Considered in* Inglis *v.* Inglis and Baxter 71

West (H.) & Son, Ltd. *v.* Shephard ([1963] 2 All E.R. 625; [1964] A.C. 326; [1963] 2 W.L.R. 1359).
  Considered in Cutts *v.* Chumley.. 89
West Ham Corpn. *v.* Charles Benabo & Sons ([1934] All E.R. Rep. 47; [1934] 2 K.B. 253; 103
  L.J.Ch. 452; 151 L.T. 119). *Doubted in* London Borough of Hillingdon *v.* Cutler 361
West Rand Central Gold Mining Co., Ltd. *v.* Regem ([1905] 2 K.B. 391; 74 L.J.K.B. 753; 93
  L.T. 207). *Applied in* Nissan *v.* Attorney-General 200
Westhoughton Urban District Council *v.* Wigan Coal and Iron Co., Ltd. ([1919] 1 Ch. 159; 88 L.J.Ch.
  60; 120 L.T. 242). *Distinguished in* Radstock Co-operative & Industrial Society, Ltd. *v.* Norton-
  Radstock Urban District Council 812
Westwood *v.* National Coal Board ([1966] 2 All E.R. 208; [1966] 1 W.L.R. 682). *Reversed.* H.L... 593
Whall *v.* Bulman ([1953] 2 All E.R. 306; [1953] 2 Q.B. 198; [1953] 3 W.L.R. 116). *Considered and
  distinguished in* Oscroft *v.* Benabo 548
White *v.* Bijou Mansions, Ltd. ([1937] 3 All E.R. 269); [1937] Ch. 610; 107 L.J.Ch. 32; 157 L.T.
  105). *Dicta of* SIMONDS, J., *approved in* Beswick *v.* Beswick 1197
—— ([1938] 1 All E.R. 546; [1938] Ch. 351; 107 L.J.Ch. 212; 158 L.T. 338). *Dicta of* SIR WILFRID
  GREENE, M.R., *approved in* Beswick *v.* Beswick 1197
Whittingham *v.* Davies ([1962] 1 All E.R. 195; [1962] 1 W.L.R. 142). *Distinguished in* Little Park
  Service Station, Ltd. *v.* Regent Oil Co., Ltd... 257
—— ([1962] 1 All E.R. 198-200; [1962] 1 W.L.R. 146-149). *Dicta of* LORD EVERSHED, M.R.,
  dissented from in Little Park Service Station, Ltd. *v.* Regent Oil Co., Ltd. 257
Williams *v.* Tenby Corpn. ((1879), 5 C.P.D. 135; 49 L.J.Q.B. 325; 42 L.T. 187). *Applied in*
  Nair *v.* Teik 34
Winstone *v.* Winstone ([1959] 3 All E.R. 580; [1960] P. 28; [1959] 3 W.L.R. 660). *Applied in*
  Des Salles d'Epinoix *v.* Des Salles d'Epinoix.. 539
Winter *v.* Inland Revenue Comrs. ([1961] 3 All E.R. 859; [1963] A.C. 249; [1961] 3 W.L.R. 1069).
  Dictum of LORD REID *applied in* Re S.B.A. Properties, Ltd. 615
Wise *v.* Kaye ([1962] 1 All E.R. 257; [1962] 1 Q.B. 638; [1962] 2 W.L.R. 96). *Considered in*
  Cutts *v.* Chumley 89
Wright *v.* Mills ([1843-60] All E.R. Rep. 842; (1859), 28 L.J.Ex. 223; 33 L.T.O.S. 152). *Applied in*
  Re Seaford (*decd.*) 458
Young *v.* Young ([1962] 3 All E.R. 120; [1964] P. 152; [1962] 3 W.L.R. 946). *Considered in*
  Northrop *v.* Northrop 961

STATUTES, ETC., NOTED

	PAGE
Administration of Justice (Miscellaneous Provisions) Act, 1933 (c. 36), s. 2 (1)	1088
Agricultural Holdings Act, 1948 (c. 63), s. 25 (1) (d) (as substituted by Agriculture Act, 1958 (c. 71), s. 3 (2))	189
Companies Act, 1948 (c. 38)—	
s. 54	953
s. 162 (1)	525
s. 169 (3)	606, 615
(4)	610, 1255
(5)	1255
s. 199	14
s. 231	1192
s. 290 (1), (4)	875
ss. 319 (4), 320	1150
s. 447	1255
Constitution of the Commonwealth of Australia, 1900 (c. 12), ss. 9, 92	433
Contracts of Employment Act 1963 (c. 49)—	
Sch. 1, para. 10 (2)	30
Sch. 2, paras. 1 (1), 3 (1)	1062
Costs in Criminal Cases Act, 1952 (c. 48), s. 2 (1)	399
County Courts Act, 1959 (c. 22), ss. 108, 109	548
Criminal Appeal Act, 1907 (c. 23), s. 4 (1) proviso (as amended by Criminal Appeal Act 1966 (c. 31), s. 4 (1))	766
Criminal Justice Act, 1925 (c. 86), s. 14 (2)	1088
Defamation Act, 1952 (c. 66), s. 3 (1)	497
Factories Act, 1961 (c. 34)—	
s. 5 (1)	293
s. 14 (1)	1072
Finance Act, 1894 (c. 30), ss. 2 (1) (c), 3 (1)	249
Finance Act, 1940 (c. 29)—	
s. 43 (1) (as amended by Finance Act, 1950 (c. 15), s. 43 (1))	173
s. 44 (1) (1A) (substituted by Finance Act, 1950 (c. 15), s. 46)	249
Finance Act, 1944 (c. 23), s. 40	249
Finance Act, 1954 (c. 44), s. 16 (3)	636
Finance Act, 1960 (c. 44), ss. 28 (1), (2) (d), 43 (4) (g)	48
Fires Prevention (Metropolis) Act, 1774, (c. 78), s. 86	62
Foreign Compensation Act, 1950 (c. 12), s. 4 (4)	986
Foreign Marriage Act, 1892 (c. 23), s. 8	426
Guardianship of Infants Acts, 1886 and 1925	1232
Highways Act, 1959 (c. 25)—	
s. 127 (c)	100
s. 275 (1)	675
Housing Act, 1957 (c. 56), ss. 16 (1), 17 (1), 23 (1), (2), 37 (1)	361
Income Tax Act, 1952 (c. 10)—	
Sch. D	926
Sch. D, Case I	143
Case II	980
Case VI	1009
s. 137	124
s. 156, Sch. E, Case 1 (as substituted by Finance Act, 1956 (c. 54), s. 10 (1), and Sch. 9, r. 7 to the Act of 1952)	579
s. 169 (1)	625
ss. 245, 248 (1), (2), (3), 254 (1), (3), (4), (5)	238
ss. 265 (1), 266, 271 (1) (c)	576
s. 298	930
s. 447 (1) (b)	625, 893
s. 457 (4)	585
Inheritance (Family Provision) Act, 1938 (c. 45), s. 1 (as amended by Intestates' Estates Act, 1952 (c. 64), s. 7, Sch. 3)	468
Land Charges Act, 1925 (c. 22)—	
s. 10 (2)	340
s. 17 (3)	340
Land Compensation Act, 1961 (c. 23), s. 16 (3) (b)	589
Landlord and Tenant Act, 1954 (c. 56)—	
s. 25 (1), (2)	916
s. 30 (1) (f)	257
s. 34	548
Lands Clauses Consolidation Act, 1845 (c. 18), s. 68	1099
Law of Property Act, 1925 (c. 20)—	
s. 56 (1)	1197
ss. 101 (1), 104 (1)	839
s. 205 (1) (xx)	1197
Law Reform (Miscellaneous Provisions) Act, 1934 (c. 41), s. 1	1
Law Reform (Miscellaneous Provisions) Act, 1949 (c. 100), s. 1	689
Legitimacy Act, 1926 (c. 60), s. 3	97
Limitation Act, 1939 (c. 21), s. 4 (1), proviso	472
Magistrates' Courts Act, 1952 (c. 55), s. 77	1253
Matrimonial Causes Act 1965 (c. 72)—	
s. 4 (3)	71
s. 5 (2)	510
s. 16 (1)	660
s. 39	426
Matrimonial Proceedings (Magistrates' Courts) Act, 1960 (c. 48)—	
s. 2 (1) (b), (h)	961
s. 6 (1) (c)	1128
Mental Health Act, 1959 (c. 72), s. 141 (2)	827
Merchandise Marks Act, 1887 (c. 28), s. 2 (1)	137

	PAGE
Metropolitan Police Act, 1839 (*c*. 47), *s*. 52	41
National Insurance (Industrial Injuries) Act 1965 (*c*. 52), *Sch*. 4, *para*. 1 (*b*)	119
Obscene Publications Act, 1959 (*c*. 66), *s*. 4	504
Offences against the Person Act, 1861 (*c*. 100), *ss*. 18, 20	671
Offices, Shops and Railway Premises Act 1963 (*c*. 41), *s*. 1 (2)	732
Police Act 1964 (*c*. 48), *s*. 51 (1)	407
Prices and Incomes Act 1966 (*c*. 73), *ss*. 28 (2), 29 (4)	1137
Purchase Tax Act 1963 (*c*. 9), *ss*. 33 (1), 34 (4)	399
Race Relations Act 1965 (*c*. 73), *ss*. 3, 6	1225
Rating and Valuation (Miscellaneous Provisions) Act, 1955 (*c*. 9), *s*. 9 (1)	317
Redundancy Payments Act 1965 (*c*. 62)—	
s. 1	1062
(2)	290, 866
s. 3 (1)	290
ss. 8 (1), (2), 13 (1), 25 (1)	30
Sch. 1 (5)	1062
Rent Act 1965 (*c*. 75)—	
s. 20 (1)	793
s. 27 (1), (2)	1103
Riot (Damages) Act, 1886 (*c*. 38), *s*. 2	1051
Road Traffic Act, 1962 (*c*. 59), *s*. 5	491
Sale of Goods Act, 1893 (*c*. 71), *s*. 48 (3)	449
Selective Employment Payments Act 1966 (*c*. 32), *ss*. 2 (2), (*b*) (*ii*), 10 (1)	732
Sexual Offences Act, 1956 (*c*. 69), *s*. 32	1133
Shops Act, 1950 (*c*. 28), *s*. 47	1291
Solicitors Act, 1957 (*c*. 27), *s*. 72	649
Statute of Frauds Amendment Act, 1828 (*c*. 14), *s*. 6	850
Supreme Court of Judicature (Consolidation) Act, 1925 (*c*. 49)—	
s. 31 (1) (*i*)	827
s. 41	270
s. 45 (1)	539
s. 99 (1) (*a*)	682
s. 162 (1), *proviso* (*b*) (*as substituted by* Administration of Justice Act, 1928 (*c*. 26), *s*. 9)	150
Town and Country Planning Act, 1947 (*c*. 51), *s*. 49 (1)	1099
Town and Country Planning Act, 1962 (*c*. 38)—	
s. 43 (1)	1041
ss. 45 (3), 47 (5), 221	246
Trade Disputes Act, 1906 (*c*. 47), *s*. 3	386
Variation of Trusts Act, 1958 (*c*. 53), *s*. 1	314
Weights and Measures Act 1963 (*c*. 31), *s*. 22 (2) (*a*)	507
Wills Act, 1837 (*c*. 26), *s*. 33	97

COMMONWEALTH AND OTHER TERRITORIES

Ceylon (Constitution) Order in Council, 1946 (*c*. 379), *s*. 55	367
Contract Ordinance, *s*. 71	492
Courts of Judicature Act 1964, *ss*. 67, 74	34
Election Offences Ordinance (*No*. 906 of 1954), *ss*. 33 (4), 36	34
Hong Kong Buildings Ordinance, 1955 (*No*. 68 *of* 1955), *s*. 5*B* (2)	1228
Hong Kong Estate Duty Ordinance, 1932 (*c*. 3), *s*. 19 (1)	1035
Industrial Disputes Act (*c*. 131), *No*. 43 *of* 1950 (*as amended by* Industrial Disputes (Amendment) Act (*No*. 62 *of* 1957), *s*. 31*B*)	367
Municipal Ordinance (*cap*. 252), *s*. 277 (1)	152
Road Maintenance (Contribution) Act, 1958-1965 (N.S.W.)	433

RULES

Matrimonial Causes Rules, 1957 (*S.I.* 1957 *No*. 619)—	
r. 40 (1), (2)	458
r. 73 (4)	1032
r. 74	426
R.S.C.—	
Ord. 2, *r*. 1	738
Ord. 6, *r*. 1	900
r. 8	738
(1)	900
Ord. 10, *r*. 1 (3), *Ord*. 12, *r*. 1	738
Ord. 16, *r*. 1 (1) (*b*)	622
Ord. 17, *r*. 5 (2)	1274
Ord. 20, *r*. 5 (2) (3)	682
Ord. 23, *r*. 1 (1) (*a*)	583
(*b*)	185
Ord. 28, *r*. 8	1146
Ord. 29, *r*. 1 (1)	539
Ord. 38, *r*. 19 (1), (5)	1253
Ord. 55, *r*. 3 (1), (2)	1232
Ord. 59, *r*. 6 (4)	792
Ord. 80, *r*. 2 (2)	1110
Ord. 91, *r*. 7 (1), (2)	1232
App. *A*, *forms No*. 1, *No*. 2	900
R.S.C. (Rev.) 1962, *Ord*. 80, *r*. 11	282
R.S.C. (Rev.) 1965, *Ord*. 80, *r*. 10	282
Town and Country Planning Appeals (Inquiries Procedure) Rules 1965 (*S.I.* 1965 *No*. 473), *r*. 12 (2)	1066

REGULATIONS

PAGE

Building (Safety, Health and Welfare) Regulations, 1948 (*S.I.* 1948 *No.* 1145), *regs.* 4 (*ii*),
    31 (1), (3)   1014
Factories (Standards of Lighting) Regulations, 1941 (*S.R. & O.* 1941 *No.* 94), *reg.* 2 (*a*), (*b*) ..   293
Legal Aid (General) Regulations, 1962 (*S.I.* 1962 *No.* 148), *reg.* 7 (*f*)   419
National Insurance (Industrial Injuries) (Benefit) Regulations 1964 (*S.I.* 1964 *No.* 504),
    reg. 2 (3) (*a*)   119

ORDERS

Coal and Other Mines (Sidings) Order, 1956 (*S.I.* 1956 *No.* 1773), *Sch., reg.* 20   593
Foreign Compensation (Egypt) (Determination and Registration of Claims) Order, 1962
    (*S.I.* 1962 *No.* 2187), *art.* 4 (1) (*a*), (*b*), *art.* 6 (1)   986
Temporary Restrictions on Pay Increases (20th July 1966 Levels) (No. 1) Order 1966 (*S.I.*
    1966 *No.* 1365)   1137
Temporary Restrictions on Pay Increases (No. 2) Order 1966 (*S.I.* 1966 *No.* 1468)   1137

MISCELLANEOUS

Road Haulage Association, Ltd.'s Conditions of Carriage, 1961, *conditions* 1 (*a*), 12 (*a*)   ..   940

WORDS AND PHRASES

	PAGE
Activity [Redundancy Payments Act 1965, s. 25 (1)]	30
Actual income from all sources	238
Ambiguity (contractual rights not taken away, employer not to be penalised, on an ambiguity)	1137
Annual payment [income tax]	625
Audi alteram partem	152
Becoming engaged to be married to a person professing the Jewish faith	1175
Beginning with the date of [computation of period of time, R.S.C., Ord. 3, r. 2, Ord. 6, r. 8 (1)]	900
Cause [Merchandise Marks Act, 1887, s. 2 (1)]	137
Caused [Agricultural Holdings Act, 1948, s. 25 (1)]	189
Church of England (" member of the Church of England or some Church abroad professing the same tenets ")	193
Conclusions	1066
Contingent creditor	615
Credit—See " Giving credit ".	
Date—See " Beginning with the date of ".	
Disbursements	1092
Fact—See " Findings of fact ".	
Findings of fact	1066
Forthwith [Housing Act, 1957, s. 17 (1)]	361
Gipsy [Highways Act, 1959, s. 127 (c)]	100
Giving credit (" after giving credit for any amount realised by the sale of materials ")	361
Goods and materials [dead body]	576
Greater hardship—See " Hardship [Agricultural Holdings Act, 1948, s. 25 (1) (d)] ".	
Hardship [Agricultural Holdings Act, 1948, s. 25 (1) (d).]	189
In connexion with the management of the company's affairs.	610
Interest in possession [Finance Act, 1940, s. 43 (1)]	173
Judicial Officer [Ceylon Constitution Order in Council, 1946, s. 55 (5)]	367
Machinery [mobile crane]	1072
Management—See " In connexion with the management of the company's affairs ".	
Member of the Church of England—See " Church of England ".	
Misfeasance	1255
Ordinarily resident out of the jurisdiction	583
Original subject-matter of the action	622
Otherwise—See " Unless the context otherwise requires ".	
Owner [Town and Country Planning Act, 1962, s. 221]	246
Paid—See " Rate of remuneration paid ".	
Penalised (employer not to be penalised on an ambiguity)—See " Ambiguity ".	
Perpetuities—See " Without transgressing the rule against perpetuities ".	
Person aggrieved [Highways Act, 1959, s. 275 (1)]	675
Place (" cease to carry on business in place where employee employed ")	290
Possession for sale [Weights and Measures Act 1963, s. 22 (2) (a)]	507
Proceedings [legal aid]	419
Public revenue	585
Purchase (" by reason only of bona fide purchase ")	249
Rate of remuneration paid	1137
Recover property [action " for the recovery of property "]	610
Regulated tenancy [Rent Act 1965]	793
Required	593
Requires—See " Unless the context otherwise requires ".	
Resident—See " Ordinarily resident out of the jurisdiction ".	
Revenue—See " Public revenue ".	
Sale—See " Possession for sale ".	
Special circumstances [appointment of administrator]	150
Structure [Rating and Valuation (Miscellaneous Provisions) Act, 1955, s. 9 (1)]	317
Subject-matter—See " Original subject-matter of the action ".	
Summarily determine the question at issue	1274
Survive	1056
Tenancy [Rent Act 1965]	793
Tumultuous [Riot (Damages) Act, 1886, s. 2]	1051
Ulterior or ultimate trusts	1175
Unless the context otherwise requires [statutory definition]	1197
Without transgressing the rule against perpetuities	1175

CORRIGENDA

[1967] 2 All E.R.

p. 196. Re MILLS' WILL TRUSTS. Line 1.7: for the words " to accure " substitute " for accruer"; p. 197, line H.6: for " but from the consequences of their own " read " but not from the consequences of their own "; p. 198, line E.4: for " and in my judgment this " substitute " in Australia."

p. 272. SLOUGH ESTATES, LTD. v. SLOUGH BOROUGH COUNCIL. Counsel for the plaintiffs: read " David Keene " instead of " David Kean ".

p. 368. UNITED ENGINEERING WORKERS UNION v. DEVANAYAGAM. Counsel: read " N. Chinivasagam (of the English Bar) " for the appellants; " Mark Fernando (of the Ceylon Bar) " for the respondent, instead of as printed.

p. 435. FREIGHTLINES AND CONSTRUCTION HOLDING LTD. v. STATE OF NEW SOUTH WALES. Counsel: read " S. G. Davies (of the English Bar) " for the interveners, the State of South Australia, instead of as printed.

p. 806. SANDERS v. PARRY. Line H.6, add: " The case was argued in London, but judgment was given at Hertford assizes ". Counsel: for " D. W. Powell " read " D. Watkin Powell (Edward Raw with him) ".

THE
ALL ENGLAND
LAW REPORTS
INCORPORATING THE
LAW TIMES REPORTS
AND THE
LAW JOURNAL REPORTS

YORKSHIRE ELECTRICITY BOARD *v.* NAYLOR.

[HOUSE OF LORDS (Viscount Dilhorne, Lord Morris of Borth-y-Gest, Lord Guest, Lord Devlin and Lord Upjohn), January 26, March 15, 1967.]

D *Damages—Measure of damages—Loss of expectation of life—Matters relevant to assessment—Man aged twenty with real prospects of successful and happy life killed instantaneously—Change in value of money since earlier decisions —Liability of employers for breach of statutory duty—Law Reform (Miscellaneous Provisions) Act, 1934 (24 & 25 Geo. 6 c. 41), s. 1.*

E A young man, aged twenty, died instantaneously as the result of an electric shock suffered in the course of his employment by the appellants who admitted liability. His mother as administratrix brought an action under s. 1 of the Law Reform (Miscellaneous Provisions) Act, 1934, claiming damages for the benefit of his estate in respect of his loss of expectation of life. The trial judge awarded £500 damages, but on appeal the Court of Appeal increased the amount to £1,000.

F **Held:** in awarding £500 damages for loss of expectation of life the trial judge had rightly had regard to the principle stated by VISCOUNT SIMON, L.C., in *Benham* v. *Gambling** that in assessing such damages very moderate figures should be chosen, and, as the trial judge had neither misapprehended the facts nor made a wholly erroneous estimate of the damage, his award should stand; moreover the sum of £1,000 awarded by the majority in the Court
G of Appeal was not a sum that could be described as moderate (see p. 6, letter B, p. 10, letter E, p. 11, letter B, and p. 12, letter I, and p. 14, letter A, post).

Per LORD DEVLIN: it would, I think, be a great improvement if this head of damage was abolished† and replaced by a short Act of Parliament fixing a suitable sum which a wrongdoer whose act has caused death should
H pay into the estate of the deceased; while the law remains as it is, I think that it is less likely to fall into disrepute if judges treat *Benham* v. *Gambling** as an injunction to stick to a fixed standard than if they start revaluing happiness, each according to his own ideas (see p. 12, letter C, post).

Benham v. *Gambling* ([1941] 1 All E.R. 7) followed.
Dictum of GREER, L.J., in *Flint* v. *Lovell* ([1934] All E.R. Rep. at pp. 202,
I 203) applied.
Decision of COURT OF APPEAL (sub nom. *Naylor* v. *Yorkshire Electricity Board* [1966] 3 All E.R. 327) reversed.

[As to the measure of damages for personal injury, see 11 HALSBURY'S LAWS (3rd Edn.) 255, para. 427; as to damages under the Law Reform (Miscellaneous Provisions) Act, 1934, s. 1, see ibid., pp. 256, 257, para. 428; and for cases

---

* [1941] 1 All E.R. 7.
† Compare per SELLERS, L.J. ([1966] 3 All E.R. at p. 330, letter D).

on the measure of damages for loss of expectation of life, see 36 DIGEST (Repl.) A
229-232, *1209-1234*.

For the Law Reform (Miscellaneous Provisions) Act, 1934, s. 1, see 9
HALSBURY'S STATUTES (2nd Edn.) 792.]

Cases referred to:

Andrews v. *Freeborough*, [1966] 2 All E.R. 721; [1966] 3 W.L.R. 242.

Benham v. *Gambling*, [1940] 1 All E.R. 275; *revsd.* H.L., [1941] 1 All E.R. 7; B
    [1941] A.C. 157; 110 L.J.K.B. 49; 164 L.T. 290; 36 Digest (Repl.)
    231, *1227*.

Davies v. *Powell Duffryn Associated Collieries, Ltd.*, [1942] 1 All E.R. 657;
    [1942] A.C. 601; 111 L.J.K.B. 418; 167 L.T. 74; 36 Digest (Repl.)
    231, *1229*.

Flint v. *Lovell*, [1934] All E.R. Rep. 200; [1935] 1 K.B. 354; 104 L.J.K.B. 199; C
    152 L.T. 231; 36 Digest (Repl.) 200, *1055*.

Rose v. *Ford*, [1937] 3 All E.R. 359; [1937] A.C. 826; 106 L.J.K.B. 576;
    157 L.T. 174; 36 Digest (Repl.) 229, *1210*.

Appeal.

This was an appeal by the Yorkshire Electricity Board from an order of the D
Court of Appeal (DANCKWERTS and SALMON, L.JJ., SELLERS, L.J., dissenting),
dated June 30, 1966 and reported [1966] 3 All E.R. 327, whereby an appeal by
the respondent, Edna Naylor (married woman) suing as administratrix of the
estate of Paul Naylor, deceased, from a judgment of ASHWORTH, J., at Sheffield
Assizes, dated Feb. 10, 1966, was allowed and his judgment was varied. The Court
of Appeal directed that judgment should be entered for the plaintiff for £1,060 E
8s. 6d. with costs in lieu of judgment for the plaintiff for £560 8s. 6d. with costs.
The deceased had been killed instantaneously in an accident at work. Liability
was admitted by his employers, the appellants. The deceased's mother, the
respondent, brought an action for damages, suing under the Law Reform
(Miscellaneous Provisions) Act, 1934, s. 1. ASHWORTH, J., in his judgment
described the deceased as follows: F

" The deceased was aged twenty years and four months at the date of his
death and was employed by the appellants as a jointer's mate. His working
prospects were favourable, and if he had lived he would soon have been sent
for special training, after which at the age of twenty-one, he would probably
have qualified for the grade of jointer. He was a young man in good health,
living happily at home, and he had had the good fortune to become engaged G
seven days before his death."

The relevant head of damage was loss of expectation of life. Under this head
ASHWORTH, J., awarded £500 and the majority of the Court of Appeal awarded
£1,000. The respondent also claimed for funeral expenses.

D. P. Croom-Johnson, Q.C., and *K. W. Dewhurst* for the appellants. H
J. F. S. Cobb, Q.C., and *Denis Lloyd* for the respondent.

Their lordships took time for consideration.

Mar. 15. The following opinions were delivered.

VISCOUNT DILHORNE: My Lords, on Apr. 23, 1964, Paul Naylor, then
aged twenty years and four months, died instantaneously as the result of an I
electric shock which he suffered in the course of his employment by the appellants,
the Yorkshire Electricity Board. In this action his mother claims as the administratrix of his estate damages for the loss of expectation of life suffered by him
and for his funeral expenses. The action was tried by ASHWORTH, J., at Sheffield
Assizes in February, 1966. He awarded £500 damages for loss of expectation
of life. The plaintiff appealed and the Court of Appeal (1) by a majority (DANCK-
WERTS, L.J. and SALMON, L.J., SELLERS, L.J., dissenting) allowed the appeal

<hr>

(1) [1966] 3 All E.R. 327.

A   and increased the amount to £1,000. From this decision the appellants now appeal.

Before the enactment of the Law Reform (Miscellaneous Provisions) Act, 1934, it was recognised that an injured person was entitled, if liability was proved or admitted, to recover damages under this head. The Act of 1934 provided that causes of action vested in a person survived after his death for the

B   benefit of his estate, so administrators of the estate can now sue for damages in respect of loss of expectation of life.

After the passage of the Act of 1934 widely varying amounts were awarded for damages for loss of expectation of life until this House in *Benham* v. *Gambling* (2) gave guidance as to the approach to be made in the assessment of damages under this head. In that case the House reduced the damages that had been

C   awarded in respect of the loss of expectation of life of a child age 2½ from £1,200 to £200. Viscount Simon, L.C., with whose opinion Viscount Maugham, Lord Russell of Killowen, Lord Wright, Lord Roche, Lord Romer and Lord Porter agreed (3), said (4) that in assessing damages under this head what had to be valued was not " the prospect of length of days, but the prospect of a predominantly happy life ". He said (4):

D
    " The age of the individual may, in some cases, be a relevant factor—for example, in extreme old age the brevity of what life may be left may be relevant ... The ups and downs of life, its pains and sorrows, as well as its joys and pleasures—all that makes up ' life's fitful fever '—have to be allowed for in the estimate. In assessing damages for shortening of life, therefore, such damages should not be calculated solely, or even mainly, on the basis

E   of the length of life that is lost ... The question thus resolves itself into that of fixing a reasonable figure to be paid by way of damages for the loss of a measure of prospective happiness."

He went on to point out (5) that " the right sum to award depends on an objective estimate of what kind of future on earth the victim might have enjoyed " and

F   said (6):

    " The main reason, I think, why the appropriate figure of damages should be reduced in the case of a very young child is that there is necessarily so much uncertainty about the child's future that no confident estimate of prospective happiness can be made. When an individual has reached an

G   age to have settled prospects, having passed the risks and uncertainties of childhood and having in some degree attained to an established character and to firmer hopes, his or her future becomes more definite, and the extent to which good fortune may probably attend him at any rate becomes less incalculable.

Lord Simon added (7):

H
    " The truth, of course, is that in putting a money value on the prospective balance of happiness in years that the deceased might otherwise have lived, the jury or judge of fact is attempting to equate incommensurables. Damages which would be proper for a disabling injury may well be much greater than for deprivation of life. These considerations lead me to the conclusion

I   that, in assessing damages under this head, whether in the case of a child or an adult, very moderate figures should be chosen."

In that case (2) their lordships were agreed that the proper figure to award

---

(2) [1941] 1 All E.R. 7; [1941] A.C. 157.
(3) [1941] 1 All E.R. at p. 14; [1941] A.C. at pp. 168, 169.
(4) [1941] 1 All E.R. at p. 12, letter A; [1941] A.C. at p. 166.
(5) [1941] 1 All E.R. at p. 13, letter A; [1941] A.C. at p. 167.
(6) [1941] 1 All E.R. at p. 13, letter B; [1941] A.C. at p. 167.
(7) [1941] 1 All E.R. at p. 13, letter E; [1941] A.C. at p. 168.

was £200 and LORD SIMON said (8) " even this amount would be excessive if **A** it were not that the circumstances of the infant were most favourable ".

Evidence was given before ASHWORTH, J., as to the extent of the fall in the value of the pound which had occurred since 1941. It was said that it was then worth two and one-half times what it is to-day. ASHWORTH, J., had regard to the depreciation in the value of the pound and approached the case on the footing that what was appropriate in 1941 is no longer appropriate to-day. **B** He said:

> " At the end of the day the court's task is to assess what I prefer to call a reasonable sum, but what some judges have called a moderate sum, in respect of the loss of this young man's expectation of life [and that] in terms of money the award of 1941 [in *Benham* v. *Gambling* (9)] would not represent a fair award in terms of money if given to-day." **C**

In other words he was saying that what had to be regarded as, to quote LORD SIMON (10), " very moderate figures " in 1941, would not be so regarded to-day. He assessed the sum to be awarded to the respondent at £500 and expressed the view that it was, if anything, on the high side because the deceased's prospects appeared to have been favourable. To this figure he applied two cross-checks **D** which led him to regard the award of £500 " as being, if anything, generous ".

In the Court of Appeal (11) DANCKWERTS, L.J. said that in *Benham* v. *Gambling* (9) the House of Lords evolved " a theory that the damages should be a strictly moderate figure, somewhere between a minimum of £200 and a maximum of £500 ". I do not find anything in the opinion of LORD SIMON (12) stating that the minimum figure should be £200 or the maximum £500. The guidance that he **E** gave was that the figure should be very moderate (10), and the passage which I have cited from his opinion shows that this House would have regarded a sum lower than £200 as appropriate in that case but for the child's favourable circumstances. DANCKWERTS. L.J., said (13) that he thought that in this case £500 was a ridiculous figure and that £1,000 could not be too much. He doubted whether it was not far too little. SALMON, L.J. (14) said in relation to *Benham* v. **F** *Gambling* (9):

> " It is plain from the language used by LORD SIMON, L.C. (15), that the court's problem was still to solve the question what in the circumstances of any particular case was the proper sum to award as compensation for the loss of prospective happiness. In assessing this sum however a very low standard of measurement was to be applied. In effect, this sum had to be **G** measured certainly not through a magnifying glass nor even through a plain glass but through the wrong end of a telescope."

Later he said (16):

> " It is, in my view, most important to observe that the House of Lords considered that in these cases damages in respect of the death of a young child should be substantially less than in the case of an adult." **H**

Although LORD SIMON said (10) that the damages should be reduced in the case of a very young child, he did not say that they should be substantially less than those awarded to an adult. His conclusion (10) was that both in the case of a child and of an adult a very moderate figure should be chosen. SALMON, L.J., also said (17): **I**

---

(8) [1941] 1 All E.R. at p. 13, letter H; [1941] A.C. at p. 168.
(9) [1941] 1 All E.R. 7; [1941] A.C. 157.
(10) [1941] 1 All E.R. at p. 13; [1941] A.C. at p. 168.
(11) [1966] 3 All E.R. at p. 330, letter G.
(12) [1941] 1 All E.R. at p. 8; [1941] A.C. at p. 160.
(13) [1966] 3 All E.R. at p. 330, letter I.
(14) [1966] 3 All E.R. at p. 333.
(15) [1941] 1 All E.R. at p. 8; [1941] A.C. at p. 160,
(16) [1966] 3 All E.R. at p. 334, letter C.
(17) [1966] 3 All E.R. at p. 334, letter I,

A   " It seems to me to be manifest from what was stated in *Benham* v. *Gambling* (18) that if the deceased in that case had been a young man in Paul Naylor's position, the House of Lords would have assessed the damages at much more than £200—probably at £400."

B   I do not see that that is manifest from anything LORD SIMON said (19).   While it may be that the House would have awarded a sum larger than £200, there is nothing to indicate that it would have awarded anything in the region of double that sum.   Indeed, unless it were true to say that £400 was at that time regarded as a very moderate figure, the inference that I draw from LORD SIMON'S opinion (19) is that it would not have done so.

C   It would seem that DANCKWERTS, L.J. (20) and SALMON, L.J. (21) are not in agreement with the reasoning and conclusion of this House in *Benham* v. *Gambling* (18), though they recognised that the decision is binding on them. That decision had been followed for twenty-six years.   This House did not say what sum should be awarded in all cases or say what was the minimum or or maximum figure that should be given.   It gave guidance as to the approach to be made when assessing damages for this loss and, while it recognised that the particular circumstances of the deceased might properly lead to a variation in the amount awarded, it held that that should be a very moderate figure. Even in these days with the drop in value of the pound I do not myself consider that £1,000 can be regarded as a very moderate sum.

D   In *Flint* v. *Lovell* (22) GREER, L.J., said (23):

E   " . . . I think it right to say that this court will be disinclined to reverse the finding of a trial judge as to the amount of damages merely because they think that if they had tried the case in the first instance they would have given a lesser sum.   To justify reversing the trial judge on the question of the amount of damages it will be necessary that this court should be convinced either that the judge acted on some wrong principle of law, or that the amount awarded was so extremely high or so very small as to
F   make it, in the judgment of this court, an entirely erroneous estimate of the damage to which the plaintiff is entitled."

In *Davies* v. *Powell Duffryn Associated Collieries, Ltd.* (24) LORD WRIGHT said (25):

G   " Where, however, the award is that of the judge alone, the appeal is by way of rehearing on damages as on all other issues, but as there is generally so much room for individual choice so that the assessment of damages is more like an exercise of discretion than an ordinary act of decision, the appellate court is particularly slow to reverse the trial judge on a question of the amount of damages.   It is difficult to lay down any precise rule which will cover all cases, but a good general guide is given
H   by GREER, L.J., in *Flint* v. *Lovell* (23).   In effect, the court, before it interferes with an award of damages, should be satisfied that the judge has acted on a wrong principle of law, or has misapprehended the facts, or has for these or other reasons made a wholly erroneous estimate of the damage suffered.   It is not enough that there is a balance of opinion or preference. The scale must go down heavily against the figure attacked if the appellate
I   court is to interfere, whether on the ground of excess or insufficiency."

If ASHWORTH, J., had awarded £1,000 by way of damages, I would have said

(18) [1941] 1 All E.R. 7; [1941] A.C. 157.
(19) [1941] 1 All E.R. at p. 8; [1941] A.C. at p. 160.
(20) [1966] 3 All E.R. at p. 330.   (21) [1966] 3 All E.R. at p. 331.
(22) [1934] All E.R. Rep. 200; [1935] 1 K.B. 354.
(23) [1934] All E.R. Rep. at pp. 202, 203; [1935] 1 K.B. at p. 360.
(24) [1942] 1 All E.R. 657; [1942] A.C. 601.
(25) [1942] 1 All E.R. at pp. 664, 665; [1942] A.C. at p. 616.

that he had not acted in accordance with the decision of this House in *Benham* v. A
Gambling (26), and that in the light of that decision he had made an entirely
erroneous estimate; and I would have thought it right to interfere with his award.

In awarding £500 I do not see that he acted on a wrong principle of law or
misapprehended the facts or made a wholly erroneous estimate of the damage
suffered. He had regard to the fall in the value of money and to what was said
in *Benham* v. *Gambling* (26). If anything, he regarded his estimate as on the B
high side. While I doubt if anyone would think, even in these days, that a
sum much in excess of £500 could be regarded as a very moderate sum, it is not
for this House to lay down what sum should be awarded in all cases for this loss
or what should be the minimum and the maximum award.

In my opinion, for the reasons which I have stated, the judgment of ASHWORTH,
J., should not have been interfered with and I would allow the appeal.   C

LORD MORRIS OF BORTH-Y-GEST: My Lords, the claim which
ASHWORTH, J., had to consider was brought by the administratrix of the estate
of a young man aged twenty, whose death on Apr. 23, 1964, admittedly took
place in circumstances which made the appellants liable to compensate him
for the fact that his life was shortened. Though it is said that his death was
instantaneous, the appellants have not sought to dispute that a valid cause D
of action vested in him. By reason of the provisions of the Law Reform (Miscellaneous Provisions) Act, 1934, that cause of action survived for the benefit of
his estate. The judge had to decide what sum of damages should reasonably
be awarded in respect of the deceased's cause of action. He lost what is usually
called his expectation of life. The loss was something personal to himself. No
one knows what life would in fact have held for him had he lived. No one will E
ever know. No one could ever know. The chances, the changes and the vicissitudes
of the future are in the future. He will not know them. No surmise can with
any measure of confidence be made whether by his untimely death he was
denied happiness or was spared unhappiness. The task of " equating incommensurables " is one that can never be satisfactorily achieved.

For assistance in the assessment of damages in a case such as the present F
one guidance was given in this House in *Benham* v. *Gambling* (26). The many
references to that decision in the judgment of ASHWORTH, J., show that he was
zealous in his endeavour to be guided by what was said in that case. In his
speech VISCOUNT SIMON, L.C. (27), while recognising that this head of claim
" is in fact incapable of being measured in coin of the realm with any approach
to real accuracy ", exhorted the courts (28) to arrive at " very moderate figures ". G
The sum of £200 awarded in that case was stated to be an amount which would
be excessive were it not for the fact that the circumstances of the infant were
most favourable. In the case of a very young child the future manifestly holds
many uncertainties. Because it was considered that in *Benham* v. *Gambling* (26),
these could be offset the award was fixed as high as £200. Though awards are not
measured by any statistical or actuarial test or mathematically by reference to H
prospective length of life there could be the prospect of a longer span of happy
life in the case of a young child whose circumstances were decided to be " most
favourable" than in the case of an older person with equally favourable
circumstances.

In a careful and reasoned judgment ASHWORTH, J., arrived at an assessment
of £500—an amount which he thought could only be defended from being I
regarded as being " on the high side " because the prospects of the young man
could be considered to have been favourable. Having first made his assessment,
he then tested his figure by a process of cross-checking.

On appeal to the Court of Appeal (29) two grounds of appeal were asserted,

---

(26) [1941] 1 All E.R. 7; [1941] A.C. 157.
(27) [1941] 1 All E.R. at p. 14, letter A; [1941] A.C. at p. 168.
(28) [1941] 1 All E.R. at p. 13, letter F; [1941] A.C. at p. 168.
(29) [1966] 3 All E.R. 327.

A viz., (i) that the award was " inadequate and insufficient in all the circumstances of the case ", and (ii) that the award was against the weight of evidence.
It is important to bear in mind the principles which guide an appellate court
in deciding whether they can properly differ from the decision of a judge (which
is so often a matter of discretion and individual judgment) as to the appropriate
figure of damages. In his well known judgment in *Flint* v. *Lovell* (30) GREER, L.J.,
B said (31):

> " To justify reversing the trial judge on the question of the amount of
> damages it will generally be necessary that this court should be convinced
> either that the judge acted on some wrong principle of law, or that the amount
> awarded was so extremely high or so very small as to make it, in the judgment
> of this court, an entirely erroneous estimate of the damage to which the
C plaintiff is entitled."

In his speech in *Davies* v. *Powell Duffryn Associated Collieries, Ltd.* (32) LORD
WRIGHT endorsed as a good general guide what GREER, L.J., had said (31) and
he said (33):

> " In effect the court, before it interferes with an award of damages,
D should be satisfied that the judge has acted on a wrong principle of law,
> or has misapprehended the facts, or has for these or other reasons made a
> wholly erroneous estimate of the damage suffered."

In what manner, then, can it be said that the decision of ASHWORTH, J., could
be assailed? In the first place, I see no ground for supposing that any wrong
principle of law was applied. The directions given in *Benham* v. *Gambling* (34)
E were considered with anxious care.

It was urged that the judge had failed to embark on a process of measurement
of damages, but had fixed an arbitrary sum. In support of this contention
reference was made to a passage in his judgment where he said:

> " It is generally accepted that there is an air of unreality about the
F matter, and for this reason in the absence of any statutory scale, awards
> are bound to be somewhat arbitrary."

The judge was, however, doing no more than to echo what LORD SIMON
had said in *Benham* v. *Gambling* (35); that in respect of this head of damage
it is impossible to make measurement in coin of the realm with any approach
to real accuracy; and who can doubt that there is an air of unreality about the
G matter? The average healthy and reasonably contented man would not barter
his expectation of life even for the most princely sum. The best that courts can
do in an enquiry of singular elusiveness is to follow the guidance given in *Benham*
v. *Gambling* (34). The judge was punctilious in doing so. He recognised and took
into account the fact that since 1941 there has been a fall in the value of money.
He had that consideration very fully in mind. Secondly, I cannot think that the
H judge misapprehended any fact. There has really been no suggestion at all
that he did. It remains to consider whether there was a " wholly erroneous "
estimate of damages. Such was one of the main submissions of the respondent.
The increased figure of damages fixed by the majority in the Court of Appeal (36)
was awarded on the basis that had the House of Lords (34) in 1941 been considering the circumstances of the deceased, they would then have fixed a sum
I of £400. I find this unconvincing. Insofar as it was said in the Court of Appeal (37)
that in *Benham* v. *Gambling* (34) the House of Lords

---

(30) [1934] All E.R. Rep. 200; [1935] 1 K.B. 354.
(31) [1934] All E.R. Rep. at pp. 202, 203; [1935] 1 K.B. at p. 360.
(32) [1942] 1 All E.R. at p. 664, letter H; [1942] A.C. at p. 616.
(33) [1942] 1 All E.R. at p. 664, letter H; [1942] A.C. at p. 617.
(34) [1941] 1 All E.R. 7; [1941] A.C. 157.
(35) [1941] 1 All E.R. at p. 14   [1941] A.C. at p. 168.
(36) [1966] 3 All E.R. 327.   (37) [1966] 3 All E.R. at p. 330, letter G.

> " evolved by a process of judicial legislation a theory that the damages A
> should be a strictly moderate figure, somewhere between a minimum of
> £200 and a maximum of £500."

I think that there was a misapprehension. I find no reference to any such figure
as £500 in *Benham* v. *Gambling* (38). The real foundation, however, of the
decision of the majority rested on the view that because the deceased in *Benham*
v. *Gambling* (38) was only 2½, and the deceased in the present case was twenty, an B
award in 1941 in reference to the deceased would probably have been double
what it was in *Benham* v. *Gambling* (38). The view was also held that the House
of Lords had laid it down that in these cases damages in respect of the death
of a young child should be " substantially " less than in the case of an adult.
I do not read the speech of LORD SIMON (39) as laying down quite so rigid a
proposition. Rather was he saying that each case must be individually considered. C
He said (40) that the court must be

> " satisfied that the circumstances of the individual life were calculated
> to lead, on balance, to a positive measure of happiness, of which the victim
> has been deprived by the defendant's negligence."

No one, of course, could fail to appreciate the range and the variety of the D
uncertainties that must beset any attempted assessment of the prospects that
someone will enjoy " a positive measure of happiness ". The very young child
may have, and often in times past had, serious uncertainties as to survival.
Apart from that there are for those of all ages the risks of accident and ill-health.
As, however, what is being examined concerns the prospects of attaining a
measure of happiness then it must often be the case that in an enquiry there E
will be more to go on in the case of an older than in the case of a younger person.
It was for that reason that LORD SIMON said (41):

> " When an individual has reached an age to have settled prospects,
> having passed the risks and uncertainties of childhood, and having in
> some degree attained to an established character and to firmer hopes, his
> or her future becomes more definite, and the extent to which good fortune F
> may probably attend him at any rate becomes less incalculable."

With all these considerations in mind I am not persuaded that had your lordships' House in 1941 been concerned with the case of the deceased the damages
would " probably " have been assessed at £400. Nor do I think that any attempted
building-up process from a starting figure of £200 is desirable. In the case of the
infant of 2½ in *Benham* v. *Gambling* (38), the sum of £200 only escaped being G
designated as " excessive " because the circumstances were found to be " most
favourable ". If an infant aged 2½ was subject to all the risks and uncertainties
of childhood, and if no view could be formed whether happiness could be
anticipated, an award might be very small. There might come a time when
prospects were more settled. It is to be observed and remembered that the H
prospects to be considered and those which were being referred to by LORD
SIMON (42) in his speech were not the prospects of employment or of social
status or of relative pecuniary affuence but the prospects of " a positive measure
of happiness " or of " a predominantly happy life ".

For all these reasons I think that the surmise that your lordships' House
would have decided on a figure of £400 in the year 1941 if the deceased's circum- I
stances had then been considered rests on insecure foundations.

What the judge did in the present case was to assess what he considered
to be a reasonable sum. He said that he proceeded " in the light of knowledge "
of what has been assessed in other cases. That, as it seems to me, was quite a

(38) [1941] 1 All E.R. 7; [1941] A.C. 157.
(39) [1941] 1 All E.R. at p. 8; [1941] A.C. at p. 160.
(40) [1941] 1 All E.R. at p. 12, letter G; [1941] A.C. at pp. 166, 167.
(41) [1941] 1 All E.R. at p. 13, letter B; [1941] A.C. at p. 167.
(42) [1941] 1 All E.R. at p. 13; [1941] A.C. at p. 168.

A proper approach. He was quite entitled, while making his own personal estimate, to bear in mind the trend of judicial thought. He was bound to follow what was laid down in *Benham* v. *Gambling* (43) with its emphatic exhortation that " very moderate figures should be chosen ". In doing so he formed his estimate. In this difficult and uncertain field I do not think that there was warrant for disturbing his estimate as having been wholly erroneous. I would therefore
B allow the appeal.

LORD GUEST: My Lords, the deceased, Paul Naylor, was killed on Apr. 23, 1964, in circumstances involving admitted fault on the part of the appellants. The only question is as to the quantum of damages to be awarded to the respondent, his mother and the administratrix of his estate, under the
C Law Reform (Miscellaneous Provisions) Act, 1934, for the loss of expectation of life of the deceased. ASHWORTH, J., after hearing evidence, awarded £500 and the Court of Appeal (44) by a majority (SELLERS, L.J., dissenting) doubled the award to £1,000. The appellants argued that the Court of Appeal (44) was not entitled to interfere with the award made by the trial judge. The jurisdiction of an appellant court to interfere with an award of damages made by a judge
D is strictly limited :

" To justify reversing the trial judge on the question of the amount of damages it will generally be necessary that this court should be convinced either that the judge acted on some wrong principle of law, or that the amount awarded was so extremely high or so very small as to make it, in the judgment of this court, an entirely erroneous estimate of the damage
E to which the plaintiff is entitled."

Flint v. *Lovell* (45) per GREER, L.J.

ASHWORTH, J., took all the relevant factors affecting the deceased into account. He was twenty years and four months at the date of his death; his working prospects were favourable; he was in good health, living at home, and had become engaged to be married seven days before his death. Having
F considered all these facts the judge, bearing in mind what had been said by VISCOUNT SIMON, L.C., in *Benham* v. *Gambling* (46), fixed what he regarded as a reasonable sum for the loss of expectation of life at £500. Having done so, he proceeded to cross check his figure in relation to the figure of £200 awarded by the House of Lords in *Benham* v. *Gambling* (46) and then to make allowance for the fall in the value of money to the extent of about two and a half times
G since 1941. He also checked his estimate by reference to similar awards made by himself and other judges over the period since 1941. I have been unable to see that there was anything which might be criticised in his approach to the problem.

The respondent, in justifying the Court of Appeal's decision (44), criticised ASHWORTH, J.'s judgment by arguing that he failed properly to measure his award of damages. I am not sure that I appreciate the significance of measurement
H in this connexion, but if " to measure " is to estimate, then the trial judge certainly made an estimate of the damages on a correct principle of law and I am quite unable to say that it was a wholly erroneous estimate. Next, it was said that his estimate was arbitrary; but if the estimate is, as it must be, of " incommensurables ", to use LORD SIMON's language in *Benham* v. *Gambling* (43), then the figure must of necessity be an arbitrary one. There is, in my judgment, no
I substance in the respondent's criticism of the trial judge's award.

It would be an easier matter, however, to criticise the approach made by the Court of Appeal in the opinion of SALMON, L.J., (47). He declined to accept that the figure of £200 fixed by the House of Lords in *Benham* v. *Gambling* (46) for a

(43) [1941] 1 All E.R. at p. 13; [1941] A.C. at p. 168.
(44) [1966] 3 All E.R. 327.
(45) [1934] All E.R. Rep. at pp. 202, 203; [1935] 1 K.B. at p. 360.
(46) [1941] 1 All E.R. 7; [1941] A.C. 157.
(47) [1966] 3 All E.R. at p. 331.

child of 2½ years was a figure which could properly be related to the figure to be **A** awarded to an adult in the prime of life. He said (48):

> " It seems to me to be manifest from what was stated in *Benham* v. *Gambling* (49) that if the deceased in that case had been a young man in Paul Naylor's position, the House of Lords would have assessed the damages at much more than £200—probably at £400."

From this basis he arrived, after allowing for a fall in the value of money since **B** 1941, at his figure of £1,000. It is by no means clear to me from the speech of LORD SIMON in *Benham* v. *Gambling* (50) what his award would have been for an adult except that in his view the case of a young child would justify a lower award, although he regarded £200 as a generous award justified by the exceptionally favourable circumstances of the child in that case. How much larger his figure **C** would have been for an adult I am unable to say. It may well be that a slightly higher award is justified in the case of an adult who has survived the dangers of childhood than for a very young child, but the variation would, in my opinion, be within a small compass and certainly not in the range of one hundred per cent. In view of the appreciable drop in infant mortality rates the expectation of life in a young child must now be much greater than it was, say, fifty years ago. . **D**
I am confirmed in my judgment by the case of *Andrews* v. *Freeborough* (51) where another division of the Court of Appeal refused to interfere with an award of £500 for the loss of expectation of life for a girl of eight.

I have, therefore, reached the conclusion that there was no ground for holding that ASHWORTH, J., made other than a proper and correct estimate of the damages to be awarded and that the Court of Appeal (52) were not justified in interfering **E** with his award. I would allow the appeal and restore the judgment of ASHWORTH, J.

LORD DEVLIN: My Lords, until the decision of this House in *Benham* v. *Gambling* (49), there was great uncertainty about the proper amount to award as damages for loss of expectation of life. In that case the trial judge had awarded £1,200 in respect of the death of a boy aged 2½ years. The Court of Appeal (53) **F** left the award undisturbed, MACKINNON, L.J., saying (54) that he could not say that £1,200 was too much because he had no idea what the proper figure was. The House (49) considered that damages for loss of expectation of life should be moderate and reduced the sum to £200. The annotator of this decision in the ALL ENGLAND LAW REPORTS said (55):

> " The position now is that, in the case of a young child, £200 is to be **G** considered as the maximum figure. It is not clear whether, in the case of an adult, the figure is to be greater or less, but, as it is in all cases to be a moderate figure, it is clear that in such a case it should not greatly exceed £200."

In fact thereafter with rare exceptions £200 was taken as the invariable figure **H** for the ordinary adult death. The House (49) had lowered the figure from what would presumably otherwise have been the standard, because of the extreme youth of the child and then raised it because of his most favourable circumstances. It has been assumed that these two factors cancel each other out. The assessment being based on an estimate of prospective happiness, the ground given by VISCOUNT SIMON, L.C., (56) for the reduction was that there was so much **I** uncertainty about a child's future that no confident estimate could be made. This is an exceptional principle to be applied in the law of damages, where difficulty in calculation is not ordinarily taken as a ground either for reducing or

---

(48) [1966] 3 All E.R. at p. 334, letter I.
(49) [1941] 1 All E.R. 7; [1941] A.C. 157.
(50) [1941] 1 All E.R. at p. 8; [1941] A.C. at p. 160.   (51) [1966] 2 All E.R. 721.
(52) [1966] 3 All E.R. 327.   (53) [1940] 1 All E.R. 275.
(54) [1940] 1 All E.R. at pp. 278, 279.   (55) [1941] 1 All E.R. at p. 8, letter A.
(56) [1941] 1 All E.R. at p. 13; [1941] A.C. at p. 168.

A for increasing the award. On the other hand, the circumstances that were considered exceptionally favourable in 1941 (being the fact that the child lived in a country village where the risk of road dangers and disease would be less than in a crowded centre and that the father was in steady employment) would not now be considered in any way out of the ordinary. However this may be, the figure has been taken as if, subject to the change in the value of money, it had been fixed by

B statute in 1941; and indeed the decision in *Benham* v. *Gambling* (57) has been described as " judicial legislation ". The current figure, which in fact the judge awarded in this case, is £500 and the evidence at the trial showed that this was almost exactly the equivalent of £200 in 1941.

Counsel for the respondent has not invited the House to re-open the basis of the assessment made in *Benham* v. *Gambling* (57); but he contends that it is wrong to

C take the figure of £200, as if it or its current equivalent had been settled for all time, and that it is the duty of the trial judge to measure out the appropriate sum in each case on the principles laid down in *Benham* v. *Gambling* (57). The Court of Appeal (58) acceded to this argument to the extent of raising the figure to £1,000.

The difficulty about the argument is that it is only in a most exceptional case

D that the principles laid down in *Benham* v. *Gambling* (57) admit of any flexibility in the result. Every assessment of general damage for physical injury, whether it causes loss of life or of a limb or of a faculty, has got to start from the basis of a conventional sum. If it did not, assessments would be chaotic. Every judge has within his knowledge, not only the figure of £500 as the conventional sum appropriate to loss of life, but a number of other conventional sums appropriate

E to losses of limbs and faculties. The conventional figure for loss of a limb or a faculty is only the starting point for a voyage of assessment which may, and generally does, end up at a different figure. To a great reader the loss of an eye is a serious deprivation; the value of a leg to an active sportsman is higher than it is to the average man. Then there is usually some additional financial loss, actual or potential, to be taken into account.

F While the loss of a single faculty, however, may be more serious for one individual than for another, the loss of all the faculties is, generally speaking, the same for all. Thus for loss of expectation of life the conventional figure has become the norm, unless the case is definitely abnormal. What, then, apart from the special case, would justify an increase or reduction in the price of happiness? No one—least of all any lawyer—can tell. The directions laid down in *Benham* v.

G *Gambling* (57) are such that, except in a strictly defined minority of special cases, the starting point for the assessment must also be the finish. In *Rose* v. *Ford* (59) LORD WRIGHT, having said that damages must be fair and moderate, foresaw that special cases might occur (60) " such as that of an infant, or an imbecile, or an incurable invalid, or a person involved in hopeless difficulties ". LORD SIMON, L.C., in *Benham* v. *Gambling* (57) elaborates on this. Except for the extremities

H of childhood and old age, prospective length of years makes no difference. Social position and worldly possessions are also irrelevant. Nevertheless the figure of £500 is, when compared with awards arising out of comparatively slight physical injury, extremely low. It is not immediately obvious why, as LORD SIMON says (61), " damages which would be proper for a disabling injury may well be much greater than for deprivation of life ". Compensation for the diminution of happi-

I ness due to the amputation of a leg cannot logically be less than compensation for happiness lost altogether. Nor is it immediately obvious why loss of happiness that is caused by prolonged unconsciousness should command higher compensation than a similar loss caused by death. The fact is that the whole of this branch of the law has been settled on what LORD WRIGHT in *Rose* v. *Ford* (62) called

(57) [1941] 1 All E.R. 7; [1941] A.C. 157.   (58) [1966] 3 All E.R. 327.
(59) [1937] 3 All E.R. 359; [1937] A.C. 826.
(60) [1937] 3 All E.R. at p. 373, letter C; [1937] A.C. at p. 850.
(61) [1941] 1 All E.R. at p. 13, letter F; [1941] A.C. at p. 168.
(62) [1937] 3 All E.R. at p. 367, letter F; [1937] A.C. at p. 841.

" the basis of convenience rather than of logic ". The law has endeavoured to A
avoid two results, both of which it considered would be undesirable. The one is
that a wrongdoer should have to pay large sums for disabling and nothing at all
for killing; the other is that the large sum appropriate to total disablement should
come as a windfall to the beneficiaries of the victim's estate. To arrive at a figure
which avoids these two undesirable results is a matter for compromise and not for
judicial determination. I cannot think that a judge derives much assistance B
either from the artificialities—inevitable when convenience is cloaked with logic
—in LORD SIMON's speech (63) or from the customary exhortations to use common
sense. It would, I think, be a great improvement if this head of damage was
abolished and replaced by a short Act of Parliament fixing a suitable sum which
a wrongdoer whose act has caused death should pay into the estate of the
deceased. While the law remains as it is, I think that it is less likely to fall into C
disrespect if judges treat *Benham* v. *Gambling* (64) as an injunction to stick to a
fixed standard than if they start revaluing happiness, each according to his own
ideas.

I would allow the appeal.

LORD UPJOHN: My Lords, in this case your lordships are concerned D
only with the question of damages for loss of expectation of life. The old common
law maxim was actio personalis moritur cum persona, so that a person who died
as the result of the tortious act of another could not claim any damages for pain,
suffering, hospital expenses or loss of earnings during the remainder of his life or
for damages for loss of expectation of life. That rule was abolished by the Law
Reform (Miscellaneous Provisions) Act, 1934. Thereafter many claims for damages E
for loss of expectation of life due to the tortious act of another came before the
courts. As SELLERS, L.J., said in his dissenting judgment in the Court of Appeal
(65), this led to many inquiries into the happiness and prospects of life of a
deceased person in order to assess the amount to be paid for the lost years. He
pointed out (66) that it became an almost impossible task and an inquiry distaste-
ful and repugnant to relatives and counsel alike. Then came the case of *Benham* F
v. *Gambling* (64) in your lordships' House where VISCOUNT SIMON, L.C., delivering
an opinion (63) with which all of their lordships agreed, gave valuable guidance
as to the principle on which damages for loss of expectation of life should be
assessed. He propounded the problem to be solved in these cases (67):

" The question thus resolves itself into fixing a reasonable figure to be
paid by way of damages for the loss of a measure of prospective happiness."   G

He then pointed out (68) that in attempting to assess damages for such loss the
judge or jury were equating incommensurables. In other words, he was really
saying that in the ordinary case the sum to be awarded by way of damages for
loss of expectation of life is necessarily a conventional sum. He then laid down
(68) a principle of law that in assessing such damages " whether in the case of a
child or an adult very moderate figures should be chosen ".   H

ASHWORTH, J., came to the conclusion in this case that the proper sum of
damages was £500. The Court of Appeal can only set aside that award and
substitute its own figure if it comes to the conclusion that the judge has acted on
some wrong principle of law or has misapprehended the facts or has for those or
other reasons made a wholly erroneous estimate of the damage suffered (see
Davies v. *Powell Duffryn Associated Collieries, Ltd.* (69), per LORD WRIGHT).   I
The judge delivered a very careful judgment and it is clear that he appreciated

(63) [1941] 1 All E.R. at p. 8; [1941] A.C. at p. 160.
(64) [1941] 1 All E.R. 7; [1941] A.C. 157.
(65) [1966] 3 All E.R. at p. 328.
(66) [1966] 3 All E.R. at p. 329, letter D.
(67) [1941] 1 All E.R. at p. 12, letter E; [1941] A.C. at p. 166.
(68) [1941] 1 All E.R. at p. 13; [1941] A.C. at p. 168.
(69) [1942] 1 All E.R. at p. 664, letter H; [1942] A.C. at p. 616.

A the facts precisely and also the principles of law that he should adopt in assessing damages, for he referred more than once to LORD SIMON's speech in *Benham* v. *Gambling* (70). So the only question is whether he made a wholly erroneous estimate in awarding damages of £500.

My lords, I think that the judge approached this matter in an impeccable way. He said:

B

    " The approach which I have endeavoured to make in this case is, first of all, to assess, in the light of knowledge of what has been assessed in other cases, what I consider to be reasonable as a sum for the loss of Paul Naylor's expectation of life, and I have then gone through a process of cross-checking that sum."

C I will refer later to the first cross-check. The second cross-check which he applied was this:

    " The other cross-check which I have applied is one based on awards made to my knowledge and by myself in the period of about ten years ago."

He then referred to a reported decision of his in which he awarded £350 to a young
D man (apparently in 1956) and then in his cross-check he added on twenty-five per cent. in respect of the fall in the value of money. So he reached the area of £400 to £450.

The first cross-check was based on the fact that the judge had before him the evidence of an expert in economics, statistics and mathematical economics who produced a table (the accuracy of which was not challenged), which showed
E that since the decision in *Benham* v. *Gambling* (71) the value of the £1 in purchasing power had fallen by about two and one-half times. Applying that table to the figures given in *Benham* v. *Gambling* (71) he found that, as a cross-check, the result came to £500, but he very rightly emphasised that that was merely a cross-check and it was not the basis on which he reached the figure of £500.

F My lords, when assessing damages which depend in part on loss of future earning capacity (not relevant in this case) the depreciation of the pound and the inevitable rise in wages may be very relevant. In relation to the assessment of damages for loss of expectation of life, however, I do not think that evidence as to the fall in the purchasing power of the pound has much relevance. For my part, though not questioning its technical admissibility, I deprecate the submission of
G such evidence in these circumstances; if tendered it is of little if any weight. It is clearly established that damages for the incommensurables with which alone your lordships are dealing, such as loss of expectation of life or (in an action by a living person) for loss of an eye or some other organ, must necessarily fall to be estimated within a bracket in justice both to the sufferer and to the tortfeasor. Over the years the conventional sum to be awarded for such head of damage
H rises no doubt, but by fits and by starts rather than by any estimation of the purchasing power of the pound, and in my view so it should be. This is a matter which is better and safely left to the experience and commonsense of judges who day by day have to judge of these matters. That was the exact approach of ASHWORTH, J., to this problem, with which I entirely agree. He fixed on £500 as a
I result of his great experience in these matters, and in my view his assessment cannot be said to be erroneous, still less wholly erroneous. The recent case of *Andrews* v. *Freeborough* (72), where the Court of Appeal refused to interfere with an award of £500 for the loss of expectation of life for a girl of eight, accords with this view.

---

(70) [1941] 1 All E.R. at p. 8; [1941] A.C. at p. 160.
(71) [1941] 1 All E.R. 7; [1941] A.C. 157.
(72) [1966] 2 All E.R. 721.

I myself think that in assessing £1,000 by way of damages the majority of the   **A**
Court of Appeal (73) fixed a sum which was too high and which could not
properly be described as moderate.

For these reasons I would allow this appeal.

Appeal allowed.

Solicitors: *Herbert Smith & Co.*, agents for *James Chapman & Co.*, Manchester   **B**
(for the appellants); *Rowley, Ashworth & Co.* (for the respondent).

[*Reported by* KATHLEEN J. H. O'BRIEN, *Barrister-at-Law.*]

C

HELY-HUTCHINSON v. BRAYHEAD, LTD. AND ANOTHER.

[QUEEN'S BENCH DIVISION (Roskill, J.), December 15, 16, 19, 20, 21, 1966.]

*Company—Director—Authority—Ostensible authority—Chairman and chief
executive of holding company signed letters giving collateral indemnity and
guarantee to plaintiff with a view to plaintiff's lending money to a company*   **D**
*controlled by the holding company—Plaintiff was director of holding company
and chairman of company to which money was to be lent—Plaintiff was not
familiar with the articles of association of the holding company and acted in
the transaction as an individual—Chairman had ostensible authority to act on
behalf of holding company—Articles of association of holding company*   **E**
*required disclosure to the board of directors' interests in contracts—Disclosure
to board not made—Whether rule in* Turquand's *case applicable—Whether
contracts of indemnity and guarantee were enforceable by plaintiff—Companies
Act, 1948 (11 & 12 Geo. 6 c. 38), s. 199.*

The second defendant, R., was chairman and chief executive of the
defendant company, which had power to appoint but had not appointed a
managing director; R., however, acted as if he were the defendant company's   **F**
managing director. R. was associated in business with the plaintiff, who
became chairman and managing director of, and had a controlling interest
in, P., Ltd., of which R. was a director. The business of P., Ltd. lay in the
electronics field, in which field of business subsidiaries of the defendant
company were also interested. During 1964 P., Ltd., which had been prosper-
ing, began to make losses, and the plaintiff guaranteed a credit of £50,000,   **G**
which P., Ltd. obtained from merchant bankers. Early in 1965 the defendant
company entered into an agreement with a view to acquiring a controlling
interest in P., Ltd.; this involved the sale of a large number of the plaintiff's
shares in P., Ltd. to the defendant company, whereby the plaintiff acquired,
s R. knew, some £70,000 in cash. In consequence of this arrangement the
plaintiff became in January, 1965, a director of the defendant company,   **H**
which advanced large sums of money to P., Ltd. and took over liability for
credits which P., Ltd. had received from a second firm of merchant bankers.
The plaintiff did not then attend board meetings of the defendant company.
On May 19, 1965, immediately following a board meeting of the defendant
company, which was the first that the plaintiff did attend, R. and the
plaintiff privately discussed the possibility of the plaintiff's providing further   **I**
money for P., Ltd. which was still in need of finance. Four documents were
then signed, of which two, written on the defendant company's headed
writing paper in the form of letters to the plaintiff, were signed by R. as
chairman of the defendant company. The first letter was expressed as an
undertaking to indemnify the plaintiff against any loss which might occur by
his having to fulfil his personal guarantee to the merchant bankers for a

---

(73) [1966] 3 All E.R. 327.

A   figure not to exceed £50,000, the consideration for this indemnity to be a
    personal loan by the plaintiff to P., Ltd. of a sum not exceeding £10,000;
    the second letter agreed that the defendant company would guarantee repay-
    ment of any moneys loaned by the plaintiff personally to P., Ltd. In reliance
    (as the court found) on the apparent authority of R. to sign these documents
    for the defendant company, the plaintiff advanced a total of £45,000 to
B   P., Ltd. between May 27 and June 3, 1965. The giving of the indemnity and
    the guarantee was not reported to the board of the defendant company. By
    art. 99* of the defendant company's articles of association, the contents of
    which were not known to the plaintiff, the director of a company was
    permitted to contract with the company without being liable to account for
    any profit made by him provided that the nature of his interest in the contract
C   was declared at a meeting of the directors as required by s. 199† of the
    Companies Act, 1948. Any interest of the plaintiff and of R. under the
    indemnity and the guarantee was not disclosed at any board meeting of the
    defendant company. On Sept. 27, 1965, the plaintiff resigned from the board
    of the defendant company. Having had to meet his obligations to the
    merchant bankers in the sum of nearly £51,000, he sought to recover both
D   the £45,000 loan to P., Ltd. and the £51,000 (subject to certain adjustments)
    from the defendant company, alternatively as damages from R. for alleged
    breach of warranty of authority.
        Held: (i) the contracts of indemnity and guarantee were enforceable by
    the plaintiff against the defendant company (see p. 29, letter B, post) for the
    following reasons—
E   (a) because, although R. had not implied authority to commit the
    defendant company to the transaction of indemnity and guarantee merely by
    reason of being the defendant company's chairman or managing director, yet
    the defendant company had knowingly allowed R. to hold himself out as
    having ostensible or apparent authority to enter into transactions such as
    those constituted by the indemnity and the guarantee, and the plaintiff had
F   relied on R.'s representation and ostensible authority in entering into the
    transaction of indemnity and guarantee and in advancing £45,000; and the
    plaintiff was entitled so to rely, since he was acting as an individual and was
    not acting in his capacity as a director of the defendant company in entering
    into the transaction of indemnity and guarantee and that transaction was
    not an unusual transaction, so that the rule in *Turquand's* case‡ was not
G   excluded (see p. 20, letter I, p. 26, letters B and G, and p. 28, letter D, post).
        Freeman & Lockyer (a firm) v. *Buckhurst Park Properties (Mangal), Ltd.*
    ([1964] 1 All E.R. 630) followed.
        Morris v. *Kanssen* ([1946] 1 All E.R. 586) and *Howard* v. *Patent Ivory
    Manufacturing Co.* ((1888), 38 Ch.D. 156) distinguished.
        (b) because the fact that the transaction of indemnity and guarantee
H   might have been effected in breach of art. 99 of the articles of association of
    the defendant company and of s. 199 of the Companies Act, 1948, did not
    render the contracts constituted by the transaction of indemnity and
    guarantee void or unenforceable (see p. 28, letter E, post).
        Toms v. *Cinema Trust Co., Ltd.* ([1915] W.N. 29) distinguished.
        (ii) further, if the plaintiff had not been entitled to recover under (i) above,
I   he would have been entitled to recover against R. for breach of warranty of
    authority to bind the defendant company to the transaction of indemnity
    and guarantee (see p. 29, letter D, post).
        [As to persons dealing with a company being bound to know its constitution,
    see 6 HALSBURY'S LAWS (3rd Edn.) 299, para. 603, pp. 430, 431, paras. 833, 834;

---

* Article 99, so far as material, is set out at p. 20, letter D, post.
† Section 199, so far as material, is set out in footnote (4) on p. 19, post.
‡ [1843-60] All E.R. Rep. 435.

and as to the rule in *Royal British Bank* v. *Turquand*, see ibid., p. 430, para. 833, **A**
text and note (*f*); and for cases, see 9 DIGEST (Repl.) 559, 560, *3701-3707, 675,
4458-4460*, and 96, 97, *428-430*. As to the statutory duty of a director of a
company to disclose his interest in contracts with that company, see 6 HALSBURY'S
LAWS (3rd Edn.) 301, 302, para. 607, and p. 321, para. 633.

For the Companies Act, 1948, s. 199, see 3 HALSBURY'S STATUTES (2nd Edn.)
618.]   **B**

Cases referred to:

> *Freeman & Lockyer (a firm)* v. *Buckhurst Park Properties (Mangal), Ltd.*, [1964]
>   1 All E.R. 630; [1964] 2 Q.B. 480; [1964] 2 W.L.R. 618; 3rd Digest
>   Supp.
> *Houghton (J. C.) & Co.* v. *Nothard, Lowe and Wills, Ltd.*, [1927] 1 K.B. 246;
>   96 L.J.K.B. 25; 136 L.T. 140; *affd.* H.L., [1927] All E.R. Rep. 97; **C**
>   [1928] A.C. 1; 97 L.J.K.B. 76; 138 L.T. 210; 9 Digest (Repl.) 505, *3330*.
> *Howard* v. *Patent Ivory Manufacturing Co., Re Patent Ivory Manufacturing
>   Co.*, (1888), 38 Ch.D. 156; 57 L.J.Ch. 878; 68 L.T. 395; 9 Digest
>   (Repl.) 684, *4510*.
> *Morris* v. *Kanssen*, [1946] 1 All E.R. 586; [1946] A.C. 459; 115 L.J.Ch. 177;
>   174 L.T. 353; *affg.* sub nom. *Kanssen* v. *Rialto (West End), Ltd.*, [1944] **D**
>   1 All E.R. 751; [1944] Ch. 346; 9 Digest (Repl.) 460, *3012*.
> *Royal British Bank* v. *Turquand*, [1843-60] All E.R. Rep. 435; (1856), 6
>   E. & B. 327; 25 L.J.Q.B. 317; 119 E.R. 886; 9 Digest (Repl.) 660,
>   *4374*.
> *Toms* v. *Cinema Trust Co., Ltd.*, [1915] W.N. 29; 9 Digest (Repl.) 548, *3611*.
> *Wright* v. *Horton*, (1887), 12 App. Cas. 371; 56 L.J.Ch. 873; 56 L.T. 782; **E**
>   52 J.P. 179; 10 Digest (Repl.) 811, *5261*.

Action.

In this action, commenced by writ dated Nov. 17, 1965, and tried in the
commercial court, the plaintiff, Richard Michael John Hely-Hutchinson, Viscount
Suirdale, chairman and managing director of Perdio Electronics, Ltd., sued the **F**
defendant company, Brayhead, Ltd. (" Brayhead ") and the second defendant,
Anthony James Richards, claiming in respect of sums amounting to some £96,000.
The claim against the defendant company was based on two documents, dated
May 19, 1965, signed by the second defendant (" Mr. Richards ") as chairman of
Brayhead, whereby it was agreed that the plaintiff should be indemnified against
certain loss and should be guaranteed in respect of the return of moneys that might **G**
be loaned by him to Perdio Electronics, Ltd. (" Perdio "). The agreement of
indemnity is referred to as document " C.23 ", and the agreement of guarantee
as document " C.26 ". Brayhead having denied the authority of Mr. Richards
to sign the two documents, the plaintiff joined Mr. Richards as second defendant,
claiming against him damages for breach of warranty of authority. The following
statement of facts is summarised from the judgment of ROSKILL, J.   **H**

In the course of 1956 the plaintiff had met Mr. Richards as a result of an
advertisement by Mr. Richards in " The Times " newspaper. Mr. Richards was
then in practice as an accountant and he had a small financial interest in Perdio
which was then a small private company of negligible business achievements. The
plaintiff acquired an interest in Perdio, ultimately the controlling interest, and
in or about 1956 he became Perdio's chairman and managing director. Mr. **I**
Richards' financial interest in Perdio increased as Perdio prospered and he
remained throughout on its board of directors. Perdio became a public company
in 1962. Some time in the early 1960's Mr. Richards and his brother became
interested in, and acquired control of another company, Surtees Investments,
Ltd., which in 1962 acquired control of " Brayhead ". Under the direction of
Mr. Richards, who became the chairman and chief executive of Brayhead, that
company expanded rapidly and came to control many subsidiary companies
having interests in many fields, including the electronics field.

A   Towards the end of 1964 Perdio's past prosperity turned into the making of
losses, and discussions which took place between the plaintiff and Mr. Richards
culminated on Jan. 1, 1965, in a document of that date called " Heads of Terms ",
which had contractual force and pursuant to which it was intended that Brayhead
should acquire some sixty per cent. of the shares in Perdio, thus obtaining
effective control. The agreement provided for the immediate sale to Brayhead
B   of 850,000 shares at 3s. 3d. per share, which was about thirty per cent. of the
issued ordinary share capital, and 750,000 of these shares were in fact sold to
Brayhead by the plaintiff, who ultimately became possessed, in consequence of
this sale, of some £70,000 in cash. In order to comply with the requirements of
the London Stock Exchange, collateral undertakings were given by the directors
of Perdio (including the plaintiff and Mr. Richards) to the firm of stockbrokers
C   concerned that the directors would buy for not less than 3s. 3d. a share any of
the remaining ordinary shares of Perdio which might be offered for sale on the
London market by the outside shareholders. As a result of the agreement the
plaintiff became a director of Brayhead on Jan. 14, 1965, and his appointment was
duly filed on Jan. 25, 1965. Prior to May 19, 1965, however, he never attended
a board meeting, and (so ROSKILL, J., found) he never at any material time read
D   or saw Brayhead's memorandum and articles of association and he remained at
all times wholly unaware of the contents of the memorandum and articles. The
plaintiff remained chairman and managing director of Perdio and Mr. Richards
remained on the board of that company.
      Due to its financial difficulties during 1964 and its need for additional working
capital, Perdio had obtained a revocable revolving acceptance credit facility
E   from the merchant bankers, Guinness Mahon & Co., Ltd. (hereinafter referred to
as " Guinness Mahon ") in the sum of £50,000, for which sum the plaintiff had
given on July 20, 1964, his own personal guarantee to Guinness Mahon. This
revolving acceptance credit facility was, however, insufficient, as were the overdraft facilities which Perdio had with its bankers. In consequence very shortly
after Jan. 1, 1965, Brayhead agreed to provide for Perdio the sum of £150,000
F   in cash, of which in the event £125,000 was advanced before May 19, 1965; and
Brayhead additionally took over as its own liability Perdio's liability to another
firm of merchant bankers, Kleinwort Benson, Ltd. By the beginning of May,
1965, Perdio's position was extremely serious; if Perdio was to be kept going
drastic action had to be taken, and there was no other source of finance than the
plaintiff and Mr. Richards. Mr. Richards knew that the plaintiff had the sum of
G   £70,000 in cash, and a discussion took place between them some three days
before May 19, 1965, at which the plaintiff, so the trial judge found, made it quite
plain to Mr. Richards that if the plaintiff were to lend his own money to Perdio,
then he had to be relieved of his liability to purchase the shares of the outside
shareholders in Perdio as also of his liability under his guarantee to Guinness
Mahon. A board meeting of Brayhead was held on May 19, 1965, which was the
H   first board meeting which the plaintiff had attended since he became a director
of Brayhead, and the minutes of this board meeting disclosed that a report was
made on the purchase of the 850,000 ordinary shares in Perdio, that the plaintiff
informed the board of the closing of Perdio's Sunderland factory, and that Mr.
Richards pointed out that Brayhead had agreed to lend £150,000 to Perdio and
had accepted responsibility for the Kleinwort Benson acceptance credits; but
I   nothing was recorded in the minutes as having been said by Mr. Richards about
what was to happen at the conclusion of the board meeting. Immediately after
the board meeting Mr. Richards and the plaintiff met in Mr. Richards' office. At
this meeting Mr. Richards and the plaintiff continued their previous discussion
about the plaintiff's giving further financial aid to Perdio. The trial judge found
that both parties were negotiating and that, when the two documents sued on
(C.23 and C.26) were signed at this meeting, the parties were contracting with
reference to the position that the plaintiff had £70,000 available but was by no
means certain that all that sum was going to be available for Perdio, and that,

subject to that sum being available, he was willing to advance money to Perdio **A**
provided that he obtained from Brayhead, viz., through Mr. Richards acting on
behalf of Brayhead, protection in respect of both the plaintiff's contingent
liability to the open market shareholders in Perdio and his guarantee to Guinness
Mahon. The trial judge found that the plaintiff had made no oral contract to lend
£70,000 without qualification, and that the provision of the £70,000 was not a
condition precedent to or a fundamental term of any liability to be assumed by **B**
Brayhead and the documents C.23 and C.26. At this meeting four documents
came into existence (C.23 to C.26 inclusive). Under C.25, which was signed by
the plaintiff, by Mr. Richards and by other directors of Brayhead who were
available and were shareholders of Perdio, the parties agreed to take up certain
Perdio shares held on the market. This document was signed first, the other parties
entering Mr. Richards' office to sign it. Under C.24, which was a separate letter **C**
to the plaintiff signed by Mr. Richards, the maximum liability of the plaintiff was
limited to £10,000 and Brayhead agreed to take up any additional shares offered.
This was a collateral agreement between, Brayhead, acting by Mr. Richards (as
the trial judge found) limiting the plaintiff's liability. The documents sued on
(C.23 and C.26) were letters written on Brayhead's headed writing paper, and
were then signed by Mr. Richards. They were as follows: **D**

[C.23]

May 19, 1965.

" Dear Lord Suirdale,

Re Perdio Electronics, Ltd.—Acceptance Credits.

This letter may be taken as an undertaking to indemnify you against any **E**
loss which may occur by you having to fulfil your personal guarantee to
Guinness Mahon & Co., Ltd., for a figure not to exceed £50,000. It is agreed
that the consideration for this indemnity will be a personal loan by you to
Perdio Electronics, Ltd. in a sum not exceeding £10,000.

Yours sincerely,
A. J. Richards, **F**
Chairman."

[C.26]

May 19, 1965.

" Dear Lord Suirdale,
It is hereby agreed that Brayhead, Ltd. will guarantee repayment of any
moneys loaned by you personally to Perdio Electronics, Ltd. It is a condition **G**
of this guarantee that at least six months' notice will be given by you to
Brayhead, Ltd., should the guarantee have to be implemented.

Yours sincerely,
A. J. Richards,
Chairman."
H
Between May 27 and June 3, 1965, the plaintiff advanced to Perdio four sums in
cash, making a total of £45,000, and the trial judge found that each of those sums
and the totality of those sums was advanced by the plaintiff because of and in
reliance on the promises apparently contained in the two documents of indemnity
and guarantee (C.23 and C.26), and further in reliance on the apparent authority
which Mr. Richards appeared to have when he signed those documents; if there **I**
were any defect in Mr. Richards' authority to sign C.23 and C.26, the plaintiff
was wholly unaware of it. On June 10, 1965, a further £17,500 was advanced by
Brayhead to Perdio, but more money was still needed. About this time, however,
the plaintiff (who had placed on deposit at Guinness Mahon some £60,000 of the
£70,000 he had received from Brayhead for his Perdio shares) found himself unable
to advance further sums because Guinness Mahon had frozen part of his bank
account. The plaintiff informed Mr. Richards of his inability to provide any sum
which might be needed above the £45,000, and on June 23, 1965, Brayhead

A advanced a further £10,000 and Mr. Richards and his brother between them a further £15,000 to Perdio.

There was a number of board meetings subsequent to the meeting of May 19, 1965, but Mr. Richards did not report at any of them the two documents of indemnity and guarantee (C.23 and C.26) which he had given to the plaintiff. On Sept. 27, 1965, the plaintiff formally resigned from the board of Brayhead. The

B plaintiff met his obligations to Guinness Mahon, amounting to nearly £51,000 including interest.

R. A. MacCrindle, Q.C., and *G. Slynn* for the plaintiff.

M. Finer, Q.C., and *R. B. S. Instone* for the defendant company and the second defendant.

C   ROSKILL, J., having stated the facts and reviewed the evidence, and having made the findings of facts previously indicated, continued: The plaintiff, Lord Suirdale, having had to meet his obligations to Guinness Mahon, claims a sum not far short of £51,000 in respect of principal and interest under document C.23 [the letter of indemnity set out at p. 18, letter E, supra]. In addition he claims a declaration that he is entitled under C.26 [the letter of guarantee, set

D out at p. 18, letter G, supra] to recover the £45,000 lent to Perdio together with interest thereon. The reason for the difference in the form of claim is simply this, that under the terms of C.26, the guarantee of the loan to Perdio, six months' notice had to be given by the plaintiff to Brayhead of his wish to have the guarantee implemented. At the date of the writ that six months had not in fact expired and, accordingly, when the points of claim were framed all that could be

E sought was a declaration; but counsel for the defendants, very properly, at an early stage of the trial made it plain that as the six months were now up there was no question but that, whatever the technical position at the time of the writ, the position under the two documents was now the same and that in order to avoid the necessity for the issue of another writ and of a consolidated action, I could treat the whole claim as being a claim for the sums just referred to.

F The defences, apart from those of which I have already disposed by my findings of fact, can, I think, be summarised in this way. First, it is said that there was in Mr. Richards at the time he signed documents C.23 and C.26 no actual authority and no ostensible or apparent authority (1). Secondly, it is said that if, contrary to the latter of those defences, there would have been ostensible or apparent authority on which a " stranger " or a " third party " could rely in accordance

G with what is sometimes called the rule in *Royal British Bank* v. *Turquand* (2), yet the plaintiff was at all times a director of Brayhead and though he had not read the articles of association he must be treated for all purposes as having been put on notice of the contents of those articles including art. 99 which (3) in turn refers to s. 199 of the Companies Act, 1948, (4) and must be taken to have been aware of any lack of authority and could not rely on the ostensible or apparent

H authority of Mr. Richards. Thirdly, and independently, it was said that on the many cases dealing with the position where a third party relies on an act done

(1) The text of the documents is set out at p. 18, letters E and G, ante.
(2) [1843-60] All E.R. Rep. 435; (1856), 6 E. & B. 327.
(3) Article 99, so far as material, is set out at p. 20, letter D, post.
(4) Section 199, so far as material, provides as follows:—

" (1) . . . it shall be the duty of a director of a company who is in any way, whether

I directly or indirectly, interested in a contract or proposed contract with the company to declare the nature of his interest at a meeting of the directors of the company.

" (2) In the case of a proposed contract the declaration required by this section to be made by a director shall be made at the meeting of the directors at which the question of entering into the contract is first taken into consideration, or if the director was not at the date of that meeting interested in the proposed contract, at the next meeting of the directors held after he became so interested, and in a case where the director becomes interested in a contract after it is made, the said declaration shall be made at the first meeting of the directors held after the director becomes so interested . . .

" (4) Any director who fails to comply with the provisions of this section shall be liable to a fine not exceeding £100."

with apparent or ostensible authority, the rule in *Turquand's* case (5) had no A
present application because the transactions in question were not " usual "
transactions within the meaning of those cases both because of their own nature
and because in entering into these contracts the plaintiff had acted in breach of
his obligations and duties under either or both art. 99 and s. 199 of the Companies
Act, 1948. It was said fourthly that by reason of the provisions of art. 99 of
Brayhead's articles of association both the plaintiff and Brayhead had no con- B
tractual capacity, or at least that the plaintiff had no contractual capacity, and
that for that reason these contracts, all else apart, were void or voidable or at least
unenforceable. Counsel for the defendants was not prepared to take his argument
to the extent of saying that these contracts were, by virtue of s. 199 or art. 99,
illegal, though he argued in the alternative that at the worst for his clients these
were unenforceable unless and until the provisions of that section or that article C
had been complied with.

Article 99, so far as relevant, reads:

" A director may contract with and be interested in any contract or
proposed contract with the company either as vendor, purchaser or otherwise, and shall not be liable to account for any profit made by him by
reason of any such contract or proposed contract, provided that the nature D
of the interest of the director in such contract or proposed contract be
declared at a meeting of the directors as required by and subject to the
provisions of s. 199 of the [Companies Act, 1948]. No director shall vote as
a director in respect of any contract or arrangement in which he shall be
interested, and if he do so vote his vote shall not be counted . . ."
                                                                          E
Within these major points which I have mentioned there is a number of other
points which have to be dealt with. The right starting point is to deal with the
question of ostensible or apparent authority. Counsel for the plaintiff did not
put ostensible or apparent authority in the forefront of his argument. He claimed
first that there was here implied authority in Mr. Richards by virtue of the
position which he occupied as chairman of directors and de facto managing F
director. It is convenient to say at this point that although, as one would expect,
the articles of association of Brayhead contain power to appoint a managing
director (see art. 90), no formal appointment of a managing director was ever
made. I have no doubt at all, however, on the evidence to which I have listened
and from what I have read in the documents, that Mr. Richards was at all times
in the position of a managing director and was running Brayhead as if he were its G
managing director, and that he was at all times its chief executive in addition to
being chairman. The question to what extent there may be implied authority in
a chairman or managing director acting as such as distinct from express authority,
so as to bind a company to acts done by him in the course of his duties as chairman
or managing director or chief executive is one of considerable difficulty and one on
which there appears to be little or no relevant authority. The conception of H
implied authority in such a person as distinct from express authority is not easy
having regard to the cases on this branch of the law on ostensible or apparent
authority. It was urged by counsel for the plaintiff that, as Mr. Richards was both
chairman and de facto managing director, there was for that reason alone implied
authority in him to do what he did. I have some difficulty in accepting that. I
would not be prepared to hold that there is implied authority in a chairman of a I
company, merely by reason of his office, to do what Mr. Richards did in this
particular case in signing C.23 and C.26. I do not think that mere status, derived
from the holding of a particular office such as chairman or managing director or
chief executive, of itself implies an authority which would not otherwise exist.
There may be cases where such an implication can be made, but I do not propose
to decide this issue on this point because I am quite satisfied, for the reasons

---

(5) [1843-60] All E.R. Rep. 435; (1856), 6 E. & B. 327.

A which I shall endeavour to give in a moment, that there was ostensible or apparent authority in Mr. Richards to do what he did. I think that for a large number of reasons.

The set-up in Brayhead is easy to envisage. It was an industrial holding company with a large number of subsidiaries. Its directors were in the main—not all, but in the main—working directors, each in charge of a section of the

B holding company's subsidiaries. One would look after electronics, another engineering, and so on. They would all come back to Mr. Richards for advice and, which is more important, for decision from time to time on matters concerning their own particular group. The final decision, and most especially on any matter concerning finance, was Mr. Richards' and nobody else's. Sometimes, I daresay, the directors persuaded him to take or to refrain from taking a particular

C step; no doubt, like any wise chief executive, he sought and obtained advice before he made up his mind; but in all these cases the final decision, I am quite satisfied, rested with him and with nobody else. If one goes through the minutes and documents which have been put before me, one can see repeated examples of Mr. Richards acting in this way. Sometimes, of course, the matter would come back to the board for formal ratification after he had committed Brayhead,

D perhaps technically without express authority. On other occasions, of which there are a number of examples in the minutes, he plainly committed Brayhead and then, as it were, reported the matter afterwards. There is a striking example of this, as counsel for the plaintiff pointed out in cross-examining Mr. Richards, in connexion with a Mr. Short and his company. It is worth noting that in connexion with the agreement to advance £150,000 to Perdio and the taking over

E of the Kleinwort Benson acceptance credits there is no reference that I can find until a much later date, May 19, 1965, to Mr. Richards having reported this or obtained formal authority to enter into these commitments. More important, perhaps, in this connexion is what is revealed by one of the early documents, that Mr. Richards, acting for Brayhead, varied the agreement of January, 1965, by a document signed by him " A. J. Richards. A director duly authorised for and

F on behalf of Brayhead, Limited ". This came to the notice of Brayhead's then solicitors who wrote a letter to Mr. Bond saying it would be necessary for the directors to ratify the signing of that document and enclosing a draft minute for this purpose. That minute, I am told by Mr. Bond, was never in fact signed. I can understand that sort of thing happening in a busy office, but the importance of the point is not that the minute was not signed, but that the whole incident is

G illustrative of the sort of thing which Mr. Richards was doing. It is just what one would expect a busy man in his position to do. I have no doubt that the board knew that he was doing this sort of thing all the time and that whenever he thought it was necessary he assumed, or purported to assume, authority to bind Brayhead and that the board allowed him to do it and acquiesced in his doing it. That is not to say, adopting the phrase used yesterday by counsel for the

H defendants, that all the directors were " Yes men ", I am sure that they were nothing of the kind. Mr. Richards was a forceful personality, he knew his own mind and, as I said earlier in this judgment, he is a man of financial acumen. He quite clearly was allowed by Brayhead to hold himself out as having ostensible or apparent authority to enter into commitments of the kind which he entered into, or purported to enter into, when he signed C.23, C.24, C.25 and C.26. As I

I have already said, the defendants have not sought to say that the commitments in C.24 and C.25 were entered into without authority.

It seems plain on the cases that if Lord Suirdale were a " third party ", as it is sometimes called, or an outside party, or a " stranger " in relation to these transactions he would prima facie be entitled to rely on the rule in *Royal British Bank* v. *Turquand* (6). I would respectfully borrow the statement of that rule from the language which Lord Simonds in turn borrowed from 5 Halsbury's

---

(6) [1843-60] All E.R. Rep. 435; (1856), 6 E. & B. 327.

LAWS OF ENGLAND (2nd Edn.) p. 423, para. 69 in his speech in *Morris* v. A
Kanssen (7), a case to which I shall refer in a moment.   His lordship said
this:

" The so-called rule in *Turquand's* case (8) is, I think, correctly stated in
5 HALSBURY'S LAWS OF ENGLAND (2nd Edn.) p. 423: ' But persons contracting with a company and dealing in good faith may assume that acts
within its constitution and powers have been properly and duly performed,   B
and are not bound to inquire whether acts of internal management have
been regular '."

The cases on this branch of the law are numerous and until recently they were by
no means easy to reconcile.   They extended over more than a century and until
the recent decision of the Court of Appeal in *Freeman & Lockyer (a firm)* v. *Buck-* C
hurst Park Properties (Mangal), Ltd. (9) were by no means easy to understand.   I
am, however, absolved from any detailed consideration of the earlier cases by the
fact that in the *Freeman* case (9) the Court of Appeal exhaustively reviewed and
analysed those earlier cases and laid down, in terms which are binding on me,
what the law applicable to this part of the case is.

_I do not want to lengthen this judgment by extensive citations from the   D
judgments of WILLMER, PEARSON and DIPLOCK, L.JJ., but there are one or two
passages from which I should quote.   Towards the end of his judgment WILLMER,
L.J., said this (10):

" The plaintiffs here rely on the fact that the second defendant [who was
the director of the defendant company concerned], to the knowledge of the
defendant company's board, was acting throughout as managing director,   E
and was therefore being held out by the board as such.   The act of the
second defendant in engaging the plaintiffs was clearly one within the
ordinary ambit of the authority of a managing director. The plaintiffs accordingly do not have to inquire whether he was properly appointed.   It is
sufficient for them that under the articles there was in fact power to appoint
him as such."   F

The end of the headnote (11) summarises another passage in the judgment of
WILLMER, L.J., (12).   After referring to three cases on this branch of the law (13)
it states that these

" are cases of unusual transactions in none of which were the plaintiffs
in a position to allege that the person with whom they contracted was
acting within the scope of such authority as one in his position would be   G
expected to possess."

PEARSON, L.J., said (14):

" On the facts as found the plaintiffs were entitled to rely on the second
defendant's ostensible authority to give them instructions on behalf of the
defendant company, because there was a holding out of the second defendant   H
by the defendant company as its agent to conduct its business within the
ordinary scope of that business. The expressions ' ostensible authority ' and
' holding out ' are somewhat vague. The basis of them, when the situation is
analysed, is an estoppel by representation."

---

(7) [1946] 1 All E.R. 586 at p. 592; [1946] A.C. 459 at p. 474.   I
(8) [1843-60] All E.R. Rep. 435; (1856), 6 E. & B. 327.
(9) [1964] 1 All E.R. 630; [1964] 2 Q.B. 480.
(10) [1964] 1 All E.R. at p. 640; [1964] 2 Q.B. at p. 497.
(11) [1964] 2 Q.B. at p. 481.
(12) [1964] 1 All E.R. at pp. 636-639; [1964] 2 Q.B. at pp. 491-495.
(13) *J. C. Houghton & Co.* v. *Nothard, Lowe and Wills, Ltd.* [1927] 1 K.B. 246; *Kredit-*
bank Cassel, G.m.b.H. v. *Schenkers, Ltd.,* [1927] All E.R. Rep. 421; [1927] 1 K.B. 826;
Rama Corpn., Ltd. v. *Proved Tin and General Investments, Ltd.,* [1952] 1 All E.R. 554;
[1952] Q.B. 147.
(14) [1964] 1 All E.R. at p. 641; [1964] 2 Q.B. at p. 498.

A DIPLOCK, L.J., in, if I may respectfully say so, a most lucid judgment summarised the relevant law in these words (15):

> " If the foregoing analysis of the relevant law is correct, it can be summarised by stating four conditions which must be fulfilled to entitle a contractor to enforce against a company a contract entered into on behalf of the company by an agent who had no actual authority to do so. It must
B > be shown: (a) that a representation that the agent had authority to enter on behalf of the company into a contract of the kind sought to be enforced was made to the contractor; (b) that such representation was made by a person or persons who had ' actual ' authority to manage the business of the company either generally or in respect of those matters to which the contract relates; (c) that he (the contractor) was induced by such representation to
C > enter into the contract, i.e., that he in fact relied on it; and (d) that under its memorandum or articles of association the company was not deprived of the capacity either to enter into a contract of the kind sought to be enforced or to delegate authority to enter into a contract of that kind to the agent."

Let me first dispose of the fourth point. There is no suggestion that what Mr.
D Richards purported to do on May 19, 1965, was ultra vires Brayhead. No such defence was pleaded and counsel for the defendants expressly disclaimed any reliance on such a defence.

Coming back to the first of DIPLOCK, L.J.'s points, I have no doubt whatever that Mr. Richards represented to the plaintiff that he had authority, on behalf of Brayhead, to enter into contracts of this kind. On his second point I have no
E doubt that Mr. Richards was, by virtue of his position as de facto managing director of Brayhead or, as perhaps one might more compendiously put it, as Brayhead's chief executive, the man who had, if I may use the words of DIPLOCK, L.J., " actual authority to manage ", and he was acting as such when he signed those two documents. I have already said that I have not the slightest doubt that the plaintiff was induced to advance the £45,000 by the representations
F which were made to him.

What is first contended in answer to those arguments is that the plaintiff was a director of Brayhead, and, as a director of Brayhead (even though there would vis-à-vis a true third party be ostensible or apparent authority) the plaintiff cannot take advantage of the rule in *Turquand's* case (16) because he is not, for the purposes of that rule, a " stranger ", or an " outsider ", or a " third party ",
G whichever phrase one chooses to use. Counsel for the defendants, naturally, based this branch of his argument on the decision of the House of Lords, to which I have already referred, in *Morris* v. *Kanssen* (17). The complex facts of that case are summarised in the headnote, which I will not stop to read. Suffice it to say that Mr. Morris, the appellant, had thought that he was a director of a company when he was not a director and he thought that he had acquired certain
H shares in that company, having along with other purported directors purported to allot them to himself. He sought to rely on the rule in *Turquand's* case (16) for the purpose of establishing rights against the respondent, Kanssen. LORD SIMONDS, who delivered the leading speech, rejected the argument—the argument appears previously to have been rejected in the Court of Appeal in the judgment of LORD GREENE, M.R., (18). After stressing (19) that Morris had been himself
I acting as a director in the allotment and issue of the shares to himself and others and that he was at all times the officer and agent of the company for that purpose, LORD SIMONDS said (20):

---

(15) [1964] 1 All E.R. at p. 646; [1964] 2 Q.B. at pp. 505, 506.
(16) [1843-60] All E.R. Rep. 435; (1856), 6 E. & B. 327.
(17) [1946] 1 All E.R. 586; [1946] A.C. 459.
(18) [1944] 1 All E.R. 751 at pp. 755, 756; [1944] Ch. 346 at pp. 356-359.
(19) [1946] 1 All E.R. at p. 592; [1946] A.C. at p. 474.
(20) [1946] 1 All E.R. at pp. 592, 593; [1946] A.C. at p. 475.

" What then is the position of the director or acting director who claims to A hold the company to a transaction which the company had not, though it might have, authorised? Your lordships have not in this case to consider what the result might be if such a director had not himself purported to act on behalf of the company in the unauthorised transaction. For here Morris was himself purporting to act on behalf of the company in a transaction in which he had no authority. Can he then say that he was entitled to assume B that all was in order? My lords, the old question comes into my mind, ' Quis custodiet ipsos custodes? '."

Later LORD SIMONDS said (21):

" Admit—as, to my mind, one must admit—that a director is not for the purpose of the rule in the same position as a stranger; then it is as immaterial how long he has been a director, as it is whether he is an idle or diligent C director, or a robust or sick director."

It must be observed in relation to the passages which I have just read that Morris, the alleged director, in doing what he did, had been acting for and on behalf of the company. As I read LORD SIMONDS' speech it was the fact that he had been acting for and on behalf of the company which disentitled him later D to turn round as allottee of the shares and seek to take advantage of the rule in *Turquand's* case (22) in his own favour.

Counsel for the defendants, at a very late stage of the trial, produced a case which perhaps more nearly supported the proposition for which he contended on this branch of his argument than any other, namely *Howard* v. *Patent Ivory Manufacturing Co., Re Patent Ivory Manufacturing Co.* (23). The facts can be E briefly stated. That company was to be formed at the instigation of a number of persons, of whom one was called Jordan and another was called Commans, and was to acquire an invention and certain related patents. The company was then formed. The consideration for the purchase was to be £36,500 payable as to £6,500 in cash to Jordan, who had become a director, and as to £30,000 by the allotment to Jordan and Commans of fully paid-up shares. The borrowing F powers of the company were limited to £1,000 at any one time. Unfortunately at a meeting at which Jordan was present as a director it was resolved that Jordan should receive (and Jordan agreed to accept) £3,000 in cash and £3,500 in certain debenture stock, which was issued in breach of the limitation on borrowing powers to which I have just referred. Later the company went into liquidation. Jordan and another sought to enforce the debentures against the liquidators. I need not G read anything in the judgment of KAY, J., until towards the end, where he said (24):

" But then a very much more serious question has been raised, and that is this. These debentures were issued by the directors, and it is said that the power of the directors to issue debentures is limited, and the limit is very plain when you look at art. 95 [his lordship read it and continued:] So that H when the directors have borrowed up to £1,000, and there are existing loans unpaid to that amount, the borrowing power of the directors is exhausted, and no more can be borrowed without the authority of a general meeting of shareholders. Then the next clause is, ' To secure the repayment of any moneys so borrowed, together with the interest, by debentures '. Therefore the directors could only issue valid debentures for moneys borrowed by I themselves, without the assent of a general meeting, to the extent of the borrowing power. Beyond that, in order to authorise themselves to borrow and to issue debentures, there must be the assent of the general meeting.

" Now in this case, unfortunately for the holders of these debentures, they are all directors, and therefore the well-known authority which makes it

(21) [1946] 1 All E.R. at p. 593; [1946] A.C. at p. 476.
(22) [1843-60] All E.R. Rep. 435; (1856), 6 E. & B. 327.
(23) (1888), 38 Ch.D. 156.   (24) (1888), 38 Ch.D. at pp. 170, 171.

A   unnecessary to see whether the internal regulations of a company have been observed or not do not apply; because, of course, the directors must be taken to know that the internal requirements of the company had not been observed in the case of these debentures. Accordingly, I am very sorry to say that I cannot treat the debentures as valid to the extent of more than £1,000."

B   The present defendants rely on this statement of the law as showing that a director dealing with a company of which he is a director must be taken for all purposes to have knowledge of the powers and obligations of and limitations on those powers under the articles. As I read LORD SIMONDS' speech in *Morris* v. *Kanssen* (25), he was expressly dealing with a case where a director, Morris, had been acting on behalf of the company in relation to the matter there in question, namely the purported allotment of shares to himself. Similarly in *Howard's*

C   case (26) the directors, including Jordan, were acting as directors on behalf of the company in connexion with the issue and allotment of the debentures to Jordan and others. Do those cases go so far, however, as to compel a court to say that where a director of a company, not acting as such but in his personal and individual capacity, makes a contract with that company which in relation to that contract acts not by that director but by another director who is in fact the

D   chairman and chief executive of that company, then the individual director is to be treated as possessed of constructive knowledge (for the plaintiff in the present case had no actual knowledge) of any defect in the authority of that other director, so as to exclude the operation of the rule in *Turquand's* case (27), notwithstanding that other director's representations as to his authority. It is quite plain that LORD SIMONDS was not dealing with such a case, because he

E   said (28):

"Your lordships have not in this case to consider what the result might be if such a director had not himself purported to act on behalf of the company in the unauthorised transaction."

Nor do I think that KAY, J., had such a case in mind.

F   The plaintiff did not act on behalf of Brayhead in relation to the allegedly unauthorised transaction. But leading counsel for the defendants and, in his admirable argument following his learned leader, their junior counsel said it was enough to exclude the operation of the rule in *Turquand's* case (27), that the plaintiff was a party to the transaction and was a director of Brayhead, even though he did not act for Brayhead. With the utmost respect to that argument

G   and the skill with which it was advanced by both counsel for the defendants, I find nothing in these cases which compels me to go so far as they have invited me to go. In some cases—and of course *Morris's* case (25) is one and *Howard's* case (26) is another—a director is quite plainly anything but a "stranger", or an "outsider", or a "third party", but I do not think that the mere fact that a director of a company makes a contract with that company in a capacity other

H   than that of a director, automatically affects him in the capacity in which he is contracting with constructive knowledge of such disabilities and limitations as he might be deemed to know were he also acting for the company in the transaction in question. As counsel for the plaintiff said in the course of his reply, to extend this doctrine in the way suggested would have very far-reaching ramifications on ordinary day-to-day business transactions and would, or might, involve very

I   often considerable enquiry before a contract could be signed what the respective position and authority was of a particular individual by whom it was proposed that a contract should be signed. I regard the decisions in *Morris* v. *Kanssen* (25) and in *Howard's* case (26) as decisions where, on the facts of those particular cases, the rights sought to be enforced by the plaintiffs concerned

(25) [1946] 1 All E.R. 586; [1946] A.C. 459.
(26) (1888), 38 Ch.D. 156.
(27) [1843-60] All E.R. Rep. 435; (1856), 6 E. & B. 327.
(28) [1946] 1 All E.R. at pp. 592, 593; [1946] A.C. at p. 475.

arose from acts done by them as directors which were so closely interwoven with A
their duties and acts as directors as to make it impossible for the directors involved
to say that they were not for all purposes to be treated as possessed of knowledge
of the limitations on their powers as directors. In the present case Brayhead's
agreement with the plaintiff had nothing to do with his duties and obligations as
a director of Brayhead. What he was doing was to agree to advance money to an
associated company of Brayhead of which he was chairman and managing director B
against a guarantee and indemnity from Brayhead, who were expected to become
the parent company of that associated company. He was acting, as I think,
otherwise than in his capacity as a director of Brayhead in making that agreement. He was acting as an individual, for it was he who was going to advance the
money in consideration of the agreement into which Mr. Richards was purporting
to enter on behalf of Brayhead. He was going to be the other contracting party. C
I think therefore that this argument fails.

Counsel for the defendants then submitted that, even assuming that he was
wrong on the point which I have just decided, this transaction was an " unusual "
transaction for the purposes of the exceptions to the rule in *Turquand's* case (29).
He put the argument in two ways: first he said that it was not the sort of transaction into which one would expect a managing director to enter in the circum- D
stances with somebody who was, in fact, also a director of the same company;
and, secondly, he sought to say that it was " unusual " by reason of the provisions of art. 99 of Brayhead's articles of association. I should emphasise that
this argument is independent of his principal submission based on art. 99. I will
deal with these points first because I can take them briefly. Counsel relied in
particular on the well-known decision of the Court of Appeal in *J. C. Houghton* E
& Co. v. *Nothard Lowe and Wills, Ltd.* (30), a case considered by the Court of
Appeal in *Freeman's* case (31), to which I have already referred. If one attempts
to look at this through the eyes of an ordinary businessman, I cannot see anything
in the least unusual in this transaction. The loan was being made by the plaintiff.
The parent company (as it was hoped Brayhead would become in relation to
Perdio) was going to give a guarantee and an indemnity. Brayhead itself had F
already made a very large investment in Perdio: it had lent money, it had
accepted obligations under the acceptance credits, and it was obviously going to
assist towards helping Brayhead's investment in Perdio if Perdio could be kept
afloat a little longer with the aid of the plaintiff's money, particularly as Brayhead
itself might be going to put in further money. Therefore, as between " usual "
and " unusual " transactions, I see no reason for thinking there was anything G
" unusual " in the transaction in the sense in which that adjective has been used
in the cases. Nor do I think that the fact that the agreements were or may have
been contracts in which the plaintiff was " interested " within the meaning of
art. 99 of Brayhead's articles of association makes that which was not commercially an " unusual " transaction " unusual " in the sense to which I have
just referred.   H

That leaves the major question under art. 99. This is, perhaps, the most difficult
point in the case, if only because one is in a field of law in which, notwithstanding
the help which I have had from learned counsel, the seas seem uncharted. Both
leading and junior counsel for the defendants, while shrinking from saying that a
contract entered into in breach, if that is the right word, of art. 99 of the articles
of the defendant company and s. 199 of the Companies Act, 1948, is illegal, boldly I
took their stand on the proposition that it was unenforceable, either because it
was void, or because it was voidable, or because there was in either or both of the
parties a want of capacity to contract. It is remarkable that, if this be the law,
there is no reflection of it in any case which learned counsel on either side has
been able to discover since the joint stock company came into existence in the
middle of the last century. Section 199 of the Act of 1948 does not itself avoid a

(29) [1843-60] All E.R. Rep. 435; (1856), E. & B. 327.
(30) [1927] 1 K.B. 246.   (31) [1964] 1 All E.R. 630; [1964] 2 Q.B. 480.

A   contract entered into in breach of the provisions of sub-s. (1) of that section, though sub-s. (4) imposes a small financial penalty on a director who fails to comply with the provisions of the section. The construction of s. 199 is itself by no means easy, though I do not think that it is necessary to discuss all the matters which have been touched on in argument in relation to this section. It may well be, as junior counsel for the defendants said, that the section is concerned

B   primarily with the duty of disclosure and with the machinery by which disclosure shall be made, rather than with the consequences on the contract itself of non-disclosure of the director's interest.

Some help by way of analogy is available from a case which counsel for the plaintiff cited to me, a decision of the House of Lords in *Wright* v. *Horton* (32), and in particular from the speech of LORD HALSBURY, L.C., (33). In that case

C   debentures in a company incorporated under the Companies Act, 1862, were issued to a director of the company. They were not registered in accordance with the requirements of s. 43 of the Act. The company having gone into liquidation and the validity of these debentures being contested by unsecured creditors, and also by debenture-holders, as to whom it was not shown that they had made any inquiry as to the charges on the company's property or the existence of a register,

D   it was held, reversing the decision of the Court of Appeal, that the mere omission to register, without concealment, did not invalidate the debentures; at all events as between the director and such creditors. LORD HALSBURY, L.C., said (33):

" Notwithstanding the high authority of JAMES, MELLISH and BAGGALLAY, L.JJ., it is impossible to acquiesce in the bald statement that there is a ' rule ' or an ' equitable principle ' that an unregistered mortgage or deben-

E   ture is invalid as against a director, without some further exposition of what the ' rule ' or the ' principle ' is by which it is rendered invalid. The statute, for very obvious reasons, in constituting a code for the regulation of trading companies, has enacted that they shall keep an account of mortgages or charges specifically affecting their property. Had the legislature thought right it might have rendered all mortgages or charges invalid unless they had

F   been entered in this account; it has not done so."

Following the language of LORD HALSBURY, L.C., it is remarkable that, if it had been the intention of the legislature to say that a contract entered into without compliance with s. 199 of the Act of 1948 should be wholly void or that the parties to it, or one of them, should be treated as possessed of no contractual capacity, it has not clearly said so. The true principle, although I accept that there is little

G   or no authority to support it, is, I apprehend, as follows. There is no rule of common law that a director cannot validly contract with a company of which he is a director. Equity ensured, however, that the company could, when appropriate, recover any profit made by the director as a result of his making such a contract with the company by reason of his fiduciary position, unless he was relieved from the obligation so to account by compliance with the relevant article

H   or statutory provision. Further, in certain cases equity would permit the company to avoid the contract. With one exception, to which I will refer in a moment, no case has been produced to me in which there has been a breath of a suggestion that a contract entered into in those circumstances is void or unenforceable. I think, therefore, that the true principle is that which I have endeavoured to state,

I   and I find support for that view in the fact that s. 199 does not itself refer to the consequences of non-compliance with sub-s. (1) and sub-s. (2) beyond the provision for the imposition of a fine in sub-s. (4). Nor do I think that art. 99 in its true construction leads to any different result.

I was referred by counsel for the plaintiff to one passage in PROFESSOR GOWER'S book on THE PRINCIPLES OF MODERN COMPANY LAW (2nd Edn.) (1957), p. 481, in which the author said:

---

(32) (1887), 12 App. Cas. 371.
(33) (1887), 12 App. Cas. at pp. 376, 377.

"... it seems clear that a breach ... brings the basic equitable principle   A
into operation; in other words, the contract is voidable by the company and
any profits made by the interested director are recoverable."

No authority was cited for that and, with all respect to the author, I venture
to think that the passage is somewhat too widely stated. The same criticism is to
be made of a passage to which counsel for the defendants referred me, at the end
of the reply of counsel for the plaintiff, in 6 HALSBURY'S LAWS OF ENGLAND   B
(3rd Edn.) p. 302, para. 609:

"A contract between a company and a director or his firm, or a company
in which he is interested as a director or shareholder even though only a
trustee of the shares, is voidable at the option of the company,"

a statement which, as counsel accepted, does not appear to be supported by all   C
the authorities cited.

In the present case Brayhead has never sought to avoid these contracts or to
claim rescission of them and, as counsel for the plaintiff pointed out, it is far too
late now for it to seek to do so, since the plaintiff has acted in reliance on the
representations made to him, and restitution to the original position as it was on
May 19, 1965, is now wholly impossible.   D

For those reasons I have come to the conclusion that there was ostensible or
apparent authority in Mr. Richards; that the board of Brayhead knew of and
acquiesced in Mr. Richards acting as de facto managing director of Brayhead;
that the plaintiff relied on the representations made to him and, relying on them,
made these advances totalling £45,000. I hold that his right to rely on those
representations is not affected by the fact that he was a director of Brayhead at   E
the time. I also hold that his rights are not affected by the fact that these contracts may have been in breach of, or at any rate without compliance with, s. 199
of the Act of 1948 or art. 99 of the company's articles. I say " may have been "
merely for this reason, that counsel for the plaintiff made no formal admission
that these contracts were caught by the article or the section. In my view these
were contracts in which technically the plaintiff was " interested " although, in   F
my view, neither is a contract of the type to which these provisions were in truth
intended to be directed. I fully accept counsel for the defendants' submission
that the court must not seek to diminish the stringent rule that directors must
fulfil their duties to their companies, and that the strict limitations on their
freedom of action to their personal advantage which have been imposed over the
years should be preserved in the interests of shareholders and the public; all   G
that goes without saying. In the present case, however, as I think I have already
said, these contracts were at least as much in Brayhead's interests and Mr.
Richards' interests as in the plaintiff's. Let there be no mistake about that.

The case to which counsel for the defendants referred me at the last moment
was a case only briefly reported, *Toms* v. *Cinema Trust Co., Ltd.* (34). It has the
great merit, particularly in this court, of being a judgment of SCRUTTON, J. From   H
a superficial reading, if I may use that phrase, SCRUTTON, J., does appear to say
that a contract made between a director of a company and that company for that
director's remuneration was void, because he disallowed the director's claim to
recover and gave judgment for the company on the counterclaim to recover that
which the director had already received from them. I will not spend time
analysing this case, since the report is so brief as to make it difficult to deduce   I
principles from it. As I understand it, the alleged contractual right to remuneration arose from an alleged board meeting at which were present the plaintiff
(who was a director) and another gentleman who was not a director. In order to
comply with the requirements of art. 25, the fact of the plaintiff's disclosure of
his interest had to be entered in the minutes of the company. This was never
done. I think that the ratio decidendi was that there was never on the facts a

---

(34) [1915] W.N. 29.

A valid agreement entered into for the director's remuneration. Notwithstanding the respect that any judgment of Scrutton, J., commands, this decision does not affect the conclusions which I have reached after the long and careful arguments to which I have listened in this case.

The result is that the plaintiff is entitled to recover from Brayhead on the indemnity with respect to his liability to Guinness Mahon which he has dis-
B charged and also to the declaration which he seeks with respect to repayment of his advances to Perdio.

It is necessary to deal with one other matter, which arises only if the conclusion which I have reached is wrong. It was said on behalf of Mr. Richards that if Brayhead was not liable, there was no claim against Mr. Richards, for breach of warranty of authority. It was said on the other side that Mr. Richards had
C warranted his authority to do what he did and that, if the plaintiff could not recover from Brayhead, he could recover from Mr. Richards that which he could not recover from Brayhead for want of Mr. Richards' authority. In my judgment that is right. I do not think that counsel for the defendants' point that there was no warranty of authority is well founded and, therefore, had I reached a different conclusion from that in fact reached I should none the less have held that the
D plaintiff was entitled to recover against Mr. Richards on the alternative claim for breach of warranty of authority. As, in my judgment, that matter does not arise I do not propose to say more about it. All the arguments to which I have listened are open elsewhere if necessary.

Judgment against Brayhead for a sum of £42,506 17s. 1d. under the indemnity and a sum of £37,413 6s. 8d. under the guarantee with interest at seven per cent. from
E *Oct. 1, 1965 and Apr. 4, 1966, respectively, with costs; judgment for the second defendant without costs.*

Solicitors: *Linklaters & Paines* (for the plaintiff); *T. W. Stuchbery & Son,* Windsor (for the defendants).

[*Reported by* K. Diana Phillips, *Barrister-at-Law.*]

DALLOW INDUSTRIAL PROPERTIES, LTD. v. ELSE.   A
SAME v. CURD.

[QUEEN's BENCH DIVISION (Lord Parker, C.J., Diplock, L.J., and Ashworth, J.)
March 7, 1967.]

Employment—Redundancy—Period of continuous employment—Change of employers consequent on sale of factory premises—Claimants employed for many   B
years by previous employers—Previous employers were manufacturers who
sold their factory premises to the present employers who bought the factory
to convert it into units for leasing—Claimants dismissed from employment
after 101 weeks with present employers—Whether transfer of trade by previous
employers to present employers—" Activity "—Whether prior employment
could be included in reckoning period of continuous employment—Contracts   C
of Employment Act 1963 (c. 49), *Sch.* 1, *para.* 10 (2)—*Redundancy Payments*
Act 1965 (c. 62), *s.* 8 (1), (2), *s.* 13 (1), *s.* 25 (1).

E. had been employed by J., Ltd., since 1936, and C. had been employed by
them since 1933.   In 1962, J., Ltd., transferred their business of manufacturing stoves to Bristol, and their premises at Luton were put up for sale, pending
which J., Ltd. used the premises for the storage of stoves manufactured by   D
them, E. being employed as a maintenance worker and C. as a security
officer.   In 1964 the premises were sold to the appellants, who carried on no
manufacturing business but who bought the premises in order to convert
them into fifteen factory units to be leased to manufacturers.   Soon after the
sale, builders began to convert the premises.   E. and C. were given notice to
terminate their employment with the appellants 101 weeks after the appell-   E
ants had bought the premises.   On appeal by the appellants against a decision
of the Industrial Tribunal awarding E. and C. redundancy payments under
the Redundancy Payments Act 1965, on the ground that the sale of the
premises by J., Ltd. to the appellants was a transfer of a trade, business or
undertaking within the meaning of Sch. 1, para. 10 (2)*, to the Contracts of
Employment Act 1963, applied by s. 8 (2)† of the Act of 1965, so that the   F
period of employment of E. and C. with J., Ltd. could be added to their
period of employment with the appellants, thus bringing them within the
104 weeks requisite period under s. 8 (1)‡ of the Act of 1965,

Held: J., Ltd. had not transferred any part of " a trade or business or an
undertaking " to the appellants, but had merely sold to the appellants some
real property which the appellants were using for a different purpose;   G
accordingly para. 10 (2) of Sch. 1 to the Contracts of Employment Act 1963
was not applicable and the periods of employment of E. and C. with J., Ltd.
could not be added to their periods of employment by the appellants, with
the consequences that E.'s and C.'s periods of employment did not satisfy
the requirement of s. 8 (1) of the Redundancy Payments Act 1965 and
that they would not be entitled to redundancy payments under s. 1 (1)   H
(see p. 32, letters H and I, and p. 34, letter A, post).

G. D. Ault (Isle of Wight), Ltd. v. *Gregory* ((Mar. 2, 1967), unreported)
applied.

Per CURIAM: the word " activity " in s. 25 (1)§ of the Redundancy Payments Act 1965, read in the context of " business . . . trade or profession ",
means the combination of operations undertaken by the corporate body,   I
whether or not they amount to a business, trade or profession in the ordinary
sense; accordingly, in order that there should be a change in the ownership
within s. 13 (1)∥ of the Act of 1965, there must be a change of ownership,

---

* Schedule 1, para. 10 (2), is set out at p. 32, letter C, post.
† Section 8 (2) is set out at p. 31, letter I, to p. 32, letter A, post.
‡ Section 8 (1), so far as material, provides: " For the purposes of s. 1 (1) of this Act
the requisite period is the period of 104 weeks ending with the relevant date . . .".
§ Section 25 (1), so far as material, is set out at p. 33, letter D, post.
∥ Section 13, so far as material, is set out at p. 33, letter B, post.

A   not merely in an asset of the business, but in the combination of operations carried on, such that what is transferred (if a part only is transferred) is a separate and self-contained part of the operations of the transferor in which the assets, stock-in-trade, etc. are engaged (see p. 33, letters G and I, post).

Appeals allowed.

B   [As to redundancy payments after a change of ownership of a business, see SUPPLEMENT to 25 HALSBURY'S LAWS (3rd Edn.), para. 945A, 7.

For the Contracts of Employment Act 1963, Sch. 1, para. 10, see 43 HALSBURY'S STATUTES (2nd Edn.) 286.

For the Redundancy Payments Act 1965, s. 8, s. 13, s. 25, see 45 HALSBURY'S STATUTES (2nd Edn.) 297, 301, 309.]

C   Case referred to:

Ault (G. D.) (Isle of Wight), Ltd. v. *Gregory*, (Mar. 2, 1967), unreported.

Appeals.

These were appeals by way of motion by the appellants, Dallow Industrial Properties, Ltd., who moved for orders that the decision of the Industrial Tribunal given on July 13, 1966, awarding the respondent, Percy Else, a redundancy

D   payment of £460 18s. 9d. and the respondent, Foster Douglas Curd, a redundancy payment of £234 7s. 6d. should be set aside. The facts are set out in the judgment of DIPLOCK, L.J.

The enactments and case noted below* were cited during the argument in addition to the case referred to in the judgment of DIPLOCK, L.J.

E   *P. R. Pain, Q.C.*, and *A. H. Hodgson* for the appellants.

Nigel Bridge as amicus curiae.

The respondents did not appear and were not represented.

DIPLOCK, L.J., delivered the first judgment at the invitation of LORD PARKER, C.J.: These are two appeals from decisions of the Industrial Tribunal under the Redundancy Payments Act 1965, and they both raise the same question

F   of law, namely, as to what is to be included in the requisite period of 104 weeks' continuous employment which is required in order to entitle an employee to a redundancy payment under the Act of 1965.

The facts of each case are quite simple. The two respondents, Mr. Else and Mr. Curd, were employed by Jacksons Industries, Ltd., who carried on the business of manufacturing stoves at, amongst other places, factory premises in

G   Dallow Road, Luton. Some time in 1962 the manufacturing business was transferred to Bristol, and the premises were put up for sale. Pending their sale, they were used by Jacksons for the storage of stoves manufactured by them, and Mr. Else was employed as a maintenance worker at the factory premises in Luton; Mr. Curd was employed as a security officer. The premises were sold in 1964, and were bought by the appellants, Dallow Industrial Properties, Ltd.

H   They carried on no manufacturing business at all; they bought the factory in order to convert it into some fifteen smaller factory units which they could lease to manufacturers, and soon after it was bought the builders began to convert the premises. Although Mr. Else had been employed by Jacksons since 1936, and although Mr. Curd had been employed by them since 1933, the respondents had in fact only been employed by the appellants after the take-over for a period

I   of 101 weeks. If they could count only that period of 101 weeks during which they were employed by the appellants, then they did not satisfy the requirements of s. 8 (1) of the Redundancy Payments Act 1965, of having been in continuous employment for a period of 104 weeks. Section 8 (2) of the Act of 1965, however, provides as follows:

" Subject to the preceding subsection, and to the following provisions of

---

* Landlord and Tenant Act, 1954, s. 23, s. 24; *Smith* v. *Anderson*, [1874-80] All E.R. Rep. 1121; (1880), 15 Ch.D. 247.

this section, the provisions of Sch. 1 to the Contracts of Employment Act **A**
1963 (computation of period of employment), and the provisions of any order
for the time being in force under s. 7 of that Act (1) in so far as it modifies that
Schedule, shall have effect for the purposes of this Part of this Act in determining whether an employee has been continuously employed for the requisite
period."

That requires one to turn to Sch. 1 to the Contracts of Employment Act 1963, **B**
and the relevant provision in that Schedule is para. 10 (1) and (2), which provides:

" (1) Subject to this paragraph, the foregoing provisions of this Schedule
relate only to employment by the one employer [the relevant employer being
the appellants, and the employment being in this case 101 weeks]. (2) If a
trade or business or an undertaking (whether or not it be an undertaking **C**
established by or under an Act of Parliament) is transferred from one person
to another, the period of employment of an employee in the trade or business
or undertaking at the time of the transfer shall count as a period of employment with the transferee, and the transfer shall not break the continuity
of the period of employment."

The question which we have to consider in these appeals is, therefore, the same **D**
question as we had to consider in a recent appeal last week, *G. D. Ault (Isle of
Wight), Ltd. v. Gregory* (2), that is to say what is meant on their true construction
by the words " If a trade or business or an undertaking . . . is transferred from one
person to another . . .". In the judgment to which I have just referred, the view
of this court as to the construction of para. 10 (2) was stated in words which I
will read, but changing the word " activity ", which I used in the course of my **E**
judgment there, because I shall have to refer to " activity " in the sense in which
it is used in the Act of 1965. It was there said:

" Where [para. 10 (2)] refers to the transfer of a trade or business, that
covers and includes the transfer of any trade, business or undertaking which
is run by the owner as a separate and self-contained part of his operations
in which assets, stock-in-trade and the like are engaged. It may be that an **F**
individual may carry on two different trades at different times, and, if
he transferred one of them, then clearly in my view it would be within
[para. 10 (2)], or he may carry on the same trade at different places, but if he
maintains it as a separate and self-contained part of his operations, as
plainly this was maintained, then in my view the transfer of that separate
part of his operations carried on in the particular trade is a transfer from one **G**
person to another of a trade or business within the meaning of para. 10 (2)."

Applying that construction of para. 10 (2) of Sch. 1 to the Act of 1963 to the
present case, it is plain that Jacksons did not transfer to the appellants any
part of their trade which was that of manufacturing stoves which was run by
them as a separate and self-contained part of their operations in which assets, **H**
stock-in-trade and the like were engaged; all that they did was to sell to the
appellants some real property which had been used for the purposes of their trade
and which the appellants were using for the purposes of an entirely different
business, namely, the management and disposition of factory premises. Reading,
therefore, the relevant provisions which are those of para. 10 (2) of Sch. 1 to the
Act of 1963, it is, I think, clear that the tribunal fell into an error in law in saying **I**
that the period of employment of the two respondents by Jacksons was to be
counted in computing whether or not they had been employed for the requisite
period.

It has, however, been argued by counsel who has appeared as amicus curiae
in these cases, because neither of the respondents has been represented, that some
different construction should be given to the words which I have cited from

(1) No order under s. 7 appears to have been made.
(2) (Mar. 2, 1967), unreported.

A   Sch. 1 to the Contracts of Employment Act 1963 because of the provisions of s. 13 of the Redundancy Payments Act 1965. I accept that s. 13 is the obverse of para. 10 (2), of Sch. 1 to the Act of 1963, for s. 13 provides for the circumstances in which, when a change occurs, a person who has been offered employment by the new employer will not be entitled to redundancy payments from the old employer. Section 13 (1) reads as follows:

B
> " The provisions of this section shall have effect where—(*a*) a change occurs (whether by virtue of a sale or other disposition or by operation of law) in the ownership of a business for the purposes of which a person is employed, or of a part of such a business, and (*b*) in connexion with that change the person by whom the employee is employed immediately before the change occurs (in this section referred to as ' the previous owner ') terminates the employee's contract of employment, whether by notice or without notice."

C

The subsequent subsections of that section provide, in effect, that the new employment by the new owner shall be treated as if it were employment by the old owner for the purposes of the sections which entitle a dismissed employee to redundancy payments.

D   Counsel's argument is really based on the definition of " business " in s. 25 (1) of the Act of 1965, which reads as follows:

> " In this Part of this Act ' business ' includes a trade or profession and includes any activity carried on by a body of persons, whether corporate or unincorporate . . ."

E   and the argument, as I understood it, was that, when one is dealing with a body of persons, whether corporate or unincorporate, one can dissect the combination of the various operations which it undertakes into a series of activities and, if an employee is employed in connexion—I use counsel's term—with any of those activities when so dissected and the transferee carries on a similar activity when so dissected, then s. 13 (1) applies to him. The actual terms in which counsel who **F**   appeared as amicus curiae put his proposition were these: any transfer of property simpliciter may be the transfer of a business or part of a business if persons have been employed by the transferor in connexion with that property. That, I think, is merely another way of saying that the activity in the sense in which it is used in s. 25 (1) can be dissected into a large number of operations which together make up the whole of the operations undertaken by the body of persons. For **G**   my part, I do not think that " activity " in s. 25 (1) of the Act of 1965 has that dissected meaning which counsel has urged. I think that, read in the context of " business . . . trade or profession ", it means the combination of operations undertaken by the corporate body, whether or not they amount to a business, trade or profession in the ordinary sense; they are there to cover such activities as charitable activities, schools, the National Trust or a statutory undertaking such as a **H**   water undertaking, which could not properly be described as a business or profession. In my view, however, they are to be read as covering the whole of the operations carried out by the body of persons. Accordingly, when one comes to s. 13 (1), where one finds a reference to a change occurring in the ownership of a business or of a part of a business, one gets the same result as one gets by the construction which we have put on para. 10 (2) of Sch. 1 to the Act of 1963. **I**   In order to come within s. 13 (1) there must be a change of ownership, not merely in an asset of a business as in this case, but a change of ownership in the combination of operations carried on by the trader or by the non-trading body of persons, and there can only be a change of ownership in a business or part of a business, including business activity in the sense which I have construed it, if what is transferred is a separate and self-contained part of the operations of the transferor in which assets, stock-in-trade and the like are engaged.

For these reasons I would allow these two appeals.

ASHWORTH, J.: I agree.   A

LORD PARKER, C.J.: I also agree.

Appeals allowed.

Solicitors: *A. V. C. Astley* (for the appellants); *Treasury Solicitor.*

[*Reported by* N. P. METCALFE, ESQ., *Barrister-at-Law.*]   B

NAIR *v.* TEIK.

[PRIVY COUNCIL (Viscount Dilhorne, Lord Pearce and Lord Upjohn), October 31,
November 1, 2, 1966, January 11, 1967.]   C

*Privy Council—Malaysia—Elections—Petition—Appeal—Interlocutory order to
strike out petition for want of service—Competency of appeal court—No
address for service left with registrar by candidate—Advertisement of petition
outside time prescribed for service—Whether appeal lay from interlocutory
order—Whether rule prescribing time limit for service was mandatory—Election Offences Ordinance (No. 906 of 1954), s. 33 (4), s. 36—Courts of*   D
Judicature Act, 1964, s. 67, s. 74.

The respondent presented an election petition claiming that the election
of the appellant to the Dewan Ra'ayat on Apr. 25, 1964, was invalid on the
ground that the appellant was disqualified at the time as not being a citizen
of Malaysia. The appellant did not (as he might have done under r. 10* of
the Election Petition Rules, 1954) appoint an advocate or solicitor to act for   E
him nor did he leave any address for service in the event of a petition against
him. The respondent in accordance with r. 10 lodged a copy of the petition
at the office of the registrar; this was done on the last day for service of the
petition allowed by r. 15*. Notice of presentation of the petition and a copy
of the petition were not served on the appellant within ten days of the presentation of the petition as required by r. 15, and the presentation of the petition   F
was not advertised in the Gazette (which was a method of service prescribed
by r. 15) until July 23, 1964, which was after the time limit enacted in r. 15
had expired. The appellant issued a summons to strike out the petition. By
order dated Sept. 26, 1964, the election judge struck out the petition on the
ground that it had not been served within the time required by r. 15. The
election judge considered that thereby he was making an interlocutory order,   G
and he gave leave to appeal. The Federal Court gave leave to appeal to the
Judicial Committee. On the questions (i) whether an appeal lay from the
election judge to the Federal Court or the Judicial Committee and (ii)
whether r. 15 was mandatory or directory,

Held: although by s. 36† of the Election Offences Ordinance, 1954, no   H
appeal would have lain against a final order, yet, by reason of s. 67‡ of the
Courts of Judicature Act 1964, taken with s. 33 (4)† of the Ordinance of 1954,
an interlocutory order could be the subject of appeal to the Federal Court
and the leave of the Federal Court to appeal conferred jurisdiction (by
virtue of s. 74§ of the Act of 1964) on the Judicial Committee (see p. 37,
letter H, and p. 38, letters E and I, post).

Harmon v. *Park* ((1880), 6 Q.B.D. 323) and *Lord Monkswell* v. *Thompson*   I
([1898] 1 Q.B. 353) applied.

Lord Strickland v. *Grima* ([1930] A.C. 285) distinguished.

---

* Rules 10 and 15, so far as material, are printed at p. 39, letters D to F, post. The rules
were enacted in Sch. 2 to the Election Offences Ordinance, 1954, and had force by
virtue of s. 42.
† Section 36 and s. 33 (4) are printed at p. 36, letters E to G, post.
‡ Section 67 is printed at p. 36, letter H, post.
§ As to s. 74, see p. 38, letter I, post.

A   (ii) rule 15 of the Election Petition Rules was mandatory, and, as there had been no personal service and service by advertisement was out of time, the election petition was a nullity (see p. 40, letters A and G, post).

Williams v. *Tenby Corpn.* ((1879), 5 C.P.D. 135) applied.

Appeal allowed.

B   [As to service of notice of presentation of an election petition in England, see 14 Halsbury's Laws (3rd Edn.) 268, para. 475; and for cases on the subject, see 20 Digest (Repl.) 188, 189, *1650, 1651.*

As to the jurisdiction in interlocutory proceedings on election petitions in England, see 14 Halsbury's Laws (3rd Edn.) 273, para. 485.]

Cases referred to:

C   *Arzu* v. *Arthurs*, [1965] 1 W.L.R. 675; 3rd Digest Supp.

Harmon v. *Park*, (1880), 6 Q.B.D. 323; 50 L.J.Q.B. 227; 44 L.T. 81; 45 J.P. 436; 20 Digest (Repl.) 188, *1648.*

Kennedy v. *Purcell*, (1888), 59 L.T. 279; 20 Digest (Repl.) 154, **892.*

Monkswell (*Lord*) v. *Thompson*, [1898] 1 Q.B. 353; 67 L.J.Q.B. 243; 77 L.T. 707; 20 Digest (Repl.) 191, *1667.*

D   *Pritchard, Re*, [1963] 1 All E.R. 873; [1963] Ch. 502; [1963] 2 W.L.R. 685; 3rd Digest Supp.

Senanayake v. *Navaratne*, [1954] 2 All E.R. 805; [1954] A.C. 640; [1954] 3 W.L.R. 336; Digest (Cont. Vol. A) 154, *906a.*

Strickland (*Lord*) v. *Grima*, [1930] A.C. 285; sub nom. *Parnis* v. *Agius*, 99 L.J.P.C. 81; 142 L.T. 386; 8 Digest (Repl.) 806, *573.*

E   *Théberge* v. *Laudry*, (1876), 2 App. Cas. 102; 46 L.J.P.C. 1; 35 L.T. 640; 8 Digest (Repl.) 806, *572.*

Williams v. *Tenby Corpn.*, (1879), 5 C.P.D. 135; 49 L.J.Q.B. 325; 42 L.T. 187; 44 J.P. 348; 20 Digest (Repl.) 188, *1650.*

Appeal.

F   This was an appeal by C. Devan Nair from an order of the Federal Court of Malaysia (Thompson, L.P., Dyed Shah Barakbah, C.J., and Tan Ah Tah, F.J.), dated May 13, 1965, allowing the appeal of the respondent, Yong Kuan Teik, from an order of the High Court of Malaya (Ismail Khan, J., sitting as the election judge), dated Sept. 26, 1964, striking out an election petition filed by the respondent.

G   *J. G. Le Quesne* and *Mervyn Heald* for the appellant.

John A. Baker for the respondent.

LORD UPJOHN: This appeal from the Federal Court of Malaysia is concerned with an election petition launched by the respondent on June 29, 1964, against the appellant, who was a candidate for election to the Dewan Ra'ayat at the election held on Apr. 25, 1964, claiming that his election was invalid on the ground that he was disqualified at the time, in that he was not at that time a citizen of Malaysia. Election Petitions are governed by Part 7 of the Election Offences Ordinance No. 9 of 1954, and by the rules made thereunder which are contained in Sch. 2 to that Ordinance.

I   The appellant alleged before the election judge (Ismail Khan, J.) that the petition had not been served on him in accordance with the rules; the judge ruled in his favour and, by order dated Sept. 26, 1964, struck out the petition. He gave leave to appeal to the Federal Court, who reached a contrary conclusion and allowed the appeal of the respondent. The Federal Court gave leave to appeal to their lordships' Board.

Two quite independent questions are raised by this appeal. First, whether any appeal to the Federal Court or to their lordships' Board is competent. Secondly, if any such appeal is competent, whether on the true construction of the rules

concerning the service of petitions the election judge was right in thinking that **A**
the relevant rule was mandatory, or whether he was rightly overruled by the
Federal Court, who held that it was directory only.

Constitutionally decisions on questions of contested elections are vested in the
assembly for which the contested election has been held, but in the course of the
nineteenth century many countries, including this country and many of Her
Majesty's possessions overseas, adopted the view that, as the deliberations of the **B**
assembly itself were apt to be governed rather by political considerations than
the justice of the case, it was right and proper that such questions should be
entrusted to the courts. This required legislation in every case, and in many cases
the right of appeal after the hearing of an election petition by an election tribunal
to which those hearings was entrusted was severely limited, clearly for the reason
that it was essential that such matters should be determined as quickly as possible, **C**
so that the assembly itself and the electors of the representatives thereto should
know their rights at the earliest possible moment. Essentially, however, the
question whether there is any limitation on the right of appeal must depend on
the terms of the enactment setting up the election tribunal. These are to be
found in s. 33 and s. 36 of the Election Offences Ordinance, 1954, which as
amended in 1959 are, so far as relevant, as follows: **D**

" 33. (1) Every election petition shall be tried by the chief justice or by a
judge of the High Court nominated by the chief justice for the purpose . . .

(4) Unless otherwise ordered by the chief justice, all interlocutory matters
in connexion with an election petition may be dealt with and decided by any
judge of the High Court. **E**

" 36. At the conclusion of the trial of an election petition the election
judge shall determine whether the candidate whose return or election is
complained of, or any other and what person, was duly returned or elected,
or whether the election was void, and shall certify such determination—

" (*a*) to the election commission in the case of an election of a person to
be a member of the Dewan Ra'ayat, a legislative assembly, the municipal **F**
council of the federal capital or of any other election that the election
commission may be authorised to conduct; or

" (*b*) in the case of any other election, to the ruler or governor of the state.
Upon such certificate being given such determination shall be final; and
the return shall be confirmed or altered, or the election commission or the
ruler or governor (as the case may be) shall within one month of such deter- **G**
mination give notice of election in the constituency, electoral ward or
electoral district concerned, as the case may require, in accordance with
such certificate."

Section 67 of the Courts of Judicature Act, 1964 of Malaysia is also important
on the question of appeals. **H**

" The Federal Court shall have jurisdiction to hear and determine appeals
from any judgment or order of any High Court in any civil matter, whether
made in the exercise of its original or of its appellate jurisdiction, subject
nevertheless to the provisions of this or any other written law regulating the
terms and conditions upon which such appeals shall be brought." **I**

On the footing that the order of ISMAIL KHAN, J., on Sept. 26, 1964, was a final
order it seems clear to their lordships that there was no right of appeal to the
Federal Court or to their lordships' Board. There was none to the Federal
Court because, although on a narrow construction of s. 36 it might be argued
that the right of appeal was thereby limited only after a hearing on the merits,
it has been established by two decisions of their lordships' Board that the section
applies to all cases where there had been a final determination of the matter

A whether it be on procedural grounds or on the merits. The first is *Senanayake* v. *Navaratne* (1), where Lord Simonds, L.C., delivering the judgment of the Board, said (2):

B
"They are satisfied that the election judge, as established by the Order in Council of 1946, was a tribunal with a jurisdiction, not only to determine finally the question whether the corrupt practices alleged in the petition had been committed but also to determine finally whether, on the true construction of the Order in Council, it was competent in the circumstances for the petitioner to maintain his amended petition."

That case was not dissimilar to that before their lordships, for the question was whether the petitioner had amended his petition within the proper time for
C service. The second is *Arzu* v. *Arthurs* (3); the petitions were dismissed on the ground that they did not state when they were served and that the first respondent had not been made a respondent thereto. Lord Pearce, delivering the judgment of the Board, said (4):

D
"Nor can they find a distinction in the fact that the dismissal of the petitions was based on procedural grounds. If the decision in this peculiar jurisdiction is to be final such finality must apply irrespective of the reasons for the decision. The fact that no evidence has been heard does not affect the general principle. The court in the present case did not refuse jurisdiction; it decided in its peculiar jurisdiction that the petitions were defective. As a result the petitions were dismissed. A dismissal based on a procedural matter is none the less a decision in an election petition, even where the
E matter has not proceeded to the hearing of evidence."

It is to be noted that in both these cases, the first from Ceylon and the second from British Honduras, the statutory provisions were for all relevant purposes indistinguishable from the provisions of s. 36.

There was no appeal to their lordships' Board for it has been settled by a long line of decisions of their lordships starting with *Théberge* v. *Laudry* (5) in 1876
F and ending with *Arzu* v. *Arthurs* (6) in 1964 that their lordships will not entertain appeals from the determination of an election judge. The reason for this was put very neatly by Lord Hobhouse in *Kennedy* v. *Purcell* (7) referring to *Théberge* v. *Laudry* (5):

G
"The decision of the judicial committee was, not that the prerogative of the Crown was taken away by the general prohibition of appeal, but that the whole scheme of handing over to courts of law disputes which the legislative assembly had previously decided for itself showed no intention of creating tribunals with the ordinary incident of an appeal to the Crown."

Nevertheless the underlying reason for this line of decisions was, as the authorities show, the recognition of the necessity for a speedy determination of an election
H issue. So if in this case Ismail Khan, J., made a final order, it was unappealable; but whether or not his order was final or interlocutory does not seem to have been canvassed in the courts below. It appears from the notes of Ismail Khan, J., on the argument before him on Sept. 26, 1964, that in striking out the petition both he and the parties considered that he was making an interlocutory order, for reference was made to s. 68 (2) of the Courts of Judicature Act 1964, which
I deals only with interlocutory appeals, and he gave leave to appeal thereunder. Whether he was right so to treat his order is a matter which their lordships do not decide; they think that it is a doubtful point and that it would have been better if in terms he had dismissed the petition, when no question could have arisen. They will assume that he was right in thinking that for the purposes of

---

(1) [1954] 2 All E.R. 805; [1954] A.C. 640.
(2) [1954] 2 All E.R. at p. 810; [1954] A.C. at p. 651.   (3) [1965] 1 W.L.R. 675.
(4) [1965] 1 W.L.R. at p. 679.   (5) (1876), 2 App. Cas. 102.
(6) [1965] 1 W.L.R. 675.   (7) (1888), 59 L.T. 279 at p. 280.

the appeal he was making an interlocutory order. This point was very properly   A
drawn to their lordships' attention by counsel for the respondent.

The question, then, is whether the general rules that their lordships have
already stated in relation to orders made in election petitions in regard to final
orders, applies to interlocutory orders. This must depend to some extent on
the true construction of s. 33 which deals with interlocutory matters. Counsel
for the appellant pressed their lordships with the words in s. 33 (4) that all   B
interlocutory matters in connexion with an election petition may be " dealt
with and decided by " any judge. It was argued that the word " decided "
meant " finally decided ", and reliance was placed on the case of *Lord Strickland*
v. *Grima* (8). That, however, was a very different case where His Late Majesty
by letters patent referred to the Court of Appeal in Malta, the highest judicial
tribunal in that island, the right to decide certain contested election matters.   C
The inference was drawn that no right of appeal was intended.   Their lordships,
however, do not think that the construction adopted in that case is really of
assistance to them in this case. Looking at s. 33 and s. 36, while it is clear that
s. 36 enacts that final orders are not subject to appeal, there are no such limiting
words in s. 33 (4), and it does not seem to their lordships there is to be found in
that section sufficient to overcome the express words of s. 67 of the Courts of   D
Judicature Act, 1964 already quoted, so as to preclude the bringing of an appeal
in an interlocutory matter. This may seem to be curious but, nevertheless,
until the law was later altered by statute the same situation arose in this country.
In *Harmon* v. *Park* (9) it was held that although an appeal from the election
judge to the Common Pleas Division on a Case Stated was final, yet on an interlocutory matter it could be considered by the Court of Appeal. This was followed   E
in *Lord Monkswell* v. *Thompson* (10). Accordingly, on the footing that the order
was interlocutory, in their lordships' opinion, it was open to the election judge
to give leave to appeal and for the Federal Court to entertain it.

While it is clear for the reasons already given that their lordships would not
entertain an appeal after a final determination of an election petition, the authorities do not cover the case of an interlocutory appeal, and their lordships must   F
examine the matter afresh. When the Federated Malay States became independent in 1957, the United Kingdom Federation of Malaya Independence Act, 1957,
by s. 3, (11), provided that Her Majesty by Order in Council might confer on the
Judicial Committee of the Privy Council jurisdiction in respect of appeals from
the Supreme Court of the Federation as might be appropriate for giving effect
to any arrangements made between Her Majesty and the Head of the Federation   G
for reference of such appeals to their lordships. Such arrangements were concluded in 1958, and by Her Majesty's Federation of Malaya (Appeals to Privy
Council) Order in Council, 1958, (12), and by the Appeals from the Supreme Court
Ordinance, 1958 of the Yang di-Pertuan Agong, it was enacted in identical terms
that, subject to any enactment or rules regulating the proceedings of the Judicial
Committee in respect of the Supreme Court, an appeal should lie from the court   H
to the Yang di-Pertuan Agong with the leave of the court " (*b*) from any inter-
locutory judgment or order which the court considers a fit one for appeal ".
The court was defined as the Supreme Court. The Federation of Malaya is now
Malaysia and the Supreme Court is now the Federal Court and the relevant
enactment is now (in identical terms) to be found in s. 74 of the Courts of
Judicature Act, 1964.   I

The Federal Court gave leave to appeal and thereby, as it appears to their
lordships, conferred on them jurisdiction to entertain this interlocutory appeal.

_____

(8) [1930] A.C. 285.   (9) (1880), 6 Q.B.D. 323.
(10) [1898] 1 Q.B. 353.
(11) 37 HALSBURY'S STATUTES (2nd Edn.) 198.   The section now has affect as provided by s. 5 of the Malaysia Act 1963, 43 HALSBURY'S STATUTES (2nd Edn.) 56.
(12) S.I. 1958 No. 426.   The order in council was applied to appeals by the Federal
Court of Malaysia by the Malaysia (Appeals to Privy Council) Order in Council 1963,
S.I. 1963 No. 2086.

A Nevertheless, their lordships would like it to be understood that they are reluctant to entertain interlocutory appeals especially in election petitions, and unless the case raised is of exceptional public and general importance the Federal Court may well think it wiser to leave the party aggrieved to apply to their lordships' Board for special leave to appeal under s. 74 (2) of the Courts of Judicature Act, 1964.

B This case, in their lordships' opinion, however, does raise a question of exceptional public importance on the proper interpretation of the rules relating to election petitions set out in Sch. 2 to the Election Offences Ordinance, 1954, and their lordships' decision may also govern the practice and procedure in other parts of the Commonwealth which have adopted a similar code of procedure.

C Their lordships now proceed to consider the second question stated at the beginning of their judgment. Section 38 of the Election Offences Ordinance, 1954, provides that every election petition shall be presented within twenty-one days of the publication of the result of the election in the Gazette. The rules principally relevant are r. 10 and r. 15.

D " 10. Any person returned may at any time, after he is returned, send or leave at the office of the registrar a writing signed by him on his behalf [sic] appointing an advocate and solicitor to act as his solicitor in case there should be a petition against him, or stating that he intends to act for himself, and in either case giving an address within the Federation at which notices addressed to him may be left, and if no such writing be left or address given, all notices and proceedings may be given or served by leaving the same at the office of the registrar . . .

E " 15. Notice of the presentation of a petition, accompanied by a copy thereof, shall, within ten days of the presentation of the petition, be served by the petitioner on the respondent. Such service may be effected either by delivering the notice and copy aforesaid to the solicitor appointed by the respondent under r. 10 of these rules or by posting the same in a registered letter to the address given under r. 10 of these rules at such time that, in the ordinary course of post, the letter would be delivered within the time above
F mentioned, or if no solicitor has been appointed, or no such address given, by a notice published in the Gazette stating that such petition has been presented, and that a copy of the same may be obtained by the respondent on application at the office of the registrar."

G The result of the election was published on June 11, 1964, and the petition was presented to the registrar of the Supreme Court as prescribed by r. 3 on June 29, 1964, within the required twenty-one days.

The appellant (13) did not avail himself of r. 10 by appointing an advocate and solicitor to act for him nor leave any address for service. As the appellant had left no address for service, the respondent in purported compliance with r. 10 lodged a copy of the petition on the registrar on the last day for service of the
H petition prescribed by r. 15.

Notice of presentation of the petition was advertised in the Gazette on July 23, 1964. This notice was clearly out of time. The first question is whether lodgment of the petition on the registrar was a sufficient compliance with the rules. That was a literal compliance with r. 10, but it appears to their lordships that in respect of service of petitions there is an inconsistency between r. 10 and r. 15; in view,
I however, of the very explicit provisions of r. 15 (which itself refers to r. 10) it appears clear to their lordships that a petition must be served in accordance with the terms of r. 15 and that service thereof merely in accordance with r. 10 is insufficient.

Rule 15 was not complied with strictly, for there was no personal service and no notice in the Gazette within ten days of the presentation of the petition. Although the Gazette is only published fortnightly, it would have been possible

---

(13) The appellant on the present appeal was the respondent to the election petition, and the respondent on the present appeal was the petitioner on that petition.

to comply with the rule by publishing it in the issue of July 9. So the whole   A
question is whether the provisions of r. 15 are " mandatory " in the sense in
which that word is used in the law, i.e., that a failure to comply strictly with the
times laid down renders the proceedings a nullity; or " directory ", i.e., that
literal compliance with the time schedule may be waived or excused or the time
may be enlarged by a judge. If the latter, it cannot be doubted that the appellant
has waived literal compliance by taking a step in the action, that is, by asking   B
for particulars of the petition.

This question is a difficult one as is shown by the conflict of opinion in the
courts below. The circumstances which weigh heavily with their lordships in
favour of a mandatory construction are: (i) The need in an election petition for a
speedy determination of the controversy, a matter already emphasised by their
lordships. The interest of the public in election petitions was rightly stressed in   C
the Federal Court, but it is very much in the interests of the public that the
matter should be speedily determined. (ii) In contrast, for example, to the rules
of the Supreme Court in this country, the rules vest no general power in the
election judge to extend the time on the ground of irregularity. Their lordships
think that this omission was a matter of deliberate design. In cases where it was
intended that the judge should have power to amend proceedings or postpone   D
the inquiry it was expressly conferred on him, see, for example, r. 7, r. 8 and
r. 19. (iii) If there is more than one election petition relating to the same
election or return, they are to be dealt with as one (r. 6). It would be manifestly
inconvenient and against the public interest if by late service in one case and
subsequent delay in those proceedings the hearing of other petitions could be
held up. (iv) Respondents may deliver recriminatory cases (r. 8) and speedy   E
service, in order that the respondent may know the case against him, is obviously
desirable so that he may collect his evidence as soon as possible.

With regard to the authorities, for the reasons given in (ii) above many of
them, such as Re Pritchard (14), do not assist the determination of this case. The
case of Williams v. Tenby Corpn. (15), which has stood the test of nearly ninety
years and seems to their lordships plainly rightly decided, strongly supports the   F
view that the provisions of r. 15 are mandatory.

On the whole matter their lordships have reached the conclusion that the
provisions of r. 15 are mandatory, and the respondent's failure to observe the
time for service thereby prescribed rendered the proceedings a nullity. With all
respect to the Federal Court their lordships cannot attribute weight to the
circumstances that the rules contained no express power to strike out a petition   G
for non-compliance with r. 15.

When there is a withdrawal by a party it is obviously desirable that the rules
should make provision for such an event and that it should receive due publicity
by publication in the Gazette but, if the proceedings never begin in any real
sense by reason of the failure to serve the petition, there seems no compelling
reason for any formal order. The election judge must, however, have an inherent   H
power to cleanse his list by striking out or better by dismissing those petitions
which have become nullities by failure to serve the petition within the time
prescribed by the rules.

For these reasons their lordships will report to the Head of Malaysia their
opinion that the appeal should be allowed and the petition of the respondent
dismissed and that the respondent should pay the appellant's costs of this appeal   I
and in the courts below.

Appeal allowed.

Solicitors: *Coward, Chance & Co.* (for the appellant); *Garber, Vowles & Co.*
(for the respondent).

[*Reported by* KATHLEEN J. H. O'BRIEN, *Barrister-at-Law.*]

---

(14) [1963] 1 All E.R. 873; [1963] Ch. 502.   (15) (1879), 5 C.P.D. 135.

PAPWORTH v. COVENTRY.

[QUEEN'S BENCH DIVISION (Winn, L.J., Ashworth and Widgery, JJ.), February 15, 16, 1967.]

Parliament—Regulation of traffic—Prevention of obstruction of streets in neighbourhood of Parliament—Assemblies—Sessional order of Parliament—Directions issued by the Commissioner of Police of the Metropolis—Validity of directions—Metropolitan Police Act, 1839 (2 & 3 Vict. c. 47), s. 52.

On Apr. 25, 1966, the appellant visited a metropolitan police station where he saw the respondent and two other police officers and informed them that the Committee of 100 proposed to hold a vigil of seven persons in Whitehall on Apr. 26. The appellant was informed that the proposed vigil would be an assembly in breach of the directions* of the Commissioner of Police, dated Apr. 21, 1966, made under s. 52† of the Metropolitan Police Act, 1839, which set out the sessional order of Parliament and directed all constables that (i) all assemblies or processions of persons should be dispersed and should not be in or proceed along any street, square or open space within a specified area (which included Whitehall) on any day on which Parliament was sitting, and (ii) they should prevent or remove any cause of obstruction within that area. On Apr. 26, 1966, the appellant and six other persons took up positions holding posters on the edge of the footway in Whitehall. They did not constitute a procession but were well spaced out and stood still. The respondent told them that he considered that they were an assembly and in breach of the directions and four of them left, but the appellant and two others remained. There was no disorder and no member of either House of Parliament was prevented from passing freely to or from Parliament. The appellant having refused to move was arrested. On appeal against conviction under s. 54, para. 9‡, of the Act of 1839 on the ground that the directions were ultra vires the power delegated by s. 52 of the Act of 1839,

Held: (i) the directions should be construed in accordance with (ii) below, and, if so construed, were not ultra vires s. 52 of the Act of 1839 (see p. 47, letters H, and p. 48, letters C and D, post).

(ii) s. 52 of the Act of 1839 was to be construed in accordance with the genus therein, viz., the prevention of disorder in the neighbourhood of the Houses of Parliament and of obstruction of streets and thoroughfares in the neighbourhood; and the words " assemblies or processions " in the directions of the commissioner should be read as meaning only such assemblies or processions as were capable of causing consequential obstruction to the free passage of members to or from the Houses of Parliament or disorder or annoyance in the neighbourhood or thereabouts (see p. 46, letter D, p. 47, letter E, and p. 48, letters C and D, post).

(iii) accordingly the matter would be remitted to determine whether the appellant and the six other people with him constituted an assembly which was capable of giving rise consequentially either to obstruction of streets and thoroughfares in the immediate neighbourhood of the Houses of Parliament, or to disorder, annoyance of a kind itself likely to lead to a breach of the peace; and, unless such an assembly were so constituted, the appellant should be acquitted (see p. 47, letter I to p. 48, letter A, and p. 48, letters C and D, post).

---

* The directions are set out at p. 42, letter F, to p. 43, letter A, post.
† Section 52 is set out at p. 46, letter G, post.
‡ Section 54, so far as material, provides: ". . . Every person shall be liable to a penalty not more than 40s., who, within the limits of the metropolitan police district, shall in any thoroughfare or public place, commit any of the following offences; (that is to say,) . . . 9. Every person who, after being made acquainted with the . . . directions which the commissioners of police shall have made . . . for preventing obstructions . . . shall wilfully disregard or not conform himself thereunto . . ."

[As to the powers of the Commissioner of Police of the Metropolis to make   A
directions for preventing obstruction in streets, see 33 HALSBURY's LAWS (3rd
Edn.) 570, 571, para. 968; and for cases on the subject, see 45 DIGEST (Repl.)
5-7, *9-11, 18, 21.*

As to the ejusdem generis rule in the interpretation of statutes, see 36 HALS-
BURY's LAWS (3rd Edn.) 397, 398, para. 599; and for cases on the subject, see
44 DIGEST (Repl.) 262, 263, *875-882.*   B

For the Metropolitan Police Act, 1839, s. 52, see 24 HALSBURY's STATUTES
(2nd Edn.) 817.]

Case referred to:

Brownsea Haven Properties, Ltd. v. *Poole Corpn.,* [1958] 1 All E.R. 205; [1958]
    Ch. 574; [1958] 2 W.L.R. 137; 122 J.P. 97; 45 Digest (Repl.) 6, *19.*   C

Case Stated.

This was a Case Stated by Miss Jean Graham Hall in respect of her adjudication
as a metropolitan magistrate sitting at Bow Street metropolitan magistrates'
court on July 5 and 15, 1966. At Bow Street metropolitan magistrates' court
a charge was made by the respondent, Vincent Coventry, a superintendent in   D
the Metropolitan Police Force, against the appellant, Andrew John Papworth,
under s. 54, para. 9, of the Metropolitan Police Act, 1839, that, on Apr. 26,
1966, at Whitehall, London, S.W.1, having been made acquainted with the
directions of the commissioner of police dated Apr. 21, 1966, under s. 52 of the
Metropolitan Police Act, 1839, for the purpose of keeping order and preventing
obstruction in the places, streets and thoroughfares and on the occasions specified E
therein, he wilfully disregarded the directions by remaining in the same street
when requested by a police officer in uniform to disperse. The following facts
were proved or admitted. On Apr. 21, 1966, the current session of Parliament
commenced and on that day the House of Commons passed a sessional order.
On the same day the Commissioner of Police of the Metropolis gave his directions
to all constables. The directions were in the following terms: F

"Procedures prohibited during the sitting of Parliament

" By virtue of the powers conferred on me by s. 52 of the Metropolitan
Police Act, 1839, I the undersigned, Commissioner of Police of the Metropolis,
do hereby give directions to all constables that during the session of Parliament the following sessional order shall be enforced:—' The passages through   G
the streets leading to the Houses of Parliament shall be kept free and open
and no obstruction shall be permitted to hinder the passage of members
to and from the Houses of Parliament and no disorder shall be allowed in
Westminster Hall or any passages leading to the Houses of Parliament
during the sitting of Parliament and there shall be no annoyance therein or
thereabouts.'   H

" And I further direct all constables in pursuance of the said order and
by virtue of my powers under the said Act: (1) that all assemblies or
processions of persons shall be dispersed and shall not be in or proceed along
any street, square or open place within the area specified hereunder on
any day on which Parliament is sitting:—South side of the River Thames
between Waterloo and Vauxhall Bridges, Vauxhall Bridge Road, Victoria   I
Street (between Vauxhall Bridge Road and Buckingham Palace Road),
Grosvenor Gardens, Grosvenor Place, Piccadilly, Coventry Street, New
Coventry Street, Leicester Square (north side), Cranbourn Street, Long Acre,
Bow Street, Wellington Street, crossing Strand and Victoria Embankment
west of Waterloo Bridge. Provided that processions may be routed along
the thoroughfares named except Victoria Embankment west of Waterloo
Bridge. (2) That they shall prevent or remove any cause of obstruction
within the area named in para. (1) hereof, so that every facility shall be

A   afforded for the free passage of members to and from the Houses of Parliament on any day on which Parliament is sitting.

Signed, J. Simpson,

21.4.66.   Commissioner of Police of the Metropolis."

On Apr. 25, 1966, at about 11.45 a.m., the appellant went to Cannon Row
B   police station and there saw Chief Superintendent Gilbert, Superintendent
Coventry and Inspector Neale. He informed the officers that the Committee
of 100 proposed to hold a vigil of seven persons in Whitehall at the junction with
Downing Street between noon and 1.00 p.m. to call attention to the situation in
Vietnam. The appellant was informed by Chief Superintendent Gilbert that the
proposed vigil of any number of persons would be an assembly in breach of the
C   commissioner's directions, a copy of which was handed to him. On Apr. 26, 1966,
at about noon, the appellant and six other persons took up positions holding
posters on the edge of the footway in Whitehall, part to the north of Downing
Street, part to the south. Read together in sequence these posters gave a message.
The persons were well spaced out and were stationary. Superintendent Coventry
went up to the seven persons and told them that he considered they were an
D   assembly, and that they were in breach of the directions if they carried out their
vigil. He handed each a copy of the directions and asked them to disperse.
Four then left. Three, the appellant, Miss Margaret Smith and Mr. Robert
Overy, remained, although still spaced out. Superintendent Coventry went
up to the appellant and asked him to move. The appellant said " No ". He was
arrested and taken to Cannon Row police station and charged. The appellant,
E   after he was charged and cautioned, made a statement in which he said, " I
understand that sessional orders are for the purpose of enabling members of
Parliament to go to and leave Parliament without being obstructed. I was
careful to co-operate with the police so that I did not cause an obstruction.
I did not prevent any member from reaching or leaving Parliament. Nor do I
see that I could have possibly done so ". The pavement on the west side of White-
F   hall where the vigil took place on Apr. 26, 1966, was broad, and Downing Street
was about twenty feet wide. There was no evidence that any lord or commoner
or other person was impeded in his access to the Houses of Parliament, or that
any member of the public was actually obstructed by the actions of the appellant
and his colleagues. All parties spoke highly of everyone's general conduct.

On behalf of the appellant it was contended that the directions made by the
G   Commissioner of Police of the Metropolis on Apr. 21, 1966, were ultra vires the
relevant section of the enabling Act, s. 52 of the Metropolitan Police Act, 1839,
and unenforceable because they sought to enforce a resolution of the House
of Commons which was not binding on the general public and had no legal
authority, and further (and primarily) because they exceeded the powers delegated to the commissioner under the enabling Act; in the alternative, the appel-
H   lant's actions and those of his colleagues did not on the facts constitute an
assembly or procession or cause of obstruction within the meaning of and in breach
of the directions. It was the appellant's main contention that the directions
exceeded the commissioner's powers and were ultra vires the enabling Act because
of the width with which they were framed, firstly in that they sought to prohibit
all assemblies and processions of whatever nature on any day on which Parliament
I   was sitting and secondly in the geographical area which they specified. On behalf
of the respondent it was contended that, quite apart from the sessional order,
the commissioner of police had power under the second part of s. 52, that dealing
with keeping order and preventing obstruction by the palaces and public offices,
etc., to give the directions which were the basis of the charges; that so far as
assemblies were concerned, the directions required them to be dispersed; that
police at the scene had no discretion but had to act in accordance with the
directions; that they did not have to wait until the assemblies had reached
large proportions and the directions relating to assemblies should be interpreted

as requiring them to prevent large assemblies; that the purpose of the directions, **A** based on the enabling section, was for keeping order as well as for preventing obstruction and that, therefore, the existence or otherwise of obstruction arising from unreasonable user of the highway was irrelevant though in fact such obstruction existed.

The magistrate held as follows:—(a) that the commissioner's directions of Apr. 21, 1966, were made by virtue of s. 52 of the Metropolitan Police Act, 1839, **B** and that, although they recited the sessional order, that order was for internal use only; (b) that the directions were not repugnant to the general law and were within the powers conferred on the commissioner by the enabling Act and not, therefore, ultra vires the Act; (c) that there was on the facts adduced before her no procession, but that the appellant and his colleagues constituted an assembly at the material time and in the material place and that the appellant **C** in then failing to move when asked was wilfully disregarding the directions. She, therefore, convicted the appellant, and fined him 40s. and the appellant now appealed.

The authority and cases noted below* were cited during the argument in addition to the case referred to in the judgment of WINN, L.J.

I. Brownlie for the appellant.   **D**
M. D. L. Worsley for the respondent.

WINN, L.J.: This is an interesting and important appeal which arises on a Case Stated by one of Her Majesty's metropolitan magistrates sitting at Bow Street metropolitan magistrates' court. At that court a charge was made by the respondent, a superintendent of the Metropolitan Police Force, against **E** the appellant, Andrew John Papworth, under s. 54, para. 9, of the Metropolitan Police Act, 1839. He was thereby charged that, on Apr. 26, 1966, at Whitehall, having been made acquainted with the directions of the commissioner of police dated Apr. 21, 1966, purporting to be made under s. 52 of the Act of 1839 for the purpose of keeping order and preventing obstruction in the places, streets and thoroughfares and on the occasions specified in the direction, he did wilfully **F** disregard the said directions by remaining in the same street when requested by a police officer in uniform to disperse. The learned magistrate heard that charge on two days in July, 1966, and convicted the appellant of the offence charged, and ordered him to pay a penalty of 40s. It is not, of course, the penalty of 40s. which makes this case important. As has been very lucidly and most helpfully and ably demonstrated to the court by counsel for the appellant, **G** it is a matter of principle and of the rights and liberties of subjects, and their immunity from having their lawful activities curbed save to the extent that Parliament has enacted, directly by legislation of its own or indirectly through powers delegated to a subordinate authority, that they shall be restricted. It is a matter of importance since it raises the fundamental question whether or not the directions to which I have referred were ultra vires the power delegated **H** by s. 52 of the Act of 1839. It is right, as well as convenient, to say at once that it is common ground that whatever happened on the relevant occasion was not disorderly; not unlawful for any reason other than the alleged contravention of the directions; did not cause any annoyance to anybody; did not in fact prevent any member of either House of Parliament from passing freely to or from Parliament; nor was the conduct of the appellant and his associates **I** anything but good mannered, restrained and gentlemanly. [HIS LORDSHIP stated the facts, and continued:] The directions themselves need not, I feel, be read in full, but certain aspects of them must be mentioned, and indeed emphasised, for the purposes of this judgment. They are, of course, set out verbatim

---

* *Pankhurst and Haverfield* v. *Jarvis*, (1910), 74 J.P. 64; *Pyx Granite Co., Ltd.* v. *Ministry of Housing and Local Government*, [1958] 1 All E.R. 625; [1958] 1 Q.B. 554; *Fawcett Properties, Ltd.* v. *Buckingham County Council*, [1960] 3 All E.R. 503; [1961] A.C. 636.

A in the Case Stated. They are headed " Processions prohibited during the sitting of Parliament ". The commissioner of police by these directions, having referred to the powers conferred on him by s. 52, gave directions:

B
" . . . to all constables that during the session of Parliament the following sessional order shall be enforced [and he then set out as a quotation the sessional order of Parliament itself as follows:]

' The passages through the streets leading to the Houses of Parliament shall be kept free and open and no obstruction shall be permitted to hinder the passage of members to and from the Houses of Parliament and no disorder shall be allowed in Westminster Hall or any passages leading to the Houses of Parliament during the sitting of Parliament and there shall be no annoyance therein or thereabouts '."

C

I break off from reading these directions to say that the court accepts as clearly right the submission of counsel for the appellant that the sessional order in question per se could have no effect outside the walls and precincts of the Houses of Parliament. It would have no extra mural restrictive force, and would be incapable of creating any offence in respect of conduct in the area outside the precincts of Parliament. I pick up again the process of examining these directions

D by saying that they were issued to all constables requiring them first to ensure:

" That all assemblies or processions of persons shall be dispersed and shall not be in or proceed along any street, square or open space within the area specified hereunder on any day on which Parliament is sitting."

E Then a number of streets are named, but there is an express proviso that along those streets, other than that part of the Victoria Embankment which lies to the west of Waterloo Bridge, that is to say nearer to Whitehall and to the Houses of Parliament, processions might be routed; on a controlled route that would mean. The commissioner further directed constables and officers:

F
" That they shall prevent or remove any cause of obstruction within the area named [the streets that are named], so that every facility shall be afforded for the free passage of members to and from the Houses of Parliament on any day on which Parliament is sitting."

Various contentions and arguments were raised before the learned magistrate; I do not take the time or trouble to read them. The learned magistrate held first that the directions were made by virtue of s. 52 of the Act of 1839, and, correctly

G in my view, added: " . . . although they recited the sessional order that order was for internal use only ". The commissioner recited the sessional order, and by so doing in my judgment he quite clearly revealed his motive for making the directions that he made; but the fact that he so revealed what his motive was does not itself amount to a declaration that he regarded himself as doing no more than give effect to the sessional order. That, in my view, would be a

H quite mistaken view of the effect of his directions. Moreover, in the directions themselves, the commissioner declared that he was making the directions in pursuance of the sessional order and by virtue of his powers under the Act of 1839, which strengthens the view that I was stating that he was not purporting to take his powers from the sessional order. Secondly, the magistrate found that the directions were not repugnant to the general law and were within the

I powers conferred on the commissioner by the enabling Act, and she held that they were not ultra vires the Act. Further, the learned magistrate held under para. (c), and this is the vital finding or holding:

" that there was on the facts adduced before me no procession, but that the appellant and his colleagues constituted an assembly at the material time and in the material place and that the appellant in then failing to move when asked was wilfully disregarding the directions."

She therefore convicted the appellant.

It seems to me beyond any doubt that these directions, being directions in A
writing contained in a document which is now before the court, are properly
to be construed by this court so as to ascertain what is their meaning. The
first of the directions uses the very wide terms:—" That all assemblies or processions of persons shall be dispersed . . ." The context of the direction is, I
venture to think, perfectly clear. It is that the streets are to be kept free and
open and that no obstruction is to be permitted to hinder the passage of members B
to and from the Houses of Parliament and no disorder or annoyance shall be
allowed to arise thereabouts, that is to say in the vicinity of Parliament, the
streets leading to the Houses of Parliament, or thereabouts. Further, in the
second direction the expression occurs:

" That they shall prevent or remove any cause of obstruction . . . so that
every facility shall be afforded for the free passage of members to and from   C
the Houses of Parliament on any day on which Parliament is sitting."

Within that context and as a matter of construction of the document as a whole,
I am of the firm opinion that the words " assemblies or processions " cannot
mean widely and literally all conceivable assemblies or processions, but must
have a more limited meaning, with no greater connotation or content than such D
assemblies or processions of persons as are capable of causing consequential
obstruction to the free passage of members to and from the Houses of Parliament
or their departure therefrom, or disorder in the neighbourhood or annoyance
thereabouts. I am myself of the opinion that, in any wider sense than that
which I have endeavoured to state, the directions would be ultra vires the powers
of the commissioner derived from s. 52 of the Act of 1839. Of course it should be E
borne in mind that this particular direction related to the neighbourhood of
Parliament; other directions relating to other neighbourhoods would stand on
their own footing. The section which, it is a matter of incidental comment, has
now been in force for a good many years and under which, it may be permissible
to take judicial notice, many directions of commissioners of police must have
been given, enacts as follows: F

" . . . . it shall be lawful for the commissioners (1) of police [that is the delegation of power] from time to time, and as occasion shall require, to make
regulations for the route to be observed by all carts, carriages, horses, and
persons, and for preventing obstruction of the streets and thoroughfares
within the metropolitan police district, in all times of public processions,
public rejoicings, or illuminations, and also to give directions to the constables G
for keeping order and for preventing any obstruction of the thoroughfares
in the immediate neighbourhood of Her Majesty's palaces and the public
offices, the High Court of Parliament, the courts of law and equity, the
police courts, the theatres, and other places of public resort, and in any
case when the streets or thoroughfares may be thronged or may be liable
to be obstructed."   H

Counsel for the appellant, in the course of the submissions to which I have
already paid tribute, drew the attention of the court to various authorities,
and in particular to *Brownsea Haven Properties, Ltd.* v. *Poole Corpn.* (2), and
especially to certain passages in the judgment of LORD EVERSHED, M.R. (3).
I do not propose to refer in any detail to this case; it suffices, I hope, for the
present purpose to say that that was a case in which a different statute fell to   I
be interpreted, and that the wording there was much less intractable for a
submission that the ejusdem generis rule must control the apparent wideness
of the wording. The enactment there relevant was the Town Police Clauses Act,
1847, s. 21 of which provides:

(1) The powers of the Commissioners of Police were made exercisable by the Commissioner of Police of the Metropolis by the Metropolitan Police Act, 1856, s. 5.
(2) [1958] 1 All E.R. 203; [1958] Ch. 574.
(3) [1958] 1 All E.R. at pp. 212, 213, 214; [1958] Ch. at pp. 596, 598, 599.

A   " The commissioners may from time to time make orders for the route
to be observed by all carts, carriages, horses, and persons, and for preventing
obstruction of the streets, within the limits of the special Act, in all times
of public processions, rejoicings, or illuminations, and in any case when the
streets are thronged or liable to be obstructed, and may also give directions
to the constables for keeping order and preventing any obstruction . . ."

B   I need not read any more.   There the court held that those words " in any case "
in the context of that section should be construed in accordance with the rule
known as the ejusdem generis rule of construction as intended only to cover
cases of the same class or genus as public processions, rejoicings or illuminations,
or possibly that they might be extended to traffic dislocation of a special or
extraordinary kind, conditions likely to attract a crowd; and this was the
C   operative decision, that they ought not to be treated as covering circumstances
of ordinary day to day traffic conditions. Counsel for the appellant in his submission put this case as somewhat analogous to that case, but recognised that he
must accept that here there were at least two genera, not only one genus. There
was a genus of time and a genus of place; possibly, he suggested, there was a
combination of those two genera forming a mixed genus of time and place of
D   which the characteristic was focus on a point of attraction.
     I am not myself familiar with any other case in which the court has been
asked to apply a rule of construction which might, I suppose, accurately be
described as the rule eorundem generum, not ejusdem generis;   recognising
the cogency of the submission, I nevertheless myself think that it is perfectly
clear that there is here a plain genus to be found in the context of s. 52, and
E   that is, for present purposes, the prevention of disorder in the neighbourhood
of the Houses of Parliament and prevention of obstruction of streets and thoroughfares within that neighbourhood by any cause of obstruction in the sense of any
act, conduct, construction of any edifice or any process of bringing persons
together, by reason of attraction through interest, which is capable of giving
rise to obstruction of the free access to, or departure from, the Houses of Parlia-
F   ment or to disorder in the neighbourhood of the houses of Parliament; it cannot
be doubted that Whitehall is in the neighbourhood. It does not seem to me to
make any difference at all, at any rate in the instant case, whether one says that
the genus of purpose for which regulations can be made is for the prevention of
disorder, for the prevention of such obstruction, as I have indicated, and the
prevention of annoyance, or whether one says that, by the express words found
G   at the end of the section, there is power given to ensure by direction that the
streets or thoroughfares in the neighbourhood of Parliament shall not be rendered
liable to be obstructed by any occurrence. It is trite to say that the best way
to put out a fire is to prevent it before it occurs, or in its very initial stage. In
the same way it is plain, in my view at least, that one of the effective ways of
preventing the obstruction, the disorder, the annoyance contemplated by the
H   section is to prevent the coming into existence of causes from which consequentially, and on a reasonable view potentially, such mischief may well arise. So
construed, I am of the opinion that these directions do not exceed the powers
granted to the commissioners by s. 52, and that they are, therefore, to the extent
that I have endeavoured to indicate, and construed in the sense in which I have
endeavoured to state that they must be construed, lawful and effective to create
I   an offence.
     Whether or not the appellant committed such an offence remains in my view
to be determined. I do not myself think that the learned magistrate has revealed
by her Case Stated that her mind was directed by the advocates before her, or
by herself, to the correct criterion for determining whether guilt has been
established of an offence against the directions. This Case, I think, should go
back to the learned magistrate for her further to find—without hearing further
evidence since that would be quite unfair to the appellant, but on the evidence
which she has already heard and in accordance with her findings of fact already

made—whether or not she is satisfied beyond a reasonable doubt that the   **A**
appellant and his colleagues—and by that, I say expressly, I mean the seven
of them who first came together in the place referred to in the Case—constituted
an assembly which was capable of giving rise consequentially either to obstruction
of streets and thoroughfares in the immediate neighbourhood of the Houses of
Parliament, or to disorder, annoyance of the kind itself likely to lead to a breach
of the peace.   Unless she is minded so to hold she will acquit the appellant;   **B**
only on the conditions which I have stated should she reaffirm the conviction
which she ordered to be entered on what I regard, on the material before me, as in
all probability a misunderstanding of the effect of the directions.

    ASHWORTH, J.: I agree.   The only point that I would wish to add
relates to the scope of s. 52 of the Metropolitan Police Act, 1839.   For the
appellant, counsel was content to say that the directions of the commissioner   **C**
were ultra vires, but was not prepared, understandably, to say precisely where the
vires should be drawn; it was enough for him to say that these directions went
outside them.   For my part, I would follow that example with the contrary
result.   I agree with WINN, L.J., that these directions properly construed were
within the vires, but I would wish to reserve, because it may occur on some   **D**
future occasion, the question what is the precise scope and effect of s. 52.

    WIDGERY, J.: I agree with both judgments and there is nothing which
I can usefully add.

Case remitted.

    Solicitors: *B. M. Birnberg & Co.* (for the appellant); *Solicitor, Metropolitan
Police* (for the respondent).   **E**

[*Reported by* N. P. METCALFE, ESQ., *Barrister-at-Law.*]

CLEARY v. INLAND REVENUE COMMISSIONERS.

  F

[HOUSE OF LORDS (Viscount Dilhorne, Lord Morris of Borth-y-Gest, Lord Guest,
Lord Upjohn and Lord Devlin), January 24, 25, March 15, 1967.]

*Surtax—Tax advantage—Counteracting—Transaction in connexion with distri-
bution of profits—Phrase including transfer of assets of company—Advantage
by receipt of sum as capital instead of dividend—Shareholders' sale of other
company's shares to company—Avoidance of surtax—Finance Act,* 1960   **G**
(8 & 9 *Eliz.* 2 c. 44), *s.* 28 (1), (2) (*d*), *s.* 43 (4) (*g*).

The appellant and her sister owned in equal shares the whole of the
issued share capital of two companies.   Each of the sisters sold to one of the
companies, which then had a balance on profit and loss account of £180,000
and £130,000 cash at bank, twenty-two thousand £1 shares in the other
company (which had an issued share capital of £50,000) for £60,500 in cash,   **H**
that being the full value of the shares ascertained on a proper valuation.
They were each served by the Commissioners of Inland Revenue with a
notice under s. 28 (3)* of the Finance Act, 1960, that an adjustment was
necessary for counteracting the tax advantage obtained by each taxpayer
by the sale, the adjustment comprising the recomputation of the liability
of each to surtax on the basis that the £60,500 consideration paid to each   **I**
taxpayer should be taken into account as if it were the net amount of a
dividend paid on the same date.   On appeal,

    Held: s. 28* of the Finance Act, 1960, applied and liability to surtax
was recomputable on the basis mentioned above, for the following reasons—
    (i) because the appellant obtained a " tax advantage " within the meaning
of that term in s. 43 (4) (*g*)† of the Finance Act, 1960, since by selling her

---

* Section 28, so far as material, is set out at p. 54, letter I, to p. 55, letter D, post.
† Section 43 (4) (*g*), is set out at p. 55, letter F, post.

A   shares she received as capital from the company the sum of £60,500 (the price of the shares) thereby obtaining "the avoidance of a possible assessment" to income tax, which might have been made on her if the £60,500 had been distributed to her by way of dividend (see p. 51, letter I, p. 53, letter I, to p. 54, letter A, and p. 54, letter C, and p. 56, letter E, post).

Dictum of LORD WILBERFORCE in *Inland Revenue Comrs.* v. *Parker* ([1966]
B   1 All E.R. at p. 415) followed.

(ii) because the tax advantage had been obtained in circumstances mentioned in s. 28 (2) (*d*) of the Act of 1960, notwithstanding that para. (*d*) predicated receipt "in connexion with the distribution of profits" of a company, since, when para. (*d*) was read with the definitions of "distribution" and "profits" in sub-s. (2), it extended to the application of the
C   company's profits or assets by paying the £60,500 and, on the true construction of sub-s. (2) (*d*), the fact that the value of the assets of the company was not diminished by the transaction did not render para. (*d*) inapplicable (see p. 52, letter I, to p. 53, letter A, and p. 53, letter I, to p. 54, letter A, and p. 57, letter D, post).

Decision of the COURT OF APPEAL (sub nom. *Inland Revenue Comrs.* v.
D   *Cleary, Inland Revenue Comrs.* v. *Perren,* [1966] 2 All E.R. 19) affirmed.

[As to the counteracting of tax advantages, see SUPPLEMENT to 20 HALSBURY'S LAWS (3rd Edn.) para. 276A.

For the Finance Act, 1960, s. 28 (1), (2), and s. 43 (4) (*g*), see 40 HALSBURY'S STATUTES (2nd Edn.) 447, 448, 465, 466.]

E   Cases referred to:

Cherry v. *International Alloys, Ltd.,* [1960] 3 All E.R. 264; [1961] 1 Q.B. 136; [1960] 3 W.L.R. 568; Digest (Cont. Vol. A) 586, *205a*.

Inland Revenue Comrs. v. *Parker,* [1966] 1 All E.R. 399; [1966] A.C. 141; [1966] 2 W.L.R. 486.

St. Aubyn (*L. M.*) v. *A.-G.* (*No. 2*), [1951] 2 All E.R. 473; [1952] A.C. 15; 21 Digest (Repl.) 50, *199*.

F   **Appeal.**

This was an appeal by the appellant taxpayer, Kathleen Sarah Cleary, from an order of the Court of Appeal (LORD DENNING, M.R., DANCKWERTS and SALMON, L.JJ.) dated Mar. 4, 1966, and reported [1966] 2 All E.R. 19, allowing the appeal of the Crown from an order of PENNYCUICK, J., dated Apr. 13, 1965
G   and reported [1965] 2 All E.R. 603, dismissing the appeal by the Crown from a decision of the Commissioners for the Special Purposes of the Income Tax Acts dated Mar. 12, 1964.

E. I. Goulding, Q.C., and *N. P. M. Elles* for the appellant.
J. A. Brightman, Q.C., J. R. Phillips and *J. P. Warner* for the Crown.

Their lordships took time for consideration.

H   Mar. 15.   The following opinions were delivered.

VISCOUNT DILHORNE: My Lords, on Feb. 14, 1963, the Commissioners of Inland Revenue gave the appellant notice, in accordance with s. 28 (4) of the Finance Act, 1960, that they had reason to believe that s. 28 of the Act of 1960 might apply to her in relation to the sale by her on or about July 24, 1961,
I   to Gleeson Development Co., Ltd. (hereafter called the G.D. Co.) of twenty-two thousand ordinary shares of £1 each in M. J. Gleeson, Ltd. (hereafter called the M.J.G. Co.).   The appellant then sent to the Commissioners of Inland Revenue a statutory declaration stating that, in her opinion, the section did not apply to her and giving the grounds for her opinion.   The matter then came before the tribunal appointed for the purpose, who held that there was a prima facie case for the commissioners proceeding.   The commissioners then served a notice under s. 28 (3) of the Act of 1960, the effect of which was to claim that the appellant was liable to surtax for the year 1961/62 on the basis that the amount of £60,500

which she received from the G.D. Co. on the sale to it of the shares in the M.J.G. A
Co. should be taken into account as if it were the net amount received in respect
of a dividend payable at the date of its receipt from which tax had been deducted.
The appellant appealed against this notice to the Commissioners for the Special
Purposes of the Income Tax Acts, who allowed the appeal. The Crown then
appealed to the High Court. PENNYCUICK, J. (1) dismissed their appeal. They
then appealed to the Court of Appeal (2), who allowed their appeal. The B
appellant now appeals to this House.

At all material times the appellant owned half the shares in the G.D. Co. and
her sister owned the other half. The issued capital of that company consisted
of two hundred thousand 1s. ordinary shares. The appellant and her sister
also owned on Dec. 31, 1960, all the shares in the M.J.G. Co., which had an
issued capital of fifty thousand £1 shares. The balance sheet of the G.D. Co. C
shows that at Dec. 31, 1960, there was a balance of £180,840 standing to the
credit of its profit and loss account. This sum represented an accumulation of
profits within the charge to income tax. On or about July 24, 1961, the appellant
and her sister each sold to the G.D. Co. twenty-two thousand shares in the
M.J.G. Co. for £60,500 cash. This was the full value of the shares held. Before
effecting this sale the appellant did not, as she was entitled to do by virtue of D
s. 28 (10) of the Act of 1960, inform the Commissioners of Inland Revenue what
she proposed to do and seek their determination that this section did not apply.
The result of this transaction was, as PENNYCUICK, J., said, that (3)

". . . . the sisters had together taken £121,000 in cash out of the [G.D. Co.].
They continued to own all the issued shares in the company, which now
held forty-four thousand shares in the [M.J.G. Co.] previously held by the E
sisters."

If the amount of £121,000 had been distributed by way of dividend, as it could
have been, each sister would have been liable to surtax in respect of the £60,500
each received. The question that has to be decided is whether by virtue of
s. 28 of the Act of 1960, they are liable to pay surtax in respect of the receipt F
of that amount notwithstanding that it was received in payment for and was
the full value of the shares they sold.

Section 28 (1), so far as material, reads as follows:

" Where—
" (a) in any such circumstances as are mentioned in the next following
subsection, and (b) in consequence of a transaction in securities or of G
the combined effect of two or more such transactions,
a person is in a position to obtain, or has obtained, a tax advantage, then
unless he shows that the transaction or transactions were carried out either
for bona fide commercial reasons or in the ordinary course of making or
managing investments, and that none of them had as their main object, or
one of their main objects, to enable tax advantages to be obtained, this H
section shall apply to him in respect of that transaction or those transactions:
. . ."

In this case the appellant at no time sought to contend that the sale of the shares
was carried out for bona fide commercial reasons or in the ordinary course of
making or managing investments; nor did she contend that the sale had
not as one of its main objects the obtaining of tax advantages. Consequently I
the section applies if the circumstances mentioned in any of the paragraphs of
s. 28 (2) existed and if in consequence of a transaction in securities the appellant
obtained or was in a position to obtain a tax advantage. A " transaction in
securities " is defined in s. 43 (4) (i) of the Act of 1960 as including

---

(1) [1965] 2 All E.R. 603; [1965] Ch. 1098.
(2) [1966] 2 All E.R. 19; [1966] Ch. 365.
(3) [1965] 2 All E.R. at p. 607; [1965] Ch. at p. 1107.

A   "... transactions, of whatever description, relating to securities, and in
particular—(i) the purchase, sale or exchange of securities, (ii) . . ., (iii) . . ."

The word " securities " is also defined in s. 43 (4) (*f*) of the Act of 1960 as including
shares.   In the light of these definitions it is clear beyond all doubt that the
sale of the shares in the M.F.G. Co. constituted a transaction in securities within
the meaning of this section.

B   A tax advantage is also defined in s. 43 (4) (*g*) of the Act of 1960 as follows:

" ' Tax advantage ' means a relief or increased relief from, or repayment
or increased repayment of, income tax, or the avoidance or reduction of an
assessment to income tax or the avoidance of a possible assessment thereto,
whether the avoidance or reduction is effected by receipts accruing in such
C   a way that the recipient does not pay or bear tax on them, or by a deduction
in computing profits or gains; "

The appellant has throughout contended that she did not obtain a tax advantage
as defined.   This contention succeeded before Pennycuick, J. (4).   He said
that (5):

"... the apparent effect of the definition so far as it is now in point is to
D   treat as a tax advantage a receipt on which, if the taxpayer had taken it
in one way, he would have paid or borne tax, but which he takes in some
other way without paying or bearing tax on it.   For this purpose it is
necessary to compare like with like; i.e., one must look at the actual transaction which comprises the receipt and see whether, by another form of
transaction producing the same result, the receipt would have been taxable.
E   One cannot for this purpose look at the actual transaction and then compare
it with a transaction which, although containing a common element, produces
a different result.   So, it seems to me, one cannot look at an actual transaction by way of sale, under which a member of a company transfers to the
company property equivalent to the amount paid by the company to the
member, and compare that transaction with a simple receipt by the member
F   from the company without consideration."

Pennycuick, J. (4) delivered his judgment before the case of *Inland Revenue
Comrs.* v. *Parker* (6) was heard in this House.   In that case Lord Wilberforce,
referring to the definition of tax advantage, said (7):

" The paragraph, as I understand it, presupposes a situation in which an
G   assessment to tax, or increased tax, either is made or may possibly be made,
that the taxpayer is in a position to resist the assessment by saying that
the way in which he received what it is sought to tax, prevents him from being
taxed on it; and that the Revenue is in a position to reply that if he had
received what it is sought to tax *in another way* he would have had to bear
tax.   In other words, there must be a contrast, as regards the ' receipts ',
H   between the actual case where these accrue, in a non-taxable way with a
possible accruer in a taxable way, and, unless this contrast exists, the
existence of the advantage is not established."

The definition does not require the contrast of like with like as Pennycuick, J.,
held (5) and to give it such an interpretation would narrow the scope of the
section considerably.   It is, I think, clear from what Lord Wilberforce
I   said (7), that Pennycuick, J.'s (5) view on this was not correct.

That the appellant received £60,500 in such a way that she did not pay or
bear tax on it, is not disputed.   It could have been distributed to her by way
of dividend and, if it had been, she would have been liable to tax.   There is
thus in this case the contrast to which Lord Wilberforce (7) referred.   It is

(4) [1965] 2 All E.R. 603; [1965] Ch. 1098.
(5) [1965] 2 All E.R. at p. 609; [1965] Ch. at pp. 1110, 1111.
(6) [1966] 1 All E.R. 399; [1966] A.C. 141.
(7) [1966] 1 All E.R. at p. 415; [1966] A.C. at p. 178, 179.

clear that in consequence of a transaction in securities she avoided a possible **A**
assessment to income tax, the possible assessment being that which would have
been made if she had received the sum by way of dividend. She therefore
obtained a tax advantage within the meaning of the section. It follows that if
the circumstances mentioned in any of the paragraphs in s. 28 (2) of the Act of
1960 were present, the section applies and the Crown is entitled to succeed.
The Crown contended that those stated in para. (*d*) of that subsection were **B**
present. That paragraph reads as follows:

" (*d*) in connexion with the distribution of profits of a company to which
this paragraph applies, the person in question so receives as is mentioned
in para. (*c*) of this subsection such a consideration as is therein mentioned:"

The material parts of para. (*c*) are as follows: **C**

" (*c*) the person in question receives . . . a consideration which either is,
or represents the value of, assets which are (or apart from anything done
by the company in question would have been) available for distribution by
way of dividend . . . and the said person so receives the consideration that
he does not pay or bear tax on it as income;"

Subsection (2) also provides: **D**

" In this subsection—
" (i) references to profits include references to income, reserves
or other assets,
" (ii) references to distribution include references to transfer or realisation (including application in discharge of liabilities), and **E**
" (iii) references to the receipt of consideration include references
to the receipt of any money or money's worth."

It was not disputed that the G.D. Co. was a company to which the paragraph
applied. The consideration for the sale of the shares received by the appellant
was money, and money which, apart from its payment by the company for the
shares, would have been available for distribution by way of dividend; and **F**
the appellant received it in such a way that she did not pay tax on it. Thus
the circumstances mentioned in paras. 28 (2) (*d*) were present if, but only if, the
appellant so received the consideration " in connexion with the distribution of
profits " of the company. It was strenuously argued that she had not done so.
It was pointed out that in exchange for the money the company had obtained
assets of equal value and that the amount available for distribution by the **G**
company had not been reduced. It was argued that there could be no distribution of the profits of a company without there being a diminution of the amount
available for distribution. Further it was submitted that, if the Crown was
right, there was a possibility of double taxation should the company distribute
by way of dividend the value of the shares which it had bought.

If one interpolates the definitions of the words " distribution " and " profits " **H**
contained in s. 28 (2), the words " in connexion with the distribution of profits "
become " in connexion with the distribution, transfer or realisation (including
application in discharge of liabilities) of profits, income, reserves or other
assets " of the company. There was a transfer by the company of profits and
of assets of the company. If the company entered into a contract to purchase
the shares for £60,500, there was also an application of profits and assets of the **I**
company in discharge of a liability. Acceptance of the appellant's contention
that there cannot be a distribution of profits without a diminution of the amount
available for distribution involves ignoring the definitions of the words " distribution " and " profits " and reading into the section a qualification which is not
there. Nor, if it be right that there is a possibility of double taxation, is there
anything in the section to exclude its application in that event. The effect of the
company's action, which was of course controlled by the two sisters who owned
all the shares, was to reduce its cash by £121,000, and, unless s. 28 applies, to

A transfer it to them without their incurring any liability to tax. In the light of the definitions of " distribution " and " profits " it is clear that the appellant so received the £60,500 in connexion with the distribution of the profits of the company. In my view, for the reasons which I have stated, the section does apply, and the Court of Appeal (8) were right to allow the Crown's appeal. In my opinion this appeal should be dismissed.

B

LORD MORRIS OF BORTH-Y-GEST: My Lords, the question in this case is whether the provisions of s. 28 of the Finance Act, 1960, apply to the appellant in respect of the transaction which was effected when she sold her shares for the sum of £60,500. It becomes necessary to extract from this somewhat sprawling section (with its buttressing extension clauses and with the interpretations denoted by s. 43) the provisions that apply in such a case as the

C present. As a result of following that process it seems to me that, subject to certain exceptions, s. 28 applies to a person where, in connexion with the distribution or transfer or realisation (including application in discharge of liabilities) of profits, or income or reserves or other assets of a company under the control of not more than five persons, and in consequence of a transaction in securities,

D he receives (so that he does not pay or bear tax on it as income) a consideration (which may include money or money's worth) which either is or represents the value of assets which are, or apart from anything done by the company in question would have been, available for distribution by way of dividend and if he is in a position to obtain or has obtained a tax advantage. Included in the meanings of a tax advantage is the meaning of a relief from income tax or the avoidance or

E reduction of an assessment to income tax or the avoidance of a possible assessment to income tax whether the avoidance or reduction is effected by receipts accruing in such a way that the recipient does not pay or bear tax on them or by a deduction in computing profits or gains.

Amongst the exceptions is one which provides that the section shall not apply to a person if the transaction in securities was carried out, and any change in the

F nature of any activities carried on by a person (being a change necessary in order that the tax advantage should be obtainable) was effected, before Apr. 5, 1960. Another exception and one of manifest importance is that the section will not apply to a person if he shows that the transaction or transactions in securities were carried out either for bona fide commercial reasons or in the ordinary course of making or managing investments and that none of them had as their main

G object or one of their main objects to enable tax advantages to be obtained. The appellant did not seek to bring herself within the last-mentioned exception. Her transaction was after Apr. 5, 1960. The company (Gleeson Development Co., Ltd.) was under the control of the appellant and her sister. The £60,500 was transferred to the appellant. It was transferred at the agreed price on the sale of the shares.

H It was submitted that, as a payment of £60,500 the company received shares which were worth that sum, there was no diminution of the value of the company's aggregate assets or of its fund of undistributed profits. There was, however, within the wide and comprehensive words of the section a transfer (or an application in discharge of liabilities) of money which formed a part of the assets of the company and which was available for distribution by way of divi-

I dend. It was submitted that even after applying the meanings denoted in the section and in s. 43 of the Act of 1960 it should not be held that there was a transfer of assets in a case where no diminution of the company's fund of profits resulted from what the company did. That, however, involves reading into the section words of qualification which are not contained in it. The company could have distributed the £60,500 by way of dividend. Though there was no declaration of a dividend or appropriation for the payment of a dividend, the money was available for distribution by way of dividend. The £60,500 was a receipt accruing

(8) [1966] 2 All E.R. 19; [1966] Ch. 365.

to the appellant in such a way that she did not pay or bear surtax in respect of **A** it.   Because the money was received in that way rather than as a distribution by way of dividend there was the avoidance or reduction of an assessment to, or the avoidance of a possible assessment to, surtax.   The very wide words of s. 28 seem to me to embrace the appellant's transaction in securities, and, as there was no endeavour to seek exclusion within the words of sub-s. (1), the result follows that the section applied to the appellant in respect of that transaction.   I **B** would dismiss the appeal.

LORD GUEST: My Lords, I have had the advantage of reading the speech prepared by my noble and learned friend VISCOUNT DILHORNE.   I have nothing to add.   I agree that the appeal should be dismissed.

LORD DEVLIN: My Lords, I concur.   **C**

LORD UPJOHN: My Lords, this appeal depends on the true construction of that complex s. 28 of the Finance Act, 1960, interpreted as it must be in the light of s. 43 of the Act of 1960.   The relevant facts are of the shortest.   At all material times the appellant, Mrs. Cleary, and her sister, Mrs. Perren, were sole and equal shareholders in two property-owning and developing companies called **D** Gleeson Development Co., Ltd. (G.D.) and M. J. Gleeson, Ltd. (M.J.G.) which had been founded by their father, Mr. Gleeson.   At Dec. 31, 1960, the balance sheet of G.D. showed an excess of assets over liabilities (omitting hundreds) of £191,000.   The assets consisted of fixed assets of £40,000, investments of a few hundred pounds, debtors of £30,000 and cash at the bank of £130,000.   Against that the issued capital and capital reserve consisted of £11,000 and profit and **E** loss account of £180,000, and this latter sum, as the Commissioners for the Special Purposes of the Income Tax Acts found, represented an accumulation of profits within the charge to income tax.   It was, therefore, quite clear that the sisters could have caused G.D. to declare a dividend which would have, in effect, extracted the sum of £130,000 from G.D. and put it in their pockets, but such dividend would have attracted surtax.   It is not surprising, therefore, that **F** that course was not pursued.   The cash was extracted from G.D. as follows. The issued capital of M.J.G. was fifty thousand shares of £1 each;   on July 24, 1961, each sister sold twenty-two thousand shares of her respective holding to G.D. for £60,500 cash.   This transaction, as the commissioners found as a fact, was a transaction for full value.   Accordingly, the cash held by G.D. was reduced by £121,000 and its investments were increased by the holding of forty-four thousand **G** shares in M.J.G., which, in reality remained under the control and ownership of the sisters.   This was a perfectly reasonable transaction which, apart from s. 28, could not have attracted any income tax.   The Crown, however, claim that the sum of £60,500 received by the appellant is, by virtue of that section, subject to surtax in her hands, and a like claim is made against Mrs. Perren which, it is agreed, shall be determined by this appeal.   **H**

It is conceded (i) that the transaction which I have briefly described was a transaction in securities within s. 28 (1) (*b*) of the Act of 1960; (ii) that the transaction was not carried out for bona fide commercial reasons or in the ordinary course of making or managing investments so as to claim the protection of the latter part of that subsection thereby afforded to the taxpayer.   For the purposes of this appeal the relevant parts of s. 28 are as follows: **I**

" (1) Where—
   " (*a*) in any such circumstances as are mentioned in the next following subsection,   and
   " (*b*) in consequence of a transaction in securities or the combined effects of two or more such transactions,
a person is in a position to obtain, or has obtained a tax advantage . . . .
this section shall apply to him in respect of that transaction or those transactions . . . .

A " (2) The circumstances mentioned in the foregoing subsection are that—
   " (c) the person in question receives, in consequence of a transaction whereby any other person—[receives] . . . a consideration which either is or represents the value of, assets which are (or apart from anything done by the company in question would have been) available for distribution by way of dividend, or is received in respect of future
B receipts of the company or is, or represents the value of, trading stock of the company, and the said person so receives the consideration that he does not pay or bear tax on it as income; or
   " (d) in connexion with the distribution of profits of a company to which this paragraph applies, the person in question so receives as is mentioned in para. (c) of this subsection such a consideration as is
C therein mentioned.
   " In this subsection—
      " (i) references to profits include references to income, reserves or other assets,
      " (ii) references to distribution include references to transfer or realisation (including application in discharge of liabilities), and
D   " (iii) references to the receipt of consideration include references to the receipt of any money or money's worth . . ."

It is not disputed that G.D. is a company under the control of not more than five persons and is, therefore, a company to which para. (d) applies.   The Crown seek to bring the transaction within para. (d) and, if that is established, it is agreed that the complicated subsequent provisions of the section apply, and that the
E appellant and her sister are bound to pay surtax on the respective sums of £60,500 which they have received.   Section 43 (4) (g) is in these terms:

   " Tax advantage means a relief or increased relief, from, or repayment or increased repayment of, income tax, or the avoidance or reduction of an assessment to income tax or the avoidance of a possible assessment thereto, whether the avoidance or reduction is effected by receipts accruing in such
F a way that the recipient does not pay or bear tax on them, or by a deduction in computing profits or gains; "

The Special Commissioners reached the conclusion that the sum of £60,500 received by the appellant from G.D. being the full value of the shares in M.J.G. sold by her to that company was not received by her either in connexion with
G a transfer of assets or otherwise so as to be received within the meaning of s. 28 (2) (d) and they allowed the appellant's appeal.   The Crown appealed and this came before PENNYCUICK, J. (9), who disagreed with the reasoning of the Special Commissioners, and held that the transaction whereby cash was paid by the company was within the transfer of the assets contemplated by para. (d). However, he dismissed the appeal on the ground that the appellant did not
H obtain a tax advantage as defined in s. 43 (4) (g) of the Act of 1960.   The Crown again appealed and the Court of Appeal (10) reversed that decision and held that the transaction fell within para. (d) and that the appellant had obtained a tax advantage as defined in s. 43 (4) (g).   Those are the problems which your lordships have to decide.
   It was submitted to your lordships that no tax advantage had been gained,
I for this transaction was merely a sale of assets to a company at their true value. Before the sale an assessment was liable to be made if G.D. paid a dividend by way of cash out of its profits available for that purpose.   After the sale a dividend might still be paid although no doubt assets would have to be sold in order to raise the necessary cash.   That is perfectly true.   It was further urged that, in contrast to *Inland Revenue Comrs.* v. *Parker* (11), there had been in this case no

(9) [1965] 2 All E.R. 603;   [1965] Ch. 1093.
(10) [1966] 2 All E.R. 19;   [1966] Ch. 365.
(11) [1966] 1 All E.R. 399;   [1966] A.C. 141.

diminution of assets at all. Cash had been diminished, but that had been **A**
replaced by other assets. That is also true. Accordingly, so it was argued, after
the transaction in question, an assessment remained possible, so that the words
of s. 43 (4) (g) of the Act of 1960 were not satisfied, and an assessment remained and
remains possible until it becomes impossible by declaration of dividend and the
reduction of the sum of profits in account (£180,000) accordingly. I should
mention here, though I think that it is irrelevant, that the danger of action by **B**
the Crown under s. 245 of the Income Tax Act, 1952, was removed by the issue
of clearance certificates in respect of the income of G.D. and of M.J.G. for the
year ended Dec. 31, 1962 (12).

My lords, this question depends on the proper construction of the words
" avoidance of a possible assessment thereto " in sub-para. (g). I think light is
thrown on the proper construction of those words by the words which follow: **C**
" whether the avoidance or reduction is affected by receipts accruing in such a
way that the recipient does not pay or bear tax on them ". Clearly avoidance
of a possible assessment was not merely directed to the reduction of the figure
of profits in account available for distribution but to the reduction of physical
assets for that purpose. In this case there was a sum of cash available for
payment of a dividend in cash; the result of the transaction was to remove the **D**
possibility of that sum of cash being used to declare a dividend. True, other
assets might be realised in the future so as to provide money for payment of a
dividend, but it seems to me quite clear that the definition is aimed at just such
a transaction as this. The sisters have managed, by a perfectly fair transaction,
to extract cash from the company without declaring a dividened, and thereby
they avoided a possible assessment on them which would have been made had a **E**
dividend been declared. Accordingly, in my judgment, this point fails.

I turn, then, to the question of the construction of s. 28 (2) (d). It was common
ground before your lordships that a transfer of cash is comprehended in the
phrase " a transfer of assets " and your lordships need not, therefore, consider the
case in your lordships' House of *L. M. St. Aubyn* v. *A.-G.* (*No. 2*) (13).

Sub-paragraph (d) of s. 28 (2) is a difficult paragraph and the difficulties are **F**
not diminished by the great breadth of the language used by the draftsman in
paras. (i), (ii) and (iii). They cannot possibly be described as definition clauses;
they are " artificial inclusion " clauses. I say " artificial " because the draftsman
has paid no attention to the proper use of language in relation to companies and
their finances which has been accepted by lawyers and accountants alike for a
very long time. For example, in para. (i) he has treated as synonymous profits **G**
which are " sums in account " (£180,000 in this case) on the left hand side of the
balance sheet with " other assets " which are physical or realisable assets on the
right hand side of the balance sheet. He seems to think " income " and
" reserves ", which are really sums in account, are properly described as other
assets. This gives rise to a degree of difficulty in the construction of the section.
Counsel for the Crown has submitted that, applying these artificial inclusion **H**
clauses, the paragraph must be spelt out as follows:

" In connexion with the distribution, transfer or realisation including
application in discharge of liabilities, of profits, income, reserves or other
assets of a company to which this paragraph applies, the person in question
so receives ... that he does not pay or bear tax on it as income ... a
consideration in money or money's worth which either is, or represents the **I**
value of assets which are (or apart from anything done by the company
in question would have been) available for distribution by way of dividend
or is received in respect of future receipts of the company or is or represents
the value of trading stock of the company."

For the purpose of this appeal I agree that para. (d) must be read in this way.

(12) The clearance certificates were issued on Feb. 13, 1964; see [1966] 2 All E.R.
at p. 20, letters G, H.
(13) [1951] 2 All E.R. 473; [1952] A.C. 15.

A The opening words of the paragraph " In connexion with the distribution of profits " I find difficult to understand, and I confess that I did not find the explanation for the presence of those words offered by counsel for the Crown very convincing. On the appellant's behalf it was submitted that the whole object of sub-s. 2 (*a*), (*b*) and (*c*) was to make it clear that the section was only dealing with a distribution of profits which diminished the assets of the company,
B as in *Parker's* case (14). It was further submitted that the definitions in sub-paras. (i) and (ii) following (*d*) in s. 28 (2) did not embrace a transfer of assets which did not result in a company's fund of profits in account being diminished. Relying on the observations of DEVLIN, L.J., in *Cherry* v. *International Alloys, Ltd.* (15), your lordships were urged to give words the meaning which best suits the scope and object of the statute without extending them to ground foreign to the
C intention.   So, it was argued, the object of para. (*d*) was to prevent the taxpayer receiving profits in an untaxed form. In this case there was no receipt of profits; it was a pure transaction of sale and purchase of shares which had nothing whatever to do with the appellant's position as a shareholder in the company.

I cannot accept these arguments. It seems to me that the wording of para. (*d*),
D expanded in the manner which I have mentioned, is literally satisfied.   There has been a transfer of assets of G.D. to the " person in question ", the appellant. The appellant has received a consideration in money, and has received it so that she does not bear tax on it as income.   Those assets which she has received are assets which would be available for distribution by way of dividend.

Finally, it was argued on the part of the appellant that the consideration
E mentioned in para. (*d*) must be a consideration of the nature mentioned in para. (*c*), that is to say, a consideration which either is or represents the value of assets which are available for distribution by way of dividend.   It was also (somewhat faintly) urged that there can be no assets or anything representing the value of assets available for distribution by way of dividend until there has been some appropriation for that purpose. With all respect to that argument I
F fail to understand it; not even the declaration of a dividend would appropriate the cash of £130,000 to that purpose. So for these reasons I agree with the Court of Appeal (16).

This may seem a harsh conclusion, as indeed it is, but this is a matter for Parliament. It must always be remembered that this section does not hit, and is not intended to hit, a bona fide commercial transaction or the management
G of investments in the ordinary course, unless a main object is to obtain a tax advantage. Furthermore, there are certain other built-in safeguards of which the taxpayer can avail himself. By virtue of s. 28 (10) the taxpayer can inform the Commissioners of Inland Revenue of his intention, and can get a ruling from them whether, in their opinion, it falls within the ambit of s. 28. Then, if the transaction is challenged by a notice given by the commissioners,
H the taxpayer can (and in this case did) file a statutory declaration by virtue of s. 28 (4), and then there is an appeal to a tribunal constituted as mentioned in s. 28 (7) who are empowered to determine whether or not there is a prima facie case for proceeding in the matter. For these reasons I would dismiss this appeal.

Appeal dismissed.

I Solicitors: *Winckworth & Pemberton* (for the appellant); *Solicitor of Inland Revenue* (for the Crown).

[*Reported by* KATHLEEN J. H. O'BRIEN, *Barrister-at-Law.*]

---

(14) [1966] 1 All E.R. 399; [1966] A.C. 141.
(15) [1960] 3 All E.R. 264 at p. 269; [1961] 1 Q.B. 136 at p. 148.
(16) [1966] 2 All E.R. 19; [1966] Ch. 365.

MOHAN AND ANOTHER *v.* REGINAM.

A

[PRIVY COUNCIL (Lord Hodson, Lord Pearce and Lord Pearson), October 19, 20, 1966, January 24, 1967.]

Privy Council—Trinidad and Tobago—Criminal law—Concerted action—Murder —Deceased struck by both appellants in course of quarrel—Uncertainty who struck fatal blow—Common purpose—Principals in first or second degree— Proof of pre-arranged plan unnecessary.

B

The appellants, R. and D., were father and son. During an altercation between D. and a mentally deficient boy, the deceased and two other men went to the boy's assistance. A quarrel developed between D. and the deceased. While the quarrel continued R. arrived with a cutlass, threatened the deceased and chased him in the direction of his (R.'s) house. As the deceased was running, D. emerged from a pepper tree in front of the house armed with a brushing cutlass and barred his way. One of the two men originally accompanying the deceased tried to rescue him. A third man arrived and was successful in shielding him, whereupon R. and D. desisted. The deceased who had minor wounds, a very severe wound on the right leg below the knee and a very severe back wound was taken to hospital, where he died. Death was caused by embolosis arising from the severe leg wound, but it was not clear whether the wound in the back was a contributory cause of death. There was no certainty as to which of the appellants inflicted either of the wounds. Both appellants were convicted of murder and sentenced to death. On appeal they contended that, unless it was proved which of them inflicted the fatal wound, it was necessary to prove that they were acting in pursuance of a pre-arranged plan. The appeal was determined on the assumption that the leg wound might have been the sole cause of death*. It could not be inferred from the evidence that the appellants had a pre-arranged plan.

C

D

E

Held: since the two appellants were attacking the same man at the same time with similar weapons and with the common intention that he should suffer grievous bodily harm, each was present and aiding and abetting the other and was guilty as a principal offender whether in the first or second degree, and the prosecution did not have to prove that the appellants were acting in pursuance of a pre-arranged plan (see p. 61, letter F, and p. 62, letter A, post).

F

R. v. *Kupferberg* ((1918), 34 T.L.R. 587) approved.

Dictum of LORD MORRIS OF BORTH-Y-GEST in *King* v. *Reginam* ([1962] 1 All E.R. at p. 819) approved.

G

Appeal dismissed.

[As to a person, present at the scene of crime and having a common criminal purpose with the principal in the first degree, being a principal in the second degree, see 10 HALSBURY'S LAWS (3rd Edn.) 298, para. 555; and for cases on the subject, see 14 DIGEST (Repl.) 91, 92, *533-542*.]

H

Cases referred to:

King v. *Reginam,* [1962] 1 All E.R. 816; [1962] A.C. 199; [1962] 2 W.L.R. 301; Digest (Cont. Vol. A) 352, *2199a*.

R. v. *Kupferberg,* (1918), 34 T.L.R. 587; 13 Cr. App. Rep. 166; 14 Digest (Repl.) 388, *3778*.

I

Appeal.

This was an appeal in forma pauperis, by special leave, from a judgment of the Court of Appeal of the Supreme Court of Trinidad and Tobago (WOODING, C.J., McSHINE and PHILIPS, JJ.A.), dated Oct. 25, 1965, dismissing an appeal by both appellants, Ramnath Mohan and Deodath Ramnath, from their conviction and sentence in the High Court (FRASER, J., sitting with a jury) dated May 24, 1965, whereby the appellants were found guilty of murder and sentenced to death.

---

* See p. 61, letter B, post.

A   *T. O. Kellock, Q.C.,* and *E. Cotran* for the appellants.
      J. G. Le Quesne and *S. G. Davies* for the Crown.

      LORD PEARSON: A man named Mootoo Sammy was wounded in an
encounter with the appellants on Sept. 21, 1964, and in consequence of one or
more of the wounds which he then received he died in a hospital in Port of Spain,
B Trinidad, on Oct. 4, 1964. The appellants were prosecuted for the murder of
Mootoo, and after trial before FRASER, J., and a jury at the Port of Spain assizes
were both on May 24, 1965, convicted of the murder and sentenced to death.
Their appeals to the Court of Appeal of Trinidad and Tobago were dismissed on
Oct. 25, 1965. Special leave to appeal was granted by your lordships' Board on
Mar. 23, 1966.

C   The main argument presented on behalf of the appellants can be summarised
as follows: (*a*) the medical evidence as recorded in the judge's notes (there being
no shorthand note of the evidence) shows that the death of Mootoo was caused,
or may have been caused, by only one of the wounds inflicted on him; (*b*) each
of the appellants was entitled to be acquitted unless it was proved either that he
inflicted the fatal wound or that the two appellants in attacking Mootoo were
D acting in pursuance of a pre-arranged plan; (*c*) the evidence left it uncertain
which of the two appellants inflicted the fatal wound; (*d*) there was no evidence
from which the jury could properly infer that the two appellants were acting in
pursuance of any pre-arranged plan; (*e*) therefore the convictions should be
set aside.

      It was also argued on behalf of the appellants that the judge had not sufficiently
E directed the jury on the issue of self-defence and had, in effect, withdrawn that
issue from the consideration of the jury. As to this argument it is enough to say
that, after full consideration of the summing-up, their lordships are of opinion, in
agreement with the judgment of the Court of Appeal, that the directions given to
the jury on the issue of self-defence were amply sufficient and that the issue was
not withdrawn from the jury.

F   As to the main argument on behalf of the appellants, counsel for the Crown
conceded that the evidence left it uncertain which of the appellants inflicted any
particular one of the wounds sustained by Mootoo, but they did not agree as to
the effect of the medical evidence with regard to the cause of the death nor as to
the absence of sufficient evidence for inferring a pre-arranged plan. The main
argument by counsel for the Crown was, however, to this effect: (*a*) on the facts
G of this case the prosecution did not have to establish that the appellants were
acting in pursuance of a pre-arranged plan; (*b*) it was sufficient for the prosecution to show, and it was shown, that the appellants were engaged in a common
act of attacking Mootoo with highly dangerous weapons described in the evidence
as " cutlasses ", and one or more of the wounds which they inflicted caused the
death; (*c*) each of them was actively participating, and aiding and abetting the
H other of them, in the attack on Mootoo, and each of them was rightly convicted
as a principal offender whether in the first or the seond degree.

      The appellants were father and son. The father, Ramnath Mohan, was in the
evidence sometimes called " Ramnath " and sometimes " Dailah ". He will
be referred to as " the appellant Ramnath ". He was at the time of the events
out of which this case arose between fifty and sixty years of age, and he had
I previously borne a good character. The son is named Deodath Ramnath in the
record, but in the evidence as summarised in the judge's notes he was called
" Deonath ". He will be referred to as " the appellant Deonath ". He was
eighteen years of age at the time of the events.

      The events took place at Warrenville, Cunupia, which is a few miles from Port
of Spain on the way to San Fernando. They took place in the early evening of
Sunday, Sept. 21, 1964, approximately at and after 8 p.m., at a time when night
had fallen but there was moonlight as well as some street lighting. The events
began outside the house of the witness Enos Davis, which is in a road called

" Robert's Trace ", and they finished outside the house of the appellant Ramnath, **A**
which is in South Main Road. The route by road from the one house to the other
was indirect: one would have to go from Davis' house westward along Robert's
Trace to the junction with South Main Road, and there turn sharply to the left
and go along South Main Road in a south-easterly direction. The two houses,
however, were less than one hundred yards apart; any loud noise outside Davis'
house would easily be heard in the appellant Ramnath's house; and there was a **B**
short cut between the two houses by a track passing over the intervening rice
field or garden land.

There was a christening party at Davis' house in Robert's Trace. When the
appellant Deonath was coming away from it he met a mentally deficient boy, and
there was an altercation between them. Three men, Mootoo and Deonarine and
Ramtahal, came out of a neighbouring house, and took the part of the boy. The **C**
appellant Deonath was accused of "wringing" the boy's hand, and a quarrel
developed between Mootoo and the appellant Deonath. The evidence is that
Mootoo " chucked " the appellant Deonath and that the appellant Deonath
" chucked him back ". Presumably the word " chucked " means pushed or
struck or threw over. The quarrel continued. So far there is no dispute as to the
facts. **D**

As to the subsequent events, different witnesses who had been in different
places testified to different parts of what had happened or what had been said,
and also there were in the evidence of the witnesses for the prosecution some
inconsistencies, as would be expected of eye witnesses giving their recollections
of a series of rapid events observed by the light of the moon or a street lamp.
Nevertheless, the witnesses for the prosecution were in substance all telling the **E**
same story, which was in outline to the following effect.

While the appellant Mootoo and Deonath were still quarrelling, the appellant
Ramnath came on the scene with a " cutlass " (also described as a " poniard ")
held behind his back. When one or more of the bystanders sought to restrain him,
he said " Where is Mootoo Sammy? I am going to open his back." Having
found Mootoo, the appellant Ramnath " ran him round " threatening him with **F**
the cutlass, and chased him along Robert's Trace to the road junction and round
the corner and along South Main Road towards the appellant Ramnath's house.
Deonarine was following some distance behind the appellant Ramnath. As
Mootoo was coming along the pavement towards the appellant Ramnath's house,
the appellant Deonath emerged from a pepper tree which was in front of that house.
He was armed with a cutlass, described as a " brushing cutlass " having a long **G**
handle and a short blade. He barred the way for Mootoo, and Mootoo turned back
or turned away. Both appellants attacked him with their cutlasses, and both
struck him. He tried to defend himself with something in the nature of an oil can
which he had picked up. Deonarine picked up a piece of wood and, in order to
rescue Mootoo, struck the appellant Deonath on the head with it. The appellant
Ramnath with his cutlass threatened Deonarine, and Deonarine ran away to **H**
escape from him. A man called Roodall came up and shielded Mootoo, and the
appellants desisted from their attack. Mootoo was taken to hospital.

He had received, together with minor wounds, a very severe wound on the right
leg below the knee and a very severe wound in the back. The pathologist, who
carried out the post-mortem examination, said " Death was due to massive
pulmonary embolosis. An embolosis may be defined as any clot or particle of fat **I**
or particle of cancer cell that becomes separated from a primary site in one part
of a vein or artery and is transported in the circulation. This was due to thrombus
arising in the deep vein of the right leg, the site of an incised wound of the right
leg. Associated with these was a wound on the right posterior chest wall severing
several ribs and cutting three with collapse of the right lower lobe of the lung."
That is a passage from the judge's notes of the evidence. From this passage and
other passages in the notes of the evidence it is clear that death was caused by the
" embolosis " arising from the severe wound in the leg, but it is not clear whether

A or not in the opinion of the pathologist the " associated " wound in the back was a contributory cause of the death. So far as appears from the notes of evidence, there is a possibility that the death may have been caused solely by the leg wound. The actual evidence may have been fuller and more definite. It may be significant that the point now principally relied on by counsel for the appellants was not argued at all in the Court of Appeal, and was only very obscurely covered (if at

B all) in the grounds of appeal to that court. The Court of Appeal said in their judgment " It was the first two major wounds which occasioned his death."

However that may be, the main argument presented on behalf of the appellants in this appeal was as stated previously, and it will be considered on the hypothesis that the death may have been caused solely by the leg wound. The question then arises whether each of the appellants can be held responsible for the leg wound,

C when it may have been inflicted by the other of them. There is conflicting evidence as to which of them struck the blow on Mootoo's leg, the evidence for the prosecution tending to show that the appellant Deonath struck it and the evidence for the defence tending to show that the appellant Ramnath struck it. There is uncertainty on that point.

Also it cannot be inferred with any certainty from the evidence that the

D appellants had a pre-arranged plan for their attack on Mootoo.

It is however clear from the evidence for the defence, as well as from the evidence for the prosecution, that at the material time both the appellants were armed with cutlasses, both were attacking Mootoo, and both struck him. It is impossible on the facts of this case to contend that the fatal blow was outside the scope of the common intention. The two appellants were attacking the same

E man at the same time with similar weapons and with the common intention that he should suffer grievous bodily harm. Each of the appellants was present and aiding and abetting the other of them in the wounding of Mootoo.

That is the feature which distinguishes this case from cases in which one of the accused was not present or not participating in the attack or not using any dangerous weapon, but may be held liable as a conspirator or an accessory before

F the fact or by virtue of a common design, if it can be shown that he was party to a pre-arranged plan in pursuance of which the fatal blow was struck. In this case one of the appellants struck the fatal blow, and the other of them was present aiding and abetting him. In such a case the prosecution do not have to prove that the accused were acting in pursuance of a pre-arranged plan.

In *R.* v. *Kupferberg* (1) the accused had in an earlier trial been acquitted on a

G charge of conspiracy, and in a later trial he was charged and convicted of aiding and abetting. Lawrence, J., in giving the judgment of the Court of Criminal Appeal, said that (2)

> " Mr. Purchase had also contended that the acquittal on the count charging conspiracy, which was framed on the same clause of the regulations as the charge of aiding and abetting of which the appellant had been found guilty,
>
H > entitled the appellant to plead autrefois acquit. That was not so, because conspiracy was not the same as aiding and abetting. The two offences had different ingredients: previous agreement was necessary in the one, but not in the other."

The same distinction was drawn, though incidentally, in *King* v. *Reginam* (3),

I where Lord Morris of Borth-y-Gest, delivering the judgment of the Board, said:

> " The view of the jury may have been that it was the appellant who struck the blow or blows that killed Peterkin, and that Yarde, being present, had been a party to a plot to kill, or being present had aided and abetted."

---

(1) (1918), 34 T.L.R. 587.
(2) (1918), 34 T.L.R. at p. 588.
(3) [1962] 1 All E.R. 816 at p. 819; [1962] A.C. 199 at p. 207.

A person who is present aiding and abetting the commission of an offence is A without any pre-arranged plan or plot guilty of the offence as a principal in the second degree.

Accordingly on the facts of this case the argument for the appellants cannot be sustained. Their lordships have humbly advised Her Majesty that the appeal be dismissed.

Appeal dismissed.   B

Solicitors: *A. L. Bryden & Williams* (for the appellants);   *Charles Russell & Co.* (for the Crown).

[*Reported by* KATHLEEN J. H. O'BRIEN, *Barrister-at-Law.*]

C

MASON v. LEVY AUTO PARTS OF ENGLAND, LTD.

[WINCHESTER ASSIZES (MacKenna, J.), November 6, 7, 8, 1966, March 1, 1967.]

Negligence—Escape—Fire—Escape to adjoining premises—Liability of occupier as such—Non-natural user of land by occupier—Yard used as store for D *machinery greased and stacked in wooden cases pending sale—Serious fire risk to adjoining occupiers—Destruction by fire of neighbour's hedge and garden plants—Whether burden of disproving negligence on occupier—Fires Prevention (Metropolis) Act, 1774 (14 Geo. 3 c. 78), s. 86.*

The defendants were dealers in spare motor parts and engines, for the storage of which they had occupied since 1956 a large yard.   In 1963 they E obtained and followed substantially the advice of the local fire brigade regarding the provision of fire fighting equipment on the site, in view of the large quantities of combustible materials there stored.   At the beginning of July, 1964, almost the whole of the yard was stacked high with wooden cases containing machinery, which as a protection against rust had been greased, oiled, or covered with greased or waxed paper; the stacked cases, F some of which had broken open, were covered with tarpaulins and some of these were torn; other inflammable materials, including petroleum, acetylene and paints, were also stored in the yard.   On July 2, 1964, about mid-day, after a period of very dry weather, a fire broke out in the yard; it was discovered at an early stage by the defendants' workmen, but neither their prompt efforts with the defendants' fire fighting equipment nor the measures G taken by the summoned fire brigades, availed to prevent the fire from escaping on the the plaintiff's adjoining property, where it destroyed trees and plants in his garden and a twelve-foot high laurel boundary hedge which screened the yard from his residence.   The cause of the fire was undetermined but was very probably a workman's cigarette.   In an action by the plaintiff claiming for the damage caused to his property by the H escape of the fire the defendants disclaimed liability on the ground, inter alia, that the fire had " accidentally begun " within s. 86* of the Fires Prevention (Metropolis) Act, 1774.

Held: (i) the defendants were not under a burden of disproving negligence on their part when seeking protection under s. 86 of the Fires Prevention (Metropolis) Act, 1774 (see p. 68, letter C, post).   I

Dictum of ASQUITH, J., in *Mulholland & Tedd, Ltd.* v. *Baker* ([1939] 3 All E.R. at p. 255) applied.

Hyman (Sales), Ltd. v. *Benedyke & Co., Ltd.* ([1957] 2 Lloyd's Rep. 601) distinguished.

(ii) the principle of law to be applied, following *Musgrove* v. *Pandelis* ([1918-19] All E.R. Rep. 589), was that a defendant would be liable (apart from questions of whether the fire was caused by a stranger or by the act

* Section 86, so far as material, is set out at p. 67, letters A and B, post.

A   of God) for a fire on his land spreading to damage his neighbour's property
if (a) the defendant had brought on to his land things likely to catch fire,
and had kept them there in such conditions that, if they did ignite, a fire
would be likely to spread to his neighbour's land, (b) the defendant did so
in the course of some non-natural use and (c) the thing ignited and the
fire spread (see p. 70, letter B, post).

B   (iii) the defendants' use of the yard was a non-natural user of the land,
having regard to the quantities of combustible material that they had
brought on it, the way in which the material was stored and the character
of the neighbourhood; and accordingly the defendants were liable (see
p. 70, letter E, post).

C   [As to the liability of an occupier of premises for damage by fire, see 28 HALS-
BURY'S LAWS (3rd Edn.) 52, 53, para. 48; and for cases on the subject, see 36
DIGEST (Repl.) 76, 77, *406-415.*

As to the rule in *Rylands* v. *Fletcher,* see 28 HALSBURY'S LAWS (3rd Edn.)
145-148, paras. 192-196; and for cases on the subject, see 36 DIGEST (Repl.)
282-299, *334-434.*

D   For the Fires Prevention (Metropolis) Act, 1774, s. 86, see 13 HALSBURY'S
STATUTES (2nd Edn.) 10.]

Cases referred to:

> *Balfour* v. *Barty-King (Hyder & Sons (Builders), Ltd., Third Parties)*, [1957]
> 1 All E.R. 156; [1957] 1 Q.B. 496; [1957] 2 W.L.R. 84; *affg.*, [1956]
> 2 All E.R. 555; [1956] 1 W.L.R. 779; Digest (Cont. Vol. A) 1159, *411b.*

E

> *Becquet* v. *MacCarthy,* (1831), 2 B. & Ad. 951; 109 E.R. 1396; 36 Digest
> (Repl.) 76, *406.*
>
> *Collingwood* v. *Home and Colonial Stores, Ltd.*, [1936] 3 All E.R. 200; 155 L.T.
> 550; 36 Digest (Repl.) 285, *342.*
>
> *Filliter* v. *Phippard,* [1843-60] All E.R. Rep. 879; (1847), 11 Q.B. 347; 17
> L.J.Q.B. 89; 10 L.T.O.S. 225; 11 J.P. 903; 116 E.R. 507; 36 Digest

F

> (Repl.) 76, *407.*
>
> *Goldman* v. *Hargrave,* [1966] 2 All E.R. 989; [1966] 3 W.L.R. 513.
>
> *Hyman (Sales), Ltd.* v. *Benedyk & Co., Ltd.,* [1957] 2 Lloyd's Rep. 601.
>
> *Mulholland & Tedd, Ltd.* v. *Baker,* [1939] 3 All E.R. 253; 161 L.T. 20; 36
> Digest (Repl.) 77, *413.*
>
> *Musgrove* v. *Pandelis,* [1918-19] All E.R. Rep. 589; [1919] 2 K.B. 43;

G

> 88 L.J.K.B. 915; 120 L.T. 601; *affg.* [1919] 1 K.B. 314; 36 Digest
> (Repl.) 76, *412.*
>
> *Perry* v. *Kendricks Transport, Ltd.,* [1956] 1 All E.R. 154; [1956] 1 W.L.R. 85;
> Digest (Cont. Vol. A) 1171, *599a.*
>
> *Read* v. *J. Lyons & Co., Ltd.,* [1946] 2 All E.R. 471; [1947] A.C. 156; [1947]
> L.J.R. 39; 175 L.T. 413; 36 Digest (Repl.) 83, *452.*

H

> *Rylands* v. *Fletcher,* [1861-73] All E.R. Rep. 1; (1868), L.R. 3 H.L. 330;
> 37 L.J.Ex. 161; 19 L.T. 220; 33 J.P. 70; 36 Digest (Repl.) 282, *334.*
>
> *Williams* v. *Owen,* [1956] 1 All E.R. 104; [1955] 1 W.L.R. 1293; Digest
> (Cont. Vol. A) 1159, *411a.*

Action.

The plaintiff in this action, Captain D. W. Mason, G.C., of Sway, Hampshire,

I   sought damages in respect of loss suffered in consequence of the destruction by
fire on July 2, 1964, of a twelve-foot high laurel hedge, which formed the boundary
for some seventy yards screening his private residence from the premises occupied
by the defendant company, Levy Auto Parts of England, Ltd., buyers and sellers
of spare motor parts and engines. The hedge, together with trees and other
plants for which the plaintiff also claimed damages, was destroyed as a result
of the escape from the defendants' 4½-acre yard on to the plaintiff's property of
a fire which had broken out amongst the stacked wooden cases of greased
machinery, together with other combustible materials, which were stored in the

yard in large quantities. In his statement of claim the plaintiff alleged, inter   A
alia, that the defendant company " so used their land by cluttering it with
combustible material closely packed that (his) land was endangered ". The
facts are set out in the judgment. The case was heard at Winchester Assizes,
but judgment was delivered in London.

The cases noted below* were cited during the argument in addition to those
referred to in the judgment.   B

G. N. *Parry* for the plaintiff.
M. *McGougan* for the defendants.

Cur. adv. vult.

Mar. 1. **MacKENNA, J.,** read the following judgment: The plaintiff,   C
Captain Mason, G.C., a retired officer of the Mercantile Marine, owns and occupies
Mill Cottage at Sway, in Hampshire. It is a small and attractive house built
forty or fifty years ago, standing in a garden of about a quarter of an acre.
Photographs show the garden before and after the fire which was on July 2, 1964.
It was at one time a pretty garden with flowers and matured trees, and a laurel
hedge some twelve feet high along the whole length of its southern boundary   D
and screening the plaintiff's property from the defendants'. The fire destroyed
this hedge and many of the plaintiff's trees and flowers.

The defendants' premises consist of a large yard with buildings, occupying a
total area of some four and a half acres. A former owner had occupied them
as a timber yard. The defendants, who acquired them in 1956, used them for
the storage of spare motor parts and engines bought as army surplus stores and   E
re-sold by them in the course of a business carried on here and elsewhere in
England. The buildings, some of which were destroyed by the fire, included
one where the machinery was re-packed for delivery to the defendants' customers,
and another which was the defendants' main office. The lay-out is shown on
the plan which was exhibited; the long side of the area marked " part of 374 "
is that adjoining the plaintiff's property. At the time of the fire almost the   F
whole of the defendants' yard up to its boundaries, including that which runs
with the plaintiff's garden, was stacked high with cases of machinery. Inside
the cases the machinery was either coated with oil or grease or wrapped in waxed
or greased papers as a protection against rust. The cases were of wood, and
some had broken open. Tarpaulins had been put over the stacks, and some of
these were torn. Flammable materials were stored for use in the defendants'   G
business, including petroleum, acetylene and paints. All these materials,
including the wooden boxes and the grease, the oil and the waxed and greased
papers, were, in the opinion of Mr. Damant, the assistant station officer at
Lyndhurst fire station, highly combustible. His evidence satisfied me that the
yard, used as it was by the defendants, was a serious fire risk to the adjoining
occupiers.   H

Officers of the local fire brigade had inspected the premises in 1963 to see
whether s. 40 of the Factories Act, 1961, which deals with means of escape in
case of fire, was being observed. The defendants asked these officers to advise
them about the provision of fire fighting equipment. The advice was given, and
the recommendations, contained in a letter of July 25, 1963, were substantially
complied with. One of the recommendations had been for the provision of a   I
one inch diameter water pipe, to be laid under the surface of the yard, and of
hoses. This was recommended—to quote the letter—" in view of the large
quantities of combustible materials stored in these premises ". There was a
difficulty about laying the pipe. Only that part of the yard where the buildings
stood had been concreted. Beyond this concreted area the foundations of the

---

* *Job Edwards, Ltd.* v. *Birmingham Navigations*, [1924] 1 K.B. 341; *Sedleigh-Denfield*
v. *O'Callaghan*, [1940] 3 All E.R. 349; [1940] A.C. 880; *Spicer* v. *Smee*, [1946] 1 All
E.R. 489; *Sturge* v. *Hackett*, [1962] 3 All E.R. 166.

A yard were of sawdust, which might not give sufficient protection to the water-pipes laid underneath it. So the writer of the letter suggested, as an alternative, the provision of water extinguishers and buckets of water at points indicated in a drawing. This alternative was adopted. The fire appliances are described, and their positions marked, on the plan exhibited by the defendants. One of the brigade's suggestions, under the heading " Housekeeping " in the letter,
B is in these words:

> " Access lanes, at least four feet wide, should be provided around all storage of timber boxes within and outside the buildings."

This requirement was not everywhere observed. Some of the lanes were much narrower than four feet.

C There was a prohibition against smoking in that part of the yard which adjoins the building where fire appliances (2) to (6) are indicated on the plan. In this building there was a special fire risk because of the use of chemicals in re-packing goods for delivery. Elsewhere in the yard, where the wooden cases were stacked, smoking was allowed. An incinerator close to the building that I have just mentioned can be seen in the plan. Sway railway station is close by the yard,
D whose main entrance is indeed in Station Road.

The weather for some time before the fire had been very dry. On the day itself, July 2, 1964, a fresh west wind was blowing. At about a quarter to one on that afternoon, three of the defendants' men were returning to the yard in a lorry. The party included Mr. Frampton, who was the driver, and a Mr. Blake. One of the men got down to open the gate. As he did so, Mr. Frampton, from the
E driver's seat, saw smoke coming up from the stacked cases in the yard, straight ahead of him as he looked through the gates, 150 yards away. The plan exhibited gives some idea of his view from the gate. From the gate-post marked on the plan a narrow passage with buildings on both sides leads to the storage area which is served at this point by roads marked " Gravel Sleeper and Plate Roads ". The smoke was seen by Mr. Frampton at the end of this passage, as he looked up
F it from the gateway. After parking the lorry, he entered the yard on foot to sound the fire alarm. The alarm is on a corner of a brick building to the left of the gateway and is marked on the plan. As he passed the main office, on his way to the alarm, he shouted to Colonel Laker through one of the office windows that there was a fire in the yard. Colonel Laker was in charge of the yard that day. After sounding the alarm, Mr. Frampton went to the canteen door, near
G the point marked (7), and called to the workers inside the canteen to come to the rescue. They were already on their way. He and some of the others got extinguishers and hurried to the fire. He reached it four or five minutes after he had first seen the smoke. There he saw that the canvas covering of one tier of cases was smouldering; there were no flames yet to be seen. He used his extinguisher, and when it was empty ran back to get another. By the time he
H returned flames were coming up. Mr. Blake was one of the other men who tried to put out the fire. He spoke of a burning tarpaulin, of " a nice bit of smoke ", and of his unavailing efforts to put out the fire with an extinguisher. A third of the firefighters, Mr. Robinson, who had come from the canteen, said that flames were visible when he used his extinguisher. After that, he and others filled buckets with water from a hose, and threw the water over those sheets which
I had not yet caught fire. By this time the fire was pretty fierce. Both Mr. Robinson and Mr. Blake and all the other witnesses for the defence who spoke about the fire put the scene of its outbreak where Mr. Frampton did, at what they called the crossroads, where the passage I have mentioned meets the " Gravel Sleeper and Plate Roads ".

In the meantime one of the office staff, on Colonel Laker's instructions, had telephoned to the fire brigade, and after making one call had put through a second. Colonel Laker himself had gone to the fire. He told me of the unavailing efforts of his men to extinguish it. Some of the hoses were used but they were quite ineffective. The water pressure was not strong enough. After a **A** short time the firefighters had to retire because of the intense heat, leaving the appliances on the spot. The first contingent of the fire brigade to reach the fire was that stationed at Brockenhurst, a subsidiary of the main branch of the service stationed at Lyndhurst. The Brockenhurst men got the call at 12.50 and reached the fire at 1.5, where they were joined soon after by the Lyndhurst men. Huge columns of smoke were emerging from the crates in the yard, and **B** tarpaulins were alight. One member of the fire brigade spoke of a fire seventy-five yards or so inside the main entrance, near the buildings which they tried to protect. Soon after their arrival, the fire brigade too had to retire from the front line of the fire because of the heat. They used their hoses, first fixing them to a hydrant outside the main gate, and later, because of a shortage of piped water, taking their supplies from a stream nearby. Their attempts to extinguish **C** the fire continued into the night. By 7.30 p.m. it was under control and by the morning extinguished. For part of the time the plaintiff's garden was used as a place from which to fight it.

Mrs. Mason, who is the plaintiff's wife, was in their house that morning with a friend, Mrs. Hollier, and from one of the upstairs windows the two ladies saw smoke in the yard. They put the point where it was seen near the south-west **D** corner of the captain's garden, which would be some distance from the point spoken to by the defendants' men. (None of these men, though questioned about it at the trial, had seen a fire at the place identified by the ladies.) There were at first no flames, the ladies said. After a little time they came downstairs to meet the plaintiff who was coming in from outside. The time, according to him, was then about a quarter or ten to one. He dialled 999 to give the alarm, **E** and found, when he got through to the fire brigade, that they had already been alerted. After telephoning, the plaintiff watched the fire. After five or ten minutes flames began to rise. From that time on, he said, the fire was out of control. None of the inmates of the plaintiff's house saw anyone fight the fire which they were watching until after the fire brigade came. None of them saw a second fire. Whether there were at the early stages two fires or only one is **F** a mystery. It is not impossible that there were two, and that each of the two sets of witnesses failed to observe the others' fire because their attention was concentrated on their own. The more likely theory is that there was only one fire, that this was at the point spoken to by the defendants' men, and that the plaintiff and his party failed to see these men using their extinguishers on this fire because of the smoke. **G**

How the fire (or fires) began is a still greater mystery. I myself asked some of the witnesses whether they could suggest any probable explanation, but all said that they could not. A theory put forward by the plaintiff was that the fire was the result of spontaneous combustion of compressed sawdust overheated by the warm weather of the previous week. Colonel Laker rejected this theory. The fire, he said, had nothing to do with spontaneous combustion, and it would **H** seem that his opinion on this point had been either formed on, or confirmed by, the advice he had received from experts. He thought that it might have been started by a spark from an engine on the nearby railway line. It could have been the sun, he said, or even a cigarette if anyone had been smoking. Mr. Damant of the Lyndhurst fire brigade thought that sparks from the incinerator were more likely to have caused the fire than spontaneous combustion. He saw none of **I** the signs he would have expected to see in the case of a spontaneous outbreak. Smoking seems to me the most likely of these causes. If it was smoking, the odds are that the smoker was one of the defendants' men who had been smoking in the yard either during the morning shift or in the midday break when the yard was not under supervision.

I come now to the law, beginning with s. 86 of the Fires Prevention (Metropolis) Act, 1774, whose obscure provisions were foreseeably invoked by the defendants. The section provides that

A   "... no action, suit or process whatever shall be had, maintained or
prosecuted against any person in whose house, chamber, stable, barn or
other building, or on whose estate any fire shall ... accidentally begin, nor
shall any recompense be made by such person for any damage suffered
thereby, any law, usage or custom to the contrary notwithstanding ..."

B   This is subject to a proviso

" that no contract or agreement made between landlord and tenant shall
be hereby defeated or made void."

By words, since repealed, the section also provided that

" if any action be brought, the defendant may plead the general issue,
and give this Act and the special matters in evidence at any trial thereupon
C   to be had."

The plaintiff takes three main points against the defendants. He says, first,
that the statute does not excuse a defendant in any case where the fire begins
by his negligence or that of any other person for whom he is responsible—a
point established in 1847 by *Filliter* v. *Phippard* (1)—and that the burden of
D   disproving negligence is on the defendant who claims the protection of the statute,
and that the defendants in this case have not discharged the burden. Secondly,
and alternatively, he says that he (the plaintiff) has discharged the burden of
proving negligence if it rests on him. If he fails on both these points, he says,
thirdly, that the statute does not apply to a fire which arises through the storage
of large quantities of combustible materials in the conditions which I have
E   described, and that a defendant is liable if a fire of this kind damages a neighbour's property on some principle analogous to that of *Rylands* v. *Fletcher* (2).

On the first point the reported cases are (it seems to me) much against the
plaintiff. In 1939, in *Mulholland & Tedd, Ltd.* v. *Baker* (3), ASQUITH, J., said that
the statute had altered the common law by which liability for escaping fire was
independent of negligence. He said that " a plaintiff must now establish
F   negligence ". FINNEMORE, J., took the same line in 1955 in *Williams* v. *Owen* (4):

" Was the fire the result of negligence on the part of the defendant or those
for whom he was responsible? It was accepted by counsel for the plaintiff
that the doctrine res ipsa loquitur did not apply, and that, therefore, he
had to prove that there was some default on the part of the defendant."

It is true that neither judge gave any reason for his opinion and that each treated
G   it as of the nature of things that the burden of proving negligence should be the
plaintiff's. There is, however, in a much earlier case, *Becquet* v. *MacCarthy* (5),
a passage in which LORD TENTERDEN, C.J., suggests a reason:

"... by the law of this country before it was altered by the statute 6 Ann.
c. 31, s. 6, if a fire began on a man's own premises, by which those of his
neighbour were injured, the latter, in an action brought for such an injury,
H   would not be bound in the first instance to show how the fire began, but the
presumption would be (unless it were shown to have originated from some
external cause) that it arose from the neglect of some person in the house."

If the purpose of the statute was to remove a presumption of negligence on the
defendant's part, as LORD TENTERDEN seems to say, it would not be unreason-
I   able to hold that the burden of proving such negligence was intended by the
statute to be put on the plaintiff who would naturally bear it. LUSH, J., in 1919,
said in *Musgrove* v. *Pandelis* (6) much the same as LORD TENTERDEN (7):

" The purpose of this legislation I would point out was to remove the

---

(1) [1843-60] All E.R. Rep. 879; (1847), 11 Q.B. 347.
(2) [1861-73] All E.R. Rep. 1; (1868), L.R. 3 H.L. 330.
(3) [1939] 3 All E.R. 253 at p. 255.   (4) [1956] 1 All E.R. 104 at p. 107.
(5) (1831), 2 B. & Ad. 951 at p. 958.   (6) [1919] 1 K.B. 314 at p. 317.
    (7) In *Becquet* v. *MacCarthy* (1831), 2 B. & Ad. at p. 958, just cited.

common law presumption that a fire which was not proved to have been   A
caused by some other person was caused or kindled by the householder, and
to free him from liability for fires accidentally begun."

If under the statute the householder may no longer be presumed to have caused
the fire, must he be presumed, even rebuttably, to have caused it negligently?
I would have said not.   One case only is in the plaintiff's favour, decided by
His Honour JUDGE WRIGHT in the county court, *Hyman (Sales), Ltd.* v. *Benedyk*   B
& Co., Ltd. (8).   However, that case is, I think, to be explained as a decision on
a bailee's liability to his bailor, which may perhaps be an exception to the general
rule prescribed by the Act of 1774.   That the Act of 1774 expressly excepted the
case of landlord and tenant does not, however, make it easy to imply any other
exceptions.   Nobody argued that any help was to be derived on this point from
the repealed provisions about the pleading of the general issue.   In my judgment   C
the plaintiff's first point fails.   There is no burden on the defendants of disproving
negligence.

Has the plaintiff proved that the defendants were negligent, which is his
second point?   Or has he brought the case within *Rylands* v. *Fletcher* (9) or any
similar principle of liability, which is his third point?   In his particulars the
plaintiff charges the defendants with providing no adequate means of detecting   D
or extinguishing fire.   I do not think that either of these charges was proved.
The defendants were under no duty to maintain a constant look-out for fire,
and this fire was in any case detected at an early stage by the defendants' workmen.   The appliances recommended by the fire brigade had been provided,
and if it proved impossible to control or extinguish the fire by these means that
is not the fault of the defendants for failing to provide more or better equipment.   E
Such appliances are, anyhow, intended only as first-aid.   That they were ineffective to control or extinguish this fire is not proof of any culpable failure to provide
more adequate equipment.   Then it is said that the crates were so closely
stacked " that there was no reasonable access between them for fire-fighting
purposes ".   This was true of some parts of the yard, but I have no reason to
suppose that if it had been otherwise this fire would have been controlled.   As I   F
see it, the plaintiff's real case against the defendants is in the allegation that
they " so used their land by cluttering it with combustible material closely
packed that the plaintiff's land was endangered ".   This, like the plaintiff's
other allegations, is put against the defendants in alternative ways, including
negligence, nuisance, allowing a dangerous thing, namely fire, to escape from
their land, and as a failure so to use their land as not to harm the plaintiff.   G

I shall consider it under the two last of these heads, beginning, as one must,
with *Musgrove* v. *Pandelis* (10) in the Court of Appeal, whose facts are too well
known to be re-told: in that case BANKES, L.J., reasoned thus (11): (a) there
were at common law three separate heads of liability for damage done by fire
originating on a man's property,

" (i) for the mere escape of the fire; (ii) if the fire was caused by the   H
negligence of himself or his servants, or by his own wilful act; (iii) on the
principle of *Rylands* v. *Fletcher* (9)."

(b) *Filliter* v. *Phippard* (12) decided that the statute did not cover the second case.
(c) BANKES, L.J., asked (13):

" Why, if that is the law as to the second head of liability, should it be   I
otherwise as to the third head, the liability on the principle of *Rylands* v.
Fletcher (9)? "

---

(8) [1957] 2 Lloyd's Rep. 601.
(9) [1861-73] All E.R. Rep. 1; (1868), L.R. 3 H.L. 330.
(10) [1918-19] All E.R. Rep. 589; [1919] 2 K.B. 43.
(11) [1918-19] All E.R. Rep. at p. 591; [1919] 2 K.B. at p. 46.
(12) [1843-60] All E.R. Rep. 879; (1847), 11 Q.B. 347.
(13) [1918-19] All E.R. Rep. at p. 591; [1919] 2 K.B. at p. 47.

A   The answer, I would have said with respect, is obvious enough.   There were not
three heads of liability at common law but only one: a person from whose land
a fire escaped was held liable to his neighbour, unless he could prove that it
had started or spread by the act of a stranger or of God.   *Filliter's* case (14)
had given a special meaning to the words " accidental fire " used in the statute,
holding that they did not include fires due to negligence, but covered only cases

B   of " a fire produced by mere chance, or incapable of being traced to any cause
(15)."   However, it does not follow that because that meaning may be given to
" accidental ", the statute does not cover cases of the *Rylands* v. *Fletcher* (16) kind,
where the occupier is held liable for the escape though no fault is proved against
him.   In such cases the fire may be " produced by mere chance " or may be
" incapable of being traced to any cause ".   BANKES, L.J., was making a dis-

C   tinction, unknown to the common law, between " the mere escape of fire "
(which was his first head) and its escape under *Rylands* v. *Fletcher* (16) conditions
(which was his third), and was imputing an intention to the legislature of exempting from liability in the former case and not in the latter.   In holding that an
exemption given (by virtue of s. 86 of the Act of 1774) to accidental fires " any
law, usage or custom to the contrary notwithstanding " does not include fires

D   for which liability might be imposed on the principle of *Rylands* v. *Fletcher* (16),
the Court of Appeal went very far.   It is, however, my duty to follow them
unless *Musgrove's* case (17) has been overruled, or unless its principle does not
apply to the facts proved here.   The case has not been overruled;   that is
certain.   In 1936, ROMER, L.J., doubted in *Collingwood* v. *Home and Colonial
Stores, Ltd.* (18) whether a garaged motor car (which was the source of the fire

E   in *Musgrove's* case (17)) fell within the class of exceptional objects to which the
Act of 1774 did not apply.   LORD WRIGHT in the same case (19) and LORD
PORTER in *Read* v. *J. Lyons & Co., Ltd.* (20) shared this doubt.   But none of
these judges questioned the ruling that there was this exceptional class.   LORD
WRIGHT said (19) that *Musgrove* (17) must be followed in any case to which
the rule applied, and in 1956 in *Perry* v. *Kendricks Transport, Ltd.* (21) PARKER

F   L.J., echoed his words.   In the meantime, in 1939, ASQUITH, J. (22) had followed
Musgrove's case (17) and rejected a defence based on the Act of 1774, and in
1956 HAVERS, J., did the same in *Balfour* v. *Barty-King* (*Hyder & Sons* (*Builders*),
Ltd., Third Parties) (23).
       What then is the principle?   As ROMER, L.J., pointed out in *Collingwood* v.
Home and Colonial Stores, Ltd. (24), it cannot be exactly that of *Rylands* v.

G   *Fletcher* (16).   A defendant is not held liable under *Rylands* v. *Fletcher* (16) unless
two conditions are satisfied: (i) that he has brought something on to his land
likely to do mischief if it escapes, which has in fact escaped, and (ii) that these
things happened in the course of some non-natural user of the land.   However,
in *Musgrove's* case (17) the car had not escaped from the land, neither had the
petrol in its tank.   The principle must be, ROMER, L.J., said (25) the wider one

H   on which *Rylands* v. *Fletcher* (16) itself was based, " Sic utere tuo ut alienum non
laedas ".   If, for the rule in *Musgrove's* case (17) to apply, there need be no
escape of anything brought on to the defendant's land, what must be proved
against him?   There is, it seems to me, a choice of two alternatives.   The first

---

I
   (14) [1843-60] All E.R. Rep. 879; (1847), 11 Q.B. 347.
   (15) Per LORD DENMAN, C.J., [1843-60] All E.R. Rep. at p. 881; (1847), 11 Q.B. at
p. 357.
   (16) [1861-73] All E.R. Rep. 1; (1868), L.R. 3 H.L. 330.
   (17) [1918-19] All E.R. Rep. 589; [1919] 2 K.B. 43.
   (18) [1936] 3 All E.R. 200 at pp. 208, 209.
   (19) [1936] 3 All E.R. at p. 206.
   (20) [1946] 2 All E.R. 471 at p. 479; [1947] A.C. 156 at p. 176.
   (21) [1956] 1 All E.R. 154 at p. 160.
   (22) *In Mulholland & Tedd, Ltd.* v. *Baker*, [1939] 3 All E.R. 253; cited at p. 67,
letter F, ante.
   (23) [1956] 2 All E.R. 555.   (24) [1936] 3 All E.R. at pp. 208, 209.
                    (25) [1936] 3 All E.R. at p. 209.

would require the plaintiff to prove (a) that the defendant had brought something **A**
on to his land likely to do mischief if it escaped, (b) that he had done so in the
course of a non-natural user of the land, and (c) that the thing had ignited and
that the fire had spread.   The alternative would be to hold the defendant liable
if (a) he brought on to his land things likely to catch fire, and kept them there in
such conditions that, if they did ignite, the fire would be likely to spread to the
plaintiff's land, (b) he did so in the course of some non-natural use, and (c) the **B**
thing ignited and the fire spread.

The second test is, I think, the more reasonable one, since to make the likelihood of damage if the thing escapes a criterion of liability, when the thing has
not in fact escaped but has caught fire, would not be very sensible.   I propose,
therefore, to apply the second test, asking myself these two questions: (i) did
the defendants in this case bring to their land things likely to catch fire, and keep **C**
them there in such conditions that if they did ignite the fire would be likely
to spread to the plaintiff's land?   If so, (ii) did the defendants do these things
in the course of some non-natural user of the land?

I have no difficulty in answering " yes " to the first of these questions, but the
second is more troublesome.   I feel the difficulty which any judge must feel in
deciding what is a non-natural user of the land, and have prepared myself for **D**
answering the question by reading what is said about it in SALMOND ON TORTS
(14th Edn.) at pp. 450-452 and in WINFIELD ON THE LAW OF TORT (7th Edn.)
at pp. 449-452.   Thus conditioned, I would say that the defendants' use of their
land in the way described earlier in this judgment was non-natural.   In saying
this I have regard (i) to the quantities of combustible material which the defendants brought on their land, (ii) to the way in which they stored them, and **E**
(iii) to the character of the neighbourhood.   It may be that these considerations
would also justify a finding of negligence.   If that is so, the end would be the
same as I have reached by a more laborious and perhaps more questionable
route.

The editor of SALMOND ON TORTS thinks that it is discreditable to our law that
the " unreal and impracticable " distinction between what is natural and what **F**
is not should be a criterion of strict liability (14th Edn. at p. 451).   For my part,
I find it no less deplorable that liability should depend, in the matter of fire, on
what a draftsman meant in Queen Anne's day by " accidental fires ".   (The
Act of 1774 re-enacts with amendments 6 Anne c. 31, s. 6.)   It is a proof of our
love of old things rather than a tribute to his drafting skill that we, and more
surprisingly our kinsmen in the Antipodes (see *Goldman* v. *Hargrave* (26)), are **G**
still governed by his phrase.

[Dealing with the measure of damages, HIS LORDSHIP then considered the
evidence of two surveyors (who were also estate agents) and of an expert in
arboriculture, and concluded that £700 was the proper figure of compensation
for the destruction of the laurel hedge, to which must be added the agreed figure
of £152 for trees and flowers destroyed.] **H**

Judgment for the plaintiff accordingly for £852.

Solicitors: *Taylor, Jelf & Co.*, agents for *Trestrail & James*, New Milton,
Hants (for the plaintiff); *Woodford & Ackroyd*, Southampton (for the defendants).

[*Reported by* K. DIANA PHILLIPS, *Barrister-at-Law.*] **I**

---

(26) [1966] 2 All E.R. 989.

A

INGLIS *v.* INGLIS AND BAXTER.

[PROBATE, DIVORCE AND ADMIRALTY DIVISION (Sir Jocelyn Simon, P.), March
22, 23, 24, 25, 26, 1965.]

B
Divorce—Practice—Co-respondent—Dismissal from suit—Adultery with co-respondent alleged—Discretion of court—No evidence against co-respondent at close of petitioner's case—Matrimonial Causes Act 1965 (c. 72), s. 4 (3).
On an application at the close of the petitioner's case that the co-respondent shall be dismissed from the suit under s. 5* of the Matrimonial Causes Act, 1950 (now s. 4 (3) of the Matrimonial Causes Act 1965) on the ground that there is not sufficient evidence against him, the court has a discretion
C
to accede or reject the application, even though at that stage there is no admissible evidence against the co-respondent (see p. 75, letter E, post).

Divorce—Adultery—Evidence—Evidence against co-respondent—Admission of adultery by wife in her answer supported by affidavit—Memorandum of appearance filed by co-respondent stating intention not to defend by denying
D
adultery—Testimony of wife at hearing showing adultery with co-respondent—Whether evidence of adultery against co-respondent.
Divorce—Condonation—Condonation by husband—Adultery by wife—Disclosure —Duty of wife to disclose all material circumstances.
The husband and wife married in 1945. Owing to a psychological barrier on the husband's part, there was no sexual intercourse between the spouses
E
after 1953. In 1954 and 1956 the wife committed adultery with the co-respondent. About the end of September, 1956, she was pregnant; she told the husband of her adultery in 1956, but not of that in 1954. The husband assumed correctly who was the father of her child and did not ask her about that or how long the affair had been going on. He had not suspected her of adultery. The husband accepted the child into the family,
F
and the spouses continued to live together as husband and wife. In 1960 the husband, who was an army officer, was posted to Malaya, and the wife and her child accompanied him. In 1961 he committed adultery with the woman named and in October, 1961, left the wife and thereafter lived with the woman named. Despite requests by the husband the wife did not sue for divorce, and in September, 1963, he petitioned for divorce on the ground
G
of the wife's adultery, asking the court to exercise discretion in his favour; he did not claim damages against the co-respondent. The wife by her answer admitted adultery in 1956, which she alleged was condoned, and supported her answer by affidavit; she sought a decree of judicial separation praying the exercise of the court's discretion. The co-respondent filed a memorandum of appearance, in which he answered " no " to the question " Do
H
you intend to defend the case by denying the charges of adultery against you and, if so, which of them? ". At the close of the petitioner's case the co-respondent applied to be dismissed from the suit on the ground that no evidence had been adduced against him. The court in its discretion under s. 5 of the Matrimonial Causes Act, 1950, rejected the application. Subsequently the wife gave evidence which satisfied the court that the co-respondent had committed adultery with the wife.
I
Held: (i) there had been no admissible evidence against the co-respondent before the close of the husband's case for the following reasons—
(a) because the co-respondent's answer in the memorandum of appearance

---

* Section 5, so far as material, reads " In any case in which, on the petition of a husband for divorce on the ground of adultery, the alleged adulterer is made a co-respondent . . . the court may, after the close of the evidence on the part of the petitioner, direct the co-respondent . . . to be dismissed from the proceedings if the court is of opinion that there is not sufficient evidence against him . . ."

should not be taken as an admission of adultery (see p. 77, letter A, and **A** p. 79, letter F, post).

Pidduck v. *Pidduck and Limbrick* ((1961), 105 Sol. Jo. 632) distinguished.

Jensen v. *Jensen and Howard* ([1964] 2 All E.R. 231) considered.

(b) because an admission by a respondent in a suit was not evidence against a co-respondent unless either it was made in his presence in such circumstances that his reaction to it made it evidence against him or it **B** was made in the witness-box (so that in either instance it would be open to challenge by him), and the jurat in the wife's answer did not satisfy the condition of being open to such challenge (see p. 79, letter D, post).

Corfe v. *Corfe* ([1960] 1 All E.R. 593) distinguished.

Redfern v. *Redfern* ([1886-90] All E.R. Rep. 524) and *A.* v. *A. and H.* ([1962] 2 All E.R. 573) considered. **C**

(ii) it was the duty of a spouse seeking forgiveness for adultery to disclose any factor which might reasonably weigh with the other spouse in deciding whether or not to forgive; if that were not done there would be no condonation unless the other spouse expressly or impliedly waived the requirement of further knowledge of any material fact, which the husband had not done; accordingly the wife, by reason of not having disclosed her **D** adultery of 1954, had failed to establish condonation of her adultery in 1956 (see p. 81, letter I, post).

Wells v. *Wells* ([1954] 3 All E.R. 491) considered.

(iii) in all the circumstances, and having regard particularly to the factors that the husband finally broke up the marriage, that the wife had committed adultery, her financial situation, the absence of prospect of reconciliation, **E** the position of the child, the prospect of continuance of the irregularity of the husband's present union if a decree of judicial separation were granted and the interests of the husband and of the woman named, the court would exercise its discretion by granting the husband a decree of divorce on the ground of the wife's adultery (see p. 82, letter G, to p. 83, letter D, post).

[Editorial Note. On the question of the wife's evidence being effective **F** as against the co-respondent, see also *Spring* v. *Spring and Jiggins* ([1947] 1 All E.R. 886).

As to the dismissal of a co-respondent from a suit for insufficiency of evidence, see 12 HALSBURY'S LAWS (3rd Edn.) 387, para. 852; and for a case on the subject, see DIGEST (Cont. Vol. A) 768, *4604c*.

As to when an admission by a respondent is evidence against a co-respondent, **G** see 12 HALSBURY'S LAWS (3rd Edn.) 239, para. 448, text and notes (*f*), (*g*). As to the concealment of material facts precluding condonation, see ibid., pp. 304, 305, para. 603.

For the Matrimonial Causes Act, 1950, s. 5, s. 32 (3), see 29 HALSBURY'S STATUTES (2nd Edn.) 395, 417, and for the replacing provisions, viz., the Matrimonial Causes Act 1965, s. 4 (3), s. 43 (2), see 45 ibid., pp. 450, 503.] **H**

Cases referred to:

A. v. *A. and H.*, [1962] 2 All E.R. 573; [1962] P. 196; [1962] 3 W.L.R. 212; Digest (Cont. Vol. A) 767, *4546b*.

Blunt v. *Blunt*, [1943] 2 All E.R. 76; [1943] A.C. 517; 112 L.J.P. 58; 169 L.T. 33; 27 Digest (Repl.) 429, *3589*. **I**

Bull v. *Bull*, [1965] 1 All E.R. 1057; [1965] 3 W.L.R. 1048; 3rd Digest Supp.

Corfe v. *Corfe*, [1960] 1 All E.R. 593; [1960] 1 W.L.R. 208; Digest (Cont. Vol. A) 768, *4617a*.

Deane v. *Deane*, (1858), 1 Sw. & Tr. 90; 28 L.J.P. & M. 23; 31 L.T.O.S. 25; 22 J.P. 180; 164 E.R. 642; 27 Digest (Repl.) 516, *4599*.

Jensen v. *Jensen and Howard*, [1964] 2 All E.R. 231; [1964] 1 W.L.R. 859; 3rd Digest Supp.

A *Pidduck* v. *Pidduck and Limbrick*, [1961] 3 All E.R. 481; [1961] 1 W.L.R. 1313;
  105 Sol. Jo. 632; Digest (Cont. Vol. A) 775, *5100b.*
 Redfern v. *Redfern*, [1886-90] All E.R. Rep. 524; [1891] P. 139; 60 L.J.P. 9;
  64 L.T. 68; 55 J.P. 37; 27 Digest (Repl.) 267, *2147.*
 Wells v. *Wells*, [1954] 3 All E.R. 491; [1954] 1 W.L.R. 1390; Digest (Cont.
  Vol. A) 744, *3301a.*
B *Young* v. *Bristol Aeroplane Co., Ltd.*, [1944] 2 All E.R. 293; [1944] K.B. 718;
  113 L.J.K.B. 513; 171 L.T. 113; *affd.*, H.L., [1946] 1 All E.R. 98;
  [1946] A.C. 163; 115 L.J.K.B. 63; 174 L.T. 39; 30 Digest (Repl.)
  225, *691.*

Petition.

C This was a petition presented on Sept. 6, 1963, by the husband for divorce
on the ground of the wife's adultery with the co-respondent. The husband did
not seek damages against the co-respondent. The wife, by her answer, admitted
certain acts of adultery, alleged that they had been condoned by the husband
and prayed for a decree of judicial separation on the ground of cruelty, desertion
and adultery by the husband. Pursuant to r. 17 (1) (as then in force) of the
Matrimonial Causes Rules, 1957, the wife filed an affidavit in support of her
D answer. Both parties prayed for relief in the exercise of the court's discretion.
The co-respondent filed a memorandum of appearance in Form 7 of Appendix 3
to the Rules of 1957 in which he answered " no " to the question " Do you intend
to defend the case by denying the charges of adultery made against you, and
if so, which of them? ", but indicated that he wished to be heard on costs. The
husband, by his reply, denied condonation, cruelty and desertion. The facts
E are stated in the judgment.

 Joseph Jackson for the husband.

 J. A. P. Hazel for the wife.

 C. J. S. French and *Mervyn Heald* for the co-respondent.

F Mar. 26. **SIR JOCELYN SIMON, P.,** having indicated the nature of the
suit and having referred to the petition and answer, said: Although it is an
issue on the pleadings whether the husband deserted the wife in October, 1961,
that has not been pursued before me. Presumably it was the husband's case
that he was entitled to withdraw by reason of the wife's adultery, which he
alleges to be uncondoned. I am quite satisfied, however, that that adultery, or
G anything that he may subsequently have discovered about it, had no effect on
his decision to withdraw from cohabitation or to remain apart from the wife.
As I have said, the point has not been argued on behalf of the husband; and I am
satisfied that not only has he committed adultery as he admits, but also he
deserted the wife in October, 1961.

 The live and contested issues which I have to determine are as follows: first,
H did the husband condone the wife's adultery? Secondly, was the husband
guilty of cruelty to the wife? Thirdly, both spouses having admittedly committed
adultery, how should the discretion vested in the court be exercised?

 The parties were married on June 25, 1945. The husband was at that time a
regular officer in the army, and the wife lived with him, so far as she was able, at
the various places in England and abroad where he was stationed. Not long
I after the marriage there supervened a singular misfortune for both parties,
which I am satisfied effectually poisoned their relationship. The husband, owing
to what is accepted as a psychological barrier, found himself less and less able
to have sexual intercourse with his wife. He consulted a doctor, in fact several
doctors, but the matter proved insusceptible to treatment, and in 1953 sexual
intercourse between husband and wife ceased entirely. The husband ascribes
no responsibility to the wife for that unhappy state of affairs; the wife ascribes no
culpability to the husband. In 1954 the wife committed adultery with the
co-respondent on four occasions. The husband had no knowledge and no suspicion

that that had happened nor was there anything to put him on suspicion. Later **A**
in that year the husband went on duty to the United States, where the wife
joined him; and the adultery may have occurred during the short period that
they were apart. Nothing was said to the husband about it. The wife thought
that the husband might have seen a letter in which the co-respondent's name
was mentioned; but I am satisfied that he was quite ignorant and quite unsuspicious that anything of an adulterous nature had occurred between the wife **B**
and the co-respondent; indeed, he was unsuspicious that she was in any way
emotionally involved with the co-respondent or any other man.

In June or July, 1956, the husband and the wife returned to England. They
were not living in a common household at that time; but that, as I understood it,
was merely due to the exigencies of the husband's army service and the difficulties
of obtaining accommodation. The husband knew that the wife had been lent **C**
the co-respondent's flat, but believed that the co-respondent was not there.
He knew, however, that the wife had been seeing the co-respondent, they having
been acquaintances since 1951. He thought nothing of it. However, shortly
after the wife's return from the United States, in fact in July, 1956, and again
in August, 1956, she committed adultery with the co-respondent on two occasions.
About the end of September she found that she was pregnant. She had contem- **D**
plated trying to procure a miscarriage, but had decided against that. She told
her husband that she was going to have a child. That was a great shock to him;
he has no idea that anything improper had been going on. The wife was under
the impression that she mentioned the co-respondent's Christian name; the
husband has no recollection of that having happened. I do not think anything
turns on it; and I do not think either party can be expected to have a clear **E**
recollection at this distance of time of events which must have taken place
under the stress of strong feeling. I say that I do not think that anything turns on
it because the husband correctly took it that it was the co-respondent who was
the father of the child; he was the only man whom the wife had been seeing to
the husband's knowledge. He did not, therefore, specifically enquire who was the
man who was responsible for her condition, nor did he ask how long the affair **F**
had been going on, nor where the adulterous connexion had taken place. He
assumed that it had been at the co-respondent's flat.

The wife put three alternatives to the husband: either she could try to get
rid of the child (by which, I think, she meant, and was understood to mean,
procure a miscarriage), or the husband could divorce her, or he could accept the
child as his own. He decided on the last; and so far as the world was concerned **G**
the spouses continued to live together as they had before. It goes further than
that: so far as they themselves were concerned they went on living as they had
before. Sexual relations between them were, unfortunately, not possible;
but in every other way they lived together as if husband and wife and the only
difference in their manner of living was that in due course they had a child.
The husband signed the register of births as the father of the child. He sent a **H**
card expressing great affection to the wife on the birth of the child; and when
he was posted to his next station at Woolwich they lived together in married
quarters.

Unhappily the relationship between them did not improve; and when the
husband went to his next two stations the wife did not join him. However, he
returned to her at Woolwich, where she had remained in quarters, at week-ends; **I**
and when he was posted to a third station at Lingfield, she joined him for a
short time. That was in July, 1960. In August or September, 1960, the husband
was posted to Malaya and the wife accompanied him with the child. He was
then in command of his regiment and she took her proper place as the wife of
the commanding officer. During the latter part of the husband's stay in the
East he met the woman named in the wife's answer, and committed adultery
with her in August, 1961. He did not at the time inform the wife. Shortly
after, in September, 1961, he returned to England by air; the wife and child

A returned by sea. They came together under the same roof in a flat at Blackheath for a week. At the end of that time, this being October, 1961, the husband told the wife that he was in love with the woman named and that he was leaving her, the wife. He did so and has since been living with the woman named; during the latter part of the period, at any rate, they have been living together as if husband and wife.

B   There ensued correspondence between the husband and wife. The husband was begging the wife in divorce him. Her letters do not make an agreeable impression; they are stridently querulous, rancorous and spiteful; but one must remember that she had been terribly hurt and humiliated. In some of those letters she was seeking that her husband should return to her; in others she was expressing her abhorrence of him. At times she seems to have been willing

C to divorce the husband provided that her financial security (to which she was fully entitled to have regard) was safeguarded; at other times she was saying that she had conscientious objection to divorce. In the end nothing came of the husband's overtures to the wife that she should divorce him; and on Sept. 6, 1963, he presented his petition in the suit.

   Before I come to the main issues there is one preliminary point with which I

D should deal. At the close of the husband's case counsel for the co-respondent applied that the latter should be dismissed from the suit under s. 5 of the Matrimonial Causes Act, 1950, (1), on the ground that no evidence had been adduced against him. I heard a careful argument based on authorities in support and in contradiction of that application. I dismissed it; because I held that the court had a discretion whether to accede to or reject such an application even

E though no evidence was at that stage admissible against the co-respondent. I gave my reasons for that course and the authority on which I founded myself. However, since the point is of some importance in the practice of this Division and since I heard able argument on it, I think it right that I should deal now with the main contentions that were put forward on either side. To the assertion on behalf of the co-respondent that there was no evidence against the co-respondent,

F counsel on behalf of the husband relied on two matters as constituting such evidence; first his memorandum of appearance and, secondly, the affidavit in support of the wife's answer.

   In the memorandum of appearance the co-respondent had been asked the question on the printed form (2): " Do you intend to defend the case by denying the charges of adultery made against you, and, if so, which of them? " He

G answered " No ". Counsel for the husband relied on *Pidduck* v. *Pidduck and Limbrick* (3), decided by Lord Merriman, P. That was a petition for divorce on the ground of adultery in which damages as well as costs were claimed from the co-respondent. It was defended. There was substantial evidence against the respondent but not against the co-respondent. But the court held (4) that the answer in the memorandum of appearance, which was in the same form in

H that case as it is in this, was tantamount to an admission of adultery by the co-respondent. The particular point has been considered in only one other reported case, *Jensen* v. *Jensen and Howard* (5). That was an undefended suit. There was evidence of an inclination to commit adultery on the part of both the wife and the co-respondent and an opportunity to commit adultery. There was evidence of a physical disturbance at night in a caravan which was consistent

I with adultery by the wife. There was a statement by the wife, which was found by the court to amount to an admission, that that physical disturbance had been caused by her committing adultery with the co-respondent. There was therefore clear evidence against the wife and sufficient evidence against the co-respondent,

(1) Now s. 4 (3) of the Matrimonial Causes Act 1965.
(2) I.e., question 4 in the Matrimonial Causes Rules, 1957, Appendix 3, Form 7.
(3) [1961] 3 All E.R. 481; [1961] 1 W.L.R. 1313; 105 Sol. Jo. 632.
(4) (1961), 105 Sol. Jo. 632. This point was not included in the reports in [1961] 3 All E.R. 481 and [1961] 1 W.L.R. 1313.
(5) [1964] 2 All E.R. 231.

quite apart from the memorandum of appearance. Nevertheless, CAIRNS, J., A
did consider the memorandum of appearance in the light of *Pidduck* v. *Pidduck and Limbrick* (6) and he said (7):

" I accept that statement from that high authority as a correct statement
of the law, and I see no reason why, if that rule applies to a co-respondent,
it should not apply to a respondent also. I feel quite sure that the late
President [LORD MERRIMAN, P.] in so enunciating the rule had no intention B
of suggesting that in the normal case of adultery the mere answer to that
question in the memorandum of appearance would be sufficient, without
more, to satisfy the court that adultery had been committed . . . If I had
only the memorandum of appearance of those two parties, I should certainly
not be prepared to say that that was sufficient proof of adultery against C
either of them; but, taken in conjunction with other matters to which I
have referred, I am satisfied that adultery is proved against the wife."

It seems to me that what CAIRNS, J., is saying is that the court is entitled to
take into account the statements in the memorandum of appearance, but that
such statements are not in themselves sufficient proof of adultery. On the
other hand, in *Pidduck* v. *Pidduck and Limbrick* (6), the statement *was* taken as D
sufficient proof of adultery. I therefore do not think that *Jensen* v. *Jensen and
Howard* (8) really reinforces *Pidduck* v. *Pidduck and Limbrick* (6) in what it was
argued on behalf of the husband that the latter case established, namely, that
such an answer in a memorandum of appearance does constitute sufficient
evidence of adultery.

Counsel for the co-respondent argued that *Pidduck* v. *Pidduck and Limbrick* (6) E
should not be followed. He said that it is inadmissible to read the question
" do you intend to defend the case by denying the charges of adultery made
against you, and, is so, which of them? " as meaning " do you admit you have
committed the adultery charged against you, and, if so, how much of it? ";
first, because that is not the question asked, and secondly, because it would be
an improper question to ask, particularly in what might appear to be an official F
document (see Matrimonial Causes Act, 1950, s. 32 (3), now repealed and re-
enacted by s. 43 (2) of the Matrimonial Causes Act 1965, and *Redfern* v. *Redfern* (9)).
Of all the reasons why a man should not intend to defend a case by denying a
charge of adultery, that he has in fact committed the adultery charged
is only one. He may, for example, be in love with the wife without having
committed adultery with her and wish the husband to get a decree rapidly so G
that he can marry her. It may be that he cannot afford to defend the proceedings against him and thinks that an order for costs would be preferable
to the expense of defending a case where possibly appearances are against him.
Moreover, adultery, being a serious matrimonial offence, must be proved beyond
reasonable doubt. That means that it is not enough that the evidence should H
be consistent with guilt; it must be inconsistent with any innocent explanation
that is reasonable. It would, therefore, be wrong to isolate the one inference
from the answer to the question in the memorandum of appearance which
suggests guilt to the exclusion of the inferences which can reasonably be drawn
which are more consonant with the intention of the question and consistent with
innocence. I think that those are formidable arguments. *Pidduck* v. *Pidduck* I
and Limbrick (6) was a case where damages were claimed. It may be that a
co-respondent is more likely to defend such a case if he has not in fact committed
adultery, so as to make the inference that LORD MERRIMAN, P., drew in *Pidduck*
v. *Pidduck and Limbrick* (6) a legitimate one. But I am satisfied that in the

---

(6) (1961), 105 Sol. Jo. 632.   (7) [1964] 2 All E.R. at p. 232.
(8) [1964] 2 All E.R. 231.   (9) [1886-90] All E.R. Rep. 524; [1891] P. 139.

A present case the co-respondent's answer in the memorandum of appearance should not be taken as an admission by him that he committed adultery.

I turn then to the second matter that counsel for the husband relied on, namely, the admission in the wife's answer that she had committed adultery with the co-respondent, which she supported on oath in the affidavit in support of the answer (10), whether or not it was necessary for her so to do.   On this

B part of the argument counsel for the husband relied on the decision of the Court of Appeal in *Corfe* v. *Corfe* (11).   There the respondent had been cross-examined by leave of the court in a way that tended to suggest that she had committed adultery, though she had not, in her evidence in chief, given evidence in disproof of adultery.   It was claimed that such a cross-examination was inadmissible in view of s. 32 (3) of the Matrimonial Causes Act, 1950.   The Court of Appeal

C dismissed the appeal.   They held that the wife had given evidence in the same proceedings in disproof of the alleged adultery within the meaning of s. 32 (3) of the Act of 1950, so as to lose the protection of that subsection.   In her answer she had denied the adultery alleged against her and her affidavit in support extended to verifying that denial.   Hodson, L.J., said (12):

D   " The wife, having sworn the affidavit, had given evidence in the same proceedings denying the adultery."

Willmer, L.J., and Harman, L.J., agreed.   It is said on behalf of the husband that if the respondent in *Corfe* v. *Corfe* (11) gave evidence " in the same proceedings " in disproof of the alleged adultery, so the wife here must have given evidence " in the same proceedings " in admission of her adultery with the

E co-respondent.   If so, it was admissible against him as evidence on oath given in the same proceedings.   To that counsel for the co-respondent replied that *Corfe* v. *Corfe* (11) must be read in the light of *A.* v. *A. and H.* (13) and that for the reasons given in that latter case I should not follow *Corfe* v. *Corfe* (11) in the present case.   He urged, secondly, that the Matrimonial Causes Rules, 1957, r. 25, constitutes a complete code (14) governing the adoption of the affidavit evidence

F in a divorce case, and the use of the affidavit in support of the wife's answer for the purpose sought here does not come within it.

I turn to consider the first point, that based on *A.* v. *A. and H.* (13).   That case was tried by Ormrod, J.   The husband by his petition charged his wife with adultery; the wife by her answer denied her adultery and verified the denial on oath.   So far, therefore, the circumstances were similar to those in

G *Corfe* v. *Corfe* (11).   The husband applied for leave to interrogate the wife as to the adultery alleged against her. It was conceded on behalf of the husband that discovery on an issue of adultery had always theretofore been refused and that the practice of refusal had been recognised as correct by the Court of Appeal in *Redfern* v. *Redfern* (15).   But it was argued that the situation was now altered by *Corfe* v. *Corfe* (11), at least where the respondent, by denying her adultery on oath,

H had lost the protection of s. 32 (3) of the Matrimonial Causes Act, 1950.   That argument was rejected by Ormrod, J.   *Corfe* v. *Corfe* (11) was, of course, binding on Ormrod, J., as it is on me, unless either it was distinguished from or inconsistent with *Redfern* v. *Redfern* (15) or given per incuriam—that is to say, given inadvertently to some statutory or regulatory provision governing the case or to some decision of high authority which, even though not directly binding in the

I

---

(10) Rule 17 (as originally prescribed) of the Matrimonial Causes Rules, 1957, required every answer containing more than a simple denial to be supported by an affidavit. This requirement was abolished on June 1, 1966, by S.I. 1966 No. 560.

(11) [1960] All E.R. 593.   (12) [1960] 1 All E.R. at p. 594.

(13) [1962] 2 All E.R. 573; [1962] P. 196.

(14) For r. 25 of the Rules of 1957 (S.I. 1957 No. 619), as amended, see 10 Halsbury's Statutory Instruments (Second Re-Issue) 240.

(15) [1886-90] All E.R. Rep. 524; [1891] P. 139.

case in point, was nevertheless so relevant that the judgment would in all proba- A
bility have been different if the decision had been in mind; see VISCOUNT SIMON
in *Young* v. *Bristol Aeroplane Co., Ltd.* (16).

It was argued before me, first, that ORMROD, J., did find an inconsistency
between *Redfern* v. *Redfern* (17) and *Corfe* v. *Corfe* (18), that he followed *Redfern*
v. *Redfern* (17) in preference to *Corfe* v. *Corfe* (18) and that I should do so too;
secondly, that ORMROD, J., found *Corfe* v. *Corfe* (18) had been decided per B
incuriam, so that he was entitled to disregard it, and that I should follow him
in that respect. As I read the judgment of ORMROD, J. (19), it proceeded as
follows. First, he ascertained the ratio decidendi of *Redfern* v. *Redfern* (17);
that was, that adultery is an offence of such gravity that it is to be treated in
much the same way as a criminal offence, so that discovery should not be ordered
in relation to it. The case, he held, did not turn on the protection given by the C
Matrimonial Causes Act, 1950, s. 32 (3) (or its statutory forerunners). It followed
that the fact that the respondent in *A.* v. *A. and H.* (19) had sacrificed the
protection of the Act by denying the adultery on oath did not, on the authority
of *Redfern* v. *Redfern* (17) render him liable to discovery on the issue of adultery.
I respectfully agree with the analysis of ORMROD, J., of *Redfern* v. *Redfern* (17)
and the conclusion which he reached. But it follows that so far there is no D
inconsistency between *Redfern* v. *Redfern* (17) and *Corfe* v. *Corfe* (18): the latter
is exclusively relevant to the situation where the statute applies, that is to say,
where a party is in the witness-box; the former, *Redfern* v. *Redfern* (17), is
exclusively relevant to a situation where the statute does not apply, that is to
say, where a party has not (or not yet) submitted himself as a witness.

Then ORMROD, J., went on to say (20) that even if he was wrong about that E
(by which I think he meant that even if *Redfern* v. *Redfern* (17) did turn on the
protection from interrogation given by the statute), *Corfe* v. *Corfe* (18), should
not be extended to interlocutory proceedings in regard to discovery and interrogatories because that would be in effect to make the respondent a compellable
witness on the issue of adultery and there is nothing in the statute which authorises such a procedure. Again I respectfully agree with him; but again I can F
see no inconsistency between *Redfern* v. *Redfern* (17) and *Corfe* v. *Corfe* (18)
arising in that regard, *Redfern* v. *Redfern* (17) being exclusively related to
interlocutory matters, *Corfe* v. *Corfe* (18) exclusively to trial proceedings.

Then he said (20) that the Court of Appeal in *Corfe* v. *Corfe* (18) was not
directed to *Deane* v. *Deane* (21). It is to be noted, however, that he did not
expressly say that that rendered *Corfe* v. *Corfe* (18) unauthoritative as being G
given per incuriam, though I think that counsel for the co-respondent was
justified in saying that that was the implication. I cannot myself believe that
the Court of Appeal, constituted as it was in *Corfe* v. *Corfe* (18) was inadvertent
to *Deane* v. *Deane* (21). That case was not binding on the Court of Appeal and
I do not believe the decision in *Corfe* v. *Corfe* (18) would have been any different
if it had been cited. *Deane* v. *Deane* (21) was decided before the Rules of the H
Supreme Court made affidavit evidence admissible in certain circumstances
and before the Matrimonial Causes Rules, 1957, r. 25, or its forerunners, was in
force. Counsel for the co-respondent argued that if *Corfe* v. *Corfe* (18) were
followed and *Deane* v. *Deane* (21) considered overruled it would be open to the
court to give a decree of divorce on the jurat of the petition. I do not agree;
it is the practice of the Division still to require oral evidence in support of a I

(16) [1946] 1 All E.R. 98; [1946] A.C. 163.
(17) [1886-90] All E.R. Rep. 524; [1891] P. 139.
(18) [1960] 1 All E.R. 593.
(19) [1962] 2 All E.R. 573; [1962] P. 196.
(20) See [1962] 2 All E.R. at p. 578; [1962] P. at p. 202.
(21) (1858), 1 Sw. & Tr. 90.

A petition except as covered by r. 25; but I can see no theoretical reason why the court should not in an exceptional case order that the affidavit in support of the petition (22) should be admitted as evidence under r. 25. In my view the statement in RAYDEN ON DIVORCE (9th Edn. (1964)), p. 612, to which I was referred, is certainly not now correct in the light of *Corfe* v. *Corfe* (23). Finally, ORMROD, J., held (24) that even if the court had a discretion to allow the proposed

B discovery (and it was not argued that the interrogatories could be administered as of right), it would be wrong in the circumstances of that case to permit them to be administered on what was a mere slip of the draftsman (25).

To sum up, I conclude on this part of the case, first, that *Redfern* v. *Redfern* (26) and *A.* v. *A. and H.* (27) were concerned with interlocutory proceedings and do not govern the present case; and secondly, that *Corfe* v. *Corfe* (23) is an authority

C which binds me unless it is distinguishable. But I think that it is. In *Corfe* v. *Corfe* (23) there was an admission on oath in the pleadings made by the party herself against whom it was held to be evidence. That is not the position here. The admission was made by the respondent and relied on as evidence against the co-respondent. The general rule is that an admission by a respondent is not evidence against a co-respondent unless either, first, it is made in the presence

D of the co-respondent in such circumstances that the reaction of the co-respondent to it makes it evidence against him, or, secondly, it is made in the witness-box. The factor common to both is that the admission to be evidence against a co-respondent must be made in such circumstances as render it open to challenge by him. Oral testimony on oath by a respondent in the witness-box fulfils that condition even if the co-respondent is not represented, because he has an oppor-

E tunity of being represented. The jurat in the wife's answer does not fulfil that condition.

Moreover, I think that there is great force in the argument of counsel for the co-respondent that r. 25 constitutes a complete code governing the adoption of affidavit evidence in divorce cases. The husband had closed his case; he did not put in the affidavit in support of the answer as part of his case. That is not a

F mere technicality, since adultery is a serious charge and must be strictly proved. The question posed was whether the husband had at the close of his case adduced evidence against the co-respondent. My conclusion is that neither the memorandum of appearance nor the affidavit in support of the wife's answer amounted to evidence of adultery admissible against the co-respondent. However, as I have said, in the exercise of my discretion I declined to dismiss the co-respondent

G from the suit; and shortly afterwards the wife gave evidence which established to my satisfaction that the co-respondent had committed adultery with her.

I now go back to the main issues in this suit. [His Lordship reviewed the evidence relating to the charge of cruelty and continued:] In my view, there was nothing in this case that could properly be described as cruelty; it is a charge that ought never to have been brought. I unhesitatingly reject it.

H I turn to the husband's charges against the wife of adultery in 1954 and 1956. Those are admitted, but the wife says that they were condoned. Condonation is the reinstatement of a spouse who has committed a matrimonial offence in his or her former matrimonial position in knowledge of all the material facts

I   (22) Rule 6 of the Matrimonial Causes Rules, 1957, which was in force at the date of the judgment and required that every petition should be supported by an affidavit, was repealed on June 1, 1966, by the Matrimonial Causes (Amendment) Rules 1966 (S.I. 1966 No. 560), r. 3, and an affidavit in support of a petition or other pleading is no longer required.
    (23) [1960] 1 All E.R. 593.
    (24) See [1962] 2 All E.R. at p. 578; [1962] P. at p. 203.
    (25) I.e., the draftsman of the affidavit in support of the answer.
    (26) [1886-90] All E.R. Rep. 524; [1891] P. 139.
    (27) [1962] 2 All E.R. 573; [1962] P. 196.

of that offence with the intention of remitting it, that is to say, with the intention A
of not enforcing the rights which accrue to the wronged spouse in consequence
of the offence.   The reason for the rule that condonation bars relief is that it
would generally be inequitable to permit a spouse who has forgiven an offence to
go back on the decision. Matrimony involves mutual obligations and rights;
a reinstatement in a matrimonial position therefore involves the enjoyment, or
the possibility of enjoyment, of those rights through approbation of the marriage; B
and the spouse who does that cannot in fairness subsequently be allowed to
reprobate it.   Therefore condonation is an absolute bar to a complaint.   As I
read s. 4 of the Matrimonial Causes Act, 1950, (28), the onus lies on the husband
here to satisfy the court that there was no condonation, though, in my view, he
has only to do that on a balance of probabilities (29).   The husband makes two
replies to the wife's allegation that her adultery was condoned.   He says, first, C
that he never reinstated the wife in her former matrimonial position; and,
secondly, that if he did so, he was in ignorance of material facts relating to her
adultery.

Did he reinstate the wife?   The alternatives suggested to him at his moment of
decision included divorcing the wife or accepting the child as his.   He chose not
to divorce the wife and thereby, in my view, advisedly remitted his right to relief D
for the wrong that she had done him.   It is true that there was no sexual intercourse thereafter, but neither had there been before for some years; and in every
other way the wife was reinstated in her position as a wife.   It is said that
animosity and unhappiness still prevailed between them, so that there was no
true reconciliation.   Nevertheless, they continued to live together for five years
after knowledge of the adultery had come to the husband, on the same uneasy E
and painful terms, unfortunately, as had subsisted before, but presenting to the
world and to their child a picture of husband and wife in a reasonable connubial
relationship.   It seems to me inescapable that there was a reinstatement sufficient
to satisfy the factum of condonation.

But what must the husband be taken to have condoned by the reinstatement?
That really involves two questions: first, did he know all the material facts F
when he reinstated the wife and, secondly, if he did not, is he nevertheless precluded from asserting that?   Any fact was material which would reasonably have
had a substantial weight with the husband in determining whether, on the one
hand, to exercise his right to repudiate the wife for the wrong which she had
done him or, on the other, to remit his right to do so.

The husband knew about the 1956 adultery; he may not specifically have been G
told the name of the adulterer, but he suspected that it was the co-respondent and
he was correct.   So far I think the case is covered by *Wells* v. *Wells* (30).   There
a wife had confessed adultery to her husband and told him that she was going to
bear a child of whom the co-respondent was the father.   She did not tell him that
adultery had taken place on more than one occasion, but he suspected that it had.
He had intercourse with her, which was, as the law then stood (31), a conclusive H
reinstatement.   He subsequently brought proceedings against his wife on the
ground of adultery, having by that time learned for certain that she had
committed adultery on more than one occasion.   The Court of Appeal held that
the husband had, nevertheless, condoned his wife's adultery and could not
complain about it.   Here, however, the husband did not know and had no suspicion

I

(28) Now s. 5 of the Matrimonial Causes Act 1965.
(29) It was held by the majority of the House of Lords in *Blyth* v. *Blyth* ([1966] 1 All
E.R. 524; [1966] A.C. 643), that the standard of proof on issues of condonation or con-
nivance was that of a balance of probabilities.
(30) [1954] 3 All E.R. 491.
(31) The law relating to condonation was altered by the Matrimonial Causes Act
1963, s. 1, s. 2 (43 HALSBURY'S STATUTES (2nd Edn.) 436, 437); see now s. 42 of the
Matrimonial Causes Act 1965 (45 HALSBURY'S STATUTES (2nd Edn.) 502).

A   of the 1954 adultery. The husband says that if he had known of it, it would have made all the difference to his decision. Counsel for the wife accepted the husband as a truthful witness: but said with great cogency that his declaration that it would have made all the difference was inconsistent with his having made no inquiries at the time, that he is now desperate for a divorce and that he knows now that this is the crux of the case. He would be superhuman, says counsel for

B   the wife, if he were unswayed by those considerations, even though unconsciously.

The husband put forward three reasons why he forgave his wife. First, he had a deep feeling of guilt; he was conscious of the injury which the wife had suffered by the psychological block which precluded him from having sexual intercourse with her; secondly, pity for the child that was on the way; and, thirdly, the effect that a divorce might have on his career (though that last consideration

C   was a subsidiary one). The husband was asked how far those factors could have been affected by learning that there was adultery in 1954 as well as in 1956. His answer was very confused, but on consideration I am not sure how fair it was to put the question to him in that way (I hasten to say that it was I who put it in that way). I think that what the husband was trying to tell me was that the adultery in 1954 would have been a new factor which would have come to balance

D   those other factors which weighed his decision in favour of forgiveness when he thought that the adultery had only occurred in 1956. I believe him when he says that if he had known of the 1954 adultery his decision would have been different. The wife was expecting to be divorced; the decision must have been made on a very narrow balance, and knowledge of the adultery in 1954, resumed in 1956, would, I think, have made it go the other way. Moreover, I think that it was

E   because the wife, consciously or unconsciously, recognised that and wanted to be forgiven that she did not tell the husband of the earlier adultery. But was it reasonable that the husband should have made the decision differently if he had known of the earlier adultery? I think that it would have been reasonable. This case is different from *Wells* v. *Wells* (32) where it was simply a question of one occasion of adultery or half a dozen. Adultery in 1956 was consistent with a

F   sudden yielding to temptation. Adultery committed in 1954, before the tour of duty in America, and resumed at the first opportunity in 1956, presents, I think, a materially different pattern.

The next question then is: is the husband by his failure to enquire how long the adultery had gone on precluded now from alleging that the 1954 adultery was a material factor? Clearly, there may be circumstances where it would be wrong

G   to allow a husband to say that he did not know a material fact which was not brought to his notice. If, for example, he said " I wish to hear no more about this ", or even if he merely indicated by his conduct that he wished to hear no more about it, it would not be right to allow him subsequently to claim that a material fact was not brought to his knowledge. Counsel for the wife put it in this way: once a confession of adultery is made there is an onus on the spouse to

H   whom it is made to make such inquiries as he thinks necessary before making his decision whether to take action or to condone. There is a passage in a footnote in Rayden on Divorce (9th Edn. (1964)) p. 250 which supports that way of putting it. But in my view it is not correct; it puts the onus the wrong way round. In my judgment the true rule is this: it is the duty of a spouse seeking forgiveness for adultery to disclose all the material circumstances of the offence, that is to

I   say, any factor which might reasonably weigh with the other spouse in deciding whether or not to forgive; if that is not done there is no condonation, unless the other spouse expressly or impliedly waives the requirement of further knowledge of any material fact. I do not think that the husband did so here. I therefore hold that there was no condonation of the 1954 adultery.

The case therefore rests in this way: the wife has proved that the husband has

---

(32) [1954] 3 All E.R. 491.

committed adultery from 1961 onwards and deserted her in 1961, remaining in A
desertion ever since. The husband has proved that the wife committed adultery
in 1954 which is uncondoned. (Though he purported to condone her 1956 adultery,
it matters not whether he can claim still to rely on it in the circumstances.) The
wife is asking for a judicial separation; the husband is asking for a divorce; both
need the exercise of the court's discretion in order to obtain relief.

Counsel for the wife urges that the wife's adultery had nothing to do with the B
break-up of this marriage; it was due to the desertion and adulterous connexion
on the part of the husband. I think that he is right. The wife, he said, is fully
entitled to ask for a judicial separation; it is a remedy that Parliament has made
available to her; she may ask for it in preference to a divorce for any reason or for
no reason. Where a wife has performed all the obligations of a marriage I agree
that she is fully entitled to insist on its maintenance even in a state of separation, C
particularly if her insistence is prompted by conscientious considerations. That,
however, is not the situation here. The wife has not performed all the obligations
of the marriage; she has committed adultery. Moreover, although I am satisfied
that she thinks that her prime motive in asking for a judicial separation in
preference to a divorce is conscientious, it is not so. I fear that the choice springs
from the unhappiness and humiliation which she has suffered and from a wish to D
injure the husband and the woman who has superseded her in his life. Certainly
the fact that it was the husband who finally broke up this marriage is a factor
to be weighed strongly in favour of the wife; but it must be weighed in connexion
and together with other factors. One such factor, which also speaks potently for
the wife, is the financial situation. Although she might be better off through a
divorce than by judicial separation in that she would then be able to claim a E
provision securing her maintenance after the death of the husband, whereas no
such provision can be made for her on a judicial separation—only provision for
his life and such rights as she might have under the Inheritance (Family Provision)
Act, 1938, (33)—there may not be the funds available in any case to make a
secured provision for her. While she remains married to the husband she has rights
on widowhood which are important to her, particularly rights as an officer's F
widow under the Royal Warrant. I therefore inquired what provision could be
made for her in the event of the factors, which I shall shortly have to weigh,
pointing on balance in favour of divorce. I have been satisfied that a provision
could be made for her—and I have had an undertaking in that regard—which
would safeguard her against any loss that she might suffer in her rights on
widowhood. The child, so far as I can see, will not be affected financially. G

With regard to the other factors that the court weighs in exercising discretion,
I had recent occasion to review them in detail in *Bull* v. *Bull* (34). I do not
propose to deal with any except those that are relevant to the present case. The
first is whether if the marriage is not dissolved there is any reasonable prospect
of reconciliation between the husband and the wife. I am quite satisfied that there
is no possibility of any such reconciliation. The relationship between the husband H
and the wife almost from the outset of the marriage has been a most unhappy
one and the husband has now formed a stable, though extra-marital, connexion
with the woman named in the wife's answer. The second is the position and
interest of any child of the family. Since there is no prospect of a reconciliation
the refusal of a decree of divorce and the granting of a decree of judicial separation
cannot possibly reconstitute for this child the family background of which she I
has been deprived. There is one other consideration which I think must weigh
in relation to the child and that is this: if a decree of judicial separation is granted
in preference to a decree of divorce, the husband will continue living in an irregular
union; and I cannot but think that it would be to the child's disadvantage to

---

(33) For the Act of 1938, as amended, see Sch. 3 to the Family Provision Act 1966.
(34) [1965] 1 All E.R. 1057.

A grow up in the knowledge of that. Thirdly, I must consider the interest of the party with whom the husband has been guilty of adultery, with special regard to their marriage. Clearly her interest will be promoted by a decree of divorce in preference to a decree of judicial separation. Fourthly, there is the interest of the husband and particularly the interest that he should be able to re-marry and live respectably. That again points in favour of a divorce. Those four considerations

B were laid down by the House of Lords in *Blunt* v. *Blunt* (35).

Next, was the husband or the wife the more responsible for the break-up of the marriage? I have already dealt with that; I think that the husband was the more responsible, and that is, of course, a pointer to the wishes of the wife being acceded to rather than his. What was the nature of the misconduct which necessitated prayers for discretionary relief? Was it, for example, with more than

C one man or woman? Was it promiscuous? Were there mitigating or aggravating circumstances on either side? The adultery of both parties was with one person only, not promiscuous. On each side, I think, there were some mitigating circumstances, particularly in the case of the wife. I do not think that any of the other factors really carry much weight in this case. Weighing these considerations as best I can, it seems to me that on balance they strongly favour this marriage

D being terminated. My judgment should make clear to anybody who subsequently has to deal with any matter arising out of this case where I think that the major blame lies.

My conclusion, therefore, is that I should reject the prayer of the answer and in the discretion of the court grant the husband a decree nisi of divorce on the ground of the wife's adultery with the co-respondent.

E

Decree nisi.

Solicitors: *Gerald Mayberry & Co.* (for the husband); *Freeman & Son* (for the wife); *Callingham & Co.* (for the co-respondent).

[*Reported by* ALICE BLOOMFIELD, *Barrister-at-Law.*]

F

G

H

———

I

(35) [1943] 2 All E.R. 76; [1943] A.C. 517.

A

R. *v.* ROADS.

[COURT OF APPEAL, CRIMINAL DIVISION (Lord Parker, C.J., Diplock, L.J., and
Ashworth, J.), February 27, 1967.]

*Jury—Verdict—Evidence of juror—Criminal trial—Jury directed that unanimous
verdict was necessary—Return of verdict in sight and hearing of all jurors* B
without protest—Evidence of juror that she disagreed with verdict inadmissible.

The applicant was charged on two counts with assaulting police officers.
In the summing-up the jury were repeatedly told that their verdict must be
unanimous. When the jury returned the foreman returned a verdict of
guilty on both counts. The clerk of the court and the trial judge asked the
question " those verdicts are the verdicts of you all? " On each occasion C
the foreman replied, " they are ". After the trial, a woman juror maintained
that at all times she was adamant that the applicant was not guilty. She
admitted that she heard the foreman give the verdict, but said that she was
too afraid to get up and protest that she was not in agreement. On application
for leave to appeal against conviction on the ground that the verdict was not
unanimous, the court was invited to receive an affidavit from the woman D
juror and, if necessary, to have her called and cross-examined.

Held: it was quite clear that the verdict was returned not only in the
presence of the juror, but also in her hearing and, accordingly, it was
impossible for the court to receive the affidavit (see p. 87, letter E, post).

Nesbitt v. *Parrett* ((1902), 18 T.L.R. 510), and dicta of BANKES, L.J., in
Ellis v. *Deheer* ([1922] All E.R. Rep. at p. 452), of LORD DENNING, M.R., E
and HARMAN, L.J., in *Boston* v. *W. S. Bagshaw & Sons, Ltd.* (see p. 88, letter
D, and p. 89, letter A, post) applied.

Application refused.

[As to the inadmissibility of evidence by jurors as to their deliberations and
intentions, see 15 HALSBURY'S LAWS (3rd Edn.) 420, para. 754, text and notes
(*f*), (*g*) and 23 ibid., 37, para. 71, text and note (*p*); and for cases on the F
subject, see 14 DIGEST (Repl.) 368, *3566-3567*; 30 DIGEST (Repl.) 292-294,
645-663.]

Cases referred to:
    Boston v. *W. S. Bagshaw & Sons, Ltd.*, p. 87, post; [1966] 1 W.L.R. 1135.
    Ellis v. *Deheer,* [1922] All E.R. Rep. 451; [1922] 2 K.B. 113; 91 L.J.K.B. G
        937; 127 L.T. 431; 86 J.P. 169; 14 Digest (Repl.) 368, *3567*.
    Nesbitt v. *Parrett,* (1902), 18 T.L.R. 510; 30 Digest (Repl.) 293, *653*.
    R. v. *Wooller,* (1817), 2 Stark. 111; 171 E.R. 589; sub nom. *R.* v. *Wooler,*
        (1817), 6 M. & S. 366; 105 E.R. 1280; 14 Digest (Repl.) 368, *3566*.

Application.

This was an application by Mortimer Joseph Galvin Roads for leave to appeal H
against his conviction on Feb. 2, 1967, at South West London Sessions before
the chairman (F. H. CASSELS, ESQ.) and a jury on one count of assaulting a
police officer in the execution of his duty, and one count of assaulting another
police officer occasioning him actual bodily harm. He was sentenced to six
months' imprisonment concurrent on each count. The facts are set out in the
judgment of the court. I

The cases noted below* were cited during the argument in addition to those
referred to in the judgment.

W. M. F. Hudson for the applicant.
A. C. L. Lewisohn for the Crown.

---

* *R.* v. *Thomas,* [1933] All E.R. Rep. 726; [1933] 2 K.B. 489; *Ras Behar Lal* v. *King
Emperor,* [1933] All E.R. Rep. 723.

A   **LORD PARKER, C.J.,** delivered the following judgment of the court:
In October, 1966, on a certain evening Detective Constables Tait and Burchall
were on patrol in a police car. As the result of a radio message, they went to
Richmond Bridge, got out of the car and went towards the towpath. They
there came on three men, one of whom, according to them, called out: " It's
the law ", and all three ran up a flight of steps pursued by the officers. Half-
B   way up the steps the last of the three men turned on the officers and a struggle
ensued. According to Detective Constable Tait, the man kicked him in the
eye; he and Detective Constable Burchall then grabbed the man and in the
struggle they fell all of them down the steps. As a result, Detective Constable
Burchall struck his head on the final impact and was injured. The man, as
indeed the other two men, made good their escape. Two independent bystanders,
C   a Mr. Steward and a Mr. Kirby, spoke of a man coming a little ahead of Detective
Constable Burchall, and of his vaulting over a gate and making his way down a
gangway and out of sight. On Oct. 15, 1966, the applicant was interviewed
and asked where he was on that night, and his answer was, and always has been,
that he was at home. He said: " It's not me. I don't like any sort of violence.
It must be somebody with a grudge against me to say it was me." In due
D   course an identification parade was held, and the applicant was picked out by
Detective Constable Tait, Detective Constable Burchall and by Mr. Stewart.
Mr. Kirby could not attend the identification parade but claimed to identify
the applicant in court. The jury were rightly told that they might not think
that Mr. Kirby's identification in those circumstances amounted to very much.
The defence was, as already indicated, that the applicant had been at home
E   all the evening, that he was suffering from migraine and had gone to bed early,
and, according to him, his wife, his mother-in-law and a Mrs. Sutton were there.
He called in support his wife and also Mr. and Mrs. Sutton.

It will be seen, as indicated by the chairman in his summing-up, that the
only issue here was one of identification. It was not contended that there had not
been an assault on both these police officers, nor that the assault on Detective
F   Constable Burchall was not one which had occasioned actual bodily harm. The
jury convicted, and, if one were to pause there, there would be really no ground
whatever for interfering in this case. There was ample evidence to support
the verdict, and it is not suggested that there was any misdirection of law or
of fact.

The reason that this case has come before the court is because of a juror who,
G   it is said, while present in court while the foreman gave the verdict of the jury,
was at all times adamant that the applicant was not guilty. She admits that
she heard the foreman give the verdict, but she says that she was too afraid
to get up and protest that she was not in agreement. Counsel for the applicant
has invited us to receive an affidavit from this juror along the lines indicated,
and, if need be, to have her called and cross-examined. This court has, however,
H   come to the clear conclusion that any evidence of that sort is wholly inadmissible.
It is unnecessary to go through all the cases in regard to this, but the court has
been referred to the case in 1902 of *Nesbitt* v. *Parrett* (1). The court there was
asked to receive an affidavit from a juror to the effect that he had not agreed
(and this was a civil action) to the amount of damages. When the foreman
mentioned the amount in court, the juror, so it was said, was so staggered with
I   surprise at its greatness that he tried to protest, but his feelings overcame him
and it was physically impossible for him to give utterance to a single word.
The Court of Appeal, consisting of Vaughan Williams, Romer and Mathew,
L.JJ., refused to receive the affidavit, and, as Vaughan Williams, L.J., said in
the course of the argument (1): " Then I am afraid he must forever keep silence."
In giving the judgment of the court, Mathew, L.J., referred to the fact that this
point had been disposed of in the course of argument, and added this (1):

---

(1) (1902), 18 T.L.R. 510.

"It had been laid down that a juryman could not be heard to complain   A
of a verdict to which he had been a party after he had left the jury box.
Here a juryman stated that he did not agree to the verdict. If that were
listened to, then in any case a juryman might raise a difficulty which it
would be impossible for the court to solve."

In 1922, in *Ellis* v. *Deheer* (2), the Court of Appeal were again concerned with
a civil case, and in the course of giving his judgment ATKIN, L.J., said (3):   B

"This was a trial by jury, and in order to determine the issues in the
action it was necessary that there should be a unanimous verdict of all the
twelve jurymen. In accordance with the ordinary practice the verdict is,
or ought to be, delivered in open court by the foreman in the presence of
the other jurymen, and if it is so delivered in their presence, and none of   C
them protest, there is a prima facie presumption that they all assented to it.
But that presumption may be rebutted."

That that may be rebutted is clear from *Ellis* v. *Deheer* (2), which was a case
where a jury came back to return a verdict at a time when another jury were
in the jurybox and as a result the foreman of the jury gave the verdict from
the witness box and the other jurors were lined up somewhere behind him.   D
What was said there was that certain jurors, although actually in the presence
of the foreman, had not been able to hear what he said, and were in fact in
disagreement. That was a case where the presumption was rebutted, as indeed
it was in *R.* v. *Wooller* (4), which was referred to by ATKIN, L.J. (5) as an example
of the presumption being rebutted. LORD ELLENBOROUGH, C.J., in *R.* v. *Wooller*
said (6):   E

"The doubt in this case is, whether all the jury did hear what was said
by the foreman on their behalf; they were not all within sight, and therefore
we have not the ordinary means in this instance which exists in others, of
knowing that the jury assented to what was propounded on their behalf by
the foreman. This distinguishes the present case from those which usually
occur, where every individual of the jury hears what is said, and has it in his   F
power to dissent; there the evidence is complete, that he knew what passed,
and his not dissenting is conclusive to show his approbation of the verdict."

BANKES, L.J., in *Ellis* v. *Deheer* said (7) that

"When a verdict is delivered in the sight and hearing of all the jury
without any protest on their part, the inference is irresistible that they   G
assented to it . . ."

and if after that there was any doubt on the matter it has been resolved by the
recent case of *Boston* v. *W. S. Bagshaw & Sons, Ltd.* (8). There LORD DENNING,
M.R., said (9):

"Once a jury have given their verdict, and it has been accepted by the
judge, and they have been discharged, they are not at liberty to say they   H
meant something different. In *Ellis* v. *Deheer* (7), BANKES, L.J., said that
'When a verdict is delivered in the sight and hearing of all the jury without
any protest on their part, the inference is irresistible that they assented to
it' . . ."

LORD DENNING, M.R., went on to give the reasons why and to refer to the   I
case to which I have referred, *Nesbitt* v. *Parrett* (10). In passing, it is to be

(2) [1922] All E.R. Rep. 451; [1922] 2 K.B. 113.
(3) [1922] 2 K.B. at p. 120; [1922] All E.R. Rep. at p. 454.
(4) (1817), 2 Stark. 111.
(5) [1922] All E.R. Rep. at p. 454; [1922] 2 K.B. at p. 120.
(6) (1817), 2 Stark. at p. 113.
(7) [1922] All E.R. Rep. at p. 452; [1922] 2 K.B. at p. 118.
(8) See p. 87, post.   (9) See p. 88, letter D, post.
                      (10) (1902), 18 T.L.R. 510.

A observed that Harman, L.J., as was pointed out in the argument in this case, was really prophetic of the present case. He said (11):

> " It would be destructive of all trials by jury if we were to accede to this application. There would be no end to it. One would always find one juryman who said: ' That was not what I meant ' and one would have to start the whole thing anew."

B So far as the present case is concerned, it is abundantly clear that the chairman was at pains to convey to this jury, no doubt because there had been a previous disagreement, that their verdict must be unanimous. On page after page of the summing-up he said that it was " for each and every one of you ", " each one of you ", " for all of you ", and then just before they retired
C he said:

> " Although you may have heard or seen that there is a possibility of the law being changed (12) so that a majority verdict may be brought in, the law has not been changed yet, and it follows therefore that, to be a verdict at all, your verdict must be unanimous, that is, you must all agree."

D Finally, not content with allowing the clerk of the court to put the usual question, "those verdicts are the verdicts of you all? " and to receive the answer, " they are ", the chairman himself said: " they are the verdicts of you all, Mr. Foreman? " and the foreman of the jury replied, " they are ".

It is quite clear in this case that the verdict was returned not only in the presence of this juror but also in the hearing of this juror, and in those circumstances, on the authorities to which I have referred, it is quite impossible for
E this court to receive the affidavit. That being the only point in the case, the application is refused.

Application refused.

Solicitors: *Edward Fail Bradshaw & Waterson* (for the applicant); *Solicitor, Metropolitan Police* (for the Crown).

F 　　　　　　　　　　　　[*Reported by* N. P. Metcalfe, Esq., *Barrister-at-Law.*]

NOTE.

G 　　　BOSTON *v.* W. S. BAGSHAW & SONS AND ANOTHER.

[Court of Appeal (Lord Denning, M.R., Harman and Diplock, L.JJ.), April 26, 27, 1966.]

Jury—Verdict—Evidence of juror—Civil trial—Defamation—Questions put to jury and their answers returned in presence of all jurors—Judgment subsequently given on those answers—Jurors wishing to change answers, as they were dissatisfied with result—Application for new trial—Affidavit by jurors that the answers were given
H *under misapprehension not admissible.*

Cases referred to:
　Cogan v. *Ebden*, (1757), 1 Burr. 383; 30 Digest (Repl.) 292, *639.*
　Ellis v. *Deheer*, [1922] All E.R. Rep. 451; [1922] 2 K.B. 113; 91 L.J.K.B. 937; 121 L.T. 431; 86 J.P. 169; 14 Digest (Repl.) 368, 3567.
　Nesbitt v. *Parrett*, (1802), 18 T.L.R. 510; 30 Digest (Repl.) 293, *653.*

Motion.
I This was an application by the plaintiff, Alfred Robert Boston, for a new trial of an action brought by him against the defendants W. S. Bagshaw & Sons, a firm of auctioneers and estate agents, and Associated Television, Ltd., for damages for alleged defamation. The appeal in the defamation action, but not the motion for new trial, was reported at [1966] 2 All E.R. 906. The facts relevant to the motion for a new trial are stated in the judgment of Lord Denning, M.R., post.

David Hirst, Q.C., and *D. Hancock* for the applicant.
Quintin Hogg, Q.C., and *F. M. Drake* for the respondents.

---

(11) See p. 89, letter A, post.
(12) See Criminal Justice Bill (Bill 141) cl. 10.

Dicta of Lord Denning MR and
Harman LJ at 88, 89 applied in
Nanan v The State [1986] 3 All
ER 248

LORD DENNING, M.R.: This is a motion for a new trial. We are told that **A** there are affidavits from all the twelve jurymen, in which they wish to go back on some of the answers given by them in open court. They were given several questions to answer. They deliberated for five hours and came back into court with answers which were as clear as could be. It is not possible that there could be any misunderstanding as to the questions or the answers. In respect of each of two publications the jury were asked: " Were the defendants actuated by malice? " To each they answered: " No ". The associate asked them, in accordance with the time-honoured practice: " Are they the answers of you all? " The foreman answered: " They are ". The answers **B** were duly recorded and they were discharged. On the next day the judge, after argument, held that on those answers the plaintiff failed and the defendants were entitled to judgment.

It appears that the jurors did not anticipate the result. They read it in the newspapers and some of them communicated with the plaintiff and his solicitors. Further inquires were made. Then all the twelve jurors made affidavits indicating that they gave those two answers under a misapprehension: that they meant to find malice: **C** and that they would, if they could, change these answers so as to say that the defendants were actuated by malice. Counsel for the applicant asks us to receive those affidavits and to order a new trial.

To my mind it is settled as well as anything can be that it is not open to the court to receive any such evidence as this. Once a jury have given their verdict, and it has been accepted by the judge, and they have been discharged, they are not at liberty to say that they meant something different. In *Ellis* v. *Deheer* (1) BANKES, L.J., said: **D**

" When a verdict is given in the sight and hearing of all the jury without any protest on their part, the inference is irresistible that they assented to it."

ATKIN, L.J., said (2) that there was a general rule—

" . . . that the court does not entertain or admit evidence by a juryman of what took place in the jury room either by way of explaining the grounds on which the jury arrived at their conclusion, or by way of statement as to what he believed **E** its effect would be."

The reasons are twofold: first, to secure the finality of decisions arrived at by the jury; secondly, to protect the jury themselves and to prevent them being exposed to pressure or inducement to explain or alter their views. If this were to be permitted, where is it to stop? After a jury have solemnly found a man " guilty " and he has been sentenced, are they to be at liberty next day to return and say they meant to find him " not guilty "? It cannot be. **F**

We were referred, very properly, by counsel for the applicant to a case in 1902, *Nesbitt* v. *Parrett* (3), where a juryman sought to say that he had not agreed to the amount of £1,100. He was staggered by it. He was taken so much aback that he could not speak at the time. The court said that they could not possibly receive it. It would be destructive of the whole system of trial by jury if we were to admit evidence of this kind.

The best case which counsel for the applicant said that he had in his favour was an old case of *Cogan* v. *Ebden* (4). When that case is looked at, it is quite clear that the **G** associate made a mistake. There were two issues in the case. Instead of asking the jury to give a verdict on each issue separately, he asked the jury to give a general verdict. He asked them: " how do you find—for the plaintiff or the defendant? " They said: " the defendant on both issues ". He ought to have asked them for a separate verdict on each of the two issues in that case, but he did not do so. That case is quite distinguishable. So are all the other cases. In some of these evidence was admitted as to what took place in open court. For instance, in *Ellis* v. *Deheer* (5) the jurymen were so placed that they could not hear what the foreman said. In other cases evidence was admitted **H** to show that a juryman was incompetent to act, as, for instance, because he did not understand the language in which the trial was conducted (6). Apart from such cases, however, I know of no case where evidence of jurors has been received to challenge the verdict.

I am quite satisfied that we cannot receive evidence from these jurors to say they meant something different from what was given in their verdict clearly expressed at the time and, indeed, assented to by them all in the presence of the judge. This motion **I** for a new trial on that ground must be refused.

---

(1) [1922] All E.R. 451 at p. 452, letter E; [1922] 2 K.B. 113 at p. 118.
(2) [1922] All E.R. Rep. at p. 454, letter I; [1922] 2 K.B. at p. 121.
(3) (1902), 18 T.L.R. 510.
(4) (1757), 1 Burr. 383.
(5) [1922] All E. R.Rep. 451; [1922] 2 K.B. 113.
(6) See *Ras Behar Lal* v. *King-Emperor*, [1933] All E.R. Rep. 723; cf. *R.* v. *Thomas*, [1933] All E.R. Rep. 726.

A   HARMAN, L.J.: I agree. It would be destructive of all trials by jury if we were to accede to this application. There would be no end to it. One would always find one juryman who said: " that was not what I meant " and one would have to start the whole thing anew. Interest reipublicae ut sit finis litium.

DIPLOCK, L.J.: I agree.

Motion dismissed.

B   Solicitors: *Gregory, Rowcliffe & Co.*, agents for *F. S. Hawthorn & Son*, Uttoxeter (for the applicant); *Collyer-Bristow & Co.*, agents for *Wilkins & Thompson*, Uttoxeter (for the respondents).

[*Reported by* F. Guttman, Esq., *Barrister-at-Law.*]

C   # CUTTS AND ANOTHER *v.* CHUMLEY AND ANOTHER.

[Queen's Bench Division (Willis, J.), February 20, 21, 22, 23, 24, 27, 1967.]

Damages—Personal injury—Amount of damages—Brain injury causing grave mental deficiency and personality change—Plaintiff aged twenty-eight, wife and mother of three children, happily married, and a talented commercial

D   *artist—Care in private institution necessary throughout rest of her life, probably about twenty-five years—Limited awareness in plaintiff of her deprivation—Element of bodily pain absent.*

Husband and Wife—Consortium—Damages—Wife injured in road accident for which defendant liable—Wife under care in institution for rest of her life, probably about twenty-five years—Total incapacity of wife to render services

E   *in the home to husband and children—Husband necessarily employing paid housekeeper to care for three children in his home—Claim for total loss of wife's services.*

The plaintiffs, husband and wife, claimed damages in respect of injuries suffered in a road accident in September, 1964, owing to the negligent driving (as the court found) of the first defendant. At the time of the accident

F   the wife was twenty-eight and mother of three young children, the youngest of whom was born shortly before the accident. Prior to the birth of her eldest child the wife had been employed as a commercial artist and it had been her intention to resume her career when the youngest child should have attained the age of five; she had exceptional artistic talents, and it was estimated that she could earn annually about £1,000 net before tax. She

G   was described as intelligent and lively, a devoted wife and mother, house-proud and fastidious, a good cook and efficient housekeeper; the plaintiffs were a devoted couple with everything to live for. As a result of her very serious injuries, physical and mental, the wife suffered a complete personality change; intellectually she was reduced to the level of a child aged three to five, and physically she was gravely disabled. The agreed medical conclusion

H   was that while her expectation of life was to the age of about fifty-five, her mental and physical disabilities were such that no improvement in her condition could be anticipated and that to maintain her present level and prevent deterioration she would need permanent care with occupational therapy and physio-therapy such as could only be provided in a private institution; the cost of maintaining her in one such institution had been

I   estimated to be about £1,092 per annum. The wife, notwithstanding her mental deficiencies, had some awareness of her plight.

The husband, whose injuries were relatively minor, claimed also damages for loss of consortium, viz. (a) for the total loss of his wife's services permanently, and (b) for the loss of her society during the period which she had already spent in hospital. As regards the loss of services, the husband had with some difficulty found a temporary housekeeper to care for the children and cook for the household, for a wage of £8 11s. 4d. a week; such help would be necessary for some years to replace the wife's services.

Held: (i) assessing the wife's damages under the heads of (a) pain and ⟶ **A**
suffering, (b) loss of the amenities of life, (c) cost of care for the rest of her
life in a private institution, (d) loss of probable future earnings, and (e) loss
of expectation of life, and recognising that the element of bodily pain was
not present, the proper award for general damages was a sum of £39,000*
(see p. 94, letter G, post).

Wise v. *Kaye* ([1962] 1 All E.R. 257) and *H. West & Son, Ltd.* v. *Shephard* ⟶ **B**
([1963] 2 All E. R.625) considered.

(ii) on his claim for damages for loss of consortium the husband would
be awarded £5,000 for the total loss of his wife's services (taking into account
the probability that he would obtain an income tax allowance in respect
of a housekeeper), and £200 for the loss of her society during the limited
period for which he had claimed (see p. 96, letter F, post). ⟶ **C**

Lawrence v. *Biddle* ([1966] 1 All E.R. 575) followed.

[As to the heads under which damages for torts causing personal injury are
assessed, and as to damages in respect of loss of expectation of life, see 11 HALS-
BURY'S LAWS (3rd Edn.) 255-257, paras. 427, 428, pp. 258-261, paras. 430-432;
and for cases on the subject, see 36 DIGEST (Repl.) 199-201, *1050-1062*, 229-232, ⟶ **D**
1209-1234, and DIGEST (Cont. Vol. A) 1190-1197, *1051a-1070d*; also 17 DIGEST
(Repl.) 101, *164, 165*, 102 *167, 168*, and DIGEST (Cont. Vol. A) 464, 465, *155a-168a*.

As to actions by a husband for loss of consortium, see 19 HALSBURY'S LAWS
(3rd Edn.) 820, 821, para. 1341; and for cases on the subject, see 27 DIGEST
(Repl.) 88, 89, *664-679*.]

Cases referred to: ⟶ **E**
Best v. *Samuel Fox & Co., Ltd.*, [1952] 2 All E.R. 394; [1952] A.C. 716; *affg.*
[1951] 2 All E.R. 116; [1951] 2 K.B. 639; *affg.* [1950] 2 All E.R. 798;
Digest (Cont. Vol. A) 680, *683*.
British Transport Commission v. *Gourley*, [1955] 3 All E.R. 796; [1956] A.C.
185; [1956] 2 W.L.R. 41; Digest (Cont. Vol. A) 462, *28a*.
Lawrence v. *Biddle*, [1966] 1 All E.R. 575; [1966] 2 Q.B. 504; [1966] 2 W.L.R. ⟶ **F**
930.
West (H.) & Son, Ltd. v. *Shepherd*, [1963] 2 All E.R. 625; [1964] A.C. 326;
[1963] 2 W.L.R. 1359; Digest (Cont. Vol. A) 119, *1053c*.
Wise v. *Kaye*, [1962] 1 All E.R. 257; [1962] 1 Q.B. 638; [1962] 2 W.L.R. 96;
Digest (Cont. Vol. A) 1191, *1053b*.
⟶ **G**
Action.
In this action, begun by writ dated Apr. 6, 1965, the first plaintiff, Juanita
Cutts, suing by her husband Thomas Larry Cutts as next friend, claimed damages
in respect of personal injuries sustained in an accident on Sept. 11, 1964, when
she was a passenger in a motor vehicle driven by her husband which came into
collision with a motor vehicle driven by the first defendant, Robert Chumley. ⟶ **H**
The second plaintiff, the said Thomas Larry Cutts, also claimed damages for
personal injuries sustained, and in addition for loss of his wife's consortium.
The plaintiffs alleged that the collision was due to the negligence of the first
defendant, alternatively to that of the second defendant, Stanley Alexander
Livitt, who was driving a motor vehicle following behind the first defendant.
Both defendants denied negligence; the first defendant having died an order ⟶ **I**
was made on Jan. 5, 1967, for the action to be carried on between the plaintiffs
and his administrator, Donald Robert Chumley, and the second defendant.

HIS LORDSHIP, WILLIS, J., having heard the evidence on liability, and
having found that the first defendant had driven negligently and was wholly

_____

* Initially the sum awarded was £39,500, including a sum of £1,000 damages for loss
of expectation of life; but this £1,000 was reduced to £500 following the decision of the
House of Lords in *Yorkshire Electricity Board* v. *Naylor* ([1967] 1 All E.R. 1). This
adjustment was made on Mar. 22, 1967, pursuant to agreement between the parties.

A responsible for the accident, then proceeded to consider the plaintiffs' background and the medical evidence in respect of the very grave injuries suffered by the first plaintiff. The following facts relevant to her injuries are summarised from the judgment. At the time of the accident the wife was a very attractive women of twenty-eight and the mother of three little boys, the youngest having been born shortly before the accident. The husband was an advertising visualiser,

B employed at a present salary of £1,850 a year gross. The wife was a rather shy, retiring person, intelligent and lively, a devoted wife and mother, house-proud and fastidious, a good cook and efficient housekeeper; they were a devoted couple with, as it seemed, everything to live for. The wife had been employed before the birth of the eldest son as a commercial artist, and she had quite exceptional artistic talents as an advertising designer, and also as a potter and a

C sculptor, and had expressed the hope of resuming her work as a free lance when the youngest child started school some five years from the date of the accident. The wife's injuries, as a result of the accident, were so severe that her life had been utterley shattered. She was taken unconscious from the scene of the accident to Battle Hospital, Reading; from there she was taken to the Radcliffe Infirmary, Oxford, for intensive care of neuro-surgeons, and remained there until

D Dec. 17, 1964. The visible injuries on admission were: multiple bruises and lacerations of the right frontal region and over the face; many small lacerations elsewhere. Epileptic fits soon developed, and convulsions continued despite controlling drugs, for ten days. She suffered a collapse of the upper lobe of the right lung which necessitated a tracheotomy. Nineteen days after the accident she opened her eyes; some $4\frac{1}{2}$ weeks after the accident a skin necrosis on the

E right thigh was excised and a consequent grafting operation, with blood transfusion, was carried out; it was not until $5\frac{1}{2}$ weeks after the injury that she made the first exclamatory sounds. After eight weeks she began to recognise her husband, but could not speak to him; a week later she began to be able to feed herself in an elementary way with her left hand, and could utter a few words and the names of her children. Her condition thereafter showed very little

F improvement, and on Dec. 12, 1964, a second lumbar encephalogram was carried out, which showed considerable brain damage. Her condition on Dec. 16, 1964, was described by Dr. Huw Griffith, and his opinion (in an agreed report) was:

"This lady's head injury was evidently of devasting severity. At three months after injury, there is virtually no evidence of left hemisphere function,

G as witnessed by the mutism, probable dementia, hemianopia and incontinence in addition to the hemiparesis. In addition, the optic nerve on the right has been severely damaged, and the eye here is probably to all intents and purposes blind. The air encephalogram demonstrated severe traumatic cerebral atrophy. This is maximal in the fronto-temporal region, and completes the picture of a very severe brain injury maximal in the left hemisphere.

H The prognosis for recovery is grim."

There were other reports by distinguished doctors to the same effect. For the following eighteen months or so Mrs. Cutts was continuously an in-patient in Windsor Hospital, interrupted by short spells in specialist institutions, mainly for occupational and physio-therapy. Periodical reports on her condition showed

I some improvement as time went on; the damage to the right eye cleared up, but otherwise the neurological results of the severe brain injury showed little real amelioration, despite all the medical, nursing and therapeutical care and skill lavished on her. In this context HIS LORDSHIP referred to what one of the doctors, Dr. Barham Carter, said at the end of a report dated Feb. 14, 1966, viz.:

"I should like to say that a great deal of this patient's improvement must have been due to her husband's continual devoted care and interest in his wife's recovery."

After six months in Banstead Place Rehabilitation Centre, Mrs. Cutts was moved A
to St. Bernard's Mental Hospital, Southall, where she had remained since
January, 1967. She had thus been an institutional patient since the accident in
September, 1964, apart from occasional visits to her family. HIS LORDSHIP
summarised, on the basis of the agreed medical reports, her present condition
to the following effect. (i) She had suffered a complete personality change.
She had become uninhibited in speech, laughed excessively, tended to be dirty B
in eating habits. At home she was unaware that the house needed cleaning
or whether the children were clean, dirty, or in trouble. Making a cup of tea
was the limit of her domestic capabilities. (ii) Intellectually she was reduced
to the level of a child aged three or five; she was unable to do any shopping,
and though she could add and subtract she could neither divide nor multiply;
she would laugh at whatever was on the television screen, and could understand C
nothing of what she read; a pathetic and touching commentary on her condition
were the letters which she had written to her husband, the writing on which
was almost indecipherable, but there was poignancy in what could be deciphered.
(iii) In regard to her physical condition, her speech had become difficult to
understand and repetitive; her right hand was useless; there was weakness
down the right side of her body; she had incontinence of urine, her facial features D
had become flaccid and heavy; for the injury to her right leg she had been
provided with a caliper but she disliked this and discarded it, and she would
shuffle unsteadily and for short distances with the aid of a tripod stick.

The second plaintiff, the husband, in addition to claiming damages for relatively
minor personal injuries suffered by him, claimed damages also for loss of his wife's
consortium. The facts relevant to this part of the action are set out in the E
judgment of WILLIS, J., at p. 96, letters A to D, post.

E. W. Eveleigh, Q.C., and *O. B. Popplewell* for the plaintiffs.
Bernard Caulfield, Q.C., and *J. W. Miskin* for the first defendant.
Tudor Evans, Q.C., and *Patrick Bennett* for the second defendant.

F

Cur. adv. vult.

Feb. 27. **WILLIS, J.**, read the following judgment, in which after reviewing
the evidence on liability he found that the accident was caused solely by the
negligence of the first defendant, and after reviewing the medical evidence
(see p. 91, letter D, ante) in respect of the injuries, mental and physical, suffered G
by Mrs. Cutts and summarising her present condition (see letters B to D, above),
he continued: The agreed medical conclusion is that Mrs. Cutts has gross mental
and physical disability, with a five per cent. chance of further epilepsy, and
will need permanent care in an institution for the rest of her life. Her expectation
of life, according to the doctors, is to the age of about fifty-five. Her present
condition will not show any improvement. Her general health is good, but H
no more can be done for her except to provide occupational therapy and physio-
therapy in order to maintain her present level and prevent deterioration, and
there is no dispute between the parties that this can be provided only in a private
institution.

It is almost impossible in the case of a person so tragically afflicted to form any
reliable view of the extent to which she appreciates and is affected by her plight, I
but although she seems to be unaware of her mental deficiencies, apart, so her
husband says, from occasions when she seems bewildered at her inability to find
the right word, she does show signs of frustration and annoyance at her physical
disabilities, particularly in relation to the caliper, which she once put into the
dustbin. She complains a great deal, and constantly points out the big scar
on her thigh, the tracheotomy scar and her right leg and useless arm. Counsel
for the plaintiffs, who has conducted this case with the moderation one expects
of him, has said that this is one of the most heart-rending and serious cases ever

A to come before the courts, and I think that there would be few who would disagree with him. I now find myself faced with the almost impossible task of assessing a sum of money which the law can recognise as fair and reasonable compensation to a young wife and mother with everything to live for, for the loss
of virtually everything which makes life worth living. It is a melancholy and
unenviable task, but I must do my best to discharge it.

B   There is no dispute that the heads under which I should consider, as I do,
the assessment of damages are: (a) pain and suffering; (b) loss of the amenities
of life; (c) cost of caring for her for the rest of her life in a private institution;
(d) loss of probable future earnings; and (e) loss of expectation of life. I am
satisfied that Mrs. Cutts is entitled to an award under each of these heads,
except that, in so far as pain should be properly distinguished from suffering,
C the element of bodily pain is absent in this case.

For a proper approach to my consideration of what should be awarded under
the heads of pain and suffering and loss of life's amenities, I have been referred
by counsel for the plaintiffs to the cases of *Wise* v. *Kaye* (1) and *H. West & Son,
Ltd.* v. *Shepherd* (2). Counsel for the first defendant, while not dissenting from
the view that those are cases which I should properly consider, invites me, on
D the other hand, to say that, bearing in mind the sort of level of damages which
has been awarded customarily in cases of quadraplegia, I should take into
account in approaching this matter the level of damages which is thrown up
by a general conspectus of such cases. With respect to counsel for the first
defendant, it seems to me an almost impossible task to try and compare one
appalling physical tragedy with another form of physical and mental tragedy,
E such as this case presents. It seems to me that, in so far as I can obtain guidance
from other cases, as I should in every circumstance wish to do, it is to the cases
of *Wise* v. *Kaye* (1) and *West* v. *Shepherd* (2) that, in the main, I should look for
help to guide me in my task. Of course, no two cases are exactly alike, and I
have to consider this case on its own facts. It is to be observed that in *Wise* v.
Kaye (1) there was no claim or award for pain and suffering in the award of
F £15,000 general damages, because of the plaintiff's state of unconsciousness.
A separate award was made by FINNEMORE, J., in that case for loss of probable
future earnings. In *West* v. *Shepherd* (2), where the results of the devasting
brain injury were not dissimilar from those in this case, PAULL, J., basing himself
on the £15,000 award in *Wise's* case (1), awarded the sum of £17,500 as general
damages, because he thought that there was some awareness in the plaintiff of
G her plight, which there was not in the case of Miss Wise, and in his doing so the
House of Lords saw no error in principle (3). By contrast, the evidence of
Mrs. Cutts' letters to her husband, in which inter alia she asks to be taken away
from the hospital, that of Dr. Agerholm of the Banstead Rehabilitation Centre,
who said that she had " too much insight " to be kept at Southall, and the
medical reports, lead me to the conclusion that Mrs. Cutts, though her physical
H injuries are not perhaps so gross as those of Mrs. Shephard, is more aware of
what she has to endure. This may be too subjective a comparison, and I prefer
to say that I think there is a substantial element of pain and suffering to be
taken into account in this case. The most important distinguishing factor,
however, in this case, which in my judgment leads inevitably to a higher award
for pain and suffering and loss of amenities than in *Shephard's* case (2) is the
I much greater expectation of life of Mrs. Cutts, and so an extension of the period
of suffering and deprivation which it is anticipated that she must endure. In
such a case PAULL, J., would have substantially increased the damages, as he
made clear in his judgment (4), and I can find nothing in the speeches of the

(1) [1962] 1 All E.R. 257; [1962] 1 Q.B. 638.
(2) [1963] 2 All E.R. 625; [1964] A.C. 326.
(3) PAULL J.'s words are referred to in [1963] 2 All E.R. at p. 627; [1964] A.C.
at p. 329.
(4) See [1963] 2 All E.R. at p. 627, letter G.

majority of their lordships in that case to indicate that they would have thought A
he would have erred in doing so.

In neither of these earlier cases did the element of maintenance in a private
institution arise, although LORD DEVLIN in *Shephard's* case (5), envisaging the
possibility, said:

" . . . twenty years in a private nursing home, which is not an impossible
thing to happen, would be a very formidable item in an award."   B

He was, of course, thinking of a higher annual sum that I have to consider,
but even with the lower figure to be considered in this case the item seems to
me a formidable one: indeed, in this case, I accept that for the rest of her life
Mrs. Cutts must be maintained in a private home or hospital. Happily, St.
Andrews, Northampton, can accommodate her now at a figure which is never   C
likely to be less than £1,092 per annum. There is additionally the question of
Mrs. Cutts' probable future earnings. The evidence of Mr. Sutton, a commercial
art consultant who had commissioned Mrs. Cutts in 1963 to do a much admired
group sculpted in copper for exhibition at Olympia, that she could earn £1,000
per annum net before tax was not seriously questioned, and I accept it. This
is a matter, however, which has many imponderables, and while I accept the   D
probability that Mrs. Cutts would have worked again as a commercial artist and
earned well had she done so, I think that the award under this head should be,
as counsel for the first defendant put it, " moderate, though not inconsiderable ".

In reaching my assessment of the figure of general damages, apart from that
for loss of expectation of life, I have kept in mind that, so far as future expenses
and loss of earnings are concerned, I should place Mrs. Cutts
                                                                                E
" in the same financial position so far as can be done by an award of money
as [she] would have been had the accident not happened."

see per LORD GODDARD in *British Transport Commission* v. *Gourley* (6).   At
the same time, I have taken into account the incidence of tax where appropriate;
the fact that Mrs. Cutts may not live her present estimated span; that she
will be receiving a lump sum now; the usual contingencies of life to which she F
would have been subject had this accident not befallen her, and, I hope, all
other matters which I should properly consider in the circumstances of this case.
At the request of all counsel, I find a separate figure for damages for loss of
expectation of life. This I assess at what I believe the Court of Appeal has said
should be the current conventional figure (7) of £1,000.   Including this figure,
the sum which I think proper to award to Mrs. Cutts in this case is £39,500, to G
which the agreed sum of £9 15s. special damage should be added.

I turn now to the claim of Mr. Cutts. This has to be considered under three
heads: his special damage; damages for the injuries he suffered in the accident;
and damages for loss of consortium. The special damage has been agreed at £1,755
and damages for his own personal injuries have been agreed at £200. The issue,
therefore, is to what, if any, damages he is entitled for loss of consortium. In so H
far as this comprises the two elements of society and services, the issue is narrowed
by counsel for Mr. Cutts having limited his claim to (a) for loss of service;
and (b) for loss of society only for the period during which Mrs. Cutts has already
been in hospital, which he concedes could not be a large sum. Counsel for the first
defendant, while conceding that such authority as there is is against him,
reserves his position that there must be a total loss of consortium before there   I
can be any award. I think he also reserves the position that, if there is to be a
claim for loss of consortium, it is limited to loss of services only. He points to

(5) [1963] 2 All E.R. at p. 638, letter I; [1964] A.C. at p. 358.
(6) [1955] 3 All E.R. 796 at pp. 804, 805; [1956] A.C. 185 at p. 206.
(7) See *Naylor* v. *Yorkshire Electricity Board*, [1966] 3 All E.R. 327; [1966] 3 W.L.R.
654; this has, however, since been reversed on appeal to the House of Lords, sub nom.
Yorkshire Electricity Board v. *Naylor* ([1967] 1 All E.R. 1), and £500, the amount
originally awarded by ASHWORTH, J., in that case, has been restored as the conventional
figure.

A the fifth submission for the defendants in the case of *Best* v. *Samuel Fox & Co., Ltd.* (8) in the Court of Appeal, and to the passages in the judgment of BIRKETT, L.J. (9), where, to take one short citation, BIRKETT, L.J., said (10): " Consortium, I think, is one and indivisible ", and to another passage in that case to the like effect. *Best* v. *Samuel Fox & Co., Ltd.* (11) was a case in which a wife claimed for loss of consortium represented by her deprivation of sexual

B intercourse, and it was held by the House of Lords (12) that no such claim lay in law. The observations of their lordships as to the law affecting a husband were therefore obiter in that case. Having the authority of statements, although obiter, from that source, it is necessary that I should refer to them. LORD PORTER (13) would have preferred that the husband's claim, being anomalous, as he thought, should be abolished rather than that it should be extended to a

C similar cause of action to a wife. But whereas LORD GODDARD (14) would have restricted the husband's claim to one for loss of services only, LORD REID (15) did not accept the views expressed in the Court of Appeal to which I have referred, and he recognised the right to claim for impairment as opposed to total loss of consortium. LORD REID's dictum on this matter can conveniently be referred to as cited in the judgment of BRABIN, J., in the case of *Lawrence* v. *Biddle*

D where he said (16):

E   " The contrary view was expressed by LORD REID when he said (15): ' I do not think that it is open to doubt that an impairment of a wife's capacity to render assistance to her husband was enough to found an action. Certainly an injury which temporarily incapacitated her was sufficient, and I cannot find any ground for the view that an injury which did not produce complete incapacity at any time was insufficient even if it resulted in serious and permanent impairment of her capacity to render services. Any such injury might well deprive the husband to a large extent of his wife's comfort and society but at no time deprive him wholly of it, and I have seen nothing to lead me to think that in such a case that impairment of the consortium must

F   be left out of account, and, if impairment of the consortium is enough, I have seen nothing to lead me to think that the destruction of a wife's capacity for sexual intercourse should not be regarded as such an impairment.' "

While it is common ground that the action for loss of consortium lies at law, however precarious may be its future existence, there would seem to be nothing

G anomalous in the claim put forward by Mr. Cutts in this case for loss of services, and such a claim, by whatever name, the Law Commission recommends should remain available to a husband and, indeed, become available to a wife (see the 11th Report of the Law Commission, para. 17 to para. 19 inclusive). I propose, therefore, with respect, for the reasons which seemed good to him, to follow BRABIN, J., (17) and I hold that in law Mr. Cutts is entitled to an award for

H impairment of consortium, the loss of services, of course, being total in this case.

---

(8) The submission referred to was reported in these terms: " if there were here any cause of action, which is denied, it can only be for total loss of the consortium, not for its partial loss, however serious, nor for its impairment. The words are ' per quod consortium amisit '." [1951] 2 K.B. 639 at p. 648.

I   (9) [1951] 2 All E.R. 116 at p. 125; [1951] 2 K.B. at p. 665.
   (10) [1951] 2 All E.R. at p. 125; [1951] 2 K.B. at p. 665; and per LORD ASQUITH OF BISHOPSTONE: " Consortium is, in my view, one and indiscerptible ", [1951] 2 All E.R. at p. 127; [1951] 2 K.B. at p. 669.
   (11) [1951] 2 All E.R. 116; [1951] 2 K.B. 639.
   (12) [1952] 2 All E.R. 394; [1952] A.C. 716.
   (13) [1952] 2 All E.R. at p. 396; [1952] A.C. at p. 728.
   (14) [1952] 2 All E.R. at p. 400; [1952] A.C. at p. 734.
   (15) [1952] 2 All E.R. at p. 401; [1952] A.C. at p. 736.
   (16) [1966] 1 All E.R. 575 at p. 578; [1966] 2 Q.B. 504 at p. 509.
   (17) In *Lawrence* v. *Biddle*, [1966] 1 All E.R. 575; [1966] 2 Q.B. 504.

Following the accident, Mr. Cutts has had to make such arrangements as he **A** could, with the help of his parents, his mother-in-law and friends, to ensure that his three young children were properly cared for and that he could continue to work. The youngest son has been at a nursery school and will remain there for some little time still, but the cost of his maintenance there is included in the agreed figure of special damage. Mr. Cutts' problem has been to find a suitable person to care for the children, run the house, cook and housekeep, and be resident **B** in a small bungalow. The difficulties of finding such a person at a reasonable salary are understandably considerable, but after eight months advertising and interviewing he has succeeded in finding a young lady, a Miss Ross. She comes from Kenya. But she wishes to go to the United States at the end of the year, although she has told Mr. Cutts that she will stay with him, so far as she can, until he replaces her. She goes to London for week-ends, during which Mr. **C** Cutts has to look after the children himself. Her wage, including the stamp, is £8 11s. 4d. a week, and she has her keep provided. I accept that such assistance is essential to Mr. Cutts to replace, so far as he can, the wife's services in the house. How long this will be necessary it is impossible to say; but Simon is barely three now, and it will be some years before such services as Miss Ross renders can reasonably be dispensed with, and thereafter for some time, as it seems to **D** me, some help in the home will be needed by Mr. Cutts, because his wife will not be there.

Since this matter must be dealt with realistically, I do not allow anything for Miss Ross' keep, but I do not under-estimate the problem of replacing her, and I take into account Mr. Cutts' evidence that most of the replies that he had were from ladies with a child or children of their own; and I do not think that **E** counsel for Mr. Cutts exaggerates when he submits that in Miss Ross Mr. Cutts has a bargain in every sense of the word. I also take into account that it seems probable that Mr. Cutts will obtain an income tax allowance of some sort in respect of a housekeeper. Although all that I have heard indicates that this was a very happy family and likely to remain so, the possibility of rupture in the future is something which, among the other intangibles of life, I must consider. **F** Also, the fact that Mr. Cutts will receive the damages at once must be allowed for. Making the best estimate I can, therefore, I think that the proper sum for me to award for loss of consortium is the sum of £5,200. Having regard to the desire of counsel for the first defendant to reserve a legal submission, I am perfectly prepared to separate this into two sums for loss of services and loss of society (18) if counsel wishes that I should do so. **G**

Judgment (19) *for the plaintiffs accordingly. Judgment for the second defendant against the plaintiffs.*

Solicitors: *Manley & Cooke* (for the plaintiffs); *Stanley & Co.* (for the first defendant); *Gardiner & Co.* (for the second defendant). ·

[*Reported by* K. DIANA PHILLIPS, *Barrister-at-Law.*] **H**

I

---

(18) Subsequently, at Counsel's request HIS LORDSHIP stated that he awarded £200 for loss of society and £5,000 for loss of services.

(19) On Mar. 22, WILLIS, J., reduced the award of £1,000 for loss of expectation of life to £500.

A

Re BRODIE *(deceased)*.
BARCLAYS BANK, LTD. *v.* DALLAS AND OTHERS

[CHANCERY DIVISION (Stamp, J.), February 17, 1967.]

Will—Lapse—Statutory exception from lapse—Residuary bequest to illegitimate child—Legitimation and death of child leaving issue before death of testatrix—

B   *Whether estate of legitimated child entitled to take gift—Wills Act, 1837 (7 Will. 4 & 1 Vict. c. 26), s. 33—Legitimacy Act, 1926 (16 & 17 Geo. 5 c. 60), s. 3.*

A testatrix, by her will dated Dec. 13, 1956, directed that after payment of debts etc., her residue should be divided equally between " my two sons, R.S. and J.D.B." At the date of the will J.D.B. was illegitimate. On Oct. 29, 1959, be became legitimated by the effect of the Legitimacy Act, 1959.

C   On June 21, 1962, he died leaving issue and on Dec. 15, 1962, the testatrix died. On the question what should happen to the half share of residue bequeathed to J.D.B.,

Held: (i) J.D.B. was a legitimated person within s. 3 (1)* of the Legitimacy Act, 1926, and was thereby entitled to take under any disposition coming into operation after the date of his legitimation as if he had been born

D   legitimate, the testatrix' will being such a disposition (see p. 99, letter G, post).

(ii) the half-share of the testatrix' residuary estate bequeathed to J.D.B. accordingly passed to his personal representatives, because—

(a) the right of a child of a testator or testatrix to dispose of property which after the child's death accrued to his estate by virtue of s. 33† of the

E   Wills Act, 1837, was an interest under a disposition for the purposes of s. 3 (1) (*b*) of the Legitimacy Act, 1926 (see p. 99, letter I, post), or

(b) if s. 3 (1) (*b*) of the Act of 1926 did not apply, J.D.B., as a child legitimated before the testatrix' death, would be entitled by virtue of s. 1 (1)‡ of the Act of 1926, since the interest of J.D.B.'s estate by virtue of s. 33† of the Wills Act, 1837, would not be within sub-s. (3) of s. 1‡ of the Act of 1926 and

F   so would not be excluded thereby (see p. 100, letter A, post).

Re Scott ([1901] 1 K.B. 228) applied.

[As to rights to property of persons legitimated by statute, see 3 HALSBURY'S LAWS (3rd Edn.) 95, 96, para. 149; and for cases on the subject, see 3 DIGEST (Repl.) 427-430, *232-249.*

G   For the Wills Act, 1837, s. 33, see 26 HALSBURY'S STATUTES (2nd Edn.) 1352. For the Legitimacy Act, 1926, s. 1, s. 3, see 2 HALSBURY'S STATUTES (2nd Edn.) 493, 495; and for the Legitimacy Act, 1959, s. 1 (1), see 39 ibid., p. 31.]

Case referred to:

Scott, Re, [1901] 1 K.B. 228; 70 L.J.Q.B. 66; 83 L.T. 613; 65 J.P. 84; 48 Digest (Repl.) 375, *3245.*

H   **Adjourned Summons.**

This was an application by originating summons dated June 16, 1965, by the plaintiff, Barclays Bank, Ltd., the sole executor of the testatrix, Eleanor Sutherland Brodie, deceased. The first two defendants, Ethel Mabel Dallas Brodie and Brian Rex Ibberson, were sued as the legal personal representatives of John Dallas Brodie, who was named as a residuary legatee of the testatrix

I   but predeceased her, and as such claimed a moiety of her estate by virtue of s. 33 of the Wills Act, 1837. The second and third defendants were Ian Oliver Anthony Dallas Brodie and Sandra Eleanor Florence Dallas Brodie who were the children of John Dallas Brodie, deceased, and claimed a moiety of the testatrix' estate as property undisposed of by the will. The fifth defendant was Roland Atkinson Sutherland who claimed one moiety of the estate as residuary

---

* Section 3 (1) is set out at p. 99, letter E, post.
† Section 33 is set out at p. 98, letter G, post.
‡ Section 1, so far as material, is set out at p. 98, letter I, to p. 99, letter A, post.

legatee and the other moiety thereof as property undisposed of by the will. The **A** application was for the determination of the following questions (i) an enquiry (which had been answered in the affirmative) whether John Dallas Brodie, deceased, was the legitimated son of the testatrix; (ii) whether the moiety of the testatrix' residuary estate by her will bequeathed to John Dallas Brodie devolved on her death:—(a) to the defendants Ethel Mabel Dallas Brodie and Brian Rex Ibberson as personal representatives of John Dallas Brodie on the **B** footing that he was the legitimated son of the testatrix or (b) to the defendants Ian Brodie and Sandra Brodie in equal shares on the like footing, or (c) to the defendant Roland Atkinson Sutherland on the footing that the testatrix left no legitimate issue, or (d) how otherwise the moiety devolved. The facts are set out in the judgment.

The case noted below* was cited during the argument in addition to the case **C** referred to in the judgment.

E. G. Wright for the plaintiff.
Martin Nourse for the first and second defendants.
L. L. Ware for the third and fourth defendants.
G. M. Godfrey for the fifth defendant.

D

STAMP, J.: On Dec. 13, 1956, Mrs. Eleanor Sutherland Brodie made her will and, after appointing executors and giving two pecuniary legacies, she devised and bequeathed all the residue of her estate to her executors subject to the payment of debts, funeral and testamentary expenses and death duties, and the legacies, with a direction to divide the residue equally between " my two sons Roland Sutherland and John Dallas Brodie ".

John Dallas Brodie was at the date of the will illegitimate. He was the illegiti- **E** mate son of the testatrix. On Oct. 29, 1959, he became legitimated by the effect of the Legitimacy Act, 1959. On June 21, 1962, he died leaving issue, and on Dec. 15, 1962, his mother died. The question is: what happens to the half share of residue given to him by the will? Does it, by the effect of s. 33 of the Wills Act, 1837, pass to his executors or is there an intestacy in respect thereof?

That question turns on the effect of the Legitimacy Act, 1926, and the **F** Legitimacy Act, 1959 in relation to s. 33 of the Wills Act, 1837, which provides as follows:

". . . Where any person being a child or other issue of the testator to whom any real or personal estate shall be devised or bequeathed for any estate or interest not determinable at or before the death of such person shall die in **G** the lifetime of the testator leaving issue, and any such issue of such person shall be living at the time of the death of the testator, such devise or bequest shall not lapse, but shall take effect as if the death of such person had happened immediately after the death of the testator, unless a contrary intention shall appear by the will."

Pausing there for a moment, it is abundantly clear that, but for the fact that he **H** was originally illegitimate, John Dallas Brodie or his personal representatives, would, on the death of the testatrix, have taken the half share of residue bequeathed to him and there would have been no lapse of the gift of that half share.

Then one comes to the Legitimacy Act, 1926. Section 1 provides:

" (1) Subject to the provisions of this section, where the parents of an **I** illegitimate person marry or have married one another, whether before or after the commencement of this Act, the marriage shall, if the father of the illegitimate person was or is at the date of the marriage domiciled in England or Wales, render that person, if living, legitimate from the commencement of this Act, or from the date of the marriage, whichever last happens. (2) Nothing in this Act shall operate to legitimate a person whose

---

* *Re Basioli (decd.), Re Depaoli, McGahey* v. *Depaoli*, [1953] 1 All E.R. 301; [1953] Ch. 367.

A father or mother was married to a third person when the illegitimate person was born."

I pause there to observe that sub-s. (2) was repealed by s. 1 (1) of the Legitimacy Act, 1959, and for the purposes of the present case s. 1 (1) of the Act of 1926 falls to be read (1) as if references to the commencement of the Legitimacy Act, 1926, were references to the commencement of the Legitimacy Act, 1959.
B It seems to me that, if there was nothing more in either of the Legitimacy Acts than that, an illegitimate child legitimated by the Act would be legitimated for all the purposes of the law, and in my judgment if the matter had to be considered in that way it would be abundantly clear that s. 33 of the Wills Act, 1837, would apply so as to render the gift to John Dallas Brodie an effective one.

C Subsection (3) of s. 1 of the Act of 1926, however, provides as follows:

" The legitimation of a person under this Act does not enable him or his spouse, children or remoter issue to take any interest in real or personal property save as is hereinafter in this Act expressly provided."

It seems to me that the very existence of that subsection underlines the point which I have just made, that sub-s. (1), construed in its ordinary sense, would
D operate to make the illegitimate child a child for all purposes, including the purpose of s. 33 of the Wills Act, 1837. It is, however, clear that sub-s. (3) prevents this happening, and one then turns to s. 3 of the Act of 1926 and finds this provision:

" (1) Subject to the provisions of this Act, a legitimated person and his
E spouse, children or more remote issue shall be entitled to take any interest—
(*a*) in the estate of an intestate dying after the date of legitimation;
(*b*) under any disposition coming into operation after the date of legitimation;
(*c*) by descent under an entailed interest created after the date of legitimation; in like manner as if the legitimated person had been born legitimate."

F There is a definition clause to which my attention was directed, but I do not think that it assists the conclusion of the present case.

The position appears to me to be this. By the effect of the Acts of 1926 and of 1959, the late Mr. Brodie was a legitimated person within s. 3 of the Act of 1926. Therefore he was, by the effect of that section, entitled to take any interest under any disposition coming into operation after the date of his legitimation in
G 1959, in like manner as if he had been born legitimate. Here, in the will of the testatrix, was a disposition which did come into operation after the date of Mr. Brodie's legitimation, and in my judgment it follows that he is entitled to take under that disposition as if he had been born legitimate.

If he had been born legitimate he would have taken under the disposition, because in my judgment s. 33 of the Wills Act, 1837, clearly so provides. The
H only argument to the contrary seems to me to be this: that since, at the date of his own death, he had only a spes successionis, he was not able to take under a disposition which did not come into operation till after his death. In my judgment the short answer to that contention is to be found in *Re Scott* (2). There the Court of Appeal held that a man was competent to dispose of property which, subsequent to his death, fell into his estate by the effect of s. 33. If a child whose
I personal representatives take by the effect of the Wills Act, 1837, can be said to be competent to dispose of the interest, the interest must, in my judgment, be one properly described in the terms of s. 3 (1) (*b*) of the Legitimacy Act, 1926, as an interest which the child is to be entitled to take. If the child is competent to dispose of the interest it can only be so if, taking it by the effect of s. 33 of the Wills Act, 1837, which refers to dispositions, he takes it under a disposition

(1) See s. 1 (2) of the Legitimacy Act, 1959.
(2) [1901] 1 K.B. 228.

within s. 3 (1) (*b*). That seems to me to be the logical answer to the question which **A**
I have to decide, but I would like to add this, that if it is wrong and s. 3 (1) (*b*)
of the Act of 1926 does not apply to an interest which a child can take under
s. 33 of the Wills Act, 1837, it must, in my judgment, inevitably follow that that
interest is not such an interest as is referred to in s. 1 (3) of the Act of 1926, and
if it does not fall within s. 1 (3), then there is nothing so far as I can see to prevent
a legitimated child taking it simply by the effect of s. 1 (1).   **B**

Order accordingly.

Solicitors: *Durrant Cooper & Hambling*, agents for *Edge & Ellison*, Birmingham (for the plaintiff); *Jaques & Co.*, agents for *Hill & Perks*, Norwich (for the
first and second defendants);   *Bird & Bird*, agents for *Sydney Mitchell & Co.*,
Birmingham (for the third and fourth defendants); *J. E. Lickfold & Sons*, agents
for *Morgan, Lugsdin & Haskins*, Birmingham (for the fifth defendant).   **C**

[*Reported by* JENIFER SANDELL, *Barrister-at-Law.*]

MILLS *v.* COOPER.   **D**

[QUEEN'S BENCH DIVISION (Lord Parker, C.J., Diplock, L.J., and Ashworth, J.),
March 8, 9, 1967.]

Highway—Obstruction—Camping by "gipsy" on highway—Information alleging
  offence in December, 1965, dismissed—Magistrates not satisfied that accused
  a gipsy—Subsequent information charging a like offence in March, 1966—   **E**
  Whether issue estoppel—Whether second information abuse of process of
  court—Highways Act, 1959 (7 & 8 Eliz. 2 c. 25), s. 127 (c).

In February, 1966, a magistrates' court dismissed an information preferred
against the respondent charging that, in December, 1965, he, being a gipsy,
did without lawful authority or excuse encamp on a highway, contrary
to s. 127* of the Highways Act, 1959, a submission of no case to answer   **F**
being upheld by the magistrates at the end of the prosecution case on the
ground that they were not satisfied that the respondent was a gipsy.   In
May, 1966, a second information was preferred against the respondent
charging a like offence in March, 1966.   Before the respondent was asked to
plead, a submission was made on his behalf that the question whether he
was a gipsy had been argued on the earlier occasion as a separate issue,   **G**
that the court had found in his favour, and that thus an issue estoppel arose
which would debar the magistrates from re-opening the question and
hearing the information.   The magistrates did not accept that contention,
since they were in doubt whether the doctrine of issue estoppel was applicable
in criminal law, but they dismissed the information on the ground that
it was oppressive and an abuse of the process of the court.   On appeal by   **H**
the prosecutor,

Held: the case must be remitted to the magistrates to continue the
hearing, because—
  (i) the doctrine of issue estoppel did not apply, since the issue determined
in the previous proceedings was that the respondent was not a gipsy in
December, 1965, whereas in the present case the issue to be determined   **I**
was whether he was a gipsy in March, 1966 (see p. 103, letter D, and p.
105, letters E and I, post).
  (ii) the word "gipsy" in the context of s. 127 (c) of the Highways Act,
1959, did not mean a member of the Romany race, but meant a person
leading a nomadic life without fixed abode (see p. 103, letter H, p.
104, letter F, and p. 105, letter I, post); accordingly being a gipsy was

---

* Section 127, so far as material, is set out at p. 103, letter F, post.

Dicta of LORD PARKER CJ and DIPLOCK LJ at 104, 105 applied in DPP v HUMPHRYS [1976] 2 All ER 497

Dictum of DIPLOCK LJ at 104 applied in ARNOLD v NATIONAL WESTMINSTER BANK [1990] 1 All ER 529

Considered in McILKENNY v CHIEF CONSTABLE [1980] 2 All ER 227

Dictum of DIPLOCK LJ at 104 approved in HUNTER v CHIEF CONSTABLE [1981] 3 All ER 727

Considered in ARNOLD v NATION WESTMINSTER BANK PLC [1988] 3 All 977

A   not an unalterable status and it did not necessarily follow from the incorrectness of an assertion of that status in December, 1965, that an assertion of that status in March, 1966, would be incorrect (see p. 103, letter I, p. 104, letter F, and p. 105, letter I, post).

Appeal allowed.

B   **[Editorial Note.** On the question of the availability of issue estoppel in criminal cases, see *Connelly* v. *Director of Public Prosecutions* ([1964] 2 All E.R. 401; sub nom. *R.* v. *Connelly*, [1963] 3 All E.R. 510).

As to issue estoppel, see 15 HALSBURY's LAWS (3rd Edn.) 181-183, para. 355; and for cases on the subject, see 21 DIGEST (Repl.) 227, 228, *234-236*; 230, *237-240*.

C   As to obstructions on highways, see SUPPLEMENT to 19 HALSBURY's LAWS (3rd Edn.), para. 456A, 2.

For the Highways Act, 1959, s. 127, see 39 HALSBURY's STATUTES (2nd Edn.) 546.]

Cases referred to:

Hoystead v. *Taxation Comr.*, [1925] All E.R. Rep. 56; [1926] A.C. 155; 94 L.J.P.C. 79; 134 L.T. 354; 21 Digest (Repl.) 249, *330.*

D   *Mraz* v. *R. (No. 2)*, (1956), 96 C.L.R. 62.   Dictum of DIPLOCK LJ at 104 applied
R. v. *Wilkes*, (1948), 77 C.L.R. 511.   in R v GOVERNOR OF BRIXTON, EX P
OSMAN (No 1) [1992] 1 All ER 108

Case Stated.

This was a Case Stated by justices of the county of Kent in respect of their adjudication as a magistrates' court sitting at Sevenoaks on May 27, 1966, when
E   the justices reserved their decision, giving it on June 10, 1966. On Apr. 27, 1966, an information was preferred by the appellant, William Leonard Mills, against the respondent, Abraham Cooper, charging that, on Mar. 13, 1966, at No Man's Land, Dane Bottom, Dunton Green, being a gipsy, he did without lawful authority or excuse encamp on a highway, contrary to s. 127 of the Highways Act, 1959. The following facts were proved or admitted. On Jan. 5, 1966,
F   an information was preferred by Leslie Alfred Feaver, an inspector of police, against the respondent, charging that on Dec. 22, 1965, at No Man's Land, Pilgrims Way West at the junction of Dane Bottom, Dunton Green, being a gipsy, he did without lawful authority or excuse encamp on a highway, contrary to s. 127 of the Highways Act, 1959, the venue referred to in that connexion, although slightly differently described, being the same as that referred to in the information dated Apr. 27, 1966, the respondent not having moved in the mean-
G   time. On Feb. 25, 1966, the magistrates' court sitting at Sevenoaks in the county of Kent heard the information. It was then contended by the respondent, inter alia, that the offence with which he was charged had four ingredients, the first of which was " being a gipsy "; that there was no statutory definition of " gipsy ", the definition of " gipsy " contained in the SHORTER OXFORD
H   ENGLISH DICTIONARY being cited; that the language of the section must not be taken to be tautologous; that there must be a technical meaning; that the rules of construction and interpretation of statutes bound the court; and that in any event whether the definition was the dictionary definition or the popular definition as contended by the appellant the evidence before the court was insufficient on this issue to support a conviction and that the information should
I   be dismissed. The court was of the opinion (i) that " being a gipsy " was an essential part of the offence, and (ii) that the evidence thereof was insufficient to support a conviction; and the information was accordingly dismissed at the close of the case for the prosecution after the submissions made, and without any evidence being given, by or on behalf of the respondent.

At the hearing before the justices on May 27, 1966, it was contended by the respondent, before he was asked to plead, that, in the course of the proceedings referred to above, the question whether the respondent was a gipsy had been argued before the court as a separate issue and that the court had determined

that issue in his favour, and, accordingly, there was an issue estoppel which **A**
would debar the justices from re-opening the question, and hearing this information.   It was also contended by the respondent further or in the alternative
that, having regard to the proceedings on Feb. 25, 1966, the present proceedings
were oppressive of the respondent and an abuse of the process of the court
and should accordingly be stayed by the justices in the exercise of their jurisdiction and discretion so to do.   It was contended by the appellant that the doctrine **B**
of issue estoppel had never been introduced into the criminal law, and did not
arise in this case.   It was further contended by the appellant that the magistrates' court sitting at Sevenoaks on Feb. 25, 1966, did not finally and conclusively determine that the respondent was not a gipsy and that, accordingly,
the present proceedings were not oppressive and it would not be an abuse of
the process of the court if the justices were to hear this second information. **C**
It was conceded by the appellant that it would be an abuse of the process of the
court if (contrary to his contention) he were seeking to re-open an issue which
had already been finally determined and that, if he were seeking so to do the
justices would have jurisdiction to stay the proceedings.

The justices dismissed the information, and the appellant now appealed.

The authorities and cases noted below* were cited during the argument in **D**
addition to the cases referred to in the judgment of DIPLOCK, L.J.

M. C. Parker for the appellant.

B. T. Wigoder, Q.C., and *S. J. Sedley* for the respondent.

LORD PARKER, C.J.: This is an appeal by way of Case Stated from a
decision of justices in the county of Kent sitting at Sevenoaks, who on May 27, **E**
1966, dismissed an information preferred by the appellant against the respondent
that he, on Mar. 13, 1966, at a place called No Man's Land, Dane Bottom, Dunton
Green, being a gipsy did without lawful authority or excuse encamp on a highway,
contrary to s. 127 of the Highways Act, 1959.   They dismissed the information
on the ground that the proceedings before them were oppressive and an abuse
of the process of the court. The decision was made in the following circumstances: **F**
at an earlier date, namely, on Feb. 25, 1966, the magistrates' court at Sevenoaks
had dismissed a similar information preferred against the respondent that he, on
Dec. 22, 1965, at the same place being a gipsy did without lawful authority or
excuse encamp on a highway.   That information was dismissed at the end of
the prosecution case on a submission of no case.   The justices in the instant case
find that the basis of that submission of no case and the reason for the dismissal **G**
of the information by the justices on that earlier occasion was that they, the
justices, were not satisfied that the respondent was a gipsy.   Accordingly, when
the present proceedings were called on and before the respondent was asked to
plead, a submission was made on his behalf that the question whether the
respondent was a gipsy had been argued before the court on the earlier occasion
as a separate issue, and that the court had determined that issue in his favour, and, **H**
accordingly, the submission went on, there was an issue estoppel which would
debar the justices from re-opening the question and hearing the information.
The justices felt unable to accept that contention, since they were left in doubt
whether the doctrine of issue estoppel was applicable in the criminal law; they
did, however, feel that, in all the circumstances, they had power to dismiss
the information on the ground that it was oppressive and an abuse of the process **I**
of the court, and they exercised their discretion so to do.

Before coming to the ground on which the justices dismissed the information,
it is necessary to consider this question of issue estoppel; indeed, counsel for

---

* SHORTER OXFORD ENGLISH DICTIONARY, "Gipsy"; *Phosphate Sewage Co., Ltd.*
v. *Molleson*, (1879), 4 App. Cas. 801;   *Welton* v. *Taneborne*, (1908), 99 L.T. 668;
New Brunswick Ry. Co. v. *British and French Trust Corpn., Ltd.*, [1938] 4 All E.R. 747;
[1939] A.C. 1;   *Sealfon* v. *United States*, (1948), 332 U.S. 575;   *Sambasivam* v. *Public
Prosecutor, Federation of Malaya,* [1950] A.C. 458;   *Connelly* v. *Director of Public Prosecutions,* [1964] 2 All E.R. 401;   [1964] A.C. 1254;   *R.* v. *Andrews,* [1967] 1 All E.R. 170.

A　the respondent before this court says, and I think rightly, that this, if anything, is really a case of issue estoppel, though he does in the alternative support the magistrates' action in dismissing the information on the ground that the proceedings were oppressive. Counsel's argument is to this effect, that, as a result of an earlier determination by a court of competent jurisdiction as between the same parties that the respondent was not a gipsy, there is a clear case of issue

B　estoppel which should be applied so as to prevent the same issue being re-litigated. He urged that, both on principle and authority, there was no reason why the doctrine of issue estoppel should not be applied in criminal cases, provided always that it is possible to ascertain exactly what issue had been in fact determined, which is rare in the case of a verdict of a jury. This, he said, was one of the rare cases in which it was possible to find out exactly what had been

C　determined, and, indeed, this had been found as a fact by the justices in the Case. For my part, I am by no means convinced, for reasons into which I find it unnecessary to go, that the doctrine as applied in civil cases has any application in criminal cases at all. I will, however, assume for the purposes of this case that it has. Even so, I am satisfied that it has no application in the present case, since the issue determined on the earlier occasion was that the respondent was

D　not a gipsy on Dec. 22, 1965, whereas the issue to be determined on the second occasion was whether he was a gipsy on Mar. 13, 1966. It was urged that the word " gipsy " should be given its dictionary meaning, as being a member of the Romany race, and that, once it was decided by a court that he was not a member of that race, the matter could not be re-litigated except in the event of there being fresh evidence which could not by reasonable diligence have been

E　adduced on the earlier hearing. Were that the true meaning of the word " gipsy ", then I think that it would be necessary to consider further the application of the doctrine of issue estoppel in criminal cases; I am, however, quite satisfied that " gipsy " in this context cannot bear that meaning.

　　Section 127 of the Highways Act, 1959, is dealing with obstruction and the depositing of things on the highway; it provides that:

F
　　" If, without lawful authority or excuse,—(*a*) a person deposits on a made-up carriageway, or on any highway which consists of or comprises a made-up carriageway within fifteen feet from the centre of that carriageway, any dung, compost or other material for dressing land, or any rubbish, or (*b*) a person deposits anything whatsoever on a highway to the interruption

G　of any user of the highway, or (*c*) a hawker or other itinerant trader or a gipsy pitches a booth, stall or stand, or encamps, on a highway, he shall be guilty of an offence . . ."

　　That a man is of the Romany race is, as it seems to me, something which is really too vague of ascertainment, and impossible to prove; moreover, it is, I think, difficult to think that Parliament intended to subject a man to a penalty in the

H　context of causing litter and obstruction on the highway merely by reason of his race. I think that, in this context, " gipsy " means no more than a person leading a nomadic life with no, or no fixed, employment and with no fixed abode. In saying that, I am hoping that those words will not be considered as the words of a statute, but merely as conveying the general colloquial idea of a gipsy. Looked at in that way, a man might well not be a gipsy on one date and yet be one on a

I　later date. I cannot think that the doctrine of issue estoppel, even if applicable at all in criminal cases, is applicable except in cases where the determination is as to something which has taken place on a particular day, or as to something like the date of a man's birth, which can never vary and has no application whatever to a state of affairs, as here, when a man may be described as a gipsy on one day, and may well not be so described on another day. In those circumstances, I think that the justices were right in so far as they did not apply the doctrine of issue estoppel.

So far as the ground on which they did dismiss the information was concerned, **A** every court has undoubtedly a right in its discretion to decline to hear proceedings on the ground that they are oppressive and an abuse of the process of the court. Once, however, one approaches this matter on the basis of the meaning of " gipsy " as a man leading a nomadic life, it is, I think, impossible to say that there were any circumstances here which entitled the justices to say that proceedings brought some two and a half months later on this issue whether the **B** respondent was a gipsy could in any sense of the word be said to be oppressive and an abuse of the process of the court. Accordingly, in my judgment this appeal succeeds and the Case should go back to the justices to continue the hearing.

DIPLOCK, L.J.: I agree that the word " gipsy " as used in s. 127 (c) of the Highways Act, 1959, cannot bear its dictionary meaning of a member of a **C** wandering race (by themselves called Romany) of Hindu origin. If it did, it would mean that Parliament in 1959 had amended the corresponding section of the Highway Act, 1835, (1) which referred to " gipsy or other person " so as to discriminate against persons by reason of their racial origin alone. It would raise other difficulties too. How pure blooded a Romany must one be to fall into the definition? The section is a penal section and should, I suppose, be strictly **D** construed as requiring pure Romany descent. As members of this race first appeared in England not later than the beginning of the sixteenth century, and have not in the intervening centuries been notorious for the abundance of their written records, it would be impossible to prove Romany origin even as far back as the sixteenth century, let alone through the earlier centuries of their peripatetic history from India to the shores of this island. The section, so far as it referred **E** to " gipsy ", would be incapable in practice of having any application at all. Confronted by these difficulties, counsel for the respondant only faintly argued that the word " gipsy " in the context of the section does not bear its popular meaning, which I would define as a person without fixed abode who leads a nomadic life, dwelling in tents or other shelters, or in caravans or other vehicles. If this meaning is adopted, it follows that being a gipsy is not an unalterable **F** status. It cannot be said " once a gipsy always a gipsy ". By changing his way of life a modern Borrow may be a gipsy at one time and not a gipsy at another. It is in the light of this meaning to be attached to the word " gipsy " that the question of any so-called " issue estoppel " must be considered in the present case.

The doctrine of issue estoppel in civil proceedings is of fairly recent and sporadic development, though none the worse for that. Although *Hoystead* v. *Taxation* **G** *Commissioner* (2) did not purport to break new ground, it can be regarded as the starting point of the modern common law doctrine, the application of which to different kinds of civil actions is currently being worked out in the courts. This doctrine, so far as it affects civil proceedings, may be stated thus: a party to civil proceedings is not entitled to make, as against the other party, an assertion, whether of fact or of the legal consequences of facts, the correctness of which is **H** an essential element in his cause of action or defence, if the same assertion was an essential element in his previous cause of action or defence in previous civil proceedings between the same parties or their predecessors in title and was found by a court of competent jurisdiction in such previous civil proceedings to be incorrect, unless further material which is relevant to the correctness or incorrectness of the assertion and could not by reasonable diligence have been adduced **I** by that party in the previous proceedings has since become available to him. Whatever may be said of other rules of law to which the label of " estoppel " is attached, " issue estoppel " is not a rule of evidence. True, subject to the qualification which I have stated, it has the effect of preventing the party " estopped " from calling evidence to show that the assertion which is the subject of the " issue estoppel " is incorrect, but this is because the existence of the " issue estoppel " results in there being no issue in the subsequent civil proceedings to

(1) Section 72.   (2) [1925] All E.R. Rep. 56; [1926] A.C. 155.

A which such evidence would be relevant. Issue estoppel is a particular application of the general rule of public policy that there should be finality in litigation.

That general rule applies also to criminal proceedings, but in a form modified by the distinctive character of criminal as compared with civil litigation. Here it takes the form of the rule against double jeopardy, of which the simplest application is to be found in the pleas of autrefois convict and autrefois acquit, B but the rule against double jeopardy also applies in circumstances in which these ancient pleas are not strictly available, and it is in connexion with the wider application that the High Court of Australia in particular in the cases cited (*R.* v. *Wilkes* (3) and *Mraz* v. *R.* (*No.* 2) (4)) has used the same expression as is used in civil proceedings: " issue estoppel ". For my part, I think with great respect that the use of this expression in criminal and civil proceedings alike may C lead to confusion, for there are obvious differences—lack of mutuality is but one— between the application of the rule against double jeopardy in criminal cases, and the rule that there should be finality in civil litigation. It is unnecessary, however, in the present appeal to inquire into the precise limits of the wider application of the rule against double jeopardy (5) to situations in which the pleas of autrefois convict and autrefois acquit are not strictly available, for it is D nowhere suggested that they are wide enough to prevent the prosecution in criminal proceedings against a defendant against whom previous criminal proceedings have been brought from making an assertion which he would not have been debarred by " issue estoppel " from making if the two sets of proceedings had been civil and not criminal.

In the present case the relevant assertion by the prosecution in the previous E criminal proceedings was: " that the respondent was a gipsy on Dec. 22, 1965 ". In the subsequent criminal proceedings in which this appeal is brought the relevant assertion by the prosecution was: " that the respondent was a gipsy on Mar. 13, 1966 ". Once it is recognised that being a gipsy is not an unalterable status but depends on the way of life which he is leading at any particular time, it is plain that the incorrectness of the assertion made in the previous proceedings F is not inconsistent with the correctness of the assertion made in the proceedings now under appeal. The magistrates, accordingly, would not have been right in holding that the prosecution were not entitled to, or were estopped from, asserting that the respondent was a gipsy on Mar. 13, 1966, and from proving it if they could.

One further observation: counsel for the respondent has contended that, even if this be so, the prosecution at the resumed hearing before the magistrates will G not be entitled to adduce any evidence which would by the exercise of reasonable diligence have been available to them at the time of the previous proceedings, and which tends to show that the respondent was already a gipsy on Dec. 22, 1965. For my part I do not think that there is any substance in this contention. Issue estoppel, as I have said, is not a rule of evidence. The prosecution will be entitled to call any evidence which is relevant to show that the respondent was a gipsy H on Mar. 13, 1966. Evidence as to his way of life before that date will be relevant, including evidence as to his way of life before as well as after Dec. 22, 1965. It matters not that such evidence might also tend to show that he was a gipsy on Dec. 22, 1965. That is not a matter to which the magistrates on the present prosecution have to address their minds. They have no jurisdiction to inquire into it.

As regards the contention that this prosecution was an abuse of the process of I the court, I have nothing to add to what my lord has already said.

ASHWORTH, J.: I agree with both judgments.

Appeal allowed. Case remitted.

Solicitors: *Sharpe, Pritchard & Co.*, agents for *A. C. Staples*, Maidstone (for the appellant); *Peter Kingshill* (for the respondent).

[*Reported by* N. P. METCALFE, ESQ., *Barrister-at-Law.*]

---

(3) (1948), 77 C.L.R. 511.   (4) (1956), 96 C.L.R. 62.
(5) Cf. *Director of Public Prosecutions* v. *Nasralla*, see p. 161, post.

FRISBY v. BRITISH BROADCASTING CORPORATION.   A

[CHANCERY DIVISION (Goff, J.), January 5, 6, 9, 10, 13, 1967.]

Copyright—Licence—Dramatic work—Alteration—Licensee has right to make
alterations except in so far as licence expressly or impliedly excludes right—
B.B.C. licensed by plaintiff, member of Screenwriters' Guild, to televise his
play—Right of B.B.C. to make alterations not expressly excluded by licence—   B
Agreement by B.B.C. with Screenwriters' Guild not to make structural altera-
tions of script without prior consent of author—B.B.C. claimed right to
excise two words from line—Whether agreement applied to licence—Whether
proposed alteration structural—Whether interlocutory injunction should be
granted.

By cl. 10* of an agreement, dated Oct. 1, 1963, made between the Screen-   C
writers' Guild and the British Broadcasting Corporation, in respect of plays
specially written for television (" the Guild agreement "), it was provided
that the B.B.C. should not without the author's prior consent make any
structural alterations, as opposed to minor alterations, in the script. In 1965
the B.B.C. commissioned the plaintiff, a member of the Guild, to write a television play for delivery by Dec. 31, 1965. In June, 1965, the plaintiff drew   D
the attention of the B.B.C.'s script editor to a line of dialogue which the
plaintiff proposed to include, and which he regarded as the pivot or key-line,
and sought assurance that it would be included in the televised production.
The plaintiff prepared and submitted to the B.B.C. a five-page synopsis,
which included the line. The plaintiff was asked to proceed on the basis
of the synopsis. By cl. 1 of the written contract between the B.B.C. and the   E
plaintiff by his agent, made in July, 1965 (" the July contract† ") in consideration of a fee (payable half on the signature of the contract and half on
acceptance by the B.B.C. of the play as suitable for television) the plaintiff
granted to the B.B.C., inter alia, the exclusive right to televise a performance
of the play once only during a period of two years from delivery of the full
script. Clause 2 of the July contract, which was comparable with cl. 9 of the   F
Guild agreement, read—" The B.B.C. will use [their] best endeavours to
state within a month from delivery of the full script whether the work is
acceptable as it stands or whether the B.B.C. [require] any alterations to be
undertaken by the writer to make the work acceptable for television use,
or whether the B.B.C. [do] not wish to proceed with the work (in which
case all rights therein shall revert to the writer and no further payments shall   G
be due from the B.B.C.) ". The July contract contained a note that its
terms accorded with those of the Guild agreement, but the July contract did
not expressly incorporate that agreement. In January, 1966, the plaintiff
delivered the full script and received the balance of his fee. By June, 1966,
at latest, the B.B.C. had accepted the script with certain agreed alterations made by the plaintiff; these did not alter the line in question. In   H
July, 1966, when the greater part of the production costs had been incurred, the B.B.C. objected to the line on the ground that it would offend the
majority of viewers and claimed the right to excise two words from it. On
motion by the plaintiff for an interlocutory injunction restraining the B.B.C.
from televising the play otherwise than in accordance with the script containing alterations made by the plaintiff,   I

Held: (i) (a) on its true construction the July contract constituted
the grant of a licence to televise the play, not a partial assignment of the
copyright in the play (see p. 114, letter E, post).

(b) a person licensed to publish copyright material had the right to make
alterations, even substantial ones, except in so far as the licence, expressly

---

* The material provisions of cl. 10 are set out at p. 109, letter F, post.

† The material provisions of the July contract are set out at p. 107, letter I, et seq.,
post.

A   or by implication, restricted that right; but the court would readily imply
a term limiting the right to make alterations (see p. 115, letters D and H,
post).

(ii) the B.B.C. were precluded from making structural alterations within
cl. 10 of the Guild agreement after acceptance of the full script because there
was a sufficient prima facie case that the Guild agreement applied, except
B   in so far as it was expressly or impliedly excluded by the July contract, and,
since cl. 2 of the July contract was spent once the script was accepted, the
Guild agreement was not in fact excluded (see p. 115, letter I, p. 116,
letter F, and p. 116, letter I, to p. 117, letter A, post).

(iii) the plaintiff had made out a prima facie case that the proposed
alteration was structural within cl. 10 of the Guild agreement, and accord-
C   ingly an interlocutory injunction would be granted (see p. 117, letter I, and
p. 118, letter G, post).

[As to the right of publishers to alter manuscripts, see 30 HALSBURY's LAWS
(3rd Edn.) 565, para. 1086; and for cases on the subject, see 37 DIGEST (Repl.)
420, 421, *37-41.*

As to the rights of licensees of copyright work, see 8 HALSBURY's LAWS (3rd
D   Edn.) 409, para. 745; and as to the distinction between a licence and an
assignment, see ibid., pp. 414, 415, para. 758.

For the Copyright Act, 1956, s. 37, see 36 HALSBURY's STATUTES (2nd Edn.) 131.]

Cases referred to:

Beswick v. *Beswick*, [1966] 3 All E.R. 1; [1966] Ch. 538; [1966] 3 W.L.R. 396.
City & Westminster Properties (1934), Ltd. v. *Mudd*, [1958] 2 All E.R. 733;
E   [1959] Ch. 129; [1958] 3 W.L.R. 312; Digest (Cont. Vol. A) 1027,
6376a.
Heilbut, Symons & Co. v. *Buckleton*, [1911-13] All E.R. Rep. 83; [1913] A.C.
30; 82 L.J.K.B. 245; 107 L.T. 769; 9 Digest (Repl.) 259, *1643.*
Joseph v. *National Magazine Co., Ltd.*, [1958] 3 All E.R. 52; [1959] Ch. 14;
[1958] 3 W.L.R. 366; 37 Digest (Repl.) 421, *41.*

F   **Motion.**

In an action commenced by writ issued on Dec. 22, 1966, Terence Frisby, the
plaintiff, claimed against the defendants, British Broadcasting Corporation
(" the B.B.C. "): (i) an injunction restraining the defendants from doing whether
by themselves their servants or agents or otherwise howsoever the following acts
or any of them, that is to say televising any performance or transmitting or
G   licensing the transmission of any recording or televising or licensing any recording
or using any recording of any rehearsal or television performance for any purpose
or making dubbings into foreign languages of the play written by the plaintiff
entitled " And Some Have Greatness Thrust Upon Them "; alternatively (ii) an
injunction restraining the defendants from doing whether by themselves their
H   servants or agents or otherwise howsoever the following acts or any of them, that
is to say televising any performance or transmitting or licensing the transmission
of any recording or televising or licensing any recording or using any recording
of any rehearsal or television performance for any purpose or to make dubbings
into foreign languages of the play written by the plaintiff entitled " And Some
Have Greatness Thrust Upon Them " otherwise than in accordance with the script
I   containing the alterations made by the plaintiff delivered by the plaintiff to the
defendants in or about June, 1966, and (iii) damages. By notice of motion dated
Dec. 22, 1966, the plaintiff gave notice that he would apply for interlocutory
injunctions until the trial of the action or further order in the same alternative
forms as (i) and (ii) set out in the writ.

The relevant television contract, dated July 6, 1965 (" the July contract "),
signed on behalf of the B.B.C. and by the plaintiff's agent, provided as follows—

" 1. In consideration of payment by the B.B.C. to the [plaintiff] or his
agent of a fee of £725 (payable half on the signature of this agreement and

half on the acceptance by the B.B.C. of the undermentioned material as   A
suitable for television) the [plaintiff] hereby grants to the B.B.C. the following
rights in the seventy-five minute television play ' The Trouble with Mary '
for delivery by Dec. 31, 1965 (hereinafter called ' the work '):—

" (i) The exclusive right to televise during a period of two years from the
date of delivery of the full script to the B.B.C. a performance of the work,
once only, simultaneously or non-simultaneously, live and/or recorded, from   B
all or any of the B.B.C.'s transmitters in the United Kingdom.

" (ii) The exclusive right to televise repeat performances of the work during
a period of two years from delivery of the script or one year from the date
of the initial B.B.C. performance, whichever be the longer, subject to
payment on broadcasting taking place of fifty per cent. of the initial B.B.C.
fee for each repeat given simultaneously or non-simultaneously, live and/or   C
recorded, from all or any of the B.B.C.'s transmitters in the United Kingdom.

" (iii) During a period of six months from the date of the initial B.B.C.
performance a right to acquire an exclusive option (which may be taken up
during a period of one year from the date of the initial B.B.C. performance)
to purchase the exclusive right to transmit or to licence the transmission of a
recording of the work in any overseas country subject to payment of a fee   D
(which shall not be returnable in any event and which shall be set off against
any subsequent payments due in respect of overseas sales under (iv) below)
to be calculated in respect of any particular countries at twenty-five per cent.
of the fee which would be payable under (iv) below if the option for those
particular countries is taken up by the B.B.C.

" (iv) In respect of those countries for which the B.B.C. has taken up an   E
exclusive option acquired in accordance with (iii) above the exclusive right
to televise or to license a recording of the work to be televised during a
period of five years from the date of the initial B.B.C. performance without
restriction as to the number of transmissions, subject to payment to the
[plaintiff] of the amounts specified below on such rights being taken up by the
B.B.C. within one year from the date of the initial B.B.C. performance . . .   F

" (v) The right to make a recording of any rehearsal or television performance of the work and to use it for the private purposes of the B.B.C.
and/or for televising excerpts therefrom in programmes of a historic or remin-
iscent nature or in trailer programmes and/or for any of the purposes specified
in (i) to (iv) above, the right to make dubbings of the recordings into foreign
languages and/or to add foreign language sub-titles for the purpose of effecting   G
sales in accordance with (iii) and (iv) above.

" 2. The B.B.C. will use [their] best endeavours to state within a month
of delivery of the full script whether the work is acceptable as it stands, or
whether the B.B.C. [require] any alterations to be undertaken by the
[plaintiff] to make the work acceptable for television use, or whether the
B.B.C. [do] not wish to proceed with the work (in which case all rights therein   H
shall revert to the [plaintiff] and no further payments shall be due from the
B.B.C.).

" 3. The [plaintiff] hereby warrants that he will not license or sell the
work for use on television in any country during a period between signature
of this agreement and six months after the date of the initial B.B.C. performance or, if the B.B.C. [exercise] rights under 1 (iii) and/or (iv) above,   I
in any of the countries in question until the expiration of such rights, and
he further warrants that the work shall be an original work which does not
infringe the copyright or any other right of any other person and further that
it contains no defamatory matter.

Date...............   Signed..............

"NOTE: The terms of this agreement accord with those agreed by the
B.B.C. with the Screen Writers Guild for specially commissioned series and
serials."

A   By an agreement dated Oct. 1, 1963, and made between the Screenwriters' Guild and the B.B.C., it was provided, so far as is material to this report, as follows:—

" 1. *Scope of agreement.* This agreement covers any complete and original play specially written for B.B.C. television having a duration of at least fifteen minutes in broadcasting time and not being a television play written

B   for schools programmes and a childrens puppet play.

" 3. *Initial B.B.C. performance.* For the payment negotiated in accordance with cl. 2 above the B.B.C. shall have the exclusive right to transmit within two years from the date of delivery of the completed script, a performance of the work, once only simultaneously or non-simultaneously, live and/or recorded, from all or any of the B.B.C. transmitters in the

C   United Kingdom."

" 9. *Delivery of Commissioned Scripts and Method of Payment.* (a) Within fourteen days of formal commissioning the B.B.C. will pay to the writer or his agent fifty per cent. of the agreed fee.

" (b) The B.B.C. shall have a period of one month from delivery to decide whether the commissioned script as delivered is acceptable as it stands, or whether it requires certain alterations to be undertaken by the writer to

D   make it acceptable for television use, or whether the script is to be abandoned altogether.

" (c) If the script is acceptable as it stands the B.B.C. shall thereupon pay to the writer or his agent the balance of the agreed fee.

" (d) If the script requires further alterations by the writer to make it

E   suitable, in the opinion of the B.B.C., for television, then the second half of the fee shall not become payable until such alterations as are required have been carried out to the satisfaction of the B.B.C. If the script is abandoned [under] (b), all rights therein shall revert to the writer and no further payment shall be due from the B.B.C.

" 10. *Alteration of Scripts.* The B.B.C. shall not without the prior consent

F   of the writer or his agent (which consent shall not be unreasonably withheld) make any structural alterations as opposed to minor alterations to the transmission script, provided that such consent shall not be necessary in any case where the writer is for any reason not immediately available for consultation at the time which in the opinion of the B.B.C. is the deadline from the production point of view for such alterations to be made if rehearsals and

G   transmissions are to proceed as planned."

The facts are stated in the judgment, infra.

P. R. Oliver, Q.C., and *C. F. Dehn* for the plaintiff.
C. A. Settle, Q.C., and *D. H. Mervyn Davies* for the B.B.C.

Cur. adv. vult.

H

Jan. 13.   **GOFF, J.**, read the following judgment: In this case the plaintiff, who is an actor, director and playwright, wrote a play specially commissioned by the defendants (" the B.B.C. ") for television and originally intended to be entitled, " The Trouble With Mary ", but afterwards called, " And Some Have Greatness Thrust Upon Them ". This contains a line by a female character

I   spoken in relation to sexual intercourse: " My friend Sylv told me it was safe standing up " followed incidentally by an ejaculation " She, eh? " by another character, a television interviewer, though his two words have not been much referred to in the argument.

The plaintiff says that the whole idea of the play germinated in his mind from his hearing about a girl in real life who spoke an almost identical line and that that very line is essential to, and indeed the climax of, the play. The B.B.C., on the other hand, say that it is of minor, if any, importance and can safely be dispensed with or modified and that, as it would or might give offence to the public, it must

be sacrificed. At one stage the argument proceeded as if they were proposing **A**
to delete the line altogether, but as appears from a letter of July 13, 1966, to
which I will refer in more detail later, what they really intend is to alter the line
by omitting the words " standing up " and also to omit the subsequent ejaculation
" She, eh? ", and at least at the hearing it was made clear that that is all that they
will do. The plaintiff is not satisfied even with that, and contends that the B.B.C.
must either include the line verbatim or not produce the play at all, and he offered **B**
at an early stage of the dispute to refund his fee if the B.B.C. adopted the alternative of abandoning the play. The B.B.C., however, said that they could not drop
the play because they had spent too much on it over and above the plaintiff's
fee and they claim the right to produce it with the modified line. In the result,
therefore, the plaintiff has brought this action claiming an injunction restraining
the B.B.C. from televising the play at all on the ground that by their conduct **C**
they have repudiated the contract with him, and, alternatively, a limited form
of injunction restraining them from omitting or altering the line.

It appears that the plaintiff first approached the script editor of B.B.C. Television, who doubted whether the line would be permitted. Therefore, early in
June, 1965, the plaintiff went and saw a Mr. Seth-Smith whose pen name is
James Brabazon, the B.B.C.'s story and script editor for their series " Theatre **D**
625 " on B.B.C. 2. The plaintiff's evidence is that he told Mr. Brabazon that the
line was of absolute and basic importance and that he was not interested in
writing the play at all if he could not have the line in the production when
televised, and that Mr. Brabazon agreed to this subject to consulting his superiors.
Mr. Brabazon, however, has deposed that all that he said was that once the
subject-matter of the play was accepted he thought that the line would be **E**
accepted as well and that the plaintiff should go ahead on that basis. He said
that he had no recollection of the plaintiff speaking of the line as of absolute
and basic importance and continued:

> " So far as I was concerned all that happened at our meeting really was
> that the plaintiff outlined his play and I suggested that he put it in writing and
> let me have it."   **F**

The plaintiff (as he says) in order to make sure that the line would be accepted
prepared a five page synopsis in which he specifically included it and submitted
this to Mr. Brabazon that same month. His evidence again is that about ten days
later Mr. Brabazon telephoned and said that he had submitted the synopsis to
" the powers that be " and they had confirmed that the play was " O.K." with **G**
the line, which would be allowed, and that Mr. Brabazon asked him to proceed
in accordance with the synopsis. Mr. Brabazon did in fact discuss the synopsis
with his superiors, a Mr. Messina, producer of plays, and a Mr. Bakewell then
Head of Plays, and he admits that he drew the latter's attention specifically to
the line. Mr. Bakewell himself confirms this and says that it is not normal
procedure for him to be asked to read a synopsis but that it is done when the work **H**
is likely to pose certain problems. He says that he read and approved the synopsis
and said that he thought the line would be probably acceptable.

Mr. Brabazon's evidence then is that following this conversation he telephoned
to the plaintiff and told him that a play would be commissioned on the basis of
his synopsis and added that the line would probably be acceptable, and he says
that he is quite certain that nothing he said would have been taken as meaning **I**
that the B.B.C. had taken any binding decision about broadcasting the line.
Mr. Walford, head of the copyright department of the defendants, which is
concerned with actually making the contracts, has admitted in his affidavit that
the B.B.C. asked the plaintiff to proceed on the basis of the synopsis, but he
argues that that did not tie them prior to having seen the play to particular
lines of dialogue or that any particular scene was offered to them in general.
As a result a formal contract on a printed form was negotiated and agreed between
Mr. Caffery, the assistant head of Mr. Walford's department, on behalf of the

A B.B.C. and Mr. Harvey Unna as agent for the plaintiff. It was signed by the former on July 6, 1965, and by the latter on July 14, and I will refer to it as the July contract. [His LORDSHIP read para. (i) and para. (ii) of cl. 1 of the July contract, also cl. 2 and the words of cl. 3 from " further warrants " to the end of that clause. These passages are at p. 108, letters B, H and I, ante. HIS LORDSHIP continued:] There was in force at the material time another agree-

B ment, which I will call the " Guild agreement ", dated October, 1963, and expressed to be made between the Screenwriters' Guild and the B.B.C. in respect of plays specially written for television. [His LORDSHIP read cl. 10 of that agreement, which is set out at p. 109, letter F, ante.] The plaintiff thereupon wrote the full script and delivered it to the B.B.C. early in January, 1966. Mr. Brabazon read this and passed it on to Mr. Messina, and the plaintiff's evidence is—and

C this is uncontradicted—that Mr. Messina telephoned him to say that the B.B.C. had accepted the script for television use, that he was delighted with it, and although it would run longer than seventy-five minutes it would be a great pity to cut it and so he would agree to it being a ninety minutes play at an increased fee, and in fact the B.B.C. did agree with Mr. Unna to pay the plaintiff an additional £100. Mr. Messina also said at this time that he would meet the

D plaintiff in about seven days' time to discuss who should direct the play.

On Jan. 10 the B.B.C. duly paid £362 10s. being the balance of the original fee and on Jan. 20 they paid the additional £100. They had by then, of course, seen the play and were clearly accepting it, and they did not take exception to the line or make any other requirements about the script, although the payment slip in respect of the £362 10s. contained a footnote saying: " Accepted subject to

E minor revisions still to be done on the script ", and the slip for the £100 had a similar note reading " Accepted subject to any necessary minor revisions ". Copies of these slips were sent to Mr. Unna, but it may be doubtful how far they could operate to reserve to the B.B.C. any right to make alterations which they did not otherwise possess, and certainly these notes could not authorise them without the plaintiff's consent to make structural alterations within the meaning

F of cl. 10 of the Guild agreement. In fact the plaintiff heard no more until June 16, 1966, when Mr. Brabazon informed him that a Mr. Gilchrist Calder had been appointed director and arranged a production conference which was held a few days later at which the whole play was very fully discussed. The plaintiff was asked to make a number of alterations, some of a fairly substantial character, but still no objection was taken to the line. The plaintiff considered that he was

G under no obligation to do this as in his view the B.B.C. had accepted the play, but he did in fact make the desired amendments and at a further meeting shortly afterwards between the plaintiff, Mr. Brabazon and Mr. Calder the revised draft was accepted, in which, of course, the line appeared unaltered. By now at any rate the B.B.C. had accepted the script after seeing it and after having it amended as required by them, and it is difficult to see how any effect the notes on the pay-

H ment slips might otherwise have had could have remained operative after this.

In April, 1966, however, a certain Mr. Savory had replaced Mr. Bakewell as Head of Plays and in the course of his duties, but not until July, he read the plaintiff's play, and at once took objection to the line. By this time the play was already cast and about to go into production and the defendants were, they say, committed for the greater part of the final cost of production, which Mr. Savory

I puts at about £6,000. Mr. Savory in his affidavit gives as his reasons for objecting (I quote):

" Having read the script the only objection I had to any part of it was the line now in dispute. I objected to the line mainly for two reasons. First, on artistic grounds, that it would shock the T.V. viewer out of his involvement in a story which up to that point he would be enjoying. Secondly, for the mass viewer any line so explicit is bound to give offence to the majority. I am not against a risqué story but there is a great difference between a

risqué line spoken to a live audience in a theatre and the same line being A
spoken in the more intimate atmosphere of home viewing. Having reached
this conclusion, I immediately informed my producer, my story editor, and
my director that the line should be removed. The director agreed with my
decision. The story editor and the producer said that they would speak to
the plaintiff. As far as I can remember they said that the author was very
attached to this particular line. This was the first time that I knew that this B
particular line had been discussed previously between the author and those
gentlemen."

Considerable argument ensued between the B.B.C. and their solicitors on the one
hand and Mr. Unna and the plaintiff's solicitors on the other, in the course of
which, by letter dated July 12, Mr. Walford, writing to Mr. Unna, said:
                                                                              C
" The amendment which we shall have to make will be very small and
in our view (and I gather that on this point you agree) could not possibly
be regarded as a ' structural alteration ' of the sort for which we have
undertaken in our agreements with the Writers' Guild to get an author's
consent. We intend to delete the four words underlined in the following
passage: Mary: ' My friend Sylvia told me it was safe *standing up* '. Interviewer: ' *She, eh?* '. Tony: ' Wrap it up, Eric. Get him out '. The dropping D
of these words will omit what some might regard as a funny gag and others
as an embarrassing reference, but will not in our drama department's view
in any way destroy the point or the development of the play."

In reply on July 13 Mr. Unna made the plaintiff's position quite clear when he
said: E

" It had been an express condition of writing the play and entering into a
licensing agreement with the [B.B.C.] that this line, which my client considers
important, should form part of the dialogue, and it was on this mutual
understanding and agreement that the commission was issued and the
contract eventually signed . . ."
                                                                              F
He concluded that letter, however, by saying:

" One last point, no doubt you will let me know the recording and transmission dates as soon as convenient. I would like to suggest that you record
the scene in dispute both in the form in which my client requires it and
in the form in which you propose to transmit it. By doing so you will at
least provide an opportunity of a later and an amicable settlement. If G
you record your version only, this opportunity will be lost."

The B.B.C. would not give way and in his next letter of July 15, 1966, in which
Mr. Walford maintained the B.B.C.'s attitude, he concluded by saying:

" As regards your last paragraph, the scheduled date for recording is
Aug. 6. No date has yet been fixed for transmission. You then ask whether
the [B.B.C.] would be willing to record the scene in dispute both in the form H
in which your client wants and in the form in which we propose to transmit
it. We are prepared without prejudice, to do this, if only in the hope that it
may help to convince [the plaintiff] of the reasonableness of our decision.
But I must make it clear that in saying this we in no way surrender our
editorial responsibility, nor should you or the author assume that because
we agree to record the version preferred by him it is for that reason likely I
to be used. I am afraid I must warn you frankly that I do not think it likely
that the [B.B.C.] will feel able to change its view in the future any more than
it can at this moment. But this, as you know, is not for lack of goodwill on
our part towards the author."

In the upshot in July or August the play was recorded both with and without the
line and towards the end of August the plaintiff was shown both versions, but no
agreement could be reached and these proceedings followed.

A   The plaintiff now moves for interlocutory relief and I have to decide what if anything should be done at this juncture. First the plaintiff says that there was a collateral agreement made by Mr. Brabazon that the B.B.C. would not delete or alter the line, but the B.B.C. deny that any such agreement was made in fact, and if it was they say that Mr. Brabazon had no authority to bind them, and in any event they submit such an agreement cannot be given in evidence because it is
B   inconsistent with the July contract.

In my judgment, the last of these reasons does not afford a sufficient answer, since where there is in truth a collateral contract, as distinct from a mere representation or assurance, it is admissible albeit it varies the main contract to which it is collateral. See the example given by LORD MOULTON in *Heilbut, Symons & Co.* v. *Buckleton* (1), where he said:

C
   " The effect of a collateral contract such as that which I have instanced would be to increase the consideration of the main contract by £100, and the more natural and usual way of carrying this out would be by so modifying the main contract and not by executing a concurrent and collateral contract."

There the collateral contract clearly varied the main contract by increasing the
D   price. See also CHITTY ON CONTRACTS (22nd Edn.) Vol. 1, para. 639:

   " Collateral terms. Extrinsic evidence may also be admitted to show a collateral agreement or warranty, and it is sometimes said that these too must not contradict express terms of the written contract. But it is sometimes possible to prove a collateral warranty or even a promise not to enforce an express term of the written agreement. The consideration for the promise
E   is the promisee's entering into the main contract. Thus, in *City & Westminster Properties (1934), Ltd.* v. *Mudd* (2) the draft of a new lease presented to a tenant contained a covenant that he would use the premises for business purposes only and not as sleeping quarters. The tenant objected to this covenant, and the landlords gave him an oral assurance that, if he signed the lease, they would not enforce it against him. The tenant signed the lease,
F   but later the landlords sought to forfeit the lease for breach of this covenant. HARMAN, J., held that the oral assurance constituted a separate collateral agreement from which the landlord would not be permitted to resile."

It is clear, however, that to succeed on this argument the plaintiff must show a contract which involves both parties intending to contract. The plaintiff may well have thought that he was making a binding contract with Mr. Brabazon on this
G   particular aspect of the matter, but Mr. Brabazon has sworn that for his part he had no such intention, and in my view that accords with probability since, although no doubt it was part of his duty to make arrangements concerning scripts, it was not his function to make independent contracts on such matters, nor indeed was it the function of the superior officers whom he consulted. Moreover, I cannot see that the plaintiff has made out a prima facie case on the question of authority.
H   Mr. Brabazon was the proper officer with whom to discuss script arrangements, but not with whom to make a binding contract which would prevent the B.B.C. from changing their plans. There is no evidence that he had actual authority; indeed the evidence is that he had not.

In para. 8 of his first affidavit, however, the plaintiff says that he verily believes that at all material times Mr. Brabazon was authorised to make the agreement
I   and give the assurance referred to, and that he had always been held out to him by the B.B.C. as authorised to approve scripts and lines in plays. However, he gives no details of this holding out and I cannot see that he has established a prima facie case that Mr. Brabazon was held out as having authority not merely to make arrangements as to scripts or even to give assurances but to bind the B.B.C. contractually not to vary or depart from those arrangements. After all,

---

(1) [1911-13] All E.R. Rep. 83 at pp. 90, 91; [1913] A.C. 30 at p. 47.
(2) [1958] 2 All E.R. 733; [1959] Ch. 129.

as the plaintiff felt so strongly about this line it would have been easy for him **A**
to have instructed his agent to make some provision about it in the contract.

I must, therefore, consider how the matter stands apart from the alleged
collateral contract, which may of course still be proved at the trial, and first it is
necessary to determine whether the July contract (3) was an assignment of the
copyright limited to the rights and places therein specified, in which case the
B.B.C.'s position would clearly be much stronger than if it be merely a licence. **B**

Counsel for the B.B.C. has relied on s. 37 of the Copyright Act, 1956, and it is
clear that there can be a partial assignment, and it is also true that no particular
form of words is necessary to constitute an assignment, but I have nevertheless
come to the conclusion that the July contract (4) is only a licence. Counsel for
the plaintiff has submitted that it must be so because cl. 3 clearly shows that the
copyright was for all purposes to remain vested in the plaintiff. However, despite **C**
the words " in any country ", and the use in the same clause of the limited expression " any of the countries in question ", in my judgment the time limit
prescribed by cl. 3 and its general context shows that it was designed to give protection only in respect of the rights conferred by cl. 1, paras. (iii) and (iv) and
must be construed as limited accordingly, so that it is not concerned with television rights in this country. **D**

Be that as it may, however, the agreement, as it seems to me, is not one designed
to vest the copyright in the defendants even pro tanto but merely to authorise
or license them to perform the work. The limitation to one performance only for
the original fee together with the much wider nature of the rights conferred in
the option under cl. 1 (iii) or to be granted under cl. 1 (iv) if the option be acquired
and exercised tell strongly in this direction. The distinction between a partial **E**
assignment and a licence must often be slender but it is real and in my judgment
the July contract is no more than a licence.

I turn next to consider what right, if any, a person licensed to perform a dramatic work has by the general law to alter that work and here the authorities
appear to be very meagre.

It is said in Copinger and Skone James on Copyright (10th Edn.), p. 258, **F**
para. 675, under the heading " Alterations in communications made to newspapers " as follows:

" Difficulties sometimes arise by reason of alterations made in the matter
communicated by correspondents and others to newspapers. It is necessary
to consider two cases. Where the author has assigned his copyright to the
newspaper his only cause of action is for the injury to his reputation or possi- **G**
bly malicious falsehood. Where, however, he has only granted a licence to
publish, it may be a term of the licence express or implied that no alteration
shall be made. If such term is a condition precedent to the licence a
publication with alterations would give rise to an action for infringement of
copyright, but if not there would merely be a right of action for breach of
contract. Apart from special contract, contributors to newspapers will **H**
probably be taken to have accepted the ordinary custom that editors may
make alterations in unsigned articles, but the court will readily imply a
term that no substantial alteration may be made to a signed article without
the author's consent,"

citing for that last proposition, *Joseph* v. *National Magazine Co., Ltd.* (5). Again **I**
on p. 359, para. 987, under the heading " Distinction between assignment and
licence ", there appears the following:

" In the case of more formal agreements the most important point to
determine is whether any copyright is to be vested in the publication or

---

(3) I.e., the written contract between the parties made in July, 1965; see p. 108, letter A,
ante.

(4) The terms of the July contract, so far as relevant, are at p. 108, letter A, ante.

(5) [1958] 3 All E.R. 52; [1959] Ch. 14.

A whether a licence only is intended . . . Other important distinctions between the rights of the parties according to whether an assignment or licence has been executed arise with regard to the publishers' right to alter the work, with regard to the liability of an assign of the publisher to royalties payable to the author, with regard to the position which arises on the publisher's bankruptcy, and with regard to the assignability of the benefit of the

B agreement by the publisher."

Then, on p. 359, para. 988, under the heading " Right to Alter " this appears:

" If a publisher be the absolute owner of the copyright, he is entitled, without the consent of the author, to publish successive editions of the work with additions and corrections, and, in bringing out new editions, may

C make such omissions and other changes in the original as will not injure the reputation of the author. Whereas, in the case of a licence, the licence may expressly or by implication only extend to publication in unaltered form, so that the publisher, if he publishes in an altered form, may commit an infringement."

It will be observed that what is there said is that the licence may expressly or

D impliedly require publication in an unaltered form or that no substantial alteration be made, which seems to connote that, in the absence of such a prohibition, the licensee has a right to make alterations, even substantial ones, and I have come to the conclusion that that is right.

Joseph's case (6) was not one of a mere licence to publish the plaintiff's article conferring a right of publication but of a contract to publish for which the

E plaintiff was paying and I think that the words of HARMAN, J., (7):

" the plaintiff was entitled to write his own article in his own style, expressing his own opinions, and was not bound to submit to have his name published as the author of a different article expressing other opinions in a different style ",

F and the reference at the foot of the page to (8)

" correction of mistakes or possibly grammatical changes which an editor may legitimately make "

must be read in that context. A licence, however, does not per se require the licensee to do anything. It merely protects him from an action for infringement. Without the licence he may not make any substantial use of the copyright

G material. If a person does that without a licence, he is liable whether he has reproduced it verbatim or made alterations, even substantial ones, but if he has a licence he can set that up as a defence equally whether he has copied verbatim or made alterations, unless and save in so far as the terms of the licence expressly or impliedly require him not to make alterations. In my judgment therefore, the law is correctly stated in the passages which I have cited from COPINGER,

H but, as there pointed out, the court will readily imply a term limiting the right to make alterations.

I must therefore next consider the effect of the contracts, and first the July contract alone. Counsel for the plaintiff has argued that there is an express provision in cl. 2 which gives the B.B.C. the right, within a month from delivery of the full script to require the writer to make alterations and negatives any other

I right, whether to make alterations themselves or to require them thereafter, and certainly negatives any right to make alterations after the B.B.C. have in fact accepted an agreed script; but I accept the argument of counsel for the B.B.C. that this clause operates only during the provisional period within which the payment of the second half of the fee remains conditional. The B.B.C. could either accept the work as it stood and so become liable to pay that second half of the

---

(6) [1958] 3 All E.R. 52; [1959] Ch. 14.
(7) [1958] 3 All E.R. at p. 54, letter A; [1959] Ch. at p. 20.
(8) [1958] 3 All E.R. at p. 54, letter F; [1959] Ch. at p. 20.

fee, or escape that by rejecting the play or requiring alterations, in which case **A** presumably they must accept the play if they be duly made, or, if not so made, they could still reject it. Once, however, they accept, then the clause is spent, and they are back in the position of licensee, having a right to make alterations unless there is something else to preclude them and, in my judgment, there is nothing else in the July contract. It is true that under cl. 2 the B.B.C. accept the work as it stands, and it might be argued that this implies an obligation to **B** produce it as it stands but in the context that in my view would give too wide an operation to cl. 2 and would in effect be making it work after the time when on my construction it is spent. There was some uncertainty in the argument at this stage because, of course, the parties could not see whether it was in their interest to argue that the position is governed only by the July contract and to reject the Guild agreement (9) until it be decided what right to make alterations there **C** would be on that basis, but the plaintiff claimed, if necessary, to be able to rely on the Guild agreement, if on no other ground, on the principle of *Beswick* v. *Beswick* (10), which is, however, proceeding to the House of Lords. In all the circumstances, I must clearly next consider whether there is a prima facie case that it should apply.

On the one hand, there is no reference to the Guild agreement in the July **D** contract at all, but only a footnote (11), and even that does not purport to incorporate the Guild agreement. On the other hand, the B.B.C., who felt constrained as a responsible public body to argue that the Guild agreement does apply, because that is the line which they have always adopted, and in any event because they might need to rely on it, said that I ought to imply a clause incorporating the Guild agreement, or, alternatively, that it establishes a usage **E** or custom in the trade or profession which gives rise to an implication that the prima facie right of a licensee to make alterations shall be limited in manner prescribed by the Guild agreement, or, thirdly, that in the last resort the contract ought to be rectified. It seems to me that, on one or other of these grounds, there is a sufficient prima facie case that the Guild agreement applies, save, of course, in so far as excluded expressly or by necessary implication. After all, it was an **F** agreement made by the B.B.C. with the representative body of the plaintiff's profession, of which he was, I understand, a member, and made for the purpose of regulating the terms on which the defendants should contract with the members; the parties clearly had it in mind when they made the July contract because it is expressly referred to in the note. The plaintiff's agent, Mr. Unna, thought that it applied (see the last paragraph of his letter of July 18, 1966) although he said that **G** it was made irrelevant by the collateral agreement, and as soon as the plaintiff consulted his solicitors they set up this very contention (see their letter of Sept. 2, 1966). What the B.B.C. thought when they made the July contract is perhaps a little obscure, because Mr. Walford in para. 6 of his affidavit has sworn categorically that

> " the view of the B.B.C. is that the Guild agreement did not legally form **H** part of any agreement with an author entered into in the terms of the printed agreement used in the plaintiff's case."

In para. 8 of his affidavit, however, he said that:

> " In the view of the [B.B.C.] it was proper to make the amendments in question if for no other reason because they were minor amendments and **I** not structural alterations within the meaning of cl. 10 referred to above."

Moreover, on the construction which I have placed on cl. 2 of the July contract, there is nothing there to exclude the provisions of cl. 10 of the Guild agreement,

(9) I.e., the agreement dated Oct. 1, 1963, made between the Screenwriters' Guild and the B.B.C. relating to plays specially written for television; see p. 109, letters A to D, ante.
(10) [1966] 3 All E.R. 1; [1966] Ch. 538.
(11) See p. 108, letter I, ante.

A since that comes into operation only after cl. 2 of the July contract has ceased to operate, and I am fortified in this view by the fact that the Guild agreement itself contains not only cl. 10 but also in cl. 9 a provision which, though not identical, is certainly comparable with cl. 3 of the July contract.

This brings me to the last main question: whether the alteration proposed is structural. This is a difficult question of fact on which there is a direct conflict
B of evidence which can only be resolved at the trial, when the expert witnesses, including the plaintiff himself, can be cross-examined, but there is a considerable body of evidence filed on behalf of the plaintiff and designed to show a prima facie case. Counsel for the B.B.C. has attacked that on five main points. First, he said that the experts had built into the play more than the plaintiff ever intended and the line was structural, if at all, only on that supposed basis. Secondly, this
C play is not a satire on the sex education of the working classes, or lack of it, or on the conditions in which they live, but on the exploitation and the hysteria of mass advertising. The satire is that Mary lost her value because of illegitimacy, illegitimate quintuplets would not be acceptable, and (so the argument runs) the line or at all events the expurgated part is not necessary. Thirdly, counsel said that the casual and sordid nature of the relationship had already appeared from
D earlier parts of the play to which he drew my attention. Fourthly, there would, he said, be sufficient in the emasculated line to justify the sudden breaking off of the television interview. Fifthly, with reference to para. 2 of the plaintiff's second affidavit, when the plaintiff says that he wanted to make this one line the pivot of the play in order to illustrate the comment he wished to make on the matters refered to in that paragraph, counsel for the B.B.C. submits that the line
E affords no such illustration. I find it not entirely easy to follow this particular point in the plaintiff's evidence, but it is just the kind of thing which calls for resolution by cross-examination.

I feel the force of these criticisms, but at this stage they do not seem to me to destroy the plaintiff's prima facie case, whatever may emerge at the trial. I have the plaintiff's own evidence as to his meaning and intent, and as to the
F necessity of this line in its unaltered form, which he has described in various places as the hinge, the necessary key line, and the pivot, and he, prima facie, would appear to be the best judge. I have too the fact that, even if the casual and loveless nature of the union may have already sufficiently appeared to the audience, still, according to the story, it was unknown to the television team and the advertisers, and this line brings it all suddenly and forcibly to their notice.
G Moreover, if the line were deleted altogether there would be nothing to account for the sudden disruption of the television interview or on which to hinge the second part of the play, and if it be left in, cut as suggested, it is a feeble and incomplete kind of statement at a point which must on any showing be an important moment in the play. The plaintiff says that the line points to the distinction between the babies being unwanted and conceived in a casual and sordid way
H on the one hand, and glamour on the other, and it may well be that this forceful line is required for this purpose, and cannot be whittled away without impairing the structure of the play. There again, though the weakened line might be thought sufficient to bring about a sudden disruption of the television programme, the line in its original form undoubtedly would. Further, although cross-examination may shed a different light on this, the analytical evidence of Lord Willis (12)
I presents to my mind a strong prima facie case, and I am also somewhat impressed by his reference to Pygmalion as showing how even a single line may be structural.

For these reasons, in my judgment, the plaintiff has made out a prima facie case for relief in the alternative form (13), but it is said that I ought not to grant him that because he has stood by and allowed the B.B.C. to incur expense, and on the balance of convenience.

---

(12) Founder of the Screenwriters' Guild, re-named, at the date of the motion, the Writers' Guild.
(13) See p. 107, letter H, ante.

Mr. Savory took over from Mr. Bakewell (14) in April, 1966, but he did not **A**
read the script of the plaintiff's play till July, by which time the play had already
been cast and was about to go into rehearsal, so that the B.B.C. were by then
committed to the greater part of the cost, and this may have been true also in
April, but as on any showing the plaintiff had drawn " the line " to the attention
of the appropriate officers of the B.B.C. and asked for their assurances that it
would be all right, and they had at least expressed no dissent and said that it **B**
would probably be all right, there can be no sin of delay or standing by which can
be laid at the plaintiff's door down to that stage. Then it is said that the plaintiff
by his agent caused or encouraged the B.B.C. to incur further expense by going
on with recording the play and indeed recording the disputed passage in two
forms. That, however, was done expressly sans prejudice, and, moreover, with
no possible illusions as to the plaintiff's contentions as he had made these abun- **C**
dantly clear not only by the letter from his agent to which I have already referred
but also by a letter which he himself wrote on July 12, 1966, to Mr. Brabazon
which reads as follows:

" As we have agreed, I leave to your and Calder's discretion the matter of
any possible cuts for artistic reasons in the following scenes. The opening
scene in the family's home: subsequent scene in the pub: the Arthur Dooth/ **D**
Pamela passion scene: the Pamela Piers scene and the Piers Mannering
scene. Also, the negotiation scene in the pub. However, I would just like to
make it clear that the permission for you to trim these scenes does not
extend to the scene when the T.V. Interviewer interviews the family on
television, and in particular anything relating to The Line in question.
As you know, I am adamant in my objections to any tampering with this **E**
scene and The Line must remain, be audible, and the character speaking it
in shot."

Apart from this, which for these reasons cannot in my judgment avail the B.B.C.,
the balance of convenience is all the other way. The B.B.C. will still probably
have adequate time to exploit their rights after the trial, and so far as they are **F**
damnified, then, if they succeed at the trial, they will have a clear case for redress
under the cross-undertaking in damages; but if I refuse interlocutory relief and
the plaintiff succeeds at the trial he will virtually be deprived of any remedy, since
it will be too late to prevent production of the play in its altered form, and it will
be difficult if not impossible for him to quantify his damages.

For these reasons, I propose to grant an injunction in the alternative and **G**
narrower form (15) until the trial or further order and to give any directions which
may be necessary to facilitate a speedy trial.

Order accordingly.

Solicitors: *Campbell, Hooper & Co.* (for the plaintiff); *William Charles Crocker*
(for the B.B.C.).

[*Reported by* JACQUELINE METCALFE, *Barrister-at-Law.*] **H**

I

---

(14) I.e., as Head of Plays, see p. 111, letter H, ante.
(15) See p. 107, letter H, ante.

Reversed. C.A. [1968] 1 All E.R. 9.

Reversed. C.A. [1968] 1 All E.R. 9.

A

R. *v.* INDUSTRIAL INJURIES COMMISSIONER, *Ex parte* CABLE.

[QUEEN'S BENCH DIVISION (Lord Parker, C.J., Diplock, L.J., and Ashworth, J.), February 27, 28, March 9, 1967.]

B *Industrial Injury—Disablement benefit—Assessment of degree of disability— Causation of each disability to be considered—Whether defect of vision in right eye due to disease after accident but before assessment was to be taken into consideration to assess greater disablement than would normally be incurred—National Insurance (Industrial Injuries) Act 1965 (c. 52), Sch. 4, para. 1 (b)—National Insurance (Industrial Injuries) (Benefit)*

C *Regulations 1964 (S.I. 1964 No. 504), reg. 2 (3) (a).*

The claimant claimed disablement benefit for industrial injury as result of an accident at work. As result of the accident he had lost his left eye. After the accident, but before the date of assessment, he contracted a disease to his right eye, which seriously impaired the vision of his right eye. This disease was not directly attributable to industrial accident.

D Under para. 1 (b) of Sch. 4* to the National Insurance (Industrial) Injuries Act 1965 the prima facie rule was that every disability was to be treated as resulting from the relevant accident, but this was subject to an exception that any disability " in so far as the claimant . . . (ii) would not have been subject thereto but for some . . . disease . . . contracted after, and not directly attributable to, that accident " was not to be treated as resulting

E from the accident. This exception could be modified by regulations. It was conceded that, unless regulations modified the exception stated in para. 1 (b) (ii), the claimant's application to the court (which was an application for certiorari to quash a decision of the tribunal on appeal from the medical appeal tribunal) must fail. The relevant regulation on which the claimant relied was reg. 2 (3)† of the National Insurance (Industrial

F Injuries) (Benefit) Regulations 1964 (referred to as " the benefit regulations "). By reg. 2 (3) (a) where " as a result of " the injury resulting from the relevant accident " the claimant may be expected, having regard to his physical . . . condition at the date of the assessment in respect thereof, to be subject to greater disabilities than would normally be incurred as a result of such an injury ", assessment of loss of faculty should be by reference to a degree of disablement set out in a schedule to the regulations.

G **Held:** in so far as the disabilities to which the claimant was subject owing to the loss of his left eye were enhanced as a result of the defect of vision in his right eye that developed after the accident, such enhancement must be ignored, because it was not attributable to the accident but was within the exception enacted in para. (1) (b) (ii) of Sch. 4 to the Act of 1965,

H which remained applicable in determining whether each " greater disability " to which reg. 2 (3) (a) of the benefit regulations referred resulted from the accident, for which purpose each disability should be considered separately; in the present case the loss of faculty resulting from the claimant's defect of vision in his right eye did not result from the relevant accident (see p. 123, letter I, to p. 124, letter A, and p. 124, letter D, post).

I
_____

* Schedule 4, para. 1, so far as material, provides: " For the purposes of s. 12 of this Act, the extent of disablement shall be assessed, by reference to the disabilities incurred by the claimant as a result of the relevant loss of faculty, in accordance with the following general principles:— . . . (b) any such disability shall be treated as having been incurred as a result of the relevant loss of faculty except that, subject to the provisions of any regulations made under para. 2 of this Schedule, it shall not be treated insofar as the claimant either— . . . (ii) would not have been subject thereto but for some injury or disease received or contracted after, and not directly attributable to, that accident . . ."

† Regulation 2 (3), so far as material, is set out at p. 123, letter F, post.

[As to disablement benefit, see 27 HALSBURY'S LAWS (3rd Edn.) 824, 825, **A** paras. 1451, 1452.

For the National Insurance (Industrial Injuries) Act 1965, Sch. 4, see 45 HALSBURY'S STATUTES (2nd Edn.) 1179.]

Application for certiorari.

This was an application by William James Cable for an order of certiorari **B** to quash a decision dated May 11, 1966, No. C.W.I. 2/66, made by a tribunal (G. OWEN GEORGE, Esq., and J. S. WATSON, Esq., Q.C., deputy commissioners; SIR ROBERT MICKLETHWAIT, Q.C., commissioner, dissenting) pursuant to the National Insurance (Industrial Injuries) Acts 1965 and 1966, whereby they ordered that the appeal of the applicant from a decision of a Medical Appeal Tribunal dated Aug. 21, 1964, be dismissed. The ground on which certiorari **C** was sought was that there was an error of law on the face of the record of the decision of the majority of the tribunal, viz., that in assessing the applicant's disablement regard was not to be had to any condition causing the applicant to be subject to greater disabilities than would normally be incurred as a result of the injury in respect of which he was being assessed if such condition occurred between the date of the relevant accident and the date of assessment, whereas **D** reg. 2 (3) of the National Insurance (Industrial Injuries) (Benefit) Regulations 1964, on its true construction provided that the degree of disablement of a claimant should be assessed on the basis whether he might be expected to be subject to greater disabilities than would normally be incurred as a result of his relevant injury having regard to his physical and mental condition at the date of the assessment, whether or not such condition first arose before or after **E** the relevant accident.

On Mar. 23, 1962, the applicant, who was then forty-seven years of age and was employed as a furnace worker, suffered burns to his face, eyes, neck and arms, when a crucible of molten metal burst. In December, 1962, the applicant's left eye had to be removed by operation, and he now wore an artificial eye attached to his glasses. It was not disputed that the loss of that eye resulted **F** from the accident. On Feb. 6, 1964, the medical board assessed the applicant's disablement at ninety per cent. The applicant informed this board that the sight in his right eye had failed suddenly in July, 1963, as a result of which he had been in hospital in September. The Minister of Pensions and National Insurance caused this assessment to be referred to the medical appeal tribunal. The tribunal had before them the report of a consultant which supported the **G** view that the deterioration of vision in the applicant's right eye could not be associated with the loss of the left eye. The tribunal did not confirm the decision of the medical board, but decided that the degree of disablement should be assessed at forty per cent. from Mar. 21, 1964, for life. The reasons for this decision were recorded as follows:—

H

" We accept [the consultant's] report of Mar. 9, 1964. We find that the disability in the right eye is due to disease contracted after the relevant accident and is not attributable to that accident or any other accident against which the [applicant] was insured under the [National Insurance (Industrial Injuries) Act, 1946]. We assess the disablement of the left eye at forty per cent. The disability of the right eye is assessed at thirty **I** per cent., but having regard to reg. 2 (5) (b) and reg. 2 (6) of the benefit regulations the assessment in respect of the right eye has no effect. There is no other disablement in fact resulting or treated as resulting from the relevant loss of faculty. We accept the Minister's submission that the provisions of reg. 2 (3) (a) and reg. 2 (4) do not apply. In the result, the disablement resulting from the loss of faculty is assessed at forty per cent. for life."

A   The applicant appealed* under the National Insurance (Industrial Injuries) Acts 1965 and 1966 (presumably under s. 42 of the Act of 1965) on, so far as relevant, the following ground, viz., that the medical appeal tribunal should have applied reg. 2 (3) (*a*) of the benefit regulations. On May 11, 1966, the commissioner's tribunal, by a majority, dismissed the appeal.

B   *D. J. Turner-Samuels* for the applicant.
   Nigel Bridge for the respondent.

Cur. adv. vult.

Mar. 9.   **DIPLOCK, L.J.**, read the following judgment: The National Insurance (Industrial Injuries) Act, 1946, which with subsequent amendments has now been consolidated in the National Insurance (Industrial Injuries) Act C   1965, was one of a series of statutes which inaugurated the welfare state. It operates in a field with which the law courts are only too familiar, that of industrial injuries, but introduces a concept which is wholly different from those which the courts apply in actions for damages for negligence or breach of statutory duty brought by an employee against his employer. The " injury benefit " and " disablement benefit " to which a claimant is entitled under the Act is not D   " compensation " for injury but money payable under the terms of a statutory contract of insurance. It bears no direct relationship to the actual loss sustained by the claimant as a result of the industrial injury and, in construing the Act, the court must be continually on guard against the fallacy of applying to the assessment of " benefit " the principles applicable to the assessment of damages or compensation—a task with which it is so much more familiar. The Act of E   1965 and the regulations made thereunder constitute a self-contained code dealing with the right to benefit. Cases about damages at common law throw no light on the meaning of that code. To refer to them as an aid to construction can only mislead.

In this case we are concerned with " disablement benefit ". The statutory chain of causation giving rise to a right to " disablement benefit " on the part F   of a claimant is (i) an accident arising out of and in the course of his employment, resulting in (ii) an injury, resulting in (iii) a loss of physical or mental faculty resulting in (iv) disablement (the Act of 1965, s. 5 (1) (*b*) and s. 12 (1)). Disablement simply means inability to do things, whether or not such inability involves the claimant in loss of earning power or additional expense (the Act of 1965, Sch. 4, para. 1 (*a*)), although the amount of the benefit is increased above what G   I shall call for convenience the basic amount if it does so (the Act of 1965, s. 13, s. 14 and s. 15). The basic amount of benefit to which the claimant is entitled depends on the " extent " or " degree " of his disablement, and the Act of 1965 provides in Sch. 4 and regulations made under that schedule how the extent or degree of disablement is to be assessed. Schedule 4 and the National Insurance (Industrial Injuries) (Benefit) Regulations 1964 (1) contain that part of the H   code which we have to construe in the present case. The disablement, the extent of which is to be assessed in accordance with the provisions of Sch. 4, is that which results from the accident in respect of which the benefit is claimed, and the complete statutory chain of causation between the relevant accident, relevant injury and the disablement being brought in by the use of the expression the " relevant loss of faculty ", as defined in s. 86 (1). For the purpose of assessing I   its extent disablement is treated in the introductory words of para. 1 of Sch. 4 as comprising a number of " disabilities ", not as a single composite " disability ". Paragraph 1 (*a*) requires the assessor, as a first step in the assessment,

---

* In theory this must have been an appeal to the Industrial Injuries Commissioner, but was made to a tribunal, the tribunal being that envisaged by s. 9 (3) of the National Insurance Act, 1966, comprising any three commissioners, and the decision of the majority was the decision of the tribunal.

(1) S.I. 1964 No. 504. The regulations have been amended by S.I. 1965 Nos. 36 and 1804 and by S.I. 1966 No. 338 (which, inter alia, amends reg. 2), but none of the amendments appear material to the decision.

to compare the mental and physical condition of the claimant at the time of the **A**
assessment with the normal mental and physical condition of a person of the
same age and sex, and to identify all the disabilities to which the claimant may
be expected to be subject, but to which a person of the same age and sex whose
mental and physical condition was normal would not be subject. The next
stage, dealt with in para. 1 (*b*), is to determine which of those disabilities results
from the relevant accident and is, therefore, to be taken into account in assessing **B**
the extent of disablement. For this purpose, each " disability " is to be considered separately. This sub-paragraph sets out the rules to be applied by the
assessor in determining whether the statutory chain of causation exists between
the relevant accident and any particular disability. These rules are to be
applied in place of any common law concepts of causation. The prima facie
rule is that every disability is to be treated as resulting from the accident. **C**
This prima facie rule is subject, however, to two exceptions, viz., any disability

> " . . . in so far as the claimant either—(i) would in any case have been
> subject thereto as the result of a congenital defect or of an injury or disease
> received or contracted before the relevant accident; or (ii) would not have
> been subject thereto but for some injury or disease received or contracted **D**
> after, and not directly attributable to, that accident "

is not to be treated as resulting from the accident. There is, however, power
by regulation to provide that a disability falling within these exceptions shall,
nevertheless, be treated as resulting from the accident. Paragraph 1 (*c*)
provides that, for the purpose of the comparison between the claimant and a
normal person required to be made by the assessor under para. 1 (*a*), no account **E**
must be taken of the particular circumstances of the claimant other than age,
sex, and physical and mental condition—a provision which underlines the
contrast between disablement benefit and the common law concepts of damages
or compensation. Paragraph 1 (*d*) provides that the extent of disablement
shall be expressed in terms of a percentage. This percentage is referred to in
para. 2 and para. 4 as the " degree of disablement ". Paragraph 2 contains **F**
the power to make regulations " further defining the principles on which the
extent of disablement is to be assessed . . . ". It is under this power that the exceptions in para. 1 (*b*) can be modified. There is also an express power to prescribe
that a particular loss of faculty shall be treated as resulting in a particular degree
of disablement. The effect of the exceptions in para. 1 (*b*), unless modified by
regulations made under para. 2, is to draw a distinction between claimants who **G**
have received or contracted an injury or disease not directly attributable to the
accident after the accident and those who have received or contracted such injury
or disease before the accident. In neither case are the disabilities which would have
resulted from the injury or disease apart from the accident to be taken into
account in assessing the extent of disablement. If, however, the injury or
disease was received or contracted before the accident, any greater or additional **H**
disabilities arising from the combined effect of the accident and the pre-existing
injury or disease are to be taken into account in assessing the extent of disablement, whereas if the injury or disease was received or contracted after the
accident, any greater or additional disabilities arising from the combined effect
of the accident and the subsequent injury or disease are not to be taken into
account in the assessment. **I**

In the present case, the injury sustained by the applicant as a result of the
relevant accident was the loss of his left eye. After the accident, but before the
date of the assessment, he contracted a disease of the right eye, not directly
attributable to the accident, which seriously impaired the vision of his remaining
eye. In consequence, at the date of the assessment he was subject to greater
or additional disabilities arising from the combined effect of the accident and
the subsequent disease to which he would not have been subject had he continued to retain the full vision of his remaining eye. It is conceded, as it must

A be, that, unless regulations made under para. 2 of Sch. 4 have modified in his favour the exceptions set out in para. 1 (*b*) of that schedule, this application for certiorari must fail. I, therefore, turn now to the relevant regulation which is reg. 2 of the National Insurance (Industrial Injuries) (Benefit) Regulations 1964. The references in this regulation are to the provisions of the Act of 1946, but, by virtue of s. 87 (2) of the Act of 1965, they are to be construed as references to

B the corresponding provisions of the latter Act. Regulation 2 (2) of, together with Sch. 2 to, the Benefit Regulations prescribes a number of particular losses of faculty which are to be treated as resulting in particular degrees of disablement. It defines each such loss of faculty by reference to the injury from which it results. Each such injury clearly involves a loss of faculty, e.g., either a loss of a part of the body, or a physical sense of an organ such as sight or hearing.

C It treats the loss of faculty resulting from each of the injuries described in Sch. 2 as giving rise to a separate disability. Some of the described injuries consist, however, of the combined loss of more than one part of the body, the loss of each of which separately constitute other described injuries. The proviso to reg. 2 (2) provides that, in such a case, the degree of disablement prescribed for the combined loss is to be treated as the degree of disablement resulting from

D the injury, and not the sum of the prescribed degrees of disablement for the separate losses. It is important to note that reg. 2 (2), which is introduced by the words " where as a result of the relevant accident ", does not purport to deal at all with the determination of which of all the disabilities to which the claimant is subject is to be treated as resulting from the relevant accident. This determination, so far as para. (2) is concerned, is left to be made in accordance

E with the principles laid down in para. 1 (*b*) of Sch. 4 to the Act of 1965. Regulation 2 (2) does not come into operation until after that determination has been made. The same, I think, is true of reg. 2 (3). This paragraph requires the assessor to depart from the degree of disablement prescribed in Sch. 2 to the regulations for a particular injury if certain conditions are fulfilled. So far as relevant it reads as follows:

F " (3) Where, as a result of the relevant accident, the claimant has suffered an injury specified in the said Sch. 2 but (*a*) as a result of that injury [that is to say the injury resulting from the relevant accident] the claimant may be expected, having regard to his physical and mental condition at the date of the assessment in respect thereof, to be subject to greater disabilities than would normally be incurred as a result of such injury ... the loss

G of faculty suffered by the claimant as a result of such injury shall be assessed by reference to the degree of disablement set against such injury in column 2 of the said Sch. 2 subject to such adjustment as may be reasonable in the circumstances of the case."

In order to determine whether the conditions specified in reg. 2 (3) (*a*) are

H satisfied, it is necessary first to make a comparison between the disabilities to which the claimant may be expected to be subject *as a result of the injury suffered by him as a result of the relevant accident* and the disabilities which would normally be incurred as a result of that injury. It is, therefore, necessary to consider each disability separately in order to determine whether or not it was incurred by the claimant as a result of the injury suffered by him as a result of

I the relevant accident.   For this purpose, one must apply the rules laid down in para. 1 (*b*) of Sch. 4 to the Act of 1965 for determining whether the statutory chain of causation exists between the relevant accident and the particular disability. This prohibits one from treating the disability as having been incurred as a result of the loss of faculty resulting from the injury suffered by the claimant as a result of the relevant accident in so far as the claimant would not have been subject to that disability but for some injury or disease received or contracted after and not directly attributable to that accident. It follows, therefore, that, in the present case, the assessor must ignore any enhancement of the disabilities to which the applicant would have been subject owing to the loss of his left **A** eye, in so far as that enhancement is due to the defect of vision in his right eye which developed after the accident. This is what the majority of the tribunal held.

I confess that, when first confronted with the words in para. (*a*) of reg. 2 (3): " Having regard to his physical and mental condition *at the date of the assessment* ", I was inclined, like SIR ROBERT MICKLETHWAIT, Q.C., in his minority opinion, **B** to take the view that the express reference to the date of the assessment did modify the provisions of para. 1 (*b*) of Sch. 4 to the Act of 1965; but these words echo the wording of para. 1 (*a*) of that schedule. They specify the date at which the assessor must look at the physical and mental condition of the claimant in order to form a view as to what are the disabilities to which the claimant may be expected to be subject during the period taken into account; but the other **C** words in reg. 2 (3) make it necessary to show the statutory chain of causation between the relevant accident and each disability, and there is nothing in the regulations which modifies the rules laid down in para. 1 (*b*) of Sch. 4 to the Act of 1965 for determining in respect of each disability whether that chain of causation exists.

I would accordingly dismiss this application.   **D**

ASHWORTH, J.: I agree.

DIPLOCK, L.J.: LORD PARKER, C.J., also agrees with that judgment.

Application dismissed.

Solicitors: *W. H. Thompson* (for the applicant); *Solicitor, Ministry of Social Security* (for the respondent).   **E**

[*Reported by* N. P. METCALFE, ESQ., *Barrister-at-Law.*]

LONDON AND THAMES HAVEN OIL WHARVES, LTD.
v. ATTWOOLL (Inspector of Taxes).

[COURT OF APPEAL, CIVIL DIVISION (Willmer, Harman and Diplock, L.JJ.),   **F** December 14, 15, 16, 1966.]

Income Tax—Income—Damages—Loss of profitable use of asset—Damage to jetty—Payment by shipowners responsible—Apportionment in negotiations with jetty owner's underwriters—Part attributed to loss of use of jetty— Capital loss or loss of profit—Income Tax Act, 1952 (15 & 16 Geo. 6 & **G** *1 Eliz. 2 c. 10), s. 137.*

The taxpayer company owned several jetties at its oil installation at which tankers bringing oil could berth for purposes of discharge. While coming alongside one of the jetties, a tanker was so negligently navigated that it struck the jetty and caused it serious damage. The physical damage necessitated repairs at a cost of £83,168, but in addition there was conse- **H** quential damage, quantified at £32,450, through loss of use of the jetty for 380 days during repair. The taxpayer company received a payment from the owners of the tanker, who limited their liability under the Merchant Shipping Acts. The amount of that payment was apportioned rateably between the physical damage and the consequential damage; the relevant amount apportioned to the consequential damage being £21,404. The **I** taxpayer company also received a payment from its insurers to make up the total of £83,168 for physical damage, against which alone the company was insured. The company was assessed to income tax on the basis that the £21,404 received in respect of consequential damage represented payment to the taxpayer company for loss of profits for being deprived of the use of the jetty and should be included in the taxpayer company's trading receipts for the relevant year. On appeal,

Held: the taxpayer company was properly assessed to income tax in

A respect of the sum of £21,404 received for consequential damage, because damages recovered in respect of the loss of the profitable use of the jetty were separate from and governed by different considerations from its physical injury and were a revenue receipt, moreover there had not been destruction of the capital asset (the jetty); and (per DIPLOCK, L.J.) it was compensation received for the company's being deprived of the amounts which

B it would have received from customers for the use of the jetty, the balance of which amounts after deducting expenses would have been credited to the profits of the company's trade in the relevant year, with the consequence that it should be treated as a revenue receipt for income tax purposes (see p. 132, letter I, to p. 133, letter A, p. 134, letter F, and p. 135, letter G, post).

C Per DIPLOCK, L.J.: where, pursuant to a legal right, a trader receives from another person compensation for the trader's failure to receive a sum of money which, if it had been received, would have been credited to the amount of profits (if any) arising in any year from the trade carried on by him at the time when the compensation is so received, the compensation is to be treated for income tax purposes in the same way as that sum of money

D would have been treated if it had been received instead of the compensation (see p. 134, letter G, post).

Decision of BUCKLEY, J. ([1966] 3 All E.R. 145) reversed.

[As to whether damages constitute income or capital receipts for income tax purposes, see 20 HALSBURY'S LAWS (3rd Edn.) 13-15, para. 8; and for cases on the subject, see 28 DIGEST (Repl.) 29, 30, *130*, *131*.

E For the Income Tax Act, 1952, s. 137, see 31 HALSBURY'S STATUTES (2nd Edn.) 134.]

Cases referred to:
Burmah Steam Ship Co., Ltd. v. *Inland Revenue Comrs.*, 1931 S.C. 156; 16 Tax Cas. 67; 28 Digest (Repl.) 45, **127*.

F *Crabb (Inspector of Taxes)* v. *Blue Star Line, Ltd.*, [1961] 2 All E.R. 424; [1961] 1 W.L.R. 1322; 39 Tax Cas. 482; Digest (Cont. Vol. A) 845, *172a*.

Ensign Shipping Co., Ltd. v. *Inland Revenue Comrs.*, (1928), 12 Tax Cas. 1169; 139 L.T. 111; 17 Asp. M.L.C. 472; 28 Digest (Repl.) 414, *1836*.

Glenboig Union Fireclay Co., Ltd. v. *Inland Revenue Comrs.*, 1922 S.C. (H.L.) 112; 12 Tax Cas. 427; 28 Digest (Repl.) 412, *1829*.

G *Gracie (Owners)* v. *Argentino (Owners), The Argentino*, (1888), 13 P.D. 191; affd., H.L., (1889), 14 App. Cas. 519; 59 L.J.P. 17; 61 L.T. 706; 42 Digest (Repl.) 937, *7290*.

Morahan v. *Archer and Belfast Corpn.*, [1957] N.I. 61.

Newcastle Breweries, Ltd. v. *Inland Revenue Comrs.*, [1927] All E.R. Rep. 287; 96 L.J.K.B. 735; 137 L.T. 426; sub nom. *Inland Revenue Comrs.* v. *Newcastle Breweries, Ltd.*, 12 Tax Cas. 927; 28 Digest (Repl.) 413, *1883*.

H *Pryce* v. *Elwood*, (1964), 108 Sol. Jo. 583.

R. v. *British Columbia Fir and Cedar Lumber Co., Ltd.*, [1932] All E.R. Rep. 147; [1932] A.C. 441; 101 L.J.P.C. 113; 147 L.T. 1; 38 Digest (Repl.) 475, **120*.

Short Brothers, Ltd. v. *Inland Revenue Comrs., Sunderland Shipbuilding Co., Ltd.* v. *Inland Revenue Comrs.*, (1927), 12 Tax Cas. 955; 136 L.T. 689;

I 28 Digest (Repl.) 412, *1831*.

Williams v. *Inland Revenue Comrs.*, [1943] 1 All E.R. 318; 112 L.J.K.B. 259; 168 L.T. 195; affd. H.L., [1944] 1 All E.R. 381, n.; 26 Tax Cas. 23; 28 Digest (Repl.) 350, *1547*.

Appeal.

This was an appeal by the Crown from a decision of BUCKLEY, J., on Apr. 27, 1966, reported at [1966] 3 All E.R. 145, allowing the taxpayer company's appeal by way of Case Stated from a decision of the Commissioners for the Special

Purposes of the Income Tax Acts that a sum of £21,404 (being part of an amount A
of about £77,876 recovered from shipowners as damages occasioned by negligent
navigation of the shipowners' vessel resulting in collision with a jetty belonging
to the taxpayer company) was a trading receipt and chargeable to income tax
accordingly.   BUCKLEY, J., held that the damage suffered by the taxpayer
company all flowed directly from physical injury to a capital asset of the taxpayer
company's business and that the compensation received was the relief, whole B
and indivisible, for that injury and this was a capital sum and not in part a
trading or revenue receipt.   By notice dated July 1, 1966, the Crown gave
notice of appeal that the determination and assessment of the commissioners
should be restored.   The grounds of the appeal were (i) that the sum of £21,404
formed part of the annual profits or gains arising or accruing to the taxpayer
company from its trade; (ii) that the sum of £21,404 was the amount of profit C
which the taxpayer company would have earned by the use of its jetty if the
jetty had not been temporarily damaged; (iii) that the sum of £21,404 was
received by the taxpayer company as compensation for an injury inflicted on its
trading, and that sum accordingly was to be substituted for the profits lost as
a result of such injury; (iv) that the judge was wrong in law in treating the
sum of £21,404 received by the taxpayer company as though it formed part of a D
whole and indivisible larger sum received by the taxpayer company as damages
for negligence, and (v) that the sum of £21,404 was the equivalent of the amount
recoverable by the taxpayer company as a separate head of damage in respect
of loss of profit of its trade.

The cases noted below* were cited during the argument in addition to those
referred to in the judgments.   E

Arthur Bagnall, Q.C., and *J. R. Phillips* for the Crown.
Hubert H. Monroe, Q.C., and *J. E. H. Pearce* for the taxpayer company.

WILLMER, L.J.: In the course of the argument this has been made to
appear to be a difficult and complicated case, but it is in fact a very simple case,
and in my judgment a very plain case.   It comes before us on appeal from a F
judgment of BUCKLEY, J. (1), given on Apr. 27, 1966, on a Case Stated by the
Special Commissioners of Income Tax in relation to an assessment to income tax
made against the taxpayer company under Case I of Sch. D for the year 1955-56
in the sum of £21,404.   This sum represented damages which had been recovered
from a wrongdoer in respect of loss of profits in connexion with the taxpayer
company's business as a wharf owner.   The Special Commissioners decided that G
this sum, recovered in respect of loss of profits, was taxable as a trading receipt.
BUCKLEY, J., came to the opposite conclusion, holding (2) that the sum recovered
was in respect of a capital loss, so that it constituted a capital receipt, and as
such was not taxable.   The Crown has now appealed to this court.

The essential facts of the case are extremely simple.   The taxpayer company
owns a number of jetties at its Thames Haven oil installation, where tankers H
bringing oil can berth for purposes of discharge.   On Apr. 22, 1953, a tanker,
while coming alongside one of these jetties, was so negligently navigated that she
struck the jetty in such a way as to cause serious damage thereto.   The physical
damage to the jetty necessitated repairs at a cost of £83,168.   In addition,
however, it is said that the taxpayer company sustained consequential damage
through loss of use of its jetty during the period while it was under repair, a I
period which amounted in all to 380 days.   That loss was quantified at the
figure of £32,450.   That figure was the result of a quite arbitrary calculation
based on a percentage of the capital cost of the jetty; but no question has

---

* *Corr* v. *Larkin*, [1949] I.R. 399; *Inland Revenue Comrs.* v. *West*, (1950), 31 Tax
Cas. 402; *West Suffolk County Council* v. *W. Rought, Ltd.*, [1956] 3 All E.R. 216; [1957]
A.C. 403; *Diamond* v. *Campbell-Jones*, [1960] 1 All E.R. 583; [1961] Ch. 22; *Thomas
McGhie & Sons, Ltd.* v. *British Transport Commission*, [1962] 2 All E.R. 646; [1963]
1 Q.B. 125; *John Mills Productions, Ltd.* v. *Mathias*, (1964), 43 A.T.C. 262.
(1) [1966] 3 All E.R. 145.   (2) [1966] 3 All E.R. at p. 153.

A been raised in this appeal with regard to the method of quantifying this damage. It may well be that it was adopted for the reason that the jetty had been only newly built, so that no figures were available to show what rate of profit would ordinarily be expected to accrue from the use of the jetty. It will be seen from the figures which I have given that the taxpayer company's total loss was £115,618. The owners of the tanker admitted liability; but they were able to limit their

B liability in pursuance of the Merchant Shipping Acts (3) to a sum of £77,876, which sum they duly paid together with the appropriate interest thereon.

The taxpayer company was insured against physical damage to its property, but was not insured against consequential damage. In these circumstances it reached an agreement with its underwriters to the effect that the sum recovered from the owners of the tanker should be apportioned rateably as between physical

C damage and the consequential damage, and that the underwriters should pay to the taxpayer company the unrecovered balance in respect of the physical damage. The final result of it all was as follows. The taxpayer company recovered in full the physical damage to its jetty, amounting to £83,168. It recovered by way of contribution towards its consequential loss the sum of £21,404, and it also recovered the sum of £2,325 by way of interest, making a

D grand total of £106,897. The question is whether that sum of £21,404 recovered from the tanker owners in part satisfaction of the claim for loss of use is taxable as a trading receipt in the hands of the taxpayer company.

In the course of the argument we have been referred to a considerable number of authorities, to some of which I shall have to refer in the course of this judgment. It seems, however, to me that the question which we have to decide is

E eminently a question of fact, which depends on the answer to the question: what did the sum of £21,404 represent? To adopt a phrase used in one of the authorities to which we have been referred, what place in the economy of the taxpayer company's business does this payment take?

I have said that the taxpayer company is the owner of these wharves and jetties, and in the ordinary way earns profits by the use of the jetties for the

F purpose of berthing tankers. In my judgment the same principles must apply to a jetty constructed for commercial use as apply to a ship which is engaged in commercial trading. In this connexion I venture to read the oft-quoted words of BOWEN, L.J., in *The Argentino,* " *Gracie* " *(Owners)* v. *Argentino (Owners)* (4) where he said:

G " A ship is a thing by the use of which money may be ordinarily earned, and the only question in case of a collision seems to me to be, what is the use which the shipowner would, but for the accident, have had of his ship, and what (excluding the element of uncertain and speculative and special profits) the shipowner, but for the accident, would have earned by the use of her."

H In this case, if there had been no collision, the taxpayer company would have had the use of its jetty, and by the use of its jetty it would ordinarily have earned profits. Having lost these profits, it was entitled to recover from the wrongdoer such a sum of money as would, so far as possible, put it back in the same position as that in which it would have been but for the collision. Owing to the tanker owners' right to limitation of liability, the amount actually recovered did not in fact provide full indemnity, but so far as it went it gave back to the taxpayer

I company part of what it could have expected to earn by the use of its jetty. If there had been no collision, the profits which the taxpayer company would have earned by the use of the jetty would plainly have been taxable as a trading receipt. Why, it may be asked, should not the same apply to the sum of money recovered from the wrongdoer in partial replacement of those profits?

(3) See the Merchant Shipping Act, 1894, s. 503, as extended by the Merchant Shipping (Liability of Shipowners and Others) Act, 1900, s. 1; 23 HALSBURY'S STATUTES (2nd Edn.) 656, 780.

(4) (1888), 13 P.D. 191 at p. 201.

In that connexion we were referred to the report of *The Argentino* (5) in the **A** House of Lords.   I should explain that that was a case where the owners of a ship damaged in collision were held to be entitled to recover the loss of profit which they would have made out of a charterparty which had been fixed, and which was lost in consequence of the collision.   In the House of Lords, however, LORD HERSCHELL pointed out (6) that, if the owners got back their ship from the repairers before the date when the charterparty voyage (if it had taken place) **B** would have been completed, they would have to give credit for any profits that they could have earned during the unexpired period.   Any such profits would clearly, I think, have constituted a revenue receipt; and it might be thought to follow from that that the damages for loss of the charterparty, against which any such actual earnings would have to be set off, should also be regarded as a revenue receipt.   **C**

In the present case, however, the judge came to the conclusion in the event that it was not possible to separate the damages recovered in respect of the loss of use of the jetty from those recovered in respect of the physical injury.   He treated the whole as damages for physical injury to a capital asset, and therefore as a capital receipt.   I am bound to say, however, that I have felt some difficulty in following the reasoning of the judge, and it does seem to me that in the course **D** of delivering his judgment he rather contradicted himself.   The judge is recorded as saying this (7):

" The damage to the taxpayer company's jetty was undoubtedly damage to a capital asset.   That damage occasioned not only the need to incur expense in repairing the physical damage, but also an interruption in the **E** profitable use of the jetty.   Both these consequences of the physical damage were natural and direct results of that physical damage.   The taxpayer company had but one cause of action against the owners of the ship which caused the damage, but the damages recoverable in respect of that cause of action involved two distinct elements requiring two distinct enquiries and calculations."   **F**

Then a little later he went on (8):

" If, in the present case, the jetty, instead of being damaged, had been entirely destroyed by an explosion, the amount recoverable as damages would have included an element related to the profitability of the jetty, but no part of such damage would, in my opinion, have fallen to be treated as a **G** matter of sound accountancy or for fiscal purposes as profit of the taxpayer company's business."

So far I wholly agree with everything that the judge said.   Then, however, he continued (9):

" Can it make any difference in this respect that, instead of being wholly **H** destroyed, the jetty was only partially damaged, and that, instead of losing all future profit from the jetty, the taxpayer company lost the profitable use of the jetty for only 380 days?   In my judgment, none.   The damage which the taxpayer company suffered all flowed directly from physical injury to a capital asset of its business, the jetty, inflicted by the negligent handling of a ship.   The amount of damages which the taxpayer company **I** might have recovered constitutes the relief, whole and indivisible, to which the company became entitled in consequence of that injury, subject only to the shipowners' statutory right to limit their liability.   Although some part of that amount related to the loss of use of the jetty for 380 days, this

---

(5) (1889), 14 App. Cas. 519.   (6) (1889), 14 App. Cas. at p. 524.
(7) [1966] 3 All E.R. at p. 151.   (8) [1966] 3 All E.R. at pp. 151, 152.
(9) [1966] 3 All E.R. at p. 152.

A   fact does not, in my judgment, make that part of the damages proper to be brought into account as a revenue receipt of the business."

It seems to me that in this passage, particularly where the judge referred to " the relief, whole and indivisible, to which the appellant became entitled ", he was forgetting what he had said (in my view quite correctly) previously (10)

B   viz., that the damages recoverable in respect of the cause of action " involved two distinct elements requiring two distinct enquiries and calculations ".

Moreover, it appears to me, with all respect to the view of the judge, that there is all the difference in the world between a total loss and a partial injury. In the case of a total loss, what can be recovered from the assumed wrongdoer is the value of that which has been lost.   If the thing lost is a ship or a jetty which is ordinarily used for the purpose of earning profits, the fact of its profit-

C   ability is an element to be considered in assessing its capital value.   In such a case the owner's right is a right to recover the value of the thing which has been lost, and this can no doubt be properly described as " whole and indivisible ", even though it includes some element of profitability of the thing lost; in such circumstances what is recovered is properly treated as a capital receipt.   Where, however, there is only a partial injury, as there was in the present case, there are

D   necessarily two elements to be considered if the owner is to be put back, so far as money can do it, in the same position in which he would have been but for the tortfeasor's wrongdoing.   First, he can recover the whole cost of repair, which is without doubt a capital receipt.   Secondly, he can also recover something in respect of the loss of use during the period of repair, which the judge, in the first of the passages which I have read, quite rightly held to be a distinct element.

E   I repeat, therefore, the question which I asked before: why should not damages recovered under this head be regarded as a trading receipt, in that they represent the trading profit which the owner would have earned if he had the use of his ship, or of his jetty?   If that is not a correct view of the law, then I would venture to say that there is something very much wrong with the law, for the consequence would be that a jetty owner, such as the taxpayer company, would

F   be better off by being subjected to a casualty of this sort (i.e., by losing the use of his jetty and recovering damages therefor) than he would be if he were able to use it continuously for the purpose of making profits.   That, as it seems to me, would be a very strange result indeed.

The taxpayer company's case has been very largely founded on the decision of the Court of Session and the House of Lords in *Glenboig Union Fireclay Co.,*

G   *Ltd.* v. *Inland Revenue Comrs.* (11).   That was a case in which a company was the lessee of a fireclay bed, part of which lay under a line belonging to a railway company.   The railway company commenced an action against the lessees of the fireclay bed to restrain them from working their fireclay under the railway, and pending the decision of the action it obtained an interdict from the Scottish court restraining the company from working under the railway.   That litigation

H   eventually went to the House of Lords, taking three years to get there, and in the event was decided in favour of the fireclay company.   The railway company thereupon exercised its statutory power to require that the part of the fireclay bed which lay under its line should be left unworked on payment of compensa-tion.   The compensation was duly paid to the fireclay company.   That company, however, presented an additional claim for damages against the railway company,

I   the damages consisting of the expense to which the company had been put during the three years' litigation in keeping open the fireclay field, and in due course the company received a sum of money by way of damages in addition to the compensation.

The question then arose whether the compensation and the damages recovered, or either of them, constituted trading receipts which rendered the company liable to tax, or whether, on the other hand, they constituted capital receipts.

---

(10) (1966) 3 All E.R. at p. 151.   (11) (1922), 12 Tax Cas. 427.

It was decided in the result that both the compensation and the damages were A capital receipts, the compensation because it was a payment made (to use the words used in the case) for the sterilisation of a capital asset, and the damages because the claim was a claim for expenditure incurred in protecting a capital asset, which turned out in the event to be unproductive because of the railway company's exercise of its statutory powers.

It seems to me that the result of that case in all the circumstances was hardly B surprising. The fireclay in which the company was interested was a capital asset, but it was a capital asset which could be turned into profit only by consuming it. When the railway company exercised its statutory powers, the fireclay company lost their capital asset; they could no longer consume the fireclay. In those circumstances it appears to me to be a natural result that the compensation recovered should be regarded as a capital receipt. It seems to C me, however, that loss of such a consumable capital asset was something very different from the loss of use of the jetty in this case; for a jetty is a thing which is enjoyed, not by consuming it, but by using it for the purpose of berthing ships.

With regard to the damages claimed in the *Glenboig* case (12), the ratio of the Court of Session decision was that the expenditure proved in the event to be D unproductive and, to use the words of the Lord President (LORD CLYDE), turned out to be a dead loss. It was, for this reason, held to be a capital loss, and the damages recovered in respect thereof were held to be a capital receipt; but LORD CLYDE at least made it clear that the result would, in his view, have been different if the expenditure had turned out to be productive, in the sense of enabling the fireclay company to resume working the fireclay, and thereby make E a profit. This appears from what he said in his opinion (13):

" If they were successful in the law courts, and the railway did not exercise the powers (14) of s. 71, the expenditure would turn out productive, at least to some extent, because it would enable the fireclay, temporarily under interdict, to be eventually worked. If, on the other hand, they were unsuccessful in the law courts, or if (notwithstanding their success) the railway F ultimately fell back on the powers of s. 71, it would turn out to be money thrown away, and the loss of the money would be attributable not to any commercial misadventure but to the exercise by the railway of the rights and powers belonging to it under statute. In the former case, the expenditure would be shown to form a proper trading expenditure, and to be a legitimate deduction from gross profit in estimating the ' profit arising or accru- G ing ' from the company's trade. In the latter case, it would be shown to be money spent without the possibility of return, and would therefore constitute just a loss of so much capital."

Once that case is fully understood, I am bound to say that I find it difficult to see how it really helps the taxpayer company in the present case.

Most of the other cases to which we have been referred seem to me to be H wholly favourable to the Crown's contention. I certainly do not find it necessary to refer to all the cases cited, but I should mention some of them. There are, for instance, the two cases referred to in the judge's judgment, *Ensign Shipping Co., Ltd.* v. *Inland Revenue Comrs.* (15) and *Burmah Steam Ship Co., Ltd.* v. *Inland Revenue Comrs.* (16). The judge himself quoted (17) at some length from the judgments in both these cases, and I do not find it necessary to set out the I quotations again.

Neither of these cases is by any means on all fours with the present case, but in so far as they are relevant they seem to me to afford a good deal of support for the Crown's contention. The first of these cases (15) related to compensation

---

(12) (1922), 12 Tax Cas. 427.   (13) (1922), 12 Tax Cas. at p. 449.
(14) Section 71 of the Scottish Railways Clauses Consolidation Act, 1845.
(15) (1928), 12 Tax Cas. 1169.   (16) (1931), 16 Tax Cas. 67.
(17) [1966] 3 All E.R. at pp. 150, 151.

A recovered by shipowners from the government for the detention of two ships by order of the government during a coal strike, and it was held by ROWLATT, J., and approved by the Court of Appeal, that the sum recovered was a sum paid to the owners in lieu of profits which the ships would have earned during the period of detention, *as if* they had been requisitioned. ROWLATT, J., was careful to point out that it was not the same as a requisition, but he dealt with
B the sum recovered *as if* there had been a requisition.

In the second case (18) the shipowners recovered from ship repairers agreed damages for exceeding the stipulated time for the repair of their ship, and those damages had been calculated by reference to the profit which the ship would have earned had she been delivered in time. That was held to be a trading receipt. That again was a case which came before the Court of Session, and the Lord President
C (LORD CLYDE) (who, it will be remembered, had also been a party to the decision in the *Glenboig* case (19)) delivered an opinion in which he said (20) that the damages were to be treated as " filling the hole " in the shipowner's trading profits which had been caused by the repairer's delay in completing the repairs. LORD CLYDE specifically referred to the *Glenboig* case (19) and then went on (21):

D
" But, as the case just referred to shows, it is very relevant to inquire whether the thing, in respect of which the taxpayer has recovered damages or compensation, is deprivation of one of the capital assets of his trading enterprise, or—short of that—a mere restriction of his trading opportunities."

I cite that sentence as stating in very succinct form the problem which has to be solved in a case of this sort.

E *R.* v. *British Columbia Fir and Cedar Lumber Co., Ltd.* (22), was a case where a timber company had taken out fire policies to cover themselves against loss of profit due to interruption of their business by fire. On a fire occurring, the question arose whether the moneys recovered under those policies should be treated as a capital or revenue receipt. The matter eventually found its way to the Privy Council, where it was decided that the sum recovered was to be
F treated as a revenue receipt. I think that the ratio of the decision is really summarised in the judgment of the Board delivered by LORD BLANESBURGH, where he said (23):

" In view of the nature and origin of the receipt, as they have traced these, their lordships have reached the conclusion that within the meaning even of the interpretation clause this receipt was ' income from a business ', and that
G in ordinary parlance it was income or gain derived from the business of the respondents which had necessarily to be brought into receipt as such in the profit and loss account of the business referred to . . ."

in the section of the statute.

That decision was referred to and followed by this court in *Williams* v.
H *Inland Revenue Comrs.* (24), which again was a case of money recovered under an assurance policy (in that case a life policy). LORD GREENE, M.R., in delivering the leading judgment, referred to the *British Columbia Lumber* case (22) and said (25):

" A manufacturer can, of course, insure his factory against fire. The receipts from that insurance will obviously be capital receipts. But supposing he goes further, as the manufacturer did in that case, and insures
I himself against the loss of profits which he will suffer while his factory is out of action, it seems to me it is beyond question that sums received in respect of that insurance against loss of profits must be of a revenue nature."

(18) (1031), 16 Tax Cas. 67.   (19) (1922), 12 Tax Cas. 427.
(20) (1931), 16 Tax Cas. at p. 71.   (21) (1931), 16 Tax Cas. at p. 72.
(22) [1932] All E.R. Rep. 147; [1932] A.C. 441.
(23) [1932] All E.R. Rep. at p. 151; [1932] A.C. at p. 450.
(24) [1943] 1 All E.R. 318; 26 Tax Cas. 23.
(25) [1943] 1 All E.R. at p. 321; 26 Tax Cas. at p. 37.

It appears from the way in which he expressed himself that that was a matter **A** about which LORD GREENE had no sort of doubt whatsoever. Unless it can be said that moneys recovered from insurers are to be viewed differently from moneys recovered from a wrongdoer, it seems to me that those cases really conclude this case in favour of the Crown's contention. It has been sought to argue that moneys received from insurers are in a different category from moneys recovered from wrongdoers; but, with all possible respect to the argu- **B** ment which has been advanced in that respect, it seems to me to be quite without foundation. In either case the question must be what the sum recovered repre- sents, and in either case the answer to that question must be that it represents profit which would otherwise have been earned by the use of the thing concerned.

I should mention also the two cases of *Morahan* v. *Archer and Belfast Corpn*. (26) and *Pryce* v. *Elwood* (27), both of which were decisions at first instance. Both **C** cases related to damages recovered from a wrongdoer for the loss of use of a motor car which had been damaged in collision, and which was ordinarily used for commercial purposes. In both cases only a very brief report is available, but in each case the judge who dealt with the matter had no difficulty in deciding that the damage recovered in respect of loss of use would constitute a revenue receipt. As I said when I started to review these cases, they all appear to me **D** to point in the same direction.

It has, however, been very strenuously argued on behalf of the taxpayer company that the £21,404 recovered from the tanker owners was really all part of the damages recovered for injury to the jetty. It was pointed out to us, quite fairly, that the jetty was not a construction which was going to be there for all time, but had a life of only some twenty-five years. Consequently, **E** because of the time occupied in effecting the repairs, it had only a depreciated value at the end of the repair period. It was submitted that it was quite irrele- vant that this part of the damages recovered was quantified by reference to loss of use, for the way in which a loss is quantified cannot affect the quality of the loss. What was said was that the sums recovered, whether from the insurers or from the wrongdoer, should be regarded as one whole, amounting in **F** total to compensation for the physical injury to the jetty. It was said, to use the phrase that was used in the *Glenboig* case (28), that during the period of repairs the jetty was a sterilised asset, just like the fireclay in that case. As I understood the argument, it was conceded that, if there had been no collision, and therefore no physical damage to the jetty, but the tanker had sunk just outside it so as to block access to it and prevent its use, a different result might **G** be arrived at. It seems to me that it would be strange indeed if the quality of the damages recovered for loss of use should be held to depend on the accidental circumstance whether or not there happened also to be physical injury to the jetty.

I think that the argument presented on behalf of the taxpayer company was. fallacious in two respects. In the first place, it appears to me to proceed on the **H** basis that the cause of action in a case such as this is the damage to the jetty. In truth, however, as was pointed out during the argument, the cause of action in a case of negligence is the injury to the plaintiff. In the present case the injury to the taxpayer company was a twofold injury. It not only suffered damage to its jetty, but it also suffered loss of the profits which it would have earned from its use. Secondly, I think that the argument which was presented **I** to us was fallacious in so far as it was sought to equate damages for loss of use of the jetty with depreciation of the capital value of the jetty. It seems to me that the two things are quite distinct.

I am left in no doubt that in this case the damages recovered in respect of the physical injury to the jetty are quite separate from, and governed by quite different considerations from, the damages which were recovered in respect of

(26) [1957] N.I. 61.   (27) (1964), 108 Sol. Jo. 583.
(28) (1922), 12 Tax Cas. 427.

A the loss of profitable use of the jetty. It appears to me that both on principle and on the authorities, to some of which I have referred, the sum recovered for loss of use of the jetty must be treated as a revenue receipt, and therefore properly taxable. For these reasons I would allow this appeal and would restore the decision of the Special Commissioners.

B   HARMAN, L.J.: Questions relating to capital and income are among points that in my experience arise no less in the region of fiscal law, in which we are here involved, than in that of inheritance, where they are as thick as autumn leaves; and it is tempting to try to classify them and to decide whether they fall on one side of the line or the other. The judge in the court below seems at one time to have been tempted to farm out the authorities in this way; but, as **C** he rightly reminds himself in his judgment (29):

> " Judges have from time to time been careful to say that no clear and comprehensive rule can be formulated, and no clear line of demarcation can be drawn, by reference to which it can be determined in every case whether the sum received should be regarded as a capital receipt or as a revenue receipt to be taken into account in arriving at the profits or gains of the **D** recipient's trade. Each case must be considered on its own facts."

As WILLMER, L.J., says, this is in the end a question of fact. How then do these facts stand? There is no doubt that the £21,404, which is the subject of this controversy, was arrived at between the parties by a highly arbitrary process based on the estimated loss of profit during the time in which the jetty was out of use. But that does not carry one much further, for as LORD BUCKMASTER **E** said in *Glenboig Union Fireclay Co., Ltd.* v. *Inland Revenue Comrs.* (30):

> " There is no relation between the measure that is used for the purpose of calculating a particular result and the quality of the figure that is arrived at by means of the application of that test."

He then went on to say that he was unable to regard the sum of money recovered **F** in that case as anything but capital money, and that it was erroneously entered in the balance sheet of the company concerned as a profit. So that so far one is not advanced any further forward by finding out how the sum has been arrived at, or in relation to what.

    The taxpayer company's case, as I have understood it, is that the total sum recovered is damages for the tanker owners' negligence—one cause of action, one **G** answer in damages—which, though measured in two ways, is none the less one sum. It argues further that this is compensation, and not profit from carrying on a trade; and this, it says, is the very antithesis of the annual profits and gains of the trade within which it must fall in order to bear tax under Case I of Sch. D, which is the claim that was made. The judge in the end (by a process which I must confess that I do not altogether follow) accepted that view. I find myself **H** unable to agree with him. It does seem to me that there is at least one valid test, viz., whether there has been the destruction of some capital asset of the company.

    That is well illustrated by the *Glenboig* case (31), with which WILLMER, L.J., has dealt in his judgment. In that case the pillar of fireclay left to support the railway, under the railway company's statutory rights, was permanently **I** lost to the mining company. That was a capital asset which had been destroyed, and therefore compensation for it was a capital receipt. Similarly, damages which they had received for maintaining the mine during the period of interdict, which turned out to be useless, was a sum of money employed in preserving what would have been (or what was at the time) a capital asset, and therefore partook of the nature of a capital receipt. Accordingly, the *Glenboig* case (31) seems to me to be a clear enough case.

---

(29) [1966] 3 All E.R. at p. 149.   (30) (1922), 12 Tax Cas. at p. 464.
(31) (1922), 12 Tax Cas. 427.

The other cases, or very many of them, are either instances of the disposal of A stock-in-trade, or money recovered under a contract, for instance, on an insurance policy made in the course of trade with a view to providing against the very event which had happened. *Newcastle Breweries* v. *Inland Revenue Comrs.* (33) dealt with goods requisitioned by the government, and *Ensign Shipping Co., Ltd.* v. *Inland Revenue Comrs.* (34) was concerned with what would have been compensation received by shipowners for compulsory detention of ships by B the government. In that case there was no destruction of the ships, which were capital assets; they were merely put out of commission. *Burmah Steam Ship Co., Ltd.* v. *Inland Revenue Comrs.* (35) related to a sum paid for delay in delivery, and that fell under the head of income as being a mere trading receipt; see the observations of LORD MORISON (36). In *R.* v. *British Columbia Fir and Cedar Lumber Co., Ltd.* (37), in the Privy Council, the receipts were C receipts under a fire insurance policy; and, as was pointed out, in so far as they were receipts for destruction of assets by fire, they were, of course, capital receipts, but in so far as they were related to loss of profit for those assets if they had not been burned, they were revenue receipts. *Crabb* (*Inspector of Taxes*) v. *Blue Star Line, Ltd.* (38) related to an insurance against late delivery of ships, and this was similar to diminution in the price of a capital asset. Lastly, D there is *Short Brothers, Ltd.* v. *Inland Revenue Comrs.* (39) where the sum received was compensation for the cancellation of a contract to build a ship, and that was held to be an ordinary trading receipt of the company's business.

On the whole, therefore, such attention as I have been able to give to the cases seems to me to show them holding a fairly consistent result when looked at in the light of the particular circumstances of each case when those are borne in E mind individually. In my opinion the judge mistook the effect of them and was wrong. I agree that his decision should be reversed, and this appeal allowed.

DIPLOCK, L.J.: I agree. The question whether a sum of money received by a trader ought to be taken into account in computing the profits or gains arising in any year from his trade is one which ought to be susceptible of solution F by applying rational criteria; and so, I think, it is. I see nothing in experience as enbalmed in the authorities to convince me that this question of law, even though it is fiscal law, cannot be solved by logic, and that, with some temerity, is what I propose to try to do.

I start by formulating what I believe to be the relevant rule. Where, pursuant to a legal right, a trader receives from another person compensation for the trader's failure to receive a sum of money which, if it had been received, would G have been credited to the amount of profits (if any) arising in any year from the trade carried on by him at the time when the compensation is so received, the compensation is to be treated for income tax purposes in the same way as that sum of money would have been treated if it had been received instead of the compensation. The rule is applicable whatever the source of the legal right H of the trader to recover the compensation. It may arise from a primary obliga-tion under a contract, such as a contract of insurance; from a secondary obliga-tion arising out of non-performance of a contract, such as a right to damages, either liquidated, as under the demurrage clause in a charterparty, or un-liquidated; from an obligation to pay damages for tort, as in the present case; from a statutory obligation; or in any other way in which legal obligations arise. I

The source of a legal right is relevant, however, to the first problem involved in the application of the rule to the particular case, viz., to identify for what the compensation was paid. If the solution to the first problem is that the com-pensation was paid for the failure of the trader to receive a sum of money, the

(33) [1927] All E.R. Rep. 287; 12 Tax Cas. 927.
(34) (1928), 12 Tax Cas. 1169.   (35) (1931), 16 Tax Cas. 67.
(36) (1931), 16 Tax Cas. at p. 76.
(37) [1932] All E.R. Rep. 147; [1932] A.C. 441.
(38) [1961] 2 All E.R. 424; 39 Tax Cas. 482.   (39) (1927), 12 Tax Cas. 955.

A second problem involved is to decide whether, if that sum of money has been received by the trader, it would have been credited to the amount of profits (if any) arising in any year from the trade carried on by him at the date of receipt, i.e., would have been what I shall call for brevity an income receipt of that trade. The source of the legal right to the compensation is irrelevant to the second problem. The method by which the compensation has been assessed in the

B particular case does not identify for what it was paid; it is no more than a factor which may assist in the solution of the problem of identification. I will not again traverse the cases. They seem to me to be directed to the solution of one or other of these two problems, which are not always distinguished in the judgments. In the course of these judgments different metaphors and similies (appropriate no doubt to the particular facts of the case) have been used. But I do

C not think that any of these conflict with the rule as I have expressed it.

In the present case the source of the legal right of the taxpayer company was its right to recover from the owners of the tanker damages for the loss caused to it by the negligent navigation of the tanker. Damages for negligence are compensatory. The company's right was to recover by way of damages a sum of money which would place it, so far as money could do so, in the same position

D as it would have been in if the negligent act had not taken place. The negligent act had two consequences: (i) it caused physical damage to the taxpayer company's jetty, and (ii) it prevented it from using its jetty for the purposes of its trade for 380 days. Each of these consequences caused it loss, first the expense to it of repairing the jetty, and secondly the loss of the balance of the amounts that it would have received from customers for the use of of the jetty, less the

E expenses it would have incurred in earning those sums during the 380 days while the jetty was out of use. For the loss sustained under each of these heads it was entitled to recover compensation from the owners of the tanker as damages for negligence. Under the second head it recovered £21,404. This is the compensasation with which the present appeal is concerned.

The solution to the first problem is that the £21,404 is identified as compensa-

F tion received by the taxpayer company from the owners of the tanker for the company's failure to receive the balance of the amounts which it would have received from customers for the use of the jetty, less the expenses that it would have incurred in earning these sums during the 380 days while the jetty was out of use. If this be the true identification, the answer to the second problem is that such balance, if it had been received, would have been credited to the

G amount of profits (if any) arising in any year from the taxpayer company's trade. Prima facie, therefore, the £21,404 is to be treated for income tax purposes in the same way.

Counsel for the taxpayer company has sought to escape this conclusion in the first instance by expressing the identity of what the compensation was paid for as the diminution in value of a capital asset, viz., the jetty, resulting from the

H physical harm done to the jetty. By that physical harm, he says, it was transformed from a jetty which (a) required no repairs, and (b) could be used for the next 380 days, into a jetty which (a) required repairs costing £83,168, and (b) could not be used for the next 380 days. I think that this analysis starts too late. It assumes that the cause of action was based on the physical harm done to the jetty and on nothing else. But I do not think that that is so. The cause

I of action was based on the loss sustained by the appellant trader by the negligent navigation of the tanker, and the loss sustained because the jetty could not be used for 380 days would have been recoverable even if there had been no physical harm to the jetty as, for example, if the tanker had sunk alongside the jetty, so preventing its use. I do not see how the identity of what the £21,404 was paid for can be affected by whether or not the loss of use was accompanied by physical damage.

An alternative way in which counsel for the taxpayer company puts it is that

the £21,404 compensation was paid to the company for not using its capital **A**
asset, the jetty. But I think that this is no more than ingenious semantics
designed to bring this case within some of the words used in *Glenboig Union
Fireclay Co., Ltd.* v. *Inland Revenue Comrs.* (40). The taxpayer company was paid
for the loss which it suffered because, owing to the wrongful act of the tanker
owners, it was unable to use the jetty, just as the taxpayer in *Ensign Shipping Co.,
Ltd.* v. *Inland Revenue Comrs.* (41) was unable to use his ship by reason of the **B**
exercise of paramount power of the Crown, in *Burmah Steam Ship Co., Ltd.* v.
Inland Revenue Comrs. (42) by the ship repairers' breach of contract, and in
R. v. *British Columbia Fir and Cedar Lumber Co., Ltd.* (43), because the taxpayer
was unable to use his premises because of the occurrence of the risk insured
against.

These cases are to be contrasted with cases where compensation is paid for **C**
the destruction or permanent deprivation of the capital asset used by a trader
for the purposes of his trade. Here the asset thereafter ceases to be one by the
use or exploitation of which the taxpayer company carries on its trade. As a
result of such destruction or deprivation the company ipso facto abandons that
part of its trade which involves the use of the capital asset of which it has been
deprived by destruction or otherwise, and profits which it would, but for its **D**
destruction, have made by its use or exploitation will thereafter no longer form
part of the profits arising from the trade which the company continues to carry
on. Even if the compensation payable for loss of the capital asset has been
calculated in whole or in part by taking into consideration what profits the
taxpayer company would have made had it continued to carry on a trade involving the use or exploitation of the asset, this does not alter the identity of what the **E**
compensation is paid for, viz., the permanent removal from its business of a
capital asset which would otherwise have continued to be exploited in the
business; see the *Glenboig* case (40).

Furthermore, even if any part of the compensation so calculated were treated
as paid for the taxpayer company's failure to receive such profits, the claim to
treat it for income tax purposes as profits from the use or exploitation of the **F**
asset would fail in the course of solving the second problem, since the use or
exploitation of the asset has ex hypothesi ceased to form part of the trade
carried on at the time of receipt. I agree with the order proposed by my lords.

Appeal allowed. Leave to appeal to the House of Lords refused.

Solicitors: *Solicitor of Inland Revenue; Slaughter & May* (for the taxpayer **G**
company).

[*Reported by* F. A. AMIES, ESQ., *Barrister-at-Law.*]

H

I

(40) (1922), 12 Tax Cas. 427.
(41) (1928), 12 Tax Cas. 1169.
(42) (1931), 16 Tax Cas. 67.
(43) [1932] All E.R. Rep. 147; [1932] A.C. 441.

A

SHULTON (GREAT BRITAIN), LTD.
v. SLOUGH BOROUGH COUNCIL.

[QUEEN'S BENCH DIVISION (Diplock, L.J., Ashworth and Paull, JJ.), March 3, 1967.]

B *Trade Mark—False trade description—Application—Time of application—*
 " Cause " to apply false trade description to goods—Manufacturer sold goods
 to retailer in August—Goods displayed by retailer in December and sold—
 Goods then short in volume or weight—Falsity of trade description at time when
 manufacturer applied it not proved—Whether false trade description applied
 at time of sale by retailer—Whether manufacturer caused retailer to apply
C *false trade description—Merchandise Marks Act, 1887 (50 & 51 Vict. c. 28),*
 s. 2 (1).

On Dec. 9, 1965 an inspector of weights and measures found three toilet articles, a deodorant stick and two bottles of skin conditioners, manufactured by the appellants and sold by them on or before Aug. 18, 1965, to S., a large department store, displayed on the premises. The inspector bought

D them and tested them. He found the deodorant stick to be below the weight and the conditioners to be below the volume marked on them. The weight and volumes had been marked on the goods by the appellants at some date before Aug. 18, 1965. The deodorant was volatile, if not properly sealed. No evidence was adduced that it did not bear the correct weight at the time of delivery to S. The conditioners were non-volatile. In early November, 1965,

E the appellants learnt that the marking on the conditioners was incorrect. They sent letters to all their customers, including S., directing their attention to the incorrect marking, and requested that the products be withdrawn from sale or display. Shortly thereafter, they sent fresh labels to re-mark the contents of the conditioners in grams and asked that a check be made of the gross weight of the product. This was admitted by S. On appeal by the

F appellants against convictions under s. 2 (1) (*d*), (*f*)* of the Merchandise Marks Act, 1887, for applying false trade descriptions and for causing them to be applied to the goods when displayed by S. on Dec. 9, 1965,

Held: (i) the words " applies any false trade description to goods " in s. 2 (1) (*d*) referred to the act of application of a false trade description, which in the present case would have been done, if done at all, by the appellants, at

G the time prior to Aug. 18, 1965, when the goods were manufactured and put in containers and not on Dec. 9, and an application of a false trade description at that date was not proved (compare p. 141, letter A, and p. 142, letters G and I, post).

(ii) the appellants had parted with the goods when they were sold to S., on Aug. 18, 1965, and they were not thereafter in a position to exercise any

H dominance or control or give any mandate to S. to do anything with the goods; accordingly the appellants had not, on Dec. 9, 1965, " caused " S., within the meaning of the word " cause[d] " in s. 2 (1) (*f*), to apply a false trade description to the goods (see p. 142, letters D, G and I, post).

Dictum of DONOVAN, J., in *Shave* v. *Rosner* ([1954] 2 All E.R. at p. 282) applied.

I **Quaere** whether the fact that goods bearing a trade description were on display in a shop would amount to the application of a trade description to the goods by the proprietors of the shop (see p. 141, letter I, post).

Appeal allowed.

[As to the application of a false trade description, see 38 HALSBURY'S LAWS (3rd Edn.) 491, 492, para. 821; and for cases on the subject, see 46 DIGEST (Repl.) 166-168, *1101-1118.*

---

* Section 2, so far as material, is set out at p. 140, letters G to I, post.

As to the meaning of " causing " in a criminal context, see 10 HALSBURY'S **A**
LAWS (3rd Edn.) 279, para. 519, text and notes (y)-(a).

For the Merchandise Marks Act, 1887, s. 2 (1), s. 5, see 25 HALSBURY'S
STATUTES (2nd Edn.) 1114, 1118.]

Cases referred to:

   McLeod (*or Houston*) v. *Buchanan*, [1940] 2 All E.R. 179; 1940 S.C. (H.L.) 17;
      29 Digest (Repl.) 538, *3693*.   **B**

   Mercer v. *Co-operative Retail Services, Ltd.*, (1963), 128 J.P. 45; 46 Digest
      (Repl.) 165, *1099*.

   Shave v. *Rosner*, [1954] 2 All E.R. 280; [1954] 2 Q.B. 113; [1954] 2 W.L.R.
      1057; 118 J.P. 364; 45 Digest (Repl.) 71, *210*.

Case Stated.
                                                                        C

This was a Case Stated by justices for the petty sessional division of Slough in
the county of Buckingham in respect of their adjudication as a magistrates'
court sitting at Slough on July 18, 1966, whereby they convicted the appellants,
Shulton (Great Britain), Ltd. of three offences under s. 2 (1) of the Merchandise
Marks Act, 1887. On May 27, 1966 three informations were preferred by the
respondents, Slough Borough Council, against the appellants charging that they   **D**
on Dec. 9, 1965, at Suters, Ltd., High Street, Slough did cause to be applied a
certain false trade description, namely " 2⅝ ozs.", to a container of Old Spice Stick
Deodorant when the actual net weight was 2 ozs. 5¾ drams, contrary to s. 2 (1)
of the Merchandise Marks Act, 1887; on the same date and at the same place
did cause to be applied a certain false trade description, namely "140 cc.", to
a bottle of Old Spice After Shave Skin Conditioner when the actual contents   **E**
were 127 cc., contrary to the same section of the same statute; and on the same
date and at the same place did cause to be applied a certain false trade description, namely "140 cc.", to a bottle of Old Spice After Shave Skin Conditioner
when the actual contents were 129 cc., contrary to the same section of the same
statute.

    The following facts were found. On Dec. 9, 1965 one Honour, an inspector of   **F**
weights and measures employed by the respondents, visited the premises of
Suters, Ltd. (" Suters ") a large department store in the High Street at Slough.
Among goods on display at Suters were (i) a container of Old Spice Stick
Deodorant manufactured by the appellants and sold by them to Suters. The
container bore a weight marking " Net Wt. 2⅝ oz."; (ii) a bottle of Old Spice
After Shave Skin Conditioner manufactured by the appellants and sold by them   **G**
to Suters. This bottle bore a content marking " 140 cc."; (iii) another bottle of
Old Spice After Shave Skin Conditioner manufactured by the appellants and
sold by them to Suters. This bottle bore the same content marking of " 140 cc.".
The inspector purchased these three articles from Suters on the same date,
returned to the Weights and Measures Department and measured the contents.
The measurements of the contents were (i) (the stick deodorant): 2 ozs.   **H**
5¾ drams. There was thus a deficiency of 4¼ drams from the weight marked;
(ii) (the first bottle of skin conditioner): 127 cc. There was thus a deficiency of
13 cc from the contents marked; (iii) (the second bottle of skin conditioner):
129 cc. There was thus a deficiency of 11 cc. from the contents marked. In each
case the appellants caused the content marking to be applied. Stick deodorants,
such as (i), are liable to evaporate if the top of the container becomes loose or if   **I**
the container for any reason ceases to be sealed. The skin conditioner material,
such as was contained in (ii) and (iii), is not liable to evaporate. The appellants
changed the marking on stick deodorants such as (i) from ounces to grams in
about March or April, 1965. Container (i) was delivered by the appellants
to Suters on or before Aug. 18, 1965, there being no deliveries of this product to
Suters after that date. The appellants at their factory made tests designed to
ensure that stick deodorant containers were properly filled and at the date of
delivery container (i) should have been of the correct weight. There was no

A evidence before the magistrates' court that it was not. The bottles of skin conditioner, (ii) and (iii), were delivered by the appellants to Suters, on or before Aug. 18, 1965, there being no deliveries of this product to Suters after that date, and were probably delivered on Aug. 18, 1965. In each case the appellants caused the relevant weight or content marking to be applied to the products before delivery to Suters and with the expectation at the time that the marking

B would remain on the products after delivery to Suters. In early November, 1965, the appellants learnt, as a result of a complaint in Kingston-upon-Thames, that the marking of 140 cc. on bottles of skin conditioner such as (ii) and (iii) was incorrect. On Nov. 5, 1965, the appellants sent to all their customers who received Old Spice products (which customers included Suters) a letter dated Nov. 5, 1965, drawing the retailer's attention to the incorrect marking of Old

C Spice After Shave Skin Conditioner and requesting that the product be withdrawn from sale and display immediately. A copy of this letter was produced to the justices and a copy was sent to Suters. A further letter dated Nov. 26, 1965, was sent to all the same customers. This letter again referred to the incorrect content marking on the skin conditioner, notified the retailer of a new content marking in grams which was to be introduced, enclosed labels with which

D to re-mark the contents of the product and asked that a check be made of the gross weight of the product. A copy of this letter was produced to the justices and a copy was sent to Suters. Suters admitted, both orally to the inspector (to whom they also sent a copy of the letter dated Nov. 26, 1965) and by a letter dated Dec. 31, 1965 to the appellants which was produced to the justices, that the appellants had previously warned them that one of the appellants' products

E bore an incorrect content marking.

It was contended by the appellants before the justices that (i) they did not cause the content markings (which were admittedly trade descriptions) to be applied to the goods on Dec. 9, 1965 at Slough but prior to Aug. 17, 1965 at their factory; (ii) in respect of the earlier date different questions of both fact and law arose (e.g. as to limitation and as to whether the markings were incorrect

F at that earlier date); (iii) a manufacturer who has once caused a trade description to be applied is not liable under s. 2 (1) of the Merchandise Marks Act, 1887, if, at an indefinite date in the future, when the goods are out of his ownership, possession and control, the description is found to be inaccurate; (iv) in respect of the informations concerning bottles of skin conditioner the appellants on Dec. 9, 1965, acted without intent to defraud within the meaning of s. 2 (1) of

G the Act of 1887 because they did not on that date intend to do the act forbidden by the statute and were actively taking all possible steps to avoid any breach of the law, and their conduct in causing the trade description in question to be applied had come to an end before Dec. 9, 1965.

It was contended by the respondent borough council that (a) the appellants had caused the weight marking to be applied to the container of Old Spice Stick

H Deodorant on Dec. 9, 1965, at Slough and had caused the content markings to be applied to the two bottles of Old Spice After Shave Skin Conditioner on Dec. 9, 1965, at Slough, the markings in question being of a continuing nature; (b) the weight marking and content markings were false and were trade descriptions within the meaning of s. 2 (1) of the Merchandise Marks Act, 1887; (c) the appellants were accordingly guilty of the offences charged unless they proved

I that they had acted without intent to defraud; (d) it would not be enough to prove that the appellants had acted without intent to defraud by proving that they had acted by error or inadvertence or without a dishonest intention or that Suters had not been deceived or prejudiced. The justices were of opinion that the appellants were guilty on all three informations for the following reasons. (i) The weight marking and content markings were false trade descriptions and the appellants caused them to be applied to the goods in question when they were displayed at Suters on Dec. 9, 1965, because it was still their responsibility on that date to have ensured that these goods were not so displaying such false

trade descriptions. The justices appreciated the steps taken by the appellants to A
put matters right before the offences took place, and the difficulties they faced
in these circumstances, which were inherent in their activities and formed part
of their trading risks in that connexion. These were absolute offences, the doing
of which supplied the mens rea (subject to certain statutory defences), the Act
of 1887 being designed to protect the public; and to have held other than that
the appellants were guilty in these circumstances would have been to have gone B
against the whole tenor of the Act of 1887 in that connexion. (ii) The words
" without intent to defraud " in s. 2 (1) of the Act of 1887 should be construed
in the same way as the words " otherwise acted innocently " in s. 2 (2) of the Act.
(iii) In construing these words " otherwise acted innocently " the justices were
guided by the judicial dicta contained in *Slatcher* v. *George Mence Smith, Ltd.**
that these words were not satisfied by proof that the accused had acted in good C
faith and had taken all precautions against committing an offence against the
Act of 1887, but must be construed as meaning that they had acted inadvertently
or under a misapprehension or mistake of fact. (iv) The justices did not find
that there was inadvertence, misapprehension, or mistake of fact by the
appellants in any of these cases; and held that the submissions of the appellants
in this respect did not go to defence, but were by way of mitigation only. D
Accordingly, they fined the appellants £30 for each of the offences.

The authority noted below† was cited during the argument in addition to the
cases referred to in the judgment of DIPLOCK, L.J.

Sir John Hobson, Q.C., and *T. H. Bingham* for the appellants.
Leonard Caplan, Q.C., and *Leo Clark* for the respondents.
                                                                          E

DIPLOCK, L.J.: The three toilet articles were sold by the appellants to
Suters, Ltd. some time before Aug. 18, 1965. On Dec. 9, 1965 an inspector of
weights and measures found these three articles among the goods on display at
Suters and purchased them. On test they were found to contain in the first case
less than the weight and the second case less than the volume marked on the containers. There was no evidence directed to the question of what the contents of F
the containers were at the time at which the articles were sold to Suters.

The charge was brought under s. 2 (1) (*d*) and (*f*) of the Merchandise Marks
Act, 1887, which section, so far as is relevant, provides:

" Every person who . . . (*d*) applies any false trade description to goods; or
. . . (*f*) causes any of the things above in this section mentioned to be done,
shall, subject to the provisions of this Act, and unless he proves that he G
acted without intent to defraud, be guilty of an offence against this Act.
" (2) Every person who sells, or exposes for, or has in his possession for,
sale, or any purpose of trade or manufacture, any goods or things to which
any forged trade mark or false trade description is applied, or to which any
trade mark or mark so nearly resembling a trade mark as to be calculated to
deceive is falsely applied, as the case may be, shall, unless he proves either— H
" (*a*) that, having taken all reasonable precautions against committing
an offence against this Act, he had, at the time of the commission of the
alleged offence, no reason to suspect the genuineness of the trade mark,
mark or trade description, and that, on demand made by or on behalf
of the prosecutor, he gave all the information in his power with respect
to the persons from whom he obtained such goods or things; or I
" (*b*) that otherwise he had acted innocently;
be guilty of an offence against this Act (1)."

Subsection (3) deals with the penalties for the offences. Before the magistrates,
the appellants contended that they did not cause the markings to be applied

---
* [1951] 2 All E.R. 388.
† BELL'S SALE OF FOOD AND DRUGS (13th Edn.) (Service Volume) 84.
(1) Section 2 (2) is printed as substituted by the Merchandise Marks Act, 1953, s. 4;
33 HALSBURY'S STATUTES (2nd Edn.) 920.

A to the goods on Dec. 9, 1965 at Slough, but prior to Aug. 17, 1965 at their factory. At the close of the prosecution case a submission was made by the appellants that no case was made out, and an opportunity was given to the prosecution, if they wished, to amend the charge under s. 100 of the Magistrates' Courts Act, 1952 in order to put a different date, namely one earlier than Aug. 18, 1965. The prosecu-tion did not accept that offer, but elected to proceed with the charge as laid

B relating to application of the mark to the goods on Dec. 9, 1965 at Suters, Ltd., Slough, the contention of the prosecution being that s. 2 (1) (*d*) created a con-tinuing offence. Before us, it has been contended by counsel for the appellants that that is not the case, and that the charge of applying a false description to goods or causing that to be done relates to the act of application of the mark, and that that act having been committed, any subsequent matters in relation to

C the use of the false trade description are dealt with by s. 2 (2) of the Act of 1887.

I have read both s. 2 (1) and s. 2 (2) and in my view, having regard to the context in which the words " applies any false trade description to goods " appear, and to the general scheme of the Act of 1887 as manifested by the description of the offences in sub-ss. (1) and (2), the phrase " applies any false description to goods " means the act of application of the false description. In

D the present case that was done, if it was done at all, by the appellants at the time when they manufactured the goods and put them into the containers. That is so far as the matter goes under s. 2 of the Act of 1887, and there is no previous authority directly on the point. There is, however, a decision of this court in *Mercer* v. *Co-operative Retail Services, Ltd.* (2) which indicates, although it is not the actual ratio decidendi of that case, that LORD PARKER, C.J., who gave the

E judgment of the court, took the same view as to the construction of the word " applies " in s. 2 (1) of the Act of 1887, which I have indicated appeals to me as the correct one. I need not read the judgment, but it contains passages (3) which make it plain that it was on that basis that the court was deciding the case.

The respondents, however, have another string to their bow in that s. 5 of

F the Merchandise Marks Act, 1887, does provide for circumstances in which a person shall be deemed to apply a trade mark. Section 5 (1) provides:

" A person shall be deemed to apply a trade mark or mark or trade descrip-tion to goods who—(*a*) applies it to the goods themselves; or (*b*) applies it to any covering, label, reel, or other thing in or with which the goods are sold or exposed or had in possession for any purpose of sale, trade, or manu-

G facture; or (*c*) places, encloses, or annexes any goods which are sold or exposed or had in possession for any purpose of sale, trade, or manufacture, in, with, or to any covering, label, reel, or other thing to which a trade mark or trade description has been applied; or (*d*) uses a trade mark or mark or trade description in any manner calculated to lead to the belief that the goods in connexion with which it is used are designated or described by that

H trade mark or mark or trade description."

The respondents submitted that as it was found in the Case that these articles were on display at Suters, Suters in addition to exposing them and having them in their possession for sale, which would be an offence under s. 2 (2) of the Act of 1887, were also guilty of the offence of applying a false trade description to

I goods under s. 2 (1) (*d*) of the Act of 1887, and it was submitted that by sending out and selling the goods to Suters with the false description on them, the appellants caused Suters to apply a false trade description to the goods.

For my part I do not find it necessary to decide whether the mere finding, in passing, that the goods were on display would amount to the offence of applying a false description to the goods on the part of Suters. That might raise a difficult question of construction in the context of the Act of 1887. It is not, however, necessary to decide that for the purposes of this case, for I am satisfied that the

---

(2) (1963), 128 J.P. 45.   (3) (1963), 128 J.P. at pp. 46, 47.

appellants cannot be said to have caused Suters to apply a false trade description   **A**
to the goods within the meaning of s. 2 (1) (*f*). " Causing " in a criminal statute
of this kind appears to me to require what it was said to require by the House of
Lords in *McLeod* (*or Houston*) v. *Buchanan* (4), and I need only refer to a passage
in the speech of LORD WRIGHT, where he said (5):

> " To ' cause ' the user involves some express or positive mandate from the
> person ' causing ' to the other person, or some authority from the former to   **B**
> the latter, arising in the circumstances of the case."

That decision, which was in a Scottish appeal, was adopted by this court in
Shave v. *Rosner* (6). The judgment of DONOVAN, J., sets out, in my view correctly,
what is required in order to constitute the offence of causing someone else to do
an act which is unlawful. DONOVAN, J., said (7):
  C

> " ' Cause ', in this context, involves, on the authorities cited, some degree
> of dominance or of control, or some express or positive mandate, that is, in
> or by the person alleged to have caused the prohibited act, and in the present
> case there was no such dominance or control, and no such mandate."

If one examines the relationship between the appellants and Suters on Dec. 9,
1965, the appellants had parted with all property, possession and control of the   **D**
goods to Suters when they sold them to Suters on Aug. 18. They were not in a
position to exercise any dominance or control or to give any express or positive
mandate to Suters to do anything with the goods at all. Nor, so far as I can see,
did they purport to do so, except that they did endeavour sometime in November
to prevent Suters from putting the skin conditioner on display with the false
trade description on it after they had found that the description was false. In   **E**
my view, therefore, even if it could be said that Suters themselves applied a false
description to the goods on Dec. 9, 1965, the alternative way in which it was
put, it cannot be said that the appellants caused them to do so. In my view
there was no offence under s. 2 (1) (*d*) and (*f*) of the Act of 1887 disclosed on the
evidence. Whether other offences might have been charged and might have been
successfully proved, I do not know. The respondents were given an opportunity   **F**
to amend the charge to a date at which it might well be said that the appellants
did apply the description to the goods, but they elected not to do so and in these
circumstances this appeal must be allowed and the conviction quashed.

    ASHWORTH, J.: I agree. I would only add that the error into which the
justices fell appears in my view quite plainly from the Case Stated where they
state their reasons. At the beginning they say: **G**

> " The weight marking and contents markings were false trade descrip-
> tions and the appellants caused them to be applied to the goods in
> question when they were displayed at Suters' shop, Slough, on Dec. 9, 1965,
> because it was still their responsibility on that date to have ensured that
> these goods were not so displaying such false trade descriptions."

  H
It was because of that reason that they found these offences proved. In my judgment there is no foundation whatever for the proposition that it was the
responsibility of the appellants to have ensured the removal of the faulty goods,
and for the reasons given by DIPLOCK, L.J., in addition to the reason that
I have just stated, I agree that this appeal succeeds.

    PAULL, J.: I agree with both judgments.   **I**

Appeal allowed. Convictions quashed.

    Solicitors: *Slaughter & May* (for the appellants); *Sharpe, Pritchard & Co.*,
agents for *Norman T. Berry*, Slough (for the respondents).

[*Reported by* S. A. HATTEEA, ESQ., *Barrister-at-Law.*]

---

(4) [1940] 2 All E.R. 179.   (5) [1940] 2 All E.R. at p. 187.
(6) [1954] 2 All E.R. 280; [1954] 2 Q.B. 113.
(7) [1954] 2 All E.R. at p. 282; [1954] 2 Q.B. at p. 117.

A   SOMMERFELDS, LTD. *v.* FREEMAN (Inspector of Taxes).

[CHANCERY DIVISION (Plowman, J.), November 30, December 1, 2, 8, 1966.]

Income Tax—Income—Damages—Loss of profit from right of pre-emption—
Breach of contract to give pre-emption over surplus stocks—Income Tax
Act, 1952 (15 & 16 Geo. 6 & 1 Eliz. 2 c. 10), Sch. D, Case I.

B   The managing director of two engineering companies, the K. company
and the taxpayer company, owned virtually the whole of the share capital
in both. In March, 1950, the K. company purchased the whole of the issued
share capital of the taxpayer company, which thus became its wholly-owned
subsidiary, and immediately afterwards it transferred its business as a
going concern to the taxpayer company under a formal agreement which
C   transferred the benefit of all pending contracts and engagements of the
business and all other property and assets of the business. The K. company
then ceased to trade. At that time the K. company had a contract with the
Ministry of Supply conferring an option to take any material known as
Sommerfeld track declared surplus by the War Office. The Ministry broke
this contract by disposing of nine thousand tons elsewhere. The K. company
D   obtained £50,000 compensation from the Ministry in respect of that breach,
the sum being computed by estimating the loss of profit on six thousand
tons (three thousand tons being made good otherwise). The Ministry
paid the sum by a cheque drawn in favour of the K. company, which endorsed
it over to the taxpayer company, for payment into its account, but the
accounts of both companies treated the sum as a loan. Ministry of Supply
E   surpluses were one of the sources of supply of the business which the
K. company sold to the taxpayer company. The taxpayer company was
assessed to tax on the £50,000 as part of the profits of its trade under Sch. D
to the Income Tax Act, 1952, and the Special Commissioners confirmed the
assessment, holding that the sum was a revenue receipt and not a loan.
On appeal,

F   *Held:* the taxpayer company was rightly assessed to tax in respect of the
£50,000 for the following reasons—

(i) because the £50,000 belonged in equity to the taxpayer company, as the
K. company would have been bound to accept for the benefit of the taxpayer
company any offer to the K. company of the nine thousand tons of Sommerfeld track if the taxpayer company wanted the material, and the £50,000
was designed to put the K. company in the same position as if the offer had
G   been made and accepted (see p. 148, letter A, post).

(ii) because the £50,000 was not a loan despite its entry as a loan in the
books of account (see p. 148, letter B, post).

(iii) because the £50,000 was a receipt of a revenue and not of a capital
nature, since it represented compensation for the loss of profit on six thousand
H   tons of material (see p. 149, letter G, post).

London and Thames Haven Oil Wharves, Ltd. v. *Attwooll (Inspector of*
Taxes) ([1966] 3 All E.R. 145), and *Bush, Beach & Gent, Ltd.* v. *Road* ([1939]
3 All E.R. 302) applied.

Appeal dismissed.

[As to whether damages constitute income or capital receipts for income tax
I   purposes, see 20 HALSBURY'S LAWS (3rd Edn.) 13-15, para. 8; and for cases on
the subject, see 28 DIGEST (Repl.) 29, 30, *130*, *131*.

As to miscellaneous receipts constituting trade receipts under Case I of Sch. D
to the Income Tax Act, 1952, see 20 HALSBURY'S LAWS (3rd Edn.) 153, 154,
para. 268; and for cases on the subject, see 28 DIGEST (Repl.) 20-49, *78-186*;
64-68, *236-259*; 71-86, *268-328*.]

Cases referred to:
Barr, Crombie & Co. v. *Inland Revenue Comrs.*, (1945), 26 Tax Cas. 406;
28 Digest (Repl.) 127, **375*.

Bush, Beach & Gent, Ltd. v. *Road*, [1939] 3 All E.R. 302; [1939] 2 K.B. 524;   **A**
    108 L.J.K.B. 801; 161 L.T. 117; 22 Tax Cas. 519; 28 Digest (Repl.)
    27, *114*.

Dewar v. *Inland Revenue Comrs.*, [1935] All E.R. Rep. 568; [1935] 2 K.B. 351;
    104 L.J.K.B. 645; 153 L.T. 357; 19 Tax Cas. 561; 28 Digest (Repl.)
    333, *1475*.

Glenboig Union Fireclay Co., Ltd. v. *Inland Revenue Comrs.*, (1922), 12 Tax   **B**
    Cas. 427; 28 Digest (Repl.) 412, *1829*.

Inland Revenue Comrs. v. *Glasgow and South-Western Ry. Co.*, (1887), 12 App.
    Cas. 315; 56 L.J.P.C. 82; 57 L.T. 570; 11 Digest (Repl.) 249, **785*.

Kelsall Parsons & Co. v. *Inland Revenue Comrs.*, (1938), 21 Tax Cas. 608;
    28 Digest (Repl.) 126, **372*.

London and Thames Haven Oil Wharves, Ltd. v. *Attwooll* (*Inspector of Taxes*),   **C**
    [1966] 3 All E.R. 145; [1966] 3 W.L.R. 325; *rvsd.* C.A., ante p. 124;
    [1967] 2 W.L.R. 743.

Mills (*John*) *Productions, Ltd.* v. *Mathias*, (1964), 43 A.T.C. 262.

Newcastle Breweries, Ltd. v. *Inland Revenue Comrs.*, [1927] All E.R. Rep. 287;
    96 L.J.K.B. 335; 137 L.T. 426; 12 Tax Cas. 927; 28 Digest (Repl.)
    413, *1883*.   **D**

Regent Oil Co., Ltd. v. *Strick* (*Inspector of Taxes*), *Regent Oil Co., Ltd.* v. *Inland
    Revenue Comrs.*, [1965] 3 All E.R. 174; [1966] A.C. 295; [1965] 3 W.L.R.
    636; 3rd Digest Supp.

Short Bros., Ltd. v. *Inland Revenue Comrs., Sunderland Shipbuilding Co., Ltd.*
    v. *Inland Revenue Comrs.*, (1927), 12 Tax Cas. 955; 136 L.T. 689; 28
    Digest (Repl.) 412, *1831*.   **E**

Smith (*John*) *& Son* v. *Moore*, [1921] 2 A.C. 13; 90 L.J.P.C. 149; 125 L.T. 481;
    12 Tax Cas. 266; 28 Digest (Repl.) 421, *1860*.

Spencer v. *Macmillan's Trustees*, 1958 S.C. 300; 37 A.T.C. 388; Digest (Cont.
    Vol. A) 463, **114a*.

Van den Berghs, Ltd. v. *Clark* (*Inspector of Taxes*), [1935] All E.R. Rep. 874;
    [1935] A.C. 431; 104 L.J.K.B. 345; 153 L.T. 171; 19 Tax Cas. 390;   **F**
    28 Digest (Repl.) 117, *450*.

Woodhouse v. *Inland Revenue Comrs.*, (1936), 20 Tax Cas. 673; 28 Digest
    (Repl.) 333, *1479*.

Case Stated.

The taxpayer company appealed to the Special Commissioners of Income Tax
against assessments to income tax made on it under the Income Tax Act, 1952,   **G**
Sch. D, Case I, in the following sums: 1950-51 £8,000; 1951-52 £8,000; 1952-53
£10,000 and 1953-54 £10,000. The question for decision was whether a sum
of £50,000 paid by the Ministry of Supply in January, 1952, by a cheque which
was issued to K. J. & A. Sommerfeld, Ltd., and endorsed over to the taxpayer
company, should be included as a revenue receipt in computing the profits
arising from the trade carried on by the taxpayer company for income tax   **H**
purposes. The taxpayer company contended as follows: (i) that the sum of
£50,000 was paid to and received by K. J. & A. Sommerfeld, Ltd., as the only
contracting party entitled to it, and thus belonged to that company and not to
the taxpayer company; (ii) alternatively that the sum was paid by way of
compromise to K. J. & A. Sommerfeld, Ltd., against which no claim was made
by or available to the taxpayer company to recover the payment, and that the   **I**
taxpayer company was not in those circumstances liable to be taxed in respect of
the sum; (iii) that the sum was a receipt of a capital nature because it had
been paid and received for the loss of: (a) the value of a contractual right at the
date of the breach of contract; (b) a source from which circulating capital could
have been obtained to earn income, or alternatively (c) an asset on which the
profit-making or commercial organisation of the business had been constructed;
(d) (if the sum was held to belong to the taxpayer company) a part of the initial
assets of the taxpayer company's business; and (iv) that the £50,000 should

A not accordingly be included as a revenue receipt in computing the profits of the trade carried on by the taxpayer company for income tax purposes.   The Crown contended: (i) that the £50,000 belonged to the taxpayer company, and (ii) that it should be included as a revenue receipt in computing the profits arising from the trade carried on by the taxpayer company for the year ended Apr. 30, 1952, assessable to income tax for the year 1953-54.

B   The commissioners held (A) that the sum of £50,000 belonged to the taxpayer company under the terms of an agreement between it and K. J. & A. Sommerfeld, Ltd., notwithstanding the way in which it was dealt with in the books of the two companies; and (B) that it was a receipt of a revenue nature.   They therefore held that the appeal failed in principle, but adjusted the assessments to the following figures: 1950-51 £3,277 (agreed capital allowances £3,277); 1951-52
C £2,677 (agreed capital allowances £2,677);   1952-53 £3,154 (agreed capital allowances £3,154);   and 1953-54 £54,359 (agreed capital allowances £5,847). The taxpayer company appealed by way of Case Stated to the High Court.

      The cases noted below* were cited during the argument in addition to those referred to in the judgment.

      R. R. D. Phillips for the taxpayer company.
D   *J. R. Phillips* for the Crown.

Cur. adv. vult.

      Dec. 8.   **PLOWMAN, J.:**   At the beginning of March, 1950, Mr. K. J. Sommerfeld owned virtually the whole of the share capital of two engineering companies, K. J. & A. Sommerfeld, Ltd. (which I shall called the K. company)
E and Sommerfelds, Ltd., the present appellant, the " taxpayer company ". Mr. Sommerfeld was also managing director of both companies.   In that month, the K. company purchased the whole of the issued share capital of the taxpayer company, which thus became its wholly-owned subsidiary.   Immediately afterwards, the K. company transferred its business as a going concern to the taxpayer company and itself ceased to trade.
F   At this time, the K. company had a contract with the Ministry of Supply under which the K. company had an option or a right of pre-emption in respect of so much of certain material known as " Sommerfeld track " which was stored at two depots, Grangemouth and Long Marston, as might be declared surplus by the War Office.   Shortly after March, 1950, the Ministry of Supply broke its contract by disposing of nine thousand tons of this Sommerfeld track elsewhere,
G and when Mr. Sommerfeld learned of this he wrote to the Ministry of Supply in the name of the taxpayer company requesting that the matter should be put right and saying that otherwise they would claim damages.   The matter was put right to the extent of about three thousand tons, and in respect of the balance the Ministry of Supply, after negotiation, paid £50,000 compensation by a cheque drawn in favour of the K. company.   The cheque was endorsed over to
H the taxpayer company and was paid into that company's account on Jan. 29, 1952.   In the books of the two companies the transaction was shown as a loan by the K. company to the taxpayer company.   The taxpayer company claimed that this £50,000 was a post-cessation receipt of the K. company, but the Special Commissioners decided that it belonged to the taxpayer company and fell to be treated as a revenue receipt in computing the profits of its trade.   From this
I decision the taxpayer company now appeals.

      The argument for the taxpayer company may be summarised as follows. First, it was submitted that the £50,000 never belonged to the taxpayer company

---

      * *J. Gliksten & Son, Ltd.* v. *Green*, [1929] All E.R. Rep. 383; [1929] A.C. 381; *Inland Revenue Comrs.* v. *Scottish Automobile and General Insurance Co., Ltd.*, (1931), 16 Tax Cas. 381; *Evans Medical Supplies, Ltd.* v. *Moriarty (Inspector of Taxes)*, [1957] 3 All E.R. 718; *Sabine (Inspector of Taxes)* v. *Lookers, Ltd.*, (1958), 38 Tax Cas. 120; *Rolls-Royce, Ltd.* v. *Jeffrey (Inspector of Taxes)*, [1962] 1 All E.R. 801; *Fleming (Inspector of Taxes)* v. *Bellow Machine Co., Ltd.*, [1965] 2 All E.R. 513.

at all. Secondly, it was submitted that, if it did, it was never available to the **A**
taxpayer company and, therefore, on the authority of such cases as *Dewar* v.
Inland Revenue Comrs. (1) and *Woodhouse* v. *Inland Revenue Comrs.* (2), is
not taxable as the taxpayer company's income. Thirdly, it was submitted
that, if the money did belong to the taxpayer company and was available to it,
the sum was in its nature a capital and not a revenue receipt. This was put in
four ways. (a) That it was the price paid for the value at the date of the breach **B**
of a contract to supply stock-in-trade, and, as such, did not enter into the
ordinary course of trade. The case on which the taxpayer company primarily
relied under this head was *Spencer* v. *Macmillan's Trustees* (3). (b) That it
was a sum paid in respect of an asset which was a right to obtain circulating
capital and not in respect of circulating capital itself. Here, the taxpayer
company relied principally on *Regent Oil Co., Ltd.* v. *Strick (Inspector of Taxes)* (4). **C**
(c) That it was a sum received for the termination of a contract which was an
asset to which the whole commercial organisation of the taxpayer company
had been related, and was in effect paid for the disruption of that organisation.
The case principally relied on here was *Barr, Crombie & Co., Ltd.* v. *Inland
Revenue Comrs.* (5). (d) Lastly, that it was a sum paid in respect of an asset
which the taxpayer company took over and paid for as part of a going concern **D**
from the K. company, and which was therefore a capital asset on the authority
of *John Smith & Son* v. *Moore* (6). From this it was argued that the money,
being received in respect of a capital asset, was itself capital.

First, then, is the question whether the £50,000 ever belonged to the taxpayer
company. At this point, I must say a little more about the facts. The option
or right of pre-emption to which I have referred is to be found in a letter dated **E**
Oct. 11, 1948, from the deputy director of disposals at the Ministry of Supply
to Mr. Sommerfeld, with a copy to the K. company. It is headed " Contract
12/sales (RE)/2553 ". That is a reference to a contract between the Ministry of
Supply and the K. company made some two years earlier for the supply of surplus
Sommerfeld track. The letter of Oct. 11 contains the following paragraph:

F

" In return for your agreement that the above mentioned contract shall be
terminated it is further confirmed that, should the material at Long Marston
and Grangemouth recently withdrawn by the War Office be re-declared
as surplus as a result of the consideration now being given to the matter,
you will be given the opportunity of purchasing such material at the prices
shown in the contract. This will be subject to satisfactory arrangements
as to payment and clearance." **G**

The transfer of the K. company's business to the taxpayer company in March,
1950, was effected by an agreement dated Mar. 19, 1950, made between the
K. company as vendor and the taxpayer company as purchaser. That agreement
first of all contains this recital:

H

" The vendor [the K. company] has for some time past carried on business
as engineers, dealers and contractors at Trench Works aforesaid and elsewhere and has agreed to sell to the [taxpayer] company the goodwill of
the said business and the assets connected therewith which are hereinafter
mentioned at the price and on the terms hereinafter contained."

Then, in the operative part, cl. 1 provides: **I**

" The vendor [the K. company] will sell and the purchaser [the taxpayer
company] will purchase the said business now carried on by the vendor as
aforesaid as a going concern as from the date hereof and the following
assets thereof, viz. . . . ."

---

(1) [1935] All E.R. Rep. 568; 19 Tax Cas. 561.   (2) (1936), 20 Tax Cas. 673.
(3) (1958), 37 A.T.C. 388.   (4) [1965] 3 All E.R. 174; [1966] A.C. 295.
(5) (1945), 26 Tax Cas. 406.   (6) [1921] A.C. 13; 12 Tax Cas. 266.

A   Then there is included the following: in para. (a), " the goodwill of the said business "; in (d),

> " the benefit of all pending contracts and engagements to which the vendor is entitled in connexion with the said business as at the date hereof including the benefits and obligations appertaining to the post-war refund of excess profits tax ";

B   and, in para. (h),

> " all other property and assets to which the vendor is entitled in connexion with the said business on the date hereof other than those expressly excluded from the sale under the provisions of cl. 2 (1) hereof."

C   Then, in cl. 2 (1) there are certain exclusions which are not material to be stated. In cl. 3 it is provided:

> " The consideration for the sale shall be as follows: (a) In respect of the assets mentioned in cll. 1 (a), 1 (b), 1 (d), 1 (f), 1 (g) and 1 (h) the sum of £100."

D   Then there are certain other considerations which I need not state. Then, in cl. 6 it is provided:

> " Upon the signing of this agreement possession of the said premises and assets shall be given to the purchaser [the taxpayer company] and the consideration under cl. 3 (a) hereof shall be paid and thereupon the vendor [the K. company] shall at the expense of the purchaser execute and do all assurances acts and things for vesting the said premises and assets in the purchaser free from encumbrances and such apportionments (if any) as may be necessary shall be made."

E   The agreement by the Ministry of Supply to pay the £50,000 was recorded in a memorandum dated Jan. 25, 1952, in the following terms. It is headed, " Memorandum of agreement. January 25, 1952 ", and it states:

F   > " Ministry of Supply agree to pay [the K. company] £50,000 which they accept in full and final settlement of their claim against the Ministry of Supply under contract 12/Sales/2553."

That is signed on behalf of the Ministry of Supply by " W. F. Jenkins, under-secretary ", and, on behalf of the K. company by Mr. K. J. Sommerfeld.

The Case Stated says this in para. 8:

G   > " We the commissioners who heard the appeal were of opinion that the undertaking given in the letter of Oct. 11, 1948, regarding material at Long Marston and Grangemouth in the event of its being redeclared as surplus was an asset of [the K. company] which came within cl. (1), para. (d) or (h), of the agreement made on Mar. 19, 1950, between that company and the [taxpayer] company, and that the sum of £50,000, notwithstanding the way in which it was dealt with in the books of [the K. company] and the [tax-

H   payer] company, consequently belonged to the [taxpayer] company."

Counsel for the taxpayer company argued that this was wrong because the benefit of the option or right of pre-emption was not assignable at all, or, if it was, then it was assignable only with the consent of the Ministry of Supply, and it was

I   common ground that no such consent was ever asked for. Let me assume, without deciding it, that this argument is right. Even so, it does not, in my judgment, follow that as between the two companies the £50,000 did not belong beneficially to the taxpayer company whatever may have been the position of those companies vis-à-vis the Ministry of Supply.

Ministry of Supply surpluses were one of the sources of supply of the business which the K. company sold as a going concern to the taxpayer company, and, if the Ministry of Supply, instead of breaking its contract, had offered the nine thousand tons of surplus Sommerfeld track to the K. company, which had ceased

to trade, the K. company would, in my judgment, have been bound under its **A**
agreement with the taxpayer company to accept the offer for the taxpayer
company's benefit if the taxpayer company had wanted the material. From this
it follows, in my judgment, that the £50,000 which was paid in order to put the
K. company in the same position as it would have been in if the offer had been
made and accepted belonged in equity to the taxpayer company.

The second question is whether the £50,000 was ever available to the taxpayer **B**
company. The short answer to this question, in my judgment, is " yes ", because
it got the money. Counsel for the taxpayer company, however, submits that it
got the money only by way of loan from the parent company, as is demonstrated
by the way the transaction was recorded in the books of the two companies. It is,
I think, plain that the Special Commissioners did not accept the evidence of the
books, and neither do I. I have already stated that in my judgment the taxpayer **C**
company had a right to the money, and, when it received it, it was, in my
judgment, entitled to keep it. The payment was not, in reality, a loan at all.

Finally comes the question whether the sum was a receipt of the taxpayer
company of a revenue or capital nature. The decision of the Special Commissioners
was as follows—and I refer again to para. 8 of the Case Stated:

> "Having reviewed in the light of the authorities cited the facts which **D**
> were before us, and in particular those as to how far the loss of the contract
> in question was material in relation to the structure of the business, we came
> to the conclusion that the sum of £50,000 was a receipt of a revenue nature."

The fact that the £50,000 was money paid as damages or compensation is not of
itself conclusive of the question with which I am concerned. Damages may be **E**
capital or income according to the circumstances in which they are paid. Broadly
speaking, it seems that damages paid to replace a capital sum are capital and
damages paid to replace income are themselves income; but it is often difficult
to determine into which category a payment falls.

Various strands of authority were collected by BUCKLEY, J., in the recent
case of *London and Thames Haven Oil Wharves, Ltd.* v. *Attwooll (Inspector of* **F**
Taxes) (7). BUCKLEY, J., said this (8):

> "Where the sum received is of the nature of compensation for the com-
> pulsory purchase of a capital asset or for an out-and-out embargo on the
> exploitation of a capital asset, it has been held to be a capital receipt and not
> revenue, although calculated by reference to the amount of profit lost; see
> *Glenboig Union Fireclay Co., Ltd.* v. *Inland Revenue Comrs.* (9), and *Inland* **G**
> *Revenue Comrs.* v. *Glasgow and South-Western Ry. Co.* (10). Where the receipt
> has been in compensation for the expropriation of stock-in-trade, it has been
> held to be a trading receipt; see *Newcastle Breweries, Ltd.* v. *Inland Revenue*
> *Comrs.* (11). Where the asset, to compensate for the loss or modification of
> which the sum is paid, is the benefit of a contract or of some right under a
> contract, a distinction has been drawn between (a) contracts which regulate **H**
> the recipient's business, or, to borrow LORD MACMILLAN's language in *Van den*
> *Berghs, Ltd.* v. *Clark (Inspector of Taxes)* (12), relate to the whole structure
> of the recipient's profit-making apparatus, in which case the receipt is not
> treated as income but as capital; and (b) contracts made in the course of
> the recipient's business, as in *Kelsall Parsons & Co.* v. *Inland Revenue Comrs.*
> (13), and *Short Brothers, Ltd.* v. *Inland Revenue Comrs., Sunderland Ship-* **I**
> *building Co., Ltd.* v. *Inland Revenue Comrs.* (14), in which case the receipt is
> treated as a revenue receipt of the trade. (See for a review of the authorities
> *Mills (John) Productions, Ltd.* v. *Mathias* (15).)

(7) [1966] 3 All E.R. 145 (revsd. see ante, p. 124).   (8) [1966] 3 All E.R. at p. 149.
(9) (1922), 12 Tax Cas. 427.   (10) (1887), 12 App. Cas. 315.
(11) [1927] All E.R. Rep. 287; 12 Tax Cas. 927.
(12) [1935] All E.R. Rep. 874 at pp. 887, 888; 19 Tax Cas. 390 at pp. 431, 432.
(13) (1938), 21 Tax Cas. 608.   (14) (1927), 12 Tax Cas. 955.
(15) (1964), 43 A.T.C. 262.

A   " Those contracts which fall within the former category can perhaps be equated with fixed physical capital assets as forming part of the basic and enduring structure within or by means of which the business is carried on, whereas contracts of the latter kind can appropriately be equated with the circulating capital or stock-in-trade of the business as belonging to a class of things, not being capital assets, by the exploitation of which, or by the

B   turning of which to account, the profit of the business is made. Not every case, however, can be classified as analogous to the sale of a capital asset on the one hand or a sale of stock-in-trade or some other transaction in the course of the recipient's business on the other. Judges have from time to time been careful to say that no clear and comprehensive rule can be formulated, and no clear line of demarcation can be drawn, by reference to

C   which it can be determined in every case whether the sum received should be regarded as a capital receipt or as a revenue receipt to be taken into account in arriving at the profits or gains of the recipient's trade. Each case must be considered on its own facts."

To this may be added the proposition that damages for breach of contract paid

D   to replace profits which the taxpayer would or might have made under the contract are prima facie a revenue receipt; see *Bush, Beach & Gent, Ltd.* v. *Road* (16).

At this point it is necessary to examine a little more closely exactly what loss it was that the £50,000 represented. This figure was negotiated at a meeting between Mr. Sommerfeld and Mr. Jenkins and Mr. Coleman of the Ministry of

E   Supply on Aug. 29, 1951. A record of what happened at that meeting is contained in para. 3 (12) of the Case Stated. There are references there to the loss of the contract and the termination of the contract, but it is plain that what the agreement was about was the loss of the profit which would have been made on approximately six thousand tons of material if it had been offered in accordance with the contract and taken up. Mr. Jenkins thought that the loss would be about

F   £4 a ton; or, say, £25,000. Mr. Sommerfeld at first suggested that it would be £30 a ton, or £180,000, but later reduced this to £22 a ton, or £132,000. After further discussion, Mr. Sommerfeld suggested a compromise at half that sum—namely, £66,000—and Mr. Jenkins then proposed £50,000, which Mr. Sommerfeld accepted. This sum therefore represented compensation for the loss of profit on six thousand tons of steel, and as such was, in my judgment, a revenue receipt.

G   The propositions and cases on which counsel for the taxpayer company relied deal, I think, with different situations from that confronting me. They seem to me to have little bearing on the present case once one reaches the conclusion that the sum paid (and here I echo LAWRENCE, J., in *Bush, Beach & Gent, Ltd.* v. *Road* (17))

H   " . . . represented profits which the appellants would or might have made under the contract, and not the purchase price of the contract itself . . ."

That, as I have said, is the conclusion which I reach, and accordingly I dismiss this appeal.

Appeal dismissed.

I   Solicitors: *Saunders & Co.* (for the taxpayer company); *Solicitor of Inland Revenue.*

[*Reported by* F. A. AMIES, ESQ., *Barrister-at-Law.*]

---

(16) [1939] 3 All E.R. 302; 22 Tax Cas. 519.
(17) [1939] 3 All E.R. at p. 305; 22 Tax Cas. at p. 523.

A

Re S. (*deceased*).

[PROBATE, DIVORCE AND ADMIRALTY DIVISION (Baker, J.), November 23, 1966.]

*Executor and Administrator—Administrator—Appointment in " special circum-
stances "—Executrix convicted of manslaughter of deceased and sentenced
to life imprisonment—Supreme Court of Judicature (Consolidation) Act,
1925 (15 & 16 Geo. 5 c. 49), s. 162 (1), proviso (b), as substituted by
Administration of Justice Act, 1928 (18 & 19 Geo. 5 c. 26), s. 9.*

B

By his will, the husband appointed his wife his sole executrix and beneficiary. In 1965, the wife was convicted of manslaughter of her husband
and sentenced to life imprisonment. On an application by the daughters
of the deceased under s. 162* of the Supreme Court of Judicature (Consolidation) Act, 1925, as amended, for letters of administration with the will
annexed to be granted to them,

C

Held: letters of administration with the will annexed would be granted
to the daughters, because there were special circumstances within s. 162 (1)
proviso (b) of the Act of 1925, as amended, to enable the court to pass over
the executrix inasmuch as she was serving a term of life imprisonment for a
felony and it was impossible for her to act as executrix (see p. 152, letter A,
post).

D

[As to grant of administration under the discretionary power of the court, see
16 HALSBURY's LAWS (3rd Edn.) 224-226, paras. 410, 411; and for cases on the
subject, see 23 DIGEST (Repl.) 174, *1953-1955.*

For the Supreme Court of Judicature (Consolidation) Act, 1925, s. 162, as
amended by the Administration of Justice Act, 1928, s. 9, see 9 HALSBURY's
STATUTES (2nd Edn.) 777.]

E

Cases referred to:

Crippen, In the Estate of, [1911-13] All E.R. Rep. 207; [1911] P. 108; 80
    L.J.P. 47; 104 L.T. 224; 22 Digest (Repl.) 274, *2772.*

Drawmer (deceased), In the Estate of, (1913), 108 L.T. 732; 23 Digest (Repl.)
    167, *1859.*

Hollington v. *F. Hewthorn & Co., Ltd.,* [1943] 2 All E.R. 35; [1943] K.B. 587;
    112 L.J.K.B. 463; 169 L.T. 21; 22 Digest (Repl.) 244, *2412.*

F

Summons.

This was a summons to show cause why letters of administration with the
will annexed in respect of the estate of the deceased should not be granted to the
applicants, his daughters, passing over the defendant, his widow who was
appointed his sole executrix. The summons was heard in chambers, and the
report is published with the permission of BAKER, J. The facts are set out in
the judgment.

G

Bruce Holroyd Pearce for the applicants.

H

BAKER, J.: The will, which was executed on July 10, 1950, not only
appoints the widow sole executrix, but also leaves all the property to her. She
is the sole beneficiary. The matter first came before the learned registrar on
an application to set aside the will, but it is clear, I think, that that is not the
proper procedure, and counsel for the applicants now asks for letters of administration with the will annexed to be granted to the applicants.

I can summarise the point thus: the widow was, on Dec. 20, 1965, convicted
at assizes of manslaughter. The affidavits make it clear that, in the course of
her trial, she admitted killing her husband. She was in fact convicted of manslaughter, not murder, on the ground of diminished responsibility; and it was
the manslaughter of her husband. Unfortunately, there are evidential difficulties in the way of establishing all this in a court of law. Counsel for the
applicants suggests that there is a way round the difficulty; that, this being

I

---

* Section 162, so far as material is set out at p. 151, letter H, post.

A a civil action, the onus of proof is different from what it would be in a criminal case. I do not think that it is necessary to decide that interesting problem, nor is it necessary to investigate the precise limits of the decision in *Hollington* v. *F. Hewthorn & Co., Ltd.* (1). In *In the Estate of Crippen* (2), the question was whether Crippen's executrix and universal legatee could obtain the grant of letters of administration to the estate of Crippen's wife for whose murder he

B had been convicted. SIR SAMUEL EVANS, P., declined to make the grant, and allowed the murdered wife's sister to take out letters of administration. In *Hollington* v. *F. Hewthorn & Co., Ltd.* (3), GODDARD, L.J., who gave the judgment of the Court of Appeal, said:

C
" SIR SAMUEL EVANS, P., admitted the conviction as proof that the husband had murdered her. The only point that was actually decided was that the fact that the husband was a convicted felon was a sufficient special circumstance to justify passing over his personal representative; and so far the decision is beyond criticism."

He then went on to disagree with SIR SAMUEL EVANS' conclusion that he could admit the conviction as prima facie evidence that Crippen had murdered his

D wife, although " the convenience of the decision is obvious ".

Logically it is difficult if not impossible to justify the decision in *In the Estate of Crippen* (2) on this ground because, as was pointed out in 1943, 59 LAW QUARTERLY REVIEW, p. 300:

E
". . . the fact that the testator, under whom the executrix was claiming, was a convicted felon was completely immaterial unless the conviction proved that he had murdered his wife. In other words, the President was not concerned with Crippen's character (as he might have been with that of the executrix), but only with the fact that he had murdered the woman whose estate was being administered."

PROFESSOR CROSS in his book on EVIDENCE (4) refers to the narrow interpretation of *In the Estate of Crippen* (2), namely, that, under s. 73 of the Court of Probate

F Act, 1857 (now s. 162 of the Supreme Court of Judicature (Consolidation) Act, 1925, as amended by s. 9 of the Administration of Justice Act, 1928) the court may pass over a named personal representative in special circumstances. This, I think, is the surest ground on which to decide the present problem. The executrix is a convicted felon. There is no difficulty about the proof of that; it is clearly established. She admitted on oath to killing, was convicted of

G manslaughter and imprisoned for life. These are proved facts. I need not go beyond them, nor am I concerned whether she was rightly convicted or imprisoned. What happens to the estate hereafter is a matter for the Chancery Division. All I am concerned with is whether, under proviso (b) to s. 162 (1) of the Act of 1925, as amended, I can say that

H
. . . by reason of . . . any other special circumstances, it appears to the court to be necessary or expedient to appoint as administrator some person other than the person who, but for this provision, would by law have been entitled to the grant of administration . . ."

This provision also applies to an executor. BARGRAVE DEANE, J., applied the comparable provisions of the Act of 1857 in *In the Estate of Drawmer* (*decd.*) (5).

I The special circumstances were that the sole executor was serving a prison sentence

(1) [1943] 2 All E.R. 35; [1943] K.B. 587.
(2) [1911-13] All E.R. Rep. 207; [1911] P. 108.
(3) [1943] 2 All E.R. at p. 42; [1943] K.B. at p. 600.
(4) CROSS ON EVIDENCE (1958) 341; (2nd Edn., 1963) 370; this passage is not in the third edition (1967), where at p. 377 note [1] the author stated that the decision in *In the Estate of Crippen* " may perhaps still be supported on the ground that the conviction as such justified the passing over of Crippin's executrix ". The third edition had not been published at the time of the hearing of the present case.
(5) (1913), 108 L.T. 732.

A

for conspiracy and refused to renounce his rights under the will. It does not seem to me to matter whether the executor or executrix refuses or agrees to renounce rights. The executrix is here serving a term of life imprisonment for a felony, and it is quite impossible for her to act as executrix. These are special circumstances within s. 162 (1) proviso (b) which entitle me without more to pass her over and grant letters of administration with the will annexed to the applicants and I so do.

B

Order accordingly.

Solicitors: *W. H. Hopkins & Co.* (for the applicants).

[*Reported by* ALICE BLOOMFIELD, *Barrister-at-Law.*]

C

DURAYAPPAH *v.* FERNANDO AND OTHERS.

[PRIVY COUNCIL (Viscount Dilhorne, Lord Guest, Lord Devlin, Lord Upjohn and Lord Pearson), December 13, 14, 15, 1966, March 9, 1967.]

D

Dictum of LORD UPJOHN at 160
applied in STEVENSON v UNITED
ROAD [1977] 2 All ER 941

Privy Council—Ceylon—Public Authority—Quasi-judicial functions—Minister's order superseding municipal council for incompetence—Rule of natural justice—" Audi alteram partem "—No opportunity given to council to be heard in defence—Whether order voidable or a nullity—Voidable only at election of council—Municipal Ordinance (cap. 252), s. 277 (1).

E

As a result of complaints against the Jaffna Municipal Council, the Minister of Local Government sent the Commissioner of Local Government to inquire into the allegations and report to him immediately. The appellant, the Mayor of Jaffna, gave the commissioner every facility, but the commissioner did not ask any questions or give any member of the council any opportunity of expressing views. He made his report orally and then in writing on May 29. On the same day the Minister made an order stating that the council was not competent to perform the duties imposed on it and that, pursuant to the powers conferred on him by s. 277 of the Municipal Council Ordinance, he directed that the council should be dissolved and superseded on May 29. On May 30, the Governor-General appointed the commissioner together with two other persons to be special commissioners to exercise, perform and discharge the duties and functions conferred on the council or the mayor by the Ordinance. The appellant took proceedings for mandates in the nature of writs of certiorari and quo warranto to quash the order of May 29 and for an interim injunction to restrain the special commissioners from exercising the functions of the council or of the appellant.

F

G

Held: (i) (a) the rule of natural justice, audi alteram partem, was applicable to a decision on the part of the Minister to make an order under s. 277 (1) on the ground of incompetence on the part of the council; accordingly, since the rule had not been observed the order of May 29, 1966, was voidable (see p. 158, letter D, and p. 160, letter C, post).

H

Sugathadasa v. *Jayasinghe* ((1958), 59 N.L.R. 457) disapproved.

(b) moreover the rule, audi alteram partem, was applicable also for the reason that a consequence of the order was to deprive the council of its property (see p. 158, letter D, post).

I

Cooper v. *Wandsworth Board of Works* ((1863), 14 C.B.N.S. at p. 194) applied.

(ii) though the order could have been held void ab initio in an action by the council, yet it was so voidable only at the election of the council, and it was not a nullity; accordingly, as the appellant, though mayor at the time, was not representing the council in these proceedings and it was not shown

A that the council could not have been petitioner, he was not entitled to
complain of the order and could not maintain the present proceedings
(see p. 160, letters B to E, post).

Dicta of LORD EVERSHED and LORD MORRIS OF BORTH-Y-GEST in *Ridge
v. Baldwin* ([1963] 2 All E.R. at pp. 87, 110) applied.

Appeal dismissed.

B

[As to the obligation of persons exercising quasi-judicial functions to observe
the rules of natural justice, see 30 HALSBURY's LAWS (3rd Edn.) 718, 719, paras.
1368, 1369; and for cases on the subject, see 38 DIGEST (Repl.) 102, 103, *732-736*.]

Cases referred to:

Capel v. *Child*, (1832), 2 Cr. & J. 558; 1 L.J.Ex. 205; 149 E.R. 235; 19
C   Digest (Repl.) 447, *2644*.

Cooper v. *Wandsworth Board of Works*, (1863), 14 C.B.N.S. 180; 32 L.J.C.P.
185; 8 L.T. 278; 143 E.R. 414; 26 Digest (Repl.) 585, *2450*.

Fisher v. *Jackson*, [1891] 2 Ch. 84; 60 L.J.Ch. 482; 64 L.T. 782; 19 Digest
(Repl.) 642, *278*.

Macfoy v. *United Africa Co., Ltd.*, [1961] 3 All E.R. 1169; [1962] A.C. 152;
D   [1961] 3 W.L.R. 1405; 3rd Digest Supp.

Nair v. *Teik*, ante p. 34; [1967] 2 W.L.R. 846.

Nakkuda Ali v. *M. F. de S. Jayaratne*, [1951] A.C. 66; 8 Digest (Repl.)
802, *562*.

R. v. *Cambridge University, Bentley's Case*, (1723), Fortes Rep. 202; Ld. Raym.
E   1334; 92 E.R. 818; 19 Digest (Repl.) 654, *316*.

R. v. *Electricity Comrs., Ex p. London Electricity Joint Committee Co. (1920),
Ltd.*, [1923] All E.R. Rep. 150; [1924] 1 K.B. 171; 93 L.J.K.B. 390;
130 L.T. 164; 20 Digest (Repl.) 202, *3*.

Ridge v. *Baldwin*, [1963] 2 All E.R. 66; [1964] A.C. 40; [1963] 2 W.L.R. 935;
127 J.P. 295; 37 Digest (Repl.) 195, *32*.

F *Sugathadasa* v. *Jayasinghe*, (1958), 59 N.L.R. 457.

Wood v. *Woad*, (1874), L.R. 9 Exch. 190; 43 L.J.Ex. 153; 30 L.T. 815;
8 Digest (Repl.) 656, *35*.

Appeal.

This was an appeal by Alfred Thangarajah Durayappah of Chundikuly,
G Mayor of Jaffna, from a judgment of the Supreme Court of Ceylon (SANSONI, C.J.,
and SIVA SUPRAMANIAM, J.) dated Sept. 22, 1966, dismissing with costs his
petition against the four respondents.   The first respondent was W. J. Fernando,
Commissioner of Local Government, Colombo, the second respondent was
N. Nadesan, an executive engineer, the third respondent was S. C. Manica
Vasagar, Assistant Commissioner of Local Government, Jaffna, and the fourth
H respondent was Murugeysen Thiruchelvam, Minister of Local Government.
By his petition, dated June 20, 1966, the appellant prayed—(i) for mandates
in the nature of writs of certiorari and quo warranto to quash an order of the
fourth respondent, dated May 29, 1966, purporting to dissolve and supersede
the Jaffna Municipal Council (herein called " the council ") and to appoint the
first three respondents as special commissioners of the council and to authorise
I them to act for the council and to have, perform and discharge all the rights,
privileges, powers, duties and functions vested in or conferred or imposed on
the council and the mayor by any written law; (ii) for an interim injunction
restraining the first three respondents from having, exercising and, or, performing any of the rights, powers, functions or duties of the council or of the mayor;
and (iii) for a declaration that the appellant as the duly elected mayor of the
council was entitled to act as such until the election of a new mayor according
to law.

The facts are set out in the judgment of the Board.

T. O. Kellock, Q.C., *M. P. Solomon* and *M. I. Hamavi Haniffa* for the appellant. **A**
E. F. N. Gratiaen, Q.C., and *Walter Jayawardena* for the first three respondents.
E. F. N. Gratiaen, Q.C., and *R. K. Handoo* for the fourth respondent, the
Minister.

LORD UPJOHN: The first and principal question in this appeal is whether
the fourth respondent who is the Minister of Local Government (who will be
referred to as the Minister) was justified in exercising his powers under s. 277 **B**
of the Municipal Councils Ordinance (cap. 252) as amended by Act No. 12 of
1959 (this Ordinance as amended will be referred to as the Municipal Ordinance)
to dissolve the Jaffna Municipal Council (hereafter referred to as " the council ")
without giving it the right to be heard in its own defence. In other words was
the Minister before exercising his powers under s. 277 bound to observe that rule
of natural justice, which is neatly and briefly stated in the recently resuscitated **C**
Latin expression " audi alteram partem ". While it was an issue in the lower
courts, it is now no longer disputed that the Minister acted in complete good
faith and that in fact he would have given the council the opportunity of being
heard but for the urgency of the case as he or his advisers regarded it, and it is
not in doubt that if he was bound to observe the principle audi alteram partem
he failed to do so. Their lordships will only state that while great urgency may **D**
rightly limit such opportunity timeously, perhaps severely, there can never be a
denial of that opportunity if the principles of natural justice are applicable.

The council was constituted under the Municipal Ordinance as the municipal
authority for the district of Jaffna, a very large and important town, and there
was thereby conferred on it all the usual powers and duties of a local authority
in their area. Only a brief review of the provisions of the Municipal Ordinance **E**
constituting these particular local authorities is necessary. By Part I the
Minister was empowered to declare any area to be a municipality, to define the
limits of any municipality so declared and to assign a name and designation to
the municipal council to be constituted for the municipality so declared (s. 2
and s. 3). The municipal council constituted for each municipality was (subject to
reserved powers irrelevant to this judgment) to be the local authority within the **F**
administrative limits of the municipality charged with the regulation, control
and administration of all matters relating to the public health, public utility
services, public thoroughfares and generally with the protection and promotion
of the comfort, convenience and welfare of the people and amenities of the
municipality (s. 4).

By Part II elaborate provisions were made for the election of councillors, **G**
their terms of office and for the election by the councillors of the mayor and
deputy mayor, from time to time. Section 34 is important:

" (1) Every municipal council shall be a corporation with perpetual
succession and a common seal and shall have power, subject to this Ordinance
to acquire, hold and sell property and may sue and be sued by such name **H**
and designation as may be assigned to it under this Ordinance.

" (2) The common seal of the council shall remain in the custody of the
commissioner, and shall not be affixed to any contract or other instrument
on behalf of the council, except in the presence of the mayor or deputy
mayor and the commissioner who shall sign their names to such contract
or other instrument in token of their presence." **I**

Section 35 and s. 37 provided for the vesting in the council of much immovable
property, waste lands, quarries, lakes and waterworks, Crown lands (made over
with sanction of the Governor-General), public parks, gardens and open spaces,
all streets, public markets and public buildings.

The following parts of the Municipal Ordinance expanded in great detail
these all important general powers and duties conferred on municipal councils
to which detailed reference is unnecessary. By Part IX (s. 185 onwards) every
municipal council was bound to establish a municipal fund and its powers and

A duties in relation thereto were elaborated.   Then by Part XII (s. 230 onwards) every municipal council was empowered to levy rates (with the sanction of the minister) on property within the municipality.

By Part XIV headed " Central Control " s. 277 (1) enacted:

B " (1) If at any time, upon representation made or otherwise, it appears to the Minister that a municipal council is not competent to perform, or persistently makes default in the performance of, any duty or duties imposed upon it, or persistently refuses or neglects to comply with any provision of law, the Minister may, by order published in the GAZETTE, direct that the council shall be dissolved and superseded, and thereupon such council shall, without prejudice to anything already done by it, be dissolved, and cease to have, exercise, perform and discharge any of the rights, privileges, powers,

C duties and functions conferred or imposed upon it, or vested in it, by this Ordinance or any other written law."

There was a general local election for councillors to the council in December of 1963 and eighteen members were by the constitution of the council elected to it for the term of three years expiring at the end of 1966.

D There is no doubt that this council went through troublous times; within the period of 2½ years of its election four mayors were successively elected, the appellant having been elected as recently as Mar. 31, 1966.   Although their lordships are not directly concerned with such matters, it may be stated as a matter of history that a number of complaints, whether justifiable or not, as to the conduct of the council and the councillors were made to the Minister.

E He therefore sent the Commissioner of Local Government to inquire into these matters with instructions to report immediately. The Commissioner of Local Government visited Jaffna on May 27 and 28, 1966, and it is fair to say that the appellant, who had been informed by the Minister of his impending visit, gave to him every facility that he required for this purpose.   He had full access to all the minutes of the council, but he did not ask anyone any questions or give

F any member of the council any opportunity of expressing their views on any matter.   His report, first orally and then in writing, was received by the Minister on May 29, who on the same day made an order stating that it appeared to him that the Jaffna Municipal Council was not competent to perform the duties imposed on it and that pursuant to the powers conferred on him by s. 277 as amended he directed that the council should be dissolved and superseded on

G May 29, 1966.   On May 30, 1966, the Governor-General appointed the first, second and third respondents to be special commissioners to exercise perform and discharge the rights privileges powers duties and functions conferred on the council or the mayor by the municipal ordinance.   This order dissolving the council is challenged by the appellant and indeed by another councillor but your lordships are not concerned with that second challenge.

H On the question of audi alteram partem the Supreme Court followed and agreed with the earlier decision of *Sugathadasa* v. *Jayasinghe* (1), a decision of three judges of the Supreme Court on the same section and on the same issue, namely, whether a council was not competent to perform its duties.   That decision (2) laid down

I " as a general rule that words such as ' where it appears to ' or ' if it appears to the satisfaction of ' or ' if the … considers it expedient that ' or ' if the … is satisfied that ' standing by themselves without other words or circumstances of qualification, exclude a duty to act judicially."

Their lordships disagree with this approach.   These various formulae are introductory of the matter to be considered and give little guidance on the question of audi alteram partem.   The statute can make itself clear on this point and, if it does, cadit quaestio.   If it does not then the principle stated by

---

(1) (1958), 59 N.L.R. 457.   (2) (1958), 59 N.L.R. at p. 471.

BYLES, J., in *Cooper* v. *Wandsworth Board of Works* (3) must be applied. He **A** said this (4):

"... a long course of decisions, beginning with *R.* v. *Cambridge University, Bentley's Case* (5), and ending with some very recent cases, establish that, although there are no positive words in the statute requiring that the party shall be heard, yet the justice of the common law will supply the omission **B** of the legislature."

If the law were otherwise then such cases as *Capel* v. *Child* (6) where the words are in fact very similar to the words of s. 277, must have been differently decided. That case is in fact an important landmark in the history of the development of the principle audi alteram partem. The solution to this case is not to be found merely on a consideration of the opening words of s. 277. A deeper **C** investigation is necessary. Their lordships were, of course, referred to the recent case of *Ridge* v. *Baldwin* (7), where this principle was very closely and carefully examined. In that case no attempt was made to give an exhaustive classification of the cases where the principle audi alteram partem should be applied. In their lordships' opinion it would be wrong to do so. Outside well-known cases such as dismissal from office, deprivation of property and expulsion from clubs, **D** there is a vast area where the principle can be applied only on most general considerations. For example, as LORD REID when examining (8) *R.* v. *Electricity Comrs., Ex p. London Electricity Joint Committee Co. (1920), Ltd.* (9) pointed out, BANKES, L.J. (10) inferred the judicial element from the nature of the power and ATKIN, L.J. (11), did the same. Pausing there, however, it should not be assumed that their lordships necessarily agree with LORD REID'S analysis (12) of **E** that case or with his criticism (13) of *Nakkuda Ali* v. *M. F. de S. Jayaratne* (14). Outside the well-known classes of cases, no general rule can be laid down as to the application of the general principle in addition to the language of the provision. In their lordships' opinion there are three matters which must always be borne in mind when considering whether the principle should be applied or not. These three matters are: first what is the nature of the property, the **F** office held, status enjoyed or services to be performed by the complainant of injustice. Secondly, in what circumstances or on what occasions is the person claiming to be entitled to exercise the measure or control entitled to intervene. Thirdly, when a right to intervene is proved, what sanctions in fact is the latter entitled to impose on the other. It is only on a consideration of all these matters that the question of the application of the principle can properly be determined. **G** Their lordships therefore proceed to examine the facts of this case on these considerations.

As to the first matter it cannot be doubted that the Council of Jaffna was by statute a public corporation entrusted like all other municipal councils with the administration of a large area and the discharge of important duties. No one would consider that its activities should be lightly interfered with. Their **H** lordships may notice here an argument addressed to them that, as this was a local authority subject to the superior power of the Minister under s. 277, the exercise of this power was a matter properly left to him as the one responsible to the legislature to whom he was answerable for his actions and he could not be responsible to the courts under the principle audi alteram partem. Their

I

(3) (1863), 14 C.B.N.S. 180 at p. 194.   (4) (1863), 14 C.B.N.S. at p. 194.
(5) (1723), Fortes Rep. 202.   (6) (1832), 2 Cr. & J. 558.
(7) [1963] 2 All E.R. 66; [1964] A.C. 40.
(8) [1963] 2 All E.R. at p. 78, letter F; [1964] A.C. at p. 76.
(9) [1923] All E.R. Rep. 150; [1924] 1 K.B. 171.
(10) [1923] All E.R. Rep. at p. 157; [1924] 1 K.B. at p. 198.
(11) [1923] All E.R. Rep. at pp. 161, 162; [1924] 1 K.B. at pp. 206, 207.
(12) [1963] 2 All E.R. at p. 78; [1964] A.C. at p. 76.
(13) [1963] 2 All E.R. at p. 79; [1964] A.C. at p. 77.
(14) [1951] A.C. 66.

A lordships dissent from this argument. The legislature has enacted a statute setting up municipal authorities with a considerable measure of independence from the central government within defined local areas and fields of government. No Minister should have the right to dissolve such an authority without allowing it the right to be heard on that matter, unless the statute is so clear that it is plain that it has no right of self-defence. However, this consideration is perhaps one

B of approach only. The second and third matters are decisive. On the second matter it is clear that the Minister can dissolve the council on one of three grounds: that it (a) is not competent to perform any duty or duties imposed on it (for brevity their lordships will refer to this head as incompetence); or (b) persistently makes default in the performance of any duty or duties imposed on it; or (c) persistently refuses or neglects to comply with any provision of law.

C   A preliminary argument was addressed to their lordships on the footing that incompetence was the equivalent of inability to perform its duties. This argument was based on certain observations in the *Sugathadasa* case (15) where the judges expressed the opinion that the council became not competent to perform the duties imposed on it when circumstances arose that rendered it incapable of performing them. It was argued that the words in the statute " not com-

D petent " were equivalent to " not able to undertake " and it was said that in the circumstances of this case it had not been shown that the council were not able to undertake their duties and so could not be found to be incompetent. Their lordships do not agree with this argument and do not think that the judges in the *Sugathadasa* case (16) intended to go as far. It may be that a council is so incompetent that it is not able to undertake anything, but inability to undertake

E its duties (which may arise from circumstances outside anyone's control) is not the test as to incompetence.

While their lordships are only concerned with the question of incompetence, the true construction of the section must be considered as a whole and its necessary intendment in the light of the common law principles already stated. It seems clear to their lordships that it is a most serious charge to allege that the

F council, entrusted with these very important duties, persistently makes default in the performance of any duty or duties imposed on it. No authority is required to support the view that in such circumstances it is plain and obvious that the principle audi alteram partem must apply.

Equally it is clear that, if a council is alleged persistently to refuse or neglect to comply with a provision of law, it must be entitled (as a matter of the

G most elementary justice) to be heard in its defence. Again this proposition requires no authority to support it. If, therefore, it is clear that in two of the three cases, the Minister must act judicially, then it seems to their lordships, looking at the section as a whole, that it is not possible to single out for different treatment the third case, namely incompetence. Grammatically too any differentiation is impossible. The section confers on the Minister a single power to

H act in the event of one or more closely allied failures, and he can only do so after observing the principle audi alteram partem. Had the Minister been empowered to dissolve the council only for incompetence and on no other ground, it might have been argued that as " incompetence " is very vague and difficult to define Parliament did not intend the principle audi alteram partem to apply, in the circumstances, but their lordships would point out that charges of inefficiency

I or failing to be diligent or to set a good example have been held subject to the principle; see *Fisher* v. *Jackson* (17). The third matter can be dealt with quite shortly. The sanction which the Minister can impose and indeed, if he is satisfied of the necessary premise, must impose on the erring council is as complete as could be imagined; it involves the dissolution of the council and therefore the confiscation of all its properties. It was at one moment faintly argued that the council was a trustee and that it was not therefore being deprived of any of its

---

(15) (1958), 59 N.L.R. at p. 475.   (16) (1958), 59 N.L.R. 457.
(17) [1891] 2 Ch. 84.

property but this argument (soon abandoned) depended on a complete miscon- A
ception of the law of corporations. A statutory corporation such as a municipal
corporation, like every trading corporation, owns its property and the corporators
have no proprietary interest in it, but like them it can deal with its property only
in accordance with its constitution. In the case of a trading company that is
laid down in its memorandum and articles of association. In the case of a
statutory corporation it is laid down in the statute, or municipal ordinance, by B
virtue of which it is incorporated, but it is important to remember throughout
that it owns its property (it may hold property as a trustee, see s. 37 of the
Municipal Ordinance, but that is quite a different matter). The council owned
large areas of land, had a municipal fund and was empowered to levy rates
from its inhabitants, though it was bound to apply them in accordance with its
constitution. In their lordships' opinion this case falls within the principle of C
Cooper v. *Wandsworth Board of Works* (18), where it was held that no man is to
be deprived of his property without having an opportunity of being heard. For
the purposes of the application of the principle it seems to their lordships that
this must apply equally to a statutory body having statutory powers, authorities
and duties just as it does to an individual. Accordingly on this ground too the
Minister should have observed the principle.   D

For these reasons their lordships have no doubt that in the circumstances of
this case the Minister should have observed the principle audi alteram partem.
The case of *Sugathadasa* v. *Jayasinghe* (19) was wrongly decided.

Had the matter remained there their lordships would have allowed the appeal
and held the order of May 29, 1966, to have been inoperative. However, during
the hearing of the appeal their lordships raised the question, not taken in the E
court below, whether the appellant was entitled to maintain this action and
appeal. This question is of some general importance. The answer must depend
essentially on whether the order of the Minister was a complete nullity or whether
it was an order voidable only at the election of the council. If the former, it
must follow that the council is still in office and that, if any councillor, ratepayer
or other person having a legimate interest in the conduct of the council likes to F
take the point, they are entitled to ask the court to declare that the council is
still the duly elected council with all the powers and duties conferred on it by
the Municipal Ordinance.

Apart altogether from authority their lordships would be of opinion that this
was a case where the Minister's order was voidable and not a nullity. Though
the council should have been given the opportunity of being heard in its defence, G
if it deliberately chooses not to complain and takes no step to protest against
its dissolution, there seems no reason why any other person should have the
right to interfere. To take a simple example to which their lordships will have
to advert in some detail presently, if in the case of *Ridge* v. *Baldwin* (20) the
appellant Ridge, who had been wrongly dismissed because he was not given the
opportunity of presenting his defence, had preferred to abandon the point and H
accept the view that he had been properly dismissed, their lordship can see
no reason why any other person, such, for example, as a ratepayer of Brighton
should have any right to contend that Mr. Ridge was still the chief constable of
Brighton. As a matter of ordinary common sense, with all respect to other
opinions that have been expressed, if a person in the position of Mr. Ridge
had not felt sufficiently aggrieved to take any action by reason of the failure I
to afford him his strict right to put forward a defence, the order of the watch
committee should stand and no one else should have any right to complain.
The matter is not free of authority, for it was much discussed in that case.
LORD REID (21) reached the conclusion that the committee's decision was void
and not merely voidable, and he relied on the decision in *Wood* v. *Woad* (22).

(18) (1863), 14 C.B.N.S. 180.   (19) (1958), 59 N.L.R. 457.
(20) [1963] 2 All E.R. 66; [1964] A.C. 40.
(21) [1963] 2 All E.R. at p. 81; [1964] A.C. at p. 80.   (22) (1874), L.R. 9 Exch. 190.

A Their lordships deprecate the use of the word void in distinction to the word voidable in the field of law with which their lordships are concerned because, as Lord Evershed pointed out in *Ridge* v. *Baldwin* (23), quoting from Sir Frederick Pollock (24), the words void and voidable are imprecise and apt to mislead. These words have well understood meanings when dealing with questions of proprietary or contractual rights. It is better, in the field where
B the subject matter of the discussion is whether some order which has been made, or whether some step in some litigation or quasi-litigation, is effective or not, to employ the verbal distinction between whether it is truly a " nullity ", that is to all intents and purposes, of which any person having a legitimate interest in the matter can take advantage or whether it is " voidable " only at the instance of the party affected. On the other hand the word " nullity " would be quite
C inappropriate in questions of proprietary or contractual rights; such transactions may frequently be void, but the result can seldom be described as a nullity. In the field now under consideration there are many cases illustrating the difference, see for example *Macfoy* v. *United Africa Co., Ltd.* (25), where it was held that a failure to comply with certain rules of the Supreme Court rendered the proceedings voidable and not a nullity. On the other side is the very recent decision of their
D lordships' Board in *Nair* v. *Teik* (26), where a failure to comply with a rule was held to make purported subsequent proceedings a nullity. Their lordships understand Lord Reid (27) to have used the word " void " in the sense of being a nullity. In the same case Lord Hodson (28) took the view that the decision of the watch committee in *Ridge* v. *Baldwin* (29) was a nullity. On the other hand, Lord Evershed (30), though he differed on the main question whether
E the principle audi alteram partem applied, devoted a considerable part of his judgment to the question whether the decision was voidable or a nullity and with this part of his judgment Lord Devlin (31) expressly stated his agreement. Lord Evershed (32) examined the case of *Wood* v. *Woad* (33) in some detail, and he reached the conclusion (34) that in *Wood* v. *Woad* (33) the question whether the purported exclusion from the association by the committee was
F void or voidable was not essential or indeed material to the claim made in the action by the plaintiffs for damages against the members of the committee. He continued, speaking of that case (35)

   " Certainly in my judgment it cannot be asserted that the judgments in the case cited, or indeed any of them, support or involve the proposition that where a body, such as the watch committee in the present case, is
G invested by the express terms of a statute with a power of expulsion of any member of the police force and purport in good faith to exercise such power, a failure on their part to observe the principle of natural justice audi alteram partem has the result that the decision is not merely voidable by the court but is wholly void and a nullity."

H Lord Morris of Borth-y-Gest also considered (36) this question and reached the conclusion that the order of the watch committee was voidable and not a nullity. He examined the question as to the nature of the relief that the party aggrieved (Ridge) would apply for, which would be that the decision was invalid

---

I (23) [1963] 2 All E.R. at p. 88, letter I; [1964] A.C. at p. 92.
   (24) Pollock on Contract (13th Edn.) 48.
   (25) [1961] 3 All E.R. 1169; [1962] A.C. 152.   (26) Ante p. 34.
   (27) [1963] 2 All E.R. at p. 81; [1964] A.C. at p. 80.
   (28) [1963] 2 All E.R. at p. 116; [1964] A.C. at p. 135.
   (29) [1963] 2 All E.R. 66; [1964] A.C. 40.
   (30) [1963] 2 All E.R. at p. 85; [1964] A.C. at p. 86.
   (31) [1963] 2 All E.R. at p. 120; [1964] A.C. at pp. 141, 142.
   (32) [1963] 2 All E.R. at pp. 86 et seq.; [1964] A.C. at p. 88 et seq.
   (33) (1874), L.R. 9 Exch. 190.
   (34) [1963] 2 All E.R. at p. 87, letter G; [1964] A.C. at p. 90.
   (35) [1963] 2 All E.R. at p. 87, letter H; [1964] A.C. at pp. 90, 91.
   (36) [1963] 2 All E.R. at p. 110; [1964] A.C. at p. 125.

and of no effect and null and void. Their lordships entirely agree with that and **A** with the conclusion which he drew from it, namely that if the decision is challenged by the person aggrieved on the grounds that the principle has not been obeyed, he is entitled to claim that as against him it is void ab initio and has never been of any effect. It cannot possibly be right, however, in the type of case which their lordships are considering to suppose that, if challenged successfully by the person entitled to avoid the order, yet nevertheless it has some limited effect **B** even against him until set aside by a court of competent jurisdiction. While in this case their lordships have no doubt that in an action by the council the court should have held that the order was void ab initio and never had any effect, that is quite a different matter from saying that the order was a nullity of which advantage could be taken by any other person having a legitimate interest in the matter. **C**

Their lordships therefore are clearly of opinion that the order of the Minister on May 29, 1966, was voidable and not a nullity. Being voidable it was voidable only at the instance of the person against whom the order was made, that is the council; but the council has not complained. The appellant was no doubt mayor at the time of its dissolution, but that does not give him any right to complain independently of the council. He must show that he is representing **D** the council or suing on its behalf or that by reason of certain circumstances—such for example as that the council could not use its seal because it is in the possession of the municipal commissioner, or that for other reasons it has been impracticable for the members of the council to meet to pass the necessary resolutions— the council cannot be the plaintiff. Had that been shown then there are well known procedures whereby the plaintiff can sue on behalf of himself and the **E** other corporators making the council a defendant, and on pleading and proving the necessary facts may be able to establish in the action that he is entitled to assert the rights of the council. That, however, is not suggested in this case. The appellant sets up the case that as mayor he is entitled to complain, but as such he plainly is not. If the council is dissolved, the office of mayor is dissolved with it and he has no independent right of complaint, because he holds no office **F** that is independent of the council. If the mayor were to be heard individually he could only deal with complaints against the council with which ex hypothesi the council itself did not wish to deal. So accordingly, it seems to their lordships that on this short ground the appellant cannot maintain this action.

For these reasons, which differ entirely from those in the court below, their lordships have humbly advised Her Majesty that the appeal should be dismissed. **G** In the circumstances, however, there will be no order as to the costs of this appeal.

Appeal dismissed.

Solicitors: *Hatchett Jones & Co.* (for the appellant); *T. L. Wilson & Co.* (for the respondents). **H**

[*Reported by* KATHLEEN J. H. O'BRIEN, *Barrister-at-Law.*]

A   DIRECTOR OF PUBLIC PROSECUTIONS *v.* NASRALLA.

[PRIVY COUNCIL (Viscount Dilhorne, Lord Guest, Lord Devlin, Lord Upjohn and
     Lord Pearson), November 21, 22, 23, 24, 1966, February 20, 1967.]

*Privy Council—Jamaica—Criminal law—Autrefois acquit—Murder—Accused
    found not guilty of murder and jury not agreed on alternative verdict of*
B   *manslaughter—Rule that jury entitled not to return a partial verdict obsolete—
    General verdict of acquittal sufficient to found plea for all alternative offences—
    Partial verdict of acquittal sufficient only for crimes in respect of which
    verdict returned—Jury not entitled to disregard judge's direction for a partial
    verdict and to return only a general verdict—Whether verdict of jury in this
    instance was a general verdict.*

C   At the trial of the accused on a charge of murder the judge left to the
jury the two issues of murder or manslaughter. The jury brought in a
verdict of not guilty of murder, but were unable to agree sufficiently as to
manslaughter and did not bring in a verdict on that issue. On the accused's
application that, as he would be entitled to maintain a plea of autrefois
acquit, it should be declared that he could not be tried again for manslaughter
D on a voluntary bill* of indictment,

    Held: (i) if a jury brought in a general verdict of acquittal on an indict-
ment the accused could thereafter maintain a plea of autrefois acquit in
respect of every crime of which he could have been convicted on that indictment; accordingly a general verdict of acquittal on an indictment for
murder would enable autrefois acquit to be maintained for manslaughter,
E but a verdict of partial acquittal would not cover by inference a crime (in this
case manslaughter) about which the jury disagreed (see p. 167, letter E, post).

    Dictum of LORD READING, C.J., in *R.* v. *Barron* ([1914] 2 K.B. at p. 574)
and of LORD MORRIS OF BORTH-Y-GEST in *Connelly* v. *Director of Public
Prosecutions* ([1964] 2 All E.R. at p. 412) considered and explained.

    (ii) the former rule that a jury were under no obligation to return any
F verdict (in this instance a partial verdict of manslaughter) other than a
general verdict, although directed to consider the alternative offence, was
inconsistent with modern practice and was obsolete; in the present case
the jury had not returned a verdict on manslaughter, so that there was no
acquittal of that offence on which to found a plea of autrefois acquit (see
p. 172, letters B and G, post).

G   *R.* v. *Baxter* ((1913), 9 Cr. App. Rep. 60) considered.

    Per CURIAM: even if there had been no obligation on the jury to return a
partial verdict, the verdict of "not guilty of murder" was not a general
verdict of acquittal and would not have enabled a plea of autrefois acquit
to be maintained in respect of manslaughter (see p. 172, letters C and F, post).

    Appeal allowed.

H   [As to proof of a plea of autrefois acquit, and as to the plea being maintainable
in respect of alternative offences, see 10 HALSBURY'S LAWS (3rd Edn.) 405-407,
paras. 737, 738; and for cases on the subject, see 14 DIGEST (Repl.) 378-387,
3700-3775.

    As to general and special verdicts and conviction of a different offence from that
charged, see 10 HALSBURY'S LAWS (3rd Edn.) 428, 429, paras. 790, 791.]

I Cases referred to:

    Bushell's Case, (1670), Vaugh. 135; Freem. K.B. 1; 89 E.R. 2; 6 State Tr. 999;
        30 Digest (Repl.) 288, *581.*

    Connelly v. *Director of Public Prosecutions,* [1964] 2 All E.R. 401; [1964]
        A.C. 1254, 1280; [1964] 2 W.L.R. 1145; 128 J.P. 418; 48 Cr. App. Rep.
        183; *affg.* sub nom. *R.* v. *Connelly,* [1963] 2 All E.R. 510; [1964]
        A.C. 1254; [1963] 3 W.L.R. 839; 3rd Digest Supp.

---

* See p. 164, letter H, post.

Side notes (right margin):

Dictum of LORD DEVLIN at 165 applied in BAKER v THE QUEEN [1975] 3 All ER 55

Dictum of LORD DEVLIN at 165 applied in MAHARAJ v A-G OF TRINIDAD [1978] 2 All ER 670

Dictum of LORD DEVLIN at 166 applied in HARRINGTON v ROOTS [1984] 2 All ER 474

Devizes Corpn. v. *Clark,* (1835), 3 Ad. & El. 506; 111 E.R. 506; 30 Digest **A**
(Repl.) 284, *528.*

Penryn v. *Corbet,* (1598), Cro. Eliz. 464; 78 E.R. 702.

R. v. *Barron,* [1914] 2 K.B. 570; 83 L.J.K.B. 786; 78 J.P. 311; 10 Cr. App.
Rep. 81; 14 Digest (Repl.) 380, *3718.*

R. v. *Baxter,* (1913), 9 Cr. App. Rep. 60; 15 Digest (Repl.) 930, *8906.*

R. v. *Bourne,* (1952), 36 Cr. App. Rep. 125; 14 Digest (Repl.) 353, *3423.*   **B**

R. v. *Charlesworth,* (1861), 1 B. & S. 460; 31 L.J.M.C. 25; 5 L.T. 150; 25 J.P.
820; 9 Cox, C.C. 44; 121 E.R. 786; 14 Digest (Repl.) 346, *3353.*

R. v. *Jameson,* [1896] 2 Q.B. 425; 65 L.J.M.C. 218; 75 L.T. 77; 60 J.P. 662;
12 T.L.R. 551; 18 Cox, C.C. 392; 13 Digest (Repl.) 281, *2531.*

R. v. *Quinn,* (1953), S.R. (N.S.W.) 21.

R. v. *Salisbury,* (1553), 1 Plowd. 100; 75 E.R. 158; 15 Digest (Repl.) 950,   **C**
9174.

R. v. *Shipley,* (1784), 4 Doug. K.B. 73; 21 State Tr. 847; 99 E.R. 774; 32
Digest (Repl.) 82, *1049.*

R. v. *Shipton, Ex p. Director of Public Prosecutions,* [1957] 1 All E.R. 206;
121 J.P. 78; sub nom. *Re Shipton,* [1957] 1 W.L.R. 259; 40 Cr. App.
Rep. 197; 45 Digest (Repl.) 106, *352.*   **D**

R. v. *Thomas,* [1949] 2 All E.R. 662; [1950] 1 K.B. 26; 33 Cr. App. Rep. 200;
14 Digest (Repl.) 383, *3735.*

Wroth v. *Wiggs,* (1592), Cro. Eliz. 276; 78 E.R. 531.

Appeal.

This was an appeal by the Director of Public Prosecutions from a judgment
and order of the Court of Appeal of Jamaica (DUFFUS, P., LEWIS and HEN-   **E**
RIQUES, JJ.A.) dated June 11, 1965, allowing an appeal by the respondent,
Patrick Nasralla, from a judgment and order of the Supreme Court (COOLS-
LARTIGUE, DOUGLAS and SHELLEY, JJ.) dated June 5, 1963, whereby an order
by SMALL, J., in the Home Circuit Court, dated Feb. 25, 1963, adjourning the
trial of the respondent for manslaughter, was declared ultra vires and void,
in contravention of the fundamental rights and freedoms granted by s. 20 (8)   **F**
of the Constitution of Jamaica*.

J. G. Le Quesne, Q.C., and *C. J. S. French, Q.C.,* for the Crown.
David Coore, Q.C. (of the Jamaican Bar) and *M. R. Hickman* for the respondent.

LORD DEVLIN: On Oct. 9, 1962, the respondent shot and killed Gilbert
Gillespie whom as an escaping felon he was attempting to arrest. On Feb. 4,   **G**
1963, he was arraigned before SMALL, J., and a jury of twelve in the Kingston
circuit court on an indictmdent charging him with murder. By a well-established
rule of the common law which the industry of counsel has shown to have originated
in *R.* v. *Salisbury* (1), it is open to a jury, if they are not satisfied of the prisoner's
guilt on a charge of murder, to convict of manslaughter. The procedure to
be followed in Jamaica on the application of this rule is laid down in the Jury   **H**
Law, s. 44. This provides that a unanimous verdict is necessary for the conviction or acquittal of any person for murder; and that after the lapse of one
hour from the retirement of the jury a verdict of a majority of not less than nine
to three of conviction or acquittal of manslaughter may be received.

SMALL, J., in his summing up left the two issues of murder and manslaughter
to the jury and they retired at 2.27 p.m. on Feb. 11. Shortly before 3 p.m.   **I**
they returned to court and after the foreman had stated that they had arrived at
their verdict, he was asked the following questions:

"The registrar: On the charge of murder, are you unanimous? A. Yes,
sir.

---

* The Constitution is set out in Sch. 2 to the Jamaica (Constitution) Order in Council,
1962, S.I. 1962 No. 1550.

(1) (1553), 1 Plowd. 100.

A   " Q.   Do you find the accused guilty or not guilty of murder?   A.   Not
guilty of murder.
        " Q.   On the charge of manslaughter, are you unanimous?   A.   No."

The judge told the jury that a majority verdict could not be received under one
hour and that they must retire again.   They returned at 4.05 p.m. when they
were asked the following questions:—
B
        " The registrar: Mr. Foreman, please stand.   On the charge of man-
    slaughter, have you arrived at a verdict?   The foreman: Yes, sir.
        " Q.   Is your verdict unanimous?   A.   No, sir.
        " Q.   How are you divided?   A.   Four for acquittal.
        " Q.   Just tell me how you are divided?   A.   Eight to four."

C   The judge told the jury that he could not accept that verdict and asked them to
retire again.   They returned at 5.17 p.m. when the foreman said that they were
still of the same mind.   The judge, being satisfied that there was no reasonable
probability that the jury would arrived at a verdict of manslaughter, discharged
them in accordance with s. 45 (1) of the Jury Law.   The indictment was endorsed
as follows: " Verdict: Not guilty of murder.   Not agreed on manslaughter—
D   Divided eight to four ".
        Section 45 (3) of the Jury Law provides that whenever a jury has been dis-
charged the judge may adjourn the case for trial at the same or a future sitting
of the circuit court.   On Feb. 25 the prosecution applied to SMALL, J., for an
order adjourning the trial on the issue of manslaughter.   The defence opposed
the application on the ground that at any further trial the plea of autrefois
E   acquit would be bound to succeed.   The judge granted the application and made
the following order:

        " In accordance with s. 45 (3) (A) cap. 186 the court adjourns the case
    for trial at the next sitting of the circuit court on the issue of manslaughter.
    Accused allowed bail in £500.   Surety £500 to appear on Apr. 17, 1963."

F   SMALL, J., made this order after hearing argument and after having apparently
formed the view that the plea of autrefois acquit was bad or at any rate that it
was not certain that it would succeed.   This, of course, did not conclude the
matter and it was open to the defence to enter and argue the plea at the further
trial.   They preferred, however, to seek relief from the Supreme Court under a
provision of the Constitution of Jamaica which is part of Ch. III entitled " Funda-
G   mental Rights and Freedoms ".   The chapter opens with an introductory
section (s. 13) reciting that " every person in Jamaica is entitled to the fundamental rights and freedoms of the individual "; and then, having specified
them generally, goes on to provide that the subsequent provisions of the chapter
shall have effect for the purpose of protecting them.   Section 20, which bears the
marginal note " Provisions to secure protection of law ", provides by sub-s. (8)
H   as follows:

        " No person who shows that he has been tried by any competent court
    for a criminal offence and either convicted or acquitted shall again be tried
    for that offence or for any other criminal offence of which he could have
    been convicted at the trial for that offence . . ."

I   Section 25 provides that any person alleging that any of the protective provisions
has been, is being, or is likely to be contravened in relation to him may apply to
the Supreme Court for redress.
        The respondent's application under s. 25 of the Constitution was heard by
the Supreme Court and dismissed on Jan. 5, 1963.   The respondent appealed
to the Court of Appeal and on June 11, 1965, his appeal was allowed.   On
Nov. 1, 1965, the Crown was granted leave to appeal to Her Majesty in Council
and now asks as appellant that the judgment of the Supreme Court should be
restored.

It is convenient to deal in the first instance with a point raised by the respon- A
dent that, whatever view be taken of the substance of the matter, the form of
SMALL, J.'s order is wrong. The respondent argues on the authority of *R*. v.
Shipton, Ex p. Director of Public Prosecutions (2) that by the verdict of the jury
proceedings on the indictment on which he had been tried were brought to an
end. In *R*. v. *Shipton* (2) the accused was tried at assizes on an indictment
containing one count charging him with manslaughter. The jury acquitted him B
of manslaughter but were unable to agree about a possible alternative verdict of
dangerous driving. The assize judge (HAVERS, J.) directed that the accused should
be re-tried on the issue of dangerous driving before the next quarter sessions. A
court of quarter sessions has jurisdiction to try the offence of dangerous driving
but not the offence of manslaughter. The recorder at quarter sessions refused
jurisdiction and the divisional court held that he was right to do so. There is C
no procedure in criminal law for the trial of an issue; an accused must be tried
on indictment. As LORD GODDARD, C.J., said (3), the recorder had no jurisdiction to try an indictment for manslaughter. He thought that it was a pity that
the assize judge had not given leave to the prosecution to prefer a voluntary
bill indicting the accused for dangerous driving, though he expressed no view
whether on such a bill the accused would have been able to plead autrefois D
acquit.

If SMALL, J.'s order is to be read as directing the trial of an issue apart from
an indictment it is plainly wrong; but, whereas in *R*. v. *Shipton* (2) the court
of quarter sessions had no jurisdiction to entertain an indictment for manslaughter,
the Kingston circuit court had jurisdiction to try an indictment for murder
and for manslaughter. Autrefois acquit is not a ground for quashing an indict- E
ment; and it can be argued that the circuit court on the further trial would be
obliged to proceed on the indictment, leaving it to the defence to enter a plea
of autrefois acquit. That plea would be bound to succeed to the extent that it
would be a good answer to the charge of murder. Whether or not it would be a
good answer to the charge of manslaughter raises the point of substance which is
now before the Board. Alternatively, it might be argued that the circuit court F
on a further trial could properly have amended the indictment by adding a count
for manslaughter and proceeding to trial on that count only.

Their lordships think it unnecessary to pronounce on the validity of these
arguments. To obtain redress under Ch. III of the Constitution the applicant
has to show that his fundamental rights have been or are likely to be infringed,
and he cannot show this if his whole case rests on a procedural fault that could G
easily be put right. The respondent has appreciated this, and accordingly in
his claim for redress has asked not only that the order of SMALL, J., should be
set aside but also for a declaration that he cannot again be tried for the offence
of manslaughter on a voluntary bill of indictment. This raises the substance of
the matter. Their lordships think that the most convenient, if not the only
correct, way of dealing with this sort of situation is by a voluntary bill; and they H
will consider this case on the assumption that this is what would have been done.

Their lordships must, however, notice briefly a point taken by the Crown
which, if sound, would require them to deal with the validity of SMALL, J.'s
order. It is argued that the order was properly made under s. 45 (3) of the
Jury Law and that by virtue of s. 26 (8) of the Constitution (which their lordships
will later consider more fully) an order so made cannot be treated as a contra- I
vention of the Constitution. This argument was rejected—their lordships
think rightly—in both courts below. As was said in the judgment of the Supreme
Court, s. 45 (3) is procedural only. An order made under it cannot diminish the
substantive rights which the accused is given by the Constitution nor affect the
efficacy of any plea that is open to him on a further trial.

(2) [1957] 1 All E.R. 206.
(3) [1957] 1 All E.R. at p. 207, letter E, see also letter G.

A   Their lordships can now leave procedural points and consider the terms of
s. 20 (8) of the Constitution.   All the judges below have treated it as a declaring
or intended to declare the common law on the subject.   Their lordships agree.
It is unnecessary to resort to implication for this intendment, since the Constitution itself expressly ensures it.   Whereas the general rule, as is to be expected in
a Constitution and as is here embodied in s. 2, is that the provisions of the
B Constitution should prevail over other law, an exception is made in Ch. III.
This chapter, as their lordships have already noted, proceeds on the presumption
that the fundamental rights which it covers are already secured to the people of
Jamaica by existing law.   The laws in force are not to be subjected to scrutiny
in order to see whether or not they conform to the precise terms of the protective
provisions.   The object of these provisions is to ensure that no future enactment
C shall in any matter which the chapter covers derogate from the rights which at the
coming into force of the Constitution the individual enjoyed.   Accordingly
s. 26 (8) in Ch. III provides as follows:

   " Nothing contained in any law in force immediately before the appointed
   day shall be held to be inconsistent with any of the provisions of this chapter;
   and nothing done under the authority of any such law shall be held to be
D   done in contravention of any of these provisions."

Notwithstanding that " law " is in s. 1 (1) of the Constitution defined as including
" any instrument having the force of law and any unwritten rule of law ", the
respondent has argued that " law " in s. 26 (8) is confined to enacted law and
excludes the common law, so that if on its true construction s. 20 (8) expresses
E the law on autrefois differently from the common law, s. 20 (8) must prevail.
In their lordships' opinion this argument clearly fails and was rightly rejected
by Lewis, J.A., in the Court of Appeal.   Thus the question to be determined
by the Board, and which was in effect determined by both courts below, is whether
at common law and at a second trial of the respondent on an indictment for
manslaughter a plea of autrefois acquit would succeed.
F   On the face of it, it would appear that such a plea is bound to fail.   Obviously
what is fundamental to autrefois acquit is a verdict of acquittal of the offence
charged.   In the verdict returned by the jury in this case there is no acquittal
of manslaughter.   Moreover, it is conceded, as it must be, that if there had been
two counts in the indictment, and a disagreement on the second count for manslaughter, there would be nothing on which to found a plea of autrefois acquit
G to another indictment for manslaughter.   The argument for the respondent is
based on high technicalities, most skilfully developed by counsel, and its success
depends on the nature and effect of a verdict, when, as in this case two offences,
a greater and a lesser, are comprised in one count.
     There are three categories of verdict in a criminal case.   The first is the general
verdict which is of conviction or acquittal on the whole count.   The second
H is the partial verdict.   When at common law or by statute a jury is empowered
to convict of a lesser or different crime to that charged in the count, they can be
asked to return partial verdicts specifying the crime to which each verdict refers.
The third category, which is not suggested as being applicable in the present case,
is the special verdict, where the jury, as Blackstone (Commentaries Vol. III,
p. 377) puts it, " state the naked facts, as they find them to be proved, and pray
I the advice of the court thereon ".
     The argument for the respondent is put in two ways.   First, it is said that the
common law of autrefois acquit is such that any verdict of acquittal, whether it
be general or partial, is sufficient to found the plea.   Reliance is placed on two
statements of the law.   One is by Lord Reading, C.J., in *R.* v. *Barron* (4)
which, as Lewis, J.A., said in the Court of Appeal " may well be considered as
explanatory of s. 20 (8) of the Constitution ".   Lord Reading said (5):

---

(4) [1914] 2 K.B. 570.   (5) [1914] 2 K.B. at p. 574.

"... the law does not permit a man to be twice in peril of being convicted   A
of the same offence. If, therefore, he has been acquitted, i.e., found to be
not guilty of the offence, by a court competent to try him, such acquittal
is a bar to a second indictment for the same offence. This rule .applies
not only to the offence actually charged in the first indictment, but to any
offence of which he could have been properly convicted on the trial of the
first indictment."   B

Again in *Connelly* v. *Director of Public Prosecutions* (6) LORD MORRIS OF BORTH-Y-
GEST stated (7) the rule in nine propositions, the second being "that a man
cannot be tried for a crime in respect of which he could on some previous indictment have been convicted ".

Neither in *R.* v. *Barron* (8) nor in *Connelly* v. *Director of Public Prosecutions* (6)
was there any question of a disagreement. In the Court of Appeal DUFFUS, P.,   C
considered this to be immaterial. He said:

" The fact that they did not agree on a verdict in respect of manslaughter
does not mean that the applicant was not in peril of conviction for
manslaughter."

DUFFUS, P., was there evidently using the word " peril " in its natural and   D
ordinary sense; but if the rule against double jeopardy and the principles of
autrefois are to produce the same result, the word " peril " must be given a more
restricted meaning. It is true that the object of the plea of autrefois is to ensure
that a man is not placed in double jeopardy. It is true also that as a general
rule, i.e., whenever the trial of an offence is concluded as it usually is, it is right
to say that the accused must not be put in jeopardy again. But what is essential to   E
the plea of autrefois acquit is proof of a verdict of acquittal of the offence alleged—
not proof that the accused was in peril of conviction for that offence. In so far
as a verdict on any count by its terms specifies an offence, it speaks for itself.
In so far as it does not, its effect may be ascertained by enquiring of what offences
comprised in that count the accused stood in peril of conviction. This is the
only relevance of the existence of peril in the popular sense of the word; it is a   F
means of interpreting the verdict.

There are certainly statements of the law which equate the plea of autrefois
acquit with the rule against double jeopardy, notably in BLACKSTONE and
other ancient and learned writers quoted in the speech of LORD MORRIS OF
BORTH-Y-GEST in *Connelly* v. *Director of Public Prosecutions* (9). They are
accurate and complete on the basis, then generally accepted, that a trial once   G
begun must end in a verdict. It was not until after *R.* v. *Charlesworth* (10) that
it was clearly established that the discharge of the jury before they have given
a verdict did not operate as an acquittal and also that a jury could properly be
discharged because of inability to agree. Thus if the statements of the rule
against double jeopardy and of the rule of autrefois are to be completely reconciled, so as to fit the case of a discharge without verdict given, whether because   H
of disagreement or otherwise, it can be done only by placing a somewhat artificial
meaning on the word " jeopardy "—what CROMPTON, J., in *R.* v. *Charlesworth* (11)
described as " jeopardy in the legal sense of the word ". In the popular sense a
man is in jeopardy of conviction from the moment he is put in charge of a jury;
and if that jury is discharged and he is put in charge of another, he is in jeopardy
again. SIR ALEXANDER COCKBURN, C.J., in *R.* v. *Charlesworth* (12) made it   I
plain that the rule against double jeopardy could not operate in that way. He
said (13):

---

(6) [1964] 2 All E.R. 401; [1964] A.C. 1254, 1280.
(7) [1964] 2 All E.R. at p. 412, letter B; [1964] A.C. at p. 1305.
(8) [1914] 2 K.B. 570.
(9) [1964] 2 All E.R. at pp. 412-414; [1964] A.C. at p. 1306.
(10) (1861), 1 B. & S. 460; 9 Cox, C.C. 44.   (11) (1861), 9 Cox, C.C. at p. 58.
(12) (1861), 9 Cox, C.C. 44.   (13) (1861), 9 Cox, C.C. at p. 53.

A   " It appears to me, when you talk of a man being twice tried, that you
mean a trial which proceeds to its legitimate and lawful conclusion by
verdict; that when you speak of a man being twice put in jeopardy, you mean
put in jeopardy by the verdict of a jury, and that he is not tried, that he is not
put in jeopardy, until the verdict comes to pass, because, if that were not so,
it is clear that in every case of defective verdict a man could not be tried a

B   second time . . ."

In their lordships' opinion this reasoning was correctly applied in the Supreme
Court and in *R.* v. *Quinn* (14), a decision of the Court of Criminal Appeal of New
South Wales which the Supreme Court followed. The Supreme Court applied
also the statement of the law in HALE's PLEAS OF THE CROWN (1778 Edn.,
Vol. 2, p. 246):

C   " If a man be acquit generally upon an indictment of murder autrefois
acquit is a good plea to an indictment of manslaughter of the same person."

Neither LORD READING, C.J. (15), nor LORD MORRIS OF BORTH-Y-GEST (16)
in the dicta relied on were addressing their minds to the distinction between a
general and a partial verdict and it was unnecessary for the purposes of these

D   dicta that they should. The passage in HALE was before both of them and
indeed LORD MORRIS OF BORTH-Y-GEST in his speech (17) quoted it in full.

In their lordships' opinion the law on this point is as stated in HALE and in
that statement the word " generally " is of vital import. If on a plea of autrefois
acquit the accused proves a general acquittal on a previous indictment, the plea
is good for every crime for which he could on that indictment have been convicted.

E   If he proves a partial acquittal, the plea is undoubtedly good for the crime
specified in the verdict of acquittal. Whether or not it is good for any other
crime must depend on the circumstances in which it is given. Their lordships
do not intend to deal exhaustively with all the consequences of partial verdicts.
It may well be that if on any count a jury have delivered partial verdicts, whether
of conviction or acquittal, on all the crimes which they have been told to consider,

F   the verdicts taken together will support a plea of autrefois acquit on any other
crime of which the accused could have been found guilty on that count. It must
depend on what inference can in the circumstances of a particular case properly
be drawn from the verdict. It is sufficient in this case to say that a partial
verdict cannot be held to cover by inference a crime about which the jury
disagreed.

G   So it is necessary for the respondent, if he is to succeed in the plea of autrefois
acquit to bring himself within the law as stated by HALE by establishing that a
verdict of acquittal of murder coupled with a disagreement on the issue of manslaughter is not a partial but a general verdict. This leads to the second part
of the argument and to a point which was not developed in *R.* v. *Quinn* (14) or in
the Supreme Court, but which was very fully considered in the closely reasoned

H   and careful judgments in the Court of Appeal. The foundation for this part of
the argument is the proposition that on an indictment for murder, while the
jury are permitted at common law to return a verdict of manslaughter if satisfied
of the accused's guilt of the lesser offence, they cannot be compelled to do so.
They have the right to deliver a general verdict of not guilty on the indictment.
If, as in the present case, they fail to deliver a verdict on manslaughter, then, so

I   it is argued, there is only one verdict on the indictment and it must therefore be
a general verdict. The reason for the failure, it is submitted, is immaterial.
A jury may fail to reach a verdict because they did not consider the matter at
all or because, considering it, they cannot agree. It does not matter, so it is
argued, which it is. Since they are acting within their rights in returning only
one verdict, they are not obliged to state their reason for choosing to take that

(14) (1953), S.R. (N.S.W.) 21.   (15) [1914] 2 K.B. at p. 574.
(16) [1964] 2 All E.R. at p. 412, letter B; [1964] A.C. at p. 1305.
(17) [1964] 2 All E.R. at p. 413; [1964] A.C. at p. 1037.

course; and if they do state it, the reason is no more a part of the verdict than a   A
rider is.　Thus the respondent argues that the verdict in his case is a general
verdict to which the law as laid down by HALE applies.

Their lordships do not doubt that it was once the law that a jury could not be
compelled to return any verdict other than a general verdict.　The law is so
stated in HAWKINS' PLEAS OF THE CROWN (8th Edn., 1824), Vol. 2, p. 619:

> " Fourthly, that it hath been adjudged, that where the jury find a man not　 B
> guilty of an indictment or appeal of murder, they are not bound to make
> any inquiry, whether he be guilty of manslaughter, etc.; but that if they
> will they may, according to the nature of the evidence find him guilty of
> manslaughter or homicide se defendendo, or per infortunium; . . ."

The passage is quoted by HERRON, J., in *R.* v. *Quinn* (18).　HAWKINS wrote in   C
1824, but the authorities he cites for his statement of the law are not later than
the sixteenth century.　In *Wroth* v. *Wiggs* (19) the jury found that the defendant
was not guilty of murder (20) " and being demanded if he was guilty of manslaughter, they answered they had nothing to do to enquire of it ", and this
notwithstanding that " the evidence was pregnant that he was guilty of manslaughter ".　The court held (20) after consultation　 D

> " that by the law the jury are not compellable to enquire of the man-
> slaughter.　Thereupon they gave their verdict as before, and the prisoner
> was discharged."

This ruling was approved in *Penryn* v. *Corbet* (21) where it was said to have
been founded on the advice of all the justices of both Benches.　In the latter
case (21) the jury found the defendant not guilty of murder but guilty of homicide.   E
It was held that this by the advice of the court they might well do; but it was
said also that (21)

> " they might if they would (if they thought him not guilty of the murder)
> have found him not guilty generally, and not have spoken of the homicide;
> and it is at their election in this case how they will give their verdict."　 F

At the time these cases were decided the jury could have been punished for
refusing to consider the issue of manslaughter, if by the law they were required to
do so.　That is the sense of the word " compellable " in *Wroth* v. *Wiggs* (20).
Since the celebrated decision in *Bushell's Case* (22) a jury cannot in this sense be
compelled to do anything.　The law is now as stated by LORD MANSFIELD, C.J.,
in *R.* v. *Shipley* (23):　 G

> " It is the duty of the judge, in all cases of general justice, to tell the jury
> how to do right, though they have it in their power to do wrong, which is a
> matter entirely between God and their own consciences."

The point, however, remains in substance the same.　Can a conscientious jury
in a case such as this ignore, without doing wrong, a judicial direction to consider   H
the issue of manslaughter?

If the rules of practice relating to the jury had not changed since Tudor times,
the jury would function very differently from the way in which it does today.
For that matter, if the jury had not by Tudor times grown out of its mediaeval
origins, it would still have been only a jury of inquest.　The jury has been shaped
over the centuries to meet the needs of criminal justice and the development
has been made by the practice of judges, often different practices by different   I
judges, until eventually a rule emerges.　*Bushell's Case* (22), which their lordships
have just cited, is one example of a great change.　It is a far cry back from the
dictum of LORD MANSFIELD in *R.* v. *Shipley* (24) to the statute 26 Hen. 8 c. 4,

---

(18) (1953), S.R. (N.S.W.) at p. 25.　　　　　　　　(19) (1592), Cro. Eliz. 276.
(20) (1592), Cro. Eliz. at p. 276.　　　　　　　　　(21) (1598), Cro. Eliz. 464.
(22) (1670), Vaugh. 135; 6 State Tr. 999.　　(23) (1784), 4 Doug. K.B. 73 at p. 170.
(24) (1784), 4 Doug. K.B. at p. 170.

A two hundred and fifty years before, authorising the punishment of jurors for giving " any untrue verdict against the King, contrary to good and pregnant evidence ministered to them " and to the days when the Star Chamber or the judges themselves regularly inflicted such punishment.

A case already cited, *R.* v. *Charlesworth* (25), affords another striking example of change.   This case is now regarded as clearly settling that a jury which cannot
B agree can properly be discharged.   LORD COKE had stated, however, in the most positive and unqualified terms, as SIR ALEXANDER COCKBURN, C.J., said (26), that a jury once sworn and charged in the case of life or member could not be discharged by the court or any other, but must give a verdict.   BLACKSTONE said that the jury could not be discharged, unless in cases of evident necessity, until they had given in their verdict.   SIR ALEXANDER COCKBURN, C.J., dealt
C with those dicta by saying (27) that the law laid down by LORD COKE was not in accordance with modern practice and that BLACKSTONE'S statement was not (27) " a true or correct exposition of the law as practised in our time ".   He said (27) also that a statement of the law as laid down by LORD HOLT was " not in conformity with modern practice ".   In the same spirit he condemned (28) the practice sanctioned by LORD HALE of permitting a juror to be withdrawn
D if the prosecution's case was incomplete so that they could have another opportunity of presenting it.   He said (29) that since LORD HALE'S time a practice to the contrary had grown up and that

> " whether it be positive law, or whether merely a regulation of practice made by the judges in the time of LORD HOLT, is to me a matter of compara-
E > tive indifference: it has been a uniform practice of the judicial authorities of this country from that time to the present, and I take it that a rata praxis like that becomes substantially a part of the law . . ."

It is therefore unwise to treat a case like *Wroth* v. *Wiggs* (30) as having settled the law for all time and it is necessary to look at how the practice has developed. It will be found that whereas the jury's right to deliver a general verdict as
F against a special has been maintained, their right to deliver a general verdict as against a partial has, their lordships think, fallen into disuse.   It is worth glancing at one or two modern authorities on the special verdict so as to point the contrast in this respect with the partial verdict, and so as to show also in what manner the jury's right to return a general verdict has been exercised. For if it be held that in the present case the jury had a right to return a general
G verdict, it will become necessary to consider whether in fact they exercised that right.

In *Devizes Corpn.* v. *Clark* (31) the corporation as plaintiffs sought relief against the defendant, who had sold meat outside the market.   The plaintiffs claimed that they were possessed of a market on Thursday and that the defendant had infringed their right by selling meat on Thursdays from his own house
H instead of from a stall in the market place for which he would have had to pay the plaintiffs.   The judge, WILLIAMS, B. (32), thought that it was doubtful as a matter of law whether the right to a market was sufficient per se to preclude the sale of meat otherwise than from the plaintiffs' stalls.   If there existed an immemorial usage to that effect, he would have had no doubt.   He therefore invited the jury to find specially whether there was or was not such a usage.
I The jury found a verdict for the plaintiffs generally; and the following colloquy then ensued (33):

---

(25) (1861), 1 B. & S. 460; 9 Cox, C.C. 44.
(26) (1861), 1 B. & S. at p. 498; 9 Cox, C.C. at p. 46.
(27) (1861), 1 B. & S. at p. 503; 9 Cox, C.C. at p. 50.
(28) (1861), 1 B. & S. at p. 500; 9 Cox, C.C. at p. 47.
(29) (1861), 9 Cox, C.C. at p. 05; 1 B. & S. at p. 504.
(30) (1592), Cro. Eliz. 276.   (31) (1835), 3 Ad. & El. 506.
(32) (1835), 3 Ad. & El. at p. 507.   (33) (1835), 3 Ad. & El. at pp. 507, 508.

WILLIAMS, B.: " Then, gentlemen, you find that in your judgment there   A
has been an immemorial usage for the corporation to demand and receive
this stallage . . . and that there was no right on the part of the individuals
to sell in a house or shop out of the market."

The Foreman: " That is not our verdict; our verdict is for the plaintiffs;
the right to the market is acknowledged on all hands; of course, our verdict
is to say that the defendant had not a right to do what he is charged with   B
doing."

WILLIAMS, B.: " Then you further find that the defendant had no
right? "

The Foreman: " I would rather not add any words."

The judge then said (34) that an express finding might prevent further litigation.
The foreman replied that the jury had been guided by the remarks of his lordship;   C
but that they desired to add nothing to their verdict. In the King's Bench a
rule to show cause why the verdict should not be set aside was discharged, all
the judges saying (35) that the jury had a right to give a general verdict only.

In the case which arose out of the Jameson Raid, *R.* v. *Jameson* (36), the bench,
obviously fearing that in a general verdict the jury might be tempted to express
their sympathy with the accused, asked for a special verdict, putting questions   D
designed to establish the facts which would lead conclusively to guilt. The
presiding judge, LORD RUSSELL OF KILLOWEN, C.J., however, told the jury (37):

" If you choose in opposition to the request which I and my brethren
make to you to refuse to answer those questions, nobody can make you
answer them."   E

In *R.* v. *Bourne* (38) the trial judge put four questions to the jury, two on each
of two counts. LORD GODDARD, C.J., in the Court of Criminal Appeal said (39):

" Special verdicts ought to be found only in the most exceptional cases,
and in this case no member of the court has been able to find that there is
any exceptional question of criminal law involved."
      F
So there is ample authority in modern times to establish that the jury is not
bound to return a special verdict. In contrast to this no case since the sixteenth
century has been cited to the Board in which a jury has asserted a right to refuse
to return a partial verdict. On the contrary, the practice has been developed
in a way which can be explained only on the footing that a jury are expected to
accept a direction to consider lesser or different offences arising out of a count   G
in the indictment in the same way as they accept the direction to consider the
offence stated in the count. The common law rule which permits a conviction
of the lesser offence has been amplified in the last one hundred years by statutes
too numerous to mention permitting the conviction of lesser and sometimes
quite different offences. In *R.* v. *Thomas* (40) HUMPHREYS, J. (41), spoke of
the cases in which the common law allowed an alternative verdict as being   H
" very rare " compared with statute. The practice of rolling up into one count a
number of different offences based on the same facts has been found a convenient
way of shortening indictments. If it meant that a jury could for any reason
that seemed good to them refuse to consider an alternative verdict with the result
that the accused would be acquitted without trial, or if it meant that where the
jury did consider it and disagreed the result would be an acquittal, the practice   I
would never have been formed. The parody of justice which it would have
produced would have been avoided by setting out all the offences in alternative

(34) (1835), 3 Ad. & El. at p. 508.   (35) (1835), 3 Ad. & El. at pp. 510-512.
(36) [1896] 2 Q.B. 425; 12 T.L.R. 551.   (37) (1896), 12 T.L.R. at p. 594.
(38) (1952), 36 Cr. App. Rep. 125.
(39) (1952), 36 Cr. App. Rep. 125 at p. 127.
(40) [1949] 2 All E.R. 662; [1950] 1 K.B. 26; 33 Cr. App. Rep. 200.
(41) [1949] 2 All E.R. at p. 667, letter H; [1950] 1 K.B. at p. 36; 33 Cr. App. Rep.
at p. 210.

A   counts. But the practice has flourished and is now ingrained in our system, and it is impossible to reconcile with it a principle formulated when the rule allowing an alternative verdict was in its infancy, when a jury was not allowed to disagree and when acquittals resulting from the shape or content of the indictment were more readily acceptable than they are today.   There are in fact very few cases today in which a jury are not, or could not be if the facts permitted it, directed to

B   consider an alternative verdict. Their lordships are unaware of any case in which it has been suggested that such a direction has any less force than any other. They are unaware of any case in which the judge has told the jury, as Lord Russell of Killowen, C.J., did in *R.* v. *Jameson* (42) that it was only a request which they could disregard if they chose. If the respondent's argument is right, counsel for the defence would always be alert to the chance of a technical acquittal

C   legitimately obtained, and would be failing in his duty to his client if he did not remind the jury that they were not obliged to consider an alternative verdict. Their lordships are unaware of any case in which counsel has taken that course, and they will note below a case in which it certainly would have been taken if it had been thought to be open.

It is usually difficult to find specific authority marking the stages in a change

D   in practice. A practice that is in keeping with current ideas of justice and convenience rapidly acquires such strength that it is unlikely to be challenged. So such authority as there is on this point is oblique. The respondent relied on a statement taken from the judgment of Lord Goddard, C.J. in *R.* v. *Shipton* (43). Lord Goddard, after reading the section of the Road Traffic Act, 1934 which makes it lawful for the jury on an indictment for manslaughter to find the

E   accused guilty of dangerous driving, said (44): "That is entirely a permissive section."   In their lordships' opinion Lord Goddard by that sentence was saying no more than that the jury were not obliged to convict of dangerous driving; he was certainly not saying that they were not obliged to consider it, if properly directed to do so.

The Crown on the other hand relied on *R.* v. *Baxter* (45). This was a case in

F   which on an indictment for murder the jury convicted the accused of manslaughter and recommended her to mercy. The defence complained that the judge ought not to have left manslaughter to the jury. In the Court of Criminal Appeal Darling, J. said (46):

> "Mr. Marshall Hall complains that the judge, in his summing up, told
> the jury that they might find her guilty of manslaughter, and indeed

G   > suggested that they should do so. It is plain that, as an advocate Mr. Marshall
> Hall might well complain of this. The jury might have thought that the
> deceased was a man of whom the world was well rid, and so have sympathised
> with the appellant, and Mr. Marshall Hall may have hoped for an acquittal
> which he ought not to have got."

H   Later Darling, J. said (47):

> "The jury were asked if they found the prisoner guilty of murder; they
> said: 'Not guilty.' Then they were asked if they found her guilty of
> manslaughter. It seems to us that it was right to put this question to them,
> for the judge finished his summing up with a reference to manslaughter;
> it is plain that, when they said she was not guilty of murder, they had not

I   > exhausted the questions they had to decide."

This was a case in which the defence had everything to gain by telling the jury that they need not consider manslaughter unless they wished to do so. Obviously

---

(42) (1896), 12 T.L.R. at p. 594.
(43) [1957] 1 All E.R. 206 at p. 207.
(44) [1957] 1 All E.R. at p. 207, letter D.
(45) (1913), 9 Cr. App. Rep. 60.
(46) (1913), 9 Cr. App. Rep. at p. 62.
(47) (1913), 9 Cr. App. Rep. at p. 63.

it did not occur to Sir Edward Marshall Hall, an advocate of the greatest A
experience at the criminal bar, that this course was open to him. Likewise
the point could not have occurred to the judges in the Court of Criminal Appeal
as an arguable one or they would not have said without qualification that the
jury had not after the acquittal of murder exhausted the questions that they
had to decide.

Their lordships conclude that the rule that a jury cannot be directed to give B
a partial verdict is inconsistent with modern practice and obsolete. This conclusion destroys the foundation of the respondent's case and of the judgments in
the Court of Appeal. Their lordships have dealt with the point at length, not
only out of respect to the Court of Appeal but also because of its practical
importance. The respondent's argument, if sound, would have led either to
remedial legislation or to an alteration throughout the Commonwealth of the C
form in which bills of indictment are presented.

Their lordships must add, however, that even if they had concluded that
there was no obligation on a jury to deliver a partial verdict, they would still
have advised Her Majesty to allow the appeal. If *Wroth* v. *Wiggs* (48) and
Penryn v. *Corbet* (49) are still the law, then, as was said in the latter case, it
is at the election of the jury how they will give their verdict. In the present D
case they were directed by the judge to consider both murder and manslaughter
and they evidently did so. When asked for their verdict on manslaughter they
did not answer, as the jury did in *Wroth* v. *Wiggs*, (50) that " they had nothing
to do to enquire of it "; nor did they politely stand on their rights as the jury
did in *Devises Corpn.* v. *Clark* (51). They said that they or the necessary majority
of them were unable to agree. If a jury are permitted to say that they will not E
enquire into an alternative offence, they must also, at least since the middle of
the last century, be permitted to say that they have enquired into it and cannot
agree about it. The two things are not the same. If they say the first, they are
asserting their right to return a general verdict and so the verdict which they
do return must be treated accordingly. If they say the second, they are returning,
as they were requested to do, a partial verdict on murder and stating their F
inability to deliver a second partial verdict on manslaughter. There is no justification for treating the first verdict of the jury in this case, which on the face of it
is partial (being " not guilty of murder "), as general when they themselves
have made it plain that they do not intend it so to be. What is required for the
plea of autrefois acquit is proof of acquittal of manslaughter, not proof of a
situation in which the jury, if they had elected otherwise than they did, might G
have acquitted of manslaughter although divided eight to four.

For these reasons their lordships will humbly advise Her Majesty to allow the
appeal. Their lordships consider that in all the circumstances each party should
pay his own costs of this appeal and of the proceedings below and they will
humbly advise Her Majesty to vary accordingly the order of the Court of Appeal.

Appeal allowed. H

Solicitors: *Charles Russell & Co.* (for the Crown); *Alban Gould, Baker & Co.*
(for the respondent).

[*Reported by* KATHLEEN J. H. O'BRIEN, *Barrister-at-Law.*]

I

---

(48) (1592), Cro. Eliz. 276.
(49) (1598), Cro. Eliz. 464.
(50) (1592), Cro. Eliz. at p. 276.
(51) (1835), 3 Ad. & El. 506.

Reversed. H.L. [1968] 1 All E.R. 121.

Reversed. H.L. [1968] 1 All E.R. 121.

A   GARTSIDE AND ANOTHER v. INLAND
          REVENUE COMMISSIONERS.

[COURT OF APPEAL, CIVIL DIVISION (Lord Denning, M.R., Harman and Salmon,
     L.JJ.), January 26, 27, 30, 31, February 1, 2, March 2, 1967.]

Estate Duty—Determination of life interest—Discretionary trust—Accumulation
B   *of surplus income—Advancement determining discretionary trust in sums*
      advanced—Whether group of objects of discretionary trust had collectively an
      " interest in possession "—Whether objects of discretionary trust each had
      an " interest in possession "—Whether interests in accumulations were to be
      regarded as separate and independent—Finance Act, 1940 (3 & 4 Geo. 6
      c. 29), *s.* 43 (1) *as amended by Finance Act,* 1950 (14 Geo. 6 c. 15), *s.* 43 (1).

C   Under the will of a testator, who died on Jan. 8, 1941, trustees held
      a quarter share of his residuary estate on discretionary trusts during his
      son's life to apply the whole or such part as they thought fit of the income
      of the quarter share towards the maintenance support or benefit of the
      testator's son and his wife and children or any of them, and to accumulate
      and invest any surplus income to the intent that the accumulations should
D   be added to the capital of the quarter share. The trusts after the son's
      death were as to capital and income for his children attaining twenty-one or,
      being female, attaining that age or marrying, and if more than one in equal
      shares absolutely. On Jan. 2, 1962, the trustees exercised, in relation to the
      capital of the quarter share (not the accumulations of income), a power of
      advancement conferred on them by the testator's will. This power was
E   exercised by two deed polls in favour of each of the twin sons of the testator's
      son, who were then about seventeen years of age; the two grandsons of the
      testator would consequently become entitled to the capital advanced on
      attaining twenty-one. On Jan. 8, 1962, the accumulation period ended.
      The testator's son died on May 8, 1963. Estate duty was claimed on the
      sums advanced, but would not become payable (having regard to the
F   terms of s. 43 (1)* of the Finance Act, 1940) unless the interest of the objects
      of the discretionary trust, determined by the advancements, was an " interest
      in possession " before the advances were made.

          Held: estate duty was exigible on the son's death in respect of the
      funds advanced because—

          (i) (per LORD DENNING, M.R.) the group of interests of the objects of the
G   discretionary trusts for the lifetime of the testator's son, or (per HARMAN,
      L.J.) the whole bundle of rights attaching during the lifetime of the testator's
      son to his one quarter share, (that is to say, both the discretionary rights and
      the right to accumulations†), was an " interest in possession " for the
      purposes of s. 43 (1) of the Finance Act, 1940, and was determined by the
      advancements (see p. 176, letters E and H, p. 177, letter C, p. 178, letter E,
H   and p. 180, letters C and E, post).

          (ii) (per SALMON, L.J.) the interest of a discretionary object of that dis-
      cretionary trust was an " interest in possession " for the purposes of s. 43 (1)
      and was determined by the advancements (see p. 183, letter H, post).

          A.-G. v. Power ([1906] 2 I.R. 272) distinguished.

          Decision of UNGOED-THOMAS, J. ([1966] 3 All E.R. 89) reversed.

I   [**Editorial Note.** The court was agreed that there was an " interest in
possession " in the advanced funds before the advancements; but there is a
divergence of view on the question whether the interest of any one object of a
discretionary trust of income is an " interest in possession "; SALMON, L.J.'s
view is stated in holding (ii) above, but HARMAN, L.J., took the view that the
interest of a member of a discretionary class of income beneficiaries was not an
interest in possession (see p. 180, letter B, post), cf., also p. 177, letter A, post.

---

     * Section 43 (1), so far as material, is printed at p. 175, letter G, post.
     † Cf., per contra, p. 178, letter D, and p. 183, letter I, post.

As to interests ceasing on death, see 15 HALSBURY'S LAWS (3rd Edn.) 13, 14, **A**
para. 22; as to settlements with reservations, see ibid., p. 23, para. 42; and for
cases on these subjects, see 21 DIGEST (Repl.) 17-22, *57-77*, 29-32, *105-118*.

For the Finance Act, 1940, s. 43, as amended, see 29 HALSBURYS' STATUTES
(2nd Edn.) 183.]

Cases referred to:

A.-G. v. *Farrell*, [1931] 1 K.B. 81; 99 L.J.K.B. 605; 143 L.T. 639; 21 Digest **B**
    (Repl.) 29, *108*.

A.-G. v. *Heywood*, (1887), 19 Q.B.D. 326; 56 L.J.Q.B. 572; 57 L.T. 271;
    21 Digest (Repl.) 29, *107*.

A.-G. v. *Power*, [1906] 2 I.R. 272; 21 Digest (Repl.) 33, **40*.

Burrell v. *A.-G.*, [1936] 3 All E.R. 758; [1937] A.C. 286; 106 L.J.K.B. 134;
    156 L.T. 36; 21 Digest (Repl.) 12, *39*.   **C**

Chaplin v. *Hicks*, [1911-13] All E.R. Rep. 224; [1911] 2 K.B. 786; 80 L.J.K.B.
    1292; 105 L.T. 285; 17 Digest (Repl.) 89, *96*.

Hodson's Settlement, Re, Brookes v. *A.-G.*, [1939] 1 All E.R. 196; [1939] Ch.
    343; 108 L.J.Ch. 200; 160 L.T. 193; 21 Digest (Repl.) 31, *117*.

Munro's Settlement Trusts, Re, [1963] 1 All E.R. 209; [1963] 1 W.L.R. 145;
    47 Digest (Repl.) 339, *3027*.   **D**

Scott v. *Inland Revenue Comrs.*, [1935] Ch. 246; 104 L.J.Ch. 91; 152 L.T. 315;
    affd., H.L., [1936] 3 All E.R. 752; [1937] A.C. 174; 106 L.J.Ch. 36;
    156 L.T. 33; 21 Digest (Repl.) 12, *38*.

Westminster Bank, Ltd. v. *A.-G.*, [1939] 2 All E.R. 72; [1939] Ch. 610; 108
    L.J.Ch. 294; 160 L.T. 432; 21 Digest (Repl.) 32, *118*.

Wrightson, Re, Wrightson v. *Cooke*, [1908] 1 Ch. 789; 77 L.J.Ch. 422; 98 **E**
    L.T. 799; 47 Digest (Repl.) 548, *4959*.

Appeal.

This was an appeal by the Commissioners of Inland Revenue from a decision
of UNGOED-THOMAS, J., dated May 27, 1966, and reported [1966] 3 All E.R. 89,
holding that estate duty was not exigible on the death of the testator's son,
John Travis Gartside, who died on May 8, 1963, in respect of sums advanced **F**
for his twin sons from a one-quarter share of a residuary trust fund, which
share was bequeathed by the testator on trusts including a discretionary trust
of income for the benefit of the deceased, his wife and children, during his lifetime, and thereafter, trusts in favour of the deceased's children at twenty-one.
The testator's will conferred a power of advancement in favour of each of the
deceased's children, extending to one half of the share of the child.   **G**

H. E. Francis, Q.C., and *J. P. Warner* for the Crown.
G. A. Rink, Q.C., and *P. W. E. Taylor* for the trustee.

Cur. adv. vult.

Mar. 2. The following judgments were read.

                                                               H

    LORD DENNING, M.R.: On Jan. 8, 1941, Thomas Edmund Gartside
died. I will call him the grandfather. He left a will by which a fourth share
of his residuary trust fund was to be applied by trustees for the benefit of his
son John (who was then unmarried) and his family (when he did marry). I will
call it the trust fund. This trust fund was to be held by the trustees on these
trusts: **I**

    (a) During the lifetime of the son John, the trustees were to pay the income
of the trust fund, or such part of it as they thought fit, on a *discretionary trust*
for the benefit of the son, his wife and children. I will call them the " discretionary
objects ". If the trustees did not distribute the whole of the income, they were
to *accumulate* the surplus income, and add it to the capital of the fund. This
addition I will call the " accumulation fund ".

    (b) After the death of the son, the trustees were to hold both the capital and
income of the trust fund, and also the accumulation fund on trust for the grand

A   sons who attained twenty-one. I will call them the " accumulation beneficiaries ".

(c) The trustees were given power at any time to make *advances* out of the trust fund to any of the grandchildren. These advances could be of sums up to one-half of the share of that grandchild in the fund.

On the death of the grandfather on Jan. 8, 1941, the trustees took possession of the trust fund. On Aug. 5, 1942, the son married. On Jan. 5, 1945, the son

B   and his wife had twin sons (the two grandsons); they had no other children. For twenty years after the grandfather died, the trustees *accumulated* all the income of the fund. They did not distribute any of it to the discretionary objects at all. None to the son or his wife or the grandchildren. Then in 1961 they paid £786 10s. 0d. to the son and £50 to his wife. Save for those two payments, they accumulated all the income of the trust fund and added it to the capital.

C   In 1962 the figures were as follows: The original trust fund stood at £93,700, earning a gross income of £6,400 a year. The income which had accumulated over the years came to £55,185. On Jan. 2, 1962, the trustees decided to exercise the power of *advancement*. The twin grandsons were then nearly seventeen years of age. The trustees advanced each of them £23,500. These advances were made out of the original trust fund. The trustees did it by two deeds poll,

D   one in favour of each grandson. By each deed poll the trustees declared that they held investments valued at £23,500 and the income thereof on trust for that grandson if he shall attain the age of twenty-one. On May 8, 1963, the son died, leaving his wife and the grandsons surviving him. Thereafter the trustees held the original trust fund (save for the advances) and the accumulation fund on trust for the two grandsons. On the son's death there was clearly a passing of

E   those funds such as to attract estate duty; but the question is whether estate duty is payable on the advances made in January, 1962, to the grandsons. On Jan. 5, 1966, the twin grandsons became twenty-one and indefeasibly entitled to the £23,500 each.

Seeing that the advances were made in favour of the grandsons before the son's death, there was clearly no passing of them at his death so as to be caught

F   by the Finance Act, 1894; but the question is whether these advances are caught by s. 43 (1) (as amended) of the Finance Act, 1940. That section was passed so as to catch dispositions made within five years of the death. These advances were made only sixteen months before the death. They are, therefore, within the time, if they are within the words. The material words for present purposes are:

G   ". . . where an interest limited to cease on a death . . . has been determined . . . in any other manner . . . after becoming an interest in possession . . . then—(a) if, had there been no . . . determination . . . the property in which the interest subsisted would have passed on the death under s. 1 of the Finance Act, 1894, that property shall be deemed by virtue of this section to be included as to the whole thereof in the property passing on the

H   death, . . ."

In order to be caught by the words, there are four requisites: 1. The objects of the discretionary trust (i.e., the son, his wife and children) must have had an " interest limited to cease " on the son's death. 2. That interest must have become an " interest in possession " before the advances were made to the

I   grandsons. 3. That interest must have been determined by the deeds poll to the extent of the amounts advanced, namely, £47,000. 4. If the interest had not been so determined, the advanced sums (of £47,000) would have passed or be deemed to pass on the son's death under s. 1 or s. 2 (1) (b) of the Act of 1894.

If requisites 1 and 2 are satisfied, it is admitted that requisites 3 and 4 are satisfied. I turn, therefore, to requisites 1 and 2.

1. *Did the discretionary objects have an " interest limited to cease " on the son's death?* This point is settled by authority. For eighty years now the courts have held that each one of the objects of a discretionary trust has an " interest "

in the trust fund, even where there is power in the trustees to withhold it and   A
accumulate the surplus for others, see *A.-G.* v. *Heywood* (1), followed in *A.-G.*
v. *Farrell* (2). These cases have stood so long and so many transactions effected
and, I may add, so many statutes passed, on the faith of them, that we must
abide by them. What is the reasoning underlying those cases? I think that
it is simply this. Every person who is an object of a discretionary trust has a
right in respect of the trust fund, even when there is power to withhold it and   B
accumulate the surplus. He has a right to be considered by the trustees as
eligible for a payment to be made to him. This right is analogous to the right
of a competitor for a prize. Like a girl who goes in for a beauty competition.
Her entry must be taken into consideration. She has no right to any of the
prizes, but she has a right to be considered as eligible for one of them: and she
will be entitled to damages if she is shut out from consideration (see *Chaplin* v.   C
Hicks (3)). By virtue of this right, she has an interest in the prize fund. Her
interest can be assessed in money. It is the damages which will be awarded to
her if she is wrongly excluded. So with the objects of a discretionary trust.
They have a right to be considered as eligible for payment. If a wife and children
were destitute and the trustees unreasonably rejected their request for payment,
I have no doubt that a court of equity would intervene to compel it. The court   D
would, if necessary, remove the trustees and appoint others who would pay
them (see *Re Wrightson, Wrightson* v. *Cooke* (4), per WARRINGTON, J.). This right
is more than a mere hope or expectation (see *Re Munro's Settlement Trusts* (5),
per WILBERFORCE, J.). It is an interest in the trust fund, though not to any
defined part of it; but the group of discretionary objects, regarded as one unit,
have an interest in the property as a whole: because all together they are the   E
only persons who have any right to the beneficial enjoyment of the income.

Once it is accepted that the group had an " interest " in the trust fund, it
was plainly an interest limited to cease on the son's death.

2. *Did that " interest " become an " interest in possession " before the advances
were made?* The expression " interest in possession " is not defined in the statutes;
but the expression " interest in expectancy " is. It is a reasonable inference   F
that an " interest in possession " is the opposite of an " interest in expectancy ".
Section 22 (1) (*j*) of the Finance Act, 1894 says that

> " the expression ' interest in expectancy ' includes an estate in remainder
> or reversion and every other future interest whether vested or contingent,
> but does not include reversions expectant upon the determination of leases."
>   G

The question, therefore, is: what is the nature of the interest of the objects of a
discretionary trust? Is it an " interest in possession " or an " interest in
expectancy "? It must be one or other. Faced with this choice, I have no
doubt what the answer is. It is not a future interest. It is an interest in possession.
Take the common case where the trustees distribute the whole of the income
to one of the objects of the discretionary trust. Just as in *A.-G.* v. *Heywood* (1)   H
the trustees paid to Edmund Peel during his life the whole income of the funds
of the settlement: and in *Burrell* v. *A.-G.* (6), the trustees applied nearly the whole
of the income (£115,000) in paying the allowance to Harry. Surely when the
whole income is paid to one of the discretionary objects, his interest is an
" interest in possession ". There is nothing future about it at all. It is actually
in hand; and he has the beneficial enjoyment of it. Next, take the case where very   I
little is paid to one of the discretionary objects, as here, when only £786 10s.
was paid to the son and £50 to the wife. No valid distinction can be drawn
between the case where the whole is paid out and only very little. The interest
of everyone who receives something is an interest in possession. Next, take

(1) (1887), 19 Q.B.D. 326.   (2) [1931] 1 K.B. 81.
(3) [1911-13] All E.R. Rep. 224; [1911] 2 K.B. 786.
(4) [1908] 1 Ch. 789 at p. 798.   (5) [1963] 1 All E.R. 209 at p. 211.
              (6) [1936] 3 All E.R. 758; [1937] A.C. 286.

A the case where some objects of the discretionary trust receive something and
others receive nothing. It seems a little difficult to say that those who get
nothing have an interest in possession; but, be that as it may, it is plain that
the group of all the discretionary objects, considered as one unit, have an interest
in possession: because some of those at least have beneficial enjoyment of it.
Lastly, take the case where the trustees distribute none of the fund to the dis-
B cretionary objects but accumulate it all for the accumulation beneficiaries.
This is the most difficult case of all; but one thing is clear, if anyone was in
possession at all, it was the group of discretionary objects taken as a composite
unit. They were the only people who could during the relevant period " obtain
any benefit from the property or have any beneficial enjoyment of it " (see
Scott v. *Inland Revenue Comrs.* (7)). That is, I think, sufficient to enable them to
C be considered as having an " interest in possession ".

In support of these views I rely on the two leading cases in the House of Lords;
Scott's case (8) and *Burrell's* case (9).   In each of those cases there was a discretionary trust with power to accumulate (or reduce capital charges).   In
each it was held that, on one discretionary trust coming to an end and being
replaced by a different trust, there was
D
" . . . a change of hands in the beneficial title *or possession* of the property
as a whole, occurring on the death . . . which constituted a passing of the
property on that death within the meaning of s. 1 of the Finance Act, 1894."

See *Scott's* case (10) per LORD RUSSELL OF KILLOWEN. It was assumed in those
cases by all concerned that the interest of the discretionary objects had, before
E the death, become an " interest in possession "; for if it had not done so, s. 5 (3)
of the Act of 1894 would have been a complete answer to the claim. Three years
later in 1940 s. 43 of the Finance Act, 1940, was passed, including the words
" after becoming an interest in possession ". Those words are an echo of s. 5 (3).
Parliament must have been using them in the same sense in both Acts. Seeing
that under the Act of 1894 a discretionary trust with power to accumulate was
F accepted as an " interest in possession ", so also it should be accepted in the Act
of 1940.

The case of *A.-G.* v. *Power* (11) is distinguishable. The son there took a vested
legal estate as tenant in common in fee, with a limitation over on his dying under
twenty-one. The trustees had power to pay maintenance to him whilst under
twenty-one. The interest of the son there (to receive maintenance at the discre-
G tion of the trustees) was ancillary to his interest as tenant in fee. The court,
therefore, looked to his primary interest as tenant in fee: and, as that had
never become an interest in possession before his death, it followed that under
s. 5 (3) the property did not pass on his death.

Reliance was placed on the definition in FEARNE'S CONTINGENT REMAINDERS
(10th Edn.), p. 2: " an estate is vested in possession when there exists a right of
H present enjoyment ". That definition is good for legal estates; but I do not
think it apposite for equitable interests. At any rate, not for the " interest "
in a discretionary trust. FEARNE would probably not have regarded it as an
interest at all; but we must do so. Being an " interest ", we have to enquire when
it is " in possession ". I think that it is in possession when the only people who
are entitled to receive the income are the discretionary objects, considered as a
I composite unit. The only alternative is to say that no one is in possession of
the income. Which is absurd. Someone must be in possession; and it is the
group as a whole. In my opinion, so long as the whole income was distributable
to the discretionary objects, it was an " interest in possession ", even though

(7) [1936] 3 All E.R. 752 at p. 756; [1937] A.C. 174 at p. 182.
(8) [1936] 3 All E.R. 752; [1937] A.C. 174.
(9) [1936] 3 All E.R. 758; [1937] A.C. 286.
(10) [1936] 3 All E.R. at p. 756; [1937] A.C. at p. 182.
(11) [1906] 2 I.R. 272.

it was not in fact distributed to them. It was an interest in possession of the A
property as a whole.

3. *Measurement.* There is an established rule that, in a discretionary trust,
the property does not pass on the dropping of one of the lives. The reason is
said to be because the interest is not capable of being measured. I am not
altogether satisfied with this reason. In the common law we measure chances.
So also I should have thought we could measure the value of the interest of one B
of the discretionary objects. Nevertheless the rule is well established; and we
were invited to say that, by parallel reasoning, when the trustees have a discretion to give all or none of the income to the discretionary objects, their interest
cannot be measured. I am not prepared to extend the special rule (about the
dropping of one life) to cover this case. I return to *Scott's* case (12) and *Burrell's*
case (13). The House of Lords held that when the discretionary trust came to C
an end, there was a passing that could be measured. So here.

4. *The accumulation beneficiaries.* That is enough to decide the case; but I
ought to mention a further point that was put to us. It was suggested that the
whole income could be considered as an interest in possession of a composite
unit, namely, a group combined of both the discretionary objects and the accumulation beneficiaries together. I do not think that this can be done. The accumu- D
lation beneficiaries did not have an interest in possession. Their interest in the
accumulation fund was future and contingent. It would only come into being
if the trustees did not pay out the whole income to the discretionary objects
but accumulated the surplus: and in any case it would not come into being
until the son died. It was an interest in expectancy only. It cannot be regarded,
even in combination with others, as an interest in possession.   E

5. *Conclusion.* I think that the provisions of s. 43 are satisfied. The interest
of the discretionary objects, after becoming an interest in possession, was determined by the advances; and is to be treated as a passing on the death. I would
allow the appeal.

HARMAN, L.J.: Thomas Edmund Gartside died in the year 1941, having F
by his will, made in 1934, bequeathed his residue to trustees on trust for sale
and to divide the proceeds into four shares. He disposed of one quarter share
on trusts stated as follows:

" Upon trust during the lifetime of my son John Travis Gartside to pay or
apply the whole or such part as my trustees shall in their absolute and uncontrolled discretion think fit of the income of such fourth share for or towards G
the maintenance support or otherwise for the benefit of my said son John
Travis Gartside or during his life for his wife or children (if any) or any one
or more exclusively of the other or others of them in such manner in all
respects as my trustees shall in their absolute and uncontrolled discretion
without being liable to account think fit and shall accumulate the surplus
(if any) of the said income by investing the same and the resulting income H
thereof in manner hereinafter mentioned To the intent that the accumulations shall be added to the fourth share and follow the destination thereof
with power nevertheless for my trustees at any time to resort to the accumulations of any preceding year and apply the same for the maintenance
support and benefit of my said son John Travis Gartside or (during his life)
any wife or children of his or any one or more of them (b) Upon trust after I
the decease of my said son John Travis Gartside both as to the capital and
income of the fourth share for all or any the children or child of my said son
who being sons or a son attain the age of twenty one years or being daughters
or a daughter attain that age or previously marry and if more than one
in equal shares absolutely [with remainder over which did not take effect.

---

(12) [1936] 3 All E.R. 752; [1937] A.C. 174.
(13) [1936] 3 All E.R. 756; [1937] A.C. 286.

A   He added] And I declare that my trustees shall have power at any
time or times to raise by sale or mortgage upon such terms as they may
think proper out of the share of and in my residuary trust fund hereby given
to any grandchild of mine any sum or sums not exceeding one half of the then
presumptive or vested share of such grandchild and to pay or apply the same
as my trustees shall think fit for the advancement or benefit of such
B   grandchild . . .''

At the date of this will the testator had four children, one of whom was the
John Gartside already mentioned.   This son married and had twin children
born on Jan. 5, 1945.   John Gartside died on May 8, 1963, leaving his widow
and twin sons surviving.   During the lifetime of the son John the discretionary
trust was exercised only in the year 1961, and then to the tune of some £850
C   partly in favour of John and partly in that of his wife.   The whole of the rest
of the income of the one-quarter share was accumulated until January, 1962,
when the trust for accumulation ran out, as from which time the income of
John's share was paid to him until his death in 1963.   In 1962 the value of the
one-quarter share was over £90,000, apart from accumulations which were
worth some £55,000 and the trustees then decided to exercise the power of
D   advancement contained in the testator's will and did so in favour of the two
twin sons by two deeds poll in like form.   The value of the sum advanced in each
case was some £23,500 and represented the total advancement that could be
made excluding accumulations under the power in the testator's will.   John
Gartside died in 1963 and thereupon the discretionary trust of income during
his lifetime came to an end, as did the residuary trust of income which arose
E   when the accumulation period ended.   There is no doubt that, excepting the two
advanced funds, the whole property including the accumulations passed on
John Gartside's death and duty was paid accordingly at the rate of sixty per cent.
This was an actual passing, the whole fund changing hands and passing to the
two twin sons of John equally on attaining twenty-one, as they did in January,
1966, but the Crown claims in addition duty on the two advanced funds.
F   Under each of these deeds poll the advanced sum was directed to be held
on trust for one of the two advanced beneficiaries if he should attain the age of
twenty-one years.   There were further provisions purporting to defer the payment
over of parts of the sum until the beneficiaries should attain twenty-five years
and thirty years of age, but these provisions were, I think, invalid and each
advanced grandchild can now call for the transfer of the whole fund to him
G   absolutely, they having attained twenty-one years of age in January, 1966.

The result of the two advances was to put an end, so far as the advanced funds
were concerned, to the discretionary trust of income during the life of John
Gartside and to all the remainders under the will of the testator.

The Crown now claims duty on the two advanced funds.   These, of course, did
not pass on John Gartside's death and the Crown must rely on the fiction set up
H   by s. 43 of the Finance Act, 1940, which has already in effect been read by LORD
DENNING, M.R., and which I need not repeat.

It is agreed that each advanced fund constituted an interest limited to cease
on the death of John Gartside which was disposed of or determined by the
advances and that, but for these advances, the advanced funds too would have
passed under s. 1 like the rest of the share.   All the conditions laid down in s. 43
I   are satisfied if, and only if, the interest which was disposed of, namely, the
advanced fund in each case, had before the disposition, that is to say the advance,
become an interest in possession.   The whole argument in this long case has
turned around these words (14).   It seems to me that the words were put in
in order to avoid it being said that the Crown could claim on future contingent
interests, a claim which the Crown has never made, a matter alluded to in *A.-G.*
v. *Power* (15), mentioned by LORD DENNING, in the judgment of PALLES, C.B.

(14) Viz., the words in s. 43 (1), " after becoming an interest in possession ".
(15) [1906] 2 I.R. at p. 281.

It is argued that to regard the interests, so to call them, of a discretionary A
class or any member of it, unless indeed the whole class can together claim
the whole income, as an interest in possession is an extraordinary view. Furthermore, the same is even more true of the interest of those beneficially entitled to
the accumulations of the unapplied portion of the income. The interests of these
taken by themselves are clearly in expectancy and not in possession. I agree then
that none of the rights taken by themselves do amount to an interest in possession B
and that even if they do, each is not an interest capable of quantification and,
therefore, on well known principles no duty is payable. In my opinion, however,
if the whole bundle of rights attaching during his lifetime to the interest of John
Gartside's one-quarter share be combined together, that is to say, both the discretionary rights and the right to accumulations, they do amount to an
interest in possession because they embrace the whole of the property. Some- C
body must have an interest in possession, for the trustees' interest may be
disregarded for this purpose and it is the passing of beneficial interests with
which the Act of 1940 is concerned. The admitted passing of the unadvanced
portion of John's share on his death rests on this basis, that the whole property
and all the interests in it passed on that event. Exactly the same thing happened
to the advanced funds on the making of the advancements; the whole bundle D
of rights in the advanced funds changed hands, all the trusts attaching to them
before the advancements came to an end, together with all the interests in them
existing before the advancements were made: and this change of hands caused
a new interest in possession to arise, and this must in my view have arisen from
the interest in possession existing immediately before the deeds were executed,
cf., the argument of LORD RUSSELL in *Burrell* v. *A.-G.* (16). I am therefore of E
opinion that there was what may properly be described as an interest in possession
in the advanced funds taken as a whole before the date of the advancements.

This is enough to settle the issue in favour of the Crown. A great many cases
were cited to us, but none of them is directly in point, and in my judgment
the question depends purely on the true construction of the Act, and its result
is in my opinion to make the Crown's claim for duty good on the two advanced F
funds. I would allow the appeal accordingly.

SALMON, L.J.: The word " interest " as used in the Finance Acts has a
wider meaning than its strict conveyancing meaning. It is now well settled that
those eligible to benefit under a discretionary trust, commonly called the " discretionary objects ", have an interest in the property from which the income, the G
subject matter of the discretionary trust, is derived. This is so notwithstanding
that there is a power of accumulation of surplus income and the trustees may never
pay to or apply for the benefit of any of the discretionary objects one penny of the
income (*A.-G.* v. *Farrell* (17)). In the present case the trustees accumulated
virtually the whole of the income. This appeal turns on whether or not the
interest of the objects of the discretionary trust set up under the grandfather's H
will was " an interest in possession " within the meaning of s. 43 (as amended)
of the Finance Act, 1940. If it was such an interest, it was certainly limited to
cease on the death of the testator's son and it was clearly determined to the
extent of the advancement of £47,000 made by the trustees out of the original
trust fund to the twin grandsons of the testator eighteen months before the son's
death. Accordingly by virtue of s. 43, the £47,000 would be deemed to have passed I
on the son's death. But for the advancement, the £47,000, like the rest of the trust
fund, would have passed or be deemed to have passed on the son's death under s. 1
or s. 2 (1) (*b*) of the Finance Act, 1894. Indeed, on the son's death duty was
admittedly due and has been paid on the whole fund less £47,000. The issue now
is whether it is payable on the £47,000.

(16) [1936] 3 All E.R. 758; [1937] A.C. 286.
(17) [1931] 1 K.B. 81.

A   In order to decide whether or not the interest of the discretionary objects was
an interest in possession, it is necessary to consider the nature of that interest.
It certainly gave the discretionary objects no right to be paid any part of the
income or to have any part of it applied for their benefit. It made them eligible
to receive or to have applied for their benefit so much of the income (if any) as
the trustees might in their discretion decide. SNELL'S PRINCIPLES OF EQUITY
B   (25th Edn.)), p. 129, in my view correctly states the position thus:

> " A discretionary trust is one which gives the beneficiary no right to any
> part of the income of the trust property, but vests in the trustees a dis-
> cretionary power to pay him or apply for his benefit such part of the income
> as they think fit . . . The beneficiary thus has no more than a hope that the
> discretion will be exercised in his favour."

C   In *A.-G.* v. *Farrell* GREER, L.J., said of a discretionary object (18):

> " He has no legal right to force the trustees to give him anything; at the
> same time he had in a colloquial sense an interest in the estate, because it
> was an estate out of which something might be allotted to him in the dis-
> cretion of the trustees."

D   GREER, L.J., concluded that that was an interest within the meaning of the
Finance Acts. In the same case ROMER, L.J., said (19) that it was rightly decided
in *A.-G.* v. *Heywood* (20), that

> " the prospect of an object of a discretionary trust sharing in the income,
> the subject-matter of the discretionary trust, is an interest of that person
> in the property from which the income is derived."

E
The only right which any discretionary object possesses in addition to his chance
or prospect is the right that the trustees shall honestly and fairly consider whether
any, and if so what, part of the income shall be allotted to him. In a sense it may
be difficult to appreciate how discretionary objects, who have only such a limited
right and only such an uncertain chance or prospect of receiving anything, can
F   be said to have any legally recognisable interest in the trust property. Once,
however, it is conceded, as on authority it must be, that they have such an
interest, it is even more difficult to see how that interest can properly be described
as an interest in expectancy. They are in possession of the right and of the chance
or prospect to which I have referred. The value of the right and of the chance or
prospect no doubt depends on how the trustees exercise their discretion; but the
G   discretionary objects at all times enjoy the right and the chance or prospect,
whatever its value may turn out to be. A person who has a vested interest to
receive money out of a trust fund on the happening of an event has only a right
in expectancy until the event occurs. On the happening of the event, his right
becomes a right in possession. The nature of his interest in the fund is determined
by the nature of his rights. When, however, a discretionary object is paid some
H   of the income, it is not in my view accurate, having regard to the nature of his
right, to say that his right is then vested in possession. He has not even then and
never has had any right to be paid any part of the income which he receives.
On the other hand, he has at all times enjoyed and been in possession of the right
and chance or prospect which I have described. It may be tempting to say that a
chance or prospect is something enjoyed in expectancy and that when it comes
I   off, it is enjoyed in possession; but this in my view is a fallacy, for when it comes
off it ceases to be a chance or prospect and is not as such enjoyed at all. By its
very nature as long as it exists it is enjoyed in possession. After the race, the owner
of the winning horse, on being asked, " have you a chance of winning? ", would
reply: " It is not a matter of my having a chance: I have now won. I always
had a chance "; or, if he were pedantic, " I was always in possession of and

---

(18) [1931] 1 K.B. at p. 101.
(19) [1931] 1 K.B. at p. 103.
(20) (1887), 19 Q.B.D. 326.

enjoyed a chance ".   On the other hand, his right to be paid by the bookmaker A
(were it a legally recognised right) would be a right in expectancy up to the moment
his horse passed the winning post, and a right in possession thereafter. The discretionary object never has a right to be paid: he has only a chance or prospect
and the very limited right, to which I have referred, of being considered for an
allotment of income.

It has long been accepted that the value of a single discretionary object's B
interest cannot be measured and that, accordingly, no estate duty is payable on
his death. This rule may be difficult to understand. As LORD DENNING, M.R.,
points out, in the common law courts, it is by no means unusual for the value of a
chance to be assessed (see e.g., *Chaplin* v. *Hicks* (21)). If a fund, the subject matter
of a discretionary trust, yields an income of £1,000 a year and there are, say, ten
discretionary objects and the trustees have throughout the years distributed C
the whole income equally amongst them, there could be no difficulty in assessing
the value of the interest of any discretionary object who died. Similarly there
would be no difficulty in assessing the value of such an interest if throughout the
years the trustees had never paid the deceased or applied for his benefit any part of
the income. Between these two extremes there are, of course, many cases in which
the task of measuring the interest would be difficult but no more difficult than the D
task of assessing the imponderables which has to be performed every day in the
common law courts. The rule, however, that, on the dropping of the life of one
of the discretionary objects, no estate duty is payable because his interest is deemed
to be immeasurable, is so well established that it is now impossible to question it.
The respondents argue that just as no estate duty is payable on the death of one
discretionary object, because his interest is immeasurable, so no estate duty is E
payable when the whole discretionary trust ceases on a death, because the
interest of the body of discretionary objects is just as immeasurable as that of
any one of them. Even if the interest of the body of discretionary objects is
immeasurable, there can be no doubt that on the discretionary trust ceasing a
benefit accrued to the grandsons under the other trust which then took effect.
If the property did not pass under s. 1, it would pass under s. 2 (1) (*b*) of the Act F
of 1894. Moreover, I agree with LORD DENNING, M.R., that the rule relating to
the dropping of a single life should not necessarily be extended to the combined
interests of the discretionary objects as a composite body. Indeed, it is clear that
when all their interests cease on a death, the property does pass and estate duty is
exigible (*Scott* v. *Inland Revenue Comrs.* (22); *Burrell* v. *A.-G.* (23)). In the latter
case virtually the whole of the income was distributed amongst the discretionary G
objects, no point was taken under s. 5 (3) of the Finance Act, 1894, and accordingly
the question whether the interests were interests in possession was not considered.
That question arises for the first time in the present case. It is to be observed that
in this case, although the respondents contended that none of the discretionary
objects had any interest in possession, they conceded that the whole estate except
the £47,000 passed on the son's death and attracted estate duty which has been H
paid. The judge (24) and the trustees in this court relied strongly on *A.-G.* v.
Power (25). I agree with LORD DENNING, M.R., that that decision is distinguishable
from the present case. Indeed, properly understood, in my view it throws no
light on the problem which confronts us, although there is a passage in the judgment which, taken out of context, appears to do so. It is true that at first sight
the position of a discretionary object, for whose benefit the trustees have power I
to apply the income from the trust property, may seem to resemble the position of
the infant for whose maintenance or benefit the trustees have power to apply
the income from the trust property; but the two positions in law are fundamentally different. In the former case we know from the authorities, to which I

---

(21) [1911-13] All E.R. Rep. 224; [1911] 2 K.B. 786.
(22) [1936] 3 All E.R. 752; [1937] A.C. 174.
(23) [1936] 3 All E.R. 758; [1937] A.C. 286.
(24) See [1966] 3 All E.R. 89 at pp. 98, 99.   (25) [1906] 2 I.R. 272.

A have referred, that the existence of the power confers an interest in the estate on the discretionary object, whereas in the latter case the existence of the power by itself confers no separate interest on the infant. His only interest is his interest in fee.

The settlement in *A.-G.* v. *Power* (26) was in an unusual form. It vested the estate in fee on the children of the marriage equally. When the eldest child was

B born, he took the whole estate in fee subject to the birth of any other child or children. On the birth of the second child, half the estate was divested from the first child and went to the second and so on. Should any child die under twenty-one, his share became divested and divided equally amongst the others. There was also a proviso that during the minority of each child, the trustees should hold the rents and profits of his share which they had power to apply for his mainten-

C ance or benefit and accumulate the surplus but not for the infant. The surplus rents and profits were not the infant's property in any event, but were " captured by the trusts of the settlement " and, together with the infant's share of the capital, would go to the other children should the infant die under the age of twenty-one. One of the children, Hubert Power, died an infant. The question was : had he an interest in possession in his share so that estate duty became payable

D on his death? The court's decision was against the Crown on the ground that the income was not the infant's income and that the provision as to maintenance gave the infant no separate interest in the estate. His only interest was his interest in fee to which the power to maintain was ancillary. PALLES, C.B., held (27) that the conveyancing form of the settlement deed made no difference in law to the reality of the situation. It was just as if the settlement had provided that the

E children should take subject to attaining the age of twenty-one

> " with such a provision for maintenance [as the actual settlement con-
> ferred] or without it, in which event a substantially similar provision would
> have been implied by the Conveyancing Act."

In such a case the Attorney-General conceded (rightly, according to PALLES,

F C.B. (27)) that no estate duty would have been payable whether or not any of the income had been applied for the infant's maintenance or benefit. The infant's only interest in the estate would have been his interest in fee, which was an interest in expectancy only. The whole case proceeded on the basis that a power in the trustees to apply income for the infant's maintenance or benefit, even if exercised, gave the infant no separate interest in the estate. The case of *A.-G.* v. *Heywood*

G (28) was not cited. Presumably because it never occurred to anyone that the position of the infant was truly analogous to that of a discretionary object. In my view the court never considered what would have been only an academic question, namely—had the power to maintain given the infant a separate interest in the estate—would such an interest have been an interest in possession or in expectancy?

H   If, which cannot now be doubted, the chances or prospects of a discretionary object and his limited right give him an interest in the trust fund, then in my judgment, for the reasons which I have already stated, the interest must be an interest in possession and not in expectancy. *A.-G.* v. *Power* (26) does not touch this point.

If, contrary to my view, the group of discretionary objects had no interest in

I possession but only an interest in expectancy, I, for my part, would feel unable to accept the Crown's contention that their interest can be combined with that of the accumulation beneficiaries so as to form a composite unit which would have an interest in possession. At the time of the advancement, the interests of the accumulation beneficiaries were indisputably interests in expectancy. To combine one group of interests in expectancy with another group of interests in expectancy

---

(26) [1906] 2 I.R. 272.   (27) [1906] 2 I.R. at p. 281.

                    (28) (1887), 19 Q.B.D. 326.

and thereby form a composite group of interests in possession involves an in- A
tellectual gymnastic feat which, no doubt, owing to a common lawyer's in-
experience of the exercise, I cannot even follow, let alone perform. In my attempt
to do so, I have found no help in the cases of *Re Hodson's Settlement, Brookes* v.
A.-G. (29), or *Westminster Bank, Ltd.* v. *A.-G.* (30), which, so far as aggregation
is concerned, seem to me to establish no more than that for the purposes of
calculating the rate of estate duty payable, the values of different classes of interest B
may be aggregated.

I do not think that it is necessary or even permissible to assume that there
must always be some person or body of persons in possession of a beneficial
interest in the trust property. If such an assumption has to be made, no doubt the
neatest solution (when no interest in possession is otherwise discernible) is to call
into existence a body in which are amalgamated all the beneficial interests in the C
trust property, because ex hypothesi it would contain the interest in possession
which is assumed to exist. I cannot, however, accept such an assumption. If,
at the date of the advancement, the interest of the discretionary objects was truly
an interest in expectancy, then in my view there could have been no beneficial
interest in possession anywhere. The whole beneficial interest would have been
in expectancy and the Crown would have failed. D

Since, however, I consider that the discretionary objects had an interest in
possession at the date of the advancement, I would allow the appeal.

*Appeal allowed. Declaration accordingly. Leave to appeal to the House Lords
granted.*

Solicitors: *Solicitor Inland Revenue; Gregory Rowcliffe & Co.*, agents for E
John Taylor & Co., Blackburn (for the trustees).

[*Reported by* F. GUTTMAN, ESQ., *Barrister-at-Law.*]

F

PRACTICE DIRECTION.

G

PROBATE, DIVORCE AND ADMIRALTY DIVISION (DIVORCE).

*Divorce—Practice—Evidence—Affidavit—Petitioner tendering evidence by affidavit
must exhibit petition and depose to truth of its contents.*

Where leave is given to tender the evidence of a petitioner by affidavit at the H
hearing of a suit, such affidavit must exhibit a copy of the petition and depose
to the truth of its contents.

By direction of the President, Apr. 5, 1967.

COMPTON MILLER
Senior Registrar.

I

---

(29) [1939] 1 All E.R. 196; [1939] Ch. 343.
(30) [1939] 2 All E.R. 72; [1939] Ch. 610.

A

SEMLER *v.* MURPHY.

[COURT OF APPEAL, CIVIL DIVISION (Lord Denning, M.R., Harman and Salmon, L.JJ.), February 13, 14, 1967.]

B
Costs—Security for costs—Nominal plaintiff—Insolvency of plaintiff—Charge by plaintiff on fruits of the action—Amount secured by charge exceeding amount claimed in action—Whether plaintiff a nominal plaintiff suing for the benefit of some other person, viz., the chargee—R.S.C., Ord. 23, r. 1 (1) (b).

The plaintiff's brother, having advanced to the plaintiff (against whom a receiving order was made in July, 1963) £8,000 to enable him to pay his debts, took a charge over all the plaintiff's assets to secure repayment of
C
the £8,000. The plaintiff brought an action in July, 1964, against the defendant to recover over £2,000 damages on the ground that the defendant had failed to fulfil a contract to buy premises and goodwill of a business from the plaintiff for £5,000, and that on their re-sale the plaintiff had obtained only £3,000 for the premises. The plaintiff, when he brought the action, gave to his brother orally a charge on the fruits of the action.
D
On Dec. 21, 1966, a receiving order was made against the plaintiff, who was insolvent. The defendant, having learnt that the plaintiff had charged the fruits of the action in favour of his brother for a total indebtedness exceeding the amount claimed in the action, applied for security for costs on the ground that the plaintiff was a nominal plaintiff within the meaning of R.S.C., Ord. 23, r. 1 (1) (b)*.

E
Held: the plaintiff was a nominal plaintiff for the purposes of R.S.C., Ord. 23, r. 1 (1) (b), for the brother alone stood to gain from the action; and since, if the action failed, the plaintiff would not be able to pay the costs to the defendant, the court would in its discretion order security for costs in the amount of £150 (see p. 187, letter F, and p. 188, letters B, D and E, post).

F
Lloyd v. *Hathern Station Brick Co., Ltd.* ((1901), 85 L.T. 158) applied.
Cook v. *Whellock* ((1890), 24 Q.B.D. 658) distinguished.
Appeal allowed.

[As to security for costs from a nominal plaintiff, see 30 HALSBURY'S LAWS (3rd Edn.) 378, 379, para. 706 (1); and for cases on the ordering of security of costs on the ground of poverty or insolvency of the plaintiff, see DIGEST (Practice)
G
907, 908, *4480-4495*.]

Cases referred to:
Cook v. *Whellock*, (1890), 24 Q.B.D. 658; 59 L.J.Q.B. 329; 62 L.T. 675; 5 Digest (Repl.) 1076, *8677.*
Cowell v. *Taylor*, (1885), 31 Ch.D. 34; 55 L.J.Ch. 92; 53 L.T. 483; 5 Digest (Repl.) 1061, *8567.*
H
Elliot v. *Kendrick*, (1840), 12 Ad. & El. 597; 10 L.J.Q.B. 42; 113 E.R. 938; Digest (Practice) 908, *4483.*
Lloyd v. *Hathern Station Brick Co. Ltd.*, (1901), 85 L.T. 158; Digest (Practice) 908, *4493.*
Rhodes v. *Dawson*, (1886), 16 Q.B.D. 548; 65 L.J.Q.B. 134; 5 Digest (Repl.) 1076, *8675.*
I
Interlocutory Appeal.

This was a motion by the defendant, James Joseph Murphy, for leave to appeal from an order of PLOWMAN, J., dated Feb. 8, 1967, dismissing the application for security for costs and for a stay or proceedings until security was given, which the defendant had made under R.S.C., Ord. 23, r. 1 (1) (b). The defendant further moved for an order, reversing that of PLOWMAN, J., for security for costs and for a stay or proceedings until the security was provided. The principal

* R.S.C., Ord. 23, r. 1 (1) (b), so far as material, is set out at p. 186, letter C, post.

ground of appeal was that PLOWMAN, J., had misdirected himself in law in   A
holding that the plaintiff was not a nominal plaintiff within the meaning of
R.S.C., Ord. 23, r. 1.   The facts are set out in the judgment of LORD DENNING,
M.R.

A. R. Campbell, Q.C., and P. Goodenday for the defendant.
M. D. Beckman for the plaintiff.

    LORD DENNING, M.R.: R.S.C., Ord. 23, r. 1 (1) (b) enables the court B
to order security for costs where

> "... the plaintiff ... is a nominal plaintiff who is suing for the benefit of
> some other person, and there is reason to believe that he will be unable to
> pay the costs of the defendants if ordered to do so ..."

The question in this case is whether the plaintiff, Mr. Semler, is a nominal C
plaintiff.

    In March, 1963, the plaintiff agreed to sell to the defendant, Mr. Murphy,
premises at 40, Highgate High Street, Hornsey, for a sum of £5,000.   Completion
was to be on Mar. 25, 1963.   It was not completed on that day.   In July, 1963,
a receiving order was made against the plaintiff.   He owed £8,000 to various D
creditors.   His brother, Mr. Maurice Semler, advanced him £8,000 so as to
clear off his debts.   The creditors were paid.   The receiving order was rescinded.
The brother took a charge on all his assets to secure the repayment of the £8,000.
Seeing that the defendant did not complete the purchase of the premises at
Highgate, the plaintiff re-sold them for some £3,000.   Thus losing £2,000 on the
re-sale.   On July 30, 1964, the plaintiff brought an action against the defendant E
claiming damages of over £2,000.   The action has been going on for a long time.
Each side blames the other for the delay.   A day has long been fixed for hearing.
It is fixed for Feb. 16, 1967, the day after tomorrow.

    Much, however, has happened recently.   Last year the plaintiff was co-
respondent in a divorce suit.   He was ordered to pay £1,500 damages and costs.
He did not pay.   The petitioner served a bankruptcy notice.   On Dec. 21, 1966, F
a receiving order was made against him.   On Jan. 26, 1967, a meeting of
creditors took place.   Immediately after that meeting it was disclosed that the
plaintiff had charged the fruits of this action.   It appears that when he started
this action in July, 1964, he at the same time gave an oral charge in favour of
his brother over the fruits of the action.   We know that the brother already had
a charge over the house for the £8,000 that he had advanced. Now he had this G
additional oral equitable charge over the fruits of this action (1).   When the
defendant found this out, he first applied for an adjournment of the case.   That
application was refused.   Now he applies for security for costs on the ground
that the plaintiff is a nominal plaintiff, and that he is really suing for the benefit of
his brother.   It is admitted that the plaintiff is insolvent.   He will be unable to
pay the costs of the defendant if he fails in the action.

    A nominal plaintiff is a man who is a plaintiff in name but who in truth sues H
for the benefit of another.   In an early case, Elliott v. Kendrick (2), a plaintiff
assigned his estate to trustees for his creditors with power to sue in his name for
his debts.   They did sue in his name.   LORD DENMAN, C.J., said (3):

---

    (1) The plaintiff claimed in the action £2,360 damages for breach of contract for the
sale of leasehold premises and the goodwill of a hairdressers' business and its stock-in- I
trade; there was a counterclaim by the defendant for £125 deposit on the basis that the
plaintiff had repudiated the contract and the defendant had accepted the repudiation.
The charge given by the plaintiff to his brother was for £5,800, and it was this sum
which was secured also by the oral charge on the fruits of the action.   The brother's
charge extended also to the plaintiff's wife's matrimonial home, but that belonged to
her; PLOWMAN, J., had intimated that the charge extending to the matrimonial home
was irrelevant, because, if the plaintiff's brother elected to go primarily against the
matrimonial home, the wife would be subrogated to the brother's rights over the fruits
of the action.
    (2) (1840), 12 Ad. & El. 597.   (3) (1840), 12 Ad. & El. at p. 598.

A   " The trustees choose to proceed in the action in the name of a party who, for their benefit, has divested himself of all means of paying the costs. I think they should give security to the defendant."

In *Lloyd* v. *Hathern Station Brick Co., Ltd.* (4), the plaintiff, being insolvent and having brought an action against the defendants, executed a deed of assignment to a trustee for the benefit of his creditors.   It was held to be the very kind of case
B   where security would be ordered.

I agree, of course, that a trustee in bankruptcy cannot be ordered to give security for costs (see *Cowell* v. *Taylor* (5): nor can a man who has had a receiving order against him (see *Rhodes* v. *Dawson* (6); nor can a bankrupt who sues for a debt arising since his bankruptcy (see *Cook* v. *Whellock* (7)).   Those cases are, however, quite distinguishable.   Here the plaintiff, at the very time when he
C   started the action, charged the whole fruits of it to his brother.   So it was only the brother who stood to gain.   The plaintiff was truly a nominal plaintiff.

Counsel for the plaintiff argued that the plaintiff was still much interested, because if this action should succeed he would probably not be made bankrupt. He said that he was employed now as a cost accountant at £2,000 a year.   The affidavit of the solicitor gave that impression; but just before the adjournment
D   we were shown the report of the Official Receiver made yesterday.   It shows that the plaintiff himself stated that

" from April, 1964, to December, 1966, he was employed as a cost accountant and his total remuneration during that period was £3,325.   He has since been unemployed."

E   That knocks the bottom out of counsel's argument.

It comes to this.   If the action succeeds, the plaintiff's brother will go off with the whole of the proceeds and let the other creditors " whistle " for their money: whereas if the action fails, the plaintiff will not be able to pay the costs of the defendant.   It is the very kind of case in which security for costs should be ordered.   It ought not to be an expensive trial.   I would order the sum of £150.
F   The action ought not to be delayed.   If this money is found within twenty-four hours by two o'clock tomorrow, the action can still stand for Thursday.   I would make the order accordingly.

HARMAN, L.J.: The plaintiff here appears to be a man of two professions, those of cost accountant and of hairdresser, but to be employed at present in neither of them, though in the very misleading affidavit to which Lord Denning,
G   M.R., has referred, we were led to believe he was making £2,000 a year in the first capacity.   That appears to be untrue.   He is unemployed.

This action arose out of a contract made as long ago as 1963 for the sale of a going concern, which was supposed to be completed promptly, the plaintiff carrying on the going concern in the interim.   The contract has never been completed and there have been bitter disputes about the why and wherefore of
H   that matter.   During the pendency of the action two receiving orders have been made against the plaintiff.   The first one was got rid of by the intervention of the plaintiff's brother, who put forward no less a sum than £8,000 to pay the creditor.   He is the largest creditor in the recent proceedings, which arose out of a receiving order made in December, 1966.   The plaintiff, at the time when his brother made this advance, gave a general charge, as I understand it, on all his
I   assets, including a house which was in the name of his wife to secure his brother's loan.   At the time when he started this action, the plaintiff orally, it is said, gave another charge to his brother specifically on the fruits of the action; and it is said that having charged the fruits of the action to his brother, he has no interest in it and the brother will take the fruits of the action if it is successful; whereas if it is a failure, nobody will be able to recover costs, it being admitted that the plaintiff is insolvent and unable to pay.

(4) (1901), 85 L.T. 158.   (5) (1885), 31 Ch.D. 34.
(6) (1886), 16 Q.B.D. 578.   (7) (1890), 24 Q.B.D. 658.

Under these circumstances it is said that he is a nominal plaintiff suing for the   A
benefit of another, namely, his brother. Now I have grave doubt about this.
The charge is not an assignment. The brother may not enforce his rights and
the plaintiff has not been adjudicated bankrupt; he has only had a receiving
order made against him. I think that those are matters of some weight, but
both my brothers feel that this does come within the rule: it is not a mere matter
of insolvency; it is not a mere matter of a receiving order; it is a matter of a   B
deliberate act of assigning the whole fruits of the action away, and that makes
him a nominal plaintiff. I am not prepared to differ from them, though with
doubt.

There still remains the question of discretion. Who has the merits in this
matter I do not know. There are great recriminations one way and the other;
but it does appear quite clear that there was a formal contract and that for a   C
long time the defendant was minded to perform it. The action has been kept
going a tremendously long time by continual interlocutory applications on the
defendant's behalf. As recently as a fortnight ago there was an application to
take the case out of the list. One cannot help suspecting that a large part of the
motive of this application is to delay the trial. If LORD DENNING, M.R.'s
proposal stands, perhaps we need not delay the trial.   D

I would agree to an order being made for £150 security. If that be produced
by two o'clock tomorrow, the matter can stay in the list where it is and be tried
on Thursday morning. If not, the matter will have to stand out and there will
be three weeks within which to produce the security for costs.

SALMON, L.J.: I entirely agree with the order proposed. For myself   E
I have no doubt but that this action is being brought for the benefit of the plaintiff's brother within the meaning of the rule and that the plaintiff is a nominal
plaintiff. The case of *Lloyd* v. *Hathern Station Brick Co., Ltd.* (8) makes it quite
plain that if the plaintiff's brother had taken an assignment, it would undoubtedly
be established in the circumstances of this case that the action was for the benefit
of the brother. The argument, as I understand it, is that the fact that the   F
brother took a charge instead of an assignment makes all the difference. It is
said to make a difference because the brother might not avail himself of his right
under the charge.

It was said also that in spite of the charge, the fruits of the action might save
this plaintiff from bankruptcy; and, after all, here was a man who was a cost
accountant earning £2,000 a year. The affidavit by his solicitor, Mr. Tarlo, was   G
clearly understood by counsel for the plaintiff to mean that the plaintiff was
earning £2,000 a year; and, quite rightly, counsel understanding it in that way,
made a great deal of this point. No-one can possibly blame counsel because
that is the precise way in which I read the affidavit. I can only hope that it
was not meant to be so understood. It is perfectly plain from what we now
know that the plaintiff is unemployed and earning nothing and that this was   H
the position at the time the affidavit was sworn.

For myself, I do not think that in the circumstances of this case any real
distinction can be drawn between a charge such as this, given contemporaneously
with the issue of the writ, and an assignment. The obvious inference is that the
charge was given to remove any risk of the fruits of the action falling into the
hands of the plaintiff's creditors. I am certainly not weakened in that view by   I
the plaintiff's statement of affairs contained in the Official Receiver's report
which we have now seen. In that statement of affairs the plaintiff sets out his
assets and liabilities. He does not include amongst his assets this claim against
the defendant, to my mind (which I hope is not too sceptical) for the obvious
reason that he is confident that if he succeeds in the action, all its fruits will
assuredly go to his brother. I have no doubt that the action is for the benefit

(8) (1901), 85 L.T. 158.

A of the plaintiff's brother and the plaintiff is only a nominal plaintiff. I can see
no benefit which the plaintiff can derive from it.

The position here is entirely different from the position existing in *Cook* v.
Whellock (9) on which the judge relied. In that case the plaintiff was suing for
rent in respect of a tenancy which had been created after the bankruptcy proceedings. Apparently there was no possible defence to the claim and the plain-
B tiff's discharge from bankruptcy was postponed until he paid 5s. in the pound.
Clearly in that case, although the claim would benefit his creditors, it would
benefit the plaintiff also because it might expedite his discharge. There is no
possible benefit of that or any other sort to the plaintiff in this case.

I agree that the appeal should be allowed.

Appeal allowed.

C
Solicitors: *Hamilton-Hill & Partner* (for the defendant); *Tarlo, Lyons &
Aukin* (for the plaintiff).

[*Reported by* F. Guttman, Esq., *Barrister-at-Law*].

D

BAILEY v. PURSER.

[Court of Appeal, civil division (Lord Denning, M.R., Harman and Salmon,
L.JJ.), February 21, 1967.]

E *Agriculture—Agricultural holding—Notice to quit—Consent of tribunal—Greater
hardship—Considerations taken into account—Hardship to persons other
than the landlord or the tenant—Landlord's death leaving insolvent estate
and widow in poverty—Sale of holding sought by son for benefit of estate—
Whether greater hardship " caused " by withholding consent—Agricultural
Holdings Act,* 1948 (11 & 12 Geo. 6 c. 63), *s.* 25 (1) (d) *as substituted by
F Agriculture Act,* 1958 (6 & 7 Eliz. 2 c. 71), *s.* 3 (2).

In 1955 Slate Hall Farm, a farm of eighty acres, and the adjoining Five
House Farm, a farm of two hundred acres, were let to the same tenant.
In 1959 the tenant bought Five House Farm from the landlord. In 1965
the landlord, who was impecunious, gave the tenant notice to quit Slate
Hall Farm in 1966, and applied to the Agricultural Land Tribunal for consent
to the operation of the notice. The landlord died in November, 1965. His
G son was granted letters of administration limited to the pending proceedings
and wanted possession of the farm in order to sell it. In March, 1966, the
tribunal gave consent on the grounds stated in s. 25 (1) (d)* of the Agricultural
Holdings Act, 1948, as substituted by the Agriculture Act, 1958, s. 3 (2),
that " greater hardship would be caused by withholding than by giving
consent to the operation of the notice ". The tribunal took into considera-
H tion the facts that the deceased landlord left debts, that his widow was
poverty stricken, and that his son had guaranteed some of his father's
liabilities, and that the son wished to sell the farm for the benefit of the
estate which would otherwise be insolvent; the tribunal also considered what
hardship would be imposed on the tenant by being dispossessed.

Held: in determining where the greater hardship lay the tribunal were
I entitled to take into consideration all persons who might be affected by the
grant or refusal of possession, and thus had rightly taken into account the
position of the widow and of the son and the fact that the estate would be
insolvent unless the farm was sold, for which purpose vacant possession
was required; the tribunal had not erred in law and their decision should
stand (see p. 192, letters C, E and H, post).

(9) (1890), 27 Q.B.D. 658.
* Section 25 (1) (d), as published, is set out at p. 191, letter B, post.

Dictum of Asquith, L.J., in *Harte* v. *Frampton* ([1947] 2 All E.R. at p. 606)   A
applied.

Per Lord Denning, M.R.: the word " caused " in s. 25 (1) (*d*) of the
Agricultural Holdings Act, 1948, as substituted, means " done ", and the
question is whether greater hardship would be done by withholding than by
giving consent (see p. 192, letter B, post).

Decision of the Queen's Bench Divisional Court ([1967] 1 All E.R. 188)   B
affirmed.

[As to consent to a notice to quit an agricultural holding, see 1 Halsbury's
Laws (3rd Edn.) 284, 285, para. 601; and for cases on the subject, see 2 Digest
(Repl.) 14-16, *61-68*.

For the Agricultural Holdings Act, 1948, s. 25 (as originally enacted), s. 30,
see 28 Halsbury's Statutes (2nd Edn.) 48, 55.   C

For the Agricultural Holdings Act, 1948, s. 25 (1), as substituted by the
Agricultural Act, 1958, s. 3 (2), see Supplement to 28 Halsbury's Statutes
(2nd Edn.), para. [56] (amended texts).]

Cases referred to:

> *Edison, The*, [1933] All E.R. Rep. 144; 149 L.T. 49; sub nom. *Liesbosch*   D
> *Dredger* v. *S.S. Edison*, [1933] A.C. 449; 102 L.J.P. 73; 17 Digest
> (Repl.) 93, *103*.
>
> *Harte* v. *Frampton*, [1947] 2 All E.R. 604; [1948] 1 K.B. 73; [1948] L.J.R.
> 1125; 31 Digest (Repl.) 709, *7962*.

Appeal.

This was an appeal by the tenant from a judgment of the Divisional Court   E
of the Queen's Bench Division, dated Nov. 24, 1966, and reported at [1967]
1 All E.R. 188, dismissing the tenant's appeal by way of Case Stated from a
decision of the Agricultural Land Tribunal, Eastern Area, dated Mar. 7, 1966,
giving consent to the operation of a notice to quit, dated Feb. 3, 1965, served
on the tenant requiring him to quit Slate Hall Farm on Feb. 4, 1966. The
tribunal decided that greater hardship would be caused by withholding than   F
by giving consent, and in reaching their decision the tribunal took into account
all the circumstances of the case, including the various matters stated in the
report of the case below (see [1967] 1 All E.R. at p. 189, letter D). The facts
are set out in the judgment of Lord Denning, M.R.

J. A. R. Finlay for the tenant.

L. A. Blundell, Q.C., and *Ronald Bernstein* for the respondent, the administrator   G
of the landlord's estate.

LORD DENNING, M.R.: Mr. William Henry Bailey owned two farms
in Hertfordshire. One was Five House Farm of nearly two hundred acres. The
other was Slate Hall Farm of some eighty acres. In 1955 he let them to Mr.
Purser, the tenant. The tenant bought the freehold of Five House Farm in 1959.   H
Since then he has been tenant of Slate Hall Farm, paying a rent of some £341 a
year. Old Mr. Bailey, if I may so describe him, evidently got into financial
difficulties. He raised money on the farm. The liability charged on it came
to £1,340 a year: whereas the rent he was getting was only £341 16s. Eventually
on Feb. 3, 1965, old Mr. Bailey gave the tenant notice to quit Slate Hall Farm
on Feb. 4, 1966.   I

Being an agricultural holding, the tenant was entitled to and did give a counter-
notice. That meant that the notice to quit would not have effect unless Mr.
Bailey got the consent of the Agricultural Land Tribunal to it. So he applied
to the tribunal for its consent; but before the tribunal heard the matter, old
Mr. Bailey died on Nov. 17, 1965. His son, Mr. Ernest Bailey, became the
administrator of his estate, but limited to the application pending before the
tribunal. That is an unusual grant of administration, but it is not challenged
before us.

The application was part heard on Jan. 31, and was concluded on Mar. 7, 1966. At that hearing the question for the tribunal was whether to give its consent. Its consent was asked for on the ground provided in the Agriculture Act, 1958, s. 3 (2), which gave a new form to s. 25 (1) of the Agricultural Holdings Act, 1948. That section says:

B
" (1) The Agricultural Land Tribunal shall consent . . . to the operation of a notice to quit an agricultural holding or part of an agricultural holding if, but only if, they are satisfied . . . (*d*) that greater hardship would be caused by withholding than by giving consent to the operation of the notice . . ."

C
The tribunal considered the matter with the greatest care. The reason why the administrator wants possession of Slate Hall Farm is that he wants to sell it. The estate is in great financial difficulty. Old Mr. Bailey left many debts. His widow is elderly and is poverty-stricken. She is on national assistance. If possession of this holding of eighty acres could be obtained, the holding could be sold with vacant possession. The proceeds of sale might be enough to pay off the debts owing by old Mr. Bailey; and it might be possible to pay some of the legacies. On the other hand, there would be some hardship on the tenant if he

D
were turned out; but he has very substantial outside interests, and the way in which he runs his farms does not inidcate that he would suffer very greatly by the loss of these eighty acres. Apparently he does quite well on the other farm of two hundred acres.

Taking all the matters into account, the tribunal felt that on the whole greater hardship would be caused by withholding consent. They gave their

E
consent to the notice to quit. The tenant asked for a Case to be stated for the opinion of the High Court. The questions of law were: (i) whether the circumstances to which the tribunal referred were capable of being taken into consideration in deciding whether there was greater hardship; (ii) whether it was within the jurisdiction of the tribunal to consent when the objective was to sell the holding in due course.

F
On the first point, although old Mr. Bailey is dead, the administrator stands in his shoes. The tribunal are entitled to consider the greater hardship, not only to the landlord himself, but to all those concerned on the landlord's side. I would interpret " greater hardship " in this section in the same way as the courts have interpreted it in the Rent Act cases, such as *Harte* v. *Frampton* (1),

G
in which Asquith, L.J., said:

" The true view, we think, is that the county court judge should take into account hardship to all who may be affected by the grant or refusal of an order for possession—relatives, dependants, lodgers, guests, and the stranger within the gates . . ."

H
Applying this interpretation, I think that the tribunal were entitled to consider the position of the elderly widow, who is on national assistance; and of old Mr. Bailey's estate which would otherwise be insolvent: and of the son, Mr. Ernest Bailey, who guaranteed a number of the liabilities of his father. I do not see that the tribunal erred at all in the matters they considered.

On the second point, it is true that the administrator wants possession in order to sell the farm with vacant possession; but I do not think that this puts him

I
out of court. In most cases, of course, it would be a great hardship on the tenant to turn him out just to enable the landlord to resell, and the application would not be likely to succeed; but there may be cases in which it is a great hardship on the landlord if he cannot realise its value. If it is a greater hardship, I think that consent can be given. Counsel for the tenant referred us to s. 30 of the Act of 1948, which goes back to the Agricultural Land Sales (Restriction of Notices to Quit) Act, 1919. That is a difficult section to understand. All I need

---

(1) [1947] 2 All E.R. 604, at p. 606; [1948] 1 K.B. 73 at p. 79.

say is that it applies only when the landlord, during the currency of a notice to quit, contracts to sell.   That is not this case.

Then counsel for the tenant took a point on causation.   He said that you have to see whether greater hardship would be " caused ", and he went on to argue that the cause of the hardship on the landlord's side was the financial embarrassment and the impecuniosity of old Mr. Bailey, not the withholding of consent to the notice to quit.   He referred to the well known case of *The Edison* (2).   That case concerns damages for tort and remoteness.   It does not seem to me to have any real relevance here.   The word " caused " in this section means " done ".   The question is whether greater hardship would be done by withholding than by giving consent.

In my judgment the tribunal can consider the hardship on each side with regard to all the attendant circumstances.   A good instance was put by SALMON, L.J., in the course of the argument.   A landlord might be on the verge of bankruptcy through no fault of his own; but he might be saved by being able to sell with vacant possession.   It would be legitimate for the tribunal to consider the hardship on him if he did not get possession: and compare it with the hardship on the tenant if he were turned out.   No doubt it is hard on the tenant here to have to go; but, after all, he did buy the other farm, and I expect that he will be one of the possible purchasers of this farm if it is sold.   At all events, the only matter for this court, as it was for the Divisional Court (3), is whether there was any error in point of law in what the tribunal have done.   For myself I see no error in point of law.

I agree with the decision of the Divisional Court (3) and I would dismiss the appeal.

HARMAN, L.J.:   I agree and for the same reasons.   I can see nothing wrong in the matters which the tribunal have taken into account and I do not see that they have left out of consideration anything which they ought to have considered.   LORD PARKER, C.J., in giving the judgment of the Divisional Court said (4):

" In the end, therefore, I am left just looking at the words in para. (*d*), words which are wholly unrestricted as a matter of language, and I can find no possible ground for limiting the word ' hardship ' in any way.   For those reasons which I have stated shortly, I think that the tribunal came to a right decision in law, . . ."

If one does not limit that word " hardship " in one of the ways which counsel for the tenant suggested, then he does not suggest that there is any reason why we should upset the tribunal's decision.   They were the tribunal of fact, and provided they proceeded on the right ground, their decision is the end of the matter. I think that they did proceed on the right ground and I would dismiss the appeal.

SALMON, L.J.:   I agree.

Appeal dismissed.

Solicitors: *Pollard, Thomas & George Martin* (for the tenant); *I. A. Landy, Laufer & Co.* (for the administrator of the landlord's estate).

[*Reported by* F. GUTTMAN, ESQ., *Barrister-at-Law.*]

---

(2) [1933] All E.R. Rep. 144 at p. 158; [1933] A.C. 449 at p. 460.
(3) Ante p. 188.
(4) Ante at p. 191.

A

Re MILLS' WILL TRUSTS.
YORKSHIRE INSURANCE CO., LTD. AND ANOTHER
v. COWARD AND OTHERS.

[CHANCERY DIVISION (Stamp, J.), March 16, 17, 22, 1967.]

B *Will—Condition—Forfeiture—Proviso for forfeiture of share of testator's residuary*
estate if not " member of the Church of England or some Church abroad
professing the same tenets "—Proviso not void for uncertainty—Methodist
Church of Australia not a church abroad professing same tenets as Church
of England.

Under the testator's will and codicils a one-eighth share of his residuary
C estate was bequeathed on trust, as regards capital, for the children of T., a
son of the testator. The trust in favour of these grandchildren of the
testator was subject to a proviso* that if a grandchild should not be a " member of the Church of England or of some Church abroad professing the same
tenets ", then such grandchild's share should be forfeited and should accrue
to other issue of the testator. T. was a member of the Methodist Church
D of Australia, and his children were baptised into, and belonged to, that
church.

Held: the grandchildren of T. were disentitled to take beneficially by
reason of the proviso which was not invalid because—

(i) the description " a member of the Church of England or of some
Church abroad professing the same tenets " was not void for uncertainty,
E since the tenets of the Church of England, being part of the law of England
by virtue of the Act of Uniformity, 1662, were not uncertain (see p. 197,
letter I, to p. 198, letter A, and p. 198, letter F, post).

(ii) the Methodist Church of Australia, being at variance with the Church
of England in regard to the doctrine of the ministry under which episcopal
ordination only was acceptable for the ministry of the Church of England,
F was not a " Church professing the same tenets " as the Church of England
(see p. 199, letter C, post).

[**Editorial Note.** This decision may be considered, in regard to bequests
subject to conditions regarding membership of the Church of England, with
Re Tegg ([1936] 2 All E.R. 878) and *Re Allen* ([1953] 2 All E.R. 898).

As to uncertain conditions as to religion, see 39 HALSBURY'S LAWS (3rd Edn.)
G 924, para. 1398; and for cases on the subject, see 48 DIGEST (Repl.) 326-328,
2815-2821.

For the Act of Uniformity, 1662, see 7 HALSBURY'S STATUTES (2nd Edn.) 583.]

Case referred to:

A.-G. v. Calvert, (1857), 23 Beav. 248; 26 L.J.Ch. 682; 29 L.T.O.S. 61; 21 J.P.
H   371; 53 E.R. 97; 8 Digest (Repl.) 423, *1135.*

Adjourned Summons.

This was an application by originating summons dated Dec. 16, 1965, by the
plaintiffs, Yorkshire Insurance Co., Ltd., and Queensland Trustees, Ltd.,
which, together with the fourteenth defendant, Pamela Philippa Gawler Mills,
were trustees of the will of Thomas Mills, deceased, dated Feb. 8, 1915, and three
I codicils thereto. The application was for the determination of the question
whether, on the true construction of the will and codicils and in the events which
had happened (a) the one-eighth share of the residuary estate, the income of
which was appropriated to George Mills, who died on Nov. 20, 1962, accrued
to the shares of the testator's children other than his daughter Mary but including
his son Thomas and their issue; (b) if the answer to (a) were in the affirmative,

---

· * There were in fact two provisos, but only the second, which disinherited noncon-
firming grandchildren of the testator, was relevant to the question decided; see, on
this point, p. 196, letter A, post.

whether on the true construction of the will and codicils thereto, the issue of **A**
the testator's son Thomas, being the fourth, fifth, sixth and seventh defendants
or one or more of them were entitled to the share which had accrued to their
late father's share; (c) if the answer to (b) were in the affirmative, whether on
the true construction of the will and codicils the fourth to the seventh defendants
were entitled to share in the accrued share equally; or (d) how else it ought to
be dealt with. There were fourteen defendants all of whom claimed to be **B**
beneficiaries entitled to an interest in the residue under the will. The facts
are set out in the judgment.

Allan Heyman for the plaintiffs.

J. D. Waite for the fourth to seventh defendants, who were Methodist grandchildren of the testator.

P. S. A. Rossdale for the eighth defendant, an Anglican grandchild of the **C**
testator.

The other defendants did not appear and were not represented.

Cur. adv. vult.

Mar. 22.   **STAMP, J.,** read the following judgment; The question which
I have to determine affects the distribution of the estate of a testator who made **D**
his will as long ago as Feb. 8, 1915. Before reading his testamentary dispositions
and propounding the question which arises, it is convenient to state some relevant
facts regarding his family.

He had nine children living at the date of his will. One of them, Mary, was
a Roman Catholic. Another, Thomas, was a Methodist. Born in 1876 Thomas
was married in 1907 by a Minister of the Methodist Church in Australia. He had **E**
four children, who are parties to this summons, born in 1908, 1909, 1911 and
1914 respectively. All of these children were baptised in the Methodist Church
of Australia to which church they still belong. Thomas died in March, 1953.

In his will and three codicils made in 1917, 1918 and 1924, the testator described himself as of Longdown Lodge, Sandhurst, Berkshire, but he must have
had property in Australia for he appointed separate trustees to that property. **F**
The Australian property was directed to be held, however, in effect on the trusts
applicable to his other property. The will, though carefully and no doubt
professionally drawn, is difficult to read because it contains no paragraphs,
numbered or otherwise and no punctuation.

By the will the testator directed his trustees to stand possessed of the stocks,
funds, shares and securities from time to time representing his residuary real **G**
and personal estate on trust to pay the annual income arising from one half part
thereof to his wife during her life, and to pay the annual income arising from one
tenth part thereof to his son, Thomas, whom I have already mentioned, during
his life and subject thereto to stand possessed of the entirety of the trust fund
and the income thereof on trust to divide the same into seven equal shares, and
to stand possessed of one of such shares on trust for each of his children, Elizabeth **H**
Coward, Alice Maud Liddell, Florence Williams, Charles Mills, George Mills,
Duncan Mills and John Gawler Mills and their issue and otherwise as thereinafter
declared. The testator then directed his trustees to pay the annual income
arising from each child's share to such child during his or her life, and after his
or her death to stand possessed of such child's share in trust for all or such one
or more exclusively of the others or other of the issues of such child at such age **I**
or time or ages or times and for such interest or interests and if more than one
in such shares and proportions and generally in such manner as such child should
by deed or will appoint and in default of and subject to every such appointment
in trust of such of the children of the same child of his as being male should attain
their majority or being female should attain their majority and if more than one
in equal shares. The testator then declared what he meant by the expression
" majority " and inserted the usual hotchpot provision and a power of advancement. There is then a provision that if there should be no child of a son or

A daughter of his to attain his or her majority, that child's share, original or accruing, should accrue to the shares of his other seven children.

There then follows a proviso which I shall refer to as " the first proviso ". It reads:

B " Provided always and I hereby declare that if at my decease or at any time thereafter any child of mine for the time being entitled in possession to any share of the income of the said trust fund shall not be a member of the Church of England or of some Church abroad professing the same tenets or who while so entitled shall cease to be a member of such Church then and in every such case such child shall only receive the income of the said share during his or her life and as from the death of such child the share or shares of such child and his or her issue shall accrue to the others or other C of my said children . . . [and he names them] . . . equally (if more than one) and so that the accrued share of each such child shall be held upon trust for him or her and his or her issue and otherwise in the same manner as is hereinbefore declared with respect to the original share of each of my said children and that every such accrued share shall during the period allowed by law until the transfer thereof to any person or persons who shall be D absolutely entitled thereto also be subject to the like forfeiture in the event aforesaid."

There then follows another proviso to which I will refer as " the second proviso ". It reads as follows:

" Provided also that if any grandchild of mine who shall become entitled E in possession to a share (whether original or accrued) of the said trust fund under any of the trusts or powers aforesaid and as to any grandchild not born in my lifetime if becoming so entitled within twenty one years after my decease shall not on so becoming entitled be a member of such Church as aforesaid then the said share or shares of such grandchild shall be forfeited and shall accrue in the same manner in all respects and subject to the like F forfeiture as is declared by the preceding clause with reference to the forfeited share of any of my children."

The provisions which I have read are the only provisions of the will to which I need refer, except that there is a direction that during the life of Mary, who was the Roman Catholic, it should be lawful for his trustees in their discretion to pay to and for the benefit of Mary out of the annual income of the trust fund such G sum or sums not exceeding twelve pounds per week as the trustees should from time to time think fit.

It will become necessary to consider what is meant by the phrase " a member of the Church of England or of some Church abroad professing the same tenets ", and more particularly whether the Methodist Church in Australia is such a church, but subject to this question the will, at least for present purposes, presents no H difficulty. It is convenient, however, before coming to the codicils, to pause and call attention to certain features of the will.

Mary, the Roman Catholic, takes no benefit except under the discretionary power to which I have referred. Thomas, the Methodist, is given a smaller share than the other seven children, and nothing at all is given to Thomas's children. Leaving aside Thomas's children for the moment, it is to be observed that the I effect of the first proviso does not in the least affect a child of the testator who is not a member of the Church of England or of some Church abroad professing the same tenets. Although the first proviso says that such a child shall only receive the income of his share during his or her life, that is all that such child was given in the first place. What the first proviso does is to disinherit the issue of such a child, and it does so, be those issue members of, what I will call for the sake of brevity, a qualifying church or not; the non-conformity of the father or mother is to be visited on the issue and not on the father or mother. It is also to be observed that in view of the terms of the first proviso the second proviso

can only operate to exclude a grandchild of the testator whose parent was a A
member of a qualifying church. The first proviso cuts out grandchildren, whether
conformist or non-conformist, being children of a non-conformist parent—and I
use the words " conformist " and " non-conformist " in a non-technical and merely
a descriptive sense.   The second proviso cuts out only non-conformist grandchildren of a conformist parent. The two provisos are separate and distinctive
in their operation and designed for different purposes.   B

I now come to the second codicil, for the first codicil is not relevant. By that
second codicil dated June 12, 1918, the testator, so far as material, says this:

" Whereas by my said will I have declared and directed my trustees to
stand possessed of my residuary real and personal estate (hereinafter referred
to as ' the said trust fund ') upon trust to pay the annual income arising
from one half part thereof to my wife during her life and to pay the annual C
income arising from one tenth part thereof to my son Thomas during his
life and subject thereto to stand possessed of the entirety of the said trust
fund and the income thereof upon trust to divide the same into seven equal
shares and to stand possessed of one of such shares upon trust for each of
my children [and he names them] and their issue and otherwise as thereinafter declared and whereas I have devised and bequeathed all my real and D
personal effects situate and being at the time of my death in the Commonwealth of Australia to my colonial trustees upon certain trusts as to payment
of the net proceeds rents profits and income to my general trustees to be
respectively held and applied by my trustees upon the above-mentioned
trusts and whereas I am desirous that the interest of my son Thomas under
this my will shall be equal to and similar in all respects to that of my other E
sons and daughters (except my daughter Mary) Now I hereby revoke the declaration and direction to my trustees as above recited of the stocks funds
shares and securities from time to time representing my residuary real and
personal estate (in my said will referred to as ' the said trust fund ') and including the net proceeds rents profits and income of my colonial estate upon
trust to pay the annual income arising from one half part thereof to my wife F
during her life and subject thereto shall stand possessed of the entirety
of the said trust fund and the income thereof upon trust to divide the same
into eight equal shares and shall stand possessed of one of such shares upon
trust for each of my children Thomas Mills, Elizabeth Coward, Alice Maud
Liddell, Florence Williams, Charles Mills, George Mills, Duncan Mills and
John Gawler Mills and their issue and otherwise as in my said will thereinafter G
declared and I declare that throughout my said will any word or words clause
or clauses having reference mention or connexion with the trust to pay the
annual income arising from one tenth part of my said trust fund to my son
Thomas shall be construed as deleted and of no effect and that throughout
my said will where mention or reference is made to my said seven children for
the word ' seven ' shall be substituted the word ' eight ' and my said will H
shall be read and construed accordingly and so that it shall be deemed to include the name of my said son Thomas and shall also be read and construed
as if the word ' Thomas ' had been inserted throughout after the word ' children ' and before the words ' Elizabeth Coward ' and I declare that the
clause in my said will as to my children being members of the Church of
England shall not apply so far as my said son Thomas is concerned and in all I
other respects I confirm my said will."

The question to be determined is whether the children of Thomas are entitled to
take. The question did not, as a practical matter, arise on Thomas's death in
1963 because, by the effect of certain hotchpot provisions in the will to which I
have not referred, nothing then became distributable. However, now on the
death of another child of the testator the provision to accrue has come into
operation and a considerable sum is to be distributed.

A   The first submission made on behalf of the children of Thomas is that the direction at the end of the codicil

"that the clause in my said will as to my children being members of the
Church of England shall not apply so far as my said son Thomas is concerned"

operates to free the children of Thomas not only from the effect of the first proviso
B   in the will but also from the effect of the second proviso, and that irrespective
of whether the Methodist Church in Australia is a church abroad professing the
same tenets as the Church of England, the grandchildren are entitled to share in
the testator's estate. The relieving declaration, to which I have just referred, is
designed, so it is said, to relieve Thomas's family from the consequences of non-
conformity. It is said that it would be to attribute to the testator a capricious
C   and unfair intention if one construed the declaration as freeing them from the
consequences of the non-conformity of Thomas but not from their own. It is
urged that the declaration at the end of the codicil is expressed in terms which
can readily be construed as referring to the trusts in favour of Thomas and his
issue. Attention was called to the lack of precision and accuracy in the terms of
the relieving declaration, and more particularly to the fact that the relieving
D   clause speaks only of the Church of England whereas the qualifying clause in
the will speaks of membership of the Church of England or of some church abroad
professing the same tenets.

Counsel for one of the Anglican granchildren in answer referred me to the first
principle of construction that in construing a will the court is to ascertain not the
intention simply but the expressed intention, and he referred me to Hawkins
E   on Wills (3rd Edn.) p. 1. In my judgment that is all that counsel really
needs. I must read the will and codicil together, and so reading them the words
of the declaration at the end of the codicil are in my judgment clear enough.
The second proviso in the will refers to the first proviso as "the preceding
clause", and the reference in the relieving provision at the end of the codicil to
"the clause in my said will as to my children being members of the Church of
F   England" points in my judgment clearly and unequivocally to the first proviso
which is in the will spoken of as "a clause" and is a provision as to the testator's
children being members of the Church of England.

The second proviso is not a provision as to the testator's children being members
of the Church of England but to the whole class of grandchildren. If anything
more were required to show that the relieving clause was directed exclusively to
G   the first proviso, it is to be found in the operative part of the relieving clause
"shall not apply so far as my said son Thomas is concerned". The declaration
in my judgment clearly applies to prevent the first proviso operating to exclude
Thomas's issue being members of the Church of England or a qualifying church on
the ground that Thomas was not such a member, but in my judgment it will not
tolerate a construction which prevents the second proviso operating to exclude
H   grandchildren, being children of Thomas, from the consequences of their own
non-conformity. Nor in my view does this construction introduce unfairness,
improbability or caprice, for if I am right in the view which I have expressed as to
the respective effects of the first and second provisos, it would not be in the least
odd of the testator by the codicil to relieve grandchildren from the consequences
of Thomas's non-conformity but from the consequences of their own.

I   This brings me to two further points relied on on behalf of the four grandchildren. It is said that the expression "a member of the Church of England
or of some Church abroad professing the same tenets" is void for uncertainty,
or, if it is not, that the expression comprises membership of the Methodist Church
in Australia which, it is urged, is a church abroad professing the same tenets as the
Church of England.

As to the uncertainty argument, I do not think it necessary to say much. The
tenets of the Church of England are part of the law of England laid down in the
Act of Uniformity, 1662, and in the Prayer Book, which derives its authority

under the law from the Act of Uniformity, 1662, to which it is annexed (1), and **A** the statute law of England. It is in my judgment impossible to hold that the expression " the tenets of the Church of England " is in the least degree uncertain. SIR JOHN ROMILLY, M.R., in *A.-G.* v. *Calvert* (2) used almost that very expression.

On behalf of the four grandchildren it was submitted that the word " tenets " is wider than the words " dogma ", " doctrine " or " faith "—and I will assume that this is so—and that the word " tenets " embraces as well the faith, the doctrine **B** and the dogma of that church. It is still in my judgment impossible to say that any of these things are uncertain in relation to the established Church of England. Pointing to the word " same " it is submitted that the reference to a Church abroad professing " the same tenets " as the Church of England introduced a degree of uncertainty which invalidates the provision. The testator, it is said, has not used the words " professing the tenets " but " professing the same tenets " **C** and one cannot say what degree of similarity must be found for a Church abroad to satisfy the description. No doubt a purist, who wished to indicate that the tenets to be professed by the Church abroad should be those of the Church of England and no others, might more appropriately have referred to " the tenets ", but the whole phrase would have had to be recast, and putting myself in the testator's armchair as he made his will in the year 1915, I cannot think that he **D** used the phrase " the same tenets " as indicating similar tenets to those of the Church of England or as indicating a Church having some of the same tenets. To attribute such an intention to him would be to attribute to him an intention to exclude from his bounty a member of any of the Christian Churches in his own country, other than the Church of England, professing tenets however similar to those of the Church of England but to include members of those Churches situate **E** abroad; to exclude certainly a member of the Methodist Church in England but to include perhaps a member of that same church professing the very same tenets, and in my judgment this would be absurd.

Reading, as I do, the words " the same tenets " as meaning the same thing as " the tenets " of the Church of England, I cannot hold that the phrase in question is uncertain, for what those tenets are is one of English law, and an inquiry into **F** the tenets of any church abroad will reveal whether those tenets are the tenets of the Church of England. I could only take the contrary view if it were shown that in 1915 there was no church abroad which answered the description.

It is not, however, necessary for me to consider whether a church abroad organ- ised on a consensual basis without ceasing to be in communion with the Church of England, though not in connexion with it, would have fallen within the description, **G** for there were unquestionably Churches abroad such as the Church of England in India which answered the description.

It is submitted in the alternative that the Methodist Church of Australia professes the same tenets as the Church of England. The evidence is that the Methodist Church in Australia has the same tenets as the Methodist Church of Great Britain, which I will call " the Methodist Church " simpliciter. That **H** Church, having broken away from the Church of England at the end of the eight- eenth century accepts the authority of Holy Scripture, the Nicene and Apostles' Creeds and the two Gospel Sacraments of Baptism and Holy Communion. What caused the breach and eventually led to the Methodists becoming a separate body and establishing a separate Church—and I refer to and accept the affidavit evi- dence of Dr. Eric Waldran Kemp—was John Wesley's claim to be able to ordain **I** men to the Christian ministry. The Church of England, of which John Wesley

---

(1) The manuscript, which at one time was thought to have been destroyed when the Houses of Parliament were burned, was subsequently found and is now placed with this Act, 14 Car. 2 c. 24; see footnote 7 HALSBURY'S STATUTES (2nd Edn.) 585. Alternative forms of service, deviating from the Book of Common Prayer, can be used by virtue of the Prayer Book (Alternative and Other Services) Measure 1965 (No. 1), see ss. 1, 2, 4-6, 45 HALSBURY'S STATUTES (2nd Edn.) 253-256.

(2) (1857), 23 Beav. 248.

A himself was a priest, accepts in its ministry only those who have received episcopal ordination. As Dr. Kemp points out, this principle is stated in the Act of Uniformity, 1662, and in the Preface to the Ordinal in the Book of Common Prayer as annexed to that Act. The Church of England adheres to the threefold ministry of bishop, priest and deacon, as the ministry has come down from the time of the Apostles.

B   " No man [and I take this from the preface to the Ordinal itself] shall be accounted or taken to be a lawful bishop, priest, or deacon in the Church of England . . . except he be called, tried, examined, and admitted thereunto, according to the form hereafter following [i.e. the Ordinal] or hath had formerly episcopal consecration, or ordination."

C Dr. Eric Wilfred Baker, who has given affidavit evidence on behalf of the four grandchildren, concedes that the two Churches are at variance on the doctrine of the ministry. The principle of episcopacy and ordination by a consecrated bishop is in my judgment clearly one of the outstanding tenets of the Church of England which distinguishes that Church from the Methodist Church. References to Her Majesty's Protestant subjects dissenting from the Church of England and

D Protestant Dissenters are to be found in Acts of Parliament in modern times, see e.g., s. 2 of the Religious Disabilities Act, 1846, and s. 2 of the Liberty of Religious Worship Act, 1855. Her Majesty's subjects, members of the Methodist Church, and so dissenting from the Church of England, are not in my judgment members of a Church professing the same tenets.

The testator when he made his second codicil considered it necessary to say

E that the clause in his will as to his children being members of the Church of England should not apply so far as his son Thomas, who was a Methodist, was concerned, no doubt because he regarded Thomas as a non-conformist or dissenter and so not a member of the Church of England or of any Church abroad professing the same tenets. In my judgment this conclusion was well founded; and if I had any doubt on the question whether the Church of England and the Methodist

F Church had the same tenets, I should nevertheless conclude, as a matter of construction of this testator's testamentary documents, all of which must be read together, that he used the phrase " some church abroad professing the same tenets " in a sense to exclude the Methodist Church abroad. As I have already said, nothing could be more absurd than to conclude that he intended to exclude from the benefits conferred by his will grandchildren who were members of the

G Wesleyan Methodist Church or the United Methodist Church in Great Britain but to include members of those churches overseas.

Declaration accordingly.

Solicitors: *Rollit, Sons & Haydon* (for the plaintiffs and the fourth to the seventh defendants); *Lipkin, Gorman & Co.* (for the eighth defendant).

[*Reported by* Jenifer Sandell, *Barrister-at-Law.*]

NISSAN v. ATTORNEY-GENERAL.   A

[QUEEN'S BENCH DIVISION (John Stephenson, J.), January 20, 23, 24, 25, 26,
February 17, 1967.]

*Crown—Prerogative—Emergency prerogative—Compensation for loss or damage
by exercise of prerogative—Treaty with independent sovereign state—Truce
force under British command established to assist sovereign power in preservation of internal peace—Occupation by British troops of hotel on territory
of that power—Whether occupation a prerogative act of Crown—Whether
an act of state of the Crown—Whether tenant of hotel, a British subject,
entitled to compensation by the Crown—Jurisdiction of the court.*

*Constitutional Law—Act of State—Emergency—Treaty with foreign independent
sovereign power—British subject hotel owner in territory of that power—
Seizure and occupation of hotel by British troops pursuant to treaty with that
power for preservation of internal peace—Claim for compensation and in
contract—Defence of act of state.*

*United Nations—Act equivalent to act of state—Peace-keeping force established
pursuant to resolution of Security Council—Position of British contingents
of United Nations force.*

On Dec. 25, 1963, the government of the Republic of Cyprus (which had
been an independent sovereign State since Aug. 16, 1960), in response to a
joint appeal by the British, Greek and Turkish governments as signatories
of a treaty of 1960 guaranteeing the constitution of Cyprus, accepted an
offer that the forces of those three governments, stationed in Cyprus and
under British command, should assist the government of Cyprus in the
restoration of peace. This " truce force " began to operate on Dec. 26, 1963.

The plaintiff was a British subject and was tenant of a hotel in Cyprus.
British troops of the truce force, acting in accordance with orders, took
possession of the hotel on Dec. 29, 1963. They remained in possession from
Dec. 29, 1963, to Mar. 27, 1964 (" the first period "). The plaintiff alleged
that on Dec. 29, 1963, the British High Commissioner in the presence of the
Secretary of State for Commonwealth Relations on behalf of the Crown
undertook that the plaintiff should be compensated so that he would suffer
no loss by reason of the occupation of the hotel. On Mar. 27, 1964, an international peace-keeping force was established in Cyprus, pursuant to resolution of the Security Council of the United Nations and with the consent
of the government of Cyprus. The legal status of this force was set out in an
agreement, the terms of which were contained in a letter from the Secretary-
General of the United Nations to the Foreign Minister of Cyprus; and
the agreement was ratified by Law No. 29, 1964, of the Republic of Cyprus.
An agreement between the United Nations and Her Majesty's government
(Cmnd. 3017) also took effect on Mar. 27, 1964. From Mar. 27, 1964 to May
5, 1964 (" the second period ") British troops continued in occupation
of the hotel. On Apr. 25, 1964, regulations for the United Nations Force
in Cyprus (UNFICYP) were issued by the Secretary-General to be effective
from May 10, 1964. These included a provision that UNFICYP was a subsidiary organ of the United Nations and that, although the members of the
force remained in their national service, they were under the authority of
the United Nations and subject to the instructions of the commander of the
force through the chain of command. By reg. 16 the Secretary-General was to
have authority for all administrative and executive matters relating to
UNFICYP and within the limits of available voluntary contributions he
was to make provision for the settlement of any claims that were not settled
by the governments providing contingents or the government of Cyprus.
The participation of the United Kingdom in UNFICYP was confirmed on
Feb. 21, 1966, by letters exchanged between the government of the United
Kingdom and the Secretary-General, constituting an agreement deemed
to have taken effect on Mar. 27, 1964 and embodying the regulations of

Reversed in part, affirmed in part.
C.A., post, p. 1238.

Reversed in part, affirmed in part.
C.A., post, p. 1238.

A   Apr. 25, 1964. On May 7, 1964, the plaintiff's flat in the hotel, of which he had retained occupation but which he had left on Mar. 17, 1964, was found by Finnish troops to have been broken into and looted before their entry. The plaintiff sued the Crown in England in respect of the occupation of the hotel, and of loss and damage resulting therefrom, claiming (i) just compensation as of right for loss or damage to the hotel and its contents, (ii) in contract for

B money due or damages and (iii) damages for trespass to chattels, being contents of the hotel but excluding the plaintiff's flat.

   On a preliminary point of law whether the action was maintainable in respect of (i) and (ii), it was conceded (a) that claim (iii) should go forward* and (b) that any claim of the plaintiff in respect of the contents of the flat or by occupation of the hotel since May 5, 1964, could be recoverable only,

C if at all, as compensation* under claim (i); and any contention that an act of state† was a good defence to a claim in tort by a British subject whether in British or foreign territory was abandoned‡.

   Held: (i) assuming that a British subject might have a right to compensation for property taken or damaged by servants of the Crown within the jurisdiction in exercise of the prerogative in an emergency not involving

D war, yet where such a prerogative right was exercised, as in the present case, in an independent sovereign State to the detriment of a British subject, the plaintiff had no such right for the following reasons—

   (a) because the acts done by British troops during the first period were not done as agents for or as acts of state of the government of Cyprus, but were done under authority derived from the Crown in the territory of an indepen-

E dent sovereign State, the Republic of Cyprus, pursuant to an agreement or treaty between the sovereign States; thus these acts were acts of state of the Crown and accordingly were acts which were not cognizable by the court (see p. 219, letters A and C, p. 221, letter G, p. 226, letter C, and p. 227, letter E, post).

   Burmah Oil Co. (Burma Trading), Ltd. v. *Lord Advocate* ([1964] 2 All E.R.

F 348) considered.

   Salaman v. *Secretary of State in Council of India* ([1906] 1 K.B. 613) applied.

   (b) because, although the occupation of the plaintiff's hotel by British troops during the second period was done under authority derived from the United Nations and not from the Crown, yet the continuation of the occupation of the hotel during the second period under the authority of the United

G Nations was occupation authorised by an act equivalent to an act of State and so was not cognizable by the court (see p. 221, letter G, p. 222, letter C, and p. 222, letter I, to p. 223, letter A, post).

   (c) because the fact that the plaintiff was a British subject did not prevent the Crown having immunity from suit in its own courts for an act of state (see p. 226, letter E, and p. 227, letter E, post).

H   *Nabob of the Carnatic* v. *East India Co.* ((1791), 1 Ves. 371); *Rustomjee* v. *Reginam* ((1876), 2 Q.B.D. 69) and *West Rand Central Gold Mining Co., Ltd.* v. *Regem* ([1905] 2 K.B. 391) applied.

   Walker v. *Baird* ([1892] A.C. 491) and *Johnstone* v. *Pedlar* ([1921] All E.R. Rep. 176) distinguished.

   (ii) assuming that an express undertaking was given to the plaintiff that

I he should be compensated for loss or damage, the alleged contract was bound up with the act of state and was not within the jurisdiction of the court (see p. 228, letter G, post).

   [As to acts of state and the position of the Crown in the conduct of foreign affairs, see 7 HALSBURY's LAWS (3rd Edn.) 263-264, para. 565; 279-282, paras. 593-598; 287, para. 606; and for cases on acts of state as affecting the court's jurisdiction, see 11 DIGEST (Repl.) 618-626, *451-501.*

---

  * See p. 208, letter D, post.   † Act of state is defined at p. 221, letter H, post.
         ‡ See p. 224. letter E, post.

As to the nature and extent of the royal prerogative, see 7 HALSBURY'S LAWS **A**
(3rd Edn.) 221, 222, paras. 463-467; and for cases on the subject, see 11 DIGEST
(Repl.) 566, 567, *41-53*.]

Cases referred to:

A.-G. v. *De Keyser's Royal Hotel, Ltd.*, [1920] All E.R. Rep. 80; [1920] A.C.
    508; 89 L.J.Ch. 417; 122 L.T. 691; *affg. Re De Keyser's Royal Hotel,
    Ltd., De Keyser's Royal Hotel, Ltd.* v. *Regem*, [1919] 2 Ch. 197; 88 **B**
    L.J.Ch. 415; 120 L.T. 396; 17 Digest (Repl.) 437, *91*.

Bowmakers, Ltd. v. *Barnet Instruments, Ltd.*, [1944] 2 All E.R. 579; [1945]
    K.B. 65; 114 L.J.K.B. 41; 172 L.T. 1; 12 Digest (Repl.) 310, *2391*.

British South Africa Co. v. *Companhia de Moçambique*, [1891-94] All E.R. Rep.
    640; [1893] A.C. 602; 63 L.J.Q.B. 70; 69 L.T. 604; 11 Digest (Repl.)
    371, *374*.   **C**

Burmah Oil Co. (Burma Trading), Ltd. v. *Lord Advocate*, [1964] 2 All E.R. 348;
    [1965] A.C. 75; [1964] 2 W.L.R. 1231; 3rd Digest Supp.

Buron v. *Denman*, (1848), 2 Exch. 167; 6 State Tr. N.S. 525; 10 L.T.O.S.
    523; 154 E.R. 450; 11 Digest (Repl.) 454, *902*, 621, *478*.

Carnatic (Nabob of) v. *East India Co.*, (1791), 1 Ves. 371; *subsequent proceedings*,
    (1793), 2 Ves. 56; 30 E.R. 521; 11 Digest (Repl.) 619, *457*.   **D**

Carr v. *Fracis Times & Co.*, [1902] A.C. 176; 71 L.J.K.B. 361; 85 L.T. 144;
    11 Digest (Repl.) 453, *895*.

Chandler v. *Director of Public Prosecutions*, [1962] 3 All E.R. 142; [1964]
    A.C. 763; [1962] 3 W.L.R. 694; 46 Cr. App. Rep. 347, H.L.; Digest
    (Cont. Vol. A) 259, *44a*.

Civilian War Claimants' Association, Ltd. v. *Regem*, [1931] All E.R. Rep. 432; **E**
    [1932] A.C. 14; 101 L.J.K.B. 105; 146 L.T. 169; 11 Digest (Repl.)
    620, *476*.

Cook v. *Sprigg*, [1895-99] All E.R. Rep. 773; [1899] A.C. 572; 68 L.J.P.C.
    144; 81 L.T. 281; 11 Digest (Repl.) 627, *502*.

Dobree v. *Napier*, (1836), 2 Bing. N.C. 781; 3 State Tr. N.S. 621; 5 L.J.C.P.
    273; 132 E.R. 301; 11 Digest (Repl.) 454, *904*, 622, *490*.   **F**

Doss v. *Secretary of State for India in Council*, (1875), L.R. 19 Eq. 509; 32
    L.T. 294; 11 Digest (Repl.) 370, *369*.

Ferdinand (Ex-Tsar of Bulgaria), Re, [1921] 1 Ch. 107; 90 L.J.Ch. 1; 11
    Digest (Repl.) 637, *610*.

Holman v. *Johnson*, (1775), 1 Cowp. 341; 98 E.R. 1120; 11 Digest (Repl.)
    325, *16*.   **G**

Johnstone v. *Pedlar*, [1921] All E.R. Rep. 176; [1921] 2 A.C. 262; 90 L.J.P.C.
    181; 125 L.T. 809; 11 Digest (Repl.) 619, *465*.

Paley (Princess Olga) v. *Weisz*, [1929] All E.R. Rep. 513; [1929] 1 K.B. 718;
    98 L.J.K.B. 465; 141 L.T. 297; 11 Digest (Repl.) 623, *496*.

Rustomjee v. *Reginam*, (1876), 1 Q.B.D. 487; *affd.* C.A., (1876), 2 Q.B.D. 69;
    46 L.J.Q.B. 238; 36 L.T. 190; 11 Digest (Repl.) 620, *474*.   **H**

Salaman v. *Secretary of State in Council of India*, [1906] 1 K.B. 613; 75 L.J.K.B.
    418; 94 L.T. 858; 11 Digest (Repl.) 613, *426*.

Secretary of State in Council of India v. *Kamachee Boye Sahaba*, (1859), 13 Moo.
    P.C.C. 22; 7 Moo. Ind. App. 476; 19 E.R. 388; 11 Digest (Repl.)
    617, *442*.

Walker v. *Baird*, [1892] A.C. 491; 61 L.J.P.C. 92; 67 L.T. 513, P.C.; 11 **I**
    Digest (Repl.) 618, *452*.

West Rand Central Gold Mining Co., Ltd. v. *Regem*, [1905] 2 K.B. 391; 74
    L.J.K.B. 753; 93 L.T. 207; 11 Digest (Repl.) 627, *503*; 16 Digest
    (Repl.) 271, *386*.

Action.

By writ issued on Mar. 2, 1966, the plaintiff, Naim Nissan, a British subject
and at all material times the tenant of the Cornaro Hotel, near Nicosia, Cyprus,

A   claimed relief from the Crown in respect of loss and damage suffered in consequence of the occupation of the hotel by United Kingdom forces during two
periods, viz., from Dec. 29, 1963, to Mar. 27, 1964 (" the first period "), and
from Mar. 27, 1964, to May 5, 1964 (" the second period "), as set out in his
statement of claim. The relief claimed, so far as material to this report is
stated at p. 206, letters E to I, post. The particulars of loss and damage,
B   pleaded in para. 16 of the statement of claim included (A) loss or destruction
of hotel furniture, equipment, etc., £32,223; (B) loss of perishable stores, £4,268;
(C) loss of personal belongings from the plaintiff's flat, £12,802; (D) loss of
profits of £5,000 to £6,000 p.a.; (E) liability of the plaintiff for rent of the hotel
at £220 per month, £5,280, and telephone accounts paid by the plaintiff in
respect of part of the occupation period, £37.

C   By an agreed order of Master Jacob on Oct. 27, 1966, questions of law raised
by the pleadings were referred for trial as a preliminary issue by a judge alone
in the Special Paper List. These questions are set out at letter G, infra.

   Nigel Bridge for the Attorney-General (plaintiff on this preliminary issue).
   P. Goodenday for the plaintiff (defendant on this preliminary issue).

                                                              Cur. adv. vult.
D
   Feb. 17.   **JOHN STEPHENSON, J.**, read the following judgment: On
Dec. 29, 1963, British troops occupied the Cornaro Hotel near Nicosia, Cyprus.
Mr. Naim Nissan was the tenant of the hotel, lived there and carried on the
business of an hotel there. He has never since been able to live there or carry
on his business there. By a writ issued on Mar. 2, 1966, he brought an action in
E   this country against Her Majesty's Attorney-General, as permitted by the
Crown Proceedings Act, 1947, claiming from the Crown the relief set out in the
statement of claim served with his writ. The Attorney-General's defence was
served on May 26, 1966. Those pleadings raised certain questions of law. On
Oct. 27, 1966, Master Jacob made an agreed order that those questions should
be speedily tried and decided as a preliminary issue, before the trial of the action,
F   by a judge alone in the Special Paper List, the defendant to be plaintiff in the
preliminary issue and all further proceedings in the action to be stayed until
the determination of the issue. The questions of law which I have accordingly
to decide are specified in the master's order in these terms:

   " (a) Whether, upon the facts pleaded in para. 3 and the first sentence
   of para. 4 of the defence, the last two sentences of the said para. 4 disclose
G   a good defence in law to all or any, and if to some only then to which, of the
   claims and causes of action pleaded by the plaintiff in respect of events
   occurring between Dec. 26, 1963, and Mar. 27, 1964; and
      " (b) Whether upon the facts pleaded in para. 5 and the first sentence
   of para. 6 of the defence, the last sentence of the said para. 6 discloses a
   good defence in law to all or any, and if to some only then to which, of
H   the claims and causes of action pleaded by the plaintiff in respect of events
   occurring on and after Mar. 27, 1964."

The claims and causes of action pleaded by the plaintiff in respect of both periods
must be considered first. I therefore read his statement of claim remembering
that for the purpose of this trial I have to treat all the facts which it alleges as
I   proved.
   " 1. The plaintiff is and was at all material times a British subject.
   " 2. At all material times from in or about August, 1958, the plaintiff
was the tenant of the Cornaro Hotel situate on the outskirts of Nicosia,
Cyprus, at the rent of £220 per month. The said hotel, which was fully
completed only in or about the end of 1960, was latterly let to the plaintiff
at the said rent under a tenancy agreement in writing dated Sept. 14, 1960,
granted to him by Ashdjian, Ltd., for a term of five years from the date
of completion of the said hotel with an option exercisable by the plaintiff

to continue the said tenancy at the said rent for a further period of five years.   A

"3. The said hotel was a luxury hotel classified as First A and the accommodation for hotel guests consisted (inter alia) of nineteen bedrooms each with its own private bathroom and various public rooms. The said hotel was decorated and equipped by the plaintiff at a cost to him of £32,000 or thereabouts, including £4,450 spent in structural alternations necessary for the purpose of carrying on the said business. In addition   B to accommodation for guests the said hotel included a self-contained flat on the first floor thereof which was occupied by the plaintiff and his family as a residence.

"4. Prior to and following on the completion of the said hotel the plaintiff carried on the said business and developed the same as a luxury hotel catering for customers of higher income groups and up to the time of the events   C hereinafter described the plaintiff had built up a substantial goodwill for the said business and the said hotel was well-known in Cyprus as a luxury hotel.

"5. During the years 1963 and 1964 Her Majesty's forces from the United Kingdom were operating in Cyprus with the consent of the government of Cyprus for the purposes of assisting in the maintenance of peace   D as between the Greek and Turkish sections of the population of Cyprus. The said operations by Her Majesty's forces did not constitute an engaging in war nor was any act carried out by them in the course of such operations in contemplation of any war in which the Sovereign was or has subsequently been engaged.

"6. On Dec. 29, 1963, a contingent of British troops forming part of Her   E Majesty's forces referred to in para. 5 hereof, without the consent of the plaintiff, took possession of the whole of the said hotel and its furniture and equipment and all the food and stores in the said hotel and all the other chattels of the plaintiff therein with the exception of the plaintiff's said private flat and three stores situate on the ground and second floors, and thenceforth the said hotel was continuously occupied by units of Her   F Majesty's said forces in succession, which said troops damaged or destroyed the whole of the furniture and equipment of the said hotel so that the same were no longer fit for use and damaged or destroyed the interior decoration of the hotel and consumed the whole of the stock of food and stores therein, and the plaintiff's said business and the goodwill thereof were thereby wholly destroyed.   G

"7. The acts referred to in para. 6 hereof were carried out pursuant to and in accordance with the orders of the General Officer Commanding Her Majesty's troops in Cyprus, a servant of the Crown, or alternatively pursuant to and in accordance with the orders of his duly authorised subordinate commander. The said acts were performed on behalf of the Sovereign in the exercise of the royal prerogative.   H

"8. The said troops continued in occupation of the said hotel and its contents until Mar. 27, 1964, and thereafter notwithstanding that the said United Kingdom force operated with or became a part of the United Nations force in Cyprus and continued in such occupation until on or about May 5, 1964, in accordance with the orders of the said General Officer Commanding or his subordinate commander and in further or continued   I exercise of the royal prerogative on behalf of the Sovereign.

"9. On or about May 5, 1964, the British troops then in occupation of the said hotel, acting on the orders of their General Officer Commanding or his duly authorised subordinate commander in further exercise of the royal prerogative on behalf of the Sovereign handed over the said hotel and its contents to a contingent of Finnish troops forming part of the United Nations force in Cyprus since which date the said hotel has been in

A   the possession of successive units of the said United Nations force and
possession thereof has never been returned to the plaintiff.

"10. On a date which the plaintiff is unable to state save that it was
between Mar. 17, 1964, and May 5, 1964, and during the period of the
occupation of the said hotel by Her Majesty's forces as aforesaid the
plaintiff's said private flat on the first floor of the said hotel was broken
B   into and its contents looted [by British troops]."

I was told by counsel for the plaintiff that the plaintiff left his flat on Mar. 17,
1964, but at all material times the hotel and its grounds were surrounded by a
barbed wire perimeter and that the flat was found by Finnish troops on May 7,
1964, to have been broken into and looted some time before their entry. Counsel
on behalf of the Attorney-General agreed that I should treat para. 10 as amended
C   by adding the words "by British troops" so that the paragraph ends with the
allegation that the flat was looted by British troops. The statement of claim
continues:

"11. In so far as may be necessary, the plaintiff will contend that the
whole of the damage sustained by him as hereinafter set out was incurred
D   during and as a result of the occupation of the hotel by Her Majesty's forces
as aforesaid.

"12. In the premises it is just and equitable that the plaintiff should
receive, and the plaintiff will submit that he is entitled to receive, compensation for the loss and damage sustained by him consequential upon the
said seizure and occupation and continued occupation and use of the hotel
E   and its contents and the consumption of food and stores and the handing
over of the said hotel as aforesaid.

"13. In the alternative, when the said H.M. forces acting under orders
as aforesaid took possession of the said hotel and its contents on Dec. 29,
1963, as aforesaid, such action gave rise to an implied undertaking by
the Crown to compensate the plaintiff in respect of the use and occupation
F   of the said hotel and its contents by Her Majesty's forces and any consequential damage sustained by the plaintiff. Further and in the alternative
at an interview with the plaintiff on Dec. 29, 1963, Sir Arthur Clark, British
High Commissioner in Cyprus, in the presence and with the acquiescence
of the Rt. Hon. Duncan Sandys, M.P., Her Majesty's Secretary of State
for Commonwealth Relations attending on behalf of the Crown, orally
G   expressly undertook that the plaintiff would be paid or compensated so
that he would suffer no loss in respect of the said seizure and occupation.
Following on the said undertaking the said troops remained in possession of
the said hotel and its contents as aforesaid. The said express undertaking
was by way of confirmation of the said implied undertaking and was in
consideration of the plaintiff's implied acceptance of the same and his
H   implied undertaking to take no action in respect of the said occupation so
long as the said promise on behalf of the Crown was implemented within
a reasonable time. In the premises the plaintiff will submit that there is a
binding contract entered into by him with the Crown under which he is
entitled to payment or compensation as aforesaid. In breach of the said
contract Her Majesty's Ministers have failed to make any payment to the
I   plaintiff in respect of the matters aforesaid. The plaintiff will claim the
sums referred to in para. 16 hereof as being monies due under the said
agreement or alternatively as damages for breach of contract.

"14. Further and in the alternative it was an implied term of the contract
referred to in para. 13 hereof that on Her Majesty's forces vacating the said
hotel the same would be handed back to the plaintiff. In breach of the said
agreement the said H.M. forces on the orders of the General Officer Commanding, as servant of the Crown, failed to deliver possession of the said
hotel back to the said plaintiff but on or about May 5, 1964, handed over

the said hotel to United Nations or Finnish forces as aforesaid and the
plaintiff has thereby suffered loss and damage.

Particulars

" The plaintiff will claim such part (if any) of the sums referred to in para.
16 hereof as are attributable to the occupation of the said hotel by United
Nations forces from May 5, 1964, onwards.

" 15. In the alternative the said conduct of the said British troops constituted a trespass upon the furniture and equipment and other chattels of
the plaintiff at the said hotel and the plaintiff has thereby suffered the
loss and damage hereinafter set out.

" 16. By reason of the said seizure and occupation and other acts of
the said H.M. forces and further and in the alternative by reason of the said
handing over by them and further and in the alternative by reason of the
said breach of contract or in the further alternative by reason of the said
trespass the plaintiff has suffered loss and damage."

Particulars of damage were then set out (see p. 203, letter B, ante). The statement of claim ended as follows:

" The plaintiff claims—

" 1. a declaration: (i) that the plaintiff is entitled to be compensated
by the Crown in respect of the seizure of the Cornaro Hotel, near Nicosia,
Cyprus, and its contents by Her Majesty's forces on Dec. 29, 1963, and
the occupation thereof by Her Majesty's forces until May 5, 1964, and in
respect of the handing over of the said hotel to United Nations forces on
May 5, 1964, all and each of which said acts were carried out in exercise
of the royal prerogative.

" (ii) That in assessing the amount of such compensation the amount payable to the plaintiff should relate to the said seizure and the occupation
of the said hotel by Her Majesty's forces (whether or not as part of the
United Nations forces) up till May 5, 1964, and the said occupation by
United Nations forces from May 5, 1964, onwards during such period that the
plaintiff as tenant would otherwise have been entitled to occupy the said
hotel (including the period of extended or new tenancy in respect of which
the plaintiff was entitled to an option) and that the amount payable to the
plaintiff shall include compensation in respect of the following matters
during the periods aforesaid . . ."

Then a number of matters are set out, and the statement of claim continues—

" 2. In the alternative a declaration that there was a valid and binding
contract between the Crown and the plaintiff whereby the Crown undertook
to compensate the plaintiff on the basis set out in para. 13 hereof and in
the terms set out in para. 14 hereof and that by reason thereof the plaintiff
is entitled to compensation and/or damages for breach of contract on the
basis set out in para. 13 and para. 14 hereof.

" 3. In the alternative a declaration that the Crown is bound to pay to the
plaintiff damages for trespass on the basis set out in para. 16 hereof or
on such other basis as the court may think fit.

" 4. Such further or other declaratory relief as the court may think fit.

" 5. The payment to the plaintiff of compensation for his said loss and
damage.

" 6. Payment of the amount found due to the plaintiff under the contract
referred to in para. 13 hereof.

" 7. Damages for breach of contract.

" 8. Damages for trespass.

" 9. Further or other relief as the court shall think fit."

There appear clearly from this statement of claim, drawn with manifest care and

A skill, distinct claims and causes of action: (i) in justice and equity to compensation as of right (para. 12: " the first claim "); (ii) in contract for money due or damages (para. 13 and para. 14: " the second claim "); (iii) in tort for trespass to chattels (para. 15: "the third claim "), which I do not treat as including the chattels in the flat because of the concession by counsel for the plaintiff, Mr. Nissan, to which I will refer later.

B By the terms of the master's order the only paragraphs in the defence relevant to the issue which I have to try are para. 3, para. 4, para. 5 and para. 6, which are in these terms:

C " 3. As a result of civil strife between the Greek and Turkish communities in the Republic of Cyprus in December, 1963, the governments of the United Kingdom, Greece and Turkey on Dec. 24, 1963, addressed the following appeal and offer of good offices to the Cyprus government: ' The British, Greek and Turkish governments as signatories of the Treaty of Guarantee of 1960, jointly appeal to the government of Cyprus and to the Greek and Turkish communities in the Island to put an end to the present disorders. They appeal to the Cyprus government to fix a suitable hour this evening for a cease-fire and to call upon both communities to observe it. The three

D governments, mindful of the rule of law, further offer their joint good offices with a view to helping to resolve the difficulties which have given rise to the present situation '. On Dec. 25, 1963, the Cyprus government issued the following communique: ' The government of the Republic of Cyprus has accepted an offer that the forces of the United Kingdom, Greece and Turkey, stationed in Cyprus and placed under British command, should

E assist it in its effort to secure the preservation of cease-fire and the restoration of peace.'."

It was agreed by counsel that the " offer " of " joint good offices " referred to in this appeal was supplemented by an offer in the terms of this communique which accepted it.

F " 4. The relevant British forces operating in the Republic of Cyprus between Dec. 26, 1963, and Mar. 27, 1964, were part of the force under British command assisting the Cyprus government in its effort to secure the preservation of cease-fire and the restoration of peace pursuant to the agreement recorded in the said communique, which is hereinafter referred to as ' the truce force '. In the premises the truce force and the British

G elements comprised therein were agents of the Cyprus government and the actions of the truce force were acts of state of the Cyprus government which are not cognizable by this Honourable Court. Alternatively the actions of the British elements were acts of state of Her Majesty on the territory of an independent sovereign power performed in pursuance of an agreement between Her Majesty and the said power which equally are not so cognizable."

H What the defence calls the truce force thus began to operate on Dec. 26, 1963, but Mr. Nissan's hotel was not occupied until Dec. 29, and I can treat the period with which the first question of law is concerned (" the first period ") as beginning on the later date.

" 5. On Mar. 4, 1964, the Security Council of the United Nations recom-

I mended the creation, with the consent of the Cyprus government, of a United Nations Peace-Keeping Force in Cyprus. By a letter of Mar. 4, 1964, the Foreign Minister of Cyprus informed the Secretary General of the consent of the Cyprus government to the creation of the said force. The said force was established on Mar. 27, 1964. The terms of an agreement concerning the legal status of the said force were set out in a letter from the Secretary-General to the Foreign Minister of Cyprus dated Mar. 31, 1964. The agreement was by its terms deemed to have taken effect from the date of the arrival of the first element of the said force in Cyprus (Mar. 27, 1964) and was

ratified by Law No. 29 of 1964 of the Republic of Cyprus. The defendant A
will refer to the agreement for its full terms and effect.

" 6. The British forces operating in the Republic of Cyprus from and
after Mar. 27, 1964, were contingents of the United Nations force aforesaid.
In the premises no action lies against the Crown in respect of any of the
actions of the said forces."

It was eventually made clear by counsel for the Attorney-General and accepted B
by counsel for Mr. Nissan that the last sentence of para. 6 covered three separate
contentions in respect of the period with which the second question of law is
concerned (" the second period "): 1. The United Nations force and the British
contingents of it were agents of the Cyprus government and their actions were
acts of state of the Cyprus government. 2. The force and its British contingents
were agents of the United Nations and their actions were " acts of state " of C
the United Nations; if they may be so described, " acts of the United Nations ".
3. The actions of the British contingent were acts of state of Her Majesty on the
territory of an independent sovereign power performed in pursuance of the
agreement between the United Nations and the Cyprus government referred
to in para. 5 of the defence and of an agreement between the United Nations
and the British government, Treaty Series No. 32 (1966), Cmnd. 3017, which D
took effect on Mar. 27, 1964. It was conceded by counsel for the Attorney-
General that the claim in trespass to the chattels in the hotel excluding the
flat must go forward even if he succeeded in his defence to the claims for compensation and in contract. Counsel for Mr. Nissan conceded that his claims in
respect of the contents of the flat and in respect of any damage caused to Mr.
Nissan by occupation of the hotel since May 5, 1964, might be recoverable as E
compensation, but not under any other head of claim.

The questions of law, therefore, which I have to try are these—(a) Do the
allegations (in para. 4 of the defence) that in the first period the acts of which
Mr. Nissan complains were either (1) acts of state of the Cyprus government
or (2) acts of state of Her Majesty on the territory of an independent sovereign
power performed in pursuance of an agreement between Her Majesty and that F
power, disclose a good defence in law to the claims (i) for compensation; (ii)
in contract? (b) Do the allegations (in para. 6 of the defence as expounded in
argument) that in the second period the acts of which Mr. Nissan complains
were either (1) acts of state of the Cyprus government or (2) acts of state of the
United Nations; or (3) acts of state of Her Majesty performed on that territory
in pursuance of an agreement between Her Majesty and the United Nations G
and an agreement between the United Nations and the Cyprus government,
disclose a good defence in law to the claims (i) for compensation; (ii) in contract?

Questions of law which arise on the statement of claim (1) for determination
in the course of deciding the preliminary issue are—(A) Whether the acts pleaded
in para. 6 were " performed on behalf of the Sovereign in the exercise of the
royal prerogative ", as alleged in para. 7 of the statement of claim. (B) Whether, H
if they were, Mr. Nissan is entitled to receive compensation for the loss and
damage they are alleged to have caused him, as alleged in para. 12. (C) Whether
the acts give rise to an implied undertaking by the Crown to compensate him,
as alleged in para. 13. (D) Whether on the facts pleaded in para. 13 an acceptance
or undertaking by Mr. Nissan ought to be implied as alleged in that paragraph.
(E) Whether, if that acceptance or undertaking ought to be implied, it would I
be a good consideration for the undertaking alleged to have been given by the
Crown and so create a binding contract to pay compensation. The question
whether the term referred to in para. 41 ought to be implied needs no answer
in consequence of the concession made on that part of the claim.

Mr. Nissan is and was at all material times a British subject, as the statement

_____

(1) The relevant paragraphs in the statement of claim are set out at p. 204, letter E,
to p. 205, letter B, ante.

A   of claim alleges. His hotel is in the Island of Cyprus which has been, since Aug. 16, 1960, the territory of an independent sovereign republic. The hotel is not in either of the two Sovereign Base Areas over which Her Majesty's sovereignty and jurisdiction remain unaffected, but it is in that part of the island over which Her Majesty no longer has any sovereignty or jurisdiction; see Cyprus Act, 1960 (2) and the Republic of Cyprus Order in Council, 1960 (3). The British

B   Nationality (Cyprus) Order, 1960 (4) is agreed to have no application to this case.

The 1960 constitution of the Republic of Cyprus was guaranteed on July 28, 1960, by the British, Greek and Turkish Governments under a treaty, and it was as signatories of that treaty of guarantee that the three governments made the appeal and offer set out in para. 3 of the defence (5). The agreement recorded in the communiqué of Dec. 25, 1963, has to be treated as completely

C   recorded in it. It was not suggested that there were any additional terms in the offer of a truce force to which I have already referred. If there are any terms not expressed in the communiqué, they can only be terms to be implied, possibly in accordance with principles less stringent than are applicable to a commercial agreement. By contrast, the agreement of March, 1964, which is referred to in para. 5 of the defence (6) ultimately contained, with effect from

D   Mar. 27, 1964, elaborate written provisions. The fact that the force occupying Mr. Nissan's hotel occupied it in each period pursuant to agreements with an independent sovereign state or with the United Nations may be enough to establish the Crown's defence of acts of state. The question whether the force occupied it as agents of that state, of the United Nations, or of neither must depend on the terms of those agreements. The express terms of the agreement

E   under which the hotel was occupied in the first period are, as I have explained, fully set out in para. 3 of the defence. I come, therefore, to the express terms of the agreements of March, 1964, under which the hotel was occupied in the second period. These terms are all conveniently set out in Cmnd. 3017, to which I have already referred (7), except Law No. 29 of 1964 (8), which is set out at Supplement No. 1, Part 1, of the Official Gazette of the Republic of Cyprus,

F   No. 327 (174) of June 25, 1964.

On Mar. 4, 1964, the Security Council of the United Nations adopted a resolution (S/5575) by which it, inter alia,

" ' Recommends the creation, with the consent of the government of Cyprus, of a United Nations peace-keeping force in Cyprus. The composi-

G   tion and size of the force shall be established by the Secretary-General, in consultation with the governments of Cyprus, Greece, Turkey and the United Kingdom. The commander of the force shall be appointed by the Secretary-General and report to him. The Secretary-General, who shall keep the governments providing the force fully informed, shall report periodically to the Security Council on its operation; Recommends that the

H   function of the force should be, in the interest of preserving international peace and security, to use its best efforts to prevent a recurrence of fighting and, as necessary, to contribute to the maintenance and restoration of law and order and a return to normal conditions; Recommends that the stationing of the force shall be for a period of three months, all costs pertaining to it being met, in a manner to be agreed upon by them, by the Governments

I

(2) 8 & 9 Eliz. 2 c. 52. For the Act, see 40 Halsbury's Statutes (2nd Edn.) 248.
(3) S.I. 1960 No. 1368. See also the Sovereign Base Areas of Akrotiri and Dhekelia Order in Council, 1960, S.I. 1960 No. 1369 and the Sovereign Base Areas of Akrotiri and Dhekelia (Boundaries) Order in Council, 1962, S.I. 1962 No. 396.
(4) S.I. 1960 No. 2215.
(5) Paragraph 3 is set out at p. 207, letters C to E, ante.
(6) Paragraph 5 is set out at p. 207, letter I, to p. 208, letter A, ante.
(7) Treaty Series No. 32 of 1966.
(8) The Legal Status of the United Nations Force in Cyprus (Ratification) Law, 1964, dated June 25, 1964.

providing the contingents and by the Government of Cyprus. The Secretary-   **A**
General may also accept voluntary contributions for that purpose; ' Subsequent resolutions of the security council have extended the mandate of the
force for successive three month periods.''

On Mar. 4, 1964, the Minister for Foreign Affairs of Cyprus informed the Secretary-
General of the United Nations of the consent of the Cyprus government to the
creation of that force in terms which are not before me. On Mar. 31, 1964,   **B**
the Secretary-General wrote to the Minister for Foreign Affairs of Cyprus as
follows:

" Sir, I have the honour to refer to the resolution adopted by the Security
Council of the United Nations on Mar. 4, 1964. In para. 4 of that resolution
the Security Council recommended the creation, with the consent of the
government of the Republic of Cyprus, of a United Nations peace-keeping   **C**
force in Cyprus. By letter of Mar. 4, 1964, the Minister for Foreign Affairs
of Cyprus informed the Secretary-General of the consent of the government
of the Republic of Cyprus to the creation of the force. The force was
established on Mar. 27, 1964. I have also the honour to refer to art. 105
of the Charter of the United Nations which provides that the organization
shall enjoy in the territory of its members such privileges and immunities as   **D**
are necessary for the fulfilment of its purposes, and to the Convention on
the Privileges and Immunities of the United Nations to which Cyprus is a
party. Having in view the provisions of the Convention on the Privileges
and Immunities of the United Nations, I wish to propose that the United
Nations and Cyprus should make the following ad hoc arrangements
defining certain of the conditions necessary for the effective discharge of the   **E**
functions of the United Nations force while it remains in Cyprus.''

The arrangements are then set out under twenty-eight headings. They number
forty-five and include:

" 1. The ' United Nations Force in Cyprus ' (hereinafter referred to as
' the force ') consists of the United Nations Commander appointed by the   **F**
Secretary-General in accordance with the Security Council resolution of
Mar. 4, 1964, and all military personnel placed under his command. For
the purpose of these arrangements the term ' member of the force ' refers
to any person, belonging to the military service of a state, who is serving
under the commander of the United Nations force and to any civilian
placed under the commander by the state to which such civilian belongs.   **G**
2. ' Cypriot authorities ' means all state and local, civil and military
authorities of the government of the Republic of Cyprus called upon to
perform functions relating to the force under the provisions of these
arrangements, without prejudice to the ultimate responsibility of the
government of the Republic of Cyprus (hereinafter referred to as ' the
government'). 3. ' Participating State ' means a Member of the United   **H**
Nations that contributes military personnel to the force . . .

International status of the force and its members.

" 5. Members of the force shall respect the laws and regulations of Cyprus
and shall refrain from any activity of a political character in Cyprus and
from any action incompatible with the international nature of their duties
or inconsistent with the spirit of the present arrangements. The commander   **I**
shall take all appropriate measures to ensure the observance of these
obligations. 6. The government undertakes to respect the exclusively international character of the force as established by the Secretary-General in
accordance with the Security Council resolution of Mar. 4, 1964, and the
international nature of its command and function . . .

Jurisdiction

" 10 The following arrangements respecting criminal and civil jurisdiction
are made having regard to the special functions of the force and to the

A   interests of the United Nations, and not for the personal benefit of the members of the force.

" *Criminal jurisdiction.* 11. Members of the force shall be subject to the exclusive jurisdiction of their respective national States in respect of any criminal offences which may be committed by them in Cyprus.

" *Civil jurisdiction.* 12. (a) Members of the force shall not be subject
B   to the civil jurisdiction of the courts of Cyprus or to other legal process in any matter relating to their official duties. In a case arising from a matter relating to the official duties of a member of the force and which involves a member of the force and a Cypriot citizen, and in other disputes as agreed, the procedure provided in para. 38 (b) shall apply to the settlement. (b) In those cases where civil jurisdiction is exercised by the courts of Cyprus with
C   respect to members of the force, the courts or other Cypriot authorities shall grant members of the force sufficient opportunity to safeguard their rights . . .

" *Military police: arrest: transfer of custody and mutual assistance.* 14. The commander shall take all appropriate measures to ensure maintenance of discipline and good order among members of the force. To this end military
D   police designated by the commander shall police the premises referred to in para. 19 of these arrangements, such areas where the force is deployed in the performance of its functions, and such other areas as the commander deems necessary to maintain discipline and order among members of the force. For the purpose of this paragraph the military police of the force shall have the power of arrest over members of the force.

E   " *Premises of the force.* 19. The government shall provide without cost to the force and in agreement with the commander such areas for headquarters, camps, or other premises as may be necessary for the accommodation and the fulfilment of the functions of the force. Without prejudice to the fact that all such premises remain the territory of Cyprus, they shall be inviolable and subject to the exclusive control and authority of the
F   commander, who alone may consent to the entry of officials to perform duties on such premises.

" *Uniform: vehicle, vessel and aircraft markings and registration: operating permits.* 21. Members of the force shall normally wear their national uniform with such identifying United Nations insignia as the commander may prescribe . . .

G   " *Privileges and immunities of the force.* 23. The force as a subsidiary organ of the United Nations, enjoys the status, privileges and immunities of the organisation in accordance with the Convention on the Privileges and Immunities of the United Nations. The provisions of art. 2 of the Convention on the Privileges and Immunities of the United Nations shall also apply to the property, funds and assets of participating states used in Cyprus
H   in connexion with the national contingents serving in the force . . .

" *Settlement of disputes or claims.* 38. Disputes or claims of a private law character shall be settled in accordance with the following provisions: (a) the United Nations shall make provisions for the appropriate modes of settlement of disputes or claims arising out of contract or other disputes or claims of a private law character to which the United Nations is a party
I   other than those covered in sub-paras. (b) and (c) following. (b) Any claim made by (i) a Cypriot citizen in respect of any damages alleged to result from an act or omission of a member of the force relating to his official duties: (ii) the government against a member of the force; or (iii) the force or the government against one another, that is not covered by paras. 39 or 40 of these arrangements, shall be settled by a claims commission established for that purpose. One member of the commission shall be appointed by the Secretary-General, one member by the government and a chairman jointly by the Secretary-General and the government. If the Secretary-General and

the government fail to agree on the appointment of a chairman, the   **A**
President of the International Court of Justice shall be asked by either to
make the appointment. An award made by the claims commission against
the force or a member thereof or against the government shall be notified to
the commander or the government, as the case may be, to make satisfaction
thereof . . . 39. All differences between the United Nations and the government arising out of the interpretation or application of these arrangements   **B**
which involve a question of principle concerning the Convention on the
Privileges and Immunities of the United Nations shall be dealt with in
accordance with the procedure of s. 30 of the Convention. 40. All other
disputes between the United Nations and the government concerning the
interpretation or application of these arrangements which are not settled
by negotiation or other agreed mode of settlement shall be referred for   **C**
final settlement to a tribunal of three arbitrators, one to be named by
the Secretary-General of the United Nations, one by the government
and an umpire to be chosen jointly by the Secretary-General and the
government . . .

" *Effective date and duration.* 45. Upon acceptance of this proposal by your
government, the present letter and your reply will be considered as con-   **D**
stituting an agreement between the United Nations and Cyprus that shall
be deemed to have taken effect as from the date of the arrival of the first
element of the force in Cyprus, and shall remain in force until the departure
of the force from Cyprus. The effective date that the departure has occurred
shall be defined by the Secretary-General and the government. The provisions of paras. 38, 39 and 40 of these arrangements, relating to the settle-   **E**
ment of disputes, however, shall remain in force until all claims arising prior
to the date of termination of these arrangements, and submitted prior to or
within three months following the date of termination, have been settled.
In conclusion I wish to affirm that the activities of the force will be guided
in good faith by the task established for the force by the Security Council.
Within this context the force, as established by the Secretary-General and   **F**
acting on the basis of his directives under the exclusive operational direction
of the commander, will use its best endeavours, in the interest of preserving
international peace and security, to prevent a recurrence of fighting and, as
necessary, to contribute to the maintenance and restoration of law and order
and a return to normal conditions."

The Minister's reply, dated the same day, was as follows: **G**

" Sir, I have the honour to refer to your letter of Mar. 31, 1964, in which
you have proposed that the Republic of Cyprus and the United Nations
should make the ad hoc arrangements contained therein which define certain
of the conditions necessary for the effective discharge of the functions of the
United Nations force in Cyprus while it remains in Cyprus. Recalling that   **H**
by letter of Mar. 4, 1964, I informed you of the agreement of the government
of the Republic of Cyprus to the establishment of the force, I now have
the pleasure to inform you in the name of the government of the Republic
of Cyprus of its full agreement on, and its acceptance of, the terms of your
letter. The government of the Republic of Cyprus agrees, furthermore, that
subject to ratification by the Republic of Cyprus, your letter and this reply   **I**
will be considered as constituting an agreement between Cyprus and the
United Nations concerning the status of the United Nations force in Cyprus.
Pending such ratification the government of the Republic of Cyprus undertakes to give provisional application to the arrangements contained in your
letter and to use its best efforts to secure the earliest possible ratification of
the agreement. In conclusion, I wish to affirm that the government of the
Republic of Cyprus, recalling the Security Council resolution of Mar. 4, 1954,
and, in particular, paras. 2 and 5 thereof, will be guided in good faith, when

A exercising its sovereign rights on any matter concerning the presence and functioning of the force, by its acceptance of the recommendation of the Security Council that a peace-keeping force be established in Cyprus."

The agreement constituted by this exchange of letters was ratified not later than June 25 by Law No. 29 (The Legal Status of the United Nations Force in Cyprus (Ratification) Law, 1964), which I need not read. On Apr. 25, 1964, forty regula-

B tions for the United Nations force in Cyprus (UNFICYP) were issued by the Secretary-General to be effective from May 10, 1964. They included:

" 1. *Issuance of regulations.* The regulations for the United Nations Force in Cyprus (UNFICYP) (hereinafter referred to as the force) are issued by the Secretary-General and shall be deemed to take effect from the date that

C the first elements of the force are placed under the United Nations commander . . .

" 2. *Authority of regulations.* The present regulations and supplemental instructions and orders issued pursuant thereto shall be binding upon all members of the force. Contravention thereof shall constitute an offence subject to disciplinary action in accordance with the military laws and regulations

D applicable to the national contingent to which the offender belongs."

Those are two of the general provisions. Chapter II begins " International Character, Uniform, Insignia, and Privileges and Immunities ", and I need only read—

" 6. *International character.* The United Nations Force in Cyprus is a subsidiary organ of the United Nations established pursuant to the resolution

E of the Security Council of Mar. 4, 1964, and consists of the commander and all personnel placed under his command by member States. The members of the force, although remaining in their national service, are, during the period of their assignment to the force international personnel under the authority of the United Nations and subject to the instructions of the commander, through the chain of command. The functions of the force are

F exclusively international and members of the force shall discharge these functions and regulate their conduct with the interest of the United Nations only in view."

Chapter III deals with authority and command in the United Nations Force in Cyprus, and I must read reg. 11, reg. 12 and reg. 13:

G " 11. *Command authority.* The Secretary-General, pursuant to authority under the resolution of the Security Council of Mar. 4, 1964, shall issue directives to the commander as appropriate. The commander exercises in the field full command authority of the force. He is operationally responsible for the performance of all functions assigned to the force by the United Nations, and for the deployment and assignment of troops placed at the

H disposal of the force.

" 12. *Chain of command and delegation of authority.* The commander shall designate the chain of command for the force, making use of the officers of his headquarters staff and the commanders of the national contingents made available by participating governments. He may delegate his authority through the chain of command. Changes in commanders of national con-

I tingents made available by participating governments shall be made in consultation among the Secretary-General, the commander and the appropriate authorities of the participating government concerned.   The commander may make such provisional emergency assignments as may be required. Subject to the provisions of these regulations, the commander has full and exclusive authority with respect to all assignments of members of his headquarters staff and, through the chain of command, of all members of the force, including the deployment and movement of all contingents in the force and units thereof. Instructions from the principal organs of the

United Nations shall be channelled by the Secretary-General through the **A** commander and the chain of command designated by him.

" 13. *Good order and discipline.* The commander shall have general responsibility for the good order and discipline of the force. He may make investigations, conduct inquiries and require information, reports and consultations for the purpose of discharging this responsibility. Responsibility for disciplinary action in national contingents provided for the force **B** rests with the commanders of the national contingents. Reports concerning disciplinary action shall be communicated to the commander who may consult with the commander of the national contingent and, if necessary, through the Secretary-General with the authorities of the participating state concerned."

Chapter IV deals with general administrative, executive and financial **C** arrangements. Regulation 16 provides:

" 16. *Authority of the Secretary-General.* The Secretary-General of the United Nations shall have authority for all administrative and executive matters affecting the force and for all financial matters pertaining to the receipt, custody and disbursement of voluntary contributions in cash or in **D** kind for the maintenance and operation of the force. He shall be responsible for the negotiation and conclusion of agreements with governments concerning the force, the composition and size of the force being established in consultation with the governments of Cyprus, Greece, Turkey and the United Kingdom, and the manner of meeting all costs pertaining to the force being agreed by the governments providing contingents and by the government of **E** Cyprus. Within the limits of available voluntary contributions he shall make provisions for the settlement of any claims arising with respect to the force that are not settled by the governments providing contingents or the government of Cyprus. The Secretary-General shall establish a special account for the United Nations force in Cyprus to which will be credited all voluntary cash contributions for the establishment, operation and main- **F** tenance of the force and against which all payments by the United Nations for the force shall be charged. The United Nations financial responsibility for the provision of facilities, supplies and auxiliary services for the force shall be limited to the amount of voluntary contributions received in cash or in kind."

Chapter V provides for the rights and duties of members of the force, and reg. 29 **G** is in these terms:

" 29. *Jurisdiction.* (a) Members of the force shall be subject to the criminal jurisdiction of their respective national states in accordance with the laws and regulations of those states. They shall not be subject to the criminal jurisdiction of the courts of the host state. Responsibility for the exercise of **H** criminal jurisdiction shall rest with the authorities of the participating state concerned, including as appropriate the commanders of the national contingents. (b) Members of the force shall not be subject to the civil jurisdiction of the courts of the host state or to other legal process in any matter relating to their official duties. (c) Members of the force shall remain subject to the military rules and regulations of their respective national states without **I** derogating from their responsibilities as members of the force as defined in these regulations and any rules made pursuant thereto. (d) Disputes involving the force or its members shall be settled in accordance with such procedures provided by the Secretary-General as may be required, including the establishment of a claims commission or commissions. Supplemental instructions defining the jurisdiction of such commissions or other bodies as may be established shall be issued by the Secretary-General in accordance with art. 3 of these regulations."

A Lastly, Chapter VII deals with the applicability of international conventions and contains one regulation:

"40. *Observance of conventions.* The force shall observe and respect the principles and spirit of the general international conventions applicable to the conduct of military personnel."

B These regulations were expressly intended, according to the Secretary-General's covering letter to the force of Apr. 25, 1964, "for the most part to continue in effect the policies and practices which have been followed in respect of the force since it came into existence " on Mar. 27, 1964, and some of them were referred to in his letter to the United Kingdom Permanent Representative to the United Nations on Feb. 21, 1966. On that date letters were exchanged between the government of the United Kingdom and the United Nations. Paragraphs C 14 and 15 of the Secretary-General's letter were as follows:

"14. It is the intention that this letter together with your reply accepting the proposals set forth herein shall constitute an agreement between the United Nations and the United Kingdom and shall be deemed to have taken effect from the date that the national contingent provided by your govern- D ment departed from its home country to assume duties with the force. It is also intended that it shall remain in force until such time as your national contingent may be withdrawn from the force either in accordance with the terms of para. 8 above or in the light of developments affecting the function- ing of the force which may render its service no longer necessary. The provisions of para. 15 relating to the settlement of disputes should remain in E force until all outstanding claims have been settled. 15. It is also proposed that all disputes between the United Nations and your government concern- ing the interpretation or application of this agreement which are not settled by negotiation or other agreed mode of settlement shall be referred for final settlement to a tribunal of three arbitrators . . ."

The reply to that was:

F "I have the honour to refer to your excellency's letter PO 210 CYPR(2) of Feb. 21, 1966, concerning the service with the United Nations force in Cyprus of the national contingent provided by the government of the United Kingdom of Great Britain and Northern Ireland. In this matter you have proposed that my government and the United Nations should enter into an agreement in accordance with the terms provided therein. My govern- G ment accepts this proposal and agrees that your letter and this reply shall constitute an agreement between the government of the United Kingdom and the United Nations . . ."

I need, I think, only add to what I have read from the Secretary-General's letter of Feb. 21, 1966, paras. 3 and 4:

H "3. I wish to express my appreciation to your government for making available a contingent to serve with the United Nations force in Cyprus. I should like to take this opportunity to bring to your attention the following considerations relating to the force, and to propose the conclusion herewith of an agreement concerning the services of your national contingent with the force. 4. The regulations referred to above affirm the international character of the force as a subsidiary organ of the United Nations and define the I conditions of service for the members of the force. National contingents provided for the force serve under these regulations."

He then directs the attention of Lord Caradon to para. 10, para. 11 and para. 12 of his letter to the Foreign Minister of Cyprus of Mar. 31, 1964 (9), and to art. 2, art. 11, art. 13, art. 29 and art. 40 of the regulations (10), all of which I have read. In para. 7 he asks for two assurances:

---

(9) The paragraphs are set out at p. 210, letter I, to p. 211, letter C.
(10) The regulations are set out at p. 213, letters C and G, p. 214, letter B, and p. 215, letters H to A, ante.

" [(i)] that the commander of the national contingent provided by your   A
government will be in a position to exercise the necessary disciplinary
authority. [(ii)] that your government will be prepared to exercise firm and
effective jurisdiction with respect to any crime or offence which might be
committed by a member of such national contingent and to report to the
United Nations in each case on the action taken."

These assurances were given in the British reply.   B

Against these facts and documents I begin by considering the nature of the first
claim (11) and the defences to it. To decide whether any of the pleaded defences
is a good defence in law to any of the claims, it is first necessary to identify, even
in these less technical days, the cause of action on which each claim rests. The
only claim in tort is the third (for trespass to goods). The first claim (for compensation) is not a claim for trespass to land. Mr. Nissan's hotel is outside the   C
realm and this court would, therefore, have no jurisdiction to entertain a claim
for trespass to it; see *British South Africa Co.* v. *Companhia de Mocambique* (12).
Indeed, it is admitted on both sides that the possession of this hotel was throughout both periods lawful, but the basis of its legality is disputed. It was on any
view permitted by the Cyprus Government and so probably justified by the law
of Cyprus, whatever the true effect (13) of Law No. 29. It was also lawful by the   D
law of England, either because it was an Act of the Crown in exercise of the
royal prerogative, as counsel for Mr. Nissan contends, or because, as counsel for
the Attorney-General says, it was, or it was authorised by, an act of state of Her
Majesty. Counsel for Mr. Nissan rests his case for prerogative compensation (the
first claim) on *Burmah Oil Co.* (*Burmah Trading*), *Ltd.* v. *Lord Advocate* (14) and
claims that the taking and destruction of property of which he complains were   E
acts carried out lawfully by, or on the authority of, the Crown in the exercise of
the royal prerogative. Such acts were not carried out in the course of actually
fighting an enemy of the Crown, nor during or in contemplation of the outbreak
of a war in which the Sovereign was, or is, engaged. If it had been the former, it
would have been battle damage and so in the opinion of all their lordships in the
Burmah Oil Co. case (14) would not give rise to any right at common law to receive   F
compensation from the Crown. If it had been the latter, it might have given rise
to such a claim, but would now be defeated by s. 1 (1) of the War Damage Act
1965 (15). The Sovereign was not, however, in 1963 or 1964, and is not now,
engaged in any war, and the hotel was taken over and damaged not in battle but
in the maintenance or restoration of peace. There was then, and it is not disputed,
no war or battle, but there was, says counsel for Mr. Nissan, an emergency   G
comparable with the emergency in which the Burmah Oil company's installations
were destroyed by an admittedly lawful act. The exercise of the prerogative in
that emergency gave those subjects of the Crown a right to receive compensation
at common law according to the decision of the majority of their lordships' House.
So, argues counsel for Mr. Nissan, this exercise of the prerogative gives this subject
the same right.   H

Two things are clear about the acts of which the Burmah Oil company and its
co-appellants complained. First, they were done on British soil within the
jurisdiction and territory of the Sovereign. Secondly, they were done during a
war in which the Sovereign was engaged. It is equally clear that the acts of which
Mr. Nissan complains were done on foreign soil outside the jurisdiction and
territory of the Sovereign, and they were not done during a war in which the   I
Sovereign was or is engaged, nor in contemplation of the outbreak of such a war.
If, therefore, they give Mr. Nissan the right to compensation which he claims,

---

(11) See p. 207, letter A, post.
(12) [1891-94] All E.R. Rep. 640; [1893] A.C. 602.
(13) The Legal Status of the United Nations Force in Cyprus (Ratification) Law,
1964, dated June 25, 1964.
(14) [1964] 2 All E.R. 348; [1965] A.C. 75.
(15) For the War Damage Act 1965, see 45 HALSBURY'S STATUTES (2nd Edn.) 1758.

A   the common law right which the House of Lords established is wide or strong or
supple enough to avoid the fatal consequences of the blow which Parliament
aimed at it in the War Damage Act 1965. Common lawyers (said counsel for the
Attorney-General) raised their eyebrows at the decision of the majority that in
such circumstances the subject had not merely a moral claim on the bounty of the
Crown for compensation, as the minority of the House thought, but a legal right
B   enforceable in the Queen's courts against the Crown as if Her Majesty were a
private individual, though generally subject to statutory restrictions which had
for the purposes of that decision to be considered not to exist in Burma. Can
their lordships really have brought to light what is really only one aspect of a
wider principle extensive enough to cover this case? Their decision ought not,
he submitted, to be extended beyond Her Majesty's jurisdiction to the territory
C   of an independent sovereign State, or, though he laid less emphasis on this, to
emergencies of peace which do not issue in war.

A common lawyer may perhaps be forgiven if, however high he may have raised
his eyebrows at the decision in the *Burmah Oil Company's* case (16), he still
rubs his eyes when he reads s. 1 (2) of the Act of 1965 (17). " Mindful of the rule
of law ", he may be expected, not indeed to advocate the cruder method of
D   reversing a decision unpopular with the executive by removing the judge who
made it and requiring from his replacement the decision which the executive
prefers, but to approach Mr. Nissan's claim with no prejudice in favour of finding
that the legislature has barred it by a section which ends in a provision so destructive not merely of the Burmah Oil company's success in the highest court of the
land but of the authority of every court of law. Mr. Nissan's claim, however,
E   can only succeed if this apparently startling decision permits it and if this at least
equally startling statute misses it. The statute undoubtedly misses it. Does the
decision permit it?

I am not, of course, hearing an application to strike out this head of claim and
I shall assume for the purpose of deciding the preliminary issue that a British
subject may have a right to compensation from the Crown for property taken or
F   destroyed or damaged by servants of the Crown in British territory within the
jurisdiction of the Crown in an emergency which does not issue in a war involving
the Crown or its territories. It may be within the prerogative of Her Majesty to
decide that there is a national or international emergency and that action must
be taken affecting the property of her subjects, indirectly in defence of her realms
and territories by helping to preserve or restore peace between nations. Their
G   lordships were concerned in the *Burmah Oil Company's* case (16) with the war
prerogative or the defence prerogative; but I am persuaded by counsel for Mr.
Nissan that their speeches do not in terms or in spirit limit the exercise of the
prerogative to defence in a sense restricted enough to exclude such an emergency
as led to the intervention of Her Majesty's and other governments in Cyprus.
Without seeking to commit the courts of this country to the doctrine that peace
H   is now indivisible, I am willing to assume in Mr. Nissan's favour that the Sovereign
may have the prerogative right, which the common law should recognise, to act
anywhere in the modern world in the interests of Her subjects, one of which may
be " the preservation of international peace and security " by contributing to the
restoration and maintenance of peace, law and order in another State. Counsel
for the Attorney-General might find it difficult on behalf of the Crown to dispute
I   that right; but what he does dispute is that its exercise to the detriment of a
British subject *in an independent sovereign State* carries with it any right to
compensation. If such detriment is suffered, it is either through an act of state

---

(16) [1964] 2 All E.R. 348; [1965] A.C. 75.
(17) Section 1 (2) provides: " Where any proceedings to recover at common law
compensation in respect of such damage or destruction have been instituted before
the passing of this Act, the court shall, on the application of any party, forthwith
set aside or dismiss the proceedings subject only to the determination of any question
arising as to costs or expenses.

for which Her Majesty is not responsible because it is not hers, or through an act   **A**
of state for which she is in truth responsible but in law not liable to answer in the
municipal courts of this country.

Although it may be logical to examine first the nature of an act of state and
whether the acts which began and continued the injury of which Mr. Nissan complains were acts of state, it will be convenient to take the submissions of counsel
for the Attorney-General in the order in which he made them and to decide first   **B**
whose acts they were in each period. Were they, as the Crown alleges, the acts of
the Cyprus government or of the United Nations? If they were the acts of the
Cyprus government, whether legislative or executive, it is clear law that they
cannot be questioned in these courts and they afford a good defence to the first
claim, even though brought by a British subject; see *Dobree* v. *Napier* (18), and
Carr v. *Fracis Times & Co.* (19). The orders of the Queen of Portugal and the   **C**
Sultan of Muscat prevented the courts from inquiring into the damage done to
the property of British subjects by Captain Napier and Captain Carr; cf. *Princess
Olga Paley* v. *Weisz* (20).

In the first period the hotel was taken over and occupied by British troops
pursuant to the agreement of December, 1963. They, from the general officer
commanding them to the lowest ranks, were servants of the Crown. They had   **D**
sworn an oath of allegiance to the Crown and were at the disposition of the Crown,
who was their head and responsible for their operations. I was referred to the
Militia Act, 1661 (13 Car. 2, c. 6), the Bill of Rights, 1688 (1 Will. & Mar. Sess.
2, c. 2), the Promissory Oaths Act, 1868 (31 & 32 Vict. c. 72) and *Chandler* v.
Director of Public Prosecutions (21), per LORD DEVLIN. It was not suggested that
the agreement of 1963 or anything else had made them the servants of the   **E**
Republic of Cyprus, as the de facto relationship of lord and servant had been
created between the Queen of Portugal and Captain Napier, who was serving
as an admiral in the Portuguese Navy (22). It was argued, however, that a species
of *agency* had been created by that agreement between one contracting party and
the armed forces of another and the taking of the hotel was within the authority
to be implied from that contractual agency. The British troops had undoubtedly   **F**
the authority of the Cyprus government to take over the hotel in the sense that
they had implied permission. But even express permission does not necessarily
create agency, otherwise the landlord would be generally responsible for the acts
of his tenant, and the owner of a motor car for the acts of anyone permitted to
drive it. Indeed, Her Majesty would be responsible for the acts of a subject who
enlisted in the service of a foreign state at war with Her Majesty by her licence   **G**
given under the Foreign Enlistment Act, 1870. If A asks or allows B to do things
for him or calls on B for help, it depends on all the circumstances whether A is
responsible as B's principal for what B does. It may be easier to fix responsibility
on A for B's acts if B has no other principal. I was pressed with the argument
that if the British commander had been an independent mercenary called in by
the Cyprus government to command a body of mercenaries, the occupation of the   **H**
hotel would have been within his authority from the Cyprus government. He
was not, however, a mercenary: he was a serving officer in Her Majesty's forces,
and the first defence pleaded in para. 4 of the defence (23) can only succeed if the
effect of the agreement pleaded in para. 3 was to substitute the government of
Cyprus for Her Majesty as the principal for whom the British elements in the
truce force were acting and to make them agents of the government of Cyprus   **I**
exclusively, not, of course, in the day to day conduct of military operations but
in such a matter as the taking over of accommodation. If they remained agents of
Her Majesty, they acted, in my judgment, within the authority they had from

---

(18) (1836), 2 Bing. N.C. 781 at p. 784.   (19) [1902] A.C. 176 at p. 177.
(20) [1929] All E.R. Rep. 513; [1929] 1 K.B. 718.
(21) [1962] 3 All E.R. 142 at p. 156; [1964] A.C. 763 at p. 807.
(22) (1836), 2 Bing. N.C. at p. 796.
(23) For para. 3 and para. 4 of the defence, see at p. 207, letters C to G, ante.

A Her when they took over and occupied the hotel, and their authority from Her Majesty to do so was not (as was suggested) inconsistent with the sovereignty of the independent Republic of Cyprus over its own territory. I hold that they did remain her agents assisting the Cyprus government, but still acting for Her Majesty's government. Counsel for the Attorney-General referred to terms in the agreement of Mar. 31, 1964 (24) and contended that their presence in that agree-

B ment made it easier to imply them in the 1963 agreement. I find it unnecessary to read any of the later terms to which he referred into the earlier agreement in order to make it intelligible or effective. If I am permitted or bound to interpret that agreement more liberally than a business contract, I still see no reason to find in it the suggested authority for this occupation. I am satisfied that in so occupying for the first period British troops were not acting as agents for the

C Cyprus government or performing acts of state for the Cyprus government.

Did the authority for their occupation change on or after Mar. 27, 1964, for the second period? The argument for the Crown would shift responsibility for the continued occupation of the hotel during this period from the government of Cyprus to the United Nations. Counsel for the Attorney-General did not abandon his contention that then also the Cyprus government was the true principal, but

D he preferred the United Nations and did not argue that both could be principals. For this period he relied not on any general agency created by the agreements of March, 1964 (including the agreement of February, 1966 (25), which took effect in March, 1964) but on specific terms creating particular agencies or giving specific authority, for instance, para. 19 of the Secretary-General's letter of Mar. 31, 1964, to the Foreign Minister of Cyprus (26); para. 3 and para. 9 of the Secretary-

E General's letter of Feb. 21, 1966, to the United Kingdom Representative (27), and reg. 11 and reg. 12 of Apr. 25, 1964 (28). Paragraph 19 he relied on mainly as creating an agency from the Cyprus government to take (in the first period) and keep (in the second) accommodation for the United Nations force. Paragraph 3 and para. 9 and reg. 11 and reg. 12 show that Her Majesty's government as a participating government made available after Mar. 27, 1964, a national con-

F tingent to serve with the United Nations force in Cyprus. The Secretary-General issued directives, including instructions from the principal organs of the United Nations, to the commander of the force appointed by the Secretary-General to exercise in the field full command of the force, and the commander is operationally responsible for the performance of all functions assigned to the force by the United Nations and may delegate his authority to the commanders of national

G contingents. Those commanders are not to be changed except in consultaton among the Secretary-General, the commander of the force, and the appropriate authorities of the participating governments. Regulation 6 declares (29) the force to be a subsidiary organ of the United Nations, and its members, although remaining in their national service, are temporarily international personnel under the authority of the United Nations and subject to the instructions of the commander,

H through the chain of command. Counsel for the Attorney-General claimed that the members of the force were temporarily servants of the commander and that his master was in turn the United Nations, who were to be treated as equivalent to an independent sovereign state. There was, after Mar. 27, 1964, no longer any occasion, he submitted, for the exercise of the Sovereign's prerogative over them or over Mr. Nissan's hotel.

I Counsel for Mr. Nissan, on the other hand, submitted that Mar. 27, 1964, brought with it no real change in the authority of the British troops to remain in

---

(24) The agreement of Mar. 31, 1964, is set out at p. 210, letter F, et seq., ante.
(25) The agreement of February, 1966, is set out at p. 215, letters C to E, ante.
(26) Paragraph 19 is set out at p. 211, letter F, ante.
(27) Paragraph 3 is set out at p. 215, letter H, ante.
(28) Regulation 11 and reg. 12 are set out at p. 213, letter G, to p. 214, letter A, ante.
(29) Regulation 6 is set out at p. 213, letters E and F, ante.

occupation of the hotel: they were still (as for the first period) at the disposal of **A** the Crown, still occupying the hotel under Crown prerogative, still serving under Queen's Regulations, and still, as para. 3 to para. 7 of the Secretary-General's letter (30) of Feb. 21, 1966, indicated, retaining their " individuality " and subject to the exclusive jurisdiction of Her Majesty's government in respect of any criminal offences committed in Cyprus and to the disciplinary authority of their own national commander. Nothing short of a statute could divest the Crown of **B** its prerogative control over them and they remained, like the troops who destroyed the Burmah Oil company's installations in Burma (31), servants and agents of the Crown and of nobody else.

The position of British contingents of a United Nations force raises, I am told, a novel and important constitutional question, although the source and extent of their authority when serving with the United Nations force are less important **C** to Mr. Nissan than the source and extent of their authority when they were part of the truce force (32) and most of the damage was done.   I have not been invited to look at the Charter of the United Nations or at the Convention on the Privileges and Immunities of the United Nations referred to in the regulations of April, 1964, or at any text book for light on the position of this contingent and its authority to act. I am asked, without objection from counsel for Mr. Nissan, to **D** look at the documents to which I have referred, and performing, not without some sense of strain, the contortion of treating the United Nations force as regulated from Mar. 27, 1964, by the regulations of April, 1964, because the agreement of Mar. 31, 1964, was adopted by the British government in February, 1966, I have come to the conclusion that on and after Mar. 27, 1964, the British troops derived their authority to occupy the hotel no longer from Her Majesty **E** but from the United Nations, and occupied it as agents of the United Nations exclusively. From that date, until they were withdrawn from service with the United Nations force, it no longer rested with the British government to say whether they stayed in the hotel or left, and the only authority which their own commander had so long as they remained members of the force to order them in or out of the hotel or any other premises required for their accommodation or the **F** fulfilment of their functions was derived from the commander of the force and through him from the United Nations. In old-fashioned language, British troops took and occupied the hotel in the Queen's name; they continued to occupy it in the name of the United Nations; they never took or occupied it in the name of the Republic of Cyprus. That conclusion would in no way impair the allegiance of British troops to the Crown, which has lent them and their services to the **G** United Nations of which the United Kingdom is a member State, or affect the sovereignty of the Crown further than it may have been affected by becoming a member of the United Nations.

It was apparently the intention of the contracting parties that the agreement between the United Nations and the Cyprus government should provide for the settlement of all claims of a private law character against the United Nations **H** force or a member of the United Nations force by means of a claims commission, including claims by a Cypriot citizen of the kind that Mr. Nissan is bringing against the Crown (33): see para. 38 (b) of the agreement. It may also have been the intention and effect of para. 38 (a) to provide for the settlement by the United Nations of his claim, whether foreseen as a possibility or not, and the intention and effect of the agreement of 1966 to recognise that provision. When, however, I look **I** at reg. 16 of the April, 1964, regulations (34), I find that para. 38 (a) of the agreement is dealing with any claims arising in respect of the force that are not settled

(30) Paragraph 3, para. 4 and para. 7 are set out at p. 215, letter H, and p. 216, letter A, ante.

(31) See *Burmah Oil Co. (Burma Trading), Ltd.* v. *Lord Advocate*, [1964] 2 All E.R. 348; [1965] A.C. 75.

(32) See p. 207, letter G, ante.

(33) Paragraph 38 (a) (b) is set out at p. 211, letter H, to p. 212, letter B, ante.

(34) Regulation 16 is set out at p. 214, letters C to F, ante.

A by the governments providing contingents or the government of Cyprus, and that leaves open the question whether this is a claim which the government of the United Kingdom will settle, whether ex gratia or ex debito justitiae. I have no information about pay and allowances or other terms of service when a British officer is " seconded " to the army of another country or when whole units of Her Majesty's forces are " seconded " (if that describes what happened here) to an

B United Nations force, and I cannot tell how far their position really resembles that of servants temporarily lent by their general employers to another master. If, however, a British officer serving with the Transjordan Frontier Force had occupied a billet in Jordan in the carrying out of his duty to police the State of Jordan, I suppose (without verifying the assumptions which underlie my illustration) that he would have been acting as agent for the King of Jordan and the Crown

C would be no more answerable in these courts for his acts than for the acts of Captain Napier (35) or Captain Carr (36). I cannot think that the authority of the United Nations over their force can differ from the authority of an independent sovereign State over its armed forces, or that what their commander orders their force to do can be questioned in these courts if orders of the same sort could not have been questioned when authorised by the Queen of Portugal (35) or the Sultan

D of Muscat (36). That may raise, or depress, the status of the United Nations, an organisation in which a number of independent sovereign States are for some purposes united, to the level of an independent sovereign State and may require that " acts of state " be extended or altered to " acts of the United Nations ". As the United Nations can, however, make agreements with such States and by such agreements establish an armed force in their territories, I find nothing

E surprising in that. It seems to me to follow that their responsibility for what their armed force did in and to Mr. Nissan's property during the second period must be the same as the responsibility of the British government for what its part of the truce force did during the first period and that if what the latter did is not cognizable by a municipal court, neither is what the former did cognizable. If it is cognizable, it is not something for which the Sovereign is responsible.

F   I next consider whether the act or acts done by the British troops in both periods were in the first period acts of state of Her Majesty and in the second acts of the United Nations equivalent to such acts of state in their legal effect. I have come to the conclusion that the actions of the British elements in the truce force of which Mr. Nissan complains were acts of state of Her Majesty on the territory of the independent sovereign Republic of Cyprus performed in pursuance of an

G agreement between Her Majesty and the republic and that they are not cognizable by this court. Counsel for Mr. Nissan submitted first, that those acts are not acts of state at all, whoever authorised them, whoever were to complain of them; secondly, that if they were acts of state, that affords no defence to Mr. Nissan's claim because he is a British subject. After considering the able arguments of counsel for the authorities they cited, I must reject both submissions. An act

H of state has been defined thus:

> " an act of the executive as a matter of policy performed in the course of its relations with another state including its relations with the subjects of that state, unless they are temporarily within the allegiance of the Crown ":

Dr. E. C. S. Wade's " Act of State in English Law " (15 British Yearbook of

I International Law (1934) 98 at p. 103) cited in 7 Halsbury's Laws (3rd Edn.) p. 279, para. 593. Such acts are done by virtue of the royal prerogative to conduct foreign policy, which is by the constitution of this country left to the Crown.

> " The prerogative is the residue of the power of sovereignty that has not been superseded or abridged or supplanted temporarily by the power of the King in Parliament "

---

(35) See *Dobree* v. *Napier*, (1836), 2 Bing. N.C. 781.
(36) See *Carr* v. *Fracis Times & Co.*, [1902] A.C. 176.

(*Burmah Oil Company's* case (37), per LORD PEARCE); and Parliament has left A
in the Sovereign's hands such typical acts of state as making treaties, declaring
war and peace or blockade, and seizing or annexing land or goods in right of
conquest, though Parliamentary sanction may be necessary in certain cases. I
regard an act of state as a prerogative act, but I do not extend the term to what
are left of the prerogative powers of the Sovereign at common law in relation to
internal government. Where the Crown pleads an act of state the courts have a B
duty to decide whether an act which has interfered with the rights of an individual
was in truth an act of state and what were its nature and extent. If satisfied that
it is in truth an act of state, it is an exercise of sovereign power which cannot be
challenged or controlled by municipal courts and their jurisdiction is ousted by
it. For the Sovereign is not answerable in her own courts for such acts of state.
So if the sovereign makes a treaty with another State, the consequences of that C
act of state are beyond the cognizance of municipal courts because they do not
administer treaty obligations between independent States; see *Salaman* v.
Secretary of State in Council of India (38), per FLETCHER MOULTON, L.J. Nor will
they, in my judgment, administer treaty obligations between an independent
State and the United Nations. This immunity of the Sovereign from the jurisdic-
tion of her own courts has been long and clearly established by many authorities, D
including: *Buron* v. *Denman* (39); *Secretary of State in Council of India* v.
Kamachee Boye Sahaba (40); *Doss* v. *Secretary of State for India in Council* (41);
Rustomjee v. *Reginam* (42), affirmed in the Court of Appeal (43) and approved
and followed by the House of Lords in *Civilian War Claimants' Association,
Ltd.* v. *Regem* (44); *Cook* v. *Sprigg* in the Privy Council (45); *West Rand Central
Gold Mining Co., Ltd.* v. *Regem* (46); and *Salaman's* case already cited (47).   E
    This immunity extends beyond the making of a treaty to the performance of
the treaty: *Rustomjee's* case, per LORD COLERIDGE, C.J. (48). Even if LUSH, J.,
may have gone too far in that case (49) in thinking that "... *all* that is done
under that treaty is as much beyond the domain of municipal law as the negotiation of the treaty itself ...", I agree with the submission of counsel for the
Attorney-General that the occupation of the hotel was an act done under the F
treaty, in performance of the treaty, and so beyond the jurisdiction of the
municipal courts. Counsel for Mr. Nissan submitted that only administrative
actions taken at a high executive level and necessary to carry out the agreements
here relied on as acts of state could share their protection. I do not have to decide
the proper limits of that protection in general or whether it extends beyond such
exalted and essential actions as could be said to be " bound up with " such G
agreements to all acts of violence authorised by the State (cf. DR. WADE's article
(50) also at p. 103); but I have no hesitation in holding that the occupation of the
hotel in December, 1963, on the orders of the general officer commanding Her
Majesty's troops in Cyprus or his duly authorised subordinate commander (para.
6 of the statement of claim (51)) was within those limits and that its continuation
under United Nations authority did not take it outside them. This seems to me to H
be supported by the statement of claim and by what is alleged of the High Commissioner and the Secretary of State for Commonwealth Relations in para. 13 of
the statement of claim (51). I therefore reject counsel's submission that what Mr.
Nissan complains of is not an act of state at all. It follows that for the second

    (37) [1964] 2 All E.R. at p. 384; [1965] A.C. at p. 148.
    (38) [1906] 1 K.B. 613 at p. 639.   I
    (39) (1848), 2 Exch. 167.   (40) (1859), 13 Moo. P.C.C. 22.
    (41) (1875), L.R. 19 Eq. 509.   (42) (1876), 1 Q.B.D. 487.
    (43) (1876), 2 Q.B.D. 69.   (44) [1931] All E.R. Rep. 432; [1932] A.C. 14.
    (45) [1895-99] All E.R. Rep. 773; [1899] A.C. 572.
    (46) [1905] 2 K.B. 391.   (47) [1906] 1 K.B. 613.
    (48) (1876), 2 Q.B.D. at p. 74.   (49) (1876), 1 Q.B.D. at p. 497.
    (50) " Act of State in English Law ", 15 BRITISH YEARBOOK OF INTERNATIONAL
LAW (1934).
    (51) Paragraph 6 and para. 13 are set out at p. 204, letters E and F, and p. 205, letters
F to I, ante.

A period possession of the hotel was authorised by an act of the United Nations equivalent to an act of state.

Counsel for Mr. Nissan says, however, that Mr. Nissan is a British subject and the defence of an act of state cannot succeed on the first claim because " between Her Majesty and one of her subjects there can be no such thing as an act of state ". That was Sir James Fitzjames Stephen's view: A History of the **B** Criminal Law of England (1883), vol. 2, p. 65, cf. p. 61; and it was treated by Lord Phillimore in *Johnstone* v. *Pedlar* (52) as finally accepted by the Privy Council in *Walker* v. *Baird* (53) and as clear law. All their lordships held in *Johnstone's* case (54) that the plea of act of state was no defence to a claim by a friendly alien resident in the United Kingdom against an officer of the Crown in respect of the seizure and detention, ratified by the Crown, of the alien's **C** personal property. Mr. Pedlar's claim was not defeated by it, nor was Mr. Baird's. Mr. Baird and his co-plaintiffs were British subjects in possession of a lobster factory in the British territory of Newfoundland. Captain Walker, the defendant, was the senior officer of Her Majesty's ships charged with putting into force and giving effect to an agreement between Her Majesty and the government of the Republic of France by which no lobster factories not in operation before a certain **D** date should be permitted unless by joint consent of the commanders of the British and French naval stations. The plaintiffs were working their too recently opened lobster factory without such consent in contravention of that agreement. Captain Walker took and kept possession of the lobster factory in accordance with the instructions of Her Majesty's government which approved and confirmed his action. The plaintiffs claimed in trespass in the Supreme Court of Newfoundland. **E** The defence pleaded that the defendant's right to possession rested on acts and matters of state arising out of the political relations between Her Majesty and the French government, that they involved the construction of treaties and that they could not be inquired into by the court. The Supreme Court held that the defence disclosed no answer. A board of no fewer than eight Privy Councillors were of the opinion that the judgment of the Supreme Court was right. The main **F** argument of the Attorney-General for the Crown in that case seems to have been that the plaintiffs as British subjects had a duty to obey the provisions of the Anglo-French Treaty as it was a treaty to prevent war and preserve peace and so akin to a treaty of peace putting an end to war. The defendant had by delegation from Her Majesty a corresponding duty to enforce obedience to the treaty for the public safety, and his acts in enforcing it were not wrongful and gave no **G** cause of action cognizable in the courts of Newfoundland. The Attorney-General did not dispute " the right of the respondents to be compensated for the loss sustained by an act of state " (55)—therein differing, if he meant literally what he is reported to have said, from his successor appearing for the Lord Advocate in the *Burmah Oil Company's* case (56)—and he conceded that other kinds of treaties could not confer on the Crown, without the sanction of Parliament, new **H** rights against its own subjects (57)—and counsel for the Attorney-General in the present case was willing to make at least as handsome a concession. The Judicial Committee, giving its advice in the judgment of Lord Herschell, rejected the main argument on the ground that the pleaded allegations did not bring the treaty within the limited class of treaties which required no such Parliamentary sanction. They, however, brushed aside as " wholly untenable ", **I** without giving reasons, the alternative suggestion that the defendant's acts could be justified as acts of state, and that the court was not competent to inquire into a matter involving the construction of treaties and other acts of state (58). The argument of counsel for the respondents was (59):

---

(52) [1921] All E.R. Rep. 176 at p. 191; [1921] 2 A.C. 262 at p. 295.
(53) [1892] A.C. 491.
(54) [1921] All E.R. Rep. 176; [1921] 2 A.C. 262.   (55) [1892] A.C. at p. 493.
(56) [1965] A.C. at p. 85.   (57) [1892] A.C. at pp. 492, 497.
(58) [1892] A.C. at p. 497.   (59) [1892] A.C. at p. 494.

". . . the right of Her Majesty to authorise an act committed by one subject **A** towards another is a question which courts have jurisdiction to determine; for as between Her Majesty and one of her subjects there can be no such thing as an act of state."

LORD PHILLIMORE was clearly justified in saying (60) that the Board accepted that argument. The lobster factory seized was, however, unlike Mr. Nissan's hotel, within the jurisdiction and territory of the Sovereign. So was Mr. Pedlar's **B** property (61). So were the destroyed installations of the Burmah Oil company, (62). But in *Johnstone's* case (63) VISCOUNT FINLAY stated it to be settled law

". . . that, if a wrongful act has been committed against the person or the property of any person, the wrongdoer cannot set up as a defence that the act was done by the command of the Crown ";**C**

that rule of law, VISCOUNT FINLAY continued, was subject to a qualification in the case of acts committed abroad against a foreigner (*Buron* v. *Denman* (64)) but that qualification had no application to any case in which the plaintiff was a British subject (*Johnstone* v. *Pedlar* (63)). VISCOUNT CAVE'S opinion was to the same effect (65). LORD ATKINSON took the same view (66) of *Walker* v. *Baird* (67) **D** and derived support for it from *Cook* v. *Sprigg* (68). LORD SUMNER implied the same limitation (69). Their lordships had not to consider the position of a British subject (or friendly alien) outside the realm, still less in foreign territories outside the jurisdiction of the Crown; but their clear and unqualified statements of the law led counsel for the Attorney-General in the present case to abandon any attempt to treat a plea of act of state as a good defence if it was pleaded against **E** a claim *in tort* by a British subject whether in British or in foreign territory.

Yet an act of state has been successfully pleaded against British subjects in some of the cases to which he referred me. *Rustomjee* (70) was a British subject; the *Dosses* (71) may have been. *Cook* (72) and his co-appellant probably were (LORD ATKINSON may have thought not: see *Johnstone's* case (73)), but the flimsy evidence of name and length of residence in Eastern Pondoland (74) suggests **F** that they were, as assumed in 7 HALSBURY'S LAWS (3rd Edn.) p. 280, para. 594, note (*l*), and in DICEY'S CONFLICT OF LAWS (7th Edn.) (1958), p. 163, note 65. *West Rand Central Gold Mining Co., Ltd.* (75) was certainly a company registered in England. *Salaman* may have been a British subject (76) (as DICEY assumes in the same note). None of these cases was cited in *Walker* v. *Baird* (67), in *Johnstone* v. *Pedlar* (77) or in *Burmah Oil Co., Ltd.* v. *Lord Advocate* (78), **G** although VISCOUNT RADCLIFFE referred there (79) to *West Rand Central Gold Mining Co., Ltd.* (75) on another point. *Walker* v. *Baird* (67) was referred to in *West Rand Central Gold Mining Co., Ltd.* (75) but not noticed in the judgments.

---

(60) In *Johnstone* v. *Pedlar*, [1921] All E.R. Rep. at p. 191; [1921] 2 A.C. at p. 295.
(61) See *Johnstone* v. *Pedlar*, [1921] All E.R. Rep. 176; [1921] 2 A.C. 262.
(62) See *Burmah Oil Co. (Burma Trading), Ltd.* v. *Lord Advocate*, [1964] 2 All E.R. **H** 348; [1965] A.C. 75.
(63) [1921] All E.R. Rep. at p. 180; [1921] 2 A.C. at pp. 271, 272.
(64) (1848), 2 Exch. 167.
(65) [1921] All E.R. Rep. at p. 182; [1921] 2 A.C. at p. 275.
(66) [1921] All E.R. Rep. at pp. 184, 185; [1921] 2 A.C. at pp. 280, 281.
(67) [1892] A.C. 491.   (68) [1895-99] All E.R. Rep. 773; [1899] A.C. 572.
(69) [1921] All E.R. Rep. at p. 189; [1921] 2 A.C. at p. 290. **I**
(70) See *Rustomjee* v. *Reginam*, (1876), 2 Q.B.D. 69.
(71) See *Doss* v. *Secretary of State for India in Council*, (1875), L.R. 19 Eq. 509.
(72) See *Cook* v. *Sprigg*, [1895-99] All E.R. Rep. 773; [1899] A.C. 572.
(73) [1921] All E.R. Rep. at p. 185; [1921] 2 A.C. at p. 281.
(74) [1899] A.C. at p. 574.
(75) See *West Rand Central Gold Mining Co., Ltd.* v. *Regem*, [1905] 2 K.B. 391.
(76) See *Salaman* v. *Secretary of State for India*, [1906] 1 K.B. 613.
(77) [1921] All E.R. Rep. 176; [1921] 2 A.C. 262.
(78) [1964] 2 All E.R. 348; [1965] A.C. 75.
(79) [1964] 2 All E.R. at p. 372; [1965] A.C. at p. 128.

A Can an act of state be a defence to a claim by a British subject in British courts? How can one reconcile *Walker's* (80) and *Johnstone's* (81) cases with the cases of *Rustomjee* (82) and *West Rand Central Gold Mining Co., Ltd.* (83) in which the principle accepted and stated without qualification in *Walker's* (80) and in *Johnstone's* case (81) was never mentioned, let alone applied?

The distinction between the two lines of authority is, counsel for the Attorney-
B General submits, a distinction between claims in tort arising out of a wrongful act, to which, if brought by a British subject, an act of state is no defence, and claims arising out of a lawful act of state, which even British subjects cannot litigate in English courts. He put forward an analogy, somewhat paradoxically, of illegality. If a cause of action arise out of a turpis causa, the court cannot enforce it, whether the illegality is pleaded or not. So if it arise out of an act of
C state, the court has no jurisdiction to entertain it and should probably decline jurisdiction whether or not invited to do so. " No court ", said LORD MANS-FIELD, " will lend its aid to a man who founds his cause of action upon an immoral or an illegal act " (see *Holman* v. *Johnson* (84)); and counsel for the Attorney-General would have to say that in this, if in no other respect, an agreement between States may resemble an immoral or illegal contract, and a plaintiff can
D enforce his rights only if he can found his claim on, for instance, a trespass or conversion outside the agreement (*Bowmakers, Ltd.* v. *Barnet Instruments, Ltd.* (85)). This claim is said to arise out of an act not immoral nor illegal but lawful, and the prerogative which makes it lawful, as both parties allege, is not the " internal " prerogative which is left in the hands of the Crown within its realms and territories, where it can be and usually is abridged or supplanted by legislative
E provisions, but the " external " prerogative which the Crown exercises in conduct-ing foreign relations and over foreign territories outside its jurisdiction, where it cannot in the nature of things be subjected to similar controls by the legislature but only to the restrictions imposed by international comity, whether in its dealing with foreign subjects or with its own.

The answer of counsel for Mr. Nissan was that the prerogative of the Crown
F applies to the relation between the Crown and its subjects (perhaps to subjects alone; see *Re Ferdinand, Ex-Tsar of Bulgaria* (86)), wherever they may be; that this claim to compensation arises out of a direct injury from a prerogative act of the Crown, as it plainly did in the *Burmah Oil Company's* case (87); that the British subjects who have been defeated by the defence of act of state were not directly injured by the Crown's servants, who indeed never had them in mind
G when acting in the way which ultimately led to interference with their rights, and that that is the true distinction between the two lines of authority. The Burmah Oil company were given a right to compensation in the courts of this country for a prerogative act which directly destroyed their property in Burma. There is, however, nothing in that case, so he argues, which suggests that the result would have been different if Burma had already become an independent sovereign state;
H the principle of that case clearly covers the first claim in this, which must accordingly succeed.

That powerful argument does not, in my judgment, prevail. Nowhere in the arguments of counsel or in the speeches of the law lords in the *Burmah Oil Company's* case (87) is an act of state ever mentioned. That is because in the exceptional course which that case took there could (apart from the question
I whether the Public Authorities Protection Act, 1893, barred the claim) be no relevance in that or any other point but one. The only issue before the House was

---

(80) [1892] A.C. 491.
(81) [1921] All E.R. Rep. 176; [1921] 2 A.C. 262.
(82) See *Rustomjee* v. *Reginam*, (1876), 2 Q.B.D. 69.
(83) See *West Rand Central Gold Mining Co., Ltd.* v. *Regem*, [1905] 2 K.B. 391.
(84) (1775), 1 Cowp. 341 at p. 343.
(85) [1944] 2 All E.R. 579; [1945] K.B. 65.
(86) [1921] 1 Ch. 107 at p. 139, per WARRINGTON, L.J.
(87) [1964] 2 All E.R. 348; [1965] A.C. 75.

whether the admittedly lawful exercise of the prerogative in territory outside the **A**
realm but still under the British Crown gave British companies registered in
Scotland a right to be compensated by the Crown for damage thereby done.
Every one of their lordships stressed the point that the law they had to apply
was the law applicable to Burma, which was then a British Crown colony, and
that law was the common law of England not curtailed by any statutory authority
and in no way materially different from the law of Scotland. They never con-   **B**
sidered whether the destruction complained of was an act of state or the carrying
out of an act of state. They were not asked to decline jurisdiction. They never
turned their minds to the position of a British company with real property on
foreign territory or to the position of the Crown acting in execution of an international agreement on foreign territory or to a claim by the one against the other
which is founded on the acts of the Crown in those circumstances. Where such a   **C**
claim is made, the Crown can, in my judgment, plead in its defence that the very
act on which the claim is based takes it out of the jurisdiction of the courts and if
the court decides that the act is an act of state, it is disabled from proceeding to
determine whether the common law gives the right claimed. Baird (88) and
Pedlar (89) did not found their claims on matters which were acts of state, but on
torts committed within the jurisdiction of municipal courts, and no treaty was   **D**
needed to give them their causes of action. In neither case was the present
position considered.

So the cases of *Walker* (88) and *Johnstone* (89) are not in conflict with this view,
although the statements of the law lords in *Johnstone's* case (89) must, if I am
right, be read subject to the qualification that even a British subject cannot make
a claim against the Crown arising out of an act of state outside British territory.   **E**
At first sight, none of the cases from which this qualification has been extracted
resembles the instant case as closely as does the *Burmah Oil Company's* case (90).
Her Majesty's government or servants annex an independent territory, the
Kingdom of Oudh, the Raj of Tanjore, Pondoland, the Transvaal; bankers in
Calcutta who are creditors of the King of Oudh, the eldest widow of the Rajah
of Tanjore, concessionaires of rights granted by the paramount Chief of Pondo-   **F**
land, a British company whose gold is seized by the government of the South
African Republic, cannot enforce a claim against the Crown or its servants in
respect of rights of action against the Sovereign of the annexed territory except
by virtue of the act of state which is pleaded against them. Those are the cases
of *Doss* (91), *Kamachee* (92), *Cook* (93), and *West Rand Central Gold Mining Co.,
Ltd.* (94). Her Majesty's government or servants annex Lahore, confiscate the   **G**
State's property and agree to pay a pension to the Maharajah. The trustee in
bankruptcy of his residuary legatee cannot enforce a claim to arrears of pension
or an account: *Salaman's* case (95). Her Majesty by a peace treaty with the
Emperor of China obtains money out of which to pay British creditors of Chinese
merchants in Hong Kong before the war (*Rustomjee* (96)), or by a peace treaty with
Germany His Majesty agrees to obtain money to satisfy civilians caused injury   **H**
or damage by the Germans in any territory: *Civilian War Claimants' Association,
Ltd.* v. *Regem* (97). The courts held that the Crown was in neither case agent or
trustee for the claimants. In the former case the plea of act of state was upheld;
in the latter, the House of Lords were content to follow the earlier without calling
on the Attorney-General for the Crown or referring to any plea of act of state.
Nearer to the present case in some respects is *Buron's* case (98), where a   **I**

---

(88) *Walker* v. *Baird*, [1892] A.C. 491.
(89) *Johnstone* v. *Pedlar*, [1921] All E.R. Rep. 176; [1921] 2 A.C. 262.
(90) [1964] 2 All E.R. 348; [1965] A.C. 75.   (91) (1875), L.R. 19 Eq. 509.
(92) *Secretary of State in Council of India* v. *Kamachee Boye Sahaba*, (1859), 13 Moo.
P.C.C. 22.
(93) [1895-99] All E.R. Rep. 773; [1899] A.C. 572.
(94) [1905] 2 K.B. 391.   (95) [1906] 1 K.B. 613.
(96) (1876), 2 Q.B.D. 69.   (97) [1931] All E.R. Rep. 432; [1932] A.C. 14.
(98) (1848), 2 Exch. 167.

A Spaniard's claim in respect of barracoons fired and slaves freed by Commander Denman was defeated by the plea that the commander's actions, though outside the terms of the Anglo-Spanish Treaty which entitled him to stop ships, had been ratified by Her Majesty and were therefore an act of state. True Buron was not a British subject, but the principle of that case was followed and applied to aliens and British subjects alike in the later cases. Aliens like Buron (99) and Kamachee

B (100) and British subjects like Rustomjee (101) and West Rand Central Gold Mining Co., Ltd. (102) had to found their claims on acts of state and that, in my judgment, is why they failed to make the Crown responsible in any of Her Majesty's courts for the acts of state pleaded. An early attempt to found a claim to relief from the courts of this country on a treaty was made in 1791, not by a British subject but by a sovereign. " Ex pacto tali non oritur actio " was how

C LORD THURLOW, L.C., put the Attorney-General's plea to his jurisdiction to try it; see *Nabob of Carnatic* v. *East India Co.* (103). Though LORD THURLOW overruled the plea, a subsequent answer on behalf of the Crown introducing another treaty led the Lords Commissioners to dismiss the Nabob's bill two years later (104) as raising matters only cognizable by the law of nations, not by a municipal court of justice; and the death of the Nabob deprived him of his appeal and the House

D of Lords of its only opportunity hitherto to pronounce directly on the validity of such a plea (104). Mr. Nissan cannot, in my judgment, succeed where the Nabob failed and litigate in this court a claim based on a treaty or treaties between sovereign States contracting separately or collectively. I prefer the principle by which counsel for the Attorney-General reconciles and distinguishes the authorities to the principle by which counsel for Mr. Nissan seeks to do so, and I hold

E that when an act of the prerogative is sued on and the defence pleads that it is, properly understood, an act of state, a court, which on its understanding of the matter finds it to be an act of state, must decline jurisdiction.

I am glad to find confirmation of this view of the law in DICEY'S CONFLICT OF LAWS (7th Edn., 1958). Rule 21 of the General Rules as to Jurisdiction is there formulated (at p. 159) as follows:

F " The court has no jurisdiction at common law to entertain an action . . . (2) where the grounds of the action involve an act of state."

At p. 163 it is stated:

" *Act of State.* Although English courts assert jurisdiction in respect of actions by governmental officials in the United Kingdom or in any of its

G colonies they will not adjudicate upon the executive or administrative actions of the United Kingdom Government or the government of any such colony against foreigners outside these areas."

In a note to that (No. 65) already referred to, I find this:

" Even British subjects cannot claim against the British or Colonial

H Government if the claim arises out of such an act of state,"

and for that *Cook's* (105) and *Salaman's* (106) cases are cited.

In this conclusion there is much irony and little comfort for the British subject in a foreign land who looks to the power of his Sovereign's prerogative for protection from foreign governments, acting separately or together, by diplomatic or

I even armed intervention on his behalf and finds the prerogative exercised to his detriment, whatever the justification may be. Moreover it is cold consolation to him to be told that what he suffers by a blow from his protector is for the general good of all the Queen's subjects, and, it may be, of the subjects of other States as well, because it is " in the interest of preserving international peace and

(99) (1848), 2 Exch. 167.
(101) (1876), 2 Q.B.D. 69.
(103) (1791), 1 Ves. 371 at pp. 389-391.
(105) [1895-99] All E.R. Rep. 773; [1899] A.C. 572.
(100) (1859), 13 Moo. P.C.C. 22.
(102) [1905] 2 K.B. 391.
(104) (1793), 2 Ves. 56.
(106) [1906] 1 K.B. 613.

security " (107). These considerations make me reach my conclusion with some **A** reluctance, tempered by the hope that a remedy for at any rate part of Mr. Nissan's loss may be found either in the provisions of para. 38 of the 1964 agreement (108) or in the bounty of the Crown. If he proves the promise alleged to have been expressly made on Dec. 29, 1963 (109) he would indeed be justified in looking to the Crown for compensation.

There remains the second claim (110) in contract, express or implied. I am not **B** deciding whether the express undertaking alleged in para. 13 of the statement of claim (109) was given. I have to assume that it was. Can it then bind the Crown? Counsel for the Attorney-General submits that it cannot, for two reasons. First, it was outside the authority of the British High Commissioner for Cyprus, even in the presence of and with the acquiescence of Her Majesty's Secretary of State for Commonwealth Relations. Compare the view taken by the Privy Council of Mr. **C** Forbes' letter in *Kamachee's* case (111); by the Court of Appeal of the promises of Captain Elliot and Sir Henry Pottinger in *Rustomjee's* case (112), and by LORD DUNEDIN and LORD MOULTON of the facts of the Crown's entry on De Keyser's Royal Hotel in *A.-G.* v. *De Keyser's Royal Hotel, Ltd.* (113). I might add to those STIRLING, L.J.'s view of the Governor-General of India's dispatch in *Salaman's* case (114). Secondly, it was not supported by any good consideration. The only **D** consideration alleged is Mr. Nissan's implied acceptance of the undertaking and his implied cross-undertaking to take no action so long as the Crown's promise was implemented within a reasonable time. If the undertaking alleged to have been given by the High Commissioner was outside his authority or unsupported by consideration, it cannot be implied. If Her Majesty is under no legal liability enforceable in her courts to pay Mr. Nissan compensation, it is difficult to see how **E** there could be any authority, or any consideration, for a promise by any servant of hers to pay it to him. There could be express authority from Her Majesty, but it is not alleged that Sir Arthur Clark or Mr. Duncan Sandys had any express authority (115). Without it the promise would be outside their authority and the implication of any such promise is not necessary but negatived; and even if the promise were authorised and could be accepted, the only consideration alleged for it **F** is not, in my opinion, necessarily to be implied from the pleaded facts without more.

It may seem unsatisfactory to decide the claim in contract without evidence at this stage. Nevertheless I am asked to say that it stands or falls with the claim to compensation and, in my judgment, it does. If I look at the alleged contract as counsel for Mr. Nissan asked me to look at alleged acts of state, it falls within the category of acts at a high executive level which might be said to be bound up **G** with the act of state. It is therefore beyond the cognizance of the court.

I therefore answer the two questions of law raised by the pleadings as follows: (a) on the facts pleaded (116) in para. 3 and the first sentence of para. 4 of the defence, the last sentence of the said para. 4 does, but the last sentence but one does not, disclose a good defence in law to all the claims and causes of action pleaded by Mr. Nissan in respect of the events occurring between Dec. 26, 1963, **H** and Mar. 27, 1964, except the claim pleaded in para. 15 of the statement of claim for trespass on the furniture and equipment and other chattels of Mr. Nissan at the Cornaro Hotel excluding the chattels in his private flat; (b) on the facts pleaded (117) in para. 5 and the first sentence of para. 6 of the defence, the last

(107) See para. 45 of the letter from the Secretary-General of the United Nations, dated Mar. 31, 1964, cited at p. 212, letters D to G, ante.   **I**
(108) The material part of para. 38 is set out at p. 211, letter H, to p. 212, letter B, ante.
(109) See para. 13 of the statement of claim, set out at p. 205, letters F to I, ante.
(110) See p. 207, letter A, ante.
(111) (1859), 13 Moo. P.C.C. at p. 84.   (112) (1876), 2 Q.B.D. at pp. 73, 74.
(113) [1920] All E.R. Rep. 80 at pp. 84 and 97; [1920] A.C. 508 at pp. 522 and 548.
(114) [1906] 1 K.B. at pp. 637, 638.
(115) See para. 13 of the statement of claim at p. 205, letters F to I, ante.
(116) For para. 3 and para. 4 of the defence, see p. 207, letters C to G, ante.
(117) For para. 5 and para. 6 of the defence, see p. 207, letter I, to p. 208, letter A, ante.

A sentence of the said para. 6 discloses a good defence in law to all the claims and causes of action pleaded by Mr. Nissan in respect of the events occurring on and after Mar. 27, 1964. In plain terms, only Mr. Nissan's claim for trespass to the goods in the public part of his hotel before Mar. 27, 1964, can go forward to trial. He cannot take any of his other claims any further in the courts of this country—unless I am wrong.

B   Subject to anything counsel may wish to say, I make no order as to the costs of this preliminary issue, including the costs of the Attorney-General's application to Master JACOB on Oct. 27, 1966.

Judgment accordingly.

Solicitors: *Treasury Solicitor*; *Edwin Coe & Calder Woods* (for the plaintiff).

C [*Reported by* K. DIANA PHILLIPS, *Barrister-at-Law*.]

Re P. (infants).

D [CHANCERY DIVISION (Stamp, J.), February 22, 23, 24, 1967.]

Ward of Court—Jurisdiction—Previous order of magistrates under Guardianship of Infants Acts, 1886 and 1925, giving custody to father—Children then in charge of local authority under fit person order—Originating summons issued by mother to make children wards of court—Exercise by magistrates of their

E *statutory jurisdiction did not fetter prerogative jurisdiction of High Court—Forum conveniens—Magistrates' order should be reconsidered in magistrates' court unless relief was sought which the magistrates were unable to give—On application to High Court under wardship jurisdiction court would enquire whether magistrates were able to give the relief sought.*

On July 2, 1963, Chelsea Domestic Court made an order giving custody

F of two children to their mother. On Sept. 18, 1963, Chelsea Juvenile Court made a fit person order putting the children in the care of the London County Council. In February, 1964, the L.C.C. put the children in the care of their mother, but on Aug. 24, 1964, they were back with the L.C.C. On Oct. 21, 1965, the Chelsea Domestic Court made an order giving custody to the father, but the children remained in the home where they had been placed by the L.C.C. The order was affirmed by the High Court

G on May 12, 1966. The fit person order was revoked on Aug. 1, 1966, the children being placed under the supervision of the Essex County Council. The mother was not a party to the proceedings revoking the order. The London Borough of Hammersmith (which for this purpose superseded* the L.C.C.) was a party and decided to appeal. It wished the children to remain in the

H home pending the appeal, but the father wanted the children in his care and in August, 1966, he began habeas corpus proceedings on which no order was made. During the hearing the mother and the London Borough issued a summons making the children wards of court. The appeal of the London Borough against the revocation of the fit person order was dismissed on Nov. 14, 1966. After the appeal the London Borough became functus officio

I and the wardship proceedings were reconstituted, the London Borough ceasing to be a plaintiff and becoming the second defendant. The questions arose, first, whether the court, in exercising its parental jurisdiction, had power to make an order which might conflict with an order made by a magistrates' court in exercise of the statutory jurisdiction under the Guardianship of Infants Acts, 1886 and 1925, and, secondly, assuming the answer to be in the affirmative whether that jurisdiction ought to be exercised or whether the court should simply make an order de-warding the children.

---

* On Apr. 1, 1965, consequent on the London Government Act 1963.

Applied in RE D (MINORS) [1973] 2 All ER 993

Distinguished in RE D (A MINOR) [1977] 3 All ER 481

Held: (i) the exercise by the magistrates' court of its limited statutory   A
jurisdiction over children did not, in the absence of express words in the
statute, fetter the power of the Chancery Division in exercising the jurisdiction of the Crown as parens patriae over wards of court, though the
wardship jurisdiction was most usefully exercised by way of supplement to
the magistrates' courts' order where that court had not the necessary power
(see p. 234, letter H, post).   B

Re Andrews (infants) ([1958] 2 All E.R. 308); Hall v. Hall ([1963] 2 All
E.R. 140) and Re H. (G.J.) (an infant) ([1966] 1 All E.R. 952) followed.

(ii) when magistrates, in exercise of their jurisdiction under the Guardianship of Infants Acts, 1886 and 1925, had made an order for custody, then,
unless relief was sought which magistrates could not give, the forum conveniens for reconsidering that order was prima facie that magistrates' court;   C
and to decide whether to entertain a wardship application the judge should
enquire into the case to the extent necessary to determine whether relief was
genuinely sought which the magistrates were unable to give, or whether there
was some very special reason for invoking the wardship jurisdiction (see
p. 236, letter I, to p. 237, letter A, post).   D

Re K. (K.J.S.) (an infant) ([1966] 3 All E.R. 154) followed.

Re S. (an infant) ([1965] 1 All E.R. 865) distinguished.

[As to jurisdiction over wards of court, see 21 HALSBURY'S LAWS (3rd Edn.)
216, 217, paras. 478, 479; and for cases on the subject, see 28 DIGEST (Repl.)
484-486, 14-26, 606, 607, 1167-1171.   E

As to the jurisdiction of the court under the Guardianship of Infants Acts,
1886 and 1925, see 21 HALSBURY'S LAWS (3rd Edn.) 213-215, paras. 473, 474;
and for cases on the subject, see 28 DIGEST (Repl.) 606-607, 1167-1171.

As to the jurisdiction of juvenile courts, see 21 HALSBURY'S LAWS (3rd Edn.)
256, para. 555.

For the Guardianship of Infants Act, 1886, s. 5, see 12 HALSBURY'S STATUTES   F
(2nd Edn.) 943.

For the Guardianship of Infants Act, 1925, s. 3, s. 5, s. 7, see ibid., p. 955,
p. 957, p. 958.

For the Children and Young Persons Act, 1933, s. 62, see ibid., p. 1015.]

Cases referred to:

Andrews (infants), Re, [1958] 2 All E.R. 308; [1958] Ch. 665; [1958] 2 W.L.R.   G
        946; 28 Digest (Repl.) 706, 2152.

H. (G.J.) (an infant), Re, [1966] 1 All E.R. 952; [1966] 1 W.L.R. 706.

Hall v. Hall, [1963] 2 All E.R. 140; [1963] P. 378; [1963] 2 W.L.R. 1054;
        Digest (Cont. Vol. A.) 933, 2152b.

K. (K.J.S.) (an infant), Re, [1966] 3 All E.R. 154; [1966] 1 W.L.R. 1241.   H

S. (an infant), Re, [1965] 1 All E.R. 33; [1965] 1 W.L.R. 94; rvsd. C.A.,
        [1965] 1 All E.R. 865; [1965] 1 W.L.R. 483; 129 J.P. 228; 3rd Digest
        Supp.

Vigon v. Vigon and Kuttner, [1928] All E.R. Rep. 755; [1929] P. 157; 98
        L.J.P. 63; 140 L.T. 407; on appeal, C.A., [1929] P. 245; 99 L.J.P. 9;
        141 L.T. 610; 27 Digest (Repl.) 664, 6290.   I

Adjourned Summons.

This was an application by the mother of two infants by originating summons
dated Aug. 24, 1966, asking that the infants be made wards of court. The defendants were the father and the London Borough of Hammersmith. The facts
are set out in the judgment. The case was heard in camera and judgment was
given in open court. The order made was an agreed order, the parties having
come to terms approved by the court.

A   *Ian McCulloch* for the mother.
    E. A. Bramall for the father.
    Raymond Walton, Q.C., *Gavin Lightman* and *Elizabeth Appleby* for the London Borough of Hammersmith.

B   **STAMP, J.:** Counsel in opening this case, which is a wardship case in which the mother asks for care and control of two infants, said, and I agree, that it raises questions of public importance, and for this reason, although the parties have come to terms that I am able to approve, I thought it right to deliver judgment in open court. The case concerns two small children, a boy now aged six and a half and a girl now aged five. During their short lives there has raged over their heads, I hope unknown to them, a storm of litigation, culminating in a
C   clash of jurisdiction the like of which I hope will never occur again.

    The father and mother were married when the father was twenty-one and the mother just sixteen, and a child was on the way. I will only set out the uncontroverted facts with as little comment as I can on the parties, because the case did not take its full course and I have heard only part of the oral evidence. It is, however, not in doubt that from the outset the marriage was an excessively
D   unhappy one and the early summer of 1963 found the marriage broken and the parties either living apart or about to live apart.

    The subsequent history cannot be understood without some reference to the legislation affecting children. The Guardianship of Infants Act, 1886, conferred power on the High Court to appoint and remove guardians of infants, and by s. 5 of that Act it was provided that the court might on the application of the mother
E   make such order as it might think fit regarding the custody of an infant and the right of access thereto of either parent, having regard to the welfare of the infant and to the conduct of the parents and to the wishes as well of the mother as of the father and might alter, vary or discharge such order on the application of either parent, or, after the death of either parent, of any guardian under the Act of 1886. The jurisdiction so conferred was conferred only in England on the
F   High Court of Justice. That Act of 1886 did not, of course, in the least entrench on the wider paternal powers exercised by this court on behalf of the Crown as parens patriae.

    By s. 3 (2) of the Guardianship of Infants Act, 1925, it is provided that when the court makes an order under s. 5 of the Act of 1886 giving custody of the infant to the mother, then, whether or not the mother is then residing with the father,
G   the court may further order that the father shall pay to the mother towards the maintenance of the infant such weekly or other periodical sum as the court, having regard to the means of the father, may think reasonable. Section 5 of the Act of 1925 enables a father or mother to appoint a guardian of an infant after his or her death and empowers the court to resolve differences between the surviving parent and the guardian as to the guardianship and custody of the
H   infant and in such a case to make an appropriate order against the surviving parent as to the payment of maintenance. By s. 7 the jurisdiction of the High Court under the two Acts ceased to be exclusive and a court of summary jurisdiction had, in effect (subject to certain exceptions immaterial in the present instance), conferred on it the same statutory powers as the High Court. By s. 7 (3), it was provided:

I   " Where on application to the court of summary jurisdiction under the Guardianship of Infants Act, 1886, as amended by this Act, the court makes or refuses to make an order, an appeal shall, in accordance with rules of the court, lie to the High Court: Provided that, where any such application is made to a court of summary jurisdiction, and the court considers that the matter is one which would more conveniently be dealt with by the High Court, the court of summary jurisdiction may refuse to make an order, and in such case no appeal shall lie to the High Court."

The appeal is to a nominated judge of this Division.

I call attention at this point to the limitations—it is no doubt a matter for the legislature to determine whether it is a defect—of the Guardianship of Infants Acts, 1886 and 1925. Only parents and guardians can apply to a magistrates' court, or indeed to the High Court, under the provisions of those Acts. The grandmother of these little children, who I am told has behaved wisely and well in this unhappy controversy, could not have applied to a magistrates' court and, more particularly, she could not, if she had been so minded, have applied to the court of magistrates known as the Chelsea Domestic Court, for that is the court which has had partial seisin of the matter, to have care and control of the children committed to her, perhaps for a limited period, nor could the London Borough of Hammersmith make any application under the Guardianship of Infants Acts, 1886 and 1925. A grandmother, uncle or aunt or other person who seeks to have the care of a child must approach another court. Nor has a court any power under the Guardianship of Infants Acts, 1886 and 1925, to give directions where a child shall reside or go to school.

The Children and Young Persons Act, 1933, provided for the setting up of courts of summary jurisdiction called juvenile courts and by s. 62 of that Act a juvenile court, if it thinks a child to be in need of care or protection, may inter alia commit him to the care of any fit person willing to undertake the care of the child. Such an order is often referred to, and conveniently referred to, as a " fit person order " and I will in the course of this judgment so refer to it. I call attention to the fact, as I am told by counsel, that a parent seeking custody of the child against the other parent cannot apply to a juvenile court for an order to that effect. There is in the relevant statute a definition (1) of a person in need of care or protection which would not normally embrace a child who has a parent or guardian capable of exercising proper care.

In the result, a situation now may arise where the juvenile court is asked to make a fit person order committing the child to the care of the third party while one of the parents has obtained an order for custody in the magistrates' court against the other. The reverse may happen. The two orders, I suppose, are not inconsistent and will operate simultaneously, for care and custody are not the same thing. The parent asking that he may have the child to live with him, however, may have to apply to the juvenile court to revoke a fit person order and to the magistrates' court to have an order against the other parent for custody and maintenance; so proceedings are duplicated. I wish, however, to guard myself against saying that there is no machinery at all to enable one court ever to deal with both applications, for I have not been addressed on the possible effect of the Matrimonial Proceedings (Magistrates' Courts) Act, 1960, in those cases in which that Act may apply.

On July 2, 1963, a magistrates' court, namely, Chelsea Domestic Court, made an order which I will refer to as the first custody order, committing custody of the two children to the mother and ordering the father to make payments to her for the maintenance of the children. The father was to have access. As a result of a complaint made by the mother to the London County Council regarding the father's conduct, the 'Chelsea Juvenile Court made a fit person order on Sept. 18, 1963, putting the children in the care of the London County Council. On Dec. 13, 1963, an order was made by the West London Magistrates' Court providing that the maintenance payments under the first custody order should be paid to the London County Council.

On a date in February, 1964, the London County Council put the children in the care of the mother and on Feb. 25, a further order was made by the West London Magistrates' Court providing that the maintenance payments under the first custody order should be paid to the court. On Aug. 17, 1964, on an application made by the mother in April of that year alleging wilful neglect to maintain,

(1) The definition in s. 61 of the Act of 1933 was repealed by the Children and Young Persons Act 1963; see now s. 2 of that Act, 43 HALSBURY'S STATUTES (2nd Edn.) 529.

A desertion and cruelty, an order was made by the Chelsea Domestic Court to that
effect and the father was ordered to make a payment of 5s. a week for the mother's
maintenance. By Aug. 24, 1964, the children were back in the care of the London
County Council and consequently on that day the West London Magistrates'
Court made an order providing that the payments of maintenance under the first
custody order should be made to the London County Council.

B On Oct. 21, 1965, the Chelsea Domestic Court, on the application of the father,
made a further order, which I will refer to as the second custody order, committing
custody of the children to the father. That order was made by a stipendiary
sitting with lay magistrates. They stated the reasons for their conclusions as
follows:

C " We considered that the husband should have custody of each of the two
children for the following reasons—(1) The present outlook for the children
was otherwise one of indefinite institutional life. (2) The wife did not in our
view want the children back. (3) The wife wanted to keep the children
away from the husband. (4) We found that the husband would have a house
provided for him by his local authority, that this would be suitable accommodation, and that he was a fit and proper person to look after the children."

D The mother appealed to the High Court against that decision, pursuant to s. 7
of the Guardianship of Infants Act, 1925, and on May 12, 1966, the appeal was
dismissed by PENNYCUICK, J., the judge nominated pursuant to that section.

I pause to observe that under the London Government Act 1963, the London
Borough of Hammersmith succeeded, on Apr. 1, 1965, to the powers and duties
E of the London County Council in all respects relevant to this case, that the London
Borough was not entitled to be heard (though I expect their representative may
have been heard) before the Chelsea Domestic Court, and the London Borough
is certainly not entitled to appeal against the decision of the Chelsea Domestic
Court. The London Borough was, however, entitled to be heard when battle
was joined on an application by the father to have the fit person order revoked.
F That question was decided on Aug. 1, 1966, by the Hammersmith Juvenile
Court and the fit person order was revoked (2).

I interrupt the chronicle of litigation to sound a happier note. In April, 1965,
the children were placed in a Church of England home far away from London,
which I will call, though that is not its name, St. X's Home, and there they have
been to this day. Two of the sisters in charge of that home and the children's
G nurse who has looked after the two children gave evidence before me. I cannot
speak too highly of the impression these dedicated people made on me, or of the
thoughtful, tolerant and wise way in which they gave their evidence. That
evidence must, I suspect, have played a substantial part in bringing the mother
and father to agree on what is now best for the children. With them I am sure
the children have been happy, in as happy and regular a home as could have been
H found for them in the circumstances which have existed, and from which I would
judge they have derived much benefit.

The mother was not a party to the proceedings in which the fit person order was
revoked by the juvenile court on Aug. 1, but she gave evidence. The London
Borough of Hammersmith, which was a party, was dissatisfied with the decision
to revoke the fit person order and decided to appeal, on the ground that a written
I statement of one of the sisters of whom I have spoken was not received in evidence, although I think that I am right in saying that she gave oral evidence
before the court. Pending the appeal, the London Borough of Hammersmith was
anxious that the status quo should not be interrupted and that children should
remain at St. X's Home; on the other hand, the borough was content that the
father, pursuant to a previous arrangement, should have the children to stay with

_____

(2) On this occasion an order was made placing the children under the supervision of
the Essex County Council for three years. This order was made by the Hammersmith
Juvenile Court.

him during part of the school holidays but exacted an undertaking from him to   A
return them to St. X's Home thereafter. He, however, commenced habeas
corpus proceedings. He wished to have the children in his care, pursuant to the
orders which he had obtained. These habeas corpus proceedings came before one
of the vacation judges on two successive days in August. On the first of them the
children were in fact in the possession of the father who was seeking the order and
on the second of them, by the time when the matter came before the judge in the   B
afternoon, the present summons had been issued and thereby the children had
become wards of this court. No order was accordingly made in the habeas corpus
proceedings. The appeal of the London Borough of Hammersmith came before
the Divisional Court on Nov. 14, 1966, and was dismissed. Leave to appeal was
refused by that court and subsequently, I understand, by the Court of Appeal.

The present summons, in which both the mother and the London Borough of   C
Hammersmith were originally plaintiffs and the father the defendant, was, I
think, in the first place intended as purely a holding measure designed to ensure
that pending the appeal to the Divisional Court the children's lives should not be
disrupted by being taken away from St. X's Home and then, if the appeal was
successful, be disrupted yet again. It is right that I should make it very clear
that the London Borough of Hammersmith has, if I may say so, acted with the   D
greatest propriety and consideration for its charges in a case which was considered
by the very experienced children's officers concerned in it as one of the most
difficult cases with which they had had to deal. Once the appeal to the Divisional
Court had been disposed of, a new situation arose, for the London Borough of
Hammersmith had become functus officio. The wardship proceedings were
accordingly reconstituted, the London Borough ceasing to be a plaintiff and   E
becoming, in accordance, as I understand it, with the view of the master, second
defendant. So the matter comes before me.

The father has an order under the Guardianship of Infants Acts, 1886 and 1925,
granting him custody of both children. That order was made as recently as
Oct. 21, 1965, when the children were at St. X's Home, where they still are. That
order was affirmed by PENNYCUICK, J., on May 12, 1966. The attempt of the   F
borough council to persuade the juvenile court to retain the fit person order has
in the meantime failed.

Two questions arise: first, has this court, in the exercise of its parental jurisdiction over children, jurisdiction to make an order which may conflict with an
order made by a magistrates' court in exercise of the statutory jurisdiction
under the Guardianship of Infants Acts, 1886 and 1925: second, assuming the   G
answer to the first question to be in the affirmative, ought that jurisdiction to be
exercised or ought the court to make an order simply de-warding the children. In
my judgment, the answer to the first question must clearly be in the affirmative:
that the exercise of a limited statutory jurisdiction over children does not, in
the absence of express words in the statute, fetter the powers of the Chancery
Division in exercising the jurisdiction of the Crown as parens patriae over wards   H
of court.

From the decision of UPJOHN, J., as he then was, in *Re Andrews (infants)* (3),
approved by the Court of Appeal in *Hall* v. *Hall* (4), it clearly appears that that
jurisdiction can, in a proper case, be most usefully exercised by way of supplement
to a magistrates' order under the Guardianship of Infants Acts, 1886 and 1925,
in circumstances where the magistrates have not the necessary power, as evi-   I
denced by *Re H. (G.J.) (an infant)* (5); though as the judge who decided that
case I would like to take this opportunity of saying that it would have been better
if, in justifying the exercise of the jurisdiction in that case, I had relied on *Hall*
v. *Hall* (4) which, I am assured by counsel who appears in this case and who also

---

(3) [1958] 2 All E.R. 308; [1958] Ch. 665.
(4) [1963] 2 All E.R. 140; [1963] P. 378.
(5) [1966] 1 All E.R. 952.

A appeared in that case, was cited to me, rather than on *Vigon* v. *Vigon and Kuttner* (6) which, on consideration, is not at all a satisfactory authority for the proposition for which I cited it.

There remains a further question, whether the jurisdiction should be exercised where a magistrates' court has made an order. In *Re K. (K.J.S.) (an infant)* (7), BUCKLEY, J., considered this very point. The mother had obtained custody of the

B infant under an order of the magistrates' court in November, 1962. In February, 1965, the father commenced wardship proceedings and asked for a better order as to access. BUCKLEY, J., pointed out that the father had his remedy by applying to the magistrates for a more specific order as to access than that which had been made. He said (8):

C " It is undesirable, in my judgment, when the magistrates have made a custody order and an order relating to access, that a party who is dissatisfied with the way in which effect is being given to that order should seek to meet that state of affairs by instituting proceedings under the Law Reform (Miscellaneous Provisions) Act, 1949, instead of going back to the magistrates who have dealt with the matter. It would be another state of affairs altogether if there were some kind of relief were sought which the magistrates could

D not provide, as, for instance, an injunction; but there is nothing of that kind here and, in my judgment, these proceedings are really quite wrong."

He had, however, in that case, before giving judgment, already heard evidence which was adduced before him.

It was submitted as a matter of principle that, in every case, this court, before

E determining whether or not to exercise its jurisdiction notwithstanding an order previously made by a magistrates' court such as was made in this case, should do as BUCKLEY, J., did and hear all the evidence, and only then decide whether to make an order or to leave the applicant to apply to the magistrates' court for a variation of its previous order. The judgments of the Court of Appeal in *Re S. (an infant)* (9) were relied on in support of that submission. I do not think that

F those judgments do in fact constrain me to adopt such an approach, but before considering them I would call attention to the difficulties and consequences which attend such a course, and these difficulties seemed to me to loom ahead in this very case.

Supposing, after hearing all the evidence tendered by the parties for the purpose of determining whether it would be right to entertain the application, the judge

G were to come to the conclusion that there was no evidence that was not before the magistrates' court, or no evidence which could not have been adduced before the magistrates, I would have thought that he could conclude then that the application before him was one which ought not to be entertained. A judge cannot, however, divide his mind into water-tight compartments. Suppose in the examination of the evidence he forms a different view of it to that adopted by the magis-

H trates. Is he then to refrain from giving effect to his conviction that the welfare and benefit of the infant, which it is his duty to secure, could better be served by an order differing from that which the magistrates thought fit to make? Surely not. Nor will the issue ever be as clear as that. Suppose in this very case it had been established before me, as in fact was not the case, by evidence which could not have been before the magistrates, that since they made their

I order there had been such a change in the father's circumstances that he was not to have a house provided by his local authority and was quite unable to provide suitable accommodation for the children. That would be a circumstance which would have justified an application to the magistrates by the mother to reconsider the matter and it would have been far better that they should have dealt with it in this way. Is the judge, having heard all the evidence and the submissions of counsel in wardship proceedings in the High Court, to say to the

---

(6) [1928] All E.R. Rep. 755; [1929] P. 157.   (7) [1966] 3 All E.R. 154.
(8) [1966] 3 All E.R. at p. 155.   (9) [1965] 1 All E.R. 865.

mother, "Although this court has jurisdiction in the matter and has heard your   A
case, I will not tell you what I think. Seek your remedy from the magistrates,
where you should have gone in the first place ". I reject a procedure which can
lead to so absurd a result.

In coming to that conclusion I have had to consider the decision of the Court of
Appeal in *Re S. (an infant)* (10), to which I have referred in passing. That case
was a very different one from the present case. The infant there had been received   B
into the care of a local authority, not under any order of a court of competent
jurisdiction but under s. 1 of the Children Act, 1948. On an application to this
court to make the child a ward and for directions as to his custody, objection was
taken as a preliminary point to the jurisdiction of the court. PENNYCUICK, J.,
held, after reviewing the authorities, that the objection was well founded and that
in truth he had no jurisdiction to entertain the application at all. At the end of   C
his judgment, he said this (11):

" For the reasons which I have given, it seems to me that this present point
is covered by authority and that the court ought not to go into the circumstances of the case. There is no halfway house. Either the court is precluded
altogether from interfering, in which case there is no purpose in going into
the facts because the court has no effective power to review the decision of the   D
local authority; or the court has some sort of power in some circumstances
to review the decision of the local authority, in which case the court must
go into the facts and exercise whatever power it possesses. For the reasons
which I have given it does not seem to me that the court does effectively
possess that power. I propose accordingly at this stage to dismiss the
application for care and control . . ."   E

The Court of Appeal (10) took a different view, holding that this court has jurisdiction and of course it followed, as PENNYCUICK, J., recognised it must, that it
was the duty of the court to go into all the relevant facts to determine what
order it ought to make, and the Court of Appeal so held. In reference, I think, to
an argument that PENNYCUICK, J., had apart from his decision that he had no
jurisdiction, exercised a discretion not to hear it in full, PEARSON, L.J. (12),   F
and DANCKWERTS, L.J. (13) (but not, I think, LORD DENNING, M.R.), made some
remarks as to the extent to which, where a child has been taken into the care of
the local authority under s. 1 of the Children Act, 1948, a judge ought to enquire
into the facts before determining whether to exercise his wardship jurisdiction,
or not. Those remarks, which were obiter, were not in the least directed to the
question, which as I see it is quite a different question; a question not even   G
discussed and far less decided in that case, namely, the question of forum conveniens. Where the question is whether proceedings are better brought in one
court or another, I have never heard it said that the court must hear the case
before determining the preliminary question: to do so would be to proliferate
litigation.

Parliament has conferred on magistrates powers under the Guardianship of   H
Infants Acts, 1886 and 1925, and, applying the decision of BUCKLEY, J., in *Re K.
(K.J.S.) (an infant)* (14), I hold that when magistrates have made an order
for custody, then unless some relief is sought which the magistrates cannot give,
the forum conveniens for a reconsideration of that order is prima facie the magistrates' court.

For the purpose of deciding whether to entertain a wardship application where a   I
magistrates' court has already made a custody order, the judge before whom the
the matter comes must enquire into the case to the extent necessary to determine
whether relief is genuinely sought which the magistrates are not empowered to

(10) [1965] 1 All E.R. 865.
(11) [1965] 1 All E.R. 33 at p. 43.
(12) [1965] 1 All E.R. at pp. 870, 871.
(13) [1965] 1 All E.R. at pp. 869, 870.
(14) [1966] 3 All E.R. 154.

A give, or whether there is some very special reason for invoking the wardship jurisdiction. The problem is akin to that which arises when wardship and divorce proceedings are both pending, the judge in this Division and the judge of the Divorce alike having jurisdiction in relation to the children of the marriage; according to my experience, that is conveniently dealt with expeditiously and cheaply by adjourning the wardship summons to a judge as a chambers summons

B at a very early stage.

In the present case no application was made on behalf of the father at any preliminary stage of these proceedings to have a stay, though he estimates—and I have no reason to think that he has miscounted them—that he has been involved in thirteen court hearings since he applied for custody in October, 1965, or if such an application was made it was not taken to a judge. It is to be deplored that the

C father should have been so involved, more particularly as he is not legally aided, as I understand it, while the mother is. When, however, the matter came before the court earlier this week, the forces were deployed with horse, foot and artillery, and witnesses had been brought up from the country. In view of the history of the matter, it seemed to me extremely likely that if I had dealt with it on a preliminary point by making an order de-warding the children, I would prob-

D ably be condemning the father to a further journey to the court of Appeal, this time on the question of whether I had acted rightly, and followed perhaps by a further trial in this court, and that in the very special circumstances which existed at that moment it would be better if I heard the case. To this course counsel for the father did not strongly demur.

BUCKLEY, J., was, I think, faced with a similar situation in Re K. (K.J.S.)

E (an infant) (15) and I hope that this will not happen again. I say, as he said, that in my judgment it is entirely wrong.

In the result, however, I am very happy to say the parties have come to terms. These terms are supported by the London Borough and are commended to me by counsel for all the parties. Although no one suggests that they are by any means perfect, I am satisfied that the court ought to give effect to them. The father

F recognises that, as he is at present situate, it would not, for reasons into which I will not go, be suitable that he should have care of the little girl, and the mother is now reconciled to the idea that the little boy should be with his father. No court can view with the least composure the separation of two little children, but again the case has features suggesting that this is the least bad course to adopt. It is mitigated by the fact that it is contemplated that the children will spend their

G school holidays together. Since the order is an agreed one I will say no more about it, but the court will now go into camera to consider the precise terms of the order which is to be made.

Order accordingly.

Solicitors: Riders, agents for Sibly, Clough & Gibb, Bristol (for the mother); Marshall & Co. (for the father); Sharpe, Pritchard & Co. (for the London Borough

H of Hammersmith).

[Reported by JENIFER SANDELL, Barrister-at-Law.]

I

---

(15) [1966] 3 All E.R. 154.

A

PRINCES INVESTMENTS, LTD. AND OTHERS *v.* INLAND REVENUE COMMISSIONERS.
CLORE *v.* INLAND REVENUE COMMISSIONERS.

[COURT OF APPEAL, CIVIL DIVISION (Willmer, Harman and Diplock, L.JJ.), December 7, 8, 9, 12, 13, 14, 1966, January 17, 1967.]

B

Surtax—Undistributed income—Direction and apportionment—Apportionment of actual income of relevant year—Actual income meaning income actually received—Sub-apportionment of excess of apportioned sum over " actual income from all sources" of company—Dividend received in relevant year, but appropriated in accounts of prior year to other purposes, not deductible in computing excess—Income Tax Act, 1952 (15 & 16 Geo. 6 & 1 Eliz. 2 c. 10), s. 245, s. 254 (1).

C

Surtax—Investment company—Apportionments and sub-apportionments—Notice of sub-apportionments—Failure to give notice of sub-apportionments to company given surtax direction—Effect—Income Tax Act, 1952 (15 & 16 Geo. 6 & 1 Eliz. 2 c. 10), s. 248 (1), (2), (3), s. 254 (3), (4), (5).

D

An investment company within the meaning of s. 257 of the Income Tax Act, 1952, which was subject to automatic apportionment of its income, had, as its only revenue producing assets, shares in a second company from the ordinary shares of which it received two dividends of £15,771 gross each, one (called dividend " A ") for 1955-56 declared on Oct. 19, 1956, and paid on Mar. 24, 1957, and the other (called dividend " B ") for 1956-57 declared on Dec. 31, 1957, and paid on Feb. 10, 1958. The investment company's financial year ended on Mar. 31, and its accounts for the year 1955-56 were signed on Nov. 1, 1956. Its liabilities included a substantial loan from its parent or holding company. In the profit and loss account of the investment company for 1955-56 (viz., for the period Apr. 1, 1955, to Mar. 31, 1956) it credited dividend " A ", thereby enabling it to show a profit for its financial year ending Mar. 31, 1956, of £8,321, although the dividend was not in fact received until nearly a year later. It appropriated this profit to reducing the previous year's debit balance on profit and loss account. In the investment company's accounts for the year ending Mar. 31, 1957, which were signed after dividend " B " had been declared on Dec. 31, 1957, the investment company credited dividend " B " to its profit and loss account, thereby showing a profit for the year ended Mar. 31, 1957, of £8,280. This, together with capital and loan interest waived by its holding company, was appropriated by the investment company in its accounts to an interim dividend for 1956-57 on its own shares of £8,050 net (£14,000 gross), which it declared and paid to its holding company, the payment being in fact made on Mar. 28, 1957. It was common ground that the investment company's accounts were properly drawn up in accordance with current principles of commercial accounting, in particular in the crediting of dividends to profit and loss account of the investment company (the payee) for the year in respect of which they were declared, although they were not actually received until a later date, payment, however, being reasonably certain to be made. It was common ground also that in computing the " actual income from all sources " of the investment company for 1956-57 (which fell to be apportioned among its members under s. 245 and s. 262 of the Income Tax Act, 1952) it was correct to include dividend " A " (as it was actually received on Mar. 24, 1957) and to exclude dividend " B " (as it was not actually received until Feb. 10, 1958). The sum so apportioned to the holding company was £14,290, and the amount of this was not in dispute. Under s. 254 (1)* there was then to be sub-apportioned among the members of the holding company the amount

E

F

G

H

I

---

* Section 254 (1), so far as material, is printed at p. 242, letter I, post.

A by which the £14,290 exceeded the amount " which has been received by . . . [the holding company] . . . out of the income as aforesaid ", viz., out of the actual income of the investment company for 1956-57. The special Commissioners excluded, from the amount to be deducted from the £14,290 in computing this excess, the £14,000 gross dividend declared and paid by the investment company on Mar. 28, 1957, on the ground that it was not paid

B " out of the actual income from all sources of the investment company for the year 1956-57 ", viz., was not paid out of dividend " A " received by the investment company on Mar. 24, 1957, although dividend " A " was, for this purpose, the only source of " actual income " of the investment company for the year 1956-57. No notice of the sub-apportionments was given to the investment company, but on the appeal it was conceded that the invest-

C ment company had been entitled to such notice. Notice of the sub-apportionments had been given to the other appellant companies, although, as the sub-apportionments did not impose liability on those companies, they had no right to receive such notices. On appeal by the holding company and the two other companies on which notices of sub-apportionments were served and by the personal taxpayer to whom the final sub-apportionment was

D made,

  Held: (i) the dividend of £14,000 gross paid by the investment company was to be treated as paid out of the funds appropriated to its payment according to the accounts of the investment company, and therefore was not paid out of dividend " A " received by the investment company, since dividend " A " had been bindingly appropriated in the accounts of the investment

E company to reducing its debit balance on profit and loss account; that appropriation, once the investment company's accounts had been made public, was binding on the investment company, because the appropriation had practical effects as regards creditors, for it showed that the assets of the investment company were increased by the amount so appropriated, as the amount would no longer be available for distribution to members (see p. 243,

F letter F, and p. 243, letter I, to p. 244, letter B, post).

  Chancery Lane Safe Deposit and Offices Co., Ltd. v. *Inland Revenue Comrs.* ([1966] 1 All E.R. 1) applied.

  (ii) the giving of notice of the sub-apportionments to the investment company was not a condition precedent to assessment (see p. 244, letter D, post).

G (iii) although the appellant companies had no right to receive notice of the sub-apportionments, and accordingly might well not be companies " aggrieved " by having notice served on them, as the sub-apportionments imposed no liability on them, yet on the true construction of s. 248 (3)* of the Income Tax Act, 1952, which conferred the right of appeal on a company aggrieved by notice of sub-apportionment, the right of appeal was

H conferred on a company that alleged that it was aggrieved (see p. 244, letters H and I, post); moreover the personal taxpayer, as a member of a company in whose name an assessment on him was made had a right to challenge the sub-apportionment (see p. 245, letters A and C, post), and accordingly the personal taxpayer's appeal would be allowed to the extent necessary to give the investment company opportunity to appeal and to

I suspend the assessment on him meanwhile (see p. 245, letter F, post).

  Burston v. *Inland Revenue Comrs.* (*No. 2*) ([1945] 1 All E.R. 687) not followed.

 [As to computation of income tax for the purposes of a surtax direction, see 20 HALSBURY'S LAWS 556-558, paras. 1082-1084; and for cases on the subject, see 28 DIGEST (Repl.) 358-368, *1580-1613.*

---

 * Section 248 (3), so far as material, provides: "A company which is aggrieved by any . . . notice of apportionment shall be entitled to appeal to the Special Commissioners . . . and those commissioners shall hear and determine the appeal . . .".

For the Income Tax Act, 1952, s. 245, s. 248, s. 249, s. 254 and s. 255, see 31 **A**
HALSBURY'S STATUTES (2nd Edn.) 232, 235, 236, 242, 243.]

Cases referred to:

Burston v. *Inland Revenue Comrs. (No. 2)*, [1945] 1 All E.R. 687; 27 Tax Cas. 1;
    28 Digest (Repl.) 395, *1739.*

Chancery Lane Safe Deposit and Offices Co., Ltd. v. *Inland Revenue Comrs.,*
    [1966] 1 All E.R. 1; [1966] A.C. 85; [1966] 2 W.L.R. 251.   **B**

Appeal.

The first, second and third taxpayer companies (respectively Princes Investments, Ltd., Princes Realisations, Ltd., and Envoy Investments, Ltd.) appealed
to the Commissioners for the Special Purposes of the Income Tax Acts against
three notices of sub-apportionments of the actual income from all sources of New
Century Finance Co., Ltd. (the " New Century Co.") made by the commissioners **C**
on June 29, 1962, under s. 254 of the Income Tax Act, 1952, for the year of
assessment 1956-57. The grounds of appeal in each case were that the amounts
sub-apportioned were excessive in so far as no allowance had been made under
s. 254 in respect of income received by the first taxpayer company out of the
actual income from all sources of the New Century Co. in that year, and received **D**
also by the second and third taxpayer companies, from the first and second taxpayer companies respectively. The taxpayer companies contended before the
commissioners: (i) that the dividend amounting to £14,000 gross (£8,050 net)
paid by the New Century Co. to the first taxpayer company during the year of
assessment 1956-57 was an amount received by the first taxpayer company out
of the income of the New Century Co. as shown by its profit and loss account for **E**
the year ended Mar. 31, 1957; (ii) alternatively that that dividend of £14,000
gross (£8,050 net) was an amount received by the first taxpayer company out
of the £14,290 statutory income of the New Century Co. for the year of assessment
1956-57; and (iii) that in either event in sub-apportioning for the purpose of s. 254
(1) the actual income from all sources of the New Century Co. through the first
taxpayer company to the second taxpayer company and Checkendon Investments, **F**
Ltd., and through the second taxpayer company to the third taxpayer company
and Checkendon Investments, Ltd., and through the third taxpayer company
to the fourth taxpayer (Mr. Charles Clore) and to Checkendon Investments, Ltd.,
only the excess of the actual income of the New Century Co. over the amount of
the dividend of £14,000 gross (£8,050 net) fell to be sub-apportioned.

The Crown contended before the commissioners: (i) that the dividend of **G**
£14,000 gross (£8,050 net) paid by the New Century Co. to the first taxpayer
company during the year of assessment 1956-57 was not an amount received
by the first taxpayer company out of the actual income from all sources of the
New Century Co. in such manner as would in the case of an individual render the
amount so received liable to be included in the statement of his total income for
the purposes of surtax within the meaning of s. 254 (1) of the Act of 1952; (ii) that **H**
the circumstance that the statutory income of the New Century Co. for the year
of assessment 1956-57 was greater in amount than the dividend of £14,000 gross
(£8,050 net) paid by the New Century Co. to the first taxpayer company was
immaterial; and (iii) that in sub-apportioning for the purposes of s. 254 (1) the
actual income from all sources of the New Century Co. from the first taxpayer
company to the second taxpayer company and Checkendon Investments, Ltd.; **I**
from the second taxpayer company to the third taxpayer company and Checkendon Investments, Ltd.; and from the third taxpayer company to the fourth
taxpayer and Checkendon Investments, Ltd., no deduction fell to be made in
respect of that dividend. The commissioners held that the dividend received
by the first taxpayer company in March, 1957, was not income paid out of the
statutory income of the New Century Co., which was the income referred to in
s. 254 of the Income Tax Act, 1952, in a surtaxable form for 1956-57 within the
meaning of s. 254 (1). They therefore dismissed the appeals and confirmed the

A sub-apportionments. The taxpayer companies appealed by way of Case Stated to the High Court.

The fourth taxpayer appealed against a notice of sub-apportionment of the income of the New Century Co. as sub-apportioned to the third taxpayer company for the year of assessment for 1956-57 to him and to Checkendon Investments, Ltd., on similar grounds. He also appealed on the ground that notices of the sub-

B apportionments were not served in accordance with s. 248 (2) of the Act of 1952. The commissioners dismissed his appeal, and he appealed by way of Case Stated to the High Court.

On Apr. 6, 1966, as reported at [1966] 2 All E.R. 832, Buckley, J., dismissed the taxpayers' appeals, holding that the apportionment and sub-apportionments were correctly made in principle. The taxpayers appealed to the Court of Appeal.

C *C. N. Beattie, Q.C.,* and *J. E. H. Pearce* for the taxpayers.
Arthur Bagnall, Q.C., J. R. Phillips and *J. P. Warner* for the Crown.

Cur. adv. vult.

Jan. 17. **DIPLOCK, L.J.**, read the following judgment of the court at the invitation of Willmer, L.J.: In one of these appeals, the fourth taxpayer, Mr.

D Clore, personally appeals against an assessment to surtax for the year 1956-57 made on him under s. 249 of the Income Tax Act, 1952, in the name of New Century Finance Co., Ltd. In the other the fourth taxpayer, in three of his corporate manifestations other than the New Century company, appeals against sub-apportionments of the income of that company, made under s. 254 of the Act of 1952, which underlie and form the basis of the figure of the amount of

E income on which the fourth taxpayer was so assessed.

The main point argued in these appeals related to the amount of the sub-apportionable income of the New Century company for the year of assessment 1956-57. The New Century company was an investment company within the meaning of s. 257 of the Act of 1952, and therefore was subject to an automatic apportionment of its income. Its only revenue producing assets were preference

F and ordinary shares in Investment Registry, Ltd. Its liabilities included a substantial loan from its holding company, Princes Investments, Ltd. Its only outgoings were interest on that loan and various management expenses. Its accounting year, although ending on Mar. 31, has been treated as if it coincided with the tax year ending on Apr. 5.

The preference dividends received by the New Century company for the

G years 1955-56 and 1956-57 can be dismissed from further consideration. In each of these years Investment Registry, Ltd., paid the dividends on its preference shares in the years for which they were declared. These dividends were credited by the New Century company to its profit and loss accounts in the years in which they were received. The amounts of the preference dividends received by the New Century company in each year were insufficient to meet the annual interest

H payable on its loan from Princes Investments, Ltd. If the dividends on the ordinary shares of Investment Registry, Ltd., had not been credited by the New Century company to its profit and loss accounts in the years 1955-56 and 1956-57 respectively, these accounts would have shown debit balances, and no profit would have been disclosed which would have justified the payment of any dividend by the New Century company itself.

I We are accordingly concerned only with the dividends declared by Investment Registry, Ltd., on its ordinary shares and by the New Century company on its own shares for the years 1955-56 and 1956-57. For 1955-56 Investment Registry, Ltd., declared an ordinary dividend of 2s. per share on Oct. 19, 1956, and paid it to the New Century company on Mar. 24, 1957. It amounted to £15,771 gross, and we will call it " dividend A ". For 1956-57 Investment Registry, Ltd., declared an ordinary dividend, again of 2s. a share, on Dec. 31, 1957, and paid it to the New Century company on Feb. 10, 1958. It, too, amounted to £15,771 gross, and we will call it " dividend B ".

In its accounts for its accounting year 1955-56 signed on Nov. 1, 1956, after **A**
dividend A had been declared by Investment Registry, Ltd., the New Century
company credited dividend A to its profit and loss account, thus showing a profit
for the year of £8,321. Its balance sheet for the previous year had shown a debit
balance on profit and loss account of £14,527, and in its balance sheet for 1955-56
it showed the profit for the year of £8,321 as applied to reduction of the previous
year's deficit on profit and loss account. This, together with an item of loan interest **B**
waived, which was appropriated to the same purpose, reduced the debit balance
on profit and loss account at the end of the accounting year 1955-56 to £1,257.

In its accounts for 1956-57, signed after dividend B had been declared by
Investment Registry, Ltd., the New Century company credited dividend B to
its profit and loss account, thus showing a profit for that year of £8,280. This,
together with some £10,000 capital and interest on its loan waived by Princes **C**
Investments, Ltd., was appropriated by the New Century company to an interim
dividend for the year 1956-57 on its own shares of £8,050 net, or £14,000 gross,
which was declared by the New Century company and paid to Princes Investments, Ltd., on Mar. 28, 1957, and to a proposed final dividend with which we are
not concerned.

It is common ground (and is also found as a fact by the Special Commissioners) **D**
that these accounts were properly drawn up in accordance with current principles
of commercial accounting. The profit and loss accounts for each year show what
we will call the " commercial profit " for the year, and the balance sheets, together
with a separate appropriation account for 1956-57, show what was done with it.

The income of a company, however, which for surtax purposes is to be apportioned among its members under Ch. III of Part 9 of the Income Tax Act, 1952, is **E**
its " actual income from all sources " (see s. 245) for the year of assessment in the
case of an investment company (s. 262 (1)), and in computing the actual income
from any source it has to be estimated in accordance with the provisions of the
Act relating to the computation of income from that source (s. 255 (3)). The
relevant difference between the computation of " actual income " from dividends
in respect of shares for a year of assessment, and the method of dealing with **F**
dividends for the purpose of ascertaining the commercial profit for the year, is
that dividends do not become " actual income " until they are actually received,
whereas they may be credited to the profit and loss account of the payee in the
year in respect of which they are declared if it is reasonably certain that they will
in due course be received. The latter was what was done on its accounts by the
New Century company in respect of both dividend A and dividend B. **G**

It is common ground that the " actual income from all sources " of the New
Century company for the year 1956-57 fell to be apportioned among its members
under s. 262 and s. 245 of the Act of 1952, and that the amount so apportioned
to Princes Investments, Ltd., viz., £14,290, was correctly computed by including
in the computation dividend A which was actually received by the New Century
company in the year 1956-57, but excluding dividend B which was not actually **H**
received until the following year.

It then became the duty of the commissioners under s. 254 (1) to sub-apportion
among the members of Princes Investments, Ltd.,

" the excess of . . . [£14,290] . . . over the amount if any which has been
received by . . . [Princes Investments, Ltd.] . . . out of the income as afore- **I**
said . . . ",

i.e., the actual income from all sources of the New Century company for the
year 1956-57. The question in dispute is whether the dividend of £14,000 gross
declared in respect of the year 1956-57, and paid to Princes Investments, Ltd.,
on Mar. 28, 1957, was received by Princes Investments, Ltd., " *out of* the actual
income from all sources of the New Century Company for the year 1956-57 ".

In stating the problem thus we are conscious of having tacitly rejected a
contention of counsel for the taxpayers that " actual income from all sources "

A for a year out of which a distribution must be received does mean the "commercial profit" for that year as shown in the accounts of the company paying the dividend, for it is the commercial profit which determines the amount available for distribution to members in the form of a dividend payable out of income. He contends that the only relevance of the provision in s. 255 (3) that,

B   "in computing, for the purpose of this Chapter, the actual income from all sources for any year . . . the income from any source shall be estimated in accordance with the provisions of this Act relating to the computation of income from that source . . . ",

is to provide a figure which is to be substituted for the actual figure of "commercial profit" appearing in the company's profit and loss accounts in order to

C determine the sum of money to be apportioned among the members under s. 245 or s. 262 (1). We are unable so to construe the relevant sections of the Act of 1952. We think that s. 254 (1) directs the commissioners, first, to ascertain what the various sources of income of the New Century company were, secondly, to compute by applying income tax principles the amount of the income of the New Century company from each source for the year of assessment, and, thirdly,

D to ascertain how much (if any) of the total amount of such income was applied by the New Century company to the payment of its own dividend for the same year of assessment.

Dividend A received by the New Century company on Mar. 24, 1957, was its only source of "actual income" for the year 1956-57 apart from preference dividends, which for reasons already stated can be ignored. As we see it, and as

E the judge (1) saw it, the only question to be answered is: "was the dividend of £14,000 declared by the New Century company and paid to Princes Investments, Ltd., on Mar. 28, 1957, paid out of dividend A?". Or, put another way: "Did or could the New Century company appropriate dividend A to the payment of its own dividend paid on Mar. 28, 1957?". We agree with the judge (2) that the answer is "No". Dividend A was no longer available for that purpose. By

F Nov. 1, 1956, the date of the New Century company's accounts for the year 1955-56, it had already been appropriated by those accounts to the reduction of the debit balance on profit and loss account. The New Century company's accounts for the year 1956-57 show that it was dividend B which was appropriated, in anticipation of its actual receipt, to the payment of the New Century company dividend of £14,000 gross on Mar. 28, 1957.

G   The fact (if it be one, for it is not so found) that the receipt by the New Century company of dividend A on Mar. 24, 1957, provided the New Century company with liquid resources which could be used for paying its own dividend of Mar. 28, 1957, is, in our view, irrelevant. A dividend is not in any relevant sense paid "out of" a source of liquid resources any more than it is paid "out of" a bank overdraft when the cash to pay it is obtained by overdrawing on a bank account.

H It is paid out of the fund appropriated to its payment as shown in the company's accounts.

It is also in our view irrelevant that the New Century company, when it had credited dividend A to its profit and loss account for 1955-56 could, if it had wished, have appropriated the credit balance on profit and loss account of £8,321 to a dividend to be declared in respect of that year, and to be paid in the year

I 1956-57. It did not do so; it chose instead to appropriate it to reducing the debit balance on profit and loss account as at Mar. 31, 1956. This was not merely as a matter of internal book-keeping. So long as it was, it would have been open to the directors to change their minds; but as soon as their decision was recorded in their published accounts (as it was on Nov. 1, 1956) the die was cast.

---

(1) [1966] 2 All E.R. 832 at pp. 839, 840.
(2) [1966] 2 All E.R. at p. 840.

As so recorded the decision had practical effects as regards creditors and mem- **A**
bers of the company. It showed the assets of the company as enhanced by £8,321,
a sum which was no longer available for distribution to its members, and was thus
available for creditors. Once this had been done, it was in our view no longer open
to the New Century company to attribute dividend A to any other purpose, or to
claim that its own dividend in the following year was paid out of it (see *Chancery
Lane Safe Deposit and Offices Co., Ltd.* v. *Inland Revenue Comrs.* (3)). On this, the **B**
sole question in the taxpayer companies' appeals, which is also raised in the fourth
taxpayer's appeal, we agree with the judge (4).

The fourth taxpayer's appeal raises an additional question. Notices of the
sub-apportionments were not served on the New Century company. The point
was taken before the commissioners that they should have been, and that the
New Century company had a right of appeal and ought to have been a party. **C**
But the commissioners ruled otherwise. The judge held (5) that on the true
construction of the Act of 1952 the New Century company ought to have been
served with notices of the sub-apportionment, and this is no longer disputed by
the Crown. Counsel for the taxpayers has contended that service of these notices
on the New Century company was a condition precedent to the making of any
assessment on the fourth taxpayer, and that the purported assessment was a **D**
nullity. We do not agree. Section 248 draws a distinction between the making of
an apportionment by the Special Commissioners and " notice of any such apportionment ". Section 249 deals with the consequences of apportionment. Under
this section, the provisions of which apply with any necessary modifications to
sub-apportionments under s. 254, the making of the apportionment and sub-
apportionments *is* a condition precedent to an assessment, but the giving of notice **E**
of them to the company is not.

What then are the consequences of failure to give to the New Century company
notice of the sub-apportionments as required by s. 248 (2)? Technically the
New Century company, which is not a party to these proceedings, although its
parent, grandparent and great-grandparent companies are, has been deprived
of a right of appeal against the sub-apportionment to which it is entitled under **F**
s. 248 (3). Having regard to the fact that the taxpayer companies, like the New
Century company, are all corporate manifestations of the fourth taxpayer,
no injustice has resulted from this. The case for the New Century company has
been exhaustively argued on behalf of the taxpayer companies, although
technically the New Century company itself is not a party to the appeal.

Another consequence, however, of what is now conceded to be the true con- **G**
struction of the Act of 1952, is that the taxpayer companies had no right to
receive notices of the sub-apportionments. No liability was imposed on them by
the sub-apportionments; the liability to surtax which resulted from the sub-
apportionments was exclusively that of the New Century company and of the
fourth taxpayer (s. 249 (3) and (4)). Nevertheless, notices were served on them
and they did appeal. It may well be that none of them was " aggrieved " by the **H**
notices served on them, and that their appeal could have been dismissed on this
ground; but this point was not taken by the taxpayer companies or the Crown
before the Special Commissioners, and is not raised in the Special Case.

We do not think that this court is bound or entitled to take this point proprio
motu as one going to the jurisdiction of the commissioners to entertain the taxpayer companies' appeal. It is true that s. 248 (3) confers a right of appeal only **I**
on a company which is " aggrieved " by a notice of apportionment or sub-apportionment; but in this context this must mean a company which *alleges* that it is
aggrieved. If it were otherwise, the commissioners would have jurisdiction to
entertain successful appeals only, for a dismissal of any appeal on the merits is a
finding that the appellant was not " aggrieved " although he had alleged that
he was.

---

(3) [1966] 1 All E.R. 1 at pp. 22, 23; [1966] A.C. 85 at pp. 130-132.
(4) [1966] 2 All E.R. at p. 841.   (5) [1966] 2 All E.R. at p. 843.

A   In any event the fourth taxpayer was clearly entitled to appeal against the assessment on him. He, too, has challenged in his appeal the validity of the sub-apportionments which form the basis of the assessment on him. Our attention has, however, been drawn to the judgment of MACNAGHTEN, J., in *Burston* v. *Inland Revenue Comrs. (No. 2)* (6), in which he held that a member who was assessed to surtax in the name of the company could not, in an appeal against

B   the assessment, challenge the validity of the apportionment on which the assessment was based. The apportionment sought to be challenged in *Burston* v. *Inland Revenue Comrs. (No. 2)* (6) had been made under a provision in the previous legislation which is reproduced with some amendment in s. 260 of the Income Tax Act, 1952, a section which does not apply to the sub-apportionments with which the present appeals are concerned; and MACNAGHTEN, J.'s judgment was

C   based in part on the special provisions as to appeals contained in the forerunner (7) of s. 260 in the form in which it then stood. Nevertheless, part of his ratio decidendi would have applied to the fourth taxpayer's appeal against the assessment on him in the present case. We think that this part of the judge's ratio decidendi (8) was clearly wrong, and we have no doubt that a member of a company on an appeal against an assessment on him in the name of the company has the

D   right to challenge the validity of any apportionment or sub-apportionment on which the assessment is based, at any rate if the company has not already done so.

What then is the right order to make on the present appeals? On the facts stated in the Case Stated in each of the two appeals the sub-apportionments were correct. This is the only question of law raised in the taxpayer companies' appeal. Their appeal should accordingly be dismissed; but technically the New

E   Century company should have been given notice of the sub-apportionments so as to afford it an opportunity to appeal itself. It is still entitled to have notice of the sub-apportionments served on it and to exercise that right. It is conceivable that it might be able to produce further relevant evidence, although it cannot, of course, re-write its accounts for the relevant years of assessment. If the sub-apportionments were varied on new evidence, this would affect the fourth

F   taxpayer's assessment. In these circumstances the fourth taxpayer's appeal should be allowed to the extent necessary to give the New Century company the opportunity of appealing, and to suspend the assessment on the fourth taxpayer in the meanwhile.

If the New Century company is not served with notice of the sub-apportionments within twenty-eight days, the fourth taxpayer's assessment should be

G   be discharged. If the New Century company, having been given such notice, does not appeal, or if its appeal is dismissed (which it must be unless fresh facts are adduced), the fourth taxpayer's assessment should be confirmed. If the New Century company's appeal is allowed, the fourth taxpayer's assessment, so far as it depends on the sub-apportionments, must be adjusted accordingly.

H   *Taxpayer companies' appeals dismissed. Fourth taxpayer's appeal allowed to the extent necessary to give the New Century company an opportunity to appeal. Fourth taxpayer's assessment meanwhile suspended.*

Solicitors: *Titmuss, Sainer & Webb* (for the taxpayers); *Solicitor of Inland Revenue.*

[*Reported by* F. A. AMIES, ESQ., *Barrister-at-Law.*]

I

---

(6) [1945] 1 All E.R. 687; 27 Tax Cas. 1.
(7) Section 15 of the Finance Act, 1939.
(8) [1966] 2 All E.R. at pp. 842, 843.

A

COURTNEY-SOUTHAN *v.* CRAWLEY URBAN DISTRICT COUNCIL.

[QUEEN'S BENCH DIVISION (Winn, L.J., Ashworth and Widgery, JJ.), February 14, March 3, 1967.]

Town and Country Planning—Enforcement notice—Service—" Owner " of land   B
—Notice served on husband of freeholder—Land used for parking cars—
Business of parking cars carried on by husband and wife jointly—Control
of business in hands of husband—Husband described himself as owner when
applying for planning permission—Whether service on husband sufficient—
Whether enforcement notice enforceable—Town and Country Planning Act,
1962 (10 & 11 Eliz. 2 c. 38), s. 45 (3), s. 47 (5), s. 221.   C

The appellant applied to the respondent council for planning permission to use, for the purpose of the storage of cars, land near Gatwick Airport which in fact belonged to his wife. The appellant and his wife jointly occupied the land, carrying on the business of parking cars there; by agreement between them the appellant exercised control over the business and received all moneys which he paid into his banking account and ulti-   D
mately divided between him and his wife. The appellant certified, on the occasion of his application for planning permission that he was the estate owner of the land in fee simple; and he subsequently so stated in evidence at a local inquiry. Planning permission was refused and his appeal to the Minister was rejected. The appellant, having continued to use the land for the same purpose, was served with an enforcement notice, addressed to him   E
by name, to discontinue the use of the land for the storage of cars. On appeal against conviction it was not disputed that proof of proper service under s. 45 (3)* of the Town and Country Planning Act, 1962, was necessary before " any person " could be convicted of an offence under s. 47 (5); but it was submitted that the justices were entitled to infer (as they had inferred) that if the land had been let at a rack rent, the appellant's wife   F
would have allowed him to receive the rent as her agent and that he would thus have been " owner " within s. 221 of the Act of 1962.

Held: the land not being let at a rack rent, the justices had not been entitled to infer from the primary facts found that the appellant's wife would have appointed him as agent to receive the rack rent if the land had been so let; accordingly the appellant was not the owner of the land within   G
s. 221 of the Act of 1962, he was not estopped from denying that he was not the owner, and service of the enforcement notice on him was not such service as complied with s. 45 (3), with the consequence that the conviction must be quashed (see p. 248, letter I, and p. 249, letter B, post).

Watts v. *Battersea Corpn.* ([1929] All E.R. Rep. 201) distinguished.

Appeal allowed.   H

[As to service of enforcement notices, see 37 HALSBURY'S LAWS (3rd Edn.) 332-334, para. 438; and for cases on the subject, see 45 DIGEST (Repl.) 345-349, *71-85.*

For the Town and Country Planning Act, 1962, s. 45, s. 47, s. 221, see 42 HALSBURY'S STATUTES (2nd Edn.) 1015, 1019, 1180.]

I

Case referred to:
Watts v. *Battersea Corpn.*, [1929] All E.R. Rep. 201; [1929] 2 K.B. 63; 98 L.J.K.B. 273; 140 L.T. 594; 93 J.P. 137; 26 Digest (Repl.) 685, *28.*

Case Stated.
This was a Case Stated by justices for the county of West Sussex in respect of their adjudication as a magistrates' court sitting at Crawley on May 19, 1966. On Apr. 27, 1966, seven informations were preferred by Reginald

---

* Section 45 (3) so far as material is set out at p. 247, letter I, post.

A William James Tridgell, clerk of Crawley Urban District Council against the appellant Edward James Francis Courtney-Southan alleging that he used the land and premises known as Tinslow Farm, Tinsley Green, Crawley, for the storage of cars associated with Gatwick Airport in contravention of an enforcement notice served on the appellant under s. 45 of the Town and Country Planning Act, 1962, by registered post on May 26, 1965. The contraventions alleged were

B the use of the land on Mar. 21, 28 and Apr. 4, 12, 18, 25 and 27, 1966, contrary to the provisions of s. 47 of the Act of 1962. The facts are set out in the judgment of WIDGERY, J.

The cases noted below* were cited during the argument in addition to the case referred to in the judgment.

C W. J. Glover for the appellant.
Alan Fletcher for the respondents.

Cur. adv. vult.

Mar. 3. **WIDGERY, J.,** delivered the following judgment of the court at the invitation of WINN, L.J.: Tinslow Farm is near Gatwick Airport and on July 30, 1963, the appellant had applied to the respondents for planning permis-

D sion to use the land for the storage of cars associated with the airport. The application was refused. On Oct. 30, 1963, the appellant made a further application for a similar use, limited in point of time, but this was likewise refused. The appellant appealed against the latter refusal to the Minister of Housing and Local Government. On making each application and on lodging his appeal to the Minister the appellant personally or by his solicitor certified that he was

E the estate owner in fee simple in respect of the whole of the relevant land and he repeated this assertion in evidence at the public inquiry held consequent on his appeal. The appeal was dismissed on its merits. On May 26, 1965, the respondents served on the appellant an enforcement notice requiring him to discontinue the use of Tinslow Farm for the storage of motor cars. The notice was addressed to the appellant by name and was duly served on him at the farm.

F Notwithstanding the notice the use of the land for storage of cars continued, and on Apr. 27, 1966, the respondents laid the informations which gave rise to the proceedings before the justices in this case. At the hearing before the justices the appellant did not seek to dispute the foregoing facts, but submitted that his wife was in fact the owner of the land and that as the enforcement notice had not been served on her it was of no effect. Accordingly, he contended that

G no offence had been committed. On the issue thus raised by the appellant the justices found the following facts: (a) that the fee simple of the land was not vested in the appellant but had at all material times been vested in his wife; (b) that no tenancy existed between the appellant and his wife who were joint occupiers of the land; (c) that the appellant and his wife jointly carried on the business of parking cars on the land but that by agreement with his wife the

H appellant exercised control over the business and received all moneys arising therefrom. These moneys were paid into the appellant's banking account and the net profits were ultimately divided between the appellant and his wife. The justices nevertheless found the case proved, convicted on each information and fined the appellant £70 on each information. The appellant appeals to this court against his conviction contending that it was wrong in law.

I By s. 45 (3) of the Act of 1962, it is provided that:

" Where the local planning authority serve an enforcement notice, the notice—(a) shall be served on the owner and occupier of the land to which it relates."

I need not read the rest of the section. By s. 47 (5) it is provided that:

---

* Doe d. Lord Macartney v. Crick, (1805), 5 Esp. 196; Ward v. Duncombe, [1893] A.C. 369.

" Where, by virtue of an enforcement notice, a use of land is required to   **A**
be discontinued . . . then if any person uses the land or causes or permits it
to be used . . . in contravention of the notice, he shall be guilty of an offence
. . ."

It is to be observed that the offence may be committed by " any person " whether
that person was himself served with the enforcement notice or not, but it has not
been disputed before this court that proper service of the notice on the owner   **B**
and occupier under s. 45 of the Act of 1962 is a condition precedent to the validity
of the notice and that proof of such service by the prosecution is necessary
before any conviction can be entered under s. 47 of the Act. In view of the history
of the matter and the appellant's repeated assertion of ownership it is not surprising that the respondents treated him as the sole owner and occupier of the
land, but no suggestion is made that any kind of estoppel can be raised against   **C**
him.   By s. 221 of the Act " owner " for the purposes of, inter alia, s. 45, is
defined as meaning:

". . . a person, other than a mortgagee not in possession, who, whether
in his own right or as trustee or agent for any other person, is entitled to
receive the rack rent of the land, or, where the land is not let at a rack rent,   **D**
would be so entitled if it were so let."

This definition is similar to that contained in s. 4 of the Public Health Act, 1875,
except that the words " entitled to receive " are substituted for " receiving ".
Under the former definition it was held that a solicitor acting in his professional
capacity and receiving rents on behalf of his client was an " owner " (see *Watts*
v. *Battersea Corpn.* (1)) but, although the solicitor was undoubtedly " receiving "   **E**
the rents, he would not be " entitled to receive " them if entitlement implies some
title to the reversion to which they were attached. An agent who receives rents
normally does so by virtue of an authority from his principal and not by virtue
of a title in himself, but if the word " entitled " in s. 221 of the Act of 1962 is to
be narrowly construed the result will be to make the reference to an agent almost
meaningless. We are prepared to assume, without so holding, for present purposes   **F**
that an agent who has been duly authorised by the reversioner vis-à-vis a tenant
to collect rents is " entitled " to receive them and may thus be an owner for
the purposes of s. 221 of the Act of 1962. On this construction of the section the
change in language adopted by the draftsman of the Act of 1962 can be explained
by a desire to bring within the definition of " owner " a person who, though
entitled to receive the rack rent, was not in actual receipt of it because for some   **G**
reason it was not in fact being paid.

In the present case the land was not let at a rack rent so that in order to show
that the appellant was the owner of Tinslow Farm it was necessary to show that
he would have been entitled to receive the rack rent if it had been so let. The
justices held that at all material times the appellant's wife allowed the appellant
to have such control over the use and management of the land that if, on May 26,   **H**
1965, the land had been let at a rack rent he would have been entitled to receive
the rack rent as agent or trustee for her. The appellant contends in this court
that the justices were not entitled to draw this inference from the primary facts
and were indulging in sheer speculation. We are forced, with some reluctance,
to agree with this view. To assume that the land is let at a rack rent is to assume
a situation wholly different from that which in fact prevailed, and the fact that   **I**
the appellant's wife allowed the appellant to control their joint business is no
ground for inferring that she would have appointed him as her rent collector, if
she had given up occupation of the land and let it at a rack rent. It was urged
on us by counsel for the appellant that the respondents were negligent in not
ascertaining the true position between the appellant and his wife before serving
the enforcement notice, but in view of the appellant's conduct this criticism is

(1) [1929] All E.R. Rep. 201; [1929] 2 K.B. 63.

A unjustified. It is illogical that a person who was actually served with such a notice can defy it with impunity merely because of a failure to serve some other person when such failure has not prejudiced him. We are concerned at the weakness in enforcement procedure which has come to light in this case, and hope that the attention of the legislature may be drawn to it. This appeal will be allowed and the appellant's convictions will be quashed.

B
Appeal allowed. Conviction quashed.

Solicitors: *Blyth, Dutton, Wright and Bennett*, agents for *Coole & Haddock*, Crawley (for the appellant); *Sharpe, Pritchard & Co.*, agents for *R. W. J. Tridgell, Clerk to the Urban District Council* (for the respondent).

[*Reported by* N. P. Metcalfe, Esq., *Barrister-at-Law*.]

C

Re HARMSWORTH (*deceased*).

BARCLAYS BANK, LTD. AND ANOTHER v. INLAND
D   REVENUE COMMISSIONERS.

[Court of Appeal, civil division (Lord Denning, M.R., Harman and Salmon, L.JJ.), February 2, 3, 6, March 1, 1967.]

Estate Duty—Exemption and remission—Purchase—Property passing by reason of purchase—Annuity bequeathed to wife on condition that she devised one
E   *moiety of fund to which she was entitled at time of husband's death to trustees of her will to be held on same trusts as husband's residue—Acceptance of conditional bequest in 1937—Disposition by widow of reversionary interest in moiety fund constituted by such acceptance—Disposition in favour of her relatives—Estate duty exigible as on a gift to them by the disposition—Finance Act, 1894 (57 & 58 Vict. c. 30), s. 2 (1) (c), s. 3 (1)—Finance Act, 1940 (3 &*
F   *4 Geo. 6 c. 29), s. 44 (1) (1A), substituted by Finance Act, 1950 (14 Geo. 6 c. 15), s. 46—Finance Act, 1944 (7 & 8 Geo. 6 c. 23), s. 40.*

By cl. 10 of his will dated May 15, 1935, a husband bequeathed to his wife during her widowhood an annuity of £5,000 on the terms that it should be conditional on his wife, within a period of three months of his death, agreeing to hold one moiety of the real property and income producing
G   investments to which she might be entitled at the time of his death on trust to retain them for her own use during her life and subject thereto to devise the moiety to the trustees of her will to be held on the same trusts as those of the husband's residuary estate. He gave his residue on trusts for his children, their spouses and issue. The husband died on Jan. 19, 1937, and his will was proved. On Apr. 7, 1937, within three months of his death,
H   the widow gave notice in writing to the three executors and four trustees of his will that she accepted the conditional annuity and agreed to observe the terms of cl. 10. She never re-married. She received the annuity, and by her will she bequeathed the moiety fund to her trustees on trusts as directed by cl. 10. She died on Dec. 1, 1963, at which date the moiety fund amounted to about £186,030 19s. A total sum of £106,915 4s. 4d. was repaid
I   by the Commissioners of Inland Revenue in September, 1966, pursuant to a decision at first instance that no estate duty was payable. On appeal by the commissioners,

Held: (i) the widow's acceptance of the conditional bequest in April, 1937, constituted a contract, and a purchase for the purposes of s. 3 (1)* of the Finance Act, 1894, that purchase being a purchase by the testator's executors implementing his bequest, and accordingly, the reversionary interest

---

* Section 3 (1), so far as material, is printed at p. 252, letter A, post.

so purchased passed on the widow's death by reason only of that purchase, **A**
thus prima facie coming within the exemption conferred by s. 3 (1) (see
p. 252, letter I, p. 253, letter B, p. 255, letters E and G, and p. 256, letter I, post).

(ii) since, however, acceptance by the widow of the conditional gift involved
a disposition by her of a reversionary interest in the moiety fund, and that
disposition was in favour of her relatives, the disposition had, by virtue of
s. 44 (1), (1A) of the Finance Act, 1940, as amended*, to be treated as a gift, **B**
although it was in fact made in return for the annuity; accordingly, as
possession and enjoyment of the property given had not been assumed by the
donees immediately on the gift being made on Apr. 7, 1937 (since the property
given was a reversionary interest), or a benefit (the annuity) had remained
to the widow, estate duty was exigible under s. 2 (1) (c) of the Finance Act,
1894, on the basis that the disposition had been a gift, the valuation of the **C**
gift being governed by s. 40 of the Finance Act, 1944, with the consequence
that a sum of £3,505 19s. was payable on the death of the widow in
respect of estate duty on the moiety fund (see p. 254, letters A, B and E,
and p. 256, letters G and I, post).

Decision of BUCKLEY, J. ([1966] 3 All E.R. 309) affirmed as to (i), but
reversed on (ii), above. **D**

[As to property passing by reason of purchase, see 15 HALSBURY'S LAWS
(3rd Edn.) 46, para. 92; and for cases on the subject, see 21 DIGEST (Repl.)
42-44, *162-178*.

As to valuation for estate duty where the consideration for a disposition
to a relative was an annuity, see 15 HALSBURY'S LAWS (3rd Edn.) 83, para. 172. **E**
For s. 38 of the Customs and Inland Revenue Act, 1881, see 9 HALSBURY'S
STATUTES (2nd Edn.) 332, 333.

For the Finance Act, 1894, s. 2 (1), s. 3 (1), the Finance Act, 1940, s. 44, and
the Finance Act, 1944, s. 40, see 9 HALSBURY'S STATUTES (2nd Edn.) 350, 353,
472, 505.

For the Finance Act, 1950, s. 46 see 29 HALSBURY'S STATUTES (2nd Edn.) 178.] **F**
Cases referred to:

A.-G. v. *Dobree*, [1895-99] All E.R. Rep. 1057; [1900] 1 Q.B. 442; 69 L.J.Q.B.
223; 81 L.T. 607; 64 J.P. 24; 21 Digest (Repl.) 42, *162*.

A.-G. v. *Earl of Sandwich*, [1922] 2 K.B. 500; 91 L.J.K.B. 757; 127 L.T. 517;
21 Digest (Repl.) 43, *173*.

A.-G. v. *Worrall*, [1891-94] All E.R. Rep. 861; [1895] 1 Q.B. 99; 64 L.J.Q.B. **G**
141; 71 L.T. 807; 59 J.P. 467; 21 Digest (Repl.) 24, *89*.

Fitzwilliam's (Earl) Agreement, Re, [1950] 1 All E.R. 191; [1950] Ch. 448;
21 Digest Repl.) 30, *112*.

Kirkness (Inspector of Taxes) v. *John Hudson & Co.*, [1955] 2 All E.R. 345;
[1955] A.C. 696; [1955] 2 W.L.R. 1135; 28 Digest (Repl.) 310, *1356*.

Lawrence (Frederick), Ltd. v. *Freeman Hardy & Willis, Ltd.*, [1959] 3 All E.R. **H**
77; [1959] Ch. 731; [1959] 3 W.L.R. 275; Digest (Cont. Vol. A)
1057, *7417po*.

New South Wales Stamp Duties Comr. v. *Perpetual Trustee Co., Ltd.*, [1943]
1 All E.R. 525; [1943] A.C. 425; 112 L.J.P.C. 55; 169 L.T. 414;
21 Digest (Repl.) 28, **27*.

Appeal. **I**

This was an appeal by the defendants, the Commissioners of Inland Revenue,
from a judgment of BUCKLEY, J., dated July 5, 1966, and reported [1966] 3
All E.R. 309, whereby it was declared that the amount of estate duty exigible
on the death of Lady Harmsworth in respect of a fund referred to as " the
moiety fund " was £334 8s. 10d. and it was ordered that the defendants repay
to the plaintiffs the sum of £106,580 15s. 6d. overpaid for estate duty in respect

---

* By s. 46 of the Finance Act, 1950; see p. 253, letter F, post.

A   of the moiety fund together with interest. By their notice of appeal the Crown
    sought a declaration that the estate duty exigible was £106,915 4s. 4d. and
    that the plaintiffs be ordered to repay to the defendants the sum of £106,580
    15s. 6d., which had been re-paid to the plaintiffs on Sept. 6, 1966, in obedience
    to the order of Buckley, J.; alternatively for a declaration that the estate
    duty exigible was £3,505 19s. and that the plaintiffs be ordered to repay
B   to the Crown the appropriate part of the said sum of £106,580 15s. 6d. The facts
    are summarised in the judgment of Lord Denning, M.R., and are set out in
    the judgment of Buckley, J.*.

    Michael Wheeler, Q.C., and *J. P. Warner* for the Crown.
    E. I. Goulding, Q.C., and *V. G. H. Hallett* for the plaintiffs.

C   *Cur. adv. vult.*
    Mar. 1. The following judgments were read.

    LORD DENNING, M.R.: Sir Leicester Harmsworth was a man of means.
    His wife, Lady Harmsworth, had considerable investments of her own. A year
    or two before his death he made a will in which he made some specific bequests,
D   but he left his residuary estate to his five children and their families. One of the
    specific bequests was this: he left his wife an annuity of £5,000 a year for her
    life; but he imposed a condition on this bequest. In order to get the annuity,
    she had to tie up one half of her own investments. This has been called the
    " moiety fund ". She was to receive the income from this moiety fund during
    her life, but she was to leave the capital of the fund by her will to her husband's
E   residuary legatees, i.e. to their five children and their families. The bequest
    was in these terms:

        " I bequeath to my wife during her widowhood a conditional annuity of
        £5,000 and I direct that the same shall be paid upon the following terms:
        " (i) The bequest shall be conditional upon my said wife within a period of
        three months of my death agreeing to hold one moiety of the real property
F   and income producing investments to which she may be entitled at the time
        of my death Upon trust to retain the same and the income thereof for her
        use during her life and subject thereto to devise and bequeath the said
        moiety to the trustees of her will to be held by such trustees upon the same
        trusts as those of my residuary estate."

    Sir Leicester Harmsworth died on Jan. 19, 1937. Within the three months Lady
G   Harmsworth accepted the condition. On Apr. 7, 1937, her solicitors wrote to
    the executors of Sir Leicester's will and to the trustees of the will and their
    solicitors saying that she accepted the conditional annuity of £5,000 on the
    terms laid down in his will.

    Lady Harmsworth lived on for nearly twenty-seven years. She died on Dec.
    1, 1963. All that time she received the annuity of £5,000 a year from her husband's
H   estate. She also did her part. She set aside one-half of her investments. That
    half was valued in 1937 at £44,310 2s. 11d. It was kept as a separate fund.
    She received the income from it during her life: and by her will she left it, as
    she was bound to do, to her husband's residuary legatees, i.e. to their five children
    and their families.

    At her death in 1963 the moiety fund had increased in value to £186,030 19s.
I   The Revenue claimed estate duty on it on the ground that the moiety fund
    passed on her death. Prima facie the moiety fund did pass under s. 2 (1) (*b*)
    of the Finance Act, 1894. The moiety fund was property in which the deceased,
    Lady Harmsworth, had a life interest ceasing on her death. The whole benefit
    accrued to the residuary legatees. So prima facie estate duty was payable on
    the whole. The duty came to £102,316 17s. 8d. Her personal representatives
    paid it; but they now say that no estate duty was payable on it and claim that

    * [1966] 3 All E.R. at pp. 311, 312.

it should be returned. They base their case on s. 3 of the Finance Act, 1894, **A**
which provides:

> " Estate duty shall not be payable in respect of property passing on the
> death of the deceased by reason only of a bona fide purchase from the person
> under whose disposition the property passes . . . where such purchase was
> made . . . for full consideration in money or money's worth paid to the **B**
> vendor . . . for his own use or benefit . . ."

In order to understand this section, I will take two illustrations: the first is
where a young man agrees to pay an old man an annuity for life on the terms
that the old man will leave the young man his house in his will. In that case,
on the old man's death, estate duty would prima facie be payable on the house
under s. 2 (1) (*a*): but under s. 3 it is not payable because the young man had **C**
purchased the house for its full value by paying the annuity. It would be unjust
that he should have to pay estate duty on a house for which he had already
given full value (see *A.-G.* v. *Dobree* (1), per DARLING, J.). The other instance
is the converse case: when a man buys a life interest in a house for full value
on the terms that it is to revert to the seller after his death, that would prima
facie be caught by s. 2 (1) (*b*): but it is exempt by s. 3 as the purchase was for **D**
full value (cf. *A.-G.* v. *Earl of Sandwich* (2)).

In the present case " the property passing on the death of the deceased " was
the moiety fund. It passed on the death of Lady Harmsworth from her to her
husband's residuary legatees. Under whose " disposition " did that property pass?
At first sight one might think it passed under the disposition which Lady Harmsworth made by her will in 1963; but that is not correct. She had bound herself **E**
as long ago as 1937 to dispose of the moiety fund to her husband's residuary
legatees. As soon as she agreed on Apr. 7, 1937, to the condition attached to the
bequest, she became under a trust to hold the moiety fund as trustee for herself
for life with an obligation to leave it to the residuary legatees after her death.
The " disposition " was her acceptance on Apr. 7, 1937, of the bequest. By that
acceptance she disposed of her reversionary interest in return for an annuity. **F**
The annuity was " full consideration in money or money's worth ". That is
admitted. The only question is: was there a " purchase " from her?

Counsel for the Crown argued that " purchase " is the converse of " sale ":
that " sale " is a transfer of property by one person to another as the result of a
contract express or implied (relying on *Kirkness (Inspector of Taxes)* v. *John
Hudson & Co., Ltd.* (3)): and that here there was no contract between Sir Leicester **G**
and Lady Harmsworth. Counsel pinned his case to this: that for a " purchase "
there must be a contract. Thus he admitted that if Sir Leicester and Lady
Harmsworth had in their lives made an agreement that he would leave her an
annuity if she would leave the moiety fund to his residuary legatees, then there
would be a " purchase " from him; or if he had, by a testamentary option in his
will, directed his executors to offer her the annuity in return for the moiety fund, **H**
and she accepted the offer, there would be a " purchase " from her. He submitted,
however, that a conditional bequest was not a contract, even when she accepted
the condition: and, therefore, there was no " purchase ".

I am disposed myself to think that there was a contract here. Sir Leicester made
an offer through his executors to his wife, just as much as if he had directed them
to make it; and she accepted it when she accepted the conditional bequest. Even **I**
if there was no contract, however, I think that there was a " purchase " within
s. 3. The meaning of " purchase " in any statute depends on the context (see
Frederick Lawrence, Ltd. v. *Freeman Hardy & Willis, Ltd.* (4)). It is obvious that
" purchase " is not used in s. 3 in any technical sense because it covers the case

---

(1) [1895-99] All E.R. Rep. 1057 at p. 1060; [1900] 1 Q.B. 422 at p. 450.
(2) [1922] 2 K.B. 500.
(3) [1955] 2 All E.R. 345; [1955] A.C. 696.
(4) [1959] 3 All E.R. 77 at p. 82; [1959] Ch. 731 at p. 746.

A where the consideration is not in money but in money's worth. I think that in this section " bona fide purchase for money or money's worth " means a " bona fide acquisition in return for a fair equivalent in money or money's worth ". So interpreted, the reversionary interest in the moiety fund here was acquired by reason of a bona fide *purchase* by Sir Leicester (through his executors) from Lady Harmsworth. It was acquired in return for the annuity. The property in it

B passed on her death by reason *only* of that purchase, seeing that but for that purchase it would probably not have passed at all, because if she had not sold the moiety fund in return for the annuity, she might have disposed of the moiety fund elsewhere long before her death.

If the matter had stopped there, there would have been no estate duty payable on the moiety fund; but now comes the second point. Lady Harmsworth made

C this disposition in favour of her relatives as well as his (being their own five children and their families). Dispositions in favour of relatives are caught by special statutory provisions. By s. 44 of the Finance Act, 1940, as originally enacted in 1940 (omitting immaterial words):

   " (1) Where a [deceased] person . . . has made a disposition . . . in favour of
   a relative of his, the creation . . . in favour of the deceased of an annuity . . .

D shall not be treated for the purposes of s. 3 . . . of the Finance Act, 1894, as
   consideration for the disposition made by the deceased."

If that section had remained unamended, it would have fitted this case exactly. Lady Harmsworth made the disposition of the moiety fund in favour of her relatives. She received the annuity in exchange for it. That is not to be treated

E as consideration for the purpose of s. 3. So s. 3 would be of no avail. Estate duty would be payable.

Section 44 was amended, however, by s. 46 of the Finance Act, 1950. This amendment was provoked by the decision of DANCKWERTS, J., in *Re Earl Fitzwilliam's Agreement* (5). As amended, the section says that:

   " (1) Any disposition made by the deceased in favour of a relative of

F his shall be treated for the purposes of s. 2 (1) (*c*) of the Finance Act, 1894,
   as a gift unless—(*a*) the disposition was made on the part of the deceased
   for full consideration in money or money's worth paid to him for his own
   use or benefit, . . .
       " (1A) Where the deceased made a disposition of property in favour of a
   relative of his, the creation or disposition in favour of the deceased of an

G annuity . . . shall not be treated for the purposes of this section . . . as
   consideration for the disposition made by the deceased."

Applying those words to this case, s. (1A) shows that the annuity is not to be regarded as consideration: and s. 1 (1) shows that the disposition by Lady Harmsworth is to be treated for the purposes of s. 2 (1) (*c*) of the Act of 1894 as a " gift ".

H This throws us back to s. 2 (1) (*c*). This is a section which incorporates by reference s. 38 of the Customs and Inland Revenue Act, 1881, as amended by s. 11 of the Customs and Inland Revenue Act, 1889. If we thread our way through the jungle of cross-references, we find the word " gift " in s. 11 of the Act of 1889. The net result is that this disposition by Lady Harmsworth on Apr. 7, 1937 (that is, much more than five years before her death) is liable to

I estate duty under s. 2 (1) (*c*) if the

   " property taken under any gift, whenever made, of which property bona
   fide possession and enjoyment shall not have been assumed by the donee
   immediately upon the gift and thenceforward retained to the entire exclusion
   of the donor, or of any benefit to him by contract or otherwise."

Applying those words, the " property " was the reversionary interest in the moiety fund. The " gift " was the disposition on Apr. 7, 1937. The " donor "

(5) [1950] 1 All E.R. 191; [1950] Ch. 448.

was Lady Harmsworth. The " donees " were the executors and trustees of Sir **A**
Leicester's will on behalf of the residuary legatees. The property is, therefore,
under s. 2 (1) (c) liable to estate duty unless the donees immediately on Apr. 7,
1937, assumed bona fide possession and enjoyment of the reversionary interest
and thenceforward retained it to the entire exclusion of Lady Harmsworth or of
any benefit to her by contract or otherwise.

Now it is plain that the donees did not assume possession or enjoyment on **B**
Apr. 7, 1937. No-one did. For the simple reason that it was a reversionary
interest, which did not become an interest in possession until Lady Harmsworth
died. It is very different from *New South Wales Stamp Duties Comr.* v. *Perpetual
Trustee Co., Ltd.* (6), where the donee assumed possession at once of the income
of the fund. In any case Lady Harmsworth was not entirely excluded. She had
the benefit of the annuity. It does not matter that the annuity was not retained **C**
out of the gift (see *A.-G.* v. *Worrall* (7)). In my opinion, therefore, the disposition
by Lady Harmsworth is to be treated as a gift liable to estate duty under
s. 2 (1) (c) of the Act of 1894.

The judge seems to have thought (8) that because the original s. 44 expressly
mentioned s. 3 of the Act of 1894 and the amended s. 44 did not do so, s. 3 still
operated to exempt the property from estate duty; but there is a simple answer **D**
to that argument. Section 3 only applies to a " purchase ": whereas under the
new s. 44 this disposition is to be treated as a " gift ". As such, it is untouched
by s. 3, and is liable under s. 2 (1) (c) to estate duty.

The valuation, however, of the " gift " is governed by s. 40 of the Finance
Act, 1944: and under that section the duty payable is only £3,505 19s. Seeing
that the executors have paid £106,915 4s. 4d., it means that £103,409 5s. 4d. is **E**
repayable to them. I would dismiss the appeal on the " purchase " point: but
allow it on the " gift " point.

HARMAN, L.J.: Sir Leicester Harmsworth, who died in the year 1937, by
his will in 1935, after appointing certain persons to be his executors and different
persons to be trustees, made by cl. 10 a conditional bequest to his wife during her **F**
widowhood of an annuity of £5,000 on terms which my lord has already stated and
I will not repeat. They are contained in cl. 10 (1) of the will. Clause 10 (2)
authorised a fund to be set aside to provide the annuity, which was by cl. 10 (3)
made payable from his death, and the fund was to fall back into his residuary
estate. The will gave the residue of the testator's estate on trust for various
relations of Lady Harmsworth, but with no benefit to her.

At the date of her husband's death Lady Harmsworth held income-producing **G**
investments, the total value of one moiety of which was agreed to be
£44,310 2s. 11d., and within three months of the death, her solicitors sent to the
executors and to the trustees a notice accepting the condition in the following
terms:

" We hereby give you notice that she [Lady Harmsworth] accepts the **H**
conditional annuity of £5,000 bequeathed to her by cl. 10 of the said will of
her late husband the said Sir Robert Leicester Harmsworth Bart, and she
agrees—(1) that she will hold one moiety of the real property and income
producing investments to which she was entitled at the time of her late
husband's death Upon trust to retain the same and the income thereof for her
own use during her life and subject thereto to devise and bequeath the said **I**
moiety to the trustees of her will to be held by such trustees upon the same
trusts as those of the residuary estate of her late husband,"

and it adds other conditions in order to suit the terms of the gift in cl. 10 (1).

Lady Harmsworth duly segregated the one-half of her estate and enjoyed the
income of it for the rest of her life. She did not re-marry and she satisfied all the

(6) [1943] 1 All E.R. 525; [1943] A.C. 425.
(7) [1891-94] All E.R. Rep. 861; [1895] 1 Q.B. 99.
(8) [1966] 3 All E.R. 309 at p. 318.

A conditions laid down in her husband's will. At the date of her death the moiety fund, so to call it, was worth £186,030 19s. and duty was paid on that sum by her executors at fifty-five per cent. Lady Harmsworth died in December, 1963, having by will bequeathed the moiety fund to be held by her trustees on the trusts declared concerning his residuary estate by her husband's will. Lady Harmsworth's executors have claimed repayment of the duty so paid from the

B Crown, and this summons has been issued under s. 10 of the Finance Act, 1894, to determine that question.

Two separate points arise here, first, whether, apart from the legislation contained in s. 44 of the Finance Act, 1940, and its amendments, the effect of s. 3 of the Finance Act, 1894, was to exempt the moiety fund from estate duty on the death of Lady Harmsworth as being or arising out of a purchase. As to this, I

C am of opinion that the judge (9) was in the right. In my judgment the transaction between Lady Harmsworth and her husband's personal representatives was in substance the same as if the testator's will had taken the form of giving his wife a testamentary option to purchase an annuity of £5,000 a year during her widowhood at the price of holding one-half of her then property on trust for his residuary legatees. Where such an option is given, executors are bound to make an offer

D in accordance with its terms to the person to whom the option is offered, and if he accepts it, a contract is at once formed between him and the executors. This was not exactly the form that the transaction took under the testator's will, but the executors were bound to offer the conditional legacy to Lady Harmsworth, as they must have done, and she was entitled to accept it as she did by the notice. It is admitted that the fact that this notice preceded the grant of probate cannot

E affect the matter. I can see no difference between the two transactions and would accordingly be prepared to hold that there was a contract and a bona fide purchase under that contract from Lady Harmsworth by the personal representatives of her husband. On this view the disposition under which the property passed was the notice given by her solicitors, as from the date of which she held the moiety fund, subject to her own life interest, on trust for the residuary legatees under

F her husband's will. It is true that the condition was that she should by her will bequeath the property, that is the legal estate in it, not to her husband's representatives but to her own, but they were to hold it on the trusts of his will. I was at one time inclined to the view that the disposition mentioned in the section was Lady Harmsworth's will, but I think on the whole that this is not so. That will only gave effect to the contract and passed the legal interest to the

G purchasers.

On this footing s. 3 of the Act of 1894 applies in that " the property ", that is the beneficial interest in the moiety fund, passed on the death of the deceased (Lady Harmsworth) by reason only of a bona fide purchase—the bona fides is not questioned—from the person (Lady Harmsworth) under whose disposition (the assent) the property passes. It is not disputed that there was full value (in

H the form of the annuity) in money paid to the vendor (Lady Harmsworth) for her own use.

If I should be wrong about the existence of a contract, I would be prepared to hold that the transaction operated by way of trust, as the judge indicated (10). So far, therefore, the taxpayer succeeds, but there arises then a further point, which I have found somewhat confusing, under s. 44 of the Finance Act, 1940.

I This section was headed: " Purchases of annuities, etc., from relatives ", and as originally drawn, read as follows:

" (1) Where a person dying after the commencement of this Act has made a disposition of property in favour of a relative of his, the creation . . . in favour of the deceased of an annuity . . . limited to cease on the death of the

---

(9) [1966] 3 All E.R. at p. 318.
(10) [1966] 3 All E.R. at p. 314.

deceased . . . shall not be treated for the purpose of s. 3 . . . of the Finance   **A**
Act, 1894, as consideration for the disposition made by the deceased."

The Finance Act, 1950, s. 46, enacted in substitution for this the following:

" (1) Any disposition made by the deceased in favour of a relative of his
shall be treated for the purposes of para. (c) of sub-s. (1) of s. 2 of the Finance
Act, 1894, as a gift unless—(a) the disposition was made on the part of the   **B**
deceased for full consideration . . . paid to him for his own use . . .

" (1A) Where the deceased made a disposition of property in favour of a
relative of his, the creation . . . in favour of the deceased of an annuity . . .
shall not be treated for the purposes of this section . . . as consideration . . ."

The result of this legislation is that the disposition by Lady Harmsworth in favour
of the relatives of her husband must be treated as a gift made without con-   **C**
sideration. It is noteworthy that whereas s. 44 (1), as originally enacted,
specifically excluded s. 3 of the Finance Act, 1894, the amended section makes
no reference to s. 3 and it was argued that the legislature must have intended to
leave s. 3 in force. I do not accept this: mention of s. 3 was not required in the
amended section. This transaction must be treated as a gift, but this gift was
made more than five years before the death of the deceased and one is remitted,   **D**
therefore, to s. 2 (1) (c) of the Act of 1894. This again refers back to the Customs
and Inland Revenue Act, 1881, as amended by s. 11 of the Customs and Inland
Revenue Act, 1889, with the words " voluntary " and " voluntarily " omitted.

Section 38 (2) (a) of the Act of 1881 as amended by s. 11 (1) of the Act of 1889
and further amended by s. 59 of the Finance (1909-10) Act, 1910, must now be
considered. By the combined effect of these, the property included in s. 2 (1) (c)   **E**
of the Act of 1894 will include any

" property taken under any gift, whenever made, of which property bona
fide possession and enjoyment shall not have been assumed by the donee
immediately upon the gift and thenceforward retained to the entire exclusion
of the donor, or of any benefit to him by contract or otherwise."

  F
As I have said, this must be treated as a gift. It is difficult to see how possession
and enjoyment of an interest in remainder can be taken immediately on the gift,
but I think that these words are satisfied because here the husband's relations as
donees became the absolute owners of the remainder from the day when the gift
was made and could dispose of it or charge it, and the donor, that is to say, Lady
Harmsworth, had no more interest in it. So far the mischief of the section is
avoided, but there remain the words " or of any benefit to him by contract or   **G**
otherwise ". Here the benefit to the donor was the annuity which she obtained
by contract or something in the nature of a contract. There was no contract
between her and the donees, but I do not think that that matters. It has long
been settled that the benefit need not be reserved out of the subject-matter of the
gift (see *A.-G.* v. *Worrall* (11)).

  H
If this be right, the Crown succeeds on the second limb of the case, though
having regard to the relaxation of s. 44 of the Act of 1940, brought about by the
Finance Act, 1944, s. 40, Sch. 3, and s. 41, only a comparatively small sum is
payable under this head. Accordingly, in my view the Crown fails on the first
point but succeeds on the second point.

     SALMON, L.J.: I agree with both the judgments which have been   **I**
delivered.

Appeal allowed in part, dismissed in part.

Solicitors: *Solicitor of Inland Revenue; Taylor, Willcocks & Co.* (for the plaintiffs).

[*Reported by* F. GUTTMAN, ESQ., *Barrister-at-Law.*]

---

(11) [1891-94] All E.R. Rep. 861; [1895] 1 Q.B. 99.

A   # LITTLE PARK SERVICE STATION, LTD. *v.* REGENT OIL CO., LTD.

[COURT OF APPEAL, CIVIL DIVISION (Sellers, Davies and Russell, L.JJ.), November 30, December 1, 5, 6, 1966, January 25, 1967.]

B   *Landlord and Tenant—New tenancy—Business premises—Opposition by land-lord—Intention to demolish and reconstruct premises—Proposed work involv-ing demolition of all buildings and replacement by others—Tenant willing to allow access for work to be carried out—Term of existing tenancy that landlord could do such work during tenancy and that tenant should allow access for it—Whether work could reasonably be done without obtaining*

C   *possession—Landlord and Tenant Act, 1954 (2 & 3 Eliz. 2 c. 56), s. 30 (1) (f).*

A petrol filling station with garages at the rear, was let on a lease, cl. 2 (23) of which provided that the tenants should " permit the lessors at any time or times during the said term . . . to make such structural and other alterations to the said premises . . . and for this purpose and for purposes connected therewith, to permit the lessors . . . and any person authorised by the lessors

D   with or without plant material or equipment to enter upon the said premises the lessors completing such work as quickly as reasonably possible and in a manner which will interfere with the lessee and his business as little as reasonably possible ". The landlord formed the intention to demolish all the buildings on the site and construct others in their place to make a modern petrol filling station and, on the termination of the tenancy granted

E   by the lease, opposed, under s. 30 (1) (f)* of the Landlord and Tenant Act, 1954, an application by the tenants for a new lease.

The trial judge found that the landlords intended to carry out this demo-lition and reconstruction at a cost of about £18,000; that they could do so without closing down the petrol filling station completely; that as a business proposition the landlords could reasonably require complete closure of the

F   station for up to a week, as this would save them about £1,000, and that the tenants were willing to let the landlords enter and carry out these works. Accordingly the trial judge decided that the landlords had not shown, as a fact, that they could not reasonably carry out these works without obtaining possession of the premises. The trial judge, however, refused the grant of a new tenancy, holding himself bound by authority so to do as, if a new

G   tenancy were granted, the landlords could not reasonably do the work as a matter of right without obtaining possession. On appeal by the tenants,

Held: the landlords had not established their ground of opposition under s. 30 (1) (f) of the Landlord and Tenant Act, 1954, to the grant of a new tenancy, and the tenants were accordingly entitled to such a grant, because—

(i) (per SELLERS and DAVIES, L.JJ.), the finding of fact that the landlords

H   had failed to show that they could not reasonably carry out the works without obtaining possession was conclusive, for on the grant of a new lease there was every reason for it to contain a provision giving facilities equal to those afforded by cl. 2 (23) of the previous lease and the landlords themselves, if they obtained possession, would probably continue the services of the filling station while reconstruction was proceeding; the test under s. 30 (1) (f)

I   was not whether the landlords could not reasonably do the work " as a matter of right " without obtaining possession (see p. 261, letters B and I, p. 263, letter A, and p. 264, letter C, post).

(ii) (per RUSSELL, L.J.) in the present case there was no inconsistency between the landlords' proposals and the grant of a new tenancy of the whole holding, the terms of such tenancy to contain appropriate provisions to enable the proposed works to be carried out (see p. 266, letter A, post).

---

* Section 30 (1) (f) is printed at p. 259, letter B, in the judgment of SELLERS, L.J.

Dicta of PARKER, L.J., in *Fisher* v. *Taylors Furnishing Stores, Ltd.*, ([1956]   A
2 All E.R. at p. 84) and of LORD DENNING, M.R., in *Jones* v. *Thomas* ((1963),
186 Estates Gazette at p. 1053) applied.

Whittingham v. *Davies* ([1962] 1 All E.R. 195) distinguished and dicta
of LORD EVERSHED, M.R. ([1962] 1 All E.R. at pp. 198-200) dissented from.
Appeal allowed.

[As to landlords' opposition to the grant of a new business tenancy on the   B
ground of proposed demolition or reconstruction, see 23 HALSBURY'S LAWS
(3rd Edn.) 893, 894, para. 1717; and for cases on the subject, see DIGEST (Cont.
Vol. A) 1051-1055, *7417p-7417pkc.*

For the Landlord and Tenant Act, 1954, s. 30 (1), see 34 HALSBURY'S STATUTES
(2nd Edn.) 414.]
                                                                               C
Cases referred to:

Betty's Cafés, Ltd. v. *Phillips Furnishing Stores, Ltd.,* [1956] 2 All E.R. 497;
    [1956] 1 W.L.R. 678; *rvsd.* C.A., [1957] 1 All E.R. 1; [1957] Ch. 67;
    [1956] 3 W.L.R. 1134; *affd.* H.L., [1958] 1 All E.R. 607; [1959] A.C. 20;
    [1958] 2 W.L.R. 513; Digest (Cont. Vol. A) 1051, *7417pa.*

Fisher v. *Taylors Furnishing Stores, Ltd.,* [1956] 2 All E.R. 78; [1956] 2 Q.B.   D
    78; [1956] 2 W.L.R. 985; Digest (Cont. Vol. A) 1052, *7417pc.*

Jones v. *Thomas,* (1963), 186 Estates Gazette 1053; 107 Sol. Jo. 395; Digest
    (Cont. Vol. A) 1055, *7417pkc.*

Whittingham v. *Davies,* [1962] 1 All E.R. 195; [1962] 1 W.L.R. 142; Digest
    (Cont. Vol. A) 1054, *7417pka.*

Appeal.   E

This was an appeal by Little Park Service Station, Ltd., tenants to Regent Oil
Co., Ltd., of a petrol filling station, against the decision of His Honour JUDGE
TALBOT, at Portsmouth county court on May 11, 1966, refusing their application,
under Pt. 2 of the Landlord and Tenant Act, 1954, for a new lease of the station.
The facts are set out in the judgment of SELLERS, L.J.

G. B. H. Dillon, Q.C., and *E. W. H. Christie* for the tenants.   F
P. R. Oliver, Q.C., and *A. J. D. McCowan* for the landlords.

                                                                Cur. adv. vult.

Jan. 25.   The following judgments were read.

SELLERS, L.J.: The appellant tenants are the lessees and occupiers of
premises at Hulbert Road, Leigh Park, Bedhampton, Hampshire, which are   G
constructed and used as a petrol filling station. The respondents, who supply
the petrol for sale by the appellants, are the owners and lessors. The buildings
and equipment were only erected in 1959 and appear to be well-constructed on a
spacious site. There is a substantial roof over the petrol pumps and to the rear
of the site there are two sets of garages. The present litigation has arisen because
the landlords seek to turn the tenants out of the premises where they carry   H
on their business, so that the present buildings may be demolished and others
constructed in their place in order that there may emerge another petrol filling
station of a different design and lay-out. The tenants rely on the Landlord and
Tenant Act, 1954, to give them protection from eviction and for a new lease to
be granted to them. At the Portsmouth county court before his Honour JUDGE
TALBOT the tenants failed in their application for a new lease. On appeal it has   I
been contended that the facts found by the judge entitled them to the lease
claimed by them and that the grounds on which the judgment went against them
cannot be sustained.

The lease, dated Oct. 14, 1960, was for twenty-one years terminable by six
months' notice at the expiration of the first five, ten or fifteen years. The landlords
gave a proper notice terminating the tenancy under the lease on Feb. 14, 1966.
The tenants called in aid the Landlord and Tenant Act, 1954, and gave notice
that they were not willing to give up possession on the date on which the tenancy

A would terminate. They proceeded by an originating summons to apply to the court for a new lease pursuant to Part 2 of the Act of 1954. The landlords opposed the application on the ground, previously intimated to the tenants, that on the termination of the tenancy they intend to demolish and reconstruct the premises and that they cannot reasonably do so without obtaining possession of the premises: that is, the landlords rely on s. 30 (1) (*f*), which is as follows:

B   " 30. (1) The grounds on which a landlord may oppose an application under sub-s. (1) of s. 24 of this Act are such of the following grounds as may be stated in the landlord's notice under s. 25 of this Act or, as the case may be, under sub-s. (6) of s. 26 thereof, that is to say: . . . (*f*) that on the termination of the current tenancy the landlord intends to demolish or reconstruct the premises comprised in the holding or a substantial part of those premises or

C   to carry out substantial work of construction on the holding or part thereof and that he could not reasonably do so without obtaining possession of the holding; . . ."

That the landlords do intend to demolish and then reconstruct the premises is conceded by the tenant. The dispute turns solely on the provision " and that he could not reasonably do so without obtaining possession of the holding ". The

D expression " the holding " means the property comprised in the tenancy (s. 23 (3)). Under s. 31 the landlord has to establish to the satisfaction of the court any ground available to him under s. 30 on which he relies. Under s. 32, if the landlord fails in his objection and the application succeeds, then there must be an order for the grant of a new tenancy of the holding. Failing agreement between the landlord and the tenant, by s. 33 the court must determine the duration of the

E new tenancy according to what is reasonable in all the circumstances; and by s. 34 provision is made for calculating the rent to be payable. Section 35 reads as follows:

    " The terms of a tenancy granted by order of the court under this Part of this Act (other than terms as to the duration thereof and as to the rent

F   payable thereunder) shall be such as may be agreed between the landlord and the tenant or as, in default of such agreement, may be determined by the court; and in determining those terms the court shall have regard to the terms of the current tenancy and to all relevant circumstances."

The Act of 1954, therefore, in the relevant provisions of Part 2, deals with the position where a tenancy has been terminated and a right to renewal has been

G established and where, by reason of the failure of the parties to agree, the court is called on to determine the terms of a new tenancy agreement; and in determining the terms other than duration and rent the court must have regard to the terms of the current tenancy and to all relevant circumstances.

The lease of Oct. 14, 1960, which, but for the Act of 1954, would have terminated on Feb. 14, 1966, demised:

H   " First all those premises more particularly described in Sch. 1 hereto together with all buildings erections and fixtures which now are or at any time during the term hereby created may be placed thereon and secondly all the equipment (hereinafter called ' the scheduled equipment ') particulars of which are contained in Sch. 2 hereto all which premises first and secondly described are together hereinafter jointly referred to as ' the said premises '

I   which expression shall be deemed to include each and every part of the said premises."

Schedule 1 reads:

    " All that piece of land on the south west side of Hulbert Road Bedhampton in the county of Hampshire which for the purpose of identification only is more particularly delineated and described in the plan attached hereto and thereon edged with pink all which said premises are known as Little Park Garage Hulbert Road Leigh Park Bedhampton aforesaid . . ."

The "holding", therefore, is the piece of land known as Little Park Garage **A** together with all buildings, erections and fixtures which were then and might later be placed thereon during the currency of the tenancy and also the pumps and other equipment referred to in Sch. 2. By cl. 2 the tenant covenanted, among other covenants:

"(5) Not to make or permit to be made any alterations to or improvements in the said premises or erect any further buildings or structures thereon **B** nor to cut maim or injure or suffer to be cut maimed or injured any of the walls or timbers thereof"; . . .

"(23) To permit the [landlords] at any time or times during the said term and at their own expense to make such structural and other alterations to the said premises as they may consider to be necessary or desirable and for this purpose and for purposes connected therewith to permit the [land- **C** lords] and their servants or agents and any person authorised by the [land-lords] with or without plant material or equipment to enter upon the said premises the [landlords] completing such work as quickly as reasonably possible and in a manner which will interfere with the [tenants] and [their] business as little as reasonably possible."

Entry by the landlords on to the premises to do work which might interfere **D** extensively with the tenants' occupancy is clearly recognised, therefore, in the current lease.

At the time of the trial the landlords had not received final approval of their proposed plans, but the judge held that it was reasonable to suppose that planning consent would be given to a fresh application which had already been submitted. He then stated correctly that the sole issue for the court was whether the land- **E** lords could reasonably carry out their intentions without obtaining possession of the whole of the premises. The judgment accepts that the landlords' plans envisage complete demolition of the existing premises and reconstruction of a new petrol filling station, a sales office, service bay and a wash area at a total cost of little under £18,000; that it would be possible to carry out the work without completely closing down the station; that if it were closed for about a week about £1,000 **F** would be saved in the cost; that as a business proposition the landlords could reasonably require the station to be closed for not exceeding a week; and that the tenants were willing to accord the landlords permission to enter and carry out the works contemplated. After reviewing the evidence and on consideration of the arguments on s. 30 (1) (f) of the Act of 1954, the judgment states:

"Dealing with the first problem, there is the factual question whether the **G** [landlords] can reasonably carry out the works without obtaining possession. A factor which I have to take into consideration is the extra cost to the [landlords] if they have to carry out the works whilst the [tenants] continue in occupation because of the great difficulty whilst the station continues to operate, whilst on the other hand I have to bear in mind that it is possible to do the work without closing. I must also consider the fact that the evidence **H** shows that this is a lucrative business for the [tenants] which they wish to carry on for such period as a new lease will allow.

"I believe I must look at this point objectively and I have reached a conclusion that, though from the [landlords'] business point of view it would be advantageous to obtain possession, it is not reasonable, in view of the **I** fact that the works can be carried out with the lease continuing, to deprive the [tenants] of their rights to renew the lease and of their business: there-fore, from a factual point of view only, the [landlords] have not shown that they cannot reasonably carry out the works without obtaining possession."

On that finding the tenants submit that the landlords had failed in their opposition and that the claim had therefore to be decided in their favour and a new lease granted. The finding was in its terms one of fact, and there was specific and clear

A   evidence to support it. I do not think that the judge, in his final conclusion, was contemplating any complete closure of the station. His view was that the extra cost, such as it was, in balance with all the other matters, did not establish that the landlords could not reasonably do the work without obtaining possession of the holding.

B   In my view, taking everything into consideration it might be hard to find a site more suitable, or a business more convenient, for a complete demolition and reconstruction whilst a tenant was in occupation and carrying on his business. The parties had recognised as much, or almost as much, when cl. 2 (23) was inserted into the lease. There would seem every reason for the new lease to be agreed or to be granted by the court to contain at least equal facilities having regard to the landlords' expressed intention. It would still leave a tenancy where

C   the tenants could carry on their business and the landlords could perform their contemplated works. I apprehend that if the landlords were to obtain possession by ousting the tenants they themselves would continue selling petrol and carrying on the services of a filling station whilst the work of demolition and reconstruction was proceeding, at least for the greater part of the work.

The claim failed, in the judge's view, because of some observations of LORD

D   EVERSHED, M.R., in *Whittingham* v. *Davies* (1). In that case the finding of fact of the county court was the opposite of the finding in the present case. JUDGE HARPER in the Whitby county court had held that the works which the landlords intended to do were substantial and could not reasonably be carried out without obtaining possession of the holding. I now take this extract from the judgment of LORD EVERSHED (2):

E   " Then comes the third part: can that work be done reasonably by the landlords without their obtaining possession of the holding? I would observe, to begin with, that, if the new tenancy is granted and thereby the tenant obtains in law the right of exclusive possession of the premises which constitute the holding, then manifestly, I should have thought, the work could not be done at all."

F   That proposition seems axiomatic, but in my view it has no application to the facts of this case and could easily be remedied by a specific provision in a new lease where a landlord sought provision to do work on the premises. Here the existing tenancy, by cl. 2 (23), did not give the tenant the right of exclusive possession of the premises, and by s. 35 of the Act of 1954 that would undoubtedly

G   be a matter for consideration in the new lease. Later in the judgment LORD EVERSHED, M.R., said (3):

" The question: what is the test, is not one, I think, that requires much exposition. The language of s. 30 (1) (*f*) is that the landlord ' could not reasonably do [the work] without obtaining possession '. I conceive that that must mean: ' could not reasonably do it as a matter of right without obtain-

H   ing possession '. The section cannot, I think, have contemplated that it might be well and good, if the tenant chose to give unspecified facilities lasting for a considerable time. The test posed, I conceive, is: assuming the work of construction could be done at all, could it in common sense reasonably be done as contemplated if a lease has been granted with the necessary consequences as a matter of possession to the tenant?."

I   LORD EVERSHED would have added the words to the provision in the Act of 1954 " as a matter of right ". With great respect, I think that that interpretation is an isolated one and unsupported. In *Betty's Café, Ltd.* v. *Phillips Furnishing Stores, Ltd.*, commencing with the decision of DANCKWERTS, J. (4), in the Court of Appeal (5) and the House of Lords (6), the question was dealt with as a question

---

(1) [1962] 1 All E.R. 195.   (2) [1962] 1 All E.R. at p. 198.
(3) [1962] 1 All E.R. at p. 199.   (4) [1956] 2 All E.R. 497.
(5) [1957] 1 All E.R. 1; [1957] Ch. 67.   (6) [1958] 1 All E.R. 607; [1959] A.C. 20.

of fact, as a practical matter viewed in the light of the work contemplated and A
the extent to which the tenant's occupancy and his business on the premises
would be interrupted or interfered with. Several other decisions treat the
question in like manner and none has applied LORD EVERSHED's test.

The subsection contemplates that demolition might be carried out with a tenant
in occupation. In limited confined premises this would rarely be possible, but the
nature and extent of other premises and of the business carried on thereon might B
make it possible, and the section seems to require implicitly that entry on to the
premises would be provided for. If no right of entry is to be contemplated it
would be idle to consider whether the work could reasonably be done without
obtaining possession of the holding.

In the next passage of his judgment (7) LORD EVERSHED criticises what PARKER,
L.J., said in *Fisher* v. *Taylors Furnishing Stores, Ltd.* (8). PARKER, L.J., had said C
(8):

> " ' He ', [that is the landlord] must further prove, not only that he intends
> to demolish or reconstruct, as there set out, but also that ' he could not
> reasonably do so without obtaining possession of the holding '. This latter
> stipulation qualifies the nature and extent of the work. If, however sub-
> stantial the operation, it can be done with the tenant still in possession D
> [that is, in possession of the holding] the landlord has not made out his
> ground of objection."

LORD EVERSHED says (7) that he agrees with that. Then the extract (7) from the
judgment of PARKER, L.J., continues (8):

> " Thus, if it is shown that the landlord intends to occupy the holding at E
> once for the purposes of his business and thereafter, while he is carrying on
> business, to do substantial work, he has not made good his ground of objection.
> For, if it is reasonably possible to do the work while he is in occupation, it
> is equally reasonably possible for him to do it while the tenant is in occupa-
> tion."

Then LORD EVERSHED explains (9) why he does not agree with that passage; but F
such conflict as there is in those passages seems to be one of fact. PARKER, L.J.'s
observations fit the present case precisely and I would invoke and apply them.

It was urged on us in the sustained argument of counsel for the landlords that
LORD EVERSHED's judgment was agreed by WILLMER and DANCKWERTS, L.JJ. (9),
and was a judgment of this court and was binding on us. The decision in *Whitting-*
ham v. *Davies* (10) upheld the county court judge's finding of fact and it does not G
appear that any question of there being no entry as a matter of right arose in
the lower court. The reasoning of LORD EVERSHED was unnecessary for the
decision and was I think extraneous to the decision and obiter. If not, it was out
of harmony with the decision of *Fisher* (11) which preceded it and in particular
with the views of PARKER, L.J. It was not accepted in *Jones* v. *Thomas* (12),
where LORD DENNING, M.R., said as follows (13): H

> " We were referred to the judgment of LORD EVERSHED, M.R., in *Whitting-*
> *ham* v. *Davies* (10) . . . He read the section as if it meant ' could not reasonably
> do it as a matter of right without obtaining possession '. I cannot quite read
> it thus. The landlord has never a right to do work of reconstruction unless
> the contract gives it to him. It seems to me that, in order to satisfy the I
> section, the landlord must show that he could not reasonably do the work
> without obtaining possession of the holding for a considerable time, so that
> the tenant would have to quit whilst the work was carried out. If the work

(7) [1962] 1 All E.R. at p. 199.
(8) [1956] 2 All E.R. 78 at p. 84; [1956] 2 Q.B. 78 at p. 92.
(9) [1962] 1 All E.R. at p. 200.   (10) [1962] 1 All E.R. 195.
(11) [1956] 2 All E.R. 78; [1956] 2 Q.B. 78.
(12) (1963), 186 Estates Gazette 1053.
(13) (1963), 186 Estates Gazette at p. 1053.

A   could be done whilst the tenant was there, putting up with the inconvenience of having workmen about the place, the requirement is not satisfied."

If *Whittingham* v. *Davies* (14) had had in the existing lease a clause such as cl. 2 (23) here, I do not think LORD EVERSHED would have made the observation which he did. If that case is one otherwise to be regarded as binding, which I doubt, it is in the matters which I have indicated clearly distinguishable from the present

B   case. The judge felt himself bound to find against the tenants' application by reason of *Whittingham's* case (14). For the reasons which I have given, I do not think that he was.

Counsel for the landlords stressed before us the necessity for the landlords to have control of the holding so that they could organise the work, have people about and place the material and equipment where they wished and with safety.

C   In his argument the word " possession " in s. 30 (1) (*f*) was in effect replaced by " control ". In my view, so to do gives a slant to the provision. Of course, the control and organisation of the work is a matter for consideration in the issue whether the contemplated work can reasonably be done without possession of the holding. It is not conclusive.

The tenants have relied on the existing lease, and it was argued below and here

D   that all the contemplated work could be done under cl. 2 (23), which it was said was wide enough to cover it. The provision to make such structural and other alterations to the said premises as they consider to be necessary or desirable does not permit of much limitation, but the landlords do not rely on the lease which is to terminate and the tenants can rely on it only in so far as cl. 2 (23) is a term of the existing lease which calls for consideration when the new lease is

E   framed.

In my judgment, the county court judge's initial finding on the facts of this case that the work could be done reasonably without the landlords obtaining possession of the holding concludes this case in favour of the tenants' application. I would allow the appeal and failing agreement would direct that the case go back to the county court to decide the terms of the new lease in accordance with the

F   Act of 1954.

DAVIES, L.J.: I agree with the judgment of SELLERS, L.J., and have very little to add.

The result of the argument advanced by counsel for the landlords would be that in the overwhelming majority of cases the concluding words of s. 30 (1) (*f*)

G   of the Landlord and Tenant Act, 1954, would be meaningless and would confer no benefit whatsoever on the tenant. Those words must contemplate that there may be cases in which works of demolition or reconstruction can reasonably be carried out by a landlord without obtaining possession of the holding, that is to say, without dispossessing the tenant; but if, as counsel for the landlords submits, any special terms of the old tenancy or to be contained in the new tenancy are to

H   be ignored and any consent by the tenant to the doing of the works is irrelevant, the landlord would always need to obtain possession in order to do the works. For with a tenant in possession under what has been called " an ordinary lease ", a landlord has, of course, no right of entry to execute such works. Thus para. (*f*) would afford no protection at all to the tenant. It is impossible to believe that the paragraph is as meaningless as that.

I   Counsel for the landlords does not shrink from this result. He agrees that it is so ; but he says that the words would apply in a case where in order to carry out the works the landlord requires possession of part only of the holding. This would lead, however, to an equally nonsensical result. For by s. 23 (3) " the holding " means " the property comprised in the tenancy ". So in such a case one of two results would follow. Either the landlord could not show that in order to carry out the works he required possession of the whole holding, and therefore

(14) [1962] 1 All E.R. 195.

the tenant would be entitled to a new tenancy under which he would have the   A
right to exclude the landlord, and thus the possibility of reasonable and desirable
development by the landlord might be frustrated or at least postponed: or,
alternatively, it would be said that, although the landlord required only a part
of the holding, nevertheless, since a tenancy must be a tenancy of the whole
holding, the tenant's claim to a new tenancy must fail.

These considerations demonstrate that the landlords' contention is wrong. It is   B
wrong because it ignores the all-important word " reasonably ". Reasonableness
is a question of fact; and, as I think, the factual approach to the interpretation
of this provision is to be found in all the authorities, even in *Whittingham* v.
Davies (15), though, of course, that case contains the observation of LORD
EVERSHED, M.R., (16) which SELLERS, L.J., has discussed (17).

The proper meaning of s. 30 (1) (*f*) is, in my opinion, that the landlord must show   C
that he cannot reasonably carry out his works with the tenant in possession;
and if, as in the present case, it is found that in fact he can, then the tenant is
entitled to a new lease. Provision would then have to be made, either by consent
or by the inclusion in the new tenancy by virtue of s. 35 of an appropriate clause,
to allow the landlord to enter in order to carry out the works.

I do not agree with counsel for the landlords' submission that, in deciding   D
whether a given case falls within s. 30 (1) (*f*), the terms of the old lease or of a
possible new lease must be ignored. For, as I have said, in the absence of some
special clause or consent by the tenant the paragraph could have no effective
application. I agree, therefore, that the appeal succeeds.

RUSSELL, L.J.: I prefer first to consider this statutory provision without   E
regard to previous cases thereon. The Landlord and Tenant Act, 1954, s. 30 (1) (*f*)
applies where a tenancy of a holding for business purposes is in the ordinary course
of events about to be terminated, in which case the holding would come to hand.
It contains a ground on which the landlord is entitled to oppose the grant by the
court on the tenant's application of a new tenancy of the holding, which grant
would of course prevent the holding coming to hand. The particular ground is   F
that on the termination of the current tenancy (a) the landlord intends (i) to
demolish or reconstruct the premises comprised in the holding, or a substantial
part of those premises or (ii) to carry on substantial work of construction on the
holding, or part of the holding: and (b) that the landlord could not reasonably
do so without obtaining possession of the holding.

The general statutory purpose is to confer on a business tenant a right to an   G
extension of his tenancy to protect his business goodwill associated with the
holding, the value of which is difficult to assess. The purpose of para. (*f*) is to
ensure that the general statutory purpose shall not hinder the ordinary course
of property development by demolition, reconstruction and construction. It
is to be expected that the statute should wherever possible achieve both those
purposes, and I approach the construction of the final sentence (under heading (a)   H
above) in that expectation.

Paragraph (*f*) envisages two situations. One is that the holding will be in hand
at the end of the current tenancy, in which case demolition, reconstruction and
construction is open to the landlord, since he will have the right to possession of
the holding. The other is that a new tenancy of the holding will be ordered by the
court, to take effect at the termination of the current tenancy: in which case the   I
landlord will not get possession of the holding or any part thereof. The final
sentence is therefore directed to the effect on the landlord's plans of the grant
of a new tenancy of the holding under the statutory powers.

One suggestion is that the final sentence of para. (*f*) is complied with in every
case involving the proposals mentioned in the earlier part, because as against a
tenant entitled to possession prima facie a landowner could have no conceivable

(15) [1962] 1 All E.R. 195.
(16) [1962] 1 All E.R. at pp. 198-200.   (17) Ante, p. 261, letters E and H.

A right to set about demolishing or reconstructing or constructing. If this were so the final sentence would have no function; but it is further argued that it has a limiting function in that it refers to possession of " the holding " which is the *whole* holding. Thus (it is said) the whole paragraph operates in this way: that if the carrying out of the landlord's proposals reasonably requires only possession of less than the whole holding, he has no valid ground of opposition to a new

B tenancy. This view does not live up to the expectation with which, as indicated, I approach the paragraph: for it would prevent a considerable amount of development, and there does not seem to be any logical reason for drawing this particular line. Apart from authority I would reject this construction of the paragraph.

What, then, is the significance and effect of the last sentence of para. (*f*)? It is not difficult to imagine a legislative thought-process on the following lines.

C This system of protection of business tenants must not interfere with proper development of property: therefore, make it a ground of opposition if the landlord intends to carry out substantial development; but may there not be cases in which development will not be inconsistent in all the circumstances with a new tenancy? Let us, therefore, seek to cover such cases by adding the final sentence of para. (*f*). (I have used the word " development " as a convenient label for the

D works of demolition, reconstruction and construction referred to in para. (*f*)). If this was the approach, the final sentence is a way of saying " and if the landlord cannot reasonably carry out the proposed works if a new tenancy is granted ".

My first instinct was to regard the establishing of the objection as something wholly detached from the terms which might be laid down for the new tenancy; but on reflection I do not see the need for this. On my reading of the final sentence

E of para. (*f*) the court must consider all the circumstances of the case, including the nature of the landlord's proposals, the nature of the tenant's business, the layout of the premises, and the question whether it would be reasonable and sensible (in the light of those other circumstances) to insert in the new tenancy provisions which would empower the landlord to carry out his proposals. These considerations will reveal whether in any particular case it is established that a new tenancy

F cannot reasonably be granted consistently with the carrying out by the landlord of his proposals, bearing always in mind that the main purpose of the legislation is to preserve the business goodwill of the tenant at the holding.

It would be easy to list examples of cases in which, with that approach, the landlord would establish his objection. Suppose a single-floor grocer's establishment, the landlord proposing to erect a block of offices in its place. His objection

G would be sustained even if the ground floor were to embrace a shop suited to a grocer: for there could not reasonably or sensibly be substituted for the existing tenancy a tenancy of what was to become a block of offices and a shop—" the holding ". It is equally possible, however, to think of cases in which substantial works of the kind envisaged by para. (*f*) could be carried out without being wholly incompatible with a new tenancy of a kind which would fulfil the purpose

H of the legislation—that is, to give to the tenant a measure of security in relation to the goodwill of his business. One is familiar in everyday life with reconstructions substantial in degree carried out over and round the sign " Business as Usual ", while fully appreciating that in truth it means " Business Not as Usual ".

If this were the correct approach, what of the present case? Here is a petrol filling station. It has an array of pumps, with a usual canopy and kiosk. It

I has, perhaps unusually, a row of lock-up garages. It has available lavatories. The landlords are a petrol company. The lease is in a common form, under which both landlords and tenants are interested in the holding as an outlet for petrol and oil. The landlords' proposals involve total transformation of the holding by way of modernisation with the sole purpose of increasing the sale of petroleum products, an outcome which will profit both landlords and tenants. If the holding comes to hand, the landlords will effect the alterations with the sensible intention of disrupting as little as possible the holding as an outlet for the sale of petrol and oil to motorists. The activities will involve some temporary inconvenience

and loss of receipts, but the purpose in the long run is to increase the turnover: A
and it is plain that the landlords do not regard the proposed alterations as in any
way inconsistent with the continuance of this holding as a filling station.

I would therefore hold that in the present case there is in all the circumstances
no inconsistency between the landlords' proposals and the grant of a new tenancy
under the statute, such tenancy to contain appropriate provisions to enable the
works to be carried out.   If that be so, then the landlords' objection, on my B
reading of s. 30 (1) (*f*) of the Landlord and Tenant Act, 1954, is not established.
In my view the appeal should be allowed and the case remitted to the county
court with a declaration that the tenants are entitled to the grant of a new
tenancy, such tenancy to include in its terms provisions authorising the landlords
to carry out the proposed works.   Other terms of the tenancy will be determined
by the county court if not agreed.   C

In so concluding I do not rely on the fact that the existing tenancy includes
cl. 2 (23) as to structural alterations; but its presence helps to demonstrate that
the landlords' proposals are not inconsistent with a tenancy of the premises as a
filling station.

Does authority prevent the conclusion to which, apart from it, I would arrive?
On the whole I think not.   I find *Whittingham* v. *Davies* (18) not altogether an D
easy case to follow.   It is clear that on any footing it was rightly decided, because
a part of the holding was under the lessor's scheme to be appropriated for the
erection of private lock-up garages for the use of tenants of the flats in the new
building to be erected.   That part of the scheme was clearly wholly inconsistent
with a new lease of " the holding " to the existing tenant thereof.   At one stage
LORD EVERSHED, M.R., seems to be saying that, if the lessor's proposals are E
such that they are inconsistent in law with the holding being the subject of any
tenancy, no new tenancy can be granted: but this would prevent the grant of a
new tenancy in every case of proposed development and make the word " reasonably " wholly inapposite: and in other parts of his judgment he seems to depart
from this approach. I share with LORD DENNING, M.R., in *Jones* v. *Thomas* (19)
an inability to accept the " inconsistent in law " approach that appears at one F
stage in LORD EVERSHED's judgment.   On the other hand I should have thought
that there was a shorter cut to the decision in *Jones* v. *Thomas* (19) than that
which was taken.   The business carried on on the holding was that of wheel-
wright, blacksmith and carpenter.   The premises comprised in the holding were
a workshop, a forge, and a roofed-in yard.   The lessor proposed (a) to convert
the workshop into a garage, (b) to pull down the forge and (c) to remove the G
roof and supports from the yard so as to incorporate it into the garden of the
landlord's adjoining property.   I do not find it easy to see how at any rate
(b) and (c) could be consistent with the grant of a new tenancy of the whole
holding designed to enable the tenant's business to be carried on thereon.

It is perhaps dangerous to attempt a general definition in such matters: but it
seems to me that the effect of the final sentence of s. 30 (1) (*f*) of the Act of 1954 H
is that if the landlord's proposals cannot reasonably be regarded as consistent
with a grant of a new tenancy of the whole holding such as will substantially
achieve continuity in the tenant's business and its goodwill in the whole holding,
then a new tenancy cannot be granted: but in determining this question it is
relevant that a new tenancy is capable of including provisions enabling the landlord to carry out his proposals.   I

*Appeal allowed: case remitted to county court to determine terms of new lease
unless agreed.   Leave to appeal to House of Lords refused.*

Solicitors: *Kingsford, Dorman & Co.*, agents for *Blake, Lapthorn, Rea &
Williams*, Portsmouth (for the tenants); *Joynson-Hicks & Co.*, agents for *Gates &
Co.*, Brighton (for the landlords).

[*Reported by* HENRY SUMMERFIELD, ESQ., *Barrister-at-Law.*]

---

(18) [1962] 1 All E.R. 195.   (19) (1963), 186 Estates Gazette 1053.

A

R. *v.* McGREGOR.

[COURT OF APPEAL, CRIMINAL DIVISION (Lord Parker, C.J., Diplock, L.J., and Ashworth, J.), March 17, 1967.]

B *Criminal Law—Evidence—Admission—Evidence of admission of accused, when giving evidence at first trial, admitted on re-trial—Cross-examination of witness as to accused's explanation at first trial—Accused not giving evidence at second trial—Whole statement should be left to jury to decide as to the truth.*

On a re-trial of the appellant on a charge of receiving stolen goods, the appellant's wife having been acquitted on the same charge at the first trial and the jury having disagreed in respect of the charge against the appellant, the trial judge allowed the prosecution to call a police officer to give evidence

C that, at the first trial the appellant had admitted that he had possession of the goods and had said that he had put them in his wife's shopping bag. A transcript of the evidence was supplied to the defence, and counsel for the appellant cross-examined the police officer to bring out further matter that the appellant had said at the first trial and, in particular, explanations how he had come into possession of the goods and how he claimed when he came into

D possession of them that he did not know that they were stolen. The appellant did not give evidence at the re-trial. In his summing-up, the trial judge made it clear to the jury that they were to consider the explanations that the appellant had given at the earlier trial, but reminded them that, the appellant not having given evidence himself, they could not be tested. On appeal against conviction on the grounds that (a) the trial judge was wrong in allowing the

E evidence of the police officer to be given because it was inadmissible, or, even if it was admissible, because it was in the circumstances of the case unfair, and (b) the prosecution having put in the admission as to possession, the whole of it must be put in and not merely a part of it, so that not only must the admission be taken to be true, the appellant not having gone into the box and denied it, but also that his explanation must be taken to be true,

F   **Held:** (i) there was no ground on which it could be said that the police officer's evidence was inadmissible, since the appellant's admissions made at the earlier trial on oath were clearly evidence of possession, which was one of the relevant matters which the prosecution had to prove (see p. 268, letter I, post); nor was the admission of the evidence unfair in the general circumstances of the administration of justice (see p. 269, letter A, post);

G   (ii) the whole statement, both the admission and the explanation, should be left to the jury to say whether the facts asserted by the appellant in his favour be true, but the jury were not obliged to accept the explanation as true even if there were no other evidence incompatible with it (see p. 269, letter E, post) (*R. v. Jones* ((1827), 2 C. & P. 629) disapproved); in the present case, as the appellant had not given evidence, and had not gone into

H the witness box to deny the truth of his earlier statement that he had put the goods into his wife's shopping bag or to verify the explanation he had given on the previous occasion, it was only natural and proper that the jury should attach greater weight to the admission than to the explanation (see p. 269, letter I, to p. 270, letter A, post).

    Appeal dismissed.

I   [As to the use of statements made by a defendant in a criminal trial, see 10 HALSBURY'S LAWS (3rd Edn.) 476, para. 871; and for cases on the subject, see 14 DIGEST (Repl.) 490, *4721-4727*.]

Case referred to:

    R. v. Jones, (1827), 2 C. & P. 629; 172 E.R. 285; 14 Digest (Repl.) 490, *4722*.

    Appeal.

This was an appeal by John McGregor against his conviction on Oct. 24, 1966, at Liverpool Crown Court before JUDGE NANCE and a jury of receiving stolen

property. He was sentenced to three years' imprisonment. He had previously **A**
stood trial at Liverpool Crown Court for the same offence jointly with his wife;
but on Sept. 30, 1966, she was acquitted and the jury failed to agree on their
verdict regarding the appellant. During the course of the second trial the prosecution were permitted to call a witness, Inspector Dean, to give evidence of answers
given by the appellant to questions put to him in cross-examination at the first
trial. Leave to appeal against conviction was given by the single judge on a point **B**
of law, viz., whether the trial judge was right in law in allowing Inspector Dean
to give the evidence which he did. The appellant also applied for leave to appeal
against sentence. The facts are set out in the judgment of the court.

J. M. Dovener for the appellant.
I. H. M. Jones for the Crown.

C

LORD PARKER, C.J., delivered the following judgment of the court:
A police sergeant stopped a motor car which was being driven by the appellant
with his wife as a passenger in the afternoon of Mar. 1, 1966. The officer said that
he had reason to believe they were in possession of stolen jewellery and asked them
to leave the car. According to him, the appellant replied: "There's some
bastards in Liverpool." In the appellant's wife's shopping bag which had been **D**
in the car was found a parcel wrapped in newspaper which in turn contained a
plastic bag in which were silver, white gold, platinum, and metal contacts which
had been stolen over a period of some three years before from the premises of the
Automatic Telephone Co. at Edge Lane, Liverpool. The appellant and his wife
were taken to the police station and, according to the police, when the appellant
was shown the parcel he said: "I knew it was there but that is all I'm saying. **E**
I want to go to Liverpool before I say any more." Again, when he was told that
the articles had been examined and of their estimated value, he said: "I know
you won't tell me, but what I want to know is how you knew it was there."

The background which gave rise to the point in this case is that there had been
a previous trial of the appellant and of his wife. His wife had been acquitted, and
the jury disagreed in respect of the charge against the appellant of receiving. In **F**
the course of the new trial, the prosecution intimated to the defence that they
proposed to call a police officer who had been present at the first trial who would
say that the appellant had admitted at that first trial that he had possession of
these goods, which is clearly one of the elements in receiving, and, indeed, had
said that he had put them in his wife's shopping bag. After considerable argument, the judge admitted that evidence, there was an adjournment, the defence **G**
was supplied with a transcript, and counsel for the appellant proceeded to cross-
examine the police officer, quite properly, to bring out further matter that the
appellant had said at the earlier trial, and, in particular, explanations how he had
come into possession of the goods and how he claimed when he came into
possession of them that he did not know that they were stolen.

The first ground of appeal is that the learned judge was wrong in allowing that **H**
evidence to be given, first, on the ground that it was, as has been said, inadmissible; and, secondly, on quite a general ground, that, even if admissible, it was in
the circumstances of this case unfair. With regard to the first point, this court
can conceive of no ground on which it could be said that this evidence was
inadmissible. It was in the nature of an admission or a confession made at the
earlier trial on oath, and it is clearly evidence of possession, one of the relevant **I**
matters which the prosecution have to prove. The most that can be said about it
is that it is a novel point; neither counsel nor any member of the court can
remember a case when this has been done, but in principle, as it seems to this
court, there is no ground whatever in such a case why the prosecution should not
give that evidence. Secondly, it is said that it was unfair. As the court understands it, counsel for the appellant says that it was unfair because it no doubt
did cut the ground from under his feet and prevented him from making a submission of no case. It is also said to be unfair in that really, if the appellant stood

A any chance, he would have to give evidence. In fact he gave no evidence at all. Unfair in that sense it may have been, but unfair in the general circumstances of the administration of justice it was certainly not. This court can see no ground to interfere with the conviction on the first point.

The second point raised by counsel for the appellant deals with the manner in which the learned judge left the admission as to possession and the explanation **B** given at the earlier trial to the jury. As we understand it, counsel for the appellant says, and says rightly, that, if the prosecution are minded to put in an admission or a confession, they must put in the whole and not merely a part of it. He then goes on from that as the next stage to rely on an old case—not necessarily the worse for that—in 1827, *R.* v. *Jones* (1), where SERJEANT BOSANQUET ruled in that case in these terms:

C   " There is no doubt that if a prosecutor uses the declaration of a prisoner, he must take the whole of it together, and cannot select one part and leave another . . ."

So far that seems quite correct. But he then goes on (2):

D   " and if there be either no other evidence in the case, or no other evidence incompatible with it, the declaration so adduced in evidence must be taken as true."

Accordingly, counsel for the appellant submits, as I understand it, that not only must the admission as to possession be taken to be true, the appellant not having gone into the box and denied it, but also that his explanation must be taken to be true. In the opinion of this court, that case of *R.* v. *Jones* (3) is no longer authority. **E** It was an old case in 1827, long before 1898 (4), and, as stated in para. 1,128 of ARCHBOLD's CRIMINAL PLEADING, EVIDENCE AND PRACTICE (36th Edn.), the better opinion seems to be that, as in the case of all other evidence, the whole should be left to the jury to say whether the facts asserted by the prisoner in his favour be true. The court is satisfied that that passage in ARCHBOLD sets out the true position.

F   That is not the end of the matter because counsel for the appellant goes on to say that, in the present case, the judge has in effect withdrawn from the jury the explanations, and has left them only with the admission. The summing-up on this matter is not as clear as it might have been, but the court is satisfied that, read as a whole, it was accurate. The judge was at pains to tell the jury that what the policeman was allowed to say as to what other witnesses—other than the **G** appellant—said at the earlier trial was in no sense evidence of the facts to which those witnesses spoke. So far that is undoubtedly true, but there are passages which would seem to suggest that they should not consider as evidence of fact the explanations which the appellant himself had given at the earlier trial. On the other hand, read as a whole, and particularly when one comes to the later passages before the jury retired, it seems to this court that the position was made **H** clear that the jury were to consider the explanations that the appellant had given at the earlier trial, but the judge reminded them that, the appellant not having given evidence himself, the explanations could not be tested.

Finally, counsel for the appellant submits that the jury ought to have been told in fact that they should give equal weight to that part of the evidence of the appellant at the previous hearing which dealt with his admission of possession **I** and with his explanations. The court cannot conceive why the jury should attach equal weight to both. The appellant not having given evidence, not having gone into the witness box to deny the truth of his earlier statement that he had put the goods into his wife's shopping bag, and not having gone into the witness box to verify the explanations which he had given on the previous occasion, it

---

(1) (1827), 2 C. & P. 629 at p. 630.   (2) (1827), 2 C. & P. at p. 630.
(3) (1827), 2 C. & P. 629.
(4) I.e., before the passing of the Criminal Evidence Act, 1898.

was only natural and proper that the jury should attach greater weight to the **A** admission than to the explanations.

For these reasons, this court is satisfied that there are no grounds for interfering with this conviction and the appeal against conviction is dismissed.

[The court refused the application for leave to appeal against sentence.]

Appeal dismissed. Application refused.

Solicitors: *Registrar of Criminal Appeals* (for the appellant); *Prosecuting* **B** *Solicitor*, Liverpool (for the Crown).

[*Reported by* N. P. METCALFE, ESQ., *Barrister-at-Law.*]

C

SLOUGH ESTATES, LTD. *v.* SLOUGH BOROUGH COUNCIL AND ANOTHER.

[CHANCERY DIVISION (Ungoed-Thomas, J.), November 21, 22, 23, 24, 25, 1966, January 25, February 16, 1967.]   **D**

Practice—Stay of proceedings—Concurrent proceedings before distinct tribunals— Election by plaintiffs held to be the appropriate course—Factors determining exercise of court's discretion—Material time at which to assess position— Appeal to Minister against planning decision—Application to High Court concurrently for declaration on validity of planning permission—Application for stay of High Court proceedings—Withdrawal of appeal to Minister after **E** *argument before High Court and before decision on staying proceedings in High Court—Duplication of proceedings in regard to issue raised in appeal to Minister—Whether abuse of process—Whether discretion to grant stay should be exercised—Supreme Court of Judicature (Consolidation) Act, 1925 (15 & 16 Geo. 5 c. 49), s. 41.*

On Oct. 17, 1945, planning permission (UL21) was granted to the plaintiffs **F** to use the Slough Trading Estate for industrial purposes conditional on subsequent approval by the local planning authority of further particulars of development. Subsequently the defendant county council replaced the first defendant as planning authority, and since 1952 UL21 had not been relied on by the plaintiffs. The first defendant wanted an undeveloped area of land to be left for car parks, but the plaintiffs did not and applied for **G** planning permission for factories and warehouses in respect of it. The Minister called in the applications (under s. 22* of Town and Country Planning Act, 1962) to determine them himself, and directed a local inquiry, which was held in January, 1966. In one instance, however, the plaintiffs applied for approval of particulars of factory development relying on UL21; the local planning authority declined to give approval, regarding UL21 as **H** being no longer effective, and it rejected the application. The plaintiffs appealed under s. 23* of the Act of 1962. The purpose of the s. 23 appeal was to decide whether UL21 remained effective. By originating summons dated Apr. 21, 1966, the plaintiffs applied to the court for a declaration to the effect (as ultimately amended) that UL21 remained effective, or that they had permission to develop for industrial purposes so that approval could not be **I** withheld merely on the ground that development ought to be for other purposes. The purpose of making this application to the court was to obtain a decision before the first appointed day† under the Land Commission Act 1967. The defendants submitted as a preliminary point that

---

* The effect of s. 22 and s. 23 is stated at p. 273, letters H and I, post.

† Apr. 6, 1967; cf. p. 276, letter F, post. See, as regards the charge to levy, s. 33 of the Land Commission Act 1967.

A   the summons should be stayed under s. 41* of the Supreme Court of Judicature (Consolidation) Act, 1925.   After argument on that point and while judgment was reserved, the plaintiffs withdrew their s. 23 appeal.   The Minister accepted the withdrawal.   A few days later the Minister decided the applications, for planning permission that he had called in; he gave permission for development for warehouses mainly but also for some fac-

B   tories, without regard to UL21.   The time for appealing from the Minister's decision expired.

Held: (i) the proper course, independently of any withdrawal of the s. 23 appeal, had been that the plaintiffs should elect which proceedings they should pursue, and that the proceedings which they elected not to pursue should be terminated (see p. 280, letters C and G, post); this had been

C   the proper course because, although (a) there was duplication between the s. 23 appeal and the High Court proceedings (though not in relation to the applications called in under s. 22 of the Act of 1962), (b) the duplication was in the circumstances vexatious, oppressive and an abuse of the process of the court and (c) there had been no undue delay on the part of the defendants in seeking a stay, yet the granting of a stay was a discretionary

D   remedy, and in this case might have caused injustice to the plaintiffs which election by them would have avoided (see p. 275, letters E and G, p. 276, letter H, p. 277, letter H, and p. 278, letter F, post).

Dicta of LORD ESHER, M.R., in *The Christiansborg* ((1885), 10 P.D. at p. 148) applied.

The Soya Margareta ([1960] 2 All E.R. 756) considered.

E   (ii) the court was entitled, when exercising its discretion over granting a stay of proceedings, to consider the relevant circumstances as at the time of exercising the discretion; and in the circumstances of the present case, but disregarding the withdrawal of the s. 23 appeal by which the court's decision was not influenced, the court would make no order on the application for a stay of the proceedings in the High Court on the plaintiffs undertaking

F   (as they offered to do) to pay the costs of these proceedings, they having run two sets of proceedings concurrently to increase their chances of getting a decision quickly (see p. 281, letters B and F, p. 276, letter F, and p. 279, letter H, post).

[As to when a stay of proceedings is granted, see 7 HALSBURY'S LAWS (3rd

G   Edn.) 171, 172, paras. 307, 308; and for cases on the subject, see 11 DIGEST (Repl.) 542-545, *1508-1531.*

For the Supreme Court of Judicature (Consolidation) Act, 1925, s. 41, see 18 HALSBURY'S STATUTES (2nd Edn.) 478; and for the Town and Country Planning Act, 1962, s. 22 and s. 23, see 42 ibid., pp. 990, 991.]

Cases referred to:

H   *Christiansborg, The,* (1885), 10 P.D. 141; 54 L.J.P. 84; 53 L.T. 612; 11 Digest (Repl.) 551, *1587.*

Edgwarebury Park Investments, Ltd. v. *Minister of Housing and Local Government,* [1963] 1 All E.R. 124; [1963] 2 Q.B. 408; [1963] 2 W.L.R. 257; 45 Digest (Repl.) 338, *48.*

Jopson v. *James,* (1908), 77 L.J.Ch. 824; 11 Digest (Repl.) 543, *1513.*

I   *St. Pierre* v. *South American Stores (Gath & Chaves), Ltd.,* [1935] All E.R. Rep. 408; [1936] 1 K.B. 382; 105 L.J.K.B. 436; 154 L.T. 546; 11 Digest (Repl.) 372, *378.*

Soya Margareta, The, Cargo Owners on Board Soya Lovisa v. *Soya Margareta (Owners),* [1960] 2 All E.R. 756; [1961] 1 W.L.R. 709; [1960] 1 Lloyd's Rep. 675; Digest (Cont. Vol. A) 257, *1531a.*

---

* For the relevant terms of s. 41, see p. 274, letter D, post.

Adjourned Summons.   A

This was an application by originating summons dated Apr. 21, 1966, by the
plaintiffs, Slough Estates, Ltd., against the defendants, Slough Borough Council
and Buckinghamshire County Council, whereby the plaintiffs asked for
declarations which were reformulated at the hearing to the following—

" A declaration that the plaintiffs have permission to erect factories   B
with ancillary services subject to the approval of such particulars as the
local planning authority may require on areas of the Slough Trading Estate
which remained undeveloped on Oct. 17, 1945, when planning permission
was granted, or alternatively on such part or parts of such areas as have
not since been developed; alternatively, a declaration that the plaintiffs
have permission to develop such areas for industrial purposes so that the
approval for the erection of factories cannot be withheld merely on the   C
ground that the land ought to be used otherwise than for industrial purposes."

The facts are set out in the judgment.

The cases noted below* were cited during the argument in addition to those
referred to in the judgment.

Douglas Frank, Q.C., *Charles Sparrow*, Q.C., *Patrick Freeman* and *David Kean* D
for the plaintiffs.

J. L. Arnold, Q.C., and *Jeremiah Harman* for the defendants.

Cur. adv. vult.

Feb. 16. **UNGOED-THOMAS, J.,** read the following judgment, in
which, after having stated the question raised by the originating summons as   E
reformulated, he continued: The plaintiffs, Slough Estates, Ltd., are the owners
of the Slough Trading Estate and have developed land there for factories to let.
On Oct. 17, 1945, planning permission was granted under the then Town and
Country Planning Act. That is a planning permission which bears the reference
" UL21 ", and has been conveniently referred to as such. This permission was
saved by the Town and Country Planning Act, 1947, and again later by the   F
Town and Country Planning Act, 1962, which replaced the Act of 1947. The
permission was to use the estate for industrial purposes subject to a condition
requiring subsequent approval by the local planning authority, which was then
Slough Borough Council, of further particulars of development. By the Act
of 1947 Slough Borough Council was replaced as local planning authority by
Buckinghamshire County Council. Since 1952, UL21 has not been relied on   G
by the plaintiffs: planning permissions for factories were obtained by them
independently of it. Slough Borough Council subsequently intimated that
they wished a substantial area of undeveloped land on the estate to be used as
car parks for those engaged on the estate, instead of as factories, and this was
not acceptable to the plaintiffs. The issue was submitted to the Minister
through applications by the plaintiffs, for planning permission, in part for   H
factories and in part for warehouses. Under s. 22 of the Act of 1962 the Minister
called in the applications for determination by himself, and in January, 1966,
a local inquiry was held. In one case, however, the plaintiff company applied
to the local planning authority, not for new permission but for approval, of
particulars of factory development pursuant to and in accordance with the

I

* *Francis* v. *Yiewsley and West Drayton Urban District Council*, [1957] 3 All E.R. 529;
[1958] 1 Q.B. 478; *Hamilton* v. *West Sussex County Council*, [1958] 2 All E.R. 174;
[1958] 2 Q.B. 286; *Pyx Granite Co., Ltd.* v. *Ministry of Housing and Local Government*,
[1959] 3 All E.R. 1; [1960] A.C. 260; *Fawcett Properties, Ltd.* v. *Buckingham County
Council*, [1960] 3 All E.R. 503; [1961] A.C. 636; *F. Lucas & Sons, Ltd.* v. *Dorking and
Horley Rural District Council*, (1964), 62 L.G.R. 491; *Biss* v. *Smallburgh Rural District
Council*, [1964] 2 All E.R. 543; [1965] Ch. 335; *Annicola Investments, Ltd.* v. *Minister
of Housing and Local Government*, [1965] 3 All E.R. 850; *Viscount Camrose* v. *Basing-
stoke Corpn.*, [1966] 3 All E.R. 161; *Wells* v. *Minister of Housing and Local Government*,
(1966), 110 Sol. Jo. 889.

A conditions subject to which UL21 had been granted. The local planning authority decided that the UL21 permission was no longer of any effect, and therefore declined approval of the particulars submitted. So the plaintiffs appealed under s. 23 of the Act of 1962 to the Minister against the failure of the local planning authority to approve the particulars. Therefore, at the January, 1966 inquiry that matter was also before the Minister.

B   No decision from the Minister on any of these applications had been made when this case came before me. Because no decision had been made by the Minister, and an early decision was wanted by the plaintiffs, these proceedings were commenced on Apr. 21, 1966. The whole object and general effect of the s. 23 appeal to the Minister was made unmistakably clear at the inquiry by counsel for the plaintiffs, with the support of counsel for the local planning

C authority. It was to raise the question whether the UL21 was an existing valid permission for factory development, which, whatever detailed distinctions might be drawn, was in substance the same question as that raised by the application before me.

In those circumstances the defendants submitted as a preliminary point that there should be a stay of the proceedings before me. The application was opened on

D Nov. 21, but as it was opened generally by the plaintiffs, and the application by the defendants for a stay was in part based on evidence to be read in the opening, the application for the stay did not come on for hearing until Nov. 23, and was not concluded until Friday, Nov. 25, when judgment was reserved. On the following Wednesay, Nov. 30, the plaintiffs wrote to the Minister to withdraw the s. 23 appeal, and on Dec. 1 the defendants wrote to the Minister contending that he,

E the Minister, would nevertheless have to consider the validity of UL21. I had been informed of what was occurring, and therefore held up my judgment and arranged for the matter to be mentioned in court on Dec. 2, when it was left for the parties to arrange for an early day for a further hearing of the application for a stay, after and in view of the reply which was expected to the plaintiffs' letter to the Minister to withdraw the s. 23 appeal. On Dec. 8 the Minister

F wrote accepting the plaintiffs' withdrawal of the plaintiffs' submissions on UL21. On Dec. 13 the Minister gave his decision on the called-in applications, granting the permission for development for warehouses mainly and also for some factories. This decision was made without regard to any planning permission under UL21. The matter next came before me on Jan. 25 when the effect of the plaintiffs' purported withdrawal of the s. 23 appeal and the Minister's decision

G without regard to planning permission under UL21 on the application for a stay of the proceedings before me was argued.

I will now refer to certain provisions of the Town and Country Planning Act, 1962. Section 14 (2) (*b*) provides that under a development order a local planning authority may give planning permission, and the development order under which the local authority in this case was enabled to give permission was the

H Town and Country Planning General Development Order 1963 (1), of which the relevant article is art. 5 (2) (i). Section 22 (1), (2), (5) and (6) provides that the Minister may give directions for applications for planning permission to be made to him, i.e., he may, as it is generally put, call in an application made to a local planning authority. Section 23 (1), (4) and (5) provides for an applicant to a local planning authority for planning permission or approval required under

I a development order to have a right of appeal to the Minister. Section 43 I mention because it is referred to in *Edgwarebury Park Investments, Ltd.* v. *Minister of Housing and Local Government* (2) to which I shall come in a moment. It provides that application may be made to the Minister to determine whether planning permission is required in the context mentioned in the section, but no application in this case was made at all under that section.

___

(1) S.I. 1963 No. 709; amended by S.I. 1964 No. 1239, 1965 No. 498.
(2) [1963] 1 All E.R. 124; [1963] 2 Q.B. 408.

Section 176 (1) (*e*) provides that the Minister's action under sub-s. (3) of that   **A**
section is not to be questioned in any legal proceedings, except as provided by
that part of the Act of 1963, which is Part 11. Subsection (3) shows (in paras.
(*a*) and (*b*) that the Minister's action referred to in sub-s. (1) (*e*) includes any
decision under s. 22 or s. 23, i.e., on called-in applications or appeals, as I have
mentioned. Section 179 (3), which is the relevant part of Part 11 referred to in
s. 176, provides that s. 179 applies to orders mentioned in s. 176 (3) and, there-   **B**
fore, of course, to the Minister's decisions on s. 22 and s. 23.   Subsection (1)
provides that when the Minister makes a deicsion, mentioned in sub-s. (3), it
can only be questioned as provided for in the Act of 1962, and that is only on the
ground either that his action was not within his powers under the Act of 1962, or
that any of the requirements of the Act of 1962 have not been complied with.

I will now deal with the application for a stay, first as it stood at the end of the   **C**
hearing in November, before the withdrawal of the s. 23 appeal from the Minister,
and afterwards I shall deal with the effect, if any, that that withdrawal should
have on any decision which I would otherwise have made. The application for
a stay is made in accordance with the proviso to s. 41 of the Supreme Court of
Judicature (Consolidation) Act, 1925, which provides that:

> " Nothing in this Act shall disable either of the said courts [that is the   **D**
> High Court or the Court of Appeal] if it thinks fit so to do, from directing
> a stay of proceedings in any cause or matter pending before it."

The jurisdiction to grant a stay is a discretionary jurisdiction. This is fundamental to this case and to my decision on it.

It is common ground that to obtain relief the defendants must establish: **E**
(i) duplication between two sets of proceedings; (ii) oppression, vexation or
abuse of the process of the court resulting from the continuation of the proceedings sought to be stayed; and (iii) the absence of any other consideration
against the relief sought such as what was suggested in this case, viz., unreasonable delay or acquiescence on the part of the plaintiffs. I will come later to
the question how far it is necessary for the defendants to establish, in order   **F**
to obtain relief, that the relief will cause no injustice to the plaintiffs.

First, then, is there duplication? This raises, first, the question whether the
Minister has power to decide the validity of the planning permission UL21.
The plaintiffs conceded, at any rate for the purposes of the hearing before me,
that the Minister has the power, even though some doubt was expressed for the
plaintiffs whether the Minister in fact has it. The plaintiffs cannot blow hot   **G**
and cold, and they eventually abided by their concession, although this would
not confer jurisdiction where there is none. The plaintiffs' suggestion was that
the decision in *Edgwarebury Park Investments, Ltd.* v. *Minister of Housing and
Local Government* (3) prevented the Minister deciding the validity of UL21.
As stated in the headnote, it was held that s. 17 of the Act of 1947, now replaced by s. 43 of the Act of 1962, to which I have referred, provided in that   **H**
case, (4):

> ". . . only a method by which a proposed developer could ascertain whether
> what he contemplated was development, and whether it was the sort of
> development for which a general permission was given by the Town
> and Country Planning General Development Order, 1950 (5), or was
> development for which he must obtain express permission."   **I**

So that section did not enable the Minister, on an application under it, to determine whether an alleged permission by the local planning authority was valid.
All the section does is to enable a ruling to be obtained conveniently within the
ambit of the section's restricted terms, and the case (3) does not establish that the

---

(3) [1963] 1 All E.R. 124; [1963] 2 Q.B. 408.
(4) [1963] 1 All E.R. at p. 124, letter H.
(5) S.I. 1950 No. 728.

A Minister cannot decide the validity of planning permission under a s. 23 appeal. Therefore the only ground for the plaintiffs' suggestion that the Minister might not have jurisdiction seems to me to be ill-founded.

The question of duplication raises, secondly, the question of the extent to which there is in fact duplication between these proceedings and the proceedings before the Minister.   The object of both proceedings, so far as they affect UL21,

B is in general, as I have indicated, to obtain a decision whether it is an existing valid permission for building factories on the Slough Estate.   The s. 23 appeal, designed to raise the question of the UL21's validity, is in form limited to the small area of land to which the appeal directly relates, but it was designed to be and will have the effect of a test case applicable generally to all the area still within UL21.   If the court were to decide in favour of the plaintiffs that UL21

C is effective to give planning permission for factory building before a decision by the Minister, it would make superfluous and nugatory not only the appeal under s. 23 but also the called-in applications under s. 22.   The s. 22 applications would be nugatory because the plaintiffs, so I am told, have interim development certificates for factories and require none for warehouses, so that the only purpose of the s. 22 applications was to obtain planning permission and not approval for

D factories and warehouses within the ambit of a planning permission.   The court's decision in the plaintiffs' favour on UL21 would mean that they had that planning permission under UL21 without having to rely on the s. 22 applications.   If the court were to decide, against the plaintiffs, that there was no existing valid planning permission for factories under UL21, then it would decide the subject of the s. 23 appeal to the Minister, but it would leave the s. 22 applications for

E planning permission as effective applications to be dealt with by him.

In view of the withdrawal of the s. 23 appeal and the Minister's decision, the s. 22 decision of the Minister stands, but this decision would not affect any decision which the court might make on the validity of the UL21 permission. If the Minister were to have decided on the s. 23 appeal, then that decision would be conclusive except subject to appeal in accordance with s. 176 and s. 179 of

F the Act of 1962, to which I have referred, on the grounds mentioned in s. 179, that the Minister had not acted within his powers or had not complied with the relevant requirements.

It therefore appears that there was duplication between the proceedings before this court and at any rate the s. 23 appeal to the Minister, and as the application is for a stay of the proceedings before this court and not the pro-

G ceedings before the Minister, it does not extend beyond proceedings which are duplicated.

So I come to the second matter which has to be established: have the defendants established that it would be vexatious, oppressive or an abuse of the process of the court for these proceedings to go on?   It is clear, as indeed is stated in a note in the SUPREME COURT PRACTICE 1967 (6) read to me, that it is prima facie

H vexatious and oppressive to sue concurrently in two British courts.   Are the Minister and this court two British courts or tribunals for this purpose?   Clearly they are both British, and, on this s. 23 appeal, the Minister has to act in accordance with the statute and quasi-judicially in accordance with our conceptions of justice.   There was no suggestion that the Minister in acting on the s. 23 appeal would act otherwise, still less that his position was such as to militate

I against his being just.   Indeed, as the plaintiffs were anxious at the time of the inquiry that the decision should be by the Minister, and not by this court, it is difficult to see how they could possibly maintain any such suggestion and, of course, such a suggestion was never for a moment contemplated.   LORD ESHER, M.R., in *The Christiansborg* (7) in a dissenting judgment, whose dissent does not affect the passage to which I shall refer, said:

---

(6) Vol. 2, para. 3359.   (7) (1885), 10 P.D. 141 at p. 148.

" Where both actions are in England in the same tribunals—because if A they are in tribunals where the proceedings are not identical or the remedies are not equally effective the law would apply which is applicable to foreign countries—prima facie it is vexatious, and therefore it would lie on the party who brings the second action to show that it was not so. But where the cases are in foreign countries, prima facie not being vexatious, the man who says it is, must prove clearly to the court that it is, and that the B person suing him in a court with ample jurisdiction would have in every respect the same chance in a foreign court which he has here, and equal facility to enforce the remedy."

So if in this case the proceedings are identical, and the remedies equally effective, prima facie the duplication is vexatious. It was not disputed that the remedies provided by the Minister's and the court's decisions are substantially equally C effective. The proceedings are different, but it was not suggested that any differences are matters of substance or relevance. No advantage was claimed for the one procedure over the other, except that it was hoped by the plaintiffs that this court might be more expeditious than the Minister, a hope which in the event was hardly put to the test, and to the extent to which it was put to the test was belied.   D

Of course, the procedures of application to the Minister and this court are not identical. LORD ESHER's reference to identity of procedure was merely as a requirement of a prima facie case of vexation, without need to consider and compare differing procedures, and of course in his reference to foreign courts he makes it clear that vexation can be established without identity of procedure. What is required in respect of the procedure is not that there should be precise identity E but that there should be such identity as does not give an advantage of substance to the procedure sought to be stayed over the procedure before the other forum, or as LORD ESHER puts it in the passage which I have read, that the tribunal should give—and I quote his words—" the same chance ". All that was relied on by the plaintiffs was the hope that this court might come to a decision more quickly than the Minister, in time to obtain the advantage of development F which would anticipate the betterment levy under the recent Land Commission Bill, since become an Act (8), as contrasted with the plaintiffs' lack of hope of a decision in such time from the Minister. (The Minister as I have said in fact made his decision on the s. 22 application before any decision of this court, though after the purported withdrawal from him of the s. 23 appeal.) Such a hope in the breast of the plaintiffs would not appear to me to constitute or turn G on a difference of procedure. In my view, the defendants, having thus discharged any onus that lay on them with regard to procedure, have established at any rate a prima facie case of vexation. Further, it seems to me that the plaintiffs were running proceedings before two tribunals concurrently to increase their chances of getting the decision by the time when they wanted it. This ground appeared from the plaintiffs' argument, but no other ground of substance H for the duplication was suggested by them. So it seems to me that this duplication, whilst it existed, was in the circumstances established before me, vexatious, oppressive, and an abuse of the process of the court.

The defendants also relied on the danger of conflicts of findings of fact between the Minister and this court if both proceedings were to continue concurrently. Under s. 176 and s. 179 of the Act of 1962 the Minister's findings of fact cannot I be questioned. I am satisfied that this danger existed and the plaintiffs admitted that it existed, at any rate on cross-examination. In view both of my being satisfied that vexation existed independently of such danger, and of the Minister eventually, in the event, not proceeding with a s. 23 appeal, I will not pause now over the details relied on by the defendants to establish danger of conflict on fact.

(8) The Land Commission Act 1967 (c. 1).

A   I come now to the third matter to be considered on an application for a stay, so far as it arises in these proceedings.   The plaintiffs suggest that the defendants are debarred from obtaining a stay by reason of unreasonable delay and acquiescence in the duplication of proceedings.   The plaintiffs agreed that they had not been prejudiced by any delay on the part of the defendants that might have occurred, and the principal if not the main ground of their objection, as I understand it, was that the defendants had indicated, so the plaintiffs stated, that

B   their objection to the proceedings in the High Court was that the court had no jurisdiction, and not that the court should stay its proceedings.

The plaintiffs' summons which started the proceedings in the High Court was issued, as I have said, on Apr. 21, 1966.   The question of a stay involved a consideration of evidence, which was not finally completed until an affidavit

C   by the plaintiffs was filed in November, 1966, in answer to an affidavit filed by the defendants in July, though I understand that the plaintiffs' affidavit was substantially completed and available to the defendants in August.

This matter came before Goff, J., on a preliminary question on June 21 when he was satisfied that there had been, until then, no undue delay on the part of the defendants.   There then occurred the only reference, before the hearing

D   before me, to this court having no jurisdiction.   On that occasion counsel for the defendants said that objection would be taken that the High Court did not have jurisdiction, but my brother, Goff, J., in his judgment was not apparently left with the impression that it was absence of jurisdiction that the defendants wished to rely on, except in so far as perhaps it might be said to result from the plaintiffs' decision to proceed in the first place before the

E   Minister on the validity of the UL21 planning permission rather than before this court, and by such election in effect to prefer the one forum over the other. For Goff, J., in his judgment mentioned that the defendants wanted to raise matters of fact relating to a submission by the defendants on election by the plaintiffs but not apparently on any submission on absence of jurisdiction.   He said of the defendants:

F   " They want to raise matters of fact relating to possible estoppel or election between remedies, the right either to go to the Minister and then appeal to this court, or to come to this court."

Moreover where election between the duplicated proceedings is appropriate, it is commonly enforced by a stay of the unelected proceedings.

G   From an affidavit filed three weeks later, on July 12, on behalf of the defendants it was clear that the defendants' submission was not that the court had no jurisdiction but that the plaintiffs were disabled by their election to appeal to the Minister to invoke the jurisdiction of this court.   The affidavit said:

        " The plaintiff has elected to submit this very question to the Minister, and cannot now seek to litigate the same point in the courts."

H   The defendants, before Goff, J., and in their affidavit, might have put their case high, but it seems to me that the defendants have established that it sufficiently raised in good time the substance of the question debated before me, and I see here no such delay, and still less acquiescence, as should deprive the defendants of such relief on this application as they should otherwise obtain.

I   I come now to the course to be taken.   A stay is a discretionary remedy, as I have said, to be exercised in accordance with well established judicial principles, and that includes the principle that it should not cause injustice to the plaintiffs. It has been repeatedly laid down that the jurisdiction should be exercised with the greatest caution, for example, by Lord Esher, M.R., in *The Christiansborg* (9). Lord Esher added (9), but apparently with reference to proceedings by a plaintiff here and abroad:

---

(9) (1885), 10 P.D. at p. 148.

" Indeed I can find no case in which the court has stayed the second   A
action without giving the plaintiff at least the right of election."

BAGGALLAY, L.J., however, in a passage recently adopted by HEWSON, J., in
The Soya Margareta (10) said (11):

" I take it to be established by a series of authorities that where a plaintiff
sues the same defendant in respect of the same cause of action in two
courts, one in this country and another abroad, there is a jurisdiction in the   B
courts of this country to act in one of three ways—to put the party so suing
to his election, or, without allowing him to elect, to stay all proceedings in
this country, or to stay all proceedings in the foreign country—it is not in
form a stay of proceedings in the foreign court, but an injunction restraining
the plaintiff from prosecuting the proceedings in the foreign country . . ."
                                                                                    C
It is, I understand, common ground that these principles stated by BAGGALLAY,
L.J., apply in this case, but if I have misunderstood that, then in any case I
make it clear that I accept them as good law.

SCOTT, L.J., in *St. Pierre* v. *South American Stores (Gath & Chaves), Ltd.* (12)
observed: ". . . In order to justify a stay two conditions must be satisfied, one
positive and the other negative." He deals under (a) with something that I   D
have already dealt with:

" (a) the defendant must satisfy the court that the continuance of the
action would work an injustice because it would be oppressive, or vexatious
to him, or would be an abuse of the process of the court in some other
way, . . ."

Then under (b) he refers to what I now come to consider: (b) The stay must   E
not cause an injustice to the plaintiff.

This consideration of not causing an injustice to the plaintiff appears to me
to be relevant in particular to the form of relief to be given. It may well be
that election would avoid injustice to the plaintiff which a mere stay might
inflict and SCOTT, L.J.'s remarks are directed in terms to a stay. If election
avoids injustice, then there is no reason why the plaintiff should not be put to   F
his election merely because a stay, if granted without election, might inflict
injustice on him. It is not, in my view, a pre-condition of putting the plaintiff
to his election that a case for a stay without injustice to the plaintiff must be
established. A stay is a discretionary remedy and not a technical or legal right
without place for discretion, and as a matter of judicial discretion it is administered
in accordance with judicial principles to achieve justice, and therefore has regard   G
to substance rather than form. Election in this context, unlike some other contexts, is similarly not a legal right but a matter of judicial discretion. It is not
a limitation on that discretion but a product of it, to be applied where its adoption
is the appropriate course for achieving a just solution. As appears from the
authorities, the court will take into consideration that a plaintiff had started one
action before another, but it does that only in the exercise of its discretion as to   H
what, if any, remedy should be applied: and such a course by the plaintiff does
not constitute a once-for-all election excluding the court from applying the remedy
of election when the case comes before it, if it thinks that that is the just and
proper course in all the circumstances.

In *The Soya Margareta* (13) the plaintiffs were restrained from continuing
proceedings in Italy concurrently with proceedings which they had taken here.   I
It was suggested in argument before me that this was based on an election which
bound the plaintiffs, and that similarly in our case the plaintiffs had elected to
proceed before the Minister. As I read *The Soya Margareta* (13), however, it did
not turn on the exercise of a once-for-all right of election by the plaintiffs, but

---

(10) [1960] 2 All E.R. 756 at p. 762.   (11) (1885), 10 P.D. at p. 152.
(12) [1935] All E.R. Rep. 408 at p. 414; [1936] 1 K.B. 382 at p. 398.
(13) [1960] 2 All E.R. 756.

A on the continuous and current readiness of the plaintiffs to abandon the Italian proceedings (14); and the references (15) made in the judgment to the plaintiffs' election, when read in conjunction with the earlier passage, emphasise, so it appears to me, the persistence of the plaintiffs' expressed preference for and election of the English forum.

In *Jopson* v. *James* (16) the Court of Appeal stayed proceedings in this country
B for relief co-extensive with the relief sought in a court in Nova Scotia. FARWELL L.J., said (17):

> " Two points appear to me to be usual on considering whether the court should have regard and defer to a jurisdiction with which it may come in conflict, or whether the court can fairly expect that other jurisdiction to defer to it. One is priority in time, and the other is the extent of the relief
C > asked for or obtainable in the other jurisdiction. Now, in the present case there is really no question that the comity between two conflicting jurisdictions ought to have been exercised by the Vice-Chancellor in favour of the Nova Scotian court. The writ in the Nova Scotian court was considerably prior in time, and the statement of claim also. The relief asked was co-extensive, and the relief obtainable was even more effective . . ."

D
These considerations, save that the decision of this court and the decision of the Minister would appear to be equally effective, if applied to our case would incline in favour of staying the proceedings before this court. They were not, however, the only considerations in that case which persuaded the court to stay the proceedings in this country, and they are not the only considerations which tell
E for or against staying the present proceedings.

When this application came before me in November it was important to the plaintiffs to have an early decision, to enable them to anticipate the contemplated betterment levy. The need for that had arisen in view of recent proposed legislation, and I was told that it had become clear to the plaintiffs only after the Minister's inquiry, although with the expert advice available to them they might
F well have been expected to have become aware of it sooner. As I have indicated, the plaintiffs held the view that the required decision would be more quickly obtained from this court than from the Minister, and this, though not in my opinion constituting a difference of procedure or other consideration which relieved the duplication of its vexatious character, yet seems to me to be a factor which justice requires should be considered in deciding what remedy should be
G applied.

The plaintiffs preferred election to a stay of the court proceedings, clearly with a view to electing in favour of going on with the proceedings before this court. This would avoid any conflict in decision between the Minister and the court, but it would not avoid the defendants having to endure a second time a contest of the same question, namely, the validity of UL21. That, however, is a tribulation
H which may occur without necessarily establishing a case for a stay in all the circumstances, and which can sometimes be mitigated though not eliminated by provision as to costs. In this case the plaintiffs indicated that they were prepared to pay for the extra costs occasioned to the defendants by the duplication of the proceedings. A somewhat similar position arose in *The Soya Margareta* (18). The plaintiffs were prepared to abandon their proceedings in Italy rather than in this
I country and to pay the costs incurred in them, but in that case the English proceedings were apparently further advanced than the Italian proceedings (19) and had advantages over them (20) so, on (inter alia) the plaintiffs giving an undertaking to pay the costs of the Italian proceedings, those proceedings were stayed (21).

(14) [1960] 2 All E.R. at p. 759, letter E.   (15) [1960] 2 All E.R. at p. 762, letter C.
(16) (1908), 77 L.J.Ch. 824.   (17) (1908), 77 L.J.Ch. at p. 829.
(18) [1960] 2 All E.R. 756.   (19) [1960] 2 All E.R. at p. 761, letter C.
(20) [1960] 2 All E.R. at p. 760, letter H, to p. 761, letter B.
(21) [1960] 2 All E.R. at p. 762, letter D to letter G.

In our case, at the time of the November hearing before me, the proceedings **A**
before the Minister were completed, apart from the decision, and so it appears to
me that the additional costs incurred by reason of the plaintiffs' duplicating by
application to this court the matter already completed under the statutory
proceedings, save only for the Minister's decision, are the costs of the litigation in
this court. These are the proceedings which duplicated the earlier proceedings,
and whose commencement when the earlier proceedings were complete, apart **B**
from the decision, caused the vexation; and it appears to me to be only fair that
any extra costs to be borne by the plaintiffs for such duplication and vexation
should be the costs of these proceedings. These costs are, of course, independent
of the costs of any appeal, as such costs might be incurred whether on appeal
from this court or on the more limited grounds of appeal from the Minister, and
would in any case be appropriately and properly dealt with not by me but by the **C**
appellate court. If judgment had been given in this court before the withdrawal
of the appeal to the Minister then in the circumstances of this case the proper
course, in my view, would have been for the plaintiffs to have been put to their
election on undertaking to pay the costs of these proceedings in the High Court.

What is the effect of the plaintiffs' withdrawal of the s. 23 appeal and the
Minister's concurrence in that withdrawal on the order which this court should **D**
make on the application now before me? There appears to be no express statutory
provision dealing with withdrawal of a s. 23 appeal, but as the appeal is for the
advantage of the person " aggrieved " who makes it, it seems to me that it is
open to the appellant to withdraw it, at any rate with the Minister's concurrence.

The Minister accepted the withdrawal and has given his decision on the s. 22
applications without regarding any planning permission under UL21. The time for **E**
any appeal against the decision of the Minister has expired. So the validity of the
UL21 planning permission is completely outside the ambit of the decision by the
Minister and of any consequential appeal or procedure established by the town
and country planning legislation.

The defendants maintain, however, that although no conflict of fact can now **F**
arise between this court and Minister they were entitled not to be vexed by the
duplication of proceedings, that the proper remedy for such vexation was a stay
of the proceedings before this court, and that the court should not countenance or
be diverted from such a conclusion by the unilateral manoeuvre of the plaintiffs
in withdrawing the s. 23 appeal from the Minister, not only after the hearing
before him but after the hearing of the application for stay before me. For my **G**
part I consider that there is great force in these submissions for the defendants,
apart from the crucial consideration that, as I have already indicated, the proper
course, independently of the withdrawal, was in my view not a stay of the
proceedings before me but, subject to proper provision as to costs, an election by
the plaintiffs of the proceedings to be pursued, coupled of course with an effective
termination of the other proceedings. **H**

It seemed to me that the defendants' submission was fortified by the concession
made for the plaintiffs that the date as at which the court should decide whether
there is a vexatious duplication and consequently grant a stay is the date of
application for a stay, though they submitted that a stay could only be until such
time as there would be no duplication; but in my view neither the submission **I**
nor the concession is correct. If there is a stay, then automatically there is no
further duplication, and if the stay has to be decided as on the date of the application for it, when duplication ex hypothesi exists, then, at any rate so far as the
court is concerned, it is the stay and not any subsequent withdrawal or similar
action of the plaintiffs that prevents duplication thereafter. Nor is it established
that once a stay is granted of one action for vexatious duplication of proceedings,
a plaintiff is entitled to have that stay lifted by halting the other action. The
lifting of the stay cannot be a matter of absolute right and it cannot be more, in

A my view, than a matter for judicial discretion, having regard to all the circumstances of the case when the application to lift it comes before the court. Moreover, if the stay may be lifted in altered circumstances then I fail to see why, if circumstances alter between the application for a stay and its determination, those circumstances which might require the lifting of the stay should be ignored when the granting of the stay is being considered, and the court go through the

B farce of granting a stay, to be followed by its lifting owing to circumstances before the court when the stay was granted. In any case, in the exercise of such a discretionary remedy as a stay, it seems to me that the court is entitled to and should consider the substance of the matter, including the relevant circumstances properly before it at the time of its decision.

In this case, however, if I would have granted a stay of the proceedings before

C me before any withdrawal by the plaintiffs of their appeal to the Minister, I would have been disinclined to change that view on account of that withdrawal. It was common ground that another s. 23 appeal to test the validity of the UL21 planning permission could be brought before the Minister and that by agreement between the parties the submissions and evidence already made on the earlier appeal to him could be treated as such for the purposes of the new appeal; and a

D stay of the proceedings before me could be granted subject to the defendants undertaking to co-operate in such a course and thus in effect undo the plaintiffs' withdrawal of the earlier appeal. To change my view that the proper course was to stay the proceedings in this court, if that had been my view, merely because the plaintiffs had withdrawn the appeal before the Minister, would in effect be for that reason to prefer, contrary to my view, election by the plaintiffs or termination of

E the proceedings before the Minister rather than the stay of the proceedings before me; and in circumstances in which the appeal could in effect be re-established without further hearing. I, for my part, regret that the plaintiffs should have seen fit to withdraw the appeal to the Minister after the hearing before me of the application to stay the proceedings in this court, with the apparent object— indeed, I understand, with the avowed object—of influencing that decision. It

F was a fait accompli effected after the hearing before me, altering the basis on which that hearing had been conducted and judgment would proceed. I wish to make it perfectly clear that it has not had the effect of influencing my decision in favour of the plaintiffs, and perfectly clear also that it has not had the opposite effect. So, as the proceedings before the Minister have been withdrawn, what I have in mind, in accordance with the decision which I have made apart from that

G withdrawal, is that, on the plaintiffs undertaking to pay the costs of these proceedings in the High Court, I shall make no order on the application for the stay: but I will hear counsel on the precise form of order and, as usual in the ordinary course, any submission that there may be on the costs of this application.

On the plaintiffs undertaking to pay the costs of the proceedings in the High Court, the court would make no order on the application for the stay.

H
Solicitors: *Kenneth Brown, Baker, Baker* (for the plaintiffs); *Sharpe, Pritchard & Co.*, agents for *Norman T. Berry, Town Clerk*, Slough, and *R. E. Millard, Clerk of the Bucks. County Council* (for the defendants).

[*Reported by* JACQUELINE METCALFE, *Barrister-at-Law.*]

DIETZ v. LENNIG CHEMICALS, LTD.   A

[HOUSE OF LORDS (Lord Reid, Lord Morris of Borth-y-Gest, Lord Pearce, Lord
Wilberforce and Lord Pearson), March 15, 16, 20, April 26, 1967.]

*Fatal Accident—Compromise—Infant not bound until settlement approved by
court—Consent order not perfected—Misrepresentation—Defendants consented to order to pay lump sum for widow and infant child not knowing that*   B
*widow was re-marrying—Widow re-married before order—Order set aside
—R.S.C. (Rev.) 1962, Ord. 80, r. 11—R.S.C. (Rev.) 1965, Ord. 80, r. 10.*

The deceased was killed as the result of an explosion at the respondents'
factory where he was employed. He was survived by a widow and an
infant son. In August, 1965, before any action was commenced, an offer
in settlement of the claim of the widow and child was accepted " subject to   C
the approval of the court ". On Oct. 13, 1965, an originating summons
was taken out, seeking the court's approval of the settlement. This was
entitled in the name of the widow, described as " (widow and administratrix
of the estate of . . . deceased) ". The widow re-married on Oct. 25, 1965,
but she did not then inform her solicitors of her re-marriage. On Nov. 12,
1965, the summons was heard and the settlement was approved. At that   D
time the legal advisers of all parties believed that the plaintiff was still a
widow. Before the order was drawn up, her solicitors became aware of
her re-marriage, they immediately informed the respondents and the order
approving the settlement was set aside.

Held: by virtue of R.S.C. (Rev.) 1962, Ord. 80, r. 11*, the validity of the
agreement for settlement, which included a claim of an infant, depended   E
on its being approved by the court; the consent of the respondents at the
hearing of the summons was induced by misrepresentation that the plaintiff
was a widow, albeit innocently induced, and therefore the order of Nov. 12,
1965, had been rightly set aside (see p. 285, letter D, p. 286, letters B,
D and E, p. 290, letters A and B, and p. 283, letter C, post).

Decision of the COURT OF APPEAL ([1966] 2 All E.R. 962) affirmed.   F

[As to the compromise of claims by persons under disability, see 30 HALS-
BURY'S LAWS (3rd Edn.) 404, para. 760; and as to the jurisdiction of the court
in regard to approving compromises on behalf of infants generally, see 21 HALS-
BURY'S LAWS (3rd Edn.) 326, para. 687; and for cases on the subject, see 36
DIGEST (Repl.) 227, *1207-1208*, and DIGEST (Cont. Vol. A) 1211, *1208c*; and
28 DIGEST (Repl.) 698-702, *2083-2120.*   G

As to taking into account changes in circumstances when assessing damages
under the Fatal Accidents Acts, see 28 HALSBURY'S LAWS (3rd Edn.) 102, para.
111.]

Cases referred to:
Avery v. *London and North Eastern Ry. Co.*, [1938] 2 All E.R. 592; [1938]   H
      A.C. 606; 107 L.J.K.B. 546; 159 L.T. 241; 34 Digest (Repl.) 312, *2299.*
Eifert v. *Holt's Transport Co., Ltd.*, [1951] 2 All E.R. 655, n.; 36 Digest (Repl.)
      226, *1200.*
Pym v. *Great Northern Ry. Co.*, [1861-73] All E.R. Rep. 180; (1863), 4 B. & S.
      396; 32 L.J.Q.B. 377; 8 L.T. 734; 122 E.R. 508; 36 Digest (Repl.) 208,
      1093.
                                                                                 I
Appeal.

This was an appeal by Doreen Dietz, formerly the widow of James Wilson,

---

* The R.S.C. (Rev.) 1962, S.I. 1962 No. 2145, came into operation on Jan. 1, 1964.
R.S.C. Ord. 80, r. 11 of 1962 corresponds to r. 10 of Ord. 80 of R.S.C. (Rev.) 1965,
S.I. 1965 No. 1776, which came into force on Oct. 1, 1966. The wording is not precisely
the same in the two rules, but, for present purposes, the effect of each rule is the same.
The terms of r. 11 of Ord. 80 of the rules of 1962 are set out at p. 285, letter E, post;
and the wording of r. 10 of Ord. 80 of the rules of 1965 is set out at p. 289, letter D,
post.

A deceased and the administratrix of his estate, from an order of the Court of
Appeal (LORD DENNING, M.R., DAVIES and RUSSELL, L.JJ.), dated May 26, 1966,
and reported [1966] 2 All E.R. 962, dismissing the appellant's appeal from an
order of VEALE, J., in chambers, dated Mar. 23, 1966, whereby an order of Master
CLAYTON, dated Feb, 9, 1966, setting aside his order of Nov. 12, 1965, was
affirmed.   The deceased left surviving him his widow, the appellant, and their
B son, Philip James, born on July 5, 1963.   The facts are summarised in the
opinion of LORD MORRIS OF BORTH-Y-GEST.

G. J. Bean, Q.C., and Barry Chedlow for the appellant.
Hugh Griffiths, Q.C., and D. E. Hill-Smith for the respondents.

Their lordships took time for consideration.

C   Apr. 26.   The following opinions were delivered.

LORD REID: My Lords, for the reasons given by your lordships I agree
that this appeal should be dismissed.

LORD MORRIS OF BORTH-Y-GEST: My Lords, on Oct. 6, 1964,
D there was an explosion at the respondents' factory at Jarrow-on-Tyne.   It
caused the death of their employee, James Wilson.   He left a widow and an
infant son who had been born on July 5 in the previous year.   On Nov. 19,
1964, solicitors wrote a letter to the respondents claiming damages for the widow
" and the dependants ".   Letters of administration were granted to the widow
on Jan. 6, 1965.

E   Thereafter discussions took place between the solicitors and insurers who were
acting for the employers, the respondents.   The discussions were with the object
of arriving at figures which would be paid and would be acceptable in respect
of damages under the Law Reform (Miscellaneous Provisions) Act, 1934, and
under the Fatal Accidents Acts.   As a result, the solicitors on Aug. 11, 1965,
wrote a letter to the insurers in the following terms:

F   " I have now received [the appellant's] instructions to accept your offer
of £10,000 subject to the approval of the court.   I am taking out the necessary proceedings and will write to you further."

That letter was acknowledged by the insurers on Aug. 18.   They noted " that
[the appellant] accepts our offer of £10,000, subject to the approval of the court ",
and they stated that they were requesting solicitors to accept service of pro-
G ceedings on behalf of the respondents.   Thereafter, an originating summons
was taken out on Oct. 13, 1965, calling on the respondents to attend before
the master in chambers on the hearing of an application for an order that, inter
alia, the agreed terms of settlement be approved.   The plaintiff was Doreen Wilson
(widow and administratrix of the estate of James Wilson deceased, the appellant).
H The originating summons was taken out pursuant to the provisions of R.S.C.,
Ord. 80, r. 12 (Annual Practice 1966).   The originating summons set out (see
R.S.C., Ord. 80, r. 12 (2)) the particulars required pursuant to s. 4 of the Fatal
Accidents Act, 1846, i.e., " of the person or persons for whom and on whose
behalf such action shall be brought and of the nature of the claim in respect of
which damages shall be sought to be recovered ".   The summons showed that
the proceedings were on behalf of the widow and the infant, that the claims were
I based on negligence and breach of statutory duty and that damages were
claimed under the Fatal Accidents Acts on behalf of the dependants of the
deceased and under the Law Reform (Miscellaneous Provisions) Act, 1934, on
behalf of the deceased.   Amongst the orders that were asked for on the summons
were the following:

    " 1.   That the following terms of settlement of the [appellant's] claim
agreed between the parties be approved and embodied in such order and that
all further proceedings be stayed upon such claim except for the purpose of

carrying the said terms into effect and that there be liberty to apply for the   A
same purpose and generally.

. . . .

" 3.   That the [respondents] do within fourteen days pay to the [appellant's] solicitor without further order the sum of £750 in satisfaction of the claim under the Law Reform (Miscellaneous Provisions) Act, 1934.

" 4.   That the [respondents] do within fourteen days pay to the [appellant's] solicitor in satisfaction of the claim under the Fatal Accidents Acts,   B
1846-1959 the further sum of £9,250 apportioned as to £8,250 for the widow of the deceased, Doreen Wilson, and as to £1,000 for Philip James Wilson, the infant son of the deceased, who was born on July 5, 1963."

There was to be a trust deed for the purpose of carrying the settlement into
effect.   C

The summons came before the master on Nov. 12, 1965.   Representatives of the respective solicitors attended.   The main purpose of the appearance was to seek the approval of the master to the terms that had been agreed.   The master gave his approval.   He then considered the terms of the draft trust deed.   With that the representative of the respondents' solicitors was not concerned: he   D
did not remain while the trust deed was under consideration.

When the summons was being heard by the master all the legal advisers were under the belief that the appellant was still a widow.   The summons described her as Doreen Wilson and as a widow.   In fact she had re-married on Oct. 25, 1965.   She had then become the wife of Albert Henry Dietz.   When this later came to her solicitors' knowledge, they immediately informed the respondents' solicitors.   The master's order had not been drawn up.   The respondents'   E
solicitors took out a summons returnable before the master, who on the hearing of it set aside his order of Nov. 12 " so far as it applied to the action of *Doreen Wilson* v. *Lennig Chemicals, Ltd.*".   From that order the appellant appealed to VEALE, J., in chambers.   He dismissed the appeal.   There was an appeal to the Court of Appeal (1) (LORD DENNING, M.R., DAVIES and RUSSELL, L.JJ.).   The
appeal was dismissed.   By leave appeal is now brought to your lordships' House.   F

The main issue which is raised is whether in August, 1965 (either on Aug. 11 or 18) there was a binding contract made between the appellant and the respondents.   On the facts of this case what was the resulting position when there was an acceptance of an offer " subject to the approval of the court "?   Was there (as the appellant contends) a binding agreement then made which was conditional on the approval of the court being given and which would only cease to be   G
effective if court approval was not given, or was there (as the respondents contend) an agreement which was not to be binding or effective unless and until the court gave its approval.   If the former, then it was said that court approval was in fact given, and it was submitted that (good faith not being challenged) the parties took the risk that there might be a change of circumstances after the date of their agreement.   There was evidence that the question of marriage was   H
not discussed between the appellant and Mr. Dietz until Oct. 11, 1965.   If the latter, then it was submitted that when the parties were before the master on Nov. 12 the position was that the respondents were then expressing their consent to the terms for which approval was being sought and were expressing it on the faith of a representation which was a misrepresentation, although an innocent one, then made on behalf of the appellant, that she was still a widow.   I

In my view, there was no binding agreement made in August.   It is important to consider the nature and the circumstances of the offer that was accepted " subject to the approval of the court ".   It was of the sum of £10,000 of which it was intended that £750 should be referable to the claim under the Law Reform (Miscellaneous Provisions) Act, 1934.   That left the sum of £9,250 for the claims under the Fatal Accidents Acts.   An action under those Acts is brought by

─────────────────────────

(1) [1966] 2 All E.R. 962.

A and in the name of the executor or administrator of the deceased. It is provided by s. 2 of the Act of 1846 that in every such action

"... the jury may give such damages as they may think proportioned to the injury resulting from such death to the parties respectively for whom and for whose benefit such action shall be brought: and the amount so recovered, after deducting the costs not recovered from the defendant, shall
B be divided amongst the before-mentioned parties in such shares as the jury by their verdict shall find and direct."

If, therefore, there is a trial with a jury it is for the jury to consider how each of the parties is situate. (See *Pym* v. *Great Northern Ry. Co.* (2)). In his speech in *Avery* v. *London and North Eastern Ry. Co.* (3) Lord Atkin pointed out (4)
C that no question of group compensation arises and (5) that the quantum of damages in respect of any one person whose claim is before the jury is not to be regarded as being a proportion of a limited sum. The result is that the claim of every person within the class of those on whose behalf action is brought calls for separate consideration. If in the present case a writ had first been issued, and if thereafter there had been discussions leading to agreement, such
D agreement would have lacked validity unless and until the approval of the court was given. This is made clear by R.S.C., Ord. 80, r. 11, which is (6) in the following terms:

" 11. Where in any proceedings (other than a matrimonial cause, an application under s. 23 of the Matrimonial Causes Act, 1950, or a claim under s. 30 of that Act) money is claimed by or on behalf of a person under
E disability, no settlement, compromise or payment and no acceptance of money paid into court, whenever entered into or made, shall so far as it relates to that person's claim be valid without the approval of the court."

The present case came within the provisions of R.S.C., Ord. 80, r. 12, the relevant parts of which are (7) as follows:

" r. 12. Where, before proceedings in which a claim for money is made
F by or on behalf of a person under disability (whether alone or in conjunction with any other person) are begun, an agreement is reached for the settlement of the claim, and it is desired to obtain the court's approval to the settlement ... the claim may be made in proceedings begun by originating summons and in the summons an application may also be made for—(a) the approval of the court to the settlement ..."

G
When, therefore, the originating summons was taken out it made a " claim " on behalf of a person under disability (i.e., the infant). If approval to the settlement were given, then all matters connected with the carrying out of the terms could conveniently be settled. (See R.S.C., Ord. 80 r. 13). If approval were not given, then directions could be given for the trial of the claim in the
H same way as they would be given if the claim had been in a writ rather than in an originating summons; but the agreement " for the settlement of the claim " would depend for its validity on obtaining the approval of the court.

All these considerations show, in my view, that when in August, 1965, acceptance was expressed " subject to the approval of the court " of an offer of £10,000, which was to include a settlement of the claim of a person under disability
I (i.e., an infant aged two), there was then no binding agreement. The consequence was that there would be an appearance before a master at which, in order that

(2) [1861-73] All E.R. Rep. 180; (1863), 4 B. & S. 396.
(3) [1938] 2 All E.R. 592; [1938] A.C. 606.
(4) [1938] 2 All E.R. at p. 594; [1938] A.C. at p. 612.
(5) [1938] 2 All E.R. at p. 595; [1938] A.C. at p. 613.
(6) See p. 289, letter D, post; the current rule is R.S.C., Ord. 80, r. 10, of R.S.C. (Rev.) 1965, S.I. 1965 No. 1776.
(7) This rule is now R.S.C. (Rev.) 1965 (S.I. 1965 No. 1776), Ord. 80, r. 11, which is in the same terms as those stated here.

he could decide whether the proposed settlement would be for the infant's benefit, **A**
all relevant matters would be stated on behalf of the parties.   The circumstances
of the mother would be of relevance and importance when considering what the
infant should receive and what terms of settlement would be for the benefit of
the infant.   If the court's approval were given, a binding agreement would result
on the basis of which certain directions could be given by the court.

As I have already stated, when the summons was being heard by the master **B**
all who were present thought that the appellant was still a widow.   The representatives of the respondents' solicitors were there to express consent to the
settlement if the master was disposed to approve it.   Their consent was given
on the basis that the appellant was a widow.   They were induced by an innocent
misrepresentation.   The misrepresentation was set out in the title of the proceedings and in the terms of the orders asked for.   No question now arises as **C**
to what effect, if any, the re-marriage of the widow should have in assessing
reasonable damages, but when she re-married the circumstances were altered
both as they might affect the amount which the infant should receive and also
as they might affect the total amount which the respondents should pay.   The
consent given on behalf of the respondents was given under a misapprehension.
I think that the master was right in not holding them to it, and was right in **D**
setting aside rather than in drawing up his order of Nov. 12.

I would dismiss the appeal.

LORD PEARCE: My Lords, I agree with the opinions of my noble and
learned friends, LORD MORRIS OF BORTH-Y-GEST and LORD PEARSON.   I would
dismiss the appeal. **E**

LORD WILBERFORCE: My Lords, I concur.

LORD PEARSON: My Lords, on Oct. 6, 1964, Mr. James Wilson, whilst
in the employment of the respondents, was killed in an accident.   He left his
widow, the appellant, and a son who was one year old.   On Nov. 19, 1964,
solicitors instructed by the appellant wrote to the respondents claiming on **F**
behalf of the appellant " and the dependants " of the deceased damages for
negligence and breach of statutory duty.   The respondents referred the claim to
their insurance company and negotiations ensued.   At an interview on May 17,
1965, the insurance company made an offer of " £10,000 including L.R.A.", i.e.,
to pay in settlement of the claims, including the claim under the Law Reform
(Miscellaneous Provisions) Act, 1934, the sum of £10,000.   On Aug. 11, 1965, the **G**
solicitors instructed by the appellant wrote to the insurance company as follows:

" Dear Sirs,
Re Wilson (decd.) v. *Lennig Chemicals, Ltd.*
I have now received [the appellant's] instructions to accept your offer of
£10,000 subject to the approval of the court.   I am taking out the necesssary
proceedings and will write to you further." **H**

The insurance company replied on Aug. 18, 1965:

" We thank you for your letter of Aug. 11 and note that [the appellant]
accepts our offer of £10,000, subject to the approval of the court."

They went on to say that they were requesting solicitors to accept service on
behalf of the respondents, and they added " perhaps you will take the necessary **I**
action ".

On a point of detail I am not sure whether the letter of Aug. 11, 1965, should
be read as saying that the offer, or that the acceptance, was " subject to the
approval of the court ".   It makes no material difference.   If the condition was
already in the offer, the acceptance by the letter of Aug. 11 would conclude the
bargain.   If the condition was introduced by the letter of Aug. 11, that letter
would be in a law a counter-offer and the letter of Aug. 18 accepting it would
conclude the bargain.   I shall refer to the bargain as " the August settlement ".

A   On Oct. 13, 1965, an originating summons was taken out on behalf of the appellant.   It named as the appellant " Doreen Wilson (widow and administratrix of the estate of James Wilson deceased) ".   It summoned the respondents or their solicitors to attend on the master on the appellant's application for an order.   In the order applied for there were ten paragraphs, including the following

B   " 1. That the following terms of settlement of the [appellant's] claim agreed between the parties be approved and embodied in such order and that all further proceedings be stayed upon such claim except for the purpose of carrying the said terms into effect and that there be liberty to apply for the same purpose and generally.

2. The particulars required pursuant to s. 4 of the Fatal Accidents Act, 1846, are as follows:

C   (*a*) Doreen Wilson, widow and administratrix of the estate of the late James Wilson; and

(*b*) Philip James Wilson born on July 5, 1963, the infant son of the widow and the said James Wilson, deceased.

(i) Damages under the Fatal Accidents Acts on behalf of the dependants of the said deceased and

D   (ii) Damages under the Law Reform (Miscellaneous Provisions) Act, 1934, on behalf of the estate of the said deceased,

in consequence of the death of the said James Wilson deceased as a result of an accident which occurred on or about Oct. 6, 1964, at the [respondents] premises at Jarrow-on-Tyne in the county of Durham, arising out of the negligence and/or breach of statutory duty of the [respondents], their servants or agents.

E

3. That the defendants do within fourteen days pay to the [appellant's] solicitor without further order the sum of £750 in satisfaction of the claim under the Law Reform (Miscellaneous Provisions) Act, 1934.

4. That the [respondents] do within fourteen days pay to the [appellant's] solicitor in satisfaction of the claim under the Fatal Accidents Acts, 1846-

F   1959, the further sum of £9,250 apportioned as to £8,250 for the widow of the deceased, Doreen Wilson, and as to £1,000 for Philip James Wilson, the infant son of the deceased, who was born on July 5, 1963.

5. That the court do approve the terms of the trust deed attached hereto.
    . . .

G   7. That the court do approve the payment by the [appellant's] solicitor of the sum set out in para. 4 to the trustees.

8. That the court do approve the payment by the [appellant's] solicitor to the widow of the amount set out in para. 3 in respect of the Law Reform (Miscellaneous Provisions) Act, 1934."

In the originating summons the appellant was referred to several times as " the H   widow "—in the heading and in paras. 2 (*a*), 4 and 8. In fact she still was a widow on Oct. 13, 1965, when the originating summons was taken out; but on Oct. 25, 1965, she married Mr. Dietz. Her solicitors were not informed of the marriage. There is no suggestion that she had any intention to deceive anybody; but the description of her as " the widow " in the originating summons remained unamended on Nov. 10, 1965, when the originating summons was served on the I   respondents' solicitors, and on Nov. 12, 1965, when representatives of the solicitors for the parties appeared before the master and gave their consent and the master made an order as asked in the originating summons. Consequently on Nov. 12, 1965, the consent was given by the solicitors' representatives on both sides, and the order was made by the master, in ignorance of the fact that the appellant had remarried.

At the beginning of December, 1965, the appellant's solicitors ascertained, in connexion with the signing of the trust deed, that the appellant had remarried and they very properly informed the respondents' solicitors.

On Feb. 8, 1966, the respondents' solicitors took out a summons, applying for **A**
the order of Nov. 12, 1965, to be set aside. The order had not been perfected.
The grounds for setting it aside were not very clearly stated in the application,
but there were (subject to the argument presented in this appeal) good grounds
for setting aside the order, as stated by DAVIES, L.J., in his judgment in the
Court of Appeal. He said (8):

" For here the consent of the [respondents] to the making of the order by **B**
the master was plainly induced by an innocent misrepresentation made on
behalf of the [appellant] by her solicitors. The misrepresentation was that
she was still a widow at the date of the order. That misrepresentation was
contained in the title of the action; it was contained in the draft trust deed;
and, indeed, it was contained in the body of the summons which asked for an
order that the sum of £9,250 should be paid to Doreen Wilson, the widow. **C**
She was nothing of the kind. I think that that was a most material representation, in the sense that if the [respondents] had known at the time that
she had re-married they would certainly have refused to consent to the
order until the financial repercussions of her marriage were ascertained."

On Feb. 9, 1966, the master made an order setting aside his order of Nov. 12,
1965. The appellant's appeal to VEALE, J., as judge in chambers, was dismissed **D**
on Mar. 10, 1966, and her appeal to the Court of Appeal (9) was dismissed on
May 26, 1966. Leave to appeal to your lordships' House was refused by the
Court of Appeal (10), but was afterwards granted by the Appeal Committee.

The argument for the appellant, who was the plaintiff in the action, has been
to this effect:
                                                                              E
(i) The August settlement was a legally binding agreement, though conditional. Each party gave a contractual promise to implement the settlement,
if the court's approval was obtained.

(ii) The August settlement was an agreement to pay and receive the sum
of £10,000 in discharge of the appellant's claims. The £10,000 was divided into
£750 under the Act of 1934 and £9,250 under the Fatal Accidents Acts; but **F**
there was no provision in the settlement as to the apportionment of the
£9,250 between the appellant and the infant. The respondents would not be
concerned with that apportionment (*Eifert* v. *Holt's Transport Co., Ltd.* (11)).

(iii) The court's approval was required only in respect of the interests of the
infant. The £9,250 was a sufficient lump sum to safeguard the interests of
the infant, if it was duly apportioned. Its sufficiency would be not **G**
diminished, but in all probability greatly enhanced, by the remarriage. The
remarriage might affect the apportionment which was approved on Nov. 12,
1965, but that would be a matter arising solely between the appellant and
the infant and would be no concern of the respondents.

(iv) When the master on Nov. 12, 1965, approved the lump sum settlement
for £10,000 (made up of £750 plus £9,250), the condition of the August **H**
settlement was fulfilled and the obligation of the respondents to pay the
£10,000 became unconditional and immediately effective.

(v) There was no new or continuing consent to be given by the respondents'
solicitors on Nov. 12, 1965, because they had already given their consent in
the August settlement. Therefore, any mistake or misrepresentation which
may have affected the minds of the respondents or their solicitors on Nov. 12, **I**
1965, would be immaterial.

Questions of some difficulty—especially as to the possibility of a person having
authority to act as agent for an infant—can be raised in relation to this argument
and were discussed on the hearing of the appeal. I should prefer, however, to
base the decision of the appeal on the terms of the August settlement read in
conjunction with certain of the rules of the Supreme Court.

(8) [1966] 2 All E.R. at pp. 964, 965.   (9) [1966] 2 All E.R. 962.
(10) [1966] 2 All E.R. at p. 965.   (11) [1951] 2 All E.R. 655, n.

A   Recently there has been a comprehensive revision of those rules, and it has been effected in two stages. There was a partial revision by a statutory instrument (12) called " The Rules of the Supreme Court (Revision) 1962 " which came into force on Jan. 1, 1964. The revision was completed by another statutory instrument (13), called " The Rules of the Supreme Court (Revision) 1965 " which came into force on Oct. 1, 1966. In the course of the revision there were

B   changes in the arrangements and numbering of the rules. It is convenient, therefore, to identify the two relevant rules by their headings. One is headed " Compromise etc. by persons under disability ", and I will call that " the compromise rule ". The other one I will call " the approval of settlement rule ".

The compromise rule is of long standing. It was in existence before the revision, and can be found in the Annual Practice, 1963 as R.S.C., Ord. 16B, r. 11 (with a

C   parenthesis which has since been omitted and could have no bearing on this case) and the notes (14) show that the rule can be traced back to the year 1909. In the Annual Practice, 1964, after the partial revision, it appeared as R.S.C., Ord. 80, r. 11, and now, after completion of the revision, it is R.S.C., Ord. 80, r. 10. It provides as follows:

D   " Where in any proceedings money is claimed by or on behalf of a person under disability, no settlement, compromise or payment, and no acceptance of money paid into court, whenever entered into or made, shall so far as it relates to that person's claim be valid without the approval of the court."

There was a suggestion made in the course of the argument that the compromise rule, if it means what it appears to say—if " invalid " means " of no legal

E   effect "—is ultra vires.   I do not accept that suggestion. When the claim of an infant or other person under disability is before the court, the court needs, for the purpose of protecting his interests, full control over any settlement compromising his claim. In my view, the making and re-making of the compromise rule were valid exercises of the rule-making power under the Judicature Acts, which is now contained in s. 99 of the Supreme Court of Judicature (Consolidation)

F   Act, 1925.

The approval of settlement rule, under which the originating summons in this case was issued, did not exist before the recent revision of the rules. It was introduced in the course of the revision and, as is stated in the notes (15) under R.S.C., Ord. 80, r. 12, of the Annual Practice, 1964:

G   " This rule is new, and its object is to make the procedure for obtaining the approval of the court to the settlement or compromise of a claim of an infant or patient simpler and cheaper. Where such a settlement or compromise is arrived at *before proceedings are begun*, this rule enables the approval of the court to be obtained and directions for the control of the money recovered to be given on an originating summons to which no appearance is required to be entered. It is no longer necessary to issue a writ and then

H   to take out a summons in the action for such approval and directions."

As this approval of settlement rule (which is now, after completion of the revision, R.S.C., Ord. 80, r. 11) merely provides a simpler and cheaper form of proceedings than was previously available, it need not be set out here.

The compromise rule is the vital one here. The August settlement contemplated and required that the approval of the court should be obtained, and therefore

I   that proceedings should be commenced, because the approval of the court cannot be obtained otherwise than in proceedings. When the proceedings had been commenced by the originating summons of Oct. 13, 1965, they were proceedings in which money—the £9,250—was claimed on behalf of the infant as well as the appellant, and therefore under the compromise rule the August settlement, so

---

(12) S.I. 1962 No. 2145.   (13) S.I. 1965 No. 1776.
(14) See now Supreme Court Practice, 1967, p. 1089.
(15) See now Supreme Court Practice, 1967, p. 1090, where the note is repeated verbatim.

far as it related to the £9,250, was not valid without the approval of the court. In A
my view, " not valid " means having no legal effect. The settlement, so far as it
related to the £9,250, in which the infant was interested, was only a proposed
settlement until the court approved it.   Either party could lawfully have
repudiated it at any time before the court approved it. It had no validity by
virtue of the parties' agreement in the August settlement. That which might
have given it validity would have been an order made by the master with the B
effective consent of the parties on Nov. 12, 1965. A new or continuing consent
of the respondents was needed, and their purported consent was vitiated by the
innocent misrepresentation to which I have referred. The master's order of
Nov. 12, 1965, was rightly set aside by his further order of Feb. 9, 1966.

It can be said either (i) that a valid agreement was made by the August settlement but it became invalid as soon as the proceedings were commenced, or (ii) C
that the agreement made by the August settlement is, as a matter of construction,
shown by the nature of its condition to be not intended to have legal effect. I
prefer (ii), as the agreement by its condition contemplated and required the
approval of the court, which would have to be obtained in legal proceedings,
which would bring the compromise rule into operation. Also I have had the
advantage of reading the opinion of my noble and learned friend, LORD MORRIS D
OF BORTH-Y-GEST, and I agree with his reasons for deciding that no binding
agreement was made in August, 1965.

I would dismiss the appeal.

Appeal dismissed.

Solicitors: *W. H. Thompson* (for the appellant);   *Berrymans* (for the
respondents). E

[*Reported by* KATHLEEN J. H. O'BRIEN, *Barrister-at-Law.*]

R. H. McCULLOCH, LTD. *v.* MOORE.

F

[QUEEN'S BENCH DIVISION (Lord Parker, C.J., Diplock, L.J., and Ashworth, J.),
February 28, 1967.]

*Employment—Redundancy—Dismissal by reason of redundancy—Intention
of employers to cease to carry on business in " place " where employee was
employed—Notice that there would be no further work in Sussex and offer
of employment in other areas—Whether dismissal by reason of redundancy—
Redundancy Payments Act* 1965 (c. 62), *s.* 1 (2), *s.* 3 (1).

The respondent was a semi-skilled worker employed in Sussex by the
appellants, who had a contract renewable annually with the Gas Board;
the respondent was employed on laying gas mains and pipes.   In April, 1966,
the work for the Gas Board ceased.   The appellants issued a notice addressed
" To all personnel in Sussex " regretting that the employers would have H
no further work in the Sussex area.   They offered " continuation of employment with similar conditions in the Reading/Aldershot area, East Midlands
area, Luton area or Scotland ", and asked employees to let the supervisor
know their intentions.   A working rule agreement was in force which
provided that, at the discretion of the employers, an operative might be
transferred during employment from one job to another.   The respondent I
claimed a redundancy payment on the footing that he was dismissed by
reason of redundancy.   By s. 1 (2) (*a*)* of the Redundancy Payments Act
1965 an employee was to be taken to be dismissed by reason of redundancy
if the dismissal was attributable wholly or mainly to the fact that his
employer intended to cease to carry on the relevant business " in the place
where " the employee was employed.

---

* The relevant terms of s. 1 (2) are set out at p. 292, letter H, post.

A   **Held:** (i) the employers' notice amounted to dismissal within the definition of s. 3 (1)* of the Redundancy Payments Act 1965, and the working rule was irrelevant in the present case for it had not been invoked (see p. 292, letters E and G, and p. 293, letter A, post).

(ii) the employers did intend to cease to carry on business in " the place where " the respondent was employed, that is, in a defined area which in
B   this instance was Sussex, and accordingly the dismissal of the respondent was attributable wholly or mainly to that fact, and therefore the respondent had been dismissed by reason of redundancy by reason of s. 1 (2) of the Act of 1965 and was entitled to a redundancy payment (see p. 292, letter I, and p. 293, letter A, post).

Appeal dismissed.

C   [As to the dismissal of an employee by reason of redundancy, see CURRENT SERVICE to HALSBURY'S LAWS (3rd Edn.), Vol. 38, para. 808C.

For the Redundancy Payments Act 1965, s. 1 (2), s. 3 (1), see 45 HALSBURY'S STATUTES (2nd Edn.) 291, 293.]

Appeal.

This was an appeal on a point of law from a decision of the industrial tribunal,
D   who held that the respondent, J. W. Moore, was entitled to a redundancy payment from his employers, R. H. McCulloch, Ltd., the present appellants.   The facts are set out in the judgment of LORD PARKER, C.J.

J. D. W. Hayman for the appellants.
J. Mitchell for the respondent.

E   **LORD PARKER, C.J.:** The respondent had been employed by the appellants for some eleven years in Sussex. The employers were civil engineers specialising in the maintenance and installation of equipment for the Gas Board.   For some ten years they had a contract renewable every year with the South Eastern Gas Board in Sussex.   The respondent, whose home was at Portslade, Sussex, was employed by the appellants as a semi-skilled worker in laying gas mains,
F   pipes, cables, drainage pipes and such like.   In April, 1966, however, the work for the South Eastern Gas Board came to an end, and there was no work in Sussex.   In those circumstances the appellants issued a notice addressed: " To all personnel in Sussex ".   It read:

" We regret that our contract with the South Eastern Gas Board Sussex area terminates Apr. 30, 1966; after this date we shall have no further
G   work in the Sussex area.   But we can offer you continuation of employment with similar conditions in the Reading/Aldershot area, East Midlands area, Luton area, or Scotland.   Would you please by return let your supervisor know your intentions. N.B.   Subsistence allowance will be paid where applicable as per working rule agreement."

H   The respondent's contention was that that notice amounted to a dismissal, that the dismissal was by reason of redundancy, and accordingly that he was entitled to a redundancy payment.   So far the matter is quite straightforward, but it so happened that at the time when the respondent was employed by the appellants, there was in fact a working rules agreement in force; in fact it had been in force since 1921.   One of the conditions laid down in para. XD (f) read:

I   " That, at the discretion of the employer, an operative may be transferred at any time during the period of his employment from one job to another."

The argument before the tribunal was that that entitled the appellants to send this respondent anywhere in England, in Scotland or Wales; accordingly his failure to continue employment on those terms amounted to a repudiation of the contract which the appellants had accepted, and as a result they had not dismissed him.

---

* Section 3 (1), so far as material, is printed at p. 292, letter D, post.

The tribunal, by a majority, overruled that submission and held:

"That the original contract of employment made eleven years ago contained in it implied conditions that the [respondent], a semi-skilled worker, was to be employed within some accessible distance of his then place of employment and that such a condition had not been negatived by the adoption of the working rules agreement."

They went on to say that quite apart from that, the majority held:

"That there was a custom in the trade for semi-skilled operatives not to be subject to such far reaching directives of the Lands End to John O'Groats type which possibly might apply to senior executive civil engineers."

For my part I do not approach this matter in the way that the tribunal approached it. I do not think that any question of implied terms or of custom need be determined, and certainly there was no evidence that this court knows of, of there being any custom. My approach is to look at the notice which was given and ask myself in the first instance: does that amount to a dismissal? The Redundancy Act 1965, s. 3 (1) provides:

"For the purposes of this Part of this Act an employee shall, subject to the following provisions of this Part of this Act, be taken to be dismissed by his employer if, but only if,—(a) the contract under which he is employed by the employer is terminated by the employer, whether it is so terminated by notice or without notice . . ."

In my judgment this notice amounted to a dismissal within the meaning of that provision. It was plainly saying: your work in the Sussex area has come to an end, we cannot afford to employ you there doing nothing, and accordingly our contract with you will be terminated on that date, and then goes on to offer in effect a new contract of employment elsewhere. As I understand it, counsel for the appellant says: that is merely employers not wielding the big stick, and that they were entitled to say: "we can direct you to one of these places under the working rules agreement", and that his failure to accept continuation of employment on those terms was a wrongful repudiation of the contract. The fact of the matter is that these employers did not seek to invoke the clause of the working rules agreement at all, and it may well be that they did not think that it would entitle them to do what it suggested. Be that as it may, they did not invoke it. This in my opinion was a plain dismissal, and the only question then is whether it was a dismissal (and I read from s. 1 (2) (a):

"attributable wholly or mainly to the fact that the employer has ceased, or intends to cease, to carry on the business for the purposes of which the the employee was employed by him [that clearly does not apply] or has ceased, or intends to cease, to carry on that business in the place where the employee was so employed . . ."

In my judgment the appellants did intend to cease to carry on businesss in Sussex where the respondent was so employed, and accordingly this was a dismissal by reason of redundancy. Counsel for the appellants has sought to say that that is a wrong approach to this matter, and that the true reading of the enactment in the circumstances of this case is to predicate that the appellants intended to cease to carry on that business in the place where the respondent was so employed, meaning thereby in a nationwide employment in England, Scotland or Wales. I find it quite impossible to read the enactment in that way. It seems to me that the words "in the place where the employee was so employed", are condescending to the particular, not necessarily one building rather than another, but to a defined area. In these circumstances, though differing from the reason given by the tribunal, I think that they arrived at the right decision, and I would dismiss this appeal.

A   **DIPLOCK, L.J.:** For the reasons given by Lord Parker, C.J., I agree that this appeal should be dismissed. Those reasons, as will be seen, depend on the terms of the notice in fact given by the appellants to its personnel in Sussex, and do not depend on the construction of the working agreement, as to which I for my part express no view.

B   **ASHWORTH, J.:** I agree.

Appeal dismissed.

Solicitors: *Taylor, Jelf & Co.*, agents for *Day, Whately & Co.*, Godalming (for the appellants); *Pattinson & Brewer* (for the respondent).

[*Reported by* R. W. Farrin, Esq., *Barrister-at-Law.*]

C

LANE *v.* GLOUCESTER ENGINEERING CO., LTD.

[Court of Appeal, civil division (Sellers, Davies and Russell, L.JJ.), March 1, **D**   2, 1967.]

Factory—Lighting—Duty of employers to secure and maintain sufficient and suitable lighting—General illumination over areas where persons are regularly employed—General illumination over other interior parts—Workman tripping over tool lying on floor in shadow of article being constructed in the factory—Shadow reducing otherwise sufficient lighting below required level **E**   *—Accident occurred before work started or other employees were in factory— Whether employers in breach of statutory duty—Whether accident entirely workman's fault—Factories Act, 1961 (9 & 10 Eliz. 2 c. 34), s. 5 (1)— Factories (Standards of Lighting) Regulations, 1941 (S.R. & O. 1941 No. 94), reg. 2 (a), (b).*

A workman at a factory came to work early and in order to switch on **F**   more light by which to read his newspaper he walked across a part of the factory floor where in working hours persons were regularly employed (although at the time no-one else was there and work had not started), and while doing so tripped over a tie-bar which had been left lying, quite properly, beside, and in the shadow of, a mixer which was under construction. Pilot lights were on which gave an illumination of more than 0·5 foot-candles at **G**   floor-level, but in the shadow of the mixer the illumination was less than 0·5 foot-candles. The workman, who could easily have switched on other lights at another switch to which there was convenient access, claimed damages from his employers for the injury that he suffered by tripping over, alleging that they were in breach of their statutory duty under s. 5 (1)* of the Factories Act, 1961, to secure and maintain " sufficient and suitable **H**   lighting . . . in every part of a factory in which persons are working or passing ". The Factories (Standards of Lighting) Regulations, 1941, reg. 2 (a)† required that " the general illumination over those interior parts of the factory where persons are regularly employed shall be not less than six foot-candles . . .", and reg. 2 (b)† required that " the illumination over all other interior parts of the factory over which persons employed pass shall **I**   when and where a person is passing be not less than 0.5 foot-candles at floor level ".

Held: the employers were not liable for breach of statutory duty under s. 5 (1) of the Factories Act, 1961, for the following reasons—

---

* Section 5 (1) is printed at p. 296, letter A, post.   It repeats the provision formerly contained in s. 5 (1) of the Factories Act, 1937.

† Regulation 2 (a) and (b) is printed at p. 296, letters C to E, post. These regulations were made under the power contained in the Factories Act, 1937, but now have effect, by virtue of s. 183 (1) of, and Sch. 6 to, the Factories Act, 1961, under s. 5 (2) of the Act of 1901.

. (i) reg. 2 (*a*) of the Factories (Standards of Lighting) Regulations, 1941,   **A**
required the standard of six foot-candles' illumination only when persons
were actually working or employed at the factory, and so its requirement
in regard to the standard of illumination did not apply at the time when the
workman tripped (see p. 297, letter A, p. 298, letter B, and p. 299, letter A,
post).

(ii) reg. 2 (*b*) did not apply to the place where the workman tripped,   **B**
because that was a place " where persons are regularly employed " and so
was an area within reg. 2 (*a*), even though no-one was working there at the
time of the accident, with the consequence that the place was not an " other
interior part " within reg. 2 (*b*) (see p. 297, letter B, p. 298, letter D, and
p. 299, letter A, post).

(iii) the standard of illumination generally was adequate and, indeed,   **C**
exceeded that required by reg. 2 (*b*), and the fact that the strength of the
light in the shadow cast by the mixer was less than elsewhere did not constitute a breach of s. 5 (1) (see p. 297, letter C, p. 298, letter G, and p. 299,
letter D, post).

(iv) it was unnecessary for the workman to cross the working area without
first switching on the other lights at the switch to which he had convenient   **D**
access, and accordingly the accident was wholly his own fault (see p. 299,
letter D, p. 297, letter H, and p. 298, letter I, post).

Per CURIAM: a shadow cast by a movable object , such as a piece of work
in progress, does not constitute a breach of reg. 2 (*b*) merely because in the
shadow the light is below the prescribed strength (see p. 297, letter C, p. 298,
letter G, and p. 299, letter D, post).   **E**

Appeal dismissed.

[As to legal obligations in regard to lighting in factories, see 17 HALSBURY's
LAWS (3rd Edn.) 103, 104, para. 171.

For the Factories Act, 1961, s. 5, see 41 HALSBURY'S STATUTES (2nd Edn.)
248.]   **F**

Appeal.

This was an appeal by the plaintiff workman, William Lane, against the
dismissal by His Honour JUDGE BULGER at Gloucester county court on Oct. 12,
1966, of his action for damages for negligence and breach of statutory duty
against his employers, Gloucester Engineering Co., Ltd.   The facts are set out
in the judgment of SELLERS, L.J.   **G**

M. E. Lewer for the plaintiff workman.

P. Fallon for the defendant employers.

SELLERS, L.J.: What this appeal is seeking is almost the consultative
opinion of this court on s. 5 of the Factories Act, 1961, and in particular on one
of the regulations made in pursuance of that section, viz., reg. 2 of the Factories
(Standards of Lighting) Regulations, 1941 (1). On the facts of this case the   **H**
plaintiff ought not to succeed even if there had been a breach of statutory duty
established. In the circumstances, to my way of thinking he brought this
misfortune on himself, and it is difficult to see how he could have thought
otherwise.

The plaintiff was a welder, some fifty-six years of age, and he had been at work
in that capacity for many years.   On Oct. 23, 1964, whilst he was in the defen-   **I**
dants' factory he met with an accident.   He had been at work in a shop in the
factory some 150 feet by 30 feet.   He worked by day in that shop.   We have
a plan of the lighting in that particular part, for it is on lighting that this complaint is made against the defendant employers.   The evidence was (and so it
would appear from the plan) that when all the lights were on the factory was
exceptionally well lit.   Down the centre there was a row of what are called strip
lights—fluorescent lights.   There were also down each side of that relatively

(1) S.R. & O. 1941 No. 94.

A narrow shop a number of tungsten lights. No one complained that when work was taking place the factory was not well lit. During the night time it was the practice to leave on three pilot lights, as they have been called (they are depicted in the plan), almost equally distributed over the ceiling of the shop. Those three strip lights gave a satisfactory light of something over 0.5 foot-candles, and the plaintiff himself said that he could read by those lights alone.

B   The day before the plaintiff's accident, work had been in progress in this shop, as one would contemplate. We do not know what the work was but I apprehend that it was taking place throughout the length and breadth of the shop.   There happened to be in one particular place at the time a commodity in course of production called a mixer, which was some seventeen feet long by five feet high and some three feet wide. For the purpose of manufacturing a

C tie-bar had been used, and it had been placed down in the working area somewhere alongside that mixer. The whole trouble here seems to have arisen, first, because of the plaintiff's particular habits and, secondly, because he had some fortnight before changed the place where he had been working in the factory. The plaintiff said that he suffered from bronchitis and that he liked to get to work early before his work was due to commence at 7.30. He liked to get there about 7.10

D and sit down and have a rest and to read. He apparently was generally the first to arrive. He had to come in (as far as is shown on the plan) along a corridor or track internally and clock in at a place just adjacent to the shop. Having done that, it had been his habit to go to his bench, which is very near the place where the switch for the tungsten lighting is situated. That he would light up, although his work was not going to start then, and it was only put on

E for the purpose of the plaintiff being able to read his paper more comfortably. He switched on those lights. There was convenient access to the place where the switch was: it was only some seven feet from the way by which he would walk to his bench.

   The plaintiff had changed his place of work some fortnight before, his place of work being then over on the far side of the entrance to the right.   On this

F morning he changed his habit—I do not think that he had ever done this before this occasion—and he thought that, instead of switching on the tungsten lighting at the switch, he would go across the distance of the shop to the wall on the other side, almost opposite where he entered, where there was the switch, not for the tungsten lighting, which was quite near to where he had come in, but for the fluorescent strip lighting. On that occasion his preference was for that.

G No doubt the lighting would all have gone on by 7.30, but although he was alone he wished to put it on for his own purposes. To make his way to the switch for the fluorescent lighting across the working floor, he chose to go (and I say that deliberately because I can see no requirement for him to go) closely adjacent to this mixer and on the side of it which was the more remote from a light.   True it was the most direct journey, but if in fact it was in shadow he could have

H looked at the other side.   He said that he did not look, although he did say there was no way that side.   He could have turned to his left and gone down the shop that way; but he chose to go straight ahead.   There was a shadow cast by this five-feet high mixer, which was being constructed, and, not looking, he tripped over the tie-bar, which was properly there in the working place for the construction of the mixer. He fell over and hurt himself, although immediately

I afterwards he got up and put the lights on (I think the fluorescent lights) and went over to his bench.

   It is for that accident that the plaintiff blames the defendants, his employers. I find it very hard to see how he could come to blame them. If anything was his own fault, that was; but in these days everyone has to seek for a remedy, and the remedy that was alleged and which has survived to this court, is that the employers were in breach of the Factories Act, 1961, s. 5. It is also said (counsel for the defendants has challenged its accuracy) that there was a breach of the Factories (Standards of Lighting) Regulations, 1941.

The "Lighting" provision (which I think came first into the Factories **A** Act, 1937) is as follows:

> "5 (1).—Effective provision shall be made for securing and maintaining sufficient and suitable lighting, whether natural or artificial, in every part of a factory in which persons are working or passing."

Under s. 5 (2) provision is made for the Minister to make regulations prescribing **B** "a standard of sufficient and suitable lighting for factories", and that brought forth in 1941 regulations. Reference has been made in particular to reg. 2 (*a*) and (*b*) and to reg. 4. These regulations read:

> "2 (*a*) The general illumination over those interior parts of the factory where persons are regularly employed shall be not less than six foot-candles measured in the horizontal plane at a level of three feet above the floor: **C** Provided that in any such parts in which the mounting height of the light sources for general illumination necessarily exceeds twenty-five feet measured from the floor or where the structure of the room or the position or construction of the fixed machinery or plant prevents the uniform attainment of this standard, the general illumination at the said level shall be not less than **D** two foot-candles, and where work is actually being done the illumination shall be not less than six foot-candles or the greatest reasonably practicable illumination below six foot-candles.
>
> "2 (*b*) The illumination over all other interior parts of the factory over which persons employed pass shall when and where a person is passing be not less than 0·5 foot-candles at floor level. **E**
>
> "4. Adequate measures shall be taken, so far as reasonably practicable, to prevent the formation of shadows which cause eye-strain or risk of accident to any person employed."

The first matter for consideration is whether the regulations apply at all to the particular circumstances of this case. The effective and operative part of the statute is s. 5, and the plaintiff is clearly entitled to rely on that. As far as I **F** can see it places the obligation no higher than the common law; but the regulations establish in the appropriate case the standard there set down. It is significant that the standard is the standard of "general illumination"; that s in reg. 2. It is "The general illumination" and it applies to "those interior parts of the factory where persons are regularly employed"; and from the association of that with s. 5 (1) it means where they are in fact at the time working **G** or being employed.

That standard is not a rigid one because of the proviso recognising that factories are not all constructed in the same way and they present their difficulties. As I understand it, the "general illumination" that is required at what might be called bench level—that is, three feet above the floor—is a general illumination of not less than six foot-candles. The proviso is necessary because in order to **H** achieve that strength of illumination at three feet above the floor, if the ceiling exceeded twenty-five feet, very high powered lighting might be required and problems might be created. The proviso recognises, therefore, that some concession can be made in that particular circumstance, and also where the structure of the room or the position or construction of the fixed machinery or plant may prevent the light flowing uniformly over on to the benches, in which **I** case "the general illumination at the said level shall be not less than two foot-candles", and where "work is actually being done" then provision is to be made for it to be six foot-candles or as near to six foot-candles as can practicably be provided.

That paragraph, reg. 2 (*a*), applied to this factory when persons were working or were employed: the other paragraph, reg. 2 (*b*), applied to "all other interior parts of the factory over which persons employed pass", and then when they do pass the strength that has to be established is 0·5 foot-candles at floor level.

A   It is submitted on behalf of the defendants that the latter paragraph does not apply to this case because reg. 2 (*a*) applies to that area.   This was a place where persons were regularly employed and any " other interior part " was not this place where the accident happened.   I think that that submission is right.   It leaves the remedy, if any, for the plaintiff to fall under the section with regard to lighting.   Whilst I say that, however, it is my view that the judge was right in his

B   interpretation that there has been no breach of either of those paragraphs and, in particular, no breach of reg. 2 (*b*), which is the one more particularly relied on.   The requirement is that it should be 0·5 foot-candles at floor level; and so it was. One could take the power of the light which was existing at that time, which was a temporary light—the pilot lights.   The three strip lights were left on, and the evidence showed that that did give that power, that general illumination,

C   of 0·5 foot-candles in that factory.

    The evidence on which the plaintiff was relying was that there was not that power to be obtained if the measurement was taken to the side within the shadow cast by the mixer which was being produced.   In my view that would be quite an erroneous application of this provision in the lighting regulations.   I think that it is clear that it is recognised that these are lights of general power to give

D   a light on the benches, or on the floor where people are passing on the floor, and that light will be interfered with by the commodity which is being worked.

    It is provided by reg. 4 that

    " Adequate measures shall be taken so far as reasonably practicable to
    prevent the formation of shadows which cause eye-strain or risk of accident
    to any person employed."

E
It seems to me that any other interpretation would make it quite unworkable, and if anyone was to be blamed for not having the requisite 0·5 foot-candle strength at any place where it was sought to be taken on the factory floor one would get fluctuating results every few minutes in the course of the day if there was one barrow or a bogey, or a number of people standing for instance, which

F   to some extent would obscure the full effect of the light falling on to the bench or the floor: it would be creating a breach of this obligation.

    That is not the correct interpretation, and I agree with the judge on that aspect of it, although it seems that the right interpretation of regs. 2 (*a*) and (*b*) is that they are referring to two separate parts at any given time and that the " other interior parts " must be contrasted with that area where people " are

G   regularly employed ".

    Turning to the " Lighting " section itself, there has been in my view no breach whatsoever by the defendants of their general obligation under s. 5 (1).   This light was quite adequate for all the purposes during the night.   It was quite a satisfactory light to have for anyone who was coming into the shop early to his work.   If it had been required to be better—and I do not think that the

H   plaintiff thought that it required to be better because he could not see where he was going—it could have been made better quite easily by the plaintiff switching on the light at the tungsten lighting switch.   That was near at hand, and he would have had all the illumination that he wanted.   He failed lamentably to look after himself.   If it had been possible to find any breach of the regulations it would have been in my opinion a highly technical breach and I should have

I   thought it was a case where the plaintiff could be said to have brought his injury on himself by failing to take care for his own safety when every facility was at hand.

    I would dismiss this appeal.

    DAVIES, L.J.:   I agree.

    The judge was of the opinion that the case fell within reg. 2 (*b*) of the Factories (Standards of Lighting) Regulations, 1941.   I agree with the argument of counsel for the defendants that the place where this accident happened, if it came within either of the paragraphs of reg. 2 (and he submits that it did not) would have

been not within para. (b) but within para. (a), for para. (a) applies to " those A
interior parts of the factory where persons are regularly employed ".

The place where the plaintiff hurt himself was certainly that; but the standard
of illumination which is prescribed in reg. 2 (a) could not have been applicable
at the moment of the plaintiff's accident, because, although the place was an
interior part of the factory where persons are regularly employed, it was not a
part of the factory (and I now quote from s. 5 (1) of the Factories Act, 1961) B
" in which persons are working . . ."   Therefore, although reg. 2 (a) would have
had prima facie application, it did not apply because nobody was working there
at the time.

That view of the matter, of course, gets rid of the obvious absurdity which
would arise if the provisions of reg. 2 (a) applied when men were not working;
for that would mean that the full lights, which the evidence showed were as good C
as daylight, would have had to be on all night.

So far as concerns reg. 2 (b), that only applies to " all other interior parts of
the factory over which persons employed pass ".   It is plain that the scene of
the accident was a part of the factory where persons are regularly employed
and, therefore, it could not fall within the words " all other interior parts of
the factory ".   Therefore, in my view, counsel for the defendants is again right D
in saying that reg. 2 (b) does not apply.   The contrast really is that reg. 2 (a)
refers to the factory floor and reg. 2 (b) applies to places other than the factory
floor—such, I suppose, as corridors, passages and so on.

I mention in passing that the proviso to reg. 2 (a), useful though it may be in
attempting to construe these not very easy regulations, has, of course, no direct
application to the facts of the present case.   For that concerns a part of the E
factory where the light source necessarily exceeds twenty-five feet and the
evidence in this case was that the light source was twenty-four feet, ten inches
high, which is less than twenty-five feet.

That being so, the plaintiff's claim must arise, if at all, under the words of the
statute, namely s. 5 (1), by which the defendant employers had to make " effective F
provision . . . for securing and maintaining sufficient and suitable lighting . . .".
It is conceded by counsel for the defendants that it would be reasonable, in
construing that provision, to refer to the standard set by reg. 2 (b), namely, that
of " not less than 0·5 foot-candles at floor level ".   As SELLERS, L.J., has pointed
out, the evidence was that, over-all, the illumination or light in this factory did
satisfy that standard: it exceeded it very slightly.   In those circumstances, it G
seems to me that the employers did make " effective provision . . . for securing
and maintaining sufficient and suitable lighting "; and it would really be quite
unreasonable to say that, owing to the presence of this machine under construction, which happened to be a fairly large one, a slight shadow cast by that machine
resulted in a breach of the statutory obligation on the part of the employers.

In my opinion, although reached from an approach somewhat different from H
that taken by the county court judge, his judgment was completely supportable
and justifiable, on the grounds which I have attempted to set out, agreeing really
in every respect with what has been said by SELLERS, L.J.

The only other point is this.   As SELLERS, L.J., has said, it is a somewhat academic exercise to interpret this statute and these regulations on the facts of the
present case.   If ever a man did bring an accident on himself, the plaintiff did.   He I
could perfectly well have switched on the tungsten lamps at the switch, which
was within a foot or two of the place where he had been working for a considerable
time.   Instead of that, he chose to embark on this passage, which turned out for
him to be perilous (though one would not have thought it ought to have been),
and to launch himself across the factory floor in order to put on the fluorescent
lights at their switch.   In my judgment, he really was the sole and only author of
his own injury; and on that ground too I would dismiss the appeal.

A   **RUSSELL, L.J.:** I also agree that the appeal fails.

The plaintiff was passing through a part of the factory where persons are regularly employed but in which no person was at the time working. The function of the regulations is to lay down, for the purposes of the duty under s. 5 (1) of the Factories Act, 1961, standards of what is "sufficient and suitable lighting"; but no part of the Factories (Standards of Lighting) Regulations, 1941, lays B down any standard for the circumstances of this case. Regulation 2 (*a*) relates to working areas—such as this: reg. 2 (*b*) in terms relates only to parts of the factory *other than* working areas. The question therefore is whether the defendants were in breach of s. 5 (1), as no standard of "sufficient and suitable lighting" exists under the regulations to meet the case.

I cannot for myself think that there was here any breach of duty under s. 5 (1): C the relative darkness where the accident happened was due only to the presence of a piece of work in progress—one of many on the floor—which in effect cast a shadow. If the standard under reg. 2 (*b*) is referred to by analogy in applying s. 5 (1) to the present case, then I think that reg. 4 should also be so referred to: and surely it is not reasonably practicable to light all individual pockets of shadow caused by movable objects up to a 0·5 foot-candle standard.

D   If there was a breach of duty under s. 5 (1), I would also put the full responsibility for the accident squarely on the shoulders of the plaintiff. It was entirely unnecessary for him to venture into the working area without turning on the tungsten lights at their switch. That switch was very near to him as he came into the factory. It was only seven feet off the ordinary gangway—that seven feet obviously (from the plan) being perfectly adequately, and up to any standards, lit E by the pilot lights. That switch was on a column practically next-door to the bench at which the plaintiff had been working up to two weeks before the accident, so he was entirely familiar with it. The tungsten lights were ample for his immediate purpose of resting with his newspaper at his bench, and the strip lighting, the switch for which was at the point for which he was aiming, was far more than was required for his purpose.

F   *Appeal dismissed.*

Solicitors: *Evill & Coleman* (for the plaintiff workman); *Cartwright, Taylor & Corpe*, Bristol (for the defendant employers).

[*Reported by* HENRY SUMMERFIELD, ESQ., *Barrister-at-Law.*]

G ———

PRACTICE DIRECTION.

CHANCERY DIVISION

H *Family Provision—Evidence—By statements exhibited to affidavits.*
Infant—Guardianship of Infants Acts—Evidence—By statements exhibited to affidavits.
Ward of Court—Practice—Evidence—By statements exhibited to affidavits.

The judges of the Chancery Division have decided that, although affidavits I can no longer be inspected without leave (R.S.C., Ord. 63, r. 4 (1) (*c*)), it is desirable that evidence in applications under the Inheritance (Family Provision) Act, 1938, and infant matters (wardship and guardianship) shall be by way of exhibited statements as heretofore.

W. F. S. HAWKINS
Chief Master
Chancery Division.
Apr. 10, 1967.

———

BUCKLAND *v.* BUCKLAND.   A

[PROBATE, DIVORCE AND ADMIRALTY DIVISION (Scarman, J.), February 19, 1965.]

Nullity—Consent to marriage—Fear—Fear must be of sufficient degree to vitiate consent, reasonably entertained and arise from some external circumstance for which petitioner not responsible.

In a case where it is alleged that the petitioner's consent to marriage has   B
been vitiated by fear, it must be shown, first, that fear of a sufficient degree to
vitiate consent was present, and, secondly, that the fear was reasonably
entertained, but, even if the fear is reasonably entertained, it will not vitiate
consent unless it arises from some external circumstance for which the
petitioner is not himself responsible (see p. 302, letters E and F, post).

H. (*otherwise D.*) v. *H.* ([1953] 2 All E.R. 1229) followed.   C

[As to consent to marriage, see 19 HALSBURY'S LAWS (3rd Edn.) 776, para. 1243;
and for cases on the subject, see 19 DIGEST (Repl.) 36, 37, *134-137.*]

Cases referred to:
    Griffiths v. *Griffiths*, [1944] I.R. 35.
    H. (*otherwise D.*) v. *H.*, [1953] 2 All E.R. 1229; [1954] P. 258; [1953] 3 W.L.R.   D
       849; Digest (Cont. Vol. A) 661, *135a.*

Petition.

This was a petition by Cyril Edwin Buckland for a declaration that the marriage
celebrated between him and Theodora Camilleri was null and void on the ground
that it lacked his consent. In the alternative, if the marriage was valid, he
petitioned for a decree of divorce on the ground of the respondent's adultery. The   E
facts are set out in the judgment.

H. B. Grant for the petitioner.

    SCARMAN, J.: In this suit the petitioner, Cyril Edwin Buckland, prays, in
the first place, for a declaration that the marriage celebrated between him and
Theodora Camilleri, a spinster, was null and void on the ground that it lacked his   F
consent. In the alternative, if the marriage be valid, he seeks a divorce on the
grounds that the respondent has committed adultery. I am satisfied, for the
reasons that I propose to give, that the petitioner is entitled to the declaration
sought. I shall, therefore, not deal with the divorce aspect of the petition.

    The petitioner was born on Aug. 13, 1932, in Malta, the son of a Maltese mother
and an English father. He lived in Malta until 1949, when, for the first time, he   G
came to England. He returned to Malta from England in October, 1952, and
remained in Malta until May 9, 1953. I am satisfied that, by Jan. 27, 1964, the
date on which he instituted his suit, he had acquired a domicil of choice in
England. I take the facts from the evidence of the petitioner. His evidence has
not been corroborated in any material particular, but, having heard and seen him
in the witness box, I am completely satisfied that he was telling me the truth,   H
and indeed the whole truth, about the matrimonial history, which has caused
him the gravest anxiety. When he returned to Malta in October, 1952, he obtained
employment as a policeman in the dockyard area. This was British employment
in the sense that he was responsible to British authority. During the period of
October, 1952, to April, 1953, he occasionally went out with a Maltese girl whom
he knew as Dora. He went out only once or twice with her; each time it was a   I
completely harmless social occasion. He knew neither her parents nor her address.
He had no sort of affectionate or improper relationship with the girl at all.
Indeed, he had not seen her at all for several months prior to the celebration of a
ceremony of marriage to which I shall later have to direct my attention. He had
no idea how old she was.

    Towards the end of April, 1953, he was suddenly called to a police station. On
arrival he was interviewed by a Maltese C.I.D. officer. He was asked a number of
questions and then charged with the offence, as he put it, of " minor corruption ".

A By that he meant that the C.I.D. officer was charging him with corrupting a young girl who was a minor. I have the benefit of seeing the way in which the subsequent charge was drafted. It was to the effect that, over a period of three months, in a public place at Cospicua and in other localities, by means of lewd acts, he had defiled the respondent, a minor of fifteen years of age. He protested his innocence. He did not even know at the time of the questioning to whom the

B the police officer was referring when he was charging him with corrupting the girl. Some time later, but not until then, he appreciated that the girl must be the girl he knew as Dora. He then spent one night in custody. Prior to being called to the police station, he had already made arrangements to return to England. He had done so because he took the view that employment opportunities were much better in England than they were in Malta. The police either knew or discovered

C that this was his intention. The police inspector accordingly confiscated his passport, cancelled his reservation for the journey to England, and informed him that he had done so. The next day the petitioner was taken to the courts and there allowed to see his solicitor. After being formally charged before the court, he was released on bail.

It is important that the advice that the solicitor gave to the petitioner should

D be stated. He asserted to the solicitor, as he had maintained to the police, that he was completely innocent of the charge of defiling the young woman; but the solicitor's advice (if the petitioner is to be believed, and I believe him) was cynical in the extreme. It was to the effect that this sort of act, that is, the defiling of young Maltese women, was a common occurrence with British serving personnel, who, having committed it, escaped to England before they could be brought to

E book; the solicitor told him that this was widely known in Malta, and resented. Accordingly, the solicitor advised him that there was no chance for him when confronted with such a charge in a Maltese court. I can only hope that the advice was nonsense. Unfortunately, the solicitor went on to say that he was certain to lose the case and that the result would very probably be a long period of imprisonment, perhaps up to two years. He added that he would have to support,

F for some fifteen to sixteen years, the child with which the young woman was believed to be pregnant. The petitioner was frightened. If such advice was given, he had every reason to be frightened. I have come to the conclusion that such advice was given, and that he believed it. Ultimately he was advised: you really have only one choice—either marry the girl or go to prison. The advice was given at a time when his passport had been confiscated and his passage to England can-

G celled by the police. It was, as he told me he felt it to be, a terrifying situation. Faced with his terrible dilemma, he did what, in my judgment, was a very reasonable thing to do. He sought the advice of his superior in the British dockyard police, a Superintendent Gerrard. The superintendent confirmed, from his point of view, the sort of advice given him by the Maltese lawyer. The petitioner was told by the superintendent: " Well, you have really only one choice:

H either marry the girl or go to prison." This must have been a terrifying moment for the petitioner. He told me that he had hoped, and obviously reasonably hoped, that his superior officer, the superintendent, might be able to do something with the Maltese authorities to get this grave and unjustified charge removed, but the superintendent felt that he could not intervene.

The petitioner then decided that he would marry the girl. Thereafter events

I happened with what I can only describe as appalling speed. He saw the police inspector and communicated to the inspector his decision to marry the girl. Arrangements were then made so that at eight o'clock in the evening of the same day he presented himself in a church in Malta, there to be married by a parish priest. The priest apparently expected the petitioner to arrive; certainly the impression conveyed to the petitioner was that the priest was expecting him and knew all about it. Then, for the first time for several months, he saw Dora—the respondent. She was accompanied by a number of persons, no doubt including her parents. They went through a ceremony of marriage in the church. They then

retired to the petitioner's mother's home where there was some sort of dis-   A
cussion, but the petitioner took very little part in it. He was completely over-
whelmed by his distress and he went on night duty in the dockyard at 11.0 p.m.,
some three hours after he had presented himself in the church for the ceremony
of marriage. He had very little to do in the next eight days with Theodora
Camilleri, although she was living at his mother's house and so was he. He was
on night duty and slept during each day. He left Malta on May 9, 1953, and has   B
never since lived with her.

The question which I have to decide is whether the ceremony of marriage, to
which the petitioner was a party, was invalid on the grounds that it lacked the
reality of consent on his part. Such a question was considered by KARMINSKI, J.,
in *H.* (*otherwise D.*) v. *H.* (1), where the wife was the petitioner. The headnote (2)
summarises accurately the effect of his decision; it says: " In the absence of   C
consent there can be no valid marriage; and fear may vitiate consent." There
was in the case no allegation made against the respondent or his agents. The
learned judge found that the petitioner's fears genuinely existed and were of
sufficient degree to negative her consent to the marriage. He also found that they
were reasonably entertained. In the course of his judgment he commented (3)
that there appeared to be no case reported where fear or duress emanated from   D
any other source than from the respondent or his servants or agents; but he did
not allow the fact that the respondent was in no way responsible for the petitioner's
fear to defeat her claim to relief. I understand the effect of KARMINSKI, J.'s
judgment to be that, in a case where it is alleged that the petitioner's consent to
marriage has been vitiated by fear, it must be shown first that fear of sufficient
degree to vitiate consent was present; and, secondly, that the fear was reasonably   E
entertained. In *Griffiths* v. *Griffiths* (4), HAUGH, J., added what may be a limitation; having said that duress or intimidation may well produce a fear that may
lead a person to marriage, he made this comment: " But if fear is justly imposed
the resulting marriage, when contracted, is valid and binding." Thus, a third
proposition may be stated to the effect that, even if the fear is reasonably entertained, it will not vitiate consent unless it arises from some external circumstance   F
for which the petitioner is not himself responsible.

The conclusion that I have reached, on the facts in the present case, is that the
petitioner agreed to marry the respondent because he was afraid and that his
fear was brought about by an unjust charge preferred against him either by the
respondent and the respondent's father, or by the respondent's father alone. The
fear which originated in this way was greatly strengthened by the advice given   G
to the petitioner by his own solicitor and by his superior officer. I am satisfied
that, when he presented himself in the church for the marriage ceremony, he
believed himself to be in an inescapable dilemma—marriage or prison; and,
fearing prison, he chose marriage. Accordingly, basing myself on the view of the
law expressed by KARMINSKI, J., in *H.* (*otherwise D.*) v. *H.* (1), I have come to the
conclusion that the petitioner agreed to his marriage because of his fears, and that   H
his fears, which were reasonably entertained, arose from external circumstances
for which he was in no way responsible. Accordingly, in my judgment, he is
entitled to a declaration that the marriage ceremony was null and void.

I would add only one further matter. The case has given me the greatest
anxiety because it is clear that, if the history which I have accepted be
true, as I believe it to be true, a very sad state of affairs has been revealed. Also,   I
if it be right, as I find it to be right, that the petitioner was brought into a state of
panic by proceedings on an unjust charge, then those who were responsible for
initiating the charge, the father and the respondent, are gravely to blame. It
was a matter of some concern to me that a matter as serious as this had to be

(1) [1953] 2 All E.R. 1229; [1954] P. 258.
(2) [1954] P. at p. 258.
(3) [1953] 2 All E.R. at p. 1232; [1954] P. at p. 267.
(4) [1944] I.R. 35 at p. 44.

A   brought before the court in a petition which had not been served in the normal
way on the respondent. For that reason I thought it necessary to look myself into
the evidence that the registrar accepted when he dispensed with the full evidence
of service which is normally required in a divorce matter. Having looked at that
evidence I am perfectly satisfied, first, that the registrar made the right order,
and, secondly, that the respondent knows all about these proceedings and has

B   chosen to disregard them, and not to challenge the allegations made against her
by the petitioner. That being so, I make the declaration sought in the petition,
namely, that the marriage celebrated between the petitioner and the respondent
on May 1, 1953, in the Collegiate and Parish Church of Cospicua, Malta, is null
and void.

Declaration accordingly.

C
Solicitors: *Duthie, Hart & Duthie* (for the petitioner).

[*Reported by* Alice Bloomfield, *Barrister-at-Law.*]

D
Re TILLEY'S WILL TRUSTS.
BURGIN *v.* CROAD AND ANOTHER.

[Chancery Division (Ungoed-Thomas, J.), February 2, 3, 7, 1967.]

Trust and Trustee—Breach of trust—Mixing trust moneys with trustee's own
E   *money—Rights of beneficiaries—Trust moneys forming part of deceased's*
estate paid into trustee's (his widow's) own bank account—Overdraft facilities
accorded by bank to widow for property dealings—Liabilities of deceased's
estate met by widow out of her own moneys—Whether beneficiary in deceased's
estate entitled to a share of the profit from widow's property dealings.

If a trustee, having regard to all the circumstances of the case objectively
F   considered, has in fact, whatever his intention, laid out trust moneys in or
towards a purchase of property, the beneficiaries are entitled to the property
purchased and any profits which it produces to the extent to which the
property has been paid for out of trust moneys (see p. 313, letter A, post).

Principle in *Lupton* v. *White* ((1808), 15 Ves. 432) considered.

The widow of a testator who died in 1932 became, on the death of her
G   co-trustee in 1941, sole trustee of the testator's will, under which she was
entitled to a life interest and, subject thereto, two beneficiaries, who were
his children but were not hers, were entitled to his estate in equal shares.
The widow engaged in many property transactions, both before and after
the testator's death; in April, 1939, she was using overdraft facilities with
her bank amounting to £22,405. Her property transactions continued
H   throughout the war years, her overdraft in January, 1945, being £23,536.
From the testator's death the widow met all liabilities of his estate (valued
for probate at £2,150) out of her own moneys. Shortly after his death she
had practically no trust moneys in hand; she paid his funeral expenses
and the estate duty, and later redeemed a mortgage, out of her own moneys.
Properties forming part of the testator's estate were realised in 1933, 1939,
I   1951 and 1952. From these the widow received a total of £2,237 which was
paid into her bank account and was mingled with her own moneys. In 1951,
and at all times thereafter, her bank account was sufficiently in credit from
her own personal contributions to it, without regard to any trust moneys
credited to it, to pay for her later property purchases. In 1959 the widow
died, her estate being valued at £94,000. The plaintiff, who was the attorney
administrator of a deceased beneficiary, M., entitled to one half of the
capital of the testator's estate subject to the widow's life interest, sued the
widow's personal representatives in 1963 for an account of the testator's

estate. On the question whether M.'s estate was entitled to half of the A
proportion of profits of purchases made by the widow to the extent that
the defendants could not show that such properties were purchased out of
the widow's own money, or was entitled only to one half of the £2,237
(interest on that amount not being in issue and the question of whether
there was a charge for the £2,237 being immaterial owing to the amount of
the widow's estate),

B

Held: on the facts the widow trustee's breach of trust had halted
at the mixing of the trust moneys (£2,237) with her own moneys, for in
reality, she had not invested the trust moneys in properties, but the trust
moneys, by being paid into her own bank account, had been applied in
reduction of any overdraft of hers for the time being, such overdraft being
the true source of the purchase money for the properties in which she invested ; C
thus the present case was not within the principle stated at p. 303, letter F, ante,
and the plaintiff was not entitled to any share in the properties in which
the widow had invested, but was entitled only to repayment of M.'s share
of the £2,237 (see p. 313, letter F, post).

Re Hallett's Estate ([1874-80] All E.R. Rep. 793) and *Re Oatway* ([1903]
2 Ch. 356) considered. D

Dictum of LORD PARKER OF WADDINGTON in *Sinclair* v. *Brougham*
([1914-15] All E.R. Rep. at p. 643) explained.

Lupton v. *White* ((1808), 15 Ves. 432) distinguished.

[Editorial Note. The principle stated at p. 303, letter F, ante, is an objective
test ; on a trustee's deliberate application of trust moneys in or towards a pur- E
chase of property the beneficiaries are entitled, a fortiori, to a similar interest in
the property purchased and any profits that it produces, but this subjective
test is, it is emphasised, not the exclusive test (see p. 313, letter D, post).

As to the consequences of a trustee's mixing trust money with his own money,
see 14 HALSBURY'S LAWS (3rd Edn.) 630, para. 1165, and 38 HALSBURY'S LAWS
(3rd Edn.) 944, para. 1633, text and notes (*g*)-(*i*), p. 1044, para. 1800, p. 1048, F
para. 1812, text and note (*s*) ; and for cases on the subject, see 47 DIGEST (Repl.)
537-539, *4848-4864*.]

Cases referred to :
> *Armory* v. *Delamirie*, (1722), 1 Stra. 505 ; 93 E.R. 664 ; 3 Digest (Repl.) 67, *83*.
> *Brown* v. *Adams*, (1869), 4 Ch. App. 764 ; 39 L.J.Ch. 67 ; 21 L.T. 71 ; 47 G
>   Digest (Repl.) 537, *4853*.
> *Cook* v. *Addison*, (1869), L.R. 7 Eq. 466 ; 38 L.J.Ch. 322 ; 20 L.T. 212 ; 47
>   Digest (Repl.) 490, *4412*.
> *Devaynes* v. *Noble, Baring* v. *Noble, Clayton's Case*, [1814-1823] All E.R. Rep. 1 ;
>   (1816), 1 Mer. 572 ; 35 E.R. 781 ; 3 Digest (Repl.) 192, *370*.
> *Gray* v. *Haig, Haig* v. *Gray*, (1855), 20 Beav. 219 ; 52 E.R. 587 ; 1 Digest H
>   (Repl.) 498, *1360*.
> *Hallett's Estate, Re, Knatchbull* v. *Hallett, Cotterell* v. *Hallett*, [1874-80] All E.R.
>   Rep. 793 ; (1880), 13 Ch.D. 696 ; 49 L.J.Ch. 415 ; 42 L.T. 421 ; 47
>   Digest (Repl.) 537, *4854*.
> *Lupton* v. *White, White* v. *Lupton*, (1808), 15 Ves. 432 ; 33 E.R. 817 ; 47
>   Digest (Repl.) 537, *4848*. I
> *Oatway, Re, Hertslet* v. *Oatway*, [1903] 2 Ch. 356 ; 72 L.J.Ch. 575 ; 88 L.T. 622 ;
>   47 Digest (Repl.) 538, *4858*.
> *Panton* v. *Panton*, (undated), cited 15 Ves. at pp. 435, 440 ; 33 E.R. 818, 820 ;
>   3 Digest (Repl.) 74, *136*.
> *Sinclair* v. *Brougham*, [1914-15] All E.R. Rep. 622 ; [1914] A.C. 398 ; 83
>   L.J.Ch. 465 ; 111 L.T. 1 ; 3 Digest (Repl.) 167, *246*.
> *Vyse* v. *Foster*, (1872), 8 Ch. App. 309 ; 42 L.J.Ch. 245 ; 27 L.T. 774 ; 47
>   Digest (Repl.) 421, *3773*.

A   **Application.**

This was an application in an action begun by writ issued on June 5, 1963, for an account of property received by the widow of the testator, Henry Tilley, as trustee of his will and for accounts generally.   The testator died on Dec. 4, 1932.   The plaintiff was the attorney administrator of the testator's deceased daughter, who died in Southern Rhodesia on Sept. 7, 1955, entitled to a half-

B   share in the testator's estate subject to the widow's life interest.   The defendants were the personal representatives of the testator's widow, who died on July 4, 1959, having been sole trustee of the testator's will since Feb. 18, 1941.   An order was made in the action on Oct. 9, 1963, for an account of the property received by the defendants as trustees of the testator's will, with liberty to apply, and it was under this liberty to apply that the matter was brought before Ungoed-

C   Thomas, J.   The summons was heard in chambers, but judgment was delivered in open court.

D. A. Thomas for the plaintiff.
J. A. Brightman, Q.C., and *L. L. Ware* for the defendants.

UNGOED-THOMAS, J.:   This is an action for an account against a

D   trustee of a will.   The plaintiff is the attorney administrator of a deceased beneficiary under that will, and the defendants are the personal representatives of a defaulting trustee who was a sole trustee for a considerable period.

On July 8, 1927, Mr. Henry Tilley, the testator, made the will.   He appointed his wife and Mr. Dinelli executors and he gave his estate on trust for sale.   He then gave his wife a life interest in the estate with remainder to his son Charles

E   and his daughter Mabel equally.   Mabel and Charles were not the children of the testator's widow.   The testator died on Dec. 4, 1932.   Probate was granted on Apr. 29, 1933, when the estate was valued for probate purposes at £2,150. On Feb. 18, 1941, Mr. Dinelli died leaving Mr. Tilley's widow the sole trustee of his will.   On July 4, 1959, Mrs. Tilley died and on Nov. 13 of that year letters of administration to her estate were granted to the defendants and the testator's

F   daughter, Mabel, who does not feature in these proceedings as she died before they commenced.   Mrs. Tilley's estate was valued for probate purposes at approximately £94,000.   On Sept. 7, 1955, Mr. Tilley's daughter Mabel died after having married.   She died in Southern Rhodesia where she was settled, and in due course the plaintiff became the attorney administrator to her estate.

On June 5, 1963, the writ in this action was issued for an account of property

G   received by the widow as trustee of the testator's will and for accounts generally. An order was made on Oct. 9, 1963, for an account of the property received by the administrators as trustees of the testator's will, with liberty to apply, and it is under that liberty to apply that this matter now comes before me.   On Apr. 6, 1965, another order was made in these proceedings appointing an accountant to inquire into and report on the widow's dealings with the trust estate

H   from Dec. 4, 1932, which was the date of the testator's death, until the widow's death on July 4, 1959.   In due course that report was made and I shall refer to it later.

The plaintiff claims that Mabel's estate should, in virtue of Mabel's half interest in the estate, subject to the widow's life interest, have half of the proportion of the profits of the purchases made by the widow to the extent to which

I   the defendants, as her legal personal representatives, cannot show that those properties were purchased out of the widow's personal moneys.   The defendants, on the other hand, say that the plaintiff is entitled only to a charge on the defendants' bank account for half the trust moneys paid into that bank account with interest, i.e., half the sum of £2,237, which is shown to have been paid into that bank account, and the interest on that amount.

I come first to the law.   The plaintiff relied on the statement of the law in Lewin on Trusts (16th Edn.) at p. 223 and some of the cases cited in support of it.   That statement reads:

" Wherever the trust property is placed, if a trustee amalgamates it   A
with his own, his beneficiary will be entitled to every portion of the blended
property which the trustee cannot prove to be his own."

Lupton v. *White*, *White* v. *Lupton* (1) is the leading case for this proposition.
In that case the defendant, an accounting party, had mixed the plaintiff's lead
ore of unascertainable amount with his own lead ore, and the reference to the case
of *Panton* v. *Panton* (2) shows that the same principle applies where moneys are   B
similarly mixed.   The principle is thus stated (3):

". . . to apply the great principle, familiar both at law and in equity, that,
if a man, having undertaken to keep the property of another distinct,
mixes it with his own, the whole must both at law and in equity be taken to
be the property of the other, until the former puts the subject under such   C
circumstances, that it may be distinguished as satisfactorily, as it might
have been before that unauthorised mixture upon his part."

Subsequently, in referring to *Armory* v. *Delamirie* (4), the case in which a jeweller
gave a trifle for a diamond ring found by a poor boy, the reason for the principle
appears. The Lord Chancellor said (5):

". . . the Lord Chief Justice directed the jury to find, that the stone was   D
of the utmost value they could find; upon this principle, that it was the
defendant's own fault, by his own dishonest act, that the jury could not
find the real value."

In *Gray* v. *Haig*, *Haig* v. *Gray* (6) SIR JOHN ROMILLY, M.R., followed *Lupton*
v. *White* (1). The principle was followed and restated thus by SIR JOHN STUART,   E
V.-C., in *Cook* v. *Addison* (7):

" It is a well-established doctrine in this court, that if a trustee or agent
mixes and confuses the property which he holds in a fiduciary character
with his own property, so as that they cannot be separated with perfect
accuracy, he is liable for the whole.   This doctrine was explained by LORD
ELDON, L.C., in *Lupton* v. *White* (1)."   F

The words in that passage " so as that they cannot be separated with perfect
accuracy " are an essential part of SIR JOHN STUART'S proposition, and indeed
of the principle of *Lupton* v. *White* (1).   If a trustee mixes trust assets with his
own, the onus is on the trustee to distinguish the separate assets and, to the
extent that he fails to do so, they belong to the trust.   The *Lupton* v. *White* (1)
line of cases does not appear to me to go further than this.   So the proposition   G
in LEWIN, which I have read, is limited to cases where the amalgam of mixed
assets is such that they cannot be sufficiently distinguished and treated separately;
it is based on the lack of evidence to do so being attributable to the trustee's
fault.

The defendants relied on *Re Hallett's Estate, Knatchbull* v. *Hallett, Cotterell*
v. *Hallett* (8), with a view to establishing that the trustee must be presumed to   H
have drawn out his own moneys from the bank account of mixed moneys in
priority to trust moneys, with the result that property bought by such prior
drawings must be the trustee's exclusive personal property.   In that case the
claim was against a bank balance of mixed fiduciary and personal funds, and it
is in the context of such a claim that it was held that the person in a fiduciary
character drawing out money from the bank account must be taken to have   I
drawn out his own money in preference to the trust money, so that the claim
of the beneficiaries prevailed against the balance of the account.   *Re Oatway,*
Hertslet v. *Oatway* (9) was the converse of this decision in *Re Hallett's Estate* (8).

(1) (1808), 15 Ves. 432.   (2) Undated, cited 15 Ves. at pp. 435, 440.
(3) *Lupton* v. *White*, ((1808), 15 Ves. at p. 437).   (4) (1722), 1 Stra. 505.
(5) Per LORD ELDON, L.C., in *Lupton* v. *White*, ((1808), 15 Ves. at p. 440).
(6) (1855), 20 Beav. 219.   (7) (1869), L.R. 7 Eq. 466 at p. 470.
(8) [1874-80] All E.R. Rep. 793; (1880), 13 Ch.D. 696.   (9) [1903] 2 Ch. 356.

A In that case the claim was not against the balance left in the bank of such mixed moneys but against the proceeds of sale of shares which the trustee had purchased with moneys which, as in *Re Hallett's Estate* (10), he had drawn from the bank account; but, unlike the situation in *Re Hallett's Estate* (10), his later drawings had exhausted the account, so that it was useless to proceed against the account. It was held that the beneficiary was entitled to the proceeds of sale of the
B shares, which were more than their purchase price but less than the trust moneys paid into the account. The law is reviewed and the principles are stated by JOYCE, J., (11). He says:

"Trust money may be followed into land or any other property in which it has been invested; and when a trustee has, in making any purchase or investment, applied trust money together with his own, the cestuis que trust
C are entitled to a charge on the property purchased for the amount of the trust money laid out in the purchase or investment. Similarly, if money held by any person in a fiduciary capacity be paid into his own banking account, it may be followed by the equitable owner, who, as against the trustee, will have a charge for what belongs to him upon the balance to the credit of the account. If, then, the trustee pays in further sums, and
D from time to time draws out money by cheques, but leaves a balance to the credit of the account, it is settled that he is not entitled to have the rule in *Devaynes* v. *Noble, Baring* v. *Noble, Clayton's Case* (12) applied so as to maintain that the sums which have been drawn out and paid away so as to be incapable of being recovered represented pro tanto the trust money, and that the balance remaining is not trust money, but represents only
E his own moneys paid into the account. *Brown* v. *Adams* (13) to the contrary ought not to be followed since the decision in *Re Hallett's Estate* (10). It is, in my opinion, equally clear that when any of the money drawn out has been invested, and the investment remains in the name or under the control of the trustee, the rest of the balance having been afterwards dissipated by him, he cannot maintain that the investment which remains represents his
F own money alone, and that what has been spent and can no longer be traced and recovered was the money belonging to the trust. In other words, when the private money of the trustee and that which he held in a fiduciary capacity have been mixed in the same banking account, from which various payments have from time to time been made, then, in order to determine to whom any remaining balance or any investment that may have been paid
G for out of the account ought to be deemed to belong, the trustee must be debited with all the sums that have been withdrawn and applied to his own use so as to be no longer recoverable, and the trust money in like manner be debited with any sums taken out and duly invested in the names of the proper trustees. The order of priority in which the various withdrawals and investments may have been respectively made is wholly immaterial. I
H have been referring, of course, to cases where there is only one fiduciary owner or set of cestuis que trust claiming whatever may be left as against the trustee. In the present case there is no balance left. The only investment or property remaining which represents any part of the mixed moneys paid into the banking account is the Oceana shares purchased for £2,137. Upon these, therefore, the trust had a charge for the £3,000 trust money paid
I into the account. That is to say, those shares and the proceeds thereof belong to the trust. It was objected that the investment in the Oceana shares was made at a time when Oatway's own share of the balance to the credit of the account (if the whole had been then justly distributed) would have exceeded £2,137, the price of the shares; that he was therefore entitled to withdraw that sum, and might rightly apply it for his own purposes; and

(10) [1874-80] All E.R. Rep. 793; (1880), 13 Ch.D. 696.
(11) [1903] 2 Ch. at pp. 359-361.
(12) [1814-23] All E.R. Rep. 1; (1816), 1 Mer. 572.   (13) (1869), 4 Ch. App. 764.

that consequently the shares should be held to belong to his estate. To **A** this I answer that he never was entitled to withdraw the £2,137 from the account, or, at all events, that he could not be entitled to take that sum from the account and hold it or the investment made therewith, freed from the charge in favour of the trust, unless or until the trust money paid into the account had been first restored, and the trust fund reinstated by due invest- ment of the money in the joint names of the proper trustees, which never **B** was done. The investment by Oatway, in his own name, of the £2,137 in Oceana shares no more got rid of the claim or charge of the trust upon the money so invested, than would have been the case if he had drawn a cheque for £2,137 and simply placed and retained the amount in a drawer without further disposing of the money in any way. The proceeds of the Oceana shares must be held to belong to the trust funds under the will of which **C** Oatway and Maxwell Skipper were the trustees."

So, contrary to the defendants' contention, it is not a presumption that a trustee's drawings from the mixed fund must necessarily be treated as drawings of the trustee's own money where the beneficiary's claim is against the property bought by such drawings. Further, *Re Oatway* (14) did not raise the question whether a beneficiary was entitled to any profit made out of the purchase of property **D** by a trustee out of a fund consisting of his personal moneys which he mixed with the trust moneys, and so the judgment was not directed to, and did not deal with, that question.

I return now to the judgments in *Re Hallett's Estate* (15). SIR GEORGE JESSEL, M.R., (16) said:

"There is no doubt, therefore, that Mr. Hallett stood in a fiduciary **E** position towards Mrs. Cotterill. Mr. Hallett, before his death, improperly sold the bonds and put the money to his general account at his bankers. It is not disputed that the money was at his bankers mixed with his own money at the time of his death; that is, he had not drawn out that money from his bankers. In that position of matters Mrs. Cotterill claimed to be **F** entitled to receive the proceeds, or the amount of the proceeds, of the bonds out of the money in the hands of Mr. Hallett's bankers at the time of his death, and that claim was allowed by the learned judge of the court below, and I think was properly so allowed."

Later SIR GEORGE JESSEL said (17):

"The modern doctrine of equity as regards property disposed of by **G** persons in a fiduciary position is a very clear and well-established doctrine. You can, if the sale was rightful, take the proceeds of the sale, if you can identify them. If the sale was wrongful, you can still take the proceeds of the sale, in a sense adopting the sale for the purpose of taking the proceeds, if you can identify them. There is no distinction, therefore, between a rightful and a wrongful disposition of the property, so far as regards the **H** right of the beneficial owner to follow the proceeds. But it very often happens that you cannot identify the proceeds. The proceeds may have been invested, together with money belonging to the person in a fiduciary position, in a purchase. He may have bought land with it, for instance, or he may have bought chattels with it. What is the position of the beneficial owner as regards such purchases? I will, first of all, take his position when the **I** purchase is clearly made with what I will call, for shortness, the trust money, although it is not confined, as I will show presently, to express trusts. In that case, according to the now well-established doctrine of equity, the beneficial owner has a right to elect either to take the property purchased, or to hold it as a security for the amount of the trust money laid out in the

(14) [1903] 2 Ch. 356.   (15) [1874-80] All E.R. Rep. 793; (1880), 13 Ch.D. 696.
(16) [1874-80] All E.R. Rep. at pp. 795, 796; (1880), 13 Ch.D. at p. 708.
(17) [1874-80] All E.R. Rep. at p. 796; (1880), 13 Ch.D. at pp. 708, 709.

A   purchase, or, as we generally express it, he is entitled at his election either
to take the property, or to have a charge on the property for the amount
of the trust money.   But where a trustee has mixed the money with his
own, there is the distinction that the cestui que trust or beneficial owner
can no longer elect to take the property . . ."

B   Pausing there, what is apparently meant is that a beneficiary cannot take the
whole property, which is the possibility with which Sir George Jessel had
just before this been dealing.   He went on (18)

"... because it is no longer bought with the trust money simply and
purely, but with a mixed fund.   He is, however, still entitled to a charge on
the property purchased for the amount of the trust money laid out in the
purchase, and that charge is quite independent of the amount laid out by
C   the trustee.   The moment you get a substantial portion of it furnished by
the trustee, using the word ' trustee ' in the sense I have mentioned, as
including all persons in a fiduciary relation, the right to the charge follows."

Here, as I read this judgment, it does not exclude the right of the beneficiary
to claim a proportion of the mixed fund.   There was no need in that case to
D   go further than the charge claimed in the case.   So again that question was
not there considered.

Later on Sir George Jessel said (19):

" When we come to apply that principle to the case of a trustee who has
blended trust moneys with his own, it seems to me perfectly plain that he
cannot be heard to say that he took away the trust money when he had a
E   right to take away his own money ... What difference does it make if,
instead of putting the trust money into a bag, he deposits it with his banker,
then pays in other money of his own, and then draws out some money for
his own purposes?   Could he say that he had actually drawn out anything
but his own money?   His money was there, and he had a right to draw it
out, and why should the natural act of simply drawing out the money be
F   attributed to anything except to his ownership of money which was at his
bankers? "

But again this was said in relation to a claim seeking to make the account liable
and not to a claim to make what was bought with the drawings liable.

In *Sinclair* v. *Brougham* (20) the decision in *Re Hallett's Estate* (21) was
considered.   Lord Parker of Waddington said (22):
G
" The principle on which, and the extent to which, trust money can be
followed in equity is discussed at length in *Re Hallett's Estate* (24) by Sir
George Jessel, M.R.   He gives two instances.   First, he supposes the case
of property being purchased by means of trust money alone.   In such a
case the beneficiary may either take the property itself or claim a lien on it
H   for the amount of the money expended in the purchase.   Secondly, he supposes
the case of the purchase having been made partly with the trust money
and partly with money of the trustee.   [I shall come back to the next
sentence later.]   In such a case the beneficiary can only claim a charge on
the property for the amount of the trust money expended in the purchase.
The trustee is precluded by his own misconduct from asserting any interest
I   in the property until such amount has been refunded.   By the actual
decision in the case, this principle was held applicable when the trust money
had been paid into the trustee's banking account.   I will add two further
illustrations which have some bearing on the present case.   Suppose the

---

(18) [1874-80] All E.R. Rep. at p. 796; (1880), 13 Ch.D. at p. 709.
(19) [1874-80] All E.R. Rep. at pp. 805, 806; (1880) 13 Ch.D. at pp. 727, 728.
(20) [1914-15] All E.R. Rep. 622; [1914] A.C. 398.
(21) [1874-80] All E.R. Rep. 793; (1880), 13 Ch.D. 696.
(22) [1914-15] All E.R. Rep. at p. 643; [1914] A.C. at p. 442.

property is acquired by means of money, part of which belongs to one **A** owner and part to another, the purchaser being in a fiduciary relationship to both. Clearly each owner has an equal equity. Each is entitled to a charge on the property for his own money, and neither can claim priority over the other. It follows that their charges must rank pari passu according to their respective amounts [again, I emphasise this]. Further, I think that as against the fiduciary agent they could by agreement claim to take the **B** property itself, in which case they would become tenants in common in shares proportioned to amounts for which either could claim a charge."

It seems to me that when LORD PARKER says in the sentence, to which I first called particular attention, that " In such a case the beneficiary can only claim a charge on the property for the amount of the trust money expended in the purchase ", he is merely contrasting the charge with the right to take the whole **C** property which is the matter with which he has just been dealing, and LORD PARKER is not, as I see it, addressing his mind to the question whether the beneficiary could claim a proportion of the property corresponding to his own contribution to its purchase. This interpretation of the passage seems to me to be the only interpretation which in principle is consistent with LORD PARKER'S view expressed at the end of the passage which I quoted, and to which I drew **D** particular attention, where the purchase is made by the trustee wholly out of moneys of two different beneficiaries. In that case he says that they are not limited to charges for their respective amounts, but are together entitled to the whole property. Nevertheless if each of two beneficiaries can, in co-operation with the other, take the whole property which has resulted in profit from the trustee's action in buying it with their money, why can they not do so if the **E** trustee himself has also paid some part of the purchase price? Moreover if two beneficiaries can do so why not one? Indeed, it was conceded in argument that the passage should be so interpreted as suggested.

In SNELL'S PRINCIPLES OF EQUITY (26th Edn.) at p. 315 the law is thus stated:

" Where the trustee mixes trust money with his own, the equities are **F** clearly unequal. Accordingly, the beneficiaries are entitled to a first charge on the mixed fund, or on any land, securities or other assets purchased with it. Thus if the trustee purchases shares with part of the mixed fund, leaving enough of it to repay the trust moneys, and then dissipates the balance, the beneficiaries' charge binds the shares; for although under the rule in *Re Hallett's Estate* (23) the trustee is presumed to have bought the shares out **G** of his own money, the charge attached to the entire fund, and could be discharged only by restoring the trust moneys. Where the property purchased has increased in value, the charge will be not merely for the amount of the trust moneys but for a proportionate part of the increased value. Thus if the trustee purchases land with £500 of his own money and £1,000 of trust moneys, and the land doubles in value, he would be profiting from his breach **H** of trust if he were entitled to all except £1,000; the beneficiaries are accordingly entitled to a charge on the land for £2,000."

For the defendants it has been rightly admitted that, if a trustee wrongly uses trust money to pay the whole of the purchase price in respect of the purchase of an asset, a beneficiary can elect either to treat the purchased asset as trust property or to treat the purchased asset as security for the recouping of the trust **I** money. It was further conceded that this right of election by a beneficiary also applies where the asset is purchased by a trustee in part out of his own money and in part out of the trust moneys, so that he may, if he wishes, require the asset to be treated as trust property with regard to that proportion of it which the trust moneys contributed to its purchase.

Does this case fall within that principle? I was referred to *Vyse* v. *Foster* (24) as

(23) [1874-80] All E.R. Rep. 793; (1880), 13 Ch.D. 696.
(24) (1872), 8 Ch. App. 309.

A establishing the proposition that if a trustee is a debtor to his trust estate, even a debtor in respect of his business, it does not mean that the beneficiaries are entitled in proportion to the amount which the debt bears to the capital of the business, or to any extent at all, to a share of the profits of the business. The present case, however, is not a case of mere omission to call in a debt owed by a trustee or, as in *Vyse* v. *Foster* (25) owed by a firm in which a trustee was a

B partner. There was in this case a mixture of funds in the bank account and property purchased out of that account; but to what extent did the property purchased represent trust moneys?

I now come to the report (26).   Paragraph 10 of the report discloses seven property transactions dealt with by Messrs. Mooring, Aldridge and Haydon, solicitors, on behalf of Mrs. Tilley before the testator's death, as well as eleven

C after the testator's death, up to October, 1937, and the report concludes " without doubt Mrs. Tilley was involved in numerous property transactions before as well as after Dec. 4, 1932 ", i.e., the date of the testator's death. In fact, it appears that she had overdraft facilities for over £22,000 in 1939 and that she died in 1959 worth £94,000, for which there appears to be no explanation other than the success of her property transactions.

D From the testator's death the widow appears to have met estate liabilities out of her own pocket and intermingled estate moneys, when received, with her own moneys. In para. 4 it is stated that

" At this point [i.e., shortly after the testator's death] it would appear that she had 7s. only of trust moneys in hand. She then proceeded to pay out of her own private funds Henry Tilley's funeral expenses and estate duty. Then

E in June, 1933, again out of her own private funds she redeemed the mortgage on the semi-detached pair of houses ' Burley ' and ' Ringwood '. At this point the trust owed Mrs. Tilley £513 18s. 11d."

In para. 9 it is said:

" It appears that, subject to any adjustments necessary following paras. 1

F and 2 of this report [with which we need not at present be concerned] Mrs. Tilley had accumulated trust moneys amounting to £2,237 11s. 7d. and over the years had throughly confused these moneys with her own private funds."

I come now in detail to what happened when Mrs. Tilley first had a balance of trust moneys in hand. After the part which I have already read from para. 4 of

G the report it is stated:

" In August, 1933, Mrs. Tilley sold the semi-detached pair of houses ' Burley ' and ' Ringwood ' and for the first time had trust moneys in hand amounting to £179 1s. 1d. Her total credit balance at the bank at this time (Aug. 16, 1933) was £838 15s. 9d. On Aug. 17, 1933 Mrs. Tilley sent Mooring, Aldridge and Haydon a cheque for £841 10s. 4d. to settle the purchase in her

H own name, of 11, Church Street, Christchurch for £1,000. Her bank balance then became overdrawn by £4 5s. 2d., so that it could be said she utilised the trust moneys in hand to complete the purchase of 11, Church Street. However, Mrs. Tilley had been overdrawn on several occasions before (once by over £250) so she obviously had overdraft facilities at least to £250 with the bank. I must also point out that her credit balance was restored again by

I Sept. 14, 1933 and by Nov. 24, 1933 exceeded the trust balance of £179 1s. 1d. and was maintained at or above this balance until April, 1935."

The report then goes on to deal with the next transaction which is described in para. 5 in these terms:

" The next transaction in trust property took place during March and April, 1939, and concerned the semi-detached pair of houses ' Stamford '

(25) (1872), 8 Ch. App. 309.
(26) I.e., the report of the accountant; see p. 305, letter H, ante.

A

and ' Middleton '. First of all Mrs. Tilley redeemed the mortgage of £400,
then she sold the property and received net sale proceeds of £482 10s. On the
completion of this transaction Mrs. Tilley had trust moneys in hand amounting to £261 11s. 1d. [i.e. of course the £179 1s. 1d. mentioned in para. 4
together with £82 10s., being the difference between the £400 which is mentioned in para. 5, as I have just quoted, and the £482 there mentioned. The
report continues] Her bank balance at this time (Apr. 21, 1939) was
£22,405 17s. overdrawn. On Apr. 24, 1939 having just received £82 10s.
' profit ' on the sale of ' Stamford ' and ' Middleton ' [the reference to profit
in that case is the net proceeds of sale after payment of the mortgage] Mrs.
Tilley sent Mooring, Aldridge and Haydon £1,956 14s. 1d. to complete the
purchase of 17/17A, High Street, Christchurch in her own name, so, as she
had such a large overdraft, it could be said that she utilised the further
£82 10s. of trust moneys to complete this purchase. [It appears that although
the £1,956 14s. 1d. was to complete the purchase, the price for the purchase
(without taking into consideration costs) was £2,050. The report in para. 5
continues] On the other hand with such large overdraft facilities, which were
utilised right through the war years, certainly until January, 1945 (when the
overdrawn balance was £23,536 1s. 6d.), it could also be said with some
justification that the £82 10s. was hardly noticed by Mrs. Tilley and would
certainly not have affected her property dealings at that time."

B

C

D

Other estate properties were sold in June, 1951, January and April, 1952 and
realised approximately £490, £750 and £735 respectively, making with the £261
already mentioned a total of approximately £2,237 trust capital received by Mrs.
Tilley. It appears, however, and is not disputed, that from before the first of
these sales, and at all relevant times thereafter, Mrs. Tilley's bank account was
sufficiently in credit from her own personal contributions to it (without regard
to any trust moneys credited to it) to pay for her later property purchases.

E

The *Lupton* v. *White* (27) principle is not applicable to this bank account as the
amount of trust moneys paid into the mixed bank account is distinguishable as
£2,237 and can be readily separated from the widow's personal moneys. In the
circumstances of this case there would be a charge on the properties purchased by
the widow out of the bank account as security for repayment of the £2,237 trust
moneys paid into her bank account in accordance with the principle in *Re
Oatway* (28), but that would be immaterial as the £2,237 is readily available out
of the widow's estate.

F

Can the beneficiary, however, claim the proportion of the proceeds of sale of
11, Church Street which £179 approximately bears to its purchase price of £1,000
and the proportion of the proceeds of sale of 17/17A, High Street for which
£82 10s. bears to the purchase price of approximately £2,050, plus costs? These
trust moneys bore a small proportion to the purchase price of the properties.
The widow had ample overdraft facilities to pay the price without relying on these
trust sums at the time of the High Street purchase, for she had an overdraft of
over £22,000 apparently within her own overdraft facilities, and presumably
properly secured, and this would make any contribution of £82 10s. negligible.
She had throughout mixed her personal finances and those of her husband's
estate, whether paying that estate's debts when it was without ready money or
paying its proceeds of sale into her account. The £179 and the £82 10s. were
clearly not trust moneys deliberately taken by Mrs. Tilley out of the trust fund
for the purpose of investing in property in her name. They merely avoided, to the
extent of their amount, the use of Mrs. Tilley's ample overdraft facilities, and in
the case of the £179 that advantage was lost after two months by her bank account
showing a credit, although it went into debit again seventeen months later.
Moreover no interest in these trust sums was lost to any other beneficiary, as the

G

H

I

A widow was herself a life tenant. All these considerations appear to me to indicate overwhelmingly that the widow was not deliberately using trust moneys to invest in or contribute towards or otherwise buy properties in her own name, and the whole course of dealing with the trust funds and the bank accounts and the properties purchased and their history, which I have mentioned, indicate that what happened was that the widow mixed the trust moneys and her own in the

B bank account but did not rely on the trust moneys for any of the purchases. If, as it was suggested for the defendants, the correct test whether a beneficiary is entitled to adopt a purchase by a trustee to which his trust moneys have contributed and thus claim a due proportion of its profits, is a subjective test, depending on the trustee's intention to use the trust moneys to contribute to the purchase, then in my view there was no such intention and the beneficiary is

C not so entitled. My conclusion about the trustee's intention, however, is based not on any direct evidence but on the circumstantial evidence which I have mentioned. If, of course, a trustee deliberately uses trust money to contribute with his own money to buy property in his own name, then I would see no difficulty in enabling a beneficiary to adopt the purchase and claim a share of any resulting profits; but the subjective test does not appear to me to be exclusive, or

D indeed adequate, if it is the only test. It seems to me that if, having regard to all the circumstances of the case objectively considered, it appears that the trustee has in fact, whatever his intention, laid out trust moneys in or towards a purchase then the beneficiaries are entitled to the property purchased and any profits which it produces to the extent to which it has been paid for out of the trust moneys. Even by this objective test, it appears to me, however, that the trust moneys

E were not in this case so laid out. On a proper appraisal of all the facts of this particular case, the trustee's breach halted at the mixing of the funds in her bank account. Although properties bought out of those funds would, like the bank account itself, at any rate if the moneys in the bank account were inadequate, be charged with repayment of the trust moneys which then would stand in the same position as the bank account, yet the trust moneys were not invested in properties

F at all but merely went in reduction of the trustee's overdraft which was in reality the source of the purchase moneys.

The plaintiff's claim therefore fails and he is entitled to no more than repayment of half the sum of £2,237, interest not being in issue. £2,237 is readily available which makes the existence of any charge for its security immaterial.

Order accordingly.

G
Solicitors: *Denton, Hall & Burgin* (for the plaintiff); *Gibson & Weldon*, agents for *Tatterall & Sturt*, Bournemouth (for the defendants).

[*Reported by* Jacqueline Metcalfe, *Barrister-at-Law.*]

NOTE.

Re LLOYD'S SETTLEMENT. LLOYD *v.* LEEPER AND OTHERS.

[CHANCERY DIVISION (Plowman, J.), December 7, 1966.]

Trust and Trustee—Variation of trusts by the court—Settlor's application—
Extension of trust for accumulation in view of possibility of settlor's death   B
terminating trust for accumulation—Deletion of power to provide fund which
might be available for meeting liability of settlor for surtax—Variation of
Trusts Act, 1958 (6 & 7 Eliz. 2 c. 53), *s.* 1.

[As to the jurisdiction of the court to vary trusts under the Act of 1958, see
38 HALSBURY'S LAWS (3rd Edn.) 1029, 1030, para. 1772; and for cases on the
subject, see 47 DIGEST (Repl.) 332-338, *2993-3018.*   C

For the Variation of Trusts Act, 1958, s. 1, see 38 HALSBURY'S STATUTES
(2nd Edn.) 1130.

For the Finance Act, 1894, s. 2 (1) (*c*), (*d*), see 9 HALSBURY'S STATUTES (2nd Edn.)
350 (cf. 29 ibid. 178, for the para. (*c*) substituted by the Finance Act, 1950, s. 46).

For s. 405 and s. 406 of the Income Tax Act, 1954, see 31 HALSBURY'S STATUTES
(2nd Edn.) 382-384.]   D

Adjourned summons.

This was an application by originating summons under s. 1 of the Variation of
Trusts Act, 1958, for approval of a proposed variation of trusts and powers contained in a settlement dated Mar. 21, 1958, and made between the settlor, Anthony
Fetherston Lloyd, of the one part and the trustees (who were the settlor and his   E
sister Dorothea Evelyn Letitia Kerr) of the other part as confirmed by a confirmatory settlement, dated Apr. 16, 1958, made between the same parties in the
same order. The variation sought was substantially the same as that embodied in
the order subsequently made (for which see p. 316, letters G and H, post). By the
settlement the settlor assigned to the trustees one equal third part of (a) a share
of the residuary estate of his father and (b) a share in the funds comprised in a   F
settlement dated Mar. 19, 1924, to both of which he would be entitled if his
sister, Barbara Palmer, should die without issue attaining a vested interest. The
relevant trusts and powers declared by the settlement were as follows:

"3. (A) On the birth hereafter and before the date of distribution of any
child of the settlor a share of the trust fund shall for the purposes hereinafter
appearing be appropriated to such afterborn child of the settlor on the footing   G
(and every prior appropriation of a share of the trust fund shall be rectified
on the footing) that such afterborn child was born before the date of this
settlement and was hereinafter named as one of the settlor's children in
addition to his or her brothers and sisters (if any) previously but hereafter
born and that all sums then already taken out of the capital for the benefit
of any of the settlor's children have to be brought into hotchpot by the share   H
of capital appropriated to such child and have to be accounted for accordingly.

" (B) All income as it accrues due before the date of distribution shall
belong and be distributed and dealt with under the provisions hereinafter contained on the footing that no child of the settlor will thereafter be born save
that all accumulations of any income to which a child of the settlor would have
been entitled if he or she attained the age of twenty-one years shall follow   I
and devolve with the capital of the settled share appropriated to such child.

" (C) Save as hereinbefore otherwise expressly provided in this clause no
person being or claiming under or in succession to a child hereafter born to
the settlor shall have any interest in or claim in respect of any property
taken out of settlement before his or her birth or any income which accrued
before his or her birth.

" (D) All income accruing whilst the date of distribution has not arrived
and no child of the settlor is living shall be accumulated by investing the

A   same and the resulting income thereof in any investments in which capital
     money is hereby or by statute authorised to be invested.
         " (E) Subject as aforesaid the trust fund and the income thereof as from the
     date of this deed shall be held in trust for such child or children of the settlor
     as shall be born before the date of distribution and attain the age of twenty-
     one years and if more than one in equal shares absolutely.

B   " (F) Provided that if there shall be no child of the settlor who shall attain
     a vested interest under the trusts hereinbefore contained the trust fund and
     the income thereof subject to the trust for accumulation aforesaid shall be
     held in trust as to one-half thereof for the settlor's neice Romilly Greer Leeper
     if she shall attain the age of thirty years and as to the other half for such of his
     nieces Virginia Francis D'este [Raborn] Catherine Henrietta Lloyd and
C   Gwyneth Susan Lloyd and nephew Jonathan David Henry Lloyd as attain
     the age of thirty years if more than one in equal shares.
         " (G) Provided that if the trusts aforesaid or either of them shall fail
     the trust fund and the income thereof subject to the trust for accumulation
     aforesaid shall be held in trust for such of the settlor's nephews and nieces
     children of his brother and of [his sister, Dorothea] as shall be born before the
D   date of distribution and attain the age of twenty-one years if more than one
     in equal shares absolutely."
         " 4. . . . (f) Power to set aside and provide out of the income of the trust
     fund a fund to answer any liability which in the opinion of the trustees
     ought to be borne by income and in particular may provide in this way for
     any liability for income tax or surtax of the settlor or any other person
E   interested in the trust fund or any part thereof.
         " (g) If under any enactment now or hereafter in force any income to which
     any person is entitled under the trusts hereof is deemed for the purposes of
     taxation to be the income of any other person power to apply the said income
     and any subsequent income accruing hereunder in the same right in payment
     of such other person's tax liability in so far as such liability is attributable
F   to the part of the said income so deemed to be his or her income for taxation
     purposes."

     The expression " date of distribution " was defined as meaning the day on which
     should expire the period of twenty-one years from the execution of the settlement
     of Mar. 21, 1958; and the expression " settlor's children " was defined as meaning
     and including all the children of the settlor who should thereafter actually be
G   born before the date of distribution.
         The settlor was born on Oct. 4, 1914. His sister, Barbara, was born on Apr. 18,
     1918. She married Noel Thomas Francis Palmer on Oct. 6, 1951. He died on
     Oct. 27, 1963, and they had no children. She was a cripple as a result of infantile
     paralysis. At the date of the summons the settlor had no children. He had
     married on Oct. 10, 1951, and his wife was fifty-seven years of age at the commence-
H   ment of proceedings. The expectation of life according to the current table of
     the Institute of Actuaries for a male of the settlor's age was 22.3 years. If the
     settlor were to survive for this period he would die in 1988.
         Of the beneficiaries who were to take under cl. 3 (F) and (G) if no child born
     to the settlor before the date of distribution attained the age of twenty-one,
     Romilly who was the only child of the testator's sister Dorothea and was the
I   first defendant, was born on Feb. 15, 1943. The settlor's nieces Virginia, Catherine
     and Gwyneth, were born on Mar. 9, 1942, Apr. 16, 1946 and Oct. 7, 1947. The
     settlor's nephew Jonathan was born on Apr. 6, 1949. In addition there was a
     niece Harriette Lucy, who was born on Mar. 28, 1959. These nieces and nephew
     were the children of the settlor's brother Henry.
         It was apprehended that if the trust for accumulation (cl. 3 (D)) was brought
     to an end by the settlor's death*, a charge to estate duty would arise by virtue

     ———————————
     * Section 164 of the Law of Property Act, 1925, as originally enacted did not specify
     the term of twenty-one years from the date of the settlement, which was the period
     provided by the settlement, as a permissible period of accumulation.

of s. 2 (1) (*d*) of the Finance Act, 1894, in respect of the interest of the adult A
beneficiaries, and that the statutory provisions for aggregation would apply
accordingly. The settlor was advised that the potential charge to estate duty under
s. 2 (1) (*d*) would be avoided if the trust for accumulation were to be varied by providing that pursuant to s. 13 of the Perpetuities and Accumulations Act 1964 the
income of the trust fund should be accumulated until the date of distribution.

Further, by a letter dated Mar. 10, 1959, from the clerk to the Special Com- B
missioners the settlor had been informed of their opinion that the settlement came
within the charge to tax imposed by s. 405 of the Income Tax Act, 1952, and by
s. 22 of the Finance Act, 1958, by reason of cl. 4 (f). The result, if this view were
to prevail, would be that the power would constitute the reservation of a benefit
for the purposes of s. 2 (1) (*c*) of the Finance Act, 1894, and although the settlor
had survived the creation of the settlement by more than five years, the trust fund C
would nevertheless be included among property passing on his death and would
be aggregated with other property so passing for the purpose of determining the
rate of estate duty.

The settlor having been advised that these possible charges to tax would be
avoided if the settlement were to be varied by deleting the powers conferred by
cl. 4 (f) and (g), made this application to the court for variation of the settlement D
in agreed terms. The first and second defendants, being adults, consented to the
proposed variation.

The cases noted below* were cited during the argument.

John Silberrad for the plaintiff, the settlor.
Hilda Wilson for the infant beneficiaries.
Peter Rees for the co-trustee, and unborn beneficiaries.   E
The adult beneficiaries, the first and second defendants, were not represented.

PLOWMAN, J., approved a variation substantially as proposed, and made
the order summarised below.

[The order of the court provided, so far as is material to be stated here, that
the trust powers and provisions which at the date of the application were com- F
prised in and constituted by the settlement of Mar. 21, 1958, as confirmed, should
be varied as follows—

(i) For the trust contained in cl. 3 (D) the following provision be substituted
" all income accruing whilst the date of distribution has not arrived and no child
of the settlor is living shall be accumulated until the date of distribution referred
to in the settlement by investing the same and the resulting income thereof in G
any investments in which capital money is hereby or by statute authorised to be
invested ".

(2) That the powers conferred upon the trustees of the settlement be modified
so that those contained in sub-cl. (f) and (g) of cl. 4 shall cease to be exercisable in
favour of the settlor or any woman for the time being his wife Provided always
that this modification shall not preclude the settlor from exercising the rights H
conferred by s. 406 of the Income Tax Act 1952 or any re-enactment or modification thereof."]

Solicitors: *Pattinson & Brewer* (for the plaintiff, the settlor); *Syrett & Sons*
(for the third to seventh defendants, the infant beneficiaries, the co-trustee and
unborn beneficiaries).

[*Reported by* JACQUELINE METCALFE, *Barrister-at-Law.*]   I

---

* *Adamson* v. *A.-G.*, [1932] All E.R. Rep. 159; [1933] A.C. 257; *Re Watts' Will
Trusts*, [1936] 2 All E.R. 1555; *Re Ransome*, [1957] 1 All E.R. 690; [1957] Ch. 348;
Re Turner's Will Trusts, [1959] 2 All E.R. 689; [1960] Ch. 122; *Re Cohen's Will Trusts*,
[1959] 3 All E.R. 523; *Re Clitheroe's Settlement Trusts*, [1959] 3 All E.R. 789; *Re Tinker's
Settlement*, [1960] 3 All E.R. 85; *Re Wills' Trust Deeds*, [1963] 1 All E.R. 390; [1964]
Ch. 219.

A

ALMOND (Valuation Officer) v. BIRMINGHAM ROYAL INSTITUTION FOR THE BLIND AND ANOTHER.

[HOUSE OF LORDS (Lord Reid, Lord Hodson, Lord Guest, Lord Pearce and Lord Upjohn), April 4, 5, 6, 26, 1967.]

B *Rates—Exemption—Structure—Blind persons' home—Principal building or only annexe or adjunct thereof—Institution with main two-storey building—Rating and Valuation (Miscellaneous Provisions) Act, 1955 (4 & 5 Eliz. 2 c. 9), s. 9 (1).*

The ratepayers, the Birmingham Royal Institution for the Blind, a voluntary organisation within the meaning of s. 30 of the National Assistance

C Act, 1948, owned and occupied a hereditament in Birmingham consisting of (i) a large, substantial permanent two-storey building; (ii) two separate permanent single-storey buildings; (iii) various smaller buildings comprising three lock-up garages, a gardener's shed and a store, all situate in extensive grounds. All the buildings were used by the ratepayers for welfare purposes under s. 29 of the Act of 1948. The valuation officer

D contended that the buildings or at least the main buildings were not structures within the meaning of s. 9 (1)* of the Rating and Valuation (Miscellaneous Provisions) Act, 1955.

Held: a restricted meaning, limiting " structure " to temporary, impermanent buildings, would not be attributed to the word " structure " in para. (c) of s. 9 (1) of the Rating and Valuation (Miscellaneous Provisions) Act,

E 1955; accordingly the large permanent two-storey building was a " structure " within that paragraph, as also were the smaller buildings, and no account was to be taken of them in ascertaining the gross value of the hereditament for rating purposes (see p. 319, letter H, p. 320, letters C and H, and p. 323, letters B and G, post).

Dicta of LORD EVERSHED, M.R., PEARCE and HARMAN, L.JJ., in *Jewish*

F *Blind Society Trustees* v. *Henning (Valuation Officer)* ([1961] 1 All E.R. at pp. 49, 52 and 54) considered.

Walker (Valuation Officer) v. *Wood* ([1962] 3 All E.R. 188) considered; dictum of BYLES, J., in *Stevens* v. *Gourley* ((1859), 7 C.B.N.S. at p. 112) not applied.

Dictum of LORD PATRICK in *Thistle Foundation* v. *Assessor for Edinburgh*

G (1963 S.C. at p. 78) approved.

Decision of the COURT OF APPEAL ([1966] 1 All E.R. 602) affirmed.

[As to structures not to be taken into account for rating purposes, see 32 HALSBURY'S LAWS (3rd Edn.) 53, 54, para. 71; and for a case on the subject, see DIGEST (Cont. Vol. A) 1292, 1293, *844b*. For the meaning of " structure " in a building Contract, see 3 HALSBURY'S LAWS (3rd Edn.) 433, para. 816, text and

H note (e).

For the Rating and Valuation (Miscellaneous Provisions) Act, 1955, s. 9 (1), see 35 HALSBURY'S STATUTES (2nd Edn.) 396.]

Cases referred to:

Jewish Blind Society Trustees v. *Henning (Valuation Officer)*, (1959), 5 R.R.C

I 103; *rvsd.* C.A., [1961] 1 All E.R. 47; [1961] 1 W.L.R. 24; 125 J.P. 107; Digest (Cont. Vol. A) 1292, *844b*.

Stevens v. *Gourley*, (1859), 7 C.B.N.S. 99; 29 L.J.C.P. 1; 1 L.T. 33; 141 E.R. 752; 38 Digest (Repl.) 247, *578*.

Thistle Foundation v. *Assessor for Edinburgh*, 1963 S.C. 73; Digest (Cont. Vol. A) 1293, *772a*.

Walker (Valuation Officer) v. *Wood*, [1962] 3 All E.R. 188; [1962] 1 W.L.R. 1060; 126 J.P. 472; Digest (Cont. Vol. A) 1295, *907a*.

* Section 9 (1) is set out at p. 318, letters F to H, post,

Appeal.   A

This was an appeal by the valuation officer from an order of the Court of
Appeal (SELLERS, DAVIES and RUSSELL, L.JJ.), dated Dec. 20, 1965 and reported
[1966] 1 All E.R. 602, allowing an appeal by the ratepayers, the first respondents,
and dismissing a cross appeal by the valuation officer from a decision of the
Lands Tribunal (ERSKINE SIMES, Esq., Q.C.), dated Jan. 8, 1965. The Lands
Tribunal allowed in part an appeal by the valuation officer from a decision of   B
the Birmingham local valuation court dated Nov. 20, 1965. The second respondents were the Lord Mayor, aldermen and citizens of the City of Birmingham.
The facts are set out in the opinion of LORD REID.

A. J. Irvine, Q.C., and *W. J. Glover* for the valuation officer.
D. G. Widdicombe, Q.C., and *J. C. Taylor* for the ratepayers.
                                                                                 C
Their lordships took time for consideration.

Apr. 26.   The following opinions were delivered.

LORD REID: My Lords, the ratepayers own and occupy property in
Birmingham consisting of a large, substantial two-storey building, two single-
storey buildings and various smaller buildings situated in extensive grounds.   D
The question in this case is whether or to what extent s. 9 (1) of the Rating and
Valuation (Miscellaneous Provisions) Act, 1955, applies to these buildings. The
local valuation court held that it applied to all of them and therefore reduced
the gross annual value of the hereditament from £1,450 to £50. The Lands
Tribunal held that the section applied to smaller buildings but not to the main
building and held the gross value to be £1,100. The Court of Appeal (1) restored E
the decision of the local court. The valuation officer now appeals and contends
that the gross value should be £1,450 or alternatively he supports the decision
of the Lands Tribunal. Section 9 (1) provides:

" (1) For the purpose of ascertaining the gross value of a hereditament
for rating purposes, no account shall be taken—(*a*) of any structure belonging
to the Minister of Health and supplied by that Minister, or (before Aug. 31,   F
1953) by the Minister of Pensions, for the accommodation of an invalid chair,
or of any other vehicles (whether mechanically propelled or not) constructed
or adapted for use by invalids or disabled persons; or (*b*) of any structure
belonging to a local health authority, or to a voluntary organisation formed
for any of the purposes mentioned in s. 28 (1) of the National Health Service
Act, 1946 (which relates to the prevention of illness, and to the care and   G
after-care of persons suffering from illness or mental defectiveness), and
supplied for the use of any person in pursuance of arrangements made under
that subsection; or (*c*) of any structure belonging to a local authority,
within the meaning of s. 29 of the National Assistance Act, 1948 (which
relates to welfare arrangements for blind, deaf, dumb and other handicapped
persons), or to such a voluntary organisation as is mentioned in s. 30 of that   H
Act, and supplied for the use of any person in pursuance of arrangements
made under the said s. 30; or (*d*) of any structure which is of a kind similar
to structures such as are referred to in para. (*a*), para. (*b*) or para. (*c*) of this
subsection, but does not fall within that paragraph by reason that it is
owned or has been supplied otherwise than as mentioned in that paragraph."

It is admitted that all these buildings are used by the ratepayers under an   I
arrangement with the local authority for the accommodation and training of
blind persons, and the only reason now put forward by the valuation officer for
holding that s. 9 (1) (*c*) does not apply is that these buildings—or at least the
main building—are not structures within the meaning of this subsection. In
order to understand the argument it is necessary to look at all the paragraphs
of the subsection.

_____

(1) [1966] 1 All E.R. 602; [1966] 2 Q.B. 395.

A   It is not difficult to understand para. (*a*). It appears that it was the practice of the Ministry to supply prefabricated garages to disabled persons who had to use invalid chairs or other vehicles. These remained the property of the Minister and were dismantled and removed when they were no longer required. Before this provision was enacted the presence of such a garage on his premises resulted in the disabled person having to pay more rates and one can readily imagine

B the grievance and protests that must have led to the enactment of this relief. It is true that the scope of this paragraph is limited to garages which are readily removable, but that is not because the word " structure " has here a limited meaning: it is because the paragraph only applies to structures which remain the property of the Minister, and a solidly built permanent structure would become pars soli and would not remain his property. The valuation officer

C argues that it is at least unusual for the same word to have different meanings in different parts of the same section. So if " structure " had a narrow meaning in para. (*a*) one would expect it to have the same narrow meaning in para. (*b*) and para. (*c*); if, however, the narrow scope of para. (*a*) is not due to a narrow meaning of " structure " but to other reasons, this argument has no force.

    Then it was said that the mere fact that the provisions of para. (*a*) precede those

D of para. (*b*) and para. (*c*) is significant; that it would be strange to progress from a paragraph of very narrow scope to others of much wider scope. There are many reasons, however, why the draftsman may have adopted this order. It is not uncommon to find that, apart from their relative importance, it has been thought proper for what one may call hierarchical reasons to put a provision affecting a Minister before one affecting a mere local authority or private associa-

E tion. Moreover the grievance which gave rise to para. (*a*) may have been much more clamant than any which gave rise to para. (*b*) and para. (*c*). Indeed it is not very easy to see why para. (*b*) and para. (*c*) are there at all. Insofar as they relieve local authorities of rates which would have been payable to themselves they achieve mere bookkeeping entries. As regards charitable organisations, s. 8 of this Act began a new scheme of general relief, and it is not obvious why

F these particular activities of such organisations should attract additional relief. At least one can assume, however, that these paragraphs would not have been enacted unless they were intended to have some substantial effect: and I find it difficult to suppose that they would ever have been enacted if they were only to have the minimal effect for which the valuation officer contends.

    Nevertheless these general considerations are of no great weight as against

G conclusions drawn from the terms of the section. I do not think that para. (*b*) raises any separate point, so I turn to an examination of para. (*c*). Parliament has imposed a duty on local authorities to make arrangements for the welfare of the blind and has permitted them to bring voluntary organisations in to these arrangements; and it has specified hostels and workshops among the matters to be covered. So one method which must have been contemplated is that the

H voluntary organisation should provide the building and staff required and the local authority should contribute to the cost. That is what has been done in the present case. In such a case few buildings are likely to be of a temporary, prefabricated or removable kind, but the contention of the valuation officer is that the subsection gives relief only for such buildings. No reason is suggested why structures of this limited kind should have been thought more worthy of

I relief than substantial buildings. The valuation officer's contention is mainly founded on the use of the two words " structure " and " supplied ".

    It is true that these are unusual words to find in such a context. One might have expected to find " building or structure "; but the valuation officer expressly refused to argue that " structure " here means a structure which is not a building. In the ordinary course " structure " is, I think, a word of very wide meaning. I cannot think of any building which could not properly be called a structure, but there are many structures which one would not normally call buildings. The valuation officer argues that here " structure " includes some

buildings but not others. He admits that the dividing line cannot be defined **A**
and that there is no single test which can be applied: one asks with regard to
each building whether it is permanent or temporary or prefabricated and whether
it is an annexe or ancillary to some larger building. So it really becomes a question
of degree. The valuation officer does not argue that in every case the building
must be both temporary or prefabricated and ancillary to another larger building:
according to the argument these are merely guides to the decision. If it was **B**
really intended that some buildings should come within the class of structures
but not others, I cannot believe that even the least competent draftsman would
have left the distinction undefined and depending on whatever inference could
be drawn from the use of the words " structure " and " supplied " and the
general framework of the subsection. We might be forced to the conclusion
that some such distinction must be made, but not because there is any indication **C**
that it was intended. One is sometimes forced to a decision of that kind because
the alternative is an absurd result or one which goes against the general intendment of the Act of 1955; but here, on the contrary, all the indications which I
have mentioned seem to me to point to an intention that " structure " should
include all kinds of buildings.

Then the word " supplied " is said to create a difficulty; but dicta to that **D**
effect appear to me to be based on a misconception of the context in which the
word is here used. The point was put in a nutshell by HARMAN, L.J., in *Jewish
Blind Society Trustees* v. *Henning* (*Valuation Officer*) (2) when he said:

> "... it seems to me monstrous to suggest that we should substitute the
> words ' this is the structure that Jack supplied ' for the words ' this is the
> house that Jack built '." **E**

I quite agree. Suppose, however, that Jack, having built the house and added
a prefabricated annexe, finds it too big for him, and, being charitably minded,
remains the occupier but makes it available by arrangement with the local
authority for the use of the blind, would anyone but an extreme purist object
to saying that he supplied the house for the use of the blind? Further, could
anyone say—true he supplied the annexe for the use of the blind but he did not **F**
supply the house? " Supplied " may not be the ideal word in this connexion—
" provided " might be better—but it is equally bad or good as regards the house
and the annexe.

I do not think it necessary to consider para. (*d*). It raises different and difficult
problems, but does not seem to me to throw any light on the present case. Nor
do I think it necessary to deal with the *Jewish Blind Society* case (3) or *Walker* **G**
(*Valuation Officer*) v. *Wood* (4) or *Thistle Foundation* v. *Assessor for Edinburgh* (5).
The decisions do not affect the present case and I have had in mind the dicta
which are relevant here. I am not to be taken as approving or disapproving of
the decisions, and anything I might say about them could only be obiter.

I would dismiss this appeal. **H**

LORD HODSON: My Lords, the question raised by this appeal is whether,
for the purposes of rating, the erections or buildings included in the hereditament,
which is described as a Technical Trainees Hostel, Offices and premises,
49, Court Oak Road, Harborne, Birmingham, are " structures " within the
meaning of the Rating and Valuation (Miscellaneous Provisions) Act, 1955, s. 9 (1).
The hereditament includes a large two-storey building of an area on the ground **I**
of some 13,000 square feet, erected in 1904, two separate single-storey buildings
of 2,699 square feet and 2,007 square feet respectively (one having a covered
access to the main building) erected in 1958, three lock-up garages totalling
1,005 square feet, a gardener's shed of 379 square feet, a store of 240 square feet
and an area of open space of about five acres. The two-storey building and the
two single-storey buildings are substantial and permanent buildings.

---

(2) [1961] 1 All E.R. 47 at p. 54.   (3) [1961] 1 All E.R. 47.
(4) [1962] 3 All E.R. 188.   (5) 1963 S.C. 73.

A   The hereditament is owned by the ratepayers, the Birmingham Royal Institution for the Blind, which used the large building as a hostel for pupils being trained in workshops, for which the two single-storey buildings were used. The large building was also used for other purposes ancillary to the work and management of the institution. The blind pupils who used the workshops were sent to the hostel by local authorities and paid for by them. The workshops were also

B   used as a centre by blind persons.

[His Lordship set out the terms of s. 9 (1) of the Act of 1955, which are printed at p. 318, letters F to H, ante, and continued:] The hereditament belongs to the ratepayers, a voluntary organisation as is mentioned in s. 30 of the National Assistance Act, 1948. Section 29 of that Act relates to welfare arrangements for blind, deaf, dumb and other handicapped persons and the hostel thereon is

C   supplied by the voluntary association for the use of blind people.

The only question is whether the erections on the land are structures within the meaning of the section, for the other requirements of the relevant subsection, s. 9 (1) (c), are admittedly complied with. The Birmingham local valuation court held that the erections should not be taken into account and reduced the gross value of the hereditament from £1,450, as entered in the valuation list,

D   to £50, the value of the land uncovered by buildings or other erections. On appeal by the valuation officer the Lands Tribunal held that with certain exceptions the erections on the land were not " structures " within the meaning of s. 9 (1) of the Act. One outbuilding not hitherto mentioned was overlooked by the Lands Tribunal but should, as is now admitted, have been excluded. Cases were stated at the request of both sides for the decision of the Court of Appeal (6)

E   which restored the decision of the local valuation court and was wholly in favour of the ratepayers.

The submission of the valuation officer is that the decision is wrong because it is based on a wrong meaning given to the word " structure " in the section. The structures of which no account is to be taken are said to be of a more modest character than a massive building like the two-storey mansion of which the hostel

F   mainly consists. To this the word " structure " is not on the face of it appropriate. The question is not an easy one, as is shown by opinions already expressed, albeit obiter, in the decisions of the courts in other cases. One would expect to find the expression " buildings or structures " to be used if buildings of every kind were intended. It is not contended that these words are mutually exclusive. " Structure " is a word which is wide enough to cover every kind of building as

G   well as hoardings and erections of various kinds which could not properly be described as buildings. Nevertheless it has sometimes been used judicially as primarily indicating something less than a permanent building, but judges have hesitated to give a definition of either word. Perhaps the nearest attempt at a definition, which lends support to the contention of the valuation officer, is to be found in the judgment of Byles, J., in *Stevens* v. *Gourley* (7). He said (8):

H   " Without, therefore, presuming to do what others have failed to do, I may venture to suggest that by ' a building ' is usually understood a structure of considerable size, and intended to be permanent, or at least to last for a considerable time."

Per contra the valuation officer argued that the word " structure " standing

I   alone without " building " connotes something not intended to be permanent or to endure for a considerable time. This conception of impermanence was, in my opinion, rightly rejected by the Court of Appeal in the case of *Walker* (*Valuation Officer*) v. *Wood* (9).

The opening words of s. 9 (1) of the Act of 1955, " no account shall be taken ", are not equivalent to complete exemption, but the widest construction of " structure " will in most cases, as in this one, reduce the rateable value to

---

(6) [1966] 1 All E.R. 602; [1966] 2 Q.B. 395.   (7) (1859), 7 C.B.N.S. 99.
(8) (1859), 7 C.B.N.S. at p. 112.   (9) [1962] 3 All E.R. 188.

negligible proportions, and this matter has impressed those who have given a **A**
narrow meaning to the word " structure ".

The dicta of LORD EVERSHED, M.R. (10), and of PEARCE (11) and HARMAN,
L.JJ. (12), in *Jewish Blind Society Trustees* v. *Henning (Valuation Officer)* (13)
emphasize the apparent absurdity which appears from the build-up of the section.
This begins in para. (*a*) with the supply by the Minister of a shed for an invalid
carriage, a relatively trivial matter, and it is to be expected that the following **B**
subsections would relate to structures which were ancillary to other buildings
and would not include the large house such as the hostel here.   It could be said
that para. (*a*) casts its shadow on the later paragraphs.   The order in which the
paragraphs appear is not, however, a safe guide.

It was suggested by analogy from another Act that the order was selected by
beginning with the Minister and descending through the local authority and **C**
voluntary organisations to the sweeping-up para. (*d*).   Maybe para. (*a*) was
first selected and the others were later added.   This may explain the artificial
use of the word " supplied ", which is used all through instead of " provided ",
a more natural word to use in the paragraphs which follow para. (*a*), although
" supplied " is appropriate to (*a*) itself.   I would agree with the learned chairman
of the Lands Tribunal who, in the *Jewish Blind Society* case (14), regarded **D**
" supplied " as synonymous with " provided ".   In this sense it is easier to
understand the meaning of all the paragraphs contained in the subsection and
meets the difficulty, relied on by the valuation officer, of treating the mansion
house on the hereditament as " supplied " by the ratepayers for the use of blind
persons.

I do not get assistance in ascertaining the meaning of the word " structure " **E**
in the subsection from the other sections of the Act of 1955.   It is, as its title
indicates, a miscellaneous provisions Act, and it is not easy to discern a pattern
from which its scope and object can be ascertained.   Section 7 gives exemption
from rates to places of religious worship.   Section 8 gave (15) a limited relief
to charities, which have a curious rating history.   At first they were treated as
exempt, not being in beneficial occupation of the hereditaments where they were **F**
situated.   Later, although rated, they were treated benevolently by local
authorities, and only of recent years has the whole rigour of the rating law been
enforced against them by the valuation officers acting on the instructions of the
Commissioners of Inland Revenue.   Section 9, as has already been noticed,
does not exempt hereditaments but says that certain matters should not be
taken into account.   Nowhere in the Act of 1955 nor in the two earlier Acts **G**
referred to in s. 9 is there to be discerned any reason for giving the word
" structure " a restricted meaning.

Like the Court of Appeal (16) in this case I cannot see where, if " structure "
has a restricted meaning, the dividing line is to be drawn, and, particularly in a
taxing or relieving statute, it is of great practical importance that a line should
be discernible.   I have referred to the idea of impermanence.   It is difficult to **H**
say what is permanent and what is temporary.   Some degree of permanence is
necessary before there can be rateability.   I would likewise reject the concept
of prefabrication which might once have indicated impermanence but scarcely
does so today when examples of the extension of prefabrication for permanent
erections continually multiply.   The sole surviving qualifying concept seems to
be that a " structure " must be an adjunct of, or ancillary to, a main building in **I**
some way.   This finds support from para. (*a*), which no doubt suggests a structure
of that kind, for the accommodation for an invalid chair provided by the Minister
would indicate something that could be taken away.

(10) [1961] 1 All E.R. at p. 48 et seq.   (11) [1961] 1 All E.R. at p. 53, 54.
(12) [1961] 1 All E.R. at p. 54.   (13) [1961] 1 All E.R. 47.
(14) [1959] 5 R.R.C. 103.
(15) Section 8 was repealed by the Rating and Valuation Act, 1961; see now s. 11
and s. 12 of that Act, 41 HALSBURY'S STATUTES (2nd Edn.) 949, 954.
(16) [1966] 1 All E.R. 602; [1966] 2 Q.B. 395.

A   The only dividing line suggested which appears logical would be to say that those erections which do not become pars soli and so can be removed are structures. Aliter if they become fixed to the freehold. I do not understand that this argument was persisted in before your lordships but in any event, although it has the merit of near-certainty, I see no justification for reading into the paragraph a definition limiting the meaning of " structure " in that way.

B   Having heard full argument on behalf of the valuation officer I am not persuaded that a restricted meaning should be given to the word " structure" notwithstanding the dicta contained in previous decisions. The leading case in the Court of Appeal (the *Jewish Blind Society Trustees* case (17)), which has been followed since, was decided on other grounds, although no doubt argument must have been addressed to it on the point now in issue.

C   I find myself in respectful agreement with LORD PATRICK who in the Scottish case (decided under parallel legislation) of *Thistle Foundation* v. *Assessor for Edinburgh* (18) said (19) that he took the view that the draftsman of the section was merely enumerating various structures which should be exempted from rating rather than illustrating what he meant by " structure ". He added (19):

D   " In the first place, I can see no intelligible reason for conferring the benefit of derating on a structure which a local authority has erected under para. (*b*) for the after-care of ill people if it is attached to a larger building devoted to another purpose, and withholding that benefit where the whole building is devoted to the charitable purposes. In the second place, the structures which may be erected under para. (*c*) expressly include workshops where the disabled may be engaged in suitable work, and hostels where

E   those so engaged may live. There is nothing in the conception of a workshop or a hostel which suggests to me that it will be an adjunct or annexe of a larger heritage. Indeed I can find no genus in the structures with which para. (*a*), para. (*b*) and para. (*c*) deal."

I should add that the actual decision in the case just cited (18), like that in the *Jewish Blind Society Trustees* case (17), turned on another point.

F   I would dismiss the appeal.

LORD GUEST: My Lords, I have had the opportunity of reading the speech of my noble and learned friend, LORD REID. I agree with him and have nothing to add.

I would dismiss the appeal.

G   **LORD PEARCE:** My Lords, I agree with the opinions of my noble and learned friends, LORD REID and LORD HODSON, and would dismiss the appeal.

LORD UPJOHN: My Lords, I have had an opportunity of reading the speech prepared by my noble and lerned friend, LORD HODSON, in this appeal. I agree with it entirely, and for the reasons he gives I would dismiss this appeal.

H   *Appeal dismissed.*

Solicitors: *Solicitor of Inland Revenue* (for the valuation officer); *Swepstone, Walsh & Son*, agents for *Scadding, Jessop & Co.*, Birmingham (for the ratepayers).

[*Reported by* KATHLEEN J. H. O'BRIEN, *Barrister-at-Law.*]

I

---

(17) [1961] 1 All E.R. 47.   (18) 1963 S.C. 73.
                     (19) 1963 S.C. at p. 78.

HARMAN PICTURES, N.V. *v.* OSBORNE AND OTHERS.

[CHANCERY DIVISION (Goff, J.), February 22, 23, 24, 27, 28, March 20, 1967.]

*Copyright—Infringement—Injunction—Interlocutory relief—Preservation of
status quo—Screenplay alleged to infringe plaintiffs' film copyright in book—
Historical subject—Common sources of material—Plaintiffs' book supplied
with others to author of screenplay—Similarities of incidents and situations
—Differences in detail—Absence of explanation by author of screenplay of
manner and extent of use of plaintiffs' book and of how he worked and for
how long—Whether interlocutory injunction should be granted and whether
limited in scope.*

*Copyright—Infringement—Injunction—Interlocutory relief—Security for fulfil-
ment of cross-undertaking—Foreign company as plaintiffs.*

The plaintiffs, a foreign company, were owners of the film copyright in a
book called " The Reason Why ", which was about the Charge of the Light
Brigade and the story behind it. During the winter of 1961-62 there were
discussions between the defendant companies and the first defendant
concerning the possibility of making an historical film. The first defendant
was provided with Kinglake's " Invasion of the Crimea ", Hibbert's
" Destruction of Lord Raglan ", and " The Reason Why ". At the end of
1962 or early in 1963 the defendant companies commissioned the first
defendant to write a screenplay on " The Charge ", and in or about January,
1964, they commissioned two people to do research. In 1963 there were
negotiations between the plaintiffs and the defendant companies for the
acquisition of the plaintiffs' rights in " The Reason Why " or for a joint film
production. These negotiations were abortive. The first defendant having
finished his screenplay, there were press announcements concerning the
defendant companies' intention to produce a motion picture entitled " The
Charge of the Light Brigade ". Comparison of the first defendant's script
and of the book showed many differences in detail, and many instances
of details common to the sources and to the script of the screenplay; but
comparison showed also similarities of detail, and a marked similarity
of the choice of incidents and that those which were common to both were
relatively important in comparison to those in the script only. The plaintiffs
brought an action for an injunction to restrain alleged infringement of
copyright and to restrain the defendants from making or producing a film
based on the first defendant's screenplay, and applied for an interlocutory
injunction to restrain the defendants from exhibiting, releasing or distributing any film based on the screenplay or assigning the copyright therein
or granting a licence in respect of it. The first defendant deposed on affidavit that he did not base his script on the book, but he gave no explanation
how he worked or for how long. His solicitor compiled a list of sources,
and the first defendant said that this identified many but not all sources of
which he availed himself; the list included the book, and the first defendant
gave no explanation of the manner and extent of his use of that work.

Held: (i) in granting or withholding interlocutory relief the court would
have regard to the balance of convenience, but the governing consideration
was the preservation of the status quo (see p. 336, letter D, post).

Donmar Productions, Ltd. v. *Bart* (p. 338, post) followed.

(ii) at this stage of the action the court did not have to determine finally
whether there had been an infringement of copyright but only whether there
was a prima facie case of infringement, and, as similarities in incidents and
situations afforded prima facie evidence of copying and the first defendant
offered no explanation but only a bare assertion that he had not based his
script on the book, an interlocutory injunction would be granted so that

A the plaintiffs' property should be protected until the trial (see p. 335, letters A and B, and p. 336, letters C and D, post).

Jarrold v. *Houlston* ((1857), 3 K. & J. 708), and dicta of CROSSMAN, J., in *Poznanski* v. *London Film Production Co., Ltd.* (1937), MacG. Cop. Cas. (1936-45) at p. 108) and of SIR RICHARD HENN COLLINS, M.R., in *Moffatt and Paige, Ltd.* v. *George Gill & Sons, Ltd. and Marshall* ((1902), 86 L.T. at

B pp. 470, 471) applied.

Pike v. *Nicholas* ((1869), 5 Ch. App. 251) distinguished.

(iii) since the plaintiffs were not within the jurisdiction, it would be made a condition of granting the interlocutory injunction that they should give security (in the sum of £10,000) towards implementing any liability that they might incur under their cross-undertaking in damages; moreover the

C defendants should have liberty to apply to discharge the injunction at any time (see p. 337, letters A and B, post).

[As to the principles governing the grant of interlocutory injunctions, see 21 HALSBURY'S LAWS (3rd Edn.) 365, 366, paras. 765, 766; and for cases on the subject see 28 DIGEST (Repl.) 749-754, *65-99.*

D As to interlocutory injunctions to restrain the infringement of copyright, see 8 HALSBURY'S LAWS (3rd Edn.) 445, 446, para. 809; and for cases on the subject, see 13 DIGEST (Repl.) 130-132, *715-737.*]

Cases referred to:

Donmar Productions, Ltd., v. *Bart,* (1964), p. 338, post.

Hogg v. *Scott,* (1874), L.R. 18 Eq. 444; 43 L.J.Ch. 705; 31 L.T. 163; 13

E Digest (Repl.) 130, *711.*

Jarrold v. *Houlston,* (1857), 3 K. & J. 708; 69 E.R. 1294; 13 Digest (Repl.) 52, *21.*

Jones v. *Pacaya Rubber and Produce Co., Ltd.,* [1911] 1 K.B. 455; 80 L.J.K.B. 155; 104 L.T. 446; 28 Digest (Repl.) 762, *166.*

Lewis v. *Fullarton,* (1839), 2 Beav. 6; 8 L.J.Ch. 291; 48 E.R. 1081; 13 Digest

F (Repl.) 61, *93.*

Longman v. *Winchester* (1809), 16 Ves. 269; 33 E.R. 987; 13 Digest (Repl.) 51, *17.*

McCrum v. *Eisner,* (1917), 87 L.J.Ch. 99; 117 L.T. 536; 13 Digest (Repl.) 111, *533.*

Macmillan & Co., Ltd. v. *Cooper,* (1923), L.R. 51 Ind. App. 109; 93 L.J.P.C. 113;

G 130 L.T. 675; 13 Digest (Repl.) 63, *106.*

Moffatt and Paige, Ltd. v. *George Gill & Sons, Ltd. and Marshall,* (1902), 86 L.T. 465; 13 Digest (Repl.) 57, *64.*

Pike v. *Nicholas,* (1869), 5 Ch. App. 251; 39 L.J.Ch. 435; 13 Digest (Repl.) 110, *514.*

Poznanski v. *London Film Production, Ltd.,* (1937), MacG. Cop. Cas. (1936-45)

H 107.

Rees v. *Melville,* (1914), MacG. Cop. Cas. (1911-16) 168.

Spiers v. *Brown,* (1858), 6 W.R. 352; 31 L.T.O.S. 16; 22 J.P. 738; 13 Digest (Repl.) 109, *510.*

Motion.

In an action commenced by writ issued on Nov. 28, 1966, Harman Pictures,

I N.V., the plaintiffs, a body incorporated and registered according to the law of the Netherlands Antilles, and the owners of the copyright (so far as concerned reproduction in cinematograph film form) of a book " The Reason Why " written by Cecil Blanche Woodham-Smith, which was a study of the background and incidents of the Charge of the Light Brigade, claimed against the defendants, John James Osborne, Woodfall Film Presentations, Ltd., and Woodfall Film Productions, Ltd., an injunction restraining the defendants and each of them by themselves, their servants or agents (a) from infringing or authorising the infringement of the plaintiff company's said copyright, (b) from making or

producing any film of or based on the screenplay " The Charge of the Light   **A**
Brigade " written by the first defendant, (c) from assigning or purporting
to assign the copyright or any part thereof in the said or any similar screenplay
or any part thereof or from granting or purporting to grant any licence in respect
of the said or any similar screenplay or from dealing with or disposing or purporting to dispose of any interest in the said or any similar screenplay or any
copies thereof.   They also claimed damages, and consequential relief.   **B**

By their notice of motion dated Jan. 16, 1967, the plaintiffs sought an order
restraining the defendants and each of them whether by themselves or by their
servants or agents until judgment in the action or further order from doing
any of the following acts, viz., (a) making or producing any film of or based
on the screenplay " The Charge of the Light Brigade " by the first defendant
or otherwise infringing or authorising the infringement of the plaintiffs' copyright   **C**
in the work " The Reason Why " by Cecil Blanche Woodham-Smith;   (b)
assigning or purporting to assign the copyright or any part thereof in the said
or any similar screenplay or any part thereof;   (c) granting or purporting to grant
any licence in respect of the said or any similar screenplay or any copies thereof.
During the hearing of the motion, counsel for the plaintiffs limited his claim so
far as interlocutory relief was concerned to an injunction restraining the defen-   **D**
dants from exhibiting or releasing or distributing any film based on the first
defendant's screenplay.   The facts are set out in the judgment.

The cases noted below* were cited during the argument in addition to those
referred to in the judgment.

Sir Andrew Clark, Q.C., and *Lord Lloyd of Hampstead* for the plaintiffs.
J. L. Arnold, Q.C., and *M. E. I. Kempster* for the defendants.   **E**

Cur. adv. vult.

Mar. 20.   **GOFF, J.**, read the following judgment: The plaintiffs are a
body incorporated and registered according to the law of the Netherlands
Antilles, and they are the owners of the copyright so far as concerns reproduction
in cinematograph film form of the well known book " The Reason Why " written   **F**
by Mrs. Woodham-Smith dealing with the Charge of the Light Brigade and the
story which lay behind it.   They produce and distribute films in association
with Mr. Laurence Harvey.   The defendant Osborne is a well known playwright
and screenwriter and is a director of and shareholder in the two defendant
companies, both of which are English companies.   They produce and distribute
films commonly known as Woodfall Films.   **G**

In 1963 there were discussions between Mr. Laurence Harvey and the late
Mr. James Woolf on behalf of the plaintiffs and a Mr. Robin Fox and Mr. Richardson a director of both the defendant companies on their behalf as to the possibilities of the defendant companies acquiring the plaintiffs' rights or concurring
in a joint production.   In his affidavit Mr. Harvey says this:

" The said Robin Fox told me that he had read the said work with admira-   **H**
tion and he further stated that both John Osborne (the first defendant in this
action) and the said Richardson had also read the said work, and that John
Osborne had expressed enthusiasm for the treatment of the subject by the
authoress and the way she had arranged her material and that the said
Richardson had expressed a keen desire to produce a motion picture based
on the said work."   **I**

These negotiations came to nothing and the defendant Osborne has written the
script for a motion picture entitled " The Charge of the Light Brigade " which

---

* *Jarrold* v. *Heywood*, (1870), 18 W.R. 279; *Smith* v. *Chatto*, (1874), 31 L.T. 775;
Preston v. *Luck*, (1884), 27 Ch. 497; *University of London Press, Ltd.* v. *University
Tutorial Press, Ltd.*, [1916] 2 Ch. 601; *Bagge* v. *Miller*, (1920), MacG. Cop. Cas. (1917-23)
179; *Smith* v. *Grigg, Ltd.*, [1924] 1 K.B. 655; *Cambridge University Press* v. *University
Tutorial Press*, (1928), 45 R.P.C. 335; *Bolton* v. *British International Pictures, Ltd.*,
(1936), MacG. Cop. Cas. (1936-45) 20.

A the defendants are proposing to produce entirely on their own account. Meanwhile the plaintiffs had been endeavouring to exploit their rights elsewhere, but their negotiations were frustrated by press announcements of the defendants' intended production.

In these circumstances the plaintiffs have brought this action in which they claim an injunction restraining the defendants and each of them by themselves,
B their servants or agents (a) from infringing or authorising the infringement of the plaintiff company's said copyright, (b) from making or producing any film of or based on the said screenplay, (c) from assigning or purporting to assign the copyright or any part thereof in the said or any similar screenplay or any part thereof or from granting or purporting to grant any licence in respect of the said or any similar screenplay or from dealing with or disposing or
C purporting to dispose of any interest in the said or any similar screenplay or any copies thereof, damages and consequential relief. They moved the court for interlocutory relief and as claimed by the notice of motion what they were seeking was an order restraining the defendants and each of them whether by themselves or by their servants or agents until judgment in this action or further order from doing any of the following acts, viz.:
D (a) making or producing any film of or based on the screenplay "The Charge of the Light Brigade" by the first defendant or otherwise infringing or authorising the infringement of the plaintiffs' copyright in the work "The Reason Why" by Cecil Blanche Woodham-Smith; (b) assigning or purporting to assign the copyright or any part thereof in the said or any similar screenplay or any part thereof; (c) granting or purporting to grant any
E licence in respect of the said or any similar screenplay or dealing with or disposing or purporting to dispose of any interest in the said or any similar screenplay or any copies thereof.

In his reply, however, counsel for the plaintiffs limited his claim so far as interlocutory relief is concerned to an injunction restraining the defendants from exhibiting any such film or releasing it for exhibition. Counsel for the defendants
F took a preliminary objection that the plaintiffs could not be entitled to interlocutory relief in any event because of delay. In my judgment, however, this is not sound. It is conceded that there could be no question of delay before the plaintiffs first saw a script, which was not until the end of October, 1966. True it is that the motion was not launched until Jan. 16, 1967, but the writ was
G issued much earlier, namely on Nov. 28. Having regard to the fact that the plaintiffs are out of the jurisdiction, I cannot see any such delay on their part as would disentitle them to interlocutory relief, particulaly as there is no suggestion anywhere in the correspondence that they were intending or appeared to be intending to abandon their rights.

Apart from this the defendants say on the merits first that both the book
H and the script deal with a common subject which is a famous event in history on which there is, as indeed there is, a wealth of non-copyright literature and information, and that they have simply drawn on this and prepared an original work of their own without making any improper use of Mrs. Woodham-Smith's book. Secondly, that in any case the appropriate relief would be not an injunction but an account of profits.
I
At the outset the plaintiffs must, of course, establish a strong prima case that the copyright in respect of which they are suing exists and that they are the owners of it, but that is conceded. It is common ground that there can be an original work entitled to protection although the subject matter is not original, but is for example, as in the present case, some well known event in history. The precise amount of knowledge, labour, judgment or literary skill or taste which the author of any book or other compilation must bestow on its composition in order to acquire copyright in it within the meaning of the Copyright Act, 1911,

cannot be defined in express terms—see per LORD ATKINSON in *Macmillan &* A
Co., Ltd. v. *Cooper* (1). There is, however, no dispute that Mrs. Woodham-Smith
displayed all these qualities in amply sufficient measure and acquired copyright
in her book, whilst the plaintiffs' title to the film rights by assignment is also
not disputed. What is much more difficult is whether the plaintiffs have made
out a sufficient prima facie case of infringement or rather intended infringement,
and before considering the facts I must refer at some length to the relevant law. B

There is no copyright in ideas or schemes or systems or methods—it is confined
to their expression; see *McCrum* v. *Eisner* (2), where PETERSON, J., said:

" ' Copyright, however, does not extend to ideas, or schemes, or systems,
or methods; it is confined to their expression; and if their expression is not
copied the copyright is not infringed.' There is, therefore, no copyright in the
idea of a recruit, coupled with ' the orders of the day '. The only copyright C
that can exist is in the expression of such an idea, and the question in all
such cases must be whether the expression of the idea has been imitated,"

There is a distinction, however, between ideas (which are not copyright) and
situations and incidents which may be; see per SWINFEN EADY, L.J., in *Rees*
v. *Melville*, where this appears (3):
                                                                              D
" In order to constitute an infringement it was not necessary that the
words of the dialogue should be the same; the situation and incidents,
the mode in which the ideas were worked out and presented might constitute
a material portion of the whole play, and the court must have regard to
the dramatic value and importance of what if anything was taken, even
although the portion might in fact be small and the actual language not E
copied. On the other hand, the fundamental idea of two plays might be
the same, but if worked out separately and on independent lines they might
be so different as to bear no real resemblance to one another."

One must, however, be careful not to jump to the conclusion that there has
been copying merely because of similarity of stock incidents, or of incidents
which are to be found in historical, semi-historical and fictional literature about F
characters in history (see *Poznanski* v. *London Film Production, Ltd.* (4)).

In such cases the plaintiffs, and that includes the plaintiffs in the present case,
are in an obvious difficulty because of the existence of common sources, as was
emphasised in *Pike* v. *Nicholas* (5). In that case the plaintiff published a book,
and the defendant afterwards published a book on the same subject, in which
he mentioned the plaintiff's book as one of the authorities consulted by him. G
The plaintiff alleged that the defendant's book was a piracy, and in proof showed
(amongst other things) that the plaintiff had referred to a large number of
authorities to which the defendant had referred. The defendant stated that
he had taken the references from a previous writer from whom the plaintiff had
taken them, and showed that he, the defendant, had referred to two authorities
not mentioned by the plaintiff; but as to two of the authorities referred to by H
the plaintiff, and also by the defendant, the defendant was unable to state
where he had found them. It was held that, under the circumstances, the defendant had not made such use of the plaintiff's book as to entitle the plaintiff to
an injunction and that an author who had been led by a former author to refer
to older writers, might, without committing piracy, use the same passages in
the older writers which were used by the former author. I

LORD HATHERLEY, L.C., said (6):

" A case of alleged piracy like this was obviously very difficult to determine

(1) (1923), 130 L.T. 675 at p. 681.
(2) (1917), 87 L.J.Ch. 99 at p. 102. PETERSON, J. was quoting LINDLEY, L.J. in
Hollinrake v. *Truswell*, [1894] 3 Ch. 420 at p. 427.
(3) (1914), MacG. Cop. Cas. (1911-16) 168 at p. 174.
(4) (1937), MacG. Cop. Cas. (1936-45) 107 at p. 111.
(5) (1869), 5 Ch. App. 251.   (6) (1869), 5 Ch. App. at pp. 259, 260.

A   when the authors took a common subject and depended upon authors open to both of them, and when portions of the one work, which were said to resemble portions of the other work, might be taken from those common authors to which each was at liberty to resort."

Then he said (7):

B   " On the other hand, the defendant had quoted an author taken from Prichard, Calpurnius Flaccus, who was not quoted by the plaintiff, and had added to his quotation a passage from Tertullian which was not inapt to the subject. These circumstances showed clearly that the defendant went to the original source, namely, Prichard, and that he got those quotations from Prichard which the plaintiff got from Prichard. Although

C   the defendant might have been led to look more minutely into Prichard than he otherwise would have done by referring to the plaintiff's work, still the plaintiff could not say, ' I, having found these passages in Prichard, will prohibit all the world, who may find the same passages, from making use of them '. The moment he had given that degree of light to the defendant which led him to refer to that common source, if the defendant did really

D   and bona fide look at that common source, he did all that this court required him to do. He must not simply copy the passage from the plaintiff's book, but having been put on to the track, and having looked at that particular part of the book which the plaintiff led him to, he was entitled to make use of every passage from that author which the plaintiff had made use of."

E   Giffard, L.J., said (8):

" The plaintiff undertook a more formidable task than was ever undertaken before in any copyright case; for there was the fact, that the two parties started with exactly the same theme to treat of. That was beyond all question. These books were written with reference to a prize that was proposed to be given by a society in Wales. They started with a desire

F   to arrive at, as nearly as possible, the same conclusion, and with a desire, no doubt, to glorify the Ancient Britons as much as could well be done. Moreover, what may be termed the platform divisions, by means of which they worked out their books, were very nearly the same, and were for the most part taken from Dr. Prichard's book, and thus they were at once found starting entirely in the same groove. Besides, their books consisted

G   mainly of results gathered from other authorities, and could not, in the true sense of the word, be treated as original, except to a very slight extent. As to this, Sir William James, V.-C., laid down most accurately in his judgment—' That there is no monopoly in the main theory of the plaintiff, or in the theories and speculations by which he has supported it, nor even in the use of the published results of his own observations.' It would, therefore,

H   at once appear that the task undertaken by the plaintiff was an almost impossible one, unless he could show that there were substantial passages either actually copied, or copied with mere colourable alteration. It would not do to show merely one or two passages, but some material part of the book must be shown to have been taken."

I   That case was, however, in some respects special, because both authors set out to achieve the same object. Moreover the defendant had been examined and cross-examined at considerable length, a very important feature absent in the present case at this stage.

Further it is to be observed that Lord Hatherley, L.C., said (9) that they did not intend to lay down any general principles which were contrary to those laid down by Sir William James, V.-C. and as appears from the note (10)

---

(7) (1869), 5 Ch. App. at pp. 262, 263.   (8) (1869), 5 Ch. App. at pp. 267, 268.
(9) (1869), 5 Ch. App. at p. 257.   (10) (1869), 5 Ch. App. at p. 260, n.

the only principle which he laid down was that the question is between a legitimate **A**
and a piratical use of an author's work, and he said (11):

" It is certainly very singular that an author should not be able to give
a single place or time when or where he consulted a high authority, and that
he should not be able to produce a single original note, extract, or quotation."

The principle stated (12) is entirely in accordance with *Jarrold* v. *Houlston* (13). **B**
The relevant parts of the headnote are as follows:

" Another person may originate another work in the same general form,
provided he does so from his own resources and makes the work he so
originates a work of his own by his own labour and industry bestowed upon
it.

" In determining whether an injunction should be ordered, the question, **C**
where the matter of the plaintiff's work is not original, is how far an unfair
or undue use has been made of the work.

" If, instead of searching into the common sources and obtaining your
subject matter from thence, you avail yourself of the labour of your predecessor, adopt his arrangement and questions, or adopt them with a colourable
variation, it is an illegitimate use. Falsely to deny that you have copied or **D**
taken any idea or language from another work is strong indication of animus
furandi."

The point in the last sentence played a large part in the actual decision in
that case, and of course I have not got that on this motion, although the plaintiffs
may seek to show it by cross-examination at the trial. However, that does not
affect the general principles stated in the other passages which I have just read **E**
from the headnote.

I must now quote from the judgment of SIR WILLIAM PAGE WOOD, V.-C. (14),
where the principles which I have mentioned are laid down:

" The really difficult question in cases of this description, where it must
be admitted that the matter is not original, is how far the author of the
work in question can be said to have made an unfair or undue use of previous **F**
works protected by copyright? As regards all common sources, he is entitled
to make what use of them he pleases; but, as LORD LANGDALE, M.R., said
in *Lewis* v. *Fullarton* (15), he is not entitled to make any use of a work
protected by copyright which is not what can be called a fair use. As regards
the question of fair use of the plaintiff's work, the defendant to a great
degree prevents inquiry. He says broadly in his affidavit, ' I deny that I **G**
copied or took any idea or language from the work of DOCTOR BREWER '.
Upon a broad statement of that description, the question of fair use is almost
excluded. He does not say he has not read the work of DR. BREWER. He
says he has not read the second edition, or seen the eleventh edition; and
that he never read the preface—a denial which, of itself, raises an inference,
that he had read the body of the work: and he denies that he has taken any **H**
idea or language from it. The only uses consistent with that statement on
the part of the defendant would appear to be these: In publishing a work
in the form of question and answer on a variety of scientific subjects he had
a right to look to all those books which were unprotected by copyright, and
to make such use of them as he thought fit, by turning them into questions
and answers. He had also a further right, if he found a work like DR. **I**
BREWER'S and, perusing it, was struck by seeing—as I think has been the
case in the present instance—that the author had been led up to particular
questions and answers by the perusal of some other work, to have recourse
himself to the same work, although possibly he would not have thought of

---

(11) (1869), 5 Ch. App. at p. 259, n.   (12) (1869), 5 Ch. App. at p. 260, n.
(13) (1857), 3 K. & J. 708. This case was also about a book entitled " The Reason
Why ", published, however, by the defendant.
(14) (1857), 3 K. & J. at pp. 714-717.   (15) (1839), 2 Beav. 6.

A   doing so but for the perusal of the plaintiff's book. Both these, I apprehend, would be perfectly fair and legitimate modes of using the plaintiff's book; and neither would be inconsistent with Mr. Philp's affidavit, that he has not copied or taken any idea or language from DR. BREWER's book. There is another sort of legitimate use which might fairly be made by Mr. Philp, although it is scarcely so consistent with what he has deposed to in his

B   affidavit. It would be a legitimate use of a work of this description if the author of a subsequent work, after getting his own work with great pains and labour into a shape approximating to what he considered a perfect shape, should look through the earlier work to see whether it contained any heads which he had forgotten . . . The question I really have to try is whether the use that in this case has been made of the plaintiffs' book has

C   gone beyond a fair use. Now, for trying that question, several tests have been laid down. One which was originally expressed, I think by a common law judge, and was adopted by LORD LANGDALE, M.R., in *Lewis* v. *Fullarton* (16), is, whether you find on the part of a defendant an animus furandi—an intention to take for the purpose of saving himself labour. I take the illegitimate use, as opposed to the legitimate use, of another man's work on

D   subject-matters of this description to be this: If, knowing that a person whose work is protected by copyright has, with considerable labour, com-piled from various sources a work in itself not original, but which he has digested and arranged, you, being minded to compile a work of a like descrip-tion, instead of taking the pains of searching into all the common sources, and obtaining your subject-matter from them, avail yourself of the labour

E   of your predecessor, adopt his arrangements, adopt moreover the very questions he has asked, or adopt them with but a slight degree of colourable variation, and thus save yourself pains and labour by availing yourself of the pains and labour which he has employed, that I take to be an illegitimate use."

F   I should also refer to *Macmillan & Co., Ltd.* v. *Cooper* in the Privy Council (17), where LORD ATKINSON in delivering the judgment of the Board quoted with approval, and as having been approved by the Court of Appeal in *Moffatt and Paige, Ltd.* v. *George Gill & Sons, Ltd. and Marshall* (18), the following passage from the judgment of SIR ARTHUR WILSON in an earlier Indian case (19). The quotation is as follows:

G   " ' In the case of works not original in the proper sense of the term, but composed of, or compiled or prepared from materials which are open to all, the fact that one man has produced such a work does not take away from anyone else the right to produce another work of the same kind, and in doing so to use all the materials open to him. But as the law is concisely stated by SIR CHARLES HALL, V.-C., in *Hogg* v. *Scott* (20), the true principle in all these cases is, that the defendant is not at liberty to use or avail

H   himself of the labour which the plaintiff has been at for the purpose of producing his work; that is, in fact, merely to take away the result of another man's labour, or, in other words, his property.' SIR ARTHUR WILSON then points out that this principle applies to maps, road books, guide books, street directories, dictionaries, to compilations of scientific work and other subjects, and considers that it applies to a selection of

I   poems. He then gives the reason why it applies to MR. PALGRAVE's GOLDEN TREASURY in the following words: ' Such a selection as MR. PALGRAVE has made obviously requires extensive reading, careful study and comparison, and the exercise of taste and judgment in selection. It is open to anyone who pleases to go through a like course of reading, and by the exercise of

(16) (1839), 2 Beav. 6.   (17) (1923), 130 L.T. at p. 680.
(18) (1902), 86 L.T. 465.
(19) *Macmillan* v. *Suresh Chunder Deb*, (1890), I.L.R. 17 Cal. 951.
(20) (1874), L.R. 18 Eq. 444 at p. 458.

A

his own taste and judgment to make a selection for himself. But if he spares himself this trouble and adopts MR. PALGRAVE's selection, he offends against the principle.' He then proceeds to quote the following passage from LORD ELDON, L.C.'s judgment in *Longman* v. *Winchester* (21), approved of by SIR WILLIAM PAGE WOOD, V.-C., in *Spiers* v. *Brown* (22): ' So in . . . a work consisting of a selection from various authors, two men might perhaps make the same selection; but that must be by resorting to the original authors, not by taking advantage of the selection already made by another.' "

B

Then in *Moffatt's* case (23) SIR RICHARD HENN COLLINS, M.R., said:

" The sources from which these works were drawn were common. It was open to anybody to compile an edition of ' As you like it ', and open to him to go to all the sources of criticism and to make selections from them. It was open to him to cull quotations from other books and to put them together as the author of the plaintiff's book has done . . ."

C

Then he said (24):

". . . but are you at liberty to apply the same principle to a series of quotations—to take the reference given by one author although he quotes such and such a passage as illustrating this particular matter—to say, ' I will just go and see if that is correctly copied or not, and if it is correctly copied I propose to introduce it with any other quotation which illustrates the particular passage, and I propose to adopt that as my own work '? That leaves out the whole merit; the felicity of the quotation; its adaptability to a particular end; its illustration of a particular characteristic. All those things enter into the choice of one quotation as apart from another. That is a process which may involve gifts both of knowledge and intelligence. The aptness of quotation does not depend on the particular page or number of lines in which it is found; and that is all you find if you obey a certain direction to go to a certain place and take it. It does not entitle you to annex the skill and judgment and taste which has dictated the selection. It does appear to have been the defendant, Mr. Marshall's view of his rights, as his counsel has put it forward for him, that if he once knew where to find the quotation then he had a right to annex it; and that if he once knew where to look and find the quotation, and if it corresponded with what the author had written, he has a right to take it. I cannot accede to that for a moment; and it seems to me that the law is clearly such as to entitle the plaintiff to complain if quotations selected and arranged by him are imitated and adopted by the defendant, Mr. Marshall."

D

E

F

G

Now I have to apply these principles to the facts of this case, always bearing in mind that this is a motion for interlocutory relief and the facts have as yet by no means been fully investigated.

Mr. Richardson in his affidavit says that during the winter of 1961-62 he and the defendant Osborne discussed the possibility of making what he describes as another historical film, which in its context postulates somewhat inaccurately that Tom Jones was an historical film, but that is not of much moment. What is important is that he says that he provided the defendant Osborne with Kinglake's " Invasion of the Crimea ", Hibbert's " Destruction of Lord Raglan " and " The Reason Why ", and that some months later the defendant Osborne confirmed his interest and singled out Captain Nolan as a fascinating character, and he goes on: " On behalf of the defendant companies I commissioned him to write a screenplay on ' the Charge ' "; which appears therefore to have been at the end of 1962 or early 1963. Mr. Richardson then says: " Also on behalf of the defendant companies I commissioned, inter alia, John and Andrew Mollo to carry out a programme of research ", and they " supplied information to Osborne and

H

I

A myself based on their researches ". John Mollo has made an affidavit himself confirming this and giving somewhat extensive information about their work, but he says that they were instructed by Mr. Richardson in or about January, 1964 and he does not say when they reported to him or to the defendant Osborne.

   Counsel for the defendants has pointed out that there is evidence of independent research in the work of the Mollos, and internal evidence in the script that the
B defendant Osborne made use of it, e.g., in the quotation from XENOPHON in scene 6. On the other hand it appears from the passages in the evidence to which I have just referred that the defendant Osborne may have been engaged on the work for something like a year before the Mollo brothers were even instructed, and one does not know how far the screenplay had taken shape or what use the defendant Osborne had made of " The Reason Why " before the Mollos came
C on the scene. In this connexion it is interesting to observe that whilst the book, the script and Kinglake all refer to two flags flying at Canroberts Hill as the signal that the enemy was approaching, the Mollos' note does not.

   Further, counsel for the defendants has drawn my attention forcefully to the following significant considerations. Captain Nolan is the principal character in the film but he is not in the book, although of course he figures largely in it, and
D moreover a considerable number of matters attributed to Captain Nolan in the film are in fact in the book, having been transposed in the film from other officers to whom they really related. Further Mrs. Woodham-Smith, even if she knew it, did not bring out that he was an Indian officer, whereas the film emphasises that fact in a fictitious posting scene in which on that very score Lord Cardigan registers instant hostility towards Captain Nolan. Indeed this is, I think, one of
E the strongest points in the defendants' argument, as the book says that Lord Cardigan was anxious to have Captain Nolan on his staff, which is a very different treatment. Again there are a number of passages in which the script is identical with the common sources whilst the book is not, or where the script is nearer to the original, notably for example at the death of Captain Nolan, where in the book his horse carries his body back through the wrong regiment, whilst the
F script has it correctly. Then the book gives the title of one of Captain Nolan's books as " Nolan's System for Training Cavalry Horses ", whereas it is really, as stated in the script, " The Training of Cavalry Remount Horses ".

   Counsel for the defendants also relied on the fact that in scene 108 the name of the transport ship is given as the " Shooting Star ", which is the name given in Mrs. Duberly's Diary at p. 54, whereas the book has " Southern Star ", see
G p. 214, but this may not have been the same ship, for at p. 156 of the book the transport is named " Shooting Star ". Perhaps more significantly, there is at least one example where it is clear that the book comes from one source and the script from another. I refer to the retreat of the Turks where the book reports them as saying " Ship, ship, ship ", which comes from Kinglake, and in the script it is " Ship, Johnny ", which comes from Mrs. Duberly's Diary. Again it
H is said that the defendants have used the Cavalry Journal extensively although it is not one of the works specified in Mrs. Woodham-Smith's bibliography.

   Counsel for the defendants has also relied in many instances on small points of detail being common to the sources and the script, e.g., again at Canroberts Hill Kinglake refers to the two flags as the " arranged signal " whereas the book says " the signal "; then for the opening of the Battle of Balaclava the book says
I that the guns in the redoubt fired, whereas Kinglake says the fort opened fire from one of its twelve pounder guns and the scenic direction in scene 237 is " Fire from one of the twelve pounder guns from the number 1 redoubt ", and again the book says at p. 246 that at the guns Captain Morris engaged the Russian officer in command, whereas the script in scene 364 reads " Morris drives his horse full at a tall Russian who seems to be a Squadron Leader ", which is what is stated in Kinglake at p. 253.

   I have read the whole of the script very carefully, however, and compared it with the book, and I find many similarities of detail there also. Thus the descrip- **A** tive direction in scene 106 gives " hogging the stage in the foreground the officers with their mothers, wives, and even young brides ", whilst the book has at p. 142: " Officers took their wives with them, some took their mothers, there were several young brides." In scene 118 " Nolan encourages the soldiers and sailors who are struggling with the terrified creatures ". The book tells us at p. 144 that " our men worked well and were ably seconded by some of the sailors ". Then there is **B** scene 136 in which Lord Lucan says: " Above my head Sir ", and the book states that Lord Cardigan went over Lord Lucan's head, and the unusual expression in scene 214 that the cavalry had been " so low in the brushwood ", which is the precise expression in the book at p. 200. Again it is prima facie not without significance that apart from the burial of Captain Nolan the play ends with the very quotation which Mrs. Woodham-Smith used to end her description of the **C** battle.

Counsel for the defendants has made a very exhaustive examination of one section of the script showing that there are many incidents recorded in the book which find no counterpart in the script, some of which are of considerable dramatic promise and which one would expect to find reproduced if copying were afoot, e.g., the Russian cavalry jeering at the inactivity of the British cavalry, and in **D** particular the fatal fourth order being first entrusted to another officer and Captain Nolan claiming the right to bear it. As counsel for the plaintiffs points out, some of these might well be accounted for as being similar to other events already in the script, and in any event abridgement was necessary, but that may not be a complete answer.

Counsel for the defendants has also analysed the quotations which are common **E** to both works and the number of incidents and situations which occur in the script only, and statistically these analyses favour him, but on comparing the book and the script I was, and remain, impressed by the marked similarity of the choice of incidents, and the relative importance of those which are common and those in the script only and by the juxtaposition of ideas, for example the incident of the issue of unwanted stable jackets is followed in the script by this line in the **F** narrative. General Airey says to Lord Cardigan and Lockwood " A triumph my Lord ", whilst in the book the same incident is followed by the review [and] was a triumph for the Lieutenant Colonel.

Captain Richard Reynolds, represented in the play by Captain Williams, was cashiered in 1840 for inciting Lord Cardigan to a duel, and the incidents of Lord Cardigan arranging to have his officers spied on and of the issue of the unwanted **G** stable jackets both occurred in 1833. In the play, though not in the book, they appear after the cashiering, but it is interesting to observe that they both still appear together and in the same order as in the book. Again, in the scene describing the assault on the farmer I find in both book and script the use of the expressions " snooks " and " guffaw " in close proximity. Moreover, as counsel for the plaintiffs has pointed out, there are a number of descriptive phrases in **H** the book which find their way either from the book or otherwise into the script, e.g., " Divine Right Tory " and " beautiful Golden Head ", and the fact that Nolan was a Captain without purchase and the reference to Hubert de Burgh as a squire.

The question remains, did the defendant Osborne work independently and produce a script which from the nature of things has much in common with the **I** book, or did he proceed the other way round and use the book as a basis, taking his selection of incidents and quotations therefrom, albeit omitting a number and making some alterations and additions by reference to the common sources and by some reference to other sources? It is, of course, impossible to arrive at a final conclusion on that question until the trial when one will have had the advantage of discovery and the witnesses, and particularly the defendant Osborne, can be cross-examined and one can evaluate the significance of the failure of either side to call any witness whom one would have expected to see.

A   It may well be that the defendants will justify themselves completely. On the other hand they may not. All that I have to determine at this stage is whether the plaintiffs have made out a prima case, taking into account, of course, all the evidence so far filed by both sides and counsel's able argument for the defendants, and if so whether in all the circumstances relevant for my consideration I ought to grant any, and if so, what relief pending the trial.

B   For this purpose and at this stage in my judgment the lack of explanation by the defendant Osborne how or when he worked and how long it took him, is of fundamental importance. All I have is a bare assertion that he did not base the script on the book. That being sworn to must, of course, be regarded seriously, but I find it impossible to think that he can have produced this large script ready for shooting (at any rate as he claims independently) without some kind of sketch

C   plan and probably extensive notes or trial drafts of the whole or parts of it. All those will emerge on discovery and may well serve either to corroborate or discredit his evidence. It is also, I think, remarkable that instead of the defendant Osborne (who knows) saying even in outline what sources he consulted and how he arrived at his selection or even taking one or two examples of common situations and giving his own explanation, he has left it to his solicitor, who does not know

D   what happened, to compile a list of sources, and the defendant Osborne then says they have truly identified many but not all of the sources of which he availed himself in each particular. That list includes " The Reason Why ", and the defendant Osborne does not say that that is wrong and it should not have been included, nor alternatively does he give any explanation of the manner and extent of his use of that work.

E   Here I would return to the judgment of CROSSMAN, J., in the *Poznanski* case (25), where he said:

   " Similarities in incidents and situations, although affording prima facie evidence that the incidents and situations in a film have been copied from the incidents and situations in a stage play, may not be sufficient to override denial of copying, coupled with an explanation of the similarities by

F   reference to other sources. What I have to consider first is whether there are such similarities between the incidents and situations in the plaintiff's play and those in the defendant's film as to make the defendant's film a reproduction of a substantial part of the plaintiff's play."

   In the end CROSSMAN, J., reached a very clear conclusion in favour of the

G   defendants before him and he said (26):

   " The plaintiffs say that there is copyright in the selection from the historical, semi-historical and fictional literature dealing with the subject-matter of the play and the film of certain incidents, certain chronology and certain characterisation, and in the treatment of such selected material, and that M. Savoir made a selection for the purpose of the play, treated and

H   selected the material in a certain way, and consequently had copyright in the selected material as so treated. They say that the authors of the film consciously or unconsciously followed M. Savoir's selection and treatment, and in so following it infringed his copyright. I think, however, that insofar as the selection of incidents, chronology and characterisation for the film and the treatment of the selected material resemble the selection and treatment

I   for the play, such resemblance may well be due to the fact that the incidents, chronology and characterisation selected for the film, and the treatment of such selected material for the film, are the most suitable for the film. I do not find myself driven to the conclusion that the selection or treatment was a copying of M. Savoir's selection and treatment. I find that if and so far as there are similarities between the play and the film, the similarities are mainly

---

(25) (1937), MacG. Cop. Cas. (1936-45) at p. 108.
(26) (1937), MacG. Cop. Cas. at p. 111.

A in ideas, which are not the subject matter of copyright, and that the treatment and development of these ideas in the film are quite different from the treatment and development in the play. The longer I consider the play and the film, the greater the differences appear to me to be."

That, however, was at the trial, but he said categorically, and this seems very important to me for present purposes, that similarities in incidents and situations do afford prima facie evidence of copying.

On the question as to the principles on which the court acts in granting or withholding interlocutory relief, I have been referred to a transcript of the judgment of UNGOED-THOMAS, J., in *Donmar Productions, Ltd.* v. *Bart* (27), where he considered that matter at length. This shows that the plaintiff must first establish a strong prima facie case for the existence of the right on which he sues. He must at least show that he is likely to succeed. If he does that, however, or if his right is not disputed, then although he must go on to show a prima case of its infringement, yet for that purpose he does not have to show that he is likely to be successful or more likely to be so than the defendant, but only that he has a case reasonably capable of succeeding. Even then the remedy is still discretionary and in exercising its discretion the court will have regard to the balance of convenience, but the governing principle is the preservation of the status quo.

Counsel for the defendants has stressed that in *Jones* v. *Pacaya Rubber and Produce Co., Ltd.* (28) cited by UNGOED-THOMAS, J., it was necessary to grant an injunction to preserve the property, since otherwise relief at the trial would have becomes impossible. I think, however, that that is really true of the present case, since distribution of a film so like " The Reason Why ", as is the first defendant's script, would render it quite impossible for the plaintiffs to exploit their copyright. Be that as it may and whilst I recognise that the plaintiffs' rights are vulnerable and would probably be lost by any independent production of a film play on the Charge of the Light Brigade, whether made by the defendants or some third party, still in my judgment the plaintiffs are entitled to have their property protected against injury by the defendants or anyone else using Mrs. Woodham-Smith's work to assist them to bring out a film ahead of the plaintiffs. Accordingly unless there be grounds based on the balance of convenience or the circumstances generally why the court in the exercise of its discretion should withhold relief, the plaintiffs are in my judgment entitled on proper terms to such an injunction as will protect their property pending the trial of the action, when the difficult question whether the defendants' script is legitimate can be properly decided.

In these circumstances, in the present case I am satisfied that I ought to grant relief in the limited form in which it is now asked which will preserve the status quo by enabling the defendants to proceed with the making of their film so that if they prove right they will not have suffered any or any appreciable loss before the time comes when they are ready to exhibit or distribute. Of course they will have wasted their money if they prove wrong, but they would be in that position if I did not injunct them because they could only go on at their peril. The plaintiffs, on the other hand, will have their property preserved pending the trial. It is true that if I were to refuse any injunction at this stage and the plaintiffs ultimately succeeded, they would be entitled to an account of the profits, and I could now put the defendants on terms to keep separate accounts and even to keep all proceeds separately from their other moneys, but as counsel for the plaintiffs rightly pointed out, the defendants might not make any or might not make such as the plaintiffs would hope to secure from their own production. True, on the other hand, that if ultimately the plaintiffs make the film they may be less successful than the defendants would be, but in my judgment if the plaintiffs are right they are entitled to control the situation and have the play made and cast as they want it.

---

(27) See p. 338, post.   (28) [1911] 1 K.B. 455.

A   I must, however, impose terms for the protection of the defendants, and that is indeed conceded by counsel for the plaintiffs. As the plaintiffs are not within the jurisdiction I must require them to give security towards implementing any liability they may incur under their cross-undertaking in damages. It is impossible to quantify that at this stage, but they have offered £10,000, which is the figure I had independently conceived in my own mind. The injunction will therefore

B   be conditional on the plaintiffs giving security in that amount to the satisfaction of the master within twenty-one days or such further time, if any, as the parties may agree or the master direct. Further, the defendants will have liberty to apply to discharge the injunction at any time. Thus if, as the matter proceeds, it looks as if the defendants will be ready to distribute before the trial, they can come back and ask to have the injunction discharged, or for more security, by

C   which time the court will be better able to estimate the amount of the loss which the defendants will suffer if they be further restrained. The defendants will also be able to come back if there be any other material change in the circumstances. As at present advised, I think that any such application should be on the usual two days' notice despite the fact that the plaintiffs are out of the jurisdiction, though there would probably have to be some adjournment, but I will hear

D   counsel on this if they wish.

       I also think that I ought to reserve the costs to the trial judge and I shall do that unless counsel make representations to the contrary. I shall give any directions that may be asked for as to liberty to apply for a speedy trial.

       [The court made an order, the agreed minutes of which were in the following

E   terms:—" UPON hearing counsel etc. and upon reading the affidavits etc. . . . and the plaintiffs by their counsel undertaking to abide by any order . . . as to damages in case this . . . court shall hereafter be of opinion that the defendants shall have sustained any by reason of this order which the plaintiffs ought to pay

       " THIS COURT doth order that the defendants and each of them be restrained by themselves or by their servants or agents, until judgment in this action or

F   further order, (a) from exhibiting releasing or distributing any film of or based on the screenplay entitled ' The Charge of the Light Brigade ' by the defendant John James Osborne a copy whereof . . . is filed . . . (b) from assigning or purporting to assign the copyright or any part thereof in the said or any similar screenplay or any part thereof or from granting or purporting to grant any licence in respect of the said or any similar screenplay or from dealing with or disposing or purporting to dispose of any interest in the said or any similar

G   screenplay or any copies thereof save that the defendants are to be at liberty to charge the same by way of mortgage in favour of any person or persons within and ordinarily resident within the jurisdiction of this court but only upon first disclosing the terms of the present order to any such person or persons and only for the purpose of raising finance to be used in making any such film as aforesaid.

       " THE SAID ORDER to be conditional on security in the amount of £10,000

H   being provided by the plaintiffs within twenty-one days hereof and to the satisfaction of a Master of the Supreme Court. Liberty to the defendants to apply at two days' notice for further security in the event of any change of circumstances.

       " Liberty to apply to fix an early date for the trial of the action. Costs of this motion to be costs in the cause."]

I   Solicitors: *Goodman, Derrick & Co.* (for the plaintiffs); *Wright & Webb* (for the defendants).

[*Reported by* JACQUELINE METCALFE, *Barrister-at-Law.*]

Applied in GALLAGHER v POST OFFICE
[1970] 3 All ER 712

A

NOTE.

DONMAR PRODUCTIONS, LTD. *v.* BART AND OTHERS.

[CHANCERY DIVISION (Ungoed-Thomas, J.), June 3, 4, 5, 1964.]

*Copyright—Assignment—Injunction—Interlocutory relief—Principle governing grant
of interlocutory injunction—Prima facie right—Preservation of status quo pending
trial.*

B

Cases referred to:
  Jones v. *Pacaya Rubber and Produce Co., Ltd.,* [1911] 1 K.B. 455; 80 L.J.K.B. 155;
      104 L.T. 446; 28 Digest (Repl.) 762, *166.*
  Lamb v. *Sambas Rubber and Gutta Percha Co., Ltd.,* [1908] 1 Ch. 845; 77 L.J.Ch.
      386; 98 L.T. 633; 9 Digest (Repl.) 351, *2248.*
  Preston v. *Luck* (1884), 27 Ch.D. 497; 28 Digest (Repl.) 834, *758.*
  Ripley v. *Paper Bottle Co.* (1887), 57 L.J.Ch. 327; 9 Digest (Repl.) 351, *2247.*
  Smith v. *Grigg, Ltd.,* [1924] 1 K.B. 655; 93 L.J.K.B. 237; 130 L.T. 697; 46 Digest
      (Repl.) 199, *1324.*

C

Motion.
This was a motion for an interlocutory injunction to restrain, until trial or further
order, the first two defendants from disposing of the copyright of a musical play
" Oliver " in motion picture form or by radio or commercial television, and to restrain
the third defendants from acquiring it or dealing with it in so far as they had acquired it.
The first defendant was the author of the musical play. The play had been produced
by the plaintiffs and was running in London and New York. The second defendants
were a private company, carrying on business as theatrical agents. The third defendants, Romulus Films, Ltd., had made an offer for the world film, radio and television
rights of the play. The fourth and fifth defendants were added in the course of the
application for the injunction as it appeared that the copyright in the play was to
some extent vested in them. By an agreement dated May 6, 1959, between the first
defendant and the plaintiffs, the plaintiffs were to have sole licence to perform " Oliver "
with living actors in Great Britain and certain other territories and the plaintiffs had
an option to acquire rights to produce " Oliver " in the United States of America and
Canada. The plaintiffs had exercised this option. Clause 11 of the agreement provided:

D

E

> " In the event of the [first defendant, i.e., the author] receiving a bona fide
> offer for the world motion picture, radio and commercial television rights, he shall
> immediately notify [the plaintiffs] of such offer and if such offer shall be unaccept-
> able to [the plaintiffs], then if [the plaintiffs] shall within ten days from the date
> of such notification submit a better bona fide counter-offer to [the first defendant]
> or shall offer to purchase such motion picture rights, radio and commercial tele-
> vision rights on the terms of the original offer [the first defendant] shall accept
> such offer of [the plaintiffs] but in default of [the plaintiffs] offering to purchase
> the motion picture, radio and television rights within such period of ten days then
> [the first defendant] shall be at liberty to accept or refuse the original offer. In the
> event of [the first defendant] accepting such offer he shall pay to [the plaintiffs]
> the share due to them under this agreement not later than ten days after their
> receipt by [the first defendant]."

F

G

On May 4, 1964, the third defendants had notice of the contents of the agreement of
May 5, 1959. On May 6, 1964, the first defendant notified the plaintiffs that he had
received an offer for the world rights. On May 13, 1964 (i.e., within the ten days) the
plaintiffs submitted an offer from Romulus Films, Ltd., which they claimed to be a
better offer. The plaintiffs accordingly contended that on May 13, 1964, the position
was crystallised by their having made a better counter-offer for the world rights. The
defendants, taking the view that the counter-offer was not a better offer, declined
the plaintiffs' offer, and on May 21, 1964, the plaintiffs issued the writ commencing
this action.

H

Sir Andrew Clark, Q.C., Michael O'Connell Stranders, Q.C., Leonard Lewis and *Dennis
Lloyd* for the plaintiffs.
  J. T. Molony, Q.C., A. J. Balcombe and *P. E. Webster* for the first, second, fourth and
fifth defendants.
  Norman C. Tapp for the third defendants.

I

UNGOED-THOMAS, J., having stated the facts leading up to the application
for an interlocutory injunction, continued: This is an interlocutory application for
relief until the hearing of the action. The principles on which this relief is granted
have been the subject of some argument before me. In 21 HALSBURY'S LAWS OF ENGLAND
(3rd Edn.) 365, para. 765 it is stated:

A   " *Prima facie case should be shown.* Where the plaintiff is asserting a right,
he should show a strong prima facie case, at least, in support of the right which
he asserts "; ...

Then in the next paragraph on p. 366, it is stated:

" Where any doubt exists as to the plaintiff's right, or if his right is not disputed,
but its violation is denied, the Court, in determining whether an interlocutory
injunction should be granted, takes into consideration the balance of convenience
B   to the parties and the nature of the injury which the defendant, on the one hand,
would suffer if the injunction was granted and he should ultimately turn out to be
right, and that which the plaintiff, on the other hand, might sustain if the injunction was refused and he should ultimately turn out to be right. The burden of
proof that the inconvenience which the plaintiff will suffer by the refusal of the
injunction is greater than that which the defendant will suffer, if it is granted,
lies on the plaintiff."

C   It is quite clear to my mind, from those two passages, that the first passage deals with
the need to assert the right which forms the basis on which the claim for relief is asked.
The second passage deals with the violation of that right and the considerations that
come into deciding whether an injunction should be granted when a violation, as
contrasted with the existence of the right, is what is in dispute.

I was referred to two cases where the existence of the right was in dispute, namely,
Preston v. *Luck* (1) and *Smith* v. *Grigg, Ltd.* (2), where it was stated that the court
had to be satisfied that there was a probability of success, or had to be satisfied that
D   there was a strong prima facie case in favour of the applicant. Both those cases, however,
were cases in which the existence of the right which formed the foundation of the
claim was in issue and were directed to that question. I was also referred to the case
of *Jones* v. *Pacaya Rubber and Produce Co., Ltd.* (3), where there was no difficulty about
the establishment of the right but the dispute was as to its infringement. There BUCKLEY,
L.J., stated (4):

E   " The question is, there being certainly a case to be tried, what is the proper
order to make? In all cases of applications for interlocutory injunctions the
governing principle is that pending the settlement of the dispute between the
parties the court will as far as possible keep matters in statu quo."

Then after referring to cases of CHITTY, J. (5), and NEVILLE, J. (6), BUCKLEY, L.J.,
added (7):

" For my part I am disposed to go further than NEVILLE, J., did in that case;
F   he seems to have treated the question as one of discretion. All injunctions are in
one sense a matter of discretion, but it is matter of right that upon proper terms
the property shall be maintained in statu quo pending the trial."

So in an application for the interlocutory injunction the applicant must establish a
probability or a strong prima facie case that he is entitled to the right of whose violation
he complains and, subject to this being established, the governing consideration is the
maintenance of the status quo pending the trial.

G   It is well-established that in deciding whether the matter shall be maintained in
statu quo regard must be had to the balance of convenience and to the extent to which
any damage to the plaintiff can be cured by payment of damages rather than by the
granting of an injunction. Of course the burden of proof lies on the applicant throughout.

[HIS LORDSHIP having said that there was no doubt about the existence of the agreement of May 5, 1959, and that any right of the plaintiffs turned on the construction
of cl. 11 of the agreement, said that the plaintiffs had established a right to transmit
a counter-offer of a third party as provided by cl. 11. HIS LORDSHIP then considered
H   the question whether the counter-offer was a better offer, and reached the conclusion
that the plaintiffs had established the rights in the sense in which they claimed them
under cl. 11 of the agreement, that it was desirable that the status quo should be
preserved until the trial and that in the circumstances the balance of convenience
was in favour of the plaintiffs.]

Interlocutory injunction granted.

Solicitors: *Goodman, Derrick & Co.* (for the plaintiffs); *Gouldens* (for the first, second,
I   fourth and fifth defendants); *Denton, Hall & Burgin* (for the third defendants).

[*Reported by* JACQUELINE METCALFE, *Barrister-at-Law.*]

---

(1) (1884), 27 Ch.D. 497.   (2) [1924] 1 K.B. 655.
(3) [1911] 1 K.B. 455.   (4) [1911] 1 K.B. at p. 457.
(5) *Ripley* v. *Paper Bottle Co.*, (1887), 57 L.J.Ch. 327.
(6) *Lamb* v. *Sambas Rubber and Gutta Percha Co., Ltd.*, [1908] 1 Ch. 845.
(7) [1911] 1 K.B. at p. 458.

OAK CO-OPERATIVE BUILDING SOCIETY
v. BLACKBURN AND OTHERS.

[CHANCERY DIVISION (Ungoed-Thomas, J.), January 19, 1967.]

Land Charge—Estate contract—Registration—Name of estate owner should be his proper, formal name—Registration of estate contract in name of " Frank David Blackburn " when true name was " Francis David Blackburn " ineffective to give protection against subsequent mortgage by estate owner— Land Charges Act, 1925 (15 & 16 Geo. 5 c. 22), s. 10 (2).

Land Charge—Search—Official certificate of search—Conclusiveness—Application for search against name of " Francis Davis Blackburn "—True name was " Francis David Blackburn "—Certificate not conclusive—Note on certificate mentioning existence of entries under name " Francis David Blackburn " and a different address—No conclusive effect—Land Charges Act, 1925 (15 & 16 Geo. 5 c. 22), s. 17 (3).

In 1958 the third defendant agreed to buy a house, 34, Union Street, Southport; she paid a deposit, entered into possession and thereafter paid agreed instalments. She had no copy of the contract. At about the end of 1959 an estate contract was registered under the Land Charges Act, 1925, s. 10 (2)* on her behalf against the name of " Frank David Blackburn ", which was intended to refer to the man who was vendor. The vendor applied subsequently to the plaintiff society for a mortgage. The plaintiff obtained an official certificate of search in the land charges register, applying for search against the name " Francis Davis Blackburn " and giving the proper description of the house. The official certificate bore a note— " No subsisting entries clearly affecting but the following entries which may or may not relate thereto appear ". Then it mentioned under names and addresses that there appeared the name " Blackburn, Francis David " and the address " 26, Crescent Road, Southport "; and a note was added saying " please note name is as given in the registration ". On the evidence the court inferred that the true name of the vendor was " Francis David Blackburn ". The plaintiff made an advance to the first defendant on mortgage. In proceedings by the plaintiff, as mortgagee, for possession,

Held: (i) the official certificate of search was conclusive under s. 17 (3)† of the Land Charges Act, 1925, that no estate contract was registered against " Francis Davis Blackburn ", but was not conclusive in regard to " Francis David Blackburn " (see p. 342, letter I, to p. 343, letter A, post).

(ii) the name of the estate owner in which under s. 10 (2) of the Act of 1925, registration of an estate contract had to be effected was his proper name and, therefore, registration of the estate contract in the name " Frank David Blackburn " was not effective under s. 10 (2) as the proper formal name was " Francis David Blackburn "; accordingly the plaintiff had shown title to possession (see p. 344, letter C, post).

Dunn v. *Chapman* ([1920] 2 Ch. 474) distinguished.

[As to registration of land charges being effected in the name of the estate owner, see 23 HALSBURY's LAWS (3rd Edn.) 57, para. 106; and as to registration constituting notice, see ibid., pp. 60, 61, para. 113; and as to the conclusiveness of an official certificate of search, see ibid., p. 98, para. 205; and for cases on that subject, see 35 DIGEST (Repl.) 312, *285*, and ante, p. 25.

For the Law of Property Act, 1925, s. 198, see 20 HALSBURY's STATUTES (2nd Edn.) 821.

For the Land Charges Act, 1925, s. 10 (2), s. 17 (3), see 20 HALSBURY's STATUTES (2nd Edn.) 1077, 1094.]

---

* Section 10 (2), so far as material, is set out at p. 343, letter C, post.
† Section 17 (3) is set out at p. 342, letter H, post.

A Case referred to:

Dunn v. *Chapman*, [1920] 2 Ch. 474; 89 L.J.Ch. 385; 123 L.T. 415; 40 Digest
(Repl.) 180, *1431.*

Adjourned Summons.

This was an application by originating summons dated June 15, 1964,
amended on Oct. 13, 1965, by the Oak Co-operative Building Society, the plaintiff,
B against (i) Francis David Blackburn, the first defendant, (ii) Southport Mortgage
Co., Ltd., the second defendant, and (iii) Phyllis Cairnwen Caines, the third
defendant. The plaintiff claimed against the defendants—1. That the defendants
and each of them should deliver up to the plaintiff the possession of the land
with the appurtenances and outbuildings thereto belonging situate and known as
34, Union Street, Southport, in the county of Lancaster. 2. That the defendants
C and each of them should pay to the plaintiff all moneys due to the plaintiff
in respect of the covenants in a legal charge made on Dec. 4, 1962, between
the first defendant of the one part and the plaintiff of the other part. 3. Payment
by the first defendant of all moneys due to the plaintiff under the covenants
contained in the legal charge. 4. That in default of the first defendant and the
plaintiff agreeing the amount due to the plaintiff an account might be taken of
D what was due to the plaintiff under and by virtue of the legal charge. 5. An
inquiry whether anything and if so what was due to the plaintiff for any costs,
charges and expenses. 6. That the legal charge should be enforced by foreclosure
or sale. 7. Delivery of possession by the third defendant to the plaintiff of the
premises No. 34, Union Street, Southport, being the premises comprised in the
legal charge. 8. The appointment of a receiver. The facts are set out in
E the judgment.

The cases noted below* were cited during the argument in addition to the
case referred to in the judgment.

D. M. Burton for the plaintiff.

B. C. Maddocks for the third defendant.

F The first and second defendants did not appear and were not represented.

UNGOED-THOMAS, J.: This is a mortgagee's application for possession
of the property, 34, Union Street, Southport. The first defendant is the mortgagor.
He is now a bankrupt. The second defendant, who does not appear before me,
was the second mortgagee and is not concerned with these proceedings. The
third defendant is a person who made a contract with the mortgagor to purchase
G the property from him. The third defendant's case is that she entered into this
contract for the purchase of the property and duly registered it as an estate
contract before the plaintiff's mortgage with the result, so she claims, that the
plaintiff is bound by that estate contract. The plaintiff's case is that, nevertheless,
the plaintiff on application for an official search of the land charges register
obtained, so far as relevant, a nil return and is therefore not bound by the
H contract for purchase or its registration. That briefly is the issue.

On Dec. 2, 1957, the mortgagor, the first defendant, purchased the property
for £1,900 and on the same day obtained a mortgage from a building society.
In January, 1958, the third defendant agreed to purchase the property from the
mortgagor. She did not consult a solicitor and she entered into some form of
agreement with the mortgagor. That form is not before me because the third
I defendant was never given a copy of it, but I am satisfied on her evidence, which
has not been subject to cross-examination, that she did enter into such an agreement, that she did enter into possession of the property in pursuance of the
agreement, that she paid a deposit and that she has since paid up to date, or
provided for, instalments in payment of the purchase money and interest on it.
In December, 1959, the third defendant consulted a solicitor and as a result
there was a registration as an estate contract of the agreement to purchase

* *Stock* v. *Wanstead & Woodford Borough Council*, [1961] 2 All E.R. 433; [1962]
2 Q.B. 479; *Du Sautoy* v. *Symes*, ante, p. 25.

which she made with the mortgagor, the first defendant. That registration **A**
was made in reference to the first defendant under the name of Frank David
Blackburn.   In October, 1962, the first defendant applied to the plaintiff for a
mortgage and in December of that year the plaintiff's then solicitor applied for
a search of the land charges register and on Dec. 3, 1962, the official certificate
of search was obtained.   The application for the search was in respect of the
land described as 34, Union Street, Southport and the Christian name and address **B**
indicated were respectively Francis Davis Blackburn, and 34, Union Street,
Southport, Lancashire.   The official certificate of the search bore a note near
the top of it " No subsisting entries clearly affecting but the following entries
which may or may not relate thereto appear ".   It then mentioned the following
entries:—in the first column under the heading " Names and Addresses " there
appears the name " Blackburn, Francis David ", not Davis, " 26, Crescent Road, **C**
Southport, Lancashire ", and there is a note alongside it which reads " Please,
note name is as given in the registration ".   Opposite that what was registered
was the then existing second mortgage on which nothing turns.

The question is, therefore, what is the effect of the third defendant's agreement
being registered in respect of the estate owner under the name of " Frank David
Blackburn " and of the application for the search being in respect of the name **D**
of " Francis Davis Blackburn ", the official certificate indicating that there
were entries which may or may not relate to this under the name of " Francis
David Blackburn ".

Section 198 (1) of the Law of Property Act, 1925, provides that the registration
of an estate contract " shall be deemed to constitute actual notice [of it] . . . to
all persons and for all purposes connected with the land affected ".   Subsection (2) **E**
provides that it applies to " instruments and matters required or authorised
to be registered under the Land Charges Act, 1925 ", which includes, under
s. 10, class C (iv) an estate contract such as the agreement made between the
first defendant and the third defendant in this case for the purchase of the
property with which we are concerned.   Section 13 (2) of the Land Charges
Act, 1925, provides—and I summarise—that an estate contract is void as against **F**
a purchaser for money or money's worth of the land charged, unless it is registered
before the completion of the purchase.   It is provided in the definition section,
s. 20 (8), that " ' Purchaser ' means any person (including a mortgagee or lessee)
who, for valuable consideration, takes any interest in land . . ."

Section 17 is the section which deals with searches, and it and s. 10 (2) are
the crucial enactments with which we are concerned in this case.   Section 17, **G**
so far as material, reads:

" (1) Where any person requires search to be made at the registry for
entries of any matters or documents, whereof entries are required or allowed
to be made in the registry by this Act, he may on payment of the prescribed
fee lodge at the registry a requisition in that behalf.

" (2) The registrar shall thereupon make the search required, and shall **H**
issue a certificate setting forth the result thereof.

" (3) In favour of a purchaser or an intending purchaser, as against persons
interested under or in respect of matters or documents whereof entries are
required or allowed as aforesaid, the certificate, according to the tenor
thereof, shall be conclusive, affirmatively or negatively, as the case may be.

" (4) Every requisition under this section shall be in writing, signed by the **I**
person making the same, specifying the name against which he desires search
to be made, or in relation to which he requires a certificate of result of search,
and other sufficient particulars."

The words " specifying the name against which he desires search to be made,
or in relation to which he requires a certificate of result of search " are crucial.
It follows, in my opinion, that the official certificate in this case was conclusive
that there was no registration of an estate contract against the name of " Francis

A Davis Blackburn ". It indicated that there was an entry against the name " Francis David Blackburn ", but it was not conclusive with regard to " Francis David Blackburn ". It merely brought the existence of that name and of an entry against it to the notice of the person who had sought a search against the name of " Francis Davis Blackburn ". Still less, of course, was it in any way conclusive in respect of " Frank David Blackburn ". If that is correct, it

B becomes necessary to consider whether or not the original registration of the estate contract by the third defendant against the name " Frank David Blackburn " was a proper and effective registration under the provisions of the property legislation.

Thus I come back to s. 10 (2) of the Land Charges Act, 1925. It provides that:

C   " A land charge shall be registered in the name of the estate owner whose estate is intended to be affected . . ."

We are not concerned with the last part of that subsection. The most important words are the words " in the name of the estate owner ". Here I have no difficulty in inferring, if inference is needed, that the true name of the first defendant is " Francis David Blackburn ". The documents of title throughout refer to

D him under that name; but it appears on the evidence that he carried on business under the name of " Frank " or " Frank David Blackburn ". The exact description in the agreement made between the first and third defendants is not established by producing that agreement because the third defendant is in no position to do so, but the registration which she effected some appreciable time later was in fact of course, as we know, in the name of " Frank David Blackburn ".

E It is urged for the third defendant that if a person is known by a particular name that is his name, but I find difficulty in accepting it in the context of this legislation. We are dealing here with title to land and it is clearly important that a person who is making a search for the registration of any charge on land should be able confidently to make that search in respect of a name corresponding to the name in which the charge should be registered. This legislation is not dealing

F with the ordinary day-to-day commercial transaction in which precision must necessarily be sacrificed to speed, but is dealing with the historically technical and intricate matter of title to land which is customarily and necessarily generally treated with greater precision. In matters of title to land precision has been habitually observed, and indeed in dealing with land and interests in land the usual course is for those matters to be entrusted to solicitors who are aware of the

G difficulties and are qualified to deal with them.

If it be important, as obviously it is, that a person applying for a search of a register should be able confidently to apply in respect of a name against which a charge would be registered, then it is important that the name of the estate owner should not be, so far as possible, subject to difficulties and doubts. That would be avoided if, as has for so very long been and is habitually in the case of

H dealings in land, the formal and proper name of that person were the name used— and in respect of which registration and search for registration were made. If that were not so, then where and how is the line to be drawn? Are abbreviated names to be searched for, e.g., " Dick " for " Richard "? Are all abbreviated names to be searched for such as " Harry " or " Hal " for " Henry "? Are names which may have nothing to do with the person's proper and formal

I name to be searched for, e.g., should a person who may be known in some places as " Jim ", although his name is neither " Jim " nor " James " but, shall we say, " Richard ", have to be searched for under all those names? If a person has aliases are all the aliases to be searched for, before a purchaser can with confidence rely on this certificate from the land registry? In this case the name " Frank " might be considered to be an abbreviation of " Francis ", though it is capable, of course, of existing as an entirely separate name independently altogether of Francis.

It was decided in the case of *Dunn* v. *Chapman* (1) that a requirement that a **A**
memorandum of registration of a lis pendens under the Judgments Act, 1839,
s. 7 should contain the name of the person whose estate was intended to be
affected thereby, was sufficiently complied with by containing his surname and
the initials of his Christian names. I am not dealing here, however, with the
adequacy of unmisleading names but with misleading differences in names; and
although it seems to me unsatisfactory that registration should be made with **B**
Christian names indicated by initials only, it is unnecessary to come to a conclusion on that for the purpose of this judgment since it is distinguishable from
the question before me.

It seems, therefore, to me that when s. 10 (2) provides that " A land charge
shall be registered in the name of the estate owner " what is contemplated is
that it shall be registered in his proper, formal names and not in any pet, familiar, **C**
nick or common forms of those names or any other names by which he may from
place to place or time to time be known.

It follows from what I have already said that in my view the registration of the
estate contract was not registered in the name of the estate owner within the
requirements of s. 10 (2) of the Land Charges Act, 1925. Apart from the consideration which I am just going to mention, I would therefore make an order **D**
for possession in favour of the plaintiff.

This case, however, has come before me apparently somewhat hurriedly, at
any rate in its last stages, and it emerged in the course of the day and indeed on
the face of the evidence, which unfortunately counsel for the third defendant had
not had adequate time to consider fully in his client's interest, that the first
defendant who had applied to the plaintiff for a mortgage on the occasion of what **E**
was apparently presumed to be the purchase of this property had in fact, as I
have already stated, purchased this property some years ago, in 1957. Questions
might arise—and the less I say about this the better, and that is why I restrict
my observations so narrowly—whether the plaintiff might be affected by notice
of matters which might conceivably enable the third defendant to rely in answer
to the plaintiff's claim on matters not affected by the operation of the property **F**
legislation to which I have referred. In those circumstances it is only proper that
the third defendant should have the opportunity with her advisers of considering
the possibility of such an answer, and I therefore would make any order for
possession subject to terms which would give them ample opportunity for such
consideration. The course I therefore propose to adopt—but if need be I will
hear counsel further on this—is to make an order for possession suspended for **G**
twenty-eight days with a provision that in the event of the third defendant wishing
to apply to have raised in this action matters other than the issue on which I have
given judgment she should have the opportunity to do so before possession, and
that in that event the order for possession should be suspended pending the final
disposal of this action. The order for possession which I would make, so
suspended, would in the event of this action raising other issues as I have **H**
indicated, be, of course, subject to any further order made with regard to it.

[After hearing counsel, HIS LORDSHIP continued:] The order for possession
shall be suspended for six weeks, with a provision for making an application
limited to its being made within fourteen days. If not made within fourteen days,
then on the expiration of twenty-eight days from the expiration of the fourteen
days, the third defendant will have to go. **I**

Order accordingly.

Solicitors: *Brown, Turner, Compton Carr & Co.*, Southport (for the plaintiff);
Brighouses, Southport (for the third defendant).

[*Reported by* JACQUELINE METCALFE, *Barrister-at-Law.*]

---

(1) [1920] 2 Ch. 474.

A   UNITED DOMINIONS TRUST (COMMERCIAL), LTD. *v.* ENNIS.

[COURT OF APPEAL, CIVIL DIVISION (Lord Denning, M.R., Harman and Salmon, L.JJ.), February 16, 17, 20, 1967.]

Hire-Purchase—Termination of agreement—Option for finance company to termi-
nate agreement for hirer's breach—Option for hirer to terminate agreement
B   *—Minimum payment clause applicable on exercise of option—Hirer returning*
car to dealers and regretting inability to pay instalments—Letter by hirer sent
at instance of finance company expressing wish to terminate agreement—
Claim by finance company under minimum payment clause—Whether option
exercised by finance company or by hirer—Whether repudiation of agreement
by hirer—Whether any sum recoverable by finance company under hire-
C   *purchase agreement.*

On Dec. 8, 1959, the hirer, who was a waterman, obtained a 1957 Jaguar motor car on hire-purchase terms. The cash price was £1,095; the initial payment was £219 and the monthly instalments were £24 9s. 1d. each. The hire-purchase agreement gave (by cl. 8) the finance company an option to terminate the agreement for the hirer's breach, and it provided (by cl. 10)—
D   " the hirer may at any time terminate the hiring by returning the goods at his own expense and risk to the [finance company] at such place as shall be appointed by the [finance company] . . .". There was a minimum payment clause (cl. 11) whereby " should the hiring be terminated by the hirer under cl. 10 hereof or by the [finance company] under cl. 8 hereof the hirer shall . . . forthwith pay to the [finance company] . . . such further sum as with the total
E   amount of any instalments previously paid hereunder with equal two-thirds of the total hiring cost . . .". When the first instalment was due there was a dock strike, and the hirer telephoned the finance company saying that he was sorry but he could not pay. Subsequently he telephoned again saying that he would like to get rid of the worry of the car, and that he had left it and the keys with the dealers. At the instance of the finance company the hirer sent
F   them a letter, dated Jan. 28, 1960, to the effect that he wished to terminate the agreement. In reply the finance company informed the hirer that under the terms of the hire-purchase agreement he had a further liability of £709 10s. 8d. In March, 1963, the finance company sued alleging that the full minimum payment under cl. 11 had become due but limiting their claim to £271 16s. In November, 1963, they amended to allege an alternative plea
G   that the hirer had repudiated the hire-purchase agreement by his letter of Jan. 28, 1960.

Held: (i) what the hirer had done did not constitute an exercise of his option under cl. 10 of the hire-purchase agreement, and the true inference from the facts was that, there having been no consensual termination of the hire-purchase agreement, the finance company should be regarded as having
H   exercised their option under cl. 8 to terminate the hire-purchase agreement for the hirer's breach; on that basis the sum payable under the provisions of the minimum payment clause (cl. 11) was a penalty and the £271 16s. was not recoverable, nor could the finance company recover the one instalment which fell into arrear in January, 1960, for they had not claimed it in their pleading and, more than six years having elapsed since it became due, any claim for
I   it was barred by lapse of time (see p. 348, letter F, p. 349, letter A, p. 350, letter E, p. 350, letter I, to p. 351, letter A, p. 351, letter I, and p. 352, letter I, post).

Bridge v. *Campbell Discount Co., Ltd.* ([1962] 1 All E.R. 385) applied.

(ii) even if there had been repudiation of the hire-purchase agreement by the hirer, the finance company had not accepted it, because, by claiming under the minimum payment clause, they had elected to treat the contract as continuing (see p. 349, letter B, p. 350, letter H, and p. 352, letter H, post).

Per LORD DENNING, M.R.; The hirer is not to be taken to exercise the

option unless he does so consciously, knowing of the consequences, and **A**
avowedly in exercise of the option (see p. 348, letter D, post).

Appeal allowed.

Cases referred to:

Associated Distributors, Ltd. v. *Hall*, [1938] 1 All E.R. 511; [1938] 2 K.B. 83;
     107 L.J.K.B. 701; 158 L.T. 236; 26 Digest (Repl.) 667, *39*.

Bridge v. *Campbell Discount Co., Ltd.*, [1962] 1 All E.R. 385; [1962] A.C. 600; **B**
     [1962] 2 W.L.R. 439; Digest (Cont. Vol. A) 648, *39a*.

Financing, Ltd. v. *Baldock*, [1963] 1 All E.R. 443; [1963] 2 Q.B. 104; [1963]
     2 W.L.R. 359; Digest (Cont. Vol. A) 650, *77d*.

Goulston Discount Co., Ltd. v. *Harman*, (1962), 106 Sol. Jo. 369.

Appeal.

C

This was an appeal by the defendant hirer from a judgment of His Honour
JUDGE GLAZEBROOK, dated July 27, 1966, at Gravesend county court giving
judgment for the plaintiff finance company for £271 16s., being the amount
claimed by the finance company (a) under a minimum payment clause in a hire-
purchase agreement on the footing that the hirer had exercised his option under
that agreement to terminate it, and alternatively (b) as damages for the repudia- **D**
tion of the hire-purchase agreement by the hirer by letter dated Jan. 28, 1960,
expressing a wish to terminate the agreement owing to inability to pay instalments. The hirer had paid into court £24 9s. 1d., being the amount of the first
instalment. The facts are set out in the judgment of LORD DENNING, M.R.

The cases noted below* were cited during the argument in addition to those
referred to in the judgments.

E

R. P. Ground for the hirer.
P. Goodenday for the finance company.

LORD DENNING, M.R.: Mr. Ennis is a waterman in the Port of London.
On Dec. 8, 1959, he obtained a 1957 Jaguar car on hire-purchase terms. The
cash price was £1,095. He paid the initial instalment of £219. The monthly **F**
instalments payable over four years were £24 9s. 1d. The first monthly instalment
was due on Jan. 8, 1960; but just at that time there was a dockers' strike which
affected his wages very adversely. He got into difficulties. He could not pay the
first instalment of £24 9s. 1d. He telephoned the finance company and said he
was sorry but he could not pay. Their representative told him to wait a little while
to see if things improved; but the strike went on. So on Jan. 26 he telephoned **G**
the finance company again. He told them that the strike was still on and he would
like to " get rid of the worry of the car ". Their representative made this note at
the time:

> " Hirer phoned to say he is unable to maintain instalments. He has seen
> Schofields [the dealers] but they are not prepared to settle on our figures. He
> has left car and keys with dealers, and will forward surrender letter on lines **H**
> suggested by me. Seems a decent bloke—worried to death."

The finance company's representative dictated to the hirer the terms of a letter
which the hirer then wrote on Jan. 28, 1960, to the finance company:

> " Dear Sir, I am writing to inform you I wish to terminate my agreement
> with you as I find I cannot fulfil the terms stated. Please find enclosed the **I**
> keys of the car and also the log book. The car is now at Schofield's Service
> Station."

In reply the finance company wrote on Feb. 2:

---

* *James Finlay & Co., Ltd.* v. *N.V. Kwik Hoo Tong Handel Maatschappij*, [1928]
2 K.B. 604; *on appeal* [1928] All E.R. Rep. 110; [1929] 1 K.B. 400; *Jewelowski* v.
Propp, [1944] 1 All E.R. 483; [1944] 1 K.B. 510; *Cooden Engineering Co., Ltd.* v.
Stanford, [1952] 2 All E.R. 915; [1953] 1 Q.B. 86; *Lombank, Ltd.* v. *Excell*, [1963]
3 All E.R. 486; [1964] 1 Q.B. 415.

A   " Dear Sir, Jaguar TRV 944. Arrears: £24 9s. 1d. January. We are in receipt of your letter of Jan. 28, informing us that you wish to terminate the above agreement and surrender our vehicle to us, and enclosing registration book and keys. Steps are accordingly being taken to repossess our property. We have to advise you that under the terms of the hire-purchase agreement that you have signed, you have a further liability of £709 10s. 8d., and it may

B   be necessary for us to apply to you for payment of this at a later date."

There was some delay in taking possession because the finance company made a mistake about the keys: but eventually on Feb. 10 they did take possession of the car. The hirer had only had it for seven or eight weeks. He had only done between 250 and three hundred miles. He and his wife had looked after the car very well and with every care during that time. The judge so found.

C   The net result is this: the finance company had received £219 by way of initial instalment. They had taken the car back within two months. Yet they demanded in addition a sum of £709 10s. 8d. They said that it was payable under the minimum payment clause, being two-thirds of the hire-purchase price. They repeated their demand every month for the next three months; but then they let the matter drop for nearly three years. On Nov. 26, 1962, they wrote again;

D   and on Mar. 27, 1963, they issued a writ in the High Court against the hirer alleging:

" The [hirer] being in arrear in payment of the first instalment of hire rental payable under the said agreement of £24 9s. 1d. by notice in writing dated Jan. 28, 1960, as he was entitled, terminated the hiring created by the said

E   agreement and surrendered the said motor car to the [finance company]. In the premises the [finance company] became entitled to the sum of £709 10s. 8d. payable under cl. 11 of the said agreement."

They, however, added that " the [finance company] nevertheless release and abandon so much of their said entitlement as exceeds the sum of £271 16s.".

The pleading stood in that form until Nov. 4, 1963, when the finance company

F   amended it so as to allege a repudiation. They alleged in the alternative that the hirer " by the said notice dated Jan. 28, 1960, evinced an intention no longer to be bound by the said agreement ", and they claimed £271 16s. damages for breach of contract. The hirer did not enter an appearance and the finance company on Dec. 10, 1963, signed judgment; but it was afterwards set aside and the matter transferred to the county court.

G   The county court judge held that the hirer had exercised the option to terminate the agreement: that the case was governed by the decision of this court in *Associated Distributors, Ltd.* v. *Hall* (1). So he gave judgment for the finance company on the ground that the minimum payment clause was available to them. Alternatively, he held that if the hirer did not exercise this option to terminate, he repudiated the contract, and that the finance company accepted

H   the repudiation when they amended their pleading in November, 1963. He said that they could recover damages for repudiation. The hirer appeals to this court.

The first point (and it is the cardinal point in the case) is whether the hirer exercised the option to terminate the hiring. The option is given by cl. 10, which provides:

I   " The hirer may at any time terminate the hiring by returning the goods at his own expense and risk to [the finance company] at such place as shall be appointed by [the finance company] in a good state of repair and in good working order and condition."

It is followed by the minimum clause, cl. 11, which provides that

" should the hiring be terminated by the hirer under cl. 10 hereof or by the [finance company] under cl. 8 hereof, the hirer shall . . . forthwith pay to the [finance company] . . . such further sum as with the total amount of any

(1) [1938] 1 All E.R. 511; [1938] 2 K.B. 83.

instalments previously paid hereunder will equal two-thirds of the total   A
hiring cost shown in the schedule as agreed compensation for depreciation
of the goods."

The cases show this. If the hiring is terminated by the finance company under
cl. 8 (which gives the finance company power to terminate for a breach by the
hirer), then cl. 11 is a penalty. The courts will not enforce it. That was decided   B
by the House of Lords in *Bridge* v. *Campbell Discount Co., Ltd.* (2). If, however,
the hiring is terminated by the hirer under the option given to him by cl. 10, there
is a decision of this court that the finance company can enforce cl. 11 in its full
rigour. They get the car back and also two-thirds of the hire-purchase price.
That was decided in *Associated Distributors, Ltd.* v. *Hall* (3), which is said to have
been followed in *Goulston Discount Co., Ltd.* v. *Harman* (4).   C

In *Bridge* v. *Campbell Discount Co., Ltd.* (5), sitting in the House of Lords, I
expressed the view that *Associated Distributors, Ltd.* v. *Hall* (3) was wrongly
decided. So did LORD DEVLIN (6). I retain that view and I think that it is open
to this court to reconsider this decision; but it is unnecessary to do so today.
For this very good reason. Accepting for the moment that *Associated Distributors,
Ltd.* v. *Hall* (3) is good law and that a hirer, by exercising the option, does commit   D
himself to paying this large sum, then I say this: a hirer is not to be taken to
exercise such an option unless he does so consciously, knowing of the consequences,
and avowedly in exercise of the option. If this were not so, the document would
be an absolute trap set to catch him. Not one hirer in a thousand reads these
small printed clauses. Even if he did, he would not understand them. When he
returns the car, he naturally assumes that is an end of the hiring and, in conse-   E
quence, an end of the instalments. He should not be held bound to make in
addition this tremendous payment—as the price of termination—unless he knows
what he is doing. In order to bind him to it, knowledge of it must be brought
home to him in fact so as to amount to a new agreement by him to pay the sum.

On the facts this case is very like *Bridge* v. *Campbell Discount Co., Ltd.* (2).
The hirer, like Mr. Bridge, said: " I am sorry but I cannot keep up the instal-   F
ments." That was not the exercise of an option such as to render him liable for
another £709. It was simply an intimation that he could no longer keep up the
instalments and he wanted the agreement brought to an end. The finance company replied saying that steps were being taken to repossess the car. This might
have been regarded as a consensual termination, with no claims on either side
save for past arrears; but that was not pleaded or argued. In the absence of a   G
consensual termination, the finance company must be taken to have terminated
the hiring under the powers given to them by cl. 8 of the agreement. That clause
says that

" should the hirer fail to pay ... any subsequent instalment ... [the
finance company] may forthwith and without any notice terminate the
hiring."   H

That is how this agreement came to an end. The finance company exercised
their right to terminate the hiring: and the hirer was content that they should
do so. On such a termination the finance company cannot rely on the minimum
payment clause: for the simple reason that they are terminating for a breach;
and in that case the minimum payment clause is a penalty and unenforceable
under the decision of the House of Lords in *Bridge* v. *Campbell Discount Co., Ltd.*   I
(2). They can recover for such breaches only as had taken place prior to the
termination. The only breach which they can establish is the non-payment of
one instalment; see *Financings, Ltd.* v. *Baldock* (7). In their pleading, however,

(2) [1962] 1 All E.R. 385; [1962] A.C. 600.
(3) [1938] 1 All E.R. 511; [1938] 2 K.B. 83.   (4) (1962), 106 Sol. Jo. 369.
(5) [1962] 1 All E.R. at p. 400, letter I; [1962] A.C. at p. 631.
(6) [1962] 1 All E.R. at pp. 401, 402; [1962] A.C. at p. 633.
(7) [1963] 1 All E.R. 443; [1963] 2 Q.B. 104.

A   they have not sued for that instalment. More than six years have elapsed since the instalment fell due. It is far too late for them to claim it now.

There remains the alternative claim for repudiation. It is said that the hirer repudiated the contract. I very much doubt myself whether his letters and his conduct should be considered as repudiation. He was simply asking for the agreement to be terminated. He was not repudiating it; but even if it be treated

B   as a repudiation, it is clear that the repudiation was never accepted by the finance company. After receiving his letter, they treated the contract as still continuing. They claimed under the minimum payment clause, which is a thing that they could not possibly have done if there had been an acceptance of repudiation. By so doing, they elected to treat it as continuing. Counsel for the finance company said they accepted the repudiation by retaking possession of

C   the car; but that was not pleaded. Nor has it ever been suggested hitherto. The county court judge said that they accepted the repudiation in November, 1963, when they amended their pleading. That was far too late. They had already evinced their intention to treat the agreement as continuing. I do not think that they can rely on the alleged repudiation.

D   If it had been a case of repudiation, the question of damages would arise. I very much doubt whether the finance company could have shown any damage at all. They had the initial instalment of £219: and got the car back after two months. Taking the figures in Glass's Guide, even after the two months, it looks as if it was worth then £900 or £1,000. That is good evidence of the sum which it might reasonably be expected to realise. Whereas they sold it to the trade for £640. I need not, however, pursue the matter. The only possible claim by the

E   finance company is on the minimum payment clause: and they cannot recover on it for the reasons which I have given.

I would, therefore, allow the appeal and enter judgment for the hirer.

HARMAN, L.J.: The finance company sued in reliance on the hire-purchase agreement, and they sued on the footing that the relevant clause was that which

F   entitled the hirer at his option to terminate the agreement; and it was said that that was what he had done. If that is right and there was no breach, then there is no penalty clause involved and the utmost rigours of the agreement might come into force which would result in a sum of over £700 being payable to the finance company. That frightened the finance company. The car had been in the possession of the hirer for only six or seven weeks. It had been very little used and had

G   been very well maintained. The finance company had had the deposit, they had the car back, and they claimed £700 in addition. They saw that that would not wear and they reduced their claim by some arbitrary process, which I do not understand, to £271. That is what they sued for, simply saying that they forgave the hirer the rest. That shows that one must regard this agreement with the greatest caution.

H   After a time the finance company came to the conclusion that there might be another way in which they could put their case. After having appeared before the master and had rather a hostile reception from him, they asked leave to amend and they amended by alleging that there had been a repudiation by the hirer of the agreement and claiming the £271 as damages for repudiation. There was nothing in the pleadings about what acceptance there was of that repudiation.

I   When the trial came on, they pinned their faith to the view that the acceptance was the amendment of the pleadings three years or more later than the alleged act of repudiation. That claim the county court judge thought was a good claim. He did not decide it on that ground: he decided it on the ground that he was bound to hold, though he did not like it, that there being no penalty because there was no breach of the agreement, the finance company were entitled to enforce the option clause, if I may so call it, by which the hirer, it was said, had terminated the agreement.

For myself I must say that if I had agreed with that view, I should have felt **A**
bound to come to the same conclusion, because I do not think that there can be
a penalty without a breach of contract, for which the penalty may be the result.
In my judgment there was never an exercise by the hirer of this so-called option.
I agree with the view of LORD MORTON OF HENRYTON in *Bridge* v. *Campbell
Discount Co., Ltd.* (8), where he said:

" I am of the opinion, however, that the appellant never had the slightest **B**
intention of exercising the option contained in cl. 6, and the terms of his
letter show that he did not have cl. 6 in mind. He frankly and simply informs
the respondents that ' I will not be able to pay any more payments on the
Bedford Dormobile '. There is no reference to any option, and I cannot
reconcile the statement just quoted with the view that he intended to exercise
an option, the terms whereof put him under an immediate obligation to pay **C**
a further large sum to the respondents. To my mind, the letter means that
the writer feels reluctantly compelled to break his agreement, and the
apologetic terms of the letter confirm me in this view. Why should the
hirer apologise so humbly, twice, if he thought that he was merely exercising
an option given to him by the agreement? "

D
Then he mentions another indication. The words quoted seem to me to be entirely
apposite to the instant case.

Here there is a different consideration. The consideration relied on by the
finance company here was the exercise of the option by giving a notice. That was
the only thing pleaded as being an exercise of the option; but under this agreement, the option, unlike that in *Bridge* v. *Campbell Discount Co., Ltd.* (9), **E**
was exercisable not by a notice but by the return of the car to the finance company; the hirer gave notice and returned it to the dealers. Therefore he did
not exercise the option. Much less did it appear that in substance it was either
in his head or in that of the finance company's representative that any use was
being made of this clause. I would not hold that he did exercise it. It would
indeed be a matter for question. The letter he wrote was written at the dictation **F**
of the finance company, and if they were going to say, after dictating to him
the terms of the letter, that he had exercised the option which caused them to
be entitled to £700 more, they were at least bound to warn him. They did not
do so because the representative himself never had such an idea in his mind.
So much for the option point.

As to the other point, I think that it may be said that the letter was the **G**
expression of a determination not to be bound any further by the agreement. If
there had been a prompt acceptance of that, I am not sure I should not have held
that there was a repudiation, because a repudiation needs both the expression of
such an intention and its acceptance on the other side. There clearly was no
acceptance on the other side. The finance company elected not to accept repudiation; they elected to treat the agreement as binding and to sue the hirer under it **H**
and not to sue him for damages for its breach. Therefore, they cannot rely on
repudiation.

There remains the possibility that they had the right to terminate, even
though the hirer had committed no fundamental breach, but a breach in that he
had not paid one instalment and they had the right to put an end to the agreement. That fits the facts best. He writes to them and says: " Would you put **I**
an end to the agreement? I cannot go on with it. I am very sorry." They, after
a couple of weeks, take the car back from where he told them that he had left
it, he having already left the keys and the log book with them. That seems to
me to be an exercise by the finance company of their rights. If that is so, that
of course does not prevent them suing for damages, but their damages are
limited to the breaches committed up to the date when they exercised their

(8) [1962] 1 All E.R. at p. 391; [1962] A.C. at p. 615.
(9) [1962] 1 All E.R. 385; [1962] A.C. 600.

A   right, as in *Financings, Ltd.* v. *Baldock* (10), to which LORD DENNING, M.R., has referred. The suggestion that damages are at large, as they might be if there had been an accepted repudiation, does not arise. The only thing to which the finance company could be entitled would be £24, the current missing instalment. For that they have never sued.

B   As to treating the £271 as damages for that breach, namely, the non-payment of one instalment, it would not be possible to succeed on that ground, even if it was otherwise valid because it would clearly be a penalty clause within the meaning of the decision of the House of Lords in *Bridge* v. *Campbell Discount Co., Ltd.* (11). Whether if there was a repudiation there would be a substantial amount of damages due as general damages, I do not propose to stop to consider. There are difficult questions involved and I prefer to leave them alone.

C   I agree with LORD DENNING, M.R., that this appeal must be allowed.

SALMON, L.J.: Clause 10 of the hire-purchase agreement gives the hirer an option of terminating the agreement in a particular way,

> " by returning the goods at his own expense and risk to the [finance company] at such place as shall be appointed by the [finance company] in
D   a good state of repair . . . "

That purports to confer a benefit on the hirer. It is, of course, a snare and delusion, because if the hirer elects to exercise the option to terminate the agreement under that clause, he finds himself liable under the following clause to pay the finance company a sum equal to two-thirds of the total hiring costs outstanding at the date of the termination—in this case, some £709. One has this rather anomalous
E   position. Suppose a hirer is one instalment in arrear and does nothing at all except perhaps intimate that he is in financial difficulty. The finance company then has power to retake the car under cl. 8 and claim two-thirds of the hiring costs under cl. 11; but in circumstances such as those, *Bridge* v. *Campbell Discount Co., Ltd.* (11) shows quite plainly that the finance company could not recover any part of the outstanding instalments under cl. 11 because the sum
F   stipulated in the clause would constitute a penalty and would accordingly be irrecoverable. If, on the other hand, the hirer terminates under cl. 10, it is, at any rate, doubtful whether the obligation specified in cl. 11 to pay two-thirds of the outstanding hiring charges is a penalty. There is, I think, much to be said for the view that this court may be bound to hold that in these circumstances it would not be a penalty and would be recoverable. Accordingly, the hirer
G   who avails himself of the option which the finance company purports to give him under cl. 10 would be doing himself a very great disservice.

Now the first question in this case is: was this hiring terminated by the hirer under cl. 10? As I have already said, this clause states precisely the manner in which the hiring may be terminated under it. The hiring cannot be terminated in any other way under that clause, not, for instance, by writing a letter.
H   On the evidence, the hirer did not terminate the hiring under cl. 10. He did not return the goods to the finance company at a place appointed by them. It is, of course, obvious that when the hirer does what this hirer did, the finance company may agree with the hirer that they will treat the agreement as terminated. The hire-purchase agreement is then terminated by that subsequent agreement made between the parties. The hirer cannot be liable to pay two-
I   thirds of the outstanding charges unless that obligation was undertaken in what I have referred to as the subsequent agreement. If one thing is clear in this case, it is this, that the hirer certainly never agreed orally or by letter that he was prepared to pay £709 or any other sum to the finance company. He did not terminate under cl. 10, and I cannot see, therefore, how there is any ground for saying that the agreement to terminate gave the finance company any right to the sum of £709 or any part of it. If there was no agreed termination, then

---

(10) [1963] 1 All E.R. 443; [1963] 2 Q.B. 104.
(11) [1962] 1 All E.R. 385; [1962] A.C. 600.

I think that the finance company must be taken to have repossessed the goods **A** under cl. 8, as they were entitled to do since the hirer was in arrear with the first instalment. As I have already stated, this would give the finance company no right to recover any part of what would then clearly be a penalty under cl. 11.

When the finance company launched the action, they were claiming solely under cl. 11. They alleged that they were entitled to two-thirds of the out- **B** standing charges, but graciously conceded that they were prepared to restrict their claim to £270 odd. That no doubt is because they lacked the hardihood to come into open court and try to extract £709 from the hirer. This would have been obviously harsh and unconscionable and the publicity of such an action would have to fail from a business point of view. And this they no doubt realised. It is to be observed in the correspondence that again and **C** again they pressed the hirer for £709, and if he had been prepared to make arrangements with them to discharge that sum over the years, there can be little doubt but that they would have collected it from him. When they found that he was not making any response satisfactory to them in relation to their request for £709, they wrote him a letter stating, quite inaccurately, that their damages were in the region of £533 and that as a concession they would restrict **D** the claim to that amount; but he still would not pay and so they came to court claiming under cl. 11 only £270, which they say is equivalent to the damage which they have suffered. It seems to me plain that they have no claim under cl. 11 of the agreement because the agreement was not terminated under cl. 10. Either it was terminated under cl. 8 (in which case cl. 11 was a penalty clause) or it was terminated under another agreement made between the parties and **E** in that other agreement no obligation was undertaken by the hirer to pay £709 or £270 or any other sum.

Then the finance company alleged by way of amendment that they could recover the £270 as damages for breach of agreement, because what the hirer did some weeks after he had had the car amounted to a wrongful repudiation of the agreement. I am inclined myself to take the same view as HARMAN, L.J., **F** that it would be very difficult for the hirer to resist the contention that what he wrote and did in fact amounted to a repudiation. A wrongful repudiation of a contract has no effect in law, however, unless it is accepted by the other party to the contract. The judge has found that the alleged wrongful repudiation was accepted by the amendment of the writ nearly four years after it took place. That means that the judge's finding is to the effect that the agreement continued **G** for a period of nearly four years before being determined by the amendment of the writ; this he found operated as an acceptance of the repudiation made four years previously. Whatever doubt there may be about any of the issues that have been raised in this case, it seems to me that there can be no doubt at all but that that finding is wholly untenable. There is no cross-notice setting up any other acceptance of the repudiation, and therefore, even if what the hirer **H** did amounts to a repudiation, as I think that it does, it was not accepted and therefore was of no effect. Accordingly, the point which has been argued as to the true basis for the assessment of the damages does not arise. The only claim that the finance company could have had would have been for the first instalment which is now more than six years overdue and which has not been claimed. **I**

In these circumstances I agree with my lords that this appeal must be allowed.

Appeal allowed. Leave to appeal to the House of Lords refused.

Solicitors: *Church, Bruce, Hawkes & Brasington*, Gravesend (for the hirer); *Edwin Coe & Calder Woods* (for the finance company).

[*Reported by* F. GUTTMAN, ESQ., *Barrister-at-Law.*]

A   GARNAC GRAIN CO., INC. *v.* H. M. F. FAURE &
FAIRCLOUGH, LTD. AND BUNGE CORPORATION.

[HOUSE OF LORDS (Lord Reid, Lord Morris of Borth-y-Gest, Lord Pearce, Lord
Wilberforce and Lord Pearson), February 13, 14, 15, 16, 20, 21, 22, 23, 27, 28,
March 1, April 26, 1967.]

B *Agent—Creation of agency—Agency for entering into contract—Circle of contracts made on same day whereby A. sold goods and subsequently re-bought
the goods from another purchaser further down the chain of buyers—Transactions designed by A. for financial reasons—Written contracts enforceable
according to their tenor—Whether buyer who re-sold to A. acted in his purchase
from a previous buyer as agent for A. as undisclosed principal—Contracts*
C *genuine, not shams.*

*Contract—Breach—Damages—Date at which damages assessed—Sale of goods
c.i.f.—Election by buyers to accept sellers' repudiation on Jan. 24—Failure
of sellers, if contract had continued, to send shipping documents, which
would have reached buyers on Feb. 4—Damages, difference between value and
contract price, assessed at Feb. 4.*

D *Contract—Repudiation—Election whether to accept repudiation—Writ issued
claiming declaration that contract valid and claiming damages for its breach
—Writ not served—Whether election to accept repudiation.*

In July, 1963, four companies entered into a chain of four successive
contracts for the sale of fifteen thousand tons of lard, for shipment to
England, each sale being at a higher price than the last and the original
first sellers being also the last purchasers. Shipment was to be in December,
E 1963/January, 1964. Owing to the financial collapse of the original sellers
the contracts could not be fulfilled. By the end of January, 1964, the
market price of lard had risen considerably. By their solicitors' letter
dated Jan. 17, 1964, the second buyers, G., claimed to rescind their contract
with F., who bought from them, on the ground that F. acted as undisclosed
F agents for the original sellers and that fraud on the part of the original
sellers entitled G. to rescind as against F. On Jan. 24, 1964, a writ was issued
by F.'s assignees against G. claiming a declaration that the contract of sale
by G. was valid and damages for its breach. This writ was not served.
By letter dated Jan. 24, 1964, the solicitors for F.'s assignees rejected
G.'s claim to be entitled to rescind; this letter did not refer to the writ.
G In an action by G. both F. and F.'s assignees counterclaimed for damages
for breach of the contract for sale. Damages were assessed on the basis
of the market price on Feb. 4, 1964, the date on which shipping documents
might have been expected to have reached F. if they had been dispatched
on Jan. 31, 1964. On appeal it was held that F. had not contracted as
agents for the first sellers, with the consequence that the question whether
H the fraud of the first sellers could be relied on by G. as a ground for rescission
of the contract with F. did not arise. On further appeal,

Held: (i) in agreeing to buy from G. and to sell to the first seller F. acted
as principals, not as agents for the first sellers (see p. 359, letter A, and
p. 355, letters D and E, post).

(ii) by the issue of the writ F.'s assignees were primarily claiming a declara-
I tion that the contract for sale was valid and accordingly, notwithstanding
the further claim for damages, F.'s assignees were not electing by the issue
of the writ to treat the contract as terminated (see p. 360, letter E, and
p. 355, letters D and E, post).

(iii) even if F.'s assignees had, by the mere issue of the writ, elected to treat
G.'s refusal to perform the contract as repudiation of it, so that the contract
was rescinded on Jan. 24, 1964, the true date for ascertaining the difference
in market price for the purpose of assessing damages would have still been
Feb. 4, 1964, because it would have been on that date that F.'s assignees

Dictum of LORD PEARSON at 358
applied in ATLAS MARITIME v AVALON
MARITIME (No 1) [1991] 4 All ER 769

Followed in SHEARSON
MACLAINE WATSON (No
3 All ER 723 LEHMAN v
2) [1990]

were deprived of the market value of the goods (see p. 360, letter G, and   **A**
p. 355, letters D and E, post).

Decision of the COURT OF APPEAL ([1965] 3 All E.R. 273) affirmed.

[As to the contractual position where the fact of a party being an agent is not
disclosed, see 1 HALSBURY'S LAWS (3rd Edn.) 228, para. 516; as to the position
arising on the fraud of principal or agent, see ibid., p. 221, para. 502; and for
cases on the subject, see 1 DIGEST (Repl.) 681-687, *2435-2456.*   **B**

As to the assessment of damages for breach of a contract for the sale of goods
by reference to the market price, see 34 HALSBURY'S LAWS (3rd Edn.) 149, 150,
para. 248; and as to mitigation of damages, see 11 HALSBURY'S LAWS (3rd Edn.)
290, 291, para. 478; and for cases on that subject, see 17 DIGEST (Repl.) 107-111,
224-248.

As to election to accept repudiation, see 8 HALSBURY'S LAWS (3rd Edn.) 204,   **C**
para. 344, text and notes (c), (d) and 34 ibid., pp. 147, 148, para. 245.]

Cases referred to:

Frost v. *Knight,* [1861-73] All E.R. Rep. 221; (1872), L.R. 7 Exch. 111;
    41 L.J.Ex. 78; 26 L.T. 77; 17 Digest (Repl.) 108, *224.*

Heyman v. *Darwins, Ltd.,* [1942] 1 All E.R. 337; [1942] A.C. 356; 111 L.J.K.B.   **D**
    241; 166 L.T. 306; 2 Digest (Repl.) 492, *435.*

Hochster v. *De la Tour,* [1843-60] All E.R. Rep. 12; (1853), 2 E. & B. 678;
    22 L.J.Q.B. 455; 22 L.T.O.S. 171; 118 E.R. 922; 17 Digest (Repl.)
    103, *174.*

Lamb (W. T.) & Sons v. *Goring Brick Co., Ltd.,* [1931] All E.R. Rep. 314;
    [1932] 1 K.B. 710; 101 L.J.K.B. 214; 146 L.T. 318; 39 Digest (Repl.)   **E**
    643, *1513.*

Megevand, Re, Ex p. Delhasse, (1878), 7 Ch.D. 511; 47 L.J. Bcy. 65; 38 L.T.
    106; 36 Digest (Repl.) 444, *151.*

Melachrino v. *Nicholl and Knight,* [1918-19] All E.R. Rep. 857; [1920] 1 K.B.
    693; 89 L.J.K.B. 906; 122 L.T. 545; 17 Digest (Repl.) 110, *242.*

Nash v. *Dix,* (1898), 78 L.T. 445; 35 Digest (Repl.) 50, *452.*   **F**

Pole v. *Leask,* (1860), 28 Beav. 562; [1861-73] All E.R. Rep. 535; *on appeal,*
    H.L., (1863), 33 L.J.Ch. 155; 8 L.T. 645; 1 Digest (Repl.) 310, *1.*

Rabone v. *Williams,* (1785), 7 Term Rep. 360, n.; 101 E.R. 1020; 1 Digest
    (Repl.) 666, *2333.*

Roper v. *Johnson,* (1873), L.R. 8 C.P. 167; 42 L.J.C.P. 65; 28 L.T. 296;
    17 Digest (Repl.) 110, *238.*   **G**

Appeals.

The main appeal was by Garnac Grain Co., Inc. (" Garnac "), the appellants,
from an order of the Court of Appeal (SELLERS, DANCKWERTS and DIPLOCK,
L.JJ.) dated June 30, 1965 (and reported [1965] 3 All E.R. 273) and a supplemental order of that court dated July 28, 1965, allowing the appeals of the
respondents, H. M. F. Faure & Fairclough, Ltd. (" Faure ") and Bunge Corpn.   **H**
(" Bunge "), defendants in an action brought by Garnac, from a judgment
of MEGAW, J., dated July 31, 1964 (reported in part, [1965] 1 All E.R. 47). By
that judgment MEGAW, J., declared that neither Faure nor Bunge were entitled
to enforce a contract dated July 15, 1963, in which Garnac were named as sellers
of fifteen thousand tons of lard and Faure were named as buyers; (ii) dismissed
the counterclaims of Faure and Bunge whereby they sought declarations that   **I**
the contract was valid and binding and an award of damages for breach thereof
by Garnac and (iii) gave judgment in favour of Bunge against Faure in the sum
of £233,259 with interest for breach of a warranty that the contract was valid
and binding on Garnac and (iv) ordered that Garnac should have one third of
their costs of the action against Faure and Bunge jointly and severally and that
Faure should pay Bunge's costs (including any payable to Garnac).

On appeal the Court of Appeal (i) granted Faure declarations that the contract
of July 15, 1963, and an assignment dated Dec. 13, 1963, under which Faure

A   assigned their rights under the contract to Bunge, were both valid; (ii) ordered that Bunge recover £254,464 with interest from Garnac; (iii) dismissed Bunge's counterclaim against Faure; and (iv) made orders as to costs, the effect of which was that Garnac were liable to pay the costs of both Faure and Bunge on all issues both in the Court of Appeal and below.

B   There was another appeal, associated with the main appeal; whereby Bunge appealed against the same order and supplemental order of the Court of Appeal; the main appeal was decisive of the associated appeal (see p. 361, letter B, post).

The facts are set out in the opinion of LORD PEARSON, post, and in the judgment of SELLERS, L.J., [1965] 3 All E.R. at pp. 275-278.

F. P. Neill, Q.C., *C. S. Staughton* and *A. D. Colman* for the appellants.

C   *A. J. L. Lloyd*, Q.C., and *A. B. R. Hallgarten* for the first respondents.
Mark Littman, Q.C., and *J. R. Bickford Smith* for the second respondents.

Their lordships took time for consideration.

Apr. 26.   The following opinions were delivered.

LORD REID: My Lords, I have read the speech of my noble and learned friend, LORD PEARSON, I agree with it and have nothing to add.   I shall therefore
D   move that these appeals be dismissed.

LORD MORRIS OF BORTH-Y-GEST: My Lords, I have had the advantage of reading the speech prepared by my noble and learned friend, LORD PEARSON.   I am in agreement with it and I would dismiss the appeals.

LORD PEARCE: My Lords, I have had the advantage of reading the
E   speech of my noble and learned friend, LORD PEARSON with which I entirely agree.   I would therefore dismiss the appeals.

LORD WILBERFORCE: My Lords, I concur.

LORD PEARSON: My Lords, there are only two questions to be dealt with, one relating to an alleged agency of a contracting party for an undisclosed
F   principal, and the other relating to the assessment of damages for breach of the contract.   In view of the length and complexity of the case counsel were requested to confine their arguments in the first instance to these two questions, postponing any argument on other questions raised in the appeal.   A similar course had been taken in the Court of Appeal (1).   In consequence of your lordships' conclusion on the agency question, the other questions became imma-
G   terial and were not argued or considered, and they will be referred to only so far as may be necessary for the purpose of explaining the course of the proceedings.

The appellants are an American corporation, named Garnac Grain Co., Inc., who will be referred to as " Garnac ".   The respondents are an English company named H. M. F. Faure & Fairclough, Ltd., who will be referred to as " Faure ", and an American corporation, named Bunge Inc., who will be referred to as
H   " Bunge ".   Two other American corporations come into the story, one being Allied Crude Vegetable Oil Refining Corpn., who will be referred to as " Allied ", and the other (playing only a minor part) being Gersony Strauss Co., Inc., who will be referred to as " Gersony ".   The litigation arose from the financial collapse of Allied, which occurred on Nov. 18, 1963, and caused very heavy losses to the merchants (including Garnac, Faure and Bunge) who had been
I   dealing with and making loans to Allied.

Allied had carried on business at Bayonne, New Jersey, as suppliers in a very large way of vegetable oils and animal fats.   They would buy oils and fats often in comparatively small quantities, from the producers in the interior of the United States; they would accumulate stocks of these commodities in tanks owned by two warehousing companies in Bayonne; and they would sell the stocks in large consignments to merchants, primarily for export to consumers overseas.   The consumers included Unilever (Raw Materials), Ltd., belonging

(1) [1965] 3 All E.R. 273; [1966] 1 Q.B. 650 at p. 658.

to the Unilever group of companies and having depots or wharves at Brom- **A**
borough (on the Mersey) and Purfleet (on the Thames) and making large purchases of the commodities from time to time.   Other consumers were governmental agencies in developing countries in Asia and Africa.   The business was
attractive to the merchants, and they were willing to fall in with suggestions
from Allied as to the transactions to be undertaken and the modes of carrying
them out.   In particular Allied, who needed finance for buying and collecting **B**
the stocks, were able to insist that the merchants, if they were to have the
business, must make loans to Allied.   The merchants made their loans normally
on the security of " revolving " warehouse receipts for specified quantities of
the commodities and in anticipation of participating in impending or projected
transactions in the commodities.   The transactions were so large that the
merchants would not wish to be " long " of the commodities, and so a sale by **C**
Allied to the merchants and a re-sale by the merchants to the consumers would be
negotiated concurrently and a " string " of purchases and sales would be arranged.
In the simplest form a string would contain only three parties—Allied as first
sellers, the merchants as buyers and re-sellers and the consumers as last buyers;
but Allied operated in complicated and devious ways and might arrange to have
more than three parties in a string.   **D**
A difficult situation would arise if the hoped-for transaction fell through,
the negotiations with the consumers being unsuccessful.   In such a situation
Faure, if they were the merchants concerned, would expect to participate in a
later transaction and might enter into a strange pair of contracts with Allied
of a circular or " back-to-back " character.   Allied would agree to sell a quantity
of the commodity to Faure at a stated price, and Faure would agree to sell a **E**
like quantity of the same commodity to Allied (or sometimes nominally to a
subsidiary company of Allied) at a higher price, which was usually $2 per ton
higher.   This circular or back-to-back transaction would give to Faure a remuneration for making their loan, in addition to the interest charged for it,
and was considered by Faure to have further advantages as a step on the way to
participation in a later transaction of a normal commercial kind and as tying the **F**
loan to trading.   Faure were used to entering into pairs of contracts of this
character with Allied, but Garnac had no experience or knowledge of them.
There was evidence that Bunge also entered into such pairs of contracts with
Allied, but apparently not in connexion with loans of money to Allied.   The
merchants dealing with Allied were making good profits and were not incurring
any serious risks so long as Allied remained solvent and able to fulfil their con- **G**
tracts.   Even if Allied became insolvent, the merchants would still be protected
(except against falls in the market price) by their warehouse receipts so long as
these were covered by actual stocks of the commodities in the warehouses.
The contract sued on was one of four contracts made on July 15, 1963, which
will be referred to as contracts A, B, C and D.   The parties were Allied, Gersony,
Garnac and Faure.   Each contract was for the sale of fifteen thousand long tons of **H**
prime steam lard complying with Unilever specifications for shipment in December, 1963, or January, 1964, at a price c.i.f. Bromborough/Purfleet and on the
conditions of contract form 34 of the London Oil and Tallow Trades Association.
Contract A was for sale by Allied to Gersony at a price of $191 per ton.   Contract
B was for sale by Gersony to Garnac at a price of $193 per ton.   Contract C was
for sale by Garnac to Faure at $195 per ton, and this was the contract sued on. **I**
Contract D was for sale by Faure to Allied at $197 per ton.   Thus Allied were
both first sellers and last buyers in this string of contracts, and the four contracts
would have formed a " circle " under cl. 14 of contract form 34, but for the fact
that in these contracts (at any rate in contract C) cl. 14 was struck out.   If cl. 14
had been retained as a clause of the contract, only price differences would have
been payable and as between buyers and sellers in the circle the non-delivery
of documents by each seller to his buyer would not have been considered a
breach of contract.   That is subject to the question, which has not been discussed

A   and on which I express no opinion, whether the insolvency of Allied would have affected the operation of cl. 14.   Without cl. 14, there would still be an expectation that the parties would be content with payment of differences, but, subject to the questions raised in the action, either party to any of these four contracts would be entitled to require literal performance of the contract by delivery of documents and payments of the price.

B   In the event things went wrong and the parties' expectations were disappointed. Allied had their financial collapse on Nov. 18, 1963, before the time for shipment (December/January) under the four contracts of July 15, 1963.   Allied were insolvent and unable to perform their contracts: they could not deliver documents in respect of lard under contract A and they could not take up and pay for documents in respect of lard under contract D.   The merchants who had been

C   lending money to Allied suffered heavy losses.   They had believed themselves to be secured, but in fact they had no security because the stocks which ought to have been in the warehouses covering the revolving warehouse receipts were not there.   Faure were in grave difficulties and came under the control of their creditor banks.   Gersony went into liquidation.   Garnac and Bunge were affected to some extent, but less severely.   There remained outstanding, subject to the

D   questions raised in the action, the rights and obligations under contract C. Faure were entitled to have the documents delivered to them by Garnac under contract C, and in default of such delivery to claim damages for non-delivery. Owing to the insolvency of Allied and Gersony, Garnac could not obtain shipping documents from Gersony, and so were unable to effect delivery to Faure.   The market price at all material times was above the contract price, because the with-

E   drawal of Allied as a large collector and supplier of lard caused a scarcity and a consequent rise in the price.

There is therefore a claim by Faure as the buyers under contract C, or by Bunge who are assignees of Faure, against Garnac for a very large sum of damages for non-delivery of the shipping documents under contract C.   Prima facie the claim is well-founded because the contract was not fulfilled.   This claim was made

F   by way of counterclaim in the action, which had been commenced by Garnac. Garnac's defence to it was that contract C was unenforceable against them, and had been or should be rescinded, on either or both of two grounds:

   (i) that Garnac were induced to enter into the contract by fraudulent misrepresentations made by Allied and by Faure, to the effect that the transaction, of July 15, 1963, was a normal commercial trans-
G   action, and that Faure were re-selling to Unilever and were not re-selling to Allied.

   (ii) that Faure in making the contract acted as agents for Allied as undisclosed principals, that Garnac were induced to enter into the contract by fraudulent misrepresentations made by Allied, and that the fraud of the undisclosed principals rendered the contract un-
H   enforceable by the agents.

It was conceded at the hearing in the Court of Appeal (2) that Bunge as assignees of Faure could not be in any better position than Faure.

At the trial before MEGAW, J., (3) Garnac failed on the first ground, because the judge held that Faure had not made any fraudulent misrepresentation, but Garnac succeeded on the second ground.   The judge decided that Faure in making

I   contract C acted as agents for Allied as undisclosed principals, that Garnac was induced to enter into the contract by fraudulent misrepresentations made by Allied, and that the fraud of the undisclosed principals rendered the contract unenforceable by the agents.   Accordingly, he gave judgment in favour of Garnac on this issue.

I will deal separately at a later stage with the question as to the assessment of damages.

---

(2) [1965] 3 All E.R. 273; [1966] 1 Q.B. at p. 658.
(0) [1005] 1 All E.R. 47, [1900] 1 Q.B. 050.

Faure and Bunge appealed to the Court of Appeal (4). Garnac did not challenge **A**
the judge's finding that Faure did not make any fraudulent misrepresentation,
and Garnac relied solely on the second ground. The Court of Appeal (4) concentrated on the issue of agency, because, if it were decided that there was no agency,
Faure and Bunge would succeed with their counterclaim and would not need to
establish their other contentions. Their principal other contentions were that
Allied had not made fraudulent misrepresentations or had not thereby induced **B**
Garnac to enter into the contract, and that Garnac had affirmed the contract.
The Court of Appeal (4) decided that there was no agency and gave judgment
accordingly in favour of Faure and Bunge on their counterclaim for damages
for breach of contract C.

Were the Court of Appeal (4) right in deciding that there was no agency?
The law to be applied is the law relating to the creation of an agency relation- **C**
ship. The cases cited included *Rabone* v. *Williams* (5); *Pole* v. *Leask* (6); *Re
Megevand, Ex p. Delhasse* (7); *Nash* v. *Dix* (8), and *W. T. Lamb & Sons* v.
Goring Brick Co., Ltd. (9). These cases illustrate the operation of the principles
involved, but do not afford any very clear description of them. Accordingly,
reference was made to textbooks, especially BOWSTEAD ON AGENCY (12th Edn.)
ch. 1, arts. 2 and 3, the AMERICAN RESTATEMENT title AGENCY (2nd Edn.) **D**
Topic 1, para. 1, and WILLISTON ON CONTRACT (3rd Edn.) vol. 2, para. 274.
There was not in the argument any dispute as to the law, and I think that so
much as is required for the purposes of the present case can be shortly stated.
The relationship of principal and agent can only be established by the consent
of the principal and the agent. They will be held to have consented if they have
agreed to what amounts in law to such a relationship, even if they do not recognise **E**
it themselves and even if they have professed to disclaim it, as in *Re Megevand,
Ex p. Delhasse* (7). The consent must, however, have been given by each of them,
either expressly or by implication from their words and conduct. Primarily
one looks to what they said and did at the time of the alleged creation of the
agency. Earlier words and conduct may afford evidence of a course of dealing
in existence at that time and may be taken into account more generally as **F**
historical background. Later words and conduct may have some bearing, though
likely to be less important. As to the content of the relationship, the question
to be asked is: " what is it that the supposed agent is alleged to have done on
behalf of the supposed principal?" In this case Faure is alleged to have entered
into contract C on behalf of Allied. That would mean that the rights acquired
and obligations assumed by Faure as a party to the contract, though enforceable **G**
by and against Faure because they contracted in their own name without disclosing agency, would belong to Allied and would be enforceable by and against
Allied, and moreover there would be other incidents of agency, such as a duty of
Faure to account and their right to be indemnified. Does the evidence show that
Allied and Faure consented to the creation of such a relationship?

With the assistance of counsel your lordships carried out a long investigation **H**
of the evidence. This was inevitable, as numerous documents and a large amount
of oral evidence had to be taken into account and carefully considered. [HIS
LORDSHIP reviewed the main points which emerged from the investigation, and
continued:] There remains the fact, which is not without importance, that on
the face of the contracts Faure were agreeing to buy from Garnac and agreeing
to sell to Allied, and were therefore acting as principals and not as agents for **I**
Allied. These were not fictitious contracts. They created contractual rights and
obligations. It was, indeed, unlikely, when the contracts were made, that the
goods would ever have to be shipped, but that was a possibility, and in the

---

(4) [1965] 3 All E.R. 273; [1966] 1 Q.B. at p. 658.
(5) (1785), 7 Term Rep. 360, n.
(6) (1860), 28 Beav. 562; *on appeal*, H.L., [1861-73] All E.R. Rep. 535.
(7) (1878), 7 Ch.D. 511.   (8) (1898), 78 L.T. 445.
(9) [1931] All E.R. Rep. 314; [1932] 1 K.B. 710.

A situation which has arisen Faure (and Bunge as their assignees) have a valid claim against Garnac for damages for the failure to ship the goods. In my view the decision of the Court of Appeal (10) that there was no agency is correct.

The other issue relates to the assessment of the damages payable by Garnac for their breach of contract in failing to ship the goods and deliver the documents. The last date for shipment was Jan. 31, 1964, and the evidence is that docu-

B ments posted on that date would have arrived on Feb. 3 or 4. Megaw, J., assessed the damages at £254,464, being the difference between the contract price and the market price on Feb. 4, which he took at $242.50 per ton. In fact, as he had decided that Garnac were not liable under contract C, he made his assessment for the purposes of a counterclaim by Bunge against Faure for damages for breach of a warranty that contract C was valid and enforceable; but he also said expressly

C that, if he had held Garnac liable for breach of contract C, he would have awarded that sum of £254,464 as damages. The Court of Appeal (10) upheld his assessment.

On this issue as to damages three points were argued on behalf of Garnac.

1. First, it was contended that no assessment could properly be made on the basis of the difference between the contract price and the market price on Feb. 4, 1964 (or any other date that might be material), because there was then no market

D in the United Kingdom for fifteen thousand tons of lard for immediate delivery, and the evidence did not reveal any other basis for assessing damages. There was evidence that at all material times (towards the end of January and early in February, 1964), one could not buy that quantity for immediate delivery in the United Kingdom. There was, however, evidence that one could buy smaller quantities—up to two thousand tons at a time—in the U.S.A. for delivery to ports

E for shipment to the United Kingdom; and there was a market price, given by one witness as 242.50 dollars and by another witness as 243.60 dollars per ton, for such purchases on Feb. 4, 1964. If one wished to buy fifteen thousand tons at those prices one would have to do so over a period. According to one witness, if one were able to buy fifteen thousand tons of lard at one time, one would have to pay a higher price. There was thus some evidence on which Megaw, J., could find

F that there was a market price and that it was 242.50 dollars per ton on Feb. 4. No argument to the effect that there was no market price proved was presented at the trial of the action. No such point was included in the " respondents' notice " given by Garnac to the Court of Appeal (10). It may have been raised in the Court of Appeal (10), but it is not mentioned in the judgments. In these circumstances I do not think that the finding of fact of Megaw, J., on this point can be

G successfully challenged.

2. Secondly, it was argued that, if the date of failure to deliver documents was the proper date for ascertaining the difference between the contract price and the market price, the date taken should have been Feb. 3 rather than Feb. 4, 1964. The evidence, given by Mr. Fornani, the Vice-President of Bunge, was this:

" Q.—When in the ordinary course of events would documents posted in

H New York on Jan. 31 reach London?

" A.—I would say, from our experience, they would reach here on the 4th.

" Q.—That was a Tuesday?

" A.—Yes. It might be sooner. I would say three days would be frequent, but four days certainly."

I I think it is clear that Megaw, J., was entitled to find on that evidence that the date of the breach of contract was Feb. 4, being the latest date on which the shipping documents might be expected to arrive.

3. Thirdly, it was argued that on the facts of this case the proper date for ascertaining the difference between the contract price and the market price was not Feb. 4 but Jan. 24, 1964, because that was the date on which Garnac's refusal to perform contract C was (as Garnac allege) accepted by Bunge as a repudiation of the contract.

Only a few documents are relevant to this point. On Jan. 17, 1964, Garnac's **A**
solicitors wrote letters to Faure and Bunge, saying that Garnac, as a result of
their investigations, were entitled to rescind and thereby did rescind the contract.
On Jan. 24, 1964, Bunge issued a writ against Garnac, claiming—

" 1. A declaration that [the contract] the benefit of which has been
assigned to the plaintiffs is valid and subsisting.
" 2. Damages for breach of such contract."   **B**

Also on Jan. 24, 1964, Bunge's solicitors wrote a letter to Garnac's solicitors, in
which they said:

" Your letter gives no grounds for your clients' claim to rescind the contract nor does it explain why this claim should be put forward at this late
stage . . . In these circumstances, we do no more than put on record that our   **C**
clients regard this claim as inherently unmeritorious and improbable and
reserve all their rights."

The writ was not served, and was not mentioned in the letter. The first question
that arises is one of construction. It is argued that by the issue of the writ,
claiming damages as well as the declaration, Bunge were accepting Garnac's
refusal to perform the contract as a repudiation of it and were claiming damages   **D**
for the wrongful repudiation. As a matter of construction I am unable to accept
this argument. It would mean that Bunge were by this writ electing to treat the
contract as terminated—that they were rescinding it (*Heyman* v. *Darwins, Ltd.*
(11), per VISCOUNT SIMON, L.C., and per LORD WRIGHT). It seems to me that the
writ, primarily claiming a declaration that the contract is valid and subsisting,
must mean that Bunge are treating the contract as remaining in force and are   **E**
refusing to treat it as terminated.

If it be assumed, however, that as a matter of construction the claims on the
writ are capable of meaning that Bunge elected to treat Garnac's refusal to perform
the contract as a repudiation of it, two further questions arise.

(i) Could the issue of the writ, without service of it, constitute an election?
The answer seems to me not clear and I am expressing no opinion.   **F**

(ii) If Bunge did on Jan. 24 by the mere issue of the writ elect to treat Garnac's
refusal to perform the contract as a repudiation of it, so that the contract was
rescinded by Bunge on Jan. 24, does that alter the date for ascertaining the difference between the contract price and the market price? If the contract continued,
the proper date for that purpose would be Feb. 4. If the contract was rescinded
by Bunge on Jan. 24, would that become the proper date? Both on principle and   **G**
on authority the answer is " No ". If the contract had been duly carried out by
Garnac, Bunge would have had the goods (to be exact, shipping documents covering the goods) on Feb. 4. By Garnac's breach of contract Bunge have been
deprived of the market value which the goods would have had on Feb. 4, and
the measure of damages is the difference between that value and the contract
price which they would have had to pay. That is the principle. It is subject to a **H**
qualification, that if the buyer had a reasonable opportunity of mitigating the
damage by buying the goods at a lower price at an earlier date (after the acceptance of repudiation but before the contract date for performance), a reduction of
the damages may be appropriate. Both the principle and the qualification are
stated in a series of cases: *Hochster* v. *de la Tour* (12); *Frost* v. *Knight* (13);
Roper v. *Johnson* (14); *Melachrino* v. *Nickoll and Knight* (15). The qualification   **I**
does not assist Garnac here. There was no proof that Bunge or Faure had any
reasonable opportunity of buying fifteen thousand tons of lard between Jan. 24
and Feb. 4 at a lower price than $242.50 per ton.

(11) [1942] 1 All E.R. 337 at pp. 340 (LORD SIMON), 350 (LORD WRIGHT); [1942]
A.C. 356 at pp. 361, 379.
(12) [1843-60] All E.R. Rep. 12 at pp. 14, 15.
(13) [1861-73] All E.R. Rep. 221 at p. 224; (1872), L.R. 7 Exch. 111 at p. 113.
(14) (1873), L.R. 8 C.P. 167.
(15) [1918-19] All E.R. Rep. 857; [1920] 1 K.B. 693.

A In my opinion, the appeal fails on the issue as to the assessment of damages as well as on the issue as to agency and should be dismissed.

I think that the appeal should be dismissed with costs, but only one set of respondents' costs should be payable by the appellants.

There is another appeal, which may be described as a precautionary appeal, by Bunge against Faure, asking that, if Garnac should succeed in the main appeal

B and the judgment in favour of Bunge against Garnac should be set aside, the alternative judgment in favour of Bunge against Faure for damages for breach of warranty should be restored. Counsel agreed that, if the main appeal were dismissed, this other appeal should be dismissed with no order as to costs. I think that that should now be done.

Appeals dismissed.

C Solicitors: *Thomas Cooper & Co.* (for the appellants Garnac); *Richards, Butler & Co.* (for the respondents, Faure); *William A. Crump & Son* (for the respondents, Bunge).

[*Reported by* Kathleen J. H. O'Brien, *Barrister-at-Law.*]

D

LONDON BOROUGH OF HILLINGDON v. CUTLER.

[Court of Appeal, civil division (Harman, Davies and Russell, L.JJ.), March 13, 1967.]

E *Housing—Demolition order—Validity—Duty to make order " forthwith " where no undertaking accepted—Order made eight months after return date on s. 16 notice—No detriment to owner—Validity of order—Whether owner who has not appealed against demolition order can resist claim for expenses on ground that order invalid—Housing Act, 1957 (5 & 6 Eliz. 2 c. 56), s. 16 (1), s. 17 (1), s. 37 (1).*

F *Housing—Demolition order—Expenses of demolition—Lump sum price for demolition arranged by local authority with contractor—Price calculated on basis that contractor should retain materials—Whether compliance with statutory requirement to give credit for amount realised by sale of materials —Housing Act, 1957 (5 & 6 Eliz. 2 c. 56), s. 23 (1), (2).*

A local authority which makes a reasonable contract with a demolition contractor that he will demolish a house subject to a demolition order and

G retain the materials, and thereby agrees to pay him a price for the demolition based on his retaining the materials, complies with its obligation under s. 23 (1)* of the Housing Act, 1957 to " enter and demolish the premises and sell the materials thereof ", and so can recover, under s. 23 (2)† of the Act of 1957, the full price paid to the contractor as " expenses incurred by an authority under [s. 23 (1)*] after giving credit for any amount realised by the

H sale of materials " (see p. 364, letter I, to p. 365, letter A, and p. 366, letters E and I, post).

On May 5, 1961, a local authority served on the owner of a house which was unfit for human habitation a notice under s. 16‡ of the Housing Act, 1957,

---

 * Section 23 (1) provides that if the premises are not demolished within the time limited by the demolition order " the local authority shall enter and demolish the

I premises and sell the materials thereof."

 † Section 23 (2) provides that " Any expenses incurred by an authority under the foregoing subsection, after giving credit for any amount realised by the sale of materials, may be recovered by them as a simple contract debt from the owners of the premises . . ."

 ‡ Section 16 (1) provides: " Where a local authority, . . . are satisfied that any house—(a) is unfit for human habitation, and (b) is not capable at reasonable expense of being rendered so fit, they shall serve upon the person having control of the house . . . notice of the time (being sometime not less than twenty-one days after the service of the notice) and place at which the condition of the house and any offer with respect to the carrying out of works, or the future user of the house, which he may wish to submit will be considered by them "

Dicta of Davies and Russell LJJ at 366 not followed in Graddage v. Haringey [1975] 1 All ER 224

giving a return date on May 31, 1961, and proposing to make a demoli- **A**
tion order on June 27, 1961. The owner attended to be heard on May 31,
and did not oppose the making of a demolition order, which was made on
June 27, and served on the owner. A dispute arose whether the demolition
order served was properly signed, but this order disappeared. On Jan. 26,
1962, the local authority made and served a further demolition order, relying
on the May 5 notice under s. 16. The owner contended that the 1962 **B**
demolition order was invalid because it had not been made " forthwith "
as required by s. 17 (1)* of the Act of 1957. The owner suffered no detriment
from, and in fact benefited by, the delay between June 27, 1961, and Jan. 26,
1962.

Held: the 1962 demolition order was not invalid because

(i) provided that no harm is done " forthwith " means " at any reasonable **C**
time thereafter ", in the circumstances the delay until Jan. 26, 1962, was
reasonable, and so the order had been made and served " forthwith " (see
p. 364, letters C and D, p. 365, letters C and H, and p. 366, letter F, post).

Brown v. *Bonnyrigg and Lasswade Magistrates* (1936 S.C. 258) followed.

(ii) (per HARMAN, L.J.) in the absence of some detriment suffered by the
person on whom the notice is served, failure to make and serve it " forth- **D**
with " does not invalidate it (see p. 364, letter F, post).

Semble (per DAVIES and RUSSELL, L.JJ.): an owner who does not appeal
to the county court against a demolition order within twenty-one days, is
precluded by s. 37 (1)† of the Act of 1957 from later raising the defence, that
the order was invalid on a ground which could have been raised on such
appeal (see p. 366, letters A and G, post). **E**

Cohen v. *West Ham Corpn.* ([1933] All E.R. Rep. 24) considered; *West
Ham Corpn.* v. *Charles Benabo & Sons* ([1934] All E.R. Rep. 47) doubted.

Appeal dismissed.

[As to when a demolition order may be made, see 19 HALSBURY'S LAWS
(3rd Edn.) 616, 617, para. 884; as to the making of a demolition order, see ibid., **F**
p. 618, para. 996; as to demolition and recovery of expenses by the local authority
see ibid., p. 619, para. 998; and as to the conclusiveness of the order if no appeal
is brought, see ibid., p. 628, para. 1012.

As to the meaning of " forthwith ", see 37 HALSBURY'S LAWS (3rd Edn.) 103,
para. 183.

For the Housing Act, 1957, s. 16 (1), s. 17 (1), s. 23 (1), (2), s. 37 (1), see 37 **G**
HALSBURY'S STATUTES (2nd Edn.) 334, 336, 341, 352.]

Cases referred to:

Brown v. *Bonnyrigg and Lasswade Magistrates*, 1936 S.C. 258; 26 Digest
(Repl.) 688, *4*.

Cohen v. *West Ham Corpn.*, [1933] All E.R. Rep. 24; [1933] Ch. 814; 102
L.J.Ch. 305; 149 L.T. 271; 97 J.P. 155; 26 Digest (Repl.) 682, *13*. **H**

Southam, Re, Ex p. Lamb, [1881-85] All E.R. Rep. 391; (1881), 19 Ch.D. 169;
51 L.J.Ch. 207; 45 L.T. 639; 45 Digest (Repl.) 260, *268*.

West Ham Corpn. v. *Charles Benabo & Sons*, [1934] All E.R. Rep. 47; [1934]
2 K.B. 253; 103 L.J.K.B. 452; 151 L.T. 119; 98 J.P. 287; 26 Digest
(Repl.) 685, *33*.

Appeal. **I**

This was an appeal by Roy Edward Cutler, the owner of certain premises in
the London Borough of Hillingdon, against the judgment of His Honour JUDGE
RUTTLE, at Uxbridge county court, on Nov. 18, 1966, awarding the local authority
the sum claimed by it, under s. 23 (2) of the Housing Act, 1957, as expenses

---

* Section 17 (1) provides: " If no such undertaking [i.e. one as to carrying out works
or future user] is accepted by the local authority . . . then, subject to the provisions of
this section, the local authority shall forthwith make a demolition order . . ."

† Section 37 (1), so far as material, is printed at p. 365, letter I, post.

A   incurred in demolishing his premises.   The facts are set out in the judgment of
HARMAN, L.J.

    M. R. Hickman for the owner.
    P. Freeman for the local authority, was not called on.

    HARMAN, L.J.: It is not possible to discuss this case on its merits, because
B   it has not got any.   It is a miserable dispute—part of a feud being carried on
by the defendant house-owner, who is the appellant, and the local authority—
which is of long standing.   What the origin of it all is we do not know, but the
result is the bringing before this court of a number of points of really insignificant
content.

    The appeal arises out of two cases (although only one is actually the subject
C   of appeal) in which the local authority sued the owner in the county court for
certain expenses arising (they said) under demolition orders which they had
made against buildings on property of the owner.   This property appears to
have been a considerable eighteenth-century house with something under an
acre of grounds; and the buildings in question were not part of the main structure
but were coach-houses or what-not scattered about in this piece of ground
D   which apparently made shelters or houses, or anyhow dwelling-places, for certain
solitary people who preferred to live alone and had nowhere else to live, and who
paid the owner not inconsiderable sums of money by way of rent for these structures.   The local authority declared these places to be unfit for human habitation:
and nobody doubts that they are unfit.   Now, they being ex concessis wholly
unfit, the Housing Act, 1957, becomes operative.   Section 16 (1), which deals
E   with " Unfit premises beyond repair at reasonable cost ", states that where
the local authority, on a report made to them, are satisfied that a house is unfit
for human habitation they are bound to serve on the " person having control
of the house " [that is the owner in this case]

    ". . . notice of the time (. . . not less than twenty-one days after the service
    of the notice) and place at which the condition of the house and any offer
F   with respect to the carrying out of works . . . which he may wish to submit
    will be considered by them."

They did serve such notices.   They served them, it is said, in the first place
on May 5, 1961, giving a return date on May 31, 1961, proposing to make demolition orders on June 27, 1961.   A dispute arose, however, about the demolition
orders, because it was said that they were sealed but not signed by the town clerk,
G   as the Act of 1957 provides that they should be (1).   When the local authority
asked for them back, to see whether this was in fact the case, they disappeared
in some way which has never been cleared up.   The owner said that he sent
them back: the local authority said they had never received them back; and the
matter remains an unsolved mystery.   At any rate, the local authority, in order
to cut the Gordian knot, served further orders on Jan. 26, 1962.   They did not
H   give any further notice under s. 16 but treated the already existing notice as
sufficient.

    The first point taken is that that invalidates the whole proceeding and that
the notices are invalid.   Under s. 16 there are various alternatives under which
the person on whom the original notice is served may submit counter-offers and
so on; but nothing of that sort happened in this case.   Therefore, under s. 17 (1),
I   no undertaking to restore or repair having been given

    ". . . then, subject to the provisions of this section, the local authority
    shall forthwith make a demolition order for the demolition of the premises
    to which the notice given under the last foregoing section relates."

Such demolition orders were made in this case.   It is said that they were void
because they were not made " forthwith ".   It is said that " forthwith " means

    (1) Section 166 (1) requires a demolition order to be under the seal of the local authority
and authenticated by the signature of their clerk.

on the next convenient opportunity, and that that would have been the moment **A**
in 1961 at which originally the demolition order—the so-called ineffective demolition order—was made, namely, June 27, 1961, and that waiting a half year after
that makes it not " forthwith ".

The first reason why I think that that is a bad point is that I cannot see that
if the local authority fail to observe the spur given to it by the statute and do not
do it forthwith that makes the whole of their notice bad in the absence of some **B**
detriment suffered by the person on whom the notice is served. It is not said
that there was such detriment here. Indeed there was an advantage, because
the owner continued to collect rents from these horrible places for a year after
he should not have been entitled to do so. Therefore I do not think that, even
if the notices were not " forthwith ", that is good enough to defeat them.

Apart from that, however, " forthwith " is not a precise time and, provided **C**
that no harm is done, " forthwith " means any reasonable time thereafter.
As was pointed out in the bankruptcy case, *Re Southam, Ex p. Lamb* (2), it
may involve action within days: it may not involve action for years—as in the
case to which we were referred where there was a three-years interval (*Brown*
v. *Bonnyrigg and Lasswade Magistrates* (3)). Here it seems to me that the county
court judge was perfectly right in saying that " forthwith " was satisfied. There **D**
was nowhere to house these people. It was very inconvenient to make an order
and then have to put it off. It was much better to leave it as was done. Consequently I think that there is nothing in the " forthwith " point at all.

Then it is argued that the statute was not complied with by the local authority
and cannot be enforced in the way it is now sought to do. For that one must
look at s. 23 of the Act of 1957, which provides (in sub-s. (1)) that if the premises **E**
are not demolished within the due time by the owner " the local authority shall
enter and demolish the premises and sell the materials thereof ", and (in sub-s. (2))
that

> " any expenses incurred by an authority under the foregoing subsection
> after giving credit for any amount realised by the sale of materials, may be
> recovered by them as a simple contract debt from the owner of the premises **F**
> . . ."

What the local authority here did, broadly speaking, was to make a contract
with a demolition contractor so that there was a bargain between him and the
proper official of the local authority that he would do the work for so much, and
would offer the price which he did offer, taking into account the fact that he
would retain any materials that emerged from the demolition which he was **G**
about to undertake. The official, who impressed the judge as a candid and
careful witness, gave evidence that, having considered what kind of value there
might be in these materials, bricks, bits of piping, baths and so forth, he thought
that he had made the best bargain he could. He asked other contractors to
tender and none of them did so, and he arrived at the two sums which were
mentioned in these two appeals. **H**

It is said by the owner that that does not involve a sale of " the materials
thereof " (see s. 23 (1)), nor does it involve giving credit " for any amount realised
by the sale of materials " (see s. 23 (2)), and that there ought to have been a price
and then another price, one against the other—namely, the price which the
contractor was to charge, and then the price for which the contractor would
purchase the materials, and that the latter price should be set against the former **I**
price. It is said that there was not really a sale here at all, but that there was
merely one lump sum contract. The county court judge came to the conclusion
that that was a perfectly competent way for the local authority to do the business.
If they had done that which the owner wanted them to do, namely, undo every
piece brick by brick, stone by stone, screw by screw, the cost of doing so would
have been exorbitant and the owner would have been much worse off. That which

---

(2) [1881-85] All E.R. Rep. 391; (1881), 19 Ch.D. 169.   (3) 1936 S.C. 258.

A they did was not only reasonable but probably much the cheapest way for the owner in which the work could be done.   The county court judge came to the conclusion that that was a sufficient compliance with the statute, and I am heartily in agreement with him on that point.

Therefore the appeal fails on both those points.   There were some subsidiary points, but, as they do not really take the case any further, I would dismiss the
B appeal on those two grounds.

DAVIES, L.J.: I agree.

So far as concerns the first point, it seems to me that the strong persuasive authority of the case to which HARMAN, L.J., has referred, namely *Brown v. Bonnyrigg and Lasswade Magistrates* (4) is really decisive as to the meaning of the word " forthwith ".   That case concerned the Housing (Scotland) Act, 1930,
C the provisions of which are in all relevant respects similar to those of the Housing Act, 1957, which are under consideration in the present appeal.   I will refer only to two passages in the judgments of their lordships in that case.   The Lord President (LORD NORMAND) said (5):

" In my opinion, the statutory injunction to proceed ' forthwith ' was
D inserted in the statute for the purpose of spurring on a local authority to a zealous and active prosecution of its duty to close houses which are unfit for human habitation, and it does not follow that delay per se, even if that delay were a trespass against that injunction, would invalidate a demolition order."

Later on LORD NORMAND said (5):

E " It is common ground that the condition of the house and other relevant conditions remained unaltered [that is, during the period of so-called 'delay'] and that delay not only has not prejudiced the owner of the house, but has enabled her to obtain the advantage of the continued occupation of the house."

F Both the other judges made observations to the like effect.   In regard to " delay " in this case, not only has there been no prejudice to the owner, but he has had a positive advantage.   The dates speak for themselves.   The " time and place " notice was dated May 5, 1961.   The matter was considered and the owner appeared on May 31 of that year.   According to the judge, he did not oppose the demolition of these dwellings (if that be an appropriate name for them).
G The original orders were made on June 27, 1961; and then this dispute arose whether or not they had been signed by the clerk.   The fresh orders were made on Jan. 26, 1962; but the actual demolition, we were told, did not take place until October, 1964.   So the owner has had all the advantage of that time; he was enabled to continue to receive the rents, and the payment by him of the costs of demolition has been considerably postponed.   It seems to me that the
H orders served on Jan. 26, 1962, were served reasonably soon, in all the circumstances of this case.

The next question was whether, the owner having failed to appeal to the county court within the time limited by the Act of 1957 for such appeals, his defence in this case is one which he is permitted to raise.   I do not wish to go into any detail in regard to that matter.   The relevant provisions, of course, are s. 20 and s. 37 of the Housing Act, 1957, which do provide for such an appeal within
I twenty-one days.   Section 37 (1) provides that

" Any notice, demand or order against which an appeal might be brought to a county court under this Part of this Act shall, if no such appeal is brought, become operative on the expiration of twenty-one days from the date of the service of the notice, demand or order, and shall be final and conclusive as to any matters which could have been raised on such an appeal . . ."

(4) 1936 S.C. 258.   (5) 1936 S.C. at p. 265.

We have had cited to us two authorities with regard to this point, one a decision **A**
at first instance, ATKINSON, J., in *West Ham Corpn.* v. *Charles Benabo & Sons* (6)
and the other a decision of this court, *Cohen* v. *West Ham Corpn.* (7).   If it were
necessary to decide this point (which, in view of the opinion which I have
formed on the first point, it is not), I am bound to say that I should have thought
that ATKINSON, J.'s decision in the later case could not stand in the light of the
decision of this court in the earlier case, which for some extraordinary reason was **B**
not, apparently, cited to ATKINSON, J., although one of the counsel who appeared
in the former case also appeared in the later one.

Another matter, on which I will touch extremely briefly, is the question that
arose under s. 23 (1) of the Act of 1957.   The concluding words are:

"... if the premises are not demolished within that time, the local authority shall enter and demolish the premises and sell the materials thereof." **C**

Counsel for the owner contends that the local authority failed to carry out their
statutory duty in that regard, in that they did not sell the materials or account
to the owner for the proceeds of sale.   That really was a question of fact for the
county court judge, who went into it very thoroughly and came to a clear conclusion.   His conclusion was that what may be conveniently called the lump **D**
sum agreement entered into between the local authority and the contractor who
did the demolition work was a real and genuine transaction and amounted to a
payment to the contractor for the work of demolition less an appropriate, or, if
you like, a notional, credit for the value of the materials, or scrap, recovered
(such as it was); and on the evidence it obviously was not very great.   In my
view, the judge came to a correct conclusion, and that point also fails. **E**

I entirely agree with HARMAN, L.J., that this appeal fails on all points and
should be dismissed.

RUSSELL, L.J.: I also agree.   The demolition orders, in the particular
circumstances of this case, were in my view served in sufficient time.   The
particular circumstance that I have in mind is that there was over an extensive
period a dispute (which in fact I do not think was really ever fully resolved) **F**
whether similar, earlier orders had been correctly signed.   I cannot think it
would be right to say that the second lot (if I may so describe them) of demolition
orders were not produced within a reasonable time, considered against that
background.   I am, alternatively, inclined to think that the validity of the
demolition orders could not be challenged on the ground on which they are
challenged, having regard to the provisions of s. 20 and s. 37 of the Housing **G**
Act, 1957, to which DAVIES, L.J., has referred.

Finally, on the question whether the local authority prejudiced its claim for
the net cost of demolition by the fact that it did not realise for an explicit sum
the materials, the purpose of the provision is that the owner is to be charged only
the net cost of demolition, and there is no doubt at all that that purpose was
fully achieved by the method that was adopted of getting the demolition con- **H**
tractor to quote a price which would reflect the value in his hands of the materials,
to which he was to become entitled under the contract.   The result of the transaction obviously was that the local authority did sell the materials to the contractor,
and that sale was for the difference between what would have been charged for
the demolition and what was in fact charged.

I think that on all those three points the appeal fails.

Appeal dismissed. **I**

Solicitors: *Lee, Bolton & Lee*, agents for *Norman E. Kelly & Son*, Watford,
Herts. (for the house-owner); *Town Clerk*, London Borough of Hillingdon (for
the local authority).

[*Reported by* HENRY SUMMERFIELD, ESQ., *Barrister-at-Law.*]

---

(6) [1934] All E.R. Rep. 47; [1934] 2 K.B. 253.
(7) [1933] All E.R. Rep. 24; [1933] Ch. 814.

A
UNITED ENGINEERING WORKERS UNION v. DEVANAYAGAM.

[PRIVY COUNCIL (Viscount Dilhorne, Lord Guest, Lord Devlin, Lord Upjohn and Lord Pearson), November 14, 15, 16, 17, 1966, March 9, 1967.]

Constitutional Law—Judicial office—Characteristics of judicial power.

B *Privy Council—Ceylon—Judicial officer—President of labour tribunal appointed by Public Service Commission—Order of tribunal for re-instatement of dismissed employee—Validity of order—Whether office of president judicial —Industrial Disputes Act (c. 131), No. 43 of 1950, as amended by Industrial Disputes (Amendment) Act (No. 62 of 1957), s. 31B—Ceylon (Constitution) Order in Council, 1946 (c. 379), s. 55.*

C   The respondent dismissed an employee, R., a member of the appellant union. On the appellant's application, under s. 31B of the Industrial Disputes Act, 1950, as amended by the Industrial Disputes (Amendment) Act, 1957, for reinstatement and other relief, a labour tribunal on Sept. 17, 1962, made an order, under s. 33 (1) (b)* for the respondent to pay R. three months' salary and to reinstate him in employment. A labour tribunal
D consisted of one person, who was designated " President ". The Ceylon Constitution Order in Council entrusted the appointment of judicial officers to a Judicial Service Commission and entrusted the appointment of public officers, other than judicial officers, to a Public Service Commission. The presidents of labour tribunals, including the president of this tribunal, were appointed by the Public Service Commission. On the question whether
E in view of s. 55† of the Constitution, by which the appointment of judicial officers was entrusted to the Judicial Service Commission, the labour tribunal had jurisdiction to entertain the application,

   Held (LORD GUEST and LORD DEVLIN dissenting): the office of president of a labour tribunal was not a judicial office within the meaning of s. 55 of the Constitution, and accordingly the order of the tribunal was not made
F without jurisdiction (see p. 376, letter F, and p. 377, letter F, post).

   Dicta of GRIFFITHS, C.J., in *Huddart Parker & Co., Proprietary, Ltd.* v. *Moorehead, Appleton* v. *Moorehead* ((1909), 8 C.L.R. at p. 357), and of LORD SIMONDS in *Saskatchewan Labour Relations Board* v. *John East Iron Works, Ltd.* ([1949] A.C. at p. 151) applied.

   Dictum of LORD SANKEY, L.C., in *Shell Co. of Australia, Ltd.* v. *Federal*
G *Comr. of Taxation* ([1930] All E.R. Rep. at p. 680) applied.

   Shell Co. of Ceylon, Ltd. v. *Pathirana* ((1962), 64 N.L.R. 71) approved.

   Richard Pieris & Co. v. *Wijesiriwardena* ((1960), 62 N.L.R. 233) and *Electric Equipment and Construction Co.* v. *Cooray* ((1961), 63 N.L.R. 164) disapproved.

   Distinctions between executive and judicial power, and characteristics
H of judicial power discussed by LORD GUEST and LORD DEVLIN (see p. 380, letter A, to p. 383, letter C, post).

   Appeal allowed.

[As to what constitutes a court in law, see 9 HALSBURY'S LAWS (3rd Edn.) 342-344, paras. 809, 810; and for cases on the subject see 16 DIGEST (Repl.) 113-115, *1-20.*
I   As to tribunals for settlement of industrial disputes in England, see 9 HALSBURY'S LAWS (3rd Edn.) 576, 577, para. 1347 and 38 ibid., 147, para. 212.]

Cases referred to:

   A.-G. of Commonwealth of Australia v. *Reginam and Boilermakers' Society of Australia,* [1957] 2 All E.R. 45; [1957] A.C. 288; [1957] 2 W.L.R. 607; Digest (Cont. Vol. A) 136, *300a.*

---

* The provisions of s. 33 (1) are indicated at p. 372, letter C, post.
† Section 55, so far as material, is summarised at p. 369, letter D, post.

Bribery Comr. (The) v. *Ranasinghe,* [1964] 2 All E.R. 785; [1965] A.C. 172; A
    [1964] 2 W.L.R. 1301; 3rd Digest Supp.
Canadian Pacific Ry. Co. v. *Toronto Corpn. and Grand Trunk Ry. Co. of Canada,*
    [1911] A.C. 461; 81 L.J.P.C. 5; 104 L.T. 724; 8 Digest (Repl.) 833,
    847.
Electric Equipment and Construction Co. v. *Cooray,* (1961), 63 N.L.R. 164.
Huddart Parker & Co. Proprietary, Ltd. v. *Moorehead, Appleton* v. *Moorehead,* B
    (1909), 8 C.L.R. 330; 8 Digest (Repl.) 756, **819.*
K. (H.) (an infant), Re, [1967] 1 All E.R. 226.
Moses v. *Parker, Ex p. Moses,* [1896] A.C. 245; 65 L.J.P.C. 18; 74 L.T. 112;
    8 Digest (Repl.) 806, *575.*
Pieris (Richard) & Co. v. *Wijesiriwardena,* (1960), 62 N.L.R. 233.
R. v. *Deputy Industrial Injuries Comr., Ex p. Moore,* [1965] 1 All E.R. 81; C
    [1965] 1 Q.B. 456; [1965] 2 W.L.R. 89; 3rd Digest Supp.
Ridge v. *Baldwin,* [1963] 2 All E.R. 66; [1964] A.C. 40; [1963] 2 W.L.R. 935;
    127 J.P. 295; 37 Digest (Repl.) 195, *32.*
Russell v. *Duke of Norfolk,* [1949] 1 All E.R. 109; 12 Digest (Repl.) 693, *5321.*
Saskatchewan Labour Relations Board v. *John East Iron Works, Ltd.,* [1949]
    A.C. 134; [1949] L.J.R. 66; 8 Digest (Repl.) 736, *284.*   D
Shell Co. of Australia, Ltd. v. *Federal Comr. of Taxation,* [1930] All E.R. Rep.
    671; [1931] A.C. 275; 100 L.J.P.C. 55; 144 L.T. 421; 8 Digest (Repl.)
    792, *507.*
Shell Co. of Ceylon, Ltd. v. *Pathirana,* (1962), 64 N.L.R. 71.
Waterside Workers Federation v. *Alexander,* (1918), 25 C.L.R. 434; 8 Digest
    (Repl.) 756, **829.*   E

Appeal.

This was an appeal by special leave from a judgment and order of the Supreme
Court of Ceylon (SANSONI, C.J., H. N. G. FERNANDO, S.P.J., and T. S. FERNANDO,
J.; TAMBIAH and SRI SKANDA RAJAH, JJ., dissenting), dated Nov. 30, 1965,
allowing an appeal by the respondent, K. W. Devanayagam, President of the
Eastern Province Agricultural Co-operative Union, Ltd., against an order of a F
labour tribunal (established under the Industrial Disputes Act (c. 131), 1950,
as amended by the Industrial Disputes (Amendment) Acts No. 14 of 1957, No. 62
of 1957 and No. 4 of 1962) dated Sept. 17, 1962, whereby the respondent was
ordered to reinstate in employment with effect from Oct. 17, 1962, a workman
named N. Rasamanickam, a member of the appellant union, and with three
months' salary. The facts, as pleaded in para. 2 of the Case for the respondent, G
were as follows. The workman had been employed by the respondent on a
monthly basis until Sept. 14, 1961, on which date he was dismissed from the
respondent's service for insubordination and disobedience. The workman
was at all material times a member of the appellant union, which was a registered
trade union. On Nov. 4, 1961, the appellant made an application on the workman's behalf under s. 31B of the Act of 1950 as amended asking for an order H
for his reinstatement and for certain other relief. These proceedings were numbered Labour Tribunal Case No. 6/9091. On Jan. 23, 1962, the respondent
filed a statement claiming that the workman's dismissal was justified. The
proceedings in this case, together with other connected cases, were heard by
Mr. F. X. J. Rasanayagam purporting to exercise jurisdiction of a labour tribunal
under Part IVA of the Act of 1950 as amended. He held as a fact that although I
the workman failed to obey an order of the manager, he was not guilty of wilful
insubordination taking into consideration the circumstances under which the
order was given. The Labour Tribunal made an order under s. 33 (1) (*b*) to
the effect previously stated.

N. Satyendra and *N. Chinivasayagam* (both of the Ceylon Bar) for the appellants.
E. F. N. Gratiaen, Q.C., Walter Jayawardena and *Mark Fernando* for the
respondent.

A   **VISCOUNT DILHORNE:** On Sept. 17, 1962, a labour tribunal at Colombo ordered the respondent to pay three months' salary to one Rasamanickam, a member of the appellant union, and to reinstate him in employment.   The respondent petitioned the Supreme Court of Ceylon that this order should be set aside.   The matter came before T. S. FERNANDO, J., who permitted the respondent to argue that the labour tribunal had no jurisdiction to make the
B   order as it had not been appointed by the Judicial Service Commission.   T. S. FERNANDO, J., reserved the matter for consideration by more than one judge, and it was heard by a bench of five judges (1) who by a majority of three to two allowed the appeal on this ground.   The appellant now appeals with special leave.

Part VI of the Ceylon (Constitution) Order in Council, 1946, is headed " The
C Judicature ".   In this Part, s. 52 provides that the chief justice and puisne judges and commissioners of assize are to be appointed by the Governor-General and are to hold office during good behaviour.   Section 53 provides for the creation of a judicial service commission, which is to consist of the chief justice, a judge of the Supreme Court and one other person who is or has been a judge of the Supreme Court, and which by s. 55 is made responsible for the appointment,
D   transfer, dismissal and disciplinary control of judicial officers.   Section 55 (5) defines a judicial officer as the holder of any judicial office, but states that it does not include a judge of the Supreme Court or a commissioner of assize. They are excluded from the definition, for they are appointed not by the Judicial Service Commission but by the Governor-General.   Section 56 makes it an offence to seek to influence the decision of the Judicial Service Commission or
E   of a member of it.

Part VII of this Order in Council is headed " The Public Service ".   Section 57 in this Part provides that save as otherwise provided in the Order, " every person holding office under the Crown in respect of the government of the Island shall hold office during Her Majesty's pleasure ".   Section 58 provides for the establishment of a Public Service Commission which by s. 60 is made responsible
F for the appointment, transfer, dismissal and disciplinary control of public officers (i.e., holders of paid offices, other than judicial offices, as servants of the Crown in respect of the government of the Island (s. 3)).

Thus the Constitution Order in Council provides for the independence of the Ceylon civil service from the executive and for the independence of the judicature from the executive and from the civil service.   No guidance is directly
G given by the Order in Council as to the meaning of the words " judicial officer " other than the definition in s. 55 (5), but it is apparent from the Order in Council that holders of judicial offices are to be regarded as members of the judicature and not of the civil service.

The presidents of labour tribunals have always been appointed by the Public Service Commission. If the majority of the Supreme Court of Ceylon are right
H in holding in this case that they are judicial officers and so should have been appointed by the Judicial Service Commission, then it follows that the acts and orders of the labour tribunals were without jurisdiction and so invalid.

At the time when the Order in Council was made, civil and criminal justice in Ceylon was administered in the Supreme Court, District Courts, the Courts of Requests and Magistrates' Courts (see Courts Ordinance c. 6, s. 3).   Those
I   discharging judicial functions in these courts are clearly holders of judicial offices, but it does not follow that they are the only holders of such offices for the legislature may create new ones.   The Bribery Amendment Act, 1958, created bribery tribunals for the trials of person prosecuted for bribery, and in *The Bribery Comr.* v. *Ranasinghe* (2) it was held that the members of a bribery tribunal held judicial offices and that, as they had not been appointed by the Judicial Service Commission, they had no power to try a person accused of bribery and to sentence him to imprisonment.

(1) (1965), 68 N.L.R. 73.   (2) [1964] 2 All E.R. 785; [1965] A.C. 172.

There is no single test that can be applied to determine whether a particular **A** office is a judicial one. In *Saskatchewan Labour Relations Board* v. *John East Iron Works, Ltd.* (3) the question was whether that labour relations board exercised judicial power and, if so, whether in that exercise it was a tribunal analogous to a superior, district or county court. LORD SIMONDS, delivering the judgment of the Board, stated (4) that their lordships, without attempting to give a comprehensive definition of judicial power, accepted the view that its broad features **B** were accurately stated by GRIFFITHS, C.J., in *Huddart Parker & Co. Proprietary, Ltd.* v. *Moorehead, Appleton* v. *Moorehead* (5), which was approved by the Privy Council in *Shell Co. of Australia, Ltd.* v. *Federal Comr. of Taxation* (6). LORD SIMONDS went on to say (4):

" Nor do they doubt, as was pointed out in the latter case, that there are many positive features which are essential to the existence of judicial power, **C** yet by themselves are not conclusive of it, or that any combination of such features will fail to establish a judicial power if, as is a common characteristic of so-called administrative tribunals, the ultimate decision may be determined not merely by the application of legal principles to ascertained facts but by considerations of policy also."

D

Earlier he had said (7):

" Nor can a more difficult question be posed (but their lordships can find no easier test) than to ask whether one court is ' analogous ' to another."

and later he added (8):

" It is as good a test as another of ' analogy ' to ask whether the subject- **E** matter of the assumed justiciable issue makes it desirable that the judges should have the same qualifications as those which distinguish the judges of the superior or other courts."

That test appears an appropriate one to apply in relation to the question now before the Board.

In *Shell Co. of Australia* v. *Federal Comr. of Taxation* (6) the Board approved **F** the definition of GRIFFITHS, C.J., in *Huddart Parker & Co.* v. *Moorehead, Appleton* v. *Moorehead* (9), when he said:

" I am of opinion that the words ' judicial power ' as used in s. 71 of the Constitution mean the power which every sovereign authority must of necessity have to decide controversies between its subjects, or between itself and its subjects, whether the rights relate to life, liberty or property. **G** The exercise of this power does not begin until some tribunal which has power to give a binding and authoritative decision (whether subject to appeal or not) is called upon to take action."

and in relation to this, LORD SANKEY, L.C., delivering the judgment of the Board, enumerated a number of negative propositions on this subject (10):

H

" 1. A tribunal is not necessarily a court in this strict sense because it gives a final decision. 2. Nor because it hears witnesses on oath. 3. Nor because two or more contending parties appear before it between whom it has to decide. 4. Nor because it gives decisions which affect the rights of subjects. 5. Nor because there is an appeal to a court. 6. Nor because it is a body to which a matter is referred by another body . . ."

I

The holder of a judicial office exercises judicial power, but the fact that some judicial power is exercised does not establish that the office is judicial. As

---

(3) [1949] A.C. 134.   (4) [1949] A.C. at p. 149.
(5) (1909), 8 C.L.R. 330 at p. 357.
(6) [1930] All E.R. Rep. 671; [1931] A.C. 275.
(7) [1949] A.C. at p. 148.   (8) [1949] A.C. at p. 151.
(9) (1909), 8 C.L.R. at p. 357.
(10) [1930] All E.R. Rep. at p. 680; [1931] A.C. at p. 297.

A TAMBIAH, J., pointed out (11) in his dissenting judgment in this case, there were in Ceylon at the time when the Constitution Order in Council was made, a number of persons and tribunals performing some judicial functions and those persons and the members of those tribunals have not been regarded as judicial officer.   He gave (11) as one instance the divisional registrar under the Kandyan Marriage and Divorce Act who, apart from his other duties, acts as a judge in
B contested divorce proceedings between Kandyans.

To determine whether the office of president of a labour tribunal is a judicial office it is necessary to consider the powers, functions and duties entrusted to those tribunals and to have regard to the test adumbrated by LORD SIMONDS in the *Labour Relations Board* case (12) by considering whether the nature of the matters those tribunals have to deal with makes it desirable that their
C presidents should have the same qualifications as judges of the ordinary courts. The long title of the Industrial Disputes Act (c. 131), No. 43 of 1950, reads as follows:

" An Act to provide for the prevention, investigation and settlement of industrial disputes, and for matters connected therewith and incidental thereto."

D That Act provided for the reference of industrial disputes to arbitration or to an industrial court.   It was amended by the Industrial Disputes (Amendment) Act, No. 62 of 1957.   By the amending Act the Commissioner of Labour was given power to refer an industrial dispute to a labour tribunal as an alternative to referring it to arbitration, and the Minister was given power to refer a minor industrial dispute to a labour tribunal as an alternative to referring it to arbitra-
E tion or to an industrial court.   On any such reference the labour tribunal has the same powers and duties as an arbitrator under the Act (s. 15A).

An industrial dispute was defined by s. 48 as meaning any dispute or difference between employers and workmen or between workmen and workmen connected with the employment or non-employment, or the terms of employment or with the conditions of labour of any person.   The Act of 1957 amended this definition
F by adding " connected with the termination of the services or the reinstatement in service of any person " and in 1962 a further amendment was made which made it clear that the definition included a dispute between an employer and a workman.

An industrial dispute may arise over a number of matters connected with employment.   In many cases, it may be the majority of cases, the dispute will
G be over wage rates and matters connected therewith.   In other cases it may be over the dismissal of a workman or workmen, and it is clear that an industrial dispute within the meaning of the Act of 1950 may arise even though the employer has done no more than exercise his legal rights.   Satisfactory provision for the settlement of industrial disputes must cover all industrial disputes whether they arise over wages or on account of the dismissal of a workman or for other
H causes.

Section 17 provides that when a dispute has been referred to arbitration by the Commissioner of Labour or the Minister, the arbitrator

" shall make all such inquiries into the dispute as he may consider necessary, hear such evidence as may be tendered by the parties to the dispute, and thereafter make such award as may appear to him just and
I equitable."

Section 24 (1) similarly provides that it is the duty of an industrial court (which consists of one or three persons (s. 22 (4))

" to which any dispute, application or question . . . is referred or made under this Act . . . to make all such inquiries and hear all such evidence, as it may consider necessary, and thereafter to take such decision or make such award as may appear to the court just and equitable."

---

(11) (1965), 68 N.L.R. at p. 104.   (12) [1949] A.C. at p. 151.

The powers and duties of an arbitrator under the Act of 1950, of an industrial **A**
court and of a labour tribunal on a reference of an industrial dispute are thus
the same.   In relation to an arbitration, the arbitrator must hear the evidence
tendered by the parties.   So must a labour tribunal on a reference.   An industrial court has to hear such evidence as it considers necessary.   In each case
the award has to be one which appears to the arbitrator, the labour tribunal
or the industrial court just and equitable.   No other criterion is laid down. **B**
They are given an unfettered discretion to do what they think is right and
fair.

Section 33 (1) of the Act of 1950 provides that any award under the Act,
whether made by an arbitrator, an industrial court or, since the Act of 1950
was amended in 1957, by a labour tribunal may contain decisions on a variety of
matters, including decisions that wages shall be paid by an employer in respect **C**
of a period of absence from work by reason of a strike or lock-out.

Section 19 provides that the award of an arbitrator is to be binding on the
persons named therein and that the terms of the award are to be implied terms
in the contract of employment between the employers and workmen bound by
the award.   Section 26 similarly prescribes that every award of an industrial
court is to be binding on the persons referred to therein and that the terms of the **D**
award are to be implied terms in the contract of employment.

The fact that the terms of the award are to be implied terms of the contract
of employment led SANSONI, C.J. (13), with whose judgment T. S. FERNANDO, J.,
agreed (14), and H. N. G. FERNANDO, S.P.J. (15), to the conclusion that the
awards were only intended to have effect in the future.   H. N. G. FERNANDO
S.P.J. said (15) that they were " concerned not with the reparation of wrongs, **E**
but instead with the determination of future terms and conditions ".   Their
lordships are unable to agree with this.   Where the terms of an award relate to
wages or holidays it is no doubt appropriate that the terms should be implied
terms of the contract of service, but the industrial dispute may be over something that has happened in the past and something unrelated to the future,
as, for instance, over the question whether wages should be paid in respect of a **F**
period of absence from work due to a strike or a lock-out or over the dismissal
of a workman who has received all to which he is legally entitled.   Section 33 (1)
expressly gives power to order the payment of wages for a period of absence due
to a strike or a lock-out and neither an arbitrator, nor an industrial court nor
a labour tribunal on a reference is restricted to awarding a dismissed workman
no more than is legally due to him, for they may consider that his legal rights **G**
give him less than is just and equitable.   It would therefore appear that the
provision in s. 19 and s. 26 that the terms of the award are to be implied terms
of the contract of employment should be read with some qualification, for the
terms of some awards may be quite inappropriate for treatment as implied terms
of the contract of service.

It is agreed that an arbitrator under the Act of 1950, a member of an **H**
industrial court and the president of a labour tribunal when a dispute is referred
to it do not hold a judicial office.   The three judges who formed the majority
in the Supreme Court in this case, SANSONI, C.J. (16), H. N. G. FERNANDO,
S.P.J. (17) and T. S. FERNANDO, J. (14) so held.

If on the examination of the powers and functions of a labour tribunal, they
are found not to differ in any material respect from those of an arbitrator or of **I**
an industrial court, then it is to be inferred that the legislature did not intend
to create and did not create, when it provided for the establishment of labour
tribunals, a different kind of office to that held by arbitrators and the members
of an industrial court.

---

(13) (1965), 68 N.L.R. at p. 86.   (14) (1965), 68 N.L.R. at p. 102.
(15) (1965), 68 N.L.R. at p. 93.   (16) (1965), 68 N.L.R. at p. 75.
                    (17) (1965), 68 N.L.R. at p. 90.

A   The amending Act of 1957 inserted Part IVA into the Act of 1950, and it is now necessary to consider the terms of the sections contained in that Part. The first section in it, s. 31A, reads as follows:

" There shall be established for the purposes of this Act such number of labour tribunals as the Minister shall determine.   Each labour tribunal
B   shall consist of one person."

Regulation 10 (2) of the Industrial Disputes Regulations made under s. 39 of the 1950 Act provides that the person constituting a labour tribunal is to be designated President of the Tribunal.

It was thus for the Minister to decide how many tribunals there should be and then for the Public Service Commission or the Judicial Service Commission to
C   make the necessary appointments.   The tribunals were established " for the purposes of this Act ", i.e., the Act of 1950.   They were therefore intended to be part of the machinery for the prevention, investigation and settlement of industrial disputes.   The legal rights and obligations of employers and workmen can be determined in the ordinary courts.   If it had been the intention of the legislature to create judicial tribunals in substitution for or as an alternative to the
D   ordinary courts for the determination of legal rights, it is to be expected that the statutory provision creating them would have indicated that.   No such inference is to be drawn from the language of s. 31A and the statement in that section that the tribunals were to be established for the purposes of the Act indicates that that was not the intention of the legislature.   That however is not conclusive, for the legislature may have provided for the creation of a judicial
E   office by attaching to that office powers and duties of a judicial character.

Section 31B (1) introduced into the Act of 1950 by the amending Act of 1957 reads as follows:

" A workman or a trade union on behalf of a workman who is a member of that union, may make an application in writing to a labour tribunal for relief or redress in respect of any of the following matters:
F   " (a) the termination of his services by his employer;
" (b) the question whether any gratuity or other benefits are due to him from his employer on termination of his services and the amount of such gratuity and the nature and extent of any such benefits;
" (c) such other matters relating to the terms of employment or the conditions of labour as may be prescribed."
G
The right given by this section to a workman and to his union acting on his behalf to apply to a labour tribunal does not depend on the existence of an industrial dispute and it is exercisable without the intervention of the Commissioner of Labour or the Minister.

The power to prescribe other matters relating to employment and conditions
H   of labour in relation to which an application can be made, has not been exercised. If it was exercised to the full, then it would seem that a labour tribunal could hear applications in respect of all, or substantially all, the matters that might form the subject of an industrial dispute.   The fact that it is at present restricted to hearing applications under s. 31B (1) relating to the termination of employment and coming within para. (a) or para. (b) above is of no significance in
I   relation to the question whether a tribunal when dealing with such applications exercises judicial power with the result that, if this were the only function of such a tribunal, the President of it would be regarded as the holder of a judicial office.

It was strongly argued on behalf of the respondent that s. 31B (1) only gives a workman the right to apply if he has a cause of action, i.e., if he is alleging a breach by his employer of the contract of service or of some obligation imposed by law on his employer.   It was thus argued that a labour tribunal when dealing with such applications discharged the functions of a court of law and was therefore to be regarded as analogous to a court. If that were the case, one **A** would not expect access to the tribunal to be limited to one party to a dispute arising out of employment. In their lordships' view this argument is not well founded and it is not right to say that a workman can apply only if he has a cause of action.

In this connexion regard must be had to two other subsections in Part IVA, s. 31B (4) and s. 31C (1). Section 31B (4) reads as follows: **B**

" Any relief or redress may be granted by a labour tribunal to a workman upon an application made under sub-s. (1) notwithstanding anything to the contrary in any contract of service between him and his employer."

Sansoni, C.J., in the course of his judgment in this case, said (18) that he thought that this provision gave the tribunal power to give relief against any harsh **C** terms that the employer might have imposed in the contract of service. H. N. G. Fernando, S.P.J., thought (19) that this subsection was intended to overcome provisions in a contract excluding an application to a tribunal. While this provision enables a tribunal to disregard harsh terms in the contract and terms excluding an application to a tribunal, it is not limited to that. It clearly provides that the relief or redress that a tribunal may grant is not to be restricted **D** in any way by the terms of the contract.

Section 31C (1) defines the powers and duties of a tribunal on an application and provides that it

" shall be the duty of the tribunal to make all such inquiries into that application as the tribunal may consider necessary, hear such evidence as may be tendered by the applicant and any person affected by the application, **E** and thereafter make such order as may appear to the tribunal to be just and equitable."

The similarity between the wording of s. 31C (1) and that of s. 17 and s. 24 is significant and striking. An arbitrator by s. 17 and an industrial court by s. 24 are required to make such an award as appears just and equitable. A labour tribunal is required to do the same on a reference (s. 15A) and also by s. 31C (1) **F** on an application. The same meaning must be given to the words " just and equitable " in these sections. Section 17 and s. 24 give an arbitrator and an industrial court unfettered discretion to do what they consider to be right and fair. Section 31C (1) gives a similar discretion to a labour tribunal on an application, and s. 31B (4) makes it clear that in doing so it is not restricted by the terms of the contract. **G**

Section 31B (1) is the gateway through which a workman must pass to get his application before a tribunal, but it is s. 31B (4) and s. 31C (1) which state the powers and duties of a tribunal on an application.

In support of his argument that a workman could apply only if he had a cause of action, counsel for the respondent drew attention to the fact that the words " relief " and " redress " are to be found in s. 5 and s. 6 of the Civil Pro- **H** cedure Code, which respectively define an action in the civil court as " a proceeding for the prevention or redress of a wrong " and an " application to a court for relief or remedy obtainable through the exercise of the court's power or authority ". It does not, however, follow that the relief or redress obtainable on an application is obtainable only where a workman has a cause of action or that it is limited to relief or redress in respect of a breach of contract or of an **I** obligation imposed by law. Section 31B (4) and s. 31C (1) show that that is not so.

Counsel for the respondent particularly relied on the wording of s. 31B (1) (b). That provides that an application can be made in relation to " the question whether any gratuity or other benefits are due . . ." He contended that the words " are due " mean " are legally due " and in support of this contention

---

(18) (1965), 68 N.L.R. at p. 78.   (19) (1965), 68 N.L.R. at p. 94.

A he cited *Richard Pieris & Co.* v. *Wijesiriwardena* (20), where T. S. Fernando, J., held (21) that they meant legally due. In that case the respondent was not represented and so the contrary view was not argued. In *Electric Equipment and Construction Co.* v. *Cooray* (22), Fernando, J., followed the *Pieris* case (20) and set aside an order of a labour tribunal for the payment of two months' wages in lieu of notice on the ground that the workman was only entitled to one

B month's wages in lieu of notice under his contract of employment and held that a labour tribunal could only award what was legally due. In neither of these cases were s. 31B (4) and 31C (1) referred to. If these decisions are right, then full effect cannot be given to these subsections for, instead of being free to order what it considers just and equitable in the way of relief or redress, a tribunal is bound by the terms of the contract and able only to order payment of what is

C legally due.

In *Shell Co. of Ceylon, Ltd.* v. *Pathirana* (23) Abeyesundere, J., held (24) that a labour tribunal had jurisdiction, on an application under s. 31B (1), to order the payment of six weeks' wages in lieu of notice instead of two weeks' wages which had been offered to the applicant in accordance with the terms of the contract of service. The judge's attention does not appear to have been drawn to the

D decisions in the *Pieris* case (20) and in the *Electric Equipment* case (25).

Section 31B (1) does not say that a workman can apply for relief in respect of the wrongful termination of his services. It merely says that he can apply in respect of the termination of his services. The omission of the word " wrongful " is significant. In their lordships' opinion the decision in the *Shell Co.* case (23) was right and the decisions in the *Pieris* case (20) and *Electric Equipment* case (25)

E were wrong.

If, as in their lordships' opinion is the case, a workman can apply for relief or redress in respect of the termination of his employment even when the termination is in accordance with the terms of his contract and not in breach of them, and the tribunal can order what it considers to be just and equitable even though that is in excess of his legal rights, it would be odd if the powers

F of a tribunal in respect of a gratuity or other benefits on the termination of his services, were limited to ordering payment of what is legally due to him. Section 31B (1) (*b*) is curiously worded. It does not say that a workman can appply for a gratuity or other benefits legally due to him, but that he can apply in respect of the question whether they are due. The question is one for the tribunal to determine and, in the light of s. 31C (1), to decide on the basis of what appears to it

G just and equitable. If s. 31B (1) (*b*) stood alone then the words " are due " might be interpreted as meaning " are legally due ", but this subsection must be read with s. 31B (4) and s. 31C (1) and, reading it with these subsections, it is clear that the tribunal's decision is not to be whether a gratuity or other benefit is legally due but whether it is just and equitable that it should be paid. It is not whether it is legally due, but whether it ought to be paid, that the tribunal

H is required to decide. In their lordships' opinion s. 31B (1) (*b*) when properly construed lends no support to the view that on an application a labour tribunal has to determine legal rights.

Counsel for the respondent also relied on the fact that s. 31B (5) provides that where a workman applies to a labour tribunal, he is debarred from any other legal remedy. It does not, however, follow from the fact that if he makes such

I an application and is consequently unable to sue in the courts, that the labour tribunal in dealing with an application exercises judicial power. If he applies to a labour tribunal, he will get what the tribunal thinks just and equitable, and he can apply even when there has been no breach of contract. If he sues in the courts, he will have to show that he has a cause of action and he can get only

---

(20) (1960), 62 N.L.R. 233.   (21) (1960), 62 N.L.R. at p. 235.
(22) (1961), 63 N.L.R. 164 at p. 165.   (23) (1962), 64 N.L.R. 71.
(24) (1962), 64 N.L.R. at p. 72,   (25) (1961), 63 N.L.R. 164.

what is legally due to him.   It is not to be inferred, from the fact that the legisla-   A
ture has prevented a duplication of claims by a workman, that a labour tribunal
deals with an application as a judicial body.

It was also argued for the respondent that the fact that, although the decision
of a labour tribunal is made final by s. 31D (1) and cannot be called in question
in any court, provision is made by s. 31D (2) for an appeal to the Supreme Court
on a question of law, shows that a labour tribunal, when dealing with an applica-   B
tion, acts as a court of law.   This, in their lordships' opinion, is not a necessary
inference from the provision of a right of appeal on a question of law.   Provision
is made in the Arbitration Acts for the determination of questions of law by the
courts, but arbitrators are not judicial officers.

SANSONI, C.J., with whose judgment (26) T. S. FERNANDO, J., agreed (27),
held (28) that a labour tribunal was not acting judicially when dealing with an   C
industrial dispute referred to it but that it was acting judicially when dealing
with an application under s. 31B (1).   It follows from his judgment that the
Public Service Commission would be the right body to appoint the president of
a tribunal, when that tribunal was required to deal with an industrial dispute,
but that the Judicial Service Commission would be required to appoint him when
it had to deal with applications.   In their lordships' view this cannot be right.   D
Each labour tribunal may have to deal with both industrial disputes and applications.   Each labour tribunal is one tribunal with one member designated the
president.   The Act creating them lends no support to the view that the president
should be appointed by a different body depending on the nature of the work
coming before the tribunal.   In determining whether or not the office of president
is a judicial office, regard must be had to all the functions such a tribunal may   E
be required to discharge.   It is one office.

While the matter is not free from difficulty and, as has been said, no single
test can be applied to determine whether an office is judicial, in their lordships'
opinion the office of president of a labour tribunal is not a judicial office within
the meaning of those words in the Constitution Order in Council.   Their reasons
for this conclusion may be summarised as follows: F

1.   Labour tribunals were established for the purposes of the Act of 1950,
namely to provide for the prevention, investigation and settlement of industrial
disputes.   The Act making provision for them did not say that they were to
perform the functions of a court in giving effect to the legal rights of workmen in
connexion with their employment.

2.   On a reference of an industrial dispute, a labour tribunal has the same   G
powers and duties as an arbitrator under the Act.   It was rightly held by the
Supreme Court that when so acting, a labour tribunal was not acting judicially
and that an arbitrator and a member of an industrial court did not hold judicial
offices.

3.   On an application, the powers and duties of a labour tribunal do not differ
from those of an arbitrator and an industrial court or a labour tribunal on a   H
reference in any material respect.   A labour tribunal, an arbitrator and an
industrial court are required to do what is just and equitable and it is expressly
provided that a labour tribunal when dealing with an application is not restricted
by the terms of the contract of employment in granting relief or redress.

In the course of hearing an application a tribunal may be informed of the
terms of the contract, but it is not restricted to giving effect to legal rights.   I

4.   The similarity of the powers and duties of a labour tribunal both in relation
to a reference and to an application points strongly to the conclusion that its
functions are not of a different character on an application to those on a reference
or to those of an arbitrator or an industrial court.

5.   By s. 31B (2), inserted into the Act of 1950 by the amending Act of 1957,
a labour tribunal was required to defer making an order on an application if it

(26) (1965), 68 N.L.R. at p. 75.   (27) (1965), 68 N.L.R. at p. 102.
                    (28) (1965), 68 N.L.R. at pp. 81, 82.

A appeared that the subject-matter of the application was under discussion with the employer until the discussion was concluded or the Minister referred the matter to an arbitrator, or to an industrial court or a labour tribunal. A new subsection was substituted for this subsection by the Industrial Disputes (Amendment) Act, No. 4 of 1962.

B Section 31B (3), introduced by the amending Act of 1957, further provides that a tribunal shall suspend its proceedings on an application if it appears that the subject-matter of the application is similar to or identical with a matter constituting or included in an industrial dispute into which an inquiry under the Act is held, or, if the facts affecting the application are facts affecting any proceedings under any other law. This subsection further provides that on the conclusion of the inquiry or of the proceedings under any other law, the tribunal

C should resume proceedings and in making its order on the application should have regard to the award or decision in the inquiry or other proceedings.

These two subsections show that, far from being established in substitution for or as an alternative to the ordinary courts, labour tribunals were created as part of the machinery for preventing and settling industrial disputes. It would indeed be novel if proceedings in a court of law were required by law to be sus-

D pended during discussions between the parties to those proceedings and if a court of law was required to have regard to awards made in respect of an industrial dispute by non-judicial persons, when making its order on an application; so novel, indeed, as to lead to the conclusion that labour tribunals were not intended to, are not required to and do not act as courts of law.

6. Applying the test adumbrated by Lord Simonds in the *Labour Relations*

E *Board* case (29), the matters with which a labour tribunal may be required to deal, both on a reference and on an application, do not make it desirable that presidents of labour tribunals should have the same qualifications as those which distinguish the judges of the superior or other courts.

Their lordships will, for the reasons stated, humbly advise Her Majesty that this appeal will be allowed and the case remitted to the Supreme Court of Ceylon

F to deal with the respondent's appeal to the court on questions of law. The respondent must pay the appellant's costs of this appeal except for the costs of the petition for special leave to appeal.

LORD GUEST and **LORD DEVLIN** delivered the following dissenting judgment: We have the misfortune to differ from the conclusions of the majority

G of our colleagues on the Board. This decision and others like it will affect the future shape of the law and in particular will help to determine whether the growing body of law which regulates industrial relations is to be administered within the judicial or within the executive sphere. We propose therefore to state without going into much detail the basis of our dissent.

It is commonplace that with respect to industrial relations the common law

H of master and servant has fallen into disuse. Disputes about conditions of employment are not usually settled by the courts in accordance with the terms, express or implied, of the contract of service. Trade unionism could no doubt have used its increased bargaining power to obtain more realistic and elaborate contracts of service within the framework of the old common law, but it preferred to use it to seek advantages irrespective of contract and enforceable not by legal

I machinery but by the threat of the strike. The law has therefore had to make a new entry into the field of industrial relations. It has had to start again from the beginning, and, as in the field of international relations, has had to make its way in by formulating methods of securing the peaceful settlement of disputes.

As Sansoni, C.J., has recorded (30), the law of Ceylon was late in entering the industrial field with the Industrial Disputes Act, 1950. The Act set up a

commissioner with the function of promoting the settlement of industrial dis- A
putes.   He was empowered to do so by means of conciliation procedure and
of arbitration when the parties agreed to submit to it.   The Act provided also
for the making and registration of collective agreements, whose terms were to
become implied terms of the contract of employment between those employers
and workmen who were covered by it.   All these were voluntary procedures,
but the Act provided also for the compulsory settlement of disputes by an   B
industrial court.   If the Minister referred a dispute to a court, the court could
make an award, whose terms like those of a collective agreement, would become
implied terms of the contract of employment.   Provision was made for the
subsequent variation of such terms at the instance of any of the parties.

The Act of 1950 thus employed the known ways of settling the ordinary trade
dispute; but it did not include any simple way of remedying a grievance which   C
an individual workman might have against his employer.   Suppose, for example,
that a workman was dismissed with such notice as the common law thinks
reasonable but which a fair-minded employer nowadays probably accepts as
inadequate; or suppose he was dismissed because of reduction in the labour
force, but without the ex gratia payment which a reasonably generous employer
would nowadays think appropriate.   The aggrieved workman in such a case   D
could seek the help of his trade union, which could threaten industrial action.
Then there might be a reference which might result in the workman obtaining
better treatment and in an award to govern similar cases in the future.   There
might be no question, however, of principle involved calling for a general award;
the case might involve nothing more than a decision on what was the fair thing
to do in the particular circumstances.   A swift way of dealing with an individual   E
grievance without calling out the whole force of trade unionism would certainly
help to promote industrial peace.   It was supplied by an amending Act, the
Industrial Disputes (Amendment) Act, No. 62 of 1957.   This Act enlarged the
definition of industrial dispute so as to make it clear that it included a dispute
or difference between an individual employer and an individual workman.   It
inserted into the Act of 1950 a new part, Part IVA, entitled " Labour Tribunals ".   F
The function of the labour tribunal is to entertain applications by a workman
for relief or redress in respect of such matters relating to the terms of employment or the conditions of labour as may be prescribed.   The particular matters
specified in the Act are those which we have already mentioned by way of example,
namely, questions arising out of the termination of the workman's services and
relating to gratuities or other benefits payable on termination.   On such matters   G
the tribunal is to make such order as may appear to it to be just and equitable.   The
workman has to make his choice between the remedy afforded by the Act and
any other legal remedy he may have; he cannot seek both.   If he goes to the
tribunal, the tribunal's order settles the matter and is not to be called in question
in any court except that there may be an appeal to the Supreme Court on a
question of law.   Any money which the tribunal orders to be paid to a workman   H
can be recovered summarily through a magistrate's court in the same manner as a
fine.

The question for the Board is whether the labour tribunal, which under the
Act is to consist of a single person, is a " judicial officer " within s. 55 of the
Constitution.   If so, he can be appointed only by the Judicial Service Commission, in which is also vested the power of transfer, dismissal and disciplinary   I
control.   If not, he is a servant of the administration to be appointed by the
Public Services Commission.   In this way there is maintained, as the Board said
in *The Bribery Comr*. v. *Ranasinghe* (31), a dividing line between the judiciary
and the executive.

It is not disputed that the labour tribunal is an office.   If the power that is
conferred on him by Part IVA derives from the judicial power of the state, then
he is a judicial officer.   It is true that judicial power can be entrusted to someone

(31) [1964] 2 All E.R. at p. 787, letter G;   [1965] A.C. at p. 190.

A who is not a judicial officer and the person so entrusted is then generally spoken of as acting quasi-judicially. So also, administrative power can be given to a judge. The character of the office depends on the character of the chief function. Apart from his function under Part IVA the labour tribunal can act as an arbitrator to whom the commissioner can with consent refer disputes (a role that before 1957 was filled by the district judge) and in the case of a minor dispute
B can act in place of an industrial court by virtue of a reference by the Minister; but these are ancillary duties that may or may not come his way. The commission that has to make the appointment has to do so before it is known whether they will or not. It is not therefore seriously contested that the character of the office of the labour tribunal must be decided by reference to the powers granted and the duties put on him by Part IVA. So the question is whether
C these powers and duties are judicial or administrative in character.

It must be remembered that this is a constitutional question so that Parliament, when it passed the amending Act of 1957, had not a free hand. It may be thought convenient that all officers under the Act should belong to the same category, and that, as Tambiah, J., suggested (32), they should be filled by persons acquainted with labour practices rather than with practice in the courts.
D On the other hand, it may be an advantage that those who are creating the law, so to speak, in the form of general awards should be different in character to those who have to apply it in individual cases; and that those who have to give just decisions in whatever sphere should come from the profession that is experienced in the administration of justice. If this were not a constitutional point, these are the sort of considerations that might be weighed in order to
E ascertain the intent of the Act; but on the constitutional point the presumed intention of Parliament can have only a very limited effect. If Parliament wants disputes under Part IVA to be settled judicially, the persons who settle them must be appointed by the Judicial Service Commission whether Parliament thinks it convenient or not. Of course, if there be any doubt about whether the language of Part IVA does or does not confer judicial power, the intent of the Act
F is relevant to determine that point: but beyond that it is immaterial.

We think with respect that there is nothing to be gained by comparing the functions of the labour tribunal with those of the industrial court on the assumption that the latter is not a judicial body. Although the language of the Act suggests strongly that the primary function of the industrial court is arbitral (we shall consider later the exact meaning of this rather dubious word) rather
G than judicial, the court is empowered to make orders affecting the existing rights of an individual workman. On the other hand there is in the case of the industrial court no provision for appeal to a court of law or for ousting the jurisdiction of a court of law on the same subject-matter. It seems to us to be unnecessary to decide whether an industrial court, when dealing with a dispute which is also within the jurisdiction of the labour tribunal, is exercising judicial power. If
H it is, we think that the exercise is ancillary to the main function of the court which is arbitral; and consequently that the officers of the court would not be judicial officers.

Thus in our opinion the question whether a body is exercising judicial power is not to be determined by looking at its functions in conjunction with those of other bodies set up by the Act, and forming a general impression about whether
I they are judicial or administrative. Nor is it to be answered by totting up and balancing resemblances between the labour tribunal and other judicial or administrative bodies. Judicial power is a concept that is capable of clear delineation. It has to be, since it is the basis of a constitutional requirement, and legislation which falls on the wrong side of the line can be completely avoided. It has been considered many times in relation to those constitutions, particularly the Australian, which provide for the separation of powers. We propose therefore to take the basic definition and consider whether or not the power of the

(32) (1965), 68 N.L.R. at p. 109.

labour tribunal falls within it.   In the authorities there is also a discussion of a   **A**
number of identifying marks distinguishing the judicial from the executive and
legislative powers and we shall consider those that appear to us to be relevant.

The accepted definition of judicial power is that given by GRIFFITHS, C.J., in
Huddart Parker & Co. Proprietary, Ltd. v. *Moorehead* (33).   It is the power

> " which every sovereign authority must of necessity have to decide con-
> troversies between its subjects, or between itself and its subjects, whether   **B**
> the rights relate to life, liberty, or property.   The exercise of this power
> does not begin until some tribunal which has power to give a binding and
> authoritative decision (whether subject to appeal or not) is called upon to
> take action."

The power of the labour tribunal clearly falls within these general terms, but it is   **C**
worth noting some particular aspects of it.

There must be a controversy about rights or, as it is sometimes put, a *lis.*
Part IVA covers controversies between a workman and his employer about
the rights arising out of that relationship.   The power of the tribunal is that of
giving a binding and authoritative decision.   In this respect the procedure is
to be distinguished from the conciliation procedures provided under the Act.   **D**

The power proceeds from the Sovereign, i.e., it is the judicial power of the State.
In this respect it is to be distinguished from the power of an arbitrator whose
authority is derived from the consent of the parties themselves.   This factor—
that it is the judicial power of the State—carries with it another consequence.
Justice can be done in an individual case without creating any principle applicable
to other cases of the same sort; but the judicial power of the State is concerned   **E**
with justice for all and that is not attained if there are inexplicable differentia-
tions between decisions in the same type of case.   The judicial power of the
State must therefore be exercised in conformity with principle.   In *Moses* v.
Parker, Ex p. Moses (34) there was vested in the Supreme Court of Tasmania
jurisdiction to deal with disputes regarding claims to grants of land.   Such
disputes had previously been dealt with by the governor on the report of commis-   **F**
sioners, the governor being " in equity and good conscience " entitled to make a
grant.   The statute which gave jurisdiction to the Supreme Court provided that
it should not be " bound by the strict rules of law or equity in any case, or by
any technicalities or legal forms whatever ".   The Board held (35) that a decision
of the Supreme Court given under the statute was not " a judicial decision
admitting of appeal ".   Explaining this case (34) in the later case of *Canadian*   **G**
Pacific Ry. Co. v. *Toronto Corpn. and Grand Trunk Ry. Co. of Canada,* (36) the
Board said that (37)

> " . . . as the tribunal from which it was desired to appeal was expressly
> exonerated from all rules of law or practice, and certain affairs were placed
> in the hands of the judges as the persons from whom the best opinions
> might be obtained, and not as a court administering justice between the   **H**
> litigants, such functions do not attract the prerogative of the Crown to
> grant appeals."

These decisions indicate the importance of the provision in the Ceylon statute
which gives a right of appeal from the tribunal on questions of law.   In *Moses*
v. *Parker* (34) the Board, after observing (35) that the court was expressly
exonerated from all rules of law, continued (35):   **I**

> " How then can the propriety of their decision be tested on appeal?
> What are the canons by which this Board is to be guided in advising Her
> Majesty whether the Supreme Court is right or wrong?   It seems almost
> impossible that decisions can be varied except by reference to some rule;

---

(33) (1909), 8 C.L.R. at p. 357.   (34) [1896] A.C. 245.
(35) [1896] A.C. at p. 248.   (36) [1911] A.C. 461.
(37) [1911] A.C. at p. 471.

A whereas the court making them is free from rules. If appeals were allowed, the certain result would be to establish some system of rules; and that is the very thing from which the Tasmanian legislature has desired to leave the Supreme Court free and unfettered in each case. If it were clear that appeals ought to be allowed, such difficulties would doubtless be met somehow."

B In the present case it is clear that appeals are allowed and the corollary is that there must be established a system of rules. It is true that the only requirement in the Act is that the orders of the tribunal must be such as appear to them to be just and equitable; but this imports a judicial discretion, albeit a very wide one. If an order was made arbitrarily, this would be, as TAMBIAH, J., says (38), a good ground of appeal. Experience shows that out of a jurisdiction of this

C sort there grows a body of principles laying down how the discretion is to be exercised and thus uniformity is created in the administration of justice. In this fashion, as was said in *Moses* v. *Parker* (39), there emerges inevitably a system of law.

This does not mean, however, that unless the tribunal from the first applies an existing system of law it cannot be judicial. The distinction is not between

D old law and new law but between law and no law. It is quite plain to us that in doing justice and equity under the Act, the tribunal will have to have regard to many novel considerations and to pay only limited regard to matters, such as the contract of employment, which under the existing law of master and servant would be determinative. The directions given to the tribunal under s. 31B (2) and (3) are, if addressed to a court of law, unprecedented and we shall consider

E them in greater detail later. Other matters to be considered are novel only in the sense that they have never been accepted as part of the common law. The power to order reinstatement, for example, conferred by s. 33 is well known to most systems of law but not to the common law. In the United Kingdom the deficiencies of the common law in this respect are gradually being made good by statutes such as the Contracts of Employment Act 1963 and the Redundancy

F Payments Act 1965. What the Ceylon statute appears to us to be doing is to substitute for the rigidity of the old law a new and more flexible system. In some such fashion English equity gave relief from the common law. Those who made equity were judges and not administrators.

Another characteristic of the judicial power is that it is concerned with existing rights, that is those which the parties actually have at the inception of the suit

G and not those which it may be thought they ought to have; it is concerned with the past and present and not with the future. This distinction between the judicial and the arbitral power has been elaborated in a number of authorities. The word " arbitral " is not used to distinguish between judge and arbitrator in the ordinary sense, for the arbitrator, like the judge, ordinarily deals with disputes about existing rights. But most industrial arbitrations are concerned with settling

H conditions of employment as they should be in the future and " arbitral " is used to describe that function. In *A.-G. of Commonwealth of Australia* v. *Reginam and Boilermakers' Society of Australia* (40), the Board, after saying (41) that " the function of an industrial arbitrator is completely outside the realm of judicial power and is of a different order ", went on to cite (42) the well known passage from the judgment of ISAACS and RICH, JJ., in *Waterside Workers*

I *Federation* v. *Alexander* (43).

". . . the essential difference is that the judicial power is concerned with the ascertainment, declaration and enforcement of the rights and liabilities as they exist, or are deemed to exist, at the moment the proceedings are

(38) (1965), 68 N.L.R. at p. 112.   (39) [1896] A.C. 245.
(40) [1957] 2 All E.R. 45; [1957] A.C. 288.
(41) [1957] 2 All E.R. at pp. 49, 50; [1957] A.C. at p. 310.
(42) [1957] 2 All E.R. at p. 50, letter A; [1957] A.C. at p. 310.
(43) (1918), 25 C.L.R. 434 at p. 463.

A

instituted; whereas the function of the arbitral power in relation to industrial disputes is to ascertain and declare, but not enforce, what in the opinion of the arbitrator ought to be the respective rights and liabilities of the parties in relation to each other."

TAMBIAH, J. (44), we think with respect, errs in supposing that because the tribunal is not administering the old law it is not giving decisions on existing rights but creating future ones. It is the statute which creates the right to equitable relief by giving to the workman the option of going to the labour tribunal to ask for it instead of taking what the common law will give him. One method of altering the law on master and servant would be to enact a new set of rules, as has been done to some extent in the United Kingdom by the statutes which we have mentioned, leaving to the court only the task of interpretation and application. Another method, frequently employed, is to give fresh powers to the court. Under the latter method the right comes into existence as soon as there is created the relationship, in this case that of employer and workman, from which it springs; it does not have to wait for life until the relief granted is spelt out in words by the court.

B

C

Another and essential characteristic of judicial power is that it should be exercised judicially. Put another way, judicial power is power limited by the obligation to act judicially. Administrative or executive power is not limited in that way. Judicial action requires as a minimum the observance of some rules of natural justice. Exactly what these are will vary with the circumstances of the case, as TUCKER, L.J., said in *Russell* v. *Duke of Norfolk* (45) in a passage which has several times been approved. Whatever standard is adopted, TUCKER, L.J., said (46), one essential is that the person concerned should have a reasonable opportunity of presenting his case. LORD HODSON in *Ridge* v. *Baldwin* (47) after quoting TUCKER, L.J.'s dictum (48), added (49):

D

E

"No one, I think, disputes that three features of natural justice stand out— (i) the right to be heard by an unbiased tribunal; (ii) the right to have notice of charges of misconduct; (iii) the right to be heard in answer to those charges."

F

These are not necessarily features of administrative decisions. The administrator is not required to be unbiased and his decision may often affect those who have no opportunity of presenting their views.

Under s. 31C (2) the labour tribunal is empowered, subject to regulations which have not yet been made, itself to lay down the procedure to be observed by it. We think that it is clear from the authorities—indeed, the contrary was not suggested —that the nature of its enquiry is such that it must act in conformity with natural justice. A recent example of the applicability of the rules in this type of case is *R.* v. *Deputy Industrial Injuries Comr., Ex p. Moore* (50). It is arguable that the rules of natural justice are not applicable at all unless there is an obligation to act judicially and that if such a limitation is imposed on the power, it must be a judicial power. LORD PARKER, C.J., said recently in *Re K.* (*H.*) (*an infant*) (51) that it may be that where there is no duty to act judicially or quasi-judicially there is no power in the court to interfere. The point was not explored, however, in argument before the Board and we shall not therefore say more than that to hold that the labour tribunal is bound by the rules of natural justice is going a long way towards holding that it is a judicial tribunal.

G

H

I

(44) (1965), 68 N.L.R. at p. 113.
(45) [1949] 1 All E.R. 109 at p. 118.
(46) [1949] 1 All E.R. at p. 118, letter F.
(47) [1963] 2 All E.R. 66 at p. 114; [1964] A.C. 40 at p. 132.
(48) [1949] 1 All E.R. at p. 118.
(49) [1963] 2 All E.R. at p. 114; [1964] A.C. at p. 132.
(50) [1965] 1 All E.R. 81 at p. 86; [1965] 1 Q.B. 456 at p. 476.
(51) [1967] 1 All E.R. 226 at p. 231, letter E.

A   Finally, there is the principle that the judicial power must be exercised so as to do justice in the case that is being tried and the judge must not allow himself to be influenced by any other consideration at all. Considerations of policy or expediency, which are permissible for the administrator, must be altogether excluded by the judge. The labour tribunal is, as we have said, empowered by the statute to enquire into matters that have hitherto been regarded as outside

B   the purview of courts of law and as relevant only to the making of collective bargains. If these enquiries, although unusual and opening up a new source of law, are all subordinate to the tribunal's task of making a just and equitable order on the workman's application for relief, well and good. If they impose on the tribunal, however, the duty of making an order that is politic or expedient rather than one which is just and equitable, then the tribunal is in effect being

C   told that it is not a judicial tribunal. To our minds this is the crucial question in this case. We must now review the provisions in the Act which are said to introduce extraneous considerations inconsistent with the judicial task.

    We do not attach importance to the fact that by s. 31A (1) labour tribunals are established for the purposes of the Act. The purposes of the Act as set out in the preamble are " the prevention, investigation and settlement of industrial

D   disputes, and . . . matters connected therewith or incidental thereto ". It is argued that this means only the arbitral settlement of industrial disputes, but this seems to us to beg the question. That was what it meant when the Act of 1950 was first drafted, because the Act then provided only for conciliation and arbitral settlement; but the preamble does not prescribe the mode of settlement and, if Parliament decided by the amending Act of 1957 to introduce judicial

E   settlement, there would be no call to alter the preamble.

    Nor do we consider that the exercise of any of the powers conferred by s. 33 requires the tribunal to act unjudicially. The power to reinstate, or to grant compensation in lieu of reinstatement, is new but there is nothing unjudicial about it. Likewise, the provision in s. 31B (4) that the tribunal may, in granting relief or redress, override the terms of the contract of service is in this branch

F   of the law startlingly new; but it is not contrary to modern ideas of justice. The idea that freely negotiated contracts should be conclusively presumed to contain just and equitable provisions began to die with the end of the nineteenth century. Long before then equity had refused to give effect to provisions in a contract which it considered to be harsh and unconscionable. From the beginning of the twentieth century legislatures all over the Commonwealth have been

G   writing terms into contracts and taking them out, whatever the parties may think about them. No doubt it is taking the process a step further to leave it to the discretion of the court to say for itself what terms of the contract it will enforce, but there is nothing in this that is contrary to principle. Indeed in this subsection the statute is doing no more than accepting and recognising the well known fact that the relations between an employer and his workman are no longer completely

H   governed by the contract of service.

    The provisions in the Act which appear to us to be questionable fall into two categories. First, there are those which may appear to divert the attention of the tribunal from the demands of justice to what may be called the politics of industrial bargaining. Secondly, there are those which seem to subordinate the new process under Part IVA to the other arbitral activities provided for by the Act.

I   If any of these provisions can fairly be construed as a direction to the labour tribunal that in framing his order he is not simply to decide what is just and equitable as between the parties but that he is also to consider what sort of order is most likely to promote industrial peace generally, and that, if the just order might give rise to conflict, he is not to make it, we should not hesitate to conclude that the labour tribunal was not a judicial body. All these provisions are, however, prima facie subordinate to the definitive words in s. 31C (1) which make it the duty of the tribunal to enquire into the application for relief and to make such order as may appear to it to be just and equitable. These words in their natural

and ordinary meaning require the tribunal to do justice between the parties to   A
the application. That is the dominating duty and the dominion can be overthrown
only if there is a strong inference from other provisions in Part IVA that justice
between the parties is not to be the only object of the order. We have to take into
consideration not only the positive words of s. 31C (1) but also the other indications, to which we have drawn attention, that the tribunal is vested with judicial
power, especially the provision for appeal to the Supreme Court and the fact that   B
the tribunal must observe the rules of natural justice. Finally, it is to be remembered that Part IVA, ousts, at the option of the workman, the jurisdiction of the
ordinary courts. It would require very strong words to satisfy us that an Act of
Parliament, which deprived the employer of his rights at common law in any
dispute which he might have with one of his workmen, offered him no alternative
way of getting justice as distinct from administrative treatment.   C

It is not in our opinion inconsistent with the dominating duty to make a just
and equitable order that the statute should prescribe the sources of equity to
which the tribunal must have regard. This in our opinion satisfactorily accounts
for the presence in the statute of two provisions which are said to require the
tribunal to have regard to extraneous considerations. The first is s. 31B (3)
which requires the tribunal before making its order to consider any relevant   D
arbitral award and then have regard to it. We can see nothing contrary to justice
in this. A good guide to what is fair and equitable in a particular case must be
furnished by settlements which bodies of employers and workmen have made or
are making in similar cases. The terms of collective bargains must be a source to
which the tribunal can properly resort. It is true that the terms of such bargains
may reflect the operation of considerations of policy or expediency which have   E
induced the assent of one side or the other; but that does not involve the tribunal
in questions of policy any more than the application of a statute involves a court
of law in the issues of policy that have led up to its enactment.

The other provision is s. 46 (4), which allows the commissioner to be present
and heard in any proceedings before the labour tribunal. If this means that the
commissioner is entitled to express his opinion on how the claim should be   F
treated, it would indeed be a serious matter to consider, for it is to be presumed
that the commissioner would concern himself with questions of general policy
rather than of individual justice. But there is no need to suppose that the function
of the commissioner is more than that of informing the court about the results of
collective bargains which, as we have said, the tribunal may properly regard as a
source of equity and of assisting the tribunal in the inquiries which it is told to   G
make about other similar proceedings.

In the second category there are two provisions in s. 31B (2) which allow the
arbitral or conciliatory procedure to take precedence over the tribunal's procedure.
One is the provision in para. (a) which requires the tribunal to give effect to any
settlement of the matter which is reached with the employer by the workman's
trade union. The other is the provision in para. (b) which requires the tribunal   H
to dismiss the workman's claim if its subject matter forms part of an industrial
dispute referred by the Minister under the arbitral provisions of the Act. This
dismissal does not preclude the workman from pursuing his rights at common law
since under s. 31B (5) they are excluded only where proceedings before the tribunal
are taken and concluded.

These provisions are designed to avoid a conflict of jurisdiction between the   I
bodies set up under the Act. It would, for example, plainly be absurd if the tribunal was to decide a dispute in favour of an applicant and the industrial court
was to decide it against him, making its decision or award under s. 19 or s. 26
a term of the applicant's contract of employment. Parliament resolves the conflict
by limiting the jurisdiction of the tribunal. It is difficult to say that this limitation is unfair since, if the workman dislikes the limitation, he need not resort to
the tribunal at all; he can, if he prefers, exercise his common law right; but

A   whether it is unfair or not is not to the point. A limitation on the jurisdiction cannot affect the quality of decisions given within the jurisdiction.

The second provision, para. (b), in terms ousts the jurisdiction of the tribunal, leaving the matter to be settled either as an industrial dispute or by the workman's action at common law. The first provision is a less obvious way of ousting the jurisdiction but that is what in substance, though not in form, it is doing. A

B   court of law has no doubt the formal power of refusing to make an order in accordance with a settlement reached by the parties, but it is a power which is exercised only in exceptional cases, as for example when one of the parties is under the protection of the court. Otherwise the court does not enquire whether the proposed settlement achieves a just result; it assumes that it does. It assumes also that counsel has authority to make a settlement on behalf of his client; if he

C   has not, it is a matter that they must settle between themselves. The Act is based on a similar assumption that a trade union has a similar authority from its members. This is evident not only in para. (a) but more significantly in s. 8 which empowers a trade union to make a collective settlement which will alter the terms of individual contracts. If para. (a) had provided that any settlement made by the applicant's trade union was deemed to be authorised by him, it would

D   have achieved the same result without affording any scope for the suggestion that the tribunal was being asked to adopt a practice not normally followed by courts of law.

Section 31B (2) is therefore removing from the jurisdiction of the tribunal disputes which Parliament considers are better settled by other means. It is true that in such settlements by other means what is thought to be politic and exped-

E   ient may play a large part. It often does in settlements of ordinary actions; but this does not inject expediency into the deliberations of the tribunal. There is nothing in s. 31B (2) which affects the duty of the tribunal under s. 31C (1) to decide in accordance with justice and equity all such matters as it has to decide.

Accordingly we conclude that the orders which the tribunal is to make under Part IVA are judgments and not administrative orders. Since the whole function

F   of the tribunal under Part IVA is to consider applications and hold enquiries which are to end in judgments, it must follow that the tribunal is a judicial tribunal and that the person constituting the tribunal is a judicial officer.

Appeal allowed.

G   Solicitors: *A. L. Bryden & Williams* (for the appellants); *Farrer & Co.* (for the respondent).

[*Reported by* KATHLEEN J. H. O'BRIEN, *Barrister-at-Law.*]

A

MORGAN v. FRY AND OTHERS.

Reversed. C.A. [1968] 3 All E.R. 452.

[QUEEN'S BENCH DIVISION (Widgery, J.), February 20, 21, 22, 23, 24, 27, 28, March 1, 2, 3, 6, 17, 1967.]

*Trade Union—Inducement to commit breach of contract—Unlawful means—
Absence of justification—Threats to call strike—No express prohibition of
strikes in contract of employment—Threats made to procure dismissal from
employment of plaintiff who had resigned from union—Plaintiff dismissed
as result of threats—Whether strike notice would lawfully have terminated
employment—Whether implied term in contract permitting strikes—Whether
union officers liable for conspiracy or intimidation—Trade Disputes Act,
1906 (6 Edw. 7 c. 47), s. 3.*

B

C

The plaintiff had been a lockman employed by the Port of London
Authority (" the P.L.A.") until his dismissal on Apr. 6, 1963. Lockmen
were a numerically small group who fulfilled a vital function and who could
have paralysed the whole port if they had decided on a stoppage of work.
The P.L.A. did not enforce a closed shop, but at all material times the
majority of its lockmen were members of the Transport & General Workers'
Union (" the transport union "). All the defendants were officers of the
transport union. The plaintiff joined the P.L.A. in June, 1959, and the
transport union two months later. In 1962, some thirty members of
the transport union, including the plaintiff, formed a break-away union called
the Union of Port Workers (" the U.P.W."). The plaintiff then allowed
his membership of the transport union to lapse. F., the regional secretary of
the transport union (the first defendant) in March, 1963, obtained from
its general executive council plenary powers enabling him to call a strike,
and informed the P.L.A. that it was his intention to exercise those powers
by instructing transport union members not to work with U.P.W. members
or with non-unionists, but to carry out their duties as far as possible without
assistance from such persons. The defendant H. attended with F. the
meetings at which F. first formulated this threat. The contracts of P.L.A.
employees contained no express ban on strikes. The plaintiff was asked
by the P.L.A. to rejoin the transport union, and when he refused he was
dismissed. He was subsequently re-admitted to membership of the transport
union, but the P.L.A. declined to re-employ him. In an action by
the plaintiff against, among others, F., the regional secretary, and H., the
district organiser, of the union (neither of whom were employed by the
P.L.A.), and against the chairman and secretary of the Poplar branch of
the union, for damages on the ground that the plaintiff's dismissal was
the consequence either of their unlawful conspiracy or of unlawful
intimidation exercised by them against the P.L.A.,

D

E

F

G

Held: (i) the claim based on alleged conspiracy failed because the
defendants' actions were not intended to injure the plaintiff, but were done
in the genuine belief that they were necessary to protect the legitimate
interests of the transport union; moreover their actions were done in contemplation or furtherance of a trade dispute as defined by the Trade
Disputes Act, 1906, s. 5 (see p. 394, letter D, post).

H

(ii) in regard to the claim based on intimidation of the P.L.A.—

I

(a) no term would be implied in the lockmen's contracts of service that
strike action consequent on refusal to work with members of the U.P.W.
would not be a breach of their contracts of service (see p. 396, letter H, post),
and

(b) F. was not protected by s. 3 of the Trade Disputes Act, 1906, against
an action at the suit of the plaintiff (as distinct from an action at the suit
of the employer, the P.L.A.) for intimidation based on his threat to induce
breaches of the lockmen's contracts of service (such threat being a threat of

A an unlawful act); accordingly, as F.'s conduct was unlawful and thus unjustifiable, the plaintiff was entitled to recover damages for intimidation as against F. (see p. 397, letters A and D, post).

Dictum of LORD PEARCE in *J. T. Stratford & Son, Ltd.* v. *Lindley* ([1964] 3 All E.R. at p. 114, letter H) applied.

Rookes v. *Barnard* ([1964] 1 All E.R. 367) followed and dictum of LORD
B DEVLIN, (ibid., at p. 398 and p. 400, letter B) considered.

(c) H. was liable as a joint tortfeasor with F., but it had not been proved that the chairman and secretary of the Poplar branch of the union were parties to F.'s acts, and accordingly they were not joint tortfeasors and were not liable (see p. 397, letter F, post).

C [As to the liability of trade union members for civil conspiracy, see 38 HALSBURY'S LAWS (3rd Edn.) 66, para. 76; and for cases on the subject, see 45 DIGEST (Repl.) 590, 591, *1459-1467*.

For the Trade Disputes Act, 1906, see 25 HALSBURY'S STATUTES (2nd Edn.) 1267.]

Cases referred to:

D *Allen* v. *Flood*, [1895-99] All E.R. Rep. 52; [1898] A.C. 1; 67 L.J.Q.B. 119; 77 L.T. 717; 45 Digest (Repl.) 280, *38*.

Crofter Hand Woven Harris Tweed Co., Ltd. v. *Veitch*, [1942] 1 All E.R. 142; [1942] A.C. 435; 111 L.J.P.C. 17; 166 L.T. 172; 45 Digest (Repl.) 534, *1175*.

Rookes v. *Barnard*, [1962] 2 All E.R. 579; [1963] 1 Q.B. 623; [1962] 3 W.L.R.
E 260; *rvsd.* H.L. [1964] 1 All E.R. 367; [1964] A.C. 1129; [1964] 2 W.L.R. 269; 45 Digest (Repl.) 590, *1464*.

Stratford (J. T.) & Son, Ltd. v. *Lindley*, [1964] 2 All E.R. 209; [1965] A.C. 269; [1964] 2 W.L.R. 1002; *rvsd.* H.L. [1964] 3 All E.R. 102; [1965] A.C. 269; [1964] 3 W.L.R. 541; 45 Digest (Repl.) 309, *228*.

Action.
F This was an action for damages brought by the plaintiff, James Patrick Morgan, against six officers of the Transport & General Workers' Union, alleging that they had procured his dismissal from employment with the Port of London Authority by conspiracy or by unlawful intimidation. The facts are set out in the judgment.

G *W. L. Mars-Jones, Q.C.,* and *Jonathan Sofer* for the plaintiff.
John D. Stocker, Q.C., and *M. Stuart-Smith* for the defendants.

Cur. adv. vult.

Mar. 17. **WIDGERY, J.,** read the following judgment: Before I begin to read this judgment may I express my indebtedness to counsel for the assistance
H which they gave me throughout a complicated case.

The plaintiff in this action was employed by the Port of London Authority (to whom I will refer as the P.L.A.) as a lockman from June, 1959, until he was dismissed on Apr. 6, 1963. He claims damages against the defendants Fry, Harrall, Mehegan and Bilson, alleging that his dismissal was the result of an unlawful conspiracy between these defendants or a consequence of unlawful
I intimidation exercised by them against the P.L.A. to secure a termination of the plaintiff's contract of service. Similar claims against the defendants Crispin and Crone were discontinued in the course of the trial.

The P.L.A. are responsible for the administration of the docks in the Port of London and Tilbury. They employ a total of some 650 lockmen to operate the gates and sluices whereby shipping enters the docks from the river. Most of the lockmen are employed in the London group of docks but about 130 work at Tilbury which is some fifteen miles away. Although a comparatively small group numerically, the lockmen fulfil a vital function and a stoppage of work amongst

them could paralyse the whole port in a very short time. Their pay and condi-   **A**
tions of service are generally regarded as good, and with one minor exception
no stoppage of work has originated amongst the lockmen in living memory.

The P.L.A. do not make membership of a trade union a condition of employment amongst lockmen, but at all material times the bulk of the men so employed
were members of the Transport & General Workers' Union (to which I refer for
brevity as the transport union). The P.L.A. welcomed this because, although   **B**
they do not wish to insist on what is popularly called a closed shop, it is a convenience to them to be able to negotiate with a single union on behalf of the
lockmen as a whole. For some time the P.L.A. had had an understanding with
the transport union, which may or may not have had the force of a contract,
that they would not recognise any body other than the transport union for the
purpose of negotiating pay and conditions of service for lockmen in their employ.   **C**

The defendants are all officials or perhaps officers of the transport union,
which is organised geographically in branches, districts, and regions. Members
of a particular trade may also be organised in trade groups within the union.
The lockmen employed by the P.L.A. were enrolled in the Poplar branch of the
union, of which branch the defendant Bilson was chairman and the defendant
Mehegan secretary. The Poplar branch came within a district organisation of   **D**
which the defendant Harrall was paid full-time district organiser, and this
district in turn came under the No. 1 region of which the defendant Fry was
regional secretary.

The transport union has copious rules which contemplate that its affairs
shall be largely controlled by democratic vote of the rank and file, but this does
not always happen in practice. The method of summoning meetings is haphazard   **E**
and they are poorly attended. No proper check is made to see that only eligible
members vote and the system is too cumbersome to provide quick decisions. In
the result the paid officials have wide powers and frequently act on their own initiative in the expectation that they will be supported by general rank and file opinion
in the union if their actions are subsequently questioned. The official policy of
the transport union was not to press for a closed shop, but in practice this policy   **F**
was subjected to the important qualification that if their members in a particular locality complained strongly at being required to work with non-unionists
the union would " back " them. This meant that, although the officers would not
normally initiate action for the removal of non-unionists, they would do so
in a particular shop or trade or area if feeling amongst their own members was
strong enough to suggest that an unofficial strike against the non-unionists was   **G**
likely. The union's ultimate weapon to secure the removal of non-unionists was,
of course, to call a strike of its own members and thus bring pressure to bear
on the employer. No union official could call a strike without obtaining what
were called plenary powers from the general executive council through Mr.
Frank Cousins, the general secretary. Having obtained plenary powers, it was
open to the official concerned to take action without reference to the members   **H**
affected though, in practice, he had to be careful to see that he carried them
with him and to this end he would frequently, though not invariably, call special
or mass meetings of members to endorse his actions.

The plaintiff, now aged thirty-one, joined the P.L.A. as a lockman on June 1,
1959, after service in the Merchant Navy. He was assigned to a lock called the
Blackwall Entrance in the London group of docks to which the P.L.A. by agree-   **I**
ment with the transport union were required to assign two foremen and eight
lockmen. The lock could in fact be adequately and safely manned by two foremen
and six lockmen. The P.L.A. did not invite the plaintiff to join a union, but he
was recruited by the transport union about two months after starting work.
He says that he had no political allegiance and did not take any interest in
union affairs until 1960 or 1961.

Two incidents occurred during 1961 and 1962 which throw light on the plaintiff's
attitude to union membership at that time. First, the lockmen at Tilbury were

A dissatisfied, because they said that they were too far removed from their branch headquarters at Poplar and were neglected by union officials. Unofficially they formed their own sub-branch which met at Tilbury and eventually about a dozen of their number set up a new union of their own called " The Port Workers Association ". The P.L.A., senior officials of the transport union and some of the more active members of the Poplar branch combined to persuade these

B men to come back to the transport union, which they did, and the incident soon blew over. The plaintiff was not directly concerned in this incident but he told me in evidence that he approved of the action taken by the transport union and did not then recognise the right of the break-away members at Tilbury to set up their own union. The second incident occurred on cup final day in May, 1962, when the plaintiff reported for duty with his shift at the Blackwall

C Entrance but work could not start because only five lockmen were present. A number of barges waiting to enter the lock were kept for nearly two hours until a sixth man appeared, but it was then 12.50 p.m. and the plaintiff and one Hammond insisted on going to their dinner although waiting barges could have been handled in under half-an-hour. This so incensed the foreman, one Curley, that he operated the lock with the remaining men, which he could safely

D do as the level of the water made it unnecessary to operate a swing bridge over the lock and thus reduced the manpower required. Mr. Hammond, however, reported the men to the Poplar branch of the union and they were fined by the branch. Mr. Curley refused to pay his fine and Hammond and the plaintiff incited other men at the lock to strike in protest at Mr. Curley's continued employment. This incident is of interest in showing that in the summer of

E 1962 the plaintiff had no scruples about striking to obtain the dismissal of a workman who no longer belonged to the transport union, and it also helps to explain why Mr. Hammond is sometimes described as a trouble-maker.

In 1962 the transport union was negotiating with the P.L.A. to settle new wage rates and terms of service for lockmen. Most of these terms were agreed without difficulty, but the P.L.A. rejected the union's claim for a 5d. per hour

F shift allowance based on the fact that the lockmen's hours varied with the tide so that they had the irregularity of hours associated with shift working. There had been pressure amongst the rank and file of the union to support this latter claim and on Sept. 9, 1962, a mass meeting of the Poplar branch, mustering 120 lockmen, voted on a motion by Mr. Hammond in favour of an unofficial strike if it was not conceded. The union officials dissuaded the men from unofficial

G action and discussions between the union and the P.L.A. were resumed on a higher level with the general manager of the P.L.A. and a Mr. Henderson, who was a national secretary of the waterways group of the union, being brought in to lead their respective teams. These discussions lead to a provisional agreement for the acceptance of a shift allowance of 3d. per hour, but a mass meeting of the Poplar branch rejected this proposal by ninety votes to fifty-five, and

H Hammond and another member of the transport union called Eric Beadle canvassed the men to support an unofficial strike to secure the full allowance of 5d.

On Oct. 25, 1962, there were further discussions between the P.L.A., led by the general manager, and the officials of the transport union, led by Mr. Henderson, but the P.L.A. were adamant and the union officials clearly formed the view

I that they should accept the offer of 3d. They accordingly called a further mass meeting of the Poplar branch for Oct. 28, at which the recommendations to settle for 3d. per hour were accepted by eighty-four votes to forty-three. Some of the men criticised the conduct of this meeting and when the result of the vote was announced some twenty or more, mostly from Tilbury and led by Mr. Beadle, walked out of the meeting in disgust. The plaintiff did not attend this meeting.

On Nov. 1, 1962, a number of lockmen, mainly from Tilbury, decided to form a new break-away union called the Union of Port Workers (to which I refer as the

U.P.W.). Mr. Beadle was elected president, one Senior, who had been active **A**
in the formation of the Port Workers Association in the previous year, was
appointed secretary and Mr. Hammond also took a leading part. All the witnesses
concerned say that formation of the U.P.W. was a spontaneous expression of
the men's dissatisfaction with the transport union's failure to press the claim
for a 5d. shift allowance, but I am left with the impression that some of the
leading spirits may have been glad of the opportunity to gain power. The **B**
strength of the U.P.W. at this time was about thirty, all of whom with five
exceptions were employed at Tilbury. Four of the five exceptions worked at
the Blackwall Entrance and included the plaintiff, Mr. Hammond and one
Atkins. The transport union rules make no provision for resignation from the
union but provide that a failure to pay thirteen weeks' subscriptions shall
exclude from membership. Most of the members of the U.P.W., including **C**
the plaintiff, merely allowed their subscriptions to the transport union to lapse,
but a few (including Mr. Beadle) wrote letters of resignation to the general
secretary, Mr. Cousins. The formation of the U.P.W. produced a reaction amongst
the members of the transport union who remained loyal to that union. Individual
members of the transport union showed no particular animosity towards members
of the U.P.W. and seem to have been content to work alongside them, but **D**
there is a good deal of evidence that members of the U.P.W. toured the docks
in an endeavour to secure recruits and that this led to protests from the more
articulate members of the transport union.

On Nov. 28, 1962, the defendant Mr. Harrall reported to the defendant Mr.
Fry in a strongly worded letter in which he said

> " I must again stress that such is the intense desire of our members to **E**
> eradicate the U.P.W. that the possibility of a dispute to obtain this cannot
> be dismissed, indeed, so much so that as some of the defectors' T. & G.W.U.
> cards are paid to the end of the quarter, the feeling of our men is that come
> thirteen weeks into the new year then something must be done."

On Jan. 18, 1963, a meeting took place between the P.L.A. and the transport **F**
union to discuss the position which had arisen. At the meeting Mr. Fry made
clear his attitude, which he has maintained throughout this matter, namely,
that the transport union would not contemplate any compromise with the
U.P.W., and that it was imperative that members of the U.P.W. should abandon
that body and rejoin the transport union. Mr. Fry was not opposed to officers
of the P.L.A. seeking to obtain this result by persuasion, but he insisted that if **G**
persuasion failed the transport union would resort to strike action to enforce
the removal of U.P.W. members from the port. I have had the advantage of
seeing Mr. Fry and I find him to be an honest and sincere man with no feelings
of personal animosity against the plaintiff. A lifetime of experience and training
in the trade union movement has taught him that small breakaway unions must
be stamped out immediately and his attitude in this case has been dictated by **H**
that creed. He sincerely believes that developments such as the formation of
the U.P.W. are injurious to the preservation of peace in the docks and that the
interest of the transport union, the men, the P.L.A. and the public are best served
by all lockmen remaining loyal members of the transport union.

As a result of this meeting Mr. Enderby, the staff relations officer of the P.L.A.,
interviewed ten of the lockmen, who were thought to be the leading spirits in the **I**
U.P.W., but no conclusive result emerged and on Feb. 11, 1963, at a further
meeting between Mr. Enderby and officers of the transport union Mr. Fry complained of the delay and again stressed that he had in mind to direct the loyal
members of his union not to work alongside members of the U.P.W. Mr. Fry
said that he was being " urged " to take such action by the loyal members of
union, but I do not think that he needed much urging. The defendant Mr. Harrall
attended these meetings and supported his superior Mr. Fry.

There were further discussions in the next three weeks but no progress was

A made, and on Mar. 6, 1963, Mr. Fry wrote to Mr. Frank Cousins seeking plenary powers for the withdrawal of labour. In this letter he accuses the U.P.W. of associating with known trouble-makers in the docks and seeks authority to direct members of the transport union " not to work with the U.P.W. and other non-trade unionists ". He justifies this request by saying that

B   " the declared aims and objects of the U.P.W. are to enroll all P.L.A. lockmen-tugmen, dredger and elevator crews and P.L.A. assistants which, if successful, would create a very powerful unit."

Mr. Fry had no basis, other than rumour, for the allegations which he made and he did not genuinely believe the truth of what he said. Even now I do not fully understand why he was prepared to embroider his report in this way, C but his underlying motive was his conviction that the U.P.W. was a menace to the transport union and to industrial peace and that it must be stamped out accordingly. Plenary powers were duly granted by the general executive council of the transport union on Mar. 8, 1963, and on Mar. 14, 1963, Mr. Fry communicated this decision to the P.L.A. in these terms:

D   " I have to advise you that on and from Monday, Apr. 1, 1963, the members of this organisation employed at Blackwall and South West India Dock will be instructed not to work with the people in the above category (U.P.W. and other non-trade unionists). They are to carry out their duties as far as possible without the assistance of these people."

At the time Mr. Fry had not obtained any formal authority from his union E members to adopt this line, nor was there evidence of feeling against members of the U.P.W. expressed by those colleagues who worked alongside them. Mr. Harrall, however, gave evidence, which I accept, that there was feeling against the U.P.W. in the London group of docks caused by the action of some of the more militant members, such as Mr. Hammond, who were going around seeking to recruit loyal members of the transport union to defect to the U.P.W. However, F Mr. Fry was satisfied that he could carry the members of his union with him and he needed no assurance beyond this. In fact the matter was raised at a meeting of the Poplar branch on Mar. 15, and of the Tilbury sub-branch on Mar. 19, and the respective minutes do not disclose any dissent from Mr. Fry's proposals.

On Mar. 25, the plaintiff was interviewed by Mr. Ryland, Mr. Enderby's G assistant, and told that his services would be terminated unless he agreed to rejoin the transport union. He declined to rejoin. Meantime, someone had pointed out to Mr. Fry that, if the P.L.A. were to discharge the recalcitrant members of the U.P.W. by Apr. 1, they would have insufficient time to give the one week's notice of dismissal required by their contract of service, and on Mar. 29 Mr. Fry told Mr. Harrall that no union action should be taken until H Apr. 8. On Mar. 29, the P.L.A. gave a week's notice of dismissal to the plaintiff, Mr. Hammond and Mr. Atkins, the remaining member of the U.P.W. employed at the Blackwell Entrance having either rejoined the transport union or made his peace with that union in some other way.

The plaintiff's claim is based on the loss which he is alleged to have suffered consequent on such dismissal and the subsequent history of the matter is relevant I only in so far as it reflects on the state of mind of the parties at this time or on the amount of damage suffered by the plaintiff.

On Apr. 3, 1963, the plaintiff, Mr. Hammond and Mr. Atkins wrote a joint letter to the P.L.A. appealing against their dismissal. The plaintiff did not draft this letter which was probably the work of Mr. Senior on behalf of all three. On Apr. 5, Mr. Enderby replied on behalf of the P.L.A. rejecting this appeal. Thereafter the plaintiff took legal advice.

Although Mr. Fry had achieved his object so far as eliminating the U P W

in the London group of docks was concerned, the position at Tilbury was un-   A
changed. He accordingly proceeded to bring similar pressure to bear on the
P.L.A. in respect of U.P.W. members at Tilbury.

Meanwhile on May 1, 1963, Mr. Hammond and the plaintiff each made formal
applications to Mr. Harrall for re-admission to membership of the transport
union. Mr. Harrall quite properly replied that such applications must be made
to the Poplar branch and that the next meeting of that branch would be held   B
on May 17. On the same day (May 1) the plaintiff had applied to the P.L.A.
for reinstatement, only to be told on May 9 that the P.L.A. did not wish to
re-employ him. The meeting of the Poplar branch held on May 17 was attended
by a number of members from Tilbury including Mr. Beadle who had rejoined
the transport union following Mr. Fry's pressure against the U.P.W. at that
port. Mr. Beadle moved that the plaintiff, Mr. Hammond and Mr. Atkins be   C
re-admitted to membership of the transport union and that Mr. Harrall endeavour
to get them re-employed with the P.L.A. and, at a poorly attended meeting,
this proposal was carried by ten votes to six. The defendant Mr. Mehegan
thereupon wrote to Mr. Harrall " appealing " against this decision. No one
suggests that the rule of the transport union gave any such right of appeal,
but Mr. Harrall in a letter dated May 27, which in my judgment does him no   D
credit at all, purported to rule that the resolution was invalid. He says that
he did this after consultation with Mr. Lucas, the regional organiser of the transport union, and the reasons for his decision are stated to be (a) that the three
men concerned were " unemployed " and that to admit them would be contrary
to established custom; (b) that the resolution rescinded an earlier resolution
of Apr. 23, 1963, and this had not been done in the orthodox manner by notice of   E
motion; and (c) that the vote had been supported by Tilbury members who had
no right to vote at the Poplar branch.

None of these reasons bears examination for a moment. The alleged custom
not to admit men not employed in the waterways group of trades could not
with justice have applied to the men in question, even if the custom existed at all.
The alleged earlier resolution of Apr. 23 is a figment of someone's imagination;   F
there is no rule requiring a notice of motion to rescind such a resolution and it is
abundantly clear that members of the Tilbury sub-branch were at this time
entitled to vote at branch meetings at Poplar, even if they rarely did so in
practice. Mr. Harrall's explanation is that this answer was dictated to him by
Mr. Lucas and that he did not agree with it, but I do not accept this explanation.
In my judgment the true explanation is that Mr. Mehegan and other Poplar   G
members had been taken by surprise by the influx from Tilbury and were annoyed
that this had led to a decision which they did not think would be favoured by
the bulk of the membership. In fact Mr. Hammond took legal advice which
brought the matter to the attention of Mr. Cousins, who promptly directed that
the resolution must be put into effect. I do not understand why Mr. Harrall
permitted himself to write this letter, still less do I understand why Mr. Fry   H
endeavoured to support this wholly indefensible attitude, as he did in a letter
to Mr. Cousins on June 7, 1963. Thanks to the intervention of Mr. Cousins the
three recalcitrants were allowed to rejoin the transport union, and on June 14
Mr. Hammond paid the arrears of union contributions due for himself, the
plaintiff and Mr. Atkins, thus completing their reinstatement as full paid-up
members. The plaintiff was not aware until later that this had been done and   I
seems to have been curiously disinterested. He made no further contributions
to the union and by October, 1963, was again excluded from membership by
reason of this default.

Meanwhile attempts were being made by some members of the transport
union to get the plaintiff, Mr. Hammond and Mr. Atkins reinstated in their old
jobs with the P.L.A. At a poorly attended meeting at Tilbury it was resolved
by eleven votes to one on June 18, 1963, that the union take firm action to
effect their reinstatement " even to the extent of a stoppage of work ", but when

A this was passed on to the P.L.A. by Mr. Harrall it was met with a blank refusal. On Sept. 30, 1963, it was resolved by eleven votes to none that the Tilbury branch apply for

> " the same plenary powers in order to obtain the re-employment of Brothers Hammond, Atkins and Morgan, as those used to obtain their dismissal "

B

and this was duly transmitted by Mr. Harrall to Mr. Fry who on Oct. 17, 1963, rejected it on the ground that

> " plenary powers were not given to obtain the dismissal of the members concerned but to support the union's membership in refusing to work with members of the U.P.W. and other non-unionists."

C

It was well within Mr. Fry's discretion to decline to support the ultimate weapon of strike action for the purpose of reinstating these three men, and I think that this was the true reason for his refusal. He would have given less cause of suspicion as to his motives if he had frankly said so at the time. In the result the plaintiff never returned to the service of the P.L.A. and eventually obtained

D other employment on terms which he says were less advantageous.

I must now amplify these findings of fact on matters which are directly relevant to the issues in this case. The plaintiff was dismissed by a lawful notice given in accordance with his contract of service. The P.L.A. dismissed the plaintiff in order to avoid the action which Mr. Fry had intimated would occur on Apr. 8, namely, a refusal of members of the transport union to work alongside U.P.W.

E members. In giving this intimation Mr. Fry had no intention of injuring the plaintiff, and he would have preferred that the plaintiff should have avoided dismissal by rejoining the transport union. His intention was not to secure the removal of the plaintiff as such, but to secure the removal of those men (if any) who insisted on remaining in the U.P.W. The decision so to act was Mr. Fry's decision alone. It has been argued by counsel for the defendants that Mr. Fry did

F no more than communicate a decision already reached by the rank and file of the union, but this is not so. Mr. Fry has much experience of the docks and with the assistance of reports from Mr. Harrall he knew the feeling of the articulate minority of shop stewards and other keen trade unionists, who might lead un-official action and through whom the voice of the members is heard. These men had long been pressing for a closed shop and the formation of the U.P.W.

G provided a focus for this feeling. Mr. Fry was confident that the articulate minority would support him and this was all that he needed to know. It may be that if he had delayed action indefinitely the local pressures would have become overwhelming, but there was no prospect in April, 1963, that the loyal lockmen at the Blackwell Entrance would walk out in defiance of the dominating influence of Mr. Hammond unless Mr. Fry gave them an official instruction

H to do so. Many of the transport union members had no strong feelings on these matters, and some actually signed a petition in support of Mr. Hammond and the plaintiff, but Mr. Fry knew that the local leaders would support him and he acted accordingly.

Mr. Harrall's part in the affair was to keep Mr. Fry informed of the feelings of the men. He was in no sense responsible for Mr. Fry's decision. On the whole

I he did his work fairly, though occasionally his reports were exaggerated by including the more extreme rumours in which he could hardly have had a genuine belief. He had no feelings or bias against the plaintiff at the material time and his letter of May 27, which I have criticised, was due to a momentary annoyance which was not typical of his general behaviour. Mr. Bilson and Mr. Mehegan merely carried out their duties as branch chairman and secretary respectively. Both approved of Mr. Fry's decision when it was communicated to them, but neither had any responsibility for it.

The plaintiff is a somewhat colourless personality who came under the influence

of Mr. Hammond. He has shown remarkably little feeling over these matters **A**
and is certainly no lockside Hampden crusading for the liberty of the individual.
Mr. Hammond was an exceedingly forceful shop steward who, as one witness
put it, " knew all the rules and regulations and could tie an ordinary layman in
knots in no time ". He insisted on the letter of the law to the annoyance of his
employers and sometimes carried this to extremes. He may well have gone
further and fomented trouble for trouble's sake, but as I have not seen him I **B**
am unwilling to express a final view as to this.

The plaintiff puts his claim in two main ways. First, it is said that there was
here a combination between the defendants wilfully to do an act causing damage
to the plaintiff in his trade, thus actionable without proof that the means
employed would have been unlawful if employed by a single individual. Secondly,
it is contended that the defendants procured the dismissal of the plaintiff by **C**
unlawful intimidation within the principles enunciated in *Rookes* v. *Barnard* (1).

Of these claims the former is easily disposed of. I have no hesitation in holding
that what was done by the defendants was done in contemplation or furtherance
of a trade dispute as defined by s. 5 of the Trade Disputes Act, 1906, and in any
event their actions were not designed to injure the plaintiff but were done in
the genuine belief that they were necessary to protect the legitimate interests **D**
of the transport union and its members. The immediate purpose of Mr. Fry and
Mr. Harrall was to put an end to the U.P.W. so far as the Port of London and
Tilbury were concerned, and their action was dictated by the sincere belief that
this would remove a threat to the transport union's power to negotiate on behalf
of the lockmen as a whole and the particular threat to industrial peace which
can be created by small breakaway unions, particularly if they get into the control **E**
of unscrupulous people.

I turn therefore to the plaintiff's second submission based on *Rookes* v.
Barnard (1). It is common ground that the Trade Disputes Act 1965 has no
application to this case. In *Rookes* v. *Barnard* (1) the plaintiff, a skilled draughtsman employed by B.O.A.C., resigned his membership of a trade union to which
employees in the design office belonged. The union had negotiated a closed shop **F**
agreement with B.O.A.C. which precluded the recruitment of non-union labour
in the design shop, but it does not appear that this prevented the employers
from retaining the services of a union member who resigned from the union.

The individual service agreements of the design staff provided that no lockout
or strike should take place but that disputes should be dealt with by a national
joint council. The members of the union in the design office nevertheless resolved **G**
that if the plaintiff was not removed from the design office " a withdrawal of
labour " by all union members would take place, and on this resolution being
communicated to B.O.A.C. by the defendants (who were union officials and
of whom two were employees of B.O.A.C.) B.O.A.C. dismissed the plaintiff by
notice. It was held in the House of Lords that the defendants had committed
the tort of intimidation and were liable to the plaintiff in damages notwith- **H**
standing that the acts complained of were done in contemplation or furtherance
of a trade dispute. LORD REID stated the issue thus (2):

> " This case, therefore, raises the question whether it is a tort to conspire
> to threaten an employer that his men will break their contracts with him
> unless he dismisses the plaintiff, with the result that he is thereby induced
> to dismiss the plaintiff and cause him loss . . ."   **I**

In the present case counsel for the plaintiff submits that if the lockmen at the
Blackwall Entrance had on Apr. 8 " refused to work with the members of the
U.P.W." they would have committed a breach of their contracts of service
with the P.L.A., and that Fry's threat to produce this result was a threat to the
P.L.A. to induce a breach of contract by the lockmen which threat induced

(1) [1964] 1 All E.R. 367; [1964] A.C. 1129.
(2) [1964] 1 All E.R. at p. 373; [1964] A.C. at p. 1166,

A the P.L.A. to dismiss the plaintiff and cause him loss. Accordingly, says counsel
for the plaintiff, the issue raised in this case is identical with that raised in *Rookes*
v. *Barnard* (3) and the plaintiff must succeed.

Counsel for the defendants has sought to distinguish *Rookes* v. *Barnard* (3)
on a number of points. He first contends that the intimidation given by Mr. Fry
to the P.L.A. was not a threat but a warning of action which was liable to occur
B by reason of the feeling of the rank and file in the union. I have already given
my grounds for rejecting this submission and in my opinion there is nothing in
counsel for the defendants' further point that Fry's requirement could have been
met without the dismissal of the plaintiff if the P.L.A. had chosen to transfer
him to another part of the port, because this, as Mr. Fry knew, was never a
practical proposition. Once the plaintiff refused to rejoin the transport union the
C P.L.A. were bound to dismiss him or face the consequences of Mr. Fry's threatened
action.

Counsel for the defendants' main submission on this aspect of the case is
that the conduct of the lockmen which Mr. Fry threatened to induce would
not have amounted to a breach of their contracts with the P.L.A. and therefore
involved no illegality. He distinguishes *Rookes* v. *Barnard* (3) by reference to the
D ban on strikes which the contract of service in that case contained and says
that in the absence of such a clause in the contract a workman who strikes after
due notice does not thereby commit a breach of contract at all. He explains this
result in one of two ways: (a) that the notice of intention to strike operated as a
lawful determination of the contract on the day for which the strike was called,
so that the withdrawal of labour did not occur until the contract was at an end;
E or (b) that the contract of service contained an implied term whereby the workman might lawfully strike after due notice, whereupon the employer might
elect whether to determine the contract or to keep it alive pending negotiations.
On either view it is submitted that the act of striking is not a breach of contract,
and that to induce a strike is not to use unlawful means for the purposes of the
tort of intimidation. When *Rookes* v. *Barnard* (4) was before the Court of Appeal
F DONOVAN, L.J., referred to this point. He said (4):

" There can be few strikes which do not involve a breach of contract
by the strikers. Until a proper notice is given to terminate their contract
of service, and the notice has expired, they remain liable under its terms to
perform their bargain. It would, however, be affectation not to recognise
that in the majority of strikes, no such notice to terminate the contract is
G either given or expected. The strikers do not want to give up their jobs;
they simply want to be paid more for it or to secure some other advantage
in connexion with it. The employer does not want to lose his labour force;
he simply wants to resist the claim. Not till the strike has lasted some time,
and no settlement is in sight, does one usually read that the employers have
given notice that unless the men return to work their contracts will be
H terminated and they will be dismissed. If a threat to break one's own contract
of service be ' unlawful ', the actual breach of it must be ' unlawful ' too. Yet
no one seems yet to have thought that a strike itself in breach of contract
is unlawful, and at this time of day I do not think that it is."

The view that a threat to a strike is not " unlawful " must presumably be treated
I as wrong in view of the decision of the House of Lords, but DONOVAN, L.J.'s
opinion that it amounts to a breach of contract is clear and I do not think that
he is referring only to strikes which occur without prior notice.

The plaintiff, however, relies on a dictum of LORD EVERSHED, in the House of
Lords where he said (5):

---

(3) [1964] 1 All E.R. 367; [1964] A.C. 1129.
(4) [1962] 2 All E.R. 579 at p. 600; [1963] 1 Q.B. 623 at p. 682.
(5) [1964] 1 All E.R. at p. 381; [1964] A.C. at p. 1180.

" . . . it has long been recognised that strike action or threats of strike   A
action (however those terms be interpreted—and I have in mind what fell
from DONOVAN, L.J. (6), in his judgment in the Court of Appeal) in the
case of a trade dispute do not involve any wrongful action on the part of the
employees, whose service contracts are not regarded as being or intended
to be thereby terminated. So much was stated by LORD WATSON in his
speech in *Allen* v. *Flood* (7) and has, as I believe, been since consistently   B
followed."

LORD EVERSHED then went on to refer to the " very important fact " that the
contract then in question contained the special embargo on strike action, and
clearly treated this as the foundation for the conclusion that the strike action
threatened was a breach of contract. If LORD EVERSHED was equating " wrongful
action " in this context with a breach of contract, I have some difficulty in   C
understanding his reference to LORD WATSON. It is true that the latter said in
Allen v. *Flood* (8):

" They were not under any continuing engagement to their employers,
and, if they had left their work and gone out on strike they would have
been acting within their right . . .",
                                                                        D
but it appears (9) that the men were employed on terms that they might leave
at the close of any day, and this is all that they appear to have been minded to do.
I can find nothing in the authorities to which I have been referred to support
the view that strike action, whether after notice or not, is other than a breach
of the contract of employment and this is confirmed by LORD DENNING, M.R.,
in *J. T. Stratford & Son, Ltd.* v. *Lindley* (10), where in regard to the " everyday   E
case where there is no special contract forbidding a strike," he says (10):

" Suppose that a trade union officer gives a strike notice. He says to an
employer ' We are going to call a strike on Monday week . . . unless you
dismiss yonder man who is not a member of the union . . .' Such a notice is
not to be construed as if it were a week's notice on behalf of the men to
terminate their employment; for that is the last thing any of the men   F
would desire . . . The strike notice is nothing more nor less than a notice
that the men will not come to work. In short, that they will break their
contracts . . ."

Counsel for the defendants points out, as did DONOVAN, L.J., that, if a strike
after notice amounts to a breach of contract, it is odd that one never hears of
workmen being sued by their employers in consequence of such breach. The   G
answer may be that such actions against individual workmen are pointless,
and a union official who induces such a breach will normally be protected from
action by the employer by the Trade Disputes Act, 1906.

In the result I must reject counsel for the defendants' argument that action
taken by the lockmen in consequence of Mr. Fry's direction would not amount
to a breach of their contracts. There may be room in some cases for the implica-   H
tion of a term such as he contends for, but, since the lockmen had contracted
on the basis of no closed shop, it would be very strange to find in the same
contract an implied term making it lawful to strike to secure that object.

Counsel for the defendants also seeks to distinguish *Rookes* v. *Barnard* (11)
on the ground that in that case the threat came from the workers themselves
and amounted to a threat that they would break their contracts, whereas Mr.   I
Fry's threat was that he would induce breaches by others. In *Stratford & Son,
Ltd.* v. *Lindley* (12) LORD DENNING, M.R., draws this distinction and appears to

(6) [1962] 2 All E.R. at pp. 594-602; [1963] 1 Q.B. at pp. 675-685.
(7) [1895-99] All E.R. Rep. 52 at p. 70; [1898] A.C. 1 at p. 99.
(8) [1895-99] All E.R. Rep. at p. 70; [1898] A.C. at p. 99.
(9) [1895-99] All E.R. Rep. at p. 84; [1898] A.C. at p. 130.
(10) [1964] 2 All E.R. 209 at pp. 216, 217; [1965] A.C. 269 at p. 285.
(11) [1964] 1 All E.R. 367; [1964] A.C. 1129.
(12) [1964] 2 All E.R. at p. 216; [1965] A.C. at p. 284.

A take the view that an inducement to break a contract in these circumstances
would be protected by s. 3 of the Trade Disputes Act, 1906, even at the suit of a
third party, but LORD PEARCE in the same case (13) takes the opposite view. In
my judgment the weight of authority is in favour of LORD PEARCE'S view, and
requires me to hold that the protection afforded by s. 3 to an act which induces
a breach of contract is of no avail when the action is brought by someone who is
B not a party to the contract and whose cause of action is based on intimidation
and not on inducing a breach of that contract simpliciter.

Finally, counsel for the defendants contends that the defendants can excuse
their conduct as being justified in all the circumstances of the case.   The
possibility of a plea of justification as an answer to a claim for intimidation was
not considered in *Rookes* v. *Barnard* (see per LORD DEVLIN (14)).   A claim by a
C party to a contract for the unlawful inducement of its breach may be met by a
plea of justification, though the circumstance in which such a plea may be
raised are not precisely defined.   (I refer to SALMON ON TORTS, (14th Edn.) at
p. 593).   If, in the present case, the defendants could justify the inducement of
a breach of the lockmen's contracts vis-à-vis the P.L.A. (otherwise than by
reliance on the Trade Disputes Act, 1906) their action would not be " unlawful "
D so as to support a claim for intimidation by the plaintiff, but when once it is
established that the defendants' conduct is unlawful as between the defendants
and the P.L.A. I can see no ground on which it can be said that the use of such
unlawful means can be justified vis-à-vis the plaintiff.

It follows that in my judgment the plaintiff is entitled to recover against
Mr. Fry; but what of the other defendants? They are liable if, and only if, they
E are joint tortfeasors in the tort of intimidation committed by Mr. Fry.   Mr.
Harrall attended the meetings with the P.L.A. at which Mr. Fry first formulated
his threat and on one occasion spoke in support of Mr. Fry. He also communicated
the terms of the proposed withdrawal of labour to the Poplar and Tilbury
branches and clearly commended Mr. Fry's actions to those branches. The fact
that he was carrying out the instructions of his superior trade union officials
F affords him no defence (*Crofter Hand Woven Harris Tweed Co., Ltd.* v. *Veitch*
(15)), and in my judgment he played a sufficiently active role to make him a
tortfeasor jointly with Mr. Fry. Counsel for the plaintiff argues that Mr. Bilson
and Mr. Mehegan are similarly implicated, but I disagree with this. Mr. Mehegan
convened, and Mr. Bilson presided over, a meeting of the Poplar branch on Mar.
15, 1963, at which Mr. Fry's proposals were considered, but although both
G favoured those proposals neither voted for them, and it is not clear from the
minutes that any sort of resolution was carried. There was such a resolution at a
later meeting on Mar. 29, 1963, but these two defendants did not vote on it and
by this time the P.L.A.'s notice to dismiss the plaintiff had already been sent.
For these reasons I am not satisfied that Mr. Bilson and Mr. Mehegan were
parties to Mr. Fry's action, and the claims against them will be dismissed.

H I turn finally to the question of damages. The plaintiff was unemployed for
some six weeks, but thereafter had a number of employments and finally became
a collector of receipts from pre-payment gas meters under one of the gas boards.
His present earnings are 6s. per week less than they would have been if he had
continued his work as a lockman, and it is agreed as a matter of arithmetic that
his loss of earnings up to Feb. 20, 1967, was £340. I have to attempt an estimate
I of how long the plaintiff would have remained in employment as a lockman,
but for the defendants' interference. He was well suited to the job, but once he
came under the influence of Mr. Hammond the P.L.A. became dissatisfied with
him. He did not seem to me to put a high value on the job because, if he had
done so, he would at least have given some thought to rejoining the transport
union to avoid dismissal. His refusal to rejoin was not due to any desire to

(13) [1964] 3 All E.R. 102 at p. 114; [1965] A.C. at p. 336.
(14) [1964] 1 All E.R. at pp. 398, 400; [1964] A.C. at pp. 1206, 1209.
(15) [1942] 1 All E.R. 142 at p. 147; [1942] A.C. 435 at p. 441.

support a moral principle, but was due to the influence of Mr. Hammond, whose motives remain obscure. There is no reason whatever to suppose that he would have remained as a lockman until he retired at sixty-five, and I think that a fair estimate of his continuance in that employment would have been five years from his dismissal. An appropriate round figure to represent his loss would be £425, and there will be judgment against Mr. Fry and Mr. Harrall for this sum.

Judgment accordingly.

Solicitors: *Lawford & Co.* (for the plaintiff); *Pattinson & Brewer* (for the defendants).

[*Reported by* MARY COLTON, *Barrister-at-Law.*]

NOTE.

R. *v.* KALINSKI.

[COURT OF APPEAL, CRIMINAL DIVISION (Lord Parker, C.J., Salmon, L.J. and Fenton Atkinson, J.), April 4, 1967.]

Criminal Law—Trial—Jury—Direction to jury—Unanimity in decision—Such direction not normally necessary.

[Editorial Note. Guidance on how a jury may be directed in regard to unanimity, if they are to be so directed, is given in *R.* v. *Davey* ([1960] 3 All E.R. 533).

As to the verdict of jurors generally and the requirement of unanimity, see 23 HALSBURY'S LAWS (3rd Edn.) 36, para. 69; and for cases on the subject, see 30 DIGEST (Repl.) 280, 281, *481-483, 485.*

As to the position if a jury do not agree, see 10 HALSBURY'S LAWS (3rd Edn.) 431, 432, para. 796.]

Application.

The applicant, Gustav Kalinski, was convicted on trial before quarter sessions of shopbreaking and larceny and was fined. He applied for leave to appeal against his conviction on the ground, among others, that the jury had not been directed that their verdict must be unanimous.

The applicant did not appear and was not represented.

LORD PARKER, C.J., in the course of delivering the judgment of the court said: It is well known that some judges do point out to juries that their verdict must be unanimous. Others do not. This court would like to make it quite clear that in the ordinary way the court will not hold that to fail to tell the jury that their verdict must be unanimous is a non-direction.

[HIS LORDSHIP dealt with other matters arising on the application, and concluded:] In the present case the court is quite satisfied that there was ample evidence to support the verdict. There is no complaint that can be properly made of the summing-up, and accordingly the application is refused.

Application refused.

[*Reported by* N. P. METCALFE, ESQ., *Barrister-at-Law.*]

A

NOTE.

R. *v.* SIMMONDS AND OTHERS.

[COURT OF APPEAL, CRIMINAL DIVISION (Sachs, L.J., Fenton Atkinson and
James, JJ.), February 27, 28, March 1, 2, 3, 6, 10, 1967.]

Criminal Law—Conspiracy—Continuing single offence—Particulars in terms of a
B   *statutory offence, prosecution for which was subject to a time limit—Whether*
time limit applied to charge of common law conspiracy so laid—Purchase
Tax Act 1963 *(c.* 9), *s.* 33 (1), *s.* 34 (4).

Criminal Law—Trial—Length—Conspiracy to defraud Revenue—Complicated
purchase tax evasions—Steps to be taken for shortening trials—Severance of
counts.

C   The trial of the accused on charges concerning evasion of purchase tax
having lasted eighty-one days and involved costs exceeding £77,000, the Court
of Appeal give guidance on what steps can be taken to avoid the recurrence
of trials of such duration and expense (see p. 402, letter D, post).

Certain accused were charged with common law conspiracy to defraud the
Crown of purchase tax, the particulars of two counts of conspiracy being in
D   the terms of s. 17* of the Finance Act, 1944. By para. 2 of Sch. 9 to the
Finance Act, 1940†, a charge for the offence enacted by s. 17 had to be
brought within three years next after the date of the offence committed.
One charge alleged conspiracy between Jan. 1, 1962 and Aug. 31, 1962, the
indictment being preferred on Mar. 24, 1965.

Held: the prosecution was not time-barred because (i) the three year
E   statutory time limit did not apply to the common law offence of conspiracy,
and (ii), even if the three year time limit had applied, the conspiracy charged
was a single conspiracy running from Jan. 1, 1962 to Aug. 31, 1962, and
therefore was continuing after Mar. 24, 1962 (see p. 404, letter I, and
p. 405, letter F, post).

R. v. *Blamires Transport Services, Ltd.* ([1963] 3 All E.R. 170) applied.
F   Appeals dismissed.

Criminal Law—Costs—Several accused—Form of order—Joint and several order
for payment—Matters to be taken into consideration in awarding costs against
particular accused—Costs in Criminal Cases Act, 1952 (15 *&* 16 *Geo.* 6
& 1 Eliz. 2 *c.* 48), *s.* 2 (1).

An order under s. 2 (1) of the Costs in Criminal Cases Act, 1952, for pay-
G   ment of costs by several accused may be joint and several in form. Such costs
should, however, be related to the costs in or about the prosecution of
individual accused; and the court would consider, first, what were the costs
of bringing the particular accused to justice and, second, would then exercise
a general discretion (see p. 406, letters B and E, post).

[As to trials of two or more defendants, see 10 HALSBURY'S LAWS (3rd Edn.)
H   415, para. 760; and for cases on the subject, see 14 DIGEST (Repl.) 253, 254,
2189-2212.

As to conspiracy to commit a statutory offence, see 10 HALSBURY'S LAWS
(3rd Edn.) 312, para. 570; and for cases on the subject, see 14 DIGEST (Repl.)
121-129, *851-911.*

As to an order on a convicted person to pay costs, see 10 HALSBURY'S LAWS
I   (3rd Edn.) 551, para. 1013; and for cases on the subject, see 14 DIGEST (Repl.)
683, *6976-6979.*

For the Costs in Criminal Cases Act, 1952, s. 2, see 32 HALSBURY'S STATUTES
(2nd Edn.) 63.

For s. 17 of the Finance Act, 1944, see 21 HALSBURY'S STATUTES (2nd Edn.)
1295; and for the Purchase Tax Act 1963, s. 33 (1), s. 34 (4), see 43 HALSBURY'S
STATUTES (2nd Edn.) 1047, 1050.]

---

* Replaced by s. 33 of the Purchase Tax Act 1963.
† Replaced by s. 34 (4) of the Purchase Tax Act 1963.

Cases referred to: A

Castro v. *R.*, [1881-85] All E.R. Rep. 429; (1881), 6 App. Cas. 229; 50 L.J.Q.B.
497; 44 L.T. 350; 45 J.P. 452; *affg.* sub nom. *R.* v. *Castro*, (1880),
5 Q.B.D. 490; *affg.* (1874), L.R. 9 Q.B. 350; 14 Digest (Repl.) 261, *2283*.

R. v. *Barnett*, [1951] 1 All E.R. 917; [1951] 2 K.B. 425; 115 J.P. 305; 35
Cr. App. Rep. 37; 14 Digest (Repl.) 231, *1933*.

R. v. *Blake*, (1844), 6 Q.B. 126; 13 L.J.M.C. 131; 8 J.P. 596; 115 E.R. 49;   B
14 Digest (Repl.) 136, *993*.

R. v. *Blamires Transport Services, Ltd.*, [1963] 3 All E.R. 170; [1964] 1 Q.B.
278; [1963] 3 W.L.R. 496; 127 J.P. 519; 47 Cr. App. Rep. 272; Digest
(Cont. Vol. A) 339, *895a*.

R. v. *Gould*, [1965] Crim. L.R. 547.

Appeals.   C

The four appellants, (1) Bernard Harry Simmonds, (2) William Holford
Barrington-Coupe, (3) Terence William Orwell and (4) Henry Cohen, and the
two appellant companies, Hampden Co. (Sales), Ltd. and Hampden Co. (Electronics), Ltd., were convicted with another accused, Conway, and four other
companies, none of whom appealed, on major counts charging conspiracy to
defraud the Crown of purchase tax and other counts against some of the accused   D
charging offences against the purchase tax legislation. Count 1 charged the four
appellants, the first appellant company, another accused and two other companies
with conspiracy between Jan. 1, 1962, and Aug. 31, 1962, to cheat and defraud
the Crown and the Commissioners of Customs and Excise of purchase tax chargeable on the delivery of wireless receiving sets. Count 2 was the same, substituting   E
Conway and another company for the second appellant, another accused and two
companies. The particulars of the conspiracies alleged in count 1 and count 2 were
in terms the offences created by s. 17 of the Finance Act, 1944. Count 3 charged
the first and second appellants, the two appellant companies, another accused
and two other companies with a similar conspiracy between June 15, 1962 and
Sept. 30, 1963. Count 4 charged the first appellant and the second appellant   F
company with fraudulent evasion of purchase tax on one transaction, involving
two hundred sets. Count 5 charged the first appellant and the same company
with furnishing a false purchase tax return with intent to deceive. Count 6
related only to Conway and another company. All the appellants and the
appellant companies were convicted on all the charges with which they were
concerned. The trial lasted eighty-one days and involved costs totalling £77,417.   G
On May 17, 1966, the appellants were sentenced as follows—the first appellant,
Simmonds, to twenty-one months' imprisonment in all and fines totalling £6,750;
the second appellant, Barrington-Coupe, to twelve months' imprisonment in all
and fines totalling £2,000; the third and fourth appellants, Orwell and Cohen, to
twelve months' imprisonment in all each and fines amounting to £3,000 each in
all. The first appellant company, Hampden Co. (Sales), Ltd., was fined £8,500   H
in all. No sentence was passed on the second appellant company, Hampden Co.
(Electronics), Ltd. The appellants appealed on the ground, among other grounds,
that the length and complexity of the trial was such that justice could not be done
to the individual appellants.

Sir Peter Rawlinson, Q.C., and *J. C. J. Tatham* for the appellants Simmonds,
Hampden Co. (Sales), Ltd. and Hampden Co. (Electronics), Ltd.   I

Muir Hunter, Q.C., and *D. A. Paiba* for the appellant Barrington-Coupe.

N. N. McKinnon, Q.C., and *N. E. Wiggins* for the appellants Orwell and Cohen.

E. S. Fay, Q.C., J. S. R. Abdela, Q.C., and *A. D. Collins* for the Crown.

Cur. adv. vult.

Mar. 10. **FENTON ATKINSON, J.,** delivered the judgment of the court
in the course of which, after setting out the charges and referring to the general
scheme of purchase tax legislation, he continued: It is of course true that a

A dominant feature of the proceedings, and a matter naturally stressed by each of the appellants' counsel in turn, was the length of the trial. So long was it that it has been stated that only once before has there been one which took longer—the *Tichborne* trial (1). It has been designated by many adjectives, such as " massive " " marathon " and " monster ", and there is no doubt that its very duration cast an inordinate burden both on the presiding judge, the jury, and all others who

B took part in the trial. This court has viewed the factor of length with grave concern. Whenever, a trial assumes such proportions the risk is greatly increased of injustice being done, because individual cases get buried under the weight of a mass of material—and there is a proportionate need for extra care in the conduct of the trial. Moreover the longer the trial the higher the chances that some jurors may become casualties or the subject of attempted subornation. Thus in the

C present case there were at the end only ten jurors left in good health, and during the concluding stages there was an attempt to bribe one of them. It is thus essential—quite apart from the factor of expense where public funds have to bear not only the cost of the prosecution but also to pay through legal aid for solicitors and two counsel for several defendants—to consider at an appropriate point in this judgment what steps can be taken to reduce to a minimum, indeed if

D possible to eliminate, the chances of a recurrence of such abnormal proceedings. For that purpose it is naturally necessary to try and analyse the main factors which led to what occurred in the present case. As a preliminary it is to be noted that the ever mounting intricacy of the legislation imposing taxes has been followed by ever increasing ingenuity on the part of numbers of persons conspiring together fraudulently to evade the taxation. Such are the complexities of these

E fraudulent schemes and the devices used in them that only too often the only way that the interests of justice can be served is by presenting to a jury with the aid of schedules an overall picture of the scheme and charging a conspiracy to cheat and defraud. Obviously every effort should be made to present instead to the jury a relatively small series of substantive offences—but that cannot always be done and this case was one of those where only a conspiracy charge can provide for the

F protection of the interests of the community when once the legislature produces intricate laws. It follows also that only too often charges of defrauding the revenue (be it of purchase tax or other tax) involve months of complex investigations: this is especially the case when, as here, several individuals and several companies are concerned, and proper records have either not been kept at all or are so kept as to present an incomplete or false picture. Such investigations necessarily involve

G the revenue officers in long multiple examinations of records, followed in turn by protracted interviews in which large numbers of questions have to be asked as to the documents under investigation. The documents themselves are often bound to be voluminous in order that the appropriate details may be established with that formality needed in a criminal trial; but a very great deal can be done and has here been done to reduce the number that have to be looked at by the jury

H by the compilation of schedules from which the overall position can readily be seen. Little, however, can be done to reduce the length of interviews.

In the present case clear and full schedules were prepared and in the end the case fully merited the comment of the trial judge (who has considerable experience in such matters) that this was a very ordinary case of a purchase tax fraud. What was it then that led the trial to extend over some eighty-one days at the Central

I Criminal Court when, incidentally, it had taken only ten days before the committing magistrates? Several factors have emerged as contributing to the result.

First, the prosecution insisted that all the six counts so interlocked that it was necessary for there to be a single trial. The presiding judge, faced with a mass of documents (including some three thousand exhibits) in the course of a busy sessions at the Central Criminal Court, had but scant opportunity to analyse

(1) I.e., *R.* v. *Castro*, (1874), L.R. 9 Q.B. 350. That trial lasted from Apr. 23, 1873, to Feb. 28, 1874.

the situation and test the view put forward by the prosecution: moreover, there A
was substantially no real effort on the part of the accused to seek any severance
between the counts. In retrospect, and of course this court realises that in some
respects it is acting with the aid of hindsight, it is quite clear that the three
individual substantive counts ought not to have been tried at the same time as
the three conspiracies. Moreover counts 1 and 2, which relate to conspiracies
ending on Aug. 31, 1962, could have been tried separately from the third con- B
spiracy (count 3) which was concerned with June 15, 1962, to Sept. 30, 1963, and
mainly involved a different method of securing the fraudulent evasion of purchase
tax. Whether to try count 3 separately would have reduced the length of the
trial subsequently is doubtful, for the necessity would have remained for providing an overall picture with the aid of the one and only credit-worthy stocktaking of Oct. 1, 1963: but some reduction in length could have been achieved C
for the benefit of the jury, albeit at the potential expense of taking up the time of
a second jury. Such severance at least merited careful consideration by the trial
judge who, if he had had the requisite knowledge at the outset, might have
considered it could with advantage have been tried separately.

It is at this point proper to turn, after consultation within the Criminal Division
of this court, to consideration of what can be done to avoid trials of this type D
being unduly prolonged, or at least to reduce the chances of a recurrence of one
of so great a duration as the present. Naturally it is the duty of prosecuting
counsel in the interests of justice as a whole to see that the case is prepared so that
it can be presented to a jury in as simple a way as is practicable. Much may
depend on their being consulted even before there are prepared those schedules
which set the pattern of the case. The court has no reason to doubt that in general E
this principle is followed, and that considerable effort in that direction was made
in the present case. The views of prosecuting counsel are, however, obviously not
a conclusive factor in such matters, even when supplemented by submissions by
counsel for the defence. Experience of recent years has demonstrated the need
for the trial judge being able to form an independent judgment on the severability
of counts. For him to be given such an opportunity involves two factors. For F
this purpose it is imperative that he be given a proper opportunity to consider
the papers before the accused are arraigned. Time must be afforded to this end,
and it must be remembered that hours thus spent may be matched by the saving
of days of trial. Then there is the question as to what can be done to assist a
judge faced with a monumental pile of papers to assess the nature of the case
without intolerable labour. If, whenever a long trial appears to be likely, arrange- G
ments were made before the committal proceedings for a transcript to be made of
the opening speech of counsel for the prosecution at those proceedings and of any
submissions made by or on behalf of the accused, so that these can be provided
for the trial judge together with the depositions and the exhibits, that would
provide him with considerable assistance. The extra cost of such transcripts
would be saved time and time again. Thus in the present case, even if such an H
examination had only resulted in counts 4, 5 and 6 being severed, a court week
costing about £750 a day would probably have been saved. Had counts 1 and 2
been severed from count 3, that again would have produced more easily manage-
able trials—at any rate if the two factors mentioned later were also appropriately
dealt with. If on examination of material before him the judge considers that the
presentation of the case in the way proposed by the prosecution involves undue I
burdens on the court in general and jurors in particular, and is for this or other
reasons contrary to the interests of justice, he has a right and indeed a duty to
ask that the prosecution recast their approach in those interests, even if a
considerable adjournment is entailed.

The next factor to be observed is the extreme length of the notes which are
customarily taken by Customs and Excise officers when conducting investigations.
This may be due to the intricate detail involved. The question, however, arises
whether it is either necessary or in the interests of justice that every word that

A   occurs in these notes be put into evidence in examination-in-chief. Obviously the notes must be made available to the defence before trial, but this court considers that there is vast scope for those engaged in the preparation of a case for trial so to bring out the evidence-in-chief as to extract the essence of the interviews without going into every word in them. This can be done in a way which will provide for the jury an account fair in all respects to the accused as well as to the

B   prosecution. In future efforts should be directed to pruning the material to be put before the jury in the first instance by the prosecution, but without, of course, imperilling the right of the defence to seek to bring in other matters which appear in the notes. In the present case the evidence of the customs and excise witnesses as given in chief occupies over five hundred pages (some 175,000 words) and the cross-examinations nine hundred pages: and that omits numbers of pages of

C   re-examination, recall and so forth. Had there been a proper pruning at the outset a great deal of this outpouring of words could have been omitted and some two or three weeks of court time saved, assuming always that a proper discretion had been exercised by counsel for the defence as to appropriate cross-examination.

Next, it seems proper in the context of what happened in the present case to refer to a matter which is, of course, generally recognised. Whilst in no way

D   detracting from counsel's duty to his client, he can and should exercise in the interests of justice as a whole a proper discretion so as not to prolong cases unnecessarily. It is no part of his duty to raise untenable points at length or to embark on lengthy cross-examination on matters that are not in truth in issue. Counsel for the Crown has told this court the estimate of the length of the case that had been formed by the prosecution before the trial commenced. This

E   estimate, arrived at in the light of previous experience of similar trials, was that the present trial might take from thirty to forty days, but not longer. This court considers he had no reason to think otherwise—even after making due allowance for all the counts being tried together and for there having been no pruning of unnecessary material from the evidence-in-chief of Customs and Excise officers. It is to be observed that submissions made to the judge in the absence of the jury

F   occupied no fewer than 334 pages (about 140,000 words); 153 pages related to " no case " submissions and 181 pages to admissibility of evidence. Of the 334 pages, 212 relate to the submissions by one counsel. Moreover, the above tally of pages does not include anything in relation to the numerous objections and submissions made in the presence of the jury—often relating to the same point more than once despite the judge having given a ruling. Where submissions are

G   made which seek to impugn long established rules of procedure or well recognised rules of law and are thus of a type to which obviously a trial judge could not give effect, there is no reason as a rule why they cannot be made briefly with a view to reserving the position for a higher court. It is, however, only right to add that the trial at present under consideration was exceptional in the respects just mentioned, and it is far from the intention of this court to seek to make any

H   general criticism affecting the majority of trials in these respects.

Having referred to the difficulties created by lengthy trials in general and to the fact that the trial now under consideration was protracted to an inordinate length, it is next necessary to consider whether in this instance any miscarriage of justice resulted. At all stages the learned judge discharged his duties with meticulous care and great patience. The attempts made in this court to impugn

I   some of his directions on points of law wholly fail. It is moreover to be noted that in each instance he, at an appropriate stage, properly crystallised the true and simple issue to the jury. Time and again he emphasised that the vital question was whether they were sure that the accused acted with intent to deceive or to cheat or to defraud. As to suggested misdirections or non-directions on fact, to some of which reference will be made later, these proved either to have no basis at all or to be trivial in the context of the summing-up as a whole.

As regards the jury, everyone must sympathise with them on the ordeal to which they were put. It is however right to mention that the calibre of juries

today can be high, and that their capacity to follow weeks of evidence should not
be under-estimated. It is, for instance, far from unknown nowadays for several
members of a jury to correct counsel or the court in the course of such a trial
should a wrong exhibit number or date be quoted. The summing-up commences
with a reference to tributes paid to this particular jury by counsel for the
prosecution and the defence, and goes on:

" Those of us who have spent our working lives in the courts and who
have been present in this court have not failed to notice with admiration
the attention and concentration which you have paid hour after hour, day
after day, week after week, and month after month."

Moreover, an examination of the transcript shows how keenly and accurately the
foreman in particular followed the case and that the above tributes were no mere
formality.

This court repeats its endorsement of the view of the trial judge that despite
its length, the case was in essence a simple one and sees no reason for considering
that it was not understood and its separate issues properly weighed by the jury,
nor does it see any other indication of a miscarriage of justice having occurred
by reason of the time the trial took.

[HIS LORDSHIP then considered the different counts, in the course of which he
referred to submissions that the prosecution was barred from proceeding on
count 1 and count 2 by lapse of time. HIS LORDSHIP said:] We turn now to
counsel for the second appellant's submission that the prosecution was barred
from proceedings on count 1 and count 2 by lapse of time. He points out that
any proceedings for an offence of evading purchase tax, whether under the Finance
Act, 1944, or the Purchase Tax Act 1963, must be commenced within three years
from the date of the commission of the offence (see s. 34 (4) of the Purchase Tax
Act 1963, replacing earlier statutory provisions to the same effect). Counsel
contends that the conspiracies charged in count 1 and count 2 were in reality
conspiracies to commit the statutory offence of evading purchase tax contrary
to s. 17 of the Finance Act, 1944, and that therefore the time limit must in law
apply. He goes on to argue that as the earliest date alleged for both conspiracies
was Jan. 1, 1962, and the information was not laid until Mar. 24, 1965, the
limitation period applied to bar further proceedings.

The proper time for such a point to be taken is on motion to quash the indictment before plea, but at that stage this novel point appears to have escaped the
attention of five leading counsel and seven junior counsel, and five firms of
solicitors representing the accused, and it was not until the thirty-seventh day of
the hearing (just two months after the trial started) that counsel first raised the
matter, having, as he explained to the judge, fallen over it one night in the dark.
He concedes that he can quote no direct authority in support of his submission
and was constrained to agree that if he is right, the criminal courts of this country
have proceeded on a mistaken view of the law for over one hundred years. He
has even gone so far as to contend that the statutory form of indictment for this
type of offence is based on a complete misunderstanding of the law.

In our view there is no substance whatever in the point. First, the accused
were not charged with the statutory offence, but with a common law conspiracy
to cheat and defraud for which no limitation period is laid down. It is to be
observed that common law conspiracies to cheat and defraud the Crown of
revenue have now been current for more than one hundred years (see *R.* v.
Blake (2)). But even if the conspiracy charged had been a conspiracy to commit
the statutory offence, it is well settled that such a charge lies even though the
accused thereby loses the protection of a time limit applicable to the statutory
offence, and becomes liable to a penalty which may far exceed the maximum for a
statutory offence (see *R.* v. *Blamires Transport Services, Ltd.* (3) and cases therein
cited).

---

(2) (1844), 6 Q.B. 126.   (3) [1963] 3 All E.R. 170; [1963] 1 Q.B. 278.

A   There is a second and even more fundamental objection to counsel's point. The whole basis of his argument is that if there were a statute of limitation which applied to conspiracy, time would run from the first moment when the conspirators agreed. He contends that even if the conspirators in this case were proved not only first to have conspired together on Jan. 1, but also to have continued in pursuance of their conspiracy to act in combination to defraud the customs
B authorities until Aug. 31, 1962, yet the only relevant date for the purpose is Jan. 1, 1962. He submits that it is only the first making of the agreement by any two of the conspirators that is relevant for this purpose. This argument is based on a complete fallacy as to the nature of conspiracy. Of course, if two men agree on a particular day to embark on a course of criminal conduct over a period of months, the offence of conspiracy is committed at the moment of agreement. But
C they remain conspirators and their conspiracy continues until either the criminal purpose has been achieved or their agreement has been brought to an end.

     The offence of conspiracy has clearly over the centuries been committed by being a member of what in the old books is referred to as a " confederacy "—that is to say being one of two or more persons acting or planning to act in concert under some agreement—be it express or implied—in pursuit of a criminal design.
D Furthermore, it is well established law that if A and B conspire together to carry on, for example, a course of fraudulent trading, C may join in (or in the older phraseology " adhere to ") the conspiracy at a later date and then A may drop out and be replaced by D. But it all remains a single conspiracy as long as all of them are for the period of their participation acting in combination to achieve the same criminal objective. This view of the law finds statutory recognition in
E the form of conspiracy count laid down in Sch. 1 to the Indictments Act, 1915, as amended by the Indictment Rules, 1916 (4) (see Archbold's Pleading, Evidence and Practice in Criminal Cases (36th Edn.) para. 4072). So on the facts of this case the period of limitation, if there had been one, would have run at the earliest only from Aug. 31, 1962, so far as Simmonds, Barrington-Coupe, Cohen and Orwell were concerned, and from the end of May, 1962, so far as Conway was
F concerned.

     Once there is exposed the patent fallacy underlying the submissions that a conspiracy can only be laid as occurring on the first day of a criminal agreement, the suggestion that in the present case it cannot be charged in relation to the overt acts that took place after Mar. 24, 1962, is simply unarguable.

     [His Lordship then turned to a submission, in support of which reliance was
G placed on *R.* v. *Barnett* (5) that as the particulars of count 1 and count 2 were in terms the offences created (6) by s. 17 of the Finance Act, 1944 the counts of conspiracy would not lie. His Lordship considered *R.* v. *Barnett* (5) and rejected the submission on the ground that the offence under s. 17 could be committed by one person, and the present case was not one where the agreement between one or more persons to do certain things was itself made a specific
H offence by statute. Having rejected a submission of alleged wrongful admission in evidence of answers to questions put to the accused by customs officers, His Lordship concluded:] It follows from what has been said in this judgment that all the appeals against conviction are dismissed.

     It only remains to deal with the question of costs. The learned judge made an order against the accused Simmonds, Barrington-Coupe, Cohen, Orwell, Conway,
I the two Hampden Companies, Barrington-Coupe, Ltd. and Master Records, Ltd. in respect of costs. He did so in these terms:

     " I make a joint and several order against all of you that you pay a sum not exceeding £15,000 towards the costs of the prosecution."

---

     (4) S.R. & O. 1916 No. 282.   For Sch. 1 to the Act of 1915, as amended, see 5 Halsbury's Statutes (2nd Edn.) 997.
     (5) [1951] 1 All E.R. 917; [1951] 2 K.B. 425.
     (6) Section 17 was repealed by the Purchase Tax Act 1963; see now s. 33 of that Act; 43 Halsbury's Statutes (2nd Edn.) 1047.

The second appellant (Barrington-Coupe) appeals against that form of order. **A**
Counsel on his behalf, first, complains of the form of order being " joint and
several " and draws attention to difficulties which might arise as between the
different accused on enforcement. Secondly, he contends that the order is not
valid in that it does not bear relation to the costs " in or about the prosecution
and conviction " of the second appellant, and by virtue of the terms of the Costs
in Criminal Cases Act, 1952, s. 2 (1) it is only in respect of the whole or part of **B**
such costs that the court can order a convicted person to pay costs (7); see *R.*
v. *Gould* (8). This court sees no objection to the order being made against a number
of accused in the form of a joint and several order. The trial court is not concerned
with matters which may arise as between the convicted persons on enforcement
of the order. There is, however, force in the other arm of the submission: more
force when the order is looked at from the point of view of the appellants Cohen **C**
and Orwell and the accused Conway, none of whom were concerned in count 3
and who do not appeal against the order, than when it is regarded from the point
of view of the first and second appellants (Simmonds and Barrington-Coupe) and
their companies. The court has been provided with figures which represent
approximately the number of pages of the transcript occupied by, and the number
of words spoken in respect of submissions made on behalf of, the various defen- **D**
dants and the evidence adduced by and on their behalf. Figures have also been
provided which indicate the time taken in closing speeches. There was a trial
within a trial in respect of one accused only. Examination of the transcript of
evidence reveals the time spent in cross-examination of the prosecution witnesses
on behalf of the various defendants. These are not the only matters which the
court takes into account in assessing what is the proper order in respect of these **E**
appellants in regard to costs, for the court is necessarily concerned first to consider generally what were the costs of bringing the particular accused to justice
(in conspiracy cases this may prove to be the entire costs of the proceedings) and
then to exercise a general discretion. Taking the whole of the available information into consideration this court, in the exercise of its discretion, considers that,
having regard to the terms of the Costs in Criminal Cases Act, 1952, the proper **F**
order as to costs is that the appellants Simmonds, Barrington-Coupe, Hampden
Co. (Electronics), Ltd. and Hampden Co. (Sales), Ltd. be ordered to pay jointly
and severally the sum of £12,500 towards the costs of the prosecution and that
the appellants Cohen and Orwell be ordered to pay jointly and severally the sum
of £2,500. Conway, Barrington-Coupe, Ltd. and Master Records, Ltd. are not
before the court, and this court cannot vary the order made against them but **G**
indicates that, had they appealed in this respect, the order against them would,
in the discretion of the court, have been that their liability for costs be joint and
several—in the case of Conway and Master Records, Ltd., with that of Cohen
and Orwell in the sum of £2,500; and in the case of Barrington-Coupe, Ltd., with
that of Simmonds, Barrington-Coupe and the two Hampden companies in the
sum of £12,500. **H**

Appeals dismissed. Orders as to costs varied.

Solicitors: *M. A. Jacobs & Son* (for the appellants Simmonds, Hampden Co.
(Sales), Ltd. and Hampden Co. (Electronics), Ltd.); *Muscatt, Nelson & Co.* (for
the appellant Barrington-Coupe); *John Wood & Co.* (for the appellants Orwell
and Cohen); *Solicitor, Customs and Excise* (for the Crown).

[*Reported by* N. P. METCALFE, ESQ., *Barrister-at-Law.*] **I**

---

(7) Section 2 (1), so far as material, provides " A court of assize . . . before which any
person is convicted may, if it thinks fit, order him to pay the whole or any part of the
costs incurred in or about the prosecution or conviction, including any proceedings
before examining justices."
(8) [1965] Crim. L.R. 547.

ROBSON AND ANOTHER *v.* HALLETT

[QUEEN'S BENCH DIVISION (Lord Parker, C.J., Diplock, L.J., and Ashworth, J.), March 7, 8, 1967.]

Police—Constable—Assault on, in execution of duty—Police officers entering garden of house and knocking on front door to inquire about alleged offence —Police sergeant invited inside and leaving when requested to do so by tenant of house—Other officers remaining in garden of house—Assault on police sergeant as he was leaving house—Other officers coming to sergeant's assistance—Assault on sergeant and officer in general mêlée—Whether officers were trespassers—Implied licence to enter garden and approach front door— Whether officers were acting in execution of duty—Police Act 1964 (c. 48), s. 51 (1).

Three police officers, a sergeant and two police constables, who were making enquiries about an offence, went in the course of their duty to the appellants' home, the house of which their father, R., was the tenant. The two police constables went through the unlocked gate and small garden and knocked at the door. The appellant T., opened the door and one of the police constables asked him whether he had been out that night, saying that they were making some enquiries. After the sergeant, who had been turning the car in which the police officers came, had come to the door, the appellant said that the sergeant could come in but not the two police constables. When the sergeant was inside the house, R. told him to get out. The sergeant proceeded to leave but, as he reached the threshold of the door, the appellant T. jumped on his back and punched him. When the door opened, the police constables who had remained outside saw the sergeant fall forwards with the appellant T. on his back. One of the constables went to the sergeant's assistance and pulled the appellant T. off; and a mêlée developed. The appellant D. came round from the back of the house and proceeded to kick and punch the other police constable; he also kicked the sergeant, and both he and the appellant T. started to punch the police constable. On appeal by the appellants from the dismissal of their appeals to quarter sessions against convictions of assaulting the police constable in the execution of his duty, contrary to s. 51 (1)* of the Police Act 1964, and on appeal by the respondent prosecutor against the quashing of the appellant D.'s conviction of assaulting the sergeant in the execution of his duty, contrary to s. 51 (1).

Held: (i) all three police officers were lawfully on the premises when they were outside the house in the garden because, like any other members of the public coming on their lawful business, they had an implied licence to walk through the unlocked gate and up to the door of the house; moreover (per LORD PARKER, C.J., and ASHWORTH, J.) when the sergeant went inside the house, the two police constables were lawfully in the garden, their licence to be there not having been revoked (see p. 412, letter D, p. 413, letter C, and p. 414, letters B and H, post).

(ii) on the sergeant's licence to be in the house being withdrawn by R., the sergeant had a reasonable time in which to leave and was not, therefore, a trespasser and was still in the execution of his duty at the time when he was assaulted; accordingly, the respondent's appeal against the quashing of the conviction of the appellant D. would be allowed and the case would be sent back to quarter sessions with a direction to dismiss the appellant D.'s appeal against his conviction of assaulting the sergeant (see p. 413, letter F, p. 413, letter I, to p. 414, letter A, and p. 414, letters E and H, post).

(iii) the two police constables were acting in the execution of their duty in coming to the assistance of the sergeant in the garden; moreover, once the

---

* Section 51 (1), so far as material, provides: " Any person who assaults a constable in the execution of his duty . . . shall be guilty of an offence . . ."

breach of the peace occurred, they were entitled to enter and be in the   A
garden for the purpose of stopping it, and accordingly the convictions of
the appellants of assault on the police constable should stand (see p. 413,
letters H and I, and p. 414, letters G and H, post).

Appellants' appeals dismissed; respondent's appeal allowed.

[As to power of entry by police, see 30 HALSBURY'S LAWS (3rd Edn.) 130, 131,   B
para. 209; as to resisting a peace officer, see 10 HALSBURY'S LAWS (3rd Edn.)
634, 635, para. 1207; and for cases on the subject, see 15 DIGEST (Repl.) 852-854,
8194-8216.

For the Police Act 1964, s. 51, see 44 HALSBURY'S STATUTES (2nd Edn.) 924.]

Cases referred to:
> *Davis* v. *Lisle*, [1936] 2 All E.R. 213; [1936] 2 K.B. 434; 105 L.J.K.B. 593;   C
> 155 L.T. 23; 100 J.P. 280; 15 Digest (Repl.) 852, *8201.*
>
> *Great Central Ry. Co.* v. *Bates*, [1921] 3 K.B. 578; 90 L.J.K.B. 1269; 126 L.T.
> 61; 36 Digest (Repl.) 51, *278.*
>
> *McArdle* v. *Wallace*, (1964), 108 Sol. Jo. 483; 3rd Digest Supp.

Case Stated.   D

This was a Case Stated by the Court of General Quarter Sessions of the Peace
for the county of Durham in respect of their adjudication of two appeals from
the decisions of the magistrates' court sitting at Gateshead in the county borough
of Gateshead on Jan. 7, 1966.   The appeals were heard on Feb. 1 and 2, 1966.

These were appeals by the appellants, Dennis Robson and Thomas Robson,
against their conviction before the magistrates' court sitting at Gateshead   E
on Jan. 7, 1966.   The appellant Dennis Robson appealed against his conviction
for having (i) on Oct. 15, 1965, in the county borough of Gateshead, assaulted
Sgt. Brian McCaffrey in the execution of his duty, contrary to s. 51 (1) of the
Police Act 1964; (ii) on the same day and at the same place, assaulted P.C.
William Burnett Paxton in the execution of his duty, contrary to the same
statute; and (iii) on the same day and at the same place assaulted P.C. Kenneth   F
Jobson in the execution of his duty, contrary to the same statute.   For each of
these offences he had been sentenced to be imprisoned for three months, the
sentences to run concurrently, and he appealed against each of the sentences.
The appellant Thomas Robson appealed against his conviction for having on
Oct. 15, 1965, in the county borough of Gateshead assaulted P.C. William Burnett
Paxton in the execution of his duty, contrary to s. 51 (1) of Police Act 1964.   G
The prosecutions were brought by the respondent, John Arthur Hallett, chief
constable of Gateshead. The following facts, so far as material to this report,
were found.   On Friday, Oct. 15, 1965, at about 11 p.m. three officers of the
Gateshead County Borough Police Force, Sgt. McCaffrey, P.C. Paxton and P.C.
Jobson, were on duty in a police van.   Just after 11.30 p.m., they received a
message, as a result of which they went to Lobley Hill Road. There they received   H
information concerning an alleged offence.   As a result they went to 28, Laurelwood Gardens to make inquiries relating to it.   Sgt. McCaffrey was driving the
van, and he stopped it at the gate of No. 20.   The two other officers alighted and
went to the door of the house.   Sgt. McCaffrey drove the van to the end of the
street (a distance of about fifty feet), turned the van and stopped it at the gate
of No. 28.   None of the officers had a warrant of any kind.   The offence under   I
investigation was a misdemeanour only and the officers at that time did not
intend to make an arrest.   No. 28 Laurelwood Gardens was a semi-detached
villa, and a council house. There was a small garden in front and a short flight
of steps led from the front door to the garden gate.   The tenant was the father
of the two appellants, Mr. Robson, senior.   P.C. Paxton knocked at the door
of the house and it was opened by the appellant Thomas Robson.   P.C. Paxton
asked him who he was and he said that he was Thomas Robson.   P.C. Paxton
asked him if he had been out that night as they were making some inquiries.

A The sister of the appellants came to the door. When the van driven by Sgt. McCaffrey returned and stopped at the gate, the appellant Thomas Robson became excited. He shouted: " I'm not going in that. I'm not going in that. What's it there for? " The sister shouted to someone upstairs. Sgt. McCaffrey alighted from the van and walked to the front door. He told the appellant Thomas Robson that no-one had any intention of locking him in the van. The

B sergeant explained why he had come and asked if he could come into the house. The appellant Thomas Robson said: " You're not putting me in that." He then said to the sergeant, " You can come in ", and, pointing to the other officers, " but not those . . . . . ". Sgt. McCaffrey stepped in and the door was closed. The other two officers remained outside. There was a passage leading from the front door to the back of the house. There was a staircase on the left and a

C living-room on the right. Sgt. McCaffrey, with the appellant Thomas Robson, went into the living-room. The sister ran upstairs calling " Dad ". Sgt. McCaffrey told the appellant Thomas Robson why he had called. Sgt. McCaffrey heard someone coming downstairs and Mr. Robson senior entered the room. As he entered, he said to the sergeant, " You get out, mister. You've no right here. I said ' Get out '." Sgt. McCaffrey immediately turned to leave. He

D said, " Righto, Mr. Robson ". He came out of the living-room and went along the passage, saying to the appellant Thomas Robson that he wanted to continue the conversation outside the front door. The appellant Thomas Robson followed him along the passage. The door was then open, and when the sergeant had almost reached the threshold the appellant Thomas Robson jumped on his back and began punching him under the ribs on the left hand side. The sergeant

E rolled half forward through the doorway and landed on his knees on the steps just outside. The place on which he fell was slightly to the right of the door, as one looked at the house from the garden gate. P.C. Paxton and P.C. Jobson had remained outside the front door when Sgt. McCaffrey went into the house. Both heard the sound of voices coming from within and both heard Mr. Robson senior tell the sergeant to get out. When the door opened, they both saw

F the sergeant fall forwards with the appellant Thomas Robson on his back. P.C. Jobson pulled the appellant Thomas Robson off Sgt. McCaffrey. The appellant Thomas Robson was struggling, and P.C. Jobson took him towards the left hand side of the house. A mêlée developed very quickly. P.C. Paxton, as soon as he saw the sergeant with the appellant Thomas Robson on his back, had gone towards him, but before he could reach him, Mr. Robson senior, came

G out of the house and began pulling at the sergeant. P.C. Paxton pulled Mr. Robson senior away towards the left side of the house. As they reached the left hand edge of the steps, Mr. Robson senior fell on his back and lay on the grass. P.C. Paxton left him and made his way to the right to help Sgt. McCaffrey. The wife and daughter of Mr. Robson senior were in the garden. Sgt. McCaffrey had now got up from the steps. The appellant Dennis Robson had been at the

H back of the house. He saw his father on the grass and he ran round the left hand side of the house shouting, " Get off the old man ". He kicked and punched P.C. Paxton several times. He kicked Sgt. McCaffrey in the privates. Both the appellants started to punch P.C. Paxton. All the members of the Robson family moved to the house and stood just inside the doorway. The father, mother and daughter were in front, the two appellants behind. P.C. Paxton

I was bleeding from a wound on the left side of the face. Sgt. McCaffrey moved towards the door to speak to Mr. Robson senior. As he did so, the appellant Dennis Robson kicked him on the left thigh. All the members of the Robson family then withdrew into the house and the door was closed. Sgt. McCaffrey went to the van and radioed for assistance. The subsequent events are not material to this report.

It was contended before quarter sessions by counsel for the appellants that: (a) even if the police were assaulted, they were not assaulted in the exercise of their duty; (b) if the appellants were not guilty of assault in the execution of their duty, they could not be found guilty of common assault on the charge as **A** laid; (c) as the house and garden of 28, Laurelwood Gardens was private property, and as the three officers had no authority from the tenant to enter, and had no warrant, they were trespassers ab initio as soon as they entered the gate. They remained trespassers while they were on the property, and at no time were they, therefore, in the execution of their duty; (d) as soon as the tenant ordered Sgt. McCaffrey to leave the house, he became a trespasser, and, if he was not a tres- **B** passer before, he became one then, and from that moment ceased to be in execution of his duty; (e) on being ordered out by Mr. Robson senior, Sgt. McCaffrey became a trespasser ab initio; (f) on hearing Sgt. McCaffrey being ordered out, P.C. Paxton and P.C. Jobson no longer had any implied right of licence if (which was denied) they ever had one to remain on Mr. Robson senior's premises, and they then became trespassers and trespassers ab initio; (g) if the appellant **C** Thomas Robson assaulted P.C. Paxton, he used no more violence than was necessary to prevent arrest, and the purported arrest was unlawful, as P.C. Paxton was attempting to arrest the appellant Thomas Robson without a warrant for a misdemeanour which he had not witnessed; (h) if the appellant Dennis Robson assaulted Sgt. McCaffrey and P.C. Paxton and P.C. Jobson, he did so in defence of his father under the reasonable belief that his father was being **D** assaulted.

It was contended by counsel for the respondent before quarter sessions that:— (a) the three police officers, in entering the premises, were not trespassers ab initio, because they had lawful business thereon; (b) if a person entered premises for the purpose of lawful business, and the proprietor ordered him off the premises, he became a trespasser, but before he did so he must first be given a reasonable **E** opportunity and time in which to leave the premises; (c) at the time of visiting the premises the three police officers had no reason to search the premises and had no intention of making an arrest. Their sole object in going to the premises was to make inquiries, for which purpose neither a search warrant nor a warrant of arrest was appropriate. Nor had they at that time evidence which would justify the issue of any such warrant; (d) Sgt. McCaffrey had been invited into **F** the house by the appellant Thomas Robson, there must be an implied authority in a son of reasonable age, on behalf of his father, to invite a person into the house and the sergeant could not thereafter, until he was ordered out of the house, have been a trespasser; (e) P.C. Paxton and P.C. Jobson were never ordered by Mr. Robson senior to leave the premises and they were at no time trespassers; (f) when the appellant Thomas Robson jumped on the back of **G** Sgt. McCaffrey he did something which amounted to a common assault, P.C. Paxton and P.C. Jobson saw him commit this common assault and it became their duty to pull the appellant Thomas Robson away. That resulted in a breach of the peace. It became the duty of P.C. Paxton and P.C. Jobson to prevent a breach of the peace and to rescue the sergeant. In so doing they were acting in execution of their duty; (g) when the appellant Dennis Robson kicked Sgt. **H** McCaffrey in the privates, the sergeant was " trying to sort the position out ". He was, therefore, acting in the execution of his duty in attempting to quell a breach of the peace which related to him; (h) when the appellant Dennis Robson kicked P.C. Jobson, the police officer was till acting in the execution of his duty, although that assault occurred a little later than the assaults on the other two officers; (i) when the appellant Thomas Robson assaulted P.C. Paxton, the **I** police officer had witnessed a breach of the peace, was justified in intervening and was in the execution of his duty when doing so; (j) the appellant Dennis Robson did not see anyone strike his father and there were no grounds for belief that his father was being assaulted; (k) even if the appellant Dennis Robson had reasonable ground for believing that his father was being assaulted, the action which he took was more than was required for the defence of his father.

The Appeal Committee were of opinion, so far as relevant to this report, as follows: (i) the three police officers, when they entered the garden of the house

A to make inquiries regarding a complaint which had been made to them, were
not trespassers; (ii) the appellant Thomas Robson had an implied authority to
allow Sgt. McCaffrey to enter the house, and when the sergeant entered in pursuance of that permission, he was not a trespasser; (iii) from the moment Mr.
Robson senior ordered Sgt. McCaffrey to leave the house, he became a trespasser
and was no longer acting in execution of his duty (the appeal committee relied
B on the last sentence of the judgment of GODDARD, J., in Davis v. Lisle*); (iv) Sgt.
McCaffrey, as a result of being ordered off the premises, was not acting in execution of his duty while he remained on the premises. He was still on the premises
when he was kicked by the appellant Dennis Robson, and such assault, therefore,
was not committed while the sergeant was acting in the execution of his duty;
(v) P.C. Paxton and P.C. Jobson were never ordered to leave the premises and
C were never trespassers; (vi) when P.C. Paxton and P.C. Jobson saw Sgt. McCaffrey
come through the doorway with the appellant Thomas Robson on his back,
and the appellant Dennis Robson striking him, they were under a duty to go
to his assistance. The mêlée which developed amounted to a breach of the
peace, and they were under a duty to quell it. The three police officers, throughout the mêlée, were doing no more than trying to separate the contestants and
D restore order. P.C. Paxton and P.C. Jobson were, therefore, acting in the
execution of their duty. P.C. Paxton was assaulted by both the appellants
when he was trying to quell the mêlée. These assaults amounted, therefore,
to assaults on him when he was acting in the execution of his duty; (vii) the
appellant Dennis Robson saw his father on the ground and reasonably thought
that he had been knocked down in the mêlée, but his subsequent actions were
E not done to protect his father. There was no-one on or assaulting his father.
His action in kicking the privates of Sgt. McCaffrey indicated his frame of
mind. P.C. Paxton, when the appellant Dennis Robson kicked and punched
him, was not beside the father and was walking away from him. There was no
justification for punching P.C. Paxton the second time; (viii) the appellant
Thomas Robson was not acting in self-defence when he punched P.C. Paxton.
F The police officer was not then endeavouring to arrest him. He was simply
trying to restore order.

Accordingly the appeal committee reversed the decision of the magistrates in
respect of the assault by the appellant Dennis Robson on Sgt. McCaffrey, confirmed their decision in respect of the assault by the appellant Dennis Robson
on P.C. Paxton and reversed their decision in respect of the assault by the
G appellant Dennis Robson on P.C. Jobson. They confirmed the sentence of
three months' imprisonment in respect of the assault on P.C. Paxton. They
confirmed the decision of the magistrates in respect of the assault by the appellant
Thomas Robson on P.C. Paxton. The appellants now appealed against the
convictions recorded against them and the respondent appealed against the
quashing of the conviction of the appellant Dennis Robson on the charge of
H assault on Sgt. McCaffrey.

The cases noted below† were cited during the argument in addition to those
referred to in the judgment of LORD PARKER, C.J.

R. A. R. Stroyan for the appellants.
Sir David Renton, Q.C., and R. R. Rawden-Smith for the respondent.

I   LORD PARKER, C.J.: On Jan. 7, 1966, at a magistrates' court sitting at
Gateshead, the appellant Dennis Robson was convicted of assaulting a Sergeant
McCaffrey in the execution of his duty, also a Police Constable Paxton, and
thirdly a Police Constable Jobson. The appellant Thomas Robson was also
convicted on one charge, namely, of assaulting P.C. Paxton in the execution of
his duty. Both the appellants appealed to quarter sessions for the county of

---

* See p. 413, letter E, post.
† Thomas v. Sawkins, [1935] All E.R. Rep. 655; [1935] 2 K.B. 249; Dumbell v.
Roberts, [1944] 1 All E.R. 326.

Durham, who upheld the conviction of the appellant Dennis Robson for assaulting A
P.C. Paxton and also the conviction of the appellant Thomas Robson for assaulting that police constable, but they quashed the convictions of the appellant
Dennis Robson for assaulting P.C. Jobson and Sgt. McCaffrey. It is from the
decision of quarter sessions that this appeal now comes to this court by way of
Case Stated, and it involves not only the appeals of the appellants against the
two convictions which remain recorded against them, but also an appeal by the B
respondent, the prosecutor, in respect of the quashing of the appellant Dennis
Robson's conviction of assaulting Sgt. McCaffrey. The appeal in respect of the
quashing of his conviction of assaulting P.C. Jobson is not pursued in this court.
[HIS LORDSHIP stated the facts, and continued:] What is said in this case, and
this is really the foundation of counsel for the appellants' argument, is that all
three police officers were trespassers ab initio; having arrived at the garden C
gate, although up till then they were acting in the execution of their duty,
making inquiries into an offence committed that night, yet the moment when
they set foot onto the steps leading up to the front door they were all three
trespassers. For my part, it is no doubt true that the law is sometimes said to
be an ass, but I am happy to think that it is not an ass in this respect, because
I am quite satisfied that these three police officers, like any other members of the D
public, had implied leave and licence to walk through that gate up those steps
and to knock on the door of the house. We are not considering for this purpose
the entering of private premises in the form of a dwelling-house, but of the
position between the gate and the front door. There, as it seems to me, the
occupier of any dwelling-house gives implied licence to any member of the
public coming on his lawful business to come through the gate, up the steps, and E
knock on the door of the house.

Counsel for the appellants has stressed the words used by ATKIN, L.J., in
Great Central Ry. Co. v. *Bates* (1). In that case, a police constable, seeing the
door of the defendants' warehouse open after dark, and in order to see that
everything was right, entered the warehouse and injured himself. It was held
that he had no legal right to enter being neither an invitee nor a licensee. ATKIN, F
L.J., in the course of his judgment said this (2):

" Now it appears to me that he had no right to enter these premises at
all, and I think that counsel for the respondent has been a little hard put to it
to defend the right of entry in these circumstances. It can hardly be suggested
that the right exists in respect of a dwelling house. If it did the privacy of
an Englishman's dwelling house would be most materially curtailed. In G
view of the limitations that have been laid down over and over again as to the
right of a constable to force a door, and as to the limitations of his powers
unless he has a warrant, or in cases of felony, it appears to me quite impossible to suggest, merely because a constable may suspect there is something
wrong, that he has a right to enter a dwelling house either by opening a door
or by entering an open door or an open window and go into the house. It is H
true that a reasonable householder would not as a rule object if the matter
was done bona fide and no nuisance was caused. But the question is whether
the constable has the right to enter."

I hope that nothing that I am saying will be thought in any way to detract from
what ATKIN, L.J., said; but we are not here considering the right to enter the I
front door of the house but merely the right to go in at the garden gate and go up
to the front door. Lastly under this head, counsel for the appellants invoked
Davis v. *Lisle* (3). It is unnecessary to go through the facts of that case in any
detail, but there is no doubt that it did involve the right of a police officer to enter
garage premises, and there are passages in the judgments in that case which in
isolation might be taken to suggest that he had no leave or licence to enter on to

(1) [1921] 3 K.B. 578.   (2) [1921] 3 K.B. at pp. 581, 582.
                 (3) [1936] 2 All E.R. 213; [1936] 2 K.B. 434.

A those premises. When one looks at the case, however, it is quite clear that it was decided on the basis that a time came when the proprietor told the police officer to leave, and, as it was put, from that moment he became a trespasser and ceased to be acting in the execution of his duty. That case, in my judgment, is no authority for saying that a police officer on his lawful business making proper inquiries has no right to enter the front gate of private premises and to go up B and knock on the front door.

Finally, it is to be observed that what I have said is fully in accord with a recent decision of this court in 1964, *McArdle* v. *Wallace* (4). Again it is unnecessary to go into the facts of that case, though it is to be observed that the court there held that a constable who entered an adjacent yard and knocked on the rear door of premises in order to rouse the occupier and make inquiries came on to those C premises with the implied authority of the occupier. The only question in that case was whether that implied leave and licence had been revoked by the occupier's son. Accordingly, in my judgment, all three police officers were lawfully on those premises while they were outside the house.

What happened then was, as I have said, that Sgt. McCaffrey was allowed to enter the house by the permission of the occupier's son. It was not suggested that D the occupier's son had no authority so to do, and, accordingly, when Sgt. McCaffrey was in the house he was lawfully in the house and was still acting in the execution of his duty. What counsel for the appellants says in regard to Sgt. McCaffrey is this, that the moment Mr. Robson senior said " Get out " he at once became a trespasser and at once, instanter, ceased to be acting in the execution of his duty. That proposition, which I confess sounds remarkable, is E based as I understand it on the last sentence in the judgment of GODDARD, J., in *Davis* v. *Lisle* (5), where he said: " He had no right to be on the premises once he had been asked to leave." In my judgment, it is quite wrong to read those words as words of a statute; they were in relation to a case where the police officer, having been plainly told to leave, was remonstrating and asserting his right to stay. In the present case, Sgt. McCaffrey was doing all he could to leave, and F was not asserting any right to stay. It seems to me that, when a licence is revoked as a result of which something has to be done by the licensee, a reasonable time must be implied in which he can do so, in this case to get off the premises; no doubt it will be a very short time, but he was doing here his best to leave the premises. Looked at in a slightly different way, it is argued that he was acting in the execution of his duty up to the very moment he was told to get out, and G one asks oneself what was he doing when he was assaulted? He was surely carrying on his duty, which was a duty to get out.

In my judgment, therefore, the respondent's cross-appeal in regard to the assault on Sgt. McCaffrey succeeds. In regard to the two remaining assaults, those by the appellants Dennis and Thomas Robson on P.C. Paxton, counsel for the appellants' case is really based on the submission that the officers were H throughout and remained trespassers. As I have already said, I think that they were lawfully on those premises when they entered them; they, as opposed to Sgt. McCaffrey, had never been told to get out, their implied licence to be there had never been revoked, and, accordingly, there they were in this little garden seeing Sgt. McCaffrey set on by the appellant Thomas Robson and a general mêlée developing. It seems to me quite impossible in those circumstances to say that I they were not acting in the execution of their duty in coming to the assistance of Sgt. McCaffrey, and also avoiding any further breach of the peace. It is really unnecessary to go further, but, even if they had been outside the gate, it seems to me that they would have had abundant right to come on to private property in those circumstances.

Accordingly, I would dismiss the appeals by the appellants, but I would send the Case back to quarter sessions with a direction that they should dismiss the

appeal by the appellant Dennis Robson against his conviction by the magistrates **A**
for assaulting Sgt. McCaffrey.

DIPLOCK, L.J.: I agree. These appeals raise three simple points on the
law of trespass on land which affect all members of the public as well as the
police officers with whom this appeal is concerned. The points are so simple
that the combined researches of counsel have not revealed any authority on them. **B**
There is no authority because no one has thought it plausible up till now to
question them. The first is this, that when a householder lives in a dwelling house
to which there is a garden in front and does not lock the gate of the garden, it
gives an implied licence to any member of the public who has lawful reason for
doing so to proceed from the gate to the front door or back door, and to inquire
whether he may be admitted and to conduct his lawful business. Such implied **C**
licence can be rebutted by express refusal of it, as in this case the Robsons could no
doubt have rebutted the implied licence to the police officers by putting up a
notice on their front gate " No admittance to police officers "; but that was not
done in this case. The second proposition is this, that when, having knocked at
the front door of the dwelling-house, someone who is inside the dwelling-house
invites the person who has knocked to come in, there is an implied authority in **D**
that person, which can be rebutted on behalf of the occupier of the dwelling-
house, to invite him to come in and so licence him to come into the dwelling-house
itself. In the present case, it was the son, the appellant Thomas Robson, and not
the father who was the occupier who invited Sgt. McCaffrey to come in. In those
circumstances, Sgt. McCaffrey, whilst in the dwelling-house on the invitation of
the son, was no trespasser. The licence, however, could be withdrawn by the **E**
father who was the person entitled to give it. He withdrew it and, on its being
withdrawn, the sergeant had a reasonable time to leave the premises by the most
appropriate route for doing so, namely, out of the front door, down the steps
and out of the gate, and, provided that he did so with reasonable expedition,
he would not be a trespasser while he was so doing. That is sufficient to give the
reasons for allowing the appeal of the prosecution in the case of the attack on **F**
Sgt. McCaffrey.

As regards P.C. Paxton and P.C. Jobson, it does not seem to me to matter
whether, when they were denied entrance at the front door, they were trespassers
in remaining in the garden if they did remain in the garden after that, because
there are two ways in which a person who enters land of another person may fail
to be a trespasser. One is leave and licence of the person entitled to possession,
to which I have already referred; the other is in the exercise of an independent **G**
right to proceed on the land. In the case of P.C. Paxton and P.C. Jobson, once a
breach of the peace was taking place under their eyes, they had not only an
independent right but a duty to go and stop it, and it matters not from that
moment onwards whether they started off on their journey to stop it from outside
the premises or from inside the premises. They were entitled, once the breach of
the peace occurred, to be on the premises for the purpose of preventing it or **H**
stopping it.

I agree with the order proposed by LORD PARKER, C.J.

ASHWORTH, J.: I agree with both judgments.

Appeals dismissed.   Cross-appeal allowed.   Case remitted in part. **I**

Solicitors: *Bentleys, Stokes & Lowless,* agents for *Thomas Magnay & Co.,*
Gateshead (for the appellants); *C. D. Jackson,* Gateshead (for the respondent).

[*Reported by* N. P. METCALFE, ESQ., *Barrister-at-Law.*]

SEAGER *v.* COPYDEX, LTD.

[COURT OF APPEAL (Lord Denning, M.R., Salmon and Winn, L.JJ.), March 13,
14, 15, April 18, 1967.]

*Equity—Confidence—Breach of confidence—Damages—Use of information
obtained in confidence—Springboard for activities detrimental to informant
—Unpatented device disclosed by inventor as alternative in course of negotiation for marketing his patented device—Patented device already on sale by
inventor's firm—Information acquired by defendant company partly private
and partly available to public—Application by defendant company for
patent, and device sold by them—Damages.*

An inventor, with whom the defendant company were negotiating for
the marketing rights of a patented carpet grip, which the inventor or his
firm made and sold to anyone who wished to buy it, endeavoured at an
interview with the defendant company's assistant general manager and with
the defendant company's sales manager to interest them in his alternative
device, which he called by a description such as "Invisigrip", which
device was not patented. The information was given in confidence. The
defendant company were not at the time interested. Subsequently, negotiations regarding marketing the patented grip having broken down, the
defendant company applied for a patent in respect of a carpet grip very
similar to the alternative device, the "Invisigrip", giving the name of the
assistant general manager as inventor. They maintained that this grip was
their own idea.

Held: the defendant company had made use, albeit honestly, of information which had been received in confidence and which was not available to
the public; they were accordingly liable for breach of confidence, and the
plaintiff was entitled to damages, assessed on basis of reasonable compensation for the use of the confidential information (see p. 418, letters B and
G, p. 418, letter I, to p. 419, letter A, and p. 419, letter B, post).

Appeal allowed.

[**Editorial Note.** It is to be observed that damages were awarded. It has
been said that, apart from liability for breach of contract, which would not
have been relevant in the present case, damages are obtainable for breach of
confidence by virtue of Lord Cairns' Act (*Saltman Engineering Co., Ltd.* v.
Campbell Engineering Co., Ltd., [1963] 3 All E.R. at p. 415, letter H).

As to the principles on which relief (by injunction) may be granted in respect
of the use of confidential information in breach of confidence, see 21 HALSBURY'S
LAWS (3rd Edn.) 395, para. 825; and for cases on the subject, see 28 DIGEST
(Repl.) 854-856, *844-875.*

For Lord Cairns' Act (viz., the Chancery Amendment Act, 1858), s. 2, see
18 HALSBURY'S STATUTES (2nd Edn.) 456.]

Cases referred to:

Cranleigh Precision Engineering, Ltd. v. *Bryant*, [1964] 3 All E.R. 289; [1965]
 1 W.L.R. 1293; 3rd Digest Supp.
Saltman Engineering Co., Ltd. v. *Campbell Engineering Co., Ltd.*, (1948),
 [1963] 3 All E.R. 413 n.; 65 R.P.C. 203; 12 Digest (Repl.) 709, 710, *5407.*
Terrapin, Ltd. v. *Builders' Supply Co. (Hayes), Ltd., Taylor Woodrow, Ltd. &
 Swiftplan, Ltd.*, [1960] R.P.C. 128; Digest (Cont. Vol. A) 940, *875a.*

Appeal.

By writ issued on July 19, 1963, the plaintiff, John Henry Seager, brought an
action against the defendant company, Copydex, Ltd., claiming an injunction
to restrain the defendant company, whether acting by themselves, their directors,
officers, servants or agents or otherwise howsoever, from (briefly stated) making
use of information supplied by the plaintiff in confidence and from selling carpet
grips in the manufacture of which information supplied by the plaintiff in confidence had been used. The plaintiff also sought an inquiry as to damages by

Considered in ENGLISH v DEDHAM
VALE [1978] 1 All ER 382

reason of the defendant company's breaches of confidence, or an account of **A**
profits, and other relief.   The breach of confidence alleged by the plaintiff
consisted in using information given by the plaintiff, concerning a carpet grip
(the " Invisigrip "), during negotiations with a view to the defendant company's
marketing the plaintiff's patented " Klent " carpet grip.

The plaintiff was the proprietor of a light engineering business and an inventor.
He invented and patented a special carpet grip, which he called the " Klent "   **B**
grip, to keep carpet down;   it was a metal strip nailed to the floor, and the
carpet was stretched over it and caught by spikes;   the inventive step lay in the
construction of the spikes.   The plaintiff also devised another carpet grip,
which he called the " Invisigrip ";   the teeth in this device were V-shaped
domed prongs.   This second, alternative, device was not patented.   As a result
of a television " Get Ahead " contest in February, 1961, in which the plaintiff   **C**
took part and showed his " Klent " grip, a Mr. Preston, who was acting secretary
and assistant general manager of the defendant company, became interested in
the " Klent " grip.   He and the sales manager of the defendant company,
Mr. Boon, negotiated with the plaintiff for the marketing of the " Klent " grip
by the defendant company.   The plaintiff himself wished to retain rights over
the " Klent " grip, so as to enter again for the next television contest.   Negotia-   **D**
tions lasted for over a year, but in the course of them, and in particular at an
interview on Mar. 13, 1962, the plaintiff disclosed to Mr. Preston and Mr. Boon
the alternative device, " Invisigrip ".   The plaintiff alleged that the disclosure
was made by means of drawings and verbal explanation and that he disclosed
the full details of manufacture and design.   Negotiations finally broke down
in May, 1962.   The further facts are summarised in the judgment of LORD   **E**
DENNING, M.R.

The action was tried before BUCKLEY, J., who dismissed it on July 14, 1966.
By notice dated Sept. 19, 1966, the plaintiff gave notice of appeal.

The plaintiff appeared in person.
P. Ford for the defendant company.

Cur. adv. vult.   **F**
Apr. 18.   The following judgments were read.

   LORD DENNING, M.R., having reviewed the course of events, and having
said that there was no doubt that the information which the plaintiff gave to
the defendant company was given in confidence, continued: Summarised, the
facts are these—   **G**
   (i) The plaintiff invented the " Klent " carpet grip and took out a patent
for it.   He manufactured this grip and sold it.   He was looking for a selling
organisation to market it.
   (ii) The plaintiff negotiated with the defendant company with a view to their
marketing the " Klent " grip.   These negotiations were with Mr. Preston, the
assistant manager, and Mr. Boon, the sales manager.   These negotiations lasted   **H**
more than a year, but came to nothing.
   (iii) In the course of those negotiations, the plaintiff disclosed to Mr. Preston
and Mr. Boon all the features of the " Klent " grip.   He also told them of an
idea of his for an alternative carpet grip with a " V " tang and strong point.
But they rejected it, saying that they were only interested in the " Klent " grip.
   (iv) Both Mr. Preston and Mr. Boon realised that the information was given   **I**
to them in confidence.   Neither of them had any engineering skills, nor had
invented anything.
   (v) As soon as the negotiations looked like coming to nothing, the defendant
company decided to make a carpet grip of their own, which was to be basically
similar to the " Klent " grip, but with spikes which would not infringe the
plaintiff's patent.
   (vi) The defendant company did in fact make a carpet grip which did not
infringe the plaintiff's patent for a " Klent " grip.   But it embodied the very

A   idea of an alternative grip (of a " V-tang " with strong point) which the plaintiff mentioned to them in the course of the negotiations.   They made an application to patent it, and gave the name of Mr. Preston as the true and first inventor.

(vii) The defendant company gave this carpet grip the name " Invisigrip " which was the very name which the plaintiff says that he mentioned to Mr. Preston and Mr. Boon in the course of the negotiations.

B   (viii) The defendant company say that their alternative grip was the result of their own ideas and was not derived in any way from any information given to them by the plaintiff.   They say also that the name of " Invisigrip " was their own spontaneous idea.

(ix) I have no doubt that the defendant company honestly believe the alternative grip was their own idea; but I think that they must unconsciously have

C   made use of the information which the plaintiff gave them.   The coincidences are too strong to permit of any other explanation.

The Law.   I start with one sentence in the judgment of LORD GREENE, M.R., in *Saltman Engineering Co., Ltd.* v. *Campbell Engineering Co., Ltd.* (1):

"If a defendant is proved to have used confidential information, directly or indirectly obtained from the plaintiff, without the consent, express or

D   implied, of the plaintiff, he will be guilty of an infringement of the plaintiff's rights."

To this I add a sentence from the judgment of ROXBURGH, J., in *Terrapin, Ltd.* v. *Builders' Supply Co. (Hayes), Ltd., Taylor Woodrow, Ltd. & Swiftplan, Ltd.* (2), which was quoted and adopted as correct by ROSKILL, J., in *Cranleigh Precision*

E   *Engineering Co., Ltd.* v. *Bryant* (3):

"As I understand it, the essence of this branch of the law, whatever the origin of it may be, is that a person who has obtained information in confidence is not allowed to use it as a springboard for activities detrimental to the person who made the confidential communication, and springboard it remains even when all the features have been published or can be

F   ascertained by actual inspection by any member of the public."

The law on this subject does not depend on any implied contract.   It depends on the broad principle of equity that he who has received information in confidence shall not take unfair advantage of it.   He must not make use of it to the prejudice of him who gave it without obtaining his consent.   The principle is clear enough when the whole of the information is private.   The difficulty

G   arises when the information is in part public and in part private.   As for instance in this case.   A good deal of the information which the plaintiff gave to the defendant company was available to the public, such as the patent specification in the Patent Office, or the " Klent " grip, which he sold to anyone who asked. But there was a good deal of other information which was private, such as, the difficulties which had to be overcome in making a satisfactory grip; the necessity

H   for a strong, sharp tooth; the alternative forms of tooth; and the like.   When the information is mixed, being partly public and partly private, then the recipient must take special care to use only the material which is in the public domain.   He should go to the public source and get it: or, at any rate, not be in a better position than if he had gone to the public source.   He should not get a start over others by using the information which he received in confidence.

I   At any rate, he should not get a start without paying for it.   It may not be a case for injunction but only for damages, depending on the worth of the confidential information to him in saving him time and trouble.

Conclusion.   Applying these principles, I think that the plaintiff should succeed.   On the facts which I have stated, he told the defendant company a a lot about the making of a satisfactory carpet grip which was not in the public domain.   They would not have got going so quickly except for what they had

(1) (1948), [1963] 3 All E.R. at p. 414, letters H, I; 65 R.P.C. at p. 213.
(2) [1960] R.P.C. at p. 130.   (3) [1956] 3 All E.R. at pp. 301, 302, letter E.

learned in their discussions with him. They got to know in particular that it   A
was possible to make an alternative grip in the form of a " V-tang ", provided
the tooth was sharp enough and strong enough, and they were told about the
special shape required. The judge thought that the information was not significant. But I think it was. It was the springboard which enabled them to
go on to devise the " Invisigrip " and to apply for a patent for it. They were
quite innocent of any intention to take advantage of him. They thought that,   B
as long as they did not infringe his patent, they were exempt. In this they were
in error. They were not aware of the law as to confidential information.

I would allow the appeal and give judgment to the plaintiff for damages to
be assessed.

SALMON, L.J., having reviewed the facts, in the course of which he said
that the case turned entirely on what occurred at the interview on Mar. 13, 1962,   C
between the plaintiff and Mr. Preston and Mr. Boon, when the plaintiff attempted
to interest them in the alternative carpet grip with a V-shaped prong, conluded:
To my mind the irresistible inference from the uncontroverted facts is that the
plaintiff disclosed his idea and explained his " Invisigrip " device to Mr. Preston
and Mr. Boon at the meeting of Mar. 13, 1962. The plaintiff, as he amply
demonstrated before us, is a very difficult man to stop talking. He was deter-   D
mined to interest Mr. Preston and Mr. Boon in " Invisigrip " and to show them
why it had advantages over all the other carpet grips with V-shaped prongs
which had previously been tried and found wanting. I hope that I am not
under-rating Mr. Preston's and Mr. Boon's powers when I conclude that they
failed to stop him. I certainly acquit them of any conscious plagiarism. In
May, 1962, when it was obvious that the " Klent " was out of their reach they   E
were admittedly casting about for a carpet grip which would not infringe the
plaintiff's patent. A grip on the " Klent " principle would present obvious
risks. Prior to the meeting of Mar. 13, 1962, they were convinced that there
was no future in any carpet grip with a V-shaped prong. That is why they were
so anxious to secure the " Klent ". At the conclusion of that meeting they
were still uninterested in a V-shaped prong. What caused them to turn to it in   F
May when all chance of securing the " Klent " had vanished? I do not think
that they consciously went through any such process of thought as " That old
man, difficult though he is, has a very inventive turn of mind. I wonder if,
after all he may have been right last March in what he claimed for his V-shaped
domed prong which has not been patented. No one has succeeded in producing
an effective V-shaped prong before, but perhaps his will work. Let us try and   G
remember what he told us about it." Nevertheless the germ of the idea and
the broad principle of the domed V-shaped prong was I am certain implanted
in their minds by the plaintiff at the interview of Mar. 13, 1962, and afterwards
subconsciously reproduced and used, if only as a springboard, to forestall the
plaintiff with " Invisigrip ". This is no reflection on their honesty, but it
infringes the plaintiff's rights. I would accordingly allow the appeal.   H

WINN, L.J., having referred to the application by the defendant company
and Mr. Preston which was filed in the Patent Office, to Mr. Preston's subsequent
evidence that he did not invent the device, and to the evidence concerning
meetings between the plaintiff and Mr. Boon and Mr. Preston and subsequently
between Mr. Boon and Mr. Sudbury, concluded: To my own mind it appears
that the proper conclusion to be drawn from all the material before the court,   I
not by any means primarily from the direct evidence, is that the plaintiff did
explain his " Invisigrip " idea to Mr. Boon and Mr. Preston; that they absorbed
what he told them; and were able to recall enough from their memories to
indicate to Mr. Sudbury (4) and Mr. Turl (4) what they wanted them to produce.

(4) Mr. Sudbury was the new products officer of Dexicon, Ltd., to whom Mr. Boon
applied to make a prototype of the defendant company's grip, the Invisigrip. The
grip was ultimately manufactured for the defendant company by another company,
British Tools and Pressings, Ltd., and Mr. Turl was the representative of that company.

A In doing so they did not, I think, realise that they were infringing a duty of confidence: I think that they did infringe it. In so holding I do not imply any condemnation of Mr. Boon or Mr. Preston as dishonest men. Mr. Preston made a most revealing statement in evidence in the court below where he said ". . . action for breach of confidence. I did not know such a thing existed . . . the only problem was that we might infringe his patent ". In my view the appeal

B succeeds.

LORD DENNING, M.R.: The court grants neither an account of profits, nor an injunction, but only damages to be assessed by the master. Damages should be assessed on the basis of reasonable compensation for the use of the confidential information which was given to the defendant company.

Appeal allowed.

C
Solicitors: *Courts & Co.* (for the defendant company).

[*Reported by* F. GUTTMAN, ESQ., *Barrister-at-Law.*]

D
R. v. AREA COMMITTEE No. 1 (LONDON) LEGAL AID AREA, Ex parte RONDEL.

[QUEEN'S BENCH DIVISION (Lord Parker, C.J., Diplock, L.J., and Ashworth, J.), March 6, 1967.]

Legal Aid—Certificate—Grant—Matters to be taken into consideration by legal aid committee in determining whether to grant or refuse certificate—View

E *taken by committee on merits conclusive in absence of fresh evidence— " Proceedings "—Appeal to House of Lords—Certiorari and mandamus against refusal of certificate not granted—Legal Aid (General) Regulations, 1962 (S.I. 1962 No. 148), reg. 7 (f).*

In considering whether to grant a civil aid certificate for any particular proceeding, the legal aid committee are entitled to take into consideration

F the nature and merits of the action as a whole, and whether or not there are reasonable grounds for pursuing that action (see p. 422, letter H, and p. 423, letter D, post).

Under reg. 7 (f)* of the Legal Aid (General) Regulations, 1962, the view which the legal aid committee take in their absolute discretion on the merits of the action is conclusive in the absence of fresh evidence (see p. 423,

G letters A and D, post).

Per CURIAM: where proceedings are referred to in the Legal Aid and Advice Act, 1949, and in the Legal Aid (General) Regulations, 1962, those proceedings are not confined to actions but involve all proceedings of an interlocutory nature (see p. 422, letter B, and p. 423, letter D, post).

H [As to the grounds for refusing a civil aid certificate, see 30 HALSBURY'S LAWS (3rd Edn.) 518, para. 976.

For the Legal Aid and Advice Act, 1949, s. 1, s. 12 and Sch. 1, see 18 HALSBURY'S STATUTES (2nd Edn.) 533, 548, 563.

For the Legal Aid (General) Regulations, 1962, reg. 7, see 5 HALSBURY'S STATUTORY INSTRUMENTS (First Re-issue) 227.]

I Case referred to:
Mills v. *Mills*, [1963] 2 All E.R. 237; [1963] P. 329; [1963] 2 W.L.R. 831; 3rd Digest Supp.

Application for certiorari and mandamus.

This was an application by Norbert Fred Rondel for an order of certiorari to bring up and quash a decision of the respondents, the Area Committee No. 1 (London) Legal Aid Area, dated Jan. 25, 1967, and for an order of mandamus

---

* Regulation 7, so far as material, is set out at p. 421, letters F to H, post.

Dictum of LORD BARKER CJ at 422 considered in MEGARITY v D J RYAN & SONS (No 2) [1980] 3 All ER 602

directed to the respondents to decide the grant of legal aid according to law. The facts are set out in the judgment of LORD PARKER, C.J.

Mark Littman, Q.C., and *L. J. Blom-Cooper* for the applicant.
Sir Peter Rawlinson, Q.C., and *John K. Wood* for the respondents.
R. J. A. Batt for the defendant in the action.

LORD PARKER, C.J.: This case has attracted a considerable amount of publicity in its various stages, and it is unnecessary to state the facts in detail. The proceedings commenced as the result of the applicant being found guilty at the Central Criminal Court in May, 1959, on a count of causing grievous bodily harm with intent. On that occasion he was defended by counsel on a dock brief. Almost six years later, in February, 1965, the applicant issued a writ claiming damages for professional negligence in connexion with the defence and delivered a statement of claim which was clearly his own draft. In May, 1965, the defendant applied to strike out that statement of claim and also to have the action dismissed on the ground that no cause of action was disclosed. The master before whom the matter came ordered the action to be dismissed. That was upheld by LAWTON, J., (1) in December, 1965, and by the Court of Appeal (2) on Oct. 20, 1966. On Dec. 1, 1966, the applicant applied to the appeal committee of the House of Lords for leave to appeal against that order of the Court of Appeal, and leave was granted. Accordingly, on Dec. 8, 1966, the applicant applied for a legal aid certificate:

" To enable me to instruct solicitor and counsel (Q.C. and junior) to appear on my behalf on an appeal to the House of Lords from the decision of the Court of Appeal dated Oct. 20, 1966, dismissing my appeal from the decision of LAWTON, J., dated Dec. 21, 1965, striking out my statement of claim. Leave to appeal to the House of Lords was given by the appeal committee of the House of Lords on Dec. 1, 1966."

That application further revealed that, at an earlier stage, namely, in January, 1966, the applicant had applied for a legal aid certificate to prosecute the action generally, and also for an emergency certificate in connexion with his appeal to the Court of Appeal. That application had been refused. Let me say at once that the matter was dealt with, as it is conceded, with great care by the legal aid committee, who received written grounds urging the grant of legal aid, and went so far, which is unusual, as to allow the applicant's solicitor to come before them and urge the grant of legal aid. On Jan. 25, 1967, however, the committee issued their decision in this form:

" Your application for legal aid has been considered and I have to inform you that the area committee have decided to refuse it for the reasons set out in para. F below. There is no right of appeal against this decision."

Paragraph F was in these terms:

" It appears unreasonable that you should receive legal aid in the particular circumstances of the case."

It is the applicant's submission before this court that that reason disclosed in para. F is bad in point of law. Accordingly, the application is made for certiorari to quash that decision as disclosing an error on the face of the record.

It is necessary to refer to one or two provisions of the Legal Aid and Advice Act, 1949, and of the Legal Aid (General) Regulations, 1962 (3). The Legal Aid and Advice Act, 1949, provides in Part 1 for new arrangements for legal aid and legal advice. Section 1 provides that:

" (1) This and the three next following sections provide for, and (save as hereinafter mentioned) relate only to, legal aid in connexion with proceedings before courts and tribunals in England and Wales, not being proceedings in

---

(1) [1966] 1 All E.R. 467.   (2) [1966] 3 All E.R. 657.
(3) S.I. 1962 No. 148.

A   which free legal aid may be given under the enactments amended by Part 2 of this Act.

    " (2) Unless and until regulations otherwise provide, the proceedings in connexion with which legal aid may be given are any proceedings of a description mentioned in Pt. 1 of Sch. 1 to this Act, except proceedings mentioned in Pt. 2 of that Schedule."

B   Reference to Sch. 1 need only be made in order to draw attention to the fact that, apart from setting out " Proceedings in any of the following courts ", naming a number of courts, it proceeds in Part 1, para. 2, to state:

    " Proceedings before any person to whom a case is referred in whole or in part by any of the said courts."

C   In connexion with excepted proceedings it sets out certain proceedings such as defamation and the like which are excepted, and also includes in Part 2, para. 6, as excepted " Proceedings incidental to any proceedings mentioned in this Part of this Schedule ".

  To return to s. 1, sub-s. (6) provides that:

    " A person shall not be given legal aid in connexion with any proceedings
D   unless he shows that he has reasonable grounds for taking, defending or being a party thereto, and may also be refused legal aid if it appears unreasonable that he should receive it in the particular circumstances of the case."

  Section 12 is the regulation making power, and by sub-s. (1):

    " The Lord Chancellor may make such regulations as appear to him neces-
E   sary or desirable for giving effect to this Part of this Act or for preventing abuses thereof."

  The regulations, which are the Legal Aid (General) Regulations, 1962, were made by the Lord Chancellor in exercise of his powers, including those under s. 12, and by reg. 7 dealt with the refusal of certificates:

F   " If an appropriate committee refuse an application for a certificate, they shall notify the applicant, stating that the application has been refused on one or more of the following grounds. . ."

  The only relevant grounds here are found in para. (*e*) and para. (*f*), but it should, perhaps, be mentioned that para. (*a*), para. (*b*), para. (*c*) and para. (*d*) deal with matters such as where the disposable income exceeds the permitted amount and
G   matters of contribution, and whether they are in fact proceedings in which legal aid can be granted. Paragraph (*e*) and para. (*f*), however, are in these terms:

    " (*e*) that the applicant has not shown that he has reasonable grounds for taking steps to assert or dispute the claim, or for taking, defending or being a party to the proceedings; or (*f*) that it appears unreasonable that he should receive legal aid in the particular circumstances of the case (whether
H   as a result of any discretion given to an appropriate committee under any provision of these Regulations or otherwise)."

  Pausing there, it is to be seen that both para. (*e*) and para. (*f*) of reg. 7 are carrying out faithfully the provisions of s. 1 (6) of the Act of 1949. Under the first limb of sub-s. (6), and now to be found in para. (*e*), an onus is put on an applicant
I   to show that he has reasonable grounds for taking the proceedings. Paragraph (*f*), on the other hand, is providing that legal aid may also be refused if it appears unreasonable, and in regard to that no onus is cast on the applicant. Further, before leaving the regulations, it is to be observed that, in certain of those regulations—and our attention has been drawn to reg. 5 (7)—reference is made to cases where the committee have a discretion to refuse, the discretion which is clearly referred to in reg. 7 (*f*). By reg. 5 (7), it is provided, inter alia, that:

    ". . . an application for a certificate shall not be approved where it appears
to the appropriate committee that only a trivial advantage would be gained

by the applicant in asserting or disputing the claim, or from the proceedings,   **A**
to which the application relates, or that, on account of the simple nature of
the claim or proceedings, a solicitor would not ordinarily be employed."

It is to be observed, however, that reg. 7 (*f*) does not refer alone to those
matters of discretion which are specifically provided in the regulations, but also
that the application may be refused if it appears unreasonable " otherwise ".

Counsel for the applicant, in his able argument before this court, begins by   **B**
submitting, and for my part I think that he is undoubtedly right, that, where
proceedings are referred to in the Act and in the regulations, those proceedings
are not confined to actions but involve all proceedings of an interlocutory nature.
I find it unnecessary to refer to all the matters to support that view.   I have
already referred to passages in Sch. 1 to the Act of 1949 from which it is to be
observed, though it cannot be an aid to construction, that the regulations them-   **C**
selves, and in particular reg. 6, are treated on the basis that proceedings here
include interlocutory proceedings.   Indeed, the matter has been determined in a
slightly different connexion by the Court of Appeal in *Mills* v. *Mills* (4).   Accordingly, counsel for the applicant asks the court to infer that, since the committee
did not refuse the application on ground (*e*), viz.,
                                                                                       D
> " that the applicant has not shown that he has reasonable grounds for
> taking steps to assert or dispute the claim, or for taking, defending or being
> a party to proceedings; . . ."

it must be assumed and inferred that the committee were satisfied by the applicant
that he did have reasonable grounds for pursuing this matter to the House of
Lords.   For my part, I think that that is really an inevitable inference to be   **E**
drawn in the circumstances, particularly when it is remembered that the House
of Lords must have felt that there really was something to look into here, and
gave leave to appeal.

The next limb, and the vital limb, in the argument of counsel for the applicant
is that, that being so, when one considers the alternative, which is ground (*f*),
one is only considering whether it is reasonable in the particular circumstances   **F**
of the case in relation to the proceeding, and he would say here, merely the
proceeding by way of appeal to the House of Lords.   Indeed, he goes further and
says that the consideration whether the applicant may succeed on the merits,
that is to say in his action as opposed to this proceeding, is wholly irrelevant to
the grant of legal aid for the purpose of this proceeding.   It really involves this,
that a plaintiff may be refused legal aid because it is thought that he has no   **G**
reasonable grounds for pursuing his claim, and yet the moment the defendant
takes action either by way of applying to have the action dismissed as disclosing
no cause of action, or maybe by applying for the determination of a preliminary
point in lieu of demurrer, then immediately the merits in the action as a whole
become quite irrelevant and the sole question is whether there is a reasonable
ground for defending a claim in the interlocutory proceeding in question.   For   **H**
my part, I find that I am quite unable to accept that argument.   It seems to me
that it is for the committee to consider the whole of the circumstances, and, in
considering whether to grant legal aid for any particular proceeding, to take
into consideration the nature of the action as a whole, and whether or not there
are reasonable grounds for pursuing that action.   If one looks at it from the
point of view of the use of public money or from the point of view of the unfor-   **I**
tunate defendant who is at risk in relation to costs when proceeded against
under legal aid, it would be quite wrong if the committee were not entitled
to take into consideration what I may call the merits of the action itself.

Finally, counsel for the applicant says that, even if the merits of the action
are not wholly irrelevant to the grant of legal aid for the specific proceeding, yet
at any rate the absence of merits is not conclusive.   He would desire this court

(4) [1963] 2 All E.R. 237; [1963] P. 329.

A to say something which would support, I imagine, a further application to the legal aid committee. For my part, I think that it follows from what I have already said that the view which the committee in their absolute discretion took on what I may call the merits of the action must be conclusive in the absence of fresh evidence. I see no half-way house. If it is relevant, as it certainly is relevant in my view, it must, I think, also be conclusive in the absence of fresh

B evidence. If the committee have decided that the action does not warrant legal aid on the merits, then I do not see how any action taken by the defendant thereafter which results in the plaintiff defending interlocutory proceedings can in any way alter their view that the action does not warrant legal aid. For those reasons, I think that this application fails and should be dismissed.

I would only add that it must be of very great satisfaction to everybody to

C know that, as counsel for the applicant has said, a number of eminent Queen's Counsel will be available from whom the applicant can choose, who will be prepared to conduct his case in the House of Lords, and also that the defendant in the action has made it possible for this to be done without strict compliance with the House of Lords rules.

D **DIPLOCK, L.J.:** I agree.

ASHWORTH, J.: I agree.

Application dismissed.

Solicitors: *Michael Zander* (for the applicant); *A. M. V. Panton* (for the respondents); *Forsyte, Kerman & Philips* (for the defendant in the action).

E [*Reported by* S. A. HATTEEA, ESQ., *Barrister-at-Law.*]

DAVEY AND OTHERS *v.* LEE.

F [QUEEN'S BENCH DIVISION (Lord Parker, C.J., Diplock, L.J., and Ashworth, J.), March 2, 1967.]

Criminal Law—Attempt—Definition of what amounts to an attempt.

An actus reus necessary to constitute an attempt to commit a crime is complete if the prisoner does an act which is a step towards the commission of the specific crime, which is immediately and not merely remotely con-

G nected with the commission of it, and the doing of which cannot reasonably be regarded as having any other purpose than the commission of the specific crime (see p. 425, letters F and H, post).

[As to what constitutes an attempt to commit a crime, see 10 HALSBURY'S LAWS (3rd Edn.) 307, 308, para. 567 text and notes (*h*)-(*j*); and for cases on the

H subject, see 14 DIGEST (Repl.) 112-117, *776-810.*]

Case Stated.

This was a Case Stated by the justices for the quarter sessions of the peace for the county of Devon on an appeal from the magistrates acting in and for the petty sessional division of Woodbury, on Apr. 15 and 18, 1966. On Feb. 11, 1966, the respondent, Ronald Archibald Lee, charged the appellants Michael John

I Davey, Michael John Rigler and Robert Rigler, that, at Sowton on Feb. 10, 1966, they jointly attempted to steal a quantity of metal, the property of the South Western Electricity Board, against the peace of our Sovereign Lady the Queen her Crown and Dignity. On Mar. 2, 1966, the magistrates in and for the petty sessional division of Woodbury in the county of Devon sitting at Exmouth on hearing the information convicted the appellants. On Mar. 9, 1966, the appellants entered notices of appeal against their convictions to the quarter sessions of the peace for the county of Devon. The following facts were found: At about 6.30 p.m. on Feb. 10, 1966, Motor Patrol Constable Jane went to the east side

Dictum of LORD PARKER CJ at 425 applied in R v MOHAN [1975] 2 All E.R 193

of the South Western Electricity Board's compound at Sowton. When the officer   A
was about one hundred yards from the compound he heard, coming from the
vicinity of the perimeter of the compound, a snipping sound and when he was
about seventy-five yards from the compound he heard a scrambling sound. The
officer saw two men by the edge of the perimeter fence of the compound. He
shone his torch and was able to identify one of the two men as being the appellant
Michael John Rigler; the officer was unable to identify the second man. At   B
about 6.50 p.m. on the same day, Wilfred Seldon saw a motor van, registered
number 21 NYA, parked without lights on a piece of private ground about half a
mile from the compound. Shortly afterwards he saw the van driven off and it
travelled thirty or forty yards before its lights were switched on. He saw two
men, of whom one was driving the van and the other was running alongside the
van at the passenger's door. At about 9.55 p.m. on the same day, the same motor   C
van was stopped by Motor Patrol Constable Manley at Barnstaple Cross which
was approximately fourteen miles from the place at which Mr. Seldon had seen
the van. The appellants were in the motor van, which was being driven by the
appellant Robert Rigler. In the pockets of the driver's door was found a pair of
wire cutters. When the wire cutters were found, the appellant Robert Rigler said
" They are wire cutters, we've been pigeon-shooting ". When asked to go to   D
Crediton police station, the appellant Robert Rigler said, " Yes, it's better to get
it cleared up now ". The motor van moved off and, after it had travelled eight to
ten yards, something was thrown from the van. On the following day, police
officers found a pair of bolt croppers in a hedge near Barnstaple Cross at about
the place at which something had been thrown from the van on the previous
night. On Feb. 11, 1966, at Exmouth police station, all the appellants gave as an   E
explanation that they had been pigeon shooting on the evening of Feb. 10, 1966.
An album of photographs was proved in evidence. The eastern end of the South
Western Electricity Board compound at Sowton was the copper store; at that
point the compound was enclosed by an outer single strand wire fence and a number of cypress trees, a fence consisting of six strands of heavy barbed wire, a
fence consisting of four strands of insulated wire and finally a chain link fence.   F
On Feb. 11, 1966, when Detective Constable Medland inspected the fences, the
outer single-strand wire fence had been cut, the barbed wire and insulated wire
fences had been cut, and the chain link fence had been cut to within a height of two
feet from its top. It was proved by forensic evidence which the justices accepted
that all four types of wire could have been cut by the bolt croppers and that only
the insulated wire could have been cut by the wire cutters. The compound con-   G
tained drums of copper, other stores, an office building and dwelling-houses.
The appellants did not give evidence. The justices were satisfied by the evidence
that the appellants intended to break and enter the compound and to steal therein
in the vicinity of the place where the fences had been attacked such copper as
was removable, with or without the use of bolt croppers, but that they were
interrupted by Motor Patrol Constable Jane when they had very nearly completed   H
the last of the steps necessary to break into the compound for the purpose of
carrying out their intention.

It was contended before quarter sessions by the appellants that there was
insufficient evidence to justify convictions on the information for the following
reasons: that the act of cutting through the fences was insufficiently proximate to
the offence of stealing metal to constitute an attempt; and that, as the compound   I
contained other stores, an office building and dwelling-houses as well as the copper
store, the act of cutting through the fences, even if it was rightly found to be an
attempt to commit some other offence, could not be held beyond reasonable doubt
to be an attempt to commit the offence charged as opposed to an attempt to
commit some other offence. It was contended before quarter sessions by the
respondent that the appellants were rightly convicted, as the act of cutting through
the fences being one on which it was open to the justices to find that they had been
interrupted could amount to an attempt and that, as the fences cut were near

A the copper store, it was open to the justices to find that the appellants had attempted to steal metal.

Quarter sessions dismissed the appeals, and the appellants now appealed.

The cases noted below* were cited during the argument.

A. Whitfield for the appellants.

S. B. Thomas for the respondent.

B LORD PARKER, C.J., having stated the nature of the appeal and the facts, continued: The point was taken before the justices, as it has been taken here, that what had occurred was nothing more than acts preparatory to the commission of an offence, and did not amount to an attempt; alternatively, it was said that it had not been proved that, if there was an attempt, it was an attempt to steal a quantity of metal; it might have been something else. To take the C last point first, it seems to me abundantly clear when one looks at these photographs that, granted an intention to break in and steal, it was clearly an intention to steal metal.

The real point taken by counsel for the appellants is that an intention to steal is not sufficient to constitute an attempt, but that there must be acts which have moved further than being merely preparatory acts. What amounts to an attempt D has been described variously in the authorities, and, for my part, I prefer to adopt the definition given in STEPHEN'S DIGEST OF CRIMINAL LAW (5th Edn., 1894), art. 50, where it says that:

"An attempt to commit a crime is an act done with intent to commit that crime, and forming part of a series of acts which would constitute its E actual commission if it were not interrupted."

As a general statement that seems to me to be right, though it does not help to define the point of time at which the series of acts begins. That, as STEPHEN said, depends on the facts of each case. A helpful definition is given in para. 4104 in ARCHBOLD'S PLEADING, EVIDENCE AND PRACTICE (36th Edn.), where it is stated in this form:

F "It is submitted that the actus reus necessary to constitute an attempt is complete if the prisoner does an act which is a step towards the commission of the specific crime, which is immediately and not merely remotely connected with the commission of it, and the doing of which cannot reasonably be regarded as having any other purpose than the commission of the specific crime."

G It seems to me that the facts of this case fully come within that test, and that the magistrates were undoubtedly right in the view they formed. I would dismiss this appeal.

DIPLOCK, L.J.: I agree. There are some branches of the criminal law in which it is permitted for justices and juries to use their common sense. I am H glad to find that I am not constrained by the authorities to say that the law of attempt is excluded from those branches. I accept the definition which LORD PARKER, C.J., has taken from the current edition of ARCHBOLD'S CRIMINAL PLEADING, EVIDENCE AND PRACTICE as a correct definition of the test to be applied, and the facts of this case fall amply within that definition.

ASHWORTH, J.: I agree.

I   *Appeal dismissed.*

Solicitors: *Vandercom, Stanton & Co.*, agents for *Toller, Oerton & Balsdon*, Barnstaple (for the appellants); *Sharpe, Pritchard & Co.*, agents for *County Prosecution Solicitor, Devon County Council* (for the respondent).

[*Reported by* N. P. METCALFE, ESQ., *Barrister-at-Law.*]

---

* *R. v. Eagleton*, [1843-60] All E.R. Rep. 363; *R. v. Roberts*, (1855), Dears. 539; *R. v. White*, [1908-10] All E.R. Rep. 340; [1910] 2 K.B. 124; *R. v. Robinson*, [1915] 2 K.B. 342.

A

COLLETT (otherwise SAKAZOVA) *v.* COLLETT.

[PROBATE, DIVORCE AND ADMIRALTY DIVISION (Ormrod, J.), June 24, 1966, January 23, April 4, 1967.]

Marriage—Foreign marriage—Validity—Essential requirements of valid marriage distinguished from procedural requirements—Foreign Marriage Act, 1892 (55 & 56 Vict. c. 23), s. 8.

B

Marriage—Validity—Declaration—British subject domiciled in England— Procedure to obtain declaration—Matrimonial Causes Act 1965 (c. 45), s. 39 —Matrimonial Causes Rules, 1957 (S.I. 1957 No. 619), r. 74.

In 1948, the husband, a British subject by birth, and the wife, who was Bulgarian by origin, were married at the British consulate in Prague in the presence of the British ambassador. The parties had since lived in England. The marriage was invalid by the lex loci contractus. No notice of the intended marriage was given in accordance with s. 2 of the Foreign Marriage Act, 1892, the notice was not filed nor entered by the marriage officer in accordance with s. 3, the consent of the wife's parents was not obtained or dispensed with as required by s. 4, no oath was taken as required by s. 7, and the marriage was not registered under s. 9.

C

D

On a petition by the wife for a decree of nullity for want of form, or, alternatively, for a declaration (under, so the court intimated*, R.S.C., Ord. 15, r. 16) that the marriage was a valid marriage, the trial judge found that the actual ceremony of marriage was properly performed and was in all essentials a marriage.

Held: (i) the prayer for the decree of nullity would be rejected because—

E

(a) if a ceremony of marriage had actually taken place which, as a ceremony, would be sufficient to constitute a valid marriage, the courts would hold the marriage valid unless constrained by express statutory enactment to hold otherwise (see p. 431, letter D, post), and

(b) s. 8† of the Foreign Marriage Act, 1892, was the crucial section, for it dealt with solemnisation and the necessary requirements of a valid marriage under the Act, whereas s. 2, s. 3, s. 4, s. 7 and s. 9 were essentially administrative or procedural and were directory rather than mandatory in nature, and, as there had been compliance with the essential requirements of s. 8, the marriage was valid (see p. 430, letter E, and p. 431, letter E, post).

F

(ii) a petitioner who was a British subject domiciled in England and who sought a declaration of validity of his or her marriage must proceed under s. 39‡ of the Matrimonial Causes Act 1965 and r. 74 of the Matrimonial Causes Rules, 1957; accordingly the wife was not entitled (under R.S.C., Ord. 15, r. 16) to a declaration that the marriage was a valid marriage (see p. 432, letter F, post).

G

Dicta of ORMROD, J., in *Kassim (otherwise Widmann)* v. *Kassim (otherwise Hassim) (Carl and Dickson cited)* ([1962] 3 All E.R. at pp. 432, 433) followed.

Garthwaite v. *Garthwaite* ([1964] 2 All E.R. 233) distinguished.

H

[As to solemnisation of marriages under the Foreign Marriage Acts, see 7 HALSBURY'S LAWS (3rd Edn.) 97, 98, para. 175; and for cases on the subject, see 11 DIGEST (Repl.) 465, *991, 992.*

As to petitions for declarations of validity of marriage, see 19 HALSBURY'S LAWS (3rd Edn.) 816, para. 1333.

I

For the Foreign Marriage Act, 1892, s. 8, see 11 HALSBURY'S STATUTES (2nd Edn.) 749.

For the Matrimonial Causes Act 1965, s. 39, see 45 HALSBURY'S STATUTES (2nd Edn.) 497.

---

* See p. 431, letter F, post.

† Section 8, so far as material, is set out at p. 429, letter A, post.

‡ The relevant terms of s. 39 are set out at p. 431, letter H, post.

A　For the Matrimonial Causes Rules, 1957, s. 74, see 10 Halsbury's Statutory
Instruments (2nd Re-issue) 275.]

Cases referred to:

Garthwaite v. *Garthwaite*, [1964] 2 All E.R. 233; [1964] P. 356; [1964] 2
　W.L.R. 1108; 3rd Digest Supp.

Greaves v. *Greaves*, (1872), L.R. 2 P. & D. 423; 41 L.J.P. & M. 66; 26 L.T.
B　745; 27 Digest (Repl.) 56, *345.*

Holmes v. *Simmons (falsely called Holmes)*, (1868), L.R. 1 P. & D. 523; 37
　L.J.P. & M. 58; 18 L.T. 770; 27 Digest (Repl.) 58, *361.*

Kassim (otherwise Widmann) v. *Kassim (otherwise Hassim)* *(Carl and Dickson
　cited)*, [1962] 3 All E.R. 426; [1962] P. 224; [1962] 3 W.L.R. 865;
　Digest (Cont. Vol. A) 233, *922a.*

C　*Plummer* v. *Plummer*, [1916-17] All E.R. Rep. 591; [1917] P. 163; 86 L.J.P.
　145; 117 L.T. 321; 27 Digest (Repl.) 57, *355.*

Taczanowska (otherwise Roth) v. *Taczanowski (Krystek cited)*, [1957] 2 All E.R.
　563; [1957 P. 301; [1957] 3 W.L.R. 141; Digest (Cont. Vol. A)
　237, *966c.*

Wright v. *Elwood*, (1837), 1 Curt. 662; 163 E.R. 231; *previous proceedings*
D　(1835), 1 Curt. 49; 27 Digest (Repl.) 49, *260.*

Petition.

This was a petition by the wife for a decree of nullity of her marriage to the
husband for want of form or, in the alternative, for a declaration that her marriage
was a valid marriage. The husband did not defend the suit. The facts are set out
E　in the judgment.

　A. L. Mildon for the wife.

　A. B. Ewbank for the Queen's Proctor.

Cur. adv. vult.

　Apr. 4. **ORMROD, J.,** read the following judgment: This is a petition by
F　Mrs. Mariana Ivanova Collett for a decree of nullity of her marriage to Mr. Alec
Leonard Collett for want of form or, in the alternative, for a declaration that her
marriage to the husband was a valid marriage. The husband entered an appearance indicating that he did not propose to defend the suit which, accordingly,
originally came before me as an undefended case. In view of the difficult questions
of law which were plainly going to arise, I adjourned the matter in order that I
G　might ask for the assistance of the Queen's Proctor. This has now been given to
me and, as always, I am very much indebted to him and to counsel who appeared
as amicus curiae on the Queen's Proctor's instructions, for his careful argument.

　The ceremony of marriage took place on Apr. 1, 1948, at the British consulate
in Prague, in the presence of the British Ambassador and the vice consul, Mr.
McLaughlin, and other persons. It was conducted by a minister of the Church of
H　Scotland, the Reverend Robert Smith, and followed the form in use in the Church
of Scotland. Mr. Smith gave evidence before me and told me that, in 1948, he was
the recognised chaplain to the British Embassy in Prague and had an English
congregation in the city. The validity of the marriage is attacked on two grounds.
It is submitted, first, that it was invalid by the lex loci contractus, that is, by the
law of Czecho-Slovakia in force on Apr. 1, 1948, and secondly, that it was not in
I　accordance with the provisions of the Foreign Marriage Act, 1892. Accordingly,
the wife claims that her marriage was void ab initio. It was conceded by the
Queen's Proctor that the marriage was not in accordance with the formalities
required by Czech law and cannot be supported by reference to the lex loci. This
was established by the evidence of Dr. Drucker, a former member of the Czech
bar. It was also agreed by counsel on both sides that this marriage could not be
supported on the basis of the Court of Appeal's decision in *Taczanowska (otherwise
Roth)* v. *Taczanowski (Krystek cited)* (1) for various reasons, of which it is necessary

_____

(1) [1957] 2 All E.R. 563; [1957] P. 301 at p. 314.

to mention only two.   In the present case, the circumstances of the parties **A**
at the time of the marriage were not such as to justify this court in departing
from the lex loci test of validity.   Moreover, the exchange of consents took place
before a minister who was not episcopally ordained.   The validity or invalidity
of this marriage, therefore, depends on the Foreign Marriage Act, 1892.

It is, accordingly, necessary to examine the facts which bear on this question.
The parties first met in Prague in 1947.   At that time the husband, who was and is **B**
a British subject by birth, was working in Prague as a free-lance journalist.   He
was twenty-five years of age and a bachelor.   The wife, who is Bulgarian by
origin, was studying at the University of Prague and acting as a correspondent
for a Bulgarian newspaper.   She was then a spinster aged nineteen.   Her home was
in Bulgaria where her father held an important post in the Government.   In the
autumn of 1947, the husband asked her to marry him, and early in 1948 she agreed **C**
to marry him.   No formal engagement took place and no plans for a wedding had
been made.   Soon after they became engaged, the communist forces took over
the government of Czecho-Slovakia and the husband was told to leave the country.
They arranged that the wife, then Miss Sakazova, should also go to London.   As
she was about to board the aeroplane at Prague, she was called to an office at the
airport and taken for interrogation to the Ministry of the Interior.   After several **D**
hours she was allowed to leave on her promise to return early next morning.   She
was met by the husband and taken to the house of some friends.   Early next
morning she was taken by the husband to the British consulate in Prague, where
hurried arrangements had been made for them to be married by the Reverend
Robert Smith, in the presence of the British Ambassador and the vice consul, Mr.
McLaughlin (who also gave evidence before me).   After a week or two they came **E**
to England where they lived together for some seventeen years as husband and
wife.   They have a girl, now aged sixteen years, and a boy now aged nearly nine
years.   Had not marital difficulties arisen, the nature of which is, of course,
irrelevant at this stage, neither party would have suggested that theirs was
anything but a valid marriage.

It is, however, submitted on behalf of the wife that this marriage is invalid for **F**
non-compliance with a number of the requirements of the Foreign Marriage Act,
1892.   These are set out in detail in the petition.   Briefly, it is said that no notice
of the intended marriage was given in accordance with s. 2;   the notice was not
filed or entered by the marriage officer in accordance with s. 3;   the consent of
the wife's parents was not obtained or dispensed with as required by s. 4;   no oath
was taken as required by s. 7;   and the marriage was not registered under s. 9. **G**
An informal certificate was provided by the Reverend Robert Smith and signed
by all those present including the parties and the ambassador.   There was extreme
urgency in view of the obvious threat to the wife, and the embassy at Prague at
that time was without the necessary forms and register because, I understand, no
marriage officer at the embassy had been appointed by a marriage warrant, and
no administrative arrangements for marriages under the Act of 1892 had been **H**
made.   Counsel for the Queen's Proctor concedes each of these examples of non-
compliance with the provisions of the statute, but contends that these are not
mandatory in nature and do not go to the question of validity.   He submits, on
the contrary, that s. 8 is the vital section, and that all the requirements of that
section were complied with in this case.   Counsel for the wife concedes that all
save one of these requirements were met, but contends that the ceremony did not **I**
take place between the hours of 8.0 a.m. and 6.0 p.m.   I am not satisfied on the
evidence that the ceremony, in fact, took place before 8.0 a.m.   It is common
ground that it took place in the morning at about 8.0 a.m., and I find on the
evidence that it took place between 8.0 a.m. and 6.0 p.m.

Section 8 (2), as amended (2), is in these terms:

---

(2) By the Marriage (Extension of Hours) Act, 1934, s. 1 (2).

A   " Every such marriage shall be solemnized at the official house of the
marriage officer, with open doors, between the hours of eight in the fore-
noon and six in the afternoon in the presence of two or more witnesses, and
may be solemnized by another person in the presence of the marriage officer,
according to the Church of England, or such other form and ceremony as the
parties thereto see fit to adopt, or may, where the parties so desire, be
B   solemnized by the marriage officer."

" Marriage officer ", is defined in s. 11 (1) as any officer authorised by a Secretary
of State under a marriage warrant or any officer authorised by regulations made
under s. 21. Apparently, in 1948 there was no officer in Prague authorised under
a marriage warrant, but by the Foreign Marriages Order in Council, 1913, (3),
art. 4, the ambassador is a marriage officer and does not need a marriage warrant
C   (this provision has been revoked by the Foreign Marriage Order 1964, (4)). The
" official house of a marriage officer " is defined (5) in s. 24 and in the order in
council to which I have referred. Article 3 provides (6) that the house in which the
ambassador resides or which is occupied by him for the purpose of his embassy
shall be deemed to be the official house of the ambassador. The consulate is,
therefore, clearly within this definition. The ceremony, therefore, took place in
D   the presence of the marriage officer at the official house of the marriage officer.
There is no evidence that the doors were not open. I am satisfied that the parties
exchanged the declarations set out in s. 8 (3). The actual rite itself is in no way
challenged. I am satisfied, therefore, that the actual ceremony of marriage was
properly performed and was in all essentials a marriage.

The question remains, however, whether the non-compliance with the
E   procedural requirements, detailed previously, renders this marriage invalid.
This matter can be approached in two ways, narrowly from the construction of
the Act of 1892 itself; and on a much broader front from a consideration of the
effects of non-compliance with procedural requirements on marriage, in English
law generally. Looking at the Act of 1892 itself, s. 1 provides that:

F   " All marriages between parties of whom one at least is a British subject
solemnized in the manner in this Act provided in any foreign country or place
by or before a marriage officer within the meaning of this Act shall be as valid
in law as if the same had been solemnized in the United Kingdom with a
due observance of all forms required by law."

I emphasise the word " solemnized ". The only section of the Act of 1892 which
G   deals with solemnization is s. 8 and, if I am right in my construction of that
section and on the facts, this marriage was " solemnized in the manner in this
Act provided ". It would be difficult to hold that a failure to comply with s. 2
in regard to notice could be fatal to the validity of the marriage since, under
art. 15 of the Order in Council of 1913, the Secretary of State can waive or modify
the requirements as to notice (7). A failure under s. 3 (which refers to filing and
H   posting of notices of intended marriages) is nothing to do with the parties and
could not reasonably be held to go to validity. If s. 4, which relates to parental
consents, goes to validity, it would be contrary to the fundamental rule of
marriages in England that absence of parental consent does not affect validity
once the ceremony has taken place. It would, in my judgment, require express
statutory provision if absence of parental consent were to affect the validity of
I   marriages under the Act of 1892. The absence of the preliminary oaths required
by s. 7 must be essentially a procedural or administrative requirement since one
of them is repeated as a declaration at the ceremony, and the other goes only to

(3) S.R. & O. 1913 No. 1270, as amended.
(4) The order of 1964, S.I. 1964 No. 926, HALSBURY'S STATUTORY INSTRUMENTS (Second
Re-Issue) 204, revoked and replaced the order of 1913 as amended. As to marriage officers,
see now arts. 19 and 20 of the order of 1964.
(5) ". . . the office at which the business of such office is transacted . . ."
(6) See now art. 3 of the order of 1964.
(7) See now art. 13 of the order of 1964.

parental consent. Lack of subsequent registration can only go to proof of the **A**
marriage, and this marriage was most amply proved before me. Finally, s. 13
seems to make it clear that the failure in at least some of the procedural requirements (as opposed to the formal requirements of solemnization) cannot go to
validity. Section 13, as amended (8), provides:

" (1) After a marriage has been solemnized under this Act it shall not be **B**
necessary, in support of the marriage, to give any proof of the residence for
the time required by or in pursuance of this Act of either of the parties
previous to the marriage, or of the consent of any person whose consent
thereto is required by law, nor shall any evidence to prove the contrary be
given in any legal proceedings touching the validity of the marriage.

" (2) Where a marriage purports to have been solemnized and *registered*
under this Act in the official house of a British ambassador or consul, . . . it **C**
shall not be necessary in support of the marriage, to give any proof of the
authority of the marriage officer by or before whom the marriage was
solemnized and registered, nor shall any evidence to prove his want of
authority, whether by reason of his not being a duly authorised marriage
officer or of any prohibitions or restrictions under the marriage regulations
or otherwise, be given in any legal proceedings touching the validity of the **D**
marriage."

It will be observed that, under sub-s. (1), solemnization alone precludes subsequent inquiry as to residence, or as to want of parental consent, whereas under
sub-s. (2), solemnization and registration precludes all inquiry as to procedural
matters and as to the authority of the marriage officer.

In my judgment, on the true construction of the Act of 1892 and the marriage **E**
regulations, s. 8 is the crucial section which deals with solemnization and the
necessary requirements of a valid marriage under the Act of 1892, whereas the
other sections to which I have referred are essentially administrative or procedural
and are directory rather than mandatory in nature. This conclusion is, in my
judgment, consistent with the general approach of English law to the question
of the formal validity of a marriage; but since there appear to be no reported **F**
authorities on this aspect of the Foreign Marriage Act, 1892, I must expand this
conclusion to some extent.

The control of the formation of marriage in this country has a long statutory
history, much of it intended to prevent clandestine marriages. The general
tendency has been to preserve marriages where the ceremonial aspects were in
order, rather than to invalidate them for failure to comply with the statutory **G**
provisions leading up to the ceremony. This is illustrated by the Marriage Act,
1823, s. 22, which (9) provided expressly that a marriage should be void for undue
publication of banns or for a defective licence if the parties " shall knowingly
and wilfully intermarry " without due publication of banns, etc. In *Wright* v.
Elwood (10), it was held that a marriage would not be held void under this section
unless both parties were cognizant of the undue publication or other defect. **H**
The Marriage Act, 1836, s. 42, contained (11) a similar provision extending to
marriages before a registrar. In *Holmes* v. *Simmons* (*falsely called Holmes*) (12)
LORD PENZANCE held that a notice of an intended marriage which omitted
certain of the husband's christian names and suppressed the fact that he was
only fifteen years of age did not affect the validity of the marriage. In *Plummer*
v. *Plummer* (13), the Court of Appeal held that, in a case of a marriage by licence, **I**
a notice in an entirely false name did not affect the validity of the marriage.

(8) By the Foreign Marriage Act, 1947, s. 4.
(9) Repealed; see now s. 25 of the Marriage Act, 1949; 28 HALSBURY'S STATUTES
(2nd Edn.) 673.
(10) (1837), 1 Curt. 662.
(11) Repealed; see now s. 49 of the Marriage Act, 1949; 28 HALSBURY'S STATUTES
(2nd Edn.) 695.
(12) (1868), L.R. 1 P. & D. 523.
(13) [1916-17] All E.R. Rep. 591; [1917] P. 163.

A   WARRINGTON, L.J., referred (14) to the Marriage and Registration Act, 1856, s. 19,
     which (15) provided certain penalties if any "valid marriage" should be had by any
     wilfully false notice, declaration or certificate, and pointed out that the legislature
     there expressly accepted that a valid marriage could be had in such circumstances.
     He expressed the principle in the concluding sentence of his judgment, where he
     observed that the consequences of a false notice was not to invalidate the marriage
B   but to expose the parties to the penalties for perjury. In *Greaves* v. *Greaves* (16),
     LORD PENZANCE held that a marriage in the parish church, intended to be by
     licence, was valid, notwithstanding the fact that the licence was not issued until
     the day after the ceremony. He said (17):

         " I understand the meaning of this provision [s. 22 of the Marriage Act,
         1823] to be that the marriage is only to be annulled if it is established
C   affirmatively to the satisfaction of the court, that at the time when the
         ceremony was solemnized both parties were cognizant of the fact that a
         licence had not issued, and being cognizant of that fact wilfully inter-
         married."

     In my judgment, the principle which emerges from the corpus of legislation
D   regulating the formation of marriages in England and from the reported cases
     arising therefrom is that, if a ceremony of marriage has actually taken place
     which, as a ceremony, would be sufficient to constitute a valid marriage, the courts
     will hold the marriage valid unless constrained by express statutory enactment
     to hold otherwise. This is consistent with the traditional concept, both of the
     common law and of the canon law, that the essence of marriage is the formal
E   exchange of voluntary consents to take one another for husband and wife. In my
     judgment, the Foreign Marriage Act, 1892, should be construed on the same
     principle. Accordingly, as all the essential requirements of s. 8 were complied
     with in this case, the marriage of the wife and the husband is, in my judgment, a
     valid marriage. If this view should prove to be wrong and this marriage be held
     to be void, I am satisfied on the facts that, at the date of the conception of each
F   of the children of the parties, both parties reasonably believed it to be valid
     within the meaning of the Legitimacy Act, 1959, s. 2.

     I must now consider the alternative prayer in the petition for a formal declara-
     tion that the marriage is a valid marriage. This prayer (as it appeared in the
     original petition), is clearly an attempt to invoke the jurisdiction of the court to
     make declaratory judgments under R.S.C., Ord. 15, r. 16. The question arises,
G   however, whether, in view of the Matrimonial Causes Act 1965, s. 39, this court
     can, or ought to, exercise this jurisdiction under the Rules of the Supreme Court
     in a case which is covered by that section. The point is of some importance
     because under s. 39 of the Act of 1965 and r. 74 of the Matrimonial Causes Rules,
     1957 (18) a special code of procedure is laid down which was not followed in this
     case. Section 39, which was formerly s. 17 of the Matrimonial Causes Act, 1950,
H   applies primarily, but not exclusively, to petitions for declarations of legitimacy.
     Under sub-s. (1), it is provided that:

         " Any person who is a British subject . . . may, if he is domiciled in England
         or Northern Ireland . . . apply by petition to the court for a decree declaring
         that . . . his own marriage was a valid marriage."

I   These provisions cover in all respects the present wife and the present petition.
     By s. 39 (6), all such petitions must be delivered to the Attorney-General, and
     by r. 74 the petitioner must apply to the registrar for directions as to what parties
     shall be served with the petition. These are important safeguards, because the

     ---

     (14) [1916-17] All E.R. Rep. at p. 594; [1917] P. at p. 172.
     (15) Repealed; not re-enacted.
     (16) (1872), L.R. 2 P. & D. 423.
     (17) (1872), L.R. 2 P. & D. at pp. 424, 425.
     (18) S.I. 1957 No. 619.

rights of third parties may be adversely affected by a declaration that a marriage **A**
is valid and, consequentially, that the children of the marriage are legitimate.
Accordingly, if the court were to exercise the jurisdiction under the Rules of the
Supreme Court and declare a marriage valid, it would enable a petitioner to obtain
what might be, in effect, a declaration of legitimacy of his or her children without
complying with the requirements of s. 39 (6) and of r. 74.

I had occasion to consider an analogous situation in *Kassim (otherwise Wid-* **B**
mann) v. *Kassim (otherwise Hassim) (Carl and Dickson cited)* (19). In that case
the question arose whether this court had the option to grant either a decree of
nullity under its matrimonial jurisdiction or a declaration under R.S.C., Ord. 25,
r. 5 (as it then was), (20) that the marriage was void. I concluded that there was
no room for the exercise of the discretionary jurisdiction founded on the Rules of
the Supreme Court. In the present case, I have come to the same conclusion, **C**
namely, that in cases covered by s. 39 the court must proceed under, and in
accordance with, that section. The reasons for so holding, which I have already
outlined, are at least as, if not more, compelling than those in *Kassim* v. *Kassim*
(21). Counsel for the wife, however, drew my attention to some observations
relevant to this point in the judgments of the Court of Appeal in *Garthwaite* v.
Garthwaite (22). WILLMER, L.J., (23) and DIPLOCK, L.J., (24) were prepared to **D**
assume that this court had jurisdiction to grant bare declarations of validity
otherwise than under s. 17 of the Act of 1950. In that case the question had been
raised but not argued whether s. 17 precluded the court from entertaining
proceedings for a bare declaration of validity in circumstances in which the
petitioner could not bring herself within the terms of that section. The court
was not considering the problem which is before me now, which is whether the **E**
wife, who is within the terms of that section, can apply for a bare declaration of
validity in a different form of proceeding and without complying with the
provisions of that section. In the *Garthwaite* case (22), the petitioner was admittedly not domiciled in England, and was seeking a declaration, not that her
marriage was valid ab initio, but that it still subsisted. The judgments in the
Garthwaite case (22) do not, therefore, bear on the present problem. **F**

In my judgment, a petitioner who is seeking a declaration that his or her
marriage is valid and who is a British subject and domiciled in England must
proceed under s. 39 of the Act of 1965. Accordingly, the wife is not entitled to
such a declaration on the present petition. The result is that I reject the prayer
for a decree of nullity and the alternative prayer for a declaration that the
marriage was valid. I should only add that, at the conclusion of the argument, in **G**
order possibly to save time and money, I gave the wife leave to file a second
petition under s. 39 of the Act of 1965, but for reasons no doubt as seem good to
her she has not seen fit to avail herself of that leave. Accordingly, I have to deal
with the petition as it stands in front of me, in which case, as I say, I refuse both
prayers, and I think that the right order will be to dismiss the petition.

Petition dismissed. **H**

Solicitors: *Pink, Marston, Birch & Delafield,* Portsmouth (for the wife);
Queen's Proctor.

[*Reported by* ALICE BLOOMFIELD, *Barrister-at-Law.*]

I

---

(19) [1962] 3 All E.R. 426 at pp. 432, 433; [1962] P. 224 at pp. 233 and 234.
(20) Now R.S.C., Ord. 15, r. 16.
(21) [1962] 3 All E.R. 426; [1962] P. 224.
(22) [1964] 2 All E.R. 233; [1964] P. 356 at p. 370.
(23) [1964] 2 All E.R. at p. 235; [1964] P. at p. 377.
(24) [1964] 2 All E.R. at p. 247; [1964] P. at p. 397.

A FREIGHTLINES AND CONSTRUCTION HOLDING, LTD. v.
STATE OF NEW SOUTH WALES AND THE COMMISSIONER
OF MOTOR TRANSPORT AND OTHERS.

B
[PRIVY COUNCIL (Lord Reid, Lord Hodson, Lord Pearce, Lord Wilberforce and
Lord Pearson), January 25, 26, 30, 31, February 1, 2, 6, 7, 8, April 10, 1967.]

*Privy Council—Australia—New South Wales—Transport—Freedom of inter-
state trade—Road charge—Provision that owners of certain vehicles having
more than a specified load capacity shall pay at a rate per ton per mile towards
compensation for wear and tear to public highways—Validity of statute—
Constitution of the Commonwealth of Australia, 1900 (63 & 64 Vict. c. 12),*
C *s. 9, s. 92—Road Maintenance (Contribution) Act, 1958-1965, (N.S.W.).*

The Road Maintenance (Contribution) Act, 1958-1965 (N.S.W.) imposed, on
owners of commercial goods vehicles with a load capacity of over four tons, a
road charge, at a rate per ton per mile of public streets travelled, towards
compensation for wear and tear to the public streets caused by such travel.
The appellants, who carried on business as inter-state carriers and owned
D commercial goods vehicles, sought a declaration that the Act was invalid
generally or invalid in respect of certain sections and schedules by virtue of
s. 92* of the Constitution.

Held: approving the decisions of the High Court of Australia in three
relevant transport cases†, the Road Maintenance (Contribution) Act,
1958-1965 (N.S.W.) was valid, because in principle a charge that really
E attempted to fix a reasonable recompence or compensation for the use of a
highway and for contribution to the wear and tear which a vehicle might be
expected to make should be sustained as consistent with the freedom s. 92
of the Constitution conferred on transportation as a form of inter-state
commerce (see p. 447, letter H, and p. 439, letter G, post).

Hughes & Vale Proprietary, Ltd. v. State of New South Wales ([1954] 3
F All E.R. 607) followed.

Dissenting judgments in *Willard* v. *Rawson* ((1933), 48 C.L.R. 316);
R. v. *Vizzard, Ex p. Hill* ((1934), 50 C.L.R. 30) and *McCarter* v. *Brodie*
((1950), 80 C.L.R. 432) applied.

Principles of majority or unanimous judgments in three decisions of the
High Court of Australia, *Hughes & Vale Proprietary, Ltd.* v. *State of New
G South Wales (No. 2)* ((1955), 93 C.L.R. 127), *Armstrong* v. *State of Victoria
(No. 2)* ((1957), 99 C.L.R. 28) and *Commonwealth Freighters Proprietary, Ltd.*
v. *Sneddon* ((1959), 102 C.L.R. 280) approved.

Appeal dismissed.

[As to trade among states of Australia being free, see 5 HALSBURY'S LAWS
(3rd Edn.) 513, 514, para. 1123, text and notes (b)-(g); and for cases on the
H subject, see 8 DIGEST (Repl.) 753, 754, *299, 300*.

For the Constitution of the Commonwealth of Australia, 1900, s. 92, see 6
HALSBURY'S STATUTES (2nd Edn.) 285.]

Cases referred to:
Allwrights Transport, Ltd. v. *Ashley*, (1962), 107 C.L.R. 662.
Armstrong v. *State of Victoria (No. 2)*, (1957), 99 C.L.R. 28.
I *Bessell* v. *Dayman*, (1935), 52 C.L.R. 215; 41 A.L.R. 145; 8 A.L.J. 469.

---

* Section 92, so far as relevant, provides: " On the imposition of uniform duties of
customs, trade, commerce, and intercourse among the States, whether by means of
internal carriage or ocean navigation, shall be absolutely free."

† The three relevant transport cases referred to above are those cases between 1955
and 1959 inclusive which are referred to at letter G, above; but the three transport
cases referred to in *Hughes & Vale Proprietary, Ltd.* v. *State of New South Wales* ([1954]
3 All E.R. 607) were those in which dissenting judgments were delivered which ultimately
were preferred (cf. [1954] 3 All E.R. at p. 613, letter F, and p. 617, letter D5), viz., the
three cases named at letter F, above

Boardman v. *Duddington*, (1959), 104 C.L.R. 456.   A

Braniff Airways v. *Nebraska State Board*, (1954), 347 U.S. 590.

Breen v. *Sneddon; Martin* v. *Sneddon*, (1961), 106 C.L.R. 406.

Capitol Greyhound Lines v. *Brice*, (1949), 339 U.S. 542.

Commonwealth of Australia v. *Bank of New South Wales*, [1949] 2 All E.R. 755;
    [1950] A.C. 235; 8 Digest (Repl.) 753, *300*.
                                                        B

Commonwealth Freighters Proprietary, Ltd. v. *Sneddon, Boland* v. *Sneddon*,
    (1959), 102 C.L.R. 280; [1959] A.L.R. 550; 32 A.L.J.R. 408; Digest
    (Cont. Vol. A) 525, *786j*.

Duncan v. *State of Queensland*, (1916), 22 C.L.R. 556; 22 A.L.R. 465; 8 Digest
    (Repl.) 761, *918*.

Gilpin (O.), Ltd. v. *Comr. for Road Transport & Tramways (N.S.W.)*, (1935),   C
    52 C.L.R. 189.

Hughes & Vale Proprietary, Ltd. v. *State of New South Wales*, [1954] 3 All E.R.
    607; [1955] A.C. 241; [1954] 3 W.L.R. 824; Digest (Cont. Vol. A)
    138, *938a*.

Hughes & Vale Proprietary, Ltd. v. *State of New South Wales (No. 2)*, (1955),
    93 C.L.R. 127.   D

James v. *Commonwealth of Australia (No. 2)*, [1936] 2 All E.R. 1449; [1936]
    A.C. 578; 105 L.J.P.C. 115; 155 L.T. 393; 8 Digest (Repl.) 753, *299*.

McCarter v. *Brodie*, (1950), 80 C.L.R. 432; [1950] A.L.R. 385; 24 A.L.J. 172;
    8 Digest (Repl.) 762, *937*.

Melbourne Harbour Trust Comrs. v. *Colonial Sugar Refining Co., Ltd.*, (1926),
    V.L.R. 140; 42 Digest (Repl.) 1121, *2515*.   E

Pelham (Lord) v. *Pickersgill*, (1787), 1 Term Rep. 660; 99 E.R. 1306; 26 Digest
    (Repl.) 321, 391.

R. v. *Vizzard, Ex p. Hill*, (1934), 50 C.L.R. 30; 40 A.L.R. 16; 7 A.L.J. 362;
    8 Digest (Repl.) 761, *914*.

Willard v. *Rawson*, (1933), 48 C.L.R. 316; [1933] A.L.R. 209; 7 A.L.J. 57;
    8 Digest (Repl.) 761, *913*.   F

Appeal.

This was an appeal by special leave from a judgment of the Full Court of the
High Court of Australia (TAYLOR, WINDEYER and OWEN, JJ.), dated May 2,
1966, upholding a demurrer by the respondents, the State of New South Wales
and the Commissioner for Motor Transport, to the statement of claim of the
appellants, Freightlines and Construction Holding, Ltd.   G

In an action against the respondents, the appellants by writ dated Mar. 8,
1966, sought a declaration that the Road Maintenance (Contribution) Act,
1958-1965 (N.S.W.) was invalid, or alternatively that certain sections and
schedules thereof were invalid, by reason of the provisions of s. 92 of the Constitution of the Commonwealth of Australia; alternatively the appellants sought a
declaration that the said Act did not validly apply in respect of motor vehicles   H
owned by the appellants and used exclusively in or for the purposes of inter-state
trade, commerce or intercourse by reason of s. 92 of the Constitution.

By order dated Dec. 21, 1966 leave to intervene was granted to T.N.T. (Sydney)
Proprietary, Ltd., another carrier of commercial goods with an interest similar
to that of the appellants. Leave to intervene on the other side was also granted
to the Commonwealth of Australia, the States of South Australia, Victoria,   I
Tasmania, Queensland and Western Australia.

William Deane, Q.C. and *M. H. McLelland* (both of the New South Wales
Bar) for the appellants.

H. A. Snelling, Q.C. (Solicitor-General for New South Wales), M. M. Helsham,
Q.C. (of the New South Wales Bar) and *Mervyn Heald* for the respondents.

K. J. Holland, Q.C. and *A. J. Rogers* (both of the New South Wales Bar) for
the interveners, T.N.T. (Sydney) Proprietary, Ltd.

A   A. F. Mason, Q.C. (Solicitor-General for the Commonwealth of Australia) and
Ivor J. Greenwood (of the Victoria Bar) for the interveners, the Commonwealth
of Australia.

   W. A. N. Wells, Q.C. (Assistant Crown Solicitor of South Australia) and S. G.
Davies (of the South Australian Bar) for the interveners, the State of South
Australia.

B   B. L. Murray, Q.C. (Solicitor-General of Victoria) and R. A. Gatehouse for the
interveners, the States of Victoria and Tasmania.

   A. L. Bennett, Q.C. (of the Queensland Bar) and R. A. Gatehouse for the
interveners, the State of Queensland.

   R. D. Wilson, Q.C. (Crown Counsel of New South Wales) and R. A. Gatehouse
for the interveners, the State of Western Australia.

C   LORD PEARCE: Since 1900 when the Constitution of the Commonwealth
of Australia was founded there have been vast changes in road transport between
the states. The roads themselves have very greatly increased in extent, elaboration, efficiency and cost of maintenance. There has been a like increase in the
extent, volume and weight of inter-state commercial traffic. The broad problem
raised by the present case and by the transport cases in general is this. To what
D   extent, if at all, can inter-state commercial transport be lawfully required by the
states (or by the Commonwealth) to contribute directly to the maintenance and
up-keep of the road system which is vital to its existence and which is constantly
and inevitably being worn away by its daily impact?

   According to the appellants, it cannot be required to make any direct material
contribution to the cost of road maintenance. Or, if it can, the contribution to the
E   cost must bear so close a relation to the actual wear and tear caused to the
particular roads by the particular vehicles on their particular journeys that for
practical purposes it would be impossible to exact it. To hold otherwise, it is
argued, would create an inroad into s. 92 which enacts that trade, commerce,
and intercourse among the states, whether by means of internal carriage or ocean
navigation, shall be absolutely free. Moreover, such an inroad would, it is said,
F   lead to the erosion of that charter of absolute freedom which s. 92 has granted
to inter-state commerce. This is the basis of the various arguments, so ably
presented by the appellants' counsel, by which he seeks to show that the legal
concept embodied in the transport cases since 1955 is wrong, and that it cannot
justify those decisions.

   The appellants, who carry on business as inter-state carriers and own com-
G   mercial goods vehicles, seek a declaration that the Road Maintenance (Contribution) Act, 1958-1965 of the State of New South Wales is invalid generally, or
invalid in respect of certain sections and schedules, by virtue of the provisions of
s. 92 of the Constitution. That Act imposes on owners of commercial goods
vehicles (with a load capacity of over four tons) a road charge at a rate per ton
per mile of public streets travelled in New South Wales towards compensation
H   for wear and tear to public streets caused by such travel. The respondents
demurred to the statement of claim. The High Court, following its own previously
decided cases, one of which had already held that the provisions of the Act in
question were valid, allowed the demurrer. On appeal to your lordships leave
to intervene was given to another carrier of commercial goods, who had an interest
similar to that of the appellants. On the other side leave to intervene was given
I   to the states of South Australia, Victoria and Tasmania, Queensland and Western
Australia. These states are closely interested, since they have enacted legislation
which is in all material respects similar to the legislation which is here attacked.

   The Commonwealth of Australia has also intervened. It has not enacted
similar legislation; but it is, equally with the states, bound by s. 92 (James v.
Commonwealth of Australia (No. 2) (1)). It is therefore concerned to maintain
an interpretation of s. 92 which will enable it to pass similar legislation with

(1) [1936] 2 All E.R. 1449; [1936] A.C. 578

regard to road maintenance charges, if it should wish to do so. It is also concerned   A
to maintain an interpretation which will support the validity of certain legislation
authorising the making of charges for aerodromes and other facilities and services
used by persons engaged in inter-state trade, commerce, and intercourse. It is
conceded by counsel for the appellants, however, that his arguments are not
directed against and do not touch this latter class of legislation.

In addition to the appellants and respondents all the interveners have by their   B
counsel made submissions on this interesting and important matter and their
lordships are much indebted for the careful arguments.

It has long been established that the words " absolutely free ", strong as they
are, cannot be read without any qualification. It is clear that s. 92 does not, for
instance, give to inter-state goods the privilege of travelling on railways or ships
without paying for their freight. Fifty years ago SIR SAMUEL GRIFFITH, C.J.,   C
said (*Duncan* v. *State of Queensland* (2)):

" But the word ' free ' does not mean extra legem any more than freedom
means anarchy. We boast of being an absolutely free people, but that does
not mean that we are not subject to law."

Those words were quoted in *Commonwealth of Australia* v. *Bank of New South*   D
Wales (3), where there was much discussion of the extent to which the words
" absolutely free " should be qualified. It was there suggested (4) by way of
general proposition that regulation of trade, commerce and intercourse among
the states was compatible with its absolute freedom, and that s. 92 is violated
only where an act operates to restrict commerce " directly and immediately as
distinct from creating some indirect or consequential impediment which may   E
fairly be regarded as remote ". It was also pointed out (5) with justice that actual
decisions on the matter were likely to be controversial and that although the
decision was one for a court of law the problems were likely to be largely political,
social or economic. This has certainly been so in the transport cases where there
have been many differences of opinion.

In the case of *Hughes & Vale Proprietary, Ltd.* v. *State of New South Wales* (6)—   F
for convenience called *Hughes & Vale No. 1* (6), the Privy Council was called on
to decide a transport case concerning the provisions of the State (Transport)
Co-ordination Act of New South Wales requiring application to be made for a
licence (which might be granted or refused at discretion by an executive official),
and various consequential provisions applying to the operators of public motor
vehicles engaged in inter-state trade. It was held that they contravened s. 92 and   G
were, therefore, invalid.

Various transport cases which had been decided by the High Court came
into question in *Hughes & Vale No. 1* (6). In none of those could it be properly
said, however, that they imposed charges for road maintenance and nothing more.
Nor on the view of the judges who upheld the validity of various acts in those
cases was it necessary to rely on the argument that they dealt with road main-   H
tenance charges. The first of these transport cases was *Willard* v. *Rawson* (7)
where the court by a majority (DIXON, J., dissenting (8)) upheld a Victorian
law requiring the registration of all motor-cars. Their lordships express no opinion
on the correctness of the case. It is, however, interesting to note that DIXON, J.,
in his dissenting judgment said (9):

" If a statute fixes a charge for a convenience or service provided by the   I
state or an agency of the state, and imposes it upon those who choose to avail
themselves of the service or convenience, the freedom of commerce may well
be considered unimpaired, although liability to the charge is incurred in

(2) (1916), 22 C.L.R. 556 at p. 573.
(3) [1949] 2 All E.R. 755 at p. 771, letter G; [1950] A.C. 235 at p. 310.
(4) [1949] 2 All E.R. at p. 771, letter H; [1950] A.C. at p. 310.
(5) [1949] 2 All E.R. at p. 772, letter A; [1950] A.C. at p. 310.
(6) [1954] 3 All E.R. 607; [1955] A.C. 241.   (7) (1933), 48 C.L.R. 316.
(8) (1933), 48 C.L.R. at p. 329.   (9) (1933), 48 C.L.R. at p. 334.

A   inter-state as well as intra-state transactions.   But in such a case the imposition assumes the character of remuneration or consideration charged in respect of an advantage sought and received."

There one has a glimpse of the concept which he subsequently developed and elaborated.

B   It is also interesting to see that Mr. Fullagar as counsel in the case argued (10) that a reason for the invalidity of the registration fee under discussion was that it was not computed according to the mileage run on the roads and that the purpose was not to maintain the highway.

Next for consideration by the Board in *Hughes & Vale No. 1* (11) came *R.* v. *Vizzard, Ex p. Hill* (12) where the High Court had considered the very same statute which was then before the Board.   The majority had held that it was C   valid, but STARKE, J., (13) and DIXON, J., (14) had dissented on the ground that it contravened s. 92.   Again in *O. Gilpin, Ltd.* v. *Comr. for Road Transport & Tramways* (*N.S.W.*) (15) and in *Bessell* v. *Dayman* (16) the majority had upheld the Act, but STARKE, J., (17) and DIXON, J., (18) had again dissented for the same reason.

The last of the transport cases considered by the Board in *Hughes & Vale No. 1* D   (11) was *McCarter* v. *Brodie* (19) where a Victorian Act, by which commercial goods vehicles could not operate on public highways unless licensed to do so under the Act, had been held by the majority to be good.   DIXON, J., (20) and FULLAGAR, J., (21) had dissented.   The Board in *Hughes & Vale No. 1* (11) upheld the dissenting judgments and thus endorsed the earlier dissenting judgments of DIXON, J., (22).   It quoted at length from the judgment of DIXON, J., in *McCarter* E   v. *Brodie* (20) and accepted his view (23) on the following six propositions as to mistakes which underlay the previous transport cases (24): The *Bank* case (25) had rejected as erroneous three of them which had often been put forward: (i) that s. 92 does not guarantee the freedom of individuals; (ii) that

F   " if the same volume of trade flowed from state to state before as after the interference with the individual trader . . . then the freedom of trade among the states remained unimpaired ";

and (iii) that

G   " because a law applies alike to inter-state commerce and to the domestic commerce of a state, it may escape objection notwithstanding that prohibits, restricts or burdens inter-state commerce."

The *Bank* case (25) had also settled
(iv) that

    " the object or purpose of an act challenged as contrary to s. 92 is to be ascertained from what is enacted and consists in the necessary legal effect H   of the law itself and not in its ulterior effect socially or economically ";

(v) that

    " the question what is the pith and substance of the impugned law, though possibly of help in considering whether it is nothing but a regulation

(10) (1933), 48 C.L.R. at p. 318.   (11) [1954] 3 All E.R. 607; [1955] A.C. 241.
I   (12) (1934), 50 C.L.R. 30.   (13) (1934), 50 C.L.R. at p. 52.
(14) (1934), 50 C.L.R. at p. 56.   (15) (1935), 52 C.L.R. 189.
(16) (1935), 52 C.L.R. 215.   (17) (1935), 52 C.L.R. at p. 219.
(18) (1935), 52 C.L.R. at p. 220.   (19) (1950), 80 C.L.R. 432.
(20) (1950), 80 C.L.R. at p. 463.   (21) (1950), 80 C.L.R. at p. 483.
(22) (1933), 48 C.L.R. at p. 334; (1934), 50 C.L.R. at p. 56; (1935), 52 C.L.R. at p. 202; (1935), 52 C.L.R. at p. 220; (1950), 80 C.L.R. at p. 463.
(23) (1950), 80 C.L.R. at p. 465.
(24) For the source of the following six propositions, see *Hughes & Vale No. 1*, [1954] 3 All E.R. at p. 621, letters, F, H, and p. 622; [1955] A.C. at p. 295.
(25) [1949] 2 All E.R. 755; [1950] A.C. 235.

of a class of transactions forming part of trade and commerce, is beside the   A
point when the law amounts to a prohibition or the question of regulation
cannot fairly arise ";

and (vi) it is erroneous to make a distinction between

" on the one hand motor-vehicles as integers of traffic and on the other
hand the trade of carrying by motor vehicles as part of commerce."   B

The carriage of goods and persons does not lie " on the circumference of the
conception of commerce " but " at or near the centre ".

In the dissenting judgments, which were thus accepted and became good law,
DIXON, J., (26) had been primarily concerned with what could *not* be done without
contravening s. 92 rather than with what *could* properly be done; and the
majority, who were thus overruled, had not, ex hypothesi (since they were content   C
with the validity of the relevant Acts), been concerned to explore such a question.
In the new light thrown on the transport cases by the decision in *Hughes & Vale
No. 1* (27), the High Court (with SIR OWEN DIXON now the chief justice) set
itself to give some obiter guidance on how far it was practicable, in conformity
with s. 92, for the states to secure financial contributions towards the large cost
of maintaining their roadways against the deterioration caused by the increased   D
and increasing demands of heavy vehicles. In *Hughes & Vale Proprietary, Ltd.*
v. *State of New South Wales (No. 2)* ((28), for convenience called *Hughes & Vale
No. 2* (28)) the particular statutes concerned were unanimously held invalid,
but the judgments deliberately dealt with the wider aspects of the situation. The
joint judgment of DIXON, C.J., McTIERNAN and WEBB, JJ., (29) describes the
problem as being one (30)   E

" which hitherto has not received consideration in this court untrammelled
by the conceptions held to be erroneous by the Privy Council in *Hughes &
Vale No. 1* (27). It is the problem of saying how far, if at all, and on what
grounds a pecuniary levy can be made directly upon inter-state transportation by road and yet leave that form of trade, commerce and intercourse
absolutely free."   F

The judgment states (31):

" In conception the distinction is clear between laws interfering with the
freedom to effect the very transaction or to carry out the very activity which
constitutes inter-state trade, commerce or intercourse and laws imposing
upon those engaged in such transactions or activities rules of proper conduct   G
or other restraints, so that it is done in a due and orderly manner without
invading the rights or prejudicing the interests of others and, where a use is
made of services or privileges enjoyed as of common right, without abusing
them or disregarding the just claims of the public as represented by the state
to any recompense or reparation that ought in fairness to be made."

The judgment goes on to point out (30) that the question cannot be dealt with on   H
the basis of the ownership of property, nor on the basis of a facility or service,
like railways, electricity, gas, or water. The roads of a state being an established
everyday means of carrying on commerce, were one of the basic assumptions of
s. 92. The judgment states (32):

" But whilst it is not possible to justify the imposition of a charge for the   I
use of the roads on the basis of property, if it includes inter-state commerce,
there are other grounds which make it possible to reconcile with the freedom
postulated by s. 92 the exaction from commerce using the roads, whether the

---

(26) (1933), 48 C.L.R. at p. 334;   (1934), 50 C.L.R. at p. 56;   (1935), 52 C.L.R. at p.
202;   (1935), 52 C.L.R. at p. 220;   (1950), 80 C.L.R. at p. 463.
(27) [1954] 3 All E.R. 607; [1955] A.C. 241.   (28) (1955), 93 C.L.R. 127.
(29) (1955), 93 C.L.R. at p. 150.   (30) (1955), 93 C.L.R. at p. 171.
(31) (1955), 93 C.L.R. at p. 160.   (32) (1955), 93 C.L.R. at p. 172.

A journey be inter-state or not, of some special contribution to their maintenance and upkeep in relief of the general revenues of the state drawn from
the public at large. The American phrase is that inter-state commerce must
pay its way. It is but a constitutional aphorism, but it serves to bring home
the point that in a modern community the exercise of any trade and the
conduct of any business must involve all sorts of fiscal liabilities from which,
B in reason, inter-state trade or business should have no immunity. Those who
pay them are not unfree, they merely pay the price of freedom. Just as any
commercial pursuit or activity must conform with the laws affecting its
incidents, notwithstanding that it may form part of inter-state commerce, so
it must discharge the fiscal liabilities which state law attaches to those
incidents. No one, for example, would say that s. 92 gave a depot or terminal
C of an inter-state air service or road transport business immunity from rates or
land tax. The aphorism, however, does not tell you where the application
of this principle stops, even under the American doctrine which allows more
latitude than our s. 92 can admit. 'The appealing phrase that "inter-
state business must pay its way" can be invoked only when we know what
the "way" is for which inter-state business must pay.'—per Frankfurter,
D L.J., in *Braniff Airways* v. *Nebraska State Board* (33). Needless to say, the
principle has no application if there is a discrimination against inter-state
commerce, if it is placed under any disadvantage in face of the state's
internal commerce. The principle has no application to impositions the
purpose of which is not to recoup the state or supply the means of providing
the services, or a relevant service, of government, but to give effect to some
E social or economic policy, as for example, to deprive road transport of an
advantage in competing with railways.

" A distinction of much importance must be maintained between impositions upon things which are only incidental to or consequential upon carrying
on the activity, as for instance a tax on the occupation of premises, a ' pay
roll ' tax, a profits tax, and impositions upon the thing itself. To exempt a
F business from the former because it has an inter-state character might go
beyond preserving freedom of inter-state trade and amount to a privilege—
'. . . to require that inter-state trade shall be protected from the ordinary
incidents of competitive business is to give—not an immunity from
interference, but a specially privileged position '."

G Their Honours then proceeded to state the solution to the problem and the
principles on which a charge for use may be based in the following way (34):

" For the purpose of that provision (s. 92) it may perhaps be said with some
confidence that, if a charge is imposed as a real attempt to fix a reasonable
recompense or compensation for the use of the highway and for a contribution
to the wear and tear which the vehicle may be expected to make, it will be
H sustained as consistent with the freedom s. 92 confers upon transportation
as a form of inter-state commerce. But if the charge is imposed on the inter-
state operation itself then it must be made to appear that it is such an
attempt. That it is so must be evident from its nature and character. Prima
facie it will present that appearance if it is based on the nature and extent
of the use made of the roads (as for example if it is a mileage or ton-mileage
I charge or the like); if the proceeds are devoted to the repair, upkeep,
maintenance and depreciation of relevant highways, if inter-state transportation bears no greater burden than the internal transport of the state and if
the collection of the exaction involves no substantial interference with the
journey. The absence of one or all of these indicia need not necessarily prove
fatal, but in the presence of them the conclusion would naturally be reached
that the charge was truly compensatory.

---

(33) (1954), 347 U.S. 590 at p. 607.   (34) (1955), 93 C.L.R. at p. 175.

" The expression ' a reasonable compensation or recompense ' is con-   A
venient but vague.   The standard of ' reasonableness ' can only lie in the
severity with which it bears on traffic and such evidence of extravagance in
its assessment as come from general considerations.   In speaking of ' relevant
highways ' it is intended to mark the importance of recognizing the size of
Australian states, as distinguished from most American states.   It is for the
use of certain roads that it is supposed the recompense is made, and not for   B
the use of roads of an entirely different character many hundreds of miles
away.   It may of course be immaterial if the charge is based on average costs
of road care, repair and maintenance, which may well give a lower rate
than if it were based on the costs in connection with the highway used.   It
does not seem logical to include the capital cost of new highways or other
capital expenditure in the costs taken as the basis of the computation.   It is   C
another matter with recurring expenditure incident to the provision and
maintenance of roads.   The judgment whether the charge is consistent with
the freedom of inter-state trade must be made upon a consideration of the
statutory instrument or instruments by and under which it is imposed.   The
fault with s. 18 (4)-(6) is that these provisions confer an authority which ex
facie gives no assurance that the charge imposed under it will conform with   D
what amount to constitutional necessities.   It is needless to consider whether
this necessarily means that the subsections are wholly void, so that it would
be unnecessary to wait to see what is done under them.   For in any case, they
fall with the licensing provisions.

"All that is conceded to the state by what has been said is authority to
exact a compensatory payment for the use of the highways notwithstanding   E
that it is a use in the course of inter-state trade."

Then after pointing out what, in their Honours' view, would *not* be a charge able
to be levied consistently with s. 92, they proceeded (35):

" But very different considerations arise when the state demands payment in respect of the use of a physical thing which the state provides   F
although under no legal obligation to provide it.   No one would doubt that, if
coal is discharged from inter-state colliers through handling equipment and
bins established by the state, the state may impose a proper charge by way of
recompense or remuneration.   But a state may build a wharf which inter-state
ships cannot well do otherwise than use.   Yet it seems undeniable that the
state can require the ships to pay wharfage provided the wharfage charge is   G
genuinely fixed as a fair and reasonable compensation for the use of the
wharf.   Government aerodromes constructed and equipped for traffic by air
may be indispensable to inter-state aerial navigation; but because charges
are levied for the use of them no one would say that air navigation among the
states is not free.   The fact is that we find nothing inconsistent with our
conception of complete freedom of inter-state trade in the exaction, for the   H
use of physical things like the foregoing, of a pecuniary charge, if in truth
it is no more than a reward, remuneration or recompense.   But when an
exaction is compulsory, it must possess characteristics which distinguish it
from a mere tax, falling upon inter-state trade.   It is for this reason that the
relation which the amount of the exaction bears to the actual use of the
facility should appear, and that there should not be evidence of an attempt   I
to achieve objects that go beyond the recovery of fair compensation for the
actual use made of the facility.   We are accustomed to the levy of charges
for the use of such things as have been given as examples, coal-handling
equipment, wharves and aerodromes, and accordingly we see in it nothing
incongruous with freedom of trade.   We are not accustomed to charges being
made for the use of ordinary bridges; but it would strike few minds that there
was any impairment of freedom of inter-state trade in placing a toll upon

(35) (1955), 93 C.L.R. at p. 177.

A   the use of some great bridge erected as a major engineering work, like that over Sydney Harbour. Must a highway be treated by the state for the purposes of s. 92 as in a different category from wharves, bridges, aerodromes and special constructional works which inter-state trade uses? A modern highway is in fact a constructional work of a very substantial character indeed. It cannot be distinguished from the facilities that have been

B   mentioned either in cost, the technical and engineering skill it demands or the general purpose it serves. It is an engineering work of a major description designed to carry heavy motor vehicles between distant places. There is little exaggeration in saying that its association with the highways of the nineteenth century is a matter of history rather than of practical identity or resemblance. But highways have in Australia a very different history from

C   wharves and analogous constructional works. At the time when s. 92 was enacted, with very few, if any, exceptions, the highways of Australia were available without charge for the use of all persons as of right. It has not always been so in England. Even before the period of statutory tolls it was competent for the Crown to grant a franchise to take tolls over a road in consideration of the grantee keeping the road in repair: see *Lord Pelham* v.

D   *Pickersgill* (36). Then of course there came the long history of turnpike roads governed by turnpike trusts constituted by statute. Is it an anterior assumption of s. 92 that the roads of a state, whatever form they take, must be available without charge to all kinds of inter-state traffic? Is such an assumption part and parcel of the freedom which the provision guarantees? To give an affirmative answer to this question implies that in reference to

E   inter-state commerce the law, that is to say the state law conferring upon the subjects of the Crown a right of free passage over highways, is unchangeable. There seems to be no constitutional reason why this should be so. What is essential for the purpose of securing the freedom of inter-state transportation by road is that no pecuniary burden should be placed upon it which goes beyond a proper recompense to the state for the actual use made of the physi-

F   cal facilities provided in the shape of a highway. The difficulties are very great in defining this conception. But the conception appears to be based on a real distinction between remuneration for the provision of a specific physical service of which particular use is made and a burden placed upon inter-state transportation in aid of the general expenditure of the state. It seems necessary to draw the distinction and ultimately to attempt to work

G   out the conception so as to allow of a charge compatible with real freedom because it is no more than a fair recompense for a specific facility provided by the state and used for the purpose of his business by the inter-state trader."

WILLIAMS, J., spoke to a somewhat similar effect (37). FULLAGAR, J., said (38):

H   " Nor is it any denial or qualification of this freedom to come and go to say that nobody is bound affirmatively to facilitate my coming and going or to supply me with the means of coming or going. Nobody is bound to provide for me a ship or an aeroplane or a motor car. Nor is anybody bound to provide for me a wharf or an aerodrome or a parking station. If a government or a governmental instrumentality does provide any of these things, it

I   is clearly entitled to make at least a reasonable charge for the use thereof, and the making of such a charge cannot be said to interfere with my freedom to come and go: cf. *Melbourne Harbour Trust Comrs.* v. *Colonial Sugar Refining Co., Ltd.* (39). This, however, is, of course, subject to the proviso that the charges made do not involve any discrimination against me as an inter-state trader or traveller. If they do, they assume at once a different aspect, and can no longer be regarded as merely charges for a service rendered. They

(36) (1787), 1 Term Rep. 660.   (37) (1955), 93 C.L.R. at p. 184.
(38) (1955), 93 C.L.R. at p. 208.   (39) (1926), V.L.R. 140.

impose a special burden on me as an inter-state trader or traveller, and they   A
do therefore interfere with my freedom to come and go . . .

"There is, however, another aspect of the matter. Large, fast moving,
and often very heavy, road vehicles provide to-day, in Europe, America and
Australia, a normal and necessary means for the transportation of goods and
passengers. Such vehicles require, for their safe, efficient and economical use,
roads of considerable width, and of a hardness and durability beyond what   B
was achieved by John McAdam. Because such roads serve, directly or
indirectly, the needs of the community as a whole, it is the natural function
of governments to provide and maintain them. That function has been
assumed in Australia by the states, acting directly or through a statutory
instrumentality, as one of their constitutional functions, though large sums
have been paid to the states by the Commonwealth for assistance in the   C
performance of this function under a series of Commonwealth Acts, of which
the latest is the Commonwealth Aid Roads Act, 1950.

"Such roads, as I have said, serve directly or indirectly the needs of the
community as a whole. But, because the users of vehicles generally, and of
public motor vehicles in particular, stand in a special and direct relation to
such roads, and may be said to derive a special and direct benefit from them,   D
it seems not unreasonable that they should be called upon to make a special
contribution to their maintenance over and above their general contribution
as taxpayers of state and Commonwealth. Among those who so use roads are
persons who use those roads exclusively for the inter-state carriage of goods
or passengers. Does s. 92 mean that such persons must be exempt from
making any contribution towards the maintenance of the roads which they   E
use? I do not think it does. It does not appear to me to be inconsistent with
anything I have said above to say that such persons may be called upon to
make a contribution towards the cost of maintaining something from which
they may fairly be regarded as deriving a benefit over and above that which
is derived by the community as a whole. In making such a contribution they
are not really paying a price for their coming and going. They are paying a   F
price for something which makes their coming and going safer, easier, or more
convenient than it would be if the highways which they use were allowed to
fall into disrepair or decay. So regarded, the exaction of a contribution
towards the maintenance of the highways of a state does not appear to me,
necessarily and of its very nature, to offend against s. 92. Such a view derives
support, I think, from the view taken in a considerable number of cases in the   G
United States, although, as has often been pointed out, there is no s. 92 in the
Constitution of the United States, and the question of the validity of such
charges arises there in connection with a constitutional doctrine which has
not been adopted here."

KITTO, J., expressed (40), and gave clear and detailed reasons for, the view
that the states could *not* validly make any charge for the use made of roads   H
by vehicles engaged in inter-state trade. TAYLOR, J., also expressed (41) similar
reasoned views but he said that in cases where by reason of their weights and
construction vehicles are calculated to work destruction of such a nature to
roads that they ought not to be on them at all, the states may validly prohibit
their use on the road. In such cases it is legitimate for the states to stipulate
for payment of a charge as a condition of relaxing such prohibition.   I

In *Armstrong* v. *State of Victoria* (*No. 2*) (42) the majority DIXON, C.J., (43)
McTIERNAN (44), WILLIAMS (44) and FULLAGAR, JJ. (45) (WEBB (46), KITTO (47)
and TAYLOR, JJ. (48) dissenting) repeated their views and amplified them. In

---

(40) (1955), 93 C.L.R. at p. 215.   (41) (1955), 93 C.L.R. at p. 225.
(42) (1957), 99 C.L.R. 28.   (43) (1957), 99 C.L.R. at p. 36.
(44) (1957), 99 C.L.R. at p. 61.   (45) (1957), 99 C.L.R. at p. 81.
(46) (1957), 99 C.L.R. at p. 74.   (47) (1957), 99 C.L.R. at p. 84.
(48) (1957), 99 C.L.R. at p. 86.

A   that case (49) the High Court had an actual statute to consider, framed within the principles adumbrated obiter in *Hughes & Vale No. 2* (50). The Act there under consideration was for practical purposes identical with the Act which is being considered in the present case. Evidence was called whose nature appears by inference from the judgments. The Act was held valid by the majority. DIXON, C.J. (51) (in his judgment with which McTIERNAN, J., agreed (52))

B   pointed out (53) that the liability to pay accrued from the actual use of the road and the amount was quantified by the length of the journey. Payment was not exacted as a condition precedent to carrying the goods or entering upon or continuing the journey. He observed (54):

C   " When it is said that a toll upon a bridge, to take the example mentioned, does not burden inter-state commerce it does not mean that the payment is not borne by the traffic or that the payment is so small that its incidence cannot be felt. It means that the payment is of such a kind that it is no impairment of the freedom of commerce or of movement if you are required to make it . . . ."

After referring (54) to tolls on bridges, charges on aerodromes, and tonnage

D   rates on ships berthing at wharves, he said (54),

" Although the payments are exacted under the authority of the law from parties engaged in inter-state commerce who must incur the charges if they are to pursue the inter-state transactions, yet there is no detraction from the freedom of inter-state commerce. The reason, as I venture to suggest, simply is that, without the bridge, the aerodromes and airways,

E   the wharves and the sheds, the respective inter-state operations could not be carried out and that the charges serve no purpose save to maintain these necessary things at a standard by which they may continue. However it may be stated, the ultimate ground why the exaction of the payments for using the instruments of commerce that have been mentioned is no violation of the freedom of inter-state trade lies in the relation to inter-state trade

F   which their nature and purpose give them. The reason why public authority must maintain them is in order that the commerce may use them, and so for the commerce to bear or contribute to the cost of their upkeep can involve no detraction from the freedom of commercial intercourse between states. It is not because the charges are consensual for plainly they are imposed by law; if the conditions are fulfilled that the law prescribes, a

G   liability arises. It is not because they are based on property. Indeed the instruments of commerce in question are public works often subject to and complicated by a combination of authorities.

" Once however it appears that, under colour of the law, the charge is imposed not for the purpose of obtaining a proper contribution to the maintenance and upkeep of the work but for the purpose of adversely

H   affecting the inter-state commerce, then whatever its guise it is called in question by s. 92 as an infringement of the freedom of trade commerce and intercourse among the states."

After incorporating a passage quoted above from the judgment in *Hughes & Vale No. 2* (55) DIXON, C.J., continued (56):

I   " The passage which as I have already said must be read into this judgment from that in *Hughes and Vale Proprietary, Ltd.* v. *State of New South Wales (No. 2)* (55) concludes with a reference to the difficulties necessarily arising in working out the distinction between, on the one hand, recompense or remuneration for the provision of a specific physical service of which

(49) (1957), 99 C.L.R. 28.   (50) (1955), 93 C.L.R. 127.
(51) (1957), 99 C.L.R. at p. 36.   (52) (1957), 99 C.L.R. at p. 61.
(53) (1957), 99 C.L.R. at p. 40.   (54) (1957), 99 C.L.R. at p. 43.
(55) (1955), 93 C.L.R. at p. 178.   (56) (1957), 99 C.L.R. at p. 47.

particular use is made and on the other hand, a burden placed on inter-   A
state transportation in aid of the general expenditure of the state. The
careful argument in this case on the part of the plaintiffs was of course not
directed to diminishing or solving the difficulties; but it had a particular
value as an exposure of latent questions to which any practical measure
must give rise. Nevertheless I am confirmed in the view that it is ' necessary
to draw the distinction and ultimately to attempt to work out the concep-   B
tion so as to allow of a charge compatible with real freedom because it is
no more than a fair recompense for a specific facility provided by the state
and used for the purpose of his business by the inter-state trader '."

WILLIAMS, J., agreed (57) and confirmed his views as set out in *Hughes &*
Vale No. 2 (58).

FULLAGAR, J., said (59):   C

" What is permissible (whether you call it a ' compensation ' or a ' recompense ' or what you will) is the exaction of a contribution towards the
maintenance of something which can be used as of right. The distinction
is, to my mind, both real and important. For, if what is permissible were
of the former character, the states must obviously be very much at large.
If, on the other hand, what is permissible is of the latter character, the   D
powers of the states are defined, and the courts have a power of investigation
and ultimate control, which can be exercised to prevent an infringement
of s. 92, the final question in each case being whether what is exacted is in
truth and in substance, and is no more than a contribution towards the
maintenance of public highways."

And again (60):   E

" Every one of the indicia (i.e., as suggested in *Hughes and Vale No. 2*) (58)
is present here. The charge is based on ton-mileage, and is thus related on
its face to the nature and extent of the use made of roads. Section 30 of
the Act requires all moneys received by the board to be paid into the
Country Roads Board fund to the credit of a special ' Roads Maintenance   F
Account ' and money to the credit of that special account is to be applied
only to the maintenance of public highways. Inter-state transport bears
no greater burden than the internal transport of the state. And the collection
of the charge involves no interference with any inter-state journey. It is
to be added that the charge is not shown to be quantitatively unreasonable
either in the sense of being out of proportion to the actual cost of main-   G
tenance or in the sense of imposing a practically prohibitive burden. It is
to be added also that the state adduced evidence to show the actual basis
on which the amount of the charge had been arrived at. Anything even
approximating to mathematical accuracy is obviously out of the question,
but the evidence does, I think, establish that there is what FRANKFURTER, J.
(in *Capitol Greyhound Lines* v. *Brice* (61)) has called ' a relationship between   H
what is demanded and what is given by the state '. It shows, I think,
that there has been a ' real attempt to fix a reasonable recompense or
compensation '."

The last of this important trilogy was *Commonwealth Freighters Proprietary, Ltd.*
v. *Sneddon* (62), which dealt with the validity of the New South Wales Act
here in question. The Act was unanimously held (62) to be valid. The learned   I
chief justice restated his previous views. He concluded (63):

" In *Armstrong's* case (64) I considered that, notwithstanding the unsatisfactory basis of the information upon which, in the circumstances I

(57) (1957), 99 C.L.R. at p. 61.   (58) (1955), 93 C.L.R. 127.
(59) (1957), 99 C.L.R. at p. 82.   (60) (1957), 99 C.L.R. at p. 83.
(61) (1949), 339 U.S. 542 at p. 550.   (62) (1959), 102 C.L.R. 280.
(63) (1959), 102 C.L.R. at p. 293.   (64) (1957), 99 C.L.R. 28.

A   have summarised, the conclusion must rest, the realities of the case clearly were that a contributory charge had been levied for the maintenance of highways sufficiently uniform in its incidence, reasonably proportionate to the wear and tear involved and otherwise conforming with the tests accepted by a majority of the judges for a charge consistent with true freedom in carrying on trade, commerce and intercourse."

B   And again (65):

" The basal reason in the distinction upon which these cases rest is that the constant flow of traffic involves equally constant recurring charges to uphold the surface on which it continues to travel and that it is no impairment of its liberty so to travel if a charge is levied commensurate C   with the use and attrition for the purpose of upholding the surface."

KITTO (66) and TAYLOR, JJ. (66) held that the court was bound by *Armstrong's* case (67) and therefore no longer dissented.

MENZIES, J. (68) did not question the rationale of *Armstrong's* case (67); but he considered (69) and refuted the argument that since the Victorian case of *Armstrong* (67) had been decided in the light of factual evidence as to the D   reasonableness of the charges as they related to the Victorian roads, this New South Wales Act could not be properly held valid without similar evidence; and that since the charges in the two acts were identical, the Victorian evidence supporting the charges gave a prima facie indication of unreasonableness, since charges which were reasonable in respect of Victoria were unlikely to be reason-E   able in respect of New South Wales. He said (70):

" Any decision that a statute is constitutional or unconstitutional, however it may have been reached, is necessarily one of law and is, in the absence of special circumstances, of binding authority.   Where such a decision has been reached simply by process of construction and comparison no difficulty arises about the binding authority of the decision in subsequent F   cases.   Where, however, the decision has depended in part upon findings of fact there is room for argument.   Where the facts which have entered into the decision were ascertained by judicial notice there would seem to be no sound reason for not according the decision the same authority as if it had depended upon nothing more than a comparison between the challenged legislation and the constitution because the only matters of which judicial G   notice can be taken are those considered too notorious to require proof, that is, matters beyond controversy.   Where, however, the facts which have entered into the decision have been ascertained from evidence there is more room for doubt whether the decision so reached has binding authority except in cases where precisely the same facts are established.   This problem, like the more fundamental problem of the place of evidence in constitutional H   cases, is not a matter for unnecessary generalization, because it is possible to envisage cases where a decision based upon findings of fact could properly be called into question, but to deal with the case in hand I am not in doubt that if after taking evidence in an action the court has decided that a state law leaves trade, commerce and intercourse among the states absolutely free and so does not contravene s. 92, its decision on that point of law so I   long as it stands puts the matter at rest.   Where a decision concerning validity has been reached upon findings of fact it would, of course, be open to the court to consider the matter again upon the representation that the significant facts are no longer as they were, but this is another matter which need not be considered here."

---

(65) (1959), 102 C.L.R. at pp. 294, 295.   (66) (1959), 102 C.L.R. at p. 296.
(67) (1957), 99 C.L.R. 28.   (68) (1959), 102 C.L.R. at p. 298.
(69) (1959), 102 C.L.R. at p. 299.   (70) (1959), 102 C.L.R. at p. 301.

Those observations seem to their lordships, with respect, to contain good sense; **A** but in this area sharply defined questions of fact in the foreground blend imperceptibly in the middle distance with the broader and more distant matters of which a tribunal may take judicial notice. Moreover as at present advised it seems to their lordships that these are matters peculiarly within the province of the High Court and they therefore make no further comment on them.

There is an interesting judgment of WINDEYER, J. (71), who had not been **B** concerned with previous transport cases, in which he examines and adopts their rationale, supporting it by its accordance with (72)

" some historic doctrines of English law and with old practices which can, I think, be regarded as in harmony with the freedom which s. 92 assures."

C

He then went on (72) to consider from medieval times the situation with regard to highways, bridges, ferries and tolls.

Three later cases were cited to their lordships, *Boardman* v. *Duddington* (73), *Breen* v. *Sneddon* (74) and *Allwrights Transport, Ltd.* v. *Ashley* (75) in which the High Court followed the same line of reasoning. They added little or nothing to the argument save in so far as the appellants' counsel claimed *Allwrights'* **D** case (75) as an indication of the undesirable lengths to which the heresy which he was attacking could go. There it was held (75) that it was not relevant that the total amount of charges collected in respect of a particular highway exceeds the amount expended on its upkeep (76). "What matters", said the joint judgment, "is that a rate is adopted by the state . . . and is expended only upon the maintenance of highways, using the word ' maintenance ' in the widest **E** sense." Thus there has been evolved a legal concept,which has become established by the authority of the High Court in several decisions. It has been worked out by careful, thoughtful judgments in which those of the learned and very distinguished chief justice SIR OWEN DIXON have naturally played the leading part. It is conceded that, broadly speaking, it is fair and reasonable in its practical effect; but the appellants rightly contend that if it offends against the charter **F** of freedom contained in s. 92 it cannot stand. Naturally counsel for the appellants largely bases his arguments on the clear and careful judgments of KITTO, J. (77) and TAYLOR, J. (78) who, as long as it was open to them, maintained that such exactions from inter-state trade were inconsistent with the absolute freedom conferred by s. 92.

Counsel for the appellants' argument runs thus. Admittedly there is some **G** qualification of the words absolutely free; and freedom of inter-state traffic under s. 92 has certain implied restrictions. Traffic must be regulated by rules; and if an exaction is truly regulatory, e.g., if registration is necessary for control of traffic and a compulsory payment for licences goes towards paying the costs of registration machinery, this does not offend s. 92. But the charge under consideration cannot be described as regulatory. Nor in fact do the supporters **H** of its validity rely on its regulatory nature. Again there is admittedly a right to charge for facilities. But this is limited to charges based on a right of property with a consequent power to exclude. Railways (or aerodromes) which are owned by the state and from which the public may by right of property be excluded are thus different from highways where the public (including inter-state traffic) go as of *right*. This right is one of which the trader is a beneficiary, and if the **I** inter-state trader can be charged for this he may be charged for all the benefits

---

(71) (1959), 102 C.L.R. at p. 302.   (72) (1959), 102 C.L.R. at p. 303.
(73) (1959), 104 C.L.R. 456.   (74) (1961), 106 C.L.R. 406.
(75) (1962), 107 C.L.R. 662.   (76) (1962), 107 C.L.R. at p. 668.
(77) (1955), 93 C.L.R. at p. 215; (1957), 99 C.L.R. at p. 84.
(78) (1955), 93 C.L.R. at p. 225; (1957), 99 C.L.R. at p. 86.

A provided to him by the state. Any charge for a right to go on the roads is irreconcilable with freedom. (See KITTO, J., *Hughes & Vale No. 2* (79); TAYLOR, J. (80)). This is a mere tax on the movement of the trader, movement which he is entitled to make as an integral and all important part of his inter-state trade.

B "If it is conceded that a person enjoys a constitutional immunity from all charges upon his going inter-state by road, I do not see how it can be asserted, without contradicting the concession, that that person is not immune from a charge imposed and measured by reference to an aspect, or a necessary incident or consequence, of his going inter-state by road."

(Per KITTO, J., *Armstrong's* case (81).)   To impose such a charge, it is argued, is inconsistent with *Hughes & Vale No. 1* (82).

C The arguments thus shortly summarised are formidable and their lordships have given them careful consideration; but in their opinion they do not invalidate the legal concept contained in the judgments of SIR OWEN DIXON, C.J., and other members of the court in the three relevant transport cases (83). The appellants' argument assumes that if the charge is not regulatory in the strict sense and is not a charge for facilities in the strict sense, it cannot be made.

D It assumes that the qualifications which admittedly have to be made in the words "absolute freedom", cannot include a charge which does not come strictly within either of those categories. It denies a right to charge towards the upkeep of something which the trader can use as of right. Yet there is admittedly a framework within which the freedom operates, a framework which one may describe in the apt words of KITTO, J., in *Breen* v. *Sneddon* (84),

E "as circumscribing an individual's latitude of conduct in the interests of fitting him into a neighbourhood—a society, membership of which entails, because of its nature, acts and forbearances on the part of each by which room is allowed for the reasonable enjoyment by each other of his own position in the same society."

F This framework partly consists of rules (and charges therefor) of strictly regulatory nature, and partly consists of charges for facilities (e.g., railways and wharves). One may ask why the framework should not also consist of a duty to contribute directly to the cost of that which the trader, while using the highway as of right, consumes by the wear and tear which he inflicts on it. The framework within which the trader's freedom operates is nowhere indicated

G with any precision or at all. Its extent is a matter of inference and common sense. Counsel for the appellants' argues in terrorem that the judgments attacked might be extended to cover charges for other matters of which the trader should properly be a beneficiary in exercising his freedom under s. 92. But the transport cases have rightly been treated in the High Court as cases in isolation from other aspects of the freedom of inter-state trade.

H Their lordships accept the judgments of SIR OWEN DIXON, C.J., and the other judgments of the High Court to the like effect in the three relevant transport cases (83) as being a correct development and exposition of the law. In their view the Act here in question is valid, and does not on the general point offend against s. 92.

Apart from their general contention the appellants relied on three subsidiary

I matters.

Counsel for the appellants argued that since the Act expressly puts a burden on commercial vehicles (or private vehicles acting commercially) as such, it

---

(79) (1955), 93 C.L.R. at pp. 221-223.   (80) (1955), 93 C.L.R. at pp. 237, 238.
(81) (1957), 99 C.L.R. at p. 86.
(82) [1954] 3 All E.R. 607; [1957] A.C. 241.
(83) (1955), 93 C.L.R. 127; (1957), 99 C.L.R. 28; (1959), 102 C.L.R. 280.
(84) (1961), 106 C.L.R. at p. 415.

discriminates against commerce and thus the burden becomes one which offends A
against the freedom under s. 92, even if a burden on all private citizens' and
traders' vehicles alike would not do so. Their lordships cannot accept that
contention. Once it is established that the charge towards the wear and tear
of the roads is allowable as part of the framework within which the freedom
of s. 92 runs, it does not cease to be so because it is put only on that section of
the transport which causes the heaviest wear and tear. If it is not a burden on B
freedom within the meaning of s. 92, it does not become one merely because it is
(on a common sense computation and with no discriminatory malice) laid on
those who may be considered the proper persons to bear it.

It was further argued that, granted the general right to impose such a charge
in certain circumstances, there was no evidence to support this particular charge
and the onus should be on the state in this connexion. Their lordships would C
refer to their comment on the passage from the judgment of MENZIES, J., quoted
above (85).

Finally it was argued (by counsel for the appellants) that since a factual
situation was necessary to the validity of these charges and since, even assuming
that it now existed, yet it might not continue to exist, the Act was invalid.
For when an Act depends for its validity on transient circumstances it is valid D
only if it refers to them; and it is invalid, if it is passed in general terms, thus
claiming a permanence to which it is not entitled. In support of this proposition
he referred to various decisions in the United States of America. The hypothesis
on which the proposition is based is that the cost of road maintenance in New
South Wales may diminish to such an extent that the charge exacted can no
longer be regarded as bearing a reasonable relationship to the cost of road E
maintenance and the wear and tear of traffic. Whether this attractive hypothesis
has sufficient relation to reality and instals into the factual situation any element
of transience, their lordships do not venture to estimate. This again seems to be
a matter peculiarly within the province of the High Court and their lordships
are content to accept their view of the matter.

For these reasons their lordships will humbly advise Her Majesty that the F
appeal should be dismissed. The appellants must pay to the respondents their
costs of this appeal.

Appeal dismissed.

Solicitors: *Rodgers, Horsley & Burton* (for the appellants); *Light & Fulton*
(for the respondents); *Winston & Co.* (for T.N.T. (Sydney) Proprietary, Ltd.); G
Coward, Chance & Co. (for the Commonwealth of Australia); *Blyth, Dutton,
Wright & Bennett* (for the State of South Australia); *Freshfields* (for the States
of Victoria, Tasmania and Queensland); *M. L. Moss & Son* (for the State of
Western Australia).

[*Reported by* KATHLEEN J. H. O'BRIEN, *Barrister-at-Law.*] H

I

---

(85) (1959), 102 C.L.R. at p. 301.

A   R. V. WARD, LTD. *v.* BIGNALL.

[COURT OF APPEAL, CIVIL DIVISION (Sellers, Diplock and Russell, L.JJ.), February
   9, 10, 17, 1967.]

Sale of Goods—Unpaid seller—Re-sale—Effect as rescission of contract of sale—
   Re-sale of part of goods sold—Right to retain proceeds of re-sale—Right
B *to sue buyer for damages for non-acceptance, but not for price—Measure of*
   damages—Sale of Goods Act, 1893 (56 & 57 Vict. c. 71), s. 48 (3).

   If an unpaid seller of goods in possession of the goods re-sells the goods, or
   part of them, as he is entitled to do under s. 48 (3)* of the Sale of Goods Act,
   1893, the contract of sale is rescinded, with the consequences that the buyer
   is discharged from any further liability to pay the price and the seller is
C entitled to retain the proceeds of the resale, whether they be greater or
   less than the contract price, and in addition to sue the buyer for damages for
   non-acceptance if the re-sale, after deducting its extra expenses, realises
   less than the contract price (see p. 452, letter H, p. 453, letter D, and p. 457,
   letters A and H, post).
      Gallagher v. *Shilcock* ([1949] 1 All E.R. 921) overruled.
D   On May 6, 1965, the plaintiff contracted with the defendant for the sale
   to the defendant of two motor cars, a Vanguard and a Zodiac, for a total
   price of £850, of which the defendant paid a deposit of £25. The defendant
   repudiated the contract. On the same day (May 6) the plaintiff's solicitors
   wrote to the defendant notifying him, among other matters, that if he failed
   to pay the balance by May 11, the plaintiff would endeavour to re-sell the
E cars. The defendant did not pay the price. On May 24, 1965, the plaintiff
   sold the Vanguard for £350. The plaintiff, having failed to sell the other
   car, subsequently brought an action against the defendant for damages,
   being the balance of the total purchase price (£475) and advertising expenses
   (£22 10s.). On appeal by the defendant against an award of such damages,
      Held: the re-sale of the Vanguard by the plaintiff, as unpaid seller, con-
F stituted a rescission of the contract of sale with the defendant; therefore the
   plaintiff was not entitled to recover the balance of the purchase price but only
   damages (£47 10s.) for loss sustained by the defendant buyer's default (see
   p. 453, letter E, and p. 457, letters G and H, post).
      Per DIPLOCK, L.J.: in modern times very little is needed to give rise to
   the inference that the property in specific goods is to pass only on delivery
G or payment (see p. 453, letter I, post).
      Appeal allowed.

   [As to re-sale under his statutory rights by a seller of goods, see 34 HALSBURY'S
   LAWS (3rd Edn.) 142, para. 235; and for cases on the subject, see 39 DIGEST
   (Repl.) 776-778, *2517-2543.*
      For the Sale of Goods Act, 1893, s. 48, see 22 HALSBURY'S STATUTES (2nd Edn.)
H 1012.]

Case referred to:
   Gallagher v. *Shilcock,* [1949] 1 All E.R. 921; [1949] 2 K.B. 765; [1949] L.J.R.
      1721; 39 Digest (Repl.) 776, *2522.*

   Appeal.
I   This was an appeal by Arnold Herbert Bignall, the buyer under a contract for
   the sale of two motor cars by R. V. Ward, Ltd., against so much of the judgment
   of His Honour Deputy Judge ELLISON, at Woolwich county court, dated Aug. 2,
   1966, as assessed the damages awarded to the seller for the buyer's breach of
   the contract of sale at £497 10s. The facts are set out in the judgment of
   SELLERS, L.J.

   M. J. Hyam for the buyer.
   A. C. Whitaker for the seller.

───
* Section 48 is printed at p. 452, letter C, post.

Applied in MOSCHI v LEP [1972] 2
All ER 393

Cur. adv. vult. A

Feb. 17. SELLERS, L.J., read the following judgment: In May, 1965, the plaintiff seller, wished to sell two motor vehicles, a Vanguard Estate car and a Ford Zodiac, for which, by advertisement, it was asking £395 and £490 respectively. The defendant buyer, who is a dealer in motor vehicles, saw the advertisement and on May 6, 1965, he went to Mr. Ward's private house. There he examined both the vehicles and then offered Mr. Ward, for the seller, £850 for the two, which was accepted. No log books were produced or even mentioned. The buyer paid £25 in cash and went off to get the balance of £825 in cash from his bank, and it was arranged that he would return with the balance of the price and pay it to Mrs. Ward. Whilst away the buyer had second thoughts. The Vanguard had been advertised as 1962 and the buyer thought that so to describe it was a misrepresentation or a misdescription. He told Mr. Ward that he would not, in the circumstances, proceed with the purchase. The buyer offered to pay £800 instead of the £850. That was refused. The buyer then offered to take the Zodiac alone for £500 and that was refused.

On the same day the seller consulted its solicitors. They wrote a letter to the buyer in which they quoted what the buyer had written on the back of one of the seller's cards:

" A. M. Bignall Purchased Vanguard Estate Ford Zodiac for sum of £850 [signed] A. M. Bignall £25 deposit paid as seen and approved."

In view of the argument before this court it is necessary to quote further from the letter. It continues:

" In view of the foregoing it is our view that ownership of the said motor cars passed to yourself. Mr. Ward further states that you left his home for the purpose of obtaining the balance of the agreed purchase price in cash, but that on your return, you informed Mrs. Ward in the absence of Mr. Ward that you did not intend to purchase the Vanguard but would only purchase the Ford which conversation you later repeated to Mr. Ward over the telephone. As mentioned above, ownership of the two cars has now passed to yourself, and all that remains is for you to collect the same, and to pay to [the seller] the balance of the agreed purchase price. We have advised [the seller] that a binding agreement has been made by you to purchase the said motor cars, and that failure by you to take possession thereof, and to pay the balance of the agreed purchase price will place you in breach of the said agreement, and will entitle them to recover against you by way of damages, such sum below the price agreed by you, should it be necessary to sell them elsewhere. In these circumstances please accept this letter as notice calling upon you to take delivery of the said cars and to pay the balance due of £825, on or before Tuesday next May 11, failing which [the seller] will consider you in breach of the said agreement, will dispose of the said motor cars for the best price [it] can obtain, and in the event of them receiving a price below that agreed by yourself, will look to you for the difference after giving credit for the £25 already paid by you."

The buyer did nothing except to consult a solicitor and to maintain that there had been misrepresentation.

On Oct. 12, 1965, the seller's solicitors wrote to the buyer's solicitor and, after denying that there had been any misrepresentation and pointing out that the buyer had inspected both vehicles before arriving at the contract, the letter continues:

" In an effort to mitigate the damage following [the buyer's] repudiation [the seller] sold the said Vanguard for £350 but [its] efforts to procure a purchaser for the Zodiac have been completely fruitless."

The Vanguard was sold on or about May 24, 1965, without any further communication to the buyer up to that date than the letter of May 6. The seller also

A endeavoured to sell the Zodiac, but it has remained unsold and in the seller's possession throughout. Apparently without any further communication between the parties, the writ in this action was taken out on Feb. 9, 1966.

That in its terms was a claim for damages, being the balance of the contract price £825 less the £350 received from the sale of the Vanguard plus £22 10s. advertising expenses in respect of the two cars since the date of the contract, a
B total of £497 10s. When the matter came before Deputy Judge ELLISON the buyer pursued two defences. First, that there had been no enforceable contract because the Vanguard, it was alleged, was a 1961 car and it had been misrepresented or described wrongly as 1962 and the buyer had rightly refused to perform the contract. The Vanguard was in fact first registered in 1962 and there was no model of this type of 1962 manufacture. The judge found no misdescrip-
C tion and no misrepresentation and that there was a binding contract on May 6, 1965. From that finding there is no appeal before us.

Secondly, the defence relied on the buyer's offer to buy the Zodiac for £500 and the seller's refusal of it and said that the seller had failed to mitigate its loss. The judgment held that this was not an unfettered offer. It was to be substituted for the contract to buy the two vehicles. This was clearly right, but judgment
D was thereupon entered for the seller for £497 10s. damages and costs. The position at the end of the trial was that the seller had the Zodiac, which had been in its complete possession throughout with the log book registered in its name, and it had also the judgment in its favour for £497 10s. This could not be right, except on the basis of a lien, to which no reference was made. The action in the lower court followed, as I think, the statement of claim and was in substance for damages
E for non-acceptance. That was the seller's proper claim, in my view, but no questions arose about the Zodiac. What had happened to it since May 6 was not investigated except that the seller had advertised it for sale unavailingly on some seven occasions between May 13 and Aug. 10, 1965. No value was placed on it at the trial. By the letter of Oct. 12 it had been offered to the buyer for £475 and he refused it.

F Throughout the trial it was assumed, as I see it, that the property had not passed to the buyer on May 6 notwithstanding the seller's solicitors' statement to the contrary. If reference had been made to the issue, which it was not, the court would have had to have regard to s. 17 and s. 18 of the Sale of Goods Act, 1893. In this court counsel for the seller stressed s. 18, r. 1, but that only applies when " a different intention " does not appear. In accordance with s. 17 (2) the
G court has to have regard in finding the intention of the parties " to the terms of the contract, the conduct of the parties, and the circumstances of the case ". The fact that the buyer after inspection agreed to buy the two vehicles on the morning of May 6, 1965, and paid £25 in cash at the time goes but little way to establishing that the parties intended the vehicles then and there to become the buyer's property. There was not even a payment by cheque. The buyer went to his bank
H to get cash and that was to be handed over to Mrs. Ward. He had not even seen the log books or inquired of their existence. No mention was made of the removal of the vehicles or of their insurance, although it is possible (no evidence was adduced) that the buyer as a dealer had some floating insurance cover.

I would hold that the property had not passed to the buyer: all that has happened since May 6, 1965, fits in with that view and is not in harmony with the
I two vehicles being transferred to the buyer when the bargain was made. The seller's remedy was rightly pursued below as damages for non-acceptance. I need not develop that further as in my view the result of this case would be the same whether or not the property had passed at the time of the sale.

As soon as the appeal was opened on behalf of the buyer against the judgment for £497 10s. counsel for the seller asked leave to amend the grounds of his cross-appeal. His contention was that the claim throughout had been for the balance of the price of the two cars bargained and sold and that the Zodiac car had been the buyer's vehicle and not the seller's since the moment of the contract of sale,

He relied on s. 48 of the Sale of Goods Act, 1893. Counsel for the seller was A
allowed to advance his argument, but I do not think that it was open to him
strictly, as it was not raised in the court below and the point of law did not arise
solely on the facts established in that court. As I have said, there was no finding,
indeed issue, whether the property had passed at the time of the agreement to
purchase. If the property did pass on May 6, the position is governed by various
sections of the 1893 Act. Neither vehicle passed into the possession of the buyer. B
The Zodiac has remained with the seller throughout and the Vanguard was sold
by it about May 22, 1965. As a binding contract has been established the seller
was an unpaid seller and by s. 39 (1) (c) had a right of resale as limited by the
Act of 1893.

Section 48 is as follows:

" (1) Subject to the provisions of this section, a contract of sale is not   C
rescinded by the mere exercise by an unpaid seller of his right of lien or retention or stoppage in transitu. (2) Where an unpaid seller who has exercised
his right of lien or retention or stoppage in transitu resells the goods, the buyer
acquires a good title thereto as against the original buyer. (3) Where the
goods are of a perishable nature, or where the unpaid seller gives notice to the
buyer of his intention to resell, and the buyer does not within a reasonable   D
time pay or tender the price, the unpaid seller may re-sell the goods and
recover from the original buyer damages for any loss occasioned by his breach
of contract. (4) Where the seller expressly reserves a right of re-sale in case
the buyer should make default and, on the buyer making default, re-sells the
goods, the original contract of sale is thereby rescinded, but without prejudice
to any claim the seller may have for damages."   E

The question on this part of the appeal is whether, if the property passed on the
sale, the Zodiac car which has not been sold remains the buyer's property so that
the action of the seller is for the price, or whether by the sale of the Vanguard the
seller has rescinded the whole contract on the buyer's breach of it so that the
ownership of the Zodiac reverted back to the seller and its remedy is in damages F
under the statute, or in effect damages for non-acceptance, giving credit for
what it has received from the sale of the goods or part thereof.

Subsection (1) and sub-s. (2) speak clearly. Subsection (4) expressly provides
" the original contract of sale is thereby rescinded ". That was necessary because
where the seller " expressly reserves a right of sale in case the buyer should make
default ", a seller who resells under such a contract would be applying and   G
affirming the contract and his action would be consistent with it. Under sub-s. (3)
no such provision of rescission is necessary, for if an unpaid seller resells he puts
it out of his power to perform his contract and his action is inconsistent with a
subsisting sale to the original buyer. Once there is a resale in accordance with
s. 48 by an unpaid seller in possession of the contractual goods the contract of sale
is rescinded, whether the sale be of the whole of the goods or a part, and in this   H
respect sub-s. (3) and sub-s. (4) fall into line. As the property in the goods reverts
on such a resale, the seller retains the proceeds of sale whether they be greater or
less than the contractual price. The probability in normal trade is that the
price would be less and give rise to a claim for damages, as for non-acceptance of
the goods.

This was the view taken in BENJAMIN ON SALE (7th Edn.), edited by JUDGE   I
KENNEDY, K.C., and 29 HALSBURY'S LAWS OF ENGLAND (2nd Edn.), p. 185,
para. 249, (1) which states:

" When the buyer, by his words or conduct, repudiates the contract, the
seller, even where the property has passed, is entitled to treat the contract
of sale as rescinded, and to re-sell the goods as an owner thereof, but without
prejudice to his right to damages in respect of any loss caused to him by the
buyer's default."

(1) See also 34 HALSBURY'S LAWS (3rd Edn.) 141, 142, para. 235.

A   Since those editions, Finnemore, J., has interpreted s. 48 (3) in *Gallagher* v.
Shilcock (2). He held that, having regard to the express provision for rescission
in s. 48 (4), where the right of resale has been reserved in the contract of sale, the
true construction of sub-s. (3) is that, where an unpaid seller, in the absence of
such a reservation, exercises his right of resale under sub-s. (3), that exercise
does not operate to rescind the contract, for the seller, in so acting, is affirming
B   the contract and ensuring that he receives the contract price.

   With every respect to that learned and very experienced judge, I think that
the construction works the other way round. The express reservation in a
contract would permit the unpaid seller to sell without acting inconsistently or in
conflict with his obligations. His conduct would not evidence a rescission by him
on the buyer's breach. Nevertheless sub-s. (4) makes the resale operate as a
C   rescission and leaves the remedy, if any loss ensues, in damages. This brings it
into harmony with sub-s. (3), which also gives a claim for damages for any loss
occasioned by the original buyer's breach of contract. If the unpaid seller resells
the goods he puts it out of his power to perform his obligation under the original
contract, that is, to deliver the contractual goods to the buyer. By the notice to
the buyer the seller makes payment of the price " the essence of the contract ",
D   as it is sometimes put. It requires the buyer to pay the price or tender it within
a reasonable time. If he fails, the seller in possession of the goods may treat the
bargain as rescinded and sell the goods. The suit for damages becomes comparable
to a claim for damages for non-acceptance of the goods where the property never
has passed. The property has reverted on the sale and the second buyer gets a
good title. The seller resells as owner. Subsection (2) expressly gives the buyer a
E   good title thereto as against the original buyer.

   On this view of the law the seller cannot recover the price of the Zodiac, which
is in the circumstances its property. It can however recover any loss which it has
sustained by the buyer's default. The parties have sensibly agreed that the value
of the Zodiac in May, 1965, was £450. The total contract price was £850, against
which the seller has received £25 in cash, £350 for the Vanguard, and has to give
F   credit for £450 for the Zodiac. To the loss of £25 must be added the sum for
advertising, which was admittedly reasonably incurred—£22 10s. The seller's
loss was therefore £47 10s.

   I would allow the appeal and enter judgment for £47 10s. in favour of the
seller in substitution for the award of the deputy judge.

G   DIPLOCK, L.J., read the following judgment: This is an appeal from a
judgment of the deputy county court judge at Woolwich county court in what
appeared to be a simple action for damages for non-acceptance of goods. The
appeal is as to quantum of damages only. Sellers, L.J., has already stated the
facts. The main issue in the action was whether it was a term of the contract
that the Vanguard should be a 1962 model. The judge held that it was not, and
H   there is no appeal from this decision. The legal consequence of this finding was
that the buyer's refusal to go on with the contract was a wrongful repudiation of
the contract. The seller could elect to treat that as rescinding the contract, giving
him an immediate right to damages for non-acceptance. Alternatively he could
hold the buyer to the contract. This he chose to do, and communicated his
intention to the buyer both orally and by a letter written by his solicitors on
I   May 6 which Sellers, L.J., has already read. That letter states the opinion of
the seller's solicitors, that the property had passed to the buyer. It was no doubt
based on s. 18, r. 1 of the Sale of Goods Act, 1893; but the governing rule is in
s. 17, and in modern times very little is needed to give rise to the inference that
the property in specific goods is to pass only on delivery or payment. I think
that I should have inferred that in this case: but I do not find it necessary to form
any final conclusion on this matter, on which the judge made no finding.

Whether or not the property had passed on May 6, 1965, the seller was only **A** liable to deliver on payment or tender of the balance of the purchase price (see the Sale of Goods Act, 1893, s. 28) and was entitled until then to retain possession, either by virtue of his lien as an unpaid seller if the property had passed (Sale of Goods Act, 1893, s. 39 (1)), or by virtue of his right to withhold delivery if the property had not passed (sub-s. (2) of the same section). In either case the unpaid seller has a right to resell the goods if he gives notice of his intention to do so and **B** the buyer does not within a reasonable time pay or tender the price (Sale of Goods Act, 1893, s. 48 (3)). The note in the current edition of CHALMERS (3) that the right of resale only arises where the seller exercises his right of lien or stoppage in transitu, that is, where the property has passed to the buyer, is in my view wrong. This subsection enables a seller in possession of the goods to make time of payment of the purchase price of the essence of the contract whether the **C** property has passed or not. The seller cannot have greater rights of resale if the property has already passed to the buyer than those which he would have if the property had remained in him.

The letter of May 6 contained notice to resell on or after May 11. Whether this was a reasonable time or not does not matter. The buyer never tendered the price, and on or before May 24 the seller resold the Vanguard for £350. He **D** advertised the Zodiac for sale, but failed to find a buyer at the advertised price, and on Oct. 12, 1965, offered to deliver it to the buyer against payment of £475, being the balance of the original purchase price of £850 for the two cars less the deposit of £25 and the £350 received on resale of the Vanguard car. The letter of Oct. 12, 1965, in which this offer was made expressed the intention of the seller to institute proceedings against the buyer for the sum of £475 " as the **E** balance of money due and payable . . . for goods bargained and sold "; but when the writ was issued on Feb. 9, 1966, the cause of action was not framed as an action for the balance of the purchase price under s. 49 (1) of the Sale of Goods Act, 1893, but as an action for damages for non-acceptance under s. 50 (1), although the particulars of damage were inappropriate to an action for damages for non-acceptance. In the particulars of damage in the statement of claim credit **F** was given, against the balance of the purchase price of £825, for the sum of £350 for which the Vanguard had been sold, but no credit was given for the market price of the Zodiac.

At the trial neither party, nor the judge, seems to have given his mind to the question of where the property in the Zodiac lay by that date. The only argument as to the quantum of damages was based on the contention that the seller ought **G** to have mitigated his damages by accepting the buyer's offer to purchase the Zodiac alone for £500 on May 6, 1965. This contention was ill-founded. At the date of that offer the contract of sale of the two cars was still in being. The offer to buy the Zodiac alone was a proposal by the buyer to rescind that contract by mutual consent coupled with an offer to enter into a fresh contract of sale of the Zodiac alone. The seller, as he was entitled to do, refused to rescind the existing **H** contract of sale at that date, and no question of mitigating his damages then arose. The deputy county court judge appears to have tacitly accepted the view that the seller was under a duty to mitigate his damage as soon as the buyer wrongfully repudiated the contract but that his rejection of the buyer's offer of £500 for the Zodiac was not a breach of that duty, as the seller was entitled to test the market before accepting any offer to buy either or both of the cars. The judge **I** awarded the seller the damages which he claimed and made no allowance for the value of the Zodiac, which the seller still retains.

If the seller, at the date of the issue of the writ, had been in a position to bring an action for the balance of the purchase price and had done so, the measure of damages awarded by the deputy county court judge would have been correct and the seller would have been entitled to retain possession of the Zodiac, by

---

(3) 14 Edn. (1963), p. 143.

A virtue of his unpaid seller's lien until the judgment was satisfied (Sale of Goods Act, 1893, s. 43 (2)). If, however, he were only in a position to claim damages for non-acceptance, which was what he did, the prima facie measure of his damages would be the difference between the contract price and the market price of the two cars (Sale of Goods Act, 1893, s. 50 (1) and (3)) and any reasonable costs, such as those of advertising, incurred by him in reselling the cars. The onus of

B proving the market price of both cars lay on the seller. The evidence of the sale of the Vanguard at £350 on May 24, 1965, was evidence of the market price of the Vanguard. Evidence of the price at which he had advertised the Zodiac but failed to sell it was some evidence that its market price was less than those figures, which ranged from £490 on May 25, 1965, to £450 on July 1, 1965. The lowest figure at which it was offered was however rather late in date, and in order to

C avoid any necessity for a new trial the parties have very sensibly agreed on a figure of £450 as the market price of the Zodiac at about the end of May, 1965. If, therefore, the seller's only right at the date of the issue of the writ on Feb. 9, 1966, was for damages for non-acceptance, the appeal must be allowed and the damages awarded reduced by £450 from £497 10s. to £47 10s.

In this court it has been contended on behalf of the seller that when an unpaid

D seller who retains possession of goods the property in which has passed to the buyer exercises his statutory right of resale under s. 48 (3) of the Sale of Goods Act, 1893, he does not thereby elect to treat the contract as rescinded, but remains entitled to recover the purchase price from the buyer although he must give credit for the net proceeds of sale of any of the goods which he has sold. Authority for this proposition is to be found in the judgment of FINNEMORE, J., in *Gallagher*

E *v. Shilcock* (4), and the question in this appeal is whether that judgment is right or not.

FINNEMORE, J., based his conclusion on his view as to the construction of s. 48 of the Sale of Goods Act, 1893, and in particular on the contrast between the express reference in s. 48 (4) to the contract's being rescinded when goods are resold under an express right of resale and the absence of any reference to rescis-

F sion in s. 48 (3); but with great respect I think that this disregards basic principles of the law of contract and that there is another explanation for the contrast between the two subsections.

Rescission of a contract discharges both parties from any further liability to perform their respective primary obligations under the contract, that is to say to do thereafter those things which by their contract they had stipulated that they

G would do. Where rescission occurs as a result of one party's exercising his right to treat a breach by the other party of a stipulation in the contract as a repudiation of the contract, this gives rise to a secondary obligation of the party in breach to compensate the other party for the loss occasioned to him as a consequence of the rescission, and this secondary obligation is enforceable in an action for damages; but until there is rescission by acceptance of the repudiation the

H liability of both parties to perform their primary obligations under the contract continues. Thus, under a contract for the sale of goods which has not been rescinded the seller remains liable to transfer the property in the goods to the buyer and to deliver possession of them to him until he has discharged these obligations by performing them, and the buyer remains correspondingly liable to pay for the goods and to accept possession of them.

I The election by a party not in default to exercise his right of rescission by treating the contract as repudiated may be evinced by words or by conduct. Any act which puts it out of his power to perform thereafter his primary obligations under the contract, if it is an act which he is entitled to do without notice to the party in default, must amount to an election to rescind the contract. If it is an act which he is not entitled to do, it will amount to a wrongful repudiation of the contract on his part which the other party can in turn elect to treat as rescinding the contract.

(4) [1949] 1 All E.R. 921; [1949] 2 K.B. 765.

Part 4 of the Sale of Goods Act, 1893, s. 38 to s. 48, deals with the rights of an A
unpaid seller both before the property in the goods has passed to the buyer and
after it has passed. The mere fact that a seller is unpaid does not necessarily
mean that the buyer is in breach of the contract or, if he is, that his breach is one
which entitles the seller to exercise his right of treating the contract as repudiated.
Section 39 (1) and (2) state what the unpaid seller's rights are in relation to the
possession of the goods before and after the property has passed to the buyer. B
Subsection (1) para. (c) provides that he shall have " a right of resale as limited
by this Act ". Section 41 to s. 47 deal in greater detail with the exercise by the
unpaid seller of his rights in relation to the possession of the goods after the
property has passed to the buyer. Section 48 deals with several topics. Subsection
(1) reads as follows:

> " Subject to the provisions of this section, a contract of sale is not   C
> rescinded by the mere exercise by an unpaid seller of his right of lien or
> retention or stoppage in transitu."

If the contract provided for delivery on a specified date, the seller's conduct in
failing to deliver on that date would put it out of his power to perform one of his
primary obligations under the contract if time were of the essence of the contract.
It was therefore necessary, or at least prudent, to provide expressly that if his D
failure to deliver were in the mere exercise of a lien or right of stoppage in transitu
it did not discharge the seller's liability to deliver the goods on tender of the contract price or the buyer's liability to accept the goods and to pay for them.

Subsection (2) deals with a different topic, videlicet the title of a new buyer to
whom the goods are resold by the seller. If the property in the goods at the time
of the resale remained in the seller, the new buyer would obtain a good title at   E
common law and would require no statutory protection. The subsection is
therefore limited to cases where the property in the goods at the time of resale
had already passed to the original buyer and provides that where the seller is in
possession of the goods in the exercise of his unpaid seller's lien or right of
stoppage in transitu the new buyer shall acquire a good title, and this is so
whether or not the seller had a right of resale as against the original buyer.   F
Subsection (3) reads as follows:

> " Where the goods are of a perishable nature, or where the unpaid seller
> gives notice to the buyer of his intention to re-sell, and the buyer does not
> within a reasonable time pay or tender the price, the unpaid seller may
> re-sell the goods and recover from the original buyer damages for any loss   G
> occasioned by his breach of contract."

This is the provision of the Act of 1893 which confers " a right of resale as limited
by this Act ", referred to in s. 39 (1) (c). The right dealt with in this subsection
is a right as against the original buyer. As a stipulation as to time of payment is
not deemed to be of the essence of a contract of sale unless a different intention
appears from the terms of the contract (Sale of Goods Act, 1893, s. 10 (1)), failure H
by the buyer to pay on the stipulated date is not conduct by him which entitles
the unpaid seller to treat the contract as repudiated. He remains liable to deliver
the goods to the buyer on tender of the contract price (Sale of Goods Act, 1893,
s. 28). Apart from this subsection, if the unpaid seller resold the goods before or
after the property had passed to the original buyer he would remain liable to the
original buyer for damages for non-delivery if the original buyer tendered the I
purchase price after the resale, and if the property had already passed to the
original buyer at the time of the resale he would be liable to an alternative action
by the original buyer for damages for conversion. The purpose of the subsection
is to make time of payment of the essence of the contract whenever the goods
are of a perishable nature, and to enable an unpaid seller, whatever the nature
of the goods, to make payment, within a reasonable time after notice, of the
essence of the contract. As already pointed out, an unpaid seller who resells the
goods before the property has passed puts it out of his power to perform his

A primary obligation to the buyer to transfer the property in the goods to the buyer and, whether or not the property has already passed, to deliver up possession of the goods to the buyer. By making the act of resale one which the unpaid seller is entitled to do, the subsection empowers the seller by his conduct in doing that act to exercise his right to treat the contract as repudiated by the buyer—that is, as rescinded: with the consequence that the buyer is discharged from any

B further liability to perform his primary obligation to pay the purchase price and becomes subject to the secondary obligation to pay damages for non-acceptance of the goods. If the contract were not rescinded by the resale, the seller would still be entitled to bring an action against the buyer for the price of the goods, although no doubt he would have to credit the buyer with the proceeds of the resale. If this were the intention of the subsection, one would have expected it

C to provide this in express terms. That it was not the intention is, however, apparent from the words used to define the remedy of the unpaid seller who has exercised his right of resale, videlicet to " recover from the original buyer damages for any loss occasioned by his breach of contract ". It is, of course, well established that where a contract for the sale of goods is rescinded after the property in the goods has passed to the buyer the rescission divests the buyer of

D his property in the goods.

Subsection (4) deals with the consequences of a resale by a seller, not necessarily an " unpaid seller " as defined in s. 38, made in the exercise of an express right of resale reserved in the contract on the buyer making default. If such an express right was exercisable after the property in the goods had passed to the buyer, its exercise might in one view be regarded as an alternative mode of

E performance of the seller's primary obligations under the contract and the resale as being made by the seller as agent for the buyer. It was therefore necessary to provide expressly that the exercise of an express power of resale should rescind the original contract of sale. That is in my view the explanation of the express reference to rescission in sub-s. (4). The absence of a similar express reference to rescission in sub-s. (3) is no sufficient ground for ascribing to sub-s. (3) a meaning

F which the actual words of the subsection would appear to contradict and which would in my view conflict with the general principles of the law of contract.

In the present case the unpaid seller resold only part of the goods which he had contracted to sell to the original buyer. This makes no difference. His primary duty under the contract was to deliver both cars to the buyer. If he delivered only one, the buyer would be entitled to reject it (Sale of Goods Act, 1893, s. 30

G (1)). By his conduct in selling the Vanguard on May 24, 1965, the unpaid seller put it out of his power to perform his primary obligation under the contract. He thereby elected to treat the contract as rescinded. The property in the Zodiac thereupon reverted to him, and his only remedy against the buyer after May 24, 1965, was for damages for non-acceptance of the two cars, of which the prima facie measure is the difference between the contract price and their market value

H on May 24, 1965.

I, too, would allow this appeal and enter judgment for the seller for £47 10s. instead of £497 10s.

RUSSELL, L.J.: I agree.

Appeal allowed. Judgment for seller for £47 10s.

I Solicitors: *Dollman & Pritchard*, agents for *Dehn, Lauderdale & Weedon*, Welling, Kent (for the buyer); *S. R. Carter* (for the seller).

[*Reported by* HENRY SUMMERFIELD, ESQ. *Barrister-at-Law.*]

A

Re SEAFORD (*deceased*).   SEAFORD *v.* SEIFERT.

[PROBATE, DIVORCE AND ADMIRALTY DIVISION (Cairns, J.), March 13, 14, 20, 1967.]

Divorce—Decree absolute—Judicial act—Application for decree and the filing of the application were one transaction—Decree relating back to beginning of day on which it was made—Matrimonial Causes Rules, 1957 (S.I. 1957 No. 619), r. 40 (1), (2).

B

Intestacy—Grant of administration—Wife's notice of application for decree nisi to be made absolute received and filed on day deceased husband found dead— Deceased dying during night before application received by registrar—Burden of proof on wife to show marriage subsisting at time of deceased's death.

C

In March, 1965, a decree nisi of divorce was granted to the plaintiff and in June, 1965, an appeal by the deceased (the plaintiff's husband) was dismissed. Some time after 5.15 p.m. on July 5, 1965, the plaintiff's solicitors posted an application to the district registry for the decree to be made absolute. Some time after about 9.0 p.m. on July 5, 1965, the deceased took an over-dose of drugs.   The letter containing the notice of application for decree absolute was delivered at 8.30 a.m. on July 6, 1965, and at 10.0 a.m. the district registrar filed the notice and endorsed the court minutes with a note that the decree had been made absolute at that time, and a certificate of decree absolute was issued.   Between 11.30 and 11.45 a.m. on the same morning, the deceased was found dead in bed.   On Jan. 21, 1966, the district registrar, having been notified by the plaintiff's solicitors that the divorce suit had abated by reason of the deceased's death on the night of July 5/6, 1965, endorsed on the certificate of decree absolute the words " ineffective, suit abated by reason of death of [deceased] before filing ". The trial judge found as a fact that the deceased died between 9.0 p.m. on July 5, 1965, and 4.0 a.m. on July 6, 1965.   An application by the plaintiff, the deceased having died intestate, for a grant of letters of administration of his estate was opposed by the defendant, the deceased's mother, on the ground that she was the only person entitled to the estate, the marriage having been dissolved before the deceased died.

D

E

F

Held: the plaintiff was not entitled to letters of administration (see p. 476, letter G, post) because—

(i) the onus was on the plaintiff to establish that the deceased died before the decree absolute took effect, viz., if the doctrine of relation back of the judicial act of making the decree applied, before midnight on July 5/6, 1965, and, on the evidence, the plaintiff failed to discharge this onus (see p. 460, letter I, to p. 461, letter A, and p. 461, letters G and I, post); and

G

(ii) the lodgment of the application for decree absolute and its filing (which under r. 40 (1), (2) of the Matrimonial Causes Rules, 1957, made the decree absolute) were to be treated as a single transaction, the filing being a judicial act, and the transaction could not be split into a non-judicial part, the application, and a judicial part, the filing; accordingly the doctrine of the relation back of a judicial act to the beginning of the day on which it was done (not, in this instance, to the time when the application was delivered at the court office) applied, and the registrar had jurisdiction to file the application on that day and by so doing made the decree absolute with effect from the beginning of that day (see p. 466, letter H, to p. 467, letter A, and p. 467, letter C, post).

H

I

Wright v. *Mills* ([1843-60] All E.R. Rep. 842) and *Kruhlak* v. *Kruhlak* (*No. 2*) ([1958] 2 All E.R. 294) applied.

Dictum of LORD COLERIDGE, C.J., in *Taunton Case, Marshall* v. *James* ((1874), L.R. 9 C.P. at p. 712) explained.

A   [As to the time when judicial acts are taken to be done, see 37 HALSBURY'S
LAWS (3rd Edn.) 102, para. 180; and for cases on the subject, see 45 DIGEST
(Repl.) 271, 272, *404-411.*

As to the effect of divorce on the death intestate of one party to the marriage,
see 16 HALSBURY'S LAWS (3rd Edn.) 399, para. 769.

For the Matrimonial Causes Rules, 1957, r. 40, see 10 HALSBURY'S STATUTORY
B INSTRUMENTS (Second Re-issue) 250.]

Cases referred to:
   B. v. B., [1961] 2 All E.R. 396; [1961] 1 W.L.R. 856; Digest (Cont. Vol. A)
      812, *6597a.*
   Clarke v. *Bradlaugh*, [1881-85] All E.R. Rep. 1002; (1881), 8 Q.B.D. 63;
C   51 L.J.Q.B. 1; 46 L.T. 49; 46 J.P. 278; 45 Digest (Repl.) 272, *411.*
   Edwards v. *Reginam*, (1854), 9 Exch. 628; 23 L.J.Ex. 165; 23 L.T.O.S. 39;
      156 E.R. 268; 45 Digest (Repl.) 271, *403.*
   Gatty (F. A.) and Gatty (P. V.) v. *A.-G.*, [1951] P. 444; 3 Digest (Repl.) 399, *12.*
   Hodgson v. *Armstrong*, [1967] 1 All E.R. 307; [1967] 2 W.L.R. 311.
   Kruhlak v. *Kruklak (No. 2)*, [1958] 2 All E.R. 294; [1958] 1 W.L.R. 606;
D   122 J.P. 360; 45 Digest (Repl.) 272, *409.*
   Lyttleton v. *Cross*, (1824), 3 B. & C. 317; 3 L.J.O.S.K.B. 2; 107 E.R. 751; 23
      Digest (Repl.) 369, *4390.*
   MacDarmaid v. *A.-G.*, [1950] 1 All E.R. 497; [1950] P. 218; 22 Digest (Repl.)
      158, *1436.*
   Porchester (Lord) v. *Petrie*, (1783), 3 Doug. K.B. 261; 99 E.R. 644; 45
E   Digest (Repl.) 271, *404.*
   R. v. *Willshire*, (1881), 6 Q.B.D. 366; 50 L.J.M.C. 57; 44 L.T. 222; 45 J.P.
      375; 15 Digest (Repl.) 885, *8538.*
   Ramsden v. *Ramsden*, (1953), unreported.
   Shelley's Case, (1581), 1 Co. Rep. 93b; Moore K.B. 136; 72 E.R. 490; 45
F   Digest (Repl.) 269, *360.*
   Stanhope v. *Stanhope*, (1886), 11 P.D. 103; 55 L.J.P. 36; 54 L.T. 906; 50 J.P.
      276; 27 Digest (Repl.) 535, *4818.*
   Swann v. *Broome*, (1764), 3 Burr. 1595; 97 E.R. 999; *affd.* H.L., sub nom.
      Broome v. *Swan*, (1766), 6 Bro. Parl. Cas. 333; 2 E.R. 1115; 45 Digest
      (Repl.) 247, *149.*
   Tabernacle Permanent Building Society v. *Knight*, [1892] A.C. 298; 62 L.J.Q.B.
G   50; 67 L.T. 483; 45 Digest (Repl.) 271, *399.*
   Taunton Case, Marshall v. *James*, (1874), L.R. 9 C.P. 702; 43 L.J.C.P. 281;
      30 L.T. 559; 38 J.P. 487; 20 Digest (Repl.) 179, *1556.*
   Warren, Re, Wheeler v. *Mills*, [1938] 2 All E.R. 331; [1938] Ch. 725; 107
      L.J.Ch. 409; 159 L.T. 17; 45 Digest (Repl.) 272, *412.*
   Wiseman v. *Wiseman*, [1953] 1 All E.R. 601; [1953] P. 79; [1953] 2 W.L.R.
H   499; Digest (Cont. Vol. A) 780, *5547a.*
   Wolfenden v. *Wolfenden*, [1947] 2 All E.R. 653; [1948] P. 27; [1948] L.J.R.
      622; 27 Digest (Repl.) 686, *6564.*
   Wright v. *Mills*, [1843-60] All E.R. Rep. 842; (1859), 4 H. & N. 488; 28
      L.J.Ex. 223; 33 L.T.O.S. 152; 157 E.R. 931; 45 Digest (Repl.) 272,
      408.
I
Application.

This was an application by the plaintiff, who was the wife of the deceased
and who claimed to be his widow, for a grant of letters of administration of the
deceased's estate. The facts are set out in the judgment.

D. J. M. Campion for the plaintiff.
J. C. Mortimer, Q.C.. for the defendant.

                                                    Cur. adv. vult.

Mar. 20. **CAIRNS, J.,** read the following judgment: John Seaford died A intestate between about 9.0 p.m. in the evening of July 5, 1965, and about 11.30 a.m. the next morning. The plaintiff was his wife and claims to be his widow, and accordingly claims a grant of letters of administration of his estate. The defendant is the mother of the deceased, and contends that his marriage to the plaintiff was dissolved before he died and claims a grant as his next of kin and the only person entitled to his estate. The only issue before me is whether B the marriage had been dissolved, or must be deemed to have been dissolved, before the deceased died.

The facts, so far as they are known, are all agreed and are as follows. The deceased was born on July 18, 1926, a German national. He came to England in 1936, and in 1947, immediately after he came of age, he became a naturalised British subject. He acquired an English domicil of choice which he never lost. C On Nov. 23, 1959, he married the plaintiff. They had no children. About 1964 he went to Scotland in the course of his employment by the United Kingdom Atomic Energy Authority. He resided thereafter at a hostel at or near Thurso. The plaintiff petitioned for divorce on the ground of the deceased's cruelty, and on Mar. 3, 1965, a decree nisi was pronounced in her favour. The deceased appealed, and on June 30, 1965, his appeal was dismissed. Some time after D 5.15 p.m. on July 5, 1965, the plaintiff's solicitors posted to the district registry at Bournemouth, where the suit was proceeding, an application for the decree to be made absolute. The deceased was alive at 9.0 p.m. on July 5. Some time during the night or in the early morning, in his bedroom at the hostel, he took an overdose of sodium amytal tablets, as a result of which he died. At 8.30 a.m. on July 6, 1965, the plaintiff's solicitors' letter containing the notice of application E for decree absolute was delivered at the district registry. At 10.0 a.m. the district registrar filed the notice and endorsed the court minutes with a note that the decree had been made absolute at that time. The same day a certificate of decree absolute was issued. Between 11.30 and 11.45 a.m. the same morning, the deceased was found dead in bed. His body was examined by two doctors, Dr. Deans and Dr. Hill, at noon. The body was cold. There was generalised F rigor mortis and fully established hypostasis. On Jan. 20, 1966, the plaintiff's solicitors gave notice to the district registrar that the divorce suit had abated " by reason of the death of the [deceased] on the night of July 5/6, 1965 ". On Jan. 21, 1966, the district registrar endorsed on the certificate of decree absolute the words " ineffective, suit abated by reason of death of [deceased] before filing " and added his signature. A similar note was placed on the court minutes. G

What is not known is the exact time of the deceased's death, and there is an issue as to the inference which ought to be drawn from the evidence of the doctors, both of whom were called for the plaintiff. Their evidence was substantially to the same effect, and was uncontradicted. They were excellent witnesses, and I accept what they told me without reservation. This makes it unnecessary for me to go through the details of their evidence. The opinions they expressed H were to the following effect. At noon on July 6, 1965, the deceased had been dead for at least six hours. Probably he had been dead for considerably longer than this. One doctor thought that it would have taken between eight and ten hours for his body to reach the condition in which it was found, and the other doctor put the period at between eight and twelve hours. Both agreed that he might have been dead for as long as twenty-four hours. At this stage I make I the finding of fact that the deceased died between 9.0 p.m. on July 5 and 4.0 a.m. on July 6, 1965. Whether it can be found that the deceased died before or after midnight must at the best depend on a very slender balance of probabilities. For the defendant, it is contended that it is impossible to decide and, therefore, the matter must depend on who has the onus of proof.

The reason why it is important to determine, if possible, whether the death occurred before or after midnight is this. The making absolute of a decree of divorce has been held to be a judicial act. There is an ancient rule of law that a judicial

A act generally relates back to the beginning of the day on which it was performed. If the deceased died on July 5, he unquestionably died before the marriage was dissolved, but if he died between midnight and 4.0 a.m. on July 6, and if the decree absolute relates back to the first moment of July 6, then the marriage must be deemed to have been dissolved before he died. In seeking to fix the time of death I am reluctant to fall back on the onus of proof unless compelled to.

B It is always a last resort and there are special difficulties about it in this case. Each side is claiming the right to administration; each is setting up an affirmative case. To say that the onus is on the plaintiff to establish her claim and that the onus is on the defendant to establish her counter-claim might lead to the absurd result that both failed—and I suppose that the estate would then be bona vacantia.

C Counsel for the defendant says that the plaintiff has to show affirmatively that she was the wife of the deceased at the time of his death. If she fails to prove this, then she loses and it must follow that the defendant is entitled to administration, because her relationship to the deceased is admitted. Counsel for the plaintiff says that, wherever the onus of proof might lie initially, he has established a prima facie case by producing the registrar's minute in the words

D " ineffective; suit abated by reason of death of [deceased] before filing ". This endorsement was made in pursuance of a registrar's direction of Oct. 12, 1953: see RAYDEN ON DIVORCE (10th Edn.). p. 891. And counsel for the plaintiff, relying on the maxim omnia praesumuntur rite esse acta, argues that the note affords him some evidence that death took place before the decree absolute took effect—which, if the doctrine of relation back applies, means that it took place

E before midnight.

No case has been cited which constitutes any direct authority on where the onus lies. In *R.* v. *Willshire* (1) LORD COLERIDGE, C.J., said of the defendant in a bigamy case,

" He thus set up the evidence of a life in 1868, which, in the absence of evidence to the contrary will be presumed to have continued to 1879."

F He was the only member of a court of five judges to enunciate this proposition, and in *MacDarmaid* v. *A.-G.* (2) HODSON, J., held that there was no presumption as to the continuance of life. In *F. A. Gatty and P. V. Gatty* v. *A.-G.* (3), KARMINSKI, J., held that, once a valid marriage was proved, it was for him who asserted that it had been dissolved to prove a valid decree. In that case, how-ever, there was no dispute that both parties to the marriage were alive at the

G time of the alleged divorce. In the absence of any clear authority, I have reached the conclusion that the onus is on the plaintiff. In coming to this decision I have considered what the position would be if the time schedule were much longer. Suppose a husband treated his wife with cruelty and then left her. For three years she hears nothing of him. Then she starts a divorce suit for cruelty and gets an order for service by advertisement. The husband never

H appears. The wife gets her decree and has it made absolute. Three years later the husband's body is found in a state of decay but nobody can say whether he has been dead six months or six years. If the wife were then to allege that she was his widow, I think that the onus would clearly be on her to establish that he had died before decree absolute. In essence, I do not consider that the problem is any different where the events took place within a few hours instead

I of being spread over several years.

If, then, the plaintiff fails to discharge the onus on her to show that she was still married to the deceased at the time of his death, I think that it follows not only that she is not entitled to administration but that she cannot effectively answer the defendant's claim. I accept the argument of counsel for the defen-dant that, if the plaintiff is unable to establish her entitlement, the defendant

(1) (1881), 6 Q.B.D. 366 at p. 369.
(2) [1950] 1 All E.R. 497; [1950] P. 218.
(3) [1951] P. 444 pp. 452, 453.

succeeds because her relationship to the deceased is conceded and there is no A
other claimant. I do not accept the argument of counsel for the plaintiff,
based on the registrar's note of Jan. 21, 1966. I do not see why greater weight
should be attached to this note than to the certificate of decree absolute. Moreover, the terms of the note, even if they can be said to constitute evidence of
death before the filing of the application for decree absolute, cannot, except by a
very strained construction, be taken to certify that death occurred before mid- B
night. Is there any other evidence which would enable me to say that the
plaintiff has discharged the onus of proof? I have anxiously considered the
evidence of the doctors and the surrounding circumstances. The strongest
medical evidence in favour of death before midnight is that of Dr. Deans who said
at the end of his evidence that covered parts of the body would feel cool, as he
found them, only after about twelve hours, and that rigor mortis would usually C
take about twelve hours to establish. On the other hand, Dr. Hill said that the
room was very warm and that this would tend to accelerate the establishment of
rigor. The evidence tends to support a time of death near or before midnight,
but I do not feel able to say that it shows that death is more likely than not to
have occurred before midnight. I have also considered whether it could be
said that a man who felt driven to take a fatal dose of sleeping tablets would be D
more likely to do it on retiring to bed than at some time during the night; but
I have decided that this is much too speculative. He may well have spent some
hours in or out of bed wrestling with whatever problems he may have had before
finally deciding to take his own life.

I am, therefore, of opinion that the plaintiff's case must fail and that the
defendant's must succeed unless I am to hold as a matter of law that, even if the E
deceased died in the early hours of July 6, 1965, the marriage was not dissolved.
This depends on whether or not this decree absolute relates back to the earliest
moment of July 6. This is a question of great difficulty, and much learning
and ingenuity has been devoted to it by counsel. The most recent and most
direct authority is *Kruhlak* v. *Kruhlak* (*No. 2*) (4). The headnote reads as
follows: F

" A married woman separated from her husband gave birth to an illegitimate child at 7.30 a.m. At 10 a.m. the same day a decree nisi of divorce
dissolving her marriage was made absolute. The father of the child was
at the time free to marry the mother, and subsequently did so. On an
application by the mother, who had meanwhile obtained a separation order
against the father, for an affiliation order in respect of the child as being a G
bastard child within s. 3 of the Bastardy Laws Amendment Act, 1872, Held:
the decree absolute, being a judicial act, dated from the earliest time of the
day on which it was made, and the child was accordingly legitimated under
s. 1 of the Legitimacy Act, 1926, by the subsequent marriage of the child's
parents; therefore, the application failed ",
                                                                                H
and the appeal to a Divisional Court of the Queen's Bench Division consisting of
LORD GODDARD, C.J., CASSELS and DIPLOCK, JJ., was dismissed. The first
judgment was given by DIPLOCK, J., and is quite short. It reads as follows (5):

" The applicant, the mother, gave birth to a girl named Joan on Dec. 2,
1953, at 7.30 a.m. On the same day a decree absolute was made in favour
of the mother's former husband from whom she had been living separate. I
The father of the child was the respondent to the summons, and they were
married on Dec. 19, 1953; that is to say, seventeen days after the birth of
the child. In the present proceedings the mother took out a summons under
the Bastardy Laws Amendment Act, 1872, s. 3, as amended, against the
father. The magistrates dismissed that summons on the ground that the
child in respect of whom the application was made was a legitimate child.

(4) [1958] 2 All E.R. 294.
(5) [1958] 2 All E.R. at p. 296.

A   They relied on the rule that where a judicial act takes place, such as the granting of a decree absolute, it dates from the earliest time of the day on which it was made; therefore, the mother and her former husband were divorced before the birth of the child at 7.30 on that day. The child is accordingly a legitimate child of the marriage of Dec. 19, 1953, by virtue of s. 1 of the Legitimacy Act, 1926. This appeal is therefore dismissed."

B   LORD GODDARD, C.J., and CASSELS, J., agreed without adding anything of relevance to my present problem. I think that this authority is binding on me, and counsel for the plaintiff has not sought to suggest the contrary. The case does not seem to have been fully argued. No authorities appear to have been cited in the Divisional Court and, indeed, the appellant's counsel made it clear that his client would prefer to lose the appeal if she could. No case has been

C   cited, however, which casts doubt on the continuing validity of the rule that a judicial act relates back to the beginning of the day, nor any case which suggests that the filing of a notice of application for decree absolute is anything other than a judicial act. I do not, therefore, consider that it is open to me to question the rightness of the decision in *Kruhlak* v. *Kruhlak* (*No. 2*) (6).

D   Counsel for the plaintiff argues, however, that *Kruhlak's* case (6) can be distinguished on two grounds. First, there was no doubt in that case that the registrar had jurisdiction to make the decree absolute; here it is said that the registrar was deprived of jurisdiction by the death. Secondly, it does not appear from the report of *Kruhlak's* case (6) when the application for decree absolute was lodged. So, said counsel, it might be assumed that it was lodged before

E   the day of filing. If that was so, there was no circumstance which stood in the way of relating back the decree absolute to the beginning of the day of filing. I am now able to say, although it was not known when I heard the argument of counsel, that the application for decree absolute in the divorce suit to which reference was made in *Kruhlak's* case (6) was lodged on the day before filing. The discovery of this fact has involved considerable research on the part of the central registry and the co-operation of the Leeds district registry, because the

F   name of Mrs. Kruhlak before she married for the second time does not appear in either of the reports of the case. I am very grateful for the trouble which has been taken and which has enabled me to see the divorce file. The name of the suit was *Ramsden* v. *Ramsden* (7), and the application for decree absolute which is on the file was stamped by the district registrar with the words " Fee paid Dec. 1, 1953 ", and then there is another stamp worded " Filed Dec. 2,

G   1953, 10 a.m." So counsel for the plaintiff puts his argument in these two ways. (i) The court can always inquire at what time a non-judicial act was done and there is no relating back of a non-judicial act. Lodging the notice is a non-judicial act. The registrar had no jurisdiction to make the decree absolute until after the lodgment. The notice of application was lodged after the death and, therefore, the registrar had no jurisdiction to entertain it. (ii) The true rule is

H   that a judicial act relates back to the earliest moment of the day on which it could have been done. The earliest moment at which a decree can be made absolute is the time of lodgment of the notice of application; therefore, this decree absolute could only relate back to 8.30 a.m. and it could be no more effective then than at 10.0 a.m. because the deceased was already dead.

I   Before discussing these arguments, it is desirable to trace the origin of the rule about relation back, to see the grounds on which it has been put and to examine certain qualifications to which it may be subject. The old rule was that a judgment was deemed to have been given on the first day of the term in which it was signed or, when signed in vacation, on the first day of the previous term: see TIDD'S PRACTICE (1828, Vol. 2), p. 935. The validity of the rule so stated was accepted in *Lord Porchester* v. *Petrie* (8), and other cases. Later,

---

(6) [1958] 2 All E.R. 294.   (7) (1953), unreported.

(8) (1783), 3 Doug. K.B. 261.

relation back to the first day of the term seems to have been abandoned but **A** relation back to the beginning of the day of the judgment remained.   Thus, in *Edwards* v. *Reginam* (9), COLERIDGE, J., said:

" The doctrine that judicial acts are to be taken always to date from the earliest minute of the day in which they are done stands upon ancient and clear authority."

B

And in *Wright* v. *Mills* (10), it was held that where judgment had been signed at 11.0 a.m. and the defendant had died at 9.30 a.m. the same morning, the judgment was regular.   Indeed, this principle goes as far back as *Shelley's Case* (11), where judgment was given at the sitting of the court on the first day of term and the party had died before the court sat, and the judgment was held good. (Nobody has suggested that this " rule in *Shelley's Case* (11) " was abolished by s. 131 of **C** the Law of Property Act, 1925.)   In some of the cases the present rule is said to be based on the doctrine that the court takes no notice of the time of day at which a judicial proceeding takes place (*Edwards* v. *Reginam* (12), per COLERIDGE, J.); or takes no notice of fractions of the day (*Wright* v. *Mills* (13), per POLLOCK, C.B.).   In other cases the basis advanced has been that judgments take precedence over other acts (for example a payment to a bank; see *Re* **D** *Warren*, *Wheeler* v. *Mills* (14)) or other events (such as death; see *Wright* v. *Mills* (15), per BRAMWELL, B.) which occurred on the same day.   Protests have been made from time to time about the legal fiction which the rule involves, for example in *Lyttleton* v. *Cross* (16), in *Wright* v. *Mills* (10) and in *Clarke* v. *Bradlaugh* (17).   Nevertheless, it has been repeatedly declared to be a well-established rule.   In *Clarke* v. *Bradlaugh* (18), it was described by BRETT, L.J., **E** as " part of common law procedure ".   It was, however, applied in the Chancery Division in *Re Warren* (14), and since *Kruhlak* v. *Kruhlak* (*No. 2*) (19) it must be taken to be part of the procedure of the Divorce Division as well.

The rule has sometimes been stated in a qualified form.   One qualification has been that the judgment relates back, " unless there is anything on the record to the contrary " (see TIDD'S PRACTICE, p. 935 and *Lord Porchester* v. **F** *Petrie* (20)).   I do not think that this qualification is applicable here.   Counsel for the plaintiff has suggested that, because of the registrar's later memorandum that the decree absolute was ineffective, there is something on the record to show that the decree did not relate back.   It can hardly be supposed, however, that the court can, of it's own motion or on the application of a party, alter the effect of a decree after it has taken effect, in the absence of some jurisdiction to **G** vary it.   Another suggested qualification has been to say that relation back takes place " unless it works injustice "; see *Lyttleton* v. *Cross* (16).   I do not, however, see that it can be said that, in the present case, the rule would work injustice.   Is there any injustice in the devolution of the property of an intestate on his mother rather than on a wife who has chosen to divorce him and the dissolution of whose marriage is almost exactly coincidental with his death? **H** If the plaintiff is held to be an ex-wife and not a widow, she is entitled to apply for some maintenance under s. 26 of the Matrimonial Causes Act 1965.   Whether she would be awarded any maintenance under that section or not I express no opinion.   Then in *Taunton Case*, *Marshall* v. *James* (21), LORD COLERIDGE, C.J., said:

I

---

(9) (1854), 9 Exch. 628 at p. 631.
(10) [1843-60] All E.R. Rep. 842;   (1859), 4 H. & N. 488.
(11) (1581), 1 Co. Rep. 93b.   (12) (1854), 9 Exch. at p. 632.
(13) [1843-60] All E.R. Rep. at pp. 842, 843;   (1859), 4 H. & N. at p. 490.
(14) [1938] 2 All E.R. 331;   [1938] Ch. 725.
(15) (1859), 4 H. & N. at p. 493.   (16) (1824), 3 B. & C. 317.
(17) [1881-85] All E.R. Rep. 1002;   (1881), 8 Q.B.D. 63.
(18) (1881), 8 Q.B.D. at p. 68.   (19) [1958] 2 All E.R. 294.
(20) (1783), 3 Doug. K.B. at p. 273.
(21) (1874), L.R. 9 C.P. 702 at p. 712.

A
" But we are here dealing with a judicial proceeding: and it is not disputed that, when a judicial proceeding has been shown to have taken place on a particular day, it must, in the absence of evidence to the contrary, be presumed to have taken place at the earliest moment of the day that it could take place."

B
To the last few words of this sentence I shall come back later. For the moment I notice the words " in the absence of evidence to the contrary ". I feel that the inclusion of these words must have been a slip on LORD COLERIDGE'S part. There is nothing in any other case to suggest that the rule creates a mere rebuttable presumption, and, indeed, in *Wright* v. *Mills* (22), *Edwards* v. *Reginam* (23) and *Kruhlak* v. *Kruhlak* (*No. 2*) (24), there was evidence as to the actual time of the judicial act.

C
There is, however, another suggested qualification on which counsel for the plaintiff strongly relies. The proposition is that the act relates back only to the earliest *possible* moment of the day. The rule was stated in this form by POLLOCK, C.B., in *Wright* v. *Mills* (25). In *Marshall* v. *James* (26), in the passage which I have already quoted, LORD COLERIDGE used similar language. Under the old rule of relation back to the beginning of the term, LORD MANSFIELD in *Swann* v.

D
Broome (27) said that a judgment could not relate back to a date before the date of the writ. In *Tabernacle Permanent Building Society* v. *Knight* (28) a passage in LORD WATSON'S speech supports the view that the judicial act cannot always be related back to the beginning of the day. This brings me to a matter which has not been referred to in any of the judicial pronouncements, with one exception, that of LORD WATSON. That is the question of the jurisdiction of the court

E
to make the order. In many of the cases this issue could not have arisen. For instance, in *Kruhlak* v. *Kruhlak* (*No. 2*) (24), there was no doubt at all that the registrar had jurisdiction to make the decree absolute on the day that he made it. *Tabernacle Permanent Building Society* v. *Knight* (28) was a case which arose because an arbitration award was published on a certain day and on the same day one of the parties to the arbitration applied to the court for a rule nisi to

F
show cause why the arbitrators should not be required to state a case, and LORD WATSON said this (29):

G
" If there had been any evidence to shew that an award was published on the same day as the order but before the latter was applied for, I should not, as at present advised, have been prepared to hold that this case was governed by the decision of the Court of Exchequer in *Wright* v. *Mills* (22). There the court had undoubted jurisdiction, and was moreover seized of the case at the time when, fictione juris, its order was held to have been made. Here the court had no process before it until the initial order was applied for; and it had no jurisdiction to grant the order, if, at the time of the application, there was a completed award."

H
This proposition seems to be right in principle and I respectfully accept it as a correct statement of the law.

I
I will now indicate briefly how counsel for the plaintiff develops the two branches of his argument. First, as to jurisdiction: r. 40 (1) of the Matrimonial Causes Rules, 1957 (30), provides that an application by a spouse to make absolute a decree nisi pronounced in his favour shall be made by lodging a notice of application in a prescribed form, and that if the registrar is satisfied of certain

(22) [1843-60] All E.R. Rep. 842; (1859), 4 H. & N. 488.
(23) (1854), 9 Exch. 628.
(24) [1958] 2 All E.R. 294.
(25) [1843-60] All E.R. Rep. at p. 843; (1859), 28 L.J.Ex. at p. 224.
(26) (1874), L.R. 9 C.P. at p. 712. (27) (1764), 3 Burr. 1595.
(28) [1892] A.C. 298 at p. 304. (29) [1892] A.C. at p. 304.
(30) S.I. 1957 No. 619.

R

matters the notice shall be filed. Rule 40 (2) provides that on the filing of the A
notice the decree shall become absolute. No other relevant means of making a
decree absolute is prescribed. Therefore, says counsel for the plaintiff, before the
decree can be made absolute there must be an effective lodging of the notice of
application. The notice of application here was posted on July 5 and received
at 8.30 a.m. on July 6, 1965. The recent case of *Hodgson* v. *Armstrong* (31) is
sufficient authority to show that the time of lodgment is not the time of posting B
nor the time the letter is opened but is the time when it is delivered at the court;
in this case 8.30 a.m. on July 6, 1965. The next step is to establish that the
lodgment is a non-judicial act. The issue of a writ has been deemed to have been
a non-judicial act (*Clarke* v. *Bradlaugh* (32)) and a fortiori it may be said that the
lodgment of the notice of application (which involves no activity on the part of
the court or any of its officers) is not a judicial act. The court will take notice C
of the time of a non-judicial act and will not give it effect before that time (see
Clarke v. *Bradlaugh* (32)). So, it is said, the lodgment could have no operation
anterior to 8.30 a.m. By that time the suit had already abated because of the
death of the deceased and could not be revived (see *Stanhope* v. *Stanhope* (33)).
Death is not a judicial act, and there is no obstacle in law to taking notice of the
fact that the death preceded the lodgment. The final step in the argument is that, D
because the lodgment was ineffective, a condition precedent to the making of the
decree absolute was wanting and, therefore, the registrar had no jurisdiction to
make the decree absolute. Therefore, it was a nullity; see *Wolfenden* v. *Wolfenden*
(34), approved by the Court of Appeal in *Wiseman* v. *Wiseman* (35), and also
B. v. *B.* (36).

Despite the eloquent logic of this argument, I do not in the end find that I can E
accept it. Most judicial acts are preceded, and usually immediately preceded, by
an application for the act to be performed. *Wright* v. *Mills* (37) is a good example.
The judicial act there was the signing of judgment. It is plain from the report
that the plaintiff had attended the office of the court to sign judgment; that is
to say, applied to the appropriate officer to enter judgment in his favour. I do
not think that judgment can be entered without such an application. If, say, in F
default of appearance, an officer of the court entered judgment without any
application being made by the plaintiff for such judgment, the judgment would
clearly be a nullity. It could have been argued just as much in *Wright* v. *Mills*
(37) as in the present case, that the application for judgment was a non-judicial
act and occurred after the abatement of the action by the death of the other
party. It was, indeed, argued (38) that signing judgment was an act of the party G
and not of the court. But this argument was not accepted. LORD WATSON (39),
in the passage which I have read, distinguished *Wright* v. *Mills* (37) as a case
where " the court had undoubted jurisdiction, and was moreover seized of the
case . . .". The distinction that LORD WATSON drew was between that type of case
and the type where, at the moment when the act alleged to be a judicial act is
performed, there is no process in being. Here, there was at all material times a H
process in being—the divorce suit. The plaintiff in her petition had prayed for
the marriage to be dissolved. I think that counsel for the defendant is right when
he submits that the lodging of the application for decree absolute and the filing
of it is to be regarded as a single transaction. It is one " judicial proceeding ",
to use the expression which was used in *Edwards* v. *Reginam* (40), and was also
used in *Marshall* v. *James* (41) in the passage that I read. A judicial proceeding I

---

(31) [1967] 1 All E.R. 307.
(32) [1881-85] All E.R. Rep. 1002; (1881), 8 Q.B.D. 63.
(33) (1886), 11 P.D. 103.
(34) [1947] 2 All E.R. 653; [1948] P. 27.
(35) [1953] 1 All E.R. 601 at p. 604; [1953] P. 79 at p. 87.
(36) [1961] 2 All E.R. 396.
(37) [1843-60] All E.R. Rep. 842; (1859), 4 H. & N. 488.
(38) (1859), 4 H. & N. at p. 490.   (39) [1892] A.C. at p. 304.
(40) (1854), 9 Exch. 628.   (41) (1874), L.R. 9 C.P. at p. 712.

A cannot be split into a non-judicial part and a judicial part. To make sense of all the authorities on the topic, the application for judgment, or for a receiving order, or for a decree absolute, has to be treated as part and parcel of the judicial act. Another way of putting it would be this. A process does not abate at death at a particular time; it abates on the day of the death unless a final order or decree absolute is made on that day. This is the joint effect of *Wright* v. *Mills* (42) and

B *Kruhlak* v. *Kruhlak* (*No. 2*) (43). In *Wright* v. *Mills* (44), POLLOCK, C.B., said:

> " In truth, however, it only amounts to this, that by the practice of the court you may inquire whether the party was alive on the day, but you shall not inquire into the precise time of death on that day; . . ."

I should not interpret this as meaning that one can never inquire into the time
C of death, but rather that one cannot inquire into the relationship between time of death and time of a court order made on the same day. This means that there is jurisdiction to make the decree absolute at any time on the day of death, and, if there is jurisdiction to make it absolute, there must be the right to apply for it to be made absolute. For these reasons, I hold that the registrar had jurisdiction to file the notice of application, thereby making the decree absolute.

D The second branch of counsel for the plaintiff's argument requires no elaboration. He relies on the authorities to which I have referred for the proposition that a judicial act relates back only to the earliest moment of the day on which the act could have been done, and says that, in this case, that moment was when the application was lodged—8.30 a.m., after the death. The answer must be the same as before. If counsel for the plaintiff's argument were right, it would mean
E that the judgment in *Wright* v. *Mills* (44) would only have related back to the time when the court office opened and the plaintiff attended to sign judgment. It would also mean that in *Kruhlak* v. *Kruhlak* (*No. 2*) (43) the Divisional Court would have been bound to inquire when the application for decree absolute was lodged; although, as I have said, the application was in fact lodged on the day before filing, it seems clear that the Divisional Court did not concern themselves
F with this circumstance. I think, therefore, that the reference to the earliest *possible* moment of the day must be taken to mean the earliest moment of the day when the court was seized of the process as a whole.

For these reasons, I conclude that the plaintiff has failed to establish that she was still married to the deceased at the time of his death. Accordingly, she is not his widow and is not entitled to a grant. Her claim being thus disposed of,
G the defendant is entitled to letters of administration and there will be a grant to her.

Order accordingly.

Solicitors: *Peacock & Goddard*, agents for *Luff, Raymond & Williams*, Wimborne Minster (for the plaintiff); *Wilkinson, Kimbers & Staddon*, agents for
H *Humphries, Kirk & Miller*, Wareham (for the defendant).

[*Reported by* ALICE BLOOMFIELD, *Barrister-at-Law.*]

I

---

(42) [1843-60] All E.R. Rep. 842; (1859), 4 H. & N. 488.
(43) [1958] 2 All E.R. 294.
(44) (1859), 4 H. & N. at p. 493.

Re BLANCH (*deceased*). BLANCH *v.* HONHOLD.

[CHANCERY DIVISION (Buckley, J.), February 20, March 6, 1967.]

Family Provision—Evidence—Deceased's state of mind admissible—Testamentary capacity not to be investigated—Feebleness of mind did not constitute a reason for deceased's action that was relevant under s. 1 (7)—*Widow not benefiting under deceased's will—Inheritance (Family Provision) Act,* 1938 (1 & 2 Geo. 6 c. 45), *s.* 1, *as amended by Intestates' Estates Act,* 1952 (15 & 16 Geo. 6 & 1 Eliz. 2 c. 64), *s.* 7, *Sch.* 3.

The plaintiff and the deceased were married on May 2, 1957, when she was seventy-one and he was sixty-eight. The marriage was successful apart from the deceased's jealous disposition. During the last few months of his life the plaintiff cared for the deceased although he gave her no money. He died on May 6, 1965. By his will the deceased appointed the defendant, who was his only surviving child and was born of his first marriage, to be his sole executrix, devisee and legatee. His net estate was of the value of about £15,000. The plaintiff's personal income was about £315 a year. The defendant was married and had two infant sons. The plaintiff sought an order for reasonable provision under the Inheritance (Family Provision) Act, 1938. Evidence had been admitted showing the deceased's state of mind.

Held: (i) under the Act of 1938 the court should consider any matter that might properly be regarded as being relevant including, in certain cases, the state of the deceased's mind and the fact that a dependant had cared for the deceased during a long mental or physical illness, and such evidence would be admissible (see p. 471, letters A and C, post).

(ii) testamentary capacity was not a matter that should be investigated on an application under the Act of 1938 and feebleness of mind could not constitute a reason for the deceased's actions which was relevant under s. 1 (7)* of the Act of 1938 (see p. 471, letter D, post).

Practice Note ([1945] W.N. 210) criticised and explained.

(iii) the deceased's irrational jealously accounted for his failure to provide for the plaintiff but this had no bearing on whether his action was reasonable or what provision the court should order for the plaintiff; having regard to the facts that the plaintiff was aged eighty-one and of slender means, and to all the other circumstances the court would order that she should receive £600 per annum during her life out of the income of the estate which on average would amount to £900 per annum, subject to a deduction in respect of the rent of the deceased's house in which the plaintiff was living (see p. 471, letter F, and p. 472, letters B and D, post).

[As to exercise of jurisdiction under the Inheritance (Family Provision) Act, 1938, by court, see 16 HALSBURY'S LAWS (3rd Edn.) 460, para. 919; and for cases on the subject, see 24 DIGEST (Repl.) 967-969, *9754-9761.*

For the Inheritance (Family Provision) Act, 1938, s. 1, as amended by the Act of 1952, see 32 HALSBURY'S STATUTES (2nd Edn.) 139, and as further amended by the Family Provision Act 1966, see Sch. 3 to the Act of 1966.]

Case referred to:

Practice Note, [1945] W.N. 210.

_____

* The Inheritance (Family Provision) Act, 1938, s. 1 (7), as amended, provides: " The court shall also, on any such application, have regard to the deceased's reasons, so far as ascertainable, for making the dispositions made by his will (if any), or for refraining from disposing by will of his estate or part of his estate, or for not making any provision, or any further provision, as the case may be, for a dependant, and the court may accept such evidence of those reasons as it considers sufficient including any statement in writing signed by the deceased and dated, so, however, that in estimating the weight, if any, to be attached to any such statement the court shall have regard to all the circumstances from which any inference can reasonably be drawn as to the accuracy or otherwise of the statement."

A   **Adjourned Summons.**

This was an application by originating summons dated Sept. 30, 1965, by the plaintiff, Madeleine Pauline Julie Blanch as the lawful widow of Thomas Alfred Blanch, deceased, under the Inheritance (Family Provision) Act, 1938, and R.S.C., Ord. 14, r. 1, for such reasonable provision as the court thought fit, subject to such conditions or restrictions if any as the court might impose, out
B of the net estate of the deceased for her maintenance. The deceased died on May 6, 1965, being then domiciled in England and leaving a will dated Aug. 15, 1964, whereof probate was granted to the defendant, Marguerite Madeleine Emilie Honhold, on Aug. 27, 1965. The facts are set out in the judgment.

The case noted below* was cited during the argument in addition to the one referred to in the judgment.

C   *Jeremiah Harman* for the plaintiff.

   J. D. Waite for the defendant.

Cur. adv. vult.

Mar. 6. **BUCKLEY, J.**, read the following judgment: This is an application under the Inheritance (Family Provision) Act, 1938, by the widow of the
D deceased. The plaintiff and the deceased were married on May 2, 1957, when he was aged sixty-eight and she seventy-one years. They had both been married before. He was a widower and she a widow. The deceased's first wife had been a French woman and was an old friend from childhood days of the plaintiff, who is also a French woman. The plaintiff lived in France until she married the deceased. The deceased's first wife died in the year 1956. At that time the
E plaintiff had promised to visit the deceased and his wife in England, as she had done on a previous occasion, and after his first wife died the deceased wrote to the plaintiff suggesting that notwithstanding that he had lost his wife she should adhere to this plan and come to visit him in England. She demurred for a time but he wrote to her frequently and eventually persuaded her to come, and in the course of that correspondence he first suggested that he and the plaintiff
F should marry.

The plaintiff came to England to visit the deceased at Easter, 1957, and shortly afterwards they were married on May 2 of that year. They made their matrimonial home at the house in which the deceased had lived with his first wife, at 25, Munster Road, Teddington, and subject to one aspect which I must mention, the marriage was a successful and a happy one. Unfortunately, how-
G ever, the deceased seems to have been a man of a jealous disposition, although an extremely affectionate man. From the beginning of the marriage this tendency to be jealous of other men in connexion with his wife demonstrated itself, but from early in 1964 this became concentrated on a young boy who was the son of friends of the plaintiff and the deceased. He was then twenty years old. It is not suggested that there was anything at fault with the plaintiff's relations
H with this young man, nor is it suggested that there was any rational basis for the deceased's jealousy of him. At the instance of the plaintiff the deceased consulted a psychiatrist, and the plaintiff says that the psychiatrist told her that in his opinion the deceased was suffering from an obsessive state of mind and a persecution complex. At any rate, it is conceded in these proceedings that the deceased's conduct in this respect was not wholly rational. Notwithstanding
I this jealousy of the boy in question, the deceased's attitude to his wife remained extremely affectionate.

In the summer of 1964 the plaintiff paid a visit to her native country to visit friends and relations there. The deceased was to have gone with her but ultimately refused to do so and he stayed in England while the plaintiff was in France. When she returned to England she found herself locked out of the matrimonial home, all the locks having been changed, and as a result of this she

---

  * *Re Borthwick (decd.)*, [1949] 1 All E. R. 472; [1949] Ch. 395.

first went to a nursing home and then found lodgings for herself, but this separa- A
tion of the plaintiff and the deceased did not last very long for, on Nov. 1, 1964,
there was a reconciliation between them and the plaintiff returned to live with
her husband. Again it is not suggested that the plaintiff was in any way to
blame for this separation; but after this event the deceased apparently became
very parsimonious in his dealings with the plaintiff. He gave her no money
and bought all the food and household things himself, but she lived with him, B
did all the cooking and cared for him and apart from this rather distressing aspect
of the deceased's attitude to his wife, the marriage remained an affectionate and
successful one.

This state of affairs, however, did not last for very long for on May 6, 1965, the
deceased died, the plaintiff having cared for him until the time of his death. His
will was dated Aug. 15, 1964, and was made while the plaintiff was in France C
and by that will the testator appointed the defendant, who is his only surviving
child of his first marriage, sole executrix, and made her sole devisee and legatee
under that will. The net estate of the testator for the purposes of the Act of
1938 is of the value of about £15,000. The plaintiff has a personal income of
only about £315 a year, consisting mainly of her old age pension. She has
virtually no capital. The defendant is a married woman with two infant sons. D
Her husband earns about £2,500 a year, but she herself apparently has no private
means. It is not suggested by the defendant that the deceased acted reasonably
in making no provision for his wife. She was married to him for some eight
years; the marriage was a happy one apart from the deceased's unhappy jealous
disposition. Notwithstanding this unfortunate circumstance and the deceased's
consequent meanness to the plaintiff in financial matters at the end of his life, E
the plaintiff stood by him and cared for him until he died.

The defendant has been willing to agree to some provision being made for the
plaintiff out of the estate, but the parties have not been able to agree as to the
amount of such provision. I should have not delayed delivering my judgment
at the end of the argument had I not been referred to a *Practice Note* (1), the
effect of which is still reflected in a note in the SUPREME COURT PRACTICE (2). F
As the *Practice Note* (1) is not very long I will read it in full:

" VAISEY, J., said that, in applications under the Inheritance (Family
Provision) Act, 1938, any suggestion of the testator's weakness of mind
ought to be excluded. He could not see the relevance of it. He was
confident that it was not an issue in such cases. He had consulted his
brother judges and he thought that he could say, without any impropriety G
that, in such cases, any suggestion of unsoundness of mind, or even want of
lucidity of mind, could not possibly be raised. It might be the reason why
the will was in a rather queer form and it might be the reason why it was
unintelligible, but it could not be one of the testator's reasons for making
the bequest. It was a lack of reason and the point ought not to be raised."
H
The master, having regard to that *Practice Note* (1), questioned whether some
of the evidence that has been filed in these proceedings ought properly to be
admitted. As VAISEY, J., apparently had consulted his brethren before he
made the statement which is recorded in the *Practice Note* (1) I thought that
perhaps it was desirable that I should consult some of my present brethren
before delivering this judgment, and I have done so. I think that the shade I
of VAISEY, J., in this court, where he sat for many years, would forgive
me if I said that in making the observations which he made on that occasion
he was speaking a little unguardedly and in wider terms than those in which he
really meant to be understood. The *Practice Note* (1) as it stands should not be
taken to be of general application. The Act of 1938 enjoins the court to have
regard to any matter or thing which in the circumstances of the case it may

(1) [1945] W.N. 210.
(2) SUPREME COURT PRACTICE, 1967.   Note to R.S.C., Ord. 99, r. 3.

A consider relevant or material (3). In certain cases there are likely to be respects in which the state of the deceased's mind may properly be regarded as relevant and material. For instance, the state of the deceased's mind may be very material to the weight to be attributed to any reasons which he may have given in his life time for failing to make provision for a dependant or for making such provision as he did make for such a dependant. Moreover, although the test

B of what must be regarded as reasonable provision for the purposes of s. 1 (1) of the Act of 1938, (4) should be an objective test, as should the test of what provision the court ought to direct to be made for a dependant, yet the test may have to be made in the light of the competing claims on the deceased's bounty. If, as I think may be the case, it is sometimes necessary to take into consideration that a dependant has devoted himself or herself to caring for the deceased during

C a long physical illness, it may be equally relevant to take into account care during a long period of mental illness, and evidence would be admissible in that respect. In either case, the fact that the dependant has devoted time and trouble to caring for the deceased may be something to which some weight should be given in assessing the moral obligations of the deceased to the dependent in question.

D If a will has been admitted to probate, testamentary capacity could not be alleged and feebleness of mind, whether amounting to or falling short of testamentary incapacity, could never, I think, be a reason for the purposes of s. 1 (7) of the Act of 1938. In my judgment, the *Practice Note* (5) should be read as indicating only that testamentary capacity, or the lack of it, is not a matter which should be investigated on an application under this Act, and that feebleness

E of mind or understanding cannot constitute a reason for the deceased's conduct which is relevant for the purposes of s. 1 (7).

In the present case I feel no doubt that the deceased's irrational jealousy accounted for his complete failure to make any provision for the plaintiff, but it is not a reason which has any bearing either on whether it was reasonable for him to fail to provide for her, or on what provision the court should order to be

F made for her, except in so far as the plaintiff's having apparently endured this state of affairs for about a year with a generous understanding may be said to be an answer to a moral claim on the deceased's bounty; I cannot say, however, that this particular aspect should, in the circumstances of this case, have very much influence on my decision. The question I ask myself is: what provision ought I to order to be made out of the estate for the plaintiff who is now eighty-one

G years of age, has very slender means, and against whom nothing is said, bearing in mind that the sole beneficiary under the deceased's will is his only surviving child and the mother of his two infant grandsons?

Evidence has been filed directed to showing that a trust fund held on trust for the plaintiff for life and on her death for the defendant absolutely could be satisfactorily invested in accordance with the Trustee Investments Act, 1961,

H and with due regard to their respective interests, so as to yield seven per cent. Since the commencement (6) of s. 3 of the Family Provision Act 1966, there is no longer any statutory requirement to limit such provision as the court may see fit to order to an estimated or notional income of the estate, but, to reach a just apportionment of the benefits in the deceased's estate, an estimate of its probable income yield may still be relevant. Where a forecast over what may

I turn out to be a fairly long period of years is required I do not think that it would be right to assume that interest rates or rates of income yield would, throughout such a period, maintain their existing level. The court has always adopted a cautious and conservative attitude in relation to such matters, but

---

(3) I.e., relevant or material in relation to the applicant; see s. 1 (6).
(4) Section 1 (1) requires the court to consider whether, in effect, the deceased has failed to make reasonable provision for, in the present case, the plaintiff.
(5) [1945] W.N. 210.   (6) Section 3 came into force on Nov. 17, 1966.

A the period with which I am concerned must, in the ordinary course, be fairly
short.

For the present purpose I feel justified in assuming that an average annual
income of about £900 per annum gross could be maintained throughout the
period.   I take into account the fact that the postponement of the defendant's
interest in capital cannot, in the normal course, be for very many years, and that
she has a husband to support her.   Taking these and the other considerations
B which I have mentioned into account, I reach the conclusion that, subject to the
point which I must mention next, the plaintiff should receive £600 a year out of
the income of the estate as from the death of the deceased, during her life or, of
course, until remarriage.

The plaintiff has, since the death of the deceased, remained in occupation of
25, Munster Road.   The yearly rental value of that property is estimated by
C the defendant at £400.   The plaintiff remained there because she had nowhere
else to go, and because she could not afford to move.   In these circumstances,
I do not think that she should be charged a full occupation rent.   Giving the
matter the best consideration that I can, I think the appropriate order for me to
make is that the plaintiff should receive, as from the death of the deceased, £350 a
year for two years or until she vacates 25, Munster Road; that thereafter she
D should receive £600 a year, and that she should be charged no occupation rent
if she vacates 25, Munster Road before May 6, 1967, which will be the end of the
two year period, but in respect of any occupation of 25, Munster Road after
that date she should pay a full occupation rent.

Order accordingly.

E Solicitors: *Sherwood, Cobbing & Williams*, Kingston-upon-Thames (for the
plaintiff); *Biddle, Thorne, Welsford & Barnes*, agents for *E. Fitzgerald-Hart & Son*,
Boroughbridge (for the defendant).

[*Reported by* JENIFER SANDELL, *Barrister-at-Law.*]

F

FOWLEY MARINE (EMSWORTH), LTD. *v.* GAFFORD.

[QUEEN'S BENCH DIVISION (Megaw, J.), February 27, 28, March 1, 2, 3, 21, 1967.]

*Limitation of Action—Land—Adverse possession—Sea-bed—Whether possession
sufficiently exclusive—Limitation Act,* 1939 (2 & 3 Geo. 6 c. 21), *s.* 4 (1),
proviso.
G
*Trespass to Land—Possession—Sea-bed—Concurrent possession by persons
having moorings placed in sea-bed—Whether exclusive possession necessary to
sustain action.*

*Water and Watercourses—Navigation—Laying and maintenance of permanent
moorings—Whether an ordinary incident of navigation—Whether common
law right exists to lay such mooring in the land of another person.*
H
The plaintiff company claimed to be the owner of a tidal creek in Chichester
harbour, that is, to be owner of the sea-bed and (presumably) of the banks,
and to be entitled to charge the defendant, a yachtsman, for a permanent
mooring which he had placed in the sea-bed in 1961.   The plaintiff company
had purchased the creek and part of the foreshore, not immediately adjacent,
in 1963.   The title shown had commenced with a conveyance of 1878*,
I evidenced by a draft indenture and by statutory declarations of 1913
stating that the actual deed of conveyance and the earlier documents of title
had been lost, and that the property had not since been mortgaged, charged,
or encumbered.   There were further conveyances in 1918 and 1950.   In 1885†
the then owner had entered into an agreement, not referred to in his statutory

A   declaration, to sell the property to an oyster fishery company. No conveyance was produced, but the owner of the creek had received shares issued
in accordance with the agreement, and there was evidence that the fishery
company had subsequently bred oysters there. The fishery company had been
wound up in 1904, and there was no evidence of what had then happened to
its assets. The statutory declarations of 1913 included one by the then
B   owner's agent, stating, among other matters, that he had collected rent from a
tenant of the creek and other property for six years prior to 1913. The creek
was used for navigation by pleasure and fishing craft, and there was evidence
that some of the owners of such craft had placed permanent moorings in the
creek at varying dates going back to before the first world war. There was no
evidence whether they had sought permission to do so. A previous owner
C   of the creek had himself had a permanent mooring there, and had given a
sailing club permission to lay six permanent moorings in return for a rent.
After 1945 the club had sold the moorings to individual members, and
permission had later been given for a further six moorings to be laid by
individual members, one of them being the defendant, who knew that such
permission had been sought and granted. The defendant's mooring (put
D   down in 1961) consisted of two heavy anchors and a mooring buoy connected
by chains. A shipyard company had also put down six permanent moorings
at varying dates and without permission. By 1963 there were at least
twenty-four and probably thirty or more permanent moorings, and evidence
showed permission only with regard to about twelve of them. The plaintiff
company then claimed an annual fee of £5 in respect of each mooring; some
E   sixteen owners paid that fee, but others, including the defendant, did not.
Harbour bye-laws of 1954 forbade the maintenance of private moorings
without the permission of the harbour-master, but the evidence was that the
harbour-master had never replied to applications for permission.

Held: (i) there was no common law right to lay or maintain permanent
moorings in another person's land without his permission (see p. 480,
F   letter B, post).

Dicta of BLACKBURN, J., in *Marshall* v. *Ulleswater Steam Navigation Co.*
((1871), L.R. 7 Q.B. at p. 172) and of FLETCHER MOULTON, L.J., in *Denaby
and Cadeby Main Collieries, Ltd.* v. *Anson* ([1911] 1 K.B. at pp. 201, 202)
followed.

(ii) the plaintiff company had not established actual exclusive possession
G   sufficient to sustain an action in trespass irrespective of the plaintiff
company's legal title to the bed of the creek (see p. 484, letter G, and p. 487,
letter G, post); accordingly neither could the plaintiff company establish
actual exclusive possession for sixty years so as to create a title against the
Crown under the statutes of limitation* (see p. 490, letter B, post).

Foster v. *Warblington Urban District Council* ([1904-07] All E.R. Rep.
H   366) followed on the first point.

Dictum of LORD WATSON in *Lord Advocate* v. *Young* ((1887), 12 App. Cas.
at p. 553) considered.

(iii) the plaintiff company had not established legal title to the property,
since, without deciding whether the Crown had ever divested itself of ownership, the proper inference on the evidence was that the property had been
I   conveyed to the oyster fishery company in 1885 but it could not be inferred
that the property had subsequently been reconveyed to the vendor from
whom the plaintiff company's title derived (see p. 488, letter F, and p. 489,
letters A and I, post).

(iv) the evidence did not establish a customary right nor justify the
presumption of lost modern grant entitling the defendant to affix permanent
moorings in the creek, as there was a lack of universality of assertion of such

* See now the proviso to s. 4 (1) of the Limitation Act, 1939; this replaced provisions
of the Crown Suits Act, 1769, s. 1, and the Crown Suits Act, 1861, s.1.

a right by those who had used the creek, and even if there had been such a A
custom it would have been destroyed by the bringing into force of the
harbour bye-laws (see p. 490, letters D and G, post).

[As to the right to fix moorings in tidal waters, see 39 HALSBURY'S LAWS (3rd
Edn.) 534-536, para. 720; and for cases on the subject, see 47 DIGEST (Repl.)
741, 742, *827-836*.

As to the right of the person in possession to bring an action for trespass, see B
38 HALSBURY'S LAWS (3rd Edn.) 744, 754, para. 1214.

For the Limitation Act, 1939, s. 4 (1), see 13 HALSBURY'S STATUTES (2nd Edn.)
1164.]

Cases referred to:

    A.-G. v. *Parmeter, Re Portsmouth Harbour*, (1811), 10 Price, 378; 147 E.R. 345; C
       on appeal, H.L. sub nom. *Parmeter* v. *Gibbs, Re Portsmouth Harbour*,
       (1813), 10 Price, 412; 47 Digest (Repl.) 709, *547*.

    A.-G. v. *Wright*, [1897] 2 Q.B. 318; 66 L.J.Q.B. 834; 77 L.T. 295; 47 Digest
       (Repl.) 741, *827*.

    Beckett (Alfred F.), Ltd. v. *Lyons*, [1967] 1 All E.R. 833; [1967] 2 W.L.R. 421.

    Denaby and Cadeby Main Collieries, Ltd. v. *Anson*, [1911] 1 K.B. 171; 80
       L.J.K.B. 320; 103 L.T. 349; 47 Digest (Repl.) 738, *801*.   D

    Fitzhardinge (Lord) v. *Purcell*, [1908] 2 Ch. 139; 77 L.J.Ch. 529; 99 L.T. 154;
       72 J.P. 276; 47 Digest (Repl.) 728, *727*.

    Foster v. *Warblington Urban District Council*, [1904-07] All E.R. Rep. 366;
       [1906] 1 K.B. 648; 75 L.J.K.B. 514; 94 L.T. 876; 70 J.P. 233; 47
       Digest (Repl.) 712, *579*.

    Hastings Corpn. v. *Ivall*, (1874), L.R. 19 Eq. 558; 47 Digest (Repl.) 709, *550*. E

    Iveagh (Earl) v. *Martin*, [1960] 2 All E.R. 668; [1961] 1 Q.B. 232; [1960] 3
       W.L.R. 210; 47 Digest (Repl.) 741, *834*.

    Lord Advocate v. *Young, North British Ry. Co.* v. *Young*, (1887), 12 App. Cas.
       544; 47 Digest (Repl.) 712, *577*.

    Lyon v. *Fishmongers' Co.*, (1876), 1 App. Cas. 662; 46 L.J.Ch. 68; 35 L.T. 569;
       42 J.P. 163; 47 Digest (Repl.) 739, *814*.   F

    Marshall v. *Ulleswater Steam Navigation Co.*, (1871), L.R. 7 Q.B. 166; 41
       L.J.Q.B. 41; 25 L.T. 793; 36 J.P. 583; 47 Digest (Repl.) 740, *825*.

    Nicholls v. *Ely Beet Sugar Factory, Ltd.*, [1931] All E.R. Rep. 154; [1931] 2
       Ch. 84; 100 L.J.Ch. 259; 145 L.T. 113; 36 Digest (Repl.) 320, *661*.

Action.   G

By writ dated Sept. 25, 1964, the plaintiff company, Fowley Marine (Emsworth),
Ltd., sued the defendant, D. Gafford, for a declaration, an injunction and
damages. By its statement of claim, as amended, the plaintiff company pleaded
that since Apr. 2, 1963, it had been owner in fee simple of certain foreshore
and mudlands and the sea bed of and surrounding the creek in Chichester Harbour
at Emsworth, Hampshire, known as Fowley Rythe and in the premises the H
waters from time to time overlying the same. The plaintiff company alleged
that since about July, 1963, the defendant, without the consent of the plaintiff
company, had laid and affixed mooring tackle to a part of the foreshore or of
the sea bed and had continued to maintain and use it for the purpose of making
fast to it his yacht; that he had by his solicitors denied the plaintiff company's
right and title to the foreshore and sea bed and waters, had refused to enter into I
the plaintiff company's usual form of licence agreement permitting him to
maintain and use the mooring and had refused to pay the plaintiff company its
annual charge of £5. The plaintiff company pleaded further that the defendant
was a trespasser on the plaintiff company's foreshore and sea bed and waters
and intended to continue his trespass unless and until restrained by the court.
The plaintiff company claimed (i) a declaration that the foreshore and sea bed
and water were its property, that the defendant had no right to lay or affix his
mooring tackle thereto or to maintain and use it until he obtained the plaintiff

A company's consent, and that the plaintiff company were entitled to demand and
receive from the defendant a reasonable charge for its consent; (ii) an injunction
restraining the defendant by himself his servants or agents from laying, fixing,
maintaining or using the mooring without the consent of the plaintiff company.
By his defence the defendant denied that the plaintiff company was or at any
time had been owner in fee simple of the foreshore or mudlands or waters, and

B pleaded that the foreshore or mudlands or water belonged to the Crown and that
the defendant had a right to moor and to lay mooring tackle at the foreshore
by custom or by prescription or by lost modern grant. The defendant counterclaimed for a declaration that he had a right by custom or prescription to moor
at and on the foreshore or mudlands or waters without any charge. By an
amended reply and defence to counterclaim the plaintiff company further

C alleged that any customary or prescriptive right which might at any material
time have been vested in the defendant, though any such right was denied,
was determined on Mar. 29, 1964, by the making of the Emsworth Harbour
Bye-laws 1963 in pursuance of the Emsworth Harbour Order 1896, and of s. 83
of the Harbours, Docks and Piers Clauses Act, 1847. By an amended defence
to counterclaim the plaintiff company denied that the defendant had the rights

D that he claimed, and alternatively alleged that his mooring tackle was first laid
at or about its present position in or about 1958 by one Dalgleish acting on his
behalf with the express oral permission of one Andrew, a director of G. A.
Andrew, Ltd., the plaintiff company's predecessor in title. The plaintiff company
pleaded further allegations about subsequent user under licence. By an amended
reply to the amended defence to counterclaim the defendant denied that he

E first laid or caused to be laid mooring tackle in or about 1958 as was alleged by
the plaintiff company. The facts are set out in the judgment.

  R. N. Titheridge for the plaintiff company.
  C. Lawson, Q.C., and *Joseph Jackson* for the defendant.

  Mar. 21. **MEGAW, J.,** read the following judgment: This action raises
F many and difficult questions of fact and of law relating to public rights and
private rights in respect of the foreshore and the sea-bed in tidal waters. I am
grateful to counsel for their careful arguments and for their thorough exploration
of the authorities which clearly involved much research, some of it in esoteric
spheres.

  Fowley Rythe is a tidal creek in a part of Chichester Harbour. The entrance to
G Chichester Harbour northwards from the English Channel passes between the
mainland of Sussex near West Wittering on the east, and the south-east tip of
Hayling Island on the west. The channel then divides into two; one channel
runs east and north to Bosham and Chichester; the other runs north. Between
Thorney Island, which is not an island, and the north-east tip of Hayling Island,
that other channel then divides, one part, called Emsworth Channel, leading

H northwards up to Emsworth, and the other part called Sweare Deep, running
north-west between the north of Hayling Island and the mainland of Hampshire.
Some eight hundred or nine hundred yards north of the junction with Sweare
Deep, Emsworth Channel again divides. The right hand portion, as one goes
north, is still called Emsworth Channel, now running slightly east of north to the
eastern portion of Emsworth town. The left hand portion runs west of north to

I near the mainland, at Western Parade in the western part of Emsworth town.
This portion is called Fowley Rythe. The total length, from the junction with
Emsworth Channel, called Fowley Point, to the dry land would appear to be
something less than one thousand yards, though no doubt towards the mainland
end the Rythe becomes, at best, an increasingly small and insignificant channel.
For a considerable part of its length, however, it can be, and is, used by pleasure
boats, for navigation and mooring, and it is also used by fishing boats. It provides
a navigable channel for small boats, for most of its length at least at most states
of the tide, and it is used as such. Some two hundred yards to the west of Fowley

Point is a small piece of land, higher than the surrounding foreshore, known as A Fowley Island. Its surface remains above water level, even at high spring tides. The area on both sides of Fowley Rythe is foreshore; that is to say, it is not overflowed by the sea at mean low tide, but is overflowed at mean high tide. It is referred to in certain documents as " mud land ". For a considerable part of its length, small pleasure boats can lie moored in the Rythe, afloat at all times.

The plaintiff company, which was incorporated in or about 1963, claims to be B the owner of, inter alia, Fowley Rythe. It purchased Fowley Rythe, and a part of the foreshore abutting Western Parade, from G. Andrew, Ltd., on Apr. 2, 1963. In or about the year 1961, the defendant, Douglas Gafford, who lives in Farnham and has been an active yachtsman for many years, put down a permanent mooring in Fowley Rythe. The mooring consists of two heavy anchors, twenty-five feet apart, placed in the bed of the creek, and joined by a chain from the C centre of which another chain is attached by a swivel. A mooring buoy is attached to that other chain. Some of the other moorings in Fowley Rythe to which I shall refer hereafter were of that nature. Others, more old fashioned, involved the embedding of heavy timbers in the banks of the Rythe. All of them required the laying of heavy objects in or on the soil of the bed or banks of the Rythe.

In July, 1963, the plaintiff company asked the defendant, as also others who D were using permanent moorings in Fowley Rythe, to pay a fee of £5 per year for a licence agreement permitting the laying, maintaining and use of the mooring. While various other persons accepted and paid, the defendant refused, and he continued thereafter to maintain and use the permanent mooring. On Sept. 25, 1964, the plaintiff company started this action, asserting that the defendant is a trespasser.   E

I accept that the primary purpose of the plaintiff company in seeking to assert a right of control in Fowley Rythe is to preserve the amenities, and in particular to prevent the chaos which would result, and which perhaps had already begun to result, from unlicensed and uncontrolled freedom on the part of the ever-increasing number of amateur yachtsmen to lay permanent moorings wherever they can find a space to do so in Fowley Rythe. It is not difficult to imagine the F friction, confusion and perhaps self-strangulation of pleasure yachting and fishing in that area which such uncontrolled freedom might soon create.

There are, indeed, bye-laws made in 1954 by the Urban District Council of Havant and Waterloo, in pursuance of statutory power under the Emsworth Harbour Order, 1896, and s. 83 of the Harbours, Docks and Piers Clauses Act, 1847. Under those bye-laws it is provided that no person shall lay down or retain G a private mooring in the harbour, which included Fowley Rythe, without first having obtained the written consent of the harbour master. On the evidence before me, however, though applications were submitted to the harbour master two years or more ago, there has been no response, positive or negative, to any application, and no sign of anything having been done. The plaintiff company says that its title is not in any way affected by the bye-laws; the harbour master H has a power of veto, but no more. Subject to the veto, the plaintiff company's rights remain unimpaired.

The plaintiff company's primary motive, I have no doubt, is to preserve the amenities; but I cannot decide this case on the basis of any view which I may hold as to the desirability of the sort of control which the plaintiff company seeks to exercise. If the plaintiff company is not in law entitled to charge for permanent I moorings in Fowley Rythe, the defendant cannot be compelled to pay a charge.

In this action the plaintiff company asserts that it is the owner in fee simple of Fowley Rythe and that the defendant is a trespasser. It claims a declaration, and an injunction and damages. The defendant denies the plaintiff company's ownership and asserts that the ownership is in the Crown. He asserts also that he has a right to moor and lay mooring tackle by custom or lost modern grant. He also claims that, irrespective of any question of ownership or customary right, the fixing of permanent moorings in the sea-bed is an ordinary incident of the

A navigation of tidal or other navigable waters, and that therefore, by the common law, he is not a trespasser in laying or maintaining permanent moorings; he claims as a navigating member of the public an absolute right to do so, whether against the plaintiff company, if it is the owner, or against the Crown, if the Crown is the owner. The defendant by counterclaim accordingly asks for a declaration of his right to moor without charge, on the basis of custom, prescription, lost
B modern grant or common-law right.

The nature and extent of the ownership claimed by the plaintiff company is ownership of the soil of Fowley Rythe; that is, the sea-bed and presumably the banks thereof, though not of the immediately surrounding foreshore along the length of the Rythe. The plaintiff company does not assert ownership of the water flowing in the tidal creek; nor does it dispute the undoubted public right
C of navigation in those waters, nor the right to do such things as it concedes are properly incidental to such navigation, including, for example, the temporary dropping of a vessel's normal anchor, as distinct from the laying of permanent moorings.

There is no doubt that prima facie ownership of the foreshore and of the sea bed of tidal rivers and creeks is in the Crown. Equally, there is no doubt that
D there can be private ownership of the foreshore and of the sea-bed of tidal waters, based on the proof or presumption of a grant from the Crown at some time or other, possibly in the remote past. In the article on Waters and Watercourses in 39 Halsbury's Laws of England (3rd Edn.), p. 509, para. 664 it is said:

" The ownership of the foreshore and bed in tidal waters is determined by the same rules as the ownership of the seashore is ascertained and
E prima facie the soil of the foreshore and bed is vested in the Crown on the presumption that it is waste of the kingdom which has not been granted."

Lord Cairns, L.C., in *Lyon v. Fishmongers' Co.* (1) refuted a view expressed in the court below that in a navigable river the soil is always in the Crown. He said:

" As to this, it may be observed that the soil of a navigable river may, as
F Lord Hale observes (2), be private property."

It is clear, and the contrary has not been contended, that the same applies to the soil of navigable creeks in the foreshore. This is confirmed by a passage in the judgment of Parker, J., in *Lord Fitzhardinge v. Purcell* (3).

At this stage I shall summarise the issues, in the order in which I propose to deal with them.
G 1. Is it, as the defendant asserts, by both his defence and his counterclaim, an ordinary incident of navigation, and thus exercisable as of right at common law by all Her Majesty's subjects as owners or navigators of vessels, that they may place permanent moorings in land belonging to, or in the possession of, some other person, without the permission of such person, whether he be the Crown or a private individual? I take this issue first because it raises a question of law of
H general importance, because it does not depend on an assessment of the evidence, and because, if it should be decided in favour of the defendant, it would be decisive of both claim and counterclaim.

2. If the answer to 1. is " No ", has the plaintiff company shown that it has possession of the bed and banks of Fowley Rythe so as to entitle it to treat the defendant as a trespasser by reason of his retention of a permanent mooring in
I Fowley Rythe without their permission? This arises because the plaintiff company says that, as against the defendant, its possession is sufficient. It does not need to show ownership or to disprove the presumption of the title of the Crown.

3. If the answer to 2. is " No ", has the plaintiff company established a good title, otherwise than under the Limitation Act, 1939, including the rebuttal of the presumption of ownership by the Crown?

(1) (1876), 1 App. Cas. 662 at p. 673.
(2) De Jur. Mar. part i, c. 3.
(3) [1908] 2 Ch. 139 at p. 167.

4. If the answer to 2. and 3. is " No ", has the plaintiff company shown a title　A
by reference to the proviso to s. 4 (1) of the Limitation Act, 1939, relating to
actions by the Crown to recover the foreshore?

5. Has the defendant, if it be necessary on the claim, and in any event on his
counterclaim, established the right to fix permanent moorings in Fowley Rythe
by virtue of a custom or prescription or a presumed lost modern grant?

The first issue raises the question: what is an " ordinary incident of naviga-　B
tion "?　Does it include the right of all members of the public owning or
navigating vessels to place fixed moorings in another person's land without his
permission?　It is to be noted that the defendant's assertion of such a right, in
this issue, is not related to any question of custom, properly so called.　It is
asserted as being part of the common law of the land, which can be abrogated or
controlled only by statute; as where Parliament has provided or authorised that　C
a port or harbour authority may control the mooring of vessels.　Otherwise, it is
said, the right is universal and unlimited, as to place (provided that the land in
question is under or beside navigable waters); as to persons exercising it (provided it is exercised in connexion with navigation); and as to time, in that it
relates to and covers fixtures in the soil which are more than merely temporary.
It is not disputed that, if the laying of permanent moorings is to be regarded as an　D
" ordinary incident of navigation ", the defendant will succeed.　The question,
therefore, is whether this is an " ordinary incident of navigation ".

The defendant's proposition is founded on words used by LORD ESHER, M.R.,
and A. L. SMITH, L.J., in *A.-G.* v. *Wright* (4).　If what was said by them means
what the defendant says that it means, and if it is properly to be treated as part
of the ratio decidendi of that case, then I am bound by it, and that would be an　E
end to the plaintiff company's claim and an establishment of the defendant's
counterclaim.　I do not regard the passages in question as more than obiter dicta.
As such they are, of course, entitled to high regard, but they are inconsistent with
other earlier and later persuasive dicta to which I shall refer.

A.-G. v. *Wright* (4) in the Court of Appeal is an appeal from a judgment of
CAVE, J., with a special jury.　The defendant was a sub-lessee of a several fishery　F
at Leigh on the river Thames, the owner being prima facie owner of the soil
underneath the fishery.　He had cut adrift craft moored by fishermen and
yachtsmen to moorings which had been fixed in the soil of the foreshore and he
had removed some of the moorings.　The report does not indicate by whom the
moorings had been so fixed, or when.　The action was brought by the Attorney-
General at the relation of a number of fishermen and yacht-owners, claiming　G
an injunction to restrain the defendant from interfering with their moorings.　The
jury found an immemorial user of the foreshore, by all persons navigating the
waters at Leigh, for fixed moorings, and they gave their verdict for the plaintiff.
Judgment was given in accordance with the verdict and an injunction was
granted.　The defendant appealed.

It would seem in those circumstances that the sole issue between the parties　H
was as to the immemorial user, perhaps in respect of particular persons or a
particular class, and certainly in respect of a particular place.　The jury would
hardly have been invited to find a verdict as to the common law of the land, which
would be the province of the judge.　That the question of local immemorial user
was the sole issue is confirmed by a passage at the beginning of the judgment of
A. L. SMITH, L.J., (5):　　　　　　　　　　　　　　　　　　　　　　　　　I

" I do not pause to inquire about the pleadings, for the case is shortly
that from time immemorial—as the jury have found on evidence that is
overwhelming—the fishermen and yacht-owners who are represented in the
information by the Attorney-General have been mooring their craft at the
place in question . . ."

That being the sole issue between the parties, anything that was said in the

(4) [1897] 2 Q.B. 318.　　　　　　　　　　　(5) [1897] 2 Q.B. at p. 322.

A judgments of the Court of Appeal, over and above their upholding of the jury's verdict as to local custom, was, in my judgment, obiter.

It is not, however, clear that LORD ESHER's words related to any right of placing moorings in another person's land. After taking judicial notice of what he said were the facts about H.M.S. Victory at Portsmouth and about yachts in Cowes Roads (statements which are criticised factually in a footnote at p. 513 of COULSON

B & FORBES ON WATERS AND LAND DRAINAGE), LORD ESHER said (6):

" There is, therefore, this mode of bringing a ship to rest and keeping her so for a time, which is within the ordinary course of navigation. This is not a right of any individual: it is a general right to use the waters for navigation in any ordinary way, and to anchor in either of the two well-known ways, either by means of an anchor or of a mooring."

C

It may be that LORD ESHER was discussing only the right of a navigator to use permanent moorings which are already there, as distinct from the right actually to place and keep moorings in some one else's land. It may be that A. L. SMITH, L.J., in passages in his judgment (7) was dealing with the same limited aspect. If, however, the judgments go further than that, I respectfully think that they are

D not only obiter, but should not be followed in that further aspect.

It would, to my mind, be quite remarkable that, if such a right had always existed at common law, there are not to be found any cases in the books, discussing and defining the right. For endless problems would necessarily have arisen as to the various aspects of the scope and limitations of the right, which would have called for decision by the courts over the centuries. Yet there appears to be no

E such case. More important is the fact that there are authoritative dicta which are flatly inconsistent with the supposed right. BLACKBURN, J., that great master of the common law, in *Marshall* v. *Ulleswater Steam Navigation Co.* (8), said in relation to rights of navigation:

" And, therefore, the rule of law is . . . that they have no right to disturb the soil covered with water [videlicet, the soil belonging to another person]

F as by permanently fixing anchors."

This authority does not appear to have been cited to the court in *A.-G.* v. *Wright* (9). Again, fourteen years after *A.-G.* v. *Wright* (9), in *Denaby and Cadeby Main Collieries, Ltd.* v. *Anson* (10), a case in which *A.-G.* v. *Wright* (9) was cited, FLETCHER MOULTON, L.J., as I understand his judgment, strongly and clearly

G rejected the conception. He said (11):

" It must be remembered that the right here claimed is one which directly affects the owner of the soil. The fact that it involves permanent occupation of the water over it would be sufficient to establish this; but in addition it involves mooring or anchoring on the land itself, which is a right much of the same character as a right to drive piles into his land for the purpose of

H fixing the position of the coal hulk. The plaintiffs therefore set up that the public have a right to do this wherever it can be shown that a section of the public is benefited thereby. I cannot find any trace of any servitude of this wide description in any legal authority or decision, and a universal silence of this kind is the strongest proof that no such common law right exists."

I This passage indicates that FLETCHER MOULTON, L.J., did not regard the judgments in *A.-G.* v. *Wright* (12) as meaning that one can, without permission and as a common law right, place permanent moorings in some one else's land as an

---

(6) [1897] 2 Q.B. at p. 321.
(8) (1871), L.R. 7 Q.B. 166 at p. 172.
(9) [1897] 2 Q.B. 318.
(11) [1911] 1 K.B. at pp. 201, 202.
(12) [1897] 2 Q.B. 318.

(7) [1897] 2 Q.B. at p. 323.

(10) [1911] 1 K.B. 171.

ordinary incident of navigation. Finally, in *Earl of Iveagh* v. *Martin* (13), A
PAULL, J., expressed the view that " the right to have a permanent mooring is
doubtful ", but he preferred the view expressed by BLACKBURN, J., in the passage
which I have previously cited (14), and he added (13): " As was said many years
ago: ' A man may not use the highway to stable his horse '."

I hold that there is no common law right to lay or maintain permanent moorings
in another person's land without his permission. Such a right may, of course, B
arise from custom or may be given by statute. Whether there is here such a
customary right I shall consider later, when I deal with the fifth issue. On the
first issue, the defendant fails.

I reach this conclusion with satisfaction. To my mind it would be little less
than fantastic that, in the absence of statute or proved local custom, the law
should allow any one navigating a ship or vessel, including every amateur C
yachtsman, to place bulky objects in another's land, without permission, and to
retain them there, presumably for ever, as being " an ordinary incident of
navigation ".

Before I consider and express my conclusions on the remaining issues, it is
desirable that I should set out the essential matters in the evidence with regard
to the plaintiff company's assertion of title to, and possession of, Fowley Rythe, D
involving also the evidence relating to the defendant's defence and counterclaim
based on custom and lost modern grant. As will be clear from what I have said
in defining the issues, the plaintiff company's primary contention is that it has
shown possession, and that possession is enough for its claim in trespass, without
having to show what has been described by counsel as a " paper title ". Nevertheless, it is desirable at this stage to set out also matters relating to the title E
claimed.

The " paper title " on which the plaintiff company relies begins with a conveyance of Jan. 26, 1878, from a Mrs. Jarman to William Henry Baldwin Castle.
The evidence of this conveyance is a draft indenture, verified by a statutory
declaration of Mr. Castle in 1913, in which he records that the actual deed of
conveyance and the earlier documents of title referred to therein had been lost. F
I see no reason to doubt that the draft indenture accurately represents a deed
made in the same terms on that date, and that the earlier documents of title
existed and were as specified therein. The property conveyed consisted of three
parcels, for which the consideration paid by Mr. Castle was £210. The parcels
were, first, just over nine acres of " mudland ", consisting of part of the foreshore immediately adjacent to which is now Western Parade, Emsworth; second, G
Fowley Island and adjoining mudland of some twenty-three acres; and, third,
" the rythe called Fowley Rythe containing five acres one rood and ten
perches ". The tracing, which I have no doubt is a reproduction of the plan
attached to the lost deed of conveyance, shows that it is the Rythe itself—the
bed and, I assume, the banks—which was conveyed in this parcel, running south-
ward and progressively widening from the mudland which constituted the first H
parcel, where the Rythe is extremely narrow, and terminating very close to
Fowley Point. The earlier transactions recited in the deed begin with a conveyance
of July 22, 1870, relating to these identical parcels.

I omit for the moment reference to a transaction in 1885, affecting the same
three parcels of land, between Mr. Castle and another, of the one part, and a
company called the Fowley Oyster Fishery Co., Ltd., of the other part; a trans- I
action on which the defendant strongly relies as destroying the plaintiff company's
" paper title ", whatever its validity might otherwise be.

The next relevant evidence in this context is in two statutory declarations,
made, respectively, by Mr. Castle on Mar. 27, 1913, and by a Mr. Fogden on
Mar. 18, 1913. Mr. Castle's declaration, as I have already stated, refers to the
1878 conveyance and to the loss of the original deed and other documents. He
states that

---

(13) [1960] 2 All E.R. 668 at p. 684; [1961] 1 Q.B. 232 at p. 273.
(14) (1871), L.R. 7 Q.B. at p. 172.

A   " I have never had occasion to deal with the said lands and hereditaments in any way and I cannot remember when I last saw the said deed and documents of title."

He asserts that he has never mortgaged, charged or encumbered the property in question. Mr. Fogden refers to the purchase by Mr. Castle in 1878 and says that Mr. Castle then instructed him, Fogden, to collect the rents and act as his agent

B   in reference to the lands bought. He asserts that during the whole of the time from 1878 to 1913 he has so managed them and that

" for some six years past James Richard Mant of High Street, Emsworth, butcher, has been the tenant of the said lands and hereditaments and has paid me rent therefor during the said period."

C   Mr. Fogden avers that Mr. Castle never mortgaged or encumbered the lands or any part of them. Neither Mr. Castle nor Mr. Fogden in their statutory declarations makes any reference to the Fowley Oyster Fishery Co., Ltd. transaction in 1885.

Mr. Castle died on June 13, 1918. His executors, by indenture dated Dec. 14, 1918, sold the same three parcels, including Fowley Rythe, to Mr. Harvey Dixon.

D   The purchase price was £17 10s. Mr. Dixon was a resident of Emsworth, and was very well known in the locality. He was chairman of the local bench of magistrates and at one time chairman of the local council. He was also a yachtsman and a member of the Emsworth Sailing Club, of which he became a flag officer, and a member of the committee and a trustee of the club property, and, I assume, so remained until his death. Mr. Dixon died on Sept. 16, 1943.

E   His executors, on Apr. 19, 1950, conveyed the same lands, consisting of the three parcels including Fowley Rythe, to G. Andrew, Ltd., the price being £100. G. Andrew, Ltd., was a private company of which Mr. William Reginald Dudley Andrew was a governing director and in which he held ninety-eight out of one hundred fully paid shares of £1 each. On Apr. 2, 1963, G. Andrew, Ltd. conveyed to the plaintiff company, for a consideration of £500, two of the three parcels

F   comprised in the earlier conveyances. Fowley Island was retained by G. Andrew, Ltd.; Fowley Rythe and the mudlands opposite to Western Parade were conveyed to the plaintiff company.

I shall have to return to questions which have arisen regarding the " paper title " when I consider the third issue (see p. 488, letter B, post). I now turn to the evidence affecting the plaintiff company's claim to have possession of Fowley

G   Rythe. So far as that is concerned, the relevant date, I apprehend, is in or about July, 1963, when the plaintiff company demanded payment from the defendant. Nevertheless, evidence of earlier facts and events is relevant on that issue, and the evidence which I am now about to summarise is relevant also on the issues of the plaintiff company's claim to title under the Limitation Act, 1939, and on the defendant's claims of customary right and lost modern grant.

H   There was an issue of fact whether the defendant knew that, before his permanent mooring was placed in Fowley Rythe, consent was sought on his behalf from Mr. Andrew as representing G. Andrew, Ltd., at that time the owner of the Rythe if the claimed " paper title " was good. Mr. Dalgleish, who was employed as a boatman by the Emsworth Sailing Club from 1924 until 1965 gave evidence for the plaintiff company. His memory was not accurate on certain questions of

I   dates. For example, he believed that certain moorings laid in Fowley Rythe by the sailing club with the express permission of Mr. Dixon were laid in 1924 or 1925. In fact, as appears from the evidence of the late Vice-Admiral Curtis, whose written statement was admitted under the Evidence Act, 1938, those moorings were laid in 1933. Apart, however, from such errors of recollection as to dates, I find that Mr. Dalgleish was a reliable and responsible witness, and, where there is conflict, I prefer his evidence as to the facts about moorings to that of other local fishermen and boatmen called as witnesses.

On the issue as to the laying of the defendant's mooring, Mr. Dalgleish says

that when the defendant asked him as to the laying of a mooring in Fowley Rythe, A
he told the defendant that he was going to get permission, and the defendant
knew that that permission would be sought from Mr. Andrew.   In cross-
examination it was put to him that he never told the defendant that he was
asking anybody's permission to put the mooring down.   Mr. Dalgleish maintained
that he did tell the defendant.   When the defendant gave evidence, he stated that
Mr. Dalgleish said " I'll see Mr. Andrew ".   When the defendant asked, " What's B
this to do with Mr. Andrew? ";   Mr. Dalgleish replied " Mr. Andrew owns
Fowley Island ".   In cross-examination, the defendant agreed that obviously
Mr. Dalgleish felt he had to see Mr. Andrew about the matter; but he, the
defendant, did not understand the alleged reference to Fowley Island, but
thought that, as he put it, " Dalgleish had some bee in his bonnet about it ", and
did not give the matter any further thought.   I have no doubt that, whatever he C
now thinks, the defendant was aware at the time that Mr. Dalgleish was going to
seek Mr. Andrew's permission to lay the mooring in Fowley Rythe, and acquiesced
in that permission being sought.

That is one matter relied on by the plaintiff company as evidencing their
possession in fact of the Rythe and also as rebutting the defendant's claim of
customary right.   It is not relied on by the defendant as creating any relevant D
right in his favour.   By his pleading he denied, indeed, that any permission had
been sought with his knowledge or authority.   So far as the plaintiff company is
concerned, there is no suggestion that it constitutes an estoppel against the
defendant, or has any similar legal effect precluding him from disputing the
plaintiff company's possession or ownership.

There is a number of other matters on which the plaintiff company relies as E
evidence of possession in fact of Fowley Rythe.

First, it relies on the conveyances which I have cited.   While these, no doubt,
constitute the background against which the plaintiff company, and its predecessors in the " paper title ", might be expected to exert possession of the Rythe, I
do not see how the existence of a " paper title " can in itself be evidence of
possession in fact.   At the most, it entitles it to bring in as relevant evidence F
things done in the way of actual possession by its predecessors in that " paper
title ".

Secondly, the plaintiff company relies on the evidence in Mr. Fogden's statutory
declaration of his letting, for a rent, to Mr. Mant, the butcher, of the properties
including Fowley Rythe for about six years before Mar. 18, 1913.   I see no reason
to disbelieve that factual statement of Mr. Fogden.   It is some evidence of actual G
possession of the Rythe by Mr. Castle, through a lessor or licensee, from 1907
until at least 1913.   Against that, evidence was given of there having been certain
other permanent moorings in the Rythe before the first war.   Mr. Dalgleish's
uncle, Mr. Mills, now aged ninety-eight, is said to have laid three sets of moorings
in the Rythe from 1884 to 1904, taking them up at the end of each sailing season
and replacing them at the start of the next season.   After 1904, he abandoned H
them.   There was, not surprisingly, no satisfactory evidence whether or not Mr.
Mills had sought or obtained the permission of any one.   There was also evidence,
which I accept, of a Mr. Swinburn, now aged seventy, of at least three moorings
having been laid in the Rythe by people whom he named, at some time before
the first war.   Again, there is no acceptable evidence whether the persons concerned had sought any one's permission.   The only other evidence given by Mr. I
Swinburn which was of any real help is that, between the first and second wars,
there were about a dozen permanent moorings, in all, in the Rythe.   That, I
think, corresponds reasonably closely with the evidence of Mr. Dalgleish.

Thirdly, further evidence of possession relied on by the plaintiff company is
that Mr. Harvey Dixon, at that time owner under the " paper title ", had had a
mooring for his own boats in Fowley Rythe.

Fourthly, the plaintiff company sought to rely on the fact, proved by Captain
Wynne-Edwards, that in or soon after 1934, he, living in Emsworth, had obtained

A permission from Mr. Dixon's estate office to build a pier over the foreshore, paying a peppercorn rent for it. The place where the pier was built was on the first parcel of land referred to in the conveyance, namely, the part of the foreshore adjacent to Western Parade. I do not think in the circumstances this piece of evidence is of any great weight in relation to the question of actual possession of the other parcel with which I am alone concerned in this action, namely Fowley Rythe.

B   Fifthly, the plaintiff company strongly relies on the evidence, which was uncontradicted and which I accept, that in 1933 (not 1924 or 1925 as Mr. Dalgleish thought) Mr. Harvey Dixon gave permission to the Emsworth Sailing Club to place six permanent moorings in Fowley Rythe, for use by members who had ocean-going boats, the members paying the club an annual fee for this use. These moorings were, apparently, sold by the club to individual members after 1945.

C There is no evidence that any one's permission was sought for the sale.

Sixthly, as I hold to be proved, after the second war, when G. Andrew, Ltd. held the " paper title ", that company, through Mr. Andrew, gave Mr. Dalgleish permission at various times to lay further permanent moorings for individual members of the sailing club, to a total of about six. I would infer that the members concerned knew of the fact that such permission had been obtained. The

D defendant's mooring was one of these. I have already held that he knew that permission was sought.

Seventhly, the plaintiff company relies on its own acts asserting possession, as evidenced by their letter of July 12, 1963, within three months or so of their assuming the " paper title ", and on the fact, as proved, that in 1963 some eleven persons paid their mooring fees, and in 1964 some sixteen persons, all in respect

E of moorings in Fowley Rythe.

I shall now summarise the evidence relied on by the defendant in these matters.

As to the plaintiff company's " seventhly " above, the defendant shows that, at the relevant date—the summer of 1963—there were other persons, occupying fixed moorings in Fowley Rythe, who have not accepted the plaintiff company's demand to pay fees therefore.

F   In their letter of July 12, 1963, the plaintiff company wrote as follows to the defendant, and no doubt to other persons using the moorings:

" A number of moorings exist in Fowley Rythe channel and it is understood that previous owners made no attempt to regulate the moorings nor incidentally to collect mooring fees from the users."

G This, the defendant says, comes at least very close to an admission that the plaintiff company's predecessors had not asserted nor exercised possession of Fowley Rythe and that the plaintiff company was not then in possession. I have already referred to the evidence about moorings before the first war. After the first war, as I accept from the evidence of Mr. Woodley, the manager since 1920 of the Emsworth Shipyard Co., Ltd., permanent moorings were laid in Fowley

H Rythe from time to time on his instructions. Some six in all were so laid, some of them probably soon after the second war. Some of them were let out at a rent by the shipyard to clients. No one's permission was sought. Mr. Woodley knew, and no doubt frequently met, Mr. Dixon and later Mr. Andrew, but he had no idea that permission was required, or that any one claimed a right to give or refuse permission. The laying and continual use of these moorings must have been known

I to Mr. Harvey Dixon and, later, to Mr. Andrew. It is true that, before 1920, one mooring appears to have been laid by the predecessor company of Mr. Woodley's company, and that Mr. Harvey Dixon was a director of that company; but I cannot draw the inference that the post-1920 moorings of the shipyard company were based on, or treated by all concerned as, an extension of some earlier permission that might conceivably have been given to some one else.

While there is a good deal of confusion in the evidence about the dates, numbers and places in the Rythe of other permanent moorings laid by other persons, it is clear on the evidence that by the summer of 1963 there were at least twenty-four

permanent moorings in the Rythe, and probably thirty or even more. Of these, A
so far as the evidence goes, only some dozen or so were laid with the permission
of the plaintiff company's predecessors. That means that, including Mr. Woodley's six moorings, at least as many again had been laid by various persons at
various times, with a complete absence of evidence either that permission had
been sought or that objection had been raised by the plaintiff company's
predecessors.   B

Having reviewed the evidence, I now come to consider the second issue, which
is whether the plaintiff company has proved possession of Fowley Rythe so that,
without more, the defendant is a trespasser.

The contention of the plaintiff company, which is I think open to it on the
pleadings although it expressly pleads ownership in fee simple, is based on a
proposition of law which can be stated in words used by PARKER, J., in *Lord*   C
Fitzhardinge v. *Purcell* (15):

> " An action of trespass is founded on possession, and in order to succeed
> the plaintiff must show possession of the lands on which the acts complained
> of were committed at the date of such acts. If possession be shown, the
> defendant is not at liberty to set up the title of a third party unless he   D
> justifies what he has done under a licence from such third party. When, how-
> ever, as in the present case, a plaintiff in trespass, not being able to prove
> actual possession, proposes to show possession at law by proving his title to
> the property, the defendant may, I think, show, if he can, that the title is
> not in the plaintiff, but in some third party."

It is not, as I understand it, challenged by the defendant that that proposition E
of law is correct. If the plaintiff company shows actual possession of the whole
bed and banks of Fowley Rythe, then the defendant, not asserting for himself
any licence from the Crown to place a fixed mooring in the Rythe, cannot put the
plaintiff company to proof of their title against the Crown. If, on the other hand,
the plaintiff company fails to show such actual possession, then they can establish
their action for trespass against the defendant only by showing " possession at   F
law ", as PARKER, J., calls it (15).

The real dispute between the parties on this issue is, I believe, primarily one of
law. For the plaintiff company it is said that it is sufficient for it to show some
evidence of possession, even though it be slight. For the defendant it is said that
the plaintiff company, before it can rely on mere actual possession as a ground
for making the defendant a wrongdoer and a trespasser, must show that it has, G
at the relevant time, exclusive actual possession.

In my judgment, on principle and authority, the defendant's contention is
right. The plaintiff company must show exclusive possession in fact, subject only
to one qualification relating to a peculiarity applicable to possession of the
foreshore and the bed of tidal waters thereon.

I see no reason why, in principle, a possession which is less than exclusive should H
be sufficient to found an action in trespass without further proof of title in the
plaintiff. In the book " POSSESSION IN THE COMMON LAW ", by SIR FREDERICK
POLLOCK and R. S. WRIGHT, J., there are numerous indications that what is
called " de facto possession ", to be relevant for such purposes as the plaintiffs
here desire, must be exclusive. Thus at p. 30, the following passage will be found:

> " What kind of acts, and how many, can be accepted as proof of exclusive   I
> use, must depend to a great extent on the manner in which the particular
> kind of property is commonly used. When the object is as a whole incapable
> of manual control, and the question is merely who has de facto possession,
> all that a claimant can do is to show that he or some one through whom he
> claims has been dealing with that object as an occupying owner might be
> expected to deal with it, and that no one else has done so."

(15) [1908] 2 Ch. at p. 145.

A   The last eight words are important.

The two authorities principally relied on by the plaintiffs are *Hastings Corpn.* v. *Ivall* (16) and *Nicholls* v. *Ely Sugar Beet Factory, Ltd.* (17). There is no doubt that these cases illustrate and apply the doctrine stated by Parker, J., in the passage which I have cited from *Lord Fitzhardinge* v. *Purcell* (18); and in the *Ely Sugar Beet* case (17) the doctrine is extended to cover nuisance as well as

B   trespass. In neither case, however, did the question of the exclusive nature of the plaintiffs' possession arise, and it was therefore unnecessary for it to be discussed.

I see no reason why exclusiveness should not at least equally be an element here, where it is asserted that the defendant is a wrongdoer simply on the basis of the plaintiff company's alleged actual possession of property, as it unquestionably is in other cases where actual possession is relevant to found a title. I shall

C   refer to two such cases, where exclusive possession was stated to be essential.

In *Lord Advocate* v. *Young, North British Ry. Co.* v. *Young* (19) Mr. Young claimed a title to the foreshore of a place called Colinswell, as against, inter alios, the Crown. For this purpose it was necessary for Mr. Young to show a prescriptive right, by possession by himself and his predecessors for twenty years, under certain Acts of Parliament. There was evidence of acts of possession,

D   but there was also evidence of what were called " encroachments " or " concurrent possessions " by other persons; in particular the collection of sea-weed and the removal of clay and stones from the foreshore. Lord Watson, in whose speech Lord Halsbury, L.C., and Lord Macnaghten concurred, said (20):

E   " These were in no proper sense the acts of the Crown; but acts of that description, although done without title, tend to derogate from the possession of the riparian proprietor, and if carried far enough will deprive possession of that exclusive character which is necessary in order to establish a prescriptive right. After careful consideration of the evidence bearing on these acts, I am satisfied that they were neither of such extent, nor of such duration in point of time, as to affect the quality of the possession had by the respondent and his predecessors. It seems to be proved that these encroachments by the

F   public (for in any view they were acts of encroachment) were not known to the proprietors of Colinswell; but I do not think that the respondent would have benefited by their ignorance if the acts had been more marked in character, or longer continued."

Foster v. *Warblington Urban District Council* (21) is a case which, curiously,

G   concerned the foreshore of Emsworth. It was a claim by one who asserted long-continued possession of oyster-beds on the foreshore for damage for nuisance consisting of the discharge of sewage. Fletcher Moulton, L.J., made it clear (22) that the " long continued enjoyment " necessary to found the plaintiff's right must be " of an exclusive character, of a right or a property ". He went on to show why, on the facts of the case, the possession was clearly exclusive in

H   character. I see no reason in logic, as I can find no basis in the authorities, for the view that any lesser extent of actual possession is sufficient for the purposes for which the plaintiffs require to use it on this issue.

The evidence which is necessary to establish possession of property must, of course, depend on the nature of the property, as was emphasised in the passage which I have cited from " Possession in the Common Law ". I accept that, as

I   regards the bed of a tidal creek, the evidence of placing permanent moorings on or in the soil may be of great importance. The exercise of rights of navigation, and the ordinary incidents thereof, are of no relevance for or against a claim for possession of the sea-bed. I accept also, in favour of the plaintiff company, since the

(16) (1874), L.R. 19 Eq. 588.   (17) [1931] All E.R. Rep. 154; [1931] 2 Ch. 84.
(18) [1908] 2 Ch. at p. 145.   (19) (1887), 12 App. Cas. 544.
(20) (1887), 12 App. Cas. at pp. 554, 555.
(21) [1904-07] 3 All E.R. Rep. 366; [1906] 1 K.B. 648.
(22) [1904-07] All E.R. Rep. at p. 378; [1906] 1 K.B. at p. 679.

contrary was not, I think, contended, that the granting of permission, by the A
plaintiff company's predecessors, to place permanent moorings can properly be
treated as consistent with, and indeed evidence of, possession by them. Much
might depend on the terms of the " permissions ", as to which there was no
evidence. For example, a " permission " might amount to a surrender for all
time of the right of the person giving permission to resume possession of the place
where the mooring was laid; and the sale by the sailing club to some of its B
members of the moorings laid with Mr. Dixon's permission might support such a
surrender, concurred in by the person who had given permission, or his successor.
I shall assume, however, that the " permissions " proved to have been given in
certain cases by Mr. Dixon and Mr. Andrew were and continued to be in the nature
of revocable licences.

I have mentioned earlier that the doctrine of exclusive possession, in relation C
to the foreshore and the beds of tidal creeks, is subject to a qualification. This is
illustrated by passages in the judgments in two cases. In *Lord Advocate* v. *Young*
(23), LORD WATSON said:

> " In estimating the character and extent of his possession it must always
> be kept in view that possession of the foreshore, in its natural state, can
> never be, in the strictest sense of the term, exclusive. The proprietor cannot D
> exclude the public from it at any time; and it is practically impossible to
> prevent occasional encroachments on his right, because the cost of preventive
> measures would be altogether disproportionate to the value of the subject."

In *Alfred F. Beckett, Ltd.* v. *Lyons* (24), RUSSELL, L.J., said:

> " It is a well known aspect of English law that in relation to the foreshore E
> a great many activities have been generally tolerated without giving rise to
> any legal right to continue them."

I do not think, however, that that qualification, which of course I fully accept,
has much relevance in a case such as the present, where the plaintiff company's
claim to have actual possession is founded to a large extent on the laying by it, or
with its permission, of permanent moorings: and the " concurrent possession ", F
to use LORD WATSON's phrase, relied on by the defendant is the laying of similar
moorings, to an equal or greater extent, by persons other than the alleged
possessors, with their knowledge and without evidence of their permission being
sought.

It is then suggested for the plaintiff company that this evidence of " concurrent
possession " may be explained as not affecting the plaintiff company's possession, G
or exclusive possession, by reference to an inference that it was done with the
tacit permission, or tolerance, of the plaintiff company's predecessors. In this
context, reliance is placed on the judgments of the Court of Appeal in *Beckett,
Ltd.* v. *Lyons* (25), already cited. In that case, the question was whether the
court should find a legal origin for a right, claimed to be enjoyed by the inhabitants
of the County Palatine of Durham, to take " sea-coal " from the foreshore, which H
had been leased by the Crown to a rural district council. The Court of Appeal held
that the evidence, while it established a local practice on so small a scale and so
limited in area as to be consistent with a licence from, and with toleration by,
the Crown, was not sufficient to support a claim as of right such as to require
the court to find a legal origin for the practice in the fiction of a lost Crown grant.
Part of the ground for the decision was, in the words of HARMAN, L.J., (26) that I
" toleration is a sufficient explanation ". HARMAN, L.J., also pointed out (27),
that none of the witnesses who gave evidence as to the practice of taking coal
was asked whether he believed himself to be exercising a legal right or was
merely doing something which he felt confident that the owner would not stop,
but would tolerate because it did no harm.

---

(23) (1887), 12 App. Cas. at p. 553.   (24) [1967] 1 All E.R. 833 at p. 847.
(25) [1967] 1 All E.R. 833.   (26) [1967] 1 All E.R. at p. 846.
(27) [1967] 1 All E.R. at p. 843.

A   I do not think that it is open to the plaintiff, who seeks to found an action for trespass on the basis, simply, of exclusive possession in himself, to nullify the evidence of equivalent acts of concurrent possession by others such as have been proved in this case, by saying that he or his predecessors must be assumed to have tolerated them because they did no harm.   No suggestion appears in Lord Watson's speech in *Lord Advocate* v. *Young* (28) which I have already cited,

B   that, if Mr. Young or his predecessors had known of extensive " encroachments ", they might be assumed, in the absence of evidence to the contrary, to have tolerated them so as to render them ineffective to defeat a claim based on exclusive possession.

The point of difference is, I think, illustrated by a question asked of Mr. Woodley in cross-examination by counsel for the plaintiff company, no doubt in

C   an effort to found an argument on *Beckett, Ltd.* v. *Lyons* (29): " If you had known that Mr. Harvey Dickson was the owner, would you have asked permission to lay the moorings? " To this Mr. Woodley necessarily answered " Yes ". The very question presupposed, however, that Mr. Harvey Dixon was the owner in law. Mr. Woodley, as I accept, had no idea that Mr. Dixon was the owner or claimed to be such.   Therefore, if Mr. Dixon was showing tolerance as regards Mr.

D   Woodley's moorings, it was what may be described as unilateral tolerance. The recipient was not aware that he was being tolerated by any one and did not act on that basis. The point in *Beckett's* case (29) was, on the other hand, that the truthful answers from the witnesses, in relation to their taking coal from the sea-shore, might well have been: " I did not think I was exercising a legal right, but I felt confident that the person with the legal right would tolerate it."

E   For the same reasons, I do not think that the plaintiff company gains support from the well-known passage in Parker, J.'s judgment in *Lord Fitzhardinge* v. *Purcell* (30) cited by Harman, L.J., in *Beckett's* case (31). Parker, J., was not there dealing with the question of possession in fact, which, as appears from the passage in the judgment already cited, the plaintiff had not proved. He was dealing with the question of an alleged legal right, relevant in *Beckett's* case (29),

F   but not relevant to the issue with which I am now concerned. In any event, I do not think that the assertion by Mr. Dixon or Mr. Andrew of a right to exclusive possession of Fowley Rythe could on the evidence in this case have been described as an " unnecessary and injurious restraint " against persons who placed permanent moorings without seeking their permission.

I hold accordingly that the plaintiff company has failed to prove actual

G   possession of the whole of Fowley Rythe of such a nature, and of sufficient exclusiveness, to establish its primary claim, arising on this second issue; namely, that because of their alleged possession the defendant is a trespasser, irrespective of their legal title to the bed and lands of the Rythe.

It follows that if the plaintiff company is to succeed it must prove its legal title, otherwise than by mere actual possession. This brings me to the third issue, the

H   plaintiff company's so-called " paper title " to Fowley Rythe.

It is, I confess, unsatisfactory that I should have to consider the plaintiff company's legal title as against the Crown in the absence of the Crown. Yet that is what is put in issue by the plaintiff company's assertion of legal title and the defendant's assertion that the title is not in the plaintiff company but is in the Crown. It would have been of assistance if the Crown had been represented, that

I   issue being raised in the pleadings; but I am told that, while both parties would have welcomed the intervention of the Crown and an approach was made to invite the Attorney-General to be joined, that invitation was declined. At one stage I had doubt whether I could properly proceed in the absence of the Crown, but I have satisfied myself, on precedent, that I can and should do so. That was the course taken by Parker, J., when he was faced with the same problem in

---

(28) (1887), 12 App. Cas. 544.   (29) [1967] 1 All E.R. 833.
(30) [1908] 2 Ch. at pp. 168, 169.   (31) [1967] 1 All E.R. at p. 843.

Lord Fitzhardinge v. *Purcell* (32). It must necessarily follow, unsatisfactory though A
it be, that while I have to decide between the plaintiff company and the defendant
whether the plaintiff company can disprove the Crown's title to Fowley Rythe,
the Crown, and I apprehend also that the plaintiff company, is not bound by the
decision as between themselves. I have to do my best to decide the question
between those who are parties to the action, in the absence of an interested
person, the Crown.   B

I have already set out the sequence of what has been called the " paper title "
(see p. 480, letter F et seq., ante), except for two matters. The first of those is that
the plaintiff company has not merely to show a title on the documents since 1870
or 1878, but it must also show a probability that before the first conveyance in
the sequence the Crown had divested itself of the ownership of the bed and banks
of this tidal creek. The second matter is that the defendant says that, even   C
assuming the first point against him, he has shown a break in the plaintiff
company's title by a transaction in 1885.

As to the first point, the plaintiff company relied on a grant by King Charles 1
to Mary and William Wandesford in the year 1628, and also on other evidence
including a tithe award of April, 1838. The Wandesford grant was considered
by the Court of Exchequer in 1811 in *A.-G.* v. *Parmeter, Re Portsmouth Harbour* D
(33), and by the House of Lords on appeal in the same case in 1813 (34). The
defendant says that those decisions in effect are authority that the Wandesford
grant is of no validity to establish a divesting of title by the Crown. The plaintiff
company says that LORD ELDON's speech in the House of Lords indicates that the
grant may be of relevance. The plaintiff company also relies on the decision of
the Court of Appeal in *Foster* v. *Warblington Urban District Council* (35), as E
authority for the proposition that the whole of the foreshore of Emsworth was
there shown to have been waste of the Manor of Warblington and hence to have
been divested from the Crown by some ancient grant to the then Lord of the
Manor—perhaps an early Earl of Emsworth. It is better, I think, that I should
express no view on the validity or relevance of the Wandesford grant or on the
other evidence and submissions on this point, since it is unnecessary to do so in F
view of my decision on the second point, and since it is undesirable, unless it be
necessary for the decision of the present action, to decide matters relating to
the title of the Crown in the absence of the Crown.

The second point is this. On Mar. 5, 1885, an agreement was made between
Mr. Henderson, Mr. Castle and Mr. Hersee, the latter as trustee for a joint stock
company, Fowley Oyster Fishery Co., Ltd., which was then about to be incorpor- G
ated. Amongst the provisions, Mr. Castle agreed to sell to the company the three
parcels of property which he had bought in 1878, including Fowley Rythe. He
was to receive as consideration fully paid shares in the new company. That company was incorporated on Mar. 9, 1885. On Mar. 31, 1885, a confirmatory agreement was executed, Mr. Castle and the Fowley Oyster Fishery Co., Ltd., being
among the parties to it. The agreement of Mar. 5, 1885, by which Mr. Castle H
undertook to sell the property to the company was scheduled to the confirmatory
agreement. The contemplated shares were duly issued, including the shares which
Mr. Castle was to receive as consideration for the sale of the property to the
company. There were sixteen shareholders in all. This shareholding is evidenced
by a certificate under the Companies Acts stating the position as at Sept. 9, 1885.

An article in a journal called the " Evening News " for Oct. 21, 1885, has been I
produced. It shows that the company had begun operations " in breeding, culti-
vating and dealing in oysters " in the property which was covered by the agreement. There is a reference to what is clearly Fowley Rythe, which is described
as " originally the store ground for wintering brood oysters ". No conveyance
of the property, including the Rythe, by Mr. Castle to the company has been
produced and none can be found. It is, therefore, left as a matter of inference

(32) [1908] 2 Ch. at p. 146.   (33) (1811), 10 Price, 378.
(34) (1813), 10 Price, 412.   (35) [1904-07] All E.R. Rep. 366; [1906] 1 K.B. 648.

A whether such conveyance as was contemplated and required by the agreement
was ever actually executed. I draw the inference that there probably was such a
conveyance. This is not only because it would have been the normal and expected
consequence of the agreement, but also because of the fact that such a conveyance
would provide a sensible explanation of the failure of Mr. Castle in 1913 to find
the 1878 deed or the earlier documents referred to therein. They would presumably
B have passed to the company, on a conveyance of the property, as documents of
title. If there was such a conveyance, it is not suggested that there was any
re-conveyance by the company to Mr. Castle thereafter. It does not, however,
matter whether or not that inference is correct. It is conceded for the plaintiff
company that, even if no conveyance was ever executed, Mr. Castle would
thereafter by virtue of the agreement have held the property, including Fowley
C Rythe, as trustee for the company, which would have been the beneficial owner.
   It is apparent that the Fowley Oyster Fishery Co., Ltd., did not prosper. Indeed
it is possible that its operations in the Emsworth Harbour area soon ceased. Its
history can be deduced only from documents filed with the registrar of companies.
From these, it appears that by August, 1889, the company's registered office,
wherever it had been originally established, was at Poole. One of the original
D shareholders, Mr. Penney, lived at Poole. By a resolution of Aug. 29, 1889, the
name of the company was changed to " Poole Oyster Fishery Co., Ltd.". Mr.
Penney was then the secretary of the company. Whether it was then carrying
on oyster activities at Poole, and if so, whether the Fowley enterprise had been
abandoned, can be a matter of speculation only. It is, however, clear that on
July 25, 1892, the Poole Oyster Fishery Co., Ltd., passed a winding-up resolution,
E on the ground that " the company cannot by reason of its liabilities, continue its
business ". Mr. Penney was appointed liquidator. On June 17, 1904, the company
was dissolved. There is no evidence what, if anything, happened to any of its
property in the winding-up. In view of the evidence of the winding-up resolution
in 1892, it is unlikely that the company's difficulties can be attributed to the
disaster which occurred in 1902, when persons who had eaten Emsworth oysters
F at a mayoral banquet in Winchester were attacked by typhoid fever. This
lamentable occurrence is referred to in *Foster* v. *Warblington Urban District
Council* (36) which I have already cited.
   The plaintiff company says that the proper inference is that at some time
between 1885 and 1904 there was an agreement between the company and Mr.
Castle, and, presumably, the other shareholders, which resulted in the Fowley
G properties, including Fowley Rythe, being regranted or released by the company
to their previous owner, Mr. Castle; so that, there having been no conveyance
to the company, the company's beneficial title under the trusteeship of Mr. Castle
was given up, and Mr. Castle again became both legal and beneficial owner,
with, presumably, adjustments affecting the financial rights of other shareholders.
I do not think that such an inference can properly be drawn. First, as I have said,
H I would infer that there was a conveyance to the company, and there was no re-
conveyance. Second, even if there were no conveyance, but Mr. Castle continued
to hold the legal title as trustee for the company, I find it impossible to draw the
inference that a subsequent agreement was made such as the plaintiff company
suggests. Mr. Castle's statutory declaration in 1913 asserts that " I have never had
occasion to deal with the said lands ". On any view, that is not correct. Whether
I or not in 1913 Mr. Castle had completely forgotten the episode of the Fowley
Oyster Fishery Co., Ltd., I am unable to infer on the documentary evidence that
the title, whether beneficial only, or legal, which passed to the company came back
to him by some unevidenced and forgotten transaction. If the company's ownership, legal or beneficial, of Fowley Rythe was not otherwise disposed of in or
before the dissolution of the company, it would, I suppose have reverted to the
Crown, as bona vacantia, as counsel for the defendant submits. Hence the
plaintiff company fails to establish their " paper title ", so far as the evidence in
this action goes.

(36) [1904-07] All E.R. Rep. 366; [1906] 1 K.B. 648.

I come to the fourth issue. The plaintiff company relies alternatively on a sub- A mission that it has a title against the Crown by reason of sixty years' adverse possession under the proviso to s. 4 (1) of the Limitation Act, 1939, relating to the foreshore, which is defined in s. 31 of the Act of 1939 to include the bed of any tidal water. As counsel for the plaintiff company was, I think, disposed to agree, if the plaintiff company cannot establish possession sufficient to support its submission on the second issue, it cannot discharge the heavier burden under the B Limitation Act, 1939. For that purpose, the plaintiff company must establish, as one element, exclusive possession at the relevant date. That it fails to do, for reasons which I have given when dealing with the second issue.

Lastly, and this is the fifth issue, the defendant both by his defence and by his counterclaim asserts that he is entitled as of right to affix mooring tackle in Fowley Rythe on the grounds of custom, prescription and lost modern grant. In C his final speech, counsel for the defendant abandoned the claim based on pre- scription, but he maintained his claim on the other two grounds. Much of the evidence and argument was directed, in part, to these matters. In view of my decision, on the plaintiff company's primary claim, that they, to succeed, have to show exclusive possession, it follows that the evidence as to concurrent possession was relevant to both issues, though with the onus of proof resting differently on D the two issues. On the issues of custom and lost modern grant the defendant fails. The evidence shows a lack of universality of assertion by those who have used Fowley Rythe over the years, of a right to fix permanent moorings, certainly as against the plaintiff company or its predecessors in the alleged " paper title ". The evidence that various persons, including, as I have held, the defendant him- self, were aware that permission had been sought from Mr. Dixon and Mr. Andrew, E and in some cases at least that such permission had been given, establishes that there was nothing like a universal assertion of a claim as of right, such as is necessary to establish a customary right or the presumption of a lost modern grant. Moreover, I consider that such a custom, apparently suggested as being applicable to the world at large—to all persons who choose to navigate in Fowley Rythe—would require to be much more closely defined and limited before it could F be justified as a custom or as the subject-matter of a grant. If it applied to the world at large and gave continuing rights to persons who had established per- manent moorings, it would soon become self-destructive so far as the public at large is concerned.

Further, if there had been such a custom earlier, it would, as the plaintiff company asserts, have been destroyed by the bringing into force of the Harbour G bye-laws under statutory authority, since a customary right for any one to lay moorings at will anywhere in the Rythe would be repugnant to the statutory con- trol given to the harbour master, whether in fact exercised or not, to prohibit the laying of moorings by any one, either in the Rythe at all, or at any particular place in it.

I have earlier held on the first issue that the right which is also asserted in the H defence and in the counterclaim for any member of the public including the defendant to put permanent moorings in any part of the foreshore or the bed of a tidal creek, irrespective of its ownership by the Crown or by a private individual, is not warranted as a part of the common law of the land.

It follows that both the claim and the counterclaim fail and that neither party is entitled to the relief claimed by him.   I

Claim and counterclaim dismissed.

Solicitors: *Waterhouse & Co.*, agents for *Glenville*, Portsmouth & Southsea (for the plaintiff company); *Wilkinson, Kimbers & Stadden*, agents for *Perkins & Harris*, Guildford (for the defendant).

[*Reported by* MARY COLTON, *Barrister-at-Law.*]

A

NOTE.

R. *v.* TUNDE-OLARINDE.

B [COURT OF APPEAL, CRIMINAL DIVISION (Lord Parker, C.J., Winn, L.J., and
Willis, J.), January 26, 1967.]

*Road Traffic—Disqualification for holding licence—Life disqualification—
Whether for certain period—Road Traffic Act, 1962 (10 & 11 Eliz. 2 c. 59),
s. 5.*

C [As to disqualification for holding or obtaining a driving licence, see 33 HALS-
BURY's LAWS (3rd Edn.) 638, 639, para. 1080; and for cases on the subject, see
45 DIGEST (Repl.) 118, 119, *409-419.*]

Appeal.
This was an appeal by John Tunde-Olarinde against that part of his sentence,
passed on him at Inner London Sessions on two counts of driving while dis-
D qualified, which ordered disqualification from driving for life.   The appellant
had been disqualified for fifteen years in July, 1960 for two offence of driving
while disqualified and four offences of driving without having in force an
insurance policy in respect of third-party risks.

P. T. S. Batterbury for the appellant.

E   **LORD PARKER, C.J.,** having stated the nature of the appeal and having
reviewed the appellant's history in regard to use of the roads, concluded: Counsel
for the appellant has argued that to disqualify the appellant for life really leaves
him little hope of driving again.   That no doubt was the intention.   The single
judge, in giving leave, questioned whether a disqualification for life was a proper
sentence in that it might be argued that the period was not certain and ascertain-
F able and thus did not enable disqualification to be reckoned by reference to it.
Under the Act (1) the court must disqualify for a period.   Granted that it
must be a period certain, this court is quite satisfied that disqualification for life
is for a period certain, and indeed courts throughout the country have been
acting on this basis for years.   The appeal is dismissed.

Appeal dismissed.

G   Solicitor: *Registrar of Criminal Appeals* (for the appellant).

[*Reported by* N. P. METCALFE, ESQ., *Barrister-at-Law.*]

H

I

---

(1) See Road Traffic Act, 1962, s. 5; 42 HALSBURY'S STATUTES (2nd Edn.) 891.

SIOW WONG FATT v. SUSUR ROTAN MINING, LTD. AND A ANOTHER.

[PRIVY COUNCIL (Lord Hodson, Lord Guest and Lord Upjohn), February 13, 14, 15, April 19, 1967.]

Privy Council—Malaysia—Compensation—Act done for another person— Expenditure on making road to mineral lands—Appellant granted prospector's B *licence—Agreement by appellant with company for sub-lease of mineral lands to company—Assignments of benefit of agreement vesting benefit in first respondents—Road to mineral lands built by respondents when they were prospectively entitled to mining rights and sub-lease by virtue of assigned agreement—Whether respondents entitled to compensation from appellant for building road, they having ceased to be entitled to the benefit of the agreement—* C *Contract Ordinance, s. 71.*

In November, 1959, the appellant was granted a prospector's licence in respect of certain mineral lands in Johore. In September, 1960, the benefit of an agreement by which the appellant was to allow a company to prospect the mineral lands and to grant a sub-lease of the lands to the company (when the lease was granted to the appellant) became vested in the first D respondents; the consideration for the agreement included paying to the appellant a tribute per ton of ore raised. Between April and December, 1961, the first respondents constructed a road, eight or nine miles long, to the mineral lands. At the time the first respondents were the owners of the mining rights in the mineral lands by virtue of the agreement. Subsequently they ceased to be so, for they settled with the assignor to them not to enforce E the assignment in their favour. On appeal in an action by the first respondents against the appellant for compensation for the cost of making the road, which they claimed under s. 71 of the Contract Ordinance, whereby a person who " lawfully does anything for another person . . ., not intending to do so gratuitously, the latter is bound to make compensation to the former in respect of . . . the thing so done ", F

Held: the relevant point of time at which to determine whether the conditions of s. 71 were satisfied was when the thing was done, and in the present case when the first respondents built the road in 1961 they were not acting for the appellant but for their own benefit, and they were intending to act gratuitously, for they were not looking to anyone for reimbursement; accordingly the conditions of s. 71 were not satisfied and the respondents G were not entitled to the reimbursement that they claimed (see p. 496, letters B, D and E, post).

Observations of LORD SIMONDS in *Governor-General in Council* v. *Madura* ((1948), L.R. 75 I.A. at p. 221) applied.

Appeal allowed.

[Editorial Note. There is no provision in the English statute law exactly H comparable to s. 71 of the Contract Ordinance; perhaps the nearest analogy is the equitable rule under which a person who in good faith incurs expense in dealing with the property of another is, in appropriate circumstances, able to resist a claim by the true owner to the extent of being allowed as against the true owner the expenses of what has been done; see 14 HALSBURY's LAWS (3rd Edn.) 530, para. 999, text and notes (g)-(i) and ibid., p. 640, para. 1180; and for cases I on this subject, see 21 DIGEST (Repl.) 452-455, *1542-1568*.]

Case referred to:

Governor-General in Council v. *Madura*, (1948), L.R. 75 I.A. 213.

Appeal.

This was an appeal from a judgment and order of the Federal Court of Malaysia, appellate jurisdiction (THOMSON, L.P., CHONG JIN, C.J., and TAN AH TAH, F.J.), dated Sept. 18, 1964, whereby the appellant, Siow Wong Fatt, was ordered to pay compensation to the first respondents, the Susur Rotan Mining, Ltd., under s. 71

A   of the Contract Ordinance, such compensation to be equivalent to all moneys expended by the respondents in respect of the appellant's mineral lands, subject to one excepted set of payments.   The judgment allowed the respondents' appeal from a judgment of the High Court of Malaysia (AZMI, J.), dated Jan. 22, 1964, in so far as it dismissed the respondents' claim for compensation under s. 71. The Kota Mining Co., Ltd., were pro forma respondents. The facts are

B   set out in the judgment of the Board.

   I. C. Baillieu and *A. M. Hill* for the appellants.
   Mervyn Heald for the respondents.

   LORD UPJOHN: This is an appeal from the order dated Feb. 18, 1965, of the Federal Court of Malaysia whereby the appellant was ordered to pay

C   compensation to the respondents under and by virtue of the provisions of s. 71 of the Contract Ordinance. It raises some difficult, though short, questions of general importance on the true construction of s. 71.

   The facts are rather complicated, but for the purposes of this appeal can be fairly briefly stated. Parts of Johore are rich in minerals which are owned by the State. The appellant (to whom their lordships will refer as Mr. Siow) had the good

D   fortune to make some discoveries in relation to a few hundreds of acres of land in the Susur Rotan district, which gave promise of bearing iron ore. Their lordships will refer to this land as the mineral lands. On Apr. 10, 1957, he applied to the relevant government authorities for a prospector's licence to prospect for minerals thereon. A licence was granted to him on Nov. 21, 1959, and by statute this gave him, in effect, the right to a first refusal of a lease to mine the mineral

E   lands. To jump ahead chronologically, issue of a mining lease for ten years at a rent of $5 per acre to Mr. Siow was duly approved by the appropriate authorities on Sept. 28, 1961, and, though not in evidence before their lordships, it is not in dispute that a lease of the mineral lands was shortly thereafter granted to him.

   It is common ground that neither the application for a prospector's licence nor the grant of such licence gave to Mr. Siow any legal or equitable estate or interest

F   in the mineral lands; but it is not in doubt that he could contractually and for consideration transmit to others the rights or expectancies which were likely to accrue to him as a result of his application in accordance with the ordinary and customary practice in relation to such matters in Johore.

   Mr. Siow was not a mining engineer and had no great resources; he was a lucky prospector, very willing to turn to quick account the discoveries which he thought

G   that he had made. On June 17, 1958, he entered into an agreement with two gentlemen trading under the style of Tang Hai Mining Co. which (as varied by supplemental agreement of Dec. 2, 1958) provided that he would allow that company to prospect the mineral lands in consideration of a cash sum then and there paid (by way of loan), and he undertook to grant to them a sub-lease if and when a lease should be granted to him in consideration of payment of further sums and

H   a tribute of 50c. per ton of iron ore raised.   On July 3, 1959, the Tang Hai Mining Co. sold their rights under the agreements just mentioned to one Shan Sai Sow. As between those parties the cash payments and tonnage tributes were increased, but nothing turns thereon.

   Shan Sai Sow then formed a company called the Kota Mining Co., Ltd. (to which their lordships will refer as Kota) and by an agreement on Dec. 4, 1959,

I   the benefits and burdens of the agreement of July 3, 1959, were thereby transferred to Kota. On Sept. 19, 1960, by an agreement made between Kota and the first respondent, Susur Rotan Mining, Ltd. (to whom their lordships will refer as Susur Rotan) Kota granted its rights under the earlier agreements to Susur Rotan in consideration of $40,000 then and there paid and a further $40,000 to be paid at a later stage (which in fact never was paid) and a tribute of $2 for every ton raised. It is clear from cll. 3 and 4 of this agreement that Susur Rotan was the company who were entitled to mine and exploit the mining lands. This would, of course, involve them in much expenditure preparatory to such exploitation,

such as the building of roads, jetties and other works, and such expenditure would   A
fall on Susur Rotan, who could not look to any other person for reimbursement of
such expenditure under or by virtue of this chain of agreements.

By the end of the year 1960 therefore the business situation may be summarised
thus. Mr. Siow had received a prospector's licence which gave him a great
advantage in that as a commercial proposition he was almost certain to receive
a mining lease in respect of the mineral lands. By a train of sub-contracts Susur   B
Rotan were entitled as a matter of substance to the benefit of the prospector's
licence and the right to a mining sub-lease of the mineral lands.

The mineral lands were virgin jungle. It would not be difficult to extract the
ore from the land for it is all on or near to the surface, but it was commercially
necessary to make a road for eight or nine miles to the nearest public road. There
had been some thought of an alternative route to the sea which would have   C
involved making a small jetty, but in the end it was decided that to build a road
was the right answer. Accordingly Susur Rotan made this road, starting in April,
1961, and finishing it in December of that year at a cost of $140,000. It is clear
that Susur Rotan did this because at this time for the reasons just mentioned,
subject to the payment of cash and a tribute, they were commercially the owners
of the mining rights granted or to be granted to Mr. Siow, though no doubt   D
through a chain of sub-leases. This has never been disputed. However, as will
appear in their lordships' judgment, Susur Rotan, at a later stage, chose to settle
their rights to exploit the mineral lands for a cash payment. The road was
completed, but Susur Rotan never started to mine the mineral lands; it was
suggested that the reason for this was due to some failure on the part of Mr. Siow
to meet his obligations, but this alleged failure has never been explored in the   E
courts below and their lordships are quite unable to accept that as proved. For
whatever reason Kota did not carry out their part of the contract with Susur
Rotan and the latter, feeling themselves aggrieved, brought an action against
Kota for specific performance of the agreement of Sept. 19, 1960, joining Mr.
Siow as another defendant, against whom they made a claim based on an alleged
oral agreement.   F

It is necessary to explore the course of this action in some detail for their
lordships heard much argument on it. Susur Rotan issued their writ on Sept. 17,
1962, and by their statement of claim they claimed (a) against Mr. Siow specific
performance of an alleged oral agreement made in a series of conversations on or
about the Chinese New Year 1961 (February, 1961) between Mr. Siow and
Susur Rotan whereby, in consideration of Susur Rotan taking such steps as would   G
enable Mr. Siow to obtain a mining lease, Mr. Siow agreed to grant to Susur
Rotan a sub-lease of the mineral lands and (b) against Kota specific performance
of the agreement of Sept. 19, 1960.

As the claim against Mr. Siow was for specific performance of an oral agreement, Susur Rotan pleaded a number of acts of part performance by them,
including the construction of the mining road already mentioned, alleged to have   H
been done in pursuance of that oral agreement. When the case came on before
Azmi, J., on Nov. 10, 1963, counsel for Susur Rotan announced that the action
between his client and Kota had been settled on the terms that Kota should pay
to Susur Rotan the sum of $30,000 in full and final satisfaction of their claim
under the agreement of Sept. 19, 1960. So the action then proceeded between
Susur Rotan and Mr. Siow. The pleadings made no mention of s. 71 nor of any   I
fact to support such claim, except such as were pleaded as acts of part performance
to support the alleged oral agreement. However it is fair to say that, in opening
the case, counsel for Susur Rotan did mention that he had an alternative claim
under s. 71 for work on the road, not, as he submitted, intended to be done
gratuitously. It is equally fair to say that during the action little was heard of that
section and the real issue, as is clear from the judgment of Azmi, J., was whether
in fact there was an oral agreement to the effect pleaded. He came to the conclusion that there was no such oral agreement as alleged or at all and he dismissed

A the action. In his judgment he did not mention s. 71. It is quite clear, however, in reading his judgment that one of Susur Rotan's main arguments had been that one of the obligations undertaken by Mr. Siow under the alleged oral agreement was to pay for the building of the road. However, all this was expressly negatived by the judge.

Susur Rotan then appealed to the Federal Court. It was strenuously argued B by Susur Rotan that the decision of Azmi, J., was wrong, and that he should have held in their favour that the alleged oral agreement was established. Alternatively it was argued on behalf of Susur Rotan that if there was no such agreement, they were entitled to compensation in respect of their expenditure on the road. This was argued without any serious objection from Mr. Siow's counsel. The Federal Court found against Susur Rotan on the alleged oral agreement, but in their favour C under s. 71 and directed an inquiry as to the sum to which they were thereby entitled.

It was argued before their lordships, though not strongly, that, as s. 71 was not pleaded nor any claim made thereunder in the writ or statement of claim, it was not open to Susur Rotan to maintain any claim under that section. It was much more strongly argued that as no facts had been pleaded, except very briefly as D particulars of part performance of the alleged oral agreement, this claim should be very carefully scrutinised, for had it been expressly pleaded then Mr. Siow might have desired to call evidence on this matter. It is not necessary to dwell on this in view of the opinion which their lordships will later express on this appeal.

Susur Rotan has not sought to challenge the findings of both courts against the E existence of an oral agreement and the sole question therefore before their lordships is whether the Federal Court were right in holding that Susur Rotan had a valid claim against Mr. Siow under s. 71 in respect of their expenditure on the road. That section is in these terms:

F " Where a person lawfully does anything for another person, or delivers anything to him, not intending to do so gratuitously, and such other person enjoys the benefit thereof, the latter is bound to make compensation to the former in respect of, or to restore, the thing so done or delivered."

That section is in terms identical with s. 70 of the Indian Contract Act on which there is some authority to which their lordships will later briefly refer.

It has been common ground before their lordships that four conditions must be G satisfied to establish a claim under s. 71. The doing of the act or the delivery of the thing referred to in the section (i) must be lawful; (ii) must be done for another person; (iii) must not be intended to be done gratuitously; and (iv) must be such that the other person enjoys the benefit of the act or the delivery.

In their lordships' judgment these matters must be answered at the time that the act is done or the thing delivered and this, their lordships think, is of funda- H mental importance. In this case the relevant time was therefore the building of the roadway in April to December, 1961.

As to the first point, it is of course clear and not in dispute that as between Mr. Siow and Susur Rotan the act was lawful, it was clearly in the contemplation of both parties that Susur Rotan should do this work.

It is the second point which in their lordships' judgment is decisive of this case. I As a matter of phraseology the section seems clear on it. To bring the section into play the person, when doing the act or delivering the thing, must do the act " for another person " or deliver some thing " to him ". So that his then present intention must be to do the act or to deliver the thing for or to another.

It was argued before their lordships, as indeed in the Federal Court (as appears from the notes of Tan Ah Tah, F.J.), that doing the act means no more than that the act must be one which in fact benefits another. It was argued that the crucial point was that, although one may do the act for one's own benefit, yet if in the end ex post facto one does not obtain that benefit but another does then

one may claim against that other under s. 71 as an act done for him. This seems A
to their lordships a complete misreading of the section. Their lordships are
fortified in their judgment by the observations of LORD SIMONDS on s. 70 of the
Indian Contract Act (*Governor-General in Council* v. *Madura* (1)).

It is clear for the reasons already given that when the road was built in 1961
it was built by Susur Rotan, though no doubt with the full knowledge, agreement
and indeed day to day approval of Mr. Siow, for Susur Rotan's own benefit, for B
under the chain of contracts they were the body who were going to exploit the
mineral lands. It was not done for another. This was indeed conceded in effect
by counsel for Susur Rotan in the Federal Court who (according to the notes of
THOMSON, L.P.), said " That we built the road for our own benefit does not
exclude the section." THOMSON, L.P., himself, though it is true in that part of
his judgment dealing with the alleged oral contract, said: C

" There was no satisfactory evidence that the making of the road would
accelerate in any way the granting of the lease to Mr. Siow. On the other
hand it was something that would have to be done some time as part of the
development of the mine, and be done at the expense of Susur Rotan as the
operating company in whatever way the sub-lease came to them."

It seems clear to their lordships that Susur Rotan fail to establish this second D
condition.

The third condition, that it must not be intended to be done gratuitously,
supports, as their lordships think, their view of the second condition, namely
that doing the act for another person must be literally construed, for it is difficult
to describe an act done for oneself as gratuitous; the adjective does not fit. Put E
rather differently, it seems clear that the act of building the road in this case was,
for the reasons just mentioned, intended to be done gratuitously for the simple
reason that at the time it was done Susur Rotan did not intend to look to another
for reimbursement of its expenditure. In their lordships' judgment Susur Rotan
also fail to satisfy this condition.

With all respect to the judgment of THOMSON, L.P., they think that he failed F
to appreciate the importance of judging of the matter at the time that the act or
delivery is performed and that it must be a non-gratuitous act performed for
another person. The condition that another must ultimately enjoy the benefit
of the act or delivery must also be satisfied, but it is only one of the four necessary
tests laid down by the section.

With regard to the fourth condition, their lordships cannot accept the argument
advanced on behalf of Mr. Siow. It was argued that his only interest in the G
mineral lands was a royalty of 50c. per ton extracted, and so he gained no benefit
from the building of the road; but it is clear on the facts, though the details are
obscure and were never fully explored, that Mr. Siow has benefited beyond that
from the building of the road.

If the other conditions of the section are satisfied, then compensation must be H
paid for that act, if the person sued has enjoyed that benefit. That compensation
must prima facie be measured by the worth of the act done. Whether or not it
ought to be modified by an assessment of the benefit enjoyed is not a matter
which their lordships propose to discuss in this judgment.

For these reasons their lordships will advise the Head of Malaysia that the
appeal should be allowed and the order of AZMI, J., be restored, and that the
first respondents pay the costs of the appellant of this appeal and in the Federal I
Court.

Appeal allowed.

Solicitors: *Lipton & Jefferies* (for the appellant); *Parker, Garrett & Co.* (for
the respondents).

[*Reported by* KATHLEEN J. H. O'BRIEN, *Barrister-at-Law.*]

---

(1) (1948), L.R. 75 I.A. 213 at p. 221.

FIELDING AND ANOTHER v. VARIETY, INCORPORATED.

[COURT OF APPEAL, CIVIL DIVISION (Lord Denning, M.R., Harman and Salmon, L.JJ.), March 6, 7, 8, 1967.]

Libel—Damages—Exemplary or punitive damages—No withdrawal of libel or apology—Conduct of defendant taken into account, although exemplary or punitive damages not to be awarded.

Malicious Falsehood—Damages—Pecuniary loss—Damages for injured feelings not recoverable—Damages reduced from £10,000 to £100—Defamation Act, 1952 (15 & 16 Geo. 6 & 1 Eliz. 2 c. 66), s. 3 (1).

A weekly periodical, " Variety ", published in New York, carried in March, 1966, an article which, after saying that the London musical theatre was a story of failure that season continued—" Both the American imports and the locally originated shows, such as ' Twang ' and ' Charlie Girl ', have been disastrous flops ". " Charlie Girl ", however, which was produced by the plaintiff, was in fact a great success. When in the United States he spoke to the editor and to the author of the article. He suggested that there should be a two-page article to put the matter right. No apology nor correction was published. The success of " Charlie Girl " in England, however, was not impaired, and the play continued running for over a year after the article was published and was still continuing. The plaintiff had hoped to take it to the United States in due course, and it was accepted that anyone who considered producing it in the United States would come first to England to see it, before deciding. The plaintiffs brought an action in England, claiming damages for libel and injurious falsehood. The defendant did not put in a defence; accordingly, falsity and malice were admitted. On appeal against an award of £5,000 for injury to the plaintiff's reputation, and £10,000 damages to the plaintiff company for pecuniary damage,

Held: (i) in regard to injurious falsehood, although by s. 3 (1) of the Defamation Act, 1952, it was not necessary in the present case to allege or to prove special damage, the plaintiff company could recover only its pecuniary loss, and the damages so recoverable would be reduced to £100, for there had been no pecuniary loss in England and prospect of production in the United States was not shown to have been adversely affected (see p. 499, letter H, p. 500, letter B, p. 501, letter E, and p. 503, letter I, post).

(ii) in regard to libel, the damages were not confined to pecuniary damage, and, although the court should not now award exemplary damages on account of the defendant's conduct, yet the court could take into account the defendant's conduct in relation to injury to the plaintiff's proper feelings; in the circumstances the award of £5,000 would be reduced to £1,500 (see p. 500, letter G, p. 501, letter G, and p. 503, letter B, post).

Dictum of LORD DEVLIN in *Rookes v. Barnard* ([1964] 1 All E.R. at p. 407) applied.

Appeals allowed.

[As to the consequences of taking advantage of s. 3 (1) of the Defamation Act, 1952, and not pleading special damage, see also *Calvet* v. *Tomkies* ([1963] 3 All E.R. 610).

As to malice and a defendant's conduct as factors in awarding damages for libel, see 24 HALSBURY'S LAWS (3rd Edn.) 115, para. 212; and for cases on the subject, see 32 DIGEST (Repl.) 195, *2083-2097*, 199, *2143-2149.*

As to damage in an action for malicious falsehood, see 24 HALSBURY'S LAWS (3rd Edn.) 130, 131, paras. 240, 241; and for cases on the subject, see 32 DIGEST (Repl.) 205, *2222*, 206, *2228-2230.*

For the Defamation Act, 1952, s. 3 (1), see 32 HALSBURY'S STATUTES (2nd Edn.) 400.]

Approved in CASSELL v BROOME [1972] 1 All E.R. 801

Cases referred to:

A

Davies v. *Powell Duffryn Associated Collieries, Ltd. (No. 2)*, [1942] 1 All E.R.
  657; [1942] A.C. 601; 111 L.J.K.B. 418; 167 L.T. 74; 36 Digest
  (Repl.) 231, *1229*.

Flint v. *Lovell*, [1934] All E.R. Rep. 200; [1935] 1 K.B. 357; 104 L.J.K.B. 199;
  152 L.T. 231; 17 Digest (Repl.) 193, *913*.

McCarey v. *Associated Newspapers, Ltd.*, [1964] 3 All E.R. 947; [1965] 2 Q.B.   B
  86; [1965] 2 W.L.R. 45; 3rd Digest Supp.

Ratcliffe v. *Evans*, [1891-94] All E.R. Rep. 699; [1892] 2 Q.B. 524; 61 L.J.Q.B.
  535; 66 L.T. 794; 56 J.P. 837; 17 Digest (Repl.) 77, *17*.

Rookes v. *Barnard*, [1964] 1 All E.R. 367; [1964] A.C. 1129; [1964] 2 W.L.R.
  269; 3rd Digest Supp.

Appeal.

C

By writ dated Apr. 5, 1966, the plaintiff, Harold Fielding, and the plaintiff
company, Harold Fielding, Ltd., sued Variety Incorporated, claiming damages
for libel and injurious falsehood contained in an article published by the defendants in a weekly periodical, " Variety ", alleged to have a circulation throughout
the United States of America, the United Kingdom, the Commonwealth and
other countries. The plaintiff was chairman and majority shareholder of Fielding   D
House, Ltd., which was the majority shareholder of the plaintiff company.
The facts are stated in the judgment of LORD DENNING, M.R., at letter H, infra,
et seq., post.

On July 18, 1966, the plaintiffs obtained interlocutory judgment against the
defendants for damages to be assessed. The plaintiffs elected that damages
for injury to feelings and reputation should be awarded on the claim for libel   E
to the plaintiff and the damages for pecuniary loss should be awarded on the
claim for injurious falsehood to the plaintiff company. Damages having been
assessed by the master, it was adjudged on Oct. 26, 1966, that the defendants
do pay to the plaintiff £5,000 and to the plaintiff company £10,000, being the
amounts of the assessed damages. By notice of appeal dated Nov. 8, 1966,
amended on Nov. 29, 1966, the defendants appealed against the assessment of   F
damages and for an order that it might be set aside and the damages might be
assessed at such sums as should be found to be just or that a new assessment
should be ordered. The grounds of appeal stated in the notice of appeal included,
among other grounds, that there was no evidence that the value to the plaintiff
company of the musical show to which the libel referred had in any way been
diminished by reason of the publication of the libel.   G

G. R. F. Morris, Q.C., and *M. E. I. Kempster* for the defendants.
Colin Duncan, Q.C., and *A. T. Hoolahan* for the plaintiffs.

LORD DENNING, M.R.: Mr. Harold Fielding, the plaintiff, is an im-
presario of distinction. In the last few years he has been responsible for a large
number of productions in the West End of London. A year or two ago he pro-   H
duced " Half a Sixpence ". It was a great success here. Then it was taken to
America where it made a great deal of money. In December, 1965, he produced
another musical show called " Charlie Girl ". It was at the Adelphi Theatre.
It was a great success too. By Jan. 3, 1966, the box office receipts at the Adelphi
Theatre constituted an all-time record for that theatre. The plaintiff and his
company (1) took advantage of this success to put an advertisement in a periodical I
called " Variety ". It is printed and published weekly in New York. It is devoted
to the theatrical profession and has a world-wide circulation. It contains notices
and descriptions of all that is happening in the theatrical world. As a result of
the advertisement, the editor and proprietors of " Variety " must have been well
aware of the great success of " Charlie Girl ".

---

(1) Harold Fielding, Ltd., the second plaintiff, called in this report " the plaintiff
company ".

A   Nevertheless, on Mar. 9, 1966, " Variety " produced an article by a writer who called himself Harm Schoenfeld. It said that the musical stage was " sick ", and that a composer called Vernon Duke had surveyed the scene in Paris, London, and the United States in the musical theatre world and found that it was " sick ". Then the article went on:

B   " The London musical theatre is a story of failure this season, Duke comments. Both the American imports and the locally originated shows, such as ' Twang ' and ' Charlie Girl ', have been disastrous flops."

That statement was true so far as " Twang " was concerned; but it was completely untrue so far as " Charlie Girl " was concerned. It ought never to have been written and inserted in this newspaper at all.

C   The plaintiff was naturally most indignant. He happened to be in New York about that time or shortly afterwards. He spoke to the editor of this periodical " Variety ". The editor roared with laughter and said: " It was nothing, Fielding." The plaintiff afterwards spoke to the writer of the article. He said it was unimportant and that he would get in touch with the plaintiff again, which he never did. One or other of them offered to put a note in the paper saying that the plaintiff had come over to the United States with a view to producing " Charlie Girl " there and negotiating a deal; but, as that was untrue, the plaintiff rejected the offer. He suggested that there should be a two-page, double spread, article in the paper to put it right; but this was refused. No correction and no apology was put in the paper at all.

    The plaintiff and the plaintiff company issued a writ claiming damages for libel and injurious falsehood. The defendants did not put in any defence. Judgment was entered against the paper for damages to be assessed. The assessment came before Master DIAMOND. He heard the evidence of the plaintiff and another witness. He awarded £5,000 to him for injury to his personal reputation. He awarded £10,000 to the company, Harold Fielding, Ltd., for pecuniary damage. The defendants appeal to this court on the quantum of the damages.

F   The parties have agreed that the damages for injurious falsehood should be awarded to the plaintiff company: and that the damages for libel should be awarded to the plaintiff personally.

    I will first consider the claim for injurious falsehood. In the old days, in order to make good such a claim a plaintiff had to show that the words were false; he had to show malice; and also had to prove special damage, which might be general loss of business (see *Ratcliffe* v. *Evans* (2)). Now by the Defamation Act, 1952, s. 3 (1) it is no longer necessary to allege or to prove special damage if the words on which the action is founded are calculated to cause pecuniary damage to the plaintiff and are published in writing or other permanent form. All the necessary elements are here admitted. It is admitted that the words were calculated to cause pecuniary damage. The question is: what pecuniary damage has been suffered? The plaintiffs on this head of claim can recover only damages for their probable money loss, and not for their injured feelings.

    One thing is clear. There is no pecuniary damage in this country. No-one suggests that the box office receipts at the Adelphi Theatre are any the less by reason of this publication. " Charlie Girl " is such a success in England that it is fully booked up already well into this present season. The only pecuniary damage that is suggested is the chance of losing a production in the United States. The plaintiff gave his evidence very accurately and very impressively. He said that " Charlie Girl " must suffer harm; but he admitted that in the general trade it is known in New York as a great success—" It is known in the entertainment circles where I am talking to them." He agreed also that anyone thinking of producing " Charlie Girl " in the United States would send someone over here to see it. He added that he was hopeful that he would be able to take it to the United States in due course, but it might have to be varied considerably. In

---

(2) [1891-94] All E.R. Rep. 699; [1892] 2 Q.B. 524.

these circumstances I cannot find any evidence to show that the chances of A
production in the United States have been adversely affected. I should have
thought that everyone of note in the theatrical profession in the United States
must know by now that " Charlie Girl " has been a great success. None of them
is likely to be influenced by those two words written as long ago as March, 1966.
I cannot go with the master in his assessment of £10,000. I would assess the
pecuniary damage from this publication at only a nominal sum which I would B
put at £100.

I must now consider the claim for libel. By describing " Charlie Girl " as a
" disastrous flop ", the defendants reflected on the plaintiff's competence. The
damages here are at large. They are not confined to pecuniary damage. At one
time in the case of libel it was the understanding of all of us that a jury (or a
judge, if it was tried by a judge) could mark the disapproval of the court by C
awarding exemplary or punitive damages. The House of Lords, however, in
Rookes v. *Barnard* (3), in a judgment delivered by LORD DEVLIN, in which the
other lords concurred, have told us that we must not give damages of an exemplary
or punitive nature. I believe the High Court of Australia has taken a different
view, but we in this court must follow what the House of Lords have told us.
So we cannot give exemplary or punitive damages. LORD DEVLIN, however, went D
on to say (4):

".. . it is very well established that in cases where the damages are at large
the jury (or the judge if the award is left to him) can take into account the
motives and conduct of the defendant where they aggravate the injury
done to the plaintiff. There may be malevolence or spite or the manner of
committing the wrong may be such as to injure the plaintiff's proper feelings E
of dignity and pride. These are matters which the jury can take into account
in assessing the appropriate compensation."

That was followed and applied in the decision of this court in *McCarey* v. *Associated Newspapers, Ltd.* (5). We can, therefore, consider the want of any excuse
or justification by this newspaper. It behaved very badly indeed. No correction,
no apology, not even to this day. Its conduct must have infuriated the plaintiff. F
He is a master in his art and profession: and yet he is treated thus. The injury
to him has certainly been aggravated by their conduct. His feelings have been
grievously wounded without any justification. For all this he is entitled to
damages; but what is the amount to be, remembering that we can no longer give
exemplary or punitive damages?

In all the circumstances we think that the sum of £5,000 which the master G
awarded is a wholly erroneous estimate. After consultation together we have
agreed to substitute the sum of £1,500. I would allow the appeal accordingly.

HARMAN, L.J.: Such experience as I have had in this court with the
subject of libel has satisfied me that when the damages are, as they say, at large,
they do present a most baffling problem. When one is trained in a different school, H
that problem is necessarily difficult because the damages bear no relation to
any calculation that you can make. They are truly, as it is said, at large. In this
court, of course, we only see them when they are said either to be too large by
a very long way or too small: and usually they represent the flights of fancy
of an incensed jury. In the present case there was no jury. There was a very
experienced master and, therefore, one must regard the dissent that at least my I
mind has felt from the beginning with some suspicion. One may not, as LORD
DENNING, M.R., has said, award swingeing or punitive damages nowadays. The
bad behaviour of the defendants must, therefore, be left out of account on that
view.

---

(3) [1964] 1 All E.R. 367; [1964] A.C. 1129.
(4) [1964] 1 All E.R. at p. 407; [1964] A.C. at p. 1221.
(5) [1964] 3 All E.R. 947; [1965] 2 Q.B. 86.

A   The defendants have indeed, so it seems to me, made the worst of every possible world. They have driven themselves, or been driven, into a position where it must be taken that they knew what they were publishing was untrue, yet they did it maliciously, that is to say intending to hurt, and then when challenged with it, they produced no apology or even a disclaimer of any sort. Naturally under those circumstances the master felt strongly against them, and so do I; but that which

B   was published, though at the time it was published it might have been a very damaging thing, has been proved by the passage of time not to have had that result at all. The box offices at the Adelphi Theatre continue to click as hard as ever they did. The run is going on. It was only three months after its production that the libel was issued. Here we are a year later and it is proved to have had no effect at all. I cannot think now that a publication a year ago in an ephemeral

C   journal, which was, as everybody now knows, entirely wrong, can have any effect at all on the financial prospects: indeed, it is admitted that they had none on the financial prospects in England; but it is said that England is a mere bagatelle. You only produce these things in England in order to put them on to the American market: there is the place where you make your money. " What a difference it might have made to us ", say the plaintiffs, " if this had never appeared." Well,

D   there is not any evidence of that either, as I see it. There is a statement by the plaintiff that he believes it must have been harmful; but that really will not do if it is not supported by any concrete evidence at all. If there was evidence that there had been negotiations before the libel and they had broken off at that point, of course damage would be seen to flow at once; but there was no such evidence. The plaintiff is at the moment very hopeful of putting this on to the

E   American stage, though he acknowledges that by reason of its Cockney origin and rather English character, a good deal of adaptation will be necessary. So in my judgment the pecuniary damages come to nothing much. I would agree with LORD DENNING, M.R., that £100 is amply sufficient for that.

So far as the plaintiff is concerned, I feel much more sympathy. I do not think I need repeat what LORD DENNING, M.R., has said about his feelings and the blow

F   to the reputation of a man in his position when an international and widely circulating journal says this his " latest darling " has been a " disastrous flop ". It turns out to be wholly untrue, but still he is entitled to quite substantial compensation. As my brothers think £1,500 is the right sum, I do not dissent from it.

I would, therefore, agree with the terms on which LORD DENNING, M.R.,

G   moves to allow this appeal.

SALMON, L.J.: I do not belong to the school that considers that damages in an action for defamation should necessarily be very moderate. There are some cases in which justice demands that the damages should be large, and in some very large indeed; but I cannot persuade myself that this is one of them. In 1935

H   GREER, L.J., said in *Flint* v. *Lovell* (6), and his words were echoed by LORD WRIGHT in *Davies* v. *Powell Duffryn Associated Collieries, Ltd.* (*No. 2*) (7), that before an appellate tribunal is entitled to interfere with an assessment of damages it must be satisfied that the damages were assessed on a wholly erroneous basis. Today, twenty-five years later, those words perhaps have a slightly archaic ring, but they enshrine a principle which is just as true as ever it was. It is not a question

I   of whether we, if we had been assessing the damages, would have assessed them at less, or even at very much less, than did the learned master. Before we can interfere we have to be satisfied that the damages awarded are wholly out of proportion to the injury suffered.

The plaintiff and the plaintiff company are of the highest standing in the

---

(6) [1934] All E.R. Rep. 200 at pp. 202, 203; [1935] 1 K.B. at p. 360.
(7) [1942] 1 All E.R. 657 at p. 664, letter H; [1942] A.C. 601 at p. 617.

theatrical world. They have earned a reputation for great ability and integrity, **A**
and they have enjoyed a large measure of success. The plaintiff presented a play
called " Half a Sixpence " that ran for eighteen months in this country to packed
houses. It then went to America where it had an even greater success, which it
is still enjoying, and it has earned and is still earning very large profits for the
plaintiff. On Dec. 16, 1965, he presented at the Adelphi Theatre in London this
play " Charlie Girl ". From the first night it was a resounding success. It played **B**
to packed houses and indeed broke all box office records at the Adelphi Theatre.
In March, nearly three months later, the defendants published in their newspaper
" Variety ", an article reviewing the stage productions for the last six months
in London, Paris and New York; and in the course of that article it said, wholly
untruly, that " Charlie Girl " was a " disastrous flop ". The language perhaps
is just as inelegant as it is inaccurate; but the meaning is fairly plain. A " disas- **C**
trous flop " is a play which runs for a few nights or perhaps a few weeks and then
all connected with it.

The plaintiff and the plaintiff company brought this action claiming damages
for libel and injurious falsehood. In the court below counsel for the plaintiffs
very sensibly elected that the damages for injury to feelings and reputation
should be awarded on the claim for libel to the plaintiff and the damages for **D**
pecuniary loss should be awarded on the claim for injurious falsehood action
to the plaintiff company. I can very well understand the plaintiff's indignation, annoyance and anxiety when he read that article in " Variety ". It
was a wholly untrue statement. It reflected certainly on his ability to " pick
a winner " and he must have felt that there was a real risk that it might damage
the box office receipts. He spoke on the telephone to the writer of the article **E**
and to the editor of the paper asking that they should publish an apology and
correction, giving him, what is called I think in the newspaper world, a " two-
page spread ". Whether he was right to ask for such a prominent retraction
is beside the point. Even if he were not, there was nothing to prevent " Variety "
doing what in fairness they ought to have done, namely, to have published
an article, equally prominent to the article, complained of apologising and **F**
correcting their mistake; but they did nothing of the kind. The materiality
of that, as far as damages are concerned, is that it not unnaturally tended to
heighten the plaintiff's irritation and annoyance. In the old days before the
decision of the House of Lords in *Rookes* v. *Barnard* (8) the fact that the defendants had not apologised or withdrawn could legitimately have been taken
into account so as to increase the damages. The plaintiff might have been **G**
awarded what are called exemplary damages. The jury might have considered
the desirability of marking their disapproval of the defendants' conduct, and
perhaps deterring them and others from repeating it, by awarding heavy damages.
We now know, however, that the fact that the defendants did not apologise
nor withdraw cannot be taken into account in those respects, but it is material
only in so far as it increased the injury to the plaintiff's feelings.   **H**

The first question, I think, that has to be dealt with is: can the award of
£5,000 conceivably be a proper amount to award under that head? For my part,
I am by no means convinced that any useful guide to the solution of such a problem can be derived from the amount that is awarded in accident cases; but it is
unnecessary to express a concluded view on that matter. What impresses me is
this, that whatever may have been the plaintiff's anxiety and annoyance at the **I**
immediate time of publication, this article had not the slightest effect on the
success of the play " Charlie Girl " at the Adelphi Theatre. As time went on
it must have been quite obvious to the plaintiff that it was having no such effect.
Everyone in the theatrical world knew and everyone who went to see the play
knew that it was being presented by the plaintiff and playing to packed houses.

---

(8) [1964] 1 All E.R. 367; [1964] A.C. 1129.

A It seems fairly obvious to me that the article cannot have had any really serious effect on the plaintiff's reputation. Nevertheless he is entitled to be compensated, as I say, for the anxiety and annoyance which he very naturally felt at the time. For my part I consider that the sum of £5,000 under that head was out of all proportion to the compensation justly payable to the plaintiff, and I agree with my lords that the right figure under that head is £1,500.

B   As for the pecuniary loss, it is conceded by the defendants, who have not put in a defence, that the article was published maliciously and that it was calculated to cause pecuniary damage. We have to approach the case on that basis. This does not, however, mean that if the evidence adduced shows (as in my view it does) that the pecuniary damage is minimal, the evidence ought to be ignored. As I have already said, it is conceded that there is no pecuniary damage suffered in

C this country, and I for my part consider that it is quite plain using one's common sense, as I think one is entitled to do, that the article has not really caused any damage to the play's prospects of being produced in America. In his evidence, which of course was entirely accepted, the plaintiff said that " Charlie Girl " was a fairly small scale British musical which was trying to establish itself in London with a view to becoming a world property. This was the same

D system as was used for ' Half a Sixpence '." In March, nearly three months after it had first been introduced, it had started well on its way to establishing itself in London. I am happy to say that it is now well established. It has been running for some sixteen months to packed houses, and even last October when the hearing took place before the master, it was booked well into 1967. It obviously is a highly successful venture and it is going to have a very long run.

E When a play has a very long run in England, those who present it, not unnaturally, have their eye on the American market where even greater profits can be made than in this country. This is so because of the much larger public which is there within reach. When a play has had a long run in London, those who present it no doubt interest themselves in finding American producers who will present the play in the United States of America; and at that stage it may even be that they do not

F have to look for them: the Americans will be scanning the London stage with a view to seeing what there is there that might be a useful commodity in America. Of course, the same thing happens vice versa when there is a success in New York. It does not necessarily follow that because a play has been successful in London, it will appeal to the American public. Tastes differ. The Americans will come here and look at the play and exercise their judgment as to whether it

G may succeed in New York in the light of their experience of American taste. They do not, however, come here to assess its prospects in the United States of America unless the play has had a very long and successful run in this country. It seems to me to be quite fanciful to suggest that when the prospective American producers come to consider this play they will take into account what was said by " Variety " a year or perhaps eighteen months previously, even if they

H remember it, which is highly unlikely. If they do remember it, they will know that it was quite untrue, because the play will then have been running to packed houses in London for eighteen months or more. It was ridiculous for " Variety " to have said it was a " flop ". It was the very antithesis of a " flop "—as everyone realises.

      However much one may deplore what was said in " Variety " last March, I

I find it impossible to persuade myself that it can really make any financial difference to the plaintiff or in any way diminish the chances of that play being produced in America. Nevertheless one has to approach the case on the basis that it is calculated to cause some pecuniary damage, but the highest figure which I think ought to be awarded under this head is £100.

      I have borne well in mind that these damages have been assessed by a master of very great experience and ability. I can only think that the explanation is that a spell was cast by the artistry of counsel for the plaintiffs' advocacy, which has on

many occasions before worked wonders. This award of £15,000 in all was a wonder   A
indeed, but one which we cannot allow to survive. I agree that the appeal should
be allowed.

Appeals allowed. Order varied to the damages of £1,500 and £100 accordingly.

Solicitors: *Denton, Hall & Burgin* (for the defendants); *M. A. Jacobs & Sons*
(for the plaintiffs).
                                                                              B
[*Reported by* F. GUTTMAN, ESQ., *Barrister-at-Law.*]

DIRECTOR OF PUBLIC PROSECUTIONS   C
v. A. AND B.C. CHEWING GUM, LTD.

[QUEEN'S BENCH DIVISION (Lord Parker, C.J., Widgery and O'Connor, JJ.),
April 13, 1967.]

Criminal Law—Obscene publications—Evidence—Expert evidence—Whether
admissible to show effect of publication on children of various ages—Obscene   D
Publications Act, 1959 (7 & 8 Eliz. 2 c. 66), s. 4.

The respondent company sold cards with chewing gum. They had in
contemplation that it was likely that the cards and copies thereof would be
sold in and with packets of chewing gum and be read and seen by children
of all ages from five upwards, and that such children would swop cards   E
among themselves in order to obtain a complete set and would, therefore,
see and read a complete set. At the trial of the respondent company on an
information charging them with having for publication for gain obscene
articles, viz., the cards, contrary to s. 2 (1)* of the Obscene Publications Act,
1959, and s. 1* (1) of the Obscene Publications Act 1964, the magistrates
refused to hear expert evidence of psychiatrists, experienced in child   F
psychiatry, as to the likely effect on children of various ages of certain of
the sets of cards taken singly and together. By s. 4 (1)† of the Act of
1959, a person was not to be convicted of an offence against s. 2 of the Act
if it was proved that publication of the article in question was justified as
being for the public good on the ground that it was in the interests of science,
literature, art or learning, or of other objects of general concern, and by
s. 4 (2)‡ it was provided that the opinion of experts might be admitted in   G
any proceedings to establish or negative that ground. On appeal by the
prosecutor against the dismissal of the information,

Held: (i) the evidence of the psychiatrists was admissible at common
law in the present case to show what sort of effect the cards, singly or together,
would have on children of different ages and what it would lead them to do,
and whether what they were led to do was a sign of corruption or depravity   H
(see p. 506, letters A and G, and p. 507, letter C, post).

(ii) s. 4 of the Act of 1959 did not make such evidence inadmissible,
because it was not dealing with evidence which might or might not be called
in regard to a tendency to corrupt or deprave (see p. 507, letter A and C,
post); accordingly, the Case would be remitted for re-hearing by a different
bench of magistrates.   I

Appeal allowed.

---

* Section 2 (1), as amended by s. 1 (1) of the Obscene Publications Act 1964, so far as
material, provides: " Subject as hereinafter provided, any person who, whether for
gain or not, publishes an obscene article or who has an obscene article for publication
for gain (whether gain to himself or gain to another) shall be liable " to certain
punishments.

† Section 4 (1), so far as material, is set out at p. 506, letter H, post.
‡ Section 4 (2) is set out at p. 506, letter I, post.

A   [As to the test of obscenity, see SUPPLEMENT to 10 HALSBURY'S LAWS (3rd Edn.), para. 1276A; and for cases on the subject, see 15 DIGEST (Repl.) 895, *8625-8631.*

For the Obscene Publications Act, 1959, s. 4, see 39 HALSBURY'S STATUTES (2nd Edn.) 273.]

Case Stated.

B   This was a Case Stated by justices for the North East London Commission Area in respect of their adjudication as a magistrates' court sitting at Romford on Sept. 13, 1966.   On July 4, 1966, an information was preferred by the appellant, the Director of Public Prosecutions, under s. 2 (1) of the Obscene Publications Act, 1959, and s. 1 (1) of the Obscene Publications Act 1964, against A. and B.C. Chewing Gum, Ltd., the respondent company, that on Mar. 31, 1966, at

C   1, Spilsby Road, Harold Hill, Romford, Essex, they had for publication for gain divers obscene articles, to wit, forty-three " bubble gum " battle cards.   The following facts were found.   On Mar. 31, 1966, the respondent company had in their possession for publication for gain a set of seventy-three cards.   The respondent company had in contemplation that, and it was likely that, (a) the cards and copies thereof would be sold in and with packets of chewing gum and

D   be read and seen by children of all ages from five upwards; (b) such children would swop cards among themselves in order to obtain a complete set of seventy-three cards and would, therefore, see and read a complete set.   Counsel for the appellant tendered expert witnesses experienced in child psychiatry to give evidence as to the likely effect on children of various ages of the forty-three cards taken singly and together.   Counsel for the respondent company sub-

E   mitted that that evidence was inadmissible.   The justices were of the opinion that counsel for the respondent company was right, and, accordingly, refused to hear the expert witnesses.

It was contended on behalf of the appellant that the forty-three cards by themselves, and more particularly when seen and read together, would tend to deprave and corrupt some, at any rate, of the children who would be likely to

F   read and see them.   It was contended on behalf of the respondent company that the cards would not tend to deprave and corrupt such children.

The justices dismissed the information, and the appellant now appealed.

The cases noted below* were cited during the argument.

J. H. Buzzard for the appellant.

G   *Sebag Shaw,* Q.C., and *J. Lloyd-Eley* for the respondent company.

LORD PARKER, C.J.:   This is an appeal by way of Case Stated from a decision of justices for the North East London Commission Area, sitting at Romford, who dismissed an information preferred by the appellant, the Director of Public Prosecutions, against the respondent company, that, on a day in March, 1966, they had for publication for gain divers obscene articles, to wit, forty-three

H   " bubble gum " battle cards, contrary to s. 2 (1) of the Obscene Publications Act, 1959, and s. 1 (1) of the Obscene Publications Act 1964.   [HIS LORDSHIP stated the facts, and continued:]   The appellant at the trial tendered expert witnesses, in the form of psychiatrists, experienced in child psychiatry, to give evidence as to the likely effect on children of various ages of the forty-three cards taken singly and together.   The justices, however, refused to hear that expert

I   evidence.   If they were wrong in so doing, then clearly this Case must go back for re-trial.

What was submitted to the justices and has been submitted to this court is that, as a general rule, a long standing rule of common law, evidence is inadmissible if it is on the very issue which the court has to determine.   For my part, and I am only dealing with this case, I cannot think that the evidence tendered was

---

* *Ramadge* v. *Ryan,* (1832), 2 Moo. & S. 421;   *R.* v. *Holmes,* [1953] 2 All E.R. 324; *John Calder (Publications), Ltd.* v. *Powell,* [1965] 1 All E.R. 159; [1965] 1 Q.B. 509.

on that very issue. There were really two matters for consideration. First, **A** what sort of effect would these cards singly or together have on children, and no doubt children of different ages, and what would it lead them to do? Secondly, was what they were led to do a sign of corruption or depravity? As it seems to me, it would be perfectly proper to call a psychiatrist and to ask him in the first instance what his experience, if any, with children was, and to say what the effect on the minds of children of different groups would be if certain types of **B** photographs or pictures were put before them, and indeed, having got his general evidence, to put one or more of the cards in question to him and ask what would their effect be on the child. For myself, I think that it would be wrong to ask the direct question whether any particular cards tended to corrupt or deprave, because that final stage was a matter which was entirely for the justices. No doubt, however, in such a case the defence might well put it to the witness that **C** a particular card or cards could not corrupt and, no doubt, whatever the strict position may be, that question coming from the defence would be allowed, if only to give the defence an opportunity of getting an answer from the expert " No ". On that ground alone, as it seems to me, the evidence in the present case was admissible.

I myself would go a little further, in that I cannnot help feeling that, with the **D** advance of science, more and more inroads have been made into the old common law principles. Those who practice in the criminal courts see every day cases of experts being called on the question of diminished responsibility, and, although technically the final question " Do you think he was suffering from diminished responsibility? " is strictly inadmissible, it is allowed time and time again without any objection. No doubt when dealing with the effect of certain things on the **E** mind science may still be less exact than evidence as to what effect some particular thing will have on the body, but that, as it seems to me, is purely a question of weight.

I said that I was confining my observations to this particular case, because I can quite see that, when considering the effect of something on an adult, an adult jury may be able to judge just as well as an adult witness called on the **F** point. Indeed, there is nothing more that a jury or justices need to know; but certainly when dealing with children of different age groups and children from five upwards, any jury and any justices need all the help that they can get, information which they may not have, as to the effect on different children. For those reasons, I think that certainly in so far as this objection is based on common law it fails. **G**

The second and perhaps the strongest point urged by counsel for the respondent company depends on s. 4 of the Obscene Publications Act, 1959, itself. It is there provided by sub-s. (1) that a person shall not be convicted of an offence against s. 2

" if it is proved that publication of the article in question is justified as being for the public good on the ground that it is in the interests of science, **H** literature, art or learning, or of other objects of general concern "

Subsection (2) provides that

" It is hereby declared that the opinion of experts as to the literary, artistic, scientific or other merits of an article may be admitted in any proceedings under this Act either to establish or to negative the said ground."

I

Counsel for the respondent company's argument is that that makes it clear that the opinion of experts is admissible only on the second ground, that is, on the ground that it is in the interests of science, literature, art or learning or of other objects of general concern for the public good, and that, accordingly, the statute itself has ruled as inadmissible evidence of experts whether something tends to deprave or corrupt. For my part, I am quite unable to accept that argument for two reasons. First, when one gets to s. 4, the time has come when the article is held to tend to deprave or corrupt, and the only question then is

A whether or not there should be a conviction, because publication may nevertheless be for the public good and, as it were, more than counterbalance the possible
tendency to deprave and, accordingly, the section is not dealing at all with
evidence which may or may not be called in regard to a tendency to corrupt
or deprave. Secondly, as it seems to me, and in any event, the very wording of
s. 4 (2) shows that the draftsman was putting it in ex abundanti cautela, bearing
B in mind the old common law principle and the various cases on the matter.

I have come to a clear conclusion that the justices were wrong in this case
and, accordingly, I would allow this appeal, and send the Case back for re-hearing
by a different bench of magistrates.

WIDGERY, J.: I agree.

C **O'CONNOR, J.:** I agree.

Appeal allowed. Case remitted.

Solicitors: *Director of Public Prosecutions* (for the appellant); *Montague & Co.*
(for the respondent company).

[*Reported by* Ellen B. Solomons, *Barrister-at-Law.*]
D

BEN WORSLEY, LTD. *v.* HARVEY.

E [Queen's Bench Division (Lord Parker, C.J., Widgery and O'Connor, JJ.),
April 14, 1967.]

*Weights and Measures—Bread—Weight—" Possession for sale "—Loaves in
dispatch area of bakery deficient in weight—Stale bread not for sale also in
dispatch area—Notice displayed that no bread was for sale till passed by
bread dispatch supervisor—Whether bread in dispatch area that had not been
F so passed was in possession for sale—Weights and Measures Act* 1963 (c. 31),
s. 22 (2) (*a*).

The respondent visited the dispatch area of the appellant company's
bakery where he found many trays of loaves on bogies. He asked the
manager of the bakery if the loaves were for sale and was told that they were
all for sale. In fact among the loaves were many returns, stale loaves not for
G sale. The respondent selected some loaves which were not returns and
weighed them. Some were under weight. Between the dispatch area and
the loading bay there was an opening with a large notice stating that no
bread in the store was for sale until it had been passed by the bread dispatch
supervisor. There was a supervisor in charge of the dispatch area whose
duty was to check-weigh the loaves by means of spot checks before they
H were passed to the loading bay. On appeal against convictions of being
in possession for sale of loaves which were under the weight, required by
Sch. 4, Pt. 4, para. 3*, of the Weights and Measures Act 1963, contrary to
s. 22 (2)† of the Act.

Held: the loaves were not in the appellant company's " possession for
sale " for the purposes of s. 22 (2) (*a*) of the Weights and Measures Act 1963
I

---

* Schedule 4, Pt. 4, para. 3, so far as material, provides: " A whole loaf of bread of a
net weight exceeding ten ounces shall be made for sale only if it is of a net weight of
fourteen ounces or a multiple of fourteen ounces: . . ."

† Section 22 (2), so far as material, provides: " Subject to the provisions of this
Part of this Act, in the case of any goods required by or under this Act . . . to be made
for sale, only in particular quantities . . . any person shall be guilty of an offence who
—(*a*) whether on his own behalf or on behalf of another person, has in his possession
for sale, sells or agrees to sell . . . any such goods . . . made otherwise than in that
quantity . . . whether the sale is, or is to be, by retail or otherwise."

until the loaves were checked and sorted out and it was decided which of   A
them were for sale (see p. 509, letters G and I, post).

Appeal allowed.

[As to the statutory weight and weighing of bread, see 39 HALSBURY'S LAWS
(3rd Edn.) 813-815, paras. 1236, 1237; and for cases on the sale of bread by
weight, see 25 DIGEST (Repl.) 128-130, *464-486.*

For the Weights and Measures Act 1963, s. 22 (2), Sch. 4, Pt. 4, para. 3, see   B
43 HALSBURY'S STATUTES (2nd Edn.) 1397, 1453.]

Case Stated.

This was a Case Stated by justices for the county of Lancaster acting in and for
the petty sessional division of Darwen in respect of their adjudication as a
magistrates' court sitting at Darwen, whereby they convicted the appellant   C
company, Ben Worsley, Ltd., bakers, of three offences against s. 22 (2) of the
Weights and Measures Act 1963, on three informations laid by the respondent,
Brian James Harvey, on Aug. 26, 1966, charging that they did have in their
possession for sale certain goods, namely three whole loaves of bread made for
sale in a quantity of one pound nine ounces, one and a half drams, one pound
ten ounces and six drams and one pound ten ounces and eight and a half drams   D
net weight respectively, these not being a quantity in which the said goods were
required by para. 3 of Pt. 4 of Sch. 4 to the Weights and Measures Act 1963,
to be made, contrary to s. 22 (2) of the Weights and Measures Act 1963. The
following facts were found. With the consent of Mr. Davies, the manager of the
appellant company, the respondent on Aug. 12, 1966, entered the bakery of the
appellant company and in the dispatch area found many trays of loaves of bread.   E
The respondent asked the manager whether the loaves on the tray were for sale,
and he replied " It's all for sale ". This reply was obviously a generalisation
because it appeared that some of the loaves were returns and not for sale. The
respondent selected some of the loaves which were not returns and which at a
later stage would pass through an opening into the loading bay and weighed
seventy, and of these loaves, the three loaves in respect of which these informa-   F
tions had been laid were respectively two ounces, fourteeen and a half drams,
one ounce seven and a half drams, and one ounce ten drams deficient in weight.
Between the dispatch area and the loading bay there was an opening which
bore a notice, size about three feet by two feet, with three inch high red lettering
on a white background which read as follows: " No bread in this store is for
sale until it has been passed by the bread dispatch supervisor." The manager   G
of the appellant company gave evidence that it was one of the duties of the
bread dispatch supervisor to check-weigh loaves by means of spot checks before
the bogies containing the loaves passed from the dispatch area to the loading bay;
the bread supervisor was not called to give evidence as to what his duties were,
neither was any evidence given that there was any weighing equipment by means
of which the spot check weighing referred to in the manager's evidence could be   H
carried out; the justices took exception to the respondent going into the bakery
to check-weigh loaves of bread with a view to prosecuting under s. 22 of the
Weights and Measures Act 1963, and particularly when this was done in a room
which contained near the opening to the loading bay the notice which has been
mentioned.

It was contended by the appellant company before the justices that no offence   I
had been committed because, at the stage of processing at which the loaves in
question were weighed by the respondent, these loaves were not " in possession
for sale " because the loaves had not been passed by the bread dispatch supervisor.

The justices found that the appellant company were in possession for sale of
the loaves in question because (i) the general function of this bakery was to bake
loaves for sale; (ii) the manager had told the respondent that all the loaves in
the dispatch area were for sale; (iii) there was no evidence that the loaves in
question were in the despatch area for any purpose other than for sale; (iv)

A despite the notice that has been mentioned on balance of probabilities no further check weighing or other processing would have been carried out on the loaves in question before they left the bakery for delivery to customers. Accordingly the justices convicted the appellant company and imposed fines of £10 in each case.

The question for the opinion of the High Court was whether the justices were
B correct in law in finding as a fact that the appellant company had in their posssesion for sale the three loaves of bread which were deficient in weight contrary to s. 22 of the Weights and Measures Act 1963.

D. G. Nowell for the appellant company.

R. C. Southwell for the respondent.

C   LORD PARKER, C.J., having stated the facts, continued: I regret that I have come to a different conclusion from the justices in this case. Of course, this was a bakery whose general function was to bake loaves of bread. It is no doubt true that Mr. Davies, the manager of the appellant company, did say that all the loaves in the dispatch area were for sale. As to that the justices cannot or ought not to attach too much weight to it, because they themselves
D point out that that statement of Mr. Davies cannot be accepted at its face value, as there was a number of returns, stale loaves, in the dispatch area, which clearly were not for sale. The justices then say that there was no evidence that the loaves were there for any other purpose than for sale, and the probability was that they would not have been checked. In my judgment that is wrong on the facts of this case. It is quite clear that although the actual processes,
E the steps in manufacture, had been completed by the time when the loaves were in the dispatch area, yet none of the loaves in that area could properly be said to be for sale until those that were for sale had been sorted out. In the first place, the stale loaves had to be removed, and secondly, unless it was a complete sham—and there is no suggestion of that—there would be spot checks of each batch of loaves as a result of which numbers of loaves might have been
F rejected, as being not proper for sale. To suggest, and this must be the result of the magistrates' finding, that every loaf produced by a bakery is immediately in its possession for sale, seems to me to be something which just would not enable the bakery to carry on its business properly at all. It is well known that in the course of baking there will be numbers of loaves which are not of the proper weight, and to come to an interpretation which will make a bakery
G commit an offence day after day is one which I would be very loath to accept.

The proper view is that loaves are not in the possession of a bakery for sale until not only the process of manufacture is complete but also they have been checked and sorted out, and it is decided which of them are for sale.

One other point was mentioned by the justices, and that was that there was no evidence of any weighing equipment. I myself can attach no importance
H to that if only for the reason that Mr. Davies was apparently not cross-examined at all when he described the duties of the bread dispatch supervisor, and accordingly the occasion never arose for the calling of any evidence as to the nature of the weighing equipment. I have come to the conclusion that this appeal succeeds, and I would allow it.

    WIDGERY, J.: I agree.

I   O'CONNOR, J.: I agree.

Appeal allowed.

Solicitors: *Church, Adams, Tatham & Co.* (for the appellant company); *Norton, Rose, Botterell & Roche,* agents for *Town Clerk, Lancashire County Council* (for the respondent).

[*Reported by* N. P. Metcalfe, Esq., *Barrister-at-Law.*]

GOSLING *v.* GOSLING.   A

Applied in WARREN v WARREN [1970] 2 All ER 159

[COURT OF APPEAL, CIVIL DIVISION (Willmer, Danckwerts and Sachs, L.JJ.),
January 18, 19, 20, February 17, 1967.]

*Divorce—Collusion—Agreements and arrangements—Consideration by the court
—Test whether likely to lead to decree contrary to the justice of the case—
Court should take into consideration what might support respondent's case*   B
*and counsel's opinion on the merits—Leave to implement agreement, but not
approval of an agreement that was collusive—Matrimonial Causes Act 1965
(c. 72), s. 5 (2).*

The parties were married in 1920 and there were no children of the marriage
living. In 1947 the husband left the wife, and thereafter there was no
cohabitation between the parties. In 1963 an inquiry agent obtained a   C
statement from the husband that he had " decided to leave my wife and in
fact left the home never to return. Since that date I have never lived
with my wife again and have no intention of returning to her at any time ".
No just cause for leaving was alleged, the only reason given being a series
of arguments and that the marriage became unhappy; there was no suggestion that the wife consented to the separation. In May, 1964, the wife   D
presented a petition for divorce on the ground of desertion to which the
husband entered a general appearance. At a meeting between the parties'
solicitors it was intimated that the husband would deny desertion and allege
constructive desertion by the wife, but the husband never filed an answer.
Originally the husband had paid the wife £3 a week maintenance, but this
was reduced to 10s. after his retirement about 1960. Payment had ceased   E
on the presentation of the petition, and in view of the wife's earnings and
capital there was no prospect of any significant amount being awarded for
maintenance or of the wife's recovering her costs of the suit. From correspondence between the parties' solicitors early in 1966 it emerged that
the parties were prepared to enter into an agreement that the husband
would no longer defend the suit, provided the wife claimed no more than a   F
nominal 1s. a year for maintenance and did not ask for costs. In October,
1966, the wife issued a summons seeking relief, asking the court to " take
into consideration for the purpose of s. 5 (2)* of the Matrimonial Causes
Act 1965 the agreement to be made between the [parties] . . . and [to] give
such directions thereon as the court thinks fit ". The question was thus
raised on preliminary application. The husband's solicitor, supporting the   G
wife's application, invited the commissioner hearing the case to look at
the husband's own statement which showed that his reason for leaving the
wife was his preference for the company of the woman with whom he had
been living for twenty years, and at counsel's opinion on the merits advising
that the defence of a consensual separation was unlikely to succeed. The
divorce commissioner did not adopt that course, but refused to approve   H
the proposed agreement on the ground that " it was impossible for me to
say on the evidence before me that a decree could not possibly be obtained
contrary to the justice of the case ". On appeal, the Court of Appeal
having allowed themselves to be informed of the contents of the husband's
statement, and of counsel for the husband's opinion on the merits,

Held: (i) the commissioner erred in law and his order could not be sup-   I
ported for the following reasons—

(a) because, although in deciding whether to grant leave to implement
an agreement which, before the Matrimonial Causes Act 1963, would have
been regarded as a collusive agreement, the crucial question was whether,
if the agreement were implemented, a decree would be granted contrary to
the justice of the case, yet the test was to make a realistic assessment of the

---

* Section 5 (2) is set out at p. 513, letter E, post.

A   probable result, viz., whether the defence that was to be abandoned was
likely to succeed, not whether the defence could not by any possibility
succeed (see p. 517, letters F and H, and p. 522, letters B and D, post).

Nash v. *Nash* ([1965] 1 All E.R. 480) and *M.* v. *M.* (*No. 1*) ([1967] 1 All
E.R. 870) considered.

(b) because the commissioner should have looked at the husband's state-
B   ment and counsel's opinion on the merits (see p. 518, letter F, and p. 524,
letter C, post).

Nash v. *Nash* ([1965] 1 All E.R. 480) approved.

(ii) notwithstanding that the proposed agreement was collusive the
circumstances were such that leave would be granted for the agreement
to be implemented; accordingly there would be a further direction that
C   the suit should be set down for hearing as undefended, at which hearing the
view of the Court of Appeal on the present application would in no way
bind the trial judge, who would have the duty of enquiring into the circumstances of the case (see p. 518, letter I, p. 520, letters B to D, p. 522, letter I,
and p. 524, letter E, post).

(iii) the court's order should not be expressed as " approving " a collusive
D   agreement, but as granting leave to implement the agreement (see p. 516,
letter F, and p. 523, letter G, post).

(iv) an application by the wife for costs of the appeal out of the legal
aid fund must fail by reason of s. 1 (4)* of the Legal Aid Act, 1964 (see p. 524,
letter G, post).

Observations on the definition of collusion (see p. 513, letter I, et seq., and
E   p. 520, letter H, et seq., post).

Appeal allowed: form of order stated (see p. 519, letter B, post).

[As to the effect of collusion on divorce proceedings, see 12 HALSBURY'S
LAWS (3rd Edn.) 300-302, paras. 594-598; and for cases on the subject, see
27 DIGEST (Repl.) 388-395, *3206-3253.*

For the Matrimonial Causes Act 1965, s. 5 (2), see 45 HALSBURY'S STATUTES
F   (2nd Edn.) 452.]

Cases referred to:
German v. *German,* (1965), 109 Sol. Jo. 353.
Head (formerly Cox) v. *Cox (Smith cited),* [1964] 1 All E.R. 776; [1964] P. 228;
[1964] 2 W.L.R. 358; 3rd Digest Supp.
G   *Iverson* v. *Iverson,* [1966] 1 All E.R. 258; [1967] P. 134; [1966] 2 W.L.R. 1168.
M. v. *M. (No. 1),* [1967] 1 All E.R. 870; [1967] 2 W.L.R. 1333.
Mulhouse (formerly Mulhausen) v. *Mulhouse (formerly Mulhausen),* [1964]
2 All E.R. 50; [1966] P. 39; [1964] 2 W.L.R. 808; 3rd Digest Supp.
Nash v. *Nash,* [1965] 1 All E.R. 480; [1965] P. 266; [1965] 2 W.L.R. 317;
3rd Digest Supp.
H   *Noble* v. *Noble and Ellis (No. 2),* [1964] 1 All E.R. 577; [1964] P. 250; [1964]
2 W.L.R. 349; *affd.* C.A., [1964] 1 All E.R. 769; [1964] P. 250; [1964]
2 W.L.R. 734; 3rd Digest Supp.
Rowley v. *Rowley and Austin and French (Cooper intervening),* [1964] 3 All E.R.
314; [1965] P. 178; [1964] 3 W.L.R. 946; 3rd Digest Supp.

Interlocutory Appeal.
I   This was an appeal by the wife against an order dated Nov. 7, 1966, and made
by His Honour JUDGE HAROLD BROWN in chambers when sitting as a special
commissioner in divorce, refusing to give approval to an agreement made between
the petitioning wife and the respondent husband pursuant to s. 5 (2) of the
Matrimonial Causes Act 1965. The grounds of appeal were: (i) that the judge

---

* Section 1 (4) reads: " An order under this section shall not be made by any court
in respect of costs incurred by the unassisted party in any proceedings in which, apart
from this Act, no order would be made for the payment of his costs."

failed to take into account relevant considerations, viz., that the defence which **A**
by the terms of the agreement the husband agreed to abandon was a defence
which had no reasonable prospect of success and that there was no real likelihood
that abandonment of the defence, if adhered to, would result in a decree contrary
to the justice of the case if such a decree were granted; and (ii) that the judge
was wrong in deciding that the agreement to abandon the defence was a bar to
the court's approval of the collusive agreement, or alternatively there was no **B**
evidence on which he could come to that conclusion.

P. G. Langdon-Davies for the wife.
A. J. D. McCowan for the husband.
J. H. Hames for the Law Society.

Cur. adv. vult. **C**
Feb. 17. The following judgments were read.

WILLMER, L.J.: The parties in this case are both over seventy years of
age, and were married as long ago as June 19, 1920. There are no children of
the marriage now living. In 1947 the husband left the wife, and there has
since been no cohabitation between the parties. Since that date the husband **D**
has lived in a house with another woman, who has acted as his housekeeper. It is
not alleged, however, that he has been guilty of adultery or of any improper
relations with this other woman.

The wife, who was a woman who earned her own living, took no action until
1963. She then, however, engaged an inquiry agent, who was able to interview
the husband and obtain a statement from him. In that statement the husband
says: **E**

" During the year 1947 . . . I decided to leave my wife and in fact left the
home never to return. Since that date I have never lived with my wife again
and have no intention of returning to her at any time."

The statement does not allege that the husband had any just cause for leaving;
the only reason given is that there was a series of arguments and the marriage **F**
became unhappy. The statement contains no suggestion that the wife consented to the separation. Armed with this confession statement, the wife
presented a petition for divorce dated Mar. 20, 1964, but not filed till May 12 of
that year. On Sept. 2, 1964, the husband obtained a legal aid certificate for
the purpose of defending the suit, and entered a general appearance. In the
following month there was an interview between the parties' solicitors, at which **G**
it appears to have been intimated by the husband's solicitor that the husband
would deny desertion and would allege constructive desertion on the part of the
wife. This was said to arise from the relationship between the wife and a man
who became a lodger with the parties in 1940, and who has been a lodger with
the wife substantially ever since; but it was not then suggested, and never has
been suggested, that there have ever been any improper relations between the **H**
wife and the lodger. In spite of the husband's solicitor's intimation of a possible
defence, however, no answer has ever been filed on behalf of the husband.

For many years after the separation the husband paid the wife £3 per week by
way of maintenance. About 1960 when the husband retired, this was reduced
to 10s. per week, but since the petition was filed no maintenance whatever has
been paid. Thanks to her own work and to the maintenance received from her **I**
husband over the years the wife has been able to accumulate a modest sum
of capital, sufficient at any rate to render her ineligible for legal aid. The
husband, on the other hand, is without means, and is substantially living on his
retirement pension. In these circumstances there can be no real likelihood of the
wife being awarded anything significant by way of maintenance, or even recovering her costs of the suit.

In early 1966 correspondence took place between the respective solicitors,
from which it emerged that the parties were prepared to enter into an agreement

A whereby, provided that the wife claimed no more than a nominal sum of 1s. per annum by way of maintenance and did not ask for costs, the husband would no longer defend the suit. In consequence a summons was issued on behalf of the wife on Oct. 13, 1966, whereby relief was sought in the following terms:

B " That the court do take into consideration for the purposes of s. 5 (2) of the Matrimonial Causes Act 1965, the agreement to be made between the [wife] and the [husband] (particulars of which are set out in the affidavit to be used in support of the said application, a copy whereof is delivered herewith) and do give such directions thereon as the court thinks fit."

The summons was heard on Nov. 7, 1966, by His Honour JUDGE HAROLD BROWN, Q.C., sitting as a special commissioner in divorce at Brighton, when he refused
C to approve the proposed agreement, but granted leave to appeal without further hearing. The commissioner gave no further directions. The wife now appeals to this court, and her appeal is warmly supported by the husband. It is apparent that both parties desire the case to be heard as an undefended suit on the terms provided by the proposed agreement.

Section 5 of the Matrimonial Causes Act 1965, is the section which defines the
D powers and duties of the court in relation to the hearing of a divorce petition. Subsection (2), under which the present application was made, is in the following terms:

E " (2) Provision may be made by rules of court for enabling the court, on application made either before or after the presentation of the petition, to take into consideration for the purposes of this section any agreement or arrangement made or proposed to be made between the parties and to give such directions in the matter as the court thinks fit; but nothing in this subsection affects any duty of the parties to disclose to the court any agreement or arrangement made between the parties in contemplation of or in connexion with the proceedings."

F In pursuance of the subsection a new rule has been made and incorporated as r. 2A of the Matrimonial Causes Rules, 1957 (1), which provides, so far as material to the present case, (a) that any application under the subsection shall be made to a judge, and (b) that the application shall be supported by an affidavit by the applicant or his solicitor setting out particulars of the agreement or arrangement in question and the grounds on which the application is made. In the present case the application was supported by an affidavit sworn by the wife's solicitor.
G Section 5 (2) of the Act of 1965 is in substance a re-enactment of a similar provision first introduced in the Matrimonial Causes Act 1963. By that Act a radical change was effected in the law relating to collusion, which became a merely discretionary bar to relief instead of an absolute bar, as it had previously been. It remains, however, the duty of the court, on hearing of a divorce petition, to inquire so far as it reasonably can whether any collusion exists
H between the parties. Since the passing of the Act of 1963 the effect of the change in the law relating to collusion, and the matters to be considered by the court on an application under what is now s. 5 (2) of the Act of 1965, have been considered in a number of cases at first instance, to some of which I shall have occasion to refer hereafter; but this is the first occasion on which any of these questions has arisen for consideration in this court. It is desirable, therefore,
I to start at the beginning, and to inquire what was, and what was not, regarded as amounting to collusion under the law as it was before 1963.

Collusion has never been the subject of any statutory definition. It is defined in RAYDEN ON DIVORCE (10th Edn.), p. 275, in terms which have since received judicial approval, as follows:

" Collusion means an agreement or bargain between the parties to a

_____

(1) S.I. 1957 No. 619. For r. 2A, which was inserted by S.I. 1963 No. 1990, see 10 HALSBURY'S STATUTORY INSTRUMENTS (Second Re-Issue) 225.

suit or their agents, whereby the initiation of the suit is procured or its   **A**
conduct provided for; but not every bargain entered into by parties to a
pending divorce suit is collusive. An essential element in a collusive
bargain is an attempt to pervert the course of justice."

Even before the passing of the Act of 1963 it was frequently held that the parties
to a divorce suit were free to enter into a sensible agreement or arrangement
with regard to ancillary matters, such as custody of children, maintenance and   **B**
so forth, even during the currency of the proceedings, provided that such agreement or arrangement did not include any term affecting the conduct of the suit.
As was said by SIR JOCELYN SIMON, P., in *Mulhouse (formerly Mulhausen)* v.
Mulhouse (formerly Mulhausen) (2):

"... it is perfectly proper—indeed it may be laudable—for the parties to   **C**
come to reasonable agreement as to damages or costs or maintenance or
custody and access or property disputes between them. Such arrangements,
once concluded, may not infrequently lead a party to feel that it is no longer
in his or her interest to contest the allegations made in the main proceedings.
But what is not permissible is to introduce as a term of the agreement or
arrangement, so that it forms part of the consideration, the abandonment   **D**
of a defence which is believed to be good."

As was pointed out by SCARMAN, J., in *Nash* v. *Nash* (3), the effect of the Act
of 1963 was to give the court power to discriminate between objectionable and
non-objectionable collusion, and in the case of the latter to confer on the court
a discretion to grant relief notwithstanding the existence of the collusion. The
Act of 1963, however, was silent as to the tests to be applied in determining   **E**
whether a particular collusive agreement should or should not properly be
regarded as objectionable, so as to necessitate the withholding of relief. It has
been left to judicial interpretation to set the standards by which this difficult
question is to be determined.

In what I believe to be the first case in which this question fell to be decided,
Head (formerly Cox) v. *Cox (Smith cited)* (4), WRANGHAM, J., directed himself as   **F**
follows:

" It is sufficient for me in this case to say that it seems to me that in
considering whether or not discretion should be exercised in respect of an
agreement of this character, the first matter to which I should direct my
attention is the question whether or not the result of such an agreement
is likely to be that a result is reached in the proceedings contrary to the   **G**
justice of the case. In other words, I must be satisfied that the court will
not, as a result of the agreement, be granting relief for a matrimonial offence
which has not occurred, or to a party who would not receive relief if the
whole of the facts were before the court. Secondly, I think I should direct
my attention to the question whether any children of the marriage, in
particular any infant children, might be prejudiced by what was being done.   **H**
Thirdly, I think I should satisfy myself that the parties in the case have
treated the court with complete and unreserved candour."

I refrain from expressing any view on the question whether, having so directed
himself, WRANGHAM, J., arrived at a correct decision on the facts of the particular
case. What he did was to sanction the abandonment by each party of charges   **I**
of cruelty made against the other, and to allow the case to proceed undefended
on a charge of adultery put forward by one party and admitted by the other.
It could be said that the adoption of this course could possibly have resulted
in a decree contrary to the justice of the case, and might amount to the court, in
effect, giving its blessing to a divorce by consent. I should desire to emphasise that,

(2) [1964] 2 All E.R. 50 at p. 56; [1966] P. 39 at p. 49.
(3) [1965] 1 All E.R. 480 at p. 482; [1965] P. 266 at p. 269.
(4) [1964] 1 All E.R. 776 at p. 777; [1964] P. 228 at p. 230.

A whatever else Parliament may have intended by the change in the law relating to collusion, it cannot have intended to introduce divorce by consent, as it were, by the back door. Such a change in the law, if it is ever to be brought about, would have to be specifically enacted in plain terms. All I am concerned with at the moment, however, is whether WRANGHAM, J., directed himself correctly in propounding the three tests which I have read.

B   These tests were accepted and followed by SIR JOCELYN SIMON, P., in *Mulhouse* v. *Mulhouse* (5), by CAIRNS, J., in *Rowley* v. *Rowley and Austin and French (Cooper intervening)* (6) and by SCARMAN, J., in *Nash* v. *Nash* (7). In the first-named case: SIR JOCELYN SIMON, P., added in relation to the first of the three tests proposed (8):

C
    " In positive terms this means that the court is likely to view benevolently an agreement which provides for the court, if satisfied on the uncontested evidence, pronouncing a judgment which would have been the likely outcome of the case if there had been no agreement and the suit had been fought out."

I am bound to say that I detect some degree of conflict between the approach of these experienced judges and the test propounded by the editors of RAYDEN ON
D DIVORCE in the definition which I have read. For, if there is no likelihood that the result of the proceedings will be contrary to the justice of the case, it will be difficult to say that there has been any attempt to pervert the course of justice, which is said by RAYDEN to be an essential element of a collusive bargain. I think that the test propounded in RAYDEN is probably somewhat too narrow, and that the true view is that *any* bargain between the spouses which contains a
E term providing for or affecting the conduct of the suit is at least potentially collusive, whether or not it can fairly be said that there has been an attempt to pervert the course of justice. At any rate, I am not prepared to differ from the views expressed by three experienced judges in the cases to which I have referred.

    In the present case, however, we are relieved from further consideration of this
F problem, for it was candidly admitted by counsel for the wife that the proposed agreement here in question is one which before the Act of 1963 would have been regarded as collusive. It is true that counsel for the husband was disposed to question whether this admission was rightly made; but I do not think that this matters, for it is the wife's application with which we are here concerned, and it is she who is seeking the directions of the court.

G   I turn now to consider the effect of s. 5 (2) of the Act of 1965, which is no doubt designed to enable the parties to a divorce suit to obtain some sort of preliminary ruling from the court before trial. I am bound to say that the subsection strikes me as a masterpiece of obscurity. It provides singularly little guidance as to what the judge hearing the application is expected to do. He is to " take into consideration " any agreement or arrangement made or proposed to be
H made; but there is nothing to indicate how he is to take it into consideration, what powers he has having taken it into consideration, what kind of directions he is expected to give, or how far his directions given at that preliminary stage are to be regarded as binding on the court which will ultimately try the suit. All that is said is that the judge is to take the agreement into consideration " for the purposes of this section ". As I have already pointed out, however,
I the purposes of the section are to define the powers and duties of the court on the hearing of the suit. So far as collusion is concerned, where this is found to exist, it is left to the judge at the trial to decide in his discretion whether relief should or should not be granted; see sub-s. (4). It cannot have been intended, I apprehend, that the exercise of the discretion thus vested in the trial judge

---

(5) [1964] 2 All E.R. 50; [1966] P. 39.
(6) [1964] 3 All E.R. 314; [1965] P. 178.
(7) [1965] 1 All E.R. 480; [1965] P. 266.
(8) [1964] 2 All E.R. at p. 55; [1966] P. at p. 47.

should in any way be fettered by such directions as may be given on the occasion **A**
of the preliminary application provided for by sub-s. (2). It is presumably
intended, however, that the judge hearing the application shall decide whether the
agreement or arrangement put forward is or is not in fact collusive, and, if it is
collusive, whether it is prima facie of the objectionable or the non-objectionable
type.

In this state of obscurity it has been left to the court to do its best by judicial **B**
interpretation to make sense of the subsection. A valiant effort to this end has
been made by SCARMAN, J., in *Nash* v. *Nash* (9), where he took the opportunity
to adjourn into court for judgment a number of summonses that had come before
him. If I venture to criticise what he said in one respect, this is no way diminishes
my admiration for the masterly way in which he grappled with the problem.
The gist of what he said as to the possible courses open to the judge on the hearing **C**
of the preliminary application is contained in the following paragraph of his
judgment (10):

" The purpose of the rule is to save time and expense by enabling parties
to obtain a ruling before trial. Such applications are no substitute for trial:
they leave undiminished the trial judge's duty of inquiry; they do not in
any way fetter his discretion. Nevertheless, on such an application the **D**
court possesses considerable powers: it may, inter alia—(i) dismiss the
petition, if of the opinion that there has already occurred, in the suit, collusion causing an ' irremediable perversion of the course of justice ' (this
power resides in the court by reason of the Matrimonial Causes Act, 1950, s. 4,
notwithstanding its amendment by the Act of 1963); (ii) require the discharge of the agreement or an undertaking that the proposals will not be **E**
implemented as a condition of allowing the suit to proceed; (iii) approve
the agreement or arrangement and give consequential directions as to the
conduct of the suit; (iv) adjourn the application to the trial judge; or
(v) simply make no order upon the application."

My only criticism of this passage is in relation to heading (iii). If the agree- **F**
ment or arrangement put forward is found not to be collusive at all, there can,
of course, be no objection to the court's " approving " it. I do not believe,
however, that it could ever be right for the court to say that it " approves " an
agreement or arrangement which is in fact found to be collusive. For, as pointed
out by SIR JOCELYN SIMON, P., in *Mulhouse* v. *Mulhouse* (11), the fact that
Parliament has seen fit to leave collusion as a discretionary bar to a decree of
divorce " tends to suggest that it is still regarded by the legislature as an inherently **G**
undesirable activity ". I mention this point because in the course of the hearing
we asked to see, and were shown, specimens of the form of order devised by the
registry for use in connexion with applications under this subsection. This
form makes provision for an order stating that the agreement or proposed
agreement is " approved " or " not approved ". No doubt this phrase is used
because of what was said by SCARMAN, J., in *Nash* v. *Nash* (9). Where the **H**
agreement is in fact found to be collusive, however, I cannot think that this is the
correct expression to use. The most that the court should do in such a case is to
" grant leave to implement " the proposed agreement.

Subject to this, I agree with SCARMAN, J.'s analysis of the courses open to the
judge who has to hear one of these preliminary applications, and I can only
express my gratitude for the guidance which he has given in relation to the **I**
task of the court in giving effect to this obscure statutory provision. After
stating his view as to the courses open to the judge hearing the application,
SCARMAN, J., went on as follows (12):

---

(9) [1965] 1 All E.R. 480; [1965] P. 266.
(10) [1965] 1 All E.R. at p. 482; [1965] P. at p. 270.
(11) [1964] 2 All E.R. at p. 54; [1966] P. at p. 46.
(12) [1965] 1 All E.R. at pp. 482, 483; [1965] P. at p. 271.

A   " The application cannot achieve its purpose of saving time and expense unless parties treat the court with the ' complete and unreserved candour ' of which WRANGHAM, J., speaks in *Head* v. *Cox* (13). The evidence in support must not only be true as far as it goes; it must reveal all that is known on the following topics: (a) the agreement or arrangement, and its intended consequences for the parties; (b) the financial circumstances of husband,

B   wife and children in sufficient detail to enable the court to form a view as to the reasonableness of the provision made for them; (c) the nature of the suit, an assessment of the strength of the parties' respective cases and available defences. On the application, the court will require to be satisfied under two heads: (i) that the agreement makes reasonable provision for maintenance, custody, access, damages, or costs, according to its subject-

C   matter; (ii) that there is nothing in the agreement or its surrounding circumstances likely to endanger the true course of justice."

With all this I wholly agree, and it remains for me only to reiterate what had already been said by SCARMAN, J., viz. (14), that

    " Such applications are no substitute for trial; they leave undiminished
D   the trial judge's duty of inquiry; they do not in any way fetter his discretion."

Further guidance on this subject has now been afforded by the recent judgment of SIR JOCELYN SIMON, P., in *M.* v. *M.* (*No. 1*) (15).

In the light of the guidance thus afforded to us, I turn to consider the circumstances of this particular case. The commissioner delivered no formal judgment

E   on the application; but he has been good enough to supply us with a note of his reasons for refusing to " approve " the agreement. In this he has given a number of reasons for thinking that, if the agreement were implemented, a decree granted to the wife *might* be contrary to the justice of the case. I have no doubt that he was right in thinking that this was the crucial question which he had to consider; but in arriving at his answer to it I think that the commissioner mis-

F   directed himself. He expressed his conclusion in these words:

    " I felt that having regard to those matters it was impossible for me to say on the evidence before me that a decree could not possibly be obtained contrary to the justice of the case."

In saying this I think that he was putting the case against the wife far too high. I do not accept that the court must be satisfied that a decree could not possibly

G   be obtained contrary to the justice of the case. If that were the standard required, no application of this kind could ever hope to succeed once the agreement was found to be collusive in any degree, and the whole procedure would be a sheer waste of time and effort. In my judgment the task of the judge hearing an application of this kind, where there is admittedly some degree of collusion, is to endeavour to make a realistic assessment of the *probable* result of the case,

H   if it were fought out, basing himself on the information that is before him, and if necessary asking for further information. He must ask himself whether the defence which it is proposed to abandon is one which would be *likely* to succeed, but he does not have to satisfy himself that the defence could not by any possibility succeed.

    This is of itself enough, in my judgment, to vitiate the commissioner's con-
I   clusion; but I think that there is a further reason for allowing the appeal. It is perfectly true that the affidavit of the wife's solicitor was not very informative with regard to the wife's reply to the defence which had been foreshadowed. In the circumstances of this case I should have expected that an affidavit would be forthcoming from the wife herself with regard to her relationship with the lodger,

(13) [1964] 1 All E.R. at p. 777; [1964] P. at p. 230.
(14) [1965] 1 All E.R. at p. 482; [1965] P. at p. 270.
(15) [1967] 1 All E.R. 870.

of which the husband complained. It was, however, open to the commissioner, **A**
when the matter was before him, to ask for further information with regard to
this aspect of the case, and if necessary to adjourn the application to enable this
information to be supplied. We have been informed that what in fact happened
at the hearing was that the husband's solicitor, who was present to support the
application, invited the commissioner to look at the husband's own statement
and at counsel's opinion on the merits. The commissioner, however, did not **B**
see fit to take this course, but proceeded to give his decision without availing
himself of this vital information. In this respect I think that he fell into error.
In this court we have thought it right to allow counsel for the husband to inform
us as to the contents of the husband's statement, and as to the effect of his
own opinion on the merits. It now transpires that the husband's statement
(which would presumably form the basis of the evidence which he would be **C**
able to give) is completely silent with regard to any complaints about the wife's
relationship with the lodger. The statement, we are told, makes it clear that
the husband's real reason for leaving his wife was simply that he preferred the
company of the woman with whom he has been living for the last twenty years.
In the light of this information it must be clear that there would be little chance
of the husband making out a case of constructive desertion, or of just cause for **D**
leaving. The only possible defence which counsel for the husband thought
might be open would be that the separation was consensual; but, for reasons
which he explained to us, he came to the conclusion that this defence would be
unlikely to succeed, and he advised accordingly.

Had this information been available to the commissioner, and had he not
denied himself the advantage of learning what there was to be said in support **E**
of the husband's case, I cannot think that he would have reached the conclusion
which he did. I entertain no doubt that it would have been proper for the
commissioner to look at the husband's statement and counsel's opinion, or at
least to allow himself to be informed of their contents, as we have done. It is
apparent from the report of *Nash* v. *Nash* (16) that, in a number of the cases
dealt with, SCARMAN, J., was informed of, and acted on, the advice given by **F**
counsel as to the party's chances of success. In this I am abundantly satisfied
that he took a right and proper course; indeed, it seems to me that, unless this
course is taken, it must be well nigh impossible in a number of cases to form any
realistic view as to the prospects of one or other party succeeding.

For these reasons I have come to the conclusion that the commissioner's
order cannot be supported. The question then arises what course we in this **G**
court should follow now that all the circumstances of the case are before us.
It is plain that any defence which the husband could put forward would be of
the most shadowy nature. In offering to abandon his defence, therefore, he
cannot be said to be giving away very much. Viewing the matter realistically
I can see no likelihood of a decree being granted contrary to the justice of the
case if the wife's petition is allowed to go undefended. Equally the wife cannot **H**
be said to be giving away very much, having regard to the husband's lack of
means, by limiting herself to a claim for nominal maintenance and by abandoning
her claim for costs. I see no ground for suspecting that the court has been
treated with anything but candour on either side. In the circumstances, notwithstanding the admission that the proposed agreement is such as would be
held to be collusive, I am of the opinion that leave should be granted to the **I**
parties to implement it.

The case may accordingly be set down for hearing in the undefended list;
but I would venture to emphasise once again that our conclusion on this preliminary application does not in any way bind the trial judge. It will still be
his duty to decide whether, on the evidence given, the wife makes out her case.
It will still be for him, in accordance with the duty imposed by the statute on the
court, to inquire into all the circumstances of the case, and in particular whether

(16) [1965] 1 All E.R. 480; [1965] P. 266.

A   any collusion exists between the parties, and to consider whether there are any circumstances which call for the exercise of discretion. In view of all that has happened, I think that it will be desirable to transfer the case from the Brighton District Registry to the Principal Registry, and to direct that the case be tried in London by one of the judges of the Probate, Divorce and Admiralty Division. In my judgment the appeal should be allowed, and I would propose that the

B   order should be in the following terms:

" This court having considered the affidavit of Mark Jeremy Calvert-Lee dated Oct. 12, 1966, the terms of the proposed agreement therein referred to and the information given by counsel directs (subject to the power and duty of the judge at the trial to make further inquiries and to make such further or other order as may be meet having regard to further material

C   thus brought to his notice) that the parties be at liberty to conclude the proposed agreement as to the conduct of the suit and to implement it and further directs that the suit be transferred from the Brighton District Registry to the Principal Registry and set down for hearing in London as an undefended cause before one of the judges of the Probate, Divorce and Admiralty Division and further directs that the said agreement be not in

D   the absence of further order a bar to the relief claimed by the petitioner [the wife]."

DANCKWERTS, L.J.: The background of this appeal is, of course, the change in the law made by the Matrimonial Causes Act 1963, which has made collusion no longer a compulsive bar to the granting of a decree of divorce, and has conferred on the court a measure of discretion in the matter. The immediate

E   subject of the appeal is the provisions of s. 5 (2) of the Matrimonial Causes Act 1965. [HIS LORDSHIP read s. 5 (2) which is set out at p. 513, letter E, ante, and continued:] It is undeniable that in this subsection the wisdom of Parliament has been expressed with particularly oracular obscurity. It is to be noticed that the sidenote to the section is " Hearing of petition ", and all the other

F   subsections are concerned with matters which arise in connexion with the hearing of a divorce petition. When the court takes into consideration on the hearing of the petition an agreement or arrangement between the parties, no particular difficulty arises. The court may consider that the agreement or arrangement is, under well settled principles, not within the description of a collusive agreement, or the court may consider that the agreement or arrangement, though collusive,

G   is not objectionable as tending to interfere with the proper administration of justice, or the court may consider that the agreement or arrangement is collusive, and as such is thoroughly objectionable. Accordingly, the court may decide that the agreement or arrangement does not prevent the court's granting a decree of divorce, or the court may decide that in view of the collusive agreement a decree must be refused.

H   When, however, the question arises on an application to the court before the hearing of the petition, either by a summons in the proceedings or on an originating summons before a petition has been presented, then difficulties arise. The court is to take into consideration the agreement or arrangement, but no hint is given in the subsection as to what the court is to do. It is to be surmised that the object of such a preliminary application is to enable the parties to

I   ascertain whether it is worth while to proceed to the hearing of a petition, or whether the agreement or arrangement is so objectionable that it is useless to proceed unless the agreement or arrangement is abandoned. Or the result may be to convert a defended petition into an undefended case. In this way, expense and delay may be avoided.

The judges of the Divorce Division have, in face of this obscurity, made a gallant attempt to give a sensible effect to the provisions of the subsection; see per SCARMAN, J., in *Nash* v. *Nash* (17) and a group of other cases decided

(17) [1965] 1 All E.R. 480; [1965] P. 266.

on the similar provisions of s. 4 (3) of the Matrimonial Causes Act 1963. The **A**
practice has been on a preliminary application before the hearing of the petition
to " approve " agreements or arrangements which were considered to be unobjectionable though having elements of collusion. Though this is a practical solution,
the objection to it is that it does not seem to be justified by the words of the
subsection, which do not in my opinion justify the use of the words " approve "
or " sanction ". The court, however, may give directions under the terms of the **B**
subsection and, in my opinion, a preferable course is that, where an agreement
or arrangement between the parties is not objectionable because it is not in fact
collusive or, where, though collusive, it is not " corrupt " (as it has been called)
in the view of the court, the court should direct that the petition may proceed to
trial, notwithstanding the agreement or arrangement, or may be set down as an
undefended petition, as the case may require.   **C**
    On the merits of the present case, if all the circumstances and information
(including counsel's opinion, see *Nash* v. *Nash* (18)) had been before the commissioner, I think that it would have appeared that the agreement between the
parties was not objectionable, and accordingly I think that the appeal should be
allowed, and that a direction should be given that the petition may proceed and
be set down as an undefended petition.   I agree with the form of order proposed **D**
by WILLMER, L.J.

    SACHS, L.J.: By virtue of s. 4 of the Matrimonial Causes Act 1963, col-
lusion ceased to be an absolute bar to a claim for relief in a matrimonial cause,
and became instead a discretionary bar.   The duty of the court to inquire
whether any collusion existed between the parties was confirmed and provision **E**
was made for rules to be made enabling the court to consider, before a cause
was tried (and indeed before a petition was presented), agreements made or
proposed to be made between the parties, and for directions in the matter then to
be given.   The above provision for rules is repeated in s. 5 (2) of the Matrimonial
Causes Act 1965.   The only relevant rules are the Matrimonial Causes (Amendment No. 2) Rules 1963 (19).   **F**
    However inartistic may be the phraseology of s. 5 (2), or of the relevant rules,
their primary purpose is to my mind plain.   In so far as that subsection and
the rules relate to pending causes, they were intended primarily to enable the
often perplexing question whether an agreement was collusive, and, if so, whether
it should in the circumstances be taken to be a bar to the relief claimed, to be at
any rate examined in chambers before the expenses of trial were incurred.   It **G**
was also clearly intended to enable appropriate directions to be given, as on a
summons for directions, in accordance with any conclusions arrived at.   The
present appeal raises far-reaching questions on how the court should approach
the first of the above matters, and also as to what should be the nature and form
of any directions that it should give.
    It is however necessary, before considering these questions, to say something **H**
as to the meaning of the word " collusion ", a matter that has been examined
in a number of decisions since the Act of 1963, but as to which it is difficult to
find a previous locus classicus with a clear cut definition. For the purposes of the
present appeal it is not necessary to give an exhaustive definition, but it is convenient here to refer to that given in the initial part of para. 12 of RAYDEN ON
DIVORCE (10th Edn.) at p. 275. The relevant words are: **I**

> " Collusion means an agreement or bargain between the parties to a
> suit . . . whereby the initiation of the suit is procured or its conduct provided
> for . . ."

That corresponds with the passage in the admirable judgment of SCARMAN, J.,
in *Noble* v. *Noble and Ellis* (*No. 2*) (20) where he says:

---

(18) [1965] 1 All E.R. 480; [1965] P. 266.
(19) S.I. 1963 No. 1990.
(20) [1964] 1 All E.R. 577 at p. 582; [1964] P. 250 at p. 257.

A   " If on a fair consideration of the circumstances, the parties intend by their agreement to match institution of suit or any aspect of its conduct with the provision of some benefit to the party instituting or in that aspect conducting the suit, there is, in my opinion, collusion."

B   It was on those statements of the law that counsel for the wife asserted throughout that the proposals in the present case were collusive, and counsel for the husband agreed that they must be frankly laid before the court. I agree generally that such agreements are collusive, and that in particular the agreement proposed here is collusive.

It is to be noted, first, that it is difficult to conceive of any agreement relating to the institution or conduct of a suit that is not intended to bring some benefit to one of the parties, and, secondly, that I have not so far introduced into the C   definition the word " corrupt ", or any adjective or phrase that could today be regarded as denigratory. I would indeed respectfully dissent from the concept that, in any case in which they do not in any way tend to pervert the course of justice, such agreements can nowadays reasonably be styled " corrupt ", to use the word that appears in so many judgments to be allocated to all agreements coming within the above statements of the law. Whether that word came to be D   applied to them somewhat over-often because of some Victorian notion of distaste for any agreement that might affect the sanctity of marriage, or simply because any bargain touching the course of proceedings was prima facie one that might interfere with the court's prerogative, need not be examined. I doubt if the cases can be reconciled on this point. One way or another, the word " corrupt " seems in course of time to have become a legal term of art in relation to collusion rather E   than a word used with the meaning normally given to it today.

In no sphere is it more necessary that legal process should, wherever practicable, be consonant with public opinion, the current needs of society (cf. per Latey, J., in Iverson v. Iverson (21)), and the standards of practice obtaining amongst practitioners of high repute, than the sphere of matrimonial causes. For many years agreements of the above type, bringing proper benefits to the parties to such F   causes, have been freely negotiated between solicitors of excellent repute. Without them the congested courts would become intolerably and unnecessarily over-worked, and the cost of legal aid grossly increased. There is much to be said in favour of the bulk of such agreements, and, so long as nothing is sought to be done which would produce a result contrary to the justice of the case, pejorative adjectives are not called for.

G   In matters relating to status, however, the court must always examine with care all arrangements as to the initiation of and the conduct of proceedings (compare the final part of s. 5 (2) of the Act of 1965 and r. 4 of the Matrimonial Causes Rules, 1957). For this reason such agreements have come, and presumably must continue to come, under the heading of collusion. I fully endorse, however, the views of Scarman, J., in Nash v. Nash (22) that such agreements H   can be divided into the unobjectionable and the objectionable. To call the former " corrupt " is a misleading use of words; that adjective should be reserved for agreements which are objectionable.

The present case relates to proceedings where the parties have been married a long time, where there has been an obvious and complete breakdown of the marriage, and where there are no children whose interests have to be safeguarded. I   Assuming that the judge in chambers is satisfied that the court is being treated with complete candour, and has had the requisite necessary material fully put before it, I consider that in such a case the true test normally to be applied when considering what does and what does not constitute objectionable collusion is a single and simple one. Looking at the case as a whole as it appears on the material before him, is the agreement one likely to produce a result

(21) [1966] 1 All E.R. 258 at p. 264; [1967] P. 134 at p. 144.
(22) [1965] 1 All E.R. 480; [1965] P. 266.

contrary to the justice of the case?   The mere fact that some valid claim A
for relief is withdrawn, or some triable defence is not pressed, is not of itself
conclusive on this point; if it were, the defended lists throughout the country
would become even more overburdened by long causes, the fighting of which
produces a gross waste of time and money without any ultimate good.

Assuming that the judge has been supplied with the appropriate material with
that fullness and candour which is essential, and assuming also that he has had, B
where necessary, the assistance of the views of counsel (or, where counsel has not
advised, solicitor), his task is not normally a difficult one. If it is reasonably clear
that the justice of the case will not be interfered with if the agreement is
implemented, he can direct that the case go forward on the basis that, on the
material before him, it will not form a discretionary bar to the relief claimed. If,
on the other hand, he is left in doubt, then he can either adjourn the summons C
for the obtaining of further material, or let it proceed to trial, without at that
stage giving such directions. If it is clear that the agreement would produce some
injustice, he can give such directions as on that basis seem appropriate; in some
cases the directions might in practice cause the proceedings to be terminated
at an early stage. In coming to his conclusions it is, of course, obvious that they
must be based on the available material, and that will not include the advantages D
of having seen witnesses and heard them cross-examined. In such circumstances
it is naturally impracticable for a judge to be certain of the correctness of his
views as to the justice of the case, but that does not mean that he cannot normally
come to a conclusion as to the probabilities; that is all that he can or need do.

Where the parties to a matrimonial cause raise a multiplicity of claims and
defences, it is of frequent occurrence in the course of a lengthy trial that at some E
stage the judge permits that cause to be determined on some claim (or claims) to
relief which can be cogently proved, whilst permitting the parties not to proceed
with some other claim for relief even if it appears to have some backing of
evidence. Similarly at trial he may permit a defence to be properly withdrawn,
providing that this is done openly, and there is no attempt to deceive the court
or to produce an overall result which does not tally with the justice of the case. F
Not infrequently in such cases both parties are granted a decree. There is no
reason why the judge in chambers, if satisfied that such results are likely to occur
at trial and to meet the justice of the case (cf. the recent judgment of SIR JOCELYN
SIMON, P., in *M*. v. *M*. (*No. 1*) (23)) cannot give directions which will produce
the same result without all the expense and user of the valuable time of men and
women that long trials involve. The importance of the costs aspect of the matter G
is rightly mentioned in *Head* (*formerly Cox*) v. *Cox* (*Smith cited*) (24) and *Nash*
v. *Nash* (25).

Finally, in relation to the question of the judge's approach to his task, it should
be mentioned that, even if the agreement itself has objectionable characteristics,
that does not necessarily preclude the court from saying that it does not form
a bar to the relief. The matter is one of discretion. It is not unknown for an H
agreement to provide by wrong methods for the right result, and instances can
even be found in the books of cases where the collusive agreement was found
objectionable, but the upshot of the case was the same as that intended by the
agreement (e.g., *German* v. *German* (26) as briefly reported). One way or another
a court must always return to the simple test of the justice of the case in relation
to the facts as a whole.   I

Having discussed the factors to be taken into consideration on a summons, it
is as well to add a word on one fundamental point. It goes, of course, without
saying that nothing in this judgment is intended to derogate from the essential
necessity of the judge at trial being satisfied that a matrimonial offence has been
committed, and of the judge hearing the summons and the trial judge being fully

---

(23) [1967] 1 All E.R. 870.   (24) [1964] 1 All E.R. at p. 778; [1964] P. at p. 232.
(25) [1965] 1 All E.R. at p. 482; [1965] P. at p. 270.   (26) (1965), 109 Sol. Jo. 353.

A   on guard against the summons procedure being used as a back door towards securing a divorce by consent where no such offence has been committed.

I now turn to the questions: what are the directions which can be given by the judge, and what form they should take. As already stated, the duty of the court to inquire into the matter of collusion has been maintained by the Act of 1963 and the successor provisions in the Act of 1965 (the onus of disproving collusion

B   seems, however, no longer to be insisted on; compare s. 4 (2) (*c*) of the Matrimonial Causes Act, 1950, and s. 5 (4) (*a*) of the Act of 1965). The marginal note to s. 5 of the Act of 1965 is " Hearing of petition ". I do not, however, think that this should deflect me from a view formed without taking into account its presence, viz., that, reading s. 5 as a whole, the provisions of sub-s. (2) enable the duty of the court as to inquiry to be in part performed by the judge hearing

C   the summons under the previously cited rules. (In declining to be influenced by the marginal note to s. 5 of the Act of 1965, I have in mind two points. First, the marginal note to the corresponding s. 4 of the Matrimonial Causes Act, 1950, reads: " Duty of court on presentation of petition ". Secondly, that for the reasons given in Maxwell on the Interpretation of Statutes (11th Edn.), p. 42, marginal notes are normally not regarded for purposes of interpretation,

D   though they may be in certain cases.)

On the other hand, no conclusion reached on the summons can affect the right of the trial court to elicit further material, or its duty in appropriate circumstances to put questions for that particular purpose. So long, however, as nothing is done to preclude the exercise of those last mentioned rights and duties, or the power of the trial court to reach, having regard to the further material, a conclusion

E   contrary to that formed by the judge on the summons, there seems to me no reason why on that summons a judge cannot give directions that the case go forward on the basis of his conclusions unless and until some further factor emerges.

The way in which the judge should state his conclusions, and the precise directions which he should then give, must vary according to the facts of the

F   case, and no doubt will evolve in due course as a matter of practice. It may well be, however, that the time has come for a rule to be framed which will at any rate give some guidance as to some of the directions that can be given. I agree that the present practice of simply stating after the hearing of the summons that the proposed agreement is " approved " seems to be open to objection. I doubt if in itself it is a direction at all, though it may be intended to give a number of

G   directions in a somewhat elliptical way. At any rate, a simple statement that the agreement was approved does not make it on the face of the order apparent that it is still open to the court further to investigate the matter at trial, and then to treat it as a bar to relief. It is, however, not necessary for me further to examine this matter as I am in full agreement with the direction proposed in this case by Willmer, L.J.

H   If the correct lines of approach to the questions arising on an application under the rules of 1963 in a pending cause are as above stated, the next question is as to how they should be applied in the present case. Some at any rate of the difficulties that arose on the summons may be due to the paucity of information put before the commissioner by the wife petitioner, who was seeking a divorce on account of her husband's desertion in 1947, in respect of which she held his

I   signed admission dated Nov. 27, 1963. The vital paragraphs in the affidavit of her solicitor read:

" (6) That the terms of the said proposed agreement are that the [wife] shall waive her claim for costs contained in the said petition and shall limit her claim therein for maintenance to the sum of 1s. per annum. Further and in consideration thereof it is provided by the said proposed agreement that the [husband] shall abstain from filing an answer alleging a defence to the said petition. (7) That I am informed by the [husband's] solicitors and verily believe that the said defence is to the effect that the [husband] denies

that he has deserted the [wife] and alleges that the [wife] has constructively   A
deserted the [husband] by reason of the [wife's] alleged relationship with one
Stacey, being a lodger at the [wife's] home from 1940 to 1945 and from 1947
to the present and still so lodging."

The wife herself filed no affidavit, and thus, so far as concerned the material put
before him by the wife, the commissioner was not unnaturally left in doubt as
to the facts and as to the real meaning of the phrase used by her solicitor in   B
para. 8 of the affidavit: "The [husband's] defence is strongly denied by the
[wife]." Unfortunately, however, he declined to consider the material the
husband's solicitor asked him to take into account, nor does he seem to have
suggested that the wife might provide further information and adjourned the
application for that purpose. He thus precluded himself from regarding information such as that which has now been placed before this court. In addition he   C
adopted an approach which, if normally followed, would stultify the whole object
of the procedure for which s. 5 (2) of the Act of 1965 provides. Instead of looking
at the probabilities of the case in the light of the material before him, the test
that he sought to apply is shown by his phrase:

"It was impossible for me to say . . . that a decree could not possibly be
obtained contrary to the justice of the case."   D

That approach is very different from one which looks at the balance of
probabilities.

For the reasons given by WILLMER, L.J., I agree that, had he let all the available
material be placed before him and then applied to it the correct tests, the proposed
agreement would have been held to be one that could be implemented provided   E
that at trial no further adverse facts were elicited by the court. Appropriate
directions would then have been given on that basis. I would accordingly allow
the appeal and make an order in the terms proposed by WILLMER, L.J. I would
add that, if it were thought fit to give further consideration to the rules, there may
be something to be said for examining whether they should not insist on some
affidavit or statement of the party making the application (not merely of the   F
solicitor), and also make express mention of the need for the relevant facts to be
fully stated.

[Following further submissions by counsel in regard to costs:]

WILLMER, L.J.: I do not find it necessary to express any view on the
question whether this appeal constitutes "separate proceedings" within the
meaning of the Legal Aid Act 1964, because I am satisfied that the application   G
for payment of the wife's costs out of the legal aid fund must in any event fail
having regard to the provisions (27) of s. 1 (4) of the Act of 1964. For reasons which
have already been fully ventilated in the course of the argument, I do not see
how in this case, apart from the Act of 1964, an order for payment of costs could
properly have been made against the assisted party, the husband. That appears
to me to be fatal to the application.   H

In those circumstances I prefer to express no view with regard to the other
arguments which have been addressed to us. These must be left for decision in
some future case where consideration of them may be necessary for the decision
of the case.

DANCKWERTS, L.J.: I agree.

SACHS, L.J.: I agree.   I

Appeal allowed. Order in terms stated by WILLMER, L.J.

Solicitors: *Blyth, Dutton, Wright & Bennett*, agents for *Coole & Haddock*,
Horsham (for the wife); *Rawlinson & Butler*, Horsham (for the husband);
Law Society.

[*Reported by* F. A. AMIES, ESQ., *Barrister-at-Law*.]

---

(27) For s. 1 (4), see footnote *, p. 511, ante.

A

Re THOMAS GERRARD & SON, LTD.

[CHANCERY DIVISION (Pennycuick, J.), April 4, 5, 6, 7, 13, 1967.]

Company—Auditors—Negligence—Standard of care and skill required in audit
—Stocktaking procedure—Alteration of invoices giving cause for suspicion
B   *—Complete examination required, rather than acceptance of managing direc-*
tor's assurance—Companies Act, 1948 (11 & 12 *Geo.* 6 *c.* 38), *s.* 162 (1).

An old-established private company carried on business as cotton spinners.
It had an issued share capital of £150,000. Its stock was taken and its
accounts were made up and audited half-yearly. From March, 1957 to
March, 1962, its annual balance sheets showed a position of stable and
C   continuing prosperity. For each year dividends of ten per cent. were paid.
A firm of accountants, K., gave each year, an unqualified auditors' report
in accordance with s. 162* of the Companies Act, 1948. In September, 1962,
it was discovered that the company's annual accounts as presented year by
year had borne no relation to its true position and that the company was
in fact insolvent. An independent firm of accountants made up a balance
D   sheet showing the company's true financial position on Nov. 22, 1962,
and on the same date the company passed a resolution for creditors' voluntary winding-up and a liquidator was appointed. Investigations showed that
C., the managing director who had conducted the day-to-day business of
the company had, since 1956, falsified the accounts, thereby concealing
the fact that in 1956-57 the company had made a small profit and thereafter
E   a heavy loss. In October, 1964, he was convicted on a number of charges
including falsification of books. The liquidator brought misfeasance proceedings against him which were compromised on payment by C. of £7,100
and costs.

C. falsified the books by three methods, viz., (a) he caused the half-yearly
stock valuation to be inflated by the inclusion of non-existing items either
F   by addition to real, or by fictitious, parcels; (b) he caused the price payable
by the company on purchases of stock made shortly before the end of each
current period of account to be included in the outgoings, not of that period,
but of the succeeding period, and (c) he caused the price payable to the
company on sales of stock made after the end of each current period
of account to be included in the receipts, not of that succeeding period of
G   account but in those of the current period. For the purpose of (b) above C.
altered the dates of invoices; the alterations were apparent and some of
them came to the notice of the auditors in the course of their audits. For the
purpose of (c) above C. tore the top copies of the invoices out of the numbered
invoice book and kept or destroyed them. In answer to the auditor's
question in the course of the audits, C. explained that such invoices came
H   in at the end of the stocktaking and it was easier to leave them out. The
auditors trusted C. and accepted his assurance that the stock taking procedure was correctly operated. There was expert accountancy evidence
that, if invoices were altered, complete examination of purchase invoices
should be made, and suppliers should be communicated with as to correct
versions.

I   The company paid income tax and profits tax on the inflated profits shown
in the annual accounts, nearly all of which was recovered on appeal to
the Special Commissioners; and the net dividends distributed were paid
either wholly or in part out of capital in certain years. The liquidator issued
a summons under s. 333 (1)† of the Companies Act, 1948, for a declaration
that such of the respondents as were partners in the firm of K. at the time
of the audits of the accounts for the years 1957 to 1962 were guilty of

---

* Section 162, so far as material, is set out at p. 534, letters C and D, post.
† Section 331 (1), so far as material, is set out at p. 533, letter F, post.

negligence and breach of duty in respect of the audits, and for payment **A** of compensation by three of the respondents, the loss being alleged under two heads, (i) the net dividends distributed otherwise than out of profits and (ii) income tax and profits tax paid by reference to non-existing profits.

Held: (i) the discovery of the altered invoices put the auditors on enquiry, and, by not thereafter investigating further (e.g., by examining the suppliers' statements and communicating with the suppliers if necessary) into the **B** purchases of stock at the end of each current accounting period and the attribution of price to the succeeding period of account, the auditors failed in their duty to exercise reasonable care and skill (see p. 536, letter I, to p. 537, letter A, and p. 537, letter D, post).

Principle stated by LINDLEY, L.J., in *Kingston Cotton Mill Co.* (*No. 2*) ([1896] 2 Ch. at p. 284) applied, but the decision in that case distinguished. **C**

(ii) the auditors' breach of duty was the direct cause of loss as regards the dividends distributed otherwise than out of available profits and as regards income tax and profits tax paid by reference to non-existent profits, and in estimating the loss tax recovered should be deducted and the costs of recovering the tax should be added; compensation should be assessed accordingly, the auditors being entitled to credit for the amount recovered **D** from C., and an inquiry as to the amount of compensation would be ordered, which inquiry would include the allocation of liability for the compensation among the members of the firm of auditors (see p. 538, letters B and H, post).

Per CURIAM: the standards of reasonable care and skill are, on the expert evidence, more exacting today than those which prevailed in 1896 when *Re Kingston Cotton Mill Co.* (*No. 2*), supra, was decided (see p. 536, letter G, **E** post).

[As to the duties and position of auditors in relation to an audit of company accounts, see 6 HALSBURY'S LAWS (3rd Edn.) 387, 388, paras. 751, 752; and for cases on auditors and their liability, see 9 DIGEST (Repl.) 587-590, *3880-3904.*

As to misfeasance summonses in respect of neglect of duty by auditors, see **F** 6 HALSBURY'S LAWS (3rd Edn.) 624, para. 1230.

For the Companies Act, 1948, s. 162, s. 333, Sch. 9, see 3 HALSBURY'S STATUTES (2nd Edn.) 588, 715, 869.]

Cases referred to:
Bolivia Republic Exploration Syndicate, Ltd., Re, [1914] 1 Ch. 139; 83 L.J.Ch.
    235; 110 L.T. 141; 9 Digest (Repl.) 185, *1198.* **G**
Kingston Cotton Mill Co. (*No. 2*), *Re,* [1896] 1 Ch. 331; 65 L.J.Ch. 290; 73
    L.T. 745; *rvsd,* C.A., [1896] 2 Ch. 279; 65 L.J.Ch. 673; sub nom.
    Re Kingston Cotton Mill Co., Ltd., Ex p. Pickering & Peasegood (*No. 2*),
    74 L.T. 568; 9 Digest (Repl.) 587, *3880.*
London and General Bank, Ltd., Re, Ex p. Theobald (*No. 2*), [1895-99] All
    E.R. Rep. 953; [1895] 2 Ch. 673; 64 L.J.Ch. 866; 73 L.T. 304; 9 **H**
    Digest (Repl.) 643, *4275.*

Adjourned Summons.

This was an application by originating summons dated Mar. 9, 1965, by Gilbert Hamer Eaves, the liquidator of Thomas Gerrard & Son, Ltd. (a company in voluntary winding-up) for the following relief; (i) a declaration that such **I** of the respondents respectively as were partners in the firm of P. & J. Kevan at the time of the audit by that firm of the balance sheets of the company for its financial periods ended Mar. 3, 1957, Mar. 8, 1958, Mar. 7, 1959, Mar. 5, 1960, Mar. 4, 1961, and Mar. 31, 1962, and the relevant accounts of the company for the periods ending on those dates were guilty of negligence and breach of duty in respect of the audit of which accounts whereby the company paid dividends out of capital or otherwise irregularly to the extent of the total of £26,254 13s. 1d. net and made payments of income tax and profits tax in excess of the liability

A therefor of the company to the extent of £56,659 6s. 6d.; (ii) an order that the
respondents Kevan William Horton and James Edward Sharman (partners in
the firm of P. & J. Kevan at all material times), pay to the liquidator compensation for such negligence and breach of duty to the extent of the aggregate of
(a) the sum of £26,254 13s. 1d.; (b) the excess of the sum of £56,659 6s. 6d. over
the amount recovered from the Commissioners of Inland Revenue; (c) the
B costs of recovering the same from the Commissioners of Inland Revenue;
(d) a sum equal to interest on the moneys so recovered while held by the Commissioners of Inland Revenue; (iii) an order that the respondent Frank Kirkham
(a partner in P. & J. Kevan until Dec. 31, 1959), pay to the applicant as such
liquidator compensation for such negligence and breach of duty to the extent
of the aggregate of (b), (c) and (d) in para. (ii) ante, and (iv) an order that the
C respondents, John Phethean Nightingale and Alwyn Charles Robert Thompson
(partners in P. & J. Kevan at all material times after Jan. 1, 1960), pay to the
applicant as liquidator compensation for negligence and breach of duty to the
extent of £26,254 13s. 1d. The facts are set out in the judgment.

The cases noted below* were cited during the argument in addition to those
referred to in the judgment.

D *Raymond Walton*, Q.C., and *J. G. Monroe* for the liquidator.

R. B. S. Instone for the respondents.

Cur. adv. vult.

Apr. 13. **PENNYCUICK, J.**: This summons is issued under s. 333 of the
Companies Act, 1948, by Mr. Eaves, the liquidator of Thomas Gerrard & Son,
E Ltd., to which I will refer as " the company ". The respondents are five individuals who during the period from Mar. 2, 1957, up till the liquidation of the
company on Nov. 22, 1962, were members of the firm of accountants known
as P. & J. Kevan, to which I will refer as " Kevans ". Two of them, Mr. Horton
and Mr. Sharman, were partners in the firm throughout that period; Mr.
Nightingale and Mr. Thompson became partners on Jan. 1, 1960; the other,
F Mr. Kirkham, ceased to be a partner on Dec. 31, 1959. The summons was tried
on points of claim with oral evidence and cross-examination.

The facts as I find them are as follows. The company was incorporated as
long ago as 1881 as a private company. It carried on at Adlington, near Chorley,
Lancashire, a well-established business of cotton spinners, specialising in the
manufacture of brocades. Its articles contained no unusual provisions. I need
G refer only to the following:

" (121) The profits of the company available for dividend and resolved to
be distributed shall be applied in the payment of dividends to the members
in accordance with their respective rights and priorities. The company in
general meeting may declare dividends accordingly. (122) No dividend shall
be payable except out of the profits of the company, or in excess of the
H amount recommended by the directors . . . (138) Auditors of the company
shall be appointed and their duties regulated in accordance with s. 159 to
s. 162 of the Act [that is, the Companies Act, 1862]. (139) The auditors'
report to the members made pursuant to the statutory provisions as to
audit shall be read before the company in general meeting, and shall be
open to inspection by any member . . ."

I During the relevant period the issued capital of the company was £150,000.
The directors were Mr. Crossfield, a businessman with other interests; Mr.
Ramsden, his personal secretary; Mr. Croston, the managing director who

---

* *Re Denham & Co.*, (1883), 25 Ch.D. 752; *Newton* v. *Birmingham Small Arms Co.,
Ltd.*, (1906), 2 Ch. 378; *Squire, Cash Chemist, Ltd.* v. *Ball, Baker & Co.*, (1911), 106
L.T. 197; *Re City Equitable Fire Insurance Co., Ltd.*, [1924] All E.R. Rep. 485; [1925]
Ch. 407; *Fomento (Sterling Area), Ltd.* v. *Selsdon Fountain Pen Co., Ltd.*, (1958), 1 All
E.R. 11; *R.* v. *Shacter*, [1960] 1 All E.R. 61; [1960] 2 Q.B. 252.

conducted the day-to-day business of the company; and Mr. Taylor, the produc- **A** tion manager. The secretary was a Mr. Heyes, Mr. Croston's brother-in-law, who at some time also became a director. He died in 1962. A Mr. Snape assisted Mr. Heyes in the later years. Mr. Crosfield and his wife together held a large block of shares. Mr. Croston held eighteen thousand shares. Mr. Croston was a well-known and respected figure in the Adlington district where he was a justice of the peace and councillor. **B**

The company's year of account ran from and to varying dates in March. Stock was taken half-yearly and the accounts were made up and audited half-yearly. The balance sheets of the company for the whole year's accounts ended on Mar. 2, 1957, Mar. 8, 1958, Mar. 7, 1959, Mar. 5, 1960, Mar. 4, 1961 and Mar. 31, 1962 were put in evidence. These show a position of stable and continuing prosperity. At Mar. 2, 1957, the company had a reserve fund of £60,000 and a **C** balance on profit-and-loss account of £82,474. Stock was put at £165,492. In each of the years which I have mentioned the profit-and-loss account showed a fair net profit, namely, 1956-57, £9,514; 1957-58, £11,798; 1959-60, £12,048; 1960-61, £14,539; and 1961-62, £11,156. For each year the directors paid an interim dividend of five per cent. and a final dividend of five per cent. making ten per cent. in all, and the company in general meeting approved those dividends. **D** The current profits were ample to provide the net amount of the dividend. At Mar. 31, 1962, the company had a reserve fund of £47,500 and the balance on profit-and-loss account was £104,605. Its stock in trade was put at £239,925. The debit balance at the bank was £43,107. The amount owing to other creditors was £138,846 and the amount owing by debtors £126,263.

For each year Kevans gave an unqualified report in accordance with s. 162 **E** of the Companies Act, 1948. I will read the report on the balance sheet as at Mar. 31, 1962:

" Auditors' report to the members of Messrs. Thomas Gerrard & Son, Ltd. We have obtained all the information and explanations which to the best of our knowledge and belief were necessary for the purposes of our audit. In our opinion proper books of account have been kept by the company **F** so far as appears from our examination of those books. We have examined the above balance sheet and annexed profit and loss account which are in agreement with the books of account. In our opinion and to the best of our information and according to the explanations given us the said accounts give the information required by the Companies Act, 1948, in the manner so required and the balance sheet gives a true and fair view of the state of **G** the company's affairs as at Mar. 31, 1962, and the profit and loss account gives a true and fair view of the profit for the year ended on that date."

Up to the end of September, 1962, the skies remained unclouded. Then came immediate and total disaster. It turned out that the company's accounts as presented year by year bore no relation to its true position and that the company **H** was in fact hopelessly insolvent. Kevans made up a balance sheet as at Nov. 5, 1962, and an independent firm of accountants, Messrs. Harry L. Price & Co., subsequently made out a balance sheet as at Nov. 22, 1962, the date of the liquidation. In the last-mentioned balance sheet the company's stock is put at £27,916 only. Its debit balance at the bank had increased to £169,442; its other creditors were put at £130,416 against debtors of £10,274; the profit and **I** loss account showed an adverse balance of £319,855, which was reduced to £272,395 by transfer of the balance to the credit of general reserve. The company passed a resolution for creditors' voluntary winding-up on Nov. 22, 1962, and Mr. Eaves, who was a partner in Harry L. Price & Co., was appointed the liquidator.

The investigations made in the first place by Kevans and thereafter by Harry L. Price & Co., showed that Mr. Croston had, at least since the year 1956-57, made a regular practice of falsifying the company's accounts, thereby concealing the

A fact that in 1956-57 the company had made a small profit and that for each
subsequent year the company had made a heavy loss, and presenting instead a
picture of steady and substantial profit. Mr. Croston was prosecuted on Oct. 10,
1964, and he was convicted at Liverpool Crown Court on a number of charges,
including falsification of books, and sentenced to five years' imprisonment. The
liquidator brought misfeasance proceedings against Mr. Croston on Jan. 17,
B 1967, and these proceedings were compromised on payment of £7,100, together
with £400 costs. These figures represent the maximum which the liquidator
considered could be recovered from Mr. Croston.

Mr. Croston falsified the company's books by three methods, which I will
now indicate. (a) Mr. Croston caused the half-yearly stock valuation to be inflated
by the inclusion of non-existing items, either by way of addition to real parcels
C or by way of fictitious parcels. The procedure of stock-taking adopted by the
company was for stock to be taken by employees in the various departments
of the company's mill. The original sheets taken by these employees were then
submitted to Mr. Croston. He collated them into a stock summary book and
gave a certificate as to the total amount. In the course of collating the original
sheets he inserted in them a number of fictitious items and then had the sheets
D retyped with the inclusion of these items. The figures entered in the stock book
represented the original figures as increased by those attributed to the fictitious
items.

(b) Mr. Croston caused the price payable by the company on purchases of
stock made shortly before the end of each current period of account to be included
in the outgoings, not of that period, but of the succeeding period. The effect of
E this manoeuvre was that in the account for the current period the stock purchased was brought in but its price was excluded. The invoices sent by the
suppliers were placed in what is known as a guard book. Mr. Croston altered the
dates of the invoices so as to transfer them from the current to the succeeding
period of account. The alterations were made either by erasing the original
date and typing in the new date or simply by crossing out the original date in
F ink and writing in the new date. The alterations were quite open in the sense
that they are immediately apparent to the eye of anyone looking at the invoices.
The invoices so altered were numerous, although a relatively small proportion
of the total invoices sent to the company by suppliers. In some instances the
original date was as much as a month before the close of the current period of
account. It will be observed that if nothing more had been done the inclusion
G of the price in the succeeding period of account would have correspondingly
reduced the company's profit for that period, but in fact the process was repeated
to a constantly increasing extent half-year by half-year for each successive
period of account.

(c) Mr. Croston caused the price payable to the company on the sales of stock
made after the end of each current period of account to be included in the
H receipts, not of that succeeding period of account but in those for the current
period. The effect of this manoeuvre was the converse of that last described.
Again it was constantly repeated. The invoices sent to customers bore the correct
date. Mr. Croston tore the top copies of these invoices out of the numbered
invoice book and kept or destroyed them.

It will be convenient to mention at this point that the procedure adopted by
I auditors for ensuring that goods purchased and their purchase price are brought
into the same period of account and likewise that goods sold and their sale
price are brought into the same period of account is known as the " cut-off "
procedure.

It is common ground that I should not in this judgment attempt to deal
with figures, some of which are complicated. It will be sufficient to say that the
total amount by which the profits of the company were inflated by the three
methods was very large. It will be remembered that the true balance sheet
as at Nov. 22, 1962, showed an adverse balance of £272,395 on profit and loss

account as against a favourable balance of £152,105 on general reserve and A
profit and loss account in the falsified balance sheet as at Mar. 31, 1962. The
company was periodically assessed to and paid income tax and profits tax on
the inflated profits as shown by its accounts. The whole of this tax, except
£3,433, has now been recovered and there may be further recoveries. The
liquidator incurred costs amounting to £2,294 on a successful appeal to the
Special Commissioners in connexion with the recovery of tax. After bringing B
in the amounts standing to the credit of general reserve on profit and loss account
the company had accumulated profits sufficient to cover the dividends paid up
to and including the year 1958-59. The liquidator confines his claim in this
respect to the years 1959-60, 1960-61 and 1961-62. The net dividends paid for
these three years were £9,187 10s., £9,187 10s. and £7,879 13s. 1d. respectively.
The explanation of the last figure is apparently that Mr. Croston himself did not C
take his dividend for 1961-62. The liquidator did not seek to establish as regards
the years prior to 1959-60 that the directors, if they had known that the company
had made a loss in the year, would not have recommended a dividend out of
accumulated profits.

The only director who gave evidence was Mr. Ramsden, whose evidence was
not of major significance. Mr. Crossfield is ill. Mr. Heyes is dead. Neither Mr. D
Croston nor Mr. Taylor was called, nor was Mr. Snape. The other witnesses who
gave evidence on the liquidator's side were the liquidator himself and his clerk,
Mr. Farnworth, who explained the falsification of the books in detail. The
company had an out-of-date and inadequate system of internal accounting.

I turn now to the steps taken by Kevans in connexion with the audit of the
company's accounts, particularly in so far as these bear on the three methods of E
falsification above mentioned. During the relevant years the audit was conducted on behalf of Kevans by Mr. Nightingale, a qualified accountant who,
as I have said, became a partner in 1960. He conducted the audit with the
assistance of Mr. Swarsbrick, a senior clerk employed by Kevans. Mr. Swarsbrick
carried out most of the detailed work of checking stock sheets, invoices, books
and so forth. Mr. Nightingale came to the mill when the detailed work was more F
or less finished and proceeded himself to complete the audit. When the audit
was complete Mr. Nightingale extracted the profit and loss account and balance
sheet from the books kept by the company.

Mr. Nightingale and Mr. Swarsbrick gave evidence. Mr. Nightingale and
Mr. Swarsbrick throughout believed Mr. Croston to be a man of the highest
integrity. Apart from the alteration of invoices under method (b) they had no G
reason to suspect otherwise. They were aware that the company's system of
accounting was inadequate. At some time before 1962 they had set about the
task of persuading various clients with inadequate systems of account to bring
these up to date. Unfortunately, their confidence in the company's standing and
probity had made them leave it to the last. They had just addressed themselves
to the improvement of the company's system in 1962 when the crash came.   H

Mr. Nightingale and Mr. Swarsbrick obtained their information as to the
various matters which arose in the course of their duty from officials of the
company, particularly Mr. Croston and Mr. Heyes. The steps regularly taken by
Mr. Nightingale and Mr. Swarsbrick in relation to the three matters in which
falsification took place were as follows. (i) Mr. Swarsbrick checked the figures
contained in the stock summary book against the stock sheets produced to him. I
Mr. Nightingale and Mr. Swarsbrick accepted Mr. Croston's assurance that
there were no other stock sheets. They took no steps with a view to ascertaining
the existence of the original sheets made out in the various departments of the
mill. Mr. Croston's assurances were given in the presence of some other official
of the company.

(ii) Mr. Swarsbrick questioned Mr. Heyes with regard to the stock situation
towards the end of each half year with a view to satisfying himself that the
price of the stock was brought into the same account as that into which the

A stock was taken. Mr. Heyes assured him that this was so. When he came on the altered invoices in connexion with the next half year's audit he asked Mr. Heyes for an explanation. Mr. Heyes stated, in Mr. Swarsbrick's words, that these had been " carried forward as not being in stock at the year's end ". Mr. Swarsbrick amplified his explanation in the following words. He was asked— " Did Mr. Heyes give you any further explanation as to which it was, or is that

B what you thought yourself? " He replied—" No, it was one or the other. It was either that the goods had not been delivered yet and the invoice was dated prior to the accounting date or in fact the goods had been delivered but had not been taken into the stock."

In addition Mr. Nightingale himself interrogated Mr. Croston with regard to the cut-off position. His evidence on these matters is as follows:

C " (Counsel for Kevans): There have been some references to the cut-off. How did that apply and how did you deal with it in relation to this company? (A) Obviously, completing the audit very soon after the year end and the half year end, the cut-off procedure must be investigated. Being fully aware of this, both from the sales side and the purchase side, I interrogated Mr.

D Croston. (Q) What did you ask him? (A) I questioned what he did about goods in stock at the end of the year for which an invoice had not been received, or conversely, an invoice which may have been received for goods which had not yet arrived; and similarly on the sales side whether there was any possibility of the sales being both in sales and in stock. He assured me, again in the presence of other directors, that he took personal charge of

E this particular problem at the end of each half year. I said: ' You have no goods inwards book,' but he inferred that he kept some sort of record for his own information and he was absolutely satisfied that the cut-off had been correctly applied both to sales and purchases. As this statement was made by a man in a management position and in the presence of other officials of the company, I accepted it. (Q) How did that statement tie in with the

F stock certificates? (A) It was on the question of stocks that the question started. I said: ' Well, Mr. Croston, are we quite sure that all the stock has been correctly taken? ', and I went through it with him. He explained to me how the method of stocktaking was done, with rough stock sheets, and then in the stock summary book; and then automatically following from that must follow the question of the cut-off on both sides. The whole thing was

G dealt with as part of the audit investigation. (Q) If in fact Mr. Croston's answers to you were false, what would have been the effect of the falsehood on the position at the beginning of the next accounting period? (A) If his answers had been false, the stock would have been wrong and he would have had a carry over of invoices into the following year which properly would relate to the previous year. (Q) Why did not the falsehoods as regards period

H (i) become exposed when you were dealing with period (ii)? (A) As has been mentioned in evidence, a lot of the invoices following the previous year and also the carry over invoices at the year end have been obviously amended with a circle in ink, the dates crossed off and, say, Mar. 31 deleted in ink and Apr. 2 put in at the top, quite obviously, and also the words ' Not in stock' written across very many invoices. We knew these invoices had been

I altered and this came out again in the question all connected with the cut-off ' Mr. Croston, we notice certain invoices are marked " Not in stock " and have the dates altered. Why? ' He would then say: 'Because it is more convenient for me to leave them out. They came in at the end of stocktaking; they came in in relation to yarns and beams and it is easier to leave them out of stock and I have them in the total.' (Q) Did you sometimes see the guard book or was it one of your assistants? (A) Mr. Swarsbrick saw the guard book. (Q) Then you yourself never saw any purchase invoices with amended dates at that time? (A) I was obviously told they existed by my senior clerk,

but whether I actually saw one—I knew altered invoices existed of the   A
nature I have mentioned."

Mr. Nightingale was content with Mr. Croston's explanation and took no further
steps to check the cut-off procedure. To use his own words:

" (Q) The reason you did not go very deeply into what happened after the
year end, or what appeared to happen after the year end in the books,   B
was because you trusted Mr. Croston's assurance that he was operating
cut-off procedure correctly. (A) Yes."

Mr. Nightingale did not make any enquiries of suppliers nor did he report the
alterations in the invoices to the board.

(iii) Mr. Swarsbrick questioned Mr. Heyes with regard to stock sold after
the end of each half year with a view to satisfying himself that the price of the   C
stock was brought into the same period of account as that in which the stock
was taken out. Mr. Heyes assured him that this was so. As appears from the
passage which I have already read. Mr. Croston gave a similar assurance to Mr.
Nightingale. Mr. Croston explained the absence of the torn-out invoices by
saying that these had been spoilt in typing and thrown away. Mr. Nightingale
accepted this explanation. As I have already said, Mr. Nightingale took no   D
further steps to check the cut-off procedure.

An accountant of high standing was called to give expert evidence on either
side, Mr. Macnamara, a partner in Kemp, Chatteris & Co. for the liquidator,
and Mr. Philp, a partner in Cooper Bros. for Kevans. Mr. Macnamara gave a
general account of the duties of auditors with particular reference to stock
valuation and cut-off procedure. He accepted the general proposition contained   E
in the handbook issued by the Council of the Institute of Chartered Accountants
in these words:

" It is the duty of the auditor of a company to arrive at an independent
professional opinion on whether the directors have properly carried out
their own duties in the preparation of accounts and their presentation to
shareholders."   F

He emphasised the importance of a sound system of internal accounting and
stated that where there is not a sound system it is the duty of the auditor to
make deeper and more extensive tests. He explained in detail the checks to be
made in relation to stock valuation and cut-off. He gave it as his view that on
discovery of the altered invoices it was the duty of Mr. Nightingale to make   G
a complete examination of all the purchase invoices, to communicate directly
with the suppliers and to inform the board. I think that I should quote his
words:

" If the invoices were altered, then undoubtedly a complete examination
should be made of all purchase invoices and, where alterations were seen,
the suppliers should be communicated with as to the correct versions.   H
At the same time, as this would be a very serious matter, the completion
of any report on the accounts should be held over and the board of directors
informed."

I accept the evidence of Mr. Macnamara. I do so without any hesitation because
Mr. Philp in cross-examination agreed with it without qualification. In his
examination-in-chief Mr. Philp gave these answers: I

" (Q) Have you as a result of your questioning of them [that is Kevans]
obtained in your opinion enough explanations to enable you as an expert
in these matters to form a view whether or not they fell short of the accepted
standards? (A) I do not think they fell short. (Q) I ask you first of all if you
have obtained enough information to enable you to form a view? (A) Yes.
(Q) And what is your view? (A) My view is that on the basis that they
checked every entry in the books and on the basis that they never accepted

A the managing director's word without it being corroborated, that they have
a proper audit."

As I understood him, however, the one substantial ground on which he sought
to exculpate Kevans was that of time. I will quote two further passages from
his evidence. Immediately after the passage which I have last read he said:

B   " I think the trouble in this case was the speed with which the directors
required the accounts to be signed. This did not give sufficient time for the
normal standard audit procedures, such as verification of statements and so
forth, to be dealt with. On the basis that they had to sign on the date, I
think the questions they asked and given the evidence they asked, were all
they could do, and if they were satisfied with the honesty of corroboration
C   of the matters by the senior and trusted official of the company, that they
did all they could do."

Then in cross-examination came this:

" (Q) . . . And your answer is that the speed with which the directors required
the accounts to be signed did not give time for the normal procedures to be
carried out? (A) Yes; the normal procedures being the checking with creditors'
D   statements that purchases were included in the right month. (Q) And similarly
presumably the debits? (A) Yes. (Q) In other words, perhaps I can take this
very shortly, you really agree with what Mr. Macnamara was saying on those
two heads, subject to the vital qualification of time? (A) I do. I do not
disagree with anything Mr. Macnamara said. (Q) You do not dispute anything
he said? (A) No. (Q) Under those heads or generally? (A) At all? "
E

I turn now to the law. The present summons is brought under s. 333 (1) of the
Companies Act, 1948, which, so far as material, provides:

" If in the course of winding-up a company it appears that any person
who has taken part in the formation or promotion of the company, or any
past or present . . . officer of the company has . . . been guilty of any
F   misfeasance or breach of trust in relation to the company, the court may,
on the application of . . . the liquidator . . . . examine into the conduct of
the . . . officer, and compel him . . . to contribute such sum to the assets
of the company by way of compensation in respect of the . . . misfeasance
or breach of trust as the court thinks just."

G It is not in dispute that for this purpose an auditor is an officer of the company.
The points of claim were amended more than once in the course of the hearing
so as to formulate the claim in the correct manner. The points of claim in their
final form, after setting out certain facts, allege the breach of duty on the part of
Kevans in the following terms:

H   " Kevans were guilty of negligence and breach in respect of the audit of
the books and accounts for the said years in that (i) they failed to check
or alternatively failed to check sufficiently the stock books and stock sheets;
(ii) they failed to take the proper steps which would have enabled them to
discover that the purchases effected by the company had been suppressed
to the extent set out in Sch. 1 annexed to these points of claim; and (iii)
they failed to take the proper steps which would have enabled them to
I   discover that the sales effected by the company had been over-stated to
the extent set out in Sch. 2 annexed to these points of claim whereby they
were guilty of breach of duty as auditors in that they made unqualified
reports on the said balance sheets and documents whereas such certificates
should (in the absence of their checks and discoveries leading to correction
thereof) have made reports appropriately qualified."

Section 147 (1) of the Companies Act, 1948 prescribes that a company must
" cause to be kept proper books of account". By s. 148 the directors must lay

a profit and loss account and balance sheet before the company in general
meeting. Section 149 (1) is in these terms:

" Every balance sheet of a company shall give a true and fair view of
the state of affairs of the company as at the end of its financial year, and
every profit and loss account of a company shall give a true and fair view
of the profit or loss of the company for the financial year."

By s. 159 (1) a company must appoint auditors. Section 162 is critical on the
present issue. It provides:

" (1) The auditors shall make a report to the members on the accounts
examined by them, and on every balance sheet, every profit and loss account
and all group accounts laid before the company in general meeting during
their tenure of office, and the report shall contain statements as to the matters
mentioned in Sch. 9 to this Act. (2) The auditors' report shall be read before
the company in general meeting and shall be open to inspection by any
member. (3) Every auditor of a company shall have a right of access at all
times to the books and accounts and vouchers of the company, and shall be
entitled to require from the officers of the company such information and
explanation as he thinks necessary for the performance of the duties of
the auditors."

I need not read sub-s. (4).

Schedule 9 which is referred to in s. 162 (1) is headed " Matters to be expressly
stated in auditors' report ", and it provides:

" 1. Whether they have obtained all the information and explanations
which to the best of their knowledge and belief were necessary for the purposes
of their audit. 2. Whether, in their opinion, proper books of account have
been kept by the company, so far as appears from their examination of
those books, and proper returns adequate for the purposes of their audit
have been received from branches not visited by them. 3. (1) Whether
the company's balance sheet and (unless it is framed as a consolidated
profit and loss account) profit and loss account dealt with by the report
are in agreement with the books of account and returns. (2) Whether, in
their opinion and to the best of their information and according to the
explanations given, the said accounts give the information required by
this Act in the manner so required and give a true and fair view (a) in the
case of the balance sheet, of the state of the company's affairs as at the end
of its financial year; and (b) in the case of the profit and loss account, of
the profit or loss for its financial year; or, as the case may be, give a true
and fair view thereof subject to the non-disclosure of any matters . . . not
required to be disclosed."

The scheme of the Act of 1948, then, is that the directors must prepare the
accounts; the auditors must make a report to the members on the accounts;
the report must contain statements on certain specified matters. It is, I think,
clear that the auditor, when he " thinks " for the purpose of s. 162 (3) what is
necessary for the performance of his duties, when he forms the " belief " mentioned in para. 1 of Sch. 9, when he forms the " opinion " mentioned in para. 2
of Sch. 9, and again when he forms the " opinion " mentioned in para. 3 (2) of
Sch. 9, must exercise reasonable care and skill. Equally if he performs these
mental operations without exercising reasonable care and skill and then proceeds
to give an unqualified statement, in other words a clean certificate, he is in
breach of his statutory duty as an officer of the company. Once the pleadings
had been brought into order, counsel for Kevans, did not, as I understood him,
contend to the contrary. It has always been the law that an auditor must
exercise reasonable care and skill and it could hardly be suggested that the effect
of the present statutory provisions is to diminish this obligation.

A   I was referred to such judicial decisions on the duties of auditors as are to be
found in the books. The most important for the present purpose is the decision
of the Court of Appeal in *Re Kingston Cotton Mill Co. (No. 2)* (1), in which it
was held (affirming the judgment of VAUGHAN WILLIAMS, J. (2)) that where an
officer of a company had committed a breach of his duty to the company, the
direct consequence of which had been a misapplication of its assets, for which
B   he could be made responsible in an action, such breach of duty was a " misfeasance " for which he might be summarily proceeded against under the
Companies (Winding-up) Act, 1890, s. 10, and it was not necessary that an action
should be brought. In that case, for some years before the company was wound
up, balance sheets signed by the auditors were published by the directors to
the shareholders in which the value of the company's stock-in-trade at the
C   end of each year was grossly overstated. The auditors relied on certificates,
wilfully false, given by J., one of the directors who was also manager, as to the
value of the stock-in-trade. Dividends were paid for some years on the footing
that the balance sheets were correct; but if the stock-in-trade had been stated
at its true value it would have appeared that there were no profits out of which
a dividend could be declared. If the auditors had compared the different books
D   and added to the stock-in-trade at the beginning of the year the amounts purchased during the year, and deducted the amounts sold, they would have seen
that the statement of the stock-in-trade at the end of the year was so large as to
call for explanation; but they did not do so. It was held (reversing the decision
of VAUGHAN WILLIAMS, J. (2)), that, it being no part of the duty of the auditors
to take stock, they were justified in relying on the certificates of the manager,
E   a person of acknowledged competence and high reputation, and were not bound
to check his certificates in the absence of anything to raise suspicion, and that
they were not liable for the dividends wrongfully paid. An auditor was not
bound to be suspicious where there were no circumstances to arouse suspicion;
he was only bound to exercise a reasonable amount of care and skill.

This decision has been so much relied on in the present case that I ought to
F   read two passages from the judgment of LINDLEY, L.J. First (3):

" I come now to the real question in this controversy, and that is, whether
the appellants have been guilty of any breach of duty to the company. To
decide this question it is necessary to consider—(1) what their duty was;
(2) how they performed it, and in what respects (if any) they failed to
perform it. The duty of an auditor generally was very carefully considered
G   by this court in *Re London and General Bank, Ltd., Ex p. Theobald (No. 2)* (4)
and I cannot usefully add anything to what will be found there. It was there
pointed out that an auditor's duty is to examine the books, ascertain that
they are right, and to prepare a balance sheet showing the true financial
position of the company at the time to which the balance sheet refers.
But it was also pointed out that an auditor is not an insurer, and that in
H   the discharge of his duty he is only bound to exercise a reasonable amount
of care and skill. It was further pointed out that what in any particular
case is a reasonable amount of care and skill depends on the circumstances
of that case; that if there is nothing which ought to excite suspicion, less
care may properly be considered reasonable than could be so considered
if suspicion was or ought to have been aroused. These are the general
I   principles which have to be applied to cases of this description. I protest,
however, against the notion that an auditor is bound to be suspicious as
distinguished from reasonably careful. To substitute the one expression
for the other may easily lead to serious error."

---

(1) [1896] 2 Ch. 279.   (2) [1896] 1 Ch. 331.
(3) [1896] 2 Ch. at p. 284.
(4) [1895-99] All E.R. Rep. 950 at pp. 956 958; [1895] 2 Ch. 673 at pp. 682,684

Re London and General Bank, Ltd. (5) should be looked at in full. Then in the A *Kingston Cotton Mill* case comes this passage (6):

" The auditors did not profess to guarantee the correctness of this item. They assumed no responsibility for it. They took the item from the manager, and the entry in the balance-sheet showed that they did so. I confess I cannot see that their omission to check his returns was a breach of their duty to the company. It is no part of an auditor's duty to take stock. No one B contends that it is. He must rely on other people for details of the stock-in-trade on hand. In the case of a cotton mill he must rely on some skilled person for the materials necessary to enable him to enter the stock-in-trade at its proper value in the balance-sheet. In this case the auditors relied on the manager. He was a man of high character and of unquestioned competence. He was trusted by every one who knew him. The learned judge C has held that the directors are not to be blamed for trusting him. The auditors had no suspicion that he was not to be trusted to give accurate information as to the stock-in-trade in hand, and they trusted him accordingly in that matter. But it is said they ought not to have done so, . . ."

LINDLEY, L.J., then gave his reasons why that was said. He concluded (7): D

" The question is whether, no suspicion of anything wrong being entertained, there was a want of reasonable care on the part of the auditors in relying on the returns made by a competent and trusted expert relating to matters on which information from such a person was essential. I cannot think there was." E

I need only quote further the well-known sentence in the judgment of LOPES, L.J. (8): " He [that is the auditor] is a watch-dog, but not a bloodhound."

This case appears, at any rate at first sight, to be conclusive in favour of Kevans as regards the falsification of the stock taken in isolation. Counsel for the liquidator pointed out that before 1900 there was no statutory provision corresponding to s. 162 of the Companies Act, 1948. That is so, but I am not F clear that the quality of the auditor's duty has changed in any relevant respect since 1896. Basically that duty has always been to audit the company's accounts with reasonable care and skill. The real ground on which *Re Kingston Cotton Mill Co. (No. 2)* (9) is, I think, capable of being distinguished is that the standards of reasonable care and skill are, on the expert evidence, more exacting today than those which prevailed in 1896. I see considerable force in this contention. G It must, I think, be that it is open, even in this court, to make a finding that in all the particular circumstances the auditors have been in breach of their duty in relation to stock. On the other hand, if this breach of duty stood alone and the facts were more or less the same as those in *Re Kingston Cotton Mill Co. (No. 2)* (9) this court would, I think, be very chary indeed of reaching a conclusion different from that reached by the Court of Appeal in *Re Kingston* H *Cotton Mill Co. (No. 2)* (9).

I return now to the three methods of falsification (see p. 529, letters B to H, ante) and will seek to apply the law as I understand it to those three methods.

(a) I think it better not to make a finding on what would be the position under this head (a) if it stood alone.

(b) I find it impossible to acquit Kevans of negligence as regards purchases of I stock before the end of each current period of account and the attribution of the price to the succeeding period of account. I will assume in their favour that Mr. Nightingale was entitled to rely on the assurances of Mr. Heyes and Mr. Croston until he first came on the altered invoices, but once these were discovered he was clearly put on inquiry and I do not think that he was then entitled to rest content

(5) [1895-99] All E.R. Rep. 953; [1895] 2 Ch. 673.　　(6) [1896] 2 Ch. at p. 286.
(7) [1896] 2 Ch.at p. 287.　　　　　　　　　　　　　　　(8) [1896] 2 Ch. at p. 288.
(9) [1896] 2 Ch. 279.

A with the assurances of Mr. Croston and Mr. Heyes, however implicitly he may have trusted Mr. Croston. I find the conclusion inescapable, alike on the expert evidence and as a matter of business common sense, that at this stage he ought to have taken steps on the lines indicated by Mr. Macnamara, that is to say, he should have examined the suppliers' statements and where necessary have communicated with the suppliers. Having ascertained the precise facts so far

B as it was possible for him to do so, he should then have informed the board. It may be that the board would then have taken some action; but whatever the board did he should in each subsequent audit have made such checks and such inquiries as would have ensured that any mis-attribution in the cut-off procedure was detected. He did not take any of these steps. I am bound to conclude that he failed in his duty. It is important in this connexion to remember that this is

C not a case of some isolated failure in detection. The fraud was repeated half-yearly on a large scale for many years. The words which I have quoted from the judgment of LINDLEY, L.J., (10) in *Re Kingston Cotton Mill Co.* (*No. 2*) are, I think, precisely in point:

D
> ". . . what in any particular case is a reasonable amount of care and skill depends on the circumstances of that case; that if there is nothing which ought to excite suspicion, less care may properly be considered reasonable than can be so considered if suspicion was or ought to have been aroused."

Here suspicion ought emphatically to have been aroused and the auditors ought to have taken the steps which I have indicated.

E (c) The position with regard to sales of stock after the end of each current period of account and the attribution of the price to the current period of account is different in an important respect, namely, that here no alteration of documents is involved. What happened, as I have said, is that Mr. Croston destroyed the copy invoices and gave a plausible though untrue explanation for their absence. Again I think that it is better not to make any finding on what would be the position under this head if it stood alone.

F It is conceded by counsel for Kevans that if breach of duty is found under any one of the three heads, the measure of compensation is the same as if breach of duty had been found under either two or all three heads. This concession is clearly right. The three heads are closely interrelated and once put on their guard under any one head the auditors ought to have taken such steps as would have ensured that a fraud under either of the other heads equally would not

G remain undetected. It is for this reason that I have thought it better not to make separate findings under heads (a) and (c). These are matters of some general importance and findings under either of them in isolation would be unnecessary and might be misleading.

As I have said, Mr. Philp, while accepting in full the evidence of Mr. Macnamara as to the duties of auditors, gave it as his opinion that in the circum-

H stances of this case Kevans were not guilty of breach of duty. The ground for this view was largely, if not wholly, as I understood him, that the directors did not give Kevans proper time in which to make their audit and that Kevans did the best they could in the time at their disposal. I do not think that this view could be supported on the facts. It is true that Kevans' audit was required by the directors to be completed on a date quite soon after the close of each period

I of account. On the other hand, they started their audit before the end of the period of account and neither Mr. Nightingale nor Mr. Swarsbrick made any complaint in evidence that they were not given sufficient time to make their audit.

However that may be, I do not think that Mr. Philp's view is good in law. The auditors of the company owe a statutory duty to make to the members a report containing certain statements. If the directors do not allow auditors time to conduct such investigations as are necessary in order to make these statements,

(10) [1896] 2 Ch. at p. 284.

the auditors must, it seems to me, either refuse to make a report at all or make an A appropriately qualified report. They cannot be justified in making a report containing a statement the truth of which they have not had an opportunity of ascertaining. Incidentally this point, as a matter of expert evidence, was not put to Mr. Macnamara.

Finally, I must consider the measure of compensation. This must consist in the loss to the company caused by Kevans' breach of duty. Loss is pleaded under B two heads, namely, (i) the net dividend distributed other than out of available profits, and (ii) income tax and profits tax assessed and paid by reference to non-existing profits, less tax recovered plus the costs of the successful appeal to the Special Commissioners. In my judgment Kevans' breach of duty was the direct cause of the loss under both these heads. Counsel for Kevans contended that in each case the action of the directors and, as regards dividend, presumably also C of the members, constituted the direct cause and broke the chain of causation; in other words, the damage, he contended, was too remote. I must consider this contention in regard to each head of loss.

(i) As events showed, the directors were willing to recommend and the members to confirm the payment of a dividend where they believed profits to be available. On the other hand, the directors could not lawfully pay, or the members approve, D a dividend unless profits were available. In the real circumstances there was no such profit. The payment of a dividend in these circumstances was the natural and probable result of the false picture which Kevans allowed the accounts to present. The volition of the directors and members was addressed to this false picture. They never addressed and could not lawfully have addressed any volition to the real picture. See in this connexion 11 HALSBURY'S LAWS OF E ENGLAND (3rd Edn.), p. 268 and the following pages, under the heading "Remoteness of Damage ", and in particular the passage at pp. 281-283. I was referred also to a sentence in the judgment of ASTBURY, J., in *Re Republic of Bolivia Exploration Syndicate, Ltd.* (11), where he said:

" I think that auditors of a limited company are bound to know or make themselves acquainted with their duties under the articles of the company F whose accounts they are appointed to audit, and under the Companies Acts for the time being in force; and that when it is shown that audited balance sheets do not show the true financial condition of the company and that damage has resulted, the onus is on the auditors to show that this is not the result of any breach of duty on their part."

(ii) Kevans' breach of duty was the direct cause of their preparing a profit and G loss account which showed a taxable profit and of the adoption by the company of that account. The charge of tax followed automatically. The directors had no choice in the matter. Fortunately, most of the tax has been recovered. It may be that the balance will be recovered; but the loss of any balance which is not recovered is the natural and probable result of Kevans' breach of duty. So is the H expenditure on the costs of proceedings for recovery.

Kevans are, of course, entitled to credit for the amount recovered from Mr. Croston.

As I have said, I am not invited to make any findings as to figures, and I propose accordingly to direct an inquiry as to the amount of the compensation. This inquiry will cover the allocation as between the individual members of the I firm of Kevans. I have not heard any argument on this last point.

Order accordingly.

Solicitors: *Gregory, Rowcliffe & Co.*, agents for *Addleshaw, Sons & Latham*, Manchester (for the liquidator); *Ince & Co.* (for the respondents).

[*Reported by* JENIFER SANDELL, *Barrister-at-Law.*]

---

(11) [1914] 1 Ch. 139 at p. 171.

A   # DES SALLES d'EPINOIX *v.* DES SALLES d'EPINOIX.

[COURT OF APPEAL, CIVIL DIVISION (Willmer and Sachs, L.JJ.), January 16, 17, 18, 1967.]

Injunction—Husband and wife—Matrimonial home—Husband's application in wife's maintenance proceedings—Husband excluded from matrimonial home
B   *—Leasehold premises in joint names—Relief sought by respondent husband not sufficiently related to wife's claim for maintenance—R.S.C., Ord. 29, r. 1 (1)—Supreme Court of Judicature (Consolidation) Act, 1925 (15 & 16 Geo. 5 c. 49), s. 45 (1).*

The parties were married in 1946 and established the matrimonial home in a maisonette held under a tenancy from year to year, initially from before
C   the marriage in the wife's name but in 1960 transferred into the joint names of the husband and wife. After a period of estrangement the husband on Nov. 4, 1966, left the wife, and, on his attempting to return on Dec. 15, he found the lock changed and when he rang the bell the wife refused to admit him. She thus admittedly excluded him from the matrimonial home. In the meantime on Dec. 1 the wife had issued an originating summons
D   seeking maintenance under s. 22 of the Matrimonial Causes Act 1965 on the ground of the husband's wilful refusal to maintain her. She intended to present a petition for divorce on the ground of cruelty. On Dec. 21, 1966, the husband issued a summons in the maintenance proceedings on which an order was made permitting him to return to the matrimonial home and granting an injunction restraining the wife from preventing him from doing
E   so. On appeal,

Held: the order made would be discharged for the following reasons—

(i) notwithstanding the generality of the wording of s. 45 (1)* of the Supreme Court of Judicature (Consolidation) Act, 1925, and of R.S.C., Ord. 29, r. 1 (1)†, it was contrary to established principle to grant the injunction as the claim to it did not arise out of, and was not incidental to, the
F   wife's cause of action for maintenance (see p. 544, letter A, and p. 546, letter G, and p. 547, letters B and F, post); moreover (per WILLMER, L.J.), the injunction sought was not necessary for protecting the husband's rights of property or his rights in relation to the wife's claim for maintenance (see p. 544, letters B and E, post).

Carter v. *Fey* ([1894] 2 Ch. 541) and *Winstone* v. *Winstone* ([1959] 3 All E.R. 580) applied.
G   (ii) in the circumstances the discretion of the court ought not to have been exercised in favour of granting the injunction (see p. 545, letter C, and p. 546, letter A, post).

Appeal allowed.

[As to the need for a defendant's application for an injunction to be connected
H   with the purpose of the plaintiff's action, see 21 HALSBURY'S LAWS (3rd Edn.) 412, para. 862 text and note (f) ; and for cases on the subject, see 28 DIGEST (Repl.) 865, *947*, 880, *1057*, *1058*.

As to extent of damage etc. which must be established to obtain an injunction, see 21 HALSBURY'S LAWS (3rd Edn.) 354, para. 742; and for cases on the subject, see 28 DIGEST (Repl.) 766-770, *204-223*. For the Supreme Court of Judicature
I   (Consolidation) Act, 1925, s. 45 (1), see 18 HALSBURY'S STATUTES (2nd Edn.) 482.]

Cases referred to:

Carter v. *Fey* [1894] 2 Ch. 541; 63 L.J.Ch. 723; 70 L.T. 786; 28 Digest (Repl.) 880, *1058*.

Jedfield v. *Jedfield*, (1960), The Times, Nov. 10.

Montgomery v. *Montgomery*, [1964] 2 All E.R. 22; [1965] P. 46; [1964] 2 W.L.R. 1036; 3rd Digest Supp.

---

* Section 45 (1), so far as material, is set out at p. 546, letter B, post.
† R.S.C., Ord. 29, r. 1 (1), so far as material, is set out at p. 542, letter A, post.

Distinguished in McGIBBON v McGIBBON [1973] 2 All E.R. 836

Morgan v. *Hart*, [1914] 2 K.B. 183; 83 L.J.K.B. 782; 110 L.T. 611; 21 **A**
      Digest (Repl.) 774, *2595*.
Scott v. *Scott*, [1950] 2 All E.R. 1154; [1951] P. 193; 27 Digest (Repl.) 84, *632*.
Silverstone v. *Silverstone*, [1953] 1 All E.R. 556; [1953] P. 174; [1953] 2 W.L.R.
      513; Digest (Cont. Vol. A) 689, *2094a*.
Winstone v. *Winstone*, [1959] 3 All E.R. 580; [1960] P. 28; [1959] 3 W.L.R.
      660; Digest (Cont. Vol. A) 811, *6542a*.   **B**

Appeal.
This was an appeal by the wife against an order of FAULKS, J., made on Jan. 11,
1967, ordering that the husband be at liberty to return to the matrimonial home
at 39, Lansdowne Road, London, W.11, on Monday, Jan. 16, 1967, on his undertaking not to molest the wife, and that the wife herself, her servants or agents be
restrained, and an injunction be granted restraining the wife, from preventing   **C**
him from so doing. The grounds of appeal were: (i) that the judge misdirected
himself in law in that he held that the husband was entitled to the injunction
claimed in proceedings under s. 22 of the Matrimonial Causes Act 1965; (ii) that
an injunction should not have been granted which was not necessary to protect
the person or property of the husband; and (iii) that on the facts proved or   **D**
admitted the order should not have been made.

B. Garland for the wife.
R. D. B. Davies for the husband.

WILLMER, L.J.: This appeal arises out of a dispute between a husband and
wife who were married as long ago as Oct. 26, 1946. At that time the wife was a   **E**
widow, who had a son then six years of age by a previous marriage. There is also
one child of the present marriage, a son born on July 19, 1947. The parties
established their matrimonial home at No. 39, Lansdowne Road in West London.
The premises there consist, as I understand it, of a maisonette which is held
under a tenancy from year to year. In fact the wife had acquired a tenancy in
her own name some time shortly before the marriage, and on the marriage the   **F**
husband went to live with her there. In or about 1960, for some reason or another,
the tenancy was transferred into the joint names of the two parties. The husband
says that he has always paid the rent and outgoings in respect of the matrimonial
home, and it is said that this amounts to about £850 a year. We are informed
that at the present moment the rent is in arrear to the extent of about £200, and
we have seen correspondence which shows that the landlord is threatening to take   **G**
proceedings for the purpose of terminating the tenancy. As I read the affidavits
of both parties, the marriage between this husband and wife was never particularly happy. For the last few years of their cohabitation it appears that they were
living virtually separate lives. They did, however, continue to reside together
until Nov. 4, 1966, when the husband left.

There is an issue between the parties whether, as the wife says, the husband   **H**
then left her for good, or whether, as the husband says, he left only for the
purpose of having a brief respite and with the intention of returning after a short
interval. He says that he did in fact attempt to return to the matrimonial home
on Dec. 15, 1966, but found that the wife had changed the lock on the door;
consequently he could not get in with his key, and when he rang the bell the wife
refused to admit him. The wife's case, as disclosed in her affidavit, is that the   **I**
husband throughout the marriage has treated her with cruelty, as a result of which
her health suffered. It has been intimated that a petition for divorce on the
ground of cruelty is in the course of preparation. In the meantime, however, on
Dec. 1, 1966, the wife commenced proceedings by originating summons seeking
maintenance on the ground of the husband's wilful neglect to maintain her.
Those proceedings are brought under what is now s. 22 of the Matrimonial Causes
Act 1965. On this appeal it is, of course, not only unnecessary but undesirable
to go into the merits of the wife's claim. It seems to me that much must depend

A on whether the wife is able to substantiate the charges which she makes against her husband; if she fails in that respect, it will obviously be difficult for her to avoid being held to be in desertion, having regard to the fact that she has refused to receive her husband back.

With regard to the figures, the husband has said that his income is in the neighbourhood of £3,300 per annum. He claims to have paid £10 per week to the

B wife since the separation, i.e., at the rate of £520 per annum. The wife has also had the advantage of living rent free in the matrimonial home. It will clearly be a matter for consideration, when the main dispute comes to be tried, whether these amounts, when they are grossed up, reveal that, so far as figures are concerned, there has been a wilful neglect to maintain the wife. I merely mention those figures in order to show the background against which this appeal falls to be

C considered.

The appeal arises in this way. On Dec. 21, 1966, the husband issued a summons seeking an order from the court permitting him to return to the matrimonial home and restraining the wife from preventing him from doing so. That summons came before Faulks, J., at the end of last term. It was then adjourned, and the matter was dealt with on the first day of the present sittings, viz., Jan. 11, 1967.

D On that occasion the judge made an order in favour of the husband substantially in the terms asked for, the husband giving an undertaking that he would not molest the wife or interfere in any way with her enjoyment of the matrimonial home. The wife now appeals to this court contending that that order was not properly made. It is argued, first, that there was no jurisdiction to make such an order in the circumstances of the present case; secondly, and in the alternative,

E that, if there was jurisdiction, the judge exercised his discretion wrongly in the light of all the facts of the case in making the order.

The argument for the wife can be summarised under three headings. First, it has been argued that an injunction can properly be granted only where it is ancillary to or comprised within the scope of the substantive relief sought in the main proceedings. In the present proceedings the only relief sought is that sought

F by the wife, viz., periodical payments based on her allegation of wilful neglect to maintain. There is not (and indeed in these proceedings I do not think that there could be) any cross-prayer by the husband; and in those circumstances it is said that there is nothing to which this application for an injunction could be ancillary. Secondly, it has been argued that an injunction can properly be granted only where it is necessary for the purpose of protecting either the person or the

G property of the party seeking it. Here it is alleged that there is no threat to the person of the husband, nor is it necessary to grant the injunction for the purpose of protecting any property rights of his. Thirdly, it has been argued that the right to seek an injunction in proceedings instituted under s. 22 of the Matrimonial Causes Act 1965, is inferentially, if not expressly, limited, having regard to s. 32 (1) of the Act of 1965. I do not think that it is necessary to read the terms

H of that section. It is sufficient to say that it is the section which makes provision authorising the court to make an order in favour of an applicant in maintenance proceedings restraining the respondent from making a disposition of his property with the intention of defeating the applicant's claim, or setting aside such a disposition if one has in fact already been made. It has been suggested (and I think probably rightly suggested) that that provision was included in the Act

I of 1965, having first appeared in the Matrimonial Causes Act 1963, in order to get over the decision of this court in *Scott* v. *Scott* (1), where it was held that there was no jurisdiction to make such an order unless and until an actual order for payment of money had already been made by the court.

On the other side it has been forcefully argued that the jurisdiction to grant an injunction which is conferred by s. 45 of the Supreme Court of Judicature (Consolidation) Act, 1925 is in the widest possible terms. That fact, it is said, is

(1) [1950] 2 All E.R. 1154; [1951] P. 193.

well recognised by the rule-making authority, for R.S.C., Ord. 29, r. 1 (1), A
provides:

"An application for the grant of an injunction may be made by any party
to a cause or matter before or after the trial of the cause or matter . . ."

Here it is said that the wife's proceedings under s. 22 of the Matrimonial Causes
Act 1965 at least constitute a " cause or matter ", and the husband is a party B
thereto. In such circumstances, it is contended, the jurisdiction to grant an
injunction cannot be denied. Secondly, it has been argued that the injunction
sought by the husband is sought in aid of his legal right to a half interest in the
matrimonial home. That circumstance, it is said, distinguishes the case from
that of *Montgomery* v. *Montgomery* (2), where it was in fact decided by ORMROD,
J., that an injunction could be granted only in support of a legal right.   C
  We have had the benefit of a very full argument on this appeal, a good deal
fuller, I suspect, than that which was presented to the judge below. Having heard
the submissions presented on both sides, I am satisfied that the argument for
the appellant wife must prevail. I do not think that it is necessary to go over all
the points which have been canvassed before us. In particular, I do not think
that it is either necessary or desirable to express any view on the question whether D
there is jurisdiction to grant an injunction in circumstances such as those of the
present case. What I do say is that I am abundantly satisfied that on the
authorities it would be contrary to well established principle to grant any such
injunction.
  In support of the argument for the wife reliance was placed (and I think rightly
placed) on the decision of WINN, J., in *Winstone* v. *Winstone* (3). That case E
actually arose out of an application by a wife for leave to present a petition for
dissolution of her marriage within three years of the date of the marriage. Such
a proceeding was, of course, a " cause or matter " which, until decided, was a
" cause or matter " pending before the court. Pending the decision of that
matter, the wife applied for an injunction restraining the husband from interfering
with her occupancy of the matrimonial home. That came before WINN, J., F
sitting as vacation judge, and it was (4):

"Held that the court's jurisdiction under s. 45 of the Supreme Court of
Judicature (Consolidation) Act, 1925, to grant injunctions was limited to
making orders within the scope of the substantive relief sought in pending
proceedings; and, as the only proceedings here pending were those seeking
leave to present a petition and the injunction sought was outside the scope G
of those proceedings, the court had no jurisdiction to entertain the
application."

In the course of delivering his judgment, WINN, J., referred to the section in the
Supreme Court of Judicature (Consolidation) Act, 1925 and made reference to
some observations of BUCKLEY, J., in *Morgan* v. *Hart* (5), which were directed
to the similar terms of the corresponding section in the Supreme Court of H
Judicature Act, 1873. The judge went on (6):

"In my view those words are to be construed and understood as limited
to the granting of an injunction ancillary to and comprised within the scope
of the substantive relief sought in the proceedings in which the application
for the injunction is made. I find myself unable to accede to the cogent and I
helpful submissions of [counsel for the wife] that once any proceedings have
been competently and effectively commenced, as these proceedings for leave
to file a petition within three years have been commenced, an injunction may
be granted for relief on a subject-matter falling outside the ambit, scope and
effect of the proceedings in which the injunction is sought."

---

(2) [1964] 2 All E.R. 22; [1965] P. 46.   (3) [1959] 3 All E.R. 580; [1960] P. 28.
(4) [1960] P. at p. 29.   (5) [1914] 2 K.B. 183 at p. 185.
      (6) [1959] 3 All E.R. at p. 581; [1960] P. at pp. 34, 35.

A   The judge consequently refused to grant the injunction.

That decision, if I may say so, seems to me to be substantially in line with the earlier decision of this court in *Carter* v. *Fey* (7). The headnote of that case reads (7):

B   " A defendant who has not filed a counter-claim cannot apply for an injunction against the plaintiff, unless the relief sought by the injunction is incident to or arises out of the relief sought by the plaintiff. If the defendant desires any other relief before the time arrives for delivery of a counter-claim, he must issue a writ in a cross-action."

That case arose out of a partnership between two persons which had been dissolved. They had been carrying on a business in partnership as wine, ale and C   spirit merchants in the city of Winchester. In the proceedings the plaintiff was claiming an injunction restraining the defendant from carrying on a business of the same kind within a radius of two miles. The defendant, without filing any defence or putting forward any counter-claim, sought an interlocutory injunction restraining the plaintiff from using his name on his vans, signboards, and so forth. The case came to this court, and LINDLEY, L.J., said (8):

D   " The defendant says that if he were not in a hurry he might put in a counter-claim, and by it claim such an injunction as he asked for in his motion. Assuming that he could do so, can he now ask for an injunction without a counter-claim and without issuing a writ of his own? He relies upon R.S.C., 1883, Ord. 50, r. 6, where it is provided that an application for an injunction may be made to the court or a judge by any party, and if it E   be made by the plaintiff it may be made either ex parte or by notice, and if it be made by any other party, then on notice to the plaintiff, and at any time after appearance by the party making the application."

I pause there to remark that that rule covered substantially the same ground as the present R.S.C., Ord. 29, r. 1. LINDLEY, L.J., went on (9):

F   " That rule at first sight appears to favour the defendant's contention; but if the defendant is right, it would be equally competent for a plaintiff to ask for an injunction for something outside the subject-matter of his action. If the defendant's application for an injunction were in any way connected with or incidental to the object and purpose of the plaintiff's action, he would have good ground for his contention; but it has really nothing to do with the relief sought by the plaintiff, and therefore, in my opinion, the defendant G   is wrong."

LOPES, L.J., said (10):

" The question is this—whether the defendant can move for an injunction against the plaintiff without filing a counter-claim or issuing a writ in a cross-action. In my opinion, he can in some cases, but only in cases where the H   defendant's claim to relief arises out of the plaintiff's cause of action, or is incidental to it."

The third member of the court, DAVEY, L.J., having referred to s. 25 (8) of the Supreme Court of Judicature Act, 1873 and to R.S.C., 1883, Ord. 50, r. 6, went on to say that it was contended (11):

I   ". . . that the words of the rule should be construed to apply to any injunction that the defendant deems himself entitled to. I do not agree with that construction. In my opinion, it must be relating to or arising out of the relief sought in the action which is before the court, and that any other injunction cannot properly be granted in the action. The defendant's cross-motion in the present case does not in my opinion fulfil that condition; it

---

(7) [1894] 2 Ch. 541.   (8) [1894] 2 Ch. at p. 544.
(9) [1894] 2 Ch. at pp. 544, 545.   (10) [1894] 2 Ch. at p. 545.
(11) [1894] 2 Ch. at p. 546.

does not arise out of the relief sought in the only action which is before the   A
court.''

It seems to me that, when one comes to apply that principle to the facts of the
present case, it simply cannot be contended that the husband's claim to relief
by way of injunction arises in any way out of the wife's cause of action, or is in
any respect incidental to it.

Furthermore, I do not think that an injunction can properly be granted except   B
where it is shown to be necessary for the purpose of protecting the applicant's
person or property. For this purpose I am prepared to accept that the husband
has a legal right in respect of his interest in the matrimonial home. The case of
Montgomery v. *Montgomery* (12), however, to which I have already referred, and
which decided that an injunction cannot be granted except in support of a legal
right, is not in my judgment authority for the reverse proposition, that, wherever   C
there is a legal right in respect of property, an injunction may be granted. There
have, of course, been many cases in which one spouse has been granted an injunction restraining the other spouse from entering or continuing to reside in the
matrimonial home. Such a case, for instance, was *Silverstone* v. *Silverstone* (13),
a decision of PEARCE, J. I refer to it only as an instance of a case where an
injunction restraining one spouse from having access to the matrimonial home   D
was granted because it was necessary for the protection of the other spouse. As
appears, however, from the decision of MARSHALL, J., in *Jedfield* v. *Jedfield* (14),
such an injunction ought to be granted only where it is really necessary for
protective purposes. In the present case there is no question of any necessity to
protect the person of the husband, and I can see no reason for granting an
injunction for the purpose of protecting such right of property as he has in the   E
matrimonial home.

The position, as I see it, is that the wife's conduct in excluding the husband
from the matrimonial home (as she admittedly did) is such as would constitute
her a deserting party, unless she is in a position to establish that she had good
cause for doing what she did. That means in practice that she will have to make
good the charges which she has brought against the husband; otherwise her   F
claim based on the allegation of wilful neglect to maintain will necessarily fail,
for no husband can be made liable to maintain a deserting wife. Even assuming
that the wife succeeds in establishing that she had just cause for excluding the
husband, the value of her occupancy of the matrimonial home will necessarily
have to be taken into account, first, in determining whether there has in fact been
a wilful neglect to provide reasonable maintenance, and, secondly, in determining,   G
if there has been wilful neglect to maintain, what is the appropriate quantum of
maintenance that ought to be ordered. I can see no ground for saying that an
injunction in favour of the husband, such as has been granted by the judge, is in
any way necessary for protecting the husband's rights of property, or his rights
in relation to the claim which is now being put forward by the wife.

We have been informed (although no note has been shown to us of what was   H
said by the judge) that he appeared to be very much influenced by the possibility
that, if the husband were to be allowed back into the matrimonial home, there
might be a chance of a reconciliation between the parties. I would be the first
to agree that that is a very laudable object; but the husband has not said in any
of his numerous affidavits that he in fact wants a reconciliation; all that he has
said is that he wants to get back into the house, so as to be able to reside in what   I
has been the matrimonial home. Furthermore, it does seem to me, in view of the
past history and of all that has happened, that a reconciliation is not in the
least likely to be promoted by the husband's return to the matrimonial home; in
fact the reverse would seem to be rather more probable.

(12) [1964] 2 All E.R. 22; [1965] P. 46.
(13) [1953] 1 All E.R. 556; [1953] P. 174.
(14) (1960), The Times, Nov. 10.

A   Lastly, I would make this observation. The whole of this dispute between these two spouses is a dispute about money. The wife wants maintenance. The husband wants to be relieved, so far as is possible, of his financial obligations. He makes no secret of the fact that his desire to get back and reside in the matrimonial home is due to the fact that he does not want to have the expense of maintaining two establishments. He says that he cannot afford to maintain two establish-

B   ments; but I am bound to say, in view of his income as it has been disclosed, and in the absence of any other responsibilities, I find that statement rather difficult to accept. In any case, however, his continued exclusion from the matrimonial home cannot, in my judgment, lead to any loss which cannot be adjusted in terms of money when all the financial arrangements between the parties come to be sorted out in the course of the present proceedings.

C   In those circumstances I have come to the conclusion that the judge erred in principle in treating this as a case in which relief by way of injunction can properly be granted. If I am wrong about that, then I would say that I am abundantly satisfied that, even if the judge had a discretion to exercise, his exercise of it in the circumstances of the present case was a wholly wrong one which cannot be supported. I would, therefore, allow the appeal and discharge the order made by

D   the judge.

SACHS, L.J.: I agree, but as we are differing from the judge of first instance it is appropriate not to confine myself merely to stating my full agreement with what has fallen from Willmer, L.J. In the first place I would like to emphasise that what the husband has here been seeking to assert is his proprietary right in

E   No. 39, Lansdowne Road. That is the right which is referred to in para. 6 of his affidavit of Dec. 19, 1966, and I have not the slightest doubt that it was solely on that ground that he based his claim to an injunction. Indeed, the whole of the persuasive submissions of counsel for the husband were founded on that particular right; wisely perhaps he neither did seek, nor apparently was prepared to seek, to submit any claim which might be construed as an attempt to enforce conjugal

F   rights.

Next, it seems right to advert to two points in the wife's affidavit which, of course, are not for the decision of this court at this time. The first is her allegation that the husband's purported desire to enforce his proprietary rights was, having regard to his conduct before the proceedings under s. 22 of the Matrimonial Causes Act 1965 were started, a mala fide exercise, the only true objective of which

G   was to defeat the wife's s. 22 claim by putting up a facade of "no desertion". Secondly, there is in the evidence before this court (as it was before the court below) a cogent medical report as to the potential adverse effect on the wife of the husband's return to No. 39, Lansdowne Road. In that behalf, too, attention may be drawn to that paragraph in the husband's affidavit of Jan. 10, 1967, in which he refers to the wife as having "always been of a nervous disposition".

H   I do not wish to express any opinion on these allegations made by the wife; but this much should be said, that neither the allegation of mala fides nor the allegation as to the potential effect on the wife of the return of the husband can be said to lack prima facie evidence. To my mind, when the court cannot examine those issues without cross-examination and further inquiry, it would be quite wrong, even if the court had the appropriate powers, to exercise its equitable

I   jurisdiction for the purpose of enforcing the return of the husband. Indeed, I would add that this is a case where one finds a husband with an annual income of £3,300 (less tax, of course) swearing his affidavits from Chesham Street and the Albany; and for my part that portion of his contentions that appears to rely on almost a plea ad misericordiam, in relation to his being unable to afford a suitable alternative residence while the s. 22 proceedings are being determined, does not appear to be unduly attractive. I have come unreservedly to the conclusion that, even if there were jurisdiction, and if in addition that it was in principle open to the husband to seek the remedy that he claims in the course of these proceedings

which originated under s. 22 of the Matrimonial Causes Act 1965, I would regard **A**
the granting of relief as a wrong exercise of judicial discretion.

It seems also clear to my mind, moreover, that in principle this court (and in
this context, of course, that includes the court of first instance) ought not even
to entertain a claim for this particular injunction. Counsel for the husband relied
on s. 45 (1) of the Supreme Court of Judicature (Consolidation) Act, 1925, which
provides :   **B**

"The High Court may grant . . . an injunction . . . by an interlocutory
order in all cases in which it appears to the court to be just or convenient
so to do."

That section is the lineal successor of s. 25 (8) of the Supreme Court of Judicature
Act, 1873, where, again omitting unessential words, one finds that the relevant   **C**
provision reads:

"An injunction may be granted by an interlocutory order of the court in
all cases where it shall appear to the court to be just or convenient that such
order should be made."

Starting from that point, and proceeding also to rely on the wording and considerable width of the provisions of R.S.C., Ord. 29, r. 1 (1), counsel for the   **D**
husband submitted that, once the husband and wife were before the court by
virtue of the s. 22 proceedings, it was open to the husband to apply to the court to
assert his proprietary right to No. 39, Lansdowne Road. Initially he put his
submissions as high as this, that once a set of matrimonial proceedings is in
existence a party thereto may obtain an injunction relating to any matter touching
the parties irrespective of whether it was one which concerned the subject-matter   **E**
of the original proceedings. At a later stage he appeared to lessen the width of
that submission by agreeing, for instance, that the husband could not in the s. 22
proceedings have sought to obtain against the wife an injunction in regard to an
unrelated libel. He continued, however, to press the argument that as regards
this proprietary right it was open to this court to grant the injunction.

To my mind the provisions of s. 45 of the Act of 1925 never have been, nor   **F**
ought they ever to be, interpreted in the somewhat uninhibited manner that
counsel for the husband favours. It is neither right for the court, nor open to the
court, to throw all normal procedural rules of practice out of the window into the
Strand because of the provisions of s. 45 and, so to speak, sit under some sort of
procedural "palm tree". Clearly any injunction sought by a defendant or
respondent to proceedings initiated by a plaintiff or applicant must bear some   **G**
appropriate relation to the subject-matter of the relief claimed in the proceedings
already initiated, proceedings which may either have been commenced, or in
certain cases may be in course of being commenced. That relationship may
naturally include, for instance, that of being molested simply by reason of
having started proceedings, but the relationship must be material and must exist.
In so far as authority need be cited to support that proposition, one finds it   **H**
consistently in such cases as have already been before the courts. Thus in *Carter*
v. *Fey* (15) the matter was discussed, and the lords justices sitting in the Court of
Appeal agreed that the relief must be associated with the subject-matter of the
defendant's claim. Having regard to what has fallen from WILLMER, L.J., I
need not refer to the individual passages in those judgments. I would however
add this, that in *Carter* v. *Fey* (15) the point arose when the plaintiff had com-   **I**
menced proceedings by due process, and the defendant had not filed a counterclaim, but was in a position so to do. Here, however, we are considering an
originating summons of the nature envisaged by the provisions of s. 22 of the
Matrimonial Causes Act 1965, and I find it extremely difficult to see how there
could in any event be what might normally be termed a counterclaim, or at any
rate a relevant counterclaim in such proceedings. One of the later authorities on

---

(15) [1894] 2 Ch. 541.

A the subject is that already mentioned of *Winstone* v. *Winstone* (16).   There Winn, J., referred to the need for any injunction claimed being on a subject-matter within the ambit, scope and effect of the proceedings already before the court.

On the material before us here the claim for an injunction cannot be said, to my mind, to fall within any of the tests propounded in the cases already cited, or

B to be in any way related to the subject-matter of the s. 22 proceedings.   I am aware, of course, of the possibility (strongly denied, though it may be, by the husband) that this claim for relief may be part of an attempt to destroy the wife's claim under s. 22.   As against that, if the wife has a claim under s. 22, she had a vested interest in it immediately before the s. 22 proceedings commenced, and the action of the husband could not destroy that vested interest.   (I would add that,

C if it was his intention by this claim for an injunction to destroy the claim under s. 22, that would have afforded abundant reason for the exercise of a discretion not to grant the relief claimed, even if it was open to the husband to come to the court for that relief.)   The possibility of the issue before the court being related to the claim under s. 22 simply because of the reason just indicated has obviously to be disregarded.   That leaves the claim to the proprietary right as being one

D that simply bears no material relation to the s. 22 proceedings.

In reaching this conclusion I have not in any way relied on the point put forward by counsel for the wife as to the suggested limiting effect of s. 32 of the Matrimonial Causes Act 1965.   On that point I am in entire agreement with what has fallen from Willmer, L.J., and wish to add nothing.   The result is that in principle this application by the husband cannot be entertained by the court in these

E proceedings.   Whether the correct phraseology is that of Lindley, L.J., in *Carter* v. *Fey* (17), where he referred to its not being competent for the defendant to make such a motion, or whether the correct phraseology is that of Lopes, L.J., in the same case, where he refers to the matter as an important question of practice, or whether one should look on the matter from the point of view of Winn, J., in the *Winstone* case (16), where he dealt with it as a matter of jurisdiction, it does

F not seem to be necessary to decide.   It is enough to say that on principle, I, like Willmer, L.J., consider the position to be clear that this court cannot entertain the husband's application.   For the reasons which I have given, I, too, would allow the appeal.

Appeal allowed.   Order appealed from discharged.

G   Solicitors: *Speechly, Mumford & Soames* (for the wife); *Hillearys* (for the husband).

[*Reported by* F. A. Amies, Esq., *Barrister-at-Law.*]

H

I

---

(16) [1959] 3 All E.R. 580; [1960] P. 28.
(17) [1894] 2 Ch. 541.

OSCROFT AND OTHERS *v.* BENABO AND ANOTHER.   A

[COURT OF APPEAL, CIVIL DIVISION (Willmer, Harman and Diplock, L.JJ.), November 28, 29, 1966.]

*Landlord and Tenant—New tenancy—Business premises—Terms of new tenancy
—Rent—Controlled sub-tenancy—All circumstances relevant to what rent
might be expected to be obtained in open market to be taken into consideration*   B
—Landlord and Tenant Act, 1954 (2 & 3 Eliz. 2 c. 56), s. 34.

*County Court—Appeal—Ground of appeal—Point of law not argued in court
below—Appeal limited to points raised in court below—Questions of fact
not appealable—County Courts Act, 1959 (7 & 8 Eliz. 2 c. 22), s. 108,
s. 109.*

Partners were tenants under a twenty-one years' lease, from Aug. 31,   C
1945, of a ground floor shop and workrooms and a first floor residential flat.
They carried on the business of radio and television engineers, and one of
the partners, T., had occupied the flat since 1948 paying a weekly rent of
£1 8s. to the partnership. By notice dated Apr. 21, 1966, the tenants
applied for a new lease. The landlords agreed that a new lease for fourteen
years should be granted, but the amount of the rent was not agreed. It   D
was agreed, however, that if the flat was decontrolled by the Rent Act, 1957,
the rent should be £712 per annum exclusive, of which £462 was to be the
rent for the shop and £250 for the flat; but if the flat remained controlled
under the Rent Restrictions Acts, then the rent should be £552 10s. per annum,
of which £90 would be the controlled rent for the flat. A qualified surveyor
gave evidence that if the flat had been separately assessed in 1956 it would   E
have had the same annual rateable value as a neighbouring flat, viz., £35.
The county court determined the rent, for the purposes of s. 34* of the
Landlord and Tenant Act, 1954, at £552 10s. per annum, finding that there
was a tenancy of the flat and that the rateable value of the flat for the year
1956 was £35 and that the rent of the flat was, therefore, a controlled rent. It
was not contended before the county court that the question whether the   F
rent was a controlled rent was irrelevant for the purposes of s. 34, but the
landlords appealed on that ground and on the grounds that it was not shown
that T. had a tenancy of the flat and that there was no evidence that the
rateable value of the flat in 1956 was £35.

Held: (i) the point of law as to the irrelevancy of a controlled rent of the
flat which was put forward by the landlords on appeal, not having been   G
taken in the county court, was not open to them on appeal, for the present
case did not raise a question going to the jurisdiction of the county court
or to illegality (see p. 552, letter A, p. 554, letter I, and p. 557, letter D,
post); moreover, even if the point were open, the county court in determining rent for the purposes of s. 34 of the Landlord and Tenant Act, 1954,
should have taken into consideration all circumstances, including the   H
existence of a statutory sub-tenancy, relevant to the question for what
rent the holding might reasonably be expected to be let in the open market
(see p. 553, letter A, p. 554, letter H, and p. 558, letter A, post).

Smith v. *Baker & Sons* ([1891-94] All E.R. Rep. 69) followed.

Whall v. *Bulman* ([1953] 2 All E.R. 306) considered and distinguished.

Rose v. *Hurst* ([1949] 2 All E.R. 24) distinguished.   I

(ii) there was evidence on which the county court could have found that
T. had a sub-tenancy and that the rateable value of the flat was £35; and
accordingly on these questions of fact the decision of the county court
should stand (see p. 553, letters E and I, and p. 555, letters C and F,
post).

Appeal dismissed.

---

* Section 34, so far as material, is set out at p. 552, letter C, post.

A   [As to the determination of rent on the grant of a new tenancy of business premises under the Landlord and Tenant Act, 1954, see 23 Halsbury's Laws (3rd Edn.) 898, 899, para. 1725; and for a case on the subject, see Digest (Cont. Vol. A) 1063, *7417ya.*

As to the ascertainment of the rateable value of premises under the Rent Act, 1957, see 23 Halsbury's Laws (3rd Edn.) 728, para. 1476; and for a case on B   the subject, see Digest (Cont. Vol. A) 1073, *7593d.*

As to appeal from a county court lying on a question of law only, see 9 Halsbury's Laws (3rd Edn.) 323, para. 784; and for cases on the subject, see 13 Digest (Repl.) 467-474, *917-977.*

For the Landlord and Tenant Act, 1954, s. 34, see 34 Halsbury's Statutes (2nd Edn.) 418.
C   For the Rent Act, 1957, s. 11, see 37 Halsbury's Statutes (2nd Edn.) 561.

For the County Courts Act, 1959, s. 108, s. 109, see 39 Halsbury's Statutes (2nd Edn.) 183, 186.]

Cases referred to:
   Abrahams v. *Dimmock*, [1915] 1 K.B. 662; 84 L.J.K.B. 802; 112 L.T. 386;
D   13 Digest (Repl.) 468, *922.*
   Glasgow Navigation Co. v. *Iron Ore Co.*, [1910] A.C. 293; 79 L.J.P.C. 83;
       102 L.T. 435; Digest (Practice) 522, *1881.*
   Postmaster-General v. *Blackpool and Fleetwood Tramroad Co.*, [1921] 1 K.B. 114;
       90 L.J.K.B. 136; 124 L.T. 365; 85 J.P. 71; 20 Digest (Repl.) 233, *142.*
   Rose v. *Hurst*, [1949] 2 All E.R. 24; [1949] 2 K.B. 372; [1949] L.J.R. 1491;
E   31 Digest (Repl.) 632, *7414.*
   Sharpe v. *Nicholls*, [1945] 2 All E.R. 55; [1945] K.B. 382; 114 L.J.K.B. 409;
       172 L.T. 363; 13 Digest (Repl.) 471, *952.*
   Smith v. *Baker & Sons*, [1891-94] All E.R. Rep. 69; [1891] A.C. 325; 60
       L.J.Q.B. 683; 65 L.T. 467; 55 J.P. 660; 13 Digest (Repl.) 467, *918.*
   Snell v. *Unity Finance, Ltd.*, [1963] 3 All E.R. 50; [1964] 2 Q.B. 203; [1963]
F   3 W.L.R. 559; Digest (Cont. Vol. A) 325, *929a.*
   Whall v. *Bulman*, [1953] 2 All E.R. 306; [1953] 2 Q.B. 198; [1953] 3 W.L.R.
       116; 13 Digest (Repl.) 450, *734.*

Appeal.
This was an appeal by the landlords, Cyril Benabo and Rebecca Lillian Orman,
G   from a judgment of deputy judge Perreth, dated July 2, 1966, delivered at Barnet county court in proceedings brought by the tenants William Thomas Oscroft, Sydney John Oscroft, and John James Thomas against the landlords under the Landlord and Tenant Act, 1954, asking for a new lease for fourteen years of the premises, No. 199, Woodhouse Road, Friern Barnet, where the tenants carried on a business in partnership as radio and television dealers and engineers.

H   *W. R. Rees-Davies* for the landlords.
   M. P. Solomon for the tenants.

   WILLMER, L.J., stated the nature of the appeal, and continued: The landlords, the present appellants, are the freeholders. The respondent tenants, who were the applicants before the county court, were tenants under a twenty-one I   years' lease dated Aug. 31, 1945, which had been granted by the appellants' predecessor in title, and which expired on June 24, 1966. By their notice dated Apr. 21, 1966, the tenants applied for a new lease, and proposed a term of fourteen years. The premises in question consist of a shop and workrooms on the ground floor and residential accommodation on the first floor. The residential accommodation on the first floor has been occupied since about the year 1948 by one of the three partners, Mr. Thomas. The evidence was that Mr. Thomas paid a rent of £1 8s. a week, which was deducted from his weekly drawings of £10. When the case came on before the deputy county court judge it appeared that

there was a measure of agreement between the parties. The deputy judge's   A
notes contain a record that the following terms were agreed:

" 1. There should be granted a new lease for fourteen years, rent review
at the end of seven years.   2. If flat [that means the residential accommodation upstairs] was decontrolled by the Rent Act, 1957, the rent should be
£712 per annum exclusive, being £462 in respect of the shop and £250 being
a reasonable rent under the Act of 1965 for the flat exclusive.   3. If the   B
flat escaped the Act of 1957 and remained controlled under the old Acts,
the rent should be £552 10s., of which £90 would be the controlled rent of the
flat."

The judge added a note of his own that: " the only issue for the court to decide
was whether or not the flat became decontrolled by the Act of 1957 ".   That was   C
the point which the judge proceeded to consider.

The first question to which he addressed his mind was whether there was a
tenancy of the flat held by Mr. Thomas, or whether it was a mere service occupancy. On that point he decided that the evidence disclosed a tenancy. The
second question which he had to consider was with regard to the rateable value
of the flat, for if that was under £40, it would not be caught by the Rent   D
Act, 1957, but the flat would still be controlled.   On this point the judge found
that the rateable value in the year 1956 (which was the operative year under
the Rent Act, 1957) was £35. He therefore concluded that it was a controlled
tenancy. Accordingly, he decided that the proper figure for the rent of the
whole premises should be £552 10s., and he gave judgment for that sum.

The main point which has been taken on this appeal has been that, owing to   E
an oversight on the part of counsel on both sides, and on the part of the judge
himself, the question which was debated before him was not a relevant question
for the purpose of deciding, under s. 34 of the Landlord and Tenant Act, 1954,
what the rent under the new lease ought to be. What has been submitted is that
under that section the sole question to be determined was at what rent the
holding might reasonably be expected to be let in the open market. It is said   F
that for that purpose the fact of the residential accommodation being sublet
under a protected tenancy would be wholly irrelevant. Consequently, it has been
contended that the case was decided on a wholly erroneous basis. It has further
been submitted that on the evidence it was not proved that Mr. Thomas did
have a tenancy of the flat; and it has also been argued that there was no
admissible evidence to support the deputy judge's conclusion that the rateable   G
value was only £35.

Those are the matters which have been ventilated on this appeal, and it
seems to me that four questions arise. 1. Is it open to the landlords, not having
taken the point below, but on the contrary having specifically invited the deputy
judge to decide the very question which he did decide, to contend that he proceeded on a wholly erroneous basis in basing his conclusion on his finding that   H
Mr. Thomas held the residential accommodation under a protected tenancy?
2. If that point is open, is it right to say that the deputy judge's finding of a
protected tenancy is totally irrelevant to the question which he had to decide
under s. 34 of the Landlord and Tenant Act, 1954?   3. Was there evidence to
support the finding that Mr. Thomas had a tenancy of the residential accommodation?   4. If so, was there evidence to support the finding that this was a   I
protected tenancy?   I will deal with those four points in that order.

As to the first point, ever since the case of *Smith* v. *Baker & Sons* (1) it has
been well settled that this court will not ordinarily entertain an appeal from a
county court unless the point raised on the appeal was raised and dealt with at
the trial. The principle on which this court acts is based on the fact that the
right of appeal from a county court is the creature of statute, and this court is

_____

(1) [1891-94] All E.R. Rep. 69; [1891] A.C. 325.

A limited by the terms of the enabling statute, which is now the County Courts Act, 1959, s. 107 to s. 114, which are the sections dealing with appeals. It is true that subsequent cases have shown that there are exceptions to this rule. One exception arises when it is made to appear to the Court of Appeal that the order made by the county court judge was made without jurisdiction. It is probably true to say that most of the cases which have arisen for decision under

B this head have arisen in relation to appeals under the Rent Acts where, of course, the jurisdiction of the county court judge to make an order is confined within strictly defined limits. Secondly, there is an exception in cases where the court is being invited to enforce an illegal contract, and of that an illustration is to be found in the case of *Snell* v. *Unity Finance, Ltd.* (2). In the present case it is conceded that the point now sought to be taken was not taken in the court below,

C and to my mind it certainly does not fall within either of these two exceptional classes of case to which I have referred; but it has been suggested that there is really a third class of exception to the rule in *Smith* v. *Baker & Sons* (3). What is said is that in the present case the effect of the course taken at the trial was to invite the court to decide the case on a completely unreal and hypothetical basis; and that is something which the court must always decline to do. In

D support of that submission we were referred to the case of *Whall* v. *Bulman* (4) as an illustration of just such a case. That was a forfeiture action in a county court, which proceeded in the county court on the basis that the defendant had, in breach of his agreement, used for living accommodation rooms which had been let to him as office accommodation. When the case came to the Court of Appeal it transpired, apparently for the first time, that the agreement contained no

E express covenant in relation to that matter, nor was there any proviso for re-entry in the event of a breach. That point had been overlooked in the county court, where the case had proceeded on the basis that the tenancy had come to an end, and the only question was as to the effect of the Rent Acts. In those somewhat unusual circumstances this court took the course of referring the case back for re-trial by the county court judge. Sir Raymond Evershed, M.R., made it

F clear in his judgment that he regarded the case as a wholly exceptional one. I think that it may be said, however, that it was left to Denning, L.J., to supply the true ratio decidendi of the court's decision. What Denning, L.J., said was this (5):

G " What, then, is to be done? This point was not taken below nor in the notice of appeal. Can this court itself take it? I think so, for the reason that the case comes before the court as if the parties had said to one another: ' Although there is no forfeiture clause, we agree that the court should treat the case as if there were one '. If the parties had knowingly made such an agreement, this court would not adjudicate on it. This court is here to try real cases, not hypothetical ones. The parties cannot agree on a false hypothesis and ask the court to adjudicate upon it."

H It is said that that is exactly the same as happened in the present case; but, with all respect, I do not think that that is so. It seems to me that *Whall* v. *Bulman* (4) was a different case from the present one. In that case the court was being invited to deal with the matter on a completely hypothetical basis of fact. Here, as it appears to me, all that can be said is that the argument below pro-

I ceeded on what is now alleged to be an erroneous view of the law. I do not think that it is a parallel case with *Whall* v. *Bulman* (4). In the present case what was tried by the judge was in no sense an unreal case. He applied his mind to the actual facts disclosed in the evidence. If he reached a wrong conclusion in law because his mind was not directed by counsel to what is now said

---

(2) [1963] 3 All E.R. 50; [1964] 2 Q.B. 203.
(3) [1891-94] All E.R. Rep. 69; [1891] A.C. 325.
(4) [1953] 2 All E.R. 306; [1953] 2 Q.B. 198.
(5) [1953] 2 All E.R. at p. 309; [1953] 2 Q.B. at p. 202.

to be the true view, that I think is not a matter which on principle can be raised **A**
for the first time in this court.   On the first point, therefore, I would hold that
it is not open to the landlords to raise their main submission for the first time
in this court.

In case I am wrong about that, however, I proceed to examine the second question which I posed.   Let me assume for the moment that the point is open in
this court.   Then is it right to say that the deputy judge's finding of a protected **B**
tenancy was irrelevant to the question which he had to decide?   That depends
on s. 34 of the Landlord and Tenant Act, 1954, the relevant part of which is in
these terms:

> " The rent payable under a tenancy granted by order of the court under
> this Part of this Act shall be such as may be agreed between the landlord
> and the tenant or as, in default of such agreement, may be determined **C**
> by the court to be that at which, having regard to the terms of the tenancy
> (other than those relating to rent), the holding might reasonably be expected
> to be let in the open market by a willing lessor, there being disregarded—
> (*a*) any effect on rent of the fact that the tenant has or his predecessors in
> title have been in occupation of the holding ..."

Then there are further paragraphs dealing with other matters to be disregarded **D**
which are not relevant in the present case.   In support of the argument put
forward by counsel for the landlords that the fact (if it be a fact) of Mr. Thomas
having a protected tenancy is irrelevant, reliance has been placed on the case of
Rose v. *Hurst* (6); but, with all respect to the argument, I do not find any great
assistance from that decision.   That was a case of a man who had a twenty-one **E**
years' lease of premises where he both carried on a shop and lived in residential
accommodation over the shop.   On the expiry of his twenty-one years' term the
tenant had the choice of either staying on as a statutory tenant under the Rent
Restriction Acts, or taking proceedings for a new lease under the Landlord and
Tenant Act, 1927.   He chose to adopt the latter alternative.   The county court
judge granted him a new lease of fourteen years at a rent considerably in excess **F**
of that which had been payable under the old lease.   The tenant appealed and
contended that the rent under his new lease ought to be at the same rate as that
under the old lease, which would have been the standard rent if he had
stayed on as a statutory tenant.   It was held by this court that, in determining
what a willing lessee would agree to give and a willing lessor would agree to
accept, no regard should be paid to the Rent Restriction Acts.   The leading judg- **G**
ment was given by DENNING, L.J., and I think that the effect of the decision is
really summed up in the last paragraph of his judgment, where he said this (7):

> " In these cases the tenant must elect between two inconsistent rights.   He
> must elect either to remain on as a statutory tenant at the standard rent,
> or to take a new lease at a rent fixed as between a willing lessor and a willing
> lessee.   He cannot have the benefit both of the new lease and of the standard **H**
> rent.   In this case he has elected to take a new lease, and so he must pay ..."

what was then the full rent.   I do not see how this really helps in the present case.
It would, of course, have been very material if Mr. Thomas personally was the
party asking for a new lease.   It may well be that in such circumstances he would
have been put to his election whether to remain on as a statutory tenant at the
standard rent, or to take a new lease at a rent to be fixed in accordance with the **I**
market value; but that is not this case.   Assuming (if I may anticipate the third
point) that Mr. Thomas is the tenant of the upper floor, he is the tenant of the
partners, and not of the landlords.   It seems to me that if he is a tenant, and if his
tenancy is a protected one, that must be a relevant circumstance to consider
when deciding what a willing lessor would be prepared to accept on the open

(6) [1949] 2 All E.R. 24; [1949] 2 K.B. 372.
(7) [1949] 2 All E.R. at p. 26; [1949] 2 K.B. at p. 377.

A market for the premises as a whole, which is what the judge has to decide in pursuance of s. 34 of the Act of 1954. In fixing what a willing lessor would be prepared to take, it seems to me that all the circumstances of the particular case, including the fact of any existing sub-tenancy, must necessarily be taken into consideration. In these circumstances I am not persuaded that the point sought to be taken in this court, even if it is open to the appellants, is a good point.

B I come then to the third question which I posed. The judge found in favour of Mr. Thomas that there was a tenancy of the residential accommodation. On the notice of appeal, as originally filed, no point was taken that what Mr. Thomas had was not a tenancy. In the course of the hearing yesterday, however, when it was sought to raise this point, we directed that the new ground should be put C into writing, and this morning we have been presented with further grounds of appeal which, after discussion, we granted leave to add. The point now taken is put in two ways, which I think really amount to the same thing, namely, that there was no evidence on which the judge could properly come to the conclusion that the residential accommodation was let by the tenants to Mr. Thomas as tenant. As to that I propose to deal with the matter very shortly by saying that D to my mind the deputy judge's notes reveal quite clearly that there was evidence on which he could come to the conclusion that what Mr. Thomas had was a tenancy. There was, of course, a possible alternative contention, which was at one stage canvassed in the course of the argument, viz., that the three tenants being partners were in law incapable of creating a protected tenancy in favour of one of their own number. That point was not taken in the court below, however, E and has not been raised by the notice of appeal even in its amended form before us. In those circumstances, as far as the third question is concerned, I come to the conclusion that there was evidence in support of the deputy judge's finding with which it is impossible for this court to interfere. It must be remembered that in this class of case there is no right of appeal on fact; the only appeal that we can entertain is an appeal on a question of law. It follows that we have F jurisdiction to interfere with a finding of fact only if we are satisfied that there was no evidence on which that finding could properly be arrived at.

I come then to the last question, as to which it has been submitted that there was no admissible evidence to show that the rateable value of the residential accommodation was within the limit prescribed by the Rent Act, 1957, so as to constitute it controlled premises. The difficulty on this aspect of the case has G been caused by the fact that the shop and the flat at No. 199, Woodhouse Road, never were separately assessed. There never was any valuation of the flat as a separate hereditament. In those circumstances the judge had to do the best that he could. He heard evidence from Mr. Taylor, who is a qualified surveyor and estate agent. Mr. Taylor had himself inspected the premises. He had also inspected the 1956 valuation list in relation to the next-door premises, No. 201, which he H said were virtually identical with No. 199. In the case of No. 201 there had been separate assessments of the ground floor shop on the one hand and the upstairs residential accommodation on the other. Mr. Taylor expressed the view that the flat at No. 199, if it had been separately assessed, would have had the same rateable value as that of No. 201, namely, £35. It has been argued that Mr. Taylor's evidence on this point was inadmissible evidence, and that the only admissible I evidence would have been that of the valuation officer. I have never succeeded in understanding how the valuation officer's opinion would have been of any greater value than Mr. Taylor's. It could only have been an opinion, since he had never had occasion to fix any rateable value for the flat at No. 199 as a separate hereditament. In my judgment there clearly was evidence on which the judge could come to his conclusion with regard to the rateable value of the flat. That, I think, concludes the questions which have arisen in this case. The result is that in my view it is not possible for us to interfere with the judge's conclusion in these proceedings, and I would accordingly dismiss the appeal.

HARMAN, L.J.: This case has taken an unfortunate course. The respon-   A
dent tenants, who are partners, took a tenancy of the property by lease in 1945
from the then landlords. At that time there was a rent controlled tenant in the top
storey, being a separate hereditament, I suppose. He later went out of possession,
so that the tenants got possession of the whole of the building, and they then
arranged that one of them should occupy the part which the statutory tenant had
vacated. The lease came to an end in June, 1966, and in due course, before the   B
arrival of that date, the tenants applied to the county court for a new lease. The
landlords were quite willing to grant a new lease, but the new rent was not agreed,
and the matter came before the deputy county court judge for him to determine
that point.

When the case was opened, counsel for the landlords announced that a measure
of agreement had been reached, and as noted by the deputy county court judge   C
the following agreed terms were propounded: that there should be a new lease
for fourteen years; that if the flat had been decontrolled by the Rent Act, 1957,
there should be a certain rental, but that if it was not decontrolled, then another
and a lower rent would be payable. It was thus agreed between the parties that
the Rent Act, 1957, was the criterion, and the only matters which the judge had
to decide were, first, had there been a tenancy in the proper sense of the word at   D
all, and secondly, was the proper rateable value attributable to the upper premises
under £40, because it was agreed that, if it was, the tenancy (if it existed) was a
controlled tenancy. The judge found the answers to both those questions in the
affirmative, and he gave judgment for the lower sum.

The matter now comes before this court, and it is said that everybody was under
a misapprehension; that the Rent Act, 1957, had nothing to do with the matter   E
at all; that under the Landlord and Tenant Act, 1954, what had to be found was
the open market value; that therefore the Rent Act, 1957, was an irrelevant
consideration, and that all that the judge had to do was to find the unencumbered
value of the holding, and without a restricted tenancy, though there was one.
It was said that *Rose* v. *Hurst* (8), made it manifestly obligatory on the judge
himself to take this point: that LORD GREENE, M.R., had pronounced in that   F
case that the Rent Acts and the Landlord and Tenant Acts were mutually
exclusive, and that therefore the controlled rent could have nothing to do with it,
and that the whole thing was dealt with under a misapprehension.

In my opinion the decision in *Rose* v. *Hurst* (8) had nothing to do with the
present case at all. That was a case in which the statutory tenant applied for a
new tenancy under the Landlord and Tenant Act, 1927, and, having applied,   G
he said that he was entitled to take advantage of the fact that he was a rent
controlled tenant, and that therefore there could be only one answer as to the
rent which he had to pay under his new lease. The court decided, not unnaturally,
that he could not have it both ways; either he was a statutory tenant, or he was
not, and if he was, he remained a statutory tenant—the two things were mutually
exclusive. That has nothing to do with the present case. The point is whether,   H
when finding the market value, the county court judge is to take into account all
the factors. If, for instance, there is a statutory tenant in possession of part of
the premises, is that a matter which he can take into account in arriving at the
open market value? It seems to me that he clearly is entitled to look at the open
market value of these premises in the condition in which they are, and with such
disadvantages as they possess as between a willing lessor and a willing lessee.   I
There is no rule, so far as I can see, to exclude the judge taking into account the
fact that there was a statutory tenancy.

However that may be, it does appear to me to be a point of law which was not
taken below and cannot be taken in this court. It is true that the case bears some
superficial resemblance to the case before SIR RAYMOND EVERSHED, M.R.,
DENNING and ROMER, L.JJ., of *Whall* v. *Bulman* (9) which has been cited to us.

(8) [1949] 2 All E.R. 24; [1949] 2 K.B. 372.
(9) [1953] 2 All E.R. 306; [1953] 2 Q.B. 198.

A As WILLMER, L.J., has explained, however, the true ratio decidendi of that case was that the court was asked to decide the question on a basis which did not exist at all, namely, that though there was no proviso for re-entry, the matter could be treated as though there were one. The court said that that was a mere abstract question on which there could not be adjudication, and therefore that the case must go back to the county court judge to remind him of the fact that,

B if there were no proviso for re-entry, an order for possession for breach of covenant could not be made. That is not this case at all, but even, if it had been an admissible consideration, I do not think that it would have carried the day because the point was not taken in the court below.

As to the question whether there was a tenancy or not, I myself would certainly have held, I think, on the evidence as we have it on the note, that there was no

C such thing; but that is a question of fact, and I do not think that it is possible to say that there was no evidence on which the judge could come to a contrary conclusion. To that contrary conclusion he came, and in my opinion it is not open to us, however much the notice of appeal is amended, to accede to an appeal on that ground, which is purely one of fact. As to the point about the rateable value, I add nothing to what WILLMER, L.J., has said. I should have come to the same

D conclusion on the rateable value point as did the deputy judge. He was not only entitled, but perfectly right, to come to that conclusion. It seems to me, therefore, that in arriving at the figure of £552, the judge was entitled so to find, more especially having regard to the agreement between the parties with which he was confronted. I would dismiss the appeal.

E **DIPLOCK, L.J.:** Counsel for the landlords has sought to sustain this appeal on a number of grounds of fact and of law, some of which were not mentioned in the notice of appeal in the form in which it was at the opening of this appeal. Of those which were mentioned this court has jurisdiction to entertain two only. The first is a question of law taken at the hearing, namely, that there was no evidence on which the deputy county court judge could find that the rateable

F value of the flat was £35 in 1956. I agree with my lords that there was evidence on which he could so find. His finding is one of fact from which there can be no appeal. The second, also taken at the hearing, is that the deputy judge admitted inadmissible evidence of the value of the flat next door. This ground has not been pursued before us.

The right of appeal from the determination of the county court under s. 34 of

G the Landlord and Tenant Act, 1954 (10), of the rent payable under a new lease of business premises is conferred and confined by s. 107 and s. 108 of the County Courts Act, 1959. Section 107 makes it clear that there is no right of appeal on any question of fact, for the proceedings do not fall within s. 109. Section 108 confers a right of appeal on some questions of law, and thus a corresponding jurisdiction on this court to entertain appeals on these questions. As long ago as

H 1891, however, the House of Lords in *Smith* v. *Baker & Sons* (11), decided that, on the true construction of the corresponding section of the County Courts Act, 1888, the right of appeal was confined to determinations by the county court judge on points of law which had been expressly raised by the parties at the hearing before him, which had at least been brought to his attention and been the subject of a ruling by him; see *Abrahams* v. *Dimmock* (12), and contrast

I *Postmaster General* v. *Blackpool and Fleetwood Tramroad Co.* (13).

The decision of the House of Lords in *Smith* v. *Baker & Sons* (11) goes to the jurisdiction of an appellate court to hear appeals from county courts on questions of law. It does not go merely to the practice of this court from which departure is permissible in exceptional cases. Even if we thought that no injustice would be done to the parties in a particular case to allow an appeal on a point of law

---

(10) Section 34, so far as material, is set out at p. 552, letter C, ante.
(11) [1891-94] All E.R. Rep. 69; [1891] A.C. 325.
(12) [1915] 1 K.B. 662.   (13) [1921] 1 K.B. 114 at p. 120.

neither raised nor ruled on in the county court, we should have no jurisdiction to **A** do so, for our only jurisdiction in the matter is conferred on us by s. 108 of the County Courts Act, 1959.

The policy of Parliament manifested by s. 107 of the County Courts Act, 1959, is to impose restrictions on any general right of appeal from county courts, and the House of Lords has construed the right of appeal which was conferred by the section in the County Courts Act, 1888 (corresponding to s. 108 in the Act of 1959) **B** as excluding any right of appeal from a determination in point of law which the county court judge has neither made, nor been asked to make. Parliament must be presumed to have known this in 1934 when it used the same words in the corresponding section of the County Courts Act, 1934, in 1954 when it conferred on the county court a new jurisdiction under s. 34 of the Landlord and Tenant Act, 1954 to determine the rent payable under a new lease granted pursuant to **C** that Act of 1954, and in 1959 when, in the County Courts Act, 1959, it re-enacted the right of appeal in similar words. To this general rule limiting the questions of law on which appeal may be brought from decisions of a county court, there are two apparent exceptions, namely, questions as to the jurisdiction of the county court to hear and determine the proceedings, or to make the order appealed against, and questions as to the legality of the subject-matter of the cause of **D** action. The reasons for these exceptions are explained in *Snell* v. *Unity Finance, Ltd.* (14). Counsel for the landlords has argued that *Whall* v. *Bulman* (15) shows that in a category of cases (apparently susceptible of no more precise definition than " exceptional "), this court can, as a matter of public policy, entertain a question of law not raised in the county court which goes neither to jurisdiction nor to legality. The judgment of SIR RAYMOND EVERSHED, M.R., in that case does **E** not perhaps state his ratio decidendi with his customary clarity and concision, but the case is explained (16) by DENNING, L.J., as being one in which the parties had invited the county court judge to decide the matter on a false hypothesis of fact, and the county court judge had done so. If this were the true view of the matter, the attack on his judgment went to his jurisdiction, for unless the power is expressly conferred by statute, English courts have no jurisdiction to determine **F** hypothetical questions and give judgment on them, even at the invitation of the parties; see *Glasgow Navigation Co.* v. *Iron Ore Co.* (17). On any other view of its ratio decidendi, the judgment of SIR RAYMOND EVERSHED, M.R., would in my view conflict with the decision of the House of Lords in *Smith* v. *Baker & Sons* (18). The chief attack on the judgment in point of law which counsel for the landlords sought to advance was that, in assessing the rent to be paid under the **G** new lease, the deputy county court judge ought not to have taken into account the fact, which he had found, that the flat on the upper floor of the premises was let to Mr. Thomas on a tenancy protected by the Rent Restriction Acts. So far from this point of law having been raised before the deputy judge, counsel for the landlords had himself intervened in the opening of the tenants' case to say that he agreed that, if the deputy judge did find that there was a protected **H** tenancy, the rent should be reduced to the lower figure which the deputy judge in fact determined, and the hearing proceeded on that basis. He has argued that he can nevertheless take the point in this court because it goes to jurisdiction. Section 34 of the Landlord and Tenant Act, 1954, on its true construction by its reference to the " open market ", he says, enjoins the deputy county court judge, in fixing the rent of the premises as a whole, to ignore the existence **I** of a protected tenancy of any part of them; and he seeks to rely on the decision of this court in *Rose* v. *Hurst* (19) in support of this proposition. Even assuming,

---

(14) [1963] 3 All E.R. 50; [1964] 2 Q.B. 203.
(15) [1953] 2 All E.R. 306; [1953] 2 Q.B. 198.
(16) [1953] 2 All E.R. at p. 309; [1953] 2 Q.B. at p. 202.
(17) [1910] A.C. 293.
(18) [1891-94] All E.R. Rep. 69; [1891] A.C. 325.
(19) [1949] 2 All E.R. 24; [1949] 2 K.B. 372.

A   however, that *Rose* v. *Hurst* (20) did so decide, the judge's error of law in failing
to apply it in the present case would not destroy his " jurisdiction " to hear
and determine the application, and to make the order which he did. Courts (even
inferior courts) have " jurisdiction " to be wrong in law; that is why we hear
appeals on questions of law and not merely applications for certiorari. A court
may lack " jurisdiction " to hear and determine a particular action or application

B   because (i) of the composition of the court (for example, the bias of the judge),
or (ii) the subject-matter of the proceedings (for example, title to foreign land),
or (iii) the parties to the proceedings (for example, diplomatic immunity); or,
although having jurisdiction to hear and determine the proceedings, it may lack
jurisdiction to make the kind of order made; *Sharpe* v. *Nicholls* (21) is an example
of this. A mere error of law, however, made by a county court judge on an

C   application of a kind which he is entitled to entertain between parties between
whom he is entitled to adjudicate, resulting in an order of a kind which he is
entitled to make, does not affect his " jurisdiction " to make the order. It is an
erroneous determination in point of law from which there may be an appeal if
the statute conferring the right of appeal so allows. As the point of law now
alleged to constitute the error in his judgment was not taken below, the statute,

D   the County Courts Act, 1959, does not so allow. Nevertheless, because at the
hearing counsel for the landlords did not simply fail to raise the point at all, but
actually expressed his agreement with the submission of law made by counsel
for the tenants that the deputy county court judge was bound to take into
account, in determining the rent under the new lease, the existence of a protected
tenancy of part of the premises, he contends that he is in a stronger position than

E   if he had not actively (though, of course, inadvertently) misled the court as to the
law applicable. He contends that in the circumstances the deputy judge was
invited by the parties to decide the case on a false hypothesis, as in *Whall* v.
Bulman (22), and that he had no jurisdiction to comply with that invitation. In
Whall v. *Bulman* (22), however, the false hypothesis was one of fact. Here the
so-called hypothesis was one of law. That makes all the difference. Any judgment

F   which is founded on an error of law is given on a false hypothesis of law. To call
an " error " a " hypothesis " does not change its nature or convert it into
usurpation of jurisdiction.

    Counsel for the landlords also sought leave to argue a further point (not raised
on his notice of appeal before the hearing) that Mr. Thomas never had a tenancy
of the upper flat; at most he had a licence to occupy. This point was raised at the

G   hearing, but as depending on a question of fact only, namely, what was orally
agreed between Mr. Thomas and his partners as to his occupancy of the flat. On
this question of fact, there is no right of appeal. The landlords were given leave
to amend their notice of appeal to contend that there was *no* evidence on which
the county court judge could so find; I agree with my lords that there was some
evidence. A question of law might have been raised whether the occupation by

H   one partner of part of the partnership premises is capable in law of giving rise to
a tenancy. No such question of law was raised at the hearing, however, and so
could not be raised here even if it had been mentioned in the notice of appeal in
any of its editions or proposed editions. In the result the only points open to the
landlords on this appeal fail. The other points of fact and of law which were sought
to be argued we have no jurisdiction to entertain. The appeal must accordingly

I   be dismissed. Lest the landlords should feel chagrined, however, that they had
lost a meritorious appeal on what may appear to them to be a mere technicality,
namely, that the point of law in their favour was not taken by their counsel at
the hearing, I may add (although for my part I regard this as strictly obiter) that
Rose v. *Hurst* (20) is in my view no authority for the proposition which counsel

---

(20) [1949] 2 All E.R. 24; [1949] 2 K.B. 372.
(21) [1945] 2 All E.R. 55; [1945] K.B. 382.
(22) [1953] 2 All E.R. 306; [1953] 2 Q.B. 198.

A

for the landlords has sought to advance. I do not think that the judge was misled as to the law. The point was a bad one, anyway.

Appeal dismissed.

Solicitors: *D. G. Segalov & Co.* (for the landlords); *Leggatt & Leggatt* (for the tenants).

[*Reported by* F. A. AMIES, ESQ., *Barrister-at-Law.*]

B

DICKSON v. THE PHARMACEUTICAL SOCIETY OF GREAT BRITAIN AND ANOTHER.

C

[COURT OF APPEAL, CIVIL DIVISION (Lord Denning, M.R., Danckwerts and Sachs, L.JJ.), December 12, 13, 14, 15, 16, 19, 1966, January 26, 1967.]

Trade—Restraint of trade—Corporation—Professional society—Resolution restraining trading activities of members—Need to establish reasonableness—Reasonableness in interests of members and of public—Reasonableness in interests of members and reasonableness in interests of public not established.

D

The objects of the Pharmaceutical Society of Great Britain, which was incorporated by royal charter in 1843, since replaced by a royal charter of 1953, included an object, which was the object relevant to the present case, " to maintain the honour and safeguard and promote the interests of the members in their exercise of the profession of pharmacy ". All registered pharmacists were required by law to be members. In general pharmacists had to trade in order to live; accordingly they had professional activities and also trading activities, the society being primarily concerned with the former activities. Limited companies could not be members nor be registered pharmacists, but they could employ registered pharmacists and could be authorised sellers of poisons under the supervision of registered pharmacists. There were 29,004 members of the society. The council of the society issued a code of conduct for the guidance of pharmacists and corporate bodies carrying on business under the Pharmacy Acts, which most pharmacists regarded as binding on them. It appointed inspectors to go round chemists' shops, who looked to see if the code of ethics was being observed and reported breaches to the council. If unable to get a breach remedied the council passed the information on to the statutory committee, a disciplinary body with powers of striking a pharmacist off the register or removing a company chemist from the register, subject to appeal to the High Court. The statutory committee gave great weight to the views of the profession on questions of misconduct and had regard to the code of ethics.

E

F

G

H

Following disquiet in the profession over possible lowering of standards of the profession through the extension of the trading of chemists beyond the pharmaceutical goods (medicines, drugs, thermometers, bandages, etc.) and traditional goods (toothpaste, lipstick, toilet articles, films, cameras, photographic equipment, etc.) to non-traditional goods (handbags, thermos flasks, greetings cards, etc.), the society, at a meeting attended by over six thousand members, passed the following resolution by 5,026 votes to 1,346: " New pharmacies should be situated only in premises which are physically distinct, and should be devoted solely to: (i) professional services, as defined [the dispensing of medicines and the sale of pharmaceutical goods]; (ii) . . . non-professional services as defined [the sale of traditional goods]; (iii) such other services as may be approved by the council [the sale of non-traditional goods]; and the range of services in existing pharmacies, or in pharmacy departments of larger establishments, should not be extended beyond the

I

A present limits, except as approved by the council." This was intended to form part of the code of ethics. Although the resolution was approved by a large majority at the meeting, some twenty-two thousand members did not vote on it. A director of Boots, Ltd., a company with 1,265 chemists' shops, including 369 selling non-traditional goods which were subject to variation, who was himself a registered pharmacist, brought an action for a declaration that the

B proposed rule was invalid and an injunction to restrain the society from acting on it.

Held: the declaration sought must be made and the injunction granted for the following reasons:

(i) if a professional body laid down a rule of conduct for its members, which was regarded as binding on them, there was jurisdiction to inquire into the

C validity of the rule and to grant a declaration as to its validity and, if it were invalid, an injunction so that members should know, as they were entitled to know, where they stood and what goods they could sell; accordingly, notwithstanding that the new rule was a rule of a " code of ethics " of a professional body, the issue was justiciable (see p. 565, letter I, p. 566, letter D, p. 568, letter H, and p. 572, letter I, to p. 573, letter A, post).

D (ii) although the society was entitled to impose restraint on trading activities of pharmacists when such restraint was reasonable in the interests of the profession and in the interests of the public, yet a rule of conduct imposing an unreasonable restraint of trade would be ultra vires and invalid, notwithstanding that the society was a body of professional men, as (per SACHS, L.J.), the majority of pharmacists engaged in retail trade (see p. 566,

E letter H, p. 567, letter F, p. 568, letter H, and p. 573, letters D and H, post).

(iii) the restraint of trade imposed by the new rule had not been agreed by all members and was thus an involuntary restraint in relation to them and would be invalid unless justified; it had not been shown that the selling of non-traditional goods distracted pharmacists from their pharmaceutical work or affected adversely the status of the profession or the number and

F quality of new entrants to the profession, and accordingly the restraint was not reasonable in the interests of the profession (see p. 567, letter B, p. 568, letter F, p. 569, letter G, and p. 573, letter I, post); further (per DANCKWERTS and SACHS, L.JJ.), the restraint was not reasonable in the public interest (see p. 569, letter A, and p. 574, letter F, post).

Gunmakers, etc. v. *Fell* ((1742), Willes 384) and *Swaine* v. *Wilson* ((1889),

G 24 Q.B.D. 252) applied.

Per LORD DENNING, M.R.: the circumstances alleged to justify the restraint should have been pleaded by the society in their defence (see p. 567, letter H, post; cf. p. 573, letter G, post).

Decision of PENNYCUICK, J., ([1966] 3 All E.R. 404) affirmed.

[Editorial Note. Disputes that are purely disputes in relation to professional

H ethics are not justiciable (*Cox* v. *Green,* [1966] 1 All E.R. 268); thus it is essential to observe the emphasis laid in the judgments in the present case on the trading activities that pharmacists had necessarily to pursue.

As to the classification of the restraints to which the doctrine against restraint of trade applies, see 38 HALSBURY'S LAWS (3rd Edn.) 16, para. 10.

As to restraint of trade being void unless reasonable in relation to parties and

I the public and the onus of proof of reasonableness, see 38 HALSBURY'S LAWS (3rd Edn.) 21, para. 15; and for cases on the subject, see 45 DIGEST (Repl.) 443-449, *271-297.***]**

Cases referred to:

Boulting v. *Association of Cinematograph, Television and Allied Technicians,* [1963] 1 All E.R. 716; [1963] 2 Q.B. 606; [1963] 2 W.L.R. 529; 45 Digest (Repl.) 543, *1229.*

City of London Case, (1610), 8 Co. Rep. 121b; 77 E.R. 658; 45 Digest (Repl.) 383, *17.*

Cox v. *Green*, [1966] 1 All E.R. 268; [1966] Ch. 216; [1966] 2 W.L.R. 369.   **A**

Eastham v. *Newcastle United Football Club, Ltd.*, [1963] 3 All E.R. 139; [1964] Ch. 413; [1963] 3 W.L.R. 574; 45 Digest (Repl.) 505, *933*.

Faramus v. *Film Artistes' Association*, [1963] 1 All E.R. 636; [1963] 2 Q.B. 527; [1963] 2 W.L.R. 504; *affd.*, H.L. [1964] 1 All E.R. 25; [1964] A.C. 925; [1964] 2 W.L.R. 126; 45 Digest (Repl.) 542, *1228*.

Gunmakers, etc. (Master, etc.) v. *Fell*, (1742), Willes, 384; 125 E.R. 1227; 45   **B**
Digest (Repl.) 464, *483*.

Hughes v. *Architects' Registration Council of the United Kingdom*, [1957] 2 All E.R. 436; [1957] 2 Q.B. 550; [1957] 3 W.L.R. 119; 7 Digest (Repl.) 471, *523*.

Jenkin v. *Pharmaceutical Society of Great Britain*, [1921] 1 Ch. 392; 90 L.J.Ch. 47; 124 L.T. 309; 13 Digest (Repl.) 274, *970*.   **C**

Kruse v. *Johnson*, [1895-99] All E.R. Rep. 105; [1898] 2 Q.B. 91; 67 L.J.Q.B. 782; 79 L.T. 647; 62 J.P. 469; 13 Digest (Repl.) 239, *639*.

Lawson, Re, (1941), 57 T.L.R. 315; 33 Digest (Repl.) 562, *273*.

Lloyd v. *Institute of Chartered Accountants*, (Oct. 11, 1961) unreported.

London Association of Shipowners and Brokers, Ltd. v. *London and India Docks Joint Committee*, [1891-94] All E.R. Rep. 462; [1892] 3 Ch. 242; 62   **D**
L.J.Ch. 294; 67 L.T. 238; 30 Digest (Repl.) 172, *229*.

Mitchel v. *Reynolds*, (1711), 1 P. Wms. 181; 24 E.R. 347; 45 Digest (Repl.) 395, *110*.

Morris (Herbert), Ltd. v. *Saxelby*, [1916-17] All E.R. Rep. 305; [1916] 1 A.C. 688; 85 L.J.Ch. 210; 114 L.T. 618; 45 Digest (Repl.) 449, *296*.

Nagle v. *Fielden*, [1966] 1 All E.R. 689; [1966] 2 Q.B. 633; [1966] 2 W.L.R.   **E**
1027.

Nordenfelt v. *Maxim Nordenfelt Guns and Ammunition Co.*, [1891-94] All E.R. Rep. 1; [1894] A.C. 535; 63 L.J.Ch. 908; 71 L.T. 489; 45 Digest (Repl.) 444, *275*.

Rossi v. *Edinburgh Corpn.*, [1905] A.C. 21; 38 Digest (Repl.) 180, **449*.

Routh v. *Jones*, [1947] 1 All E.R. 758; 45 Digest (Repl.) 495, *822*.   **F**

Swaine v. *Wilson*, (1889), 24 Q.B.D. 252; 59 L.J.Q.B. 76; 62 L.T. 309; 54 J.P. 484; 45 Digest (Repl.) 527, *1118*.

Appeal.

The defendant society, the Pharmaceutical Society of Great Britain, was incorporated by royal charter and its objects included the advancement of chemistry and pharmacy and " to maintain the honour and safeguard and   **G**
promote the interests of its members in their exercise of the profession of pharmacy ". In 1954 it appointed a committee to study the state of pharmaceutical practice. In 1961 the committee made its report. In it the committee divided activities other than the general professional practice of pharmacy into three categories: (i) professional, (ii) non-professional but traditionally associated with pharmacy and (iii) other activities. It stated: **H**

" (19) In connexion with (i) the following share in greater or lesser degeee the scientific and professional characteristics of pharmaceutical general practice and can be regarded as natural concomitants: the supply of veterinary medicines, infant and invalid foods, sickroom appliances, agricultural, horticultural and industrial chemicals, scientific apparatus, surgical   **I**
appliances, and instruments, electro-medical and actino-therapeutic apparatus and services involving chemical, biochemical and bacteriological analysis. In connexion with (ii) the supply of perfumes, cosmetics and toilet requisites and of photographic materials, apparatus and services has always been closely associated with pharmacy. The nature of these goods and services is such that pharmacists have been the most appropriate and convenient persons to engage in their supply, a fact which is responsible for pharmacies being the main suppliers. In principle no objection can be

A	taken to the continuation of the association of these activities with pharmaceutical practice. In connexion with (iii) it is doubtful whether there are any other activities which in general can be regarded as consistent with the practice of pharmacy if carried on to a significant extent in an establishment which is not clearly departmentalised, that is to say, conducted with separate accommodation, stock and staff involving a pharmacist in personal super-

B	vision. It may well be that in country districts it is in the public interest that goods which normally would not be regarded as suitable should be sold in pharmacies, but this need not affect the general rule."

	The council considered the report and convened a special general meeting of the society on July 25, 1965, which by a large majority passed a resolution in the

C	terms of a motion put before it. The effect of the resolution was that new pharmacies should be situated in physically distinct premises and should be devoted solely to (i) professional services, (ii) non-professional services within the limits recommended in the report and (iii) such other services as might be approved by the council. The range of services in existing pharmacies, or in pharmacy departments of larger establishments, should not extend beyond

D	existing limits except as approved by the council.

	The plaintiff, Mr. Robert Campbell Miller Dickson, was a member of the defendant society and the retail director of Boots Pure Drug Co., Ltd. On June 23, 1965, he issued a writ against the defendant society, and its president, Mr. James Cecil Bloomfield, the second defendant, suing in his capacity as a member of the society. In his statement of claim he claimed declarations: (a) that the motion

E	then due to come before the meeting of members was not within the powers, purposes or objects of the defendant society; and (b) that it was not within the powers, purposes or objects of the society (i) to enforce or carry out or attempt to enforce or carry out the provisions of the motion; (ii) to regulate, prescribe or impose restrictions as to or to attempt to regulate, prescribe or impose restrictions as to the places or premises in which new pharmacies might be situated or the

F	physical structure of new pharmacies; or (iii) to regulate, prescribe or restrict the services which might be provided by or the classes or descriptions of goods which might be supplied from or sold in new pharmacies or in existing pharmacies or in the pharmacy departments of large establishments. It was alleged that the motion if passed would in practice operate as a rule in restraint of trade affecting the members of the society engaged in the retail pharmacy trade, was contrary to public policy and was illegal and void. The plaintiff also claimed an injunction

G	restraining the defendant society from enforcing or carrying out or acting on the motion. The defendants in their defence did not admit certain allegations in the statement of claim, including the allegation that in practice the motion would operate as a rule in restraint of trade. They did not plead justification of any such restraint of trade on the ground of reasonableness. On June 23, 1966, as reported

H	at [1966] 3 All E.R. 404, PENNYCUICK, J., gave judgment for the plaintiff, holding that the motion constituted a restraint of trade which could be supported only if the defendants had established reasonableness in the interests of the parties (the defendant society and its members), and as they had not done that the restraint was contrary to public policy and an injunction must be granted to restrain the carrying out of the motion.

I	The defendants appealed to the Court of Appeal on the following grounds. 1. That the judge, having rightly found (a) that the motion complained of in the statement of claim was not itself capable of forming the subject-matter of a declaration or injunction; (b) that a statement on matters of professional conduct issued by the defendant society, in which the substance of the motion was intended to be incorporated, consisted of rules of professional conduct, not constituting bye-laws or having themselves any compulsive force, which were regarded by most members as binding in honour, erred in law and misdirected himself in holding that the motion in conjunction with all or any of the following

U

intended actions by the defendant society in respect of the motion gave rise to a   A
justiciable issue. 2. That the plaintiff had no locus standi to maintain an action
for relief in respect of the motion on the ground that its effect was in restraint of
trade of third parties, viz., Boots Pure Drug Co., Ltd., and its subsidiaries. 3.
That if and in so far as the judge held that the doctrine of restraint of trade
applied to a rule of professional conduct, binding in honour only, he erred in law
and misdirected himself. 4. That the judge, having rightly found that the motion   B
was within the objects of the defendant society, as expressed in its charter of 1953,
erred in law and misdirected himself in holding that, by reason of the application
of the doctrine of restraint of trade, the motion together with the intended action
of the defendant society thereon fell outside such objects; or constituted such an
improper exercise of the corporate powers of the defendant society as entitled the
court to interfere by declaration or injunction; and further and in any event   C
the judge erred in law and misdirected himself in failing to hold that, independently of the charter, the defendant society had power to pass and act on
the motion complained of by virtue of the powers impliedly conferred on it
by the Pharmacy Act, 1954, and further or alternatively by virtue of its
status as a professional body. 5. That the judge erred in law and misdirected
himself in holding that the following circumstances brought such rules of   D
professional conduct within the doctrine of restraint of trade; (a) the fact
that the defendant society attempted to persuade members to observe such
rules, and expended money for that purpose; and (b) the initiation by the
defendant society in the last resort of proceedings before the statutory committee;
further that there was no evidence before the judge that the two matters constituted a restraint of trade; and further that the judge erred in holding as he did   E
in that he treated rules having merely evidential value in proceedings before the
statutory committee as if they were rules enforceable proprio vigore in such
proceedings. 6. That the judge erred in law and misdirected himself in holding
that the motion was contrary to public policy and void unless the defendants
pleaded and proved circumstances rendering it reasonable " in the interests of
the parties, i.e., the society and its members ", in that (a) the question of reason-   F
ableness in the interests of the parties did not arise in relation to an alleged
restraint of trade which was not contractual; (b) reasonableness in the interests
of the parties, if it arose at all, arose only for decision by the statutory committee
or on appeal therefrom by the High Court on the facts of a particular case; (c)
further or alternatively, all relevant circumstances being before the court, the
question of such reasonableness (if it arose) was one of law for the court, and the   G
judge should have decided it, and should have decided it in favour of the defendants. 7. That, if the matters complained of in the statement of claim did give
rise to a justiciable issue, and in the circumstances found by the judge the motion
did constitute a restraint of trade within the doctrine, the judge erred in law and
misdirected himself in failing to decide whether the alleged restraint was reasonable in the public interest and further in failing to decide, on the facts and circum-   H
stances proved or admitted before him that the restraint was not proved to be
contrary to the public interest. 8. That the judge erred in law and misdirected
himself in holding that the council of the defendant society was not entitled to
give effect to the resolution passed on the motion, at least for the purpose of giving
(a) guidance to members of the defendant society as to their conduct, and (b)
assistance to the statutory committee in deciding, pursuant to its duty under   I
s. 8 of the Pharmacy Act, 1954, what did and what did not constitute misconduct.
9. That the judge erred or alternatively wrongly exercised his discretion in
granting an injunction the effect of which was to restrain the statutory committee
of the defendant society from carrying out its statutory duties pursuant to the
Pharmaceutical Society (Statutory Committee) Order of Council, 1957* in regard

---

* S.I. 1957 No. 754.

A to any complaint relating to or involving the suitability of new pharmacy premises or goods or services supplied from any pharmacy premises.

The plaintiffs served a cross-notice of intention to rely on the following grounds additional to those relied on by the court below: (i) that the motion scheduled to the order of PENNYCUICK, J., and the enforcement or carrying out or attempting to enforce or carry out the provisions of the motion were not calculated to main-

B tain the honour and safeguard and promote the interests of the members in their exercise of the profession of pharmacy; and (ii) that, if and so far as the question of reasonableness arose, the motion or the carrying out or enforcement of its provisions, or any attempt at such carrying out or enforcing, was unreasonable in the public interest.

C *N. N. McKinnon, Q.C., R. I. S. Bax, Q.C.*, and *I. S. Warren* for the defendants.
R. J. Parker, Q.C., F. P. Neill, Q.C., and *G. M. Waller*, for the plaintiff.

Cur. adv. vult.

Jan. 26. The following judgments were read.

LORD DENNING, M.R.: The defendant society, the Pharmaceutical
D Society of Great Britain, controls the professional activities of pharmacists; but pharmacy is not like other professions. A man cannot live on pharmacy alone. He has to go into trade to pay his way. He is both pharmacist and trader; and then he is called a " chemist ". He keeps a chemist's shop where he sells many things. The question is how far the defendant society can control his trading activities.

E We are all familiar with the traditional pattern of a chemist's shop. When you go in there is on one side of the shop a qualified man dressed in a white coat. He is a registered pharmacist. He dispenses doctors' prescriptions; and from his counter he sells medicines and drugs, thermometers and bandages, and all needs for the sick. Those are called " pharmaceutical goods ". On the other side there are shop girls dressed in their neat overalls. At their counters they sell toothpaste, lipstick, and all articles of toilet; also films, cameras and photographic
F equipment. Those are called " traditional goods ".

This traditional pattern is being eroded. Nowadays, when you go into a chemist's shop, you will often see goods on sale which are quite outside the traditional range; handbags, thermos flasks, greeting cards, gifts, and such like. These are called " non-traditional goods ". They are usually displayed with
G discretion and play a subsidiary role. They do not detract from the general character of the shop as a chemist's shop; but in some of the bigger shops these " non-traditional goods " assume a major role. You will there find that a large part of the space is devoted to the sale of books, gramophone records, even wines and spirits. So that the shop loses its individual character as a chemist's shop. It becomes part of a general emporium.

H Many pharmacists of the old school are alarmed at this new tendency. They fear that it will lower the standards of the profession and the esteem in which it is held. They desire to put a brake on it. They propose to do it, not by controlling the *size* of a chemist's shop but by controlling the *kind* of goods sold in chemists' shops. They wish to see a rule of conduct of the profession to this effect: that every *new* chemist's shop should confine itself to traditional goods and have its
I separate entrance from the street; and that every *existing* chemist's shop should confine itself to *traditional* goods and not go beyond, except that it can keep its *present* range of non-traditional goods. This rule is to be observed and not departed from except with the approval of the council of the defendant society.

The proposal has aroused much controversy; so much so that the defendant society called a special general meeting to consider it. It was held at the Royal Albert Hall on July 25, 1965. Over six thousand members attended. The president put a motion to the meeting. It was in these terms:

" *New pharmacies* should be situated only in premises which are physically

distinct, and should be devoted solely to: (i) professional services, as defined   A
in para. 19 of the report of the committee on the general practice of pharmacy.
[These services are the dispensing of medicines and the sale of pharmaceutical
goods.] (ii) within the limits recommended in the report, non-professional
services, as defined in para. 19 of the report. [These are the sale of traditional goods.] (iii) such other services as may be approved by the council.
[These are the sale of non-traditional goods.] And the range of services in   B
existing pharmacies, or in *pharmacy departments of larger establishments*
should not be extended beyond the present limits, except as approved by the
council."

The motion was carried by the large majority of 5,026 against 1,346. The defendant society has, however, over twenty-nine thousand members. So there are
more than twenty-two thousand members whose views are unknown. Boots   C
Pure Drug Co., Ltd. oppose the proposal. They have 1,265 chemist's shops.
Some 869 are traditional. Some 369 are non-traditional. The policy of Boots,
Ltd., is to vary the range of goods in their shops as occasion demands. Thus they
used to provide libraries. This no longer pays. They have replaced them with
gramophone records and gift departments. They wish to continue this policy.
So one of their directors, Mr. Dickson, the plaintiff, who is himself a registered   D
pharmacist, has brought proceedings against the defendant society to declare that
the proposed new rule is invalid and for an injunction to prevent the society
from acting on it. An application was made for an interim injunction but no
injunction was granted, because the defendant society agreed not to act on the
new rule until the matter had been determined by the courts. The case raises
three issues. (i) Is it a justiciable matter? (ii) Is the scheme beyond the powers   E
of the defendant society? (iii) Is it an unreasonable restraint of trade? In order
to determine these points, we must first consider the constitution of the defendant
society.

1. *The Pharmaceutical Society of Great Britain.* The defendant society was
incorporated by royal charter in 1843, now replaced by a royal charter of Dec. 31,   F
1953. The society is recognised in several Acts of Parliament as representing the
profession. Its objects are

" to advance chemistry and pharmacy; to promote pharmaceutical education and the application of pharmaceutical knowledge: to maintain the
honour and safeguard and promote the interests of the members in their
exercise of the profession of pharmacy: to provide relief for distressed   G
persons being members,"

etc. The society is governed by a council of twenty-one elected members who
have power to make bye-laws in furtherance of the objects of the society, subject
to the approval of the Privy Council.

All registered pharmacists are members of the defendant society. The statute   H
so provides; but a limited company cannot be a member, nor can it be a registered
pharmacist. Nevertheless a limited company can carry on a chemist's business. It
can employ registered pharmacists. It can be an authorised seller of poisons so
long as it is under the superintendence of a registered pharmacist: and provided
also that its premises are registered under the Pharmacy Acts. In that way these
" company chemists " come under the jurisdiction of the defendant society.   I
There is a disciplinary body for pharmacists and company chemists. It is
constituted by statute and is called the statutory committee. It has a legal
chairman appointed by the Privy Council and five other members appointed by
the defendant society. It can inquire into charges of misconduct against a
registered pharmacist or an officer of a company chemist. If it finds the charge
proved, it can strike the pharmacist off the register or, in the case of a company
chemist, it can order that its premises be removed from the register. There is a
right of appeal from the statutory committee to the High Court.

A   2. *The Code of Ethics.* In order to implement the proposed new rule, the council proposes to include it in the code of ethics. The official description of this code is:

> " A statement upon matters of professional conduct issued by the council of the Pharmaceutical Society of Great Britain for the guidance of pharmacists and corporate bodies carrying on business under the Pharmacy Acts."

B   The council emphasises that

> " this statement is not primarily a basis for applying compulsion but a means of assisting pharmacists to discharge the moral obligation resting upon them."

Despite these disclaimers, the evidence shows that this code has compelling force. Most pharmacists regard it as binding on them. The council appoints inspectors C who go round to chemists' shops. These inspectors have statutory functions, but in addition they look to see whether the code of ethics is being observed. If they notice a breach, they report it to the secretary of the defendant society. He seeks, by persuasion, to get the breach remedied. If persuasion fails, he passes the information on to the statutory committee. That committee is charged to consider whether there has been

D   " such misconduct . . . as in the opinion of the statutory committee renders the person unfit to have his name on the register . . ."

In deciding on misconduct, the statutory committee will give great weight to the views of the profession; see *Re Lawson* (1). In particular, it will have regard to the code of ethics. It may treat a breach of the code as evidence of misconduct. That is shown by a case in 1950 about advertising. The legal chairman of the statutory E committee, Mr. Gerald Gardiner, Q.C., speaking of the code of ethics, said:

> " Whilst it is for us to form our own view of what is proper professional conduct, we should naturally at all times pay great regard to the views of the profession itself, as expressed by the council and members of the society."

No doubt the statutory committee is an independent tribunal. It may reject F the code; or on appeal the High Court may do so; compare *Hughes* v. *Architects Registration Council of the United Kingdom* (2); meanwhile, however, unless and until the code is rejected by higher authority, it is regarded as binding on pharmacists and corporate bodies: i.e., binding not only on those who agree to it, but also on those who disagree. As such it is—for them—their law; see *London Association of Shipowners and Brokers, Ltd.* v. *London and India Docks Joint* G *Committee* (3), per Lindley, L.J.

    3. *Is it a justiciable matter?* If a pharmacist or company chemist should object to the proposed new rule, there is a remedy open to him. He can ignore the rule, sell what goods he likes, fight the issue before the statutory committee, and if need be appeal to the High Court. If a case were pending before the statutory committee, the courts would leave it to the committee to decide, subject to appeal; H see the decision of Wilberforce, J., in *Lloyd* v. *Institute of Chartered Accountants* (4) and *Cox* v. *Green* (5).

    I do not think, however, that that is the only remedy. In my opinion if a professional body lays down a rule of conduct for its members, which is regarded as binding on them, then the courts of law have jurisdiction to inquire into the validity of the rule. As with the old guilds, so also with modern professional bodies. I Their rules are only valid if they come within the powers granted to them by their charter. Suppose the defendant society were to make a rule that it would not admit a woman to membership: so that no woman could ever become a registered pharmacist. I have no doubt that the court would intervene and declare the rule

---

(1) (1941), 57 T.L.R. 315.
(2) [1957] 2 All E.R. 436; [1957] 2 Q.B. 550.
(3) [1891-94] All E.R. Rep. 462 at p. 466; [1892] 3 Ch. 242 at p. 252.
(4) (Oct. 11, 1961), unreported.
(5) [1966] 1 All E.R. 268; [1966] Ch. 216.

to be invalid and compel the defendant society to admit her; see *Nagle* v. **A** *Fielden* (6). Take trading activities. Some professions have a rule prohibiting a member from carrying on a trade. That may be reasonable in the case of a profession like the legal profession; but it would be quite unreasonable in the case of the pharmaceutical profession. Suppose the defendant society were to make a rule that no pharmacist should sell any goods other than pharmaceutical goods. Such a rule would put nearly every pharmacist out of business, because no **B** pharmacist can make a living except by selling other goods. Such a rule would be unreasonable and bad. Any member affected could bring an action for a declaration that it was invalid and an injunction to restrain the society from seeking to enforce it. He would not have to wait until he was brought before the statutory committee. He could bring his action at once so as to know where he stood; see *Rossi* v. *Edinburgh Corpn.* (7). Not only a member, but a party interested could **C** bring it, such as a company chemist (see *Boulting* v. *Association of Cinematograph, Television and Allied Technicians* (8)), for the company is just as much affected as a member (see *Eastham* v. *Newcastle United Football Club, Ltd.* (9)).

So also with this proposed new rule under which the council seeks to forbid the selling of non-traditional goods. The persons affected are entitled to know where they stand. In opening a new chemist's shop or extending their existing **D** lines, they are entitled to know what goods they can sell. They should not be left in uncertainty. The courts can grant a declaration that the proposed rule is valid or is not valid; and, if invalid, it can grant an injunction to prevent the council carrying it into effect.

4. *Is it ultra vires?* The objects of the defendant society are set out in the charter of 1953. The only relevant object is **E**

" to maintain the honour and safeguard the interests of the members in their exercise of the profession of pharmacy."

At the time when the charter was granted, it was well known that all retail pharmacists carried on a trade as well as a profession. Yet the objects were expressly confined to " their exercise of the *profession* of pharmacy ": i.e., to **F** the profession itself and not to the trade. That shows that the defendant society is concerned with the professional activities of the pharmacists and not with their trading activities. This distinction existed under the old charter of 1843 and is retained by the new charter of 1953. In *Jenkin* v. *Pharmaceutical Society of Great Britain* (10) the defendant society sought to regulate the hours of business, the wages and conditions of employment of pharmacists, and the prices charged for **G** goods. PETERSON, J., held that this was beyond its powers. The society accepted this decision. In consequence a trade union was formed called the National Pharmaceutical Union to control the trading activities.

Nevertheless I do not think that the defendant society is powerless in regard to trading activities. If and in so far as the trading activities of pharmacists are inconsistent with, or derogate from, the proper practice of the profession, then the **H** society has power to intervene to safeguard the interests of the profession. The society can impose restraint on trading activities when such restraints are reasonable in the interests of the profession and reasonable in the interests of the public; but it cannot impose unreasonable restraints. Unreasonableness in restraint of trade is only a particular category of ultra vires; see *Faramus* v. *Film Artistes' Association* (11), per DIPLOCK, L.J., approved in the House of Lords (12), **I** by LORD EVERSHED and LORD PEARCE. So in order to determine ultra vires, we must turn to the question of unreasonableness. This I now do.

---

(6) [1966] 1 All E.R. 689; [1966] 2 Q.B. 633.   (7) [1905] A.C. 21.
(8) [1963] 1 All E.R. 716 at pp. 725, 733; [1963] 2 Q.B. 606 at pp. 629, 643.
(9) [1963] 3 All E.R. 139 at pp. 155, 156; [1964] Ch. 413 at pp. 442-445.
(10) [1921] 1 Ch. 392.
(11) [1963] 1 All E.R. 636 at p. 651; [1963] 2 Q.B. 527 at p. 556.
(12) [1964] 1 All E.R. 25 at pp. 30, 31; [1964] A.C. 925 at pp. 943, 945.

A   5. *Restraint of trade.*   The proposed new rule restricts the trading in non-traditional goods.   To this restraint the judge below applied the principles applicable to *contracts* in restraint of trade. He cited the familiar cases of *Nordenfelt* v. *Maxim Nordenfelt Guns & Ammunition Co.* (13) and *Herbert Morris, Ltd.* v. *Saxelby* (14). He held that the defendant society ought to have pleaded that the restraint was reasonable in the interests of the parties: and as this was not
B   pleaded, the society failed in their defence.

     I approach the case somewhat differently. The restraint which is imposed by this new rule is not a voluntary restraint, such as is contained in a contract. It was not agreed to by all the members. There are 29,004 members. Only 5,026 voted for it. 1,346 voted against it. Some 22,632 did not vote at all. Yet these 22,632 will be bound by the new rule. So will the company chemists who are not
C   members at all. So far as all these are concerned, it is an *involuntary restraint.* In the great case of *Mitchel* v. *Reynolds* (15) PARKER, C.J., drew a distinction between voluntary restraints (i.e., by agreement of the parties) and involuntary restraints (i.e., against, or without, a man's own consent). Instances of involuntary restraints are those contained in bye-laws by chartered societies (see *Gunmakers, etc.* v. *Fell* (16)) and rules made by a friendly society (see *Swaine* v. *Wilson* (17)).
D   These involuntary restraints fall under the general principle of the common law that all restraints of trade (which the law so much favours), if nothing more appear, are bad. It is for the party who imposes the restraint to set forth in his pleading the circumstances on which he relies. Once the circumstances are established, it is a question of law for the judge to decide whether they do or do not justify the restraint; see the concluding words of PARKER, C.J., in *Mitchel* v.
E   *Reynolds* (18), the judgment of WILLES, C.J., in the *Gunmakers'* case (19), the opening words of LORD PARKER OF WADDINGTON in *Herbert Morris, Ltd.* v. *Saxelby* (20), and the judgment of LORD GREENE, M.R., in *Routh* v. *Jones* (21).

     There is no case in the books where this principle has hitherto been applied to professional bodies; but I see no reason why they should be exempt. If the council of a professional body should make a rule which is in restraint of trade,
F   it is as much subject to the law of the land as anyone else. It must set forth the circumstances which justify the restraint. The courts will then decide whether it is valid or not. It is valid if it is reasonable in the interests of the profession and also reasonable in the interests of the public; but it is invalid if it is unreasonable. It is different with trade unions, but that is only because Parliament has in their case sanctioned restraints of trade, no matter how unreasonable they may be
G   (see *Faramus* v. *Film Artistes' Association* (22), per LORD PEARCE). The professions, however, have no exemption. If they impose restrictive practices on their members, they must be prepared to justify them. In this respect the principles of the common law run parallel with the statutory provisions of the Restrictive Trade Practices Act, 1956.

     In the present case I think that the defendant society ought to have set forth
H   in its pleading the circumstances which justify the restraint; but I would not wish the case to go off on a pleading point. The circumstances on which it relies were fully canvassed before the judge and we should consider them.

     In considering whether the new rule is reasonable in the interests of the profession of pharmacy, the first suggestion was that the selling of non-traditional goods *distracted* pharmacists from their pharmaceutical work so that they were
I   unable to supervise it properly; but this was not supported by the evidence. The judge found that there was no evidence that so far there had in fact been any

   (13) [1891-94] All E.R. Rep. 1; [1894] A.C. 535.
   (14) [1916-17] All E.R. Rep. 305; [1916] 1 A.C. 688.
   (15) (1711), 1 P. Wms. 181.   (16) (1742), Willes, 384 at p. 388.
   (17) (1889), 24 Q.B.D. 252.   (18) (1711), 1 P. Wms. at p. 187.
   (19) (1742), Willes, at pp. 388, 389.
   (20) [1916-17] All E.R. Rep. at p. 315; [1916] 1 A.C. at p. 704.
   (21) [1947] 1 All E.R. 758 at p. 763.
   (22) [1964] 1 All E.R. at pp. 32, 33; [1964] A.C. at pp. 946-949.

greater want of supervision in shops which sold non-traditional goods than in those which did not do so. The second suggestion was that the selling of non-traditional goods affected the number and quality of *new entrants* into the profession; but this again was not supported by the evidence. The judge found that there was no evidence that, so far, any prospective entrants were in fact influenced in their choice of career by the range of goods sold in retail shops. The third suggestion was that the selling of non-traditional goods affected the *status* of the pharmacist. The judge left this out of account because, with one exception, the defendant society's witnesses laid no emphasis on it. I think that I can see why. The selling of non-traditional goods does not affect status any more than the selling of traditional goods. The president of the defendant society himself is not only a pharmacist selling toilet articles and photographic goods; he is also an ophthalmic optician supplying spectacle frames and spectacles. The chairman of the ethical committee sells wines and spirits. The secretary of the Liverpool branch sells greeting cards and thermos flasks. When the leaders of the profession themselves go into trade in this way, it is difficult for them to say that it affects status.

If it were shown that the selling of non-traditional goods affected the profession adversely to a greater extent than traditional goods, there might be some justification for restraining it; but there was no evidence to that effect. In any case, if the circumstances were such as to afford any justification, the proposed rule is not a reasonable way of dealing with the mischief. It is too arbitrary and capricious. If a chemist in one town sells handbags and greeting cards, why should not the chemist in the next town sell them also? If he is meeting fresh competition in toilet articles and films, why should he not switch over to thermos flasks and electric blankets? I know that under the proposed new rule the council is given a dispensing power; but it is in truth a licensing power giving it power to say in what goods a person shall or shall not trade. That is placing too arbitrary a power in its hands. The courts cannot uphold it.

For all these reasons the new rule is not reasonable in the interests of the profession. This makes it unnecessary for me to consider whether it is reasonable in the interests of the public. I have considerable doubt whether it is reasonable. If pharmacists are to be confined to traditional goods, it might lead to fewer pharmacies only available at great distances. Enough to say that in my opinion the restraint of trade contained in the proposed new rule is unreasonable: and being unreasonable it is ultra vires the defendant society.

6. *Conclusion*. I expect that most people, when they go for their medicines, would prefer to go to an old-time chemist's shop with its green and red carboys in the window; but that is no longer possible. The chemist has to go into trade in order to live; and, once he goes into trade, it is for him to decide what goods he shall sell. His colleagues cannot say to him: " You must trade in these goods and not in those." That would be too great an interference with his freedom. I would dismiss this appeal.

DANCKWERTS, L.J.: I agree so thoroughly with the judgment of LORD DENNING, M.R., that I was minded not to write a judgment of my own. I will, however, add a few observations to the analysis by LORD DENNING and the conclusions which he has reached. As LORD DENNING has said in his own words and I add in mine, to my mind the moral of this case is that pharmacists cannot live by drugs alone. They would have to close their businesses if they were not able to sell the traditional goods to which LORD DENNING has referred, and to sell, at least in many cases, the non-traditional goods which the public has become accustomed to buy in " chemists' shops ". In this country the chemist's shop has not become the social centre that it has become in the United States of America, in which the teenage population gather for ice-cream sodas and other such things, and gossip. It is undoubtedly, on the evidence, however, a convenience to the general public to be able to buy cosmetics (which are traditional goods) and many

A other classes of goods. This, of course, applies particularly to multiple stores such as Boots and Timothy Whites and Taylors. It would, in my opinion, plainly be contrary to the interests of the public if chemists or pharmacists had to close down for financial reasons, and it obviously would be against the interests of the pharmacists if this should occur.

B The position is, in my opinion, put with the greatest clarity in *Gunmakers, etc.* v. *Fell* (23), per Willes, C.J. He said:

C "The general rule is that all restraints of trade (which the law so much favours), if nothing more appears, are bad. This is the rule which is laid down in that famous case of *Mitchel* v. *Reynolds* (24), which is very well reported ... But to this general rule there are some exceptions; as first that if the restraint be only particular in respect to the time or place, and there be a good consideration given to the person restrained, a contract or agreement upon such consideration so restraining a particular person may be good and valid in law, notwithstanding the general rule; and this was the very case of *Mitchel* v. *Reynolds* (26), where such a bond was holden to be good. So likewise if the restraint appear to be of a manifest benefit to the public, such a restraint by a bye-law or otherwise may be good. For it is to be considered

D rather as a regulation than a restraint; and it is for the advantage and not the detriment of trade that proper regulations should be made in it. And it is plain by the recitals of this charter granted to the Gunmakers' Co. that this was the very purpose for which this corporation was created."

And in the *Gunmakers'* case (25) the bye-law was held to be bad.

E These are the principles on which the defendant society's proposals must be judged. As has been pointed out by Lord Denning, M.R., the evidence given at the hearing does not support the arguments based on inconvenience or inefficiency or other interference with pharmacists in their professional work. The test must be: are the proposals in the interests of pharmacists and not contrary to the public interest? Of course, the rules or principles of professional bodies very

F often do involve restraints of trade. But these restraints are justified either by preventing undesirable operations by the members or to protect them in their livelihood, and to prevent the public with whom they have to deal being deprived of efficient and honourable service. They still have to be justified on the principles to which I have referred.

G In my opinion the proposals fail, in both these respects, to justify the restrictions which they attempt to impose. For the reasons which I have previously mentioned, they are not in the interests of the members of the defendant society, and they do not comply with the interests of the public. In the result they are invalid. I also would dismiss the appeal.

SACHS, L.J.: The profit-making activities carried on in chemists' premises

H in this country are dispensing, mainly dispensing doctors' prescriptions, the sale of pharmaceutical goods as defined in para. 24 of the report of July, 1961, from which stemmed the motion of July 25, 1965, and the sale of non-pharmaceutical goods. The first two activities involve the pharmacist in charge in responsibilities which have led to the passing of a number of Acts which, whatever their title (Pharmacy Act, Pharmacy and Poisons Act, or Pharmacy and Medicines Act), I

I will refer to simply by the years in which they were passed, and to the practice of pharmacy evolving into a profession. The second activity, however, also involves trading in many items with which those Acts are not concerned. The third activity, selling non-pharmaceutical goods, whether traditional or non-traditional, is naturally one outside the ambit of the Acts. The motion of July 25, coupled with the steps which the defendant society wishes to take to secure its implementation, I will refer to as "the scheme".

(23) (1742), Willes at pp. 388, 389.   (24) (1711), 1 P. Wms. 181.
(25) (1742), Willes 384.

It is as well at the outset to mention that no one who has read the voluminous A
documentation put before the court can doubt but that the raising of the status
of pharmacists is a fundamental objective of the scheme. It is an objective which
the defendant society has been pursuing over a great many years by seeking to
impose ethical restrictions on the conduct of those engaged in pharmaceutical
service. By the scheme it is sought to impose restrictions on the design of new
pharmacies, i.e., any premises which may in future be used for pharmaceutical B
services but have not so far been thus used; to restrict the ranges of non-pharmaceutical goods that may be sold at new pharmacies; and also, by different
criteria, to restrict the ranges of such goods sold in existing pharmacies.   Those
restrictions are not based on some ratio of the area to be used for pharmaceutical
services and the sale of pharmaceutical goods in relation to the area used for the
sale of other goods; nor on any ratio of the staff to be used as between those C
activities; nor on the quality of the non-pharmaceutical articles to be sold by
retail trade; nor on those articles having characteristics which might (as in
the case of livestock) be noxious to or otherwise detrimentally affect some
pharmaceutical range of goods.
      Counsel for the defendants with his usual frankness stated in the course of
his opening address that in the very long term the defendant society hoped to D
produce a situation comparable with that obtaining in certain countries across
the Channel, where, according to some of the evidence, legislation precludes the
sale at pharmacies of household goods—and where dispensing is more remunerative (i.e., costs more).   In other words, it appears that the scheme may be the
first step towards excluding in the long run from pharmacies all ranges of non-
pharmaceutical goods—or at any rate all goods other than those at present E
referred to as " traditional goods " (many of these naturally did not exist when
the defendant society was incorporated by its charter of 1843).
      No one who himself belongs to a profession can be otherwise than sympathetic
to the attempts of another body of men to raise the status of their members.
Subject to one rather important consideration, the higher the standard the better
for the public.   That consideration may arise thus.   The higher the standard F
of qualifications and ethics is raised, the higher will be the remuneration which
they may reasonably expect, irrespective of whether the standard is strictly
necessary for the tasks in hand: and the more their opportunities to earn money
by retail sales are restricted, the greater will be the difficulty in making a pharmaceutical service business economically attractive, and thus the less may
become the number of pharmacies available to the public and the higher the G
dispensing charges which individuals or the National Health Service may have to
pay to enable pharmacies to be economically viable.
      One of the objects of the defendant society as set out in the charter of 1843
was " the protection of those who carry on the business of chemists and drug-
gists "; but in *Jenkin* v. *Pharmaceutical Society of Great Britain* (26), PETERSON,
J., decided, inter alia, that a proposal by the defendant society " to regulate H
the prices at which members may sell their goods " was ultra vires, and remarked
(27) that he found it

> " . . . impossible to suppose that when a charter of 1843 incorporating
> such a society as the defendants' for the purpose of advancing pharmacy,
> promoting education and providing a benevolent fund also enabled it to
> protect members who carried on the business of chemists and druggists   I
> . . . that it was intended to legalise by royal charter a combination in restraint
> of trade."

Since, at any rate, that decision, matters relating to the trading interests of
owners of pharmacies have been dealt with by the National Pharmaceutical
Union.

---

(26) [1921] 1 Ch. 392.   (27) [1921] 1 Ch. at p. 402.

A   The precise terms of that union's constitution were not before the court. Their nature, however, is clear from the copy of pp. 456 and 457 of the " Pharmaceutical Journal " of Nov. 20, 1920. Moreover, it was stated at the Bar that the constitution of the union and the statements of its objects were, so far as is material, substantially the same as the draft that appears at p. 457. If that be so, one of its objects includes " the imposition of restrictive conditions on the
B conduct of the business of chemists and druggist ", as well as a large number of other objects concerned with trading.

    The defendant society has not sought at any stage before the passing of the motion of July, 1965, to contest the validity of the above judgment of PETERSON, J.; nor is there any evidence of any attempt of the society since then to exercise functions stated by that judgment to be ultra vires. There is nothing in the
C new charter that relates to trading activities and this seems to be a deliberate omission consistent with the objects of the defendant society no longer including the above cited phrase which appeared in the charter of 1843.

    The current charter is dated Nov. 19, 1953, and came into force on Dec. 31, 1953—the same date as the Pharmacy Act, 1953 (repealed in 1954) came into effect. In essence it replaced the whole of the charter of 1843 (and the later
D supplemental charters) in all respects

> " except in so far as it incorporates the society and authorises them to have a common seal and to sue and be sued "

(cl. 2). The charter of 1953 was not confirmed by statute, though that of 1843 had been so confirmed by s. 1 of the Pharmacy Act, 1852 and other legislation—
E now all repealed. By cl. 6 of the charter of 1953 the defendant society's members are

> " all such persons as are for the time being registered pharmacists within the meaning of the Pharmacy and Poisons Act, 1933."

Its objects are of a type common amongst professional bodies and include one

F > " to maintain the honour and safeguard and promote the interests of the members in their exercise of the profession of pharmacy."

The charter itself provides for the making of bye-laws generally (cl. 17) for purposes which have no relation to those for which provision is made in the Pharmacy Act, 1954 (see s. 16) or any other Act.

    On behalf of the defendant society it was much pressed that it was as regards
G the scheme in the same position as some authority acting under statutory powers, in that it was in some ways buttressed by statute. Having examined both the Acts and the charter of 1953 I can find no warrant for such a submission. On the contrary, in relation to the relevant matters it is in my view in no different position from any other society incorporated by charter. In that behalf it is to be observed that, although the legislature must at all material times have been
H well aware of the trading activities of owners of pharmacies and of the fact that over the last forty years or so there has existed a union concerned with those activities, none of the relevant provisions of the Acts and none of the current bye-laws, as approved by the Privy Council, touch retail trading in any goods other than those specific pharmaceutical goods mentioned in the Acts themselves. Nor do those provisions or bye-laws touch the construction of pharmacy premises :
I the only control of the premises is that which enables those of a body corporate to be struck off the register of premises if its officer or employee is liable to be struck off the register of pharmacists. It is against the background of the preliminary matters mentioned above that there falls to be considered the various points which have been raised at the trial of this action and during the appeal to this court.

    The first issue canvassed in this court and at first instance (28) was as to whether the motion itself is within the scope of the defendant society's objects

---

(28) [1966] 3 All E.R. 404.

as expressed in the charter, assuming the scheme not to be in improper restraint **A**
of trade.   That it was intended in aid of the honour of the profession is obvious,
and thus to promote the interest of members in the exercise of that profession.
Similarly, the matters which PETERSON, J., held ultra vires in *Jenkins*' case (29)
were intended to be intra vires the then charter; but intention, even if
reasonable, is not enough.

I do not, however, find it necessary finally to decide this issue, but, in view of **B**
the considerable discussion both at first instance and before this court, and having
in mind the possibility that the matter may be taken further, it seems right to
express my considerable doubts whether the motion is intra vires—quite
apart from the restraint of trade points.   Firstly, it does not seem to have
concerned itself with an appropriate target.   To draw a line in relation to
trading activities that does not concern itself with the quality of the goods **C**
sold, or the effect on the pharmaceutical service of selling them, seems curiously
irrelevant.   What is it in point to preclude a pharmacist from selling high class
binoculars or first class watches—but to allow him to sell cheap cameras or the
like toileteries?   Secondly, the design of new pharmacies, if it has no relation
to the physical needs of a pharmaceutical service, likewise seems irrelevant.
The vast combined space that may be needed in a single hall by a big store for **D**
the sale of non-pharmaceutical goods such as toileteries and photographic wares
would be permissible—however modest the available pharmaceutical service
and however restricted the range of pharmaceutical goods: but the relatively
small area required in village premises where it was sought to sell a few watches
in addition to pharmaceutical goods would have to be partitioned off.

Thirdly, one must look at the composite effect of the motion, coupled with the **E**
discretion left to the council to make exceptions.   When asked how this would
affect the opening of new pharmacies in villages or small towns, counsel for the
defendant society said that no doubt the particular needs of such places would
be regarded when an application was made to sell additional ranges of goods
so that a pharmacy might be economically viable.   To my mind that would
produce in effect a sort of licensing system by which the council would decide **F**
what was needed in the light of evidence of local requirements.   The council
has, however, been given no powers to act as a licensing authority—and, whether
or not it is reasonable that such an authority should exist, the council would be
stepping well outside its powers in seeking to act as such (cf. *Rossi* v. *Edinburgh
Corpn.* (30)).   Moreover, unqualified control of the design of premises is a function
which likewise has not been allocated to it.   **G**

Lastly, the scheme seeks in a rather devious way to put the defendant society
in the position to exercise those powers and objects over trading interests which
it deliberately abjured after the *Jenkin's* decision (29) and which have no place
amongst the objects set out in the charter of 1953.

The next issue raised is whether the matters for which the plaintiff seeks a
remedy by way of declaration are justiciable.   It is clear that the scheme is **H**
intended to be enforced by strong pressure on the part of the council—a pressure
exercised by aid of reports from inspectors and by correspondence inducing
compliance.   On precedent a ninety per cent. compliance (perhaps even more)
can be thus secured without resort to any form of process, and it may be a very
long time before the council seeks to risk embarking thereon, especially if it
prefers first to secure a wide compliance by other means.   **I**

It is obviously essential that a man faced with the prospect of such pressure
should be enabled at the earliest practicable opportunity to regulate his business
affairs with knowledge of what in law are his rights.   Uncertainty and stagnation
are to be deplored in business matters.   For the reasons given by LORD DENNING,
M.R., I entirely agree that the courts can in this type of case in their discretion

(29) [1921] 1 Ch. 392.
(30) [1905] A.C. 21.

A grant such declarations or such injunctions as may in the circumstances be meet, so that the owner of a chemist's business can ascertain what is his position and may not have to endure the harassment of unjustified pressure.   For instance, to take an obvious example, one has only to look at *Hughes* v. *Architects' Registration Council of the United Kingdom* (31), where a professional body had sought to enforce a rule that for the same man conduct which was permissible on Dec. 31,

B 1955, had become misconduct on Jan. 1, 1956.   Had Mr. Hughes either himself or with others similarly affected by the rule sought in advance of Dec. 31, 1955, a declaration that the relevant rule was unreasonable and invalid, no doubt such a declaration would have been made.   Had he desired before the end of 1955 to obtain a decision of the courts how he stood about closing down part of his activities, it would have been utterly wrong for him to have been unnecessarily

C under harassment until the date the matter came before the tribunal.   I would only add that in such cases the fact that the defendant society is in its own view attempting to " do good " is not normally in point.

One can thus come to the question on which to my mind this case turns. Is the scheme in improper restraint of trade?   If it is in improper restraint, the scheme is, of course, ultra vires.   That it is in restraint of trade is, despite the

D submissions made for the defendant society, obvious.   It forbids a man selling articles from his premises.   Is the restraint imposed improper?   The books emphasise time and again that a subject is at common law free to engage in any non-noxious trade as and where he wills.   Any restraint imposed on trade (other than by legislative action—of which there is no lack) has to be justified. A royal charter cannot of itself justify a restraint—at any rate, where there is

E no antecedent custom (*City of London Case* (32)), and the mere fact that the restraint is imposed pursuant to the objects of such a   charter likewise cannot justify it

By what test can a restraint be justified and on whom does the onus of justification lie?   The trial judge held (33) that two tests had to be satisfied: first, was it reasonable between the parties (i.e., the defendant society and its members);

F the second was the public interest.   He further held that, as regards the first, the onus lay on the defendant society; as to the second it lay on the plaintiff.   He further held (34) that, as the defendant society had not pleaded that it was reasonable between the parties and refused so to plead, its case fell to the ground (compare *Gunmakers, etc.* v. *Fell* (35)) and he thus need not consider the public interest issue.   It would be a matter of regret if this case had to turn on a pleading

G point: and it is not necessary that it should.   Nor, on the facts as they have emerged from the oral evidence and the bulky documentation, is there any need to resort to the questions of onus of proof or even to discuss them except in relation to the pleadings.   Accordingly, I turn to the points canvassed with exemplary care before this court.

Taking first the submission that the law as to restraint of trade does not apply

H in this case because the defendant society is in essence a body of professional men, I see no warrant for acceding to it.   The case is concerned with a body, the bulk of whose members ever since it was founded have engaged in retail trade and whose present members intend to continue so to do.   In relation to that activity they are clearly amenable to the general law of the country in relation to trading.   How far the law as to restraint of trade can by analogy extend to a

I profession that does not engage in trade is a different matter.   The next question is whether the scheme is one which imposes an unreasonable restraint as between the defendant society and its members.   Does it pass the first of the two tests propounded by Pennycuick, J. (33)?   On the material before this court, I agree entirely on this point with the view expressed by Lord Denning, M.R., for the reasons he has given.

---

(31) [1957] 2 All E.R. 436; [1957] 2 Q.B. 550.
(32) (1610), 8 Co. Rep. 121b.   (33) [1966] 3 All E.R. at p. 407.
(34) [1966] 3 All E.R. at p. 411.   (35) (1742), Willes, 384.

Having regard, however, to the course the trial took at first instance in relation **A**
to this issue, I prefer to rest my judgment primarily on conclusions, reached
without hesitation, on the public interest issue—the second of the two tests.
It is right, however, to add that as regards the first test I find it very difficult
to see how, even if the course of the trial at first instance had been different, any
further material could have emerged which could derogate from the cogency of
that discussed in the judgment of LORD DENNING, M.R. **B**

As regards the public interest, I have already stated that it does not in the
present case matter where the onus lies. In view of the submissions based on
Kruse v. *Johnson* (36), I should, however, mention that that case does not seem
to me to afford guidance here; partly because the scheme does not in my view
stem from any statutory grant of powers and partly because the facts in *Kruse's*
case (36) were so very different. Much of the evidence and even more of the **C**
arguments in this court touching public interest related to the position of multiple
shop owners such as Boots and to great departmental stores such as Harrods.
Such establishments were said to be concerned with between one quarter and
one third of the turnover in pharmaceutical goods, and thus to form an important
element in the pharmaceutical world. No less important, however—and may
be even considerably more important—are the great number of pharmacies **D**
established in communities where the multiple shop companies do not operate.
To cause the only village chemist's business not to be economically viable or to
prevent a second chemist opening in some slightly larger area could be a serious
detriment to the community. Counsel for the defendants asked the court not
to take a " Boots' eye " view of public interest and I for one readily accede to
that request. **E**

On the facts such attempts as were made to show affirmatively that the public
resorting to pharmacies would gain from the change failed in the way which LORD
DENNING, M.R., has mentioned. The defendant society's main point collapsed at
the end of the proceedings of June 17 in the trial court. Once it cannot be shown
that the existing pharmaceutical service is such that the particular changes
envisaged by the scheme would benefit the public, the way lies the more easily **F**
open to those who assert that the scheme is not in the public interest. The trial
judge made no finding on this issue, but the evidence coupled with the findings
of fact, express and implicit, made by him in other parts of his judgment leads
me to the conclusion that the scheme is against the public interest for the following
reasons.

First, the result of the scheme if fully enforced would be to increase the number **G**
of smaller pharmacies that would close for economic reasons. (Incidentally it
would lessen the proportion of smaller pharmacies to those owned by the large
multiple pharmacy companies and the larger general stores: but that is perhaps
beside the point). Secondly, because the scheme would in due course lessen
the profitability of many—may be a high proportion—of the larger businesses
which include a pharmaceutical service, it would in the long run tend to diminish **H**
the prospects of such salaries being paid to pharmacists as best attract new
entrants into the profession, and in addition to increase the prices charged for
dispensing to private customers and the National Health Service alike. Thirdly
(though this overlaps with other grounds), it would tend against the opening of
new pharmacies and also the ability of existing pharmacies to compete with each
other and to meet the wishes of the public, wishes which must vary according **I**
to what other shops are available in the locality. Finally, there can be taken
into account some of those factors discussed when considering the ultra vires
issue, viz., the curious irrelevancy of main facets of the particular scheme to the
improvement of pharmaceutical service; and the undesirability of imposing
anything in the nature of a licensing system except under legislation.

These factors to my mind far outweigh any advantage gained by increasing

---

(36) [1895-99] All E.R. Rep. 105; [1898] 2 Q.B. 91.

A the status of pharmacists—assuming that such advantage can (contrary to my view) be said to be produced, and assuming, too, that it is relevant. Having come to the conclusion that the restraint in trade imposed by the scheme is improper, it follows that for the reasons already stated I agree that this appeal should be dismissed.

There remains, however, an important matter which has been canvassed as
B germane to some of the issues determined, but which does not call for a decision in this case; it is, however, as well to mention it lest otherwise it should be said to have been implicitly decided. I refer to the position of the statutory committee, which has to determine what is misconduct under the provisions of the Acts vis-à-vis any rulings by or guidance given by the council of the defendant society or its ethical committee as to the conduct of its members. Counsel for
C the defendant society and counsel for the plaintiff both stressed the independence of the statutory committee—indeed, that was one of the few points on which counsel were agreed.

The council of the defendant society is in the difficult position of having to discharge functions placed on it by two rather different types of instrument— a series of statutes passed for the protection of the public, and a charter for the
D furtherance of the interests of what is now a profession. The two sets of functions are not necessarily fully coterminous. It follows that there may be a distinction between that conduct which an ethical committee would regard as undesirable between men independently carrying on a profession and conduct which would result in an employee of a multiple stores being unfit to carry on his duties in its pharmaceutical department. The distinction is all the more relevant when it
E is borne in mind that the stores are not members of the defendant society but are yet liable to have their premises struck off the register: and also that the Acts contain no reference to trading in non-pharmaceutical goods, although when they were passed it was well known that trading in such goods was normally carried on in pharmacy premises. It is this potential distinction that may well lie at the root of the attempts of the council in 1963 to influence the decisions
F of the statutory committee on advertising, and its determination to enforce its ethical policies whatever might or might not be the rulings of the committee as to what constituted misconduct under the Acts. Whether that be so or not, however, the potential distinction exists and may one day come before the courts for resolution.

So far as the present case is concerned, it merely underlines the importance
G of a member of the defendant society being able to resort to the courts, so that he may know where he stands at law when pressure is being applied by the society to enforce some ethical code to the detriment of his business. I prefer, however, to make it plain that nothing in this judgment is intended to decide whether, if the scheme had been intra vires the charter, it would necessarily be enforceable under the provisions of s. 3 of the Pharmacy Act, 1954—that type of point is
H for the future. Nor is anything in my judgment intended to assert that the inspectors of the defendant society have any statutory right to enter premises for the purpose of enforcing any rules other than one strictly pertaining to the defendant society's functions under the Acts.

Appeal dismissed. Leave to appeal to the House of Lords granted.

Solicitors: *Lamartine, Yates & Lacey* (for the defendants); *Seaton Taylor & Co.*
I (for the plaintiff).

[*Reported by* F. A. Amies, Esq., *Barrister-at-Law.*]

BOURNE (Inspector of Taxes) *v.* NORWICH CREMATORIUM, LTD. A

[CHANCERY DIVISION (Stamp, J.), March 6, 7, 1967.]

Income Tax—Allowance—Industrial building or structure—Crematorium— Expenditure incurred in construction of furnace chamber and chimney tower of crematorium—Whether furnace chamber and chimney tower industrial building or structure—Whether dead human bodies " goods and materials "— Income Tax Act, 1952 (15 & 16 Geo. 6 & 1 Eliz. 2 c. 10), s. 265 (1), s. 266, s. 271 (1) (c).

The taxpayer company owned a crematorium which comprised a memorial garden, a chapel and front porch and cloisters, and the furnace chamber and chimney tower, these latter having been built in 1936-37 at a cost of £2,157. In the tower and chamber human corpses were reduced to ashes, which were then disposed of in accordance with the instructions of the deceased or his representatives. The taxpayer company was assessed to income tax in respect of its trade under Case I of Sch. D to the Income Tax Act, 1952, and it claimed an annual allowance under s. 266 on expenditure incurred on the construction of the furnace chamber and chimney tower.

Held: the consumption by fire of the dead body of a human being was not " the subjection of goods or materials to any process ", and so the furnace chamber and chimney tower were not within the definition of an industrial building or structure in s. 271 (1) (c)* of the Income Tax Act, 1952; the taxpayer company was not, therefore, entitled to the allowance that it claimed (see p. 578, letter I, post).

Appeal allowed.

[As to what are industrial buildings for the purposes of initial and other income tax allowances, see 20 HALSBURY'S LAWS (3rd Edn.) 483, para. 919; 494-501, paras. 947-963; and for cases on the subject of such allowances and balancing charges, see 28 DIGEST (Repl.) 310, *1356-1358*; for allowances in respect of cemeteries and crematoria, see 20 HALSBURY'S LAWS (3rd Edn.) 520, 521, paras. 998-1001; and for cases on the subject, see 28 DIGEST (Repl.) 145, *554, 555*.

For the Income Tax Act, 1952, s. 265 (1), s. 266, s. 271 (1) (c), see 31 HALS-BURY'S STATUTES (2nd Edn.) 255, 257, 264; and for s. 271, as amended, see Vol. 1 of the SUPPLEMENT to 31 HALSBURY'S STATUTES (2nd Edn.) para. [273] Amended Texts.]

Cases referred to:

Inland Revenue Comrs. v. *Saxone, Lilley & Skinner (Holdings), Ltd.,* [1967] 1 All E.R. 756; [1967] 1 W.L.R. 501.

R. v. *Slade,* (1888), 21 Q.B.D. 433; 57 L.J.M.C. 120; 59 L.T. 640; 52 J.A. 599; 2 Digest (Repl.) 372, *491*.

Case Stated.

The taxpayer company, Norwich Crematorium, Ltd., appealed to the General Commissioners of Income Tax for Norwich City against an assessment to income tax under Case I of Sch. D to the Income Tax Act, 1952, in the sum of £8,500 in respect of the profits of a crematorium for 1964-65. The question for decision was whether the furnace chamber and chimney tower of the taxpayer's crematorium were industrial buildings or structures for the purpose of Chapter I of Part 10 of the Act so as to entitle the taxpayer to an annual allowance under s. 266 of the Act of 1952 in respect of expenditure incurred by the taxpayer on the construction of the tower and chamber. The commissioners found on the evidence that the furnace chamber and chimney tower were used for the subjection of goods or materials to a process and accordingly the taxpayer was entitled to annual allowances under s. 266. The assessment was accordingly determined at

---

* Section 271 (1), so far as material, is set out at p. 577, letter F, post.

A £8,588 less capital allowances of £1,551. The Crown appealed by way of Case Stated to the High Court.

Heyworth Talbot, Q.C., and J. R. Phillips for the Crown.

J. P. Graham, Q.C., and M. R. Stewart-Smith for the taxpayer.

B **STAMP, J.:** Her Majesty's inspector of taxes appeals by way of Case Stated under the Income Tax Act, 1952, s. 64, against a decision of the General Commissioners for the division of Norwich City. By that decision the commissioners allowed a claim under s. 266 of the Income Tax Act, 1952, for an annual allowance in respect of expenditure incurred by the taxpayer on the construction of a furnace and chimney tower at the taxpayer's crematorium near Norwich. The question arises on an assessment to income tax on the taxpayer in the sum of

C £8,500 for the income tax year 1964-65.

Part 10 of the Act of 1952 conferred relief from income tax for certain capital expenditure. Chapter I of Part 10 is headed, " Industrial buildings and structures, etc.". Section 265 (1), which is the first section which appears in that chapter, confers allowances, called initial allowances, equal to a proportion of the expenditure incurred by a taxpayer before an appointed day (which was in fact a date

D in 1946),

> ". . . on the construction of a building or structure which is to be an industrial building or structure occupied for the purposes of a trade carried on either by him . . ."

or by such a lessee as is there mentioned. Section 266 grants relief by way of

E annual allowance to a taxpayer entitled to an interest such as is there described in an industrial building or structure, such annual allowance to be of an amount equal to a proportion of the capital expenditure incurred on the construction of the building or structure. Section 271 defines what is meant by an industrial building or structure and, so far as material for present purposes, it reads as follows:

F > " (1) Subject to the provisions of this section, in this chapter, ' industrial building or structure ' means a building or structure in use . . . (c) for the purposes of a trade which consists in the manufacture of goods or materials or the subjection of goods or materials to any process; . . ."

The question is whether the furnace chamber and chimney tower is an industrial

G building or structure within the definition so as to qualify for an annual allowance.

The facts of the case as found by the commissioners are these. The taxpayer is a public company incorporated on Apr. 5, 1935, under the Companies Act, 1929, and it carries on the trade of the disposal of the human dead by cremation. It is assessed on its profits under Case I of Sch. D. The profits for the year 1964-65 were agreed at £8,588, less capital allowances of £1,508; subject to the further

H claim for capital allowances under appeal. The crematorium owned by the taxpayer is at Horsham Saint Faiths, in Norfolk, and comprises a memorial garden and buildings therein. The buildings include a chapel and front porch, cloisters, and the furnace chamber and chimney tower. The furnace chamber and chimney tower were built in 1936-37 at a cost to the taxpayer of £2,157.

In the tower and chamber human corpses are reduced to ashes, which are

I disposed of in accordance with the instructions of the deceased or his representatives. Sometimes they are scattered, sometimes handed to the deceased's family and sometimes put into caskets to be placed in a permanent memorial. A brochure issued by the taxpayer is attached to and forms part of the Case Stated. The brochure describes with illustrations the cloisters furnished with tablets as memorials to those whose ashes repose in the gardens, the chapel with its organ where the funeral services are held, and the gardens of charming appearance which, with the buildings, occupy a site some sixteen acres in extent in the Norfolk countryside.

Counsel for the Crown is entitled in my judgment to say, looking at that **A** description, that the taxpayer's trade, for trade it is for the purposes of income tax, consists of all those services and facilities which enable the obsequies of the human being to be carried out with that reverence and decorum which is demanded by a civilised society. I would say at once that my mind recoils as much by the description of the bodies of the dead as " goods or materials " as it does from the idea that what is done in that crematorium can be described as **B** " the subjection of " the human corpse to a " process ". Nevertheless the taxpayer so contends, and I must examine that contention.

" Goods or materials " is, it is contended, a phrase of the widest import embracing all things animate and inanimate. " Goods " itself, urges counsel for the taxpayer, is a word of the widest import, and he calls my attention to the fact that, for the purposes of s. 40 of the Metropolitan Police Courts Act, 1839, that expression **C** has been held to include dogs; see *R.* v. *Slade* (1). Counsel goes on to say that, if contrary to his submission human remains are not goods, then the shroud and coffin containing those human remains are properly so described. Regarding the latter submission, I can only say that I do not think it is the purpose of the taxpayer or of his trade to subject coffins and shrouds to consumption or incineration by fire.   **D**

Little reliance is placed, perhaps wisely, on the word materials, but it is submitted that the whole phrase " goods and materials " is a phrase as wide as one can find. On that part of the argument I can only say that, although the human body is no doubt material in the same sense that all things visible are material, there is in my judgment something in the word " materials ", in the plural, which forbids the construction of the phrase " goods and materials " **E** that is urged on me. In my judgment it would be a distortion of the English language to describe the living or the dead as goods or materials. The argument, of course, goes on inevitably to this: that just as " goods and maeterials " is wide enough to embrace, and does embrace, all things animate and inanimate, and so includes the dead human body, so the other words to which a meaning must be given, namely " subjection ". and " process ", are words of the widest import. **F** Parliament cannot, so the argument as I understood it runs, have intended to exclude from the definition a process whereby refuse or waste material is destroyed or consumed by fire and, putting it crudely, for it can only be put crudely, the consumption by fire of the human body is a process. I protest against subjecting the English language, and more particularly a simple English phrase, to this kind of process of philology and semasiology. English words derive colour from those **G** which surround them. Sentences are not mere collections of words to be taken out of the sentence, defined separately by reference to the dictionary or decided cases, and then put back again into the sentence with the meaning which you have assigned to them as separate words, so as to give the sentence or phrase a meaning which as a sentence or phrase it cannot bear without distortion of the English language. That one must construe a word or phrase in a section of an **H** Act of Parliament with all the assistance one can from decided cases and, if one will, from the dictionary, is not in doubt; but having obtained all that assistance, one must not at the end of the day distort that which has to be construed and give it a meaning which in its context one does not think it can possibly bear. What has to be decided here is whether what is done by the taxpayer, viz., the consumption or destruction by fire of the dead body of the human being, is within **I** the phrase, " the subjection of goods or materials to any process ". I can only say that, having given the matter the best attention that I can, I conclude that the consumption by fire of the mortal remains of homo sapiens is not the subjection of goods or materials to a process within the definition of " industrial building or structure " contained in s. 271 (1) (c) of the Income Tax Act, 1952.

I have not adverted to an alternative argument which counsel for the Crown

---

(1) (1888), 21 Q.B.D. 433.

A foreshadowed but which has not been developed and has not been the subject of debate, whether the trade of the taxpayer could in any event be said to " consist of " cremation: a debate which would be complicated by the provisions of s. 271 (2), and in which the recent decisions of the House of Lords in *Inland Revenue Comrs.* v. *Saxone, Lilley & Skinner (Holdings), Ltd.* (2) would not be irrelevant. The appeal must in my view be allowed.

B   *Appeal allowed.*

Solicitors: *Solicitor of Inland Revenue*; *Mills & Reeve* (for the taxpayer).

[*Reported by* F. A. AMIES, ESQ., *Barrister-at-Law.*]

C   POOK (Inspector of Taxes) *v.* OWEN.

[CHANCERY DIVISION (Stamp, J.), February 28, March 3, 1967.]

*Income Tax—Deduction in computing profits—Expenses—Medical practitioner—
General medical practitioner practising at his residence and also holding*
D *part-time appointments at hospital fifteen miles away—Hospital work as
obstetrician and anaesthetist—Emergency cases—Expenses of travel by car
to and from hospital—Whether expenses deductible—Income Tax Act, 1952
(15 & 16 Geo. 6 & 1 Eliz. 2 c. 10), s. 156, Sch. E, Case 1, as substituted by
Finance Act, 1956 (4 & 5 Eliz. 2 c. 54), s. 10 (1), and Sch. 9, r. 7 to the Act
of 1952.*

E The taxpayer carried on practice as a general medical practitioner at his residence at Fishguard and also held part-time appointments as obstetrician and anaesthetist with a hospital board at a hospital at Haverfordwest fifteen miles away. Under the terms of his appointments he was on stand-by duty as an obstetrician one week-end a month and as an anaesthetist on Monday and Friday nights and one week-end a month. His work was
F concerned with emergency cases at the hospital and he had to be accessible by telephone. On receipt of a telephone call from the hospital, his responsibility for the patient began immediately, and he gave instructions to the hospital staff and usually set out immediately for the hospital by car, although he might advise treatment by telephone and await a further report, not every call requiring a visit to the hospital. He claimed to deduct the
G expenses of travelling to and from the hospital from the emoluments of his appointments on which he was assessed to income tax under Sch. E,

Held: the travelling expenses were not deductible from the taxpayer's emoluments of his appointments as computed for income tax purposes, because they were not money expended " wholly, exclusively and necessarily in the performance " of his duties under r. 7* of the rules applicable to
H Sch. E to the Income Tax Act, 1952, but were personal to himself as he chose to live fifteen miles from the hospital (see p. 582, letter G, post).

Ricketts (Inspector of Taxes) v. *Colquhoun* ([1926] A.C. 1) applied.

Appeal allowed.

[**Editorial Note.** The position where the medical practitioner held part-time appointments in conjunction with private practice, with the consequence that
I assessments fell to be made both under Sch. D and Sch. E, was considered in *Mitchell* v. *Ross* ([1961] 3 All E.R. 49).

As to deduction in respect of travelling expenses in computing assessable emoluments, see 20 HALSBURY'S LAWS (3rd Edn.) 327, 328, para. 600; and for cases on the subject, see 28 DIGEST (Repl.) 242-247, *1059-1099*.

For s. 156 of the Income Tax Act, 1952, as amended, see SUPPLEMENT to **31**

(2) [1967] 1 All E.R. 756.
* Rule 7 is set out at p. 581, letter F, post.

Affirmed. C.A. [1968] 1 All E.R. 261.

Affirmed. C.A. [1968] 1 All E.R. 261.

HALSBURY'S STATUTES (2nd Edn.), para. [158] Amended Texts; and for r. A
7 of Sch. 9 to the Act of 1952, see 31 HALSBURY'S STATUTES (2nd Edn.) 524.]

Case referred to:

    Ricketts (Inspector of Taxes) v. *Colquhoun*, [1925] 1 K.B. 725;   *affd*. H.L.,
        [1926] A.C. 1;   95 L.J.K.B. 82;   134 L.T. 106;   10 Tax Cas. 118;   28
        Digest (Repl.) 242, *1059*.
                                                                      B
Case Stated.

The taxpayer, Dr. David Norman Howell Owen, appealed to the General
Commissioners of Income Tax for Kemes in Pembrokeshire against the following
assessments made on him under Sch. E to the Income Tax Act, 1952:   1962-63
(additional assessment) employment, etc., £412 plus superannuation disallowed
£39, £451;   1963-64, employment, etc., £1,481, less superannuation £48, £1,433. C
The taxpayer contended before the commissioners: (i) that his duties under his
part-time appointments under the South West Wales Hospital management
committee (which were all connected with emergency cases at the committee's
hospital at Haverfordwest) commenced when he received a telephone call from
the hospital and that his journeys to and from the hospital were wholly,
necessarily and exclusively in the performance of the duties;   (ii) that under D
r. 7 of Sch. 9 to the Act of 1952 there should be deducted from the emoluments
of his appointments assessed on him the costs of journeys made between his
residence and the hospital, being £150 for 1962-63 and £123 for 1963-64.   The
Crown contended before the commissioners that the taxpayer's place of employment during the relevant period was the hospital, that in travelling to and from
the hospital he was not performing the duties of his office or employment and E
that accordingly the expenses of the journeys should not be deducted from the
emoluments.

The commissioners decided that the taxpayer's duties commenced at the
moment when he was first contacted by the hospital authorities and thereafter
his travelling expenses to and from the hospital or to and from an emergency
were wholly, exclusively and necessarily incurred or expended in the duties of F
that office.   They therefore allowed the appeal and determined the assessments
at the agreed figures on that basis of £301 and £1,310.   The Crown appealed by
way of Case Stated to the High Court.

J. R. Phillips for the Crown.

J. R. Cherryman and *G. J. Topham* for the taxpayer.

                                                        Cur. adv. vult. G

Mar. 3. **STAMP, J.:** This is an appeal by the inspector of taxes by way of
Case Stated under s. 64 of the Income Tax Act, 1952, against a decision of the
General Commissioners for the division of Kemes in Pembrokeshire.   The matter
arises out of assessments to income tax made on the taxpayer under Sch. E
to the Act for the years 1962-63 and 1963-64.   The taxpayer holds a part-time H
appointment with the South West Wales Hospital management committee at a
hospital in Haverfordwest.   He also carried on practice as a general medical
practitioner at his residence at Fishguard some fifteen miles away.   He is assessed
on his emoluments from the hospital under Sch. E.   He seeks to deduct from his
emoluments the expenses of travelling between the hospital and his residence, and
claims that on the particular facts of the case he is entitled to do so on the ground I
that those expenses were in the years in question expenses which are deductible
under the terms of r. 7 of the Rules applicable to Sch. E.

The facts found by the General Commissioners are set out in para. 3 of the
Case Stated, from which it appears that the taxpayer holds part-time appointments with the South West Wales Hospital management committee as obstetrician and anaesthetist at the Pembroke County War Memorial Hospital at
Haverfordwest.   There is a scarcity in the area of persons duly qualified to do this
work.   Under the terms of these appointments he is on stand-by duty at the

A following times: as obstetrician, one week-end a month; as anaesthetist, on Monday and Friday nights and one week-end a month. During these periods he is required to be accessible by telephone. All his work in connexion with these appointments is concerned with emergency cases at the hospital. On receipt of a telephone call from the hospital he gives instructions to the hospital staff (e.g., to prepare the patient for an operation). Usually he then sets out immediately B to the hospital by car. Sometimes he advises treatment by telephone and then awaits a further report. Not every telephone call results in a visit to the hospital. Sometimes the telephone call is received when he is out on his medical rounds and not thus necessarily at his house. His responsibility for a patient begins as soon as he receives a telephone call.

Under the terms and conditions of service of hospital, medical and dental C staffs, the hospital management committee pays to the taxpayer travelling expenses at a fixed rate per mile for journeys between Fishguard and the hospital at Haverfordwest. Expenses are not payable for a single journey in excess of ten miles and the taxpayer bears the cost of the additional five miles himself. In 1962-63 he made about 140 journeys to the hospital and the expenses payments reimbursed to him from the hospital for the outward and return journeys totalled D £100, leaving him to bear the balance of £50. The sum of £100 is included in the sum of £412 assessed for that year under Sch. E. In 1963-64 he made about 115 journeys and received by way of reimbursement of his expenses £82, which is included in the assessment for 1963-64, leaving him to bear the balance of £41. At all times the taxpayer is on call for obstetric " flying squad " duties, which means that he may be called to attend an obstetric emergency in any part of E Pembrokeshire. Such calls are rare. The taxpayer seeks to deduct the whole cost of travelling incurred; i.e., for 1962-63, £150 and for 1963-64, £123.

Rule 7 of the Rules applicable to Sch. E provides as follows:

" If the holder of an office or employment of profit is necessarily obliged to incur and defray out of the emoluments thereof the expenses of travelling in the performance of the duties of the office or employment or of keeping and F maintaining a horse to enable him to perform the same, or otherwise to expend money wholly, exclusively and necessarily in the performance of the said duties, there may be deducted from the emoluments to be assessed the expenses so necessarily incurred and defrayed."

The commissioners, finding as a fact that the taxpayer's duties commenced at G the moment he was first contacted by the hospital authorities, concluded that his travelling expenses to and from the hospital or to and from an emergency were wholly, exclusively and necessarily incurred or expended in the duties of his office. I should perhaps emphasise at this point that the Case does not raise any question regarding the expenses connected with the " flying squad " duties referred to in the Case, and the existence of those duties is not relevant except in order to H indicate the terms of his employment and the manner in which the taxpayer's duties had to be performed.

If the matter was res integra one might think that an expense of travelling which a particular individual in the particular circumstances in which he finds himself is necessarily obliged to incur in order to perform the duties of his office was an expense which he was entitled to deduct from his emoluments within the I meaning of the rule. That in effect was the view taken by Warrington, L.J., in the leading case of *Ricketts* (*Inspector of Taxes*) v. *Colquhoun* (1), where the Recorder of Portsmouth, a barrister living and practising in London, sought to deduct from his emoluments as recorder his travelling expenses between London and Portsmouth. That view was, however, rejected in the House of Lords and, as I understand the law as laid down by the House of Lords in that case, it is that the rule comprehends only those expenses which each and every occupant of the

_____

(1) [1925] 1 K.B. 725; 10 Tax Cas. 118.

particular office is necessarily obliged to incur in the performance of the duties A
of that office: i.e., expenses imposed on each holder by the very fact that he
holds, or ex necessitate of, that office. It does not extend to include expenses
which an individual has to incur mainly or only because of circumstances in
relation to his office which are personal to himself or are the result of his own
volition. The House of Lords also held in *Ricketts* v. *Colquhoun* (2) that in relation
to travelling expenses a further test of admissibility had to be passed, i.e., that B
it must be shown that the expenses were incurred in the performance of the
duties of the office.

The taxpayer in the present case claims that the travelling expenses are within
the rule. He points in particular to the finding that his duties commence at the
moment when he is first contacted by the hospital authorities, to the instructions
which he gives on the receipt of a telephone call from the hospital, to the advice C
as to treatment which he sometimes gives on the telephone without immediately
following it up by a visit to the hospital, to the fact that his responsibility begins
as soon as he receives a telephone call and, for good measure, to the fact that he
may be called out to attend an obstetric emergency in any part of Pembrokeshire.
He claims accordingly that the travelling expenses are incurred in travelling in
the performance of the duties of his office. He claims that the office is a peripatetic D
office and that there are two places where the duties of the office are performed,
viz., his residence at Fishguard and the hospital. Alike when he is travelling to
the hospital as when he is returning from it he is performing the duties of his
office. His duty, so the argument runs, is to be on call, to answer the call and to
return to be on call again—and so no doubt it is, and he cannot perform his duty
as matters stand without incurring these expenses. If " necessarily " in r. 7 E
meant necessarily

" in regard to the circumstances of the individual concerned, the holder
of the office, and in regard to the ordinary usages of mankind "

—I quote the language of WARRINGTON, L.J., in *Ricketts* v. *Colquhoun* (3) rejected
by the House of Lords—then the taxpayer would in my judgment bring himself
within the rule. The expenses of travelling between Fishguard and Haverfordwest F
are not, however, in my judgment, expenses which the holder of the offices of
obstetrician and anaesthetist at the hospital at Haverfordwest is obliged to incur
by the very fact that he holds those offices. They are not incurred ex necessitate
the office, and accordingly not in my judgment within the rule. The holder of the
offices if he lived in Haverfordwest would not incur them. The travelling expenses
are not expenses imposed on each holder of those offices ex necessitate of the G
offices, but personal to the taxpayer himself because he happens to live, or chooses
to live, fifteen miles away from the hospital at Haverfordwest. Whatever duties
he performs at Fishguard or travelling between Fishguard and Haverfordwest he
does not perform ex necessitate of his office or have to perform them there.

Taking the view I do it is not necessary for me to consider as a separate question H
whether the expenses satisfy the further additional test of being incurred " in
the performance of the duties of the office ". I am very sorry for the taxpayer in
this case, but the words of the statute are, as has often been pointed out, very
rigid. The commissioners in my view clearly came to a wrong conclusion as a
matter of law, and I must allow the appeal.

Appeal allowed. I

Solicitors: *Solicitor of Inland Revenue*; *Le Brasseur & Oakley* (for the taxpayer).

[*Reported by* F. A. AMIES, ESQ., *Barrister-at-Law.*]

---

(2) [1926] A.C. 1; 10 Tax Cas. 118.
(3) [1925] 1 K.B. at pp. 735, 736; 10 Tax Cas. at p. 128.

A

NOTE.

APPAH v. MONSEU.

[Queen's Bench Division (Swanwick, J.), April 21, 1967.]

B

Costs—Security for costs—" Plaintiff ordinarily resident out of the jurisdiction "
—Action for breach of promise of marriage—Plaintiff a Ghanaian national
resident in England since 1956—Plaintiff stated intention to return to Ghana
if suitable employment available—Security sought on re-trial of action—
Court not satisfied that plaintiff ordinarily resident out of jurisdiction—
R.S.C., Ord. 23, r. 1 (1) (a).

C

[As to when security for costs may be ordered, see 30 Halsbury's Laws
(3rd Edn.) 378-380, para. 706, text and note (e); and for cases on the subject,
see Digest (Practice) 909-911, *4496-4520*.]

Cases referred to:

D

Jelic v. Co-operative Press, Ltd., [1947] 2 All E.R. 767; 2nd Digest Supp.
Lewis v. Lewis, [1956] 1 All E.R. 375; [1956] 1 W.L.R. 200; Digest (Cont.
    Vol. A) 240, *1024b*.
Macrae v. Macrae, [1949] 2 All E.R. 34; [1949] P. 397; [1949] L.J.R. 1671;
    113 J.P. 342; 27 Digest (Repl.) 693, *6629*.

Interlocutory application.

E

This was an application for security for costs in an action for damages for
breach of promise of marriage brought by Miss Mercy Ogoniwa Appah, a citizen
of Ghana, against the defendant, Monsieur Guy Monseu, a Belgian doctor. The
application for security for costs was made by the defendant. The plaintiff
had been resident in England since 1956 and (according to the pleadings) was
working as, inter alia, a free-lance broadcaster. The action was tried before
John Stephenson, J., and a jury on Mar. 2, 3, 6, 7, 8 and 9, 1967. The jury

F

were unable to agree on a verdict and, the parties being unwilling in all the
circumstances to accept a majority verdict, a re-trial was ordered. The plaintiff
appeared in person both at the trial and on the applications subsequently made
to Paull, J., with a view to fixing the date for the re-trial, on one of which
occasions she remarked that at the conclusion of the proceedings she had an
intention of returning to Ghana. In an affidavit now before the court on the

G

present application of the defendant (under R.S.C., Ord. 23, r. 1 (1) (a)*) for
security for costs of the re-trial, the plaintiff stated in effect that what she intended
to do (dependent, the court presumed, to some extent on the outcome of the
case) was to make some enquiries to see whether a suitable position in Ghana
would be available and whether she could return there, and if so, whether she
could obtain a booking with a shipping company; the booking of a passage

H

would probably take a considerable time.

Cyril W. F. Newman for the defendant.
The plaintiff appeared in person.

SWANWICK, J., having stated the nature of the application and having

I

reviewed the course of events consequent on the disagreement of the jury,
as summarised supra, continued: The application is made by the defendant
under R.S.C., Ord. 23, r. 1 (1) (a), on the ground " that the plaintiff

---

* R.S.C., Ord. 23, r. 1 (1) provides, so far as material: " Where, on the application
of a defendant to an action or other proceeding in the High Court, it appears to the
court—(a) that the plaintiff is ordinarily resident out of the jurisdiction, . . . then if,
having regard to all the circumstances of the case, the court thinks it just to do so,
it may order the plaintiff to give such security for the defendant's costs of the action
or other proceedings as it thinks just."

is ordinarily resident out of the jurisdiction ". It is supported by his affidavit A
in which he testifies to a statement that the plaintiff made and further to various
facts (to which I need not refer in detail) suggesting that the plaintiff is in financial
difficulties, or at least in a very weak financial position, and that solicitors
applied successfully to be taken off the record because she had not been able to
meet her commitments with regard to costs to them. It is also suggested that
she is unlikely to succeed in this action; and it is submitted to me that there is B
hardship on the defendant in this case, who is a Belgian doctor, who has since
married someone else, and is a man of some means but comparatively limited
means.

The first question is whether the defendant brings himself within the terms of
R.S.C., Ord. 23, r. 1 (1) (a), on the ground "that the plaintiff is ordinarily resident
out of the jurisdiction ". I have been referred, in particular, to two authorities. C
The first of those is *Jelic* v. *Co-operative Press, Ltd.* (1) which was decided in the
Court of Appeal. That case dealt with a rule that was in slightly different terms,
different in this respect, that it read (2):

"A plaintiff ordinarily resident out of the jurisdiction may be ordered
to give security for costs, though he may be temporarily resident within the
jurisdiction."   D

That rule expressly distinguished between somebody ordinarily resident and
somebody temporarily resident out of the jurisdiction. This express distinction
has not been repeated in the present rule, but it is urged that the words " ordinarily resident " retain the same meaning. In *Jelic's* case (1), it was held that a
foreigner who had been in England for two years and did not intend to leave E
could be held to be ordinarily resident in England and not merely temporarily
resident.

The other relevant authority to which I was referred is *Lewis* v. *Lewis* (3),
which was decided on a very narrow point in the divorce jurisdiction by WILLMER,
J., the question being whether a wife, who had left Australia and embarked on
a vessel in order to come to England to live permanently there, could be said to F
have started her ordinary residence in England at the time she set foot on the
ship rather than the time she set foot on the shore, and it was held that she could.
It was a very special matter; but a passage was quoted from the judgment of
SOMERVELL, L.J., in the case of *Macrae* v. *Macrae* (4), in which he said that
ordinary residence could be changed in a day, and that when somebody cut his
connexion with a place, such as by disposing of his house, and made arrangements to have his home somewhere else, and there were indications that the place G
to which he moved was the place at which he intended to make his home for an
indefinite period, then as from that date he was ordinarily resident in that place.

I do not think that either of those authorities specifically covers the position
which has arisen in this case. This is that the plaintiff has been resident in
England since 1956, and that, although she is minded to leave this country at H
the conclusion of this case, that is somewhat of a provisional decision depending
on whether she can obtain suitable employment in Ghana, presumably at a
suitable wage, and can make arrangements to go back there. I am not satisfied,
in those circumstances, that it can be said, according to the wording of R.S.C.,
Ord. 23, r. 1 (1) (a), " that the plaintiff is ordinarily resident out of the jurisdiction ". Those words are in the present tense; I am not satisfied that she is I
ordinarily resident out of the jurisdiction. If, however, I am wrong about that,
it still would remain a matter of discretion for me.

The whole of the trial has taken place in circumstances in which the position
of the plaintiff and her intentions at the conclusion of the case could have been

(1) [1947] 2 All E.R. 767.
(2) The rule referred to, R.S.C., Ord. 65, r. 6A, was revoked by the R.S.C. (Revision)
1962 and re-enacted in different form in R.S.C., Ord. 23, r. 1 (1) (a).
(3) [1956] 1 All E.R. 375.
(4) [1949] 2 All E.R. 34 at p. 36; [1949] P. 397 at p. 403.

A investigated had it been thought fit, and only at this stage, and because, as an unrepresented person, she makes a chance remark in the course of an application to PAULL, J., is this point now seized on. I have considered the whole of the circumstances: I have considered the question of the position of the defendant and the position of the plaintiff and, although I realise that there may be hardships, yet, having the discretion that I have, I do not think that it would be
B right in the circumstances of this case, that I should order security. The application is therefore refused.

Application dismissed.

Solicitors: *Simmonds, Church, Rackham & Co.* (for the defendant).

[*Reported by* K. DIANA PHILLIPS, *Barrister-at-Law.*]

C

LUSH (Inspector of Taxes) *v.* COLES.

[CHANCERY DIVISION (Stamp, J.), March 2, 3, 8, 1967.]

Income Tax—Income—Bounty—Civil Defence Corps—"Public revenue"—Bounty paid to members of Civil Defence Corps out of local authority funds—Local authority being partly reimbursed from central government funds—
D *Whether bounty paid out of public revenue and thus exempted from tax by the Income Tax Act,* 1952 (15 *&* 16 *Geo.* 6 *c.* 6 *&* 1 *Eliz.* 2 *c.* 10), *s.* 457 (4).

Considered in CALDICOTT v VARTY [1976] 3 All ER 329

The taxpayer was a member of the Civil Defence Corps set up as a Civil Defence force for Great Britain, a Crown service, pursuant to the Civil Defence Act, 1948 and a warrant of the designated Secretary of State. The corps consisted of volunteers enrolled by the Secretary of State or by
E authorities or persons authorised by him, and was organised in local divisions by local authorities under his direction. The taxpayer was a member of class A, which consisted of members who had undertaken to serve for a period of three years and to perform duties by way of advanced training or otherwise. He had become entitled as a member of officer rank to a bounty of £15 for 1963-64 in return for undertaking to perform those duties for at
F least forty-five hours in the aggregate, the bounty being paid by the local authority, who were reimbursed a fixed proportion by the government. He was assessed to income tax on the £15 under Sch. E to the Income Tax Act, 1952, but claimed exemption on the grounds that it was paid in consideration of training as a member of the reserve and auxiliary forces of the Crown.

Held: the taxpayer was assessable to tax in respect of the bounty because
G it was not paid "out of the public revenue" within the meaning of those words in the exempting provision, s. 457 (4)* of the Income Tax Act, 1952, as public revenue connoted the public revenues of the kingdom and not the receipts of a local authority (see p. 587, letter I, to p. 588, letter A, and p. 588, letter C, post).

Semble: the Civil Defence Corps may be one of the reserve and auxiliary
H forces of the Crown within s. 457 (4) (see p. 587, letter H, post).

Appeal allowed.

[As to the exemption from income tax of sums payable as bounty to members of reserve and auxiliary forces, see 20 HALSBURY'S LAWS (3rd Edn.) 353, para. 647; and for cases on deductions in computing income of officers of the armed forces, see 28 DIGEST (Repl.) 245, *1082, 1083*.

I For the Civil Defence Act, 1948, see 26 HALSBURY'S STATUTES (2nd Edn.) 450.

For the Consolidated Fund Act, 1816, see 21 HALSBURY'S STATUTES (2nd Edn.) 31; and for the Public Revenue and Consolidated Fund Charges Act, 1854, s. 1, see ibid., 148.

For the Income Tax Act, 1952, s. 457 (4), see 31 HALSBURY'S STATUTES (2nd Edn.) 434; and for s. 17 of the Finance Act, 1962, see 42 ibid., 357.]

Case Stated.

The taxpayer, John William Coles, appealed to the General Commissioners of

---

* Section 457 (4) is set out at p. 587, letter C, post.

Income Tax for Kettering, Northamptonshire, against a further assessment of **A**
£15 in respect of a civil defence bounty made on him for 1963-64 under Sch. E
to the Income Tax Act, 1952. The question for determination was whether a
Civil Defence Corps bounty of £15, which the taxpayer as a senior officer of class
A of the Civil Defence Corps had qualified to receive for training during a year,
was exempt from the charge under Sch. E by the terms of s. 457 (4) of the Income
Tax Act, 1952. The commissioners decided that the Civil Defence Corps was a **B**
reserve and auxiliary force of the Crown within the meaning of s. 457 (4) and that
the bounty came within the subsection and was accordingly not to be regarded
as income for any tax purposes. They therefore discharged the assessment. The
Crown appealed by way of Case Stated to the High Court.

J. R. Phillips for the Crown.
The taxpayer appeared in person.   **C**

Cur. adv. vult.

Mar. 8. **STAMP, J.**: This is an appeal brought by the inspector of taxes
by way of Case Stated under s. 64 of the Income Tax Act, 1952, against a decision
of the General Commissioners for the Kettering division of Northamptonshire,
whereby an assessment to income tax under Sch. E for 1963-64 on the taxpayer, **D**
Mr. John William Coles, in the sum of £15, was discharged. The sum of £15 was
a sum which Mr. Coles received as a Civil Defence Corps bounty. The question
for determination is whether that sum so received is by the effect of s. 457 (4)
of the Income Tax Act, 1952, exempt from income tax. Although the amount
is small, the case affects a very considerable number of people who loyally give
their service to the Civil Defence Corps.

The Civil Defence Corps was set up pursuant to the provisions of the Civil **E**
Defence Act, 1948, and a warrant (1) of the designated Secretary of State as a
Civil Defence force for Great Britain. Civil defence is conveniently described in
some notes, appended to the Stated Case, issued under the aegis of the Home
Office and the Scottish Home Department, as the defence of the country by any
means short of military action against the effects of hostile attack (2). The Civil **F**
Defence Corps consists of volunteers enrolled by the Secretary of State or by such
authorities or persons as he may authorise to act, local divisions of the corps being
organised by local authorities under his direction and the conditions of service
being such as he may from time to time promulgate. By the effect of the Civil
Defence Corps (Organisation and Bounty) Warrant 1962, (3) every member of the
Civil Defence Corps other than a recruit shall be a member of class A or class B, **G**
or of the reserve of the corps. Eligibility for service in class A or class B is that
the person concerned shall either have passed a test or tests approved by the
Secretary of State or hold a senior officer rank. Paragraph 3 of the warrant of
1962 provides that class A of the corps shall consist of eligible members of the
corps who: (a) have undertaken to serve therein for a period of three years and
to perform duties by way of advanced training or otherwise, and (b) have been **H**
accepted for service therein by the Secretary of State.

By para. 10 of the warrant of 1962 it is provided, under the cross-heading
" Bounty ", as follows:

" 10 (1) Where a member of class A of the corps on undertaking to serve
therein for a period of three years, further undertook to perform such duties
as are mentioned in para. 3 of this warrant and required of him for at least **I**
forty-five hours, in the aggregate, in each year of that period, then, on
completion of each of those years, he shall be entitled to a bounty, if, in the
year in question, he performed all the duties required of him or performed

(1) The Civil Defence Corps Warrant, 1949; 4 HALSBURY'S STATUTORY INSTRUMENTS
(First Re-Issue) 73.
(2) Compare the definition in s. 9 (1) of the Act of 1948; see 26 HALSBURY'S STATUTES
(2nd Edn.) 457.
(3) The warrant was published in the London Gazette for Oct. 19, 1962, and is
summarised in 4 HALSBURY'S STATUTORY INSTRUMENTS (First Re-Issue) 120.

A   duties required of him for at least forty-five hours in the aggregate.

" (2) The amount of the bounty shall be: (a) in the case of a member holding a junior or senior officer rank on the completion of the year in question £15."

Paragraph 10 then goes on to specify the amount of bounty receivable in other cases. The taxpayer, having duly qualified under para. 10 (1) and (2) (a), received
B   a bounty of £15, and this is the amount which was assessed for tax on him under Sch. E for the year 1963-64, and this is the assessment to which I have referred and which is the subject of this appeal. Section 457 (4) of the Income Tax Act, 1952, is in the following terms:

" The sums known as training expenses allowances payable out of the
C   public revenue to members (whether men or women) of the reserve and auxiliary forces of the Crown, and the sums payable by way of bounty out of the public revenue to such members in consideration of their undertaking prescribed training and attaining a prescribed standard of efficiency shall not be treated as income for any income tax purposes."

Section 457 contains something of a hotchpot of provisions exempting from
D   income tax various payments made to members of the forces of the Crown formerly contained in several sections of earlier Finance Acts. Subsection (4) itself is taken directly from, and is a re-enactment of, s. 27 of the Finance Act, 1947, which it is to be observed came into operation at a time before the Civil Defence Corps had come into being. The present sub-s. (4) is in terms identical with s. 27 of the Act of 1947, subject only to the omission of a comma which
E   appears in the earlier section—an omission which leaves another comma oddly placed, but appears not to affect the meaning of the exempting provision.

For the purposes of this appeal it is common ground, first, that the sums known as " training expenses allowances " referred to in the first limb of sub-s. (4) are not paid to members of the Civil Defence Corps; second, that the Civil Defence Corps is a Crown service; third, that the civil defence bounties are paid out of
F   local authority funds, the local authority being reimbursed a fixed proportion of them out of, to use a neutral expression, central government funds; and, fourth, that the bounties paid to members of the Civil Defence Corps are payable " in consideration of their undertaking prescribed training and attaining a prescribed standard of efficiency " as specified in the second limb of the subsection.

On behalf of the Crown it was submitted that the Civil Defence Corps is not
G   one of " the reserve and auxiliary forces of the Crown " referred to in sub-s. (4). In the ordinary meaning of the English language, so it is said, the word " force " implies an armed body of men, and a reference in a statute to the forces of the Crown is a reference, so it is urged, to the armed forces of the Crown which the Civil Defence Corps is not. A number of statutes in which the word " force " was used with the latter significance were called to my attention. Further, it is said
H   that a reserve force and an auxiliary force means a reserve or auxiliary force of the armed forces of the Crown. The Civil Defence Corps is, so the argument runs, neither a reserve nor an auxiliary force, for it is autonomous and separate. It is, in my judgment at least, doubtful whether these contentions are in general well-founded. I would have thought that in an appropriate context a force of the Crown might well comprehend a force which is not an armed force, and it is not
I   in my view an abuse of the English language to describe the police as a force. Again, in an appropriate context the expression " reserve and auxiliary forces " might well be used to comprehend an unarmed, autonomous force separate altogether from the armed forces, but held behind the armed forces as a defence to defend or protect the population and property of the realm from the worst consequences of the piercing of the first or earlier lines of defence, or a force whose duty was to act in a capacity auxiliary to that of the armed forces.

I, however, prefer not to decide the case on those grounds, because the further or alternative contention of the Crown that these civil defence bounties are not

payable " out of the public revenue " and are accordingly not within the **A**
contemplation of the subsection is in my judgment correct.

It was submitted by the taxpayer that the expression " out of the public
revenue " was wide enough to include payments made by a local authority out
of its funds subject in part to reimbursement out of central government funds.
In my judgment this latter submission is not well-founded.   " The public
revenue " is an ancient term of art dating at least from the year 1816 when by **B**
the Consolidated Fund Act, 1816 (56 Geo. 3 c. 98) all the public revenues of Great
Britain and Ireland " were consolidated into one Consolidated Fund of the
United Kingdom ".   The expression " public revenue " then became the natural
way of describing all the public revenues, and my attention has been directed
to the Public Revenue and Consolidated Fund Charges Act, 1854 (17 & 18 Vict.
c. 94), whereby certain charges and payments therein referred to were described **C**
as " charged on or made payable out of the several branches of the public
revenue ".   The expression " the public revenue " is also used by text-book
writers to describe, and in my judgment signifies, the public revenues of the
kingdom, and not the receipts or revenues of a local authority.   Money which is
payable by a local authority out of its funds cannot in my judgment be appropriately described as " payable out of the public revenue ", and it can in my **D**
judgment make no difference that the local authority receives reimbursement of
the money either in whole or in part out of the public revenue.

My attention was called to the fact that in sub-ss. (1), (2) and (5) of s. 457, which
re-enact s. 30 (1) of the Finance Act, 1946, s. 28 of the Finance Act, 1947, and
s. 24 of the Finance Act, 1951, respectively, there is the use of the expression
" out of moneys provided by Parliament ".   The argument is that those words **E**
are used in contradistinction to the description " out of the public revenue "
which must accordingly receive a wider significance.   There is, however, no evidence
that there were at the date in 1947 when the forerunner of sub-s. (4) was
introduced into the Income Tax Acts any " training expenses allowances " or
" bounties " payable otherwise than out of the funds of the central government,
which militates against the view that the words " out of the public revenue " **F**
were used to embrace a wider class of payments.   It may well be that the two
expressions used in the subsections have a different significance, but in each of the
subsections which speak of " moneys provided by Parliament " that phrase is
used in relation to sums payable under schemes " out of moneys provided by
Parliament "; and I would assume until the contrary was shown, which it was
not, that the schemes themselves referred to the moneys payable thereunder as **G**
provided, or to be provided, " out of moneys provided by Parliament ", and that
is in my judgment a sufficient explanation of the difference between the expression
" out of the public revenue " and " out of moneys provided by Parliament ".
Moreover, since the Civil Defence Corps was not constituted until after 1947, it
is not surprising that Parliament in that year should have used language
inappropriate to cover bounties payable to members of that corps. **H**

This concludes the matter in favour of the Crown, and it is not necessary for
me to consider whether in truth the payments by way of bounty to members of
the Civil Defence Corps can properly be described as payable in consideration of
their undertaking prescribed training and attaining a prescribed standard of
efficiency within the meaning of sub-s. (4), or whether the whole expression " in
consideration of their undertaking prescribed training and attaining a prescribed **I**
standard of efficiency " can be construed as providing for two alternative qualifications.   I am extremely sorry for the taxpayer in this case, but I must allow the
appeal and the assessment must be restored.

Appeal allowed.

Solicitor: *Solicitor of Inland Revenue.*

[*Reported by* F. A. AMIES, ESQ., *Barrister-at-Law*].

A   **Re CROYDON DEVELOPMENT PLANS 1954 and 1959.**
    HARRISON v. LONDON BOROUGH OF CROYDON.

[CHANCERY DIVISION (Pennycuick, J.), March 7, 8, 1967.]

*Declaration—Jurisdiction—Hypothetical question—Basis of assessing compensa-
tion for compulsory acquisition of land—Whether planning permission might*
B   *reasonably have been expected to be granted—Question of factual nature,
not question of construction—Absence of jurisdiction—Originating summons
set aside—Exclusivity of jurisdiction of Lands Tribunal over disputes as to
compensation—Land Compensation Act, 1961 (9 & 10 Eliz. 2 c. 23), s.
16 (3) (b).*

The plaintiff owned properties in respect of which the defendant London
C   Borough of Croydon had made a compulsory purchase order that had been
duly confirmed. Notice to treat was given on Apr. 30, 1965, and the assessment of compensation had been referred to the Lands Tribunal. By virtue
of s. 16 (3) (b)* of the Land Compensation Act, 1961, if land was allocated
on the current development plan to two or more uses, it was to be assumed,
when assessing compensation, that planning permission would be granted
D   for any development for which it might reasonably be expected to be
granted. The land in question was marked on the development plan as
"primarily for shopping and other business". The plaintiff applied by
originating summons for declaratory relief to determine whether compensation should be assessed on the assumption that planning permission would
have been granted in respect of the land for office development. A govern-
E   ment White Paper, published on Nov. 4, 1964, indicated that land within
the metropolitan area should not be used for office development except in
certain conditions. On Aug. 5, 1965, the Control of Office and Industrial
Development Act 1965 was enacted; this was retrospective to Nov. 5, 1964,
as regards the metropolitan region. The defendant borough sought to have
the originating summons set aside on the ground that the court had not
F   jurisdiction to deal with the matters that it raised. It was not contested
that under s. 1† of the Act of 1961 disputes as to compensation were determinable by the tribunal and that as regards compensation the jurisdiction
of the court was excluded.‡

Held: the question raised by the summons, whether on Apr. 30, 1965,
planning permission might have been expected to be granted for office
G   development, was not a question of construction but was a hypothetical
question of a factual nature constituting one of the factors to be taken
into account by the tribunal in assessing compensation; and accordingly
the summons did not raise any issue determinable by the court and would
be set aside (see p. 591, letter I, and p. 592, letter H, post).

[As to what questions are determinable on originating summons, and as to
H   future questions, see 30 HALSBURY'S LAWS (3rd Edn.) 304, para. 559 note (q);
and for cases on the subject, see DIGEST (Practice) 709-711, *3040-3055.*

As to the jurisdiction of the Lands Tribunal to determine compensation on
compulsory acquisition of land, see 10 HALSBURY'S LAWS (3rd Edn.) 169, 170,
paras. 293, 294, and p. 228, para. 424.

For the Land Compensation Act, 1961, s. 1, s. 14, s. 16, see 41 HALSBURY'S
I   STATUTES (2nd Edn.) 44, 57, 60.]

Procedure Summons.

The plaintiff, Florence Louisa Harrison, applied by originating summons
dated Dec. 29, 1966, for the determination of the question whether on the true
construction of the Land Compensation Act, 1961, and the words "Central
area primarily for shopping and other business" as marked on the Croydon

---

* Section 16 (3) is set out at p. 590, letter I, to p. 591, letter B, post.
† Section 1 is set out at p. 590, letter G, post.
‡ See p. 591, letter G, post.

development plan dated June 19, 1954, as amended by the Croydon development **A**
plan first quinquennial review dated 1959, it was to be assumed for the purpose
of assessing compensation payable on the compulsory acquisition of the plaintiff's
land (within the said central area) in accordance with the Croydon (East-West
Flyover) Compulsory Purchase Order 1963, that planning permission would be
granted in respect of the land for office development.   The defendants, the
London Borough of Croydon, applied by summons dated Jan. 19, 1967, for the **B**
originating summons to be set aside on the ground that the court had no jurisdiction to deal with the matters raised therein.   The facts are set out in the
judgment.   The cases noted below* were cited during the argument.

 A. P. Fletcher and *R. P. Ground* for the applicant corporation.
 K. R. Bagnall for the plaintiff.

 PENNYCUICK, J.:   I have before me a summons on the part of the **C**
London Borough of Croydon, which is the defendant in the present matter,
seeking an order that the originating summons itself be set aside on the ground
that the court has no jurisdiction to deal with the matters raised therein.

 The originating summons is issued by Miss Florence Louisa Harrison as
plaintiff, the borough being the defendant.   The summons is intituled:

 " In the matter of the Land Compensation Act, 1961, and In the Matter **D**
 of the Croydon Development Plan dated June 19, 1954, and In the matter
 of the Croydon Development Plan First Quinquennial Review dated 1959
 and In the matter of numbers 2 to 12 (even numbers) Sheldon Street, 60 to
 69 (inclusive) Wendle Street, and 21 to 29 (odd numbers) Scarbrook Street
 in the London Borough of Croydon and In the matter of the Croydon
 (East-West Flyover) Compulsory Purchase Order 1963." **E**

 The facts, so far as now material, may be stated very shortly.   The plaintiff,
Miss Harrison, is the owner of the properties mentioned in the title to the summons.
The corporation has made a compulsory purchase order in respect of those
properties, and that order has been duly confirmed.   Notice to treat was given
on Apr. 30, 1965, and the matter of compensation has been referred to the **F**
Lands Tribunal.   The question at issue between the plaintiff and the corporation
is the basis on which compensation is to be assessed.   I need read only two or
three sections in the Land Compensation Act, 1961, in order to make the issue
raised by the present summons intelligible.   Section 1 reads as follows:

 " Where by or under any statute (whether passed before or after the
 passing of this Act) land is authorised to be acquired compulsorily, any **G**
 question of disputed compensation and, where any part of the land to be
 acquired is subject to a lease which comprises land not acquired, any question
 as to the apportionment of the rent payable under the lease, shall be referred
 to the Lands Tribunal and shall be determined by the tribunal in accordance
 with the following provisions of this Act."

Section 14 (1) reads as follows: **H**

 " For the purpose of assessing compensation in respect of any compulsory
 acquisition, such one or more of the assumptions mentioned in s. 15 and
 s. 16 of this Act as are applicable to the relevant land or any part thereof
 shall be made in ascertaining the value of the relevant interest."

Section 16 (3) reads as follows:

 " If the relevant land or any part thereof (not being land subject to com- **I**
 prehensive development) consists or forms part of an area shown in the

* *Wolverhampton New Waterworks Co.* v. *Hawkesford,* (1859), 6 C.B.N.S. 336; *Gas-*
light and Coke Co. v. *Holloway,* (1885), 52 L.T. 434; *Barraclough* v. *Brown,* [1895-99] All
E.R. Rep. 239;   [1897] A.C. 615;   *Barwick* v. *South Eastern and Chatham Ry. Cos.,*
[1921] 1 K.B. 187;   *Pyx Granite Co., Ltd.* v. *Ministry of Housing and Local Government,*
[1959] 3 All E.R. 1;   [1960] A.C. 260;   *Re Purkiss' Application,* [1962] 2 All E.R. 690;
Punton v. *Ministry of Pensions and National Insurance (No. 2),* [1964] 1 All E.R. 448;
Angosam Finance Co., Ltd. v. *Oxby,* [1964] 1 All E.R. 791;   [1965] Ch. 390;   *Mount-*
garret v. *Claro Water Board,* (1964), 15 P. & C.R. 53; *Re Rowton Houses, Ltd.'s Leases,*
[1966] 3 All E.R. 996.

A   current development plan as an area allocated primarily for a range of two
     or more uses specified in the plan in relation to the whole of that area, it shall
     be assumed that planning permission would be granted, in respect of the rele-
     vant land or that part thereof, as the case may be, for any development
     which—(a) is development for the purposes of a use of the relevant land or
     that part thereof, being a use falling within that range of uses, and (b) is
B   development for which planning permission might reasonably have been
     expected to be granted in respect of the relevant land or that part thereof,
     as the case may be."

     In the present case the properties in question are not land " subject to compre-
     hensive development " but they form part of an area shown in the current
     development plan as under the description " central area primarily for shopping
C   and other business ".

     The present summons asks this question:

        " Whether on the true construction of the Land Compensation Act, 1961,
     and the words ' central area primarily for shopping and other business ' as
     marked on the Croydon Development Plan dated June 19, 1954, as amended
     by the Croydon Development Plan First Quinquennial Review dated
D   1959 it is to be assumed—for the purpose of assessing compensation payable
     on the compulsory acquisition of the plaintiff's land (within the said central
     area) in accordance with the Croydon (East-West Flyover) Compulsory
     Purchase Order 1963—that planning permission would be granted in respect
     of the said land for office development."

E   It will be seen that that question is related to s. 16 (3) of the Act of 1961, the
     question being whether development for office purposes is development " for
     which planning permission might reasonably have been expected to be granted in
     respect of " the properties.

     I should mention one other matter. The government published a White Paper
     on Nov. 4, 1964, indicating an intention that land within the metropolitan area
F   should not be used for office development, except in certain conditions. That
     White Paper was published before the notice to treat. That notice was given,
     as I have stated, on Apr. 30, 1965. Subsequently on Aug. 5, 1965, there was
     enacted the Control of Office and Industrial Development Act 1965, which is
     expressed by s. 3, as regards the metropolitan region, to be retrospective to Nov.
     5, 1964.

G   The corporation now seeks to have the whole summons set aside on the ground
     that the court has no jurisdiction to deal with the matters raised by it. It is not
     in dispute that under s. 1 of the Land Compensation Act, 1961, the determination
     of disputed compensation is entrusted to the Lands Tribunal, and as regards
     the amount of compensation the jurisdiction of the court is excluded. Counsel
     for the plaintiff, however, contends that s. 16 (3) raises an issue which can and
H   should be determined by the court.

     It then becomes necessary to consider exactly what is the nature of the question
     raised by the summons. The question is not one of construction of the Act of 1961
     itself, so far as I can see; nor certainly is it a question of construction of the
     words " primarily for shopping and other business " contained in the develop-
     ment plan. The question is whether, if there had been no compulsory purchase
I   of the properties, development for office purposes is one for which planning
     permission might reasonably have been expected to be granted on Apr. 30,
     1965. If there had in fact been no compulsory purchase it is perfectly clear
     that this court would not have answered such a question, on the ground that the
     question was hypothetical and on the ground that the question did not raise
     any justiciable issue between the plaintiff and the corporation. Those two
     grounds run into one another.

     In fact, having regard to the compulsory purchase order, there is no question
     of planning permission being actually granted in respect of the properties. The

significance of the question raised by the summons, as appears from the words **A**
of the summons, lies wholly in the effect of the answer to the question as a
factor in the assessment of compensation. It seems to me that this circumstance
so far from rendering the question one which this court should answer is another
and conclusive reason why the court should not answer it. Indeed, the court
has no jurisdiction to do so. Any question of disputed compensation falls, under
s. 1 of the Act of 1961, within the exclusive jurisdiction of the Lands Tribunal, **B**
and it cannot, it seems to me, be open to the court to determine in isolation one
factor in the computation of the compensation.

Counsel for the plaintiff contended that the originating summons seeks a
declaratory judgment within the terms of R.S.C. Ord., 15, r. 16. It seems to me
that the summons does not seek a declaratory judgment on anything but a
hypothetical question, the sole significance of the answer to that question being **C**
concerned with the amount of the compensation.

Counsel for the plaintiff then said that the summons raises a question as to
the basis legal principle on which compensation is to be assessed. He said that
the question is the effect of s. 16 (3) in the light of the circumstances which
existed at the date of the notice to treat. So far as I can see there is no question
of law raised by the summons. The question is not one on the construction of **D**
s. 16 but of what might have been expected to happen had there not been a
compulsory purchase order. That is in the nature of a hypothetical question of
fact.

Counsel for the plaintiff contended that the question raised by the summons is
analogous to a question of title, and he pointed out that a question of title will
certainly be answered by the court. It seems to me, however, that this is not a **E**
true analogy. The present question concerns the amount of compensation. A
question of title concerns the person to whom the compensation is to be paid and
does not, except perhaps indirectly, concern the amount of the compensation.

Counsel for the plaintiff raised what he expressed to be a subsidiary question
of law. That question resulted from the order of events which I have mentioned,
namely the issue of the White Paper before and the passing of the Act of 1965 **F**
after the date of the notice to treat. The question is, he says, should one ignore
the existence of the White Paper as at the date of the notice to treat? It seems
to me, however, that this is simply a factor which has to be taken into account
in answering the hypothetical question raised by s. 16 (3), i.e., might it reasonably
have been expected that at the date of the notice to treat planning permission
for office development would have been granted. **G**

I was referred to a number of authorities in which the court has or has not
regarded its jurisdiction as being excluded by the terms of a particular statute.
It seems to me that none of those cases has any direct bearing on the present
case and that it would not be useful for me to cite them.

I conclude that the question raised by this summons is simply a hypothetical
question constituting one of the factors which must be taken into account by **H**
the Lands Tribunal in determining the amount of the compensation, and that the
summons raises no issue which should or can be determined by this court.

It is worth mentioning in conclusion that there is an appeal from the Lands
Tribunal on any question of law (1), so that if the plaintiff considers that the
tribunal misdirects itself in any respect in the assessment of compensation then
the plaintiff will have a remedy by way of appeal from the decision of the tribunal. **I**

I propose accordingly to make an order setting aside the originating summons.

Order accordingly.

Solicitors: *Sharpe, Pritchard & Co.*, agents for *Town Clerk*, Croydon (for the
applicant corporation); *Woolley & Whitfield* (for the plaintiff).

[*Reported by* JENIFER SANDELL, *Barrister-at-Law.*]

(1) See the Lands Tribunal Act, 1949, s. 3 (4); 28 HALSBURY'S STATUTES (2nd Edn.)
322; and R.S.C., Ord. 61, r. 1.

A   SMITH (*formerly* WESTWOOD) *v.* NATIONAL COAL BOARD.

[HOUSE OF LORDS (Lord Reid, Lord Hodson, Lord Guest, Lord Pearce and
Lord Upjohn), April 12, 13, 17, 18, May 23, 1967.]

B   *Mine—Railway above ground—Bank of spoil placed less than three feet from
track—Loose material on route for shunter going in course of duty from one
point to another—Route, formerly safe, obstructed and side of bank sloping
steeply towards track—Shunter not warned—Shunter preceding train, slipped
on bank, fell between railway wagons and was killed—Whether negligence
on part of employers of shunter—Whether shunter " required " in the course
of his duty to pass on foot over that material or between it and the line—
Whether breach of statutory duty—Whether contributory negligence by shunter*
C   *—Coal and Other Mines (Sidings) Order, 1956 (S.I. 1956 No. 1773), Sch.
reg. 20.*

The deceased, who was an experienced shunter employed by the respondents, was walking along a walk-way accompanying a railway train; he was
walking by the side of the track to a point where he was to uncouple wagons
from the train, and, as shunter, was in charge of the wagons. He had his
D   back to the train, which was backing in the direction that he was walking,
and he was preceding the train. After he had gone some twenty to twenty-
five yards the train overtook him; he fell between the second and third
wagons and was killed. The House of Lords inferred that the deceased
had almost reached a point on the walk-way where there was a mound or
bank of loose débris, which had a flat top and a steep slope coming right down
E   to within three feet of the track of rails, that the deceased tried to climb the
slope to escape the train and that he slipped and fell. The mound of débris
was the result of a bulldozing operation carried out by the respondents.
Regulation 20* of the Coal and Other Mines (Ridings) Regulations, 1956,
provided that the manager of a mine should make and secure the efficient
carrying out of arrangements whereby, if material was placed at a distance
F   less than three feet from the track of rails of a line and " any person employed
at the mine is required . . . to pass on foot over that material or between
it and the line ", the material was so placed that he could pass without
being exposed to risk of injury by traffic on the line. By reg. 9† if any
person employed at a mine might be exposed to risk of injury by reason
of vehicles pushed by a locomotive, the person in charge of those vehicles
G   should accompany or precede the leading vehicle. On appeal by the
deceased's widow in an action against the respondents for negligence or
breach of statutory duty,

Held: (i) (LORD GUEST dubitante) the respondents were liable for negligence in that they had allowed a normally safe route to become blocked by
a dangerous obstruction and had not warned those who would be likely to use
H   the route (see p. 595, letter F, p. 597, letter A, p. 598, letter B, p. 600, letter I,
and p. 605, letter H, post; cf., p. 599, letter F, post).

(ii) in reg. 20 of the Coal and Other Mines (Sidings) Regulations, 1956, the
word " required " did not mean " ordered " or " instructed ", and (LORD REID
not deciding on this ground) the respondents were in breach of statutory
duty under reg. 20 because, in the circumstances, the deceased was
I   " required " to use the way which he followed, although he was not ordered
to pass over the bank of débris (see p. 598, letter A, p. 599, letters A and D,
p. 600, letter I, and p. 605, letter F, post; cf., p. 596, letter F, post).

Dictum of LEWIS, J., in *Henaghan* v. *Rederiet Forangirene* ([1936] 2 All
E.R. at p. 1433) applied.

(iii) (LORD HODSON and LORD UPJOHN dissenting) there was contributory

---

* Regulation 20 is printed at p. 596, letters C and D, post.
† Regulation 9, so far as relevant, is set out at p. 597, letter G, post.

negligence on the part of the deceased and his share of responsibility for   **A**
his injury was twenty-five per cent. (see p. 597, letter B, p. 600, letter B,
and p. 602, letter G, post; cf., p. 598, letter F, and p. 605, letter G, post).

Per LORD REID: such regulations as the regulations of 1956 are not
intended to codify the whole common law duties of the employer in the
sphere in which they operate (see p. 596, letter H, post).

Decision of the COURT OF APPEAL (sub nom. *Westwood* v. *National Coal*   **B**
Board [1966] 2 All E.R. 208) reversed.

[As to railway lines above ground at a mine, see 26 HALSBURY'S LAWS (3rd
Edn.) 658, para. 1270.

As to liability for accidents to railway servants, see 31 HALSBURY'S LAWS
(3rd Edn.) 656, para. 1019; and for cases on the subject, see 38 DIGEST (Repl.)   **C**
297-299, *66-76*.

For a summary of the Coal and Other Mines (Sidings) Order, 1956, see 14
HALSBURY'S STATUTORY INSTRUMENTS (First Re-Issue) 89.]

Cases referred to:
   Henaghan v. *Rederiet Forangirene*, [1936] 2 All E.R. 1426; 24 Digest (Repl.)
      1029, *50*.   **D**
   Hutchinson v. *London & North Eastern Ry. Co.*, [1942] 1 All E.R. 330; [1942]
      1 K.B. 481; 111 L.J.K.B. 369; 166 L.T. 228; 38 Digest (Repl.) 297, *68*.

Appeal.

This was an appeal by Kathleen Smith (formerly Westwood) as administratrix
of the estate of her deceased husband, Frank Westwood, from an order of the
Court of Appeal (SELLERS and SALMON, L.JJ., DANCKWERTS, L.J., dissenting)   **E**
dated Feb. 17, 1966, and reported sub nom. *Westwood* v. *National Coal Board*
([1966] 2 All E.R. 208), allowing the appeal of the respondents, the National
Coal Board, from a judgment of BAKER, J., at Leeds Assizes, dated July 12, 1965,
whereby the appellant was awarded damages under the Fatal Accidents Acts,
1846 to 1959, and the Law Reform (Miscellaneous Provisions) Act, 1934, for
personal injuries resulting in the death of the deceased. BAKER, J., found   **F**
that the respondents were negligent at common law and were in breach of their
statutory duty under the Coal and Other Mines (Sidings) Regulations, 1956,
reg. 20. He rejected an allegation of contributory negligence on the part of
the deceased and awarded damages of £5,000 (an agreed amount) in favour
of the appellant. The facts are set out in the opinion of LORD UPJOHN, at
p. 602, letter H, et seq., post.   **G**

P. Stanley Price, Q.C., and *H. G. Bennett* for the appellant.
J. F. S. Cobb, Q.C., and *P. J. M. Kennedy* for the respondents.

Their lordships took time for consideration.

May 23. The following opinions were delivered.

   H

   LORD REID: My Lords, this is an action for damages in respect of the
death of a shunter, Frank Westwood, in the course of his employment by the
respondents at Whitwood Colliery, Yorkshire. On the morning of Apr. 14, 1964,
three wagons in one of the colliery sidings had to be moved to another siding.
These sidings ran east and west fanning out to the east. The wagons were in a
siding to the north of the yard and had to be moved to the south-most siding   **I**
no. 5. The deceased coupled the wagons to a diesel locomotive which pulled
them westwards. Then another man changed points there and the locomotive
pushed the wagons back towards no. 5 line. The deceased meanwhile crossed
the other lines to the points for no. 5 line and made sure that they were set
correctly. The place on no. 5 line where he was to have uncoupled the wagons
was about one hundred yards east of these points. At that time the leading
wagon was a good distance to the west of these points and the train was moving
at seven or eight miles an hour. The deceased walked off in advance of the

A train towards the place where he was to uncouple the wagons. When he had gone some twenty or twenty-five yards, however, the train overtook him and he fell between the second and third wagons and was killed.

The first question is whether the evidence is sufficient to prove how he came to fall between these wagons. The main defence at the trial was that the deceased was not walking in front of the train at all but was "pole riding", and fell from

B his shunter's pole which he was using for that purpose, but that was disproved. The points lever for the no. 5 line was on the south side of it, and the normal route from there to the point where the wagons were to be uncoupled had been by a walk-way on the south side of no. 5 line. The deceased was last seen by the engine driver walking on that walk-way: then the wagons in front of the engine driver interrupted his view. There was a large mound of débris to the south of

C no. 5 line and some time before the accident a bulldozing operation had moved part of this, so that a bank was made with a flat top and a steep slope of loose débris, which came right down to the south side of the line at about the point where the evidence showed that the deceased had fallen between the wagons. It seems to me to be highly probable that the deceased must have almost reached this point when the train overtook him, and he must have tried to mount the bank

D to get out of the way of the train and have slipped and fallen back below the coupling of the second and third wagons. Indeed any other possibility seems to me to be extremely unlikely. If the bank and steep slope had not been there, he would have been quite safe on the old walk-way while the train overtook and passed him. So the presence of the débris displaced by the bulldozer certainly contributed to the accident, and the question is whether this involved negligence

E on the part of the respondents' servants.

An employer, or those for whom he is responsible, must always have in mind not only the careful man but also the man who is inattentive to such a degree as can normally be expected; and it is common experience that, if one is accustomed to pass along a safe route, one may be less attentive than when going where one has not been before. So an employer who allows a normally safe

F route to become blocked by a dangerous obstruction without warning those who may use it will in my view be guilty of negligence, at least unless the obstruction is so obvious that even an inattentive man would notice it in time to avoid danger. If it is not as obvious as that and it contributes to an accident, the man may be guilty of some contributory negligence but some share of the blame must fall on the employer.

G That is I think this case. When the deceased left the no. 5 points it was obvious that there was another equally convenient route open to him. The bank left by the bulldozer tailed off near the points, and the bulldozer had left a broad and easy track over the top of it, which sloped gently up from the points. So the deceased could have walked up this track with safety. The respondents' case is that it was so obvious that this was the proper way to go that no one would

H have expected an experienced shunter to go along the old walk-way; but I am not at all convinced that that was so. This aspect of the case received little attention at the trial. The appellant was concentrating on a regulation to which I shall come later, and the respondents were concentrating on their case that the deceased had been pole riding. None of the admirable photographs produced illustrates this matter clearly, and there is little evidence about it. It may be

I that, if the deceased had looked very carefully, he would have seen that the normal route was impassable some twenty yards ahead of him, though I am not quite sure about that. I cannot, however, hold that he was negligent in starting off on the normal walk-way, or that the respondents were entitled to assume that everyone having occasion to go that way would take the track over the bank.

Before the deceased actually reached the obstruction he must have noticed it. He was then in some difficulty, because there would then be a steep bank of loose material on his right, which he would have to surmount in order to reach the bulldozer track, and he could easily slip on it. He knew that the train was just behind him and his only safe course was to stop and let it pass him. BAKER, J., found that the deceased was not guilty of contributory negligence, largely because he had said " nor is there any evidence that he realised or indeed ought to have realised that the train was upon him ". I cannot agree with that. As shunter he was in charge of the train; he knew roughly where it was; and a man of his experience must have known that it was overtaking him. There was a strong wind, but even so one might think that he would hear it. In my opinion the deceased was negligent in trying to scramble up the bank so near the train, but I do not think that he should be held to have been more than twenty-five per cent. to blame.

The appellant's main case was that the accident had been caused by the respondents' breach of reg. 20 of the Coal and Other Mines (Sidings) Regulations, 1956, (1) which provides:

" 20. The manager of every mine shall make and secure the efficient carry-ing out of arrangements whereby, in every case in which any material is placed (otherwise than on ground ordinarily used for the stocking of material) at a distance less than three feet from the track of rails of a line and any person employed at the mine is required in the course of his duty to pass on foot over that material or between it and the line, that material is so placed in such manner that—(a) every such person can so pass without being exposed to risk of injury by traffic on that line; and (b) if that material extends (whether continuously or not) for a distance exceeding sixty feet measured parallel with that line, there are provided at intervals not greater than sixty feet adequate spaces or recesses in that material."

I have described how the bank of débris extended almost to the actual rail of siding no. 5. The respondents' case is that the deceased was not required to pass over it. In my view " required " does not mean expressly instructed. If a man's duty requires him to be at point A and then to proceed from there to point B, he is required to go from A to B by a reasonable route, and, if there is more than one reasonable route, an employer who gives no directions to the man cannot say that he was not required to go by either: both must be safe. I have already dealt with the choice which the deceased had to make when he left the no. 5 points. If he was not then bound to realise that the old walk-way was unsafe, it was reasonable for him to walk along it at least up to a point, and I think that he was therefore, at least up to that point, " required " to use this route within the meaning of the regulation. When, however, it became obvious that to proceed farther along that route was unsafe, was he still " required " to use it? I would think not, if at that point there was another safe and convenient route still open to him.

This case has been argued on the footing that a regulation such as this is in-tended to codify the whole common law duty of the employer for the sphere in which it operates. I do not think that that is the purpose of such regulations. They prohibit certain specified dangerous practices under penalty; but it often happens that the facts of a particular case do not clearly come within the limited terms of the regulation. In such a case I see no need to strain the words of the regulation. The common law can deal with the case.

This regulation is not at all easy to interpret. It appears to assume that, if a space of three feet from the track of rails of a line is made safe, a person can pass over that space without being exposed to risk of injury by traffic on that line; but it appears that the engine of this train overhangs the line by some two feet, and it is difficult to see how a person passing on the one foot remaining is not exposed to risk of injury. The substance of this regulation goes back at least to 1906 and things may have been different then; but I find it difficult to believe that mere compliance with this regulation will ensure safety to-day.

(1) S.I. 1956 No. 1773; the regulations are set out in a schedule to the Coal and Other Mines (Sidings) Order, 1956.

A   Suppose that a man overtaken by a train moves farther than three feet from the line in order to be well clear of the engine and then slips at a point more than three feet from the line. Does the regulation assist him? That may have happened in the present case. I think it better to decide this case on the common law rather than attempt to deal with these obscurities; but if the regulation does apply, I think that there would still be contributory negligence and the assessment of
B liability would be the same.

    I would allow this appeal and restore the order of BAKER, J., subject to a deduction of twenty-five per cent. from the damages which he awarded.

    LORD HODSON: My Lords, here, as so often in a fatal accident case, there is uncertainty as to the manner in which the deceased met with the accident
C which brought about his death. SELLERS, L.J., in the Court of Appeal (2) found himself unable to find the necessary degree of probability to accept the learned judge's finding how the event happened. DANCKWERTS and SALMON, L.JJ., (3), however, and, as I understand it, all your lordships are prepared to accept the judge's conclusion as being more than conjecture and being based on a high degree of probability. I also accept the conclusion. In my opinion, the essential
D feature of the finding of fact is that it is highly probable that the deceased must have almost reached the point on the walk-way by the side of the no. 5 line where a steep slope of loose débris came right down to the side of the line, when the train which he was accompanying in pursuance of his duty as a shunter overtook him. At this point, I think, he must have tried to climb the bank to escape the train, slipped and fallen between the second and third wagons.

E   The next question which falls to be decided is whether the accident was caused by the respondents' breach of reg. 20 of the Coal and Other Mines (Sidings) Regulations, 1956. [HIS LORDSHIP read reg. 20, which is set out at p. 596, letters C and D, ante, and continued:] I think that the material was placed " at a distance less than three feet from the track " and that the deceased was " required in the course of his duty to pass on foot over that material or between it and the line ".
F The word " required " does not mean specifically ordered, but it does involve that the use of the route was reasonable in proceeding on the journey which the person employed was making.

    The respondents contended that the deceased was not required to pass over the obstruction, as he could easily have reached the destination of his train from the point where he had to adjust the points without going anywhere very near to
G the obstruction. In this connexion I think reg. 9 has a bearing on the case. This regulation reads:

    " 9. In every case in which any person employed at a mine is or might be exposed to risk of injury by reason of the movement on a line of two or more other vehicles pushed by a locomotive, the person in charge of those other vehicles shall—(*a*) accompany or precede the leading vehicle, watch the
H line ahead of it, and give any warning which may be requisite for the purpose of minimising that risk . . .;"

    True that the train which the deceased was accompanying was proceeding at the rate of seven or eight miles an hour, about double the normal walking pace. Nevertheless, I think that he was carrying out a duty covered by reg. 9 and was accordingly " required " to pass the way he did in the sense of the regulation in
I order to accompany or precede his train. Indeed, it is admitted in the defence that the deceased was accompanying the train in the course of his employment. True that the regulation is not easy to construe, for a space of three feet from the track is insufficient to enable a man to pass safely between a running train and stacked material, since a train overlaps the intervening space by $1\frac{1}{2}$ feet in the case of wagons and two feet in the case of the engine.

---

(2) [1966] 2 All E.R. 208 at p. 210
(3) [1966] 2 All E.R. at p. 211, letters B and C; p. 213, letter A.

The fact that the regulation as drawn, appears to be insufficient to provide any   A
adequate means of safety does not, in my opinion, justify the conclusion that it
does not apply to the facts of this case. Concluding, as I do, that the deceased
was " required " to use the way which he followed and that it was obstructed as
described, I think that the breach of regulations is established and this was a
cause of the accident.

I agree with my noble and learned friend, LORD REID, that the finding of   B
negligence at common law is justified by the evidence and having nothing to
add to his opinion on this topic.

I would not, however, impute any contributory negligence to the deceased
himself in the absence of any evidence, as I think, to support such a finding. I
approach the case on the lines followed by LORD GREENE, M.R., in *Hutchinson*
v. *London and North Eastern Ry. Co.* (4). He said: C

"... I do not think it is right, in cases of this kind, where there is a defence
of contributory negligence in an action based on breach of a statutory rule,
designed, as I have said, to protect men as much from their own carelessness
as from anything else, to draw inferences unfavourable to a deceased man
and impute to him all those elements the absence of which would negative   D
any negligence on his part."

I do not think that it is enough to say that the deceased was an experienced and
capable shunter and must have known of the danger of being overtaken by his
train, whether or not the high wind prevented him hearing it approach. All this
is true, but he found himself in a predicament and took a course which on the
face of it does not seem to have been foolhardy or unreasonable. He made for   E
the bank of loose material, failed to retain his foothold because the loose material
gave way and fell under the train. If the bank had not given way, he would have
been able to continue on his way ready to meet the train at the end of its journey.
He was making for his destination in a way which appears to have been the most
direct. I am not prepared to make a finding against him of negligence because
he did not, when he became aware of the danger, stop, lie down or take other   F
action which we now know, or think that we know, would have saved his life.

I would allow the appeal and restore the judgment of BAKER, J.

LORD GUEST: My Lords, there is bound to be a certain amount of speculation as to the precise manner in which an accident happened when a workman
is killed instantaneously in circumstances where there is no eye witness of the   G
occurrence. In this case, however, although no one saw the accident, there is a
certain amount of real evidence which has been conveniently demonstrated on a
plan, and from which it is possible to draw a certain inference. I am not disposed
to differ from the conclusion arrived at by BAKER, J., and concurred in by
DANCKWERTS (5) and SALMON, L.JJ., (6) as to the probable explanation of the
accident, particularly in the absence at this stage of the case of any suggestion   H
by the respondents that the deceased met his death while pole riding. The
explanation given by DANCKWERTS, L.J., (5) is that when the deceased got near
to the point where the space between the bank and the rails narrowed to less than
three feet he must have tried to get up on the bulldozed track which was only
two feet above the level of the rails and slipped on the sloping bank and fallen
between the passing wagons and so met his death.   I

If the accident happened in this manner, it opens the way for the application
of reg. 20 of the Coal and Other Mines (Sidings) Regulations, 1956, and it leaves
only for consideration the question whether the deceased was " required " in
the terms of that regulation " in the course of his duty to pass on foot over that
material " (i.e. material placed at a distance less than three feet from the track

---

(4) [1942] 1 All E.R. 330 at pp. 334, 335; [1942] 1 K.B. 481 at p. 486.
(5) [1966] 2 All E.R. at p. 211, letters B and C.
(6) [1966] 2 All E.R. at p. 213, letter A.

A of rails) " or between it and the line ". The word " required " must take its meaning from the context. It is conceded that it does not mean " ordered " (see *Henaghan* v. *Rederiet Forangirene* (7), per LEWIS, J.), nor do I think that it means that it was a matter of necessity for the workman to pass that way, or that, in other words, there was no other way open to him. There were alternative routes for him to take. He could have proceeded direct from the northern sidings by

B crossing the rails to the reservoir, but it was reasonable for him to proceed to the western end of line no. 5 in order to check the points. He could have proceeded on the opposite side of the line to the mound of material, the left side, but this was not a very convenient approach having regard to the proximity of line no. 4 to line no. 5. He would have had to walk part of the way between the rails of line no. 4 and thereafter his passage would be made difficult by the proximity of the

C projecting sleepers on line no. 4 to the sleepers on line no. 5. On the other hand, the right-hand side of the line in approaching the reservoir was the normal and usual way for shunters to accompany their trains. It was the side out of which the driver of the engine would be looking. The deceased could have surmounted the material by proceeding along the bulldozed track, but this was rough and found by the trial judge to be dangerous to walk on. I am content to adopt the

D test of " required " as being whether it was reasonably incidental to the performance of the deceased's duty as a shunter. So judged, my view is that the deceased was " required " in the terms of reg. 20. Whether, in fact, he was fulfilling a statutory duty under reg. 9 by accompanying or preceding the train is not to the point, if what he was doing was reasonably incidental with the performance of his duties as a shunter. For these reasons I have reached the conclusion that the

E respondents were in breach of reg. 20 and that a causal connexion between the breach and the accident has been established.

    In the view which I take of the breach of statutory duty by the respondents it is unnecessary for me to deal with the common law case of negligence. I should say, however, that I would have had more difficulty than the rest of your lordships in holding the respondents in breach of their common law duty not to expose the

F deceased to unnecessary risk.

    On the question of contributory negligence the judge acquitted the deceased. He gives his reasons as follows:

    " He did not realise what the danger was as he walked along until he came to the point where he met disaster. He may not have heard or realised that the train was so close upon him, and trying to extricate himself from the

G   danger, or indeed unknowing that he was in such danger because of the overhang of the trucks and the narrowness of the way, he was trapped in this funnel and knocked over or brushed by the train and fell between the wagons, as I have tried to indicate."

    Earlier in his judgment the judge said " I think this is almost a classic trap ". If that view was justified on the evidence, then I can understand the learned

H judge acquitting the deceased of contributory negligence; the idea of a trap and of contributory negligence are mutually inconsistent. If the deceased could not have appreciated that he was in an area of danger then, clearly, there was no contributory negligence; but this was the case of an experienced and capable shunter. He knew that the train proceeding from behind him at seven to eight miles per hour would overtake him somewhere in the region of the mound of

I material. The mound of material must have been obvious to him, although he might not have appreciated the exact amount of clearance which its proximity to the line would give him. If the accident happened where the trial judge found, the deceased had put himself into a position similar to that between the rails and in which he was in danger of being hit by the approaching train. There was an elementary precaution which he could have taken to ensure his safety, namely, to stop and look behind to see where the train was, and if it was as close as it must

(7) [1936] 2 All E.R. 1426 at p. 1432.

have been, to stand back and allow it to pass. The defect in BAKER, J.'s reasoning A
on this aspect of the case is that he says that there is no evidence that the deceased
realised, or indeed ought to have realised, that the train was on him as he went
into the narrow gap between the material and the line. My view is that if the
deceased did not assure himself that the train was not on him, then he neglected
an elementary precaution for his own safety. Notwithstanding the view of the
trial judge, which of course is entitled to great weight, I am unable to acquit the B
deceased of any negligence, and I would agree that the degree of contributory
negligence should be twenty-five per cent. I would therefore allow the appeal
and restore the judgment of BAKER, J., subject to a deduction from the damages
awarded of twenty-five per cent.

LORD PEARCE: My Lords, the respondents were, in my opinion, negligent C
at common law. The walk-way where the deceased was killed was a normal route
for him to use. He was the shunter accompanying the train; this was both
admitted in the pleadings and shown by the evidence. The pole-riding theory
was rejected by the judge and must be discarded. It was argued that the deceased
should not have used that part of the walk-way since he should, by the time when
he arrived at the points lever, have seen the obstruction and the necessity of the D
alternative route on top of the bank; but there is no adequate evidence to show
that this was obvious from the points lever. Nor is there any photograph (out of
the many which the respondents provided) to show what was the view from that
place. If a normal route for employees is rendered dangerous by employers, they
should make that fact clear according to the circumstances and see that the
existence of the alternative route is obvious to employees. Here nothing was done E
to show that an alternative route should be taken. There was no indication, nor
was it obvious, just where the suggested alternative route should depart from the
walk-way.

It must have been known to the respondents that to have an obstructed or
treacherous surface close to the line might be dangerous to those who had to walk
alongside, since it might cause them to stumble into a passing train. I think that F
this is clear by inference from the evidence; and the mere existence of reg. 20
of the Coal and Other Mines (Sidings) Regulations, 1956 would further bring this
fact to the attention of the respondents.

The bull-dozing operations had for a space of four or five yards made the surface
of the walk-way adjacent to the line both obstructed and treacherous. It was
this fact which caused the accident. For the main outline of the accident is clear G
enough on a balance of probabilities. It is the details which are inscrutable.
Whatever were the details, I am satisfied, as was the judge, that it was the
spoil adjacent to the line which caused the accident. The deceased must have
tried to pass over the spoil either by going diagonally across it or scrambling
horizontally up it in order to get away from the train. He must have slipped or
fallen or rolled down the bank on to the line. H

Why, it is argued, should the respondents have anticipated such an unfortunate
and unlikely coincidence of events or foreseen any real danger? Granted, however,
a knowledge that there should not be treacherous surfaces adjacent to the line,
since they might cause men to stumble in to passing trains, the present coincidence
was but a particular example of that general danger. The possible injury being
so serious and the removal of the danger so easy, the respondents were negligent I
in not removing it or taking some other steps to prevent the danger.

Moreover, the respondents were, I think, in breach of reg. 20. The spoil was
" material placed . . . at a distance of less than three feet from the track ". But
was the deceased " required in the course of his duty to pass on foot over that
material "? In my opinion, he was. Under reg. 6 there had to be a competent
person in charge of the movement of the train. The deceased was the shunter in
charge. As such he was accompanying the train under reg. 9. His duty was to
accompany or precede the leading vehicle, watch the line, and give any requisite

A warning. True it is that his duty related to " every case in which any person employed at a mine is or might be exposed to risk of injury by the reason of the movement ... of ... vehicles " and that at the relevant moment there was nobody in the vicinity who might be injured. I cannot, however, accept the argument that this fact caused any break in his duty. If any employee had suddenly rushed on to the line from some concealed spot, it would have been the duty of the

B deceased to take instant avoiding action. Although the need for action was intermittent, the duty was continuous. Once it is conceded (as it must be and was conceded in the defence) that he was " accompanying " the train, it can be said that he was " required to pass on foot " by any route that was normal to a shunter accompanying a train on that particular track. The walk-way on the right (where the accident happened) was a normal route for such a shunter.

C What, then, was the duty of the respondents with regard to the material placed within three feet of the track? They must secure the efficient carrying out of arrangements whereby the material is placed in such a manner that every person required to pass over it or between it and the line can do so without being exposed to risk of injury by traffic on the line. It was argued that there is great difficulty as to the meaning of the regulation, because the engine in parts overhangs the

D walk-way by two feet and therefore, it was said, the three feet cannot give safety. In the Court of Appeal (8) this caused much debate; but the evidence does not deal with this difficulty. Moreover Mr. Hilton, the manager, who should know, appears to have considered in his evidence that it is possible for the train to pass a man safely when he is in the three feet walk-way. The respondents' counsel asked him: " I am asking you to assume he is in the three feet where the train

E can pass him perfectly safely? " Mr. Hilton, without demurring, answered " In that case I should stand until the train had gone past ". The regulation is apparently drafted on the basis that safety can be attained in the three feet walk-way provided that its surface is good so that a man is not caused to stumble or forced by its obstruction to go nearer to the line; and the material has to be so placed that he is not endangered. Additionally, if there is more than sixty feet

F of it alongside the line, there must be at intervals of not more than sixty feet " adequate spaces or recesses in that material ". Those recesses clearly must extend a good deal further than three feet from the line. As a matter of common sense it seems that they must be there as temporary additional refuges, while a train is passing, for men who are embarrassed by tools or who have to pass one another, or who by their numbers cannot be conveniently accommodated on the

G three foot which has to be available all along the line. The regulation is badly drafted, but its sense is clear in so far as it clearly intends that the surface of the material should not be treacherous or obstructive within three feet of the line, presumably so that the men shall not stumble into or have their attention diverted from the traffic. The spoil at the scene of the accident came almost to the line itself, and contrary to the regulation no arrangements had been made whereby it

H was so placed that a man could pass over it or between it and the line without being exposed to risk of injury by traffic. As a result of this breach the accident occurred.

As to contributory negligence, the main contention of the respondents at the trial was that the deceased had been pole-riding, which would indeed have been negligent. When this was rejected, there remained the more general allegation

I that he " failed to select a path for himself which was safe and which afforded a secure foothold, or failed to look where he was going and failed to take care for his own safety ". Since he was dead he could not give evidence. Therefore, as a matter of justice one should not make any findings against him which his answers might reasonably have dispelled. If, however, the evidence points to his negligence and there do not appear to be any reasonable and likely explanations which could acquit him of negligence, the respondents, also as a matter of justice, are entitled to a finding of contributory negligence.

(8) [1966] 2 All E.R. 208.

I acquit the deceased of any negligence in not diverging from the walk-way A
at the points lever. At that distance it is not sufficiently shown that he should
have noticed the obstruction. Moreover, the natural perspective, by which the
line and the bank would normally appear to be converging into the distance,
might help to disguise the fact that the obstruction was encroaching on the walk-
way; but when he approached the actual place where the obstruction was, it
must have been plain to see. He then had to decide whether to walk right in to B
the line or scramble up over the spoil. He knew that the train, of which he himself
was in charge and which he could control by his signals, was behind him and was
about to approach. He was an experienced shunter who knew the perils. He was
aware no doubt, as were the respondents, of the danger of stumbling on a treacherous surface close beside the rails. He could then have stopped for a few seconds
in the unobstructed walk-way, which he had hitherto been traversing, until the C
train went by; or he could at that point have scrambled up the bank at a safe
distance from the line. In either event prudence dictated that he should look
round and see where the train was. Had he done so, it does not seem reasonably
possible that he would have been killed. Instead, either he proceeded in the very
narrow gap between the spoil and the line and then tried to scramble up horizontally at the last moment or he proceeded diagonally across the loose spoil D
within three feet of the line and slipped sideways. Either course was risky, as
he must have seen and known if he was keeping a good look out as a man should
when there is a train somewhere behind him on the line.

The judge, with natural sympathy, excuses him on various grounds. He may
not have heard or realised that the train was so close on him; but why did he
not turn round and look? There was no trouble in doing so, and any careful E
man would look round before doing anything (with a train in his rear) that might
result in his getting too near the line. Assuming that he had not already walked
negligently into the danger area, he could then have remained immobile until
the train passed. He may have been trying, it was said, to extricate himself from
the danger or not have known he was in danger because of the overhang of the
trucks and the narrowness of the way, and he was trapped in the funnel and F
knocked over by the train. But as an experienced shunter he well knew the
overhang of the trucks, and he could plainly see the narrowness of the way. The
judge says that he was trapped in the funnel; but whatever be his view from the
points lever he could plainly see the obstruction when he came to it; and, if he
kept a good look out as he should have done (knowing that his train was coming
on behind him), he must have realised that the path was narrowing and driving G
him too close to the line. Making all allowances for the absence of his evidence I
cannot see any reasonable possibility that could acquit him wholly of negligence.
I would assess his blame at one quarter and deduct that proportion from the
agreed damages.

I would allow the appeal.
                                                                            H
    LORD UPJOHN: My Lords, this appeal is concerned with the liability
of the respondents, the National Coal Board, in respect of an accident at about
8.45 a.m., on Apr. 14, 1964, to one of their employees, Frank Westwood, a
shunter engaged in shunting operations at the service sidings at Whitwood Colliery
who was run over and killed by the shunting train of which he was in command.
No one saw the accident or can describe exactly how it happened, and therefore I
the first matter to be considered is, on the balance of probabilities, how the
accident occurred. The day was fine, although there was a strong wind blowing
from the north, but there was no other shunting operation going on that morning
and the only engine working at the siding was the one under the deceased's
command. It was a diesel engine driven by one Ellis, and the story starts when
the shunting engine, pulled three coal wagons from no. 1 siding, which was the
most northern of the sidings, down to the weighbridge about 150 yards away to
the south-west, where the bridge man was able to alter the points so that the

A engine could push the wagons back to sidings no. 4 and no. 5 on the south side of the siding. While this was being done, the deceased crossed from no. 1 siding to the points lever dividing sidings no. 4 and no. 5 to see whether he had correctly altered the points so that on its return journey the engine and wagons would travel over the points on to no. 5 siding, which was the southernmost of the sidings. The object of the operation was to bring these three wagons, which

B contained ash, opposite to a reservoir further to the east, where their contents would be delivered into the reservoir. The deceased checked the points and satisfied himself that he had, in fact, altered them correctly. By this time the shunting engine pushing the three wagons in front of it was coming up fast behind him at about eight miles an hour, or roughly twelve feet per second. The deceased, as was usual both in general and in respect of this particular siding, walked on

C the right-hand side of the line no. 5 at a speed of between three and four miles an hour or about four to five feet per second. On the right of the fifth siding was a bank of spoil from the mine. Until quite recently that bank had been near but not too close to the fifth siding, so that there had been always a perfectly clear walk-way on the right of the siding for a shunter, to get to the reservoir. Recently, however, the respondents, with a view to seeing whether this spoil,

D mainly of shale, could be used for other purposes, caused a bulldozer to carry some of it away for experiment. This left at a few feet to the right of the fifth siding a reasonably safe level walk for a shunter though, as the learned judge pointed out, this was purely fortuitous, as its primary purpose was to explore the quality of the shale.

The action of the bulldozer, however, caused some of the shale to spill over to-

E wards the fifth siding. At a point between twenty and twenty-five yards from the points lever already mentioned this overspill came, so far as one can tell, right up to the line and formed a loose, entirely unpacked, slope or bank of about forty-five degrees up to the bulldozed track about two feet higher than the rails, thus obstructing the previous safe walk-way. This fifth siding was only used as an emergency siding and it was not disputed that it was only used perhaps once or

F twice a month, so that the deceased, who had been a shunter there for about a year and admittedly a good, careful, hardworking man, would not have been on this siding after the bulldozer had altered the bank of spoil. It was equally admitted that no one had ever told him that as a result of this bulldozing job the walk-way to the right of the fifth siding was obstructed. All we know of the accident is this: that Mr. Ellis, approaching the points pushing the three wagons

G in front of him, saw the deceased as usual walking on the right-hand side of the rail, obviously accompanying the train with a view to uncoupling the wagons when they got opposite to the reservoir. Mr. Ellis' view was then obstructed because of a slight bend in the line which, having regard to the wagons in front of him, prevented him from seeing the deceased. All that we know is that, at a point just beyond where this bank of spoil had spilled over close to the rail,

H the deceased was thrown under the front wheels of the third wagon and killed.

I agree with Danckwerts, L.J. (9), with whom Salmon, L.J. (10), also agreed, that the reconstruction of this accident is not difficult; it is perfectly plain on the balance of probabilities that the deceased walked forward in front of the train on the right-hand side of the rails and that the train was catching him up quite fast. Personally I think that, by the time when he was close to the point where

I the spoil slope or bank was down to the rails, it was probable that the leading wagon had passed him or, at any rate, was abreast of him. But it is not necessary to make any finding about that. It is quite plain that he then saw that his walk-way on the right of the rails was obstructed by this new slope or bank of spoil, and so he did what any young man of thirty-seven, especially with a shunting pole in his hand, would do. He climbed up this easy slope (it was only two feet high) and then for some reason he slipped and fell, most probably

(9) [1966] 2 All E.R. at p. 211, letters B and C.
(10) [1966] 2 All E.R. at p. 213, letter A.

because this spoil, being purely loose overspill from the sides of the bulldozer, **A** let him down and so he fell under the wheels of the third of the three wagons and was killed.

The appellant, who is his widow, claims damages against the respondents for breach of statutory obligation and for negligent breach of duty at common law.

Before setting out the relevant statutory duties, I should say that the real **B** defence of the respondents at the trial was that the deceased, though in command of his train, was following a known, though illegal, practice among shunters of " pole-riding ". This defence failed and has not been pursued before your lordships; but, as the evidence of the respondents was in the main directed to this issue, it is not surprising that the evidence on the issues that your lordships have to consider, to which I shall refer in a moment, is somewhat scanty. **C**

The statutory obligation is reg. 20 of the Coal and Other Mines (Sidings) Regulations, 1956. [HIS LORDSHIP read the regulation, which is set out at p. 596, letters C and D, ante, and continued:] It is clear and admitted that this was ground not ordinarily used for the stocking of material and that the spoil had encroached to within three feet from the tracks of the line. It is clear, too, that the deceased could not pass over that loose material or between it and the line without being **D** exposed to risk of injury by traffic on the line, for the spoil which had fallen down was not packed in any way to make it safe for a shunter in the course of his duties to pass along his accustomed walk-way. So the sole question is whether the deceased, who was employed at the mine, was " required in the course of his duty to pass on foot over that material or between it and the line ". The first question, therefore, is whether it can be established that the deceased was **E** " required " to pass over the three-foot space. It has been held, and in my opinion rightly, by LEWIS, J., in *Henaghan* v. *Rederiet Forangirene* (11) that the use of the word " required " does not mean " ordered ". The test must be whether it was reasonable for him in the course of his duty to proceed in the way in which he did. I shall return to this matter a little later. The position really was that the deceased, a shunter, capable, experienced and careful was in charge **F** of the engine. He did not follow it down to the points where Mr. Parker was in charge because it was quite unnecessary for him to do so. It is quite true that reg. 9 of the regulations of 1956 compelled him to accompany the locomotive and other vehicles where the locomotive was pushing those vehicles, but of course the locomotive was, in fact, pulling them down to the weighbridge where Mr. Parker was going to change the points. It would have been a complete waste of **G** time for the train to have slowed down to permit the deceased to have accompanied it to the weighbridge, especially as there was no other activity going on at the siding at that time. When Mr. Parker had altered the points and the train was coming back on to the track sidings no. 4 and no. 5 the locomotive was pushing; and so the deceased, having checked that he had altered the points correctly to get the wagons on to this little used siding no. 5, was then, in his **H** customary way, leading the train (catching him up as I have described) in order to get them to the reservoir where he would uncouple the wagons.

Now, the first argument on behalf of the respondents was that having reached the points lever some twenty-five yards from the obstruction where the deceased was killed, he should have seen that it was so obvious that the walk-way, which he was accustomed to use, was obstructed, that he should have done one of two **I** things: either have crossed over the points, which he could have done because the train was then fifteen to twenty yards behind him, and walked up on siding no. 4, or taken this new bulldozed track which I have already described. Had it been established that his normal route to the right of siding no. 5 was plainly and obviously obstructed, I should myself see much force in the argument that he

_____

(11) [1936] 2 All E.R. at p. 1433.

A was not " required ", within the meaning of the regulation, to go on the right-hand side of the rail when two other ways were open to him. But for my part I do not accept the premise. I do not think that anyone who has been accustomed to take the normal course on the right of this emergency siding, as it was admitted the deceased must have done twelve to twenty-four times within the last twelve months, is to be criticised, still less to be held legally liable, for failing to spot the

B fact that some twenty-five yards ahead there was this two-foot sloping bank, no more, which would obstruct his way. So I reject that view. Then SALMON, L.J., (13) was of opinion that the deceased was not really in charge of the train for the purposes of reg. 9, and that he could perfectly well have walked straight from no. 1 siding to the reservoir and was not, therefore, required to go to the right of no. 5 siding. He might possibly have done that in all the circumstances of the case

C without much criticism, but he did not. This careful man was in charge of the train and he was, in the terms of reg. 9, accompanying or preceding the leading vehicle, and I find myself quite unable to agree with SALMON, L.J.'s observations on this point (12). So I think that the deceased was quite properly, lawfully and as was " required " of him, pursuing the route that he had been accustomed to pursue on siding no. 5.

D   Then, as he approached the point where the slope of spoil was coming down to the line and, as I think, he probably found the leading wagon passing him, he found himself in a dilemma, for he could not pursue his well-known, accustomed and normal route any longer. So what did he do? As I have already said, I think that he did what any young active man of thirty-seven, with a five feet nine inches pole in his hand would have done. He did not stop and wait for the train

E to pass him: had he done that, he would be alive today. He tried to scramble up the bank and in some way which we do not know he was let down, because it was loose spoil, and he fell to his death. I cannot myself think that the respondents can be excused from liability because he did that. It seems to me clear that the respondents have quite plainly failed to comply with r. 20 and this failure caused his death.

F   Then as to contributory negligence. I cannot myself think that the deceased was in any way to blame for taking the emergency action that I have described, though I cannot agree with BAKER, J., in thinking that the deceased may not have heard or realised that the train was overtaking him at this moment. It is very well settled that a man, pursuing his normal and usual course and finding his progress suddenly obstructed by some unexpected and unnotified action of

G his employer, which is far from obvious until he is right on it, is not to be criticised and found guilty of contributory negligence by taking the wrong course in the emergency, unless it was an obviously stupid one. He was not to blame, in my opinion, for doing what he did; the respondents were wholly to blame for leaving a small innocent-looking two feet high and apparently easily surmountable bank which in fact was treacherous and utterly unsafe.

H   As to negligence at common law, I myself am of the opinion that the respondents are also legally liable. Their duty is not to expose their employees to any unnecessary risk. For their own purposes they sent up a bulldozer on to the bank of spoil to see whether the shale was worth recovering, and the result of that was that it overspilt on to the bank near the rail, rendering that which had been a previously perfectly safe walk-way into a dangerous, if not impossible, one. It was said that

I the manager would have to be a paragon of virtue to spot this, and that any shunter who is naturally used to seeing obstructions on the sidings in the course of his duty must be expected to deal with that. I entirely disagree. On this little used siding there had always been a perfectly clear walk-way, no warning had been given, and I cannot see why any shunter should be expected to be alive to the new difficulty, especially as it was in a sense a small one. My previous observations on contributory negligence also apply and I shall not repeat them. I

_____

(12) [1966] 2 All E.R. at p. 213.

therefore agree with the judgments of BAKER, J., and DANCKWERTS, L.J., (13).　**A**
I would allow the appeal and restore the learned judge's judgment in toto.

Appeal allowed.

Solicitors: *White & Leonard & Corbin, Greener*, agents for *Raley & Pratt*,
Barnsley (for the appellant); *D. H. Haslam*, agent for *C. M. H. Glover*, Doncaster
(for the respondents).

B

[*Reported by* KATHLEEN J. H. O'BRIEN, *Barrister-at-Law.*]

Re TRAVEL & HOLIDAY CLUBS, LTD.

[CHANCERY DIVISION (Pennycuick, J.), March 21, 22, 1967.]　　　**C**

*Company—Winding-up—Compulsory winding-up—Board of Trade's application
　—Just and equitable—Evidence—Inspectors' report—Report admissible—
　Sufficiency as evidence—Misconduct or fraud—Order made on consideration
　of report alone when uncontradicted by evidence adduced by company—
　Companies Act, 1948 (11 & 12 Geo. 6 c. 38), s. 169 (3).*

A petition was presented by the Board of Trade under s. 169 (3)* of　　**D**
the Companies Act, 1948, seeking an order for the winding-up of a company.
The petition alleged that the Board of Trade had appointed inspectors
under s. 168 of the Companies Act, 1948, to investigate and report on the
affairs of the company and that the inspectors had made a final report from
which it appeared expedient to present the petition in accordance with
s. 165 (*b*) (i)†, by reason of circumstances suggesting that the manager of　**E**
the company's business had been guilty of misconduct towards the company.
It further alleged that the company was insolvent and that it was just and
equitable that the company should be wound up. The inspectors had
heard oral evidence and examined the books of the company. Their findings
fully bore out the allegations of misconduct. The report was in evidence
at the hearing of the petition. Formal affidavits were filed in support of　**F**
the petition and an affidavit by an expert was also filed. A joint affidavit
was filed by the inspectors exhibiting their report and summarising certain
findings. The company filed no evidence in answer and was not represented
at the hearing of the petition.

Held: the court was entitled to look at the inspectors' report and, being
satisfied from the report, in the absence of any evidence to the contrary　**G**
adduced by the company, that, on the basis of the findings in the report,
the company was insolvent and that it was just and equitable for it to be
wound up, the court would make the winding-up order sought (see p. 608,
letter F, and p. 609, letter G, post).

Re A.B.C. Coupler and Engineering Co., Ltd. (No. 2) ([1962] 3 All E.R. 68)
not followed.　　**H**

[As to appointment of inspectors by the Board of Trade, see 6 HALSBURY'S
LAWS (3rd Edn.) 388–393; paras. 753–760; and for cases on investigations by
the Board of Trade, see 9 DIGEST (Repl.) 627, *4187-4190*.

For the Companies Act, 1948, s. 165, s. 169 (3), see 3 HALSBURY'S STATUTES
(2nd Edn.) 590, 594.]

I

Case referred to:

　A.B.C. Coupler and Engineering Co., Ltd. (No. 2), Re, [1962] 3 All E.R. 68;
　　[1962] 1 W.L.R. 1236; Digest (Cont. Vol. A) 188, *5944a.*

Petition.

This was a petition presented by the Board of Trade under s. 169 (3) of the

---

(13) [1966] 2 All E.R. at p. 211.
* Section 169 (3) is set out at p. 607, letter H, post.
† Section 165, so far as material, is set out at p. 607, letter G, post.

A Companies Act, 1948, seeking an order for the compulsory winding-up of Travel & Holiday Clubs, Ltd. The facts are set out in the judgment.

J. P. Warner for the petitioner, the Board of Trade.

PENNYCUICK, J.: This is a petition presented by the Board of Trade whereby the Board of Trade seeks an order for the compulsory winding-up of
B Travel & Holiday Clubs, Ltd., to which I will refer as "the company". The petition contains, amongst others, the following allegations. The company was incorporated in January, 1964, and the nominal capital of the company was £5,000; the shares have at all times been held as to forty-nine thousand by Henry Whitfield and as to the remaining one thousand by his wife. The objects for which the company was established were to carry on a tourist agency.

C   "On Aug. 14, 1964, your petitioners, in exercise of the powers conferred on them by s. 165 (*b*) of the Companies Act, 1948, appointed William McLaren Howard, Q.C., and John Peter Landau, certified accountant (hereinafter called 'the inspectors') to investigate and report on the affairs of the company.
      "On May 4, 1966, the inspectors made a final report to your petitioners
D under s. 168 of the said Act. From such report it appeared to your petitioners expedient to present this petition by reason of circumstances suggesting that a person concerned with the management of the company's affairs, namely Patrick Collis, who was the manager of its business, had in connexion therewith been guilty of misconduct towards the company, in that he (unknown to Mr. Whitfield)—(a) had received from McLelland, Pope &
E Langley, Ltd., a company which he (the said Patrick Collis) employed as air brokers to the company, sums amounting in the aggregate to about £1,600, of which he did not give any satisfactory explanation to the inspectors, and (b) had allowed McLelland, Pope & Langley, Ltd., to make unreasonably high profits out of their business of arranging air transport on behalf of the company.
F   "The company is insolvent and unable to pay its debts. In the circumstances, it is just and equitable that the company should be wound up."

I will read part of two sections from the Companies Act, 1948.

      "165. Without prejudice to their powers under the last foregoing section, the Board of Trade—. . .(*b*) may do so [investigate the company's affairs] if it appears to the Board that there are circumstances suggesting—(i) that its
G business is being conducted with intent to defraud its creditors or the creditors of any other person or otherwise for a fraudulent or unlawful purpose or in a manner oppressive of any part of its members or that it was formed for any fraudulent or unlawful purpose.
      "169 (3). If, in the case of any body corporate liable to be wound up under this Act, it appears to the Board of Trade, from any such [inspector's]
H report as aforesaid that it is expedient so to do by reason of any such circumstances as are referred to in sub-para. (i) or (ii) of para. (*b*) of s. 165 of this Act, the Board may, unless the body corporate is already being wound up by the court, present a petition for it to be so wound up if the court thinks it just and equitable that it should be wound up or a petition for an order under s. 210 of this Act or both."
I The report referred to is, of course, a report made by inspectors appointed under s. 165. The report prepared by Mr. Howard and Mr. Landau is in evidence. They heard oral evidence and examined the books of the company. Their findings fully bear out the allegations as to the content of their report, which is contained in para. 6 of the petition; that is to say, they found that Mr. Collis had received sums amounting to £1,600 from air brokers and that he allowed the air brokers to make unreasonably high profits.
      The Board of Trade, having considered that report, came to the conclusion

that it was expedient, by reason of such circumstances as are referred to in **A**
s. 165 (*b*) (i), to present a petition for the company to be wound up by the court.
In support of the petition, there has been filed, apart from the formal affidavit
verifying the petition, an affidavit by a Mr. Willis, who is managing director
of M. K. Kendall, Ltd., travel agents and air brokers, establishing, by way
of expert evidence, that the normal commission payable to brokers is something
in the order of five per cent. to 7½ per cent. There has also been filed a joint **B**
affidavit by Mr. Howard and Mr. Landau, the inspectors, exhibiting their report
and summarising certain findings. I will refer again to that affidavit in a few
moments. The company filed no evidence in answer and has not been represented
on the hearing of the winding-up petition.

Apart from a difficulty provided by the decision in *Re A.B.C. Coupler and
Engineering Co., Ltd.*, (*No. 2*) (1), I should myself have found no difficulty in **C**
making a winding-up order as sought on the petition. When one looks at
s. 169 (3), that subsection contains two requirements: first, it must appear
to the Board of Trade, from the report, that it is expedient, by reason of the
specified circumstances, to present a winding-up petition; and, secondly,
the court must think it just and equitable to make a winding-up order. The
subsection contains no other requirement.   **D**

In the present case it has appeared to the Board of Trade expedient to present
a winding-up petition, and it seems to me plainly just and equitable to make the
order on that petition. It so seems to me on two grounds: first, that I have
before me a report made by two inspectors acting in a statutory fact-finding
capacity, on oral evidence and examination of books, which report finds misconduct and is not contradicted by any evidence adduced on behalf of the **E**
company; and, secondly, on the ground that the company, as appears from the
report, is wholly insolvent. Given those two circumstances, I cannot see why
it should not be just and equitable for me to make a winding-up order.

So far as the admissibility of the report is concerned, I should have thought
that, being a report made by persons in a statutory fact-finding capacity, the
court must be entitled to look at it and act on it; unless it is challenged on behalf **F**
of the company. It seems to me that I could properly consider it just and equitable for the company to be wound up on the basis of the report so far as it makes
out misconduct in the conduct of the company's affairs, quite apart from the
matter of insolvency.

The difficulty which has arisen stems from the decision of BUCKLEY, J., in
Re A.B.C. Coupler and Engineering Co., Ltd. (No. 2) (1). In that case a petition **G**
to wind up a company was presented by the Board of Trade under s. 169 (3)
of the Companies Act, 1948, and the evidence filed in support of the petition
consisted of three affidavits sworn by an official of the Board of Trade. One
was the statutory affidavit required by r. 30 of the Companies (Winding-up)
Rules, 1949 (2), and another exhibited the inspectors' reports concerning the
company and two other related companies. The third affidavit exhibited the **H**
signed copies of the inspectors' reports as to each of the three companies, and
in it the deponent stated that he believed that the facts set out in all the reports
were true and that the opinions contained in the said reports were the opinions
of the inspectors. On the question whether the evidence filed was sufficient
to support the charges contained in the petition it was held that where grave
charges were levelled against individuals in a winding-up petition, or where the **I**
case was one of complexity turning on the conduct of persons more or less in
the relationship of partners in a company, the court would not in the exercise
of its discretionary jurisdiction be satisfied with prima facie evidence but would
require the petitioner to substantiate his case more fully; that in such cases it
would require, where practicable, the evidence of witnesses with direct knowledge
of the matters to which they were testifying, and on which they could be cross-
examined, and which conformed to the ordinary rules of the admissibility of

---

(1) [1962] 3 All E.R. 68.   (2) S.I. 1949 No. 330.

A evidence; that the evidence in that case was not sufficient to support the charges levelled in the petition since it was all hearsay evidence, and that, accordingly, the petition would be dismissed.

The argument before the learned judge went on the footing that the affidavit evidence was admittedly hearsay evidence, but it was sufficiently strong hearsay evidence to justify an order being made. For example, BUCKLEY, J., said (3):

B require the petitioner to substantiate his case more fully; that in such cases it

C
" Counsel for the petitioners said that it was not incumbent on [the petitioners] to prove the irregularities which they suggested had occurred, as a plaintiff would have to prove those irregularities in proceedings against defaulting directors for misfeasance, but that what the petitioners should prove to the satisfaction of the court was circumstances that suggested a probability that there had been misconduct which made a winding-up just and equitable."

D
The point was not, as I read this judgment, taken on behalf of the Board of Trade, which is now made on the present petition, that the report of the inspectors stands in a wholly different position from ordinary affidavit evidence and represents the conclusions made by a statutory fact-finding body, after hearing oral evidence and examination of the books. I find that argument convincing. It seems to me that it would not be in accordance with the apparent intention of the section that where inspectors appointed under the Act have made a report, the court should not be entitled to look at that report and accept it not as hearsay evidence, but as material of a different character altogether and should have to be satisfied anew by evidence of the ordinary nature as to the facts found in the report.

E
I have great hesitation in taking a different view on this matter from BUCKLEY, J. I do so, however, with less hesitation because the point now advanced on behalf of the Board of Trade was not advanced before him in that case.

To avoid misunderstanding, I should say that an entirely different position would arise if in such a case the company sought to challenge, by way of evidence, the findings at which the inspectors had arrived. It may very well be that in such a case the company would be entitled to re-open the matters on which the inspectors had made their findings, and the result of that would, I think, be that this court, in its winding-up jurisdiction, would have to consider those issues afresh. I merely mention that by way of reservation. It does not arise in the circumstances of the present case, where the company has not seen fit to appear at all or adduced any evidence or addressed any argument to the court. As I have said, in the absence of any further evidence, I cannot see why, on a proper construction of the section, I should not have regard to the findings of the inspectors as contained in their report and, on the basis of that report and in the absence of any further evidence, come to the conclusion that it is just and equitable that the company should be wound up.

F

G

H
I would only like to mention one further matter. In the present case the inspectors have themselves sworn an affidavit. That appears to correspond to a hint thrown out by BUCKLEY, J., in Re A.B.C. Coupler Engineering Co., Ltd. (No. 2) (4). Again I hesitate extremely to express a different view from BUCKLEY, J., but it does seem to me undesirable that inspectors who have conducted an enquiry in a statutory fact-finding capacity should have to give evidence of their findings on which they would be liable to be cross-examined.

I
In all the circumstances, for the reasons which I have given, I propose to make a compulsory order in this case.

Order accordingly.

Solicitor: *Solicitor, Board of Trade.*

[*Reported by* JENIFER SANDELL, *Barrister-at-Law.*]

---

(3) [1962] 3 All E.R. at p. 71.   (4) [1902] 3 All E.R. at p. 74.

A

S.B.A. PROPERTIES, LTD. *v.* CRADOCK AND OTHERS.

[CHANCERY DIVISION (Goff, J.), April 4, 5, 1967.]

Company—Investigation by Board of Trade—Action begun by Board of Trade in plaintiff company's name consequent on inspector's report—Damages for negligence for breach of duty sought—Payment of balance alleged to be due from bank on current account claimed—Application by defendant bank to stay and strike out proceedings—No allegation of fraud or other such misconduct on the part of the bank—Winding-up petition pending against plaintiff company—Action not authorised by s. 169 (4)—Application adjourned until after hearing of winding-up petition—Companies Act, 1948 (11 & 12 Geo. 6 c. 38), s. 169 (4).

B

The Board of Trade brought an action in the name of the plaintiff company against three individuals and the defendant bank, claiming a declaration that payment to the defendant B. of a sum of £44,600 standing to the credit of the plaintiff company with the defendant bank was a misapplication of the plaintiff company's money. There was a consequential claim for damages in respect of the alleged misapplication and as against the defendant bank a further claim of damages for negligence. There was an alternative claim against the defendant bank for a sum of £44,602 17s. 5d. allegedly due to the plaintiff company on current account. This amount was made up of an existing credit balance of £2 17s. 5d. enlarged by a notional re-credit of the £44,600 paid by the defendant bank to B. The action was brought in purported pursuance of power conferred by s. 169 (4)* of the Companies Act, 1948. A petition for the winding-up of the plaintiff company had been presented by the Board of Trade and was to be heard within a few days after the summons next mentioned. On a summons by the defendant bank that all further proceedings be stayed and the action be dismissed for want of authority to sue in the plaintiff company's name,

C

D

E

Held: (i) the defendant bank was entitled to succeed on its application for the following reasons—

(a) the words " or other misconduct " in s. 169 (4) of the Companies Act, 1948, should be construed ejusdem generis with the reference to fraud and misfeasance immediately preceding them in sub-s. (4), but no moral turpitude was alleged against the defendant bank (see p. 612, letter F, and p. 613, letters D and E, post).

F

(b) the words " in connexion with . . . the management of the plaintiff company's affairs " in s. 169 (4) were too narrow to include merely acting as the plaintiff company's bankers; and accordingly the neglect alleged against the defendant bank was not within the scope of sub-s. (4) (see p. 613, letter I, post).

G

(c) the action was for the recovery of damages for negligence or breach of duty, and was not " for the recovery of any property " within s. 169 (4); moreover, even if the plaintiff company's balance on current account were enlarged by re-crediting the £44,600, the claim to recover the plaintiff company's balance on current account would merely be a claim to enforce payment of a debt, not to recover property (see p. 614, letter F, post).

H

(ii) although the action was brought in the plaintiff company's name without authority, the court would not strike it out forthwith but, having regard to the pending winding-up petition, would adjourn the application until after the hearing of the winding-up petition (see p. 615, letter E, post).

I

Principle in *East Pant Du United Lead Mining Co., Ltd.* v. *Merryweather* ((1864), 2 Hem. & M. 254) applied.

Dictum of JENKINS, L.J., in *Danish Mercantile Co., Ltd.* v. *Beaumont* ([1951] 1 All E.R. at p. 929) considered.

---

* The terms of s. 169 (4) are set out at p. 612, letter E, post.

A   [As to proceedings by the Board of Trade, see 6 HALSBURY'S LAWS (3rd Edn.) 391, 392, para. 759.

For the Companies Act, 1948, s. 169 (4), see 3 HALSBURY'S STATUTES (2nd Edn.) 594.]

Cases referred to:

B
    Danish Mercantile Co., Ltd. v. *Beaumont*, [1951] 1 All E.R. 925; [1951] Ch. 680; 1 Digest (Repl.) 456, *1066*.

    East Pant Du United Lead Mining Co., Ltd. v. *Merryweather*, (1864), 2 Hem. & M. 254; 71 E.R. 460; 9 Digest (Repl.) 608, *4038*.

    Johnson (B.) & Co. (Builders), Ltd., Re, [1955] 2 All E.R. 775; [1955] Ch. 634; [1955] 3 W.L.R. 269; Digest (Cont. Vol. A) 183, *5467a*.

C
    Kingston Cotton Mill Co. (No. 2), Re, [1896] 2 Ch. 279; 65 L.J.Ch. 673; sub nom. *Re Kingston Cotton Mill Co., Ltd., Ex p. Pickering and Peasegood (No. 2)*, 74 L.T. 568; 9 Digest (Repl.) 587, *3880*.

    St. Aubyn (L. M.) v. *A.-G. (No. 2)*, [1951] 2 All E.R. 473; [1952] A.C. 15; 21 Digest (Repl.) 49, *199*.

    Thomas v. *Marshall (Inspector of Taxes)*, [1953] 1 All E.R. 1102; [1953] A.C. 543; [1953] 2 W.L.R. 944; 28 Digest (Repl.) 282, *1252*.

D
Procedure Summons.

By a writ dated Mar. 8, 1966, the plaintiff, S.B.A. Properties, Ltd., claimed against all the defendants (Francis Richard Cradock, Alfred Bieber, John Leonard Burden and the Bank of Nova Scotia) (a) a declaration that the payment to the third defendant, on or about Apr. 28, 1960, of the sum of £44,600 forming

E   part of the amount standing to the credit of the plaintiff company on current account with the defendant bank and the further payment of the like sum on or about the same day by the third defendant to the first defendant (in two sums of £26,816 and £17,784 respectively) were, respectively, misapplications of moneys of the plaintiff; and (b) damages in respect of such misapplications. Further or in the alternative the plaintiff company claimed against the defendant bank

F   damages for negligence. The plaintiff company claimed also against all the defendants an order for the payment by the defendants to the Board of Trade of the amount of the expenses of and incidental to the investigation into the affairs of the plaintiff company by an inspector appointed by the Board.

By its statement of claim served on Dec. 9, 1966, the plaintiff company did not repeat the claim for a declaration made in the writ, but claimed against all defen-

G   dants damages in respect of the alleged misapplication of moneys and, further or alternatively, damages for alleged negligence against the defendant bank. In addition a further alternative claim was included in the statement of claim against the defendant bank for payment of a sum of £44,602 17s. 5d. alleged to be due by the defendant bank to the plaintiff company on current account. The basis of this claim, stated in para. 14 of the statement of claim, was that the defendant

H   bank had no sufficient authority to debit the plaintiff company's account with the said sum of £44,600 paid to the third defendant and remained indebted to the plaintiff company in respect of that sum. Apart from that sum, the balance standing to the credit of the plaintiff company's account with the defendant bank was £2 17s. 5d., making thereby a total allegedly due to the plaintiff company from the defendant bank on current account of £44,602 17s. 5d.

I   On Nov. 27, 1963, the Board of Trade in pursuance of powers conferred by s. 165 (b) of the Companies Act, 1948, had appointed an inspector to investigate the affairs of the plaintiff company and to report thereon. The inspector made his report on Feb. 3, 1966, and from such report, so it was alleged in the statement of claim, it appeared to the Board of Trade that this action ought in the public interest to be brought by the plaintiff company. The presentation of a petition for the winding-up of the plaintiff company is mentioned in the judgment at p. 614, letter G, post). By a summons dated Mar. 9, 1967, the defendant bank applied for (i) an order that all further proceedings in the action be stayed and

that the action be dismissed on the ground that it had been commenced and was A
being maintained without the authority of the plaintiff company or other lawful
cause; and (ii) an order that the solicitor to the Board of Trade as the solicitor
purporting to act for the plaintiff company pay the bank its costs of the action
including the costs of the application to be taxed as between solicitor and own
client. The facts are set out in the judgment.

Jeremiah Harman for the Bank of Nova Scotia.   B
J. P. Warner for the plaintiff company.

   GOFF, J.: This is a procedure summons issued by the fourth defendant,
the Bank of Nova Scotia, in an action brought in the name of S.B.A. Properties,
Ltd. by the Board of Trade against three individuals, F. R. Cradock, A. Bieber
and J. L. Burden, who are alleged to have misapplied £44,600 of the plaintiff C
company's money by means of cheques passing through current accounts of the
plaintiff company and the defendants Cradock and Burden with the defendant
bank. The action was so brought in purported pursuance of the powers given to
the Board of Trade by s. 169 (4) of the Companies Act, 1948. The defendant bank,
which is one of standing and reputation, claims that, whether or not it has
incurred any liability to the plaintiff company, the case, so far as it is concerned, D
does not fall within the subsection and by this summons seeks to stay all further
proceedings against it in the action. The question is one of construction of the
subsection which I will now read.

   " If from any such [inspectors'] report as aforesaid it appears to the Board
   of Trade that proceedings ought in the public interest to be brought by any
   body corporate dealt with by the report for the recovery of damages in respect E
   of any fraud, misfeasance or other misconduct in connexion with the promotion or formation of that body corporate or the management of its affairs, or
   for the recovery of any property of the body corporate which has been misapplied or wrongfully retained, they may themselves bring proceedings for
   that purpose in the name of the body corporate."

Counsel for the defendant bank has submitted on its behalf that the words " or F
other misconduct " must be construed ejusdem generis and that they, therefore,
embrace only cases involving some degree of moral turpitude. Indeed, he says
that this is a classical case for the application of that rule. He reinforces this
submission by reference to s. 333 which, he says, although more limited with
respect to the persons against whom a remedy is available, is wider in terms of
subject-matter and yet it has been held that that section does not cover mere G
common law negligence and, a fortiori, therefore, s. 169 (4). He points to the use
in s. 333 of the words " or become liable or accountable for any money or
property of the company ".

   Counsel for the Board of Trade, on behalf of the plaintiff company, says that
there is no reason for placing a narrow construction on the words in s. 169. Indeed,
the public interest to which it expressly refers requires a liberal one. He too relies H
on comparison with s. 333 and submits that mere negligence was excluded by the
courts in their construction of that section and its predecessors because they must
not be so construed as to cover any misconduct by an officer of the company as
such. He relies on a passage in the judgment of LOPES, L.J., in *Re Kingston Cotton
Mill Co. (No. 2)* (1). The relevant passage was cited by SIR RAYMOND EVERSHED,
M.R., in *Re B. Johnson & Co. (Builders), Ltd.* (2) and is as follows: I

   " ' The learned judge in the court below held that misfeasance covered
   any misconduct by an officer of the company as such for which such officer
   might have been sued apart from the section. In my judgment this is too
   wide. It would cover any act of negligence—any actionable wrong by an
   officer of a company which did not involve any misapplication of the assets

---

(1) [1896] 2 Ch. 279 at p. 288.
(2) [1955] 2 All E.R. 775 at p. 782; [1955] Ch. 634 at p. 650.

A   of the company. The object of this section of the Act is to enable the liquidator to recover any assets of the company improperly dealt with by any officer of the company, and must be interpreted bearing that object in view. It doubtless covers any breach of duty by an officer of the company in his capacity of officer resulting in any improper misapplication of the assets or property of the company.' "

B   Then, so the argument runs, when the legislature introduced the words " or other misconduct " into s. 169 (4) or its predecessor, it must have had this in mind and have intended to include any legal wrong provided it satisfied the further condition of being in connexion with the management of the company's affairs. Further, counsel for the Board of Trade says the limitation of the section by reference to moral turpitude would create an impossible position, as there would be no precise or fixed standard by which to judge that question.

C   I see no reason to construe s. 169 (4) either particularly strictly or particularly liberally. I think that it is simply a matter of the ordinary meaning of the words which the legislature has used. Now it is to be observed that the subsection does not say " or any misconduct ", but " or other misconduct ", and, in my judgment, I ought to accept the construction of counsel for the defendant bank. One does not have to define moral turpitude. It is easy to recognise when one sees it. The conception of other misconduct ejusdem generis with fraud and misfeasance is, in my judgment, sufficiently clear and precise, and I ask myself why should the legislature refer specifically to fraud and misfeasance if it really meant any breach of duty?

E   If I am right so far, the defendant bank is entitled to succeed on this part of the argument because there is really no allegation in the statement of claim of anything wrong on its part other than negligence or breach of duty as a banker. There is no suggestion of anything approaching fraud or misfeasance or other misconduct as I have construed that expression. I was at one time somewhat concerned with the allegation in para. 12 of the statement of claim that the defendant bank was party or privy to the misapplication of the £44,600. That is, of course, denied; but I am not trying the action and, if that were an allegation of something within the ambit of s. 169 (4), that would be sufficient for the plaintiff company. However, I cannot construe that in vacuo. I must have regard to the whole context and tenor of the pleading and I observe that even the words themselves do not allege that the defendant bank was party or privy to any fraud or misfeasance but only to the misapplication of the money.

G   Even, however, if I be wrong so far, still I cannot bring myself to think that the wrongful acts or neglects of the defendant bank were in connexion with the management of the plaintiff company's affairs. It is true that the words are " in connexion with " and not " in ", and counsel for the Board of Trade has submitted that any kind of nexus between the wrong and the management would suffice. He agreed, however, that the mere fact of acting as the plaintiff company's bankers would not amount to acting in connexion with the management of its affairs. He said that the payment out of the plaintiff company's funds is part of that management and if the defendant bank actively participates in that payment, it brings itself within the subsection. However, acting as the plaintiff company's bankers must inevitably involve active participation in this sense in the payment out of the plaintiff company's moneys whenever it uses the banking account for that purpose, and it seems that one gets back to where one started. In truth, in my judgment, whatever the words " in connexion with " may embrace, they are altogether too narrow to include merely acting as the plaintiff company's bankers, even negligently, or honouring cheques drawn without authority, which is all that is alleged in this case.

There remains the second part of s. 169 (4) of the Companies Act, 1948:

" . . . or for the recovery of any property of the body corporate which has been misapplied or wrongfully retained . . . "

Here counsel for the defendant bank argues that there must be specific property **A**
to be recovered and that the subsection cannot apply to an action to make a bank
liable to replace money which it has, so it is said, wrongly debited to the
company's account. In many contexts money is property, and he concedes that
this subsection would apply to an action to recover specific money as, for example,
a bag of sovereigns or currency notes, but he submits that the words do not
comprehend a bank balance. In this connexion counsel for the defendant bank **B**
has relied, not as a direct authority but as some indication of the meaning to be
attributed to the words, on what was said by LORD SIMONDS in the revenue case
of *St. Aubyn (L. M.)* v. *A.-G. (No. 2)* (3), supported as he was by LORD OAKSEY and
LORD NORMAND, although LORD RADCLIFFE and LORD TUCKER took a different
view. That was a case on the Finance Act, 1940, and was subject, therefore, to
the rule that there is no intendment about such Acts; moreover the words of the **C**
section were different, namely, " makes a transfer of any property ". I do not
derive much assistance from this case, particularly as in *Thomas* v. *Marshall
(Inspector of Taxes)* (4) LORD MORTON OF HENRYTON made it clear that LORD
SIMONDS' speech had been intended to apply only to the particular case before
him.

I come back to the words of s. 169 (4) of the Companies Act, 1948, which refer **D**
on the one hand to an action for damages for fraud, misfeasance or other misconduct, and on the other hand to an action to recover property. Apart from the
alternative claim to payment, this action is in form a claim for damages, not to
recover property, and, in my judgment, it is so in substance also. What the
plaintiff company seeks is not to recover its property but damages for negligence
or breach of duty. This is not a tracing action. Even the alternative is not, in my **E**
judgment, a claim to recover property which has been misapplied. It proceeds
on the footing that the payment by Mr. Cradock to the plaintiff company was
rightly made, but that the payment by the plaintiff company to Mr. Burden was
not, and that the latter should, therefore, be disregarded, leaving the otherwise
small credit balance on the plaintiff company's account enlarged by the £44,600.
This, however, simply results in the banker-customer relationship of debtor and **F**
creditor. Even if the claim to enforce payment of that debt can be said to be an
action to recover property, it is not, in my judgment, recovering property
misapplied.

In my judgment, therefore, as things stand, the defendant bank must succeed,
but counsel for the Board of Trade has argued that inasmuch as the Board of
Trade has presented a petition under s. 169 (3) for the winding-up of the plaintiff **G**
company, which petition is to be heard next Monday, I ought to stand this matter
over to see if an order be made and, if so, whether a liquidator when appointed
will ratify or adopt the action. He relies on the well-settled rule that when an
action is commenced on behalf of a company and without its authority, the court
will not strike it out forthwith but will itself convene or allow to be convened a
general meeting of the company or a meeting of the directors to consider whether **H**
to adopt the action, and so too it will wait if the company is about to be wound up,
as exemplified in *East Pant Du United Lead Mining Co., Ltd.* v. *Merryweather*
(5), and to some extent by *Danish Mercantile Co., Ltd.* v. *Beaumont* (6). The latter
case was, in any event, different on the facts because the liquidator had actually
been appointed and had ratified before the application to strike out was heard,
but JENKINS, L.J., said (7):   **I**

" The relevant passage [in BUCKLEY ON THE COMPANIES ACTS (12th Edn.)
p. 169] for the present purpose is in these terms: ' (6) If the case be one in
which the company ought to be plaintiff, the fact that the seal is in the
possession of the adverse party will not necessarily preclude the intending

(3) [1951] 2 All E.R. 473 at p. 485; [1952] A.C. 15 at p. 32.
(4) [1953] 1 All E.R. 1102 at p. 1106; [1953] A.C. 543 at p. 558.
(5) (1864), 2 Hem. & M. 254.   (6) [1951] 1 All E.R. 925; [1951] Ch. 680.
(7) [1951] 1 All E.R. at pp. 929, 930; [1951] Ch. at p. 686.

A   plaintiffs from using the company's name. Neither will it be necessary to obtain the resolution of a general meeting in favour of the action before the writ is issued. In many cases the delay might amount to a denial of justice. In a case of urgency the intending plaintiffs may use the company's name, but at their peril, and subject to their being able to show that they have the support of the majority. In an action so constituted, the court may give

B   interlocutory relief, taking care that a meeting be called at the earliest possible date to determine whether the action really has the support of the majority or not.' That passage, where it refers to the calling of a meeting, accords with the well-settled practice of the court in cases in which, in proceedings brought by a company, a dispute arises as to the authority with which the company's name has been used as plaintiff. It is common practice

C   in such cases to adjourn any motion brought to strike out the company's name with a view to a meeting being called to see whether the company desires the action to be brought or not."

Counsel for the defendant bank submits, on the other hand, that the principle does not apply to the present case because nobody purported to act for the plaintiff company and there is nothing to ratify. The Board of Trade claimed the statutory power to sue in the name of the plaintiff company which, in my judg-

D   ment, they did not possess as against the defendant bank, and it is submitted that the defendant bank is, therefore, entitled to have the action stayed, and one cannot treat the Board of Trade as simply dropping out leaving this an action brought by the Board's solicitor on behalf of the company but without authority. However, the action is an action brought in the name of the plaintiff company;

E   the plaintiff company and not the Board of Trade is the plaintiff, and the action is so brought without authority. It seems to me that the case does fall within the principle and, accordingly, there being a winding-up petition pending, I ought to adjourn this matter until after the hearing of that petition. I will hear counsel as to the length of any such adjournment.

F   *Order that the summons be adjourned until seven days after the hearing of the winding-up petition.*

Solicitors: *Simmons & Simmons* (for the Bank of Nova Scotia); *Solicitor, Board of Trade* (for the plaintiff company).

[*Reported by* JENIFER SANDELL, *Barrister-at-Law.*]

G

Re S.B.A. PROPERTIES, LTD.

[CHANCERY DIVISION (Pennycuick, J.), April 24, 25, 1967.]

Company—Winding-up—Compulsory winding-up—Board of Trade's applica-
tion—Evidence—Cross-examination—Affidavit of official of Board of Trade

H   *—Application by bank, defendant in action brought by Board of Trade in the*
name of that company, for an order for cross-examination of official on
affidavit—Action previously held to have been brought without authority—
Application by defendant bank for stay of proceedings in the action stood over
pending hearing of winding-up petition—Whether bank was a contingent
creditor of company by reason of possible future order for costs—Whether bank,

I   *to which no present debt was owed by company, had locus standi to appear on*
winding-up petition.

An action was instituted in the name of a company as plaintiff by the Board of Trade pursuant to s. 169 (3)* of the Companies Act, 1948. On application of the defendant bank, one of four defendants, the action was held to have been brought in the name of the company without authority. The court, however, did not stay the action but stood it over pending the presentation of a petition for the compulsory winding-up of the company, since the

* Section 169 (3) is set out at p. 620, letter A, post.

liquidator, if the compulsory winding-up order were made, might be in a　**A**
position to prosecute the action. The bank was not a creditor of the company
for a present debt. On the hearing of the winding-up petition the bank
sought, under R.S.C., Ord. 38, r. 2 (3), an order for cross-examination of an
official of the Board of Trade on his affidavit filed in the winding-up
proceedings.

　　Held: the bank was not a contingent creditor* of the company in respect　**B**
of the costs that the bank had already incurred in the action, because, the
action having been brought without authority, the company was not at
present liable to costs and the possibility that the liquidator might ratify
the bringing of the action, and that his ratification would relate back to its
commencement, did not render the bank a contingent creditor of the
company at the present time; and accordingly the bank had no locus standi　**C**
on the winding-up petition and, for that reason, as also in exercise of the
court's discretion under R.S.C., Ord. 38, r. 2 (3), the order for cross-
examination sought would not be made (see p. 619, letters A to C, and G, post).

　　Dictum of LORD REID in *Winter* v. *Inland Revenue Comrs.* ([1961] 3 All
E.R. at p. 859, letter E) applied.

　　　　　　　　　　　　　　　　　　　　　　　　　　　　　　　　　　　　　　D
*Company—Winding-up—Compulsory winding-up—Board of Trade's applica-
tion—Just and equitable—Evidence—Inspector's report—Report admissible
—Sufficiency as evidence—Misconduct or fraud—Order made on considera-
tion of report alone when uncontradicted by evidence adduced by company—
Companies Act, 1948 (11 & 12 Geo. 6 c. 38), s. 169 (3).*

　　A petition was presented by the Board of Trade pursuant to s. 169 (3)† of　**E**
the Companies Act, 1948, for the compulsory winding-up of a company. The
petition was based on a report which the Board of Trade obtained from an
inspector appointed under s. 165 of the Act of 1948, in which it was found
that a sum of £44,600 had been taken from the resources of the company.
The company was not represented at the hearing of the petition.

　　Held: under s. 169 (3) the court could treat an inspector's report, not as　**F**
evidence in the ordinary sense, but as material on which, if it were not
challenged, the court could make a winding-up order on the ground that it
was just and equitable to do so, and, as the circumstances appearing from
the inspector's report in the present case showed were ample to justify the
making of a winding-up order, the court would make the order sought (see
p. 621, letters F and H, post).
　　　　　　　　　　　　　　　　　　　　　　　　　　　　　　　　　　　　　　G
　　Re Grosvenor & West-End Railway Terminus Hotel Co., Ltd. ((1897), 76
L.T. 337) distinguished.

　　Re Travel & Holiday Clubs, Ltd. (ante, p. 606) followed.

　　[As to the presentation of a winding-up petition consequent on investigations
by the Board of Trade, see 6 HALSBURY'S LAWS (3rd Edn.) 391, para. 759; and
for cases on investigations by the Board of Trade, see 9 DIGEST (Repl.) 627,　**H**
4187-4190.

　　As to notice of intention to appear on the hearing of a winding-up petition, see
6 HALSBURY'S LAWS (3rd Edn.) 548, 549, para. 1055.

　　As to the court's discretion over ordering the attendance of a witness for
cross-examination, see 15 HALSBURY'S LAWS (3rd Edn.) 463, para. 834.

　　For the Companies Act, 1948, s. 169 (3), see 3 HALSBURY'S STATUTES (2nd　**I**
Edn.) 594.]

Cases referred to:
　　Grosvenor & West-End Railway Terminus Hotel Co., Ltd., Re, (1897), 76 L.T.
　　　　337; 9 Digest (Repl.) 627, *4187*.
　　Travel & Holiday Clubs, Ltd., Re, ante, p. 606.

---

* Compare s. 224 (1) of the Companies Act, 1948.
† Section 169 (3) is set as at p. 620, letter A, post.

A Winter (Executors of Sir Arthur Munro Sutherland (decd.)) v. Inland Revenue
Comrs., [1961] 3 All E.R. 855; [1963] A.C. 235; [1961] 3 W.L.R. 1062;
21 Digest (Repl.) 62, 242.

Petition.

This was a petition presented by the Board of Trade pursuant to s. 169 (3) of
the Companies Act, 1948, for the winding-up by the court of S.B.A. Properties,
B Ltd. A preliminary point was first heard, the Bank of Nova Scotia, which was
fourth defendant in the action brought by the Board of Trade in the name of
the company, certain proceedings in which are reported at p. 610, ante, seeking
an order under R.S.C., Ord. 38, r. 2 (3) for the cross-examination of a witness
on behalf of the Board of Trade.

The cases noted below* were cited during the argument in addition to those
C referred to in the judgment.

Jeremiah Harman for the Bank of Nova Scotia (on the preliminary point).
J. P. Warner for the Board of Trade.

PENNYCUICK, J.: The present petition is presented by the Board of
Trade under the power conferred by s. 169 (3) of the Companies Act, 1948, and
D is for the compulsory winding-up of the company, S.B.A. Properties, Ltd. There
is pending an action in the Chancery Division intituled " 1966 S.No.1161 ", the
plaintiff being the company, and the defendants being three individuals named
Mr. Cradock, Mr. Bieber and Mr. Burden and the Bank of Nova Scotia as fourth
defendant. The writ in the action states that the action is brought in the name
of the plaintiff by the Board of Trade pursuant to s. 169 (4) of the Companies
E Act, 1948. In the course of the action there have been disputes between the Board
of Trade and the bank. In March, 1967 the bank issued a summons to stay the
action on the ground that the Board of Trade had no power under s. 169 (4) to
bring this action in the name of the company against the bank. That procedure
summons was heard by GOFF, J., (1) who acceded to the bank's application in
principle. He did not, however, stay the proceedings but stood them over pending
F the hearing of the present petition on the footing that, if an order was made on
the petition, then there would be a liquidator of the company who would be in a
position to prosecute the action, and who would or might be in a position to
ratify what had already been done. That is the present state of affairs.

The petition was presented on Mar. 13. It was supported by the usual statutory
affidavit. There was also a short affidavit by Mr. Williams, Assistant Official
G Receiver, exhibiting the report which he had made on the instructions of the
Board of Trade. There was then an affidavit by Mr. Sykes, a solicitor acting on
behalf of the bank, in which he set out the history of the matter and also made a
considerable number of complaints as to the manner in which the Board of Trade
has been carrying on the present action. Those complaints are made partly in
the affidavit itself and partly by reference to a bundle of correspondence. I will
H now read para. 6 and part of para. 7 of that affidavit:

" 6. Counsel for the Board of Trade had applied for such an adjournment
... [i.e. before GOFF, J.,] ... upon the ground that if the company was wound-
up by this Honourable Court and the Official Receiver was appointed
liquidator, the Official Receiver could and probably would ratify the action
of the Solicitor to the Board of Trade and, on behalf of the company, adopt the
I action. The bank most strongly objects to this suggestion. As appears above
the company has no monies in hand; the Official Receiver would be bound to
look to the Board of Trade for his solicitor and own client costs of the action;
in the result the Board of Trade, which has been held to have no power to
bring this action against the bank in its own right, would nonetheless be

---

* *Re British Equitable Bond and Mortgage Corpn., Ltd.*, [1910] 1 Ch. 574; *Re Duffy*
(decd.), [1948] 2 All E.R. 756; [1949] Ch. 28; *Re William Hockley, Ltd.*, [1962] 2 All
E.R. 111.

(1) The proceedings on this summons are reported at p. 610, ante.

financing out of public funds the same action, although under what power   A
the board can so expend public money is unclear to me. Such a result would
be oppressive to the bank by enabling the action to be continued against it
despite the decision on the point raised by the procedure summons. The
events upon which the claim against the bank is allegedly based took place
some seven years ago and evidence is obviously difficult to obtain when
dealing with so stale a claim.   B

" 7. The bank is a prospective or contingent creditor of the company for
the bank's costs of the action if the bank's defence is successful. The costs of
the action to date amount to approximately £750 and I estimate, if the action
comes to trial and lasts three or four days, as seems likely, that the bank's
party and party costs will exceed £4,000."

He says that he knows of " no other reason for presentation of this petition than   C
to enable the action to be carried on against the bank ".

Finally, Mr. Deane, a chief executive officer in the office of the Solicitor to the
Board of Trade, filed an affidavit in answer. I need not refer at any length to that
affidavit. It contains the Board of Trade's answers to the various allegations as to
the manner as to which it has carried on the action. I should, I think, state that he
gives reasons, quite apart from the conduct of the action, why in the opinion of   D
the Board of Trade a liquidator should be appointed. On the hearing of the
present petition the company is not represented. The bank is, however,
represented by counsel and he seeks an order under R.S.C., Ord. 38, r. 2 (3) for
the cross-examination of Mr. Deane on his affidavit. I have now to deal with
that preliminary point.

Counsel for the Board of Trade opposes the application and does so primarily   E
on the ground that the bank has no locus standi to appear on the hearing of this
petition. It is not in dispute that the only persons entitled to appear on the
hearing of a winding-up petition are the company, its creditors and its contributories. It is further not in dispute that for this purpose a person is a creditor _
only if he is a creditor either for a present debt, or for a prospective debt or for a
contingent debt. It is not suggested that the bank is a creditor either for a present   F
debt or for a prospective debt in the sense in which that word is used here. What
is contended by counsel for the bank is that the bank is a creditor for a contingent
debt.

The nature of a contingent debt was considered by the House of Lords in
Winter (Executors of Sir Arthur Munro Sutherland (decd.)) v. *Inland Revenue Comrs.*
(2), in which the majority held that a contingent liability was a liability which,   G
by reason of something done by the person bound, would necessarily arise or
come into being on an event or events which might or might not happen. This is
what was said by LORD REID (3) with which LORD GUEST's definition (4) accords.
In order that one may have a contingent debt one must find that there has been
something done by the person bound. The question then is what, if anything,
has already been done.   H

Counsel for the bank goes on to contend that the bank is a creditor for a
contingent debt consisting of the costs which it has already incurred. At first
sight it seems quite clear that the company is under no liability for those costs
because, as GOFF, J., has held, the writ was issued in the name of the company
without any authority, and accordingly the company is at the moment under no
such liability in respect of costs. Counsel, however, contends that, if the liquidator   I
ratifies the proceedings taken in the name of the company without authority,
then the ratification will relate back, so that the action will have been from the
beginning the action of the company; and, accordingly, if the company fails in
the action the costs from the beginning of the action will be payable by the
company, and the liability will arise in that future event as the result of what was

(2) [1961] 3 All E.R. 855; [1963] A.C. 235.
(3) [1961] 3 All E.R. at p. 859, letter E; [1963] A.C. at p. 249.
(4) [1961] 3 All E.R. at p. 867, letter I; [1963] A.C. at p. 262.

A   done by the company when it issued the writ, bearing in mind the retrospective effect of ratification.

That is an attractive argument, but I do not think that I ought to accept it. I must look at the matter as it stands today. As things stand today, it is admitted that the company is not, and never can be, apart from ratification, under any liability for the costs already incurred. That being the position

B   I do not think that I ought to regard the bank as a contingent creditor of the company. As things are today, nothing has been done by the company which can give rise to such a contingent liability, and I do not think that I am entitled to look to the future and say that, if something is done in the future, then that something will relate back so as to produce the notional result that the company has already done something which in fact it had not done at the date of the

C   hearing of the petition. I recognise that the Board of Trade has stated its expectation that the liquidator, if appointed, will in all probability ratify what was done in the name of the company. Even so I do not think that I would be justified in saying that the bank is at this stage a contingent creditor of the company. It is not in dispute that any liability which the company may, through its liquidator, incur towards the bank in the course of proceedings after the commencement of

D   the winding-up, does not represent a contingent liability for the present purpose. In the circumstances it seems to me that the bank is not a creditor of the company for the purpose of this petition.

I should add that, if the bank had established that it was a creditor, I am very far from being persuaded that this is a case in which it would have been right for me in the exercise of my discretion under R.S.C., Ord. 38, r. 2 (3) to direct

E   cross-examination of Mr. Deane at the instance of the bank. The issue with which I am concerned is whether this company should be wound up. The matter which have been raised on behalf of the bank in Mr. Sykes' affidavit are all matters relating to the action. The bank complains of the manner in which the Board of Trade has carried on the action. It complains of the expenditure of public funds on the prosecution of the action and it complains of

F   the Board of Trade's intention, if able to do so, to ratify the commencement of the action in the name of the company. More specifically it complains of certain matters relating to particulars and discovery. The evidence which has been filed on either side on these matters does not seem to me to be directly relevant to the question whether it is just and equitable that the company should be wound up on the petition of the Board of Trade, and I do not think that, if I have a discretion

G   in this matter, I ought to exercise it by allowing cross-examination on those matters. They are only very indirectly relevant to the question which I will have to decide, namely, whether the winding-up order should be made. Their relevance is to the action rather than to the question whether the company should be put into liquidation.

I am not invited by counsel for the Board of Trade to exclude counsel for the

H   bank from being heard on the present petition, and whether or not he has, strictly, a locus standi so to be heard, I will certainly allow him to say whatever he wants on the petition, but I do not think that I ought to allow cross-examination.

[The bank intimated that it did not wish to take further part in the proceedings on the winding-up petition.]

I   Apr. 25. PENNYCUICK, J., having heard the application for compulsory winding-up of the company, said: This petition is presented by the Board of Trade pursuant to s. 169 (3) of the Companies Act, 1948, for the winding-up of S.B.A. Properties, Ltd., to which I will refer as " the company ". The petition is based on a report which the Board of Trade obtained from an inspector appointed under the provisions of s. 165 of the Act of 1948. The inspector made a report into the details of which it is unnecessary to go. It will be sufficient to say that in the course of that report he found that the sum of £44,600 had been taken away from the resources of the company in a manner which he indicates.

Section 169 (3) of the Companies Act, 1948, is in these terms:

"If, in the case of any body corporate liable to be wound up under this Act, it appears to the Board of Trade, from any such [inspectors'] report as aforesaid that it is expedient so to do by reason of any such circumstances as are referred to in sub-para. (i) or (ii) of para. (b) of s. 165 of this Act, the board may, unless the body corporate is already being wound up by the court, present a petition for it to be so wound up if the court thinks it just and equitable that it should be wound up or a petition for an order under s. 210 of this Act or both."

I had to consider the application of that subsection in *Re Travel & Holiday Clubs, Ltd.* (5). In that case I held that on a petition presented by the Board of Trade under s. 169 (3) the court was entitled to look at the inspectors' report and act on it in the absence of any other evidence. In the present case the inspectors' report, if one is entitled to look at it, provides, it seems to me, clear grounds for holding that it is just and equitable that the company should be wound up. If I have jurisdiction to do so, I propose on the evidence to make the order.

On the hearing of this petition counsel for the Board of Trade called my attention to a case which had escaped notice on the hearing of the *Re Travel & Holiday Club, Ltd.'s* (5) petition, namely *Re Grosvenor and West-End Railway Terminus Hotel Co., Ltd.* (6). That is a decision of the Court of Appeal given in 1897 which was heard on the terms of the Companies Act, 1862, and in particular the provisions contained in s. 56 and the subsequent sections of that Act. Section 56 gave the Board of Trade power to appoint an inspector to examine into the affairs of any company on application made by the members of the company. The provisions of the Act of 1862 conferred no power on the Board of Trade to take any step consequent on the inspectors' report corresponding to the powers which are conferred on the Board of Trade by s. 169 of the Act of 1948. In particular, the Board of Trade had no power under the Act of 1862 to present a petition. The headnote in the case stated that an examination into the affairs of a joint-stock company by an inspector appointed by the Board of Trade under s. 56 of the Companies Act, 1862, was not a proceeding of such a nature that prohibition could lie in respect of it either to the Board of Trade or to the inspector. That was the actual decision of the Court of Appeal, but all the three judgments contain certain observations as to the functions of the inspector and the admissibility of evidence of the report which he makes. I will refer to those passages in the judgments. LORD ESHER, M.R., said (7):

"What is the nature of that inquiry? The object of the inquiry which the Board of Trade has authority to order under s. 56 is to examine into and ascertain facts to enable the inspector to make a report of his opinion to the Board of Trade. That is all . . .: The examination is to be made for the purpose of making a report, and that report when made has no legal effect with regard to anyone, and cannot be used as evidence against anyone. The inquiry held by the inspector is not a judicial inquiry, and has nothing in the nature of a judicial determination . . . The report will not be evidence in a court of justice of the existence of any fact mentioned in it; it binds no one and has no effect upon anyone or any company. It is not a judicial inquiry, and even if he should overstep the authority which he has he would not be liable to a writ of prohibition."

LOPES, L.J., said (8):

". . . the inquiry before the inspector is not a judicial proceeding at all. Can it be said that this inquiry is in any respect a judicial proceeding? Sections 56 to 61, inclusive, of the Companies Act, 1862, appear to me to embody a certain scheme or code for obtaining information by means of the inspector appointed by the Board of Trade. It is to be observed that all that

---

(5) Ante, p. 606.
(7) (1897), 76 L.T. at p. 338.
(6) (1897), 76 L.T. 337.
(8) (1897), 76 L.T. at p. 339.

A   the inspector can do is to make a report to the board. The board cannot do anything when it has received the report. The report itself is not evidence of anything contained in it . . . It is clear to my mind that this cannot be said to be a judicial proceeding."

Finally, CHITTY, L.J., said (9):

B   " The object of s. 56, and the supplementary sections of the Companies Act, 1862, is simply to afford to a minority of a company constituted under the Act an opportunity for obtaining information which they could not otherwise obtain. The beginning and the end of the duty of an inspector appointed under s. 56 is to examine and report. He does not occupy a quasi-judicial position. The proceedings before him are not judicial in any

C proper sense of the term. There is no court, and no judge, nor anyone assuming to constitute a court, or exercising a jurisdiction which he does not possess, or exceeding any jurisdiction which he has. As has been pointed out, the whole business begins and ends with the inquiry and report. The report cannot be made the foundation of any subsequent action, it is merely evidence of the opinion of the inspector. He is nothing more than an inspector as he

D is described in the Act."

The question which counsel for the Board of Trade has very fairly put before me is whether there is anything in that case which invalidates the decision which I gave in *Re Travel & Holiday Clubs, Ltd.* (10). He contends that there is not and I agree with him.

The decision in *Re Grosvenor and West-End Railway Terminus Hotel Co., Ltd.*

E (11) is to this effect: first, that the function of the inspector is to make an inquiry and report and not to come to a judicial decision. That, I think, is still the same today. Then it is said that the report of the inspector is not evidence in a court of law of the existence of any fact mentioned in it. Again, so far as that goes, that is still true today; but that is by no means the end of the matter.

What one is concerned with under s. 169 (3) is whether the court can treat the

F inspectors' report, not as evidence in the ordinary sense, but as material on which, if it is not challenged, the court can proceed to make a winding-up order on the ground that it is just and equitable so to do. It seems to me that the whole tenor of s. 169 (3) is to that effect. This consideration, namely whether the report could be regarded by a court as material on which to make a winding-up order, was not, and could not have been, in the minds of the Court of Appeal in *Re*

G *Grosvenor and West-End Railway Terminus Hotel Co., Ltd.* (11) because at that time under the Act of 1862 the Board of Trade, as was stated more than once in the judgments, had no power to take any further step on the report; in particular, it could not present a winding-up petition. The minds of the Court of Appeal in that case, which was an application for an order of prohibition, could not have been addressed to the circumstances which arise under s. 169 (3)

H and I do not think that I am obliged to treat anything that was said in that case as prohibiting me from taking into account as material, on a winding-up petition, the report of an inspector appointed by the Board of Trade. As I have said, the circumstances contained in the report, as long as I can look at it at all, are ample to justify the making of a winding-up order, and I propose to do so.

Order accordingly.

I   Solicitors: *Simmons & Simmons* (for the Bank of Nova Scotia); *Solicitor, Board of Trade.*

[*Reported by* JENIFER SANDELL, *Barrister-at-Law.*]

---

(9) (1897), 76 L.T. at p. 339.
(10) Ante, p. 606.
(11) (1897), 76 L.T. 337.

A

STANDARD SECURITIES, LTD. *v.* HUBBARD AND ANOTHER.

[CHANCERY DIVISION (Pennycuick, J.), February 14, 1967.]

Practice—Third party procedure—Notice—Relief connected with the " original subject-matter of the action "—Specific performance of agreement to sell land to vendors sued for specific performance of their subsequent sale of land— Whether third party notice valid—R.S.C., Ord. 16, r. 1 (1) (b).

B

By an agreement dated Jan. 24, 1957, the third party agreed to sell certain premises to the two defendants. By an agreement dated May 29, 1963, the defendants agreed to sell the same premises to a company, which then assigned the benefit of the agreement to the plaintiff. The agreement of Jan. 24, 1957, remained uncompleted. The plaintiff issued a writ against the defendants seeking specific performance of the agreement of May 29, 1963. By a third party notice issued under R.S.C., Ord. 16, r. 1*, addressed to the third party the first defendant claimed specific performance of the agreement dated Jan. 24, 1957. The third party applied to have the third party notice set aside.

C

Held: the " original subject-matter of the action " for the purposes of r. 1 (1) (b) of R.S.C., Ord. 16 was the agreement of May 29, 1963, being an agreement for the sale of the premises, and the relief claimed against the third party, being specific performance of the agreement of Jan. 24, 1957, for the sale of those premises to the defendants, was relief related to or connected with the agreement of May 29, 1963, for the defendants could not perform that agreement unless the agreement of Jan. 24, 1957, were performed, and both agreements would normally be completed by a single instrument; accordingly the matter was within R.S.C., Ord. 16, r. 1 (1) (b) and the third party notice would not be set aside (see p. 624, letters A, C and E, post).

D

E

[As to claims against a third party, see 30 HALSBURY'S LAWS (3rd Edn.) 445, para. 838; and for cases on the subject, see DIGEST (Practice) 451, 452, *1384, 1385.*]

F

Procedure Summons.

By an agreement dated Jan. 24, 1957, Telesurance, Ltd., the third party, agreed to sell certain premises to the defendants, Lafayette Ronald Hubbard and Sidney John Parkhouse. By an agreement dated May 29, 1963, the defendants agreed to sell the same premises to Rathbone Holdings, Ltd. By an assignment dated Feb. 7, 1964, the latter assigned the benefit of the agreement to the plaintiff, Standard Securities, Ltd. On July 4, 1966, the plaintiff issued a writ against the defendants seeking specific performance of the agreement of May 29, 1963. By a third party notice issued under R.S.C., Ord. 16, r. 1 (1), dated Sept. 21, 1966, addressed to Telesurance, Ltd., the defendant Hubbard claimed specific performance of the agreement of Jan. 24, 1957. This was a summons dated Jan. 17, 1967, by the third party seeking to set aside the third party notice.

G

H

The cases noted below† were cited during the argument.

C. A. Brodie for the third party.
J. D. Waite for the defendants.

PENNYCUICK, J.: By an agreement dated Jan. 24, 1957, Telesurance, Ltd., the third party, agreed to sell to the defendants, namely Lafayette Ronald Hubbard and Sidney John Parkhouse (who, apparently, took no part in this action), certain premises known as 35, Fitzroy Street, London. By an agreement dated May 29, 1963, the defendants agreed to sell the same premises to a company known as Rathbone Holdings, Ltd. By an assignment dated Feb. 7, 1964, Rathbone Holdings, Ltd., assigned the benefit of the last mentioned agreement

I

---

* R.S.C., Ord. 16, r. 1, so far as material, is set out at p. 623, letters C to E, post.
† *Pontifex* v. *Foord*, (1884), 12 Q.B.D. 152; *Birmingham and District Land Co.* v. *London and North Western Ry. Co.*, (1886), 34 Ch.D. 261.

A to the plaintiff company, Standard Securities, Ltd. The agreement of Jan. 24, 1957, remains uncompleted.

On July 4, 1966, the plaintiff issued a writ against the defendants, seeking specific performance of the agreement dated May 29, 1963. By a third party notice dated Sept. 21, 1966, addressed to the third party, the defendant Hubbard claimed against the third party specific performance of the agreement dated

B Jan. 24, 1957. No point is taken on the present application by reason of the fact that the third party notice is given only by the defendant Hubbard and not also by the defendant Parkhouse.

On Jan. 17, 1967, the third party took out the present summons, seeking that the third party notice be set aside. The third party notice was given under the terms of R.S.C., Ord. 16, r. 1 (1) which reads as follows:—

C

" (1) Where in any action a defendant who has entered an appearance—(*a*) claims against a person not already a party to the action any contribution or indemnity; or (*b*) claims against such a person any relief or remedy relating to or connected with the original subject-matter of the action and substantially the same as some relief or remedy claimed by the plaintiff; or (*c*) re-

D quires that any question or issue relating to or connected with the original subject-matter of the action should be determined not only as between the plaintiff and the defendant but also as between either or both of them and a person not already a party to the action; then, subject to para. (2), the defendant may issue a notice in Form No. 20 or 21 in Appendix A . . . containing a statement of the nature of the claim made against him and,

E as the case may be, either of the nature and grounds of the claim made by him or of the question or issue required to be determined."

The origin of the rule in its present form is explained in the note at p. 197 of the SUPREME COURT PRACTICE, 1967. Under the 1875 rules, there was a corresponding order in very wide terms. By the R.S.C., 1883, the order was varied

F so as to confine it to claims for contribution or indemnity. Then, again, in 1929, the rule was amended so as to widen it by the inclusion of the matter now contained in para. (*b*) and para. (*c*) of R.S.C., Ord. 16, r. 1 (1). The rule has stood substantially unamended since 1929, though the wording of the substantive paragraphs is not exactly the same.

The objects of the rule are (as explained in the note on p. 198 in the SUPREME

G COURT PRACTICE, 1967, and the cases there cited) to prevent multiplicity of actions and to enable the court to settle disputes between all parties to them in one action and to prevent the same question from being tried twice with possibly different results. There have been a great number of decisions under the rule as it stood limited to claims for contribution and indemnity, but it appears that there have been no decisions on the scope of the rule as it now stands, that is,

H in particular, under para. (*b*) and para. (*c*) of the rule.

To return to the present case, counsel for the third party contends that the claim sought to be raised against the third party cannot be brought under any of the three paras. (*a*), (*b*) and (*c*) in r. 1 (1). He said, candidly, that the point is a purely technical one, but, of course, if the point is well-founded one must give effect to it.

I Counsel for the defendants does not rely on para. (*a*), which refers to claims for contribution or indemnity, and I say no more about that. He does rely on para. (*b*) and para. (*c*) and, in particular, he relies on para. (*b*). The first question which arises on the construction of para. (*b*) is what is meant by the original subject matter of the action. Now it seems to me that in the present case the original subject-matter of the action is the agreement dated May 29, 1963, for the sale of 35, Fitzroy Street by the defendants to (by assignment) the plaintiff at the price and on the terms specified in that agreement.

Counsel for the third party said that the original subject matter of the action

is simply the agreement dated May 29, 1963. I do not think that one can in that **A**
way abstract the agreement from the contents of the agreement.

Counsel for the defendants says that the original subject matter of the action
is the physical premises, namely 35, Fitzroy Street. Again, I do not think that
that is right. I think that the subject matter of the action is neither the agreement
in abstraction from its content, nor the premises in isolation from the agreement,
but the agreement being an agreement for the sale of those premises.   **B**

The question then is, are the claims for relief or remedy, claimed against the
third party, related to or connected with the agreement dated May 29, 1963?
The relief or remedy claimed against the third party is specific performance of
the agreement dated Jan. 24, 1957, for the sale of the same premises, that agreement being still uncompleted. Now is that relief or remedy connected with the
agreement of May 29, 1963? It seems to me that on any ordinary use of language it **C**
is so related and connected. In the first place, the defendants will be able to perform the agreement of May 29, 1963, only if they are first able to obtain the relief
or remedy which they seek against the third party, viz., performance of the agreement dated Jan. 24, 1957. In the second place, in the ordinary course of conveyancing the two agreements for sale will be completed by a single instrument, in
which the three parties concerned will join and the execution of that instrument **D**
will be one of the matters which will be secured by the order for specific performance in the present action. It is, of course, possible to complete the two
agreements by separate conveyances, but that would be contrary to conveyancing practice; it would also involve payment of double stamp duty.

In those circumstances, I find it impossible to say that the relief or remedy
against the third party does not relate to or is not concerned with the subject- **E**
matter of the present action. It has not been suggested that the relief or remedy
sought by the third party proceedings is not substantially the same in any
relevant sense as the relief or remedy claimed by the plaintiff against the defendants. In each case the party concerned is claiming specific performance of a
contract for the sale of this property.

I would add that para. (c) does not appear to me to be applicable. I do not **F**
think that there is any single question or issue relating to or connected with the
original subject matter of the action which ought to be determined, not only
as between the plaintiff and the defendants, but also between either of them and
the third party.

I was referred to certain cases under the rules as they stood between 1883 and
1929. I do not think that it would be useful to go into those further or to consider **G**
what is an interesting question, whether, in those particular cases, the decisions
would have been different had the rules stood as they stand today. I propose,
therefore, to dismiss the summons to set aside the third party notice.

Application dismissed.

Solicitors: *J. A. Wall* (for the third party); *Signy & Co.* (for the defendants). **H**

[*Reported by* JENIFER SANDELL, *Barrister-at-Law.*]

A

CAMPBELL AND ANOTHER
(TRUSTEES OF DAVIES'S EDUCATIONAL TRUST)
v. INLAND REVENUE COMMISSIONERS.

[COURT OF APPEAL (Lord Denning, M.R., Harman and Salmon, L.JJ.), February 8, 9, 10, 13, 1967.]

B *Income Tax—Annual payments—Covenanted payments to charity—Common intention that covenanted payments should be used by charity to buy goodwill of covenantor's educational establishment—Plan to convert tutorial establishment to educational trust—Covenanted payments not pure bounty and thus not annual payments—Income Tax Act, 1952 (15 & 16 Geo. 6 & 1 Eliz. 2 c. 10), s. 169 (1), s. 447 (1) (b).*

C   In order to put Davies's, a first class place of education owned by a company, Davies's (Tutors), Ltd., on a permanent basis, three of the principals who were directors of the company set up a charitable trust. Under the trust the trustees (a director and the secretary of the company) were to hold the trust fund on charitable trusts for the promotion of education. On the following day the company executed a deed of covenant in which it

D agreed with the trustees to pay them annually for seven years out of the general fund of the company's taxed income a sum equal to eighty per cent. of its net profits. A few days later the two trustees formed a second company which agreed by deed to purchase the goodwill of Davies's (Tutors), Ltd. for £50,000 (a fair price) by five instalments of £10,000 each year, and on completing payment of the full sum to buy all the company's premises and

E equipment at a fair market valuation by an independent valuer. It was the common intention of all concerned that the covenanted payments would be used by the trustees to buy the business of Davies's (Tutors), Ltd., whose equity shareholders would in due course receive a fair but not excessive price for its assets. The trustees claimed repayment of tax on the first two instalments paid by the first company under the covenant.

F   **Held:** (i) as, for the reasons stated in (a) and (b) below, the covenanted payments were not annual payments within s. 169 (1) or s. 447 (1) (b) of the Income Tax Act, 1952, the trustees were not entitled to recover the income tax deducted therefrom—

      (a) (per LORD DENNING, M.R., and HARMAN, L.J.) because the income received by the trustees under the covenant was committed, even though by a

G private understanding, to a purpose which benefited the covenantors (see p. 629, letters F and I, and p. 630, letter E, post).

      (b) (per SALMON, L.J.), because each covenanted payment to the trustees became subject to a trust that it should be dealt with in accordance with the common intention, and for that reason, though whether the obligation was legal or only moral did not really matter, could not be regarded as pure

H bounty and thus lacked the character necessary to constitute an " annual payment " for income tax purposes (see p. 631, letters E and G, and p. 633, letter B, post).

      (ii) (per HARMAN, L.J.), moreover the covenanted payments would not be applied for charitable purposes only within s. 447 (1) (b) of the Act of 1952, as there was a counter-benefit to the covenantor (see p. 630, letter I, post;

I cf. p. 629, letter H, post).

      Inland Revenue Comrs. v. *City of London Corpn.* (*as the Conservators of Epping Forest*) ([1953] 1 All E.R. 1075), and *Inland Revenue Comrs.* v. *National Book League* ([1957] 2 All E.R. 644) applied.

      Decision of BUCKLEY, J. ([1966] 2 All E.R. 736) affirmed on rather different grounds.

      [As to what are annual payments for income tax purposes, see 20 HALSBURY'S LAWS (3rd Edn.) 362-364, para. 666; and for cases on the subject, see 28 DIGEST (Repl.) 169-176, *678-709.*

Affirmed. H.L. [1968] 3 All E.R. 588.

For the Income Tax Act, 1952, s. 169 (1), s. 447 (1), see 31 HALSBURY'S A
STATUTES (2nd Edn.) 162, 427.]

Cases referred to:

Hanbury (decd.), Re, Comiskey v. Hanbury, (1939), 38 Tax Cas. 588.

Howe (Earl) v. Inland Revenue Comrs., [1918-19] All E.R. Rep. 1088; [1919]
    2 K.B. 336; 88 L.J.K.B. 821; 121 L.T. 161; 7 Tax Cas. 289; 28 Digest
    (Repl.) 351, 1549.   B

Inland Revenue Comrs. v. City of London Corpn. (as the Conservators of Epping
    Forest), [1953] 1 All E.R. 1075; [1953] 1 W.L.R. 652; 117 J.P. 28;
    34 Tax Cas. 293; 28 Digest (Repl.) 171, 690.

Inland Revenue Comrs. v. National Book League, [1957] 2 All E.R. 644; [1957]
    Ch. 488; [1957] 3 W.L.R. 222; 37 Tax Cas. 455; 28 Digest (Repl.)
    175, 708.   C

Taw and Torridge Festival Society, Ltd. v. Inland Revenue Comrs., (1959), 38
    Tax Cas. 603; Digest (Cont. Vol. A) 882, 708a.

Appeal.

The taxpayers appealed to the Special Commissioners of Income Tax against
the refusal by the Commissioners of Inland Revenue of claims made by the   D
taxpayers under s. 447 (1) (b) of the Income Tax Act, 1952, for exemption from
income tax chargeable for 1960-61 and 1961-62 on payments received by the
taxpayers under a deed of covenant dated Mar. 30, 1961. The questions for the
commissioners' decision were: (i) whether payments made under the deed of
covenant were annual payments within the meaning of s. 447 (1) (b); and (ii)
if so, whether those payments had been applied to charitable purposes only within   E
the meaning of the subsection. The taxpayers contended before the commissioners
that the payments were annual payments forming part of the income of a trust
established for charitable purposes only, that the income was applied to charitable
purposes only and that the taxpayers were therefore entitled to exemption. The
Crown contended before the commissioners: (a) that the disputed payments were
not paid by the paying company, Davies's (Tutors), Ltd., without conditions or   F
counter-stipulations and were not " pure income profit " in the hands of the
taxpayers; (b) that they were received by the taxpayers subject to an obligation,
legal or practical, to use them for the benefit of the company; (c) that accordingly
they were not annual payments within s. 447 (1) (b); (d) that they were not
applied to charitable purposes only within s. 447 (1) (b), being applied, inter alia,
for the benefit of the company by securing the sale of assets and goodwill of their   G
business; and (e) that the exemption claimed had been properly refused. The
commissioners found that the deed of covenant under which the payments were
made was entered into on a clear understanding both by the covenantor company
and the shareholders of the company and by the taxpayers that the payments
would be used to buy the covenantor company's business. They held, therefore,
that the understanding was a condition or counter-stipulation attached to the   H
deed of covenant not falling within the class of incidental privileges which might
be enjoyed by a donor to a charity, and that the disputed payments were not
annual payments.

On Apr. 6, 1966, as reported at [1966] 2 All E.R. 736, BUCKLEY, J., dismissed
the taxpayers' appeal by way of Case Stated against the decision of the commissioners, holding that the payments were not income in the hands of the   I
trustees and were therefore not annual payments within s. 447 (1) (b) of the Act
of 1952, although the (so held) contractual obligation of the trustees to apply the
payments towards the purchase of the covenantor company's business did not
deprive them of the character of bounty, and although if annual payments they
would have been applied for charitable purposes. The taxpayers appealed to the
Court of Appeal.

Desmond C. Miller, Q.C., S. I. Simon and Margot Hoare for the taxpayers.
E. I. Goulding, Q.C., J. R. Phillips and J. P. Warner for the Crown.

A   LORD DENNING, M.R.: " Davies's " is a first class place of education. It was founded by Mr. Vernon Davies in 1927 and turned into a private limited company in 1946, called Davies's (Tutors), Ltd. The founder died unexpectedly in 1952, leaving his interest to his widow. Since that time Davies's has been run by three of the principals, Mr. Campbell, Mr. McBride and Mr. Hall. They are directors of Davies's (Tutors), Ltd., and, together with Mrs. Davies, hold most of
B   the shares. In 1961 they were all anxious to establish Davies's on a permanent basis. So they decided to set up a charitable trust for the purpose. The idea was that the trust should buy from Davies's (Tutors), Ltd. the goodwill, premises and equipment of Davies's; and then carry it on for the years to come. They consulted their solicitor, Mr. Fairfax-Jones, and their accountant, Mr. C. A. Barber; and, under their advice, executed various documents to implement the
C   plan. One of these documents was a seven-year covenant in favour of the charitable trust. The object was to enable the trust to recover tax on the payments under the covenant. That is a perfectly legitimate thing to seek to do. Every charity in the country benefits in this way by seven-year covenants. The question is whether it has succeeded in this case.

The facts are stated in the Special Case. Suffice it for me to reduce them to the
D   essentials:

1. *The charitable trust for education.*—On Mar. 29, 1961, a charitable trust was formed under the name " The Davies's Educational Trust ". The first trustees were Mr. Campbell (a director and shareholder in Davies's (Tutors), Ltd.) and Mr. Fairfax-Jones (a solicitor and the secretary of Davies's (Tutors), Ltd.). There was to be a trust fund of moneys thereafter to be received by the trustees: and
E   the trustees were to hold the fund on charitable trusts for the promotion of education; with power (amongst other things) to purchase, acquire and carry on schools and tutorial establishments.

2. *The seven-year covenant.*—On Mar. 30, 1961, Davies's (Tutors), Ltd. executed a deed of covenant whereby they agreed with the trustees of the charitable trust that

F
       " the company will out of the general fund of taxed income of the company annually on Apr. 5 in every year for a period of seven years . . . pay to the trustees . . . such a sum as will equal in amount eighty per cent. of the "

net profits of the company. The remaining twenty per cent. was retained to meet profits tax. So the covenant was in effect to pay *all* the net profits of Davies's
G   (Tutors), Ltd. (after deducting profits tax) to the trustees for the next seven years. These net profits came to about £12,500 a year.

3. *The purchase of Davies's by the trustees.*—On Apr. 4, 1962, the two trustees formed themselves into a company called Davies's Educational Developments, Ltd. Its authorised capital was £100, of which two shares of £1 each were issued, one to each trustee. I will call it Davies's Developments, Ltd. On Apr. 5, 1962,
H   Davies's Developments, Ltd., by deed agreed to purchase from Davies's (Tutors), Ltd. the goodwill of Davies's. The value of the goodwill was put at £50,000 (which was a fair price), and Davies's Developments, Ltd., were to buy it by five instalments of £10,000 a year. As soon as the £50,000 had been paid, Davies's Developments, Ltd. agreed to buy from Davies's (Tutors), Ltd. all their premises and equipment at a fair market valuation by an independent valuer.

I   4. *The understanding.*—The evidence established quite clearly that, when Davies's (Tutors), Ltd. entered into the deed of covenant of Mar. 30, 1961, *an understanding* had been reached between all concerned that the covenanted payments would be used by the trustees to buy the business of Davies's (Tutors), Ltd., as a going concern. The intention of all the parties was that Davies's in its present form should be perpetuated in the hands of an educational trust; and that the equity shareholders of Davies's (Tutors), Ltd. should in due course receive a fair but not excessive price for the assets of that company.

5. *The income of the trust.* The trustees received the first two instalments under

the deed of covenant (due on Apr. 5, 1961, and Apr. 5, 1962) amounting to **A**
£25,831 12s. 2d. The trustees applied this money, as to £10,000 in part purchase
of the goodwill of Davies's (Tutors), Ltd., and as to £11,900 in the purchase of the
trade fixtures of that company.

The question is whether the trustees of the charitable fund are entitled to
repayment of tax in respect of the first two instalments which they have received
under the deed of covenant. This claim to repayment arises out of the provisions **B**
of the Income Tax Act, 1952, s. 123 (1), s. 169 (1) and s. 447 (1) (*b*). They are so
familiar that I will not read them again. Suffice it to say that a trust established
for charitable purposes only is entitled to exemption from tax

> "in respect of any yearly interest or *other annual payment*, forming part of
> the income of . . . [the] trust . . . so far as the same are applied to charitable   **C**
> purposes only."

The Davies's Educational Trust is admittedly a trust established for charitable
purposes only. So the two points are: (i) Were the payments under the deed of
covenant " annual payments " forming part of the income of the trust? (ii) Were
they applied to " charitable purposes only "?

It is a common practice nowadays for a man to make a seven-year covenant **D**
in favour of a charity. The object is to enable the charity to recover tax from
the Revenue. The theory on which it works is best shown by an illustration.
Take a man who has a taxable income of £1,000 a year. He is taxed on the whole
of the £1,000 at the standard rate of 8s. 6d. in the pound. It comes to £425. Now
suppose he makes a covenant in favour of his parochial church council to pay
them £10 a year for seven years. He is entitled to deduct tax at source before he **E**
pays the church council. He deducts tax at 8s. 6d. in the pound, which comes
to £4 5s. and pays the church council £5 15s. a year. Now that £10 a year payable
under the covenant is really the income of the church council. If you look at
it from their point of view, it is £10 a year coming to them forming part of their
income. Being their income, it ceases to be the income of the payer. So the £10
a year becomes the income of the church council, thus reducing the income of the **F**
payer to £990. Now you do not subject any income to tax twice over. That
means that, when he pays tax on the full £1,000, he pays it both on his own income
of £990 and on the church council's income of £10. In so far as he pays tax on the
£990, he pays it on his own account. It is over and done with. In so far as he
pays tax on the £10, he pays it on behalf of the church council. The church
council have suffered tax by deduction of £4 5s. at source; but, being a charity, **G**
the church council are not liable to tax on that £10. They are exempt. They can,
therefore, recover it from the Revenue.

That illustration points the moral of this whole case. In order to be an " annual
payment " within these sections, the payment must be such that it can be truly
regarded as the income of the recipient taxable by deduction at source. Typical
instances are mentioned in the statute. " Yearly interest " can be illustrated **H**
by interest payable on loans. " Annuities " can be illustrated by annuities
granted by will or obtained by purchase from an insurance company. The words
" other annual payments " are ejusdem generis. They are payments which recur
each year in which nothing remains to be done by the recipient except to receive
the money. The recipient is not to supply goods or services or give or do anything
in return for the payment. If he does so, it is no longer an " annual payment ".   **I**
This appears from *Earl Howe* v. *Inland Revenue Comrs.* (1), and *Re Hanbury*
(*decd.*), *Comiskey* v. *Hanbury* (2). In *Inland Revenue Comrs.* v. *City of London
Corpn.* (*as the Conservators of Epping Forest*) (3) LORD NORMAND indicated that a
sum would be an " annual payment " if it was paid " without conditions or

---

(1) [1918-19] All E.R. Rep. 1088; 7 Tax Cas. 289.
(2) (1939), 38 Tax Cas. 588.
(3) [1953] 1 All E.R. 1075 at p. 1085; 34 Tax Cas. 293 at p. 324.

A counter-stipulations out of taxed income "; and this was adopted by LORD
EVERSHED, M.R., as a good guide in *Inland Revenue Comrs.* v. *National Book*
League (4).

Counsel for the taxpayers submitted that LORD NORMAND was referring only
to conditions or counter-stipulations which were *legally enforceable*; and he argued
that, even where there was only a *private understanding* that the covenantor

B should receive a counter benefit (which was not legally enforceable), it was
nevertheless an " annual payment ". I cannot accept this submission in the least.
A seven-year covenant is nullified for tax purposes by a private understanding,
just as much as by a contractual stipulation. Take the common case of a covenant
by a father to pay his son, who is over twenty-one, £400 a year. If it is wholly
the son's income without reservation, it is an " annual payment "; but if there

C is a private understanding that the son should return it or part of it to his father
in cash or in kind, then it is not an " annual payment " so as to qualify for tax
benefits. The Final Report of the Royal Commission on the Taxation of Profits
and Income, 1955, Cmnd. 9474, over which LORD RADCLIFFE presided made a
caustic reference to private understandings of this kind. It said:

D " We feel little doubt that a number of such understandings do exist and
that they are no better than a fraud on the system."

See para. 159.

In the present case the judge held that there was a legally binding obligation
on the trustees to use the sums in paying for the purchase of Davies's. I decline
to go into the question whether it was legally binding or not. I care not one way

E or the other. There was, as the commissioners found, a clear understanding that
they should be so used. That is enough. The moneys payable by the covenantors
were being returned to them as part payment of the purchase price. It is said
that it was a fair price and is no different from their buying another school; but
I think that there is all the difference in the world. By having the money returned
to them, even in payment of the price, the covenantors were receiving a counter

F benefit. Suppose a man gives a covenant for seven years to his old school, and in
return there is a private understanding that his son, who is a dunce, will be given
a place. The sum payable under the covenant does not qualify as an " annual
payment ", even though he pays the full fees for his son. The return benefit
disqualifies. It cannot be ignored except when it is minimal and negligible; see
the *National Book League* case (5), per MORRIS, L.J., and *Taw and Torridge*

G *Festival Society, Ltd.* v. *Inland Revenue Comrs.* (6).

The judge was influenced by the fact that the trustees were bound to apply the
payment for the purchase of a capital asset. I do not think it matters that it was
to be applied for the purchase of a capital asset. Income is none the less income,
even though it is used to buy a capital asset. Its character is determined at the
time of its receipt. The important thing is that it was committed to a purpose

H which benefited the covenantors, even if only by a private understanding. That
takes it out of the category of an " annual payment ".

This makes it unnecessary to consider whether it was applied for charitable
purposes only. All I would say is that, seeing that it was applied in part for the
purpose of a counter-benefit for the covenantors, I do not see how it can be said
to have been applied for charitable purposes only. In my opinion, therefore, the

I sums payable under the seven-year covenant were not " annual payments ".
Davies's (Tutors), Ltd. are not entitled to deduct tax from the payments. The
trustees are not entitled to claim back anything from the Revenue. I would,
therefore, dismiss the appeal.

HARMAN, L.J.: There are occasions, even in Revenue cases, when what
one comes to look for is substance and not form. Here were corporators owning

---

(4) [1957] 2 All E.R. 644 at p. 648; 37 Tax Cas. 455 at p. 470.
(5) [1957] 2 All E.R. at p. 652; 37 Tax Cas. at p. 475.
(6) (1959), 38 Tax Cas. 603.

a first class educational business which paid eight hundred per cent. on its ordinary A
shares and made a living also for the majority shareholders. It paid tax, of course,
like any other commercial concern. The object of the corporators was to sell this
business at its full value without losing control of it. They left it to their
accountant to find the best means, and what we have is his plan, which smells a
little of the lamp. His plan was: (i) to sell the goodwill to a concern still controlled
by the vendors: (ii) to find the price out of the profits of the business: (iii) to get   B
back the income tax which was being paid by the vendors, thus accelerating the
payment of the purchase money.

What were the steps taken to carry it out? The first was that a trust was set
up, a trust for educational purposes only, and therefore a charitable trust, but as
its name implies, it was to be tied to Davies's, the name of the business. The
object of the charitable trust was to take over the business from Davies's. The   C
second step in this was the covenant which the company entered into the day after
its formation, which was a covenant for seven years to pay eighty per cent. of its
profits to the trust. The third step was that the trust was to use the money to
pay for the business. I care not at all, like LORD DENNING, M.R., whether this
was a legally binding transaction or merely one that was morally binding on
everybody. After all, all the participators in this scheme were on one side of the   D
table. They were the corporators in this business. They were the people who were
making a living out of it and who were hoping to get a good price for it. There is
nothing wrong with that; but it makes a formal agreement quite unnecessary,
because it was to everybody's interest and it was everybody's intention to carry
it out in this way if it would get back the company's income tax. The fourth step
was that the trust, being a charity, was to apply to get back the income tax   E
payable by the vendors and return it to the vendors directly it was got back and
so hasten the payment of the purchase price.

It is on this last rock that the ship founders. If I pay my college at Oxbridge
income payments over seven years, these are annual payments, because I expect
and get no returns from my outlay. If I make conditions, such as a free place
for my son, no tax is reclaimable. Judge the present case by this test. The   F
covenantor makes his payment to the trust. Everyone concerned knows the object
of it; it is to get back the payments as instalments of the purchase money for the
business—it is to recover through the trust the tax it has paid and return it to
themselves as further instalments. No doubt when the seven years are up, there
is to be a further covenant on a further understanding that the covenanted sums
will go to pay for the vendors' physical assets, freeholds and leaseholds. The   G
prospect is that no-one in this business will pay any tax for years. It is a splendid
scheme. Meanwhile the business will remain under the control of the majority
shareholders and provide them with salaries as managers of the business. It is
almost too good to be true. In law quite too good to be true. It won't do.

That is enough in my opinion to deal with this appeal. I follow the judge (7)
until he reaches this point precisely; but his further reasoning I cannot follow,   H
and so far as I can follow it, I do not accept it; but it makes no difference.

As to the second point, that the payments were applied for charitable purposes
only, being payments made to buy an educational business, when looked at it is
essentially the same point at a different stage. The payments to be made by the
covenantor are not in my opinion for charitable purposes only because they are
paid in pursuance of the understanding that they shall be devoted to the purchase   I
of the business. Therefore it does not matter that the business is an educational
business and therefore within the objects of the charitable trust, because the
objects of the charitable trust are not wholly charitable in this case but to pay
for a business, of which they themselves are the controllers. On both points,
therefore, I would dismiss the appeal.

SALMON, L.J.: [I have heard it said that golf is essentially an easy game

(7) [1966] 2 All E.R. 736; [1966] Ch. 439.

A   made difficult. It seems to me that the question that arises in this case is essentially an easy question made difficult. It has been made difficult only by the irrelevant complexities and ingenuity under which it has been almost submerged.

The company, Davies's (Tutors), Ltd., covenanted to pay eighty per cent. of its annual profits to a charitable trust called the Davies's Educational Trust

B   for a period of seven years. The company deducted income tax from those profits before paying them to the trust. The trust seeks to recover the tax that has been so deducted. The covenant was part of an arrangement found by the Special Commissioners to have been made between the directors and shareholders in the company and the trustees. There were only two trustees; one was a director of the company and the other was the company's secretary. It was the common

C   intention of all those persons, as found by the Special Commissioners, and part of the arrangement between them, that every penny paid under the deed of covenant to the trustees should be returned to the company enriched by the tax that had been recovered, and that in return the company would transfer all its assets to the trust. The first asset to be so acquired was to be the company's goodwill valued at some £50,000. It is conceded that there was a moral obligation

D   on the trustees to return the money to the company in the way which I have indicated, but it is argued that there is no legal liability on them to do so. There was, of course, no formal agreement between the parties interested because, as Harman, L.J., has said, they were all on the same side of the fence; their interests were common and there was no need for any formal agreement.

I myself agree, however, with the judge (8) that each payment became the

E   subject of a trust in the hands of the trustees and they were under an equitable duty to deal with those payments in accordance with the common intention of all the parties and the arrangements made between them. I should think it very remarkable if, in the highly unlikely event of the trustees using the money that they received in breach of the understanding and for the purpose, say, of financing a school which was in competition with one of the schools belonging to the

F   company, the Court of Chancery would be unable to intervene. I have no doubt that it would intervene to prevent what I think would be a clear breach of trust; but in my view it does not matter very much whether there was such a trust in respect of the money paid under the covenant or whether there was merely a moral obligation on the part of the trustees to return it. In no circumstances can it be regarded as pure bounty.

G   The case for the taxpayers, as I understand it, is that the money which they received is an " annual payment " within the meaning of those words in the Income Tax Act, 1952 (9) despite the fact that that money is to be returned to the company; this, they say, is so because it is returned in payment for the company's assets and the price being paid for the assets is a fair and reasonable price. In order for the money paid under the covenant to constitute " annual

H   payments " in the hands of the trustees so that they can recover the tax that has been deducted, it is clearly established by such authorities as *Inland Revenue Comrs.* v. *City of London Corpn. (as the Conservators of Epping Forest)* (10) and *Inland Revenue Comrs.* v. *National Book League* (11) that the money must have been paid to the trustees without " conditions " or " counter-stipulations " or as a " pure gift " or " pure bounty ". There may well be cases in which it would

I   be difficult to decide whether what was paid to a trust was by way of pure gift or whether there were any counter-stipulations which prevented the money from being a pure gift or pure bounty. But this in my view is not one of those cases. Every penny which the charity received it had to return to those who gave it. It was certainly under a moral duty to do so, and in my view would be committing

---

(8) [1966] 2 All E.R. at p. 745; [1966] Ch. at p. 460.
(9) See s. 169 and s. 447 (1) (*b*).
(10) [1953] 1 All E.R. 1075; 34 Tax Cas. 293.
(11) [1957] 2 All E.R. 644; 37 Tax Cas. 455.

a breach of trust should it fail to do so. It seems to me to be entirely beside the A
point that, once the trustees had returned the money, they were going to receive
in exchange an asset which would be of the same value as the money being
returned.

May I illustrate this point by an example? A enters into a covenant to pay a
charitable trust, B, £10,000 a year for seven years. He does so, deducting tax.
There is an understanding between A and B that B will pay £70,000 back to A as B
consideration for a house which A will then transfer to B. As I understand the
argument of counsel for the taxpayers, providing the house is worth the £70,000,
that is all right: the payments by A to B are pure bounty. If, however, the house
is worth only, say, £10,000, counsel concedes that it would be ridiculous to regard
the money paid by A to B as bounty. To my mind, however, the value of the
house would be wholly irrelevant to the question with which we are concerned. C
A is not giving away any money; he is getting it back, plus the tax which he has
deducted from it. What he is giving away is the house. Suppose the circumstances
postulated, but that the house is worth £200,000. If anyone asked the question:
What was A's bounty to B, no-one would think of saying that A had made a gift
to B of £70,000. Any ordinary man would say that it was true that A had, for
some mysterious reason, parted with that sum less tax and received it back plus D
the tax but he had not given it away. He had been much more charitable than if
he had given away a mere £70,000. What he had done in fact was to give away a
property worth £200,000. So here, the most that can be said in favour of the
taxpayers is that the company is in fact giving away its assets to the trust—
certainly its goodwill. Unfortunately, from the point of view of everyone
concerned, except the Commissioners of Inland Revenue, that gift does not E
afford them any tax advantage.

There is only one other point which I should like to mention and it is this.
According to the findings in the Case, the goodwill, which was the first asset to be
" purchased ", has been correctly valued at £50,000. The Case is not, however,
particularly illuminating on this point, because it does not deal with the circumstances in which the goodwill could be said to be worth £50,000. When a business F
is sold, the usual form of the transaction is for the shares in the company carrying
on the business to be sold either on a profit earning basis or on an assets value
basis; and one of the assets, of course, is the goodwill. In the present case there
is no question of selling the company's shares to the trust. The idea was for the
company to transfer its assets to the trust. One of those assets was the goodwill
valued at £50,000. Naturally if all the assets are made over and the company G
transferring them is a company such as this is, with a good name and a good
profit record, the goodwill is no doubt worth a lot of money. When the goodwill
is included amongst the assets sold, there is in the ordinary course always a
covenant by vendors not in future to trade under the same name or any name like
it and quite often a covenant against competing with the purchasers. Having
had some experience of contracts relating to the sale of assets of a business, I H
confess that I have never heard of anyone finding a purchaser who was prepared
to buy goodwill alone. As far as I can see, the purchaser would be getting
absolutely nothing—however valuable the goodwill might be if acquired with the
other assets and subject to the usual covenants. In the present case the company
can still carry on the business under the old name. The trust gets no share of the I
profit; it gets nothing except the chances of making some use of the goodwill if
and when it receives sufficient money from the company to acquire the company's
other assets with which the business is carried on. These include a large number
of very valuable freehold and leasehold premises. It is inconceivable that any
sane person entering into an ordinary commercial transaction would buy goodwill
in such circumstances. It seems to me, although perhaps it is not very relevant,
that in this respect also the company and its corporators were, no doubt perfectly
properly, receiving a real benefit by reason of this arrangement. They were

A receiving cash down for goodwill in circumstances in which it would be unsaleable on the open market.

However that may be, once the so-called benefactor is parting with his money under a covenant on the basis that the money is to come back to him, it seems to me to be obviously impossible, in any circumstances, to regard the payment of the money by the so-called benefactor as pure bounty. I agree that the appeal B should be dismissed.

Appeal dismissed. Leave to appeal to the House of Lords refused.

Solicitors: *J. S. Fairfax-Jones* (for the taxpayers); *Solicitor of Inland Revenue.*

[*Reported by* F. A. Amies, Esq., *Barrister-at-Law.*]

C

NOTE.

THE LUCILE BLOOMFIELD.

D   Owners of the M.V. Ronda v. Owners of the
S.S. Lucile Bloomfield.

[Court of Appeal, civil division (Willmer, Danckwerts and Winn, L.JJ., assisted by Capt. G. P. McGraith and Capt. L. M. Hill, D.S.C., R.N.R., Trinity Masters), February 27, 28, March 1, 1967.]

E *Shipping—Collision—Apportionment of liability—Differentiation between vessels involved not possible—Whether appellate court would interfere with decision.*

[As to the apportionment of liability for damage in collision actions, see 35 Halsbury's Laws (3rd Edn.) 696-698, para. 1047; and for cases on the subject, see 42 Digest (Repl.) 915, 916, *7098-7105.*

For the Maritime Convention Act, 1911, s. 1, see 23 Halsbury's Statutes F (2nd Edn.) 830.]

Cases referred to:
  British Aviator, The, [1965] 1 Lloyd's Rep. 271.
  British Fame (S.S. or Vessel) (Owners) v. *S.S. or Vessel Macgregor (Owners)*
    [1943] 1 All E.R. 33; [1943] A.C. 197; 112 L.J.P. 6; 168 L.T. 193;
G   74 Lloyd L.R. 82; 42 Digest (Repl.) 913, *7085.*
  Peter Beroit, The (1915), 85 L.J.P. 12; 114 L.T. 147; 13 Asp. M.L.C. 203;
    42 Digest (Repl.) 885, *6735.*

Appeal.

This was an appeal by the defendants, owners of the American vessel, Lucile Bloomfield, from a decision of Karminski, J., given on July 22, 1966 and reported H (but on the question of costs only) at [1966] 3 All E.R. 294, in respect of a collision with the plaintiffs' vessel Ronda, which occurred on Oct. 1, 1963 at about 10.23/24 p.m. The Ronda, a Norwegian motor vessel, was inward bound for Le Havre from New York and the Lucile Bloomfield was outward bound from Le Havre to Antwerp. The collision was more or less at right angles and both vessels sustained damages. The collision took place in the approaches to the port of I Le Havre in an area where the Le Havre pilot cutter was normally to be found cruising. At the time of the collision the Lucile Bloomfield had just disembarked her pilot, while the Ronda was manoeuvring to pick up her pilot to take her to port. The Ronda was holed and water entered. She succeeded in getting into port where she later sank.

In giving judgment in the action brought by the plaintiffs, the owners of the Ronda, Karminski, J., found that the collision was caused by bad look-out on both sides. If the Lucile Bloomfield had seen the Ronda approaching in time, instead of two minutes before the collision, she would not have gone full steam

Dictum of Winn LJ at 635 explained in The Annemiese [1970] 2 All ER 29

ahead but would have gone as hard astern as she could straight away and avoided A
a collision. Similarly, if the Ronda had kept a proper look-out she would have
seen the Lucile Bloomfield far earlier than she did and by a simple helm action
would have cleared her by a safe distance. He held both vessels to blame and
apportioned the liability equally between them. He gave judgment in favour
of the plaintiffs for half of their damages and half of their costs as he could find
no mathematical formula to distinguish on his findings of fact the culpability B
between the two vessels. The defendants did not put in any counter-claim in
the action. They appealed, contending that the Lucile Bloomfield ought not to
have been found to blame at all, or alternatively, if she was to blame, her share
of the blame should have been a great deal smaller than that attributed to her.

J. V. Naisby, Q.C., and Gerald Darling for the defendants.

B. C. Sheen, Q.C., and R. F. Stone for the plaintiffs.   C

WILLMER, L.J., having reviewed the facts and referred to the arguments
and to the decision in the court below, continued: We have, of course, been
referred to the House of Lords decision in *Owners of S.S. British Fame* v. *Owners
of S.S. Macgregor* (1). It is enough to say that the House of Lords made it clear
that an appellate court should be slow to interfere on a mere question of apportion- D
ment of blame as between two wrongdoing vessels. It may very well be that, if
the learned judge in this case had seen fit to divide the responsibility between
the two vessels in a way rather more favourable to the Lucile Bloomfield, it
would have been difficult for this court to interfere; but he did not do so. He saw
witnesses from both sides, and he came to the conclusion, in his discretion, that
in all the circumstances it was not possible to differentiate between the two vessels. E
I think that that is a conclusion with which it is particularly difficult for this court
to interfere, especially having regard to s. 1 (1), proviso (a) of the Maritime
Conventions Act, 1911, which provides that:

" If, having regard to all the circumstances of the case, it is not possible to
establish different degrees of fault, the liability shall be apportioned equally."
        F

What is meant by " establishing different degrees of fault " in that context was
discussed as long ago as 1915 in the House of Lords in the case of *The Peter
Benoit* (2), extracts from the speeches in which have been read to us this morning.
I need not refer again to what was said, except to remind myself that the grounds
for differentiating between two wrongdoers must be supported by evidence and
proved as a matter of judicial determination; it is not enough that the court G
should have a general leaning in favour of one side rather than the other. In
those circumstances, taking what I hope is a broad view of the case, I am not
persuaded that we ought to interfere with the judge's decision (3) in this case.
I would therefore dismiss the appeal.

DANCKWERTS, L.J.: I agree with the judgment of WILLMER, L.J.,
and I think that the learned judge (3) reached a right conclusion. It is plain that H
the substantial cause of the collision was the failure of both ships to keep a proper
lookout. There may have been errors of navigation which occurred during the
last few minutes, but they were due, it seems to me, to the general reason which
I have mentioned. It is quite clear to me that, on the principles stated in *The
British Aviator* (4), we ought not to interfere with the apportionment of blame
made by the judge, and I also would dismiss the appeal.   I

WINN, L.J.: I have made up my mind that I should agree to the dismissal
of this appeal, and with the judgment delivered by WILLMER, L.J. Since I have
not seen fit to refrain during the hearing of the appeal from certain indications

(1) [1943] 1 All E.R. 33; [1943] A.C. 197.
(2) (1914), 114 L.T. 147; 13 Asp. M.L.C. 203.
(3) [1966] 3 All E.R. 294.
(4) [1965] 1 Lloyd's Rep. 271 at pp. 277, 278.

A of my own personal impression as to what happened on the night in question, and who caused it to happen, I think it only frank that I should make it clear that I have expressed my agreement for two reasons. First, I have had regard to the cogent effect of *Owners of S.S. British Fame* v. *Owners of S.S. Macgregor* (5), to which WILLMER, L.J., has just referred. Secondly, and rather more particularly, because it has been brought home to me once more what is the practice of

B the Admiralty Division about the application of proviso (*a*) to s. 1 of the Maritime Conventions Act, 1911. I say " once more " because I was a party to the judgment in *The British Aviator* (6). I then expressed my complete agreement within, I note, a month or six weeks of my becoming a member of the court. When I look again now at that section, I observe (and I think it is right that I should say this) a perfectly clear indication that the primary task of the court is to apportion

C liability according to fault. This is followed by the proviso that if the court finds it not possible to apportion different degrees of fault, the court is to declare an equal distribution of fault. It is, therefore, as a matter of construction, a condition precedent to a declaration that liability be apportioned equally that the court has found it impossible to establish different degrees of fault. To my mind that is not the same thing as saying that where different degrees of fault cannot be

D established, then the liability should be equal. When LORD ATKINSON, in *The Peter Benoit* (7) in 1915, spoke of the need to justify differentiation between the blameworthiness of two vessels, and of the need that there should be " a clear preponderance of culpability ", those words may not mean more than this, that one is not to seek to distinguish a mere five per cent., $7\frac{1}{2}$ per cent. and ten per cent., by way of distinction, and that it is only where there is a marked distinction

E of material amount that it is right to depart from fifty per cent. WILLMER, L.J., himself in *The British Aviator* (6) spoke of a rather different matter, not of the need to have a clear preponderance of responsibility. He said (8) (and I respectfully agree with what he then said):

" I think that in plain language what the proviso means is that, whatever the ground may be for attributing different degrees of fault, it must be a
F ground which is proved by cogent evidence . . ."

I venture to think that the court should never act on any particular ground when deciding how liability should be imposed or distributed unless such ground has been proved by cogent evidence. WILLMER, L.J., then went on to say (8): " . . . if that is not so, the old Admiralty rule of equal division continues to

G prevail." I now more clearly appreciate than before that what has happened historically is that the language of s. 1 of the Maritime Conventions Act, 1911, and more particularly of the proviso, has been construed against a background of pre-existing practice so as to give to the meaning of the words a restrictive, narrow and (as I venture to think) unduly narrow construction of the language used by Parliament. I agree that the appeal should be dismissed.

H *Appeal dismissed.*

Solicitors: *Hill, Dickinson & Co.* (for the defendants); *Ingledew, Brown, Bennison & Garrett* (for the plaintiffs).

[*Reported by* F. A. AMIES, ESQ., *Barrister-at-Law.*]

I

(5) [1943] 1 All E.R. 33; [1943] A.C. 197.
(6) [1965] 1 Lloyd's Rep. 271.
(7) (1915), 114 L.T. 147; 13 Asp. M.L.C. 203.
(8) [1965] 1 Lloyd's Rep. at p. 277.

TAPPER (Inspector of Taxes) *v.* EYRE.   A

[CHANCERY DIVISION (Stamp, J.), March 1, 1967.]

Income Tax—Allowance—Investment allowance—Mini van licensed for carriage
of goods and used solely for purposes of business of radio engineer—
Advertisements relating to business on the sides of the van—Van of a type
commonly used as private vehicle and suitable to be so used—No modification   B
made to van—Whether van qualified for an investment allowance—Finance
Act, 1954 (2 & 3 *Eliz.* 2 *c.* 44), *s.* 16 (3).

The taxpayer, a radio and electrical engineer, purchased an Austin mini
van at a cost of £400 for the purposes of delivering, repairing and maintaining
television sets, and also for the purposes of his business as an electrical
engineer.   No modification had been made to the van, but there were   C
advertisements relating to the taxpayer's trade on its side, and it was fitted
with a roof rack for the purpose of carrying equipment and materials,
including television aerials used in connexion with the taxpayer's business.
It had a " C " licence.   There was evidence that many persons used
Morris and similar vans only for private purposes and without possessing a
" C " licence.   The General Commissioners of Income Tax held that the van   D
was new machinery and plant qualifying for an investment allowance under
s. 16 (3)* of the Finance Act, 1954.   On appeal,

Held: the mini van did not qualify for an investment allowance, since it
was excluded by the proviso† to that subsection, there being no evidence that
it was " of a type not commonly used as private vehicles and unsuitable to be
so used " within the meaning of those words in the proviso (see p. 638,   E
letter H, post).

Appeal allowed.

[As to investment allowances in respect of motor vehicles, see 20 HALSBURY'S
LAWS (3rd Edn.) 495, para. 947, text and note (*m*); and for a case on the subject
of investment allowances, see DIGEST (Cont. Vol. A) 874, *480a.*

For the Finance Act, 1954, s. 16 (3), as amended, see Vol. 1 of the SUPPLEMENT   F
to 34 HALSBURY'S STATUTES (2nd Edn.), para. [328] Amended Texts.]

Case referred to:

> *Bourne* (*Inspector of Taxes*) v. *Auto School of Motoring* (*Norwich*), *Ltd.*, (1964),
> 42 Tax Cas. 217; 3rd Digest Supp.

Appeal.

The taxpayer, Roy Eyre, appealed to the General Commissioners of Income   G
Tax for Wayland, Norfolk, against an assessment to income tax under Case I
of Sch. D to the Income Tax Act, 1952, in the sum of £3,800, in respect of the
profits of his business as a radio and television dealer for 1965-66.   The question
for decision was whether expenditure incurred in the purchase of an Austin
mini van used in connexion with the business qualified for an investment
allowance under s. 16 (3) of the Finance Act, 1954.   The commissioners held   H
that the vehicle was machinery or plant qualifying for the allowance under the
subsection.   The Crown appealed under s. 64 of the Income Tax Act, 1952, by
way of Case Stated to the High Court.

J. R. Phillips for the Crown.

The taxpayer did not appear and was not represented.   I

STAMP, J.: The matter arises on an assessment to income tax under Case I
of Sch. D in the sum of £3,800 in respect of the respondent taxpayer's profits of
his business as a radio and television dealer for the income tax year 1965-66.   The
question which falls to be decided is whether expenditure incurred on the provision
of a new road vehicle used in connexion with the taxpayer's business qualified
for an investment allowance under s. 16 (3) of the Finance Act, 1954.

---

* Section 16 (3), so far as material, is set out at p. 637, letter C, post.
† The proviso is set out at p. 637, letter E, post.

A   The General Commissioners who heard the appeal decided that question in favour of the respondent taxpayer.   Before stating the facts it is perhaps convenient that I should refer to s. 16 of the Finance Act, 1954.   Section 16 (1) provides:

B   " In the cases provided for by this section, an allowance (in this Act referred to as an ' investment allowance ') shall be made in respect of capital expenditure on new assets incurred after Apr. 6, 1954."

Section 16 (2) deals with the amounts of the investment allowances and nothing turns on the provisions of that subsection.   Section 16 (3), as amended (1) provides:

C   " An investment allowance equal to three-tenths of the expenditure shall be made in addition to an initial allowance under Chapter 2 of the said Part 10 in respect of expenditure on the provision of new machinery or plant, and any provision of the . . . Income Tax Acts applicable to initial allowances under that chapter, so far as it is applicable in relation to allowances for new assets, shall apply also to investment allowances under this subsection . . ."

subject to certain exceptions to which I need not refer.

D   It is common ground in this case that the motor car in question is new machinery or plant within the meaning of the subsection to which I have just referred.   The subsection, however, is followed by a proviso to which I must now refer, and which gives rise to the difficulty in this case.   The proviso is in the following terms:

E   " Provided that no investment allowance shall be made under this subsection in respect of expenditure incurred on the provision of road vehicles unless they are of a type not commonly used as private vehicles and unsuitable to be so used or are provided wholly or mainly for hire to or for the carriage of members of the public in the ordinary course of a trade."

It is not suggested that the road vehicle in this case is provided wholly or mainly for hire to or for the carriage of members of the public in the ordinary course of a

F   trade, and the question which the commissioners had to determine was whether the road vehicle with which they were concerned fell within the provision that it was " of a type not commonly used as private vehicles and unsuitable to be so used ".   Both qualifications must be fulfilled in order that an investment allowance for the road vehicle may be claimed.

G   The facts are set out in para. 3 of the Case Stated and were found in the following terms:

" . . . (a) the [taxpayer] was a radio and electrical engineer;   (b) in the year to Feb. 28, 1965, the [taxpayer] had purchased an Austin mini van at a cost of £400 for the purposes of delivering, repairing and maintaining radio and television sets, and also for the purposes of his business as an electrical

H   engineer;   (c) no modifications whatever had been made to the said van; there were advertisements relating to the [taxpayer's] trade on the sides of the said van and it was fitted with a roof rack for the purpose of carrying equipment and materials, including television aerials, used in connection with the [taxpayer's] business;   (d) the said van was licensed for the carriage of goods and the [taxpayer] held a current ' C ' licence for that purpose.   The

I   said van was used solely for the purposes of the [taxpayer's] business and was one of its assets.   For private purposes the [taxpayer] made use of his own private car."

There was some evidence by a Mrs. Burgess that she owned a Morris—not an Austin, but a Morris—van which was used solely for private purposes.   She did not use it for business purposes, although she did use it as transport to and from her place of employment.   She had bought it because it was cheaper and handier than a saloon car, since the van had more room at the back of the seats.   The van

(1) By the Finance Act, 1959, s. 21 (2), Sch. 1, para. 5 and the Finance Act 1963, s. 33.

was registered as a private vehicle and did not carry a " C " licence. She also   A
knew several other owners of similar vans who used them only for private
purposes.

I will read the contentions of the taxpayer before the commissioners because,
although he was represented by a chartered accountant at that hearing, he does
not appear before me. The commissioners set those contentions out in the
following terms: B

   " It was contended by Mr. Arthur Edmund Shaw, chartered accountant,
on behalf of the [taxpayer] that investment allowances had been granted by
the Inland Revenue for many years but a new policy had now appeared
restricting such allowance to large vans, as it was alleged that the mini van
had now acquired a private user status. He claimed, however, that this could
not apply to the [taxpayer's] user of this vehicle. He referred to the case of   C
Bourne (Inspector of Taxes) v. Auto School of Motoring (Norwich), Ltd. (2) . . .
where it was held that the respondent was entitled to investment allowance
in respect of Ford Anglia saloon motor cars carrying a permanent name
plate and adapted for dual control. He further contended that having
previously agreed allowances in respect of such vehicles, i.e., mini vans, the
inspector was not entitled to change the interpretation of the law but that   D
the law itself would require to be amended."

I need not notice the arguments and contentions on behalf of the inspector of
taxes, but I must refer to the findings of the commissioners. They are these:

   " We, the commissioners who heard the appeal, found that although
many of these vehicles were used as private motor vehicles, they were   E
primarily business vehicles. They were not subject to purchase tax and if
members of the public took advantage of the regulations to acquire cheap
vehicles, this should not deprive business users for whom the vehicles were
intended of an investment allowance which had previously been granted for
such vehicles. We determined the appeal in favour of the [taxpayer] in the
sum of £3,708 less capital allowances £1,535."   F

The commissioners' finding that many of these vehicles were used as private
motor vehicles was no doubt based on figures contained in a schedule to the Case,
which shows that of all the small Austin and Morris vans first licensed in 1964,
only thirty-six per cent. had been licensed as goods vehicles, the remainder
being licensed as other vehicles under para. 2 (c) of Sch. 5 to the Vehicles (Excise)
Act, 1962. If the figures for the small Austin vans are taken separately, the   G
proportions are substantially the same. As I have indicated, in order to qualify
for an investment allowance for a road vehicle, the road vehicle must be of a
type—I emphasise the word " type "—not commonly used as private vehicles
and must also be of a type unsuitable to be so used.

With all respect to the commissioners, it does not seem to me that they had
any evidence before them on which they could possibly hold that the vehicle in   H
question was of such a type or had either of the qualities required in order to
qualify for an investment allowance. On the contrary, such evidence as the
commissioners had, it seems to me, in both respects, points entirely in the opposite
direction. So far as regards the reference to Bourne v. Auto School of Motoring (2)
referred to in the Case Stated, it seems to me that that case was concerned with
quite a different problem, viz., whether a vehicle fitted with dual control, and so   I
I would have thought not commonly used and very unsuitable to be used as a
private vehicle, passed the necessary tests.

Appeal allowed.

Solicitor: Solicitor of Inland Revenue.

[Reported by F. A. AMIES, ESQ., Barrister-at-Law.]

---

(2) (1964), 42 Tax Cas. 217.

A   CITYLAND AND PROPERTY (HOLDINGS), LTD. *v.* DABRAH.

[CHANCERY DIVISION (Goff, J.), March 17, 20, 1967.]

Mortgage—Collateral advantage—Premium—Charge on mortgagor's house on occasion of expiration of lease and his purchase of freehold from landlords—
B   *Loan of £2,900 by landlords—Purchase price £3,500—£600 provided by mortgagor—Sum charged by mortgage £4,553, payable by seventy-two equal monthly instalments—Premium (£1,653) included in the sum charged—On default whole of money lent and premium would become due—Mortgagor in default—Mortgagees sought to enforce mortgage—Whether charge should stand as security for premium as well as for moneys lent—Whether interest should be allowed.*

C   The defendant was formerly a tenant of the plaintiffs, and, when his lease expired, he purchased the freehold of the demised property for £3,500 from the plaintiffs. He provided £600 from his own resources and arranged with the plaintiffs for the balance of £2,900 to be left on mortgage and secured by a charge on the property. The charge, dated Apr. 6, 1965, provided that in consideration of the loan of £2,900 the defendant as beneficial owner charged
D   the property to the plaintiffs with the payment of £4,553 (the additional £1,653 being a premium) to be paid by seventy-two equal monthly instalments of £63 4s. 8d. By virtue of the charge, if default in paying an instalment were made, the whole of the principal and the premium would become due. The premium amounted to fifty-seven per cent. of the loan; or, if the instalments were treated as repayment of money lent with interest, the rate
E   of interest on completion of the instalments would be nineteen per cent. The defendant made default, and the plaintiffs took proceedings to enforce the charge by possession or sale, and sought payment of the principal and interest.

        Held: in the circumstances of this case, having regard to the fact that the loan was a secured loan, to the size of the premium, to the fact that both
F   loan and premium would become due on default in paying instalments, and to the high rate of interest which complete payment over the period the instalments would represent, the collateral advantage by way of premium for which the charge provided was unreasonable, and the charge should stand as security only for the principal lent and interest thereon at a rate which, for the purposes of the present case only, would be seven per cent. (see p. 647,
G   letter I, to p. 648, letter A, and p. 648, letters C and G, post).

        Kreglinger v. *New Patagonia Meat and Cold Storage Co., Ltd.* ([1911-13] All E.R. Rep. 970) followed.

        Per CURIAM: if the charge should have stood as security for the premium as well as the advance, the court would not have allowed interest in addition (see p. 648, letter D, post).
H
        [As to a collateral benefit as a clog on the equity of redemption, see 27 HALSBURY'S LAWS (3rd Edn.) 236, 237, para. 425; and as to collateral benefits which may be enforced, see ibid., p. 237, para. 426; and for cases on the subject, see 35 DIGEST (Repl.) 358, 359, *618-628*; and for cases on bonuses, see ibid., 407, *1022-1026.*

I   As to payment of interest, see 27 HALSBURY'S LAWS (3rd Edn.) 202, para. 342; and for cases on the subject, see 35 DIGEST (Repl.) 738, *4057-4063.*]

Cases referred to:
        Broad v. *Selfe*, (1863), 2 New Rep. 541; 9 L.T. 43; 11 W.R. 1036; 35 Digest (Repl.) 358, *621.*
        Carey v. *Doyne*, (1856), 5 I. Ch. R. 104; 35 Digest (Repl.) 738, **1988.*
        Chambers v. *Goldwin*, (1804), 9 Ves. 254; 1 Smith, K.B. 252; 32 E.R. 600; 35 Digest (Repl.) 420, *1127.*
        Howard v. *Harris*, (1683), 1 Vern. 100; 23 E.R. 106; 35 Digest (Repl.) 270, *17.*

Considered in MULTISERVICE BOOK-BINDING V MARDEN [1978] 2 All ER 489

James v. *Kerr*, (1889), 40 Ch.D. 449; 58 L.J.Ch. 355; 60 L.T. 212; 53 J.P. 628; A
35 Digest (Repl.) 358, *620*.

Kerr's Policy, Re, (1869), L.R. 8 Eq. 331; 38 L.J.Ch. 539; 35 Digest (Repl.)
738, *4061*.

Kreglinger v. *New Patagonia Meat and Cold Storage Co., Ltd.*, [1911-13] All E.R.
Rep. 970; [1914] A.C. 25; 83 L.J.Ch. 79; 109 L.T. 802; 35 Digest
(Repl.) 280, *20*.   B

Mainland v. *Upjohn*, (1889), 41 Ch.D. 126; 58 L.J.Ch. 361; 60 L.T. 614; 35
Digest (Repl.) 407, *1026*.

Mendl v. *Smith*, (1943), 112 L.J.Ch. 279; 169 L.T. 153; 35 Digest (Repl.)
738, *4063*.

Potter v. *Edwards*, (1857), 26 L.J.Ch. 468; 35 Digest (Repl.) 407, *1022*.

Sterne v. *Beck*, (1863), 1 De G.J. & Sm. 595; 32 L.J.Ch. 682; 8 L.T. 588; 20 C
Digest (Repl.) 544, *2533*.

Adjourned Summons.

This was an application by originating summons dated July 22, 1966, by the
plaintiff mortgagees, Cityland and Property (Holdings), Ltd., against the
defendant, James Dabrah, whereby the plaintiffs claimed (i) payment of all
moneys due to the plaintiffs under the covenant contained in a legal charge dated D
Apr. 6, 1965 whereby the defendant charged to the plaintiffs the property known
as 69, Mansfield Road, London, N.W.5; (ii) that in default of the plaintiffs and
defendant agreeing the amount due to the plaintiffs, an account might be taken;
(iii) payment of interest at £5 per cent. per annum on the said amount from the
date when the same so became due, and (iv) possession of the mortgaged property.
The facts are set out in the judgment.   E

The cases noted below* were cited during the argument in addition to those
referred to in the judgment.

J. M. E. Byng for the plaintiffs.
J. H. G. Sunnucks for the defendant.

   GOFF, J.: In the end the matter comes down to a somewhat small compass. F
The first point taken on behalf of the defendant was that this was not a legal
mortgage. That was an argument intended to be based on the absence from the
legal charge of the words " by way of legal charge "; but it is quite clear that, in
the case of registered land, there is no necessity for those words to appear in the
charge. Section 25 of the Land Registration Act, 1925 provides:

   " (1) The proprietor of any registered land may by deed—(*a*) charge the G
registered land with the payment at an appointed time of any principal sum
of money either with or without interest; . . .

   " (2) A charge may be in any form provided that—(*a*) the registered land
comprised in the charge is described by reference to the register or in any
other manner sufficient to enable the registrar to identify the same without
reference to any other document; (*b*) the charge does not refer to any other H
interest or charge affecting the land which—(i) would have priority over the
same and is not registered or protected on the register, (ii) is not an overriding
interest."

Section 27 (1) provides:

   "A registered charge shall, unless made or taking effect by demise or I
sub-demise, and subject to any provision to the contrary contained in the
charge, take effect as a charge by way of legal mortgage."

Counsel for the defendant conceded that, in view of those sections, he could

---

* *Thompson* v. *Hudson*, (1869), L.R. 4 H.L. 1; *Protector Endowment Loan and Annuity
Co.* v. *Grice*, (1880), 5 Q.B.D. 121; *Booth* v. *Salvation Army Building Association,ʼLtd.*,
(1897), 14 T.L.R. 3; *Dunlop Pneumatic Tyre Co., Ltd.* v. *New Garage and Motor Co., Ltd.*,
[1914-15] All E.R. Rep. 739; [1915] A.C. 79; *Campbell Discount Co., Ltd.* v. *Bridge*,
[1962] 1 All ER. 385; [1962] A.C. 600.

A not maintain this objection. What the position would be if it had been un-registered land was in the circumstances not argued, and I therefore refrain from saying anything on that point one way or the other. The charge being a legal mortgage, the plaintiffs are entitled to possession as legal mortgagees, and I so order.

B The mortgage came about in these circumstances, that the defendant was the tenant of the plaintiffs and when his lease expired he desired to purchase the freehold from them. The price was £3,500 and he was able to provide out of his own resources £600 and no more, and the balance was, therefore, left on mortgage and secured by the charge to which I have referred. That charge is in these terms:

C " In consideration of £2,900 (the receipt whereof is hereby acknowledged) . . . [that was the amount lent] . . . I, James Dabrah [the defendant] of 69 Mansfield Road, N.W.5 in the county of London . . . as beneficial owner here-by charge the land comprised in the title above mentioned with the payment to Cityland and Property (Holdings), Ltd. [the plaintiffs] on Apr. 6, 1965 of the sum of £4,553 . . . [which is an additional sum of £1,653] . . . and the [defendant] covenants with the [plaintiffs] to repay to the [plaintiffs] the

D said sum of £4,553 by seventy-two equal monthly instalments of £63 4s. 8d. the first of such payments to be made on May 6, 1965 and thereafter on the 6th day of each of the successive seventy-one months and if and so long as the provisions of this deed and the covenants and obligations on the part of the [defendant] herein expressed or implied shall have been observed and performed the [plaintiffs] shall accept payment of the said principal sum by

E instalments and in the manner aforesaid provided however that should the [defendant] be able to repay at any time in less than seventy-two months from the date hereof the balance then outstanding of the said sum of £4,553 the [plaintiffs] will grant to the [defendant] on such payment a pro rata dis-count on the sum of £4,553 based on the terms upon which such sum is now assessed provided further that notwithstanding anything hereinbefore

F contained the power of sale under this charge shall be deemed to arise on July 6, 1965."

Then there were certain covenants which are not material, and in view of my decision that the plaintiffs are legal mortgagees I do not have to pursue the question of sale any further.

G The next point taken by the defendant was a purely technical one, that the plaintiffs in their evidence had failed to comply with the requirements of R.S.C., Ord. 88 and, in particular, r. 6. In the evidence filed in support of the applica-tion there were undoubtedly deficiencies, but, in my judgment, those were cured by an affidavit in reply and that technical objection fails.

That left one main matter and one subsidiary matter. The main matter is that

H the defendant says that the terms of the mortgage are unreasonable and oppres-sive and ought not to be enforced beyond the repayment of the original sum advanced with interest at five per cent. to date of payment; and the subsidiary matter is that the plaintiffs claim in addition to the loan and the premium interest at that rate on the balance from time to time outstanding of the aggregate of the loan and premium.

I No evidence was filed to show any harsh, unconscionable or unfair dealing beyond such, if any, as appears from the terms of the mortgage itself; but the defendant first mounted an argument based on the proviso that if the lender were able to repay within six years, the borrowers would allow a pro rata discount. The defendant said that he did not know the basis on which the premium was calculated, and when he sought to ascertain it during the proceedings, the plaintiffs refused to tell him, and he said that that created an element of uncertainty and prejudiced him in the matter of redemption. Indeed, in the affidavit in reply Mr. Kirch, on behalf of the plaintiffs, said that his company

were advised that the reason why the principal sum of £4,553 was charged on the A
land is not relevant to these proceedings. However, no evidence was filed to show
that there was, in truth, no basis on which that sum was calculated and that it
was purely arbitrary. If there had been such evidence, it would have imported
an element of uncertainty and I would have had to consider what effect that would
have on the rights of the parties; but, as I have said, there was no such evidence.

Further, the defendant was not in a position to redeem. On the contrary, he B
was in default from a very early stage. If he had offered to redeem and the plaintiffs had refused or neglected to inform him how the proviso operated, and what
sum, therefore, was required on redemption, he would have been entitled to bring
a redemption action and obtain the required information, either on discovery or
by an order for an account, or, if need be, by a special order for an inquiry.
As counsel for the plaintiffs has persuaded me, however, the proviso does not C
operate, when, so far from offering to redeem within the six years, the defendant
is in default and the plaintiffs are enforcing their rights, and in my judgment,
therefore, the defendant can make nothing of that point.

Then the defendant presented a much more formidable argument, that the
large premium which brought the loan of £2,900 up to no less than £4,553 was in
itself harsh and unconscionable, and such a collateral advantage as a court of D
equity would not allow. In support of the mortgage counsel for the plaintiffs
referred me first to the case of *Potter* v. *Edwards* (1). In that case the loan was
£700 and a premium of £300 was held good, but KINDERSLEY, V.-C., who decided
that case, said (2):

" It is true that, in an ordinary case, where there is a mortgage for £1,000,
and it is proved that £700 only has been advanced, the court will only allow E
it to stand for £700, but in this case there is uncontradicted evidence of an
arrangement to a different effect,"

and there was evidence that the security was of an unsatisfactory nature and the
arrangement was made on that account. If, of course, that stood as an ordinary
rule it would defeat the plaintiffs because no evidence was led in this case to show F
any particular reason why the premium should be charged and, indeed, in the
passage from the evidence which I have read, the plaintiffs contended that that
was irrelevant. That case was decided, however, shortly after the repeal of the
usury laws and the doctrines of equity in this regard grew very largely from
analogy to those laws, and at the time of the decision in *Potter* v. *Edwards* (1) the
precise way in which the equitable doctrines were developed after the repeal of G
those Acts had not been determined.

I was then referred to the case of *Mainland* v. *Upjohn* (3), where again the
premium was upheld but the decision to that effect was again based on the security
being of a speculative character. The headnote is (3):

" Where advances have been made by a mortgagee to a mortgagor upon
security of a speculative character, such as a building estate, the court will, H
in taking the account in a redemption action, allow to the mortgagee sums
actually deducted by him for commission or bonus at the times of making
the advances, provided the deductions were made as part of the mortgage
contract, under a bargain deliberately entered into by the parties while on
equal terms and knowing perfectly well what they were doing, and without
any improper pressure, unfair dealing, or undue influence on the part of the I
mortgagee: the court treating the transaction in each case as amounting in
fact to the payment of the whole amount of the advance to the mortgagor
and the return of a certain part of it to the mortgagee as a consideration for
the accommodation."

KAY, J., said (4):

---

(1) (1857), 26 L.J.Ch. 468.   (2) (1857), 26 L.J.Ch. at p. 469.
(3) (1889), 41 Ch.D. 126.   (4) (1889), 41 Ch.D. at p. 136.

A   " I have now to deal with that which is the material part of this case, and
it raises a question of very considerable interest and importance, namely,
what sort of collateral advantage can a mortgagee stipulate for and take
from his mortgagor, now that the usury laws have been abolished by the
Act of 1854 (17 & 18 Vict. c. 90)? Before that time it was very well settled
that collateral advantages could not be insisted upon by a mortgagee. There

B   are many ways in which the equity to redeem was defended by stringent
provisions laid down by the court which created that equity. Among them
there was first of all this: that the amount stated in the mortgage deed to be
advanced was never conclusive. The mortgagor, or anybody claiming under
him, was always at liberty to show, if he could, that that amount had not
been actually all advanced."

C   Again, KAY, J., having quoted from LORD ELDON (5), said (6):

" I read that for this reason, that LORD ELDON there, although no doubt
one objection he makes to these exactions was that they tend to usury, still
does not rest his objection entirely upon that ground. He says, besides, that
they are oppressive, and are exactions that a mortgagee is not allowed to

D   make. It is a very interesting question indeed, and one which I certainly
do not consider is at present finally settled, how far the abolition of the laws
against usury has affected this jurisdiction, or the extent to which the court
will exercise its jurisdiction, as between mortgagor and mortgagee. I had
occasion recently in *James* v. *Kerr* (7) to refer to one case which has occurred
since the abolition of the usury laws, namely, the case of *Broad* v. *Selfe* (8),

E   which was decided in the year 1863."

Then KAY, J., said of that case (9):

" LORD ROMILLY, M.R., said this (10): ' The contract in this case was
only a contract of mortgage to the extent of £200 principal and the interest
upon it; but not beyond this. His Honour thought that the cases referred
to by Mr. Roberts '—including *Chambers* v. *Goldwin* (11), which I have

F   already mentioned—' and several others which he had consulted, showed the
principle that the court would not permit a person, under the colour of a
mortgage, to obtain a collateral advantage not belonging or appurtenant to
the contract of mortgage. Although this principle, in its origin, probably had
reference to the usury laws, it went, in His Honour's opinion, beyond them,
and was not affected by their repeal.' There we have a most emphatic state-

G   ment by a very experienced judge that, in his opinion, the stipulation for a
collateral advantage by way of bonus to be paid when the mortgage debt is
paid off is a thing which is not permitted between mortgagor and mortgagee,
notwithstanding the abolition of the usury laws. The mortgage in that case
was dated, as I have said, in 1861, considerably after the usury laws were
abolished."

H   Then KAY, J., referred to *Potter* v. *Edwards* (12) and continued thus (13):

" Then KINDERSLEY, V.-C., says that he thinks the whole £1,000 must be
paid before the mortgage can be redeemed. So that there I have the distinct
authority of a judge who, although the point was not argued, was a very
accomplished lawyer, and from whose mind, if there had been anything in

I   the question, the point certainly could not have been absent—that, upon a
loan of money on a risky security, it is legitimate, between mortgagor and
mortgagee, to deduct from the actual amount a very considerable bonus—
in that case as much as £300 out of £1,000; and that where that is deliberately

---

(5) From *Chambers* v. *Goldwin*, (1804), 9 Ves. 254 at p. 271.
(6) (1889), 41 Ch.D. at p. 138.   (7) (1889), 40 Ch.D. 449.
(8) (1863), 11 W.R. 1036; 2 New Rep. 541.   (9) (1889), 41 Ch.D. at p. 139.
(10) (1863), 11 W.R. at p. 1037.   (11) (1804), 9 Ves. 254.
(12) (1857), 26 L.J.Ch. 468   (13) (1889), 41 Ch.D. at pp. 141, 142.

done, and the parties completely understand one another, the mortgagor A
cannot afterwards reopen it, but is bound to let his property remain as a
security, not for the money he actually received, but for the larger sum
expressed to have been advanced. I am told that no case can be found in
which *Potter* v. *Edwards* (14) has been cited since, except one, which did not
determine the same point. But the case has found its way into the textbooks, and I find it cited as an authority in MR. FISHER'S work on MORT- B
GAGES. Accordingly, if this be an alteration in existing law, it is an alteration
which has the sanction of a judge of very considerable position: but it does
not appear whether the mortgage in that case was a mortgage made after
the abolition of the usury laws, for the date of it is not given in the report,
and the only reference in the report to the usury laws is in the argument, in
which it was said that there was no breach of the usury laws in the trans- C
action. Possibly it may have been a mortgage before the usury laws were
abolished [in fact it was not] and the learned judge seems to have thought
that, whether the usury laws existed or not, there was nothing in a transaction
of that kind which was obnoxious to any law recognised in these courts as
between mortgagor and mortgagee."

Pausing there, there was a state of uncertainty but both the cases were cases D
in which there was evidence to show that the security was defective, and in the
first case which I cited it was stated as the ordinary rule that a premium could
not be maintained. The matter was clarified, however, in the case of *Kreglinger*
v. *New Patagonia Meat and Cold Storage Co., Ltd.* (15). The headnote is (16):

" There is now no rule in equity that a mortgagee cannot stipulate in the E
mortgage deed for a collateral advantage to endure beyond redemption,
provided that such collateral advantage is not either (i) unfair and unconscionable, or (ii) in the nature of a penalty clogging the equity of redemption, or (iii) inconsistent with or repugnant to the contractual or equitable
right to redeem."

The collateral advantage in that case, which was a transaction between two large F
trading concerns, was an agreement that for a period of five years from the date
thereof the borrowing company would not sell sheep skins to any person other
than the lenders so long as the latter were willing to buy at the best price offered
by any other person, and further, that the borrowing company should pay to the
lenders commission on all sheep skins sold by the company to any other person.
VISCOUNT HALDANE, L.C., in that case said (17): G

" The principle was thus in early days limited in its application to the
accomplishment of the end which was held to justify interference of equity
with freedom of contract. It did not go further. As established it was
expressed in three ways. The most general of these was that if the transaction
was once found to be a mortgage, it must be treated as always remaining a
mortgage and nothing but a mortgage. That the substance of the transaction H
must be looked to in applying this doctrine, and that it did not apply to cases
which were only apparently or technically within it, but were in reality
something more than cases of mortgage, *Howard* v. *Harris* (18) and other
authorities show. It was only a different application of the paramount
doctrine to lay it down in the form of a second rule that a mortgagee should
not stipulate for a collateral advantage which would make his remuneration I
for the loan exceed a proper rate of interest. The legislature during a long
period placed restrictions on the rate of interest which could legally be
exacted. But equity went beyond the limits of the statutes which limited

(14) (1857), 26 L.J.Ch. 468.
(15) [1911-13] All E.R. Rep. 970; [1914] A.C. 25.
(16) [1914] A.C. at p. 25.
(17) [1911-13] All E.R. Rep. at p. 974; [1914] A.C. at pp. 36, 37.
(18) (1683), 1 Vern. 190.

A   the interest, and was ready to interfere with any usurious stipulation in a mortgage. In so doing it was influenced by the public policy of the time. That policy has now changed, and the Acts which limited the rate of interest have been repealed.   The result is that a collateral advantage may now be stipulated for by the mortgagee provided that he has not acted unfairly or oppressively, and provided that the bargain does not conflict with the third

B   form of the principle.   This is that a mortgage (subject to the apparent exception in the case of family arrangements, to which I have already alluded) cannot be made irredeemable, and that any stipulation which restricts or clogs the equity of redemption is void.   It is obvious that the reason for the doctrine in this form is the same as that which gave rise to the other forms.   It is simply an assertion in a different way of the principle

C   that once a mortgage always a mortgage and nothing else."

LORD PARKER OF WADDINGTON, opening his speech, said (19):

" The respondents in this case are appealing to the equitable jurisdiction of the court for relief from a contract which they admit to be fair and reasonable and of which they have already enjoyed the full advantage.   Their title

D   to relief is based on some equity which they say is inherent in all transactions in the nature of a mortgage.   They can state no intelligible principle underlying this alleged equity, but contend that your Lordships are bound by authority.   That the court should be asked in the exercise of its equitable jurisdiction to assist in so inequitable a proceeding as the repudiation of a fair and reasonable bargain is somewhat startling, and makes it necessary to

E   examine the point of view from which courts of equity have always regarded mortgage transactions.   For this purpose I have referred to most, if not all, of the reported cases on the subject, and propose to state shortly the conclusions at which I have arrived."

It will be seen that LORD PARKER regarded the transaction in that case as being fair and reasonable and, indeed, it was admitted so to be.   Then LORD PARKER

F   said (20):

" I now come to the particular class of mortgages to which I have already referred that is to say, mortgages to secure borrowed money.   For the whole period during which the Court of Chancery was formulating and laying down its equitable doctrines in relation to mortgages there existed statutes strictly limiting the rate of interest which could be legally charged for

G   borrowed money.   If a mortgagee stipulated for some advantage beyond repayment of his principal with interest, equity considered that he was acting contrary to the spirit of these statutes, and held the stipulation bad on this ground.   There thus arose the rule so often referred to in the reported decisions, that in a mortgage to secure borrowed money the mortgagee could not contract for any such advantage.   There was said to be an equity to

H   redeem on payment of principal, interest, and costs, whatever might have been the bargain between the parties, and any stipulation by the mortgagee for a further, or as it was sometimes called, a collateral advantage came to be spoken of as a clog or fetter on this equity.   It is of the greatest importance to observe that this equity is not the equity to redeem with which I have hitherto been dealing.   It is an equity which arises ab initio, and not only on

I   failure to exercise the contractual right to redeem.   It can be asserted before as well as after such failure.   It has nothing to do with time not being of the essence of a contract, or with relief from penalties, or with repugnant conditions.   It is not a right to redeem on the contractual terms, but a right to redeem notwithstanding the contractual terms, a right which depended on the existence of the statutes against usury and the public policy thought to be involved in those statutes.   Unfortunately, in some of the authorities this

(19) [1911-13] All E.R. Rep. at p. 979; [1914] A.C. at pp. 46, 47.
(20) [1911-13] All E.R. Rep. at pp. 983, 984; [1914] A.C. at pp. 54-56.

right is spoken of as a right incidental to mortgages generally, and not   A
confined to mortgages to secure borrowed money. This is quite explicable
when it is remembered that a loan is perhaps the most frequent occasion
for a mortgage. But it is, I think, none the less erroneous. I can find no
instance of the rule which precludes a mortgagee from stipulating for a
collateral advantage having been applied to a mortgage other than a mortgage
to secure borrowed money, and there is the authority of LORD ELDON in   B
Chambers v. *Goldwin* (21) for saying that this rule was based on the usury
laws. The right (notwithstanding the terms of the bargain) to redeem on
payment of principal, interest, and costs is a mere corollary to this rule, and
falls with it. It is to be observed that stipulations for a collateral advantage
may be classified under two heads. First, those the performance of which is
made a term of the contractual right to redeem, and, secondly, those the   C
performance of which is not made a term of such contractual right. In the
former case in settling the terms on which redemption was allowed the
Court of Chancery entirely ignored such stipulations. In the latter case, so
far as redemption was concerned, the stipulations were immaterial, but it
is said that in both cases the Court of Chancery would have restrained an
action at law for damages for their breach. This is possible, though I can   D
find no instance of its having been done, but clearly on a bill for an injunction
to restrain an action at law the plaintiff would have to show some equity
entitling him to be relieved from his contract, and such equity could, I
think, have been based only on the usury laws, or the public policy which
gave rise to them. The last of the usury laws was repealed in 1854, and
thenceforward there was, in my opinion, no intelligible reason why mortgages   E
to secure loans should be on any different footing from other mortgages. In
particular, there was no reason why the old rule against a mortgagee being
able to stipulate for a collateral advantage should be maintained in any form
or with any modification. Borrowers of money were fully protected from
oppression by the pains always taken by the Court of Chancery to see that
the bargain between borrower and lender was not unconscionable.   F
Unfortunately, at the time when the last of the usury laws was repealed, the
origin of the rule appears to have been more or less forgotten, and the cases
decided since such repeal exhibit an extraordinary diversity of judicial
opinion on the subject. It is little wonder that, with the existence in the
authorities of so many contradictory theories, persons desiring to repudiate
a fair and reasonable bargain have attempted to obtain the assistance of   G
the court in that behalf. To one who, like myself, has always admired the
way in which the Court of Chancery succeeded in supplementing our common
law system in accordance with the exigencies of a growing civilization, it is
satisfactory to find, as I have found on analysing the cases in question, that
no such attempt has yet been successful. In every case in which a stipulation
by a mortgagee for a collateral advantage has, since the repeal of the usury   H
laws, been held invalid, the stipulation has been open to objection, either (i)
because it was unconscionable, or (ii) because it was in the nature of a penal
clause clogging the equity arising on failure to exercise a contractual right to
redeem, or (iii) because it was in the nature of a condition repugnant as well
to the contractual as to the equitable right.''

Finally, LORD PARKER summed the matter up (22) where he said that he invited   I
their lordships

   '' to hold, that there is now no rule in equity which precludes a mortgagee,
   whether the mortgage be made upon the occasion of a loan or otherwise, from
   stipulating for any collateral advantage, provided such collateral advantage
   is not either (i) unfair and unconscionable, or (ii) in the nature of a penalty

---

(21) (1804), 9 Ves. at p. 271.
(22) [1911-13] All E.R. Rep. at pp. 986, 987; [1914] A.C. at p. 61.

A   clogging the equity of redemption, or (iii) inconsistent with or repugnant to the contractual and equitable right to redeem."

The matter is stated in 27 HALSBURY'S LAWS OF ENGLAND (3rd Edn.) p. 238, para. 428, as follows:

". . . but a contract for payment to the mortgagee of a bonus in addition to the sum advanced is valid if the bonus is reasonable and the contract was
B   freely entered into by the mortgagor."

It follows from those authorities that the defendant cannot succeed merely because this is a collateral advantage, but he can succeed if, and only if, on the evidence the bonus in this case was, to use the language of LORD PARKER (23), ". . . unfair and unconscionable ", or, to use the language of HALSBURY (24), " unreasonable ", and I therefore have to determine whether it was or was not.
C   In doing that I have to consider all the circumstances. Unlike the facts in the *Kreglinger* case (25), this was not a bargain between two large trading concerns. It was the case of a man who was buying his house and a man who was obviously of limited means, because he was unable to find more than £600 towards the purchase, whereas in evidence filed for another purpose the plaintiffs have stated that all the other persons who had purchased property from the company
D   had been able themselves to finance or to arrange finance for the purchases. The premium which was added to the loan was, as I understand, no less than fifty-seven per cent. of the amount of the loan. I do not think that it is really open to the plaintiffs to justify this premium as being in lieu of interest because they claim interest on the aggregate of the loan and the premium; but, even if it be, then, taking the mortgage as a six-year mortgage—and, of course, they bound
E   themselves not to call it in within that time if the instalments were duly paid— it would still represent interest at nineteen per cent which is out of all proportion to any investment rates prevailing at the time. Moreover, it was expressly provided by the charge that, on default, the whole should immediately become due.

F   Now, it is clear on the authorities, notably *Sterne* v. *Beck* (26), that if one has a debt or creates a debt by making a loan, and one provides for repayment by instalments, a proviso that the whole should become due on default is not bad as a penalty or otherwise; but where one adds a premium and one provides that the whole of the premium shall also become due, that, in my judgment, is a different matter. The plaintiffs have been at pains to point out that the concession allowed by way of discount to the borrower, if he offered to redeem within the six
G   years, would not apply if he defaulted and they sought to enforce the mortgage. Reasonableness, fairness and conscionability depend on all the circumstances, and in my judgment I am entitled to weigh as a factor that if default were made, the premium could become payable forthwith; and I am told that the effect of that would be to make interest, in effect, at the rate, on the facts of the present case, of thirty-eight per cent.
H   I further have this to bear in mind, that this was not an unsecured loan: a security was being offered with a reasonable margin, not, it is true the one-third/ two-thirds margin that one usually expects in trustee investments, but still the defendant provided £600 and there was that margin in the property to secure the plaintiffs. I think that they would have been entitled to charge a higher rate of interest than the normal market rate or a reasonable premium comparable there-
I   with, but nothing like the extent of nineteen per cent. looked at as an interest rate, or fifty-seven per cent. looked at as a capital sum; and it must be borne in mind that this premium was so large that it forthwith destroyed the whole equity and made it a completely deficient security. If default were made and all that had been secured was the principal and interest, it was likely that on any

(23) [1911-13] All E.R. Rep. at p. 987; [1914] A.C. at p. 61.
(24) Vol. 27, p. 238, para. 428.
(25) [1911-13] All E.R. Rep. 970; [1914] A.C. 25.
(26) (1863), 1 De G.J. & Sm. 595.

exercise of the plaintiffs' powers as mortgagees, there would be a surplus for the **A**
mortgagor, but this premium destroyed any possibility of that, and it also made
the security which was offered deficient.

For these reasons in my judgment this was not reasonable, and on the equity
as now defined in *Kreglinger's* case (27) I can and ought to interfere.

The plaintiffs relied by analogy on the Moneylenders Act (28) under which
interest in excess of forty-eight per cent. is deemed to be harsh and unconscionable, **B**
and said that this is nothing like that. Even in the case of the Moneylenders Act
a less rate of interest may be held on the facts harsh and unconscionable; but if it
exceeds forty-eight per cent., it is deemed so to be; but, far more important
than that, moneylending transactions are in their nature speculative and often
without any security whatsoever. This was a mortgage on security, and on
security in which there was a reasonable margin of equity for the protection of the **C**
plaintiffs as mortgagees. In my judgment, therefore, all that the plaintiffs are
entitled to enforce is the amount now outstanding in respect of principal and
interest, after bringing into account the payments which have been made.

Having reached that conclusion the subsidiary point is no longer material, but
I should add that had I thought that the mortgage should stand as a security for
the advance and the premium, I would certainly not have allowed interest in **D**
addition. True it is as a general rule that a mortgage debt carries interest in the
absence of an express provision, but that is because, as stated in the Irish case
of *Carey* v. *Doyne* (29), approved in *Re Kerr's Policy* (30), it would be inequitable
to allow redemption without payment of interest; or, as it was put in *Mendl* v.
Smith (31), interest is allowed unless there is any contractual right or equity
to exclude it. In my judgment this large premium would exclude the ordinary **E**
rule and I would not have allowed interest in addition.

It remains only to say something on the rate of interest. When the plaintiffs
were claiming interest on the aggregate of the loan and the premium, they
suggested five per cent., and the defendant has embraced that; but I think that
that is too low a rate. If one is charging interest on the actual loan one ought at
least to give market rates and possibly, in the circumstances of this case, some- **F**
what more. I have not been addressed on the rate of interest. As at present
advised I propose to allow six per cent. and I will hear either counsel, if they wish
to make representations that it ought to be greater or less.

[After submissions.]

Having heard argument on the question of interest, I do not accept the submission that it should be 9½ per cent. but I think that my initial idea of six per **G**
cent. was too low and I will fix it at seven per cent., as the rate which I have
chosen for this case on its own facts; the rate has no bearing on what would be
the proper rate for any other case.

Declaration accordingly.

Solicitors: *Travers Smith, Braithwaite & Co.* (for the plaintiffs); *Donald W.* **H**
Plunkett (for the defendant).

[*Reported by* JACQUELINE METCALFE, *Barrister-at-Law.*]

I

---

(27) [1911-13] All E.R. Rep. 970; [1914] A.C. 25.
(28) See Moneylenders' Act, 1927, s. 10; 16 HALSBURY's STATUTES (2nd Edn.) 392.
(29) (1856), 5 I.Ch.R. 104.
(30) (1869), L.R. 8 Eq. 331.   (31) (1943), 112 L.J.Ch. 279.

A

Re FULD (*deceased*).

[PROBATE, DIVORCE AND ADMIRALTY DIVISION (Scarman, J.), March 3, 22, 1967.]

Costs—Taxation—Common fund basis—Client giving notice to act in person and seeking to vet solicitor's bills of cost before lodgment for taxation—Lien of solicitor for costs—Probate action—Client a defendant in action—Fund

B *held by plaintiffs for defendant client's costs—Form of order—Solicitors Act, 1957 (5 & 6 Eliz. 2 c. 27), s. 72.*

The applicants were four firms of solicitors who at different times acted for L., one of fourteen defendants in a lengthy probate action. Probate of the deceased's will and first codicil was granted and costs, including the costs of L., were ordered " to be taxed on a common fund basis, if not

C agreed " and to be paid out of the estate. In the result, L. had succeeded in the action. A sum of £45,000 was directed to be raised by the plaintiffs out of the estate and allocated proportionately between the parties on estimates of their costs. The sum of £1,000 was thus held by the plaintiffs' solicitors in respect of the costs of L. Immediately before the date of an appointment before the registrar to give directions as to taxation of costs, L. filed a

D notice of appearance in person. L. declined to bring in her solicitors' bills of costs unaltered, reserving the right to withhold the bills either wholly or partly, alleging that she had claims against the solicitors for negligence or breach of duty in the conduct of the litigation. L. had no resources out of which to pay her solicitors' costs, if they were not paid out of the estate. Some of her solicitors had been financed by legal aid. The applicants applied

E to the court for an order that their proper costs on taxation be paid out of the estate, each seeking in effect to conduct the taxation themselves so far as it concerned their respective bills, and relying on solicitors' lien.

Held: although in the present case there was a fund, subject to the solicitors' lien and to s. 72* of the Solicitors Act, 1957, yet in the exercise of this discretionary jurisdiction for the protection of solicitors, the court must

F have regard also to the client's rights; accordingly the court would not make the order sought, but would order that the plaintiffs should make no payment on account of costs to L. without giving fourteen days' notice to the applicants of intention to do so, that the applicants should be at liberty to apply to the court for directions, in which case no payment on account of costs was to be made to L. without the leave of the court, and that the

G £1,000 held by the plaintiffs' solicitors should be paid into and remain in court until further order (see p. 654, letter H, p. 655, letter B, and p. 656, letter I, to p. 657, letter A, post).

Dictum of SIR GEORGE JESSEL, M.R. in *Emden* v. *Carte* ((1881), 19 Ch.D. at p. 318) considered.

Re Margetson and Jones ([1897] 2 Ch. 314) distinguished.

H [As to a solicitor's lien for his costs, see 36 HALSBURY'S LAWS (3rd Edn.) 173, para. 237; and for cases on the subject see 43 DIGEST (Repl.) 284, 285, *3002-3010.*

As to a charging order for costs, see 36 HALSBURY'S LAWS (3rd Edn.) 184-187, paras. 252-254; and for cases on the subject see 43 DIGEST (Repl.) 318, 319, *3331-3341.*

As to solicitors and own client taxation under the Solicitors Act, 1957, see

I 36 HALSBURY'S LAWS (3rd Edn.) 164, 165, para. 221; and for cases on the subject see 43 DIGEST (Repl.) 240-244, *2508-2579.*

---

* Section 72, so far as material, provides: " Any court in which a solicitor has been employed to prosecute or defend any suit, matter or proceeding may at any time declare the solicitor entitled to a charge on the property recovered or preserved through his instrumentality for his taxed costs in reference to that suit, matter or proceeding, and may make such orders for the taxation of the said costs and for raising money to pay, or for paying, the said costs out of his said property, as they think fit and all . . . acts done to defeat, or operating to defeat that charge shall . . . be void as against the solicitor."

For the Solicitors Act, 1957, s. 68, s. 72, see 37 HALSBURY'S STATUTES (2nd A
Edn. 1109, 1116.]

Cases referred to:

Bibby (James), Ltd. v. *Woods (Howard, Garnishee)*, [1949] 2 All E.R. 1;
  [1949] 2 K.B. 449; 21 Digest (Repl.) 747, *2355*.

Bryant, Ex p., (1815), 1 Madd. 49; 56 E.R. 19; 43 Digest (Repl.) 303, *3178*.

Campbell v. *Campbell and Lewis*, [1941] 1 All E.R. 274; 43 Digest (Repl.) B
  302, *3168*.

Emden v. *Carte*, (1881), 19 Ch. 311; 51 L.J. 371; 45 L.T. 328; 43 Digest
  (Repl.) 326, *3402*.

Margetson and Jones, Re, [1897] 2 Ch. 314; 66 L.J.Ch. 619; 76 L.T. 805;
  43 Digest (Repl.) 307, *3218*.

Mason v. *Mason and Cottrell*, [1933] All E.R. Rep. 859; [1933] P. 199; 102 C
  L.J.P. 91; 149 L.T. 346; 27 Digest (Repl.) 562, *5150*.

Mercer v, *Graves*, (1872), L.R. 7 Q.B. 499; 41 L.J.Q.B. 212; 26 L.T. 551;
  43 Digest (Repl.) 314, *3294*.

Ross v. *Buxton*, (1889), 42 Ch.D. 190; 58 L.J.Ch. 442; 60 L.T. 630; 54 J.P.
  85; 43 Digest (Repl.), 309, *3247*.

Summons.   D

This was an application by summons by four firms of solicitors who represented
the respondent, Miss Peta Ledivitch, at different times in the course of a probate
action in which the plaintiffs, Phillip Harry Hartley and John Popham Blows,
sought probate in solemn form of the will and codicil of Peter Harry Fuld,
deceased. Miss Ledivitch was one of fourteen defendants. Probate was granted of E
the will and first codicil, and the costs of some of the defendants, including Miss
Ledivitch, and the costs of an appeal by her were ordered to be paid out of the
estate. After the appeal Miss Ledivitch acted in person, and thereby became
responsible for the carriage of her solicitors' bills of costs. Miss Ledivitch reserved
the right to withhold her solicitors' bills of costs from submission for taxation,
either wholly or partially, in effect reserving the right to vet the charges herself F
before the bills were brought in. The applicant solicitors applied to the court for
an order that their proper costs and charges be taxed and paid out of the estate to
them or for such further or other order as the court might think just for their
protection and for preventing Miss Ledivitch from depriving them of their costs.
The facts are set out in the judgment.

S. Goldblatt for the applicant solicitors.   G
R. J. Parker, Q.C., and *G. M. Waller* for the plaintiffs.
Miss Peta Ledivitch appeared in person.

SCARMAN, J.: On Feb. 8, 1965, the court began the hearing of this action,
in which the plaintiffs sought probate of the will and first codicil of Peter Harry
Fuld. The deceased was a wealthy man, having very substantial assets in H
England, but the greater part of his fortune was situate in Germany. There
were fourteen defendants to the action, some of whom sought to establish the
validity of three further codicils. Miss Peta Ledivitch was the tenth defendant.
After a hearing of ninety-two days, the court by a judgment which was delivered
on Nov. 1, 1965, (1) admitted to probate the will and first codicil but rejected
the three further codicils. The result represented a victory for, amongst others,
Miss Ledivitch. She had an interest given her by the will in the income accruing I
from the residuary estate—an interest which, at least so far as the English
assets are concerned, is protected by the court's decision. She tells me, however,
that litigation is still pending in the courts of Karlsruhe in the Federal Republic
of Germany. On Nov. 22, 1965, the court heard argument as to costs and ordered
that the costs of some of the defendants, including those of Miss Ledivitch,
were to be paid out of the estate and " to be taxed on a common fund basis,

(1) [1965] 3 All E.R, 776,

A if not agreed ". Notwiths: ng her victory, Miss Ledivitch, on Dec. 30, 1965, gave notice of appeal, appare   y believing that the true will of the deceased was some instrument other than t   , which had been admitted to probate. One other defendant, who was interest· in the three rejected codicils, also gave notice of appeal. In February, 1966, Miss Ledivitch's appeal was dismissed and on July 28, 1966, the other defendant's appeal was dismissed on terms which have

B been made a rule of court. These terms included a provision that Miss Ledivitch's costs of the appeal be taxed on a common fund basis and paid out of the estate. On July 15, 1966, PAYNE, J., ordered that the administrators pendente lite raise £45,000 out of the estate, that the plaintiffs' solicitors obtain bills of estimates of costs from the solicitors of parties concerned and, on approval of such bills by a registrar, pay out the sum of £45,000 proportionately to the bills so approved.

C In due course, the parties, including Miss Ledivitch who was then represented by Lawrence Alkin & Co., solicitors, one of the present applicants, agreed to a distribution of the £45,000 which included £1,000 for Miss Ledivitch. Owing to the dispute between Miss Ledivitch and her solicitors, this sum is still held by the plaintiffs' solicitors who wish to have directions as to its disposal. During the proceedings in the action, Miss Ledivitch sometimes appeared in person

D and at other times was legally represented. In all, nine different firms of solicitors appeared on the record as having at different times represented Miss Ledivitch. Of these nine firms, six were privately instructed by Miss Ledivitch; the others were instructed under the legal aid scheme. Four of the firms privately instructed now apply to the court for an order that their proper costs and charges be taxed and paid out of the estate to them, or for such further or other order as the court

E may think just for their protection and for preventing Miss Ledivitch from depriving them of their costs.

After the final hearing in the Court of Appeal, the parties and their advisers turned their attention to costs. At this time, Lawrence Alkin & Co., solicitors, were still acting for Miss Ledivitch. An appointment was arranged for Dec. 9, 1966, at which the registrar was to give directions with regard to the taxation

F of the various bills of costs in the action. At this appointment the registrar observed that some parties had, in the course of the proceedings, changed their solicitors. Accordingly, it was agreed that it would be convenient in such cases if the successive solicitors involved filed and supported their own bills in respect of costs which had been incurred by the party in question while represented by the particular solicitor. One such party was, of course, Miss Leditivch.

G She, however, had on Dec. 8, i.e., the day previous to the appointment, filed notice of acting in person. Accordingly, the registrar told her that she had technically made herself responsible for the carriage of all the solicitors' bills for costs incurred on her behalf. He suggested to her that, as a litigant in person, she would find it very much simpler if all the solicitors who had acted for her were left to submit and deal with their individual bills. There is no doubt that

H the registrar believed that Miss Ledivitch accepted his suggestion. She clearly raised no objection, but she now refuses to allow the course suggested by the registrar to be taken. The registrar at the same time gave general directions as to the time-table for taxation, indicating that bills of costs were to be brought in not later than Feb. 17, 1967, and that taxation was to take place in April.

I On Dec. 19, 1966, Miss Ledivitch wrote to Mr. Trevor, one of the solicitors concerned, in these terms:

" As you have been on the books as representing me (although under the mistaken belief that you were an independent solicitor and not acting for other parties involved in the action), I would like to know if you intend to present me with a bill."

Meanwhile, his firm (Trevor, Reid & Co.) lodged their bill for taxation but, through an unfortunate oversight, failed to send any copy of it to Miss Ledivitch.

Accordingly, at the end of January, 1967, she again asked for their bill and on   A
Jan. 27 they replied in these terms:

> " We would confirm that in this matter we have, in fact, along with the
> other parties to this action, lodged a bill for taxation covering the period
> during which we acted on your behalf and this will doubtless be dealt with
> in due course. To the extent that any part of our charges and disbursements
> is not allowed on taxation against the estate, an account would remain to   B
> be rendered to you, although we trust that such amount will, in fact, be
> limited to a comparatively small sum."

Not unnaturally, this letter failed to satisfy Miss Ledivitch because it failed to
include a copy of the bill that had been lodged. On Jan. 30, 1967, therefore,
Miss Ledivitch wrote asking to receive the bill, and, in the course of her letter,   C
used these words:

> " May I remind you that before bills are lodged with the court, that they
> must be seen and agreed by the party for whom you were acting, in this
> case myself. I must ascertain that you acted on my instructions and I
> can only do this by examining your bill and the documents put forward
> by you to support such a bill . . . It will be up to me to defend the bill that   D
> you present and I cannot do this without a proper knowledge of what
> services you rendered to me."

The solicitors replied on Feb. 2 asserting that their bill had been lodged for
taxation, in accordance with the registrar's directions, on an appointment when
Miss Ledivitch was present, and purporting to include a copy of the bill that had   E
been lodged. They made it clear that she could see all the relevant papers and
correspondence if she wished to do so, but they failed to enclose the bill. By
Feb. 8 Miss Ledivitch had seen the bill and such papers and correspondence as
were still in the possession of the solicitors. In a letter written on that date
she asked for " a little clarification of the bill ". She was certain, she said,
that the solicitor had acted in good faith, though she believed he was mistaken   F
as to her desires and wishes, and said: " Although I do not dispute your right
to be paid for work which you might have done, the question remains, by whom ? "
She went on to ask that the solicitor make the position clear in the bill of costs
" and then the taxing master will decide how much of your bill I must pay
and also how much might be rightly debited " against another defendant. It
is clear from the letter that Miss Ledivitch was not disputing the right of the   G
solicitor to lodge a bill, but was protesting against the contents of the bill.
According to the affidavit of Mr. Trevor, the other solicitors concerned had
either already lodged, or were about to lodge, their bills covering the periods
during which they had acted for Miss Ledivitch.

Since the appointment of Dec. 9, 1966, there have been various appearances
by one or more of the parties concerned in this application before the registrar   H
or one of the taxing officers of the Probate Division. I need only refer to an
appointment before the registrar on Feb. 2, 1967. This appointment was attended
by Mr. Trevor and by Miss Ledivitch. The registrar took the view that Miss
Ledivitch, having filed notice of change to act in person on the day prior to the
summons for taxing directions, was alone entitled to bring in the bills of costs,
to attend thereon and to receive a certificate for costs in her favour. The
registrar asked Miss Ledivitch whether she would undertake to bring in the bills   I
of costs, complete and unaltered. She replied that she would give no such undertaking and that she reserved the right to withhold the bills either in toto or to a
partial extent. Mr. Trevor asked for an opportunity to argue the matter fully,
to which request the registrar acceded. He then gave Miss Ledivitch an appointment for Mar. 2, when the matter could be argued and he could give such further
directions as might be necessary. This appointment was vacated by Miss Ledivitch
at some time prior to Feb. 10, but the registrar directed that it should nevertheless

A be retained so that the matter might be fully ventilated. In fact, however, the registrar cancelled the appointment, as the parties were to attend on this application on the morning of Mar. 3.

Miss Ledivitch has filed no evidence. She indicated more than once during the hearing that she disputed some of the statements of fact to be found in Mr. Trevor's affidavit; but the facts which I have set out are clearly established

B and, in my judgment, suffice to enable me to reach a decision on this application. If corroboration were needed as to her attitude towards the taxing proceedings, it was available in what she said to the court during argument. She maintained before me her right to withhold the bills from taxation either in toto or to a partial extent. She did not, however, dispute the retainer of the applicant solicitors, all of whom have appeared on the record as her solicitors at different

C times. Her concern was to emphasize that their bills covered services not rendered to her, or that in various ways they had been guilty of neglect or breach of duty to her in the conduct of the litigation as her solicitors. I have not investigated these allegations, and make no finding on them.

From the facts which I have stated I draw the following inferences. First, Miss Ledivitch has no intention of surrendering control of the inter partes

D taxation of her costs. Secondly, while not disputing the applicant solicitors' right to some costs, she intends to submit for this taxation only such bills as meet with her approval. Thirdly, she believes that she has claims against her solicitors and maintains that they require investigation before she can decide on the bills to be submitted on her behalf to the plaintiffs' solicitors and the court for taxation. Fourthly, by her actions and present attitude she is preventing

E the inter partes taxation of her costs from proceeding on the basis of the solicitors' bills so far lodged. It would be wrong, however, to draw the inference that she is embarked on a policy deliberately to deprive her solicitors of their legitimate costs. She has grievances, genuine or fancied, which she wants investigated but which have not yet been investigated. Finally, Miss Ledivitch has at present available to pay her solicitors no resources other than her fund of

F taxed costs represented by the orders of November, 1965, and July, 1966; and there is no indication that she is likely to have, in the reasonably near future, any sufficient resources other than this fund.

Miss Ledivitch submits, as a matter of law, that the order that her costs be taxed and paid out of the estate is her order. She argues that she has the right to determine what bills, if any, shall be lodged for taxation, and that she may,

G if she chooses, refrain from proceeding with the taxation or enforcing the order for costs. The solicitors do not dispute her analysis but submit that there comes a point at which the court will interfere to protect them. They submit that this point has been reached, and that, unless the court intervenes, Miss Ledivitch will deprive them of access to the one fund from which they have any reasonable chance of getting paid.

H As security for payment of his remuneration, a solicitor has what is commonly called a lien on a sum of money which comes into existence owing to his exertions. In *James Bibby, Ltd.* v. *Woods (Howard, Garnishee)* (2) LORD GODDARD, C.J., commented that, in this connexion, the term " lien " was a misnomer. He added (3):

I   " That was made clear by the judgment of COCKBURN, C.J., in *Mercer* v. *Graves*, where COCKBURN, C.J., said (4): ' There is no such thing as a lien except upon something of which you have possession . . . although we talk of an attorney having a lien upon a judgment, it is in fact only a claim or right to ask for the intervention of the court for his protection, when, having obtained judgment for his client, he finds there is a probability of the client depriving him of his costs.' "

(2) [1949] 2 All E.R. 1 at p. 3, letter H; [1949] 2 K.B. 449 at p. 453.
(3) [1949] 2 All E.R. at pp. 3, 4; [1949] 2 K.B. at p. 453.
(4) (1872), L.R. 7 Q.B. 499 at p. 503.

In *Mason* v. *Mason and Cottrell* (5) LORD HANWORTH, M.R., referring to *Mercer* A
v. *Graves* (6), said:

> " The nature of a solicitor's lien is pointed out in the course of that case.
> It is merely a right to claim the equitable interference of the court, who may
> order that the judgment obtained by the solicitor's client do stand as
> security for her costs and that payment of such an amount as will cover them
> be made to the solicitor in the first instance. That lien is one which prevails B
> over a fund which is in sight; the right is one which, so to speak, cannot
> prevail at large."

By their application, therefore, the solicitors are claiming, at this stage, the
equitable interference of the court. If they are to obtain the assistance of the
court, they must first show that there is a fund in sight. It is well settled that C
costs payable by one party to another are a fund which can be made the subject
of a charge in favour of the party's solicitor; see *Campbell* v. *Campbell and
Lewis* (7). It is immaterial that the costs are ordered, as in the present case,
to be paid personally to the client. In *Ex p. Bryant* (8) it was argued against
the solicitor that the order directed that the costs should be paid to the client
personally. The Vice-Chancellor gave the argument short shrift (9): D

> " This is an attempt to deprive the solicitor of his lien for his costs . . .
> Though the order was personal and the costs directed to be paid to List,
> it was not meant, nor can it have the effect, to deprive him of his lien. I
> do not wish to relax the doctrine as to lien, for it is to the advantage of
> clients as well as solicitors; for business is often transacted by solicitors
> for needy clients, merely on the prospect of having their costs under the E
> doctrine as to lien."

It might, however, be argued that there is no fund in sight before taxation has
determined the amount of it. As a matter of common sense, the fund has been
in sight, at least since the court's order for the payment of these costs became
final by dismissal of the appeal proceedings. Is it to be suggested, merely because
the client has not ascertained the amount of the fund by agreement or taxation, F
that there is no fund? If this were the law, the client would indeed be able
to deprive the solicitor of his lien, which, as was emphasised in *Ex p. Bryant* (8),
it is the policy of the law to protect. The cases stress that the solicitor's right
is to the exercise by the court of an equitable jurisdiction. It would be an absurdity
if such a jurisdiction could be stultified by the failure of the client to take the
steps necessary to realise the solicitor's security. Equity looks on that as done G
which ought to be done—the old maxim has validity in such circumstances.

In my opinion, therefore, there is a fund over which the lien may prevail,
and the court has jurisdiction at this stage to intervene. The question, therefore,
becomes one of the exercise of discretion in the particular circumstances of the
case. I must bear in mind that it is unlikely that without the aid of the fund
Miss Ledivitch will be able, within any reasonable period of time, to pay her H
solicitors. Of her many solicitors, some were financed by legal aid; her income
from the residue of the estate may not come to hand for some time yet (proceedings
are still pending in Germany); she has, if she is to be believed, suffered a serious
business reverse in Italy where she was, until recently, living. The solicitors'
prospect of recovery of their costs, without recourse to the fund, is, I would
think, a dim one. I must also bear in mind that Miss Ledivitch's insistence on I
herself conducting the inter partes taxation and " vetting " the bills lodged
by her solicitors is holding up the ascertainment of the amount of the fund
available as security for the solicitors' costs. Nevertheless, the court in its
legitimate concern for the solicitor must not disregard the rights of the client.
Inter partes taxation, even on a common fund basis, is not to be confused with

---

(5) [1933] P. 199 at p. 214; [1933] All E.R. Rep. 859 at p. 868.
(6) (1872), L.R. 7 Q.B. 499.   (7) [1941] 1 All E.R. 274.
(8) (1815), 1 Madd. 49   (9) (1815), 1 Madd. at p. 52

A   a solicitor and own client taxation. Miss Ledivitch is entitled to have a bill from each solicitor delivered to her, in accordance with the requirements of s. 68 of the Solicitors Act, 1957. She is entitled to have these bills taxed, and is not liable to pay her solicitors until that taxation is completed. Further, she alleges that she is entitled to damages from one or more of the solicitors for negligence or breach of duty.

B   In these circumstances, the duty of the court is to intervene only if it be necessary for the solicitor's protection, and then only to the extent necessary to safeguard his lien. The intervention, if the court thinks it right to intervene, must not prejudice the rights of the client. The solicitors, in effect, seek now to conduct the inter partes taxation, so far as it concerns their respective bills, and to be paid directly by the estate the costs thus taxed. In pressing the court

C   to make this order at this stage, counsel for the solicitors relied on two cases, and on the language of s. 72 of the Solicitors Act, 1957 (10), under which a court may, in certain circumstances, declare a solicitor to be entitled to a charge on property recovered or preserved through his instrumentality.

    The first case was *Ross* v. *Buxton* (11). In that case, the trustee in bankruptcy of the solicitor obtained from the court (a) an order for the taxation of the

D   solicitor's bill against his client, who was plaintiff in the action, so as to ascertain the balance due from client to solicitor, and the amount of the lien; and (b) an order on the defendant's solicitors to pay such sum as was sufficient to discharge the lien. What had happened was that the plaintiff, acting without his solicitor, had settled the action for £50, which was the amount the defendant had paid into court in satisfaction of the claim. The plaintiff's solicitor gave notice to the

E   defendant's solicitors not to pay any money to the plaintiff until his costs were paid. Yet, although they had notice, they arranged for the £50 in court to be paid out to themselves, whereupon they paid it over to the plaintiff. It is to be noted of the case that the order for payment in discharge of the lien was to be effective only after the ascertainment of the amount due by taxation of the solicitor's bill against his own client, the plaintiff. The decision is, therefore of

F   no help to the applicant solicitors, for in the present case there has been no solicitor and own client taxation. On the contrary, the decision supports the view that no order for payment ought to be made until after such a taxation.

    The next case to which counsel for the solicitors referred me was *Re Margetson and Jones* (12). Mr. and Mrs. Pugh were engaged in litigation with their former solicitor, Mr. Jones. The litigation concerned a dispute over a bill of costs

G   delivered by Mr. Jones. In this litigation the Pughs retained Mr. Margetson to act for them. After the litigation had reached the stage of an order for taxation, Mr. Margetson heard no more until he learnt that his clients, who were impecunious, had accepted a small sum direct from Mr. Jones in settlement. Mr. Margetson recovered judgment against the Pughs in the Mayor's court for his costs but it was not satisfied. Thereafter Mr. Margetson sought an order enabling him

H   to continue the Pughs' litigation against Jones by completing the taxation left unfinished by reason of the settlement. KEKEWICH, J., commented that (13):

> " There is an apparent anomaly in allowing Mr. Margetson to continue proceedings which he cannot proceed with in the name of his clients and which they themselves have stopped, they having withdrawn the retainer."

I   Nevertheless, he made an order that the costs incurred by Mr. Margetson in the litigation should be taxed and paid by Mr. Jones. The foundation of the order was the finding that it was (14):

> " . . . a distinct case of a cheat, and that what was done on the part of Mr. Jones was done with the intention of cheating Mr. Margetson of his costs."

---

(10) Section 72, so far as material is set out in footnote (*) on p. 649, ante.
(11) (1889), 42 Ch. 190.   (12) [1897] 2 Ch. 314.
(13) (1897) 2 Ch. at p. 321.   (14) [1897] 2 Ch. at p. 320.

The case is to be distinguished from the present, first, because I am unable to   **A**
infer from the evidence an intention on the part of Miss Ledivitch either to cheat
or to deprive her solicitors of their proper costs: secondly, because in *Margetson's*
case (15) there was no doubt about the amount of the Pughs' indebtedness to
him on account of his costs (and he had judgment) whereas Miss Ledivitch is
vigorously challenging the extent of her indebtedness to the applicant solicitors
and there has been no ascertainment of the amount due to them. Nevertheless,   **B**
the case does show how extensive are the powers of the court to protect and enforce
a solicitor's lien for his costs on the fruits of litigation won by his exertions.

In his reliance on the terms of s. 72 of the Solicitors Act, 1957, counsel for the
solicitors emphasised that under its provisions the court could make at any
time a charging-order in favour of a solicitor who had acted in his client's litigation.
This is clearly so; and the charging-order may be accompanied by an order   **C**
for the taxation of the solicitor's costs. But it is plain that the charge and any
consequential order for its enforcement by payment must be limited to costs
properly incurred. As SIR GEORGE JESSEL, M.R., remarked in *Emden* v. *Carte* (16),
when discussing an earlier section to the same effect (s. 28 of the Attorneys and
Solicitors Act, 1860):

> " It is the duty of the judge in making an order to limit the order to the   **D**
> costs properly incurred, and to direct taxation of the costs properly incurred."

I accept the analogy of s. 72. Indeed, one way in which the court may enforce a
solicitor's lien is to act under the section. Whether the court, therefore, is intervening in the exercise of its inherent jurisdiction to protect the solicitor, or
proceeding under s. 72 of the Act of 1957, the same considerations apply. In   **E**
either case the court must limit its order to costs properly incurred. How can
a solicitor's proper costs in a contentious matter be ascertained in the absence
of agreement, save by taxation of the bill which he delivers to his client? Counsel
for the solicitors submits that the amount of an inter partes taxation—even, as
here, on a common fund basis—cannot be more than the amount due on a
solicitor and own client taxation. No doubt, this is generally true but, it cannot be   **F**
confidently asserted to be so in this case. For there are matters which Miss
Ledivitch claims would substantially reduce her solicitors' entitlement to costs.
They have not been investigated and, until they are, the court cannot be certain
what, if anything, is owing to the solicitors on account of their costs. Accordingly,
I refuse at this stage to make an order either entrusting the inter partes taxation
to the solicitors or requiring the plaintiffs to pay the costs so taxed to the
solicitors. It might well prejudice the contentions that the client would wish to   **G**
urge on a solicitor and own client taxation; it might also embarrass her in the
prosecution of her claims for damages. Furthermore, there would be great
practical difficulties in allowing the solicitors, against the will of their client,
to conduct an inter partes taxation.

Nevertheless, the court can intervene at this, or indeed, at any stage to protect   **H**
the solicitor, though its order must be adjusted to the particular circumstances
operating at the time it is made. In my judgment, the solicitors in this case are
entitled to have the fund, which is the security for their costs, protected, even
though neither the amount of the fund nor the amount of their costs has yet
been ascertained. Accordingly, I order that the plaintiffs are to make no payment
on account of costs to Miss Ledivitch, without giving the applicant solicitors
fourteen days' notice of their intention so to do, and that the applicant solicitors   **I**
are to have liberty to apply to the court for directions, in which event no payment
on account of costs is to be made to Miss Ledivitch without the leave of the
court. If the applicants wish to have a solicitor and own client taxation, they
may apply at the conclusion of this judgment, and I will hear them and Miss
Ledivitch. If, after such taxation, Miss Ledivitch should be dragging her heels
on the inter partes taxation, it may be that the court could then make the sort

---

(15) [1897] 2 Ch. 314.   (16) (1881), 19 Ch.D. 311 at p. 318.

A of order which the solicitors—in my opinion prematurely—are seeking today. Finally, I direct that the £1,000 held by the plaintiffs' solicitors on account of Miss Ledivitch's costs be paid into court, and remain in court, until further order.

Order accordingly.

B [*After discussion a further order was made, by consent, that the solicitors should be at liberty to lodge bills of costs for taxation as between solicitor and client under s. 69 of the Solicitors Act, 1957, such bills to be lodged and to be delivered to Miss Ledivitch within fourteen days; order for taxation of the bills so lodged.*]

Solicitors: *Trevor, Reid & Co.* (for the applicant solicitors); *Clifford Turner & Co.* (for the plaintiffs).

[Reported by ALICE BLOOMFIELD, *Barrister-at-Law.*]

C

FITZPATRICK v. BATGER & CO., LTD.

D [COURT OF APPEAL, CIVIL DIVISION (Lord Denning, M.R., Salmon and Winn, L.JJ.), March 17, 1967.]

Practice—Want of prosecution—Dismissal of action—Inordinate delay without excuse.

On Dec. 13, 1961, the plaintiff suffered personal injuries from an accident in the course of his employment by the defendants. On Feb. 7, 1963, a
E writ was issued and the defence was delivered on Apr. 19, 1963. In June, 1963, negotiations took place between the parties about a settlement of the action, the defendants making an offer which the plaintiff refused. Nothing more was done until February, 1965, when the defendants made a slightly larger offer in settlement of the plaintiff's claim which was again refused. These negotiations ended in March, 1965. Finally, on Jan. 27, 1967,
F the plaintiff's solicitors wrote a letter seeking to revive the action, whereupon the defendants took out a summons to dismiss the action for want of prosecution, no summons for directions having been taken out by the plaintiff. It was not disputed that the delay was the fault of the plaintiff's solicitor. On appeal by the defendants from an order allowing the action to be revived on payment into court of security for costs,
G **Held:** there had been such inordinate delay without excuse that the action would be dismissed for want of prosecution (see p. 658, letter F, and p. 659, letter F, post).

Appeal allowed.

[As to dismissal of actions for want of prosecution, see 30 HALSBURY'S LAWS (3rd Edn.) 410, 411, para. 771.]

H Cases referred to:

Reggentin v. *Beecholme Bakeries, Ltd.,* (1967), 111 Sol. Jo. 216.
Ward v. *James,* [1965] 1 All E.R. 563; [1966] 1 Q.B. 273; [1965] 2 W.L.R. 455; 3rd Digest Supp.

Interlocutory Appeal.

I This was an appeal by the defendants from an order of BROWNE, J., dated Feb. 17, 1967, dismissing their appeal from an order of Master DIAMOND dated Feb. 9, 1967, ordering that the action by the plaintiff against the defendants be dismissed for want of prosecution unless the plaintiff gave security for costs within twenty-one days in the sum of £30 and served a summons for directions within seven days thereafter. The facts are set out in the judgment of LORD DENNING, M.R.

J. R. Phillips for the defendants.
P. H. Ripman for the plaintiff.

Z

LORD DENNING, M.R.: In this case the plaintiff, Mr. Michael Fitz- A
patrick, on Dec. 13, 1961, was working in the premises of his employers the
defendants, Batger & Co., Ltd., making toffee. He was helping to carry a bowl
of hot toffee across the floor when he fell. Some of the toffee splashed over his
hand and leg. He was off work for several weeks and sought damages against
his employers. He obtained legal aid in October, 1962. Solicitors on his behalf
issued a writ on Feb. 7, 1963. Up to that stage there was no undue delay. The B
defence was delivered on Apr. 19, 1963. In June, 1963, there was a discussion
without prejudice. The insurance company were ready to offer the sum of £300
in settlement; but the plaintiff and his advisers did not accept that sum. Then
this action went to sleep for some eighteen months or more. The solicitor's
clerk had left the firm and it was overlooked. In February, 1965, the plaintiff's
solicitor revived the claim. Again the defendants were ready to pay £300 in C
settlement. They went further. They offered a modest increase on £300. The
plaintiff and his advisers did not accept the offer. The negotiations ended on
Mar. 2, 1965. The matter went to sleep again for nearly two years. Then the
London agents of the plaintiff's solicitor wrote a letter seeking to revive it.
Thereupon the defendants took out a summons to dismiss the case for want of
prosecution. R.S.C., Ord. 25, r. 1 (4), provides that, if the plaintiff does not D
take out a summons for directions (as he did not in this case), the defendant
himself may do so or he can apply for an order to dismiss the action. The master
and the judge allowed it to be revived if £30 was paid into court as security
for costs. The defendants appeal to this court. They say that a peremptory
order should be made to dismiss the action.

Only last week, in *Reggentin* v. *Beecholme Bakeries, Ltd.* (1), I said that it is E
the duty of the plaintiff's adviser to get on with the case. Public policy demands
that the business of the courts should be conducted with expedition. Just
consider the times here. The accident was on Dec. 13, 1961. If we allowed this
case to be set down now, it would not come on for trial until the end of this
year. That would be some six years after the accident. It is impossible to have
a fair trial after so long a time. The delay is far beyond anything which we F
can excuse. This action has gone to sleep for nearly two years. It should now
be dismissed for want of prosecution.

I know that this is a matter for the discretion of the judge, but I am satisfied
that he was wrong; and, following our ruling in *Ward* v. *James* (2), we can
interfere. This will not prejudice the plaintiff personally. He has, as far as I
can see, an unanswerable claim against his solicitor for his neglect. The damages G
will be at least the sum of £300 which was offered in settlement. I would allow
the appeal and order that the action stand dismissed.

SALMON, L.J.: I entirely agree. The defence was delivered as long ago as
April, 1963. Some further particulars of the statement of claim were delivered in
July, 1963. The accident which the plaintiff is alleged to have suffered as a result of H
the defendants' negligence occurred as long ago as December, 1961. From July, 1963,
until February, 1965, the plaintiff's solicitor did nothing at all to get on with the
action. It is conceded that the reason for this very serious delay was the fault
of one of the plaintiff's solicitor's clerks. Then in February and March, 1965,
the plaintiff's solicitor apparently woke up for a while and there were some without
prejudice negotiations with the defendants. In the course of those negotiations,
the defendants' solicitors repeated an offer which they had made as long ago as I
June 25, 1963, to pay the plaintiff £300. Indeed, they went further and indicated
that they would be prepared to pay rather more than £300. That offer was
refused. Again nothing happened at all so far as the plaintiff's solicitor was
concerned for nearly two more years, i.e., until the beginning of 1967. It is not

---

(1) (1967), 111 Sol. Jo. 216.
(2) [1965] 1 All E.R. 563; [1966] 1 Q.B. 273.

A disputed that that gross delay was the fault of the plaintiff's solicitor which I, for my part, cannot think has been satisfactorily explained. I am happy to say that, in the vast majority of cases, these actions are brought on for trial quite promptly. I have great sympathy with many solicitors in the difficulties which they have to face in litigation of this kind; but grossly inordinate delay of the kind which has occurred in this case is quite inexcusable and ought not to
B be tolerated.

It is of the greatest importance in the interests of justice that these actions should be brought to trial with reasonable expedition. It is not only in the interests of defendants that this should be done, but it is perhaps even more in the interests of plaintiffs themselves. It is said in this case that the action ought not to be dismissed, because the defendants might have taken out a summons to
C dismiss for want of prosecution much earlier than they in fact did. They no doubt, however, were relying on the maxim that it is wise to let sleeping dogs lie. They had good reason to suppose that a dog which had remained unconscious for such long periods as this one, if left alone, might well die a natural death at no expense to themselves; whereas, if they were to take out a summons to dismiss the action, they would merely be waking the dog up for the purpose of
D killing it at great expense which they would have no chance of recovering. I am not surprised that they did not apply earlier, and I do not think that the plaintiff's advisers should be allowed to derive any advantage from that fact.

The plaintiff is not being deprived of compensation because, as LORD DENNING, M.R., has said, unless, as seems fantastically unlikely, he was urging his solicitor not to get on with the case, he has an unanswerable claim against him for negligence.
E How much he will recover I do not know, but it certainly could not be less than the £300 which was offered to the plaintiff's solicitor, first in June, 1963, and then later in February and March, 1965. I am quite satisfied that, in the circumstances of this case, where there has been such grossly inordinate delay without any real excuse, the discretion below was wrongly exercised. As far as this case is con-
F cerned—each case must turn on its own facts and circumstances—I have no doubt but that the proper order is to dismiss the action for want of prosecution. I would allow the appeal accordingly.

WINN, L.J.: I agree completely with both the judgments delivered by my lords and would add little. SALMON, L.J., has used the expression " grossly
G inordinate delay ". I respectfully adopt that expression, and express my own view that the delay in this case is utterly inordinate compared even with other bad instances which distort the present pattern of procedure in personal injury cases, as revealed by the forty-three personal injury claims set down for trial in the High Court during the month of January, 1967. In the present case the period of time which has elapsed since delivery of defence is forty-seven months
H up to now. Twenty-one out of the forty-three cases that I have mentioned were running-down cases, and in them the period of time between delivery of defence and setting down averaged five months. In four only of those twenty-one cases did the delay exceed nine months; in most of the twenty-one cases the period fell between two months and eight months. In the twenty-two industrial injury cases the average period between delivery of defence and setting down was
I ten months. In twelve of those cases there was an application for particulars and particulars were delivered. There is one other set of figures, which I will mention because it does confirm the expression of opinion that this delay is inordinate. Of those same forty-three cases, the time between accident and setting down averaged 29·6 months. In the case of running-down actions it was only 27·5 months. In both sets of cases the interval between accident and writ was sixteen months. It follows that taking the average of all the personal injury cases, 13·6 months elapsed between writ and setting down. In the case of the running-down

cases it was eleven months between writ and setting down. This case compares   **A**
very badly with those.

I agree that this appeal should be allowed.

Appeal allowed. Action dismissed.

Solicitors: *Milners, Curry & Gaskell* (for the defendants); *Harold Kenwright
& Cox*, agents for *W. Timothy Donovan* (for the plaintiff).

  B

[*Reported by* F. GUTTMAN, ESQ., *Barrister-at-Law.*]

FOARD v. FOARD.

[PROBATE, DIVORCE AND ADMIRALTY DIVISION (Payne, J.), April 4, 1967.]   **C**

*Divorce—Maintenance of wife—Secured maintenance—Token order—Substantive
order should be based on evidence as to earnings, means, assets and circumstances of parties—Token sum of £10 ordered to be secured to the wife for life—
Matrimonial Causes Act 1965 (c. 72), s. 16 (1).*

A decree absolute having been granted to the wife, the husband re-   **D**
married. He had no earning capacity and lived on pensions, but he owned a
freehold bungalow. On an application by the wife for, inter alia, secured provision, the registrar ordered the husband, under s. 16 (1)* of the Matrimonial
Causes Act 1965, to secure for the wife a charge of £1,000 on the bungalow
to provide an income for her during her life but only from the date of the
death of the husband. On appeal by the husband,

Held: (i) in making the order the registrar had attempted to make a   **E**
present assessment of the future fortunes of the wife and the ability of the
husband to pay without having any reliable evidence for the purpose, and
this was not justified, even though there was power under s. 31 of the Act of
1965 to vary an order for secured provision, since an assessment of maintenance should be based on evidence of earnings, means, assets and   **F**
circumstances of the parties (see p. 663, letter F, and p. 664, letter C, post).

Principle stated by SIR BOYD MERRIMAN, P., in *Chichester* v. *Chichester*
([1936] 1 All E.R. at p. 273) applied.

(ii) a token order for secured provision could, however, be made, and
accordingly the registrar's order would be varied by ordering the provision
of a sum of £10 to be secured to the wife for her life until further order and   **G**
charged on the bungalow, registration in respect of the charge to be effected
at the land registry; as a consequence the wife would be able to apply for a
variation of the secured provision under s. 31 of the Act of 1965, if that
became advisable, or, if the bungalow were not disposed of in the husband's
lifetime and he did not leave a reasonable provision for the wife after his
death, she might apply under s. 26 of the Act of 1965 (see p. 664, letters   **H**
E, H and I, and p. 665, letter B, post).

Appeal allowed.

[As to the power to order a gross or annual sum by way of permanent maintenance, see 12 HALSBURY'S LAWS (3rd Edn.) 430, para. 966; as to principles
applying to secured maintenance, see ibid., pp. 435, 436, para. 981; and for
cases on the subject, see 27 DIGEST (Repl.) 628, 629, *5894-5897*.   **I**

For the Matrimonial Causes Act 1965, s. 16, s. 26 and s. 31, see 45 HALSBURY'S
STATUTES (2nd Edn.) 468, 483, 488.]

Cases referred to:
Chichester v. *Chichester*, [1936] 1 All E.R. 271; [1936] P. 129; 105 L.J.P. 38;
    154 L.T. 375; 27 Digest (Repl.) 617, *5768*.

---

* Section 16 (1), so far as material, is set out at p. 662, letter I, to p. 663, letter A,
post.

A   *Shearn* v. *Shearn*, [1930] All E.R. Rep. 310; [1931] P. 1; 100 L.J.P. 41; 143
      L.T. 772; 27 Digest (Repl.) 629, *5897*.

Appeal.

This was an appeal by the husband from that part of an order of the senior
registrar, dated Jan. 11, 1967, ordering the husband to secure to the wife for
her life a charge of £1,000 on the freehold property owned by him at 18, Hamilton
B   Road, Hunton Bridge, Kings Langley, Hertfordshire. The facts are set out in
the judgment. The summons was heard in chambers, but judgment was delivered
in open court.

J. A. P. *Hazel* for the husband.
T. A. C. *Coningsby* for the wife.

C   *Cur. adv. vult.*

Apr. 4. **PAYNE, J.**, read the following judgment: On Jan. 11, 1967, the
senior registrar ordered, first, that the husband should pay to his wife, Verna
Sybil Foard, as from July 5, 1966, maintenance at the nominal rate of 1s. per
annum and, secondly, that the husband should secure for the wife a charge of
D   £1,000 on freehold property 18, Hamilton Road, Hunton Bridge, Kings Langley
in the county of Hertford, to provide an income for the wife during her life but
only from the date of death of the husband. The husband now appeals against the
second part of the order. No objection is taken to the first part of the order as
it is common ground that the wife cannot, at the present time, owing to the
relative financial position of the parties, establish a right to more than a nominal
E   payment.

The husband and wife were married on July 30, 1955, when the husband was
aged sixty-three years and the wife twenty-five years. The child born on Apr. 15,
1949, was adopted by the parties on May 25, 1962, and is a child of the family.
She is now aged eighteen and is a trainee nurse. On Feb. 8, 1965, the wife filed a
petition for dissolution of the marriage on the ground of cruelty. The suit was
F   not defended; a decree nisi was pronounced on Apr. 1, 1966, and on July 5, 1966,
the decree was made absolute. On Nov. 16, 1965, an order was made that the
husband should pay 15s. per week for maintenance of the child until Apr. 5, 1966,
when she would be almost seventeen. At the hearing of the petition the wife
was given leave to amend the prayer in the petition by adding to the prayer for
maintenance a prayer for secured provision. Affidavits were filed by the husband
G   and by the wife in support of, and in opposition to, the application for maintenance and secured provision. The wife, who is now thirty-six years of age, is a
qualified nurse earning about £10 per week. The husband, who is now seventy-
four years of age, is partially disabled and unemployed. He has no earning
capacity and lives on two retirement pensions, a small sum of interest from a
building society and a supplementary pension from the Ministry of Social
H   Security—a total income of about £6 per week. He has a capital asset which is
the foundation for the present proceedings, namely, a freehold bungalow, 18,
Hamilton Road, Hunton Bridge, Kings Langley, which he values at about
£3,250 and the wife values at about £5,000. The husband also has an account
in a building society amounting to about £450, and £20 in premium bonds. On
Dec. 30, 1966, the husband married a young woman aged twenty-seven who was
I   a qualified nurse. She has two children aged 2½ years and nine months for whom
she receives maintenance from the children's father.

In those circumstances the application for maintenance and secured provision
came before the senior registrar, and it was apparent that the wife on her figures
could not establish a claim to any immediate weekly, monthly or annual maintenance. The learned registrar accordingly, recognising her right to maintenance
if the relative financial resources of the parties changed, ordered the payment of
maintenance at the rate of 1s. per annum during their joint lives until further
order. He then made the order appealed against for the purpose of securing some

income to the wife after the death of the husband. It seems reasonably clear that   A
the registrar had in mind that, during the lifetime of the husband, the bungalow
might be sold and the proceeds devoted in one way or another to the benefit of
the second wife and her children, or, alternatively, that, on the death of the
husband, the bungalow or any proceeds of sale, or investments of those proceeds,
might pass under the husband's will or, on intestacy, to the second wife. There is
conflicting evidence about the husband's intentions. He has said that he does not   B
want to sell the bungalow but that economic circumstances may compel him to
do so. The wife alleges that he has recently spent money on improvements.
Before his re-marriage he was certainly indicating that he intended the wife to
have the property after his death and had spoken of putting it into joint names
during their lifetime.

The argument of counsel for the husband can be summarised as follows: that   C
the order of the learned registrar is wrong in principle; that the registrar has not
made an order for securing provision properly so called, but has in effect ordered
provision out of the estate of the husband after his death and has given security
in the meantime; that the registrar has sought to anticipate an order under s. 26
of the Matrimonial Causes Act 1965.

The purpose of the present statutory provisions can be more clearly appreciated   D
after a brief study of the early legislation. Under the Matrimonial Causes Act,
1857, s. 32, the court had power to order only secured provision by way of
maintenance. In the preamble to the Matrimonial Causes Act, 1866, it was
stated:

> ". . . it sometimes happens that a decree for a dissolution of marriage is
> obtained against a husband who has no property on which the payment of   E
> any such gross or annual sum can be secured, but nevertheless he will be able
> to make a monthly or weekly payment to the wife during their joint lives . . ."

Accordingly, by that Act, the alternative of weekly or monthly maintenance
unsecured was introduced, and by the Matrimonial Causes Act, 1907, s. 1, the
court was empowered to make both orders concurrently. This position continued   F
under the Supreme Court of Judicature (Consolidation) Act, 1925, s. 190, and
s. 19 of the Matrimonial Causes Act, 1950. The relevant part of s. 19 (2) read as
follows:

> " On any decree for divorce or nullity of marriage the court may, if it
> thinks fit, order that the husband shall, to the satisfaction of the court,
> secure to the wife such gross sum of money or annual sum of money for any   G
> term not exceeding her life, as, having regard to her fortune, if any, to the
> ability of her husband and to the conduct of the parties, the court may
> deem to be reasonable . . ."

There followed provision for reference to one of the conveyancing counsel of the
court to settle a deed or instrument, if necessary. Section 19 (3) dealt with
monthly or weekly unsecured maintenance. At that time there was no power to   H
order payment of a lump sum outright to the wife. Furthermore, unless provision
had been made for the divorced wife in the lifetime of the husband, she had no
means of securing maintenance for herself after his death.

The lot of the divorced wife was materially improved by recent legislation.
New provisions were included in the Law Reform (Miscellaneous Provisions)
Act, 1949, the Matrimonial Causes (Property and Maintenance) Act, 1958 and   I
the Matrimonial Causes Act 1963. These are now to be found in the Matrimonial
Causes Act 1965. Section 16 (1) of the Act of 1965 provides:

> " On granting a decree of divorce or at any time thereafter . . . the court
> may, if it thinks fit . . . make one or more of the following orders—(a) an
> order requiring the husband to secure to the wife, to the satisfaction of the
> court, such lump or annual sum for any term not exceeding her life as the
> court thinks reasonable having regard to her fortune (if any), his ability and

A   the conduct of the parties; (*b*) an order requiring the husband to pay to the wife during their joint lives such monthly or weekly sum for her maintenance as the court thinks reasonable; (*c*) an order requiring the husband to pay to the wife such lump sum as the court thinks reasonable."

B   Section 26 of the Act of 1965, replacing s. 3 of the Matrimonial Causes (Property and Maintenance) Act, 1958, enables a former spouse who has not re-married to obtain reasonable provision out of the net estate of a deceased husband or wife, if on an application the court is satisfied that it would have been reasonable for the deceased to make provision for the survivor's maintenance and that the deceased has made no provision, or has not made reasonable provision, for the survivor's maintenance. Section 31 and s. 27 enable any orders made for provision of the former spouse under s. 16 or s. 26 to be varied or discharged. Section 32

C   enables a person to restrain a former spouse from disposing of property in order to defeat a claim for financial relief or to avoid a transaction already completed with that intention. The wife in this case cannot claim any provision under s. 26 until after the death of the husband, and she could not, in my opinion, obtain an order under s. 32 restraining the husband from selling the property because she has no, or no reliable, evidence that the husband intends to dispose of the

D   property. Still less has she any evidence of any intention on his part to defeat any claim to financial relief on her part. She has no more than the suspicion, however well-founded, that the effect of the husband's re-marriage may be to prejudice any future claim by her.

The learned registrar in the circumstances has acted under s. 16 (1), and has assessed the claim of the wife against the husband at (a) the nominal annual sum

E   of 1s. payable forthwith and for their joint lives and (b) the income on the gross sum of £1,000 during her life as from his death at an uncertain date in the future. The registrar's object as stated in the order was to provide an income for the wife from the date of death of the husband. In my opinion, the registrar has tried to attain the very laudable object of protecting the wife against the risk that the husband may sell the house and deprive her of any security for the future.

F   My reason for differing from the registrar is that he has attempted to make a present assessment of the future fortunes of the wife and the ability of the husband to pay without any reliable evidence for the purpose. It is not possible to say now what would be reasonable secured provision for the wife on the death of the husband, or what claim she might be able to establish under s. 26 if she pursued that remedy after his death. Guidance for the solution of the problem

G   of assessing maintenance and secured provision is to be found in the judgment of Sir Boyd Merriman, P., in *Chichester* v. *Chichester* (1). The passage which I wish to read is as follows:

"If there is any principle in this matter, it is this, that, whatever the old Ecclesiastical proceedings with regard to alimony and maintenance may have been—and I must not be thought to be excluding alimony to main-

H   tenance at any rate so far as our present jurisdiction is concerned—it is based upon the statute of 1925, reproducing, of course, the earlier Matrimonial Causes Acts. I think the only principle to be observed is that one should follow the statute. The statute is this: ' On any decree for divorce or nullity '—I am not reading all the words—' the court may secure to the wife such gross sum of money or annual sum of money for any term, not

I   exceeding her life, as having regard to her fortune, if any, to the ability of her husband '—that means his ability to pay, of course—' and to the conduct of the parties, the court may deem to be reasonable '. That is the first thing we are directed to do, or directed that we may do. The other is this: that in divorce or nullity ' the court may, if it thinks fit, by order, either in addition to or instead of an order under sub-s. (1) '—that is an order for security—' direct the husband to pay to the wife during the joint lives of the

husband and the wife such monthly or weekly sum for her maintenance and   A
support as the court may think reasonable '.   It is perfectly obvious, therefore, so it seems to me, that there is no such thing as deciding first what the
proportion is and then how much of that shall be secured.   What one
has to decide on the whole matter, having regard to the considerations which
the statute directs one to take into account, is whether there shall be any
security at all, and, if so, whether it shall be a gross sum of money or any   B
annual sum of money, and for what term, or whether there shall be nothing
at all secured, and then, whether one orders security or not, order in substitution for security or in addition to security what reasonable sum shall be
paid.   One has to take all the circumstances of the case into account and
arrive at a proper solution having regard to the factors which are mentioned
in the statute.''   C

It seems to me to follow that the court at the time of assessment must have
evidence as to the earnings, means, assets and circumstances of the parties.
The learned registrar in the present case has assessed the current maintenance at a
nominal figure having regard to the present circumstances; has looked into the
future, wherein the relative positions of the parties can only be the subject of
conjecture, and has sought to make an assessment accordingly.   There may be   D
vital or material changes in the circumstances of the wife or of the husband
between the present time and his death.   The fact that the order for secured
provision can now be varied under s. 31 of the Act of 1965 is of real importance
to the parties, but it does not, in my view, justify an assessment which is not
supported by available evidence.
    Fortunately, the object which the learned registrar had in mind can be attained.   E
Just as in appropriate circumstances a nominal order can be made for annual
maintenance, so a token order for secured provision can be made and this can be
varied under s. 31 if or when there is evidence on which an assessment can be
made.   In LATEY ON DIVORCE (14th Edn.), p. 253, the following passage appears:

    " The powers of the court were clearly defined in *Shearn* v. *Shearn* (2),   F
    wherein it was decided, inter alia, (1) An order for security cannot be left
    open for future consideration.   It must be made or withheld at the same
    time as the award or refusal of an order for periodic payments . . .''

Then there is a footnote:

    " (*o*) But there seems to be nothing in the statute to prevent a token
    order being made for security as in the case of the joint lives order, and   G
    since the change in the law effected by the Law Reform (Miscellaneous Pro-
    visions) Act, 1949, whereby a security order is variable, the court has made
    token orders of security.''

I shall, accordingly, vary the registrar's order by ordering the provision of a
nominal sum to be secured and charged on the property.   The charge must be   H
registered at the land registry so that notice will be given to the wife in the event
of any disposition of the property.   If the husband disposes of the bungalow
during his lifetime it will be known what capital is available and what proposal
he has for its investment.   The then present circumstances of the wife, the
husband and his family will be ascertainable.   The wife will be able to apply for
a variation of the present order, if that course is advisable on the evidence, and   I
it may be that the most satisfactory order at that time will be the payment of a
reasonable lump sum under s. 16 (1) (*c*) of the Act of 1965 in final discharge of
the husband's liability.   One of the matters which I have in mind in view of the
small sum involved is the advantage of avoiding a deed or instrument and the
necessity of referring the matter to conveyancing counsel.   If the property is not
sold during the husband's lifetime and if the husband does not make reasonable
provision for her, the wife may be advised to make a claim against the estate

_____

    (2) [1930] All E.R. Rep. 310; [1931] P. 1.

A   under s. 26; that will depend on all the circumstances subsisting at that time. If the net estate does not exceed £5,000, the court may order that provision be made by way of a lump sum payment under s. 26 (3). It is provided in s. 26 (4) that, on any application under that section, the court should have regard, inter alia, to any order made under s. 16 (1), so that the order which I am now making will be before the court on any subsequent application either to

B   vary or for maintenance out of the estate.

A suitable nominal lump sum would, I think, be £10. The appeal will, accordingly, be allowed and the registrar's order varied. The order will read:

"It is ordered that the [husband] do pay, or cause to be paid to the [wife] as from July 5, 1966, maintenance for herself during their joint lives until further order at and after the rate of 1s. per annum less tax payment

C   monthly, and it is further ordered that the [husband] do secure to the [wife] for her life until further order the gross sum of £10 to be charged upon the freehold property 18, Hamilton Road, Hunton Bridge, Kings Langley, in the county of Hertford."

Appeal allowed.

D   Solicitors: *Sharpe, Pritchard & Co.* (for the husband); *Denis Hayes* (for the wife).

[*Reported by* ALICE BLOOMFIELD, *Barrister-at-Law.*]

E

BOYS *v.* CHAPLIN.

[QUEEN'S BENCH DIVISION (Milmo, J.), March 1, 2, 3, 22, 1967.]

Conflict of Laws—Tort—Damages—Remoteness of damage—Accident in Malta between servicemen normally resident in England but stationed in Malta—Action in England—Whether damages to be assessed in accordance with

F   *English or Maltese law.*

The plaintiff was injured in a motor accident in Malta caused by the negligence of the defendant. Both the plaintiff and the defendant were normally resident in England, but at the time of the accident they were serving with the British forces stationed in Malta. The damages recoverable by Maltese law could not have included compensation for pain or suffering,

G   and would in the circumstances of the present case have been £53, the amount of the agreed special damage, but, if estimated in accordance with English law, would be £2,250 and the £53 special damage.

Held: the tort being admitted and actionable in England, remoteness of damage did not fall to be determined according to the lex locus delicti, and damages should be assessed in accordance with English law (see p. 668,

H   letter A, and p. 670, letter F, post).

Machado v. *Fontes* ([1897] 2 Q.B. 231) followed.

[As to the measure of damages for torts committed abroad, see 7 HALSBURY'S LAWS (3rd Edn.) 86, para. 157; and for cases on the subject, see 11 DIGEST (Repl.) 449, 450, *878-884.*]

I   Cases referred to:

Canadian Pacific Ry. Co. v. *Parent*, (1914), Q.R. 24 K.B. 193; *on appeal,* [1917] A.C. 195; 11 Digest (Repl.) 427, *369.*

Kendrick v. *Burnett*, (1897), 25 R. (Ct. of Sess.) 82; 11 Digest (Repl.) 454, *478.*

M'Elroy v. *M'Allister*, 1949 S.C. 110; 11 Digest (Repl.) 452, *475.*

Machado v. *Fontes*, [1897] 2 Q.B. 231; 66 L.J.Q.B. 542; 76 L.T. 588; 11 Digest (Repl.) 450, *882.*

Moxham (M.), The, (1876), 1 P.D. 107; 46 L.J.P. 17; 34 L.T. 559; 3 Asp. M.L.C. 191; 11 Digest (Repl.) 370, *372.*

Affirmed. C.A. [1968] 1 All E.R. 283.

Affirmed. C.A. [1968] 1 All E.R. 283.

Naftalin v. *London, Midland & Scottish Ry. Co.*, 1933 S.C. 259; 8 Digest **A**
      (Repl.) 118, *531*.
Phillips v. *Eyre*, (1870), L.R. 6 Q.B. 1; 10 B. & S. 1004; 40 L.J.Q.B. 28; 22
      L.T. 869; *affg.* (1869), L.R. 4 Q.B. 225; 11 Digest (Repl.) 451, *888*.

Action.

In this action the plaintiff, David Malcolm Boys, claimed damages for personal
injuries which he sustained in Malta on Oct. 6, 1963, when a motor scooter on   **B**
which he was a pillion rider was in collision with a motor car driven by the
defendant, R. E. Chaplin. The facts are set out in the judgment.

J. M. Cope for the plaintiff.
Tudor Evans, Q.C., and *D. J. Hyamson* for the defendant.

Mar. 22.   **MILMO, J.,** stated the nature of the action and continued: **C**
Although a defence was delivered denying negligence on the part of the defendant
and alleging that the accident was caused by the negligence of the driver of the
scooter, by letter dated Jan. 27, 1967, these pleas were abandoned and, for the
purposes of the action, it was admitted that the collision in question was solely
caused by one or more of the acts or omissions set out in the particulars of
negligence alleged against the defendant in the statement of claim. The sole   **D**
issue was, therefore, that as to damages, and this was itself simplified by an
agreement of the special damage at £53 and a further agreement of the medical
evidence. Apart from the actual figures, the fundamental difference between the
parties is whether the damages fall to be assessed under the law of Malta or that
of England.

Both the plaintiff and the defendant are normally resident in this country. At   **E**
the time of the accident they were both serving in the armed forces of the Crown,
the plaintiff in the Royal Air Force and the defendant in the Royal Navy. They
were both stationed in Malta and it could not be said that they had gone there of
their own accord and volition, unless it is to be said that anyone who joins the
forces and submits to the discipline of the forces must thereby be deemed to give
his irrevocable consent to go voluntarily to any part of the world to which he   **F**
may be ordered. I mention this aspect of the matter because of the possible
distinction to be drawn between a cause of action arising out of a breach of
contract in a foreign country and one arising out of a tort in a foreign country,
for whereas in the former case it can be said that in the absence of agreement to
the contrary the parties must be assumed to have agreed that their rights and
obligations under the contract shall be governed by the local law, no such   **G**
agreement or consent could be implied in the circumstances of the present case.

Evidence was given on each side as to the measure of damages in tort under
Maltese law. I am very doubtful whether the distinguished witness who was
called on behalf of the plaintiff and whose evidence was given before an examiner
was, strictly speaking, qualified to testify as to Maltese law. On the other hand,
a retired judge of the Court of Appeal of Malta was called on behalf of the   **H**
defendant, and I prefer his evidence as to the relevant provisions and principles
of Maltese law.

The damages for personal injuries recoverable by a plaintiff under Maltese law
are very strictly limited and, broadly speaking, are confined to what our courts
would treat as special damages; nothing is recoverable for pain or suffering or for
loss of amenity, whether past or future, or for any problematical, as distinct from   **I**
certain, future financial loss. The relevant provisions relating to damages in tort
in Malta are to be found in para. 1088 of the Civil Code, as amended, which reads
as follows:

" (1) The damage which is to be made good by the person responsible in
accordance with the foregoing provisions shall consist in the actual loss which
the act shall have directly caused to the injured party, in the expenses which
the latter may have been compelled to incur in consequence of the damage, in

A the loss of actual wages or other earnings, and in the loss of future earnings arising from any permanent incapacity, total or partial, which the act may have caused. (2) The sum to be awarded in respect of such incapacity shall be assessed by the court, having regard to the circumstances of the case, and, particularly, to the nature and degree of incapacity caused, and to the condition of the injured party."

B I am satisfied that all that a plaintiff is entitled to recover under the law of Malta is (i) actual financial loss directly suffered, (ii) expenses which he has been compelled to incur, (iii) the amount of wages which he has actually lost and (iv) a sum in respect of future loss of wages which he can actually prove will occur. He cannot recover anything in respect of pain and suffering in itself and as distinct from its economic effect on him. In a case in Malta where there is evidence C of a possible future incapacity arising from the injury, the court will make provision in its order to enable the plaintiff, in the event of such incapacity materialising, to come back and recover in respect of it, but, as long as it is potential only, the plaintiff can recover nothing for it.

If the plaintiff's present claim is to be adjudicated on by application of the law of Malta, I am satisfied that he is not entitled to recover more than £53, the D sum agreed for the special damage. Counsel for the plaintiff was unable to point to any head of damage recoverable under Maltese law, as I have found such law to be, which is not covered by this figure of £53. The figure is low because the plaintiff continued to receive his full pay until he was discharged from the R.A.F. in consequence of his injuries and some five years short of his normal discharge date, but he at once obtained other, and much more remunerative, employment E in civil life. There was no evidence that as a result of the accident he will be certain to sustain any further financial loss, and the possibility that he may do so is not something which would be taken into consideration in quantifying his damages under the law of Malta. On the other hand, it was common ground that the injuries which the plaintiff sustained were serious, and were such as would entitle him to substantial damages at English law.

F At the date of the accident the plaintiff was twenty-two years of age and had served six years of a twelve years engagement in the R.A.F. He ranked as a junior technician, and, but for the accident and his consequent discharge, would have sat for his corporal technician's certificate, which is a qualification in electronics recognised in civil engineering circles.

In the accident the plaintiff sustained a fractured skull and was unconscious G for three days thereafter. He has been rendered wholly and permanently deaf in his right ear. Due to damage to the labyrinth on the right side, his sense of balance has been substantially impaired; he loses his balance on turning sharply or closing his eyes or on going into a dark room. The right side of his face is partially paralysed and he suffers from watering of the right eye when he eats. The headaches from which he suffered have improved, but he still has them about H twice a week. Further improvement in his condition is unlikely. As to the duration of his treatment, he was detained in hospital in Malta until Dec. 19, 1963, when he was returned to England, where he remained an in-patient in the R.A.F. Hospital at Wroughton until Apr. 7, 1964. He received further out-patient treatment and was eventually discharged from the Royal Air Force on June 5, 1964.

The plaintiff, on being discharged from the Royal Air Force, almost immediately I found employment as an electronic engineer, and it is improbable that his disabilities will have any effect in future on his actual earning capacity, though there is a possibility that they may do so. Nevertheless, on any view, the total loss of hearing in one ear and an impaired sense of balance are serious incapacities for a young man with all his adult life in front of him. They may well result in his sustaining further injuries in the future which he would not have sustained had he been in full possession of all his protective senses. Moreover, it is not a trivial matter that one should have to endure headaches on an average twice a week for the rest of one's existence. Taking everything into consideration,

including the drop in the value of sterling, I assess the general damages which A
the plaintiff would be entitled to recover if English law is applied at £2,250.

It is the contention of the plaintiff that he is entitled to recover from the
defendant in this action precisely the same damages as he would have recovered
had the accident occurred in England. He relies on the decision of the Court of
Appeal in *Machado* v. *Fontes* (1), which has stood for some seventy years and has
been constantly applied and acted on during that period, with the result that B
plaintiffs in the courts of this country have been enabled to recover damages for
torts committed elsewhere which they would not have been able to recover in the
courts of the countries where they were committed.

It is, in these circumstances, necessary to look closely into the decision in
Machado's case (1). The action was brought in England to recover damages for
an alleged libel on the plaintiff said to have been published in Brazil. The C
defendant sought leave to amend his defence by adding the following plea (1):

" Further the defendant will contend that if (contrary to the defendant's
contention) the said pamphlet has been published in Brazil, by the Brazilian
law the publication of the said pamphlet in Brazil cannot be the ground of
legal proceedings against the defendant in Brazil in which damages can be
recovered, or (alternatively) cannot be the ground of legal proceedings against D
the defendant in Brazil in which the plaintiff can recover general damages
for any injury to his credit, character, or feelings."

It is to be observed that two alternative allegations were contained in this plea—
(i) that no damages could be recovered in Brazil, and (ii) that no general damages
could be recovered in Brazil.

The matter came before the Court of Appeal on an interlocutory appeal from E
the order of the judge in chambers giving leave to make the amendment. The
argument was that this plea was bad and afforded no answer to the claim because
it did not state that the act complained of could not be the subject of criminal
proceedings in Brazil—indeed, it appears to have been conceded that libel was a
criminal offence in Brazil. The court upheld this contention, holding that the
plea was absolutely bad and should be struck out. In the course of his judgment, F
Lopes, L.J., said (2):

" It then follows, directly the right of action is established in this country,
that the ordinary incidents of that action and the appropriate remedies ensue.
Therefore, in this case, in my opinion, damages would flow from the wrong
committed just as they would in any action brought in respect of a libel G
published in this country."

Rigby, L.J., said (3):

" It is not really a matter of any importance what the nature of the
remedy for a wrong in a foreign country may be . . . We start, then, from
this: that the act in question is prima facie actionable here, and the only
thing we have to do is to see whether there is any peremptory bar to our H
jurisdiction arising from the fact that the act we are dealing with is
authorised, or innocent, or excusable, in the country where it was committed.
If we cannot see that, we must act according to our own rules in the damages
(if any) which we may choose to give."

In a closely reasoned argument, for which I am much indebted, counsel for the I
defendant submitted that in an action brought in our courts in respect of a tort
committed outside the jurisdiction, all questions as to the remoteness of damage,
as distinct from the actual assessment or measure of damage, fell to be determined
under the lex loci delicti, and that the application of this principle precluded the
plaintiff in the present action from recovering any sum beyond the special
damages agreed at £53.

(1) [1897] 2 Q.B. 231.   (2) [1897] 2 Q.B. at p. 234.
                (3) [1897] 2 Q.B. at pp. 235, 236.

A   He based his argument on three contentions. First, he said that the decision in
Machado's case (4) was in direct conflict with at least two other decisions of equal
authority, and invited me not to follow that decision. Secondly, he argued that
the ratio decidendi in *Machado's* case (4) fell far short of the proposition contended
for by the plaintiff, and that the passages in the judgment relied on by the
plaintiff were obiter dicta which were not good law and should not be followed.
B   Thirdly, he invited me to say that *Machado's* case (4) was a peculiar and special
one because, since there was no civil remedy for libel in Brazil, there could be no
question of applying the local law as to the damages recoverable and therefore,
once the English court recognised a right of action, there was no law to apply in
relation to the damages other than the lex fori.

Dealing with the first of the above contentions, it was said that the judgments
C   in *Machado* v. *Fontes* (4) were in conflict with those of the Court of Exchequer
Chamber in *Phillips* v. *Eyre* (5), despite the fact that they purport to follow and
indeed to be founded on that decision. It was also said that they conflict with the
Court of Appeal decision in *The M. Moxham* (6). I am unable to see that this is so.

Phillips v. *Eyre* (5) was a case in which the plaintiff sought relief in the form
of damages in tort in respect of certain acts of the Governor of Jamaica committed
D   in Jamaica in the course of dealing with disturbances in that colony. A number of
points of law fell to be determined, and it was held, inter alia, that, in order to give
rise to an action in tort in this country founded on an act committed outside the
jurisdiction, it was not necessary that such act should give rise to a civil remedy
sounding in damages in the place where committed, provided that the act was
not an innocent act in that place. In the argument addressed to me it was not
E   suggested that this principle was wrong, but it was argued that the decision in
Machado's case (4) conflicted with *Phillips* v. *Eyre* (5) in another respect.

In *Phillips* v. *Eyre* (5) it was held that in deciding whether or not the act of the
defendant complained of was lawful in the place where committed, regard must
be paid and effect given to an Act of Indemnity promulgated in Jamaica purporting to release and discharge the defendant from all liability to the plaintiff in
F   respect of the acts complained of in the action. It was said that in consequence
Phillips v. *Eyre* (5) is authority for the proposition that in cases such as the
present one, in determining whether any, and, if so, what, damages are recoverable
in an English court, the lex loci delicti must be applied. I cannot agree that this
is a correct interpretation of *Phillips* v. *Eyre* (5), and plainly the lords justices in
Machado's case (4) took the same view. I think that all that *Phillips* v. *Eyre* (5)
G   decided in this connexion was that in determining whether a particular act was
or was not justifiable in the place where committed, regard must be had and
effect given to local legislation legalising and making justifiable, albeit retroactively, such act in such place. Nor am I able to see that the decision in *The M.
Moxham* (6) conflicts in any way with *Machado* v. *Fontes* (4). The issue was
whether the defendants, who were the owners of the ship M. Moxham and were
H   sued in England in respect of damage done by the ship in Portuguese waters
owing to the negligence of her master and crew, were liable in tort to the plaintiffs.
At English law the defendants would, of course, have been vicariously liable for
the torts of their servants, but at Portuguese law there was no such liability. The
court held that since the defendants had not committed any act in the locus
delicti for which they were liable either criminally or civilly, they had a good
I   defence to the action brought against them in England.

The second point argued on behalf of the defendant was that the ratio decidendi
in *Machado's* case (4) was a very narrow, and indeed a very technical, one; and
that, if and in so far as the court dealt with the damages (if any) which the
plaintiff might be entitled to recover at the trial, the observations were obiter
dicta and should not be followed by me. In my judgment, this contention is

_____

(4) [1897] 2 Q.B. 231.   (5) (1870), L.R. 6 Q.B. 1.
                        (6) (1876), 1 P.D. 107.

untenable, and I am confident that if it had been advanced to the lords justices **A** who decided *Machado's* case (7), they would have been more than a little surprised. The court decided that the proposed plea was wholly irrelevant and could afford no answer to the plaintiff's claim. If the point which it was sought to raise had been relevant on the issue as to damages, the amendment would have had to have been allowed, for, in the absence of such amendment, it would not have been open to the defence to take the point at the trial. Without the amend- **B** ment, the defence could not have been allowed to support the contention raised in the alternative that the damages recoverable in Brazil excluded general damages, or, indeed, to call any evidence as to Brazilian law which might have a bearing on the damages.

I think that the third point taken on behalf of the defendant in relation to *Machado* v. *Fontes* (7) is manifestly fallacious. The argument, as I understand it, **C** is that it was only because there was no lex loci delicti applicable in relation to damages that the lex fori was to be applied. In the first place, as I have already pointed out, there was an allegation, albeit in the alternative, that if any damages were recoverable, they were restricted to special damages. Secondly, the logical consequence of no damages being recoverable beyond those recoverable under the lex loci delicti—and this is the defendant's basic contention—is that no **D** damages at all are recoverable if under the lex loci no damages are recoverable, and not that the damages then become at large.

The decision in *Machado* v. *Fontes* (7) has not been followed in a number of Scottish cases; see *Kendrick* v. *Burnett* (8), *Naftalin* v. *London, Midland & Scottish Ry. Co.* (9), *M'Elroy* v. *M'Allister* (10). It has not met with the unqualified approval of the authors of some English text books, and in particular has **E** been criticised by PROFESSOR CHESHIRE in his PRIVATE INTERNATIONAL LAW (7th Edn.). Further, in the judgment of the Judicial Committee of the Privy Council in *Canadian Pacific Ry. Co.* v. *Parent* (11), VISCOUNT HALDANE said:

" It is not necessary to consider whether all the language used by the English Court of Appeal in the judgments in *Machado* v. *Fontes* (7) was sufficiently precise."   **F**

Counsel for the defendant was, however, unable to direct my attention to any judgment binding on an English court in which the validity of the decision in *Machado* v. *Fontes* (7) has been queried, and in my judgment that decision is fatal to the contention of the defendant in the present case.

For the foregoing reasons, there must be judgment for the plaintiff for £2,250 general and £53 special damages, making a total sum of £2,303.   **G**

Judgment for the plaintiff for £2,303.

Solicitors: *Roche, Son & Neale*, agents for *Buss, Cheale & Co.*, Tunbridge Wells (for the plaintiff); *Gascoin & Co.* (for the defendant).

[*Reported by* MARY COLTON, *Barrister-at-Law.*]   **H**

I

---

(7) [1897] 2 Q.B. 231.   (8) (1897), 25 R. (Ct. of Sess.) 82.
(9) 1933 S.C. 259.   (10) 1949 S.C. 110.
(11) [1917] A.C. 195 at p. 205.

A

R. *v.* HAZELTINE.

[COURT OF APPEAL, CRIMINAL DIVISION (Salmon, L.J., Fenton Atkinson and Brabin, JJ.), April 21, 1967.]

B *Criminal Law—Trial—Plea—Plea of guilty to a lesser offence—Charge of wounding with intent—Plea of guilty to unlawful wounding not accepted by prosecution—Accused tried on charge of wounding with intent—Jury returned verdict of not guilty—Accused sentenced for unlawful wounding—Only one plea to any one count—Plea was, therefore, not guilty—Conviction quashed —Offences against the Person Act, 1861 (24 & 25 Vict. c. 100), s. 18, s. 20.*

C The appellant, when arraigned on an indictment, pleaded not guilty to count 4, which charged wounding with intent to do grievous bodily harm contrary to s. 18* of the Offences against the Person Act, 1861; but he pleaded guilty to unlawful wounding†. The prosecution refused to accept the plea of guilty to the lesser offence, and the appellant's trial proceeded accordingly, the jury being told that he had pleaded not guilty to count 4. The appellant gave evidence to the effect that what he did was done in self-defence or by accident. In regard to count 4 the jury were asked merely for a verdict of guilty or not guilty. They found the appellant not guilty. He was, however, sentenced for unlawful wounding. On appeal,

D

Held: there could be only one plea to any one count in respect of which an accused was put in charge of a jury, and in the present case that plea was " not guilty "; accordingly, when the jury returned their verdict the appellant was acquitted, and the conviction would be quashed (see p. 673, letter H, and p. 674, letters B and I, post).

E *R. v. Cole* ([1965] 2 All E.R. 29) explained and distinguished.

Per CURIAM: in such a case as this it is open to the prosecution to call evidence before the jury to the effect that the accused has pleaded guilty to unlawful wounding and to make the point that it is inherent in such a plea that he admits that what he did was unlawful and malicious; such an admission is wholly inconsistent with the defence that what he did was done by accident or in self-defence (see p. 674, letter C, post).

F

[**Editorial Note.** The distinction, where an indictment contains separate counts charging wounding with intent and alternatively unlawful wounding, is drawn at p. 673, letter E, post, but it is intimated that it is not desirable always to include both counts (see p. 674, letter E, post).

G As to a plea of guilty to a lesser offence, see 10 HALSBURY'S LAWS (3rd Edn.) 408, para. 742 text and note (*d*); and for cases on the subject, see 14 DIGEST (Repl.) 285, *2609, 2610.*

As to conviction of unlawful wounding on charges of more serious offences, see 10 HALSBURY'S LAWS (3rd Edn.) 735, 736, para. 1411, text and note (*t*).

H For the Offences against the Person Act, 1861, s. 18, s. 20, see 5 HALSBURY'S STATUTES (2nd Edn.) 793, 795.]

Case referred to:
R. v. Cole, [1965] 2 All E.R. 29; [1965] 2 Q.B. 388; [1965] 3 W.L.R. 263; 129 J.P. 326; 49 Cr. App. Rep. 199; 3rd Digest Supp.

I

---

* Section 18, so far as material, provides: " Whosoever shall unlawfully and maliciously by any means whatsoever wound or cause any grievous bodily harm to any person . . . and being convicted thereof shall be liable . . . to be kept in penal servitude for life . . ."

† I.e., contrary to s. 20 of the Offences against the Persons Act, 1861, which provides: " Whosoever shall unlawfully and maliciously wound or inflict any grievous bodily harm upon any other person, either with or without any weapon or instrument, shall be guilty of a misdemeanour and being convicted thereof shall be liable . . . to be kept in penal servitude . . .". Under s. 5 of the Prevention of Offences Act, 1851, a person charged with an offence under s. 18 may be convicted of an offence under s. 20.

Appeal.

The appellant Clifford Hazeltine appealed by leave of the single judge against his conviction at Surrey Assizes on Feb. 14, 1967, of unlawful wounding. BLAIN, J., sentenced him to nine months' imprisonment. Leave to appeal was granted on the ground that the appellant, whose plea of guilty to unlawful wounding was not accepted by the prosecution or the trial judge, was acquitted on count 4 (wounding with intent to do grievous bodily harm) of an indictment on which as a whole he was placed in the jury's charge and then sentenced on the basis of the unaccepted plea. The facts are set out in the judgment of the court.

The authorities and cases noted below‡ were cited during the argument in addition to the case referred to in the judgment of the court.

D. M. Cheatle for the appellant.
P. M. Griffith for the Crown.

SALMON, L.J., delivered the following judgment of the court: This appeal raises a novel point of law, which arises in this way. The appellant was arraigned on an indictment containing a number of counts, the only material one being count 4 under which he was charged with wounding with intent to do grievous bodily harm contrary to s. 18 of the Offences against the Person Act, 1861. When he was called on to plead to that count he said " Not guilty but guilty to unlawful wounding ". The Crown, however, refused to accept that plea and he was put in charge of the jury on count 4, the jury being told that he had pleaded not guilty to that count. At the end of the case, the jury retired and they returned a simple verdict of not guilty to that count. He was then sentenced by the learned judge to nine months' imprisonment for unlawful wounding. It was argued on behalf of the appellant that in these circumstances the judge had no power to sentence him and should have ordered him to be discharged.

I will now state the material facts. It appears that on Friday, Dec. 23, 1966, at about 8.30 p.m. a young man called Frank Bullen and a young woman were together in Bridge Street, Leatherhead. The appellant walked towards them with another man who was tried with him. This other man, according to the evidence of Frank Bullen which was corroborated by the young woman, grabbed Bullen by the lapels of his coat and said, " Give me some money. I want another pint ". Bullen said he had not got any money, whereupon the other man punched him on the nose and then rained blows on him drawing blood. According to Bullen he was attacked at the same time from behind and the blows that were struck to the back of his head also broke the skin and drew blood. The evidence of Bullen was corroborated, as I have said, by his companion and also to a very large extent by a passer-by. When the appellant went into the witness box he told a story which was wholly inconsistent with the admission inherent in his plea of guilty to unlawful wounding. He said in effect that his companion and Bullen were fighting, he stepped in to separate the two of them and Bullen kicked him in the groin and he struck out at Bullen; what he did was done either in self defence or else by accident. If that story were true or if it might have been accepted as being possibly true, then clearly he was not guilty of wounding with intent, nor guilty of unlawful wounding.

The evidence against the appellant was quite overwhelming. Nevertheless the point of law remains to be decided. It is clear that there can be only one plea to any one count in respect of which a man is put in charge of the jury. If an accused man says that he admits certain ingredients of the offence charged in the count but not others, that is a plea of not guilty. It is possible, however, when an accused is tried for wounding with intent, for the jury to find him not guilty of wounding with intent but guilty of unlawful wounding, and it is also possible,

‡ 14 HALSBURY'S STATUTES (2nd Edn.) 924; ARCHBOLD'S CRIMINAL PLEADING, EVIDENCE AND PRACTICE (36th Edn.), paras. 404, 426, 574, 2652, 2664. *R.* v. *Forde*, [1923] All E.R. Rep. 477; [1923] 2 K.B. 400; *R.* v. *Soanes*, [1948] 1 All E.R. 289; *R.* v. *Kelly*, [1965] 3 All E.R. 162; [1965] 2 Q.B. 409.

A having regard to s. 39 (1) of the Criminal Justices Administration Act, 1914, for a man accused of wounding with intent, to plead not guilty to that offence but guilty to unlawful wounding. The section reads as follows:

> " Where a prisoner is arraigned on an indictment for any offence, and can lawfully be convicted on such indictment of some other offence not charged in such indictment, he may plead not guilty of the offence charged in the
B > indictment, but guilty of such other offence."

Prior to that statutory provision, it was not possible for an accused to plead guilty to unlawful wounding when charged with wounding with intent, but it was and always has been possible for a jury, when a man is charged with wounding with intent, to return a verdict of unlawful wounding. So before the Act of 1914
C the position was that an accused man might be saying " Of course I am guilty of unlawful wounding but I had no intention of doing grievous bodily harm ", the prosecution might be satisfied that a plea of that kind ought to be accepted and the judge might be so satisfied, yet a great deal of unnecessary time and money had to be wasted by holding a full dress trial in order to obtain a verdict from the jury which the prosecution, the defence and the judge were satisfied
D was the only proper verdict in the circumstances.

This court has no doubt but that s. 39 (1) of the Act of 1914 was introduced so as to remove this anomaly which resulted in the great waste of time and money to which I have referred. In the view of this court, however, that statutory provision did not get rid of the rule that there can be but one plea to one count should the trial proceed on that count. Accordingly, if an accused pleads not
E guilty to wounding with intent but guilty to unlawful wounding and counsel for the prosecution or the judge takes the view that that plea ought not to be accepted and the trial proceeds, the plea of guilty to unlawful wounding is deemed to be withdrawn and the only plea is the plea of not guilty to wounding with intent. It is then for the jury to consider the evidence and at the end of the case to say quite simply either that the accused is not guilty or is guilty of wound-
F ing with intent or that he is not guilty of wounding with intent but is guilty of unlawful wounding.

A case such as this is quite different from a case such as *R.* v. *Cole* (1) where there were two counts in the indictment, one charging a serious offence, one a lesser offence. That case lays down the correct procedure to be followed where an accused pleads guilty to the count charging the lesser offence and not guilty to the count charging the more serious offence. If the plea to the less serious
G offence is not accepted, the accused will then be put in the charge of the jury only on the more serious count. If he is acquitted on that count, he will then be sentenced on the count to which he has pleaded guilty. If, on the other hand, he is convicted on the more serious count, the proper course is for the judge to allow the count to which he has pleaded guilty to remain on the file and not to proceed to sentence him on that count. In the present case, however, there
H was but one count which is indivisible and the only effective plea to that count in respect of which the appellant was put in charge of the jury was the plea of not guilty. At one stage of the summing-up the learned judge explained the position with complete accuracy to the jury. He told them that they could find the appellant not guilty of anything or if they were satisfied, beyond a reasonable doubt, that he was guilty of wounding with intent, they could find
I him guilty of that offence, or if they were satisfied beyond a reasonable doubt that he was guilty of unlawful wounding but not satisfied about the intent, then they could find him guilty of unlawful wounding. Towards the end of the summing-up, however, he appears to have told the jury that since the appellant pleaded guilty to unlawful wounding in the first instance, it was unnecessary for them to consider that matter. When the jury were asked for their verdict on count 4 they were asked merely whether they found him guilty or not guilty

(1) [1965] 2 All E.R. 29; [1965] 2 Q.B. 388.

on that count and they said not guilty. They were not asked whether they A found him guilty of unlawful wounding and they certainly did not do so. Unfortunately in this particular case the plea which he had offered of guilty to unlawful wounding, as a plea, was a nullity. Therefore the jury having found him not guilty, he should have been allowed to go. It is an unfortunate result because the appellant has clearly no shred of merit.

The conclusion, however, is inescapable, that there cannot be more than one B effective plea to any count in respect of which an accused is put in charge of the jury. The only effective plea here was a plea of not guilty. The court desires to make this plain should a case of this kind arise in the future: it is open to the prosecution to call evidence before the jury to the effect that the accused has pleaded guilty to unlawful wounding and to make the point that it is inherent in such a plea that he admits that what he did was unlawful and malicious. C Such an admission is wholly inconsistent with a defence that what he did was done by accident or in self-defence. If the accused gives evidence and sets up a defence which is wholly inconsistent with the admission which he has already made, then he should be cross-examined by the prosecution on that admission. He should be asked, for example, " If the story you are now telling the jury is true, namely that you were acting purely in self-defence, why did you an hour D ago admit in this very court that you were guilty of unlawful wounding? ", a question which most accused might find very difficult to answer. Although in this case the technicalities of the law lead to a very unmeritorious person escaping from what on any view was a lenient sentence, in practice this is highly unlikely to arise in the future if the prosecution adopt the course which has just been indicated. Nor in the opinion of this court does this decision make it E desirable in the future always to add a count under s. 20 of the Offences against the Person Act, 1861, when the indictment contains a count under s. 18. It is difficult to see how any advantage could be gained from so doing. Suppose the accused were to plead guilty to the s. 20 count and not guilty to the s. 18 count. If on his trial, he were to raise a defence of accident or self-defence to the s. 18 count, the only answer he could make to the question which we have F indicated should be put to him in cross-examination would be that he did not understand the nature of his pleas of guilty to the count under s. 20. Were there any real possibility that this might be true, he would be allowed, even at that stage, to withdraw his plea and the trial would proceed on both counts— so the position would, in reality, be just the same as if there had been only the count under s. 18. G

In the present case, the members of the jury were in court but unsworn when the admission was made which is inherent in a plea of guilty to unlawful wounding; no evidence was called before them of the admission and when the appellant who made it had the effrontery to put up this defence, he was never asked a word in cross-examination about why he had pleaded guilty to unlawful wounding, and thereby in reality admitted that the blows had not been struck in H self-defence or by accident. Moreover it is plain from the form of the question put by the jury after they had retired that if they had been asked, they would unhesitatingly have found the appellant guilty of unlawful wounding. However that may be, this court is clearly of the opinion that unfortunately no course is open here other than to uphold the contention made on behalf of the appellant and the appeal is allowed accordingly. I

Appeal allowed. Conviction quashed.

Solicitors: *Registrar of Criminal Appeals* (for the appellant); *Wontner & Sons* (for the Crown).

[*Reported by* N. P. METCALFE, ESQ., *Barrister-at-Law.*]

A   PHILLIPS *v.* BERKSHIRE COUNTY COUNCIL.

[QUEEN'S BENCH DIVISION (Lord Parker, C.J., Widgery and O'Connor, JJ.),
   April 17, 18, 19, 1967.]

*Highways—Street—Private street works—Appeal to quarter sessions—" Person
   aggrieved "—Resolution of county council, being both highway authority
   and street works authority, for making up street—Quashed by order of magis-*
B *trates' court—Appeal by council to quarter sessions—Whether council a
   " person aggrieved " within Highways Act, 1959 (7 & 8 Eliz. 2 c. 25),
   s. 275 (1).*

A county council were both highway authority and street works authority*
for the purposes of the Highways Act, 1959, in relation to a street within
C a rural district. A magistrates' court having quashed a resolution for
making up part of the street, the council appealed to quarter sessions, who
allowed their appeal. The consequence of quashing the resolution would
have been that the cost of making up the street would have fallen on the
council as highway authority and not on the frontagers. On a preliminary
question whether the council were " a person aggrieved " by the order of
D the magistrates' court and thus were entitled to appeal to quarter sessions
under s. 275 (1)† of the Act of 1959,

   Held: the council were a " person aggrieved " within s. 275 (1) of the
Highways Act, 1959, with the consequence that appeal lay from the magistrates' court to quarter sessions because—
   (i) if the order of the magistrates' court stood, the council would be left
E with a legal burden, viz., that of discharging the cost of making up the
street, which a contrary order of the justices would have removed (see p. 679,
letters B and C, post).

   R. v. *Nottingham Quarter Sessions, Ex p. Harlow* ([1952] 2 All E.R. 78)
applied.

   R. v. *London Sessions Appeal Committee, Ex p. Westminster City Council*
F ([1951] 1 All E.R. 1032) distinguished.
   (ii) the council should not be regarded for present purposes as two separate
entities, the street works authority and the highway authority, but as a single
entity, and accordingly the fact that as street works authority no burden
fell on the council did not preclude them from being a " person aggrieved "
(see p. 679, letters D and F, post).

G *R.* v. *Boldero, Ex p. Bognor Regis Urban District Council* ((1962), 60 L.G.R.
292) applied.
   Appeal dismissed.

   [As to meaning of " person aggrieved " in enactments, see 25 HALSBURY'S
LAWS (3rd Edn.) 293, 294, para. 569, text and note (*h*); and for cases on the
subject, see 4 DIGEST (Repl.) 201, *1803-1806*; 26 DIGEST (Repl.) 483, *1695*; 32
H DIGEST (Repl.) 611, *1926*; 36 DIGEST (Repl.) 367, *46*; 38 DIGEST (Repl.) 190,
191, *178-181*; 45 DIGEST (Repl.) 24, *68*, 340, *55*, 354, *105, 106*; DIGEST (Cont.
Vol. A) 155, *917b*.
   For the Highways Act, 1959, s. 1 (3), s. 213 (2), s. 275, see 39 HALSBURY'S
STATUTES (2nd Edn.) 412, 638, 688.]

Cases referred to:
I *R.* v. *Boldero, Ex p. Bognor Regis Urban District Council*, (1962), 60 L.G.R. 292;
      Digest (Cont. Vol. A) 639, *2061a*.
   R. v. *London Sessions Appeal Committee, Ex p. Westminster City Council*,
      [1951] 1 All E.R. 1032; 115 J.P. 350; sub nom. *R.* v. *London Quarter
      Sessions, Ex p. Westminster Corpn.*, [1951] 2 K.B. 508; 26 Digest
      (Repl.) 483, *1695*.

───
* See s. 213 (2) definition of " street works authority " and s. 1 (3) of the Highways
Act, 1959; see p. 677, letter I, post.
† Section 275 (1) is set out at p. 677, letter F, post.

R. v. *Nottingham Quarter Sessions, Ex p. Harlow,* [1952] 2 All E.R. 78; [1952] A
2 Q.B. 601; 116 J.P. 397; 38 Digest (Repl.) 212, *334.*

Case Stated.

This was a Case Stated by Berkshire Quarter Sessions sitting at Reading on
Feb. 7, Mar. 28, 29 and 31, and May 3, 1966, when they heard an appeal by
the respondents, Berkshire County Council (" the council ") against a deter- B
mination by the Forest Magistrates' Court sitting at Bracknell of objections
by the appellant, Stanley Julius Phillips, to a proposal by the council to execute
street works in an alleged private street, namely that known as Sadlers Lane,
from its junction with Reading Road A.329 southwards for a distance of 353
yards or thereabouts (referred to as the material part of Sadlers Lane) on the
ground that such alleged private street was not a private street. The magistrates' C
court determined that Sadlers Lane was not a private street and quashed
the resolution of approval and the specification plan sections estimate and
provisional apportionment relating thereto and ordered that the council should
pay to the appellant 150 guineas costs. On Feb. 7, 1966, quarter sessions heard
as a preliminary point a submission on behalf of the appellant that the council
had no right of appeal to a court of quarter sessions against the determination D
of the magistrates' court and on Mar. 28, 1966, quarter sessions ruled against
this submission. On Mar. 28, 29 and 31, quarter sessions heard the appeal and
on May 3, 1966, allowed it and ordered that the appellant should pay the costs
thereof and in the court below incurred by the council. The appellant requested
the quarter sessions to state a Case for the opinion of the High Court, and the
following Case was accordingly stated. E
On the hearing of the preliminary point the following facts were proved or
admitted. The material part of Sadlers Lane is and was at all times material
to the proposal in the rural district of Wokingham. The council are and were
at all such times the street works authority within the meaning of Part 9 of the
Highways Act, 1959, for streets in such rural district. The sections of the Act
of 1959 referred to therein as " the Code of 1892 " apply and at all such times F
applied in the rural district. The council are and were at all such times the
highway authority within the meaning of the Act of 1959 for (with immaterial
exceptions) the highways within such rural district. The appellant is and was
at all such times the owner of the properties fronting Sadlers Lane named in his
notices of objection to the proposal. The requisite procedural steps appropriate
to the making of the proposal and the making and the hearing of objections G
thereto were duly followed.
It was contended for the council before quarter sessions on the preliminary
point that the council were a person aggrieved within s. 275 (1) of the Act of
1959. It was contended for the present appellant, when before quarter sessions,
on the preliminary point that the council were not a " person " and were not
susceptible to being a person aggrieved within s. 275 (1) of the Act of 1959; H
and that if they were susceptible of being a person aggrieved, they were not in
fact aggrieved except by the order for costs, and in that event the appeal should
be limited to the question of costs.
Quarter sessions came to the following conclusions—(a) that the council
were entitled to appeal under s. 275 (1) of the Act of 1959 and (b) that the material
part of Sadlers Lane was a private street. I
The cases noted below* were cited during the argument in addition to those
referred to in the judgment of WIDGERY J.

A. E. Holdsworth for the appellant.
Kenneth Jones, Q.C., and *R. M. A. C. Talbot* for the council.

---

* *R.* v. *Surrey Quarter Sessions, Ex p. Lilley,* [1951] 2 All E.R. 659; [1951] 2 Q.B. 749;
Ealing Corpn. v. *Jones,* [1959] 1 All E.R. 286; [1959] 1 Q.B. 384; *R.* v. *Dorset Sessions
Appeal Committee, Ex p. Weymouth Corpn.,* [1960] 2 All E.R. 410; [1960] 2 Q.B. 230.

A   **WIDGERY, J.**, delivered the first judgment at the invitation of LORD PARKER, C.J.: This is an appeal by Case Stated from quarter sessions for the county of Berkshire who, on May 3, 1966, allowed an appeal by the respondents, Berkshire County Council (" the council ") from an order of justices sitting at Bracknell, who in turn, on Nov. 24, 1965, had quashed a resolution, specification and accompanying documents passed by the council for the making-up of part

B   of a road in their county called Sadlers Lane at Wokingham. The appropriate procedure under the Highways Act, 1959, in this area is contained in that group of sections called the " Code of 1892 ". It was common ground from the start that the procedural matters which sometimes give difficulty in the application of this code were all correctly performed in this case, and throughout the litigation, both in the two courts below and in this court, the sole question at issue

C   has really been whether the portion of Sadlers Lane which the council sought to make up was, in fact, a private street; it being, of course, necessary that the relevant portion of the lane should be a private street in order to give jurisdiction to use these powers at all. A private street is defined in s. 213 of the Highways Act, 1959, as meaning a street not being a highway maintainable at the public expense. No one has doubted that Sadlers Lane is a street, and so the issue is

D   further confined to the question " was it or was it not a highway maintainable at the public expense? " Authority shows that when this issue is raised the onus is on the council to show that the street was a private street and, therefore, that it was not maintainable at the public expense.

          Before quarter sessions a preliminary point was taken by the appellant, the frontager, to the effect that no appeal lay from the justices to quarter sessions

E   in a matter of this kind. Quarter sessions ruled that jurisdiction lay in them and, accordingly, the point was taken again in this court. In an interim decision this court has indicated that jurisdiction does lie in quarter sessions in such a case. I must first give my reasons for supporting the view that that jurisdiction exists. The provision in the Highways Act, 1959, material to this point is s. 275 (1), which provides that:

F   " Where a person aggrieved ·by an order, determination or other decision
          of a magistrates' court under this Act is not by any other enactment
          authorised to appeal to a court of quarter sessions he may appeal to such a
          court."

          The order made by the justices in this case was clearly an order made by a

G   magistrates' court, and no other provision for appeal to quarter sessions is provided. Accordingly, the issue here, which is one which has troubled the courts on previous occasions, is whether the council were " a person aggrieved " for the purposes of this section. Before proceeding to consider this in detail, I should say that counsel for the appellant has submitted that the council are not " a person " within the meaning of the definition. He does that, as I understand it,

H   to keep the point open, and has not sought to press it in this court. I content myself by saying that as a matter of construction I am quite satisfied that the council are " a person ", and one can, therefore, proceed to the more difficult question of whether they are " a person aggrieved ".

          This question must involve some consideration of what the practical consequences are of the order of the magistrates going in one way or in the other.

I   The practical consequences can, I think, be summarised in this way. The land in question is in the rural district of Wokingham and in the administrative county of Berkshire, and in a rural district in such a county the council (who are the county council) are the street works authority for the purposes of the Highways Act, 1959. One gets that from s. 213 of the Act of 1959. Also in such a situation the council are the highway authority for all highways within the rural district, and that comes from s. 1 (3) of the Act of 1959.

          ˎ The power to undertake street works under the Code of 1892 is, as I read it, a purely discretionary power. It cannot, therefore, be said that the street works

authority are in any way bound to exercise the powers given to them, nor can it A
be said that the council as the highway authority were in any case bound to
carry out street works on the somewhat elaborate scale which is envisaged in
this case. The highway authority as such are bound to maintain (which includes
repair) the highway, if it is repairable at public expense, and no doubt can do
what are popularly called street works at their own expense if they wish, justifying
their action as being a proper act of improving the highway. In summary, there- B
fore, if this road is repairable at public expense the council must repair it and do
whatever work they deem necessary on it at their own expense and cannot charge
the frontagers at all. On the other hand, if this road is not repairable at public
expense, the council have no duty to repair it at all and can, by using the appropriate procedure, require street works to be done at the expense of the frontagers.
As a matter of fact, therefore, if the decision of the justices in this case stood it C
would result in the council having to shoulder the expense of repair, whatever
that might be, and having no right to require works to be done by the frontagers.

Does that make them for present purposes a person aggrieved? The principle
is not altogether easy to state, because there is a somewhat bewildering mass of
authority, or so I have always found it, on this point; but it is well established
that cases may arise in which a local authority, frustrated in its legitimate purpose D
by an order of justices, is nevertheless not aggrieved in any strict or legal sense. I
do not propose to add to the present volume of authority by any detailed consideration of these matters, but an example may usefully be quoted, and the example
I would choose is the case of *R.* v. *London Sessions Appeal Committee, Ex p.*
Westminster City Council (1). In that case the Westminster City Council had
power to license street traders and cancel their licences, with a right of appeal to E
the justices. In that instance the city council, having cancelled a licence and the
licence-holder having gone to the justices by way of appeal, the justices reversed
the city council's decision and ordered the reinstatement of the licence. That
was a clear case in which the city council had been frustrated in its legitimate
purpose, but it was held that it was not a person aggrieved by the justices' action
because no legal burden was thrown on it as a result of the order, nor was it left F
to bear any legal burden which might otherwise have been removed from its
shoulders. By contrast to that, to show the other side of the coin, as it were, there
is the case of *R.* v. *Nottingham Quarter Sessions, Ex p. Harlow* (2). The headnote
of that case reads:

" Where a local authority in pursuance of its powers and duties as sanitary
authority under s. 75 (1) of the Public Health Act, 1936, has served a notice G
and requirement on the owner or occupier of premises for the provision of a
dustbin, and a court of summary jurisdiction has set aside the notice without
making an order for costs against the local authority, that body is ' a person
aggrieved ' by the decision of the court of summary jurisdiction within the
meaning of s. 301 of the Public Health Act, since such decision places on the
local authority the legal burden of carrying out its duties in some other way. H
It has consequently a right of appeal to quarter sessions against the order of
the court of summary jurisdiction."

The principle involved is stated in the judgment of the court given by PARKER, J.,
as follows (3):

" Accordingly, once the court of summary jurisdiction in the present case I
had declared null and void the notice and requirement to the applicant,
as agent for the owners, to provide a dustbin, the respondent council would
have to fulfil its duties in some other way. It would either have to provide
a dustbin itself, or serve a notice on the occupier requiring him to do so with
the risk of being taken by the occupier to the court, and having to incur,

(1) [1951] 1 All E.R. 1032; [1951] 2 K.B. 508.
(2) [1952] 2 All E.R. 78; [1952] 2 Q.B. 601.
(3) [1952] 2 All E.R. at p. 80; [1952] 2 Q.B. at p. 605.

A   and possibly to pay, costs. In other words, the council is left with a legal
burden which, if the order of the court of summary jurisdiction had not been
made, the council would have discharged. In these circumstances the council
is, in our view, ' a person aggrieved '."

Applying that principle to the present case, and disregarding for a moment
counsel for the appellant's argument that the council are here in a sense two bodies
B   exercising two separate powers, the position as I see it would be that if as a result
of the justices' order the council were saddled with the expense of repairing this
road and unable to pass to the frontagers the cost of doing street works the council
would be assuming, or left with, a legal burden of a kind which a contrary order
before the justices would have removed from them. This burden cannot be dismissed as being too remote because it was the direct and inevitable consequence
C   of the order. Subject, therefore, to counsel for the appellant's point, to which I
have already briefly referred, it seems to me this case falls squarely within the
last-mentioned decision and that the council would be " a person aggrieved ".

Counsel for the appellant's final argument is that one cannot, as it were, set off
gains which the council obtain as street works authority against losses which it
suffers as highway authority. Accordingly, he says that as street works authority
D   they are in no sense aggrieved, because as street works authority no burden
falls on them; and on that footing he would contend that there was no right of
appeal in the present case. In my judgment it is quite wrong to regard the
council as being two entities for this purpose. It is wrong to regard the street
works authority referred to in the Act of 1959 as being a separate person, because
no authority can ever be the street works authority simpliciter. The scheme of
E   the Act of 1959 was to parcel up those provisions which are conveniently referred
to as the street works provisions and give them either to the county council or
to the county district council according to the circumstances prevailing in the
area. As a matter of draftsmen's shorthand this has been done by referring to
the recipient of these powers as the street works authority and then proceeding
to say in a given case which of the established local authorities shall be the street
F   works authority and thus be recipient of the powers. In the absence of authority
I would myself hold without hesitation that one can in this case look at the totality
of the council's powers and duties. There is, in fact, however, authority which
supports that view. It is to be found in the case of R. v. Boldero, Ex p. Bognor
Regis U.D.C. (4). This was a case in which the street works authority was an
urban district council, and the headnote reads in these terms:
G
    " An urban district council, as street works authority, passed resolutions
    under s. 174 (1) and (2) of the Highways Act, 1959, that certain streets be
    sewered and approving the necessary specifications, plans and apportionment.
    A number of objections were referred to the justices who considered that the
    proposed works were unreasonable and quashed the resolutions of approval.
H   The council appealed to quarter sessions and it was contended on behalf
    of one of the objectors that the council was not a person ' aggrieved ' by the
    decision of the justices within s. 275 (1) of the Highways Act, 1959, and,
    therefore, had no right of appeal. Quarter sessions held that it had no juris-
    diction and dismissed the appeal. The council applied for an order of
    mandamus to compel quarter sessions to hear and determine their appeal.
    Held, allowing the application, that no distinction could be drawn between
I   the functions of an urban district council as a public health authority under
    the Public Health Act, 1936, and its functions as street authority under the
    Highways Act, 1959; and that since the decision of the justices quashing the
    resolutions cast on the council the legal burden of carrying out its duty to
    sewer, the council was ' aggrieved ' within s. 275 (1) of the Act of 1959 by
    that decision and, accordingly, had a right of appeal."

Counsel for the appellant very properly points out that the facts of that case were
_____
(1) (1960), 60 L.G.R. 909.

somewhat unusual in that the duty referred to was the duty of sewering, and it is A
the fact that an urban district council has under the Public Health Act, 1936,
an independent duty to sewer. It follows, therefore, that here the work which
would be entailed under the Public Health Act, 1936, was identical so far as
sewering was concerned with that under the Private Street Works Act, 1892.
It seems to me, however, that that does not make any difference to the principle
which I would seek to apply here, and I have no hesitation in saying for my part B
that the preliminary point taken was a false one, that the council were aggrieved
to the extent and for the reasons which I have given and that quarter sessions
were entirely right in hearing the appeal.

[His Lordship then reviewed the evidence and relevant inclosure award on
the question whether Sadlers Lane was a highway maintainable at the public
expense, and concluded:] In my judgment there was no ancient highway over C
this road, it has been ever since 1843 a road repairable at private expense; and
all the other considerations being satisfied, the quarter sessions had, I think, no
alternative but to find, as they did, that this was a private street and to make the
order which they made. In my judgment, therefore, this appeal should be
dismissed.

    O'CONNOR, J.: I agree on both the preliminary point and on the sub- D
stantive points in the appeal with the judgment which has just been delivered by
WIDGERY, J.

    LORD PARKER, C.J.: I also agree and have nothing to add.

Appeal dismissed.

Solicitors: *Harris, Chetham & Co.* (for the appellant); *Sharpe, Pritchard & Co.,* E
agents for *E. R. Davies,* Reading (for the respondent).

[*Reported by* N. P. METCALFE, ESQ., *Barrister-at-Law.*]

 F

NOTE.

FREEDMAN v. FREEDMAN.

[PROBATE, DIVORCE AND ADMIRALTY DIVISION (Ormrod, J.), April 12, 1967.] G

Injunction—Husband and wife—Restraining wife from molesting husband—
Wife's petition for judicial separation—Husband's application for injunction
to restrain molestation—Husband of sufficient means to live elsewhere than
in matrimonial home, but choosing to remain there—Injunction not granted.

[As to injunctions in matrimonial causes, see 12 HALSBURY'S LAWS (3rd Edn.) H
477, para. 1067; and for cases on the subject, see 27 DIGEST (Repl.) 683, *6518-*
6528.]

Summons.

This was a summons by the husband, respondent to a petition brought by his
wife for judicial separation, asking for an injunction restraining her from attacking, molesting, threatening or in any wise interfering with him. The summons I
also asked for an injunction restraining the wife from remaining in the
matrimonial home, but this relief was not pursued at this hearing of the summons.

M. H. Jackson-Lipkin for the husband.
M. Levene for the wife.

    ORMROD, J., having stated the nature of the application, continued:
The situation, so far as this application is concerned, is that the wife has filed
a petition for judicial separation on the ground of cruelty. I have looked at

A the contents of the petition, and it is not necessary for me to say any more than that it reveals, if it is true, a long period of quarrelling, bickering and fighting between the husband and wife. The husband has filed an answer in which he asks for a dissolution of the marriage on the ground of cruelty, and he alleges certain acts of violence by her, throwing things about and bad language. He now applies to the court to exercise its powers to grant an injunction to

B restrain the wife from molesting him. By his evidence, apart from a general reference to his answer which he swears to be true (it is difficult to see what option he had in that regard) he merely refers, after many general allegations, to one specific occasion on Feb. 23, 1967, when there was a violent scene between husband and wife. They, of course, are still living in the same house. That scene continued on the following day. It is quite clear on the evidence that

C the immediate cause of the scene was the fact that the husband had given the wife much less money than she thought she was entitled to under the court order. I have not gone into the precise details of this, but it does appear that she may have had some reasonable ground for complaining. The husband, I gather, misunderstood or was misinformed by his accountant of the effect of the order, and so there may have been a genuine misunderstanding on that occasion. It

D certainly not unnaturally gave rise to a formidable row. That is the only specific incident that is put before me in evidence. There is reference to another incident at the husband's shop. He was not there, and it seems to me that that was a squabble between some lady who was looking after the shop and the wife.

In those circumstances, I am asked to exercise the very far-reaching powers of

E this court to grant injunctions against molestation. Now no one, I hope, more fully realises than I do the enormous value of this power of this court to restrain molestation in proper cases. It makes all the difference in the world, as I well know from my experience at the Bar, to people who are momentarily at any rate under grave pressure and in grave trouble. It is a most valuable power, but it has to be exercised in my judgment reasonably and sensibly.

F There is an obvious tendency these days to ask the court to invoke this power very much too light-heartedly, for there are often lists of these summonses for hearing every week, and I think that the time has come when the court really should take a more careful look at them.

This case strikes me as being an example of a case in which the court should refuse to exercise its power to grant an injunction. The husband owns shops

G and, I gather, houses. What his financial position is, I do not know precisely, but he is apparently well enough off to take himself for a holiday skiing in Switzerland, and, if he chooses to endure the insults of his wife because he is determined to go on living with her in the matrimonial home, then he must make his choice. He is obviously in a position, if he wants to, to do what most sensible people who find themselves in matrimonial misery do at some stage when the misery

H becomes intolerable: they get out. As far as I am able to understand, there is nothing whatever to stop the husband leaving the matrimonial home, except that he does not want to; and that does not seem a very good reason for his invoking the exercise of the court's ultimate powers of injunction. I say that for this reason. The only power that the court has got to enforce an injunction, if it is broken, is to commit; and is it conceivable that I would commit the wife

I for continuing to squabble with the husband because he chooses to remain in the matrimonial home? The answer is obviously not. I am not going to commit a woman to prison because she continues to squabble with her husband. Therefore, it would be most unwise for me to grant an injunction which would probably lead to that result.

It is quite obvious from the history of these two people—for there have been summonses in the Southend magistrates' court by every member of the family apparently in the neighbourhood—that they will go on fighting so long as they are under the same roof. The husband is in a position to remove himself or to

stay according to his assessment of the situation, and in my judgment he must   A
take his own remedies first.

This is, to my mind, the perfect example of a situation in which the court will
not grant an injunction. Accordingly, the summons is dismissed with costs.

Application dismissed.

Solicitors: *Rudd, Moorfoot & Davenport*, Southend-on-Sea (for the husband);   B
Menassé, Ralph Freeman & Tobin (for the wife).

[*Reported by* ALICE BLOOMFIELD, *Barrister-at-Law.*]

MITCHELL *v.* HARRIS ENGINEERING CO., LTD.   C

[COURT OF APPEAL, CIVIL DIVISION (Lord Denning, M.R., Davies and Russell,
L.JJ.), April 12, 13, 26, 1967.]

*Practice—Parties—Adding or substituting party as defendant—Amendment of
writ to change defendant from H.E. Co. (Leeds), Ltd. to H.E. Co., Ltd.—
Limitation period expired—Whether rule of court permitting amendment*   D
*was ultra vires—Whether leave to amend was just—Supreme Court of
Judicature (Consolidation) Act, 1925 (15 & 16 Geo. 5 c. 49), s. 99 (1) (a)—
R.S.C., Ord. 20, r. 5 (2) (3).*

The new rule*, R.S.C., Ord. 20, r. 5 (2) (3), which permits amendment of
a party's name on, e.g., a writ, notwithstanding that the effect will be to
substitute a new party after the limitation period has expired, is not ultra   E
vires (see p. 686, letters G and I, and p. 687, letter I, post).

The plaintiff was employed by H.E. Co., Ltd. at their Tunbridge Wells
works. On Aug. 27, 1963, he had an accident at work and was injured. He
claimed damages from his employers. On Aug. 9, 1966, a writ was issued on
his behalf. When the writ was drafted the name H.E. Co., Ltd. was inserted
as defendants. A junior clerk of the solicitors was sent to Somerset House   F
to search the register. He searched the register of English companies and
found the name of an English company, H.E. Co. (Leeds), Ltd. He inserted
" (Leeds) " in the name of the defendant on the writ before it was issued.
H.E. Co., Ltd. was in fact incorporated in Northern Ireland. It and H.E. Co.
(Leeds), Ltd. had the same directors and secretary. The three year limitation
period expired on Aug. 27, 1966. On Sept. 28, 1966, the writ was served on   G
the English company; the endorsement showed that the accident was
alleged to have occurred at the Tunbridge Wells works, which were the
Irish company's works. On appeal from an order allowing the plaintiff to
amend the writ, under R.S.C., Ord. 20, r. 5, by substituting the Irish company
as defendants,

Held: there had been a genuine mistake, which had not misled the   H
defendants, and accordingly the amendment was rightly allowed (see p. 686,
letters H and I, and p. 688, letter E, post).

Appeal dismissed.

[Editorial Note. The decision that R.S.C., Ord. 20, r. 5 is intra vires, in
effect affirms the like conclusion reached in *Rodriquez* v. *Parker* ([1966] 2 All E.R.
349, see at p. 364, letters C, E).   I

Reported decisions which are negatived or qualified by the new R.S.C., Ord. 20,
r. 5, include *Weldon* v. *Neal* ((1887), 19 Q.B.D. 394); *Mabro* v. *Eagle Star &
British Dominions Insurance Co., Ltd.* ([1932] All E.R. Rep. 411); *Marshall* v.
London Passenger Transport Board ([1936] 3 All E.R. 83); *Batting* v. *London*

---

* Rules 4 and 5 of R.S.C., Ord. 20 were substituted by R.S.C., 1964, S.I. 1964 No. 1213,
r. 7, which came into operation on Oct. 1, 1964. Rule 5 of Ord. 20, as so substituted,
was consolidated into the R.S.C. (Rev.) 1965, S.I. 1965 No. 1776, with effect from Oct. 1,
1966.

Applied in LIFF v PEASLEY [1980] 1
All ER 623   Considered in YEW BON TEW v
                                                             KENDERAAN BAS MARA [1982]
                                                             3 All ER 833

A *Passenger Transport Board* ([1941] 1 All E.R. 228); *Hilton* v. *Sutton Steam Laundry* ([1945] 2 All E.R. 425) and *Davies* v. *Elsby Brothers, Ltd.* ([1960] 3 All E.R. 672). The allowance of correction of a misnomer in *Whittam* v. *W. J. Daniel & Co., Ltd.* ([1961] 3 All E.R. 796) is in line with the decision in the present case.

As to misjoinder of parties, see 30 HALSBURY'S LAWS (3rd Edn.) 394, 395, para. 735; and for cases on the subject, see DIGEST (Practice) 405, 406, *1062-1076*.

B As to amendments being refused formerly on the ground that they would defeat the statutes of limitation, see 24 HALSBURY'S LAWS (3rd Edn.) 200, 201, para. 358, and 30 ibid., p. 34, para. 72.

As to the power to make rules of court, see 9 HALSBURY'S LAWS (3rd Edn.) 422, 423, para. 973.

For the Supreme Court of Judicature (Consolidation) Act, 1925, s. 99 and
C Sch. 1, see 18 HALSBURY'S STATUTES (2nd Edn.) 511, 518.]

Cases referred to:

A.-G. v. *Sillem*, (1864), 10 H.L. Cas. 704; 33 L.J.Ex. 209; 10 L.T. 434; 44 Digest (Repl.) 200, *135*.

Batting v. *London Passenger Transport Board*, [1941] 1 All E.R. 228; 38 Digest (Repl.) 150, *1053*.

D *Davies* v. *Elsby Brothers, Ltd.*, [1960] 3 All E.R. 672; [1961] 1 W.L.R. 170; 32 Digest (Repl.) 617, *1961*.

Hill v. *Luton Corpn.*, [1951] 1 All E.R. 1028; [1951] 2 K.B. 387; 115 J.P. 340; 32 Digest (Repl.) 614, *1939*.

Hilton v. *Sutton Steam Laundry*, [1945] 2 All E.R. 425; [1946] K.B. 65; 115 L.J.K.B. 33; 17 L.T. 31; 23 Digest (Repl.) 64, *552*.

E *Mabro* v. *Eagle Star & British Dominions Insurance Co., Ltd.*, [1932] All E.R. Rep. 411; [1932] 1 K.B. 485; 101 L.J.K.B. 205; 146 L.T. 433; 32 Digest (Repl.) 618, *1967*.

Marshall v. *London Passenger Transport Board*, [1936] 3 All E.R. 83; 32 Digest (Repl.) 620, *1984*.

Pontin v. *Wood*, [1962] 1 All E.R. 294; [1962] 1 Q.B. 594; [1962] 2 W.L.R.
F 258; 32 Digest (Repl.) 615, *1941*.

Weldon v. *Neal*, (1887), 19 Q.B.D. 394; 56 L.J.Q.B. 621; 32 Digest (Repl.) 620, *1981*.

Interlocutory Appeal.

By writ issued on Aug. 9, 1966, the plaintiff claimed damages for personal
injuries and consequential loss suffered as the result of an accident which occurred
G on or about Aug. 27, 1963, " at the defendants' premises situate at Longfield Road, Tunbridge Wells ", in the county of Kent owing to the negligence or breach of statutory duty of the defendants, their servants or agents. The defendants named in the writ were " Harris Engineering Co. (Leeds), Ltd.".

By order dated Jan. 27, 1967, JAMES, J., dismissed an appeal from an order of
MASTER JACOB dated Nov. 29, 1966, granting leave to the plaintiff under R.S.C.,
H Ord. 20, r. 5, to amend the writ and all subsequent proceedings by substituting Harris Engineering Co., Ltd. for Harris Engineering Co. (Leeds), Ltd. By notice of appeal dated Feb. 13, 1967, the defendants appealed from the order of Jan. 27, 1967, for an order discharging so much of the order of Nov. 29, 1966, as gave leave to the plaintiff to amend the writ and subsequent proceedings.

I *A. J. Bateson* for the defendants.
Esyr Lewis for the plaintiff.

Cur. adv. vult.

Apr. 26. The following judgments were read.

LORD DENNING, M.R.: Two associated companies have very similar names. One company is called Harris Engineering Co., Ltd., the other company is called Harris Engineering Co. (Leeds), Ltd. Harris Engineering Co., Ltd. states on its notepaper that its head office is at York Works, Browning Street, London,

S.E.17. It has factory premises at Tunbridge Wells, Kent. Strangely enough, A
it is not an English company. It is a company incorporated in Northern Ireland.
It gives its address for service in England as York Works, Browning Street,
London, S.E.17. Harris Engineering Co. (Leeds), Ltd. is a company incorporated
in England; its registered office is at York Works, Browning Street, London,
S.E.17. The two companies have common directors and a common secretary.

The plaintiff, Mr. Mitchell, was employed by Harris Engineering Co., Ltd. at B
their works at Tunbridge Wells. On Aug. 27, 1963, he fell and hurt himself. His
solicitors claimed damages from his employers, who passed it on to their insurers.
The claim was disputed. There was great delay in pursuing it, and nearly three
years had passed before the plaintiff's solicitors issued a writ. When the solicitors
drafted the writ, they inserted the name of the defendants, " Harris Engineering
Co., Ltd., whose registered office is situate at York Works, Browning Street "; C
but then they sent a junior clerk along to Somerset House. He searched the
English register of companies and found only the company " Harris Engineering
Co. (Leeds), Ltd.", with its registered office situate at York Works, Browning
Street. He assumed very naturally that this must be the correct name of the
defendants and altered the draft by inserting " (Leeds) ". It did not occur to
him to search the register for companies incorporated in Northern Ireland: D
because that was a separate register, and he never thought that the defendants
would be in that register. If he had looked in that register, he would have seen
the Harris Engineering Co., Ltd. incorporated in Northern Ireland.

Accordingly, on Aug. 9, 1966, the plaintiff's solicitors issued a writ naming
" Harris Engineering Co. (Leeds), Ltd." as defendants. The indorsement was in
these words: E

> " The plaintiff's claim is for damages for personal injuries and conse-
> quential loss suffered as a result of an accident which occurred on or about
> Aug. 27, 1963, at the defendants' premises situate at Longfield Road,
> Tunbridge Wells in the county of Kent, owing to the negligence and/or
> breach of statutory duty of the defendants, their servants and agents."

F

The three years period of limitation expired on Aug. 27, 1966. Four weeks later,
on Sept. 28, 1966, the plaintiff's solicitors served the writ by registered post
addressed to " Harris Engineering Co. (Leeds), Ltd." at York Works, Browning
Street. That was the address of both companies. It was received by the secretary,
or someone in his place, who acted on behalf of both these companies. On reading
the indorsement, he must have realised that the claim was intended for the com- G
pany which employed the plaintiff at the Tunbridge Wells works. He sent it on
to the insurance company. They took the point that the writ was issued against
the wrong company. It was issued against " Harris Engineering Co. (Leeds),
Ltd.", whereas it should have been issued against " Harris Engineering Co.,
Ltd.".

At first the plaintiff's solicitors tried to amend the writ without getting the H
leave of the court. They thought they could do it under R.S.C., Ord. 20, r. 1.
They struck out the word " Leeds ", so that the defendants appeared as " Harris
Engineering Co., Ltd."; but thereupon Harris Engineering Co., Ltd. said that
it was not permissible to make that amendment without leave, as it was substituting a party. The plaintiff acknowledged that to be true: and in return applied
under R.S.C., Ord. 20, r. 5, for leave to amend the writ by substituting " Harris I
Engineering Co., Ltd." for " Harris Engineering Co. (Leeds), Ltd.". The
defendants objected to this being done. They said that " Harris Engineering
Co., Ltd." had a statutory defence because the period of limitation had expired:
and that the writ should not be amended so as to deprive them of that right.
The plaintiff said that R.S.C., Ord. 20, r. 5 was a new rule made especially to
meet such a case as this; but the defendants then said that the rule was ultra
vires.

The new R.S.C., Ord. 20, r. 5, so far as material, is in these terms:

A   " (2) Where an application to the court for leave to make the amendment mentioned in paras. (3), (4) or (5) is made after any relevant period of limitation current at the date of issue of the writ has expired, the court may nevertheless grant such leave in the circumstances mentioned in that paragraph if it thinks it just to do so.

" (3) An amendment to correct the name of a party may be allowed under

B   para. (2) notwithstanding that it is alleged that the effect of the amendment will be to substitute a new party if the court is satisfied that the mistake sought to be corrected was a genuine mistake and was not misleading or such as to cause any reasonable doubt as to the identity of the person intending to sue or, as the case may be, intended to be sued.

" (4) An amendment to alter the capacity in which a party sues (whether

C   as plaintiff or as defendant by counterclaim) may be allowed under para. (2) if the capacity in which, if the amendment is made, the party will sue is one in which at the date of issue of the writ or the making of the counterclaim, as the case may be, he might have sued.

" (5) An amendment may be allowed under para. (2) notwithstanding that the effect of the amendment will be to add or substitute a new cause of

D   action if the new cause of action arises out of the same facts or substantially the same facts as the cause of action in respect of which relief has already been claimed in the action by the party applying for leave to make the amendment."

Counsel for the defendant submitted to us that this new R.S.C., Ord. 20, r. 5 (2), (3), (4) and (5) was beyond the powers of the rules committee. Their powers are

E   defined by s. 99 (1) (a) of the Supreme Court of Judicature (Consolidation) Act, 1925. It enables rules of court to be made

" For regulating and prescribing the procedure (including the method of pleading) and the practice to be followed in the Court of Appeal and the High Court . . ."

F   Counsel for the defendants says that this section enables the rule committee to regulate the machinery of litigation, but it does not enable the courts to alter or take away existing rights or make new rights, and he cited A.-G. v. Sillem (1). Furthermore, he says that the rules of court are subordinate legislation which cannot alter, vary or contradict an Act of Parliament, and in particular cannot alter the statute of limitations.

G   Prior to the new rule, there was a long line of authority which said that, once a person had acquired the benefit of a statute of limitations, he was entitled to insist on retaining that benefit: and, what is more, the court would not deprive him of that benefit by allowing an amendment of the writ or of the pleadings. For instance, there was a case where a firm called Elsby Brothers turned themselves into a company called Elsby Brothers, Ltd. An injured workman, within

H   the three years permitted by the statute, issued a writ against " Elsby Brothers ". After the three years, he discovered his mistake and sought to amend by substituting " Elsby Brothers, Ltd." as defendants. He was not allowed to do so (see Davies v. Elsby Brothers, Ltd. (2)). Another case was where a man had been killed and his widow claimed compensation under the Fatal Accidents Acts. She brought an action within the one year permitted by the statute against the

I   employers; but she described herself in the writ " as administratrix " of her husband's estate, when she had not then taken out letters of administration. When the mistake was discovered she sought to amend the writ by striking out the words " as administratrix "; but the one year had by that time expired, and she was not allowed to do so (see Hilton v. Sutton Steam Laundry (3)). Other instances are Weldon v. Neal (4), where an amendment was not allowed to

---

(1) (1864), 10 H.L. Cas. 704.   (2) [1960] 3 All E.R. 672.
(3) [1945] 2 All E.R. 425; [1946] K.B. 65.
(4) (1881), 19 Q.B.D. 394.

substitute a new cause of action, and *Mabro* v. *Eagle Star & British Dominions* A
Insurance Co. (5), where an amendment was not allowed to substitute a new
plaintiff.

Some of the judges in those cases spoke of the defendant having a " right " to
the benefit of the statute of limitations: and said that that " right " should
not be taken from him by amendment of the writ; but I do not think that was
quite correct. The statute of limitations does not confer any right on the defen- B
dant. It only imposes a time limit on the plaintiff. Take the statute here in
question. It is s. 2 of the Limitation Act, 1939, as amended by s. 2 (1) of the Law
Reform (Limitation of Actions, &c.) Act, 1954. It says that in the case of actions
for damages for personal injuries for negligence, nuisance or breach of duty " the
action shall not be brought " after the expiration of three years from the date on
which the cause of action accrued. In order to satisfy the statute, the plaintiff C
must issue his writ within three years from the date of the accident. There is
nothing in the statute, however, which says that the writ must at that time be
perfect and free from defects. Even if it is defective, nevertheless the court may,
as a matter of practice, permit him to amend it. Once it is amended, then the
writ as amended speaks from the date on which the writ was originally issued and
not from the date of the amendment. The defect is cured and the action is brought D
in time. It is not barred by the statute (see *Hill* v. *Luton Corpn.* (6); *Pontin*
v. *Wood* (7)).

In my opinion, whenever a writ has been issued within the permitted time, but
is found to be defective, the defendant has no right to have it remain defective.
The court can permit the defect to be cured by amendment: and whether it
should do so depends on the practice of the court. It is a matter of practice and E
procedure. As such it can be altered by the rule committee under s. 99 (1) (*a*)
of the Act of 1925. That is what has been done by R.S.C., Ord. 20, r. 5 (2), (3),
(4) and (5). Rule 5 (3) has removed the injustice caused by the decision in *Davies*
v. *Elsby Brothers, Ltd.* (8). Rule 5 (4) has removed the injustice caused by *Hilton*
v. *Sutton Steam Laundry* (9). Rule 5 (5) has removed the injustice caused by such
cases as *Marshall* v. *London Passenger Transport Board* (10) and *Batting* v. F
London Passenger Transport Board (11).

In my opinion, therefore, the rule was within the powers of the rule committee,
and the attack on it fails. It is a most beneficial provision which enables the courts
to amend proceedings whenever the justice of the case so requires. The
amendment relates back to the date of the issue of the writ.

Once this rule, R.S.C., Ord. 20, r. 5, is held to be within the powers of the rule G
committee, there is the further question whether the court in its discretion should
grant the amendment. The master and the judge thought that the amendment
should be granted: and I agree with them. It is a very proper case for amendment. It was a genuine mistake by the plaintiff's solicitors; and the secretary
of the two companies must have realised it as soon as he read the writ and the
indorsement.   H

I can well understand the defendants taking the point. They thought that the
claim was so shadowy and so stale that it would be a good thing to stop the
action at the outset; but the point is not a good one. They must fight the case
on the merits. I would dismiss the appeal.

DAVIES, L.J.: I agree with what LORD DENNING, M.R., has said and with
the judgment which RUSSELL, L.J., is about to deliver and do not wish to add I
anything.

(5) [1932] All E.R. Rep. 411; [1932] 1 K.B. 485.
(6) [1951] 1 All E.R. 1028; [1951] 2 K.B. 387.
(7) [1962] 1 All E.R. 294; [1962] 1 Q.B. 594.
(8) [1960] 3 All E.R. 672.
(9) [1945] 2 All E.R. 425; [1946] K.B. 65
(10) [1936] 3 All E.R. 83.
(11) [1941] 1 All E.R. 228.

A   RUSSELL, L.J.: I will call the appellant, Harris Engineering Co., Ltd.,
the " Irish company ", and Harris Engineering Co. (Leeds), Ltd., the " Leeds
company ".

Master JACOB and JAMES, J., on appeal, have under R.S.C., Ord. 20, r. 5 (2)
and (3) given leave to amend the writ by deleting the word " Leeds " from the
name of the defendants (i.e., substituting the name of the Irish company for that
B of the Leeds company), and there has been consequential alteration of the
address to an address for service of Mr. Buteaux at York Works.

The Irish company appeals on the grounds: (a) that R.S.C., Ord. 20, r. 5 (2)
and (3) are ultra vires the rule-making power as dealing with a matter of the
substantive rights of the Irish company against whom no writ was issued within
three years of the accident; (b) that in the present case there was no " mistake "
C within r. 5 (3); and (c) that discretion was wrongly exercised in allowing the
amendment, in that it should not have been thought " just " to do so within
r. 5 (2).

R.S.C., Ord. 20, r. 5 was first introduced in 1964. [HIS LORDSHIP read r. 5 (2)
and (3), which are set out at p. 685, letters A and B, ante, and continued:] Until
1961, if by amendment a defendant was substituted, the proceedings were deemed
D to be commenced when the amended writ was served on him, so that this question
of affecting his position in relation to the statute of limitations could not arise.
(It is still the same under the County Court Rules, 1936, except in a case where
someone turns up and demands or volunteers to be substituted as defendant.)
There was in the Rules of the Supreme Court apparently a gap of two years
between the disappearance of that provision of R.S.C., Ord. 16, r. 11 and the
E introduction of R.S.C., Ord. 20, r. 5.

On the question of ultra vires, I accept that the Rules of the Supreme Court are
limited to matters of practice and procedure, which have been said to be con-
vertible terms. Section 99 of the Supreme Court of Judicature (Consolidation)
Act, 1925 is concerned with such matters and is in Part 4 which is cross-headed
" General Provisions as to Trial and Procedure ". It is quite clear that a rule of
F court cannot in terms alter the period of time laid down by a statute within which
an action must be brought; but it seems to me to be equally clear that the
circumstances in which a litigant may amend his existing proceedings, for
example by addition or substitution of defendants, are essentially a matter of
practice or procedure. Nor does it appear to me that the Order made conflicts
with the law contained in the statute of limitations, notwithstanding that, if the
G amendment had been refused, a defence would have been available to the Irish
company under that statute in a different action. The statute says that an action
founded on tort shall not be brought after the expiration of three years from the
date on which the cause of action accrued. The torts alleged in the present case by
the writ are torts of breach on Aug. 27, 1963, of common law and statutory duty
at premises at Longfield Road, Tunbridge Wells, and the action was brought
H within three years of the alleged event. It was argued that before the amendment,
the Irish company had a sure shield under the statute and the amendment
removed that shield; but its sure shield under the statute was one which was
available to it in another action should one be brought out of time. Its shield in
the present proceedings was not the statute, but the fact that it was not yet a
defendant in them. That shield could be taken away by the procedural power of
I permitting amendment of these proceedings. For these reasons, which appear
to me preferable to those based on the conception of statutes of limitation as
procedural in character for the purposes of private international law, I do not
consider R.S.C., Ord. 20, r. 5 (2) and (3) to be ultra vires.

We were referred to a number of cases in which the courts have declined to
permit amendments which would have the effect of depriving a party of the ability
which he would have in any fresh proceedings to take advantage of the statute of
limitations. It was urged that these were based on an inability in point of substantive law to deprive a person of a right conferred on him by the statute of

limitations than on a settled practice. Various locutions were used in these cases,   A
some expressly referring to practice, others pointing (but not, I think, conclusively) in the direction of " defeating " the statute. See, e.g., GREER, L.J.,
and SCRUTTON, L.J., respectively, in *Mabro* v. *Eagle Star & British Dominion
Insurance Co., Ltd.* (12). I take these cases to have been decided, however, on
grounds of settled practice, albeit attributable to the parties' positions vis-à-vis
the statute of limitation. So far as I am aware, no judge said that it would be   B
outside the jurisdiction of the court to allow the amendment in question: and if
it were thought to be a question of substantive law, this would surely have been
the immediate and short answer to the application to amend.

I turn to the next point, whether the present case is within the language of the
rule. I think that it is. The amendment sought involves the correction of the
name of the defendant, albeit that it is alleged, and correctly so, that it also   C
involves the substitution of the Irish company for the Leeds company. Moreover,
there was in my view a genuine mistake by the junior clerk on the facts stated,
though it is true that with a greater degree of diligence, and perhaps with a lesser
degree of self reliance, he would not have made it. It is suggested that mistake
here means error without fault: but I do not see why the word should be so
narrowly construed. It was not misleading, because when the writ was served, it   D
was served on Mr. Buteaux, secretary to both companies, who could not have
failed to observe, since the accident alleged was at the Irish company works, that
the Irish company was intended to be the defendant. Moreover, the mistake did
not mislead the Irish company into thinking it was clear of liability on Aug. 27,
1966. It would have thought so (if at all) without the mistake.

Finally, should the judge and the master have thought it just to allow the   E
amendment? I am not prepared to say that they were wrong in so thinking. It
was urged in particular that the plaintiff would have an action in negligence
against his solicitors if the amendment were not permitted, and that this tips the
scale when balancing deprivation of the plaintiff of his action in tort against
deprivation of the Irish company of a defence of limitation. I do not think so.

I would dismiss the appeal.   F

Appeal dismissed. Leave to appeal to the House of Lords refused.

Solicitors: *Tucker, Turner & Co.* (for the defendants); *Evill & Coleman* (for
the plaintiff).

[*Reported by* F. GUTTMAN, ESQ., *Barrister-at-Law.*]   G

H

I

(12) [1932] All E.R. Rep. 411; [1932] 1 K.B. 485.

INDYKA v. INDYKA.

[HOUSE OF LORDS (Lord Reid, Lord Morris of Borth-y-Gest, Lord Pearce, Lord Wilberforce and Lord Pearson), March 6, 7, 8, 9, 13, 14, May 23, 1967.]

Divorce—Foreign decree—Decree granted to wife in Czechoslovakia—Residence of wife in territory of foreign court for more than three years preceding application for divorce there—Husband domiciled in England—Avoidance of limping marriages—Public policy—Recognition of foreign decree pronounced before the commencement of s. 1 of the Law Reform (Miscellaneous Provisions) Act, 1949 (12, 13 & 14 Geo. 6 c. 100).

In 1938 the husband married his first wife. Both were Czech nationals domiciled in Czechoslovakia. The husband joined the Czech army in 1939. Later he joined the Polish forces and at the end of the war of 1939-45 he was demobilised in England. He acquired a domicil of choice in England in 1946. His first wife remained throughout in Czechoslovakia. Under Czech law nationality formed the relevant basis for divorce jurisdiction. On Jan. 18, 1949, the marriage of the husband and the first wife was dissolved on her application by decree of a court in Czechoslovakia. The Law Reform (Miscellaneous Provisions) Act, 1949, s. 1 (1)*, which allowed a wife in England to obtain a divorce after three years residence, came into force in December, 1949. In 1959 the husband re-married in England. In proceedings by his second wife for divorce he contended that his re-marriage was void, as the English court would not recognise the decree of the Czech court in January 1949.

Held: the dissolution of the first marriage by the Czech decree of Jan. 18, 1949, would be recognised by the English court, with the consequence that the second marriage was valid, for the following reasons—

(i) because the first wife had been residing for more than three years in Czechoslovakia before the decree, and the fact that the decree preceded the Act of 1949 should not prevent its recognition, after that Act, on the principle that the English courts should recognise a jurisdiction which they themselves then claimed by virtue of s. 1 of the Act of 1949* (see p. 707, letter G, p. 717, letter H, p. 727, letters E and H, and p. 730, letter B, post; cf., p. 693, letter F, and p. 703, letter D, post).

Travers v. *Holley and Holley* ([1953] 2 All E.R. 794) approved.

(ii) because, there being substantial connexion between the first wife and Czechoslovakia (where she had lived all her life, had married, and had had her matrimonial home), recognition of the decree should be accorded on the basis (LORD REID not deciding on this ground) of her Czech nationality, which nationality the husband also had or had had (see p. 708, letter C, p. 718, letter A, p. 726, letter F, p. 727, letter E, p. 731, letter I, to p. 732, letter A, and p. 703, letter D, post); or (per LORD REID) recognition of the decree should be accorded on the ground that the first wife had had her matrimonial home in Czechoslovakia and had continued to reside there (see p. 703, letter D, post).

Decision of the COURT OF APPEAL ([1966] 3 All E.R. 583) affirmed.

Divorce—Foreign decree—Recognition by English court—Basis of recognition—Domicil—Nationality—Residence—Relaxation, as regards foreign decrees, of the rule that domicil was the only test of jurisdiction in divorce.

The law governing recognition by English courts of the divorce decrees of foreign courts being largely judge-made law, and the purpose of the rule laid down in *Le Mesurier* v. *Le Mesurier* ([1895-99] All E.R. Rep. 836) that domicil should be the sole test of jurisdiction having never achieved the universality intended and having been eroded by statute and change of

---

* Now s. 40 (1) (*b*) of the Matrimonial Causes Act 1965; 45 HALSBURY'S STATUTES (2nd Edn.) 499, 500.

circumstances, some departure from the strictness of that rule in its appli- **A**
cation to recognition of foreign decrees should be made; accordingly
guidance is given by the House of Lords on the extent of relaxation of the
rule which is acceptable, and this may be summarised as follows—

(1) The basic rule remains that English courts continue to recognise
foreign divorce decrees if, and only if, these are granted or recognised by
the court of the husband's domicil (see p. 726, letters B and C, p. 706, **B**
letter E, p. 707, letter D, and p. 717, letter B, post; cf. p. 731, letter A, post).

(2) Recognition may, nevertheless, be extended to divorce decrees of
foreign courts granted on the basis of nationality of both spouses (see
p. 708, letter C, p. 718, letter A, p. 726, letter G, and p. 731, letter A, post;
cf., p. 703, letter B, post).

(3) Recognition may, perhaps, be extended to divorce decrees of foreign **C**
courts on the basis of nationality separately acquired by a wife living apart
from her husband (see p. 731, letter A, p. 717, letter E, and p. 726, letter G,
post).

(4) Recognition should not be so extended to decrees obtained by fraud
or which offend against substantial justice, or unless there is such real and
substantial connexion between the petitioner and the court exercising **D**
jurisdiction as shows that the petitioner is not resorting to that jurisdiction
merely for convenience in obtaining a decree that, e.g., the court of the
domicil would not grant (see p. 706, letter C, p. 715, letter I, p. 727, letter
C, and p. 731, letters B and C, post).

(5) Apart from recognition on the principle of *Travers* v. *Holley and Holley*
([1953] 2 All E.R. 794), non-domiciliary residence seems not to be acceptable **E**
as a qualification for recognition of a foreign divorce decree (compare p. 702,
letter I, to p. 703, letter A, p. 726, letter H, and p. 731, letter E, post).

[**Editorial Note:** The present decision is not a decision on what should be
the basis in private international law of the divorce jurisdiction of the English
courts, but only on what should be the basis of recognition by the English courts
of decrees of divorce obtained in foreign countries. All opinions, except that of **F**
LORD REID, accept as deserving such recognition a decree made by a foreign
court in exercise of jurisdiction based on nationality, as distinct from domicil,
or (per LORD MORRIS OF BORTH-Y-GEST, see p. 708, letter C, post) on citizenship.
LORD REID would accord recognition to the divorce decree of the court of the
matrimonial home (see p. 702, letter H, post). Such extension of the basis of
recognition of foreign divorce decrees as this decision envisages is for the courts **G**
to work out in future cases, subject, of course, to any Act of Parliament enacting
law on this subject.

As to the recognition by English courts of foreign decrees of divorce, see
7 HALSBURY'S LAWS (3rd Edn.) 112, 113, para. 200; and for cases on the subject,
see 11 DIGEST (Repl.) 481-483, *1079-1097.*]

H

Cases referred to:
    Armitage v. *A.-G., Gillig* v. *Gillig,* [1906] P. 135; 75 L.J.P. 42; 94 L.T. 614;
        11 Digest (Repl.) 483, *1094.*
    Armytage v. *Armytage,* [1895-99] All E.R. Rep. 377; [1898] P. 178; 67 L.J.P.
        90; 78 L.T. 689; 11 Digest (Repl.) 475, *1052.*
    Arnold v. *Arnold,* [1957] 1 All E.R. 570; [1957] P. 237 [1957] 2 W.L.R. 366; **I**
        Digest (Cont. Vol. A) 244, *1094a.*
    A.-G. for Alberta v. *Cook,* [1926] All E.R. Rep. 525; [1926] A.C. 444; 95
        L.J.P.C. 102; 134 L.T. 717; 11 Digest (Repl.) 472, *1030.*
    Bater v. *Bater,* [1906] P. 209; 75 L.P.P. 60; 94 L.T. 835; 11 Digest (Repl.)
        482, *1087.*
    Bowie (or Ramsay) v. *Liverpool Royal Infirmary,* [1930] All E.R. Rep. 127;
        [1930] A.C. 588; 99 L.J.P.C. 134; 143 L.T. 388; 11 Digest (Repl.)
        339, *109.*

A   *De Montaigu* v. *De Montaigu*, [1913] P. 154; 82 L.J.P. 125; 109 L.T. 79;
    11 Digest (Repl.) 473, *1040*.

Dolphin v. *Robins*, (1859), 7 H.L. Cas. 390; 29 L.J.P. & M. 11; 34 L.T.O.S. 48;
23 J.P. 725; 11 E.R. 156; *affg.* sub nom. *Robins* v. *Dolphin*, (1858),
1 Sw. & Ir. 37; *subsequent proceedings*, sub nom. *Robins* v. *Dolphin*,
(1860), 1 Sw. & Ir. 518; 11 Digest (Repl.) 356, *252*.

B   *Dunne* v. *Saban* (*formerly Dunne*), [1954] 3 All E.R. 586; [1955] P. 178;
    [1954] 3 W.L.R. 980; Digest (Cont. Vol. A) 245, *1097a*.

Fenton v. *Fenton*, [1957] V.L.R. 17.

Formosa v. *Formosa*, [1962] 3 All E.R. 419; sub nom. *Gray* (*otherwise Formosa*)
v. *Formosa*, [1963] P. 259; [1962] 3 W.L.R. 1246; Digest (Cont. Vol.
A) 248, *1107a*.

C   *Forster* v. *Forster and Berridge*, (1863), 3 Sw. & Ir. 151; 32 L.J.P.M. & A. 206;
    9 L.T. 148; 164 E.R. 1231; *subsequent proceedings*, (1863), 4 B. & S.
    187; 32 L.J.Q.B. 312; 8 L.T. 661; 122 E.R. 430; 27 Digest (Repl.)
    475, *4122*.

Garthwaite v. *Garthwaite*, [1964] 2 All E.R. 233; [1964] P. 356; [1964] 2
W.L.R. 1108; 3rd Digest Supp.

D   *Harvey* v. *Farnie*, (1880), 5 P.D. 153; *affd.* C.A., (1880), 6 P.D. 35; *affd.*
    H.L., (1882), 8 App. Cas. 43; 52 L.J.P. 33; 48 L.T. 273; 47 J.P. 308;
    11 Digest (Repl.) 481, *1084*.

Herd v. *Herd*, [1936] 2 All E.R. 1516; [1936] P. 205; 105 L.J.P. 108; 155
L.T. 355; 11 Digest (Repl.) 351, *201*.

Keyes v. *Keyes and Gray*, [1921] P. 204; 90 L.J.P. 242; 124 L.T. 797; 11
E   Digest (Repl.) 467, *1003*.

Lack v. *Lack*, [1926] S.L.T. 656.

Le Mesurier v. *Le Mesurier*, [1895-99] All E.R. Rep. 836; [1895] A.C. 517;
64 L.J.P.C. 97; 72 L.T. 873; 11 Digest (Repl.) 468, *1011*.

Lepre v. *Lepre*, [1963] 2 All E.R. 49; [1965] P. 52; [1963] 2 W.L.R. 735;
Digest (Cont. Vol. A) 248, *1101c*.

F   *Levett* v. *Levett*, [1957] 1 All E.R. 720; [1957] P. 156; [1957] 2 W.L.R. 484;
    Digest (Cont. Vol. A) 245, *1094b*.

Lord v. *Colvin*, (1859), 4 Drew. 366; 28 L.J.Ch. 361; 32 L.T.O.S. 377; 62
E.R. 141; *subsequent proceedings* (1860), 1 Drew. & Sm. 24; 3 L.T. 228;
11 Digest (Repl.) 333, *65*.

Lord Advocate v. *Jaffrey*, [1920] All E.R. Rep. 242; [1921] 1 A.C. 146; 89
G   L.J.P.C. 209; 124 L.T. 129; 11 Digest (Repl.) 356, *253*.

Mountbatten (*Marquess of Milford Haven*) v. *Mountbatten* (*Marchioness of
Milford Haven*), [1959] 1 All E.R. 99; [1959] P. 43; [1959] 2 W.L.R.
128; Digest (Cont. Vol. A) 241, *1024e*.

Niboyet v. *Niboyet*, (1878), 4 P.D. 1; 48 L.J.P. 1; 39 L.T. 486; 43 J.P. 140;
H   11 Digest (Repl.) 469, *1021*.

Ogden v. *Ogden*, [1904-07] All E.R. Rep. 86; [1908] P. 46; 77 L.J.P. 34;
·   97 L.T. 827; 11 Digest (Repl.) 357, *260*.

R. v. *Lolley*, (1812), Russ. & Ry. 237; 11 Digest (Repl.) 486, *1108*.

Robinson-Scott v. *Robinson-Scott*, [1957] 3 All E.R. 473; [1958] P. 71; [1957]
3 W.L.R. 842; Digest (Cont. Vol. A) 246, *1097c*.

I   *Ross* v. *Ellison* (*or Ross*), [1930] A.C. 1; 96 L.J.P.C. 163; 141 L.T. 666;
    11 Digest (Repl.) 335, *81*.

Salvesen (*or Von Lorang*) v. *Austrian Property Administrator*, [1927] All E.R.
Rep. 78; [1927] A.C. 641; 96 L.J.P.C. 105; 137 L.T. 571; 11 Digest
(Repl.) 478, *1069*.

Schibsby v. *Westenholz*, [1861-73] All E.R. Rep. 988; (1870), L.R. 6 Q.B. 155;
40 L.J.Q.B. 73; 24 L.T. 93; 11 Digest (Repl.) 505, *1220*.

Shaw v. *Gould*, (1868), L.R. 3 H.L. 55; 37 L.J.Ch. 433; 18 L.T. 833; 11
Digest (Repl.) 481, *1081*.

Stathatos v. *Stathatos*, [1913] P. 46; 82 L.J.P. 34; 107 L.T. 592; 11 Digest A
    (Repl.) 472, *1039*.

Travers v. *Holley and Holley*, [1953] 2 All E.R. 794; [1953] P. 246; [1953]
    3 W.L.R. 507; Digest (Cont. Vol. A) 240, *1023a*.

Udny v. *Udny*, (1869), L.R. 1 Sc. & Div. 441; 11 Digest (Repl.) 326, *22*.

Wall v. *Wall*, [1949] 2 All E.R. 927; [1950] P. 112; 11 Digest (Repl.) 468, *1020*.

Wilson v. *Wilson*, (1872), L.R. 2 P. & D. 435; 41 L.J.P. & M. 74; 27 L.T. 351; B
    11 Digest (Repl.) 468, *1010*.

Winans v. *A.-G.*, [1904-07] All E.R. Rep. 410; [1904] A.C. 287; 73 L.J.K.B.
    613; 90 L.T. 721; *revsg.* sub nom. *A.-G.* v. *Winans*, (1901), 85 L.T. 508;
    11 Digest (Repl.) 329, *41*.

Appeal.   C

The appellant husband, Rudolph Fransisyck Indyka, and his first wife, Helena
Indyka, who were both Czech nationals domiciled in Czechoslovakia, were
lawfully married there on Jan. 16, 1938. After the German invasion of Czechoslovakia in September, 1938, the appellant joined the Czech army; subsequently
he served with the Polish army in the Middle East and in Italy and came to
England in 1946. He decided to remain in England and acquired in 1946 an
English domicil of choice, which he thereafter retained. The first wife remained   D
resident in Czechoslovakia. On Jan. 18, 1949, the District Court of Ostrava in
Czechoslovakia granted the first wife a decree of divorce on the ground of deep
disruption of marital relations; the decree became final fourteen days later. On
Mar. 20, 1959, the appellant married the respondent, Rose Indyka, at a register
office in the county of Kent. On Aug. 7, 1964, the second wife presented a petition   E
for divorce from the husband on the ground of his cruelty. The husband denied
the alleged cruelty and by his amended answer averred that he was not lawfully
married to the second wife because the decree of Jan. 18, 1949, purporting to
dissolve his marriage to the first wife, was of no effect in England, and that the
first wife was alive at the time of his marriage to the second wife. At the hearing
of the suit on Jan. 27, 1966, it was agreed that the issue in which the validity of   F
the English marriage was in question should be determined first. The trial judge
found (see [1966] 1 All E.R. 781) that the decree of Jan. 18, 1949 was not valid
in English law and rejected the prayer in the second wife's petition, decreeing on
the husband's answer that the English marriage was null and void.

This was an appeal from the judgment of the Court of Appeal (LORD DENNING,
M.R., and DIPLOCK, L.J.; RUSSELL, L.J., dissenting) dated July 13, 1966, and   G
reported [1966] 3 All E.R. 583, whereby the Court of Appeal allowed the second
wife's appeal from an order made on Feb. 4, 1966, by LATEY, J., dismissing her
petition for divorce as previously stated.

D. G. A. Lowe, Q.C., and *B. H. Anns* for the wife.
G. H. Crispin, Q.C., and *M. P. Picard* for the husband.
                                                                               H
Their lordships took time for consideration.

May 23. The following opinions were delivered.

    LORD REID: My Lords, the husband is a citizen of Czechoslovakia. He
married his first wife there in January, 1938. Both were then domiciled there.
On the outbreak of war he joined the Czech army. Later he joined the Polish   I
forces commanded by General Sikorski. At the end of the war he came to England,
was demobilised here and decided to remain in England. He became domiciled
in England in 1946. In 1948 the first wife petitioned for divorce in Czechoslovakia,
where she had resided throughout, and on Jan. 18, 1949 decree of divorce was
granted by the appropriate court of that country on the ground of deep disruption
of marital relations, but on the application of the wife no declaration of guilt was
incorporated in the judgment. It is not disputed that under the law of Czechoslovakia the Czech court had jurisdiction and this was a valid decree of divorce.

A   Some time later the husband heard about this divorce. He believed that it was valid and that he was free to remarry. In 1959 he married the respondent (the second wife) who was an English woman domiciled in England. In 1964 the second wife petitioned for divorce on the ground of cruelty. In his defence the husband, no doubt acting on legal advice, alleged that the Czech divorce was invalid and that, therefore, his second marriage was invalid. LATEY, J., (1)

B   accepted this contention and pronounced decree of nullity of the second marriage. On appeal his decision was reversed by the Court of Appeal (2) (LORD DENNING, M.R., and DIPLOCK, L.J., RUSSELL, L.J., dissenting).

This case raises the general question of the extent of the right or duty of the courts of England to recognise a foreign decree of divorce which is valid in the country where it was pronounced. The essential facts are that when the first wife

C   began proceedings and obtained her decree both she and her husband were, according to our law, domiciled in England. But both were citizens of Czechoslovakia, their home was there after they married until he left it and the wife had resided in that country all her life. It is not clear from the evidence whether jurisdiction under Czech law depended on the nationality of the parties, or the residence of the wife or both, but clearly it had nothing to do with domicil in our

D   sense. The question is whether your lordships are precluded by English law from recognising this foreign decree by the mere fact that at the relevant time the parties were domiciled in England. I accept for the purposes of this case the present doctrine of English law that during the subsistence of a marriage the wife cannot have a domicil different from that of her husband. This rule may (or may not) be " the last barbarous relic of a wife's servitude " (per LORD DENNING, M.R.,

E   in *Formosa* v. *Formosa* (3)), but to alter it might have wide repercussions and I think that this matter had better be left to Parliament.

Inevitably the argument before LATEY, J., (1) and the Court of Appeal (2) turned on the application of the decision in *Travers* v. *Holley and Holley* (4). In my opinion the decision in that case was right, but I think that it must be based on wider grounds than those adopted by the Court of Appeal (4)—on grounds

F   which the operation of the rule stare decisis would have prevented that court from adopting. In that case the spouses married in England and emigrated to New South Wales where the husband acquired a domicil of choice. On the outbreak of war he joined the Australian forces and later transferred to the British army. In 1944 the wife, alleging desertion, was granted decree of divorce in New South Wales. The court here had to decide whether that divorce could

G   be recognised as valid in this country. It was alleged that, before proceedings were begun in New South Wales, the husband had abandoned his domicil of choice and reacquired his English domicil of origin, and that therefore, even if the New South Wales court still had jurisdiction under the law there, we could not recognise the validity of its decree. The Court of Appeal held (4), however, that, even if he had so abandoned his Australian domicil, that did not prevent us from

H   recognising the New South Wales decree.

In order to understand the reason given it is necessary to start from *Le Mesurier* v. *Le Mesurier* (5). The court in *Travers* v. *Holley and Holley* (4) accepted, as they were bound to do, the general proposition that that case established that the domicil of the husband at the time when proceedings are begun is the sole test of jurisdiction for divorce, and that it followed from that that an English

I   court cannot recognise a decree of divorce granted in another country unless the husband was, according to our ideas, domiciled in that country when the proceedings began. The Court of Appeal (6) relied, however, on the fact that Parliament had enacted, by s. 13 of the Matrimonial Causes Act, 1937, that

---

(1) [1966] 1 All E.R. 781.   (2) [1966] 3 All E.R. 583.
(3) [1962] 3 All E.R. 419 at p. 422, letter C; [1963] P. 259 at p. 267.
(4) [1953] 2 All E.R. 794; [1953] P. 246.
(5) [1895-99] All E.R. Rep. 836; [1895] A.C. 517.
(6) [1953] 2 All E.R. at p. 796; [1953] P. at pp. 250, 251.

" Where a wife has been deserted by her husband . . . and the husband was   A
immediately before the desertion . . . domiciled in England and Wales, the
court shall have jurisdiction for the purposes of any proceedings under
Part 8 of the [Supreme Court of Judicature (Consolidation) Act, 1925],
notwithstanding that the husband has changed his domicil since the
desertion . . ."

This Act, of course, did not apply to New South Wales and it made no reference   B
to recognition of foreign divorces; but it so happened that an earlier Act of the
legislature of New South Wales had given to wives deserted there an almost
identical right to petition there. HODSON, L.J., said, referring to the English
Act of 1937, (7):

" It seems to me, therefore, that Parliament has cut the ground from   C
under the argument put forward on behalf of the husband. If English
courts will only recognise foreign decrees of divorce where the parties are
domiciled in the territory of the foreign court at the time of the institutions
of proceedings, because that is the jurisdiction which they themselves claim,
what is the situation when the courts of this country arrogate to themselves
jurisdiction in the case of persons not domiciled here at the material date?   D
It must surely be that what entitles an English court to assume jurisdiction
must be equally effective in the case of a foreign court . . .
" I would say that where, as here, there is in substance reciprocity, it
would be contrary to principle and inconsistent with comity if the courts
of this country were to refuse to recognise a jurisdiction which mutatis
mutandis they claim for themselves. The principle laid down and followed   E
since the *Le Mesurier* case (8) must, I think, be interpreted in the light of
the legislation which has extended the power of the courts of this country
in the case of persons not domiciled here."

SOMERVELL, L.J., dealt briefly with this matter. He said (9):

" On principle it seems to me plain that our courts in this matter should   F
recognise a jurisdiction which they themselves claim. I do not myself really
understand on what grounds it was submitted that the result should be
otherwise."

JENKINS, L.J., had dissented on another point, but he stated his agreement on
this point (10).
Before I comment on these reasons I think that I should trace the subsequent   G
development of the *Travers* v. *Holley and Holley* (11) doctrine. Most of the
subsequent cases arose out of the farther extension of the jurisdiction of the
English courts enacted by the Law Reform (Miscellaneous Provisions) Act, 1949,
which provided in s. 1 (now incorporated in s. 40 of the Matrimonial Causes
Act 1965) that

" The High Court in England shall have jurisdiction in proceedings by a   H
wife for divorce, notwithstanding that the husband is not domiciled in
England, if (*a*) the wife is resident in England and has been ordinarily
resident there for a period of three years immediately preceding the
commencement of the proceedings . . ."

At first there was a tendency to require that the foreign statutory provisions must
within narrow limits correspond with the English statutory provisions if the   I
foreign divorce was to be recognised. The English statutes give no additional
rights to husbands and it was held in *Levett* v. *Levett* (12) that a foreign decree

_____

(7) [1953] 2 All E.R. at p. 800; [1953] P. at pp. 256, 257.
(8) [1895-99] All E.R. Rep. 836; [1895] A.C. 517.
(9) [1953] 2 All E.R. at p. 797, letter A; [1953] P. at p. 251.
(10) [1953] 2 All E.R. at p. 797; [1953] P. at p. 251.
(11) [1953] 2 All E.R. 794; [1953] P. 246.
(12) [1957] 1 All E.R. 720; [1957] P. 156.

A granted to a husband did not come within the scope of the *Travers* v. *Holley and Holley* (13) doctrine. HODSON, L.J., said (14) that this was

"accurately summarised by DAVIES, J., in the later case of *Dunne* v. *Saban* (*formerly Dunne*) (15) as follows: '. . . the observations in *Travers* v. *Holley* (13) decide that this court will recognise the right of [foreign] courts to encroach upon the principle of domicil only to the extent to which this court also does '."

B

Then difficulties arose in cases where the wife had in fact resided for over three years in the country where she obtained a divorce from a husband domiciled elsewhere, but where the courts of that country exercised jurisdiction on some quite different ground from residence of the wife for three years or more, e.g., on the ground of the nationality of the spouses. This problem was solved by
C KARMINSKI, J., in *Robinson-Scott* v. *Robinson-Scott* (16). He said (17):

"I believe that the true question to be answered in this case is whether the courts of this country can recognise a foreign decree where in fact the wife was resident in the territory of the foreign court for three years immediately preceding the commencement of the proceedings there, even though
D the jurisdiction of the foreign court was based on different grounds. In my view this question has not yet been asked or answered by our courts . . . In my view the correct answer to the question which I have asked myself is this: where in fact there has been three years' residence by a wife in the territory of the foreign court assuming jurisdiction in a suit for dissolution, the English court should accept that as a ground for exercising jurisdiction, because it
E would itself accept jurisdiction on proof of similar residence in England."

That has now become recognised in practice as a proper test for recognition of a foreign divorce granted to a wife.

I can now return to consider the reasoning in *Travers* v. *Holley and Holley* (13). In the the first place the English courts did not "arrogate to themselves juris-
F diction in the case of persons not domiciled here ". They were required by Parliament to exercise that jurisdiction. So the argument must be that, whenever Parliament requires the court to exercise a new jurisdiction, it thereby requires or authorises the court to recognise the validity of a farther class of foreign decrees which the courts would not previously have recognised. I find that very difficult to reconcile with the provisions of the Matrimonial Causes (War Marriages)
G Act, 1944. That Act applied (s. 1 (2)) to marriages between a husband domiciled abroad and a wife domiciled in England before the marriage and celebrated between Sept. 3, 1939, and an appointed day, and it conferred on the court jurisdiction in relation to them (s. 1 (1)) " as if both parties were at all material times domiciled in England ". The Act went on to deal with recognition: it provided by s. 4 that a decree granted under its provisions or by virtue of any
H substantially corresponding law in any part of His Majesty's dominions (18) should " by virtue of this Act be recognised in all British courts, whether within or without His Majesty's dominions other than Dominion courts ". Suppose there had been a substantially similar law in a foreign country, or a wife had obtained a decree abroad in circumstances which if they had occurred in England would have given the English court jurisdiction under the Act of 1944, would the doctrine
I of *Travers* v. *Holley* (13) have applied? Or would the fact that the Act expressly required recognition in certain cases exclude recognition in other cases to which

---

(13) [1953] 2 All E.R. 794; [1953] P. 246.
(14) [1957] 1 All E.R. at p. 723, letters A and B; [1957] P. at p. 161.
(15) [1954] 3 All E.R. 586 at p. 592; [1955] P. 178 at p. 190.
(16) [1957] 3 All E.R. 473; [1958] P. 71.
(17) [1957] 3 All E.R. at p. 478; [1958] P. at pp. 87, 88.
(18) Viz., His Majesty's dominions outside the United Kingdom

the doctrine would apply? When the Act of 1944 came to an end (19) and was re- A
placed by s. 1 of the Act of 1949, the latter Act was silent as to recognition. Did
this mean that any limitation as to recognition contained in the Act of 1944
disappeared so as to give full rein to the *Travers* v. *Holley* (20) doctrine, or did
it mean that for the future Parliament did not intend that the extended jurisdiction in the Act of 1949 should be accompanied by any widening of the existing
rules as to recognition of foreign decrees?   B

That, however, is only a minor difficulty. The decision in *Travers* v. *Holley* (20)
was based on reciprocity and comity. Reciprocity appears to me to mean that
we should say—if you will recognise that we have this jurisdiction we will recognise that you have a similar jurisdiction. I do not think that this was ever regarded
as the test and it certainly could not be under the wider *Travers* v. *Holley* (20)
doctrine as stated in the passage which I have quoted from KARMINSKI, J. (21). C
Comity is a word of many meanings, but for several reasons the meaning which
it appears to have in *Travers* v. *Holley* (20) does not appear to me to be a satisfactory basis for recognition. Comity has never been the basis on which we
recognise or give effect to foreign judgments. This was made clear by BLACKBURN,
J., in *Schibsby* v. *Westenholz* (22), where he said:

> " We were much pressed on the argument with the fact that the British   D
> legislature has, by the Common Law Procedure Act, 1852, s. 19 conferred
> on our courts a power of summoning foreigners, under certain circumstances,
> to appear, and, in case they do not, giving judgment against them by default.
> It was this consideration principally which induced me at the trial to enter-
> tain the opinion which I then expressed and have since changed. We think
> that if the principle on which foreign judgments were enforced was that which   E
> is loosely called ' comity ', we could hardly decline to enforce a foreign
> judgment given in France against a resident in Great Britain in circum-
> stances hardly, if at all, distinguishable from those in which we, mutatis
> mutandis, might give judgment against a resident in France; but it is quite
> different if the principle be that which we have just laid down."

The *Travers* v. *Holley* (20) doctrine would not lead to a rational development   F
of the law. Too frequently when Parliament is legislating to remove a particular
injustice the provisions of the Bill are drafted as narrowly as possible to achieve
that result, so that they introduce an anomaly into the existing law rather than
making any general reform. The main reason for this is that such piecemeal
changes can be enacted more speedily with less demands on the time of Parlia-   G
ment than a more general reform would require. Parliament has in mind only
the particular circumstances in this country, and it would be quite unrealistic
to suppose that when Parliament entrusts a new jurisdiction to our courts it
has any intention to affect our rules for the recognition of foreign judgments.
With rare exceptions Parliament has left the courts free to develop those rules,
and I see no reason why, by adopting the doctrine of *Travers* v. *Holley* (20) we   H
should tie that development to what Parliament has done with quite a different
object in view.

To adopt this doctrine with regard to the Act of 1949 would, in my view, lead
to very undesirable consequences. The Act of 1949 entitles any wife who has
resided here for three years to sue for divorce. An Italian or a citizen of the
Republic of Ireland may come to this country accompanied by his wife to take   I
up a three or four years' appointment, there being no question of their acquiring
an English domicil or even making their home here. If the husband commits a

(19) The Act has not been repealed, but by s. 1 (4) of the Act of 1949 the issues in
any proceedings in which the court has jurisdiction by virtue of s. 1 of the Act of 1944
are to be determined in accordance with the law which would be applicable thereto
if both parties were domiciled in England at the time of the proceeding.
(20) [1953] 2 All E.R. 794; [1953] P. 246.
(21) [1957] 3 All E.R. at p. 478, letter D; [1958] P. at pp. 87, 88.
(22) [1861-73] All E.R. Rep. 988 at p. 991; (1870), L.R. 6 Q.B. 155 at p. 159.

A matrimonial offence the wife can petition for divorce as soon as she has resided here for three years. Probably Parliament never really intended such a result but it is the necessary result of the terms of the Act. This hardly accords with comity in any sense, and it creates what has come to be known as a " limping marriage ", because such a decree of the English court would rightly be refused recognition in the country of their nationality and domicil. It might have to be B recognised in Scotland because the courts of one part of the United Kingdom could hardly refuse to recognise something done in another part of the United Kingdom in the exercise of a power given by the Parliament of the United Kingdom. But other countries would be free to disregard it and probably many would refuse to recognise it. Then take the converse case. An Englishman accompanied by his wife takes a three years' appointment in one of the hundred C odd countries of the United Nations where divorce is granted on some flimsy pretext or perhaps merely on request, but they have no intention of making their home there. If the wife, after residing there for three years, gets such a divorce are the English courts really to be bound to recognise its validity? I can see no answer to that if we accept the *Travers* v. *Holley* (23) doctrine as it is at present being applied; and the result would be the same if an English wife went to such a D country, for the purpose of getting a divorce, resided there for three years, perhaps obtaining employment there, and then returned here with her decree. So I propose to consider whether there is not some more satisfactory basis for supporting the decision in *Travers* v. *Holley* (23) and the cases which have followed on it.

The main obstacle is the ratio of *Le Mesurier's* (24) case; but before dealing E with that, it may be of assistance to look at the position before that case was decided. In England domicil had never been the ground of jurisdiction of the ecclesiastical courts in cases of nullity, divorce a mensa et thoro or other matters. This depended on residence or on the place of celebration of the marriage. In Scotland, where divorce a vinculo has been competent since the reformation, the grounds of jurisdiction were much the same. Domicil was brought in to solve F the conflict between the English and Scots' courts with regard to marriages celebrated in England. The English courts tended to regard them as indissoluble by any court anywhere: the Scots' courts held that a short residence in Scotland was sufficient to give them jurisdiction to dissolve any marriage. *Shaw* v. *Gould* (25) decided that the English courts would not recognise a Scots' divorce when the residence in Scotland did not involve the acquisition of a Scots' domicil. I do not G think that this was a far reaching decision, but Lord Westbury's observations are important. He referred to (26):

">. . . such a sentence as by the comity of nations (that is by the general principles of jurisprudence which are recognised by the Christian states of Europe) has an extra territorial effect and authority."

H Later he referred to (27):

">. . . the best established rules of universal jurisprudence, that is to say . . . those rules which, for the sake of general convenience and by tacit consent, are received by Christian nations and observed in their tribunals. One of these rules certainly is, that questions of personal status depend on the law of the actual domicil."

I Then after quoting Rodenburg he said (27):

">" This position, that universum jus, that is, jurisdiction which is complete and ought to be everywhere recognised, does, in all matters touching the

---

(23) [1953] 2 All E.R. 794; [1953] P. 246.
(24) [1895-99] All E.R. Rep. 836; [1895] A.C. 517.
(25) (1868), L.R. 3 H.L. 55.
(26) (1868), L.R. 3 H.L. at p. 81   (27) (1868), L.R. 3 H.L. at p. 82.

personal status or condition of persons, belong to the judge of that country   **A**
where the persons are domiciled, has been generally recognised."

I am afraid that these observations required qualification in several respects.
In the first place it is clear from the whole passage that the jurists whom he
quotes were using domicil in the sense of habitual residence and not in the stricter
sense in which it has been interpreted by more recent decisions of this House. I
do not know whether these jurists dealt with the case of a wife separated from   **B**
her husband and living in a different state; but our reports show that it was at
one time commonly thought that, as it was a wife's duty always to be with her
husband, she could not be heard to say that she resided elsewhere (even if that
involved no fault on her part) and thereby spoil the symmetry of the law. Even
as regards English law, LORD WESTBURY can hardly have thought that all questions involving status, e.g. nullity, must be decided by the court of the domicil.   **C**
More important, however, LORD WESTBURY has ignored the notorious fact that
at least the older jurists were much more inclined to state the law as they thought
it ought to be than to investigate the law as it was in fact administered in the
very numerous states or jurisdictions into which Christian Europe was then
divided: any such investigation would have been laborious and might have been
impracticable. I think that I am right in saying that by 1868 nationality had   **D**
become more important than domicil in many of these jurisdictions; but much
weight was clearly given to LORD WESTBURY'S observations (28) by the Board
which decided *Le Mesurier's* case (29).

The statute which gave to the English court jurisdiction to decree divorce
a vinculo made no reference to domicil and for a considerable time it remained
doubtful whether domicil in England was essential. The arguments either way   **E**
were developed in *Niboyet* v. *Niboyet* (30) where by a majority the Court of Appeal
held that residence was sufficient. JAMES, L.J., said (31):

" I do not think that I am overruling any English case . . . in laying down
that where and while the matrimonial home is English, and the wrong is
done here, then the English jurisdiction exists and the English law ought to   **F**
be applied."

He had said earlier (32):

" It would be very desirable no doubt that a judicial decree of dissolution
of a marriage affecting the status of husband and wife, a decree in rem, should
be if possible recognised by the courts of every other country according to the
principles of international comity. But is such a result possible? Would any   **G**
French court recognise the dissolution of a French marriage because the
French husband had been minded to establish his domicil in England? "

The dissenting judgment of BRETT, L.J. (31), is important and it illustrates some
of the difficulties involved if domicil is to be the only ground of jurisdiction.
He said (33):   **H**

" By the universal independence of nations each binds by its personal
law its natural born subjects and all who may become its subjects. By
the universal consent of nations everyone who elects to become domiciled in
a country is bound by the laws of that country, so long as he remains
domiciled in it, as if he were a natural born subject of it."

I do not know where he found this universal consent, but that would not be   **I**
sufficient for this purpose. If domicil being the sole test of jurisdiction is to be
founded on international consensus, it would be necessary to add that by universal
consent each nation ceases to hold bound by its personal law any of its natural

---

(28) (1868), L.R. 3 H.L. at pp. 81, 83.
(29) [1895-99] All E.R. Rep. 836; [1895] A.C. 517.
(30) (1878), 4 P.D. 1.   (31) (1878), 4 P.D. at p. 9.
(32) (1878), 4 P.D. at p. 8,   (33) (1878), 4 P.D. at p. 12.

A born subjects who chooses to become domiciled in another country. But that
BRETT, L.J., did not and could not say. Then he said (34):

  " The status of marriage is the legal position of the married person as such
  in the community or in relation to the community. Which community is it
  which is interested in such relation? None other than the community of which
  he is a member, that is the community with which he is living as a part of it
B . . . That is the community in which he is living at home with intent that
  among or in it should be the home of his married life. But that is the place of
  of his domicil."

But by the law of England the " home of his married life " is not the domicil
of a native of another country, unless

C   " prolonged residence in England was accompanied by an intention . . .
  to choose England as his permanent home in preference to the country of his
  birth. The law requires evidence of volition to change."

(per LORD MACMILLAN in *Bowie (or Ramsay)* v. *Liverpool Royal Infirmary* (35)).
Then BRETT, L.J., saw the difficulty if the husband leaves his wife in the home of
his married life and acquires another domicil. He said (36):

D   " The case of an adulterous husband deserting his wife by leaving the
  country of his domicil and assuming to domicil himself in another might
  seem to raise an intolerable injustice; but we cannot help thinking that
  in such a case, if sued by his wife in the country in which he had left her, he
  could not be heard to allege that that was not still the place of his married
  home, i.e. for the purpose of that suit, of his domicil."
E
Nevertheless, by an application of the case of *Le Mesurier* (37) a husband (or
rather the King's Proctor) was in fact heard to allege just that. Then BRETT,
L.J. (36), prayed in aid American authority without noticing that there the wife
can have a separate domicil for divorce; and his theory led him to say (38) that
the rule for judicial separation must be the same as the rule for divorce.
F I can now come to *Le Mesurier's* case (37). The husband, a member of the
Ceylon Civil Service, resided in Ceylon and had his matrimonial home there,
but he was not domiciled there. The Ceylon court held that they had no jurisdiction to entertain his petition for divorce and he appealed to the Privy Council.
LORD WATSON, giving the judgment of the Board, said (39):

  " It is not doubtful that there may be residence without domicil sufficient
G to sustain a suit for restitution of conjugal rights, for separation, or for
  aliment; but it does not follow that such residence must also give jurisdiction
  to dissolve the marriage."

Then he rejected the Scottish view that there could be a matrimonial domicil
short of domicil in the full sense partly on the ground that it was not precisely
defined. I am bound to say, however, that I would in many cases find it easier
H to say what amounted to a matrimonial home than to say whether there was
that animus manendi necessary to create a domicil of choice. Then he dealt
with the view of various jurists and included (40) a quotation from BAR (41):

  " A decree of divorce therefore, pronounced by any other judge than a
  judge of the domicil or nationality, is to be regarded in all other countries as
I inoperative."

Unfortunately the words " or nationality " appear to have escaped the notice

(34) (1878), 4 P.D. at p. 13.
(35) [1930] All E.R. Rep. 127 at p. 132; [1930] A.C. 588 at p. 598.
(36) (1878), 4 P.D. at p. 14.   (37) [1895-99] All E.R. Rep. 836; [1895] A.C. 517.
(38) (1878), 4 P.D. at p. 19.
(39) [1895-99] All E.R. Rep. at p. 842; [1895] A.C. at p. 531.
(40) Section 173 GILLESPIE'S TRANSLATION, p. 382.
(41) [1895-99] All E.R. Rep. at p. 845; [1895] A.C. at p. 538.

of their lordships. Then having referred to the leading English authorities A
LORD WATSON said (42):

" Their lordships have in these circumstances, and upon these considerations, come to the conclusion that, according to international law, the domicil
for the time being of the married pair affords the only true test of jurisdiction
to dissolve their marriage."

Then he quoted (42) a passage from the judgment of LORD PENZANCE in *Wilson* v. B
Wilson (43):

" Different communities have different views and laws respecting matrimonial obligations, and a different estimate of the causes which should justify
divorce. It is both just and reasonable, therefore, that the differences of
married people should be adjusted in accordance with the laws of the com- C
munity to which they belong, and dealt with by the tribunals which alone
can administer those laws. An honest adherence to this principle, moreover,
will preclude the scandal which arises when a man and woman are held to be
man and wife in one country and strangers in another."

My first comment is that, although the English courts honestly adhered to that
principle until Parliament had to intervene, that did not in fact preclude the D
scandal of limping marriages; and the reason is not far to seek. From the wording
of the judgment it seems to me that in laying down this test their lordships must
have thought that they were keeping in line with the practice in other civilised
countries; but in fact they were not. Their view has been followed in the Commonwealth, but so far as I know nowhere else. So far as I have any knowledge
of the matter the position appears to be (and to have been in 1895) that most E
European countries attach more importance to nationality or sometimes residence, and in the United States most if not all the states by permitting the wife
to have a separate domicil for this purpose do not regard the court of the
husband's domicil as the only court which has jurisdiction. But I would find it
surprising if their lordships really thought that they were keeping in line with other
countries. It is just possible that they were actuated by the hope, common F
in Victorian times, that if England showed the way others would see the light
and follow: if so, any such hope has been grievously disappointed.

That this decision has had most unfortunate consequences can hardly be denied.
Parliament has found it necessary to encroach on it on many occasions. It was
enacted by the Matrimonial Causes (Dominion Troops) Act, 1919, that where a
marriage was contracted during the war by a member of H.M. Forces domiciled G
in any of His Majesty's dominions the court in that part of the United Kingdom
where the marriage took place should have jurisdiction. Then in *Keyes* v. *Keyes
and Gray* (44), it was held that the courts in India had no jurisdiction to grant
divorce to persons resident but not domiciled there, although such divorces
had been regularly granted there for fifty years: and again Parliament had
immediately to put this right by the Indian Divorces (Validity) Act, 1921, which H
was followed by the Indian and Colonial Divorce Jurisdiction Act, 1926. Then
in *Herd* v. *Herd* (45), where a husband domiciled here had left his wife and acquired
a domicil of choice in America, it was held that the English court had no jurisdiction to entertain her petition for divorce; and that had to be put right by
the Act of 1937 to which I have already referred. Then during the last war it
was found necessary to pass the Act of 1944 to which I have already referred and I
later to replace it by the Act of 1949.

There must surely be something wrong with a rule which has required such
frequent remedial intervention by Parliament; but can we do anything about
it? I think that we can and should. It is true that it has frequently been approved

---

(42) [1895-99] All E.R. Rep. at p. 847; [1895] A.C. at p. 540.
(43) (1872), L.R. 2 P. & D. 435 at p. 442.
(44) [1921] P. 204.
(45) [1936] 2 All E.R. 1516; [1936] P. 205.

A in this House, and, but for these interventions by Parliament, I should have great doubt whether it would be proper for this House sitting judicially to depart from it; but I would draw a distinction between the rules which govern the jurisdiction of our courts and the rules which determine the extent to which we should recognise foreign decrees. The former are statutory; although the Matrimonial Causes Act, 1857 did not mention domicil, the later Acts are all drafted on the **B** assumption that domicil was the only ground of jurisdiction under it. Obviously we cannot revise an Act of Parliament: the most that we can do is to suggest matters which might be borne in mind when an amending Bill is being drafted and passed. But Parliament has rarely intervened in the matter of recognition of foreign matrimonial decrees. The existing law is judge-made and I see no reason why that process should stop. I do not attach great importance to the fact **C** that *Le Mesurier* (46), was dealing with jurisdiction and not recognition, because I think that their lordships must have intended their rule to apply to both, and I think that it has commonly been accepted as applying to both.

The essence of the rule in *Le Mesurier* (46) is that there should be only one test, and only one court with jurisdiction to apply it, and the purpose was to avoid limping marriages. That essence has been permanently destroyed by **D** Parliament and that purpose was never achieved. There are now two general grounds of jurisdiction in this country—domicil and residence of the wife irrespective of any domicil which she has or ever had. So I see nothing to prevent our adding additional ground for recognition besides domicil. But the common law has not been built up by judges making general pronouncements: it has been built by the rational expansion of what already exists in order to do justice in particular **E** cases.

When we apply our test of domicil at present we neither recognise the validity of the ground on which the foreign court had jurisdiction under its law, nor do we pay any heed to the ground on which that court granted decree of divorce. What we do is to make our own investigation into the facts to see whether, according to our law, the husband was domiciled within the jurisdiction of the **F** foreign court. If he was, we recognise the decree no matter on what ground that court claimed to have jurisdiction and no matter on what ground the decree was granted. If he was not, we refuse to recognise the decree. I would not in general depart from that method of approach. It would be most invidious if we were to say that we approve of some of the grounds on which foreign courts claim jurisdiction but do not approve of others, or if we were to say that we approve of some **G** of the grounds on which they decree divorce but do not approve of others. Moreover I would certainly not be in favour of recognising as valid all the various grounds on which foreign countries claim jurisdiction, still less all the various grounds on which they grant divorces. Parliament has power to do that if ever it should desire to do so, but I would not think it proper for the courts to do it.

I can see no difficulty in making one comparatively small change, because **H** some English authorities and present Scottish practice both point in that direction. I have already quoted the passage from the judgment of Brett, L.J., in *Niboyet* (47) where he states his view that a husband who leaves his wife could not deprive her of her remedy by then acquiring another domicil; and it appears from what is said in *Herd's* case (48) that the English courts were applying that rule until they were stopped by a too loyal adherence to the ratio in *Le Mesurier* (46). Moreover **I** that rule is of ancient origin in Scotland. Two centuries ago Erskine wrote (Inst. I. 6. 44):

" Action might perhaps be sustained at the suit of the innocent party against the deserter, though not residing in this Kingdom, upon evidence adduced that the desertion was wilful, and that the defender left the kingdom,

---

(46) [1895-99] All E.R. Rep. 836; [1895] A.C. 517.
(47) (1878), 4 P.D. at p. 14.   (48) [1926] 2 All E.R. 1516; [1926] P. 205.

and still remains abroad, from a deliberate purpose of abandoning the   **A**
conjugal society, lest such wrong should be left without a remedy."

That view has been accepted and the existing law is stated in WALTON, HUSBAND
AND WIFE (3rd Edn.) p. 384:

" It is a matter of daily practice that divorce for desertion is granted
when the facts point to the husband having gone abroad animo manendi.
There are dicta to the effect that the same rule applies when the husband   **B**
has been guilty of adultery in Scotland and has afterwards abandoned his
Scottish domicil."

Le Mesurier's case (49) has not been held in Scotland to prevent that practice
from continuing and therefore it has not been thought necessary to enact for
Scotland a counterpart of s. 13 of the Act of 1937. So it would seem proper at   **C**
least to hold that, where a husband leaves his wife in the matrimonial domicil
and she has by the law of that country a right to obtain a divorce which accrued
before he changed his domicil but only sues for 'and obtains her divorce thereafter,
we ought to disregard that change of domicil and recognise the foreign decree.

Nevertheless I think that we must go farther than that. First, with regard to
residence there are many references in English and Scots' authorities to the   **D**
matrimonial home, and matrimonial domicil, and the community with which the
spouses are most closely connected, and with all respect to the Board in *Le
Mesurier* (49) I do not think that there would often be any real difficulty in
determining where the spouses' matrimonial home was or with what community
they were most closely associated. There may, of course, be cases where they
have never settled down anywhere: even if intending to reside in a particular   **E**
place for some considerable time they may abstain from associating themselves
in any way with the community there and remain nomads. Everyone must have
a domicil, but not everyone has a real home. In such cases we would have to fall
back on domicil. It would be quite wrong to exclude domicil as a test, but, once
we get rid of the idea that there can only be one test and that there can never be
jurisdiction in more than one court, it seems to me to be very much in the public   **F**
interest that there should be some other test besides that of domicil. If a man of
English origin goes to another country and intends if possible to remain there for
his working life, it seems to me to be quite wrong that the question whether the
English court or the court of that other country has jurisdiction to dissolve his
marriage should depend on the difficult question whether he does or does not
intend to return to England when he retires. He may not know himself; and if   **G**
proceedings are raised by his wife, she may be still less able to supply the answer.
Indeed if he has left her she may not know where he is, let alone whether he has
acquired some new domicil. On the other hand, it does not seem right that if the
spouses go to a country where divorce is easy, intending to stay there for only
a few years and then to return home, either spouse should be entitled to take
advantage of their short stay to obtain a divorce on trivial grounds.   **H**

I think that the need would best be met by reviving the old conception of the
matrimonial home and by holding that, if the court where that home is grants
decree of divorce, we should recognise that decree. In this matter I can see no
good reason for making any distinction between the husband and the wife. If we
recognise a decree granted to the one, we ought equally to recognise a decree
granted to the other; but if the husband leaves the matrimonial home and the   **I**
wife remains within the same jurisdiction I think that we should recognise a
decree granted to her by the court of that jurisdiction. I find much more difficulty
in accepting the view that if a wife parts from her husband and goes to live by
herself in a new jurisdiction, her residence there, whether for three years or any
other period, must necessarily be accepted as sufficient to require us to recognise
a decree granted to her. It would certainly be reasonable that, where such a wife

(49) [1895-99] All E.R. Rep. 836; [1895] A.C. 517.

A is habitually resident within that jurisdiction and has no present intention of
leaving it, we should recognise a decree granted to her there; but I do not wish
to go farther than that without fuller consideration in an appropriate case.
 There is one other matter which I should mention and which may require
consideration by the legislature or by the courts. In many countries jurisdiction
depends on nationality, indeed one might almost say that in half the world domicil
B in one form or another prevails and in the other half nationality. If they are to
live in peaceful co-existence it may be necessary to take note of this, and then
it may be necessary to extend some protection to a wife who retains British
nationality on marrying a foreigner and to foreigners who come under the
protection of our law by establishing their home here; but on these questions I
prefer to express no opinion.
C Finally, it is well recognised that we ought not to alter what is presently understood to be the law if that involves any real likelihood of injustice to people who
have relied on the present position in arranging their affairs. But I have been
unable to think of any case, and counsel have been unable to suggest any case,
where such injustice would result from what I have invited your lordships to
accept.
D I would dismiss this appeal on the grounds that the Czech decree dissolving
the husband's first marriage ought to be recognised as valid because the first wife
to whom it was granted had had her matrimonial home in Czechoslovakia and
had continued to reside there after her husband left, and that the fact that he
acquired a domicil of choice in England before the wife raised proceedings in her
country does not prevent that recognition.

E
 LORD MORRIS OF BORTH-Y-GEST: My Lords, though the legislature has from time to time since 1857 defined and specified the grounds on which
our courts will decree a dissolution of marriage, it has in the main, though subject
to certain relatively recent statutory enactments, been left to the courts to decide
the basis on which they will undertake jurisdiction. It has largely been left to
F the courts to decide whether and when decrees of dissolution granted in the courts
of other countries will here be recognised. A problem as to recognition has arisen
in the present case. The persons affected may for convenience be referred to as
the husband, the first wife and the second wife. The appellant husband believing
himself to be free to marry, " married " the respondent (his second wife) on
Mar. 20, 1959. They lived together. She asserts that he treated her with cruelty
G and, by a petition dated Aug. 7, 1964, prayed for dissolution by reason of it. The
husband by his answer dated Nov. 24, 1964, denied the charge. Then some time
later (on June 18, 1965), he amended his answer by saying that he was never
married to the second wife at all. He said that the first wife, a Czech lady, whom
he had married in Czechoslovakia on Jan. 16, 1938, was still alive and that a
decree of dissolution which she had obtained in Czechoslovakia on Jan. 18, 1949,
H was invalid and was of no effect in England because on the latter date he was
domiciled in England. He prayed that it might be declared that his marriage to
the second wife was null and void. LATEY, J., (50) held him entitled to a decree
so declaring. The cruelty allegations were not heard. On appeal the Court of
Appeal (51) by a majority set aside the order of the learned judge but gave leave
to appeal to your lordships' house.
I The question as to the validity of the " marriage " between the husband and
the second wife calls, therefore, for a decision as to whether the decree of Jan. 18,
1949, should here be recognised. If it should, then the wife's petition of Aug. 7,
1964, can eventually be heard. If it should not, then the wife has no marriage to
seek to dissolve.
 After hearing evidence the judge (50) held that the Czech decree was valid
according to Czech law and became final fourteen days after Jan. 18, 1949. The

decree recorded that the parties had married on Jan. 16, 1938, and that the first **A**
wife (who was the petitioner) was a Czechoslovak citizen. She sought her decree
on the grounds of " deep disruption of marital relations " caused, according to
her allegation, by the fact that the husband had left her on Sept. 1, 1939, and had
not returned to her since that date and had not shown any interest in her and was
at the time of her petition of unknown abode. She did not apply for his guilt to
be declared in the judgment of the court. Evidence was given that he had left **B**
her on Sept. 1, 1939, and had not since then sent any news. The decree recorded:

" As follows from the facts established, obviously no marital union has
existed between the parties for more than nine years, during which time the
[husband] has expressed no intention of preserving the marital union and of
carrying out the obligations imposed on him by s. 91 and s. 92 of the Marriage
Law. He has not given the [first wife] any news regarding himself and does **C**
not show any interest in her."

There was evidence before the English court that the Czech courts assume
jurisdiction to dissolve decrees on the basis of the parties being Czechoslovakian
citizens. The husband was not heard by the Czech court and the decree recited
that his abode was unknown. (It was, however, expressly stated in the present **D**
proceedings that no point was being taken that the Czech decree lacked validity
because the husband was not served.) The Czech court appointed a curator to
represent the husband. The husband's evidence in the English court was that he
learned of the Czech decree subsequent to its making: his mother (who was in
Czechoslovakia) telephoned him and told him about it.

In the English court the husband gave evidence, but neither party adduced **E**
evidence from the first wife. The judge held that the husband had joined the
Czech army when Czechoslovakia was invaded and that, on the occupation of
that country, he with many others had crossed the border into Poland and served
with the Polish army: that he was captured by the Russians and imprisoned in
Siberia until he was released to serve with the Polish army under General Sikorski:
that he served in the Middle East and in Italy and came to England in 1946. **F**
LATEY, J., held as follows (52):

" Throughout these years he was anxious, but unable, to communicate
with the first wife. On arrival in England, he was offered the choice of
returning to Czechoslovakia or remaining in England. He was still domiciled
in Czechoslovakia. He chose to remain and settle in England where he has
stayed ever since. There is no dispute that, by so doing, he acquired a **G**
domicil of choice in England in 1946, and that he has remained domiciled
here ever since. I so find."

LATEY, J., further held as follows (53):

" Neither party has adduced evidence from the first wife in person or by
affidavit or statement. I do not say that in any way critically, for one knows **H**
the serious practical difficulties. I accept, however, as wholly honest and
reliable the husband's evidence that he wanted to be reunited with the first
wife in 1946, that he wrote suggesting either that she join him in England or
that he join her in Czechoslovakia, and that she wrote saying that she would
not live with him again, that she had thought him dead and that she had
someone else with whom she was living and by whom she had a child. He did **I**
not desert his first wife. On the contrary I am satisfied that she deserted
him."

It appears, therefore, that on the findings of fact in the English court the findings
of the Czech court were incorrect. Nevertheless, the Czech decree was a good
decree by Czech law. The ground on which it was given, i.e., " deep disruption
of marital relations ", though one not recognised by English law, and though

(52) [1966] 1 All E.R. at p. 782, letter F.
(53) [1966] 1 All E.R. at p. 782, letter H.

A not supported by any " declaration of guilt ", was a sufficient ground. It is, however, a somewhat disturbing circumstance that the Czech court, hearing only the first wife, accepted her version of the facts while the English court, hearing only the husband, accepted his version of the facts. Each version contradicted the other.

The learned judge was bound by the decision in *Travers* v. *Holley and Holley*
B (54) and he proceeded to consider whether he could apply it. The husband was domiciled in Czechoslovakia until 1946. He then acquired a domicil of choice in England. Could it be said that he then deserted his first wife in Czechoslovakia so that, had there been jurisdiction in the Czech court, comparable to that laid down by s. 13 of the Matrimonial Causes Act, 1937, she could have entertained a suit for dissolution? On the findings of fact of the English court that could not be
C said. On an application of the principle adopted in *Travers* v. *Holley* (54) the judge would, however, have recognised the Czech decree on the basis that the wife had residence for over three years in Czechoslovakia, save for the fact that the decree was made in the early part of 1949 whereas the Law Reform (Miscellaneous Provisions) Act, 1949, was not enacted until Dec. 16, 1949.

The immediate question which is raised in the appeal is whether the Czech
D decree should be recognised. Various issues present themselves for consideration. Is the principle of *Travers* v. *Holley* (54) to be upheld? If it is, can the Czech decree be recognised on an application of it? Can the decree be recognised on some broader principles and how should they be stated?

Subject to certain exceptions made by statute the basis on which the English courts assume jurisdiction in proceedings for divorce is that of domicil. This has
E been the result of judicial decisions. Over many years there was some vacillation, but in the end the test of domicil as the basis for jurisdiction came to be accepted. The law might have developed quite differently. The views of the majority in the Court of Appeal in *Niboyet* v. *Niboyet* (55) might have prevailed; but since the case of *Le Mesurier* v. *Le Mesurier* (56) the test of domicil has prevailed. Thus in *Salvesen (or von Larang)* v. *Austrian Property Administrator* (57) LORD
F PHILLIMORE stated clearly in his speech (58) that the law of England recognises the competence and the exclusive competence of the court of the domicil to decree dissolution of a marriage, or, as LORD HALDANE expressed it (59), " the court of the domicil is the true court of jurisdiction ". Other matters have likewise been the result of judicial decision. The courts have laid down what is meant by domicil: see *Winans* v. *A.-G.* (60); *Ross* v. *Ellison (or Ross)* (61); *Bowie (or*
G *Ramsay)* v. *Liverpool Royal Infirmary* (62). So have they decided that a wife takes her husband's domicil and cannot have a separate domicil of her own.

Although it was as a result of judicial pronouncements that the principle of domicil was recognised as the basis of jurisdiction, implied statutory recognition of this has followed. Thus domicil was mentioned in the Matrimonial Causes (Dominions Troops) Act, 1919, and when by s. 13 of the Matrimonial Causes Act,
H 1937 (now s. 40 (1) of the Matrimonial Causes Act 1965) provision was being made to assist deserted wives, the court was given jurisdiction to entertain certain proceedings by a wife, " notwithstanding that the husband is not domiciled in England ", if she has been deserted by him or if he has been deported from the United Kingdom, provided that he was domiciled in England immediately before the desertion or deportation. So also when s. 1 of the Law Reform (Miscellaneous
I Provisions) Act, 1949, was enacted (now s. 40 (1) (*b*) of the Act of 1965) the court was given jurisdiction to entertain certain proceedings (for divorce or nullity of

----

(54) [1953] 2 All E.R. 794; [1953] P. 246.   (55) (1878), 4 P.D. 1.
(56) [1895-99] All E.R. Rep. 836; [1895] A.C. 517.
(57) [1927] All E.R. Rep. 78; [1927] A.C. 641.
(58) [1927] All E.R. Rep. at pp. 87, 88; [1927] A.C. at p. 665.
(59) [1927] All E.R. Rep. at p. 82; [1927] A.C. at p. 654.
(60) [1904-07] All E.R. Rep. 410; [1904] A.C. 287.
(61) [1930] A.C. 1.   (62) [1930] All E.R. Rep. 127; [1930] A.C. 588.

marriage) by a wife notwithstanding that the husband is not domiciled in England, **A** if she is resident in England and has resided in England for a period of three years immediately preceding the commencement of the proceedings (provided that the husband is not domiciled in any other part of the United Kingdom or in the Channel Islands or the Isle of Man).

All this shows, and the express statutory exceptions only serve to emphasise, that the principle is firmly embedded in English law that jurisdiction to entertain **B** divorce proceedings is founded on domicil. The present case is, however, concerned only with questions of recognition of foreign decrees. In this field there have been some statutory provisions and many judicial decisions. It is too late, in my view, to urge that recognition should be limited to cases where by statute provision is made for it. So also it is, in my view, too late to urge that recognition of a foreign decree should in any event and, apart from other considerations, be limited to **C** cases where such decrees have been based on grounds which are grounds for a decree of dissolution in this country. Recognition should, however, always be subject to the proviso that the foreign decree is not vitiated by fraud nor contrary to natural justice (compare *Lepre* v. *Lepre* (63)). In his speech in *Salvesen's* case (64) LORD HALDANE said (65):

"Our courts, . . . never inquire whether a competent foreign court has **D** exercised its jurisdiction improperly, provided that no substantial injustice according to our notions has been committed."

It has followed from the acceptance of domicil as the basis for assuming jurisdiction in England that, if a husband and wife are domiciled in another country and if there is a decree of divorce in that country, it will here be recognised. There has been no insistence that the grounds for a decree in the other country should **E** conform or correspond to those laid down in England (see *Bater* v. *Bater* (66)). The principle underlying such recognition may have been that it was felt that confidence could be reposed in courts that acted and proceeded in like manner as the English courts and whose conceptions were in accord with those of the English courts. Faith in the dominance of the domicil principle was shown in the decision **F** in *Armitage* v. *A.-G.*, *Gillig* v. *Gillig* (67), where it was held that a decree obtained elsewhere than in the country of the domicil of the parties would be recognised if it would be recognised by the court of the country where the parties were domiciled at the time of the proceedings. No separate domicil in a wife would, however, be recognised (*Lord Advocate* v. *Jaffrey* (68) and *A.-G. for Alberta* v. *Cook* (69)).

If there was some underlying principle or notion that, where other countries **G** based their jurisdiction in the same way as did England, their decrees should be recognised, then the views expressed in *Travers* v. *Holley* (70) would seem to follow quite naturally. Ever since 1899 it had been the law in New South Wales that a deserted wife who was domiciled in New South Wales when the desertion began should not be deemed to have lost her domicil by reason only of her husband having thereafter acquired a new foreign domicil. After the enactment **H** in England of s. 13 of the Act of 1937 why should the English court not recognise a jurisdiction which, mutatis mutandis, they claim for themselves?

In his powerful judgment in *Fenton* v. *Fenton* (71) O'BRYAN, J., takes the point (72) that in the years before 1895 (when *Le Mesurier's* case (73) was decided), though the English courts were assuming jurisdiction on the basis of what was regarded as the matrimonial domicil of the parties, they were insisting that **I**

---

(63) [1963] 2 All E.R. 49; [1965] P. 52.
(64) [1927] All E.R. Rep. 78; [1927] A.C. 641.
(65) [1927] All E.R. Rep. at p. 85; [1927] A.C. at p. 659.
(66) [1906] P. 209.   (67) [1906] P. 135.
(68) [1920] All E.R. Rep. 242; [1921] 1 A.C. 146.
(69) [1926] All E.R. Rep. 525; [1926] A.C. 444.
(70) [1953] 2 All E.R. 794; [1953] P. 246.   (71) [1957] V.L.R. 17.
(72) [1957] V.L.R. at p. 19.   (73) [1895-99] All E.R. Rep. 836; [1895] A.C. 517.

A   foreign decrees would only be recognised if granted by a country where the parties had in a strict sense their domicil. The courts were proceeding on the basis that certain " rules of universal jurisprudence " were established, pursuant to which question of personal status depended on the law of the " actual domicil ". Lord Watson in his judgment in *Le Mesurier* (74) followed what had been said in 1868 in the case of *Shaw* v. *Gould* (75), that a decree of a foreign

B   tribunal would be valid if the parties were domiciled within its jurisdiction. In *Shaw* v. *Gould* (75) Lord Westbury referred to (76) the " comity of nations " in terms of being " the general principles of jurisprudence which are recognised by the Christian states of Europe ". Again (77) in referring to

     " those rules which, for the sake of general convenience and by tacit consent are received by Christian nations and observed in their tribunals "

C

he said (77) that included in such rules " certainly is, that questions of personal status depend on the law of the actual domicil ".

    If, however, the view of English law was established by 1895 and continued thereafter to be that only domicil (by the law of which status is determined) could be the foundation for assuming divorce jurisdiction, with the corollary that

D   there could be recognition of a foreign decree if the domicil of the husband (and, therefore, of the wife) was in the foreign country, it seems to me that a vital change was made when the basis for assuming jurisdiction was altered. Even if the decision in *Travers* v. *Holley* (78) was new law, I would consider that it was both reasonable and desirable. If a deserted wife may obtain a decree in England under the conditions laid down in 1937 (and now contained in s. 40 (1) (*a*) of the

E   Act of 1965) it seems to me to be reasonable to recognise a decree granted in another country in the exercise of a comparable jurisdiction. So also if jurisdiction is exercised in England on the basis of three years' residence by a wife if the conditions of s. 40 (1) (*b*) are satisfied, it seems to me to be reasonable to recognise a decree granted to a wife in another country that accepts jurisdiction in similar circumstances. These significant statutory exceptions to the rules which

F   previously adhered so closely to domicil as the basis and the only basis for jurisdiction would seem to justify, if not to require, recognition of decrees of dissolution granted in another country in the exercise of a jurisdiction similar to or, I would say, substantially similar to, that exercised by the court in England. I would, therefore, approve the decision in *Travers* v. *Holley* (78). Nor do I see any reason why after the passing of the Law Reform (Miscellaneous Provisions) Act, 1949,

G   our courts should not recognise the decree of the Czech court on the basis that though made before December, 1949, it was made by the court of a country in which the wife had been ordinarily resident for three years. The issue which the judge tried in the present case was whether the husband had been free to marry in March, 1959. In my view, he was free to marry because after December, 1949, our courts were entitled to treat the Czech decree of January, 1949, as having

H   dissolved the husband's first marriage.

    The years of conflict between 1939 and 1945 witnessed movements of combatants and others to and from different countries on a scale that would not have been expected in the calmer days of peace. In the present era the speed and ease of transport gives rise to conditions that differ widely from those obtaining in the latter part of the last century. All this means that, if recognition of foreign decrees

I   is closely circumscribed, there will be increasing numbers of cases where a person is to be regarded in one country as married and in another country as not married. It can well be understood that, when our courts were saying that domicil and nothing but domicil could be the basis for jurisdiction, a decree in a country where there was no domicil was regarded as barren and valueless; but the changes made in 1937 and 1949 were far-reaching, and domicil thereafter no longer occupied

---

(74) [1895-99] All E.R. Rep. at p. 840;   [1895] A.C. at p. 527.
(75) (1868), L.R. 3 H.L. 55.   (76) (1868), L.R. 3 H.L. at p. 81.
(77) (1000), L.R. 3 H.L. at p. 83.   (78) [1953] 2 All E.R. 794; [1953] P. 246.

its role of being essential. Before the time of those changes we recognised a **A** foreign decree, if the husband was domiciled in the country. Now that we assume jurisdiction if a wife has been ordinarily resident in England for three years, I can see no reason why we should not recognise a decree made in some other country where the wife was resident for three years. Once, however, the rigidity of insistence on domicil has been displaced, the question must be asked whether it is reasonable only to recognise decrees where the foreign jurisdiction is founded **B** on rules which mutatis mutandis are like ours. There is peril in assuming that only our rules are rational and justifiable. Looking back on the course of judicial decisions it is readily seen that though doctrine evolved one way, it might quite easily have evolved another way. This leads me to the view that no essential or fundamental superiority of our basis for jurisdiction can be claimed over all others. While in the present case I would support recognition of the Czech decree **C** on the basis adopted by the majority in the Court of Appeal (79), I would also support it on a wider basis. The evidence was that the Czech court accepted jurisdiction on the ground that both the parties were and always had been Czechoslovakian citizens. The first wife at the time when she presented her petition in Czechoslovakia undoubtedly had a real and substantial connexion with that country. I see no reason why the decree of the Czech court should not **D** in those circumstances be recognised. There may, in other cases, be further and different bases for recognition. The Royal Commission on Marriage and Divorce (1951-5), (80) while pointing out (see para. 797) that no two witnesses were exactly agreed on a solution of the problem of the basis of recognition, stated that there was general endorsement of the principle that the English court should at least recognise the competence of a court of another country to grant a decree of **E** divorce in the exercise of a jurisdiction similar to that which the English court itself exercises, no matter on what basis such latter jurisdiction is founded. The commission favoured a wide measure of recognition being given to divorces obtained in other countries and suggested two guiding principles, (i) that there should be reciprocity of treatment, so that recognition should be given to a divorce obtained in the exercise of a jurisdiction substantially similar to that **F** exercised by the English and Scottish courts and, (ii) that due regard should be paid to the personal law of the parties, so that recognition should be given to a divorce which has been granted in accordance with, or which would be recognised by, the personal law. A number of specific possible suggestions were recorded. Unless by legislation some code can be enacted the courts will be left to deal with problems as and when they arise. I would decide the present case in the way **G** that I have set out.

I would dismiss the appeal.

LORD PEARCE: My Lords, We are here concerned with the problem of " limping marriages ". Perhaps " unilateral marriages " is a better description since it brings home more clearly the harshness and absurdity of a situation where one spouse is held in the bonds of a marriage to which there is no other party, **H** while the former partner is free and able to marry again. Of course, when there is such a remarriage, the unilateral spouse may be able to take subsequent proceedings based on adultery; but this may be fraught with difficulty and expense. From the view of public policy and common sense there is something wrong with any law to the extent to which it fosters such a situation. Yet it is not easy to see how the problem should be solved. It depends on the interplay **I** of jurisdiction and recognition of foreign decrees among the nations. It is a matter for each country to decide, both in respect of what marriages or parties its courts will assume jurisdiction and also what decrees of divorce by foreign courts it will recognise. It may recognise all or none or take some intermediate position. In this it will be largely influenced by public policy. The boundaries which it sets for answering each of the problems need not necessarily coincide; but insofar as

---

(79) [1966] 3 All E.R. 583.   (80) Cmd. 9678.

A it confines its recognition more narrowly than its jurisdiction, it is adding to the sum of unilateral marriages. Thus the definition of jurisdiction should be closely related to that of recognition; and in *Le Mesurier* v. *Le Mesurier* (81) this fact was appreciated.

In 1857 the English courts for the first time were enabled by statute to grant divorce. When they dealt with ordinary English couples, born, bred and living

B in England, no problem of jurisdiction or of recognition would arise; but it was inevitable that there must be other less normal cases in which one or both of these problems would need to be faced. The Matrimonial Causes Act, 1857, however, gave no guidance on either. One cannot doubt that these problems were deliberately left for the courts to work out a solution. Moreover, see the observation of SIR CRESSWELL CRESSWELL in 1863 in *Forster* v. *Forster and Berridge* (82):

C " I should have been very glad indeed if the legislature had said that the court had no jurisdiction except over persons domiciled in England. When LORD CAMPBELL was Lord Chancellor, I asked him to bring in a bill to settle the question and to define my jurisdiction; but he said, ' I cannot do it. Whenever that question is raised it must be decided on legal principles. It cannot be defined '."

D On jurisdiction to grant divorce our courts were for some time in doubt what attitude they should adopt. In *Niboyet* v. *Niboyet* (83) the matter was still in the balance; but the scales there came down by a majority in favour of residence as the test of jurisdiction. This had been the test in the ecclesiastical courts whose jurisdiction had been handed on to the High Court; but those courts had only

E had the power to grant what was in effect a judicial separation, and the novel power to grant divorce gave rise to different considerations. Two of the judgments (84) in the Court of Appeal adopted residence as the test of jurisdiction. BRETT, L.J., (85) however, came to a contrary conclusion, which was later adopted by the courts; but he erroneously went so far (86) as to disallow, even in suits for judicial separation, jurisdiction on the ground of residence; a view which was

F never adopted by the courts (see *Armytage* v. *Armytage* (87)). The majority decision in *Niboyet* (83), though not expressly overruled, was superseded by a concept of the matter which was set out at length by LORD WATSON in a judgment in the Privy Council in *Le Mesurier* (81). This concept was thereafter adopted by the courts; but the foundations of the concept were in one respect faulty at the time and have in other respects been undermined by changes in the subsoil and by deliberate statutory demolitions.

G The Privy Council (81) was looking for a rule which would accord with the law of nations, the jus gentium, and would provide one universal world-wide test. It accepted as the law of England LORD WESTBURY's view in *Shaw* v. *Gould* (88), a recognition case,

H ". . . that the tribunal of a foreign country having jurisdiction to dissolve the marriages of its own subjects, is competent to pronounce a similar decree between English subjects who were married in *England*, but who before or at the time of the suit are permanently domiciled within the jurisdiction of such foreign tribunal, such decree being made in a bona fide suit without collusion or concert . . ."

LORD WATSON said (89):

I " On the other hand a decree of divorce a vinculo, pronounced by a court whose jurisdiction is solely derived from some rule of municipal law peculiar

(81) [1895-99] All E.R. Rep. 836; [1895] A.C. 517.
(82) (1863), 3 Sw. & Ir. 151 at p. 155.   (83) (1878), 4 P.D. 1.
(84) See the judgments of JAMES and COTTON, L.JJ., (1878), 4 P.D. at pp. 3, 20.
(85) (1878), 4 P.D. at p. 9.   (86) (1878), 4 P.D. at p. 19.
(87) [1895-99] All E.R. Rep. 377; [1898] P. 178.
(88) (1868), L.R. 3 H.L. at p. 85.
(89) [1895-99] All E.R. Rep. at p. 840; [1895] A.C. at p. 528.

to its forum, cannot, when it trenches upon the interests of any other   A
country to whose tribunals the spouses were amenable, claim extra-territorial
authority."

After a long examination of English and Scottish cases which were in a discordant
and unsatisfactory condition, the Board came to the conclusion (90) " that the
domicil for the time being of the married pair affords the only true test of jurisdiction to dissolve their marriage ".   The Board adopted the words of LORD   B
PENZANCE in *Wilson* v. *Wilson* (91):

" Different communities have different views and laws respecting matrimonial obligations, and a different estimate of the causes which should
justify divorce. It is both just and reasonable, therefore, that the differences
of married people should be adjusted in accordance with the laws of the
community to which they belong, and dealt with by the tribunals which   C
alone can administer those laws. An honest adherence. to this principle,
moreover, will preclude the scandal which arises when a man and woman are
held to be man and wife in one country, and strangers in another."

That hope has not been fulfilled. Why is this?

In the first place, the Board (92) in concluding that domicil was the only true   D
test according to international law, wholly disregarded nationality. The two
ancient writers on international law to which the judgment referred said nothing
of nationality. This was natural, since it was not until the beginning of the last
century that the test of nationality, as determining a man's personal law, spread
throughout Europe from France; but the Board also quoted (93) " BAR, the
latest continental writer on the theory. and practice of international private   E
law " as saying " the judge of the domicil or nationality is the only competent
judge " and

" a decree of divorce, therefore, pronounced by any other judge than a
judge of the domicil or nationality, is to be regarded in all countries as
inoperative."

Yet the judgment proceeded to ignore nationality; and if (as we are told by   F
junior counsel for the wife from his useful researches) there was at the beginning
of this century a fairly even division between the numbers of those persons
whose personal law was determined by nationality and those whose personal law
was determined by domicil, the belief that a test founded on domicil was or could
be universal was erroneous.

Moreover, even between this country (and Scotland) and the other countries   G
who regarded domicil as the test, a gap widened.   In *Lord* v. *Colvin* (94) SIR
RICHARD KINDERSLEY, V.-C., had defined domicil as (95)—

" That place . . . in which he has voluntarily fixed the habitation of
himself and his family, not for a mere special and temporary purpose, but
with a present intention of making it his permanent home, unless and until   H
something (which is unexpected, or the happening of which is uncertain)
shall occur to induce him to adopt some other permanent home."

Probably this definition would have still sufficed when *Le Mesurier* (92) was
decided.   Owing, however, to the decisions in *Winan* v. *A.-G.* (96) and *Bowie*
(or *Ramsay*) v. *Liverpool Royal Infirmary* (97) our word " domicil " unfortunately
attained a meaning which it did not have at the time of *Le Mesurier's* case (92),   I
and which it has never had in other countries. (This no doubt was partly

---

(90) [1895-99] All E.R. Rep. at p. 847; [1895] A.C. at p. 540.
(91) (1872), L.R. 2 P. & D. at p. 442.
(92) [1895-99] All E.R. Rep. 836; [1895] A.C. 517.
(93) [1895-99] All E.R. Rep. at p. 845; [1895] A.C. at p. 538.
(94) (1859), 4 Drew. 366.   (95) (1859), 4 Drew. at p. 376.
(96) [1904-07] All E.R. Rep. 410; [1904] A.C. 287.
(97) [1930] All E.R. Rep. 127; [1930] A.C. 588.

A   influenced by the special situation existing between England and Scotland with
its interplay of long-term residents.)   As a result, the differences of married
people often have to be adjusted in accordance with the community to which
they " do *not* belong ".   Until this rigid view of domicil is modified so as to accord
more nearly with the views of other countries who look to domicil as the test, it
will give rise to constant difficulties.

B   The problem of domicil was considered not only by the Standing Committee
on Private International Law (98) but also by the Royal Commission on
Marriage and Divorce, 1951-1955, whose report was published in 1956 (99).
The recommendations of both favoured an abolition of the doctrine of revival of
domicil of origin and a presumption, inter alia, that where a person has his home
in a country he should be presumed to live there permanently.   These would go
C   some little way to bridge the gap between England (and Scotland) and other
nations.   The view of the minority of the standing committee, wisely perhaps,
would have gone further.   For present purposes, however, and until a question of
domicil comes before your lordships' House, one must accept the strict test
applied in *Bowie's* case (100) and acknowledge the existence of the wide gap that
lies between our concept of domicil and that of other countries.

D   Further, it is a principle of English law that the wife acquires the husband's
domicil and that she cannot, even when separated under a decree of judicial
separation (*A.-G. for Alberta* v. *Cook* (101)) acquire a domicil of her own choice.
It was obvious that great hardship could be caused to a wife by this rule.   A
husband could always change his domicil, but a wife could not.   She could obtain
relief only in the courts of the husband's domicil which (according to our notions)
E   might be in some distant land, though he had married her in England and set up
his home here; or he might desert her, leave this country, and revert to or acquire
some distant domicil or even a domicil whose whereabouts she did not know;
and she was powerless to prevent her domicil from following his changes.   Many
of the domicil countries (particularly in the United States of America) have
avoided this hardship by allowing to a wife a separate domicil, but we have not
F   adopted this concept.

These difficulties were emphasised by the first world war when wives who had
in this country married soldiers coming to it from abroad found themselves
unable to obtain a divorce in our courts.   The Matrimonial Causes (Dominion
Troops) Act, 1919, broke the rigidity of the jurisdiction rule in *Le Mesurier* (102)
in order to give a right to bring matrimonial proceedings in our courts where a
G   marriage had been contracted in the United Kingdom by a member of His
Majesty's forces domiciled in His Majesty's possessions or protectorates.   It
made no discrimination between men and women.

The Scots' courts, which had for centuries allowed divorce on the ground of
desertion, adopted the sensible rule in general that their courts had jurisdiction
to entertain an action for divorce by a wife on the ground of desertion if her
H   husband was domiciled in Scotland at the time of leaving her, since after a cause
of action has arisen a husband is not entitled (by changing his domicil) to subject
his wife to the jurisdiction of the court of another country (see *Lack* v. *Lack* (103).
Sir Gorell Barnes, P., giving the judgment of the Court of Appeal in *Ogden* v.
Ogden (104) adopted (obiter) a somewhat similar line:

   " If the country of the husband's domicil refuse to recognise the marriage,
I   and, therefore, cannot and will not entertain a suit for divorce against him,
the justice and reasonableness of the international rule just mentioned cease
to be apparent, and the wife having no right of suit whatever against the

---

(98) Seventh Report, March 1963 (Cmnd. 1955), and First Report, 1954 (Cmd.
9068).
(99) Cmd. 9678, see paras. 816-818.
(100) [1930] All E.R. Rep. 127; [1930] A.C. 588.
(101) [1926] All E.R. Rep. 525; [1926] A.C. 444.
(102) [1895-99] All E.R. Rep. 836; [1895] A.C. 517.   (103) [1926] S.L.T. 656.
(104) [1904-07] All E.R. Rep. 80 at p. 105; [1908] P. 46 at p. 82.

husband in his country, and having been left in the country of her original   A
domicil where the marriage was celebrated and is recognised as binding upon
both her and him, it would seem reasonable to permit her to sue in the latter
country for the dissolution of the tie which is recognised therein, though not
in the foreign country, in case she has grounds of suit which would entitle
her to a divorce if her husband had been domiciled in her country; in other
words, to treat her as having a domicil in her own country which would be   B
sufficient to support a suit. No general rule of law would then really be
infringed. The necessities of the case would call for the intervention of the
courts of her own country in order to do her justice and release her from a tie
recognised in the one country though not in the other."

This dictum was adopted as a basis for giving relief to wives whose husbands
were domiciled elsewhere; first, by BARGRAVE DEANE, J., in *Stathatos* v. *Stathatos*   C
(105) and secondly, by SIR SAMUEL EVANS, P., in *De Montaigu* v. *De Montaigu*
(106). Unfortunately this dictum of the Court of Appeal (107) was subsequently
(*Herd* v. *Herd* (108)) held to be erroneous, in view of the two later cases of LORD
Advocate v. *Jaffrey* (109) and *A.-G. for Alberta* v. *Cook* (110). So, in 1937 there had
to be statutory provision in s. 13 of the Matrimonial Causes Act, 1937, to help
deserted wives, whose husbands were domiciled here immediately before the   D
desertion but had since changed their domicil, by enabling them to obtain a
divorce from our courts. Thus, again, the rigidity of the jurisdiction rule in
Le Mesurier (111) was broken by statute.

In the second world war, as in the first world war, the Matrimonial Causes
(War Marriages) Act, 1944, gave a relief somewhat similar to that given in 1919.
The jurisdiction of the High Court was extended irrespective of domicil to all   E
marriages (with certain exceptions) celebrated between Sept. 3, 1939, and the
appointed day (which was in fact June 1, 1950), where the husband was not and
the wife was at the time of the marriage domiciled in England. There were also
similar provisions relating to Scotland. This was a further serious inroad on the
jurisdiction rule in *Le Mesurier* (111).

After the war it was obvious that yet a further infraction of the rule was neces-   F
sary in order to deal with the changed circumstances of life in general. Both
before, during and after the war many refugees and immigrants had come to
this country, some hoping to return one day to their own land, some acquiring
here a domicil of choice. Some were wives who had come here apart from their
husbands. The world had become more shifting and mobile than it was in the
last century. Moreover, divorce had become much more common and easier to   G
obtain. In actual figures it had, as one can see from the figures published in the
report of the Royal Commission on Marriage and Divorce, increased a hundred-
fold. In the last century if a wife was deserted by her husband, whether domiciled
here or not, she was tied to him until he died. Now society in this and many other
countries was no longer content with that situation. She must be freed to live a
normal life; and it was felt that on the grounds of morals, humanity and con-   H
venience she should be able to obtain divorce in the country where she genuinely
lived. So there was granted to wives who had resided here for three years a right,
regardless of domicil, to seek divorce in our courts. This was the final Parliamentary demolition of the foundations which underlay the rule in *Le Mesurier*
(111); and it was substantial. In respect of one sex the rule, so far as it concerns
jurisdiction, has now, virtually, ceased to exist.   I

In this state of affairs the Court of Appeal in *Travers* v. *Holley and Holley* (112),

(105) [1913] P. 46.   (106) [1913] P. 154.
(107) [1904-07] All E.R. Rep. 86; [1908] P. 46.
(108) [1936] 2 All E.R. 1516; [1936] P. 205.
(109) [1920] All E.R. Rep. 242; [1921] 1 A.C. 146.
(110) [1926] All E.R. Rep. 525; [1926] A.C. 444.
(111) [1895-99] All E.R. Rep. 836; [1895] A.C. 517.
(112) [1953] 2 All E.R. 794; [1953] P. 246.

A decided that a decree of divorce given in the courts of New South Wales against a husband who was domiciled in England should be recognised in our courts. In New South Wales there was a statute which made, with regard to deserted wives, a provision corresponding with s. 13 of our Act of 1937. The court held that it would be contrary to principle and inconsistent with comity if the courts of this country refused to recognise a jurisdiction which, mutatis mutandis, they claimed
B for themselves. It is argued that they were wrong in so deciding.

The problem of recognition has given rise to many combinations and permutations of difficulty, and there has been a large number of cases on the subject, especially in recent years. (See RAYDEN (10th Edn.) pp. 66-83, where the subject is dealt with in detail and the various cases are usefully collected.)

In view of the recognition rule established by inference from *Le Mesurier* (113)
C and by various authorities, the Court of Appeal in *Travers* v. *Holley and Holley* (114) were not able to take an untrammelled view of the matter. If they were to loosen the rigidity of the recognition rule, they could do so only by relying on the jurisdictionary infractions made by Parliament into the rule in *Le Mesurier* (113) as justifying a wider recognition of foreign decrees. Thus, they gave as their ratio that comity demanded a recognition of decrees granted under circum-
D stances in which we ourselves would grant them. If one amplifies the reasoning slightly by saying that Parliament's infractions were an acknowledgment that an undiluted application of the rule in *Le Mesurier* (113) would, in a changed world, no longer work, and that a similar common sense acknowledgement was thereby justified in respect of recognition, I think that it is valid reasoning. It would be insular and unreasonable to maintain that one should in the interests
E of universality and international law (which was the avowed object of the rule in *Le Mesurier* (113)) refuse to acknowledge decrees given on the same basis as those which one is giving oneself. If comity be allied to common sense and a desire to make things work, one should not, while taking rights over the subjects of other countries who reside here, refuse to acknowledge the rights of other countries to do likewise. That had been one part of the basis of *Le Mesurier* (113);
F and for that reason, though not a case of recognition, it was rightly considered as laying down, obiter, that only decrees of the courts of domicil should be recognised. For its reasoning treats the limitation of jurisdiction to the court of the domicil and the limitation of recognition of decrees to those of the court of the domicil as being two sides of the same coin. Divorce, being at that time severely restricted in this country, it was natural that a very restricted and
G protected view should also be taken of recognition.

We have to look at *Le Mesurier* (113) afresh to see how much of it survives or should survive in a changed world. So far as jurisdiction is concerned, the alterations created by Parliament have been so many and so great that it must, I think, now be left to Parliament to deal with the matter. The Royal Commission on Marriage and Divorce (115), for the reasons there set out, made various
H recommendations on this subject, but these have not yet been adopted. So far as recognition is concerned, Parliament has, apart from certain reciprocal arrangements within the Commonwealth under the Colonial and Other Territories Divorce Jurisdiction Acts, 1926 to 1950, (116), and the Matrimonial Causes (War Marriages) Act, 1944, refrained from intervening; and it is for the courts to decide what decrees they will recognise, bearing in mind the policy of Parliament in
I extending jurisdiction and the social necessities that, in this country as in others, underlay that policy.

---

(113) [1895-99] All E.R. Rep. 836; [1895] A.C. 517.
(114) [1953] 2 All E.R. 794; [1953] P. 246.
(115) Cmd. 9678 (1956); see paras. 848 et seq., and App. IV, para. 7.
(116) These are the Acts enumerated in s. 6 (2), (4) of the Act of 1950; see 29 HALSBURY'S STATUTES (2nd Edn.) 142.

Up to the date of *Travers* v. *Holley and Holley* (117) the broad general principle   A
adopted by English and Scots' law had been that recognition should be given to
divorce obtained in another country only if the husband and wife were domiciled
in that country when the proceedings started. To this rule, however, there had
been one sound and valuable exception laid down by *Armitage* v. *A.-G., Gillig* v.
Gillig (118), namely, that a divorce obtained in a country other than that in which
the parties were domiciled should receive recognition if it would be accepted as   B
valid by the court of the country in which the parties were domiciled at the time
of the proceedings. The English view being that the court of domicil should be
regarded as having the closest connexion with the parties, the views of that court,
as shown either by its own decree or by its acknowledgement of the decrees of
other countries, should on general principles decide the matter.

There is an interesting article by DEAN ERWIN GRISWOLD in the HARVARD   C
LAW REVIEW, vol. 65, p. 227, published before *Travers* v. *Holley and Holley* (117)
was decided, but not in fact cited to the court (see HARVARD LAW REVIEW,
vol. 67, p. 826, n. 17), in which DEAN GRISWOLD deals with the various difficulties
and arrives at the same conclusion as that which the Court of Appeal reached.
He writes:

> " It is my suggestion that the applicable conflict of laws rule should be   D
> that a divorce should be recognised in the forum when it was granted under
> circumstances which are those under which the forum will itself grant a div-
> orce; in other words that the recognition rule applied by a court should
> follow, and indeed be a reflection of, its jurisdictional rule. You will note that
> I am not contending that every state should recognise any divorce granted in
> any other Anglo-American state. I am not suggesting, for example, that   E
> British courts must recognise all of the divorces granted in Nevada or else-
> where in the United States. I am merely contending that New South Wales
> should recognise a divorce granted to a deserted wife in England when New
> South Wales would itself grant a divorce to a deserted wife in New South
> Wales under the same circumstances. It makes no difference whether the
> statutory provision proceeds in terms of residence or in terms of the deserted   F
> wife retaining a separate domicil. It is the factual situation which is import-
> ant. If the facts are such that the court of the forum would have jurisdiction,
> on proper cause, to grant a divorce, then it is my submission that it should
> recognise a divorce granted elsewhere on the basis of the same facts regardless
> of any question of domicil."

In 1956 the Report of the Royal Commission on Marriage and Divorce dealt with   G
the difficulties created by refusal to recognise foreign decrees. It assumed that
Travers v. *Holley and Holley* (117) was good law. It reads (Cmd. 9678, para. 848):

> " As we have said, we are in favour of a wide measure of recognition
> being given to divorces which have been obtained in other countries. We
> think that there should be two guiding principles. In the first place there   H
> should be reciprocity of treatment; recognition should be given to a divorce
> which has been obtained in the exercise of a jurisdiction substantially similar
> to that exercised by the English and Scottish courts. Secondly, due regard
> should be paid to the personal law of the parties; recognition should therefore
> be given to a divorce which has been granted in accordance with, or would be
> recognised by, the personal law. In some cases both principles would apply,   I
> in others the one, or the other, but not both."

To narrow the ground of recognition accorded by *Travers* v. *Holley and Holley* (117)
might cause grave difficulties in respect of those who may have remarried on the
strength of it; but even more important it would create unnecessary hardship
and difficulty in the future. Counsel for the husband, while attacking the decision,
admitted frankly that common sense and practical benefit were all in its favour.

---

(117) [1953] 2 All E.R. 794; [1953] P. 246.   (118) [1906] P. 135.

A It has worked well and it has removed much hardship. In my opinion it would be wrong to overrule or narrow it; one should rather broaden it, and regard our own jurisdiction as only an approximate test of recognition with a right in our courts to go further, when this is justified by special circumstances in the petitioner's connexion with the country granting the decree.

It has been said that it allows a wife to go abroad in order to secure a divorce
B which she could not have got by remaining here; but that is not likely to be a frequent occurrence. The difficulty of all divorce problems is that when a humane society provides relief in certain circumstances for those whose intolerable situation demands relief, it is always liable to be abused by the encroachment of undeserving people, who do not really need it and could preserve their marriage if they tried a little harder. So it is a question of degree and common sense how
C far one shall withhold relief of hardship because of its possible abuses. In the rare cases where a wife goes to the length of living abroad for three years and getting a divorce, one may console oneself with the thought that nothing could hold the marriage together and that to maintain its form unilaterally is merely a sham. It has come to be realised that in a modern world marriages cannot be compelled to work by Act of Parliament or decrees of restitution. The greatest help that
D the law can give to the maintenance of marriage is by encouraging the centripetal and discouraging the centrifugal forces of a married pair, by not making it too easy for them to part while providing dissolution in circumstances which demand relief. For that reason, I would regard the possibilities of wives going abroad for three years to secure relief as insufficient to outweigh the advantages of the rule in *Travers* v. *Holley and Holley* (119).

E Moreover, there are two further considerations that reinforce this view. First, the refusal to recognise the decree obtained by a wife who has gone to live abroad gives little support to marriage in general. The punishment of the unilateral husband who remains in this country will do little to deter the wife from seeking her own freedom. Secondly, and even more important, the recognition of a decree given abroad to a wife resident there (though by our law she is domiciled in this
F country) fits in with the scheme of the many domicil countries which not unreasonably allow a wife to have a domicil of her own apart from that of her husband. (See also the recommendation of the Royal Commission on Marriage and Divorce, Cmd. 9678, para. 825, that our jurisdiction should be extended to wives who can show that, had they been single women, they would be held to have acquired a domicil in England, and that when a wife who before the marriage had an English
G domicil is separated from her husband and resident here, she should be deemed to have (for the purpose of divorce proceedings) a separate English domicil).

It may fairly be said that *Travers* v. *Holley and Holley* (119) creates an untidy recognition situation in its differentiation between men and women; but the situation between men and women is, for social reasons, inherently untidy in the field of matrimonial jurisdiction. He is in control of her domicil. Moreover,
H she is frequently dependent on him for the support of herself and their children. If he can by residing abroad for three years obtain a decree which is recognised in this country, it will terminate his matrimonial obligations and debar his former wife from seeking financial relief in our courts. Unless Parliament introduces some machinery for granting such relief while acknowledging the foreign severance of the marriage tie, I see no practical means of putting men and women on the same
I basis with regard to recognition of decrees; and there are other difficulties. The inherent differences between the situations of the wife and the husband are acknowledged by the discrimination between them which Parliament has adopted in dealing with jurisdiction.

I think, however, that our courts should reserve to themselves the right to refuse a recognition of those decrees which offend our notions of genuine divorce. They have done so when decrees offend against substantial justice,

and this, of course, includes a decree obtained by fraud. I think, however, that   **A**
it also includes or should include decrees where a wife has gone abroad in order
to obtain a divorce and where a divorce can be said not to be genuine according
to our notions of divorce.   On this point (though not otherwise) I think that
the grounds of divorce and questions of collusion can also be considered as
throwing light on the matter.   In the United States of America there is a reservation of this kind, in their recognition of foreign decrees.   Where jurisdiction   **B**
is taken on one day's residence and divorce is granted on incompatibility of
temperament (as in the State of Chihuahua—see *Mountbatten (Marquess of
Milford Haven* v. *Mountbatten (Marchioness of Milford Haven)* (120)), it is clear
that a court is simply purveying divorce to foreigners who wish to buy it;   and
that does not accord with our notions of genuine divorce.   No doubt there may
be difficult border line cases; but I feel sure that our judges could distinguish   **C**
reasonably in practice between those jurisdictions which purvey divorces to
the foreign market and those who are genuinely trying to make laws for the
divorce of its citizens (including its genuine residents) to whom its duty lies.

I appreciate the force of the able judgment given by O'BRYAN, J., in *Fenton*
v. *Fenton* (121), but I am not convinced by it so far as this country is concerned;
and it is to this country alone that my own observations are directed, since   **D**
this difficult problem of recognition contains so large an element of public policy.

The decision in *Travers* v. *Holley and Holley* (122) was usefully amplified by
Mr. Commissioner LATEY, Q.C., in *Arnold* v. *Arnold* (123), and by KARMINSKI, J.,
in *Robinson-Scott* v. *Robinson-Scott* (124).   The latter cited DEAN GRISWOLD'S
article (125) in support of his judgment (126).   He decided that:

"Where in fact there has been three years' residence by a wife in the   **E**
territory of the foreign court assuming jurisdiction in a suit for dissolution,
the English court should accept that as a ground for exercising jurisdiction
because it would itself accept jurisdiction on proof of similar residence in
England.   It is not essential for recognition by this court that the foreign
court should assume jurisdiction on the grounds laid down by s. 18 of the
Matrimonial Causes Act, 1950.   It is sufficient that facts exist which would   **F**
enable the English courts to assume jurisdiction."

In the former case (*Arnold* (124)) Mr. Commissioner LATEY, Q.C., adopted the
view (obiter) that the fact that in a foreign court some lesser period suffices
to found jurisdiction is beside the point if in fact there had been, say, two
years' residence or more, or even less, and the residence is genuine and bona
fide and not merely for the purpose of getting a divorce in a convenient court (127).   **G**

"The necessity laid down by statute in England for three years' residence,
in the case of a wife whose husband is domiciled abroad, is probably due
to the notion that our courts could not be used for the convenience of
birds-of-passage and that the court had to satisfy itself that the petitioning
wife had chosen her home in England, though by operation of law her   **H**
domicil was that of her husband domiciled abroad, and living either abroad
or in England."

This view did not commend itself to KARMINSKI, J., in *Robinson-Scott* (128),
who thought that three years' residence in fact before the proceedings was
essential.   I would prefer to keep that matter open to be worked out by the
courts, since there is something to be said for either view.   **I**

(120) [1959] 1 All E.R. 99; [1959] P. 43.   (121) [1957] V.L.R. 17.
(122) [1953] 2 All E.R. 794; [1953] P. 246.
(123) [1957] 1 All E.R. 570; [1957] P. 237.
(124) [1957] 3 All E.R. 473; [1958] P. 71.
(125) 65 HARVARD LAW REVIEW at p. 231.
(126) [1957] 3 All E.R. at p. 478; [1958] P. at p. 88.
(127) [1957] 1 All E.R. at p. 576, letter A; [1957] P. at p. 253.
(128) [1957] 3 All E.R. at p. 478; [1958] P. at p. 87.

A   In *Mountbatten* (129), however, DAVIES, J., rightly refused (130) to apply the principle of *Armitage* (131) to the wife's court of residence, since, though we acknowledge its right to grant her a divorce, in appropriate cases there seems no adequate reason to regard it as the arbiter on her personal law in other respects.

  Thus recognition can no longer be confined to decrees of the court of domicil, though that is the primary court to which one should look. Moreover, even
B at the time of *Le Mesurier* (132) nationality could not properly be ignored; and in my opinion decrees of the court of nationality, when jurisdiction is taken on the ground of nationality, should be recognised. The Report of the Royal Commission on Marriage and Divorce (Cmd. 9678, paras. 856, 857) reads:

    " 856. It must be accepted that the courts in a number of countries assume jurisdiction to grant a divorce if the husband is a national of that country
C   whatever his domicil may be. To refuse recognition to a divorce obtained in such circumstances is to increase the number of ' limping marriages ' and to cause hardship to the persons affected. To recognise such decrees is to promote a better understanding in the international sphere and possibly to secure wider recognition of English and Scottish decrees of divorce granted on the basis of domicil . . .
D   " 857. We recommend, therefore, that recognition should be given in England and Scotland to the validity of a divorce (i) which has been obtained, whether judicially or otherwise, by a spouse in accordance with the law of the country of which both husband and wife were nationals, or of which either the husband or the wife was a national at the time of the proceedings, or (ii) which would be granted recognition by the law
E   of that country."

  There we have the advantage of a fuller investigation of the question of nationality than the Board had before them in *Le Mesurier* (132). Moreover, in my view, our courts should recognise nationality to the extent suggested by the Royal Commission. This would have produced a different and more satis-
F factory result in the case of *Levett* v. *Levett* (133).

  On the facts of the present case I accept the view of the majority of the Court of Appeal (134) that the marriage in 1959 was good although the Czecho-slovakian divorce was granted in 1949, a few months before this country extended its jurisdiction by allowing resident wives to obtain divorce in our courts. The ground of recognition rests not on any exact measure of our own
G jurisdiction, but on the wider ground of public policy in which our own juris-diction is a most important element. The facts which made it right for our courts to have wider jurisdiction and give wider recognition existed at the date of the Czech decree, even though those facts did not until a few months later result in the statute by which this country took wider jurisdiction. When once the appreciation of these facts has been brought home to our courts by Parlia-mentary extension of their jurisdiction, their recognition should be retrospective.
H Also, if our courts were asked in 1959, at the date of the marriage, whether the husband was free to remarry, how could public policy tolerate the answer, " No, because, although we have for ten years been ourselves taking similar jurisdiction in such a case as this, we did not start to do so until a few months after the date of the Czechoslovakian decree "? In my opinion the question
I whether a foreign decree should be recognised should be answered by the court in the light of its present policy, regardless (within reason) of when the decree was granted.

  There are further reasons which, in my opinion, compel the recognition of the decree. Both parties to the marriage were nationals of Czechoslovakia

---

(129) [1959] 1 All E.R. 99; [1959] P. 43.
(130) [1959] 1 All E.R. at p. 118, letter B; [1959] P. at p. 83.
(131) [1906] P. 135.   (132) [1895-99] All E.R. Rep. 836; [1895] A.C. 517.
(133) [1957] 1 All E.R. 720; [1957] P. 156.   (134) [1966] 3 All E.R. 583.

(and incidentally domiciled there as well until 1946), the matrimonial home **A**
was there, the petitioning wife resided there all her life, and their courts took
jurisdiction there on the ground of nationality. Undoubtedly the country of
the nationality was the predominant country with regard to the parties to this
marriage, and as such its decree ought to be recognised in this country.

On the fact of the present case there is, fortunately, no tragic issue either
way, and I do not think it necessary to discuss them; but on the wider issue **B**
there can be much unhappiness caused by unilateral marriage. It is not possible
wholly to avoid it, but it is the duty of the courts to do their best to reduce it.

I would dismiss the appeal.

LORD WILBERFORCE: My Lords, the issue in these proceedings is
whether the appellant husband's marriage to his second wife in 1959 was valid, **C**
as she claims, or, as the husband contends, was void because of the subsistence of
a prior marriage between the husband and Helena Indyka, to whom he was
married in 1938 and to whom I shall refer as "the wife". This depends on
whether recognition ought to be given by English courts to a decree of divorce
made by the District Court of Ostrava in Czechoslovakia on Jan. 18, 1949, on
the application of Helena Indyka, dissolving her marriage with the husband on **D**
the ground of deep disruption of marital relations.

There can be no doubt that the crude facts speak strongly in favour of recognition. The divorce was granted by a court of the nationality of both spouses, and
under Czech law, as an expert proved at the trial, nationality is the relevant
connecting factor for purposes of divorce. Czechoslovakia is the country in which
the spouses last lived together as man and wife: it is the country in which the **E**
wife continued to reside after cohabitation ceased. The reality of the connexion
between the law of Czechoslovakia and the marriage cannot be doubted, whether
regarded in itself, or by comparison with the only alternative system of law,
namely, English law. No point, I should add, is taken by the husband regarding
service or notice, or the lack of either, of the Czechoslovakian proceedings.

What then, it may be asked, is the obstacle to recognition, or what reason is **F**
there for asserting that it is the courts of this country which alone should dissolve
this marriage? The answer that is given is that England has, since 1946, become
the domicil of the husband: that this necessarily involves attributing an English
domicil to the wife, and that, since the law of this country admits domicil as the
exclusive basis for jurisdiction in divorce, recognition must be refused to the
Czech decree. This argument involves as its logical consequence that English **G**
law forces on the wife the necessity of following her husband to whatever foreign
country he may select as his domicil of choice, which she might or might not have
means of identifying, and to which she might well find it impossible to go, and
taking proceedings against him there under a—to her—foreign law. She would
be obliged to do this because a foreign law, to which she has never submitted,
into which it cannot in any sense be said that she married, substitutes for the law **H**
of her nationality, which is the connecting factor accepted by her country, a law
based on domicil. It must be a powerful principle of law which compels these
conclusions.

The principle in question is that of the exclusive authority of the law of the
domicil, meaning in relation to a married woman the domicil of her husband, a
principle fastened on English law by the case of *Le Mesurier* v. *Le Mesurier* (135). **I**

It would be tedious here to restate the process by which this decision of the
Judicial Committee of the Privy Council, in an appeal from Ceylon, established,
after an interval of thirty-eight years during which vacillations were found in
the law, that the jurisdiction of the English matrimonial court to dissolve
marriages under the Matrimonial Causes Act, 1857, was based exclusively on an
English domicil. There are a number of loci classici in which this is lucidly

(135) [1895-99] All E.R. Rep. 836; [1895] A.C. 517.

A explained (for examples *Wall* v. *Wall* (136), per PEARCE, J., *Garthwaite* v. *Garthwaite* (137), per DIPLOCK, L.J., and DEAN GRISWOLD in 65 HARVARD LAW REVIEW, p. 193). The jurisdiction of the English courts to dissolve marriages is not in issue here, and though this House may be free to review the matter, it would not be right to use the present as an occasion for reconsidering whether the accepted doctrine requires modification and, if so, in what direction. The issue

B which we have to face is narrower, namely, whether an English court can and ought to recognise a decree granted to a married woman by a court other than that of England, being the country in which her husband is domiciled.

  Le Mesurier (138) is of concern in this because it has been treated as establishing the rule that domicil is also the only basis on which recognition can be given to foreign decrees of divorce. So far as it does so, its correctness is directly in issue

C and this House is both entitled and bound to examine its validity.

  Before doing so, it is necessary to refer to earlier English decisions bearing on the recognition of foreign decrees of divorce. Some of these are decisions of this House, and, to the extent to which they were followed by *Le Mesurier* (138), they may be invoked to add authority to that case. In fact examination of them shows that, apart from any right which we now have to depart from them, they

D have left entirely open the question whether recognition should be given or refused to decrees of courts other than that of the parties' (i.e., the husband's) domicil.

  The earliest of these is *Dolphin* v. *Robins* (139) where the validity of a Scottish decree of divorce came in question in the English probate court. Recognition of the decree was refused, on the ground that the parties were not bona fide domiciled

E in Scotland, but had only resorted there for the purpose of obtaining a divorce. In other words, no proper basis for the jurisdiction of the Scottish courts was shown. This decision was followed in *Shaw* v. *Gould* (140), the leading nineteenth century authority, in which speeches of considerable learning were delivered in the House. The case was an English appeal in which it became necessary to consider the validity of a Scottish decree of divorce. The parties were at the time of

F the marriage domiciled in England but the husband was induced, by a gift of money and the promise of more, to go to Scotland so as to establish the necessary domicilium fori and the wife obtained a decree of divorce there. The decision was that there was no bona fide domicil in Scotland, that (as in *Dolphin* v. *Robins* (139)) the parties had merely resorted there so as to found jurisdiction and that the divorce could not be recognised. The basis on which foreign decrees of

G dissolution of marriage are recognised was examined in most detail by LORD WESTBURY. A judgment could not, he said, (141) claim extra-territorial authority unless it be pronounced " in accordance with rules of international public law ". He then referred (142) to the writings of HUBER, RODENBURG and BOULLENOIS. HUBER he quoted in order to show that one country cannot by its laws interfere with the institutions of another. Judicial divorce was not possible in England at

H the time the Scottish decree was obtained (i.e., in 1846) and it could not be allowed that persons domiciled in England should resort to Scotland for the sole purpose of getting released from an English marriage and so evading the laws under which they lived (143).

  " When they return to the country of their domicil, bringing back with them a foreign judgment so obtained, the tribunals of the domicil are entitled

I or even bound to reject such judgment as having no extra-territorial force or validity."

  I quote this passage as showing the type of situation with which LORD WESTBURY

---

(136) [1949] 2 All E.R. 927; [1950] P. 112.
(137) [1964] 2 All E.R. 233; [1964] P. 356.
(138) [1895-99] All E.R. Rep. 836; [1895] A.C. 517.
(139) (1859), 7 H.L. Cas. 390.   (140) (1868), L.R. 3 H.L. 55.
(141) (1868), L.R. 3 H.L. at p. 81.   (142) (1868), L.R. 3 H.L. at pp. 81, 83
                (143) (1868), L.R. 3 H.L. at p. 82.

was dealing—resorting to a foreign jurisdiction for the purpose of obtaining a **A**
divorce not obtainable under the domestic law and returning with it to the
country of domicil. The rule of public policy (for that is what it is) that he stated
has relevance today and I shall return to it.

That such a decree should not be recognised is all that the case decides; but
LORD WESTBURY's reasoning went beyond this limited conclusion and
undoubtedly influenced the later development of the law. The proposition which **B**
he was concerned to establish was that questions of personal status depend on the
law of the domicil, and it was to demonstrate this that he made reference to
foreign writers and to STORY's CONFLICT OF LAWS. In this part of his argument
he had a limited objective, which was to refute the opinion (to us evidently
erroneous, but in 1868 still widely accepted as following from *R.* v. *Lolley* (144),
and indeed agreed to by the Vice-Chancellor) that as to the dissolubility of a **C**
marriage regard was to be had to the lex loci contractus, i.e., that an " English "
marriage could be dissolved only in England. With none of this argument is there
any need now to disagree. What is important is that he was not concerned to
lay down any exclusive right of recognition for decrees made by courts of the
domicil. This limitation of the decision appears even more clearly from the opinion
of LORD COLONSAY (145). After dealing with the case of " resorting " to a foreign **D**
jurisdiction in the same manner as LORD WESTBURY he went on to say (146):

> "... if you put the case of parties resorting to Scotland with no such view,
> and being resident there for a considerable time, though not so as to change
> the domicil for all purposes, and then suppose that the wife commits adultery
> in Scotland, and that her husband discovers it and immediately raises an
> action of divorce in the court in Scotland, ... and that he proves his case **E**
> and obtains a decree, which decree is unquestionably good in Scotland, and
> would, I believe, be recognised in most other countries, I am slow to think
> that it would be ignored in England merely because it had not been
> pronounced by the Court of Divorce here."

I have referred at some length to *Shaw* v. *Gould* (147) because it is, in spite of **F**
its age (a debilitating factor in private international law), better entitled than
others to be regarded as of authority in relation to the recognition of foreign
decrees of divorce. Without in any way seeking to whittle down its effect or
authority, it may fairly be said that as a decision it is dealing with a special
type of case: that of " resorting " so as to found jurisdiction, and that, so far
as its reasoning goes, it makes clear that opinion had not in 1868 hardened **G**
against giving recognition to decrees of divorce unless granted by the courts
of the domicil. It leaves us free to consider whether there are cases in which
that should be given.

The other case which it is necessary to mention is *Harvey* v. *Farnie* (148).
The question there was again whether recognition should be given to a Scottish
decree of divorce. The marriage was celebrated in England between a husband
then domiciled in Scotland and a wife then domiciled in England. In spite of **H**
Shaw v. *Gould* (147), which one would have thought had laid *Lolley's* case (144)
to rest, most of the judgments are concerned to show that jurisdiction in divorce
is based on domicil and does not depend on the lex loci contractus. No more
than its predecessors did it seek to limit the right of recognition to decrees granted
by the court of the husband's domicil.

It was in this state of the law as regards recognition that the Judicial Com- **I**
mittee delivered the opinion in *Le Mesurier* (149). *Le Mesurier* (149) was not a
case concerned with recognition at all, but it would not be right merely to
dispose of what was then said as obiter dicta. For not only have later cases on

---

(144) (1812), Russ. & Ry. 237.   (145) (1868), L.R. 3 H.L. at p. 88.
(146) (1868), L.R. 3 H.L. at p. 96.   (147) (1868), L.R. 3 H.L. 55.
(148) (1880), 5 P.D. 153; *affd.* (1880), 6 P.D. 35; *affd.* (1882), 8 App. Cas. 43.
(149) [1895-99] All E.R. Rep. 836; [1895] A.C. 517.

A recognition made it a ground of their decision, but also the reasoning itself rests on the hypothesis that a common legal structure can be found to contain both the domestic jurisdiction of English courts and recognition by them of foreign decrees.

The opinion of the Board, and I forbear from quotation since the conclusion is now well accepted, was based on a theory of a jus gentium—meaning a body of
B doctrine common to civilised states—under which " domicil " is mutually and generally accepted as the exclusive jurisdictional basis. The convenience of this doctrine is obvious: for, if it were in all situations true and if it were generally accepted, there would in relation to each marriage be one and only one jurisdiction competent to decree dissolution, a jurisdiction moreover (assuming that " domicil " was given both a common and a sensible interpretation) which
C could normally be that with which the spouses could be taken to have identified themselves. Recognising the attractive simplicity of this, one may say that even in 1895 the basic assumption was insecure. For even then " domicil " as a connecting factor had in many states given way to the rival basis of nationality. Lord Watson, indeed, quotes from Bar (probably the second edition of his work on private international law of 1892) these words (150) " in actions of
D divorce . . . the judge of the domicil or nationality is the only competent judge ". But the reference to nationality does not seem to have struck his attention: at least he makes no further reference to it.

Since 1895 the hypothesis of a jus gentium based on " domicil " as the sole and commonly accepted basis of jurisdiction in divorce has been seriously weakened.

E   First, in *Udny* v. *Udny* (151) Lord Westbury was able to say (152):

" The civil status [of each individual] is governed universally by one single principle, namely, that of domicil . . . it is on this basis that the personal rights of the party, that is to say, the law which determines his majority or minority, his marriage, succession, testacy, or intestacy, must depend. International law depends on rules which, being in great measure derived
F   from the Roman law, are common to the jurisprudence of all civilised nations . . ."

This uniformity has, however, largely dissolved. Important differences as to the meaning of " domicil " have emerged both as between common law and civil law systems, and at least within the former, between one country and
G   another. By contrast with the American conception (from which via Story it mainly seems to have been derived) the English has increased in rigidity and in divergence from any necessary relation to the real considerations on which matrimonial disputes ought to be adjudicated. Lord Penzance in a much quoted passage (*Wilson* v. *Wilson* (153)) said (154):

" It is both just and reasonable, therefore, that the differences of married
H   people should be adjusted in accordance with the laws of the community to which they belong and dealt with by the tribunals which alone can administer those laws."

Developments in English law, however, particularly since *Winans* v. *A.-G.* (155), and its persistent refusal to allow a separate domicil to a married woman even if separated from or abandoned by her husband, have meant that " domicil "
I   frequently does not represent the community to which people belong.

Second, it is now well accepted that domicil is not the only or commonly accepted " connecting factor " in matters of status or personal law: nationality is one which many states consider appropriate. (See Dr. Cheshire's article in 61 Law Quarter Review, p. 352, and Rabel, Conflict of Laws.)

---

(150) [1895-99] All E.R. Rep. at p. 845;   [1895] A.C. at p. 538.
(151) (1869), L.R. 1 Sc. & Div. 441.   (152) (1869), L.R. 1 Sc. & Div. at p. 457.
(153) (1872), L.R. 2 P. & D. 435.   (154) (1872), L.R. 2 P. & D. at p. 442.
   (155) [1904-07] All E.R. Rep. 410;   [1904] A.C. 287.

Third, occasions of conflict between domestic jurisdictions in matrimonial   **A**
matters have multiplied. Visiting forces in two world wars brought about a
large number of mixed marriages and these have been added to by displacements
of population leaving one spouse in a different country from that to which
the other has moved, often, even if willing, unable to move there. Problems
arising from these situations have forced themselves on the attention of the
courts and it is of interest to follow their reactions. Broadly it can be said that,   **B**
though on occasions, mainly in undefended cases, judges have shown themselves willing to depart from the strictness of the domicil principle, they have
ultimately felt compelled to return to it. But, and this is significant, too, there
have been many occasions where, after they have done so, Parliament has
intervened, and while nominally maintaining the principle has grafted exceptions
on to it to take account of realities.   **C**

I. *Le Mesurier* (156) established that parties resident in Ceylon could only
obtain a divorce in the country of their domicil, a rule which logically applied to
all British domiciled persons residing anywhere in the British Empire. It was
some time before Parliament interfered, and not till a similar case relating to
Indian divorces had come before the English court. In *Keyes* v. *Keyes and
Gray* (157), the parties were domiciled in England but resident in India. The   **D**
High Court of Lahore had granted a divorce in reliance on the Indian Divorce
Act, 1869. SIR HENRY DUKE, P., declared the divorce to be invalid. In his
judgment he referred to the fact that in three earlier cases decided in England
it had been assumed that Indian decrees of divorce between British subjects
(presumably domiciled in England) were valid, and to a passage in DICEY'S
CONFLICT OF LAWS where that author had expressed the opinion that divorces   **E**
in India could be given on a residence basis. SIR HENRY DUKE, P., held, however,
that this doctrine, appearing to rest on the Court of Appeal decision in *Niboyet*
v. *Niboyet* (158) had been superseded by *Le Mesurier* v. *Le Mesurier* (156).
After this and similar divorces had been retrospectively validated by Parliament,
the Indian and Colonial Divorce Jurisdiction Act, 1926, (159) empowered courts
in India or elsewhere in His Majesty's dominions, as laid down by order in council,   **F**
to grant divorces to persons domiciled in the United Kingdom as if they were
domiciled in the territory in question. While domicil was thus, nominally, or
notionally, retained as the basis, jurisdiction was exercisable on the ground
of *residence* of the petitioner at the time of presenting his petition and of *last
residence together by the parties*. The substantive law to be applied was English
law. This Act was applied by order in council (160) to various territories and to   **G**
Ceylon in 1936.

II. As regards war marriages, in the 1914-18 war the Matrimonial Causes
(Dominion Troops) Act, 1919, gave power to United Kingdom courts to grant
matrimonial relief in effect to British wives marrying in the United Kingdom
any member of H.M. Forces domiciled in any British possession or protectorate
to which the Act might be applied as if the parties were domiciled in the United   **H**
Kingdom. This jurisdiction could not be exercised, however, if the parties had
resided together in the country of the husband's domicil. Thus the Act sanctioned
a breach of the principle of unitary jurisdiction at the place of the husband's
domicil.

III. Meanwhile English courts had been concerned with the problem of
women, domiciled in England at the time of their marriages, married to foreigners   **I**
domiciled elsewhere. Such a case was *Ogden* v. *Ogden* (161): the respondent's

---

(156) [1895-99] All E.R. Rep. 836; [1895] A.C. 517.
(157) [1921] P. 204.   (158) (1878), 4 P.D. 1.
(159) 3 HALSBURY'S STATUTES (2nd Edn.) 1158.
(160) See 4 HALSBURY'S STATUTORY INSTRUMENTS (First Re-Issue) 278-280 " Divorce
Jurisdiction within the Commonwealth ".
(161) [1904-07] All E.R. Rep. 86; [1908] P. 46.

A first husband had obtained a nullity decree in France, the country of his nationality and of his domicil. The judgment of Sir Gorell Barnes, P. (later Lord Gorell), in the Court of Appeal contained two important passages. In the first he said (162) that it was no real exception to the principle of recognition of divorces granted by the court where the parties are domiciled that

B   " in cases where a wife has been deserted in the country of the domicil by her husband in circumstances entitling her to sue for divorce it has been held that she might sue in the courts of the country of the domicil notwithstanding the fact that the husband has left the country and might possibly have done so with the intention of acquiring a domicil in another country. The decree in such a case is justified, either by considering that the husband cannot be heard to say that he has changed his domicil, or, as

C   some have thought, that the wife must ex necessitate be entitled to treat the country of the previous matrimonial domicil as still being the country of her domicil, and to require its courts to do justice to her, because otherwise it would be impossible for a wife so situated to obtain a decree, as the respondent might keep changing his abode from place to place, asserting that he had abandoned his original domicil, and any domicil with which

D   it were sought to fix him."

From the Report of the Royal Commission on Divorce in 1912 (163), of which Lord Gorell was chairman, it appears that the cases which he had in mind were undefended cases. In the second passage Lord Gorell suggested (164) that where the court of the husband's domicil had declared the marriage to be void, thereby making her a wife in her country but not in his, the English court

E   might dissolve her marriage on the basis that the foreign court had relieved her of any obligation to observe the domicil of her husband. These observations are stated to rest on considerations of justice, in circumstances in which the reasonableness of the international rule, as to the unity of domicil, ceases to be apparent. This seems good sense and a basis of sound law.

F   A number of other pronouncements by judges relating to the position of wives deserted by or separated from their husbands can be found in the cases. I refer to some of these, though these were not authoritative at the time, so as to show that even under the prevailing authority of Le Mesurier (165) another current of opinion continued to run to which ultimately Parliament gave recognition.

G   In Armytage v. Armytage (166), Gorell Barnes, J., said this (167):

        " The court does not now pronounce a decree of dissolution where the parties are not domiciled in this country except in favour of a wife deserted by her husband, or whose husband has so conducted himself towards her that she is justified in living apart from him, and who up to the time when she was deserted or began so to be justified was domiciled with her husband

H   in this country, in which case, without necessarily resorting to the American doctrine that in such circumstances a wife may acquire a domicil of her own in the country of the matrimonial home, it is considered that in order to meet the injustice which might be done by compelling a wife to follow her husband from country to country he cannot be allowed to assert for the purposes of the suit that he has ceased to be domiciled in this country."

I In this he was following what had been said in Niboyet v. Niboyet (168):

        " The case of an adulterous husband deserting his wife by leaving the country of his domicil and assuming to domicil himself in another, might

(162) [1904-07] All E.R. Rep. at p. 101; [1908] P. at p. 78.
(163) Cmd. 6478.
(164) [1904-07] All E.R. Rep. at p. 103; [1908] P. at pp. 82, 83.
(165) [1895-99] All E.R. Rep. 836; [1895] A.C. 517.
(166) [1895-99] All E.R. Rep. 377; [1898] P. 178.
(167) [1895-99] All E.R. Rep. at p. 380; [1898] P. at p. 185.
(168) (1878), 4 P.D. at p. 14.

seem to raise an intolerable injustice; but we cannot help think that in   A
such case if sued by his wife in the country in which he had left her, he
could not be heard to allege that that was not still the place of his married
home, i.e., for the purpose of that suit, of his domicil.''

The interest of this is that it was said by BRETT, L.J., whose dissenting judgment
has been taken to have prevailed over those of the majority. Similar observations
by SIR GORELL BARNES, P., were made in *Bater* v. *Bater* (169).   B

Again the rule of the single and exclusive authority of the court of the domicil
reasserted itself in the courts. After SIR GORELL BARNES, P.'s, observations
in *Ogden* v. *Ogden* (170) had been followed in two undefended cases, in each
case of English wives married to foreigners domiciled abroad (*Stathatos* v.
Stathatos (171), *De Montaigu* v. *De Montaigu* (172)), BUCKNILL, J., reverted to
the old principle in *Herd* v. *Herd* (173). In doing so he followed two decisions   C
of which mention must be made.

(i) *Lord Advocate* v. *Jaffrey* (174) was a decision of this House in a Scottish
appeal. It was not a matrimonial case but one of succession. The husband
having from a Scottish domicil of origin acquired a domicil of choice in
Queensland, Australia, it was sought to establish, on the death of his wife   D
who had remained in Scotland, that she had retained a Scottish domicil
by reason of the fact that her husband's conduct would have justified a
decree of judicial separation. No such decree had in fact been obtained,
so the proposition was plainly untenable, but their lordships expressed
clear opinions that during the subsistence of the marriage no distinct domicils
as between husband and wife could exist.   E

(ii) *A.-G. for Alberta* v. *Cook* (175) was a decision of the Privy Council
in an appeal from the Supreme Court of Alberta. Reversing the decision
of the Supreme Court (whose judgment nevertheless contained some persuasive reasoning) a strong Board held that (176)

"a decree of judical separation . . . does not enable the wife to acquire
a domicil different from that of her husband *and thus* [my italics]   F
entitle her to sue for a divorce in a court other than that of her husband's
domicil.''

The injustice there existing was glaring since the husband, after separating
from the wife had drifted from one place to another and eventually disappeared, so that his domicil could not be ascertained.

                                                                                G

It is hardly surprising that the Canadian Parliament intervened and by the
Divorce Jurisdiction Act, 1930, enabled a wife deserted by her husband who
had been living apart for two years or more to seek divorce in the province
where the husband was domiciled immediately prior to the desertion.

Consequent on *Herd* v. *Herd* (173) Parliament in this country found it necessary
to intervene to provide a remedy for deserted wives. In doing so, it was following   H
an initiative which had long since been taken in a number of Commonwealth
countries. Starting with the Victoria Divorce Act, 1889, New South Wales
in 1892, New Zealand in 1898, Tasmania in 1919, Western Australia in 1911,
Queensland in 1923, Southern Australia in 1928, had all in slightly differing forms
enacted legislation enabling wives deserted by their husbands to sue for divorce
in the state where they were domiciled before desertion. With regard to this   I
legislation DICEY in his CONFLICT OF LAWS (2nd Edn. 1908), after expressing
his opinion that both divorces granted under the Indian Divorce Act and those
granted under Colonial Acts would be valid in England and throughout the

(169) [1906] P. at p. 211.   (170) [1904-07] All E.R. Rep. 86; [1908] P. 46.
(171) [1913] P. 46.   (172) [1913] P. 154.
(173) [1936] 2 All E.R. 1516; [1936] P. 205.
(174) [1920] All E.R. Rep. 242; [1921] 1 A.C. 146.
(175) [1926] All E.R. Rep. 525; [1926] A.C. 444.   (176) [1926] A.C. at p. 444.

A British dominions, continues that if such divorces are admitted to have extra-territorial effect, English courts will " probably be driven to relax the rigidity of the rule that divorce jurisdiction depends wholly on domicil ".

In the United Kingdom, legislation corresponding to these Colonial Acts was passed in 1937 (the year, one may note, in which almost complete equality as to the substantive law of divorce was established), although a Bill in similar
B terms had been laid before Parliament in 1921. The Matrimonial Causes Act, 1937, s. 13 while (as before) nominally preserving both the jurisdictional rule and the unity of domicil, enabled wives to bring matrimonial proceedings in cases of desertion by, or deportation of, the husband.

This legislative trend was continued and carried further by two later Acts. The Matrimonial Causes (War Marriages) Act, 1944, made, in relation to the
C second world war, similar provisions as regards wives domiciled in the United Kingdom as had been made by the earlier Act of 1919. It did not apply to marriages celebrated after May 31, 1950. Of more general importance and relevance was the Law Reform (Miscellaneous Provisions) Act, 1949. This Act, which came into force on Dec. 16, 1949, conferred (177) on the High Court in England divorce jurisdiction in cases where the wife has been resident in England
D for three years immediately prior to the commencement of proceedings, provided that the husband is not domiciled elsewhere in the United Kingdom. It is to be noted that there is no requirement either that the wife should be a British subject, or that she should previously have been domiciled in England, so that the jurisdiction can be invoked by foreigners on the basis of three years' residence only, whatever the purposes or circumstances of that residence may be. A
E somewhat similar provision had been enacted in New Zealand in 1930 (Divorce and Matrimonial Causes (Amendment) Act, 1930, s. 3).

These developments, in my opinion, have made such extensive breaches in the unitary domicil theory which formed the premise of the *Le Mesurier* (178) decision as to make it impossible any longer to maintain that there is a positive and rigid rule of English private international law that foreign decrees of divorce
F will be recognised only if granted by the court of the husband's domicil. The principle stated by that case, and followed, no doubt quite correctly, by the courts in the intervening period, now, so far as it relates to the recognition of foreign decrees, calls for modification. I have previously examined the decisions of this House which preceded *Le Mesurier* (178), and I need add only that I do not regard the decision of this House in *Salvesen (or Von Lorang) v. Austrian*
G *Property Administrator* (179) as adding any further strength or scope to the opinion of the Judicial Committee. What departure, then, from the latter ought now to be made?

My Lords, it is tempting, and in accordance with the empirical tradition, to confine oneself to the case now for decision: to proceed from case to case, until the occasion for a fresh generalisation arrives, is certainly a sound method,
H and, at the other extreme, to attempt a comprehensive statement of the circumstances in which recognition should be given to foreign decrees, would be a task of great difficulty. When, however, we are called on, as here, to depart from an accepted rule, some endeavour must be made to state some principle, even though of only partial application, on which the departure may be founded. I should make it clear that this appeal, and the following observations, relate
I only to decrees of dissolution of marriage.

To start with it must be accepted that a close relation exists between the domestic jurisdiction of English courts on the one hand and the principles of recognition of foreign decrees on the other. How close this should be is a matter to which I shall return when I come to consider *Travers v. Holley and Holley* (180),

---

(177) See s. 1 (1) of the Act of 1949.
(178) [1895-99] All E.R. Rep. 836; [1895] A.C. 517.
(179) [1927] All E.R. Rep. 78; [1927] A.C. 641.
(180) [1953] 2 All E.R. 794; [1953] P. 246.

but there must be some relation. This is because a person's status, even when A some foreign element is involved, ought so far as possible to depend on one system, so as to avoid what LORD PENZANCE in *Wilson* v. *Wilson* (181) called the scandal of differing status in different countries.

Secondly, it is necessary at the present time (i.e., until the law is changed by Parliament or, so far as that is possible, by the judges) to start from the foundation that the jurisdiction of the English courts as regards dissolution of marriage B rests, subject to specific statutory exceptions in favour of wives, on domicil. It is further necessary, in my opinion, for the purposes of this case to accept that in English law a married woman cannot acquire a domicil separate from that of her husband: to alter this rule would involve a number of consequences in relation to other matters than divorce which would be beyond what is appropriate for the decision of this case, and can probably be done only by Parliament. C

Consistently with the first principle, the basic rule should be preserved that English courts should continue to recognise foreign decrees of divorce if, and only if, these are granted (or recognised—see *Armitage* v. *A.-G.* (182), by the court of the husband's domicil.

There are two possible directions in which (as shown by the matters to which I have referred) departure might be made from the strictness of these principles. D

1. Recognition might, in appropriate circumstances, be given to the factor of nationality, whether of both parties, or conceivably of one party, to the marriage.

2. Recognition might be given to decrees given on a residence basis, either generally, or in the particular case of wives living apart from their husbands where to subject them uniquely to the law of their husband's domicil would E cause injustice, and where the jurisdiction of the court of the country of residence is appropriate.

As regards the first of these, the relevance of nationality as a connecting factor in certain cases may, in principle, be accepted. In individual situations, however, many factors are involved: nationality (and the complexities of F " British nationality "), sometimes double nationality, or statelessness, and, especially as regards non-unitary states, these may be combined in different ways with residence or with domicil. The present case is one in which, in combination with other factors, the nationality factor (of both spouses) appears to me to be relevant on the question of recognition. In other cases the nationality of one spouse may be similarly relevant at least in relation to the quality of G residence, where jurisdiction is based on residence. Beyond this, at the present, I am unable to define the situations in which nationality may be taken into account.

As regards the second of these, although it may be possible without any general change in the law by Parliament for judicial decision to allow recognition generally to decrees based on the non-domiciliary residence of the spouses, H to do so in the present context appears to me to go further than is justified by the considerations advanced before us. On the other hand, it is my clear opinion that the particular departure from the rule, or tyranny of the domicil which I have mentioned (above, 2), is justified and is long overdue.

If it be said that it is illogical, or asymmetrical, to sanction a breach in the domicil rule in favour of wives and not in favour of husbands, then the answer I must be that experience has shown (and has so convinced our own and other legislatures) that it is the wife who requires this mitigation, that the nature of what is required has been clearly shown, and that (with the possible exception of the case where he is respondent to a wife petitioner and desires to cross petition) no corresponding case has been shown to exist as regards the husband. He retains his domicil and the right to change it. All that this development does is

(181) (1872), L.R. 2 P. & D. at p. 442.
(182) [1906] P. 135.

A remove an inequitable inequality arising from the anachronistic dependence
of the wife for her domicil on her husband.

How far should this relaxation go? In my opinion, it would be in accordance
with the developments that I have mentioned and with the trend of legislation
—mainly our own but also that of other countries with similar social systems
—to recognise divorces given to wives by the courts of their residence wherever
B a real and substantial connexion is shown between the petitioner and the country,
or territory, exercising jurisdiction. I use these expressions so as to enable the
courts, who must decide each case, to consider both the length and quality of
the residence and to take into account such other factors as nationality which
may reinforce the connexion. Equally they would enable the courts (as they
habitually do without difficulty) to reject residence of passage or residence, to
C use the descriptive expression of the older cases, resorted to by persons who
properly should seek relief here for the purpose of obtaining relief which our
courts would not give. I draw support in this from the opinion of *Le Mesurier* v.
Le Mesurier (183) where it was said (184):

D " Bona fide residence is an intelligible expression, if, as their lordships
conceive, it means residence which has not been resorted to for the mere
purpose of getting a divorce which was not obtainable in the country of
domicil."

Applying the principle stated to the facts of this case, without recapitulation,
the conclusion easily emerges that the Czechoslovakian divorce of 1949 should be
recognised.   •

E Finally, as to *Travers* v. *Holley and Holley* (185). I do not find it necessary
to discuss either the case itself, or those which have followed it, in detail, since
I am in general agreement with what my noble and learned friend, Lord Reid,
has said about it. The decision itself is clearly unexceptionable and it has
provided a working rule which, though not without some process of refinement,
has proved, if not its logic, at least its utility in the courts. It is only when it is
F invoked to lay down a cast iron rule that the courts' power and duty to recognise
foreign decrees of divorce follows by implication from amendments to the domestic
law as to divorce jurisdiction that I begin to find difficulties. For I am unwilling
to accept either that the law as to recognition of foreign divorce (still less other)
jurisdiction must be a mirror image of our own law or that the pace of recognition
must be geared to the haphazard movement of our legislative process. There
G is no reason why this should be so, for the courts' decisions as regards recognition
are shaped by considerations of policy which may differ from those which influence
Parliament in changing the domestic law. Moreover, as a matter of history, it
is the law as to recognition which has led and that as to domestic jurisdiction
which has followed, and Parliament, by refraining from legislating as to recognition (as with minor exceptions it has done) must be taken to have approved
H this divergence. So I would not regard the *Travers* v. *Holley and Holley* (185)
rule as amounting to more than a general working principle that changes in
domestic jurisdiction should be taken into account by the courts in decisions
as to what foreign decrees they will recognise.

If the principles of recognition of foreign decrees of divorce are placed on the
more general basis which I have suggested (rather than being governed by the
I quasi-mathematical application in reverse of domestic legislation) I have no
fears that uncertainty will be introduced into the law. The courts are well able
to perform the task of examining the reality of the connexion between the
resident petitioner wife and the jurisdiction invoked, bearing in mind, but not
being rigidly bound by, the developments of domestic jurisdiction. In so acting,

---

(183) [1895-99] All E.R. Rep. 836; [1895] A.C. 517.
(184) [1895-99] All E.R. Rep. at p. 846; [1895] A.C. at p. 538.
(185) [1953] 2 All E.R. 794; [1953] P. 246.

I am convinced that they are more likely to reach just, and to avoid artificial, **A** results.

I would dismiss the appeal.

LORD PEARSON: My Lords, the former system of law, regulating the exercise of divorce jurisdiction by the English courts and their recognition of divorces granted in other countries as valid in England, was a compact and **B** symmetrical system, and I think that the main principles can be shortly stated as follows:

1. Jurisdiction in divorce was based exclusively on domicil, so that—(*a*) an English court would not grant a divorce unless the parties were domiciled in England, and (*b*) a divorce granted by a court of another country would not be recognised as valid in England unless the parties were domiciled in **C** that country or the divorce would be recognised in the country of their domicil.

2. " Domicil " had the meaning given to it in the English case-law, including *Winans* v. *A.-G.* (186) and *Bowie* (*or Ramsay*) v. *Liverpool Royal Infirmary* (187).

3. The wife's domicil was always the same as that of her husband, so that **D** (*a*) she could not have a separate qualification for suing for divorce in England, and (*b*) a divorce obtained by her in a court of some other country by virtue of a separate qualification would not be recognised as valid in England.

The domicil referred to is, of course, domicil at the relevant date, which is, I suppose, the date of the commencement of the proceedings, but it does not have **E** to be defined for the purpose of the present appeal.

The former system was found to be, or became, unrealistic and disadvantageous in a number of respects. Many countries have taken nationality rather than domicil as the basis of divorce jurisdiction. Some of the countries which take domicil as the basis of divorce jurisdiction have a less exacting concept of domicil —more simply and directly related to the idea of a settled home or permanent **F** residence—than the concept established by the English case-law. Some countries have allowed the wife in certain situations to have a separate qualification for suing for divorce. The discordance between the principles of the former system in this country and the actual practice of other countries was productive of " limping " marriages: the parties might be still married according to the law of England, though divorced according to the law of some other country or **G** countries. There was conspicuous hardship in the case of a deserted wife living in England and having her husband domiciled in some other country.

Also there have been relevant changes in general conditions. There is greatly increased mobility. There have been transfers of population and extensive displacements of persons as well as normal migration. There is more international trade and international travel. Divorces have become far more frequent, **H** so that the stability of marriage has been diminished. Another new element is the prevalence of retirement pensions, which may render the application of the very exacting concept of domicil more difficult in relation at any rate to matrimonial jurisdiction, because it may quite often happen that a man intends to keep his home, earn his living and bring up his family over a period of many years in one country and yet to go to another country when he retires on pension. **I**

The disadvantages of the former system, aggravated or at any rate made more manifest by changes in general conditions, have led to corrective legislation. The enactments dealing specially with war-time or post-war situations or with particular Commonwealth problems would not necessarily affect the validity of the general principles on which the former system was founded, because those

(186) [1904-07] All E.R. Rep. 410; [1904] A.C. 287.
(187) [1930] All E.R. Rep. 127; [1930] A.C. 588.

A principles might be still generally correct though needing some exceptions of a temporary or otherwise limited character. There are, however, two enactments having such generality and permanence that they must be regarded as affecting the general principles of the system. One of these enactments, relating primarily to the case of the deserted wife, began as s. 13 of the Matrimonial Causes Act, 1937, and was re-enacted as s. 18 (1) (a) of the Matrimonial Causes Act, 1950

B and is now contained in s. 40 (1) (a) of the Matrimonial Causes Act 1965. The other of these enactments, relating to a wife who has resided in England for three years, began as part of s. 1 of the Law Reform (Miscellaneous Provisions) Act, 1949, and was re-enacted as s. 18 (1) (b) of the Matrimonial Causes Act, 1950, and is now contained in s. 40 (1) (b) of the Act of 1965. These two enactments strike at the roots of the former system. An English court will now in some cases

C grant a divorce although the parties are not domiciled in England, and will now in some cases grant a divorce on the basis that the wife has, separately from her husband, a qualification of her own for suing for divorce.

These enactments, however, relate only to the exercise of jurisdiction by the English courts. They contain no provision as to the recognition in England of the validity in England of divorces granted in other countries. In fact the law relating

D to such recognition is almost entirely judge-made law; but it does not follow that the law relating to such recognition must remain unaffected by the statutory changes in the basis of the exercise of divorce jurisdiction by the English courts.

I think that as a minimum the principle of Travers v. Holley and Holley (188) must be applied in this case.

E   " On principle it seems to me plain that our courts in this matter should recognise a jurisdiction which they themselves claim "

(per Somervell, L.J., (189))

"... it would be contrary to principle and inconsistent with comity if the courts of this country refused to recognise a jurisdiction which mutatis

F mutandis they claim for themselves "

(per Hodson, L.J., (190)). No doubt the principle should be regarded as a general principle, not to be applied as a cast iron rule in every case without regard to the character of the relevant English legislation. The jurisdiction exercised by the English courts under the two enactments to which I have referred (now contained in s. 40 (1) of the Matrimonial Causes Act 1965) is, how-

G ever, of a general and apparently permanent character—not related to special or transient conditions—and there is no evident reason for refusing recognition to divorces granted in other countries in cases where, mutatis mutandis, jurisdiction would be exercised by the English courts under either of those two enactments. The principle applies if the facts are such as would, mutatis mutandis, confer jurisdiction on the English courts, even though the court in the other country

H may have claimed jurisdiction on some other basis (Robinson-Scott v. Robinson-Scott (191)).

In the present case the first wife, when she obtained her divorce from the husband had been resident for more than three years, in fact all her life, in Czechoslovakia. She obtained her divorce in February, 1949, some months before the passing of the Law Reform (Miscellaneous Provisions) Act, 1949,

I which made three years' residence in England a qualification for a wife to sue for divorce in England. The husband married or purported to marry the second wife in 1959, about ten years later. On what sequence of dates can the Travers v. Holley and Holley (188) principle be applied? There are arguments to the contrary

---

(188) [1953] 2 All E.R. 794; [1953] P. 246.
(189) [1953] 2 All E.R. at p. 797; [1953] P. at p. 251.
(190) [1953] 2 All E.R. at p. 800; [1953] P. at p. 257.
(191) [1957] 3 All E.R. at p. 478; [1958] P. at p. 88.

as stated in the judgment of LATEY, J., (192) at first instance and the minority A judgment of RUSSELL, L.J., in the Court of Appeal (193), but on the whole I think that an affirmative answer should be given for the reasons stated in the judgments of LORD DENNING, M.R., (194) and DIPLOCK, L.J., (195) in the Court of Appeal and in the opinions of my noble and learned friends, LORD MORRIS OF BORTH-Y-GEST and LORD PEARCE.

Thus, my first ground for dismissing the appeal is that the first wife had been B living in Czechoslovakia for more than three years and the *Travers* v. *Holley and Holley* (196) principle applies, although the Czech court did not base their jurisdiction on residence and although the divorce in Czechoslovakia preceded by a few months the passing of the Act of 1949.

I also think that wider considerations are involved in this appeal. So long as the former system prevailed, it was a symmetrical system: the domicil of the C parties was the one and only basis on which any court anywhere could properly exercise divorce jurisdiction: therefore, the basis for recognising divorces granted in other countries was of necessity exactly coincident with the basis for exercising jurisdiction in this country. Now the former system is no longer maintainable. It has been undermined and discredited by its disadvantages and the changes in general conditions and the passing of the two enactments to which I have referred. D It no longer stands in the way of a realistic and reasonable view being taken of the range of cases in which validity should be accorded in England to divorces granted in other countries.

At this stage I am conscious of the lack of the apparatus of law reform—issuing a questionnaire and awaiting considered replies to it, receiving memoranda, hearing oral evidence, collecting statistics and obtaining information as to the E systems prevailing in other countries. We have had, however, valuable assistance from counsel, and there is a great deal of information set out in the Report of the Royal Commission on Marriage and Divorce, presented in 1956 (197). The Royal Commission made recommendations for legislation on the subject of the recognition of divorces granted in other countries. Since then there has not been any legislation implementing those recommendations or otherwise providing for such F recognition. In the meantime the courts have to operate. There is a practical need for some guidance to be given by your lordships' House, even if it can only be given in rather general terms. I am not intending to say that there necessarily ought to be legislation, but only that in the absence of legislation it is appropriate that there should be some general guidance from this House.

There is the plain fact that divorce jurisdiction is exercised on different bases G in different countries. It cannot be said that the English basis—of domicil according to English case law plus the two enactments in favour of wives—is the only reasonable basis. Domicil according to a less exacting definition would be a not unreasonable basis and would have some advantages. The basis of nationality would in a great many cases give the same result as any basis of domicil, and it has the advantage of simplicity, and it seems to have been in use H in many countries for many years. Nationality, however, is not available as a basis for use by federal and other nations which contain states, provinces or countries having the same nationality but separate divorce jurisdictions. Such nations will naturally use domicil as their basis, or they might use some residential qualification falling short of domicil. Therefore, unless the nations now using nationality as their basis are willing to change it (which is not indicated), there I must be in the international sphere at least two different bases of jurisdiction being used. The duality is in that sense inevitable, and in any case it exists, and it should not be ignored.

---

(192) [1966] 1 All E.R. at p. 782.   (193) [1966] 3 All E.R. at p. 591.
(194) [1966] 3 All E.R. at p. 584.   (195) [1966] 3 All E.R. at p. 587.
(196) [1953] 2 All E.R. 794; [1953] P. 246.   (197) Cmd. 9678.

A   It seems to me that, subject to appropriate limitations, a divorce granted in another country on the basis of nationality or on the basis of domicil (whether according to English case law or according to a less exacting definition) should be recognised as valid in England. Also if the law of the other country concerned enables a wife living apart from her husband to retain or acquire a separate qualification of nationality or domicil for the purpose of suing for divorce, and the

B   jurisdiction has been exercised on the basis of that qualification, that would not, normally at any rate, be a reason for refusing recognition.

One obvious limitation is that a decree obtained by fraud or involving grave injustice should not be recognised. In addition there is a limitation which can only be indicated in rather general terms, and I will gratefully borrow some phrases. In the words of my noble and learned friend, Lord Wilberforce,

C   there must be a real and substantial connexion between the petitioner and the country or territory exercising jurisdiction. In the words of my noble and learned friend, Lord Pearce, the court must be not " simply purveying divorce to foreigners who wish to buy it ". In the words of Mr. Commissioner Latey, Q.C., the courts must not be used " for the convenience of birds of passage " (Arnold v. Arnold (198)). An alleged domicil can be fictitious: the petitioner may have

D   declared his intention to settle permanently in the country concerned, but the evidence may show that he was only resorting there temporarily in order to obtain a divorce. Similarly a nationality might be acquired temporarily for the purpose of obtaining a divorce. Also nationality might perhaps in some circumstances be regarded as insufficient to found jurisdiction, if there was no longer any real and substantial connexion between the petitioner and the country of his or her

E   nationality.

As to the validity in England of divorces granted in other countries on the basis of a merely residential qualification, I feel that there is a difficulty. As a matter of general principle, I would have thought that mere residence, falling short of domicil according to the less exacting definition, ought not to be a sufficient qualification. The broad distinction is between a person who makes his home in a

F   country and a person who is a mere sojourner there. A person may be appointed to some diplomatic or military or commercial post in a foreign country and serve there for three or more years without becoming either dissociated from the community of his home country or associated with the community of the foreign country. His wife may be in the same position. There is, however, the second of the enactments referred to above, the one now contained in s. 40 (1) (b) of the

G   Act of 1965, which enables a wife after three years' residence in England, to sue for divorce, whatever may be the nationality or domicil of her husband and herself or of either of them. The principle of Travers v. Holley and Holley (199) then requires that a divorce obtained in a foreign country by a wife who has resided in that country for three years or more should be recognised as valid in England. On the facts of this case the question whether recognition should be extended to a

H   divorce granted on the basis of any other residential qualification—for example a husband's residence for three years or more, or a wife's residence for some period less than three years—does not need to be decided and I prefer to express no opinion on it except that there is a difficulty.

In my view, the divorce obtained by the first wife in Czechoslovakia in February, 1949, should be recognised as having been valid in England in 1959,

I   so that the husband was free to marry and did validly marry the second wife in 1959. Such recognition should be given on two grounds. First, the Travers v. Holley and Holley (199) principle should be applied as mentioned above. Secondly, the divorce was granted in Czechoslovakia on the basis of the first wife's proved Czechoslovakian nationality, and there was no lack of real and substantial connexion with Czechoslovakia. The first wife had lived there all her life, and had

(198) [1957] 1 All E.R. at p. 576; [1957] P. at p. 253.
(199) [1953] 2 All E.R. 794; [1953] P. 246.

been married there, and had her matrimonial home there and was left there by the   A
husband. There is no suggestion that she had any intention or desire to go to any
other country. The husband had originally Czechoslovakian domicil and
presumably also nationality. There is a finding that he acquired an English
domicil of choice in 1946, but there is no finding or evidence that he acquired any
new nationality.

I would dismiss the appeal.   B

Appeal dismissed.

Solicitors: *Schindler & Co.* (for the husband); *Boxall & Boxall*, agents for
Boys & Maughan, Margate (for the wife).

[*Reported by* KATHLEEN J. H. O'BRIEN, *Barrister-at-Law.*]

C

MINISTER OF LABOUR v. MORGAN.

[QUEEN'S BENCH DIVISION (Lord Parker, C.J., Widgery and O'Connor, JJ.),
April 20, 1967.]

D

*Selective Employment Tax—Refund—Sub-postmaster employing two women
wholly in the handling of money and clerical work—Whether employees
engaged in non-qualifying activities carried on for office purposes—Offices,
Shops and Railway Premises Act* 1963 (c. 41), *s.* 1 (2)—*Selective Employment Payments Act* 1966 (c. 32), *s.* 2 (2), (*b*) (ii), *s.* 10 (1).

The respondent was the sub-postmaster of a private sub-post office   E
where he employed two ladies, whose activities were the ordinary activities
of a post office with the exception that no telegraph facilities were afforded
to the public. The activities included the selling of stamps, postal and
money orders, savings stamps and insurance stamps, dealing with savings
bank deposits and pensions and issuing licences. The respondent paid
selective employment tax in respect of the two employees. The sub-post   F
office was an establishment engaged by way of business under s. 2 (2) (*a*)*
of the Selective Employment Payments Act 1966, wholly in activities
covered by minimum list heading 707† in Ord. XIX of the Standard
Industrial Classification and the two employees engaged wholly in the
activities of the establishment and formed for the purposes of s. 2 (2) (*b*) (i)*
of the Act of 1966 more than half of those employed there. By s. 2 (2)   G
(*b*) (ii)* of the Act of 1966, an applicant for a refund of selective employment tax had to show that more than half of such employees were not so
employed wholly or mainly in non-qualifying activities, which, by s. 10 (1)‡
of the Act of 1966 included activities carried on for office purposes within the
meaning of s. 1 (2)§ of the Offices, Shops and Railway Premises Act 1963,
which included clerical work and handling money. On appeal by the   H
Minister of Labour from a decision of the Industrial Tribunal that the
respondent was entitled to a refund of the selective employment tax under
s. 2 (1)* of the Act of 1966 which he had paid in respect of the two employees,

Held: the respondent was not entitled to a refund of the selective
employment tax for the following reasons—

(i) because the proper approach to s. 2 of the Act of 1966 was to look at   I
the occupation of each person and see what activities were involved and then
to consider whether that person was wholly or mainly engaged in non-
qualifying activities (see p. 737, letter D, post); and

---

* Section 2, so far as material, is set out at p. 734, letters A to C and E, post.
† Heading 707, so far as material, reads: "All post office establishments . . . and
other telephone or telegraph services."
‡ Section 10 (1), so far as material, is set out at p. 735, letter D, post.
§ Section 1 (2), so far as material, is set out at p. 735, letters H and I, post.

A   (ii) because applying that approach, the whole of the work of the two
employees was the handling of money and clerical work within the meaning
of office purposes in s. 1 (2) of the Act of 1963 and these were " non-qualifying activities " as defined in s. 10 (1) of the Act of 1966 and accordingly
the requirements of s. 2 (2) (*b*) (ii) of the Act of 1966 were not satisfied
(see p. 736, letter F, post).

B   Appeal allowed.

[As to selective employment tax, see SUPPLEMENT to 33 HALSBURY'S LAWS
(3rd Edn.) para. 479A.

For the Offices, Shops and Railway Premises Act 1963, s. 1, see 43 HALSBURY'S
STATUTES (2nd Edn.) 189.

C   For the Selective Employment Payments Act 1966, s. 2, s. 10, see 46 HALS-
BURY'S STATUTES (2nd Edn.) 171, 182.]

Appeal.

This was an appeal by the appellant, the Minister of Labour, from a decision
of the Industrial Tribunal, dated Jan. 17, 1967, whereby it was decided that the
establishment of the respondent, Alban Morgan, satisfied the requirements of
D s. 2 (2) (*a*) and (*b*) of the Selective Employment Payments Act 1966. The grounds
of the appeal were that the decision was wrong in law in that (a) the Industrial
Tribunal misdirected themselves as to the proper construction of the expression
" office purposes " within the meaning of s. 10 (1) of the Selective Employment
Payments Act 1966, and s. 1 (2) of the Offices, Shops and Railway Premises Act
1963; and (b) on the evidence more than half of the employed persons employed
E in any employment in the respondents' establishment were so employed wholly
or mainly in non-qualifying activities, viz., activities carried on for office purposes; and that accordingly the respondent's establishment did not satisfy
the requirements of s. 2 (2) (*a*) and (*b*) of the Selective Employment Payments
Act 1966. The facts are set out in the judgment of LORD PARKER, C.J.

F   *The Solicitor-General (Sir Dingle Foot, Q.C.), P. E. Webster, Q.C.,* and *G. Slynn*
for the appellant.

John Wilmers, Q.C., and *Brian Galpin* for the respondent.

LORD PARKER, C.J.: The respondent, Mr. Morgan, was at all material
times the sub-postmaster at premises at 54, Bounces Road, London, N.9; it
G was a private sub-post office unassociated with the common form of sub-post
office which has a village shop or tobacconist as well. In that sub-post office
he employed two lady employees. Their activities, as found by the tribunal,
were the ordinary activities of a post office with the exception that there were
no telegraph facilities afforded to the public. The activities included the selling
of stamps, postal orders, money orders, dealing with savings bank deposits,
H selling savings stamps and insurance stamps, issuing licences and dealing with
pensions. In respect of those two employees the respondent paid selective
employment tax.

The question that arises in this appeal is whether he is entitled, under the
Selective Employment Payments Act 1966, to a refund of the tax which he
has paid in respect of each of those two employees. He applied to the Industrial
I Tribunal, who, on Jan. 17, 1967, decided that he was entitled to a refund. It is
against that decision that the appellant, the Minister of Labour, now appeals on
what has to be a point of law. This being the first case under the Act of 1966 that
has reached this court, it is convenient to read the relevant provisions. Section 1
deals with the payment of what is called selective employment premium; that
is not only a refund in respect of the tax paid in respect of any person, but a
premium in addition. Section 2 is dealing with refund of the tax alone; s. 3,
s. 4, s. 5 and s. 6 deal with special cases, which do not come within s. 1 and s. 2.
Section 2 (1) provides that:

"Where an employer has paid selective employment tax for any contri-   A
bution week in respect of a person in an employment to which this section
applies, then, subject to the provisions of s. 7 of this Act, the appropriate
Minister shall make to the employer in respect of that person and that
week a payment of an amount equal to the tax paid."

Subsection (2) then deals with cases to which that provision applies, and it   B
provides that:

"Subject to sub-s. (6) of this section, this section applies to any employment which, not being employment to which s. 1 of this Act applies, is
employment in, or carried out from, an establishment where—(a) the
establishment is engaged by way of business wholly or partly in activities
such as are mentioned in any one of paras. (a) to (e) of sub-s. (3) of this   C
section; and (b) subject to sub-s. (4) of this section, more than half of the
employed persons employed in any employment in, or carried out from,
that establishment—(i) are so employed wholly or mainly in connexion
with those activities; and (ii) are not so employed wholly or mainly in non-
qualifying activities . . ."

It is unnecessary to read any further in that subsection. Pausing there, it will   D
be seen that, before a refund can be obtained, the employer must first show
that the employment was in, or carried out from, an establishment engaged
by way of business wholly or partly in activities which are mentioned in certain
paragraphs of sub-s. (3). The only relevant provision in sub-s. (3) is to be found
in para. (a) (iv), which provides that:

"(3) The activities referred to in sub-s. (2) (a) of this section are—(a)   E
activities falling under any of the following minimum list headings in the
Standard Industrial Classification, namely—. . . (iv) any heading in Order
XIX (which relates to transport and communication) other than heading
709 . . ."

This is legislation by reference, and the Standard Industrial Classification is a   F
production of the Central Statistical Office first issued in 1948, and varied from
time to time. That classification is based on industries as opposed to occupations.
All persons, whatever their occupations, whether administrative work, technical
work, clerical work and so on, employed in a "Unit" of industry are employed
in the industry to which the "Unit" is classified. The classification itself comes
under a number of so-called orders, and each industry under each order has   G
what is called a minimum list heading. Order XIX, which is the order referred
to in s. 2 (3) (a) (iv), is an order headed "Transport and Communication". It
covers railways; it covers road passenger transport, including bus and tramway
service, taxis and private-hire cars; it covers road haulage contracting, sea
transport, port and inland water transport, air transport, and finally, under
minimum list heading 707, "Postal Services and Telecommunications". I say   H
"finally" because, although there is a minimum list heading 709 entitled
"Miscellaneous Transport Services and Storage", that is specifically excepted
by sub-s. (3) (a) (iv) and, accordingly, there is no doubt that, in the present case,
as was conceded before the Industrial Tribunal and before this court, this sub-
post office was an establishment engaged by way of business wholly in activities
mentioned in sub-s. (3), to wit, wholly engaged in postal services.   I

To return to s. 2 (2), once that is established, then before a refund can be
obtained two further conditions have to be satisfied. The first (sub-s. (2) (b) (i))
is that more than half of the employed persons employed in any employment
in, or carried out from, that establishment are so employed wholly or mainly in
connexion with those activities. Pausing there, if, as in this case, the establishment itself is wholly, as opposed to partially, engaged by way of business in
activities which qualify, then everybody employed in employment carried out
in that establishment is clearly wholly employed in connexion with those activities.

A   In other words, that first condition follows from the finding that the establishment in question is wholly engaged in the qualifying activities. It would only really have to be further considered where the establishment was only partly engaged in those activities. Again, to come back to this case, it is quite clear that these two ladies were engaged wholly in connexion with the activities of the establishment and that they formed more than half of those engaged there.

B   The applicant for the refund has, however, to prove the further matter set out in s. 2 (2) (*b*) (ii), namely, to repeat the words, that

"... more than half of the employed persons employed in any employment in, or carried out from, that establishment—. . . . (ii) are not so employed wholly or mainly in non-qualifying activities . . ."

C   In order to understand what is meant by "non-qualifying activities" one turns next to s. 10 (1), the interpretation section. There one finds the definition of "non-qualifying activities". I will first read the whole of the definition:

"'non-qualifying activities' means—(*a*) activities carried on for office purposes within the meaning of s. 1 (2) of the Offices, Shops and Railway Premises Act 1963, other than drawing and other than such activities
D   falling under minimum list heading 486 or under sub-head 1 of minimum list heading 702 in the Standard Industrial Classification; or (*b*) activities by way of the carriage of goods by road in connexion with a business—(i) by the person carrying on that business; or (ii) where that person is a company, by an associated company; or (*c*) activities by way of the sale of goods."

E   Subject to a possible relevance of para. (*c*) "activities by way of the sale of goods", the sole question for the purposes of this appeal is whether these two ladies who formed more than half of those employed in the establishment were, or were not, wholly or mainly employed in activities carried on for office purposes within the meaning of that Act of 1963. This is another piece of legislation by reference, in a form which I think has probably given rise to the difficulties in
F   which the tribunal found themselves, because the Act of 1963 is an Act dealing with office premises; it is dealing with buildings and making provision for the health, safety and welfare of persons employed in office and shop premises. It is in connexion with that Act, concerned with the welfare of people working in buildings, that this definition of "office purposes" arises. It arises in this way. Section 1 (1) of the Offices, Shops and Railway Premises Act 1963, provides:

G   "The premises to which this Act applies are office premises, shop premises and railway premises, being (in each case) premises in the case of which persons are employed to work therein."

Having stated that general scope of the Act, it then goes on in s. 1 (2) to provide definitions, and the first is "office premises", which is defined as follows:

H   "(*a*) 'office premises' means a building or part of a building, being a building or part the sole or principal use of which is as an office or for office purposes."

Having used that expression "for office purposes", it was necessary to go on and define in connexion with the use of the building what was meant by "office purposes". It is defined thus:

I   "(*b*) 'office purposes' includes the purposes of administration, clerical work, handling money and telephone and telegraph operating."

As it seems to me, the Selective Employment Payments Act 1966, is quite clearly not dealing with premises at all; it is dealing with activities. Accordingly, when there is imported this definition by reference "for office purposes", it seems to me quite clear that the matters which are included for office purposes must be read as activities, and these activities include here clerical work and handling of money. I do not mention others because those, as it seems to me,

are the two relevant activities. Finally, by s. 1 (2) (c) of the Act of 1963, " ' clerical   A
work ' includes writing, book-keeping, sorting papers, filing " and further matters
to which I need not refer.

Having stated that, I will return to s. 2 (2) of the Act of 1966, and one sees
the framework of that Act. Having arrived at an establishment engaged by way
of business wholly in certain qualifying activities, it follows from that that
all the persons employed there are employed in connexion with those activities.   B
They will cover any amount of different occupations—maybe the office boy,
the cleaner, up to the senior employees in the establishment. The applicant for a
refund has then, in order to get a refund, to show that more than half of all
those present there were not employed wholly or mainly in these non-qualifying
activities. Of course, in many cases there is no difficulty at all. It will be found
that, within the premises, there will be separate offices, the managing director's   C
office, the accounting office and so on, where it is easy to count heads of those
who are engaged in the non-qualifying activities. Equally, as it seems to me,
there will be many cases when a man's occupation will involve a number of
activities, somewhat one might call qualifying activities and some non-qualifying,
and at that stage one gets into a question of fact and degree, asking oneself,
looking at the occupation of the man: is it shown that he is not wholly or mainly   D
engaged in the non-qualifying activities?

Coming back to the present case, and approaching it de novo and in the
light of what I consider to be the proper approach, it seems to me inevitable
that one should find that both these ladies were engaged wholly, or mainly—
I think wholly—in non-qualifying activities. It might, of course, be said that
part of their activity consisted in selling, the selling of stamps, postal orders   E
and so on, the selling, in other words, of goods, but that could not assist the
respondent because the selling of goods is treated as a non-qualifying activity.
Probably the true view, however, is that, in so far as they were, to use a general
expression, selling anything, they were really collecting revenue and handling
that revenue. It seems to me that the whole of their work would be covered
by the expression " clerical work, handling money ". Accordingly, I find   F
myself differing from the Industrial Tribunal. The way in which the tribunal
approached this matter is not altogether clear, but I am persuaded by counsel
for the appellant that the true view here is that the tribunal were really saying
that these two ladies were mainly engaged in the handling of money and clerical
work, but nevertheless they felt that the handling of money or the clerical work
which would be a non-qualifying activity was such as could not properly be said   G
to come under the heading " office purposes ". They say this:

"We consider that the words ' office purposes ' as the heading of the
definition cannot be entirely forgotten when one deals with the acts which
are said to comprise it. Here in this sub-post office, we consider, the ladies
are engaged, in the ordinary sense of the word, not in ' office purposes ' but
in providing the services which are provided by a post office. The office   H
side of the post office is that side of it which is carried out by [the respondent],
it is the keeping of the accounts, doing the clerical work, making the returns."

They go on:

"Having regard to the fact that these phrases ' handling money ',
' writing ', do appear in a definition of office purposes, we consider that that   I
general definition still governs the particular operations which fall under it;
although these words describe action which shows that something is done
for office purposes. If the handling of money, or the writing, is done for
something which obviously is not for office purposes, then the mere grammatical sense of the words cannot be taken to represent the intention of the
legislature in this regard. The intention of the legislature here was to make
sure that where persons obtained a refund they can only do so if more
persons are engaged on the service or operation with which the establishment

A   is mainly concerned than with the mere administration of the establishment. Here we come to the conclusion that more of the employees—in fact all the employees of this sub-post office—are engaged in providing the services of the sub-post office; they are not engaged in the administration of the post office. We consider that the words ' handling money ' and ' writing ' in the definition of ' office purposes ' do not apply because the handling of money

B   and the writing which is done by these ladies has no connexion whatsoever with what can be called office purposes; those acts are essentially associated with the service which is performed in this sub-post office."

I confess that I have sympathy with the tribunal in their approach, but I do not think myself that their test in this matter is warranted. It suggests that, before one can have a non-qualifying activity of this sort, it must be, as it were,

C   isolated, the sort of case where one gets somebody whose sole job is sitting in an office doing the accounts, writing letters and so on. It may be that they have been led into that approach by the words " office purposes ", which, as I have already said, are words used really in connexion with the use of a building. In my judgment, there is no warrant for approaching the matter in that way, but

D   one has to look at the occupation of each person and see what activities are involved, and then ask oneself at the end whether that person is wholly or mainly engaged in a non-qualifying activity.

I should mention one other matter. It was urged before us by counsel for the respondent, that, if this be right, this is a case where, to put it colloquially, Parliament has given on the one hand and taken away with the other, and he

E   points out, what I think is really conceded, that " postal services ", which is one of the headings in Ord. XIX of the Standard Industrial Classification, can only apply in relation to s. 2 of the Act of 1966 as regards the private post office either with or without the grocery shop. That arises because s. 3 of the Act of 1966, to which I have not referred, is in fact dealing with the Postmaster-General and what I might call the public post office. Counsel's point is that here are postal

F   services specifically being included as an activity which could attract a refund, and yet if the argument on the other side is right, they can never get a refund because everyone engaged in that sub-post office of the type we are considering will be engaged on non-qualifying activities. There is some force in that argument, but the force is dissipated largely, if not wholly, when one realises that this is again legislation by reference; that this document " Standard Industrial Classi-

G   fication " was drawn up for quite different purposes at a time when there was no selective employment payment, and when it had never been decided that the public post office would be dealt with quite separately, and, perhaps what is more important, " postal services " is not the one form of activity which is to attract refund; it is in fact only one item in the other items dealt with in Ord. XIX to which I have already referred. In my judgment, there is not sufficient

H   weight in counsel for the respondent's contention to lead me to construe the section in any other way.

I would allow this appeal.

WIDGERY, J.: I entirely agree, and there is nothing which I can usefully add.

I   **O'CONNOR, J.:** I agree.

Appeal allowed.   Leave to appeal to Court of Appeal granted.

Solicitors: *Solicitor, Ministry of Labour; Munro, Pennefather & Co.* (for the respondent).

[*Reported by* N. P. Metcalfe, Esq., *Barrister-at-Law.*]

THE GNIEZNO.

A

Owners of the Motor Vessel Popi v. Owners of Steamship or Vessel Gniezno.

[Probate, Divorce and Admiralty Division (Brandon, J.), March 2, 3, 6, 7, 1967.]

Admiralty—Practice—Appearance—Writ in rem not served on defendants— Notice of counterclaim filed by defendants—Writ time-expired when appearance entered—Whether appearance effective—Whether notice of counterclaim effective to raise a counterclaim—R.S.C., Ord. 2, r. 1, Ord. 6, r. 8, Ord. 10, r. 1 (3), Ord. 12, r. 1.

B

On Mar. 7, 1963, a collision occurred between the Popi, owned by the plaintiffs, and the Gniezno, owned by the defendants. The damage to the Popi was less than the damage to the Gniezno. On Feb. 26, 1965, a writ in rem was issued by the plaintiffs against the defendants (the " Popi's action "). No step was taken to serve the writ. Extension of the two year time limit under s. 8* of the Maritime Conventions Act, 1911, to Nov. 7, 1965, having been agreed by the plaintiffs, the defendants and the cargo owners of the Gniezno issued a writ in rem on Nov. 3, 1965, against the owners of the Popi (the " Gniezno's action "). On Nov. 30, 1966, the solicitors for the owners of the Popi intimated that they had no authority to accept service of the writ in the Gniezno's action. The writ in the Gniezno's action was renewed by order of the Admiralty registrar, the Popi not having been within the jurisdiction, and the writ remained current at all material times. Although the writ in rem issued in the Popi's action by the plaintiffs had not been served and the time limit for its service had expired, the defendants, on Dec. 19, 1966, entered appearance voluntarily in the Popi's action and filed a notice of counterclaim. The plaintiffs in the Popi's action moved for an order that the appearance and notice of counterclaim be set aside and that the counterclaim was not maintainable, and that the defendants sought an extension of time under s. 8 of the Act of 1911 to allow them to pursue their counterclaim.

C

D

E

F

Held: (i) in regard to the entry of appearance—

(a) in principle, and on the wording of R.S.C., Ord. 12, r. 1† and R.S.C., Ord. 10, r. 1 (3)‡, a defendant was entitled to appear voluntarily to a writ which had not been served on him, at any rate while the writ was current for service (see p. 744, letter C, and p. 745, letter D, post).

G

Dictum of Cross, J., in *Pike* v. *Michael Nairn & Co., Ltd.* ([1960] 2 All E.R. at p. 186) followed.

(b) further, although the writ was not valid for service (see R.S.C., Ord. 6, r. 8§) by the time when the defendants voluntarily entered appearance, their appearance was valid, because the writ remained a writ and the provisions of the rules which rendered the writ invalid for service when time had expired were for the defendants' benefit and could be waived (see p. 746, letter I, and p. 747, letter E, post).

H

Sheldon v. *Brown Bailey's Steel Works, Ltd.* ([1953] 2 All E.R. 894) applied.

(ii) in regard to the notice of counterclaim—

(a) a counterclaim could be raised only by a proceeding recognised or directed by rules of court (see p. 754, letter C, post).

I

(b) although in the Admiralty court a practice of filing notices of counterclaims had grown up, such a notice could not raise a counterclaim contrary to (a) above, and thus the notice of counterclaim in the present case was ineffective (see p. 755, letter I, and p. 756, letters B and I, post).

---

* Section 8, so far as material, is set out at p. 758, letter I, to p. 759, letter B, post.
† R.S.C., Ord. 12, r. 1, so far as material, is set out at p. 743, letter H, post.
‡ R.S.C., Ord. 10, r. 1, so far as material, is set out at p. 743, letter E, post.
§ R.S.C., Ord. 6, r. 8, so far as material, is set out at p. 745, letter F, post.

A   (c) accordingly, the notice of counterclaim would be set aside pursuant to
R.S.C., Ord. 2, r. 1* or under the inherent jurisdiction of the court to set
aside any irregular proceeding (see p. 758, letter A, post).

The Saxicava ([1924] P. 131) followed.

Bildt v. *Foy* ((1892), 9 T.L.R. 34) and *The Fairplay XIV* ([1939] P. 57)
considered.

B   (iii) no order ought to be made either on the plaintiff's motion for an
order that the counterclaim was not maintainable or on the defendants'
motion for an extension of time (see p. 759, letter I, post).

[As to appearance to a writ in rem, see 1 HALSBURY'S LAWS (3rd Edn.) 80, 81,
para. 168; as to service of such a writ, see ibid., p. 79, para. 165.

As to a counterclaim in an action in rem, see ibid., p. 89, para. 193; and for
C   cases on the subject, see 1 DIGEST (Repl.) 218, 219, *1068-1072*.]

Cases referred to:

Battersby v. *Anglo-American Oil Co., Ltd.,* [1944] 2 All E.R. 387; [1945]
K.B. 23; 114 L.J.K.B. 49; 171 L.T. 300; 2nd Digest Supp.

Bildt v. *Foy,* (1892), 9 T.L.R. 34; *on appeal,* C.A., 9 T.L.R. 83; 40 Digest
D   (Repl.) 466, *513.*

Fairplay XIV, The, [1939] P. 57; 108 L.J.P. 65; 62 Lloyd L.R. 108; 1 Digest
(Repl.) 218, *1072.*

Fell v. *Christ's College, Cambridge,* (1787), 2 Bro. C.C. 278; 29 E.R. 153.

General Railway Syndicate, Re, Whiteley's Case, [1900] 1 Ch. 365; 69 L.J.Ch.
250; 82 L.T. 134; 1 Digest (Repl.) 11, *95.*

E   *Heaven* v. *Road and Rail Wagons, Ltd.,* [1965] 2 All E.R. 409; [1965] 2 Q.B.
355; [1965] 2 W.L.R. 1249; 3rd Digest Supp.

Kerley, Son and Verden, Re, [1900-03] All E.R. Rep. 858; [1901] 1 Ch. 467;
70 L.J.Ch. 189; 83 L.T. 699; Digest (Practice) 312, *371.*

Oulton v. *Radcliffe,* (1874), L.R. 9 C.P. 189; 43 L.J.P.C. 87; 30 L.T. 22;
16 Digest (Repl.) 139, *212.*

F   *Pike* v. *Michael Nairn & Co., Ltd.,* [1960] 2 All E.R. 184; [1960] Ch. 553;
[1960] 2 W.L.R. 897; 3rd Digest Supp.

Salybia, The, [1910] P. 25; 79 L.J.P. 31; 101 L.T. 959; 11 Asp. M.L.C. 361;
1 Digest (Repl.) 218, *1070.*

Saxicava, The, [1924] W.N. 59; *on appeal,* C.A., [1924] P. 131; 93 L.J.P. 66;
131 L.T. 342; 16 Asp. M.L.C. 324; 1 Digest (Repl.) 218, *1071.*

G   *Sheldon* v. *Brown Bayley's Steelworks, Ltd.,* [1953] 2 All E.R. 894; [1953]
2 Q.B. 393; [1953] 2 W.L.R. 542; 3rd Digest Supp.

Motions.

This was a motion by the plaintiffs, the owners of the Panamanian motor vessel
Popi, and a cross-motion by the defendants, the owners of the Polish steamship
Gniezno, in an Admiralty action in rem arising out of a collision between the
H   two vessels (hereinafter called the " Popi's action "). The following facts are
taken from the judgment.

On Mar. 7, 1963, there was a collision in the South Kattegat between the
Popi and the Gniezno. On May 2, 1963, the owners of the two vessels exchanged
guarantees to provide security for their respective claims. Both the guarantees
were given by the West of England Steamship Owners' Protection and Indemnity
I   Association, Ltd. The guarantee in respect of the claim of the owners of the
Popi was in these terms:

" In consideration of your releasing and/or refraining from arresting
or otherwise detaining the above vessel or any other vessel in the same
ownership in connexion with the above incident, we hereby undertake to pay
you on demand any sums not exceeding £15,000, plus interest and costs, if
any, which might be agreed between the parties or adjudged to be due to

* R.S.C., Ord. 2, r. 1, is set out at p. 757, letters C to E, post.

you in respect of the above incident from the owners of the above vessel   A
by the High Court of Justice in England."

The reference to " the above vessel " was to the heading of the guarantee where
the name of the vessel, Gniezno, appeared. The other guarantee was mutatis
mutandis in the same terms except that the sum guaranteed was larger, £45,000.
On Apr. 6, 1964, the solicitors for the plaintiffs wrote to the insurers of the
Gniezno asking for an estimate of the Gniezno's claim, and this request was   B
repeated in a further letter dated June 8, 1964. On Sept. 28, 1964, the insurers
of the Gniezno sent a rough estimate of the claim. On Feb. 17, 1965, the insurers
of the Gniezno asked the solicitors for the plaintiffs for a three months' extension
of the two year time limit under s. 8 of the Maritime Conventions Act, 1911,
and on Feb. 22, 1965, the solicitors for the plaintiffs granted an extension on
condition that the insurers of the Gniezno agreed English jurisdiction. On   C
Feb. 26, 1965, the solicitors for the plaintiffs issued a writ in rem in the Popi's
action against the defendants for damages caused by the collision, the property
proceeded against being the Gniezno. The solicitors for the plaintiffs also
issued a second writ against the defendants in their capacity as owners of numerous
sister ships. The solicitors for the plaintiffs took no steps to serve either writ,
nor did they make any request to the defendants or their insurers to instruct   D
solicitors to accept service of either writ. Between February and September,
1965, negotiations took place between the solicitors for the plaintiffs and the
defendants or their representatives. On Oct. 4, 1965, the London agents of
the defendants asked for a further extension of time to Nov. 7, 1965, and this
was agreed to by the solicitors for the plaintiffs on the telephone. On Oct. 15,
1965, the insurers of the Gniezno wrote to the solicitors for the plaintiffs giving   E
a final specification of their claim, and indicating that a delegation was coming
to England which they hoped would be able to settle the dispute. On Oct. 21,
1965, the solicitors for the plaintiffs replied suggesting that the question of
liability should be settled first. On Nov. 3, 1965, the solicitors for the defendants
and the cargo owners issued a writ in rem against the plaintiffs for damages
caused by the collision, the property proceeded against being the Popi (herein-   F
after called the " Gniezno's action "). Nothing happened after that for a
substantial period. Then, on Oct. 26, 1966, the solicitors for the defendants
wrote to the solicitors for the plaintiffs asking them to accept service of the writ
in the Gniezno's action. The letter was in these terms:

    " We have been instructed to act on behalf of owners of the vessel Gniezno
and owners of cargo lately laden on board her. We have been informed   G
that our clients' vessel was involved in a collision with the Popi on Mar. 7,
1963, in the southern part of the Kattegat and that you are acting on behalf
of the owners of the Popi. We were also informed that time limit was
extended until Nov. 7, 1965. This being the final extension we were instructed to issue a writ on behalf of the owners of the Gniezno and cargo
against your clients, owners of the Popi. This writ was issued on Nov. 3,   H
1965, and as time is approaching for the last day of service we should be
pleased to hear that you have authority to accept service and enter an
appearance thereto."

On Nov. 1, 1966, the solicitors for the plaintiffs replied to that letter as follows:

    " We thank you for your letter of Oct. 26 and confirm our telephone   I
conversation of today when we told you that we did not have authority to
accept service and enter an appearance. We are asking our clients for
instructions about this. We shall be pleased if you will accept this letter
as our agreement to the writ you have issued remaining valid until such
time as we receive instructions. In the event of our clients telling us that
we are not to accept service then the writ shall remain valid for one week
after we give notice of this to you so that you may then take steps as necessary for the validity of the writ to be further preserved. We confirm your
having told us that the writ you have issued is in rem naming the owners of

A　the ship Gniezno and her cargo as plaintiffs and the owners of the Popi as defendants. We shall be pleased if you will let us have a sight of the writ as early as possible."

On Nov. 30, 1966, the solicitors for the plaintiffs wrote a further letter:

B　" We would refer to our letter of Nov. 1 which we presume reached you safely. Our instructions do not permit us to accept service of the writ which you issued. In these circumstances we agree that the writ shall remain valid from one week from today's date so that you may take such steps as you consider necessary for the validity to be further extended."

On Dec. 6, 1966, the Admiralty registrar, on an ex parte application by the solicitors for the defendants and her cargo owners, renewed the writ in the C　Gniezno's action for six months, viz., until June 3, 1967. The renewal was made mainly on the ground that the Popi had not been within the jurisdiction of the court since the issue of the writ. On Dec. 29, 1966, the solicitors for the defendants entered an appearance in the Popi's action despite the fact that the writ in that action had not been served. On the same day the same solicitors filed a notice of counterclaim on behalf of the defendants. The document was headed D　in the action in the ordinary way and read as follows:

" Take notice that the defendants, the owners of the steamship or vessel Gniezno counterclaim against the owners of the motor vessel Popi in respect of their loss and/or damage occasioned by a collision between the Gniezno and the Popi which took place in the southern area of the Kattegat in the month of March, 1963."

E　The document was addressed " To the plaintiffs and to Messrs. Holman, Fenwick & Willan, their solicitors or agents ". The memorandum of appearance and a copy of the notice of counterclaim was served on the solicitors for the plaintiffs.

The notice of motion by the plaintiffs, dated Feb. 13, 1967, was for an order in the following terms:

F　" (i) That the defendants' appearance or purported appearance and any service or purported service of the writ deemed to be effected thereby be set aside; (ii) That the defendants' notice of counterclaim dated Dec. 29, 1966, be set aside; (iii) That the counterclaim by the defendants was not maintainable."

G　The notice of motion gave the grounds for the application as follows:

" (i) That the defendants were not entitled to enter an appearance to the writ unless and until the plaintiffs served or purported to serve the writ on the defendants. (ii) At the date of the defendants' appearance or purported appearance to the writ the said writ was not valid for service. (iii) A notice of counterclaim is not a document the filing or service of which H　is directed or recognised by the rules of this Honourable court and is in consequence a nullity and/or has no effect. (iv) A counterclaim cannot be commenced by filing or serving a notice of counterclaim but only by a proceeding directed or recognised by the rules of this Honourable court. (v) The claim to which the notice of counterclaim relates is not maintainable by reason of s. 8 of the Maritime Conventions Act, 1911."

I　The notice of cross-motion by the defendants, dated Feb. 22, 1967, read as follows:

" Take notice that the court will be moved on Tuesday, Feb. 28, 1967, at 10.30 or so soon thereafter as counsel can be heard, by counsel for the above-named defendants that if and so far as it may be necessary this Honourable court will extend the period under s. 8 of the Maritime Conventions Act, 1911, so as to allow the defendants to pursue their counterclaim in this action."

No grounds for relief were given in the notice.

The cases noted below* were cited during the argument in addition to those   A referred to in the judgment.

J. Franklin Willmer and *J. C. Tylor* for the plaintiffs.

N. A. Phillips for the defendants.

BRANDON, J. stated the facts and continued: The purpose of the two motions is as follows. The plaintiffs' damage is less than the defendants' damage,   B and the plaintiffs would be content to leave the loss arising from the collision to lie where it has up to now fallen. For that reason they have taken no steps to effect service of the writ in either of their actions hoping that the actions would die. The defendants are not content with that situation, and are anxious to prosecute their claim in one way or another. Their first idea was to go on with their own action, the action which I have called the Gniezno action. That   C idea was frustrated by the refusal of the solicitors for the plaintiffs to accept service of the writ. To get over that, the defendants have tried to counterclaim in the plaintiffs' action. For this purpose they entered an appearance in the action although the writ had not been served, and at the same time they filed and served a document called a notice of counterclaim. By these steps they hoped to create a situation where, even if the plaintiffs did not proceed with their   D claim, they, the defendants, could proceed with their counterclaim. The plaintiffs' attitude is that they would like to discontinue their action, but only if they can be sure that the defendants cannot go on with their counterclaim. The object of the plaintiffs' motion is, therefore, to get the ruling of the court on the question whether the defendants are, or are not, in a position of counterclaimants so as to be able to go on with their counterclaim irrespective of discontinuance   E by the plaintiffs. The plaintiffs contend that the defendants are not in that position. The plaintiffs take the further point that, even if the defendants are in principle in the position of counterclaimants, their counterclaim is out of time under the Maritime Conventions Act, 1911, and is, therefore, not maintainable. The defendants also desire to have decided the question whether they are entitled to go on with a counterclaim even if the plaintiffs discontinue. They   F claim that they are so entitled, and they also ask by their cross-motion for an extension of the time to counterclaim if such an extension be necessary, which they do not admit.

I propose to deal with the main question first, that is to say, the question whether the counterclaim can go on even if the plaintiffs discontinue. That question, it may be said, is not in terms raised by either motion, but both counsel   G have stated on behalf of their respective clients that it is the principal question on which they desire the ruling of the court, and, in those circumstances, I think that it is desirable that the court should give the ruling for which the parties ask. I shall deal later with the question of the time-bar, if any, under the Maritime Conventions Act, 1911.

The plaintiffs' contentions on what I have called the main question fall under   H two heads. The first is that the appearance was not valid because it was made voluntarily to an expired writ. I use the word " voluntarily " in this connexion to mean an appearance without previous service, and I use the expression " expired writ " to mean a writ, the validity for the service of which has expired under the relevant rule of court. The second contention is that the notice of counterclaim is an ineffective proceeding not authorised by rules of court. On   I those grounds the plaintiffs ask that both the appearance and the notice of counterclaim be set aside. I shall deal with each of those two contentions in turn, taking the question of the validity of the defendants' appearance first. On this it appears to me that two points arise for determination; first, can a

---

* *The North American*, (1859), Sw. 466; *The Espanoleto*, [1920] P. 223; *The Alnwick*, [1965] 2 All E.R. 570; [1965] P. 357.

A defendant in an action appear voluntarily during the currency of the writ; secondly, can he do so after the writ has expired and has not been renewed? I shall discuss the first question first, namely, whether a defendant can appear voluntarily during the currency of the writ.

First of all I shall consider the wording of the relevant rules. The issue of a writ in an action of this kind is covered by two rules, R.S.C., Ord. 5, r. 2 (a),

B which is a rule of general application, and R.S.C., Ord. 75, r. 3 (1), which is a rule relating particularly to Admiralty actions in rem. R.S.C., Ord. 5, r. 2, provides:

" Subject to any provision of an Act, or of these rules, by virtue of which any proceedings are expressly required to be begun otherwise than by writ, the following proceedings must, notwithstanding anything in r. 4, be begun

C by writ, that is to say, proceedings—(a) in which a claim is made by the plaintiff for any relief or remedy for any tort, other than trespass to land . . ."

R.S.C., Ord. 75, r. 3 (1) provides:

" An action in rem must be begun by writ; and the writ must be in Form No. 1 or 2 in Appendix B, whichever is appropriate."

D Service of the writ is also governed by two rules, R.S.C., Ord. 10, r. 1, which is of general application, and R.S.C., Ord. 75, r. 8, which is of particular application to Admiralty actions in rem. R.S.C., Ord. 10, r. 1 provides:

" (1) Subject to the provisions of any Act and these rules, a writ must be served personally on each defendant by the plaintiff or his agent. (2) Where

E a defendant's solicitor indorses on the writ a statement that he accepts service of the writ on behalf of that defendant, the writ shall be deemed to have been duly served on that defendant and to have been so served on the date on which the indorsement was made. (3) Where a writ is not duly served on a defendant but he enters an unconditional appearance in the action begun by the writ, the writ shall be deemed to have been duly served

F on him and to have been so served on the date on which he entered the appearance . . ."

R.S.C., Ord. 75, r. 8 provides:

" (1) Subject to para. (2), a writ by which an action in rem is begun must be served on the property against which the action is brought except . . ."

G There follow sub-para. (a) and sub-para. (b), which provide two exceptions which I need not read. Then:

" (2) A writ need not be served on the property or registrar mentioned in para. (1) if the writ is deemed to have been duly served on the defendant by virtue of Ord. 10, r. 1 (2) or (3)."

H Appearance to a writ is governed by R.S.C., Ord. 12, r. 1, which provides:

" (1) Subject to para. (2) and to Ord. 80, r. 2, a defendant to an action begun by writ may . . . enter an appearance in the action and defend it by a solicitor or in person . . . (3) An appearance is entered by properly completing the requisite documents, that is to say, a memorandum of appearance, as defined by r. 3, and a copy thereof, and handing them in at, or sending them by post to, the appropriate office . . ."

I In the absence of authority, I should have thought that the wording of R.S.C., Ord. 12, r. 1, was wide enough to cover a case of appearance without previous service. There is nothing in the wording of the rule itself to suggest that the right to appear which is conferred is limited to cases where there has been previous service of the writ. That view which I should form on the wording of R.S.C., Ord. 12, r. 1, appears to me to be supported by the wording of R.S.C., Ord. 10, r. 1 (3), which expressly contemplates appearance by a defendant without there having previously been due service of the writ on him.

It is argued on behalf of the plaintiffs that R.S.C., Ord. 10, r. 1 (3), only applies   **A**
to a case of bad service as distinct from no service, that is to say, that a defendant
would be entitled to appear where a plaintiff had made an ineffective and irregular
attempt to serve a writ on him, but would not be entitled to appear when no
attempt to serve a writ had been made at all. I do not think that this is a
natural and right construction of R.S.C., Ord. 10, r. 1 (3). I think that the
wording of the rule means this, that, in any case where there has not been due   **B**
service, a defendant may enter an unconditional appearance and, if he does so,
it will have the effect stated. It seems to me that any case where there has
not been due service comprehends a case where there has not been any service
at all, and I do not see any reason for reading R.S.C., Ord. 10, r. 1 (3), in the
narrow way in which the plaintiffs invite me to do. On the wording of the rules,
therefore, for the reasons which I have given, I am of opinion that a defendant   **C**
is entitled to appear to a writ even though it has not been served on him, at any
rate while the writ is current for service.

This view at which I have arrived by reference to the wording of the rules
appears to me to be supported by a number of authorities. I was referred to
three cases in which the matter has been considered. These are *Fell* v. *Christ's
College, Cambridge* (1), *Oulton* v. *Radcliffe* (2) and *Pike* v. *Michael Nairn & Co.,*   **D**
Ltd. (3). I do not think that it is necessary for me to examine these cases in
detail. It will be sufficient for me to read a short passage from the judgment
of CROSS, J., in *Pike* v. *Michael Nairn & Co., Ltd.* (4), where the learned judge
said:

> " The service of the process of the court is made necessary in the interests   **E**
> of the defendant so that orders may not be made behind his back. A
> defendant, therefore, has always been able to waive the necessity of service
> and to enter an appearance to the writ as soon as he hears that it has been
> issued against him, although it has not been served on him (see *Fell* v.
> *Christ's College, Cambridge* (1), *Oulton* v. *Radcliffe* (2))."

In my respectful opinion, that is a correct statement of the law which I ought to   **F**
follow. According to a note (5) in the SUPREME COURT PRACTICE, 1967, R.S.C.,
Ord. 10, r. 1 (3), was introduced comparatively recently in order to give effect
to the principle established in the authorities to which I have referred. It is,
of course, difficult to know why the rule committee should at any time introduce
any particular rule, but it seems to me a reasonable inference that that was the
reason. Looking at the matter as one of principle, it seems to me that a defendant   **G**
ought to have the right to enter a voluntary appearance in this way so that in
any case where an action is hanging over him he may take steps to have it dismissed. Under the present rules there is no obligation to serve a writ earlier
than within twelve months, and even then a plaintiff may, if he shows cause,
obtain a renewal of the writ ex parte. In this way a defendant may have an
action, the existence of which is known to him, hanging over him for a very   **H**
considerable period. It seems to me desirable in principle that a defendant,
faced with such a situation, should be able to obtain some finality. There is a
passage in the judgment in one case which was cited to me which is not consistent
with the view that I have formed and it is right that I should refer to it. The
case is *Heaven* v. *Road and Rail Wagons, Ltd.* (6). The matter before the court
was an application to renew a writ after it had expired. I do not for a moment   **I**
question the decision of the learned judge on that application or the reasons
which he gave for it, but there is a passage towards the end of his judgment,

---

(1) (1787), 2 Bro. C.C. 278.   (2) (1874), L.R. 9 C.P. 189.
(3) [1960] 2 All E.R. 184; [1960] Ch. 553.
(4) [1960] 2 All E.R. at p. 186; [1960] Ch. at p. 560.
(5) See SUPREME COURT PRACTICE 1967, p. 61.
(6) [1965] 2 All E.R. 409; [1965] 2 Q.B. 355.

A relied on by counsel for the plaintiffs, which seems inconsistent with what CROSS,
J., said in *Pike* v. *Michael Nairn & Co., Ltd.* (7). MEGAW, J., said (8):

"So far, it is the issue of the writ which is in question, the technical
bringing of the action. It is left to the rules of court to deal with the next
stage: the service of the writ, which, so far as the defendant is concerned,
is the effective start of the proceedings. Not till then does the defendant
B have any opportunity of invoking the assistance of the court or of trying,
if he be so minded, to ensure reasonable expedition in having his alleged
liability defined and thereafter determined. The rules of court provide
twelve months—a not ungenerous time, it might be thought—within which
the plaintiff can hold up proceedings by not serving his writ."

C I do not think that the learned judge can have had present to his mind the
question whether in certain cases a defendant may not appear voluntarily
without a writ being served on him. In particular, I feel certain that he cannot
have had cited to him the authorities to which I have referred, or otherwise I do
not think that he would have expressed himself in the way in which he did.
While I entertain the greatest respect for any judgment of MEGAW, J., I do
D not think that I can treat his observations in that case, which did not form the
ground of his decision, as casting doubt on the correctness of those authorities.
My conclusion, therefore, on the plaintiffs' first point is that in principle a defendant can appear voluntarily to a writ which has not been served on him, anyhow,
while the writ remains valid for service.

I have, however, to consider the plaintiffs' second point which is this: although
E it may be open to a defendant to appear during the currency of the writ, it is
not open to him to appear when the writ has expired. The argument for the
plaintiffs on this point is based on the wording of R.S.C., Ord. 6, r. 8, and R.S.C.,
Ord. 10, r. 1 (3), the argument being that, if the writ is not valid in the hands of
the plaintiff for service on the defendant, then equally it cannot be valid for
the purpose of a notional service effected by a voluntary appearance. R.S.C.,
F Ord. 6, r. 8, deals with the duration and renewal of a writ and provides:

"(1) For the purpose of service, a writ (other than a concurrent writ) is
valid in the first instance for twelve months beginning with the date of its
issue and a concurrent writ is valid in the first instance for the period of
validity of the original writ which is unexpired at the date of issue of the
concurrent writ. (2) Where a writ has not been served on a defendant, the
G court may by order extend the validity of the writ from time to time for
such period, not exceeding twelve months at any one time, beginning with the
day next following that on which it would otherwise expire, as may be
specified in the order, if an application for extension is made to the court
before that day or such later day (if any) as the court may allow . . ."

I have already read R.S.C., Ord. 10, r. 1 (3). That is a rule, it will be recollected,
H which provides that, where a defendant enters an unconditional appearance,
although the writ has not been duly served on him, the writ shall be deemed to
have been duly served on him on the day on which he entered the appearance.

In order to decide whether this is a good argument or not, it is necessary
to consider the effect of R.S.C., Ord. 6, r. 8. This rule is a revised rule, and
such authorities as there are on the matter, apart from the case decided by
I MEGAW, J., to which I have referred, relate to an earlier rule in slightly different
terms. It seems to me to have been established by a decision of the Court of
Appeal that, under the old rule at any rate, a writ which has expired is not a
nullity; it is only invalid for the purpose of service by the plaintiff on the defendant. That was decided by the Court of Appeal in *Sheldon* v. *Brown Bayley's
Steel Works, Ltd.* (9). The Court of Appeal in that case did not consider to

---

(7) [1960] 2 All E.R. at p. 186; [1960] Ch. at p. 560.
(8) [1965] 2 All E.R. at p. 416; [1965] 2 Q.B. at p. 366.
(9) [1953] 2 All E.R. 894; [1953] 2 Q.B. 393.

be correct a statement in an earlier decision of the same court (10) that an **A**
expired writ was a nullity.   SINGLETON, L.J., said (11):

" I do not regard it as strictly accurate to describe a writ which has not
been served within twelve months as a nullity.   It is not as though it had
never been issued.   It is something which can be renewed.   A nullity cannot
be renewed.   The court can grant an application which results in making
it just as effective as it was before the twelve months' period had elapsed.   **B**
I do not think that the court had in mind what had been said in *Re Kerly,
Son and Verden* (12), to which I have referred.   Moreover, it was not necessary for the decision of the court in *Battersby* v. *Anglo-American Oil Co.,
Ltd.* (13) to consider this.   The question was whether the court would exercise the discretion which it had under R.S.C., Ord. 64, r. 7, to renew a writ
when the renewal would deprive a defendant of the benefit of a limitation   **C**
which had accrued, and the judgment was to the effect that discretion
ought not to be exercised in such circumstances.   If the writ had been a
nullity, there would have been no point in considering whether the court
should exercise its discretion to renew it.   The position under Ord. 8, r. 1,
is that the writ is not in force for the purpose of service after the twelve
months' period had run.   It is still a writ.   The unconditional appearance   **D**
by the second defendants is a step in the action.   It amounts to a waiver
with regard to service.   It prevents the second defendants from being
able to contend successfully that the service on them is bad."

DENNING, L.J., discussing the service of an expired writ, said (14):

" If it was an irregularity, then the irregularity was waived by the uncon-   **E**
ditional appearance.   But if it was a nullity, then it could not be waived at
all.   It was not only bad, but incurably bad.   In determining the question,
it is important to notice that, even after twelve months have expired, the
writ can be renewed.   This is not done under R.S.C., Ord. 8, r. 1, for that only
permits renewal before the twelve months have expired.   It is done under
R.S.C., Ord. 64, r. 7, which is the general rule permitting enlargement of time   **F**
. . . Now, if a writ can be renewed after the twelve months have expired, that
must mean that it is not then a nullity.   There are other reasons, too, why
the writ cannot be considered a nullity.   Suppose a defendant, who is
served after the twelve months, deliberately enters an unconditional
appearance and goes to trial.   It may be that it is a case where no statute
of limitation avails him and he does not think it worth while to object to the   **G**
service of the writ, because he knows that it would only mean the issue of a
fresh one.   Could he thereafter turn round and say that all the proceedings
were void on the ground that the writ was a nullity?   Clearly not.   That
shows that the service out of time was only an irregularity which could be
waived."

That decision was on the old R.S.C., Ord. 8, r. 1, and R.S.C., Ord. 64, r. 7.   As   **H**
I have said, the present rule, R.S.C., Ord. 6, r. 8, is in somewhat different terms,
but I have come to the conclusion that there is no material difference between
the effect of the new rule and the old rule as regards the status of an expired
writ.   I consider that the decision of the Court of Appeal, to which I have
referred, binds me to hold that an expired writ is still a writ, although it is not
available to the plaintiff for service on the defendant if the defendant chooses   **I**
to take the point.   On the other hand, the defendant can, if he likes, waive
the point.   In that case the service of an expired writ will be good service.

(10) In *Battersby* v. *Anglo-American Oil Co., Ltd.*, [1944] 2 All E.R. at p. 389;   [1945]
K.B. at p. 29.
(11) [1953] 2 All E.R. at p. 896; [1953] 2 Q.B. at p. 400.
(12) [1900-03] All E.R. Rep. 858 at p. 860; [1901] 1 Ch. 467 at pp. 471, 478.
(13) [1944] 2 All E.R. 387; [1945] K.B. 23.
(14) [1953] 2 All E.R. at p. 897; [1953] 2 Q.B. at p. 401.

A   If a defendant can waive the right to complain of a writ being served on him out of time, I do not see in principle why he should not also be entitled to waive the requirement of service itself not only while the writ is current, but also after it has expired. The essential point seems to me to be that the requirements in the rules relating to service are requirements made for the protection or benefit of the defendant, and that, because of that, if the defendant wishes to

B   waive any of those requirements, he can do so. It is clear from *Sheldon's Case* (15) that a defendant can accept service of an expired writ although the plaintiff could not impose service of it on him. I cannot see why, if a defendant can appear voluntarily before the twelve months have elapsed, he is not also entitled to do so after the twelve months have elapsed. It has been objected by counsel for the plaintiffs that, if this is so, a defendant could enter a voluntary

C   appearance many, many years after the issue of the writ and, as I understood him, thereby cause considerable embarrassment. I think that the answer to that is that, if a plaintiff wishes to put an end to an action which he has begun, he can do so by discontinuing. The rule relating to discontinuing (16) is in very wide terms, and enables a plaintiff to discontinue an action at any time, until after service of the defence on him, without leave. It is true that, in that

D   event, he has to pay the defendant's costs, but that is only reasonable if he has started proceedings and caused the defendant to incur costs, and it seems to me that, if a plaintiff chooses to leave an action on foot after he has instituted it, he has no right to complain that it remains on foot for certain purposes of the defendant as well as for his own purposes. I, therefore, decide this second point also against the plaintiffs and hold that the defendants' appearance in this case

E   is valid although made voluntarily to an expired writ.

     I now turn to the second main matter, the validity of the notice of counterclaim. On this the plaintiffs take the following points. First of all they say that the only way in which a defendant can gain the status of a counterclaimant is by serving a defence and counterclaim on the plaintiff at the proper time and that, until that is done, his status is that of defendant simpliciter and not counter-

F   claimant. Secondly, the plaintiffs say that, even if there are certain exceptional cases under the rules where it is possible for a defendant to gain the status of a counterclaimant at some earlier stage of an action, it is not possible for him to do so by filing or serving a notice of counterclaim; that is a proceeding neither directed nor recognised by rules of court and is, therefore, a nullity. The defendants, on the other hand, contend that service of a notice of counterclaim, though

G   admittedly not directed or recognised by rules of court, is in accordance with a long standing practice in collision cases in the Admiralty court, and should, therefore, be accepted as a valid proceeding conferring on a defendant the status of counterclaimant. It is difficult to know what language to use to describe the initiation of a counterclaim. It is a curious circumstance that, in other kinds of proceedings, there is first a document which begins the proceedings and later

H   another document in the nature of a pleading setting out in detail the matters relied on. For instance, in an action the plaintiff issues a writ and then delivers a statement of claim, and in third-party proceedings a defendant issues a third party notice and later a third party statement of claim. In the case of a counterclaim, however, there is no provision for two documents in that way; the whole matter seems to be combined, in general at any rate, in one proceeding, namely,

I   service of a defence and counterclaim. Whether it is desirable that this should be so or not is a matter that may, perhaps, deserve consideration. There are various expressions one can use to describe the initiation of a counterclaim. One can talk about beginning a counterclaim or setting up a counterclaim or raising a counterclaim or bringing a counterclaim, and, indeed, a variety of expressions have been used at different times in different rules of court. It seems

---

(15) [1953] 2 All E.R. 894; [1953] 2 Q.B. 393.
(16) R.S.C., Ord. 21, r. 2.

to me that the expression most apt to describe the initiation of a counterclaim, A
as distinct from the delivery of a pleading containing a counterclaim, if there be
any distinction, is " raising a counterclaim ", and I propose, for convenience, to
use that expression hereafter in that sense.

The plaintiffs, in support of their argument, rely on the terms of the Supreme
Court of Judicature (Consolidation) Act, 1925, s. 39, and of the rules relating to
counterclaims, R.S.C., Ord. 15, r. 2 and r. 3. Section 39 (1) of the Supreme Court B
of Judicature (Consolidation) Act, 1925, provides:

> " The court or judge shall have power to grant to any defendant in respect
> of any equitable estate or right or other matter or equity, and also in respect
> of any legal estate, right or title claimed or asserted by him—(a) all such
> relief against any plaintiff or petitioner as the defendant has properly claimed
> by his pleading, and as the court or judge might have granted in any suit   C
> instituted for that purpose by that defendant against the same plaintiff
> or petitioner . . ."

Counsel for the plaintiffs contends that that shows that a counterclaim may only
be raised by a pleading. I do not think that that necessarily follows. The first
part of the subsection refers to a right being claimed or asserted by a defendant. D
Paragraph (a) then goes on to give to the court power to grant to a defendant who
has claimed or asserted a right all such relief as may be properly claimed by his
pleading. It seems to me that the subsection contemplates, at least to some extent,
two stages in regard to a counterclaim. First, the claiming or asserting of a right,
and, secondly, the delivery or service of a pleading on which relief is to be granted,
and it seems to me that it leaves it to rules of court to prescribe exactly how the E
counterclaim is to be, first, asserted and, secondly, pleaded. The plaintiffs'
contentions gain more support in my view from the terms of R.S.C., Ord. 15,
r. 2 and r. 3. R.S.C., Ord. 15, r. 2, provides:

> " (1) Subject to r. 5 (2), a defendant in any action who alleges that he has
> any claim or is entitled to any relief or remedy against a plaintiff in the action
> in respect of any matter (whenever and however arising) may, instead of   F
> bringing a separate action, make a counterclaim in respect of that matter;
> and where he does so he must add the counterclaim to his defence . . . (3) A
> counterclaim may be proceeded with notwithstanding that judgment is given
> for the plaintiff in the action or that the action is stayed, discontinued or
> dismissed . . ."

Then R.S.C., Ord. 15, r. 3, which deals with counterclaims against additional G
parties, provides:

> " (1) Where a defendant to an action who makes a counterclaim against
> the plaintiff alleges that any other person (whether or not a party to the
> action) is liable to him along with the plaintiff in respect of the subject-
> matter of the counterclaim, or claims against such other person any relief
> relating to or connected with the original subject-matter of the action, then, H
> subject to r. 5 (2), he may join that other person as a party against whom
> the counterclaim is made. (2) Where a defendant joins a person as a party
> against whom he makes a counterclaim, he must add that person's name to the
> title of the action and serve on him a copy of the counterclaim; and a person
> on whom a copy of a counterclaim is served under this paragraph shall, if
> he is not already a party to the action, become a party to it as from the time I
> of service with the same rights in respect of his defence to the counterclaim
> and otherwise as if he had been duly sued in the ordinary way by the party
> making the counterclaim . . ."

Then there are other provisions where that is dealt with in detail. It is to be
observed that R.S.C., Ord. 15, r. 2, talks about " making " a counterclaim, and it
prescribes the method of making it, that is to say, by adding a counterclaim to
the defence. The argument for the plaintiffs is that that is the only method

A prescribed for making a counterclaim, and that there is no method prescribed for raising a counterclaim at some earlier stage in the action. I am not entirely convinced that R.S.C., Ord. 15, r. 2 (1), does not contemplate something at an earlier stage. It is not easy to construe. I shall read it again. It says:

B
" Subject to r. 5 (2), a defendant in any action who alleges that he has any claim or is entitled to any relief of remedy against a plaintiff in the action in respect of any matter (whenever and however arising) may, instead of bringing a separate action, make a counterclaim in respect of that matter; and where he does so he must add the counterclaim to his defence."

C This contemplates an allegation of the existence of a counterclaim at some stage, so far as I can see, anterior to the stage of making the counterclaim, but it is not clear whether the allegation there referred to is an allegation outside the proceedings or an allegation within the proceedings. It is, however, right to say that, under the rule, the mode by which the counterclaim is to be made is by the service of a counterclaim added to the defence. It follows from that that a defendant cannot, under that rule, make a counterclaim until a statement of claim has been served on him because it is not until then that he can serve a
D defence.

One of the difficulties about this matter is that these rules to which I have just referred are new rules, and such authorities as there are on the matter relate to earlier rules in somewhat different terms. The previous rules which were relevant were R.S.C., Ord. 19, r. 3, and R.S.C., Ord. 21, r. 16. I take these from the Annual Practice, 1963, being the last Annual Practice in which they
E appeared. R.S.C., Ord. 19, r. 3, read as follows:

" Subject to the provisions of r. 15 of Ord. 21, and subject also to r. 3A of this order, a defendant in an action may set-off, or set up by way of counterclaim against the claims of the plaintiff, any right or claim, whether such set-off or counterclaim shall have the same effect as a cross-action, so as to enable the court to pronounce a final judgment in the same action, both
F on the original and on the cross-claim."

R.S.C., Ord. 21, r. 16, provided as follows:

" If, in any case in which the defendant sets up a counterclaim, the action of the plaintiff is stayed, discontinued, or dismissed, the counterclaim may nevertheless be proceeded with."

G It will be observed that the expression used in both rules is " set up a counterclaim ". That expression disappeared in the new rules which use the expression " make a counterclaim ", and there is a large number of other rules in the present rules besides those to which I have already referred which use the expression " make a counterclaim ". Such authorities as there are relate to the old rules, and it is necessary, therefore, to examine them with some care because one has
H to consider whether they apply having regard to the change of wording in the new rules. I have considered that matter, and the conclusion which I have come to is that, although there has been some change in the wording of the rules, including the substitution of the word " make " for the words " set up ", the authorities on the old rules ought to be regarded as applicable also to the new rules. I am not satisfied that the alterations were intended to make any real change in the
I position with regard to raising a counterclaim. The present R.S.C., Ord. 15, r. 2 (3), simply says:

" A counterclaim may be proceeded with notwithstanding that judgment is given for the plaintiff in the action or that the action is stayed, discontinued or dismissed."

It seems to me, however, implicit in that new rule, even though the words " make " or " set up " are not used, that what is permitted to be proceeded with must be something which already has an existence; in other words, a defendant can

proceed with a counterclaim only if he has first raised a counterclaim. Accord- A
ingly, I regard the authorities to which I am now about to refer as guiding me, not
only in relation to the effect of the old rules, but also in relation to the effect of
the new rules.

The first case is *Bildt* v. *Foy* (17). I do not propose to examine the case in
detail, but, as I understand the decision of the Divisional Court, it was that, where
in R.S.C., Ord. 14 proceedings the defendant relies in his affidavit in opposition to B
summary judgment on a counterclaim, he has set up a counterclaim within the
meaning of the rules then in force. The decision of the Divisional Court was
appealed to the Court of Appeal, and it is right to say they decided the case and
affirmed the decision of the Divisional Court on a ground other than that to which
I have just referred. They seem further to have entertained some doubt whether
the Divisional Court's view of the matter was correct, but they did not dissent C
from the view of the Divisional Court, still less did they overrule it. It seems to
me, therefore, that the decision of the Divisional Court, subject to any point
arising from the changes in the rules, remains binding on me. The decision in
Re General Railway Syndicate, Whiteley's Case (18) is on the same lines as *Bildt* v.
Foy (17), and I regard those two decisions as indicating that a counterclaim can
be raised by the filing of an affidavit in accordance with the rules in Ord. 14 D
proceedings. If that is right, it means that, in such a case, there is a raising of a
counterclaim at an earlier stage than the service of any pleadings.

The next cases which have to be looked at are Admiralty cases, the first of
which is *The Salybia* (19). In that case, an action was discontinued before anything
had been done to raise a counterclaim at all, but after it had been discontinued a
counterclaim was intimated by letter. The court held that in those circumstances E
no counterclaim had been set up or could be proceeded with. That decision is
not surprising because there had been discontinuance before anything was done
with regard to the counterclaim. SIR JOHN BIGHAM, P., said (20):

"The real question which the defendants wish to raise by their application
for an order against the plaintiffs to deliver a preliminary act is: whether
they are in a position to proceed with a counterclaim, notwithstanding the F
discontinuance of the action by the plaintiffs. I think the application is wrong
in form, for I do not see how the plaintiffs, who are foreigners, are to be
compelled to deliver a preliminary act for the purpose of the intended
counterclaim, nor do I know what will happen if they refuse or neglect to
deliver such a document. But I prefer to deal with the substance of the
matter. I think it is clear that if a defendant has already 'set up' a counter- G
claim in an action, a plaintiff has no power to prevent the trial of that
counterclaim by discontinuing the action. That appears by Ord. 21, r. 16 . . ."

and the learned President set out the rule. He went on (20):

"But the question is whether in this case a counterclaim ever was 'set
up', for there is no authority for the contention that a counterclaim can be H
set up after 'the case' has ceased to exist. I am of opinion that no counterclaim ever was set up. A counterclaim can only be born of a living action.
The letter of Nov. 4 was written after the action had been wholly discontinued
and when 'the case' had gone. If *Bildt* v. *Foy* (17) be good law, I think it is
distinguishable on the ground that there the counterclaim was mentioned
while the action was still alive, whereas here it was not mentioned until I
after the action was dead. I doubt, moreover, whether a mere casual reference to an intention to prefer a counterclaim can be described as setting up a
counterclaim at all. I think the registrar was right in refusing the
application."

---

(17) (1892), 9 T.L.R. 34; on appeal, 9 T.L.R. 83.   (18) [1900] 1 Ch. 365.
(19) [1910] P. 25; 11 Asp. M.L.C. 361.
(20) [1910] P. at p. 27; 11 Asp. M.L.C. at p. 362.

A   The next case is *The Saxicava* (21). This case seems to me to be of great importance in connexion with the matter which I have to decide. I will read the
headnote (22):

> " This summons, adjourned into court for argument, came before the court
B   on appeal from the refusal of the assistant Admiralty registrar to make
any order on the defendants' application that the plaintiffs be ordered to
file a preliminary act. The summons was taken out to raise the question
whether a counterclaim had been sufficiently ' set up ' within the meaning
of the Rules of the Supreme Court so as to enable the defendants to proceed
with it after the plaintiffs had given notice of discontinuance of their action.
It appeared that on Sept. 12, 1923, a collision took place between the Greek
steamship Despina, belonging to the plaintiffs, and the steamship Saxicava,
C   belonging to the defendants, the Anglo-Saxon Petroleum Co., Ltd. On
Sept. 13 the plaintiffs instituted an action in rem in the Vice-Admiralty Court
at Gibraltar, but after correspondence between the respective solicitors it
was withdrawn. On Sept. 14 the defendants issued a writ in rem in this
country against the owners of the Despina, but as the Despina had been
sunk and her owners were foreigners the action was not proceeded with. On
D   Sept. 17 the owners of the Despina and her master, officers and crew issued
a writ in personam in the action now in question against the Anglo-Saxon
Petroleum Co. In this action the defendants desire to set up a counterclaim,
and it was admitted by the plaintiffs' solicitors that they were aware that
the defendants intended to put forward a counterclaim, but on Jan. 5, 1924,
the plaintiffs filed a notice of discontinuance of the action. Thereupon the
E   defendants took out a summons for an order that the plaintiffs should be
ordered to file their preliminary act, so that the counterclaim might be
preserved and proceeded with."

I must say that I do not see how the filing of a preliminary act would have helped,
because a statement of claim would have been necessary before a defence and
counterclaim could have been delivered; but, be that as it may, the court went
F   on to deal with the substance of the matter. Sir Henry Duke, P., gave a reserved
judgment which is reported as follows (23):

> " It was contended that on the correspondence between the respective
solicitors the plaintiffs must be held to have undertaken to give bail, or the
substitute for bail, to meet a counterclaim by the defendants. The burden
G   of proof as to that was upon the defendants, and they had not satisfied that
burden. It was, therefore, necessary to consider whether, apart from any
agreement between the parties, the plaintiffs were bound under the rules to
deliver a preliminary act. The cases of *Bildt* v. *Foy* (24); *The Salybia* (25)
and *Re General Railway Syndicate, Whiteley's Case* (26), had been referred to,
but it was not suggested that they concluded the matter. When the rules
H   were referred to, it seemed to him that the intention of the framers was that
a counterclaim should be set up by a pleading, and that when, in Ord. 21,
r. 16, it was provided that ' If, in any case in which the defendant sets up a
counterclaim, the action of the plaintiff is stayed, discontinued, or dismissed,
the counterclaim may nevertheless be proceeded with ', what was meant
was that a counterclaim might be proceeded with when the defendant
I   set up the counterclaim in the cause. The possibility of setting up a counterclaim arose under the Supreme Court of Judicature Act, 1873, s. 24. The
rules which were made to carry into effect the provisions of the sections of the
Act had not substantially been changed, at any rate in recent times. [The

(21) [1924] W.N. 59; on appeal, [1924] P. 131; 16 Asp. M.L.C. 324.
(22) [1924] W.N. at p. 59.
(23) [1924] W.N. at pp. 59, 60; 16 Asp. M.L.C. at p. 325.
(24) (1892), 9 T.L.R. 34; on appeal, 9 T.L.R. 83.
(25) [1910] P. 25; 11 Asp. M.L.C. 361.   (26) [1900] 1 Ch. 365.

President read R.S.C., Ord. 19, r. 3, and continued:] All the subsequent   **A**
rules with regard to the setting-up of a counterclaim had their genesis in
the general rule, which related to the setting-up of a counterclaim in the
action by pleadings, so that judgment might be given upon it, and Ord. 21,
r. 10, directed that a counterclaim should be set up in the defence. In this
case there was nothing ' in the cause '. The question was whether correspondence not establishing agreement as to bail, but giving express notice of   **B**
a counterclaim, was sufficient to set up a counterclaim. In his opinion, it
would be entirely contrary to the plain meaning of the rules, or any extension
of them which was consistent with their general tenour, to hold that a
counterclaim might be set up by notice outside the action, without any
setting of it up by any proceedings in the action. The result was that the
appeal must be dismissed."   **C**

SIR HENRY DUKE, P., did not decide that the only way a defendant could set up
a counterclaim was by delivering a counterclaim added to a defence, although
in part of his judgment he seemed to indicate that he thought that that might
be the position. Another part of his judgment seems to indicate that he also
thought that, if a plaintiff gave or undertook to give bail in respect of a counterclaim intimated by a defendant, a counterclaim might thereby be set up and be   **D**
able to be proceeded with. He did not, of course, decide that, because he held
that it was not shown that an undertaking to give bail had been given, but he
appears at least to have kept the point open. The only matter that he decided
was that a letter outside the action could not set up a counterclaim. That decision
was appealed and was unanimously affirmed by the Court of Appeal (27). The
reasoning of the lords justices, however, does not seem to have been exactly   **E**
the same. According to the headnote, two members of the court, BANKES, L.J.,
and SCRUTTON, L.J., decided that a counterclaim must at least be set up by some
proceeding which is directed or recognised by the rules and in respect of which
there is a record on the files of the court. I am not sure that that headnote is
a correct interpretation of the judgment of SCRUTTON, L.J., and I think it necessary to examine rather more closely the grounds on which each member of the   **F**
court based his decision. BANKES, L.J., referred (28) to *Bildt* v. *Foy* (29) and
Re General Railway Syndicate (30), without apparent disapproval, and he seems
to have been willing to accept as correct what had been decided in those cases,
namely, that in summary proceedings under R.S.C., Ord. 14, a counterclaim
could be set up by a defendant by means of an affidavit. Earlier in his judgment,
after referring to various rules in which the expression " set up " is used, he said   **G**
this (31):

" But it seems to me that ' set up ' can only refer to some step in the proceedings which is either directed by or recognised by the rules, because
it is in reference to such matters only that the rules are dealing; and when
it speaks of setting up a defence it must mean set up in some proceeding which   **H**
is recognised or directed by the rules. Under Ord. 14 the proceeding is by way
of affidavit, but when one comes a stage further and refers to pleadings it
seems to me that Ord. 21, r. 16, in speaking of ' setting up ', must refer to a
setting up in a pleading, or, at any rate, in some proceeding which is recognised or directed by the rules, and which becomes part of the record, or something which is filed in the court."   **I**

It seems to me that BANKES, L.J., was there saying that, for a document to be
enough to set up a counterclaim it must satisfy two requirements: firstly, it
must be a proceeding recognised or directed by rules of court, and, secondly, it
must be filed as part of the record of the court. I say " two requirements ",

(27) [1924] P. 131; 16 Asp. M.L.C. 324.
(28) [1924] P. at p. 136; 16 Asp. M.L.C. at p. 328.
(29) (1892), 9 T.L.R. 34; on appeal, 9 T.L.R. 83.
(30) [1900] 1 Ch. 365.   (31) [1924] P. at p. 135; 16 Asp. M.L.C. at p. 328.

A   because that is the way he stated it, but I rather think that Bankes, L.J., regarded the two requirements as linked together because he seems to be taking the view that, if the proceeding was directed or recognised by rules of court, then there would be something on the record of the court relating to it. There are, however, these two elements in the requirements which he specifies. Scrutton, L.J., in his judgment also referred to the various rules, and he said (32):

B

" It appears to me that setting up a counterclaim must be done by something which is recorded in the court. I do not think it is necessary to decide in this case whether setting it up in an affidavit under Ord. 14 as a defence to a claim, or as a reason why execution should not issue or judgment be given on a claim, is ' setting up ' a counterclaim or not, because there is nothing of that sort in this case, but it seems to me clear that one cannot extend it

C

to a mere notice from the defendant to the plaintiff. I am not certain whether the learned counsel who argued this case contended that oral notice would do. Here we have solicitors communicating with each other over the telephone and disagreeing as to what has happened. One is the in realms of uncertainty, and the rules limit dealing with counterclaims to matters in respect of which there is a record on the files of the court."

D

It seems to me that the emphasis in Scrutton, L.J.'s judgment is on there being a record on the files of the court rather than on there being a proceeding directed or recognised by the rules of court. But counsel for the plaintiffs argued that, while that might be so on a literal interpretation of the part of the judgment which I have read, if the judgment is read as a whole Scrutton, L.J., was really

E   saying very much the same as Bankes, L.J. I am not sure of that. I feel that Scrutton, L.J., was committing himself slightly less than Bankes, L.J., and was content to decide the case on the simple ground that the intimation of a counterclaim by means outside the cause could not amount to a setting up of a counterclaim. Sargant, L.J., seems to me to have gone further than both the other members of the court. He said (33):

F

" Order 21, r. 16, deals with the setting up of a counterclaim and refers to some definite step in the proceedings, but I do not think that the phrase ' sets up ' is satisfied by a general intimation outside the proceedings of the intention of the defendant to proceed by way of counterclaim. The phrase ' sets up ' in that rule must have the same meaning as in the immediately preceding rule, and in the other rules to which Scrutton, L.J., has referred,

G   r. 10 and r. 11. Each of these rules, as it seems to me, is a definite legal step in the delivery of the counterclaim, which is, for the purpose of the counterclaim, the commencement of the action. I agree with the view, which I think was indicated by Bankes, L.J., that in the case of an affidavit under Ord. 14, the setting up there is a setting up for the purpose of the particular proceeding contemplated by that order, and I do not think myself that the

H   filing of the affidavit under Ord. 14 could be a setting up of the counterclaim for any purpose except the purpose of replying to the plaintiff's attempt to get judgment. It seems to me that in the rules as to pleadings under Ord. 21 the setting up of the counterclaim means the delivery of the counterclaim according to the rules."

Sargant, L.J., as it seems to me, was there saying that the only way to set up

I   a counterclaim for the purpose of being in a position to proceed with it after discontinuance by the plaintiff was by the delivery of a defence and counterclaim. He was, therefore, going further than either Bankes, L.J., or Scrutton, L.J., thought it necessary to go. Indeed, I think that it is implicit in his judgment that he did not agree with the grounds of decision of the Divisional Court in *Bildt* v. *Foy* (34).

---

(32) [1924] P. at p. 138; 16 Asp. M.L.C. at p. 329.
(33) [1924] P. at pp. 138, 139; 16 Asp. M.L.C. at pp. 329, 330.
(34) (1892), 9 T.L.R. 34.

It is my duty to try to find in the judgments of the Court of Appeal the true   **A**
ratio decidendi, and the position, as I see it, is that at least two of the lords
justices, BANKES and SARGANT, L.JJ., were of opinion that a counterclaim
could only be set up by a proceeding recognised or directed by rules of court.
BANKES, L.J., appears to have thought that that might include a proceeding
authorised or directed by the rules other than the delivery of a defence and
counterclaim itself, and he obviously had in mind the situation that arises   **B**
in summary proceedings under R.S.C., Ord. 14. SARGANT, L.J., on the other
hand, appears to have thought that there had to be delivery of a defence and
counterclaim. Since two members of the court held what was, to the extent stated
at least, a common view, I feel that I am bound by it. Accordingly, I feel that
I must regard the decision of the Court of Appeal in *The Saxicava* (35) as a binding
decision that a counterclaim can be raised only by a proceeding recognised or   **C**
directed by rules of court.

It was argued for the defendants that, even if that be the true interpretation
of the judgment in that case, the judgments went further than was necessary for
the decision of the case and were, therefore, obiter. It was said that the only
decision necessary was that a proceeding outside the cause giving rise to nothing
on the record of the court was not enough to set up a counterclaim. I agree that   **D**
that was all that was necessary in order to determine the case before the Court of
Appeal, but it seems to me that I must examine and consider myself bound by
the reasons given by the lords justices in their judgments, even although those
reasons went somewhat further than was strictly necessary. I, therefore, do not
regard myself free to hold that a proceeding not authorised or directed by the
rules of court can be effective to raise a counterclaim.   **E**

The last case which needs to be looked at is *The Fairplay XIV* (36). I think that
the most convenient way of stating the facts is to read that part of the judgment
of SIR BOYD MERRIMAN, P., which relates to them, after which I shall read some
of the observations later in the judgment which deal with the point with which I
am concerned. SIR BOYD MERRIMAN, P., said (37):

" This is a motion by the defendants, who have appeared in the action   **F**
in rem between the owners of the motor yacht Snowbird and the owners
of the tug Fairplay XIV, to be allowed to prosecute a counterclaim notwithstanding the provision of s. 8 of the Maritime Conventions Act, 1911.
The circumstances are that on Sept. 4, 1936, there was a collision in German
waters between the Snowbird and this tug, or her tow. The precise circumstances of the collision have not been gone into on this motion and will form   **G**
a subject of investigation in the action. But I am told that after the collision
there was a certain amount of negotiation in Germany in the course of which
the owner of the Snowbird put forward his claim. There were discussions
as to limitation, and so forth, but it is not very clear, on what I have been
told, to what extent, if any, the tug-owners put forward any detailed counterclaim. Whatever the position was at the time, however, nothing further was   **H**
done in the sense that no proceedings were taken by either side in the German
courts, and, apparently, the matter had gone to sleep. But on some date in
July, 1937, the owner of the Snowbird did give instructions to his London
solicitors that a look-out was to be kept for the tug in case she came into
English waters, and that, if she did so, an action in rem was to be started.
Faithful to their instructions, the solicitors had a very vigilant look-out   **I**
kept, and on her arrival in these waters on Aug. 23, 1938, they got information through Lloyd's signal station, and, practically on her arrival in an
English port, a writ was issued and her arrest effected. Meanwhile the
Snowbird herself, which had been sunk by the collision, had been salved
in circumstances which made her a constructive total loss, and I am told that

---

(35) [1924] P. 131; 16 Asp. M.L.C. 324.   (36) [1939] P. 57.
(37) [1939] P. at pp. 59, 60.

A   she was broken up some time ago. As far as the defendants were concerned, therefore, there was at no material time a res against which they could take action. Whether it was that they did not wish to sue in Germany, or that they preferred to ' let sleeping dogs lie ' unless and until they were attacked, they have not, in fact, taken any action against the plaintiff. But now that their ship has come to this country, and been arrested in an action

B   which has been constituted in this court, they wish to be allowed to proceed by way of counterclaim. The arrest having taken place on Aug. 23, it is plain that they had eleven days from the time when they were attacked in which they would have been in time to take any proceedings that they might be advised to take. Mr. Willmer does not, of course, dispute that they could have put themselves in order by issuing a cross-writ at any time between Aug.

C   23 and Sept. 4, and if they had done so no question would have arisen, and this motion would have been unnecessary. Instead of which, all that they actually did was to enter an appearance in the action against them, and that they did on Aug. 31, five days before the period of two years had elapsed."

Further on in his judgment Sir Boyd Merriman, P., said (38):

D   " These defendants, as soon as they were attacked, ought to have done one of two things. They ought to have issued a cross-writ before Sept. 4, which would have put them in time, or, if time had permitted, have put in a counterclaim. Now in fact, in the ordinary course of procedure they could not counterclaim by Sept. 4 because the plaintiff's statement of claim had not been delivered. It would have needed some special order to accelerate

E   the pleadings to enable them to proceed in time. I have no doubt that, if any such application had been made, the answer would have been: ' Why do you not take out a cross-writ and then the matter can be dealt with on the cross-writ.' But in neither sense had they in fact instituted proceedings on their claim before Sept. 4."

    I am not in this connexion concerned with the matter which was before Sir

F   Boyd Merriman, P., in that case, namely, whether it was a proper case for the grant of an extension. The relevance of the judgment is in the part which I have just read where Sir Boyd Merriman, P., indicated that it would not have been practicable for the defendants to set up a counterclaim because that stage of the proceedings would not have been reached in time. It seems to me clear that, if Sir Boyd Merriman, P., had thought that there was some other way in which a

G   counterclaim could have been set up, for instance, by the service or filing of a notice of counterclaim, or some other document put on the file of the court, he would not have expressed himself in the way in which he did. It seems to me that he was viewing the matter through the eyes of one who thought that the way to raise a counterclaim, and the only way to raise a counterclaim, was by the delivery of a defence and counterclaim at the appropriate stage in the action. It may

H   be said, of course, that the point was not argued before him, and it seems clear that he did not have in mind the authorities on R.S.C., Ord. 14 procedure nor, I think, the position that can arise when steps are taken by a defendant at an early stage of a collision action to get security for a counterclaim. But the judgment does indicate a view, to my mind, that a counterclaim can in general only be raised by delivery of a defence and counterclaim; it is, at any rate, entirely

I   inconsistent with the view that a counterclaim can be raised at an early stage by a document called a notice of counterclaim.

    I now have to consider the argument raised by the defendants that there has been a long practice in the Admiralty court to file notices of counterclaim, and that it ought to be recognised as a proper practice even though it is not authorised or directed by rules of court. It is always difficult when a practice is alleged to establish with any degree of certainty the facts with regard to it. However, from

(38) [1939] P. at p. 61.

inquiries which I have made of the registry, who have been able to investigate the A
situation at any rate since 1925, it is clear that, from time to time, notices of
counterclaim have been filed in collision actions. I think that it would be right
to say that there has grown up a practice, though not a general practice, of filing
such documents. It also seems to me that it is in many ways a convenient practice, in that it puts on the record of the court for the information both of the court
and the plaintiff that the defendant intends to make a counterclaim. But I feel B
bound to hold in the light of the authorities to which I have referred that, however
convenient the practice may be, such a notice cannot be a raising of a counterclaim so as to enable a defendant to proceed with his counterclaim even though
the plaintiff discontinues. It seems to me that the notice of counterclaim does
not satisfy the test laid down by at least two of the lords justices in *The Saxicava*
(39). It follows that, in my view, the notice of counterclaim is of no effect in C
raising a counterclaim in this case.

I have already indicated that there may be exceptional cases where a counterclaim is raised at a stage in an action earlier than the stage of service of a defence
and counterclaim. One such case is in proceedings under R.S.C., Ord. 14, and
another such case seems to me to be where the defendant in an Admiralty action
seeks to obtain security for an intended counterclaim by the arrest of the plain- D
tiff's ship or by the obtaining of bail in order to avoid such arrest. That case,
as I indicated earlier, appears to have been present to the mind of SIR HENRY
DUKE, P., in *The Saxicava* (40), when he referred to the contention that there
had been an undertaking by the plaintiff to give bail. The raising of a counterclaim at an early stage in this way seems to me to be contemplated by the rules
relating to the arrest of a plaintiff's vessel by a defendant, certainly the old rule E
and I think also the new rule. The old rule which was in force until the beginning
of 1964 was R.S.C., Ord. 5, r. 16, and I am clear that that rule contemplated the
arrest of a plaintiff's ship in respect of a counterclaim by a defendant at an early
stage of the action. It was treated as having that effect in the practice books;
see, for example, WILLIAMS AND BRUCE (2nd Edn. 1886), p. 265, (3rd Edn. 1902),
p. 275; see also 1 HALSBURY'S LAWS (3rd Edn.), p. 74. The rule provides for the F
filing of an affidavit by the defendant to lead the warrant of arrest, and it seems
to me that the effect of that affidavit in relation to the raising of a counterclaim
may well be the same as the effect of the affidavit in R.S.C., Ord. 14 proceedings,
to which reference has already been made. The new rule is R.S.C., Ord. 75, r. 5.
This has different wording, and it is certainly arguable that, under the new rule,
arrest at an early stage of the action is not contemplated; but I feel very doubtful G
whether it was ever intended to change the position in this respect in 1964.
Under the new rule, as under the old, the defendant can, in my view, by following
the process laid down in the rule, arrest a plaintiff's ship at an early stage in
respect of a counterclaim. It may well be, moreover, that, where a defendant has
availed himself of this right of arrest at an early stage, he should be held to have
thereby raised a counterclaim, and so to be in a position to proceed with that H
counterclaim despite discontinuance by the plaintiff. If that be a right view of
the law, then this constitutes a second exception to the general state of affairs
along with the exception arising in summary proceedings under R.S.C., Ord. 14.
I do not, however, think that it is necessary to decide any of these matters in this
case. The defendants here do not claim to have raised a counterclaim by virtue
of an affidavit filed under R.S.C., Ord. 14, nor do they claim to have raised a I
counterclaim by virtue of an affidavit filed under R.S.C., Ord. 75, r. 5, and it is,
therefore, not necessary to determine what would be the position if they were so
claiming. It is enough for me to say that, following *The Saxiclava* (39), the procedure which they have adopted, namely, the filing of a notice of counterclaim,
was ineffective to raise a counterclaim.

The question remains what relief, if any, the plaintiffs are entitled to in the light

---

(39) [1924] P. 131; 16 Asp. M.L.C. 324.   (40) [1924] W.N. 59; 16 Asp. M.L.C. 324.

A of my decision that the notice of counterclaim is ineffective. It has been argued on behalf of the defendants, as I understand it, that the more ineffective the notice of counterclaim is the less need there is to do anything about it, and that the filing of a document which is not authorised by rules of the court is a harmless, administrative matter which ought to be left to stand. I have not heard full argument whether the filing of this document is an irregularity within the mean-

B ing of the relevant rule or not. Irregularities are now dealt with by R.S.C., Ord. 2, r. 1, which provides:

" (1) Where, in beginning or purporting to begin any proceedings or at any stage in the course of or in connexion with any proceedings, there has, by reason of any thing done or left undone, been a failure to comply with the requirements of these rules, whether in respect of time, place, manner, form

C or content or in any other respect, the failure shall be treated as an irregularity and shall not nullify the proceedings, any step taken in the proceedings, or any document, judgment or order therein. (2) Subject to para. (3), the court may, on the ground that there has been such a failure as is mentioned in para. (1), and on such terms as to costs or otherwise as it thinks just, set aside either wholly or in part the proceedings in which the failure

D occurred, any step taken in those proceedings or any document, judgment or order therein or exercise its powers under these rules to allow such amendments (if any) to be made and to make such order (if any) dealing with the proceedings generally as it thinks fit. (3) The court shall not wholly set aside any proceedings or the writ or other originating process by which they were begun on the ground that the proceedings were required by any of these

E rules to be begun by an originating process other than the one employed."

It might be said that the filing of the notice of counterclaim was not within r. 1 (1) of R.S.C., Ord. 2, because it was not a failure to comply with the requirements of the rules, but rather the doing of something not covered by the rules at all. I think, however, that that would be rather a narrow construction to put on

F r. 1 (1) of R.S.C., Ord. 2. It seems to me that, if a party proceeds in a matter in a way not authorised by the rules, then there has been in that respect a failure to comply with the rules. If the rules prescribe a particular way of raising a counterclaim and a defendant uses a different way, it seems to me that, in that respect, there has been a failure by him to comply with the requirements of the rules within the meaning of r. 1 (1) of R.S.C., Ord. 2. Under r. 1 (2), the court may either

G set aside or give leave to amend if an amendment is appropriate. There is, however, one mandatory provision in r. 1 (3) of R.S.C., Ord. 2, and that is that the court is not wholly to set aside proceedings simply because the wrong form of originating process has been used.

I have considered whether it could be said that the defendants in this case, by serving a notice of counterclaim, have, within the meaning of R.S.C., Ord. 2,

H r. 1 (3), taken proceedings by the wrong originating process. It seems to me, however, that what is contemplated by R.S.C., Ord. 2, r. 1 (3) is that the court shall not set aside proceedings where a party, out of a number of recognised methods of beginning proceedings, chooses the wrong one, where, for instance, instead of beginning proceedings by writ, he begins them by originating summons, or, instead of by petition, by originating motion, and so on. It does not

I seem to me to contemplate a case where, instead of beginning proceedings by the prescribed method of process, a party uses a form of process which is not prescribed for any kind of proceedings whatever; for example, I do not think that, if a party begins an action by issuing, instead of a writ, an application for a driving licence, R.S.C., Ord. 2, r. 1 (3), would prevent the court from setting aside the application for a driving licence. I do not think that it can have that meaning. It follows that, in my view, on the proper construction of R.S.C., Ord. 2, r. 1, the court has power to act in this case either by setting aside or by giving leave to amend. No application has been made to amend, and it is difficult

to see how this document can be amended at this stage of the proceedings so as A
to produce any useful result. In these circumstances, it seems to me that the
right course for the court to take in order to protect the interests of the plaintiffs
is to set aside the notice of counterclaim pursuant to R.S.C., Ord. 2, r. 1. If I
am wrong in the view which I have taken on the construction of R.S.C., Ord. 2,
r. 1, then I am of opinion that the court has inherent jurisdiction to set aside a
proceeding as irregular as this.   B

I ought before leaving this part of the case, in deference to the authors concerned, to refer briefly to what is said about the making of a counterclaim in
BRITISH SHIPPING LAWS, Vol. 1, ADMIRALTY PRACTICE. In para. 252, after a
reference to R.S.C., Ord. 75, r. 5 (1), the following passage appears:

" It is to be noted that a defendant may arrest at any time after he has
appeared if he has a counterclaim. He does not have to wait until pleadings,   C
but, if he does not, he must serve a notice of counterclaim before arresting."

Then in para. 267 it is said:

" It may be convenient here to reiterate that a defendant who has
entered appearance and who has a counterclaim has a right of arrest of the
plaintiff's property similar to that which the plaintiff has against the defen-   D
dant's property. This is provided for in Ord. 75, r. 5 (1), and although from
the wording of the rule it may appear that this right of arrest does not
arise until after the defendant has delivered his defence and counterclaim,
this is not the case, for provided the defendant has given to the plaintiff's
solicitors notice of counterclaim setting out briefly the nature of the defendant's cause of action on the lines of a general indorsement to an Admiralty   E
writ in rem, he may then proceed to issue a warrant of arrest and deliver
it to the marshal for execution in the manner described with regard to the
plaintiff, supra. This is in practice hardly ever necessary owing to the fact
that Admiralty writs are issued by solicitors who are well aware of a defendant's rights in this respect; consequently if the plaintiff's property comes
within the jurisdiction and the defendant has a right of arrest there is no   F
difficulty in persuading the plaintiff to give bail."

The authors are quite right in that last observation, because I am told that no
defendant has arrested a plaintiff's ship for some forty years. As will be clear
from my judgment, I do not disagree with the view expressed in that work
that a defendant has a right under R.S.C., Ord. 75, r. 5, to arrest a plaintiff's
ship at an early stage. The only statement from which I dissent is the statement G
that it is necessary for a defendant, in order to exercise that right, to serve a notice
of counterclaim. It seems to me that the old R.S.C., Ord. 5, r. 16, and the present
R.S.C., Ord. 75, r. 5, lay down the procedure to be followed in such a case, and,
provided that that procedure is followed and the appropriate affidavit is filed to
lead the warrant of arrest, then the right to arrest can be exercised. For the
reasons which I have given, I shall order that the notice of counterclaim in this H
case be set aside.

I now pass to the question of the time-bar under the Maritime Conventions
Act, 1911, s. 8. As I have indicated, the plaintiffs by their motion ask for an order
that a counterclaim is not maintainable, and the defendants by their cross-
motion ask that, if it be necessary to extend the time, the court should extend it.
Section 8 of the Maritime Conventions Act, 1911, provides as follows: I

" No action shall be maintainable to enforce any claim or lien against
a vessel or her owners in respect of any damage or loss to another vessel,
her cargo or freight, or any property on board her, or damages for loss of
life or personal injuries suffered by any person on board her, caused by the
fault of the former vessel, whether such vessel be wholly or partly in fault,
or in respect of any salvage services, unless proceedings therein are commenced within two years from the date when the damage or loss or injury

A   was caused or the salvage services were rendered . . . Provided that any
court having jurisdiction to deal with an action to which this section relates
may, in accordance with the rules of court, extend any such period, to such
extent and on such conditions as it thinks fit, and shall, if satisfied that there
has not during such period been any reasonable opportunity of arresting the
defendant vessel within the jurisdiction of the court, or within the territorial
B   waters of the country to which the plaintiff's ship belongs or in which the
plaintiff resides or has his principal place of business, extend any such period
to an extent sufficient to give such reasonable opportunity."

So there is a two-year period for claims of the kind made in this action and the
court may extend that period for good cause in certain cases and must extend it
in other cases. It is conceded that the expression " action " in s. 8 includes a
C   proceeding by counterclaim. If it were not conceded, I should so hold, for it
seems to me to follow from the decision in *The Fairplay XIV* (41) to which I have
referred. There is no provision in the Maritime Conventions Act, 1911, comparable
with s. 28 of the Limitation Act, 1939, whereby for limitation purposes the date
of a counterclaim is taken as the date of the writ. It follows that, in this case,
apart from any extension, the time for either side to claim or counterclaim in
D   respect of the collision expired on Mar. 6, 1965. There was, however, an agreed
extension, so far as the defendants were concerned, to Nov. 7, 1965. The position,
therefore, is that any action begun or counterclaim raised by the defendants
after that date, namely, Nov. 7, 1965, is prima facie out of time under the statute,
and can only be maintained if the court grants an extension of time. It follows
that, if the present action were to proceed to the stage where a defence and
E   counterclaim were delivered, that counterclaim would prima facie be out of time;
but it is to be observed that the writ in the Gniezno's action was issued within
the period of two years as extended by agreement, and that, therefore, if that
action was proceeded with, the claim in it would not be out of time. It is also
to be observed that the writ in that action is still in force, having been renewed
by the order of the Admiralty registrar, to which I referred earlier.
F   It seems to me that the plaintiffs' application and the defendants' cross-
application in regard to this matter ought to be taken together. If I had held
that the defendants have already, by virtue of the notice of counterclaim, done
what was necessary, apart from any question of time-bar, to raise a counterclaim,
then it would have been necessary to adjudicate on the merits of the application
to extend the time; but, if my view is right that no effective counterclaim has yet
G   been raised, it does not seem to me that it is necessary to come to any decision
on what would be the right course to take if such a counterclaim either had been
raised or could clearly be seen to be about to be raised. It would not be right for
me to express any final view on the question whether there is any method open
to the defendants of raising a counterclaim, apart from any question of time-bar,
if the plaintiffs take no further step in the action. I will only say that there are
H   obviously difficulties in their way. Unless I were persuaded either that there was a
counterclaim or that there was likely to be one which could be proceeded with, I
should not think it necessary to determine the question of extension at all. On
this ground alone, therefore, it seems to me that no order ought to be made
on either the plaintiffs' application for an order that a counterclaim is not
maintainable or the defendants' application for an extension of time, if necessary.
I   There is, however, a further reason why I consider that no order ought to be
made on either of these applications, and that is that the Gniezno's action is
still in being. The writ was issued in time and it is still valid for service, and it
has been indicated by counsel for the defendants that consideration is being given
to the taking of whatever steps may be possible or appropriate to proceed with
that action. Some of the steps which have been discussed as being possible or
appropriate include application by the defendants to amend the writ so as to

(41) [1939] P. 57.

make it a writ in personam, and a further application to serve the writ as so
amended on the plaintiffs out of the jurisdiction. It would be wrong for me to
express any view on the merits of such applications. It will be sufficient for the
court to deal with the merits of such applications if and when they are made. But
in view of the fact that the defendants have open to them the possibility at least
of proceeding with an action which is in time, I do not think that there is any
need to give them leave, even if the merits otherwise warranted it, to proceed
with a counterclaim in this action. On this ground also, therefore, no order need
be made

I wish to make it clear that, in not making any order on the application of either
party with regard to the time-bar, I am not shutting out any further applications
by either party if the situation should change. This is an interlocutory decision,
not a final decision, and, if the circumstances should change because of any steps
taken by either party, if the situation should change in the sense that either a
counterclaim were effectively raised or there was an obvious prospect that one
would be effectively raised, then the situation would be different from what it is
now, and I wish to make it quite clear that it would be both possible and appropriate for the parties to make further applications in regard to the matter. I
think that that covers all the matters raised in these motions.

Motions dismissed.

Solicitors: *Holman, Fenwick & Willan* (for the plaintiffs); *Waltons, Bright
& Co.* (for the defendants).

[*Reported by* N. P. METCALFE, ESQ., *Barrister-at-Law*.]

R. P. DOOBAY AND OTHERS *v.* MOHABEER.

[PRIVY COUNCIL (Lord Gardiner, L.C., Viscount Dilhorne and Lord Wilberforce),
January 11, 12, February 21, 1967.]

*Privy Council—Guyana—Hire-purchase—Warranty—Mill, known to be defec-
tive, purchased under hire-purchase agreement—Obligation on owner to remedy
defects—Failure to remedy defects—Delivery of mill taken by hire-purchasers
—Expenses incurred in installing mill—Measure of damages for breach of
contract by failing to remedy mill's defects.*

The appellant hire-purchasers entered into a contract to acquire from the
respondent owner a rice mill at a price of $14,500, of which $3,000 was
payable as a deposit and the remainder was payable by instalments initially
of $2,000 each. The rice mill was of Japanese manufacture and was not, as
the hire-purchasers knew, in working order. The owner was responsible for
remedying the defect, it being contemplated that experts should be brought
from Japan to put the mill in order. The mill was useless to the hire-
purchasers unless the defects were remedied. The hire-purchasers laid a
concrete foundation, spending $1,500 on it. They bought a Lister engine at
a cost of some $3,500. They took delivery of the mill. They paid $5,000,
including the deposit and thereafter paid no more. The defects were not
remedied, and the hire-purchasers were unable to get them remedied. The
hire-purchase agreement was not determined by the owner, and the legal
relation of the parties remained that of bailor and bailee. The owner sued for
the balance of the price ($9,500) and the hire-purchasers counterclaimed for
damages. Relevant clauses of the contract included cl. 4, whereby the hire-
purchasers agreed to keep the mill in working order and repair, but only the
owner or the owner's agents were permitted at the hire-purchasers' expense
to effect the repairs, and cl. 8, which provided that—" When the hiring is

A　terminated the [hire-purchasers] shall not on any ground whatsoever be entitled to any allowance, credit, return or set-off for payments previously made." A sum of $240 damages awarded to the hire-purchasers on their counterclaim was not in dispute. On appeal from an order awarding the owner $9,500 and the hire-purchasers damages of $240,

Held: the owner was entitled to the $9,500 claimed and the hire-purchasers

B　were entitled to damages on their counterclaim, such damages amounting to $16,240, for the following reasons—

(i) the hire-purchasers had paid money and had assumed obligation to pay further instalments for an article from which they derived no benefit, and so their damages would be such sum as would compensate them for that loss; cl. 8 of the contract did not disentitle them to recover the $5,000 that they

C　had paid because on the true construction of cl. 8 the word " terminated " therein referred to termination pursuant to either of two prior clauses of the contract, cl. 1 or cl. 6, and thus did not extend to the present case (see p. 764, letter H, and p. 765, letters A to C, post).

Charterhouse Credit Co., Ltd. v. *Tolly* ([1963] 2 All E.R. 432) applied.

(ii) accordingly the hire-purchasers were entitled to recover by way of

D　damages $5,000 paid to them together with the $9,500 payable to the owner on his claim, and the hire-purchasers were further entitled to $1,500 in respect of installation costs and to the sum of $240 (making in all $16,240), but they were not entitled to damages in respect of the Lister engine (see p. 765, letters H and I, post).

Appeal allowed in part.
E

[As to damages for loss caused to a hirer of chattel through defects, see 2 HALS-BURY'S LAWS (3rd Edn.) 123, 124, paras. 237 text and note (*b*), 239.

As to the implied condition of fitness in hire-purchase contracts, see 19 HALS-BURY'S LAWS (3rd Edn.) 532, 533, para. 858; and for cases on the subject, see 26 DIGEST (Repl.) 666, *35*, *36*, and DIGEST (Cont. Vol. A) 648, 649, *43a, 43b.*]
F

Cases referred to:

Charterhouse Credit Co., Ltd. v. *Tolly,* [1963] 2 All E.R. 432; [1963] 2 Q.B. 683; [1963] 2 W.L.R. 1168; Digest (Cont. Vol. A) 649, *43b.*

Helby v. *Matthews,* [1895-99] All E.R. Rep. 821; [1895] A.C. 471; 64 L.J.Q.B. 465; 72 L.T. 841; 60 J.P. 20; 26 Digest (Repl.) 660, *14.*

G　*Yeoman Credit, Ltd.* v. *Apps,* [1961] 2 All E.R. 281; [1962] 2 Q.B. 508; [1961] 3 W.L.R. 94; Digest (Cont. Vol. A) 648, *43a.*

Appeal.

This was an appeal by the appellants, R. P. Doobay and others, from a judg-ment of the British Caribbean Court of Appeal, which varied the order of the Supreme Court of British Guiana (CRANE, J.), in respect of a rice mill purchased

H　by the appellants from the respondent Mohabeer for $14,500 on a hire-purchase agreement dated Sept. 27, 1961. The mill was not in working order at the time of purchase. The appellants had paid $5,000 under the agreement, namely a deposit of $3,000 and one instalment of $2,000, but refused to pay further instalments on the grounds that the respondent had committed a breach of warranty in not carrying out his undertaking to have the mill put in working order by his

I　expert. The respondent sued for the balance of $9,500. The appellants, while not denying the claim, counterclaimed for $9,800 for breach of contract or as special damages. The Court of Appeal upheld the claim for $9,500 in favour of the respondent but varied the order of CRANE, J., by reducing the damages awarded to the appellants on the counterclaim to $240. The appellants appealed. The facts are set out in the opinion of the Board.

K. M. McHale for the appellants.

A. T. Davies, Q.C., and *J. G. Leach* for the respondent.

LORD WILBERFORCE: This is an appeal by the defendants in the A
action, from a judgment of the British Caribbean Court of Appeal. That court
varied the judgment of CRANE, J., in the Supreme Court of British Guiana by
reducing from $3,500 to $240 the amount awarded to the appellants against the
plaintiff, who is respondent on this appeal, on the appellants' counterclaim. The
Court of Appeal upheld the judgment of the trial judge for $9,500 in favour of the
respondent. The appellants appeal against both parts of the Court of Appeal's B
decision. The proceedings arose out of a transaction concerning a rice mill, the
property of the respondent. The first appellant, R. P. Doobay (to whom their
lordships will for convenience refer as " the appellant "), who acted throughout
and gave evidence on behalf of his partners, the other appellants, went, together
with a Mr. Angus Whyte, himself a rice miller and owner of a similar mill, to see
the mill at the respondent's premises in September, 1961. It is not clear from the C
evidence whether the appellant paid one visit or two or (if one) on which exact
date the visit was made. The appellant was shown the mill, which was a one ton
multi-stage machine manufactured by the Japanese firm Sikoko and called a
Kyowa mill: it included a separator. The mill was not in working order, but the
respondent told the appellant that two experts were coming from Japan to put
it in good working order. The appellant decided to buy it and signed three D
documents, of which, in the event, only the third is material. The first, dated
Sept. 14, 1961, was a letter to the respondent stating that the appellant agreed
to buy the mill for $14,500 to be paid in certain instalments. The second, dated
Sept. 27, 1961, was headed " Receipt " and acknowledged payment of $3,000 in
part payment of $14,500, the purchase price for the mill. This document set out
the dates on which the balance was to be paid, and stated that the mill was sold E
and delivered " as is and where is to-day ", and that a proper hire-purchase
agreement was to be made at a later date, on which the receipt would be null and
void. It was signed by the respondent and the three partners. A hire-purchase
agreement was in fact prepared and entered into (being the document next
referred to), and it has not been disputed that thereafter the receipt ceased to
have effect. No reliance was placed on it before their lordships.   F

The hire-purchase agreement bore the date of Sept. 27, 1961, though in fact
it was signed somewhat later. It was a hiring agreement, in what is commonly
known as the *Helby* v. *Matthews* (1) form, with an option for the hirers to become
the owners of the mill by full payment at any time during the hire. The price of
the mill was stated to be $14,500 and the balance of this amount, after deducting
the down payment of $3,000, was to be paid as to $2,000 on Nov. 25, 1961, G
$2,000 on Apr. 16, 1962 and $7,500 on November [sic] 1962. The agreement
contained a number of usual clauses, including a statement that the hirers were
bailees only and giving the owner power to retake on default: but it is necessary
to refer specifically to two. By cl. 4 the hirers agreed to keep the mill in good
working order and repair, but only the owner or the owner's agents were
permitted (at the hirers' expense) to effect the repairs. By cl. 8 it was provided H
that:

" When the hiring is terminated the hirer shall not on any ground whatsoever be entitled to any allowance, credit, return or set-off for payments
previously made."

An argument was based on this clause which it will be necessary to consider. I
Soon after the signature of this agreement, the appellant took delivery of the
machine and, with the help of Mr. Angus Whyte, installed it at the partnership
factory: for this purpose he laid a concrete foundation spending, according to his
evidence, $1,500 in all, including workmanship. He also bought a Lister engine
to propel the mill at a cost of some $3,500. A few months later he paid an instal-
ment of $2,000, but this was not before he had a conversation with the respondent

(1) [1895-99] All E.R. Rep. 821; [1895] A.C. 471.

A in which, answering the appellant's complaint that the mill could not be got to work, the respondent said that the experts were coming from Japan. The experts never did come: a Mr. Neville, sent by the respondent, tried to make it work but failed; the appellant contacted the agents for another Japanese firm in British Guiana who were unable to help, and the mill in fact never operated properly. The appellant offered to return the mill and to leave the respondent

B with the $5,000 he had received, but this offer was rejected. After a solicitor's letter, the writ was issued on Dec. 5, 1962.

In view of the course taken by the proceedings, some reference is required to the pleadings. The statement of claim, as amended, claimed $9,500 as the balance due on the hire-purchase agreement of Sept. 27, 1961, i.e., the purchase price ($14,500) less the deposit ($3,000) and the first instalment ($2,000). The appellants

C delivered a defence and counterclaim. By the defence they admitted the hire-purchase agreement, said that they had spent $9,800 for the installation and in acquiring the engine for the mill, alleged that the mill never operated, and that the respondent undertook to get his expert to rectify the mill and was guilty of breach of warranty. Then " by way of set-off and counterclaim " the appellants repeated the main averments of the defence (which included those above referred

D to) and claimed:

> 1. $9,800 as damages for the breach of the said agreement and, in the alternative,
> 2. As special damages: (*a*) $5,000 paid as advance for the mill; (*b*) $1,500 for installation; (*c*) $3,300 for the Lister engine.

E At the trial before CRANE, J., the judge held that it was for the appellants to begin. The appellant himself gave evidence. In addition to proving the matters pleaded, he said that he had put eighty bags of padi, obtained from two customers, into the mill but that it broke up the rice. He had to pay these customers $8 per bag. He called Mr. Angus Whyte, who supported his evidence as to the failure of the mill to work, and a Mr. Algoo, one of the two customers, who had given

F to the appellant, and been paid for, thirty bags of padi which the mill had damaged. The judge found that the mill was delivered in a state of disrepair with a promise that it would be rectified later by an expert. He held that the appellants had never determined the bailment and that they had no answer to the respondent's claim, but that they were entitled to sue for damages. He disallowed the appellants' claim for $5,000 on the ground that this was excluded

G by cl. 8 of the hire-purchase agreement. Of the other two sums claimed he allowed that for $3,500 [sic] as the purchase price for the Lister engine, but not that for $1,500, which he considered " had not been properly established ". He disallowed a claim for $640 paid to customers in respect of damaged rice both on the ground that it had not been pleaded and because it was not recoverable as damages. He gave judgment for the respondent on the claim for $9,500 and for

H the appellants on the counterclaim for $3,500.

Both sides appealed against this judgment. The Court of Appeal took the view that the appellants had not repudiated the agreement and that at the trial they had taken the position that " they had purchased the mill and had elected to keep it ". They held that the appellants were liable for the unpaid instalments and that, there being no total failure of consideration, they could not recover the

I $5,000 which they had paid. The respondent was liable for damages for breach of warranty, but no claim had ever been made for the cost of putting the mill in good working order. The installation of the mill and the provision of an engine were the appellants' responsibility and they could not recover in respect of these items. The court awarded $240 in respect of damaged rice, even though this had not been pleaded, but disallowed all the three sums specifically claimed in the counterclaim.

In the present appeal it has not been seriously disputed that the appellants have no answer to the claim for $9,500 nor that, in principle, they are entitled to

recover damages for breach of warranty. The only issue is as to the measure of **A**
such damages having regard (inter alia) to the pleadings. The first point to
establish is the legal relationship between the appellants and the respondent at
the date of the writ. This appears to their lordships to admit of no doubt. The
hiring agreement had not been determined by the owner of the mill, nor had the
hirers become the purchasers of it by an exercise of their option. The relation
remained therefore that of bailor and bailee. Their lordships are of opinion that **B**
the Court of Appeal were under a misapprehension when they held that at the
trial the appellants had taken the position that they had purchased the mill.
They had not, it is true, repudiated the hire-purchase agreement, as they might
well have done, but they had never taken the necessary steps to convert themselves from hirers to purchasers. The property in the mill remained, and remains,
in the owner—the respondent, and the damages which the hirers are entitled to **C**
recover must be calculated on the basis of a failure by the owner to comply with
his obligation to put the mill in working order.

The correct measure of these damages is not, in the view of their lordships, the
cost of so doing. This might well have been the case had the property in the mill
passed to the appellants and had the appellants lost their right to return it to
their vendor (see *Charterhouse Credit Co., Ltd.* v. *Tolly* (2), per Upjohn, L.J.). **D**
This, however, was not so; the property remained in the owner of the mill.
Moreover, though in some cases of hire-purchase, damages based on the cost of
repairing the article hired may be appropriate (see *Yeoman Credit, Ltd.* v.
Apps (3), which their lordships merely quote by way of example without entering
into the grounds for the decision), that is not necessarily always so: regard must
be had to the nature of the article hired, the defects in it and how they arose, **E**
and the character of the owner's obligation to make them good. The contract
in this case was unusual. It was not one for the hire-purchase of an article which
turned out to be defective, contrary to the expectation of the hirer or to the
bargain; the article was known to be defective and was hired as such together
with a contractually assumed obligation by the owner to remedy the defects.
Further, the defects were such that, unless they were remedied, the mill was **F**
useless to the hirers. Finally, to remedy the defects was a matter for which the
owner was wholly responsible: the evidence shows that neither the hirers themselves, nor such persons as the hirers were able to consult in British Guiana, were
able to make the mill work, and indeed the contract itself (cl. 4) expressly
deprived the hirers of the right themselves to undertake repairs. All this underlines the essential character of the owner's obligation to put the mill in repair, **G**
an obligation which it was contemplated he would carry out through experts to
come from Japan. It is in relation to these circumstances that the damages
recoverable by the appellants must be assessed. They have paid money, and
assumed an obligation to pay further instalments, for an article from which they
have derived and can derive no benefit whatever; the only damages which can
compensate them for this are such as correspond in amount with the loss they **H**
have sustained which includes, in the first place, these sums. Their lordships
find support for this approach to the measure of damages in the case of *Charterhouse Credit Co., Ltd.* v. *Tolly* (4). There the trial judge had awarded damages
based on the cost of remedying the defects, but the Court of Appeal decided that
the hirer was entitled to reimbursement of all moneys paid or payable, less a
deduction for the use of the defective article. In that case the plaintiff company **I**
had terminated the hiring midway, but this, though reducing the amount due to
the plaintiff (and so ultimately recoverable by the hirer) makes no difference in
principle. The decision also shows that a defendant may recover all money paid
or payable by him even though he has not taken steps to repudiate the agreement.

Before considering whether, consistently with the pleadings, damages ought to

(2) [1963] 2 All E.R. 432 at p. 443; [1963] 2 Q.B. 683 at p. 711.
(3) [1961] 2 All E.R. 281 ; [1962] 2 Q.B. 508.
(4) [1963] 2 All E.R. 432; [1963] 2 Q.B. 683.

A   be awarded on this basis it is necessary to deal with the argument, already
mentioned, based on cl. 8 of the hire-purchase agreement. The judge held that
this clause prevented the appellants from recovering the $5,000 which they had
already paid. Their lordships cannot agree with this. The clause, by its initial
words, operates " when the hiring is terminated ". Prima facie these words
would seem to contemplate some action by one or other of the parties putting an
B   end to the agreement, and not to a mere expiry of the period of the hiring. That
this is so is, in their lordships' view, conclusively confirmed by other references in
the agreement to " termination ". Thus cl. 6 confers on the owner power
summarily to terminate the hiring and cl. 1 of the owner's agreement refers to
termination by the hirer. The word " terminated " in cl. 8 must refer to these
specific cases, neither of which has in fact occurred, and to these cases only. The
C   clause therefore affords no defence to the appellants' claim for recovery of their
money.

It remains to consider the pleadings. They were described by the Court of
Appeal as uninspired, and their lordships would be inclined to agree that the
counterclaim was not so drafted as to cover damages based on the cost of repair.
But, as regards the measure of damages which their lordships think appropriate,
D   the matter stands otherwise. In the first place, as regards the $5,000 which the
appellants had actually paid, this is both claimed specifically under the heading
of special damages, and appears to be included within the sum of $9,800 claimed
as general damages. Such difficulty as there is relates to the further sum of
$9,500 due on the hire-purchase agreement to the respondent, and for which he is
entitled to judgment on the claim. In law, this sum is precisely comparable with
E   the sum of $5,000; the two together represent the hiring instalments paid or due
by the appellants which, through the respondent's default, have been lost to them.
In their lordships' view both sums ought to be considered as included in the
appellants' claim. The appellants had stated in their defence reasons why they
should not be liable for the outstanding $9,500: the allegations there contained
were repeated in the counterclaim. Taken together, the appellants' case was
F   clear enough: it was that they were not liable to the respondent for anything
and he was liable to repay them $5,000. This could be made good either by
rejecting the respondent's claim for $9,500 and awarding the appellants $5,000 on
the counterclaim; or, should the respondent be held entitled to judgment for
$9,500 on his claim, by awarding both sums to the appellants on their counter-
claim. To interpret the counterclaim in this way involves no hardship to the
G   respondent; the facts on which the appellants were relying were fully pleaded,
and on any view of the matter the respondent was faced with the appellants'
contention that they owed him nothing and, per contra, claimed $5,000 back
from him. Their lordships therefore hold the appellants entitled, on their counterclaim, to $14,500 in respect of their commitments under the hire-purchase agree-
ment. It is hardly necessary to add (since the counterclaim can only have been
H   brought on this basis) that the respondent remains the owner of the machine
and the appellants cannot now take steps to make themselves the owners of it.

With regard to the other sums claimed: the appellants are not, in their lordships' opinion, entitled to $3,300 or any sum in respect of the Lister engine: they
have the engine, the purchase of it is not shown to have involved any loss, and
the claim was rejected in the Court of Appeal. With regard to the cost of installing
I   the mill, the appellants are, in principle, entitled to damages, since such expenditure has been thrown away. The trial judge seems to have accepted this, but held
that the figure claimed—$1,500—had not been properly established. The
appellant, however, gave evidence about this expenditure; as recorded in the
judge's note he said " the cost of the installation was $1,500 including workman-
ship ", and no challenge to this by cross-examination seems to have been made,
nor did the judge give any reasons for holding the sum excessive. In these
circumstances, the right course, in their lordships' view, is to award to the

appellants the sum claimed. There is no cross-appeal as regards the sum of $240   A
awarded to the appellants.

Their lordships will therefore humbly advise Her Majesty that the judgment
of the British Caribbean Court of Appeal ought to be varied by entering judgment
for the appellants on their counterclaim for $16,240. The judgment on the claim
will stand. The respondent must pay the costs of this appeal.

Appeal allowed in part.   B

Solicitors: *Garber, Vowles & Co.* (for the appellants); *Simmons & Simmons*
(for the respondent).

[*Reported by* KATHLEEN O'BRIEN, *Barrister-at-Law.*]

C

R. *v.* O'REILLY.

[COURT OF APPEAL, CRIMINAL DIVISION (Salmon, L.J., Fenton Atkinson and
Brabin, JJ.), April 11, 1967.]   D

Criminal   Law—Trial—Summing-up—Evidence—Corroboration—Rape—Iden-
tity—Scientific evidence identifying accused as assailant—Corroboration
not mentioned in summing-up, but jury directed to disregard evidence of com-
plainant and another and to consider scientific evidence on issue of identity—
Sufficiency of the direction—Criminal Appeal Act, 1907 (7 *Edw.* 7 *c.* 23),   E
s. 4 (1) *proviso, as amended by Criminal Appeal Act* 1966 (*c.* 31), *s.* 4 (1).

A man made two unsuccessful attempts to rape a woman on a dark night.
One L. heard the woman scream and saw her lying on the ground with the
man molesting her. A few days later the appellant was put on an identification parade and L. picked him out as the man whom he saw assaulting the
woman. The woman complainant was unable to identify him, but later in   F
the police court and at the trial she said that she recognised his voice and face
and that he was the man who had assaulted her. The appellant was charged
with attempted rape. The issue was one of identity. Forensic scientific
evidence showed that the mohair fibres found on the appellant's clothes
were identical with the mohair fibres with which the complainant's coat was
made, and that blue nylon fibres found on the appellant's shirt were identical   G
with those of which the complainant's knickers were made. In summing-up
the jury were told it would be dangerous to convict if the direct evidence
stopped at that of the complainant and L.; the jury were directed to consider the scientific evidence alone and whether that carried conviction to
their minds. No mention was made of corroboration. A correct direction
was given on the onus of proof and the ingredients of the offence. On appeal   H
against conviction,

Held: although in sexual cases it was a rule that a jury should be warned
of the danger of convicting without corroboration and the warning should
be given in terms which a jury could understand, yet in the present case the
jury had been told to disregard the evidence of the complainant and L.
on the issue of identity and to approach their verdict on the basis of the   I
scientific evidence; this direction was unexceptionable, notwithstanding
that the word " corroboration " was not used, for it required the jury to consider the independent testimony that identified the appellant with the
offence; moreover the case was one where the proviso to s. 4 (1) of the
Criminal Appeal Act 1907, as amended, should be applied if necessary (see
p. 768, letter G, and p. 769, letters A to C, and G, post).

R. v. *Trigg* ([1963] 1 All E.R. 490) considered and distinguished.

Appeal dismissed.

A   [As to corroboration in sexual cases, see 10 HALSBURY'S LAWS (3rd Edn.) 462, para. 850; and for cases on the subject, see 14 DIGEST (Repl.) 543, 544, *5271-5279*; 15 DIGEST (Repl.) 1014, *9991-9993*.]

Cases referred to:

    R. v. *Beck*, (1896), unreported.

    R. v. *Clynes*, (1960), 44 Cr. App. Rep. 158; Digest (Cont. Vol. A) 379, *5276b.*

B   *R.* v. *Sawyer*, (1959), 43 Cr. App. Rep. 187; Digest (Cont. Vol. A) 379, *5276a.*

    R. v. *Slater*, (1909), unreported.

    R. v. *Trigg*, [1963] 1 All E.R. 490; [1963] 1 W.L.R. 305; 127 J.P. 257; 47   Cr. App. Rep. 94; Digest (Cont. Vol. A) 379, *5276c.*

Appeal.

C   This was an appeal by John Joseph O'Reilly against his conviction at Hertfordshire Quarter Sessions on Nov. 18, 1966, before the deputy chairman (OWEN STABLE, Q.C.) and a jury of attempted rape. He was sentenced to thirty months' imprisonment. The facts are set out in the judgment.

  The case noted below* was cited during the argument in addition to those referred to in the judgment of the court.

D   *D. A. Hollis* for the appellant.

  R. J. Lowry for the Crown.

    SALMON, L.J., delivered the following judgment of the court: The complaint made against the summing-up is that the learned deputy chairman did not warn the jury that it would be dangerous to convict without corroboration of the complainant's evidence. The complainant, Mrs. Reid, was walking home on the
E evening of Aug. 27, 1966, when at about 11.55 at night she was attacked by a man who carried her into an alleyway and there made a determined and brutal, but unsuccessful, attempt to rape her. She fought him off and he made a similar attempt a little later on. That was her evidence. A Mr. Lake was called, who said that he heard a woman scream, he ran to the place from where he had heard the screams coming and there he saw Mrs. Reid lying on the ground with a man on
F top of her molesting her with his hands round her throat. He said that at that particular spot the light was quite good. A few days later the appellant was put on an identification parade and Mr. Lake picked him out as the man who had been attacking Mrs. Reid. Mrs. Reid was quite unable to identity him; but later in the police court and at the trial she said she recognised his voice and his face and that the appellant was the man. The police examined the clothes that were
G being worn by the appellant on the night in question and also Mrs. Reid's clothes. On the appellant's clothes were found strands of mohair and strands of blue nylon which were not part of the fabric of the clothing which he was wearing. On Mrs. Reid's clothes there were found some viscous rayon fibres. All these different lots of fibres were sealed into separate packages by the police and sent to the forensic science laboratory. Mr. Grieve from that laboratory examined the
H various fibres and gave evidence. He said that these fibres had been put under an exceptionally powerful microscope that magnified them 450 times. As for the viscous rayon fibres that were found on Mrs. Reid's clothes, these were identical, according to Mr. Grieve, with fibres of material from which the appellant's jacket was made. It was said on his behalf that this jacket is not a very special jacket and that there may have been other men wearing the same
I sort of jacket with the same sort of viscous rayon fibres. According, however, to Mr. Grieve, when they were blown up—as we have already said to 450 times their true size—the fibres were absolutely identical. This would have been impossible, according to Mr. Grieve, unless the fibres all came from the same garment or two different garments which had been made by the same machine, probably in the same batch. The mohair fibres found on the appellant's clothes were identical with the mohair fibres from which Mrs. Reid's coat was made;

----

  * *R.* v. *Parry*, [1962] Crim. L.R. 37.

and the blue nylon fibres found on the appellant's shirt were identical with the **A**
blue nylon fibres of which Mrs. Reid's knickers were made. The appellant said
that his wife had a mohair skirt; but when his wife was called she denied that
her skirt was made of mohair and said it was a cotton mix. Mr. Grieve said
that although it was impossible to be certain without examining the skirt under
a microscope in his view it was, as Mrs. O'Reilly said, a cotton skirt. The
appellant said that the blue nylon fibres could have, and did, come from his **B**
wife's underclothes, but Mrs. O'Reilly when she gave evidence admitted that
she had no blue nylon knickers and that her underclothing was all made either
of black nylon or of white cotton.

In the course of his summing-up, the learned deputy chairman told the jury
that if the case had stopped at the direct evidence of Mrs. Reid and Mr. Lake,
to which I have already referred, he would have warned them that it was **C**
dangerous to convict. The reason for this is obvious. Identity is always, or
very often, a matter of considerable doubt. He probably had the *R.* v. *Slater* (1)
and *R.* v. *Beck* (2) cases in mind. The most honest, candid and reliable witnesses
can easily make mistakes about identity. The learned deputy chairman, no
doubt with that in mind, said to the jury: well, if the case had merely stopped
with Mrs. Reid and Mr. Lake then it would probably have been dangerous to **D**
convict. He asked the jury to consider the case on the basis that none of that
direct evidence had been given, that it had been a very dark night, and that
no one could have seen who Mrs. Reid's attacker was, and he asked them to
consider the scientific evidence alone, to which reference has already been made;
and he said to them that it might be, and it was entirely a matter for them, that
that scientific evidence looked at by itself might carry conviction to their minds. **E**
His direction on the onus of proof and the ingredients of attempted rape was
clear and accurate. He made it plain to the jury that they could not convict
unless convinced beyond any reasonable doubt of the appellant's guilt.

As I have said, the complaint here is, so it is said, that there was no warning
to the jury about the necessity for corroboration. At the trial the whole issue
was identity. The defence never challenged Mrs. Reid's evidence that someone **F**
had attempted to rape her and, indeed, one can see it would have been very difficult to do so, particularly as Mr. Lake came on the scene when the woman was
screaming, her clothes in disarray, with a man on top of her with his hands round
her neck. The whole case was fought on the issue as to whether this appellant was
that man. Undoubtedly it is the rule that in sexual cases the jury must be warned
of the danger of convicting without corroboration. This rule does not depend on **G**
any legal theory but on long practical experience which has shown that where
there is no corroboration in such cases it is indeed dangerous to convict; and this
applies certainly no less strongly in cases where identity is in issue: *R.* v. *Sawyer*
(3); *R.* v. *Clynes* (4). It applies too whether the point is or is not taken on behalf
of the defence. Accordingly the warning must obviously be given (i) where
there is no evidence of corroboration, and (ii) where there is evidence capable of **H**
corroborating the complainant but which the jury might conclude does not
amount to corroboration. The vast majority of cases fall into one or other of
these two categories. It may perhaps seem strange that where evidence is called
which, if accepted, indisputably must amount to corroboration, it is, according
to the present state of the law, always necessary to tell the jury how dangerous
it would have been to convict if there had been no such evidence. That, however, **I**
is what was decided in the case of *R.* v. *Trigg* (5). The rule that the jury must
be warned does not mean, however, that there has to be some legalistic ritual
to be automatically recited by the judge, that some particular form of words or
incantation has to be used and, if not used, the summing-up is faulty and the

---

(1) (1909), unreported.   (2) (1896), unreported.
(3) (1959), 43 Cr. App. Rep. 187.   (4) (1960), 44 Cr. App. Rep. 158.
            (5) [1963] 1 All E.R. 490.

A conviction must be quashed. The law, as this court understands it, is that there should be a solemn warning given to the jury, in terms which a jury can understand, to safeguard the accused.

In this case the learned deputy chairman gave such a warning although he never used the magic word " corroboration "; and it is doubtful if the jury would have understood what it meant if he had. Indeed, when the actual word is used **B** it is necessary for the court to tell the jury what it does mean. In the view of this court this summing-up is impeccable. If one looks at the substance of what the deputy chairman said, he clearly told the jury that it would be wholly unsafe to convict on the evidence of Mrs. Reid alone. Indeed, he went much further than that. He told them that it would have been unsafe to have convicted on the evidence of Mrs. Reid and the evidence of Mr. Lake had that evidence not **C** been supported by the scientific evidence. It would be reducing the law to a farce if because the word " corroboration " was not used it should be said that there is some vice in a summing-up of that kind. No criticism could be made if the deputy chairman had used the ordinary formula and had said to the jury: " It is, I am bound to warn you, very dangerous in a sexual case to convict on the uncorroborated evidence of the complainant; you should look for some inde- **D** pendent testimony which tends to show not only that the offence was committed but also that it was committed by the accused. In this particular case if you believe Mr. Lake you may think that his evidence is corroboration, and strong corroboration, of what she says. The same applies to the scientific evidence. On the other hand, even without Mr. Lake and Mr. Grieve, if you were completely convinced beyond a doubt of the accused's guilt by the evidence of Mrs. Reid **E** alone you would be entitled to convict on her uncorroborated evidence, bearing in mind my warning that it would be dangerous to do so. But here, of course, that danger does not exist, because there is the evidence of Mr. Lake and Mr. Grieve which, if true, amounts to corroboration. Its weight is a matter for you."

That would have been an unexceptionable direction to the jury, but one far more unfavourable to the appellant than the direction in fact given by the deputy **F** chairman when he said, in effect, it would be unsafe to convict on Mrs. Reid's evidence and Mr. Lake's evidence alone. Disregard it. Approach the case on the basis of the scientific evidence. Then he stated quite plainly what the scientific evidence was. The scientific evidence was overwhelming, as it sometimes is. It seems to this court inconceivable that any jury on that evidence, whatever the form of direction given to them, could have come to any conclusion save that **G** beyond any sort of doubt at all this man was guilty. Accordingly, if there was any fault in this summing-up—which this court confesses that it is quite unable to detect—this court would without hesitation have come to the conclusion that this is one of those exceptional cases in which the proviso (6) should be applied, since there is no possibility of any miscarriage of justice. The appeal is accordingly dismissed.

H
Appeal dismissed.

Solicitors: *Registrar of Criminal Appeals* (for the appellant); *Julius White & Bywaters*, agents for *Penman, Johnson & Ewins*, Watford (for the Crown).

[*Reported by* N. P. Metcalfe, Esq., *Barrister-at-Law.*]

I

---

(6) I.e., the proviso to s. 4 (1) of the Criminal Appeal Act, 1907, as amended by s. 4 (1) of the Criminal Appeal Act 1966.

R. *v.* CRIMINAL INJURIES COMPENSATION BOARD,   A
Ex parte LAIN.

[QUEEN'S BENCH DIVISION (Lord Parker, C.J., Diplock, L.J., and Ashworth, J.),
March 9, 10, April 20, 1967.]

*Certiorari—Criminal Injuries Compensation Board—Compensation awarded
under prerogative, not under statute—Jurisdiction of High Court to issue*   B
certiorari.

A police constable was shot in the face by a suspect, whom he was about to
question, and became blind in the left eye. He applied to the Criminal
Injuries Compensation Board for compensation under the scheme*. He was
offered and accepted an interim award of £300. Not many days later he was
found dead, his death being at his own hands but attributable to the original   C
injury. His widow accordingly became entitled to the interim award and
she applied also on behalf of herself and her children for compensation. On
this application a single member of the board made a final award of £300.
The widow applied for a hearing before three members of the board. The
three members decided that not only national insurance payments but also
payments from the police fund should have been deducted in assessing her   D
award, as these latter were payments from public funds within para. 13 of
the scheme*. As these amounts exceeded the £300 final award, the three
members made a nil award in its place. The widow applied for certiorari to
quash their decision. The scheme was not statutory but was debated in
Parliament and, after amendment, was announced in both Houses. The
board were appointed by the Secretary of State and administered on behalf   E
of the executive government moneys granted by Parliament to the Crown.
The authority of the board to grant compensation derived, therefore, from the
prerogative act of the Crown.

Held: (i) in determining what compensation, if any, to award to an
applicant the board were performing a quasi-judicial function affecting the
public, lawful authority for which derived from the prerogative; the court   F
had jurisdiction, by way of prerogative order, to supervise the discharge of
these functions notwithstanding that the board did not derive their authority
from statute and that their administrative functions, by way of payment,
were the distribution of bounty (see p. 777, letter F, p. 778, letters E and
H, p. 781, letter I, p. 782, letter F, and p. 784, letter C, post).

Re Clifford and O'Sullivan ([1921] 2 A.C. 570) distinguished, and dictum   G
of ATKIN, L.J., in *R. v. Electricity Comrs., Ex p. London Electricity Joint
Committee Co.* ([1923] All E.R. Rep. at p. 161) explained.

R. v. Manchester Legal Aid Committee, Ex p. R. A. Brand & Co., Ltd.
([1952] 1 All E.R. 480) applied.

(ii) in the present case, however, the decision of the tribunal of three
members disclosed on the face of it no error of law and certiorari would not   H
be granted (see p. 776, letter H, p. 777, letter A, p. 778, letter H, and
p. 782, letters G and I, post).

Per LORD PARKER, C.J.: application to the tribunal of three members
was not an appeal, but an application de novo (see p. 777, letter A, post).

[As to compensation for victims of crimes of violence, see SUPPLEMENT to 10
HALSBURY'S LAWS (3rd Edn.), para. 1020A.   I

As to whether certiorari will lie in respect of non-statutory tribunals, see 11
HALSBURY'S LAWS (3rd Edn.) 55-57, para. 114; ibid., 128-130, para. 239; and
for cases on the subject, see 16 DIGEST (Repl.) 443, 444, *2502-2504,* 446-448,
2522-2557.]

---

* The scheme was set out in a White Paper (Cmnd. 2323) which, as amended, was
announced in Parliament on June 24, 1964; further amendments were announced on
Aug. 3, 1965. The relevant paragraphs are set out at p. 774, letter G, and p. 775, letter G,
post, in the judgment of LORD PARKER, C.J.

A Cases referred to:

Clifford and O'Sullivan, Re, [1921] 2 A.C. 570; 90 L.J.P.C. 244; 126 L.T. 97; 16 Digest (Repl.) 433, *2364*.

Nixon v. A.-G., [1930] 1 Ch. 566 at p. 581; 99 L.J.Ch. 259; 143 L.T. 176; *affd. on other grounds*, [1930] All E.R. Rep. 487; [1931] A.C. 184; 100 L.J.Ch. 70; 144 L.T. 249; 44 Digest (Repl.) 195, *82*.

B R. v. Boycott, Ex p. Keasley, [1939] 2 All E.R. 626; [1939] 2 K.B. 651; 108 L.J.K.B. 657; 19 Digest (Repl.) 610, *117*.

R. v. Electricity Comrs., Ex p. London Electricity Joint Committee Co., [1923] All E.R. Rep. 150; sub nom. R. v. Electricity Comrs., Ex p. London Electricity Joint Committee Co. (1920), Ltd., [1924] 1 K.B. 171; 93 L.J.K.B. 390; 130 L.T. 164; 88 J.P. 13; 16 Digest (Repl.) 433, *2381*.

C R. v. Manchester Legal Aid Committee, Ex p. R. A. Brand & Co., Ltd., [1952] 1 All E.R. 480; [1952] 2 Q.B. 413; 5 Digest (Repl.) 1083, *8733*.

R. v. Postmaster-General, Ex p. Carmichael, [1928] 1 K.B. 291; 96 L.J.K.B. 347; 137 L.T. 26; 91 J.P. 43; 16 Digest (Repl.) 464, *2834*.

R. v. Treasury Lords Comrs., (1872), L.R. 7 Q.B. 387; 41 L.J.K.B. 178; 26 L.T. 64; 36 J.P. 661; 16 Digest (Repl.) 343, *1214*.

D R. v. Woodhouse, [1906] 2 K.B. 501; 75 L.J.K.B. 745; 95 L.T. 367, 399; 70 J.P. 485; *revsd. on other grounds*, H.L., sub nom. Leeds Corpn. v. Ryder, [1907] A.C. 420; 76 L.J.K.B. 1032; 97 L.T. 361; 71 J.P. 484; 16 Digest (Repl.) 443, *2504*.

Motion for certiorari.

E This was an application by way of motion by Margaret Rose Lain for an order of certiorari to bring up and quash a decision of the Criminal Injuries Compensation Board on July 7, 1966, being a decision of three members (SIR WALKER CARTER, Q.C., SIR RONALD MORISON, Q.C., and C. P. HARVEY, ESQ., Q.C.), reducing to nil the amount of compensation previously awarded by a single member (E. D. SUTCLIFFE, ESQ., Q.C.), to her and her children, under the scheme F for compensation for victims of crimes of violence approved by Parliament as a result of a White Paper (Cmnd. 2323). The applicant had applied for compensation on the death of her husband, a police constable, in the following circumstances. The police constable had been shot in the face by a suspect whom he was about to question, and had applied to the board for compensation and had accepted an interim award of £300. Not many days later he had taken his own G life, but it was conceded that his death was attributable directly to the injury that he had sustained. The applicant thus became entitled to the £300 awarded to him, and she also applied after his death for compensation in her own right and on behalf of her children. On this application she had been awarded the further £300 by the single member of the board.

The single member of the board decided that—

H 1. It was right under para. 5 of the scheme* that the board should entertain the application by the widow on her own behalf and on behalf of the children; being satisfied that the injuries suffered by the deceased, including his death at his own hand, were directly attributable to a criminal offence.

2. The cheque for £300 was properly offered to the personal representative of the deceased, the interim award in that amount having been offered to and I accepted by the deceased before he died. The widow was the person solely entitled to the estate, and in assessing compensation that sum of money should be taken into account as an asset of the estate.

3. Under para. 11† of the scheme the board were bound in assessing compensation by the principles applied under the provisions of the Fatal Accidents Acts,

---

* See p. 775, letter A, post.
† See p. 775, letter B, post.

1846 to 1959. Under para. 13*, the amount of compensation must be reduced   A
by the amount of any payments from public funds accruing as a result of the
death.

The single member took a basic dependency of £12 a week, reduced under
para. 13 of the scheme to £3 a week by the deduction of £9 national insurance
pension and allowances for the widow and her children. He applied a twelve
year purchase and discounted the end figure to £1,600. The benefit accruing to   B
the widow from her entitlement to the estate he assessed at £1,000, to which he
added the £300 interim award. In the result he made a final award of £300, which
he apportioned as to £50 for each of the three children and as to the balance of
£150 to the widow. In making his award, the single member did not deduct the
amount payable to the widow by way of ordinary or special police pension or by
way of gratuity. Although he did not doubt that such pensions and gratuities   C
were payments from public funds, he took the view that the purpose of para. 13
of the scheme was to ensure that benefits under the national insurance Acts
should be taken fully into account, and that it was not intended to affect pensions
such as police pensions. These in his opinion were left to the board to be considered on general legal principles, and he drew attention to the anomaly of
having to make a deduction in the case of the death of a public servant, and no   D
deduction in the case of the death of a private employee. The widow did not
accept the single member's decision and asked for a hearing before three members
of the board.

The three member tribunal accepted the single member's reasoning and
conclusions summarised in paras. 1.-3., ante, but found it impossible to allow
this claim. They found that in addition to a national insurance widow's pension   E
of £4 per week the widow was receiving a widow's special pension of £282 16s. 7d.
per annum and had also been awarded a gratuity of £2,210. The evidence before
them was that this special pension and gratuity would be paid out of the police
fund which was built up partly out of local rates and partly out of exchequer
grants. They agreed with the single member that these were payments from public
funds accruing as a result of the officer's death to his widow; but they found   F
themselves unable to conclude, as the single member had concluded, that they
were not covered by para. 13, of the scheme equally with the national insurance
widow's pension. At the hearing before them no attempt was made on behalf of
the widow to support the single member's reasoning. On the contrary it was
contended vigorously that both the national insurance widow's pension and the
payments from the police fund were payments from public funds within the   G
meaning of para. 13 and that the single member had misdirected himself in drawing a distinction between them. He ought, it was argued, to have held that,
although all these payments were covered by the relevant words of that paragraph, para. 13 itself had no application to this claim. The argument ran as
follows: (a) The scheme must be regarded as "subordinate legislation" within
the meaning attached to that term in 36 HALSBURY'S LAWS (3rd Edn.) 476-478,   H
paras. 723, 724; (b) as such, it must be construed with the same strictness as
would be applied if it were an Act of Parliament (36 HALSBURY'S LAWS (3rd
Edn.) 493, para. 745); (c) under para. 9 of the scheme compensation would be
assessed on the basis of common law damages "subject to what is said in the
following two paragraphs"—i.e., paras. 10 and 11, but not para. 13; (d) para. 11
referred to the Fatal Accidents Acts, 1846 to 1959 and said that "the amount of   I
compensation will be governed by the same principles as under those provisions";
(e) s. 2 of the Act of 1959 provided that:

"(1) In assessing damages in respect of a person's death in any action
under the Fatal Accidents Act, 1846, . . . there shall not be taken into
account any insurance money, benefit, pension or gratuity which has been
or will or may be paid as a result of the death."

And "benefit" was defined as including benefit under the National Insurance

* See p. 775, letter D, post.

A Acts; (f) para. 13 of the scheme was expressed to apply only " where applicable ", and in view of the clear language of para. 9 and para. 11 it was obviously not applicable in a case such as this.

The three member tribunal were unable to accept this argument. They could not agree that the scheme was to be classed as subordinate legislation. It was not legislation at all; it conferred no legal rights on anyone; it was intended merely
B as an experiment which, in the light of its working over the next few years, might lead to legislation in the future. It was made clear in the House of Commons debate of May 5, 1964, that the intention of what is now para. 13 was to ensure that claimants would not be compensated out of public funds twice over—which would be the result of accepting the argument advanced. Full value must in their opinion be given to all the paragraphs of the scheme, and
C para. 13 could be reconciled with paras. 9 and 11 on the basis that " the amount of compensation " had first to be assessed on the lines laid down in paras. 10 and 11, and that, once this amount had been determined, it became their duty to make the deductions specified in paras. 12 and 13. It followed in their view that the words " where applicable " must be treated as surplusage. In the light of this conclusion there must be deducted from any award which they would
D otherwise make to the widow not only the capitalised value of her national insurance widow's pension, but also that of her pension from the police fund and her gratuity of £2,210 from the same source. In addition there must be deducted the £300 which she had already received under their interim award. Since the total of these sums exceeded the amount of compensation which they (or indeed the single member) would have considered appropriate to the case, they were
E unable to sanction any further payment. The three member tribunal had not overlooked the claims on behalf of the deceased's dependant children. In addition, however, to the pensions and gratuity already mentioned the widow was receiving a total of £151 18s. 4d. per annum from the police fund in respect of her children as well as a widowed mother's allowance from the ministry for the three younger children at the standard rate of £5 2s. per week which would cease
F when the children attained the age of sixteen. Henceforth, until the children were of working age, they would be dependent on their mother instead of on their father. But the total of all payments from public funds above mentioned appeared to them to be sufficient to provide for the dependancy as well as to compensate the mother.

The applicant's grounds for seeking an order of certiorari were as follows:
G that the decision of the tribunal was wrong in law for the following amongst other reasons: (i) The tribunal wrongfully assumed or exercised a power to reduce or set aside, adversely to the claimant, an original award made in her favour by the single member. (ii) No power was conferred by paras. 17 and 18 of the scheme that would permit the variation of an award by a single member of the board, so as to reduce the compensation directed by a single member of the
H board to be payable to an applicant under the scheme. (iii) The tribunal was entitled only to dismiss an appeal and so to uphold the original award of the single member or to allow an appeal so as to increase the compensation payable under the scheme. (iv) the tribunal wrongfully or excessively reduced the sum that should have been awarded as compensation under the scheme in that they—(a) failed to assess and compute the compensation to be awarded wholly in accord-
I ance with the same principles as were laid down in the Fatal Accidents Acts, 1846 to 1959 as required by para. 11 of the scheme; (b) deducted in whole or in part from the compensation to be awarded the benefits receivable under the National Insurance Acts; (c) deducted from the compensation to be awarded in whole or in part the pensions and gratuity payable under the Police Pensions Regulations, 1962; (d) wrongfully applied para. 13 of the scheme in their computation of the sum to be awarded; (e) assessed a figure for dependency which was too low to be in accord with the principles of the Fatal Accidents Acts, 1846 to 1959; (f) failed to comply with the principles of the Fatal Accidents

Acts, 1846 to 1959 by making erroneous and/or excessive deductions from the **A** compensation to be awarded in respect of assets included in the estate of the deceased. (v) The tribunal failed to act in accordance with the principles of natural justice in that they failed to state in their written decision sufficiently or at all the calculations or reasoning which underlay their award. (vi) In the premises the applicant was and at all material times had been entitled under the rules of the scheme to be awarded compensation in respect of the death of her husband **B** substantially in excess of the nil final payment awarded by the tribunal and was entitled to a final payment to be determined in accordance with the principles set out in para. 3 thereunder and contained in the Fatal Accidents Acts, 1846 to 1959.

The cases noted below* were cited during the argument in addition to those referred to in the judgment.   **C**

R. E. G. Howe, Q.C., and *J. K. Toulmin* for the applicant.
Nigel Bridge for the respondent board.

Cur. adv. vult.

Apr. 20. The following judgments were read.

LORD PARKER, C.J.: The Criminal Injuries Compensation Board came **D** into existence in the following circumstances. In March, 1964, the government set out in a White Paper proposals for compensating victims of violence and persons injured whilst assisting the police. The White Paper proposed an experimental and non-statutory scheme under which compensation would be paid ex gratia. The scheme was to be administered by the board who were to be provided with money through a grant-in-aid out of which payments would be **E** made when the board was satisfied that compensation was justified. Debates on the proposals took place in the House of Commons on May 5 and in the House of Lords on May 7, 1964. As a result a number of amendments were made in the scheme and the amended scheme was announced in both Houses of Parliament on June 24, 1964. Further amendments to the scheme were announced by the Home Secretary in the House of Commons on Aug. 3, 1965. This amended scheme, **F** so far as is material to these proceedings provided as follows:

" 1. The compensation scheme will be administered by a body to be known as the Criminal Injuries Compensation Board which will be appointed by the Home Secretary and the Secretary of State for Scotland, after consultation with the Lord Chancellor. The chairman will be a person of wide legal experience, and the other members, of whom there will initially be five, will **G** also be legally qualified . . .

" 2. The board will be provided with money through a grant-in-aid out of which payments will be made to applicants for compensation where the board are satisfied, in accordance with the principles set out below, that compensation is justified. Their net expenditure will fall on the votes of the Home Office and the Scottish Home and Health Department. **H**

" 4. The board will be entirely responsible for deciding what compensation should be paid in individual cases and their decisions will not be subject to appeal or to ministerial review. The general working of the scheme will, however, be kept under review by the government, and the board will submit annually to the Home Secretary and the Secretary of State for Scotland a full report on the operation of the scheme, together with their **I** accounts. The report and accounts will be open to debate in Parliament . . .

" 5. The board will entertain applications for ex gratia payment of

---

* *R.* v. *Winchelsea Corpn.*, (1673), 2 Lev. 86; *R.* v. *Roupell*, (1776), 2 Cowp. 458; *R.* v. *Treasury Lords Comrs.*, (1835), 4 Ad. & El. 286; *R.* v. *Legislative Committee of Church Assembly, Ex p. Haynes-Smith*, [1928] 1 K.B. 411; *R.* v. *London County Council, Ex p. Entertainments Protection Association, Ltd.*, [1931] 2 K.B. 215; *Nakkudi Ali* v. *Jayaratne*, [1951] A.C. 66; *R.* v. *Disputes Committee of National Joint Council for the Craft of Dental Technicians, Ex p. Neate*, [1953] 1 All E.R. 327; [1953] 1 Q.B. 704.

A   compensation in those cases where: (a) the applicant, or, in the case of an application by a spouse or dependent (see para. 11 below) the deceased, suffered personal injury directly attributable either to a criminal offence . . .

     " 9. Subject to what is said in the following two paragraphs, compensation will be assessed on the basis of common law damages and will take the form of a lump sum payment, rather than a periodical pension. More than one

B   payment may, however, sometimes be made—for example, where only a provisional medical assessment can be given in the first instance.

     " 11. Where the victim has died, no compensation will be payable for the benefit of his estate, but the board will be able to entertain claims from his spouse and dependants. For this purpose, compensation will be payable to any person entitled to claim under the Fatal Accidents Acts, 1846 to 1959,

C   or, in Scotland, under the corresponding Scottish law. The amount of compensation will be governed by the same principles as under those provisions . . ."

     " 12. The board will consider whether, because of provocation or otherwise, the victim of the crime bears any share of responsibility for it, and in accordance with its assessment of the degree of responsibility will reduce the

D   amount of compensation or reject the claim altogether.

     " 13. Where applicable, the compensation will also be reduced by the amount of any payments from public funds accruing, as a result of the injury or death, to the benefit of the person to whom the award is made.

     " 17. The initial decision whether the application should be allowed (and, if so, what amount of compensation should be offered), or should be rejected

E   will normally be taken by one member of the board, who will communicate his conclusions to the applicant; if the applicant is not satisfied with that decision, whether because no compensation is offered or because he considers the amount offered to be inadequate, he will be entitled to a hearing before three other members of the board, excluding the one who made the initial decision. It will, however, also be open to the single member, where he

F   considers that he cannot reach a just and proper decision, himself to refer the application to three other members of the board for hearing.

     " 18. At the hearing, it will be for the applicant to make out his case; he and a member of the board's staff will be able to call, examine and cross-examine witnesses. The board will reach their decision solely in the light of the evidence brought out at the hearing, and all the information before them

G   will be available to the applicant. While it will be open to the applicant to bring a friend or legal adviser to assist him in putting his case, the board will not pay the costs of legal representation. They will, however, have discretion to pay the expenses of witnesses whose attendance is considered to be necessary."

     The applicant in this case is the widow of a police constable who on Feb. 19, 1965,

H was shot in the face by a suspect whom he was about to question, as a result of which he developed a sudden total blindness of the left eye. He applied to the board for compensation and, the prognosis for the recovery of sight in the left eye being uncertain, he was offered and accepted an interim award of £300. About a week later he was found dead in his home from gun shot wounds and it is conceded that his death at his own hand was directly attributable to the original

I injury. The applicant being solely entitled to the deceased's estate thereupon became entitled to the £300 interim award and she further, as she was entitled to do under the scheme, applied in her own right and on behalf of the children for compensation. This application in the course of the normal practice came before a single member of the board who, taking into consideration the interim award paid to the applicant, made a final award of a further £300. In arriving at this figure the single member made a deduction in respect of the national insurance pension and allowance for the widow and children, but made no deduction for the amount payable to the widow by way of ordinary or special police pension or

by way of gratuity. Whilst accepting that the latter were " payments from   **A**
public funds " within para. 13 of the scheme, he nevertheless considered that it
could not have been the intention that such payments, as opposed to the national
insurance payments, should be deducted in arriving at the compensation payable.
The applicant, considering that the amount of this final award was inadequate,
asked for and was granted a hearing before three other members of the board.

By a decision in writing dated July 7, 1966, the three members held, inter alia,   **B**
that not only the national insurance payments but also the payments from the
police fund should have been deducted and since the total of these payments
exceeded the amount of the compensation which was considered appropriate
they made a nil final award in the place of the £300 awarded by the single member.

It is in these circumstances that counsel for the applicant now submits that the
decision of the three members discloses errors of law on the face of their decision   **C**
and asks that an order of certiorari should issue to quash the decision.

Logically the first question is whether the board are a body of persons amenable
to the supervisory jurisdiction of this court, but it is convenient to deal first with
the alleged errors assuming for this purpose that the court has jurisdiction. The
first point made by counsel for the applicant was that the board were wrong in
law in deducting any part of the payments receivable whether by way of national   **D**
insurance or police pensions. The argument quite shortly was that under para. 9
of the scheme the compensation is to be assessed on the basis of common law
damages " subject to what is said in the following two paragraphs ". Turning to
the second of these paragraphs, para. 11, it is clear that a widow's compensation
is to be assessed as under the Fatal Accidents Acts, 1846 to 1959, and under
s. 2 of the Act of 1959 no part of the payments in question would be deductible.   **E**
That, says counsel for the applicant, is an end of the matter. For my part, I am
quite unable to accept that contention, which would render para. 12 and para. 13
of the scheme of no effect. It is I think clear that paras. 9 to 13 inclusive must
be read together as forming the code by which compensation is to be assessed.
Paragraph 9 lays down the starting point, how, what I may call, gross compensation is to be assessed, subject to the limitations in para. 10, and then para. 12   **F**
and para. 13 provide for deductions in certain circumstances. It may be that
the words " where applicable " in para. 13 are mere surplusage, but to treat
them as such is to be preferred to a construction which would render para. 13
of no effect. It was urged that it could not have been the intention of the scheme
that a dependant of a police officer should be worse off than a dependant of a
private employee such as a detective employed by a large store, but I can see   **G**
nothing incongruous in such a result. Counsel for the applicant further submitted,
although not with much confidence, that payments out of the police fund were
not " payments from public funds ". Both the single member and the three
members held that they were, and I can see no reason to disagree with their
findings as a matter of law. Indeed this point was expressly disowned by the
applicant at the hearing before the three members.   **H**

The second alleged error on the face of the decision is that the three members
had no power to reduce the award of £300 by the single member to a nil award.
On an appeal on the ground that the amount awarded by the single member is
inadequate the three members, it is said, can only allow the appeal and increase
the award or dismiss the appeal leaving the award of the single member untouched.
This contention, however, is based on the premise that the " hearing " is an   **I**
appeal and that the three members are an appellate tribunal. It is true that the
board have laid down " Notes on Procedure " in which the three members are
referred to as an " Appellate Tribunal " but in my judgment para. 17 of the
scheme does not support this view. Under that paragraph the application will
normally come forward and be dealt with by a single member on paper and
without a hearing. If, however, the applicant is dissatisfied or the single member
so desires the application can be referred to three other members for decision

A after a hearing. This is in no sense an appeal, but merely a renewal of the application and I can see nothing wrong in the three members hearing and deciding the application de novo. Accordingly in my judgment the decision discloses no error of law on its face.

I come back now to the question whether the board are a body of persons amenable to the supervisory jurisdiction of this court. Counsel for the board

B submits that the board are not and bases his submission on the well-known words of Atkin, L.J., in *R.* v. *Electricity Comrs., Ex p. London Electricity Joint Committee Co.* (1), where he stated the jurisdiction of this court in these terms:

" Wherever any body of persons having legal authority to determine questions affecting the rights of subjects, and having the duty to act

C judicially, act in excess of their legal authority, they are subject to the controlling jurisdiction of the King's Bench Division, exercised in these writs."

Counsel contends that in the present case these conditions are not fulfilled in that (i) the board are not a body of persons having " legal authority " in the sense of having statutory authority; and (ii) the board are not a body of persons

D having authority " to determine questions affecting the rights of subjects " in that a determination of the board gives rise to no enforceable rights, but only gives the applicant an opportunity to receive the bounty of the Crown. In invoking Atkin, L.J.'s definition, however, it must be remembered that the words used were in relation to a case of a statutory tribunal and where the question was, inter alia, whether a statutory tribunal as opposed to an inferior

E court was amenable to the jurisdiction. The definition was no wider than was necessary for the purposes of that case and was not in my judgment intended to be an exhaustive definition.

I can see no reason either in principle or in authority why a board, set up as this board were set up, should not be a body of persons amenable to the jurisdiction of this court. True the board are not set up by statute but the fact that

F they are set up by executive government, i.e., under the prerogative, does not render their acts any the less lawful. Indeed, the writ of certiorari has been issued not only to courts set up by statute but also to courts whose authority was derived, inter alia, from the prerogative. Once the jurisdiction is extended, as it clearly has been, to tribunals as opposed to courts, there is no reason why the remedy by way of certiorari cannot be invoked to a body of persons set up

G under the prerogative. Moreover the board, though set up under the prerogative and not by statute, had in fact the recognition of Parliament in debate and Parliament provided the money to satisfy the board's awards. Counsel for the board strongly relied on *Re Clifford and O'Sullivan* (2), in which it was held by the House of Lords that prohibition would not lie because the military tribunal in question had no legal authority. In my judgment, however, that was a very

H special case in which, in the course of armed rebellion, military tribunals were set up to put down force by force. In other words their activities were altogether outside the field of law now under consideration. As Atkin, L.J., himself said in the *Electricity Commissioners'* case (3), " . . . the so-called courts were not claiming any legal authority other than the right to put down force by force . . . "

With regard to counsel for the board's second point I cannot think that

I Atkin, L.J., intended to confine his principle to cases in which the determination affected rights in the sense of enforceable rights. Indeed in the *Electricity Commissioners'* case (4) the rights determined were at any rate not immediately enforceable rights since the scheme laid down by the commissioners had to be approved by the Minister of Transport and by resolutions of Parliament. The commissioners nevertheless were held amenable to the jurisdiction of this

---

(1) [1923] All E.R. Rep. 150 at p. 161; [1924] 1 K.B. 171 at p. 205.
(2) [1921] 2 A.C. 570.   (3) [1923] All E.R. Rep. at p. 161; [1924] 1 K.B. at p. 206.
(4) [1923] All E.R. Rep. 150; [1924] 1 K.B. 171.

court. Moreover, as can be seen from *R.* v. *Postmaster-General, Ex p. Carmichael* (5) A
and *R.* v. *Boycott, Ex p. Keasley* (6) the remedy is available even though the
decision is merely a step as a result of which legally enforceable rights may be
affected. The position as I see it is that the exact limits of the ancient remedy
by way of certiorari have never been, and ought not to be, specifically defined.
They have varied from time to time, being extended to meet changing conditions.
At one time the writ only went to an inferior court. Later its ambit was extended B
to statutory tribunals determining a lis inter partes. Later again it extended to
cases where there was no lis in the strict sense of the word, but where immediate
or subsequent rights of a citizen were affected. The only constant limits throughout were that the body concerned was under a duty to act judicially and that
it was performing a public duty. Private or domestic tribunals have always
been outside the scope of certiorari since their authority is derived solely from C
contract, that is from the agreement of the parties concerned. Finally, it is to
be observed that the remedy by order of certiorari has now been extended (see
R. v. *Manchester Legal Aid Committee, Ex p. R. A. Brand & Co., Ltd.* (7)), to
cases in which the decision of an administrative officer is arrived at only after
an inquiry or process of a judicial or quasi-judicial character. In such a case
this court has jurisdiction to supervise that process.   D
    We have, as it seems to me, reached the position when the ambit of certiorari
can be said to cover every case in which a body of persons, of a public as opposed
to a purely private or domestic character, has to determine matters affecting
subjects provided always that it has a duty to act judicially. Looked at in this
way the board in my judgment comes fairly and squarely within the jurisdiction
of this court. The board are, as counsel for the board said, " a servant of the E
Crown charged by the Crown, by executive instruction, with the duty of distributing the bounty of the Crown ". The board are clearly, therefore, performing
public duties. Moreover the board are quite clearly under a duty to act judicially,
and indeed no argument to the contrary has been presented. They are to consist
of a chairman of wide legal experience and five other members who are legally
qualified (see para. 1 of the scheme). It is charged with assessing compensation F
on the basis of common law damages save as varied by the scheme (see paras.
9 to 13). Its procedure involves the examination and cross-examination of
witnesses, and it is provided that the burden is on the applicant to make out his
case and that the decision shall be arrived at solely in the light of the evidence
brought out at the hearing (para. 18). Finally, I cannot think that the position
created by the setting up of the board is any different from what the position G
would have been if the Home Secretary had provided that he himself, after a
judicial process, should decide whether and if so what compensation should
be paid in any particular case. He would then, as it seems to me, have been
himself amenable to certiorari in relation to the judicial process. In the result
I hold that this court has jurisdiction to inquire into the decision of the board
in order to see whether there is on the face of the record any error of law and, H
having done so, I hold that there is no such error. Accordingly I would dismiss
the application.

    DIPLOCK, L.J.: The question of jurisdiction raised by this application
is one of novelty and importance. The Criminal Injuries Compensation Board
are not constituted by statute or statutory instrument but by act of the Crown, I
that is the executive government, alone. The board administer on behalf of the
executive government moneys granted by Parliament to the Crown for distribution by way of compensation to persons who have suffered personal injury
directly attributable to criminal offences, the prevention of crime or the appre-
hension of offenders. So far there is nothing novel about this. If the matter

---

(5) [1928] 1 K.B. 291.
(6) [1939] 2 All E.R. 626; [1939] 2 K.B. 651.
(7) [1952] 1 All E.R. 480; [1952] 2 Q.B. 413.

A rested there no person would have any right to obtain any payment out of those moneys which would be enforceable in courts of law by action or controllable by prerogative writ.

The matter does not, however, rest there. The executive government announced in Parliament and published to intending applicants a document called " The Scheme ". It took the form of a statement expressed in the future tense of how

B the distribution of compensation to applicants would be carried out. It stated that the board would entertain applications for payment of compensation where specified conditions were fulfilled, and laid down the procedure for the determination by the board of such applications. That procedure at any rate bears all the characteristics of a judicial or quasi-judicial procedure; and the board, when determining applications in accordance with that procedure, are clearly

C performing de facto quasi-judicial functions, that is, acting as an inferior tribunal. The board's authority to do so is not derived from any agreement between Crown and applicants but from instructions by the executive government, that is, by prerogative act of the Crown. The appointment of the board and the conferring on the board of jurisdiction to entertain and determine applications, and of authority to make payments in accordance with such determinations, are acts

D of government, done without statutory authority but none the less lawful for that.

The jurisdiction of the High Court as successor of the court of Queen's Bench to supervise the exercise of their jurisdiction by inferior tribunals has not in the past been dependent on the source of the tribunal's authority to decide issues submitted to its determination, except where such authority is derived solely from agreement of parties to the determination. The latter case falls within the

E field of private contract and thus within the ordinary civil jurisdiction of the High Court supplemented where appropriate by its statutory jurisdiction under the Arbitration Acts. The earlier history of the writ of certiorari shows that it was issued to courts whose authority was derived from the prerogative, from royal charter, from franchise or custom, as well as from Act of Parliament. Its recent history shows that as new kinds of tribunals have been created,

F orders of certiorari have been extended to them too and to all persons who under authority of government have exercised quasi-judicial functions. True, since the victory of Parliament in the constitutional struggles of the seventeenth century, authority has been generally if not invariably conferred on new kinds of tribunals by or under Act of Parliament and there has been no recent occasion for the High Court to exercise supervisory jurisdiction over persons

G whose ultimate authority to decide matters is derived from any other source. I see no other reason, however, for holding that the ancient jurisdiction of the court of Queen's Bench has been narrowed merely because there has been no occasion to exercise it. If new tribunals are established by acts of government, the supervisory jurisdiction of the High Court extends to them if they possess the essential characteristics on which the subjection of inferior tribunals to the

H supervisory control of the High Court is based.

What are these characteristics? It is plain on the authorities that the tribunal need not be one whose determinations give rise directly to any legally enforceable right or liability. Its determination may be subject to certiorari notwithstanding that it is merely one step in a process which may have the result of altering the legal rights or liabilities of a person to whom it relates. It is not even essential

I that the determination must have that result, for there may be some subsequent condition to be satisfied before the determination can have any effect on such legal rights or liabilities. That subsequent condition may be a later determination by another tribunal (see *R.* v. *Postmaster General, Ex p. Carmichael* (8); *R.* v. *Boycott, Ex p. Keasley* (9)). Is there any reason in principle why certiorari should not lie in respect of a determination where the subsequent condition which

---

(8) [1928] 1 K.B. 291.
(9) [1939] 2 All E.R. 626; [1939] 2 K.B. 651.

must be satisfied before it can affect any legal rights or liabilities of a person   A
to whom it relates, is the exercise in favour of that person of an executive discretion as distinct from a discretion which is required to be exercised judicially?

Counsel for the board submits that there is. He contends that what distinguishes the Criminal Injuries Compensation Board from all other inferior tribunals
to which certiorari has issued in the past is that a determination of the board,
whether allowing or refusing an application for compensation, is incapable of   B
having any effect on any legally enforceable rights or liabilities of the applicant.
Whatever the determination of the board, it lies solely within the discretion
of the executive government whether or not to pay, out of monies provided by
Parliament for compensating victims of crimes of violence, any sum to any
individual, irrespective of whether he has applied to the board or not and of
what the board has determined. So far as an applicant is concerned a deter-   C
mination of the board is a mere *brutum fulmen*, even though he may have a
strong expectation of finding a crock of gold where the lightning ends. For
the way in which it exercises *its* discretion as to the way in which the moneys
voted by Parliament are to be distributed, the executive government, acting
in this case through the Home Secretary, is responsible to Parliament alone.
I would accept that, even after money had been granted by Parliament on the   D
faith of " The Scheme " as communicated to Parliament in answer to a Parliamentary question, the executive government could alter its instructions to the
board as set out in " The Scheme " in any way that it chose, and that the High
Court would have no jurisdiction to call in question the executive government's
power to do so. I would also accept that the executive government was entitled,
as by " The Scheme " it has expressly chosen to do, to make payments of com-   E
pensation to applicants ex gratia and not as a matter of legal right. Its decision
to do so was taken in the exercise of a purely administrative discretion, which
the High Court has no jurisdiction to control. The concept of ex gratia payments
by the Crown to subjects is a familiar one. It gives rise to no rights in the unpaid
subject to enforce payment by civil action for a money judgment or a declaration
of rights (see *Nixon* v. *A.-G.* (10)) or by prerogative order of mandamus (see   F
R. v. *Treasury Lords Comrs.* (11)). It does not, however, follow from this, as
counsel for the board contends, that so long as the instructions given by the
executive government to the board require the board to act judicially, the
board are answerable only to the executive government for the way in which
they exercise their judicial functions and are free from any control by the High
Court. The authority relied on for this contention is *Re Clifford and O'Sullivan* (12).   G
It was dealing, however, not with a new constitutional development in time of
peace, but with one of the most ancient constitutional principles in time of peril
—" inter arma silent leges ". The so-called military tribunals with which that
case was concerned were operating in circumstances of armed rebellion in
Ireland and were aiding the military commander in exercising his right to repel
force by force, by advising him as to its exercise in particular cases. The speeches   H
in the House of Lords were directed to acts which were outside the field of law
altogether, and any general observations which are to be found in them must in
my view be read in that context and not as necessarily applicable to inferior
tribunals lawfully constituted and making, in time of peace, decisions which are
capable of affecting legally enforceable rights or liabilities of subjects.

In the present case we are concerned with an inferior tribunal lawfully con-   I
stituted in time of peace by an act of government. It may be a novel development in constitutional practice to govern by public statement of intention made
by the executive government instead of by legislation. This is no more, however,
than a reversion to the ancient practice of government by royal proclamation,
although it is now subject to the limitations imposed on that practice by the
development of constitutional law in the seventeenth century. The relevant

---

(10) [1930] 1 Ch. 566 at p. 587.   (11) (1872), L.R. 7 Q.B. 387.

(12) [1921] 2 A.C. 570.

A limitation is that, save within the narrow field still left to the prerogative legislative power (for example, declaration of war or blockade), a proclamation cannot deprive any subject of any rights to which he is entitled at common law or by statute, or grant to him any immunities to which he is not so entitled.   The only limitation, however, on the power of the executive government to confer benefits on subjects by way of money payments is a practical one, to wit, the

B necessity to obtain from Parliament a grant in aid for that purpose.   Such a grant was obtained in the present case and confirmed by the annual Appropriation Acts.   True it is that having obtained the grant the executive government was not under any obligation enforceable by the courts to distribute any part of it to any particular subject or at all.   It could have withheld or made payments in accordance with its unfettered and arbitrary executive discretion.   It chose,

C however, to adopt the method of appointing a board on which it conferred two distinct functions, one judicial in character, the other administrative.   The judicial function was to determine in accordance with specified principles whether any particular applicant should be offered any money payment and, if so, how much.   The administrative function was to make payments to applicants in accordance with such determinations.   " The Scheme " not only constituted

D and defined the authority of the board to make such payments but also, as published to applicants, was a lawful proclamation stating the conditions required to be satisfied by subjects seeking payments of compensation and requiring them as a condition precedent to the receipt of any payment to submit their claims to adjudication by the board in the exercise of the board's judicial functions. It was on the faith of the proclamation that the application to the board with

E which the present case is concerned was made.

As was pointed out by this court in *R.* v. *Manchester Legal Aid Committee, Ex p. R. A. Brand & Co., Ltd.* (13) the mere fact that the ultimate result to which an administrative process leads is left to the discretion of the executive government does not prevent an earlier stage in the process from being quasi-judicial in character, and, where this is so, the High Court has jurisdiction to

F exercise supervisory control over that stage by certiorari.   The High Court can be deprived of that jurisdiction either directly by Act of Parliament or indirectly by the elimination of any quasi-judicial stage by the organ of government which has lawful authority to determine what form the administrative process shall take.   So long, however, as the quasi-judicial stage in the administrative process persists the High Court's power of control of it by certiorari continues.   In cases

G which have hitherto come before this court the organ of government which has had the lawful authority to determine the form which the administrative process shall take has been either Parliament itself or Her Majesty in Council or a Minister or other officer of the executive government, in each case acting under powers conferred by Parliament.   In the case of compensation for crimes of violence, however, the organ of government which has lawful authority to

H determine the form which the administrative process shall take for the distribution of compensation is, for the reasons I have stated, the executive government itself without need for any other authority from Parliament than is implied in its grant of moneys for that purpose.

I see no reason in principle why the fact that no authority from Parliament is required by the executive government to entitle it to decide what shall be the

I form of the administrative process under which compensation for crimes of violence is paid, should exempt the board from the supervisory control by the High Court over that part of its functions which are judicial in character.   No authority has been cited which in my view compels us to decline jurisdiction. Certainly applicants have an interest in the proper performance by the board of their judicial functions.   Moreover, despite counsel for the board's reference to the bounty of the Crown with its nostalgic echoes of Maundy Thursday, so

---

(13) [1952] 1 All E.R. at p. 489;   [1952] 2 Q.B. at pp. 428, 429.

has the public whose money the board distributes to the tune of nearly £1,000,000 A
a year. True it is that a determination of the board that a particular sum by way
of ex gratia payment of compensation should be offered to an applicant does not
give the applicant any right to sue either the board or the Crown for that sum.
It does not follow, however, that a determination of the board in favour of
an applicant is without any legal effect on the rights of the applicant to whom
it relates. It makes lawful a payment to an applicant which would otherwise B
be unlawful. The moneys which the board are authorised to distribute are held
by the board in a fiduciary capacity, and " The Scheme " defines and limits
the board's authority to make any payment out of them to anyone. It makes
a determination by the board, in the exercise of the board's judicial functions,
that an offer of a particular sum to a particular applicant is justified, a condition
precedent to the board's authority in the exercise of the board's administrative C
functions to make any payment to that applicant. Any payment made by the
board to any person contrary to those instructions, that is, without a prior
determination that an offer of that sum to the payee is justified in accordance
with the principles laid down in the scheme, would constitute a breach of duty
by the board as agents of the Crown and could be recovered by the Crown from
the recipient as money had and received—at any rate if he had notice of the D
breach. It may be that if, as counsel for the board contends, the payment is
mere bounty without any consideration in the eye of the law, notice to the
recipient of the breach of duty is unnecessary: but, however, that may be,
the publication of " The Scheme " to the applicant would constitute notice of
the limitations on the board's authority to make payments.

I do not find it necessary for the purposes of this case to express any view E
whether certiorari would lie in respect of a determination which was incapable
of having any effect on legal rights in any circumstances. It is, however, in my
opinion quite sufficient to attract the supervisory jurisdiction of the High Court
to quash by certiorari a determination of an inferior tribunal made in the exercise
of its quasi-judicial powers, that such determination should have the effect of
rendering lawful and irrecoverable a payment to a subject which would other- F
wise be unlawful and recoverable. I would, therefore, hold that we have jurisdiction to entertain the present application for an order of certiorari against
the Criminal Injuries Compensation Board.

Having said that, I do not find it necessary to add anything to what LORD
PARKER, C.J., has already said about the alleged errors on the face of the board's
determination. I agree that no error is disclosed and having entertained the G
application, I too would dismiss it.

ASHWORTH, J., whose judgment was read by LORD PARKER, C.J.: In
these proceedings the applicant seeks an order of certiorari to remove into this
court and quash an order or decision of the Criminal Injuries Compensation
Board (hereinafter called " the board ") whereby the earlier decision of a single H
member of the board awarding compensation in the sum of £300 was reversed
and her application for compensation was rejected altogether. The grounds on
which the applicant now seeks relief are set out in the statement filed pursuant
to R.S.C., Ord. 53, r. 1, but it is unnecessary for me to deal with them in detail,
as I agree with my lords that for the reasons already given they do not establish
the applicant's claim to the relief sought. These proceedings however involve I
another issue of considerable importance, namely, the question whether this
court has in any event jurisdiction by means of an order of certiorari to review
a decision of the board.

The nature of the remedy by way of certiorari has been discussed in many
cases and to my mind one of the most helpful passages is to be found in the
judgment of FLETCHER MOULTON, L.J., in R. v. Woodhouse (14). The decision

(14) [1906] 2 K.B. 501.

A of the Court of Appeal in that case was reversed in the House of Lords (15), but Fletcher Moulton, L.J.'s observations about the remedy were not criticised. He said (16):

B " The writ of certiorari is a very ancient remedy, and is the ordinary process by which the High Court brings up for examination the acts of bodies of inferior jurisdiction. In certain cases the writ of certiorari is given by statute, but in a large number of cases it rests on the common law. It is frequently spoken of as being applicable only to ' judicial acts', but the cases by which this limitation is supposed to be established show that the phrase ' judicial act ' must be taken in a very wide sense, including many acts that would not ordinarily be termed ' judicial '. For instance, it is evidently not limited to bringing up the acts of bodies that are ordinarily

C considered to be courts . . . Other instances could be given, but these suffice to show that the procedure of certiorari applies in many cases in which the body whose acts are criticised would not ordinarily be called a court, nor would its acts be ordinarily termed ' judicial acts '. The true view of the limitation would seem to be that the term ' judicial act ' is used in contrast with purely ministerial acts. To these latter the process of certiorari does not

D apply, as for instance to the issue of a warrant to enforce a rate, even though the rate is one which could itself be questioned by certiorari. In short, there must be the exercise of some right or duty to decide in order to provide scope for a writ of certiorari at common law."

So far as the board are concerned I have no doubt that they are under a duty

E to act judicially when they are considering applications for compensation, and I do not think that counsel for the board would seek to argue to the contrary. It is true that when the board consider such applications there is no lis before them, but the idea that a duty to act judicially can only arise if a lis exists has long since been discarded; see *R.* v. *Manchester Legal Aid Committee, Ex p. R. A. Brand & Co., Ltd.* (17). In passing, I note that the scheme under which

F the board function provides (18) in para. 18 that at the hearing it will be for the applicant to make out his case and that he and a member of the board's staff will be able to call, examine and cross-examine witnesses. Further, it provides that the board will reach their decision solely in the light of the evidence brought out at the hearing. It would of course be going much too far to say that every person or body called on to exercise some right or duty to decide (to use Fletcher

G Moulton, L.J.'s words (16)) is amenable to an order of certiorari. If persons agree that issues which have arisen or may arise between them are to be referred to an arbitrator or a body of persons, this court will not entertain an attempt to obtain relief by means of a prerogative order. In other words private or domestic tribunals are outside the range of an order of certiorari. The fact that such tribunals are not amenable to such an order does not, however, take

H one far towards solving the problem whether in the present case the board are so amenable, since it cannot be suggested that they are a private tribunal constituted by agreement between the parties who may appear before them. It was contended by counsel for the board that before this court has jurisdiction to entertain an application for an order of certiorari, it must be shown that the tribunal in question has either been constituted by Act of Parliament or derives

I its jurisdiction from common law, and reliance is placed on passages in the speeches of Viscount Cave and Lord Sumner in the case of *Re Clifford and O'Sullivan* (19). In the present case it is plain that the board do not derive their jurisdiction from common law, and it is equally plain that they have not been

(15) Sub nom. *Leeds Corpn.* v. *Ryder*, [1907] A.C. 420.
(16) [1906] 2 K.B. at pp. 534, 535.
(17) [1952] 1 All E.R. at pp. 488, 489; [1952] 2 Q.B. at p. 428.
(18) For para. 18, see p. 775, letter G, ante.
(19) [1921] 2 A.C. at pp. 583 and 589 respectively.

constituted by Act of Parliament. They were set up by the executive after the **A** proposal to set them up had been debated in both Houses of Parliament, and the money needed to satisfy their awards is drawn from sums provided by Parliament. It can therefore be said that their existence and their functions have at least been recognised by Parliament, which to my mind has a two-fold consequence: in the first place it negatives any notion that the board are a private tribunal and secondly it confers on the board what I may call a public or official character. **B** The number of applications for compensation and the amounts awarded by the board alike show how greatly the general public are affected by the functioning of the board.

It is a truism to say that the law has to adjust itself to meet changing circumstances and although a tribunal, constituted as the board, has not been the subject of consideration or decision by this court in relation to an order of **C** certiorari, I do not think that this court should shrink from entertaining this application merely because the board have no statutory origin. It cannot be suggested that the board have unlawfully usurped jurisdiction: they act with lawful authority, albeit such authority is derived from the executive and not from an Act of Parliament. In the past this court has felt itself able to consider the conduct of a Minister when he is acting judicially or quasi-judicially and **D** while the present case may involve an extension of relief by way of certiorari I should not feel constrained to refuse such relief if the facts warranted it. In the familiar passage from the judgment of ATKIN, L.J., in *R.* v. *Electricity Comrs.* (20) there are included the words: " affecting the rights of subjects " and counsel for the board contended that they constitute an insuperable obstacle to any relief by way of certiorari, because nobody has any legal right to compensation. **E** He argued with force that the payment of compensation is expressly declared to be ex gratia: it is bounty and nothing else. For my part I doubt whether ATKIN, L.J., was propounding an all-embracing definition of the circumstances in which relief by way of certiorari would lie. In my judgment the words in question read in the context of what precedes and follows them, would be of no less value if they were altered by omitting " the rights of " so as to become **F** " affecting subjects ". I regard the duty to act judicially, in a public as opposed to a private capacity, as the paramount consideration in relation to relief by way of certiorari.

I need only refer to one other matter. Somewhat tentatively counsel for the board suggested that while this court might perhaps have jurisdiction if the board acted non-judicially, it could not correct errors in law, if made by **G** the board. I cannot myself see any justification for thus limiting the jurisdiction of this court. If the board are amenable at all to certiorari, they are amenable in full, and there is no room, so to speak, for half relief. For these reasons I am of opinion that this court had jurisdiction to entertain the application but that on the facts the application fails.

Application refused. **H**

Solicitors: *Russell Jones & Walker* (for the applicant); *Treasury Solicitor* (for the respondent board).

[*Reported by* N. P. METCALFE, ESQ., *Barrister-at-Law.*]

I

---

(20) [1923] All E.R. Rep. at p. 161; [1924] 1 K.B. at p. 205. The passage is set out at p. 777, letter C, ante.

A

BRITISH ROAD SERVICES, LTD. *v.* ARTHUR V. CRUTCHLEY & CO., LTD. (FACTORY GUARDS, LTD., Third Parties).

[LIVERPOOL WINTER ASSIZES (Cairns, J.), February 20, 1967.]

B *Independent Contractor—Negligence—Liability of employer for negligence of independent contractor—Warehouseman—Security patrols for guarding warehouse provided by independent contractor—Patrolman negligent— Whether negligence for which independent contractor vicariously responsible attributable also to warehouseman—Whether warehouseman liable as bailee.*

C The plaintiffs transported by road a lorry load of whisky worth about £9,000. They arranged with the defendants for them to receive the whisky at their warehouse. It was unloaded from the lorry and loaded on to a trailer in the warehouse, where it stood for some hours and where passers-by could see it. The trailer was left standing in the warehouse hitched to a tractor unit, ready to be driven out early the following morning to the docks. The warehouse was guarded at night by security patrol, for which the defendants contracted with the third parties. Normally the patrolman visited the D premises four times nightly, and the system of guarding gave a sufficient standard of security. On this night, however, the patrolman visited the warehouse three times only, his last visit finishing at 2.18 a.m. The fourth visit, if he had made it, would have been at about 5 a.m. During the night at a time which, so the court inferred, would have been not long after the patrolman's third visit, thieves broke into the warehouse through the roof, E cut the stout bolts on the door, opened it from inside and drove off the vehicle loaded with the whisky. The plaintiffs, having compensated the owners for the loss of the whisky, sued the defendants for the amount, and the defendants claimed against the third parties. The court found that the patrolman was negligent in not making a fourth visit, that the third parties were vicariously responsible for his negligence and that the defendants were F negligent in allowing the load of whisky to stand a number of hours where it could be seen by passers-by. The court inferred that the theft was the work of a gang, that a watch would have been kept on the warehouse so that the arrival of the lorry would have been noted, and that the theft was likely to have been completed by 3.30 a.m.

G **Held:** (i) the negligence of the patrolman for which the third parties were vicariously responsible was to be attributed also to the defendants (see p. 790, letter H, post); nevertheless the defendants had discharged the onus, which was on them, of showing that the negligence did not cause the loss, because, if the patrolman's fourth visit had been made, it would have been made at 5 a.m., which would have been too late to prevent the theft or to H enable the whisky to be recovered (see p. 790, letter I, and p. 791, letters H and I, post).

(ii) the defendants were not liable for their own negligence in leaving the trailer for some hours where passers-by could see it, because the probability was that the warehouse was being watched and the unloading of the lorry would have revealed the presence of the load of whisky, with the consequence that the negligence did not cause the loss (see p. 791, letter D, post).

I [As to the onus of proof where goods entrusted to a bailee are lost, see 2 HALSBURY'S LAWS (3rd Edn.) 117, 118, para. 227; and for cases on the subject, see 3 DIGEST (Repl.) 78, 79, *161-168*.

As to liability for the negligence of independent contractors, see 28 HALSBURY'S LAWS (3rd Edn.) 23, 24, para. 21.]

Cases referred to:
Adams (Durham), Ltd. and Day v. *Trust Houses, Ltd.*, [1960] 1 Lloyd's Rep. 380; 3rd Digest Supp.

Reversed, C.A. [1968] 1 All E.R. 811.

Cassidy v. *Ministry of Health*, [1951] 1 All E.R. 574; [1951] 2 K.B. 343; 33 **A**
    Digest (Repl.) 534, *112.*

Coldman v. *Hill*, [1918-19] All E.R. Rep. 434; [1919] 1 K.B. 443; 88 L.J.K.B.
    491; 120 L.T. 412; 22 Digest (Repl.) 176, *1609.*

Dalton v. *Angus*, [1881-85] All E.R. Rep. 1; (1881), 6 App. Cas. 740; 50
    L.J.Q.B. 689; 44 L.T. 844; 46 J.P. 132; *affg.* S.C. sub nom. *Angus* v.
    Dalton (1878), 4 Q.B.D. 162; 34 Digest (Repl.) 198, *1394.* **B**

Houghland v. *R. R. Low (Luxury Coaches), Ltd.*, [1962] 2 All E.R. 159; [1962]
    1 Q.B. 694; [1962] 2 W.L.R. 1015; Digest (Cont. Vol. A) 46, *71a.*

Hughes v. *Percival*, [1881-85] All E.R. Rep. 44; (1883), 8 App. Cas. 443; 52
    L.J.Q.B. 719; 49 L.T. 189; 47 J.P. 772; *affg.* S.C. sub nom. *Percival* v.
    Hughes (1882), 9 Q.B.D. 441; 7 Digest (Repl.) 317, *323.*

Tarry v. *Ashton*, [1874-80] All E.R. Rep. 738; (1876), 1 Q.B.D. 314; 45 **C**
    L.J.Q.B. 260; 34 L.T. 97; 40 J.P. 439; 34 Digest (Repl.) 205, *1437.*

Action.

This was an action by British Road Services, Ltd., the plaintiffs, to recover as
damages the money which they had paid to indemnify the owners of a consignment of whisky which was stolen from the defendants' warehouse on July 29/30,
1963, on the ground that the loss was caused by the defendants' breach of contract **D**
or negligence. The defendants, Arthur V. Crutchley & Co., Ltd., denied liability
and claimed against the third parties, Factory Guards, Ltd., who had contracted
to provide certain security services at the warehouse, indemnity or contribution
in respect of any liability by the defendants to the plaintiffs. The facts are set out
in the judgment.

E

R. H. Forrest, Q.C., and *R. R. Leech* for the plaintiffs.
D. B. McNeill, Q.C., and *F. D. Paterson* for the defendants.
A. Rankin for the third parties.

    CAIRNS, J.: On July 29, 1963, the plaintiffs, British Road Services, Ltd.,
brought by lorry from Edinburgh to Liverpool, a load of two hundred cases of
whisky worth more than £9,000. The whisky was to be put on board two ships **F**
lying at Merseyside Docks. Because it was convenient to the plaintiffs for the
final stage of transport to the docks to be handled by other carriers, they arranged,
as they had often done before, for the defendants, Arthur V. Crutchley & Co.,
Ltd., to receive the whisky at their warehouse in Cotton Street, Liverpool, for
later conveyance to the docks. The whisky was unloaded from the plaintiffs'
lorry and loaded on to a trailer in the warehouse. There was some difficulty about **G**
getting it accepted by the ships that day, so it remained on the trailer in the
warehouse overnight. The trailer was left standing in the warehouse, hitched to
a tractor unit, facing one of the warehouse doors, ready to be driven out soon after
the opening of the warehouse at half past six on the morning of July 30. During
the night thieves broke in through the roof, succeeded in opening the warehouse
door from the inside and drove away the articulated vehicle to a disused warehouse **H**
a few hundred yards away. There they transferred the load to a vehicle of their
own and drove off to an unknown destination. Only a few cases of whisky have
been recovered. The plaintiffs have indemnified the consignors in full against
their loss. They now claim damages from the defendants, alleging that the loss
was caused by their breach of contract or negligence. The defendants deny
liability. The defendants have a contract with the third parties, Factory Guards, **I**
Ltd., for the third parties to supply certain security services at the Cotton Street
warehouse. The defendants say that this contract was broken and the service
negligently performed, and so they claim from the third parties indemnity or
contribution in respect of any liability which they may be under to the plaintiffs.
    It is first necessary to consider what was the contract between the plaintiffs
and the defendants. The plaintiffs have a printed form of conditions of sub-
contracting, and they say that a copy of this was sent to the defendants in
January, 1960, and governed the terms of business between them thereafter. The

A defendants deny that they ever received this document and say that in any case they are not subcontractors as that term is understood in the transport industry. Moreover, they say that their course of business with the plaintiffs had always been to accept goods for carriage only on their own conditions, contained in the printed conditions of carriage of Road Haulage Association, Ltd.

B On the occasion in question there was no contract between them and the plaintiffs until two delivery notes were presented at the office at Cotton Street and stamped " Received under A.V.C. conditions ". I am not satisfied that the defendants ever received the plaintiffs' form of conditions and in any case I think that on whatever terms the goods were tendered to them, they made a counter-offer by stamping the delivery notes with the words that I have mentioned. By then handing over the goods the plaintiffs' driver, on behalf of the plaintiffs,

C accepted this counter-offer. If that is wrong, then in my view the parties were never ad idem as to any special terms of contract and the defendants' duties in respect of the goods were the common law duties of a bailee for reward. Since Road Haulage Association, Ltd.'s conditions contain no term which would limit or extend their responsibility, it is immaterial whether these conditions were applicable or not. In my judgment the duty of the defendants was the duty to

D exercise reasonable care of the goods according to all the circumstances of the case; see *Houghland* v. *R. R. Low (Luxury Coaches), Ltd.* (1).

It is convenient at this point to give a short description of the way in which the entry and theft was accomplished, so far as is known. For this description I am indebted to the evidence of Detective Officer Pugh who took part in the investigation into the crime. I am glad to say that he was allowed to give his account of

E the matter without any technical objections, though he probably had no first hand knowledge of some of the matters about which he spoke. As to the reliability of his conclusions, based in part on his expert knowledge of the ways of criminals, I have no doubt. The officer said that the crime was probably committed between 3 and 6 a.m., and the most likely part of that period was the first hour. It was unlikely that a ladder had been used. Probably one man had climbed by means of

F a drainpipe or otherwise on to an adjoining building, had made a perilous journey over several roofs, had then broken the glass of the skylight and descended to the floor by climbing along the gantry of a crane and down one of its supports and had then gone to the door near which the goods were standing. He had cut the very stout bolts of the locks on the door with a powerful cutting instrument, and then opened the door to a so-called " wheelman " who would be waiting outside.

G The vehicle would then be driven away to the disused warehouse in the neighbourhood. The time taken from start to finish would be about eight minutes. The time up to the driving away of the reloaded goods would be about three-quarters of an hour. Such a crime could be carried out only by a highly skilled and determined gang, who would have made long preparations for it. A blue-print of the premises would be prepared. The day to day operations of the warehouse and the system

H of night time protection would be carefully observed. Watch would be kept for the arrival of some sufficiently attractive goods and their position in the warehouse would be noted. The thieves would have been prepared to face any obstacles in the way of watchmen, guard dogs or alarm signals. " Nothing that occurs to me ", said the officer, " would have stopped them ". The loss was discovered when the warehouse was opened at about half past six on the morning of July 30.

I The main ways in which the defendants are said to have failed in their duty are the following:

1. They kept the goods in a warehouse with a glass skylight which could be broken so that entry could be effected.

2. They had no system of alarm bells nor any more modern alarm system.

3. They employed no nightwatchman nor guard dogs, but were content to

(1) [1962] 2 All E.R. 159; [1962] 1 Q.B. 694.

arrange with the third parties to send a mobile patrolman—a so-called security   **A**
officer—to make four short visits during the night.

4. Through the third parties, they were negligent in making only three visits
during the night in question, omitting a visit at about 5 a.m. which might have
been of great importance in preventing or interrupting the unlawful entry or
in recovering the goods.

5. They kept the loaded trailer standing most of the day in the warehouse on   **B**
July 29, visible from the street.

6. They left the trailer hitched to a tractor unit in the most convenient position
for driving it away once the doors had been opened.

7. They allowed a ladder to be available in a yard attached to the premises.

There is no substantial dispute about what the servants of the defendants and
the third parties did or omitted to do. The questions which arise are: (a) Does the   **C**
conduct complained of amount to negligence? (b) Are the defendants responsible
for any negligence on the part of the third parties or their servants? (c) On whom
does the onus lie to establish that any negligence which occurred did or did not
cause or contribute to the loss? (d) Did any negligence which occurred cause or
contribute to the loss?

In approaching question (a) great emphasis is laid by the plaintiffs on the fact   **D**
that the load concerned was an exceptionally valuable one and exceptionally
attractive to thieves. These are certainly circumstances which must be taken
into account in deciding whether the precautions adopted by the defendants were
such as to constitute reasonable care of the goods. A reasonably careful man
might leave a lorry load of gravel unguarded in the street, but everybody agrees
that a lorry load of whisky should never be left unattended in a public place. On   **E**
the other hand it cannot be said that a warehouseman must always adopt extra
precautions when he has a particularly tempting consignment on his premises. If
his normal precautions are such as any reasonable person would consider to be
adequate security against theft, then he need take no additional measures to
protect particularly valuable goods. Furthermore, nobody can be expected to go
to such lengths as will make theft virtually impossible. To provide the same   **F**
degree of security as is provided, say, for the gold in Fort Knox would be beyond
the powers of the ordinary warehouse keeper. It has to be remembered that every
addition to safety costs money and in the interests of his customers as well as
his own interests the person whose business includes the safeguarding of goods
has to draw a reasonable balance between the degree of risk and the cost of
reducing it.   **G**

With these criteria in mind I turn to consider the various ways in which the
defendants are said to have failed in their duty of care.

1. As to the building itself, counsel on behalf of the plaintiffs did not in his
final speech invite me to say that it was insufficiently strong. It was described
by witnesses for the plaintiffs without serious challenge, and in substance with the
concurrence of the police officer, as one of the best warehouses in the north of   **H**
England and much better than average for security. The skylight was extremely
difficult of access and was glazed with reinforced glass. Moreover it was some
twenty-eight feet above the floor level and the descent from it to the floor would
be a most hazardous undertaking. Unless the building were to be deprived
altogether of daylight it is difficult to see how a safer window could have been
furnished. All walls and doors were mostly solidly constructed and I do not find   **I**
that the building was in any way deficient.

2. The detective officer said that there were two possible alarm systems which
might have been used to give the alarm when the skylight was approached or
broken. One was an alarm bell outside the premises. Such a bell is normally
exposed and could easily be stuffed with some soft material to prevent its ringing.
Recently cages have been devised which will make this more difficult. They
had been introduced a few years before 1963, but had not come into general use.
The other system is a type of silent alarm connected by telephone to police

A headquarters which would be costly to install and operate and would be justified only if highly valuable goods were regularly stored. Having regard to the great difficulty of access to the skylight and the high cost of installing any really efficient alarm system to guard it, I do not consider that it was negligent to refrain from installing one.

3. The traditional method of guarding a place at night is to have a night watch-
B man on duty. The traditional night watchman is an elderly and not very active man. In recent years several companies have offered a service of mobile patrols to take the place of night watchmen. The third parties are such a company and in 1963 were a well established company regarded as offering a good service. The system is that a patrolman visits the premises usually four times during the night. On different nights he comes at different times so that the thief never knows when
C he may arrive. He has a key to the premises, goes in and makes a tour of an agreed route. At a number of fixed points on the route he operates a numbered key, chained to the wall, on a clock which he carries and thereby records on a tape that he has visited that point at a recorded time. The police regard this system as an improvement on the method of employing a night watchman. The patrolmen are young and athletic men and their credentials are checked before
D they are taken on. No doubt greater security would be provided if more frequent visits were paid and greater still if a man of the same quality were on the premises all night and made frequent tours recorded on a clock. But the supply of suitable men is limited. Qualifications required are similar to those needed for a police officer, and the Liverpool police force is five hundred under strength. The cost would be very heavy. Guard dogs are rarely used at premises such as the defen-
E dants' and are not difficult for skilled intruders to silence. In my judgment the steps taken by the defendants for the patrolling of these premises were well up to the standard generally accepted as sufficient.

4. Unfortunately on the night in question the patrolman, Mr. Collins, who was charged with the duty of visiting the Cotton Street warehouse, paid only three visits instead of four, the last visit finishing at 2.18 a.m. On none of those visits
F did he go to every one of the check points. He gave evidence and put forward some sort of explanation of his failure to make four proper inspections, but he totally failed to convince me that he had any proper appreciation of the serious-ness of his duties or that he exercised anything like reasonable diligence in performing them. He was negligent and the third parties, as his employers, are responsible for his negligence.

G 5. In my view it was unwise of the defendants to advertise the presence of a load of whisky by allowing it to stand for a number of hours in their warehouse where passers-by could see it. This must be regarded as negligence on their part.

6. There were good business reasons for leaving the trailer hitched to its unit and near the door so as to be ready for a quick departure in the morning. Moreover, a risk which also exists in premises such as the defendants' and which it is at least as
H necessary to guard against as theft is fire, and the more easily vehicles can be moved the less difficult it is to deal with a fire if one breaks out. In my view the defendants were entitled to believe that their premises were so secure that it was unnecessary for them, as reasonable persons, to take steps to hem in this vehicle so as to make it more difficult for it to be moved out of the door.

7. I do not propose to discuss how the ladder came to be where it was because
I I am satisfied that it was not used by the criminals at all.

In addition to the matters with which I have dealt one or two other parts of the defendants' procedure were relied on by the plaintiffs as constituting negligence. For example, their using for communication with the docks a radio-telephone system. I am satisfied that these other matters were in accordance with usual practice and were not negligent. I, therefore, reach the conclusion that there was no negligence, except in two respects. I am conscious that in other respects the degree of caution exercised by the defendants was by no means the maximum that might have been employed. It is always easy after a loss has occurred to

think of ways in which security might have been improved. No bailee is required **A**
to provide ideally safe conditions of storage. £9,000 is a substantial value, but
there must be many shops and warehouses, and indeed some private houses,
where goods of comparable value are held in far less secure conditions without
anybody supposing that insufficient care is being taken of them. It is the standard
of the reasonable business man, not that of the ultra-cautious person, that is the
test.   **B**

As I have found that there was some negligence on the part of a servant of the
third parties, I will next consider question (b), that is, whether that negligence is
to be attributed to the defendants. For reasons which will hereafter appear it is
unnecessary for me to express any concluded opinion about this and it does seem
to me to be a most difficult question in law. No case has been cited to me in which
the court has had to consider whether the bailee's duty of care is fulfilled by **C**
appointing an apparently competent independent contractor or whether he is
liable for the negligence of his independent contractor's servants. In tort the
tendency has been to extend the liability of a principal for negligence of independent contractors. In *Cassidy* v. *Ministry of Health* (2) DENNING, L.J., said (3):

> " I take it to be clear law, as well as good sense, that, where a person is
> himself under a duty to use care, he cannot get rid of his responsibility by **D**
> delegating the performance of it to someone else, no matter whether the
> delegation be to a servant under a contract of service or to an independent
> contractor under a contract for services. LORD BLACKBURN laid that down
> on many occasions (see *Tarry* v. *Ashton* (4), *Dalton* v. *Angus* (5), *Hughes* v.
> *Percival* (6)) and so have other great judges."

    E

In *Adams (Durham), Ltd. and Day* v. *Trust Houses, Ltd.* (7), Mr. Fenton
Atkinson, Q.C., commissioner of assize, had to consider whether a bailee was
responsible for a loss due to the fraudulent act of his servant. He was not concerned with independent contractors, but he reached his conclusion on grounds
which seem to me to be applicable to independent contractors as much as to
servants. He said (8):   **F**

> " It seems to me that the duty to take reasonable care to keep that car
> safe rested on the defendants and they delegated that duty to Atkinson, and
> they are responsible to the plaintiffs, not so much as being vicariously
> responsible for the torts of Atkinson driving about the streets, but on the
> basis that they had entrusted to him the fulfilment of their own contractual
> duty, and that duty was not performed, and for that breach of contract, apart **G**
> from any special condition, in my view they are liable to the plaintiffs."

On the whole, though not without doubt, I consider that the defendants must
accept responsibility for the negligence of the third parties.

Question (c). It is clear law that where goods in the custody of a bailee are lost,
the bailee is liable for damages to the bailor unless he can prove that the goods
were not lost through any negligence for which he is responsible. During the **H**
argument I was inclined to think that although this rule relieved the bailor from
having to prove negligence, it did not relieve him, if negligence were established,
from having to prove the causal connexion between the negligence and the loss.
However, counsel on behalf of the defendants conceded that the onus was on him
to prove that any negligence which occurred did not cause the loss. Having
considered the case of *Coldman* v. *Hill* (9) I am satisfied that he was right to make **I**

---

(2) [1951] 1 All E.R. 574; [1951] 2 K.B. 343.
(3) [1951] 1 All E.R. at p. 586; [1951] 2 K.B. at p. 363.
(4) [1874-80] All E.R. Rep. 738; (1876), 1 Q.B.D. 314.
(5) [1881-85] All E.R. Rep. 1; (1881), 6 App. Cas. 740.
(6) [1881-85] All E.R. 44; (1883), 8 App. Cas. 443.
(7) [1960] 1 Lloyd's Rep. 380.
(8) [1960] 1 Lloyd's Rep. at p. 386.
(9) [1918-19] All E.R. Rep. 434; [1919] 1 K.B. 443.

A this concession. It is sufficient to quote one sentence from the judgment of
SCRUTTON, L.J., (10):

> " It was his duty as bailee to prove that his breach of duty did not cause
> the loss, not the plaintiff's duty to show that it did."

B It is, of course, unnecessary for the defendants to prove with certainty that their
breach of duty did not cause the loss. It is sufficient if they can prove that it
probably did not.

The two breaches of duty that I have attributed to the defendants are their
keeping the load exposed in their warehouse during daylight on July 29, and the
failure to carry out fully the patrolling of the premises during the night. As to
the first of these matters, Detective Officer Pugh expressed the opinion that a

C gang such as the one that must have carried out this crime could quite easily
have discovered the arrival of this whisky at the defendants' warehouse. Clearly
they must have been on the lookout for something of the kind. No normal
precautions would have concealed it from them. For such a gang the continued
exposure of the load was neither here nor there. The strong probability is that
they had somebody on the watch to note the arrival of the load and to see

D whether it left before nightfall. The load had to be exposed while it was transferred
to the trailer and, if anything, any efforts to conceal it would only have emphasised
the value attached to it. As to the negligence of the patrolman, first of all no
importance is to be attached to his careless performance of his first three tours of
inspection. Nobody suggests that the theft had already occurred by 2.18 a.m.
The strength of the plaintiffs' case is that the fourth visit would normally have

E been made at about 5 a.m., that it is possible that a visit at that time would have
interrupted the criminals, and even if it did not, seeing that the theft probably
occurred before that hour, would have enabled the alarm to be raised much earlier
than it was, so as to offer a much better chance of recovery.

In *Coldman* v. *Hill* (11) the breach of duty was a failure to report a theft of
cattle promptly, and the plaintiff succeeded because the defendant could not

F prove that a prompt report would not have enabled the cattle to be recovered.
In the present case a great deal turns on when the crime was committed. Nobody
can say with certainty, but Detective Officer Pugh says the most probable time
was between 3 and 4 a.m. But for this evidence I should have taken the view
that it was likely to be earlier. A study of the record of the security officer's
visits in June, 1963, indicates that the interval between one visit and the next

G was usually about two hours or more, though sometimes considerably less, and
on at least one occasion it was only a few minutes over an hour. The natural
time to choose to break in would be as soon as possible after the patrolman's
visit and if for some reason it was impracticable for the thieves to break in before
three o'clock, one would expect them to do so at the earliest possible moment
thereafter. Certainly they would wish to have the operation completed before

H half past three, for thereafter the patrolman might arrive at any moment. In
my judgment it is a strong probability that the theft was completed by that hour
and accordingly that the goods were on the thieves' own vehicle and setting out
on the next stage of their journey by a quarter past four. Since the next visit,
if it had been paid at all, would probably have been paid at about five, and since
there was certainly no breach of duty in failing to visit before that hour, I am

I satisfied that the breach of duty did not cause or contribute to the loss. The
raising of the alarm at or shortly after five o'clock would have been far too late
to put a police cordon round the district or to offer any substantial prospect of
recovering the goods.

For these reasons I am of the opinion that the plaintiffs' claim against the
defendants fails and accordingly the question of any claim over against the third
parties does not arise, nor is it necessary for me to decide whether a limitation of

---

(10) [1918-19] All E.R. Rep. at p. 442, letter I; [1919] 1 K.B. at p. 458.
(11) [1918-19] All E.R. 434; [1919] 1 K.B. 443.

liability contained in the defendants' terms of contract was applicable. I will, **A**
however, state, in case it should become relevant hereafter, that in my view the
limitation clause was part of the contract between the plaintiffs and the defendants and that nothing had occurred between them to constitute a waiver of that
clause in relation to whisky.

Judgment for the defendants against the plaintiffs with costs, and for the third **B**
party against the defendants without costs.

Solicitors: *Herbert J. Davis, Berthen & Munro*, Liverpool (for the plaintiffs);
Herbert Smith & Co. (for the defendants); *Peace & Darlington*, Liverpool (for
the third parties)

[*Reported by* K. B. EDWARDS, ESQ., *Barrister-at-Law.*]

C

NOTE. **D**

BRITISH ROAD SERVICES, LTD. *v.* ARTHUR V. CRUTCHLEY & CO., LTD. (FACTORY GUARDS, LTD., Third Parties).

[COURT OF APPEAL, CIVIL DIVISION (Lord Denning, M.R., Davies and Russell,
L.JJ.), May 3, 1967.] **E**

*Court of Appeal—Respondent's notice—Service on third party—Leave not
required—R.S.C., Ord. 59, r. 6 (4).*

[As to a respondent's notice on an appeal to the Court of Appeal, see 30 HALS-
BURY'S LAWS (3rd Edn.) 466, 467, para. 880.

For R.S.C., Ord. 59, r. 6, see SUPREME COURT PRACTICE 1967, p. 750.] **F**

Case referred to:
Salmon, Re, Priest *v.* Uppleby, (1889), 42 Ch.D. 351; 61 L.T. 146; 47 Digest
(Repl.) 455, *4050.*

Application.
This was an application to the Court of Appeal by the defendants, Arthur
V. Crutchley & Co., Ltd., by notice dated Apr. 27, 1967, for leave to serve the **G**
third parties, Factory Guards, Ltd. with a respondent's notice, for directions
in regard to the service of the notice of appeal on the third parties and for leave
to serve the notice out of time. The plaintiffs, British Road Services, Ltd.,
had given notice of appeal, dated Apr. 12, 1967, addressed to the defendants
and to the third parties and to their respective solicitors; and the defendants
by a respondent's notice dated Apr. 28, 1967, addressed to the plaintiffs and to **H**
the third parties, and their respective solicitors, gave notice of intention to
contend on the hearing of the appeal that the judgment of CAIRNS, J. (reported
at p. 185, ante) should be affirmed on grounds specified in the respondent's notice,
being grounds other than those relied on by the trial judge (see R.S.C., Ord. 59,
r. 6 (2)*).

I

---

* R.S.C., Ord. 59, r. 6, provides, so far as is material: " (1) A respondent who, not
having appealed from the decision of the court below, desires to contend on the appeal
that the decision of that court should be varied . . . must give notice to that effect.
(2) A respondent who desires to contend on the appeal that the decision of the court
below should be affirmed on grounds other than those relied upon by that court must
give notice to that effect specifying the grounds of that contention . . . (4) Any notice
given by a respondent under this rule . . . must be served on the appellant, and on all
parties to the proceedings in the court below who are directly affected by the contentions of the respondent, and must be served— . . . (b) in any other case, within twenty-
one days, after the service of the notice of appeal on the respondent."

A   *J. S. Mason* for the defendants.
  G. H. G. Williams for the plaintiffs.
  P. H. Ripman for the third parties.

  LORD DENNING, M.R.: We think that we should make clear the
proper practice on appeals in actions where there are third parties. If the plaintiff
B has lost in the court below and appeals in this court seeking to make the defendant liable: and then the defendant (as respondent) serves a respondent's
notice in which he seeks (if he is held liable to the plaintiff) to recover indemnity
or contribution from the third party: then in such case the respondent is entitled,
without leave, to serve the notice on the third party. The third party is a person
who is " directly affected by the contentions of the respondent " within R.S.C.,
C Ord. 59, r. 6 (4) and should be served with the respondent's notice. Furthermore,
the respondent can and should annex to the notice when he serves the third
party the notice of appeal. That is necessary in order that the third party should
know what the appeal is about.
  The case of *Re Salmon, Priest* v. *Uppleby* (1), is no authority to the contrary.
It only applies to the present R.S.C., Ord. 59, r. 3 (5) (which deals with a notice
of appeal by an appellant). It has no application to a respondent's notice under
D R.S.C., Ord. 59, r. 6 (4). Nowadays if a respondent desires to claim over against
a third party, he can serve a respondent's notice without leave. In this case
therefore, there is no need for the defendants to apply for leave to serve the third
parties. The defendants are entitled without leave to serve the third parties with
the respondent's notice (together with a copy of the notice of appeal, which they
have themselves received). They are in time and should do so today.
E So far as the costs are concerned, as it turns out that this is an unnecessary
application, I am afraid that the defendants must pay the costs of the other
parties.

Application dismissed.

F Solicitors: *Herbert Smith & Co.* (for the defendants); *Herbert J. Davis, Berthen
& Munro,* Liverpool (for the plaintiffs); *Peace & Darlington,* Liverpool (for the third
parties).

[*Reported by* F. GUTTMAN, ESQ., *Barrister-at-Law.*]

(1) (1889), 42 Ch.D. 351.

G
BROWN *v.* CONWAY.

[COURT OF APPEAL, CIVIL DIVISION (Sellers, Diplock and Russell, L.JJ.), February
6, 7, March 7, 1967.]

BAILEY *v.* SPARK AND ANOTHER.

[COURT OF APPEAL, CIVIL DIVISION (Sellers, Diplock and Russell, L.JJ.), February
H 7, March 7, 1967.]

HODGSON *v.* GODFREY.

[COURT OF APPEAL, CIVIL DIVISION (Sellers, Diplock and Russell, L.JJ.), February
14, March 7, 1967.]

*Rent Restriction—Possession—Succession to statutory tenancy—Tenancy protected
I   by Rent Acts, 1920-1939 coming to an end before commencement of Rent Act of
    1965—Widow succeeding as statutory tenant—Death of widow before
    commencement of Act of 1965—Claim for possession against child resident
    with widow for over six months before her death—Claim heard after commence-
    ment of Act of 1965—Whether child's occupation protected by Act of 1965—
    " Tenancy "—" Regulated tenancy "—Rent Act 1965 (c. 49), s. 20 (1).*

  In each of three cases the contractual tenant of an unfurnished dwelling
house of such rateable value that it was controlled by the Rent Acts, 1920
to 1939, died, in two instances after the tenancy had become a statutory

tenancy, and left surviving him a widow who became statutory tenant by
virtue of s. 12 (1) (g) of the Increase of Rent and Mortgage Interest (Restrictions) Act, 1920. In each case the widow died before Dec. 8, 1965 (the date
on which the Rent Act 1965 came into force) and a child who had been
living with her in the house for more than six months before her death
survived her. In actions for possession by the landlords, tried after Dec. 8,
1965, each child relied on the provision of s. 20 (1)* of the Act of 1965 that
" Where the tenancy of a dwelling house has come to an end before the
commencement of this Act and the tenancy would have been a regulated
tenancy had this Act been then in force, then—(a) no order for possession
of the dwelling house shall be made which would not be made if this Act had
come into force before the termination of the tenancy . . .".

Held: s. 20 (1) did not apply and so the landlord was entitled to
possession, because the words " the tenancy " throughout s. 20 (1) referred
to the contractual tenancy of the father which, when it came to an end, was
(and would have been had the Act of 1965 then been in force) a " controlled "
tenancy and not a " regulated " one (see p. 797, letters C and G, p. 799,
letters F and I, and p. 802, letter I, post).

Remon v. *City of London Real Property Co., Ltd.* ([1921] 1 K.B. 49)
distinguished.

Per DIPLOCK, L.J.: " tenancy " unqualified by any adjective where it
appears in s. 20 or elsewhere in the Rent Act 1965, means a contractual
tenancy (see p. 799, letter I, post).

Per DIPLOCK and RUSSELL, L.JJ.: s. 13† of the Rent Act 1965 has no
retroactive effect of itself (see p. 798, letter I, and p. 800, letter I, post).

Appeals allowed in the cases of *Brown* v. *Conway* and *Bailey* v. *Spark
and Another.*

Appeal dismissed in the case of *Hodgson* v. *Godfrey.*

[As to succession to a statutory tenancy, see SUPPLEMENT to 23 HALSBURY'S
LAWS (3rd Edn.) para. 1590.

For the Rent Act 1965, s. 1, s. 13, s. 20, see 45 HALSBURY'S STATUTES (2nd
Edn.) 822, 833, 839.]

Case referred to:

Remon v. *City of London Real Property Co., Ltd.,* [1921] 1 K.B. 49; 89 L.J.K.B.
    1105; 123 L.T. 617; 31 Digest (Repl.) 638, *7455.*

Appeals.

Brown v. *Conway.*

This was an appeal by Arthur Brown, a landlord of a flat at 3, Oxford Road,
London, against the dismissal by His Honour JUDGE REGINALD CLARK at
Clerkenwell county court on May 12, 1966, of his action against the defendant,
C. D. Conway, for possession of the flat, and damages for trespass therein.

E. Campbell-Salmon for the landlord.
I. E. Jacob for the defendant.

Bailey v. *Spark and Another.*

This was an appeal by Thomas Bailey, landlord of a house at 87, Central Road,
Dearham, Cumberland, against the dismissal by His Honour JUDGE MADDOCKS
at Workington and Cockermouth county court on Aug. 11, 1966, of his action
against the defendants, Fred Spark and his wife Gwendoline Spark, for possession
of the house and mesne profits.

M. Pearson for the landlord.
The defendants did not appear and were not represented.

---

* Section 20 (1) is set out at p. 796, letter I, to p. 797, letter A, post.
† Section 13, so far as material, is set out at p. 796, letters F to H, post.

A   *Hodgson* v. *Godfrey.*

This was an appeal by the defendant, Miss H. M. Godfrey, against the decision of Deputy Judge Ellison, at Cambridge county court on Sept. 23, 1966, dismissing her appeal against the order of the registrar who had made an order for possession of 97 Norwich Street, Cambridge, in favour of the landlord, James Frederick Hodgson.

B   *A. L. Figgis* for the defendant.
Henry Palmer for the landlord.

                                       Cur. adv. vult.

Mar. 7, 1967. The following judgments were read.

C   **SELLERS, L.J.:** These three appeals were heard separately, but all parties who were before the court (the defendants Spark did not appear) agreed that it would be convenient if the court gave one judgment to cover the three cases as each case raised precisely the same point. The three plaintiffs were landlords seeking possession of residential premises and the defendants were resisting it. Each dwelling-house was within the rateable value of premises to which the Rent Acts applied before 1965.

D   In *Brown's* case the father of the defendant had been the contractual tenant of the top flat at No. 3, Oxford Road, London, on a weekly unfurnished tenancy until his death in 1964. On his death his widow, who had been living with her husband, remained in occupation as a statutory tenant. The widow died on Nov. 13, 1965, leaving in the flat her son, the defendant, who had resided there throughout his life, I think, and certainly for at least the six months prior to the widow's death.

E   In *Bailey's* case the father of the female defendant, one John Ritson, had been the contractual tenant of a dwelling-house No. 87, Central Road, Dearham, Cumberland, from about 1936 and by reason of a notice of increase of rent under the current Rent Acts this became a statutory tenancy and passed to his widow about seven years ago. Mrs. Ritson died on June 12, 1965, and the two defendants, who are husband and wife and who had resided with the wife's mother for at least six months, have continued in occupation.

F   In *Hodgson's* case the defendant's father had been a contractual tenant of 97, Norwich Street, Cambridge, for a time. On Feb. 23, 1961, he had become a statutory tenant by reason of a notice of increase of rent under the current Rent Acts, and on his death on Dec. 30, 1964, Mrs. Godfrey, his widow, succeeded to the statutory tenancy. She died on Sept. 18, 1965, and her daughter, who had lived with her mother for at least six months, has continued to occupy the premises.

G   If the three respective mothers, occupying as statutory tenants, had lived on until Dec. 8, 1965, it is conceded that the three separate defendants would have had a good claim to remain in occupation as " second successors " under the Rent Act 1965, and no order for possession could have been made against them.

H   The respective plaintiffs, the landlords, claim possession on the ground that each tenancy has terminated and that the defendants are trespassers who have acquired no right to occupation under the Rent Act 1965.

In *Brown's* case His Honour Judge Clark and in *Bailey's* case His Honour Judge Maddocks found in favour of the defendant's contention and each refused an order for possession. In *Hodgson's* case Deputy Judge Ellison upheld the decision of the registrar of the Cambridge county court, who had made an order for possession in favour of the landlord.

I   We have been told by counsel that there are known to be six decisions (including these three) in the county courts on the effect of the Rent Act 1965, in the respect here in issue and that the judgments so far are evenly divided, three one way, three the other. It is, I think, to be regretted that an Act, which bears so closely on the lives of people, affecting the very home in which they live, should be capable of producing such opposite interpretations in the courts.

The Rent Act 1965 came into force on Dec. 8, 1965. By s. 1 it brought within **A**
the control of the courts residential premises of a much higher rateable value than
had been the case before, although, as the rateable values had increased considerably, some at least of the premises might previously have been under control
when a lower rateable value applied. The tenancy of premises brought within
the control of the courts by the Act was designated a " regulated tenancy ", in
contrast to a tenancy already under control, to which I will hereinafter refer as a **B**
" controlled tenancy ". Section 1 (4) and (7) of the Rent Act 1965 provide:

" (4) In this Act ' regulated tenancy ' means—(a) a tenancy to which
the Rent Acts apply by virtue of this section; or (b) a statutory tenancy
arising on the termination of such a tenancy as is mentioned in para. (a) of
this subsection . . . (7) Nothing in this section shall affect the application of **C**
the Rent Acts to a tenancy to which they apply apart from this section."

The effect seems to be that the expression " regulated tenancy " does not embrace
the existing controlled tenancy. The statutory tenancies are therefore in two
classes. The new " regulated tenancy " was created separately, it would seem,
because provisions were made for these tenancies to have their rents adjusted to a
fair rent by the courts, whereas the then existing " controlled tenancy " of **D**
premises of lower rateable value had already been subject to control in respect of
increases in rent and rates by various Acts.

Another purpose of the Act of 1965 was to take one stage further the right of a
member of a family to continue in the tenancy, if the specified qualifications were
fulfilled. Ever since the Increase of Rent and Mortgage Interest (Restrictions)
Act, 1920, by reason of s. 12 (1) (g), on the death of the original tenant of premises **E**
to which the Rent Acts applied, whether a contractual tenancy or one which had
become a controlled tenancy, there have been provisions for one successor. After
one successor the tenancy could be terminated by the landlord.

Section 13 of the Rent Act 1965 made provision for two successors in these
terms:

F

" (1) The following provisions of this section shall apply on the death of
the tenant under a statutory tenancy (in this section referred to as the first
successor) whose right to retain possession by virtue of the Rent Acts arose on
the death of the person who had been the tenant under a tenancy to which
those Acts applied. (2) If either—(a) the first successor leaves a widow who
was residing with him at his death; or (b) the first successor is a woman or **G**
leaves no such widow but a member of his family was residing with him for
not less than six months immediately before his death, the widow or member
of the first successor's family (or, if more than one, such of them as may in
default of agreement be decided by the county court or, in Scotland, the
sheriff) shall be the second successor for the purposes of this section and,
except in the case mentioned in sub-s. (5) of this section, the right to retain **H**
possession by virtue of the Rent Acts shall pass to him."

In order to obtain for themselves the tenancy which they would have acquired
if their respective mothers had lived up to Dec. 8, 1965, instead of dying on
June 12, Sept. 18, and, the latest in date, Nov. 13, 1965, all the tenants relied
particularly on s. 20 (1), which is as follows:

I

" Where the tenancy of a dwelling-house has come to an end before the
commencement of this Act and the tenancy would have been a regulated
tenancy had this Act been then in force, then—(a) no order for possession of
the dwelling-house shall be made which would not be made if this Act had
come into force before the termination of the tenancy; and (b) where a court
has made an order before the commencement of this Act but the order has
not been executed, the court, if of opinion that the order would not have
been made if this Act had been in force, may, on the application of the

A   person against whom it was made, rescind or vary it in such manner as the
court thinks fit for the purpose of giving effect to this Act."

The opening words, " Where the tenancy of a dwelling-house has come to an end
before the commencement of this Act ", are fulfilled in all the present cases; but
the requirement continues—" and the tenancy would have been a regulated
tenancy had this Act been then in force ". Certainly the tenancy which would
B   have come into being had the Act of 1965 been in force would have been a
" regulated tenancy ", and some of the county court judges have regarded that
to be the requirement of the section in order to make the provisions of s. 13
retrospective. That construction involves the word " tenancy " being used in
two different senses in the same subsection, and I think that it must be rejected.
    The question more clearly is, would these tenancies which have come to an end
C   have been " regulated tenancies " (if the Rent Act 1965 had been in force) whilst
the mothers were each enjoying occupation as the successors of their respective
husbands under the old provisions whereby the tenancies were controlled?

It seems strange that such circumstances as exist here should have been overlooked when a retroactive look was being made as in s. 20. Section 13 when it
came into force was to apply to all statutory tenancies, the existing " controlled
D   tenancy " and the new " regulated tenancy ". The " controlled tenancy ",
covering the lowest rateable-valued property, had retained protection for some
forty-five years and would seem more deserving of retroactive effect than the
higher rated premises newly coming under control. However, one cannot read
the Act of 1965 back into the preterminating period unless the conditions of
s. 20 (1) are fulfilled.
E   By s. 13 (3) the " second successor " obtains a " regulated tenancy "—that is,
one subject to the " fair rent " adjustment by the provisions of the Act of 1965—
even though the terminating tenancy had been a " controlled tenancy ". In
such a case, sub-s. (3) (*a*) provides:

    " this Act shall apply in relation to the regulated tenancy as if the last
F   rental period beginning before the death of the first successor had been a
    contractual period . . ."

In these cases that would apply because each tenancy had long since ceased to be
a contractual tenancy, but it would not operate, I think, to make the terminating
tenancy a " regulated tenancy " to which s. 20 could be applied. It would bring
the newly emerging " second successor " tenancy into line for the purpose of the
G   fair rent provisions. The existing tenancy itself would not be a " regulated
tenancy " because it would already be subject to the existing Rent Acts.
    Counsel for the tenant Miss Godfrey, in particular, submitted in his argument
that a statutory tenancy is, on the authorities, the tenancy of the dwelling-
house and continues to be the same tenancy notwithstanding that the tenant may
change in the manner authorised by the appropriate Acts. Therefore he submitted
H   that if the Act of 1965 had been in force the dwelling-house would have retained
its tenancy. It would have been a regulated tenancy and it matters not that it
was not a regulated tenancy before it came to an end. He also relied on the
approach made to this particular protective legislation in *Remon* v. *City of
London Real Property Co., Ltd.* (1).
    I am not satisfied that the legislature intended that persons in the category of
I   these three defendants were to be excluded from the benefit of s. 13, and it may
well be that counsel are right in stating that, if these defendants have not been
provided for, they should have been and it was so intended. Although I have
seen no reason for their exclusion when those in the higher valued houses are
catered for and am tempted to construe the provisions as widely to that end as
possible, I find myself in agreement with my brethren on these two submissions
of counsel and do not wish to add anything to their reasons for rejecting them.

(1) [1921] 1 K.B. 49.

In the result, the appeals in *Brown* v. *Conway* and *Bailey* v. *Spark* succeed and   A
the appeal in *Hodgson* v. *Godfrey* fails. Orders will be made accordingly, including
the incidence of costs on which there was a separate head of appeal in *Hodgson*
v. *Godfrey*.

      DIPLOCK, L.J. (read by SELLERS, L.J.): These three appeals against the
judgments of county court judges in the first two cases refusing and in the third
case making an order for possession of dwelling-houses to which the Rent Acts   B
applied before the coming into force of the Rent Act 1965, raised the same point
of law. In each case the father of the tenant had been originally the contractual
tenant of the dwelling-house and on the father's death his widow, the defendant's
mother, had, by virtue of the definition in s. 12 (1) (*g*) of the Increase of Rent and
Mortgage Interest (Restrictions) Act, 1920, become entitled to retain possession of
the dwelling-house by virtue of the Rent Acts, 1920 to 1939. In each case the   C
mother died before Dec. 8, 1965, when the Rent Act 1965 came into force, and
the defendant was residing with her for not less than six months before her death.
On the mother's death the defendant had no right under the Rent Acts, 1920 to
1939 to remain in possession of the dwelling-house. Those Acts did not recognise
any right of what is now known as a " second successor ". On the death of the
mother each defendant became a trespasser in the dwelling-house and remained   D
so at least until Dec. 8, 1965, when the Rent Act 1965 came into force.
Nevertheless each continued wrongfully in possession until that date.

      The only question in these appeals is whether the Rent Act 1965 did give to
them a right to retain possession thereafter—i.e., to convert their wrongful
possession into a statutory tenancy. The Rent Act 1965, by s. 1 (1) and (2),
extended the application of the Rent Acts, 1920 to 1939 (referred to in the Act   E
as " the Rent Acts ") to every tenancy of a dwelling-house of which the rateable
value did not exceed in Greater London £400 and elsewhere in Great Britain
£200; but by sub-s. (7) nothing in s. 1 was to affect the application of the
Rent Acts to a tenancy to which they applied apart from that section.   Accordingly on the termination, after the coming into force of the Rent Act 1965, of a
contractual tenancy brought within the Rent Acts, 1920 to 1939 by s. 1 of the   F
Act of 1965, a statutory tenancy arose if the contractual tenant or his successor
retained possession. By s. 1 (4) a " regulated tenancy " was defined to mean:

      " (*a*) a tenancy to which the Rent Acts apply by virtue of this section; or
      (*b*) a statutory tenancy arising on the termination of such a tenancy as is
      mentioned in para. (*a*) of this subsection."
                                                                            G
In order to distinguish a " regulated tenancy " from a contractual tenancy or a
statutory tenancy to which the Rent Acts, 1920 to 1939 applied apart from the
section, I shall call the latter a " controlled tenancy ".   The distinction is
important, for the provisions relating to the regulation of the rent payable under
a " regulated tenancy " differ materially from the provisions relating to the
regulation of rent payable under " controlled tenancies ".
                                                                            H
      Section 13 of the Rent Act 1965 contains a new provision applicable to both
" regulated tenancies " and " controlled tenancies " which gives to persons in the
position of the defendants (who are referred to as " second successors ") a right
to retain possession by virtue of the Rent Acts, 1920 to 1939, but provides by
sub-s. (3) that any such person shall be tenant under a " regulated tenancy "
even though the statutory tenancy of the first successor to which the second   I
successor succeeded was a " controlled tenancy ". Subsection (4) amends the
definition of " tenant " in the Rent Acts, 1920 to 1939 so as to include a " second
successor " in addition to the first successor who was already included in the
definition by s. 12 (1) (*g*) of the Act of 1920.

      I find it impossible to discern in the wording of s. 13 an intention that the
section should have any retroactive effect. I should take this view on the construction of the section itself, but it is reinforced by the presence in the Act of 1965 of
s. 20, which contains express provision as to the retroactive effect to be given to

A   the statute. This, in my view, leaves no room for any implication that any other section such as s. 13, which confers new rights on tenants or on landlords, was intended in itself to confer such rights retroactively. These appeals, in my view, accordingly turn on the application of s. 20 to the facts of the case. Section 20, so far as is relevant, reads as follows:

B   " (1) Where the tenancy of a dwelling-house has come to an end before the commencement of this Act and the tenancy would have been a regulated tenancy had this Act been then in force, then—(*a*) no order for possession of the dwelling-house shall be made which would not be made if this Act had come into force before the termination of the tenancy; and (*b*) where a court has made an order before the commencement of this Act but the order has not been executed, the court, if of opinion that the order would not have
C   been made if this Act had been in force, may, on the application of the person against whom it was made, rescind or vary it in such manner as the court thinks fit for the purpose of giving effect to this Act.

      " (2) A person who retains possession by virtue of this section shall be deemed to do so under a statutory tenancy arising on the termination of a tenancy to which the Rent Acts applied by virtue of s. 1 of this Act, and the
D   terms as to rent and otherwise of that tenancy shall be deemed to have been the same, subject to any variations the court may specify, as those of the tenancy mentioned in sub-s. (1) of this section."

To come within the section at all a tenancy of a dwelling-house must: (i) have come to an end before Dec. 8, 1965, and (ii) be of such a character that if the Rent
E   Act 1965 had been in force when it came to an end it would have been a " regulated tenancy "—that is to say, neither a " controlled tenancy " nor one to which the Rent Acts, 1920 to 1939 would not apply—by virtue of s. 1 of the Rent Act 1965. " The tenancy " mentioned in sub-s. (1) as having come to an end before the commencement of the Act means a contractual tenancy.

      Throughout the Act of 1965 a clear distinction is drawn between a " tenancy "
F   and a " statutory tenancy " arising on the termination of a tenancy. By the interpretation section of the Act of 1965, s. 47, " statutory tenancy " has the same meaning as in the Housing Repairs and Rents Act, 1954, where " statutory tenancy " is defined, by s. 49 (1), as follows:

      " ' Statutory tenant ' means a tenant (as defined in para. (*g*) of sub-s. (1)
G   of s. 12 of the Act of 1920) who retains possession by virtue of the Rent Acts and not as being entitled to a tenancy, and ' statutory tenancy ' shall be construed accordingly."

By the same s. 47 " tenant " and " tenancy " have the same meanings as in the Act of 1920, which also takes us to s. 12 (1) (*g*) of the latter Act. In that section, while on the one hand " tenant " is given an extended meaning, which includes
H   a first successor and has from the earliest cases decided under the Rent Acts been construed as including a " statutory tenant " as later defined in the Act of 1954, on the other hand " tenancy " is not given an extended meaning corresponding to that given to " tenant " and has never been construed as including a " statutory tenancy " as defined in the Act of 1954. It is true that in a number of judgments to which our attention was drawn by counsel for the tenant in the
I   appeal in *Hodgson* v. *Godfrey* the statutory tenancy arising on the termination of a contractual tenancy has been described as being the same tenancy, but expressions such as this have been used merely as a convenient way of referring concisely to the effect of s. 15 (1) of the Act of 1920, and not as a matter of construction of the word " tenancy " where it appears in the Rent Acts. " Tenancy " unqualified by any adjective where it appears in s. 20 or elsewhere in the Rent Act 1965, means, in my view, a contractual tenancy. In each of the present appeals " the tenancy " mentioned in s. 20 (1) is the original contractual tenancy from which the occupation of the defendant derived.

It has been argued that the expression " the tenancy " in sub-s. (1) is used in **A**
one sense where it appears for the first time and the third time but in a different
sense where it appears for the second time, and that where it appears for the
second time it means ' the statutory tenancy of which the person against whom an
order for the possession of the dwelling-house is sought would have been tenant
if the Rent Act 1965 had been in force when the tenancy first referred to came
to an end '. Quite apart from this involving construing " tenancy " as " statutory **B**
tenancy ", which for the reasons already given is in any event impermissible, to
construe a single expression " the tenancy " as having a meaning which changes
and then reverts to its original meaning when used three times in the same
sentence seems to me to be quite impossible. The reference in sub-s. (2) to " the
tenancy mentioned in sub-s. (1) of this section " would also seem to confirm that
there is only one tenancy mentioned in sub-s. (1).   **C**

It has been argued that to construe s. 20 as I have done would have the result
that it would operate retroactively to give to second successors to tenancies which
were not " controlled tenancies " rights to retain possession while denying such
rights to second successors to " controlled tenancies " and Parliament cannot have
intended so capricious a result. I do not find it necessary to express any opinion
whether the section has this result in the case of tenancies which were not **D**
" controlled tenancies " before the Rent Act 1965 was passed. First successors
without any fresh contractual tenancy remaining in possession of dwelling-houses
which were not subject to " controlled tenancies " had only been protected from
eviction since Dec. 17, 1964, (2), and Parliament may well have overlooked the
possibility of there being second successors in possession by Dec. 8, 1965. Section
20 (2) would not be apt in the case of any successor remoter than the first successor **E**
retaining possession on the termination of a contractual tenancy. I can see no
indication of any clear intention of Parliament which would justify our giving to
the expression " the tenancy " in s. 20 (1) a meaning other than that which, as
I have indicated, I think that it clearly has.

I would allow the first two appeals and dismiss the third.

F

RUSSELL, L.J.: In each of these cases the premises were subject to
control under the Rent Acts before 1965. Accordingly they did not involve
" regulated tenancies " under the Rent Act 1965, because a regulated tenancy is
one to which the Rent Acts were made to apply by virtue of s. 1 of the Act of 1965,
and this does not include one to which by reason of its low rateable value the
Rent Acts already applied. In each case the occupation had been successively by **G**
a father, and on his death before the operative date of the Act of 1965 by his
widow, and since her death, also before that date, by a child. Under the Rent
Acts the widow was entitled to remain in possession as successor to the husband,
but no such right was conferred on the child or on anyone else as a second successor
to the widow. Under the Act of 1965 the child would, if the widow had survived
the operative date, be entitled to remain in possession as second successor; see **H**
s. 13. The question is whether the Act of 1965 has not only introduced the idea
of a second successor but has also done so in some sense retrospectively in cases
such as these with the result that the child can resist an order for possession.

The language of s. 13, taken by itself, in no way indicates retrospective operation. Subsection (1) enacts that the provisions of the section " *shall* apply *on* the
death " of the first successor: that a person " *shall* be the second successor "; **I**
and that the right to retain possession " *shall pass* to him ". Putting these
together, the section is saying that a possessory right *shall pass* to B. *on* A.'s
death, which is wholly inappropriate to a case in which A. is already dead without
any possessory right having devolved on B., who became merely the former
licensee of a former statutory tenant. Nor can I accept the suggestion that
s. 13 (4) has a retrospective flavour: it only extends an existing statutory

(2) See the Protection from Eviction Act 1964; 44 HALSBURY'S STATUTES (2nd Edn.)
688.

A definition of " tenant " to include a second successor and says nothing about the time from which such extension operates.

I turn then to the transitional provisions contained in s. 20 in order to see whether they apply to a second succession in existing control cases such as these: or, if they do not, whether they compel one to the conclusion that s. 13 not-withstanding its terms must be construed to apply in some sense retrospectively
B to them.

Conditions precedent to the applicability of s. 20 (1) are (a) that the *tenancy* of a dwelling-house has come to an end before Dec. 8, 1965, and (b) that the *tenancy* would have been a regulated tenancy had the Act of 1965 been in force when that tenancy came to an end. If the conditions precedent are fulfilled the section operates after Dec. 7 to prevent orders for possession or the execution of orders
C for possession that would not have been ordered had the Act come into force before the termination of the *tenancy*. Subsection (2) confers a status on the person thus protected from eviction by deeming him to retain possession after Dec. 7 under a *statutory tenancy* arising on the termination of a *tenancy* to which s. 1 of the Act of 1965 applies the Rent Acts (that is to say a regulated tenancy), with terms the same as those of the *tenancy* mentioned in sub-s. (1).

D In my judgment there is only one *tenancy* referred to in the conditions precedent to the applicability of s. 20, and that is a contractual tenancy in the regulated rateable value group. The Act of 1965 distinguishes between a tenancy (which is contractual) and a statutory tenancy (which is not). Section 1 (1) and sub-s. (2) in combination bring under regulated control a *tenancy* of a dwelling-house under certain value limits but above existing control limits. Subsection (4) defines a
E " regulated tenancy " as a *tenancy* which is brought under regulated control by s. 1 *or a statutory tenancy* arising on the termination of *such a tenancy.* Subsection (5), looking ahead to the machinery for regulating rents in such cases, again distinguishes between a *tenancy* which is brought under regulated control by s. 1 and a *statutory tenancy* which may follow it, and labels the former in terms a *contractual tenancy.* Section 11 has the same approach, in dealing with existing
F controlled tenancies as either a *tenancy* or a *statutory tenancy* arising on the determination of *such a tenancy.*

Section 20 cannot therefore have any application to any of these three cases, since in none of them was there ever a contractual tenancy in the value group of regulated tenancies. This seems to me the plain and simple meaning and effect of the section.

G An argument was advanced on s. 20 based on the fact that by s. 13 (3) a second successor's statutory tenancy is to be a regulated tenancy, whether the preceding tenancy was a regulated tenancy or one under old control. What was said was this. Authority establishes that a statutory tenancy is the same tenancy as that which preceded it. Therefore if the Act of 1965 had been in force the one tenancy *would* have been a regulated tenancy. Even if (which I do not necessarily accept)
H authority did so establish, this argument cannot be supported. For one thing it involves inserting the words " or become " after the words " would have been ". In any event s. 20 (1) is directed first to the fact of a contractual tenancy having come to an end and secondly to the hypothetical impact of the Act of 1965 on the tenancy at that moment: in none of the three cases before us could it be said that that impact would have resulted in a regulated tenancy. In fact
I in two cases the contractual tenancy had come to an end long before the father died: and in the third case on the father's death the widow's statutory tenancy as successor could not have been a regulated tenancy.

Finally, it was argued that s. 20, in cases of tenancies in the regulated value group, would operate to protect a person in the position of the defendants in these cases: that it would be capricious of the legislature to do this in the regulated group but not in the old control group: and that therefore there is ground for extracting from s. 13 a retrospective operation notwithstanding its language. As at present advised I think that it is probably correct to say that s. 20 operates

after Dec. 7 to protect a person still in occupation as " second successor " though **A**
the first successor died before Dec. 8. Section 20 is plainly primarily aimed at
affording protection after Dec. 7, 1965, to an ex-contractual tenant in the
regulated value range who has succeeded in resisting eviction that long and to
confer on such person a statutory tenancy. I observe that a possession order
against such a person could have been suspended for up to twelve months under
the Protection from Eviction Act 1964, s. 2. In such a case it appears to me that **B**
his widow remaining in occupation would also be within the protection of s. 20: if
the Act of 1965 had been in operation before the determination of the husband's
contractual tenancy, s. 1, by applying the Rent Acts, would have not only
protected the husband thereafter but also his widow on his later death. I observe
that the widow was also within s. 2 of the Act of 1964, though not a child unless
there was no widow. What then of a child? It seems to me that if the Act of 1965 **C**
had come into operation before the husband's contractual tenancy ended, not
only would s. 1 have conferred on the widow a statutory tenancy (so that the condition precedent contained in s. 13 (1) would have been fulfilled) but also the
rest of the section would have made the child a second successor: therefore the
hypothesis in s. 20 (1) (a) would have existed and the protection of s. 20 would
have extended to the child. However, even if this view be correct, I cannot see **D**
that it can entitle us to read s. 13 as retrospective in its operation—as referring
to a case where a " second succession " has already taken place before the Act.
Indeed to do so would, it seems to me, lead to a conflict between s. 13 and s. 20
in one respect. Section 13 applies to both existing control and to new regulation
cases. If s. 13 is to be given a retrospective construction in existing control cases
—as is suggested—it must bear the same construction in new regulation cases. **E**
That would mean that on Dec. 8, 1965, s. 13 would simply confer on the child in
a " regulated " case " the right to retain possession by virtue of the Rent Acts "
and the position of " a tenant under a regulated tenancy "; but s. 20 would
deem that same child to retain possession under a statutory regulated tenancy on
terms as to rent and otherwise of the previous contractual tenancy " subject to
any variations the court may specify ". **F**

Assuming there to be the difference between regulated cases and old control
cases in relation to " second successions " before the Act of 1965, it seems far
more likely that such a " second succession " was brought within s. 20 in regulated
cases by accident rather than design: if it was by design I find it impossible to
suppose that the same retrospective effect would not in express terms have been
given—either in s. 13 or elsewhere—to second successions in old control cases **G**
where the relevant facts were perhaps more likely to exist. It was in this
connexion suggested that Parliament might in such last cases have been relying
on the courts to deal with s. 13 in a spirit which they displayed in *Remon* v. *City
of London Real Property Co., Ltd*. (3). That was, however, a totally different type
of case in which this court was able to give a loose or stretched construction to
words such as " tenant " and " let " to include a tenant holding over after **H**
termination of his tenancy because otherwise, in the language of SCRUTTON, L.J.
(4), " the whole purpose of the Act would have been defeated ", and " If this
was not so every . . . tenant for whose benefit the Acts were obviously framed,
was outside the Act ".

Accordingly, in my judgment s. 20 has no operation in the present cases which
were not cases of regulated tenancies, and further s. 13 cannot be construed so as **I**
to apply to cases that would have been second succession cases had the first
successor died after the Act of 1965 came into operation but where the first
successor in fact died before that date. The appeal in the first two cases should be
allowed and possession ordered, and the appeal in the third case should be
dismissed.

---

(3) [1921] 1 K.B. 49.
(4) [1921] 1 K.B. at p. 58.

A   *Appeal in Brown* v. *Conway allowed. Order for possession in six weeks from Mar. 7, 1967. Terms of order as to damages for trespass to be agreed between counsel.*

Appeal in Bailey v. *Spark and Another allowed. Order for possession on Apr. 20, 1967, and for payment of mesne profits at the rate of 13s. 7d. per week from June 12, 1965, to date when possession given.*

B   *Appeal in Hodgson* v. *Godfrey dismissed.*

Solicitors: *Trott & Gentry* (for the landlord Brown); *D. H. P. Levy & Co.* (for the defendant Conway); *Beachcroft & Co.*, agents for *Curwen & Co.*, Workington (for the landlord Bailey); *Francis & Co.*, Cambridge (for the defendant Godfrey); *Downham & Co.*, Maidenhead (for the landlord Hodgson).

C   [*Reported by* Henry Summerfield, Esq., *Barrister-at-Law.*]

SANDERS *v.* PARRY.

D   [Hertford Assizes (Havers, J.), February 13, 14, 15, 16, 17, March 22, 1967.]

Master and Servant—Duty of servant—Fidelity—Solicitor employing assistant solicitor—Implied term that assistant solicitor would serve solicitor with good faith and fidelity—Assistant solicitor accepting offer from important client of solicitor to take lease of premises owned by client and to do client's
E   *legal work—Assistant solicitor leaving solicitor's employment and entering into agreement with client to undertake all legal work for client for seven years—Whether breach of agreement with solicitor.*

In January, 1964, the plaintiff, a solicitor, entered into an agreement with the defendant to employ the defendant as assistant solicitor. The plaintiff had an important builder client, T., and in correspondence with the
F   defendant before the defendant commenced work with him, the plaintiff referred to the fact that one of T.'s conditions for remaining with the plaintiff was that the plaintiff would replace the defendant's predecessor with someone as efficient as he was. It was an implied term of the agreement between the plaintiff and the defendant that the defendant would serve the plaintiff with good faith and fidelity. The agreement was made in contemplation
G   of the possibility of a partnership if terms could be agreed; but the agreement contained no provision restricting the defendant from practising in a limited area for a period of years after he left the plaintiff's employment. After the defendant commenced employment with the plaintiff at the plaintiff's office in the town where T. carried on his business, the defendant did T.'s legal work on behalf of the plaintiff. In June, 1964, negotiations
H   took place over the question of a partnership between the plaintiff and the defendant, but the defendant's bank would advance him money to purchase a share in the partnership only if T. would give an assurance that he would remain a client of the partnership for a definite period. T. was not prepared to give such an undertaking. In October, 1964, the defendant handed to the plaintiff a letter from T. in which T. wrote that the defendant had
I   applied for a lease of the upper part of his premises and that T. had accepted the defendant as a tenant. T. further said in the letter that instructions to act for him would in future be sent to the defendant, and asked that all the files relating to T.'s business should be handed over to the defendant. The defendant gave the plaintiff the notice required by the agreement. The defendant left the plaintiff's employment, moved to the premises which T. had acquired and entered into an agreement with T. and his three companies that, for a period of seven years, the defendant should undertake all the legal work of T. and his companies and that, during that period, T.

would not instruct any other solicitor in connexion with any legal work with-   **A**
out the defendant's consent. S., the plaintiff's secretary in his branch
office where the defendant worked, left when he did. He had offered her
work as his secretary about ten days before he left; she accepted. In an
action by the plaintiff for damages for breach by the defendant of the
agreement between them, the trial judge found that it was not established
that the defendant's agreement with T. was initiated by the defendant.   **B**

Held: (i) the defendant in entering on his agreement with T. was guilty
of breach of the duty, implied by law in the service agreement, that the
defendant would serve the plaintiff with good faith and fidelity (see p. 808,
letter D, post).

Dicta of LORD GREENE, M.R., and of MORTON, L.J., in *Hivac, Ltd.* v. *Park
Royal Scientific Instruments, Ltd.* ([1946] 1 All E.R. at pp. 353, 354, 356, 357)   **C**
applied.

(ii) the defendant was also in breach of contract with the plaintiff in that
the defendant's offer to S. caused her to leave the plaintiff's service (see
p. 807, letter B, post).

(iii) the plaintiff was entitled to substantial damages for the defendant's
breach at (i) above, and to nominal damages of 40s. for his breach at (ii) above   **D**
(see p. 807, letter B, and p. 809, letter I, post).

[As to the nature of a servant's duties during his employment, see 25 HALS-
BURY'S LAWS (3rd Edn.) 462, para. 894; and for cases on the subject, see 34
DIGEST (Repl.) 146, 147, *1005-1009*.]

Cases referred to: **E**
Chaplin v. *Hicks*, [1911-13] All E.R. Rep. 224; [1911] 2 K.B. 786; 80 L.J.K.B.
    1292; 105 L.T. 285; 17 Digest (Repl.) 89, *96*.
Hivac, Ltd. v. *Park Royal Scientific Instruments, Ltd.*, [1946] 1 All E.R. 350;
    [1946] Ch. 169; 115 L.J.Ch. 241; 174 L.T. 422; 34 Digest (Repl.)
    146, *1009*.
Lamb v. *Evans*, [1893] 1 Ch. 218; 62 L.J.Ch. 404; 68 L.T. 131; 34 Digest   **F**
    (Repl.) 152, *1047*.
Wessex Dairies, Ltd. v. *Smith*, [1935] All E.R. Rep. 75; [1935] 2 K.B. 80;
    104 L.J.K.B. 484; 153 L.T. 185; 34 Digest (Repl.) 146, *1006*.

Action.
This was an action by the plaintiff, Frederick Orpen Sanders, who at all   **G**
material times practised as a solicitor under the firm name of Sanders
Penman & Co., against the defendant, David John Parry, for damages for
breach of contract, viz., an agreement entered into on or about Jan. 2, 1964, by
the plaintiff with the defendant to employ him as assistant solicitor at a salary
of £2,000 per annum. There was to be a trial period of three months, and
thereafter the defendant's employment would be terminable by one month's   **H**
notice on either side. The agreement was admitted, and the defendant did not
dispute that it was an implied term of the agreement that he would serve the
plaintiff with good faith and fidelity. The agreement was made in contemplation
of the possibility of a partnership if terms could subsequently be agreed. The
defendant commenced employment with the plaintiff on Mar. 16, 1964, and
remained in that employment until Oct. 21, 1964, when he was dismissed by the   **I**
plaintiff. After his dismissal the defendant set up in practice at Grays, Essex,
where he had formerly been working in the plaintiff's office, and a Mrs. Stanford,
who had formerly been employed by the plaintiff in his office at Grays, left that
employment and took employment with the defendant. The main breach of
contract that was alleged by the plaintiff was that, between July, 1964, and
October, 1964, the defendant entered into an agreement with a Mr. Tully, an
important client of the plaintiff, whereby it was provided that the defendant
should leave the plaintiff's employment and should set up in practice on his own

A   at Grays in premises to be leased to him by Mr. Tully and thereafter would
carry out for Mr. Tully the whole of the type of work, or the main part of the
work, which formerly the plaintiff had been doing for Mr. Tully. The defendant
contended that the offer which he accepted came from Mr. Tully, that the defendant did not initiate it, and that he did not commit any breach of the implied
term of good faith and fidelity.

B   The plaintiff was admitted as solicitor in June, 1950, and in 1956 had opened
branches at Grays and Brentwood in Essex. At the end of March, 1963, he
advertised for an assistant solicitor, whom he wished to employ to take charge of
his office at Grays, where the work for Mr. Tully was done. The defendant
answered the advertisement. The defendant was admitted as a solicitor in
March, 1961, and was anxious to get experience of private practice. The agree-
C   ment which was reached between the plaintiff and the defendant contained no
provision restricting the defendant from practising in a limited area for a period
of years after he left the plaintiff's employment. In correspondence with the
defendant in January, 1964, the plaintiff referred to their builder client, that is
to say, to Mr. Tully, expressing the hope that he would remain with them. This
letter continued—

D   " One of the conditions of [Mr. Tully's] remaining is that I replace Mr.
    Penman by someone who is as efficient as he is, so I hope you will fit the
    bill. You will find he is also setting up as an estate agent, and I have
    offered him the premises next door to my office, which he will probably
    accept."

E   After the defendant started work on Mar. 16, 1963, in the Grays office, he did
work on behalf of the plaintiff for Mr. Tully, to whom the defendant gave
complete satisfaction. On Oct. 19, 1964, the defendant handed to the plaintiff
at the Grays office a letter from Mr. Tully in these terms—

        " I have to inform you that [the defendant] has applied for a lease of the
    upper part of my premises at Orsett Road, Grays, and after careful con-
F   sideration I have accepted him as a tenant. Obviously instructions to act
    for me will be sent to him, at the same time I will ensure that some future
    work will be channelled into your office at 14, London Road. I would
    like to retain the cordial atmosphere that exists between me and your
    Mr. Alderson and Mr. Gorman but am of the firm opinion that as [the defen-
    dant] has handled my business so successfully a further disruption of my
    affairs would be hardly beneficial to my business at this time. I would be
G   obliged if you would immediately hand to [the defendant] all the files
    relating to my business."

The plaintiff had not previously had any idea that an agreement had been made
between Mr. Tully and the defendant. The plaintiff and the defendant had been
negotiating a partnership, and the plaintiff had supplied accounts up to 1962-63
H   for inspection by the defendant, but they had not yet discussed the terms. The
plaintiff asked the defendant—" Why did you do this when we were negotiating
a partnership? " The defendant did not answer. When the defendant handed
the letter to the plaintiff, he told the plaintiff that it was not accurate; the
defendant also asked the plaintiff to take a month's notice, and told the plaintiff
that a Mrs. Stanford, who worked in the office as his private secretary, was
I   dissatisfied and that the defendant had offered her employment with him.
        In evidence the defendant testified that about the middle of June, 1964, he
had raised the question of a partnership with the plaintiff. A figure had not
been discussed, but the defendant had asked for accounts to be supplied in respect
of the current year, but they were not available being still with the accountants.
At this time the defendant did not contemplate any possibility that Mr. Tully
might employ him personally. The defendant approached Mr. Spain, the manager
of the bank at which the plaintiff and the defendant and Mr. Tully banked, to see
whether an advance would be available to purchase a share in the partnership.

The bank manager said that an advance would be considered, though possibly **A**
not of the sum that the defendant would require, if an assurance could be obtained
from Mr. Tully that his business would remain with the partnership between
the plaintiff and the defendant when formed. The defendant saw Mr. Tully
after this, and told him that the bank manager was prepared to consider an
advance if Mr. Tully could give an assurance that he would remain a client of
the partnership for a definite period. Mr. Tully was not prepared to give such **B**
an undertaking. According to the defendant, Mr. Tully said that he was purchasing premises at Orsett Road, where he intended to carry on an estate agency
business, and he would like to have a solicitor occupying the same premises
doing his professional work for him; and that Mr. Tully then said that, if the
defendant would like the job, he could have it, but that he must not say anything
to the plaintiff about it at that stage. The defendant's evidence was that he **C**
said to Mr. Tully that he would have to consider it. A week later he told Mr.
Tully that he would like to accept the offer, and that he would like an assurance
from him that his business would remain with him, the defendant. Mr. Tully
agreed to give such an assurance. In regard to Mr. Tully's letter, which the
defendant handed to the plaintiff on Oct. 19, 1964, the defendant said that he
told Mr. Tully that he had not applied for a lease. According to the defendant, **D**
Mr. Tully said that he did not like the plaintiff and that the real reason could not
be put into writing, so he thought that that was the best way of doing it in the
circumstances.

On Oct. 20, 1964, the plaintiff told the defendant to take over a case at Chelms-
for Assizes from another employee, Mr. Alderson. The defendant declined, and the
plaintiff, having come over to the Grays office, told the defendant to clear out. The **E**
defendant refused to go until he got the file of Mr. Tully's business, which eventually was handed over to him. An apportionment was made for the amount
which was or might become due in respect of that account, and the defendant
gave a cheque for the amount. He took with him the file and the deeds. On
Oct. 21, 1964, the defendant left the plaintiff and went to the premises at
Orsett Road, which Mr. Tully had acquired and from which he was carrying on **F**
his estate agent's business. An agreement was entered into between three
companies which Mr. Tully controlled, Mr. Tully and the defendant, by which
it was agreed that the defendant should for a period of seven years from the date
thereof undertake all the legal work of the companies and of Mr. Tully and
should be paid for it according to the scales of costs appropriate thereto at the
time at which the work should be carried out. The agreement provided that **G**
the companies and Mr. Tully would not during the period instruct any other
solicitor or firm of solicitors in connexion with any legal work without the
defendant's consent.

Mrs. Stanford also left the plaintiff's employment and joined the defendant on
Oct. 26, 1964. She had been employed with the plaintiff for five years. On
Oct. 19, 1964, she gave the plaintiff a week's notice. In evidence she said that **H**
the defendant did not persuade her to leave, but that she was leaving anyhow.
About ten days before Oct. 19, the defendant had told her that he was going to
work for Mr. Tully and that he would require a secretary, and that he would be
very pleased if she would like to be that secretary. The defendant said in evidence
that Mrs. Stanford had said that she would like to accept that.

J. P. Comyn, Q.C., R. J. S. Harvey and *D. W. Powell* for the plaintiff.   **I**
Joseph Dean for the defendant.

HAVERS, J., having stated the nature of the action, and having reviewed
the evidence of the witnesses, particularly that of the defendant and of Mrs.
Stanford, and having said that there was a breach of the defendant's agreement
with the plaintiff by reason of the circumstances in which Mrs. Stanford left
the plaintiff's employment, continued: In my view, there was a duty on the
defendant, when Mrs. Stanford told him that she was dissatisfied, to have reported

A that to his principal and so to have given him an opportunity of seeing what he could do to meet any complaint that Mrs. Stanford had, so that she could remain with him.   She said that she was not in any hurry to go; but then the defendant made this offer to her, which she accepted, and it was only when this offer was made that she gave her notice.   In my view, it was the duty of the defendant to have reported this dissatisfaction of the secretary to his principal in order

B to give him an opportunity, as far as he could, to satisfy her.   Instead of forwarding his principal's interests he was concerned only in promoting his own. He made this alternative offer to Mrs. Stanford which she accepted and it was as a result of that alone that she left the plaintiff and joined the defendant. That was, in my view, a breach of contract, and in respect of that breach of contract, the plaintiff is entitled to nominal damages of 40s.

C There was another matter, and that was that the defendant had approached Mr. Gorman, who was also an employee of the plaintiff.   The defendant offered him a job at an increased salary plus a percentage, and this offer was conditional on the defendant buying the practice at Grays.   The defendant said that he asked Mr. Gorman, if he, the defendant, bought the practice at Grays, whether he would be prepared to stay with the possible mention of an increased salary

D and percentage bonus, but that he had not seriously considered buying that practice.   If that was so, what was the point in offering Mr. Gorman a job? The plaintiff suggests that the defendant was probably sounding out Mr. Gorman in an endeavour to see whether he would possibly come with the defendant.

The first thing that I have to decide is this.   Did the defendant solicit Mr. Tully in any way with regard to that agreement?   The defendant could hardly

E be surprised if the plaintiff took that view when the defendant handed him the letter on Oct. 19, 1964, in which Mr. Tully said:

"I have to inform you that [the defendant] has applied for a lease on the upper part of my premises at Orsett Road, Grays, and after careful consideration I have accepted him as a tenant."

F The plaintiff said that he went to see Mr. Tully on Oct. 19 and Mr. Tully told the plaintiff that the defendant had approached Mr. Tully and had said that he was going, and that, to prevent him going, Mr. Tully had said that he would give the defendant a job.   On the other hand I have the evidence of the defendant, Mr. Spain and Mr. Tully as to the events which preceded the agreement between Mr. Tully and his companies and the defendant, that at that time the defendant was still negotiating with the plaintiff as to the partnership and that he had

G approached Mr. Spain to see if the plaintiff could get an advance of money. Mr. Spain said that the bank could advance money only if there was an assurance that Mr. Tully's work would remain with the partnership, and it was then that the defendant approached Mr. Tully and asked for that assurance and he did not get it.   Although I have a good deal of suspicion about this, I am unable to say, on a balance of probabilities, that the agreement was initiated by the

H defendant.

The next point that arises is this.   If the agreement with Mr. Tully was not initiated by the defendant, but if he accepted, during the subsistence of his agreement with the plaintiff, an offer made by Mr. Tully, was that a breach of the agreement?   In my view, there was a duty at all times during the subsistence of that agreement on the defendant to protect his master's interests, especially

I to do his best to retain Mr. Tully as a client of his master, and, having regard to the letter to which I have already referred (1), there was a duty on the defendant to look after and protect Mr. Tully's interests on behalf of the plaintiff.   In accepting this offer the defendant was not protecting his master's interests, for he made no effort to try and retain Mr. Tully as a client of his master.   The defendant was placing himself in a position in which there was a conflict of interests between him and his principal, and he was looking after his own interests

---

(1) Viz., the plaintiff's letter of January, 1964; see p. 805, letter D, ante.

to the detriment of his master's interests. He was knowingly, deliberately and   **A**
secretly acting, setting out to do something which would inevitably inflict
great harm on his principal. There being a duty on the defendant to protect
the interests of his principal, then, if Mr. Tully had expressed any dissatisfaction
as to the position, the defendant should have found out any grievance which Mr.
Tully thought he had and should have gone to the plaintiff, who was the defendant's principal. It may well be that there was a misunderstanding in Mr.   **B**
Tully's mind about the affair with Mr. Penman, and, if the defendant had gone
to the plaintiff about this, there might well have been an opportunity for him
and Mr. Tully to have sorted it out and to have cleared up the misunderstanding.
I think that there was what was accurately described by counsel for the plaintiff
as a " conspiracy of silence " between the defendant and Mr. Tully. The defendant said that, if he disclosed the existence of this agreement at once to his   **C**
principal, he would betray Mr. Tully's confidence, and so he was silent in the
interests of Mr. Tully and to his principal's detriment. It apparently never
occurred to the defendant that, while he was still employed by the plaintiff, he
could not discuss any offer Mr. Tully made; he could not possibly do that until
his agreement with the plaintiff was terminated. I am satisfied that, in accepting
the offer, by such conduct the defendant was guilty of breach of duty in regard   **D**
to the agreement, implied therein by law, that the defendant would serve the
plaintiff with good faith and fidelity.

On looking at the authorities I am supported by *Wessex Dairies, Ltd.* v. *Smith*
(2), where these words of A. L. SMITH, L.J., are quoted (3):

> " ' I think that it is a necessary implication which must be engrafted on
> such a contract that the servant undertakes to serve his master with good   **E**
> faith and fidelity. That is what was said in *Lamb* v. *Evans* (4), and I
> entirely agree with it '."

When this matter was considered later in *Hivac, Ltd.* v. *Park Royal Scientific
Instruments, Ltd.* (5), LORD GREENE, M.R., said this:

> ". . . it has been said on many occasions that an employee owes a duty of   **F**
> fidelity to his employer. As a general proposition that is indisputable.
> The practical difficulty in any given case is to find exactly how far that
> rather vague duty of fidelity extends."

Then he said this (6):

> ". . . he . . . may be, disabling himself from performing his duties to his
> real employer and placing himself in an embarrassing position."   **G**

Later he said (7):

> ". . . ' During the subsistence of the contract of service and during his
> master's time the servant has to look after, not his own interests, but those of
> his master.' "

There is also this passage (8):   **H**

> " On the other hand, it would be deplorable if it were laid down that a
> workman could consistently with his duty to his employer, knowingly,
> deliberately and secretly set himself to do in his spare time something
> which would inflict great harm on his employer's business."

In the judgment of MORTON, L.J., there is this short passage (9):   **I**

---

(2) [1935] All E.R. Rep. 75 at p. 78; [1935] 2 K.B. at p. 88.
(3) In *Robb* v. *Green,* [1895] 1 Q.B. 315 at p. 320; see also [1895-99] All E.R. Rep.
1053 at pp. 1056, 1057.
(4) [1893] 1 Ch. 218.
(5) [1946] 1 All E.R. 350 at p. 353; [1946] Ch. 169 at p. 174.
(6) [1946] 1 All E.R. at p. 354; [1946] Ch. at p. 174.
(7) [1946] 1 All E.R. at p. 354; [1946] Ch. at p. 175, quoting GREER, L.J., in *Wessex
Dairies, Ltd.* v. *Smith*, [1935] 2 K.B. at p. 84; [1935] All E.R. Rep. at p. 76.
(8) [1946] 1 All E.R. at p. 356; [1946] Ch. at p. 178.
(9) [1946] 1 All E.R. at p. 357; [1946] C.h at p. 180.

A

"... but I do say that in my view the obligation of fidelity subsists so long as the contract of service subsists, and even in his spare time an employee does owe that obligation of fidelity."

These cases seem to me, to give support to the view which I have taken, that, in entering on that agreement with Mr. Tully, the defendant was committing a breach of the duty of fidelity and good faith he owed to the plaintiff.

B

Now I have to assess damages. What the plaintiff has lost is a chance; he has lost the chance of retaining the work of Mr. Tully. This question of the assessment of damages of a lost chance was considered in *Chaplin* v. *Hicks* (10). In the course of his judgment, VAUGHAN WILLIAMS, L.J., said (11):

C

" I do not agree with the contention that, if certainty is impossible of attainment, the damages for a breach of contract are unassessable."

Then a little later on, he said (11):

" But the fact that damages cannot be assessed with certainty does not relieve the wrong-doer of the necessity of paying damages for his breach of contract."

D

Then there is this passage in the judgment of FLETCHER MOULTON, L.J. (12):

" But in most cases it may be said that there is no recognised measure of damages, and that the jury must give what they think to be an adequate solatium under all the circumstances of the case."

FARWELL, L.J., said this (13):

E

" Now, the expression ' almost to a certainty ' means that the contemplated event is very probable, and the fact that it is very probable only increases the amount of damages which a jury would give."

This breach by the defendant deprived the plaintiff of the opportunity of retaining Mr. Tully's work. It might well have been that he would have continued to handle the work, and that he would have kept it if the defendant had acquired a

F

partnership in this firm or had remained an assistant solicitor with the firm. It may well be that, if the defendant had gone on—and it was only a question of arranging terms with the plaintiff—Mr. Tully might well have accepted the defendant as a partner and have been quite happy to let the firm carry on with the work. The defendant said that it was this personal animosity which Mr. Tully had towards the plaintiff which was of very great importance; he had only

G

seen the plaintiff once and Mr. Penman normally did the work for him. Having seen Mr. Tully in the witness-box, I am satisfied that, in the way of business, he would not allow any sort of personal animosity to interfere. I am satisfied, therefore, that the breach of duty deprived the plaintiff of the chance of retaining Mr. Tully as a client. I have to consider the figures. I estimate that the gross fees for twelve months would be £4,680. I was told that the figure put on office

H

expenses was about fifty-four per cent., so, therefore, profit for the twelve months' period would be in the neighbourhood of £2,000. Estimating as reasonably as I can, and doing the best that I can, I think that a proper sum to award in all the circumstances of the case would be £500. There will be judgment for the plaintiff for £500 for that breach, and 40s. for the other breach in connexion with Mrs. Stanford.

Judgment for the plaintiff.

I

Solicitors: *Sanders, Penman & Co.*, Brentwood (for the plaintiff); *Roney & Co.* (for the defendant).

[*Reported by* MARY COLTON, *Barrister-at-Law.*]

(10) [1911-13] All E.R. Rep. 224; [1911] 2 K.B. 786.
(11) [1911] 2 K.B. at p. 792; [1911-12] All E.R. Rep. at p. 227.
(12) [1911] 2 K.B. at p. 796; [1911-13] All E.R. Rep. at p. 229.
(13) [1911] 2 K.B. at p. 799; [1911-13] All E.R. Rep. at p. 231.

BENTWORTH FINANCE, LTD. v. LUBERT AND ANOTHER.   A

[COURT OF APPEAL, CIVIL DIVISION (Lord Denning, M.R., Salmon and Winn, L.JJ.), March 21, 1967.]

Hire-Purchase—Agreement—Implied condition—Log book—Motor car let on hire-purchase but log book not delivered—Hirer consequently did not licence and did not use—Suspensive condition—Contract not enforceable and instalments not recoverable as no log book provided.

Hire-Purchase—Indemnity—Implied condition that log book should be provided on hire-purchase of motor car—Log book not delivered—Contract unenforceable by finance company—Agreement to indemnify finance company against loss or damage arising from hire-purchase agreement being unenforceable inapplicable.

By a hire-purchase agreement the plaintiffs let a second-hand motor car to the first defendant on terms under which she was to pay twenty-four monthly instalments of £18 6s. 10d.   The second defendant agreed to indemnify the plaintiffs against all loss or damage which they might suffer arising out of or consequent on their having entered into the agreement or which might arise from the agreement being unenforceable against the hirer.   The first defendant obtained a car from dealers, who had since disappeared.   The car was left outside the first defendant's house, but no log book was with it. She did not get it licensed and did not use it.   After some months the plaintiffs re-possessed the car, and sued the defendants for instalments and for the cost of repairs to the car which was damaged.

Held: (i) it was an implied condition of the hire-purchase agreement that the log book should be supplied, and until it was supplied there was no contract and no instalment became due (see p. 811, letter E, and p. 812, letter C, post).

(ii) the loss or damage that the plaintiffs suffered did not arise from the hire-purchase agreement being unenforceable, but from the plaintiffs allowing the car to be delivered by the dealers without the log book (see p. 812, letters B and C, post).

[As to the duty of the owner to deliver goods let on hire-purchase, see 19 HALSBURY'S LAWS (3rd Edn.) 536, para. 864, and as to implied terms in hire-purchase agreements, see ibid., pp. 531, 532, para. 855; and for cases on the subject see 26 DIGEST (Repl.) 665, 666, *31-36.*]

Appeal.

This was an appeal by the plaintiffs, Bentworth Finance, Ltd., from a judgment of His Honour JUDGE McINTYRE, given on Oct. 25, 1966, at Wandsworth County Court dismissing the plaintiffs' action for £91 14s. 2d. arrears under a hire-purchase agreement and damages for breach of the agreement limited to £50. The action was brought against the first defendant, Mrs. Lubert, as the hirer; and was brought, as against the second defendant, Albert Mathieson, under an indemnity dated June 17, 1965, whereby the second defendant agreed to indemnify the plaintiffs against any loss suffered by them consequent on their having entered into the hire-purchase agreement with the first defendant.   The facts are set out in the judgment of LORD DENNING, M.R.

H. K. Woolf for the plaintiffs.   I

P. K. J. Thompson for the defendants.

LORD DENNING, M.R.: In June, 1965, the first defendant, Mrs. Lubert, signed a hire-purchase agreement.   By it the plaintiffs, Bentworth Finance, Ltd., purported to let to her an Austin car on hire-purchase.   The cash price was £475. She paid £120 down in cash.   There were to be twenty-four monthly instalments of £18 6s. 10d. per month, the first instalment being payable on July 21, 1965. The second defendant, Mr. Mathieson, signed an indemnity form.   A car was

A delivered to the first defendant. At any rate it was left outside her house; but she says that she did not use it, as it was not licensed and there was no log book with it. So she could not get it licensed or pay the tax. Nor could she use it on the road. She did not pay the instalments. In December, 1965, the plaintiffs re-took the car and sued for the instalments. They discovered that it had been damaged and needed repair. By an amendment they sued for the
B cost of repairs.

The judge said that in this transaction there was an implied condition that there should be a log book and that the hirer would not become liable unless and until it was handed over. I think that he was right. It is the common understanding of people that, if a car is bought or is taken on hire-purchase, the log book will be provided. There is a great difference between the price of a car
C *with* the log book and the price of a car *without* the log book. The absence of it gives rise to suspicion that the seller has a doubtful title. In short, the log book, although not a document of title, is very good evidence of title. It is a practical necessity also for the hirer to have the log book. He has to produce it in order to get the car licensed, so as to be on the road; or else he has to explain its absence, so as to get a duplicate.

D There was evidence supporting this condition. Early in August two young men, said to be from the plaintiffs, came to see about the car. Mr. Lubert told them: " We have not got the log book. We cannot licence the car and pay the tax until we get the log book." The young men said that it would come within a day or two. Mr. Lubert said: " We are ready to pay the instalments if you produce the log book." But they never did produce the log book. In the
E circumstances I think that the contract did not come into operation. The provision of the log book was a condition on which the very existence of the contract depended. It was, in technical language, a suspensive condition. Until the log book was provided, there was no contract of hire-purchase at all. No instalments, therefore, fell due.

There was some evidence that the car got damaged in December, 1965. Exactly
F how does not appear. The plaintiffs claim £50 damages on account of it. They relied on a clause on the back of the hire-purchase agreement; but, as the contract did not come into operation until the log book was provided, this clause did not come into operation at all.

It seems to me very important, as it did to the judge, that the court should uphold the necessity for a log book in these transactions. The dealers appear to
G have disappeared. The judge said:

" We all know that there is a big market in stolen cars and log books in South London, that the dealers sounded like rogues selling from a bombed-site pitch and their disappearance roused the greatest suspicion as to their title to this car and therefore to the plaintiffs' title to the one that reached
H the first defendant and her husband. A genuine log book was therefore of great importance to the first defendant and she could not be blamed for not even applying for a duplicate in the particular circumstances of this case."

I entirely agree with those observations. It seems to me that she was not bound
I to apply for a duplicate. That is only available, as counsel for the plaintiffs said, if it is shown that the original was lost, destroyed or mutilated. The first defendant was not bound to go and make any such plea to the licensing authorities. She was entitled to say to the dealer or the plaintiffs: " Produce the log book. Until you do, there is no contract." There may, of course, be circumstances in which the condition may be waived by taking delivery of the car and using it; but no such waiver was proved here.

Then counsel for the plaintiffs argued that even if the first defendant were not liable, nevertheless the second defendant was liable. He signed a form of indemnity which was annexed to the hire-purchase agreement. Under it he **A** agreed to indemnify the plaintiffs

" against all loss, damage or expense which you may suffer and all claims, costs or expenses made against you or incurred by you in any way arising out of or consequent upon your having entered into such agreement howsoever arising including such loss or damage as aforesaid which may arise from the said agreement being unenforceable against the hirer." **B**

Counsel for the plaintiffs submitted that the loss or damage arose from the plaintiffs' entering into the agreement or from its being unenforceable. I do not think that their claim is good. The loss or damage did not arise from those causes. It arose from other matters altogether. It arose from the plaintiffs allowing the dealers to hand over the car without the log book. I think that the judge came to a right decision in this case and I would dismiss the appeal. **C**

 SALMON, L.J.: I agree.

 WINN, L.J.: I also agree.

Appeal dismissed.

Solicitors: *H. Stock & Co.* (for the plaintiffs, the finance company); *V. J. Gersten* (for the defendants). **D**

[*Reported by* F. GUTTMAN, ESQ., *Barrister-at-Law.*]

RADSTOCK CO-OPERATIVE & INDUSTRIAL SOCIETY, LTD. **E**
v. NORTON-RADSTOCK URBAN DISTRICT COUNCIL.

[CHANCERY DIVISION (Ungoed-Thomas, J.), February 14, 15, 16, 17, March 9, 1967.]

Nuisance—Sewer—Obstruction to flow of river caused by pipe of sewer constructed by local authority beneath river bed but becoming exposed as river bed washed away—Damage to plaintiffs' property from eddies caused—Sewer not **F** *out of repair—Whether any breach of duty to plaintiffs by statute or common law established—Covenant, in lease demising sewerage rights, that local authority would not interfere with flow of water in river—Benefit of covenant not assigned to plaintiffs subsequently becoming riparian owners—Statutory powers of sewage disposal overriding lease.*

In 1907 the defendants' predecessors in title, Radstock Urban District **G** Council, obtained by agreement under s. 14 of the Public Health Act, 1875, a lease for ninety-nine years enabling them to provide a sewer across the River Somer. By cl. 14 of the lease the council covenanted with the lessor (which term was defined to include assigns) that the council would not interfere with the flow of water in the river. The sewer was built and the relevant part of it was laid across and in the bed of the River Somer. The **H** sewer vested by statute in the council and had since remained vested in them or their successors, the defendants, as local authority, the relevant statutory provisions* overriding pro tanto the lease. Subsequently the plaintiffs acquired from the freeholder first (in 1915) the lease and later (in 1953) the freehold of land including the relevant part of the bed of the River Somer. There was no assignment of the benefit of cl. 14 of the lease of 1907 to the **I** plaintiffs. Without any fault on the part of the council or the defendants the bed of the river became washed away, and the pipe of the sewer became exposed. The exposed pipe caused eddies in the flow of water which damaged the plaintiffs' property. In August, 1965, the plaintiffs sued the defendants for an injunction and damages. Their claim was put on three grounds, (a)

---

* The relevant provisions are, in particular, s. 13 and s. 14 of the Act of 1875; s. 15 (1) (iii), s. 20 and s. 31 of the Public Health Act, 1936; see p. 817, letters A to C, G and H, and p. 818, letter B, post.

A   nuisance at common law by interference with the flow of water in the river
to the plaintiffs' riparian property, (b) that the water was injuriously affected
within s. 331* of the Public Health Act, 1936, by being diverted by the
defendants' pipe with consequential damage to the plaintiffs, and (c) breach
of cl. 14 of the lease of 1907. On a preliminary point whether, on the
facts pleaded, the plaintiffs were entitled in law to the relief claimed,

B   **Held:** the plaintiffs were not so entitled, and accordingly the action
would be dismissed, for the following reasons—

(i) in order to fix the defendants with liability in nuisance by interference
with the flow of water, a failure of duty on their part to the plaintiffs must
be established, but the sewer had been lawfully laid and remained in good
order, and to construct the sewer on the river bed in a manner which did not

C   affect the flow of water was not open to objection on the ground that some
change might occur outside the sewer which would cause it in future to
affect the flow of water; moreover, the duty under s. 23† of the Public Health
Act, 1936, did not impose on the defendants duty to maintain the land or
conditions outside the sewer (see p. 821, letter C, p. 822, letter A, p. 823,
letter F, and p. 825, letter D, post).

D   *Moore* v. *Lambeth Waterworks Co.* ((1886), 17 Q.B.D. 462) followed.
Dictum of LORD BLACKBURN in *Orr Ewing* v. *Colquhoun* ((1877), 2 App.
Cas. at pp. 861, 862) applied.

(ii) s. 331 of the Public Health Act, 1936, did not create any liability
additional to nuisance at common law, and nuisance was not established
for the reason stated at (i) above (see p. 825, letters F and H, post).

E   *Roberts* v. *Gwyrfai District Council* ([1899] 2 Ch. 608) distinguished.
(iii) cl. 14 of the lease of 1907 did not constitute a condition of the exercise
of some right by the defendants non-compliance with which would be
restrained if the right were exercised; moreover by virtue of the Public
Health Act, 1936, the defendants were not dependent on the terms of the
lease for conveying sewage but could rely on their overriding statutory

F   powers (see p. 826, letters F and G, post).
Westhoughton Urban District Council v. *Wigan Coal and Iron Co., Ltd.*
([1919] 1 Ch. 159) distinguished.

[As to duties arising in relation to the diversion or obstruction of water in
streams, see 28 HALSBURY'S LAWS (3rd Edn.) 162, para. 231, text and note (*l*);
39 ibid., 523, para. 693; and for cases on the subject, see 47 DIGEST (Repl.)

G   656-666, *162-252.*
As to freedom from liability for acts done in the exercise of statutory powers
without negligence, see 30 HALSBURY'S LAWS (3rd Edn.) 690, 691, p. 694, para.
1335 (express proviso preserving liability for nuisance); and for cases on the
subject, see 38 DIGEST (Repl.) 13-18, *49-77.* As to the need to establish negligence in an action in respect of statutory sewage disposal, see 31 HALSBURY'S

H   LAWS (3rd Edn.) 223, para. 325.
As to the vesting and maintenance of public sewers, see 31 HALSBURY'S
LAWS (3rd Edn.) p. 200, para. 294, p. 209, para. 304; and as to the construction
of sewers crossing watercourses, see ibid., p. 206, para. 299.]

Cases referred to:

I   *Baron* v. *Portslade Urban District Council,* [1900] 2 Q.B. 588; 69 L.J.Q.B. 899;
83 L.T. 363; 38 Digest (Repl.) 161, *28.*
Coverdale v. *Charlton,* (1878), 4 Q.B.D. 104; 48 L.J.Q.B. 128; 40 L.T. 88;
43 J.P. 268; 26 Digest (Repl.) 344, *621.*
Dudley Corpn., Re, [1881-85] All E.R. Rep. 565; (1881), 8 Q.B.D. 86; 51
L.J.Q.B. 121; sub nom. *Dudley Corpn.* v. *Earl of Dudley's Settled
Estate Trustees,* 45 L.T. 733; 40 J.P. 340; 41 Digest (Repl.) 41, *280.*

* Section 331 is set out at p. 818, letter D, post.
† Section 23, so far as material, is set out at p. 817, letter I, to p. 818, letter A, post.

Dunne v. *North Western Gas Board*, [1963] 3 All E.R. 916; [1964] 2 Q.B. 806; **A**
    [1964] 2 W.L.R. 164; Digest (Cont. Vol. A) 626, *93a.*

Great Central Ry. Co. v. *Hewlett*, [1916-17] All E.R. Rep. 1027; [1916] 2 A.C.
    511; 85 L.J.K.B. 1705; 115 L.T. 349; 38 Digest (Repl.) 6, *14.*

Greenock Corpn. v. *Caledonian Ry. Co.*, [1916-17] All E.R. Rep. 426; [1917]
    A.C. 556; 86 L.J.P.C. 185; 117 L.T. 483; 81 J.P. 269; 36 Digest
    (Repl.) 166, *885.*   **B**

Hickman v. *Maisey*, [1900] 1 Q.B. 752; 69 L.J.Q.B. 511; 82 L.T. 312; 26
    Digest (Repl.) 326, *449.*

Manchester Corpn. v. *Farnworth*, [1929] All E.R. Rep. 90; [1930] A.C. 171;
    99 L.J.K.B. 83; 94 J.P. 62; sub nom. *Farnworth* v. *Manchester Corpn.*,
    142 L.T. 145; 38 Digest (Repl.) 38, *193.*

Moore v. *Lambeth Waterworks Co.*, (1886), 17 Q.B.D. 462; 55 L.J.Q.B. 304; **C**
    55 L.T. 309; 50 J.P. 1756; 38 Digest (Repl.) 41, *213.*

Orr Ewing v. *Colquhoun*, (1877), 2 App. Cas. 839; 26 Digest (Repl.) 326, *442.*

Roberts v. *Gwyrfai District Council*, [1899] 2 Ch. 608; 68 L.J.Ch. 757; 81 L.T.
    465; 64 J.P. 52; 36 Digest (Repl.) 332, *754.*

Sedleigh-Denfield v. *O'Callaghan*, [1940] 3 All E.R. 349; [1940] A.C. 880;
    164 L.T. 72; sub nom. *Sedleigh-Denfield* v. *St. Joseph's Society for* **D**
    Foreign Missions, 109 L.J.K.B. 893; 36 Digest (Repl.) 316, *629.*

Smeaton v. *Ilford Corpn.*, [1954] 1 All E.R. 923; [1954] Ch. 450; [1954] 2
    W.L.R. 668; 118 J.P. 290; 38 Digest (Repl.) 162, *32.*

Seymor's Case, (1612), 10 Co. Rep. 95b; 77 E.R. 1070; 38 Digest (Repl.)
    794, *103.*

Thompson v. *Brighton Corpn., Oliver* v. *Horsham Local Board*, [1894] 1 Q.B. 332; **E**
    63 L.J.Q.B. 181; 70 L.T. 206; 58 J.P. 297; 26 Digest (Repl.) 420, *1292.*

Tithe Redemption Commission v. *Runcorn Urban District Council*, [1954]
    1 All E.R. 653; [1954] Ch. 383; [1954] 2 W.L.R. 518; 118 J.P. 265;
    19 Digest (Repl.) 531, *3670.*

Tunbridge Wells Corpn. v. *Baird*, [1896] A.C. 434; 65 L.J.Q.B. 451; 74 L.T.
    385; 60 J.P. 788; 26 Digest (Repl.) 345, *624.*   **F**

Westhoughton Urban District Council v. *Wigan Coal and Iron Co., Ltd.*, [1919]
    1 Ch. 159; 88 L.J.Ch. 60; 120 L.T. 242; 33 Digest (Repl.) 825, *876.*

Ystradyfodwg and Pontypridd Main Sewerage Board v. *Bensted (Surveyor of*
    Taxes), [1906] 1 K.B. 294; affd. C.A., [1907] 1 K.B. 490; affd. H.L.,
    [1907] A.C. 264; 76 L.J.K.B. 876; 97 L.T. 141; 71 J.P. 425; 28 Digest
    (Repl.) 5, *3.*   **G**

Action.

This was an action commenced by writ issued on Aug. 6, 1965, by the plaintiffs, Radstock Co-operative and Industrial Society, Ltd., against the defendants,
Norton-Radstock Urban District Council, who were the local authority for that
urban district for the purposes of the Public Health Act, 1936. By their amended **H**
statement of claim, re-served on Feb. 21, 1967, the plaintiffs pleaded, among
other matters, that they were owners of premises at Radstock which consisted
of a bakery shop and other buildings and included a bridge carrying a private
carriageway over the River Somer for the use of the plaintiffs. They pleaded
that the defendants had laid a sewer in 1904 by virtue of powers conferred by
the Public Health Act, 1875, through the land of the plaintiffs, under an agree- **I**
ment dated Aug. 26, 1904, between Earl Waldegrave, the plaintiffs' predecessor
in title, and the defendants, and under a lease dated Mar. 15, 1907, between the
same parties, and that the sewer was vested in the defendants under the Public
Health Act, 1936; that the sewer was laid across land of the plaintiffs and across
the river, and was laid in the bed of the river; that it was a term of the lease by
cl. 14, that " the council will not interfere with the flow of or pollute the water
in the River Somer ". The plaintiffs pleaded the demise to them of the premises
by lease dated June 1, 1915, by Earl Waldegrave, and that in 1915 the plaintiffs

A constructed a bridge in the same line as the sewer in such manner as to make the bridge independent of the sewer and to avoid interference therewith. The plaintiffs pleaded their purchase of the reversion on Apr. 10, 1953, to their premises, including the bed and banks of the river within their boundaries. They pleaded that the sewer was now above the level of the bed of the river and by reason thereof the water flowing along the course of the river was obstructed

B and eddies and forces of water in the river created by or resulting from the obstruction had eroded the banks of the river and undermined and damaged the bridge of the plaintiffs. The plaintiffs claimed (a) £3,500 damages in respect of injury to the bridge and other adjacent property; and (b) an injunction restraining the defendants from continuing the sewer above the bed of the river. By an order made on July 15, 1966, by GOFF, J., the following question was

C set down for hearing before trial, pursuant to R.S.C., Ord. 33, r. 3, viz., whether on the footing that all the allegations of facts contained in the statement of claim could be proved the plaintiffs could as a matter of law be entitled to damages or an injunction.

The cases noted below* were cited during the argument in addition to those referred to in the judgment.

D *Douglas Frank*, Q.C., and *H. Parrish* for the plaintiffs.
Raymond Walton, Q.C., and *W. H. Goodhart* for the defendants.

Cur. adv. vult.

Mar. 9. **UNGOED-THOMAS, J.**, read the following judgment: This
E application raises a preliminary question for decision under an order made on July 15, 1966. The question is whether, on the footing of the facts alleged in the statement of claim, the plaintiffs are entitled in law to an injunction or damages as claimed.

The plaintiffs' complaint is of obstruction to the flow of a river caused by a sewer vested in the defendants resulting in eddies which damaged the plaintiffs'
F property. The sewer was laid long ago in the river bed where it was harmless but in recent years part of the river bed has been washed away exposing the pipe to the flow of the water and so we have the eddies complained of. The river is the River Somer in Somerset, and the plaintiffs' damaged property is riparian property and a bridge.

Between 1904 and 1907 the defendants' predecessors in title, the Radstock
G Urban District Council, sewered their district. On Mar. 15, 1907, the council took from the plaintiffs' predecessor in title, Earl Waldegrave, a lease to enable them to provide for a sewer without resorting to compulsory powers. The lease gave power to convey sewage by specified sewers, maintain the sewerage system and enter specified lands for that purpose. The council had powers to take the lease under s. 14 of the Public Health Act, 1875, to which I will come later. The

H lease is expressed to be made between Earl Waldegrave

"(. . . hereinafter called ' the lessor ' which expression shall where the context admits include his heirs assigns and successors in title or other the person or persons for the time being entitled to receive the rent hereby reserved . . .) "

I and, of course, the urban district council. The operative part provides that

---

* *Reg.* v. *Pratt*, (1855), 4 E. & B. 860; *Taylor* v. *Oldham Corpn.*, (1876), 4 Ch.D. 395; *Bathurst Borough* v. *Macpherson* [1874-80] All E.R. Rep. 703; (1879), 4 App. Cas. 256; *Rolls* v. *St. George the Martyr, Southwark, Vestry*, (1880), 14 Ch.D. 785; *Strettons' Derby Brewery Co.* v. *Derby Corpn.*, [1891-94] All E.R. Rep. 731; [1894] 1 Ch. 431; *A.-G.* v. *Conduit Colliery Co.*, [1895] 1 Q.B. 301; *A.-G.* v. *Tod Heatley*, [1895-99] All E.R. Rep. 636; [1897] 1 Ch. 560; *Gerrard* v. *Crowe*, [1920] All E.R. Rep. 266; [1921] 1 A.C. 395; *Fisher* v. *Ruislip-Northwood Urban District Council and Middlesex County Council*, [1945] 2 All E.R. 458; [1945] 1 K.B. 584; *Railway Executive* v. *West Riding of Yorkshire County Council*, [1949] 1 All E.R. 836; [1949] Ch. 423.

"... in consideration of the expense incurred and to be incurred by the   A
council in constructing and making the approach road sewage tanks
buildings pipes ..."

and so on, the lessor—that is Earl Waldegrave—demises to the council various
matters mentioned in the lease, including as fourthly mentioned,

" Full and free power and liberty to convey sewage and waste water   B
from the town and district of Radstock aforesaid and such other districts
as the council may from time to time elect to drain under the hereditaments
shown on the said plan hereto annexed and thereon coloured blue, (a) by
means of continuous lines ... of pipes ..."

and so on as therein mentioned.   It also demised, as it expressed it, full power
to maintain the pipes and other works and full power to enter on specified   C
pieces of land for such purposes.   The habendum provides that the "... land
powers liberties and premises ..." conveyed to the council should be held for
ninety-nine years from June 24, 1904, for the purposes of the disposal of the
sewerages which were there mentioned.

The lease contains covenants by the council with the lessor amongst other
things by cl. 5 to construct the sewage works therein mentioned and maintain   D
them, and by cl. 14, amongst other things, it is provided, "... the council will
not interfere with the flow of or pollute the water in the River Somer ".   There
is also at the end of the lease a proviso in a common form that if the rent is
unpaid or default is made in the performance or observance of any of the covenants, it should be lawful for the lessor to re-enter and remove the sewer pipes
and the other works, and that thereupon the grant and demise should determine.   E
The sewers were built, and the relevant part of the sewer is the part marked
M—N on the land coloured blue on the plan annexed to the lease.   This part
of the sewer, M—N, is part of the sewerage system which the lease contemplated.
It is common ground that the lease is valid only in so far as it is not contrary to
the Public Health Acts—as it is not possible to contract out of those statutes—
and that, therefore, for example, the clause in the lease (to which I referred)   F
for re-entry on non-payment of rent or breach of covenant is void: and under
s. 13 of the Public Health Act, 1875, and s. 20 of the Public Health Act, 1936, to
which I will refer later, sewers on construction vested and have since remained
vested under the statutes in the defendants or their predecessors in title, independently of the lease, which the statute overrides.

On June 1, 1915, a lease of the plaintiffs' premises mentioned in the statement   G
of claim was granted by Earl Waldegrave to the plaintiffs and the premises so
granted included relevant parts of the river bed of the River Somer.   There is
no reference in this lease to the sewer, but, in fact, on the lease plan there is
shown across the river a line corresponding to that part of the M—N line on the
plan of the 1907 lease.

On Apr. 10, 1953, the Waldegrave Estates Co., which was the successor in   H
title to Earl Waldegrave, conveyed to the plaintiffs the fee simple of the property
comprised in the 1915 lease to them.   There was no reference in this conveyance
to the 1907 lease to the council, and there was no express assignment of the benefit
of cl. 14 of that lease (which I have mentioned) by which the council covenanted
not to interfere with the flow of or pollute the water in the River Somer.   The
lease and conveyance to the plaintiffs were, in effect, of all relevant rights of   I
property except such as were included in the 1907 lease to the council or vested
by statute in the local authority.

The bed of the stream, without fault on the part of the defendants, has to
some extent been washed away with the results which I have already mentioned,
and so on Aug. 6, 1965, the writ in this action was issued.

I will now refer first to the relevant statutory provisions which are contained
in the Act of 1875, which was the Act in operation at the time of the 1907 lease,

A and to the Act of 1936 which replaced it. Section 13 of the Act of 1875 provided that sewers on their construction vested in the local authority. It read:

" All existing and future sewers within the district of a local authority, together with all buildings, works, materials and things belonging thereto [subject to exceptions which I will not mention] shall vest in and be under the control of such local authority . . ."

B
Section 14 authorised the local authority, inter alia, to take the lease, as it expressed it, ". . . respecting a sewer . . .". It provided:

" Any local authority may purchase or otherwise acquire from any person any sewer, or any right of making or of user or other right in or respecting a sewer . . ."

C
The rest of the section I need not read.

Section 15 imposed on the local authority an obligation to make, to maintain and repair sewers. Section 16 gave them powers to make sewers over land including in land water. Section 18 gave them power to alter and discontinue sewers. Section 19 provided that local authorities should cause sewers not to be a nuisance, and it was in these terms:

D

" Every local authority shall cause the sewers belonging to them to be constructed covered ventilated and kept so as not to be a nuisance or injurious to health, and to be properly cleansed and emptied."

Section 308 provided compensation for the exercise of powers under the Act, and s. 332 provided that a local authority was not authorised to affect water injuriously except with the consent in writing of the person entitled to prevent it, and was in these terms:

E

" Nothing in this Act shall be construed to authorise any local authority to injuriously affect any reservoir canal river or stream or the feeders thereof or the supply quality or fall of water contained in any reservoir canal river stream or in the feeders thereof, in cases where any body of persons or person would, if this Act had not passed, have been entitled by law to prevent or be relieved against the injuriously affecting such reservoir canal river stream feeders or such supply quality or fall of water, unless the local authority first obtain the consent in writing of the body of persons or person so entitled as aforesaid."

F

G The Public Health Act, 1936, which came into force on Oct. 1, 1937, imposes, by s. 14, a duty on the local authority to provide sewers. By s. 15 (1) (iii) it is provided that a local authority may take a lease of a sewer. It is in less wide terms than the terms of the corresponding s. 14 of the Act of 1875, but this is doubtless due to the fact that in the meantime s. 157 of the Local Government Act, 1933, gave power to the local authority to lease land for any of their purposes,

H and this made the wide terms of s. 14 of the Act of 1875 superfluous.

Section 20 of the Act of 1936 continues the vesting of sewers already vested in the local authority and provides that leased sewers are also so to vest. It is in these terms:

" (1) All sewers within the meaning of the Public Health Act, 1875, and sewage disposal works which, by virtue of the provisions of that Act, were immediately before the commencement of this Act vested in a local authority, shall continue to be vested in them, and there shall also vest in them . . . (*b*) all sewers and sewage disposal works constructed by them at their expense, or acquired by them."

I

Section 22, corresponding to s. 18 of the Act of 1875, provides that a local authority may alter or close a public sewer, and s. 23, corresponding to s. 15 of the Act of 1875, imposes a duty to maintain sewers and that reads:

" It shall be the duty of every local authority to maintain, cleanse and

empty all public sewers vested in them, subject, however, to their right A
under the next succeeding section to recover in certain cases the expenses,
or a part of the expenses . . ."

I need not refer to the next section. Section 31, corresponding to s. 19 of the
Act of 1875, provides that the local authority is so to discharge its functions as
not to create a nuisance, and it reads:

" A local authority shall so discharge their functions under the foregoing B
provisions of this Part of this Act as not to create a nuisance."

This Part of the Act (Part 2), of course, deals with sewers. Section 331, corresponding to s. 332 of the Act of 1875, provides that the Public Health Act, 1936,
does not authorise a local authority to affect injuriously water without the
consent of the person entitled to prevent or be relieved against it, and that section C
reads:

" Nothing in this Act shall authorise a local authority injuriously to
affect any reservoir, canal, watercourse, river or stream, or any feeder
thereof, or the supply, quality or fall of water contained in, or in any feeder
of, any reservoir, canal, watercourse, river or stream without the consent
of any person who would, if this Act had not been passed, have been entitled D
by law to prevent, or be relieved against, the injurious affection of, or of the
supply, quality or fall of water contained in, that reservoir, canal, watercourse
river, stream or feeder."

The statement of claim has been attacked for the defendants not on matters
which can be cured by amendment but on the substance of the case which it is
designed to present. It states by para. 1 that the plaintiffs are the owners E
of premises, which it describes, in the urban district of Norton-Radstock and
that such premises include a bridge over the River Somer. It states in para. 2
that the defendants are the local authority for this urban district for the purposes
of Part 2 of the Public Health Act, 1936. Paragraph 3 reads:

" The defendants laid a sewer in 1904 by virtue of their powers in the F
Public Health Act, 1875, through the land of the plaintiffs under an agreement dated Aug. 26, 1904, between Earl Waldegrave (the predecessor in
title of the plaintiffs) and the defendants and under a lease dated Mar. 15,
1907, between the same parties and the said sewer is vested in the defendants
under s. 20 of the Public Health Act, 1936."

Paragraph 4 reads: G

" The said sewer was laid across the land of the plaintiffs and across the
said river between the points 35 and 36 marked on the plan attached to the
said lease and was laid in the bed of the said river and it was a term of cl. 14
of the said lease that ' the council will not interfere with the flow of or pollute
the water in the River Somer '." H

Then it alleges, by para. 5, the lease of June 1, 1915, by which Earl Waldegrave
demised the premises to the plaintiffs. Paragraph 7 has since been amended,
and, as amended, provides:

" On Apr. 10, 1953, the plaintiffs purchased and there was conveyed to
them by Earl Waldegrave the freehold reversion of the said premises which I
premises included the bed and the banks of that part of the said river
which was within the boundaries of the said premises."

Then by amendment there is a new para. 9 which reads:

" The plaintiffs contend that the defendants are liable to the plaintiffs as
follows:—(i) In nuisance at common law. (ii) In negligence for failure to
exercise their statutory powers to avoid the creation of a nuisance or an
injury to the plaintiff. (iii) For breach of the aforementioned covenant

A   (viz., cl. 14 of the 1907 lease).   (iv) For breach of the provisions of s. 331 of the Public Health Act, 1936."

Then follows the old para. 9 which is amended to be para. 10 and alleges:

B   " The said sewer is now above the level of the bed of the river and by reason thereof the water flowing along the course of the said river is obstructed and eddies and forces of water in the said river created by or resulting from the obstruction have eroded the banks of the said river and undermined and damaged the said bridge of the plaintiffs referred to in para. 1 and para. 8 hereof."

Then the statement of claim gives particulars of that damage.

C   The allegation of negligence in para. 9 (ii) of the statement of claim is directed to alleging negligence, in so far as it is a necessary ingredient in establishing in the circumstances of this case—which I will consider later—nuisance for which the defendants may be held responsible.   As appears from para. 9 of the statement of claim and the plaintiffs' case as presented before me, the whole basis of that case is obstruction or interference with the flow of the river by the defendants' sewer.   The plaintiffs' case was eventually put in three ways.   It was said that the defendants were liable (i) in common law nuisance constituted by obstruction

D   or interference by the defendants' pipe with the flow of water to the plaintiffs' riparian property; (ii) because the water was " injuriously affected " within s. 331 of the Act of 1936 by being diverted by the defendants' pipe, with consequential damage to the plaintiffs; (iii) for breach of cl. 14 of the 1907 lease not to " interfere with the flow of . . . the water in the River Somer ".

E   The defendants submitted a short answer to all these three ways of putting the plaintiffs' case.   They submitted that " obstruction ", " interference ", " injuriously affecting " all involve doing something to the pre-existing situation as contrasted with a mere change in that situation leading to the obstruction, interference or injuriously affecting.   They said that it was the flow that washed away part of the bed of the river and then battered against the sewer, and not

F   the sewer that washed away the bed and then battered against the flow of the river.   Certainly the sewer lay harmlessly in the bed and it was not it nor the defendants that took off its covering which led to the trouble.   The validity of the plaintiffs' submissions does not, however, turn exclusively on the dictionary meaning of " obstruction ", " interference " or " injuriously affecting " without regard to the nature of the responsibility or liability for such occurrences.   The

G   submissions, therefore, cannot in my view be satisfactorily considered apart from the law on the liability for these occurrences.

So I turn to the law.   First, it will be convenient to consider the nature of the defendants' and the plaintiffs' interests in, and rights relating to, the sewer.   I take it to be now well-established that what vests in the local authority in respect of a sewer is not an easement but a " material thing ", land, " a hereditament " capable of actual occupation and consisting of the pipe and what it

H   encloses.   The local authority has even a right of subjacent support for the pipe. This hereditament vests for an estate in fee simple.   The estate in fee simple is a determinable fee subject to defeasance on the hereditament ceasing to be a sewer: but this does not prejudice the whole fee simple vesting in the local authority and there is no reversion or remainder on the determination of the local authority's interest, but merely a right in the person through whose land the local authority's

I   sewer hereditament exists to have that hereditament back on such determination.   (See *Coverdale* v. *Charlton* (1), a highway case; *Re Dudley Corpn.* (2), on subjacent support; *Ystradyfodwg and Pontypridd Main Sewerage Board* v. *Bensted (Surveyor of Taxes)* (3); *Tithe Redemption Commission* v. *Runcorn Urban District Council* (4); Note to *Seymor's Case* (5).)

(1) (1878), 4 Q.B.D. 104.   (2) [1881-1885] All E.R. Rep. 565; (1881), 8 Q.B.D. 86.
(3) [1906] 1 K.B. 294 at p. 308; [1907] 1 K.B. 490 at p. 499; [1907] A.C. 264 at p. 268.
(4) [1954] 1 All E.R. 653 at pp. 656, 661; [1954] Ch. 383 at pp. 398, 406.
(5) (1612), 10 Co. Rep. 95b.

The plaintiffs submitted that the defendants' property in a sewer was analogous **A** to an authority's property in a highway, and that the land in a highway vests in a highway authority subject to the vesting being limited to such rights of property as are necessary for the highway authority to carry out its statutory powers and duties.   This submission was a partial reflection of the more comprehensive argument advanced and rejected in *Tithe Redemption Commission* v. *Runcorn Urban District Council* (6).   In support of this submission words from LORD **B** HERSCHELL's speech in *Tunbridge Wells Corpn.* v. *Baird* (7) were quoted, namely:

"... it seems to me that the vesting of the street vests in the urban authority such property and such property only as is necessary for the control, protection, and maintenance of the street as a highway for public use."

C

Those words were used, however, in the context of a case dealing with rights in subsoil and with the extent of physical land which vests, and were not addressed to the nature of the rights within the material thing which does vest.   Further, *Hickman* v. *Maisey* (8), relied on for the plaintiffs, went on the footing that the soil of the highway was vested in the plaintiff and was never directed to the question of vesting in the local authority.   The submission is, in my view, **D** contrary to the authorities which I have mentioned and appears to me to be founded on a confusion between what vests and the purpose for which it vests. That land vests for a purpose makes it no more in the case of a local authority than of a charity or a limited company the purpose that vests and not the land.

I come now to the first way in which the plaintiffs put their case, namely, that the defendants are liable in common law nuisance, constituted by obstruction **E** or interference by the defendants' pipe with the flow of water to the plaintiffs' riparian property.   The defendants argue that as the flow is affected not by any change of any kind in the defendants' hereditament—namely the sewer— whether in use, situation or otherwise, there is no such nuisance or ground of liability in tort as is known to the law.   It was said that to incur liability for nuisance in respect of a property there must be more than continuation of a **F** property in exactly the same state without change at all on it.   In support, reference was made to definitions or descriptions of nuisance in SALMOND ON TORTS (13th Edn.), p. 182, CLERK AND LINDSELL ON TORTS (12th Edn.), para. 1213, and the speech of LORD ATKIN in *Sedleigh-Denfield* v. *O'Callaghan* (9); and certainly it is not contended by the plaintiffs that these definitions covered their first submission, so that I need not pause to consider them.

Other cases were mentioned to which I must refer.   First, I quote from the **G** headnote of *Moore* v. *Lambeth Waterworks Co.* (10), approved in all the speeches in the House of Lords in *Great Central Ry. Co.* v. *Hewlett* (11).   The headnote states:

" A fire-plug had been lawfully fixed in a highway by the defendants. Originally the top of the fire-plug had been level with the pavement of the **H** highway, but in consequence of the ordinary wearing away of the highway the fire-plug projected half an inch above the level of the pavement.   The fire-plug itself was in perfect repair.   The plaintiff, whilst passing along the highway, fell over the fire-plug and was hurt:—Held, that, as the fire-plug was in good repair, and had been lawfully fixed in the highway, no action by the plaintiff would lie against the defendants."

I

It would seem to me to have been an obvious truism that it does not follow that, because nobody else may be liable for the damage to the plaintiffs, therefore the defendants must be liable.   LORD ESHER, M.R., said (12):

---

(6) [1954] 1 All E.R. 653;   [1954] Ch. 383.   (7) [1896] A.C. 434 at p. 442.
(8) [1900] 1 Q.B. 752.
(9) [1940] 3 All E.R. 349 at p. 360;   [1940] A.C. 880 at p. 897.
(10) (1886), 17 Q.B.D. 462.   (11) [1916-17] All E.R. Rep. 1027;   [1916] 2 A.C. 511.
(12) (1886), 17 Q.B.D. at p. 466.

A
  " Now it is said that if the fire-plug had not been in the highway, the wearing down of the roadway was not sufficient to make the road so out of repair, as to render the authority having the care of it indictable. That is true."

Then he said (13):

B
  " I think that no action will lie by this plaintiff against the road authority; but it does not follow that because no action will lie against the road authority, therefore he can maintain an action against the defendants who have done no wrong."

To fix liability on the part of the defendants it must be established that they have failed in a duty to the plaintiffs, a duty cast on them by law, whether statute or common law. LINDLEY, L.J., said (14):

C

  " Suppose, for example, the pipes of this waterworks company to be somewhat below the level of the surface, and a storm to carry the whole of the surface away, so as to leave their pipes uncovered and projecting: I take it that the company could not be indicted for a nuisance for having the pipes so exposed, although the pipes might be an obstruction to the traffic. It appears to me, however, apart from authority, that the plaintiff has not shown, that these defendants have either by a matter of commission or omission neglected any duty which is cast upon them by law."

D

LORD ESHER, M.R., commented (15):

  " ' If the road is worn down, are they to mend the road? ' Ir was answered ' No, they cannot mend the road '. Then what are they to do? Why, they must cut down the fire-plug; as the road wears down, they must keep cutting down the fire-plug. That seems to be a curious liability to put upon the waterworks company."

E

It would, with respect, seem to me too to be a curious liability to put on the sewerage authority to move the sewer which might well prejudice the sewage system or, perhaps, restore the bed of the river which in this case belongs to the plaintiffs themselves.

F

  The plaintiffs did not suggest that the defendants should make good their own river bed, but they did suggest that they should remove the sewer. What duty is there on the defendants that can result in their having to take such a course? In *Moore* v. *Lambeth Waterworks Co.* (16) it was decided that there was no such analogous duty. The essential and distinctive circumstance there was as stated by LINDLEY, L.J. (17) and quoted with approval by LORD WRENBURY in *Great Central Ry. Co.* v. *Hewlett* (18):

G

  " ' The plug itself was not out of repair, and there was nothing the matter with it. It had not grown. It had not changed in any way '."

The same may be said of the sewer in our case, and that is similarly the essential and distinctive circumstance on which the defendants rely. In *Thompson* v. *Brighton Corpn.*, *Oliver* v. *Horsham Local Board* (19), the principle of *Moore* v. *Lambeth Waterworks Co.* (16) was applied to the case of a sewer. In that case a sewer grating projected above the level of a highway because the road had worn away and injured a horse which stumbled against it. A. L. SMITH, L.J., said (20):

H

I

  ". . . as long as the gratings lawfully and properly put down remained in perfect order, *Moore* v. *Lambeth Waterworks Co.* (16), in this court, has decided there is no breach of duty in the defendants in leaving the gratings alone."

---

(13) (1886), 17 Q.B.D. at p. 467.   (14) (1886), 17 Q.B.D. at p. 470.
(15) (1886), 17 Q.B.D. at p. 466.   (16) (1886), 17 Q.B.D. 462.
(17) (1886), 17 Q.B.D. at pp. 469, 470.
(18) [1916-17] All E.R. Rep. at p. 1033; [1916] 2 A.C. at p. 526.
(19) [1894] 1 Q.B. 332.   (20) [1894] 1 Q.B. at p. 342.

In our case the sewers were indisputably lawfully and properly put down and   A
remained in perfect order.

In *Greenock Corpn.* v. *Caledonian Ry. Co.* (21) the law in Scotland, equally
applicable in England, on the liability of a person who interferes with a natural
watercourse was thus stated by LORD FINLAY, L.C. (22):

> " That principle is—that if a person chooses upon a stream to make a
> great operation for collecting and damming up the water, for whatever   B
> purpose, he is bound, as the necessary condition of such an operation, to
> accomplish his object in such a way as to protect all persons lower down the
> stream from all danger. He must secure them against danger. It is not
> sufficient that he took all the pains which were thought at the time necessary
> and sufficient. They were exposed to no danger before the operation. He
> creates the danger and he must secure them against danger, so as to make   C
> them as safe notwithstanding his dam as they were before."

There was, however, clearly from the very outset and throughout interference
by the dam in that case with a natural watercourse, whereas here the pipe in its
bed, in the position from which it was not moved, constituted no interference
at all.   D

The plaintiffs relied on *Roberts* v. *Gwyrfai District Council* (23). In that case
the plaintiff as lower riparian owner was held entitled to an injunction restraining
the defendants from taking water from a lake whereby the flow of water in the
stream through the plaintiff's mill should be diminished, thereby injuriously
affecting, within s. 332 of the Public Health Act, 1875, the common law right
of the plaintiff to the accustomed flow. In that case SIR NATHANIEL LINDLEY,   E
M.R., said (24):

> " The right of the plaintiff as the owner and occupier of his mill is to have
> the water flow down the stream, which has its origin in the lake, in the
> accustomed way. That right is subject to the rights of the other riparian
> proprietors higher up the stream; but, subject to those rights, there is no
> right whatever to alter the flow of the water in its old accustomed way.   F
> If it is said that the alteration of the old flow is an improvement, that is a
> matter of opinion. There is no right to interfere with the accustomed flow of
> the water."

Then he said (25):

> " In my opinion these rights have been infringed, for, although [counsel   G
> for the defendants'] view is that the defendants are not entitled to do what
> they have done, they have in fact most materially altered the flow of the water
> to which the plaintiff is entitled."

A little later he said (26):

> " ' It is a matter quite immaterial whether, as riparian owner of Wayte's
> tenement, any injury has now been sustained or has not been sustained by   H
> the respondents. If the appellants are right, they would, at the end of
> twenty years, by the exercise of this claim of diversion, entirely defeat the
> incident of the property, the riparian right of Wayte's tenement. That is a
> consequence which the owner of Wayte's tenement has the right to come
> into the Court of Chancery to get restrained at once, by injunction, or declara-
> tion, as the case may be '."   I

---

(21) [1916-17] All E.R. Rep. 426; [1917] A.C. 556.
(22) [1916-17] All E.R. Rep. at pp. 430, 431; [1917] A.C. at p. 569 (quoting from
Lord Justice-Clerk HOPE in *Kerr* v. *Earl of Orkney* (1857), 20 Dunl. (Ct. of Sess.)
298 at p. 302).
(23) [1899] 2 Ch. 608.   (24) [1899] 2 Ch. at p. 612.
(25) [1899] 2 Ch. at p. 614.
(26) [1899] 2 Ch. at p. 614, quoting from LORD CAIRNS, L.C., in *Swindon Waterworks
Co.* v. *Wilts and Berks Canal Navigation Co.*, (1875), L.R. 7 H.L. 697 at p. 705.

A In that case, unlike the case before me, there was from the first an active interference with the flow of the water, and what the defendants did was never authorised under statute or otherwise. There was a clear, active interference with the plaintiff riparian owner's right to the unaltered flow of water which, though no actual damage had been sustained, might, if unrestrained, develop into a prescriptive right and thus convert what the defendants never had any right

B to do, into a right to the prejudice of the plaintiff's rights as riparian owner. The case thus does not affect the decisions already cited and is irrelevant to the submission for the defendants that for the defendants to incur liability in nuisance there must be more than the continuation of the property in exactly the same state without change at all on it.

In *Orr Ewing* v. *Colquhoun* (27) a Scottish case, it was decided that the appel
C lants had no right to execute any works which would interfere with or obstruct the navigation of a navigable river, and that the works complained of—in fact a bridge—did not do so. Lord Blackburn said (28):

"I think it clear law in England, that, except at the instance of a person (including the Crown) whose property is injured, or of the Crown in respect of an injury to a public right, there is no power to prevent a man making an
D erection on his own land, though covered with water, merely on a speculation that some change might occur that would render that piece of land, though not now part of the water way, at some future period available as part of it. I think that the land being covered by water is in such a case a mere accident, and that the defenders are as much at liberty to build on the bed of the river (if thereby they occasion no obstruction) as they would be to build on
E an island which might at some future period be swept away."

This passage indicates to my mind that to place or build something on a river bed which does not affect the flow of water is not open to objection on the ground that some change might occur, otherwise than in that thing, that might in the future cause it to affect the flow: and that such a change if it were to occur would
F make it no more open to objection than a change which swept away an island on which an erection was built.

In *Sedleigh-Denfield* v. *O'Callaghan* (29), the headnote, inter alia, states:

"On the respondents' land was a ditch in which at a later date was placed a pipe or culvert for carrying off rain water, the pipe not being laid by the respondents, or with their knowledge or consent, and thus by a trespasser.
G They, however, subsequently became aware, through their servants, of its existence and they in fact used it for the draining of their fields."

The crucial consideration in this case was that an artificial work, namely the pipe or culvert, replaced the former course of water and interfered with and impeded its flow and thus caused a nuisance, by flooding, to neighbours. Viscount Maugham said (30):
H
". . . there is no doubt that, if an owner of land for his own convenience diverts, or interferes with, the course of a stream, he must take care that the new course provided for it shall be sufficient to prevent mischief from an overflow to his neighbours' land, and that he will prima facie be liable if such an overflow should take place."

I Then he referred to some cases and later he said (31):

"The distinction between a natural use of land, or of water flowing through it, and the consequences of constructing some artificial work on land which alters the flow of water and causes damage to a neighbour has been drawn in a number of cases."

(27) (1877), 2 App. Cas. 839. (28) (1877), 2 App. Cas. at pp. 861, 862.
(29) [1940] A.C. at p. 880.
(30) [1940] 3 All E.R. at p. 354; [1940] A.C. at p. 888.
(31) [1940] 3 All E.R. at p. 354; [1940] A.C. at p. 889.

The passage (32) on continuing or adopting a nuisance was also referred to, but A in our case it is not disputed that if there is such a nuisance as alleged at all, then the defendants are liable for it.   The issue in this case turns on the existence of nuisance, and not on continuation or adoption.   So the *Sedleigh-Denfield* case (33) is in the same line of authority for the present purposes as *Greenock Corpn.* v. *Caledonian Ry. Co.* (34).

It was accepted for the plaintiffs that in consequence of s. 31 of the Public B Health Act, 1936, they had no remedy in nuisance against the defendants in the absence of negligence by them. (Reference was made to *Smeaton* v. *Ilford Corpn.* (35) and *Dunne* v. *North Western Gas Board* (36)).

The plaintiffs suggested, however, that the burden of proving absence of negligence lay on the defendants and they based this suggestion on observations of VISCOUNT SUMNER in *Manchester Corpn.* v. *Farnworth* (37).   That was a C claim for nuisance by fumes from electric works and the particular dispute which immediately led to the observations was whether the defendant had taken reasonable means and precautions to avoid the consequences.   That was clearly a matter within the peculiar knowledge in the first place, at any rate, of the defendants and to that extent the burden of proof would naturally lie on them. LORD SUMNER's observations were made on a somewhat differently worded D section, and the defendants submitted that it did not follow that the overall burden of proving absence of negligence in the circumstances of this case lay on the defendants.   If, however, the defendants were correct, it would only mean for present purposes that the plaintiffs would have to allege negligence and in so far as they do have to allege it, it is accepted for present purposes as alleged by the amendment to the statement of claim.   Therefore this question E as to where the burden of proof lies ceases to be material for present purposes, for which it is assumed that the facts which the plaintiffs allege in the statement of claim are established.

The alleged negligence relied on by the plaintiffs before me was stated to be having " knowledge or means of knowledge of the nuisance and the ability to abate it ".   This statement was exposed to the comment for the defendants F that it begged the question of nuisance in the plaintiffs' own favour, because it assumed the nuisance in which negligence itself was an essential factor.   I take the plaintiffs to have meant, however, that the negligence consisted of having knowledge or means of knowledge of the facts which, apart from negli- gence, would constitute nuisance for which the defendants would be liable, and failing to exercise the means available to abate it.   Even so stated, however, G the proposition is subject to substantial limitations.   It does not, of course, decrease the need to establish common law nuisance independently of negligence, but adds the requirement of negligence in addition to what would constitute common law nuisance, before the defendants can be fixed with liability.   There was clearly no nuisance or negligence in the laying of the pipe, nor, indeed, is it alleged or suggested that there was any such nuisance or negligence in any way H until part of the river bed was washed away years later.   So at one stage of the argument it was stated for the plaintiffs that the " nuisance relied on is inter- ference by the defendants with the flow of the river by failing to abate the consequences to the plaintiffs of that interference ".   I confess to some little difficulty in appreciating how failing to abate the consequence of interference can, of itself, constitute interference.   In order to constitute nuisance or other I liability in tort the failure to abate must be more than mere omission " to abate the consequences " and must amount to failure to carry out an obligation to abate.   That obligation, however, can only arise if the unabated interference

(32) [1940] 3 All E.R. at p. 358; [1940] A.C. at p. 894.
(33) [1940] 3 All E.R. 349; [1940] A.C. 880.
(34) [1916-17] All E.R. Rep. 426; [1917] A.C. 556.
(35) [1954] 1 All E.R. 923 at p. 936; [1954] Ch. 450 at p. 477.
(36) [1963] 3 All E.R. 916; [1964] 2 Q.B. 806.
(37) [1929] All E.R. Rep. 90 at p. 97; [1930] A.C. 171 at p. 187.

A causes the nuisance or if there is, independently of it, a duty to the plaintiffs on the part of the defendants to abate.

The plaintiffs sought to establish such a duty to abate on the ground that the defendants were under an obligation, as they put it, to " manage " the sewer. The defendants are under an obligation under s. 23 of the Public Health Act, 1936, to maintain the sewer, but it is not failure to maintain the sewer in the sense of
B keeping it in proper condition that has caused the trouble in this case. So the plaintiffs contended that the obligation to maintain included the obligation to " manage including managing in such a way as to avoid nuisance if that is possible consistent with the statutory duty of providing a sewer system," and for this the plaintiffs relied on the observations of LORD HALSBURY, L.C., in *Baron* v. *Portslade Urban District Council* (38). When examined, however, the
C observations, as was acknowledged, established the very opposite so far as they went and were sought to be applied to this case, namely that liability there was based not on the obligation to " maintain " sewers, but to " cleanse " them, and that the word " manage " was used not as an extension of the meaning of " maintain " but in a sense narrower even than " maintain ", namely to " cleanse ". I fail to see that the statutory obligation to " maintain " the sewer involves any
D such extended obligation to maintain lands or conditions outside the sewer, as the plaintiffs suggest, or that it involves obligations to third parties like the plaintiffs who are complete strangers to the sewer. Certainly I am not aware of any argument of any substance advanced for the plaintiffs to the contrary.

So in my view the plaintiffs fail on their first way of putting their case, and I come to their second way of putting it—that the water was " injuriously affected "
E within s. 331 of the Public Health Act, 1936, by being diverted by the defendants' pipe. That section provides that nothing in the Act of 1936 authorises the local authority injuriously to affect water without the consent of the person entitled to prevent it or be relieved against it—and there was no such consent here.

The defendants concede that this section takes liability for " injuriously
F affecting " water out of the requirement, under s. 31, of negligence in any relevant nuisance. On the other hand, however, s. 331 does not create any nuisance additional to nuisance under common law—it just restores the common law position in respect of liability for " injuriously affecting water ". What is meant by " injuriously affecting water "? The side note is in these terms, " Works affecting water rights ", and the plaintiffs submitted that the section
G did not apply to damage to riparian land through interference with the flow of water. I need not, however, consider this submission, for in so far as the plaintiffs can rely on this section to exclude the requirement of negligence in any nuisance as the basis of the remedies which they claim, it seems to me that such exclusion is immaterial, for reasons already appearing in my observations on the plaintiffs' first way of putting their case. This second way of putting their
H case can carry the plaintiffs' case no further for present purposes than the first way since negligence is now in any case alleged in the statement of claim; and it must in my view fail for the reasons already canvassed.

The plaintiffs' claim is, thirdly, founded on breach of cl. 14 of the 1907 lease ". . . not to interfere with the flow of . . . the water in the River Somer ".

It is common ground that there was no express assignment of the benefit of
I this clause to the plaintiffs. The plaintiffs suggested that they were entitled to the benefit of it as a restrictive covenant whose benefit ran with the reversion. The plaintiffs are not entitled, however, to the reversion—the fee simple in the sewer is vested in the defendants under the statute which has overriding effect; and though subject to determination, it admits of no reversion as already explained. Further, the covenant in cl. 14 of the lease is with the lessor as defined at the beginning of the lease as including " his heirs assigns and successors in title or other the person or persons for the time being entitled to

(38) [1900] 2 Q.B. 588.

receive the rent hereby reserved ". The plaintiffs are not the lessor, his heirs, **A** assigns or successors in title to the hereditament constituted by the sewer. Nor is it alleged or sought to be alleged by amendment of the statement of claim or otherwise that they are " entitled to receive the rent hereby reserved ", and I am told that in fact liability for payment of rent was amicably terminated many years ago. Nor was the benefit of the covenant annexed to any land.

The plaintiffs, however, claim that any interference by the defendants with **B** the flow of the water was contrary to the terms on which the lease was made, that the defendants cannot take advantage of the lease without complying with its terms, and that the plaintiffs as successors in title of Earl Waldegrave, the lessor, are entitled to enforce these terms. Of course, as I have already indicated, the plaintiffs are not successors in title of Earl Waldegrave as lessor of the hereditament constituted by the sewer or of any land to which the benefit of the **C** covenant was annexed. The plaintiffs, however, called in aid *Westhoughton Urban District Council* v. *Wigan Coal and Iron Co., Ltd.* (39). In that case the defendants' right to let down the surface of land was subject to a condition for payment of compensation, and therefore their right to let down was a qualified right, namely a right to let down subject to compensation. Apart from this qualified right the plaintiffs were entitled to the surface free from any right to **D** let it down; and under the qualified right there could be no letting down at all of the surface without compensation. It, therefore, necessarily followed that the only right enforceable as against the surface owners, the plaintiffs, was not an absolute right to let down the surface, but the qualified right to let down with compensation. It was in those circumstances that it was held that the plaintiffs were entitled to restrain the letting down of the surface by the defendants in the **E** absence of compensation. The right not to have the surface let down was unquestionably a right attached to the surface and an aspect of the ownership of the surface whose owner the plaintiffs were. Further, cl. 14 in this case is very differently worded from the condition in the *Westhoughton* case (39), and, in my view, does not constitute a condition at all, and this difference also is sufficient of itself, apart from any other consideration, to make the *West-* **F** *houghton* case (39) inapplicable.

Even if cl. 14 were a condition which the plaintiffs were entitled to enforce as a term on which the lease was granted, the defendants, by virtue of the statutory vesting in them of the fee simple of the sewer under the statutory provisions which, admittedly, override the lease, would not be dependent on the lease for conveying sewage through the sewer. So they would not be restricted by **G** cl. 14 as a condition qualifying their powers to convey sewage and subjecting them to the relief sought in this action. Clause 14 might, nevertheless, well take effect as a covenant but, as a covenant, it would only be effective as between the original parties to the lease or between the defendants as lessees and an express assignee of the benefit of the covenant, which the plaintiffs are not.

The overall conclusion, therefore, is that the defendants are entitled to succeed. **H**

Action dismissed (under R.S.C., Ord. 33, r. 7) with costs.

Solicitors: *Taylor, Willcocks & Co.*, agents for *Kent, Rathmell & Young*, Radstock, Somerset (for the plaintiffs); *Knapp-Fishers*, agents for *Faulkner, Creswick & Gould*, Bath, Somerset (for the defendants).

[*Reported by* JACQUELINE METCALFE, *Barrister-at-Law.*]   **I**

---

(39) [1919] 1 Ch. 159.

A

MOORE *v.* COMMISSIONER OF METROPOLITAN POLICE AND OTHERS.

[COURT OF APPEAL, CIVIL DIVISION (Danckwerts and Sachs, L.JJ.), April 28, 1967.]

B *Court of Appeal—Interlocutory appeal—Leave to appeal—Order refusing leave to bring proceedings in respect of acts done in pursuance of Mental Health Act, 1959—Whether order interlocutory or final—Whether leave to appeal necessary—Supreme Court of Judicature (Consolidation) Act, 1925 (15 & 16 Geo. 5 c. 49), s. 31 (1) (i)—Mental Health Act, 1959 (7 & 8 Eliz. 2 c. 72), s. 141 (2).*

C An order of a judge refusing an applicant under s. 141 (2)* of the Mental Health Act, 1959, leave to bring proceedings against persons in respect of acts done by them in pursuance of the Mental Health Act, 1959 is an interlocutory, not a final, order, and so, by virtue of the Supreme Court of Judicature (Consolidation) Act, 1925, s. 31 (1) (i)†, no appeal lies against such an order without the leave of the judge or of the Court of Appeal.

D

[As to appeals to the Court of Appeal against interlocutory orders, see 30 HALSBURY'S LAWS (3rd Edn.) 452, para. 855; as to what is an interlocutory judgment or order, see 22 ibid., pp. 742-746, paras. 1606-1609; and for cases on the subject, see 30 DIGEST (Repl.) 153, 154, *65-87.*

As to leave to bring proceedings in respect of anything done under the Mental E Health Act, 1959, see 29 HALSBURY'S LAWS (3rd Edn.) 435, 436, para. 847, text and notes (*a*)-(*e*).

For the Supreme Court of Judicature (Consolidation) Act, 1925, s. 31 (1) (*i*), see 5 HALSBURY'S STATUTES (2nd Edn.) 360.

For the Mental Health Act, 1959, s. 141 (2), see 39 ibid., p. 1075.]

Case referred to:
F *Cathcart, Re,* [1893] 1 Ch. 466; 33 Digest (Repl.) 676, *1242.*

Preliminary Point of Law.

On an appeal by George Okwudili Moore, an applicant under s. 141 of the Mental Health Act, 1959, for leave to bring proceedings against the Commissioner of Metropolitan Police, West Park Hospital Epsom, Dr. Enfield, Dr. McManus, Wandsworth Borough Council, Mr. Biswamber, Mr. Gonzalez, and others, against G the refusal by WILLIS, J., in chambers, on Mar. 22, 1967, of his application for leave to bring the proceedings, counsel for some of the proposed defendants objected that the applicant could not appeal without the leave of WILLIS, J. (which had been refused) or of the Court of Appeal.

D. D. H. Sullivan for the hospital.
H *P. E. Webster,* Q.C., for Dr. Enfield, Dr. McManus and Wandsworth Borough Council.

The applicant appeared in person.

DANCKWERTS, L.J.: Section 141 (2) of the Mental Health Act, 1959, provides that

I   " No civil or criminal proceeding shall be brought against any person in any court in respect of any such act [the acts referred to being acts in pursuance of the particular Act of 1959] without the leave of the High Court, and the High Court shall not give leave under this section unless satisfied that there is substantial ground for the contention that the person to be proceeded against has acted in bad faith or without reasonable care."

The question is whether the applicant, Mr. Moore, is entitled to proceed, without

---

* Section 141, so far as material, is printed at letter I, supra.
† Section 31 (1), so far as material, is printed at p. 828, letter D, post.

first obtaining leave from us, with the appeal which he wishes to make from a **A**
decision of WILLIS, J., in chambers dated Mar. 22, 1967, on an application under
s. 141 (2) for leave to bring an action which the applicant wishes to bring against
a number of persons. WILLIS, J., by an order of Mar. 22, 1967, refused leave to
bring the proceedings. Also, when WILLIS, J., was asked about leave to appeal
from his decision, he said that if leave was not required for an appeal of course
the applicant could proceed but that, if leave was required, then he, WILLIS, J., **B**
refused leave.

That is the position, and a preliminary objection is taken now to the applicant's
appeal, both by one counsel on behalf of some of the defendants and by another
counsel on behalf of another defendant, on the ground that, leave having been
refused by WILLIS, J., the leave of this court, the Court of Appeal, is required
before the applicant can proceed with his appeal. That depends on whether the **C**
order in these proceedings refusing leave to bring the action is a final order or
whether it is an interlocutory order.

Section 31 (1) of the Supreme Court of Judicature (Consolidation) Act, 1925,
provides as follows:

" No appeal shall lie . . . (*i*) without the leave of the judge or of the Court
of Appeal from any interlocutory order or interlocutory judgment made or **D**
given by a judge, except in the following cases . . .":

and then several cases are set out, none of which applies to the present matter.
The question is whether this is an interlocutory order or whether it is a final order,

It seems to me fairly clear that it is an interlocutory order; but the applicant
has been relying on a note on p. 735 of the SUPREME COURT PRACTICE, 1967, **E**
against the side number " 59/1/12 ", which is in these terms:

" Mental health. Appeal lies to the Court of Appeal from an order of
the judge (Judicature Act, 1925, s. 26 (2) notwithstanding s. 31 (1) (*h*),
Re Cathcart (1); Mental Health Act, 1959, s. 111)."

What is referred to as the subject of the decision in *Re Cathcart* (1) is the provision
now made by s. 111 of the Act of 1959. Section 111 is a different section from **F**
s. 141. Section 111 is concerned with appeals to the judges appointed for the
purpose in the Chancery Division from the Master of the Court of Protection, and
appeals from those judges to the Court of Appeal. The note is correct in respect
of those cases; but it does not apply to s. 141, and *Re Cathcart* (1) is no authority
in regard to s. 141. The ordinary rules apply to the proceedings referred to in
s. 141 of the Mental Health Act, 1959. Thus the matter comes within the pro- **G**
visions of s. 31 (1) of the Act of 1925. I am completely satisfied that this is an
interlocutory matter and, therefore, it is a case where leave from us to proceed
is required before this appeal can be maintained. Therefore I decide against the
applicant on this preliminary point.

SACHS, L.J.: I agree. I have some sympathy with the approach of the **H**
applicant on this matter when he submits that an order barring a set of proceedings has the appearance of being something final; but orders of this type have,
over a considerable period, been held to be interlocutory—for instance orders
striking out a statement of claim for being vexatious are held to be interlocutory.

It may well be that the reason for this is basically that one is dealing with a
set of proceedings and not with a right; but it can also be said that there are many **I**
cases (of which this is typical) where it would be against the tenor of the Supreme
Court of Judicature (Consolidation) Act, 1925, or other legislation that there
should be an undue proliferation of appeals when they are matters of a nature
that requires the leave of the court before they get into any list.

I entirely agree that, on the authorities, and for the reasons given by
DANCKWERTS, L.J., this particular case is one of those which should be regarded as

(1) [1893] 1 Ch. 466.

A being interlocutory within the provisions of the Act of 1925, and that leave to appeal is required.

Preliminary objection upheld.

[The applicant then applied for leave to appeal. The court, having considered the application, were not satisfied that there was substantial ground for the contention that the proposed defendants had acted in bad faith or without
B reasonable care, and so refused leave.]

Leave to appeal refused.

Solicitors: *Nigel Ryland* (for the hospital); *Hempsons* (for Dr. Enfield and Dr. McManus); *Town Clerk*, Wandsworth (for the Wandsworth Borough Council).

[*Reported by* Henry Summerfield, Esq., *Barrister-at-Law.*]

C

JAMES *v.* HEPWORTH & GRANDAGE, LTD.

[Court of Appeal, civil division (Sellers, Davies and Russell, L.JJ.), February
D   28, March 1, 1967.]

Safe System of Working—Extent of master's duty—Duty to give information or advice—Availability of protective clothing—Notice advising workman of availability and advising him to wear it—Workman unable to read, but master unaware of this—Foundry—Injury from molten metal—Probability that protective clothing would not have been used.

E   The plaintiff, who was employed by the defendants as a metal spinner, had to pour molten metal into a channel to feed it into a metal spinning machine. If he took insufficient care molten metal might splash on to his legs or feet. The employers provided goggles, safety spats, gloves and aprons for workmen who asked for them, but left it to the individual workman to ask for and wear them if he wished. The foreman, who had trained the
F plaintiff, and the foundry superintendent both considered it undesirable to wear spats, because of the risk that molten metal might be trapped by them instead of being shaken off. Of the twenty-four workmen in the shop very few wore spats. In the shop were two large notices stating what protective clothing was available, and that it "should be worn for your personal safety". The workman was, unknown to the employers, unable to read.
G He had not been told about the safety spats during his training, but had noticed the two workmen wearing them. He did not, however, enquire about them or about the notice. He wore gloves and goggles, but never asked for, or wore, safety spats. While at work he was injured by molten metal. The injury would not have occurred had he been wearing safety spats. In an action by the workman against his employers for damages for
H this injury,

Held: the employers had not been negligent, and so the workman's claim failed, for each of the following reasons—

(i) because the employers had fulfilled their duty at common law by providing spats, informing workmen that they were there, and letting them make their choice, even though the plaintiff was, unknown to them,
I unable to read the relevant notices (see p. 831, letters D and I, and p. 833, letters C and D, post).

(ii) because the only inference which could be drawn from the plaintiff's failure to enquire about the notices or the spats which he saw, and from the fact that only few out of the twenty-four wore the spats, was that even if the plaintiff had been told that spats were available he would not have worn them before the accident (see p. 832, letters D and F, and p. 833, letters D and G, post).

Appeal allowed.

[**Editorial Note.** On holding (i) the present decision follows, in effect, **A**
Qualcast (Wolverhampton), Ltd. v. *Haynes* ([1959] 2 All E.R. 38), extending
the principle to circumstances where the plaintiff workman, unknown to the
employer, could not read the relevant notices; on holding (ii) the present
case should be considered with *Nolan* v. *Dental Manufacturing Co., Ltd.* ([1958]
2 All E.R. 449, holding (i)), where a like result was reached on similar reasoning,
it being held that causation was not established because the workman would not **B**
have used the protective clothing.

As to a master's duty to provide effective supervision and take reasonable
safety precautions, see 25 HALSBURY'S LAWS (3rd Edn.) 513, 514, para. 980;
and for cases on the subject, see 34 DIGEST (Repl.) 240-250, *1760-1811*.]

Appeal.

This was an appeal by Hepworth & Grandage, Ltd., the employers of Alfred **C**
James, a workman who was injured while pouring molten metal in their factory,
against the decision of His Honour JUDGE SUDDARDS, at Bradford county
court on Oct. 26, 1966, awarding the workman £170 16s. 8d. damages for this
injury in his action against the employers for common law negligence. The
facts are set out in the judgment of SELLERS, L.J.

W. A. Macpherson for the employers.   **D**
P. R. Pain, Q.C., and *J. M. Roberts* for the workman.

SELLERS, L.J.: The defendant employers appeal from a decision against
them in the Bradford County Court in which His Honour JUDGE SUDDARDS
found in favour of the plaintiff, a workman with the defendants, in respect of
a relatively trivial accident which justified, if it was to succeed, a total award **E**
of £170 16s. 8d. damages. The judge, no doubt familiar with the locality, found
in his judgment that

"The [employers] are one of the most safety-conscious firms in the
district, if not the most safety-conscious, and they had gone to the length
of hanging two notices in the shop in the plainest terms offering all safety **F**
equipment free."

Those notices are relative to the facts of this case.

The plaintiff workman is a Jamaican, apparently a fine big man so that he
had to have exceptionally large sized gloves and goggles. I do not know how
long he had been over in this country but he had been with the defendant
employers for some four years at the time of his accident, and for the previous **G**
six months he had done the task at which he met with this unfortunate
accident. That was described as the task of a metal spinner, which involved
pouring molten metal into a channel or guide in order to feed it to a rotating
or spinning machine for the purpose, I apprehend, of making metal liners.
That place of pouring was said to be about two feet above ground level. When,
six months before, he had transferred to this department, the workman had **H**
had no less than four weeks' instruction in what is apparently not a very complicated task; but it requires care because it is the handling of molten metal,
which is dangerous. He was employed on piece work and the task he was on, if
not done with complete care, might result in some of the metal splashing about
and possibly dropping on to a man's legs or feet.

It was as far back as Dec. 18, 1963, after six months at the work, that the **I**
workman was pouring the molten metal into this machine in the customary way
when some splashed and dropped on to one foot and leg and caused one or two
burns, happily not of a very serious nature.

Eventually, for those injuries and the resultant loss the workman claimed
damages against his employers. The allegation against them (a familiar one in
these courts) is that they did not provide spats or gaiters, which some regard as
a protection against such an occurrence as happened here. The employers
denied any breach of duty and the matter resolved itself in the following way.

A The employers did provide spats, which were available on the premises, and they put up two notices, both in similar terms. The one before us is in these terms:

> " The following items of protective clothing are available for issue free of charge: Goggles: safety spats: gloves: aprons. They should be worn for your personal safety. Safety boots are available at cost price."

B

Now to the ordinary workman in the factory that was about as clear a notice as could be given. On the photograph the colours in which it is displayed are not revealed but it may well be that the words " They should be worn for your personal safety " were in red or some outstanding colour: the rest seems to have been in black. It was not known to the employers, and I cannot see

C any reason why it should have been known to them, that (as the plaintiff workman said) he could not read. For the four years during which he had been in the factory that apparently had been undetected. He could speak and could understand, and no one had noticed that he was not able to communicate in the ordinary way.

It is on that aspect of the case that the judge has found in the workman's

D favour. The judge has found that the spats were provided—there is no doubt that they were available—but he thought that the workman was in a peculiar position; and the judge discriminated in his favour. In my view that was to impose a higher standard and a greater duty of care than the common law of this country requires. The employers gave adequate notice to those working in the factory by reason of this particular notice board. Not only that: the

E position in this factory was that there were probably some twenty-four people, at the most, sometimes less, working there and the majority did not wear spats, but at least two workmen did. The spats have not been produced here—they ought to have been: they were in the court below—but they are of such a distinctive type that I apprehend that no one could be unaware that they were a form of protective clothing. The workman was there: they were available for

F him to see them; he said that he had seen them, and I cannot think that they did not convey to his mind that that was yet another device that he could have had if he wished it. He could have made some enquiry about it. In fact he provided himself with the safety boots, and he was supplied with goggles and with gloves.

Some point was made about the form of instruction given to this workman.

G In the four weeks that he was being trained it was not suggested to him that he should wear spats and for the very good reason that the instructor, the foreman, Mr. White, had taken the view—as indeed did many others in this factory, and the courts are aware that it is the view in other factories too—that there were disadvantages in wearing spats, and some took the view that the disadvantages were greater than the advantages. Mr. White thought that it was better not to

H wear them. They were not only uncomfortable and the feet got very hot but there was a danger, he thought, as did others including Mr. Hylton, who was the superintendent, of the metal remaining longer on the skin, if any should fall, because it might get trapped between the top part of the spats and the body, whereas with loose trousers hanging over without the spats it was thought that would be more likely to throw off any metal which had been splashed over.

I That is a point of view which I should have thought was certainly one that could be reasonably entertained.

The position with regard to the employers in those circumstances was that they should make provision for the spats, inform people that they were there, and let them make their choice. That was done, and it would be too harsh a view to say that there was any failure on the part of the employers to perform their common law duty.

It was argued by counsel for the workman that something in the workman's favour can be derived from the fact that he was not initially instructed in the

use of spats or told expressly that they were available. I have given a reason   **A**
why they were not mentioned by Mr. White, who instructed him; but from
then on during a period of six months it must have been apparent to the workman
that spats were available because people were wearing them. He could have
made some enquiries about them, and I cannot see why he in the particular
circumstances should be put in any better position than his comrades with regard
to the notice.   **B**

Assuming that there had been a breach of duty, then the following question
would arise. If everything had been done that could possibly have been done,
if individual attention had been given to the workman and he had been asked to
make his choice expressly whether he would wear spats or not, what are the
probabilities as to what he would have done? Looking at this evidence as charitably as I can and having regard to what others were doing and the fact that   **C**
the workman himself did not apparently, according to his evidence, enquire
as to what the notice which was there was about and whether it had anything
to do with him or his work, and did not make any enquiries of his colleagues
who were wearing spats as to what they were for and why they wore them,
and having regard to the large number who did not wish to wear spats, I think
that on the probabilities and on the balance of all the factors, if everything   **D**
had been done that could have been done, as I have said, it is improbable that
the workman would have been wearing spats at the time. In those circumstances
there can be no claim for damages in this case.

The judge did not deal with this last point, which is a vital one. There are in
a variety of industries a good many articles which are thought by some—not
thought so strongly or even at all by others—to be of a protective character.   **E**
It is not altogether to be condemned that certain articles of protective clothing
or protective equipment are to be thought by some to possess at least as many,
perhaps more, disadvantages than advantages so that they do not wish to wear
them for their own safety. It would be wrong for the plaintiff to recover in every
case. The right finding here was that the position of the workman would have
been just the same, with regard to the protective clothing which he has alleged   **F**
should have been supplied, if it had been supplied. It would not have been worn
by him. The appeal should be allowed and judgment entered for the employers.

     DAVIES, L.J.: I agree. There was obviously a duty on the employers
to take reasonable care for the safety of their workmen. In the context of this
case, what is said is that there was a duty on them to provide these protective   **G**
spats, to inform the workmen of that provision, and to give the workmen the
option to wear the spats if they so wished. There is no question but that spats
were provided; but it is said that the plaintiff workman, in the circumstances
of this case, was not informed of their provision and, therefore, was not given
any opportunity of exercising his own choice in the matter.

The notice to which SELLERS, L.J., has referred (there were at least two of   **H**
them) was in the plainest possible terms and in large capitals; but it so happens
that, according to the evidence, this workman could not read. On the other
hand, as SELLERS, L.J., has said, the workman admitted that he saw a couple
of fellow-workmen wearing spats; and he does not deny that he saw the notice.
He could perfectly well have asked somebody to tell him what was contained
in the notice; but apparently he did not do so.   **I**

If it were not for the fact of the existence of this notice, I cannot help feeling
that there would have been no conceivable case here for the workman. The
important words of the notice are perhaps these: " They should be worn for
your personal safety ". It has more or less been argued for the workman that,
in the light of that notice—which obviously represents the view of the management of this factory—the wearing of spats is almost compulsory.

If the notice board had stood alone, the workman might have a very strong
case; but, as I think, it is quite impossible to give to this notice the sort of

A effect which is sought to be given to it, in the light of the evidence of Mr. White, the night shift foreman, and Mr. Hylton, the superintendent of the foundry. Mr. White had been night shift foreman for eight years and had worked for about twenty-eight years in the department. Mr. Hylton had been some twenty-six years in the employers' employ. Without referring to it in detail, the substance of the evidence of both those gentlemen was that, so far from its being

B desirable that spats should be worn for the operation that the workman was conducting, the wearing of spats was, in practice, not only unnecessary but undesirable. It is really quite impossible, in my view, to set against that evidence of those two very experienced men the ex post facto view of the workman himself in court, three years or more after he had had his accident, that "spats are safer ".

C Like SELLERS, L.J., I cannot see, in the circumstances of this case, that there was any breach of duty here by the employers towards the workman. Quite apart from that, it is clear on the evidence, in view of the statistics to which SELLERS, L.J., has adverted, that, even if the workman had known (which he says that he did not know) about the possibility of wearing spats, the overwhelming probability is that, like nearly all the men in this foundry, he would

D not in fact have worn them.

I therefore agree that the appeal succeeds.

RUSSELL, L.J.: I agree that the appeal succeeds. It is argued that the employers, when training the workman for this work, ought to have drawn his special attention to the availability of safety spats (although there are large notices doing this in the shop, partly, I understand, in lettering in the warning

E colour red) just *in case* he (a) could not read and (b) had not bothered to ask anyone else what the notice or notices said.

I cannot accept that this burden should be put on the employers. I would also in deciding whether spats were reasonably necessary for the safety of the workman in this particular task, have inclined, in assessing the whole of the

F evidence, to the view that the evidence of Mr. White and Mr. Hylton outweighs the evidence of the existence of the notice stating that " Safety spats " (among other things) " should be worn for your personal safety ". Indeed, on the actual evidence of Mr. White and Mr. Hylton there is much to be said for the view that this was, as is the case with some of the rules which various industries lay down, a counsel of perfection and not a statement of what was reasonably

G necessary for safety.

In any event I am quite clear that if the availability of safety spats had been specifically brought to the workman's notice, then, on balance of probability, he would not have used them. Only two out of the twenty-four in this shop ever wore them; and if the two people most likely to have mentioned them had been asked about them—that is, Mr Hylton and Mr. White—they would

H have discouraged their use by the workman. On this head of the case, I am not impressed at all by the fact that after the accident the workman did wear spats, and said in evidence that he thought them " safer ". My reason for not being impressed by this is that he was burned in circumstances in which he would *not* have been burned if he had been wearing spats, and it therefore throws no light on what action he would have taken originally had the availability of

I spats been actually brought to his attention.

Appeal allowed. Judgment entered for defendants.

Solicitors: *Ward, Bowie & Co.*, agents for *A. V. Hammond & Co.*, Bradford (for the employers); *W. H. Thompson* (for the workman).

[*Reported by* HENRY SUMMERFIELD, ESQ., *Barrister-at-Law.*]

Re EARL OF MIDLETON'S WILL TRUSTS.
WHITEHEAD v. MIDLETON (EARL).

[CHANCERY DIVISION (Stamp, J.), April 6, 7, 10, 11, 12, May 12, 1967.]

Will—Gift—Donee—Person who on death of present Earl should succeed to the earldom—Heir presumptive had no interest in property so given.

A testator bequeathed income of his residuary estate (viz., income accruing after the death of his widow and during the lifetime of the present Earl of Midleton) to the person who on the death of the present Earl should succeed to the earldom and attain the age of twenty-one years or, if there were no such person, to the person who should succeed to the viscountcy and attain that age.

Held: no real distinction lay between a gift to the heir of a living person and a gift to the person who on the death of a living person should succeed to his title; accordingly the income passed as on intestacy of the testator (see p. 838, letter I, to p. 839, letter A, post).

Re Parsons, Stockleigh v. *Parsons* ((1890), 45 Ch.D. 51) applied.

Re Duke of St. Albans' Will Trusts ([1962] 2 All E.R. 402) not followed.

[**Editorial Note.** In accordance with the rule nemo est haeres viventis the expectation of a person to succeed to property as the heir or next-of-kin of another person is a spes successionis, not a title to or interest in property; see 32 HALSBURY'S LAWS (3rd Edn.) 326, 327, para. 506, and 18 ibid., pp. 376, 377, para. 716; and for cases on the subject see 38 DIGEST (Repl.) 841, 842, *538-544*, and 48 ibid., pp. 31, 32, *165-187*.

For the Trustee Act, 1925, s. 31, see 26 HALSBURY'S STATUTES (2nd Edn.) 94; and for the Law of Property Act, 1925, s. 175, see 20 ibid. 789.]

Cases referred to:

Dursley (Lord) v. *Fitzhardinge*, (1801), 6 Ves. 251; 31 E.R. 1036; 22 Digest (Repl.) 607, *6995*.

Parsons, Re, Stockley v. *Parsons*, (1890), 45 Ch.D. 51; 59 L.J.Ch. 668; 62 L.T. 929; 38 Digest (Repl.) 841, *539*.

St. Albans' (Duke) Will Trusts, Re, Coutts & Co. v. *Beauclerk*, [1962] 2 All E.R. 402; [1963] Ch. 365; [1962] 3 W.L.R. 206; Digest (Cont. Vol. A) 1300, *657a*.

Adjourned Summons.

This was a summons, dated Sept. 19, 1966, by the plaintiff, John William St. John Whitehead, the trustee of the will dated Aug. 22, 1940, and the two codicils thereto, dated May 9, 1941, and Dec. 1, 1941, of the Right Honourable William St. John Freemantle, First Earl of Midleton, deceased (" the testator "), who died on Feb. 13, 1942, for the determination by the court of certain questions of construction. There were six defendants, all of whom claimed to be beneficially interested under the trusts of the will and codicils. The first defendant was the Right Honourable George St. John, Second Earl of Midleton; he was the present Earl, was the eldest son of the testator and was known during his father's lifetime as Viscount Dunsford.

By his will the testator directed his trustees to hold his residuary estate on trust to pay the income to the first defendant during his life and after his death on trust, as to both capital and income, for the person who should then succeed to the title of Earl of Midleton on his attaining the age of twenty-one years, but if no one should then succeed to that title and attain that age, for the person who should then succeed to the title of Viscount Midleton on his attaining the age of twenty-one years. The testator further directed that the income should be paid to the first defendant only so long as he should not sell the mansion house of Peper Harow and eight hundred acres of the land settled therewith or lease the mansion house for a term exceeding seven years, and that on such a sale or lease the income should be accumulated during the remainder of the life

A of the first defendant or for twenty-one years from the testator's death, whichever should be the shorter period, and that after the expiration of that period his residuary estate and the income thereof should be paid or transferred to the person who, if the first defendant were dead, would under the trusts thereinafter expressed then be entitled thereto.   By a second codicil the testator revoked the bequest of income to the first defendant and bequeathed the same income to his

B wife, the Countess of Midleton, during her life, and after her death bequeathed " the same upon the like trusts as are contained in my said will after the death of " the first defendant.

The first defendant sold the mansion house.   The income of the testator's residuary estate was paid to his widow, the dowager Countess of Midleton, until her death on June 2, 1966.   The first defendant, who had been married twice but

C had had no child, was seventy-nine years old at the time of the present application. If he died, not being survived by a male child, the earldom would become extinct. The viscountcy, however, would not lapse but would (as matters stood) vest in the sixth defendant, who was a second cousin of the first defendant.

The second question raised by the summons was whether the income of the testator's residuary estate arising after the death of the testator's widow and

D until the death of the first defendant (a) was payable to the person or persons who would be entitled to the capital of the said residuary estate if the first defendant had died immediately before such income arose or (b) was properly undisposed of by the testator's will and codicils and devolved as on the intestacy of the testator or (c) was held on some other and if so what trusts.

E
D. J. Nicholls for the plaintiff.
J. E. Vinelott for the first defendant.
E. W. Griffith for the second to fifth defendants.
E. G. Nugee for the sixth defendant.

STAMP, J.: I have already held that the revocation by the codicil of the bequest of income of the testator's residuary estate contained in the will and the

F bequest in the codicil of " the same upon the like trusts as are contained in my said will after the death of my said son George St. John Viscount Dunsford " operate alike only over the income bequeathed to the latter, and that the codicil does not affect the trusts of capital contained in the will.   Upon what trusts then is the income accruing after the death of the testator's widow held during the residue of the life of the present Earl?   In the terms of the codicil it is held on the

G like trusts as are contained in the will after the death of the present Earl.   The only trust contained in the will after the death of the present Earl is the trust to pay or transfer the residuary estate to the person who shall then succeed to the title of Earl of Midleton on his attaining twenty-one or if no such person to the person who shall then succeed to the title of Viscount Midleton on his attaining twenty-one.   In my judgment the conclusion is inescapable that by the codicil

H the testator has bequeathed the income on that trust. The effect of this conclusion I will consider in a moment, but I must first refer to the argument to the contrary advanced by counsel for the sixth defendant.

It was provided by the will that the payment of income of the residuary estate to the present Earl should be made only so long as he should not sell the mansion house of Peper Harow and certain land, and that on such a sale the income was

I to be accumulated during the remainder of the life of the present Earl or for a period of twenty-one years reckoned from the testator's death, whichever should be the shorter period, and after the expiration of the period the trustees were directed to pay or transfer the residuary estate and the income to the person who, if the present Earl were dead, would " under the trusts hereinbefore expressed then be entitled thereto ".   The present Earl did in fact sell the mansion house, so that if his life interest had not been revoked by the codicil the trust for him would in the terms of the will, apart from the effect of s. 106 of the Settled Land Act, 1925, have come into operation. Counsel for the sixth defendant invites me to

hold that, when the codicil speaks of the like trusts as are contained in the A
testator's will after the death of the present Earl, it is referring to the trust
declared in the event of the present Earl selling the mansion house and that the
trust by reference to which the gift of income in the codicil is made is the trust for
" the person who if my said eldest son were dead would under the trusts hereinbefore expressed then be entitled thereto ". Faced by the fact that his client was
not at the expiration of twenty-one years from the death of the testator the person B
who would, if the present Earl had then been dead, have been so entitled, counsel
for the sixth defendant invites me to hold that the income is payable to the
person who is for the time being the person who, if the present Earl had died at
the moment when the income accrued, would have been entitled to the residuary
estate. In my judgment the words of the codicil do not tolerate such a construction. The only trust following the sale of the mansion house which could possibly C
be described as a trust contained in the will after the death of the present Earl
is the trust arising if the period of accumulation thus specified determines by the
death of the present Earl. If that trust, however, is to be given any meaning in
relation to that event, it must, because the present Earl would in fact be dead, be
construed as a trust not for the person who would, if the present Earl were dead,
be the person entitled " under the trusts hereinbefore expressed " but for the D
very person so entitled on the death of the present Earl under the trusts aforesaid, that is to say, on trust for the person who then succeeds to the earldom or
failing such a person to the person who succeeds to the viscountcy.

I hope that I have done justice to the argument advanced, for I confess having
a difficulty in construing the codicil as referring to provisions in the will which
could no longer take effect by reason of the revocation of the gift of income con- E
tained in the codicil itself. The arguments were supported by calling in aid the
words in the codicil " the like trusts ", but although I accept the proposition that
that phrase is an elastic phrase which can to some extent be stretched and pulled
to fit the meaning which one derives from other relevant provisions in a will, it
is not a phrase which may be stretched and pulled so as to give effect to a guess
which one has made as to what the testator intended. And where, as here, there F
is simply a bequest on the like trusts as are contained in the will after the death
of the present Earl there is in my judgment no escape from the conclusion that
the reference is to the very trusts so contained and not to some trusts which one
may think are like them or which the testator might, if he had thought about it,
have wanted to insert.

I conclude, therefore, that the income of the residuary estate as well as the G
capital is held on trust for the person who, on the death of the present Earl,
succeeds to the earldom and attains the age of twenty-one or if there is no such
person for the person who succeeds to the viscountcy and attains that age.

Counsel for the sixth defendant submits that if this is so his client, who is the
heir presumptive to the viscountcy, has now an interest in the capital of the
residuary estate contingent on his surviving the present Earl and there being no H
son of the present Earl to obtain a vested interest; and that since the income is
similarly held that contingent interest can properly be said to carry the intermediate income within s. 31 (3) of the Trustee Act, 1925. Therefore, so the
argument runs, s. 31 (1) of the Trustee Act, 1925, applies and the income is
accordingly payable to the sixth defendant. It would be odd if for the purpose of
s. 31 a distinction had to be drawn between a single gift of capital and income to I
A. contingently on his attaining twenty-one and two separate gifts, one of capital
and the other of the intermediate income each to A. contingently on his attaining
twenty-one, on the ground that in the former case the gift of capital did, but in
the latter it did not, carry the intermediate income. I think, however, that the
point is there and that it is not elucidated by the terms of s. 175 of the Law of
Property Act, 1925, which provide, so far as material, that a contingent bequest
of property shall carry the intermediate income of that property " except so far
as such income . . . may be otherwise expressly disposed of ". The argument that

A s. 31 of the Trustee Act, 1925, is applicable was, raised, however, only at a late
stage of the case, and because I can decide this case without deciding that question
or the possible further question whether the interest of a possible future son of the
present Earl would not be a " prior interest " to that of the heir presumptive so
as, by the effect of s. 31 (1) of the Trustee Act, 1925, to preclude that section from
applying at all, I prefer to express no opinion on it. This I am able to do because

B there is, in my judgment, a more fundamental objection to the submission that the
heir presumptive has a contingent interest in the estate. In my judgment he has
no such interest, nor any interest at all.

A gift to A., if on the death of B. he shall be heir of B. or one of the next of
kin of B. or shall then have some other specified characteristic, confers on A. a
present interest called contingent and which becomes vested if, on the death of

C B., A. has the required characteristic. On the other hand, a gift to whomsoever
shall at the death of B., a living person, be the heir of B. or one of the next of kin
of B., or shall then have some other specified characteristic in my judgment
confers no interest on anyone until the death of B., when one enquires who has
the required characteristic. A gift in equal shares to the persons who at the death
of B. shall be members of the Athenaeum Club no more confers an interest,

D contingent or otherwise, on the present members of the club who may hope to
remain members until the death of B. than it does on all those other persons in the
world who may hope to be elected in the meantime and remain members at the
death of B. Neither class has during the life of B., even if B. be in articulo mortis,
more than a hope of being or becoming one of the designated class, spes
successionis.

E   In *Lord Dursley* v. *Fitzhardinge* (1), Lord Eldon, L.C., said:

" The case of *Smith* v. *A.-G.* (2) went upon this; that the next of kin of the
lunatic had no interest whatever in the property. Put the case as high as
possible; that the lunatic is intestate; that he is in the most hopeless state,
a moral and physical impossibility, though the law would not so regard it,
that he should ever recover, even, if he was in articulo mortis, and the bill

F   was filed at that instant, the plaintiff could not qualify himself as having any
interest in the subject of the suit. The case of an heir apparent was very
properly put by Lord Chief Justice De Grey in his most luminous judgment. Upon that occasion he said, he never liked equity so well as when it
was like law. The day before I heard Lord Mansfield say, he never liked
law so well as when it was like equity; remarkable sayings of those two

G   great men, which made a strong impression on my memory. Lord Chief
Justice De Grey said, that at law the heir apparent cannot have the writ
de ventre inspiciendo in the life of his ancestor; as for that purpose he must
be verus haeres. If the ancestor was in a fever, a delirium, having made
no will, and it was not possible for him to recover, still the law would look
upon him as mere heir apparent, having nothing but an expectation which

H   is different from an expectancy in the legal sense, and as having no interest
whatever upon that ground."

The result of the English authorities is summarised by Kay, J., in *Re Parsons,
Stockley* v. *Parsons* (3), at the beginning of a detailed and considered judgment
in the course of which he examined those authorities. He said this (4):

I   " The question is whether she had then a contingent title. It is indisput-
able law that no one can have any estate or interest, at law or in equity,
contingent or other, in the property of a living person to which he hopes to
succeed as heir at law or next of kin of such living person. During the life
of such person no one can have more than a spes successionis, an expectation
or hope of succeeding to his property. The law is the same where there is a
limitation by will or settlement of real or personal property to the heir or

(1) (1801), 6 Ves. 251 at p. 260.   (2) In Chancery, 1777, unreported.
(3) (1890), 45 Ch.D. 51.   (4) (1890), 45 Ch.D. at p. 55.

statutory next of kin of a living person. During his life no one can say, ' I   A
have a contingent estate or interest as possible heir or next of kin '; just as
in the first case no one can have more than an expectation or hope of being
heir or next of kin. It makes no difference that the limitation is not to the
actual heir or next of kin, but to the persons who would be heir or next of
kin if the ancestors were to die at some future time. Until that time arrives
there is no one who can say he has anything beyond a hope or expectation."   B

Were it not for the decision in *Re Duke of St. Albans' Will Trust, Coutts & Co.
v. Beauclerk* (5), I would not have had any doubt that a gift to the person who
shall succeed to a particular title on the death of a living person was in the like
case to a gift to the heir or next of kin of a living person, for I can see no difference
in principle. But *Re Duke of St. Albans' Will Trust* (5) is, I think, a decision to the   C
contrary. The facts in that case were these. The tenth Duke of St. Albans had
given certain estates to the use of every successive son of his own for life with
remainder to the sons of that son in tail male, and his will then went on as follows:

" and on failure of such issue to the use of the person who on my death or
failure of my male issue (which shall last happen) shall become Duke of St.
Albans in tail male."   D

The tenth Duke died and his eldest son the eleventh Duke died without issue.
The tenth Duke had two other sons, the second of whom, Osborne, was at the
date of the judgment the twelfth Duke, had no issue and was eighty-seven years
of age. The person who at the date of the judgment would become the thirteenth
Duke on the death of the twelfth Duke without issue was the defendant, Charles
Beauclerk. The question was whether, during the life of the twelfth Duke,   E
Charles Beauclerk had such an interest as enabled him to disentail pursuant to
s. 15 of the Fines and Recoveries Act, 1833. In the way in which the matter was
dealt with this depended on whether Charles Beauclerk was " an actual tenant
in tail, whether in possession, remainder, contingency, or otherwise " within the
meaning of that section. Throughout the judgment of the learned judge he
assumed that Charles Beauclerk had a contingent interest, and at the end of his   F
judgment, referring to an argument based on *Re Parsons, Stockley v. Parsons* (6),
he said this (7):

" But for the present purpose there is a difference between the position of
an heir in the sense of the next in blood to a living person and the position
of an heir in the sense of a presumptive or contingent successor to a title.   G
The interest of Charles Beauclerk under this settlement is not as heir in the
sense of the nearest in blood to the tenth or twelfth Duke but as the possible
successor to the dukedom, and I can see no reason why a person should not
have a contingent interest in property created by reference to the event of
succession to a title."

I, of course, accept that a person may have a contingent interest in property   H
created by reference to the event of succession to a title, e.g., a gift to A. if he
shall succeed to the title. I am unable to accept, however, the distinction between
a gift to the heir of a living person, which is, or was, no more nor less than a gift
to him who on the death of that person succeeds to his undevised freehold estate
of inheritance, and a gift to him who on the death of that person succeeds to his
title. Such distinction as there may be is in my judgment a distinction without a   I
difference and I must prefer the decision and reasoning in *Re Parsons, Stockley
v. Parsons* (6) to that in *Re Duke of St. Albans' Will Trusts* (5).

Since there is, in my judgment, at present no person contingently interested,
or interested at all, in the capital or income under the trusts of the will and

(5) [1962] 2 All E.R. 402; [1963] Ch. 365.
(6) (1890), 45 Ch.D. 51
(7) [1962] 2 All E.R. at p. 405; [1963] Ch. at p. 372.

A codicil, and since the period allowed for an accumulation, if an accumulation would have been appropriate, has expired, it is an irresistible conclusion that the income falls to be dealt with as if the testator had died intestate in respect thereof.

Declaration accordingly.

Solicitors: *Warrens* (for the plaintiff and the first and fourth defendants);
B *Roney & Co.* (for the second and third defendants); *Charles Russell & Co.* (for the fifth defendant); *Joynson-Hicks & Co.* (for the sixth defendant).

[*Reported by* Jenifer Sandell, *Barrister-at-Law.*]

C

PROPERTY AND BLOODSTOCK, LTD. *v.* EMERTON.
BUSH *v.* PROPERTY AND BLOODSTOCK, LTD.

[Chancery Division (Ungoed-Thomas, J.), March 7, 8, 9, 10, 22, 1967.]

D *Mortgage—Sale—Leasehold property—Covenant by lessee in lease not to assign —Contract for sale by lessee's mortgagee—Condition that sale subject to mortgagee's obtaining consent to assignment of lease to purchaser—Date fixed by contract for completion passed—Mortgagee obtained order for possession —Lessee tendered redemption moneys before time for delivering possession under the order arrived—Lessee applied for a stay of proceedings for possession,*
E *and brought an action to redeem the mortgage—Whether contract for sale put an end to the right of redemption—Law of Property Act, 1925 (15 & 16 Geo. 5 c. 20), s. 101 (1), s. 104 (1).*

In January, 1964, a twenty-one years' lease of an inn was granted. It contained a lessee's covenant not to assign the premises. The lessee charged the leasehold premises to a mortgagee. Notice requiring payment of principal
F moneys secured by the mortgage was given to the lessee in April, 1965, and, the mortgagee's power of sale having arisen, the mortgagee contracted on Sept. 26, 1966, to sell the leasehold premises to a purchaser. The date fixed by the contract for completion was Oct. 24, 1966. The sale was expressed (by condition (j)) to be subject to the vendor's obtaining the consent of the landlords to the assignment of the lease to the purchaser.
G The mortgagee having obtained an order for possession, the lessee in January, 1967, before the delivery of possession had to be made under the order, tendered redemption moneys. In the present proceedings the lessee* sought a stay of the order for possession and redemption of the mortgage.

Held: (i) on the true construction of the contract for sale, and in particular of condition (j), obtaining the landlords' consent was not a condition
H precedent to the formation of a contract of sale and creation of the relation of vendor and purchaser between the mortgagee and the purchaser (see p. 849, letter F, post); accordingly the date by which the landlords' consent had to be obtained was the date at which title had in fact to be established, not the date stated in the contract as the date fixed for completion (see p. 848, letter D, post).

I *Ellis* v. *Rogers* ((1885), 29 Ch.D. 661) and *Day* v. *Singleton* ([1899] 2 Ch. 320) applied.

Aberfoyle Plantations, Ltd. v. *Cheng* ([1959] 3 All E.R. 910) and *Re Sandwell Park Colliery Co.* ([1928] All E.R. Rep. 651) considered and distinguished.

(ii) therefore, as an unconditional contract for sale by a mortgagee precluded

---

* The lessee had in fact executed a deed of assignment to a trustee in favour of creditors; moreover, the lease had been granted to the lessee and his wife jointly; but they held on trust for the lessee (see p. 841, letter H, post). These matters are not referred to in the headnote, with a view to simplicity, for they did not affect the principle decided.

the mortgagor's right of redemption, the lessee in the present case had   A
been precluded since the date of the contract for sale from exercising the
right of redemption (see p. 844, letter H, and p. 849, letter I, post).

    Lord Waring v. *London and Manchester Assurance Co., Ltd.* ([1934] All
E.R. Rep. 642) followed.

[As to when a mortgagee may be restrained from exercising his power of sale,
see 27 HALSBURY'S LAWS (3rd Edn.) 301, 302, para. 566; and for cases on the   B
effect of sale on an equity of redemption, see 35 DIGEST (Repl.) 587-588, *2596-
2598.*

    For the Law of Property Act, 1925, s. 101, s. 104, see 20 HALSBURY'S STATUTES
(2nd Edn.) 655, 665.]

Cases referred to:
    Aberfoyle Plantations, Ltd. v. *Cheng,* [1959] 3 All E.R. 910; [1960] A.C. 115;   C
        [1959] 3 W.L.R. 1011; Digest (Cont. Vol. A) 1309, *909a.*
    Bain v. *Fothergill,* [1874-80] All E.R. Rep. 83; (1874), L.R. 7 H.L. 158;
        43 L.J.Ex. 243; 31 L.T. 387; 39 J.P. 228; 40 Digest (Repl.) 287, *2392.*
    Blaiberg v. *Keeves,* [1906] 2 Ch. 175; 75 L.J.Ch. 464; 95 L.T. 412; 40 Digest
        (Repl.) 76, *585.*   D
    Day v. *Singleton,* [1899] 2 Ch. 320; 68 L.J.Ch. 593; 81 L.T. 306; 31 Digest
        (Repl.) 429, *5556.*
    Ellis v. *Rogers,* (1885), 29 Ch.D. 661; 53 L.T. 377; 40 Digest (Repl.) 280,
        2335.
    Sandwell Park Colliery Co., Re, Field v. *The Co.,* [1928] All E.R. Rep. 651;
        [1929] 1 Ch. 277; 98 L.J.Ch. 229; 10 Digest (Repl.) 824, *5389.*   E
    Smith v. *Butler,* [1900] 1 Q.B. 694; 69 L.J.Q.B. 521; 82 L.T. 281; 40 Digest
        (Repl.) 266, *2232.*
    Torrance v. *Bolton,* (1872), L.R. 14 Eq. 124; 41 L.J.Ch. 643; 27 L.T. 19; *on
        appeal,* 8 Ch. App. 118; 42 L.J.Ch. 177; 27 L.T. 738; 37 J.P. 164;
        40 Digest (Repl.) 73, *557.*
    Waring (Lord) v. *London and Manchester Assurance Co., Ltd.,* [1934] All E.R.   F
        Rep. 642; [1935] Ch. 310; 104 L.J.Ch. 201; 152 L.T. 390; 35 Digest
        (Repl.) 587, *2598.*

Motions.

On Nov. 3, 1966, Property and Bloodstock, Ltd. commenced proceedings
(" the possession proceedings ") by originating summons against Philip John
Emerton for possession of leasehold property known as Boulters Inn, Boulters   G
Lock, Maidenhead, Berkshire, comprised in a lease dated Jan. 3, 1964, made
between the Borough of Maidenhead as landlords and Harris Fitzroy Duyland
Bush and Doris Marjorie Bush (his wife) as tenants. Mr. and Mrs. Bush were
trustees of the leasehold property for Mr. Bush. The leasehold property was
charged by deed dated Jan. 3, 1964, in favour of Property and Bloodstock, Ltd.
(" the mortgagee ") to secure repayment of the sum of £10,500 with interest.   On   H
Dec. 9, 1966, it was ordered that Philip John Emerton (who was trustee under
a deed of assignment by Mr. Bush in favour of creditors) should within twenty-
eight days after service of the order deliver up possession to the mortgagee.   On
Jan. 16, 1967, tender was made of the money due under the mortgage, but
refused.   On Jan. 17, 1967, Harris Fitzroy Duyland Bush and Philip John
Emerton commenced proceedings by writ (" the redemption proceedings ")   I
against (i) the mortgagee, (ii) Arthur James Cressy, to whom the mortgagee
had contracted on Sept. 26, 1966, as mortgagee to sell the property, and (iii)
Doris Marjorie Bush claiming, inter alia, redemption of the legal charge of
Jan. 3, 1964, and an injunction to restrain the mortgagee and the purchaser
from completing by assignment the contract of Sept. 26, 1966.

By two notices of motion, both dated Jan. 17, 1967, the defendant in the
possession proceedings and the plaintiffs in the redemption proceedings sought
an order that pending the trial of the second action, the order for possession

A obtained on Dec. 9, 1966, should be stayed; they sought also an order in the redemption proceedings to restrain the mortgagee and the purchaser from taking any step towards completing the contract of Sept. 26, 1966.   It was agreed that the motions should be treated as the trials of the actions.   The facts are set out in the judgment.

B *A. L. Price* for Harris Fitzroy Duyland Bush and Philip John Emerton.
Arthur Bagnall, Q.C., and *M. Nesbitt* for Property and Bloodstock, Ltd.
N. C. H. Browne-Wilkinson for Arthur James Cressy.
D. M. Burton for Doris Marjorie Bush.

Cur. adv. vult.

Mar. 22.   **UNGOED-THOMAS, J.,** read the following judgment: There
C are two motions before me which it is agreed should be treated as the trial of the actions.   They both raise the same main question, namely whether a mortgagee's duly made contract for sale of mortgaged leasehold premises was prevented from terminating the mortgagor's right of redemption by a provision under its special conditions of sale that ". . . the sale is subject to the vendor obtaining the consent of the . . ." lessor to the assignment of the lease to the purchaser.

D The first action is by originating summons and is by the mortgagee, Property and Bloodstock, Ltd. against Philip John Emerton (the trustee of a deed of assignment made by the mortgagor), for possession of the mortgaged leasehold premises.   The motion in this action is, pending the trial of the second action, to stay an order for possession obtained by the mortgagee, as first mortgagee, on Dec. 9, 1966.   The second action is by writ, by the mortgagor, Harris Fitzroy
E Duyland Bush, and Mr. Emerton, against the first mortgagee and Arthur James Cressy, who has entered into a contract with the mortgagee to purchase the leasehold premises, and Doris Marjorie Bush, the wife of the plaintiff Mr. Bush, and trustee with him and for him of the mortgaged premises and a chargee of Mr. Bush's beneficial interest in the premises.   This second action is for redemption of the legal charge made in favour of the first mortgagee.

F On Jan. 3, 1964, the Borough of Maidenhead granted Mr. and Mrs. Bush a lease of Boulters Inn, Maidenhead, for twenty-one years from Apr. 14, 1962, at the yearly rent therein mentioned.   The lease contained a covenant by the tenants ". . . not to assign underlet or part with the possession of the demised premises or any part thereof ".   On the same day Mr. and Mrs. Bush executed a legal charge of the premises in favour of the mortgagee and assigned the goodwill of the business and benefit of all licences held by the tenants in connexion
G therewith to the mortgagee, subject to a proviso for redemption.

By a legal charge of Feb. 15, 1965, Mr. Bush charged his beneficial interest in the leasehold property to secure a payment to Mrs. Bush.   In a further legal charge of Apr. 21, 1965, to which Mr. and Mrs. Bush were parties, it was recited that they held the lease on trust for Mr. Bush.   By an assignment of Apr. 21,
H 1965, Mr. Bush declared that he would henceforth stand possessed of, inter alia, his leasehold property on trust for Mr. Emerton, and it was provided that Mr. Emerton should, for the purpose of realising the trust property, have power to carry on and manage Mr. Bush's business, and Mr. Bush irrevocably appointed Mr. Emerton his attorney for executing the trusts of the deed.   Mr. Emerton went into possession of the leasehold premises and has since had possession of them and carried on the business of an innkeeper there.

I On Apr. 23, 1965, the mortgagee gave notice requiring payment of the mortgage principal and interest so that, ever since, the mortgage principal has been required to be repaid.   On Sept. 26, 1966, the contract for sale by the mortgagee to Mr. Cressy, which I have mentioned, was entered into.   This contract is in a printed form and the operative part reads as follows:

" Memorandum.   It is hereby agreed that Property & Bloodstock, Ltd. . . . is the vendor and that Arthur James Cressy . . . is the purchaser of the property described in the accompanying particulars of sale, at the

price of £25,000 subject to the accompanying conditions of sale, and that the
purchase shall be made and completed according to the said conditions of
sale, so far as the same are applicable to a sale by private treaty."

Then it is signed by the parties and a reference is made to the purchase money
and deposit.

The particulars referred to are particulars of Boulters Inn, Maidenhead, being
the premises comprised in the lease which I have mentioned.   There was no
mention in this contract for sale of goodwill at all.   Then there was, under the
heading " Special conditions of sale ", a number of printed and typewritten
conditions and to some of these I shall refer.

" (a) The sale is subject to the following conditions and to the conditions
known as the National Conditions of Sale (17th Edn.) so far as the latter
conditions are not inconsistent with the following conditions; . . . [(c) provided
for payment of a deposit;] (d) The completion shall be on Oct. 24, 1966;
(e) The vendor is selling as mortgagee; . . . (g) The property is sold with the
benefit insofar as the vendor is capable of assigning the same of a licence
dated Apr. 10, 1958, made between the mayor aldermen and burgesses of
the borough of Maidenhead of the one part and Peter Calver Reeves of the
other part for the exclusive selling ice cream and refreshments on Ray
Mill Island in consideration of payment of the yearly sum of £25.   [(h) provided for the sale being with vacant possession on completion;] (i) The
vendor will use its best endeavours but without incurring any personal liability
to assist the purchaser in obtaining at the purchaser's expense a transfer
to the purchaser or its nominee of all licences and renewals of licences necessary in relation to the business of a licenced victualler and innkeeper carried
on upon the property.   [Then comes the crucial condition] (j) The sale
is subject to the vendor obtaining the consent of the mayor aldermen
and burgesses of the borough of Maidenhead to the assignment of the said
lease to the purchaser."

The National Conditions of Sale, which are printed on the form, provide by
condition 10 (I) as follows:

" Where the interest sold is leasehold for the residue of an existing term
the following provisions of this condition shall apply."

Then sub-cl. (5) reads:

" The sale is subject to the reversioner's licence being obtained, where
necessary.   The fee for such licence shall be paid by the vendor, but, if the
licence cannot be obtained, the vendor may rescind the contract on the same
terms as if the purchaser had persisted in an objection to the title which the
vendor was unable to remove."

That, in effect, refers back to condition 8 (6) of the National Conditions which
reads as follows:

" If the purchaser shall persist in any objection to the title which the
vendor shall be unable or unwilling, on reasonable grounds, to remove, and
shall not withdraw the same within ten days of being required so to do,
the vendor may, subject to the purchaser's rights under s. 42 and s. 125 of the
Law of Property Act, 1925, by notice in writing to the purchaser or his
solicitor, and notwithstanding any intermediate negotiation or litigation,
rescind the contract."

Then sub-cl. (7) provides:

" Upon such rescission the vendor shall return the deposit, but without
interest, costs of investigating title or other compensation or payment, and
the purchaser shall return the abstract and other papers furnished to him."

Condition 22 of the National Conditions of Sale provides for time being made of the
essence of the contract upon service of a notice in writing, and sub-cl. (2) of that
condition reads:

A   " Upon service of such notice as aforesaid it shall become and be a term of the contract, in respect of which time shall be of the essence thereof, that the party to whom the notice is given shall complete the contract within twenty-eight days after service of the notice (exclusive of the day of service): but this condition shall operate without prejudice to any express right of either party to rescind the contract in the meantime."

B   On Oct. 24, 1966, came the date fixed for completion under the contract.   On Nov. 3 the possession proceedings by originating summons were commenced. On Dec. 9 an order was made for possession to be given up by Mr. Emerton to the mortgagee within twenty-eight days after service of the order.   On Jan. 16, 1967, before the expiration of the twenty-eight days, the mortgagor tendered the money due under the mortgage: it was disputed whether it was the correct

C   amount, but this discrepancy was not relied on as material to the argument developed before me.   On Jan. 17, 1967, the redemption proceedings by writ were commenced, and on the same day the two notices of motion to which I have referred and which are now before me were given.

I come now to the law.   First, I will deal with the statute law, and then with the case law which bears on the issue;   and secondly, with the construction of the contract for sale in this case and the application of that law to it.   The relevant

D   statute law is in the Law of Property Act, 1925, s. 101 (1) (i), which confers on a mortgagee the power of sale when the mortgage money has become due, and s. 104 (1), which provides that a mortgagee who so sells can by deed convey the property sold.   They provide:

E   " 101.—(1) A mortgagee, where the mortgage is made by deed, shall, by virtue of this Act, have the following powers, to the like extent as if they had been in terms conferred by the mortgage deed, but not further (namely): —(i) A power, when the mortgage money has become due, to sell, or to concur with any other person in selling, the mortgaged property, or any part thereof, either subject to prior charges or not, and either together or in lots, by public auction or by private contract, subject to such conditions respecting

F   title, or evidence of title, or other matter, as the mortgagee thinks fit . . .

" 104.—(1) A mortgagee exercising the power of sale conferred by this Act shall have power, by deed, to convey the property sold, for such estate and interest therein as he is by this Act authorised to sell or convey or may be the subject of the mortgage, freed from all estates, interest, and rights to which the mortgage has priority, but subject to all estates, interests,

G   and rights which have priority to the mortgage."

It is common ground that a contract of sale which is absolute or, in other words, unconditional, precludes the right of redemption in accordance with the decision in *Lord Waring* v. *London and Manchester Assurance Co., Ltd.* (1), but there was argument as to the precise scope of the basis of that decision and as to how much

H   further it went.   In that case the mortgagor's contention was that there was a distinction between a contract for sale and a sale and that (2) " the equity of redemption is not barred by sale till the moment of completion ".   The counter submission was (3) " The contention [that is the contention of the mortgagor] confuses power to sell with power to convey.   Conveyance is simply the machinery by which the legal title is passed . . ."   Crossman, J., in his judgment stated (4):

I   "The contract is an absolute contract, not conditional in any way, and the sale is expressed to be made by the company as mortgagee."

There was argument whether " not conditional in any way " meant, as the mortgagee before me contended, not conditional on the mortgagor's right to redeem, or, alternatively, not subject to a condition precedent to the formation

(1) [1934] All E.R. Rep. 642; [1935] Ch. 310.
(2) [1935] Ch. at p. 314.   (3) [1935] Ch. at p. 316.
(4) [1934] All E.R. Rep. at p. 644; [1935] Ch. at p. 317.

of the contract, or, on the other hand, as the mortgagor before me contended, not **A** subject to a condition whose fulfilment is dependent on a third party where the failure to fulfil the condition terminates the contract. The contract to which CROSSMAN, J., referred was a contract of sale and it was the contract of sale itself which he described as " not conditional in any way ". This necessarily means that it was the contract of sale itself which was not conditional; but a contract of sale is not itself grammatically or properly described as conditional **B** because it contains terms which amount to conditions, but only because it is itself subject to a condition.

The judge made it clear that the unconditional contract for sale in that case was an exercise of the power of sale and bound the mortgagor, and he gave his reasons for that (5):

" In my judgment, s. 101 (1) (i) of that Act, which gives to a mortgagee **C** power to sell the mortgaged property, is perfectly clear, and means that the mortgagee has power to sell out and out, by private contract or by auction, and subsequently to complete by conveyance; and the power to sell is, I think, a power by selling to bind the mortgagor. If that were not so, the extraordinary result would follow that every purchaser from a mort- gagee would, in effect, be getting a conditional contract, liable at any time **D** to be set aside by the mortgagor's coming in and paying the principal, interest, and costs. Such a result would make it impossible for a mortgagee, in the ordinary course of events, to sell unless he was in a position to promise that completion should take place immediately or on the day after the contract, and there would have to be a rush for completion in order to defeat a possible claim by the mortgagor. It seems to me impossible seriously **E** to suggest that the mortgagor's equity of redemption remains in force pending completion of the sale by conveyance. The only effect of the conveyance is to put the legal estate entirely in the purchaser: that follows from s. 104 (1) of the Law of Property Act, 1925, which provides that a mortgagee shall have power to convey the legal estate; and the whole legal estate can be conveyed free from all estates, interests, and rights to which **F** the mortgage has priority."

He thus concluded a little later (6):

" The result in the present case is that the sale effected by the contract, assuming, for the moment, that there is no objection to it on any other ground, binds the mortgagor, and that it is too late after the sale for him to **G** tender the mortgage money and become entitled to have the property reconveyed to him."

I emphasise the words " the sale effected by the contract ". In that case the contract for sale was not subject to any condition, whether prerequisite to the formation of the contract or to any contract which was to effect a sale. It is crucial to this judgment that the contract for sale, being absolute and not subject **H** to a condition itself, effected a sale. So, to my mind, it decided that a contract for sale, not subject to a condition whose fulfilment is prerequisite to the forma- tion of a contract of sale and, therefore, to effecting a sale which such a contract automatically effects, in the exercise of the power of sale within s. 101 (1) of the Law of Property Act, 1925, is binding on the mortgagor and therefore precludes the right of redemption, as long, of course, as the contract for sale exists. Con- **I** versely, any condition which was not a prerequisite to the formation of a contract for sale effecting a sale, which such a contract effected, would not prevent the contract being a binding contract for sale and, therefore, effecting a sale in the exercise of a statutory power of sale and thus precluding the right of redemption.

In *Ellis* v. *Rogers* (7) all the members of the Court of Appeal, COTTON, BOWEN and FRY, L.JJ., in disagreeing obiter with KAY, J., treated as a matter of title

(5) [1934] All E.R. Rep. at pp. 644, 645; [1935] Ch. at pp. 317, 318.
(6) [1934] All E.R. Rep. at p. 645; [1934] Ch. at p. 318.   (7) (1885), 29 Ch.D. 661.

A   the obtaining of the landlord's consent to the assignment of premises the subject
of an agreement for a lease containing a qualified provision against assignment
without his consent; and they therefore treated consent as not required until
good title had to be established.   In that case there was no express condition
at all dealing with the landlord's consent, either in the sense of a condition as a
prerequisite to the formation of a contract of sale, or in the sense of a term of the
B   contract of sale.   So the case goes towards establishing that, in the absence of
provision indicating the contrary, the obtaining of a landlord's consent to the
assignment of a lease containing a provision against assignment without consent
is a matter of title and that the consent need not be shown until good title has
been established.

   In *Aberfoyle Plantations, Ltd.* v. *Cheng* (8), a Privy Council case, the vendors
C   agreed to sell land to part of which they had title, but part of which was subject
to seven leases which had expired and to which the vendors, therefore, had no
title, although they were, in fact, negotiating for a renewal of the leases.   Clause 1
of the agreement provided that " Subject to the condition contained in cl. 4 the
vendor will sell and the purchaser will buy " the whole property.   Clause 4
was in these terms:

D   " The purchase is conditional on the vendor obtaining at the vendor's
   expense a renewal of the seven (7) leases described in the schedule hereto
   so as to be in a position to transfer the same to the purchaser and if for any
   cause whatsoever the vendor is unable to fulfil this condition this agreement
   shall become null and void and the vendor shall refund to the purchaser
   the deposit or deposits already made under cl. 2 hereof notwithstanding
E   anything contained in cl. 10 hereof."

   Clause 10 reads:

   " If from any cause (other than the vendor's default) the purchase shall
   not be completed on Apr. 30, 1956 . . . as herebefore provided then this
   agreement shall become null and void and the deposit or deposits already
F   made will be forfeited."

   The time for completion was fixed (first by the contract, and afterwards by
arrangement between the vendor and purchaser at a later date).   By the date
so fixed the vendors, through no fault of their own, had not obtained a renewal
of the leases, and the purchaser brought the action for return of the deposits
which he had paid.   He succeeded because in the absence of express provision
G   it was held that the date fixed for completion was the date by which the condition
was to be fulfilled.

   It seems quite clear to me that there was a binding agreement, namely the
agreement containing the clauses to which I have referred: and it was, none the
less a binding agreement, despite the condition contained in cl. 4 and the reference
to that condition in cl. 1.   Thus, for example, Lord Jenkins, delivering the
H   judgment, asked (9):

   " Within what period of time did the agreement . . . require the condition
   contained in cl. 4 to be performed? "

   Clause 4 itself, because it was part of the binding agreement, governed what was
to happen if the vendor was unable to fulfil the condition.   And in accordance
with *Day* v. *Singleton* (10), an authority to which I will next refer, the vendor
I   was under a duty to the purchaser to try to fulfil the condition, a duty arising
by implication from the agreement because he had entered into a binding agreement with the purchaser.   Nevertheless, Lord Jenkins referred (11) to the
agreement as a " conditional agreement "; and he explained (11) what he meant
by " conditional agreement ", namely, " an agreement providing, subject to

---

(8) [1959] 3 All E.R. 910; [1960] A.C. 115.
(9) [1959] 3 All E.R. at p. 914; [1960] A.C. at p. 124.
(10) [1899] 2 Ch. 320.
(11) [1959] 3 All E.R. at p. 911; [1960] A.C. at p. 124.

the condition therein mentioned, for the sale . . .''. This itself indicates that there   **A**
is a binding agreement and that the condition attaches not to that agreement but
to the sale for which the agreement provides. He quoted (12) the judgment of
MAUGHAM, J. in *Re Sandwell Park Colliery Co., Field* v. *The Co.* (13). In that
case there was a contract for the sale of property containing a clause, cl. 14, that
" This contract and the sale hereby agreed to be made is subject to the same
being approved and sanctioned by the court " without a date being fixed for   **B**
obtaining such approval. It was held that the court's approval had to be
obtained before the date fixed for completion. The quotation (14) from
MAUGHAM, J., referred to the condition as ". . . ' a condition upon which the
validity of the contract as one sale (sic: q. " one of sale ") depends ' ". This
quotation again indicates that the condition is not a condition on which the
validity of the contract for all purposes depends but only its validity in so far   **C**
as it is, in LORD JENKINS'S words already quoted (15), ". . . providing, subject
to the condition therein mentioned, for the sale . . .". Moreover, when a little later
in the passage quoted (14) MAUGHAM, J., refers to, " ' . . . the very existence of
the mutual obligations is dependent on the performance of the condition ' ",
it seems to me that the mutual obligations there referred to are the mutual obligations arising out of the contract, not as a contract in all its aspects, but as a   **D**
contract of sale and, necessarily, as a contract of sale establishing the relationship of vendor and purchaser as indicated in the *Waring* case (16). Similarly, in
the *Sandwell Park* case (17), MAUGHAM, J., said:

> " Clause 14 of the contract must be regarded as a condition precedent
> which had to be satisfied before the contract would be binding [and he added   **E**
> the significant qualification] as a contract for sale."

This analysis appears to me to be confirmed by LORD JENKINS' statement (18)

> ". . . that the reason for taking the date fixed for completion by a con-
> ditional contract of sale as the date by which the condition is to be fulfilled
> appears to their lordships to be that, until the condition is fulfilled, there
> is no contract of sale to be completed, and, accordingly, that, by fixing a   **F**
> date for completion, the parties must by implication be regarded as having
> agreed that the contract must have become absolute through performance
> of the condition by that date at latest."

The reference to " the contract " towards the end refers back to " contract of
sale " twice mentioned earlier in the quotation. As he says that, until the
condition is fulfilled, there is no contract of sale to be completed, and as we   **G**
have seen that there is a binding contract, the distinction is drawn between the
binding contract and the contract for sale which the binding contract provides
shall arise only on the fulfilment of the condition. It is only on that contract for
sale arising on the fulfilment of the condition that there comes into existence a
contract for sale establishing the relationship of vendor and purchaser of the
land thus agreed to be sold. And where the binding contract fixes a date for   **H**
completion and provides that the contract of sale establishing the relationship of
vendor and purchaser shall arise on the performance of a condition, that condition,
in the absence of other express provision, has to be fulfilled by the date fixed for
completion where such a date is fixed.

Day v. *Singleton* (19) dealt with the duty of a vendor of a leasehold interest to
obtain a landlord's consent where assignment could not be made without consent.   **I**

---

(12) [1959] 3 All E.R. at pp. 914, 915; [1960] A.C. at pp. 125, 126.
(13) [1928] All E.R. Rep. 651; [1929] 1 Ch. 277.
(14) I.e., the quotation in *Aberfoyle Plantations, Ltd.* v. *Cheng*, [1959] 3 All E.R.
at p. 915; [1960] A.C. at p. 126.
(15) [1959] 3 All E.R. at p. 911; [1960] A.C. at p. 124.
(16) [1934] All E.R. Rep. 642; [1935] Ch. 310.
(17) [1928] All E.R. Rep. at p. 653; [1929] 1 Ch. at pp. 281, 282.
(18) [1959] 3 All E.R. at p. 915; [1960] A.C. at p. 126.
(19) [1899] 2 Ch. 320.

A The vendor contracted to sell a lease containing a covenant against assignment without the landlord's consent, and the contract contained the provision, " The title of the above premises [which, of course, were the subject of the sale] to be satisfactory and subject to landlord's consent to transference of lease ". I take this to mean that title was to be subject to the landlord's consent, and not that the contract of sale itself was to be subject to it so as to preclude the relationship

B of vendor and purchaser arising until the consent had been obtained, i.e., that the consent was to be a matter of title and not a prerequisite to the formation of a contract of sale creating a vendor and purchaser relationship. Accordingly, Sir Nathaniel Lindley, M.R., said (20) that it was not necessary for the vendor to obtain the consent ". . . until the time for completing the assignment . . . had arrived "; that is, as I read it, " until the time for actual completion had

C arrived ", and that therefore the obtaining of the consent was a matter of title and not a condition prerequisite to the formation of a contract of sale and the relationship of vendor and purchaser.

No date was fixed for completion, and the vendor gave notice to rescind the contract. The vendor, however, had made no effort to obtain the landlord's consent before he gave notice and it was therefore held that he was liable to the

D purchaser in substantial damages for breach of duty to the purchaser to try to obtain the landlord's consent, and not merely to return of deposit, interest and costs of investigating the title in accordance with the rule in *Bain* v. *Fothergill* (21) limiting damages for failure to show good title to land. So the case (22) decided that where there is a contract for sale of a lease containing a covenant against assignment without the landlord's consent, then, although it is provided

E that title shall be subject to the landlord's consent, the vendor is under a duty to the purchaser to try to obtain that consent, and that substantial damages, and not merely *Bain* v. *Fothergill* (21) damages, as in the case of failure to show good title, are recoverable for breach of that duty. It seems to me that a fortiori where the creation of the contract for sale itself and the creation thereby of a vendor and purchaser relationship is subject to the landlord's consent (and thus where it

F would hardly even be arguable that the consent was a mere matter of title in which damages are limited as in *Bain* v. *Fothergill* (21)), that then the vendor is under a duty to the purchaser to try to obtain that consent and substantial damages are recoverable for its breach: and certainly no distinction was sought to be made in argument before me about such duty and damages arising where merely title, on the one hand, or contract of sale itself on the other hand, was subject to the

G landlord's consent.

In *Smith* v. *Butler* (23) an agreement for sale of leasehold property was entered into containing a clause that " the agreement was entered into on the condition that the mortgagee would consent to the transfer of the existing loan to the [purchaser] ", being a loan secured on the property by a subsisting mortgage. The purchaser treated the contract as at an end before the date fixed for com-

H pletion, and, therefore, before the date by which consent need be obtained. It was held that the purchaser was (as Romer, L.J., indicated (24)), in breach of contract, and therefore could not recover his deposit. It appears that in the light of the *Aberfoyle* case (25), this case was decided on the basis that the condition about consent was a condition precedent to the formation of a contract of sale creating the relationship of vendor and purchaser.

I It thus seems to me to follow from these cases that in an agreement providing for a sale of leaseholds, whether title on the one hand or the creation of contract of sale establishing the relationship of vendor and purchaser on the other hand, is made subject to obtaining the landlord's consent, the first mentioned agreement

---

(20) [1899] 2 Ch. at p. 327.
(21) [1874-80] All E.R. Rep. 83; (1874), L.R. 7 H.L. 158.   (22) [1899] 2 Ch. 320.
(23) [1900] 1 Q.B. 694.   (24) [1900] 1 Q.B. at p. 699.
(25) [1959] 3 All E.R. 910; [1960] A.C. 115.

is itself a binding agreement between the parties to it and creating binding con-   **A**
tractual obligations between them, whose breach would sound in substantial
damages. If, however, what the agreement provides for is that the contract of
sale and, therefore, the relationship of vendor and purchaser thereby created was
subject, as a condition precedent, to the formation of the contract of sale and,
therefore, the relationship of vendor and purchaser, to the landlord's consent,
then in the absence of other express provision the date by which that consent has   **B**
to be obtained is the date fixed for completion where the agreement fixes that
date. But if what the agreement provides for is that title and not the creation of
a contract of sale is subject to that consent being obtained, then that consent
has to be forthcoming by the date at which title has to be established, normally
actual completion.

In the light of these decisions I come to the contract in this case. The crucial   **C**
question, in view of these decisions, is whether condition (j) in the contract
providing: " The sale is subject to the vendor obtaining the consent of . . ." the
landlord, is a condition precedent to the formation of a contract of sale (and of the
relationship of vendor and purchaser thereby created), or is a matter of title
arising within a contract of sale. In other words, is the contract a contract
providing for sale to be effected by a contract of sale on the condition being   **D**
fulfilled, or is it itself a contract of sale effecting a sale as, for example, in the
Waring case (26)? If the contract is a contract of sale establishing the relationship
of vendor and purchaser and condition (j) and the consent are, therefore, a
matter of title, then the mortgagee vendor is not limited to the date fixed for
completion, namely Oct. 24, 1966, to obtaining that consent. If, however, the
contract is not a contract of sale but a contract providing for sale to be effected   **E**
by a contract of sale on condition (j) being fulfilled, then condition (j) is not a
matter of title but a condition precedent to the formation of a contract of sale,
so that the vendor mortgagee is limited to the date fixed for completion for
obtaining the consent. The answer turns on the construction of the contract.

The contract is in a printed form embodying the National Conditions of Sale.
The operative part is introduced by the word, " Memorandum ", and is followed   **F**
by the words, " It is hereby agreed that " the mortgagee company " is the
vendor and that " Mr. Cressy " is the purchaser ". The words " vendor " and
" purchaser " are not inserted as defined expressions, but as words in their
ordinary substantive meaning, and by the quoted words it is recorded and agreed
that the mortgagee is already the vendor and that Mr. Cressy is already the
purchaser when the contract is signed. " Vendor " may be used to describe a   **G**
person offering for sale and " purchaser " to describe a person seeking purchase:
but this would not be their likely meaning, particularly in their present context.
The quoted words suggest that the contract itself was intended to acknowledge
and agree that there was a vendor and purchaser relationship between the
parties when the contract was signed. The operative part then provides that the
parties are vendor and purchaser of the property,   **H**

". . . subject to the accompanying conditions of sale, and that the
purchase shall be made and completed according to the said conditions of
sale . . ."

It is the function of conditions of sale to state the terms on which the property
is sold and to deal, in particular, with matters of title (see *Torrance* v. *Bolton* (27);   **I**
Blaiberg v. *Keeves* (28)). Reference to obtaining a landlord's consent would be
more readily expected in the conditions of sale if it were a matter of title than if
it were a precondition to the formation of a contract of sale. If it were such a
precondition it would be more readily expected in the operative part or the body
of the contract or memorandum.

Here, however, in condition (j) the sale is made " subject " to the vendor

(26) [1934] All E.R. Rep. 642; [1935] Ch. 310.
(27) (1872), L.R. 14 Eq. 124 at p. 130.   (28) [1906] 2 Ch. 175 at p. 184.

A   obtaining the landlord's consent. Although "subject" might suggest a condition precedent to the sale, the operative part itself uses the word "subject" in stating that it is agreed that the mortgagor is the vendor and Mr. Cressy the purchaser of the property "subject to the accompanying conditions of sale". Moreover, none of those conditions, whether special or general, is, apart from the questionable case of condition (j), a condition precedent to the formation of a

B   contract of sale and the creation of the relationship of vendor and purchaser at all. In para. (a) of the special conditions it is similarly said that "The sale is subject to the following conditions . . .", none of which is a condition precedent to the contract of sale, except questionably condition (j). And in general condition 10 it is said that "The sale is subject to the reversioner's licence being obtained, where necessary", and in that condition the word "subject" does

C   not convert the obtaining of the licence from a matter of title into a condition precedent to the formation of the contract of sale, nor was it suggested that the quoted words made general condition 10 such a condition precedent.

The operative part does, however, provide that "the purchase shall be made and completed according to the said conditions of sale", and it is arguable that this provision that "the purchase shall be made" according to the conditions

D   means that the contract of purchase shall be entered into according to those conditions which include condition (j). The printed form, however, would still so read even though there were no such condition as condition (j), which is the only condition which it is suggested might be precedent to the formation of a contract of sale; and "purchase" and "made" do not have the precise meaning of "contract of purchase" and "entered into": they may well refer

E   to the process of effecting the purchase by carrying out the contract of purchase, and this appears to me to be the preferable interpretation in this context.

My conclusion, therefore, is that condition (j) is not a condition precedent to the formation of a contract of sale, and the creation of the relationship of vendor and purchaser between the mortgagee and Mr. Cressy, and that, therefore, the mortgagee was not limited to Oct. 24, 1966 to obtaining the landlord's consent.

F   The mortgagor, however, contended that, even so, the mortgagee was limited to a reasonable period after the date fixed for completion, namely Oct. 24, to obtain their consent and that such a period had expired. It was not suggested that the date fixed for completion was of the essence of the contract, and in view of (inter alia) general condition 22 providing for time being made of the essence of the contract, this is not surprising. Moreover, although it was contemplated

G   that the business of a licensed victualler would continue to be carried on at the premises, the subject of this sale which has been canvassed before me was the leasehold and not the business. It appears that the reason for the licence not being given for, at any rate, an appreciable part of the time since Oct. 24, has been due to the very issue between mortgagor and mortgagee litigated in these proceedings; and it seems to be common ground that it cannot be said that the licence cannot

H   be obtained. However that may be, counsel for the mortgagor stated that he did not rely on any circumstances (other than the mere passing of time) as relevant to making the passing of time since Oct. 24 unreasonable. In my view it would be wrong to conclude that, in the circumstances, the passing of time since Oct. 24 makes the omission to obtain the licence unreasonable.

My conclusion, therefore, is that the mortgagor fails in his submissions and

I   that since the contract of Sept. 26, 1966 he has not had and has not now a present right of redemption.

Declaration accordingly.

Solicitors: *Kidd, Rapinet, Beck & Co.*, agents for *Kidd, Rapinet, Badge & Co.*, Slough (for Harris Fitzroy Duyland Bush and Philip John Emerton); *Burton & Ramsden* (for Property and Bloodstock, Ltd.); *Partridge, Moss & Co.*, Teddington (for Arthur James Cressy); *Clarke, Square & Co.* (for Doris Marjorie Bush).

[*Reported by* Jacqueline Metcalfe, *Barrister-at-Law.*]

A

W. B. ANDERSON & SONS, LTD. AND OTHERS
v. RHODES (LIVERPOOL), LTD. AND OTHERS.

[LIVERPOOL ASSIZES (Cairns, J.), February 21, 22, 23, 24, March 3, 1967.]

Negligence—Duty to take care—Statement—Reply to enquiry—Representation of
credit-worthiness of purchaser—Wholesaler and commission agent's buyer   B
purchasing in vegetable market for third party—Negligence by manager of
wholesaler in not informing buyer about state of account of third party with
wholesaler—Whether wholesaler owed duty of care to prospective vendor to
the third party.

Misrepresentation—Credit—Negligence—Oral representation—Whether defence
of absence of writing maintainable under Statute of Frauds Amendment Act,   C
1828 (9 Geo. 4 c. 14), s. 6.

The plaintiff companies and the first defendant, R., Ltd., which was an
established company of good repute, carried on business as wholesalers in the
Liverpool fruit and vegetable market; R., Ltd. sometimes acted also as
commission agents. The manager of a newly incorporated company, T., Ltd.,
in April, 1965, called on J., the manager of R., Ltd., and bought some   D
potatoes from R., Ltd. for cash. J. made no enquiry about T., Ltd. In the
following weeks T., Ltd. bought more potatoes from R., Ltd., but on credit.
The market rule was that payment should be made within seven days after
invoice. Some payments were made by T., Ltd. to R., Ltd., but the account
fluctuated and at material times there was always more than £2,500 owing
by T., Ltd. to R., Ltd. Customers' accounts were not at this time sufficiently   E
reviewed by R., Ltd., and in consequence of this Reid, R., Ltd.'s salesman
and buyer, was not informed by J. or by R., Ltd.'s book-keeper of the state
of account with T., Ltd. In May, 1965, the method of business between R.,
Ltd. and T., Ltd. changed to a commission basis. Reid ordered potatoes
from the plaintiffs, and sales were entered as, or amended to be, sales to
T., Ltd. In answer to enquiries made by four of the plaintiffs to Reid when   F
he ordered potatoes for T., Ltd., Reid replied in words such as " they are
all right ", which the court found to mean that T., Ltd. was credit-worthy.
Reid's replies were made in good faith without negligence on his part. But
for J.'s and R., Ltd.'s book-keeper's negligence in their handling of R.,
Ltd.'s accounts, they would have known at the material times the extent of
T., Ltd.'s indebtedness to R., Ltd. They did not, however, know this. T.,   G
Ltd. became insolvent and was unable to pay for potatoes purchased and
delivered to T., Ltd. by the four plaintiffs. In an action by the four plaintiffs
and others against R., Ltd., Reid and J., for damages for negligence in
representing that T., Ltd. was credit-worthy,

Held: the four plaintiffs were entitled to recover as against R., Ltd. (but
not against Reid or J.*) damages for their loss in giving credit on sales of   H
potatoes to T., Ltd., for the following reasons—

(i) a duty of care existed between R., Ltd. and the four plaintiffs in relation
to representations made by Reid acting as R., Ltd.'s servant or agent, because
the representations concerned business transactions whose nature made clear
the gravity of the enquiries and the importance and influence attached to the
answers, and because none of the plaintiffs would have been willing to sell to   I
T., Ltd. on credit but for the assurance that T., Ltd. was credit-worthy (see
p. 857, letter A, and p. 862, letter C, post).

Hedley Byrne & Co., Ltd. v. *Heller & Partners, Ltd.* ([1963] 2 All E.R. 575)
applied.

(ii) the negligence of J. and R., Ltd.'s book-keeper in not informing Reid
about the state of R., Ltd.'s account with T., Ltd. was negligence for which

---

* As regards the claim against J., see p. 856, letter I, post.

A R., Ltd. was vicariously responsible, and accordingly the breach of the duty
of care owed by R., Ltd. to the four plaintiffs as stated at (i) ante was established, although Reid himself was not negligent in making the representations
(see p. 856, letter C, p. 857, letter B, p. 862, letter E, and p. 865, letter F,
post).

B (iii) s. 6* of the Statute of Frauds Amendment Act, 1828, did not constitute
a defence to a claim based on negligence and, therefore, although the oral
representations of Reid were representations as to the credit of T., Ltd.,
s. 6 did not apply to them for they were not made fraudulently (see p. 865,
letter E, post).

Banbury v. Bank of Montreal ([1918-19] All E.R. Rep. 1) applied.

C [As to negligence and the arising of a duty to take reasonable care in relation
to physical injury, see 28 HALSBURY'S LAWS (3rd Edn.) 3, para. 1, p. 7, para. 4,
pp. 20, 21, para. 17; and for cases on the subject, see 36 DIGEST (Repl.) 12-18,
34-79, and pp. 27, 28, *113-120*.

As to innocent misrepresentation not giving rise to a right of action for damages,
see 26 HALSBURY'S LAWS (3rd Edn.) 857, para. 1594; and for cases on the subject,
see 35 DIGEST (Repl.) 55, *481, 482*; but see now Misrepresentation Act 1967, s. 2.

D As to the defence of absence of writing where an action is brought on a representation as to credit, see 26 HALSBURY'S LAWS (3rd Edn.) 870, 871, para. 1615;
and for cases on the subject, see 26 DIGEST (Repl.) 31-34, *187-204*.

For the Statute of Frauds Amendment (Lord Tenterden's) Act, 1828, s. 6, see
4 HALSBURY'S STATUTES (2nd Edn.) 660.]

E Cases referred to:

Banbury v. Bank of Montreal, [1918-19] All E.R. Rep. 1; [1918] A.C. 626;
87 L.J.K.B. 1158; 119 L.T. 446; 36 Digest (Repl.) 14, *59*.

Candler v. Crane, Christmas & Co., [1951] 1 All E.R. 426; [1951] 2 K.B. 164;
36 Digest (Repl.) 17, *75*.

Clay v. A. J. Crump & Sons, Ltd., [1963] 3 All E.R. 687; [1964] 1 Q.B. 533;
[1963] 3 W.L.R. 866; Digest (Cont. Vol. A) 75, *486b*.

F Derry v. Peek, [1886-90] All E.R. Rep. 1; (1889), 14 App. Cas. 337; 58 L.J.Ch.
864; 61 L.T. 265; 54 J.P. 148; 35 Digest (Repl.) 27, *187*.

Donoghue (or McAlister) v. Stevenson, [1932] All E.R. Rep. 1; [1932] A.C. 562;
101 L.J.P.C. 119; 147 L.T. 281; 36 Digest 85, *458*.

Everett v. Griffiths, [1920] 3 K.B. 163; 89 L.J.Ch. 929; 123 L.T. 280; 84
G J.P. 161; affd. H.L., [1921] 1 A.C. 631; 90 L.J.K.B. 737; 125 L.T. 230;
85 J.P. 149; 33 Digest (Repl.) 709, *1659*.

Fish v. Kelly, (1864), 17 C.B.N.S. 194; 144 E.R. 78; 43 Digest (Repl.) 116,
1054.

Haslock v. Fergusson, (1837), 7 Ad. & El. 86; 6 L.J.K.B. 247; 112 E.R. 403;
26 Digest (Repl.) 32, *192*.

H Hedley Byrne & Co., Ltd. v. Heller & Partners, Ltd., [1961] 3 All E.R. 891;
[1962] 1 Q.B. 396; [1961] 3 W.L.R. 1225; affd. H.L., [1963] 2 All E.R.
575; [1964] A.C. 465; [1963] 3 W.L.R. 101; Digest (Cont. Vol. A)
51, *1117a*.

Heilbut, Symons & Co. v. Buckleton, [1911-13] All E.R. Rep. 83; [1913] A.C.
30; 82 L.J.K.B. 245; 107 L.T. 769; 9 Digest (Repl.) 259, *1643*.

I Heskell v. Continental Express, Ltd., [1950] 1 All E.R. 1033; 17 Digest (Repl.)
131, *380*.

Low v. Bouverie, [1891-94] All E.R. Rep. 348; [1891] 3 Ch. 82; 60 L.J.Ch. 594;
65 L.T. 533; 35 Digest (Repl.) 34, *258*.

Nocton v. Lord Ashburton, [1914-15] All E.R. Rep. 45; [1914] A.C. 932; 83
L.J.Ch. 784; 111 L.T. 641; 43 Digest (Repl.) 115, *1038*.

Robinson v. National Bank of Scotland, 1916 S.C. (H.L.) 154; 26 Digest (Repl.)
33, *63*.

---

* Section 6 is set out at p. 862, letter F, post.

Shiells v. *Blackburne*, (1789), 1 Hg. Bl. 158;   126 E.R. 94;   3 Digest (Repl.)   A
71, *111*.

Stradling v. *Morgan*, (1560), 1 Plowd. 201;   75 E.R. 308;   44 Digest (Repl.)
222, *387*.

Swann v. *Phillips*, (1838), 8 Ad. & El. 457;   7 L.J.Q.B. 200;   112 E.R. 912;   26
Digest (Repl.) 32, *194*.

Wilkinson v. *Coverdale*, (1793), 1 Esp. 74;   12 Digest (Repl.) 251, *1945*.   B

Woods v. *Martins Bank, Ltd.*, [1958] 3 All E.R. 166;   [1959] 1 Q.B. 55;   [1958]
1 W.L.R. 1018;   3 Digest (Repl.) 182, *324*.

Action.

The seven plaintiff companies, referred to as Anderson, Roberts, Ellwood,
Skenes, Wood, North Western and Pollard respectively, and the first defendant,   C
Raymond E. Rhodes (Liverpool), Ltd. (" Rhodes ") were importers and wholesalers doing business in the fruit and vegetable market in Liverpool.   The first
defendant sometimes also acted as commission agents.   The second defendant,
Reid, was employed by Rhodes as a salesman and buyer, and the third defendant,
Jones, was the manager of Rhodes.   Each plaintiff entered into a contract
with Taylors (Corn and Produce), Ltd. (" Taylors "), for the sale of potatoes by   D
the plaintiff concerned to Taylors.   Taylors were incorporated on Mar. 26, 1965,
and were compulsorily wound up on a petition presented on July 15, 1965;
they were insolvent.   They took delivery of the potatoes sold but were unable
to pay for them.   The plaintiffs brought an action for damages against the
defendants on the ground of negligence in making representations, as alleged,
leading the plaintiffs to enter into transactions with Taylors in the belief that   E
Taylors were worthy of credit.   The facts are set out in the judgment.

Andrew Rankin for the plaintiffs.
R. R. Leech for the defendants.

Cur. adv. vult.

                                                                                  F
Mar. 3.   **CAIRNS, J.,** read the following judgment: In this action there
are seven plaintiffs and three defendants.   Each plaintiff is a company carrying
on business as importers and wholesalers in the Liverpool fruit and vegetable
market.   I shall refer to them respectively as Anderson, Roberts, Ellwood, Skenes,
Wood, North Western, and Pollard.   The first defendant is a company carrying
on similar business to the plaintiffs and sometimes acting as commission agents—   G
I shall call them Rhodes.   The second defendant, Reid, was at the material times
employed by Rhodes as a salesman and buyer.   The third defendant, Jones, was
Rhodes' manager.   The cause of all the trouble was a company called Taylors
(Corn and Produce), Ltd., whose headquarters were at Bolton, and to whom I
shall refer as Taylors.   They are not a party to the action.   Each plaintiff makes
a separate claim against Rhodes and against Reid and Jones, alleging that it was   H
led by the defendants to believe that Taylors were worthy of credit.   Each plaintiff
entered into a contract with Taylors, Rhodes acting as agents for Taylors, and
either Reid or Jones acting on behalf of Rhodes, for the sale of a quantity of
potatoes.   Some plaintiffs entered into more than one such contract.   The potatoes
were all delivered, but none of them were ever paid for.   Taylors was a " mush-
room " company, which was incorporated on Mar. 26, 1965, with a capital of   I
£100, traded in April, May and June, 1965, and was compulsorily wound up,
insolvent, on a petition presented on July 15, 1965.   Each claim depends in the
main on representations alleged to have been made by Reid or Jones to an
officer or servant of a plaintiff.   In each case I have to decide what was said and
whether it constituted a representation that Taylors was deserving of credit.
There is no allegation of fraud against any defendant.

The important question of law which arises is whether there was any duty of
care resting on the defendants.   Is the doctrine enunciated in the House of Lords

A   in *Hedley Byrne & Co., Ltd.* v. *Heller & Partners, Ltd.* (1) applicable here? If there was a duty of care it is hardly disputed that the duty was broken. If any plaintiff makes out a prima facie case, then comes the question whether its claim is barred by s. 6 of the Statute of Frauds Amendment Act, 1828, (2) usually known as Lord Tenterden's Act. That section provides that a representation as to credit is not actionable unless in writing. None of the representations relied

B   on in this case was in writing, and at first sight that might look like a short answer to all the claims. In *Banbury* v. *Bank of Montreal* (3) the House of Lords, however, gave a restricted meaning to the section, holding that it applied only to fraudulent representations. The question is whether that case is still to be taken to exclude negligent representations from the operation of the section notwithstanding the *Hedley Byrne* case (1).

C   Apart from the case based on representations, the plaintiffs make a series of other allegations of negligence against the defendants. The gist of these other allegations is that the defendants knew that the plaintiffs would be influenced by Rhodes' own good reputation in the market to give credit to Taylors, and that the defendants, therefore, owed a duty to the plaintiffs to take care to learn about Taylors' reliability and to inform the plaintiffs of their findings. These con-

D   tentions are based on *Donoghue (or McAlister)* v. *Stevenson* (4) and *Clay* v. *A. J. Crump & Sons, Ltd.* (5). I can dispose of this part of the plaintiffs' claims straight away. *Clay* v. *A. J. Crump & Sons, Ltd.* (5) is a case like most, if not all, of the cases following *Donoghue* v. *Stevenson* (4) on personal injuries. In *Hedley Byrne & Co., Ltd.* v. *Heller & Partners, Ltd.* (1), although counsel for the appellants in that case relied strongly on *Donoghue* v. *Stevenson* (4) in his argument, it was not

E   on those bases that the House of Lords reached their conclusion, and four of their lordships expressly rejected the idea that *Donoghue* v. *Stevenson* (4) had any direct bearing on the case (see per LORD REID, (6) LORD HODSON, (7) LORD DEVLIN, (8) and LORD PEARCE (9)). If the doctrine of *Donoghue* v. *Stevenson* (4) does not directly impose any duty on the maker of the representation, I do not see how it can possibly impose a duty on a trader, apart from any representation

F   he may make, to enquire about another trader's credit and give information about it to persons who may deal with that other trader. In my view, if the plaintiffs are to succeed at all, it must be on the basis of representations made to them.

The history of the matter may be summarised as follows. Early in April, 1965, less than a fortnight after Taylors was incorporated, one Cookson, manager of

G   Taylors, called on Jones in Rhodes' office to buy some potatoes. The only introduction which he brought with him was a printed card bearing his company's name, and Jones, who had never seen him before and never heard of Taylors, made no enquiries about that company. He sold him for cash a small lot of potatoes at the price of £44 4s. During the following weeks, Rhodes continued to supply potatoes to Taylors, but on credit. The custom of the market is that

H   accounts are payable seven days after invoice. In practice, nobody insists on absolutely prompt payment, but payment is expected to be made within the next two or three weeks at the latest, and a new customer, and particularly one who had given no sort of references, would normally be allowed less latitude. Taylors did make payments to Rhodes from time to time, but by May 14, they had had goods to the value of £6,242 which had not been paid for, and of this sum £5,080

I

(1) [1963] 2 All E.R. 575; [1964] A.C. 465.
(2) Section 6 is set out at p. 862, letter F, post.
(3) [1918-19] All E.R. Rep. 1; [1918] A.C. 626.
(4) [1932] All E.R. Rep. 1; [1932] A.C. 562.
(5) [1963] 3 All E.R. 687; [1964] 1 Q.B. 533.
(6) [1963] 2 All E.R. at p. 580; [1964] A.C. at p. 482.
(7) [1963] 2 All E.R. at p. 596; [1964] A.C. at p. 506.
(8) [1963] 2 All E.R. at p. 608; [1964] A.C. at p. 525.
(9) [1963] 2 All E.R. at p. 615; [1964] A.C. at p. 536.

was currently due in the sense that more than seven days had elapsed since **A**
invoice. Thereafter, the state of the account fluctuated, but at all material times
there was something over £2,500 overdue. It is conceded on behalf of the defendants that these were excessively large outstandings, and if anybody in Rhodes'
office had realised the amount of them Taylors would not have been considered
to be meeting their obligations satisfactorily. Unfortunately, there was at the
time great slackness in the working of Rhodes' accounting system; books were **B**
not being kept up-to-date, statements were not being regularly despatched to
customers, and normal steps were not being taken to review the state of customers'
accounts. Apparently there was pressure of business, and the office was under-
staffed. Responsibility must rest on Jones, Rhodes' manager, and on O'Connor,
Rhodes' book-keeper. If they had known the true state of affairs, they would
have told Reid. Reid himself had no responsibility for collecting payments or **C**
for studying the accounts. He would expect to have been told if a customer was
not paying regularly.

From about the middle of May, 1965, Rhodes began to do business with
Taylors on a different basis. Instead of selling their own goods to Taylors they
acted as commission agents, effecting contracts on the market between Taylors
and other suppliers on the basis that they themselves would receive a commission **D**
from Taylors. They say that the reason for this change was that they wished to
reduce their turnover. On May 14, came the first of the transactions involved in
this action, which was with the first plaintiff, Anderson. Scott was a salesman
employed by Anderson; he knew Rhodes and knew Reid as their buyer. Reid
approached Scott and made an enquiry about potatoes, resulting in the sale of
149 bags. Up to then Scott had supposed the purchaser to be Rhodes, but when **E**
he came to make out a delivery order Reid asked him to make it out in the name
of Taylors. Scott said, " Are they reliable? I have never heard of them ". Reid
replied, either, " They are all right ", or " They are quite all right ". He probably
added, " We have had business transactions with them ". Scott says that Reid
continued: " If they do not pay you, we will ", but Reid denies this. Scott says
that if in answer to his enquiry about Taylors' reliability, Reid had said, " I do **F**
not know ", he would not have accepted Taylors as purchasers. Reid agrees that
if he had given this answer he would not have expected Scott to be willing to
book the goods to Taylors. They were so booked, and in due course they were
delivered. The price, £239 2s., remains outstanding. A week later, Anderson's
senior salesman, Caloe, sold another one hundred bags of potatoes to Reid, at
first booking them to Rhodes but later, at Reid's request, altering the name to **G**
Taylors. Caloe knew about the earlier transaction, but made some enquiry of
Reid about the standing of Taylors as a result of which Reid said they were big
potato people with large canteen orders. The price of the one hundred bags was
£130. Thus, Andersons' total claim is for £369 2s. damages. There were two sales
by the second plaintiff, Roberts, one on May 20, of 360 bags, and one on May 24,
of four hundred bags. Their total claim is for £874 13s. 4d. Both sales were **H**
negotiated by Reid with Puddifer, a director and manager of Roberts. A feature
of this case is that the potatoes were obtained by Roberts from J. & J. Lyons,
auctioneers, who have the reputation of insisting on prompt payment. There was
a conflict of evidence whether Lyons were brought into direct contractual relations with Taylors. I do not think that they were, though I am satisfied that
certain conversations were conducted on the basis that they were. I do not think **I**
that anybody was trying to mislead the court about this—businessmen often
conduct their affairs in ways which pay little heed to exact legal relationships.
On the first sale, the goods were first booked to Rhodes, but Reid later asked
Puddifer to book them to Taylors. Puddifer says that he enquired: " Is he a
good account and a good payer? " adding, " Lyons require payment within
seven days and if they are not paid by Taylors we should have to pay, and I will
have to get it off Taylors or you ". And he says that Reid answered, " He is a

A good account and a good payer ". Reid did not recollect any part of this conversation and denied that he had ever used the expressions " good account " or good payer ". He said that he had probably said that Taylors were all right. The sale on May 24 went through without any further material conversation. The sale by the third plaintiff, Ellwood, was one of 134 bags of potatoes at the price of £167 10s. and was negotiated by Reid with Ellwood's salesman, Taylor,

B on May 21. This Mr. Taylor has no connexion with the Taylors' company. This Mr. Taylor says that he asked Reid what kind of firm Taylors were and Reid replied that they supplied canteens and were a good account. Reid denies this.

The fourth plaintiff, Skenes, sold thirty cases of potatoes on May 24, and thirty-five cases on May 25, at a total price of £132 10s., the transaction being effected between Reid and Skenes' salesman, Tilston. Tilston told me that he

C made no enquiries about Taylors' standing, (a) because he thought that as they were introduced by Reid they would be all right, and (b) because he himself had not been long with Skenes' and did not know that Taylors were a new customer.

The fifth plaintiff, Wood, made five sales to Taylors on various dates from May 26 to June 9, involving altogether potatoes to the value of £688 18s. 6d. The first four sales were certainly negotiated by Reid with Wood's salesman,

D Revell, and although Reid denies that the last one was, I accept Revell's evidence that it was. Again, Taylors' name was first mentioned after the bargain had been made and Revell asked if they were all right. Reid replied, " They are all right and we have served them a number of times ". No further enquiry was made on the later occasions. The sixth plaintiff, North Western, sold two hundred baskets of potatoes to Taylors on May 27, at a price of £190, their salesman

E Lymer acting for North Western and Reid for the purchasers. When the bargain had been made, Lymer started to write the name Rhodes on the delivery order, but Reid stopped him and said " No, Taylors ". Lymer said, " I do not know them; are they all right? " Reid said, " Yes; I have just purchased two hundred for them from Melda Fruit: everybody gives them credit ". Melda Fruit was in fact a firm who at first booked an order in the name of Taylors, but later had it

F changed to Rhodes. I am not, however, satisfied that Melda had required this change before the purchase from North Western. Moreover, so many merchants had by this time given credit to Taylors that I do not think that the statement " everybody gives them credit " was misleading. These further statements were, however, no more than corroborative details intended to back up the assurance that Taylors were all right.

G Finally, the seventh plaintiff, Pollard, through a Mr. Pollard, one of their directors, sold to Taylors on June 2, 1965, one hundred barrels of potatoes at the price of £163 6s. 8d. Reid had nothing to do with this transaction. Mr. Pollard says it was negotiated by Jones. Jones denies this entirely. I prefer Mr. Pollard's evidence and accept his account of the conversation which took place. He says that when the bargain had been fixed he asked Jones if the goods were to be

H booked to him, that is, to Rhodes, and he replied, " No, Taylors ". Pollard asked their address and if they were all right to invoice goods to; Jones replied, " They are all right and we do business with them ourselves ".

[His LORDSHIP referred to the reliability of the evidence of the witnesses and discussed what meaning should be attached to the phrase " they are all right " used in relation to Taylors, and continued:] Apart from evidence as to some

I special meaning of the words, " they are all right ", I should without doubt construe them as meaning, " they are credit-worthy "; and, having considered all the various interpretations advanced, I adhere to the view that this is their real meaning. The question whether the speaker is bound to give a careful answer or merely an honest answer is a separate question, and is a question of law. So is the question whether if there is a duty of care, it rests solely on the individual who spoke the words, or rests also on his employer on whose behalf he speaks. Having arrived at my construction of the words, I consider that in general the person to whom they are spoken is entitled to understand them in the sense of that construction, whatever the speaker may have meant by them. If, A however, the hearer does in fact understand them in a weaker sense, then he cannot rely on the true sense. If he thought that he was being told only that Reid knew nothing against Taylors, he could have no complaint if Reid in fact knew nothing against Taylors even though he ought to have known.

I now make these findings of fact. But for their negligence in handling the accounts, Jones and O'Connor would have known before May 14 that Taylors B were not credit-worthy, but they did not become aware of that fact until much later, and possibly not until a cheque of Taylors was dishonoured on about June 8. Because of their negligence, Reid was not warned that Taylors were unworthy of credit. If he had been so warned he would not have told sellers that Taylors were all right, and some, at any rate, of the sales which he negotiated would not have been effected. Reid was not negligent because he was entitled to C assume that if Taylors were not meeting their liabilities he would have been warned of this by Jones and O'Connor.

It is now necessary to apply these findings to the various transactions.

Anderson's case: Scott says that he interpreted Reid's words to mean merely: " I have been dealing with Taylors and nobody has told me to stop." This was true. Further, Scott says that he relied not on the representation, but on the D guarantee given by Reid. For both of those reasons I am of opinion that Anderson's claim fails. They are in no better position in relation to the second transaction than to the first because nothing further was said to Caloe which could assist.

Roberts' case: I accept that the transaction was brought about by the representation that, " He is a good account and a good payer ", and that this representa- E tion was made by reason of the negligence of Jones and O'Connor in failing to discover and inform Reid that Taylors were bad payers.

Ellwood's case: The representation was that Taylors' was a good account and the consequences are similar to those in Roberts' case.

Skene's case: No representation was made at all, and this case fails.

Wood's case: The representation was there all right: this was a misrepresenta- F tion and the consequences are similar to Roberts' case.

North Western's case: On the affirmative answer to the question " Are they all right? ", this is exactly similar to Wood's case.

Pollard's case: Here Jones, and not Reid, was the buyer. His representation that Taylors were all right was certainly at least negligent. Mr. Pollard, however, said that he expected an honest answer and no more. Pollard is in this difficulty; G if they got an honest answer they cannot complain; if they did not get an honest answer they cannot succeed here because they have not alleged fraud, and if they had and had proved it their claim could have been met by Lord Tenterden's Act. So Pollard's claim fails.

I now have to consider whether Roberts, Ellwood, Wood and North Western have a cause of action in negligence. Was there a duty of care lying on Rhodes H or on Jones in respect of the representations made by Reid? From the way in which the statement of claim is drawn, I am not sure whether it was intended to claim against Jones in respect of any representations made by Reid. If it had been so intended, I should have expected to see an allegation that Jones was negligent in not informing Reid of the state of the accounts between Rhodes and Taylors, and there is no such allegation. Assuming, however, that it was so I intended, I do not think that a claim against Jones can succeed. It was not as his servant or agent, but as Rhodes' that Reid was acting, and there is no evidence of any instructions from Jones to Reid such as might have made him liable as the actual author of the representations. Jones ought to have known that enquiries about Taylors' conduct were likely to be made of Reid, and ought to have informed himself and thereafter informed Reid of the state of the accounts, but there is no evidence that he ever knew of the representation being made, and in the circumstances he cannot in my view be held responsible for that. Rhodes, on

A the other hand, were Reid's employers, and I am satisfied that he acted as their servant or agent in making the representation. Further, Jones and O'Connor were also servants of Rhodes, and it was through their negligence in failing to keep Reid properly informed that the representations came to be made. Rhodes are, therefore, prima facie liable in damages to four of the plaintiffs provided they owed these plaintiffs a duty of care in respect of the representation.

B   Under the law as it was understood to be before *Hedley Byrne & Co., Ltd.* v. *Heller & Partners, Ltd.* (10) was decided in the House of Lords, there could be no liability for negligent misrepresentation unless there was a contractual duty of care. The actual decision in the *Hedley Byrne* case (10) was that the plaintiffs could not succeed because the representations made to them were expressly made without responsibility, but all the law lords agreed that in some circum-
C stances there could be a liability in tort for negligent misrepresentation. An academic lawyer might be prepared to contend that the opinions expressed by their lordships about liability for negligent misrepresentation were obiter, and that *Candler* v. *Crane, Christmas & Co.* (11) is still a binding decision. In my judgment that would be an unrealistic view to take. When five members of the House of Lords have all said, after close examination of the authorities, that a
D certain type of tort exists, I think that a judge of first instance should proceed on the basis that it does exist without pausing to embark on an investigation of whether what was said was necessary to the ultimate decision. While, however, there was unanimity as to the existence in some circumstances of a legal duty of care in making representations, it is by no means clear that there was unanimity as to what those circumstances were. All agreed that mere casual remarks made
E on a social occasion gave rise to no such duty. All agreed that a formal expression of opinion by a professional man, made in such circumstances that a person not in contractual relations with that man was intended to act on it, might give rise to the duty. But is a statement by a business man, made without any formality and without any immediate opportunity for investigation and construction, capable of raising the duty?

F   To show how difficult this question is, I will cite two passages in judgments in the Court of Appeal, each of which received expressions of approval in the House of Lords, and then some passages from speeches in the House of Lords itself. In his dissenting judgment in *Candler* v. *Crane, Christmas & Co.* (12), DENNING, L.J., said:

G   " Let me now be constructive and suggest the circumstances in which I say that a duty to use care in making a statement does exist apart from a contract in that behalf. First, what persons are under such duty? My answer is those persons, such as accountants, surveyors, valuers and analysts, whose profession and occupation it is to examine books, accounts, and other things, and to make reports on which other people—other than their clients—rely in the ordinary course of business. Their duty is not merely a duty to use care in
H their reports: they have also a duty to use care in their work which results in their reports. Herein lies the difference between these professional men and other persons who have been held to be under no duty to use care in their statements, such as promoters who issue a prospectus: *Derry* v. *Peek* (13) (now altered by statute [Companies Act, 1948, s. 43]), and trustees who answer inquiries about the trust funds: *Low* v. *Bouverie* (14). Those persons
I do not bring, and are not expected to bring, any professional knowledge or skill into the preparation of their statements. They can only be made responsible by the law affecting persons generally, such as contract, estoppel, innocent misrepresentation or fraud. It is, however, very different with

(10) [1963] 2 All E.R. 575; [1964] A.C. 465.
(11) [1951] 1 All E.R. 426; [1951] 2 K.B. 164.
(12) [1951] 1 All E.R. at pp. 433, 434; [1951] 2 K.B. at pp. 179, 180.
(13) [1886-90] All E.R. Rep. 1; (1889), 14 App. Cas. 337.
(14) [1891-94] All E.R. Rep. 348; [1891] 3 Ch. 82.

persons who engage in a calling which requires special knowledge and skill.   A
From very early times it has been held that they owe a duty of care to those
who are closely and directly affected by their work, apart altogether from any
contract or undertaking in that behalf. Thus FITZHERBERT, in his NEW
NATURA BREVIUM (1534) 94D, says that: '. . . if a smith prick my horse
with a nail . . . I shall have my action upon the case against him, without
any warranty by the smith to do it well . . . for it is the duty of every artificer   B
to exercise his art rightly and truly as he ought.' This reasoning has been
treated as applicable not only to shoeing smiths, surgeons and barbers, who
work with hammers, knives and scissors, but also to shipbrokers and clerks
in the Custom House who work with figures and make entries in books,
'. . . because their situation and employment necessarily imply a competent
degree of knowledge in making such entries . . .'; see *Shiells* v. *Blackburne* (15),   C
per LORD LOUGHBOROUGH, which was not referred to by DEVLIN, J., in
Heskell v. *Continental Express, Ltd.* (16). The same reasoning has been
applied to medical men who make reports on the sanity of others; see *Everett*
v. *Griffiths* (17). It is, I think, also applicable to professional accountants.
They are not liable, of course, for casual remarks made in the course of
conversation, nor for other statements made outside their work, or not made   D
in their capacity as accountants (compare *Fish* v. *Kelly* (18)); but they are,
in my opinion, in proper cases, apart from any contract in the matter, under
a duty to use reasonable care in the preparation of their accounts and in the
making of their reports."

In the *Hedley Byrne* case (19) this passage was approved by LORD DEVLIN (20)
and by LORD PEARCE (21), and none of the other three members of the House   E
dissented from it.

Now, in his judgment in the Court of Appeal in the *Hedley Byrne* case (22),
PEARSON, L.J., said:

"Apart from authority, I am not satisfied that it would be reasonable to
impose on a banker the obligation suggested, if that obligation really adds
anything to the duty of giving an honest answer. It is conceded by counsel   F
for the plaintiffs that the banker is not expected to make outside inquiries to
supplement the information which he already has. Is he then expected, in
business hours in the bank's time, to expend time and trouble in searching
records, studying documents, weighing and comparing the favourable and
unfavourable features and producing a well-balanced and well-worded report?
That seems wholly unreasonable. Then, if he is not expected to do any of   G
those things, and if he is permitted to give an impromptu answer in the
words that immediately come to his mind on the basis of the facts which he
happens to remember or is able to ascertain from a quick glance at the file or
one of the files, the duty of care seems to add little, if anything, to the duty
of honesty. If the answer given is seriously wrong, that is some evidence—
of course, only some evidence—of dishonesty. Therefore, apart from   H
authority, it is to my mind, far from clear, that the banker, in answering such
an inquiry, could reasonably be supposed to be assuming any duty higher
than that of giving an honest answer."

In the House of Lords this passage found favour with LORD MORRIS OF BORTH-
Y-GEST (23) and LORD HODSON (24). To cite all the relevant passages from the   I

(15) (1789), 1 Hy. Bl. 158 at p. 162.
(16) [1950] 1 All E.R. 1033 at p. 1042.
(17) [1920] 3 K.B. 163 at pp. 182, 217.
(18) (1864), 17 C.B.N.S. 194.
(19) [1963] 2 All E.R. 575; [1964] A.C. 465.
(20) [1963] 2 All E.R. at p. 611; [1964] A.C. at p. 530.
(21) [1963] 2 All E.R. at p. 617; [1964] A.C. at pp. 538, 539.
(22) [1961] 3 All E.R. 891 at p. 902; [1962] 1 Q.B. 396 at pp. 414, 415.
(23) [1963] 2 All E.R. at p. 594; [1964] A.C. at p. 503.
(24) [1963] 2 All E.R. at p. 600; [1964] A.C. at pp. 512, 513.

A speeches in the House of Lords in the *Hedley Byrne* case (25) would overwhelm
this judgment, and I confine myself to a few quite short quotations. LORD
REID said (26):

B "The most obvious difference between negligent words and negligent
acts is this. Quite careful people often express definite opinions on social or
informal occasions, even when they see that others are likely to be influenced
by them; and they often do that without taking that care which they would
take if asked for their opinion professionally, or in a business connexion."

After quoting a passage from *Robinson* v. *National Bank of Scotland* (27), LORD
REID said this (28):

C "This passage makes it clear that LORD HALDANE did not think that a
duty to take care must be limited to cases of fiduciary relationship in the
narrow sense of relationships which had been recognised by the Court of
Chancery as being of a fiduciary character. He speaks of other special
relationships, and I can see no logical stopping place short of all those
relationships where it is plain that the party seeking information or advice
was trusting the other to exercise such a degree of care as the circumstances
D required, where it was reasonable for him to do that, and where the other
gave the information or advice when he knew or ought to have known that
the inquirer was relying on him. I say 'ought to have known' because in
questions of negligence we now apply the objective standard of what the
reasonable man would have done. A reasonable man, knowing that he was
being trusted or that his skill and judgment were being relied on, would, I
E think, have three courses open to him. He could keep silent or decline to give
the information or advice sought: or he could give an answer with a clear
qualification that he accepted no responsibility for it or that it was given
without that reflection or inquiry which a careful answer would require: or
he could simply answer without any such qualification. If he chooses to
adopt the last course he must, I think, be held to have accepted some
F responsibility for his answer being given carefully, or to have accepted a
relationship with the inquirer which requires him to exercise such care as the
circumstances require."

LORD MORRIS OF BORTH-Y-GEST said (29):

G "My Lords, it seems to me that if A assumes a responsibility to B to
tender him deliberate advice, there could be a liability if the advice is
negligently given. I say 'could be' because the ordinary courtesies and
exchanges of life would become impossible if it were sought to attach legal
obligation to every kindly and friendly act. But the principle of the matter
would not appear to be in doubt. If A employs B (who might, for example,
be a professional man such as an accountant or a solicitor or a doctor) for
H reward to give advice and if the advice is negligently given there could be a
liability in B to pay damages. The fact that the advice is given in words
would not, in my view, prevent liability from arising. Quite apart, however,
from employment or contract there may be circumstances in which a duty
to exercise care will arise if a service is voluntarily undertaken. A medical
man may unexpectedly come across an unconscious man, who is a complete
stranger to him, and who is in urgent need of skilled attention: if the medical
I man, following the fine traditions of his profession, proceeds to treat the
unconscious man he must exercise reasonable skill and care in doing so."

Later on, LORD MORRIS continued (30):

---

(25) [1963] 2 All E.R. 575; [1964] A.C. 465.
(26) [1963] 2 All E.R. at p. 580; [1964] A.C. at pp. 482, 483.
(27) 1916 S.C. (H.L.) 154 at p. 157.
(28) [1963] 2 All E.R. at p. 583; [1964] A.C. at p. 486.
(29) [1963] 2 All E.R. at pp. 588, 589; [1964] A.C. at pp. 494, 495.
(30) [1963] 2 All E.R. at p. 589; [1964] A.C. at p. 495.

" To a similar effect were the words of LORD LOUGHBOROUGH in the
much earlier case of *Shiells* v. *Blackburne* (31) when he said: '. . . if a man
gratuitously undertakes to do a thing to the best of his skill . . ., an omission
of that skill is imputable to him as gross negligence.' Compare also *Wilkinson*
v. *Coverdale* (32). I can see no difference of principle in the case of a banker.
If someone who was not a customer of a bank made a formal approach to
the bank with a definite request that the bank would give him deliberate
advice as to certain financial matters of a nature with which the bank
ordinarily dealt the bank would be under no obligation to accede to the
request: if, however, they undertook, though gratuitously, to give deliberate
advice (I exclude what I might call casual and perfunctory conversations)
they would be under a duty to exercise reasonable care in giving it."

Later on, LORD MORRIS said (33):

" Leaving aside cases where there is some contractual or fiduciary relationship there may be many situations in which one person voluntarily or
gratuitously undertakes to do something for another person and becomes
under a duty to exercise reasonable care. I have given illustrations. Apart
from cases where there is some direct dealing, there may be cases where one
person issues a document which should be the result of an exercise of the skill
and judgment required by him in his calling and where he knows and intends
that its accuracy will be relied on by another."

Further on, LORD MORRIS said (34):

" There is much to be said, therefore, for the view that if a banker gives
a reference in the form of a brief expression of opinion in regard to credit-
worthiness he does not accept, and there is not expected from him, any
higher duty than that of giving an honest answer."

LORD HODSON said (35):

" I do not think that it is possible to catalogue the special features which
must be found to exist before the duty of care will arise in a given case, but
since preparing this opinion I have had the opportunity of reading the speech
which my noble and learned friend, LORD MORRIS OF BORTH-Y-GEST, has
now delivered. I agree with him that if in a sphere where a person is so
placed that others could reasonably rely on his judgment or his skill or his
ability to make careful inquiry such person takes it on himself to give
information or advice to, or allows his information or advice to be passed on
to, another person who, as he knows, or should know, will place reliance upon
it, then a duty of care will arise."

LORD DEVLIN said (36):

" I have had the advantage of reading all the opinions prepared by your
lordships and of studying the terms which your lordships have framed by way
of definition of the sort of relationship which gives rise to a responsibility
towards those who act on information or advice and so creates a duty of care
towards them. I do not understand any of your lordships to hold that it is
a responsibility imposed by law on certain types of persons or in certain sorts
of situations. It is a responsibility that is voluntarily accepted or undertaken,
either generally where a general relationship, such as that of solicitor and
client or banker and customer, is created, or specifically in relation to a
particular transaction. In the present case the appellants were not, as in
Woods v. *Martins Bank, Ltd.* (37), the customers or potential customers of

(31) (1789), 1 Hy. Bl. at p. 162.
(32) (1793), 1 Esp. 74.
(33) [1963] 2 All E.R. at p. 590; [1964] A.C. at p. 497.
(34) [1963] 2 All E.R. at pp. 594, 595; [1964] A.C. at p. 504.
(35) [1963] 2 All E.R. at p. 601; [1964] A.C. at p. 514.
(36) [1963] 2 All E.R. at pp. 610, 611; [1964] A.C. at pp. 529, 530.
(37) [1958] 3 All E.R. 166; [1959] 1 Q.B. 55.

A   the bank. Responsibility can attach only to the single act, i.e., the giving of the reference, and only if the doing of that act implied a voluntary undertaking to assume responsibility. This is a point of great importance because it is, as I understand it, the foundation for the ground on which in the end the House dismisses the appeal. I do not think it possible to formulate with exactitude all the conditions under which the law will in a specific case imply

B   a voluntary undertaking, any more than it is possible to formulate those in which the law will imply a contract. But in so far as your lordships describe the circumstances in which an implication will ordinarily be drawn, I am prepared to adopt any one of your lordships' statements as showing the general rule; and I pay the same respect to the statement by DENNING, L.J., in his dissenting judgment in *Candler* v. *Crane, Christmas & Co.* (38) about

C   the circumstances in which he says a duty to use care in making a statement exists."

A little later LORD DEVLIN continued (39):

"I shall therefore content myself with the proposition that wherever there is a relationship equivalent to contract, there is a duty of care. Such a relationship may be either general or particular. Examples of a general

D   relationship are those of solicitor and client and of banker and customer. For the former *Nocton* v. *Lord Ashburton* (40) has long stood as the authority and for the latter there is the decision of SALMON, J., in *Woods* v. *Martins Bank, Ltd.* (41) which I respectfully approve. There may well be others yet to be established. Where there is a general relationship of this sort, it is unnecessary

E   to do more than prove its existence and the duty follows. Where, as in the present case, what is relied on is a particular relationship created ad hoc, it will be necessary to examine the particular facts to see whether there is an express or implied undertaking of responsibility."

And LORD PEARCE said (42):

"The true rule is that innocent misrepresentation per se gives no right to

F   damages. If the misrepresentation was intended by the parties to form a warranty between two contracting parties, it gives on that ground a right to damages (*Heilbut, Symons & Co.* v. *Buckleton* (43)). If an innocent misrepresentation is made between parties in a fiduciary relationship it may, on that ground, give a right to claim damages for negligence. There is also, in my opinion, a duty of care created by special relationships which, though

G   not fiduciary, give rise to an assumption that care as well as honesty is demanded.

"Was there such a special relationship in the present case as to impose on the respondents a duty of care to the appellants as the undisclosed principals for whom National Provincial Bank, Ltd. was making the inquiry? The answer to that question depends on the circumstances of the transaction. If,

H   for instance, they disclosed a casual social approach to the inquiry, no such special relationship or duty of care would be assumed (see *Fish* v. *Kelly* (44)). To import such a duty the representation must normally, I think, concern a business or professional transaction whose nature makes clear the gravity of the inquiry and the importance and influence attached to the answer."

I   Now, the Rhodes' position was certainly not that of professional advisers such as DENNING, L.J., was considering, and there seems no reason why they should be

---

(38) [1951] 1 All E.R. at p. 433; [1951] 2 K.B. at p. 179.
(39) [1963] 2 All E.R. at p. 611; [1964] A.C. at p. 530.
(40) [1914-15] All E.R. Rep. 45; [1914] A.C. 932.
(41) [1958] 3 All E.R. 166; [1959] 1 Q.B. 55.
(42) [1963] 2 All E.R. at p. 617; [1964] A.C. at p. 539.
(43) [1911-13] All E.R. Rep. 83; [1913] A.C. 30.
(44) (1864), 17 C.B.N.S. 194.

expected to spend time in " reading documents, weighing and conferring favour-   A
able and unfavourable features and producing a well-balanced and well-worded
report " any more than the banker to whom PEARCE, L.J., directed his attention.
On the other hand, Rhodes' opinion was clearly asked " in a business connexion ",
to use LORD REID's phrase. The advice was not " casual and perfunctory ", and
there was " some direct dealing " between the parties: these are expressions used
by LORD MORRIS. I think that it can be said that the plaintiffs could reasonably   B
rely on the judgment and skill of Rhodes. Here I am quoting LORD HODSON, and
I think there was an element of which LORD DEVLIN speaks—" a relationship
equivalent to contract . . ." Finally, to use a test suggested by LORD PEARCE;
the representation here concerned a business transaction whose nature made clear
the gravity of the enquiry and the importance and influence attached to the
answers. I say that this test was satisfied, because it is clear that none of the   C
plaintiffs would have been willing to sell to Taylors unless they had been assured
that Taylors were " all right ", or something to the same effect. I do not think
that DENNING, L.J., intended to lay down that the duty of care could arise only
in the case of professional men, and if he did this would not be consistent with
the view of at least three of the law lords in the *Hedley Byrne* case (45).   There
was no necessity (in connexion with the transactions that I am considering) to   D
read many documents or to weigh and consider favourable or unfavourable
factors, or at least there would have been no such necessity if Rhodes had kept
their accounts in a reasonably careful manner, as I consider the enquirers were
entitled to assume that they did.

I reach the conclusion that the duty of care did exist here, but it was not
complied with, and that unless some special defence is open to Rhodes, four of   E
the plaintiffs are entitled to damages from them. The special defence that has
to be considered is that in s. 6 of Lord Tenterden's Act. The words of the section
are as follows:

"No action shall be brought whereby to charge any person upon or by
reason of any representation or assurance made or given concerning or relating to the character, conduct, credit, ability, trade, or dealings of any other   F
person, to the intent or purpose that such other person may obtain credit,
money, or goods upon [it] unless such representation or assurance be made in
writing, signed by the party to be charged therewith."

In *Banbury* v. *Bank of Montreal* (46), it was unanimously held by the House of
Lords that this section applied only where the representation was fraudulent. The   G
law lords based their decision partly on the history of the section. Because s. 4
of the Statute of Frauds (1677) made a promise to answer for a debt, default or
miscarriage of another unenforceable unless in writing, a custom grew up in the
profession of alleging a fraudulent representation as to credit in order to circum-
vent the statute. Apparently juries, displaying their traditional anxiety to find
verdicts in favour of plaintiffs, were easily induced to find fraud where no real   H
fraud existed. To put an end to this practice, LORD TENTERDEN introduced the
bill containing this section, and it was passed by Parliament. In *Banbury's*
case (46) the House of Lords, taking the view that the section was ambiguous,
interpreted it narrowly, according to the presumed intention of Parliament to
overcome a particular grievance; so they held that it applied only to fraudulent
representation.   I

In *Banbury's* case (46) the action was framed in negligence. At that time it was
supposed that a duty of care in respect of a representation could arise only under
a contract. It is instructive to read two passages from the argument. The first
sentence of the argument on behalf of the plaintiff appellant is (47):

(45) [1963] 2 All E.R. 575; [1964] A.C. 465.
(46) [1918-19] All E.R. Rep. 1; [1918] A.C. 626.
(47) [1918] A.C. at p. 629.

A   " If a person carrying on a business or profession takes upon himself to give advice on a matter as to which he has or professes special skill or knowledge in the way of that business or profession, in such circumstances that the person advised relies upon that special skill or knowledge, he is under a duty to that person to use due care in advising him."

B   The other passage is in the course of the argument on behalf of the respondent (48):

" No case can be found in the books where an action for negligence in giving gratuitous advice has been maintained, whether the advice be given by a person possessing special knowledge of the subject or not. The duty which it is alleged the bank owed to the appellant can arise in this case only if there is shown a valid contract to be careful."

C   Three members of the House held that in the circumstances there was no contractual duty of care. The minority held that there was evidence on which the jury were entitled to find that there was such a duty. So, in the view of the majority, the point under Lord Tenterden's Act did not really arise for decision. Nevertheless *Banbury's* case (49) has always been considered to be authority for the proposition that Lord Tenterden's Act only applies to fraudulent

D   misrepresentation.

It is argued with force before me by counsel for the defendants that all that the House of Lords can really be considered to have decided in *Banbury v. Bank of Montreal* (49) is that Lord Tenterden's Act did not apply to a representation made in breach of contractual duty of care. Now, before 1828 it had been realised that an action might be found in tort for negligence by making a representation

E   as to credit. The pleaders of the day would no doubt have framed their statements of claim in negligence with a still greater confidence in being able to persuade juries to make a finding of negligence and so defeat the Statute of Frauds and LORD TENTERDEN would have included this inclination among the mischiefs to be suppressed. Further, it is contended for the defendants that to hold that a

F   fraudulent oral misrepresentation is not actionable in tort, while a negligent oral misrepresentation is so actionable, is an absurdity. What possible sense can there be in making the author of a representation liable in negligence, but relieving him if he can establish that he perpetrated a fraud?

As against this, it is said for the plaintiffs that to distinguish for the purposes of the Act of 1828 between tortious and contractual negligence is a still greater

G   absurdity, and passages in the speeches in *Banbury's* case (49) are relied on as showing that the Act of 1828 applies to actions for fraudulent representation only and not to actions for breach of any duty of care. The principal passages which are relied on in that action are these:

LORD FINLAY, L.C., said (50):

" In my opinion an action of this nature does not fall within s. 6 of Lord

H   Tenterden's Act at all. The action is for the breach of the duty which it is alleged the bank had undertaken of advising the appellant, and not for misrepresentation."

Then LORD FINLAY said (51):

" Section 6 appears to me, upon its plain meaning to be confined to actions

I   brought upon misrepresentations as such, and not to bar redress for failure to perform any contractual or other duty... These words appear to me to have no such effect. The present action is not brought either ' upon ' or ' by reason of '

---

(48) [1918] A.C. at p. 635.
(49) [1918-19] All E.R. Rep. 1; [1918] A.C. 626.
(50) [1918-19] All E.R. Rep. at p. 5; [1918] A.C. 639.
(51) [1918-19] All E.R. Rep. at p. 6; [1918] A.C. 640.

any misrepresentation. It is based upon the alleged existence of a duty to   A
take reasonable care in advising the plaintiff, and is neither ' upon ' nor ' by
reason of ' any misrepresentation.''

Later LORD FINLAY said (52):

" Subject to these considerations a banker may, as such, give advice on
investments to a customer who consults him, or, indeed, to any one who   B
comes to him for advice, and whom he chooses to advise. If he undertakes to
advise, he must exercise reasonable care and skill in giving the advice. He is
under no obligation to advise, but if he takes upon himself to do so, he will
incur liability if he does so negligently.''

LORD ATKINSON said (53):
                                                                              C
" On the contrary, I think, for reasons I shall give presently, that Lord
Tenterden's Act only applies to fraudulent representations, not to an
innocent representation such as Galletly is alleged to have made.''

And later on he said (54):

" No new statute was required at the time the Act was passed to deal with   D
innocent representations. This statute was, I think, designed to deal with
false and fraudulent representations and those alone, and, being of that
opinion, I think that, despite the generality of the words ' Any representation or assurance ', I am, acting on the principle of interpretation of statute
laid down in *Stradling* v. *Morgan* (55), bound to construe the Act so as to carry
out the intention of the legislature which passed it, and to hold that it only   E
applies to representation and assurances of this latter character and to those
alone.''

LORD PARKER OF WADDINGTON said (56):

" On the other hand, it must be remembered that the only representation
which itself gives rise to a cause of action on the part of a person injured   F
thereby is a fraudulent representation. An innocent representation, except
possibly as raising an estoppel or implication of contract, has in itself no legal
effect at all. It being possible, therefore, to give the words of the section a
wider or a narrower meaning, it is quite in accordance with sound principles
of construction to examine into the abuses which the Act was intended to
remedy, and such examination is all in favour of the narrower meaning . . .   G
Lastly, until the present case no attempt appears to have been made to
construe the section to include actions for negligence. It is true that in
Haslock v. *Fergusson* (57) and in *Swann* v. *Phillips* (58) the section was held
applicable to actions of assumpsit; but if these cases be examined it will be
found (i) that the representation sought to be proved was fraudulent; and
(ii) that the plaintiff might have brought an action for fraud though he elected   H
to proceed in assumpsit. Whether rightly or wrongly decided, these cases
have no bearing on the present question, for it is common ground that
Mr. Galletly acted honestly throughout. In my opinion, Lord Tenterden's
Act does not apply to an action for breach of a duty to take care.''

                                                                              I
(52) [1918] A.C. at p. 654.
(53) [1918-19] All E.R. Rep. at p. 11; [1918] A.C. at p. 669.
(54) [1918-19] All E.R. Rep. at p. 20; [1918] A.C. at p. 693, 694.
(55) (1560), 1 Plowd. 201 at p. 204.
(56) [1918-19] All E.R. Rep. at pp. 26, 27; [1918] A.C. at p. 707.
(57) (1837), 7 Ad. & El. 86.
(58) (1838), 8 Ad. & El. 457. [The only authority for regarding the cause of action
as assumpsit appears to be the use of that word in Adolphus & Ellis's head-note. Pleadings, argument, and judgments all treat the action as being on the case for deceit.]

A And LORD WRENBURY said at the beginning of his speech (59): " This is not an
action for fraud. It is an action for negligence and breach of duty." LORD
WRENBURY quotes BRAMWELL, B., (60) as saying (61):

" . . . ' the effect of the statute is that a man should not be liable for a
fraudulent representation as to another person's means unless he puts it down
in writing and acknowledges his responsibility for it by his own signature.'

B   " These being the authorities, the question to be answered is: Does s. 6 of
Lord Tenterden's Act apply to an innocent misrepresentation? In my
opinion it does not. The words of the section are ' to charge any person upon
or by reason of any representation ' &c. The words ' charge any person upon
any representation ' point, I think, plainly to an action for deceit. To main-
C tain such an action there must be fraud, and there must be damage. If these
two are satisfied, nothing more is required. Fraud is the cause of action.
The charge is made upon the tort committed by the fraudulent misrepresentation. The same is not true of an innocent representation. An innocent
representation per se constitutes no cause of action."

It appears to me that the effect of these citations as a whole is this. An action for
D fraudulent misrepresentation as to credit is an action on the representation and
is barred by Lord Tenterden's Act unless in writing. An action in respect of a
negligent misrepresentation is not an action on the representation and is an
action for breach of a duty of care. This reasoning is not based on deriving a duty
of care from a contract. LORD FINLAY speaks of " any contractual or other
duty ". LORD PARKER says that the Act of 1828 does not apply to a " duty to
E take care ". LORD WRENBURY says that negligence is the cause of action. The
conclusion is that an action for breach of a duty of care in making a representation
is not barred by the Act of 1828. In my judgment I am bound by this decision
and must hold that Lord Tenterden's Act affords no defence here. Accordingly,
I give judgment for Roberts for £874 13s. 4d.; judgment for Ellwood for £167 10s.;
judgment for Wood for £688 18s. 6d.; judgment for North Western for £190. All
F those judgments will be against Rhodes alone. I give judgment for all three
defendants against Anderson, Skene and Pollard.

Judgment accordingly.

Solicitors: *William Rudd, Freeman & Getley*, Liverpool (for the plaintiffs);
Banks, Kendall, Taylor & Gorst, Liverpool (for the defendants).

G   [*Reported by* K. B. EDWARDS, ESQ., *Barrister-at-Law.*]

H

I

---

(59) [1918-19] All E.R. Rep. at p. 27; [1918] A.C. at pp. 710.
(60) In *Swift* v. *Jewsbury*, (1874), L.R. 9 Q.B. 301 at p. 316.
(61) [1918-19] All E.R. Rep. at p. 28; [1918] A.C. at pp. 712, 713.

A

ARNOLD v. THOMAS HARRINGTON, LTD.

[QUEEN'S BENCH DIVISION (Lord Parker, C.J., Widgery and O'Connor, JJ.),
April 13, 14, May 11, 1967.]

*Employment—Redundancy—Work of a particular kind—Fitter operating garage's
emergency breakdown service—Fitter occupying flat rent-free in part of business
premises connected with another side of employer's business—Sale by
employers of that side of the business and of premises which contained flat
—Notice given to fitter to terminate employment and vacate flat—Subsequent
offer by employers of re-employment as fitter refused—Emergency breakdown
service discontinued—Whether fitter entitled to redundancy payment—
Redundancy Payments Act 1965 (c. 62), s. 1 (2).*

B

C

The appellant was employed by the respondents as a motor fitter. His work
included operating an emergency breakdown service on alternative nights
and week-ends. For this purpose he was required to live in a flat where the
respondent's business was carried on. This flat was in premises where the
body-building side of the business, not the garage side of the business, was
carried on. He occupied the flat rent-free under an agreement with the
respondents which excluded the relation of landlord and tenant. The respondents decided to sell the body-building side of their business. For this they
required vacant possession of the premises: accordingly they gave the
appellant four weeks' notice terminating his employment in June, 1966, and
requiring vacant possession of the flat. They offered him re-employment
as a fitter but without free accommodation. The appellant refused. The
respondents discontinued their emergency breakdown service, as none of their
fitters lived near enough to the garage. They employed another fitter in place
of the appellant. On appeal from a decision of the industrial tribunal that the
appellant had not been dismissed by reason of redundancy, and accordingly
was not entitled to a redundancy payment,

D

E

Held: the work which the appellant was required to do was that of fitter,
and the work of the emergency breakdown service was not " work of a
particular kind " for the purposes of s. 1 (2) (*b*)* of the Redundancy Payments
Act 1965; the work on which the appellant was employed as fitter had not
come to an end and the respondents had shown that the appellant's dismissal
was not attributable wholly or mainly to matters specified in para. (*a*) or
para. (*b*) of s. 1 (2) and thus was not dismissal by reason of redundancy (see
p. 869, letters B, D and E, and p. 870, letter A, post).

F

G

Dictum of WIDGERY, J., in *North Riding Garages, Ltd.* v. *Butterwick* ([1967]
1 All E.R. at p. 647) considered and explained.

Appeal dismissed.

[As to dismissal of employee by reason of redundancy, see SUPPLEMENT to
38 HALSBURY'S LAWS (3rd Edn.), para. 808C.

For the Redundancy Payments Act 1965, s. 1, see 45 HALSBURY'S STATUTES
(2nd Edn.) 290.]

H

Case referred to:
North Riding Garages, Ltd. v. *Butterwick*, [1967] 1 All E.R. 644; [1967] 2
W.L.R. 571.

I

Appeal.

This was an appeal by the appellant, George Reginald Arnold, by notice
dated Dec. 9, 1966, against a decision of the Industrial Tribunal sitting at Gresse
Street, London, given on Oct. 11, 1966, and notified to the appellant on Nov.
11, 1966, whereby they decided that the appellant's dismissal from the employment of the respondents, Thomas Harrington, Ltd., by notice given on May 27,

---

* Section 1 (2), is set out at p. 868, letter B, post.

A 1966, was not by reason of redundancy under s. 1 of the Redundancy Payments Act 1965, and that, accordingly, the appellant was not entitled to redundancy payments. The facts are set out in the judgment of the court.

    L. S. Shields for the appellant.

    J. G. Hull for the respondents.

Cur. adv. vult.

B

    O'CONNOR, J., read the following judgment of the court at the invitation of LORD PARKER, C.J.: The respondents, Thomas Harrington, Ltd., had two sides to their business which were carried on in separate but adjacent premises, a repairing and servicing garage and a body building business. As part of the garage side of the business the respondents operated an emergency breakdown

C service outside normal business hours, including week-ends, in conjunction with the A.A. and the R.A.C. The appellant, George Reginald Arnold, is a skilled motor fitter who was employed in the garage side of the business. From 1964 onwards he was required to be on duty to operate the emergency breakdown service on alternate nights and alternate week-ends. By an agreement made on Mar. 2, 1964, between the appellant and the respondents it was provided

D that (and I read only the relevant parts):

> " Whereas the [appellant] is in the employment of the [respondents] and for the proper performance of his duties in such employment it is essential that he should occupy the premises hereinafter described it has been agreed as hereinafter appears
> Now it is hereby agreed as follows:—

E > 1. The [appellant] whilst in the said employment and for the proper and efficient discharge of his duties in the said employment is hereby required during the term of such employment to occupy the premises known as Flat One, 274, Old Shoreham Road, Hove, Sussex (hereinafter called ' the premises ') . . .
> 5. Nothing herein contained shall create the relationship of landlord and

F > tenant between the parties hereto
> 6. The occupation of the premises by the [appellant] is a condition of his employment with the [respondents] and the right of the [appellant] to occupy the premises shall cease upon the termination of the [appellant's] said employment or upon the [appellant] being transferred to another place of business of the [respondents] (after employment ceases occupier can have

G > up to a maximum of a month to move)."

This flat was situated in the premises where the body building side of the business was carried on. Part of his remuneration for operating the emergency breakdown service was described by the respondents as an ex gratia incentive bonus of 10s., 15s., or £1 per caller, depending on distance. In May, 1966, the respondents decided to sell off the body building side of their business and for this purpose

H they required vacant possession of the premises including the flat occupied by the appellant. To achieve this result they gave four weeks' notice to the appellant on May 27, 1966, terminating his employment on June 24 and requiring him to vacate the flat. On June 23 the respondents offered to re-employ the appellant, an offer which in fact was an offer to continue to employ him as a fitter in the garage but without free accommodation. The appellant refused. The respondents

I took on another fitter as soon as they could find one, but, as none of their fitters lived close enough to the garage, they discontinued the emergency breakdown service hitherto carried on.

    The appellant claimed that he had been dismissed by reason of redundancy. Section 1 of the Redundancy Payments Act 1965, provides that:

> " (1) Where on or after the appointed day an employee who has been continuously employed for the requisite period—(*a*) is dismissed by his employer by reason of redundancy . . . then, subject to the following

provisions of this Part of this Act, the employer shall be liable to pay to him
a sum (in this Act referred to as a ' redundancy payment ') calculated in
accordance with Sch. 1 to this Act.

" (2) For the purposes of this Act an employee who is dismissed shall
be taken to be dismissed by reason of redundancy if the dismissal is attributable wholly or mainly to—(a) the fact that his employer has ceased,
or intends to cease, to carry on the business for the purposes of which the
employee was employed by him, or has ceased, or intends to cease, to carry
on that business in the place where the employee was so employed, or (b)
the fact that the requirements of that business for employees to carry out
work of a particular kind, or for employees to carry out work of a particular
kind in the place where he was so employed, have ceased or diminished or
are expected to cease or diminish."

Section 9 of the Act of 1965 provides for reference of disputes to the Industrial
Tribunal and by s. 9 (2) for the purposes of any such reference an employee who
has been dismissed by his employer shall, unless the contrary is proved, be
presumed to have been so dismissed by reason of redundancy.

The reasons given by the tribunal for refusing the claim were as follows:

" The [appellant] was employed as a motor fitter with the respondents
with effect from Mar. 7, 1955. He ceased to be employed on June 24, 1966.
His employment was terminated by the respondents in a letter dated May
27, 1966. It was the case for the [appellant] that he was entitled to a
redundancy payment because the work for which he was employed had
ceased and the alternative employment offered to him was unsuitable in that
it involved the loss of a rent free flat and the loss of certain additional
earnings which accrued to him by reason of his employment on alternate
weekends. This weekend employment arose solely out of his occupation of
the flat. He estimated the loss of his earnings as £6 or £6 10s. per week.
This sum included a notional value of £4 per week for the tenancy of the
flat. The respondents contended that this was not a case of redundancy.
The work on which the [appellant] was employed had not come to an end and
the sole reason for giving him notice of dismissal was their desire to obtain
possession of the flat. He would under the terms of his new contract have
continued to work for them as a fitter. His job was filled immediately, albeit
with some difficulty owing to the shortage of skilled mechanics. The tribunal
found as a fact that the work on which the [appellant] was mainly engaged
had not ceased and that therefore there was no redundancy within the
meaning of s. 1 of the Redundancy Payments Act 1965. The tribunal are
further of the opinion that the sole reason for giving notice of dismissal
was the desire by the respondents to obtain possession of the flat. If there
is no redundancy the question of alternative employment under s. 2 (3)
and (4) of the Act does not arise. The tribunal came to their decision with
some reluctance because in their view the [respondents] did not, when giving
the [appellant] notice, treat him with that candour to which he was entitled
after so long a service. The [appellant] contended that he was a resident
fitter in that he could be called upon every alternate weekend to do additional
work and that that work was no longer available and that therefore he was
redundant. The tribunal take the view that the weekend work formed
only a very small part of the work done by the [appellant] and that his
dismissal was not attributable wholly or mainly to the cessation of that
work. His main work as a fitter had not ceased and it was not contemplated
that it would cease."

Although it is nowhere expressly stated in the reasons for the decision it is
implicit that the tribunal found that the dismissal of the appellant was not
attributable wholly or mainly to the fact that the requirements of the business

A for employees to carry out work of a particular kind had ceased or diminished.

On behalf of the appellant counsel submitted that the particular work for which the appellant was employed was that of a resident-fitter evidenced by the fact that as a term of his employment he was required to occupy the flat; that as the respondents decided to dispose of the building in which the flat was situated and had no other living accommodation in or near to the premises in

B which to house a resident-fitter it must follow that the requirements of the business for a resident-fitter had ceased. We find ourselves unable to accept this submission. The work which the appellant was employed to do was that of a fitter. The form of the agreement by which he was permitted to occupy the flat so long as he remained in the respondents' employment is in common form to give expression to an underlying agreement that the relationship of landlord

C and tenant should not be created between the parties; see cl. 5 of the agreement (1). There is nothing in that agreement which required the appellant to do any work of any particular kind. The reality of the matter is that the free flat was part of the appellant's remuneration and there was clear evidence to show that the requirements of the business for employees to carry out work of the particular kind, namely, that of a fitter had not ceased or diminished.

D Counsel for the appellant next submitted that the operation of the emergency breakdown service was itself work of a particular kind which could only be carried out by an employee housed in or near to the garage premises; that when the respondents decided to put it out of their power to provide accommodation they accepted that this work would cease, albeit temporarily, and that it must follow that the requirements of the business for employees to carry out

E work of that particular kind had ceased within the meaning of s. 1 (2) (*b*) of the Act of 1965. Before this submission can succeed it is essential to show that the operation of the emergency breakdown service was " work of a particular kind " within s. 1 (2) (*b*) of the Act of 1965. We are satisfied that it was not. The work was that of a motor fitter and the operation of the emergency breakdown service was no more than a requirement that that work should be done as and when

F necessary outside normal working hours. It was a condition of the appellant's employment which did not alter in any way the nature of the work, which remained the work of a fitter in the garage business. Reading the judgment of this court in *North Riding Garages, Ltd.* v. *Butterwick* (2) WIDGERY, J., said:

G " It is, we think, important to observe that a claim under s. 1 (2) (*b*) is conditional on a change in the requirements of the business. If the requirement of the business for employees to carry out work of a particular kind increases or remains constant, no redundancy payment can be claimed by an employee, in work of that kind, whose dismissal is attributable to personal deficiencies which prevent him from satisfying his employer. The very fact of dismissal shows that the employee's services are no longer

H required by his employer . . ."

This last statement is correct in the majority of cases but in the present case it is only so in the widest sense, namely, that if there was no other way of getting possession of the flat the respondents were prepared to run the risk of having to dismiss the appellant and look for another skilled fitter. It must not be forgotten that before a dismissal can be one by reason of redundancy it must be attributable

I wholly or mainly to the matters set out in s. 1 (2). At the hearing before the tribunal it was for the respondent employers to show that this dismissal was not so attributable. In the present case the tribunal held that they had done so, for it found, on ample evidence, that the sole reason for dismissing the appellant was the desire of the respondents to obtain possession of the flat. In our judgment

(1) See p. 867, letter F, ante.
(2) [1967] 1 All E.R. 644 at p. 647.

the tribunal came to a correct decision that the appellant was not dismissed by **A**
reason of redundancy and this appeal is dismissed.

Appeal dismissed.   Leave to appeal to the Court of Appeal refused.

Solicitors: *W. H. Thompson* (for the appellant);   *J. S. Lumsdon* (for the
respondents).

[Reported by N. P. METCALFE, ESQ., Barrister-at-Law.] B

<hr>

PUBLIC TRUSTEE v. KENWARD.

C

[CHANCERY DIVISION (Buckley, J.), March 7, 8, 1967.]

*Res Judicata—Extent—Issues in action—Administration action—Order for
account and inquiry as to defendant's indebtedness to estate—Certificate by
master of amount due from defendant—Fresh action by judicial trustee of
estate to recover amount—Application for summary judgment—Defendant* **D**
*seeking to raise counterclaim in action that certain assets referred to in
certificate were partnership assets in which he was interested—Claim not
made by him at time of taking account—Defendant debarred from counterclaiming in action on ground of res judicata.*

The defendant and his wife carried on a farming business in partnership.
She made a will whereby she appointed the defendant and her brother the **E**
executors.   She died in June, 1957, and probate was granted to the two
named executors.   The defendant was advised, so he alleged, that the
accounts of the partnership should be adjusted by the transfer of the land
out of the partnership to become assets of the testatrix' estate.   Difficulties
having arisen, proceedings were begun in June, 1961, for administration of
the estate by the court.   Pursuant to an order made on Mar. 21, 1962, an **F**
account was taken and an inquiry was made as to the indebtedness of the
defendant to the estate.   The master certified the defendant's indebtedness
to the estate as £8,549 7s. and that £412 11s. 11d. ought to be allowed to him
by way of set-off.   There were references in the particulars in a schedule to
the certificate to adjustments necessary in connexion with the partnership
in the farming business.   In 1964 the Public Trustee was appointed sole **G**
judicial trustee of the will in place of the existing trustees, and an order was
made for the Public Trustee to take proceedings to recover from the
defendant the sum of £8,136 15s.   In an action for this purpose by the
Public Trustee the defendant, on a summons under R.S.C., Ord. 14, r. 1
for summary judgment, alleged that he wanted to counterclaim that the land
was partnership assets and that he had an interest therein.

    Held: the counterclaim belonged to the subject-matter of the account and **H**
inquiry directed by the order of Mar. 21, 1962, and, as the defendant had not
then put forward any claim to set-off whatever sum should be found due to
him as a partner on taking the partnership accounts, and as his evidence then
filed had implied acceptance that the land was part of his wife's estate, he
was debarred from counterclaiming in the action that the land was partnership assets, for that matter was res judicata; and accordingly the plaintiff **I**
was entitled to judgment (see p. 874, letters G and I, and p. 875, letter A,
post).

    Dicta of WIGRAM, V.-C., in *Henderson* v. *Henderson* ([1843-60] All E.R.
Rep. at pp. 381, 382) and of SOMERVELL, L.J., in *Greenhalgh* v. *Mallard*
([1947] 2 All E.R. at p. 257) applied.

    [As to estoppel and res judicata, see 15 HALSBURY'S LAWS (3rd Edn.) 181-183,
para. 355; and for cases on the subject, see 21 DIGEST (Repl.) 244-250, *306-333.*]

A Cases referred to:

    Caird v. *Moss*, (1886), 33 Ch.D. 22; 55 L.J.Ch. 854; 55 L.T. 453; 21 Digest (Repl.) 240, *295*.

    Greenhalgh v. *Mallard*, [1947] 2 All E.R. 255; 45 Digest (Repl.) 302, *191*.

    Henderson v. *Henderson*, [1843-60] All E.R. Rep. 378; (1843), 3 Hare 100; 1 L.T.O.S. 410; 67 E.R. 313; 21 Digest (Repl.) 244, *306*.

B **Summons.**

    This was a summons dated Nov. 17, 1966, by the plaintiff, the Public Trustee, for an order that he be at liberty to enter final judgment under R.S.C., Ord. 14, r. 1 in an action against the defendant, Peter Trayton Kenward, for £8,136 15s., the amount claimed in the statement of claim to be owing to the plaintiff as judicial trustee of the estate of the defendant's wife. The facts are set out in
C the judgment.

    Martin Nourse for the plaintiff.

    J. A. Moncaster for the defendant.

    BUCKLEY, J.: The defendant's wife made a will whereby she appointed the defendant and her brother to be her executors, and she gave her residue on
D terms that the income of half of it should be paid to the defendant for his life; and subject to that interest she gave the capital and income to her three children, who are infants, in equal shares contingently on their attaining the age of twenty-one years. She died in June, 1957, and probate was granted to both the executors named. However, owing to difficulties which arose between the executors in relation to the indebtedness of the defendant to the estate of his wife, proceedings
E were commenced by originating summons in June, 1961, which in the first instance asked for administration of the lady's estate by the court and for a scheme of maintenance in respect of her children. That summons was amended in 1964 to ask for determination of the question whether the trustees of the will of the testatrix ought to take any, and if so what, steps to recover the whole or any part of a sum of £8,136 15s. owed by the defendant, Captain Kenward, to the estate,
F and that it might be determined what should be done if the whole or any part of that sum were not recovered from him, and other consequential relief.

    On that summons an order was made on Mar. 21, 1962, the defendant not objecting, whereby an account was directed to be taken of the indebtedness of the defendant to the estate and an inquiry as to what, if any, sum ought to be allowed to him by way of set-off against the amount which might be certified on
G the taking of the account. That order was made on evidence which included an affidavit of the testatrix' brother, Col. Eyres Monsell, who was an executor of her will, in the course of which he stated at para. 9 that at the date of her death the testatrix owned a freehold farm, Rays Farm, on which she and the defendant carried on a farming business as partners in equal shares. In para. 12 the deponent said that
H

    " Despite continuous negotiation over several years it has not proved possible to reach any agreement with Capt. Kenward either as to the amount which he accepts as representing his indebtedness to the estate or as to the discharge of that indebtedness."

    That was the problem which the account and inquiry were presumably intended
I to solve. The defendant filed an affidavit in which in para. 8 he said:

    " Although the farm was carried on at a loss and the executors were obliged to find further moneys to enable it to be carried on, I would respectfully submit that the fact that I continued to carry on the farm and to devote my whole time and attention to it, not only without remuneration but at a loss to myself, resulted in benefit to the testatrix' estate."

    He went on to say that the testatrix purchased the farm buildings and 167 acres of land in 1952 for £14,500, that the farm buildings and eighty-seven acres were

sold in 1959 for £10,250 and a further twenty-six acres were sold in the year 1962   **A**
for £3,531. He pointed out that the executors therefore had received £13,750 for
part of the farm as against the purchase price of £14,500 for the whole. He said
that an offer for a further forty acres had been refused at £8,000 and as regards
a further fourteen acres, which had not been offered for sale, that he considered
£2,800 could be obtained. On this basis he said there had been a capital appreciation amounting to £10,500. " This position . . .", he said, ". . . could not, in my   **B**
view, have been attained if I had not continued to run the farm as a going
concern ". Reading that affidavit with the affidavit of Col. Eyres Monsell, his
co-executor and co-trustee, to which I referred earlier, it would seem, certainly
at first impression, that the defendant was not disputing that the land formed
part of his wife's estate.

The account and inquiry was taken by the master who, in due course, certified   **C**
that the defendant's indebtedness to the estate was a sum of £8,549 7s. and that
a sum of £412 11s. 11d. ought to be allowed to him by way of set-off. Particulars
of those sums are set out in a schedule to the certificate, and in two of the items
in that schedule there are references to adjustments necessary to be made between
the defendant and the estate in connexion with the partnership relating to the
farming business.   **D**

By a further order of Nov. 20, 1964, PLOWMAN, J., appointed the Public
Trustee sole judicial trustee of the will of the testatrix in place of the defendant
and his brother-in-law. He ordered the Public Trustee to take proceedings against
the defendant to recover the sum of £8,136 15s. owed by the defendant to the
estate of the testatrix. That is the sum found due on the certificate, less the
amount proper to be set off so found on the certificate of the master. It was   **E**
ordered that the Public Trustee should be authorised to compromise the proceedings, if the defendant paid £4,000. The court directed that any judgment obtained
against the defendant for the sum of £8,136 15s. should not be enforced for a sum
in excess of £4,000, and that to the extent that the sum of £8,136 15s. should not
be recovered the deficit should be borne by capital and as between the infant
defendants in equal shares.   **F**

The Public Trustee consequently issued his writ in this action on July 27, 1966,
claiming £8,136 15s., and he applies under R.S.C., Ord. 14, r. 1 (1) for summary
judgment. The defendant resists that application on the ground, as he alleges,
that the land on which the farming business was carried on formed an asset of the
partnership and that in consequence he is entitled to an interest in the proceeds
of sale of that land. He says that he was advised by solicitors dealing with the   **G**
administration of the testatrix' estate that it would be disadvantageous for death
duty purposes if the testatrix' share in the land was treated as personalty rather
than realty and that he was advised by the solicitors that the partnership accounts
should be adjusted by the transfer of the land out of the partnership. He says
that he agreed to this, but that it was represented as being a mere legal technicality
to change the character of the assets in the testatrix' estate. He says that he did   **H**
not understand that it would have the effects which had since been claimed by
his co-executor, namely that the land and all the capital profits relating to it
became assets of the estate in which he as a partner had no interest. He says that
the consequences of his agreeing to this only gradually became clear to him during
the course of the administration proceedings, when the master debited him with
all the losses on the farm. He says that he appeared before the master in person,   **I**
but it appears that he did at that time have solicitors. They may not have represented him before the master, although the certificate given by the master
would seem to indicate otherwise. He says that his solicitors then advised him
that he need not worry about the master's certificate too much, because he could
mention any matters he wanted to to the judge later. Accordingly the master
made the certificate in the form that he did. When the matter came before
PLOWMAN, J., it seems that the defendant's solicitor was unfortunately unwell
and that the defendant was consequently without the benefit of his advice. The

A judge then told him that he was no longer in a position to challenge the certificate. He says that later he took counsel's advice and he was advised by counsel that there was no use in attempting to appeal against the judge's order, i.e. PLOWMAN, J.'s order of Nov. 20, 1964, but that he, the defendant, should wait until the Public Trustee attempted to do what he calls " enforce the certificate ", which I think means recover the sum of £8,136 15s. shown by the certificate to be due
B from the defendant, which is the occasion of this action.

The defendant seeks in this action, therefore, to counterclaim that the land on which the farming operations were carried on forms an asset of the partnership and that he has an interest in that land as one of the partners and in the proceeds of sale. He quantifies his claim in his affidavit as a half share of the profits on realising the land, £4,791, the sum of £417, which he claims he has expended on
C improving the land or maintaining it since his wife's death, and the sum of £144 which he claims to be entitled to by virtue of his right to receive the income of one half of the residue. Those amounts total £5,352. He does not dispute his liability for the balance of £2,784 15s.

The Public Trustee on this application claims that the defendant is estopped by the doctrine of res judicata from raising this counterclaim, and alternatively
D he says that the proper form in which to pursue the claim which the defendant is anxious to pursue would be in the administration proceedings and not by way of counterclaim in this action.

I have been referred to *Greenhalgh* v. *Mallard* (1) where SOMERVELL, L.J., in the Court of Appeal says this (2):

E   " I think that on the authorities to which I will refer it would be accurate to say that res judicata for this purpose is not confined to the issues which the court is actually asked to decide, but that it covers issues or facts which are so clearly part of the subject-matter of the litigation and so clearly could have been raised that it would be an abuse of the process of the court to allow a new proceeding to be started in respect of them."

F He then cites a passage from the judgment of WIGRAM, V.-C., in *Henderson* v. *Henderson* (3) as follows:

". . . I believe I state the rule of the court correctly, when I say, that where a given matter becomes the subject of litigation in and of adjudication by, a court of competent jurisdiction, the court requires the parties to that litigation to bring forward their whole case, and will not (except under special circumstances) permit the same parties to open the same subject of
G   litigation in respect of matter which might have been brought forward as part of the subject in contest, but which was not brought forward only because they have, from negligence, inadvertence, or even accident, omitted part of their case. The plea of res judicata applies, except in special case, not only to points upon which the court was actually required by the parties to form an opinion and pronounce a judgment, but to every point which properly
H   belonged to the subject of litigation, and which the parties, exercising reasonable diligence, might have brought forward at the time."

The fact that, when an action is brought by A against B, B might in the same proceedings have raised a counterclaim against A relating to some quite different cause of action, but does not do so, will not, I think, estop B from pursuing that
I claim in subsequent litigation. That seems to me to appear clearly from *Caird* v. *Moss* (4), where a claim for rectification of an agreement was said not to be barred as res judicata by litigation on the agreement itself.

However, the question in the present case must be whether it is right to regard the claim which the defendant now wants to raise as something which properly

(1) [1947] 2 All E.R. 255.
(2) [1947] 2 All E.R. at p. 257.
(3) [1843–60] All E.R. Rep. 378 at pp. 381, 382.
(4) (1886), 33 Ch.D. 22.

belonged to the subject-matter of the account and inquiry directed by the order   A
of Mar. 21, 1962. If it were a matter which can be said properly to have belonged
to that investigation of the relative rights of the defendant and the testatrix'
estate, then the fact that the defendant, whether it be by inadvertence or accident
or as the result of his being unwisely advised or lacking advice, did not raise the
point on any of those grounds would be no justification for allowing him to raise
it now. Therefore, I must look with care at precisely what it was that the court   B
directed at that time should be the subject-matter of the inquiry.

The account was to be an account of the defendant's indebtedness to his wife's
estate, and the inquiry was to be an inquiry as to what sum ought to be allowed
to him by way of set-off. No general accounts and inquiries were directed such as
would be found in a full administration order. Had there been such accounts and ·
inquiries one would, of course, have been an inquiry as to the assets of the estate   C
and another as to the liabilities of the estate. Those accounts and inquiries would
have clearly thrown up the position as to what the relations between the defendant and the testatrix were with regard to the land on which the farming operations were conducted. A right of set off, of course, strictly can only exist where
the amount set off is a liquidated amount and is to be set off against some other
ascertained or ascertainable amount.   D

At the time this inquiry was taken there was no indication what the value of the
defendant's interest in the land on which the farming operations were conducted,
assuming his claim that that land was a partnership asset is well founded,
amounted to; the amount had not been liquidated. On the other hand, it is
manifest from the nature of the case and the evidence filed on the originating
summons that the object of this account and inquiry was to arrive at finality   E
between the defendant and the estate of the testatrix. Its object was to discover
what sum he ought to bring into the estate. It was open to him on the taking of
the inquiry to say " in addition to these various items already quantified which I
claim to be entitled to set off, I also claim to be entitled to set off whatever sum
may be found to be due to me as a partner of my wife on taking partnership
accounts between us ", or he could have said " I claim to set off whatever part   F
of the proceeds of sale of the land ought to be paid to me on a proper adjustment
of the accounts between my wife's estate and myself in respect of the land ".
He did not put forward any suggestion at that time that the land was a partnership asset. On the contrary, as I have pointed out, the evidence which he filed
does not dispute the statement in the evidence which he was answering that the
land belonged to the testatrix, but puts forward a claim for consideration on the   G
ground that he has done things which have increased the value of that land and
benefited the estate. It seems to me that his evidence there was framed in a way
which clearly implied that he accepted that the land was part of his wife's estate.

I am conscious that, if I decide that as a result of the doctrine of res judicata
he is in these circumstances excluded from now putting forward his claim that
the land was a partnership asset, I am in a sense shutting him out from the judg-   H
ment seat. I am oppressed, however, by the certainty that I feel that the order
of Mar. 21, 1962 was intended to arrive at finality with regard to his liabilities to
the testatrix' estate and the liabilities of her estate to him, with a view to the
proper administration of the estate and the proper ascertainment of the assets
of which it consisted. His time for putting forward his claim to an interest in
this land and to a claim against the estate in respect of something related to the   I
land was at the time the inquiry was taken leading to the master's certificate.
It was something that, in the language of WIGRAM, V.-C., (5) belonged to the
subject of that inquiry and which the defendant, if he had exercised reasonable
diligence, could have brought forward at that time.

With the wisdom of hindsight, one would have desired that the inquiry had been
framed in rather different language, had one known that this sort of point was
going to be raised in future. The parties, and in particular the defendant,

(5) [1843–60] All E.R. Rep. at pp. 381, 382.

A had, however, every reason to understand that the inquiry was directed to
discovering any sort of claim which he could put forward to reduce or counterbalance his indebtedness to his wife's estate, whether it would in strictness then
be called a present right of set-off or not. On these grounds, I think that as he
did not then put forward this claim he is now barred from doing so on the ground
that the matter is in fact res judicata. Accordingly I think that the right course
B is that I should direct that judgment be entered for the plaintiff in the sum of
£8,136 15s.

Judgment accordingly.

Solicitors: *Church, Adams, Tatham & Co.*, agents for *Day & Yewdall*, Leeds
(for the plaintiff); *Gibson & Weldon*, agents for *Burley & Geach*, Bishop's Waltham
C (for the defendant).

[*Reported by* JENIFER SANDELL, *Barrister-at-Law.*]

D

Re CORNISH MANURES, LTD.

[CHANCERY DIVISION (Pennycuick, J.), April 26, 1967.]

*Company—Winding-up—Voluntary winding-up—Account of winding-up to
be made up by liquidator so soon as the affairs of the company are fully
E   wound-up—Sufficient if account made up fully so far as liquidator is aware
—Final meeting convened—Subsequent receipt of surtax demand—Sum
retained to meet surtax and note of explanation sent with account—Account
and return registered—Consequent dissolution of company—More than two
years after dissolution application made under s. 352 for declaration that
winding-up was void—Registration of account and return effective and dis-
F   solution valid—Companies Act, 1948 (11 & 12 Geo. 6 c. 38), s. 290 (1), (4).*

A company went into liquidation and its undertaking was transferred to a
new company. The old company was indebted to the new company in a
sum of about £8,701 and this debt was waived by the directors of the new
company. The ultimate result of the waiver was that the sum of £8,701
found its way into the pockets of Mr. and Mrs. T. who together owned all
G   the shares in the old company. A day or two after the final general meeting
of the old company on July 18, 1964, the liquidator of the old company
received a surtax notice which had been delayed in the post. A sum of
money was retained to meet surtax, pursuant to a direction under s. 245 of
the Income Tax Act, 1952, and any balance was to be remitted to the
contributories. The liquidator appended a note to his return of the holding
H   of the final winding-up meeting, explaining the position. The Registrar
of Companies registered the account and return on July 21, 1964. The
surtax was paid on Oct. 9, 1964. Under s. 290 (4)* of the Companies Act,
1948, a company is deemed to have been dissolved on the expiration of three
months after the registration of the liquidator's return (viz., in this case, on
Oct. 21, 1964); and by s. 290 (1)† the liquidator's making up of his account
I   of the winding-up is to be done " as soon as the affairs of the company are
fully wound up ". In September, 1966, the new company went into a
creditors' voluntary winding-up. On a motion by the liquidator of the
new company by notice dated Nov. 18, 1966 (i.e., more than two years
after Oct. 21, 1964) for a declaration under s. 352 (1)‡ of the Act of 1948
that the dissolution of the old company was void.

---

* Section 290 (4) is set out at p. 877, letter F, post.
† Section 290 (1) is set out at p. 877, letter I, to p. 878, letter A, post.
‡ Section 352 (1) is set out at p. 877, letter H, post.

Held: the requirement of s. 290 (1) of the Companies Act, 1948, that the **A**
affairs of a company should be " fully wound up " before the account was
made up was sufficiently complied with so soon as the affairs were fully
wound up so far as the liquidator was aware; in the present case, when the
liquidator made up his account before the final meeting he had fully dealt
with the affairs of the old company so far as he was aware, and accordingly
the registration of the account and the return was effective under s. 290 (4), **B**
with the consequences that the notice of motion under s. 352 was out of time,
as the old company had been dissolved more than two years previously, and
that there was no jurisdiction to make the declaration sought (see p. 880,
letters D to E, F and I, post).

   Re London and Caledonian Marine Insurance Co. ((1879), 11 Ch.D. 140)
and *Re Pinto Silver Mining Co.* ((1878), 8 Ch.D. 273) considered. **C**

[As to the dissolution of a company in voluntary winding-up, see 6 HALS-
BURY's LAWS (3rd Edn.) 756, 757, paras. 1529, 1530; and as to the court's
power to declare dissolution void, see ibid., p. 757, para. 1532; and for cases on
the dissolution of companies, see 10 DIGEST (Repl.) 1102, 1103, *7614-7630.*

   For the Companies Act, 1948, s. 290 and s. 352, see 3 HALSBURY's STATUTES
(2nd Edn.) 683, 726.] **D**

Cases referred to:
   London and Caledonian Marine Insurance Co., Re, (1879), 11 Ch.D. 140;   40
      L.T. 666; 10 Digest (Repl.) 1103, *7617.*
   Pinto Silver Mining Co., Re, (1878), 8 Ch.D. 273; 47 L.J.Ch. 591; 38 L.T. 336;
      10 Digest (Repl.) 1102, *7616.* **E**

Motion.

This was a motion by notice dated Nov. 18, 1966, by Cornish Manures (1963),
Ltd. (the " new company ") by its liquidator, the new company being in a
creditors' voluntary winding-up, for a declaration that the dissolution of Cornish
Manures, Ltd. (the " old company " from which the new company had acquired
its business) was void, and that the applicant or the liquidator or any creditor **F**
or contributory of the old company might be at liberty to apply to the court in
the proceedings to determine any question arising in the voluntary winding-up
of the old company as there might be occasion. The dissolution of the old
company took place on Oct. 21, 1964. The facts are set out in the judgment.

   The case noted below* was cited during the argument in addition to the cases
referred to in the judgment. **G**

   Allan Heyman for the applicant, the liquidator of the new company.
   M. Essayan for the respondent, the liquidator of the old company.

   PENNYCUICK, J.: This motion relates to a company known as Cornish
Manures, Ltd., to which I will refer as " the old company ". The motion is
made by the liquidator of a company known as Cornish Manures (1963), Ltd., **H**
to which I will refer as " the new company ". The motion seeks a declaration
that the dissolution of the old company is void, with certain consequential
relief.

   The old company was incorporated in 1940. The whole of its assets were held
by Mr. Joseph Morris Turner and his wife. On Feb. 18, 1963, the old company
passed a special resolution placing the company in members' voluntary winding- **I**
up and a Mr. G. H. M. Webb was appointed the liquidator of the old company.
At about the same time the undertaking of the old company was transferred to
the new company on certain terms. The details of that transaction will be
found in an affidavit sworn by Mr. Webb in which he corrects certain statements
made by the liquidator of the new company. The new company took over the
stock-in-trade of the old company. The new company discharged and took
over the old company's overdraft at its bank, but the amount of that overdraft

   * *Tolhurst* v. *Associated Portland Cement Manufacturers (1900), Ltd.,* [1902] 2 K.B. 660.

A was higher than the amount which fell to be paid by the new company for the stock-in-trade. In the event—and as the result of certain cross entries in the account into which it is not necessary to go—the old company remained indebted to the new company in the sum of £8,701 2s. 2d. The old company had a considerable surplus of assets. On Mar. 3, 1964, a letter was addressed to the liquidator of the old company by the directors of the new company in the following
B terms:

> "As directors and shareholders of Cornish Manures (1963), Ltd., we hereby give you notice that we have waived the sum of £8,701 2s. 2d. due from you as liquidator of Cornish Manures, Ltd."

Exactly why the new company thought it right in that way to waive a debt
C owing to the new company by the old company is not clear, and neither of the counsel concerned on this motion has sought to defend the transaction. On the face of it the transaction represents a simple gift by the new company to the old company.

The new company did not prosper and on Sept. 28, 1966, a resolution was passed for a creditors' voluntary winding-up of the new company. It will be seen that the ultimate result of the waiver of the debt of £8,701 was that that
D sum found its way into the pockets of Mr. and Mrs. Turner in the liquidation of the old company, instead of those of the creditors of the new company in the liquidation of that company. It is for that reason that the liquidator of the new company seeks to have the liquidation of the old company re-opened.

The liquidator of the old company proceeded with that liquidation. A final
E meeting of the old company was held on July 18, 1964. The liquidator of the old company made an account pursuant to the provisions of s. 290 of the Companies Act, 1948, and sent that account, with the return mentioned in the section, to the Registrar of Companies. The registrar registered the account on July 21.

It follows in accordance with the provisions of s. 290, unless there is any more to it, that the old company is to be deemed to have been dissolved on Oct. 21,
F 1964. Section 290 (4) is in these terms:

> "The registar on receiving the account and either of the returns hereinbefore mentioned shall forthwith register them, and on the expiration of three months from the registration of the return the company shall be deemed to be dissolved."

Notice of the present motion was given on Nov. 18, 1966. It will be seen that
G that is a date outside the expiration of two years from the date of dissolution of the old company.

Section 352 (1) of the Companies Act, 1948, under which the motion is brought, is in these terms:

> "(1) Where a company has been dissolved, the court may at any time within two years of the date of the dissolution, on an application being made
H for the purpose by the liquidator of the company or by any other person who appears to the court to be interested, make an order, upon such terms as the court thinks fit, declaring the dissolution to have been void, and thereupon such proceedings may be taken as might have been taken if the company had not been dissolved."

I On the face of it, the two years having elapsed since dissolution, the present motion is out of time and the court has no jurisdiction to make an order on it.

Counsel for the liquidator of the new company contended that nonetheless the court has jurisdiction by reason of this fact, that when the liquidator of the old company made up his final account he had not yet fully wound up the affairs of the company, so that he acted prematurely in sending in the final account. Section 290 (1) is in these terms:

> "Subject to the provisions of the next following section, as soon as the affairs of the company are fully wound up, the liquidator shall make up an

account of the winding-up, showing how the winding-up has been conducted   A
and the property of the company has been disposed of, and thereupon shall
call a general meeting of the company for the purpose of laying before it
the account, and giving any explanation thereof.''

When one looks at the liquidator's return of the final winding-up meeting one
finds that he had retained a balance of £8,954, and one finds an entry at the
foot of the return in these terms '' A surtax direction under s. 245 Income Tax   B
Act, 1952—£6,165 10s.''   At the end of the return comes this note:

'' The balance carried down, as shown on p. 3 overleaf [the balance of
£8,954] could not be paid to the contributories ... at the time of the final
meeting a quorum not being present, and further, due to the strike of Post
Office workers at the time, it was not possible to obtain a payable order   C
from the liquidation branch of the Board of Trade before seven days of the
date of the meeting had elapsed.   Since the date of the final meeting, a
notice dated July 13, 1964, also delayed due to the Post Office workers'
strike has been received from the Special Commissioners of Income Tax,
under s. 250 (1) of the Income Tax Act, 1952, in respect of surtax on the
contributories.   The Special Commissioners state that the amount of surtax   D
will be about £2,800, but that it will not be possible to assess the precise
liability for a considerable time.   In the circumstances, therefore, a deed
of undertaking to pay is to be executed as between the contributories and the
liquidator, after which the balance carried down less £2,800 will at once
be remitted to the contributories, and as soon as the surtax has been assessed,
which will be a maximum of £2,800, this sum will be remitted to the Inland   E
Revenue and any small balance remaining thereafter to the contributories
less costs of the deed of undertaking.''

According to that note, what happened was that the liquidator made his arrangements for final winding-up at the date of the final meeting, but he did not know
until a day or two afterwards, owing to a delay in the post, that there was a
surtax demand for approximately £2,800.   He subsequently swore an affidavit   F
which shows how the matters were dealt with.   The surtax was paid on Oct. 9.
There are some other very small payments and then what remained was paid
over to Mr. Turner.

Is there then on those facts any reason for saying that the company was not
dissolved three months after the registration of the return?

I was referred to two cases in the Court of Appeal as to the meaning of words   G
in the Companies Act, 1862, comparable to those in s. 290 (1).   The first case
is *Re Pinto Silver Mining Co.* (1), in which case HALL, V.-C., held as follows (2):

'' It appears to me that this company cannot be deemed dissolved, at
least as regards the petitioner and the other unsatisfied creditors of the
company.   Section 142 is only capable of being acted upon as soon as the
affairs of the company are fully wound up.   Such was not the case when   H
the meeting in question was held and the return made.''

The Court of Appeal reversed that decision.   JAMES, L.J., said this (3):

'' This case must have been decided under some misapprehension as to
the facts.   The first point raised is whether the court has any jurisdiction
to make a winding-up order after a dissolution of the company under a   I
voluntary winding-up, and I much doubt whether there is any such jurisdiction.   Where there has been a de facto winding-up; liquidators appointed;
the accounts of the liquidators laid before a meeting, as required by the
Companies Act, 1862, s. 142; a return duly made to the registrar, and the
statutory period of three months elapsed, it would need a great deal of

(1) (1878), 8 Ch.D. 273.
(2) (1878), 8 Ch.D. at p. 282.
(3) (1878), 8 Ch.D. at pp. 283, 284

A   argument to satisfy me that the court can go behind the return. The
provisions of the Act as to dissolution would be of very little value if a
creditor could, after that period, come and open the whole matter because,
through mistake, some formality had been omitted, some creditor had not
come in, or some asset had been left undiscovered. The only case in which
it is desirable that what has been done should be undone is where there
B   has been a fraud by which some one is injured."

COTTON, L.J., said this (4):

" It is urged that the company has not been completely wound up, and
therefore s. 143 does not apply. It is not necessary to give any opinion
as to what is to be done where there has been a substantial non-compliance
with the provisions of the Act, but the mere fact that there are debts remain-
C   ing unpaid is no such non-compliance, otherwise an insolvent company
could never be dissolved . . ."

I will return in a moment to that case.

The other case is *Re London and Caledonian Marine Insurance Co.* (5). The
headnote is as follows:

D   " The court has no jurisdiction to make an order for winding-up a company
which has been voluntarily wound up and dissolved under s. 142 and s. 143
of the Companies Act, 1862, unlesss the dissolution can be impeached on
the ground of fraud."

Again JAMES, L.J., gave the first judgment. He made these statements in the
E   course of his judgment (6):

" I have considered this case, and it seems to me that in all respects
it is governed by the decision of this court in *Re Pinto Silver Mining Co.* (7).
Of course, when a question has been decided by the court once it ought not
to be re-argued on immaterial distinctions which practically make no more
difference to the real subject-matter of the decision than the name of the
F   parties to the suit; and what was decided in the case to which I have
referred was, that we could not put upon these words, ' as soon as the
affairs of the company are fully wound up ', the construction contended
for, namely, to make that a condition precedent and construe it to mean
that everything had been done which was to be done. We are of opinion
that those words could not mean that if there were a single asset outstanding
G   or a single debt unpaid, the affairs of the company were not to be considered as wound up."

After giving some instances he went on (8):

" We must put some practical and sensible meaning on the words, and
in my opinion they mean ' as far as the liquidators can wind them up ';
that is, when the liquidator has done all that he can to wind up the company,
H   when he has disposed of the assets as far as he can realise them, got in the
calls as far as he can enforce them, and paid the debts as far as he is aware of
them, and has done all that he can do in winding-up the affairs, so that he
has completed his business so far as he can, and is functus officio. Then it
is his duty to call a meeting, to give in his account of the affairs of the
company, and to make a return to the registrar under the Act. We thought
I   that was the meaning of ' fully winding-up ', and that being so, we thought
there was no power to go behind the dissolution except in the case which I
suggested as a possible case—the case of absolute fraud—fraud which the
company could be fixed with. If there were a case of that kind, then very

(4) (1878), 8 Ch.D. at p. 285.
(5) (1879), 11 Ch.D. 140.
(6) (1879), 11 Ch.D. at p. 143.
(7) (1878), 8 Ch.D. 273.
(8) (1879), 11 Ch.D. at pp. 143, 144.

likely the whole thing might be set aside; that is to say, it might, on **A**
proper proceedings being taken, be made clear that the whole winding-up
was null and void, and then the company would be restored again to its
position, subject to claims of creditors and contributories, or any other persons
who might have rights to enforce or equities to be adjusted in relation to the
company.   But in the absence of any case of fraud of that kind it seems
to me that the court has no jurisdiction whatever."   **B**

I respectfully think that there is a certain hiatus in the reasoning of JAMES,
L.J., in those two cases. He first said that the meaning of the words is " as far as
the liquidators can wind them up " and explains that as meaning that the
liquidator must have done all that he could to wind up the company.   Then by
way of antithesis he takes the case of what he describes as " absolute fraud ".
There is, I think, an intervening area, that is to say, the area in which there is **C**
no fraud but the liquidator calls the final meeting before he has done all that
he can do to wind up the company.   It is to that point which COTTON, L.J.,
directed the comment which I have read out from his judgment in *Re Pinto
Silver Mining Co.* (9).   However, I do not think that I am concerned in the
present case, on the facts, with that particular difficulty.   It is quite clear from
the judgments in both cases that the section cannot be construed as meaning **D**
that the affairs of the company must in fact have been fully wound up.   It is
at least sufficient that they should have been fully wound up so far as the
liquidator is aware.

In the present case it appears, from the note which I have read on the return
of the final winding-up meeting, that when the liquidator made out his final
account he had, so far as he was aware, fully dealt with the affairs of the com- **E**
pany and that he had discharged all liabilities of which he was aware.   What
happened was that owing to a delay in the post notice of a further liability
came in a day or two afterwards.   I do not think that in those circumstances
it is possible to say that the final meeting was not duly held in accordance with
s. 290.   On the contrary, the case seems to me to fall clearly within the reasoning
in the two cases which I have cited.   That being the position, I do not think **F**
that there can be any doubt that the registration was effective under s. 290 (4)
and accordingly that the period of three months then began to run.

I abstain from expressing any view as to what would be the position if a
liquidator, having knowledge that he had not fully dealt with the affairs of the
company in a material respect, nonetheless called a final meeting.   It may be
that in the absence of fraud the registration would still be effective, but I am not **G**
concerned to decide that point.

Counsel for the liquidator of the new company very naturally drew attention
to the irregularities in the winding-up of the affairs of the old company, and in
particular pointed out that the liquidator did not in his return make any note
as to the £8,701 odd which it appeared was owing to the new company.   He did
not, however, seek to set up any case of fraud, and I do not think that I am **H**
concerned to take that point any further.

So far as the present application is concerned, the position is that the registration was effective under s. 290 (4).   Accordingly, the old company was dissolved
upwards of two years before the date of the present notice of motion.   The
notice of motion is out of time and I have no jurisdiction to exercise any discretion
in the matter.   **I**

Motion dismissed.

Solicitors: *Isadore Goldman & Son* (for the applicant, the liquidator of the
new company); *Simmons & Simmons*, agents for *Jackson & Ryan*, King's Lynn
(for the respondent, the liquidator of the old company).

[*Reported by* JENIFER SANDELL, *Barrister-at-Law.*]

---

(9) (1878), 8 Ch.D. at p. 285.

Re E. (an infant).

[COURT OF APPEAL, CIVIL DIVISION (Willmer, Danckwerts and Winn, L.JJ.), March 2, 3, 1967.]

Ward of Court—Jurisdiction—Alien children—Child, a girl of seven subject to custody order of foreign court, removed from jurisdiction of that court and brought to England—Custody of child previously taken from mother by foreign court and given to father—Father killed in motor accident—Child willingly making her home with father's sister in England—Temporary custody of child awarded by foreign court to mother after father's death—Comity—Special circumstances—Whether care and control of child, made a ward of court in England, should be given to father's sister.

American citizens were married in 1958 and made their home at Albuquerque, New Mexico, in the United States. In September, 1959, a daughter was born. Nine months later, in June, 1960, the mother obtained a divorce from the father on the ground of incompatibility, and also an order for the custody of the daughter. But in March, 1962, a further order was made transferring custody to the father, with limited rights of access to the mother, on the ground that it was said that the mother was not a fit and proper person to have custody, apparently because of her record of association with other men. Later the same year the father executed a document in which he said that he did not regard either the mother or her parents as suitable persons to have the custody of his daughter and expressed the wish that her aunt, his sister living in England, should take over the child's custody in the event of his decease. For three and a half years he looked after his daughter and in August, 1965, he brought her to England on a holiday trip. They stayed with his sister, who promised to look after the child in the event of the father's death. In December, 1965, the father was killed in a road accident. The child was in the car, and was taken to hospital, but she was not seriously injured. His father, the child's grandfather, who knew of the father's wishes, immediately telephoned to the child's aunt to fly from Europe to New York, where he met her with the child, whom he had brought from the hospital. The mother, who had meanwhile remarried and was living in Portland, Oregon, having failed to prevent the removal of the child, obtained a court order requiring the grandfather and others to deliver the child to her maternal grandmother and enjoining them from removing the child from the United States. Before the order could be served, although it was known to the grandfather and apparently the sister, the child's aunt, she had left for England with the child. The child had welcomed her aunt in New York with open arms, and had made her home with her in England. The child's mother obtained a further court order in America awarding her temporary custody of the child, and subsequently came to England. In May, 1966, the child was made a ward of court on the aunt's application, and she, the plaintiff in the proceedings, applied to the court for and was given care and control of the child subject to access by the mother. In giving that decision the trial judge condemned the conduct of the grandfather and the plaintiff in removing the child to England, and held that the English court must pay regard to the orders of the proper foreign court unless satisfied beyond reasonable doubt that to do so would inflict serious harm on the child, but found that the plaintiff stood in the relation of mother to the child and that to take the child away from her would be utterly disastrous for the child. On appeal,

Held: (i) although where a child, who was already subject to the order of a foreign court, was removed from the jurisdiction of that court regard should be paid to the order of the foreign court unless to do so would inflict serious harm on the child, yet the trial judge had rightly held that he had himself to decide on the child's future, rather than to abdicate responsibility

by implicitly undertaking to abide by a decision of the foreign court (see   A
p. 885, letter I, and p. 887, letters C, G and I, post).

(ii) in the circumstances, and particularly in view of the fact that the only
home which the child had known in the United States had been effectively
destroyed by her father's death, the findings of the trial judge that the
plaintiff had come to be in the relation of mother to the child and that it
would be disastrous to take the child away from the plaintiff should stand,   B
and with them his direction that the plaintiff should have care and control
of the child (see p. 886, letters C and H, and p. 887, letters F, H and I, post).

Decision of CROSS, J., ([1967] 1 All E.R. 329) affirmed.

[As to custody disputes affected by conflict of laws, see 7 HALSBURY'S LAWS
(3rd Edn.) 126, 127, para. 227; as to the infant's welfare being paramount, see 21
ibid., pp. 193, 194, para. 428; and for cases on the subject of welfare of infants,   C
see 28 DIGEST (Repl.) 614, 615, *1205-1218.*]

Case referred to:

H. (*infants*), *Re*, [1965] 3 All E.R. 906; *affd.* C.A., [1966] 1 All E.R. 886;
[1966] 1 W.L.R. 381.

Appeal.   D

' This was an appeal by the defendant against an order of CROSS, J., dated
Dec. 2, 1966, and finally sealed on Jan. 16, 1957, reported at [1967] 1 All E.R.
329, ordering that an infant, Diana, the niece of the plaintiff, should remain
a ward of court and that she should remain in the custody, care and control of
the plaintiff. The defendant, the mother of Diana, sought an order that Diana
should no longer remain a ward of court, that her custody, care and control should   E
be committed to the defendant, and that she should be at liberty to be returned
to the United States of America. The grounds of appeal were: (i) that the order
was against the weight of the evidence; (ii) that the judge failed to take sufficiently
into account the orders of the American courts in favour of the mother; (iii) that
he failed to take sufficiently into account the circumstances in which Diana
came to be brought into the jurisdiction of the Court of Appeal; (iv) that he   F
failed to take sufficiently into account Diana's age, nationality and former
country of residence; (v) that he failed to give sufficient weight to considerations
of public policy, comity of nations and the jurisdiction of the American court;
and (vi) that his decision was wrong or that he exercised his discretion wrongly.

J. P. Comyn, Q.C., and V. K. Winstain for the appellant, Diana's mother.

S. W. Templeman, Q.C., and A. J. Blackett-Ord for the respondent, Diana's   G
aunt.

WILLMER, L.J.: This is an appeal against a judgment (1) of CROSS, J.,
given on Dec. 2, 1966, in wardship proceedings relating to a young American girl,
who is now resident in this country. The ward, to whom I will refer as " Diana ",
is some 7½ years old, having been born on Sept. 4, 1959. The plaintiff in the pro-   H
ceedings is the ward's aunt, the sister of the ward's deceased father. She is a
married woman resident in this country. She commenced these proceedings by
originating summons on May 9, 1966. The defendant is Diana's mother. She is
an American citizen by birth, is now married to an American citizen, and is
normally resident in Portland, Oregon.

After a hearing which lasted for a number of days, during which the judge   I
heard a considerable amount of oral evidence, as well as having a number of
affidavits before him, he came to the conclusion that Diana should remain a
ward, and that care and control of her should be committed to her aunt, the
plaintiff. The mother now appeals to this court, asking in the first place that that
order be reversed, and that the care and control of Diana should be granted
to her. Alternatively, it is contended on her behalf that no order should have

(1) [1967] 1 All E.R. 329.

A been made, but that it should have been left to the court in New Mexico, of which
Diana is already a ward, to determine who should have her care and control.

The real difficulty of the case is caused by the fact that Diana was brought to
this country by her aunt from the United States of America in circumstances
amounting to something very like an act of kidnapping; certainly she was brought
to this country in defiance of an existing order of the court of New Mexico. That
B is a circumstance which, not unnaturally, is very much relied on by the mother
in presenting her case. There is quite a long history behind this case, the facts of
which have been very fully set out in the judgment of the judge (2). I do not
think that it is either necessary, or indeed desirable, for me to recite them all
again in detail. I shall do my best to summarise what seem to me the salient
facts.

C Diana's parents, who were both American citizens, married on May 2, 1958,
and they made their home in a place called Albuquerque in New Mexico. The
mother had been married before, her previous husband having been resident in
Illinois. He had obtained a divorce against her in February, 1958, and he had also
obtained an order for the custody of the two children which she had by that
marriage. Diana was born in September, 1959; nine months later, on June 27,
D 1960, the mother obtained a divorce from the father in New Mexico on the ground
of incompatibility, which is a ground for divorce in that state. The case was dealt
with by JUDGE REIDY, sitting in Albuquerque. On the same occasion, and from
the same judge, the mother obtained an order for the custody of the infant, Diana.

On Mar. 27, 1962, the same judge made a fresh order on the application of the
father, transferring the custody of Diana to him and taking it away from the
E mother, the ground of that order being that the mother was said not to be a fit
and proper person to have the custody of a small child. The reason why the judge
came to that conclusion was apparently because of the mother's record of association with other men. By the same order the mother was granted certain limited
rights of access, but that access was not to extend to staying overnight. The
mother appealed against that decision to the Supreme Court of New Mexico,
F but her appeal was dismissed.

Later in the same year, on Aug. 1, 1962, the father executed a rather unusual
document, in which he set out his wishes with regard to what was to happen to
Diana in the event of his premature death. Having regard to the events which
followed, it seems almost uncanny that the father should have taken the trouble
to set out his wishes in that way. The gist of what he said in that document was
G that he did not regard either the mother or the mother's parents as suitable
persons to have the custody of Diana. He expressed the wish that his sister (the
present plaintiff, Diana's aunt), who was then already married and living in
England, should take over the custody of Diana in the event of his own decease.

From the time that he obtained the order from JUDGE REIDY till the end of
1965, a period of something like three and a half years, the father in fact looked
H after Diana, and was father and mother to her. In August, 1965, he brought
Diana to this country on a holiday trip, in the course of which they stayed with
the plaintiff. He took the opportunity then of extracting a promise from the
plaintiff that in the event of his death she would look after Diana. In the meantime the mother, in or about June, 1965, had married again. She went after the
marriage to live with her present husband in Portland, Oregon, which we are
I told is about three thousand miles from Albuquerque where Diana was.

On Dec. 28, 1965, a most tragic event occurred when the father was killed in a
motor accident. Unhappily, the child Diana was with him at the time in the car,
and actually saw her father killed. She herself received no serious injury, but was,
of course, very emotionally upset and was taken to hospital in a place called
Durango, which lies just over the border of New Mexico in the state of Colorado.
Following this tragic event, things happened very quickly. The father's father,

---

(2) [1967] 1 All E.R. at pp. 330-336.

Diana's grandfather, was very concerned to see that his son's wishes about Diana, **A** of which he was well aware, should be carried out. He therefore himself telephoned to the aunt, who was then in the course of a holiday on the continent of Europe, and arranged for her to fly at once to New York for the purpose of taking over the custody of Diana. He then himself travelled to Durango; he himself, I understand, is ordinarily resident in New Jersey. He had with him his attorney. Together they went to the hospital where Diana was, and somehow or other succeeded in spiriting her away out of hospital, which they did on Dec. 30, 1965. **B** Having thus collected Diana, the grandfather flew with her direct to New York, so as to be ready immediately for the plaintiff when she arrived from Europe.

In the meantime, however, the mother also had heard of what had occurred. She flew south from Portland, Oregon, and met her own parents, who themselves were concerned as to the future of the child, Diana. They failed to prevent the **C** grandfather from removing Diana in the way that I have described. They accordingly made an application to JUDGE REIDY, and on Jan. 3, 1966, obtained an order from him directed, amongst other people, to the grandfather and to his attorney, requiring them to deliver Diana to her maternal grandmother, and enjoining them from removing Diana from the United States. By the time that the order was made, the grandfather and Diana were already in New York. **D** The plaintiff arrived there on the following day, viz., Jan. 4. Before the order made by JUDGE REIDY could be served on them, the plaintiff, with Diana, was able to obtain a flight, and flew first to Montreal and then to England, starting on Jan. 6 and arriving in England on Jan. 7.

I have said that the order of JUDGE REIDY had not been served on them at the time of the plaintiff's leaving; but it is abundantly clear that the grandfather **E** knew of it, and it seems probable, as I understand the judge's judgment, that the plaintiff also knew of it. Reliance has been placed on the fact that a flight via Montreal was arranged, instead of a direct flight to London, and it has been suggested that this was done because a flight to Montreal ranks as an internal flight, and would not require the production of any passports, which might have led to the asking of awkward questions. Against that it is said, however, that the **F** choice of a flight to Montreal was made for a very different reason, viz., that there was a transport strike on in New York at the time, and that it was easier and more convenient to take the flight via Montreal, which would start from Newark airport.

On Jan. 10, 1966, after the departure of the plaintiff and Diana, JUDGE REIDY in Albuquerque made a further order, whereby he awarded the temporary custody **G** of Diana to the mother. CROSS, J., having referred in his judgment to this order, said (3):

" In awarding temporary custody to the mother JUDGE REIDY was not, of course, deciding that on the merits of the case she ought to have custody rather than [the present plaintiff and her husband]. His view, with which, if I may say so with respect, I entirely concur, was that the matter **H** ought to have been brought before him, and that the action of [the grandfather] and [his attorney], was grossly improper. He gave temporary custody to the mother, as a weapon which she might conceivably be able to use in order to put the child back before him so that he could decide on the child's future."

I

Later the judge said (4):

" One cannot say what he would have decided. But, difficult as the decision would have been, he was the one person in the world in a position to make it with full knowledge of all the relevant facts; and if the decision had gone against her, the mother would have had the consolation of knowing that the decision had been made by an American judge in the American courts. All

(3) [1967] 1 All E.R. at p. 335.
(4) [1967] 1 All E.R. at p. 336.

A   that has been rendered impossible by the action of [the grandfather] and [his attorney]."

I venture to quote those passages from the judgment of the judge in order to show that he was very fully alive to the desirability of the question of Diana's future being decided by the court in Albuquerque. If I may say so, I wholly agree with the observations which the judge there made.

B   Having obtained that order, the mother was not in a position to do anything about it. She is not, I understand, a wealthy woman. She had not the funds to follow Diana across the Atlantic. She did ascertain by telephone that the child was in fact in England, and was with the plaintiff. So for some months she saved and borrowed money until she could afford the fare across the Atlantic. Eventually she was able to come to this country in early May, 1966, and, having come to this

C   country, she duly met the plaintiff and Diana. It was in those circumstances that the plaintiff, being afraid that the mother might herself in her turn try to kidnap Diana, commenced the present proceedings, as a result of which Diana became a ward of court. It is, I think, right to say that counsel for the mother on this appeal has not sought to make any secret of the fact that it was the mother's private intention, if she could, to do that very thing, viz., kidnap the child and

D   take her back to America.

I think that it remains only to say, by way of summarising the facts, that, when Diana's father was killed, the only home which the child had ever known was destroyed. She is, however, very devoted to her aunt, and the evidence, as accepted by the judge, was that she welcomed her aunt with open arms when they met in New York after the tragedy (5). It appears that she has in fact eventually

E   settled down quite happily in this country in her new home, and is going to school. I say " eventually " because there is no doubt that Diana was in a very emotional state, and for some time at least she was inclined to be difficult, and suffered from nightmares, and so forth.

On those facts I think that the judge was faced with a peculiarly difficult problem. On the one hand he quite rightly felt that it was his duty to condemn in the

F   most forthright terms the conduct of the grandfather, and to a lesser extent that of the plaintiff, in smuggling Diana out of the United States in defiance of an order made by the court of the domicil of which Diana was already a ward. On the other hand, he also had to consider as the first and paramount consideration the welfare of Diana. I do not think that it was at all an easy matter, in the very unusual circumstances of this case, to maintain a correct balance between these

G   conflicting considerations.

At the outset of his judgment, after expressing his concern at what he described as the growing tendency, which has recently been apparent, of kidnapping children in this way and removing them from the jurisdiction of a foreign court, the judge proceeded as follows (6):

H   " The courts in all countries ought, as I see it, to be careful not to do anything to encourage this tendency. The substitution of self help for due process of law in this field can only harm the interests of wards generally, and a judge should, as I see it, pay regard to the orders of the proper foreign court unless he is satisfied beyond reasonable doubt that to do so would inflict serious harm on the child."

I   First of all, I would like to say, by way of comment on that passage, that I wholly agree with, and would wish to support, everything that the judge said about the duty of all courts not to countenance behaviour of the kind there referred to. The other comment that I would make on it is that it seems to me that in that passage the judge was giving himself exactly the same direction as he had previously given himself in the earlier case of Re H. (infants) (7). That was a case

(5) [1967] 1 All E.R. at p. 334, letter H.
(6) [1967] 1 All E.R. at p. 330.
(7) [1965] 3 All E.R. 906.

which undoubtedly did have a number of features in common with the present   A
case; but it was different in one very essential respect, viz., that in that case
both the father and mother were alive, and both of them had settled homes in the
state of New York. In that case it was the mother who had smuggled the children
out of the state of New York and brought them to this country in defiance of
an order of the New York court. The judge there came to the conclusion that the
children would come to no harm if he ordered their immediate return to their   B
father's home in New York, and he accordingly made an order that they should be
so returned so that the New York court could decide as to their future. There
was an appeal to this court (8) from the decision of the judge (9) in that case, but
we in this court upheld his decision.

As I have said, this case is radically different in that very essential respect,
for here the only home that the child Diana has ever known in the United States   C
had been effectively destroyed by her father's death. In the present case, therefore, the effect of transferring care and control of Diana to her own natural mother
would necessarily be to uproot her from the new home in this country in which
she has now happily settled down, to take her away from her aunt, who has more
or less established a relationship of mother to the child, and to transfer her to
surroundings which would be wholly strange to her, viz., in Portland, Oregon.   D
It might be different if the child was to go back to Albuquerque where, I suppose,
she might find herself among her own friends and some of her own people; but,
of course, in Portland, Oregon, she would be a complete stranger.

In those circumstances, the judge, having asked himself substantially the
same question as he had asked himself in the previous case of *Re H.* (*infants*) (9),
arrived in this case at the opposite answer. What he said, having referred to the   E
conduct of the grandfather in taking the child away from the hospital, was this (10):

" But, however much one may disapprove of his action—and I am very far
indeed from condoning it—one cannot shut one's eyes to the results which have
flowed from it. Having heard [the plaintiff] in the witness-box, I have no
doubt whatever that she stands in the relation of mother to Diana, and that   F
to take Diana away from her would be utterly disastrous for the child."

To be fair to the mother, I do not read this as meaning that the judge took an
adverse view of her. On the contrary, he rather went out of his way to pay tribute
to the mother for the way in which she had behaved; he described her as " a
woman of charm and intelligence "; but it is also fair to say that he did bear in
mind the strictures which had been made about her moral behaviour in the past.   G
What the judge was concerned with in using the word " disastrous ", I think,
was the danger of taking the child away from the plaintiff, having regard to the
relationship which had been built up between them. To take the child away from
the plaintiff would involve removing her from the only home which she now knows,
and setting her adrift in wholly strange surroundings.

In view of the judge's finding that it would be disastrous for the child to take   H
her away, it is indeed difficult to see what order he could properly have made
other than the one that he did. We invited counsel for the mother to direct our
attention to any evidence which there might be tending to rebut this finding
of the judge; but in answer to that invitation, the only reply which counsel was
able to give was that the judge ought never to have got into the position of asking
himself that question at all. What was submitted was that the proper course   I
would have been to adjourn the case, though maintaining the wardship in being
for the time being, without forming (and certainly without expressing) any
view as to the merits of the case, or as to the effect on the child, so as to give time
and opportunity for the whole matter to be thrashed out and decided by JUDGE

(8) [1966] 1 All E.R. 886.
(9) [1965] 3 All E.R. 906.
(10) [1967] 1 All E.R. at p. 337.

A REIDY in the court at Albuquerque. That point had been argued also before CROSS, J., and he dealt with it in this way (11):

B
"... counsel for the mother suggested that a possible solution would be for me to leave Diana here for the time being while asking the New Mexico court to decide on her future and implicitly undertaking to abide by its decision. That to my mind would be to abdicate my responsibility. In cases of this sort, either the child must go back or this court must decide on its future. As *Re H.* (*infants*) (12) shows, unless there are compelling reasons to the contrary, the child ought to be sent back, but here in my judgment there are such reasons."

C Let me say that in my judgment the judge dealt with this submission in the proper way. I am abundantly satisfied that he was right, and indeed was only carrying out the duty entrusted to him, in himself considering what would be the effect on Diana of such order as he might be disposed to make. As I have said, he gave himself the same direction that he gave himself in the earlier case, and I think that in doing so he asked himself the right question.

D Once he had decided, as he did, that it would be " disastrous " to take Diana away from the plaintiff and from the only home that she now knows, I think that he was not only entitled but also bound to say so in no uncertain terms, and to give effect to his view, as he did, by directing that the plaintiff should have the care and control of the child. I cannot refrain from expressing my sympathy with the mother, who has fought valiantly to recover care and control of her own daughter. I have no doubt that in the course of doing so she has subjected herself to a good deal of expense and hardship in her efforts. I feel sympathy all the more

E because I fully recognise the obvious difficulties, on geographical grounds, in making any satisfactory provision for the mother having regular access; but in view of the judge's finding as to the effect of removing Diana from the care and control of the plaintiff, I do not think that any other decision was open to him. In those circumstances in my judgment the appeal must be dismissed.

F   **DANCKWERTS, L.J.:** I agree. In cases of this kind, where the welfare of an infant is concerned, and there are conflicting views as to what is best for the infant's welfare and future, the decision is always a difficult one. CROSS, J., had also, however, decided the earlier case of *Re H.* (*infants*) (13), on which great reliance was placed by counsel on behalf of the mother, and in that case his decision to send the two boys back to the United States was upheld by the Court of

G Appeal (12) The judge indeed said (11) that unless there were compelling reasons to the contrary, the proper course would be that the child should go back to the United States, but he found that there were such reasons in the present case, and I agree with him. There is no doubt on the evidence in the case that the plaintiff, Diana's aunt, had become a mother to the child, and it does appear that in the past the defendant mother had not really been very much of a mother to her.

H I am satisfied that the judge reached the right conclusion that it would now be disastrous to Diana to remove her from the care of the plaintiff and send her back to the United States. In my judgment the judge's decision was the right one, and I also would dismiss the appeal.

     WINN, L.J.: I agree completely with the judgments delivered by my lords,
I and do not think that I can usefully add anything.

Appeal dismissed.

Solicitors: *Crane & Hawkins* (for the mother); *Roney & Co.* (for the aunt).

[*Reported by* F. A. AMIES, ESQ., *Barrister-at-Law.*]

---

(11) [1967] 1 All E.R. at p. 338.
(12) [1966] 1 All E.R. 886.
(13) [1965] 3 All E.R. 906.

CHALCOTS DEVELOPMENTS, LTD. *v.* DE GRAY.   A

[COURT OF APPEAL, CIVIL DIVISION (Sellers, Diplock and Russell, L.JJ.), February 15, 16, 1967.]

Landlord and Tenant—Tenancy—Grant—Invalid notice to quit to furnished sub-tenant expiring at midnight of Mar. 25—Removal of furniture by tenant earlier on Mar. 25—Cesser of tenant's interest at midnight on Mar. 25—Sub-tenant remaining in occupation—Subsequent valid notice to quit given by landlord to sub-tenant—Claim by sub-tenant that the tenancy had become an unfurnished tenancy.

The tenant of a house, unfurnished, let one room in the house, furnished with furniture belonging to the tenant, to a sub-tenant on a weekly sub-tenancy. The freeholder, the tenant's landlord, gave the tenant notice to quit expiring on Apr. 30, 1965, and granted a lease of the house to the plaintiffs. In December, 1965, the plaintiffs wrote to the tenant a letter which they believed to grant her licence to remain in the house and to collect rents from sub-tenants; but the letter was held in fact to create a tenancy expiring with Mar. 25, 1966. On Feb. 26, 1966, the tenant gave the sub-tenant notice to quit on Mar. 25, 1966. This notice, being for one day less than four weeks, was invalid*, although the plaintiffs, the tenant and the sub-tenant all thought that it was valid. On Mar. 25, 1966, the tenant removed her furniture from the sub-tenant's room, but the sub-tenant, who had brought in some furniture of her own, remained in occupation of the room; she paid no rent in respect of the period after Mar. 18. The plaintiffs had bought the tenant's furniture from her, and did not realise that she had removed her furniture from the sub-tenant's room. On Mar. 29, 1966, the plaintiffs requested the sub-tenant, by letter, to leave. As the plaintiffs could not find their copy of the notice to quit which the tenant had served on the sub-tenant, they sent the sub-tenant, on Apr. 19, 1966, a proper four week notice to quit the room " on May 21, 1966, or at the end of the next complete four weeks of the tenancy after the date thereof ". With this notice to quit the plaintiffs sent a covering letter stating that this notice was without prejudice to the notice which had expired on Mar. 25, and demanding one week's rent up to Mar. 25, and mesne profits thereafter. After this notice had expired the plaintiffs brought an action against the sub-tenant, claiming possession of the room, alleging that the sub-tenant had had a furnished tenancy which had been determined by the Apr. 19 notice to quit, arrears of rent up to May 21, and mesne profits from then on. Later, on June 6, 1966, a letter was written on behalf of the sub-tenant to the plaintiffs stating that the furniture in the room was the sub-tenant's and so her tenancy was not furnished, asking what rent the plaintiffs wanted, and offering to pay " a reasonable rent on an unfurnished basis ". The plaintiffs replied by letter on June 7 that the letting had been furnished and that they saw no reason why a lower rent should be fixed. The sub-tenant contended that by reason of the removal of the tenant's furniture on Mar. 25 before the expiry, at midnight, of the invalid notice to quit, alternatively by reason of the plaintiffs' letter of Apr. 19 and the subsequent conduct already described, the sub-tenant had become tenant to the plaintiffs of the room on an unfurnished tenancy, and so could claim the protection of the Rent Acts.

Held: no such unfurnished tenancy had come into existence, and the plaintiffs were entitled to possession, because

(i) the common misapprehension that the notice to the sub-tenant to quit on Mar. 25 was valid, by reason of which the tenant removed her furniture and the sub-tenant assented to its removal, could not turn the furnished sub-tenancy into an unfurnished one (see p. 891, letters C and I, and p. 892, letter I, post).

---

* By virtue of the Rent Act, 1957, s. 16; 37 HALSBURY'S STATUTES (2nd Edn.) 567.

A   (ii) on the facts it was not established and could not be inferred that a new unfurnished tenancy was created after Mar. 25, 1965, between the plaintiffs as landlords and the sub-tenant as tenant (see p. 891, letter G, and p. 892, letters F and I, post).

Appeal dismissed.

B   [As to the change of a tenancy from a furnished to an unfurnished letting, see 23 HALSBURY'S LAWS (3rd Edn.) 750, 751, para. 1506; and for cases on the subject, see 31 DIGEST (Repl.) 652-655, *7558-7576*.]

Appeal.

This was an appeal by Mrs. Y. De Gray, who had been sub-tenant to a previous tenant of a room in a house now let to the plaintiffs, Chalcots Developments, Ltd., C against the order of His Honour JUDGE CURTIS RALEIGH, made at Bloomsbury county court on Sept. 16, 1966, that she give possession of the room to the plaintiffs. The facts are set out in the judgment of DIPLOCK, L.J.

G. V. Owen for the appellant sub-tenant.
Michael Albery, Q.C., and *L. A. Marshall* for the plaintiffs.

D   **DIPLOCK, L.J.**, delivered the first judgment at the request of SELLERS, L.J.: This is an appeal from a judgment of His Honour JUDGE CURTIS RALEIGH at Bloomsbury county court by which he ordered the appellant sub-tenant, Mrs. De Gray, to give up possession of a room on the first floor of 132, King Henry's Road, N.W.3 and referred a claim for mesne profits and rent to the registrar.

The premises 132, King Henry's Road are in Hampstead and form part of a E large estate, belonging to Eton College, which is now in process of development by the plaintiffs. The room occupied by the sub-tenant is in a house of which a Mrs. Drummond-Hay was originally tenant at the time when she let the room to the sub-tenant; Mrs. Drummond-Hay was a tenant of Eton College, the free-holders. Her tenancy of the house was determined by notice to quit given by the freeholders on Oct. 30, 1964, and expiring six months after that date—that is to F say on Apr. 30, 1965. In the meantime the freeholders had entered into a lease of the premises to the plaintiffs. The plaintiffs did not require possession of the house immediately and some negotiations took place between them and the tenant as a result of which they wrote to the tenant on Dec. 1, 1965, a letter by which they agreed to the tenant's remaining in possession of the house until Mar. 25, 1966. The plaintiffs were under the impression—which persisted, I G think, up to the date of the trial—that by that letter they did not create in the tenant any interest in the premises but merely licensed her to occupy them and to collect the rents from any sub-tenants. However, at the hearing the county court judge found that the effect of that letter was to grant to the tenant a leasehold interest for a term of years certain expiring on Mar. 25, 1966.

The sub-tenant occupied the room under a furnished weekly tenancy. On H Feb. 26, 1966, she received a notice to quit from the tenant requiring her to quit the premises on Mar. 25, 1966. As 1966 was not a leap year, that notice (as everyone now accepts) was an invalid notice, because it was one day short of the required four weeks' notice. On Mar. 25, however, on the instructions of the tenant, and in the belief that the notice was a valid one, removal men came round and removed the furniture. The sub-tenant was present at the time. She I too was under the impression that the notice was a valid notice to quit; and the furniture was removed. In anticipation of its removal, of which the sub-tenant had been warned about a fortnight before, she had already brought into the room some furniture of her own; and she remained in possession of the room. However, at midnight on Mar. 25/26, 1966, the tenant's interest in the room ceased and, consequently, so did the sub-tenancy of the sub-tenant. However, the sub-tenant remained in possession—in law, as a trespasser—after Mar. 25. On Mar. 29, 1966, a letter was written to her by the plaintiffs asking her to quit the premises.

At this time, as I have said, the plaintiffs were under the impression that the   **A** tenant had been merely their licensee and that any tenancy which the sub-tenant had had after May, 1965 had been a tenancy from the plaintiffs—and, of course, a furnished tenancy; but the plaintiffs were unable to find the notice to quit that the tenant had served and accordingly, on Apr. 19, in order to make their position secure (as they thought), they sent to the sub-tenant two documents, one a notice to quit which was in these terms: **B**

" Dear Madam. 132, King Henry's Road, N.W.3. As your landlords, we hereby give you notice to quit and deliver up to us, or to whom we may appoint, on May 21, 1966, or at the end of the next complete four weeks of the tenancy after the date hereof, possession of the premises being one room on the first floor at the above-mentioned address."

  C

With that there was a covering letter, of which I should read perhaps one or two passages. It started:

" Further to our letter of Mar. 29, we understand that you are still in occu-pation at the above address notwithstanding the fact that the notice to quit recently served on you expired on Mar. 25, 1966. As you are aware, you are not entitled to be re-housed and we require possession of the property   **D** forthwith. Without prejudice to the former notice served on you, we are enclosing herewith a further formal notice and trust that you will make every effort to secure suitable alternative accommodation without further delay. We understand that no rent, which was previously payable at the rate of £3 11s. 6d. per week, has been paid in respect of any period since Mar. 18. To date therefore outstanding rent of £3 11s. 6d. and mesne profits, payable   **E** after the expiry of the notice to quit and accruing at the same rate as rent, of £10 14s. 6d. are due to us."

It will be observed from that letter that it was written in the belief that the plaintiffs were the landlords of the sub-tenant and had been the landlords of the sub-tenant under a furnished tenancy, and also in the belief at that time that that tenancy had been duly determined by a valid notice to quit on the previous   **F** Mar. 25: thus, it will be seen, the plaintiffs demanded rent up to Mar. 25 and mesne profits thereafter.

The sub-tenant had in the meantime been consulting a legal advice centre and had apparently informed them for the first time of the events of Mar. 25, when the tenant had removed the furniture from the flat. On June 6, 1966, which was after the plaint was issued, the legal advice centre wrote to the plaintiffs a letter,   **G** of which I need read, I think, only the two middle paragraphs.

" She [the sub-tenant] informs us that the furniture at present on the premises is her own, and therefore the tenancy is not a furnished one, and she wishes to know what rate you propose to fix the rent at, in view of this fact. She says she is willing to pay a reasonable rent on an unfurnished basis."

  H

The plaintiffs replied, by letter on June 7, saying that the letting had been a furnished tenancy and that they saw no reason why the rent should be fixed at a lower rate.

Shortly before those letters the plaint had been issued in the Bloomsbury county court, in which the plaintiffs claimed as landlords under a furnished   **I** tenancy of the room. In addition to claiming possession, for which they relied on their notice to quit of Apr. 19, they claimed arrears of rent at £3 11s. 6d. up to May 21, and mesne profits at the same rate after that date. That, as I say, was issued in the belief that it was a furnished tenancy. The sub-tenant did not obtain, or indeed seek, any legal representation in the county court, although invited and requested to do so by the plaintiffs: she conducted her own case. In the result, the judge had to consider (as he has always to do under the Rent Acts) whether there was any defence to the claim for possession and mesne profits. He

A   came to the conclusion that there was not and, accordingly, ordered possession to be given, and mesne profits and arrears of rent to be ascertained.

In this court the sub-tenant has been represented by counsel, who has put forward with great skill every argument that can be put forward against the judgment of the court court judge. He has put her case in two ways, only the first of which was disclosed (at any rate to me) in the revised grounds of appeal

B   put forward. That was this: that, though the sub-tenancy of the sub-tenant from the tenant started as a furnished tenancy, yet it had ceased to be a furnished tenancy and had become an unfurnished tenancy at the moment at which the furniture had been removed by the tenant's agents, and that, accordingly, for a period of perhaps twelve hours before the sub-tenant's interest in the room expired she was a tenant under an unfurnished tenancy and accordingly entitled

C   to the protection of the Rent Acts. Authorities were read to us in an endeavour to show that, in circumstances like these, what was a furnished tenancy before had become, for the last twelve hours of its life, an unfurnished tenancy. I do not find it necessary to refer to those authorities in detail. That contention, it seems to me, is quite wrong and, indeed, hardly arguable.

There was, however, an alternative way in which the case was put which must

D   be considered. Counsel for the sub-tenant has contended that the plaintiffs by their letters of Apr. 19 and conduct thereafter created a new unfurnished tenancy of the premises, between themselves as landlords and the sub-tenant as tenant. For such a tenancy to be created, it would be necessary to find that the plaintiffs and the sub-tenant had agreed on the terms of the tenancy and to the establishment of the relationship of landlord and tenant on unfurnished terms. If the

E   sub-tenant had paid rent to the plaintiffs, which she did not, difficult considerations might have arisen; but it seems to me plain, on the documents which I have read, that there was no such agreement. The letters and notice to quit of Apr. 19 were sent in the belief that there was subsisting a furnished tenancy. That belief was erroneous in two respects: first, the tenancy had come to an end on Mar. 25, and secondly, after that date there was no furniture of the landlord's

F   in the house. If those letters are to be regarded as an offer at all, it was an offer of a furnished tenancy of the room at the rent of £3 11s. 6d. a week; and it was plainly rejected on the sub-tenant's behalf by the letter of June 6 (which I have read), which stated that there was no furniture in the house and made a counter-offer to take an unfurnished tenancy, which was refused by the letter of June 7.

I can see no ground and no material on which it is possible to say that a new

G   unfurnished tenancy was created after Mar. 25, when the sub-tenant's interest under her sub-lease with the tenant came to an end. I would accordingly dismiss the appeal.

There is, however, one comment which I should make and which may involve some minor change in the order made by the county court judge. The plaint, being based on the belief that the plaintiffs were the landlords before Mar. 25,

H   did claim rent for the period from Mar. 18 to Mar. 25, a sum to which they are clearly not entitled. After that date it may be that their claim would be more correctly described as damages for use and occupation rather than mesne profits; but that does not matter.

RUSSELL, L.J.: I agree.

I   The sub-tenant first contends that the removal of the furniture on Mar. 25, 1966, turned a furnished sub-tenancy, which was bound to end at midnight with the ending of the tenancy out of which it derived, into an unfurnished sub-tenancy, the result being that the superior landlords (that is to say the plaintiffs) found themselves at midnight saddled with a protected tenancy of this one room. I have no hesitation (without referring to the authorities cited) in saying that this is a bad point. The furniture was removed, and the sub-tenant assented to its being removed, because it was thought (erroneously, by a margin of one day) that the intermediate landlord (that is to say, the tenant) had given a valid notice to determine the furnished sub-tenancy such as justified the removal of the **A** furniture on that day. It seems to me that misapprehension on both sides cannot effect the transmutation suggested, quite apart from the fact that the sub-tenant had paid the rent for the *furnished* tenancy up to midnight on Mar. 25/26—though she was able later in fact to stop the cheque.

The alternative contention is based on the correspondence and the form of the claim and is, as I understand it, as follows. Granted that the furnished sub- **B** tenancy remained such until midnight on Mar. 25/26, it then necessarily came to an end with the end of the intermediate tenancy; but thereafter the documents (it is said) show the plaintiffs asserting themselves to be landlords of the sub-tenant, and the sub-tenant asserting herself to be tenant of the plaintiffs. This, it is said, could only refer to a new tenancy starting on Mar. 26 which ex hypothesi must be unfurnished and so protected.   **C**

Now all that was written and done by the plaintiffs is quite easily explained. They acted on the assumption that the sub-tenant was *their* tenant of the furnished room from a date in 1965 and that a letter to the tenant constituted the latter not tenant of the house, with the sub-tenant as sub-tenant under the tenant, but licensees or managers on the plaintiffs' behalf. In this they were wrong in law, as has been held by the county court judge. The other relevant point is that **D** the plaintiffs thought that they were buying for £15 the furniture in the defendant's room in situ, and had no idea that it had been removed (we do not know where) under the aegis of the tenant's housekeeper. These matters, to my mind, explain fully every step and statement on the plaintiffs' part as having no connexion whatever with an agreement made after Mar. 25 with the sub-tenant for the grant of an unfurnished tenancy. Nor was the sub-tenant's conduct **E** consistent with such an agreement, for we find the second (or what might be called the longstop) notice to quit answered by an enquiry from the sub-tenant what was the rent proposed? In the circumstances it seems to me it would be quite unjustified to find or to infer the creation of a new unfurnished tenancy between the plaintiffs and the sub-tenant after Mar. 25.

The fact that the plaintiffs' pleading and claim was based on the same **F** erroneous view of the letter to the tenant does not in any way affect my view on this point. Nor does the fact that the order refers to the registrar for determination the plaintiffs' claim for arrears of rent and mesne profits. It is clear from the county court judge's judgment that the plaintiffs have in fact no claim for arrears of rent: there is only a claim for damages for trespass since Mar. 25. Whether there should be any alteration in the order in this regard, I am not for the moment **G** quite sure. Counsel for the plaintiffs has not asked for an alteration. If (which I do not suppose for a moment) nothing can be awarded under the phrase " mesne profits " unless there has been a relation of landlord and tenant, I dare say the plaintiffs' development budget will stand it. The sub-tenant has some furniture of her own in the room but has been living elsewhere since July, 1966. The order for possession made by the county court was to take effect in October, 1966. In **H** those circumstances, it seems to me that a short period of, say, fourteen days will amply suffice as further suspension of the possession order.

SELLERS, L.J.: I am in entire agreement with the judgments of both my lords and do not propose to add anything to them.

The appeal therefore will be dismissed and with the concession of the plaintiffs an order will be made for possession in fourteen days from to-day.   **I**

Appeal dismissed. Order for possession in fourteen days.

Solicitors: *Peter Mallack & Co.* (for the sub-tenant); *Michael Conn & Co.* (for the plaintiffs).

[*Reported by* HENRY SUMMERFIELD, ESQ., *Barrister-at-Law.*]

A

INLAND REVENUE COMMISSIONERS *v.* EDUCATIONAL GRANTS ASSOCIATION, LTD.

[COURT OF APPEAL, CIVIL DIVISION (Lord Denning, M.R., Harman and Salmon, L.JJ.), February 14, 15, 16, 1967.]

B *Income Tax—Charity—Selection of beneficiaries—Preferential application of income for private class—Company established for charitable educational purposes—Main income from another company by way of covenanted payments—Major part of income applied towards education of children associated with covenantor company—Public benefit essential to charitable purpose— Whether income applied to charitable purposes only—Income Tax Act, 1952*
C *(15 & 16 Geo. 6 & 1 Eliz. 2 c. 10), s. 447 (1) (b).*

Educational Grants Association, Ltd., a company incorporated by guarantee, had as its principal object: " To advance education in such ways as shall from time to time be thought fit and in particular by making grants to or for the benefit of and for the education of all such persons as shall be considered likely to benefit from education at a preparatory, public or other
D independent school, including boarding schools, and at technical colleges." This association was conceded by the Crown to be established for charitable purposes only. The association's income was to be applied for its objects. Its memorandum of association had seven signatories who were the chairman, four directors and two solicitors of a limited company. The company entered into a seven-year covenant to pay the association annually £3,000
E less tax, and the chairman and his brother each made it a donation of £5,000. The association informed the company that the association would consider applications in respect of children of employees or former employees of the company and of its associated companies, and a circular was issued by the company to its staff in the higher salary range and to departmental managers. Applications were received and in the first five years grants were
F made exclusively for company employees' and ex-employees' children, though the association also made some payments to educational institutions. Thereafter the association made grants also to other children but in four successive years grants for company employees' and ex-employees' children constituted seventy-five to eighty-five per cent. of the whole. The association applied for repayment of the tax deducted by the company from its annual £3,000
G payment under the seven-year covenant.

Held: in so far as income received by the association was applied for the education of children of employees or former employees of the company, with which the association was in fact connected, the income was not applied for a purpose that in law was a charitable purpose, because the purpose lacked the necessary public element; accordingly the requirement of s. 447
H (1) (b)* of the Income Tax Act, 1952, that income should be applied for charitable purposes only was not satisfied, and the association was not entitled to recover income tax deducted from the covenanted sums paid by the company, notwithstanding the concession that the association was established for charitable purposes only (see p. 897, letter B, p. 898, letter I, to p. 899, letter A, and p. 899, letters D and H, post).
I *Oppenheim* v. *Tobacco Securities Trust Co., Ltd.* ([1951] 1 All E.R. 31) applied.
Decision of PENNYCUICK, J. ([1966] 3 All E.R. 708) affirmed.

[As to the exemption of charities from income tax under Sch. D to the Income Tax Act, 1952, see 20 HALSBURY'S LAWS (3rd Edn.) 606, 607, para. 1182; and for cases on the subject, see 28 DIGEST (Repl.) 315-323, *1373-1423*; DIGEST (Cont. Vol. A) 509, *1405a.*

---

* Section 447 (1) (b), so far as material, is set out at p. 895, letter I, post.

For the Income Tax Act, 1952, s. 447, see 31 HALSBURY'S STATUTES (2nd Edn.) A
427.]

Cases referred to:

    Caffoor (Mohamed Falil Abdul) (Trustees of the Abdul Gaffoor Trust) v. *Comr. of Income Tax, Colombo*, [1961] 2 All E.R. 436; [1961] A.C. 584; [1961] 2 W.L.R. 794; Digest (Cont. Vol. A) 88, *66.*

    Campbell (Trustees of Davies's Educational Trust) v. *Inland Revenue Comrs.*, B
[1966] 2 All E.R. 736; [1966] Ch. 439; [1966] 2 W.L.R. 1448; *affd.* C.A., ante, p. 625; [1967] 2 W.L.R. 1445.

    Compton, Re, Powell v. *Compton*, [1945] 1 All E.R. 198; [1945] Ch. 123; 114 L.J.Ch. 99; 172 L.T. 158; 8 Digest (Repl.) 330, *123.*

    Jones v. *Williams*, (1767), Amb. 651; 27 E.R. 422; 8 Digest (Repl.) 322, *64.*

    Koettgen, Re, Westminster Bank, Ltd. v. *Family Welfare Association Trustees*, C
[1954] 1 All E.R. 581; [1954] Ch. 252; [1954] 2 W.L.R. 166; Digest (Cont. Vol. A) 93, *126a.*

    Oppenheim v. *Tobacco Securities Trust Co., Ltd.*, [1951] 1 All E.R. 31; [1951] A.C. 297; 8 Digest (Repl.) 321, *55.*

    Watcham v. *A.-G. of East Africa Protectorate*, [1918-19] All E.R. Rep. 455; [1919] A.C. 533; 87 L.J.P.C. 150; 120 L.T. 258; 17 Digest (Repl.) D
48, *563.*

Appeal.

The taxpayer association appealed to the Special Commissioners of Income Tax against the refusal by the Inland Revenue Commissioners of its claim under s. 447 (1) (*b*) of the Income Tax Act, 1952, to exemption from income tax under E
Sch. D for the years 1958-59, 1959-60, 1960-61, and 1961-62. The questions for decision were: (i) whether certain payments made to the taxpayer association by Metal Box Co., Ltd. under a deed of covenant dated July 16, 1954, were annual payments from which income tax was properly deductible; and (ii) if the payments were such annual payments, whether certain payments to individuals made by the taxpayer association were applications of its income for charitable F
purposes only within the meaning of s. 447 (1) (*b*) of the Act of 1952, so as to entitle the taxpayer association to the exemption claimed. It was admitted on behalf of the Crown that the taxpayer association was a body of persons established for charitable purposes only. After hearing the contentions of the parties, the commissioners held that the payments by Metal Box Co., Ltd., to the taxpayer association were annual payments from which tax was properly deductible and G
that the taxpayer association's grants to individual children were applications of the taxpayer association's income for charitable purposes only. The Crown appealed by way of Case Stated to the High Court. Only the second point was argued. On July 13, 1966, as reported at [1966] 3 All E.R. 708, PENNYCUICK, J., allowed the Crown's appeal, holding that seventy-five to eighty-five per cent. of the taxpayer association's income had been applied to the education of children H
by virtue of their connexion with Metal Box Co., Ltd., that the income had accordingly not been applied by way of public benefit and that it was not " applied to charitable purposes only ". The taxpayer association appealed to the Court of Appeal.

    Heyworth Talbot, Q.C., *H. Major Allen*, Q.C., and *P. W. I. Rees* for the taxpayer association.   I

    E. I. Goulding, Q.C., *J. R. Phillips* and *J. P. Warner* for the Crown.

    LORD DENNING, M.R.: On Nov. 1, 1953, a company was formed called the Educational Grants Association, Ltd. (the taxpayer association). It was limited by guarantee. The seven gentlemen who subscribed to the memorandum of association were all closely connected with Metal Box Co., Ltd., being the chairman of that company, four of its directors and two of its solicitors. The principal object of the association was:

A   " To advance education in such ways as shall from time to time be thought
fit and in particular by making grants to or for the benefit of and for the
education of all such persons as shall be considered likely to benefit from
education at a preparatory, public or other independent school, including
boarding schools, and at technical colleges . . ."

B   There were other ancillary objects. All income was to be applied for the objects
of the taxpayer association. It was not to be distributed or given away by way of
profit.

Under the articles the affairs of the taxpayer association were to be managed by
a council of management. There were three members of the council. They were
all three directors of Metal Box Co., Ltd. On Nov. 30, 1953, the council met.

C   The taxpayer association had no money: but it was reported to the council that
a grant would shortly be made to the association by Metal Box Co., Ltd. The
council then arranged for applications to be made for the benefit of " Metal Box
children " (by which I mean children of employees or former employees of
Metal Box Co., Ltd., and of its associated companies). They told their secretary
to inform Metal Box Co., Ltd. that they would consider applications in respect of

D   Metal Box children. On Mar. 1, 1954, a circular was sent out from the office of
the managing director of Metal Box Co., Ltd. It went to the staff in the higher
salary range and to the managers of the various departments of Metal Box Co.,
Ltd. The circular said that:

    " As Metal Box Co., Ltd. subscribes to the [taxpayer] association, the
    council of management have stated that they will be prepared to consider

E   (inter alia) applications made on behalf of children of employees of Metal
    Box Co., Ltd."

Following the circular, the taxpayer association received applications on behalf
of several Metal Box children. On Apr. 15, 1954, they considered five of these
applications. They also made an estimate of the income which they would
require. It was £2,500 to £3,000 a year. No doubt that estimate was conveyed

F   to Metal Box Co., Ltd.; for we find that three months later Metal Box Co., Ltd.
entered into a seven-year covenant for £3,000 a year. By deed dated July 16,
1954, Metal Box Co., Ltd. covenanted with the taxpayer association

    " that for a period of seven years from the date hereof it will pay annually
    to the association the sum of £3,000, less income tax."

G   In 1955 Sir Robert Barlow, the chairman of Metal Box Co., Ltd., made a donation
of £5,000 to the taxpayer association, and his brother did the same.

For the first five years—1954 to 1958—all the grants for individuals were made
for the benefit of Metal Box children, and no other children. The taxpayer association made some payments to educational institutions, such as Christ's Hospital.
After the first five years—from 1959 onwards—the taxpayer association has made

H   a few grants to young people who were not Metal Box children, but the majority
of grants have been to Metal Box children. The figures show that in the year
1958-59 no less than eighty-five per cent. of the whole of the taxpayer association's income was devoted to the education of Metal Box children. In the year
1959-60 it was eighty-five per cent. In the year 1960-61 if was seventy-six per cent.;
and in the year 1961-62 it was eighty-five per cent.

I   The question is whether the seven-year covenant qualifies for repayments of
tax. This depends on s. 447 (1) (*b*) of the Income Tax Act, 1952, which provides:

    " Exemption shall be granted from tax . . . (*b*) in respect of any yearly
    interest or other annual payment, forming part of the income of any body of
    persons or trust established for charitable purposes only . . . so far as the
    same are applied to charitable purposes only."

The first requisite is that the taxpayer association must be " established for
charitable purposes only ". That means that it must be established for advancing

education exclusively for the public benefit; and not for private benefit, in whole **A** or in part. Looking at the memorandum of association by itself, without outside aid, I should have thought that the objects clause was ambiguous on this point. The memorandum says the object is " to advance education ". The judge implied after " education " the words " for the public benefit "; but you can just as well imply the words " for the public or private benefit ". Seeing that the words of the document are ambiguous, it is permissible to look at what was done under it **B** (see *Watcham* v. *A.-G. of East Africa Protectorate* (1)). If the taxpayer association used its funds for advancing education in the private sphere as well as in the public sphere, I should presume that the members were acting lawfully within their powers rather than unlawfully in dereliction of them. But at this stage I will not pursue the point. Suffice it to say that the Crown has conceded that this association was a body of persons established for charitable purposes only.   **C**

The second question is whether the payments under the covenant were " annual payments " such as to qualify for exemption from tax. We have just considered those words in *Campbell (Trustees of Davies's Educational Trust)* v. *Inland Revenue Comrs.* (2). If these payments were made out of pure bounty, they qualify for exemption; but if they were made in the expectation of a benefit in return, whether arising out of contract or of private understanding, they would **D** not qualify for exemption. The Special Commissioners for the Purposes of the Income Tax Acts found here that there was no agreement or understanding, whether contractual or otherwise, or any counter stipulation in favour of Metal Box Co., Ltd. The Crown has not appealed against that finding. So these payments qualify as " annual payments ".

There remains the third question, whether the " annual payments " were **E** " applied to charitable purposes only ". If and in so far as they were applied for advancing education exclusively for the public benefit, they were applied for charitable purposes. If and in so far as they were applied for advancing education in the private sphere, however, they were not applied for charitable purposes. Thus far it is easy to state; but when we come down to earth, we run into diffi-culties. A long line of cases show that a trust is for the public benefit if it is for **F** the benefit of the community or a section of the community. The inhabitants of a named place are a section of the community for this purpose; but the employees of a particular company or companies are not. It follows that, if a man sets up a trust *for the children of the inhabitants of Bournville*, it will be held to be for the public benefit; but if he sets up a trust *for the children of those employed by Cadburys, Ltd.* at Bournville, it will be held to be for private benefit. In each case **G** the beneficiaries will probably be identical, but in point of law the one trust is charitable and the other is not. There is no logic in it. LORD MACDERMOTT pointed that out in his dissenting speech in *Oppenheim* v. *Tobacco Securities Trust Co., Ltd.* (3). Shorn of logic, we can only go by the decided cases. So we come to this. If funds are applied to found a closed scholarship, available only to boys from a particular school, those funds are applied for charitable purposes **H** only. If, however, funds are applied to found a closed scholarship, available only to boys whose fathers are employed by a particular company, they are not applied for charitable purposes.

Accepting this distinction, albeit illogical, I turn to the present case. The greater part of these funds were applied to advance the education of Metal Box children, i.e., the children of employees or former employees of Metal Box Co., **I** Ltd. The judge said (4):

" The inference is inescapable that this part of the taxpayer's income— i.e., seventy-five per cent. to eighty-five per cent.—has been expended for the

---

(1) [1918-19] All E.R. Rep. 455; [1919] A.C. 533.
(2) Ante, p. 625.
(3) [1951] 1 All E.R. 31; [1951] A.C. 297.
(4) [1966] 3 All E.R. 708 at p. 719; [1967] Ch. 123, at p. 144.

A   benefit of these children by virtue of a private characteristic; i.e., their connexion with Metal Box Co., Ltd. Such an application is not by way of public benefit."

The remaining fifteen per cent. to twenty-five per cent. was applied for children unconnected with Metal Box Co., Ltd., and for educational institutions. Those
B   are conceded to be for the public benefit. So we have a case where part of the income was applied for the private benefit of Metal Box children (which is not charitable) and the other part for the public benefit (which is charitable). In so far as the income was applied for Metal Box children, it was not applied for charitable purposes and does not qualify for exemption. The commissioners took a different view. They seem to have been influenced by the decision of UPJOHN,
C   J., in *Re Koettgen, Westminster Bank, Ltd.* v. *Family Welfare Association Trustees* (5); but that has to be read subject to the doubts thrown out by LORD RADCLIFFE in *Mohamed Falil Abdul Caffoor (Trustees of the Abdul Gaffoor Trust)* v. *Comr. of Income Tax, Colombo* (6). In my opinion we are compelled by *Oppenheim's* case (7) to hold that the application for Metal Box children was not charitable.

D   Counsel for the taxpayer association in his forceful argument said that, if this conclusion were right, it would mean that every payment made for the benefit of a Metal Box child was ultra vires, being beyond the powers of the taxpayer association. I do not accept this view. The Crown's concession (that the taxpayer association was established for charitable purposes only) may not have been correct. As SALMON, L.J., observed in the course of the argument, if anyone were
E   to suggest that the council of management was acting ultra vires, the answer would be that, on a fair reading of the memorandum of association, it can apply the funds, not only for the public benefit, but also for private benefit. So it can apply the funds for the benefit of Metal Box children as well as other children. It is true that in law this is not a charitable purpose; but it is a good purpose. The council, very properly, is providing these funds for the children of employees;
F   but it is not a case in which it can obtain repayments of tax from the Revenue. I, therefore, agree in substance with the decision of the judge and I would dismiss this appeal.

   HARMAN, L.J.: It has become not uncommon for large modern corporations to look after the children and the dependants of their employees. It is part of a good employer's view of his duties in these days, and it is natural, if such a
G   project be favoured by the board of directors, that they should look out for the most economical way of spending their money. It is out of this that there have grown the not very infrequent cases, as I understand it, in recent years, of which *Oppenheim* v. *Tobacco Securities Trust Co., Ltd.* (7) is the prime example. Here we have another one. Metal Box Co., Ltd. is a very large organisation with many subsidiary companies, particularly abroad, and it occurred to a member of the
H   board of that company that it would be a good thing to provide further education for the children of its employees, particularly those who were abroad and on whom it was a great burden no doubt to send their children home to be educated. So he began to consider how this could best be brought about and no doubt he took a good deal of advice. The result was that there was set up this company, the respondent taxpayer association in this appeal, Educational Grants Association,
I   Ltd., a company limited by guarantee and with objects which, it has been agreed so far as this case is concerned, are exclusively charitable objects.

   Now it has been the attempt of our generation to define " charity ". A number of very able people a few years ago sat down to try and do it, but it defeated all

_____

(5) [1954] 1 All E.R. 581; [1954] Ch. 252.
(6) [1961] 2 All E.R. 436; [1961] A.C. 584.
(7) [1951] 1 All E.R. 31; [1951] A.C. 297.

of them and they retired in disorder. Nobody has ever got further than LORD A
CAMDEN, L.C.'s definition, I think, in *Jones* v. *Williams* (8), in which he said:
" Definition of charity; a gift to a general public use, which extends to the poor
as well as to the rich." The word " public " there runs through all the charity
cases; but even to this there is an exception, because there are the poverty cases
which stick out like a sore thumb from the general rule. It has been well settled
since LORD GREENE, M.R.'s classic judgment in *Re Compton, Powell* v. *Compton* B
(9) that the public element is essential. LORD SIMONDS has said that, if one
speaks about a trust for education in the atmosphere of charitable works, one
means education in the public domain and not private education.

When this case began before the commissioners, it was argued for the Crown
that there was an element in the covenant by Metal Box Co., Ltd. with the
charitable body which caused the payments not to be " annual payments " C
within s. 447 of the Income Tax Act, 1952. The commissioners decided that there
were no strings tied to that covenant and that the payments made under it were
" annual payments "; and against that the Crown did not appeal. That of course
gave away a great deal; and for myself I am not sure that I should have agreed
with that view. I think that if one looks at the genesis of this scheme and looks
at the objects of the scheme, it was in essence a plan to educate the children of D
Metal Box employees; and, if it was that, I feel some doubt whether these
payments are " annual payments " within the meaning of the section.

However, in this court we are not concerned with that. We are only concerned
with the second part of the conundrum, viz., whether the application of the fund,
committed under the covenant to the taxpayer association, was for charitable
purposes only: viz., public charitable purposes. Counsel for the taxpayer associa- E
tion says that one must not add words to the memorandum, and I agree. When,
however, one gets to the actions of the taxpayer association, which are a question
of fact, one must remember that charity, if it is to be charity only, must be
confined to the public domain. I do not myself subscribe to the view of LORD
DENNING, M.R., that one can construe a modern document by looking to what
was done under it. That I regard, with all deference to him, as a heresy. One can F
only construe an ancient document in that way. However that may be, I do not
think that there is any ambiguity here. Public charity was meant; and if that
be the argument, that argument succeeds. Public education alone is a charity.
When one comes to the application, which is a question of fact from which
inferences are to be drawn, I draw the same inference, and I feel bound to draw
it, as the judge below (10). One starts with the estimate of the income required. G
How could the council estimate the income required for an educational purpose
unless it was looking for the ambit over which that purpose was to be directed.
The question obviously was—how much shall we need to educate the probable
Metal Box candidates? £3,000 a year was chosen for that purpose. Similarly,
great care was taken not to circularise people beyond, so to speak, the family.
Counsel for the taxpayer association said that any small charity must limit its H
advertising or circularisation, and with that I would agree; but in this the board
and the council were more or less the same people. Care was taken not to let it
leak out too far. Circularisation was among the higher ranks of the Metal Box
employees. Similarly the candidates who were put forward to the board by the
secretary, who was the secretary of Metal Box Co., Ltd. and of the charitable
body, were to a great predominance Metal Box children: in fact for the first I
years they were only Metal Box children. There have since been four children, I
think, outside altogether, and there have been some institutions.

Taking all the facts which the commissioners state, I cannot help being driven
to the conclusion that the application of this money was directed and guided into
the dependants of the Metal Box employees. If that be so, I do not think that

---

(8) (1767), Amb. 651.
(9) [1945] 1 All E.R. 198; [1945] Ch. 123.
(10) [1966] 3 All E.R. 708; [1967] Ch. 123.

A it is a charity. However large the link may be, one may not have a charity from an educational point of view if the nexus between the objects is one single person, one single company or one single family. The section of the public may be extremely small. The employees in the case of *Oppenheim* (11) were extremely large. There are no doubt many here. It does not matter about size. It is the connecting link between them that matters.

B   I started hearing this case feeling that this was an object with which we ought to sympathise, and of course one does sympathise with the motives of big companies who seek to make the lot of their employees more attractive and to raise the standard generally of those who help them by helping with the education of their children. As the argument went on, however, it seemed to me that no company of this sort, no more than an individual, ought to be able to educate its

C dependants at the expense of the state. It is an admirable thing that children of employees should have a higher education, but I do not see why on the whole that should be at the expense of the taxpayer. However, I do not, I hope, follow my sympathies in this case. I follow what I think to be the true rule. Counsel for the Crown said that he could put his argument in a nutshell. He should have said he could put it in a " metal box "; and that really is the whole of this case. I

D would dismiss this appeal.

    SALMON, L.J.: With some reluctance, but with no doubt, I agree that this appeal must be dismissed for the reasons given by my lords. Charity in law has a restricted, but no very well defined, meaning. I certainly am not prepared to attempt a definition. All that I can say with reasonable certainty is that charity

E in law does not include the kind of charity that begins at home. In order for the " annual payment " to enjoy exemption from income tax under s. 447 (1) (*b*) of the Income Tax Act, 1952, it must be shown (i) that the educational trust was established only for the purpose of advancing the education of the public or a sector of the public, viz., for charitable purposes only, and (ii) that the annual payments were applied for charitable purposes only, viz., only for the purpose of

F advancing the education of the public or a sector of the public. In the present case it is admitted that the taxpayer association has complied with the first requirement.   The question is whether it has complied with the second requirement.

    The House of Lords has decided in *Oppenheim* v. *Tobacco Securities Trust Co., Ltd.* (11) that the class specified in the objects clause of a trust deed is not a sector

G of the public if the only nexus between the members of the class is that they are in the employment of a particular employer, and that accordingly an educational trust established for the benefit of the children of employees or former employees is not a charitable trust. It follows from that decision, by which we are bound, that, if the objects clause in the memorandum in the present case had been in the form in which it was in that case, the taxpayer association would not have been a

H charitable trust, for it would not have been established for charitable purposes only. If a trust established for the purpose of making grants for the education of children of employees or former employees of Metal Box Co., Ltd. would not be established for charitable purposes only, it seems to me to follow, as the night follows the day, that annual payments applied for the purpose of educating the children of employees or former employees of the company are not applied to

I charitable purposes only. I do not mean that any child of a Metal Box employee is necessarily excluded from the ambit of this beneficence. If it had been shown, for example, that by chance a few such children had been amongst the members of the general public to have benefited from the grants, I should not have thought that that was in any way breaching the requirement that the annual payments must be applied for charitable purposes only. The trouble in this case is that, when one looks at all the facts which have been recited by my lords and which I need

---

(11) [1951] 1 All E.R. 31; [1951] A.C. 297.

A not repeat, one is driven to the same inescapable conclusion as was the judge (12), viz., that seventy-five to eighty-five per cent. of the annual payments were in fact not applied for the benefit of a sector of the public but for the benefit of children of employees or former employees of Metal Box Co., Ltd. as such. Unless one makes nonsense of s. 447 (1) (b) and construes the words at the end of the paragraph, " to charitable purposes only ", as having a different meaning from the

B words " for charitable purposes only " in the middle of the paragraph, I cannot see any way in which it would be possible to decide this case in favour of the taxpayer association and in conformity with the decision in the *Oppenheim* case (13). It would involve the absurdity of holding that what the trust is in fact doing is being done for charitable purposes only, although, if the trust had been established to do that very thing, it would not have been established for charitable purposes only. I think that the decision of the House of Lords in the

C *Oppenheim* case (13) leads necessarily to the conclusion that this appeal must be decided against the taxpayer association.

All I want to add is this. I share the doubt of LORD DENNING, M.R., about the meaning of the objects clause. I too would doubt whether it was not perhaps ambiguous—whether its language was not wide enough to allow the payments to be applied for non-charitable educational purposes. As for the other matter

D (about which my lords have differed), viz., whether what was done afterwards throws any light on what the intention was at the time when the deed was settled, this matter does not arise for decision and I prefer to express no view about it. I agree that the appeal should be dismissed.

Appeal dismissed. Leave to appeal to the House of Lords granted.

E Solicitors: *Allen & Overy* (for the taxpayer association); *Solicitor of Inland Revenue*.   [*Reported by* F. A. AMIES, ESQ., *Barrister-at-Law*.]

TROW *v.* IND COOPE (WEST MIDLANDS), LTD. AND ANOTHER.

F [COURT OF APPEAL, CIVIL DIVISION (Lord Denning, M.R., Harman and Salmon, L.JJ.), March 9, 10, May 2, 1967.]

Time—Computation—Duration of specified period—Period " beginning with the date of . . ."—Writ of summons issued on Sept. 10, 1965, and served on Sept. 10, 1966—Validity of writ for the purpose of service for twelve months beginning with the date of its issue—Whether service out of time—R.S.C.,

G *Ord. 6, r. 8 (1).*

Practice—Rules of court—Forms prescribed by rules—Note on form inconsistent with order—Time for service of writ prescribed by order inconsistent with note on writ—Order prevails—R.S.C., Ord. 6, r. 1, r. 8 (1), App. A, forms No. 1, No. 2.

H The plaintiff was injured in an accident on Sept. 11, 1962. On Sept. 10, 1965, at 3.5 p.m. she issued a writ claiming damages for personal injuries, alleging breach of statutory duty and negligence. The note below the teste of the writ, which bore date Sept. 10, 1965, read: " This writ may not be served more than twelve calendar months after the above date unless renewed by order of the court." By R.S.C., Ord. 6, r. 8 (1)* a writ was valid

I for the purpose of service for twelve months beginning with the date of its issue. The writ was served on the defendants on Sept. 10, 1966, before 3.5 p.m. On appeal from an order setting aside service of the writ as being invalid for not being effected within the time allowed by R.S.C., Ord. 6, r. 8 (1), it was admitted that the writ was served within the time stated in the note on the writ.

---

(12) [1966] 3 All E.R. 708; [1967] Ch. 123.
(13) [1951] 1 All E.R. 31; [1951] A.C. 297.
* R.S.C., Ord. 6, r. 8 (1), so far as material, is set out at p. 909, letter F, post.

Applied in Re LYMPNE INVEST-
MENTS [1972] 2 All ER 385

Applied in HAMMOND v HAIGH
[1973] 2 All ER 289

Applied in HAMMOND v
CASTLE [1973] 2 All ER 289

Dicta of HARMAN and SALMON LJJ
at 908, 909 applied in HEATH v
LONGMAN [1973] 2 All ER 1228

A   **Held:** (i) the word " date " in the phrase " beginning with the date " in R.S.C., Ord. 6, r. 8 (1) meant " day ", and, as the law did not for present purposes take account of fractions of a day, the time of day when the writ was served was immaterial (see p. 904, letter C, p. 907, letter I, and p. 912, letter D, post).

Lester v. *Garland* ((1808), 15 Ves. 248) applied.

B   (ii) (LORD DENNING, M.R., dissenting) the period prescribed by R.S.C., Ord. 6, r. 8 (1) as " beginning with the date " included the day on which the writ was issued, and accordingly the period for service of the writ expired with Sept. 9, 1966, and the writ was not served within the time allowed by the rule (see p. 908, letter F, and p. 911, letter E, post; cf. p. 905, letter G, post).

C   *Hare* v. *Gocher* ([1962] 2 All E.R. 763) and *Sidebotham* v. *Holland* ([1891-94] All E.R. Rep. 617) applied.

Goldsmiths' Co. v. *West Metropolitan Ry. Co.* ([1900-03] All E.R. Rep. 667) distinguished.

Pugh v. *Duke of Leeds* ((1777), 2 Cowp. 714) considered and distinguished.

(iii) (LORD DENNING, M.R., dissenting) the rule (R.S.C., Ord. 6, r. 8 (1))

D   prevailed over the note on the writ; and accordingly the writ was rightly set aside as having been served out of time (see p. 907, letter G, p. 909, letter C, and p. 913, letter E, post; cf. p. 906, letter D, post).

Per HARMAN, L.J. (SALMON, L.J., concurring; LORD DENNING, M.R., contra) the phrases " beginning with " and " beginning from " mean two opposite things (see p. 908, letter I, and p. 909, letters G and H, post;

E   cf. p. 904, letter I, post).

Per SALMON, L.J. (LORD DENNING, M.R., concurring) the words " commencing on " a certain date are indistinguishable from the words " beginning with " a certain date (see p. 911, letter A, post; cf. p. 904, letter I, post).

Decision of BLAIN, J. ([1967] 1 All E.R. 19) affirmed.

F   [As to the inclusion or exclusion of first and last days in the computation of prescribed periods of time, see 37 HALSBURY'S LAWS (3rd Edn.) 92-99, paras. 161-173; and for cases on the subject, see 45 DIGEST (Repl.) 252-257, *195-250*.

As to the service and renewal of writs within the proper time, see 24 HALSBURY'S LAWS (3rd Edn.) 199, 200, para. 357, and 30 ibid., p. 303, para. 558; and for cases on the subject, see 32 DIGEST (Repl.) 623, 624, *2001-2013*, DIGEST (Practice) 311, 312, *358-368*, and 3rd DIGEST SUPP.]

G   Cases referred to:

Baker v. *Bowketts Cakes, Ltd.*, [1966] 2 All E.R. 290; [1966] 1 W.L.R. 861; Digest (Cont. Vol. B) 502, *2022Aa*.

Campbell v. *Strangeways*, (1877), 3 C.P.D. 105; 47 L.J.M.C. 6; 37 L.T. 672; 42 J.P. 39; 45 Digest (Repl.) 270, *393*.

Gelmini v. *Moriggia*, [1911-13] All E.R. Rep. 1115; [1913] 2 K.B. 549; 82

H   L.J.K.B. 949; 109 L.T. 77; 32 Digest (Repl.) 389, *179*.

Goldsmiths' Co. v. *West Metropolitan Ry. Co.*, [1900-03] All E.R. Rep. 667; [1904] 1 K.B. 1; 72 L.J.K.B. 931; 89 L.T. 428; 68 J.P. 41; 45 Digest (Repl.) 257, *247*.

Hare v. *Gocher*, [1962] 2 All E.R. 763; [1962] 2 Q.B. 641; [1962] 3 W.L.R. 339; 126 J.P. 395; 45 Digest (Repl.) 257, *250*.

I   *Holman* v. *Elliott*, [1944] 1 All E.R. 639; [1944] 1 K.B. 591; 113 L.J.K.B. 459; 170 L.T. 373; 36 Digest (Repl.) 226, *1204*.

Lester v. *Garland*, (1808), 15 Ves. 248; 33 E.R. 748; 45 Digest (Repl.) 254, *211*.

Marren v. *Dawson Bentley & Co., Ltd.*, [1961] 2 All E.R. 270; [1961] 2 Q.B. 135; [1961] 2 W.L.R. 679; 45 Digest (Repl.) 252, *196*.

Pugh v. *Duke of Leeds*, (1777), 2 Cowp. 714; 48 E.R. 1323; 45 Digest (Repl.) 262, *288*.

Russell v. *Ledsam*, (1845), 14 M. & W. 574; 14 L.J.Ex. 353; 5 L.T.O.S. 495; 153 E.R. 604; 45 Digest (Repl.) 257, *245*.

Seignorett v. *Noguire*, (1705), 2 Ld. Raym. 1241; 92 E.R. 318.   A

Sidebotham v. *Holland*, [1891-94] All E.R. Rep. 617; [1895] 1 Q.B. 378; 64
    L.J.Q.B. 200; 72 L.T. 62; 31 Digest (Repl.) 488, *6136*.

Stewart v. *Chapman*, [1951] 2 All E.R. 613; [1951] 2 K.B. 792; 115 J.P. 473;
    45 Digest (Repl.) 113, *385*.

Young v. *Higgon*, [1835-42] All E.R. Rep. 278; (1840), 6 M. & W. 49; 9
    L.J.M.C. 29; 4 J.P. 88; 151 E.R. 317; 45 Digest (Repl.) 254, *214*.   B

Interlocutory Appeal.

This was an appeal by the plaintiff, Mrs. Christina Trow, from an order of
BLAIN, J., made on Oct. 28, 1966 (reported [1967] 1 All E.R. 19) allowing the
appeal of the defendants from a decision of the district registrar of Hanley given
on Oct. 17, 1966. BLAIN, J., set aside service of the writ of summons on the   C
defendants and all subsequent proceedings in the action on the ground that
service of the writ was out of time. The grounds of appeal were—(i) that the judge
erred in law in holding that the writ was not valid for the purpose of service when
served; (ii) that he erred in law in holding that the period of twelve months
beginning with the date of issue of the writ expired at midnight on the day
preceding the first anniversary of the issue of the writ for the purpose of R.S.C.,   D
Ord. 6, r. 8; (iii) that he erred in law in holding that the decision in *Hare* v.
Gocher ([1962] 2 All E.R. 763) was decisive of the issue on the appeal before him;
(iv) that he erred in law in not giving effect to, or in not taking sufficiently into
account, the note on the form of writ which was prescribed by R.S.C., Ord. 6,
r. 1 and App. A, viz., " this writ may not be served more than twelve calendar
months after the above date unless renewed by order of the court "; (v) that he   E
erred in law in holding that R.S.C., Ord. 3, r. 2 (1), (2) did not apply to the
service of a writ or the provisions of Ord. 6, r. 8; and (vi) that he erred in law
in setting aside service of the writ in this action, as the defendants' summons
had not asked for service of the writ to be set aside, and that he erred in law in
granting them leave to amend their summons, or that he exercised his discretion
to grant leave for such amendment on a wrong principle by virtue of R.S.C.,   F
Ord. 12, r. 9, which required that any application for an order for service of writ
to be set aside should be made within fourteen days of entry of a conditional
appearance, in that the defendants had not made any application for such
service to be set aside within such period.

G. Slynn for the plaintiff.
E. B. Gibbons, *Q.C.*, and *S. Tumim* for the defendants.   G

Cur. adv. vult.

May 2. The following judgments were read.

LORD DENNING, M.R.: Every practitioner knows that a writ must be
served within twelve months of the date on which it was issued; but how is that   H
twelve months to be calculated? What is the last day—the very last day—on
which it can be served? That is the question which we have to decide today. It
is very like a period of limitation. Every practitioner knows in personal injury
cases that a writ must be issued within three years of the date on which the cause
of action accrued; but how is that three years to be calculated? What is the last
day—the very last day—on which the writ can be issued? The answer to each   I
of these questions depends, no doubt, on the precise wording of the enactment in
each case; but the wording is not nearly so precise as it could be or should be.
It does not say whether the time is to be " inclusive " of the day of the date or
" exclusive " of it. The two questions are so much inter-related that I propose
to consider both of them, especially as the facts here illustrate both.

On Sept. 11, 1962, at Kidsgrove the plaintiff, Mrs. Trow, was crossing the yard
of the Queen's Head Inn when she fell and hurt herself. If she wished to sue for
damages, she had to bring the action within three years. The statute of limitation

A   says that an action for personal injuries shall not be brought " after the expiration of three years *from* the date on which the cause of action accrued " (see
s. 2 (1) of the Limitation Act, 1939, as amended by s. 2 (1) of the Law Reform
(Limitation of Actions, &c.) Act, 1954). The cause of action accrued on Sept. 11,
1962. What was the last day of three years " *from* that date "? Was it Sept. 10,
1965, or Sept. 11, 1965? CHANNELL, J., would have said that it was Sept. 10, 1965

B   (see *Gelmini* v. *Moriggia* (1)). HAVERS, J., would have said that it was Sept. 11,
1965 (see *Marren* v. *Dawson Bentley & Co., Ltd.* (2)). I think that HAVERS, J.,
was right, for reasons which I will give later. The last day for issuing a writ was
Sept. 11, 1965.

The issue of the writ:

C   The solicitors for the plaintiff issued the writ in time. They issued a writ on
Sept. 10, 1965, one day before the last day. They issued it against the defendants
who owned the Queen's Head Inn and their manager. They issued it out of the
Hanley District Registry. The registrar stamped on it the court seal and noted
on it the time " 3.5 p.m." on Sept. 10, 1965.

The service of the writ:

D   If the plaintiff wished to serve that writ on the defendants, she had to serve it
within twelve months of the date of issue—Sept. 10, 1965. What was the last
day of the twelve months? Was it Sept. 9, 1966, or Sept. 10, 1966? It was very
important for the solicitors for the plaintiff to make sure of the day: because if
they let the twelve months expire without serving the writ, that was the end of
it: for there would be very little chance of getting it renewed (see *Baker* v.

E   *Bowketts Cakes, Ltd.* (3)).

The note on the writ:

The writ itself stated the last day for service. On the face of the writ there was
in large letters the words: " Witness, Gerald Baron Gardiner, Lord High
Chancellor of Great Britain, Sept. 10, 1965." Immediately below those words
there was this note: " This writ may not be served more than twelve calendar

F   months *after* the above date unless renewed by order of the court." That was an
official note which was contained in the prescribed form of writ and was of equal
force to a rule of court (see s. 225 of the Supreme Court of Judicature (Consolidation) Act, 1925 (4), R.S.C., Ord. 6, r. 1, and App. A, form 1).   Everyone
agrees that, on the wording of that note, the last day for service was Sept. 10,
1966.

G   The solicitors for the plaintiff served the writ in time, according to the note.
On Saturday, Sept. 10, 1966, at one minute before midday, they left a copy of
the writ at the registered office of the defendants in Burton. At eleven minutes
before one o'clock they served the manager personally at the Queen's Head Inn.

The rule of court:

The defendants admit that, according to that note, the writ was served in time;

H   but they point to a rule of court which, they say, gives a different result. It is
one of the new rules which came into force on Oct. 11, 1964. It is R.S.C., Ord. 6,
r. 8 (1), which provides:

" For the purpose of service, a writ . . . is valid in the first instance for
twelve months beginning *with* the date of its issue . . ."

I   The defendants say that under that rule, in calculating the twelve months, the
day of the date of issue must be included. You must, therefore, include Sept. 10,
1965, in the twelve months. You thus arrive at Sept. 9, 1966, as the last day for
service of the writ. The defendants say that the note on the writ is wrong and
should be rejected. The judge accepted that contention for reasons which are
reported (5). So according to the rule the service here was a day too late.

---

(1) [1911-13] All E.R. Rep. 1115; [1913] 2 K.B. 549.
(2) [1961] 2 All E.R. 270; [1961] 2 Q.B. 135.   (3) [1966] 2 All E.R. 290.
(4) By s. 225 " rules of court " includes forms.   (5) [1967] 1 All E.R. 19.

In this situation it is necessary to analyse the wording of R.S.C., Ord. 6, r. 8 (1)   **A**
in some detail. This I proceed to do. No help is to be gained from R.S.C., Ord. 3,
r. 2, because no act is " required " to be done. Nor is anything to be gleaned by
looking at the old rule and the old note. They were differently worded with great
precision and gave rise to no difficulty (see *Holman* v. *Elliott* (6)).

Date:

It was suggested for the plaintiff that the word " date " should be construed   **B**
as meaning " time ", so that the twelve months ran from 3.5 p.m. on Sept. 10,
1965, to 3.5 p.m. on Sept. 10, 1966: and that the service was good as it was
before that time. In support of this suggestion, reference was made to the
SHORTER OXFORD DICTIONARY, which gives one of the meanings as " the precise
time at which anything takes place ".

I cannot accept this suggestion. When we speak of the *date* on which anything   **C**
is done, we mean the date by the calendar, such as: " The *date* today is May 2,
1967." We do not divide the *date* up into hours and minutes. We take no account
of fractions of a *date*. If authority were needed for so obvious a proposition, it
can be found in the judgment of LORD MANSFIELD, C.J., in *Pugh* v. *Duke of
Leeds* (7). Speaking of the date of delivery of a deed, he said:

   D

> " For what is ' the date '? The date is a memorandum of the day when
> the deed was delivered: in Latin it is ' datum ': and ' datum tali die ' is,
> delivered on such a day. Thus in point of law, there is no fraction of a day:
> it is an indivisible point . . . ' Date ' does not mean the hour or the minute,
> but the day of delivery: and in law there is no fraction of a day."

Applying these words, we must take no account of the time, 3.5 p.m. We must   **E**
regard the writ as issued on Sept. 10, 1965, just as if that date were an indivisible
point. The whole day of the date of issue must either be *included* or *excluded* in
calculating the twelve months. If it is *included*, then, in point of fact, the period
for service is less than twelve months by a few hours. If it is *excluded*, it is more
than twelve months by a few hours. Which is it to be? I may add that a similar
situation arises with the period of limitation. The " date " on which the cause   **F**
of action accrues is either *included* or *excluded* in the three years.

" *With* " *or* " *from* " :

It was suggested that the words " beginning *with* " have a different meaning
from the words " beginning *from* ", in this way: In calculating twelve months
beginning *with* the date of issue, you *include* that date in the twelve months (as
was done in *Hare* v. *Gocher* (8)): whereas in calculating twelve months beginning   **G**
from the date, you *exclude* it (as was done in *Marren* v. *Dawson Bentley & Co.,
Ltd*. (9)).

I acknowledge that those cases warrant this distinction between the preposi-
tions " with " and " from "; but it is far too subtle for my liking. It is one of
those nice distinctions in which lawyers delight. They are out of touch with the
common man. If a man contracts to build a house in twelve months beginning   **H**
with the date when the first sod is turned, it is just the same as if he said twelve
months beginning *on* or *from* that date. You may well say that that date is to be
included in either case: but you cannot say that it is *included* in one case and
excluded in the other. For this purpose " with ", " from " or " on " a date are
equivalent expressions. It has been so held. First in a case decided by HOLT, C.J.,
in 1705 called *Seignorett* v. *Noguire* (10), and recited more fully by LORD MANS-   **I**
FIELD, C.J., in *Pugh* v. *Duke of Leeds* (11). By a contract a partnership was to
continue for four years to begin *from* the date of the contract. The declaration
described the contract as four years to begin *with* the date of the contract. It was
held that there was no variance (11).

---

(6) [1944] 1 All E.R. 639; [1944] 1 K.B. 591.   (7) (1777), 2 Cowp. 714 at p. 720.
(8) [1962] 2 All E.R. 763; [1962] 2 Q.B. 641.
(9) [1961] 2 All E.R. 270; [1961] 2 Q.B. 135.
(10) (1705), 2 Ld. Raym. 1241.   (11) (1777), 2 Cowp. at p. 722.

A   ". . . the whole court held, that to aver that a contract was to commence
' with the day of the date ', was the same thing as to aver that it commenced
' from the day of that date '."

(As it happens, in that case they held that the day of the date was to be *included*.)
Secondly, in *Sidebotham* v. *Holland* (12), a man granted a yearly tenancy " commencing *on* May 19, 1890 ".   Lindley, L.J., said (13) that no distinction had
B   ever been drawn between tenancies commencing " on " a particular day and
" from " the same day. They were equivalent expressions. " Any distinction
between them for such a purpose as this is far too subtle for practical use . . ."

I reject, therefore, the distinction between " with " and " from " and turn to
consider whether the day of the date should be included or not. Until 1808 there
was a tendency to include the first day and exclude the last day: and I confess
C   that would be my own impression, apart from authority. Then, however, there
came the leading case of *Lester* v. *Garland* (14), which considers cases like the
present where a period is fixed within which a person must do something or take
the consequences. Sir William Grant, M.R., said that (15)

". . . it would be more easy to maintain, that the day of an act done, or an
D   event happening, ought in all cases to be excluded, than that it should in all
cases be included."

His reasoning was afterwards adopted by many great judges in the nineteenth
century, including Lord Tenterden and Parke, B., and the earlier cases were
disapproved. By the time we get to the twentieth century, Mathew, L.J., was
able to say in this court that

E   " The rule is now well established that when a particular time is given,
from a certain date, within which an act is to be done, the day of the date
is to be excluded,";

see *Goldsmiths' Co.* v. *West Metropolitan Ry. Co.* (16), which was followed by Lord
Goddard, C.J., in *Stewart* v. *Chapman* (17). Finally, in 37 Halsbury's Laws
F   of England (3rd Edn.), pp. 92-99, we find all the cases analysed and the rule
stated at p. 95, para. 168:

" The general rule in cases in which a period is fixed within which a person
must act or take the consequences is that the day of the act or event from
which the period runs should not be counted against him."

This general rule clearly applies to the statutes of limitation (when the plaintiff
G   must issue his writ within three years *from the date* of the accrual of the cause of
action). The first day is not counted in the period. If an accident happens on
Nov. 8, 1954, the last day is Nov. 8, 1957 (see *Marren* v. *Dawson Bentley & Co.,
Ltd.* (18)). Likewise I would apply the general rule to R.S.C., Ord. 6, r. 8 (1). In
calculating the twelve months I would not count the date of issue of the writ. If
the writ is issued on Sept. 10, 1965, I would say the last day for service is Sept. 10,
H   1966. This interpretation has the great merit that it brings the rule of court into
accord with the note. The rule committee approved the note as well as the rule.
They never intended the one to be repugnant to the other. If you wish to discover
what they meant by the rule, you can look at the note. It is their own dictionary.

Repugnancy:

I   My brothers, however, think that the general rule is excluded here by the words
" beginning with ". They fasten on the word " with " and say that it is different
from the word " from ". They hold that, on the wording of the rule, the date of
issue is to be included in the computation. Let me assume that they are right. It

---

(12) [1891-94] All E.R. Rep. 617;   [1895] 1 Q.B. 378.
(13) [1891-94] All E.R. Rep. at p. 620;   [1895] 1 Q.B. at p. 384.
(14) (1808), 15 Ves. 248.   (15) (1808), 15 Ves. at p. 257.
(16) [1904] 1 K.B. 1 at p. 5;   [1900-03] All E.R. Rep. 667 at p. 669.
(17) [1951] 2 All E.R. 613;   [1951] 2 K.B. 792.
(18) [1961] 2 All E.R. 270;   [1961] 2 Q.B. 135.

means that there is a repugnancy between the rule of court and the note on the A
writ. Under the rule the last day is Sept. 9, 1966, and under the note it is Sept. 10,
1966. Which is to prevail? The note is the thing on which people act. It is a
positive direction which every solicitor has before him when he serves his writ.
He is told clearly that he has twelve months after the date of issue. Surely he is
entitled to rely on that note. It has been issued by the rule committee for his
instruction, intending that he should act on it. If that note is to be discarded as B
repugnant, it would be nothing less than a trap for him. He would never dream of
looking up the rules to see if the note was correct. Not one solicitor in a thousand
would do so. He would go by the note. Rather than lead him into a trap, I would
let the note prevail over the rules of court.

Any other view would lead to great inconvenience. It would mean that every
form of writ now in existence has got on it a false note. There is a danger of people C
being misled unless it is amended. Are all the existing forms to be called in and
reprinted? Are we to put everyone to all this trouble just for the sake of a single
word—" with " instead of " from "? It is carrying formalities much too far. I
suppose there is an alternative—to amend the rule so as to read " from " instead
of " with "; but even that will take some time. I would prefer to let the note
explain the rule: and, if need be, prevail over the rule. After all, it is the note D
which most people go by—and not the rule. Every solicitor has the note before
him: he may not have the rule. I would allow this appeal and hold that this writ
was served in time.

HARMAN, L.J. (read by Salmon, L.J.): By the indorsement on the writ
in this action the plaintiff claims in the alternative against two defendants E
damages arising out of an accident when she tripped or slipped in the yard of the
Queen's Head Inn, Kidsgrove, Staffordshire, on Sept. 11, 1962. The breaches
alleged are breaches of statutory duty under the Occupiers' Liability Act, 1957:
alternatively, the negligence of the defendants or one of them. The writ was
issued at 3.5 p.m. on Sept. 10, 1965, out of the Hanley District Registry, that is
to say, just in time to preserve the right of the plaintiff from the mischief of the F
Limitation Act, 1939, s. 2, as amended. This gives a period of three years " after
the expiration of three years from the date " of the accident. It is to be noted
that the phrase here is " after ", so that time does not begin to run until a day
after the event occurs and this no-one now doubts, though it was not always so,
as appears from the case of *Lester* v. *Garland* (19)—per Sir William Grant, M.R.

Having issued this writ, the plaintiff's advisers pursued their dilatory tactics G
and did not serve it on either defendant until Sept. 10, 1966, service in each case
being earlier than 3.5 p.m. The defendants entered conditional appearances and
applied to set aside the writ as being served out of time. This was a mistake. The
proper application to make was to apply to set aside service of the writ, but the
judge (20) before whom the application came treated the application as amended
so as to be such an application, and he decided, contrary to the view taken by H
the district registrar, that the writ was served out of time and that service should
be set aside. The plaintiff appeals.

The modern rule governing the length of time during which a writ is valid is
R.S.C., Ord. 3, which is headed " Time ". Rule 2 provides that

" (1) Any period of time fixed by these rules . . . for doing any act shall be
reckoned in accordance with the following provisions of this rule. (2) Where I
the act is required to be done within a specified period after or from a specified
date, the period begins immediately after that date. (3) Where the act is
required to be done within or not less than a specified period before a specified
date, the period ends immediately before that date."

R.S.C., Ord. 6, r. 1 provides that every writ must be " in form No. 1 . . . in
App. A ". Rule 7 (3) provides that issue of a writ takes place on its being sealed

---

(19) (1808), 15 Ves. 248   (20) [1967] 1 All E.R. 19.

A by an officer of the office out of which it is issued. Rule 8, which is headed
"Duration and renewal of writ", provides:

> "(1) For the purpose of service, a writ . . . is valid in the first instance for
> twelve months beginning with the date of its issue . . ."

So far, it seems to me, the position is clear. R.S.C., Ord. 3, r. 2 does not deal with
B the words " beginning with the date " but with a period after or from or before
a date, and therefore has no application. R.S.C., Ord. 6, r. 8 limits the validity
of a writ for the purpose of service to twelve months " beginning with the date
of its issue ", and I cannot doubt that for that purpose the date with which the
period begins is the date of the writ's issue. That date in this case was Sept. 10,
1965. Beginning with that date and counting a period of twelve months carries
C one to the end of Sept. 9, 1966. On this footing the writ here was served out of
time.

R.S.C., Ord. 6, r. 8 is part of the 1962 revision and was taken from R.S.C.,
Ord. 8, r. 1 of 1875. That order was headed " Original writ in force for twelve
months " and provided by r. 1:

> "No original writ of summons shall be in force for more than twelve
D months from the day of the date thereof, including the day of such date . . ."

This is inelegant but clear. It shows that from 1875 until 1962 the first day was
to be included. The rule committee seem to have been conscious of the inelegance
and to have thought that it was enough to use the words " beginning with the
date ", but I cannot suppose that the framer of the rule thought that by this
alteration he was altering the law, nor do I think that he did so. If he had wished
E to do so, he might have used the words " beginning from the date ", but as he
chose to say " with " and not " from ", it seems to me that no alteration was
intended.

When one looks at form no. 1 of the forms of writ in App. A to the rule before
the 1962 revision one finds on that form the following:

> "Memorandum to be subscribed on the writ. N.B. This writ is to be
F served within twelve calendar months from the date thereof . . . including the
> day of such date, and not afterwards."

Thus the form of the writ prescribed by the old appendix agrees with the wording
of R.S.C., Ord. 8, r. 1, and no difficulty is encountered.

The difficulty arises from the revised form of writ introduced by the 1962
G revision where these words appear: " Note:—This writ may not be served more
than twelve calendar months after the above date . . ." This points clearly enough
to a period of twelve months excluding the day of the writ's issue. The two seem
to me to be quite inconsistent and the question is which is to govern the other.
In my judgment the rule must govern and not the note. It is true that R.S.C.,
Ord. 6, r. 1 prescribes that every writ must be in the form in the appendix so that
H a writ today must carry the note. It is said that the two provisions have an equal
force, and it was argued, though for a reason obscure to me, that the note ought
to override the rule because the writ as issued would otherwise be misleading, but
as counsel for the defendants pointed out, the note is directed rather to the
person issuing the writ than to the person on whom it is served, and it is the
former who would be deceived rather than the latter.

I As to the word " date ", I think that counsel for the defendants was again right
in saying that this word means a division of time shown on the calendar and does
not refer to any particular time of the day. It was further argued for the plaintiff
that as a writ comes into existence only when it is sealed (see R.S.C., Ord. 6,
r. 7), and as this writ was not sealed till 3.5 in the afternoon, it would not in the
morning of the day of its issue have been in existence and therefore its duration
would be less than twelve months, and it was said that R.S.C., Ord. 6, r. 8 showed
that twelve months validity was laid down, but this I think is a fallacy. The rule
does not say " valid for twelve months " but " valid for twelve months beginning

with the date of its issue ". Thus the validity of the writ is to last over a period of   A
twelve months beginning with its date, that is to say, from the first moment of
its date. It is common in leases, for instance, to talk of a term of so many years
from a back date, and this is no more than that.

It was further argued that it was the duty of the court, if possible, to reconcile
the rule and the note so as to make them consistent one with the other, and that
this could be done by splitting the day and leaving the writ valid up to 3.4 p.m.   B
on Sept. 10, but I can see no warrant for this. The law does not as a rule take
account of fractions of the day unless there is some necessity for it, as for instance
in the dog licence case (*Campbell* v. *Strangeways* (21)), and there is no such
necessity here. That case turned on the fact that the dog licence was taken out
during the day in question. It was therefore clear that during so much of that day
as preceded the issue of the licence, the dog was not licensed. During the rest of   C
the day the dog was licensed. It was therefore necessary to split the day into the
period before and the period after the issue of the licence. To construe it otherwise would be to fly in the face of the facts because it was certainly true that
during part of the day the dog was unlicensed and during the subsequent part of
the day it was licensed. Accordingly, " date " in that case must mean " time ",
but in the absence of any such necessity, " date " and " time " are in contra-   D
distinction one from the other. " Date " is the whole period of twenty-four hours
and " time " is the moment during that period which is critical. This is no
warrant, therefore, for holding that in the absence of necessity, " date " and
" time " can be treated as the same thing. Moreover, in the present rules, as
SALMON, L.J.'s judgment shows, " date " and " time " are clearly distinguished.
I do not think that we should be justified in reading the words as if they were   E
" beginning with the time " of its issue.

Modern authority tends to prefer a method of calculation which excludes the
first day (see *Stewart* v. *Chapman* (22)); but this is only a general rule, and
PARKE, B., is quoted (23) as saying in *Russell* v. *Ledsam* (24):

" The usual course in recent times has been to construe the day exclusively,   F
whenever anything was to be done in a certain time after a given event or
date . . ."

There, however, the word used is " after " and I see no escape from the conclusion
that where the word " with " is used, the first day is included.

LORD DENNING, M.R., considers that this is to draw too fine a distinction and
does not accord with commonplace ideas, but I cannot agree that to regard   G
" with " and " from " as opposite one to the other is a fine distinction or one
which the ordinary man would not understand and I do not think that this is a
lawyer's quibble. The case before LORD MANSFIELD, C.J. (*Pugh* v. *Duke of
Leeds* (25)) in which he cites *Seignorett* v. *Noguire* (26), was decided many years
before the case before SIR WILLIAM GRANT, M.R. (*Lester* v. *Garland* (27)) in the
days when it was considered to be the rule that the first day should be included.   H
If that were so, of course the expressions " from the date " and " on the date "
and " beginning with the date " were all equivalent because all were construed
inclusively. At least since the decision of SIR WILLIAM GRANT, M.R., the rule, if
there be a rule, is the other way and it follows that " beginning with " and
" beginning from " mean two opposite things. In any event the ordinary
meaning of the language of the rule should be followed unless there is something   I
to show that it should not.

The judge cited (28) and relied on the decision of the Divisional Court in *Hare*
v. *Gocher* (29), where the words were " beginning with the commencement of

---

(21) (1877), 3 C.P.D. 105.   (22) [1951] 2 All E.R. 613; [1951] 2 Q.B. 792.
(23) [1951] 2 All E.R. at p. 618; [1951] 2 Q.B. at p. 798.
(24) (1845), 14 M. & W. 574 at p. 582.   (25) (1777), 2 Cowp. 714.
(26) (1705), 2 Ld. Raym. 1241.   (27) (1808), 15 Ves. 248.
(28) [1967] 1 All E.R. at pp. 22, 23.   (29) [1962] 2 All E.R. 763; [1962] 2 Q.B. 641.

A this Act " and " beginning with the date on which it is passed ". WINN, J.,
giving the first judgment came to the conclusion that the phrase " beginning
with . . ." was especially used in the Act there in question (30) in order to avoid
any equivocation and to exclude the ordinary rule. It was argued before us that
this decision was unnecessary having regard to a phrase in the Interpretation
Act, 1889, to which the court's attention was not drawn and which made it
B unnecessary to construe the words " beginning with ". I cannot accept this. It
may be true that there was another reason supporting the decision of the court,
but the court did not rely on it and was simply construing the words " beginning
with " in their ordinary meaning, and this, as it seems to me, is the right way to
construe the rule.

I can only think that the framer of the note in the new form of writ made an
C unfortunate error, but that he did not annul the rule (R.S.C., Ord. 6, r. 8), nor
by the side wind of a note alter the law.

It seems to me most improbable that it was intended to alter what had been
the accepted practice ever since 1875 by a note, and by a note, moreover, inconsistent with the rule which, after all, must prevail, say the note what it may. It
is no doubt inconvenient that the forms of writ now in existence do contain this
D inconsistency, but that can be put right by the rule committee and the temporary
inconvenience cannot in my opinion be used as an argument for construing the
word " with " as if it was the word " from ", which is the effect produced by
the judgment of LORD DENNING, M.R. I am of opinion that the judge (31) was
perfectly right in the conclusion which he reached and I would without hesitation,
with all due deference to the contrary view of LORD DENNING, M.R., dismiss
E this appeal.

SALMON, L.J.: This appeal raises questions of difficulty concerning the
true construction of R.S.C., Ord. 6, r. 8 (1) which provides that:

" For the purpose of service, a writ . . . is valid in the first instance for
twelve months beginning with the date of its issue . . ."

F Is the date of the issue of the writ in this case Sept. 10, 1965, or 3.5 p.m. on
Sept. 10, 1965? Does the time for service expire at midnight on Sept. 9, or at
midnight on Sept. 10, or at 3.5 p.m. on Sept. 10, 1966? Ordinarily the law takes
no account of fractions of a day unless there is some special reason for doing so,
as there was, e.g., in *Campbell* v. *Strangeways* (32). Equally, if an act is required
to be done within a given time from or after a certain day, that day is not now
G ordinarily included in the calculation of the time (*Young* v. *Higgon* (33); *Goldsmiths*' *Co.* v. *West Metropolitan Ry. Co.* (34); *Stewart* v. *Chapman* (35)). This
rule is also embodied in R.S.C., Ord. 3, r. 2 (2), but it has no application here. It
cannot in any way affect the meaning of the words " for twelve months beginning
with the date of its issue ". This writ was issued on Sept. 10, 1965 at 3.5 p.m.
The twelve-month period beginning with the date of its issue must necessarily in
H my view have begun either at the first moment of Sept. 10 or at 3.5 p.m. on that
day. It cannot have begun on the following day.

September 10 begins immediately after midnight on Sept. 9 and finishes at
midnight on Sept. 10. This is self-evident. Accordingly if the date of the issue
of the writ was Sept. 10, 1965, the validity of the writ for the purpose of service
began with Sept. 10, 1965 and expired twelve months later with Sept. 9, 1966.
I Counsel for the plaintiff, in his most attractive and able argument, contended
that if this were right, it would follow that the writ would be valid for service
immediately after midnight of Sept. 9, 1965, that is to say, many hours before its
issue, and that this would be absurd. I do not think, however, that any such

(30) The Caravan Sites and Control of Development Act, 1960.
(31) [1967] 1 All E.R. 19.   (32) (1877), 3 C.P.D. 105.
(33) [1835-42] All E.R. Rep. 278; (1840), 6 M. & W. 49.
(34) [1900-03] All E.R. Rep. 667; [1904] 1 K.B. 1.
(35) [1951] 2 All E.R. 613; [1951] 2 K.B. 792.

absurdity arises. The word " writ " in the rule must mean a writ which has been   **A**
issued because ex hypothesi a writ cannot be served until it is issued. Indeed
until then it has no real existence. The rule measures the time within which such
a writ is valid for service; and that time is a period of twelve months measured
from a moment before the writ was issued. There is nothing novel in such a
procedure. As HARMAN, L.J., points out, it is a common place for the term of a
lease to be measured from a date before the lease itself came into existence. No   **B**
doubt it follows that a plaintiff will never have a full twelve months within which
to serve his writ but only twelve months less a few hours. If, on the other hand,
one were to read the rule as meaning that the writ was valid for service for twelve
months beginning with the day after the date of its issue, it would follow that the
writ could not be served on the day of its issue—which might seem a little surprising. I cannot, however, accept that, if words have any meaning, " beginning   **C**
with the date of its issue " can be construed to mean the same as " beginning
with the day after the date of its issue ".

The judge relied (36) strongly on the views expressed by WINN, J., and concurred in by LORD PARKER, C.J., and BRABIN, J., in *Hare* v. *Gocher* (37). In that
case the court was considering whether the applicant had made his application
within the time prescribed in the Caravan Sites and Control of Development   **D**
Act, 1960. The question was whether the application had been made within the
two month period " beginning with the commencement of this Act ". The Act
came into operation " at the expiration . . . of one month beginning with the date
on which it is passed ". WINN, J., had no difficulty in finding that these words
required the day on which the Act was passed to be included in the computation
of time. Counsel for the plaintiff points out that the attention of the court was not   **E**
drawn to s. 36 (2) of the Interpretation Act, 1889 which specifically provides that
when a statute is expressed to come into operation on a certain day, it comes into
operation immediately on the expiration of the previous day. He says that this
section made the decision in *Hare* v. *Gocher* (37) inevitable without its being
necessary to consider the meaning of the words " beginning with the date " in
the Act of 1960. This is, no doubt, true but it does not detract from the weight   **F**
to be attached to the views expressed in that case. Nor do I consider that these
views are in any way inconsistent with *Pugh* v. *Duke of Leeds* (38) or *Sidebotham*
v. *Holland* (39). Indeed, in my opinion, they are supported by those authorities.
In *Pugh's* case (38) the question for decision was whether a term of years expressed
to commence " from the day of the date " of a lease included or excluded that
day. It was held that the word " from " might have either meaning and that its   **G**
true construction depended on the intention of the parties to be gathered from
the context in which the word was used. There were many authorities to which
LORD MANSFIELD, C.J., referred in which the word had been construed one way
and the other; amongst them was *Seignorett* v. *Noguire* (40). In that case it was
held that " from the day of the date " included that day and therefore meant
the same as " commencing with the day of the date ". It was treated as self-   **H**
evident that " commencing with the day of the date " included that day. LORD
MANSFIELD approved that decision, and held in *Pugh's* case (38) that the word
" from " included the date of the lease. The tendency until *Lester* v. *Garland* (41)
was to construe " from " as being inclusive. The tendency since then has been
to the contrary. I cannot, however, accept that this can alter what in my view
is and always has been the clear meaning of the words " commencing with the   **I**
date ". Any period of time to be calculated as commencing or beginning with a
certain day must include that day.

(36) [1967] 2 All E.R. at pp. 22, 23.
(37) [1962] 2 All E.R. 763; [1962] 2 Q.B. 641.
(38) (1777), 2 Cowp. 714.
(39) [1891-94] All E.R. Rep. 617; [1895] 1 Q.B. 378.
(40) (1705), 2 Ld. Raym. 1241.
(41) (1808), 15 Ves. 248.

A   In *Sidebotham* v. *Holland* (42) the plaintiff agreed to let a house to the defendant as a yearly tenant " commencing on May 19, 1890 ". The words " commencing on " a certain date are to my mind indistinguishable from " beginning with " a certain date. The question was whether a six months' notice to quit expiring on May 19 was a good notice. The point taken on behalf of the defendant was that the notice expired one day too late, since the year expired at midnight on May 18.

B   LINDLEY, L.J., with whom LORD HALSBURY agreed, held (43) that May 19

> " must be treated as the first day of the tenancy . . . The tenancy cannot, therefore, be treated as commencing on May 20 to the exclusion of May 19."

Nevertheless he thought that for the purpose of a notice to quit, no distinction should be drawn between a tenancy commencing " on " a certain date and one commencing " from " such a date. He concluded that, although a notice for
C   May 19 would have been correct since it expired with the conclusion of the year, yet on the old authorities a notice expiring on the anniversary of the day on which the tenancy commenced was equally correct. Certainly such a notice had never been held to be invalid. A. L. SMITH, L.J., said (44):

> " I cannot hold . . . that when a written agreement states that a person
D   shall become a yearly tenant ' commencing on May 19 ', that it means that he shall become such a tenant ' commencing on the day after May 19 ' . . ."

Although he expressed doubts, he did not, however, dissent (having regard to the state of the authorities on notices to quit) from the decision of the court that a notice to quit is valid even if it expires on the anniversary of the day on which the tenancy began. We are not here considering a notice to quit. R.S.C., Ord. 6,
E   r. 8 (1) states expressly that a writ is valid for service in the first instance for a period of twelve months beginning with the date of its issue. *Sidebotham* v. *Holland* (44) seems to me to re-affirm what has never hitherto been doubted, namely, that when a period of time is required to be calculated as beginning on or with a certain date, that date must be included in the calculation.

    There can be no doubt about how the law stood in relation to the service of the
F   writ between 1875 and the date of the new rule. The old R.S.C., Ord. 8, r. 1 provided that no original writ should

> " be in force for more than twelve months from the day of the date thereof, including the day of such date . . ."

This language is certainly clear. I fancy that its apparent inelegance is due to the
G   fact that those who drafted it were very much alive to the dictionary definition of the word " date " and were anxious completely to forestall one of the arguments which has been so persuasively advanced on the plaintiff's behalf in the present case. This argument was founded on the NEW OXFORD and the SHORTER OXFORD DICTIONARY definition of the word " date " as " the precise time at which anything takes place or is about to take place ". I cannot think that a
H   complete alteration in the law would have been attempted by using words in R.S.C., Ord. 6, r. 8 (1) which seem to me, at any rate at first sight, to leave it unchanged. Had any alteration been intended it would have been so easy for the rule to have stated that the writ should be valid for issue " for twelve months beginning with the time of its issue " or simply " beginning with its issue " or " beginning with the day immediately following the date of the issue " or even
I   " beginning from the date of its issue ".

    Whilst it is in my view impossible to read R.S.C., Ord. 6, r. 8 (1) as meaning that the period of twelve months shall run from the beginning of the day after the date on which the writ was issued, it is possible, having regard to the dictionary definition of the word " date ", to read the rule as meaning that the twelve months period shall run from the precise minute of the day on which

---

(42) [1891-94] All E.R. Rep. 617; [1895] 1 Q.B. 378.
(43) [1891–94] All E.R. Rep. at p. 619; [1895] 1 Q.B. at p. 382.
(44) [1891-94] All E.R. Rep. at p. 621; [1895] 1 Q.B. at pp. 386, 387.

the writ was issued. The real difficulty is to decide whether the framers of the new   **A**
rule intended completely to alter the law or to leave it alone and merely to tidy
up the apparent inelegance of the language of the old rule, without perhaps
appreciating the surprising dictionary definition of " time " which I think may
have accounted for the language of the old rule. I say " surprising " because, if I
asked anyone the date when the judgments were delivered in this case, he would
reply " On May 2, 1967 " and not " Between 10 and 10.45 a.m. on May 2, 1967 ";   **B**
nor do I think that he would have any difficulty in saying, if asked, that today's
date began at midnight yesterday and ends at midnight tonight. Similarly, if I
asked anyone the date of his birth or his marriage, he would not dream of including
in his answer the precise times at which he was born or married. This, I think,
is because the common law is only following the practice of the common man in
taking no notice of fractions of a day unless there is some special reason for   **C**
doing so. When there is such a special reason, it is usual both in common parlance
and in the rules (as I shall presently show) to refer specifically to the time and
the date.

In my view counsel for the defendants is quite right in saying that whatever
the strict dictionary definition may be, the word " date " is generally understood as meaning a twenty-four hour division of time shown on the calendar.   **D**
I do not think that it is used in any other sense in R.S.C., Ord. 6, r. 8 (1). It
would I think be unrealistic to suppose that it means a particular time on a
given day when no ordinary person would so understand it. R.S.C., Ord. 6,
r. 8 (2) also lends some support to this view. This provides for the extension of
the validity of a writ

        E

  " for such period, not exceeding twelve months at any one time,
beginning with the day next following that on which it would otherwise
expire . . ."

The twelve months' extension runs from the expiration of the period within
which the writ could originally have been served. This seems to show that, just
as the extended period begins with a day, so the original period ends with a day.   **F**
Otherwise there would be a hiatus of some hours between the original period and
the new period; in which event it would hardly be accurate to describe the new
period as an extension of the old.

The chief difficulty that arises in this case lies in the fact that the construction
which I feel constrained to put on R.S.C., Ord. 6, r. 8 (1) is wholly inconsistent
with the note on the form of the writ prescribed by R.S.C., Ord. 1, r. 9, Ord. 6,   **G**
r. 1 and App. A. The former note on the old writ was wholly consistent with the
old rule. This new note, however, which is undoubtedly part of the form of the
writ, reads:

  " This writ may not be served more than twelve calendar months after
the above date unless renewed by order of the court."

        H

Thus, whilst R.S.C., Ord. 6, r. 8 (1) includes the date of service, the note on
the writ excludes it.

Clearly R.S.C., Ord. 1, r. 9, Ord. 6, r. 1 and App. A, which prescribe the form
of the writ (including the note) should, if possible, be reconciled with R.S.C.,
Ord. 6, r. 8 (1); but in my view no such reconciliation is possible. If the words
" the above date " in the note could be read as meaning the precise time at   **I**
which the writ was issued, it might perhaps be possible to read the word " date "
in R.S.C., Ord. 6, r. 8 (1) as referring to the precise time at which the writ was
served. The difficulty is, however, that the note immediately follows the words
on the writ: " Witness, Gerald Baron Gardiner, Lord High Chancellor of Great
Britain the   day of   196 ." Accordingly it follows that the date referred
to in the note on the writ in the present case is Sept. 10, 1965, and not any
particular time on that day.

There is also this further point. R.S.C., Ord. 6, r. 7 (3) provides that the

A   " Issue of a writ takes place on its being sealed by an officer of the office out of which it is issued."

Whilst R.S.C., Ord. 63, r. 3 provides:

" (1) Any document filed in the Central Office in any proceedings must be sealed with a seal showing the date on which the document was filed.

B   (2) Particulars of the time of delivery at the Central Office of any document for filing [and] the date of the document . . . shall be entered in books kept in the Central Office for the purpose."

These rules appear to draw a clear distinction between time and date. The writ must be sealed with a seal showing its date but the books kept in the Central Office must contain an entry showing not only its date but also its time. It is C true that the practice has grown up of writing below the seal on the writ the precise time at which it was filed; but this cannot alter the meaning of the rules, which use " time " and " date " to denote different things.

Since I have come to the conclusion, for the reasons which I have stated, that the note on the writ is irreconcilable with R.S.C., Ord. 6, r. 8 (1), it is necessary to choose between them. The note is intended in my view as no more than a guide D or sign-post to indicate the course which should be followed in order to comply with the requirements of R.S.C., Ord. 6, r. 8 (1). By an unfortunate oversight this sign-post is pointing in the wrong direction. It cannot, however, affect the clear requirement of R.S.C., Ord. 6, r. 8 (1). The road north leads northwards even when the sign-post has been turned round in the opposite direction. I have no doubt but that that rule, which explicitly states the time within which the E writ is valid for service, must prevail over the note on the writ. This no doubt makes for great inconvenience until the note or the rule is altered by the rule committee. Accordingly, if I could persuade myself that there is any ambiguity in the rule, I would gladly resolve the ambiguity by reference to the note and resolve it in the sense which has commended itself to LORD DENNING, M.R. Unfortunately, however, I can find no such ambiguity. It is no doubt a pity that F this inconvenience should arise from the use in the rule of the word " with " instead of the word " from "; but even the shortest single word can affect the whole meaning of any enactment. I do not think that the proposition that a period stated " as beginning with " a certain date does begin on that date depends on any fine distinction, legal subtlety or empty formality. In my view it depends on the plain and natural meaning of ordinary English words. This G court has no power to rectify the rule; it cannot change the words in which it is expressed—however convenient it might be to do so.

It follows that in my view the time for service in the present case expired at midnight on Sept. 9, 1966, and, since the writ was not served until the following day, its service was invalid. I would accordingly dismiss the appeal.

Appeal dismissed.   Leave to appeal to the House of Lords refused.

H   Solicitors: *Waterhouse & Co.*, agents for *Nelson & Steele*, Kidsgrove, Staffs. (for the plaintiff); *Preston, Lane-Claypon & O'Kelly*, agents for *Hollinshead & Moody*, Stoke-on-Trent (for the defendants).

[*Reported by* F. GUTTMAN, ESQ., *Barrister-at-Law.*]

NOTE.   A

THE FAIRPORT (No. 4)*.

VOGIATZIS AND OTHERS *v.* OWNERS OF STEAMSHIP FAIRPORT
(MOSCHAKIS AND ANOTHER INTERVENING).
                                                                 B
[PROBATE, DIVORCE AND ADMIRALTY DIVISION (Karminski, J.), May 1, 1967.]

*Admiralty—Practice—Action in rem—Priorities—Caveat payment entered by
second mortgagees—Second mortgagees had issued writ, Folio 117, in April,
1966—Caveat lapsed in May, 1966—Order regarding priorities made in
July, 1966, in present action, Folio 62, in absence of second mortgagees—
Funds, representing proceeds of sale of vessel, still in court—Whether court*   C
*would vary its order at the instance of interveners, the second mortgagees, so as
to allow adjudication on priority as between them and necessaries men and all
other persons interested in the proceeds of sale.*

[As to caveat against payment in an Admiralty action in rem, see 1 HALSBURY'S
LAWS (3rd Edn.) 84, 85, para. 179; and for cases on the subject, see 1 DIGEST
(Repl.) 264, *1650-1654.*]   D

Cases referred to:
    Acrux, The, [1961] 1 Lloyd's Rep. 471; 3rd Digest Supp.
    Leoborg, The (No. 2), [1963] 2 Lloyd's Rep. 268, 441; [1964] 1 Lloyd's Rep.
        380; 42 Digest (Repl.) 659, *4120.*
    Markland, The, (1871), L.R. 3 A. & E. 340; 24 L.T. 596; 1 Asp. M.L.C. 44;   E
        1 Digest (Repl.) 264, *1650.*
    Stream Fisher, The, [1926] All E.R. Rep. 513; [1927] P. 73; 96 L.J.P. 29;
        136 L.T. 189; 17 Asp. M.L.C. 159; 26 Lloyd L.R. 4; 1 Digest (Repl.)
        264, *1654.*

Motion.

This was a motion by interveners, Mrs. Mina Moschakis and Mrs. Irene Manos,   F
for an order that an order made by KARMINSKI, J., on July 26, 1966, with regard
to priorities in respect of the fund in court (the proceeds of sale of the Panamanian
steamer " Fairport ") be varied so as to order that the priority of the claims of
the necessaries men, Barclay Curle & Co., Ltd. and Robb Moore & Neill, Ltd., be
reserved and that the priority of claims as between the interveners, the necessaries
men and all other persons interested in the proceeds of sale of the Fairport be   G
determined either in an action 1966 Folio 117, in which the interveners were
plaintiffs, or in such other action as might be just and convenient. The facts are
set out in the judgment. Previous proceedings in May, 1966, were reported at
[1966] 2 All E.R. 1026.

    A. E. J. Diamond for the interveners.
    N. Bridges-Adams for the necessaries men.   H

    KARMINSKI, J.: This matter comes before me in the form of a motion on
behalf of interveners, Mrs. Moschakis and Mrs. Manos, for an order that an order
made by me in July, 1966, with regard to priorities (1) be varied so as to order
that the priority of the claims of the necessaries men, namely, Barclay Curle &
Co., Ltd. and Robb Moore & Neill, Ltd. be reserved, and that the priority of   I
claims as between the interveners, Barclay Curle & Co., Ltd., Robb Moore &
Neill, Ltd. and all other persons interested in the proceeds of sale of the Fairport
be determined either in action 1966 Folio 117, in which the present interveners
are plaintiffs, or in such other action as may be just and convenient. When the
matter came before me on priorities in July, 1966, the plaintiffs in Folio 117,

---

* *The Fairport (No. 2)* is reported in [1966] 2 Lloyd's Rep. 7, and *The Fairport (No. 3)*
in [1966] 2 Lloyd's Rep. 253.
  (1) See *The Fairport (No. 3),* [1966] 2 Lloyd's Rep. 253.

A that is the interveners, were not present or represented. What happened,
briefly, was this. They had issued a writ setting out their claim as second
mortgagees of the ship and claiming the necessary relief on Apr. 9, 1966. Quite
shortly after that their statement of claim was filed in the same month. A caveat
had been entered earlier, but had in fact expired in May, 1966. On the practice
as it stands, the caveat having expired, there was no duty at all on the Admiralty
B registry to give any notice to the interveners nor did they do so. But immediately
after my order was made, it was drawn to the attention of the interveners'
solicitors that the order had been made, and that orders had been made for
payment out of the proceeds of sale. There is no doubt that the failure to renew
the caveat was an oversight on the part of the solicitors advising those parties,
though the oversight was in the circumstances not a serious one in the sense that
C it was the kind of oversight which even a careful lawyer might have made in the
general way of his business. It is important here to realise that they had not been
inactive until after my order of July, 1966. They had taken the necessary steps
of issuing a caveat originally, of issuing a writ and of filing a statement of claim;
it was only later that the slip or oversight of failing to renew the caveat occurred.
If the caveat had been renewed, as it should have been, this difficulty would not
D have arisen; they would have been notified of the application before me on
priorities and they would, I doubt not, have been represented and put their
case forward.

The origin of the present practice seems to have come from *The Markland* (2),
a case decided in 1871 by SIR ROBERT PHILLIMORE. The facts of that case are
very different from the present. SIR ROBERT PHILLIMORE said in his judgment (3):

E "With regard to the fact that the order for payment in this case was
actually signed by me, I cannot hold that upon that ground the court is
functus officio. The court has not parted with the funds; and, after it has
been apprised that by so doing it would be inflicting an injustice upon parties
who have a prior legal claim over those funds, it would be strange indeed if
the court had not power to prevent the execution of the order. I am clear
F that I have power, and ought to exercise it, to prevent the execution of that
order, the effect of which would be to do a wrong to a party who has
established priority in his claim."

The learned judge went on to direct a new form of warning when a caveat was
entered. An important part of that decision, as I understand it, is that where, as
G here, the court has not parted with the fund, it has not completed its duty of
adjudicating between the parties. In other words, it is not functus officio and,
where the result of doing nothing might be to inflict an injustice, then it must
act. Over fifty years later the matter in a different form came before BATESON, J.,
in *The Stream Fisher* (4). In that case, BATESON, J., said this (5):

H "Again, *The Markland* (2) is a useful case when dealing with these matters;
because in that case a suitor had obtained a decree, but payment out had
not been made, and the decision was this: ' The rule that the court will give
priority to the suitor who first obtains a decree applies only as between
claimants in pari conditione. Where, in a suit in rem, a decree has been made
per incuriam for the payment of money out of the proceeds in court to
satisfy the claim of the plaintiff, the court may, before the money has been
I paid, revoke or vary the decree.' That case points to the fact that, so long
as the court has possession of the proceeds, it will see that they are properly
distributed."

That is the position here, and I am urged by counsel for the necessaries men to
pay particular attention to the fact that it is the duty of applicants who want to

---

(2) (1871), L.R. 3 A. & E. 340.   (3) (1871), L.R. 3 A. & E. at p. 343.
(4) [1926] All E.R. Rep. 513; [1927] P. 73.
(5) [1926] All E.R. Rep. at pp. 518, 519; [1927] P. at p. 84.

vary an order to act quickly. He relies on two recent decisions of HEWSON, J., *The* **A**
Acrux (6) and *The Leoborg* (*No. 2*) (7). HEWSON, J., pointed out and emphasises in
both those cases the necessity of acting quickly. I desire to say nothing which
would in any way diminish the urgency of these repeated warnings; on the other
hand it is, perhaps, not irrelevant to consider that one of counsel for the necessaries men's clients, Robb Moore & Neill, Ltd., have not yet got judgment. They
were still in that state in July, 1966, when I made the order that I did. While **B**
appreciating in full the need for acting quickly, I have to remember that this is a
somewhat unusual case in which there have been difficulties in getting opinions on
Panamanian law as to the validity of the mortgage which has been put in issue.
The main thing which impresses me, however, is the duty of this court not to
abstain from further action when there is a fund in court, and where the result
of such abstention may be to create an injustice. I appreciate that the fault, if **C**
that is not too harsh a word, in this matter is the failure of the solicitors to renew
the caveat; but I cannot think that that would justify me in virtually depriving
the plaintiffs in Folio 117 of their remedy, and I do not propose to do so. What I
intend to do here is to vary my order so as to allow the matter to be decided on
its merits as between the alleged second mortgagees and the necessaries men on a
future application as to priorities. That can be done in one of two ways; it can **D**
be dealt with at the hearing, whenever that may be, of Folio 117, or it could be
reserved by the trial judge at the conclusion of that case to be determined later.
I do not propose to go further into that and I vary my own order in that sense.

Order accordingly.

Solicitors: *Gerald Samuels* (for the interveners); *Norton, Rose, Botterell &* **E**
Roche (for the necessaries men).

[*Reported by* N. P. METCALFE, ESQ., *Barrister-at-Law.*]

COMMERCIAL PROPERTIES, LTD. *v.* WOOD. **F**

[COURT OF APPEAL, CIVIL DIVISION (Harman, Davies and Russell, L.JJ.), March
14, 1967.]

*Landlord and Tenant—Notice to quit—Business premises—Date for which
statutory notice may be given—Monthly tenancy—Rent payable monthly in
advance on first day of each calendar month—Landlord's notice to terminate
on eleventh day of month—Effect—Landlord and Tenant Act, 1954 (2 & 3* **G**
Eliz. 2 c. 56), s. 25 (1), (2).

A tenancy of business premises was continued, by virtue of the Landlord
and Tenant Act, 1954, s. 24*, as a monthly tenancy with rent payable
monthly in advance on the first day of each calendar month. On Oct. 4, 1965,
the landlord gave a notice in the prescribed form, in accordance with s. 25 **H**
of the Act of 1954, specifying Apr. 11, 1966, as the date on which the tenancy
was to come to an end.

Held: the notice, being a valid notice for termination of the tenancy
within the period allowed by s. 25 (2)† of the Landlord and Tenant Act, 1954,
effectively terminated the tenancy on Apr. 11, 1966 (see p. 918, letter I,
and p. 919, letters D and F, post).

Scholl Mfg. Co., Ltd. v. *Clifton* (*Slim-Line*), *Ltd.* ([1966] 3 All E.R. 16) **I**
applied.

[As to a landlord's notice to terminate a business tenancy, see 23 HALSBURY'S
LAWS (3rd Edn.) 889, para. 1711; and for cases on the subject, see DIGEST
(Cont. Vol. A) 1024, *6111Aa, 6111Ab, 6111Ac.*

---

(6) [1961] 1 Lolyd's Rep. 471.   ((7 [1963] 2 Lloyd's Rep. 269, 441.
* Section 24 (1), so far as material, is printed at p. 918, letter B, post.
† Section 25, so far as material, is printed at p. 918, letters D and F, post.

A   For the Landlord and Tenant Act, 1954, s. 24 (1), s. 25, see 34 Halsbury's
Statutes (2nd Edn.) 409, 410.]

Case referred to:

Scholl Mfg. Co., Ltd. v. *Clifton (Slim-Line), Ltd.*, [1966] 3 All E.R. 16; [1966]
3 W.L.R. 575;

B   **Appeal.**   *monthly.*

This was an appeal by the defendant tenant, Thomas Urwin Wood, from the
judgment of His Honour Judge Ifor Lloyd, at Wandsworth county court on
Oct. 6, 1966, ordering him to give possession of the premises, No. 248, Balham
High Road, comprised in his tenancy to the plaintiff landlord, Commercial
Properties, Ltd.   The defendant held the premises, which comprised a cellar,

C   lock-up shop, shop, back room, kitchen and scullery on the ground floor and six
rooms, bathroom and lavatory on the upper floors, on a monthly tenancy.   They
had been let to him by a tenancy agreement dated Feb. 19, 1940, made between the
plaintiff landlord and the defendant, for three and a half years from Apr. 1, 1940,
and thereafter from month to month, except for the cellar and lock-up shop, which
were let to him on a monthly tenancy as from Aug. 1, 1946.   The defendant

D   occupied the premises for the purpose of his business as a café proprietor.   Notice
to terminate the defendant's business tenancy on Apr. 11, 1966, was given
under s. 25 of the Landlord and Tenant Act, 1954.   This notice was dated Oct. 4,
1965, and was served on that day; it was in Form 7 prescribed by the Landlord
and Tenant (Notices) Regulations, 1957, S.I. 1957 No. 1157.   The defendant
admitted that Part 2 of the Landlord and Tenant Act, 1954, applied to the

E   premises, and, at the hearing before the county court judge, conceded that the
notice was a valid notice complying in form with the provisions of s. 25 of the
Act of 1954.   No common law notice to terminate the contractual tenancy on
the first day of a month was given.   No oral evidence was given before the county
court judge, the matter being argued on the law and the documents admitted
before the court.   In concluding his judgment the county court judge said that

F   he preferred to base it on the view that s. 25 of the Act of 1954 varied the contractual provision as to the giving of a notice to quit and substituted a statutory
notice; and that the plaintiff landlord had terminated the tenancy in the only
way open to a landlord in the case of premises to which Part 2 of the Act of
1954 applied.   His Honour accordingly made an order for possession in six
weeks and for mesne profits to the date of the hearing, Sept. 19, 1966, when

G   judgment was reserved.

G. R. F. Morris, Q.C., and *E. F. Monier-Williams* for the tenant.

L. A. Blundell, Q.C., and *S. Ibbotson* for the landlord, were not called on to
argue.

H   **HARMAN, L.J.:**   The appellant tenant's tenancy of 248, Balham High
Road began some years ago under a lease and, before any relevant date, had
become a monthly tenancy of the whole of the house determinable by a notice
coinciding with the month.   These were business premises, and it was admitted
that Pt. 2 of the Landlord and Tenant Act, 1954, applied.

On Oct. 4, 1965 the landlord served a notice on the tenant in the statutory form

I   to terminate the tenancy on Apr. 11, 1966.   Why the landlord chose that particular period does not appear, but it has caused the trouble which has arisen here.   It
could have been avoided (as the landlord admitted) by making the notice coincide
with the end of the month or the beginning of another one; but that was not done.
It is said that, it being a contractual term of this tenancy that it should end
with the last day of the month, any notice must have not only the statutory
quality of lasting six months but also the contractual quality of ending on the
right day, and that this notice does not have that effect, and is ineffective for its
purpose.

The answer to this point is that, as I pointed out in *Scholl Mfg. Co., Ltd.* v.   A
Clifton (Slim-Line), Ltd. (1) (and I think DIPLOCK, L.J., pointed it out rather more
clearly (2)) there is only one tenancy under the Landlord and Tenant Act, 1954:
there is not a statutory tenancy, as there is under the Rent Acts. The tenancy
is one: the notice to quit is one. The Act of 1954 itself provides the answer quite
clearly. Section 23, with which Pt. 2 begins, provides that that Part applies to
any tenancy where the property comprises premises occupied for the purpose of   B
a business. Section 24 (1) provides in terms:

" A tenancy to which this Part of this Act applies shall not come to an end
unless terminated in accordance with the provisions of this Part of this
Act . . ."

That is quite categorical. It is stated in clear terms that in the case of any   C
tenancy to which this Part of the Act of 1954 applies the tenancy shall not come
to an end unless there is a statutory termination of it, and it is a statutory
termination alone, so far as the landlord is concerned, which can bring the
tenancy to an end. There is a saving for the tenant's right, but none for the
landlord's. Section 25 (1) shows how this statutory right of the landlord to
terminate the tenancy is to operate; i.e.:

D

" by a notice given to the tenant in the prescribed form [that prescribed
form was employed here] specifying the date at which the tenancy is to
come to an end . . ."

and then that is defined.

Now if that were all, any kind of notice would apparently do. All one has to do
is to serve a notice in the prescribed form stating the date and there is an end.   E
When one looks at s. 25 (2) one finds that the notice has to be between six and
twelve months in duration. So that shows that, whatever else there may be in
the contract, between six and twelve months' notice must be given. Subsection (3)
and sub-s. (4) seem to me to clinch the matter, because they go on to give protection which otherwise would not be given to a tenant. Subsection (3) provides
that where the contract provides for more than a six-monthly notice one prolongs   F
the statutory length of notice pro tanto; and sub-s. (4) reads:

" In the case of any other tenancy, [that is, a periodic tenancy] a notice
. . . shall not specify a date of termination earlier than the date on which . . .
the tenancy would have come to an end by effluxion of time."

Both those subsections seem to me to postulate that a notice under the Act of   G
1954 is the way, and is the only way, of putting this tenancy to an end. I think
that the county court judge dealt with this matter admirably in his judgment.
He said:

" Was the effect of the s. 25 notice of Oct. 4, 1965, that it terminated the
tenancy for all purposes or only for the purposes of the Landlord and Tenant
Act, 1954? In my opinion it terminated it for all purposes."

H

In one more passage he said:

" Where a valid statutory notice under s. 25 has been given, that in my
view determines the tenancy just as effectively as a contractual notice would
have done but for the Act."

In both those statements I concur, and I think that the county court judge was   I
perfectly right.

A further point was taken, for the first time in this court, which had to do with
the fact that rent under this particular lease was payable in advance. It was
payable monthly in advance on the first of each month. It is said that giving a
notice for a day other than the first of the month disturbs without warranty the

(1) [1966] 3 All E.R. 16 at p. 18.   (2) [1966] 3 All E.R. at pp. 19, 20.

A   contractual obligation on the parties to pay and receive respectively rent at that date and no other, and that therefore that shows that, at any rate where rent is payable in advance, one must choose a date to make one's six-months' notice coincide with the date when the rent would become payable—the principle suggested being that no more disturbance of the contractual relations of the parties is to be assumed than is necessary to give validity to the statute. I

B   cannot take that as a serious point. It is quite true that it would be tidier, where the rent is payable in advance on the first of each month, if the landlord made his notice coincide with the date when rent became due; but that so slender an inconvenience should cut down the plain words of the statute is a thing I cannot accept at all.

C   I do not deal with the cases which counsel for the tenant cited to us, for I think that that is not necessary. The statute itself gives the answer.

I would dismiss the appeal.

DAVIES, L.J.: I entirely agree with what Harman, L.J., has said and also with the full and clear judgment of the county court judge; and I do not wish to add anything.

D

RUSSELL, L.J.: I also agree. Section 24 (1) of the Landlord and Tenant Act, 1954 ousts the ordinary methods by which a landlord can terminate a tenancy such as this. It provides that

" A tenancy to which this Part of this Act applies shall not come to an end unless terminated in accordance with the provisions of this Part of this

E   Act . . ."

Section 25 (1), so far as concerns termination by a landlord, in perfectly general terms says that he may terminate a tenancy " by a notice given . . . in the prescribed form specifying the date at which the tenancy is to come to an end . . .". That is perfectly wide in its language, and I see no reason for narrowing it in

F   any way by reference to what was the contractual method of determining a tenancy until the Landlord and Tenant Act, 1954, stepped in and made it irrelevant.

Section 25 (2) contains the definition of the limitation of what the date of termination is to be: the notice must be given " not more than twelve nor less than six months before the date of termination specified therein ". It is argued

G   that one should construe sub-s. (1) in a narrow sense so as not to interfere with the ordinary contractual rights. Therefore it is said that in a case such as this—particularly when the rent is payable in advance—the only date which can be selected under sub-s. (1) is one of the periodic dates appropriate to the monthly tenancy; but this seems to me to be entirely contradicted by the rest of the section, which demonstrates that the legislature considered that sub-s. (1) was to be construed in its full apparent width; because in sub-s. (3) there is a provision

H   by which, if one has, in effect, a tenancy under which one has to give more than six months' notice to quit, then the landlord must give at least that length of notice and it is not sufficient for him to give the six months which is provided for under sub-s. (2). That shows as plainly as anything that without that special provision sub-s. (1) would have allowed the landlord to ride rough-shod over that

I   contractual position.

Similarly, sub-s. (4) provides that if one has a term of years, then the notice may not be given under sub-s. (1) to expire before the end of that term of years by effluxion of time. Again that shows quite plainly the width which was attributed by the legislature to the language of sub-s. (1).

This is a reasonably clear point, in which the county court judge was quite right. One cannot help feeling sympathy for the tenant, who, because his then advisers apparently did not pay sufficient attention to the time limits for application for a new tenancy, missed his chance. On the other hand, if the tenant's

arguments are successful, as I understand it, he does not admit that the landlord **A**
has any power *now* to give a one-month notice, because, he says, that these are
business premises and that the landlord must start again at square one.

Appeal dismissed.

Solicitors: *Barlow & Co.* (for the tenant); *R. A. Roberts* (for the landlord).

[*Reported by* HENRY SUMMERFIELD, ESQ., *Barrister-at-Law.*] **B**

TALBOT *v.* TALBOT.

[COURT OF APPEAL, CIVIL DIVISION (Harman, Davies and Russell, L.JJ.), March **C**
  15, 16, 1967.]

*Will—Option—Purchase—Gift of option to purchase land at reasonable valuation
—No express reference in will to trustees fixing what the price should be—
Whether option valid—Inquiry to be held to fix reasonable price.*

A testator directed that his son John should have the option of purchasing
the testator's farm T. and eleven acres at a reasonable valuation and that **D**
his son Joseph should have the option of purchasing his farm P. and six acres
at a reasonable valuation. There was no uncertainty as to the land affected.

Held: the options to purchase at a reasonable valuation were valid and
enforceable, and, in the absence of agreement on the price, the court would
direct an inquiry to fix the price by valuation (see p. 923, letter D, p. 924,
letters C and G, and p. 925, letter H, post); the price should be ascertained **E**
as at the time of the testator's death but, in making the valuation, regard
should be had to events subsequent to the testator's death (see p. 923, letter
I, p. 924, letter H, and p. 925, letter G, post).

Dictum of SIR WILLIAM GRANT, M.R., in *Milnes* v. *Gery* ((1807), 14 Ves.
at p. 407), and *Gaskarth* v. *Lord Lowther* ((1805), 12 Ves. 107) applied.

Per RUSSELL, L.J.: the sons were entitled to know before they exercised **F**
their options the result of the valuation, so that they might see whether their
financial situations justified them in exercising the options (see p. 925, letter
B, post; cf., p. 923, letter F, post).

Decision of BURGESS, V.-C. ([1967] 1 All E.R. 601) affirmed.

[**Editorial Note.** The present was not a case where the will had provided **G**
special machinery for making the valuation and the machinery had broken
down; in such a case the court will not fill the lacuna (see p. 925, letter F, post).

As to the creation of options to purchase by will, see 39 HALSBURY'S LAWS
(3rd Edn.) 912, para. 1383; and for cases on the subject, see 48 DIGEST (Repl.)
56-58, 404-417.]

Cases referred to: **H**

Bwllfa and Merthyr Dare Steam Collieries (1891), Ltd. v. *Pontypridd Waterworks
    Co.,* [1900-03] All E.R. Rep. 600; [1903] A.C. 426; 72 L.J.K.B. 805;
    89 L.T. 280; 11 Digest (Repl.) 136, *199.*

Gaskarth v. *Lord Lowther,* (1805), 12 Ves. 107; 33 E.R. 41; 40 Digest (Repl.)
    221, *1801.*

Harmsworth (decd.), Re, Barclays Bank, Ltd. v. *Inland Revenue Comrs.,* [1966] **I**
    3 All E.R. 309; [1966] 3 W.L.R. 1077; *on appeal,* C.A., ante p. 249.

Milnes v. *Gery,* (1807), 14 Ves. 400; 33 E.R. 574; 2 Digest (Repl.) 505, *513.*

Morgan v. *Milman,* (1853), 3 De G.M. & G. 24; 22 L.J.Ch. 897; 20 L.T.O.S.
    285; 43 E.R. 10; 44 Digest (Repl.) 44, *309.*

Radnor (Earl) v. *Shafto,* (1805), 11 Ves. 448; 32 E.R. 1160; 48 Digest (Repl.)
    56, *404.*

Vickers v. *Vickers,* (1867), L.R. 4 Eq. 529; 36 L.J.Ch. 946; 36 Digest (Repl.)
    628, *1922.*

(left margin) Distinguished in ROBINSON v COLLINS [1975] 1 All ER 321

A   *Waite* v. *Moorland*, (1865), 13 L.T. 91; *on appeal*, (1866), 14 L.T. 649; 12 Jur. N.S. 763; 48 Digest (Repl.) 57, *410*.

Appeal.

On a petition by the plaintiffs, who were the executors and trustees of the will, dated Dec. 4, 1953, of Peter Talbot (deceased), by which he purported to give options of purchasing at a reasonable valuation two farms to his sons John and
B   Joseph, the first and second defendants, Burgess, V.-C., as reported at [1967] 1 All E.R. 601, decided that both options were valid and effectual, and directed a special inquiry to ascertain the reasonable valuation of each farm. The third, fourth, fifth, and sixth defendants, children of the testator and residuary legatees under his will, now appealed from this decision of Burgess, V.-C. The facts are set out in the judgment of Harman, L.J.
C

P. A. *Ferns* for the third, fourth, fifth and sixth defendants.

D. B. *Mallard* for the plaintiffs.

B. C. *Maddocks* for the first and second defendants.

HARMAN, L.J.: This is an appeal from a decision of Burgess, V.-C., (1)
D   given on July 19, 1966, at the Chancery Court of the County Palatine of Lancaster. It concerns the will of one Peter Talbot, who died in May, 1964, and whose will was proved in January, 1965, by the two petitioners (as they were in the court below), one of those being a brother and the other being a daughter. All the defendants to the petition were similarly children of the testator. He singled out two of them, John and Joseph, primarily as the objects of his bounty, in this sense, that each of those two was resident in a house that belonged to him, paying
E   a rent and farming some land that went with it, and it was apparently the testator's wish that the two boys who lived on these two farms should have the first refusal, enabling them to live there, but that they should pay the proper price so that they could not get any further advantage, the price falling into residue and being split among all the children equally. There has arisen an unfortunate family dispute over this matter. It probably arises from the fact
F   that this is land potentially of very much rising value, and it may well be that if John and Joseph or either of them can exercise the option given by the testator's will he might get a great profit to the disadvantage of his brothers and sisters, and of course that immediately arouses family jealousy and one can see the difficulty. However that may be, nothing very much has been done. There have been, we are told, family discussions—family disputes—and they have all come
G   to nothing because no price can be agreed on for these two holdings. Consequently the executors—whose interests themselves are conflicting, one of them being interested to see the option exercised, the other the other way—have quite properly been advised that they should put the matter into the hands of the court, and they, in the manner still current in the Palatine Court, petitioned the court for an answer to the disputed question, which, as set out in the petition, was:
H   whether, on the true construction of the will, the options to purchase thereby granted are valid and, if so, on what basis and by whom the properties comprised therein ought to be valued? Burgess, V.-C., (1) has decided that by saying that the options are valid and that, as there is no agreement about the method of ascertaining the value at which the options are to be exercised, the court will take the matter into its hands; and he has directed a special inquiry as to the proper
I   value to be put on each of these two holdings for the purposes of the options.

Against that the children other than John and Joseph appeal. Principally they say (and really this is the pith and marrow of their plea) that this is a contract too vague to be entertained or specifically enforced by the court. I say " contract " because a testamentary option is something which potentially can become a contract on its exercise at any time by the person holding the option, and so the principles of contract seem to me to apply to it, because the person getting a

(1) [1967] 1 All E.R. 601.

property under a testamentary option gets it by exercising the option and
entering into a contract in that behalf with the executors. That was decided (if
there is need for authority) by this court the other day in *Re Harmsworth (decd.)*,
Barclays Bank, Ltd. v. *Inland Revenue Comrs.* (2)—now on the way to the House
of Lords.

The will was not in a very ordinary form. The testator made provision for his
wife (who, however, predeceased him), and gave his executors £10 each. He then
went on:

"... on the death of my wife I direct that my son John ... shall have
the option of purchasing Thorn Bush Farm and approximately eleven acres
at a reasonable valuation, providing he allows my brother James ... to
reside at Thorn Bush Farm for the remainder of his life [James is one of the
executors] and I direct that my son Joseph ... shall have the option of
purchasing Porch Farm and approximately six acres at a reasonable valuation should Joseph refuse the option then it shall be offered to my son John
should he refuse then it shall be offered to my son Ralph should he refuse
then it shall be offered to my son Geoffrey ... Should John refuse the
option on Thorn Bush Farm and the options on Porch Farm be refused then
I direct that the rejected farm or farms along with the field approximately
three and a half acres situate on the north-west side of Slag Lane with the
remainder of my effects whatsoever shall be sold and the proceeds divided
in equal shares between my children ":

and then they are named. There is no difficulty about the subject-matter of the
two options: I need not go into that. Everybody agrees what " Porch Farm "
and " Thorn Bush Farm " and the other " three and a half acres " refer to
when the testator mentions them. The words which arouse the controversy are,
of course, " at a reasonable valuation ", and the question is whether that is
sufficient direction to induce the court specifically to perform any agreement
which might arise out of it.

Of course a contract for the sale of land must state a sufficient description of the
land and it must state either the price or the agreed method of arriving at
the price, and that, in my judgment, is enough. One will find that stated in all the
text books. I take first SUGDEN, and I quote from the Fourteenth Edition—the
author being still LORD ST. LEONARDS, as he had then become. He wrote this,
in para. 32 on p. 287: " If an agreement be made to sell at a fair valuation, the
court will execute it although the value is not fixed." Now that is a perfectly
categorical, plain statement; and the author, himself no mean authority, supports
it by a note which refers to *Milnes* v. *Gery* (3), to which BURGESS, V.-C., referred
(4). That went off on a different point but it is a judgment of SIR WILLIAM
GRANT, M.R., himself a very great authority. He said this (5):

" The case of an agreement to sell at a fair valuation is essentially different ... In that case no particular means of ascertaining the value are
pointed out: there is nothing, therefore, precluding the court from adopting
any means, adapted to that purpose."

In *Milnes* v. *Gery* (3) the exact means had been pointed out by the testator: that
is to say, there were to be two arbitrators and an umpire. Those means broke
down, and SIR WILLIAM GRANT came to the conclusion that the court, where the
means pointed out by the testator had broken down, would not create others as
that would be something which the court had no jurisdiction to do, but that,
where the matter was left open, as SIR WILLIAM GRANT said, and no machinery
was provided, there is no reason why the court should not step in and lend its
benevolent aid. That seems to me to be good sense and good law.

---

(2) Ante, p. 249.   (3) (1807), 14 Ves. 400.
(4) [1967] 1 All E.R. at pp. 602, 603.   (5) (1807), 14 Ves. at p. 407.

A   I turn to another work of authority, WILLIAMS ON VENDOR AND PURCHASER (4th Edn.), p. 47:

> " The parties to the contract and the property to be sold must therefore be sufficiently described, and the price, or the means of ascertaining it, be stated."

B   For that, again, *Milnes* v. *Gery* (6) is cited. Then there is a note about the difference between sale of chattels and sale of real estate. In the course of that note the author wrote this:

> " An express agreement to buy land at its fair value is, however, valid, and would, it seems, be specifically enforced ":

and for that he cited SIR WILLIAM GRANT, and LORD CRANWORTH, L.C., in a
C   dictum in *Morgan* v. *Milman* (7). That is very high authority.

Lastly, I look at DART ON VENDOR AND PURCHASER (8th Edn.), p. 222:

> " A general agreement to sell ' at a fair valuation ' may be enforced; and the court will, if necessary, direct a reference to ascertain the price."

Then the author went on to refer to the distinction made in *Milnes* v. *Gery* (6).

D   Therefore there is good authority for saying that an option to purchase " at a fair valuation " or " at a fair price " is an option which the court will enforce; and it seems to me that these words " at a reasonable valuation " are the same as saying " at a fair price ". In other words, the will means that the first and second defendants are not to have any monetary advantage over their brothers, because the fair price is to be divided among all of them equally; and it is only
E   the shift in values brought about by urbanisation which has caused the difficulty in this case.

The first and second defendants have not hitherto exercised their options, and their plea is that they are entitled to know what is the reasonable valuation before they make up their minds. There is a direction that they are to have an option to buy at a formula. The formula is, " a reasonable valuation ". The doubt that
F   has assailed my mind is whether they must exercise their option first and the " reasonable valuation " is to follow or whether they are entitled to say to the trustees " Let us arrive first at the reasonable valuation and then we will tell you whether we will buy ". The two things really ought to work out at the same result, but they may not, and these two sons, being cautious people, say " We want to know what we are in for: before we buy the pig take it out of the poke."

G   Then arises the question about how one arrives at " a reasonable valuation ". It does not necessarily mean that the trustees alone have the right to do the valuing or cause the valuing to be done. It does not say that. The valuation has got to be " reasonable ". The means of arriving at it would have to be agreed by everybody concerned. BURGESS, V.-C. (8), has quite properly cut the Gordian knot by saying that in the event the court must do it for them, and the court will on
H   its side hear the evidence of a valuer, or perhaps two valuers for all I know, called in the inquiry, and each of them of course can use what he knows now or what he knows at the date when the valuation is made to arrive at the purchase price. The valuation is to be made, according to BURGESS, V.-C.'s order, as at the death of the testator. There is no appeal about that, and it is justified, I feel, because the right to have the land at the option accrued at that date; but that
I   does not mean, or it will not mean, when valuation comes, that the valuers are to draw blinkers over their eyes or to shut their eyes to the fact that some time has passed since the testator's death and very likely the lands have very much increased in value since: they are entitled to say what, to-day, knowing what they do, and discounting back for the three years, is the proper market value of these farms. That being so, I am of opinion that BURGESS, V.-C., arrived at the right conclusion.

---

(6) (1807), 14 Ves. 400.   (7) (1853), 3 De G. M. & G. 24.
            (8) [1967] 1 All E.R. at p. 604.

Certain other authorities were cited which were quite in point but I need not **A** go elaborately into them. There was the celebrated case, *Earl of Radnor* v. *Shafto* (9)—celebrated for this reason, that, though LORD ELDON, L.C., is celebrated for his doubts, this is the classic expression of them, because he prefaces his judgment by saying (10) that he had had doubts about the construction of the particular will for twenty years; and it had been in course of administration all that time. He came down quite clearly to the view that it was a thing that the **B** court would do—to put a reasonable price on land in a proper case. He did not do so in that case, for reasons into which I do not think I need go; but the passage (11) quoted in full by BURGESS, V.-C., (12) (which I shall not repeat) shows what LORD ELDON thought; and that adds to the authority, if need be, that an option to buy " at a fair price ", like an agreement " at a fair price ", is an enforceable agreement, an enforceable option, which the court will execute, **C** and if the parties cannot arrive at the fair price the court has means to do it for them in the way that BURGESS, V.-C., has done.

I, therefore, would dismiss this appeal.

DAVIES, L.J.: I agree. I would add to the authorities cited by HARMAN, L.J., two other passages on the effect which the courts have in the past given to a **D** form of words similar to the form which appears in this will. The first one is in *Gaskarth* v. *Lord Lowther* (13) and I would refer, again, to words of LORD ELDON, L.C., (14):

" The answer to the objection, that the offer of Raincock's estate at a fair valuation is too loose, and goes no farther than treaty, is, that it is not unfrequent to have the price ascertained by a third person . . . or, if that **E** person cannot ascertain it, by a reference to the master: all the other terms except the price alone, being agreed upon."

The other passage (and the only other passage to which I will refer) is in the case to which HARMAN, L.J., referred, *Morgan* v. *Milman* (15), where LORD CRANWORTH, L.C., said: **F**

" I confess that upon principle, as well as upon authority, the court cannot here, as it appears to me, take upon itself to do that [that is, to provide the machinery]. If, indeed, there had been an agreement that the price should be that which was to be ascertained upon a fair valuation, then the court might interfere."

G

It is perfectly well established by those dicta, and by the text books to which HARMAN, L.J., has referred, that that is the correct view.

Counsel for the third to sixth defendants sought to argue before this court, as I understood his submission, that the words " a reasonable valuation " are different from " a fair valuation " or " a fair price ". I confess that I was unable to appreciate the difference. It seems to me that in a context such as this the **H** words manifestly mean the same thing.

Apart from that, agreeing, as I do, with what HARMAN, L.J., has said, I do not think that I can usefully add anything.

RUSSELL, L.J.: I also agree. The option is a right or benefit conferred by the will, and the duty of the trustees or executors as such was to take what steps **I** were necessary to give effect to such a benefit so conferred. They should address their minds to the question what was a reasonable valuation, bearing in mind, of

---

(9) (1805), 11 Ves. 448.   (10) (1805), 11 Ves. at p. 453.
(11) (1805), 11 Ves. at pp. 454, 455.
(12) [1967] 1 All E.R. at pp. 603, 604.
(13) (1805), 12 Ves. 107.   (14) (1805), 12 Ves. at p. 113.
                    (15) (1853), 3 De G., M. & G. at p. 34.

A course, as trustees the interests both of the option beneficiaries and of residue;
but they are not, under this will, made the arbiters of what " a reasonable
valuation " is, and if they and the option beneficiaries dispute (as they have done)
on the quantum, it must, it seems to me, be referred to and ascertained by the
court. I do not see that it is necessary or required that the option beneficiary
should exercise his option on the basis of the formula. He should be entitled, and

B I consider is entitled, to exercise his option also on the *result* of applying the
formula: that is to say, he is entitled to know before he exercises his option how
the formula works out so that he may see whether his financial situation justifies
his committing himself. There does not seem to me to be any uncertainty in this
matter: I take the reasonable valuation to be the same as the fair price, or fair
valuation, or proper valuation.

C   I do not accept the proposition that a valid contract inter vivos cannot be
made to sell land " at a fair value ". I do not recall any case which was cited
which said so. On the contrary, as has been pointed out, SIR WILLIAM GRANT,
M.R., in *Milnes* v. *Gery* (16) stated that it could. Also to the same effect was
Gaskarth v. *Lord Lowther* (17), where the offer that was made was in these terms:

D   " I have since your agreeing to purchase bought a small estate of the late
Mr. Raincock's in front of my house . . . I offer that at a fair valuation."

In the course of the litigation a decree was made and the master was directed " to
set a value on the estates of Gaskarth, in the decree described as the estates
purchased of Mr. Raincock ". In due course the master valued that estate at
£1,700. Up to that stage it was either decided or assumed on all hands that that

E was a perfectly valid and enforceable contract when an offer in that form was
accepted. There was possibly also an indication to the same effect in *Morgan* v.
Milman (18): and it seems to have been assumed on all hands in *Waite* v.
Morland (19), and in the text books on the subject, to which reference has
already been made.

    Of course the courts will not fill a lacuna where specific machinery has been

F set up for valuation and that machinery breaks down, except perhaps in the case
of the valuation of matters ancillary to a main sale, such as timber or fixtures;
but in the present case no machinery has been set up: all that has been laid down
is the formula of " reasonable valuation ".

    Finally, it seems to me to be proper to value as at death, although it is admitted
by counsel that knowledge of subsequent developments affecting value should be

G imputed to the person notionally valuing as at the death, on the lines, I suppose,
of *Bwllfa and Merthyr Dare Steam Collieries (1891), Ltd.* v. *Pontypridd Waterworks
Co.* (20).

    So, if I may conclude my views: First, the option might be exercised " blind "
before the formula of " reasonable valuation " is worked out, but, in my judgment,
need not be exercised until the formula is worked out. Second, " reasonable

H value " is the same as " fair value " or " fair price ", and this formula would not
be too uncertain even in an inter vivos contract. Third, if there be not agreement
on the figure, the court may and should determine it. It is not a question of the
machinery provided breaking down, when the court may not substitute other
machinery. No machinery was provided—merely a formula, which the court can
construe and apply. Fourth, the date for valuation is the death. The will, I

I think, is to be construed as offering the property with effect from the death; but
it is admitted that subsequent developments may be considered in that valuation.
Lastly, the option must be exercised, I take it, within a reasonable time after the
formula is worked out.

---

(16) (1807), 14 Ves. at p. 407.
(17) (1805), 12 Ves. 107.
(18) (1853), 3 De G. M. & G. 24.
(19) (1866), 14 L.T. 649.
(20) [1900-03] All E.R. Rep. 600; [1903] A.C. 426.

I agree that the decision of BURGESS, V.-C., (21) was right and with the order   **A**
he made, and that the appeal fails.

Appeal dismissed.

Solicitors: *Gregory, Rowcliffe & Co.*, agents for *Edward L. Alker & Ball*, Wigan
(for the third, fourth, fifth and sixth defendants); *Hamlins, Grammer & Hamlin*,
agents for *Thomas R. Dootson & Co.*, Leigh (for the plaintiffs); *Sharpe, Pritchard* **B**
& Co., agents for *Ackerley, Heaton & Pigot*, Wigan (for the first and second
defendants).

[*Reported by* HENRY SUMMERFIELD, ESQ., *Barrister-at-Law.*]

C

MASON (Inspector of Taxes) *v.* INNES.

[COURT OF APPEAL, CIVIL DIVISION (Lord Denning, M.R., Davies and Russell,
L.JJ.), April 28, May 1, 2, 1967.]

D

*Income Tax—Profits—Author—Gift of rights in unpublished book to father—
Whether author taxable on value of rights—Income Tax Act, 1952 (15 & 16
Geo. 6 & 1 Eliz. 2 c. 10), Sch. D.*

The taxpayer, a well-known and successful author, who was about to
publish a new book, assigned the rights in the book (valued at £15,425) to his
father by way of gift. The taxpayer's expenses of travelling to the Persian **E**
Gulf to gather material for the book were allowed as a deduction from his
income for income tax purposes, and it was found that the writing of the book
and the disposal of the rights took place in the course of the carrying on by
the taxpayer of his profession as an author. The taxpayer, whose earnings
were assessed to income tax on a cash basis (viz., actual receipts less actual
expenditure), was assessed to tax on the estimated value of the rights in the **F**
book assigned to his father as if it were the taxpayer's income.

Held: the taxpayer was not chargeable to income tax on the gift which he
made of copyright in his book (see p. 928, letter I, p. 929, letter I, and p.
930, letter B, post).

Sharkey (Inspector of Taxes) v. Wernher ([1955] 3 All E.R. 493)
distinguished.   **G**

Per LORD DENNING, M.R.: the principle of *Sharkey* v. *Wernher** does not
extend beyond the cases of traders who keep stock-in-trade and whose
accounts are or should be kept on an earnings basis but a professional man
comes within the general principle that when nothing is received there is
nothing to be brought into account (see p. 928, letter F, post; cf., p. 929,
letter H, post). **H**

Decision of GOFF, J., ([1967] 1 All E.R. 760) affirmed.

[As to what constitute trade receipts for income tax purposes, see 20 HALS-
BURY'S LAWS (3rd Edn.) 149-158, paras. 262-276; 240-243, paras. 442-444; and
for cases on the subject, see 28 DIGEST (Repl.) 71-86, *268-328;* 154-158, *594-623.*

For the Income Tax Act, 1952, s. 471, see 31 HALSBURY'S STATUTES (2nd Edn.) **I**
445.

For the Finance Act, 1960, s. 32, see 40 HALSBURY'S STATUTES (2nd Edn.) 452.]

---

(21) [1967] 1 All E.R. 601.
* [1955] 3 All E.R. 493; the principle for which the Crown contended, as applied to
the present case, is that the appropriation of an asset, which has been produced in the
course of a trade or profession, to the trader's or professional man's own purposes,
amounts to a realisation of that asset or receipt of its value, so that he must bring it
into account for income tax purposes (see p. 928, letter D, post).

A Cases referred to:

  Carson (Inspector of Taxes) v. *Peter Cheyney's Executor*, [1958] 3 All E.R. 573;
    [1959] A.C. 412; [1958] 3 W.L.R. 740; 38 Tax Cas. 240; 28 Digest
    (Repl.) 155, *598.*

  Petrotim Securities, Ltd. (formerly Gresham Trust, Ltd.) v. *Ayres (Inspector of
    Taxes)*, [1964] 1 All E.R. 269; [1964] 1 W.L.R. 190; 41 Tax Cas. 389;

B   3rd Digest Supp.

  Sharkey (Inspector of Taxes) v. *Wernher*, [1955] 3 All E.R. 493; [1956] A.C. 58;
    [1955] 3 W.L.R. 671; 36 Tax Cas. 275; 28 Digest (Repl.) 74, *280.*

Appeal.

 This was an appeal from a decision of GOFF, J., dated Dec. 9, 1966, and reported
[1967] 1 All E.R. 760, dismissing the appeal of the Crown from the order of the
C Special Commissioners of Income Tax discharging an additional assessment of
income tax made against the taxpayer in respect of all the rights in his book
" The Doomed Oasis ", of which the taxpayer had executed an assignment to
his father by way of " natural love and affection " on Apr. 4, 1960. The market
value of the rights assigned was £15,425. It was contended by the Crown that
the taxpayer should be charged to income tax in respect of that sum, although he
D had not received any money for the rights assigned, but had given them away.

 Hubert H. Monroe, Q.C., and *J. R. Phillips* for the Crown.
 R. E. Borneman, Q.C., and *R. A. Watson* for the taxpayer.

  LORD DENNING, M.R.: The taxpayer, Mr. Hammond Innes, is a writer
of distinction who has for many years carried on the profession of an author.
E He has written many novels and travel books. He has kept his accounts on a
cash basis and has submitted these to the Revenue for tax purposes. On the one
side, he has included his receipts from royalties and so forth. On the other side,
he has included the expenses of his travels overseas to gather material; the
expenses of his study at home; and a small salary to his wife for her work for
him. In this case we are concerned with one particular novel which he wrote
F called " The Doomed Oasis ". It was based on material which he had gathered
in the Persian Gulf in 1953. He started to write it in September, 1958, and
worked on it up till 1959. He charged all the expenses in his accounts for those
years. In 1960 he was about to publish it; but he felt that he would like to do
something to support his father who had retired on modest resources. So the
taxpayer decided to transfer the copyright in the book, " The Doomed Oasis ",
G to his father as a gift. By an assignment made on Apr. 4, 1960, he assigned to his
father " in consideration of natural love and affection " the copyright, performing rights and all other rights in " The Doomed Oasis ". The question arises
whether he is liable to tax on the value of those rights in " The Doomed Oasis ".
If he had sold the rights at that time in 1960 their market value would have been
£15,425. The Crown says that that sum ought to be brought into his accounts and
H that he should be taxed on it, although he did not receive a penny for the rights
because he had given them away. I may add that the taxpayer had also before
publication assigned rights in two others of his novels, one to his mother and the
other to his mother-in-law. So a like question may arise there.

 I start with the elementary principle of income tax law that a man cannot be
taxed on profits that he might have, but has not, made: see *Sharkey (Inspector
I of Taxes)* v. *Wernher* (1). At first sight that elementary principle seems to cover
this case. The taxpayer did not receive anything from " The Doomed Oasis ".
In the case of a trader there is, however, an exception to that principle. I take
for simplicity the trade of a grocer. He makes out his accounts on an " earnings
basis ". He brings in the value of his stock-in-trade at the beginning and end of
the year: he brings in his purchases and sales; the debts owed by him and to
him; and so arrives at his profit or loss. If such a trader appropriates to himself

---

(1) [1955] 3 All E.R. 493; 36 Tax Cas. 275.

part of his stock-in-trade, such as tins of beans, and uses them for his own **A**
purposes, he must bring them into his accounts at their market value. A trader
who supplies himself is accountable for the market value. That is established by
Sharkey v. *Wernher* (2) itself. Now, suppose that such a trader does not supply
himself with tins of beans, but gives them away to a friend or relative. Again he
has to bring them in at their market value. That was established by *Petrotim*
Securities, Ltd. (*formerly Gresham Trust, Ltd.*) v. *Ayres* (*Inspector of Taxes*) (3).   **B**

Counsel for the Crown contends that that exception is not confined to traders.
It extends, he says, to professional men, such as authors, artists, barristers and
many others. These professional men do not keep accounts on an " earnings
basis ". They keep them on a " cash basis ": by which I mean that on one side
of the account they enter the actual money which they expend; and on the other
side they enter the actual money which they receive. They have no stock-in-   **C**
trade to bring into the accounts. They do not bring in debts owing by or to them,
nor work in progress. They enter only expenses on the one side and receipts on
the other. Counsel for the Crown contended that liability to tax did not and
should not depend on the way in which a man keeps his accounts. There is no
difference in principle, he says, between a trader and a professional man. He
stated his proposition quite generally in this way. The appropriation of an asset,   **D**
which has been produced in the ordinary course of a trade or profession, to the
trader's or professional man's own purposes, amounts to a realisation of that
asset or the receipt of its value, and he must bring it into account. I cannot
accept this proposition. Suppose an artist paints a picture of his mother and gives
it to her. He does not receive a penny for it. Is he to pay tax on the value of it?
It is unthinkable. Suppose he paints a picture which he does not like when he   **E**
has finished it and destroys it. Is he liable to pay tax on the value of it? Clearly
not. These instances—and they could be extended endlessly—show that the
proposition in *Sharkey* v. *Wernher* (4) does not apply to professional men. It is
confined to the case of traders who keep stock-in-trade and whose accounts are,
or should be, kept on an earnings basis, whereas a professional man comes within
the general principle that, when nothing is received, there is nothing to be   **F**
brought into account.

I would add only that the legislature seems to have acted on this footing.
Section 471 of the Income Tax Act, 1952, applies where an author has spent more
than twelve months in writing a book and sells it for a lump sum. He can
" spread " the lump sum over two or three years: so that his tax on it does not
fall all in one year. That provision only applies to lump sums received by him.   **G**
If the legislature had thought he was liable for the market value of books given
away, surely they would have extended the " spread " to those cases also.

Take next the case of *Carson* (*Inspector of Taxes*) v. *Peter Cheyney's Executor*
(5). The House of Lords held that when an author dies or discontinues his
profession, he is not taxable on moneys received after the date of discontinuance.
That was altered by s. 32 of the Finance Act, 1960. He now becomes chargeable   **H**
on sums arising from his profession, even though he receives them after he has
discontinued it. This provision does not apply when he gives a book away. If
the legislature had thought he was chargeable on its value, I should have thought
it would have covered that case too.

I hold that the taxpayer is not chargeable with tax on gifts which he makes of
copyright in his books. I think that Goff, J., (6) and the Commissioners came to   **I**
a right decision. I would dismiss this appeal.

DAVIES, L.J.: I agree. It is not in dispute that there is no specific provision
in tax legislation to cover the present case. What is sought by the Crown in this

(2) [1955] 3 All E.R. 493; 36 Tax Cas. 275.
(3) [1964] 1 All E.R. 269; 41 Tax Cas. 389.
(4) [1955] 3 All E.R. 493; 36 Tax Cas. 275.
(5) [1958] 3 All E.R. 573; 38 Tax Cas. 240.

(6) [1967] 1 All E.R. 760.

A case is to extend what is said to have been the principle in *Sharkey (Inspector of Taxes)* v. *Wernher* (7) to what I, like LORD DENNING, M.R., regard as being an entirely different set of circumstances. I, too, think that it is very remarkable that if the Crown were right in the present case, the result would inevitably follow that there could be no spread-over over a period of two or, as the case may be, three years under the provisions of s. 471 of the Income Tax Act, 1952. If the

B taxpayer is assessable on the sum of £15,000 odd (which is the agreed figure for the value of the copyright in this work) then, as I understand it, he would have to pay income tax, and of course, surtax, on the whole of that sum on the basis of its having been earned in one year. That strikes one as being a very remarkable state of affairs.

The position of a novelist was adverted to in the speech of LORD KEITH OF

C AVONHOLM in *Carson (Inspector of Taxes)* v. *Peter Cheyney's Executor* (8), where he said this:

> " I turn, accordingly, to consider what is involved in the professional activities of an author during his life. An author writes books generally for profit or in the hope of profit. It is only when they make a profit that any question of assessing him on the profits of a profession can arise. It is

D only by exploiting the work of his brain and his pen that he can make any professional income."

The contention on behalf of the Crown in this case is that although the tax-payer has not made, and will not in the present state of affairs ever make, any profit out of the copyright in this work, he must be deemed to have made the

E profit of £15,000 odd because he could have made that profit if he had not given the rights away to his father. That seems to me to be an extraordinary extension of anything that was said in *Sharkey* v. *Wernher* (7). I should refer to the words of LORD RADCLIFFE in *Sharkey* v. *Wernher* (9), on which great reliance was placed by the Crown. In this passage of his speech LORD RADCLIFFE was dealing with the difference on the facts of that case between a cost of production valuation

F and a market valuation, and he said this (9):

> ". . . it seems to me better economics to credit the trading owner with the current realisable value of any stock which he has chosen to dispose of without commercial disposal than to credit him with an amount equivalent to the accumulated expenses in respect of that stock. In that sense, the trader's choice is itself the receipt, in that he appropriates value to himself

G or his donee direct instead of adopting the alternative method of commercial sale and subsequent appropriation of the proceeds."

I agree with LORD DENNING, M.R., that that principle which was enunciated on the facts of that case, which was really concerned with the method of valuation rather than with anything else, can be applied only to a trader or to a person whose accounts are made up on an earnings basis and who has stock-in-trade

H which he may, other than in a commercial manner, transfer to himself or for no consideration to a third party. If the position contended for by the Crown in this case ought to be the law, it seems to me that in the years which have elapsed since 1954 when *Sharkey* v. *Wernher* (7) was decided, provision should have been made to that effect by legislation in the various Acts that have been passed by Parliament. For those reasons, in addition to what has been said by LORD

I DENNING, M.R., I agree that this appeal should be dismissed.

RUSSELL, L.J.: The Crown accepts that it is a general principle of income tax law that a man is taxed on the basis of what he receives and not on what he might have received. The Crown says, however, that the principles which led to the decision in *Sharkey (Inspector of Taxes)* v. *Wernher* (7) lead inevitably

---

(7) [1955] 3 All E.R. 493; 36 Tax Cas. 275.
(8) [1958] 3 All E.R. at p. 584; 38 Tax Cas. at p. 267.
(9) [1955] 3 All E.R. at p. 506; 36 Tax Cas. at p. 307.

to a decision in favour of the Crown also in the present case. I cannot accept that. **A** *Sharkey* v. *Wernher* (10) was dealing with a disposal of stock-in-trade by a trader whose annual profits were computed on an earnings basis, the stock-in-trade being a necessary part of the computation. The copyright and other rights in the book now in question in no sense formed stock-in-trade of the taxpayer, and before the assignment to his father they had no part in any computation of profits and gains. For tax purposes his annual profits were computed on a cash **B** basis. It seems to me that the Crown is trying to impose tax, on the one hand, by computation on a cash basis and, on the other hand, by computation on an earnings basis, thus seeking to mix oil and water. In the end, however, I am entirely unable to see that the decision in *Sharkey* v. *Wernher* (10) pushes us to the length suggested and I decline to travel that length without being forced to.

Appeal dismissed. Leave to appeal to House of Lords granted, on condition that **C** *that Crown pay both sides' costs in the House of Lords and leave the orders as to costs in the courts below undisturbed.*

Solicitors: *Solicitor of Inland Revenue* (for the Crown); *Field, Roscoe & Co.* (for the taxpayer).

[*Reported by* F. A. AMIES, ESQ., *Barrister-at-Law.*] **D**

MACSAGA INVESTMENT CO., LTD.
v. LUPTON (Inspector of Taxes).

[COURT OF APPEAL, CIVIL DIVISION (Lord Denning, M.R., Harman and Salmon, **E** L.JJ.), February 7, 8, March 15, 1967.]

Income Tax—Allowance—Machinery or plant—Wear and tear—Sub-lease of building containing heating equipment and lifts—Sub-lessors were property investment company and sub-lessee was a government department—Full repairing covenant by sub-lessee—Machinery likely to require replacement **F** *during currency of sub-lease—Whether allowance available only where machinery and plant used for trade—Whether sub-let on terms that burden of wear and tear fell directly on sub-lessor—Income Tax Act, 1952 (15 & 16 Geo. 6 & 1 Eliz. 2 c. 10), s. 298.*

The taxpayer company, a property investment company, sub-let a building to a government department for a period of thirty-five years from June 24, **G** 1958. The sub-lessee entered into a full repairing covenant. The building contained heating equipment, lifts and other fittings (" the equipment "). The anticipated life of the heating equipment and lifts was twenty-five years, so that it was probable that the sub-lessee would have to replace them during the currency of the sub-lease. The taxpayer company claimed an allowance under s. 298 (1)* of the Income Tax Act, 1952, on account of the **H** wear and tear of the equipment.

Held: (i) s. 298 (1) applied only to machinery or plant used for a trade, and, as none of the equipment was used for the purpose of a trade, the taxpayer company were not entitled to the allowance which they claimed (see p. 932, letters E and F, p. 934, letters E and H, p. 936, letter F, and p. 937, letter F, post).

(ii) moreover (per HARMAN and SALMON, L.JJ.), the obligation to replace **I** such items of the equipment as during the term sub-demised would be replaced in all probability by the sub-lessee fell on the sub-lessee, and accordingly the items were not let, for the purposes of s. 298 (1), on such terms that the burden of their wear and tear fell directly on the taxpayer company (see p. 934, letter I, to p. 935, letter B, and p. 939, letter F, post).

---

(10) [1955] 3 All E.R. 493; 36 Tax Cas. 275.
* Section 298 (1), so far as material, is set out at p. 932, letter C, post.

A   Observations of LORD DENNING, M.R., and SALMON, L.J., on the meaning of the words " wear and tear " in s. 298 (1) of the Income Tax Act, 1952, and whether they meant depreciation (see p. 932, letter H, et seq., and p. 937, letter I, et seq., post; cf., p. 935, letter C, post).

Decision of PENNYCUICK, J., ([1966] 3 All E.R. 375) affirmed on different grounds.

B   [As to tax allowances to lessors and lessees of machinery and plant, see 20 HALSBURY'S LAWS (3rd Edn.) 494, paras. 945, 946; and for cases on the subject, see 28 DIGEST (Repl.) 135, 136, *508, 515*.

For the Income Tax Act, 1952, s. 298, s. 299, see 31 HALSBURY'S STATUTES (2nd Edn.) 290.]

C   Cases referred to:

Boarland (Inspector of Taxes) v. *Pirie, Appleton & Co., Ltd., Stem Co., Ltd.* v. *Hyett*, [1940] 1 All E.R. 539; [1940] 1 K.B. 841; 109 L.J.K.B. 440; 23 Tax Cas. 547; *affd.*, C.A. [1940] 3 All E.R. 306; [1940] 2 K.B. 491; 109 L.J.K.B. 967; 163 L.T. 276; 23 Tax Cas. 547; 28 Digest (Repl.) 135, *508*.

D   *Hall (John) Junior & Co.* v. *Rickman*, [1904-07] All E.R. Rep. 946; [1906] 1 K.B. 311; 75 L.J.K.B. 178; 94 L.T. 224; 28 Digest (Repl.) 135, *509*.

Hinton (Inspector of Taxes) v. *Maden & Ireland, Ltd.*, [1959] 3 All E.R. 356; [1959] 1 W.L.R. 875; Digest (Cont. Vol. A) 874, *480a*.

Union Cold Storage Co., Ltd. v. *Simpson (Inspector of Taxes)*, *Union Cold Storage Co., Ltd.* v. *Ellerker*, [1938] 4 All E.R. 673; *revsd.* C.A., [1939]

E   2 All E.R. 94; [1939] 2 K.B. 440; 108 L.J.K.B. 681; 160 L.T. 515; 22 Tax Cas. 547; 28 Digest (Repl.) 136, *515*.

Appeal.

This was an appeal by the taxpayer company against the decision of PENNY-CUICK, J., dated July 6, 1966, dismissing their appeal against the decision of the Special Commissioners of Income Tax, given on Aug. 19, 1964, refusing their

F   claim under s. 298 of the Income Tax Act, 1952, for an allowance in respect of wear and tear of machinery or plant for the year 1960-61. The taxpayer company held a building lease of a London site and, when the building was completed, sub-let the whole of it to the Minister of Works for thirty-five years from June 24, 1958. Among other equipment the building contained lifts, which the sub-lessee replaced in 1960, and central heating. The expected life of the lifts was twenty-

G   five years. The questions for the commissioners' decision were (i) whether certain heating equipment, lifts, sprinklers, incinerators and fittings were machinery or plant within the meaning of s. 298 (1); and if they were, whether they were let on such terms that the burden of their wear and tear fell directly on the taxpayer company as lessor so as to entitle the company to the allowance claimed under the section. The commissioners found that those items of equipment were not in

H   use in any trade and they held that they were not, therefore, machinery or plant within the meaning of s. 298 (1). PENNYCUICK, J., held that s. 299 of the Act of 1952 applied, and, since it was common ground that s. 298 and s. 299 could not both apply, s. 298 did not apply.

Heyworth Talbot, Q.C., *H. Major Allen*, Q.C., and *B. Pinson* for the taxpayer company.

I   *Hubert H. Monroe*, Q.C., and *J. R. Phillips* for the Crown.

Cur. adv. vult.

Mar. 15. The following judgments were read.

LORD DENNING, M.R.: The facts appear in the Case Stated (1) and I need only summarise them. On Dec. 11, 1958, Macsaga Investment Co., Ltd. (" the taxpayer company ") sub-let to the Minister of Works a block of offices

---

(1) See [1966] 3 All E.R. 375 at pp. 376, 379; [1967] Ch. 167 at pp. 168, 169.

called Southbridge House, Park Street, S.E.1 for thirty-five years from June 24, **A**
1958, at a rent of £55,000 a year. It contained heating equipment (by oil-fired
burners with circulating water), lifts (three of them), sprinklers, incinerators and
fittings. All these formed part of the premises sub-let to the Minister. The tenant
entered into a full repairing covenant to keep the premises in good and substantial
repair. There was no exception for " fair wear and tear ". The anticipated life
of the heating equipment and lifts was only twenty-five years: so it was probable **B**
that the tenant during the sub-lease would have to renew them. In point of fact
the original lifts were not satisfactory and the tenant installed new ones in 1960,
two years after the beginning of the sub-lease.

The question is whether the taxpayer company, in computing their profits, are
entitled to an annual wear and tear allowance in respect of heating equipment,
lifts, sprinklers, incinerators and fittings. This depends on the true construction **C**
of s. 298 (1) of the Income Tax Act, 1952, which provides:

" Where machinery or plant is let upon such terms that the burden of the
wear and tear falls directly upon the lessor, there shall be made to him, for
each year of assessment, an allowance on account of the wear and tear of so
much of the machinery or plant as is in use at the end of the year . . ."

The first point: **D**

The first point is whether, in order to qualify for an annual allowance, the
machinery and plant must be in use in a trade. In my opinion s. 298 applies
only to machinery or plant which is in use for the purpose of a trade. The section
is one of the group of sections, s. 279 to s. 304, which are concerned with machinery
and plant used by a person in carrying on a trade. Section 279 deals with the **E**
case where the trader himself owns the machinery and plant and uses it in his
trade. Section 298 and s. 299 deal with the case where the trader does not own
the machinery and plant but hires it on lease from the owner. Section 299 by
express words contemplates the carrying on of a trade. Section 298 does so by
implication. The judge (2) did not feel able to make this implication; but I
think that it should be made. I find myself in agreement with the Special **F**
Commissioners on this point.

In this case it is plain that none of the items was in use for the purpose of a
trade at all. The taxpayer company were not traders. They were a property
investment company. The ministry were not traders. They were a government
department. Not being used for a trade, the items do not qualify for an annual
allowance at all. The Special Commissioners, in case they were wrong on this **G**
first point, went on to consider the second point. So did the judge (3). I propose
to do the same.

The second point:

The second point is whether " the burden of the wear and tear " fell on the
taxpayer company. This point depends on the meaning of the " wear and
tear " of machinery and plant in s. 298. This is a phrase which runs through all **H**
the provisions about annual allowances from 1878 onwards. Section 12 of the
Customs and Inland Revenue Act, 1878 is the parent section which is re-enacted,
with intervening amendments, in s. 280, s. 298 and s. 299 of the Income Tax
Act, 1952. I think that " wear and tear " in these sections means " depreciation ".
The position can be tested by taking four instances.

First, take a trader who has himself bought and owns the machinery and plant **I**
with which he carries on his trade. It is a capital asset. He expends money in
keeping it in good repair. He can deduct the cost of these repairs in computing
the profits of his trade; but in spite of all these repairs, it diminishes in value. It
may have a working life of only ten years, at the end of which it is worth nothing.
It is a wasting asset. In 1878 the legislature said that he could deduct an " annual
allowance " to cover that depreciation in capital value. The deduction was made

(2) [1966] 3 All E.R. at pp. 379-382; [1967] Ch. at pp. 176-179.
(3) [1966] 3 All E.R. at p. 382; [1967] Ch. at p. 179.

A each year by taking an agreed percentage of prime cost. In a case in 1906 the percentages over the years came to more than one hundred per cent. of prime cost and still the trader was allowed to go on deducting a percentage; see *John Hall Junior & Co.* v. *Rickman* (4). In the next year Parliament intervened to prevent him from deducting in total any more than the actual cost.

B In cases of that kind (when the trader owns the machinery and plant) there is no difficulty. The trader deducts the cost of repairs to arrive at his profits and he gets, in addition, an annual allowance for depreciation. If, however, you look at the sections, you will find that the word " depreciation " is not used at all. The phrase used is " wear and tear ". In s. 12 of the Act of 1878 and r. 6 (1) of the Rules applicable to Sch. D in the Income Tax Act, 1918, the annual allowance is given for " the diminished value by reason of wear and tear ". In this context

C it clearly means " diminished value by reason of depreciation ". Likewise in s. 280 of the Act of 1952 an allowance is made to the trader " on account of the wear and tear ", clearly meaning on account of depreciation.

Secondly, take a trader who does not own the machinery and plant but hires it from the owner on the terms that the tenant must maintain it and deliver it over in good condition at the end of the lease. Its working life is, say, good for ten

D years: but the lease is only for five years. The trader expends money in keeping it in good repair. He can deduct the cost of those repairs in computing his profits of the trade. But meanwhile the machinery and plant has depreciated in value. At the end of the five years when the owner gets it back, it may be worth only half as much as at the beginning. Who is to get the annual allowance for depreciation? Good sense requires that the owner should get it, because he is the one who

E has suffered the capital loss; but on the original wording of s. 12 of the Act of 1878 and r. 6 (2) of the Act of 1918, the lessee got the annual allowance for depreciation because he was by the terms of the lease " bound to maintain " it. That appears from *Union Cold Storage Co., Ltd.* v. *Simpson (Inspector of Taxes), Union Cold Storage Co., Ltd.* v. *Ellerker* (5), where the lessee got the allowance, even though the lessor made all the capital renewals. This was put right in the

F next year by s. 22 of the Finance Act, 1940 which did not give the lessee the annual allowance unless the commissioners were satisfied that " the burden of the wear and tear of the machinery or plant will in fact fall directly " on the lessee. I think that " wear and tear " is there used in the same sense as in my first illustration where a trader is himself the owner. It means depreciation. I am confirmed in this view by *Boarland (Inspector of Taxes)* v. *Pirie, Appleton &*

G *Co., Ltd., Stem Co., Ltd.* v. *Hyett* (6). That concerned a factory. The tenant was under full repairing covenants and sought to get the deduction for depreciation. He was not allowed it. WROTTESLEY, J., said (7) that it was absurd

" that a tenant, who, unlike an owner, does not himself ultimately bear the loss due to depreciation should, nevertheless, be given a measure of relief as though he did bear that burden."

H This court (8) agreed with his reasons and affirmed his decision. It was a decision on a different statute; but the absurdity is the same. It would be absurd that the tenant should get the annual allowance for depreciation when he does not suffer the loss due to depreciation.

Thirdly, take again the case of a trader who is a lessee of machinery, but the working life of the machinery is ten years and the lease is twenty years. The

I trader expends money every year in keeping it in repair. It wears out after ten years. He expends money in the tenth year in getting a new machine. He can deduct the whole cost of it in computing his profits. Is he entitled to the annual allowance as well? Clearly not. The lessor should get the annual allowance on

(4) [1904-07] All E.R. Rep. 946; [1906] 1 K.B. 311.
(5) [1939] 2 All E.R. 94; 22 Tax Cas. 547.
(6) [1940] 1 All E.R. 539; on appeal, [1940] 3 All E.R. 306; 23 Tax Cas. 547.
(7) [1940] 1 All E.R. at p. 543; 23 Tax Cas. at p. 554.
(8) [1940] 3 All E.R. 306; 23 Tax Cas. 547.

the original machinery (because he has suffered the depreciation) and, when it is   A
replaced, neither should get an annual allowance on the replacement (because the
tenant has deducted the cost in computing his profits).

Fourthly, take the case where a lessor lets machinery and plant to a trader on
the terms that the lessor will do all repairs and renew it whenever it wears out.
In such a case the lessor will usually himself be a trader. He deducts the cost of
repairs in computing his profits and he gets the annual allowance on his capital   B
expenditure on the original item and on renewals. That is fair enough. The case
falls within s. 298 (1) because the burden of the " wear and tear ", i.e., the depreciation, falls on him and he has to renew the capital asset; see *Hinton (Inspector of
Taxes)* v. *Maden & Ireland, Ltd.* (9). It is similar to the first instance which I
have taken.

If the machinery and plant in this case were in use in a trade, it would fall   C
within the third instance above. The burden of the " wear and tear " would fall
on the sub-lessors (the taxpayer company) and they would be entitled to the
annual allowance on it. I would agree with the Special Commissioners on this
point.

Conclusion:

Those two points are the only questions of law raised in the Case Stated and   D
discussed before us. I refrain from discussing any other point. I find myself in
agreement with the Special Commissioners on both points and in disagreement
with the judge (10). In the result, however, the taxpayer company are not
entitled to an annual allowance and I would dismiss the appeal.

HARMAN, L.J. (read by SALMON, L.J.): I concur with both my brethren   E
in holding that this appeal should be dismissed. I concur with each of them in
founding this opinion on the view that the articles of machinery comprised in the
sub-demise of the leasehold property in question, Southbridge House, Park
Street, S.E.1, are not " machinery or plant " within the meaning of s. 298 and
s. 299 of the Income Tax Act, 1952. A study of Part 10 of the Act of 1952 shows
that it gives various reliefs in respect of industrial buildings and structures and   F
the whole Part is entirely devoted to trade. It is true that a study of the Part
shows that there can be something described as machinery or plant in a building
where no trade is carried on, but a clear distinction is made between machinery
or plant so employed and machinery or plant employed in an industrial structure
devoted to trade. The judge (11) seems to have construed the two sections in
isolation, and not finding the word " trade " in s. 298 (1)—" so much of the   G
machinery or plant as is in use [in the trade] at the end of the year "—he declined
to import the words in square brackets. If that be right, s. 298 and s. 299 do not
cover the same ground because the latter expressly speaks of " a person by whom
the trade is carried on ". This seems not only to refer to the section where it
appears, but being " the trade " and not " a trade ", refers back to the preceding
section. Again the two sections, as everybody agreed at the hearing, cover the   H
whole field, but on the judge's view (11) s. 298 would apply whether or no a trade
were carried on but s. 299 only in the latter event. In order to make these two
sections work at all, they must be applied to the same subject-matter, namely,
the subject-matter of a demise in which trade is carried on either by lessor or
lessee. This is enough to determine the appeal.

The claim made here was for wear and tear during the year 1960-61. When one   I
looks at the facts, the machinery then in use in the building was not the machinery
demised by the underlease at all but other machinery installed by the sub-lessee
at his own expense because he was dissatisfied with the lift installed at the time
of the demise. Moreover, the evidence was that the life of these new lifts, and still
more of the older ones which they replaced, was likely to be a good deal shorter

(9) [1959] 3 All E.R. 356.
(10) [1966] 3 All E.R. 375; [1967] Ch. 167.
(11) [1966] 3 All E.R. at pp. 379-382; [1967] Ch. at pp. 176-179.

A than the term of the sub-lease and it seems clear that when they wear out, the Crown as sub-lessee will be bound under the terms of the sub-lease to replace them at its own expense. Under these circumstances I am unable to see how it can be maintained on behalf of the taxpayer company that under the terms on which the machinery was let, the taxpayer company could be entitled to an allowance in respect of the year 1960-61, for the burden of replacing the machinery would

B fall, as it had in fact fallen, on the Crown as sub-lessee. It is to be observed that the Crown, not being a trader, could never make a claim under s. 299. I, therefore, agree with my brother SALMON, L.J., on what he calls his third point, this point not being dealt with by LORD DENNING, M.R.

On the vexed question on which my brothers differ, I do not propose to decide. It is a purely hypothetical question which cannot arise because there is no

C machinery or plant to which it can apply, and I do not find it profitable to enquire whether, if a state of things existed which cannot exist, a right could arise in favour of the sub-lessor which could not arise in favour of the sub-lessee because of the fact to which I have already alluded, that s. 299 is expressly confined to the case of a person carrying on the trade.

D   SALMON, L.J.: On Dec. 11, 1958, the taxpayer company granted a full repairing underlease to the Minister of Works of an office block known as South-bridge House in South East London for a period of thirty-five years from June 24, 1958. These premises contained fixed equipment consisting, amongst other things, of certain lifts and boilers. No trade or business has ever been carried on in Southbridge House, nor do the taxpayer company carry on the business

E of letting machinery or plant or any business other than that of a property investment company. The taxpayer company contend that on the true con-struction of s. 298 of the Income Tax Act, 1952, the equipment to which I have referred is " machinery or plant ", that it is deemed to be used for the purpose of a trade carried on by them, and that " the burden of the wear and tear thereof falls directly upon " them. The taxpayer company, accordingly,

F contend that they are entitled to the allowance granted by the section.

The three questions which have been canvassed on this appeal are:

1. Is the meaning of the words " machinery or plant " in s. 298 of the Income Tax Act, 1952 confined to equipment used for the purpose of a trade? Or, put in a slightly different way, does the section grant any allowance in respect of machinery or plant which is not in fact used for the purpose of a trade?

G   2. What do the words " burden of the wear and tear " mean?

3. Does this burden fall on the taxpayer company?

The first question:

If s. 298 is read in isolation, the construction for which the taxpayer company contend as to the meaning of " machinery or plant " might well be right. I do

H not consider, however, that it is permissible to look at this section in isolation. It must be looked at within the framework in which it appears and in the light of the manifest policy of the Act of 1952. This section is one of a group of sections in Chapter 2 of Part 10 of the Act of 1952 dealing with reliefs for certain capital expenditure in relation to machinery and plant. It seems to me to be plain that the whole chapter is dealing with nothing but allowances in respect of equipment

I used in trade. There can, I think, be no doubt (and indeed it is conceded) that every section in this chapter other than s. 298 refers only to equipment so used. The essential characteristics of the words " machinery or plant ", whenever mentioned in this chapter of the Act of 1952, is that they are used in trade. Section 279 and s. 280 deal respectively with the initial allowance and annual allowance to be made to a trader who has incurred capital expenditure on the provision of machinery or plant used for the purposes of his trade. Section 281 to s. 291 deal with the various methods of calculating such allowances by way of limitation and otherwise. Section 292 to s. 296 deal with balancing allowances and charges. All

these sections are concerned with the trader who has spent his capital in acquiring   A
machinery or plant used for the purposes of his trade. They are followed by a
series of sections (including s. 298 and s. 299) described in the Act of 1952 as
supplemental to them. It seems to me that at this stage the legislature, satisfied
that it has dealt with the allowances to be made to the trader who has himself
expended capital in the acquisition of machinery or plant used for the purposes
of his trade, goes on to consider to whom such allowances should be made when   B
machinery or plant which is used by a trader for the purposes of his trade has
been let to him. Should the allowance be made to the lessee trader himself or to
the lessor? The criterion (with which I will deal when considering questions 2 and
3) depends on the incidence of the burden of wear and tear. Section 298 lays down
the conditions under which the allowance should be made to the lessor; s. 299
those under which it should be made to the lessee. Clearly the allowance cannot   C
be made to both the lessor and the lessee. The sections are mutually exclusive
and must be read together in order to understand what is included in and excluded
from each. For this purpose the scheme of the Act of 1952 is the same as that of
the statutes it replaces but it is more elaborate than any of them. These statutes
are the Customs and Inland Revenue Act, 1878, the Income Tax Acts of 1918 and
1945, and the Finance Act, 1949. I will read the relevant words of both the   D
subsections of s. 298 of the Act of 1952:

> " (1) Where machinery or plant is let upon such terms that the burden of
> the wear and tear thereof falls directly upon the lessor, there shall be made
> to him, for each year of assessment, an allowance on account of the wear and
> tear of so much of the machinery or plant as is in use at the end of the
> year . . . (2) The preceding provisions of this Chapter shall apply in relation   E
> to any such lessor of machinery or plant as is mentioned in sub-s. (1) of this
> section as if the machinery or plant were, during the period of the letting,
> in use for the purpose of a trade carried on by him . . ."

In my judgment the words " machinery or plant " in sub-s. (1) apply only to
equipment used in a trade. The whole scheme of Chapters 1 and 2 of this Part   F
of the Act of 1952 is to grant allowances solely in respect of trade and kindred
occupations. Chapter 1 deals with allowances in respect of industrial buildings,
viz., buildings in which a trade is being carried on. Chapter 2 (the one with which
we are concerned) deals with allowances in respect of machinery or plant used
in trade carried on in such industrial buildings. As I have already indicated, it is
in my view an essential characteristic of " machinery or plant " that it is used in   G
trade. Accordingly, in my judgment equipment which is not used in a trade
cannot be " machinery or plant " within the meaning of those words in sub-s. (1)
of s. 298. It is only if the equipment is used in a trade and is therefore " machinery
or plant " within sub-s. (1) that sub-s. (2) can come into operation. In such a case
sub-s. (2) deems that it is the lessor who is carrying on the trade in which the
machinery or plant is being used and applies the preceding provisions of Chapter 2   H
to the lessor. It does not in my view deem that a trade is being carried on when
in fact it is not.

Section 299 is complementary to s. 298 and shows when the allowance is to be
granted to the lessee instead of the lessor. The opening words of s. 299, " where
machinery or plant is let to the person by whom *the* trade is carried on . . .", in
my view support the construction which I have put on s. 298. " The trade " is   I
the trade in which the machinery or plant is being used. Moreover, there would
seem to be no reason why the allowance in respect of the lifts and boilers should
in no event be payable to the sub-lessee (the Minister) unless a trade is being
carried on on the premises but may be payable to the sub-lessors (the taxpayer
company) even if no trade is being carried on there.

There can be no doubt but that before the deeming provision was first
introduced by s. 20 (2) of the Income Tax Act, 1945, the allowances for machinery
or plant were confined to equipment used in trade. Paragraph (5) of r. 6 of the

A Rules applicable to Cases 1 and 2 of Sch. D to the Income Tax Act, 1918, was the precursor of s. 298 (1) of the Act of 1952. In that paragraph an essential characteristic of " machinery or plant " undoubtedly was that it was used in trade, although trade was not specifically mentioned in para. (5). This paragraph followed para. (2), which dealt with the allowances to the trader lessee; para. (2) and para. (5), together with all the other paragraphs of r. 6, made it plain that

B r. 6 was concerned with nothing but allowances in respect of equipment used in trade. In the Act of 1952 the order of the provisions dealing with allowances to the lessee trader and the lessor are reversed, s. 298 replacing para. (5) and s. 299 replacing para. (2). Clearly in my view the words " machinery or plant " in s. 298 (1) have the same meaning as they had in the old para. (5) of r. 6 and are given no different meaning by the language of sub-s. (2) of s. 298.

C What then is the purpose of the deeming provision in sub-s. (2) of s. 298 of the Act of 1952, if it has only the limited meaning which I put on it? Its purpose is obvious, for it is expressly stated in sub-s. (2) itself. It is to make all the preceding provisions of Chapter 2 of Part 10 of the Act of 1952 apply as if the machinery or plant, which ex hypothesi is in use in trade, were in use for the purpose of a trade carried on by the lessor; but for this deeming provision many of the preceding

D provisions would not apply. For example, the limit on annual allowances is stated in s. 288 to be governed, amongst other things, by

> " any initial allowance, relevant exceptional depreciation allowances or scientific research allowances given in respect of the machinery or plant *to the person by whom the trade is carried on,* and to any annual allowances for previous years of assessment given in respect of the machinery or plant *to*

E *that person . . .*"

so that the aggregate amount of the allowances will not " exceed the actual cost *to that person* of the machinery or plant . . .". Accordingly, unless the lessor were deemed to be the person by whom the trade was carried on by the lessee in those cases in which the lessor is entitled to the annual allowances, there might be no

F limit to the amount of the allowances he could recover.

For these reasons I agree with the findings of the Special Commissioners as to the meaning of machinery or plant in s. 298, namely, that the lifts and boilers, etc. at Southbridge House, not being used in trade, are not " machinery or plant " within the meaning of s. 298 and that, therefore, the Crown is entitled to succeed. The judge (12) took a contrary view on this question. Nevertheless he

G found in favour of the Crown because he decided the second and third questions stated at the beginning of this judgment against the taxpayer company. The Special Commissioners took a different view from the judge (12) on these two questions. Having regard to the conclusion which I have reached on the first question, it follows that in my judgment the appeal should be dismissed.

It is therefore unnecessary to decide the second and third questions. Neverthe-

H less out of respect for the very able arguments that were addressed to us on those questions, I will briefly consider them.

The second question:

What is the meaning of the words " the burden of the wear and tear " in s. 298? The taxpayer company contend that these words mean something quite different from a mere obligation to maintain and keep in repair. They say that the words

I cover depreciation in value in so far as it cannot be made good by maintenance in good and substantial repair. It is undoubtedly true that however well machinery and plant may be maintained, it will eventually reach the end of its useful life and will have to be replaced. I understand the taxpayer company to say that where this burden falls on lessors, they are entitled to the allowance under s. 298 notwithstanding that the obligation to keep the machinery in good repair lies on the lessees. The taxpayer company contend that it would be absurd that

---

(12) [1966] 3 All E.R. 375; [1967] Ch. 167.

lessees who can claim the cost of repair as a deductible expense should also be   **A**
allowed the capital allowance under s. 299. Even assuming that this would be
absurd, it does not help to solve the problem. Machinery and plant are often, and
perhaps more usually, let separately and not, as in the present case, as part of a
building. In such a case it is the lessor's trade to let machinery and plant. When
machinery or plant is let separately, not infrequently it is on the terms that the
lessor shall be responsible for its maintenance. Thus, in such a case, even if the   **B**
taxpayer company's construction of the words, " the burden of the wear and
tear " be correct, the essential absurdity, if it be an absurdity, would still exist.
The lessor could deduct the expense of the maintenance in calculating his profits
or gains and would also be entitled to a capital allowance under s. 298 (1). Whatever may be the true meaning of " the burden of wear and tear ", the expense
incurred in maintenance may be deductible by the same person as the one   **C**
entitled to the grant relating to capital expenditure.

It is conceded that under the Income Tax Act, 1918, in its original form, the
question whether the allowance in respect of the diminished value by reason of
wear and tear should be granted to the lessor or lessee depended on which of them
was bound by the terms of the letting to maintain the machinery in good repair.
The taxpayer company contend, however, that the law in this respect was altered   **D**
by the proviso to para. (2) of r. 6 of the Rules applicable to Cases 1 and 2 of
Sch. D added by s. 22 of the Finance Act, 1940. The proviso read as follows:

> " Provided that this paragraph shall not apply to any machinery or plant
> unless the commissioners having jurisdiction in the matter are satisfied,
> having regard to all the relevant circumstances of the case, that the burden
> of the wear and tear of the machinery or plant will in fact fall directly upon   **E**
> that person."

The taxpayer company's argument is that the proviso was introduced to ensure
that the lessee should not get the grant unless the burden of compensating the
lessor for depreciation in value or of replacing the machinery when it became
useless fell on the lessee. This seems to me a little unlikely, since when machinery   **F**
is let separately, as it usually is, in my experience it is almost unheard of for the
lessee to undertake the obligation of compensating the lessor for depreciation in
value in ordinary use, still less of replacing it should it become useless or wear out
in normal use. In my view the proviso was added to para. (2) of r. 6 in 1940 solely
to remove the anomaly created by the decision of this court in *Union Cold
Storage Co., Ltd.* v. *Simpson (Inspector of Taxes), Union Cold Storage Co., Ltd.* v.   **G**
Ellerker (13). In that case the obligation to maintain in good repair had been
undertaken by the lessees but in fact discharged by the lessors. This court held
that the lessees were nevertheless entitled to the allowance. In my view the
legislature thereupon intervened solely to ensure that notwithstanding that
lessees undertook the obligation to maintain the machinery in good repair, they
should not receive the allowance unless " the commissioners . . . are satisfied   **H**
that . . . the burden of the wear and tear . . . will *in fact* fall directly upon
[them] ". This seems to me to equate " the burden of the wear and tear " with
the obligation referred to in para. (2), " to maintain . . . and deliver over in good
condition at the end of the lease ". The amended para. (2) of r. 6 with its proviso
is in effect reproduced in s. 299. Nevertheless the taxpayer company contend
that even if they are wrong as to the effect of the proviso to para. (2) introduced   **I**
in 1940 and reproduced in s. 299, the law was changed by the Income Tax Act,
1945, and that this change was carried into the Income Tax Act, 1952, by the
alteration of the language used in para. (5) of r. 6

> " Where the machinery or plant is let upon such terms that the burden of
> maintaining and restoring it falls upon the lessor "

to the language of s. 298 (1)

---

(13) [1939] 2 All E.R. 94; 22 Tax Cas. 547.

A   " Where machinery or plant is let upon such terms that the burden of the wear and tear thereof falls directly upon the lessor . . ."

B   The taxpayer company say that this alteration of language shows that the legislature intended that the right to the allowance should no longer depend on the incidence of the obligation to maintain in good repair but on the circumstances to which I have already referred. This seems to me to read altogether too much into the alteration in language, particularly having regard to the construction I put on the proviso to para. (2) of r. 6 and to s. 299. If the legislature had intended to alter the law in the sense for which the taxpayer company contend, the use of the words " wear and tear " would have been singularly inept. They have long been understood in relation to a covenant to repair " fair wear and tear excepted ". Moreover, depreciation in value of a capital asset does not by any

C   means necessarily depend on wear and tear. Such an asset irrespective of wear and tear may greatly depreciate in value should it become obsolete or obsolescent.

The taxpayer company seek to rely on *Boarland* (*Inspector of Taxes*) v. *Pirie, Appleton & Co., Ltd., Stem Co., Ltd.* v. *Hyett* (14). That case, however, turned on the true construction of s. 15 of the Finance Act, 1937, which related to allowances in respect of industrial premises. The crucial words being considered were " the

D   whole burden of any depreciation " in sub-s. (5) of s. 15 and not the words " the burden of the wear and tear ", certainly not in their context in the legislation referring to allowances in respect of plant and machinery. Moreover, in the *Boarland* case (14) the covenant to keep in repair was not a full repairing covenant. It excluded liability for " general failure of structure ". I do not think that any assistance can in the instant case be derived from that authority. For the reasons

E   which I have indicated, I cannot accept the taxpayer company's submissions as to the meaning of the words " the burden of the wear and tear " in s. 298.

The third question :

Even if the taxpayer company were right on question 1 and on their construction of the words, " the burden of the wear and tear ", they could not in my view

F   succeed on this appeal, since the burden, in the circumstances of this case, would fall on the sub-lessee, the Minister of Works. The Special Commissioners have found as facts that the " life of the existing lifts is about twenty-five years " and that " the boilers have an expected life of twenty-five years ". The under-lease was for thirty-five years and contained a full repairing covenant. Accordingly, the obligation to replace the lifts and boilers and the burden of the

G   depreciation in their value must fall on the sub-lessee. It was argued, though somewhat faintly, that the lifts and boilers might last longer than anticipated and might still be in use at the expiration of the underlease. Anything, I suppose, is possible, but the facts in a civil case are decided on a balance of probabilities. Moreover the courts are bound by the Special Commissioners' findings of fact. On those findings the lifts and boilers sub-let to the Minister would have to be

H   replaced by the Minister or his successors in title. It may be that the replacement lifts and boilers may not have as long a life at the end of the underlease as had the original lifts and boilers which happened to be new at the commencement of the sub-lease. This, however, in my view, is irrelevant and is in any event a circumstance which should have been taken into account when the rent was fixed.

I   I would accordingly dismiss the appeal.

Appeal dismissed.   Leave to appeal to the House of Lords granted.

Solicitors: *Glover & Co.* (for the taxpayer company);   *Solicitor of Inland Revenue.*

[*Reported by* F. A. Amies, Esq., *Barrister-at-Law.*]

_____

(14) [1940] 1 All E.R. 539; 23 Tax Cas. 547.

GARNHAM, HARRIS & ELTON, LTD. *v.* ALFRED W. ELLIS   A
(TRANSPORT), LTD.

[QUEEN's BENCH DIVISION (Paull, J.), April 11, 12, 13, 1967.]

Carriers—Contract—Carriage of goods—Exception clause—Notification of loss
out of time allowed by exception clause—Carriage sub-contracted without
permission of consignor and without making proper enquiries about sub-   B
contractor—Valuable load of copper wire, untraceable if stolen—Power to
sub-contract carriage of such load not conferred by contract—Load lost,
probably by theft by sub-contractor—Whether contractor liable in the circum-
stances for conversion—Road Haulage Association, Ltd.'s Conditions of
Carriage, 1961, conditions 1 (a), 12 (a).

The plaintiffs regularly sent copper wire from London to their associated   C
company in Glasgow, and frequently employed the defendant carriers for
that purpose. The contracts with the defendants were oral, and it was
accepted by the parties that the conditions of carriage of the Road Haulage
Association, Ltd., were applicable. Copper wire was a valuable load, easy
to steal and untraceable when stolen. On Dec. 4, 1964, the plaintiffs orally
contracted with the defendants for them to carry copper wire worth   D
£3,775 9s. 1d. to the associated company in Glasgow, and gave the defendants
a delivery order in their favour for the collection of the copper wire from
the persons in possession of it. Without informing the plaintiffs the defendants arranged with a man unknown to them, who gave the name of Wallace
Transport of Stirling, to transport the copper wire, and, without making
enquiries concerning him or any firm of that name, handed over the delivery   E
order to him. The defendants knew, so the court found, that the plaintiffs
would not have consented to sub-contracting to a stranger without making
proper enquiries. The copper wire was collected on Dec. 8, but was never
delivered to the associated company. Wallace Transport was in fact non-
existent and the number of the stranger's lorry was a false number. On
Jan. 6/7 the plaintiffs became aware that the copper wire had not been   F
delivered. They notified the defendants, but notification was two days after
expiry of the time allowed by condition 12 (a)* of the conditions of carriage,
which excluded a contractor's liability in the absence of notice, the term
" contractor " being defined by condition 1 (a)† to include a person carrying
goods under a sub-contract with the contractor. The plaintiffs sued for the
return of the copper wire or its value, or damages for breach of contract or   G
for conversion.

Held: (i) having regard to the nature of the load and its value, the
defendants had not power to sub-contract the carriage without the plaintiffs'
consent (see p. 944, letter I, post).

(ii) the sub-contracting in the present case was a deliberate interference
with the plaintiffs' rights amounting to a conversion of the goods, to which   H
condition 12 (a) afforded no defence, and accordingly the plaintiffs were
entitled to recover damages for conversion (see p. 944, letter I, post).

Dictum of DIPLOCK, L.J., in *Morris* v. *C. W. Martin & Sons, Ltd.* ([1965]
2 All E.R. at p. 735) considered and applied.

[As to personal performance of contracts, see 8 HALSBURY's LAWS (3rd Edn.)
161, para. 275; and for cases on the subject, see 12 DIGEST (Repl.) 660-664,   I
5122-5148.

As to an exception clause in a contract of carriage not protecting against
fundamental breach, see 4 HALSBURY's LAWS (3rd Edn.) 155, 156, para. 412;
cf., 11 ibid., p. 393, para. 641 text and note (*f*).

As to the liability of a bailee for unauthorised acts, see 2 HALSBURY's LAWS
(3rd Edn.) 116, para. 225 text and notes (*j*), (*k*).]

---

* Condition 12 (a) is set out at p. 942, letter I, post.
† Condition 1 (a) is set out at p. 942, letter I, to p. 943, letter A, post.

A Cases referred to:

> Caxton Publishing Co., Ltd. v. Sutherland Publishing Co., Ltd., [1938] 4 All E.R.
> 389; [1939] A.C. 178; 108 L.J. Ch. 5; sub nom, Sutherland Publishing
> Co., Ltd. v. Caxton Publishing Co., Ltd. (No. 2), 160 L.T. 17; 13 Digest
> (Repl.) 128, 680.
>
> Coggs v. Bernard, (1703), 2 Ld. Raym. 909; 92 E.R. 107; 3 Digest (Repl.)

B > 64, 52.

> Davies v. Collins, [1945] 1 All E.R. 247; 114 L.J.K.B. 199; 172 L.T. 155;
> 3 Digest (Repl.) 102, 287.
>
> Morris v. C. W. Martin & Sons, Ltd., [1965] 2 All E.R. 725; [1966] 1 Q.B.
> 716; [1965] 3 W.L.R. 276; 3rd Digest Supp.

C **Action.**

This was an action begun by a writ dated Jan. 19, 1966, by the plaintiffs
Garnham, Harris & Elton, Ltd., against the defendants, Alfred Ellis (Transport)
Ltd., for damages in respect of the loss of copper wire worth £3,775 9s. 1d. By
their statement of claim the plaintiffs pleaded, among other matters, that on
Dec. 4, 1964, the defendants agreed that they would for reward collect and
D carry copper wire for the plaintiffs from London to Glasgow; that on or about
Dec. 8, 1964, the defendants, by some agent unknown to the plaintiffs, collected
the copper wire from two addresses in London but that, despite request, the
defendants had failed to deliver up the copper wire. In the alternative, so the
plaintiffs alleged, the defendants on about Dec. 8, 1964, caused some thief
unknown to the plaintiffs, but falsely holding himself out to be acting on behalf
E of carriers known as Wallace Transport of Stirling to collect the copper wire,
and that they did so without making any sufficient enquiries as to the bona
fides of the thief, whereby the defendants were in fundamental breach of their
contract with the plaintiffs. The plaintiffs further pleaded that in the alternative
the defendants converted the copper wire to their own use by, in effect, handing
to the thief documents entitling him to collect the copper wire and thereby
F enabling him to steal it. The plaintiffs accordingly claimed the return of the
copper wire or £3,775 9s. 1d., its value; alternatively £3,775 9s. 1d. damages
for fundamental breach of contract; and in addition interest from Dec. 8, 1964
under the Law Reform (Miscellaneous Provisions) Act, 1934. By their defence
the defendants admitted the contract and that the copper wire was collected
on Dec. 8, 1964 by the defendants' agent and had not been delivered. They
G denied the alleged conversion and fundamental breach of contract and alleged
that it was an express term of the contract between the plaintiffs and the
defendants that the defendants should in no circumstances be liable for non-
delivery of the goods unless the defendants were advised within twenty-eight
days after receipt by them of the goods (see condition 12 (a) of the conditions
of carriage of the Road Haulage Association, Ltd., p. 942, letter I, post); and
H that the plaintiffs did not advise the defendants of non-delivery until more than
twenty-eight days had elapsed after receipt of the goods by the defendants'
agent.

The following facts are summarised from the judgment. The plaintiffs
regularly sent loads of copper wire from London to Glasgow to an associated
company called Actid, Ltd. For that purpose the plaintiffs frequently entered
I into contracts with the defendants, who were carriers. These contracts were
oral and were made by the plaintiffs' traffic manager, Mr. Bowen, enquiring of
the defendants if they could carry a particular load and by the defendants'
accepting the obligation. Mr. Bowen's contracts were made orally with Mr.
Birkley, the transport manager of the defendants. On acceptance the plaintiffs
would send to the defendants delivery orders authorising the persons in whose
possession the copper wire was to hand it over to the defendants. The delivery
orders were limited to delivery to the defendants by name, A. W. Ellis (Transport)
Ltd. The plaintiffs accepted that the conditions of carriage of the Road Haulage

Association, Ltd. attached to the particular contract in issue between them and **A**
the defendants. Copper wire was in fact about the easiest and most valuable
of all carriers' loads to steal; once it was stolen it was quite untraceable. It
could be described as " the gold of thieves ". It was essential from the plaintiffs'
point of view that they should engage reliable firms of haulage contractors who
would employ reliable drivers. The plaintiffs did not know that the defendants
ever sub-contracted their contracts, and would not have agreed to a general **B**
right for the defendants to sub-contract. The trial judge (PAULL, J.) accepted
Mr. Bowen's evidence that if he had been told that the defendants proposed to
sub-contract the contract, he would have asked who the sub-contractors were,
and would have checked as to the standing of the proposed sub-contractors;
if, for example, their names were not in the Transport Guide he would have
taken the contract away and employed other carriers. In the present instance **C**
Mr. Birkley, without informing the plaintiffs, telephoned the London representative of Rowe Transport of Ayrshire, but found that they were unable to carry
the copper wire. Later an unknown man telephoned, gave the name of Wallace
Transport of Stirling and said that Road Transport had given the name of the
defendants who wanted to sub-contract for goods going to Glasgow. In fact
there was no such firm as Wallace Transport and the address given was false. **D**
Mr. Birkley asked the man to come to his office and handed over the delivery
orders to collect the copper wire from two London firms. Mr. Birkley did not
check on the firm name that the stranger gave and did not check whether the
vehicle that the stranger brought had a carrier's licence and did not even take
its number. He was content when the stranger said that he had an insurance
policy and a driver's licence, even though the stranger could not produce these **E**
documents. A representative of one of the two firms from whom the copper wire
was collected on Dec. 8, 1964, took the number of the vehicle that collected it.
The number was found to be false. There was no immediate checking of particular
loads of copper wires sent by the plaintiffs to Actic, Ltd.; but every two months
or so a check was made. By Dec. 31 it was found that Actic, Ltd. was short by
thirteen tons. By Jan. 6/7, 1965 it was discovered that the missing load of copper **F**
wire was the one of which delivery was taken on Dec. 8, 1964. This was the
plaintiffs' first loss of copper wire. Notice of the loss was given to the defendants,
but thirty days, rather than the twenty-eight specified by condition 12 (a) of the
conditions of carriage, after delivery of the copper wire to the stranger.

Quintin Hogg, Q.C., and *F. M. Drake* for the plaintiffs.
R. P. Smith, Q.C., and *F. A. Martineau* for the defendants.   **G**

PAULL, J., having stated the facts and reviewed the evidence, continued:
The defence is based on the Road Haulage Association, Ltd.'s conditions of
carriage. On Mr. Bowen's evidence the plaintiffs accept that they must be
deemed to form part of the contract between the parties, but it must be remembered that they are not particular conditions relating to this contract only, but **H**
are general conditions drawn up to cover an innumerable variety of contracts.
The condition relied on is condition 12, which, so far as is material, states:

" The contractor shall in no circumstances whatsoever be liable:—(a).
For non-delivery (however arising) of a consignment or any part thereof
unless he is advised of the non-delivery at the forwarding or delivery depot
within twenty-eight days and receives the detailed claim for the value of **I**
the goods within forty-two days after receipt of the consignment by the
contractor to whom the same was handed by the consignor; . . ."

The date of the receipt of the copper wire by the man calling himself Wallace
Transport was Dec. 8, 1964, but this condition must be read in conjunction
with condition 1. Condition 1, so far as material reads:

" In these conditions of carriage (hereinafter called ' these conditions ')
(a) ' contractor ' (unless the context forbids) includes the contractor's

A servants and agents and any person or persons carrying goods under a sub-contract with the contractor . . .''

Non-delivery of the copper wire was notified to the defendants thirty days after the goods were collected, that is, two days out of time. This defence is clearly a good one unless the plaintiffs can establish that there was a conversion of the goods by the defendants or what is called a fundamental breach of the

B contract between the parties. DIPLOCK, L.J., in *Morris* v. *C. W. Martin & Sons, Ltd.*, (1), said:

" One of the common law duties owed by a bailee of goods to his bailor is not to convert them, i.e., not to do intentionally in relation to the goods an act inconsistent with the bailor's right of property therein (see *Caxton Publishing Co., Ltd.* v. *Sutherland Publishing Co., Ltd.*, (2) per LORD PORTER).

C This duty, which is common to all bailments as well as to other relationships which do not amount to bailment, is independent of and additional to the other common law duty of a bailee for reward to take reasonable care of his bailor's goods. Stealing goods is the simplest example of conversion; but, perhaps because in his classic judgment in *Coggs* v. *Bernard* (3), SIR JOHN HOLT, C.J., discusses the circumstances in which bailees are liable to

D their bailors for the loss of goods stolen not by the servant of the bailee but by a stranger, some confusion has, I think, arisen in later cases through failure to recognise the co-existence of the two duties of a bailee for reward: to take reasonable care of his bailor's goods and not to convert them—even by stealing.''

E Clearly the conditions of a contract do not apply to an act of conversion by the party in whose possession the goods are, unless indeed, as would be most unlikely, there were express conditions to cover such an act, but mere non-delivery, however caused, is not in my judgment in itself sufficient to amount to conversion. As to the fundamental breach, it seems to me that that cannot arise in this case unless there was a conversion, and that a conversion can only arise if the

F circumstances under which Mr. Birkley gave the collector of the copper wire authority to collect it were such that the giving of that authority was outside any authority which Mr. Birkley had as to the manner in which he might deal with the goods. It was agreed that for this purpose Mr. Birkley was the alter ego of the defendants.

Two questions arise: (i) under the terms of the contract, could Mr. Birkley sub-contract for the carriage without express consent of the plaintiffs? (ii) If

G yes, must Mr. Birkley have known, or ought he to have known, that he was sub-contracting in a manner quite outside the contemplation of the parties when the contract was entered into? In other words, in a manner so reckless that no reasonable man could think that he was fulfilling the contract by allowing the man who called to collect the goods. It has been said by DAVIES, L.J., in

H another case (4) that condition 1 of these conditions gives the right to sub-contract. It may well be that in the circumstances of that case that was correct, but in this case at any rate I cannot think that that is so. The word " contractor " was not used in what may be called the body of this contract—that is, in any words passing between Mr. Bowen and Mr. Birkley. Moreover condition 1 starts with the words: " In these conditions ", thus limiting the meaning to

I the conditions and not incorporating that meaning into the body of the contract even if the word " contractor " had been used in the body of the contract. The words " in these conditions " limit the meaning, so that it can be read only in relation to the conditions which are then set out. Now these conditions are concerned with the rights and liabilities of " the contractors ", and condition 1

(1) [1965] 2 All E.R. 725 at p. 735; [1966] 1 Q.B. 716 at p. 732.
(2) [1938] 4 All E.R. 389 at pp. 403, 404; [1939] A.C. 178 at p. 202.
(3) (1703), 2 Ld. Raym. 909.
(4) Compare *John Carter (Fine Worsteds), Ltd.* v. *Hanson Haulage (Leeds), Ltd.*, [1965] 1 All E.R. at p. 122, letter F.

is quite consistent with notice being given to the consignor that, if the contractor A
by express or implied power does sub-contract, then the sub-contractor has the
same rights and liabilities as the contractor himself. In my judgment the words
in this case do not give any authority to sub-contract.

The next question is the power to sub-contract. As LORD GREENE, M.R.,
said in *Davies* v. *Collins* (5):

> " Whether or not in any given contract performance can properly be   B
> carried out by the employment of a sub-contractor must depend on the
> proper inference to be drawn from the contract itself, the subject matter
> of it, and other material surrounding circumstances."

Normally, undoubtedly, I should hold that a contract of carriage may be sub-
contracted. In the course of the argument I put to counsel for the defendants
the question: If this had been a load of gold and known to be such by both   C
parties, would there have been a right to sub-contract? His answer was " no ",
and clearly that is because of the nature of the load. This load was, to the
knowledge of both parties, the " gold of thieves ", in other words, the sort of
cargo that every gang of lorry thieves, and every lorry thief, will strive with every
nerve to steal, and, as Mr. Bowen put it, it has become much too common for
such loads to disappear. If necessary, I am prepared to hold that in any contract   D
for the carriage of such goods there must be some express words, preferably in
the body of the contract, giving a carrier the right to sub-contract. If the
consignor signs such a contract he knows he has given the right to sub-contract.
If there are no such words, then I think that Mr. Bowen was expressing the
view of consignors of such goods generally when he said:

> " We must find reputable firms of haulage contractors with whom to   E
> contract. We have half-a-dozen of such contractors. If I am told that
> a contractor cannot do it himself, I require to know the name of the
> sub-contractor. Then I check, and either I agree or, if I do not agree, I give
> the contract to another of our contractors. I had no idea that without
> my consent this contract would be sub-contracted."   F

He would never have consented to a general right to sub-contract such a load,
and in my view that applies to all cases where well-known companies who have
to arrange for the carriage of this type of goods enter into contracts with carriers.
Quite apart from this aspect of the case, in my judgment Mr. Birkley knew
quite well what answer he would have received if he had telephoned Mr. Bowen
and said: " I propose to give this load over to a complete stranger; the name   G
he has given me is not in the ABC Guide; he could produce no insurance
certificate and no driving licence; I do not know if he has an A licence and I
have not found anyone for whom he has done any work; I have not even seen,
let alone checked, the number of his lorry or seen whether that lorry has any
firm's name or any name upon it." Mr. Birkley knew, I think, that if he had
said that to Mr. Bowen, not only would the answer have been a horrified " no ",   H
but also Mr. Birkley's company would promptly have been cut off the list of
authorised carriers.

In my judgment therefore I hold first of all that there was no right to sub-
contract at all, and that secondly the manner of the sub-contracting was such
that it amounted to a deliberate interference, without justification, in a manner
inconsistent with the rights of the plaintiffs, and by reason of that deliberate   I
interference with their rights, the plaintiffs are entitled to succeed in conversion.
I therefore give judgment for the plaintiffs.   *Judgment for plaintiffs.*

Solicitors: *Herbert Barron & Co.* (for the plaintiffs); *Doyle Devonshire & Co.,*
agents for *Molineaux, McKeog & Cooper,* Newcastle-upon-Tyne (for the
defendants).

[*Reported by* MARY COLTON, *Barrister-at-Law.*]

(5) [1945] 1 All E.R. 247 at p. 250.

A   CHADWICK v. BRITISH TRANSPORT COMMISSION.

[QUEEN's BENCH DIVISION (Waller, J.), April 24, 25, 26, May 12, 1967.]

Damages—Remoteness of damage—Mental shock—Rescuer helping voluntarily at scene of railway accident with many casualties—Subsequently suffering prolonged and disabling nervous shock—Whether injury too remote.

B *Negligence—Rescue—Railway collision causing many casualties among passengers —Rescuer voluntarily assisting in rescue work—Whether duty of care owed to rescuer—Rescuer subsequently suffering prolonged mental shock.*

In December, 1957, C. was about forty-four years old and since 1945 had been successfully engaged in a window-cleaning business and taking an interest in social and charitable activities in his community. In 1941 when

C he was twenty-eight years old, he had suffered some psycho-neurotic symptoms, but he had not suffered from them for sixteen years thereafter and he was not (so the court found) someone who would be likely to relapse under the ordinary stresses of life. On Dec. 4, 1957, immediately following a collision between two railway trains on a line a short distance from his home, C. voluntarily took an active part throughout the night in rescue

D operations at the scene of the accident, in which ninety persons had been killed and many others were trapped and injured. As a result of the horror of his experience at the scene of the accident C. suffered a prolonged and disabling anxiety neurosis necessitating hospital treatment. In an action brought by C. and continued after his death by his widow as his personal representative it was conceded by the defendants that the accident was

E caused by negligence for which they were legally responsible, but liability to C. in damages was denied.

Held: the defendants were in breach of duty to C. and his illness was suffered as a result of that breach, with the consequence that his personal representative was entitled to recover damages, for the following reasons—

(i) it was reasonably foreseeable in the event of such an accident as had

F occurred that someone other than the defendants' servants might try to rescue passengers and might suffer injury in the process; accordingly the defendants owed a duty of care towards C. (see p. 952, letter A, post).

Ward v. T. E. Hopkins & Son, Ltd. ([1959] 3 All E.R. 225) followed.

(ii) injury by shock to a rescuer, physically unhurt, was reasonably foreseeable, and the fact that the risk run by a rescuer was not exactly the same

G as that run by a passenger did not deprive the rescuer of his remedy (see p. 951, letters C and D, p. 952, letter B, post).

(iii) damages were recoverable for injury by shock notwithstanding that the shock was not caused by the injured person's fear for his own safety or for the safety of his children (see p. 951, letter A, post).

Principle laid down in Hay (or Bourhill) v. Young ([1942] 2 All E.R. 396)

H applied.

Dulieu v. White & Sons ([1900-03] All E.R. Rep. 353) and *Owens v. Liverpool Corpn.* ([1938] 4 All E.R. 727) considered.

(iv) as a man who had lived a normal busy life in the community with no mental illness for sixteen years, there was nothing in C.'s personality to put him outside the ambit of the defendants' contemplation so as to

I render the damage suffered by him too remote (see p. 953, letters A and B, post).

Dictum of LORD WRIGHT *in Hay (or Bourhill) v. Young* ([1942] 2 All E.R. at pp. 405, 406) distinguished.

[As to remoteness of damage in negligence claims and as to damages for emotional shock, see 11 HALSBURY's LAWS (3rd Edn.) 270, 271, para. 448, pp. 277-280, paras. 458-461, and 28 ibid., pp. 98, 99, paras. 106, 107; and for cases on the subject, see 17 DIGEST (Repl.) 122, 123, *333-339*, and 36 DIGEST (Repl.) 195-197, *1030-1039*.]

As to intervening acts by the plaintiff and the defence of " volenti non fit   A
injuria ", and as to liability where human intervention by way of rescue operations may be anticipated, see 28 HALSBURY'S LAWS (3rd Edn.) 29, 30, para. 26,
note (d), pp. 82-84, paras. 87, 88, note (h), and 11 ibid., pp. 282, 283, paras.
467, 468; and for cases, see 36 DIGEST (Repl.) 150-152, *781-799*.]

Cases referred to:

Brandon v. *Osborne Garrett & Co., Ltd.*, [1924] All E.R. Rep. 703; [1924]
     1 K.B. 548; 93 L.J.K.B. 304; 130 L.T. 670; 36 Digest (Repl.) 191, *1008*.

Donoghue (or M'Alister) v. *Stevenson*, [1932] All E.R. Rep. 1; [1932] A.C. 562;
     101 L.J.P.C. 119; 147 L.T. 281; 36 Digest (Repl.) 85, *458*.

Dulieu v. *White & Sons*, [1900-03] All E.R. Rep. 353; [1901] 2 K.B. 669;
     70 L.J.K.B. 837; 85 L.T. 126; 36 Digest (Repl.) 197, *1038*.   C

Hambrook v. *Stokes Brothers*, [1924] All E.R. Rep. 110; [1925] 1 K.B. 141;
     94 L.J.K.B. 435; 132 L.T. 707; 36 Digest (Repl.) 196, *1035*.

Hay (or Bourhill) v. *Young*, [1942] 2 All E.R. 396; [1943] A.C. 92; 111 L.J.P.C.
     97; 167 L.T. 261; 36 Digest (Repl.) 16, *66*.

Hughes v. *Lord Advocate*, [1963] 1 All E.R. 705; [1963] A.C. 837; [1963]
     2 W.L.R. 779; Digest (Cont. Vol. A) 1143, *89a*.   D

King v. *Phillips*, [1953] 1 All E.R. 617; [1953] 1 Q.B. 429; [1953] 2 W.L.R.
     526; 17 Digest (Repl.) 123, *339*.

Overseas Tankship (U.K.) Ltd. v. *Morts Dock & Engineering Co., Ltd.* (The
     Wagon Mound), [1961] 1 All E.R. 404; [1961] A.C. 388; [1961] 2
     W.L.R. 126; [1961] 1 Lloyd's Rep. 1; Digest (Cont. Vol. A) 1148, *185a*.
     E

Owens v. *Liverpool Corpn.*, [1938] 4 All E.R. 727; [1939] 1 K.B. 394; 108
     L.J.K.B. 155; 160 L.T. 8; 17 Digest (Repl.) 123, *337*.

Smith v. *Johnson & Co.*, (1897), *cited in*, [1895-99] All E.R. Rep. at p. 270;
     [1897] 2 Q.B. at p. 61; 66 L.J.Q.B. at p. 496; 76 L.T. at p. 494; 36
     Digest (Repl.) 197, *1036*.

Vaughan v. *Taff Vale Ry. Co.* (1860), 5 H. & N. 679; 29 L.J.Ex. 247; 2 L.T.   F
     394; 24 J.P. 453; 157 E.R. 1351; 36 Digest (Repl.) 6, *8*.

Wagner v. *International Ry. Co.*, (1921), 232 N.Y. Rep. 176.

Ward v. *T. E. Hopkins & Son, Ltd.*, [1959] 3 All E.R. 225; [1959] 1 W.L.R. 966;
     Digest (Cont. Vol. A) 1189, *1016a*.

Wilkinson v. *Downton*, [1895-99] All E.R. Rep. 267; [1897] 2 Q.B. 57; 66
     L.J.Q.B. 493; 76 L.T. 493; 17 Digest (Repl.) 122, *334*.   G

Action.

In this action for damages for personal injuries commenced by writ issued on
Dec. 2, 1960, Henry Chadwick of 161 Albyn Road, Deptford, S.E.8, claimed
damages for prolonged mental shock and consequent loss suffered by him as a
result of his voluntary participation in rescue operations throughout the night   H
of Dec. 4/5, 1957, at the scene of the railway accident (commonly known as
the Lewisham railway disaster) in which as a result of two trains coming into
collision ninety persons were killed and many seriously injured. Following
on his death in December, 1962 (from causes unconnected with the accident)
the action was by leave of the court under an order dated Dec. 19, 1963,
continued by his widow, Ellen Chadwick, as administratrix of his estate,   I
claiming damages on behalf of the estate pursuant to the provisions of the
Law Reform (Miscellaneous Provisions) Act, 1934. The defendants, the British
Transport Commission, admitted that the accident was due to their negligence but denied that this was a breach of duty towards Mr. Chadwick and
pleaded in defence the maxim " volenti non fit injuria "; the defendants
denied that Mr. Chadwick suffered any injuries, loss or damage as alleged and
did not admit that any of them resulted from the defendants' negligence. The
facts are set out in the judgment.

A   The cases noted below* were cited during the argument in addition to those referred to in the judgment.

Hugh Griffiths, Q.C., and *Philip Otton* for the plaintiff widow.
Tudor Evans, Q.C., and *A. C. Goodall* for the defendants.

Cur. adv. vult.

B   May 12. **WALLER, J.:** This action is brought by the plaintiff as personal representative of her late husband for damages for personal injuries which she says were caused by the Lewisham train disaster on Dec. 4, 1957. The cause of action, if there is one, therefore arose nearly ten years ago. Counsel for the plaintiff has frankly said that he can give no satisfactory explanation for the delay, but also has said that the letter before action was written on Dec. 19, 1958. The
C   difficulties of trying a case long after the event are increased in this instance by the fact that the original plaintiff died on Dec. 20, 1962; his private practitioner, who would have been an important witness, has died; the doctor who attended him at hospital has died, and the consulting psychiatrist who attended him has retired from practice. Such delay in bringing proceedings to court without any satisfactory explanation may cause injustice to the plaintiff, it undoubtedly
D   creates the impression of great prejudice to the defendants, and it makes the task of the tribunal very difficult. The reasons for the delay I will consider at a later stage. Meanwhile I must do my best to arrive at a conclusion about the facts.

The defendants have been extremely co-operative and as a result I have had a number of contemporary documents in the form of hospital case notes from the two hospitals attended by the late Mr. Chadwick and, in spite of the delay,
E   I am left in no doubt about Mr. Chadwick's medical history and the diagnosis of his condition.

The description of the events of Dec. 4, 1957, and of the deceased's, Mr. Chadwick's, part in those events cannot be supported by contemporary documents and the court must therefore rely on the recollection of witnesses going back 9½ years. As I shall indicate, however, those events were of so calamitous
F   a nature that the recollections of those involved are probably more reliable than one would usually expect after 9½ years. On Dec. 4, 1957, just before 6 o'clock in the evening, there occurred at Lewisham a very serious railway accident. In bad weather conditions two trains collided, as a result of which ninety persons were killed. Mr. Chadwick the original plaintiff, went to the scene to do what he could to help. He worked there all night. The present
G   plaintiff's case is that whereas before the accident he was a cheerful busy man carrying on a window cleaning business and with many spare time activities, after the accident by reason of the shock of his experiences that night he became psycho-neurotic, he no longer took the interest in life which he had taken and he was unable to work for a considerable time. Damages are claimed for the shock he sustained and for the consequences. The defendants, whilst admitting that the
H   train collision was caused by their negligence, deny liability, and I must therefore determine the facts before dealing with the difficult issues involved.

Mr. and Mrs. Chadwick lived at 161, Albyn Road, Lewisham. They had lived there since December, 1945. Mr. Chadwick was a window cleaner and carried on a window cleaning business. He was a public spirited person who used to help with whist drives; he was a governor of three local schools and was a
I   member of the local chamber of commerce. On Dec. 4, 1957, about 6 o'clock

---

* *Pugh* v. *London, Brighton and South Coast Ry. Co.*, [1896] 2 Q.B. 248; *Re Polemis and Furness, Withy & Co., Ltd.*, [1921] All E.R. Rep. 40; [1921] 3 K.B. 560; *Haynes* v. *G. Harwood & Son*, [1934] All E.R. Rep. 103; [1935] 1 K.B. 146; *Roe* v. *Minister of Health*, [1954] 2 All E.R. 131; [1954] 2 Q.B. 66; *Schneider* v. *Eisovitch*, [1960] 1 All E.R. 169; [1960] 2 Q.B. 430; *Smith* v. *Leech Brain & Co., Ltd.*, [1961] 3 All E.R. 1159, [1962] 2 Q.B. 405, *Warren* v. *Scruttons*, [1962] 1 Lloyd's Rep. 497; *Doughty* v. *Turner Mfg. Co., Ltd.*, [1964] 1 All E.R. 98; [1964] 1 Q.B. 518; *Boardman* v. *Sanderson*, [1964] 1 W.L.R. 1317; *Haley* v. *London Electricity Board*, [1964] 3 All E.R. 185; [1965] A.C. 778.

in the evening there was a railway accident at Lewisham when in poor visibility a   A
moving train ran into the back of a stationary train and ninety persons were
killed. The accident happened some two hundred yards from the Chadwick's
house. Mr. Chadwick was told of the accident by his wife and he immediately
ran out of the house to help. Mrs. Chadwick did not see him again until 3 o'clock
in the morning, when he came in, covered with mud, with blood on his hands and
clutching a small golliwog brooch which he gave to Mrs. Chadwick to look after.   B
He went out again and did not return until 6 o'clock in the morning. He was in a
mess with blood and the like. He would not go to bed and he was upset and
shaking. The golliwog brooch belonged to a small boy, three years of age, who had
been killed in the accident.

Mrs. Taylor, who was a passenger in one of the trains and who sustained dis-
located hips, a fractured pelvis, a fractured thigh and severely lacerated legs,   C
gave evidence and described how she was trapped up to the waist as a result
of this accident. She said that there was a young girl beside her and a man
suspended above her on his hands taking his weight. There was another railway
carriage on top and a young girl hanging out of the window screaming. Mrs.
Taylor was afraid that the other carriage would come on top of her. Then,
she said, Mr. Chadwick came; he was cheerful and gave comfort to Mrs. Taylor.   D
After going round to the other side, he told Mrs. Taylor that her legs were broken,
and then a light was produced and Mrs. Taylor saw above her a girl impaled on a
girder and saw her own left leg was, as she said, mangled and scarlet with blood.
In another phrase, she described herself as being on a sea of bodies, including a
man underneath her who was dead, and she also described how there was a hand
sticking out which caught hold of Mr. Chadwick's jaw as he went past. Mr.   E
Chadwick was a fairly small man, and the doctor who was attending at that
particular part of the accident used Mr. Chadwick to crawl into the wreckage
where he, the doctor, was too big to go and he got Mr. Chadwick to give an
injection to Mrs. Taylor. In spite of the great time difficulty, I am quite satisfied
that Mrs. Taylor was giving an accurate account and that the scene of this
catastrophe was such as would not normally be seen. During the time that   F
Mrs. Taylor saw him, she described Mr. Chadwick as a most courageous man,
very cheerful and encouraging, who allayed the fears of those around Mrs.
Taylor.

Mr. Chadwick, before the accident, had been running a successful window
cleaning business together with his wife. They had started that business in 1945.
He took an interest in social and charitable activities and was, as one witness   G
said, " a hard-working little man ". He had a happy disposition and got on
extremely well with people. After the accident, he started sleeping badly,
waking up in the night and talking of the little boy whom he had seen. Mrs.
Chadwick found that he was not sleeping and about Christmas time, that is to
say four or five weeks after the accident, he stopped working. He was shaking.
Mrs. Mills, another witness, whom Mr. Chadwick had helped with whist drives,   H
also described how she saw him change. She first noticed him shaking about
five weeks after the accident, and there is no doubt that a marked change was
noticed within a few weeks of the accident. Mr. Chadwick consulted his doctor,
who prescribed tablets; but eventually in May, 1958, he went to the Miller
General Hospital. The doctor who attended him there (Dr. Grace) has retired
and is not available, but the whole of the hospital notes have been made an exhibit   I
in this case. Mr. Chadwick was treated for a gastric ulcer, the history showing
that he was saying that he had lost weight since the Lewisham train disaster,
and eventually on July 27, 1958, he had an operation for this ulcer. By Oct. 2,
Dr. Grace was describing his condition as anxiety neurosis, mentioning the
Lewisham train disaster and noting that " the effects of the incident have been
considerable as regards his psychological state ". [HIS LORDSHIP referred to
the medical evidence afforded by the hospital notes, stated that on Jan. 8, 1959,
Mr. Chadwick was admitted to Belmont Hospital as an in-patient, to evidence

A afforded by hospital notes there, and to the oral evidence of Dr. Kendall, consultant in neurology to the South West Regional Hospital Board, which included Belmont hospital. Dr. Kendall never saw Mr. Chadwick, but saw the hospital notes, and was of opinion that the train disaster caused Mr. Chadwick's condition. His LORDSHIP said that he accepted the evidence of Dr. Kendall and continued:] I find that Mr. Chadwick was a man who had suffered psycho-neurotic symptoms

B in 1941 when he was twenty-eight years old; that for the next sixteen years he suffered no such symptoms; that although he was a man who might break down under stress, having regard to his age, he was not someone who would be likely to relapse under the ordinary stresses of life and that this illness was a major stress reaction, or what used to be called a "catastrophic neurosis", due to stress of quite unusual proportions, namely, his experiences in the Lewisham

C train disaster. I also accept Dr. Kendall's evidence that this is something which is known to result from major catastrophes such as earthquakes, fires, floods and major accidents or disasters. Furthermore, although there was clearly an element of personal danger in what Mr. Chadwick was doing, I think that I must deal with this case on the basis that it was the horror of the whole experience which caused his reaction. This case raises a number of unusual issues and I am

D greatly indebted to counsel for both parties for the helpful arguments which they have addressed to the court. In order to determine whether or not the defendants are liable to the plaintiff for damages in this case, there are five questions, the answers to which have been the subject of argument. These are: (i) Are damages recoverable for injury by shock where the injured man's shock is not caused by fear for his own safety or the safety of his children? (ii) Is fore-

E seeability of injury by shock a necessary ingredient? (iii) Did the defendants owe a duty to Mr. Chadwick who was not their servant but had come to their aid? (iv) Would the fact that the risk run by the rescuer was not precisely that run by the passenger deprive the rescuer of his remedy? (v) Was Mr. Chadwick of such extraordinary susceptibility that he ought not to have been in the contemplation of the reasonable man?

F   Dealing with the first question—Are damages recoverable for injury by shock where the injured man's shock is not caused by fear for his own safety or for the safety of his children? The earliest authority to which I wish to refer is *Dulieu* v. *White & Sons* (1). That was a point of law decided on the pleadings. The plaintiff had sustained a shock when the defendants' van was driven into the bar in which the plaintiff was serving. The decision was that of a divisional court

G consisting of KENNEDY and PHILLIMORE, JJ., and the court held that the action would lie. The reasoning of the two judgments was on different lines and KENNEDY, J., but not PHILLIMORE, J., was inclined to think that the shock must be one arising from a reasonable fear of immediate personal injury to oneself, and he said (2):

H   " It is not, however, to be taken that in my view every nervous shock occasioned by negligence and producing physical injury to the sufferer gives a cause of action. There is, I am inclined to think, at least one limitation. The shock, where it operates through the mind, must be a shock which arises from a reasonable fear of immediate personal injury to oneself. A. has, I conceive, no legal duty not to shock B.'s nerves by the exhibition of negligence towards C., or towards the property of B. or C. The limitation

I was applied by WRIGHT and BRUCE, JJ., in the unreported case of *Smith* v. *Johnson & Co.* (3), referred to by WRIGHT, J., at the close of his judgment in *Wilkinson* v. *Downton* (4). In *Smith* v. *Johnson & Co.* (3) a man was killed by the defendant's negligence in the sight of the plaintiff, and the plaintiff became ill, not from the shock produced by fear of harm to himself, but

---

(1) [1900-03] All E.R. Rep. 353; [1901] 2 K.B. 669.
(2) [1901] 2 K.B. at p. 675; [1900-03] All E.R. Rep. at p. 357.
(3) (1897), cited in [1895-99] All E.R. Rep. at p. 270; [1897] 2 Q.B. at p. 61.
(4) [1895-99] All E.R. Rep. 267 at p. 270; [1897] 2 Q.B. 57 at p. 61.

from the shock of seeing another person killed. The court held that this   A
harm was too remote a consequence of the negligence. I should myself, as I
have already indicated, have been inclined to go a step further, and to
hold upon the facts in *Smith* v. *Johnson & Co.* (5) that, as the defendant
neither intended to affect the plaintiff injuriously nor did anything which
could reasonably or naturally be expected to affect him injuriously, there
was no evidence of any breach of legal duty towards the plaintiff or in regard   B
to him of that absence of care according to the circumstances which WILLES,
J., in *Vaughan* v. *Taff Vale Ry. Co.* (6) gave as a definition of negligence."

So it does seem, however, that KENNEDY, J.'s limitation is made following
Smith v. *Johnson & Co.* (5) because the defendant did not do " anything which
could reasonably or naturally be expected to affect [the plaintiff] injuriously ".
In other words, he was imposing the limitation which he did impose on the grounds   C
of unforeseeability.

Then came the case of *Hambrook* v. *Stokes Brothers* (7), in which the majority
of the Court of Appeal did not apply KENNEDY, J.'s dictum to a case of injury
by shock where the shock arose out of a mother's fear of injury to her children.

I next consider the case of *Hay* (or *Bourhill*) v. *Young* (8), the well known
case of the Edinburgh fish wife. Except in the speech of LORD RUSSELL OF   D
KILLOWEN (9), there is no disapproval of the majority of the Court of Appeal
in *Hambrook* v. *Stokes Brothers* (7). LORD MACMILLAN said this (10):

> " It is no longer necessary to consider whether the infliction of what is
> called mental shock may constitute an actionable wrong. The crude view
> that the law should take cognizance only of physical injury resulting from
> actual impact has been discarded, and it is now well recognised that an   E
> action will lie for injury by shock sustained through the medium of the eye
> or the ear without direct contact. The distinction between mental shock
> and bodily injury was never a scientific one, for mental shock is presumably
> in all cases the result of, or at least accompanied by, some physical disturb-
> ance in the sufferer's system, and a mental shock may have consequences
> more serious than those resulting from physical impact. In the case of   F
> mental shock, however, there are elements of greater subtlety than in the
> case of an ordinary physical injury and these elements may give rise to
> debate as to the precise scope of legal liability."

With the exception of the speech of LORD RUSSELL there are no observations
placing any particular limitation on the kind of shock for which damages will
be recoverable. I do not see any objection in principle to damages being recover-   G
able for shock caused other than by fear for one's own safety or for the safety
of one's children. One only too frequently comes across the case of a man with
a trivial industrial injury which subsequently produces genuine neurotic symptoms not due to fear but due to other causes. It would seem anomalous if serious
mental illness accompanied by a trivial injury would entitle a man to compensation but if there were no trivial injury it would not. I should also mention   H
the case of *Owens* v. *Liverpool Corpn.* (11), which was a case where the plaintiff
recovered damages for shock not due to fear for personal safety or for the safety
of children. There is nothing in this decision which is inconsistent with the view,
which I have expressed, and although some disapproval of the decision was
expressed by some of their lordships in *Hay* (or *Bourhill*) v. *Young* (8), in my
opinion there is nothing in this disapproval (12) inconsistent with the view that   I

(5) (1897), cited in [1895-99] All E.R. Rep. at p. 270; [1897] 2 Q.B. at p. 61.
(6) (1860), 5 H. & N. 679 at p. 688.
(7) [1924] All E.R. Rep. 110; [1925] 1 K.B. 141.
(8) [1942] 2 All E.R. 396; [1943] A.C. 92.
(9) [1942] 2 All E.R. at p. 402, letters B, C; [1943] A.C. at p. 103.
(10) [1942] 2 All E.R. at p. 402; [1943] A.C. at p. 103.
(11) [1938] 4 All E.R. 727; [1939] 1 K.B. 394.
(12) See the speeches of LORD THANKERTON, LORD WRIGHT and LORD PORTER in
[1942] 2 All E.R. at pp. 400, 406 and 408, 409; [1943] A.C. at pp. 99, 110, 114-116.

A I have formed. In my opinion, therefore, provided that the necessary requisites of liability are there, shock, other than fear for oneself or children, causing injury, may be the subject of a claim for damages.

The second question which I have to consider is: Is foreseeability of injury by shock necessary? The House of Lords in *Hay (or Bourhill)* v. *Young* (13) considered a number of matters in deciding whether or not the defendant owed
B a duty to the plaintiff and in deciding that the plaintiff was outside the area of contemplation, one of the matters considered, particularly by LORD WRIGHT, was the foreseeability of injury by shock. In *King* v. *Phillips* (14) DENNING, L.J., said in the passage which was later quoted with approval by VISCOUNT SIMONDS in *Overseas Tankship (U.K.) Ltd.* v. *Morts Dock & Engineering Co., Ltd. (The Wagon Mound)* (15), that

C   "... there can be no doubt since *Hay (or Bourhill)* v. *Young* (13) that the test for liability for shock is foreseeability of injury by shock."

I therefore must ask myself whether injury by shock was foreseeable in this case. The scene described by Mrs. Taylor was the kind of thing to be expected if trains collided as these did and it was one which could, in my view, properly
D be called gruesome. In my opinion, if the defendants had asked themselves the hypothetical question: " If we run one train into another at Lewisham in such circumstances that a large number of people are killed, may some persons who are physically unhurt suffer injury from shock?", I think that the answer must have been " Yes ".

The third question is: Did the defendants owe a duty to the plaintiff who was
E not their servant but who had come to their aid? The test is: What ought the defendants to have foreseen? In the case of *Ward* v. *T. E. Hopkins & Son, Ltd.* (16), the Court of Appeal were considering the circumstances in which defendants owe a duty to rescuers. MORRIS, L.J., said this (17):

    " The first stage in the proof of the claim involves proof that the defendant company were negligent towards their employees, the second that such
F   negligence caused such employees to be in peril, the third that this could reasonably have been foreseen, and the fourth that it could also have been reasonably foreseen that someone would be likely to seek to rescue them from their peril and might either suffer injury or lose his life. In the classic words of LORD ATKIN in *M'Alister (or Donoghue)* v. *Stevenson* (18): ' You must take reasonable care to avoid acts or omissions which you can reason-
G   ably foresee would be likely to injure your neighbour '. Neighbours are those persons (18) ' who are so closely and directly affected by my act that I ought reasonably to have them in contemplation as being so affected when I am directing my mind to the acts or omissions which are called in question '. So in this case it is said that, if the defendant company negligently caused or permitted their servants to be placed in dire peril in a gas-filled well, it
H   ought reasonably to have been contemplated that some brave and stalwart man would attempt to save their lives. In the eloquent words of CARDOZO, J., in *Wagner* v. *International Ry. Co.* (19): 'Danger invites rescue. The cry of distress is the summons to relief. The law does not ignore these reactions of the mind in tracing conduct to its consequences. It recognises them as normal. It places their effect within the range of the natural and probable.
I   The wrong that imperils life is a wrong to the imperilled victim; it is a wrong also to his rescuer'."

In the present case, the defendants were negligent towards their passengers.

---

(13) [1942] 2 All E.R. 396; [1943] A.C. 92.
(14) [1953] 1 All E.R. 617 at p. 623; [1953] 1 Q.B. 429 at p. 441.
(15) [1961] 1 All E.R. 404 at p. 415; [1961] A.C. 388 at p. 426.
(16) [1959] 3 All E.R. 225.   (17) [1959] 3 All E.R. at p. 230.
(18) [1932] All E.R. Rep. 1 at p. 11; [1932] A.C. 562 at p. 580.
(19) (1921), 232 N.Y. Rep. 176 at p. 180.

As a result, passengers were injured and put in peril. All of that could reasonably A have been foreseen. It could also be foreseen that somebody might try and rescue passengers and suffer injury in the process, and in my opinion the defendants owed a duty to Mr. Chadwick who was within the area of contemplation.

The fourth question is: Would the fact that the risk run by the rescuer was not precisely that run by the passenger deprive the rescuer of his remedy? This is a point taken by counsel for the defendants. In my opinion, once the possibility B of rescue occurs, the precise manner of rescue is immaterial. See, for example, the case which I have just mentioned, *Wagner* v. *International Ry. Co.* (20), where the rescuer was doing something which was quite different from that which was involved by those in the train; and see also *Brandon* v. *Osborne Garrett & Co., Ltd.* (21). The very fact of rescue must, in my view, involve unexpected things happening. I have already indicated, however, that in my C view injury by shock was foreseeable from this accident and therefore it can be said that the risk was not different. It is not necessary that the defendants should be able to foresee every step which leads to the injury. In *Hughes* v. *Lord Advocate* (22), the way in which the accident happened was said to be unforeseeable, but the House of Lords held that as the danger was foreseeable the defendants were liable, although the steps by which the danger occurred were D unforeseeable. I am inclined to think in this case that if the defendants had thought about it, they ought to have foreseen the possibility of a rescuer suffering from shock, but in my view it is sufficient to say that shock was foreseeable and that rescue was foreseeable.

The fifth question is: Was Mr. Chadwick of such extraordinary susceptibility that he ought not to have been in the contemplation of the reasonable man? E LORD WRIGHT in *Hay (or Bourhill)* v. *Young* said (23):

" What is now being considered is the question of liability, and this, I think, in a question whether there is duty owing to members of the public who come within the ambit of the act, must generally depend on a normal standard of susceptibility. This, it may be said, is somewhat vague. That is true; but definition involves limitation, which it is desirable to avoid further F than is necessary in a principle of law like negligence, which is widely ranging and is still in the stage of development. It is here, as elsewhere, a question of what the hypothetical reasonable man, viewing the position, I suppose ex post facto, would say it was proper to foresee. What danger of particular infirmity that would include must depend on all the circumstances, but generally, I think, a reasonably normal condition, if medical evidence is G capable of defining it, would be the standard. The test of the plaintiff's extraordinary susceptibility, if unknown to the defendant, would in effect make the defendant an insurer. The lawyer likes to draw fixed and definite lines and is apt to ask where the thing is to stop. I should reply it should stop where in the particular case the good sense of the jury, or of the judge decides." H

LORD WRIGHT went on to rule out of contemplation a pregnant fish wife who was (24) " completely outside the range of the collision ".

Modern medicine recognises mental illness in a variety of forms. As I mentioned earlier, neurosis of one kind or another is a frequent visitor to the courts in claims for damages for personal injuries. The community is not formed of normal citizens, but with all those who are less susceptible or more susceptible to I stress to be regarded as extraordinary. There is an infinite variety of creatures, all with varying susceptibilities. Mr. Chadwick was a man who had lived a normal busy life in the community with no mental illness for sixteen years.

(20) (1921), 232 N.Y. Rep. 176.
(21) [1924] All E.R. Rep. 703; [1924] 1 K.B. 548.
(22) [1963] 1 All E.R. 705; [1963] A.C. 837.
(23) [1942] 2 All E.R. at pp. 405, 406; [1943] A.C. at p. 110.
(24) [1942] 2 All E.R. at p. 406, letter C; [1943] A.C. at p. 111.

A   He was, said Dr. Kendall, not likely to relapse under the ordinary stresses of life. Indeed, the evidence showed that during those sixteen years he had on one occasion been attacked by a gang of youths with bicycle chains, without any mental illness or injury resulting. This illness, according to Dr. Kendall, is a sufficiently common accompaniment of catastrophes to be given a name (25). In my opinion, there was nothing in Mr. Chadwick's personality to put him

B   outside the ambit of contemplation. I have come to the conclusion, therefore, that the defendants were in breach of the duty they owed to Mr. Chadwick and that the illness which he suffered as a result of that breach was one for which he was or, in this case, his personal representative, entitled to recover. Mrs. Chadwick is therefore entitled to damages against the defendants.

This illness started in early 1958 and required hospital treatment for approxi-

C   mately six months in 1959. Thereafter Mr. Chadwick was able to work but was never the same man as he had been before the accident. He died from causes unconnected with the accident in December, 1962. He lost wages as a result of this illness and, giving credit for his earnings and for half the sickness benefit, the total comes to £935 3s. 6d. In addition, for the misery and discomfort for what must have been the greatly diminished pleasure in life and for his

D   periods of treatment in hospital, I would assess the general damages at £600, making a total of £1,535 3s. 6d. for which the plaintiff is entitled to recover.

Judgment for the plaintiff.

Solicitors: *James & Charles Dodd* (for the plaintiff); *M. H. B. Gilmour* (for the defendants).

[*Reported by* K. DIANA PHILLIPS, *Barrister-at-Law.*]

E

SOUTH WESTERN MINERAL WATER CO., LTD. v. ASHMORE.

F   [CHANCERY DIVISION (Cross, J.), May 1, 2, 3, 4, 5, 1967.]

Company—Shares—Purchase of shares with financial assistance of company—Debenture to be issued by subsidiary company as security for purchase price of its shares from parent company—Agreement with a view to effecting a purchase by defendant of the business and assets of parent company—Major part of purchase price intended to be paid over a period of years and to be secured by

G   *charge—Mode of effecting purchase infringed s. 54—Issue of debenture an integral term of agreement—Rights of parties to agreement in view of effect of s. 54—Companies Act, 1948 (11 & 12 Geo. 6 c. 38), s. 54.*

After the death of the controlling shareholder of M., Ltd., oral arrangements were made between the defendant and directors of M., Ltd., one of whom was solicitor to the deceased shareholder's executors, with a view to the

H   defendant's buying the business assets of M., Ltd. for £42,500. Of that sum £6,000 was to be paid forthwith and the defendant was to have eight years in which to pay the balance of £36,500, which was to be secured by a charge. The defendant was to acquire the business assets of M., Ltd., but not shares of that company, and was to take possession of the assets forthwith. Since he would need a company by which to run the business, it was also arranged

I   that S., Ltd., a wholly owned subsidiary of M., Ltd., should be made available for this purpose. S., Ltd. had no assets and was not carrying on business. On June 5, 1965, the day following that on which the oral arrangements were made, the defendant signed an agreement prepared by the solicitor director of M., Ltd. with a view to carrying the arrangements into effect. This agreement was made between M., Ltd. and the defendant and provided for the payment of the £6,000, for the defendant to have an option to purchase the shares of S., Ltd. for £36,500, and for the £36,500 to be secured by a

---

(25) I.e. " catastrophic neurosis ", referred to at p. 949, letter B, ante.

debenture on the assets of S., Ltd. repayable in eight years. The provision   A
for issue of the debenture thus infringed s. 54 of the Companies Act, 1948,
but the persons concerned were unaware of this at that time. The defendant
took possession of the assets and ran the business, in the course of which he
contracted liabilities. In January, 1966, the infringement of s. 54 came to the
attention of M., Ltd. M., Ltd. by letter of their solicitors informed the
defendant that the proposed debenture would infringe s. 54, claimed payment   B
of the £36,500 in cash, and subsequently served notices with a view to
rescission of the agreement if the £36,500 were not paid.

Held: (i) the fact that the granting of the debenture would infringe s. 54
of the Companies Act, 1948, did not render the whole agreement of June 5,
1965, null and void (see p. 958, letter B, post).

(ii) it was an integral term of the agreement of June 5, 1965, that there   C
should be a debenture, and the defendant was under no obligation to pay
on terms that were substantially different, nor were M., Ltd. entitled to
retain the £6,000 on rescission of the agreement; in the circumstances the
right of each party to the agreement was to ask the court to decree restitutio
in integrum on equitable terms (see p. 958, letter D, and p. 960, letters B, C
and D, post).   D

[As to the prohibition of a company's providing financial assistance for the
purchase of its own shares, see 6 HALSBURY'S LAWS (3rd Edn.) 170, 171, para. 358;
and for cases on the subject, see 9 DIGEST (Repl.) 651, *4327-4330*.

For s. 54 of the Companies Act, 1948, see 3 HALSBURY'S STATUTES (2nd Edn.)
507.]   E

Action.

This was an action brought by South Western Mineral Water Co., Ltd. (" the
mineral company ") by writ issued on Apr. 1, 1966, in which the mineral company
sought relief against the defendant, Brian Wilkinson Ashmore, on the basis of
rescission of an agreement, dated June 5, 1965, between the mineral company   F
and the defendant, or of the discharge of the agreement by breach on the part of
the defendant. The relief claimed was possession; and alternatively the mineral
company claimed specific performance of the agreement on the footing that a
sum of £36,500, forming part of the purchase price under the agreement, should
be paid on completion.

The following narrative is summarised from the judgment of CROSS, J. The   G
mineral company had been controlled and managed in recent years by a Mr.
Munckton, who died in 1963; most of the shares in the mineral company were
held by his executors, or his widow or his married daughter, but the chairman of
the mineral company, a Mr. Pettit, held two hundred shares. The mineral
company had a wholly owned subsidiary, Solent Products, Ltd., which had no
assets and, at the time of the agreement previously mentioned, was not carrying   H
on any business. On June 4, 1965, at a meeting between the defendant, a Mr.
Hawkins, who was solicitor to the executors and a director of the mineral
company, and Mr. Fletcher, who was an accountant and a director of the mineral
company, it was agreed orally that the defendant would give £42,500 for the
business assets of the mineral company, excluding certain assets not material to
this report. The defendant was to pay £6,000 down, but was to have eight years
to pay the balance of £36,500, interest being payable on the balance from time-   I
to-time outstanding at eight per cent. The £36,500 was to be secured by an
effective charge. The defendant was to take possession of the assets forthwith.
As he would need a company through which to run the business, Solent Products,
Ltd. was to be made available for that purpose. On June 5, 1965, the defendant
signed an agreement, prepared by Mr. Hawkins, expressed to be between the
defendant of the one part and the mineral company of the other part. The
material terms of this agreement were—

A   " Whereby in consideration of the sum of £6,000 payable by [the defendant] as to £1,000 in cash on the signing hereof and as to £5,000 by way of undertaking to pay the same . . . within thirty days [the mineral company] agree to grant an option to [the defendant] to purchase the total shareholding of [their] subsidiary company, Solent Products, Ltd., for the sum of £36,500.

B   " It is further hereby agreed as follows: (i) Completion date shall be on or before June 15, 1965. (ii) The purchase price of £36,500 shall be secured by way of a fixed and floating debenture on the assets of Solent Products, Ltd. repayable in a period of eight years from the date hereof and carrying interest on the outstanding balance thereof from time to time at the rate of £8 per cent. per annum. The debentures shall be secured by a personal

C guarantee by [the defendant] supported by the deposit by [the defendant] of securities acceptable to [the mineral company] to the value of £9,000, such securities to be deposited with [the mineral company's] solicitors . . . (iii) The assets of Solent Products, Ltd. and of [the mineral company] included in the sale are as follows . . . [the assets included a factory site at Bourne-

D mouth, a factory site at Swanage, both of which were owned by the mineral company, and the benefit of a lease of a factory at Southampton, which apparently belonged to Mr. Munckton before his death, but of which the beneficiary was prepared at the instance of the mineral company to grant a lease to the defendant] . . . (d) All motor vehicles, plant, machinery, stock and containers used in connexion with [the mineral company's business at Bournemouth, Southampton and Swanage] as at June 1, 1965; (e) The

E benefit of all contracts of [the mineral company]; (f) The benefit of all trade marks owned by [the mineral company] and the right to use the trade name of ' South Western Mineral Water Company, Ltd.' and the right to hold out Solent Products, Ltd. as carrying on the business in succession to [the mineral company]. (iv) The [mineral company] will pay in full [their] creditors as at June 1, 1965, and [their] debtors shall be assigned to Solent Products, Ltd.

F as at that date. The purchase price of the said debtors shall be secured by further debenture bearing interest of £1 per cent. per annum above Bank rate on the balance of [the debts] collected by [the defendant] as certified by the auditors [of the mineral company] from time to time. Such debenture shall be repaid in full within twelve months from the signing hereof. (v) The benefit and burden of the existing hire-purchase agreement with Distillers,

G Ltd., shall be assigned to [the defendant]. (vi) [The defendant] shall be entitled to the net rents and profits of the business carried on by [the mineral company] with effect from June 1, 1965."

His Lordship, CROSS, J., having observed that Solent Products, Ltd., notwithstanding the terms of this agreement, had no assets at the time, intimated that the issue of the debenture for which cl. (ii) provided would infringe s. 54 of the

H Companies Act, 1948, though the transaction could have been carried out differently in a manner which would not have infringed that enactment. HIS LORDSHIP found on the evidence that the parties concerned did not have s. 54 in mind at the time. HIS LORDSHIP further observed that it was wrong for the mineral company to purport to give the defendant the right to use its own registered name, South Western Mineral Water Co., Ltd.

I   On June 8, 1965, the defendant went into possession and started to run the business which had formerly been that of the mineral company. On the same day a mandate to National Provincial Bank, Ltd. was executed. The mandate was headed with the name of Solent Products, Ltd. and was as follows—

     " We give below for your records the full names and signatures of the director and signing officials of this company."

The mandate was signed by the defendant, who described himself as the chairman, and by Mr. Buchanan, who was the defendant's accountant and was described as

director, and by Mr. Hawkins and a Mr. Warren, each of whom was said to be a A
director. At that time the chairman and directors of Solent Products, Ltd. were
Mr. Pettitt, Mrs. Foster, a daughter of Mr. Munckton, and Mr. Fletcher. HIS
LORDSHIP observed that if blame attached to anyone in connexion with the
signing of this mandate, it would be to Mr. Hawkins, who was the only solicitor
engaged in the transaction. The sale was not completed on July 15 by the
execution of the debentures, and the £5,000 was not paid within the thirty B
days for which the agreement provided, but it was paid early in October, 1965.
On Oct. 12, 1965, there was a meeting at the offices of the mineral company
which was attended by Mr. Pettitt, Mr. Fletcher and Mr. Hawkins, and by the
defendant and Mr. Buchanan. The purpose of the meeting was to resolve a
question about liability to make refunds on returned mineral water containers,
and also to complete the agreed transaction. At a fairly late stage at the meeting C
Mr. Fletcher intimated on behalf of the mineral company that it was not prepared
to complete. A subsequent letter, dated Oct. 20, 1965, from Mr. Hawkins to Mr.
Buchanan showed, however, that notwithstanding the meeting the transaction
was likely to go through. Difficulty then arose over the mandate given to the
bank, the bank having requested authority of the mineral company and of the
directors of Solent Products, Ltd. if the bank were to settle cheques signed D
by the defendant on Solent Products, Ltd.'s account, since the bank had become
aware that the defendant and his colleagues were not the chairman and directors
of that company. Mr. Fletcher had not previously heard about the mandate,
and a meeting was held of the directors of the mineral company, which resulted
in Mr. Hawkins and Mr. Fletcher resigning their directorships.

At a meeting of the board of the mineral company on Jan. 14, 1966, Mr. E
Pettitt's son, who was a solicitor, raised the question whether s. 54 of the Companies Act, 1948, would be infringed by issuing the debenture for which the
agreement provided. The defendant joined the meeting later. He was not
told of the question as to s. 54 at that time, but was asked whether he would be
prepared to pay £36,500 at once. He had, apparently, been in negotiation
for resale of some of the properties at a profit, and was willing to try to sell F
properties and raise the £36,500 if he could, if only because that would avoid his
liability to pay eight per cent. interest. Alternatively he was anxious that the
transaction should be completed by the company executing the debenture and
his receiving the conveyances. The mineral company took counsel's opinion
who advised that cl. (ii) of the agreement infringed s. 54, and that Solent Products,
Ltd. could not grant the debenture envisaged. On Feb. 10, 1966, having received G
counsel's opinion, the solicitors for the mineral company, who were Mr. Pettitt's
firm, wrote to the defendant as follows—

" You are aware that we have been instructed to act for [the mineral
company] . . . you are also aware that our clients have been much concerned
at the delay in completion, which still continues despite your repeated
assurances that the matter will be completed at an early date. In view of this H
delay and the present unsatisfactory position our clients have taken the
opinion of leading counsel who advises [inter alia] that the proposal for a
debenture to be given to secure the purchase price of £36,500 would contravene s. 54 of the Companies Act, 1948, and therefore be illegal. The [mineral
company] cannot allow the present state of affairs to continue any longer
and unless, therefore, within seven days from this date the purchase price is I
paid in cash or £36,500 deposited in cash in the joint names of yourself and
ourselves at . . . [a bank], the [mineral company] will be compelled to
resume possession of [their] business and assets and will require a full
account of your dealing therewith whilst in possession thereof."

On this letter HIS LORDSHIP observed that the people really in default at that
time were the mineral company, not the defendant; and, that Mr. Hawkins
and the mineral company were responsible for the position in regard to s. 54.

A His LORDSHIP described the letter as an unfortunate one in the circumstances for the mineral company to write. The defendant's solicitor was in hospital at that time, and his firm replied by letter dated Feb. 17, 1966, accepting that probably the agreement contravened s. 54, but maintaining that the oral agreement reached by the parties did not contravene that section; they further stated that the mineral company were not entitled to payment of the sum of
B £36,500 forthwith, nor were they entitled to resume possession of the business and premises occupied by the defendant.

On Feb. 22, 1966, the mineral company served two notices on the defendant. The first, addressed to the defendant, read—

C " Take notice that [the mineral company] who is vendor under a contract entered into by your election to exercise the option granted by an agreement dated June 5, 1965, for the purchase of the total shareholding of Solent Products, Ltd. and of the assets specified in cl. (iii) of the said agreement for the sum of £36,500 is willing and ready to execute and to cause and procure all other necessary parties (if any) to concur in proper transfers, conveyances and assignments . . . to you or otherwise as you may direct of the property comprised in the said contract . . . and that [the mineral company] now
D call on and require you forthwith to tender for execution such transfers, conveyances and assignments and to pay the said purchase money [i.e., the £36,500] and further that if you fail to comply with this notice within twenty-eight days from the date hereof [the mineral company] will then treat the said contract as at an end and be at liberty to resell the said property or any part thereof or hold you liable to make good to [them] such loss, costs,
E damage and expenses as may be incurred by [them] by reason of your default in performing the said contract."

His LORDSHIP observed that that notice proceeded on a misconceived view of the legal position and was a nullity; since the defendant was under no obligation to pay £36,500 down. A separate notice was also addressed to the defendant,
F which read—

" Take notice that [the mineral company] hereby revoke the licence under which you have been let into possession of the business of Solent Products, Ltd. and of the other assets comprised in cl. (iii) of an agreement dated June 5, 1965, and made between yourself of the one part and [the mineral company] of the other part and hereby require you to deliver up
G possession of the same to [the mineral company]."

On Apr. 1, 1966, the mineral company issued the writ beginning this action. The cases noted below* were cited during the argument.

Raymond Walton, Q.C., and *J. M. E. Byng* for the mineral company.
J. H. Hames for the defendant.

H ─────────────────────────────────────

* *Right d. Lewis* v. *Beard*, (1811), 13 East. 210; *Doe d. Gray* v. *Stanion*, [1835-42] All E.R. Rep. 290; *Doe d. Tomes* v. *Chamberlaine*, (1839), 5 M. & W. 14; *Walker* v. *Jeffreys*, (1842), 1 Hare 341; *Burgess* v. *Boetefeur*, (1844), 7 Man. & G. 481; *Pickering* v. *Ilfracombe Ry. Co.*, [1861–73] All E.R. Rep. 773; (1868), L.R. 3 C.P. 235; *Greenwood* v. *Turner*, [1891-94] All E.R. Rep. 190; [1891] 2 Ch. 144; *Kearney* v. *Whitehaven*
I *Colliery Co.*, [1891-94] All E.R. Rep. 556; [1893] 1 Q.B. 700; *Unsworth* v. *Jordan*, [1896] W.N. 2; *Berners* v. *Heming*, [1925] All E.R. Rep. 557; [1925] Ch. 264; *Berg* v. *Sadler and Moore*, [1937] 1 All E.R. 637; [1937] 2 K.B. 158; *Public Trustee* v. *Pearlberg*, [1940] 2 All E.R. 270; [1940] 2 K.B. 1; *Bowmakers, Ltd.* v. *Barnet Instruments, Ltd.*, [1944] 2 All E.R. 579; [1945] K.B. 65; *Victor Battery Co., Ltd.* v. *Curry's, Ltd.*, [1946] 1 All E.R. 519; [1946] Ch. 242; *Fox* v. *Hunter-Paterson*, [1948] 2 All E.R. 813; *Dennis & Co., Ltd.* v. *Munn*, [1949] 1 All E.R. 616; [1949] 2 K.B. 327; *Wheeler* v. *Mercer*, [1956] 3 All E.R. 631; [1957] A.C. 416; *Brown Jenkinson & Co., Ltd.* v. *Percy Dalton (London), Ltd.*, [1957] 2 All E.R. 844; [1957] 2 Q.B. 621; *Sajan Singh* v. *Sardara Ali*, [1960] 1 All E.R. 269; [1960] A.C. 167; *Australian Blue Metal, Ltd.* v. *Hughes* [1962] 3 All E.R. 335; [1963] A.C. 74.

CROSS, J., having reviewed the facts down to and including the meeting on   A
Jan. 14, 1966, when the question of the effect of s. 54 of the Companies Act, 1948
was first raised (see p. 956, letter E, ante), stated that it was probably desirable
for him at that stage to give his view of the position resulting from the effect of
s. 54 on the agreement of June 5, 1965, and continued:] I do not take the view
that the fact that the granting of this debenture would be a criminal offence by
Solent Products, Ltd., made the whole of the agreement of June 5, 1965,   B
absolutely null and void so that the court will not allow anybody to rely on any
of its provisions. No case that has been cited to me suggests that I am obliged
to arrive at so ridiculous a conclusion. The position, was, I think, that if the
mineral company were prepared to waive the obligation of Solent Products,
Ltd., to provide the debenture and were prepared to complete the transaction
on the footing that they merely had the personal undertaking of the defendant   C
to pay the £36,500 over eight years with eight per cent. interest secured only by
the £9,000 securities and without any charge on the assets taken over by Solent
Products, Ltd., they were at liberty to enforce the agreement on that basis.
In fact, however, the mineral company say that an integral part of the arrangement was that there should be a debenture. I think that they are right on that
point. It was so substantial a part of the consideration that, though they could   D
waive it and enforce the contract without it if they liked, the defendant could
not compel them to complete on that basis. Alternatively, I think that the
defendant, if he was willing to waive the period of eight years for the payment of
the purchase money which was inserted obviously for his convenience, and pay
the £36,500 down, he was at liberty to do so. I do not think the mineral company could have refused to accept the money and, quite clearly, they would   E
not have refused. The defendant, however, was unwilling or unable to pay it.

But the mineral company contended that they could compel the defendant
to pay £36,500 down. That appears to me to be an untenable argument. When
the agreement says:

"The purchase price of £36,500 shall be secured by way of a fixed and
floating debenture on the assets of Solent Products, Ltd., repayable in a   F
period of eight years,"

it means to my mind that the purchase price is not payable in any other way
without the defendant's consent. It would be odd to say that he was under a
personal obligation to pay on terms which were different from the terms of the
debenture which was to secure the payment. It is plain to my mind that in
the earlier part of the agreement where the mineral company agrees to grant   G
an option to the defendant to purchase the shareholding of Solent Products,
Ltd., for the sum of £36,500, one must read in the words "to be satisfied and
only satisfied in the manner hereinafter provided", so that it is not the case that
the mineral company could compel the defendant to pay the £36,500 down.

[HIS LORDSHIP then referred to the letter of Feb. 10, 1966 (see p. 956, letters G
to I, ante), and the reply thereto on the defendant's behalf, and to the notices   H
dated Feb. 22, 1966 (see p. 957, letters C to G, ante). Having intimated that no
claim for rectification was before the court, and that it was immaterial whether the
defendant was in the position of a licensee or of a tenant at will in relation to
assets comprised in the agreement of June 5, 1965, HIS LORDSHIP continued:]
There are, however, serious objections to the second notice to the defendant,
dated Feb. 22, 1966. How is it to be construed? How was the defendant meant to   I
construe it in relation to the other document which was served contemporaneously with it? The other document, which was nugatory, though presumably
the mineral company thought that it had some effect, told the defendant to pay
the purchase price within twenty-eight days. Did the second notice require
him to deliver up possession forthwith, within twenty-eight days, even though
he was prepared to complete in accordance with the other document? That
is one possible construction though the mineral company say that it is not the
right one. They say that "forthwith" merely meant with all reasonable

A speed and certainly did not involve the defendant's giving up possession within the twenty-eight days. Then was he to consider this second notice as ancillary to the first and as being a statement that if he failed to pay at the end of the twenty-eight days they then would resume possession because of his failure to pay? Or was he to regard it, as the mineral company say it was intended, as an entirely independent notice demanding possession within a reasonable time

B even if the first notice was nugatory? Whatever the mineral company intended, I certainly do not think that their intention was made plain to the defendant by these notices.

[HIS LORDSHIP then referred to the letter of the defendant's solicitors dated Feb. 22, 1966, and the reply thereto, and having read extracts from the letter of the defendant's solicitors dated Mar. 16, 1966, setting out their view of the

C legal position, continued:] The position really was this. The mineral company could not call on the defendant to pay the £36,500 down, but he could not compel them to go on with the agreement of June 5, 1965, without the debenture; and if he was not in fact himself prepared to pay £36,500 down, this agreement, though it was not a nullity, was not in the circumstances enforceable by either party. Therefore, the only thing to do was to reach some agreement for a

D restitutio in integrum or some agreement varying the original agreement. If the parties could not arrive at any agreement, then it would be necessary for one or other party to go to the court and ask the court to cut the Gordian knot somehow or other and that would obviously involve the giving up of possession by the defendant. In the letter dated Mar. 16, 1966, I do not think that the defendant was entirely facing up to that difficulty. He was apparently claiming

E to continue to remain in possession although the contract could not be completed according to its terms because neither party would waive the provisions in it which were in their favour.

The writ in this action was issued by the mineral company on Apr. 1, 1966. In that writ they set out the agreement and the entry by the defendant into possession and the notices, and they claim that the defendant failed to comply with the

F first notice and on that basis they claim that they were entitled either to rescind the agreement or that it was discharged by the breach of the defendant. They then set out the second notice and they say the defendant failed to deliver up possession and they claim possession and alternatively they claim specific performance. Incidentally, they applied under R.S.C., Ord. 14 (B) for a summary order for possession, but that application was dismissed.

G The defence says that the mineral company cannot be entitled to specific performance on the terms on which they are asking for it, that is, payment of £36,500 down. The defendant further says that he has never been in breach and that there was no effective notice determining the licence or tenancy at will, and he asks that the action should be dismissed.

During the time that the case has taken to come on for trial, the defendant

H has continued in possession. He admits that he collected a number of the book debts, which he was entitled to do under the contract, and it appears also that he has contracted a good many liabilities for goods supplied to the business which he has been running for which he has not paid. A number of the dissatisfied creditors have issued writs against the mineral company because the goods were apparently ordered in the name of the mineral company. In that connexion one

I will remember the extraordinary cl. iii (f) in the agreement of June 5, 1965, (1), under which the mineral company purported to give the defendant the right to use the trade name of the mineral company. One does not know what the outcome of the actions between the creditors and the mineral company will be. It may be that in some or all of the cases the mineral company could show that the defendant was not their agent to contract any liability, but one can well understand the anxiety of the mineral company as to their position. It appears,

(1) See p. 955, letter E, ante.

too, that Solent Products, Ltd., is in difficulties and that a winding-up petition   A
has been presented against it.

It is plain that having regard to the view which I have formed on the construction of the agreement, many of the claims made by the mineral company in these
proceedings are unjustified.   They cannot claim specific performance of the
agreement on the terms which they suggest, the payment of £36,500 down.
As the first notice of Feb. 22 was nugatory, they cannot say that they have any   B
right to rescind the contract because of the defendant's failure to comply with
it.   Nor has it been discharged by the breach by the defendant.   As I have
said, at that date the defendant was not in breach and any claim for damages
against the defendant is, I think, out of the question.   The right of either party
in the circumstances, if no agreement could be reached, was to come to the court
and ask the court to decree some sort of restitutio in integrum on equitable   C
terms.

I should now deal with one question of principle on the terms of the restitutio
in integrum.   It was suggested on behalf of the mineral company that at all
events they would be entitled to keep the £6,000 paid for the option on the ground
that there was not a total failure of consideration for the payment of it.   They
say that the contract was not an absolute nullity, and that it was possible for   D
the defendant, if he was prepared to waive the eight-year period for payment
of the purchase money and produce the £36,500 at once, to force the mineral
company to accept it.   I do not think that such a meagre right as that affords
any equitable title in the mineral company to retain the £6,000.   Any restitutio
in integrum which I decree in the circumstances must be on equitable terms
and it would be unfair that they should retain that sum.   On the other hand it   E
must be a term of the restitutio that the defendant should go out of possession
and allow the mineral company to resume possession of the business and the
properties.   It was argued by the defendant that the plaintiffs were claiming a
right to possession on the basis of their second notice which was no more valid
than the first and that, therefore, the action should be dismissed.   To my mind
serious criticisms can be levelled against the second notice.   It was, I think,   F
difficult for the defendant to know, when he received it, exactly what it meant.
Be that as it may, by Mar. 16, 1966, before the writ was issued, the defendant on
his side had made his position clear and was putting forward a claim which was
untenable, namely, that although he could not carry out the agreement by
granting the debenture and although he could not compel the mineral company
to accept any other security, he was nevertheless entitled to remain in possession.   G
If he had put forward the argument that he had not received reasonable notice
in sufficient time to go out, that the word " forthwith " was ambiguous and that
he must have a number of months to get out, then the position would have
been different.   But in view of the attitude which the defendant adopted considerably before the writ was issued I would not be justified in dismissing this
action.   H

What I propose to do is to declare, that in the circumstances the agreement
entered into is unenforceable on either side and that the parties must be restored
as far as possible to their former positions.   If the parties cannot agree the
terms of a restitutio in integrum in the light of what I have said the matter must
be mentioned to me again.

Liberty to apply accordingly.   I

Solicitors: *Robins, Hay, Long & Gardiner*, agents for *Rawlins, Davy & Wells*,
Bournemouth (for the mineral company);   *Muscatt, Nelson & Co.* (for the
defendant).

[*Reported by* JACQUELINE METCALFE, *Barrister-at-Law.*]

A

NORTHROP v. NORTHROP.

[Court of Appeal, civil division (Willmer, Diplock and Winn, L.JJ.), April 17, 18, 19, May 11, 1967.]

B *Magistrates—Husband and wife—Maintenance—Wilful neglect to maintain— Consensual separation—Implication of agreement by husband to support wife as well as child to the extent to which wife precluded by her obligations to child from supporting herself—Maintenance order on ground of husband's neglect to maintain wife, as distinct from child—Matrimonial Proceedings (Magistrates' Courts) Act, 1960 (8 & 9 Eliz. 2 c. 48), s. 2 (1) (b).*

C *Magistrates—Husband and wife—Maintenance—Wilful neglect to maintain— Consensual separation—Neglect to maintain child—Court's power to found on that neglect an order for provision for the wife, in addition to maintenance for the child—Provision such as to enable wife to discharge obligations to child impairing her earning power—Matrimonial Proceedings (Magistrates' Courts) Act, 1960 (8 & 9 Eliz. 2 c. 48), s. 2 (1) (b), (h).*

D On a complaint by the wife that the husband had deserted her and that he had been guilty of wilful neglect to provide reasonable maintenance for herself and for an infant child of the marriage, the justices found in effect that the spouses' parting was a consensual separation, and the finding was upheld on appeal. The justices also found that the husband had been guilty of wilful neglect to maintain both the wife and the child, and they made an order that the husband should pay maintenance at the rate of £5 a

E week in respect of the wife and £2 a week in respect of the child. On appeal,

Held: (i) (Willmer, L.J., dissenting from this ground) a matrimonial order could be made, on the ground of wilful neglect to provide reasonable maintenance for the child, containing provision not only under s. 2 (1) (h) of the Matrimonial Proceedings (Magistrates' Courts) Act, 1960, for maintenance of the child at a rate not exceeding 50s. weekly, but also under

F s. 2 (1) (b) for payment of such weekly sum, not exceeding £7 10s., as the court considered reasonable by way of supplement to the wife's own resources so as to enable her properly to provide for the needs of the child (see p. 975, letters B and D, p. 976, letters B and C, p. 977, letter I, and p. 979, letter G, post: cf., p. 968, letter F, post); the case would, therefore, be remitted to the justices to decide (a) whether there had been wilful neglect to provide reasonable maintenance for the child as distinct from the wife, and (b) whether

G and to what extent the wife had been precluded by her obligations to the child from earning sufficient to support herself and the child (see p. 976, letters G and I, and p. 977, letter G, and p. 979, letter I, post).

Young v. *Young* ([1962] 3 All E.R. 120) considered.

Dicta of Lord Merriman, P., in *Kinnane* v. *Kinnane* ([1953] 2 All E.R.

H at p. 1146), cited by Marshall, J., in *Cooke* v. *Cooke* ([1960] 3 All E.R. at p. 46), and in *Starkie* v. *Starkie (No. 2)* ([1953] 2 All E.R. at p. 1522), applied.

(ii) on a consensual separation it might be right to imply an agreement by the husband to support, not only an infant child of the marriage, but also the wife to the extent to which her earning capacity was impaired by the discharge of her obligations to the child, and where such an agreement was

I implied maintenance for the wife (as distinct from provision for the wife to enable her to discharge obligations to the child) could be ordered under s. 2 (1) (b) of the Act of 1960; accordingly the case would be remitted to the justices to decide whether such a term should be implied as would justify the finding of wilful neglect to maintain the wife (see p. 970, letters D to H, p. 977, letters B to H, and p. 978, letter H, post).

Baker v. *Baker* ((1949), 66 (pt. 1) T.L.R. 81) and *Kinnane* v. *Kinnane* ([1953] 2 All E.R. 1144) applied on this point.

Per Winn, L.J., Diplock, L.J., concurring: any wife who has not been

guilty of a matrimonial offence, whether she is still living with her husband   A
or has separated from him consensually, is entitled to provision under
para. (*b*) as well as para. (*h*) of s. 2 (1)* of the Matrimonial Proceedings (Magistrates' Courts) Act, 1960, in a matrimonial order, if she has established her
right to such an order under s. 1 (1) for wilful neglect (see p. 976, letter C,
and p. 977, letter I, post).

Decision of the DIVISIONAL COURT ([1966] 3 All E.R. 797) affirmed on   B
(ii), but over-ruled on (i), p. 961, ante.

[**Editorial Note.** In considering this decision there should be had in mind
throughout the distinction between the grounds on which a matrimonial order
may be made (s. 1 (1) of the Act of 1960) and the content of the order when made
(s. 2 (1)); regard should also be had to the emphasis laid by DIPLOCK, L.J.,
on a wife's right to payment for herself, i.e., provision under s. 2 (1) (*b*),   C
where she is supporting a child of the family, without imposing on her the
legal obligation of having first to establish implication of an agreement
by the husband at the time of their separation to provide reasonably for her to
enable her to maintain the child (see p. 977, letter I, to p. 978, letter B, and
p. 978, letter D, post).

As to consensual separation, see 12 HALSBURY'S LAWS (3rd Edn.) 484, para.   D
1080; and for cases on the subject, see 27 DIGEST (Repl.) 343, 344, *2840-2860*.

As to wilful neglect to maintain a child, see 12 HALSBURY'S LAWS (3rd Edn.)
482, para. 1077; and for cases on the subject, see DIGEST (Cont. Vol. A) 819, 820,
6720b, 6721a, 6721c.

For the Matrimonial Proceedings (Magistrates' Courts) Act, 1960, s. 2, see
40 HALSBURY'S STATUTES (2nd Edn.) 399.]   E

Cases referred to:

Baker v. *Baker*, (1949), 66 (pt. 1) T.L.R. 81; 27 Digest (Repl.) 82, *630*.

Chapman v. *Chapman*, (1951), C.A., Apr. 4, unreported.

Cooke v. *Cooke*, [1960] 3 All E.R. 39; [1961] P. 16; [1960] 3 W.L.R. 807;
124 J.P. 433; Digest (Cont. Vol. A) 820, *6721c*.

Kinnane v. *Kinnane*, [1953] 2 All E.R. 1144; [1954] P. 41; [1953] 3 W.L.R.   F
782; 117 J.P. 552; Digest (Cont. Vol. A) 819, *6721a*.

Lilley v. *Lilley*, [1959] 3 All E.R. 283; [1960] P. 158 at p. 169; [1959] 3
W.L.R. 306; 123 J.P. 525; Digest (Cont. Vol. A) 667, *6196a*.

National Assistance Board v. *Parkes*, [1955] 3 All E.R. 1; [1955] 2 Q.B. 506;
[1955] 3 W.L.R. 347; *affg.*, sub nom. *Stopher* v. *National Assistance*
Board, National Assistance Board v. *Parkes*, [1955] 1 All E.R. 700;   G
[1955] 1 Q.B. 486; [1955] 2 W.L.R. 622; Digest (Cont. Vol. A) 687,
1809a

Naylor v. *Naylor*, [1961] 2 All E.R. 129; [1962] P. 253; [1961] 2 W.L.R. 751;
125 J.P. 358; Digest (Cont. Vol. A) 816, *6684a*.

Pinnick v. *Pinnick*, [1957] 1 All E.R. 873; [1957] 1 W.L.R. 644; 121 J.P. 256;   H
Digest (Cont. Vol. A) 674, *636ba*.

Starkie v. *Starkie (No. 2)*, [1953] 2 All E.R. 1519; [1954] 1 W.L.R. 98; 118
J.P. 59; Digest (Cont. Vol. A) 819, *6720b*.

Stringer v. *Stringer*, [1952] 1 All E.R. 373; [1952] P. 171; 116 J.P. 102;
Digest (Cont. Vol. A) 674, *636b*.

Vaughan v. *Vaughan*, [1963] 2 All E.R. 742; [1965] P. 15; [1963] 3 W.L.R. 964;   I
127 J.P. 404; Digest (Cont. Vol. A) 824, *6755g*.

Young v. *Young*, [1962] 3 All E.R. 120; [1964] P. 152; [1962] 3 W.L.R. 946;
Digest (Cont. Vol. A) 730, *3037b*.

Appeal and cross-appeal.

The husband appealed and the wife cross-appealed, and served a cross-notice
in respect of the husband's appeal, against an order of a Divisional Court of the

---

* Section 2 (1), so far as material, is set out at p. 972, letters F to H, post.

A Probate, Divorce and Admiralty Division (Sir Jocelyn Simon, P., and Karminski, J.) given on Oct. 28, 1966, and reported at [1966] 3 All E.R. 797. The
husband sought an order that that part of the judgment of the Divisional Court
should be rescinded whereby it directed that the justices of the petty sessional
division of Brighouse Borough in the West Riding of Yorkshire should rehear and
consider further matters concerning the wife's complaint made to them that the
B husband had wilfully neglected to provide reasonable maintenance for the wife
and her infant child; and also an order varying the judgment by setting aside
the order of the justices made on Jan. 13, 1966, adjudging that he had been
guilty of wilfully neglecting to provide such maintenance. The grounds of
appeal were: (i) that, there being no or alternatively no sufficient evidence on
which the Divisional Court could find that the husband had wilfully neglected
C to provide reasonable maintenance for the wife or for her infant child, the court
ought to have set aside the order of the justices and not directed a further
hearing of the complaint by the justices; (ii) that the Divisional Court was
wrong in law in holding that the husband could be found guilty of wilfully
neglecting to provide reasonable maintenance for the wife as well as for the
infant child if it were proved that the husband had in fact wilfully neglected
D to provide reasonable maintenance for the child, and notwithstanding the fact
that the separation between the husband and the wife was a consensual one,
with no agreement that the husband accepted any liability for the maintenance
and support of the wife; (iii) that the Divisional Court was wrong in law on the
proved and admitted facts in not holding that the wife had deserted the husband
on and ever since Feb. 11, 1964.

E   The wife by her cross-notice gave notice of her intention to contend that the
part of the judgment of the Divisional Court should be rescinded by which it
directed that the justices should rehear and consider further matters concerning
the wife's complaint, and that it should be varied by dismissing the husband's
appeal against the justices' decision to the Divisional Court.

   By her cross-appeal the wife sought an order rescinding that part of the
F judgment of the Divisional Court whereby it dismissed the wife's appeal against
the finding of the justices that the husband had not deserted the wife, and that
the judgment should be varied by adjudging that the husband had deserted
the wife on and ever since about Feb. 11, 1964. The grounds of the wife's appeal
were: (i) that the Divisional Court was wrong in law in dismissing the wife's
appeal; (ii) that on the facts the Divisional Court should have allowed the
G wife's appeal and have ordered that the husband had deserted the wife on and
ever since about Feb. 11, 1964.

   C. T. Reeve, Q.C., and *N. Taylor* for the husband.
   D. G. A. Lowe, Q.C., and *B. H. Anns* for the wife.

                                                            Cur. adv. vult.

H   May 11. The following judgments were read:

   WILLMER, L.J.: In this case we had before us an appeal and cross-appeal
against a judgment of the Divisional Court (1) of the Probate, Divorce and
Admiralty Division consisting of Sir Jocelyn Simon, P., and Karminski, J.,
given on Oct. 28, 1966, on cross-appeals brought by husband and wife respectively
against an order of Jan. 13, 1966, made by the justices of the petty sessional
I division of Brighouse Borough. The proceedings arose out of a complaint by the
wife that her husband had deserted her on Feb. 11, 1964, and had been guilty
of wilful neglect to provide reasonable maintenance for herself and the infant
child of the marriage. The justices found that the alleged desertion was not
proved, but that the husband was guilty of wilful neglect to maintain both the
wife and the child. They accordingly made an order that the husband should
pay maintenance at the rate of £5 per week in respect of the wife and £2 per
week in respect of the child.

Against this order the husband appealed on the grounds (i) that the justices A
were wrong in law in finding him guilty of wilful neglect to maintain either the
wife or the child, and (ii) that the wife ought to have been held to be in desertion.
There was also a complaint as to the quantum of maintenance ordered, but this
has not been proceeded with. The wife appealed on the ground that the
justices were wrong in not holding the husband guilty of desertion. The Divisional
Court (1) dismissed both parties' charges of desertion, but allowed the husband's B
appeal to the extent of remitting to the justices for further findings of fact the
wife's complaints of wilful neglect to maintain herself and the child. In this
court each party has again contended that the other was in desertion. Both
parties also appeal against the order remitting the question of maintenance
to the justices for further findings of fact, the husband on the ground that there
was no sufficient evidence to justify the finding that he had been guilty of any C
wilful neglect to maintain either the wife or the child, the wife on the ground that
the justices' finding to that effect was right and ought to have been sustained.

The material facts can be briefly stated. The parties were married in September,
1944, and, after residing for some two years in Cambridge, made their home in
Halifax. There are two children of the marriage, a son born in 1944, who is
now self-supporting, and a daughter born in 1953, who is still at school. There D
had been previous periods of separation, but the final parting took place on
Feb. 11, 1964. It is common ground that on that occasion, following a quarrel,
the wife told the husband to go. The husband took her at her word and left,
not without some assistance from the wife, who packed his bag for him, looked
up the time of his train, and even gave him money for the journey. The husband
went back to Cambridge, where he has lived ever since with his sister. The E
wife and the two children have remained in the matrimonial home at Halifax.
From the time of the parting until a date well after the first hearing of the wife's
summons (which was adjourned by the justices to enable the possibility of a
reconciliation to be explored) the husband paid £2 per week for the maintenance
of the younger child, but he paid nothing for the maintenance of the wife until
an interim order was made against him. Following the separation the wife on F
three occasions, Feb. 24, Mar. 2 and Sept. 16, 1964, wrote to the husband suggesting that he might return to her. In March, 1964, both parties instructed solicitors,
and a considerable correspondence ensued between the solicitors, in the course
of which each party put forward proposals for a reconciliation. The wife's
solicitors were inviting the husband to return to the matrimonial home in Halifax,
which the husband was unwilling to do. The husband's solicitors suggested that G
the wife should join the husband in Cambridge, where it was said that the husband
was willing to provide accommodation, but this the wife refused to do. In the
event, therefore, nothing came of the negotiations, and the parties have remained
apart ever since February, 1964. The wife's summons, whereby she complained
of desertion and of wilful failure to maintain herself and the younger child,
came on for hearing in July, 1964, when it was adjourned, and an interim order H
for maintenance was made. The summons was eventually restored and disposed
of on Jan. 13, 1966, when the wife's complaint of desertion was dismissed, but
the order complained of was made on the ground of wilful neglect to maintain
both wife and child.

It will be convenient to deal first with the issue of desertion, as to which the
justices in their reasons made the following findings: I

" (ii) Our view about the parting on Feb. 11, was that both parties were
in the wrong, the wife in telling the husband to leave and persisting in
telling him, and the husband in taking her at her word. We thought that
before that the parties were only existing together and that both were
satisfied to part, but at the same time there was really nothing between
them that could not have been put right by sensible discussion. (iii) Both

(1) [1966] 3 All E.R. 797.

A   parties made subsequent offers to resume cohabitation, but they were half-hearted on both sides; we did not think they were sufficiently clear for either side to rely on them as establishing desertion; they had ceased to cohabit, and the only definite place where they could resume cohabitation was the matrimonial home."

B   The Divisional Court (2) interpreted the justices' conclusions as amounting to a finding that the initial separation was consensual, and that the offers made on either side to resume cohabitation, being half-hearted, were not to be regarded as genuine.

[HIS LORDSHIP stated the contentions of the husband and of the wife on the issue of desertion, and concluded:] I agree with the view expressed by the Divisional Court (3) that the questions at issue, the nature of the parting and C   the bona fides of the subsequent overtures, were essentially matters of fact for the justices, and that there was ample material to support their conclusions.   In my judgment the Divisional Court (2) were right in refusing to interfere with those conclusions, and were right also in concluding that they amounted in effect to a finding of consensual separation.

I turn then to consider the question whether the finding of the justices that D   the husband was guilty of wilful neglect to maintain both wife and child can be supported on the basis that the separation was consensual, and that there was no desertion on the part of either spouse.   Where only husband and wife are concerned it has been repeatedly held that a husband consensually separated from his wife is under no liability to maintain her, unless the agreement to separate is found to be subject to an express or implied term that the husband E   is to provide maintenance for the wife.   This was decided by the Divisional Court in *Baker* v. *Baker* (4) (a decision twice approved obiter in this court); in *Chapman* v. *Chapman* (5) in 1951 and in *Lilley* v. *Lilley* (6) and followed on frequent occasions by the Divisional Court, notably in *Stringer* v. *Stringer* (7) and *Pinnick* v. *Pinnick* (8).   It has not been argued in the present case that those decisions were wrong, and for my part I see no reason to doubt the rule which F   they established.   The question raised by the present case is whether the rule applies where the wife is left with a dependent child to look after.   There was no evidence in this case of any express agreement by the husband to provide maintenance, but it remains open for consideration whether the circumstances of the separation were such that an agreement to provide maintenance is to be implied.

G   It is not suggested (and I do not think that it could be contended) that a dependent child's right to be maintained could be affected by any agreement between the parents.   The only ground on which the finding of wilful neglect to maintain the child has been attacked is that the husband did in fact at all material times pay £2 per week for her maintenance.   Since this was precisely the amount which the justices awarded for the maintenance of the child there H   could not, it is said, be any justification for the finding of wilful neglect to maintain her.   As to this, I agree with the view of the Divisional Court (9) that the justices may well have thought that £2 per week for the child was appropriate in the context, but only in the context, of £5 per week for the wife.   It could well be that, if the husband can successfully challenge the order in favour of the wife, the finding of wilful neglect to maintain the child and the amount awarded I   for her maintenance should be reconsidered.

The crucial questions for decision, therefore, are: (i) whether the finding of wilful neglect to maintain the wife can stand, and (ii) whether, even without such a finding, the wife is nevertheless entitled to an award of maintenance.

(2) [1966] 3 All E.R. 797.   (3) [1966] 3 All E.R. at p. 799, letter B.
(4) (1949), 66 (pt. 1) T.L.R. 81.   (5) (1951), C.A., Apr. 4, unreported.
(6) [1959] 3 All E.R. 283; [1960] P. 158 at p. 169.
(7) [1952] 1 All E.R. 373; [1952] P. 171.
(8) [1957] 1 All E.R. 873.   (9) [1966] 3 All E.R. at p. 800.

Before considering these questions further it is well to refer to the provisions A of the relevant statute, which is the Matrimonial Proceedings (Magistrates' Courts) Act, 1960. By this Act the previous Summary Jurisdiction (Separation and Maintenance) Acts, 1895 to 1949, were repealed and substantially re-enacted, though with certain amendments, one of which is of importance in the present case. The scheme of the Act of 1960 is as follows. By s. 1 (1), various matri- monial offences are listed which, if committed by one spouse, entitle the other B spouse to apply by way of complaint to a magistrates' court for an order under the Act. These include, in para. (h), the case where a husband

"has wilfully neglected to provide reasonable maintenance for the wife or for any child of the family who is, or would but for that neglect have been, a dependant."

C

Section 2 (1) provides that on hearing a complaint under s. 1 by either of the parties to a marriage

"the court may make an order (in this Act referred to as a 'matrimonial order') containing any one or more of the following provisions ..."

There follows a list of the orders which it is competent for the court to make, and these include the following, which are relevant to the present case: D

"(b) a provision that the husband shall pay to the wife such weekly sum not exceeding £7 10s. as the court considers reasonable in all the circumstances of the case; ... (d) a provision for the legal custody of any child of the family who is under the age of sixteen years; ... (h) a provision for the making by the defendant or by the complainant or by each of them, for the maintenance of any child of the family, of payments by way of E a weekly sum not exceeding in the case of payments by either one of the parties in respect of any one child the sum of 50s."

The paragraph goes on to provide that such payments are to be made to any person to whom the legal custody of the child is for the time being committed by the order.   F

Under the legislation previously in force it was not competent for the court to make an order in respect of the custody or maintenance of a child unless the complaining spouse established his or her ground of complaint and obtained an order thereon; but under s. 4 (1) of the Act of 1960 it is now competent for the court to make an order in respect of a child even though the complaining spouse fails to make good his or her complaint. It is now provided that, where the G court has begun to hear a complaint, then, whether or not the court makes the order for which the complaint is made, the court may make a matrimonial order containing any provision such as is mentioned in paras. (d) to (h) of s. 2 (1). This is clearly a very wide provision. On the face of it it would seem that, in a case where a wife's only complaint is of wilful neglect to provide reasonable maintenance for a child of the family under s. 1 (1) (h), even though the court H declines to make the order for which the complaint is made (which means, I suppose, that there is no finding of wilful neglect to maintain), the court may nevertheless make an order for the maintenance of the child under s. 2 (1) (h). This may seem an odd result, but since it is of no material relevance to the present case (in which the wife put forward two other complaints), it is not necessary to discuss the matter further.   I

The argument put forward on behalf of the wife is that, once she has established good ground for any of the complaints listed in s. 1 (1) of the Act of 1960, she is entitled to obtain any of the orders which it is competent for the court to make in her favour under s. 2 (1). The argument is founded on some observations made obiter by LORD MERRIMAN, P., and assented to by PEARCE, J., in Kinnane v. Kinnane (10), and on the decision of the Divisional Court in Starkie v. Starkie (No. 2) (11). In the former case the justices had dismissed a wife's complaint

(10) [1953] 2 All E.R. 1144; [1954] P. 41.   (11) [1953] 2 All E.R. 1519.

A of desertion, but made an order on the ground of wilful neglect to maintain that
the husband should pay the wife maintenance both for herself and for her child.
The husband appealed against the order for maintenance, and the wife cross-
appealed against the dismissal of her complaint of desertion.   In the course of
his judgment LORD MERRIMAN, P., said (12):

B   ". . . any sum awarded for the maintenance of the wife, and any sum
ordered to be paid to the wife for the support of the children is, as it always
has been, an order for the wife.   Speaking generally, any of these orders,
as I read the code, can only be made if it is established that one of the
complaints made by the wife under the code is found to be proved.   In
other words, I reject the argument that an order cannot be made in favour
of the wife for maintenance of the wife unless it is founded on wilful refusal
C to provide reasonable maintenance for her or, put the other way, that, if the
only legitimate finding is that there has been wilful neglect to provide reasonable maintenance for the infant children whom the husband is legally
liable to maintain, no order for maintenance of the wife can be made.   I do
not think that that is the law.   It may be that the amount which a court
thinks reasonable as an award in favour of a wife may depend on whether
D the neglect has been of the wife or of the children or both, but, in my opinion,
the right to make an order is established when once the justices are satisfied
that any one of the complaints set out in the Act of 1895, s. 4, is proved."

LORD MERRIMAN, P., however, went on to say that he did not think that the case
could be decided solely on that ground, but that the justices' order should be
sustained on two other grounds, viz., (i) that, if the separation was consensual,
E it could be only on the basis that the husband undertook to continue to support
the wife and child, and (ii) that on the facts found by the justices the husband
was in desertion, so as to entitle the wife to an order on that ground. PEARCE, J.,
agreed with these conclusions.

The only case in which, on proof of a husband's wilful neglect to maintain her
child, a wife has been held entitled to an order for maintenance for herself is
F *Starkie* v. *Starkie* (*No. 2*) (13).   In that case the justices found that the separation was consensual, and that there was no agreement express or implied for the
husband to pay maintenance.   They nevertheless made a finding of wilful
neglect to maintain both wife and child, and awarded 20s. per week for the wife
and 30s. per week for the child.   The Divisional Court came to the conclusion
that the finding of wilful neglect to maintain the wife could not stand; but they
G held that failure on her part to obtain a finding of wilful neglect to maintain
herself did not bar her from proving wilful neglect to maintain the child.   On
proof of that the wife was entitled, following the doctrine enunciated in *Kinnane*
v. *Kinnane* (14), to obtain any of the orders permissible under the Act then in
force, including an order for maintenance of herself; but, since she had failed
to establish that there was any wilful neglect to maintain herself, the discretion
H of the justices in awarding her maintenance for herself should have been exercised
in recognition of that fact.   As the justices had awarded the maximum sum
then permissible for the maintenance of the child, the wife ought to receive by
way of maintenance for herself only the nominal sum of 1s. per week.

In later cases, notably *Cooke* v. *Cooke* (15), *Naylor* v. *Naylor* (16) and *Young*
v. *Young* (17), the Divisional Court, as it was bound to do, has accepted as
I correct the doctrine enunciated in *Kinnane* v. *Kinnane* (14) and applied in
Starkie v. *Starkie* (*No. 2*) (13).   In none of the later cases, however, did the point
actually arise for decision, nor has the question ever been considered in this
court.

---

(12) [1953] 2 All E.R. at p. 1146; [1954] P. at pp. 43, 44.
(13) [1953] 2 All E.R. 1519.   (14) [1953] 2 All E.R. 1144; [1954] P. 41.
(15) [1960] 3 All E.R. 39; [1961] P. 16.   (16) [1961] 2 All E.R. 129; [1962] P. 253.
            (17) [1962] 3 All E.R. 120; [1964] P. 152.

I think that the time has come to decide whether the view expressed in A
Kinnane v. *Kinnane* (18) is right. For my part I do not think that it is. Without
undermining a great deal of well-established authority I do not think that it is
possible to say that, on proof of any of the offences listed in s. 1 (1) of the Act
of 1960, a wife is entitled to any of the orders specified in s. 2 (1). For instance,
it has been repeatedly held that a non-cohabitation order cannot properly be
made where the complaint found to be proved is one of desertion; but, if the B
view contended for be well founded, it would be competent for the justices to
make such an order not only in a case of desertion, but also on a finding of wilful
neglect to maintain the wife or even a child. I cannot think that Parliament
intended any such thing. Again, it is well established that a wife who has herself
been found guilty of a matrimonial offence (apart from adultery, which is the
subject of a special provision in s. 2 (3) of the Act) is not entitled to obtain a C
maintenance order for herself. The reason for this has been said to be that

" a wife's right to maintenance under the legislative code with which we
are here concerned has been approximated to a wife's right to maintenance
at common law ";

see per SIR JOCELYN SIMON, P., in *Young* v. *Young* (19). A wife who was guilty D
of a matrimonial offence, for instance, desertion, was prior to the Act of 1960 not
even entitled to an order for the maintenance of her children; see *Naylor* v.
Naylor (20). As now decided, however, in *Vaughan* v. *Vaughan* (21), this disability has since been removed by s. 4 (1) of the Act of 1960. In my judgment
the true effect of the Act of 1960 is that, on proof of one of the offences listed in
s. 1 (1), a wife is entitled under s. 2 (1) to such an order as is relevant to that E
offence. Thus, if she proves that there has been a wilful neglect to provide maintenance for herself, she is entitled under para. (*b*) to an order for maintenance
for herself. If all that she proves, however, is a wilful neglect to maintain her
child, she is in my view restricted to the remedy provided by para. (*h*). If it be
thought that this involves socially undesirable consequences, the remedy lies
with Parliament, and should not be the subject of " judicial legislation ". F
For these reasons I have come to the conclusion that *Starkie* v. *Starkie* (*No. 2*)
(22), based as it was on LORD MERRIMAN's observations in *Kinnane* v. *Kinnane*
(18), was wrongly decided. It follows that I feel bound to reject the main argument
put forward on behalf of the wife.

I have ventured to state my reasons for this conclusion at some length because
my lords, while they agree with me in thinking that the appeal should be dismissed G
and the case remitted to the justices as directed by the Divisional Court (23),
take a different view on this particular point. I would conclude what I have to
say on this part of the case by making two observations. One is that it was not
on the ground now contended for on behalf of the wife that the Divisional Court
(23) in fact remitted the case to the justices for further findings of fact.
I will turn in one moment to consider what the Divisional Court (23) did in fact H
decide. The other observation is that, if I thought that the argument now
presented on behalf of the wife were right, I should regard the Divisional Court's
order remitting the case to the justices as plainly wrong. On the basis of the
wife's argument there would be nothing worthy to be remitted. Assuming the
wife to be entitled to maintenance for herself on mere proof of wilful neglect to
maintain the child, the only remaining question would be one of quantum, as to I
which the court should be slow indeed to interfere with the award made by the
justices, who had all the figures before them.
I come now to consider what the Divisional Court (23) actually did decide. I

---

(18) [1953] 2 All E.R. 1144; [1954] P. 41.
(19) [1962] 3 All E.R. at p. 126; [1964] P. at p. 160.
(20) [1961] 2 All E.R. 129; [1962] P. 253.
(21) [1963] 2 All E.R. 742; [1965] P. 15.
(22) [1953] 2 All E.R. 1519.   (23) [1966] 3 All E.R. 797.

A   must preface what I have to say by remarking that, while I wholly agree with
the conclusion at which they arrived, in the course of reaching that conclusion
they propounded what seems to me to be an erroneous view of the law. In order to
make that good, I must, in justice to the Divisional Court, quote at some length
from the judgment of the court which SIR JOCELYN SIMON, P., delivered. He
said (24):

B   " This parting has been found to be a consensual one, so that the wife is
    not precluded from a finding of wilful neglect to maintain her, as she might
    have been if there had been a finding that she was in desertion; see *Young*
    v. *Young* (25). Where, on a consensual parting, without any stipulation
    exonerating the husband from supporting a dependent child, there has been
    wilful neglect to maintain such child, the court may make a finding of wilful
C   neglect to maintain the wife; see *Kinnane* v. *Kinnane* (26) and *Starkie* v.
    Starkie (*No. 2*) (27), explained in *Cooke* v. *Cooke* (28); see also *Young* v.
    Young (29). This rule is clearly established in our view; though the reason
    for it is not developed in the authorities. In our judgment, it arises out of
    the close identification of interest between mother and dependent child; so
    that a failure to maintain the child throws the obligation on to its mother
D   and amounts to a wilful neglect to maintain her, notwithstanding that
    there is no stipulation to maintain her in the separation agreement."

With the greatest possible respect to the Divisional Court I cannot accept this
statement as accurate. Neither in *Kinnane* v. *Kinnane* (26) nor in *Starkie* v.
Starkie (*No. 2*) (27) was it decided that where nothing more is proved than
wilful neglect to maintain a child, the court may make a finding of wilful neglect
E   to maintain the wife. The so-called " rule " is that which I have previously
stated, viz., that, where there has been wilful neglect to maintain the child, the
court may make an order that the husband shall pay maintenance not only for
the child, but also for the wife. This, even if it were right, however, would not
mean (as the Divisional Court said) that failure to maintain the child " amounts
to a wilful neglect to maintain " the wife. After observing (30) that the £2 per
F   week which the justices ordered the husband to provide for the child's maintenance was in the context of the wife receiving £5 per week, SIR JOCELYN SIMON, P.,
continued (30):

    " Moreover, what we have found to be the explanation of *Kinnane* v.
    Kinnane (26), *Starkie* v. *Starkie* (*No. 2*) (27) and *Cooke* v. *Cooke* (28) leads us
G   to assent to counsel's further submission."

Since I do not agree with the Divisional Court's explanation of the three cases
cited, I cannot agree that this furnished any valid ground for the conclusion which
SIR JOCELYN SIMON, P., proceeded to state. Nevertheless, I do for my part wholly
agree with that conclusion, but I do so not because of the so-called rule in *Kinnane*
v. *Kinnane* (26); I agree on the entirely different ground which SIR JOCELYN
H   SIMON, P., next proceeded to state. His judgment continued (30):

    ". . . where a husband and wife enter into an agreement to live apart and
    their family includes a child who needs a mother's personal care to an extent
    which precludes her from earning sufficient income to support herself, it is a
    necessary implication that the husband agrees to support, not only the child,
    but also the wife, in whole or in part, while living in a state of separation (the
I   extent depending on the degree of impairment of the wife's earning capacity
    by the discharge of her obligations to the child). We think that this is borne

---

(24) [1966] 3 All E.R. at pp. 799, 800.
(25) [1962] 3 All E.R. at p. 126; [1964] P. at pp. 160, 161.
(26) [1953] 2 All E.R. 1144; [1954] P. 41.
(27) [1953] 2 All E.R. 1519.
(28) [1960] 3 All E.R. 39; [1961] P. 16.
(29) [1962] 3 All E.R. at p. 126; [1964] P. at p. 160.
(30) [1966] 3 All E.R. at p. 800.

out by consideration of the extreme case of an unweaned child; the obliga-   A
tion to support such a child can, in ordinary circumstances, only be discharged
by supporting the mother.''

Then, omitting a paragraph which is not relevant for present purposes, SIR
JOCELYN SIMON, P., continued (31):

     " It is on this ground that we think that the finding of the magistrates   B
that the husband was guilty of wilful neglect to maintain his wife, notwithstanding that the separation was a consensual one without apparently
any stipulation as to the maintenance of the wife, is capable of being
sustained. To be so sustained, however, there would have to be a further
finding of fact, namely—that the wife *was* reasonably precluded from
supporting herself, in whole or in part, by her necessary obligations to the
child. Since this point was never argued before the magistrates, they have   C
naturally made no finding on it. We, therefore, think that the finding that
the parting was and continued to be a consensual one must stand; but that
the question of wilful neglect to maintain the wife must be remitted to the
magistrates for the purpose of investigating the question of fact which we
have indicated, and on the basis of their finding determining whether there
has been wilful neglect to maintain the wife.''   D

With all this I wholly agree. Where it is proved that, by reason of her obligations
towards her child, a wife is reasonably precluded from supporting herself, in whole
or in part, it is in my judgment permissible to draw the inference that the consensual agreement to separate is subject to an implied term whereby the husband
agrees to support not only the child, but also the wife. If so, any breach of such   E
implied term may entitle the wife to a finding of wilful neglect to provide maintenance for herself as well as the child. This was one of the two grounds on which
Kinnane v. *Kinnane* (32) was actually decided by the Divisional Court. The
difficulty in the present case, as pointed out by SIR JOCELYN SIMON, P., is that
the justices made no finding as to the question whether, and if so to what extent,
the wife was precluded from supporting herself by reason of her obligations to   F
the child. Only when the necessary facts with regard to this have been found
will it be possible to determine whether the consensual separation of the parties
is to be regarded as subject to an implied term requiring the husband to support
the wife as well as the child. Unless the findings of fact are such as to justify the
implication of such a term, I do not think that the finding against the husband
of wilful neglect to maintain the wife can stand. It is for the justices to determine   G
whether, in all the circumstances of the case, such a term ought to be implied so
as to justify the finding of wilful neglect to maintain the wife, and if so what
amount should be ordered to be paid to the wife in respect thereof under s. 2
(1) (*b*).

     I have endeavoured to state what I conceive to be the question to be deter-
mined with some precision because I think that it is important, if the case is to   H
be remitted to the justices, that they should clearly understand exactly what it is
that they are required to decide. I think that the question, as I have stated it, is
exactly in accordance with the conclusion of the Divisional Court (33). Although,
for the reasons which I have given, I cannot agree with all the grounds on which
they based their conclusion, I am satisfied that the Divisional Court (33) did in
the event reach the right conclusion in remitting the question of wilful neglect   I
to maintain the wife for further findings of fact by the justices. I would
accordingly dismiss the appeal and cross-appeal.

     WINN, L.J., read the next judgment at the request of WILLMER, L.J.:
The magistrates of the petty sessional division of Brighouse Borough sitting on
Jan. 13, 1966, had before them three complaints by the wife, who is the respon-
dent in this court, and also cross-appeals. The first complaint was that her

---

(31) [1966] 3 All E.R. at p. 800.   (32) [1953] 2 All E.R. 1144; [1954] P. 41.
(33) [1966] 3 All E.R. 797.

A husband had deserted her on Feb. 11, 1964; she also complained that he had
been guilty of wilful neglect to maintain (a) herself, (b) the infant child of the
marriage, a girl now some thirteen years of age. The magistrates found that the
alleged desertion was not proved, but made findings affirming each of the other
complaints and ordered the husband to pay £5 a week to the wife and £2 a week
for the child. The order of the magistrates was drawn up in the form of a recital
B of the complaints, including

"has been guilty of wilful neglect to provide reasonable maintenance for
his said wife and for her infant child Jean Margaret whom he was then and
now is legally liable to maintain",

and the statement "it is adjudged that the said complaint is true". It is therefore
clear that the magistrates found that the husband had been guilty of wilful
C neglect to maintain the wife, and that they intended by their order to require him
to pay £5 a week for her maintenance.

Both husband and wife appealed to the Divisional Court (34) of the Probate,
Divorce and Admiralty Division and their appeals were determined on Oct. 28,
1966, by SIR JOCELYN SIMON, P. and KARMINSKI, J., who concurred in a single
judgment of the court. The essential facts are fully set out in the judgments of
D the Divisional Court (34) and WILLMER, L.J. They do not require to be here
repeated. It suffices to say that the Divisional Court (34) thought, in my opinion
quite rightly, that the case should be dealt with on appeal on the basis that
there was an unimpugnable finding by the magistrates that the parting of the
husband and wife, which took place in February, 1964, was a consensual parting,
the nature of which never changed. I entirely agree that there was ample
E material to support these conclusions, and that neither the Divisional Court nor
this court should interfere with them. It follows that the wife has not been
guilty of any matrimonial offence. The question for decision by this court is what
rights she has having regard to that vital circumstance, as well as to the fact
that she has no financial resources of her own other than a restricted ability to
earn a small income of the order of £3 a week.
F The course of development of the legislation enabling wives to obtain from
justices orders requiring their husbands to make payments to them has tended
to liberalise the assistance thus provided for them and any child of the marriage.
Under the Summary Jurisdiction (Married Women) Act, 1895, s. 4, a wife could
apply only on proof of an assault, of defined gravity, or desertion, persistent
cruelty or wilful neglect to maintain her or her children and that she had been
G thereby compelled to leave her husband. On finding any such complaint
established the court could make a non-cohabitation order equivalent to a judicial
separation, commit the custody of any child under sixteen to the wife, and order

" . . . that the husband shall pay to the applicant personally, or for her
use, to . . . such weekly sum not exceeding £2 as the court shall, having
H regard to the means both of the husband and wife, consider reasonable."

The £2 limit was raised to £5 by s. 1 (1) of the Married Women (Maintenance)
Act, 1949. Section 6 of the Act of 1895 provided:

"No orders shall be made under this Act on the application of a married
woman if it shall be proved that such married woman has committed an
act of adultery: Provided that the husband has not condoned, or connived
I at or by his wilful neglect or misconduct conduced to such act of adultery."

Section 7 provided that any existing order should be discharged on proof that
the woman in whose favour it was made had subsequently committed an act
of adultery.

The Licensing Act, 1902, made the Act of 1895 applicable to a case where a
wife could show that her husband was an habitual drunkard and, for the first
time, gave a husband a right to apply to the court if his wife was an habitual

(34) [1966] 3 All E.R. 797.

drunkard for, inter alia, custody of any child of the marriage. In 1920 the· A
Married Women (Maintenance) Act, 1920 enacted that, where an order made or
varied thereafter committed any child to the custody of the wife, it might
include a provision that the husband should pay to the wife or another person
a weekly sum not exceeding 10s. for the maintenance of such child up to the
age of sixteen. The 10s. limit was increased by the Act of 1949 to 30s. and the
age limit to twenty-one years.   B

By the Summary Jurisdiction (Separation and Maintenance) Act, 1925, the
condition that the wife must have been caused to leave her husband by his cruelty
or neglect was abolished, and additional grounds of complaint were introduced,
including persistent cruelty to a child; this ground was also made available to a
husband. By s. 2 of the Act of 1925 it was provided that, if a wife in whose
favour an order had been made committed adultery, the order should not be C
discharged if in the opinion of the court the adultery was conduced to by failure
of the husband to make payments under the order which he was able to make,
and that, if the order was discharged, the court might none the less order custody
of any child to remain with the wife, and order the husband to pay to her or
another person for the maintenance of each such child a weekly sum not exceeding 10s. up to the age of sixteen. The limit of 10s. was increased to 30s. by the D
Guardianship and Maintenance of Infants Act, 1951.

The statute which now governs the matter is the Matrimonial Proceedings
(Magistrates' Courts) Act, 1960. Section 1 (1) of that Act, so far as material,
provides as follows:

" A married woman . . . may apply by way of complaint to a magistrates'
court for an order under this Act against the other party to the marriage on E
any of the following causes of complaint arising during the subsistence of
the marriage, that is to say, that the defendant . . . (h) being the husband
has wilfully neglected to provide reasonable maintenance for the wife or for
any child of the family who is, or would but for that neglect have been, a
dependant . . . "

Section 2 (1) of the statute provides, so far as is material, as follows: F

" Subject to [matters not here material] on hearing a complaint under the
said s. 1 by either of the parties to a marriage the court may make an order
. . . containing any one or more of the following provisions: . . . (b) a
provision that the husband shall pay to the wife such weekly sum not
exceeding £7 10s. as the court considers reasonable in all the circumstances
of the case . . . (h) a provision for the making by the defendant or by the G
complainant or by each of them, for the maintenance of any child of the
family, of payments by way of a weekly sum not exceeding in the case of
payments by either one of the parties in respect of any one child the sum
of 50s. being—(i) if and for so long as the child is under the age of sixteen
years payments to any person to whom the legal custody of the child is H
for the time being committed by the order . . . "

Section 2 (3) (b) of the Act of 1960 preserved the bar against a wife who has
committed adultery not condoned or connived at or conduced to by wilful neglect
or misconduct. Section 4 of the Act of 1960 enables a court which is not prepared
to make the order for which complaint is made to make " a matrimonial order "
providing for custody or care of a child, and access, and for payment by husband I
or wife of a weekly sum not exceeding 50s. for the maintenance of each such
child.

In *Young* v. *Young* (35) (the only relevant reported case of which the court is
aware decided since the Act of 1960 came into force), SIR JOCELYN SIMON, P.
observed (36) that under a line of decisions relating to the earlier legislation
enacted in 1895 and amended in 1902, 1920 and 1925,

---

(35) [1962] 3 All E.R. 120; [1964] P. 152.
(36) [1962] 3 All E.R. at p. 126; [1964] P. at p. 160.

A   " . . . a wife's right to maintenance under the legislative code with which
     we are here concerned has been approximated to a wife's right to main-
     tenance at common law . . ."

     I pause to comment that strictly a wife had no right at common law to obtain
     from her husband, by action or otherwise, any payment of money, nor did the
B   Married Women's Property Act, 1882, give her any such rights. The most which
     she could do was to pledge his credit; compare per LORD GODDARD, C.J., in
     Stopher v. *National Assistance Board, National Assistance Board* v. *Parkes* (37),
     where he also said:

         " The legislature, therefore, provided that, where a man has deserted his
         wife or failed to supply her with proper maintenance, justices can make an
C   order. If, however, the parties separated by mutual consent and have
         parted on the terms that the husband was not to maintain the wife, the
         husband is not guilty of wilful refusal to maintain the wife."

     Whether or not on a true analysis the decisions to which SIR JOCELYN SIMON, P.,
     was referring in *Young* v. *Young* (38) have produced, as he said, a position approxi-
     mating to the position of a wife at common law does not require consideration
D   in this appeal, nor is their propriety now in question. What is clear is that the
     court has not tended to take a liberal view of the statutory rights of the wife.
     SIR JOCELYN SIMON, P., recognised that the court had held that a deserting
     wife, or a wife who had committed any actual matrimonial offence, was disen-
     titled to an order for maintenance in her favour, whereas the statute of 1895
     itself (and the later statutes) specifically singled out only adultery as a bar to a
E   claim for maintenance.

     In *Cooke* v. *Cooke* (39) LORD MERRIMAN, P., referring to the statutory provisions
     earlier than those of 1960, analysed their effect in a passage (40) which, although
     obiter for the purposes of the decision of the court in that case, appears in my
     respectful opinion to be correct and of direct relevance in the present appeal.
     I desire to adopt what he there said, though I would point out that he cannot
F   have had in mind (since it was not relevant in the case) the change of law enacted
     in s. 2 of the Act of 1925:

         " On the one hand there is the effect of a finding of adultery upon any
         order in respect of wilful neglect to maintain the child. About that . . .
         there could be no argument at all. Section 6 of the Summary Jurisdiction
G   (Married Women) Act, 1895, would be conclusive, because no order can be
         made under the Act on the complaint of a married woman if it shall be
         proved that such married woman has committed an act of adultery, with the
         saving proviso about condonation . . . Seeing that an order in respect of
         wilful neglect to provide reasonable maintenance for a child is an order
         made in favour of the wife, no such order could possibly be made if
H   adultery has been committed. In *Starkie* v. *Starkie (No. 2)* (41), on the
         other hand, we were dealing with a case in which the wife had disabled
         herself from getting an order for wilful neglect to maintain herself by the
         fact that, as we held, the separation was consensual, and was without any
         agreement, express or implied, that the husband should nevertheless main-
         tain her as a separated wife. We held that that did not affect the husband's
I   liability to maintain the child, and, therefore, that he could be held to have
         neglected to maintain the child."

     MARSHALL, J., said (42) that he fully agreed with a passage which he extracted

     ───

     (37) [1955] 1 All E.R. 700 at pp. 705, 706; [1955] 1 Q.B. 486 at p. 496.
     (38) [1962] 3 All E.R. 120; [1964] P. 152.
     (39) [1960] 3 All E.R. 39; [1961] P. 16.
     (40) [1961] P. at pp. 21, 22; [1960] 3 All E.R. at pp. 42, 43.
     (41) [1953] 2 All E.R. 1519.
     (42) [1960] 3 All E.R. at p. 46; [1961] P. at p. 26.

from the judgment of LORD MERRIMAN, P., in *Kinnane* v. *Kinnane* (43) where   A
the latter said (44):

" . . . any sum awarded for the maintenance of the wife, and any sum
ordered to be paid to the wife for the support of the children is, as it always
has been, an order for the wife. Speaking generally, any of these orders, as
I read the code, can only be made if it is established that one of the complaints made by the wife under the code is found to be proved. In other   B
words, I reject the argument that an order cannot be made in favour of the
wife for the maintenance of the wife unless it is founded on wilful refusal to
provide reasonable maintenance for her, or, put the other way, that, if the
only finding is that there has been wilful neglect to provide reasonable
maintenance for the infant children whom the husband is legally liable to
maintain, no order for maintenance of the wife can be made. I do not   C
think that is the law. It may be that the amount which a court thinks
reasonable as an award in favour of a wife may depend on whether the
neglect has been of the wife or of the children or both, but, in my opinion,
the right to make an order is established when the justices are satisfied
that any one of the complaints set out in the Act of 1895, s. 4, is proved."
                                                                               D
MARSHALL, J., himself added (45):

" On the view that I take of s. 4, wilful neglect to provide reasonable
maintenance for a child is a separate complaint."

I respectfully agree with that passage from *Kinnane* v. *Kinnane* (44) and with
the view expressed by MARSHALL, J.   E

In my opinion those views apply a fortiori to the position under the Matrimonial Proceedings (Magistrates' Courts) Act, 1960, for the reasons: (a) that the
provision which may now be made by the court for the support or maintenance
of any child is to be expressly so framed as to secure that any payment ordered
is paid to the person, or local authority, to whom is entrusted, under an order
for custody or otherwise, for the time being, the care of that child, and is clearly   F
received by such person, who may in a given case be the father or some relative
other than the mother, or the local authority, in the capacity of custodian on
behalf of the child; (b) on the other hand, where the court includes in its order
any provision for payment to the wife, this is not to be fixed " having regard to
the means both of the husband and wife ", but is to be simply a provision

" that the husband shall pay to the wife such weekly sum not exceeding   G
£7 10s. as the court considers reasonable in all the circumstances of the
case."

It is plain that the existence of an infant child needing care from its mother,
and the extent of the care needed, and the requirements in the form of accommodation due to the existence of the child and the effect of such matters on the
earning capacity of the mother, are all relevant circumstances of the case within   H
the meaning of s. 2 (1) (*b*) of the Act of 1960. It is noteworthy also that, under
the Act of 1960, a wife may have made against her a provision in like terms
requiring her to pay a weekly sum to her husband if his earning capacity is
impaired.

An analysis of these modern provisions was given in *Young* v. *Young* (46) by
SIR JOCELYN SIMON, P. He there posed the question: I

" Would failure to provide reasonable maintenance for the child give
jurisdiction to make a maintenance order in favour of a wife who would not
otherwise be entitled?"

(43) [1953] 2 All E.R. 1144; [1954] P. 41.
(44) [1953] 2 All E.R. at p. 1146; [1954] P. at p. 43.
(45) [1960] 3 All E.R. at p. 46; [1961] P. at p. 26.
(46) [1962] 3 All E.R. at p. 125; [1964] P. at p. 159.

A Having then set out the terms of s. 1 (1) (*h*) of the Act of 1960, and having noted that *Cooke* v. *Cooke* (47) established that failure to maintain the wife and failure to maintain the child are two quite separate grounds of complaint, he proceeded to consider the terms of s. 2 (1) (*b*) and (*h*) and said (48):

B " On the face of these provisions it would appear that once the offence of wilful neglect to provide reasonable maintenance for a child has been committed under s. 1 (1) (*h*), any of the orders specified under s. 2 (1) could be made, including a maintenance provision for the wife."

C With the substance of that passage I entirely agree, but respectfully take leave to doubt whether those references to " a maintenance order in favour of the wife " and " a maintenance provision for the wife " are precisely accurate, since it does not seem to me that a payment ordered to be made under s. 2 (1) (*b*) of the Act of 1960 should properly be regarded always as a payment of " maintenance " for the wife. Such a payment will clearly constitute maintenance for the wife wherever there is no child, and may well, where it is ordered to be made by reason of the existence of a child whom the husband has not properly maintained, provide some margin over and above the needs of the child beneficial to

D the wife. I prefer, however, to regard a' sum ordered to be paid under this sub-s. (2) (1) (*b*), on the specific ground that the husband has been found guilty of neglect to maintain the child under s. 1 (1) (*h*), as being a payment the purpose or reason for which is no more precisely specified than that it is considered by the court " reasonable in all the circumstances of the case ". There may be very little difference in substance between the view there expressed by SIR JOCELYN

E SIMON, P. (and amplified by him in a passage which I am about to quote) and the view which I have endeavoured to express; but there is this distinction, as it seems to me, that, if the court concentrates its attention on the needs of the child in respect of maintenance, then it is likely that the payment to the wife (to which she becomes entitled merely because the child has not been properly maintained) will not be greater in amount than the sum reasonably necessary

F to enable her, in all the circumstances, to make proper provision for the needs of the child. SIR JOCELYN SIMON, P., said in *Young* v. *Young* (49):

" Even where the husband's misconduct alone leads to the break-up of the marriage, the wife may nevertheless be disentitled to an order for her own maintenance on the ground of his wilful neglect to maintain her. She may, for example, have such income of her own that the husband was

G justified, whatever his misconduct, in refusing to maintain her. But if he were guilty of wilful neglect to maintain the child of the marriage, the wife would be entitled to an order for maintenance of the child on that ground. Moreover, if subsequently she lost her own source of income, she would be able, in my view, to secure a variation of the original order based on her husband's wilful neglect to provide reasonable maintenance for the

H child, so as to provide for her own maintenance, and this would be so whether or not the original order provided nominally for her maintenance."

With that passage I express my respectful concurrence. However, towards the end of the same passage SIR JOCELYN SIMON, P., went on to consider a case in which a wife had been guilty of desertion or of cruelty, and there he said (50):

I " The husband cannot be convicted of wilful neglect to provide reasonable maintenance for her in those circumstances. He could, however, be guilty of wilful neglect to provide reasonable maintenance for the child of the family. Is it open to the court to make an order also for the maintenance of the wife in such circumstances? In my view the answer is No."

---

(47) [1960] 3 All E.R. 39; [1961] P. 16.
(48) [1962] 3 All E.R. at p. 125; [1964] P. at p. 159.
(49) [1962] 3 All E.R. at p. 125; [1964] P. at p. 160.
(50) [1962] 3 All E.R. at p. 126; [1964] P. at p. 160.

With this latter passage I find myself unable fully to concur, though reading it   A
strictly it is, I agree, correct in stating that in those circumstances no order
could be made with the object of providing maintenance for the benefit of the
wife.   In my opinion, however, it would be open to the court in such a case to
make under the Act of 1960, over and above any order providing under para.
(*h*) for the maintenance of the child, an order under para. (*b*) of s. 2 (1) for
payment to the wife of such sum as was reasonable in all the circumstances of   B
the case, having regard (a) to any need that there may be to supplement her
own resources sufficiently to enable her properly to provide for the needs of the
child, and (b) to the fact that she is a wife who has been guilty of a matrimonial
offence.   As I have already indicated, I think that there is an a fortiori case of
statutory entitlement of any wife who has not been guilty of a matrimonial
offence whether she is still living with her husband or has separated from him   C
consensually to a provision under para. (*b*) as well as para. (*h*).

This view is in accord, subject to the same semantic point about the term
" maintenance ", with a passage in LORD MERRIMAN, P.'s judgment in *Starkie*
v. *Starkie* (*No. 2*) (51).   Having referred to the decision in *Baker* v. *Baker* (52),
quoted with approval in this court in *Chapman* v. *Chapman* (53), LORD MERRIMAN,
P., said (51):   D

> " The separation was consensual, and there was no agreement, express or
> implied, to maintain the wife.   In my opinion, therefore, the finding of wilful
> neglect to provide reasonable maintenance for the wife cannot stand.   That
> is not, however, the end of the case.   We pointed out in *Kinnane* v. *Kinnane*
> (54) that the wife would be entitled, if she established a complaint of wilful   E
> neglect to provide reasonable maintenance for her infant child whom the
> husband was legally liable to maintain, to any order permissible under the Act
> of 1895, s. 5, and the Married Women (Maintenance) Act, 1920, s. 1 (1), and
> containing, of course, a provision giving her the custody of the child.   We
> also pointed out that the establishment of that complaint might entitle her
> to an order for maintenance, not limited to any sum which was awarded in   F
> respect of the child of which she was given the custody.   But, at the same
> time, we pointed out that if she failed to establish wilful neglect to maintain
> herself, the discretion of the justices as to the amount to be awarded must
> be exercised in recognition of the fact that she had failed to establish that
> matter."

For the reasons which I have endeavoured to indicate, I am of the opinion that   G
the justices were entitled to order this husband to make a payment to this wife
of an amount in excess of the limit, fixed by the current statute, of 50s. a week as
a provision for the child, but I consider (as did the Divisional Court (55)) that the
matter should be remitted to the magistrates for the purpose of their deciding a
further question.

In my judgment the further question which they should now decide is not, as   H
the Divisional Court (55) thought, only whether there has been wilful neglect to
maintain the wife, but also the question whether there has been such neglect to
maintain the child, and if so what is the sum which, in all the relevant circumstances, it is reasonable that the husband should be ordered to pay to the wife
over and above such sum as he is ordered to pay as a provision for the child.   As
the Divisional Court stated (55), they will require to find as a fact whether, and to   I
what extent, the wife has been precluded by her necessary obligations to the
child from earning sufficient to provide for the child and to support herself in

(51) [1953] 2 All E.R. at p. 1522.
(52) (1949), 66 (pt. 1) T.L.R. 81.
(53) (1951), C.A. Apr. 4, unreported.
(54) [1953] 2 All E.R. 1144; [1954] P. 41.
(55) [1966] 3 All E.R. 797.

A conditions enabling her properly to care for the child, including suitable accommodation for the child. They must consider anew whether there has been neglect to maintain the wife, but if they dismiss that complaint they will apply themselves to the other question which I have stated.

The Divisional Court (56) rested their judgment primarily, as I understand it, on the view that where there is a consensual parting of parents who have a child B or children, there is (at any rate in the absence of an express contrary stipulation) a term of the agreement to separate necessarily to be implied in it that the husband agrees with his wife to support not only the child but also the wife to such extent as her earning capacity may be impaired by the discharge of her obligations to the child. Apart from rejecting the adverb " necessarily " in favour of, for example, " possibly ", or such a phrase as " it may be right to imply ", I am not disposed C myself to dissent further from that view which stems from the decision in *Baker* v. *Baker* (57) (albeit from an obiter dictum therein) and has sociological merits whether or not it stands on firm theoretical ground. I find it a less satisfactory ground for supporting the right of a wife, who is the mother of a child or children, to receive, after consensual parting, a payment pursuant to para. (*b*) of s. 2 (1) of the Act of 1960 than the direction which, on my construction of it, the Act D itself contains that a magistrates' court may so order. Furthermore, because of the statutory provisions it is wholly unnecessary, in the case of a wife who has a child in her custody, to resort to any such legal fiction. Implied terms are insubstantial foundations for such essential rights, and are not readily found in the area of matrimonial relationships, of which it has so often been said that the parties do not regard themselves as contracting the one with the other, or seeking E to define their legal rights and duties. The fundamental objection to reliance on an implied term is that it must surely be excluded in any case where any intention to accept it has been expressly repudiated, or is inconsistent with contemporaneous conduct. Nor do I favour the idea that any rule of law should be invoked to construct a contract by which a husband is to be deemed, unconsciously, to have bound himself to make payments, for an indefinite period, of amounts F which, as relevant circumstances change, may substantially vary.

I think that the wife respondent to this appeal succeeds in substance, since the question ought still to be left to the justices whether or not the appellant husband impliedly agreed with her to maintain her despite the separation. If so, they may see fit to order maintenance to be paid under s. 2 (1) (*b*); they should understand that this is a question of fact, and that there is no necessary implication that he G did so agree. As a separate matter they must decide whether there has been wilful neglect to maintain the child, and if so what weekly sums the husband should be ordered to pay on this ground under s. 2 (1) (*b*) and (*h*) respectively; the total cannot exceed £10. I do not give any indication as to the amount which should be ordered. I would add that the court has settled the precise questions which are to be sent to the magistrates. These will be handed down in H due course. They are as follows:

1. Is it to be inferred that the husband agreed to maintain the wife? If so, did his failure to do so amount to wilful neglect to maintain the wife?

If the answer to this question is Yes, the order is to stand. If the answer to this question is No, then

I 2. In respect of his wilful neglect to maintain the child, what weekly sums should the husband be ordered to pay to the wife (a) under s. 2 (1) (*b*); (b) under s. 2 (1) (*h*)?

DIPLOCK, L.J.: I agree with the judgment of WINN, L.J., and specifically with his formulation of the two questions to be considered by the magistrates when the case is remitted to them; but I go further than he does. I reject entirely

---

(56) [1966] 3 All E.R. 797.   (57) (1949), 66 (pt. 1) T.L.R. 81.

any suggestion that a wife who is supporting a child of the family has no right   **A**
to any order for payment to be made to her under s. 2 (1) (*b*) of the Matrimonial
Proceedings (Magistrates' Courts) Act, 1960, unless the agreement between the
spouses to separate contains an express or implied term that the husband should
provide some financial support for the wife as well as the child. I do so with
great diffidence for it involves differing from WILLMER, L.J., and both members
of the Divisional Court (58), all of whom have great experience in this field of law,   **B**
whereas I had none either at the Bar or as a judge of the High Court. In the
Court of Appeal, however, I have seldom heard sustained citation of authorities
on matrimonial causes without an uneasy feeling that family rights form a branch
of the law into which the courts have introduced esoterism where Parliament
intended only simplicity. The authorities which have been relied on in the
present case are no exception, but unfortunately, so far as concerns wilful neglect   **C**
to maintain a child, I see nothing in them which requires us to resort to any
concept of implied terms of an agreement made between husband and wife, or
which prevents us from looking at the current statute which governs the matter,
seeing what it says, and applying it to the facts of this case.

It is important to distinguish between the grounds on which a matrimonial
order may be made, which are set out in s. 1 (1) of the Act of 1960, and the   **D**
provisions which may be contained in such an order, which are set out in s. 2 (1).
Among the grounds on which a matrimonial order may be made is that the
husband " has wilfully neglected to provide reasonable maintenance for the wife
or for any child of the family ". Wilful neglect connotes a failure by the husband
to perform a duty which was recognised at common law.

At common law a husband was under a duty to provide his wife not with money,   **E**
but with necessaries. This duty was not directly enforceable by the wife by action
against her husband, but was recognised by her implied authority to pledge his
credit for necessaries, an authority which could not be withdrawn if they were
living apart in circumstances which entitled the wife to refuse to live with him,
and the husband did not provide her with sufficient funds to enable her to maintain herself. But her right to pledge her husband's credit for necessaries was an   **F**
inadequate remedy for the separated wife whose husband's credit was not pledge-
worthy. That is why the Summary Jurisdiction (Married Women) Act, 1895,
was passed; but where the circumstances were such that the wife was not entitled
to refuse to live with her husband and the separation was simply by mutual
consent of the spouses, the husband was entitled, as he was when she was living
with him, to withhold her authority to pledge his credit, for her remedy and her   **G**
duty was to return to him. Unless, therefore, he had expressly or impliedly
agreed to do so, the husband was under no duty to provide her with reasonable
maintenance in cash or in kind so long as they were living apart simply by mutual
consent, and he could not be guilty of wilful neglect to do so. At any rate, I
think that I am constrained by the authorities which my lords have cited so
to hold.   **H**

It follows that in the present case one question which the magistrates must
consider is whether or not it was an implied term of the agreement (perhaps
" mutual acquiescence " is a better description) under which the spouses
separated that the husband should provide any, and if so what, maintenance for
the wife herself. Unless they find that there was such an implied term, their
finding of wilful neglect to provide reasonable maintenance for the wife cannot   **I**
stand.

There is an alternative ground, however, on which they may order a weekly
sum to be paid by the husband to the wife. Where there was an infant child, the
husband's duty to maintain the child was recognised at common law, although
it was not directly enforceable by action on behalf of the child. This duty was

---

(58) [1966] 3 All E.R. 797.

A not brought to an end by separation of the spouses by mutual consent, nor could any agreement between husband and wife release him from it. Accordingly, a husband can be found guilty of wilful neglect to provide reasonable maintenance for a child of the family who is living with his wife from whom he has separated pursuant to a mutual agreement which contains no term express or implied that he should provide any financial support for either the wife or the child, and
B even though it contains an express term that the wife will maintain the child at her own expense. If he is guilty of such wilful neglect to provide reasonable maintenance for the child who is living with the wife, there is power in the magistrates to make a matrimonial order. Such order may include provision that the husband shall pay to the wife a weekly sum not exceeding £7 10s. In the statute the weekly sum is not expressed to be for the maintenance of the wife.
C The only limitation on the power to order such payment is that the sum shall be such " as the court considers reasonable in all the circumstances of the case ".

A circumstance which is always relevant is that the husband, whether or not he is also under any duty to maintain his wife, is under a duty to make sufficient financial provision for the proper maintenance of the child as long as the child is living with the wife. The child must be clothed, housed and tended by the wife.
D This will involve her in direct expense for food and clothing, etc., for the child. It may involve her indirectly in additional expense for more costly accommodation than would be adequate for herself if living alone. It may also involve her in loss of earnings in so far as her ability to undertake paid employment is restricted by the child's need for her personal care. Provision for the husband to pay or to contribute to these expenses of the wife and to recoup her in whole or in part for her lost earnings may be made by ordering payment of a weekly sum under
E s. 2 (1) (b) of the Act of 1960. Alternatively, as respects expenses, if the magistrates make an order giving legal custody of the child to the wife, provision for the husband's payment of, or contribution to, these may be made by ordering payment of a weekly sum to the wife under para. (b) of s. 2 (1) of the Act of 1960, or partly under para. (b) and partly under para. (h). Since, however, payments
F made under para. (h) are for the maintenance of the child, and are held by the wife in a fiduciary capacity to be expended on his maintenance, she can be recouped for her loss of earnings only under para. (b).

Subject to the limits of £7 10s. under para. (b) and £2 10s. under para. (h), a reasonable weekly sum to cover these direct and indirect expenses and loss of earnings represents the maximum which the magistrates, exercising their dis-
G cretion judicially, can order the husband to pay under these two paragraphs where the spouses are separated by mutual agreement without any express or implied term that the husband shall give financial support to the wife. It does not follow that in all cases the magistrates should award the maximum. The wife, too, is under a concurrent duty to maintain the child as is recognised by para. (h). It is therefore proper, even in the absence of any express agreement as to how the
H expenses of maintaining the child are to be borne, to take into consideration her means as well as those of her husband, and to determine to what extent (if any) they exceed what is needed for her own reasonable maintenance and, if they do, how much it would be reasonable for her to contribute towards the cost of maintaining the child. They should give effect to this by reducing the amount ordered to be paid by the husband under para. (b) or para. (h), or both.
I In the present case the wife's means would not justify any reduction on these grounds. It is, I think, clear, however, that the magistrates did not direct their minds to the considerations outlined above. I agree that the case should be remitted to them to find by how much the direct and indirect expenses incurred by the wife in feeding, clothing and housing the child, and the loss of earnings sustained by her by reason of the necessity for her to tend the child, exceed the weekly sum of £2 which they have awarded under s. 2 (1) (h). The amount of this excess, provided it is reasonable having regard to the means of the husband, is the

amount which he should be ordered to pay to the wife under s. 2 (1) (b) in respect A
of his failure to provide reasonable maintenance for the child.

*Appeal and cross-appeal dismissed. Case remitted to magistrates for further
findings of fact and their answers to questions by the court set out at end of judgment
of* WINN, L.J.

Solicitors: *Vizard, Oldham, Crowder & Cash and Robertson, Martin & Co.,* B
agents for *Wild, Hewitson & Shaw,* Cambridge (for the husband); *Jaques & Co.,*
agents for *Rhodes, Thain & Thomas,* Halifax (for the wife).

[*Reported by* F. A. AMIES, ESQ., *Barrister-at-Law.*]

———————

C

MURRAY (Inspector of Taxes) *v.* IMPERIAL CHEMICAL INDUSTRIES, LTD.

[COURT OF APPEAL, CIVIL DIVISION (Lord Denning, M.R., Davies and Russell, D
L.JJ.), April 5, 6, 7, 10, 1967.]

*Income Tax—Profits—Computation of profits—Capital receipts—Licences for
manufacture of Terylene in foreign countries—Covenants of licensor not to
manufacture or licence manufacture there—Lump sum payments for covenants
—Whether capital or income—Income Tax Act, 1952 (15 & 16 Geo. 6 & 1* E
Eliz. 2 c. 10), Sch. D, Case 2.

The taxpayer company held an exclusive licence under patents for the
manufacture and exploitation of Terylene, and also owned ancillary patents
of their own. The taxpayer company granted exclusive sub-licences for the
lives of the major patents, and exclusive licences under the ancillary patents,
to five European companies in return for payment of agreed royalties. The F
royalties were revenue receipts subject to tax. In addition the taxpayer
company covenanted not to manufacture or sell Terylene or products of a
similar character in the country concerned. The consideration for these
" keep-out " covenants, to take one typical instance, was a " net capital
sum " of £400,000 payable by six equal instalments. The instalments were,
substantially, payable annually. The taxpayer company were not dealers G
in patent rights or patent licences.

Held: the £400,000 payable for the " keep-out " covenant was capital
and was received as capital by the taxpayer company, and thus was not
chargeable to income tax although it was payable by annual instalments,
because it was in effect part payment for an exclusive licence for the whole
life of patent rights, viz., for an outright disposal of the whole of a capital
asset (the patent rights of the country concerned) of the taxpayer company, H
and because the £400,000 had no reference to, and was payable irrespective
of there being, any user of the licence (see p. 983, letters F and G, p. 984,
letter H, and p. 985, letter E, post).

Inland Revenue Comrs. v. *British Salmson Aero Engines, Ltd.* ([1938]
3 All E.R. 283) and dicta of LORD GREENE, M.R., in *Nethersole* v. *Withers*
(*Inspector of Taxes*) ([1946] 1 All E.R. at p. 716) applied. I

Decision of CROSS, J. ([1967] 1 All E.R. 369) affirmed.

[As to capital profits not constituting profits for income tax purposes, see 20
HALSBURY'S LAWS (3rd Edn.) 149, 150, para. 263; and for cases on the subject,
see 28 DIGEST (Repl.) 25-27, *105-115,* and cf. (on trading expenses) ibid., 115-124,
431-480.

For the Income Tax Act, 1952, Sch. D, Case 1, see 31 HALSBURY'S STATUTES
(2nd Edn.) 116, 122-126.]

A　Cases referred to:

　Inland Revenue Comrs. v. British Salmson Aero Engines, Ltd., British Salmson
　　　Aero Engines, Ltd. v. Inland Revenue Comrs., [1937] 3 All E.R. 464;
　　　affd. C.A., [1938] 3 All E.R. 283; [1938] 2 K.B. 482; 107 L.J.K.B.
　　　648; 159 L.T. 147; 22 Tax Cas. 29; 28 Digest (Repl.) 120, 461.

　Nethersole v. Withers (Inspector of Taxes), [1946] 1 All E.R. 711; 28 Tax Cas.
B　　　501; affd. H.L., sub nom. Withers (Inspector of Taxes) v. Nethersole,
　　　[1948] 1 All E.R. 400; [1948] L.J.R. 805; 28 Tax Cas. 501; 28 Digest
　　　(Repl.) 155, 600.

　Rustproof Metal Window Co., Ltd. v. Inland Revenue Comrs., [1947] 2 All E.R.
　　　454; [1947] L.J.R. 1479; 177 L.T. 657; 29 Tax Cas. 243; 28 Digest
　　　(Repl.) 438, 1916.

C　**Appeal.**

　This was an appeal by the Crown from a decision of Cross, J., dated Nov. 1,
1966 and reported [1967] 1 All E.R. 369, upholding the determination of the
Commissioners for the Special Purposes of the Income Tax Acts on an appeal
by the taxpayer company against assessments under Case 1 of Sch. D to the
Income Tax Act, 1952, for the years 1958-59 and 1960-61, and a claim by the
D　taxpayer company under s. 341 of the Act for the year 1955-56, for an adjustment
of its liability for that year by reference to a loss. The question for determination was, in substance, whether certain sums received under covenants (" the
' keep-out ' covenants ") contained in agreements by the taxpayer company
with nine foreign companies in consideration of the sale of manufacturing and
selling rights of Terylene were trading receipts for income tax purposes. The
E　commissioners held that none of the disputed payments except one-half of those
under the agreement with two Japanese companies and those under the agreement with two Polish companies were receipts falling to be included in the
Case 1 computation of the taxpayer company's profits.

　Arthur Bagnall, Q.C., and J. R. Phillips for the Crown.
　Heyworth Talbot, Q.C., and N. P. M. Elles for the taxpayer company.
F
　　　　　　　　　　　　　　　　　　　　　　　　　　　Cur. adv. vult.

　　　LORD DENNING, M.R.: In the 1950s, the taxpayer company, Imperial
Chemical Industries, Ltd., were exploiting a new fibrous material which they called
Terylene. They manufactured it on a large scale at Wilton, but they could not
make enough to meet the world demand. So they granted exclusive licences to
G　foreign companies in various countries. In each licence they covenanted that
they would not themselves enter the market for that country. They covenanted
to " keep out " of that country. In return for these " keep-out " covenants, they
received considerable sums of money from the overseas companies. The question
is whether these sums are part of the profits of the taxpayer company which should
be brought into tax. The amount of tax involved is over £1 million.

H　　The detailed facts are set out in the Case Stated and in the report of the
hearing before Cross, J. (1). I need only pick out the salient points. The
master patents for Terylene were owned by the Calico Printers' Association
(" C.P.A."), who granted the taxpayer company an exclusive licence to
exploit them and to grant sub-licences to others. The ancillary patents were
owned by the taxpayer company themselves but they were unable themselves
I　to exploit the world market for Terylene. So they granted sub-licences to
five European companies and two Japanese companies. A typical sub-licence
was that granted by the taxpayer company to a Dutch company covering
the Netherlands and Belgium. (i) The taxpayer company granted to the
company an exclusive licence to use the major patents (owned by C.P.A.)
in return for a royalty based on the net invoice value of the Terylene products
sold or utilised. (ii) The taxpayer company granted an exclusive licence to use
the ancillary patents (which they owned) in return for a royalty of £10,000 a

――――――――――――――――――――――――――――――――――
　(1) [1967] 1 All E.R. 369 at pp. 370-376.

year for ten years. (iii) The taxpayer company agreed to provide " know-how ". **A**
No separate consideration was stated for " know-how ", because they expected
to get their return by way of the royalties coming in sooner. (iv) The taxpayer
company agreed to " keep-out " of the Netherlands, Belgium, and, in addition,
Luxembourg, and not to operate there in the patented article Terylene or in
products similar to Terylene for the period of the patent and a little longer. In
return for this " keep-out " covenant, the licensee agreed to pay the sum, des- **B**
cribed as a capital sum (2), of £400,000 payable by six equal annual instalments,
but the licensee had the option of discharging the annual instalments by one
payment. The terms for the Japanese company were similar except that the
" know-how " and " keep-out " covenants were combined together in return for
a capital sum of £103,500. This was attributed by the Special Commissioner as to
one half for " know-how " and one half for the " keep-out " covenant. This **C**
apportionment was accepted by the Crown.

The question for decision is as to the £400,000 payable for the " keep-out "
covenant by annual instalments. Was it a trading receipt and taxable as part
of the income of the taxpayer company or was it a capital receipt which is not
taxable? In considering this question, I would point out that this " keep-out "
covenant is not a covenant " in gross ". It does not stand by itself. It is ancillary **D**
to the grant of a licence. Its effect can best be understood by remembering the
different kinds of licence with which we are familiar. An ordinary " licence "
is a permission to the licensee to do something which would otherwise be unlawful.
It leaves the licensor at liberty to do it himself and to grant licences to other
persons also. A " sole licence " is a permission to the licensee to do it, and no one
else, save that it leaves the licensor himself at liberty to do it. An " exclusive **E**
licence " is a permission which is exclusive to the licensee, so that even the
licensor himself is excluded as well as anyone else. A " keep-out " covenant is a
covenant which bolsters up an exclusive licence. It makes express that which
would otherwise be implied. The licensor covenants expressly with the licensee
that he will not enter on the domain which he has granted to the licensee. In the
present case the " keep-out " covenants are somewhat wider than the exclusive **F**
licence in area, time and products; but this makes no difference to the tax position.
The receipts by the taxpayer company bear the same character—capital or
income—no matter whether the " keep-out " covenant is co-extensive with the
licence or somewhat wider than it. In these circumstances I do not think that it
would be correct to consider a " keep-out " covenant as a thing by itself. The
essence of the transaction in each case is that the taxpayer company granted to **G**
the foreign company an exclusive licence to use the patents in the country
concerned for the term of the patents and, in return received remuneration in the
shape of: (a) a royalty payable on the net invoice value of products sold or utilised.
(This was for use of the master patents of C.P.A.) (b) A royalty of a fixed sum
payable each year. (This was for use of the ancillary patents of the taxpayer
company.) (c) A lump sum payable by instalments over six years. (This was said **H**
to be for the " keep-out " covenant.)

Now the taxpayer company are not dealers in patent rights or patent licences.
When they granted this exclusive licence, they were to my mind disposing of a
capital asset. If this had been an assignment of patent rights, there could be no
doubt that the taxpayer company would be disposing of a capital asset. I see no
difference in this regard between an assignment of patent rights and the grant of **I**
of an exclusive licence for the period of the patent. It is the disposal of a capital
asset. But this does not determine the quality of the money received. A man may

---

(2) Article X (2) of the agreement between the taxpayer company and the Dutch
company (A.K.U.), for which see [1967] 1 All E.R. at pp. 372, letters B et seq., provided
so far as material—" In consideration for the [keep-out] covenants by [the taxpayer
company] the licensee will pay to [the taxpayer company] in sterling in London a net
capital sum of £400,000. The said capital sum of £400,000 shall be payable in six equal
instalments of £66,666 13s. 4d. . . . ".

A dispose of a capital asset outright for a lump sum, which is then a capital receipt. Or he may dispose of it in return for an annuity, in which case the annual payments are revenue receipts. Or he may dispose of it in part for one and in part for the other. Each case must depend on its own circumstances; but it seems to me fairly clear that if and in so far as a man disposes of patent rights outright (viz., by an assignment of his patent, or by the grant of an exclusive licence) and

B receives in return *royalties* calculated by reference to the actual user, the royalties are clearly revenue receipts. If and in so far as he disposes of them for *annual payments* over the period, which can fairly be regarded as compensation for the user during the period, then those also are revenue receipts (such as the payment of £2,500 a year over ten years in *Inland Revenue Comrs.* v. *British Salmson Aero Engines, Ltd.* (3), and, of course, the royalties of £10,000 a year in the present

C case). If and in so far as he disposes of the patent rights outright for a *lump sum*, which is arrived at by reference to *some anticipated quantum of user*, it will normally be income in the hands of the recipient (see the judgment of LORD GREENE, M.R., in *Nethersole* v. *Withers (Inspector of Taxes)* (4), approved by VISCOUNT SIMON in the House of Lords (5)). If and in so far, however, as he disposes of them outright for a *lump sum* which has *no reference* to anticipated user, it will normally

D be capital (such as the payment of £25,000 in the *British Salmson* case (3)). It is different when a man does not dispose of his patent rights, but retains them and grants a non-exclusive licence. He does not then dispose of a capital asset. He retains the asset and he uses it to bring in money for him. A lump sum may in those cases be a revenue receipt (see *Rustproof Metal Window Co., Ltd.* v. *Inland Revenue Comrs.*, per LORD GREENE, M.R. (6), who emphasised that it was

E a non-exclusive licence there). Similarly a lump sum for " know-how " may be a revenue receipt. The capital asset remains with the owner. All he does is to put it to use.

Applying these criteria, in the present case it is quite clear that the royalties for the master C.P.A. patent and the royalties for the ancillary patents of the taxpayer company were revenue receipts. That is admitted. So far as the

F lump sum is concerned, I regard it as a capital receipt, even though it is payable by instalments. I am influenced by the facts: (i) that it is part payment for an exclusive licence, which is a capital asset; (ii) that it is payable in any event irrespective of whether there is any user under the licence; even if the licensees were not to use the patents at all, this sum would still be payable; (iii) that it is agreed to be a capital sum payable by instalments and not as an annuity or a

G series of annual payments. In these circumstances I am quite satisfied that the lump sum was a capital receipt and the taxpayer company are not taxable on it. I find myself in entire agreement with the judgment of CROSS, J. (7), and I would dismiss the appeal.

DAVIES, L.J.: I agree. A clear statement of the law on this matter is to

H be found in a passage in LORD GREENE, M.R.'s judgment in *Nethersole* v. *Withers (Inspector of Taxes)* (8), to which LORD DENNING, M.R., has referred. It may be convenient perhaps to quote that passage. LORD GREENE, having referred to *Inland Revenue Comrs.* v. *British Salmson Aero Engines, Ltd.* (3), proceeded in these terms (8):

I " This decision is a clear authority, so far as this court is concerned, that a lump sum payment received for the grant of a patent licence for a term of years may be a capital and not a revenue receipt; whether or not it is so

---

(3) [1938] 3 All E.R. 283; 22 Tax Cas. 29.
(4) [1946] 1 All E.R. 711 at p. 716; 28 Tax Cas. 501 at p. 512.
(5) [1948] 1 All E.R. 400 at p. 403; 28 Tax Cas. at p. 518.
(6) [1947] 2 All E.R. 454 at p. 459; 29 Tax Cas. 243 at p. 270.
(7) [1967] 1 All E.R. 369.
(8) [1946] 1 All E.R. at p. 716; 28 Tax Cas. at p. 512.

must depend on any particular facts which, in the particular case, may throw **A**
light upon its real character, including, of course, the terms of the agreement
under which the licence is granted. If the lump sum is arrived at by reference
to some anticipated quantum of user it will, we think, normally be income in
the hands of the recipient. If it is not, and if there is nothing else in the case
which points to an income character, it must, in our opinion, be regarded as
capital. This distinction is in some respects analogous to the familiar and **B**
perhaps equally fine distinction between payments of a purchase price by
instalments, and payment of a purchase price by way of an annuity over a
period of years.''

One might add that the case to which LORD GREENE was referring there, the
British Salmson case (9), in many respects has similarities to the one at present
before this court. As LORD DENNING, M.R., has said, that passage in LORD **C**
GREENE's judgment was quoted and approved by VISCOUNT SIMON in the House
of Lords in the same case (10). As I think CROSS, J., applied the law, as one would
have expected, with complete accuracy in the present case, I would refer to a
passage in his judgment, where he said this (11):

" The contention of the Crown before me, as before the commissioners, **D**
was that the various agreements were simply the mode in which the taxpayer
company chose to exploit some of its patent rights in the course of its trade
and that the lump sum payments were simply part of the total consideration
for all the obligations undertaken by the taxpayer company. Even if there
were no authority on the point, I, for my part, would not have accepted this
argument. The rights which the taxpayer company possessed in the C.P.A. **E**
patents and its own ancillary patents were not part of its circulating capital
but were fixed capital assets of its business. If it had sold those rights in
different countries outright for capital sums, those sums could not have been
treated as trading receipts. But the agreements in question contained in
substance dispositions of the whole interest of the taxpayer company in the
patents in the various countries supported by the ' keep-out ' covenants. A **F**
transaction of that sort does not seem to me to be in the least like the impart-
ing of ' know-how ' for reward, and, if the parties chose to arrange that part
of the consideration received by the taxpayer company should take the form
of a capital payment, and be attributed to the ' keep-out ' covenants, I do not
see why that part should not be capital for tax purposes.''

I agree with that. Counsel for the Crown conceded, as I understood his sub- **G**
mission, that if the transaction in the present case had taken the form of an out-
and-out assignment by the taxpayer company of their patent to the Dutch
company, the Japanese company, or various other companies, for a lump sum,
payable by instalments or not, that would be a capital receipt. It seems to me
that the present transaction is in substance the same as that. This was a sub-
licence of the patent for the whole of the life of the patent. That seems to me to **H**
be in the same shoes as the sort of transaction which the Crown conceded would
result in a capital receipt and not a revenue receipt. I therefore agree that the
judgment of CROSS, J. (12), was correct in every respect, and I would dismiss the
appeal.

    RUSSELL, L.J.: Without doubt the exclusive licences under the C.P.A.
patents, and the allied but subsidiary taxpayer company's patents, were fixed **I**
capital assets of the taxpayer company. They were in fact the foundation of the
Fibre Division. The Crown admits that if, to take the agreement with A.K.U.,
the Dutch company, touching Holland and Belgium as an example, the taxpayer
company had assigned to A.K.U. the C.P.A. exclusive licences and their own

(9) [1938] 3 All E.R. 283; 22 Tax Cas. 29.
(10) [1948] 1 All E.R. at p. 403; 28 Tax Cas. at p. 518.
(11) [1967] 1 All E.R. at p. 377.
(12) [1967] 1 All E.R. 369.

A patents in relation to those countries on the same terms of payment, the sum of £400,000 would have been not a revenue receipt but a receipt on capital account arising from a disposition of fixed capital assets. Similarly in the other contracts the subject of this appeal. The Crown contends, however, that the outcome is the exact opposite because the taxpayer company granted only sub-licences under the C.P.A. exclusive licences and licences under their own patents, and have,

B therefore, not disposed of or realised their fixed capital assets. In considering whether the taxpayer company have made such a disposition, however, regard must be had to the reality of the situation. Taking again the Dutch and Belgian example, before the agreement with A.K.U., the taxpayer company, by virtue of their exclusive licences from C.P.A. and their own subsidiary patents, had the right for the whole life of the patents (a) to make, use and vend in those countries

C in accordance with the patents, and (b) to prevent all others from so doing. It was that group of rights that constituted the whole value of this part of the taxpayer company's fixed capital from which profits were to be expected to grow. The result of the contract with A.K.U. was that the whole of this group of rights was disposed of for ever by the taxpayer company and effectively vested in A.K.U. In exchange the taxpayer company acquired a contractual obligation

D on the part of A.K.U. to pay a sum of £400,000, and in addition royalties related directly to the extent of user in the case of the C.P.A. patents and consisting of an annuity in the case of their own patents. The taxpayer company had deprived themselves completely of all ability thereafter to turn that part of their fixed capital to account whether by direct use of the inventions, or by licensing for reward. They had effectively transferred that ability to another; and that ability

E had been that part of their fixed capital. The substance of the matter was that the taxpayer company disposed of a part of their fixed capital in part for a sum (£400,000) which of itself, unlike the royalties, did not bear the stamp of a revenue receipt. I entirely agree with CROSS, J. (13) on this point.

Since this in my view wholly disposes of the appeal, I prefer to say nothing either way on the alternative method of putting the case for the taxpayer, which

F was the ground on which the Special Commissioners decided the case, viz., that the taxpayer company deprived themselves for a period by the agreement of the right or ability or potential ability to make, use and vend " agreement products " in, for example, Holland and Belgium; that this right or ability was part of their fixed capital; and that the £400,000 was expressly under the contract the consideration for this deprivation. As CROSS, J., pointed out (14), however, and

G indeed the Crown urged, this aspect of the case was ancillary to the whole disposition of the patent rights, and indeed a sine qua non of such disposition, especially in the possible event of the patents proving vulnerable or of a new method being discovered by the taxpayer company, and, therefore, cannot affect adversely the taxpayer company's contentions on the first point. I also would dismiss the appeal.

H *Appeal dismissed. Leave to appeal to the House of Lords refused.*

Solicitors: *Solicitor of Inland Revenue; J. S. Copp* (for the taxpayer company).

[*Reported by* F. A. AMIES, ESQ., *Barrister-at-Law.*]

I

---

(13) [1967] 1 All E.R. at p. 377.
(14) [1967] 1 All E.R. at pp. 376, 377.

ANISMINIC, LTD. v. THE FOREIGN COMPENSATION COMMISSION AND ANOTHER.

[COURT OF APPEAL, CIVIL DIVISION (Sellers, Diplock and Russell, L.JJ.), January 16, 17, 18, 19, 20, 23, 24, 25, 26, 27, 30, 31, February 1, March 23, 1967.]

Certiorari—Jurisdiction—Principle—Statutory tribunal's decision—No certiorari provision in statute—Error going to jurisdiction distinguished from error within jurisdiction—Review of decision for error of law apparent on face of record and within jurisdiction excluded by no certiorari provision—Error going to jurisdiction, however, would render tribunal's decision a nullity notwithstanding no certiorari clause.

A tribunal authorised by statute to make a determination must form an opinion on, among other questions, (a) whether in order to proceed with the inquiry the case before the tribunal is of a kind into which the tribunal is empowered by statute to inquire, and if so (b) whether the facts premised by statute to establish legal consequences are established; if error in (a) is made (viz., an " error going to the jurisdiction ") the tribunal's determination is a nullity, but if error in (b) is made (viz., an " error within jurisdiction "), the determination remains effective, for the tribunal has jurisdiction to be wrong as well as to be right. An error within jurisdiction, if it is an error in law apparent on the face of the record, can be controlled by certiorari, unless the statute excludes jurisdiction by certiorari (viz., contains a " no certiorari clause "); but, even if the statute does contain a no certiorari clause, the High Court will still have jurisdiction to decide whether the tribunal's determination is a nullity by reason of an " error going to juris-diction ", whether that error is of fact or of law (see p. 995, letter D, p. 995, letter F, p. 996, letters B and I, p. 990, letter G, and p. 1008, letter E, post).

R. v. *Shoreditch Assessment Committee, Ex p. Morgan* ([1908-10] All E.R. Rep. 792) and *Ex p. Bradlaugh* ((1878), 3 Q.B.D. 509) considered.

Certiorari—Statutory tribunal—Determination of tribunal to be final—Application to Foreign Compensation Commission—Application of a kind into which the commission had jurisdiction to inquire—Alleged error of commission in construing Order in Council—No power in court to substitute the court's opinion on construction for the commission's—Foreign Compensation (Egypt) (Determination and Registration of Claims) Order, 1962 (S.I. 1962 No. 2187), art. 4 (1) (a), (b), art. 6 (1)—Foreign Compensation Act, 1950 (14 Geo. 6 c. 12), s. 4 (4).

A company, Anisminic, owned a mining business in Egypt which, at the time of the Suez incident in 1956, was sequestrated under the provisions of a proclamation of the Egyptian government. It was sold by the sequestrator to an Egyptian organisation, T.E.D.O. Anisminic refused to recognise the sale. In November, 1957, Anisminic entered into an agreement with T.E.D.O. and the sequestrator to sell the whole of Anisminic's business in Egypt to T.E.D.O. for £500,000. In 1959 a compensation fund was established under the Egypt-ian compensation agreement* out of which compensation was to be made in respect of property sequestrated in Egypt. Distribution of the compensation was regulated by the Foreign Compensation Act, 1950, and the determination of claims was regulated by the Foreign Compensation (Egypt) (Determina-tion and Registration of Claims) Order, 1962. The matters to be established in respect of claims were prescribed by arts. 4 (1), 6 (1), and 8†. By s. 4 (4) of

---

* See p. 998, letter I, post.

† Articles 4 (1), 6 (1) and 8, so far as relevant, provide: " 4. (1) The Commission shall treat a claim under this Part [Part 3] of the Order as established if the applicant satisfies them of the following matters:—(a) that his application relates to property in Egypt which is referred to in Annex E; (b) if the property is referred to in para. (1) (a)

(*Continued at foot of p.* 987.)

A   the Act of 1950 the determination by the commission of any application made to them under the Act was not to be called in question in any court of law. By a provisional determination on May 8, 1963, the commission decided that Anisminic had failed to establish a claim under art. 4 or art. 6. It was conceded that the proceedings before the commission were an application to them under the Act of 1950. On appeal from a judgment in an action by

B   Anisminic declaring that the commission's determination was a nullity, the proceedings being treated‡ as if they were for certiorari,

Held: it being conceded that Anisminic's application was a case of the kind into which the commission had jurisdiction to inquire, the commission's determination whether the matters requisite to establish Anisminic's claim had been established was final, and the court had no power to substitute the

C   court's opinion as to that for the commission's opinion, even if the court were to consider that the commission's determination had proceeded on an error in law (of which, however, the court was not satisfied), for that error would have been an error within the commission's jurisdiction (see p. 992, letter A, p. 1001, letter D, p. 1006, letter F, p. 1007, letter B, and p. 1008, letter C, post).

Davies v. *Price* ([1958] 1 All E.R. 671) applied.

D   *Board of Trustees of Maradana Mosque* v. *Badi-Ud-Din Mahmud* ([1966] 1 All E.R. 545) criticised.

Per DIPLOCK, L.J.: where the only function of an inferior tribunal is to make a determination, and the right to enforce, or to order enforcement of, the liability to which the determination is a condition precedent is conferred on other persons, I doubt whether any action for a declaration lies against the

E   inferior tribunal (see p. 1007, letter G, post).

Appeal allowed.

[**Editorial Note.** In considering the effect of a " no certiorari clause " in relation to an error of law within a tribunal's jurisdiction, regard must be had to s. 11 of the Tribunals and Inquiries Act, 1958, which, however, was not applicable to the particular determination considered in the present case.

F   As to the quashing of decisions of inferior tribunals for want of jurisdiction, see 1 HALSBURY'S LAWS (3rd Edn.) 142, para. 268; and for cases on the subject, see 16 DIGEST (Repl.) 467-475, *2862-2940.*

As to certiorari being excluded by statute, see 11 HALSBURY'S LAWS (3rd Edn.) 137, para. 257; and as to the exclusion being inapplicable where the inferior tribunal acts without jurisdiction, see ibid., p. 138, para. 260; and for

G   cases on these subjects, see 16 DIGEST (Repl.) 490-496, *3124-3191.*

As to the power to make declaratory judgments, see 22 HALSBURY'S LAWS (3rd Edn.) 747-749, para. 1610; and for cases on the subject, see 30 DIGEST (Repl.) 168-171, *192-219.*

(Continued from foot of p. 986.)

H   or para. (2) of Annex E—(i) that the applicant is the person referred to in paragraph (1) (*a*) or in para. (2), as the case may be, as the owner of the property or is the successor in title of such person; and (ii) that the person referred to as aforesaid and any person who became successor in title of such person on or before Feb. 28, 1959, were British nationals on Oct. 31, 1956, and Feb. 28, 1959 . . .

" 6. (1) The commission shall treat a claim under this Part [Part 4] of the Order as established if the applicant satisfies them of the following matters:—(a) that his application relates to property in Egypt in respect of which no claim can be established under

I   Part 3 of this Order and which had been lost, injured or damaged after Oct. 30, 1956, and before Feb. 28, 1959, as a result of Egyptian measures; (b) that he was the owner at the time of such loss, injury or damage or is the successor in title of such owner; and (c) that the owner at the time of the loss, injury or damage and any person who became successor in title of such owner on or before Feb. 28, 1959, were British nationals on Oct. 31, 1956, and Feb. 28, 1959.

" 8. If the applicant satisfies the commission of all the matters specified in art. 6 of this Order other than that the loss, injury or damage was the result of Egyptian measures, the commission shall register the claim and report thereon to Her Majesty's Principal Secretary of State for Foreign Affairs in such manner as he shall direct."

‡ See p. 996, letter D, and p. 1007, letter C, post.

For the Foreign Compensation Act, 1950, s. 1, s. 2, s. 3, s. 4, see 29 HALSBURY'S **A**
STATUTES (2nd Edn.) 146, 147, 148; and for the Foreign Compensation Act, 1962,
s. 1, see 42 ibid., 190.

For the Tribunals and Inquiries Act, 1958, s. 11, see 38 HALSBURY'S STATUTES
(2nd Edn.) 211.]

Cases referred to: **B**

Bank Voor Handel en Scheepvaart, N.V. v. *Administrator of Hungarian Property*,
    [1954] 1 All E.R. 969; [1954] A.C. 584; [1954] 2 W.L.R. 867; 2 Digest
    (Repl.) 269, *614*.

Board of Education v. *Rice*, [1911-13] All E.R. Rep. 36; [1911] A.C. 179; 80
    L.J.K.B. 796; 104 L.T. 689; 75 J.P. 393; 19 Digest (Repl.) 630, *206*.

Bradlaugh, Ex p., (1878), 3 Q.B.D. 509; 47 L.J.M.C. 105; 38 L.T. 680; 42   **C**
    J.P. 583; 16 Digest (Repl.) 495, *3183*.

Davies v. *Price*, [1958] 1 All E.R. 671; [1958] 1 W.L.R. 434; Digest (Cont.
    Vol. A) 16, *74a*.

Maradana Mosque (Board of Trustees) v. *Badi-Ud-Din Mahmud*, [1966] 1 All
    E.R. 545; [1967] A.C. 13; [1966] 2 W.L.R. 921; Digest (Cont. Vol. B)
    234, **8a*.
                                                                              D
R. v. *Bolton*, [1835-43] All E.R. Rep. 71; (1841), 1 Q.B. 66; 10 L.J.M.C. 49;
    5 J.P. 370; 113 E.R. 1054; 16 Digest (Repl.) 468, *2876*.

R. v. *Fulham, Hammersmith and Kensington Rent Tribunal, Ex p. Hierowski*,
    [1953] 2 All E.R. 4; [1953] 2 Q.B. 147; [1953] 2 W.L.R. 1028; 117 J.P.
    295; Digest (Cont. Vol. A) 1110, *8122b*.

R. v. *Minister of Health, Ex p. Glamorgan County Mental Hospital (Committee* **E**
    of Visitors), [1938] 4 All E.R. 32; 102 J.P. 497; sub nom. *R.* v. *Minister
    of Health*, [1939] 1 K.B. 232; 108 L.J.K.B. 27; 159 L.T. 508; 33 Digest
    (Repl.) 706, *1649*.

R. v. *Nat Bell Liquors, Ltd.*, [1922] All E.R. Rep. 335; [1922] 2 A.C. 128; 91
    L.J.P.C. 146; 127 L.T. 437; 16 Digest (Repl.) 469, *2897*.

R. v. *Shoreditch Assessment Committee, Ex p. Morgan*, [1908-10] All E.R. Rep. **F**
    792; [1910] 2 K.B. 859; 80 L.J.K.B. 185; 103 L.T. 262; 74 J.P. 361;
    38 Digest (Repl.) 671, *1216*.

Rustomjee v. *Reginam*, (1876), 1 Q.B.D. 487; *affd.* C.A. (1876), 2 Q.B.D. 69;
    46 L.J.Q.B. 238; 36 L.T. 190; 16 Digest (Repl.) 271, *388*.

Appeal.

This was an appeal by the Foreign Compensation Commission and Cecil Frank **G**
Cooper, the legal officer appointed by the commission, against an order of
BROWNE, J., made on July 29, 1966, declaring that a provisional determination
of the commission made on May 8, 1963, was made without or in excess of jurisdic-
tion and was a nullity, and declaring that a further provisional determination of
June 21, 1963, was also a nullity. HIS LORDSHIP also declared that the commission
were under a statutory duty to treat as established under art. 4 of the Foreign **H**
Compensation (Egypt) (Determination and Registration of Claims) Order,
1962, the claim of the respondent company, Anisminic, Ltd. (herein called
" Anisminic "), in respect of the whole of Anisminic's former property in Egypt.

The essential facts are shortly stated at p. 1001, letters F to I, post. Before Oct. 30,
1965 Anisminic, then known as The Sinai Mining Co., Ltd., carried on the business
of mining manganese in the Sinai Peninsula under mining leases or concessions **I**
granted by the Egyptian government. In the claim which they afterwards made
to the commission they valued their property in Egypt at that date at about
£4½ million, but that figure was not admitted by the commission. Under the
agreement which Anisminic made with the Egyptian authorities on Nov. 23,
1957 (see p. 1001, letter H, post), Anisminic received £500,000 out of the proceeds
of ore produced from their former mines, but as matters stood they would not
receive anything out of a sum of £27,500,000 paid by the government of the
United Arab Republic, or the additional moneys provided by Parliament, forming

A   the Egyptian Compensation Fund*. On July 30, 1963, Anisminic issued the writ
commencing the action against the present appellants. In that action Anisminic
claimed five declarations, and a sixth alternative declaration, but it was conceded
at the hearing that amendments would be needed in the wording of any declarations which might be made at the trial, and the nature of the declarations actually
made has been indicated at p. 988, letter G, ante. By their defence delivered
B   on Nov. 18, 1963, the then defendants pleaded that the High Court had no
jurisdiction to entertain the action.

S. W. Templeman, Q.C., Nigel Bridge and *C. D. Cochrane* for the appellants.
R. J. Parker, Q.C., and *F. P. Neill, Q.C.,* for Anisminic, Ltd.

Cur. adv. vult.

C   Mar. 22. The following judgments were read.

SELLERS, L.J. (whose judgment was read by RUSSELL, L.J.): The
extensive judgments of BROWNE, J., in the Queen's Bench Division and of
DIPLOCK, L.J., in this court, which I have already had an opportunity of reading,
permit me to turn almost at once to my conclusions on this appeal, in so doing
adopting as widely as possible the surveys in the judgments of these two learned
D   judges, including their statements of the facts and the issues.

The plaintiffs, Anisminic, Ltd. (" Anisminic "), have appealed from a decision,
unfavourable to them, of the Foreign Compensation Commission. BROWNE, J.,
entertained the appeal and made a declaration favourable to Anisminic notwithstanding that s. 4 (4) of the Foreign Compensation Act, 1950, provides that

E   " The determination by the commission of any application made to them
under this Act shall not be called in question in any court of law."

Further, the Tribunals and Inquiries Act, 1958, constituted a council on tribunals
and provided for appeals to the courts from decisions of, or on appeal from,
certain tribunals; required the giving of reasons for certain decisions of tribunals
and ministries, and extended the supervisory powers of the High Court.
F   Section 11 (1) enacts:

" As respects England and Wales or Northern Ireland, any provision in
an Act passed before the commencement of this Act that any order or
determination shall not be called into question in any court, or any provision
in such an Act which by similar words excludes any of the powers of the High
Court, shall not have effect so as to prevent the removal of the proceedings
G   into the High Court by order of certiorari or to prejudice the powers of the
High Court to make orders of mandamus . . ."

It is to be noted, however, that s. 11 (3) expressly stipulates that sub-s. (1) shall
not apply to any order or determination of the Foreign Compensation Commission. Those are clear and emphatic statutory provisions and the question in this
case is whether the courts can disregard them and if so in what circumstances
H   and to what extent.

This action seeks declarations which undoubtedly call in question the determination by the Foreign Compensation Commission of an application made to the
tribunal under the Act of 1950. Nothing relevant to the appeal turns on the fact
that the determination was provisional. The application was in proper form,
the proceedings were regularly conducted, and the tribunal, properly constituted,
I   reached a reasoned decision which it made available to the parties, as I am
inclined to think, unnecessarily and perhaps undesirably.

On what, then, is this action at law based? It is alleged that the commission
have misconstrued the terms of the Order in Council (1) stipulating the matters
to be proved by an applicant in order to establish a claim. They have, it is said,

---

* See, as to this fund, p. 997, letter C, post.
(1) See the Foreign Compensation (Egypt) (Determination and Registration of
Claims) Order, 1962, S.I. 1962 No. 2187, e.g., arts. 4, 5.

required more to be proved than the order warrants or considered matters which A
do not arise on a true construction of the order and have failed to make the proper
order when the requirements of the order had been fulfilled by the applicants.
Anisminic did not shrink from submitting that whether the commission had so
erred or not could not be ascertained until the facts, the relevant statutes and
orders had been fully analysed and considered. Consequently both courts, here
and below, have been subjected to a complete consideration of all the matters B
which arose before the commission, as well as the ample authorities dealing with
the circumstances in which the courts have interfered with the decisions of
inferior tribunals where there has been a statutory clause similar, or with the
like effect, to s. 4 (4) of the Act of 1950.

I am of opinion that the courts cannot substitute their views on the construction of the Order in Council for that of the commission, who alone have to be C
satisfied that a claim has been established. A determination may in the view of
some be wrong either in fact or in law but it may none the less be a determination.
The Foreign Compensation Commission is not an inferior court administering
the general law of the land. It is a special commission of selected commissioners
called on in its present relevant jurisdiction to adjudicate on claims made by
applicants to participate in a sum of £27,500,000 (supplemented by moneys D
provided by Parliament) which the government have received from the Egyptian
government following the events at Suez in 1956.

War and confiscation and their aftermaths had brought about confusion,
complications and uncertainties with regard to property and rights. The government had negotiated this sum in the interests generally of British nationals who
had suffered loss, and any distribution of that sum was at the government's E
discretion and decision. By Orders in Council provisions were made as to the
qualifications of claimants and the entitlement to participate in the funds. This
involves the commission in ascertaining what are the requirements to substantiate
a claim. It is an inherent and indeed the initial part of their adjudication to
construe the relevant Order in Council and then to review an applicant's claim
and to reach their determination on it. The commission have been entrusted F
under the Act of 1950 with this special and defined task, and having regard to the
nature and the purpose of their adjudication Parliament has decreed that their
decision shall be final. The wisdom of this is established, rather than defeated, by
the nature and the extent of these proceedings and the inevitable delay so far
involved. What the commission had to do was to determine the application made
to them. I think that it would be a travesty to say that they have not done so. G
I am in general agreement with what DIPLOCK, L.J., has so fully said in the judgment which he is about to read and, like him, I do not find any satisfactory
reason or authority to support Anisminic's endeavour to re-open this matter
before the courts.

The submission for Anisminic has been that the commission acted without
jurisdiction in that its decision refusing the claim was wrong in law and invalid H
and therefore a nullity.

The question of jurisdiction is determinable at the commencement, not at the
conclusion, of the inquiry. The test on jurisdiction, in the only sense in which it
is relevant here, is whether the commission had power to enter on the inquiry
and make a determination; not whether their determination was right or wrong
in fact or in law.   I

" The question of jurisdiction does not depend on the truth or falsehood
of the charge, but on its nature; it is determinable on the commencement,
not at the conclusion, of the inquiry; and affidavits, to be receivable, must
be directed to what appears at the former stage and not to the facts disclosed
on the progress of the inquiry " :

per LORD DENMAN, C.J., in *R.* v. *Bolton* (2). DIPLOCK, L.J., has enumerated four

(2) [1835-42] All E.R. Rep. 71 at p. 73; (1841), 1 Q.B. 66 at p. 74.

A respects in which the authority or " jurisdiction " of a tribunal to determine matters submitted to it is limited. With these I agree. It was not suggested that any of these conditions has been infringed. The commission were properly constituted. They held an inquiry in accordance with the statutory requirements and in a judicial manner. Anisminic's claim related to the subject-matter of the commission's authority to determine. The commission reached a conclusion and

B determined the claim. They did not fail in regard to any condition precedent to their adjudication.

I do not question BROWNE, J.'s classification in his detailed and helpful review of the many authorities cited to him and to us. I apprehend that such a citation will rarely be necessary in the future as the Tribunals and Inquiries Act, 1958, will readily enable the appropriate court to exercise an appellate or at least a

C supervisory control over a wide field.

It is when the judge concluded by saying, as he did, that if he were right in his view that the commission's decision was wrong s. 4 (4) of the Foreign Compensation Act, 1950, does not oust the jurisdiction of the court, that I would with respect disagree. His view was formed, as he said, after much hesitation. Unless established authority clearly requires such a conclusion, this does not seem to me

D to be a case where the courts should strive to disregard the statutory provision that the determination should not be called in question in any court of law, which prohibition received further emphasis by the Tribunals and Inquiries Act, 1958. The courts, it is true, have not looked with favour on legislative provisions for ousting the jurisdiction of the court but if the words of prohibition in the Act of 1950 are to be given the meaning which they clearly express, as I read them, they

E do not admit of any qualification or distinguish one part of the commission's task from another. In the performance of their duties the commission may have to construe innumerable statutes, orders, contracts and documents of many kinds, some English, some foreign, and I see no reason for excepting from their adjudication the Order in Council (3) whose terms, as they understand them, direct their administration.

F The argument for Anisminic in both courts has somewhat remarkably been based fundamentally on *Ex p. Bradlaugh* (4). It was submitted that the commission had gone outside their jurisdiction because they had asked themselves the wrong questions or had required one too many questions or had answered the relevant questions correctly and failed to give proper effect to their answers. The *Bradlaugh* case (4) has been referred to in some later cases and the general

G observations of MELLOR, J., (5) that

> " It is well established that the provision taking away the certiorari does not apply where there was absence of jurisdiction "

have been quoted and accepted, but in my view the case and the decision provide no secure foundation for a case such as the present. It concerned a hearing in a

H magistrates' court in a matter penal in nature. The form of the order did not reveal that the magistrate had been satisfied of all the matters the relevant statute required. It seems to have been the form of the order rather than the substance of the matter which was involved.

I agree with DIPLOCK, L.J.'s observations on the other three cases on which the judge mainly relied: *R. v. Shoreditch Assessment Committee, Ex p. Morgan*

I (6); *R. v. Fulham, Hammersmith and Kensington Rent Tribunal, Ex p. Hierowski* (7); and *Board of Trustees of Maradana Mosque* v. *Badi-Ud-Din Mahmud* (8). In my view they fall short of establishing a principle applicable here.

(3) The Foreign Compensation (Egypt) (Determination and Registration of Claims) Order, 1962, S.I. 1962 No. 2187.
(4) (1878), 3 Q.B.D. 509.
(5) (1878), 3 Q.B.D. at p. 513.
(6) [1908-10] All E.R. Rep. 792; [1910] 2 K.B. 859.
(7) [1953] 2 All E.R. 4; [1953] 2 Q.B. 147.
(8) [1966] 1 All E.R. 545; [1967] A.C. 13.

In the present case, in my judgment, it fell to the commission and to them alone   A
to construe the Order in Council which directed the matters which had to be
established to their satisfaction by applicants claiming to share in the fund. I do
not think that BROWNE, J., had any jurisdiction to consider whether the
commission were right or wrong in their conclusion, nor has this court.

I feel no temptation to express a view on the reasoning of the minute of
adjudication which, I think, was unnecessarily revealed to Anisminic and which   B
alone has given rise to these sustained submissions.

Anisminic seized an early opportunity and made a bargain direct with the
Egyptian authorities, which they thought at the time would preclude them from
any further relief such as they now claim. They may not therefore command
much sympathetic consideration, but I apprehend that the machinery of government could operate, if thought fit by the government, to rectify any decision of   C
the commission which proved unjust in the administration and distribution of
the funds available.

I would allow the appeal and would dismiss the action.

DIPLOCK, L.J.: As has been foreshadowed in the judgment of SELLERS,
L.J., which has just been read, the judgment which I am about to read is very
long and very tedious, and it is perhaps unfortunate that it could not be handed   D
down but must be read viva voce. However, I will undertake that lengthy task.

Section 4 (4) of the Foreign Compensation Act, 1950, provides that

" The determination by the [Foreign Compensation Commission] of any
application made to them under this Act shall not be called in question in
any court of law."
                                                                                   E
In this action the plaintiffs (" Anisminic ") sought to call in question in the High
Court what purports to be a determination by the commission of an application
by Anisminic to establish certain claims to participate in compensation paid by
the government of the United Arab Republic to the government of the United
Kingdom. If the decision of the commission to which the action relates was " a
determination by the commission of an application made to them under the   F
Act " within the meaning of the subsection, a simple man could be forgiven for
thinking that BROWNE, J., had no right to make any declaration about it. I
think so too; and since it is conceded that proceedings before the commission
in which their decision was made were " an application made to them under
the Act ", the only ground on which it can be called in question in any court of
law is that it was not a " determination " of that application. That is what this   G
appeal is about.

Stated thus, the answer to the only question in this appeal depends on the true
construction of the Foreign Compensation Act, 1950, and the Orders in Council
made under it, and I venture to think that a similar question of construction of a
statute has been involved in each of the relevant cases in which the High Court
has been invited to intermeddle with decisions of " inferior tribunals "—an   H
expression in which I include not only all courts of law other than the Supreme
Court of Judicature and the House of Lords but also all other tribunals and
persons on whom authority has been conferred by statute to decide disputes
between two or more parties or claims by a subject to a right against or exempt-
tion from a liability or duty to the Crown. There are many such cases. In its
113 foolscap pages the judgment under appeal cites and summarises a representa-   I
tive selection of them which have been decided in the last century and a quarter.
Although the reports contain many other cases on this topic the judge's survey
is sufficiently complete and thorough to save me the necessity of any general
citation of authority. These cases abound with references to " error " and to
" jurisdiction ", to " error of fact " and to " error of law ", to error " going to
jurisdiction " and to " error within jurisdiction "; and these expressions are
not always used in the same sense in one case as in another. We must, I think,
go back to first principles and start by analysing and defining our terms.

A   Lawyers are concerned with facts only in so far as those facts may have legal consequences, that is, give rise directly or indirectly to a right or liability in any individual which the executive branch of government will or may enforce. There must be some person to decide in a case affecting any individual: first, what are the facts that exist, and secondly, what are the legal consequences of those facts. It is not necessarily the same person who decides both those matters, even in the

B   first instance (for example, trial by jury), but for the purposes of the present appeal we may confine our attention to cases where it is. That person must state what his decision is. Since it is the legal consequences that matter, his statement of his decision will always disclose his view as to the legal consequences of the facts which he thinks exist, but it will not necessarily disclose what those facts are.

C   Lawyers, when they talk of " error ", whether of " fact " or of " law " in such a statement, are dealing not with absolutes but with the opinions of human beings. A statement that there exist particular facts which give rise to specified legal consequences is " right " if it is made by a person to whose opinion as to the existence or non-existence of those facts, and as to their legal consequences, effect will be given by the executive branch of government. Such a statement

D   from being " right " may become " wrong ", however, if subsequently a contrary statement is made by some other person to whose opinion as to the legal consequences of those facts effect will be given by the executive branch of government in substitution for that of the person who made the first statement. It is then the later statement that is " right "; but it may be that effect will be given to the substituted opinion of such other person as to the legal consequences of facts

E   only, and not as to the existence or non-existence of the particular facts which give rise to those legal consequences. In that event the original statement that particular facts exist remains " right " and must be so treated by the person to whose substituted opinion as to the legal consequences of facts effect will be given.

   Legal consequences of facts depend on whether the particular facts which exist

F   are of a kind which conforms with a description which expresses a general idea or " universal " in the Aristotelean sense. To state that there exist particular facts which fall within that description is to make a statement about the legal consequences of those particular facts. Thus, to state of an individual, John Bull, that he is a " British national " is to state a legal consequence of the existence of other facts particular to John Bull which bring him within the description

G   " British national ", such as that he was born in the United Kingdom, or that he was born elsewhere but was granted a certificate of naturalisation by the Secretary of State. Those other facts particular to John Bull may or may not be set out in the statement. If the statement is made by a person to whose opinion as to the existence or non-existence of the facts particular to John Bull, and as to the legal consequences of those facts as respects his British nationality, effect will be given

H   by the executive branch of the government, and there is another person to whose substituted opinion as to the legal consequences of those particular facts effect will be given, but no effect will be given to his substituted opinion as to the existence or non-existence of the facts particular to John Bull, the question whether the statement can ever be said to be " wrong " depends on whether the particular facts are set out in the original statement. If they are, it is possible

I   to say that the maker of the statement has made a mistake in stating the legal consequences of the particular facts, and this is called an " error of law "; but if the particular facts are not set out it is impossible to say this. The bare statement that " John Bull is a British national " is a statement that there exist facts particular to John Bull of which the legal consequence is that he is a British national. It can only be said to be wrong if there is some person to whose substituted opinion as to the existence or non-existence of facts particular to John Bull as well as to their legal consequences effect will be given.

   Where, as in the present appeal, the description of the kind of facts which give

rise to legal rights or liabilities is contained in legislation, a statement by a person   **A**
to whose opinion effect will be given that facts particular to an individual fall
within that description is, perhaps anomalously, treated in English law as a
statement of the legal consequences of those particular facts, even though the
description itself does not appear to involve what would, in any other context, be
regarded as legal concepts. This is what is meant by the rule that the construction
of a statute is always a question of law. So, if there is some person to whose substi-   **B**
tuted opinion as to the legal consequences of the particular facts effect will be
given, and he states his opinion that the particular facts stated to exist do not fall
within the description contained in the legislation, the original statement is
" wrong " and the error is an " error of law ".

" Jurisdiction " is an expression which is used in a variety of senses and takes
its colour from its context. In the present appeal, as in most of the authorities   **C**
which have been cited, we are concerned only with statutory jurisdiction in the
sense of an authority conferred by statute on a person to determine, after inquiry
into a case of a kind described in the statute conferring that authority and
submitted to him for decision, whether or not there exists a situation, of a kind
described in the statute, the existence of which is a condition precedent to a right
or liability of an individual who is party to the inquiry, to which effect will or   **D**
may be given by the executive branch of government. A determination made
pursuant to such statutory authority is thus a statement made by a person to
whose opinion effect will be given by the executive branch of government that a
situation of the kind described in the statute exists. I have used the word
" situation " to cover both facts and the legal consequences of facts, for the
description in the statute of the situation may be a description of the kind of facts   **E**
the existence or non-existence of which is to be determined or a description of
legal consequences to which facts give rise, or a combination of both types of
description. But because of the rule that the construction of a statute is always
a matter of law, whatever type of description is used in the statute, the determination will always be or include a statement of the legal consequences of particular
facts which in the opinion of the maker of the statement exist, whether the   **F**
particular facts are set out in the statement or not. Authority to make such a
determination thus always includes authority to decide some questions of law.

The authority to determine whether a described situation exists is to be
distinguished from an additional authority which is often conferred on the same
person to make an order, of a kind described in the statute, requiring the executive
branch of government to give effect to the right or liability to which the deter-   **G**
mination that such situation exists is a condition precedent. This additional
authority where it exists is also included in the expression " jurisdiction ", and
some of the cases cited deal with it under that name; but we are not concerned
with that kind of authority in the present appeal.

The authority or " jurisdiction " to determine whether a situation of a kind
described in a statute exists is limited to a number of respects: **H**

(i) The person or persons by whom it is exercised must possess the qualifications laid down in the statute. In addition, unless it is otherwise provided
in the statute either expressly or by necessary implication, the presumed
intention of Parliament is that one of the qualifications is absence of bias.

(ii) The determination must be preceded by inquiry. The nature of the
inquiry, any conditions precedent to the inquiry, and the procedure to be   **I**
adopted in the inquiry, may be laid down expressly in the statute. In the
absence of express provision to the contrary, the presumed intention of
Parliament is that the inquiry shall be conducted in accordance with the
rules of natural justice. A convenient summary of the relevant rules is to be
found in the speech of LORD LOREBURN, L.C., in *Board of Education* v.
Rice (9).

(9) [1911-13] All E.R. Rep. 36; [1911] A.C. 179.

A   (iii) The case in which the determination is made must be one of the kind described in the statute. The statute may define the kind of cases which it confers authority on a person to determine in a number of different ways. The description will necessarily include words identifying the person or class of persons who are entitled to initiate the inquiry leading to the determination and probably the other person or class of persons (if any) who are

B   entitled to be parties to the inquiry. It will also necessarily contain a description of the subject-matter of the determination, that is, of the kind of dispute or claim to be determined.

(iv) The determination must state whether a situation of the kind described in the Act exists or not in the case of the individual to whom the determination relates.

C   If any of these conditions is not complied with, the statement is not a " determination " within the authority conferred by the statute and effect will not be given to it by the executive branch of government.

The person authorised to make the determination must necessarily form an opinion whether each of those conditions is complied with, in order to embark on

D   and to proceed with the inquiry and to make the determination; but his opinion whether they are or not is not one to which effect will be given by the executive branch of government. If it is " wrong " in the opinion of a person to whose opinion whether or not any of the conditions are complied with effect will be given by the executive branch of government, the error is an " error going to the jurisdiction " of the inferior tribunal, and the purported determination is a

E   nullity. This is not the substitution of the opinion of one person to whose opinion effect will be given for that of another to whose opinion effect would have been given but for such substitution. It is the first statement of any opinion to which effect will be given by the executive branch of government. This is what distinguishes it from the case of a determination made where all these conditions are complied with, and to which effect would be given by the executive branch

F   of government but for the fact that the determination contains a statement as to the legal consequences of particular facts which in the opinion of the maker exist, and such statement is " wrong " in the opinion of some other person to whose substituted opinion as to the legal consequences of particular facts effect will be given by the executive branch of government. The error is then an " error within jurisdiction ".

G   In the present appeal we are concerned with the " jurisdiction " not only of a particular inferior tribunal, the Foreign Compensation Commission, but also with that of the High Court itself. The High Court too is the creation of statute and its " jurisdiction " is statutory, although the principal statute, the Supreme Court of Judicature (Consolidation) Act, 1925, confers that jurisdiction in part by reference to the jurisdiction formerly exercised by the courts of common

H   law before the Supreme Court of Judicature Act, 1875. In relation to determinations of inferior tribunals the former court of Queen's Bench exercised jurisdiction of two kinds. It was the person whose opinion, whether the conditions limiting the authority of the inferior tribunal to make a statement which purported to be a determination were fulfilled, would be given effect to: that is to say, it corrected " errors going to the jurisdiction " of the inferior tribunal.

I   It was also the person to whose opinion about the legal consequences of particular facts found to exist by the inferior tribunal effect would be given in substitution for that of the inferior tribunal: that is to say, it corrected " errors within jurisdiction ". In exercising its own jurisdiction to correct " errors going to jurisdiction " of an inferior tribunal, the court of Queen's Bench was making the first effective statement whether or not particular facts existed which had the legal consequences of fulfilling the conditions limiting the authority of the inferior tribunal. It could therefore make its own inquiry into the existence or non-existence of the particular facts. It could correct " errors of fact " as well

as " errors of law " in the opinion formed by the inferior tribunal as to whether   A
or not the conditions limiting its authority to make a determination were fulfilled.
In exercising its own jurisdiction, however, to correct " errors within jurisdiction " of the inferior tribunal, the court of Queen's Bench could only correct
" errors of law ", because it was not the person to whose opinion about the
existence or non-existence of particular facts effect would be given in substitution
for that of the inferior tribunal. Consequently, where the particular facts which   B
in the opinion of the inferior tribunal existed were not set out in the statement
of their determination but only the legal consequences of those facts, the " errors
of law ", if any, could not be detected by the court of Queen's Bench. It was
only where the particular facts were set out in the statement that that court could
form an opinion as to the correctness of the statement of the inferior tribunal
about the legal consequences of those facts. It could correct only " errors of law   C
on the face of the record ".

The procedure by which the court of Queen's Bench exercised its own jurisdiction to correct " errors within jurisdiction " of an inferior tribunal was by
certiorari. This was also the commonest procedure by which it exercised its own
jurisdiction to correct " errors going to jurisdiction " of an inferior tribunal.
Although the present appeal is in an action for a declaratory judgment, it has   D
been treated for the purposes of argument as if it were brought in proceedings for
certiorari and I, too, shall deal with it on this basis.

We are concerned with a statute passed after the jurisdiction of the former
court of Queen's Bench had been transferred to the High Court of Justice. Where
a statute passed after 1875 confers or imposes on any individual, when a situation
described in the statute exists, a new right or a new liability which the executive   E
branch of government will enforce, it is a question of construction of that statute
(a) whether jurisdiction to determine whether or not that situation exists in the
case of a particular individual is conferred on the High Court or on some inferior
tribunal and, if on the latter, (b) whether or not jurisdiction is conferred on the
High Court to correct the determination of the inferior tribunal for " errors within
jurisdiction ". If the statute contains no express provision as to (a), the intention   F
of Parliament is presumed to be that the High Court shall have jurisdiction to
determine whether the described situation exists or not. The statute thus confers
on the High Court a new jurisdiction which it would not otherwise have. If,
however, the statute does contain express provision conferring jurisdiction on
some inferior tribunal to determine whether or not the described situation exists
there is no room for this presumption, and the High Court has no concomitant   G
jurisdiction to make such a determination itself. Even where this is the case,
however, the intention of Parliament as to (b) is presumed to be that the High
Court shall have jurisdiction to correct the determinations of the inferior tribunal
for " errors within jurisdiction ", unless the statute contains provisions which
expressly deprive the High Court of jurisdiction of this kind. Provisions of this
type, of which s. 4 (4) of the Foreign Compensation Act, 1950, is an example, I   H
shall call " no certiorari clauses ". Since, however, a determination of an inferior
tribunal that the described situation exists or does not exist, if made in compliance
with the conditions laid down in the statute, will affect legally enforceable rights
or liabilities of an individual, whereas if it is not made in compliance with such
conditions it will be a nullity and have no such effect, neither an express provision
conferring jurisdiction on an inferior tribunal to make such a determination nor a   I
" no certiorari clause " will deprive the High Court of its jurisdiction to correct
a purported determination of the inferior tribunal for " error going to the jurisdiction " of the inferior tribunal and to decide whether the statement of the
inferior tribunal, which purports to be a determination, is a nullity or not.

It is common ground in the present appeal that s. 4 (4) of the Foreign Compensation Act, 1950, has the effect of a " no certiorari clause " and deprives the High
Court of any jurisdiction to correct any determination of the Foreign Compensation Commission for " errors within jurisdiction ", even though they are " errors

A of law on the face of the record ". We must therefore look at the legislation, that is to say the Act of 1950 itself and any statutory instruments made in pursuance of it, to see what are the conditions limiting the jurisdiction of the commission to make determinations.

The Act of 1950 provides in s. 1 for the constitution of the Foreign Compensation Commission, but does not itself confer any jurisdiction on the Commission.

B This is done by Orders in Council made under the Act of 1950. Such Orders in Council may be made (10), inter alia,

> " if Her Majesty's Government in the United Kingdom enter into . . . an agreement with the government of any foreign country providing for the payment of compensation by the latter government . . ."

C The agreement of Feb. 28, 1959 (11) (which I will call " the Egyptian Compensation Agreement ") did provide for the payment of £27,500,000 compensation by the government of the United Arab Republic to the United Kingdom government, which thereupon became entitled to make Orders in Council providing (inter alia):

(*a*) " for the registration by the commission of claims to participate in such

D compensation, and for the making of reports by the commission with respect to such claims " (12);

(*b*) " for the determination of such claims by the commission " (13);

(*c*) " for defining the persons who are to be qualified, in respect of nationality or status, to make applications to the commission for the purpose of establishing such claims as aforesaid, and for imposing any other conditions to be fulfilled

E before such claims can be entertained " (14);

(*d*) " for prescribing the matters which have to be established to the satisfaction of the commission by persons making such applications " (15);   and

(*e*) " for any supplementary and incidental matters for which provision appears to His Majesty to be necessary or expedient " (16).

Although under the Egyptian Compensation Agreement the £27,500,000 was

F expressed to be paid to the United Kingdom in full and final settlement of claims by United Kingdom nationals against the government of the United Arab Republic and its nationals, no United Kingdom national would have had at common law any legally enforceable right against the United Kingdom government to recover any part of the compensation fund received by the United Kingdom government (*Rustomjee* v. *Reginam* (17)). Any right to participate in

G the compensation would therefore be a new right created by the Act of 1950 and Orders in Council made under it, and the High Court would have no jurisdiction to determine whether a situation existed in the case of a particular individual which gave rise to a right in him to participate in the compensation, if the Act of 1950 or Orders in Council made under it were expressly to confer such jurisdiction on some inferior tribunal.

H By the provisions which I have quoted the Act of 1950 does authorise the making of Orders in Council conferring this jurisdiction on the commission. In those provisions " claims " means claims by a person to participate in the compensation fund. These are the claims which, if an Order in Council so provides, are to be " determined " by the commission.   " Applications " made to the commission under the Act of 1950 are applications made by a person for the

I purpose of establishing his claim to participate in the compensation fund.   A " determination " by the commission of any application made to them under

---

(10) See s. 3 of the Foreign Compensation Act, 1950.
(11) Treaty Series No. 35 of 1959; Cmnd. 723. Further sums for compensation were provided by H.M. Government; see the Foreign Compensation Act, 1962, s. 1 and note thereto in 42 HALSBURY'S STATUTES (2nd Edn.) 190.
(12) Act of 1950, s. 3 (*a*).   (13) Act of 1950, s. 3 (*b*).
(14) Act of 1950, s. 2 (2) (*a*) applied by s. 3 (*c*).
(15) Act of 1950, s. 2 (2) (*b*) applied by s. 3 (*c*).
(16) Act of 1950, s. 3 (*e*).   (17) (1876), 1 Q.B.D. 487.

this Act of 1950, which by s. 4 (4) of the Act of 1950 " shall not be called in **A** question in any court of law ", therefore includes a statement by the commission of their opinion that an applicant's claim to be entitled to participate in the compensation fund has or has not been established. The kind of situation, the existence or non-existence of which is to be determined by the commission, is thus described in the Act of 1950 in terms of legal consequences only. It is for the commission to decide whether in the case of any applicant they are of opinion that **B** facts exist which give rise to those legal consequences, but, whether they state such facts or not, it is their opinion that the applicant's claim to participate in the compensation fund is established or is not established to which effect will be given by the executive branch of government and the High Court has no jurisdiction to substitute its own contrary opinion for it.

A determination by the commission that an applicant's claim to participate in **C** the compensation fund is established or is not established must, of course, comply with the conditions with respect to such determinations laid down in the Act of 1950 and Orders in Council. The Act of 1950 makes provision for imposing by Orders in Council or by rules of procedure made by the Lord Chancellor under s. 4 (2) of the Act of 1950, limitations of the four types listed earlier in this judgment, on the jurisdiction of the commission to make determinations. **D**

First: the determinations must be made by the appropriate number (18) of members of the commission duly appointed under s. 1 of the Act of 1950. It is not suggested that this condition was not fulfilled in the present case. Secondly: it must have been preceded by an inquiry conducted by the commission in accordance with the rules (19). It is common ground that this condition too was fulfilled. The Act of 1950 does provide for Orders in Council to be made imposing **E** conditions to be fulfilled before a claim can be entertained by the commission. The only condition imposed in the relevant Order in Council under this power, however, is that the application shall be made in accordance with the rules (see para. 9 of the Foreign Compensation (Egypt) (Determination and Registration of Claims) Order, 1962 (20)), and this condition was fulfilled. Thirdly: the application must be one of the kind described in the Act of 1950 or Order in **F** Council; and fourthly: the determination must state whether a situation of the kind described in the Act of 1950 or Order in Council exists or not in the case of the applicant.

The Act of 1950 itself requires that the application must be an application made by an applicant " for the purpose of establishing a claim " to participate in the compensation fund but for a more detailed description of the application one **G** must look at the Order in Council itself. For the description of the kind of situation which the determination must state exists or does not exist in the case of the applicant one must also look at the Order in Council. It is important to bear in mind, however, that any provision in the Order in Council " prescribing the matters which have to be established to the satisfaction of the commission by persons making such application " is not a description of the kind of applications **H** in which the commission have jurisdiction to make determinations, but a more detailed description of the kind of situation the existence or non-existence of which in the case of the applicant they have jurisdiction to determine.

I turn then to the Order in Council; but, in order to construe it, it is necessary first to say something about the Egyptian Compensation Agreement which is referred to in the recitals to the Foreign Compensation (Egypt) (Determination **I** and Registration of Claims) Order, 1962. The Egyptian Compensation Agreement was originally made on Feb. 28, 1959. Its terms were revised on Aug. 7, 1962, by an exchange of Notes (21). It was made in the following circumstances:

---

(18) See s. 4 (1) of the Act of 1950, and the Foreign Compensation (Administrative and Financial Provisions) Order in Council, 1950, S.I. 1950 No. 1193, art. 1.

(19) See the Foreign Compensation Commission (Egyptian Claims) Rules, 1959, S.I. 1959 No. 640, as amended.

(20) S.I. 1962 No. 2187.   (21) See Cmnd. 1820.

A   During the Suez incident the Egyptian government took measures against the property in Egypt of British nationals. These measures included the sequestration of such property and its management by sequestrators, who were empowered in some cases to sell the property, and did so. The Proclamation, No. 5 of 1956, under which these measures were taken did not purport to deal with the ultimate disposal of the property or of the income derived from it during sequestration or

B of the proceeds of sale of properties sold by the sequestrators. So far as the proclamation was concerned, the property and the income and proceeds of sale thereof were to remain in the possession of the sequestrators, whose duties were described as being to represent the British nationals concerned. Legal proceedings if brought by them were in the name of and on behalf of the British national for whom they were acting. The Proclamation appears to have been made by the

C Military Governor-General under powers vested in him during the existence of a " state of emergency ". Whether under Egyptian law the British owners would in the absence of further legislation have been entitled to the return of the property or its income or any proceeds of its sale at the end of the state of emergency we do not know, nor do we know whether subsequent legislation purporting to deprive the British owners of any title to such property, income or proceeds of sale without

D adequate compensation would have been valid under the Egyptian constitution. At any rate no such legislation appears to have been passed by Feb. 28, 1959. The Proclamation suspended the right of access of British nationals to Egyptian courts, but I see no reason for assuming that the Proclamation deprived the owners permanently of all title in Egyptian law to the property, income or proceeds of sale in the possession of the sequestrators or of a right to recover

E compensation from the sequestrators for any loss sustained as a result of their mismanagement of the property during the period of sequestration. Thus it does not seem to me that any misuse of language is involved, while the Proclamation remained in force, in describing the owner of the sequestrated property as having " claims " against the Egyptian government for the return of the property and the income thereof or any proceeds of sale at the end of the emergency, or for

F compensation for its mismanagement by the sequestrators, although such claims could not be pursued in the Egyptian courts during the emergency. At any rate, they were subsequently described as " claims " in the Egyptian Compensation Agreement.

    I also see no reason for supposing that the owner's title to the property, and any claims which he might have against the sequestrators for mismanagement,

G were in Egyptian law rights of a kind which were incapable of being assigned to third parties. An assignment made in Egypt, and probably one made to an Egyptian national anywhere, without the consent of the Minister of Finance or the sequestrator, would be void under art. 3 and art. 12 of the Proclamation, but one made with such consent would appear clearly to be valid. Whether consent was needed to an assignment made outside Egypt to a person who was not an

H Egyptian national may be doubtful. It depends on the view which Egyptian courts would take of the ambit of art. 3. It follows that I see no reason for holding that a British national who was the owner of property in Egypt under sequestration was not entitled under Egyptian municipal law to rights against the Egyptian government and the sequestrators which were capable of being assigned, and to which the assignee might, without abuse of language, be called

I a " successor in title " of the original owner.

    It is, to say the least, debatable whether these measures taken by the Egyptian government were contrary to international law. So far as they relate to property they were based on what are broadly the same principles as those applied in our own Trading with the Enemy Acts and regulations in World Wars I and II, though they were less Draconian, if I am right in construing them as leaving the beneficial title in the owner instead of converting it into a mere " spes successionis ", as the majority of the House of Lords held our own legislation did

(*Bank Voor Handel en Scheepvaart, N.V.* v. *Administrator of Hungarian Property* **A** (22)). If the Suez incident can be equiparated to a state of war between Egypt and Great Britain (which publicists may debate) there would seem to be an arguable case that the Egyptian government was entitled in international law to adopt the measures provided for in the Proclamation.

Measures of this kind taken by one belligerent against the property in its own territory of enemy nationals may well cease to be justifiable when a state of war **B** between the belligerents comes to an end. The normal practice, where there has been a formal declaration of war, is for provision to be made in the treaty of peace for what is to be done by each government about the enemy property which has been subjected to such measures; and this, despite the absence of any formal declaration of war, is what was done in the present case by the Egyptian Compensation Agreement. In making agreements of this kind a government is exercising **C** its right in international law to adopt and to settle claims by persons who are its nationals at the date of the agreement against the government of another state which is party to the agreement. Such claims may be claims to rights recognised by the municipal law of the other state but which the person entitled to the right is prevented from enforcing, as for instance by a procedural disability precluding him from access to the courts (deni de justice); or they may be claims to rights **D** not recognised by the municipal law of the other state, if failure to recognise such rights is contrary to international law. Failure to recognise a right to adequate compensation for property confiscated by the government is often asserted as constituting grounds for a claim of the latter kind.

So far as is relevant to the present appeal the Egyptian Compensation Agreement adopted and settled two types of claims on the part of British nationals **E** against the Egyptian government, that is to say, claims to the return of property under sequestration and claims for damage to property sustained as a result of sequestration. In general, measures of sequestration were to be terminated at the date of the agreement and the property or its proceeds of sale were to be returned. There were excluded, however, from the obligation to return them certain properties of named British nationals which had been sold under the **F** Proclamation and which were referred to in Annex " E " to the agreement. Claims in respect of these properties were to be settled and all liability of the Egyptian government or Egyptian nationals in respect of them discharged on payment by the Egyptian government to the British government of the compensation fund of £27,500,000. Claims for damage to property sustained as a result of sequestration were also to be settled and all liability for them discharged on **G** payment of the compensation fund. These were the only two types of claims in settlement of which the £27,500,000 was paid. In the original agreement of Feb. 28, 1959, the claims in respect of property referred to in Annex " E " which were to be settled by the payment of the compensation fund were limited to claims in respect of such property as was sold under the Proclamation; but by the exchange of Notes of Aug. 7, 1962, the definition of these claims was altered **H** so as to cover any claims in respect of properties in Egypt of British nationals named in Annex " E ", without any express reference to whether or not the properties had been sold under the Proclamation.

The provisions of the Order in Council which are most germane to this appeal are known by heart by everyone in this court and I will not bother to read them out (23). The words in para. (*a*) and para. (*b*) of art. 4 (1), in paras. (*a*), (*b*) and (*c*) **I** of art. 6 (1), and the words in art. 8 " all the matters specified in art. 6 of this order other than that the loss injury or damage was the result of Egyptian measures " describe the various situations which the commissioners must be of opinion exist in the case of a particular applicant if they are to determine that his claim, under Part 3 or Part 4 of the order of 1962, to participate in the compensation

---

(22) [1954] 1 All E.R. 969; [1954] A.C. 584.
(23) The relevant provisions are set out in footnote (†), pp. 986, 987, ante.

A fund is established and the loss with respect to it assessed, or is to be registered and reported to the Secretary of State as the case may be.

They bristle with expressions which are descriptive of legal consequences and thus involve " questions of law ", quite apart from the anomalous rule referred to earlier in this judgment that the question whether particular facts fall within the description contained in legislation of the kind of facts which give rise to legal

B rights and liabilities is treated as a statement of the legal consequences of those particular facts and is itself a " question of law ". Thus, to take art. 4 (1) (*a*) and (*b*) alone, " property in Egypt " and " successor in title " are examples of expressions which in any context are descriptive of legal consequences of the existence of particular facts, and the words " which is referred to in Annex E " qualifying the expression " property in Egypt " contain an additional description

C of the kind of facts to which the particular facts whose existence has the legal consequences described by the expression " property in Egypt " must also conform in order that the claim may be established.

These are but illustrations of the many " questions of law " about which the commission must form an opinion as to the answer, in order to arrive at a decision whether the applicant has satisfied them that a situation described in paras.

D (*a*) and (*b*) of art. 4 (1), or paras. (*a*), (*b*) and (*c*) of art. 6 (1), or the words which I have quoted in art. 8, exists in the case of that applicant. To answer such " questions of law " is a necessary incident of their jurisdiction to determine whether a claim made in an application is established or not. The High Court has no jurisdiction to substitute its own opinion as to the answer to any of these " questions of law " for the opinion of the commission, so as to lead to a different

E determination as to whether the claim is established or not. Even if the High Court thought that the commissioners' answers were erroneous, the error would be an " error within jurisdiction ".

The relevant facts about the property to which Anisminic's application related are set out in detail in BROWNE, J.'s judgment. For the purposes of this appeal it is sufficient to say that the property comprised a mining business in Egypt

F owned by Anisminic on Oct. 31, 1956, which was sequestrated under the provisions of Proclamation No. 5 of 1956. While under sequestration it sustained war damage inflicted by the armed forces of Israel, which I will call " Israeli war damage ". After sustaining such damage, it was purportedly sold on Apr. 29, 1957, by the sequestrator to an Egyptian organisation, T.E.D.O. under the powers of sale conferred by the Proclamation. Subsequently the Egyptian govern-

G ment as lessor purported to terminate Anisminic's mineral leases. Anisminic refused to recognise this purported sale as effective to divest them of their property in the assets of their mining business and threatened legal action to recover the products of its mines exported from Egypt. These threats were not without effect, and on Nov. 23, 1957, Anisminic entered into an agreement with T.E.D.O. and the sequestrator whereby Anisminic purported to sell to T.E.D.O.

H the whole of their business as carried on and situate in Egypt for the sum of £500,000 to be paid to Anisminic. In the opinion of the commission the effect of this agreement was also to transfer to T.E.D.O. any claims which Anisminic might have under Egyptian municipal law against the Egyptian government or the sequestrator arising out of the sequestration or any acts or omissions of the sequestrator.

I By their provisional determination of May 8, 1963, the commission determined that Anisminic had failed to establish any claim under art. 4 or art. 6 of the Order in Council, but that their claim in respect of the war damage inflicted by the Israeli armed forces was fit for registration under art. 8 of the order. On the face of it this provisional determination, for which no reasons were given, was a " determination " which the commission had jurisdiction under the Act of 1950 to make. Nevertheless Anisminic, despite the provisions of s. 4 (4) of the Act of 1950, attempted to call it in question in the High Court by bringing the present action against the commission for declarations. In that action there was disclosed

another document, a " minute of adjudication ", in which the commission had   **A**
recorded for their own use the reasons which had led them to form the opinion
stated in their provisional determination.

Broadly speaking Anisminic's case was, and still is, that the particular facts
about the property to which their application related that were found by the
commission to exist were of the kind described in para. (*a*) and para. (*b*) of art. 4
(1), and that accordingly the commission were under a statutory duty to treat the   **B**
claim as established. To state the proposition so baldly, however, exposes it to the
immediate answer that under the provisions of the Act of 1950 and the Order in
Council it is the commission who have to be satisfied that the particular facts are
of the kind described and that it is to their opinion on this matter and not to any
substituted opinion of the High Court that effect will be given by the executive
branch of government. In attempting to escape from this answer Anisminic's   **C**
contentions have in the course of the argument been put in three different ways.
First: that in the inquiry which preceded their determination the commission
considered matters which they had no jurisdiction to consider—they asked
themselves the wrong question. Secondly: that they treated as conditions
precedent to a claim under the Order in Council matters which were not conditions precedent. Thirdly: that the provisional determination either by itself   **D**
or read with the minute of adjudication shows that the commission were satisfied
of all the matters set out in para. (*a*) and para. (*b*) of art. 4 (1).

On analysis, however, all these arguments are three different ways of saying the
same thing. It is apparent from their minute of adjudication that the commission
were of opinion that T.E.D.O., which was never a British national, became the
" successor in title " to Anisminic before Feb. 28, 1959, and that accordingly the   **E**
requirement of art. 4 (1) (*b*) (ii) was not satisfied in the case of Anisminic's claim
under Part 3 of the order. It is less apparent, but said to be discernible on a close
analysis of the minute of adjudication, that the commission were of opinion that
no applicant could establish a claim under art. 4 or art. 6 unless he had a claim
against the Egyptian government on Feb. 28, 1959. These are the two " errors "
which it is contended the commission made. The judge was of opinion that on   **F**
a true construction of the Order in Council " successor in title " meant universal
successor only, so that there could never be a " successor in title " of a person
referred to in para. 1 (*a*) or para. 2 of Annex " E " so long as the person so referred
to was in existence. He was also of opinion that on the true construction of the
order the commission were in error in thinking that no applicant could establish
a claim under art. 4 or art. 6 unless he had a claim against the Egyptian govern-   **G**
ment on Feb. 28, 1959. As a result of these two errors in the construction of the
order he considered that the commission had asked themselves two questions,
neither of which had they jurisdiction to consider, videlicet: (i) " Had Anisminic a successor in title? "; and (ii) " Had Anisminic a claim against the
Egyptian government on Feb. 28, 1959 ? ". This is the way of putting Anisminic's
argument that the judge accepted.   **H**

As respects the second of these questions which it is alleged the commission
asked themselves, however, the argument in this court has also been presented
in the alternative way, videlicet, the commission had treated the existence of a
" claim " by the applicant against the Egyptian government on Feb. 28, 1959, as
a condition precedent to the existence of a " claim " to participate in the
compensation fund.   **I**

The third way in which the argument has been put is more devious: namely,
the minute of adjudication discloses that the commission were satisfied that
Anisminic was a person referred to in para. 1 (*a*) of Annex " E " so that, as
Anisminic was the applicant, the requirements of art. 4 (1) (*b*) (i) were also
satisfied. Their provisional determination that Anisminic's claim in respect
of the Israeli war damage was fit for registration under art. 8 shows that they
were satisfied of all the matters specified in art. 6 except that the damage was
the result of Egyptian measures. They were therefore satisfied that the property

A to which Anisminic's claim related was " property in Egypt " (see art. 6 (*a*))
of which Anisminic was the owner at the time of the damage (see art. 6 (*b*)) and
that there was no non-British national who became " successor in title " of
Anisminic on or before Feb. 28, 1959, that is, that the requirements of art.
4 (1) (*b*) (ii) were also satisfied. This leaves only the requirements of art. 4 (1) (*a*)
to be satisfied : and since the only identification contained in Annex " E " of
B the property referred to therein was by the name of its owner and Anisminic
was a person referred to in Annex " E " the " property in Egypt " to which
Anisminic's claim related must have been " property in Egypt " which is referred
to in Annex " E " within the meaning of art. 4 (1) (*a*). The commission must
therefore have been of opinion that all the requirements of art. 4 (1) (*a*) and (*b*)
(i) and (ii) were satisfied ; and their statutory duty was to treat Anisminic's
C claim as established. A determination which accepts the claim in respect of the
Israeli war damage as fit for registration under art. 8 while rejecting the claim
under art. 4 cannot, it is argued, be arrived at by any construction put on the
words " claim ", " property in Egypt ", or " successor in title ", for all these
expressions are common to art. 4 and art. 6 and incorporated by reference in
art. 8 itself. The commission, even if they had jurisdiction to decide matters of
D construction, cannot have reached their determination as a result of construing
the Order in Council but must have asked themselves some quite different
question which they had no jurisdiction to consider.

  The fallacy in the first and second ways of putting Anisminic's argument lies,
I think, in a confusion between the description in the statute of the kind of case
into which an inferior tribunal has jurisdiction to inquire, and the description
E in the same statute of the kind of situation the existence or non-existence of
which that tribunal has jurisdiction to determine. If the inferior tribunal, as a
result of its misconstruing the statutory description of the kind of case into
which it has jurisdiction to inquire, makes a purported determination in a case
of a kind into which it has no jurisdiction to inquire, its purported determination
is a nullity. The question which it has to put to itself before entering on the
F inquiry and to which, for the reasons already explained, its answer is *not* conclusive, is : " Is this a case of the kind described in the statute ? ". If the tribunal's
opinion is that it is, and the High Court's opinion is that it is not, the tribunal's
" error going to jurisdiction " in giving the wrong answer to the right question
may equally well be accounted for by saying that the tribunal's answer shows
that they must have asked themselves the wrong question. To say this does not
G advance the matter or change the character of the " error ".

  It is not suggested, however, that Anisminic's application was not a case of
the kind into which the commission had jurisdiction to inquire. They accordingly
were bound to ask themselves the question : (i) " What are the particular facts
relating to Anisminic that exist ? " and (ii) " Do these particular facts conform
to the description of a situation which is contained in art. 4 (1) (*a*) and (*b*) (i)
H and (ii) of the Order in Council ? ", and to both those questions the commission's
answer is conclusive. Any " error " which the High Court thinks they made in
the answer is an " error within jurisdiction ".

  In order to answer the second question they have to form an opinion of the
meaning of the words used in the description of the situation, for their opinion
whether the particular facts conform to that description must depend on the
I meaning which in their opinion is borne by the words by which the situation
is described. If they have formed the opinion that an expression used in the
description such as " successor in title " of a particular person includes an
assignee of that person, and the High Court is of opinion that it does not, the
error is nevertheless an " error of law within the jurisdiction " of the inferior
tribunal. Such an error must always have the consequence that in considering
whether the particular facts conform to the description, the tribunal will ask
itself the question : " Is there an assignee of that particular person ? " ; so that it
may be said that in coming to their determination the tribunal has asked itself

the wrong question. This can be said, however, of any error of construction of A the statutory description of the situation the existence of which the inferior tribunal has jurisdiction to determine, and to say it does not advance the matter or change the character of the " error ".

I think that it can be inferred from what is said in the minute of adjudication that the commission were of opinion that on the true construction of the Order in Council an applicant, in order to establish a claim to participate in the com- B pensation, must have had a claim against the Egyptian government on Feb. 28, 1959, either in his own right or as assignee of a person previously entitled to a claim; although this opinion would seem to be either part of the reasoning which supported the construction which it adopted of the expression " successor in title ", or a statement of a consequence of adopting that construction of " successor in title ", rather than an independent ground of their determination. C Assuming, however, that this was the opinion of the commission and that it was erroneous in the opinion of the High Court, it was an " error of law within jurisdiction ", and its character is not altered by describing its consequence as the commission asking themselves the wrong questions: " Did the applicant have a claim against the Egyptian government on Feb. 28, 1959 ? " or by saying, as one equally well could, that by requiring a negative answer to that question D the commission wrongly treated the existence of a claim vested in the applicant against the Egyptian government on Feb. 28, 1959, as a condition precedent to the establishment of a claim to participate in the compensation fund.

The third way in which Anisminic's argument has been put is intended to evade the conclusion that, if the commission were in " error ", their error was an error of construction of expressions in the Order in Council which they had E jurisdiction to construe. The argument is founded on the alleged inconsistency in determining that there was no claim established under art. 4 or art. 6 of the Order in Council but that there was a claim fit for registration under art. 8. This inconsistency, if there be one, cannot be deduced from the provisional determination itself. There is nothing which is inconsistent per se in determining that a claim is not established under art. 4 or art. 6 but is fit for registration F under art. 8. Indeed those are the only circumstances in which a claim is regis- trable under art. 8. Anisminic is thus driven to rely on the minute of adjudication to show that there was an inconsistency; but they must take the minute of adjudication as they find it. It is clear that what the commission were applying their mind to was the true construction of arts. 4, 6 and 8 of the Order in Council, and that this in their opinion fell to be construed in the light of the Egyptian G Compensation Agreement referred to in the recitals to the order and by the specific reference to Annex " E " in art. 4 (1) (a) itself. The minute of adjudication does not, however, dissect those articles into their component words and phrases, nor does it explicitly disclose what meaning the commission thought should be attached to any individual words or phrases other than the expression " successor in title ".   The alleged inconsistency is based on two premises, one of fact, H videlicet that the commission construed " claim ", " property in Egypt " and " successor in title " in the same sense in art. 4 and art. 6, and one of logic, videlicet that if they did so, this necessarily led to the conclusion that if the claim in respect of Israeli war damage was registrable under art. 8, the remainder of the claim was established under art. 4; but neither premise can be shown to be true.   The commission may have construed these words and phrases I differently in art. 4 and art. 6 respectively. If they did and in the opinion of the High Court were wrong in doing so, this would be an " error within jurisdiction ". Moreover, even if the commission construed these words and phrases in the same sense in art. 4 and art. 6 the alleged conclusion does not necessarily follow as a matter of logic. If the commission were of opinion that " successor in title " included a person to whom there had been assigned before Feb. 28, 1959, the original claim of the former owner of the property, whether the claim so assigned

A was one against the Egyptian government in respect of which a claim to participate in the compensation fund was sought to be established under art. 4 or art. 6,
or was one against some other government or person in respect of which registration under art. 8 was claimed, there would be no inconsistency in their determination. One claim might be assigned and the other not; and this, so far as it
is possible to discover the detailed reasoning of the commission from their minute
B of adjudication (which was never intended for publication), is the opinion which
the commission held. It is an opinion as to the true construction of the Order
in Council and if erroneous is an " error within the jurisdiction ".

The judge, as I have said, took the view that the minute of adjudication
disclosed that the commission had misconstrued the Order in Council both as to
the meaning of " successor in title " and as to the necessity for an applicant
C to be a person who had a claim against the Egyptian government on Feb. 28,
1959, or a " successor in title " of such person; and that these were " errors
going to the jurisdiction ". His ratio decidendi is summarised in two sentences
of his judgment:

> " In my judgment the commission has no jurisdiction to consider under
> art. 4 (1) any other question than those which sub-para. (a) and sub-para. (b)
D of that paragraph on their true construction require them to consider, and if
> satisfied of those matters they are under a satutory duty to treat the claim as
> established and have no jurisdiction to do anything else . . . It follows that,
> if the commission wrongly construes art. 4 (1) (a) or (b) as requiring them
> to consider something which on their true construction those two paragraphs
> do not require to be considered before the claim is established, they act
E without jurisdiction or in excess of jurisdiction."

In reaching his conclusion that despite s. 4 (4) of the Act of 1950 the High Court
was entitled to substitute its opinion as to the meaning of para. (a) and para. (b)
of art. 4 of the Order in Council for that of the commission, the judge relied
particularly on four cases on which I must briefly comment: R. v. Shoreditch
F Assessment Committee, Ex p. Morgan (24); Ex p. Bradlaugh (25); R. v. Fulham,
Hammersmith and Kensington Rent Tribunal, Ex p. Hierowski (26); and Board
of Trustees of Maradana Mosque v. Badi-Ud-Din Mahmud (27). The Shoreditch
case (24) seems to me to be a simple example of a case in which a condition
precedent to the inferior tribunal's entering on an inquiry (namely the making
of a provisional valuation list by a valuer) was not fulfilled. Bradlaugh's case (25)
G contains a wholly unexceptionable statement by SIR ALEXANDER COCKBURN,
C.J., that a " no certiorari clause " does not apply where the inferior tribunal
has exceeded the limits of its jurisdiction; but, with great respect to that strong-
minded lord chief justice, I am unable to follow his process of reasoning from
that principle to the actual decision of the court in Bradlaugh's case (25). The
real objection was to the form of the order made by the magistrate, in that
H he omitted to recite that he was satisfied of one of the matters of which he was
required by the statute to be satisfied before making the order which he made.
The Rent Tribunal case (26) was a case in which the inferior tribunal had already
fixed a rent for premises. The only kind of application which the statute gave
them jurisdiction to entertain in relation to premises for which a rent had been
already fixed, was an application to alter the rent so fixed owing to subsequent
I change of circumstances. The tenant made an application to the tribunal not
to alter the rent already fixed, but to fix it ab initio, and this the tribunal purported to do. The matter was complicated by the fact that the landlord by his
answer asked the tribunal to alter the rent already fixed owing to subsequent
change of circumstances and this the tribunal did have jurisdiction to do; but

---

(24) [1908-10] All E.R. Rep. 792; [1910] 2 K.B. 859.
(25) (1878), 3 Q.B.D. 509.
(26) [1953] 2 All E.R. 4; [1953] 2 Q.B. 147.
(27) [1966] 1 All E.R. 545; [1967] A.C. 13.

it was apparent from the facts that the tribunal had purported to determine **A**
the tenant's application and to fix the rent ab initio. The *Maradana Mosque*
case (28), a decision of the Privy Council in which none of the English cases
was cited, was mainly decided on the ground that the inferior tribunal, the
Minister of Education, had not observed the rules of natural justice in the
inquiry which preceded his order; but the Judicial Committee did deal
briefly with an alternative contention that the Minister had acted in excess of **B**
jurisdiction (29):

> " in that he failed to consider the right questions and failed to make
> decisions which were the requisite foundation for an order . . ."

I must confess that I find difficulty in reconciling this part of the judgment
of the Privy Council with previous authorities. They appear to have considered **C**
that if in their opinion there was no evidence on which the Minister could properly
come to the decision which he reached this was an " error going to jurisdiction ".
So to hold, however, is contrary to the statement of LORD SUMNER in another
decision of the Privy Council in *R.* v. *Nat Bell Liquors, Ltd.* (30) which has
hitherto been regarded as an authoritative pronouncement on the history and
scope of the jurisdiction of the High Court in proceedings to certiorari. They
appear also to have regarded the Ceylon statute as one which did not give the **D**
Minister any jurisdiction to construe the words in the statute which described
the matters of which he was to be satisfied. That may have been the effect of
that particular statute, but as a general proposition it is contrary to decisions
of English courts which are binding on us. The two most recent of these
decisions, both in the Court of Appeal, to which BROWNE, J., was not referred,
are *R.* v. *Minister of Health, Ex p. Committee of Visitors of Glamorgan County* **E**
Mental Hospital (31) and more particularly *Davies* v. *Price* (32). The ratio
decidendi of the latter case, as stated in the judgment of PARKER, L.J., with
which the two other members expressed their agreement, was that an error by
the inferior tribunal in construing the statutory description of the matters on
which it was to be satisfied was an " error within jurisdiction " and could not **F**
be corrected by the High Court if it disagreed with that construction.

In my judgment, therefore, BROWNE, J., had no jurisdiction to consider
whether or not the commission has misconstrued that part of the Order in
Council which prescribed the matters which have to be established to the satisfaction of the commission by persons making applications for the purpose of
establishing claims to participate in the compensation fund. **G**

For my part I find nothing in the subject-matter of the kind of claims which
the commission were authorised to determine which makes it unlikely that
Parliament should have intended to entrust to the commission exclusive authority
to decide what that part of the Order in Council meant. The expressions used in
that part of the order do not relate to any rights previously enjoyed by applicants
under English law but to events in Egypt which give rise to a newly created **H**
statutory right of a different character, namely to participate in the compensation fund. To determine their meaning may involve, as the argument in this
appeal has demonstrated, considering questions of Egyptian municipal law, of
the private international law of England and of Egypt, of public international
law and the interpretation of an international agreement—matters on which
it may well be thought that judges of the High Court are not the sole depositaries **I**
of wisdom and learning, and on which in the interests of the timeous distribution
of the fund among the numerous persons entitled to participate, the decision of
the commission might well be final. In this particular instance I have, as I
think, no jurisdiction to question the decision of the commission or to examine

(28) [1966] 1 All E.R. 545; [1967] A.C. 13.
(29) [1966] 1 All E.R. at p. 549, letter F; [1967] A.C. at p. 22.
(30) [1922] All E.R. Rep. 335; [1922] 2 A.C. 128.
(31) [1938] 4 All E.R. 32 at pp. 35, 36; [1939] 1 K.B. 232 at p. 245.
(32) [1958] 1 All E.R. 671 at p. 676.

A the construction which they placed on art. 4 (1) (*a*) and (*b*), art. 6 (1) (*a*), (*b*) and (*c*) and art. 8 of the Order in Council; but as we have heard full argument on the matter and as BROWNE, J., has expressed his view that the commission erred in the construction they placed on these articles, I think it only fair to say by way of obiter dictum that for the reasons indicated at various points in the earlier part of this judgment I am far from satisfied that the commission did
B misapply these articles in determining Anisminic's application, although their minute of adjudication may not express their reasons in precisely the same terms as those which I should myself have chosen.

I have dealt with this appeal as if it were brought in proceedings for an order for certiorari. It is in fact brought in an action for a declaratory judgment, and if I were not prepared to allow it on the ground already discussed I should
C have wished to hear argument on the question whether the High Court has any jurisdiction to make declarations in an action brought against an inferior tribunal in a case of this kind.

The jurisdiction of the High Court to give declaratory judgments is limited to declaring the existence of legally enforceable rights or liabilities. This will in many cases afford an alternative procedure for questioning a determination
D of an inferior tribunal on the grounds that it was made without jurisdiction and is therefore a nullity. Thus if it purports to impose on a person a liability enforceable by the executive branch of government, its enforcement will inevitably interfere with that person's common law rights. In such a case, instead of waiting for his common law rights to be infringed he may take the initiative by bringing an action in the High Court against the person who would be entitled
E to enforce, or to order or authorise the enforcement of, that liability if the determination were valid, for a declaration that the purported determination is a nullity. The defendant to such an action is not the inferior tribunal as such but the person by whom the purported liability is enforceable, that is, the person against whom an action for tort would lie if the purported liability were enforced. It may well be that the inferior tribunal has in addition to its quasi-judicial
F function of making determinations, the administrative function of enforcing them or ordering or authorising their enforcement, and where this is so the inferior tribunal may be an appropriate defendant in its administrative capacity to an action for a declaration. Where its only function, however, is to make a determination and the right to enforce or to order the enforcement of the liability to which the determination is a condition precedent is conferred on
G other persons, I doubt whether any action for a declaration lies against the inferior tribunal itself. If the liability to which the determination is a condition precedent were enforced there would be no right of action against the inferior tribunal on the part of the person against whom the liability was enforced; and I find difficulty in seeing how the High Court has jurisdiction to make a declaration against a defendant in respect of conduct by him which could never
H give rise to a cause of action against him by the plaintiff or by him against the defendant. The only remedy against the inferior tribunal itself in such a case would, I think, be by certiorari.

Similar difficulties would seem to me to lie in the way of any action for a declaration brought by a claimant to a right created by statute in respect of a purported determination by an inferior tribunal that he is not entitled to such
I right, when the tribunal's determination that he is entitled to the right is a condition precedent to the enforcement of it by him. So long as there has been no determination that the claimant is entitled to the right there is nothing capable of giving rise to any cause of action against the person against whom the right would be enforceable; and if the inferior tribunal's purported determination of non-entitlement is a nullity, this still leaves nothing capable of giving rise to any cause of action against the person against whom the right would be enforceable, and thus capable of being the subject-matter of a declaration against him. The conduct of the inferior tribunal itself in making the

purported determination, whether it is a nullity or not, is not capable of giving   A
rise to any cause of action against it on the part of the claimant. His only remedy
against it would be by certiorari and mandamus.

However, this objection has not been taken on behalf of the commission and
as I would allow the appeal it is unnecessary to decide it. Equally, however,
it must not be thought that this judgment is any authority for the proposition
that the High Court has jurisdiction to make a declaration in an action against   B
an inferior tribunal that its determination is a nullity in all cases where
proceedings for an order of certiorari or mandamus would lie.

RUSSELL, L.J.: When is a determination not a determination? That is
the question. Or rather, when is a determination which a court of law would
consider to be erroneous not a determination at all? If it be a determination   C
by the commission of a claim, its correctness cannot be questioned in any
court of law: the statute says so: the commission is ex hypothesi " right " for
the purposes for which it is established, and the fact that a judge or judges would
come to a different conclusion simply means that for those purposes they would
be " wrong ". Judicial views would have no more relevance than those of the
clientèle of Carnaby Street. To speak in general terms of an " error of law "   D
by the commission is but a convenient misnomer. The only ground on which
the courts may be approached is an assertion that for some reason the purported
determination of a claim by the commission was not such a determination at all.

I have studied the close analysis in the judgment of DIPLOCK, L.J., of this
branch of the law in general, and its application to this case in particular, and
I do not feel that I can usefully say much more than that I am entirely in agree-   E
ment with that judgment. I also think that a crucial passage in the judgment
of BROWNE, J., is where he said,

" In my judgment, the commission has no jurisdiction to consider under
art. 4 (1) any other questions than those which sub-para. (a) and sub-para.
(b) of that paragraph on their true construction require them to consider,
and if satisfied of those matters they are under a statutory duty to treat   F
the claim as established and have no jurisdiction to do anything else."

In the course of determination of a claim, however, it is for the commission to
decide on " their true construction " and not a court.

From my general agreement with the judgment of DIPLOCK, L.J., I exclude
his references to jurisdiction to give declaratory judgments: not because I   G
disagree, but because I have not addressed my mind to the matter.

I add this. To some it may seem strange or even obnoxious that prospects
of compensation for damage suffered should be subjected to infallible error by
the commission: or indeed that any tribunal (excepting always the House of
Lords) should be infallible in error. (I am not asserting that the commission did
err in this case.) In all mundane matters requiring decision or adjudication,   H
however, there must as a practical matter be an appropriate level at which a
question must be finally resolved. In the particular field now under review it
does not seem to me in any way inappropriate that the commission should be at
that level: and that was the view of the legislature when the Tribunals and
Inquiries Act, 1958, was enacted. In substance the executive is dealing broadly
with matters not strictly matters of right, and the time-consuming precision   I
of the ordinary judicial processes may well be out of place. In terms (now no
doubt outdated) of field artillery, a quadrant elevation to the nearest twenty-five
yards is a work of supererogation if you are working off a one-inch map. Moreover, if it were to appear to the executive that in a particular case injustice had
been done, correction by Order in Council is available, subject only to approval
by Parliament.

Lastly it is to be observed that Anisminic, when they entered into agreement
with the sequestrator and T.E.D.O., assumed (as was frankly admitted) that

A they would get nothing more as a result of any treaty, having decided to " go it alone ".   This fact makes no contribution whatever to my opinion on this case: but I think it should be known by the man in the street—Carnaby or other.

Appeal allowed.   Leave to appeal to House of Lords granted.

B Solicitors: Treasury Solicitor; Linklaters & Paines (for Anisminic, Ltd.).

[Reported by HENRY SUMMERFIELD, ESQ, Barrister-at-Law.]

C SCOTT (Inspector of Taxes) v. RICKETTS.

[COURT OF APPEAL, CIVIL DIVISION (Lord Denning, M.R., Davies and Russell, L.JJ.), April 4, 5, 1967.]

Income Tax—Profits—Estate agent—Casual profit—Gratuitous payment for
D consenting to a deal between a company and a society, the client of the estate agent—Compensation for withdrawal of any claim that the estate agent might have—No legal basis for any claim—Company taking over land under negotiation—Estate agent's intended acquisition of an interest in the land as an investment—Whether compensation taxable as a casual profit—Income Tax Act, 1952 (15 & 16 Geo. 6 & 1 Eliz. 2 c. 10), Sch. D, Case VI.

E The taxpayer, an estate agent, was concerned in complicated negotiations regarding three sites, a co-operative society's bombed site, which the local authority proposed to acquire compulsorily, an alternative site that the local authority was prepared to lease to the society, and a third site which the taxpayer found for the society.   At one stage the taxpayer proposed to form a company with his father to take over the alternative site.   The taxpayer approached R., Ltd. with a proposal that R., Ltd. should develop the
F alternative site jointly with him.   In the end the society acquired the third site, the local authority acquired the bombed site and the company, R., Ltd., acquired the alternative site.   The taxpayer was paid for his professional services.   In addition, however, R., Ltd. paid him £39,000 in consideration of his withdrawing any claim that he might have to participate in the alternative site.

G **Held:** the payment of the £39,000 was not an annual profit or gain within Case VI of Sch. D, s. 123 of the Income Tax Act, 1952, for the words " profits or gains " in Case VI did not include either a sum received on the sale of an asset or in settlement of a legally enforceable claim; and similarly a sum paid by way of compromise of a claim such as that which the taxpayer with-
H drew, even though the claim was not a legally enforceable claim, had not the quality of being a profit or gain within Case VI (see p. 1011, letter I, p. 1012, letter A, p. 1013, letter G, and p. 1014, letter C, post).

Decision of CROSS, J. ([1966] 3 All E.R. 791) reversed.

[As to capital payments and casual profits of a trade for income tax purposes, see 20 HALSBURY'S LAWS 287-289, paras. 526, 527; and for cases on the subject,
I see 28 DIGEST (Repl.) 216-221, 913-954.

For the Income Tax Act, 1952, Sch. D, Case VI, see 31 HALSBURY'S STATUTES (2nd Edn.) 116.]

Cases referred to:

Jones v. Leeming, [1930] All E.R. Rep. 584; [1930] A.C. 415; 99 L.J.K.B. 318; 143 L.T. 50; 15 Tax Cas. 333; 28 Digest (Repl.) 22, 87.

Ryall v. Hoare, Ryall v. Honeywill, [1923] All E.R. Rep. 528; [1923] 2 K.B. 447; 92 L.J.K.B. 1010; 129 L.T. 505; 8 Tax Cas. 521; 28 Digest (Repl.) 216, 917.

Appeal.   A

This was an appeal by the taxpayer, Norman Edward Ricketts, from a judgment of Cross, J., given on July 25, 1966, and reported [1966] 3 All E.R. 791,
whereby he allowed an appeal by the Crown by way of Case Stated from a determination of the Commissioners for the Special Purposes of the Income Tax Acts,
made on July 15, 1964, reducing the taxpayer's assessment on the basis that a
sum of £39,000 paid to the taxpayer in the circumstances stated at p. 1010, letter B
E, to p. 1011, letter C, post, was a gratuitous payment of a non-revenue nature,
and was not an annual profit, or gain assessable under Case VI of Sch. D, s. 123
of the Income Tax Act, 1952.

Hubert H. Monroe, Q.C., and *M. P. Nolan* for the taxpayer.
Arthur Bagnall, Q.C., and *J. R. Phillips* for the Crown.
                                                                               C
   LORD DENNING, M.R.: Mr. Ricketts, the taxpayer, is an auctioneer and
estate agent in Bristol. In 1959 a company called Ravenseft Properties, Ltd.
paid him the sum of £39,000. The question is whether he is taxable on it or not.
The Crown sought to charge him under Case I or Case II of Sch. D. It said that
it was part of the profits of his trade or profession. That claim was rejected by
the Special Commissioners. The Crown accept their decision on that point. D
Alternatively, the Crown sought to charge him under Case VI of Sch. D. It said
that the £39,000 was an " annual profit or gain " not falling under any other head.
The Special Commissioners rejected this claim. They held that the £39,000 was a
gratuitous payment of a non-revenue nature. The judge (1) reversed their decision.
He held that the £39,000 was taxable under Case VI as an annual profit. The
taxpayer appeals to this court.   E
   The facts relating to it are set out in the Special Case and in the report (2). I
need only summarise them here.
   The Bristol Co-operative Society employed the taxpayer in very complicated
negotiations with the Bristol Corporation. The Bristol Co-operative Society's
shop in Castle Street had been destroyed by bombs. The corporation proposed to
acquire that site compulsorily for £575,000. Having been bombed out of Castle F
Street, the co-operative society had a strong claim that the corporation should
provide them with another site. The corporation realised this and offered to let
the co-operative society a site in Merchant Street for ninety-nine years at a rent
of £25,000; but before that deal went through, the taxpayer discovered a site
called the Jacey site which would suit the co-operative society much better. It
was half the rent of the proposed Merchant Street site. So the co-operative society G
got the taxpayer to negotiate for the Jacey site in his own name. If they were
successful in getting the Jacey site, they would not need the Merchant Street site.
So the taxpayer proposed that he, with his father, should form a company to take
over the Merchant Street site. About the same time, however, there was another
company interested in the Merchant Street site called Ravenseft Properties, Ltd.
(" Ravenseft "): and it was proposed that they might come in jointly with the H
taxpayer and his father in acquiring it. Eventually a settlement was reached
whereby: (i) the corporation paid over £500,000 to the co-operative society for
the old Castle Street site; (ii) the corporation let the Jacey site to the co-operative
society; (iii) the corporation let the Merchant Street site to Ravenseft Properties,
Ltd. The co-operative society paid the taxpayer's fees for his professional services
in these respects. These fees were included in his profits and gains, and he has I
paid tax on them; but, in addition to that remuneration, Ravenseft also paid
him a sum of £39,000. The reason for this payment appears to be as follows. The
parties thought that the taxpayer had some sort of claim to an interest in the
Merchant Street site. The reason was because at one stage in the negotiations it
was proposed that he should take over the Merchant Street site, either on his own
or jointly with Ravenseft. In the result Ravenseft took over the site themselves,

───────────────────────────────

(1) [1966] 3 All E.R. 791.
(2) [1966] 3 All E.R. at pp. 792, 793.

A and the taxpayer was left with no interest in it. His ensuing claim may have been a business claim, a moral claim, or a legal claim; but whatever it was, he was bought out for £39,000. The reason for this payment was stated in this way in a letter of Nov. 18, 1958, from Ravenseft to the taxpayers:

B " In consideration of your withdrawing any claim you might have had to participate, and accepting the settlement between the Bristol Corporation and the Bristol Co-operative Society, Ltd. on the terms outlined above and agreeing at our request to execute such documents as we may be advised are necessary to record such withdrawal and acceptance, we are prepared to compensate you for the loss of your investment on the following basis;"

C and then there follow terms under which the sum of £39,000 was to be payable to the taxpayer. The taxpayer signed the letter accepting that proposal. So he withdrew any claim he might have had to participate in this proposed investment in return for the sum of £39,000. The one point now is whether this £39,000 is chargeable under Case VI. That Case is a " sweeping up " provision. It catches " annual profits or gains " which have not been caught by the other provisions. It is difficult to construe and we have to go by the decided cases.

D In *Ryall* v. *Hoare, Ryall* v. *Honeywill* (3), Rowlatt, J., staked out the guidelines: and there have been other cases following it. Some things are clear. " Annual " profits does not mean profits which are made year by year. It is satisfied by profits made in one year only. " Profits and gains " include remuneration for work done, services rendered, or facilities provided. They do not include gratuitous payments which are given for nothing in return. Nor do they include profits in the nature of capital gains. So they do not include gains made on purchase and sale of an asset. Such gains (except for recent legislation) are only taxable if the transaction was an adventure in the nature of trade.

E The crux of the present case is that the taxpayer had no legal ground to be paid anything. All he had—to use the judge's words (4)—was " a moral claim or a nuisance value ". Ravenseft paid him £39,000 in order that he should not feel aggrieved: and to get rid of any possible claim. If they had paid this sum over to him as a gratuitous payment, it would not have come within Case VI; but because it was " dressed up " as a contract—to use the judge's own words (5) —he has held that it is caught by Case VI. I do not think that that is right. Take the case where a man has a good legal claim which he agrees to forego in return for a sum of money, such as a claim for personal injuries which is compromised by payment of a lump sum. That is not an annual profit or gain within Case VI.

G It is the sale of an asset—namely, his legal claim—for a price. Next, suppose that the man has a claim which he believes to be good but which is in fact unfounded— and he agrees to forego it in return for a sum of money. It might be a claim for personal injuries when he has no evidence of negligence. It is not strictly an " asset ", because it would not stand up in the courts; but the compromise is binding. The payment has the same quality as if the claim were well-founded. It

H is not an annual profit or gain within Case VI. Finally, take a man who has a moral claim but knows that he has no legal claim. He tries it on so as to see if the defendants will pay him something. They agree to buy him out so as to save the cost of fighting it. It seems to me that the payment for tax purposes has the same quality as that in a compromise. It is not an annual profit or gain within Case VI.

I The judge seems to have thought (6) that, as the payment was made under a contract, that was enough to bring it within Case VI. I cannot agree with him. It must be a contract for services or facilities provided, or something of that kind. The present case is rather like *Jones* v. *Leeming* (7), in the House of Lords.

---

(3) [1923] All E.R. Rep. 528 at p. 529; 8 Tax Cas. 521 at p. 525.
(4) [1966] 3 All E.R. at p. 796, letter H.
(5) [1966] 3 All E.R. at p. 796, letter E.
(6) [1966] 3 All E.R. at p. 796.
(7) [1930] All E.R. Rep. 584; 15 Tax Cas. 333.

If the sum was taxable at all, it was taxable as part of the profits of the taxpayer's   **A**
trade or profession. Once that is negatived, it becomes simply a sum received in
compromise of a disputed claim, whether legal or moral makes no difference.

I think that this case does not fall within Case VI. I would allow the appeal and
restore the decision of the commissioners.

DAVIES, L.J.: In the course of expressing my agreement with the judgment   **B**
which has been delivered by LORD DENNING, M.R., I would add a few facts as to
the history of this matter.

In January, 1957, a letter was written to the taxpayer by his solicitors which
referred to a draft agreement between the Bristol Co-operative Society and the
taxpayer, whereby the co-operative society's interest in the Merchant Street site
was to be transferred to the taxpayer with a view to it being retransferred to   **C**
people described as " your intended ultimate purchasers ". That was a company
which the taxpayer had been proposing to form, as LORD DENNING has said, to
develop the Merchant Street site. By that time the taxpayer had already
approached Ravenseft Properties, Ltd. (" Ravenseft ") through Mr. Kerr, who was
acting for them, with the proposal that the Merchant Street site should be
developed jointly by Ravenseft and the taxpayer or his associates. On Aug. 28,   **D**
1958, a letter was written on behalf of Ravenseft by Mr. Kerr to the taxpayer
in which these two passages occur. The first is:

> " My clients [that is Ravenseft] will, as previously agreed, undertake to
> conclude satisfactory arrangements with yourself in respect of the joint
> development of the Merchant Street site, such arrangements to be the subject
> of separate negotiations."   **E**

Further on in the same letter a note of warning is sounded:

> " With regard to item 3 above [that is the passage which I have just read]
> which concerns your own private investment and the meeting with my
> clients in 1956 when it was agreed between you to form a joint investment
> company, I think that I should point out that my clients have already intim-
> ated to me that because of the new site area now involved, it may be more   **F**
> convenient to them to develop on their own. They may ask you to consider
> disposing of your interest. In these circumstances it would be their intention
> to offer you a capital sum for the loss of your investment."

Then it appears that subsequent to that letter, the co-operative society had—and
I quote from the Case Stated—   **G**

> " indicated to Ravenseft that, in the society's view, the agreement of
> [the taxpayer], in his private capacity, to the proposed settlement should be
> obtained, because of the understanding relating to the Merchant Street site
> which had been reached at the end of 1956."

Then finally I quote the passage, to which LORD DENNING has already referred,   **H**
in the letter of Nov. 18, 1958, in which these words occur:

> " Clearly, of course, if a lease is granted to this company [that is Ravenseft]
> of the Merchant Street site, any expectation which you might have had of
> participating in the development of the site and retaining a personal invest-
> ment will be defeated. In consideration of your withdrawing any claim you
> might have had to participate, and accepting the settlement between the   **I**
> Bristol Corporation and the Bristol Co-operative Society, Ltd. on the terms
> outlined above and agreeing, at our request, to execute such documents as
> we may be advised are necessary to record such withdrawal and acceptance,
> we are prepared to compensate you for the loss of your investment on the
> following basis."

Then the payment of the £39,000 is specified.

It seems to me that the payment made by Ravenseft to the taxpayer in those
circumstances was either a gratuitous payment or a payment for the buying of

A the taxpayer's possible claim. The Special Commissioners came to the conclusion that it was a gratuitous payment. The judge thought otherwise, and I am in agreement with him on that point. The judge expressed his conclusion in these words (8):

B " I cannot see, therefore, how the payment can properly be described as a gratuitous payment. But equally I fail to see how it can be described as the purchase price of any asset owned by the taxpayer. What he had was a moral claim or a nuisance value, whichever way you like to put it, and that cannot properly be described as an asset susceptible of being sold, even though it may in fact yield money. In this case the money which the taxpayer received from it was not a gratuitous payment but a payment under a contract in consideration of his consent to the deal between the Ravenseft company C and the society and I can see no reason why it should not be taxed as a casual profit under Case VI."

With the first part of that, as I have said, I agree. The second I cannot accept. It does not matter, as I think, whether the taxpayer had any real or legally enforceable claim or not. It is perfectly plain from the short passages which I have D read, that the parties were negotiating on the basis that he had a claim. Whether a moral claim, whether a commercial claim, or whether a claim under some sort of gentlemen's agreement, matters not. They were proceeding on the basis that he had a claim, and that in those circumstances it was right and proper, and no doubt, in view of the taxpayer's position and experience, expedient, that he should be persuaded to waive or give up any such rights as he thought that he had or E the other parties thought that he had. It is perfectly true that the payment made to him was a payment made under a contract; but the only contract was the contract by Ravenseft to pay and by the taxpayer to accept payment in return for the giving up of such rights as the taxpayer might or might not have.

There was some suggestion at one time (though I do not think it was very seriously advanced) that it might be said that the taxpayer's undertaking to sign F any necessary documents to implement his agreement might be the consideration for the payment, and that therefore in some sort of way the payment was a payment for services to be rendered or things to be done in the future. Of course, however, the signing of any such document as might be thought necessary would be in exactly the same position as the execution of a conveyance on the sale of a piece of land.

G In my judgment, without referring to any authorities, it is clear that this was not in any sort of form an annual receipt of a profit or gain. It was the buying out, as I have said, of the taxpayer's claim.

I would only add in conclusion, that which I might perhaps have said at the commencement, that there is no suggestion whatsoever on the part of the Crown that what was done in the circumstances of this case was done dishonestly or H done for the purpose of evading tax. The contention of the Crown is that what was done did in fact bring the transaction within the scope of Case VI.

For these reasons, in addition to what LORD DENNING has said, I agree that this appeal should be allowed.

RUSSELL, L.J.: I also agree that this appeal succeeds. I think that the proper view is that this payment was, as it purported to be made in the contract I letters, for the withdrawal by the taxpayer of his claim to be entitled to an interest in an investment in the development of the Merchant Street site. This was not a legally enforceable claim, but one which clearly in this business world was considered a strong non-legal claim which was well worth the substantial payment made for its withdrawal. If it had been a legal claim, it is plain that £39,000 would be outside Case VI. It would be payment received by way of realisation of an asset and, as such, would lack the quality of income for tax purposes

(8) [1966] 3 All E.R. at p. 796.

which is necessary to come within annual profits and gains under that head. A
The Crown says that this cannot apply to a case where there is no legal right;
and CROSS, J., said (9):

". . . I fail to see how it can be described as the purchase price of any asset
owned by the taxpayer. What he had was a moral claim or a nuisance value,
whichever way you like to put it, and that cannot properly be described as
an asset susceptible of being sold, even though it may in fact yield money." B

I think, however, with respect, that that does not solve the question before us,
which is whether the receipt has the quality of income. It seems to me that for this
purpose there is a true analogy between a sum received on the sale of an asset,
or a sum received in settlement of a legally enforceable claim (or, I may add, one
arguably legally enforceable), and a sum received, as here, in payment for the
withdrawal of a moral or business-world claim, a spes acquisitionis such as this. C
By such analogy I think that the sum paid is not shown to have the quality of
income necessary to attract tax and is, therefore, not within Case VI.
    The appeal, therefore, succeeds.

                    Appeal allowed. Leave to appeal to the House of Lords refused.

    Solicitors: *Robbins, Olivey & Lake*, agents for *Burges, Salmon & Co.*, Bristol D
(for the taxpayer); *Solicitor of Inland Revenue.*

                        [*Reported by* F. A. AMIES, ESQ., *Barrister-at-Law.*]

DONAGHEY v. BOULTON & PAUL, LTD.
E
[HOUSE OF LORDS (Viscount Dilhorne, Lord Reid, Lord Hodson, Lord Guest and
Lord Pearson), May 1, 2, 3, 4, June 20, 1967.]

*Building—Building regulations—Roof—Roof work—Fragile materials covering
roof—Fall through hole in roof under repair—Liability of contractors to
servant of sub-contractor—Employee of sub-contractors falling through gap
whilst re-positioning asbestos sheet—Crawling boards provided but not used* F
*—Foreman of contractors and of sub-contractor present but neither ensured
that crawling boards used—Building (Safety, Health and Welfare) Regulations, 1948 (S.I. 1948 No. 1145), reg. 4 (ii), reg. 31 (1), (3).*

    The respondents were sub-contractors of a company which had undertaken
work that included repairing the roof of an aircraft hangar. The repair
of the roof had been sub-contracted to the respondents. Part of this work G
of repair was carried out by servants of the respondents, and part was
sub-contracted by the respondents to P. O'Brien & Co. The respondents
provided the necessary materials and safety apparatus, but P. O'Brien & Co.
supplied the labour. The appellant, who was employed by P. O'Brien & Co.,
was engaged in carrying out repairs to the roof of the hangar by replacing
damaged asbestos sheets. The roof was constructed with a number of H
ridges running cross-wise. The apex of each ridge was sixty-two feet from
the ground, the slope of each ridge finishing at a gutter fifty feet from the
ground and then sloping upwards to the next ridge. The slope of the roof
where the appellant was working was twenty-two degrees. There was no
evidence that the roof was slippery or as to the state of the weather. By
para. (1) of reg. 31* of the Building (Safety, Health and Welfare) Regulations, I
1948, where work was done on a sloping roof and, taking into account the
pitch, the nature of the surface, and the state of the weather, a person was
likely to slip down or off the roof, suitable precautions had to be taken
to prevent his so falling. By para. (3) of reg. 31 where work was being done
on roofs covered with fragile materials (as this roof was) " through which "

---

(9) [1966] 3 All E.R. E.R. at p. 796.
    * Regulation 31, so far as material, is printed at p. 1017, letter H, and p. 1024, letter
D, post.

A a person was liable to fall, crawling boards were to be provided and used. Crawling boards were available on the ground in the present case, but they were not on the roof and were not used. Whilst the appellant and another workman were re-positioning one of the re-laid asbestos sheets, the appellant lost his balance and fell through an open space in the roof (not through the asbestos sheeting) to the ground, thereby sustaining serious injuries.

B At the time of the accident the respondents' foreman was in charge, and it was part of his job to see to the sheeting, but he left it to P. O'Brien & Co.'s foreman to use his own judgment as he was a qualified man. P. O'Brien & Co. were without means and uninsured. On appeal in an action for damages for personal injuries against P. O'Brien & Co. and the respondents, the claim against the respondents being based on alleged breach of statutory

C duty under reg. 31,

   Held: (i) the respondents were liable to the appellant in damages for breach of statutory duty, because—

   (a) the respondents had not divested themselves of control over the execution of the work and consequently the work was being " performed " by them within the meaning of reg. 4 (ii)* of the Building (Safety, Health

D and Welfare) Regulations, 1948; accordingly they were under statutory duty to comply with the requirements of reg. 31 (see p. 1020, letter I, p. 1022, letter A, p. 1023, letters G and I, p. 1026, letter I, and p. 1031, letters F and G, post).

   Decision of PEARSON, J., in *Mulready* v. *J. H. & W. Bell, Ltd.* ([1952] 2 All E.R. 663) approved; principal ratio decidendi of the Court of Appeal

E in the same case ([1953] 2 All E.R. 215) disapproved.

   (b) the respondents were in breach of reg. 31 (3) as crawling boards were not used; and the appellant was entitled to the benefit of that enactment since the mischief against which it was directed was the risk of an injury to an employee workman from a fall from the roof, and the fact that the accident had not happened in precisely the way contemplated by reg. 31 (3),

F as the fall had been through an open space not through fragile material, did not exclude the respondents' civil liability (see p. 1019, letters G to I, p. 1025, letter E, p. 1026, letter C, p. 1028, letter G, p. 1030, letter G, and p. 1031, letter G, post).

   Gorris v. *Scott* ((1874), L.R. 9 Exch. 125) and *Ginty* v. *Belmont Building Supplies, Ltd.* ([1959] 1 All E.R. 414) distinguished.

G (ii) reg. 31 (1) did not apply, because it was directed to the risk of slipping down or off a roof and falling from the edge of the roof and not, as in the present case, falling through a hole in the roof (see p. 1018, letter F, p. 1024, letter C, p. 1026, letter I, p. 1029, letter F, and p. 1031, letter G, post).

   Per CURIAM: although the point that reg. 31 (1) did not apply in the circumstances of this case was not taken before the trial judge, the Court

H of Appeal had been right in allowing it to be raised on appeal before them (see p. 1024, letter A, p. 1026, letter I, p. 1028, letter H, and p. 1031, letter G, post).

   Decision of the COURT OF APPEAL (sub nom. *Donaghey* v. *P. O'Brien & Co.* ([1966] 2 All E.R. 822) reversed on holding (iii) of that report, viz., as regards reg. 31 (3), affirmed on holding (ii), viz., as regards reg. 31 (1), and approved

I on holding (i) of that report, viz., allowing the contention regarding reg. 31 (1) to be raised; and reversed, in the result, as regards liability.

   [As to safety provisions for roof work under building regulations, see 17 HALSBURY'S LAWS (3rd Edn.) 127, para. 206 notes (*k*), (*l*); and for cases on the subject, see 24 DIGEST (Repl.) 1075, *327*; 1077, *333, 334*; 1081, *361-363*.

   For the Building (Safety, Health and Welfare) Regulations, 1948, reg. 4, reg. 31, see 8 HALSBURY'S STATUTORY INSTRUMENTS (1st Re-Issue) 189, 202.]

   ---

   * Regulation 4, so far as material, is printed at p. 1027, letters C and D, post.

Cases referred to: A

    Bailey v. *Ayr Engineering & Constructional Co., Ltd.*, [1958] 2 All E.R. 222;
        [1959] 1 Q.B. 183; [1958] 2 W.L.R. 882; Digest (Cont. Vol. A) 604,
        353a.

    Ginty v. *Belmont Building Supplies, Ltd.*, [1959] 1 All E.R. 414; Digest (Cont.
        Vol. A) 597, *333a.*

    Gorris v. *Scott*, (1874), L.R. 9 Exch. 125; 43 L.J.Ex. 92; 30 L.T. 431; 2 Digest   B
        (Repl.) 365, *459.*

    Grant v. *National Coal Board*, [1956] 1 All E.R. 682; [1956] A.C. 649; [1956]
        2 W.L.R. 725; 33 Digest (Repl.) 901, *1332.*

    Hughes v. *Lord Advocate*, [1963] 1 All E.R. 705; [1963] A.C. 837; [1963]
        2 W.L.R. 779; Digest (Cont. Vol. A) 1143, *89a.*

    Mulready v. *J. H. & W. Bell, Ltd.*, [1952] 2 All E.R. 663, *varied*, C.A., [1953]   C
        2 All E.R. 215; [1953] 2 Q.B. 117; [1953] 3 W.L.R. 100; 24 Digest
        (Repl.) 1075, *327.*

    Overseas Tankship (U.K.), Ltd. v. *Morts Dock & Engineering Co., Ltd., The
        Wagon Mound (No. 1)*, [1961] 1 All E.R. 404; [1961] A.C. 388; [1961]
        2 W.L.R. 126; [1961] 1 Lloyd's Rep. 1; [1961] A.L.R. 569; Digest
        (Cont. Vol. A) 1148, *185a.*   D

    Public Works Comrs. v. *Angus & Co., Dalton* v. *Angus & Co.*, [1881-85] All
        E.R. Rep. 1; (1881), 6 App. Cas. 740; 50 L.J.Q.B. 689; 44 L.T. 844;
        affg. sub nom. *Angus* v. *Dalton*, (1878), 4 Q.B.D. 162; 34 Digest (Repl.)
        198, *1394.*

Appeal.

This was an appeal by Eddie Donaghey from an order of the Court of Appeal   E
(WILLMER, DAVIES and RUSSELL, L.JJ.), dated May 25, 1966, and reported sub
nom. *Donaghey* v. *P. O'Brien & Co.* in [1966] 2 All E.R. 822, allowing the appeal
of the respondents, Boulton & Paul, Ltd., from a judgment of JAMES, J., given
at Bedford Assizes on Feb. 3, 1966, whereby the appellant was awarded £13,873
1s. 2d. damages for personal injuries against his employers, P. O'Brien & Co.,
and the respondents.   F

In an action commenced by writ dated Nov. 5, 1962, the appellant alleged
negligence and breach of statutory duty under reg. 31 of the Building (Safety,
Health and Welfare) Regulations, 1948, against the employers and the respondents.   The employers entered an appearance and filed a defence but, being
uninsured and without funds, took no part in the trial and allowed the appellant's
claim against them to go by default.   Negligence was not established at the   G
trial as against the present respondents, but it was found that they were in breach
of statutory duty under reg. 31 (1).   Contributory negligence on the part of the
appellant was established at the trial, he being held to be twenty-five per cent.
at fault.   The facts are set out in the opinion of VISCOUNT DILHORNE.

R. E. G. Howe, Q.C., and *J. F. Kingham* for the appellant.   H
J. D. May, Q.C., and *F. M. Drake* for the respondents.

Their lordships took time for consideration.

June 20.   The following opinions were delivered.

    VISCOUNT DILHORNE: My Lords, on Feb. 3, 1962, the appellant, who
was in the employ of a firm called P. O'Brien & Co., fell from the roof of an   I
aircraft hangar then in course of construction and as a result suffered serious
injuries.   P. O'Brien & Co. were employed by the respondents, who were themselves sub-contractors of another company, to do work on the roof of the hangar,
and one of the tasks on which they were engaged was covering the roof with
asbestos sheeting.

At the time of the accident the appellant was engaged with a man called
Mr. Crean in removing some of the asbestos sheets which had been damaged
as a result of gales and in replacing them with others.   The roof of the hangar was

A so constructed that the ridge of the sloping roof did not go along the length of the hangar but with the ridges running across the hangar. The apex of each ridge was sixty-two feet from the ground. Except at the ends of the hangar the slope of the roof was only twenty-two degrees. The slope from the ridge of the roof finished at a gutter, fifty feet from the ground, and from that gutter the roof sloped upwards to the next ridge. At the time of the accident the

B appellant and Mr. Crean were working on a part of the roof where the slope was twenty-two degrees.

They had removed the damaged sheets and relaid the lowest tier next to the gutter when P. O'Brien's foreman noticed that one of the relaid sheets was out of place. He thereupon told the appellant and Mr. Crean to put it right. To do so Mr. Crean stood on the asbestos roof covering to one side of the sheet

C that had to be moved. The appellant stood on the other side of that sheet with one foot on an angle iron purlin which formed part of the roof structure uncovered as a result of their removal of the sheets, and with his other foot on the asbestos sheeting. Behind him was an open space created by their removal of the asbestos sheets. They had some difficulty in moving the sheet which was out of place and, when it came free, the appellant lost his balance and fell through the open space

D in the roof to the ground.

He brought an action against his employers and against the respondents alleging negligence and breach of statutory duty, alleging failure to comply with the Building (Safety, Health and Welfare) Regulations, 1948 (1). P. O'Brien & Co. entered an appearance, filed a defence but did not appear at the trial. It was said that they were without funds and not insured against claims

E such as that brought by the appellant. The action was tried by JAMES, J., at Bedford Assizes in February, 1966. He held that P. O'Brien & Co. were guilty of negligence and of breach of statutory duty and that no case of negligence was established against the respondents but that they, too, were guilty of a breach of statutory duty. He assessed the damages at £18,497 8s. 2d. and, holding that the appellant was one-quarter to blame, and the respondent and P. O'Brien &

F Co. three-quarters to blame, he gave judgment against them for £13,873 1s. 2d.

From that judgment the respondents appealed to the Court of Appeal (2). If P. O'Brien & Co. are without funds and were not insured, the appellant will only recover compensation for the serious injuries which he received if he succeeds in this appeal. It is perhaps a matter which should receive consideration by the legislature whether employers who employ men to do work of the character of

G that on which the appellant was engaged should not be required to insure against claims of the nature brought by the appellant, for in the absence of insurance an injured workman may not get the compensation to which he is entitled.

The appellant in his statement of claim alleged breach of a number of regulations but in this appeal it is necessary to refer in detail only to reg. 31. That is headed " Roof Work ". It contains a number of paragraphs. Regula-

H tion 31 (1), which JAMES, J., held had not been complied with, reads as follows:

" Where work is done on the sloping surface of a roof and, taking into account the pitch, the nature of the surface, and the state of the weather, a person employed is likely to slip down or off the roof, then unless he has adequate hand-hold or foothold or is not liable to fall a distance of more than six feet six inches from the edge of the roof, suitable precautions shall be

I taken to prevent his so falling."

The appellant also alleged a breach of reg. 31 (3). [HIS LORDSHIP read the materials words of reg. 31 (3) which are set out at p. 1024, letter D, post, and continued:] JAMES, J., in his judgment said that he did not think that reg. 31 (3) had " got anything to do with this accident and in so far as it is relied on the [appellant] fails in respect of that ". He did not find that there had been a

(1) S.I. 1948 No. 1145.
(2) [1966] 2 All E.R. 822.

breach of any of the other regulations. Relying on *Mulready* v. *J. H. & W.*   A
Bell, Ltd. (3), JAMES, J., held that the respondents did not discharge themselves
from the duty of complying with reg. 31 (1) by employing P. O'Brien & Co. and
that the respondents' breach of duty was not coincidental with the appellant's
breach of duty, so that the appellant was not debarred by the decision in *Ginty*
v. *Belmont Building Supplies, Ltd.* (4) from recovering damages.

The respondents appealed to the Court of Appeal (5) and there sought to   B
contend that reg. 31 (1) did not apply. This had not been argued before JAMES,
J., though the contention had not been expressly abandoned. The Court of
Appeal (5) allowed this contention to be put forward, and it is now submitted
that they were wrong to do so.

Although in some cases the application of reg. 31 (1) may depend on evidence
as to the nature of the surface, the state of the weather and the absence of   C
adequate hand-holds or footholds, in other cases it will be clear without any
such evidence that the regulation does not apply.

In my opinion, this case is within the latter category. If it came within the
former, then the Court of Appeal (5) would have been wrong to allow this contention to be put forward. There is no dispute about how the appellant came
to fall from the roof. He did not slip on the roof and fall down it. The pitch   D
of the roof was very slight. Even if he had slipped on the roof and fallen down
it, he would have fallen into the gutter at the bottom and would not have fallen
to the ground. Regulation 31 (1) is, in my opinion, directed to ensure that proper
precautions are taken to prevent a person working on a sloping roof who is likely
to slip down or off the roof from falling from the edge of the roof where that
edge is more than six feet six inches from the ground. It was contended on   E
behalf of the appellant that in this regulation the edge of the roof did not mean
the bottom edge and that it sufficed if the appellant had fallen from any edge of
the roof, and so it was sufficient if he fell from the edge of the open space through
which he went and that was more than that distance from the ground. I am
not able to agree with this contention. It seems to me quite contrary to the
intent and meaning of the regulation. On this roof, with its very slight slope   F
terminating in the gutter in the valley between two of the sloping roofs. there
was, in my opinion, no duty to comply with reg. 31 (1). No precautions required
to be taken to prevent a man from slipping down and falling to the ground from
the bottom edge of the roof, for that terminated in the gutter.

The Court of Appeal (6) reached the same conclusion, but they appear to have
based their decision at least partly on the fact that no evidence was given at   G
the trial that the roof was slippery or as to the state of the weather, etc. I do
not agree that the regulation does not apply for these reasons. In view of the
fact that the application of reg. 31 (1) was not contested at the trial, it is not
surprising that no evidence was called on these matters.

The appellant contended before the Court of Appeal (5) that JAMES, J., had
misdirected himself in law in relation to reg. 31 (3) and should have held that the   H
respondents were in breach of this regulation. As to this WILLMER, L.J.,
said (6):

" The judge dismissed this contention in a very summary manner, holding
that reg. 31 (3) had not anything to do with this accident. In my judgment
the learned judge was plainly right, and I hope that I may be forgiven if I
too deal with this point very shortly. I do not doubt that asbestos is a fragile   I
material, and it is perfectly true that the [appellant's] work necessitated
his passing over it and working above it. I think it is plain, however, that
the mischief against which reg. 31 (3) is directed is the risk of a collapse of
the fragile material causing the workman to fall through it. There is no
evidence in the present case of any collapse of the asbestos sheeting, nor did

---

(3) [1953] 2 All E.R. 215; [1953] 2 Q.B. 117.   (4) [1959] 1 All E.R. 414.
(5) [1966] 2 All E.R. 822.   (6) [1966] 2 All E.R. at p. 830, letter C.

A the plaintiff fall through it.   He fell through a hole where there was in fact no asbestos sheeting."

Two questions have to be considered in relation to this regulation.   First, should it have been complied with and, secondly, if it should have been and was not, was breach of it the cause of the appellant's fall?

B In my opinion, the regulation did apply.   Work was being done on a roof covered with fragile materials through which a person was liable to fall more than ten feet, and the appellant and Mr. Crean were working above such fragile materials.   Consequently suitable and sufficient ladders, duck ladders or crawling boards should have been provided and used.   They were not.   Crawling boards were available on the ground, but they were not on the roof and they were not used.   In my opinion, there was a breach of this regulation.

C In the opinion of Mr. Rimmer, the expert witness called for the appellant, an adequate supply of crawling boards would have been a proper precaution for work on this roof.   The appellant in evidence said that if there had been a crawling board there he would have used it as it would have been more safe; and that he would not have fallen through the open space in the roof as the crawling board would have been wide enough to stop him going through it.

D James, J., holding that reg. 31 (1) applied, held that suitable precautions as required by that regulation were not taken as no crawling boards or other suitable materials were used.   He gave judgment against P. O'Brien & Co. on the ground that their negligence in allowing work to be done on the roof without any crawling boards or ladders being used and against that firm and the respondents on the ground that there had been failure to take sufficient precautions by the use of crawling boards to prevent the appellant falling, and so non-compliance with reg. 31 (1).   In the light of this evidence and this finding it is not possible to say that the breach of reg. 31 (3) was not the cause of the accident.

E Willmer, L.J., held (7) that the mischief at which reg. 31 (3) was directed was the risk of the collapse of the fragile material causing the workman to fall through it.   As the appellant had not fallen through it but through an open space, Willmer, L.J., held that the regulation did not apply.   If, when he lost his balance, the appellant had fallen on and through the asbestos sheeting, then, if I understand Willmer, L.J.'s judgment correctly, he would have held that the regulation applied.

F This is, I think, taking too narrow a view of the regulation.   It is intended to provide for the safety of workmen working on or above fragile roofs and the risk to which it is directed is the risk of falling from such roofs.   Regulation 31 (1) is directed to the risk of a man slipping down a sloping roof and falling off its edge. In my opinion, reg. 31 (3) should have been complied with.   It was not.   If it had been and a crawling board had been used by the appellant, it may be that he would not have lost his balance, or, if he did, as he himself said, that he would not have fallen through the hole.

G In *Gorris* v. *Scott* (8), the mischief at which the regulation was directed was the spreading of disease, not the prevention of the sheep being swept overboard. That is a very different case from this.   Here, as a result of the breach of reg. 31 (3), the appellant sustained injuries as a result of the kind of accident, namely, a fall from the roof, at which that regulation is directed, and, in my view, it matters not that when he fell he did not happen to fall on and through the fragile material.

H

I I now turn to the question : on whom lay the duty of complying with reg. 31 (3); did it rest on the respondents?   The answer to this question depends on reg. 4 of the Building (Safety, Health and Welfare) Regulations, 1948.   [His Lordship read the material terms of reg. 4, which are set out at p. 1027, letters C and D, post, and continued :]   The duty to comply with reg. 31 thus falls on every contractor

---

(7) [1966] 2 All E.R. at p. 830, letter D.
(8) (1874), L.R. 9 Exch. 125.

and employer who undertakes any of the operations to which this regulation A
applies in relation to any work, act or operation performed or about to be performed by such contractor or employer. " Undertaking any of the operations "
may mean performing them or may mean undertaking by a contract to carry
them out. In my view, it matters not, in this case, which is the correct
interpretation. If any contractor or employer comes within the ambit of this
regulation by contracting and in that sense undertaking certain operations, he is B
only under a duty under (i) to comply with such of the requirements of the
regulations there mentioned as affect any workmen employed by him, and under
a duty under (ii) to comply with such of the requirements of the regulations there
mentioned as relate to work performed or about to be performed by him. The
answer to the question, were the respondents under a duty to comply with
reg. 31 (3), thus depends on whether the work on the fragile roof on which the C
appellant was engaged was performed by them.

   Now, the head contractors had contracted with the respondents for the execution of certain works. If control over the execution of such work rested with
the respondents and not with the head contractors, then it could not be said
that the work was performed by the head contractors. Similarly, if the respondents had contracted with P. O'Brien & Co. that they should put the sheeting D
on the roof and control over the execution of that work rested solely with them,
the respondents would not, in my opinion, by virtue of reg. 4 be under any
duty to comply with reg. 31 (3).

   In this case the evidence given by a Mr. Gregory, a foreman erector in the
employment of the respondents and called by them as a witness, leads me to
the conclusion that the respondents by their contract with P. O'Brien & Co. E
had not divested themselves of control over the roofing of the hangar. The
respondents provided all the materials for the roofing. Mr Gregory said that
most of the roofing was done by O'Brien & Co.; that " some was done by Walker
and his men " (that was " another gang "), and that some was done " by
another gang also from King's Lynn. They did belong to Boulton Paul's ".
Mr. Gregory also in examination-in-chief was asked the following questions: F

   " Q. Of all the men engaged on that roof work on the hangar, for O'Brien's,
   for Walker's and for [the respondents], who was the man on the site who
   was the senior, top, foreman of all of them to keep an eye on what was going
   on?
   " A. We did have one supervisor on site but he left previous to the
   accident.   G
   " Q. Apart from that?
   " A. I was."

Later in the examination-in-chief he was asked if he knew exactly what O'Brien's
men were doing at the time of the accident and he said that he did; and he was
asked: H

   " Q. Had you told them to do it or had you left it to them?
   " A. No I, left it to his own judgment because he was a qualified man to
   do the job as regards sheeting."

Mr. Gregory was there referring to O'Brien's foreman. This answer shows that
he regarded it as part of his job to see to the sheeting and that he left it to O'Brien's I
foreman, not because it was their job with which he was not concerned, but
because O'Brien's foreman was a qualified man whom he could trust. Although
the actual labour on the roof may have been provided by a number of gangs, of
which P. O'Brien & Co.'s may have been one, with the materials provided by
the respondents, this last answer satisfies me that the respondents had not by
their contract with P. O'Brien & Co. divested themselves of control over the
execution of the work and that consequently the work was being performed by
them within the meaning of reg. 4.

A   James, J., and the Court of Appeal (9) did not consider this question, as they were bound by the decision in *Mulready* v. *J. H. & W. Bell, Ltd.* (10).   In this House it was open to the respondents to contend, and they did contend, that that case was wrongly decided.   In that case the plaintiff claimed damages for injuries which he sustained as a result of falling from the roof of a high building. The defendants, J. H. & W. Bell, Ltd., had undertaken to supply and fix metal

B   sheeting and to install three ventilators on the roof.   They had agreed with two brothers, named Keating, that they should supply the plant, materials and tackle and that the Keating brothers should carry out the work of fixing the roof sheeting and ventilators in position.   The plaintiff was employed by the Keating brothers.   Pearson, J., held (11) that the sub-contract between the defendants and the Keatings was of a very partial and minor character and that

C   the defendants remained in effective charge and control of the work.   On that ground he held (11) that the duty was imposed on them by reg. 4 of the Building (Safety, Health & Welfare) Regulations, 1948, to comply with reg. 31 and, as they had not done so, he gave judgment for the plaintiff.

The defendants appealed and the Court of Appeal (10) dismissed the appeal. Lord Goddard, C.J., in the course of delivering the judgment of the court said

D   (12) that while Pearson, J.'s judgment could be supported on the grounds stated by him, the court were prepared

"   . . . to decide the case on the ground that J. H. & W. Bell, Ltd. were the contractors who had agreed with the building owners to do the work, to perform the work on the roof and fix the ventilators.   Accordingly, we do not see how it makes any difference whether they chose to perform it by

E   their own workmen or by means of a sub-contract.   We cannot doubt that they had undertaken to perform the work . . ."

It cannot be doubted that J. H. & W. Bell, Ltd. had undertaken with the building owners operations to which reg. 31 applied.   They clearly came within the opening words of reg. 4.   Unless the terms of their contract with the building

F   owners prohibited them from doing so, they could have entered into a sub-contract for the complete execution of the work which they had undertaken to do and thereby deprived themselves of effective charge and control of the work, retaining the right to sue for breach of contract if the sub-contractors failed to fulfil their obligations.   If they had entered into such a contract, it could not, in my opinion, be said that the work was " performed or about to be performed " by them.

G   Regulation 4 (ii) only applies when the work is performed or about to be performed by a contractor or employer.   Until then no duty to comply with reg. 31 arises.

The Court of Appeal (10) relied on the observations of Lord Blackburn in *Public Works Comrs.* v. *Angus & Co., Dalton* v. *Angus & Co.* (13), where he said:

H   "   . . . a person causing something to be done, the doing of which casts on him a duty, cannot escape from the responsibility attaching on him of seeing that duty performed by delegating it to a contractor.   He may bargain with the contractor that he shall perform the duty and stipulate for an indemnity from him if it is not performed, but he cannot thereby relieve himself of liability to those injured by the failure to perform it . . ."

I   In that case the owner of land was under a duty not to deprive his neighbour's land of support.   He could not by contract divest himself of that duty.   In *Mulready's* case (10) the question was whether the defendants ever came under

---

(9) [1966] 2 All E.R. 822.
(10) [1953] 2 All E.R. 215; [1953] 2 Q.B. 117.
(11) [1952] 2 All E.R. 663 at p. 665.
(12) [1953] 2 All E.R. at p. 218, letter A; [1953] 2 Q.B. at p. 125.
(13) [1881-85] All E.R. 1 at p. 26; (1881), 6 App. Cas. 740 at p. 829.

a duty to comply with reg. 31 and they did not come under that duty unless the   **A** work was " performed or about to be performed " by them.

In my view, *Mulready's* case (14) was rightly decided by PEARSON, J. (15), and I do not agree with the additional grounds on which the Court of Appeal (14) affirmed his decision.

Counsel for the respondents also relied on the decision in *Ginty* v. *Belmont Building Supplies, Ltd.* (16). In that case PEARSON, J., held (17) that there was   **B** a fault by the employers because through their employee crawling boards were not used, but that fault of the employer consisted of and was co-incident with that of the plaintiff and in substance the accident was due to the fault of the plaintiff in breach of, and in defiance of, his instructions and of regulations which were well known to him. PEARSON, J., gave judgment, therefore, for the defendants. I think that JAMES, J., and the Court of Appeal (18) were right in holding that   **C** this decision did not apply to the facts of this case.

In my opinion, for the reasons which I have stated, this appeal should be allowed and the judgment of JAMES, J., restored.

LORD REID: My Lords, the appellant was not employed by the respondents and he was not injured by the negligence of any servant of the respondents.   **D** He can only succeed if he can show that the respondents were in breach of a statutory regulation and that that breach caused his accident. He relies on regs. 4 and 31 of the Building (Safety, Health and Welfare) Regulations, 1948.

The first question is whether the respondents had any duty under reg. 4 to comply with reg. 31. A firm of contractors, not parties to this case, had undertaken certain work which included repair work on the roof of a large hangar at   **E** Luton Airport. They had then sub-contracted for that repair work with the respondents. Part of that work was being performed by the respondents' servants but they made a further sub-contract with a small firm, P. O'Brien & Co. We do not have the terms of that sub-contract and it may not have been in writing; but it is clear that the substance of it was that O'Brien supplied labour for the fixing of asbestos sheets on the roof while the respondents supplied the   **F** necessary materials and safety apparatus. The appellant was employed by O'Brien on this work. He seeks damages from the respondents because, although O'Brien was clearly liable, O'Brien was not insured and has no means. [HIS LORDSHIP read the relevant part of reg. 4, which is set out at p. 1027, letters C and D, post, and continued:] It is not disputed that the respondents were a contractor within the meaning of this regulation, and that, if they were " performing "   **G** the work in the course of which the appellant was injured, they were bound to comply with the regulations specified; but they say that they were not performing this work, because it was being performed by O'Brien and his servants. They say that the case of *Mulready* v. *J. H. & W. Bell, Ltd.* (14) was wrongly decided.

In *Mulready's* case (14), as in this case, the defendants had sub-contracted for certain work on a roof and the plaintiff was employed by the sub-contractor. My   **H** noble and learned friend, LORD PEARSON, who was the trial judge, held (19) that this was a sub-contract of a very partial and minor character and that the defendants had remained in effective charge and control of the work. For that reason he held (20) that they were undertaking the building operation and performing the work in the course of which the plaintiff was injured. The Court of Appeal (14), however, added reasons which went much farther. They held   **I** that a duty was cast on the contractors by reg. 4 which they could not avoid by sub-contracting.

---

(14) [1953] 2 All E.R. 215; [1953] 2 Q.B. 117.
(15) [1952] 2 All E.R. 663.
(17) [1959] 1 All E.R. at p. 428.
(18) [1966] 2 All E.R. 822.
(19) [1952] 2 All E.R. at p. 664, letter H.
(20) [1952] 2 All E.R. at p. 665, letter E.

(16) [1959] 1 All E.R. 414.

A   The Court of Appeal (21) relied on the well-known statement by LORD BLACK-
BURN in *Public Works Comrs.* v. *Angus & Co.*, *Dalton* v. *Angus & Co.* (22):

"... a person causing something to be done, the doing of which casts on
him a duty, cannot escape from the responsibility attaching on him of seeing
that duty performed by delegating it to a contractor."

B   There, however, the position was that the landowner clearly owed a duty to his
neighbour not to withdraw support from his building, and the question was
whether it was any answer to say that he had employed a competent contractor
to carry out the work which withdrew the support. Here the position is quite
different. The question is whether any duty under reg. 4 ever attaches to a contractor who, by sub-contracting before the work is begun, puts the sub-contractor
C   in complete charge of the work. The Court of Appeal (23) appear to have assumed
that it does, but, in my view, this must depend on the proper construction of the
regulation.

In the first part of reg. 4 " undertaking " might mean carrying out an operation, or it might mean entering into a contract which requires the operation to be
carried out. I shall assume that it has the latter meaning; but there is nothing
D   unusual or improper in sub-contracting, and " undertaking " cannot carry the
implication that the contractor must be treated as having undertaken to employ
only his own servants to carry out the operations. The duty is to comply with
such of the requirements of (in this case) reg. 31 as relate to " any work, act or
operation performed or about to be performed " by the contractor. So no duty
can arise until work is about to be performed by the contractor; and, if the extent
E   of his sub-contracting is such that he never in any real sense " performs " the
work, I do not see how the contractor can be under any duty under this provision.
These regulations have the practical purpose of promoting safety, and it is right
that duties under them should attach to all who take part in the performance of
the work; but I can see no ground for attaching an artificial meaning to
" performing " work so that a contractor is deemed to perform work merely
F   because he has employed a sub-contractor to do it. That would be creating
vicarious liability for no useful purpose so far as safety is concerned : for, if the
contractor has no right under his contract with the sub-contractor even to
supervise the sub-contractor's operations, he cannot do anything to promote
safety. I am, therefore, of opinion that *Mulready's* case (24) was rightly decided
on the grounds stated by my noble and learned friend, LORD PEARSON (25), but
G   that the additional grounds stated by the Court of Appeal (24) are unsound.

Then the question arises whether, on the facts of this case, the respondents
were performing or taking part in the performance of the work or operations in
the course of which the appellant was injured. Not only were the respondents
responsible for seeing that materials and safety apparatus were available when
required, but the respondents' foreman says that he was there " to keep an eye
H   on what was going on ". This is not surprising because there were several gangs
working on the roof and it is hardly credible that each gang was entitled to do its
work as and when it pleased. This foreman says that he and O'Brien's men were
working in conjunction with each other. He left technical decisions to O'Brien's
foreman because O'Brien's man was an expert in this field and the respondents'
foreman was not. That, however, is what normally happens when the subordinate
I   alone is an expert. I think that, as in *Mulready's* case (24), this was, to use the
words of my noble and learned friend, a sub-contract of a very partial and
minor character. So the respondents were responsible for complying with the
requirements of reg. 31.

(21) [1953] 2 All E.R. at p. 218, letter D; [1953] 2 Q.B. at p. 125.
(22) [1881-85] All E.R. at p. 26; (1881), 6 App. Cas. at p. 829.
(23) [1966] 2 All E.R. 822.
(24) [1953] 2 All E.R. 215; [1953] 2 Q.B. 117.
(25) [1952] 2 All E.R. 663.

Before JAMES, J., it was not contended that reg. 31 (1) did not apply. This **A** matter was raised before the Court of Appeal (26) and I think that that court rightly allowed the point to be taken. In my view, this provision has no application to this case: it only applies if the workman is likely to slip down or off the roof and liable to fall a distance of more than six feet six inches " from the edge of the roof ". It was not contended that the appellant was liable to fall from the edge of the roof in the ordinary sense. Where he was working two roofs of two **B** bays sloped down to meet at a gutter and if he had slipped down the roof he would have slipped to this gutter and not have fallen at all. He fell, however, through an opening in the roof and it is said that the edges of this opening were edges of the roof. I do not agree. Openings in the roof are dealt with in reg. 30, and in reg. 31 I see no reason to extend the ordinary meaning of " edge of the roof " to include the edge of a hole in the roof. **C**

Regulation 31 (3) raises a more difficult point. Regulation 31 (3) is as follows:

" (3) Where work is being done on or near roofs or ceilings covered with fragile materials through which a person is liable to fall a distance of more than ten feet—

(a) where workmen have to pass over or work above such fragile materials, suitable and sufficient ladders, duck ladders or crawling boards, **D** which shall be securely supported, shall be provided and used;

(b) prominent notices stating that the coverings are fragile shall be affixed to the approaches thereto.

Provided that sub-para. (b) shall not apply as respects glass coverings."

It was not denied that this roof was of fragile material and it could hardly be **E** denied that, although the appellant in fact fell through a hole in the roof, he might from the place where he was working have fallen on to and through a part of the roof. That was sufficient to bring this provision into operation, and therefore there was a duty to see that crawling boards or one of the other things specified should be provided and used. The respondents had provided crawling boards somewhere on the ground nearby. The appellant wanted to use them, but he was **F** dissuaded or prevented by O'Brien's foreman. There is uncontradicted evidence that their use might well have prevented this accident, and I would therefore hold it proved that failure to use them involved a breach of the respondents' duty to comply with this regulation, and that that breach caused this accident; but it is argued that that is not sufficient to make the respondents civilly liable to the appellant.

First, the respondents rely on *Ginty* v. *Belmont Building Supplies, Ltd.* (27). **G** One might be pardoned for thinking that the result reached in that case was obvious. The employer had done all that he could to prevent breach of a regulation, but his servant disobeyed his orders, acted in breach of the regulation, was injured as a result, and then claimed damages from the employer. Of course he failed; the accident was entirely his own fault. But that bears no resemblance **H** to the present case. The respondents brought in O'Brien as sub-contractor, but, for the reasons which I have given, they remained bound to comply with the regulations and therefore liable to be sued for damage caused by a breach. The main cause of the breach which caused this accident was the fault of O'Brien's foreman. I find nothing in the authorities to entitle the respondents to disregard the fault of this foreman and succeed on the false basis that the appellant was **I** solely to blame for the breach and the accident caused by it.

Then the respondents rely on *Gorris* v. *Scott* (28). There a regulation required that pens should be provided in any vessel in which animals were imported. Sheep were carried in a vessel without there being such pens, and it was alleged that as a result the sheep were swept overboard by the sea; but it was clear that

---

(26) [1966] 2 All E.R. 822.
(27) [1959] 1 All E.R. 414.
(28) (1874), L.R. 9 Exch. 125.

A the purpose of the regulation was to prevent the spread of disease: it had nothing to do with the safety of the animals. KELLY, C.B., said that (29):

> ". . . when the damage is of such a nature as was not contemplated at all by the statute, and as to which it was not intended to confer any benefit on the plaintiffs, they cannot maintain an action founded on the neglect."

B Later he said (30):

> " But, looking at the Act, it is perfectly clear that its provisions were all enacted with a totally different view: there was no purpose, direct or indirect, to protect against such damage; . . . all the purposes enumerated being calculated and directed to the prevention of disease, and none of them having any relation whatever to the danger of loss by the perils of the sea . . .
C the damage complained of here is something totally apart from the object of the Act of Parliament, and it is in accordance with all the authorities to say that the action is not maintainable."

PIGOTT, B., said (31):

> " The legislature never contemplated altering the relations between the
D owners and carriers of cattle, except for the purposes pointed out in the Act; . . . its object was not to regulate the duty of the carrier for all purposes but only for one particular purpose."

I entirely agree with that decision: but it was dealing with something very different from the present case. Here one of the main objects of the Factories Act, 1961 was to promote safety: and the sole purpose of the regulations was to
E prevent men working on a roof from falling to the ground. It is one thing to say that, if the damage suffered is of a kind totally different from that which it is the object of the regulation to prevent, there is no civil liability. It is quite a different thing, however, to say that civil liability is excluded because the damage, though precisely of the kind which the regulation was designed to prevent, happened in a way not contemplated by the maker of the regulation. The difference is com-
F parable with that which caused the decision in *Overseas Tankship (U.K.), Ltd. v. Morts Dock & Engineering Co., Ltd., The Wagon Mound (No. 1)* (32) to go one way and the decision in *Hughes* v. *Lord Advocate* (33) to go the other way.

In deciding against the appellant on reg. 31 (3) WILLMER, L.J., said, with the the approval of the other members of the court (34):

> " I think it is plain, however, that the mischief against which reg. 31 (3)
G is directed is the risk of a collapse of the fragile material causing the workman to fall through it."

I do not think that that is quite right. The mischief against which the whole regulation is directed is the risk of injury from a fall from the roof, not the risk of collapse of the material. These regulations were made under, inter alia,
H s. 60 of the Factories Act, 1937, and that section provided that where the Secretary of State was satisfied that any process was " of such a nature as to cause risk of bodily injury to persons employed in connexion therewith " he might make regulations to meet the necessity of the case. Regulation 31 requires various precautions in various circumstances in which persons are likely to be injured in certain ways. I do not see why, however, it should follow that a person
I must be injured in precisely one of these ways before he can recover damages. Suppose a man is standing on a fragile roof near a hole in the roof. There is a breach of the regulation because crawling boards or similar apparatus have not been provided and used. Then he falls because there were no crawling boards. If he falls to his right he falls through the hole. If he falls to his left he falls

(29) (1874), L.R. 9 Exch. at p. 128.   (30) (1874), L.R. 9 Exch. at pp. 129, 130.
(31) (1874), L.R. 9 Exch. at p. 130.
(32) [1961] 1 All E.R. 404; [1961] A.C. 388.
(33) [1963] 1 All E.R. 705; [1963] A.C. 837.
(34) [1966] 2 All E.R. at p. 830, letter D.

through the fragile material. Is the law so absurd that if he falls to his right he   **A**
cannot recover damages, whereas if he falls to his left he can? It appears to me to
be a wrong approach to put each separate provision in each separate regulation
in a watertight compartment, and then to say that a man must be injured in
precisely the way contemplated in that separate provision before he can recover
damages.

That a person is to be entitled to recover damages for injury caused by a breach   **B**
of this kind of regulation is an inference which the courts have drawn from various
Acts of Parliament. They were passed for the benefit of employees and it is
inferred that Parliament intended that a person injured by reason of a breach of
their provisions or of provisions in regulations made under them should have a
civil remedy. It would seem odd to go on and infer that Parliament intended to
withhold this benefit from every person who, though his injury was caused by a   **C**
breach, did not suffer that injury in precisely the way contemplated in the statute
or regulation. I am not prepared to attribute any such intention to Parliament.

The respondents rely on the decision in *Bailey* v. *Ayr Engineering & Constructional Co., Ltd.* (35). There a regulation required a working place to be
" covered in such manner as to protect any person who is working in that place
from being struck by any falling material or article ". The plaintiff was working   **D**
in an open shaft in a building under construction when he was hit by a falling
block of masonry. His action for damages failed. PARKER, L.J., held (36) that
this regulation did not apply to material which had become part of the structure
and affixed to the freehold. I am not concerned whether that was right or wrong:
I shall assume it was right; but he appears to have held that the defendants were
in breach because they had not provided any covering. He said (37):   **E**

> " Accordingly this is a case where they cannot say that they were not in
> breach of the regulation at all, because it was their duty to take steps
> to put up some umbrella, albeit only an umbrella designed to prevent
> materials and débris and tools from falling down. Be that as it may, and
> assuming, as I do, that they were in breach, it was not that breach which   **F**
> caused the injuries in this case, but the fact that this block of masonry, some-
> thing which is completely outside the regulation, fell in the way I have
> described."

I think that he meant that, even if there had been an umbrella sufficient to
comply with the regulation, this block was so heavy that it would have crashed
through that umbrella and injured the plaintiff in just the same way. If that   **G**
was his meaning then the breach did not cause the injury and the case does not
touch the question which I have been considering. The respondents argue that
PARKER, L.J., meant that, even if compliance with the regulation would have
prevented this block of masonry from breaking through the covering and injuring
the plaintiff, still he could not recover damages for his injury although it would
then have been caused by the breach. If he did mean that then I would not   **H**
agree with him.

I would allow this appeal.

LORD HODSON: My Lords, I agree that this appeal should be allowed
for the reasons stated by my noble and learned friend, LORD REID. I add some
remarks of my own since I was a party to the decision of the Court of Appeal in
Mulready v. *J. H. & W. Bell, Ltd.* (38) upon which the appellant relies. In that   **I**
case the court upheld the decision of PEARSON, J. (39) partly on the ground
stated by him that the head contractors, Bell Ltd., were still in effect in charge
and control. He held that they were undertaking the building operations and

(35) [1958] 2 All E.R. 222; [1959] 1 Q.B. 183.
(36) [1958] 2 All E.R. at p. 226, letter B; [1959] 1 Q.B. at p. 188.
(37) [1958] 2 All E.R. at p. 226, letter F; [1959] 1 Q.B. at p. 188.
(38) [1953] 2 All E.R. 215; [1953] 2 Q.B. 117.
(39) [1952] 2 All E.R. 663.

A performing the act of fixing the ventilators within the meaning of reg. 4. Likewise I agree that the respondents to this appeal were on the facts of this case " performing " the operations in the course of which the appellant was injured. In *Mulready's* case (40), however, the court in construing reg. 4 held that the word " perform " in reg. 4 of the Building (Safety, Health and Welfare) Regulations, 1948, has a wider meaning sufficient to cover vicarious performance of the

B work by a sub-contractor and impose liability on a head contractor who subsequently took no part in the work.

In order to understand the argument it is necessary to set out reg. 4, which provided (41) as follows:

" 4. It shall be the duty of every contractor and employer of workmen who is undertaking any of the operations to which these regulations apply—

C (i) to comply with such of the requirements of regs. 5-30, 66 (1) in so far as it relates to the protection of the hoistway, 73, 75, 77, 80-84, 89, 90 (1), 91, 92, 93 and 95 as affect any workman employed by him; provided that the requirements of the said regulations shall be deemed not to affect any workman if and so long as his presence in any place is not in the course of performing any work on behalf of his employer or is not expressly or impliedly

D authorised or permitted by his employer; (ii) to comply with such of the requirements of regs. 31-33, 74 (1), (2), (3), (4) and (5), 76, 78, 79, 88, 90 (2), 94, 96 and 97 as relate to any work, act or operation performed or about to be performed by such contractor or employer of workmen; . . ."

The difference between paras. (i) and (ii) is striking. Paragraph (i) deals with

E regulations as affecting any workmen employed by every contractor and employer of workmen. Paragraph (ii) does not deal with workmen but demands compliance with the requirements of such of the regulations as relate to any work, act or operation performed by such contractor or employer of workmen.

There is thus an argument for the construction of the word " perform " so as to extend to cover a contractor who is not actually doing any works but had

F agreed with the building owners to do the work. On the other hand, manifestly inconvenience and possibility of injustice may arise, especially where there is a chain of contractors and sub-contractors, each of whom had undertaken to do the work. These considerations suggest a narrower construction of the word " perform " as being appropriately applied to the person who is physically performing the work. The employer, not the contractor, unless he is involved in the per-

G formance, must take the precautions. The wide construction of " perform " involves that every person who enters into a contract and undertakes to do any part of the work is deemed to be performing it although he sub-contracts it. This construction is not, I think, consistent with the division of duties set out in reg. 4. I am of opinion on reconsideration that the only person liable under para. (ii) is he who physically " performs " the operation and accordingly revise

H my previous opinion. On this construction of the word " perform " the well known statement on duty contained in LORD BLACKBURN'S speech in *Public Works Comrs.* v. *Angus & Co., Dalton* v. *Angus & Co.* (42) has no application.

I have nothing to add on reg. 31 (1) which has been found by the Court of Appeal (43) to have no application to this case.

Regulation 31 (3) is in a different position. JAMES, J., and the Court of Appeal

I (44) treated this regulation as inapplicable because it was aimed at preventing a different sort of accident from that which befell the appellant. [HIS LORDSHIP read reg. 31 (3), which is set out at p. 1024, letter D, ante, and continued:] In support of the contention of the respondents reliance is naturally placed on the leading case of *Gorris* v. *Scott* (44), which decided that when a statute creates a

---

(40) [1953] 2 All E.R. 215; [1953] 2 Q.B. 117.

(41) The regulation is printed as originally made, but all the regulations enumerated therein except regs. 5-33 and 80-84 were revoked in 1961.

(42) [1881-85] All E.R. at p. 26; (1881), 6 App. Cas. at p. 829.

(43) [1966] 2 All E.R. 822.   (44) (1874), L.R. 9 Exch. 125.

duty with the object of preventing a mischief of a particular kind, a person who, **A**
by reason of another's neglect of the statutory duty, suffers a loss of a different
kind, is not entitled to maintain an action in respect of such loss. Applying the
principle to this case, WILLMER, L.J., said (45):

" I think it is plain, however, that the mischief against which reg. 31 (1)
is directed is the risk of a collapse of the fragile material causing the workman to fall through it."   **B**

This of course is true, but the mischief really contemplated is the risk of a fall a
distance of more than ten feet and this need not take place in precisely the way
with which the wording of the regulation appears to deal.

I think that guidance is to be found in a decision of your lordships in the case
of *Grant* v. *National Coal Board* (46). This was an action for damages based on a **C**
breach of s. 49 of the Coal Mines Act, 1911, which prescribed: " The roof and
sides of every travelling road . . . shall be made secure . . ." A mineworker
was injured by the derailment of a bogie in which he was riding when it struck
some stone which had fallen from the roof of the travelling road. It was held
that the accident was one against which the legislation was designed to protect
him, notwithstanding that the accident happened in a manner not contemplated **D**
by the Act of 1911, viz., injury caused by the direct impact of material falling
from the roof. Applying *Gorris* v. *Scott* (47) it was pointed out in your lordships'
House that there was in that case a complete difference in kind in the mischief
aimed at, namely, the prevention of the introduction and spread of contagious
disease among animals, not their protection from perils of the sea, whereas in the
case under consideration, although the primary danger was that of being crushed **E**
or hurt by a fall of stone, yet there are other risks of a like nature which may
follow from a fall of stone which may imperil the safety of the workers. Such a
risk is the risk of a derailment as happened and caused the injury. In dealing
with *Gorris* v. *Scott* (47) where the object of the enactment was of a kind totally
different from the safety of workpeople, my noble and learned friend, LORD
REID, pointed out that if the enactment in that case implied civil liability, it **F**
was a very different thing to say that, where the object of the enactment is to
provide safety, the implication is that liability only arises if the injury occurs in a
particular way. I think that, although the matter is not free from difficulty, as
the judgments delivered on the subject of reg. 31 (1) show, yet reg. 31 (3) applies
to this case.

Agreeing as I do that the absence of crawling boards was a cause of the **G**
accident, the only remaining question is whether on the line followed by PEARSON,
J., in *Ginty* v. *Belmont Building Supplies Ltd.* (48), the accident should be attributed solely to the fault of the appellant. I cannot accept that this authority
has any relevance to this case and see no reason to disturb the finding of liability
and the proportion of blame fixed by the trial judge. I would accordingly allow the
appeal and restore the order of JAMES, J.   **H**

    LORD GUEST: My Lords, the Court of Appeal (49) have held that although
the point was not taken before JAMES, J., it was open to the appellants before
them (now the respondents in this House) to take the point that reg. 31 (1) of
the Building (Safety, Health and Welfare) Regulations, 1948, did not apply to
the circumstances of this case. In that I think that they were right. I cannot
see that any prejudice was caused to the appellant in this point being raised for **I**
the first time in the Court of Appeal (49). Sufficient of the circumstances of the
accident had been investigated to enable a decision to be made on the applicability
of the regulation.

(45) [1966] 2 All E.R. at p. 830, letter D.
(46) [1956] 1 All E.R. 682; [1956] A.C. 649.
(47) (1874), L.R. 9 Exch. 125.   (48) [1959] 1 All E.R. 414.
        (49) [1966] 2 All E.R. 822.

A   On the substantial question whether reg. 31 (1) did in fact apply, again I think that the Court of Appeal (55) were right in holding that it was not applicable. The regulation is in the following terms:

> " Regulation 31:

B
> " (1) Where work is done on the sloping surface of a roof and, taking into account the pitch, the nature of the surface, and the state of the weather, a person employed is likely to slip down or off the roof, then unless he has adequate handhold or foothold or is not liable to fall a distance of more than six feet six inches from the edge of the roof, suitable precautions shall be taken to prevent his so falling . . ."

Before the obligation to comply with the regulations arises certain conditions must be present:

C
    (i) work must be done on the sloping surface of a roof,
    (ii) taking into account the pitch of the roof, the nature of the surface, the state of the weather, a person is likely to slip down or off the roof. Then, if these conditions are present and unless there is adequate hand hold or foothold, or the person is not liable to fall more than six feet six inches from the edge of the roof,

D suitable precautions must be taken to prevent " his so falling ". This latter expression I construe as " falling from the edge of the roof ". The Court of Appeal (55) doubted whether condition 2 was satisfied, but I am not prepared to take this point against the appellant, as I think that it was assumed at the trial that by reason of one or other of the factors mentioned the appellant was liable to slip down off the roof. There was at any rate no contrary evidence for the respondents.

E The question then arises, against what circumstances had the suitable precautions to be taken—and the answer must be according to the regulation " to prevent him falling from the edge of the roof ". What in fact happened was that the appellant fell through a hole in the roof, which had been made by the temporary removal of some asbestos sheeting. The edge of the roof cannot in the context in my view comprise the sides of the hole in the roof. The distinction is made between

F the roof and the edge of the roof in reg. 31 (4) where both " the roof " and " the edge of the roof " are separately referred to. The precautions which have to be taken are not specified as precautions to prevent the person falling through the hole in the roof but to prevent him falling from the edge of the roof. Regulation 30 makes provision for accessible openings in roofs or floors which have to be protected.

G Regulation 31 (3) was summarily dismissed by James, J., and the Court of Appeal (50) gave it scant consideration. Willmer, L.J., with whose judgment Davies and Russell, L.JJ., agreed, took the view (51) that the mischief against which reg. 31 (3) was directed was the risk of the collapse of the fragile material causing the workman to fall through and that as the accident happened, not through the appellant falling through the fragile material but through a hole

H in the roof where there was no asbestos sheeting, the accident was not caused by a breach by the respondents of reg. 31 (3). I am afraid that I cannot agree with this construction of the regulation. [His Lordship read reg. 31 (3), which is set out at p. 1024, letter D, ante, and continued:] The operative part of reg. 31 (3) is that where workmen have to pass over or work above fragile materials, certain precautions have to be provided and used, such as ladders and crawling boards.

I The circumstances under which these precautions have to be taken are further defined in the opening words of reg. 31 (3) where the degree of fragility of the material is described as " materials through which a person is liable to fall a distance of more than ten feet " and the work is being done on or near roofs or ceilings covered with these materials. The stage is thus set in the opening sentence of reg. 31 (3) for the circumstances in which the precautions have to be taken. There is no doubt on the evidence that work was being done near roofs covered with material of the necessary fragility. There is no doubt that the appellant had

---

(50) [1966] 2 All E.R. 822.   (51) [1966] 2 All E.R. at p. 830.

to pass over these materials. In fact he was standing on an asbestos sheeting when **A**
he fell. There is no doubt that the precautions desiderated were not provided and
used and that if they had been used the accident would probably not have
happened. In the circumstances there was plainly a breach of reg. 31 (3). The
causal relation between the breach and the accident has been established.

It is said that the mischief against which reg. 31 (3) was designed was men
falling through fragile materials in roofs, and as the appellant did not fall through **B**
the fragile materials, the regulation does not apply. I cannot follow this argument.
The regulation was designed for the safety of men working on the roof, and the
mischief against which the regulation was designed was men falling from the roof.
(See *Grant* v. *National Coal Board* (52).) Whether the fall took place through the
roof or from a hole in the roof seems to be immaterial. In my opinion undue
importance has been attached by the Court of Appeal (53) to the phrase " through **C**
which a person is liable to fall a distance of more than ten feet ". It does not
denote the mischief against which the regulation is designed, but merely describes
the degree of fragility of the materials and the distance of a possible fall as circumstances which must exist before the regulation applies. To construe the regulation
according to the respondents would mean that if the workman put his foot through
the asbestos sheeting material and fell to the ground he could appeal to the **D**
regulation, but if he overbalanced off the asbestos sheeting and fell ten feet to the
ground he could not recover. Such an unreasonable result cannot, I think, have
been contemplated by the regulation. I cannot see any justification for the view
that before the regulation can apply the accident must have happened by the
man falling through the fragile materials. The precise way in which the accident
happened is not material if the accident which happened was the type of accident **E**
against which the regulation was designed. (See *Hughes* v. *Lord Advocate* (54).)

The strongest case relied on by the respondents was *Gorris* v. *Scott* (55). The
facts were that the defendant shipowner undertook to carry the plaintiff's sheep
from a foreign port to England. On the voyage some of the sheep were washed
overboard by a failure on the part of the defendant to take a precaution required
by the Contagious Diseases (Animals) Act, 1869. It was held that the plaintiff **F**
was not entitled to recover on the ground that the object of the statute was to
prevent the spread of contagious disease among animals and not to protect them
against the perils of the sea. The mischief against which the Act was designed
was expressed to be the introduction or spread of contagious or infectious diseases
among animals in Great Britain, and the accident of being washed overboard was
a different kind of mischief altogether against which the statute was not designed. **G**
In the present case the general purpose of the Building (Safety, Health and Welfare) Regulations, 1948, was to secure the safety of the men working, and the
mischief against which reg. 31 was designed was men falling from the roof. This
was the type of accident which happened and the regulation therefore applies to
the respondents.

A further question arises on the submission by the respondents that even if **H**
there was a breach of reg. 31, this regulation did not apply to them, as they had
sub-contracted for the work to be performed by P. O'Brien & Co., originally the
first defendants. This involves a consideration of reg. 4 (ii). [HIS LORDSHIP
read the relevant terms of reg. 4 (ii), which are set out at p. 1027, letter D, ante,
and continued:] The Court of Appeal (53) dismissed this argument, expressing
themselves bound, as they were, by the decision in *Mulready* v. *J. H. & W. Bell,* **I**
Ltd. (56). The respondents invited this House to overrule *Mulready* v. *J. H. &
W. Bell, Ltd.* (56). In that case the head contractor employed a sub-contractor
who failed to comply with reg. 31 of the Building (Safety, Health and Welfare)
Regulations, 1948. The Court of Appeal held (56) that the head contractor, even
though he had no knowledge of the breach of statutory duty, remained liable in

---

(52) [1956] 1 All E.R. 682; [1956] A.C. 649.   (53) [1966] 2 All E.R. 822.
(54) [1963] 1 All E.R. 705; [1963] A.C. 837.   (55) (1874), L.R. 9 Exch. 125.
                (56) [1953] 2 All E.R. 215; [1953] 2 Q.B. 117.

A damages to a workman employed by the sub-contractor who sustained injuries as a result of the breach. The present case and *Mulready* (57) really turn on a proper interpretation of reg. 4 (ii), the relevant part of which has already been quoted. The argument which succeeded in *Mulready's* case (57) was that if a duty was cast on the head contractor to perform the work, he cannot avoid it by sub-contracting. This assumes, however, that a duty is cast on the head con-

B tractor to perform the work. Lord Goddard, C.J., said (58) that the head contractor had agreed with the building owner to perform the work on the roof and that it did not matter whether they chose to perform it by their own workmen or by means of a sub-contract. With respect to the members of the Court of Appeal (57), that is to give too wide a meaning to the word " performed ". The head contractor, although he may undertake the operation with the building owner,

C does not perform the work if he divests himself of the control and direction of the work by employing a sub-contractor. For these reasons I consider that the ratio of decision as expressed by the Court of Appeal (57) was wrong. The trial judge (Pearson, J.), had decided the case (59) in the plaintiff's favour on a more narrow ground, namely, that in view of the control exercised by the head contractor he could be regarded as performing the work in question. On the facts of that case

D I think that he was right. The question is whether the facts in the present case can justify a similar conclusion. The difficulty is that this aspect of the matter was really never considered in the courts below as they were bound by *Mulready* (57) and the evidence is very meagre. However, there was certain evidence by Mr. Gregory, the respondents' foreman erector. G. Taylor Brandon were the main contractors and the respondents were the main roof contractors. They had sub-

E contracted some of the roof work to P. O'Brien & Co. (formerly first defendants) the appellant's employers. All the materials and safety equipment were purchased by the respondents who supplied the labour, some of which was sub-contracted to P. O'Brien & Co. and some to another firm. Mr. Gregory nevertheless was the senior man on the spot responsible to the respondents for supervising the work on the roof. In these circumstances it can fairly be said that the respon-

F dents had not divested themselves of the control and direction of the roof work and that they were " performing " the work in the terms of reg. 4 (ii). It follows that, in my view, the respondents are liable in damages for breach of statutory duty to the appellant.

On the question whether the case of *Ginty* v. *Belmont Building Supplies, Ltd.* (60) affords any protection to the respondents, I agree with the rest of your

G lordships in thinking that the case has no application to the facts of this case.

I would allow the appeal and restore the judgment of James, J.

LORD PEARSON: My Lords, I concur and have nothing to add.

Appeal allowed.

H Solicitors: *T. D. Jones & Co.*, agents for *Tearle & Herbert Jones*, Luton (for the appellant); *Denis Hayes*, agent for *John G. Clayton & Co.*, Luton (for the respondents).

[*Reported by* Kathleen J. H. O'Brien, *Barrister-at-Law.*]

I

---

(57) [1953] 2 All E.R. 215; [1953] 2 Q.B. 117.
(58) [1953] 2 All E.R. at p. 218, letter A; [1953] 2 Q.B. at p. 125.
(59) [1952] 2 All E.R. 663.   (60) [1959] 1 All E.R. 414.

EDWARDS v. EDWARDS.

[PROBATE, DIVORCE AND ADMIRALTY DIVISION (Sir Jocelyn Simon, P., and Cairns, J.), January 25, 1967.]

Divorce—Appeal—Divisional Court—Appeal from order of magistrates' court—Time for appealing—Extension of time—Factors material to exercise of court's discretion to extend time—Matrimonial Causes Rules, 1957 (S.I. 1957 No. 619), r. 73 (4).

On Apr. 15, 1964, a magistrates' court refused a husband's request that his wife's complaint alleging persistent cruelty on his part should be adjourned to permit him to obtain legal representation. The husband was adjudged guilty of persistent cruelty and a separation and maintenance order was made. By r. 73 (4) of the Matrimonial Causes Rules, 1957, notice of appeal had to be served within twenty-one days from the date of the order. On Jan. 25, 1967, the husband sought leave of the Divisional Court to appeal out of time on the ground that the magistrates' court should have given him the help that s. 61 of the Magistrates' Courts Act, 1952 envisaged but had not done so, and also on other grounds. Two counsel had advised the husband that his appeal was not likely to succeed. The justices' reasons were given either at the end of 1965 or in January, 1966.

Held: the court not being satisfied that there was good reason to suppose there had been a miscarriage of justice, leave to appeal out of time would be refused (see p. 1034, letters H and I, post).

Per CURIAM: stipulations which Parliament has laid down as to time are to be observed unless justice clearly indicates that they should be relaxed (see p. 1034, letter B, post).

[Editorial Note. This decision should be considered with that in *Finding v. Finding* ([1939] 2 All E.R. 173).

As to the time for appealing from magistrates' courts in matrimonial cases, see 12 HALSBURY'S LAWS (3rd Edn.) 509, para. 1116 text and note (*o*).

For the Magistrates' Courts Act, 1952, s. 61, see 32 HALSBURY'S STATUTES (2nd Edn.) 469.

For the Matrimonial Causes Rules, 1957, r. 73 (4), see 10 HALSBURY'S STATUTORY INSTRUMENTS (Second Re-Issue) 273.]

Appeal.

This was an appeal brought out of time by the husband against a decision of the Barnet justices on Apr. 15, 1964, when they adjudged him guilty of persistent cruelty and made a separation and maintenance order. The facts are set out in the judgment of SIR JOCELYN SIMON, P.

A. B. Hidden for the husband.

J. F. Kingham for the wife.

SIR JOCELYN SIMON, P.: This is an appeal brought out of time against a decision of the Barnet justices of Apr. 15, 1964. On that date, they adjudged that the husband had been guilty of persistent cruelty to the wife and made a separation and maintenance order. The maintenance was subsequently varied as to quantum; but the husband now seeks leave to appeal out of time against the principal decision, on the following grounds. First, that the justices wrongly exercised their discretion in refusing him an adjournment so that he might obtain legal representation before them. Secondly, that they did not give him the help which was statutorily incumbent on them under the Magistrates' Courts Act, 1952, s. 61, the relevant part of which reads:

" Where in any domestic proceedings ... it appears to a magistrates' court that any party to the proceedings who is not legally represented is

A   unable effectively to examine or cross-examine a witness, the court shall ascertain from that party what are the matters about which the witness may be able to depose or on which the witness ought to be cross-examined, as the case may be, and shall put, or cause to be put, to the witness such questions in the interests of that party as may appear to the court to be proper."

B   The husband seeks to say that the justices wrongly failed to comply with that section.   Thirdly, that the justices wrongly ruled out evidence which he could have given and now wishes to give.   Fourthly, that such evidence and other evidence which he could have given and now wishes to give would, in all probability, have led the justices to a contrary conclusion from that to which they came.   And, fifthly, that they misdirected themselves on the law and on the evidence before them, so that generally the decision does not stand up to examination.

C   I am far from convinced that any of these objections has any validity.   However, we have not heard full argument on that and I express no concluded opinion. It is, however, necessary to form a provisional view, for this reason.   The appeal is very long delayed and out of the necessary time; and if it were clear that the decision of the justices was in all probability wrong, that would be a factor to weigh with us in exercising our discretion whether to extend the time for appealing.

D   I turn to consider, then, what is the principal obstacle in the way of the husband before he ever gets to the substance of his appeal—namely, that the appeal must be brought within twenty-one days, whereas this appeal was brought well over twenty-one months, after the adjudication.   We have had from counsel for the husband an able and agreeable argument in which everything has been advanced on behalf of the husband which could be said, and he has thereby put the court in his debt.   Nevertheless, I am firmly of opinion that it would be quite wrong in the present case to extend the time for appealing.

E   All adjudication, like every piece of social engineering, is a compromise between a number of desiderata, not all of which are easily made consistent.   There should, first, be the fullest and truest assessment of all relevant facts.   There must, however, secondly, be some protection of individual privacy and liberty. Thirdly, and most relevant of all to this application, it is desirable that disputes within society should be brought to an end as soon as is reasonably practical and should not be allowed to drag festeringly on for an indefinite period.   That

F   last principle finds expression in a maxim which English law took over from the Roman law: it is in the public interest that there should be some end to litigation.   The principle, for example, applies in the doctrine which is known to lawyers as res judicata: in other words, once there is a decision on a matter by a competent court, it is binding on all courts of similar jurisdiction.   It is exemplified, too, in the various Limitation Acts.   It is also to be found in the stipulations in our codes of civil procedure as to the time within which procedural

G   steps must be taken.   As long ago as Magna Carta, King John was made to promise not only that justice should not be denied but also that it should not be delayed; and there have been times in our history when various courts have come under severe criticism for their procedural delays.

H   Courts are manned by and rely on the services of human beings, trained and conscientious, but still liable to error.   Parliament has therefore erected a structure to correct error, so far as is reasonable, by way of appeal, and indeed in certain limited circumstances by way of re-hearing.   Even so, any lawyer must be aware that litigants sometimes feel that justice has not been done to their case; and it certainly would be unfair to dismiss all such persons as harbouring the fantasies and lack of balance of Miss Flite.   It is true the justice done is often only rough justice.   The answer to that is that delayed adjudication, for all its possible advantages in ampler or more certain elucidation of fact or law, is generally liable itself to entail injustice.

So far as procedural delays are concerned, Parliament has left a discretion in the A
courts to dispense with the time requirements in certain respects. That does
not mean, however, that the rules are to be regarded as, so to speak, antique
timepieces of an ornamental value but no chronometric significance, so that lip
service only need be paid to them. On the contrary, in my view, the stipulations
which Parliament has laid down or sanctioned as to time are to be observed unless
justice clearly indicates that they should be relaxed. An example of such B
relaxation that comes readily to mind is where legal aid has been made available
to a party before this court. In order that parties shall have equal access to
the courts, Parliament has provided that those who cannot themselves finance
their legal representation shall receive public aid to that end; but with the
object of ensuing fiscal equity and public economy, Parliament has also laid
down a strict procedure whereby that legal aid is to be obtained. It not infre- C
quently happens that this procedure involves an appellant before this court
being out of time: in such circumstances, however, we readily grant an extension
of time.

The provision relevant to the present application is contained in Matrimonial
Causes Rules, 1957 (S.I. 1957 No. 619), r. 73 (4):

> " The notice of motion shall be served and the appeal entered within D
> twenty-one days from the date of the order, calculated from the time at
> which the order is signed or otherwise perfected . . ."

It would be sufficient to say that that rule has statutory force. It is, however,
right to add that it is based on thoroughly good sense. This court can only
operate with the co-operation of the court from whose decision the appeal is
brought. It is required, for example, of the latter court that they should provide E
us with a statement of the facts that they have found and of the reasons for
their decision; but after a considerable lapse of time the adjudicating body
cannot recapitulate such matters with any pretence of reality. For example,
in the present case, the decision was made on Apr. 15, 1964, and it was not until
the end of December, 1965, or the beginning of January, 1966, that the justices F
gave their reasons.

It is against that general background that I consider the facts of the present
case.

[HIS LORDSHIP then reviewed the facts of the case, pointing out that after the
justices had given their decision two counsel in succession had advised the
husband that an appeal was not likely to succeed, and continued]: G

The second matter that weighs with me is that after the hearing, the husband
had what is described in the certificate of delay as a " long conference " with his
then counsel (who was not the counsel who had originally advised against his
chance of success immediately after the hearing). This second counsel indicated
that he endorsed the opinion given by the previously instructed counsel.

If I were satisfied that there was good reason to suppose that there had been H
a miscarriage of justice here, speaking for myself, I would be strongly disposed,
notwithstanding all the disadvantages and notwithstanding the great delay,
to entertain this appeal. I am, however, not so satisfied; and in my view we
should refuse leave to extend the time for entering this appeal.

    CAIRNS, J.: I agree that in all the circumstances of this case leave to
appeal out of time should not be given, and I base that conclusion on the reasons I
which SIR JOCELYN SIMON, P., has so fully given, to which I have nothing to
add.

Leave to appeal out of time refused.

Solicitors: *Neve, Son & Co.*, Luton (for the husband); *Derrick Bridges & Co.*
(for the wife).

[Reported by ALICE BLOOMFIELD, Barrister-at-Law.]

A

MOLLER AND ANOTHER *v.* COMMISSIONER OF ESTATE DUTY.

[PRIVY COUNCIL (Viscount Dilhorne, Lord Hodson, Lord Guest, Lord Upjohn and Sir Hugh Wooding), March 9, 13, June 7, 1967.]

B

Privy Council—Hong Kong—Estate duty—Appeal from commissioner's decision —Gift inter vivos of shares—Claim for estate duty in respect of shares— Donees not executors of donor's will—No account delivered by donees in respect of shares—Whether condition of appealing that duty should be paid or security should be given for it—Hong Kong Estate Duty Ordinance, 1932 (c. 3), s. 19 (1).

C

The respondent claimed estate duty on shares that had been the subject of a gift by the deceased in his lifetime to his four sons, of whom the appellants were two. The claim was disputed. None of the sons had delivered any account or affidavit within the meaning of the Hong Kong Estate Duty Ordinance, 1932, nor had the respondent called for any account from any of them. None of the sons was executor of the deceased's will. By s. 19 (1)* of the Ordinance any person aggrieved by the decision of the respondent had, as

D

a condition of appealing to the Hong Kong Supreme Court, either to pay or to give security for the duty claimed. By s. 11 (9)† of the Ordinance, when the respondent had ascertained the amount of duty payable in respect of any accounts delivered to him, he was to notify the accountable person of his decision, and by s. 11 (12)‡ the respondent could call on the accountable person to disclose property which ought to have been disclosed but had not been disclosed, and to deliver an account and to pay the duty. The respon-

E

dent claimed that the procedure laid down by s. 19 (1) applied to the appellants.

Held: until the accountability of the donees was determined, the respondent had no power to call on them to deliver an account (or affidavit) under s. 11 (12) of the Estate Duty Ordinance, 1932, and it was only after an account had been delivered that the respondent could reach a decision notifiable

F

under s. 11 (9) and only after he had made such a decision did s. 19 (1) become applicable; it was accordingly essential before s. 19 (1) applied that the respondent must have had accounts delivered to him, and, as no accounts had been delivered by the appellants, s. 19 was not applicable and the appellants were not subject to having to pay or to give security for the duty

G

as a condition of appealing (see p. 1038, letter H, and p. 1040, letter F, post).

Appeal allowed.

[**Editorial Note.** The provision of the Finance Act, 1894, that is comparable to s. 19 (1) of the Hong Kong Estate Duty Ordinance is s. 10 (1) of the Finance Act, 1894 (9 HALSBURY'S STATUTES (2nd Edn.) 372), but its terms are essentially different for such purposes as those of the present decision.

H

As to appeal against decisions of estate duty commissioners with respect to claims for estate duty, see 15 HALSBURY'S LAWS (3rd Edn.) 155, 156, para. 319.]

Appeal.

This was an appeal from a judgment of the Full Court of Hong Kong (RIGBY, HUGGINS and JENNINGS, JJ.), dated June 22, 1966, on a Special Case under Ord. 9, r. 8 of the Hong Kong Code of Civil Procedure, holding that s. 19 of the

I

Hong Kong Estate Duty Ordinance, 1932, applied to the appellants, Eric Blechynden Moller and Ralph Blechynden Moller, who disputed and denied the validity of a claim made for estate duty by the respondent, the Commissioner of Estate Duty, and any liability for estate duty on the subject-matter of the claim. The facts are set out in the judgment of the Board.

---

* Section 19 (1) is set out at p. 1036, letter I, to p. 1037, letter C, post.
† Section 11 (9) is set out at p. 1037, letter F, post.
‡ Section 11 (12) is set out at p. 1037, letter I, post.

E. I. Goulding, Q.C., and *J. E. Vinelott* for the appellants.   A

S. W. Templeman, Q.C., and *D. A. O'Connor* (of the Hong Kong Bar) for the respondent, the commissioner.

LORD GUEST: This appeal raises a procedural point relating to a claim by the respondent for $46,423,149, being as to $23,920,000 for estate duty on property valued at $46,000,000 and as to the balance interest thereon. Nils Eric B Amelon Moller died in Singapore on Mar. 13, 1954, and probate of his will was issued by the Supreme Court of Hong Kong on Mar. 28, 1955. He left a wife, four sons, two of whom are appellants in this appeal, and two daughters. None of the sons was an executor of the deceased's will. Before his death, the deceased had, on May 15, 1940, transferred certain shares in eleven Shanghai registered companies to his four sons. The transfers were acknowledged by the deceased C in a memorandum of gift executed on the same day. On Aug. 19, 1940, the four sons transferred the shares to Mollers Trusts, Ltd., a company incorporated in Shanghai under the Hong Kong Companies Ordinance, 1932. On Sept. 30, 1941, by a deed of undertaking and guarantee which recited the memorandum of gift, the four sons covenanted to pay to the deceased during his life and after his death to his wife during her life the sum of £1,000 per month, and Mollers Trusts, Ltd. D covenanted, inter alia, to pay the monthly sums if the sons defaulted in payment. Estate duty is payable in Hong Kong on, inter alia, property taken under a disposition made by the deceased purporting to operate as an immediate gift inter vivos if bona fide possession and enjoyment shall not have been assumed by the donee immediately and thenceforward retained to the entire exclusion of the donor or of any benefit to him by contract or otherwise.   E

It is on this basis that the respondent, the Commissioner of Estate Duty for Hong Kong, claims that estate duty is payable on the death of the deceased on the shares in Mollers Trusts, Ltd. in virtue of s. 5 and s. 6 (1) (c) of the Estate Duty Ordinance. The basis of the respondent's claim is that, in terms of s. 6 (1) (c), the shares were taken under a gift by the deceased of which property bona fide possession and enjoyment was not assumed by the donee immediately on the gift F and thenceforward retained to the entire exclusion of the donor or of any benefit to him by contract or otherwise. The appellants have at all times disputed that any estate duty is payable on the deceased's death in respect of the shares either under s. 5 or s. 6 (1) (c) of the Estate Duty Ordinance. With these and other objections this appeal is not concerned.

The parties are in dispute whether the appeal procedure provided by s. 19 of G the Estate Duty Ordinance is applicable in the circumstances under which the appellants deny the validity of the claim for estate duty and any liability to estate duty on the shares. The question of the applicability of s. 19 was submitted by a Special Case under Ord. 9, r. 8 of the Code of Civil Procedure for the decision of the Supreme Court of Hong Kong. That Case contained a statement (in para. 2 (vii)), which, in their lordships' opinion, is of cardinal importance in H this appeal in these terms:

" No account or affidavit within the meaning of the Estate Duty Ordinance has been delivered by any of the four sons or called for by the [respondent] in regard to the said shares and none of the four sons has ever paid any estate duty in connexion with the death of the deceased on the said shares or at all."   I

The Full Court of Hong Kong (consisting of RIGBY, HUGGINS and JENNINGS, JJ.), to which the Special Case had been remitted, decided, on June 22, 1966, that s. 19 was applicable. The appellants appealed by leave to the Board.

It is at the outset necessary to quote in full the provisions of s. 19 (1) of the Estate Duty Ordinance which is in the following terms:

" Any person aggrieved by the decision of the commissioner with respect to the amount of estate duty payable on an affidavit or account or with

A   respect to the repayment of any excess duty or to any claim for additional
duty by the commissioner, and whether he is aggrieved on the ground of the
value of any property or the rate charged or otherwise, may, on payment of,
or giving security for, as hereinafter mentioned, the duty claimed by the
commissioner or such portion of it as is then payable by him, appeal to the
Supreme Court within three months from the date of the decision and the
B   amount of the duty shall be determined by the Supreme Court and if the duty
is less than that paid to the commissioner the excess shall be repaid. Where
the value as alleged by the commissioner of the property in respect of which
the dispute arises does not exceed one hundred thousand dollars, the appeal
under this section shall be to the Supreme Court in its summary jurisdiction."

C   It will be noted that the person aggrieved must, as a condition precedent to his
appeal to the Supreme Court, either pay or give security for the duty claimed by
the commissioner. Every executor has to specify in accounts annexed to an
affidavit for the commissioner all the property in respect of which estate duty is
payable on the death of the deceased, and is accountable for the estate duty in
respect of all the property of which the deceased was competent to dispose at
D   his death (s. 11 (4)) and has to pay the estate duty in respect of that property on
delivering the affidavit for the commissioner (s. 9 (2)). Where property passes
on the death of the deceased and his executor is not accountable therefor, inter
alios every person to whom any property so passes for any beneficial interest in
possession is accountable for the estate duty on that property and has to deliver
to the commissioner an account specifying the property in question (s. 11 (5)).
Those accountable are required to pay the duty due on such property on delivering
E   the account (s. 9 (4)). It is the commissioner's duty to check the accounts and
affidavits delivered to him (s. 11 (8)), and it is only if no payment has been made
on delivery of the accounts and affidavits or less has been paid than he thinks is
due, or no payment has been made on property on which liability to duty arises,
that a claim by the commissioner for estate duty can arise.

F   Their lordships now approach the critical subsections of s. 11 which are in the
following terms:

" (9) When the commissioner has ascertained the amount of estate duty
payable in respect of any accounts delivered to him in pursuance of this
Ordinance he shall notify the accountable person of his decision by means of
a certificate in the prescribed form. If such amount exceeds the amount of
estate duty already paid in respect of the said accounts the accountable
G   person shall forthwith pay the excess to the commissioner.

" (10) In every case in which the commissioner is satisfied that too much
estate duty has been paid, the excess shall be repaid by him.

" (11) Where the accountable person discovers that for any reason too little
estate duty has been paid he shall forthwith deliver to the commissioner a
further account, verified by oath, and shall at the same time pay the differ-
H   ence between the estate duty chargeable according to the true value of the
estate and the estate duty already paid.

" (12) Where the commissioner discovers that any property which ought
to have been disclosed by affidavit or account has not been so disclosed he
shall notify the accountable person and call upon him to disclose such
property and pay the estate duty thereon, and the accountable person shall,
I   within one month of the giving of such notice by the commissioner, deliver an
original or a further account, as the case may require, disclosing such
property, and shall at the same time pay the estate duty thereon."

The decision of the commissioner under sub-s. (9) is, it is important to note, a
decision as to amount, the amount of duty payable " in respect of any accounts
delivered to him ". If no accounts have been delivered to him, he has no power
to decide the amount of duty. He may decide that too little has been paid by an
accountable person either on an original account delivered to him or on a further

account delivered under sub-s. (11). He may, by virtue of sub-s. (12), call on an A
accountable person to disclose property which ought to have been disclosed by
affidavit or account and has not been, and that person has then to deliver an
original or further account disclosing that property. If he does so, sub-s. (8)
applies and, after checking the account, the commissioner is able to give his
decision as to the amount of duty payable in respect of that account by virtue
of sub-s. (9).   B

Turning now to s. 19 (1), it appears that the provisions of that subsection relate
back to, and follow the sequence of, the subsections just quoted from s. 11. The
first category is of persons aggrieved by the decision of the commissioner " with
respect to the amount of estate duty payable on an affidavit or account ". Such
persons may be an executor who is accountable under s. 11 (4) and a non-
executor who is accountable under s. 11 (5). In each case the " decision " of C
the commissioner in respect of accounts delivered to him is made under s. 11 (9)
by notifying the accountable person of his " decision by means of a certificate
in the prescribed form ". So far it is clear that it is only the amount of the estate
duty which is the subject of appeal procedure under s. 19 (1). The second category
of persons aggrieved under s. 19 (1) is those aggrieved by the decision of the
commissioner " with respect to the repayment of any excess duty " under D
s. 11 (10). This again would relate to the amount of the duty; the appeal would
be by a person aggrieved by the decision of the commissioner on a claim for
repayment of duty as to the amount of the excess. Finally, the third category of
persons aggrieved is those aggrieved by the decision of the commissioner with
respect " to any claim for additional duty by the commissioner ". This would
cover the case envisaged in s. 11 (12), where the commissioner discovers that E
property which ought to have been disclosed by affidavit or account has not been
disclosed. He notifies the person accountable, and the latter has to deliver an
original or further account. In each of these three categories of persons aggrieved
the person accountable has to deliver an account to the commissioner and the
commissioner can only act under s. 11 (9) after he has ascertained the amount
of estate duty payable in respect of accounts delivered to him " in pursuance F
of this ordinance ", and then and then only does he notify his decision to the
accountable person by means of a certificate in the prescribed form. The delivery
of accounts to the commissioner is a prerequisite to his making a decision. It is
to be noted that the commissioner's powers under s. 11 (12) can only be exercised
against an accountable person—that is to say, against an executor (which by
definition includes an administrator) who is made accountable expressly by G
s. 11 (4) of the ordinance or, for example, against a person to whom property has
passed in circumstances such as are prescribed by s. 6 (1) (c). Where, as here,
however, a serious issue has been joined between the commissioner and donees
of property whether any such circumstances can be established, the ordinance
confers no authority on him to decide that the donees are accountable. Until
their accountability has been determined, he has no power to call on them H
under s. 11 (12).

The duty is clearly " additional duty " under s. 11 (11) and (12), and it may be
that the third category was inserted ex abundante cautela to make it clear that
those persons aggrieved have an equal right of appeal with the first category of
persons aggrieved. Whether that be so or not, it is plain that s. 19 (1) only comes
into play when the commissioner has made a " decision " under s. 11 (9), and he I
can only make a decision after an account has been delivered to him by an
accountable person. His authority to make a " decision " is conferred only by
s. 11 (9) and by s. 26 (2) which deals with a separate matter. Although it would
have sufficed, if only the first category was in s. 19 (1), to give any person aggrieved
by the commissioner's decision as to the amount due on the accounts the right of
appeal, the draftsman wanted to make it clear beyond all doubt that s. 19 (1)
gave a right of appeal against all the decisions under s. 11. To do so, he gave
an express right not only as to decisions on the accounts but also as to repayment

A of excess and also to a decision with respect to any claim for additional duty. The section is not very happily drafted, but the appeal is with regard to his decision with respect to a claim for additional duty and his decision with respect to any such claim is his decision on the account delivered pursuant to a claim under s. 11 (12). It cannot be anything else than on an account or affidavit. Further, as it is clear beyond doubt that the first two categories relate only to amount, it

B would be very odd if the third category went far wider and included questions of liability or accountability.

The respondent contended that s. 19 was applicable to the circumstances of this case and that the appellants must, as a condition of their appeal being heard, pay or give security for the duty, unless excused by s. 19 (3). He argued that the letter of Mar. 18, 1966, together with the letter of Apr. 14, 1966, both sent to the

C appellants' solicitors, the first of which enclosed a " revised assessment memo-randum " setting out details of the duty and interest demanded amounting to $46,432,149.60, constituted a decision of the respondent with respect to a claim for additional duty by the respondent under s. 19 (1). This, he argued, was a sufficient compliance by the respondent with s. 11 (12) calling on the person accountable to disclose the property and pay the duty. In the first place, " a

D decision with respect to any claim for additional duty " is not an apt description of what the respondent has done. A decision to prefer a claim is not a decision with respect to a claim which implies the existence of a claim at the time of the decision. In the second place, the respondent has acted before the second part of s. 11 (12), namely, the delivery by the accountable person of an account has been complied with. To read the subsection in the way in which the respondent

E commissioner does would give the commissioner an option of calling on the accountable person to pay without delivering an account, in which case the appeal procedure of s. 19 (1) might or might not be applicable according to the proper construction of s. 19 (1), or of waiting for the delivery by the accountable person to the commissioner of an account, in which case the appeal procedure of s. 19 (1) would, ex concessis, be applicable. Their lordships are unable to con-

F strue s. 11 (12) so as to import in the circumstances of this case a decision of the respondent on a claim for additional duty.

It was also argued for the respondent that the word " otherwise " to be found in s. 19 (1) in conjunction with the requirement that the person must be aggrieved by the decision of the commissioner with respect to any claim for additional duty indicated that something other than amount was intended and was in fact

G applicable to a dispute as to liability. Their lordships are not satisfied that this is necessarily so. It may be that, where the commissioner has acted under s. 11 (12) and the accountable person has delivered an account, there might be a dispute whether the account disclosed property on which estate duty was payable, a question not raising the value of the property or the rate of duty. In any case, however, their lordships do not consider that the use of the word " otherwise "

H in the context can enlarge the otherwise plainly restrictive scope of the section.

The provisions of s. 19 are penal against the subject for it compels him to pay or provide security for the amount of duty claimed as a condition of appeal against the decision of the Crown and must, therefore, be construed against the Crown in cases of doubtful construction. These provisions (if applicable) at all events where, as in this case, any obligation to account, still less to pay any duty, is

I denied, impose a great hardship on the subject; this is, indeed, the main reason for the appeal before your lordships, for the appellants have been compelled to provide a large security which they maintain is crippling if they have to continue to provide it for the number of years which the substance of the dispute may take to determine. Section 11 and s. 19 can and must literally be applied, harsh though they may be, to cases where the subject has submitted to a degree of accountability by rendering an account acknowledging some liability to account (their lordships would emphasise these latter words) on which the commissioner has some material provided by the subject to enable him to reach a " decision "

based on the subject's own documents. Their lordships cannot see, however, how   **A**
the sections can, as a matter of construction, be applied to cases where no such
liability to account is admitted and no accounts have been delivered. Having
regard to para. 2 (vii) of the Special Case to which reference has already been
made in this judgment, it seems to their lordships that these sections have no
application to the facts of this case. The respondent has power by means of
ordinary Crown process to recover estate duty where liability to the duty is   **B**
contested, and this would presumably be the method of procedure which the
commissioner would adopt in order to establish that the persons charged are
accountable. Their lordships are satisfied that this question cannot be decided
within the framework of s. 19 (1).

The judges in the Supreme Court were not at one in giving their reasons for
their decision. RIGBY, J., President of the Full Court, had considerable hesitation   **C**
in agreeing with his brethren. His doubt was whether the ordinance could be
construed as to make the respondent the judge in his own cause for the purpose
of arbitrarily imposing a liability to duty on the taxpayer. This is precisely the
ground on which JENNINGS, J., based his judgment when he said:

> " Power is given to the commissioner in s. 11 (12) of the ordinance to
> require an accountable person to disclose within a month such property   **D**
> which the commissioner discovers ought to have been disclosed by affidavit
> or account and at the same time to pay the estate duty thereon. In my view
> this power authorises the commissioner to decide what property, which has
> not been disclosed by affidavit or account, ought to have been so disclosed
> and to assess forthwith the duty payable thereon, and consequently
> empowers him to decide questions of liability as well as quantum in respect   **E**
> of additional duty."

Their lordships can see no warrant in the ordinance for any such wide power being
given to the commissioner. HUGGINS, J., agreed that the respondent had proceeded " somewhat informally " under s. 11 (12), and that he did not follow
strictly the provisions of this section. He expressed the view that it did not matter   **F**
that there was no account delivered before the respondent made his decision. As
their lordships have already indicated, they regard a strict compliance with
s. 11 (9) and (12) as necessary, and that it is essential that, before there is decision
by the respondent under s. 19 (1), he must have had the accounts delivered to him.

Their lordships desire to add that s. 11 (9) requires the respondent to notify
his decision " by means of a certificate in the prescribed form ". They were
informed that no certificate had been prescribed under s. 25 of the ordinance.   **G**
There was in this case no decision of the respondent contained in a certificate
and, until the form of the certificate has been prescribed, it is difficult to see how
there can be any valid notification of the respondent's decision against the subject.
If this point had been taken by the appellants either in the court below or in
their Case, it might well have been a factor decisive against the respondent.
Their lordships, however, do not base their decision on this ground, but it serves   **H**
to reinforce their view that there is a necessity for formality and a strict
compliance with the terms of s. 11.

Their lordships will humbly advise Her Majesty that the appeal should be
allowed and that the decision of the Full Court of Hong Kong, dated June 22,
1966, should be reversed and that the question of law for the opinion of the court
in the Special Case, dated May 23, 1966, should be answered in the negative. No   **I**
order for costs was made by the Full Court by agreement of parties, but the
respondent must pay the appellants' costs of the appeal before the Board.

Appeal allowed.

Solicitors: *Norton, Rose, Botterell & Roche* (for the appellants); *Charles Russell
& Co.* (for the respondent).

[*Reported by* KATHLEEN J. H. O'BRIEN, *Barrister-at-Law.*]

A

WELLS AND OTHERS v. MINISTER OF HOUSING AND LOCAL GOVERNMENT AND ANOTHER.

[COURT OF APPEAL, CIVIL DIVISION (Lord Denning, M.R., Davies and Russell, L.JJ.), April 13, 14, 17, 18, May 11, 1967.]

B

Town and Country Planning—Development—Permission for development— Determination whether permission needed—Application for determination— Implicit in application for planning permission—Letter of local planning authority that proposed erection of plant could be regarded as permitted development sufficient determination—Bye-law consent granted subsequently for larger plant—Warning against acting on bye-law consent before planning approval deleted from consent form—Whether deletion on bye-law consent amounted to determination that planning permission not required—Town and Country Planning Act, 1962 (10 & 11 Eliz. 2 c. 38), s. 43 (1).

C

In December, 1962, the applicants, who were builders' merchants and who had for many years made concrete blocks in a building thirty-two feet high, applied to the local planning authority for planning permission to erect a concrete batching plant twenty-seven feet six inches high. As the proposed plant was not for a process that the applicants had previously carried on it might have needed planning permission. The local planning · authority replied by letter dated Mar. 1, 1963, stating that the works proposed could be regarded as permitted development under Class VIII of the Town and Country Planning General Development Order, 1950, and that, therefore, it was not proposed to take any further action on the application. The applicants did not erect the twenty-seven feet six inches high plant, but decided to build one forty-eight feet high. Thinking that that plant would be covered by the letter of Mar. 1, 1963, they applied only for bye-law consent, writing on the application form " Permitted development consent granted Mar. 1, 1963 ". On Jan. 23, 1964, the local authority granted the bye-law consent and, on the official notification, deleted the words " No action should be taken hereunder till the approval of the town planning authority and licensing authority have been obtained ". The applicants erected the forty-eight feet high plant but, as a result of complaints by local residents, the local planning authority served an enforcement notice requiring the applicants to take the plant down.   On appeal and cross-appeal to the Court of Appeal,

D

E

F

Held: (i) (RUSSELL, L.J., dissenting) the letter of Mar. 1, 1963, was a valid determination by the local planning authority under s. 43* of the Town and Country Planning Act, 1962, and was irrevocable, the local planning authority being entitled to make a determination under s. 43 without a formal written application and an application for planning permission implying an invitation to determine under s. 43 that no planning permission was necessary (see p. 1045, letter B, and p. 1046, letters F and I, post).

G

H

(ii) the enforcement notice in respect of the forty-eight feet high plant was good, because in order to satisfy s. 43 there must be a positive statement in writing by or on behalf of the local planning authority that planning permission was not required (see p. 1045, letters C and E, p. 1047, letter A, and p. 1051, letter B, post).

I

Appeal and cross-appeal dismissed.

[As to applications to determine whether planning permission is required, see 37 HALSBURY'S LAWS (3rd Edn.) 273-275, para. 372.

---

* Section 43 (1), so far as material, provides: " If any person who proposes to carry out any operations on land, or to make any change in the use of land, wishes to have it determined whether the carrying out of those operations, or the making of that change, would constitute or involve development of the land, and, if so, whether an application for planning permission in respect thereof is required . . . he may . . . apply to the local planning authority to determine that question ".

For the Town and Country Planning Act, 1962, s. 43, see 42 HALSBURY'S A
STATUTES (2nd Edn.) 1013.]

Cases referred to:

City & Westminster Properties (1934), Ltd. v. Mudd, [1958] 2 All E.R. 733;
    (1959) Ch. 129;   [1958] 3 W.L.R. 312;   Digest (Cont. Vol. A) 1027,
    6376a.

Howell v. Falmouth Boat Construction, Ltd., [1951] 2 All E.R. 278; [1951] A.C. B
    837; 21 Digest (Repl.) 399, 1260.

Inglis v. John Buttery & Co., (1878), 3 App. Cas. 552; 17 Digest (Repl.) 268,
    717.

Robertson v. Minister of Pensions, [1948] 2 All E.R. 767;   [1949] 1 K.B. 227;
    [1949] L.J.R. 323; 21 Digest (Repl.) 399, 1259.

Sassoon (M. A.) & Sons, Ltd. v. International Banking Corpn., [1927] A.C. 711; C
    96 L.J.P.C. 153; 137 L.T. 501; 17 Digest (Repl.) 364, 1705.

Appeal and cross-appeal.

This was an appeal by the applicants, Alfred Laming Wells, A. L. Wells &
Son, Ltd. and A. L. Wells & Son (Premix), Ltd., from an order of the Divisional
Court of the Queen's Bench Division (LORD PARKER, C.J., SALMON, L.J., and D
WIDGERY, J.), dated Nov. 15, 1966, allowing the applicants' appeal from a
decision of the first respondent, the Minister of Housing and Local Government,
dismissing, by letter dated Apr. 19, 1966, their appeal against an enforcement
notice served on them by Leatherhead Urban District Council, the second
respondents, on behalf of the local planning authority, to the extent that the
matter be remitted to the Minister for reconsideration. The Minister cross- E
appealed asking that the order of the Divisional Court be set aside.   The first
applicant was the managing director of the second applicants and a director
and chairman of the third applicants. The enforcement notice was addressed
to the applicants as being the owner and occupier or a person interested in the
land and premises known as A. L. Wells & Son, Ltd., Builders Merchants Yard
and Premises, Garland Road, Leatherhead, Surrey.   The facts are set out in the F
judgment of LORD DENNING, M.R.

Douglas Frank, Q.C., and Lord de Mauley for the applicants.
S. C. Silkin, Q.C., and Nigel Bridge for the respondents.

                                                                Cur. adv. vult.
May 11. The following judgments were read.
                                                                              G

    LORD DENNING, M.R.: There is a large builder's yard at Leatherhead.
It is set in the midst of a residential area close to the playing-fields of St. John's
School and not far from the Leatherhead by-pass.   The builder's yard covers
over three acres and has several buildings on it.   It is occupied by a firm of
builders' merchants.   For many years they have made concrete blocks there
in a building which is thirty-two feet high.   The applicants undoubtedly have H
" existing use " rights which enables them to carry on their existing processes
without getting planning permission.   They are also entitled to erect a new
structure for use in those processes, provided it does not exceed fifty feet in height
and does not materially affect the external appearance; see Class VIII of the
General Development Order (1).

    In December, 1962, the applicants proposed to erect in the yard a " concrete I
batching plant ".   This is a plant in which concrete is mixed ready for use; and
then, whilst wet, is taken round in lorries to building sites in the district.   The
proposed plant was only to be twenty-seven feet six inches high and did not

_____

(1) See Class VIII in Sch. 1, Pt. 1 to the Town and Country Planning General Develop-
ment, 1950, S.I. 1950 No. 728 (Pt. 1); 21 HALSBURY'S STATUTORY INSTRUMENTS (First
Re-Issue) 103, which was revoked and replaced on May 1, 1963, by Class VIII in Sch. 1,
Pt. 1 to the like-named order of 1963, S.I. 1963 No. 709.

A   materially affect the external appearance; but the process was not an *existing* process. It was a *new* process which the applicants had not carried on before. So it might not come within Class VIII and might need planning permission. At any rate, in order to clear up any difficulties, the architect, on Dec. 21, 1962, applied to the Leatherhead Urban District Council (who are the delegates of the planning authority) for planning permission. He enclosed a drawing of the

B   proposed batching plant twenty-seven feet six inches high and added that

> ". . . the plant is sited so that it is screened by existing trees and has been designed so that the height of the structure is lower than the existing workshops . . . Subject to planning permission being obtained, bye-law permission will be sought regarding details . . ."

C   On Mar. 1, 1963, the council surveyor replied to the architect:

> ". . . I am now instructed to inform you that the works proposed can be regarded as ' permitted development ' under Class VIII of the Town and Country Planning Development Order, 1950 . . . and it is therefore not proposed to take any further action on your application. My council have, however, asked me to request your co-operation in arranging for a scheme of

D   > tree planting to be carried out along the southern boundary of your site in order to preserve the amenities of the locality. I note that you will be supplying bye-law details in due course."

The applicants did not, however, erect the twenty-seven feet six inches plant. They changed their minds and decided to build a much higher plant which was forty-eight feet high. This was so high that it would materially affect the external

E   appearance. It did not satisfy the conditions of Class VIII, and on that account, beyond all doubt, it needed planning permission; but the architect did not appreciate this. He thought that this bigger plant was covered by the previous letter of Mar. 1, 1963. So he only applied for bye-law consent (2). On Dec. 30, 1963, he filled in a form of application for bye-law consent enclosing a plan of the new proposed forty-eight feet plant. At the foot of the form there was a printed

F   notice saying:

> " Applications for consent under the Town Planning Acts should be made on a separate form available at the council offices on request."

The architect, however, thought that this did not apply in this case. He wrote on the form: " Permitted development consent granted Mar. 1, 1963." The

G   council and their officers seem to have been under the same misapprehension as the architect. The council, on Jan. 23, 1964, granted the bye-law consent; and when they sent out the official notification, the following words on the form were deleted with a line drawn through them:

> " No action should be taken hereunder till the approval of the town planning authority and licensing authority has been obtained."

H   Although deleted, those words were still legible. The person who deleted them must have thought that planning permission was not necessary in this case. Hence he struck out the words which said that planning approval should be obtained. This deletion no doubt confirmed the architect in his belief that no planning permission was necessary. He told the applicants that they could safely go ahead and erect the forty-eight feet plant. So the applicants, believing

I   that no planning permission was necessary, erected the forty-eight feet plant. At once the residents complained. No doubt they objected to the appearance, but their main grievance was the nuisance and annoyance caused by the traffic. The big lorries came in and out along their residential roads with ready-mixed

---

(2) This was an application to the Engineer and Surveyor's department of Leatherhead Urban District Council, dated Dec. 30, 1963, headed " New Streets and Buildings ", giving notice of an intended new building, viz., the concrete batching plant. It was noted " Permitted Development Consent granted Mar. 1, 1963 ", on the top of the second folio.

concrete. Faced with these complaints, the local council took action. On A
Feb. 26, 1965, they served an enforcement notice requiring the applicants to
take down the forty-eight feet plant. The applicants appealed to the Minister
of Housing and Local Government. He upheld the enforcement notice. They
appealed to the Divisional Court. The judges were divided in opinion. The
majority (LORD PARKER, C.J., and WIDGERY, J.), allowed the appeal in part and
remitted the matter to the Minister for reconsideration. SALMON, L.J., would B
have allowed the appeal altogther and quashed the enforcement notice. Both
sides appeal to this court.

1. *The twenty-seven feet six inches plant.*—In the letter of Mar. 1, 1963, the
council said that the twenty-seven feet six inches plant could be regarded as
permitted development under Class VIII. The applicants rely on that letter.
They say that it amounted to a determination under s. 43 of the Town and C
Country Planning Act, 1962, that no planning permission was required; and that
this determination cannot be revoked. The Minister says that it was no such thing.
In order for there to be a valid determination under s. 43, there must be, he says,
a written application for the purpose, either by itself or combined with an application for planning permission; and that, in the absence of a written application,
the letter of Mar. 1, 1963, was of no effect. The Minister goes so far as to say that, D
even if the applicants on the faith of the letter had erected the twenty-seven feet
six inches plant, the planning authority could have come along with an enforcement notice and compelled them to take it down. Pressed on the point, counsel
for the Minister said that the letter of Mar. 1, 1963, was of no effect unless the
architect followed it up by a formal application under s. 43: " Will you please
determine whether planning permission is required? ", and received the answer: E
" None is required." I cannot believe that that is correct. If we were to require
the applicants to go through such a formality, it would be a work of supererogation. Nay more, it would be a trap. Anyone receiving such a letter as that of
Mar. 1, 1963, would think that that was enough. He would not dream of doing
more. Nor should he be bound to do so.

Now I know that a public authority cannot be estopped from doing its public F
duty, but I do think that it can be estopped from relying on technicalities; and
this is a technicality, to be sure. We were told that for many years the planning
authorities, including the Minister himself, have written letters on the same lines
as the letter of Mar. 1, 1963. It has been their practice to tell applicants that no
planning permission is necessary. Are they now to be allowed to say that this
practice was all wrong and their letters were of no effect? I do not think so. I G
take the law to be that a defect in procedure can be cured, and an irregularity
can be waived, even by a public authority, so as to render valid that which would
otherwise be invalid. Thus, in *Robertson* v. *Minister of Pensions* (3), an assurance
(that Colonel Robertson's disability was accepted as attributable to war service)
was held binding on the Crown, even though it was given independently by the
War Office instead of the Ministry of Pensions. And in *Howell* v. *Falmouth* H
Boat Construction, Ltd. (4), a defect in the licence (about the cocktail bar) was
disregarded by the House of Lords (5). So also Sir Alexander Turner's edition of
SPENCER BOWER ON ESTOPPEL BY REPRESENTATION, pp. 136-137. So here the
position is this. On Dec. 21, 1962, the applicants made in writing an application
for planning permission. They made no written application for a determination
under s. 43 of the Act of 1962; but that omission was only a defect in procedure. I
It did not prevent the planning authority from considering the matter if they
thought fit. If they decided that it was unnecessary, they were entitled to
tell the applicants so. Once the planning authority determined that no planning
permission was necessary, and told the applicants so, that was a determination

(3) [1948] 2 All E.R. 767; [1949] 1 K.B. 227.
(4) [1951] 2 All E.R. 278; [1951] A.C. 837.
(5) [1951] 2 All E.R. at p. 284; [1951] A.C. at p. 848.

A within s. 43, even though there had been no formal application before them for that purpose.

I hold, therefore, that the letter of Mar. 1, 1963, was a valid determination under s. 43; and, as such, it was irrevocable by the planning authority, just as is a planning permission. I put it on the ground that the planning authority waived any formal application and determined the matter straight away. Another way

B of putting it would be to say that the application for planning permission contained an implied invitation to the planning authority to make a determination under s. 43, if they thought fit to do so, holding that no permission was necessary. Whichever way it is put, however, it comes back to this: the planning authority are entitled to make a determination under s. 43 without the necessity of a formal written application.

C 2. *The forty-eight feet plant.* This stands on a different footing. There was no application for planning permission at all, only an application for bye-law consent. There was no statement by the council that no planning permission was necessary, only the deletion of a sentence in the bye-law approval. I cannot regard this deletion as a determination under s. 43. The general rule is that you do not look at words that have been deleted. They are struck out and are to be treated as if

D they were not in the document at all; see *Inglis* v. *John Buttery & Co.* (6), per LORD HATHERLEY, L.C., and *M. A. Sassoon & Sons, Ltd.* v. *International Banking Corpn.* (7), per VISCOUNT SUMNER. There may be exceptions to the general rule; but none of them would enable us to elevate this deletion into a positive determination that no planning permission was necessary. Ready as I am to waive irregularities and procedural defects, I think that to satisfy s. 43 there must be

E at least a positive statement in writing by or on behalf of the planning authority that no planning permission is necessary. Otherwise there would be no certainty at all in these important matters. In the absence of such a statement, I hold that planning permission was necessary for the forty-eight feet plant. It was not obtained. The enforcement notice in that respect is good.

3. *The matters to be considered.* In considering the appeal, the Minister ought

F to have taken into consideration the fact that the applicants had in their favour an irrevocable determination that, in respect of the twenty-seven feet six inches plant no planning permission was necessary. He seems to have ignored it. It seems that the traffic would be just as great a nuisance with the twenty-seven feet six inches plant as with the forty-eight feet plant. In those circumstances he might have allowed the forty-eight feet plant to remain. In the circumstances

G I think that the case should be remitted to him to take it into account.

I find myself in substantial agreement with the views of LORD PARKER, C.J., and WIDGERY, J., and would dismiss the appeal and the cross-appeal.

DAVIES, L.J.: The written application made by the applicants on Dec. 21, 1962, under cover of the letter of the same date, was an application for planning

H permission and nothing else. It is the contention of the Minister of Housing and Local Government that, on such an application, the planning authority has no power to determine under s. 43 of the Town and Country Planning Act, 1962, that an application for planning permission is not required. Before such a determination can be made, it is said, it is essential that a written application in that behalf should have been made in accordance with art. 5 (4) of the General Development Order (8), either as a separate application or as a part of an application for

I planning permission. This submission is supported by reference to various provisions of the Act of 1962 and, in particular, to s. 22 (2) and s. 181 (3). By s. 43 (2), the provisions of s. 22 are incorporated into what may be called the determination procedure; and what is said is that, in the absence of a written

(6) (1878), 3 App. Cas. 552 at p. 558.
(7) [1927] A.C. 711 at p. 723.
(8) I.e., art. 5 (4) of the Town and Country Planning General Development Order, 1950, S.I. 1950 No. 728 (Pt. 1); 21 HALSBURY'S STATUTORY INSTRUMENTS (First Re-Issue) 91. See now art. 5 (4) of the like-named order of 1963, S.I. 1963 No. 709.

application for a determination, it would be impossible for the Minister to exercise A
his powers under s. 22 to " call in " to himself such an application. Similarly, it
is pointed out that s. 181 (3) draws a marked distinction between an application
for planning permission and an application for determination under s. 43.

There can be no doubt that there are difficulties; but, in my view, one must
look at this matter realistically. We have been informed by counsel that it has
been the practice not only of planning authorities but also of the Minister himself B
when dealing with planning applications to make on occasions a s. 43 determination. There can be no doubt whatsoever that, by their letter of Mar. 1, 1963, the
planning authority purported to determine that planning permission was not
required. I will forbear to repeat the terms of that letter as it has already been
read by LORD DENNING, M.R. Nothing could be plainer than those terms; and
it is reasonably clear from the later documents of Dec. 30, 1963, and Jan. 23, 1964, C
that both the applicants and the planning authority were of the opinion that this
was the position. To my mind, it is really fantastic to suggest that, on receipt of
the letter of Mar. 1, 1963, the applicants ought either to have submitted a written
application for a determination or else to have appealed against the planning
authority's failure to deal with the planning application by means of a grant or
refusal of permission. If the applicants had taken either of these courses, I D
imagine that the planning authority might well have been displeased and might
have thought that the applicants had taken leave of their senses. It was sought
to be suggested that the planning authority would have in mind quite different
considerations when considering an application for a determination from those
which would be relevant to an application for planning permission. It is, of course,
true, as counsel for the Minister pointed out, that a planning decision is a policy E
decision and that a determination is quasi-judicial. It seems to me, however, that,
in the great majority of cases, the two matters are closely commingled and that
the question whether planning permission is required is a preliminary to the
question whether permission should be granted.

At the end of it all I find myself in complete agreement with LORD DENNING
and the majority of the Divisional Court. Unless a written application for a F
determination is made, then there is, of course, no duty on the planning authority
to make any such determination; but in a planning application there must be
taken to be an implied invitation to the planning authority to determine, if they
are of that opinion, that planning permission is not required. It is as if the
applicant were to send with his planning application a letter to the effect that, if
the planning authority were of the opinion that permission was not required, he G
would be glad to be informed of that fact. Although there is no prescribed form
for a s. 43 application, it could hardly, I think, be said that such a letter could
amount to a written application under s. 43. I have had the opportunity of
reading in advance the judgment which RUSSELL, L.J., is about to deliver. It
has to be acknowledged that the considerations which he advances on the
interpretation and implementation of the Act of 1962 are, of course, weighty; H
but, with respect, despite them I remain, in the light of the practice hitherto
from time to time adopted, of the opinion which I have expressed above.

In my judgment, therefore, the letter of Mar. 1, 1963, was a determination
under s. 43 and the cross-appeal fails.

Like LORD DENNING and the majority of the Divisional Court, I take exactly
the opposite view as to the effect of the documents of Dec. 30, 1963, and Jan. 23, I
1964. The application of Dec. 30, 1963, was not a town planning application; it
was a public health one. It was not an application for planning permission or for
a determination. It was based on a complete misapprehension that permitted
development had been granted (to use the words of the letter) by the letter of
Mar. 1, 1963, and that, therefore, no determination or permission was necessary.
The determination of Mar. 1, 1963, was that no permission was required for the
erection of the twenty-seven feet six inches structure; and it is admitted by the
applicants that, whatever the effect of that determination, it cannot assist them

A as to the forty-eight feet structure. Moreover, it is quite impossible to treat the
bye-law permission of Jan. 23, 1964, containing as it does the erasure of remark
No. 1, as an express determination that planning permission was not required.
In my judgment, therefore, the appeal also fails.

I would add that it is not easy to see on what ground the Minister treated the
history of the twenty-seven feet six inches structure and the document of Mar. 1,
B 1963, as irrelevant to his consideration of the appeal to his discretionary power
under s. 46 (1) (*a*). I should have thought that these matters were highly relevant,
despite the fact that the applicants did not in fact erect the twenty-seven feet
six inches structure. Also relevant, in my view, would be the fact that the
applicants were misled by the planning authority into incurring the expense of
erecting the forty-eight feet structure, that, if they are to reduce it to twenty-
C seven feet six inches, there will be much more expense, and that, according to the
evidence before the inspector, a twenty-seven feet six inches structure would
result in even heavier road traffic than does the forty-eight feet one. The weight
of all these matters is, of course, a matter for the Minister.

RUSSELL, L.J.: Among the decisions which from time to time have to be
D made by the appropriate authority under the Town and Country Planning Act,
1962, are two types which differ radically from each other in character. One is a
decision on an application for planning permission, which involves in the main the
application of policy and perhaps taste in the discretion of the decider. The other
is a decision, called a determination under s. 43 (1), whether proposed operations
on land, or a proposed change of its use, (a) would constitute or involve develop-
E ment, and, if so, (b) whether an application for planning permission in respect
thereof is *required* having regard to the provisions of the development order.
Such a determination does not involve discretion or policy or taste; it is an adjudication on the law as applicable to determined facts, and in theory at least there is
in any case only one correct determination. It may be further remarked that grant
of planning permission and a favourable determination under s. 43 in respect of
F the same proposals may differ greatly in their effects. An example was given of a
baker's shop with a proposed change to a butcher's shop. The determination
would be favourable, even if the shop use had been initiated only two years before
without a planning right to do so; but it would not protect the butcher's shop from
an enforcement notice within the next two years. Aliter, if planning permission
were given for a butcher's shop. Again, if planning permission is given for some
G proposal, it represents a policy view of the responsible authority; a favourable
determination might represent something quite contrary to the policy view. If
the landlowner was selling to someone who wished to buy in order to put the land
to a particular industrial use, the planning permission would be a far stronger
assurance to the purchaser that he would be able to achieve and retain his object
and that he was not likely to be faced with a revocation or discontinuance order
H and left without the factory he wanted but only with land and a compensation
claim.

With those preliminary remarks I approach first the question whether there was
a s. 43 determination favourable to the twenty-seven feet six inches concrete
batching plant by virtue of the letter of Mar. 1, 1963, from the local planning
authority following the application for planning permission in respect of that
I project. This question arises (on the cross-appeal) because, if there was no later
determination in respect of the forty-eight feet plant, but there was a determination in respect of the twenty-seven feet six inches plant, the Minister of Housing
and Local Government, in deciding on the proper action to be taken in respect
of the former, should (it is said) have directed his mind to the fact that a twenty-
seven feet six inches plant could be lawfully substituted for a removed forty-eight
feet plant unless there were a discontinuance order or revocation with consequent
compensation. I have no doubt that, if there had been an application for a
determination under s. 43 in respect of the twenty-seven feet six inches project,

accompanying or as part of the application for planning permission, that letter   A
would have been a notification of a favourable determination. In substance it
says: " Your proposals, though involving development, do not require an
application for planning permission, having regard to the provisions of the
development order." It goes on to indicate that the local planning authority
does not propose to take any *further* action; which suggests that it has taken *some*
action, which could only be a determination, and that it was purporting to treat   B
the application for planning permission as an application for a s. 43 determination. Moreover, the form of the letter indicates that the local planning authority
had not considered at all the planning aspects of the proposal, but only that which
I have described as the judicial question. The applicants could, of course, on
receiving this letter have pressed their application for planning permission or
could, after the lapse of the requisite time, have appealed from a deemed refusal   C
of that application. If they had pressed their application for planning permission,
the local planning authority might have refused it on amenity grounds.

For the Minister, it is urged that the letter cannot have been a determination
under s. 43 because an application in writing for such a determination, invoking
the judicial jurisdiction, is, under the statute and development order, an essential
preliminary to an effective determination, one that cannot be waived by the   D
local planning authority and one that the local planning authority cannot estop
itself from asserting did not exist. The statutory provisions start with s. 43 (1)
which is *all* about *applications* for a determination. It enables a person to make an
application to the local planning authority if he wishes to have determined the
question whether (i.e., whether or not) his proposals would involve development
and (if so) whether (i.e., whether or not) planning permission is required under   E
the Act of 1962 and the development order. This application for such determination may be made either as part of an application for planning permission
or without such last-mentioned application.   Under the development order,
the application for a determination must be in writing (9); and this must be so
whether or not it is part of an application for planning permission. A mere
application for planning permission cannot, therefore, carry with it an implied   F
application for a s. 43 determination in respect of the same proposal. There are
other cogent reasons why there cannot be an implied application for a determination. A landowner may, of course, not want a determination by the local planning
authority at all. The development order (10) requires that such an application
should be forwarded to the local borough or district council, and, if that council is
not the planning authority, it must forward it to the local planning authority,   G
which would in such case no doubt be the county council. The purpose of
this provision is that, in every case, the local council shall know what applications
are being made to the local planning authority before any decision is reached.
Under the development order (11), the local planning authority may be required
to supply the Minister with information with respect to an application for a
determination.   H

Section 43 (2) provides for the consequences of an application under s. 43 (1)
and of any determination made thereon by incorporating with any necessary
modifications certain sections relating to applications for planning permission.
Of these, it is to be observed that s. 19 (4) and (5) envisage the keeping of a
register of applications open to public inspection. Section 22 provides for the
possibility of an application being called in by the Minister. Section 24, in   I
connexion with appeals, provides for an assumed refusal of an application if
nothing is done by the local planning authority within a limited time; as applied
to an application for a determination, this must assume determination in a sense
adverse to the applicant. Section 181 deals separately with appeals to the High

(9) See art. 5 (4) of the Town and Country Planning General Development Order,
1963, S.I. 1963 No. 709.
(10) See art. 5 (5) of the above order.
(11) See art. 5 (11) of the above order.

A Court from decisions by the Minister on applications under s. 43, either on appeal from a determination by the local planning authority, or on an application for a determination called in by the Minister; sub-s. (3) in particular stresses that an application under s. 43 as part of an application for planning permission is something separate and severable to which alone s. 181 applies.

B Not only do these matters negative any possibility of an implied application for a determination, but it appears to me that they indicate that the ability to make a valid determination is dependent on an application for a determination having been made. I point in particular to these matters already mentioned. If the county council, as local planning authority, could make a valid determination in circumstances akin to the present, the safeguard of local interests afforded by the need to send applications through the local authority would be sidetracked.

C Similarly, the requirement (if imposed) on the local planning authority to give to the Minister information of any application under s. 43 would be sidetracked. Again, the power of the Minister to call in any such application would be side-tracked. In the Divisional Court, WIDGERY, J., considered that, because deter-minations under s. 43 can have wide-reaching effects, it is necessary that some element of formality be attached to them. He considered it necessary that an

D application should be made to the local planning authority

" so that the matter is brought before the local authority's attention in such a way as to make it clear to them that they are being asked to determine the question under the section [though specific reference to the section was not necessary]. Nothing less than that I think would do . . ."

E With all that I agree; WIDGERY, J., then concluded, however, that every applica-tion for planning permission had implicit in it not an application for a s. 43 determination of the proposals, but an invitation, should the local planning authority consider the facts justified such a course, to the local planning authority to treat the application for planning permission as an application for a determina-tion. He further stated that the questions involved in a determination under

F s. 43 are brought before the local planning authority in a serious way, because, in considering an application for planning permission, they are bound to direct their attention and minds to the question whether planning permission is required or not.

I think, with respect, that this exposition contains two serious defects. First, it means that an applicant who has no desire for a determination and has not

G applied for one, and who may prefer to test the judicial question otherwise, may find himself saddled with an adverse determination and subsequent appeal pro-cedures. Secondly, it is not correct to say that, on an application for planning permission, the local planning authority is bound to consider the questions posed by s. 43. I have already remarked that there is a great difference between the question of grant or refusal of planning permission and the judicial question under

H s. 43, and a great difference in the effects of the answers to the questions. It would not be right to say that the local planning authority, having formed a " favour-able " view on the s. 43 question, is entitled to ignore the question of planning permission: in the present case, as already remarked, there was a deemed refusal of the application for planning permission because of the inaction thereon of the local planning authority. LORD PARKER, C.J., agreed with WIDGERY, J. SALMON,

I L.J., had, he considered, a slightly different approach. He considered that no application for a determination was ever necessary, but that a determination could validly always be made on an application for planning permission at the will of the local planning authority. This conclusion suffers, I think, from the same defects. There is no doubt that the Divisional Court was led to the answer given by what appeared to be the absurd situation that a letter formally asking for confirmation of the letter of Mar. 1, 1963, as a determination, followed by a confirmation, would have cured the matter; though the machinery appropriate to a s. 43 application would, I think, have to be applied to the letter asking

confirmation. SALMON, L.J., in particular referred to the "unreality" of the A
situation. But "unreality" is not necessarily a description of a state of affairs
which denies its legal existence; it begs the question whether the problem is not
posed within technical and artificial confines. If the definition of an apparatus
requires the cart to be pushed by the horse, it is no valid criticism of a correct
statement made about the apparatus that the statement puts the cart before the
horse.   B

In this court, LORD DENNING, M.R., considers that the requirement of an application in writing for a determination can be waived by the local planning
authority, which will cure a mere defect in procedure or irregularity; or,
alternatively, that the application for planning permission contained an implied
invitation to make a determination under s. 43 but only (as I understand it) in a
sense favourable to the applicant. For the reasons that I have given, which show, C
it seems to me, that an actual application in writing is an essential part of the
machinery for determinations, I cannot agree with this conclusion. The local
planning authority is not a free agent to waive statutory requirements in favour
of (so to speak) an adversary; it is the guardian of the planning system. Nor do
I find myself able to accept the notion of an invitation to determine the judicial
question but only if the determination is one way. DAVIES, L.J., takes the same D
attitude, regarding anything else as unrealistic. In truth I think, with great
respect, that these views stem in large measure from a natural indignation that a
practice, which seems to have grown up since the system in this form was
introduced in 1947, should operate merely as a trap for the unwary landowner.
The question is, however, one of law not to be decided by a thoroughly bad
administrative practice. Suppose shortly after the Town and Country Planning E
Act, 1947, a mere application for planning permission reaching the Minister
either on appeal from a refusal by the local planning authority or called in;
suppose that the Minister wrote a letter on the lines of the March, 1963, letter. If
that were in law a determination (though never applied for), the local planning
authority would be entitled to dispute its correctness in law in the High Court
under s. 181. What in such case would have been the answer in the High Court F
when the landowner, unwilling to be a litigant in the High Court, took a preliminary point that the proceedings did not lie because he had neither wished for
nor applied for a determination and the Minister could not have made one unless
one was applied for? I do not think that in such case the landowner would have
been told that his point was unsound either because (a) the Minister was entitled
to waive the need for any application, thus precipitating the unwilling landowner G
into High Court proceedings, or because (b) all unknown to the landowner he had
impliedly invited the Minister to make a "favourable" determination and thus
precipitated himself into High Court proceedings under a section which in terms
was limited to cases of applications for s. 43 determinations.

On the footing that the March, 1963, letter was a determination for the purposes
of s. 43, however, I entirely agree that it is a factor relevant to the Minister's H
decision, and that he should reconsider the matter in the light of the fact that the
local planning authority has determined that the applicants have a right to erect
and operate the twenty-seven feet six inches project; though it may not alter his
decision.

Turning to the applicants' contention that the grant of building bye-law
approval for the forty-eight feet project constituted a favourable determination I
under s. 43 in relation to that project, I agree that it was not. The application
purported to be only a bye-law application, and the reference in it to the previous
"permitted development" serves only to show that the applicants considered
(and indeed were asserting and reminding) that neither planning permission nor
a favourable determination were required. I cannot see that this can be taken to
be in effect a question. Nor can the approval be considered a determination. It
was in express terms pursuant to the powers conferred by and for the purposes of
the Public Health Acts. Reliance was placed on the deleted but still legible first

A of the Remarks, which warned against acting on the faith of the approval without getting town planning permission. Whether the deletion of words may be used in aid of construction of other parts of a document may be doubtful; deleted words are intended not to exist, even though not illegibly erased. As to this, see the cases referred to by HARMAN, J., in *City & Westminster Properties (1934), Ltd.*
B v. *Mudd* (12). I am quite confident, however, that deleted words cannot stand up by themselves as a positive statement of the contrary. An additional last moment argument was based on a failure by the local planning authority to comply with s. 64 (2) of the Public Health Act, 1936, and some speculative notes in LUMLEY'S PUBLIC HEALTH, but it did not bear examination.

I would have allowed the cross-appeal, and I concur in dismissing the appeal.

C *Appeal and cross-appeal dismissed.   Leave for the Minister to appeal to the House of Lords refused.*

Solicitors: *Tuck & Mann and Geffen & Co.* (for the applicants); *Solicitor, Ministry of Housing and Local Government.*

[*Reported by* F. GUTTMAN, ESQ., *Barrister-at-Law.*]

D ----

J. W. DWYER, LTD. *v.* RECEIVER FOR THE METROPOLITAN POLICE DISTRICT.

E [QUEEN'S BENCH DIVISION (Lyell, J.), May 1, 2, 1967.]

Riot—Damage—Compensation—Four robbers entering shop and threatening occupants—Incident not attracting the attention of anyone outside the shop—Whether assembly " tumultuous " as well as riotous—Whether police authority liable to pay compensation—Riot (Damages) Act, 1886 (49 & 50 Vict. c. 38), s. 2.

F   At about 9.40 a.m. on a Saturday morning the plaintiffs' jewellery shop and pledge department were entered by four men who threatened two employees and a customer with iron bars, and proceeded to effect a robbery. The manager's wife, who was upstairs, heard an unusual noise and on entering the shop to investigate was similarly threatened.   The men then took property from the shop to a waiting van and, within a very short time,
G had left.   Although a certain amount of noise and commotion was caused it did not attract the attention of anyone outside the shop, nor was it heard by the proprietor of the shop next door.   On a claim by the plaintiffs against the Receiver for the Metropolitan Police District under s. 2* of the Riot (Damages) Act, 1886,

Held: the claim failed because the thieves had not satisfied the require-
H ment of s. 2 that they should be assembled tumultuously as well as riotously, a tumultuous assembly being one where the rioters were in such numbers and such a state of agitated commotion and were so acting that the forces of law and order should have been well aware of the threat which existed and have taken steps to prevent damage being caused (see p. 1055, letters A and H, post).

I   *Field* v. *Metropolitan Police Receiver* ([1904-07] All E.R. Rep. 435) considered.

[As to compensation for riot, see 30 HALSBURY'S LAWS (3rd Edn.) 86, 87, para. 145; and for cases on the subject, see 37 DIGEST (Repl.) 207-209, *116-134.*

For the Riot (Damages) Act, 1886, s. 2, see 18 HALSBURY'S STATUTES (2nd Edn.) 96.]

----

(12) [1958] 2 All E.R. 733 at p. 739 et seq; [1959] Ch. 129 at p. 140 et seq.
* Section 2 (1) is set out at p. 1053, letter E, post.

Case referred to: A

    Field v. *Metropolitan Police Receiver*, [1904-07] All E.R. Rep. 435; [1907]
        2 K.B. 853; 76 L.J.K.B. 1015; 97 L.T. 639; 71 J.P. 494; 37 Digest
        (Repl.) 207, *122*.

Action.

This was an action for damages brought by the plaintiffs, J. W. Dwyer, Ltd.,
against the defendant, the Receiver for the Metropolitan Police District, claiming   B
under s. 2 of the Riot (Damages) Act, 1886, compensation for damage suffered
at the plaintiffs' premises at High Street North, Manor Park, London, on the
occasion of a robbery there. The facts are set out in the judgment.

    R. M. O. Havers, Q.C., *J. G. Leach* and *R. R. S. Fisher* for the plaintiffs.
    David Hirst, Q.C., and *C. F. Dehn* for the defendant.
                                                                                                       C

    LYELL, J.: The robbery occurred on May 26, 1962, at about twenty
minutes to ten in the morning. It was a Saturday. On that morning, Mr. Ward,
who was the manager of the shop and who lived in a maisonette or flat immediately above the shop, at about nine o'clock, came down the internal staircase
which leads from his flat to the back part of the shop. The front part of the
shop was used for the sale of jewellery and the back part was what was described   D
as the pledge department. Customers who wished to visit the jewellery department in the ordinary way would enter from the front door which gives on to
High Street North. There was a separate entry from an alleyway running
alongside the premises by which immediate entry could be had to the pledge
department. Mr. Ward came down from the flat, opened the safe and started
to dress the shop window with trays and rings and other retail stock which he   E
took from the safe. According to his custom, he then left the safe unlocked.
At about half-past nine he heard a knock on the front door, which was still
locked. That was a knock given in accordance with custom by a Mr. Frederick
Healey, who was an assistant in the pledge department. The practice was that
he should knock on the door and then Mr. Ward would know that he was to
open the side door leading to the pledge department to enable Mr. Healey to   F
get in. On his arrival, Mr. Healey raised the shutters and at about twenty-five
minutes to ten the shop was opened for business.

The first customer in the retail department came in a few minutes later with
a watch for repair. This was a Mrs. Hooper, who is a regular customer. While
she was still in the jewellery department in the front part of the shop, according
to Mr. Healey, a man rushed in to the jewellery department. At about the same   G
time three other men came in through the side door leading to the pledge department. All of them were hooded, and all of them were armed with iron bars.
The man who came in through the main door, and who appears to have been
the leader said: " It's a hold up ". The three people who were then in the shop,
Mr. Ward, the manager, Mr. Healey, the assistant, and Mrs. Hooper were all in
their several ways immobilised by threat of the use of the iron bars—whether this   H
was by action or words I know not, and I do not think that it matters; I am
satisfied that they were immobilised under threat of force. Mr. Healey and
Mr. Ward were made to sit behind the counter in the pledge department; Mrs.
Hooper was made to go behind the counter immediately to the left of the front
door and stand with her face to the wall. One or more of the three men, as soon
as they entered the shop, had jumped or scrambled over the counter to get at   I
the safe and to get at the drawers which held the pledges taken in the pledge
department. At that stage, Mrs. Ward, who was upstairs and who, perhaps
not unnaturally, was very much on the qui vive for such an incident, as her
husband had been seriously attacked on a previous occasion, heard the unaccus-
tomed noise of somebody, as she thought, coming over the counter, and she came
down the stairs. This was an act of considerable courage. As soon as she
opened the door at the bottom of the internal staircase leading from the flats to
the pledge department she saw three men rushing about. She was seized by the

A   arm, and she, too, was told that if she did not keep quiet she would " get it ", and was threatened by one of them with the iron bar which he held. She also was forced to sit down between her husband and Mr. Healey behind the counter. The men, urged by the leader, who kept telling them to hurry, proceeded to collect and to carry pledges, money and other articles from the safe out of the premises to a van, and within a very short time all was over and the men went.

B   That there was a commotion, a bustle and a certain amount of talking—not, I think, probably above the average tone of voice—is undoubted; but the whole incident appears to have happened without attracting the attention of anybody outside the premises. I have no evidence of anybody having noticed anything untoward going on in the shop or immediately outside it. The proprietor of the next door shop heard no unusual noises. That may have been due to the fact that

C   there was a substantial brick wall between the two sets of premises; but if there had been a great uproar, I think it probable that he might well have noticed it. Those are the facts of the incident.

The plaintiffs claim that they are entitled to recover such part of their loss as was not covered by insurance, and which is agreed to amount to £468 15s. 10d., as compensation due to them under s. 2 of the Riot (Damages) Act, 1886. That

D   section reads as follows:

> " (1) Where a house, shop, or building in any police district has been injured or destroyed, or the property therein has been injured, stolen or destroyed, by any persons riotously and tumultuously assembled together, such compensation as hereinafter mentioned shall be paid out of the police rate of such district to any person who has sustained loss by such injury,

E   > stealing or destruction; but in fixing the amount of such compensation regard shall be had to the conduct of the said person, whether as respects the precautions taken by him or as respects his being a party or accessory to such riotous or tumultuous assembly, or as regards any provocation offered to the persons assembled or otherwise."

F   Subsection (2) deals with the question of who may claim where the loss has in part or in whole been compensated for by insurers, and provides that in such circumstances the person who has suffered the loss initially shall not be entitled to claim, but the insurer is entitled to stand in his shoes and make a claim as if he himself had suffered the injury and loss.

The question which I have to decide is whether the loss, quantified, as I have said, at £468 15s. 10d., which it is admitted that the plaintiffs suffered, is a loss

G   which arises from the goods, the subject of the loss, having been stolen by any persons riotously and tumultuously assembled together.

It is submitted that the facts are such that it is not proved that the loss was caused by persons who were riotously or, alternatively to riotously, tumultuously assembled together. On behalf of the defence, counsel for the defendant reserves the right to argue in another court, if necessary, that the facts which I have

H   recounted do not amount to showing that the four persons who committed the robbery were riotously assembled; but he accepts that in this court, having regard to the authorities, that argument is not open to him.

The five elements of a riot, as laid down by the Divisional Court in the case of *Field* v. *Metropolitan Police Receiver* (1) are as follows. First, there must be at least three persons involved in the assembly. Here I find as a fact that there

I   were four. Secondly, they must have assembled with a common purpose. The whole story makes it clear that they came together for one purpose, namely, to rob the plaintiffs. Thirdly, the execution of the common purpose must have taken place. Here again, the common purpose was clearly executed. Fourthly, there must be an intent on the part of the number of persons to help one another, by force if necessary, against any person who might oppose them in the execution of the common purpose. When four men, each armed with an iron bar, come in, the inevitable inference is that they had the intention of using force if any

(1) [1904-07] All E.R. Rep. 435 at p. 437; [1907] 2 K.B. 853 at p. 860.

of the three people in the shop at the time of their arrival had attempted to A
oppose them. Fifthly, there must be force or violence, not merely used in and
about the common purpose, but displayed in such a manner as to alarm at least
one person of reasonable firmness and courage. I have the evidence of all the
persons present in the shop on that occasion that they were alarmed; and, even
if I had not had their direct evidence, I should have had no hesitation in holding
that the conduct of these four men was such as to alarm persons of reasonable B
courage. All the elements of riot, therefore, are established, and I have no
hesitation in finding that the loss was caused by four men who were riotously
assembled.

The real question in this case, however, is whether they were not merely
riotously, but were also tumultuously, assembled. Counsel for the plaintiffs
rests his case on a passage from HAWKINS' PLEAS OF THE CROWN (8th Edn.), C
bk. 1, c. 28, heading 4, p. 513, to the effect that:

"A riot seems to be a tumultuous disturbance of the peace by three
persons or more assembling together of their own authority with an intent
mutually to assist one another against any who shall oppose them in the
execution of some enterprise of a private nature and afterwards actually
executing the same in a violent and turbulent manner to the terror of the D
people whether the act intended were of itself lawful or unlawful."

He maintains that " tumult " and " tumultuous action " is in itself an essential
ingredient of riot, and that, once riot is proved, the adding of the word " tumultuously " is a mere surplusage and adds nothing to what is required in order to
satisfy the provisions of s. 2 of the Riot (Damages) Act, 1886; that if on the
facts here there is sufficient to prove riot, then there is ipso facto enough to prove E
tumult. Alternatively, he puts the argument that when the Act says " riotously
and tumultuously ", on a true construction of the section the word " and "
should be read as " or " and that it is enough if he proves one or the other.

In my judgment, the second of these contentions cannot be accepted, because
it was intended only to give compensation where a crime was committed, and the
use of the phrase " riotous or tumultuous ", which occurs further on in the F
subsection, can be explained on wholly other grounds and is no support for the
argument that it is enough either to show riot or tumult in order to be
entitled to succeed in a claim for compensation. The phrase " riotous or tumultuous " in the subsection is used in connexion with the factors which are to be
taken into account in deciding how much compensation should be paid to a
person who has proved the basic requirements of the subsection: namely, that G
he has suffered a loss by the activities of persons assembled riotously and tumultuously. The words are:

" in fixing the amount of such compensation regard shall be had to the
conduct of the said person [that is the plaintiff] whether as respects the
precautions taken by him or as respects his being a party or accessory to
such riotous or tumultuous assembly, or as regards any provocation offered H
to the persons assembled or otherwise."

Those words appear to me, in general, to point to the court which has to assess
the amount of compensation being entitled to reduce the amount of compensation
if it came to the conclusion, to put it compendiously, that the plaintiffs had in
some way brought their loss on themselves or contributed towards bringing it I
on themselves. The disjunctive use of " riotous or tumultuous " can be
explained by the fact that an assembly may well start by being tumultuous and
only after a time become riotous, as well. Parliament, I think, may well have
had in mind that if one joined a group which was a tumult, and so swelled it,
one might be thought (for it is only a matter to be taken into account) to be
encouraging or making more probable the conversion of what was merely a
tumultuous assembly into an assembly that became riotous, and to that extent
it might be a factor to be taken into account in considering how much compensation the plaintiffs should be entitled to receive. I further view that use of the

A phrase " riotous or tumultuous " as supporting the view that where the words " riotously and tumultuously " are used earlier in the subsection they are intended to be cumulative; that " tumultuous " is not merely an addition with no force, but adds an additional concept to what is required before compensation can be allowed. The view that these words are to be treated as cumulative in effect, and as introducing separate concepts into the requirements on which a claim to compensation is to be based, is, in my judgment, supported by the history which lies behind this section.

Before I turn to that, I pause to consider what the concepts are which arise in one's mind when the noun, adjective or adverb, " tumult ", " tumultuous " or " tumultuously ", are applied to an assembly. I would not attempt to give a full definition of any of those words, but it seems to me that all of them bring a certain impression to one's mind. When those words are applied to an assembly of persons, the impression is that the assembly should be of considerable size; that it should be an assembly in which the persons taking part are indulging in agitated movement; an excited, emotionally aroused assembly; excitement or emotion common to the members of the assembly; and generally, though not necessarily, accompanied by noise. I agree with the submissions which have been made, that it is a question of degree whether any assembly of people can properly be said to be acting tumultuously.

I now turn to consider both the meaning of the words and the question whether the words " riotously and tumultuously " from their history are to be read as cumulative requirements, differing in character. Until very recently the victims of crime had in general, no claim to be compensated for the injury they suffered as a consequence of the crime. Compensation for loss caused by a riot was a special case. This raises the question: why was it made a special case? If a crowd of people collect in angry and threatening fashion this should become obvious to the local forces of order, and it would then become their duty to prevent the crowd from becoming a riot. This is a duty which has been recognised for centuries, and which until the nineteenth century was put on the local administrative area, the hundred or wapentake, or whatever name it might be called; and there was a duty on them to compensate for damage which was done by persons assembled riotously and tumultuously. The Act of 1886, in fact, did no more than modernise the mode of obtaining compensation and transferred the burden from the inhabitants of the hundred or wapentake to the local police authority. There is nothing secret or furtive about a crowd of people who are acting riotously and tumultuously. It seems to me that the right to compensation from public funds was given because public authority had failed to protect the public who were menaced by a threat which was, or ought to have been, obvious to the forces of law and order as they existed from time to time. In my judgment, the word " tumultuously " was added to " riotously " for the specific reason that it was intended to limit the liability of compensation to cases where the rioters were in such numbers and in such state of agitated commotion, and were generally so acting, that the forces of law and order should have been well aware of the threat which existed, and, if they had done their duty, should have taken steps to prevent the rioters from causing damage.

Applying those criteria to the facts of this case, in my judgment, it fails. Though there was no doubt a commotion and some degree of noise in the shop, the activities of the rioters attracted no attention outside. They were few in number, and the whole activity was on too small a scale to be properly described as a " tumult ". For these reasons, the claim fails, and there will be judgment for the defendant.

Judgment for the defendant.

Solicitors: *Attenboroughs* (for the plaintiffs); *Lee, Bolton & Lee* (for the defendant).

[*Reported by* MARY COLTON, *Barrister-at-Law.*]

A

Re ALSOPP (*deceased*). CARDINAL *v.* WARR AND OTHERS.

[COURT OF APPEAL, CIVIL DIVISION (Lord Denning, M.R., Davies and Russell, L.JJ.), May 3, 4, 1967.]

Will—" Survive "—Gift to such of children of granddaughter as shall survive testator—Testator eighty years old at date of will—Granddaughter married for five years at that time—One child born in his lifetime and living after his death, others born after his death.

B

By his will dated May 17, 1898, the testator, who was then about eighty years old, devised his property at Stone to his granddaughter Sarah and her husband James for their joint lives and the life of the survivor of them and after the survivor's death " unto and equally between such of [their] children as shall survive me and attain the age of twenty-one years and the issue of such of them as shall die previously . . .". The testator also devised other estates on entail for the children, whenever born, of the granddaughter. The testator died on Jan. 6, 1899. At the time of his death Sarah and James had been married for five years. They had a daughter, Fanny, and had had a son who had died soon after birth. After the testator's death they had six more children, four of whom were still living. Sarah survived her husband and died in March, 1959; five of her children were living at her death, of whom Fanny was one.

C

D

Held: the property at Stone became divisible on the death of Sarah in equal shares among all her children who attained twenty-one and the estates of any such children as had predeceased her, for the following reasons—

E

(i) (per LORD DENNING, M.R.; RUSSELL and DAVIES, L.JJ., not deciding on this ground) because by using the word " children " the testator showed an intention that all his great-grandchildren, children of Sarah, whether born before of after his death should share equally, and, rather than produce a capricious result, the word " survive " should be read as meaning " be living after me " (see p. 1059, letter C, post).

F

(ii) (per RUSSELL and DAVIES, L.JJ.), having regard to the particular circumstances and provisions of the will in this case the testator's gift of the property at Stone to " such of [their] children . . . as shall survive me and attain the age of twenty-one " should be read as a gift to " such of [their] children . . . as shall (in the case of those born in my lifetime) survive me and (in any case) attain the age of twenty-one " (see p. 1060, letters F and I, post).

G

Dictum of LORD RUSSELL OF KILLOWEN in *Elliot* v. *Joicey* ([1935] All E.R. Rep. at p. 582) considered.

Re Clark ([1864] 3 De G.J. & Sm. 111) considered.

Appeal allowed.

H

[As to the meaning of the word " survive " in wills, see 39 HALSBURY'S LAWS (3rd Edn.) 1044, 1045, para. 1566; and for cases on the meaning of " survive ", see 49 DIGEST (Repl.) 1124-1128, *10,427-10,465.*]

Cases referred to:

Castle, Re, Public Trustee v. Floud, [1948] 2 All E.R. 927; [1949] Ch. 46; [1949] L.J.R. 610; 49 Digest (Repl.) 1128, *10,464.*

I

Clark's Estates, Re, (1864), 3 De G.J. & Sm. 111; 46 E.R. 579; 49 Digest (Repl.) 1126, *10,438.*

Elliot v. Joicey, [1935] All E.R. Rep. 578; [1935] A.C. 209; 104 L.J.Ch. 111; sub nom. Re Joicey, Re Joicey v. Elliot, 152 L.T. 398; 49 Digest (Repl.) 743, *6965.*

Gee v. Liddell, (1866), L.R. 2 Eq. 341; 35 L.J.Ch. 640; 55 E.R. 1053; 49 Digest (Repl.) 1125, *10,436.*

A   *Hodgson* (*decd.*), *Re, Hodgson* v. *Gillett*, [1952] 1 All E.R. 769; 49 Digest
        (Repl.) 1125, *10,437*.

      Re Sing, Sing v. *Mills*, [1914] W.N. 90; 49 Digest (Repl.) 1125, *10,429*.

      Appeal.

      This was an appeal by the first defendant from an order of PLOWMAN, J.,
dated July 19, 1966, by which it was declared that on the true construction of the
B   will of the testator, James Allsop, the testator's property at Stone in the county
of Kent on the death of the survivor of the joint life tenants was given to the
third defendant, Fanny Ida Knight absolutely. The plaintiff was Lucy Ellen
Cardinal who claimed to be beneficially entitled to a share under trusts contained
in a devise in the will, and the first and second defendants were William Thomas
Warr and Wilfred James Giblin, the trustees of the devise. The fourth defendant
C   was Archibald Henry Warr and the fifth defendant was Bertha May Giblin, the
wife of the second defendant. All the parties, other than the second defendant,
were children of the testator's granddaughter Sarah. The third defendant was
the only child of Sarah born in the testator's lifetime who survived him. Two
children of Sarah born after his death predeceased her after attaining the age of
twenty-one. The facts are set out in the judgment of LORD DENNING, M.R.

D   *J. L. Jopling* for the first defendant.

      J. H. L. Leckie for the second defendant.

      E. A. Seeley for the third defendant.

      J. H. G. Sunnucks for the plaintiff.

      The fourth and fifth defendants did not appear and were not represented.

E   **LORD DENNING, M.R.:** Nearly seventy years ago, on May 17, 1898, the
testator, a man named James Allsop, made his will. He was then aged about
eighty. He had a granddaughter Sarah, who had been married for five years to
James Warr. This young couple were in their early twenties. They had at that
time a daughter Fanny, aged four. No doubt they hoped to have more children.

      The testator had property at Stone in Kent. In his will he left this property
F   to the young couple, Sarah and James, for their lives, and afterwards to their
children. Eighteen months later, on Jan. 6, 1899, the testator died. The young
couple, Sarah and James, continued living at Stone and had six more children.
They lived to a good old age. Eventually James died on Jan. 4, 1958, and Sarah
died on Mar. 22, 1959. Five of their children are still living. One of them is Fanny,
who was four years old when the testator died. She is now seventy-three. The
others were born after his death. They are in their sixties and fifties.

G   The question is: what is to happen to the property at Stone? Does it all
belong to Fanny or does it go to all the children to be divided equally between
them? This depends on the meaning of the word " survive " in the testator's
will. It was obviously drafted by a lawyer. The words were these:

H   " I devise all my property at Stone in the county of Kent to James Warr
      and the said Sarah Ida Bowyer Warr during their joint lives and the life of
      the survivor of them and after the decease of such survivor I give the same
      unto and equally between such of the children of the said James Warr and
      Sarah Ida Bowyer Warr as shall survive me and attain the age of twenty-one
      years and the issue of such of them as shall die previously such issue taking
      nevertheless the share only which his, her or their parents would have taken
I   if he or she had survived me and attained the age of twenty-one years and if
      more than one in equal shares as tenants in common."

The crucial words in the will are: " I give the same unto and equally between
such of the children of James and Sarah as shall survive me and attain the age of
twenty-one years." It is said that the word " survive " has only one proper
meaning. It means a person who is living at the death of the testator and continues
living afterwards. This is supported by the case of *Elliot* v. *Joicey* (1), where LORD
RUSSELL OF KILLOWEN said:

    (1) [1935] All E.R. Rep. 578 at p. 582; [1935] A.C. 209 at p. 218.

"The word 'surviving', however, which in my view, according to its ordin-   A
ary meaning requires that the person who is to survive shall be living both
at and after a particular point of time . . ."

Applying this meaning, it is said that the only child who "survived" the
testator was Fanny, because she was the only child who was living at his death.
She was then four. The others were not then born. So they did not "survive"
him. The judge has accepted this view.   B

Although that is the ordinary meaning of the word "survive", there are a
number of authorities which show that that meaning is capable of being displaced
if it leads to a capricious result which can never have been intended by the
testator. In some contexts it may mean simply "live after". The principal
authority is a case in this court in 1864, *Re Clark's Estate* (2). William Clark
made a gift by his will to   C

"all and every the children, of the said Maria Clark, who shall survive
me, equally to be divided between them."

Maria Clark at the time when William Clark died was about twelve years old.
She married nine years later and had seven children. KINDERSLEY, V.-C., held
that none of them took under the will of William Clark because none of them   D
was living at his death. They did not "survive" him. The Vice-Chancellor said
that the disposition was capricious, but that that was no ground for giving the
word "survive" a different meaning. That decision was overruled by this court.
KNIGHT BRUCE, L.J., with whom TURNER, L.J., concurred, said (3):

"I am of opinion that we may without impropriety hold the words 'who
shall survive me' to mean 'who shall be living after me' . . ."   E

That case was followed by EVE, J., in *Re Sing, Sing* v. *Mills* (4). He said that the
word "survive" was "capable of either of the meanings 'outlive' or 'live
after', and the meaning to be allocated in a particular case must be determined
by the context in the surrounding circumstances which the court was entitled to
regard". In that case he held that "survive" meant "live after".

Those cases were considered by ROXBURGH, J., in *Re Hodgson (decd.)*, *Hodgson*   F
v. *Gillett* (5), and he in effect declined to follow them. A testator left property in
trust

"for such of the child or children of the said [Captain Hodgson] who shall
survive me and . . . shall attain the age twenty-one years."

At the date of the testator's death Captain Hodgson was a bachelor. After the   G
testator's death Captain Hodgson married and had children. ROXBURGH, J.,
held that his children did not come within the bequest. They did not "survive"
the testator because they were not living at the time of his death. He realised
that this was contrary to the testator's intention. He said that the will "operates
in a most capricious manner". He invited an appeal, and said that (6)

". . . in a matter of this sort it is the duty of a judge of first instance to   H
tread the conservative path, hoping, perhaps, that a higher court will be
able to deal more radically with the situation."

There was, however, no appeal. The case, I suppose, was settled.

In my opinion *Re Hodgson* (5) was wrongly decided. I prefer to follow the
decision of this court in *Re Clark* (2), for this simple reason—that the object of
the court in construing a will is to discover the intention of the testator. I do not   I
think that his intention is to be discovered by looking at the literal meaning of
the words alone. That has led, times out of number, to the frustration of his
intentions. You must look at the will in the light of the surrounding circumstances. Eschewing technical rules and literal interpretation, you must look to see

---

(2) (1864), 3 De G.J. & Sm. 111.   (3) (1864), 3 De G.J. & Sm. at p. 115.
(4) [1914] W.N. 90.   (5) [1952] 1 All E.R. 769.
          (6) [1952] 1 All E.R. at p. 774, letter E.

A simply what the testator intended. If you find that a literal interpretation gives rise to a capricious result which you are satisfied the testator can never have intended, then you should reject that interpretation and seek for a sensible interpretation which does accord with his intention. It is sometimes said that a testator can be capricious if he likes. Yes, if you are sure that he intended to be; but you should not impute capriciousness to him merely to justify yourself in

B giving the words a literal interpretation. That is the reason why this court in *Re Clark* (7) rejected the literal meaning of " survive ".

Looking at the will here, it is obvious to me that by using the word " children " the testator intended that all his great-grandchildren (the children of James and Sarah) should share equally, including those born before his death and also those born afterwards. He did not mean that the one child then alive (Fanny)

C alone should take, else he would have said so. There is another point. If Fanny had married and had a child and died before she was twenty-one, that child would undoubtedly have taken Fanny's share. It would be remarkable if that child (a great-great-grandchild) should take the property to the exclusion of the great-grandchildren. Rather than impute such capriciousness to the testator, I would interpret " survive me " here as meaning " live after me ": just as the court did

D in *Re Clark* (7): so that the bequest includes all the great-grandchildren.

I am pleased to find that RUSSELL, L.J., has reached the same result by a different route. I will leave him to explain it himself: for he can do it far better than I could do. It means, I believe, implying quite a lot of words into the will. Implying words is, of course, only another way of effectuating the testator's intention. For myself I care not by which route the result is reached, so long as

E effect is given to the obvious intention of the testator—which was to benefit all his great-grandchildren equally, and not Fanny alone. I would, therefore, allow the appeal.

RUSSELL, L.J.: At the time when he made his will in 1898 the testator was seventy-nine years old. His granddaughter, Mrs. Warr, was a young woman,

F married five years before, with a daughter who was four years old and having had also a son who, had he not died very soon after his birth, would have been two years old. There was no reason to suppose that she would not have any more children; and indeed she had six more, all conceived after the testator died in 1899, the first five of whom were born by the year 1909, and the sixth (possibly an unexpected bonus) in 1917. In another part of his will the testator, towards the

G end of his disposition of estates other than those now in question, included an entail, true somewhat low in a series, on the sons and daughters (i.e. whenever born) of Mrs. Warr. These are some of the circumstances in which it is to be ascertained whether in his disposition of his Stone property the testator, having given life interests therein to Mrs. Warr and her husband, has limited the remainders primarily to those only of their children who should be born in his,

H the testator's, lifetime.

It seems to me that there is no doubt about some things. First, in my view the phrase " who shall survive me " has as its plain and natural meaning a reference to those persons who should be born (or, by what is described as a fiction, in some circumstances en ventre sa mère) before the writer's death and who continue to live thereafter. I think to include in the phrase those who never

I in any sense coincided in life with the writer is to depart from the proper meaning of the phrase. Secondly, it would be clearly capricious for the testator in this case to select for his bounty only those children of Mrs. Warr who happened to appear on the scene in his terminal years, and most improbable that he should do so. Thirdly, such selectiveness in the Stone disposition would fit ill with the lack of it in the other disposition, to which I have referred. Fourthly, a testator is entitled to be capricious, and some are. Lastly, testamentary dispositions have to be

---

(7) (1864), 3 De G.J. & Sm. 111.

ascertained from the intentions displayed by what has been written, in the light, **A** of course, of the surrounding circumstances.

Now we have been invited to construe " shall survive me ", not in its plain and natural sense, as pointing to those born in the testator's lifetime, but as meaning " shall not pre-decease me ". I for myself am not able to take that step. I do not find myself able to agree that *Re Clark's Estate* (8) forces me to take that step. As to *Re Sing, Sing* v. *Mills* (9), it was always the salutary practice when I **B** was at the Bar to ignore Weekly Notes reports on matters of construction. I do not propose to enlarge on that aspect of the case.

From this it will be seen that I do not find myself wholly in agreement with LORD DENNING, M.R.; but this, it seems to me, does not conclude the matter at all. The matters to which I have already referred point very strongly against an intention to restrict the class to one so limited as has been suggested; and to **C** those matters may be added the curiosity, as was pointed out in argument, that if the class be so limited, it could permit a great-great-grandchild of the testator born after his death to participate, while forbidding any great-grandchild of the testator born after his death to participate. When the testator uses in the substitutionary provision the word " them "—" the issue of such of them "—he is necessarily referring to all the children of Mr. and Mrs. Warr as a class. It seems **D** to me that the testator and the draftsman had in mind all children of the Warr's as the class, attainment of the age of twenty-one being the requirement for participation, and wished to provide for the two events which would lead to exclusion of a child from the class to the benefit of other members and to the detriment of the issue of persons thus excluded. One of those could apply to great-grandchildren born in the testator's lifetime, namely, death in his lifetime; **E** the other would be of general application, namely, death under the age of twenty-one.

Viewed thus, it seems to me that the reference to " as shall survive me " may be read not as restricting the class to the capricious and improbable limits suggested, but as applicable only to those to whom it could apply, namely, those born in his lifetime and those to whom alone the question of survival or non- **F** survival would be relevant. Thus read, the provision is the equivalent of saying " such of the children of the Warr's as shall (in the case of those born in my lifetime) survive me and (in any case) attain the age of twenty-one ". The rest of the provision, that is to say, the substitutionary provision, would fit that concept perfectly well.

It was suggested that it would make the words " survive me and " wholly **G** superfluous, but I do not think that that is correct; and indeed it was accepted that it was not correct because without them the issue of a twenty-one years old great-grandchild dying in the testator's lifetime would not be within the substitutionary gift.

For those reasons, which are quite obviously particular and peculiar to the actual will now before us, I would also allow the appeal and declare that the **H** property became divisible on the death of the surviving parent in equal shares among all the children of the Warr's who attained the age of twenty-one or their estates if already dead.

> **DAVIES, L.J.:** I agree with the result and with the reasons given by RUSSELL, L.J. I should like to add a word or two, however, on the other ground on which the judgment of LORD DENNING, M.R., principally proceeded, that is **I** to say, the meaning of the word " survive ".
>
> The authorities start with the case of *Re Clark's Estate* (8) in 1864 where this court took the view that has been primarily contended for by counsel for the first defendant in the present case, namely, that the words " who survives me " or " survivors " embrace not only those who were alive at the nominated date

(8) (1864), 3 De G.J. & Sm. 111.   (9) [1914] W.N. 90.

A but those of the same class who came into existence subsequently. Curiously
enough, two years later in 1866 there was the decision of LORD ROMILLY, M.R.,
to which we have been referred, *Gee* v. *Liddell* (10), in which he said:

> B ". . . I think that this result ought not to induce the court to give any
> other than the ordinary meaning to the words used by the testator; and
> my opinion is, that the meaning of the word ' survive ' or ' survivor '
> imports that the person who is to survive must be living at the time of the
> event which he is to survive."

LORD DENNING has referred to the words of LORD RUSSELL OF KILLOWEN in
Elliot v. *Joicey* (11) where the learned lord said:

> C " The word ' surviving ', however, which, in my view, according to its
> ordinary meaning requires that the person who is to survive shall be living
> both at and after a particular point of time, ought, as it seems to me, to be
> governed by the same considerations as those which have been applied to the
> word ' living ', where the event postulated has been that there should be a
> child living at a particular point of time, e.g. at its father's death."

In 1949 JENKINS, J., in the case of *Re Castle, Public Trustee* v. *Floud* (12), plainly
D took the same view as that which I am now suggesting is the correct one as to
the meaning of the word " survive " or " surviving ", though the learned judge
in that particular case was able to base his judgment on a slightly different ground,
as there was there the question of surviving not only the death but also a
subsequent event.

In the case of *Re Hodgson* (*decd.*), *Hodgson* v. *Gillett* (13), to which reference
E has already been made, ROXBURGH, J., took the view that the case in the House
of Lords, *Elliot's* case (14), to which I have referred, was authoritative on this
point. He said (15):

> F ". . . I am of the view that, now the prima facie meaning of the words has
> been so authoritatively determined, more care is required in drawing
> inferences from the surrounding circumstances than would have been
> necessary if the words had been held not to have a prima facie meaning."

There may be, as has rightly been pointed out, surrounding circumstances, or there
may be a context which can put on the word " survive " or " survivor " a
different meaning from that which it would normally import. In the absence of
such circumstances or context, however, the meaning of the word " survivor "
G is that indicated by LORD RUSSELL OF KILLOWEN in *Elliot's* case (15). It means
that the survivor must be in existence at and live after the date of the postulated
event. The word cannot in my view, with the utmost respect to the views
expressed by LORD DENNING, M.R., include a person who comes into existence
subsequently.

For the reasons given by RUSSELL, L.J., I entirely agree that this appeal
H succeeds.

Appeal allowed. Declaration accordingly.

Solicitors: *Kinch & Richardson*, agents for *T. G. Baynes & Sons*, Dartford (for
the first and second defendants); *Badham, Comins & Main*, agents for *Baily &
Goff*, Dartford (for the third defendant); *Rowley Ashworth & Co.* (for the plaintiff).

[*Reported by* F. GUTTMAN, ESQ., *Barrister-at-Law*.]

I

---

(10) (1866), L.R. 2 Eq. 341 at p. 344.
(11) [1935] All E.R. Rep. at p. 582; [1935] A.C. at p. 218.
(12) [1948] 2 All E.R. 927; [1949] Ch. 46.
(13) [1952] 1 All E.R. 769.
(14) [1935] All E.R. Rep. 578; [1935] A.C. 209.
(15) [1952] 1 All E.R. at p. 773.

PEARSON AND ANOTHER *v.* WILLIAM JONES, LTD.   A

[QUEEN'S BENCH DIVISION (Lord Parker, C.J., Waller and Swanwick, JJ.), June 5, 1967.]

Employment—Redundancy—Amount of redundancy payment—Statement of terms of employment referred normal working hours to works rules—Works rules stated normal working hours to be forty hour week—Overtime worked—Whether   B
overtime obligatory under national agreements—Whether overtime working to be taken into account in assessing redundancy payment—Redundancy Payments Act 1965 (c. 62), s. 1, Sch. 1 (5)—Contracts of Employment Act 1963 (c. 49), Sch. 2, paras. 1 (1), 3 (1).

Two transport drivers, formerly employed by the respondent company, claimed that redundancy payments, which had been paid to them, should   C
have been computed on an average that would take into account overtime worked (viz., should have been assessed in accordance with para. 3 of Sch. 2*
to the Contracts of Employment Act 1963). Paragraph 3 applied only " if there are no normal working hours " for the employee when employed under the contract of employment. The written statement of terms of employment of the appellant drivers stated that their normal working hours were in   D
accordance with the works rules. The works rules stated " forty hour week "
and that any overtime was in accordance with national agreements currently in force. The national agreements provided that when overtime was necessary certain provisions should apply, which included that no union workmen should be required to work more than thirty hours' overtime in any four weeks and, further, that the employers had the right to decide when   E
overtime was necessary. On an appeal from a decision of the Industrial Tribunal that there was no obligation on the appellants to work overtime, and that overtime working should not be taken into account in assessing their redundancy payments.

Held: the appellants had normal working hours, viz., the " forty hour week ", and their redundancy payments fell to be assessed accordingly under   F
para. 1 (1) of Sch. 2† to the Contracts of Employment Act 1963 as applied by para. 5 of Sch. 1 to the Redundancy Payments Act 1965; moreover (per WALLER and SWANWICK, JJ.) overtime working was not obligatory on the appellants, or (per LORD PARKER, C.J.) even if it were, the amount of the appellants' weekly pay would have fallen to be computed, for the purpose of calculating their redundancy payments, under para. 1 (1) of   G
Sch. 2 to the Act of 1963 (see p. 1065, letters A, E and G, post).

[As to the amount of redundancy payments, see SUPPLEMENT to 38 HALSBURY'S LAWS (3rd Edn.), para. 808F.

For the Redundancy Payments Act 1965, s. 1, Sch. 1, para. 5, see 45 HALSBURY'S STATUTES (2nd Edn.) 290, 338.

For the Contracts of Employment Act 1963, Sch. 2, paras. 1 (1), 3 (1), see   H
43 HALSBURY'S STATUTES (2nd Edn.) 287, 288.]

Appeal.

This was an appeal by two appellants, John Herbert William Pearson and Ronald Arthur Workman, from a decision of the Industrial Tribunal, given on Nov. 28, 1966, determining that the amount of the redundancy payments of   I
the appellants were correctly computed on the basis of the amount of a week's pay being the amount for normal working hours of a forty hour week, not taking into account overtime. By notice dated Jan. 11, 1967, the appellants gave notice of motion for an order that the tribunal's decision might be discharged and that in lieu thereof it might be ordered that for the purpose of calculating the redundancy payments to be made to the appellants the amount of a week's pay in

---

* Schedule 2, para. 3 (1), is set out at p. 1064, letter H, post.
† Schedule 2, para. 1 (1) is set out at p. 1064, letter E, post.

A   the case of each appellant should be computed in accordance with para. 3 of
Sch. 2 to the Contracts of Employment Act 1963. The existing assessment of
the appellants' redundancy payments had been calculated on the basis of a
week's pay for normal working hours in accordance with para. 1 (1) of Sch. 2
to the Act of 1963. Among the grounds of appeal were that the tribunal was
wrong in law in finding that by the terms of the appellants' contracts of service

B   they were not obliged to work overtime at the discretion of the respondent
employers, William Jones, Ltd.; and that the tribunal was wrong in law in
finding that the combined effect of the National Agreements between the Confederation of Shipbuilding and Engineering Unions and the Engineering Employers Federation and of the respondents' works rules was that normal working
hours of each appellant were forty hours per week. The facts appear from the

C   judgment of WALLER, J.

>   *J. Mitchell* for the appellants.
>   *Adrian Hamilton* for the respondent company.

    WALLER, J., delivered the first judgment at the invitation of LORD
PARKER, C.J.: This is an appeal under s. 9 of the Tribunals and Inquiries Act,

D   1958 (1) against a decision of the Industrial Tribunal given in London on Nov.
28, 1966. There was before the tribunal an application by the two appellants,
for an increase in the amount of redundancy pay which had been given to them
when they became redundant with the respondent company. The appellants
were both transport drivers; both of them had been paid redundancy payments
calculated on their years of service, on their age and on a weekly wage based on a

E   forty hour normal working week. They claim that the payment should have
been based on an average which took into account the hours of overtime which
they had been working, and the figures showed that they had been working a
considerable amount of overtime during the preceding years. The overtime had
varied somewhat. There was a time when it consisted mainly of lorries being
sent out on necessary repair work for the earth-moving machinery which the

F   respondent company used to hire out. One instance was an occasion when
it became necessary for the respondent company to send a lorry with spares
to Birmingham and, when the drivers showed disinclination to go, the foreman
said ' somebody has to go ' and someone did go. More recently, however,
that work had fallen off, and the overtime mainly consisted of work on
Saturday mornings and occasional days when extra work was done during the

G   week. The appellants both claim that under the contract under which they were
working, overtime work was compulsory, that they did overtime work and, for
reasons which I shall go into in a moment, that overtime work had to be included
in the normal working week. Paragraph 2 of the written statement of the terms
of employment, as required by s. 4 of the Contracts of Employment Act 1963
read:

H   " Normal Working Hours. Your normal working hours and the terms and
conditions relating to such hours are in accordance with the works rules."

  The works rules state, by para. 1 (a) " forty hour week in all departments ", and
then set out (in para. 1 (b)) the days on which work has to be done. Paragraph
5 of the works rules, which has the heading " Overtime ", reads:

I   " Any overtime working is in accordance with the provisions of the
national agreements currently in force between the Engineering Employers
Federation and the Confederation of Shipbuilding and Engineering Unions."

  It is therefore necessary to turn to the provisions of those national agreements
to ascertain what is there provided. Clause (j) is the relevant clause of the
national agreements and, so far as matters for the purposes of this case, provides:

---

  (1) Section 9 (38 HALSBURY'S STATUTES (2nd Edn.) 207) was made applicable by the
Tribunals and Inquiries (Industrial Tribunals) Order 1965, S.I. 1965 No. 1403.

"The federation and the trade unions agree that systematic overtime is deprecated as a method of production and that when overtime is necessary the following provisions shall apply, viz.: No union workman shall be required to work more than thirty hours' overtime in any four weeks after full shop hours have been worked, allowance being made for time lost through sickness, absence with leave or enforced idleness . . . It is agreed that the employers have the right to decide when overtime is necessary, the workpeople or their representatives being entitled to bring forward under the provisions for avoiding disputes any cases of overtime they desire discussed. Meantime, the overtime required shall be proceeded with."

It is on those terms in that context that the appellants in this case base their claim.

The Redundancy Payments Act 1965 s. 1 entitles persons made redundant to redundancy payments. It is unnecessary to refer to the detailed provisions of that Act. Schedule 1 sets out the method of calculating redundancy payments; and by para. 5, reference has to be made to Sch. 2 to the Contracts of Employment Act 1963. This case depends very much on the application of that schedule, and it is necessary to quote certain of the paragraphs in that schedule, because the arguments in this case depend on them. Paragraph 1 of Sch. 2 to the Act of 1963 reads:

"(1) For the purposes of this schedule the cases where there are normal working hours include cases where the employee is entitled to overtime pay when employed for more than a fixed number of hours in a week or other period, and, subject to the following subparagraph, in those cases that fixed number of hours (in this paragraph referred to as ' the number of hours without overtime ') shall be the normal working hours.

"(2) If in such a case—(a) the contract of employment fixes the number, or the minimum number, of hours of employment in the said week or other period (whether or not it also provides for the reduction of that number or minimum number of hours in certain circumstances), and (b) that number or minimum number of hours exceeds the number of hours without overtime, that number or minimum number of hours (and not the number of hours without overtime) shall be the normal working hours."

Paragraph 1 (2) does not apply in this case because it applies solely where the regular hours to be worked each week under the terms of a contract are regular hours in excess of the normal working hours, that is to say, some of the hours are to be paid at one rate and others, perhaps four or ten or whatever the number of hours may be, are to be paid at an overtime rate. That has no application to this case.

The other paragraph of Sch. 2 to the Act of 1963 which is important in this case is para. 3 (1) which reads

"This paragraph shall apply if there are no normal working hours for the employee when employed under the contract of employment in force in the period of notice."

Counsel for the appellants submits that the words in the statement of terms of employment which I quoted earlier, "normal working hours", are relevant only for the purposes of calculating pay. Normal working hours were there stated to be in accordance with the works rules, para. 1 (a) of which stated " forty hour week in all departments ". Counsel submits that that does not mean normal working hours for the purposes of Sch. 2 to the Contracts of Employment Act 1963 and says that it is there purely for the purpose of calculating pay. He submits that in this case there are no normal working hours for the employees within the union meaning of para. 1 (a), and that, therefore, para. 3 (1) of Sch. 2 to the Contracts of Employment Act 1963 applies. Counsel for the appellants says that this case does not come within Sch. 2, para. 1 (1), and that therefore

A it is necessary to take the average of the hours worked over a period of twelve weeks (2) up to the time when notice was given.

In my view it is impossible in this case to say that the words " normal working hours " in the statement of the terms of employment are not the same as the " normal working hours " which are referred to in para. 1 (1) of Sch. 2 to the Act of 1963. Here the employee was required to work forty hours each week;

B he might work overtime as well, but he was in any event entitled to be paid for forty hours. It is therefore impossible to say that those are not the normal working hours which are referred to in para. 1 (1). Accordingly, it is not possible to apply the provisions of para. 3 (1), which paragraph applies only if there are no normal working hours. If the construction for which counsel for the appellants contended were to be adopted, the employer would not be under an obligation

C to provide the purported hours work per week, yet the contract requires him to do so.

Even if para. 3 of Sch. 2 to the Act of 1963 did apply, however, counsel for the respondent company has submitted that cl. (j) of the national agreements already quoted, does not impose on the individual workman an obligation to work overtime. He says that the Industrial Tribunal were perfectly right when

D they came to that conclusion. He says that cl. (j) is one which is specifically referring to the situation which exists between the Federation of Employers and the Trade Unions, and he stresses the fact that throughout the paragraph the wording is such as to be permissive only. He says that in order that overtime should be compulsory there should be either an express term that the employee shall work overtime or, possibly, an implied term to that effect. There is no such

E provision in this contract. In my view, counsel for the respondent company is right in saying that an obligation to work overtime cannot be spelt out of this contract. For those reasons I would dismiss this appeal.

SWANWICK, J.: I agree.

LORD PARKER, C.J.: I also agree. Before the tribunal, the question seems
F to have been solely whether the working of overtime here was obligatory. It seems to be conceded that, if it was obligatory, then the appellants were right in their contention as to the quantification of the redundancy payments. On the whole, as at present advised, I think that the tribunal came to a right conclusion, but I find it unnecessary to decide that definitely, having regard to the fact that I am persuaded that, even if the working of overtime was obligatory, in the
G present case it came clearly within para. 1 (1) of Sch. 2 to the Contracts of Employment Act 1963. Accordingly, only the normal working hours, in this case forty, fell to be taken into consideration in the calculation.

Appeal dismissed.

Solicitors: *Pattinson & Brewer* (for the appellants); *Barlow, Lyde & Gilbert*
H (for the respondent company).

[*Reported by* S. A. HATTEEA, ESQ., *Barrister-at-Law.*]

I

---

(2) See para. 3 (2) of Sch. 2 to the Contracts of Employment Act 1963.

LORD LUKE OF PAVENHAM *v.* MINISTER OF HOUSING AND LOCAL GOVERNMENT AND ANOTHER.

[COURT OF APPEAL, CIVIL DIVISION (Lord Denning, M.R., Davies and Russell, L.JJ.), May 4, 5, 1967.]

Town and Country Planning—Development—Permission for development—Appeal—Appeal to Minister—" Findings of fact " by inspector accepted by Minister, but not inspector's "conclusions " or recommendation—No opportunity afforded to applicant to make further representations—Appeal dismissed by Minister—Application to quash Minister's decision—Whether inspector's conclusions were also findings of fact—Town and Country Planning Appeals (Inquiries Procedure) Rules, 1965 (S.I. 1965 No. 473), r. 12 (2).

A mansion house in a village was demolished. On the other side of the road, but outside the perimeter of the village, was a walled garden, which formerly was the kitchen garden of the mansion house. The respondent applied to the local planning authority for permission to build a house within the walled garden. The planning authority refused permission, and gave as their reason that the proposal would constitute an undesirable form of isolated and sporadic development outside the limits of the village in an area where no further development should be permitted other than that which was essential for agricultural purposes. The respondent appealed and the Minister appointed an inspector to hold an inquiry. The inspector's report included findings of fact, which were followed by two paragraphs headed " conclusions ". The first of these paragraphs began " 39. Bearing in mind the above facts I am of the opinion that . . .". The " conclusions " were followed by the inspector's " recommendation ", which was that the appeal be allowed. In the Minister's letter of decision the Minister stated that he accepted the inspector's findings of fact, but was unable to agree with the inspector's conclusions or with his recommendation. The Minister dismissed the appeal. Before reaching his decision the Minister did not give the respondent opportunity to make further representations. On appeal from an order quashing the Minister's decision,

Held: the Minister, in reaching his decision disagreeing with the inspector's conclusions and recommendation, had not differed from the inspector on a finding of fact within r. 12 (2)* of the Town and Country Planning (Inquiries Procedure) Rules, 1965, and accordingly had not been bound under that rule to afford the respondent an opportunity to make representations in writing (see p. 1070, letters B and D, and p. 1071, letters F and H, post).

Decision of LAWTON, J. ([1967] 1 All E.R. 351) reversed.

[As to challenging a decision of the Minister as to the control of development, see 37 HALSBURY'S LAWS (3rd Edn.) 331, 332, para. 437, and as to appeal to the Minister from a decision of the local planning authority, see ibid., p. 331, para. 436; and for cases on planning permission applications, see 45 DIGEST (Repl.) 335-340, *33-55.*

For the Town and Country Planning Act, 1962, s. 23, see 42 HALSBURY'S STATUTES (2nd Edn.) 991.

For the Town and Country Planning Act, 1959, s. 33, see 39 HALSBURY'S STATUTES (2nd Edn.) 1208.]

Appeal.

This was an appeal by the Minister of Housing and Local Government from an order of LAWTON, J., dated Dec. 7, 1966, and reported [1967] 1 All E.R. 351, whereby the decision of the Minister dated Feb. 24, 1966, dismissing the appeal of the applicant from the decision of the Bedford Rural District Council refusing the applicant planning permission for the erection of a dwelling house on land at Garden House, Pavenham, was quashed.

A   The grounds of appeal were (i) that the judge was wrong in law in holding that the Minister in arriving at his decision had differed from the inspector holding an inquiry as to a finding of fact made by the inspector within the meaning of r. 10 of the Town and Country Planning (Inquiries Procedure) Rules, 1962; (ii) that the judge misconstrued r. 10 by holding in effect that the Minister was not at liberty to give a decision at variance with any recommendation of the

B   inspector without affording the parties an opportunity to make representations, save where he differed from the inspector on a matter of law, and (iii) that on the true construction of para. (2) (*a*) of r. 10 that paragraph had no application to an expression of an opinion by the inspector as to the planning considerations which ought to be applied or as to the weight of such considerations in their application to the subject before him, which the inspector gave as his reasons

C   for making his recommendations, and that on such construction there was no failure by the Minister to comply with r. 10.   The respondent to the present appeal gave a respondent's notice dated Feb. 3, 1967, that he would rely on each of certain grounds set out in his amended notice of motion.   These included, among other grounds, that (a) the Minister failed to comply with requirements of s. 17 of the Town and Country Planning Act, 1962, by failing to have regard

D   adequately or at all to certain findings of fact (called " conclusions " in his inspector's report) whereby the present respondent's interests had been substantially prejudiced, and (b) that the Minister failed to comply with relevant requirements in that, contrary to r. 11 of the rules of 1962, or r. 13 of the corresponding rules of 1965, all or some of the reasons given by him in notifying his decision were not good and sufficient reasons, whereby the present respondent's interests

E   had been substantially prejudiced.   The facts are set out in the judgment of Lord Denning, M.R.

S. O. *Silkin, Q.C.,* and *Nigel Bridge* for the Minister.
A. B. *Dawson* for the respondent, Lord Luke of Pavenham.

LORD DENNING, M.R.: There is a small village in Bedfordshire called

F   Pavenham.   There used to be a mansion house there, but it has been demolished and is being replaced by other houses.   On the other side of the road there is an old walled garden.   It used to be the kitchen garden of the mansion house. It is about one acre in extent.   It is owned by Lord Luke of Pavenham and he seeks permission to build a house there.   The local planning authority refused permission for this reason:

G   " The proposal would constitute an undesirable form of isolated and sporadic development outside the limits of the village of Pavenham in an area where no further development should be permitted other than that which is essential for agricultural purposes."

In other words, the proposed building was outside the village " envelope " and

H   should not be permitted.   Lord Luke appealed to the Minister of Housing and Local Government under s. 23 of the Town and Country Planning Act, 1962. The Minister appointed an inspector to hold an inquiry.   It was held.   The inspector made his report.   He recommended that permission be granted.   The Minister, however, disagreed with the inspector's recommendation.   The Minister thought that Lord Luke's proposal was undesirable.   He, therefore, confirmed

I   the decision of the local planning authority and dismissed the appeal.
Prima facie the decision of the Minister was final (see s. 23 (5) of the Act of 1962); but it was open to Lord Luke to question the Minister's decision if he could show that any of the relevant requirements had not been complied with (see s. 179 (1) of the Act of 1962).   Lord Luke did question the validity of the Minister's decision.   He said that the relevant requirements had not been complied with in that the Minister had differed from the inspector on findings of fact and that the Minister ought to have notified him (Lord Luke) of the difference and given him an opportunity of making representations to him: and had not

done so. LAWTON, J., upheld (1) this contention and quashed the Minister's A decision. The Minister appeals to this court.

The relevant requirement in this regard is contained in the Town and Country Planning (Inquiries Procedure) Rules 1965, (2) and in particular r. 12 (2), which provides:

" Where the Minister differs—(a) from the appointed person on a finding of fact . . . and by reason thereof is disposed to disagree with a recommenda- B tion made by the appointed person, he shall not come to a decision which is at variance with such recommendation without first notifying the applicant . . . and affording [him] an opportunity of making representations in writing within twenty-one days . . ."

The general question is whether the Minister did differ from the inspector " on a C finding of fact ". To determine it we must see what the inspector's findings were. In a section headed " Findings of fact ", the inspector stated:

" I find the following facts. 1. The site is included in an area of no nota- tion in the approved county development plan [that means it was not set aside for development]. 2. The site is about 380 yards north of the main village street of Pavenham and on the western side of an unclassified road D leading northwards to Felmersham. 3. The site is a garden having an area of about 1·037 acres and is surrounded by a wall about twelve feet high: the wall was built over a hundred years ago in hand-made red brickwork and is well maintained. 4. The site is in the northern part of the grounds of the garden house which was built over a hundred years ago and originally the gardener's cottage of the mansion house which stood on land formerly E part of Pavenham Bury estate opposite. 5. On higher ground opposite the site and on the eastern side of the road are a mediaeval church, an old and large stable block converted into an attractive residence and detached houses of an estate under construction on the site of the original mansion house. 6. To the north and south of the site is farmland rising away from the site; farmland has a frontage to the western side of the road for about F 840 feet southwards from the garden house. 7. Residential planning permission has been given for about twenty-one acres of land having a frontage to the eastern side of the road for about 1,250 feet southwards from the church."

Then there are a series of paragraphs dealing with traffic questions which do not arise now. I will read next: G

" 12. In December, 1961, the planning authority adopted a village classifi- cation system, which is to be included in the quinquennial review of the development plan. 13. Pavenham is classified as a village which it is intended will remain substantially unaltered both as to size and character; and where it is not expected that any significant amount of new develop- ment will be permitted." H

Those are the inspector's findings of fact. In a section headed " Inspector's Conclusions ", the inspector stated:

" 39. Bearing in mind the above facts I am of the opinion that, whilst not in the built-up area of Pavenham, the site is exceptional in that it is clearly defined by a tall and fine-looking wall and forms part of a long I established group of buildings which contribute to the attractive character of the village independent of distance. A well-designed house within the

(1) [1967] 1 All E.R. 751.
(2) S.I. 1965 No. 473. These rules came into operation on Apr. 1, 1965. They super- seded the Town and Country Planning (Inquiries Procedure) Rules, 1962 (S.I. 1962 No. 1425), which were in operation at the time of the application for planning permission (Nov. 27, 1964). The inspector's report was dated Jan. 5, 1966, and the Minister's decision was dated Feb. 24, 1966.

A   walled garden would, far from harming the countryside, add to the existing charm of its setting and could not be said to create a precedent for allowing development on farmland to the north or south."

Finally, the inspector stated his " Recommendation ":

B   " 41. I recommend that the appeal be allowed subject to the condition that the siting, design and external appearance of the building and the means of access thereto shall be as may be agreed with the local planning authority, or, in default of agreement, as shall be determined by the Minister."

That was very favourable to Lord Luke, but the recommendation was not accepted by the Minister. In his letter of decision the Minister wrote:

C   " The Minister accepts the inspector's findings of fact but is unable to agree with the conclusion he draws from them or with his recommendation. The council's policy for Pavenham is that apart from the sites which have already received planning permission, the village should remain substantially unaltered in size and character. The appeal site is outside the built-up part of the village and fronts the western side of a minor country road

D   running north from the main village street. Apart from the single dwelling, ' Garden House ', immediately to the south of the site, the surrounding land on this side of the road is open and undeveloped. It is considered that a house on the appeal site, although it would be within a walled garden, would be sporadic development in open countryside on the western side of a road which apart from the existing cottage to the south is at present free of

E   building. It would appear furthermore that there is no shortage of land suitable and approved for building to meet the housing needs of the village. For these reasons your client's proposal is considered undesirable and the Minister has decided to dismiss the appeal."

Did the Minister differ from the inspector on a finding of fact? In answering this question it is essential to draw a distinction between findings of fact by the

F   inspector and an expression of opinion by him on the planning merits. If the Minister differs from the inspector on a finding of fact, he must notify the applicant, in accordance with the rules, before coming to his decision; but if the Minister differs from the inspector on the planning merits, he can announce his decision straight away without notifying the applicant beforehand.

In the present case the inspector has divided his report into sections headed

G   " Findings of fact ", " Inspector's conclusions " and " Recommendation "; but I do not think that this division is sacrosanct. We must look into them and see which of his findings are truly findings of fact and which are expressions of opinion on planning merits . All the findings which are headed " Findings of fact " numbered 1 to 12 are undoubtedly findings of fact. So also the finding 13 which states the intention of the planning authority. The inspector's " Con-

H   clusions " in para. 39 are partly findings of fact and partly expressions of opinion. The inspector stated a *finding of fact* when he said:

" The site is exceptional in that it is clearly defined by a tall and fine-looking wall and forms part of a long established group of buildings which contribute to the attractive character of the village independent of distance."

I   The inspector expressed his *opinion on planning merits* when he stated:

" A well designed house within the walled garden would, far from harming the countryside, add to the existing charm of its setting and could not be said to create a precedent for allowing development on farmland to the north or south."

Now turning to the Minister's decision letter, the question is whether he differed from the inspector on a finding of fact. The decision letter is not happily expressed. The Minister said that he was unable to agree with the " conclusions " drawn by the inspector. At one time I thought that the Minister was

disagreeing with the whole of para. 39. If he disagreed with the first sentence A
that " the site is exceptional in that it is clearly defined ", etc., I should have
thought that he was differing on a finding of fact; but I do not think that he
was really differing from it. That sentence is only a summary of the previous
findings of fact. The Minister's difference was only on the second sentence that
" a well-designed house would . . .", etc. He was differing from that expression
of opinion by the inspector. The Minister took the view that a house would be B
" sporadic development " which would harm the countryside. That was a
difference of opinion on a planning matter. The Minister was entitled to come
to a different conclusion on such a matter without the necessity of notifying
Lord Luke, or giving him an opportunity of making representations.

I must say that I have considerable sympathy with Lord Luke. The inspector's report was very much in his favour; but it must be remembered that the C
Minister has the responsibility for planning policy. In order to preserve our
countryside he has adopted a policy of setting out an " envelope " for each
village. Development is permitted within the " envelope " and not outside it.
If one person is allowed to build outside, it will be difficult to refuse his neighbour.
So the Minister must be strict. This is planning policy, and nothing else. The
courts have no authority to interfere with the way in which the Minister carries D
it out.

I do not think that the Minister was in breach of the relevant requirements.
I would, therefore, allow this appeal and restore the Minister's decision.

DAVIES, L.J.: I agree. The description which the inspector gives to the
various parts of his report is not, of course, conclusive; but it is not without E
some importance, I think, to remind oneself of the opening words respectively of
paras. 38 and 39 of his report. Paragraph 38 has the cross heading: " Findings
of fact ", and commences: " I find the following facts ". Paragraph 39 is
headed: " Inspector's conclusions " and commences with the words: " Bearing
in mind the above facts, I am of the opinion that . . . ". As I say, that is not
conclusive; but I think that it is pretty clear from those words what the inspector F
thought that he was doing.

I agree with junior counsel for the Minister's analysis of the framework of
the report. Leaving out the earlier parts, there are first his findings of fact,
secondly, his planning conclusions on those findings of fact, and, thirdly and
lastly, his recommendation to the Minister in the light of those conclusions.
LAWTON, J., in the court below unfortunately went wrong where he said (3)— G
and I will alter his references to the rules to those which we have been considering
in this case:

" Rule 13 requires (4) the Minister to send the interested parties either a
copy of the inspector's report or a summary of, and I quote: ' [his] conclusions and recommendations '. The word ' conclusions ' in this context is
apt to describe both proven and observed facts and the inferences to be H
drawn from them. As r. 12 (1) refers (5) only to ' findings of fact ' and
' recommendations ', it seems to me that the words ' finding of fact ' in that
context include ' conclusions ' in the sense indicated above."

The judge is saying there that the conclusion falls into the category of findings
of fact. I take the opposite view. If conclusions are either to be put in the
category of findings of fact or recommendations, I think that they would be I
more properly included in the latter, as they are the inspector's reasons on the
facts for his final recommendation.

There is this third point, which was adverted to by junior counsel for the
Minister, that if the words " findings of fact " in the rule include any planning

---

(3) [1967] 1 All E.R. at p. 357, letter C.
(4) Rule 13 was formerly r. 11 of the Town and Country Planning Appeals (Inquiries
Procedure) Rules, 1962 (S.I. 1962 No. 1425).
(5) Rule 12 (1) was formerly r. 10 (1) of the rules of 1962.

A   conclusion, the rule would apply in every case where the Minister differed in the upshot from the view taken and recommended by the inspector.

I will refer to one other passage in the judgment of the judge, right at the end, where he said this (6):

B   " To my sense of justice this seems particularly apt when the Minister is inclined to the opinion that the inspector has gone wrong in applying the proven planning policy to the proven and observed facts."

This is precisely apposite in the present case.   That is the function of the Minister, and that is what he did here.   I am quite satisfied that he was not differing in any respect from the findings of fact reached by the inspector.

In conclusion I would refer once more to para. 39 of the inspector's report,
C   bearing in mind that what the Minister said in his decision letter was:

" The Minister accepts the inspector's findings of fact but is unable to agree with the conclusions he draws from them or with his recommendation."

The material paragraph, para. 39, starts, as I have said before:

" Bearing in mind the above facts I am of the opinion that, whilst not in
D   the built-up area of Pavenham, the site is exceptional in that it is clearly defined by a tall and fine-looking wall and forms part of a long established group of buildings which contribute to the attractive character of the village independent of distance."

Those are all facts.   They are merely a recapitulation in substance of the facts already set out in para. 38.   Then occur these words:

E   " A well-designed house within the walled garden would, far from harming the countryside, add to the existing charm of its setting and could not be said to create a precedent for allowing development on farmland to the north or south."

Those last few lines, I think, are not facts at all.   They are an expression of the inspector's opinion and of the reason why he comes to the conclusion that permis-
F   sion ought to be given.   In my judgment the applicant in this case completely failed to show that the Minister in any respect differed from the findings of fact reached by the inspector at the inquiry.   I agree that the appeal succeeds.

RUSSELL, L.J.:   I also agree.   The question is whether the conclusions of the inspector are findings of fact for the purposes of the rule.   The con-
G   clusion in para. 39 does state some facts which are already set out in para. 38. Those facts were accepted by the Minister.   The important part of para. 39, however, is the expression of opinion by the inspector on the planning aspect of the proposal.   All the Minister is doing is not agreeing with the inspector.   He is not in my judgment differing on a finding or inference of fact.   It is argued that a finding of fact must be everything contained in the inspector's report except
H   a finding of law or of mixed fact and law or perhaps an assessment of the balance of good over evil.   I cannot accept that, and I agree with the criticism which has been levelled against the passages of the judge's judgment (7).

Anything else would lead to this result, that substantially in every single case in which the Minister concluded differently from the inspector, the procedure of r. 12 (2) of the Rules of 1965 would perhaps be put into operation, because
I   whenever the Minister disagrees with the recommendation of the inspector, it, I think, necessarily follows that he does not assent to the conclusion and reasons which led the inspector to make the recommendation.   Not only would that approach lead to administrative inconvenience, but also it seems to me, as junior counsel for the Minister pointed out, it would mean that r. 12 (2) would be largely otiose : for it would only need to say that whenever the Minister is disposed to dis-agree with the recommendation, then he must notify the party of his disagreement

(6) [1967] 1 All E.R. at p. 357, letter G.
(7) [1967] 1 All E.R. at p. 357.

and afford him an opportunity to make representations in writing: there would **A**
seem to be no purpose in confining that machinery to a case where he is only
disposed to disagree with a recommendation by reason of the fact that he differs
from the appointed person on a finding of fact.   If the phrase " finding of fact "
is to be construed so as to embrace substantially everything to be found, except a
question of law, in the inspector's report, it would, as I have indicated, really
make the reference to a finding of fact meaningless.   **B**

Appeal allowed.

Solicitors: *Linklaters & Paines* (for the applicant); *Solicitor, Minister of
Housing and Local Government.*

[*Reported by* F. GUTTMAN, ESQ., *Barrister-at-Law.*]

C

BRITISH RAILWAYS BOARD *v.* LIPTROT.

[HOUSE OF LORDS (Viscount Dilhorne, Lord Reid, Lord Hodson, Lord Guest **D**
and Lord Pearson), February 8, 9, May 8, 9, 10, June 20, 1967.]

*Factory—Dangerous machinery—Mobile crane—Failure to fence—Gap between
rotating body and wheel—Injury to workman trapped in gap—Crane part of
factory equipment containing machinery—Mobility of crane did not exclude
it from Factories Act, 1961 (9 & 10 Eliz. 2 c. 34), s. 14 (1).*

The respondent was a slinger employed by the appellants, who occupied   **E**
a scrap metal yard which was a factory within the meaning of s. 175 (2) (*b*)
of the Factories Act, 1961. A mobile crane with a hook or magnet was used
to lift scrap metal after sorting and to place it in a railway truck. The crane
was mounted on a four-wheeled chassis, the wheels of which were covered
with rubber, and the body of the crane was mounted on a vertical shaft
fitted in the centre of the chassis. It was capable of moving under its own   **F**
power. The driver, from his cab at the offside of the body, controlled the
jib and the lifting and lowering of metal. After loading he had to slew the
jib which projected from the body, in order to unload. The body revolved
with the jib. There was a gap between the bottom of the body and the chassis
where wire sometimes got caught. When this happened the slinger normally
told the driver to stop the crane, and the slinger then removed the wire.   **G**
The respondent observed a piece of wire which was caught, but he did not
follow the normal practice. While he was in a position where it was impossible
for the driver to see him and was trying to free the wire, the driver slewed
the jib, and the respondent was caught by the revolving body of the crane
and was squeezed against one of the chassis wheels. In a claim for damages
for personal injuries for negligence and breach of statutory duty the respon-   **H**
dent alleged that the gap between the body of the crane and the wheel was
a dangerous part of the machinery and was not securely fenced, contrary
to s. 14 (1)* of the Factories Act, 1961. By reason of the course of proceedings
in the courts below the appellants were precluded from contending that,
if the mobile crane were within s. 14, the part of the crane which caused
the accident was not a " dangerous part of any machinery " or that the   **I**
accident was not caused or partly caused by any failure to fence it.

Held: the appellants were liable for breach of statutory duty under
s. 14 of the Factories Act, 1961, because—
(i) s. 22 to s. 27 of the Act of 1961 were not such an exclusive and complete
code relating to cranes and other machines as would lead to the consequence
that cranes should be excluded from being within the scope of s. 14 on

---

* Section 14 (1) is printed at p. 1076, letter C, post.

A its true construction (see p. 1076, letter I, p. 1077, letter C, p. 1079, letter H, p. 1082, letter B, p. 1084, letter I, and p. 1086, letters D to F, post).

Carrington v. *John Summers & Sons, Ltd.* ([1957] 1 All E.R. 457) approved.

(ii) the crane was part of the factory equipment and its mobility did not exclude it from the scope of s. 14; accordingly s. 14 applied to dangerous parts of machinery contained in the mobile crane and, as the appellants were

B precluded from contending that the part of the crane which caused the accident was not a dangerous part of machinery, the respondent was entitled to damages (see p. 1078, letter H, p. 1079, letter C, p. 1081, letters F and G, p. 1083, letters E and F, p. 1085, letter F, and p. 1087, letter F, post).

Cherry v. *International Alloys, Ltd.* ([1960] 3 All E.R. 264) overruled.

Decision of the COURT OF APPEAL (sub nom. *Liptrot* v. *British Railways*

C *Board* [1966] 2 All E.R. 247) affirmed, but not on the same ground.

[**Editorial Note.** The course of proceedings had precluded the raising of certain contentions before the House of Lords; these contentions are enumerated as 2-4 at p. 1075, letter H, post, and are briefly indicated at p. 1072, letter I, ante. Consequently the House, while emphasising that s. 14 did not require " machines "

D but only " dangerous parts of any machinery " to be securely fenced, was precluded from deciding what particular part of the mobile crane was a dangerous part of machinery. Although it is settled by the present decision that a mobile machine that is part of factory equipment is not outside the scope of s. 14 by reason of its mobility, yet there still remains, in future cases, possibility of disputing whether the particular part of machinery which causes an accident

E is a dangerous part of machinery and as such is required, by virtue of s. 14, to be securely fenced. The distinction between accidents, which may be described as traffic accidents, and factory accidents resulting from unfenced machinery, is clearly drawn, e.g., at p. 1087, letters D to F, post.

As to what is machinery for the purposes of the Factories Act, 1961, see 17 HALSBURY'S LAWS (3rd Edn.) 70-76, paras. 122-126; and for cases on the

F subject see 24 DIGEST (Repl.) 1052-1062, *202-254*.

For the Factories Act, 1961, s. 14 (1) see 41 HALSBURY'S STATUTES (2nd Edn.) 256.]

Cases referred to:

Carrington v. *John Summers & Sons, Ltd.*, [1957] 1 All E.R. 457; [1957] 1 W.L.R. 504; Digest (Cont. Vol. A) 591, *254a.*

G *Cherry* v. *International Alloys, Ltd.*, [1960] 3 All E.R. 264; [1961] 1 Q.B. 136; [1960] 3 W.L.R. 568; Digest (Cont. Vol. A) 586, *205a.*

Miller v. *William Boothman & Sons, Ltd.*, [1944] 1 All E.R. 333; [1944] K.B. 337; 113 L.J.K.B. 206; 170 L.T. 187; 24 Digest (Repl.) 1091, *418.*

Parvin v. *Morton Machine Co., Ltd.*, [1952] 1 All E.R. 670; [1952] A.C. 515; 116 J.P. 211; 24 Digest (Repl.) 1059, *239.*

H *Quintas* v. *National Smelting Co., Ltd.*, [1961] 1 All E.R. 630; [1961] 1 W.L.R. 401; Digest (Cont. Vol. A) 585, *201c.*

Summers (John) & Sons, Ltd. v. *Frost*, [1955] 1 All E.R. 870; [1955] A.C. 740; [1955] 2 W.L.R. 825; 24 Digest (Repl.) 1055, *217.*

Appeal.

I This was an appeal from a judgment of the Court of Appeal (WILLMER and SALMON, L.JJ., DANCKWERTS, L.J., dissenting) dated Mar. 1, 1966, and reported [1966] 2 All E.R. 247, allowing an appeal by the respondent, Thomas Liptrot, from a judgment of BARRY, J., given on Oct. 11, 1965 at Manchester Assizes, whereby he dismissed the respondent's claim against the appellants, the British Railways Board. The respondent claimed damages in an action alleging negligence and breach of statutory duty on the part of the appellants in failing to fence dangerous machinery contrary to s. 14 of the Factories Act, 1961, as a result of which, so the respondent alleged, he sustained injuries on May 24, 1962,

in the course of his employment as a slinger at the appellants' locomotive works   A
at Horwich, near Bolton, Lancashire.

Marven Everett, Q.C., and *P. C. Corcoran* for the appellants.
G. Heilpern, Q.C., and *A. M. Prestt* for the respondent.
Their lordships took time for consideration.
June 20.   The following opinions were delivered.

B

   VISCOUNT DILHORNE: My Lords, on May 24, 1962, the respondent
met with an accident when employed by the appellants as a slinger in their
scrap metal yard at Horwich in Lancashire. Scrap metal is sorted there and then
lifted by a mobile crane and placed in a railway truck. The yard is in the open
but by virtue of s. 175 (2) (*b*) of the Factories Act, 1961, is a factory for the
purposes of that Act.   C
   The mobile crane is mounted on a four-wheeled chassis, the wheels of which
are covered with rubber. The body of the crane is mounted on a vertical shaft
fitted in the centre of the chassis. The crane driver sits at the offside front of
the body. The crane can travel over the ground under its own power and is
then driven by the driver from his cab, from which he also controls the movement
of the jib and the lifting and lowering of material by the crane. The jib and the   D
body of the crane can be made to revolve in a full circle above the chassis.
   The scrap metal is lifted by a hook or by a magnet. On May 24 the magnet
was in use. The jib of the crane projects from the body and, when a load of
scrap metal has been lifted, the crane driver has to slew the jib so as to unload
the metal in a railway truck.
   When the jib is slewed, the body of the crane revolves with it. There is a   E
narrow space between the bottom of the body of the crane and the chassis
over which the body revolves. When wire was lifted, it was sometimes subjected
to tension with the result that, when the wire broke or came free, it sprung up
and got caught between the body and the chassis of the crane. When this
happened, the normal practice was for the respondent to tell the crane driver
to stop the crane and then for him to remove the wire.   F
   On May 24 wire had got caught in this space on three occasions before the
accident. On each of these occasions the normal practice was followed. Then
the respondent saw that another piece of wire, a short piece, had got caught.
He saw that the magnet of the crane was on the ground and he thought that
he would have time to free the wire before a load of metal was picked up and
the body of the crane revolved. He stood between the rear wheels of the chassis,   G
close to the nearside rear wheel, in a position in which it was impossible for the
driver of the crane to see him. He leant forward and put his arm into the space
between the body of the crane and the chassis to try and free the wire. While he
was engaged on this, the crane driver slewed the jib with the result that the
respondent was caught by the edge of the body of the crane as it revolved and
squeezed against the nearside rear wheel of the chassis.   H
   He commenced an action against the appellants claiming damages for the
injuries he had received and alleging negligence and a breach of statutory duty.
In his statement of claim it was, inter alia, alleged that:

   "The trapping point between the body of the said crane and the said wheel,
   being a dangerous part of the said machine, was not securely fenced;
   negligently and/or contrary to s. 14 of the said Act."   I

The appellants by their defence denied negligence and breach of statutory duty
and alleged that the accident was solely caused, or alternatively was contributed
to, by the negligence of the respondent.
   The action was tried by BARRY, J., at Manchester Assizes in October, 1965.
He held that negligence on the part of the appellants was not established.
This finding was not challenged by the respondent in the Court of Appeal (1)

   (1) [1966] 2 All E.R. 247; [1966] 2 Q.B. 353.

A or in this House. With regard to the claim under the Factories Act, 1961, Barry, J., said that counsel for the respondent had referred to s. 27 of the Act

" and said, as this referred to cranes and working gear and as the machine which caused this accident was a crane, it was in fact machinery within the meaning of s. 14 and thus it required to be fenced."

B Barry, J., then said:

" Without the slightest hesitation, I follow the decision of Streatfeild, J., in the case of *Carrington* v. *John Summers & Sons, Ltd.* (2). The effects of that decision were that if that crane was machinery within the meaning of s. 14, then the meaning of that section would apply to it, despite the most specific requirements of s. 27 . . . I am also satisfied, applying the
C somewhat stringent tests laid down, that this was a dangerous part of the machinery."

Barry, J., did not state in any greater detail what was the part of the machinery that he was satisfied was dangerous or what was the part to which counsel referred when he said that it required to be fenced. In view of the allegation in the statement of claim, to which I have referred, it is to be presumed that
D Barry, J., and counsel were referring to what was called in that document the trapping point between the body of the crane and the wheel.

Barry, J., then went on to consider whether the mobile crane was machinery to which s. 14 of the Act of 1961 applied. He held in the light of the decision in *Cherry* v. *International Alloys, Ltd.* (3) " with very considerable hesitation " that it was not. He consequently gave judgment for the appellants, but said
E that if they had been at fault he would have held them one-third to blame and the respondent two-thirds to blame. He assessed the damages in the neighbourhood of £2,000 in addition to the special damage.

The respondent appealed to the Court of Appeal (4). The appellants did not serve a cross notice but towards the end of the hearing in the Court of Appeal (4) sought leave to do so to challenge the judge's finding that there was
F a dangerous part of the machinery. The Court of Appeal (4) did not think that it was right to grant such leave at such a late stage. The Court of Appeal (4) (Willmer and Salmon, L.JJ., Danckwerts, L.J., dissenting) allowed the appeal holding that the Factories Act, 1961, applied to a crane used in a factory.

From this decision the appellants now appeal. In para. 3 of their case it is said that the following points arise for decision:
G
" 1. Was the mobile crane which was involved in the accident which occurred . . . machinery within the meaning of s. 14 of the Factories Act, 1961?

" 2. If it was, was the part of the said mobile crane which was involved in the respondent's accident a part of the machinery in the appellants'
H factory within the meaning of the said section?

" 3. If it was, was the part where the respondent was injured a dangerous part of the machinery . . .?

" 4. On the facts as found by the trial judge was the respondent the sole author of his own misfortune? "

The second and third questions divide into two the question which the appellants
I were not permitted to argue in the Court of Appeal (4), namely, whether what has been called the trapping point constituted a dangerous part of machinery. In their lordships' view it was not open to the appellants to argue this question before them. The appellants, not having given a cross notice, did not argue in the Court of Appeal (4) that the respondent was solely to blame for the accident and, in their lordships' opinion, it was not open to them to put forward that contention before them.

(2) [1957] 1 All E.R. 457.   (3) [1960] 3 All E.R. 264; [1961] 1 Q.B. 136.
(4) [1966] 2 All E.R. 247; [1966] 2 Q.B. 353.

So initially the only question for decision by this House was whether the **A** mobile crane was machinery within the meaning of s. 14 of the Act of 1961. After the argument had proceeded for some time, the appellants sought to raise the question which had been raised before the trial judge, whether, as s. 27 of the Act of 1961 specifically related to cranes, they were to be regarded as excluded from the ambit of s. 14. Leave was given to the appellants on terms to advance this argument. **B**

Part 2 of the Factories Act, 1961, is headed: " Safety (General Provisions) ". The first section in this Part, s. 12, relates to prime movers, s. 13 to transmission machinery and s. 14 to other machinery. Section 14 (1) reads as follows:

" Every dangerous part of any machinery, other than prime movers and transmission machinery, shall be securely fenced unless it is in such a position or of such construction as to be as safe to every person employed **C** or working on the premises as it would be if securely fenced."

It is to be noted that this subsection is expressed to apply to every dangerous part of *any machinery* which is in a factory as defined by s. 175 (2) of the Act of 1961.

The immediately following sections deal with a variety of matters. Section 22 **D** deals with hoists and lifts generally; s. 23 with hoists and lists used for carrying persons; s. 24 with teagle openings and similar doorways; s. 25 (1) provides that the hoists and lifts to which s. 22 and s. 23 apply are those which have a platform or cage the direction of movement of which is restricted by a guide or guides. Section 25 (4) gives the Minister power by order to direct that a requirement of s. 22, s. 23 and s. 24 shall not apply if he is satisfied that it would be **E** unreasonable in the special circumstances of the case to enforce it. Section 26 deals with chains, ropes and lifting tackle and s. 27 with cranes and other lifting machines as defined in s. 27 (9).

It was contended that s. 22 to s. 27 are to be regarded as containing all the requirements imposed by the Factories Act, 1961, in relation to hoists, lifts, cranes and other lifting machines. In support of this contention it was pointed **F** out that s. 22 (4) required every hoistway or liftway to be efficiently protected by a substantial enclosure fitted with gates of such a character as to prevent, when the gates are shut, any person falling down the way or coming in contact with any moving part of the hoist or lift, and it was argued that this amounted to a requirement to fence. Further, s. 22 (7) provides that, inter alia, every hoist or lift shall be so constructed as to prevent any part of any person or any **G** goods carried on the hoist or lift from being trapped between the counterbalance weight and any other moving part of the hoist or lift. Counsel for the appellants submitted that any person trapped between the counterbalance weight and any other moving part was trapped by a dangerous part of the machinery. He argued that as the Minister could by order dispense with the requirement to comply with s. 22 (4) and (7), it would be anomalous if an employer, relieved by the order of **H** the Minister from complying with these requirements, was none the less liable to prosecution and to a claim for damages for breach of s. 14 (1) if he failed to fence securely against any person coming in contact with any moving part of the hoist or lift (s. 22 (4)) or being trapped between the counterbalance weight and any other moving part of the hoist or lift (s. 22 (7)). He therefore argued that s. 14 (1) was not intended to apply to hoists or lifts and that s. 22 to s. 27 con- **I** stituted a complete code of the requirements imposed by the Act in relation to hoists, lifts, cranes and other lifting machines.

While appreciating the force of the argument based on s. 25 (4) in relation to hoists and lists, it is not, in my opinion, necessary in this case to decide whether it is well founded. Section 27 which applies to cranes contains no provision similar to that of s. 25 (4). The Minister has no power by order to say that any of the requirements of that section shall not apply where he is satisfied that it is unreasonable that they should. Further, s. 27 does not contain any

A provision which can be interpreted as a requirement to fence. If this section
is to be regarded as containing all the requirements that the Act imposes in
relation to cranes, then there is no duty to fence securely every dangerous part
of any machinery in a crane. In *Carrington* v. *John Summers & Sons, Ltd.* (5)
Streatfeild, J., had to decide the same question. He refused (6) to hold that
s. 24 of the Factories Act, 1937 (now replaced by s. 27 of the Act of 1961)

B   " laid down a complete set of rules applicable to cranes and other lifting
    machines and, therefore, superseded, so far as cranes and lifting machines
    were concerned, the general provisions with regard to the fencing of
    dangerous machinery that are laid down in s. 14."

   In my view, Streatfeild, J., was right in so holding and Barry, J., rightly
C rejected this contention in this case. In my opinion, this contention of the
appellants is not well founded.
   The only other question for decision in this appeal is whether the Factories
Act, 1961, applies to mobile cranes. I cannot accept the argument advanced
before Barry, J., by counsel for the respondent that, as cranes are dealt with
in s. 27, it follows that they are machinery within s. 14.

D   In *John Summers & Sons, Ltd.* v. *Frost* (7) Lord Morton of Henryton
pointed out that the words " dangerous machine " are not used in s. 14. It is
not, in my opinion, to be assumed that every part of a machine is a part of
machinery. That word is not defined in the Factories Act, and its ordinary
meaning must be given to it. A crane can be described as a machine but no
one would say that the seat on which the crane driver sits was part of the
E machinery of the crane; nor would it be right to describe the body of a motor
car as part of the machinery of a car.
   In relation to s. 14 the question is not whether it is a machine to which that
section applies but whether there is any part of machinery which is dangerous
if not securely fenced. In this case it was not open to the appellants to contend
before your lordships that the respondent's injuries were not caused by a part
F of the machinery of the crane or that, if they were, that part was not a dangerous
part if not fenced. If it had been open to them to do so, the respondent would,
I think, have had considerable difficulty in satisfying me that the wheel of the
chassis and the body of the crane were part of the machinery of the crane. The
finding of Barry, J., on this not having been challenged, the appeal has to be
determined on the basis that the respondent's injuries were caused by a dangerous
G unfenced part of the machinery though, if the finding had been challenged,
that might have been held not to be the case.
   Despite this finding, Barry, J., held that s. 14 did not apply to a mobile
crane. As I have said, he based this conclusion on the decision in *Cherry* v.
International Alloys, Ltd. (8). In that case an experienced mechanic suffered
injuries through his hand slipping while he was adjusting the oil feed of a petrol-
H driven Lister truck and coming in contact with the fan which cooled the engine.
   The truck which had three wheels was used in a factory for carrying and
removing materials. Sellers, L.J., in the course of his judgment said (9):

      " But if this truck is machinery to which the Act applies, so is an ordinary
    motor car while in the factory, at least if used for factory purposes, and
    that no one, I would have thought, could have described as factory
I   machinery."

and, applying a common sense approach, Sellers, L.J., held that the truck was
not machinery to which s. 14 was intended to apply. It was, he said, a vehicle.

(5) [1957] 1 All E.R. 457.
(6) [1957] 1 All E.R. at p. 459, letter F.
(7) [1955] 1 All E.R. 870 at p. 874, letter E; [1955] A.C. 740 at p. 754.
(8) [1960] 3 All E.R. 264; [1961] 1 Q.B. 136.
(9) [1960] 3 All E.R. at p. 266, letter E; [1961] 1 Q.B. at p. 144.

PEARCE, L.J., said (10) that if the provisions of the Act of 1937 applied to Lister **A** trucks " lorries or motor cars that came to visit the factory would be caught by those provisions ". He went on to say that (10):

" . . . one may fairly assume that trucks were not in the mind of the draftsman. Trucks are self-contained units and the dangers that they create are different dangers from those caused by factory machinery with which the Act was primarily concerned. The danger of being run over or **B** knocked down is wholly different from the dangers that arise in factories from catching, cutting, pinching and crushing."

He further said (11) that a Lister truck would not normally be described as machinery and posed the question: if an ordinary man would not consider the truck as coming within the classification of machinery, was the judge compelled to hold otherwise? He held that the judge was not and that he was right in **C** deciding that the truck was not machinery. DEVLIN, L.J., said (12) that, in his judgment, the object of the Factories Act, 1937, was not " to make safety provision for vehicles, which may travel inside or outside a factory, or for plant and machinery inside them " and that the wide meaning of the words of s. 14 should be cut down to exclude vehicles. Relying on this decision (13) counsel **D** for the appellants argued strongly that the mobile crane which could move over the ground and along roads under its own power was also to be regarded as a vehicle and outside the ambit of s. 14.

I regret that I am unable to agree with the views expressed in and the ratio decidendi of *Cherry* v. *International Alloys, Ltd.* (13). In my opinion, the object of the Factories Act, 1961, is to make safety provisions for those employed in, **E** or who work in, factories. To that end every dangerous part of any machinery in a factory requires to be securely fenced. That is an absolute obligation except as in the section mentioned and subject to its proviso (see *John Summers & Sons, Ltd.* v. *Frost* (14) per VISCOUNT SIMONDS). This obligation does not depend on whether the machinery is a fixed part of the equipment of the factory or is on wheels and capable of moving under its own power from one part of the **F** factory to another or outside the factory.

While it would not be right to describe a vehicle as machinery, it may contain machinery; and if the vehicle forms part of the equipment of the factory, then, in my opinion, s. 14 imposes an absolute obligation, subject to the proviso in that section, to fence securely every dangerous part of the machinery that it contains. In *Cherry's* case (13), the fan which caused the injuries was, if not **G** part of a prime mover coming within s. 12 of the Act of 1961 part of the machinery in the truck coming within s. 14. The question was not, as I see it, whether the Lister truck was machinery to which the Act of 1961 applied but whether, as it was part of the equipment of the factory, it contained machinery which required to be fenced. Lorries and cars which came to visit a factory would not, in my opinion, be part of its equipment and the Act of 1961 would not apply to them. **H** I can see no valid reason for excluding any part of the equipment of a factory which contains machinery from the operation of the Act of 1961 on the ground that it is mobile or can be described as a vehicle. In my opinion, *Cherry's* case (13) was wrongly decided.

WILLMER, L.J., in the present case (15) distinguished it from *Cherry's* case (13) on the ground that in *Cherry's* case (13) the truck was basically a vehicle and in **I** this case the piece of equipment was basically a crane and that it constituted part of the factory machinery. DANCKWERTS, L.J., delivering a dissenting

---

(10) [1960] 3 All E.R. at p. 267, letter E; [1961] 1 Q.B. at p. 146.
(11) [1960] 3 All E.R. at pp. 267, 268; [1961] 1 Q.B. at pp. 146, 147.
(12) [1960] 3 All E.R. at p. 269, letter D; [1961] 1 Q.B. at pp. 148, 149.
(13) [1960] 3 All E.R. 264; [1961] 1 Q.B. 136.
(14) [1955] 1 All E.R. at p. 872, letter D; [1955] A.C. at p. 751.
(15) [1966] 2 All E.R. 247; [1966] 2 Q.B. 353.

A judgment, expressed the opinion (16) that the crane was not " properly within the meaning of ' factory machinery ' contained in the Factories Act, 1961, and in particular in s. 14 . . ." SALMON, L.J., said (17):

> " The sole question that arises on this appeal is whether a mobile mechanically operated crane used in a factory of this kind is a machine to which the Act of 1961 applies."

B He expressed the view (18) that a mobile crane used in a factory was " much closer in its character to a piece of factory machinery than it is to a motor vehicle such as a Lister truck ".

As I have indicated, in my view the question that has to be decided is not whether the crane is a machine to which the Act of 1961 applies, but whether, if it is part of the equipment of the factory, it contains machinery. If it does,
C then s. 14 (1) applies in relation to that machinery. It is not, therefore, necessary to determine whether the piece of equipment is basically a vehicle.

For the reasons which I have given, in my opinion the majority of the Court of Appeal (19), though I am not able to agree with their reasons, came to the right conclusion in this case. In my opinion this appeal should be dismissed.

D   **LORD REID:** My Lords, this case is concerned with the proper construction of s. 14 of the Factories Act, 1961, which requires dangerous parts of machinery to be securely fenced. The appellant contends that this section does not apply to cranes, or in any event that it does not apply to a mobile crane such as was instrumental in causing injury to the respondent.

There can be no doubt that prior to 1937 the statutory provisions which
E required fencing did apply to cranes. The appellant's argument is founded on the fact that, in the Factories Act, 1937, and again in the Act of 1961, there are separate sections dealing with hoists and lifts and with cranes and other lifting machines. These sections set out a number of safety provisions but there is nothing in either of them about fencing dangerous parts of machinery. On the other hand there is nothing expressly excluding s. 14. The argument is
F that these sections were intended to be complete codes in themselves, and that it is left to the Minister to make regulations about fencing for cranes, etc., if he thinks that necessary. This seems to me to be so improbable that before I would accept it I would have to be satisfied that there is some provision in these sections which is inconsistent with s. 14, or which at least makes it difficult to apply s. 14. The most that can be said, however, is that the Minister is given
G power to direct that certain requirements of these sections shall not apply in certain circumstances and that he could use this power in such a way as to produce a conflict with s. 14. Perhaps he could; but if s. 14 does apply one is entitled to assume that he would not do so, unless he has also power to modify the provisions of s. 14 and uses it to produce a coherent result. In my view, there is no substance in the appellants' argument on this matter and I have
H no hesitation in holding that s. 14 does apply to cranes and other apparatus mentioned in these two sections.

The second question is much more difficult. The appellants' main argument is that the provisions of s. 14 cannot be applied to machinery in vehicles and that this mobile crane was a vehicle. It is mounted on a chassis with four rubber tyred wheels, and the chassis can be driven and steered in the same way as an
I ordinary heavy motor vehicle. The crane consists of an ordinary jib which can be operated from a cab by means of machinery which is enclosed in a large square metal box or casing, and it is mounted on the chassis in such a way that it can be rotated as a whole on the chassis. When the crane is rotated there are clearances of some six inches between the bottom of the casing and the tops of each of the wheels. The respondent's accident occurred in an open railway

---

(16) [1966] 2 All E.R. at p. 254, letter F; [1966] 2 Q.B. at p. 367.
(17) [1966] 2 All E.R. at p. 255, letter A; [1966] 2 Q.B. at p. 367.
(18) [1966] 2 All E.R. at p. 256, letter A; [1966] 2 Q.B. at p. 369.
(19) [1966] 2 All E.R. 247; [1966] 2 Q.B. 353.

yard where metal scrap was being sorted and the crane was used to lift and **A**
move this scrap. It is admitted that the provisions of s. 151 (1) (ii) of the Act
of 1937 (repeated in the Act of 1961 (20)) applied to this yard, so that it must
be held to be a factory; and I am satisfied that this crane must be held to have
been part of the equipment of that "factory". So if the respondent's injury
was caused by any breach of s. 14 he must succeed.

The respondent very foolishly put himself in a position where the rotation **B**
of the crane on its chassis caught him between the bottom of the rotating casing
and the top of one of the wheels of the chassis. Even if s. 14 applies it is not at
all clear to me what was the dangerous part of the machinery which ought
to have been fenced, or how any breach of s. 14 caused the accident. The trial
judge said no more than "I am also satisfied, applying the somewhat stringent
tests laid down, that *this* was a dangerous part of the machinery". Probably **C**
this matter was not closely argued. It is not at all clear what "this" was.
By reason of the course which this case has taken since the trial, however, the
appellants are not now in a position to contest this finding, and we must take it
that some unspecified part of the machinery of this vehicle was dangerous and
that failure to fence it caused the accident.

The object of s. 14 is to protect persons in a factory from danger which would **D**
exist if dangerous parts of the machinery were not fenced, and the words:
"Every dangerous part of any machinery other than prime movers and transmission machinery" (which are dealt with in other sections) are quite unlimited.
So I would find it hard to suppose that the draftsman (or Parliament) in fact
intended that there should be licence to keep in a factory any machinery of
which dangerous parts were not fenced. If, however, there are compelling **E**
reasons for excluding certain kinds of machinery from the scope of s. 14, then
they must be excluded. In *Parvin* v. *Morton Machine Co., Ltd.* (21) it was held
that the section did not apply to machinery which was in the course of being
manufactured in the factory. LORD NORMAND said (22):

"But the context must be looked at and I find in the context supplied
by s. 12 and s. 13 compelling reasons for construing the word 'machinery' **F**
in s. 14 (1) as denoting only machinery used for production."

It appears from later passages in his opinion that he gave a wide meaning to
the phrase "used in production": he was contrasting machinery in course of
manufacture with machinery kept in the factory as part of its equipment. So
the question here is whether there is any compelling reason for excluding from
the scope of s. 14 machinery in vehicles (or in certain kinds of vehicles) which **G**
are part of the equipment of a factory. Mechanically propelled vehicles of
various kinds have long been part of the equipment of many factories: indeed
it would be difficult to carry on business there efficiently and economically
without them.

In *Cherry* v. *International Alloys, Ltd.* (23), a mechanic, while adjusting part **H**
of the engine of a Lister truck while it was running, sustained injury to his hand
from coming in contact with the revolving fan. Normally the fan had a guard but
it had been removed. Breach of s. 14 was alleged. In defence it was not denied
that the unfenced fan was dangerous, and it was not said to be impracticable
to fence the fan during this operation. The defence which succeeded was that
the machinery of this truck was not machinery within the scope and meaning **I**
of s. 14. Lister trucks were three-wheeled vehicles in common use in large factories
for carrying material from one part of the factory to another, and the truck was
certainly part of the normal equipment of the factory. So far as I can see the
only relevant difference between it and the crane in the present case was that the

(20) See s. 175 (2) (*b*) of the Act of 1961.
(21) [1952] 1 All E.R. 670; [1952] A.C. 515.
(22) [1952] 1 All E.R. at p. 671, letter H; [1952] A.C. at p. 521.
(23) [1960] 3 All E.R. 264; [1961] 1 Q.B. 136.

A Lister truck had no lifting mechanism and was a smaller and lighter vehicle. The main grounds of this decision were, I think, that such vehicles would not normally be classed as factory machinery: that if this truck were within the scope of s. 14 so would be any vehicle driven in to the factory: and that the dangers involved in a vehicle moving about in the factory were of a wholly different character from those to which s. 14 refers. I cannot read this decision

B as limited to those vehicles which contain no machinery other than that required to propel the vehicle. Take for instance a fork lift machine: it is small and mobile, but it also contains machinery for lifting its load off the ground. I think that on the reasoning in *Cherry's* case (24) it would be excluded from the scope of s. 14; and I do not see how size can make a difference.

Section 14 deals with dangerous parts of machinery. Sometimes one finds

C in the authorities references to dangerous machines; but that is not what the section says, and to ask the question—is this machine dangerous?—can easily lead to error. A vehicle is a dangerous machine in the sense that, if it is driven in a dangerous manner, it may run into someone and injure him. What, then, are the dangerous parts of the machine? It is not the parts of the machine which are dangerous but the machine as a whole; if one had to specify dangerous

D parts, presumably in the case of an ordinary motor car they would be the bumper, the mudguards and the grille or casing which in more modern cars is found in front of the radiator, but they are not parts of the machinery at all. Of course it would be impossible to fence against this kind of danger; but s. 14 is not dealing with this kind of danger; it is dealing with parts of machinery where danger arises from their not being fenced and is obviated by fencing. So it appears to

E me that the fact that vehicles in motion create a kind of danger which does not exist with stationary or fixed machinery is no reason for not requiring the fencing of parts of the machinery in vehicles which are dangerous whether the vehicle is in motion or not. In *Cherry's* case (24) the vehicle was not in motion when the accident occurred and it was caused by the kind of danger which is found in both fixed and mobile machinery and which can be removed

F by fencing. I am therefore of opinion that *Cherry's* case (24) was wrongly decided.

In the present case the crane was not in motion as a vehicle when the accident occurred. We must take it that there was a part of its machinery which was dangerous when the crane was being used but the vehicle on which it was mounted was at rest, and that failure to fence that dangerous part caused this accident. For the reasons which I have given I could not support the grounds

G of judgment of the majority of the Court of Appeal (25), but in my view they reached the right result. I would therefore dismiss this appeal.

LORD HODSON: My Lords, this appeal resurrects a question which was decided as long ago as 1957 by Streatfeild, J., in *Carrington* v. *John Summers & Sons, Ltd.* (26). It was contended before him that the comparison of sections

H (27) of the Factories Act, 1937 (now the Factories Act, 1961) dealing with dangerous parts of machinery and the requirement that they should be fenced, with s. 24 of the Factories Act, 1937 (now s. 27 of the Factories Act, 1961), showed that the later section laid down a complete set of rules applicable to cranes and other lifting machines. Hence it was said that the general provisions with regard to fencing of dangerous parts of machinery were to this extent superseded.

I The learned judge held, and I agree with him, that there is nothing in the language of the statute to justify the submission that the general provisions cannot exist side by side with the special provisions relating to cranes, etc. These later provisions relate to special aspects of the dangers which arise from the use of

(24) [1960] 3 All E.R. 264; [1961] 1 Q.B. 136.
(25) [1966] 2 All E.R. 247; [1966] 2 Q.B. 353.
(26) [1957] 1 All E.R. 457.
(27) Viz., ss. 12, 13, 14 of the Factories Act, 1937, which were compared with s. 24, the comparison beginning with s. 10 of the Factory and Workshop Act, 1901 (see [1957] 1 All E.R. at p. 459, letter F).

cranes, principally dangers which arise from their movement rather than from **A** the dangerous character of their individual parts. The mere fact that the Minister may make regulations dealing with cranes under s. 76 of the Act of 1961 does not, of itself, support the contention that there is an exclusive and complete code. It would be otherwise if he had made regulations which conflicted with s. 14. As was pointed out in *Miller* v. *William Boothman & Sons, Ltd.* (28) regulations may be made by the Secretary of State (29) modifying the absolute **B** obligation imposed by s. 14. Nothing of the kind has happened here and I have no difficulty in rejecting this special argument advanced on behalf of the appellants.

The main point of appeal, however, was that the mobile crane which was involved in the accident giving rise to the appeal was not machinery at all within the ambit of s. 14, so that no question arose as to any dangerous part **C** requiring to be fenced. The distinction between a dangerous part of machinery which requires to be fenced and dangerous machinery is illustrated by the sections referred to in the first argument relating to cranes which may in themselves be regarded as potentially dangerous in use. It is important to emphasise that the point that the mobile crane was not machinery was the only point raised on the appeal, apart from the one which I first dealt with, and was the only **D** point which was raised and argued before the Court of Appeal (30).

The question which may well be the real question which ought to be determined in this case, namely, " Was the part of the machinery where the respondent was injured a dangerous part? " was never argued and your lordships are not concerned with it. The appellants are concerned to support the opinion expressed by BARRY, J., at the trial of the action, and confirmed by DANCKWERTS, **E** L.J. (dissenting) in the Court of Appeal that the machinery here involved, being a mobile crane on wheels, was not within the provisions of s. 14 at all.

That all machinery in a factory is not covered by the section is exemplified by *Parvin* v. *Morton Machine Co., Ltd.* (31) which decided that machinery manufactured in the factory is not included. Any machinery which is part of the equipment of the factory is, however, within the ambit of the section unless for **F** some reason it is to be excluded.

Why, then, should the mobile crane be excluded? The appellants lean heavily on the authority of the case of *Cherry* v. *International Alloys, Ltd.* (32), a decision of the Court of Appeal which decided that a Lister truck used in a factory for carrying and removing materials produced therein was not, on a commonsense construction of s. 14 of the Factories Act, 1937, " machinery " to which the section **G** applied. The approach of the court was, I think, that it would be absurd so to regard motor cars and such like, which are no doubt dangerous if they run into people but not dangerous in themselves as machinery. Taking the view that the trucks were not " machinery ", they did not consider the question whether the dangerous part of the truck which caused the injury to the plaintiff ought to have been fenced. The circumstances were that the plaintiff was making an adjustment **H** to the truck with the engine running and was injured by the fan which was at the time of the accident revolving unguarded. It was conceded that, if the vehicle was machinery, there had been a breach of s. 14 and the plaintiff was entitled to recover. The principle of construction relied on in the Court of Appeal was that set out in MAXWELL ON THE INTERPRETATION OF STATUTES (10th Edn.) at p. 60 when dealing with the interpretation of general words and phrases. **I** DEVLIN, L.J., cited this passage (33):

---

(28) [1944] 1 All E.R. 333; [1944] K.B. 337.
(29) The functions of the Secretary of State were transferred to the Minister of Labour and National Service (Transfer of Functions (Factories, etc.), Acts) Order, 1946 (S.R. & O. 1946 No. 376), art. 2, and are now exercisable under the Act of 1961 by the Minister of Labour.   (30) [1966] 2 All E.R. 247; [1966] 2 Q.B. 353.
(31) [1952] 1 All E.R. 670; [1952] A.C. 515.
(32) [1960] 3 All E.R. 264; [1961] 1 Q.B. 136.
(33) [1960] 3 All E.R. at p. 269, letter A; [1961] 1 Q.B. at p. 148.

A   " While expressing truly enough all that the legislature intended, they frequently express more, in their literal meaning and natural force: and it is necessary to give them the meaning which best suits the scope and object of the statute without extending to ground foreign to the intention. It is, therefore, a canon of interpretation that all words, if they be general and not express and precise, are to be restricted to the fitness of the matter."

B   Devlin, L.J., then concluded (34) that in accordance with this principle the wide meaning of the words should be cut down so as to exclude vehicles.

It is quite true that the obvious dangers of a self-contained unit moving about a factory are very different from those connoted by dangerous parts of machinery, but it does not follow that mobility is the test. It is, as Salmon, L.J., pointed out in this case (35), a novel principle that in a matter of this kind mobility spells immunity and it cannot be that, if a machine is part of the factory equipment, it can no longer have dangerous parts because it is on wheels.

C   The appellants sought to restrict " machinery " in s. 14 to that which was capable of being put in motion or in use by means of a prime mover either directly or through transmission machinery, being machinery used for or incidental to a purpose of a factory as defined in s. 175 of the Act of 1961. They sought to exclude mobile machines with the characteristics of vehicles, even if they perform other functions such as lifting or carrying. The difficulties and absurdities of applying this test of exclusion are obvious, since if a crane is machinery when fixed on a concrete or other base it cannot be the less so because it is mounted on a travelling chassis.

D   The majority of the Court of Appeal (36) distinguished *Cherry's* case (37) on its facts, but I think that it is necessary to go further and to conclude that *Cherry's* case (37) was wrongly decided. It was decided on the concession that there was a dangerous part of the truck, namely, the unfenced fan, and not on the basis that the truck had no dangerous parts. Dangerous parts of machinery, not danger in movement of the whole machinery, are the considerations to which s. 14 is directed. Although machinery may, as in *Parvin's* case (38), be sometimes outside the purview of the section, there is no reason to exclude a machine which is part of the factory equipment simply because it is on wheels. Like Danckwerts, L.J., in this case I find it difficult to appreciate the real distinction between *Cherry's* case (37) and this case simply because of the absence of lifting machinery in the one case and the presence of it in the other.

E

F

G   This particular point has seldom been dealt with in other cases where equipment of a similar nature to a mobile crane has been assumed to be machinery within the meaning of the section, but there is one reported case where there was a division of judicial opinion. In that case, *Quintas* v. *National Smelting Co., Ltd.* (39), a ropeway carrying buckets was under consideration, and for myself I find it difficult to see how that could be excluded from the ambit of s. 14. The ropeway there described is a single piece of apparatus of which a part may be dangerous and within the scope of the section.

H

For the reasons that I have given I would dismiss this appeal.

LORD GUEST: My Lords, this case has had a somewhat chequered history before it reached this House. The outstanding question whether the respondent's accident was caused by a breach of statutory duty by the appellants of s. 14 of the Factories Act, 1961, has been bedevilled by a concession made by the appellants before the Court of Appeal (36). While contesting that the mobile crane involved in the accident was machinery within the meaning of s. 14, it was

I

(34) [1960] 3 All E.R. at p. 269, letter E; [1961] 1 Q.B. at p. 149.
(35) [1966] 2 All E.R. at p. 256, letter D; [1966] 2 Q.B. at p. 369,
(36) [1966] 2 All E.R. 247; [1966] 2 Q.B. 353.
(37) [1960] 3 All E.R. 264; [1961] 1 Q.B. 136.
(38) [1952] 1 All E.R. 670; [1952] A.C. 515,
(39) [1961] 1 All E.R. 630,

conceded on their behalf that, if the crane was machinery, the accident was **A**
caused by the failure to fence, under s. 14, dangerous parts of the machinery.
The appellants were held to this concession when the case first came before the
House last February and they were not allowed to take the point. This left the
House in the unenviable position of having to decide the question whether the
mobile crane was machinery on an assumption that the parts were dangerous.
It, therefore, became impossible to test the soundness of the appellants' argu- **B**
ments without analysing their implications to the full extent. I think it is
unfortunate for the respondent and also for the decision of the case that the House
cannot enter into the question of the dangerous nature or otherwise of the parts
involved; but if parties will be so unenterprising as to concede points which are
eminently arguable in order apparently to have a decision on wider issues, I
suppose that they must face the consequences. The development of the law, **C**
however, may be impeded by such a course of action.

Since the case was last before the House a new point has emerged which is set
out in the supplemental case for the appellants. This is that s. 27 of the Factories
Act, 1961, provides a complete code for the safety of cranes and that if a lifting
machine is a crane, whether stationary or mobile, then the fencing provisions of
s. 14 have no application and the occupier fulfils his duty if he complies with **D**
s. 27. I regard this argument as untenable. The history of the factory legislation
since 1889 entirely negatives such a contention. Under the Factory and Workshop
Act, 1878, the fencing of certain machinery was dealt with in s. 5 and s. 6. By
s. 5 (1) every hoist or teagle near to which any person was liable to pass or to be
employed had to be securely fenced. Dangerous machinery was dealt with in
s. 6 and this was by means of a notice by a factory inspector. In the Factory **E**
and Workshop Act, 1901, by s. 10 (1) (*a*) hoists and teagles had to be securely
fenced, and by s. 10 (1) (*c*) for the first time there was a requirement that all
dangerous parts of machinery must be fenced. This section was carried forward
by s. 14 of the Factories Act, 1937. In that Act appeared s. 22 dealing with the
construction and maintenance of hoists and lifts, and s. 24, which provided that
all parts and working gear of every lifting machine must be of good construction **F**
and properly maintained. Sections 14 and 24 were repeated in s. 14 and s. 27 of the
Factories Act, 1961. Thus the fencing of hoists and teagles as such, provided for
in the original Factory and Workshop Act, 1878, s. 5 (1), disappeared from
modern factory legislation. It would be a strange result if their fencing was not
elsewhere provided for; but that would be the effect of the appellants' argument
if sound. In my view, the fencing of hoists and teagles, if they have dangerous **G**
parts, is provided for in the general fencing provisions of s. 14 of the Act of 1961.
Thus the dangerous parts of machinery in cranes must be fenced.

The effect of the appellants' argument would be that a dangerous part of the
crane machinery could remain unfenced without any infringement of s. 14. This
would go far to defeat the purposes of the Factories Act, 1961, to provide safety
provisions. There is nothing to distinguish certainly a static crane from other **H**
machinery and, if some portions are unfenced, they may be dangerous. The
appellants suggested that the remedy lay in the Minister's power under s. 76 of
the Factories Act, 1961, to make regulations applying such of the fencing provisions as were appropriate to cranes, both mobile and static. If, however, the
fencing provisions prima facie apply to cranes, I cannot see the necessity for the
Minister to complicate the matter by making regulations. My view is that s. 27 **I**
provides a code for construction and maintenance of cranes and that s. 14, which
is general in its terms, provides for the fencing of dangerous parts of cranes for
the safety of the workmen. STREATFEILD, J.'s decision in *Carrington* v. *John
Summers & Sons, Ltd.* (40) was right.

The substantial point argued for the appellants was that as the mobile crane
was a vehicle, the fencing provisions of s. 14 were not applicable. " Machinery "

---

(40) [1957] 1 All E.R. 457.

A is defined in s. 176 as including a driving-belt; but looked at in isolation a crane is prima facie machinery in the ordinary sense of the word, whether it be mobile or static. For the purposes of this argument it was conceded that a static crane was " machinery ". What, then, is there about a mobile crane which takes it out of the category of machinery within the meaning of s. 14? *Parvin* v. *Morton Machine Co., Ltd.* (41) was relied on by the appellants. In that case this House

B held that s. 14 did not apply to machinery manufactured in the factory, but it was limited to machinery which might be broadly described as " factory equipment ". The reason for the decision was that to apply s. 14 to manufactured machinery would result in inconsistencies and anomalies which cannot have been contemplated by Parliament. The ratio decidendi of this case cannot, therefore, assist the appellants, except insofar as showing that all machinery in a factory is

C not machinery within the meaning of s. 14. Then, why should mobility take machinery out of s. 14? *Cherry* v. *International Alloys, Ltd.* (42) was strongly relied on by the appellants. There a Lister three-wheeled petrol driven truck which ran about the factory floor was held not to be machinery in an action where an operative had his hand injured by coming in contact with the unfenced fan in the engine. There are substantial differences between the Lister truck in that case

D and the mobile crane in the present. The Lister truck was not engaged in any factory process. The mobile crane was engaged in the factory process of sorting pieces of scrap metal in the yard and was, in my view, clearly part of the factory equipment (see s. 175 (2) (*b*) of the Act of 1961). To that extent Barry, J., was in error, in my view, in equiparating the two vehicles. The difficulty about the decision in the *Cherry* case (42) is, however, that it appears to have proceeded

E on the view of the matter by the Court of Appeal that a vehicle is not machinery within the meaning of s. 14 even though it is in a factory. Devlin, L.J., expressed this most clearly when he said (43) that the wide meaning of the word " machinery " in s. 14 should be cut down so as to exclude vehicles. If this is the ratio of the decision I cannot agree with it. There is nothing about the mobility of a vehicle which can exclude it from the conception of " machinery ". If the

F vehicle is engaged in a factory purpose or incidental thereto, then if it contains machinery which may have dangerous parts it falls within s. 14. If it could have been said that the construction of vehicles was such that it was quite inappropriate that their parts should be fenced while the vehicle was in motion, that might have been a good ground for holding that s. 14 was inapplicable; but no such conclusion could be made. It is at this point that it is embarrassing to have to

G deal with this aspect without considering whether there were on this crane dangerous parts which required fencing. I must make it clear, as Salmon, L.J., did in the Court of Appeal (44), that I must not be taken as deciding that the parts involved in the accident were dangerous parts of machinery within the meaning of s. 14. As I have already said, this was conceded by the appellants and the point is not now open. It is sufficient to say that in my judgment the mobile

H crane was machinery and that the appellants failed in their duty to fence it, which was a cause of the accident.

    I would dismiss the appeal.

    LORD PEARSON: My Lords, owing to the course of the proceedings at first instance and in the Court of Appeal (45), the scope of this appeal is restricted.

I The only contention now open to the appellants is to the effect that s. 14 of the Factories Act, 1961, was not applicable to this crane or any part of it. The appellants are precluded from contending that, if s. 14 were so applicable, the part of the crane which caused the plaintiff's accident would not be a " dangerous part of any machinery " within the meaning of s. 14. Thus three questions, which

---

(41) [1952] 1 All E.R. 670; [1952] A.C. 515.
(42) [1960] 3 All E.R. 264; [1961] 1 Q.B. 136.
(43) [1960] 3 All E.R. at p. 269, letter E; [1961] 1 Q.B. at p. 149.
(44) [1966] 2 All E.R. at p. 256, letter E; [1966] 2 Q.B. at pp. 369, 370.
(45) [1966] 2 All E.R. 247; [1966] 2 Q.B. 353.

might have been of some interest and perhaps difficulty, are not raised for **A**
consideration in this appeal. They are as follows: (i) Which part of the crane
should be considered to have caused the accident? (ii) Was that part of the crane
" part of the machinery " within the meaning of s. 14? (iii) If so, was it a
" dangerous part " within the meaning of s. 14? Thus, if s. 14 on its true construction could be applied to a part of this crane, it must be assumed that the part,
whichever it was, that caused the accident was a " dangerous part of any **B**
machinery " within the meaning of s. 14 and that it ought to have been fenced
and that the fencing would have prevented the accident. I have for convenience
referred to the part as causing the accident, but it might be more correct to say
that the failure to fence it caused the accident.

Being thus confined to the contention that s. 14 on its true construction could
not be applied to this crane or any part of it, the appellants have put forward **C**
two arguments in support of that contention.

First, they have argued that s. 27 of the Act forms a complete code containing
all the Act's requirements relating to cranes and excluding the application of
s. 14 to any crane or any part of any crane. The answer to this argument was
concisely stated by STREATFIELD, J., in the passage relied on by BARRY, J., in
his judgment in this case. In *Carrington* v. *John Summers & Sons, Ltd.* (46) **D**
STREATFEILD, J., referring to s. 24 of the Factories Act, 1937, which was the
predecessor of s. 27 of the Act of 1961, said:

" Section 14 applies in general to the fencing of dangerous parts of
machinery. Section 24 deals specially with cranes and lifting machines, but
deals with them from the point of view of their construction, their rails in so
far as they are travelling cranes, the loads which they are to carry, their **E**
inspection, and, in the case of overhead travelling cranes, their method of
operation, and that is all. Neither in the authorities nor in s. 24 itself,
comparing it with s. 10 of the Act of 1901 or otherwise, can I find any
justification for the submission that s. 24 of the Act of 1937 cannot exist side
by side with s. 14, and I do not think that the existence of s. 24 prevents the
operation of s. 14 if s. 14 is otherwise appropriate." **F**

The appellants' second argument has been that, because the crane was mobile
and therefore was a vehicle or analogous to a vehicle, s. 14 was not applicable to
the crane or any part of it. They relied on the decision of the Court of Appeal in
Cherry v. *International Alloys, Ltd.* (47) as an authority in their favour.

I would agree to this extent, that for very simple reasons of common sense there **G**
must be some limitation of s. 14 in relation to vehicles and mobile machines. The
function of a vehicle is to convey goods or passengers from place to place, and one
of the functions of a mobile machine is to move from a place where it is no longer
wanted to a place where it is wanted. A vehicle or mobile machine when in
motion may run into somebody or run a wheel over somebody's foot, and in that
sense is dangerous; but if it had to be securely fenced so as to eliminate this **H**
danger, it could not be moved at all and thus could not perform its function. It
is true that the obligation under s. 14 is absolute, so that, if the requirement that
some dangerous part of machinery must be securely fenced renders the machinery
unusable, the requirement must nevertheless be given its full operation even
though the effect is to prohibit the use of the machinery (*John Summers & Sons,
Ltd.* v. *Frost* (48)). It would, however, be absurd to suppose that Parliament **I**
intended to prohibit the use of vehicles and mobile machines as factory equipment.
Some escape from that absurd supposition must be found in order to give effect
to the presumable intention of Parliament.

It is of some help to notice that s. 14 refers not to a dangerous machine but to a
" dangerous part of any machinery ". It can be argued that a danger arising

(46) [1957] 1 All E.R. at p. 459, letter G.
(47) [1960] 3 All E.R. 264; [1961] 1 Q.B. 136.
(48) [1955] 1 All E.R. 870; [1955] A.C. 740.

A merely from the normal use of the entire machine is outside the scope of the section. There is, however, the contrary argument that the entire machine is "machinery", and parts of it, e.g., the bumpers and the wheels, are dangerous parts because they may strike somebody, and therefore they have to be securely fenced. Then the fencing is dangerous and has to be securely fenced, and so on ad infinitum.

B I think that the better way of escape from the absurd supposition, that no vehicle or mobile machine can lawfully be used as factory equipment, is to consider the nature of the danger contemplated, and intended to be guarded against, by s. 14. The section is not contemplating, or intended to guard against, traffic accidents. In *Cherry* v. *International Alloys, Ltd.* (49) Pearce, L.J., said:

C "It is clear that the provisions of the Act and s. 14 itself are not apt for application to trucks and lead to some unreasonable results; and one may fairly assume that trucks were not in the mind of the draftsman. Trucks are self-contained units and the dangers that they create are different dangers from those caused by factory machinery with which the Act was primarily concerned. The danger of being run over or knocked down is wholly different from the dangers that arise in factories from catching, cutting, pinching and

D crushing."

That last sentence may not contain a complete list of the kinds of factory accidents, but it does point the contrast between the danger of factory accidents and the danger of traffic accidents. A part of this mobile crane would not be a "dangerous part of any machinery" merely because it might strike somebody in

E a traffic accident.

That implied exemption does not go far enough to sustain the appellants' argument in this case. The accident suffered by the respondent was in its nature a factory accident, as he was caught in the "nip" between the stationary wheel and the moving box or casing, and he suffered injury by crushing. A vehicle or mobile machine may contain some machinery, of which a part is dangerous if not

F securely fenced. Then s. 14 applies. For instance, the crane in the present case presumably contained machinery for raising and lowering and slewing the jib, and parts of such machinery would be dangerous if they had not been fenced in by the box or casing. As has been stated above, the part of the crane which caused injury to the respondent is assumed to have been part of some machinery and to have been dangerous because it was not fenced, and it follows from these assumptions

G that the appellants are liable to the respondent for their breach of statutory duty in failing to fence that part of the crane.

Accordingly, in my opinion, the appeal fails and should be dismissed.

I think also that the decision in *Cherry* v. *International Alloys, Ltd.* (50) was wrong, because the accident in that case was not a traffic accident caused by the movement of the vehicle but was a factory accident caused by absence of fencing

H round a dangerous part of the machinery contained in the vehicle, which was factory equipment.

Appeal dismissed.

Solicitors: *M. H. B. Gilmour* (for the appellants); *Gibson & Weldon*, agents for *John Whittle, Robinson & Bailey*, Manchester (for the respondent).

[*Reported by* Kathleen J. H. O'Brien, *Barrister-at-Law.*]

I

---

(49) [1960] 3 All E.R. at p. 267, letter E; [1961] 1 Q.B. at p. 146.
(50) [1960] 3 All E.R. 264; [1961] 1 Q.B. 126.

R. *v.* WILSON.   A

[COURT OF APPEAL, CRIMINAL DIVISION (Lord Parker, C.J., Salmon, L.J., and Widgery, J.), May 11, June 6, 1967.]

Criminal Law—Indictment—Committal to quarter sessions for trial—No indictment preferred before quarter sessions—Remitted to assizes for trial—Indictment preferred at assizes containing charge not before quarter sessions— Accused lawfully indicted—Administration of Justice (Miscellaneous Provisions) Act, 1933 (23 & 24 Geo. 5 c. 36), s. 2 (1).

B

Quarter Sessions—Direction for trial at assizes—Jurisdiction under commission of the peace—Indictment first preferred at assizes—Accused lawfully indicted and tried—Criminal Justice Act, 1925 (15 & 16 Geo. 5 c. 86), s. 14 (2).

On Jan. 13, 1966, the appellant was committed for trial to quarter sessions on two charges of indecent assault and one of assault occasioning actual bodily harm. On Feb. 14, 1966, his solicitors wrote to the clerk of the peace at quarter sessions stating that his defence would not be ready in time and asked for the case to be sent for trial to the next assizes. In due course an indictment was preferred at assizes. This indictment added a count charging grievous bodily harm with intent. No indictment had been preferred at quarter sessions. On appeal against conviction,

C

D

Held: the power of quarter sessions under the commission of the peace to remit a case for trial at assizes if it was more fit to be tried there, which power was extended by s. 14 (2)* of the Criminal Justices Act, 1925, did not depend on a bill of indictment having been first preferred at quarter sessions; accordingly the appellant's trial had been lawfully remitted to assizes, he had been " lawfully indicted " there for the purposes of s. 2 (1)† of the Administration of Justice (Miscellaneous Provisions) Act, 1933, and his conviction should stand (see p. 1091, letters E and H, post).

E

Dictum of AVORY, J., in *R.* v. *Holmen* ([1918] 2 K.B. at p. 864) applied.

[As to power to transmit cases to or from assizes or quarter sessions, see 10 HALSBURY'S LAWS (3rd Edn.) 378, para. 685; ibid., p. 394, para. 715, note (*s*); 25 HALSBURY'S LAWS (3rd Edn.) 286, para. 551; and for cases on the subject, see 33 DIGEST (Repl.) 277, *1046*, *1047*, 286, *1140*.

F

For the Criminal Justice Act, 1925, s. 14, see 14 HALSBURY'S STATUTES (2nd Edn.) 942.

For the Assizes Relief Act, 1889, s. 3, see 5 HALSBURY'S STATUTES (2nd Edn.) 916; and for the Administration of Justice (Miscellaneous Provisions) Act, 1938, s. 11, see ibid., 1121.

G

For the Administration of Justice (Miscellaneous Provisions) Act, 1933, s. 2, see 5 HALSBURY'S STATUTES (2nd Edn.) 1067.]

Cases referred to:

R. v. *Holmen*, [1918] 2 K.B. 861; 88 L.J.K.B. 30; 119 L.T. 682; 83 J.P. 4; 13 Cr. App. Rep. 184; 33 Digest (Repl.) 286, *1140*.

H

R. v. *Wetherell*, (1819), Russ. & Ry. 381; 168 E.R. 855; 33 Digest (Repl.) 277, *1046*.

Appeal and application.

This was an appeal by Peter Joseph Wilson against his conviction on Mar. 24, 1966, at Leeds Assizes before ASHWORTH, J., and a jury, on three counts of an indictment, viz., on count 1 and count 4, each of which charged him with indecent assault, and on count 2, which charged causing grievous bodily harm with intent. He was sentenced to two years' imprisonment on count 1, to seven years' imprisonment on count 2, and to two years' imprisonment on count 4. The last two terms of imprisonment (viz., seven years on count 2 and two years on count 4), were to run concurrently, but their total (seven years) was to be

I

---

* Section 14 (2) is set out at p. 1090, letter F, post.

† Section 2 (1), so far as material, is set out at p. 1091, letter C, post.

A　consecutive to the two years on count 1, making nine years in all. The prisoner also applied for leave to appeal against sentence.

The authorities and case noted below* were cited during the argument in addition to the cases referred to in the judgment of the court.

W. M. Howard, Q.C., and *R. H. K. Frisby* for the appellant.

Anthony Harmsworth, Q.C., and *R. D. Ranking* for the Crown.

B

June 6.　**WIDGERY, J.,** read the following judgment of the court at the invitation of LORD PARKER, C.J.: The first matter with which the court has been concerned is an application by the appellant for leave to appeal against conviction on the merits. This was an exceedingly bad case. It concerned two young girls aged fifteen. In the case of the first girl, the appellant, according to the

C　girl's evidence, asked her in the street if she would like a lift in his car. She unwisely accepted; he took her off to a remote spot and then assaulted her. He kicked her, took off her clothes, and inserted something in her back passage, and generally treated her extremely badly. The case of the second girl was even worse; again he picked her up in his car, took her to a remote moor, took most of her clothes off, lashed her with a belt, striking her repeatedly on the

D　breasts and abdomen. A doctor who examined her described the result of the assault as showing a very considerable degree of violence, and added: " I have never seen such signs of violence in forty-five years' experience." In his application the appellant has persisted in his innocence and criticised the evidence given in the court below, but this court, after careful examination of the summing-up, is quite satisfied that the issues were fully and fairly left to the jury, and

E　there is no ground whatever for giving leave to appeal on the merits. These were two very grave assaults. It is quite clear that he is a menace to society, and it is horrifying to think of what girls might suffer at his hands. His application for leave to appeal against sentence is refused.

The substantial matter is a point of law. He had been committed for trial on Jan. 13, 1966, on two charges of indecent assault and one of assault occasioning

F　actual bodily harm and, as each of these charges was within the jurisdiction of quarter sessions, he was committed to the North Riding Quarter Sessions. On Feb. 14, 1966, the appellant's solicitors wrote to the clerk of the peace to say that the defence would not be ready in time for the next ensuing quarter sessions and asking that the case should be " sent for trial to the next assize at York ". On Feb. 21, 1966, the clerk of the peace replied that the chairman

G　of quarter sessions had agreed to the case being remitted to Leeds assizes and in due course an indictment containing an additional count of causing grievous bodily harm with intent was preferred at Leeds assizes. No indictment had been preferred at quarter sessions.

The appellant now appeals to this court on a point of law, contending that as no indictment had been preferred against him in the court of quarter sessions

H　to which he was committed there was no jurisdiction to try him at assizes and that the proceedings in that court were a nullity. Sections 9 to 11 of the Magistrates' Courts Act, 1952, give committing magistrates a wide choice from which to select the court to which an accused person may be committed (1) and it is clear that a committal to assize would have been justified in this case under s. 11. The Act of 1952 is understandably silent as to a change of venue when

I　once a committal order has been made, because this will not normally be the concern of the committing justices, but the magistrates' order is not necessarily final and there are powers under which a subsequent change of venue may be ordered. We have been referred to the commission of the peace which contains a proviso that

---

* 5 HALSBURY'S STATUTES (2nd Edn.) 1067; 14 HALSBURY'S STATUTES (2nd Edn.) 942; 32 HALSBURY'S STATUTES (2nd Edn.) 429-431; *R.* v. *London Sessions Chairman*, (1953), 37 Cr. App. Rep. 148.

(1) See 32 HALSBURY'S STATUTES (2nd Edn.) 429-431.

" if a case of difficulty . . . shall happen to arise then let judgment in **A**
no wise be given thereon before you . . . unless in the presence of one of our
justices appointed to hold the assizes in the aforesaid county "

and, although the literal meaning of these words does not seem to contemplate a
power for quarter sessions to remit a case of difficulty to assizes, it has for some
time been recognised that they have this effect. Thus in *R. v. Holmen* (2) a **B**
prisoner was committed for trial to quarter sessions where an indictment containing fifteen counts was preferred, but, after a number of these counts had been
disposed of and the jury had disagreed on a further six, the recorder transmitted
the indictment to assizes in order that the prisoner might be tried again on those
latter counts. In giving the judgment of the Court of Criminal Appeal AVORY, J.,
said (3):
                        C

" The recorder, when the jury disagreed on the charges of larceny, remitted the case to the assizes. He had ample power to do that. On behalf
of the appellant it is contended that the recorder, having embarked on the
inquiry, had no jurisdiction to remit the indictment to the assizes. The
power exists under the commission of the peace, and is to be exercised in
any case in which the court of quarter sessions is of opinion that the case is **D**
more fit to be tried at the assizes than at quarter sessions."

It is to be observed that in *R. v. Holmen* (2) an indictment had been preferred
at quarter sessions, but it is also clear that a new indictment was preferred at
assizes and the court rejected an argument that this new indictment was a
nullity.

Another power for quarter sessions to direct that a trial shall take place at **E**
assizes is to be found in s. 14 (2) of the Criminal Justice Act, 1925, which provides:

" (2) When for any reason whatsoever the trial of a person who has
been committed to be tried for an indictable offence before a court of assize
or quarter sessions for any place is either not proceeded with or not brought
to a final conclusion before that court, it shall be lawful for that court, if in **F**
its discretion it thinks it convenient so to do with a view either to expediting
the trial or re-trial or the saving of expense or otherwise and is satisfied that
the accused will not thereby suffer hardship, to direct that the trial or re-
trial of the accused shall take place before a court of assize or (if the offence is
within the jurisdiction of a court of quarter sessions) before a court of
quarter sessions, for some other place."
                        G
There is nothing in this subsection to indicate that an indictment must be preferred in the court to which the accused was committed before a direction is
given by that court for trial elsewhere, and at first sight it might appear that
this provison covered the present case. The section, however, contemplates that
the court making the order shall have jurisdiction in one " place ", and that the
court to which the trial is to go shall have jurisdiction in another place, and this **H**
is not an apt description of the jurisdiction of county quarter sessions and assizes
in the same county. It would be surprising if the power of quarter sessions to
direct a trial at assizes outside the county were wider than that relating to a
trial within the county, and we think that the draftsman of this section assumed
that adequate powers within a county already existed by virtue of the commission
of assize and the commission of the peace respectively and was seeking to extend **I**
those powers to convenient courts in neighbouring counties or places.

There are other powers under which a change of venue may occur, but these
do not depend on an order made by the court to where the accused was committed and they do not appear to be relevant on the facts of the present case.
Thus by s. 3 of the Assizes Relief Act, 1889, a prisoner committed in custody to
quarter sessions who is not tried at the sessions may apply to the assize judge for

(2) [1918] 2 K.B. 861.
(3) [1918] 2 K.B. at p. 864.

A trial at assizes or discharge from custody, and under s. 11 (3) of the Administration of Justice (Miscellaneous Provisions) Act, 1938, the High Court has power to order a change of venue whenever this is expedient in the interests of justice. By R.S.C., Ord. 79, r. 2, it is provided that on any such order of the High Court being made " the indictment (if it has been preferred) " shall be transmitted to the court at which the trial is to take place.

B It is nevertheless contended that where quarter sessions direct that a case committed to the sessions shall be tried at assizes no jurisdiction to try the case exists except on an indictment preferred at the sessions. The Administration of Justice (Miscellaneous Provisions) Act, 1933, which abolished the grand jury, provides in s. 2:

C " (1) Subject to the provisions of this section, a bill of indictment charging any person with an indictable offence may be preferred by any person before a court in which the person charged may lawfully be indicted for that offence . . . (2) Subject as hereinafter provided no bill of indictment charging any person with an indictable offence shall be preferred unless either— (a) the person charged has been committed for trial for the offence . . ."

D then follow irrelevant alternatives. Counsel for the appellant submits that a person cannot be " lawfully indicted " otherwise than in the court to which he has been committed but, in our judgment, a person can be lawfully indicted within the meaning of s. 2 (1) in any court in which he can lawfully be tried, that is to say, in the court to which he was committed or in any other court to which his trial has been lawfully directed under any of the provisions for change of venue to which we have referred. The fact that s. 2 (2) (a) refers to committal for

E trial generally and not to committal to a particular court strongly supports this construction of the section and we have been referred to no authority to the contrary.

Alternatively counsel for the appellant submits that the existence of an indictment preferred in the court to which the accused was committed is a necessary pre-requisite to a transfer of the trial to another court since there will

F otherwise be nothing in existence on which the transfer can operate. No authority is cited in support of this proposition, but our attention has been drawn to the fact that in many of the old cases in which a change of venue was ordered an indictment had been preferred in the court from which the transfer was being made (see for example R. v. Wetherell (4)). In our judgment this argument approaches the matter on the false assumption that a committal

G for trial invests the court to which the prisoner was committed with some kind of proprietary right of which the bill of indictment is a document of title. When a change of venue is lawfully ordered there is no right of property to be transferred and the order is simply an administrative direction by a competent authority for the trial to take place in a different court. There is accordingly no inherent reason why the absence of a bill of indictment should provide an obstacle to the

H making of the order. In our judgment, therefore, the ancient power of quarter sessions (as extended by s. 14 (2) of the Criminal Justice Act, 1925) to remit a case to the assizes is not dependent on a bill of indictment being first preferred at the sessions. The ancient power exits as AVORY, J., put it (5) when the case in question "is more fit to be tried at the assizes than at quarter sessions" and the extended power applies in the circumstances specified in s. 14 (2). In view

I of the congestion of the lists the rule of practice must always be observed whereby quarter sessions consult with the assize judge concerned, through the usual channels, before making any such order. For these reasons this appeal is dismissed. The court made its order at the last sitting (6).

[Counsel for the appellant applied for leave to appeal to the House of Lords.]

(4) (1819), Russ & Ry. 381.
(5) [1918] 2 K.B. at p. 864.
(6) At the hearing of the appeal on May 11, 1967, the court intimated that the appeal would be dismissed, the court's reasons to be given at a later date.

LORD PARKER, C.J.: The court has carefully considered this application A for leave to appeal to the House of Lords. There is no ground which this court can certify to involve a point of general public importance save for the one dealt with this morning by this court. If the appellant desires to appeal to the House of Lords on that point, the court will certify under s. 1 of the Administration of Justice Act, 1960, that a point of law of general public importance is involved but will refuse leave to appeal. The point on which this court will B certify can be stated in the following terms: whether, there having been no indictment at quarter sessions, the trial at assize was a nullity. Leave to appeal is refused.

Application and appeal dismissed. Leave to appeal to the House of Lords refused.

Solicitors: *Waterhouse & Co.*, agents for *T. I. Clough & Co.*, Bradford (for the C appellant); *Collyer-Bristow & Co.*, agents for *Thorpe & Co.*, Scarborough (for the Crown).

[*Reported by* N. P. METCALFE, ESQ., *Barrister-at-Law.*]

D

SALE CONTINUATION, LTD. *v.* AUSTIN TAYLOR & CO., LTD.

[QUEEN'S BENCH DIVISION (Paull, J.), May 31, June 1, 8, 1967.]

E

Bank—Documentary credit—Irrevocable credit—Selling agents opening for their foreign principals, timber exporters, an irrevocable credit with merchant bankers on sale of a shipment of timber to foreign buyers—Application for the credit included an undertaking by selling agents to provide funds to meet drafts on the credit—Draft accepted by merchant bankers—Documents of title to timber shipment delivered by merchant bankers to selling agents to enable them to collect price—Trust receipt given by selling agents—Merchant bankers went into liquidation and ceased to honour acceptances—Selling agents collected purchase price but did not provide funds for merchant bankers —Selling agents bought dishonoured draft from exporters for its face value— Whether liquidator of merchant bankers entitled to recover amount of draft from selling agents.

F

G

Selling agents in London (the defendants) contracted on May 14, 1965, on behalf of exporters in Malaysia (the N. company) to sell timber to importers in Belgium, the property in the goods to be deemed to pass on their shipment subject to the vendors' lien on them for the unpaid purchase price, payment to be made through a named Belgian bank. In respect of this shipment the selling agents applied on May 19 for, and obtained from merchant H bankers (the plaintiffs), an irrevocable credit in favour of the N. company to be available by draft drawn on the merchant bankers by the N. company, the draft to be accompanied by the documents of title to the goods as collateral security. The selling agents' application contained the following printed words: " In consideration of your opening this credit we engage to provide you with funds to meet disbursements thereunder as soon as you I receive advice that payment has been made . . ." The merchant bankers, on about May 25, instructed a bank to advise the N. company in writing of the opening of the irrevocable credit. These instructions stated that " upon presentation of the [documents of title] to us . . . we confirm that we shall place the value of such documents at your disposal ninety days after sight D/A ". On July 15, 1965, a draft for the permitted amount, maturing in accordance with the letter of credit on Oct. 28, 1965, was drawn by the N. company and accepted on July 27 by the merchant bankers, who on July 30,

A   1965, delivered to the selling agents the documents of title relating to the shipment of timber, in order that the selling agents might present them to the Belgian bank and collect the purchase price. The selling agents gave the merchant bankers a " trust receipt " stating that " we acknowledge the receipt of [the documents of title] relating to the . . . goods (now in pledge to you as security for advances) . . . we undertake to hold the

B   documents of title and the said goods when received (and the proceeds thereof when sold) as trustees for you . . . further to pay to you the proceeds of sale without deduction of any expenses . . . immediately upon receipt thereof ". On Aug. 12, 1965, a receiver and manager of the merchant bankers was appointed by mortgage debenture-holders, having a charge on all the merchant bankers' assets, and on Sept. 8, 1965, the receiver gave notice of

C   this fact to the selling agents. Subsequently to Aug. 12, 1965, the selling agents, having delivered the documents of title to the Belgian buyers, received payment for the timber, but, knowing that the merchant bankers had ceased to honour acceptances, the selling agents did not pay the money to the merchant bankers. On Sept. 28, 1965, the merchant bankers went into voluntary liquidation and their assets were insufficient fully to discharge their

D   liabilities. On Oct. 28, 1965, the draft drawn by the N. company was presented to the merchant bankers and was returned dishonoured. In March, 1966, the selling agents purchased the dishonoured draft from the N. company for its amount, and sent the dishonoured draft to the liquidator of the merchant bankers. The merchant bankers now sued the selling agents for the money that they had received from the Belgian buyers.

E   **Held:** by reason of (i)-(iii) below the merchant bankers were not entitled to recover the amount of the dishonoured draft from the selling agents (see p. 1098, letter H, post)—

(i) by the contract between the selling agents and the merchant bankers for the opening of the irrevocable letter of credit by the merchant bankers they were under an obligation, implied in the contract, to honour drafts

F   properly presented under the letter of credit, provided that the selling agents put the merchant bankers in funds to meet their " disbursements " (see p. 1097, letter A, post), the word " disbursements " meaning money which had in fact been paid out (see p. 1096, letter F, post).

(ii) thus the merchant bankers were under contractual obligation to the selling agents to honour at maturity (Oct. 28, 1965) the N. company's draft

G   that the merchant bankers had accepted, and by reason of the appointment of the receiver and the voluntary liquidation the merchant bankers had evinced an intention not to fulfil that obligation; accordingly the selling agents were discharged from the mutual obligation to provide funds to meet the disbursement on the draft (see p. 1097, letter H, post).

(iii) on the draft accepted by the merchant bankers being dishonoured

H   by them the N. company were entitled (a) to cancel the pledge of the documents of title, which they had made by sending the documents to the merchant bankers, (b) to return the draft for cancellation and (c) to claim the purchase money from the selling agents who were the N. company's agents; moreover, there had been no breach of trust by the selling agents in parting with the documents of title to the buyers and recovering the purchase price,

I   for the trust receipt contemplated that this should be done (see p. 1098, letter F, post).

[As to the nature of commercial letters of credit, and as to the mode of using them, see 2 HALSBURY'S LAWS (3rd Edn.) 214, para. 398, pp. 221, 222, para. 411; and for cases on letters of credit, see 3 DIGEST (Repl.) 282-285, *846-858*.

As to pledges by sellers and buyers of goods, see 29 HALSBURY'S LAWS (3rd Edn.) 216, para. 405; and as to an unpaid seller's lien on the goods, see 34 HALSBURY'S LAWS (3rd Edn.) 122, 123, para. 198.]

A

Case referred to:

   Bank of the United States v. *Seltzer*, (1931), 251 N.Y.S. 637; 233 App. Div. 225.

Action.

In this action begun by writ issued on July 1, 1966, the plaintiffs, Sale Continuation, Ltd., a company in voluntary liquidation since Sept. 28, 1965, but prior to that date carrying on business as merchant bankers under the name of Sale & Co., claimed £3,652 0s. 11d. as monies payable to them by the defendants, Austin Taylor & Co., Ltd., London, timber agents and brokers, in respect of irrevocable credits opened and drafts accepted by the plaintiffs at the defendants' request between May and June, 1965, and/or damages for breach of trust constituted by four " trust receipts ", of which two were dated July 30, 1965 and two were dated Aug. 5, 1965. The judgment reported here deals with one only of the four transactions, which were the subject of the writ and statement of claim, viz., a transaction in respect of an irrevocable credit which was opened in favour of the Nenasi Sawmill Co. of Kuala Lumpur, Malaysia. The facts, which were the subject of an agreed statement of facts, are summarised in the judgment.

B

C

J. L. Arnold, Q.C., and *J. M. Rankin* for the plaintiffs, the merchant bankers in liquidation.

J. M. Shaw, Q.C., and *J. G. C. Phillips* for the defendants, the selling agents.

D

Cur. adv. vult.

June 8. **PAULL, J.,** read the following judgment: This action raises certain questions of law arising out of the fact that the plaintiffs are merchant bankers in liquidation. The questions raised are questions on which there is no authority, at least not in this country. The facts, which are all agreed, are contained in an exhibit of the plaintiffs and those essential for my decision can be stated quite shortly.

E

The defendants are the selling agents for a number of foreign manufacturers and traders. In the matter material to this judgment the defendants were acting as selling agents for a company of timber exporters of Kuala Lumpur, Malaysia, called Nenasi Sawmill Co. (hereinafter called " Nenasi "). By a contract dated May 14, 1965, the defendants as agents for Nenasi sold to Messrs. A. Goeminne-Bois, a Belgian firm of timber importers, certain hardwood to be shipped to Antwerp, the documents to be presented through the Banque de Bruxelles at Ghent for payment. The property in the goods was to be deemed to have passed to the buyers when the goods were shipped, subject to the vendors' lien for unpaid purchase price. That contract having been entered into, the defendants approached the plaintiffs, asking the plaintiffs to open an irrevocable credit in favour of Nenasi for £1,870 (plus or minus ten per cent.). That application was in writing. By the application the irrevocable credit was to be available by a draft drawn by Nenasi on the plaintiffs, the draft to be accompanied by the usual documents of title. This application contained, inter alia, the following printed words:

F

G

H

" In consideration of your opening this credit, we engage to provide you with funds to meet disbursements thereunder as soon as you receive advice that payment has been made . . . and you are authorised to debit our account without previous notice to us. As regards each draft which you may accept we engage to provide you with funds to meet such draft. All commission interest charges and expenses relative hereto are for our account and you are hereby authorised to debit our account in respect thereof. In the event of our failing to provide for such drafts or disbursements and of the bank's selling the relative goods . . . we undertake to pay on demand the amount of any deficiency on such sale . . . The drafts are to be secured by the due endorsement and delivery as collateral security to the bank of the above-mentioned documents . . ."

I

A   I do not think that I need refer to this application further, save to say that it is agreed that interest was to be charged to the defendants on any draft from the date of acceptance to the date of the plaintiffs receiving the purchase price of the wood. The plaintiffs, having received this application, sent a letter addressed to the manager of the Eastern Bank, Ltd., in London, asking the bank to advise Nenasi that an irrevocable credit had been opened in their favour and giving
B   details thereof. This letter contains the following words:

> " Upon presentation of the documents to us as set out above . . . we confirm that we shall place the value of such documents at your disposal ninety days after sight D/A."

I do not think that anything further in that letter need be referred to. A copy
C   of this letter was sent to the defendants.

On July 15, 1965, a draft under the letter of credit was drawn on the plaintiffs for the sum of £2,045 18s. Under the terms of the letter of credit this draft would become payable by the plaintiffs on Oct. 28, 1965. The draft was of course accompanied by the necessary documents of title required by the letter of credit. The plaintiffs accepted the draft and handed the documents of title to the
D   defendants on July 30, 1965, in order that the defendants could present the documents to the Belgian bank and collect the purchase price. The plaintiffs obtained from the defendants a receipt headed " Trust Receipt ". The material parts of that receipt are as follows:

> " We hereby acknowledge the receipt of the under-mentioned documents of title relating to the under-mentioned goods (now in pledge to you as
E   security for advances) to be held by us on the following terms and conditions: We undertake to hold the documents of title and the said goods when received (and the proceeds thereof when sold) as trustees for you . . . Further to pay to you the proceeds of sale without deduction of any expenses . . . immediately upon receipt thereof."

F   The documents of title were duly delivered by the defendants to the buyers and the defendants received payment in respect of the goods sold under contract. This money was received after the matters which I am about to refer to had occurred.

On Aug. 12, 1965, a receiver and manager of the plaintiffs was appointed by the holders of a mortgage and debenture dated Aug. 4, 1965. By a letter
G   dated Sept. 8, 1965, the receiver gave notice of this fact to the defendants stating that the holders had a charge on the whole of the assets of the plaintiffs, and saying that the defendants might consider it inadvisable to make any payment to the holders of bills of exchange accepted by the plaintiffs under letters of credit. By letter dated Sept. 10, 1965, the defendants pointed out that certain acceptances by the plaintiffs had not been paid by them and suggested that the
H   acceptances should be sent by the defendants' principals to the defendants, who would hand them to the receiver in exchange for trust receipts that the plaintiffs held and that the defendants would then pay the moneys due on the drafts to their principals. This offer was not accepted by the receiver. The plaintiffs went into voluntary liquidation on Sept. 28, 1965, and it is one of the agreed facts in the case that the assets of the plaintiffs are not sufficient to
I   discharge their liabilities.

On Oct. 28, 1965, the draft drawn on the plaintiffs by Nenasi under the letter of credit was returned to Nenasi dishonoured. The defendants on Mar. 7, 1966, remitted to Nenasi the sum collected by them from the purchasers (£2,045 18s.) as the purchase price for the dishonoured draft. Having received the dishonoured draft from Nenasi the defendants sent it to the liquidator who has since that date had the draft in his possession.

This action also covers three other transactions similar to the one with which I have dealt in detail, the only difference being that the defendants instead of

purchasing the drafts paid them supra protest for honour. I understand that in A
these, or in one or two of these, transactions the liquidator has refused to accept
the drafts but it is agreed by both parties that the position in law in these transactions is indistinguishable from the one that I have set out and, that being
so, I do not intend to complicate this judgment by any reference to them. I
was informed that this action is a test action, and that there are other transactions somewhat similar to these in which the drafts have not been returned B
or offered to the plaintiffs. I have refused to consider what may be the effect
of this additional fact, as it does not arise in the case before me, and the position
in law must depend on the precise facts relating to such transactions.

I now come to the questions of law arising from the facts which I have outlined. The defendants admit that if the obligation on the part of the plaintiffs
duly to honour the draft forms no part of the contract between the plaintiffs C
and the defendants, then the defendants have no answer to this claim. The
plaintiffs contend that that is the true position; that the consideration for the
payment of the charges, commission and interest referred to in the application
form is the opening of the letter of credit and acceptance of the drafts. Once,
say the plaintiffs, the draft has been accepted, the matter of the payment of the
draft is purely a matter between the drawer of the draft and the bank as the D
acceptor. The acceptance gives rise to obligations to the drawer but does not
give rise to any obligation to the defendants. In support of this contention
the plaintiffs draw attention to the words in the application: " In consideration
of your opening this credit." In my judgment those words state the consideration for the defendants providing funds to meet disbursements under the credit
opened, the funds having to be provided as soon as the plaintiffs know that E
payment has been made. I reject the argument that the word " disbursements "
means disbursements which will become, or may become, due under the letter
of credit. " Disbursements " seems to me clearly to mean money which has in
fact been disbursed, i.e., paid out. No money has been disbursed by the plaintiffs
under the credit which was opened.

The obligation of the defendants with regard to any draft which the plaintiffs F
have accepted is to provide funds to meet that draft—an obligation which arises
before the draft is met—and the first question which arises is whether in those
circumstances there does not arise towards the defendants an obligation by the
plaintiffs to meet the drafts. It seems to me that one can test this matter quite
simply. Bankers have not the exclusive right of issuing letters of credit. Assume
that a stranger approached the defendants and informed the defendants that he G
was prepared to issue irrevocable credits and to accept drafts under such credits
at " cut rates ". Clearly the first question the defendants would ask is: " What
guarantee is there that you will meet the drafts after we have put you in funds? "
If the stranger replied: " That is no concern of yours. My only obligation to
you is to accept the drafts," one would think that the quite obvious reply would
be: " What are you taking about? For how long do you think we shall remain H
agents for foreign principals if we arrange for drafts to be accepted by persons
who do not meet them? " Similarly, if the defendants were purchasers, the
reply would be: " For how long do you think we could go on trading if it became
known that we arranged for drafts to be accepted by people who do not meet
them? " In my judgment it is an essential element in the contract between
the plaintiffs and the defendants that there was an implied term that, provided I
the defendants put the plaintiffs in funds to meet any accepted draft, the plaintiffs
would in fact honour the accepted draft. That term is necessary to give business
efficacy to the contract. Under the old way of looking at implied terms the answer
to the officious bystander would be: " Of course." It may well be, however,
that if the defendants did not put the plaintiffs in funds then, as between the
plaintiffs and the defendants, there is no obligation to meet the accepted draft
although there would be as between the drawer and the plaintiffs.

I therefore hold that under the terms of the contract there was an obligation

A by the plaintiffs to the defendants to honour drafts properly presented under the letter of credit, provided that the defendants put the plaintiffs in funds so to do.

In the American case of *Bank of the United States* v. *Seltzer* (1) (of which I have been provided with a photostat copy) the Supreme Court of the United States on very similar facts to the present case held that non-payment by the

B bank due to the Superintendent of Banks taking possession of the bank (the equivalent of a receiver and manager being appointed) constituted a failure of consideration towards Mr. Seltzer who was in the same position as the defendants are in in this case. I confess I do not like this way of looking at the matter so far as English law is concerned. There is certainly no total failure of consideration, nor does counsel for the defendants contend that there is. At least

C part of the consideration moving from the plaintiffs to the defendants is the opening of the letter of credit and the acceptance of the drafts. Indeed the plaintiffs contend that these two matters constitute the whole of the consideration. Whether there are any, and if so what, consequences to a partial failure of consideration has not so far as I know been explored in English law in a matter such as this.

D Having found that the promise to honour the draft, provided the plaintiffs were put in funds by the defendants, formed part of the terms of the contract between the plaintiffs and the defendants, I would ask myself the question: did the plaintiffs before the date when the defendants should have put them in funds evince an intention not to fulfil that term of the contract even if put in funds by the defendants, and if so, did that release the defendants from their

E obligation to provide funds for the fulfilment of that term? Counsel for the plaintiffs argues that the plaintiffs have never evinced an intention not to fulfil their obligation to honour the draft. The situation he says is merely that the law has stepped in and ordered that the payment should be by way of proof in the winding-up proceedings. Moreover, says counsel for the plaintiffs, even if there was the evincing of such an intention it would not be an intention to

F repudiate the contract. It would merely be to break one term of the contract, and that is not sufficient to enable the defendants to refuse to fulfil their part of the bargain. In my judgment clearly the obligation of the plaintiffs to the defendants was to honour that draft on the date when it matured, i.e., Oct. 28, 1965, and to honour means to pay in full, not merely to give to the drawer a right to make a claim for the payment of the money or part of the money on

G a future date. The appointment of the receiver and manager on Aug. 12, 1965, and the commencement of the winding up on Sept. 28, 1965, seems to me clearly to have given notice both to the defendants and the holders of the draft that the plaintiffs would be unable to honour the draft on the due date, especially when these facts are coupled with the fact that on Sept. 8, 1965, the receiver and manager gave notice to the defendants that there was in existence a mortgage

H and debenture dated Aug. 4, 1965, giving the holders a charge on the whole of the assets of the company. I have therefore no hesitation in finding that the plaintiffs did evince an intention not to fulfil that term of their contract with the defendants. If that be so, then it seems to me that whatever other consequences may follow from the evincing of such an intention it clearly gets rid of the obligation of the defendants under the contract to provide the plaintiffs

I with the funds necessary to honour the draft. They are mutual obligations under the contract and no obligation to provide funds to meet the drafts can arise if it is known in advance that the drafts are not going to be met. Indeed, if necessary, I should be prepared to hold that the evincing of that intention was a repudiation of the contract, the honouring of the draft being an essential part of the bargain, but I do not think that I need make that finding.

I now pass to considering the effect of the trust receipt. There is no doubt

_____

(1) (1931), 251 N.Y.S. 637.

that the defendants would not have obtained the documents of title had they A
not signed the trust receipt. The bank itself could and, I am told, in many
transactions did themselves collect the money due from the sale of the goods.
Do the defendants therefore hold the monies received from the purchasers in
trust for the plaintiffs so that whatever happens in connexion with the draft
the defendants are bound to pay to the plaintiffs the monies received by them
from the purchasers? On the face of the trust receipt that would appear clearly B
to be so; but ought one, so to speak, to go behind the face of the document?
One starts by saying that the position here is not the usual position where the
customer of the bank is the buyer of the goods. In such a case the seller parts
with his ownership in the documents as soon as he sends the documents to the
bank. His right is to be paid the draft. The ownership of the goods passes
to the buyer but the bank has the possessory title of a pledgee as against the C
buyer. He has that title until the buyer puts the bank in funds in respect of the
draft and discharges his liability for interest payable in respect of the draft.
If the pledgor does not do so, the bank has the usual right of a pledgee to sell
as if he were the owner.

In this case by the terms of the contract with the buyers, entered into by their
agents (the defendants), Nenasi parted with their property in the goods for all D
purposes when the goods were shipped, except for their vendors' lien for the
unpaid purchase price and when Nenasi sent the documents to the plaintiffs
Nenasi retained that lien as against the buyers. Having that lien they pledged
the documents to the plaintiffs, who took them as security against not receiving
the purchase price before they had to honour the draft, subject to the buyers'
right to demand them as soon as they paid for the goods. The application states E
that the drafts are to be secured by the delivery of the documents of title as
collateral security. Now the essence of a pledge is that it is security against
either an immediate advance or against a present liability to make a future
payment. The trust receipt contemplated that the defendants would part with
the documents to the Belgian buyer and recover the purchase price. It was no
breach of trust to do so. In my judgment the same principle applies to the F
money as applies to the obligation to put the plaintiffs in funds before the
maturity date of the draft. Once the draft is dishonoured (or notice of intention
not to honour given) Nenasi is entitled to cancel the contract of pledge by
returning the draft for cancellation and claiming the purchase money from their
agents the defendants. It is as though a pawnbroker having received the pledge
and given his pawn ticket to the pledgor refused to hand over the sum agreed G
to be lent. The pledgor can say: " Very well, here is your pawn ticket. Hand
me back my goods." In this case " the goods " (being the documents of title, or
rather the money received for them) were already in the hands of the pledgor.

For these reasons, in my judgment the plaintiffs fail on their claim in this
action and the defendants' counterclaim does not arise. The defendants are
entitled to their costs of the action. H

Judgment accordingly.

Solicitors: *Ashurst, Morris, Crisp & Co.* (for the plaintiffs); *H. A. Crowe
& Co.* (for the defendants).

[*Reported by* K. Diana Phillips, *Barrister-at-Law.*]

A

JOLLIFFE *v.* EXETER CORPORATION.

[COURT OF APPEAL, CIVIL DIVISION (Lord Denning, M.R., Davies and Russell, L.JJ.), May 8, 9, 1967.]

B

Compulsory Purchase—Compensation—Injurious affection—Construction of by-pass—Stopping-up order for existing street made by Minister of Transport, in exercise of statutory powers under which there was not liability for compensation—Street in which claimant owned garage and filling station became cul-de-sac—Whether claimant entitled to compensation for injurious affection—Lands Clauses Consolidation Act, 1845 (8 & 9 Vict. c. 18), s. 68—Town and Country Planning Act, 1947 (10 & 11 Geo. 6 c. 51), s. 49 (1).

C

The plaintiff was the owner of a garage and filling station in C. Street. C. Street was a busy street used by traffic to avoid the centre of the city. The defendant corporation, as highway authority, intended to make a by-pass which was to go across C. Street at right angles so that C. Street would become a cul-de-sac. For constructing the intended by-pass the defendant corporation needed further land and made a compulsory purchase order under s. 214 of the Highways Act, 1959, on May 24, 1960, which was confirmed by the Minister of Transport on Feb. 27, 1962. The land to be acquired was not the plaintiff's, but was near to it on the other side of C. Street. In connexion with the planned by-pass the Minister made a stopping-up order on June 6, 1962, under s. 49 of the Town and Country Planning Act, 1947, in relation to C. Street. The plaintiff claimed compensation under s. 68* of the Lands Clauses Consolidation Act, 1845, on the ground that his land was injuriously affected.

D

E

Held: the " works " referred to by s. 68 of the Act of 1845 were those authorised on the land compulsorily acquired, these works did not cause damage to the plaintiff's land and accordingly the plaintiff was not entitled to compensation under s. 68; the injury to the plaintiff was due to the stopping-up of C. Street, which was a separate step for which the statute, the Town and Country Planning Act, 1947, did not provide compensation (see p. 1101, letters G and I, and p. 1102, letters F and I, post).

F

Decision of LAWTON, J. ([1967] 1 All E.R. 258) reversed.

[As to compensation for injurious affection, see 10 HALSBURY'S LAWS (3rd Edn.) 147, para. 256; and for cases on the subject, see 11 DIGEST (Repl.) 148-152, *271-289.*

G

As to the condition of compensation that injury must arise from the execution of the works, see 10 HALSBURY'S LAWS (3rd Edn.) 159, 160, para. 278.

As to the Minister's power to stop up highways, see 19 HALSBURY'S LAWS (3rd Edn.) 97, para. 142.

For the Lands Clauses Consolidation Act, 1845, s. 68, see 3 HALSBURY'S STATUTES (2nd Edn.) 919; and for the Acquisition of Land (Authorisation Procedure) Act, 1946, s. 1, Sch. 2, see ibid., pp. 1065, 1081.

H

For the Town and Country Planning Act, 1947, s. 49, see 25 HALSBURY'S STATUTES (2nd Edn.) 558, 559, and for the superseding provisions of s. 153, s. 156 of the Town and Country Planning Act, 1962, see 42 ibid., 1120, 1124.

For the Highways Act, 1959, s. 214, see 39 HALSBURY'S STATUTES (2nd Edn.) 640.]

I

Appeal.

This was an appeal by the defendants, the City of Exeter Corporation, from a judgment of LAWTON, J., dated Nov. 10, 1966, and reported [1967] 1 All E.R. 258, whereby it was declared that the plaintiff was entitled to compensation under s. 68 of the Lands Clauses Consolidation Act, 1845, for the injurious affection caused to his land and premises known as Gayton's Garage,

---

* Section 68, so far as material, is set out at p. 1101, letter C, post.

Coombe Street in the City of Exeter, caused by the execution of the works of **A**
construction of a highway on land acquired under the City of Exeter (Coombe
Street—James Street) Compulsory Purchase Order, 1960. The plaintiff served a
respondent's notice that he would contend that the judgment should be affirmed
on the further ground that his right to compensation arose on the publication on
Apr. 4, 1962, of the compulsory purchase order and was not destroyed, defeated
or affected by the subsequent coming into effect of the Stopping-up of Highways **B**
(City and County of the City of Exeter) (No. 3) Order, 1962.

The cases noted below* were cited during the argument.

A. de Piro, Q.C., and *L. F. Read* for the defendant corporation.
D. P. Kerrigan, Q.C., and *A. B. Dawson* for the plaintiff.
Nigel Bridge as amicus curiae on behalf of the Minister of Transport.

C

LORD DENNING, M.R.: The plaintiff, Mr. Jolliffe, had a garage and
filling station in Coombe Street, Exeter. It was a busy street because it was
much used by traffic to avoid the centre of the city. So he did a good trade
there; but the defendant corporation then decided to make an inner by-pass
road to take this traffic. This new by-pass road was to go straight across Coombe
Street at right angles. In order to construct it, the Minister of Transport **D**
made an order stopping-up Coombe Street. The defendant corporation also
needed land for the new by-pass road. They already owned a good deal of
land there, but they compulsorily acquired some more. They did not take any
of the plaintiff's land but they took somebody else's land on the other side of
Coombe Street. They then built the new inner by-pass road. It went across
Coombe Street at a height of about ten feet above the previous level. The **E**
result was that plaintiff's garage and filling station was no longer on a busy
throughfare, but on a cul-de-sac. On this account he now claims a declaration
against the defendant corporation that he is entitled to compensation.

The defendant corporation realised that the plaintiff's trade had been injured;
and they have done what they can to help him. They have let to him two pieces
of land, one on either side of the new by-pass. He has put a filling station there. **F**
No doubt he does a good trade. He is charged a proper rent for those two
pieces. He says that his use of these two pieces does not affect his claim for
compensation. That is correct. If he is entitled to compensation, it is not
affected by the fact that the defendant corporation have let him those two
pieces of land.

In considering the plaintiff's claim for compensation, it is necessary to dis- **G**
tinguish between the stopping-up of the highway (Coombe Street) and the
compulsory acquisition of land.

In order to stop up the highway, the Minister of Transport made an order
under s. 49 of the Town and Country Planning Act, 1947. It was contained
in the Stopping-up of Highways (City and County of the City of Exeter (No. 3)
Order, 1962, (1), and was dated June 6, 1962. It authorised the stopping-up of **H**
various streets in Exeter, including this part of Coombe Street. It is important
to observed, however, that the Act of 1947 contains no provision for compensation. In this respect the Act is like the old Highway Act, 1835. The legislature
provided for local inquiries and confirmation by quarter sessions; but did not
provide for compensation. Under that Act the stopping-up might ruin a man's
trade, but he could recover no compensation. So here, the stopping-up of **I**
Coombe Street may damage the plaintiff's trade in that street, but he can recover
no compensation on that account.

In order to acquire the land they needed, the defendant corporation, as highway authority, made an order under s. 214 (1) of the Highways Act, 1959. They

---

* *Imperial Gas Light and Coke Co.* v. *Broadbent* (1859), 7 H.L. Cas. 600; *Caledonian
Ry. Co.*, [1843-60] All E.R. Rep. 900; *Caledonian Ry. Co.* v. *Walker's Trustees*, [1881-85]
All E.R. Rep. 592; (1882), 7 App. Cas. 259.

(1) S.I. 1962 No. 1276.

A made a compulsory purchase order on May 24, 1960, and it was confirmed by the Minister of Transport on Feb. 27, 1962; but it is important to notice that none of the plaintiff's land was acquired. The defendant corporation already owned most of the land which they needed for the new inner by-pass road. All they needed in the vicinity of Coombe Street were two parcels of land. These two parcels were shown coloured pink on the plan. They are near to the plaintiff's

B garage but on the opposite side of the street. They were not part of the street but alongside it.

The statutes provide that, if a person is injuriously affected by a compulsory acquisition (of other land, not his own), then he is entitled to compensation. The provisions are very complicated. They start with the Acquisition of Land (Authorisation Procedure) Act, 1946, s. 1 and Sch. 2. Those provisions incor-

C porate the Lands Clauses Consolidation Act, 1845. That brings in s. 68 of the Lands Clauses Act, 1845. It provides compensation

"... in respect of any lands, or of any interest therein which shall have been taken for or injuriously affected by the execution of the works ..."

The plaintiff is, therefore, entitled to compensation for injurious affection due to

D the execution of the works. What are the "works"? The works are the works authorised by the "Special Act". The "Special Act" is defined by the Act of 1946 as the "enactment under which the purchase is authorised and the compulsory purchase order". In this case that is s. 214 (1) of the Highways Act, 1959, and the compulsory purchase order. The works authorised by those provisions are the works on the pink land, and not the works in Coombe

E Street itself. The result is this. If the road works executed on the two parcels of pink land had injuriously affected the plaintiff's land, he would have been entitled to compensation; but it is apparent that the works on those two parcels (taken by themselves) did not affect the plaintiff's land at all. They were near Coombe Street, but not across it. So they did not affect the use of Coombe Street. The thing which affected the plaintiff's land was the stopping-up of the

F highway: for which there is no compensation.

Counsel for the plaintiff argued that in the present case the "works" authorised were the whole of the inner by-pass road round Exeter. He went so far as to say that if the compulsory acquisition had been of a parcel of land several hundred yards away from Coombe Street—on the other end of the by-pass —the plaintiff would have had a right to compensation. I do not think that

G that is correct. The authorised "works" here were only the works on the pink land. It was not those works which caused the damage to the plaintiff.

I may add this. It is quite possible that this pink land might have been acquired by agreement. If that had been so, counsel for the plaintiff admitted that no compensation would be payable. It would be very strange if a compulsory purchase order made all the difference.

H The judge (2) decided in favour of the plaintiff on the ground that

"... the stopping-up of the highway was nothing more than a step in the execution of the authorised works—a step which the defendants counselled and procured the Minister to take."

I am afraid that I take a different view. The stopping-up of the highway was a

I separate step altogether. It was not done in the execution of the authorised works, i.e., the works on the pink land. It was done by the Minister under a separate statute. The injury to the plaintiff would have been just as great if the highway had been stopped up by a barrier without any road works at all.

In my opinion the injury to the plaintiff was done by the stopping-up of the highway, for which the statute has not provided compensation. He must rest content with the advantageous site which has been let to him on the by-pass.

---

(2) [1967] 1 All E.R. 258 at p. 261, letter I.

I would allow this appeal, refuse the declaration asked, and enter judgment **A** for the defendant corporation.

DAVIES, L.J.: I agree. The judge obviously saw the difficulty that the stopping-up of Coombe Street was done by the order of the Minister under s. 49 of the Town and Country Planning Act, 1947. He resolved the question in these words (3):

    B

> " In my judgment the stopping-up of the highway was nothing more than a step in the execution of the authorised works—a step which the defendants counselled and procured the Minister to take. Having counselled and procured that step they must take responsibility in law for it. Part of that responsibility is to pay compensation to those whose premises have been injuriously affected. This responsibility is placed on the defendants by reason of the provisions of the Highways Act, 1959, s. 222, and the Acquisition of Land (Authorisation Procedure) Act, 1946, the combined effect of which is to apply s. 68 of the Lands Clauses Consolidation Act, 1845. In my judgment it matters not that the Minister himself, when making the stopping up order exercised powers under s. 49 of the Town and Country Planning Act, 1947, with the result that he was not himself bound to pay anyone compensation. He was doing no more than giving help to the defendants when they asked for help."

    C

    D

I respectfully say that I cannot agree with the judge in his conclusion. It is a novel doctrine that, if the Minister exercises a power which he can exercise without incurring a liability to pay compensation to anybody, the fact that the exercise of that power is done at the request of a local authority imposes an obligation on them and places them under a liability to pay compensation. What was done by the Minister when he made the stopping-up order was done under the power given to him by s. 49; and the stopping-up could not in any sense be said to be works authorised by the special Act, which was, of course, the compulsory purchase order. I agree that the appeal should be allowed.

    E

    F

RUSSELL, L.J.: I also agree that the appeal should succeed. The injury complained of results from the fact that Coombe Street ceased to be a through road. If I may quote from the statement of claim:

> " 6. In or about the month of June, 1962, a length of Coombe Street adjacent to the junction of that street and James Street was closed permanently in accordance with the order referred to in para. 4 hereof [viz., the stopping-up order made by the Minister]. 7. Thereafter the new highway was constructed across the closed length of Coombe Street."

    G

This seems to me really to establish the contention of the defendant corporation that the execution of the works authorised, that is to say the construction of the highway, did not have any injurious effect on the plaintiff's property. The damage was already done. Coombe Street, before a pick or spade had been laid on the works, had been turned into a cul-de-sac so far as the plaintiff was concerned. It is perfectly true that the stopping-up order would not have been made, nor would the road have been stopped up, were it not for the fact that the defendant corporation proposed to execute the highway works; but it cannot therefore be said that the execution of the works authorised by the compulsory purchase order injuriously affected the plaintiff's land.

    H

    I

The judge managed, as he said (4), to " look at the events in the round ", which I take it means the equivalent of taking a broader than broad view of the case, and was able to conclude, as I understand it, that since the proposals to execute the highways works were a sine qua non of the stopping-up, therefore he could come to the conclusion that the injurious affection was caused by the

---

(3) [1967] 1 All E.R. at pp. 261, 262.
(4) [1967] 1 All E.R. at p. 262, letter B.

A actual execution of the authorised works.   I am not able myself to approach the decision of this case in the same generous spirit and I too would allow the appeal.

Appeal allowed.   Leave to appeal to the House of Lords refused.

Solicitors: *Sharpe, Pritchard & Co.*, agents for *Gilbert H. Stephens & Sons*, Exeter (for the defendant corporation); *Amery-Parkes & Co.*, agents for *G. D.*
B *Cann & Hallett*, Exeter (for the plaintiff); *Treasury Solicitor*.

[*Reported by* F. Guttman, Esq., *Barrister-at-Law.*]

C CROFTON INVESTMENT TRUST, LTD. *v.* GREATER LONDON RENT ASSESSMENT COMMITTEE AND ANOTHER.

[Queen's Bench Division (Lord Parker, C.J., Widgery and O'Connor, JJ.), April 10, 1967.]

D *Rent   Restriction—Rent—Regulated   tenancy—Fair   rent—Scarcity   element—*
Evidence of capital value not conclusive basis of fair rent—Whether rent assessment committee entitled to act on their own knowledge in regard to scarcity element—Whether committee bound to notify intention to determine fair rent eliminating scarcity element so as to give opportunity for evidence on scarcity to be called—Rent Act 1965 (c. 75), s. 27 (1), (2).

E In January, 1966, a tenant of a small dwelling house at Welling, Kent, applied for the registration of a fair rent.   His tenancy was for 7½ years from Jan. 10, 1964, at a rent of £250 per annum for the first five years and £275 per annum, for the remainder of the term.   He was responsible for rates and repairs.   The rent officer's determination of fair rent, which was notified to the landlords, was £180 per annum exclusive of rates.   His determination
F stated that the house was a small, cheaply constructed terraced house which would have sold, when built in the 1934-36 period, for about £350.   The landlords objected in writing, and the matter was referred to the rent assessment committee.   At the hearing on Sept. 23, 1966, a surveyor gave evidence for the landlords that a fair rent would be £300 per annum.   His estimate was based on capital value, viz., present day cost of building, £1,945, and in
G addition site value.   Building land in that neighbourhood fetched £15,000 an acre, from which he deducted twenty-five per cent. for scarcity element, and thus reached a total cost of £3,700 as the vacant possession price.   On a full repairing lease a rent of £300 per annum would give a return of eight per cent. The committee inspected the exterior of the property, and taking into account the element of scarcity in the locality, determined the fair rent pursuant to
H s. 27* (1), (2) of the Rent Act 1965 at £200 exclusive of rates, the tenant being responsible for repairs and other outgoings.   On appeal†,

Held: the committee had not erred in law and their determination should stand for the following reasons—

(i) because the committee were entitled to act on their own knowledge in respect of scarcity of such houses to let in the locality (see p. 1108, letter E, and p. 1110, letters A and C, post).

I Dictum of Lord Goddard, C.J., in *R. v. Brighton and Area Rent Tribunal, Ex p. Marine Parade Estates (1936), Ltd.*, ([1950] 2 K.B. at pp. 420, 421) applied.

(ii) because the question of the scarcity element was apparent to the landlords from the rent officer's determination of the rent and there was

* Section 27, so far as material, is set out at p. 1106, letter F, to letter H, post.
† Appeal lay under s. 9 of the Tribunals and Inquiries Act, 1958, as applied by the Tribunals and Inquiries (Rent Assessment Committees) Order 1065, 10g. 4.

no reason why the committee, before making their determination, should
have informed the parties of the committee's intention to proceed directly
to determining a fair rent eliminating the scarcity element (see p. 1109,
letter G, and p. 1110, letters A and C, post).

(iii) because, although the committee appeared to have been mistaken
in thinking that the surveyor had made no deduction in respect of scarcity
element, for, though construction costs eliminated that element, a deduction
had in fact been made in estimating site value, yet the court was not satisfied
that the error would have made any difference, since evidence of capital
value was not conclusive but was useful principally as a guide to an upper
rent limit, and thus the landlords would still not have discharged the burden,
which was on them, of showing that the determination by the committee
was of an amount below the fair rent (see p. 1109, letter I, and p. 1110,
letters B and C, post).

Appeal dismissed.

[As to determination by rent assessment committee, see SUPPLEMENT to 23
HALSBURY'S LAWS (3rd Edn.) para. 1571B, 5; and for a case on the subject,
see 31 DIGEST (Repl.) 676, 7702.

For the Rent Act 1965, s. 26, s. 27, Sch. 3, see 45 HALSBURY'S STATUTES
(2nd Edn.) 843, 864.]

Case referred to:

R. v. *Brighton and Area Rent Tribunal, Ex p. Marine Parade Estates (1936),*
     Ltd., [1950] 1 All E.R. 946; [1950] 2 K.B. 410; 114 J.P. 242; 31 Digest
     (Repl.) 676, 7702.

Appeal.

This was an appeal by the appellants, Crofton Investment Trust, Ltd., against
a decision of the first respondents, the Rent Assessment Committee for Greater
London, given on Sept. 23, 1966, whereby they reduced the rent of one of the
appellants' properties, 235, Yorkland Avenue, Welling, Kent, which was let to
the second respondent, Desmond William Johnson, on a lease for 7½ years from
Jan. 10, 1964, at a rent of £250 a year for the first five years and at a rent of £275
a year for the remaining two and a half years, the second respondent to be responsible for the general and water rates and for internal and external decorations
and repairs. The grounds of the appeal included the following: (a) That the first
respondents failed to consider, or failed properly to consider, the evidence
before them; (b) that the first respondents took into consideration matters
which they ought not to have considered and wrongfully failed to take into consideration matters which they ought to have considered; (c) that there was no
evidence of " scarcity " within the ambit of s. 27 of the Rent Act 1965; (d) that
the appellants' evidence before the first respondents was unchallenged and uncontradicted; (e) that the determined fair rent of £200 per annum exclusive bore
no relation whatsoever to the market selling value or the replacement cost of
the premises, as to which there was no dispute; (f) that there was no evidence
of any element of scarcity in the locality; that the first respondents ought not
to have taken such element into account, in the absence of evidence; (g) that the
determined fair rent bore no relationship whatsoever to the relevant facts;
and (h) that the first respondents arrived at a determination of fair rent regardless of the facts and of the evidence. The facts are set out in the judgment of
LORD PARKER, C.J.

The case noted below† was cited during the argument in addition to the one
referred to in his judgment.

---

† R. v. *Paddington and St. Marylebone Rent Tribunal, Ex p. Bell London and
Provincial Properties, Ltd.,* [1949] 1 All E.R. 720; [1949] 1 K.B. 666.

A   *Leonard Caplan, Q.C.*, and *Harry Lester* for the appellants.
   Nigel Bridge as amicus curiae.
   The first respondents did not appear and were not represented.
   The second respondent appeared in person.

   LORD PARKER, C.J.: This is an appeal from a decision of the Rent
B Assessment Committee for Greater London given on Sept. 23, 1966, whereby the
rent for one of the appellants' properties was reduced considerably. It is an appeal,
as it has to be, on a point of law, and as this is the first case which has been
brought before this court, it is convenient to refer to such parts of the statute as
are relevant to these proceedings. The statute is the Rent Act 1965, which by s. 1
applies the Rent Acts to certain tenancies, such a tenancy being referred to as a
C " regulated tenancy ". Section 22 provides for registration areas being set up for
the purposes of the Act of 1965, and enables the Minister for every registration
area to make a scheme providing for, in effect, rent officers for the area.
Subsections (1) and (2) of s. 26 provide that:

   " (1) The rent officer for any area shall prepare and keep up to date a
register for the purposes of this Act and shall make the register available for
D inspection in such place or places and in such manner as may be provided by
the scheme made for the area under this Part of this Act or, in Scotland, as
the Secretary of State may direct. (2) The register shall contain, in addition
to the rent payable under a regulated tenancy of a dwellinghouse—(*a*) the
prescribed particulars with regard to the tenancy; and (*b*) a specification of
the dwellinghouse."

E Subsection (5) of s. 26 provides that:

   " Schedule 3 to this Act shall have effect with respect to applications for
the registration of rents and the procedure to be followed on such
applications . . ."

Turning to Sch. 3, it is provided by para. 1 that:

F   " An application for the registration of a rent for a dwelling-house may
be made to the rent officer by the landlord or the tenant, or jointly by the
landlord and the tenant . . ."

The procedure is then dealt with in para. 4 and the following paragraphs. In the
case of objections or representations against the registering of a particular rent,
the first procedure is that to be found in para. 7, which in argument has been
G referred to as the negotiating procedure. The rent officer has the landlord and
tenant before him and does try to see, in effect, whether agreement can be arrived
at. Then in para. 8 it is provided that:

   " After considering, in accordance with the preceding paragraph, what
rent ought to be registered or, as the case may be, whether a different rent
ought to be registered, the rent officer shall, as the case may require,—(*a*)
H determine a fair rent and register it as the rent for the dwelling-house; or
(*b*) confirm the rent for the time being registered and note the confirmation
in the register; and shall notify the landlord and the tenant accordingly . . ."

Provision is made for either the landlord or the tenant to register an objection
in writing, and in such event the matter is referred to a rent assessment committee. It is unnecessary to refer to it in any detail but rent assessment commit-
I tees are set up by s. 25 of the Act of 1965 and the provisions of Sch. 2. By para.
9 (1) of Sch. 3: " If such an objection is received " the rent officer is to deal with
the matter as there laid down. Paragraphs 10, 11 and 12 then go on to set out the
procedure before a rent assessment committee. They are in the nature of rules or
regulations of procedure. It is necessary to read them in a little detail. They
provide:

   " 10. The rent assessment committee to whom a matter is referred under
para. 9 of this schedule may by notice in the prescribed form served on the

                                                       . oo

A

landlord or the tenant require him to give to the committee, within such period, not less than fourteen days from the service of the notice, as may be specified in the notice, such further information, in addition to any given to the rent officer in pursuance of para. 4 of this schedule, as they may reasonably require and shall serve on the landlord and on the tenant a notice specifying a period, not less than fourteen days from the service of the notice, during which either representations in writing or a request to make oral representations may be made by him to the committee.

B

" 11. Where within the period specified under the preceding paragraph, or such further period as the committee may allow, the landlord or the tenant requests to make oral representations the committee shall give him an opportunity to be heard either in person or by a person authorised by him in that behalf, whether or not that person is of counsel or a solicitor.

C

" 12. The committee shall make such inquiry, if any, as they think fit and consider any information supplied or representation made to them in pursuance of para. 10 or para. 11 of this schedule and—

(a) if it appears to them that the rent registered or confirmed by the rent officer is a fair rent, they shall confirm that rent; (b) if it does not appear to them that that rent is a fair rent, they shall determine a fair rent for the dwelling-house;

D

and shall notify the landlord and the tenant and the rent officer accordingly; and on receiving the notification the rent officer shall, as the case may require, either indicate in the register that the rent has been confirmed or register the rent determined by the committee as the rent for the dwelling-house."

E

The only other provision of the Act of 1965 to which it is necessary to refer is s. 27, the side-note to which is " Determination of fair rent ". By sub-s. (1) it is provided that:

" In determining for the purposes of this Act what rent is or would be a fair rent under a regulated tenancy of a dwelling-house regard shall be had, subject to the following provisions of this section, to all the circumstances (other than personal circumstances), and in particular to the age, character and locality of the dwelling-house and to its state of repair."

F

Pausing there, though for my part I think that it matters not for the purposes of this case, it is clear that the rent officer and then the committee are applying a subjective test. It is the fair rent for the particular house concerned in all the circumstances other than personal circumstances. Then s. 27 (2) provides that:

G

" For the purpose of the determination it shall be assumed that the number of persons seeking to become tenants of similar dwelling-houses in the locality on the terms (other than those relating to rent) of the regulated tenancy is not substantially greater than the number of such dwelling-houses in the locality which are available for letting on such terms."

H

It is quite clear that Parliament desired to cut down all the circumstances referred to in sub-s. (1) in the sense that where there was a substantially greater number of tenants than of premises available who were willing to pay what is called scarcity value, that that element of scarcity shall not be taken into account. Finally, by reg. 4 of the Tribunals and Inquiries (Rent Assessment Committees) Order 1965 (1), s. 9 of the Tribunals and Inquiries Act, 1958, which provides for appeals on points of law to this court from certain tribunals is applied to rent assessment committees.

I

Turning to the facts of this case, Mr. Johnson, the second respondent to this appeal, had taken a lease of premises known as 235, Yorkland Avenue, Welling in the county of Kent, that lease commencing on Jan. 10, 1964, being for 7½ years, the rent payable being £250 for the first five years of the term, and £275

(1) S.I. 1965 No. 2151.

A   for the remainder of the term. He, as tenant, was to be responsible for the general and water rate, and, which was more important, for all interior and exterior decorations and repair. On Jan. 6, 1966, as he was entitled to do, he applied to the rent officer for registration of a fair rent for the premises, and suggested that the rent, bearing in mind his covenants to repair, should be £104 per annum. The matter went before the rent officer and his decision was given on Jan. 31, and

B   was before the committee, but, as is more important, had been, very properly, sent to the appellants for their comments. The rent officer's decision was in this form:

    " This property falls under the lower price group where, in this vicinity, it carries the greatest scarcity element. It is a very small, cheaply constructed terrace house and one which would have sold when built, in the

C   1934-36 period, for about £350. The largest bedroom is only twelve feet by nine feet. Access to bedroom No. 3 is through bedroom No. 1. The property has been reasonably well maintained . . . Taking into account the type of property, the locality and other circumstances mentioned above, I consider that a fair rent for this property to be £180 per annum exclusive, as the tenant is responsible for all repairs as specified in the 7½ year lease from

D   Jan. 10, 1964."

    The appellants being dissatisfied with that condition appealed, as they were entitled to, to the rent assessment committee and the matter came on for hearing on Sept. 23, 1966. There are notes kept by the secretary to the committee of that hearing, but I find it unnecessary to refer to them in any detail. It is sufficient to say that the appellants, before the committee and before this court,

E   called a Mr. Selby, a very experienced surveyor, who knew this locality. His view of the fair rent for these premises, on the basis still that the tenant bore the cost of all repairs, was £300 per annum. He arrived at that, not by way of comparison with other properties in the neighbourhood or quite generally as the result of his own experience, but by arriving at a capital value based on construction costs, and then giving the speculator, the builder, a fair interest on his money. Quite

F   shortly, he put forward for the building on present day costs, including management and builder's costs but excluding site value, the figure of £1,945; to that had to be added site value. His view was that building land in that neighbourhood fetched £15,000 per acre, but bearing in mind that that would undoubtedly include a scarcity element, he thought it right to deduct from that twenty-five per cent., and applying that to the plot in question he arrived at a figure of total

G   cost of £3,695, which he rounded off as £3,700, as he put it a vacant possession price. He pointed out that £300 per annum on a full repairing lease would give an investor eight per cent. on his money, which he felt under present conditions an investor would require for an outlay of capital in this area.

    The respondent committee in their written decision of Sept. 23, 1966 said this:

H   " (i) [Counsel for the appellants] referred in his speech to sub-s. (2) of s. 27 of the [Rent Act 1965] and said that in considering the meaning and effect of the words ' not substantially greater ' the committee was bound to inquire whether ' the number of persons seeking to become tenants was not substantially greater than the number of dwelling-houses available for letting '. The committee is satisfied that such, indeed, is the case in the locality in

I   question."

    It is quite clear, I should have thought, though not perhaps very happily worded, that the committee were fully satisfied that there were a substantially greater number of persons seeking to be tenants than there were dwellings available for letting. They go on in para. (ii) to say:

    " The committee took notice of the fact that the house is extremely small. It is an inside house in a terrace of four houses. One of its bedrooms can only be entered through another bedroom. The committee also noted that the

tenant's liability under the repairing covenants of the lease (which was **A**
expressed to be for a term of $7\frac{1}{2}$ years) was extremely heavy and was
estimated by the [appellants] at some £50 p.a. thus, the effective rent was
substantially higher than the contractual rent. (iii) The [appellants] called
evidence to the effect that a fair selling price today for the property with
vacant possession was approximate £3,700. [The witness] also said that in
estimating the cost of building a similar property today he had allowed for a **B**
scarcity element of twenty-five per cent. In the committee's view, however,
no actual deduction in respect of scarcity is evident in either the estimated
selling price or in his estimate of the capital vacant possession value (also
£3,700). The committee considered that whilst evidence of capital values of
property is useful in considering a fair rent, it is by no means conclusive.
(iv) The committee having inspected the exterior of the property and having **C**
taken into account, inter alia, the element of scarcity in the locality has
decided that a fair rent would be £200 p.a. exclusive. (v) The committee,
therefore, determined a fair rent at £200 p.a. exclusive of rates, the tenant
being responsible for repairs and other outgoings in accordance with the
terms of the lease and that this rent should take effect from the date of the
tenant's application to the rent officer." **D**

I confess that having read that, one asks oneself where it can be said that this
committee erred in law. Counsel for the appellants has put it in two ways; he
has two main points, with a subsidiary third one. His first point is that there was
no specific evidence, oral or written, before the committee that there was a
substantially greater number of persons willing to become tenants in this locality
than there were premises to let available. He said there was no evidence of that, **E**
yet in para. (iv) of the decision which I have read they found that there was. For
my part I am quite satisfied that this committee, that is to say a committee of
this sort under a procedure which is clearly to be intended to be informal and not
to be carried through with the precision of a court of justice, is fully entitled to
act, as it has been said, on their own impression and on their own knowledge. It
is idle in my view to think of gentlemen manning this committee and sitting **F**
maybe day after day without acquiring experience and knowledge of conditions
in the locality, and to say that they should shut their eyes to what they know
of their own knowledge, and act only on such evidence as may or may not be put
before them, seems to me to reduce the matter to absurdity. A very similar matter
to this was considered by this court in proceedings under the Landlord and
Tenant (Rent Control) Act, 1949. In *R.* v. *Brighton and Area Rent Tribunal,* **G**
Ex p. Marine Parade Estates (1936), Ltd. (2), the tribunal concerned had, and it is
unnecessary to go through it, to adopt very much the same procedure as the
respondent committee in the present case. LORD GODDARD, C.J., when giving
the first judgment, with which the others concurred, said this (3):

" Therefore it seems to me, the tribunal must be able to act on their own
impression and on their own knowledge; otherwise the thing would come to **H**
a standstill altogether. The procedure which I have indicated can work only
if the tribunal can act in that way and on their own inspection, if they like to
make an inspection, of the premises, or on any information which they
themselves may have. If witnesses are tendered, I have no doubt that it is
the duty of the tribunal to hear them. If they are tendered and cross-
examination is desired, it is the duty of the tribunal to allow that cross- **I**
examination. Then, if the other side wish to call evidence to answer it, it is,
again, their duty to allow it. But, I repeat, it is quite obvious that these
tribunals can act without having any evidence before them at all: neither
party need appear; neither party need file any statement in writing unless
he likes; a tenant can merely ask the tribunal to fix a proper rent; if he does,
the landlord can appear, stay away, submit any statement, or, of course, call
any evidence he likes."

(2) [1950] 1 All E.R. 946; [1950] 2 K.B. 410.   (3) [1950] 2 K.B. at pp. 420, 421.

A   It seems to me that every word of LORD GODDARD in that case is equally applicable to proceedings before a rent assessment committee. Indeed, counsel as amicus curiae points out that the rules of procedure, as I have called them, in Sch. 3 to the Rent Act 1965, provide specifically that the committee shall make such inquiries if any as they may think fit. If they are entitled to make inquiry of someone of some fact, from someone who does not give evidence before them,

B   surely they are entitled to inquire of themselves as to matters within their own knowledge.

The second way in which counsel for the appellants puts his case is that even if they are entitled to act on their own knowledge, yet here rules of natural justice, or to put it more simply, fairness, demanded that before they approached the matter as they did in para. (iv) of their decision, namely to proceed directly

C   to a fair rent eliminating a scarcity element, they should have so informed the appellant landlords' representative in order to enable the appellant landlords' representative to deal with the point and to call evidence, if need be, that there was not a substantially greater number of prospective tenants than there were premises. For my part I am quite clear that whenever a new point emerges, something which might take a party by surprise or something which the committee

D   have found out and of which the parties would have no knowledge, fairness would clearly dictate that they should inform the parties and enable them to deal with the points. Indeed, if as a result of an inquiry made pursuant to para. 12 of Sch. 3 some such point emerged, again it would be right so to inform the parties to give them an opportunity of dealing with the matter. So far I agree with counsel for the appellants, but I fail to see how that principle has any application

E   to the facts of this case. It was clear to everybody that one of the real questions here was whether there was a scarcity element in the rent found by the respondent committee; indeed the rent officer in his decision which I have already read said: " This property falls under the lower price group where, in this vicinity, it carries the greatest scarcity element." That decision was very properly sent to the appellants for their comments. They made their points; I find it unnecessary to

F   refer to the letters and the points made. It is sufficient to say that they were alive to the point made by the rent officer; they never, when given an opportunity to deal with it, denied what he had said, and at the hearing they never called evidence to negative that. Bearing in mind that it was a point of which they were aware from the very beginning, and which quite clearly was a vital point in the case, I can find no reason whatever why fairness in this case dictated that

G   the committee, before stating their findings to that effect, should have given the appellant landlords' representative an opportunity of dealing with it.

The third and subsidiary point arises on para. (iii) of the decision and reasons. I have read it already; it does appear to say that, in the committee's view, Mr. Selby had made no actual deductions in this case in respect of scarcity. If that means what it says, then I think that they misunderstood Mr. Selby's evidence,

H   because in arriving at his figure of £3,700, what he called vacant possession value, he had been at pains, first to use construction costs, which eliminated all scarcity element, and secondly in adding the site value, had made what he thought was the appropriate deduction of twenty-five per cent. to take care of the scarcity element. As I say, I think the tribunal were wrong in the view which they took of Mr. Selby's evidence; but having said that, I am by no means convinced, and

I   the burden here is on the appellants, that if they had understood Mr. Selby's evidence, as I think we understand it now, it would have made the slightest difference. As they point out, evidence of capital value, though useful, is by no means conclusive. As it seems to me, the proper view was that his fair rent of £300 was really the maximum having regard to a brand new property, whereas what the respondent committee were concerned with was this house built in 1934 to 1936 with a very heavy cost of maintenance. I cannot see any error of law in the approach of this committee, and I would dismiss this appeal.

WIDGERY, J.: I agree. Before the rent assessment committee the A appellants' principal argument was that the capital value of their investment calculated on the construction cost basis was £3,700, and that no return less than £300 per year would be a fair return on that investment. This approach, sometimes called the contractor's theory, has an honoured place in rating practice, but is rarely if ever put forward as providing an accurate guide to the rent which parties will agree in the case of a dwelling, still less to what is a fair rent in the B special circumstances of the Rent Act 1965. At best the contractor's test will normally do no more than indicate an upper limit above which it is unlikely that negotiating parties would fix the rent, and far from being, as counsel for the appellants submitted, a floor below which the rent should not be fixed, in my opinion it tends to be a ceiling above which the rent should not go.

O'CONNOR, J.: I agree and I have nothing to add.　　　C

Appeal dismissed.

Solicitors: *D. Gross* (for the appellants); *Solicitor, Ministry of Housing and Local Government* (as amicus curiae).

[*Reported by* N. P. METCALFE, ESQ., *Barrister-at-Law.*]

Re L.

[PROBATE, DIVORCE AND ADMIRALTY DIVISION (Ormrod, J.), June 28, October 21, 1966, May 8, 9, June 1, 1967.]

Divorce—Infant—Jurisdiction—Powers exercisable by Divorce Division where proceedings properly initiated there in relation to a child—Paternity of child in issue—Blood test.

A judge sitting in the Probate, Divorce and Admiralty Division has all the powers which are available to any judge of the High Court in relation to children or any other matter; and although proceedings to make a child a ward of court must be started in accordance with the provisions of the Rules of the Supreme Court and, in compliance with s. 56 of the Supreme Court of Judicature (Consolidation) Act, 1925, will be assigned to the Chancery Division, yet if proceedings in relation to a child have been properly initiated in the Probate, Divorce and Admiralty Division, it is not necessary to have recourse to the Chancery Division to invoke powers which are derived from the court's jurisdiction over wards (see p. 1117, letter G, post).

R. v. *Gyngall* ([1893] 2 Q.B. 232) applied.

Andrews v. *Andrews and Sullivan* ([1958] 2 All E.R. 305), *Re Andrews (infants)* ([1958] 2 All E.R. 308), *Re A.-H. (infants)* ([1962] 3 All E.R. 853) and *Hall* v. *Hall* ([1963] 2 All E.R. 140) distinguished.

Divorce—Custody—Paternity of child in issue—Custodial jurisdiction—Power of judge in Probate, Divorce and Admiralty Division to order blood test—Power of Official Solicitor as guardian ad litem to refuse consent—R.S.C., Ord. 80, r. 2 (2).

A mother is entitled to have her child blood-grouped if she wishes, unless and until restrained by an order of the court from so doing; a fortiori the court having full parental powers over the child can also authorise a doctor to take blood for forensic purposes (see p. 1119, letters H and I, post).

W. v. *W. (No. 4)* ([1963] 2 All E.R. 841) distinguished.

In 1958, ten years after the marriage of the husband and the wife, a child was born to the wife. Two years or so previously the wife had met the party cited. Since 1956 the wife had been committing adultery with the party cited, unknown to the husband. In December, 1963, the wife petitioned for divorce. In May, 1964, the husband filed an answer alleging adultery by the wife with the party cited. Both the petition and the answer contained prayers for the custody of the child. In October, 1964, the wife left the

A   husband, taking the child with her. In November, 1964, the wife and the party cited confessed their adultery, which they then stated began in 1964. In March, 1965, the husband first became aware that he might not be the father of the child. In July, 1965, a decree nisi was made at the hearing of the case undefended on the husband's answer, and an issue of the paternity of the child was directed. The wife and the party cited then admitted

B   that they had committed adultery since 1956. The child was a defendant to the issue of paternity, and the party cited was a party to that issue. The adult parties to the issue desired that the child's blood group should be ascertained, and each of the adults was willing to submit to serological examination. An order for the child's blood group to be taken having been refused at a hearing of the paternity issue on June 28, 1966, as the child's

C   guardian ad litem did not consent and by reason of the presumption of legitimacy of a child born in wedlock, the matter was adjourned generally* for consideration of the position under the custodial jurisdiction.

     Held: the child's interests would be best served by taking all available steps to remove doubts about her paternity; the court would order that the child should be serologically examined, the child's blood sample not

D   to be taken until the three adult parties to the issue had submitted to serological examination (see p. 1124, letter I, to p. 1125, letter A, and p. 1126, letter C, post).

     Per CURIAM: (i) once a guardian ad litem has been appointed for a child, it would be most undesirable for a parent to arrange for a serological examination without an order of the court, or at least without the consent of the

E   guardian ad litem if he is prepared to waive the necessity for an order (see p. 1121, letter H, post).

     (ii) a consent by the guardian ad litem to a child being blood-grouped in custody proceedings cannot be regarded as something required or authorised by R.S.C., Ord. 80, r. 2 (2)†, to be done " in the ordinary conduct of [the] proceedings "; but for such a consent to be a valid procedural step, the

F   sanction of the court would be required (see p. 1120, letter I, to p. 1121, letter A, post), and the decision whether or not a child should be submitted to psychiatric, medical or serological examination ultimately rests with the court (see p. 1121, letter E, post).

     Dictum of CROSS, J., in *Re S. (an infant)* ([1967] 1 All E.R. at p. 209) applied.

G   [As to orders for custody of children, see 12 HALSBURY'S LAWS (3rd Edn.) 392, para. 868.]

Cases referred to:

     A.-H. (infants), Re, [1962] 3 All E.R. 853; [1963] Ch. 232; [1962] 3 W.L.R. 1430; Digest (Cont. Vol. A) 933, *2152a.*

H   *Andrews (infants), Re*, [1958] 2 All E.R. 308; [1958] Ch. 665; [1958] 2 W.L.R. 946; 28 Digest (Repl.) 706, *2152.*

     Andrews v. Andrews and Sullivan, [1958] 2 All E.R. 305; [1958] P. 217; [1958] 2 W.L.R. 942; 28 Digest (Repl.) 710, *2191.*

     B. v. A.-G. (N.E.B. intervening), [1965] 1 All E.R. 62; [1965] P. 278; [1965] 2 W.L.R. 871; Digest (Cont. Vol. B) 50, *170a.*

I   *Birchall, Re, Wilson v. Birchall*, (1880), 16 Ch.D. 41; 44 L.T. 113; 28 Digest (Repl.) 701, *2104.*

     Cammell v. Cammell, [1964] 3 All E.R. 255; [1965] P. 467; [1964] 3 W.L.R. 791; Digest (Cont. Vol. B) 366, *4460a.*

     H. v. H., [1966] 3 All E.R. 560; Digest (Cont. Vol. B) 377, *5822d.*

     H. v. H. (H., by his guardian, intervening), [1966] 1 All E.R. 356; sub nom. *Holmes v. Holmes*, [1966] 1 W.L.R. 187; Digest (Cont. Vol. B) 354, *2673a.*

---

* See p. 1112, letter H, post.

† R.S.C., Ord. 80, r. 2 (2) is set out at p. 1120, letter H, post.

Hall v. *Hall*, [1963] 2 All E.R. 140; [1963] P. 378; [1963] 2 W.L.R. 1054;   A
    Digest (Cont. Vol. A) 933, *2152b.*

MacGowan v. *Middleton*, (1883), 11 Q.B.D. 464; 52 L.J.Q.B. 355; 40 Digest
    (Repl.) 443, *314.*

Official Solicitor v. *K.,* [1963] 3 All E.R. 191; [1965] A.C. 201; [1963] 3 W.L.R.
    408; Digest (Cont. Vol. A) 933, *2149b.*

Pickett v. *Bristol Aeroplane Co., Ltd.,* (1961), The Times, Mar. 17.   B

R. v. *Gyngall,* [1893] 2 Q.B. 232; sub nom. *Re Gyngall,* 62 L.J.Q.B. 559;
    57 J.P. 773; sub nom. *R.* v. *Gyngall, Re Hausherr (otherwise Austen),*
    69 L.T. 481; 28 Digest (Repl.) 485, *25.*

Rhodes v. *Swithenbank,* (1889), 22 Q.B.D. 577; 58 L.J.Q.B. 287; 60 L.T. 856;
    28 Digest (Repl.) 700, *2097.*

Robinson v. *Robinson,* [1963] 3 All E.R. 813; [1965] P. 39; [1964] 2 W.L.R.   C
    138; Digest (Cont. Vol. A) 810, *6527c.*

Russell v. *Russell,* [1924] A.C. 687; 93 L.J.P. 97; 131 L.T. 482; 27 Digest
    (Repl.) 318, *2649.*

S. (an infant), Re, [1967] 1 All E.R. 202; [1967] 1 W.L.R. 396.

Stocker (by her next friend) v. *Stocker (otherwise Woodruff, by her guardian),*
    [1966] 2 All E.R. 147; [1966] 1 W.L.R. 190; Digest (Cont. Vol. B) 350,   D
    2267b.

Thain, Re, Thain v. *Taylor,* [1926] All E.R. Rep. 384; [1926] Ch. 676; 95
    L.J.Ch. 292; 135 L.T. 99; 28 Digest (Repl.) 614, *1214.*

W. v. *W. (No. 4),* [1963] 2 All E.R. 386; sub nom. *W.* v. *W.* [1964] P. 67;
    [1963] 3 W.L.R. 540; *affd.* C.A., [1963] 2 All E.R. 841; sub nom.
    W. v. *W.,* [1964] P. at p. 72; [1963] 3 W.L.R. 540; Digest (Cont. Vol. A)   E
    703, *2267a.*

Issue.

This was an issue directed to be tried as to the paternity of a child born on
Feb. 8, 1958, during the continuance of the marriage between the husband and
the wife. The issue was directed at the hearing of the petition on July 9, 1965,
as an undefended case on the husband's answer before His Honour JUDGE   F
BARRINGTON sitting as commissioner in divorce. At that hearing the commissioner
granted a decree nisi of divorce against the wife on the ground of her adultery
with the party cited. The child and the party cited were parties to the issue as to
paternity. The issue came on for hearing before ORMROD, J., on June 28, 1966, in
the circumstances stated at p. 1114, letters E to G, post, on facts that were agreed
and are summarised at p. 1113, letter H, post. ORMROD, J., decided that on the   G
paternity issue the court would have to declare, in view of the fact that the Official
Solicitor as guardian ad litem of the child declined to consent to the child's blood
group being taken and by reason of the presumption of legitimacy of a child born
in wedlock, that the child was the child of the husband and the wife. ORMROD, J.,
thereupon adjourned the matter generally, until the question of custody should
be resolved, at which stage the court might have power to direct that the blood   H
group of the child, whose welfare would then be the paramount consideration,
should be taken.

The wife in her petition and the husband in his answer both prayed for the
custody of the child. The material passages of the judgment of ORMROD, J., at
the hearing of the paternity issue on June 28, 1966, are set out in a note to this
report at pp. 1126, 1127, post.   I

The cases noted below* were cited during the argument in addition to those
referred to in the judgment.

---

* CRAIES STATUTE LAW (6th Edn.), p. 123; WINFIELD ON TORT (7th Edn.) p. 29;
Duggan v. *Duggan,* (1859), 29 L.J.P.M. & A. 159; *Re McGrath (infants),* [1893] 1 Ch. 143;
Thomasset v. *Thomasset,* [1891-94] All E.R. Rep. 308; [1894] P. 295; *M.* v. *M.,* 1926 S.C.
778; *Gilbert* v. *Gilbert and Boucher,* [1928] P. 1; *Re Turner's Will Trusts,* [1936] 2 All E.R.
1435; [1937] Ch. 15; *Grey* v. *Inland Revenue Comrs.,* [1959] 3 All E.R. 603; [1960] A.C. 1;
Montgomery v. *Montgomery,* [1964] 2 All E.R. 22; [1965] P. 46.

A   *R. J. A. Temple, Q.C.*, and *Gerald Kidner* for the wife.

     Joseph Jackson, Q.C., and *Margaret Booth* for the husband.

     Gerald Kidner for the party cited.

     J. P. Comyn, Q.C., and *Bruce Holroyd Pearce* for the Official Solicitor as guardian ad litem for the child.

Cur. adv. vult.

B

     June 1. **ORMROD, J.**, read the following judgment. The question has arisen in this paternity issue whether the court has power to direct that the blood group of the child who is the subject of the issue shall be ascertained, in order that the court may reach its decision in the light of all the available evidence. It is not disputed that such evidence is relevant and may well be conclusive of C   the issue which the court has to try. Indeed, without this evidence the court cannot, in fact, determine which of the two men concerned is the father of this child and will be obliged to fall back on the presumption of legitimacy which is as likely to be wrong as right. In this case, the question is thrown into the sharpest possible focus. The husband, the wife and the party cited have all expressed, through their solicitors and counsel, not only their willingness to D   submit themselves to serological investigation to determine their respective blood groups but have also expressed their wish that the child's blood should be investigated in the same way. Neither of the men is claiming or disclaiming paternity, and the mother is not putting forward a positive case either way. All three of them are genuinely anxious to know which of the two men is the natural father of this child. None of them is interested in the results of the E   application of the legal presumption, since none of them wish to establish or evade their legal obligations to this child. Since the wife and the party cited intend to marry as soon as his marriage is dissolved, there is no question of bastardising this child in any meaningful sense. In fact, the true issue before the court is whether this child is a legitimate child of the husband and wife or will become a legitimated child of the wife and the party cited when they marry. F   The only obstacle standing in the way of the determination of this issue is the refusal of the child's guardian ad litem, the Official Solicitor, to consent to the child's blood being investigated. I have stated the position in this way, not because I intend any criticism of the Official Solicitor's action; indeed, for reasons which I will develop later I am very doubtful, after hearing the further argument in this case, whether the guardian ad litem has authority to give or withhold G   consent in such a case; but because, in my judgment, it is an accurate formulation of the problem which the court is now required to resolve and concentrates attention on the true considerations on which my judgment must be based.

     I shall confine my statement of the facts out of which this problem has arisen to those which are immediately relevant, in the hope of preserving, so far as I can, the anonymity of all concerned. The child in question was born in 1958, H   ten years after the marriage of the husband and the wife. The party cited met the wife and soon afterwards the husband in 1956. Apart from a fleeting suspicion about the intentions of the party cited in the early stages of their acquaintance, the husband had no idea that the wife had been committing adultery with the party cited from about 1956 onwards, and never for a moment doubted that he was the father of this child. The friendship between the I   husband, the wife and the party cited and his wife continued unchanged, but by 1963 relations between husband and wife, which had begun to cool off from about 1956, became increasingly unhappy and divorce was discussed between them. On Dec. 5, 1963, the wife presented a petition for dissolution alleging adultery between the husband and his present wife. On May 1, 1964, the husband filed his answer denying adultery and alleging adultery by the wife and the party cited from 1956. In October, 1964, the wife left her husband taking the child with her and went to live with the party cited. The wife in her petition described the child as a child of the family and prayed for an order for her custody

and for maintenance for her. In his original answer, the husband did not A
dispute paternity of the child whom he still believed to be his child and sought
custody of her. In November, 1964, the wife and the party cited made written
confessions of their adultery in which they stated that their adultery had started
in January, 1964. In March, 1965, the husband for the first time became aware
that he might not be the father of this child. This possibility emerged obliquely.
I am told that, in the course of proceedings in the magistrates' court between the B
party cited and his wife, the party cited admitted that he had been committing
adultery since 1956 with the wife in this case and asserted that he was the father
of her child who was born in 1958. In consequence, in April, 1965, the husband
amended his answer, to put the paternity of the child in issue. In due course the
wife abandoned her petition and the suit came on for hearing as an undefended suit
on the husband's answer on July 9, 1965, before His Honour JUDGE BARRINGTON, C
who granted the husband a decree nisi on the ground of the wife's adultery
with the party cited and at the same time directed that an issue be tried as to the
paternity of the child. On Sept. 1, 1965, the wife and the party cited swore
affidavits in which they admitted that they had been committing adultery since
1956, and that their written confessions were incomplete. They were, in fact,
untrue in that they contained a statement that adultery had commenced in 1964. D
On Dec. 1, 1965, the Official Solicitor was appointed guardian ad litem of the
child and was given leave to intervene on her behalf. On Mar. 4, 1966, a formal
order was made for the trial of this issue. The child was made a defendant
to the issue and the party cited was made a party to the issue.

This issue first came on for hearing before me on June 28, 1966. At the outset,
counsel for the husband and junior counsel for the wife submitted that the E
child's blood group should be ascertained. I was informed by counsel that both
the husband and the wife and the party cited earnestly desired this to be done,
and that each of them was willing to submit to serological examination. The
husband, through counsel, stated that his attitude to the question of custody in
particular, and of access in a lesser degree, depended on whether or not he was
the father of the child. In the circumstances of this case, this is a reasonable F
attitude, for no reasonable man would wish to take a child from the care of the
child's mother and the child's natural father when they are living together and
intending to marry. Nor would most men feel justified in insisting strongly on
access to such a child, no matter how fond he might have become of the child,
or the child of him, if such access were opposed by the mother. On the other
hand, if the husband is the father, he would naturally wish at least to maintain G
and, if possible, develop his ties with the child. At the hearing in June, 1966,
and again at the re-hearing all the relevant facts were agreed. Sensibly, to save
costs and to ensure that all the facts were before the court, the three adult
parties exchanged their proofs of evidence and have agreed that these should be
used as evidence. All three adults admit that, at the time of the conception of
this child, the wife was having sexual intercourse with both the husband and H
the party cited with and without contraceptives and at about the same frequency.
In this case, therefore, no dispute divides the three adults concerned, and none
of them seeks to gain anything out of this litigation except the knowledge of
their real relationship with this child to which all three attach great importance.
To this end all wish to avail themselves of the assistance which scientific methods
now offer.   I
At the first hearing, junior counsel for the Official Solicitor, on instructions,
was unable to assent to their request that the child should be blood-grouped, which
is, of course, essential to the scientific determination of paternity. As I have
already stated, no criticism of the Official Solicitor's decision can be made. The
three adult parties accordingly turned to the court, asking for an order that the
child be blood-grouped. At that hearing, I was of the opinion, in the light of
the decision of the Court of Appeal in W. v. W. (No. 4) (1), that the court had

(1) [1963] 2 All E.R. 841; [1964] P. 67 at p. 72.

A   no power to order a child to be blood-grouped, in the context of an issue as to paternity, and that, accordingly, the decision lay with the guardian ad litem to give or withhold his consent. At the same time I foresaw that great difficulties might arise in this case at the custody stage and that, as suggested by SIR JOCELYN SIMON, P., in *H.* v. *H.* (2), the powers of the court in its custodial jurisdiction, which were not considered in *W.* v. *W.* (*No. 4*) (3), might well be wider than in

B   ordinary litigation inter partes. Holding the view, as I do, that questions relating to the welfare and upbringing of a child should be based as far as possible on facts, and that decisions relating to people's lives should not be confused by the artificial results of the application of legal presumptions, I adjourned the hearing for full argument on the relevant powers of the court in its custodial jurisdiction. My purpose in taking this course was to avoid the absurd position

C   which would arise if the court, having declared on the presumption in the paternity issue the child to be the child of the husband and wife, then proceeded at the custody stage to order the child to be blood-grouped, only to discover that she was in fact the daughter of the party cited. At the same time I gave the husband leave to make his decree nisi absolute. I have now had the advantage of hearing this matter fully argued by leading counsel for the husband and the

D   wife and for the Official Solicitor, and I am sincerely grateful to all three counsel for their great assistance in this difficult and very important enquiry.

Two questions have to be decided, first whether the court has power to order or authorise the child to be blood-grouped; and, secondly, if the answer to the first question is affirmative, whether the court ought in its discretion so to order. It will also be necessary to consider the whole question of consent in this context.

E   Following DIPLOCK, L.J., in *W.* v. *W.* (*No. 4*) (4), I shall try to avoid the word " jurisdiction " in this connexion and speak of the court's " power ", or lack of power, to make the order in question, because the former is used in different senses in different contexts and ideas associated with its other usages are apt to cause confusion.

Counsel for the wife based his argument on the wording of the Matrimonial

F   Causes Act 1965, s. 34, and submitted that the words in sub-s. (1)

> " the court may make such order as it thinks just for the custody, maintenance and education of any relevant child "

should be construed as widely as possible, and that, so construed, they were wide enough to give the court power to order a child to be blood-grouped if this was thought to be necessary in the circumstances of a particular case to enable

G   the court to make a just order under this section. He pointed out that the language of this section of the Act of 1965 differs in detail from the wording in the corresponding sections in the earlier Acts dealing with matrimonial causes, in that the phrase " for custody ", etc., has taken the place of the phrase " with respect to the custody ", etc., in s. 26 (1) of the Matrimonial Causes Act, 1950 and in its predecessors. Counsel for the wife submitted that, in accordance

H   with the established rule for the construction of consolidating enactments, it is to be presumed that Parliament intended no substantial change in the law unless such intention clearly appears from the new wording. He, therefore, submitted that an order that a child be blood-grouped was an order " in respect to custody ". He also argued that this section be construed as widely as posssible since the court's primary duty was to regard the interests of the child as paramount:

I   *Cammell* v. *Cammell* (5), and *Robinson* v. *Robinson* (6). Counsel for the husband adopted and expanded this submission, but also put his case on a much wider base. He submitted that the first question should be answered in the light of all the powers of the High Court in relation to children, not only under the Matrimonial Causes Act 1965, but also under the court's jurisdiction over children

(2) [1966] 3 All E.R. 560 at p. 563.   (3) [1963] 2 All E.R. 841; [1964] P. 67 at p. 72.
(4) [1963] 2 All E.R. at p. 845; [1964] P. at p. 79.
(5) [1964] 3 All E.R. 255 at p. 258; [1965] P. 467 at p. 471.
(6) [1963] 3 All E.R. 813 at p. 815; [1965] P. 39 at p. 43.

generally, i.e., the powers exercised by the court on behalf of the Crown as　**A**
parens patriae. In other words, counsel argued that, for present purposes,
it was necessary to consider whether a judge could make such an order in wardship proceedings. He submitted that the court had power so to order and that I,
sitting as a judge of the Probate, Divorce and Admiralty Division, had all the
powers of a judge of the High Court and could, accordingly, make the order for
which he asked. Counsel for the Official Solicitor conceded that a judge in　**B**
wardship proceedings could probably order a child to be medically examined
for the purpose of ascertaining his blood-group, but contended that a judge
sitting in this Division had no such power and was confined to the powers contained in or to be derived from the Matrimonial Causes Act 1965, s. 34, which were
not wide enough to enable the court to make such an order and that, accordingly,
the decision in *W*. v. *W*. (*No. 4*) (7) applied. He, therefore, contended that there　**C**
was no power in the present case to make the order for which the adult parties
are asking.

In my judgment, counsel for the Official Solicitor's contention cannot be
supported because it is in conflict with the express provisions of the Supreme
Court of Judicature Act, 1873, which were repealed and substantially re-enacted
by the Supreme Court of Judicature (Consolidation) Act, 1925. Section 3 of　**D**
the Act of 1873 provided that the then existing separate courts of higher jurisdiction should be " united and consolidated together ", and thereafter should
constitute one Supreme Court of Judicature. By s. 16, the jurisdiction of, inter
alia, the High Court of Chancery and the Court for Divorce and Matrimonial
Causes was transferred to and vested in the High Court. This section is now
represented by s. 18 and s. 21 of the Act of 1925. Section 2 (3) of the Act of　**E**
1925 provides that all the judges of the High Court, save as expressly provided,
shall have " equal power, authority and jurisdiction ". Finally, by s. 4 (4),
which was added by the Administration of Justice Act, 1928, s. 6, all jurisdiction
vested in the High Court belongs to all Divisions alike, although without prejudice
to the provisions of the Act relating to distribution of business. The scheme of
this legislation is very explicitly stated in these sections. The purpose of the　**F**
Judicature Acts was first to unite the hitherto separate High Courts into one
body and then to sub-divide the work " for the more convenient despatch of
business ". For this express purpose, the three Divisions which exist today
were created by what is now s. 4 (1) of the Act of 1925, and the business of the
courts is assigned to the three Divisions in accordance with s. 56 of that Act.
One of the primary purposes of this legislation was to put an end to the necessity　**G**
for litigants to take proceedings in two or more courts in the same dispute in
order to obtain the remedies or take advantage of the practice available in one
court but not in the other (*MacGowan* v. *Middleton* (8), per BRETT, M.R.). This
would be precisely the result in this case if the submission of counsel for the
Official Solicitor were right. One or other of the parties would have to initiate
proceedings in the Chancery Division to obtain the order which it is conceded　**H**
that the Chancery judge could make, and then return to this court with the
evidence so obtained. This is directly contrary to the decision of the Court of
Appeal in *R*. v. *Gyngall* (9), in which LORD ESHER, M.R., pointed out that the
judges of the Queen's Bench Division, dealing with a writ of habeas corpus in
respect of a child properly exercised the jurisdiction of the old Court of Chancery.
He said (10):　　　　　　　　　　　　　　　　　　　　　　　　　　　　　**I**

" The present case arises after the Judicature Act, and the proceedings are
in the Queen's Bench Division. The effect of that Act is, as I have often
said, not to invent a new jurisdiction or to create new rights, but to alter the
mode of procedure; and, there having been before two independent jurisdictions, one common law and the other equity, the Act in effect provides

(7) [1963] 2 All E.R. 841; [1964] P. at p. 72.
(8) (1883), 11 Q.B.D. 464 at p. 468.
(9) [1893] 2 Q.B. 232 at p. 240.　　　　　　　(10) [1893] 2 Q.B. at pp. 239, 240.

A   that, if a person proceeds in the Queen's Bench Division under the common law jurisdiction, and it turns out that the case raises questions to which the Chancery jurisdiction is applicable, the Queen's Bench Division judges are not to send the suitor to a Chancery Court, but are to exercise the Chancery jurisdiction themselves. If such a case as this has arisen before the Judicature Act, the Queen's Bench judges, not finding any such misconduct

B   as would affect the parent's right, would have been bound to say that, as between the parent and the person who had the custody of the child, the right to the custody of the child belonged to the parent; but, if they had seen that, although there was nothing to limit the right of the parent as against the other person, there were circumstances calling for the exercise of the Chancery jurisdiction, they might have stayed their hands and given time

C   for an application to be made to the Court of Chancery to exercise its authority in the matter. Under the Judicature Act, the Queen's Bench Division judges are not to do that, but are to exercise the Chancery jurisdiction themselves. In the present case I do not think that the mother has been guilty of any misconduct which as between her and other people has derogated from her right to the custody of the child. Under these circumstances,

D   I do not think that the judges of the Queen's Bench Division assumed to exercise the common law jurisdiction. I think that they rightly assumed to exercise the other and independent jurisdiction, viz., that of the Court of Chancery. The existence of that jurisdiction is beyond dispute."

In my judgment, counsel for the Official Solicitor's submission is untenable in the light of this decision, which was cited with approval by the House of Lords in

E   *Official Solicitor* v. *K.* (11), in which LORD HODSON said:

". . . there can now be no doubt that there is no difference in the jurisdiction exercised by the various divisions of the High Court."

Counsel for the Official Solicitor, however, relied on four recent cases, namely, *Andrews* v. *Andrews and Sullivan* (12), *Re Andrews* (*infants*) (13), *Re A.-H.* (*infants*)

F   (14), and *Hall* v. *Hall* (15). All four of these cases arose out of much the same situation. In all of them properly constituted proceedings had been started in both the Chancery Division and in this Division relating to children. The judgments in all four cases were concerned with problems arising from the concurrent jurisdiction of two Divisions of the High Court and cannot be used to support an argument in favour of the exclusive jurisdiction of one.

G   In my judgment, therefore, a judge sitting in this Division has all the powers which are available to any judge of the High Court in relation to children or any other matter. This does not, however, mean that a child could be made a ward of court by proceedings in this Division. Such proceedings must be started in accordance with the provisions of the Rules of the Supreme Court and, in compliance with s. 56 of the Act of 1925, will be assigned to the Chancery Division.

H   If, however, proceedings in relation to a child have been properly initiated in this Division, it follows that it is not necessary to have recourse to the Chancery Division to invoke powers which are derived from the court's jurisdiction over wards. This is subject to one qualification. Under R.S.C., Ord. 91, r. 1, the court may give leave to make the infant a defendant to the originating summons asking that he be made a ward of court. The infant in such a case is a party to

I   the proceedings. In the normal course in this Division, the child is not a party to the proceedings. In certain circumstances, this may be a relevant consideration. In cases like the present, however, this does not arise because, in accordance with the practice in this Division, the child was made a defendant to the issue

---

(11) [1963] 3 All E.R. 191 at p. 207; [1965] A.C. 201 at p. 236.
(12) [1958] 2 All E.R. 305; [1958] P. 217.
(13) [1958] 2 All E.R. 308; [1958] Ch. 665.
(14) [1962] 3 All E.R. 853; [1963] Ch. 232.
(15) [1963] 2 All E.R. 140; [1963] P. 378.

by the order of Dec. 1, 1965. In *W.* v. *W.* (*No. 4*) (16), however, the child was not **A**
a party to the proceedings, although, I suppose, steps might have been taken to
obtain leave for the child to intervene in those proceedings. It follows, therefore,
that, if counsel for the Official Solicitor's concession was rightly made, the answer
to the first question is in the affirmative, i.e., the court has power in these proceedings to order the child to be blood-grouped. Accepting, as I do, counsel for
the husband's broader submission, it becomes unnecessary to examine further **B**
counsel for the wife's argument based on the construction of the relevant provisions of the Matrimonial Causes Act 1965. Naturally, this is no reflection
on his careful submission; it is merely an attempt to shorten what is inevitably
a lengthy judgment.

Notwithstanding his concession, however, counsel for the Official Solicitor
asked me to consider and decide whether the court has this power over one of its **C**
wards. Since this is the kernel of this case and may vitally affect the interest of a
child, I think that I ought to do so but I approach the task with diffidence. I
have not had the advantage of hearing argument against the proposition, nor
have I the experience of the judges of the Chancery Division in this particular
field. Moreover, so far as I am aware, there is no direct authority on the point.
Before going further into this aspect of the matter, however, I must consider **D**
whether the decision of the Court of Appeal in *W.* v. *W.* (*No. 4*) (16) is binding on
me in this case and compels me to hold that there is no power in any circumstances
to order blood tests to be made in order to provide evidence on the question of
paternity.

In *W.* v. *W.* (*No. 4*) (16), the husband, who was the petitioner in a nullity
suit alleging that at the date of the marriage the wife was pregnant by another **E**
man, applied for an order that the wife and child should submit to blood tests
in order that their blood-groups might be determined. Since the husband
conceded that he had had sexual intercourse with the wife about the time of
conception, the only way in which he could establish his case was to attempt to
prove by evidence of the blood-groups of himself, his wife and the child that he
was not the father of the child. It was submitted on his behalf that Parliament, **F**
having created this ground for a decree of nullity, must be taken to have authorised compulsory blood tests. That submission was rejected by CAIRNS, J., at
first instance (17), and was not pursued in the Court of Appeal (16). Next it
was said that authority to make such an order could be derived from R.S.C.,
Ord. 50, r. 3, (18), which gives the court power to order inspection of any property
or thing which is the subject-matter of the dispute and to authorise the taking **G**
of samples or the making of experiments. In the Court of Appeal, WILLMER
and DIPLOCK, L.JJ., rejected this submission, as had CAIRNS, J., on the ground
that it did not extend to taking blood samples. It was finally argued that the
power could be derived from r. 24 of the Matrimonial Causes Rules, 1957 (19),
which deals with medical inspections in nullity cases based on incapacity but
this argument was also rejected. The ratio decidendi of this decision is, I think, **H**
that to perform a blood test which involves puncturing the skin and removing
some blood would be " an assault " (per CAIRNS, J. (20)), or " prima facie . . .
an unlawful act " (per WILLMER, L.J. (21)), or " a very serious interference with
personal liberty and rights " (per DANCKWERTS, L.J. (22)) unless such procedure
was consented to by the person concerned or authorised by law, and no such
authority could be found in any enactment or rule applicable in that case. This **I**

---

(16) [1963] 2 All E.R. 841; [1964] P. at p. 72.
(17) [1963] 2 All E.R. 386; [1964] P. 67.
(18) See now R.S.C., Ord. 29, r. 2, r. 3.
(19) S.I. 1957 No. 619. For r. 24, as subsequently amended by S.I. 1963 No. 989, see
10 HALSBURY'S STATUTORY INSTRUMENTS (Second Re-Issue) 239.
(20) [1963] 2 All E.R. at p. 388; [1964] P. at p. 71.
(21) [1963] 2 All E.R. at p. 843; [1964] P. at p. 74.
(22) [1963] 2 All E.R. at p. 845; [1964] P. at p. 78.

A   reasoning is consistent with an earlier decision of the Court of Appeal in *Pickett v. Bristol Aeroplane Co., Ltd.* (23), referred to by Sir Jocelyn Simon, P., in *H.* v. *H.* (24), in which it was held that the court had no power to order a plaintiff in an accident case to submit to medical examination against his wish. The special powers of the court in relation to children were not considered in *W.* v. *W.* (*No. 4*) (25), so that it is not an authority against the existence of the powers

B   with which I am concerned in this case. If there is such a power, a blood sample taken pursuant to an order of the court would be a lawful act, and *W.* v. *W.* (*No. 4*) (25) would not apply. Similarly, if by some means a valid consent could be given on behalf of the child, there is nothing in the judgments in *W.* v. *W.* (*No. 4*) (25) to prevent it. I, accordingly, hold that the decision in *W.* v. *W.* (*No. 4*) (25) does not preclude me from considering the powers of the court in this

C   regard in relation to children.

     The problem in the present case arises, not from the refusal by the child to consent but from her incapacity to consent. Two different aspects of consent are here involved and must be distinguished. On the one hand the child as such cannot, herself, give the consent necessary to render lawful the doctor's action in taking a sample of blood. On the other hand the child cannot consent as a

D   litigant to waive her right (if any) to refuse to submit to this procedure. In normal circumstances the person who lawfully authorises a physical interference with a child, which might otherwise be technically in law an assault, is the parent of the child or some other person in whom parental rights are invested. In the event of a dispute between the parents over some therapeutic procedure to the child, the ultimate arbiter between them would be the court which, in properly

E   constituted proceedings, could undoubtedly authorise the parent in favour of the procedure to instruct the doctor to carry it out and enjoin the other parent from interfering, or forbid the procedure and enforce its prohibition by injunction. Alternatively, the court could itself authorise the procedure since, in the words of Lord Esher, M.R., in *R.* v. *Gyngall* (26), the court acts:

F   " as being the guardian of all infants, in the place of a parent, and as if it were the parent of the child, thus superseding the natural guardianship of the parent."

In the present case, therefore, the mother, as the one undoubted parent and the parent who had de facto control of the child, could lawfully authorise any therapeutic procedure recommended by the child's doctor, including the taking of specimen blood for blood-group determination. Does the fact that this determin-

G   ation is being made for forensic rather than therapeutic purposes affect the mother's right to authorise the doctor to take the samples? No such contention has been put forward in argument in this case, and I know of no authority which imposes any such limitation on her. In the absence of such authority I am prepared to hold that she is entitled to have her child blood-grouped if she wishes, unless and until restrained by an order of the court from so doing. (The position

H   of the putative father may be different because, ex hypothesi, his parenthood is in issue. If he objected to the child being blood-grouped, it would presumably be open to him to apply to the court for an order restraining the mother from authorising the doctor to perform the blood test and for the court in the exercise of its discretion to decide whether to permit or restrain her.) If, therefore, the mother can authorise the doctor to take blood for forensic purposes, a fortiori the

I   court having full parental powers over the child can also authorise the doctor to do so. Whether and in what circumstances the court will make such an order is another matter which I must consider later.

     The matter can be approached in another way. It has never been suggested that the court, in a case concerning the welfare of a child in either Division, could

(23) (1961), The Times, Mar. 17.
(24) [1966] 3 All E.R. 560 at p. 562.
(25) [1963] 2 All E.R. 841; [1964] P. at p. 72.
(26) [1893] 2 Q.B. at p. 239.

not order the child to be medically examined.   Such orders are made from time   **A**
to time in proper cases in both Divisions.   Usually the purpose of such examination is related to the health of the child, but by no means always.   From time
to time medical examinations, both physical and psychiatric, are ordered for
the express purpose of yielding evidence to be used to resolve the disputes
between the parents.   The purpose of such examination is, of course, ultimately
to assist the court to arrive at the wisest decision in the interests of the child.   **B**
One example of such an examination was considered by CROSS, J., in *Re S.
(an infant)* (27) in a most helpful judgment to which I shall return later.   It
follows, therefore, that the court can authorise a doctor to carry out a serological
examination on the child in the present case unless there is some rule of law which
prevents the court from ordering a medical examination for purely forensic
purposes.   I know of no such rule but it, of course, goes without saying that no   **C**
court would order such an examination unless it were satisfied that it was a
necessary step to enable the court to reach the wisest possible decision as to the
best interests of the child.

I now turn to consider the other type of consent, which I might call the forensic
consent.   Hitherto I have been dealing with situations where the child, although
deeply concerned with the results of the litigation, is in a passive role.   I must   **D**
now consider the position when the child, represented by a guardian ad litem,
is an active party to the proceedings.   Two questions arise, first, whether the
guardian ad litem can consent to the child being medically examined for the
purpose of the litigation and, secondly, whether if he refuses his consent, the
court is bound by his refusal.   Again, I am in a field which is almost barren of
authority.   Counsel for the Official Solicitor argued that the Official Solicitor   **E**
is, in effect, at one and the same time the child's guardian ad litem, the child's
legal adviser and the child herself speaking with an adult voice.   He would say
that, once the guardian ad litem is appointed, the child, together with the guardian,
becomes equivalent to an adult party, the guardian taking the necessary decisions
and acting for the child.   It would, I am sure, be a mistake to infer from this
submission that the Official Solicitor as guardian ad litem is seeking to assert a   **F**
right to oust the court's ultimate discretion in such matters.   The purpose of
putting it forward was to clarify the issues now before the court.   In ordinary
civil litigation, the guardian ad litem is not appointed by the court but is
nominated by the opposing party.   In cases concerning the custody and welfare
of the child, the guardian ad litem is appointed by an order of the master in the
Chancery Division, or by a registrar in this Division, under r. 56 of the Matri-   **G**
monial Causes Rules, 1957.   This rule also applies to any proceedings in this
Division to which the child is not a party in the sense of a respondent, co-respondent or party cited, but in which the court considers that the child ought to be
separately represented.   The powers and duties of a guardian ad litem are
defined in R.S.C., Ord. 80, r. 2 (2), in these words:

> " Subject to the provisions of these rules, anything which in the ordinary   **H**
> conduct of any proceedings is required or authorised by a provision of these
> rules to be done by a party to the proceedings shall or may, if the party is a
> person under disability, be done by his next friend or guardian ad litem."

This includes the right to consent, for example, to evidence being given on
affidavit and to other procedural steps, but if the guardian ad litem does anything   **I**
beyond the mere conduct of the proceedings it must be for the benefit of the
child or done with the sanction and approval of the court: *Rhodes* v. *Swithenbank* (28) and see the notes to R.S.C., Ord. 80, r. 2, at para. 80/2/14 in the SUPREME
COURT PRACTICE, 1967.

In my judgment, a consent by the guardian ad litem to a child being blood-
grouped in such a case as this cannot be regarded as something required or
authorised by the Rules of the Supreme Court to be done " in the ordinary

(27) [1967] 1 All E.R. 202.   (28) (1889), 22 Q.B.D. 577 at p. 578.

A conduct of [the] proceedings ". For such a consent to be a valid procedural
step, the sanction of the court would be required. But what is the position
when the guardian ad litem refuses to seek the approval of the court? A guardian
ad litem cannot compromise an action without the approval of the court, but it
is clear that the court cannot sanction a compromise against the wishes of the
guardian. The court, however, retains the ultimate right to remove him (*Re*
B *Birchall, Wilson* v. *Birchall* (29)). So far I have been considering the position
of a guardian ad litem in ordinary civil litigation to which the infant is a party.
In custodial cases, the position is different because the court is not dealing with
an ordinary lis inter partes but is exercising its parental jurisdiction, whether
the proceedings are instituted by an originating summons in the Chancery
Division or by a petition in this Division. In such cases, in my judgment, the
C ultimate decision must rest with the court. In *Re S. (an infant)* (30), Cross, J.,
said in relation to psychiatric examinations of children in custody cases for
purposes which were primarily forensic rather than therapeutic:

"When a child is made a ward no important step in the child's life can
be taken without the court's consent. To my mind the examination of the
ward by a psychiatrist with a view to the report being put in evidence in
D the case is such a step. If both sides agree that an examination is necessary
and agree on the person or persons to conduct it then normally no doubt
there would be no reason for the court to refuse to follow their wishes. If
they disagree, however, then it would seem right that the Official Solicitor
should be appointed guardian ad litem of the ward—as was done in this case—
and that he should decide, subject to the views of the judge, whether or
E not an examination is needed."

In my judgment, those observations are precisely in point here and show that
the decision whether or not the child should be submitted to psychiatric, medical
or serological examination ultimately rests with the court. In many cases
where the parents and the guardian ad litem are in agreement that an examination
F should be performed, or the purpose of the examination is essentially ancillary
to the matters in issue and of no great significance either to the child or to the
issue, reference to the court may not be necessary, but I find it difficult to imagine
a case in which the decision whether or not a child should be blood-grouped will
not be of major importance and difficulty. To impose such a decision on the
guardian ad litem is an altogether unreasonable responsibility, and it is unjust
G to the other persons concerned that so vital a matter should depend on his
ipse dixit.

As I have said before, in my view there is at present no rule of law or practice
which prevents a parent who is so minded from taking a child to a doctor for
serological examination, unless the other parent or the guardian ad litem has
obtained an order of the court prohibiting it. On the other hand, once a guardian
H ad litem has been appointed, it would be most undesirable for a parent to arrange
such an examination without an order of the court, or at least without the
consent of the guardian if he is prepared to waive the necessity for an order.
There is one other point which was raised in argument with which I must
deal briefly. It was suggested, rather tentatively, that the Official Solicitor as,
if I may so put it, part of the apparatus of the court, has a duty not to withhold
I material facts from the court. I do not think that there is any justification
for adding this particular straw to the burden which the Official Solicitor carries
so valiantly and uncomplainingly for the court in these cases. His primary
duty, it seems to me, is to see that the child's interests are fully safeguarded
and to help the court to arrive at the best and wisest decision so far as the child
is concerned. In the present case, his duty is to present, by evidence and
argument, the case for the child. In some cases he may think that the child is
more likely to benefit than otherwise from a serological examination. In others,

as in this case, he may take the opposite view. The decision, however, in my A
judgment, rests with the court. It remains only to add that the guardian ad
litem has no parental or quasi-parental powers or obligations to the child, which
is another reason why, if the parents object, the authority of the court is required
for a medical examination of the child.

I now turn to the extremely difficult question, whether to exercise the power
to direct that this child be examined serologically. The answer must depend on B
two classes of consideration, those which are of general application and those
which are peculiar to this case. In the end, the decision must be taken in
accordance with the principle that the interests of the child are the paramount
but not the exclusive consideration, the interests of the parents being entitled
also to be considered (*Re Thain, Thain* v. *Taylor* (31)). Among the general
considerations are the nature of the examination itself, the evidential value of the C
result of such examination, and the propriety of making such an order in the
light of the general policy of the law in matters of this kind.

No evidence has been filed in this case relating to the procedure involved in a
serological examination or to the evidential value of the results of it, but at the
same time no point is taken on behalf of the child that anything objectionable
is involved in the procedure itself or that the result would not be of value to the D
court in arriving at the best decision for the future welfare of this girl, and in
deciding which of the two men concerned in her life is her true father. The
nature of this examination and the validity of the results of it were put before
the court in some detail in *Stocker* (*by his next friend*) v. *Stocker* (*otherwise Woodruff,
by her guardian*) (32) by the well-known serologist, Dr. Grant. As appears
from the judgment of KARMINSKI, J., in that case, and indeed it is a matter of E
general knowledge in these days, evidence of blood-groups can successfully
exclude a proportion of men, wrongly supposed to be the father of a given child.
According to an article contributed by Dr. Grant to the most up-to-date text-book
on this subject, MODERN TRENDS IN FORENSIC MEDICINE, 1967, the probability
of excluding such a supposed father is now seventy-one per cent. Where the
question at issue is which of two known men is the father, the probability that F
one will be excluded by this test is presumably even higher. The test is obviously
of great evidential value and, as I have said, without such evidence a factual, as
opposed to a presumptive, determination of this child's paternity is an impossibility. It is within my own knowledge that the procedure involved in the
examination is no more than a pin prick and the removal of a very small quantity
of blood. (If, however, any of the parties wished afterwards to file evidence on G
either of those matters and to make further submissions to me on them, I should
accede to their request before making any order in this case.) Subject to that,
I am satisfied that there is nothing in the procedure involved in the examination
which would justify the court in refusing the application of the adult parties in
this case.

The propriety of making the order asked for in this case depends on a resolution H
of two conflicting principles. On the one hand, from feudal times to the present
day the courts have gone to great lengths to protect the legitimacy of children
born or conceived in wedlock. On the other hand, in the words of LORD SUMNER
in his dissenting speech in *Russell* v. *Russell* (33):

" My lords, my own view is that in the administration of justice nothing
is of higher importance than that all relevant evidence should be admissible I
and should be heard by the tribunal that is charged with deciding according
to truth. To ordain that a court should decide upon the relevant facts
and at the same time that it should not hear some of those relevant facts
from the person who best knows them and can prove them at first hand seems

(31) [1926] All E.R. Rep. 384; [1926] Ch. 676.
(32) [1966] 2 All E.R. 147.
(33) [1924] A.C. 687 at p. 748.

A　to me to be a contradiction in terms. It is best that truth should out and that truth should prevail."

Lord Sumner, of course, recognised that his principle must yield if there is an existing rule of law which actively excludes the type of evidence under consideration or if the court has no power to order such evidence to be made available, as in W. v. W. (No. 4) (34). Two methods have been used by the court to protect

B　the legitimacy of children. The first is the presumption of law that the husband is the father of any child born or conceived during the subsistence of the marriage, coupled with the requirement that this presumption can only be rebutted by proof to the contrary beyond reasonable doubt. The second was, but no longer is, the exclusion of any evidence by the spouses themselves tending to prove that sexual intercourse had not taken place between them at the relevant time. In

C　early days, nothing short of proof that the husband was beyond the four seas during the nine months of the wife's pregnancy sufficed. Later, proof that the parties were living apart under a sentence of the ecclesiastical courts was sufficient to reverse the onus of proof, but not that they were living apart under a deed of separation. The rule prohibiting the spouses from giving evidence of non-access, and thus bastardising the issue born after marriage, was vigorously

D　re-stated by the House of Lords in Russell v. Russell (35), but was finally abrogated by the Law Reform (Miscellaneous Provisions) Act, 1949, s. 7, which is now s. 43 (1) of the Act of 1965, because in a changing society it was felt to be not only an anachronism but a source of grave injustice, an example of which is to be found in B. v. A.-G. (N.E.B. intervening) (36).

E　The question which I have to consider is whether this presumption now requires me, in exercising my discretion, to refuse to order this child to be blood-grouped so as to preserve to her the benefit of it. In the days when it was first formulated and during the succeeding centuries, the legal incidents of bastardy were extremely serious. The bastard was literally a fillius nullius in the eyes of the law. Moreover, until the development of serological techniques during the last twenty years or so, proof or disproof of paternity was exceptionally hazardous unless there was

F　very clear independent evidence of non-access by the husband. The presumption was thus the only reasonable solution of the dilemma and it was jealously guarded by the court in the interests of the child. Today, the attitude towards illegitimacy and the legal incidents of being born a bastard have changed to a remarkable degree. The courts are no longer preoccupied with property rights, but are increasingly required to make adjudications which vitally affect the intimate

G　personal and private lives of the litigants who appear before them. In most of these cases today property rights are, at most, ancillary to the important personal issues. I have already made the point that it is a misuse of language to speak of " bastardising " this child, and that the real issue to be determined is to which family she belongs. The Legitimacy Act, 1959, which introduced legitimation per subsequens matrimonium into the law of England in the fullest sense, i.e., by

H　applying it to children whose parents were not free to marry at the date of their births, has created an entirely new situation which justifies and, in my judgment requires, the court to look closely at our traditional attitudes and to consider whether some relaxation of them is not required to take account of the realities of the new situation. When these social changes are accompanied by scientific developments which provide an invaluable evidential tool to help in the solution

I　of problems such as the present, to decline to use the tool in deference to tradition is to run the risk of imposing a restriction on the ability of the court to do justice which it is difficult to justify. I respectfully agree with the observation of Cairns, J., in W. v. W. (No. 4) (37) that the modern policy of the law is to favour the production of any cogent evidence which will help to establish the true

(34) [1963] 2 All E.R. 841; [1964] P. at p. 72.
(35) [1924] A.C. 687.
(36) [1965] 1 All E.R. 62; [1965] P. 278.
(37) [1963] 2 All E.R. at p. 387; [1964] P. at p. 69.

paternity of a child. In my judgment therefore, subject always to the interests A
of the child, there is no reason in principle for refusing to take advantage of the
evidence which serology can provide or for declining to exercise such powers as
the court may have to make it available, more particularly as there is nothing to
prevent parents from having the child examined in this way, at any rate before
the guardian ad litem appears on the scene, and from adducing the results in
evidence (*Stocker* v. *Stocker* (38), *H.* v. *H.* (*H., by his guardian, intervening*) (39)). B

I have also considered two other points of general application which were
put to me by counsel. These are whether it would be objectionable to compel the
child to provide evidence, and the problem of enforcing such an order. On the
first point, it would be wrong to speak of making the child give evidence against
herself because, ex hypothesi, the order would not be made if the court considered
it contrary to her interests. Moreover, there is nothing inherently objectionable C
in making a party or even a witness give evidence which is to his disadvantage.
This is one of the purposes of discovery of documents and particularly of interrogatories. If by chance the guardian ad litem or the child were in possession of a
report containing the result of a serological examination on the child undertaken
for some other purpose, it would have to be produced on discovery. So far as
enforcement is concerned, the court would undoubtedly reconsider and even D
rescind its order if it subsequently appeared that the child was refusing to allow
the doctor to take a blood sample. If the guardian or other party charged with
carrying out the order declined to obey it, the effective sanction would be the
hostile inference, which, in the absence of a reasonable explanation, the court
might draw, as it has always done from a refusal to submit to an examination by
the medical inspectors in cases of nullity on the ground of incapacity. This is E
not the place to consider whether the strength of the presumption is in any way
affected by a refusal by an adult party to submit to a blood test, but the question
may have to be decided sooner or later.

I now turn to the considerations peculiar to this case. It is quite clear on the
evidence that it is impossible to identify the father of this child without the
assistance of a blood test. Paternity could not be more doubtful. This is important F
because, unless it is clearly shown on the evidence that there is good reason to
doubt that the husband is the father of the child, it would not, in my view, be
right to order a serological investigation of the child. Furthermore, in this case,
whatever the child's present attitude may appear to be, she herself must be aware
of this doubt. For six years she was brought up as the daughter of the husband.
Now she is living as the daughter of the party cited. The inference which I draw G
from the evidence is that she now thinks of the party cited as her father. The
probability is that she will complete her childhood and adolescence as a daughter
of the family of the party cited and her mother. I recognise that, at present, the
question of paternity is not agitating her. In my experience, it would be unwise
to suppose that this state of affairs will continue indefinitely. As she grows older,
she is bound to wonder who her true father is and who are her aunts, uncles, H
grandparents and so on. One of the facts which distinguish this case from others
is that this girl has lived so long in the husband's family that she cannot avoid
such doubts. Whatever her present attitude may be, there may come a time in
her adolescence when her relations with her mother or the party cited, or both,
become strained and the temptation will be strong for her, or even for the party
cited, to challenge his paternity. Even in adult life she may suffer great anxiety I
over this question, and this will interfere in the long run with the normal development of the father-child relationship between her and the party cited. The policy
of letting sleeping dogs lie is sound only so long as the dog remains asleep. When
the dog may be awakened as easily as in this case, it is almost certainly unsound.

For these reasons, I would have come to the conclusion without much doubt
that the child's interests would be best served by taking all available steps now to

---

(38) [1966] 2 All E.R. 147.   (39) [1966] 1 All E.R. 356.

A   remove the doubts about her paternity. I have, however, been provided by the Official Solicitor with two reports by Dr. Newton, a child psychiatrist and director of the St. Marylebone Child Guidance Clinic, who has interviewed the child and the three adults. In the second of these, he expresses the opinion that the child should not have a blood test. He gives two reasons for this opinion. In the first place, he thinks that it will cause her some emotional disturbance and that she

B   will have to be told about the doubts as to her paternity or deceived about the purpose of the blood test. For reasons which I have given I cannot believe that she is not aware of this doubt now. In two or three years she will be reaching puberty and, if she has no doubts at present, she will certainly have them then. Dr. Newton's second reason is that the examination may show that the party cited is not her father which will be a severe shock to her, and that, in those

C   circumstances, the husband will insist on having access to her which will disturb her greatly. If it were open to me to take no action in relation to this question of paternity, I could understand Dr. Newton's second reason. Unfortunately, the result of accepting Dr. Newton's advice will be that the child will be presumed to be the child of the husband, and I shall be obliged to make a declaration accordingly and shall have to approach the question of access by the husband from that

D   starting point. It does not, of course, follow that access would be ordered whatever the outcome of the serological examination but, assuming that it is thought desirable that there should be no access, the best way of ensuring that end would be to establish that the party cited is her father. The husband in those circumstances would be willing to withdraw from the child's life altogether. Dr. Newton makes two other points. He says that there is a possibility that the blood-groups

E   will demonstrate that neither the husband nor the party cited is the father. This is true in theory but I agree with Dr. Newton that in this case this possibility can, for practical purposes, be excluded. The mother alone can know the truth as to this, and she is before the court pressing for an examination of the child. His other point is that there is little doubt that, as she grows up, the child will want the question of her paternity settled, but he suggests deferring the examination

F   of her blood until she herself can decide. I do not think that any good purpose is served by putting such an onus on a young person, nor, I imagine, are all the adults likely to fall in with such a suggestion. For these reasons and with natural hesitation, since I am differing from Dr. Newton, I have come to the conclusion that it is in this child's best interests that a serological examination should be carried out on her now. I am certainly not convinced that it is in her interests to

G   postpone it or that there should be a declaration that she is the husband's daughter if she in fact is the child of the party cited. In any event, it would not be a proper exercise of the court's duty to grant a formal declaration of legitimacy while making arrangements at the same time for evidence to be recorded which may later be used to demonstrate that the declaration was contrary to the fact.

     I have also to consider the interests of the husband and wife and of the party

H   cited, not only in so far as their relations with the child in the future are concerned, but also as individuals. The mother's position, if no examination is permitted, is invidious. She can only rely on her capacity to make herself believe that the party cited is the father, assuming as I do that this is the outcome for which she is hoping at present. If, however, her relations with the party cited should deteriorate in the future, her doubts and his will become increasingly corrosive.

I   The husband's predicament if no tests are done must be very unpleasant. Is he to struggle to keep contact with the child or to cut his losses? The frustration of having to make that decision in ignorance of the true facts when he knows that his uncertainty could in all probability be ended by the blood test, is an unreasonable burden to put on him unless it is clearly necessary to do so in the child's interests. The same considerations apply, mutatis mutandis, to the party cited. I have no doubt in my own mind that each of these four people concerned in this case will have a better chance of developing healthy and normal emotional relationships between themselves and with other people on the basis of the truth rather than on the basis of a doubt which three of them now know, and the fourth   **A** one day will know, can in all probability be removed quite simply. The irrelevance of the presumption of legitimacy to this situation requires no emphasis.

There only remains the position of the court which, if the examination is not made, will be charged with the duty of deciding the question of custody and access. Custody in this case is no problem, but I should personally feel the gravest difficulty in deciding whether to permit or refuse access to the husband so long as   **B** I do not know whether he is the father or not. I can conceive of similar situations in which the question of blood relationship would not be important because of other factors which were more significant. In this case it is the key to the husband's attitude to access.

For all these reasons, I am prepared to order that this child shall be serologically examined. I can do it, I think, in one of two ways, either by directing that the   **C** mother be at liberty to have the child examined in this way, or by ordering her, the mother, or the Official Solicitor to arrange for the examination to be done. In either case it would be a term of my order that the child's blood sample is not to be taken until after the three adults have submitted themselves to the doctor who will undertake the examination and have permitted him to take samples of their blood.   **D**

Order accordingly.

Solicitors: *Breeze, Benton & Co.* (for the wife and the party cited); *Lipson, Rimney & Co.* (for the husband); *Official Solicitor.*

[*Reported by* ALICE BLOOMFIELD, *Barrister-at-Law.*]

  E

NOTE.

In his judgment at the initial hearing of the paternity issue on June 28, 1966, ORMROD, J., after saying that the issue produced in the most precise and unclouded way the prob-   **F** lem of paternity testing by blood groups or by any of the later tests which were now avail- able, and after briefly referring to the course of events and intimating that it had first appeared to the husband in March, 1965, that there might be doubts about his paternity of the child, continued: In this case there is no dispute whatever between the parties as to the facts. It is agreed between husband and wife that they were having sexual inter- course at the relevant time and that there were no contraceptives being used between them. It is accepted by the husband, parallel with this, that the wife was in fact com- mitting adultery with the party cited. Thus there is no conceivable possible way of   **G** determining whether this child is the child of the husband or the child of the party cited save by the use of blood group tests in one form or another. It is clear that the presumption is that the child was the child of the husband and wife. It is plain that there is literally no evidence to rebut that presumption and the only question, therefore, is once more—" Is the court to act on the presumption knowing quite well that in this case at best the chances of the presumption being right are fifty/fifty? "—which is not a very encouraging basis for doing justice or pronouncing a finding of paternity.

Now the situation is that all three adults are extremely anxious to know the true   **H** paternity of this child. They are all prepared to submit themselves to blood tests, and so no question arises of my making by my power, or lack of power an order for them to submit to blood tests. The only fly in the ointment, if I may put it that way without disrespect, is that the Official Solicitor, who appears as guardian, has declined on behalf of the child to submit the child to that blood test. That is a decision which the Official Solicitor himself must take as the guardian, and I should be the last person in the world to underestimate the extreme difficulty of that decision. He has to consider all the   **I** circumstances of the case from the point of view of each individual child when this issue arises. He has, I suppose, to bear in mind on the one hand the extreme importance to anybody of being a legitimate child of married parents; the value of the birth certificate which is ex facie in order, and all the manifold anxieties and worries that arise in people who are illegitimate. On the other hand he has to weigh up, I suppose, because it is his decision, not mine, how important it is for this child to know her true father. Sometimes I fear that lawyers under-estimate the importance of people knowing their true parents, tending rather to exaggerate the advantages of so-called legitimacy, but I do not think that formal legitimacy is a compensation for severe doubt as to legitimacy; but there it is, the decision has to be taken by him. In the vast majority of cases he must take the view

A that it is in the interests of the child that its legitimacy should be maintained, and it can
only be the odd case where there would be manifest advantages in establishing that the
child was the child of the other man. Here I think we are back to the crucial issue, which
is this: the court, being unable on its own with its present powers to order blood tests,
has to operate on the basis of presumptions, and the guardian of the child is thrown into
an appalling dilemma in trying to make what is a wholly unreal decision; trying to say
what is for the benefit of this child before he, on behalf of the child, gives or withholds
consent to a blood test. A more impossible problem it would be difficult to think of;

B that justice as between three adults should depend, as it must depend as the law stands,
on a decision in this particular case whether it is in the interests of the child to cast light
on or withhold light from the problem, is one which is so unreal that it is almost impossible
to take rationally. So I do not have any complaint whatever against the view which the
Official Solicitor takes, that in the present state of the law he must support the child of
whom he is guardian, and if he takes the view that it is in the interests of the child that the
presumption should operate in the child's favour, that is good enough for me; it must be,

C and I accept it. However, if ever a case illustrates the extreme necessity for some
statutory power in the court to enable this sort of problem to be resolved, it is this case.
There are three people at this moment actively worried and actively anxious as to the
paternity of this child, and one day, not very soon and not very far away, there will be
a fourth person desperately anxious to know who is her father, and that is this child;
but none of them can resolve the problem and I am driven by the operation of this
presumption to make a decision which will be binding, as far as I can see, on all three

D parties and possibly the child as well, when all of us know perfectly well that the basis
of my decision has only a fifty per cent. chance of being right. That is the situation which
the present state of the law produces, and it is not for me to do anything other than
administer the law as it is.

That being so, I have to declare that this child is a child of the husband and the wife:
but when the issue of custody has to be decided, it may be virtually impossible to know
what decision to make without knowing the true paternity of this child; and it is at that
stage, so it seems to me, that the court may have to consider whether there is not power

E in custody cases to at any rate request the guardian to submit the child to a blood test.
I will not go into it because the matter is not before me, but what I think I shall do in this
case is that I shall adjourn drawing an order in these proceedings until the custody issue
is decided, and I am going to do that for the following reason. I believe the decisions of
the court should be based, so far as possible, on facts, and that decisions relating to
people's lives should not be confused by legal presumptions producing possibly highly
distorted results, and I am, therefore, not going to tie my hands, or the hands of anybody
else who has to deal with the question of custody by imposing on them what I regard as

F a highly artificial decision as to the paternity of this child. I, therefore, adjourn generally
the issue of paternity until the question of custody has been resolved, when one can look
at the whole thing anew, and this time, in those proceedings, with the interests of the
child paramount. It is perfectly clear that the decree ought to be made absolute;
moreover these proceedings have held up the decree for a long time, although I do not
think that the actual making of the decree would help the wife very much immediately,
but I suppose it may help the husband. I shall direct that the husband may apply for

G the decree absolute within seven days of today. I shall reserve the matter to myself
and I ask for a welfare officer's report.

A

BOULD *v.* BOULD (by her Guardian).

[PROBATE, DIVORCE AND ADMIRALTY DIVISION (Sir Jocelyn Simon, P., and Orr, J.), April 11, May 8, 1967.]

Magistrates—Husband and wife—Maintenance order—Interim order—Appeal to High Court from order of magistrates—Whether High Court has power to ante-date interim order—Matrimonial Proceedings (Magistrates' Courts) Act, 1960 (8 & 9 Eliz. 2 c. 48), s. 6 (1) (c).

B

There is no power in the Divisional Court to ante-date an interim order made under s. 6 (1) (c) of the Matrimonial Proceedings (Magistrates' Courts) Act, 1960 (see p. 1130, letters G and H, post).

[As to interim orders, see SUPPLEMENT to 12 HALSBURY'S LAWS (3rd Edn.) title DIVORCE, para. 1087B.

C

For the Matrimonial Proceedings (Magistrates' Courts) Act, 1960, s. 6, see 40 HALSBURY'S LAWS (2nd Edn.) 407.]

Cases referred to:

 McLellan v. *McLellan*, [1954] 1 All E.R. 1; [1954] P. 138; [1953] 3 W.L.R. 1139; Digest (Cont. Vol. A) 676, *636h.*

D

 Meyer v. *Meyer*, [1957] 2 All E.R. 546; [1957] 1 W.L.R. 927; 121 J.P. 424; Digest (Cont. Vol. A) 823, *6755b.*

 Pigott v. *Pigott*, [1957] 3 All E.R. 432; [1958] P. 1; [1957] 3 W.L.R. 781; Digest (Cont. Vol. A) 677, *636o.*

 Starkey v. *Starkey*, [1954] 1 All E.R. 1036; [1954] P. 449; [1954] 2 W.L.R. 907; 118 J.P. 279; Digest (Cont. Vol. A) 822, *6755a.*

E

Appeal.

This was an appeal by the husband from a separation order and a maintenance order in favour of the wife and their child made by the Leek justices on Oct. 13, 1966, the justices having found that the husband had deserted the wife and been guilty of wilful neglect to maintain her and the child. On Apr. 11, 1967, the Divisional Court set aside the orders and ordered a re-hearing. The question then arose whether the Divisional Court had jurisdiction to ante-date an interim maintenance order which they proposed to make to Oct. 13, 1966.

F

R. H. Tucker for the husband.
J. I. Murchie for the wife.

G

 SIR JOCELYN SIMON, P.: This is a case which this court originally heard on Apr. 11, 1967, by way of appeal from a decision of the Leek justices of Oct. 13, 1966. The justices on that date had before them four complaints by the wife: that she had been treated with persistent cruelty; that she had been constructively deserted by the husband; and that he had been guilty of wilful neglect to maintain her and their child. The justices dismissed the charge of persistent cruelty, but found desertion and wilful neglect to maintain the wife and child proved. They made a separation order, and a maintenance order in favour of the wife and the child. The husband appealed against that order. There was no cross-appeal. For reasons that were stated by ORR, J., on Apr. 11, 1967, and in which I concurred, we set aside the orders of the justices and ordered a re-hearing. To elucidate that part of the order which has not been directly in question today, I record that it is conceded that, on the re-hearing, the complaints of wilful neglect to maintain the child, as to which counsel for the husband on Apr. 11, 1967, made (as he put it) a " technical " concession, and of persistent cruelty, as to which there was no cross-appeal, will be open to the court of re-hearing for investigation and adjudication.

H

I

After the order for re-hearing that I have described, there arose discussion whether an interim order should be made; and, with the concurrence of counsel, we proposed to make an order in the following form: to set aside the original

A order of Oct. 13, 1966; to order a re-hearing before a different panel of the same justices; and to make an interim maintenance order as to £2 a week for the child (as to which no question arises) and as to £1 a week for the wife as from the date of the original order of Oct. 13, 1966, credit to be given for any sum that had been paid by the husband. However, before the order was drawn up it occurred to the members of the court that there might be no jurisdiction thus to ante-date

B an interim order. We therefore gave instructions that the order should not be drawn up and that the case should be set down again so that we might have the assistance of counsel's argument on that point.

The power of this court to order interim maintenance is under s. 6 of the Matrimonial Proceedings (Magistrates' Courts) Act, 1960. The relevant portion reads:

C
" (1) Where in the case of any complaint made to a magistrates' court under s. 1 of this Act— . . . (c) . . . on an appeal under s. 11 of this Act from . . . a matrimonial order on the complaint, the High Court . . . orders that the complaint shall be re-heard by a magistrates' court, . . . the High Court, may make an [interim] order . . .

D
" (3) . . . an interim order . . . shall cease to be in force on whichever of the following dates occurs first, that is to say—(a) the date, if any, specified for the purpose in the interim order; (b) the date of the expiration of the period of three months beginning with the date of—(i) the making of the interim order . . .."

Counsel for the husband has drawn our attention to a number of authorities
E which make it clear that, on the proof of the matrimonial offence of wilful neglect to maintain in the High Court under what is now s. 22 of the Matrimonial Causes Act 1965, or of a matrimonial offence in the magistrates' court under what is now the Matrimonial Causes (Magistrates' Courts) Act, 1960, there is power to back-date the consequent maintenance order. In the High Court it can at least be backdated to when the originating summons was taken out; see *McLellan* v.
F *McLellan* (1), considered by the Court of Appeal in *Pigott* v. *Pigott* (2) without any sign of disapprobation on this point. In the case of the courts of summary jurisdiction, on the finding of a matrimonial offence the maintenance order can be similarly backdated. There seems to have been some judicial doubt as to the exact date from which the maintenance order can be made to run—whether it be the date when the Divisional Court on appeal finds an offence proved; or,
G secondly, the date of the original hearing of the magistrates' court dismissing (wrongly, in the subsequent view of the Divisional Court) an allegation of a matrimonial offence; or, thirdly, the date of the complaint; or fourthly, the date of the matter of complaint (which may be the date when an offence of wilful neglect to maintain was first perpetrated: see, for example, *Starkey* v. *Starkey* (3); *Meyer* v. *Meyer* (4)).

H
However, the researches of counsel throw no light on whether there is any authority as to power to ante-date an interim order made under s. 6 of the Act of 1960 (this was a new provision). Under those circumstances, counsel for the husband has put his argument on principle and construction; and counsel for the wife has not found himself able to gainsay it. Counsel for the husband puts his argument under two heads. First, he says that there is a vital distinction
I between an interim order and the principal order, in that the latter pre-supposes the finding of a matrimonial offence; so that the authorities on the ante-dating of final orders are of no assistance when it comes to the question of determining whether there is power to ante-date an interim order. The only difficulty which

(1) [1954] 1 All E.R. 1; [1954] P. 138.
(2) [1957] 3 All E.R. 432 at p. 436; [1958] P. 1 at p. 7.
(3) [1954] 1 All E.R. 1036; [1954] P. 449.
(4) [1957] 2 All E.R. 546.

I feel about that is that, in *McLellan* v. *McLellan* (5), one of the arguments that A weighed with KARMINSKI, J., was the analogy of alimony pending suit, which can be ante-dated and is, indeed, habitually ante-dated, to the date of the presentation of the petition. It is true, as counsel for the husband has argued, that that embodies long-standing practice and that the power to award alimony pending suit has received statutory recognition on the basis of pre-existing practice. However, if that argument stood alone, I would have doubt whether we ought to B accede to it. Secondly, counsel for the husband argues, and in my view most cogently, that to assume power to ante-date interim orders would be in effect to drive a coach and horses through the provisions of s. 6 (1) of the Act of 1960. Paragraph (*a*) of that subsection deals with the power of a magistrates' court, in contra-distinction from this court, to make interim orders. It provides that a magistrates' court may make an interim order if it adjourns the hearing of a C complaint for a period of more than one week. The obvious intention of that paragraph is to provide for the wife's support during the time that a hearing stands adjourned for some substantial period. It would certainly seem contrary to its purpose to involve the immediate accumulation of arrears at a time when liability has not yet been determined. Counsel for the husband puts the argument even more forcefully when he comes to s. 6 (3) (*b*), which I have already read, D whereby the interim order shall come to an end at the expiration of three months from its making. The effect of ante-dating might be that an interim order could be made which would effectively have expired by the date of its making; indeed, if we ourselves in this case had made an interim order dating from Oct. 13, 1966, it would have already expired on the date on which we purported to pronounce it. It may be urged that a construction whereby there is no power to ante-date E interim orders might cause hardship to a wife who has been wrongly left without support and who may have run up debts; and, so far as appeals are concerned, it is far from infrequent for a husband to cease paying under an order which is subject to appeal. It is a partial answer to that—although not, I think, a complete answer—that, if a matrimonial offence is finally determined to have been perpe-trated by the husband, there is great flexibility in the ante-dating, on the F authorities that have been cited to us. I say that such an answer may be incomplete, in view of the financial circumstances of parties who come before magistrates' courts; so that the backdating of the final order may fail to elicit any relevant support for the wife. It may be, therefore, that there is a lacuna here which might merit the attention of the Law Commission or Parliament— whether there should not at least be some power in this court or a court appealed G from to order interim maintenance pending an appeal. That, however, would be a matter for legislation; and it seems to me that the argument on principle and construction put forward by counsel for the husband and not controverted by counsel for the wife is correct, and that there is no power in this court to ante-date an interim order.

It is, therefore, agreed that the order which should be drawn up is an order H for interim maintenance as to £1 for the wife a week, and as to £2 a week for the child as from Apr. 11, 1967, credit to be given for any sums paid since that date.

ORR, J.: I agree.

Order accordingly.

Solicitors: *Bower, Cotton & Bower*, agents for *Bowcock & Pursaill*, Leek (for the I husband); *Kennedy's*, agents for *Blagg, Son & Masefield*, Cheadle (for the wife).

[*Reported by* ALICE BLOOMFIELD, *Barrister-at-Law.*]

---

(5) [1954] 1 All E.R. 1; [1954] P. 138.

A   LAWRY *v.* LAWRY.

[COURT OF APPEAL, CIVIL DIVISION (Willmer, Diplock and Winn, L.JJ.), April
20, 21, 1967.]

*Divorce — Decree — Mutual decrees — Dissolution of marriage and judicial
    separation—Course not to be commended.*

B   Although in the exercise of the court's discretion it may be theoretically
possible to grant mutual decrees, viz., a decree of dissolution of marriage
to one party and a decree of judicial separation to the other (the latter decree
covering the interim period until the decree of divorce is made absolute and
then lapsing, but surviving if that decree is never made absolute), that
course is not to be commended, and is in conflict with the views of the Court
C   of Appeal expressed in *Crawford* v. *Crawford* ((Nov. 30, 1964), unreported)
(see p. 1132, letter I, and p. 1133, letter B, post).

Appeal dismissed.

[As to decrees of divorce generally, see 12 HALSBURY'S LAWS (3rd Edn.)
390-392, paras. 863-867; and for cases on the subject, see 27 DIGEST (Repl.)
551-553, *5015-5039.*]

D   Cases referred to:

Crawford v. *Crawford*, (Nov. 30, 1964), C.A., unreported.
Muscato v. *Muscato*, (1967), 111 Sol. Jo. 332.

Appeal.

The wife appealed against an order made by SIR JOCELYN SIMON, P., on
Nov. 30, 1966, granting the husband petitioner a decree nisi of dissolution of
E   marriage in the exercise of the court's discretion. She sought a decree of judicial
separation, or alternatively an order that the suit be reheard. Grounds of appeal
included: (i) that the decision of SIR JOCELYN SIMON, P., that the wife had
treated the husband with cruelty was wrong in law and against the weight of
the evidence; (ii) that SIR JOCELYN SIMON, P., misdirected himself in law when
exercising the discretion of the court in order to grant the husband a decree of
F   dissolution of marriage in disregarding the fact, as he found, that the husband
had deserted the wife without reasonable excuse before the wife's alleged cruelty
to the husband; (iii) that on the facts found by SIR JOCELYN SIMON, P., he
ought to have rejected the prayer of the petition and granted the wife a judicial
separation on the prayer of her answer on the ground of the husband's desertion
or adultery.

G   *A. B. Hollis* for the wife.
        R. E. Hammerton for the husband.

WILLMER, L.J.: This is a wife's appeal against a judgment given by
SIR JOCELYN SIMON, P., on Nov. 30, 1966, whereby he pronounced a decree nisi
of divorce in favour of the husband on the ground of cruelty on the part of the
H   wife. In granting that decree SIR JOCELYN SIMON exercised his discretion in
favour of the husband, having regard to the fact that the husband had admittedly
committed adultery and, as found by SIR JOCELYN SIMON, had also been guilty
of desertion. He dismissed a cross-prayer contained in the wife's answer whereby
she sought a decree of judicial separation on the ground of the husband's adultery
and desertion. The adultery which the wife charged in her answer was the same
I   as that which was admitted by the husband in his own discretion statement, and
I do not think that there is any issue about that. The husband had also alleged
in his reply, but SIR JOCELYN SIMON did not accept, that his adultery was
conduced to by the wife's cruelty.

The parties were married on Mar. 3, 1928. There are four children of the
marriage, all of whom are now grown up. Two of them, however, do enter into
the picture in the sense that they were residing at home during part of the period
which is material to this case. At all material times the matrimonial home was
at 89, Welbeck Road, Carshalton. As SIR JOCELYN SIMON, P., found (and as the

evidence made clear) this was never a happy marriage, and there were frequent   A
quarrels between the spouses. In 1946, shortly after his return from war service,
the husband left the wife and took a resident post elsewhere. He obtained employment as residential maintenance man at a club. He held that job, as I understand it, for about five years. He then obtained other employment at a sugar
refinery, but he continued to live separate and apart from his wife. SIR JOCELYN
SIMON found that the husband's conduct in leaving the wife in 1946 in this way   B
amounted to desertion. There has been no cross-notice of appeal, and it must
therefore be taken that that finding is not now challenged.

In 1956, having been away for ten years, the husband returned to the matrimonial home. He quite frankly admitted, however, that he did so, not with any
idea of effecting a reconciliation with his wife, but because he wanted to keep an
eye on the youngest child, who was a boy then about eleven years of age. He   C
was not exactly well received by his wife, and it would appear that she was no
more desirous than he was of effecting a reconciliation. They never slept together
again. After a matter of two months or so, the wife gave up performing any
wifely duties for the benefit of the husband, and from that time right up to the
present day these two unfortunate people have continued to reside under the
same roof, but living entirely separate lives. SIR JOCELYN SIMON found that   D
from 1956 onwards they were living in a state of separation, but that that
separation was brought about by the mutual consent of the two parties. I see no
reason to take any different view of the relationship between the parties.

[HIS LORDSHIP reviewed the facts, held that it was impossible to interfere
with SIR JOCELYN SIMON's finding of cruelty by the wife, referred to the wife's
second ground of appeal, viz., that SIR JOCELYN SIMON had misdirected himself   E
in exercising his discretion in favour of the husband, and continued:]   SIR
JOCELYN SIMON had well in mind the extent of the husband's responsibility for
the break-up of the marriage; but he was faced with a position in which the
public interest is very much involved. He had to balance the consideration of
respect for the sanctity of marriage (which is of particular importance in the
present case in view of the wife's conscientious objection to divorce) against the   F
public interest which is involved in the question whether it is right to keep in
being a marriage which has so obviously and so hopelessly and completely broken
down. This, after all, has not been a marriage in anything except name for
more than twenty years. It was, I apprehend, a difficult decision to make.
Had the wife been herself asking for a decree of dissolution, I apprehend that
SIR JOCELYN SIMON, P., would probably have granted a decree in her favour,   G
and perhaps only a decree in her favour, though he could, of course, have granted
mutual decrees. As the wife was not asking for such a decree, however, he was
faced with a difficult choice when he came to exercise his discretion. It was
very much a matter for him. I cannot see that he erred in any way in principle,
and I am far from feeling able to say that his exercise of his discretion was so
plainly wrong that this court would be justified in interfering.   H

[HIS LORDSHIP referred to the third ground of appeal, that SIR JOCELYN
SIMON conducted himself in such a way that justice was not seen to be done, and
continued:] In the result I can see no reason for interfering with SIR JOCELYN
SIMON's judgment in so far as he found the wife guilty of cruelty. Nor do I think
that any good reason has been shown for interfering with the way in which he
exercised his discretion.   I

I venture to mention one further point in relation to the exercise of discretion.
It would, I suppose, have been theoretically possible to grant mutual decrees in
the exercise of discretion, i.e., a decree nisi of dissolution to the husband and a
decree of judicial separation to the wife. Counsel for the wife has not, however,
argued in favour of this, and I mention the point only because of the decision of
CAIRNS, J., in *Muscato* v. *Muscato* (1) in which that very course of granting mutual

(1) (1967), 111 Sol. Jo. 332.

A   decrees was taken. He took that course apparently on the basis that, although as soon as the decree nisi of divorce was made absolute the decree of judicial separation would lapse, it would nevertheless cover the interim period and would, of course, survive if in the event the decree of divorce never was made absolute. I am bound to say, however, that it is not a course which commends itself to me, and it is a course which appears to be in conflict with the views

B   which were expressed by this court in *Crawford* v. *Crawford* (2) to which we were referred yesterday in the course of the argument. In the circumstances I can see no ground for interfering with the judgment of Sir Jocelyn Simon, P., and I would accordingly dismiss the appeal.

     DIPLOCK, L.J.: I, too, would dismiss the appeal.

C   **WINN, L.J.:** I agree completely and that the appeal should be dismissed.

     Appeal dismissed. Leave to apply forthwith for decree nisi to be made absolute.

     Solicitors: *C. H. Stanley Smith*, Carshalton (for the wife); *Rodgers, Horsley & Burton* (for the husband).

                              [*Reported by* F. A. Amies, Esq., *Barrister-at-Law.*]

D

DALE *v.* SMITH.

[Queen's Bench Division (Lord Parker, C.J., Widgery and O'Connor, JJ.), April 12, 1967.]

Criminal Law—Soliciting for immoral purposes—Persistent importuning by
E   *male person in public place for immoral purposes—Evidence of more than one invitation—Use of word of pleasantry interpreted as invitation—Such interpretation permissible as word had been used on previous day coupled with undoubted act of importuning—Sexual Offences Act, 1956 (4 & 5 Eliz. 2 c. 69), s. 32.*

     On the evening of Feb. 12, 1966, the appellant, who was the deputy
F   headmaster of a school, spoke to two or three groups of youths at a railway station. He kept bumping into two of the youths saying " Hello " or " Bumped into you again ", and asked one of them if he would like to look at some sexy photographs. On the following evening, the two youths were waiting at the station and when one of them went to the public lavatory the appellant was there and said " Hello " to him. The appellant then went
G   to a café, looked into a window and saw a boy of about ten years old. He went into the café, sat opposite the boy and talked to him, and showed him an object which might have been a piece of paper or cardboard, whitish in colour. The appellant and the boy left the café together and the three youths followed. As a result of something which the appellant said to him, the boy left the appellant who then went into a coffee bar. One of the youths
H   followed him and requested him to go to the police station. At the police station the appellant was searched and forty-five indecent photographs were found on him which he said he had found in a lavatory at the station. On appeal against conviction of persistently importuning in a public place for immoral purposes, contrary to s. 32* of the Sexual Offences Act, 1956,

     Held: the appellant had been rightly convicted, because, apart from the
I   undoubted invitation to the small boy, the justices were entitled to treat the evidence of the appellant's saying " Hello " to the youth in the public lavatory as a separate importuning, since the same word had been used the evening before and was then followed by an importuning by asking one of the youths if he wanted to look at some sexy photographs (see p. 1136, letters D to F, post).

     Appeal dismissed.

---

(2) (Nov. 30, 1964), unreported.
* Section 32, so far as material, is set out at p. 1135, letter H, post.

[As to soliciting by a male person, see 10 HALSBURY'S LAWS (3rd Edn.) 676, **A**
para. 1294; and for a case on the subject, see 15 DIGEST (Repl.) 899, *8672.*

For the Sexual Offences Act, 1956, s. 32, see 36 HALSBURY'S STATUTES (2nd
Edn.) 233.]

Case Stated.

This was a Case Stated by the justices for the city of Bradford in respect of
their adjudication as a magistrates' court sitting in the city of Bradford on   **B**
Mar. 8 and 10, 1966. On Feb. 14, 1966, an information was preferred by the
respondent, Charles Frederick Smith, against the appellant, Lincoln Dale, that
on Feb. 13, 1966, being a male person, the appellant importuned for immoral
purposes in Forster Square Railway Station, Bradford, contrary to s. 32 of the
Sexual Offences Act, 1956. On the same day the respondent preferred a
complaint against the appellant that, on Feb. 13, 1966, the appellant behaved in   **C**
a manner likely to cause a breach of the peace. The information and the complaint were heard together on Mar. 8 and the following facts were found. The
appellant was a schoolmaster and deputy headmaster of a school in Leeds and
Facts resided at 145, Stainbeck Lane, Leeds. He was of hitherto good character.

On Saturday, Feb. 12, 1966, at about 7.0 p.m., the appellant was at the
Forster Square Railway Station in Bradford. The appellant was sitting on a   **D**
seat and he was then seen to go up to and speak to two or three different groups
of youths present in the station. When spoken to, the first of those groups
moved away and the appellant went to another group. The appellant then
followed two youths, Clowes and Holliday, who gave evidence before the justices,
about the station for about an hour. He kept bumping into them saying
" Hello " or " Bumped into you again ", or expressions of that sort. Clowes **E**
and Holliday left the station. The appellant followed them, and, coming up to
Holliday, who was then standing apart from Clowes, asked if he " wanted to look
at some sexy photographs ". Holliday replied " Get lost " and the appellant
then walked away. Clowes and Holliday followed him for ten to fifteen minutes
with the intention of speaking to a police officer, but lost sight of the appellant.
On the following day, Sunday, Feb. 13, 1966, the appellant was again at the   **F**
railway station in Bradford at about 7.0 p.m. The two youths were also present
looking out for the appellant " to get him, give him a good hiding ". Clowes
went into the toilet where he saw the appellant who said " Hello ", and Clowes
left the toilet. The appellant went to the neighbourhood of the café which was
on the station adjoining the main entrance. In that café, although the serving
of meals had been discontinued, was sitting a young boy of about ten years old. **G**
The appellant first looked in at the boy, then entered the café and sat opposite to
him at a table. He took something from his pocket and showed it to the boy.
That object was whitish, measuring about four inches by three inches and could
have been a piece of paper or cardboard. The appellant spoke to the boy for
about two or three minutes and then left the café followed by the boy. Both
went into Forster Square, then to the bottom of Bolton Road, then up Stott   **H**
Hill behind the Cathedral. They kept looking back and were in fact followed by
Clowes, Holliday and another witness, Illingworth. While crossing the road the
appellant said something to the boy who ran away down Church Bank back
towards the city. The appellant continued to walk on and went to a coffee bar.
The three witnesses followed the appellant to the coffee bar and, after waiting
outside for about fifteen minutes, Illingworth went in and asked the appellant   **I**
to go to the police or two youths would beat him up. The appellant leapt up
and ran from the coffee bar but was called back by the waitress since he had not
paid. He paid his bill and then went back to the station followed by the three
witnesses, and was asked to go to the police office. He kept saying that he did
not know what Illingworth was talking about. The police were called. Complaints were made in the presence of the appellant and he replied " I thought it
in reverse. I thought they were following me ". Both the youths were at
this time agitated and angry. The appellant said he did not mind being searched.

Police called and

A At the police station the appellant was searched and on him were found forty-five indecent photographs which included photographs of male persons indulging in homosexual practices. The appellant said that he found these in a lavatory at the station. The appellant made a voluntary statement under caution to a police officer. He gave no evidence before the justices, but called two witnesses as to character. When the prosecution sought to tender evidence

B of the events of Feb. 12, 1966, it was contended by the defence that such evidence was inadmissible since it referred to Feb. 12, an occasion not alleged in the charge. It was contended on behalf of the prosecution that that evidence was admissible to show guilty intent. The evidence was admitted. When the prosecution sought to introduce evidence of the finding of the photographs, the defence contended that such evidence was inadmissible in any event, and in particular

C since there was no evidence that the appellant had produced them to any person. The prosecution contended that their appearance coincided with the object shown to the boy in the café. The justices were also mindful of the fact that, on the previous evening, the appellant had offered to show " some sexy photographs " to the witness Holliday and that this had been admitted in evidence. At the commencement of the resumed hearing on Mar. 10, 1966, the prosecutor

D sought to amend the information, by inserting the word " persistently " in front of the word " importuned ". The defence contended that that was not a proper amendment, since (a) the information before the court disclosed no offence known to the law, (b) it would be wrong to allow an amendment after substantially the whole of the prosecution evidence had been heard, and (c) no amendment could be retrospective without causing injustice. The prose-

E cution submitted that the amendment was in accordance with s. 100 of the Magistrates' Courts Act, 1952. The amendment was permitted. The defence declined the offer of an adjournment, nor did they apply to recall any witness for cross-examination. The case had been conducted throughout on the basis of " persistent " importuning. At the conclusion of the evidence it was sub-mitted on behalf of the appellant that the evidence did not disclose any offence,

F as there was no evidence in respect of Feb. 13, 1966, of importuning, or persistently importuning, or behaviour likely to cause a breach of the peace.

The justices found the appellant guilty of both offences and imposed a fine of £20 in respect of the information and bound him over for twelve months in the sum of £25 to be of good behaviour on the complaint. The appellant now appealed.

G *C. R. Dean*, Q.C., and *G. Baker* for the appellant.
J. F. S. Cobb, Q.C., and *I. S. McLean* for the respondent.

LORD PARKER, C.J.: This is an appeal on a Case Stated from a decision of justices for the city of Bradford, who convicted the appellant of an offence contrary to s. 32 of the Sexual Offences Act, 1956, which provides that " it is an

H offence for a man persistently to . . . importune in a public place for immoral purposes ". [His Lordship stated the facts, and continued:] Before the justices several points were taken. It was said in the first instance that the evidence of what had happened on the day before, namely, on Feb. 12, 1966, when quite clearly there was an importuning of Holliday, was inadmissible. The justices, as I think quite rightly, ruled that it was admissible to negative any innocent

I approach and conversation the next day with the little boy of ten, and, indeed, counsel for the appellant quite rightly has not persisted in this court in that objection. Then again objection was taken at the trial to the admission of the photographs. That again has not been persisted in here, and quite rightly because, on the authorities, those photographs were plainly admissible, even if there was not evidence that the small cardboard object shown to the small boy was one of these photographs. Finally, objection was taken to the fact, and this may have given rise to the trouble in this case, that the information omitted the word " persistently " and had merely alleged an importuning for immoral

purposes in the railway station on Feb. 13. The justices quite properly over- A
ruled that objection, and again it is not persisted with because quite clearly
there was no prejudice to the appellant, the whole case was conducted on the
basis of an offence under s. 32 of the Act of 1956 where the only offence is
persistent importuning, and they had ample powers by reason of s. 100 of the
Magistrates' Courts Act, 1952, to allow, as they did, an amendment.

The sole point taken by counsel for the appellant is that there must be a B
persistent importunity, and, whatever the word " persistent " means, it must, so
he says and I think rightly, mean a degree of repetition, of either more than one
invitation to one person or a series of invitations to different people. He says
that, on the evidence here, there was only an importuning of one person, namely,
the boy of ten, and in his case no evidence of any persistency in the sense of a
repetition of invitations to that boy. As I said, if the prosecution had been C
alive to this, they might well have alleged a persistent importuning over Feb.
12 and 13, in which case there really would have been no defence whatever in
this case. However, counsel is entitled to take the point, and this court must
deal with it.

In my judgment, there was evidence, though only just evidence, of more than
one invitation. Apart from the undoubted invitation to the small boy, there D
was this evidence of what happened in the toilet when the appellant said " Hello "
to Clowes. It is said by counsel for the appellant that that was just a pleasantry
addressed to a man whom he already knew, or at any rate knew by sight. On
the other hand, it was open as it seems to me to the justices to give a different
interpretation to that, in the sense that it was the same word that had been used
to, amongst others, Holliday the day before, which was followed in the case of E
Holliday undoubtedly by an importuning when he was asked whether he wanted
to look at some sexy photographs. It seems to me that the justices were entitled
to treat that evidence as a separate importuning which will give two importunings
on that day, Feb. 13, which, in my judgment, would be enough to support this
charge. Accordingly, I would dismiss the appeal.

F

WIDGERY, J.: I agree.

O'CONNOR, J.: I agree.

Appeal dismissed.

Solicitors: *Waterhouse & Co.*, agents for *T. I. Clough & Co.*, Bradford (for the
appellant); *Wilkinson, Howlett & Moorhouse*, agents for *Town Clerk*, Bradford G
(for the respondent).

[*Reported by* R. W. FARRIN, ESQ., *Barrister-at-Law.*]

A ALLEN *v.* THORN ELECTRICAL INDUSTRIES, LTD.
GRIFFIN *v.* RECEIVER FOR THE METROPOLITAN POLICE
DISTRICT.

[COURT OF APPEAL, CIVIL DIVISION (Lord Denning, M.R., Danckwerts and Winn,
L.JJ.), June 12, 13, 14, 1967.]

B *Master and Servant—Wages—Restrictions on pay increases—No increase above*
" rate of remuneration paid " before relevant date—Restriction to rate con-
tracted to be paid, as distinct from amount actually paid—Prices and Incomes
Act 1966 (c. 73), s. 28 (2), s. 29 (4)—Temporary Restrictions on Pay Increases
(20th July 1966 Levels) (No. 1) Order 1966 (S.I. 1966 No. 1365)—Temporary
Restrictions on Pay Increases (No. 2) Order 1966 (S.I. 1966 No. 1468).

C On July 12, 1966, employers agreed a wage increase of £1 weekly as from
Apr. 1, 1966, and another £1 weekly as from Apr. 1, 1967. The increase was
to be paid so soon as was administratively possible. On July 20, 1966, before
it was administratively possible to pay the increase, the Prime Minister
called for a standstill on prices and incomes. Accordingly the employers did
not pay the increase. An employee recovered judgment for his increase.
D On Nov. 2, 1966, s. 29 of the Prices and Incomes Act 1966 was applied
by Order to remuneration for work done under contracts of employment
that included terms of the agreement of July 12. Section 29 (4)* forbade
payment of remuneration " at a rate which exceeds the rate of remuneration paid " by the employer for the same kind of work before the relevant
date, viz. July 20, 1966.

E On July 14, 1966, a different employer agreed to pay draughtsmen in his
employ a salary at a revised and increased scale as from Jan. 1, 1965. The
arrears were to be paid at the end of August, 1966, and the increased salary
was to continue thereafter. On July 20, 1966 the standstill was announced.
The employer did not pay the increase. An employee subsequently recovered
judgment for the increase. On Nov. 24, 1966, an Order applied s. 28 (2)† of
F the Prices and Incomes Act 1966 to the contract of employment. On Nov.
24, 1966, the employer paid the increase up to Oct. 31, 1966, and not long
after paid the increase up to Nov. 23, 1966. Section 28 (2) forbade the
payment of remuneration " at a rate which exceeds the rate of remuneration
paid " by the employer for the same kind of work before the relevant date,
viz., Nov. 24, 1966, when the Order applying s. 28 (2) came into force.
G On appeals in the actions to recover amounts of increases,

---

* Section 29, so far as relevant, provides: " (3) The Secretary of State may, . . .
by order apply this section to remuneration under contracts of employment for any
kind of work. (4) An employer shall not pay remuneration to which this section applies
for work for any period while the order is in force at a rate which exceeds the rate of
remuneration paid by him for the same kind of work before July 20, 1966, by any
amount unless—(*a*) the appropriate Minister has given his consent in writing to an excess
H of that amount or of a greater amount, or (*b*) the order authorises an excess of that
amount, or of a greater amount." The Order, S.I. 1966 No. 1365, provided, by art. 2,
that s. 29 should apply to remuneration under contracts of employment for work of
the description specified in the Schedule to the order. The schedule specifies work
performed under any contract of employment the terms of which included, expressly
or by implication, all or any of the terms of the verbal agreement entered into on July
12, 1966, by or on behalf of Thorn Electrical Industries, Ltd.

I † Section 28, so far as material provides as follows: " (1) The Secretary of State may
by order apply this section to remuneration under contracts of employment for any
kind of work to be performed wholly or substantially within the United Kingdom . . .
(2) An employer shall not pay remuneration to which this section applies at a rate
which exceeds the rate of remuneration paid by him for the same kind of work before
the date of the coming into force of the order applying this section to that description
of remuneration by any amount . . ." The Order, S.I. 1966 No. 1468, provided, by
art. 2, that s. 28 should apply to remuneration under contracts of employment for
work of the description specified in the schedule to the Order. The Schedule specified
work for any period while the Order was in force performed by persons employed as
draughtsmen under the Receiver for the Metropolitan Police District.

Held: the words " rate of remuneration paid " in s. 29 (4) and s. 28 (2)   A
of the Prices and Incomes Act 1966 meant the rate contracted to be paid,
or the rate payable or applicable in respect of the employee concerned, not
the sum actually paid by way of remuneration immediately before the
relevant date; accordingly the employee, in each case, was not precluded
by s. 29 (4) or by s. 28 (2) from recovering the agreed wage increase and was
entitled to judgment accordingly (see p. 1142, letter D, p. 1143, letter D,   B
and p. 1144, letter I, post).

Per LORD DENNING, M.R.: no man's contractual rights are to be taken
away on an ambiguity in a statute; nor is an employer to be penalised on
an ambiguity (see p. 1142, letter E, post).

Appeals allowed.

C

[**Editorial Note.** The dictum quoted above may be remembered with that
of LORD SIMONDS in *L.N.E.R.* v. *Berriman* ([1946] 1 All E.R. at p. 270, letter G),
" a man is not to be put in peril upon an ambiguity ", which expressed a rule
of construction applicable to penal statutes. Those words were quoted and
relied on again by the House of Lords in *Fawcett Properties, Ltd.* v. *Buckingham
County Council* ([1960] 3 All E.R. 503, see e.g., at pp. 507, letters G, H, p. 517,   D
letter B). The same approach is here applied to a statute interfering with
contractual rights.

As to the interpretation of words in a statute in their popular sense, see 36
HALSBURY's LAWS (3rd Edn.) 392, para. 587; as to the construction of ambiguous
expressions, see ibid., 408, 409, para. 617; and as to the construction of penal
statutes, see ibid., 415, 416, para. 631; and for cases on these subjects respectively,   E
see 44 DIGEST (Repl.) 204-210, *159-249*, 216-218, *307-337*, 220, 221, *367-382*
and 321-323, *1522-1579*.

For the Prices and Incomes Act 1966 s. 28 and s. 29, see 46 HALSBURY's
STATUTES (2nd Edn.) 797, 798.]

Cases referred to:
  Chippendale v. *Holt*, (1895), 65 L.J.Q.B. 104; 73 L.T. 472; 29 Digest (Repl.)   F
    141, *817*.
  Eddystone Marine Insurance Co., Re, Ex p. Western Insurance Co., [1892]
    2 Ch. 423; 61 L.J.Ch. 362; 66 L.T. 370; 29 Digest (Repl.) 141, *816*.
  Gether v. *Capper*, (1855), 15 C.B. 696; 139 E.R. 599; 24 L.J.C.P. 69; *affd.*,
    Ex. Ch. (1856), 18 C.B. 866; 25 L.J.C.P. 260; 27 L.T.O.S. 298; 139
    E.R. 1613; 41 Digest (Repl.) 164, *92*.
                                                                                G

Appeals.
  The first appeal was by the plaintiff, Leonard Herbert Allen, from a judgment
of His Honour JUDGE GRANVILLE SMITH given at Edmonton County Court
on Jan. 18, 1967, dismissing Mr. Allen's claim for payment by the defendants
of an increase of salary due to Mr. Allen for a period from Nov. 2, 1966, until   H
Nov. 16, 1966, and continuing thereafter. By notice of appeal dated Feb. 24,
1967, Mr. Allen sought an order that the judgment should be reversed and that
judgment might be entered for him for the sum of £2 due to him up to Nov. 16,
1966. The grounds alleged in the notice of appeal were that the county court
judge was wrong in law in holding that s. 29 of the Prices and Incomes Act 1966
and the Temporary Restrictions on Pay Increases (20th July 1966 Levels)
(No. 1) Order 1966 made thereunder prohibited Mr. Allen from recovering the   I
increase in salary due to him from the defendants, Thorn Electrical Industries,
Ltd., and that the county court judge wrongly interpreted s. 29. By a respondent's
notice dated Mar. 16, 1967, the defendants gave notice that the judgment should
be affirmed on the following additional grounds—(i) s. 29 (4) required (subject
to exceptions (*a*) and (*b*) therein mentioned) that an employer should not pay
remuneration to which the section applied for work for any period while an
order made under the section was in force at a rate which exceeded the rate of

A   remuneration paid or payable by him before July 20, 1966, for the same kind of work and (ii) Mr. Allen's increase in salary was not payable before July 20, 1966, and the county court judge erred in failing so to hold.

In the second appeal the plaintiff, Douglas Henry Griffin, appealed by notice of appeal dated Mar. 15, 1967, from the judgment of His Honour JUDGE BARRING-TON, given on Mar. 6, 1967, dismissing Mr. Griffin's claim for a sum of £2 14s. 4d.

B   and for a declaration that his monthly salary payable by the defendant, the Receiver for the Metropolitan Police District, was £163 13s. 4d. gross, and for a further declaration regarding deductions from pay, not material to this report. The grounds of appeal included, among others, the following—(i) that the rate of remuneration claimed by Mr. Griffin did not exceed the rate paid to him by the defendant in respect of the same kind of work done by the plaintiff before

C   the date of coming into force of the Temporary Restrictions on Pay Increases (No. 2) Order 1966; and (ii) that the county court judge failed to direct himself that the terms of the Prices and Incomes Act 1966 and of the Order did not expressly or by necessary implication require a construction which would result in the taking away without compensation of Mr. Griffin's existing private right to his contractual remuneration nor require a construction which involved altering

D   the clearly established principle of law that a servant is entitled to remuneration in accordance with the terms of his existing contract with his master; and (iii) that the county court judge erred in law in holding that the word " paid " in s. 28 (1) of the Act of 1966 was not ambiguous and in that he did not construe the word " paid " as meaning " payable ".

E   *S. N. McKinnon*, Q.C., and *R. Ashton* for the plaintiff, Mr. Allen.

R. I. Threlfall, Q.C., and *R. O. Havery* for the defendants, Thorn Electrical Industries, Ltd.

Sir Andrew Clark, Q.C., and *D. J. Turner-Samuels* for the plaintiff, Mr. Griffin.

P. L. W. Owen, Q.C., and *R. I. Kidwell* for the defendant, the Receiver for the Metropolitan Police District.

F   *J. Newey* appeared as amicus curiae.

LORD DENNING, M.R.: Mr. Allen is a charge hand supervisor employed by Thorn Electrical Industries, Ltd. He is a member of a trade union called the Association of Supervisory Staffs, Executives and Technicians. On Tuesday, July 12, 1966, before any " wage freeze " was announced, there was an agreement

G   between the employers and the union. The employers agreed to increase the salary of 120 men, including Mr. Allen. His salary had been, in round figures, £20 a week. The agreement was to increase it by £1 to £21 a week from Apr. 1, 1966, and a further increase of £1 a week to £22 a week from Apr. 1, 1967. That was a binding contract under which Thorn Electrical Industries, Ltd., were bound to pay those increases of £1 a week. The union representatives asked:

H   " When will it be implemented? ". The employers replied: " As soon as adminis-tratively possible." The next pay day was Friday, July 15, 1955, but it was not administratively possible to calculate all the back pay, tax, and so forth, by that Friday. So the payment was deferred until the next pay day, namely, Friday, July 22, 1966; but two days before that day arrived there was an important announcement. On July 20, 1966, the Prime Minister went to the House of

I   Commons and called for a standstill on prices and incomes. There should be no increases. He said that the government would rely in the first instance on volun-tary action, but intimated that they would, if necessary, seek compulsory powers to enforce the standstill. Thorn Electrical Industries, Ltd., responded to the call. They did not pay the increase of £1 which they had promised to Mr. Allen. They went on paying £20 a week instead of the increased £21; but they had no legal warrant for non-payment, and Mr. Allen went to court to prove it. He sued for the increase of £1 a week from Apr. 1, 1966, and got judgment for it. It came to £21 up to Aug. 26, 1966. Thorn Electrical Industries, Ltd., paid it.

Now comes the point. The government sought and obtained compulsory A
powers to enforce the standstill. On Aug. 12, 1966, there was passed the Prices
and Incomes Act 1966. On Oct. 6, 1966, Part 4 was brought into operation (1).
On Nov. 1, 1966, the Secretary of State made an Order called the Temporary
Restrictions on Pay Increases (20th July 1966 levels) (No. 1) Order, 1966 (2).
It was aimed expressly at the agreement made on July 12, 1966, between Thorn
Electrical Industries, Ltd., and the union. It applied s. 29 (4) which forbade the B
employers paying the men at a rate greater than they were *paid* before July
20, 1966. Note the word " *paid* ". Thorn Electrical Industries, Ltd., say that
on the previous pay day, July 15, they only *actually paid* Mr. Allen £20. They
were, therefore, forbidden to pay him any more. Whereas Mr. Allen says that
on that day, July 15, his rate of remuneration was *by contract* £21 a week, and
he should receive it. The case depends on the true construction of s. 29 (4) of C
the Act of 1966, which provides that

" An employer shall not pay remuneration to which this section applies
for work for any period while the Order is in force at a rate which exceeds
the rate of remuneration paid by him for the same kind of work before July
20, 1966 . . ."

Before I consider the law in this case, I will state the facts of the next case. D

Mr. Griffin is a senior draughtsman employed under the Receiver for the
Metropolitan Police District. For some time there were negotiations about the
salary of draughtsmen. Pending a final agreement Mr. Griffin was receiving
salary on an interim scale of £1,742 a year; but eventually on July 14, 1966,
agreement was reached on revised scales (3). Mr. Griffin was to receive an E
increase, so as to bring up his salary for the year beginning Jan. 1, 1965, to
£1,900 a year, and for the year beginning Jan. 1, 1966, to £1,974 a year. The
agreement expressly stated that

" payment of the revised scales, together with arrears, will be made
with the salaries for August, 1966."

Accordingly, the receiver was bound *by contract* to pay to Mr. Griffin on Aug. 31, F
1966, all the back salary and all his current salary at the increased rate of £1,974
a year; and, thereafter to go on paying him at that increased rate.

Soon afterwards, before any compulsory powers were given, the Treasury
took action. They issued directives to all departments prohibiting payment
of any increases in wages and salaries. The receiver, accordingly, issued a notice
on Aug. 12, 1966, in which he said: " The prohibition includes increases arising G
from agreements already concluded but not yet paid." So Mr. Griffin did not
get the increase on Aug. 31, 1966, which he had been promised. Nor did he get
the increase in current salary thereafter.

That was, I fear, a breach of contract by the receiver. It was no doubt
justified by the economic conditions of the country at the time, but it was not
justified by law. No legal warrant existed for non-payment. Accordingly, Mr. H
Griffin brought an action to enforce his right. On Nov. 2, 1966, he issued a
summons in the county court against the receiver asking for £341, being the
arrears of his back pay, and current salary up to Oct. 31, 1966, at the increased
rate. There was no defence in law to that action, but still the receiver did not pay.
He never did pay any of the increased salary until after an order was made
under the Prices and Incomes Act 1966. This order, the Temporary Restrictions I
on Pay Increases (No. 2) Order 1966 (4), was made on Nov. 23, 1966, and came

(1) By the Prices and Incomes Act 1966 (Commencement of Part IV) Order 1966,
S.I. 1966 No. 1262.   (2) S.I. 1966 No. 1365.
(3) By R.O. Establishment Branch Notice No. 59/66 revised substantive scales of
pay were to take effect as from Jan. 1, 1965, and to supersede the interim scales published
in notice No. 68/65. The scales of Jan. 1, 1965, attracted the 1966 3½ per cent. central
pay increase, and the scales effective from Jan. 1, 1965, and Jan. 1, 1966, were set out
in the appendix to Notice No. 59/66. They were there headed " National Rates ".
(4) S.I. 1966 No. 1468.

A and unfair that it seems to me clear that such a construction cannot be correct. It cannot be right and it cannot be the intention of the legislature that the position of the employee and his right to receive the higher rate of remuneration should be dependent on the amount of the money in the office safe or the time required by the mechanics of administration for the calculation of the sums due to the individual employees. These statutory provisions are penal and are

B designed to interfere with rights of contract and the pre-existing legal position of free citizens of this country. Well-established principles, therefore, apply to the situation. Existing legal rights are not to be taken away except by clear words in the statute. If two constructions are possible, the construction which produces unreason and hardship is to be avoided, and the construction which interferes with the legal rights of the subject to a lesser extent and produces

C the less hardship is to be preferred.

On this footing, in my opinion, it is clear that the word " paid " must bear its " popular and ordinary sense " (as it has sometimes been described) so that actual payment is not required and it is sufficient that the amount is due at the material moment from the employer to the employee. The terms of the two sections clearly are directed to " the rate of remuneration " payable at the material time

D and are not directed to the amounts which are handed over by the employer in cash. The rate of remuneration payable is ascertainable, whereas the amounts handed over in cash may be affected by purely accidental matters. Accordingly, I would allow the appeal in each of the two cases.

WINN, L.J.: I too agree that each of these appeals should be allowed.

E I desire to add very little for myself. I do feel constrained to deal with one point which arises more particularly in Mr. Allen's appeal; that is the proper construction of s. 29 (4) of the Prices and Incomes Act 1966 which reads:

" An employer shall not pay remuneration to which this section applies for work for any period while the order is in force at a rate which exceeds the rate of remuneration paid by him for the same kind of work before

F July 20, 1966, by any amount unless . . ."

In Mr. Allen's appeal (and rather less prominently in Mr. Griffin's appeal) the question was argued whether those words " before July 20, 1966 ", which ought I think to be regarded as amounting to an adverbial phrase, should be taken to qualify the verb " paid " or should be taken, somewhat ungrammatically without expansion to qualify adjectivally the phrase " for work ". In Mr. Griffin's appeal

G the like point arises on s. 28 (2), where the relevant words are

" which exceeds the rate of remuneration paid by him for the same kind of work before the date of the coming into force of the order applying this section . . ."

For my part I have no doubt whatsoever that the words should be related to the

H verb " paid ", and that it is not proper to adopt the alternative construction of this section which depends on the insertion of the word " done " or " performed " after the word " work ", so as to make it read " the same kind of work done " or " performed " " before July 20 " in s. 29, and " the same kind of work done " or " performed " " before the date of the coming into force of the order " in s. 28. I say that not only because the construction contended for by counsel

I for Mr. Griffin and by counsel for Mr. Allen does violence to the proper use of the English language by confusing adverbial and adjectival phrases, but because it is clear, I think, that the draftsman intended, and Parliament must be taken to have intended, to use the expression " remuneration paid ", whatever that expression itself means, as the criterion of legality or illegality of a payment made during the period laid down by the section and the relevant order.

Having said that, which means rejecting any comparison between the two kinds of work, that is to say, work done before and after July 20, in the one case, and the date of the order, in the other, I would suggest that the draftsman,

in using the word " work " in the second line of s. 29 (4), used it only because A
s. 29 relates to work, whereas s. 28 refers to contracts of employment. In
other words, s. 29 is dealing with the subject-matter of jobs or jobs done otherwise than under a continuing contract of employment and otherwise than
as services. If that be accepted, then there is no manifest contradiction between
the first two lines of s. 29 (4) and the fourth line. It is no longer necessary
to suppose that the first two lines refer to work done and the fourth line to work B
at or before a certain time, since the subject-matter of the section is to control
remuneration *for work*.

Having disembarrassed the problem to that extent, I turn to consider the
much more important, and indeed vital, question in each of these appeals: what
is the meaning of the word " paid "? As my lords have already said (and I crave
leave to add what emphasis I can to what they have said), what the section is C
concerned with is *rate* of remuneration, and it is essential to concentrate on, not
only the presence of that word in each of the relevant sections, but also the
emphasis which by the casting of the form of the section is given to the concept
of *rate*. Now, in my opinion, whatever may have been the understanding of a
" literate or learned pedant ", a rate of remuneration is something quite different
from remuneration and something quite different from that which is paid as D
remuneration on any particular occasion for any particular job, piece of work or
contractual service. I am myself, I think, by past experience perhaps, more
readily able to see than such a " pedant " writing in an ivory tower, that the
rate is something which is far more important in controlling economic changes
for the country than that which is paid on any particular occasion. Some men,
when they come to be paid on pay day, are only going to draw a pound or two E
against a £20 rate of remuneration. Men work short weeks because there is a
football game or other attraction in the neighbourhood: other men are sick, or
regard themselves as sick, perhaps for reasons for which they themselves carry
primary responsibility on any particular morning, or on any particular day in a
working week. Each one of those men, including men who are actually, if I may
use the colloquial expression, " on the sick " for the week in question, will draw F
less than their colleagues who are doing the same job under the same conditions
in that particular week. In other cases men will be provided with lodgings.
Contractors going about the country on building sites and erecting bridges,
will in some cases provide lodgings for the men, in which case men may suffer
deductions from their pay to cover the provision of such facilities. The result
is that the men in each of those categories will be paid on a given pay day less G
than their job commands as the rate of remuneration. What is important to
have regard to is the rate of remuneration.

Now the long title to the Act of 1966, which is informative, or is intended to be,
refers, inter alia, to " enforcing a temporary standstill in prices or charges or terms
and conditions of employment ". In my view Parliament in the sections which
we have had to consider was dealing with terms and conditions, and terms and H
conditions comprise the rate of remuneration which a particular job commands
or is paid by a particular employer, or more generally as the result of wage
council decisions affecting individuals working for multiple employers. It appears
to me that really the meaning of the word " paid " in both of these sections is
either that which each of my lords has given to it—and I do not dissent at all
from their judgments in this respect—or it is, as I myself respectfully prefer to I
put it, the same as " applicable " or " prevailing " or " established ". It is the
de facto rate of remuneration at the relevant time, and in each of these cases the
de facto rate of remuneration, the agreed rate, the contractually agreed rate, if
you please, or the actual prevailing, established, applicable rate, is that for which
the respective plaintiffs contend in these actions. I think that no prohibition is
effectively imposed—I do not pause to consider what may have been the intention
of the draftsman—which prevents the employer from continuing to pay that
prevailing, established, applicable rate of remuneration.

A   It is right, in deference to counsel for Mr. Griffin, that I should deal with one particular submission he made, and that is that it does not matter, on the construction of the statute, when payment is made, even if " paid " be given its strictest sense. I do not think that I made clear why I find myself unable to accept this further and very minor submission which he made. It is for this reason, that even on the assumption that " paid " means actually paid and even
B   if it can be said that the proper construction is to refer the date in each case to the doing of the work rather than the date it is paid for, nevertheless no benefit can be derived by his client from that interpretation because, by force of s. 25 (7), it is only a payment actually made before the relevant date which is brought into account so as to enhance the previous rate or actual remuneration.

It is perhaps noticeable and worth mentioning that, when the receiver and the
C   Home Secretary dealt with the previous position, they chose to refer to " scales " which appears to me to be very much the same thing as rates.

One last opinion I express which has more general application than to these two appeals, and that is that I must reject as quite untenable any submission, such as I understood counsel for the Receiver for the Metropolitan Police District to make, that if in any case one finds (a) that a statute is worded ambiguously in
D   any particular respect, and (b) finds also clear indications aliunde that Parliament intended that they should have the strictest and most stringent meaning possible, the court is then compelled to construe the section in the sense in which Parliament would have desired it to take effect, by giving the words their most stringent possible meaning. On the contrary I think that the right view is, and as I understand it always has been, that in such a case of ambiguity, it is resolved
E   in such a way as to make the statute less onerous for the general public and so as to cause less interference, than the more stringent sense would, with such rights and liberties as existing contractual obligations. I think that both these appeals should be allowed.

Appeals allowed.

F   Solicitors: *W. H. Thompson* (for the plaintiff Allen); *Bristows, Cooke & Carpmael* (for the defendants Thorn Electrical Industries, Ltd.); *Gaster & Turner* (for the plaintiff Griffin); *Lee, Bolton & Lee* (for the defendant Receiver for the Metropolitan Police District); *Treasury Solicitor.*

[*Reported by* F. GUTTMAN, ESQ., *Barrister-at-Law.*]

Re OLD WOOD COMMON COMPENSATION FUND. ARNETT *v.* MINISTER OF AGRICULTURE, FISHERIES AND FOOD AND OTHERS.

[CHANCERY DIVISION (Goff, J.), May 2, 1967.]

Practice—Originating summons—Continuance of proceedings as if begun by writ—Plaintiff seeking inquiry what common rights, and who commoners, were, and declarations regarding compensation fund—Plaintiff uncertain of his own legal position—Action to proceed as if begun by writ so that issues might be clarified—R.S.C., Ord. 28, r. 8.

The plaintiff applied to the court by originating summons issued in November, 1964, for a declaration that a sum of about £165, which represented compensation payable to commoners by reason of requisition of a common in the world war of 1939-1945, was held on trust for persons found to be entitled thereto in the proceedings instituted by the summons, and for determining whether the compensation was payable to the plaintiff, who claimed to have rights of common, among other persons. The plaintiff also sought an inquiry to ascertain who the present commoners were and the rights of common, and declaration of rights over the common. The plaintiff desired to add parties, and obtained leave to amend. On the question whether an order should be made under R.S.C., Ord. 28, r. 8*, contrary to the plaintiff's wish, that the action should proceed as if begun by writ,

Held: the plaintiff's legal position being uncertain, the issues should be clarified by pleadings and discovery and an order would be made that the proceedings should continue as if they were an action begun by writ not by originating summons (see p. 1149, letters H and I, post).

[As to rights of common of the lord of the manor and of commoners, see 5 HALSBURY'S LAWS (3rd Edn.) 348, 355, 362, paras. 800, 801, 816, 830; and as to when procedure by originating summons is appropriate, see 30 HALSBURY'S LAWS (3rd Edn.) 303, 304, para. 559.

For the Commons Registration Act 1965, see 45 HALSBURY'S STATUTES (2nd Edn.) 70.]

Case referred to:

> *Robertson* v. *Hartopp*, (1889), 43 Ch.D. 484; 59 L.J.Ch. 553; 62 L.T. 585; 11 Digest (Repl.) 42, *583*.

Adjourned summons.

The plaintiff, Wilfred Leonard Arnett, applied by originating summons dated Nov. 6, 1964, for certain relief, the relief first claimed being—

" 1. A declaration that the first defendant, the Minister of Agriculture, Fisheries and Food, holds a sum of money (hereinafter called " the compensation fund ") representing compensation payable in respect of the compulsory requisitioning under the provisions of the Defence Regulations, 1939, and the Agriculture (Miscellaneous War Provisions) Act, 1940, of a part of Old Wood Common in Worcestershire as trustee of the compensation fund on trust for the person or persons found to be entitled thereto in these proceedings."

The plaintiff applied by the summons also for further relief, as set out at p. 1147, letters G to I, and p. 1148, letter A, post. He applied subsequently to the master for leave to amend the summons by adding further defendants and by striking out certain paragraphs. Leave for these purposes was granted, and as to this there was no dispute. The master, however, further ordered, pursuant to R.S.C., Ord. 28, r. 8, that the action should proceed as if begun by writ. The originating summons was

---

* The terms of R.S.C., Ord. 28, r. 8 (1) are set out at p. 1140, letter C, post.

A adjourned on this point into court as a procedure summons at the request of the plaintiff.

E. H. W. *Christie* for the plaintiff.

G. W. *Seward* for the defendants.

GOFF, J.: This is a proceeding of a somewhat unusual nature, the purpose

B of which is to ascertain the nature and extent of the various rights of common over a common known as Old Wood Common in Worcestershire. The plaintiff claims to have rights of common as lord of the manor. He did at one time claim to be the owner of the common, but there seems to be some technical difficulties in the way of his establishing his title, and he does not at the moment, at all events, pursue that claim. At present his claim to have rights of common

C is not disputed, but he proposes to add other defendants, and I cannot say for certain whether they will admit or dispute his rights. However, he maintains that the common is being overgrazed and that that is the result of wrongful actions on the part of some persons who are either exercising rights of common, though they have none, or are using the common more extensively than they ought; but he does not know which persons are offending, or in what way.

D In argument, the plaintiff said that there being cogent evidence of overgrazing, it must follow that there was wrongful action on somebody's part, but I am not satisfied that that is so because I see that in *Robertson* v. *Hartopp* (1), to which my attention was drawn for another purpose, the common was being overgrazed by commoners who were apparently exercising lawful rights, although that state of affairs may have arisen in that case through the lord of the manor, or his

E mortgagees, wrongfully enclosing and digging up part of the common. Be that as it may, the plaintiff wishes to ascertain what competing rights there are.

During the war, and for a number of years thereafter, the common was requisitioned, as a result of which there is payable to the commoners a small sum of compensation which amounts to about £165. The plaintiff has fastened on that as one way of determining the question which he wishes to have decided.

F He has entitled the proceedings " In the matter of a compensation fund held by the Minister of Agriculture, Fisheries and Food ", and by the originating summons he asks for a declaration that the defendant Minister holds a sum of money, being the compensation money, as trustee on trust for the person or persons found to be entitled thereto in these proceedings. Then the plaintiff asks by his summons:

G "2. Whether the compensation fund is payable by the [Minister] as such trustee (a) to the plaintiff and such other persons as can show that they have subsisting rights of common upon Old Wood Common, and (b) if so payable to whom and in any and if so what proportions, or (c) is held upon some other and if so what trusts.

H "3. If the answers to questions 2 (a), (b) and (c) above or any of them indicate that Old Wood Common is subject to subsisting rights of common so as to entitle the commoners, if any, to a share in the compensation fund, and, if necessary, (a) an inquiry as to the persons who are commoners and the holdings in respect of which they are entitled to rights of common and the rights of common, if any, appurtenant thereto; (b) an inquiry as to the proportions, if any, in which such persons are entitled to share in the compensation fund; (c) all consequential and necessary directions as to the

I basis and form of such inquiry and in particular an order that no person . . .",

and then follow some words designed to preclude certain persons from being heard on the inquiry. Counsel for the plaintiff admits that that limitation may be too wide. Then independently of the fund the summons asks

(1) (1889), 43 Ch.D. 484.

A

" 4.   Such declarations as to the rights of the parties hereto other than the [Minister] in over or upon Old Wood Common as may be found upon inquiry to be just or as the plaintiff may be found entitled to upon the evidence in support of this application."

So far as the summons is founded on the compensation fund, it is to be observed that the decision would not technically, at any rate, resolve the question who are now entitled to rights of common, or what their rights are, because the only issue would be who was dispossessed by the requisition order.   It is clear, however, that any answer to that question must throw great light on the question who are now the commoners, as the rights of common of those dispossessed by the requisitioning would be appendant or appurtenant to some holding.

B

I was somewhat concerned whether proceedings would lie where the plaintiff does not come and say " I know what my rights are and certain persons are infringing them ", but comes and says " I do not know what my rights are but if they are ascertained by an inquiry it will then emerge that some person or persons are infringing them ".   In *Robertson* v. *Hartopp* (2), to which I have already referred, whilst the matter came to trial and an injunction was granted against the lord of the manor, an issue comparable with that which arises in the present case was dealt with by directing an inquiry to be conducted by a referee. I think that there is no objection to the proceedings on the ground of their inherent nature, but in any case there is no application to strike them out at this juncture.   So that is not a matter which I have to decide.

C

D

The plaintiff, however, wishes leave to amend, first, by adding further defendants, which the master granted, and as to which there is no dispute; and secondly to amend the originating summons by striking out certain paragraphs, which I did not read, which deal with the plaintiff's position as lord of the manor. Such leave was granted; indeed general leave to amend the originating summons was given, and again if the proceedings are to continue as proceedings by originating summons, no objection is taken to that leave.   An order was further made by the master, however, pursuant to R.S.C., Ord. 28, r. 8:

E

" that the action proceed as if begun by writ.   Leave to restore for directions as to pleadings and otherwise when all parties intended by the plaintiff to be added as defendants have been so added and have entered appearances or time for appearance has expired."

F

The plaintiff is dissatisfied with that, and the matter has therefore been adjourned into court as a procedure summons on that question.   A further objection was taken at one stage, or foreshadowed by the defendants, namely that this issue ought to be decided under the Commons Registration Act 1965 and that the proceedings should be stayed accordingly.   Counsel for the defendants has conceded that he cannot properly pursue that point, at any rate at this juncture, because of the question about the compensation moneys, if for no other reason, and therefore that point also is not before me.   He says however, that there is really no trust fund here at all, merely a debt.   The question is not on what trusts the fund is held or who are the beneficiaries under the trust but who are the creditors.   That, for what it is worth, is sound, but it does not necessarily mean that the proceedings should not continue under an originating summons with a view to an inquiry because the question who the creditors are depends on the major premise " who are, or were at the material time, the commoners ". Counsel has argued that this is a case which raises a serious dispute of fact, and that therefore it is convenient that the case should proceed as if it were a writ action.   He relies indirectly upon R.S.C., Ord. 5, r. 4 which says what proceedings are appropriate to be begun by originating summons.   R.S.C., Ord. 5, r. 4 (2) is in these terms:

G

H

I

" Proceedings—(a) in which the sole or principal question at issue is, or

A   is likely to be, one of the construction of an Act or of any instrument made
under an Act, or of any deed, will, contract or other document, or some
other question of law, or (*b*) in which there is unlikely to be any substantial
dispute of fact, are appropriate to be begun by originating summons . . .''

Conversely, so the argument runs, as in these proceedings there is likely to be a
substantial dispute of fact, they are not appropriate proceedings to be com-
B   menced or carried on by originating summons and therefore I ought, under
R.S.C., Ord. 28, r. 8 to direct that they proceed by writ. That rule provides:

" (1) Where, in the case of a cause or matter begun by originating summons, it appears to the court at any stage of the proceedings that the
proceedings should for any reason be continued as if the cause or matter
had been begun by writ, it may order the proceedings to continue as if the
C   cause or matter had been so begun and may, in particular, order that any
affidavits shall stand as pleadings, with or without liberty to any of the
parties to add thereto or to apply for particulars thereof."

I do not have to be satisfied that the proceedings were wrongly commenced by
originating summons, and indeed, with the exception of certain proceedings
D   which must be begun by writ, there is a general paragraph in R.S.C., Ord. 5,
r. 1 that, subject to the provisions of any Act and of the rules, proceedings may
be begun by writ, originating summons, motion or petition. I do have to consider, however, whether for any reason the proceedings should be continued as
if the matter had been begun by writ.

Counsel for the plaintiff's reply to that argument is that there will be serious
E   questions of fact at some stage but not at this stage. He says that the serious
dispute of fact will arise when one comes to the inquiry, and that the matter
should proceed to trial with a view to an order for an inquiry on the proceedings
as at present constituted, i.e., by originating summons; the issues can be clarified,
if need be, at the inquiry stage by points of claim and defence. I am not satisfied
that that is a sound answer. In the first place, so far as the so-called compensa-
F   tion fund is concerned, the form in which relief is sought is not simply to ask for
an inquiry and then some relief arising out of the inquiry, but to ask specific
questions, whether the compensation fund is payable to the plaintiff and such
other persons as can show that they have subsisting rights of common, and if so
payable to whom and in any and if so what proportions, or whether the fund is
held upon some other and if so what trusts. The inquiry is asked for only if the
G   answers to those questions indicate that the Old Wood Common is subject to
subsisting rights. That may be a matter of form but quite apart from that it is
difficult to say that the questions of fact must be confined to a later stage in the
action, particularly when there are other defendants to be added and one does
not know precisely what attitude they will adopt. However, be that as it may,
R.S.C., Ord. 28, r. 8 (1) says " should for any reason be continued ", and it
H   seems to me that, in this somewhat unusual application where the plaintiff says
" I do not really know what the position is ", the issues ought to be clarified as
early as possible, and that therefore there ought to be pleadings followed by
discovery based on the pleadings. The defendants will then have an opportunity of seeing precisely what is said against them and how far it is specific or
general, of considering whether they would wish to consent to or oppose an
I   inquiry, whether they wish to set up their own rights in defence, whether indeed
they may want to apply to strike out the whole or some part of the claim on the
footing that it discloses no cause of action or is embarrassing, and whether they
wish to claim particulars. In a case where the plaintiff's position is so uncertain
as this, it is eminently desirable that the matter should proceed as a writ action
and not by orginating summons.

In arriving at this conclusion I would point to one thing in particular. The
affidavit in support says that the common is wholly situate in Tenbury Foreign
and that the basis of the plaintiff's claim is on common rights appurtenant to

Manor Farm. The whole of Manor Farm is within Tenbury Foreign. Counsel for   A
the defendants tells me that there may be questions in this case whether the
rights are limited to Tenbury Foreign or whether they extend beyond the area
so described. He submits that that is wholly a question of law, but it seems to
me that it may well be a question in part of law and in part of fact. In any event,
there ought to be pleadings so as to show precisely why the plaintiff says that
the rights are limited to Tenbury Foreign and exactly what Tenbury Foreign is.   B

For these reasons it seems to me that this is a case where proceedings should
continue as if they had been begun by writ, and I therefore make the same order
as was proposed to be made by the master (3).

Order accordingly.

Solicitors: *L. Dawson & Co.* (for the plaintiff); *Bower, Cotton & Bower*,
agents for *Norris & Miles*, Tenbury (for the defendants).   C

[*Reported by* JENIFER SANDELL, *Barrister-at-Law.*]

D

Re WILLIAM HALL (CONTRACTORS), LTD.

[CHANCERY DIVISION (Plowman, J.), May 23, 24, 25, June 2, 1967.]

*Company—Winding-up—Fraudulent preference—Memoranda of deposit of title
deeds to secure indebtedness to bank—Undertaking therein to execute legal
mortgage as required by bank—Shortly before company went into creditors'
voluntary winding-up bank required company to execute legal charges—*   E
*Proviso in each of legal charges that bank could determine what part of total
liability to bank should be deemed secured by legal charge and what part not
so secured—Whether a fraudulent preference—Companies Act, 1948 (11 & 12
Geo. 6 c. 38), s. 320.*

Mortgage—Sale—Appropriation of proceeds of sale—Secured creditor of company   F
*in creditors' voluntary winding-up realised security and appropriated pro-
ceeds to satisfying non-preferential part of company's indebtedness—Secured
creditor, a bank, also creditor for preferential indebtedness in respect of
moneys advanced — Whether appropriation valid against liquidators—
Companies Act, 1948 (11 & 12 Geo. 6 c. 38), s. 319 (4).*

On May 8, 1951, W.H. (Contractors), Ltd. (" the company "), executed   G
four memoranda of deposit of title deeds in favour of Lloyds Bank, Ltd.
(" the bank "), each charging a different property with payment to the
bank on demand of the company's indebtedness, but in all other material
respects each was in the same form and each was to cover indebtedness up
to £1,500. Clause 3 provided that when required by the bank, the company
would execute a legal mortgage of the premises, and cl. 4 provided that the
mortgage or charge should authorise the exercise of the statutory power   H
of sale without notice. Each memorandum was duly registered under
s. 95 of the Companies Act, 1948, on May 25, 1951.

On Jan. 9, 1964, when the company was on the brink of liquidation, the
bank demanded payment under all four memoranda, and at the same time
sent round to the company for execution four charges by way of legal
mortgage, which the company executed on Jan. 10. Clause 8 of each legal   I
charge contained a proviso (ii) whereby if the total liability of the company
exceeded the maximum limit the bank might conclusively determine what

---

(3) The order made by the master was as follows: " ORDER pursuant to R.S.C.,
Ord. 28 r. 8 that the action proceed as if begun by writ. Leave to restore for directions as to pleadings and otherwise when all parties intended by the plaintiff to be added
as defendants have been so added and have entered appearances or the time for
appearance has expired."

A   part of such total liability not exceeding the limit aforesaid should be
deemed secured by the deed and what part or parts thereof should be deemed
not so secured.   These legal charges were not registered under s. 95 of the
Act of 1948.   On Feb. 4, 1964, the company went into a creditors' voluntary
liquidation and joint liquidators were appointed.   At that date the company
was indebted to the bank in the sum of £7,921 15s. 6d.   Of that sum £2,274

B   1s. 7d. was preferential under s. 319 (4) of the Act of 1948, and the balance
of £5,647 13s. 11d. non-preferential.   In July the bank, in exercise of its
power of sale as mortgagees, sold all the properties comprised in the four
legal charges for £5,779 19s.   The bank appropriated this sum first in
discharge of the non-preferential part of its total claim, i.e., £5,647 13s. 11d.,
leaving a surplus of £132 5s. 1d. available in part satisfaction of the bank's

C   preferential claim, thereby reducing that claim to £2,141 16s. 6d.   The
company's assets were sufficient to pay its preferential debts in full, but
there would be a large deficiency as regards its ordinary unsecured creditors.
         On Dec. 15, 1964, the bank lodged a proof for the balance, £2,141 16s. 6d.,
of its preferential debt.   The liquidators rejected the proof on the ground
that the bank was not entitled to appropriate the proceeds of sale so as to

D   satisfy wholly the non-preferential indebtedness, and alternatively alleged
that the legal charges were invalid as fraudulent preferences.
         Held: (i) the bank was entitled to appropriate the proceeds of sale of
the mortgaged properties to paying the non-preferential part of the company's indebtedness to the bank (see p. 1159, letter E, post).
         Ex p. Hunter ((1801), 6 Ves. 94), *Re Medley, Ex p. Glyn* ((1840), 1 Mont.

E   D. & De G. 25), *Re Bulmer, Ex p. Johnson* ((1853), 3 De G. M. & G. 218),
Re Foster, Ex p. Dickin ((1875), L.R. 20 Eq. 767) and *Re Fox & Jacobs* ([1894]
1 Q.B. 438) followed.
         (ii) the company's intention in executing the legal charges was to carry
out its pre-existing obligation under the memoranda of deposit, and accordingly their execution, notwithstanding the terms of proviso (ii) to cl. 8 of

F   each of the legal charges, did not amount to a fraudulent preference of the
bank within s. 320 of the Companies Act, 1948 (see p. 1159, letter G, post).

         [As to proof by secured creditors, see 6 HALSBURY'S LAWS (3rd Edn.) 668,
669, para. 1322, and 2 ibid., 498, 499, para. 985; and for cases on the subject,
see 4 DIGEST (Repl.) 411, *3667-3674.*

G   As to the application of moneys received by a mortgagee generally, see 27
HALSBURY'S LAWS (3rd Edn.) 428, para. 844; and for cases on the subject, see
35 DIGEST (Repl.) 714, 715, *3815-3823.*
         As to appropriation by creditors of payments to them, see 8 HALSBURY'S
LAWS (3rd Edn.) 216, 217, para. 368.
         For the Companies Act, 1948, s. 319 (4), s. 320, see 3 HALSBURY'S STATUTES

H   (2nd Edn.) 700, 702.]

Cases referred to:
         Arkley, Ex p., (1791), Cooke's Bankrupt Laws (5th Edn.), p. 126.
         Bonacino, Re, Ex p. Discount Banking Co., (1894), 1 Mans. 59; 4 Digest
               (Repl.) 412, *3684.*
         Bulmer, Re, Ex p. Johnson, (1853), 3 De G.M. & G. 218; 22 L.J.Bcy. 65;

I   21 L.T.O.S. 109; 43 E.R. 86; 4 Digest (Repl.) 411, *3667.*
         Cunard Steamship Co., Ltd. v. *Hopwood,* [1908] 2 Ch. 564; 77 L.J.Ch. 785;
               99 L.T. 549; 10 Digest (Repl.) 813, *5278.*
         Foster, Re, Ex p. Dickin, (1875), L.R. 20 Eq. 767; 44 L.J.Bcy. 113; 33 L.T. 37;
               4 Digest (Repl.) 411, *3669.*
         Fox & Jacobs, Re, Ex p. Discount Banking Co. of England and Wales, [1894]
               1 Q.B. 438; 63 L.J.Q.B. 191; 69 L.T. 657; 4 Digest (Repl.) 412, *3686.*
         Havard, Ex p., (1790), Cooke's Bankrupt Laws (5th Edn.), p. 124.
         Hunter, Ex p., (1801), 6 Ves. 94; 31 E.R. 955; 4 Digest (Repl.) 411, *3671.*

London, Windsor and Greenwich Hotels Co., Re., Quartermaine's Case, [1892]   A
1 Ch. 639; 61 L.J.Ch. 273; 66 L.T. 19; 10 Digest (Repl.) 1002, *6880*.

Mason, Re, Ex p. Sharp, (1844), 3 Mont. D. & De G. 490; 4 Digest (Repl.)
411, *3673*.

Medley, Re, Ex p. Glyn, (1840), 1 Mont. D. & De G. 25; 4 Digest (Repl.)
488, *4292*.

Morel (E. J.) (1934), Ltd., Re, [1961] 1 All E.R. 796; [1962] Ch. 21; [1961]   B
3 W.L.R. 57; Digest (Cont. Vol. A) 50, *915a*.

Savin, Re, (1872), 7 Ch. App. 760; 42 L.J.Bcy. 14; 27 L.T. 466; 4 Digest
(Repl.) 412, *3685*.

Thompson v. Hudson, (1871), 6 Ch. App. 320; 24 L.T. 301; 12 Digest (Repl.)
544, *4129*.

Young v. English, (1843), 7 Beav. 10; 13 L.J.Ch. 76; 49 E.R. 965; 35 Digest   C
(Repl.) 715, *3821*.

Adjourned Summons.

This was an application by Lloyds Bank, Ltd. (" the bank ") by originating
summons dated Dec. 10, 1965, against Walter Matthewson and John Stanley
Armstrong, the joint liquidators of William Hall (Contractors), Ltd. (" the company "), a company in voluntary liquidation, whereby the bank, who claimed to   D
be a creditor of the company, sought an order reversing the decision of the joint
liquidators (contained in a notice dated Nov. 6, 1965) rejecting the proof of debt
of the bank (sworn on Dec. 15, 1964) wherein was claimed a sum of £2,141 16s. 6d.
as ranking preferentially for dividend under s. 319 (4) of the Companies Act, 1948.
The notice of rejection intimated that the liquidators were willing to admit the
said proof for dividend only as an unsecured debt or alternatively partly as a   E
preferential debt and partly as an unsecured debt, according to the proportions
indicated in the notice (see p. 1154, letter I, to p. 1155, letter A, post). Further,
the notice of rejection alleged that a cl. 8 proviso (ii) of the bank's legal charges,
all of which were in similar form, was invalid as against the liquidators as a
fraudulent preference. The facts are set out in the judgment.

The cases noted below* were cited during the argument in addition to those   F
referred to in the judgment.

Raymond Walton, Q.C., and *M. W. Jacomb* for the bank.
Muir Hunter, Q.C., and *David Graham* for the liquidators.

Cur. adv. vult.

June 2.   **PLOWMAN, J.**, read the following judgment: The question in   G
this case is whether, in the liquidation of a company, a secured creditor who has
realised his security for less than the total amount of his debt, part of which is
preferential, can appropriate the proceeds of sale to that part of his debt which
is not preferential, so as to leave his preferential claim unaffected.

It arises in this way. The company, William Hall (Contractors) Ltd., banked   H
at the Gateshead branch of Lloyds Bank, Ltd. On May 8, 1951, the company
executed four memoranda of deposit of title deeds in favour of the bank. Each
charged a different property at " Two Ball Lonnen ", Newcastle-upon-Tyne, with
the payment to the bank on demand of the company's indebtedness; but in all
other material respects each was in the same form, a printed bank form, identified
as S.3 (1936). The memoranda contained the following clauses: I

---

* *Ex p. Cawthorne*, (1815), 19 Ves. 260; *Seaton v. Twyford*, (1870), L.R. 11 Eq. 591;
Whitley v. Challis, [1892] 1 Ch. 64; *Farmer v. Pitt*, [1902] 1 Ch. 954; *Cornbrook Brewery
Co., Ltd. v. Law Debenture Corpn., Ltd.*, [1903] 2 Ch. 527; *affd.* C.A., [1904] 1 Ch. 103;
Re Johnson Johnson, [1904] 1 K.B. 134; *Seymour v. Pickett*, [1905] 1 K.B. 715; *Re
Johns, Worrell v. Johns*, [1928] All E.R. Rep. 662; [1928] Ch. 737; *Re Drabble Brothers*,
[1930] All E.R. Rep. 450; [1930] 2 Ch. 211; *Peat v. Gresham Trust, Ltd.*, [1934] All E.R.
Rep. 82; [1934] A.C. 252; *Re M. Kushler, Ltd.*, [1943] 2 All E.R. 22; [1943] Ch. 248;
Re Baker, [1954] 2 All E.R. 790; *Re Cutts (a bankrupt)*, [1956] 2 All E.R. 537; *Re White
Rose Cottage*, [1965] 1 All E.R. 11; [1965] Ch. 940; *Re Eric Holmes (Property), Ltd.*,
[1965] 2 All E.R. 333; [1965] Ch. 1052; *Re Trabrice, Ltd.*, (1967), unreported

A   " 3. I undertake that when required by the bank I or my representatives and all other necessary parties will at my own expense or at the expense of my estate execute to the bank or as they shall direct a legal mortgage of (or in the case of registered land a registered first charge upon) the premises comprised in the said deeds and writings or such other mortgage or charge as the bank may require upon my interest in the premises including my

B   vendor's lien in the event of any such sale as aforesaid but such legal or other mortgage or charge shall not merge or extinguish the charge hereby created.

" 4. Such mortgage or charge shall authorise the exercise of any statutory power of sale without notice at any time and without any such demand as aforesaid and shall contain all usual clauses for the benefit of the bank as

C   the bank may reasonably require.

" 6. The total amount recoverable hereunder shall not exceed £1,500 (in addition to (i) interest thereon at the current rate from six months prior to the date of demand for repayment of the money and liabilities hereby secured, and (ii) any money advanced for the purposes set out in s. 88 (3) of the Stamp Act, 1891, and (iii) costs), but so that the limit hereby imposed

D   shall not apply to or prejudice the full enforcement of any liability of mine or of my estate to the bank independently of this present memorandum."

On May 25, 1951, particulars of the four memoranda of deposit were duly registered under s. 95 of the Companies Act, 1948 (1).   On Jan. 9, 1964, when the company was on the brink of liquidation, the bank demanded payment under all

E   four instruments and called on the company to execute legal mortgages pursuant to their agreement.   At the same time the bank sent round to the company for execution four legal charges in the usual bank printed form then current.   These were executed by the company on the following day, Jan. 10.   Each of the four legal charges contained in cl. 1 a covenant by the company with the bank to pay and in cl. 2 a charge by way of legal mortgage; and then in cl. 8 there was

F   the following provision:

" The total amount recoverable hereunder shall not exceed £1,500 (in addition to (i) interest thereon at the current rate from six months prior to the date of demand for repayment of the money and liabilities hereby secured, and (ii) any money advanced for the purposes set out in s. 88 (3)

G   of the Stamp Act, 1891, and (iii) costs):   PROVIDED that—(i) the aforesaid limit of recoverability shall not in any way prejudice or affect any right of the bank independently of this deed to recover the total sum due from the [company] on any such account or in any such manner as hereinbefore mentioned or any excess of such total sum over and above the limit aforesaid.   (ii) If the total liability of the [company] exceeds the said limit the

H   bank may conclusively determine what part of such total liability not exceeding the limit aforesaid shall be deemed secured by this deed and what part or parts thereof shall be deemed not so secured."

These legal charges were not registered under s. 95 of the Companies Act, 1948, the bank taking the view that registration was unnecessary, having regard to the decision in *Cunard Steamship Co., Ltd.* v. *Hopwood* (2).

I   On Feb. 4, 1964, the company went into a creditors' voluntary liquidation, and the two respondents to this summons, Mr. Matthewson and Mr. Armstrong, were appointed joint liquidators.   At that date the company was indebted to the bank in the sum of £7,921 15s. 6d.   It is common ground that of that sum the sum of

---

(1) For s. 95 of the Companies Act, 1948, see 3 HALSBURY'S STATUTES (2nd Edn.), p. 533.

(2) [1908] 2 Ch. 564.

£2,274 1s. 7d. is preferential under s. 319 (4) of the Companies Act, 1948 (3), the A
balance of £5,647 13s. 11d. being non-preferential.

In July, 1964, the bank, in exercise of its power of sale as mortgagees, sold all
the properties comprised in the four legal charges for the sum of £5,779 19s. net.
The bank claims to appropriate this sum of £5,779 19s. first in discharge of the
non-preferential part of its total claim, that is to say the sum of £5,647 13s. 11d.
This leaves a surplus of £132 5s. 1d. available in part satisfaction of the bank's B
preferential claim, thereby reducing that claim to £2,141 16s. 6d. I should add
that the company's assets are sufficient for payment of all its preferential debts
in full, but that there will be a large deficiency as regards its ordinary unsecured
creditors.

On Dec. 15, 1964, the bank lodged a proof for the sum of £2,141 16s. 6d., and
in para. 1 of the affidavit in support of that proof the bank official who swore C
it says this:

" That the company was at the date of the commencement of the winding
up, Feb. 4, 1964, and still is, justly and truly indebted to Lloyds Bank, Ltd.,
in the sum of £2,141 16s. 6d., for moneys advanced and for interest accrued
due thereon and for commission and other usual bankers charges."
D
That statement is perhaps not completely accurate because, while it is true that
the company was indebted to the bank in the sum of £2,141 16s. 6d., that was
not the whole sum for which the company was indebted. Then the deponent
goes on to say

" for which sum or any part thereof I say that I have not, nor hath
Lloyds Bank, Ltd. or any person by their order, to my knowledge or belief, E
for their use, had or received any manner of satisfaction or security
whatsoever."

Then in the particulars of account annexed to that affidavit there appears the
following against the date February, 1964:

" Balance of overdrawn banking account of William Hall (Contractors),
Ltd., at Lloyds Bank, Ltd., Gateshead branch as at the date of the appoint- F
ment of a liquidator £7,921 15s. 6d. *Less* net proceeds of the sale of freehold properties known as Two Ball Lonnen, Newcastle £5,779 19s. showing
a balance of £2,141 16s. 6d."

against which there are the words " All of which is claimed as preferential for
wages." On Nov. 6, 1965, the liquidators rejected that proof, and by their
notice of rejection they say:
G
" We have this day [Nov. 6, 1965] rejected your proof of debt . . . and
we are only willing to admit the said proof for dividend as an unsecured
debt, *alternatively* as a proof partly for a preferential debt and partly for an
ordinary unsecured debt as hereinafter appears. And take notice that the
following are the grounds of our said rejection: 1. You have appropriated H
the nett proceeds of the freehold properties held by you as security for all
the indebtedness of the company, in satisfaction first of the whole of the
company's ordinary unsecured indebtedness to you, viz., £5,647 13s. 11d.
and you have only appropriated the balance thereof, namely, £132 5s. 1d.,
towards your said preferential indebtedness [it is common ground that that
is what the bank had done]. 2. Such appropriation is erroneous in point of I
law and is prejudicial to the interests of the general body of creditors.
3. You are under a duty to appropriate the said nett proceeds of sale of your
security (a) in satisfaction first of the whole of the company's said aggregate
preferential indebtedness of £2,274 1s. 7d. and only as to the balance
remaining, viz., £3,505 17s. 5d., towards the company's ordinary unsecured
indebtedness, leaving you an ordinary unsecured creditor for £2,141 16s. 6d.

(3) For s. 319 (4) of the Companies Act, 1948, see 3 HALSBURY'S STATUTES (2nd Edn.),
p. 700.

A   *Alternatively* (b) by apportioning the same between the company's aggregate preferential indebtedness and its ordinary indebtedness, according to the following formula: Preferential=£2,274 1s. 7d. over £7,921 15s. 6d., multiplied by £5,779 19s.=£1,659 4s. 8d., leaving you a preferential creditor for £614 16s. 11d. and an ordinary unsecured creditor for £1,526 19s. 7d."

B   Then para. 4 of the notice of rejection in the form in which it was amended during the hearing before me, is as follows:

" 4. In so far as you seek to justify your said appropriation of the whole of the said nett proceeds of sale of the security to the ordinary unsecured indebtedness of the company by virtue of the terms of four mortgages granted to you by the company each dated Jan. 10, 1964, (i) the said
C   mortgages were not duly registered pursuant to s. 95 of the Companies Act, 1948; further or alternatively (ii) the company executed the said mortgages in circumstances which amounted to a fraudulent preference of yourselves within the meaning of s. 320 of the said Act, and the said mortgages are accordingly invalid against us as liquidators, and do not confer on you any such right of appropriation as you contend for and the same are accordingly
D   void against ourselves as liquidators."

On Dec. 10, 1965, the bank issued the summons which is now before me and by which the bank asks for—

" An order that the decision of the said joint liquidators contained in notice dated Nov. 6, 1965, rejecting the proof of debt of the applicant Lloyds Bank, Ltd. sworn on Dec. 15, 1964, in the voluntary winding-up of
E   the above named company wherein is claimed the sum of £2,141 16s. 6d. ranking preferentially for dividend under s. 319 (4) of the above mentioned Act, and stating that they are only willing to admit the said proof for dividend as an unsecured debt or alternatively partly as a preferential debt and partly as an unsecured debt, may be reversed, and that the whole of the said sum may be admitted for dividend as a debt ranking preferentially under
F   the said s. 319 (4)."

Counsel for the bank puts its case in three ways. First, he submits that there is a general principle of law, on which the bank is entitled to rely, to the effect that a secured creditor is entitled to apply his security in discharge of whatever liability of his debtor that he may think fit. In pursuance of this right, the bank says
G   that it is entitled to appropriate the proceeds of sale of the mortgaged properties in the first place in discharge of its non-preferential claim, leaving it free to prove for the whole of the preferential part of its claim, less the small surplus from the proceeds of sale.

Secondly, counsel submits that in the alternative the bank had an equitable right to make this appropriation. The steps in this argument are these. First,
H   the agreement to give a legal mortgage was at all material times specifically enforceable; secondly, on a decree of specific performance the bank would have been entitled to a legal mortgage containing the provision which is in fact contained in cl. 8 (ii) of the legal charges which were executed, and such provision was therefore always implicit in the memoranda of deposit; thirdly, that provision confers an express right to appropriate in the manner in which the bank
I   seeks to appropriate.

Thirdly, counsel submits that in the further alternative the bank has an express right to make the appropriation under cl. 8, proviso (ii) itself. The advantage to the bank of its second submission over its third is that it obviates any difficulty or argument which might otherwise arise by reason of the non-registration of the legal charges.

In reply to counsel for the bank's first submission, counsel for the liquidators disputes the existence of any such general principle as that on which the bank relies, or, more accurately perhaps, he contends that if any such statement of law is to be found in the cases, it is so hedged about with exceptions and qualifica- **A** tions that it cannot be exalted to the status of a general proposition.

I turn, therefore, to the authorities. The foundation for counsel for the bank's submission was the case of *Ex p. Hunter* (4), which was decided by LORD ELDON, L.C., in the year 1801, when the law as to what debts were provable in a bankruptcy and what were not differed from the law on that subject today. The headnote to that case is as follows (4): **B**

> " Though unliquidated damages cannot be proved under a commission of bankruptcy, yet, if the demand is partly of that nature, and partly liquidated, as the difference of price upon a re-sale, the creditor, having a security, may apply it first to the former, then to the latter, and may prove the residue. Lien under the usual condition at an auction, that, if the vendee should fail to complete his purchase, the vendor should be at **C** liberty to re-sell, and the vendee pay the expenses and make good the deficiency, etc."

The facts in that case were these. Vendors sold certain estates by auction to one Jenkins for £4,670. Jenkins failed to complete and the vendors put the property up for sale by auction again. Jenkins again became the purchaser at the same figure and again failed to complete. The conditions of sale provided that if the **D** purchaser failed to comply with the conditions, the deposit should be forfeited, and that the vendors should be at liberty to resell and recover from the purchaser any deficiency together with all expenses. Jenkins then went bankrupt, and the vendors resold for £2,950. It is stated (5):

> " The petitioners attempted to prove a debt of £1,349 11s. 4d. in respect of the difference upon the re-sale and the expenses; including the following **E** articles: Auctioneer's charges upon the re-sale £70 11s.; interest £99 11s. 7d.; auctioneers' charge £44 10s.; moiety of auction duty £36 17s. 6d; solicitor's charges £30 18s. 6d. The amount of the deposits, and £200 paid by Jenkins on account, were deducted from the proof. The commissioners rejecting the proof, the prayer of the petition was, that they might be ordered to receive **F** it."

LORD ELDON, in the course of his judgment, said this (6):

> " This is a sale under a contract for the purchase of an estate; by which the purchaser became owner of the estate and the seller parted with it. The condition, in case the purchaser should fail to complete his contract, that there shall be a re-sale, and the purchaser shall make good the loss **G** and answer the expenses, forms a lien upon the estate for the purchase-money. It is in some respects like a mortgaged estate, sold to pay the mortgage-money: and the residue is the debt to be proved; but, strictly speaking, it is not in the nature of a mortgage; for if the second sale produced more than the original purchase-money, the purchaser, who had violated his agreement, could not call for an account of the surplus; or if **H** he was really a mortgagor: but the vendor contracts for this; that if the second sale produces less, he shall be considered as a mortgagee; and shall be a creditor for the rest. With respect to the objection to this proof, the difference between the sums produced by these sales is a clear liquidated debt. As to some items of the account, I agree, they could not be proved: but considering the equity of the vendors, they may have the effect by a **I** circuitous mode. I remember an instance of a mortgage made as an indemnity against acceptances of cash advanced by the mortgagee. Some of the bills had been paid before the bankruptcy: but he was under acceptances of bills floating at the time of the bankruptcy, which were not capable of being proved: but he had a right to model his security; applying it first to those bills, which he could not prove. Upon the authority of those cases

(4) (1801), 6 Ves. 94.   (5) (1801), 6 Ves. at p. 95.

(6) (1801), 6 Ves. at pp. 97, 98.

A then the vendors in this case have a right to apply the sum, produced by the last sale, first in payment of those articles, which it is just they should receive, but which they could not prove under the bankruptcy; and those articles being taken out of that sum will leave the sum capable of being proved. In that circuitous way therefore they are entitled to prove."

B The next case in this line of authority is *Re Medley, Ex p. Glyn* (7) which was decided in the year 1840 in the Court of Review. The head-note to that case is this:

" One of two bankrupts, W.M. [that was William Medley] being a partner in another firm of M. & S. [Medley & Scott] gave a security to the petitioners for any monies that might become due, either from the house of the bank-
C rupts, or from the firm of M. & S. Held, that the proceeds of the security might be applied, first in discharge of the debt due from the firm of M. & S.".".

In that case it was argued on behalf of the petition, that is to say on behalf of the secured creditors, as follows (8):

" The estate of William Medley was security for the payment of any debts, which might become due either from himself, or from him and A. O.
D Medley [that was the other bankrupt] or from Medley and Scott. It has been decided, that where a creditor has two debts owing by a bankrupt, the one proveable and the other not proveable, he may model any security which he holds, first in liquidation of the unproveable debt, and then of the proveable one, and may prove the residue of the latter debt against the estate of the bankrupt; *Ex p. Hunter* (9). The same doctrine had been also
E previously held in *Ex p. Havard* (10). We say, therefore, that all the monies, which have been realized from the security given by William Medley, should first be applied in discharge of the debt due to the petitioners from Medley and Scott.   The surety cannot interfere, until his entire obligation is discharged."

F That argument appears to have been accepted by the court, because the judgment is reported as follows (11):

" No right of appropriation by the assignees, on behalf of the estate of the surety, can arise, until the whole debt is paid. The equities due to the separate estate of William Medley will be best preserved, by allowing this fund to be appropriated to the debt due from Medley and Scott, for which the
G separate estate of William Medley is liable."

The third case was in the year 1853 and is the case of *Re Bulmer, Ex p. Johnson* (12). I do not propose to go into the facts of that case, but it is important as showing that *Ex p. Hunter* (13) was regarded as laying down a general principle. The headnote states this, among other things (12):

H " The general doctrine is, that a creditor holding a security is entitled to apply it in discharge of whatever liability of the bankrupt debtor he may think fit."

That is a reproduction of what LORD CRANWORTH, L.C., said (14), and I propose to refer only to a very short passage. LORD CRANWORTH said (14):

I " The question must therefore be dealt with on the footing of there being in the existing state of things no special agreement regulating the appro-
priation of the fund; and in such a case the doctrine of the court is clear, that the creditor holding a security is entitled to apply it in discharge of whatever liability of the bankrupt he may think fit.   The authorities

(7) (1840), 1 Mont. D. & De G. 25.   (8) (1840), 1 Mont. D. & De G. at p. 27.
(9) (1801), 6 Ves. 94.   (10) (1790), COOKE'S BANKRUPT LAWS (5th Edn.), p. 124.
(11) (1840), 1 Mont. D. & De G. at p. 28.   (12) (1853), 3 De G.M. & G. 218.
(13) (1801), 6 Ves. 94.   (14) (1853), 3 De G.M. & G. at p. 235.

referred to on this subject in the argument are conclusive; I allude particu-   **A**
larly to the case of *Ex p. Hunter* (15) and to the two cases of *Ex p. Havard* (16)
and *Ex p. Arkley* (17)."

The fourth case referred to by counsel for the bank was the case of *Re Foster,
Ex p. Dickin* (18). I again cite the case for the statement of general principle.
The headnote is as follows (18):

     B

" A creditor of two partners was also a creditor of one of the partners
separately and the title deeds of separate estate of that partner were
deposited with him to secure both the joint and the separate debts. The two
partners filed a joint liquidation petition, and the partner whose separate
estate was mortgaged also filed a separate liquidation petition. The
security having been realised: Held, that the creditor was entitled to appor-   **C**
tion the produce of the realisation between his joint and separate debts in
whatever way was most for his advantage, and that, to enable him to exercise this option, he was entitled to apply to the court, under s. 104 of the
Bankruptcy Act, 1869, to have a dividend on the joint estate declared before
the declaration of a dividend on the separate estate."

Sir James Bacon, C.J., had this to say (19):   **D**

" The case is not incumbered by any sort of difficulty. Nothing is more
clear than the law upon this subject, that a creditor who has a security which
he has a right to apply to one or other of two debts due to him, can exercise
that right in any way he thinks fit."

The words that I have just quoted " which he has a right to apply to one or   **E**
other of two debts due to him ", mean, I think, no more than this, that the
creditor cannot appropriate the security to a debt which is not covered by it;
and that is a proposition which counsel for the bank does not seek to challenge.

Finally on this part of the case counsel for the bank referred to *Re Fox &
Jacobs, Ex p. Discount Banking Co. of England and Wales* (20). I will read the
headnote, which must now be read subject to s. 66 of the Bankruptcy Act, 1914.
It is as follows (20):   **F**

" Section 23 of the Bankruptcy Act, 1890—which provides that where a
debt has been proved upon a debtor's estate with interest, such interest shall
for the purposes of dividend be calculated at a rate not exceeding five per
cent. per annum—does not prevent a secured creditor, who has realised or
assessed the value of his security, from allocating such value in discharge   **G**
of the interest, even although such interest is at a higher rate than five per
cent. per annum, and proving for the principal or balance of principal due
to him."

Counsel for the secured creditor argued thus (21):

" A secured creditor is entitled to allocate the assessed value of his
security in whatever way he pleases: *Ex p. Hunter* (15); *Re Medley, Ex p.*   **H**
Glyn (22); the Bankruptcy Act, 1883, Sch. 2, rr. 9 and 11. The company,
therefore, were entitled to allocate the £150 to the interest due to them,
although the rate was above five per cent., and to prove for the balance of
principal . . ."

Vaughan Williams, J., referred to this matter at the end of his judgment, where   **I**
he said this (23):

" I have only to add that the general right of a secured creditor to
allocate his security to that part of his debt in respect to which he had no

---

(15) (1801), 6 Ves. 94.   (16) (1790), Cooke's Bankrupt Laws (5th Edn.), p. 124.
(17) (1791), Cooke's Bankrupt Laws (5th Edn.), p. 126.
(18) (1875), L.R. 20 Eq. 767.   (19) (1875), L.R. 20 Eq. at p. 769.
(20) [1894] 1 Q.B. 438.   (21) [1894] 1 Q.B. at pp. 439, 440.
(22) (1840), 1 Mont. D. & De G. 25.   (23) [1894] 1 Q.B. at p. 442.

A   right of proof was not disputed by the counsel for the trustee. *Ex p. Hunter* (24) and *Re Medley, Ex p. Glyn* (25) are authorities under former statutes for this proposition."

Now, with that citation of authority extending over nearly a century, counsel for the bank has in my judgment made good his general proposition. In the cases
B   which were cited by counsel for the liquidators that general proposition, as far as I can see, was never challenged. I will mention some of the cases. *Re Savin* (26), *Re London, Windsor and Greenwich Hotels Co., Quartermaine's Case* (27) and *Re Bonacino, Ex p. Discount Banking Co.* (28) decided that a secured creditor could not use his security to satisfy a debt for which, in the absence of a surplus, he could not prove at all, namely interest after bankruptcy. Here, however,
C   there is no doubt that the bank has a right to prove for the balance of its debt; the only question is whether it can do so as a preferential creditor. *Re Mason, Ex p. Sharp* (29), and *Young v. English* (30), were cases in which the court inferred from the circumstances an intention by a debtor who made a payment to his creditor to appropriate that payment in a particular way. In the present case, the debtor made no payment to the creditor. *Thompson v. Hudson* (31) was a case in which it was held as a matter of construction that the parties had agreed
D   to a particular appropriation. *Re E. J. Morel (1934), Ltd.* (32) was a case concerning s. 31 of the Bankruptcy Act, 1914, and had nothing to do with the rights of a secured creditor.

I can see nothing in these cases which prevents the bank from appropriating the proceeds of the properties which it has sold to the non-preferential part of its debt, and I hold that in doing so it has done what it was in law entitled to do.
E   This makes it unnecessary for me to consider the validity of counsel for the bank's alternative submissions, but there is one matter involving questions of fact on which I should state my conclusion in case this matter should go further. Counsel for the liquidators submitted that if (contrary to my opinion) the bank were wrong on the first point, the provision contained in cl. 8, proviso (ii) of the legal charges amounted to a fraudulent preference of the bank and is accordingly
F   void under s. 320 of the Companies Act, 1948. I reject this submission and find as a fact that the benefit of that provision was not given to the bank with a view to giving it a preference. In my judgment the company's intention in executing the legal charges was simply to carry out its pre-existing obligation under the memoranda of deposit. In these circumstances, I make an order in the terms of the summons (33).
G

Order accordingly.

Solicitors: *Cameron, Kemm, Nordon & Co.* (for the bank); *Gush, Phillips, Walters & Williams*, agents for *John J. Neesham & Co.*, Newcastle-upon-Tyne (for the liquidators).

[*Reported by* JACQUELINE METCALFE, *Barrister-at-Law.*]
H

I   (24) (1801), 6 Ves. 94.
(25) (1840), 1 Mont. D. & De G. 25.
(26) (1872), 7 Ch. App. 760.
(27) [1892] 1 Ch. 639.
(28) (1894), 1 Mans. 59.
(29) (1844), 3 Mont. D. & De G. 490.
(30) (1843), 7 Beav. 10.
(31) (1871), 6 Ch. App. 320.
(32) [1961] 1 All E.R. 796; [1962] Ch. 21.
(33) See p. 1155, letter D, ante.

Re LEEK (*deceased*). DARWEN *v.* LEEK AND OTHERS.   A

[CHANCERY DIVISION (Buckley, J.), April 6, 7, 28, 1967.]

Trust and Trustee—Uncertainty—Discretionary trust—Power of selection, bare power not coupled with duty to select—Class of beneficiaries including persons considered to have moral claim on deceased—Impracticability of ascertaining beneficiaries—Power exercisable on several occasions and thus possibly beyond perpetuity limit—Whether void for uncertainty or perpetuity—Trust of proceeds of endowment assurance under pension scheme—Whether resulting trust for deceased.

L., who was managing director of a company arranged for the company to effect at its own cost an endowment assurance policy on his life providing for payment of £18,807 on his death before attaining sixty-five; the arrangement included a term that his salary should be reduced by £1,000 per annum, which was the amount of the yearly premium on the policy. The arrangement was recorded in a letter dated Dec. 1, 1956, which stated that the policy would be expressed as being effected by the company as trustee for L. and held in trust subject to the conditions set out in the letter. These conditions included provision for L. being deprived of benefit in certain eventualities, e.g., if he left the company's employment of his own free will. The letter provided that the policy moneys on the death of L. should be held by the company on trust (referred to as " the first trust ") for the benefit " of such one or more of the following persons as the company in its absolute discretion shall decide namely [L.'s] wife, children or other issue or such other persons that the company may consider to have a moral claim upon [L.] ", or on trust (referred to as " the second trust ") " failing them upon trust for the benefit of such one or more of the statutory next-of-kin in both cases in such shares and in such manner as the company in its absolute discretion shall decide ". The policy was effected in September, 1957; and in November, 1957, L. made a will whereby he appointed the plaintiff his executor and left his entire estate to his widow. L. died on Dec. 18, 1959, leaving surviving him his widow and three unmarried children, his two parents, a brother and two sisters. The policy moneys were paid by the insurers and were held by L.'s executor pending the determination of the validity of the trusts set out in the letter of Dec. 1, 1965.

Held: (i) the first trust was not void for uncertainty as it did not impose a duty to make a selection but merely conferred a discretionary power to do so and it was possible for the company to have selected a potential beneficiary whom any reasonable man would recognise as having a moral claim on L. (see p. 1165, letter G, and p. 1166, letter B, post).

Re Gestetner ([1953] 1 All E.R. 1150) and observations of SIR RAYMOND EVERSHED, M.R. in *Re Allen (decd.)* ([1953] 2 All E.R. at p. 901) applied.

(ii) the first trust, however, was void on the ground of perpetuity as it created a power of selection that might be exercised beyond the perpetuity period, for the company could exercise its discretion so as to create successive interests and on several occasions, and thus could postpone deciding on the destination of capital for longer than the rule against perpetuities would allow (see p. 1166, letters F and H, post); and the second trust, being dependent on the first trust, also failed by reason of perpetuity.

(iii) on the true construction of the letter of Dec. 1, 1956, and of the policy, having regard in particular to the references to the policy being held in trust for L., the rule in *Hancock* v. *Watson* ([1900-03] All E.R. Rep. 87) applied, despite the provisions contemplating forfeiture of L.'s benefits in certain circumstances; accordingly the policy moneys formed part of L.'s estate (see p. 1167, letter F, post).

Re Cohen's Will Trusts ([1936] 1 All E.R. 103) distinguished.

Per CURIAM: if all trusts under the arrangement made by L. had failed,

A   there would have been a resulting trust in favour of the company, not in favour of L., since the premiums were paid by the company, which could not be regarded as having paid them as L.'s agent (see p. 1167, letter G, post).

[**Editorial Note.** This decision has been approved in *Re Gulkenkian's Settlement Trusts*, post.

B   As to the certainty of objects to be benefited by a trust and to discretion being given to trustees as to which objects are to be benefited, see 38 HALSBURY'S LAWS (3rd Edn.) 835, 836, paras. 1399-1401; and for cases on the subject see 47 DIGEST (Repl.) 58, 59, *419-423*.

As to the rule against perpetuities, see 29 HALSBURY'S LAWS (3rd Edn.) 281-283, paras. 567-571; and for cases on the subject see 37 DIGEST (Repl.) 55, C 56, *1-13.*]

Cases referred to:

Allen (decd.), Re, Faith v. *Allen*, [1953] 2 All E.R. 898; [1953] Ch. 810; [1953] 3 W.L.R. 637; *subsequent proceedings*, [1954] 1 All E.R. 526; [1954] Ch. 259; [1954] 2 W.L.R. 333; 48 Digest (Repl.) 303, *2660.*

D *Cohen's Will Trusts, Re, Cullen* v. *Westminister Bank, Ltd.*, [1936] 1 All E.R. 103; 49 Digest (Repl.) 841, *7910.*

Gestetner (decd.), Re, Barnett v. *Blunika*, [1953] 1 All E.R. 1150; [1953] Ch. 672; [1953] 2 W.L.R. 1033; 37 Digest (Repl.) 411, *1400.*

Gibbard (decd.), Re, Public Trustee v. *Davis*, [1966] 1 All E.R. 273; [1967] 1 W.L.R. 42.

E *Hain's Settlement, Re, Tooth* v. *Hain*, [1961] 1 All E.R. 848; [1961] 1 W.L.R. 440; 47 Digest (Repl.) 60, *444.*

Hancock v. *Watson* [1900-03] All E.R. Rep. 87; [1902] A.C. 14; 71 L.J.Ch. 149; 85 L.T. 729; 47 Digest (Repl.) 115, *823.*

Inland Revenue Comrs. v. *Broadway Cottages Trust, Inland Revenue Comrs.* v. *Pennylands Trust*, [1954] 3 All E.R. 120; [1955] Ch. 20; [1954] 3 W.L.R. 438; 47 Digest (Repl.) 48, *315.*

F *Ogden, Re, Brydon* v. *Samuel*, [1933] All E.R. Rep. 720; [1933] Ch. 678; 102 L.J.Ch. 226; 149 L.T. 162; 48 Digest (Repl.) 479, *4339.*

Rucker v. *Scholefield*, (1862), 1 Hem. & M. 36; 32 L.J.Ch. 46; 71 E.R. 16; 37 Digest (Repl.) 366, *1030.*

Saxone Shoe Co., Ltd.'s Trust Deed, Re, Re Abbott's Will Trusts, Abbott v. *Pearson*, [1962] 2 All E.R. 904; [1962] 1 W.L.R. 943; Digest (Cont. G Vol. A) 102, *1030a.*

Sayer Trust, Re, MacGregor v. *Sayer*, [1956] 3 All E.R. 600; [1957] Ch. 423; [1957] 2 W.L.R. 261; 37 Digest (Repl.) 4041, *1332.*

Adjourned Summons.

This was an application by originating summons dated Oct. 25, 1966, by H the plaintiff, the Right Hon. Cedric Percival, Baron Darwen, for the determination of the following questions and for the following relief, viz: (i) whether the plaintiff as executor held the sum of £17,890 6s. 8d. paid consequent on the death of Colonel Ivan George Elmer Leek, deceased, under a policy of assurance on the life of the deceased, dated Sept. 25, 1957, effected by the defendant company, Dosco Overseas Engineering, Ltd. (" the company "), I with the North British and Mercantile Insurance Co., Ltd. (declared by a letter dated Dec. 1, 1956, from the company to Col. Leek): (a) on trust for the benefit of such one or more of them, the defendant Hilda Leek (the widow of the deceased), the defendants Adrian Elmer Leek, Nigel Leek and Miranda Leek (the children of the deceased) and such other persons as the company might consider to have had a moral claim on the deceased in such shares and in such manner as the company should in its absolute discretion decide; or (b) on trust for the benefit of such one or more of the first four defendants (as the statutory next-of-kin of Col. Leek) in such shares and in such manner as the company should in its

absolute discretion decide, or (c) on trust for the plaintiff as the personal repre- A
sentative of Col. Leek; or (d) on trust for the company beneficially; or (e) on
some other and if so what trusts; (ii) if and so far as necessary execution of
the trusts.   The facts are set out in the judgment.

The cases noted below* were cited during the argument in addition to those
referred to in the judgment.

A. J. Balcombe for the plaintiff executor   B
G. M. Godfrey for the first defendant, the widow.
P. J. Millett for the second, third and fourth defendants.
J. P. Brookes for the company.
H. E. Francis, Q.C., and *J. P. Warner* for the Crown.

Cur. adv. vult. C

Apr. 28.   **BUCKLEY, J.**, read the following judgment: On July 17, 1956,
the late Lt.-Col. Ivan George Elmer Leek was appointed managing director of
the fifth defendant company, Dosco Overseas Engineering, Ltd. (which I shall
call " the company "), at a salary of £4,000 per annum plus commission on sales.
Thereafter, Col. Leek, having become aware of the tax relief allowed in respect
of approved pension schemes under s. 388 of the Income Tax Act, 1952, nego- D
tiated with the North British and Mercantile Insurance Co., Ltd. (which I shall
call " the insurers ") the policy, to which I shall refer in more detail in a minute,
and secured the approval of the board of directors of the company to an arrangement recorded in a letter dated Dec. 1, 1956, from the company to himself.
It was thereby provided that the company should at its own cost effect with
the insurers a non-profit endowment assurance on Col. Leek's life in a sum of E
£18,807 payable in the event of his dying before his sixty-fifth birthday, which
was defined as the normal retirement date, and providing a provision on his
retirement in survival of that date of £1,880 14s. per annum. The letter recorded
that the policy would be expressed as being effected by the company as trustee
for Col. Leek and would be held by the company in trust subject to the conditions
set out in the letter. Those conditions included provisions for the commutation F
of Col. Leek's benefits under the arrangement in certain eventualities, and the
following " death benefit " provisions, from which I read only that part of
para. 6 which was applicable to the events which happened.

" Death benefit.   There shall be payable in the event of your death
(a) while in the company's service and before the normal retirement date
the sum assured under the policy. [I pass over sub-paras. (b) and (c), and G
read on] All sums arising out of (a) (b) and (c) above shall be held by the
company upon trust for the benefit of such one or more of the following
persons as the company in its absolute discretion shall decide namely your
wife, children or other issue or such other persons as the company may
consider to have a moral claim upon you or failing them upon trust for the
benefit of such one or more of the statutory next-of-kin in both cases in such H
shares and in such manner as the company in its absolute discretion shall
decide."

The questions for decision in this case relate to the interpretation and validity
of that provision.

In accordance with that arrangement, the company, on Sept. 25, 1957, effected I
a policy on Col. Leek's life with the insurers. In the policy the company was
described as the assured " as trustee for the person whose life is assured "—
that is, for Col. Leek. The policy was expressed to be issued in accordance with
the terms of the letter of Dec. 1, 1956. The arrangement was initiated on the
footing that as from Dec. 1, 1956, Col. Leek's salary as managing director of

---

* *Lassence* v. *Tierney*, [1843-60] All E.R. Rep. 47; *Re De Sommery*, [1921] 2 Ch. 622;
Re Coxen, [1948] 2 All E.R. 492; [1948] Ch. 747; *Innes (Inspector of Taxes)* v. *Harrison*,
[1954] 1 All E.R. 884.

A   the company should be reduced by £1,000 per annum, being the amount of the yearly premium on the policy. It was also subject to the formal approval of the Inland Revenue being obtained. Col. Leek's salary was in fact reduced accordingly. Inland Revenue approval of the scheme was obtained on Oct. 18, 1957. Col. Leek died on Dec. 18, 1959, aged forty-nine, whilst still managing director of the company. By his will he appointed the plaintiff to be his executor,

B   and left all his property to his widow, the first defendant. He left three children, the second, third and fourth defendants, who are all unmarried. Both his parents, a brother and two sisters also survived him. In due course the insurers paid to the company a net sum of £17,890 6s. 8d., being the sum of £18,807 assured by the policy less £916 13s. 4d., the balance of the current year's premium from Jan. 1, 1960, to Nov. 1, 1960. On Mar. 1, 1960, the directors of the company resolved

C   that the whole of the policy moneys should be applied to the benefit of the first defendant, and on Mar. 16, 1960, the company paid the sum of £17,890 6s. 8d. to the plaintiff who at present holds the fund. The Commissioners of Inland Revenue have been joined as the sixth defendants because, if this fund forms part of Col. Leek's estate, duty will be payable in respect of it on his death. If, on the other hand, it forms no part of his estate, no duty is payable. By the originating

D   summons, the plaintiff asks whether he holds the fund in question

> "(a) Upon trust for the benefit of such one or more of [the first, second, third and fourth defendants] and such other persons as [the company] may consider to have had a moral claim upon [Col. Leek] in such shares and in such manner as [the company] shall in its absolute discretion decide; or (b) upon trust for the benefit of such one or more of [the first four defendants as the statutory next-of-kin of Col. Leek] in such shares and in such manner as [the company] shall in its absolute discretion decide; or (c) upon trust for himself as the personal representative of [Col. Leek] or (d) upon trust for [the company] beneficially; or (e) upon some other and if so what trusts."

E

F   The Crown contend that the relevant trusts set out in that part of the letter of Dec. 1, 1956, which I have read fall into two parts: (i) a trust for such one or more of the following persons as the company should decide, namely, Col. Leek's wife, children or other issue, or such other persons as the company might consider to have a moral claim on him; and (ii) a trust for such one or more of Col. Leek's statutory next-of-kin as the company should decide. The first of these trusts, they say, is void on the alternative grounds of uncertainty or perpetuity. The

G   second, they say, cannot arise in the events which have happened, as there has been no failure of objects or potential objects of the first trust. In these circumstances, the Crown submit that the fund results to the estate of Col. Leek under the rule in *Hancock* v. *Watson* (1) or, alternatively, because, as they contend, Col. Leek provided the consideration for the policy.

   On the question of uncertainty, the Crown submit that the company's power of

H   selection under the first trust is not merely a power but is a trust or a power coupled with a duty, under which the company is bound to distribute the fund subject only to a discretion conferred on the company to select the particular members of the specified class of potential beneficiaries who shall benefit. The authorities establish that different considerations apply to a case in which a power to select beneficiaries is coupled with a duty to make such selection and to distri-

I   bute the fund accordingly from those applicable where there is no such duty, the power of selection being a bare power, or what has been called a power collateral. In the first type of case, the class of potential beneficiaries from whom selection is to be made must be so defined and of such a kind that the donee can identify every possible object of his power of selection. This need arises from the fact that the power, being of a fiduciary character, will only be accepted as validly conferred if, in the event of the donee failing in his duty, the court can execute the trust and carry the intention of the donor into effect. This the court can only do if

_____

(1) [1900-03] All E.R. Rep. 87; [1902] A.C. 14.

the whole class of potential beneficiaries can be ascertained, for the court will not   A
exercise the discretion vested in the donee but will execute the trust by distributing the fund amongst all the members of the class. In the second type of case,
exemplified by *Re Gestetner (decd.), Barnett* v. *Blunika* (2), the objects of the power
need not be so defined or of such a kind that the donee of the power can identify
them all. It is only necessary that the qualification to benefit is such that it will
be possible to say of a particular individual selected for benefit that he does or   B
does not possess the qualification.

The cases to which I have been referred may be said, I think, to fall under five
heads. (i) Where the language of the disposition or declaration of trust is such
that it imposes a clear duty on the donee of the power of selection to distribute
the fund amongst some at least of the specified class of potential beneficiaries, the
discretion conferred on the donee extending merely to selection and not to   C
deciding whether or not to select. *Re Ogden, Brydon* v. *Samuel* (3), is such a case,
and so on construction of the instrument there under consideration is *Re Saxone
Shoe Co., Ltd.'s Trust Deed* (4). In a case of this kind there is no room for a gift
in default of selection, though there may be a gift on total failure of members
of the specified class. (ii) Where the fund is given on trust for all or such one or
more of the members of a specified class of potential beneficiaries as the donee   D
of the power selects, without any gift in default of selection, as in *Inland Revenue
Comrs.* v. *Broadway Cottages Trust* (5) and *Re Hain's Settlement, Tooth* v. *Hain* (6).
In such cases the power may be more aptly described as a power of exclusion than a
power of selection, for the language demonstrates an intention that all the potential
beneficiaries shall benefit unless the donee of the power of selection in the exercise
of his discretion picks out particular members of the class to benefit. (iii) Where   E
the fund is given on trust for such one or more members of a specified class of
potential beneficiaries as the donee of the power selects with a gift in default of
selection, as in *Re Gestener (decd.)* (2). In such cases the presence of the gift in
default demonstrates that the donor did not intend to impose a duty on the donee
to make a selection in any event but contemplated that he might not elect to do
so. (iv) Where the fund is given on trust for such of certain specified objects as   F
the donee of the power selects without any gift in default of selection, but in
terms which make it clear that whether any and, if so, which of the objects shall
benefit is left entirely to the discretion of the donee of the power, as in cl. 4 of the
deed under consideration in *Re Sayer Trust, MacGregor* v. *Sayer* (7). In such a
case the permissive character of the power may be so clearly expressed that the
absence of any gift in default of its exercise cannot influence its construction.   G
(v) Where the fund is given on trust for such of certain specified objects as the
donee of the power selects in terms which are not manifestly either permissive or
mandatory and without any gift in default of selection, where the absence of any
gift in default may aid the construction of the gift for the benefit of the specified
class of objects as conferring a power coupled with a duty to make a selection.
The decision on cl. 6 of the deed under consideration in *Re Sayer Trust* (7), if it   H
does not fall within class. (i), can be placed under this head.

The problem being one of interpretation, every case must depend on its own
circumstances, the question in every case being whether there is a trust or fiduciary
duty to distribute amongst members of a specified class of objects, the only
discretion given to the donee being to decide which particular objects shall
benefit, or whether there is a trust only for such members, if any, of a specified   I
class of objects as the donee shall select. In cases which fall within (i), (ii) and

---

(2) [1953] 1 All E.R. 1150; [1953] Ch. 672.
(3) [1933] All E.R. Rep. 720; [1933] Ch. 678.
(4) [1962] 2 All E.R. 904.
(5) [1954] 3 All E.R. 120; [1955] Ch. 20.
(6) [1961] 1 All E.R. 848.
(7) [1956] 3 All E.R. 600; [1957] Ch. 423.

A (v) p. 1164, ante, the discretion or power will be treated as coupled with a duty, and in cases within (iii) and (iv) as a bare discretion or power.

How, then, should the trust which I have read from the letter of Dec. 1, 1956, be construed? Counsel for the Crown says that the first trust should be interpreted as imposing a duty to make a selection. It is true that in one sense at least it is mandatory. It provides that the fund shall be held in trust for certain

B objects; but for what objects? For such one or more of a specified class of potential beneficiaries as the company in its absolute discretion shall select. I can find in this language no express imposition of a duty to make a selection, but merely of a duty to hold the fund in trust for such objects of the power, if any, as the company may select. The words " shall decide ", as a matter of grammar and of the natural meaning of the English language, do not, in my judgment,

C have any mandatory force. Counsel for the Crown, however, relies on the absence of any gift in default of selection to reinforce his argument. In other words, he says, in effect, that this case falls within the fifth of the classes of case which I have enumerated. This involves consideration of the second trust, introduced by the words " or failing them ". Counsel say that these words mean, " If there shall be no widow, children or issue of Col. Leek and no person whom the company

D may consider to have a moral claim on him ". If counsel's construction of the first trust is right, then I think his construction of the words " or failing them " would also clearly be right, but as a matter of language the words seem to me as aptly—and, indeed, I think more naturally—to bear the meaning, " failing any such one or more of the specified class of objects as the company shall decide "; that is to say, to be equivalent to " in default of selection ". It is perhaps a

E little surprising that the second trust also confers on the company a power of selection. This fact indicates that the parties supposed that the company would have no difficulty in ascertaining whether the event on which the second trust was to take effect—the event indicated by the words " failing them "—had or had not occurred. There would be likely to be little difficulty in the company ascertaining whether Col. Leek left a widow or issue surviving him. There would be likely to

F be considerable difficulty in the company ascertaining that he left no one surviving him who could be said to have a moral claim on him. It seems to me improbable that the parties could have intended that the company should have to satisfy itself on this latter point before acting under the second trust. This reinforces my primary view that the words " failing them " are more likely to have been intended to have the sense of " in default of selection " than the sense

G contended for by counsel for the Crown. If this view is right, the case falls into class (iii) (for which, see p. 1164, letter E, ante), and the first trust should not be construed as importing a duty to make a selection, but as merely conferring a discretionary power to do so. In my judgment, this is the proper construction of the language used.

Nevertheless, says counsel for the Crown, the first trust is void for uncertainty

H because the qualification of being a person having a moral claim on Col. Leek is too indefinite. In this connexion, I was referred to *Re Gibbard (decd.), Public Trustee* v. *Davis* (8) and the earlier case in the Court of Appeal of *Re Allen (decd.) Faith* v. *Allen* (9), both of which counsel seeks to distinguish on the ground that a decision whether a particular person has a moral claim on another is a more subjective judgment than a decision whether one man is an old friend of another or whether a

I person is a member of the Church of England and an adherent to the doctrines of that Church. Where the discretion under consideration is not coupled with a duty, the same precision of definition is not required as where the discretion is coupled with a duty. It is only necessary that the qualification to benefit should be sufficiently clearly defined and of such a nature that there is a reasonable possibility of the donee of the discretion selecting a beneficiary of whom it could be clearly said that he, at any rate, satisfied the qualification, no matter how difficult it might be in more marginal cases to decide one way or the other. See in this

(8) [1966] 1 All E.R. 273.   (9) [1953] 2 All E.R. 898; [1953] Ch. 810.

connexion the observations of SIR RAYMOND EVERSHED, M.R., in *Re Allen* (*decd.*)   A (10). I see no reason to think that in the present case the company might not have found and selected some potential beneficiary whom any reasonable man would recognise as having a moral claim on Col. Leek. The concept of one person having a moral claim on another is not, in my judgment, so imprecise, nor does it invoke so wide a variety of individual judgments, as to introduce such uncertainty to the first trust as to justify my coming to the conclusion that it   B fails for uncertainty.

I turn now to the question of perpetuity. It is common ground that a special power of appointment exercisable beyond a perpetuity period commencing from the creation of the power is void. That principle is applicable to the power of selection under the first trust in the present case. The donee of the power is a corporation, and may continue in existence for longer than a life in being at the   C commencement of the trust and twenty-one years thereafter. The question, therefore, is whether on the true construction of the letter of Dec. 1, 1956, the company could exercise the discretion later than twenty-one years after the death of Col. Leek, whose life seems to be the only available life in being when the trust was created by which to measure the appropriate perpetuity period, bearing in mind that he was about forty-five years and ten months old at Dec. 1, 1956, and   D might have remarried or had more children after the commencement of the trust and yet have died before his sixty-fifth birthday. It would have been unlikely but not impossible that a second wife might have been born after Dec. 1, 1956. It is common ground that under the first trust the company could create successive interests and could, for instance, decide that Col. Leek's widow or any of his children should have a life interest only in the fund or some part of it. The Crown   E contend that the company could in accordance with the terms of the trust exercise the discretion from time to time so that it could, for instance, determine that a child should have a life interest in the fund or a part of it, and could postpone deciding how the capital should be used until the death of that child. As the class of objects includes remoter issue of Col. Leek than children, this process could be continued indefinitely. If this is the effect of the trust, it is clearly bad for   F perpetuity. On the other side, it is argued that the company is bound to make its decision within a reasonable time after the discretion becomes exercisable, and certainly within twenty-one years of Col. Leek's death. If, as is conceded, the company could in the exercise of this discretion create successive interests, I can see no reason for holding that the discretion must be exercised, if at all, once and for all, and not piecemeal on a series of occasions. If it can be exercised on   G several occasions, there seems to me to be no good reason (apart from the perpetuity rule) for holding that the company must decide the ultimate destination of the capital of the fund within any particular period. There would be nothing unreasonable in postponing a decision about the destination of the capital until the end of a limited interest in the income. It follows that in my opinion the first trust fails for perpetuity.   H

If the construction which I have adopted of the words " failing them " is right, the second trust is clearly dependent on the first trust and must also fail in consequence of the failure of the first trust on the ground of perpetuity. If I have misconstrued those words and they import total failure of objects of the first trust, there has been no such failure and the second trust cannot come into operation. On either view, if I am right in holding that the first trust fails, both   I the first and the second trusts have wholly failed. Is there, in consequence, a trust for the estate of Col. Leek under the rule in *Hancock* v. *Watson* (11) or a resulting trust to his estate or a resulting trust to the company? Counsel for the company contends that on the true construction of the letter of Dec. 1, 1956, and of the policy there is no initial trust in favour of Col. Leek on which other trusts are engrafted by the subsequent provisions of the letter. He

(10) [1953] 2 All E.R. at p. 901; [1953] Ch. at p. 817.
(11) [1900-03] All E.R. Rep. 87; [1902] A.C. 14.

A   contends that the trust in favour of Col. Leek is coupled with the later provisions so as to form one system of trusts (see per SIR WILLIAM PAGE WOOD, V.-C. in *Rucker* v. *Scholefield*, (12)). He draws attention to the fact that the letter says that the policy would be only " expressed " as being effected by the company as trustee for Col. Leek and goes on to say, " and will be held by the company in trust subject to the conditions set out in the paragraphs which follow ". Those para-
B   graphs provided for benefits to accrue to Col. Leek. They also provided for his being deprived of any benefit in certain eventualities; viz., if of his own free will Col. Leek left the company's employment before his sixty-fifth birthday, or if he was dismissed for fraud or misconduct, whereon the company was to be entitled to surrender the policy and retain the proceeds. Under another paragraph the company reserved the right to amend or discontinue the arrangement after
C   due notice, but without prejudice to any benefits then accured. Finally, the letter provided that in certain events Col. Leek's benefits would be reduced. These provisions, counsel for the company says, are inconsistent with Col. Leek's having the residual beneficial interest in the policy and the company being merely a trustee. I cannot, however, accept that, when the letter said the policy would be expressed as being effected by the company as trustee for Col. Leek,
D   that was intended to be a mere formality having no operative effect. If this were the case, both the letter and the policy would, in my judgment, be most misleading. The present case appears to me to be quite unlike *Re Cohen's Will Trusts, Cullen* v. *Westminister Bank Ltd.*, (13), on which counsel for the company relied. There, a testator gave his residue equally amongst several named children subject to the provisions and directions thereinafter contained. LUXMOORE, J. held that the
E   reference to equal division amongst the children did not constitute a gift but an enumeration of the number of shares into which the fund was to be divided, of which trusts were then declared. Here, no analogous operation can be given to the references to the policy being held in trust for Col. Leek in the letter and in the policy. The fact that the engrafted provisions contemplate forfeiture of Col. Leek's benefits in certain circumstances and contemplate the company
F   obtaining a measure of benefit in that event does not seem to me to be inconsistent with the case being one to which the rule in *Hancock* v. *Watson* (14), can apply. In my judgment that rule does apply in the present case, with the result that the policy moneys now form part of Col. Leek's estate.

     Had I taken a different view and reached the conclusion that all trusts under the arrangement had failed, I should have held that a resulting trust arose in favour
G   of the company and not in favour of Col. Leek's estate, for the premiums were paid by the company. True, Col. Leek forewent an equivalent amount of his salary, but the consideration for his doing so was the arrangement as a whole. It would, in my judgment, be impossible to regard the company as having paid the premiums as his agent. I shall accordingly make a declaration in the terms of para. (i) (c) of the originating summons (15).

H

Order accordingly.

     Solicitors: *Beale & Co.* (for the plaintiff and the first to the fifth defendants); *Solicitor of Inland Revenue.*

[*Reported by* JENIFER SANDELL, *Barrister-at-Law.*]

I

---

(12) (1862), 1 Hem. & M. 36 at p. 41.
(13) [1936] 1 All E.R. 103.
(14) [1900-03] All E.R. Rep. 87; [1902] A.C. 14.
(15) See p. 1162, letter A, ante.

PARRY v. CLEAVER.

A

[COURT OF APPEAL, CIVIL DIVISION (Lord Denning, M.R., Salmon and Winn, L.JJ.), March 15, 16, May 9, 1967.]

Damages—Measure of damages—Loss of earnings—Pension—Compulsory contributory police pension—Whether pension should be taken into account when assessing damages for loss of earnings.

B

A police officer, while on point duty directing traffic, was severely injured by the negligence of a driver of a motor car. As a result of his injuries the police officer was discharged for disablement. During his service contributions to a compulsory pension scheme were deducted from his pay, and his employers notionally contributed to the pension fund. He became entitled as of right to a pension from the police pension fund.

C

Held: in assessing the police officer's damages for loss of earnings caused by the defendant's negligence the police pension must be taken into account by way of diminution of the police officer's loss, for the compulsory pension was not independent of the terms of his employment, but was part of his earnings and was not lost (see p. 1172, letter B, p. 1173, letter B, and p. 1174, letter G, post).

D

Browning v. *War Office* ([1962] 3 All E.R. 1089) and *Parsons* v. *B.N.M. Laboratories, Ltd.* ([1963] 2 All E.R. 658) applied.

Per SALMON, L.J.: nothing in the present decision necessarily affects a plaintiff's position under a voluntary pension scheme (see p. 1173, letter D, post).

Appeal allowed.

E

[As to collateral benefits in assessing damages, see 11 HALSBURY'S LAWS (3rd Edn.) 240, 241, para. 408; and for cases on the subject, see 17 DIGEST (Repl.) 80, 81, *27-38.*]

Cases referred to:

 Bradburn v. *Great Western Ry. Co.,* [1874-80] All E.R. Rep. 195; (1874), L.R. 10 Exch. 1; 44 L.J.Ex. 9; 31 L.T. 464; 17 Digest (Repl.) 108, *222.*

F

 British Transport Commission v. *Gourley,* [1955] 3 All E.R. 796; [1956] A.C. 185; [1956] 2 W.L.R. 41; Digest (Cont. Vol. A) 462, *28a.*

 British Westinghouse Electric and Manufacturing Co., Ltd. v. *Underground Electric Rys. Co. of London, Ltd.,* [1911-13] All E.R. Rep. 63; [1912] A.C. 673; 81 L.J.K.B. 1132; 107 L.T. 325; 17 Digest (Repl.) 108, *226.*

G

 Browning v. *War Office,* [1962] 3 All E.R. 1089; [1963] 1 Q.B. 750; [1963] 2 W.L.R. 52; Digest (Cont. Vol. A) 1194, *1061b.*

 Foxley v. *Olton,* [1964] 3 All E.R. 248, n.; [1965] 2 Q.B. 306; [1964] 3 W.L.R. 1155; Digest (Cont. Vol. B) 567, *1062b.*

 Havery v. *Sharman,* (Feb. 28, 1964), unreported.

 Jones v. *Gleeson,* (1965), 39 A.L.J.R. 258.

H

 Judd v. *Board of Governors, Hammersmith, West London and St. Mark's Hospitals,* [1960] 1 All E.R. 607; [1960] 1 W.L.R. 328; Digest (Cont. Vol. A) 1194, *1061a.*

 Monmouthshire County Council v. *Smith,* [1956] 2 All E.R. 800; [1956] 1 W.L.R. 1132; 120 J.P. 417; *affd.* C.A., [1957] 1 All E.R. 78; [1957] 2 Q.B. 154; [1957] 2 W.L.R. 33; 121 J.P. 63; Digest (Cont. Vol. A) 301, *4595b.*

I

 Parsons v. *B.N.M. Laboratories, Ltd.,* [1963] 2 All E.R. 658; [1964] 1 Q.B. 95; [1963] 2 W.L.R. 1273; 44 Digest (Repl.) 243, *668.*

 Smith v. *Canadian Pacific Ry. Co.,* (1963), 41 D.L.R. (2d) 249; 45 W.W.R. 170; Digest (Cont. Vol. A) 1200, **1942j.*

Appeal.

This was an appeal by the defendant, Anthony Cleaver, from a judgment of JOHN STEPHENSON, J., given on Oct. 4, 1966, awarding the plaintiff, Reginald

H.L. [1969] 1 All E.R. Reversed. 555.

A Parry, £16,580 15s. 2d. damages for personal injuries caused by negligence of the
defendant. Of this amount a sum of £12,000 was attributable to the plaintiff's
financial loss. The trial judge decided that the plaintiff's police pension, to which
he was entitled as of right under a compulsory contributory pension scheme, should
be disregarded in assessing the damages to be awarded to him. The facts are set
out in the judgment of LORD DENNING, M.R.

B
E. W. Eveleigh, Q.C., and *E. Sanderson Temple* for the defendant.
Geoffrey Howe, Q.C., and *M. T. B. Underhill* for the plaintiff.

Cur. adv. vult.

May 9. The following judgments were read.

C
LORD DENNING, M.R.: Reginald Parry, the plaintiff, was born on
Oct. 25, 1927. He joined the Cheshire Police Force on Dec. 14, 1950, when he was
twenty-three. Twelve years later on Jan. 4, 1963, he was on point-duty directing
traffic. He was knocked down by a motor car and severely injured. He sustained
a fracture of the base of the skull and his left leg was broken in several places. It
was due to the negligence of the driver of the car, the defendant, Anthony Cleaver.
Liability is admitted. The only question is what is the proper compensation. So
D far as pain and suffering and loss of amenities are concerned, the judge has awarded
£3,500. There is no appeal on that point. The contest is as to the compensation
for financial loss, especially having regard to the Police Pensions Regulations.
The Police Pensions Regulations, 1962 (1) (made under the Police Pensions Act,
1948) provide for compulsory contributions to a pension fund, out of which the
E policeman is entitled as of right to a pension on being discharged for disablement.
The question is whether in assessing his compensation this contributory pension
is to be taken into account.

In order to assess the compensation, the dominant rule of law is that the injured
party should receive such a sum of money as will put him in the same position
as he would have been in if he had not received the injuries (see *British Transport
F Commission* v. *Gourley* (2), per EARL JOWITT). I turn, therefore, to consider what
the position of the plaintiff would have been if he had not been injured. It was
as follows. His salary as a police officer at the time of the accident came to
£21 18s. 3d. a week. Out of this sum he contributed £1 3s. 1d. to the police pension
fund. The police authorities contributed notionally £3 a week. If he had not
been injured he would have served in the police force until he had done twenty-five
G years' service: and he would have retired at the age of forty-eight. He would
then have received a retiring pension of £10 a week for the rest of his days. On
retirement at age forty-eight he would have obtained work as a clerk in civilian
employment. He would have continued in it until age sixty-five, when he would
have retired with a civilian pension as well as a police pension.

Now I will state how his position has changed owing to the accident. He re-
H mained on full pay from the date of the accident, Jan. 4, 1963, until June 30,
1964, when he was discharged owing to his incapacity. He was then aged thirty-
six. On his discharge he was entitled as of right (and not of discretion) to a
police pension of £3 18s. 4d. a week for the rest of his days. Two months later, on
Oct. 6, 1964, he obtained work as a clerk in civilian employment at £13 16s. a
week. Out of this sum he contributed 14s. 8d. a week to his employers' pension
scheme. His employers contributed 5s. a week. He was in this employment at
I the date of the trial on July 19, 1966, and is likely to continue in it until the age
of sixty-five. He will then retire and receive a civilian pension of £5 13s. 6d. a
week for the rest of his days.

Those are, of course, only rough forecasts. There are many unknown contingencies to be reckoned with. He might die at an early age owing to extraneous
causes altogether. He might get other employment; and so forth. I will make

(1) S.I. 1962 No. 2756 as amended.
(2) [1955] 3 All E.R. 796 at p. 799; [1956] A.C. 185 at p. 197.

allowances later for those contingencies. Meanwhile the task is to assess the **A**
financial loss on the forecasts which I have given. It falls into four periods.

Period 1.

This is the period from the date of the accident (Jan. 4, 1963) to the date of
trial (July 19, 1966). During this period the plaintiff received his full salary and
allowances up to July 30, 1964, when he was discharged. So he suffered no **B**
financial loss in that period. Then from July 30, 1964, to the trial on July 19,
1966, he suffered loss owing to the lower pay he received in civilian employment.
As against his police pay of £21 18s. 3d. a week, he received only civilian pay of
£13 16s. a week. In addition to his civilian pay, he received his police pension of
£3 18s. 4d. a week (which he would not have received if he had stayed in the
police). If you take the police pension into account, his loss for this period comes **C**
to £661 14s. 6d.; but if you ignore it, his loss comes to £1,080 15s. 2d.

Period 2.

This is the period from the date of trial (July 19, 1966) to the time when he
would have retired from the police force at the age of forty-eight after twenty-
five years' service (December, 1975). He suffers loss during this period owing to
the lower pay which he receives in civilian employment. As against his police **D**
pay of £21 18s. 3d. a week, he receives only civilian pay of £13 16s. a week, but he
receives his police pension of £3 18s. 4d. a week. If you take the police pension into
account, his loss for this period comes to £2,131; but if you ignore it, his loss
comes to £4,059.

Period 3.

This is the period from age forty-eight (when he would have retired from the **E**
police force) till his retirement from civilian employment at age sixty-five. He
suffers no loss of wages during this period because he would have earned the same,
being in the same civilian employment in any case: and the same amount
(£13 16s. a week) as he would have done even if he had suffered no accident. His
loss is, therefore, the difference between what his police pension would have been **F**
at age forty-eight if he had not been injured (£10 a week) and the police pension
which he in fact receives on earlier discharge at age thirty-six (£3 18s. 4d. a
week). If you take into account this pension of £3 18s. 4d. a week, his loss for this
period comes to £5,252; but if you ignore it, his loss comes to £8,170.

Period 4.

This is the period on retirement at age sixty-five from civilian employment till **G**
the assumed age of seventy-five. His loss is the difference between the police
pension if he had not been injured (£10 a week) and the combined police and
civilian pensions he in fact receives (£3 18s. 4d. a week police pension and £5 13s.
6d. a week civilian pension). It is conceded that the civilian pension must be
taken into account. The question is whether the police pension of £3 18s. 4d.
is also to be taken into account. If it is taken into account, this loss comes to **H**
£170. If it is ignored, his loss comes to £2,200.

In each of those periods the question arises: is the police pension of £3 18s. 4d.
a week to be taken into account? or is it to be ignored? or is it to be apportioned so
that you ignore the portion attributable to his own contributions and deduct the
portion attributable to his employers' contributions? There are cases in support
of each view.   **I**

(i) According to *Judd* v. *Board of Governors of Hammersmith, West London and
St. Mark's Hospitals* (3), the police pension is to be ignored for periods 1 and 2
(when he would have still been serving in the police), but it is to be taken into
account for periods 3 and 4 (when he would have retired). This was the view
adopted by JOHN STEPHENSON, J., in the present case.

---

(3) [1960] 1 All E.R. 607.

A   (ii) According to *Monmouthshire County Council* v. *Smith* (4) and the unreported case of *Havery* v. *Sharman* (5) the police pension is to be taken into account in all periods 1, 2, 3 and 4.

(iii) According to the Saskatchewan case of *Smith* v. *Canadian Pacific Ry. Co.* (6), the police pension is to be apportioned so that the portion attributable to the man's own contributions is to be ignored in all four periods, whereas the

B   portion attributable to his employers' contributions is to be taken into account.

(iv) According to the High Court of Australia, the police pension is to be ignored altogether, see *Jones* v. *Gleeson* (7).

We had occasion to consider the principles relating to this subject in *Browning* v. *War Office* (8). The general rule is that the injured party should give credit for all sums which he receives in diminution of his loss; save that there are

C   exceptional cases (such as insurance benefits) for which he need not give credit.

The plaintiff says that a contributory pension stands on the same footing as insurance benefits. Ever since *Bradburn* v. *Great Western Ry. Co.* (9), insurance benefits have been ignored. The reason is sometimes said to be because the man has paid for them himself out of his own money: and that it is unfair that he should have to bring into account that which he has bought himself. If this be

D   the true reason underlying *Bradburn's* case (9), I would agree that it applies equally to a contributory pension. The pension has been paid for, in part by his own contributions, and in part by the employer's contributions. In so far as it is paid for by his own contributions, it is a direct payment by the man. In so far as it is paid for by the employer's contributions, it is an indirect payment by the man: because it is paid by the employer on his behalf and is an indirect

E   addition to his wages.

I am afraid I cannot accept this as the reason for *Bradburn's* case (9). If it were correct, it would mean that unemployment benefit would have to be ignored also; because that is paid for in part by a man's own contributions and in part by his employer's contributions. It has been held, however, that unemployment benefit must be deducted (see *Parsons* v. *B.N.M. Laboratories, Ltd.* (10); *Foxley*

F   v. *Olton* (11)). It would also mean that the police pension of £3 18s. 4d. a week would never have to be brought into account in any of the periods: whereas it is admitted that it has to be deducted in periods 3 and 4, as was done in *Judd's* case (12). Similarly, his civilian pension of £5 13s. 6d. a week would have to be ignored: whereas it is admitted that it has to be deducted in period 4.

I would adopt as the reason for *Bradburn's* case (9) that given by VISCOUNT

G   HALDANE, L.C.:

" The reason of the decision was that it was not the accident, but a contract *wholly independent of the relation between the plaintiff and the defendant* which gave the plaintiff this advantage."

See *British Westinghouse Electric and Manufacturing Co., Ltd.* v. *Underground*

H   *Electric Rys. Co. of London, Ltd.* (13). This is much the same reason as that on which LORD REID said that insurance benefits are to be excluded. He said that it was because they are " completely collateral " (see *British Transport Commission* v. *Gourley* (14)).

Applying these tests to the present case, the contract for a contributory

I
(4) [1956] 2 All E.R. 800; *affd.* [1957] 2 Q.B. 154; [1957] 1 All E.R. 78.
(5) (Feb. 28, 1964), unreported.   (6) (1963), 41 D.L.R. (2d) 249.
(7) (1965), 39 A.L.J.R. 258.   (8) [1962] 3 All E.R. 1089; [1963] 1 Q.B. 750.
(9) [1874-80] All E.R. Rep. 195; (1874), L.R. 10 Exch. 1.
(10) [1963] 2 All E.R. 658 at pp. 670, 675, 676, 683, 684; [1964] 1 Q.B. 95 at pp. 122, 130, 131, 143, 144.
(11) [1964] 3 All E.R. 248, n.; [1965] 2 Q.B. 306.
(12) [1960] 1 All E.R. 607.
(13) [1911-13] All E.R. Rep. 63 at p. 70; [1912] A.C. 673 at p. 690.
(14) [1955] 3 All E.R. at p. 809; [1956] A.C. at p. 214

pension was not " wholly independent " of his employment. Nor was it " com- **A**
pletely collateral ". It was part and parcel of his employment. He was compelled
to pay contributions and was entitled as of right to the pension. The case is,
to my mind, indistinguishable in principle from *Browning's* case (15) (the disability pension) and *Parsons* v. B.N.M. *Laboratories, Ltd.* (16) (unemployment
benefit). In both of those cases the pension or benefit was part and parcel of the
terms of employment and was receivable as of right. It had to be taken into **B**
account. So here in all four periods the pension has to be taken into account.

The figures are therefore:

		£	s.	d.
Period 1 (special damages)		661	14	6
Period 2 (loss till retirement at age forty-eight)		2,131	0	0
Period 3 (loss from age forty-eight to retirement at age				
sixty-five)		5,252	0	0
Period 4 (loss from age sixty-five)		170	0	0

C

The last three figures (totalling £7,553) must be scaled down so as to allow for
contingencies and give effect to the fact that payment is made at once, i.e. to
reduce them to present value. I would scale them down to a total of £3,776 10s. **D**

The final figure is then £3,500 for pain and suffering and loss of amenities;
£661 14s. 6d. for special damages: and £3776 10s. for future financial loss. A
total of £7,938 4s. 6d.

I would allow the appeal accordingly.

SALMON, L.J. (read by WINN, L.J.): This appeal raises a number of
interesting and important questions, most of which are entirely open in the House **E**
of Lords but all of which are, in my view, concluded so far as this court is concerned by *Browning* v. *War Office* (15), and *Parsons* v. B.N.M. *Laboratories,
Ltd.* (16). However attractive some of the views expressed in DONOVAN, L.J.'s
dissenting judgment in the former case may be, it seems to me that we are bound
to hold that the plaintiff's pension of £3 18s. 4d. a week must be taken into
account in calculating the loss which he has suffered as a result of the defendant's **F**
negligence.

I do not think that either of the authorities to which I have referred is distinguishable in principle. In the latter case the plaintiff had made compulsory
contributions out of his wages to his unemployment benefit. This court held that
the amount he had received in unemployment benefit should be taken into account
in calculating what he had lost while unemployed. In the former case it is true **G**
that the plaintiff had made no contribution out of his wages to his pension,
whereas in the present case the plaintiff made a compulsory contribution of
£1 3s. 1d. out of his notional weekly wages of £21 18s. 3d. and the police authorities
(his employers) made a notional weekly contribution of £3 a week towards his
pension; but in my view this is immaterial. The pension scheme was compulsory. So long as the plaintiff was employed by the police authorities he could **H**
receive no more than £20 15s. 2d. a week, i.e. £21 18s. 3d. less £1 3s. 1d. No doubt
he earned by his services the £3 a week notionally contributed by his employers—
but during his employment he could never have received any part of this sum. In
exactly the same way the plaintiff in *Browning's* case (16) earned by his services
whatever sum must notionally have been contributed by his employers (the
U.S.A. Authorities) to produce his pension, but he could never have received any **I**
part of that sum whilst employed in the U.S.A. Army. If £y is what a man takes
home as wages, it can make no real difference under any compulsory pension
scheme whether a contribution of £x a week towards a pension is described
say as to ¼ £x as the servant's contribution, and as to ¾ £x as the master's contribution, or whether the whole of £x is described as the master's contribution, or
vice versa. At the end of the week the servant receives exactly the same amount

(15) [1962] 3 All E.R. 1089; [1963] 1 Q.B. 750.
(16) [1963] 2 All E.R. 658; [1964] 1 Q.B. 95.

A of money. In no circumstances can he receive more than the amount of his net salary during his employment. He receives nothing more until his employment ends and then only in accordance with the provisions of the pension scheme. To say that, but for the pension scheme, he might have received more money during his employment is entirely speculative and perhaps of little practical significance. As things were, there was no possibility of his doing so. Accordingly, since in

B *Browning's* case (17) the plaintiff's loss was held to be the capitalised value of the army salary which he was prevented from earning less the capitalised value of his army pension and present earnings, it follows that in the present case the plaintiff's loss must be calculated on the same basis.

It may be difficult to draw any real distinction in principle between a case such as the present and *Bradburn* v. *Great Western Ry. Co.* (18), in which the plaintiff

C had insured against the event brought about by the defendant's negligence. For my part I am not particularly impressed by the fact that the contract of insurance was " wholly independent of the relation between the plaintiff and the defendant ". Be that as it may, this point was canvassed in *Browning's* case (17) and decided against the plaintiff. We are bound by that decision. I wish to make it plain that nothing in the present decision, or the authorities which compel me to reach it,

D necessarily affects a plaintiff's position under a voluntary pension scheme. Whether, in such a case, the plaintiff must bring the pension into account, and if so whether he should be credited with the amount of his voluntary contributions, is a point which I regard as completely open and about which I express no opinion. Nor do I desire to express any view about the method of calculating the value of pension rights laid down in Winn, L.J.'s judgment. I must not be

E taken as agreeing with it.

I agree that damages for financial loss other than the special damages must be scaled down as proposed by Lord Denning, M.R. (and indeed substantially accepted by counsel on behalf of the plaintiff) in order to give effect to the fact that the plaintiff is to be paid a lump sum now.

I adopt the figures set out in Lord Denning, M.R.'s judgment and the final

F result of £7,938 4s. 6d. I would allow the appeal accordingly.

WINN, L.J.: The only matter of substance raised by this appeal is the question whether in the calculation of the plaintiff's estimated monetary loss for the period beginning with the date of his compulsory retirement from the police force regard ought to be had to the pension of some £203 per year for life which then became payable to him pursuant to the terms of his service. This

G pension is not in my view to be regarded as subject to any material risk of discretionary abolition or reduction. I think that the point of principle is concluded in this court by *Browning* v. *War Office* (17) and *Parsons* v. *B.N.M. Laboratories, Ltd.* (19).

The issue between the parties was not so wide as the question which I have stated, since counsel for the plaintiff conceded that in respect of the period

H beginning in January, 1976, when the plaintiff would on the findings of the judge have been retired on pension if he had not been injured by the negligence of the defendant, this pension falls to be set off, in the calculation, against the pension of £515 which he would then have drawn from the police force. I have tried hard but unsuccessfully to appreciate any distinction in this respect between the two periods before and after December, 1975, other than the obvious difference that

I the plaintiff would have been drawing pay in the earlier one and in the later a pension.

Taking the hypothesis that the plaintiff had served in the police until December, 1975, both he and, notionally, his employers would have paid annually in the meantime contributions to the police pensions fund : the £515 per annum pension represents, in a loose sense, the product or return for all those contributions :

(17) [1962] 3 All E.R. 1089; [1963] 1 Q.B. 750.
(18) [1874-80] All E.R. Rep. 195; (1874), L.R. 10 Exch. 1.
(19) [1963] 2 All E.R. 658; [1964] 1 Q.B. 95.

none will have been made since the plaintiff retired. By bringing into reckoning **A** the £515 for the period beginning with 1976, as though it had been so provided, the plaintiff is not only allowed the full benefit, for that period, of what his employers would have contributed, but has not been debited with the contributions he would have made up to December, 1975. The defendant did not expressly raise this point, but I myself think that it should be taken into account.

In my opinion where the effect of an actionable event is (a) to deprive the **B** injured person of a vested right to a future pension of £x a year for life beginning from date A, provided that he has contributed £y a year up to that date, and (b) to bring into payment a smaller pension of £z from an earlier date B, then the true measure of monetary loss in this specific respect is the present capital value of an annuity of £x from date A reduced by the present value of £y payable from date B to date A, less the present capital value of an annuity of £z from date B. **C** The court may or may not in any particular case have the valuable help of an actuary: if not, it has long been used to make its own, no doubt cruder, assessment on this basis.

In my opinion this measure is to be applied wherever (i) the plaintiff claims damages for loss of earnings from an employment, (ii) the pensions in question are payable by virtue of a term of that employment. It will have no application **D** where a plaintiff, being already retired or otherwise independent of gainful employment before the accident, makes no claim for loss of earnings: nor, of course, and this was common ground, in any case where this head of damages may be inappropriate because post-accident earnings exceed the earnings of the plaintiff before he was injured. Damages for pain, loss of mobility, or enjoyment of life are different in kind from damages for monetary loss; the two are not to be **E** set off.

It has been cogently argued by counsel for the plaintiff that any benefit derived from insurance is the sole property of the insured and should not rebound in any way to the advantage of a tortfeasor who injures him; I agree with the proposition so stated, for which, of course, *Bradburn* v. *Great Western Ry. Co.* (20) is authority. I do not consider, however, that it should be applied or has ever been **F** applied to insurance provided in the form of pension or otherwise as part of the employment remuneration or consideration for which a plaintiff ex hypothesi a claimant for loss of earnings from that employment, has worked before suffering the actionable injury. It is relevant to observe, though not in itself a conclusive reason, that such insurance is not derived from an act of volition of the plaintiff in his private sphere deciding to take out and pay for a policy of insurance. **G**

In my judgment where a plaintiff asserts that a tort has deprived him of the whole or part of what he formerly earned from an employment, we must reduce his claim to the extent not only of all he is earning or able to earn in another employment but also of all that his former employment still produces in the form of pension as a set-off against lost earnings, no less than against loss of a potential pension. **H**

Counsel for the plaintiff further submitted that the plaintiff's pre-accident earnings should be notionally written up by adding the contributions made by his employers and by himself to the pensions fund. I have already pointed out that the £515 annuity item comprises these, notionally, in respect of the period subsequent to 1975 but my more general reason for rejecting the concept is that it is unrealistic and quite impracticable for the court to apply. **I**

I think that broadly speaking the defendant's bases of contention should apply and would allow the appeal by reducing the total damages to £7,938 4s. 6d.

Appeal allowed. Leave granted to appeal to the House of Lords.

Solicitors: *H. Smith*, Manchester (for the defendant); *Russell, Jones & Wacker* (for the plaintiff).

[*Reported by* F. GUTTMAN, ESQ., *Barrister-at-Law.*]

---

(20) [1874-80] All E.R. Rep. 195; (1874), L.R. 10 Exch. 1.

A   *Re Pilkington's Will Trusts* ([1961] 2 All E.R. 330) and *Pilkington* v.
Inland Revenue Comrs. ([1962] 3 All E.R. 622) distinguished.

[As to uncertain conditions as to religion attached to gifts, see 39 HALSBURY'S
LAWS (3rd Edn.) 924, para. 1398, and for cases on the subject, see 48 DIGEST
(Repl.) 302-304, *2656-2663.*

B   As to conditions precedent and subsequent, see 39 HALSBURY'S LAWS (3rd Edn.)
915, 916, para. 1387; and for cases on the subject, see 48 DIGEST (Repl.) 290,
2568-2570.

As to application of the rule against remoteness to powers, see 29 HALSBURY'S
LAWS (3rd Edn.) 325-332, paras. 646-665.]

Cases referred to:

C   *Allen (decd.), Re, Faith* v. *Allen,* [1953] 2 All E.R. 898; [1953] Ch. 810; [1953]
         3 W.L.R. 637; 48 Digest (Repl.) 303, *2660.*
A.-G. v. *National Provincial and Union Bank of England,* [1923] All E.R. Rep.
         123; [1924] A.C. 262; 93 L.J.Ch. 231; 131 L.T. 34; 8 Digest (Repl.)
         397, *892.*
Blaiberg, Re, Blaiberg v. *Marquise de Andia Yrarrzaval,* [1940] 1 All E.R.
D   632; [1940] Ch. 385; 109 L.J.Ch. 166; 162 L.T. 418; 48 Digest (Repl.)
         320, *2773.*
Burton's Settlement Trusts, Re, Public Trustee v. *Montefiore,* [1955] 1 All E.R.
         433; [1955] Ch. 348; [1955] 2 W.L.R. 452; 47 Digest (Repl.) 113, *816.*
Clayton v. *Ramsden,* [1943] 1 All E.R. 16; [1943] A.C. 320; 112 L.J.Ch. 22;
         168 L.T. 113; 48 Digest (Repl.) 320, *2774.*
E   *Eyre, Re, Eyre* v. *Eyre,* (1883), 49 L.T. 259; 37 Digest (Repl.) 396, *1273.*
Hancock v. *Watson,* [1900-03] All E.R. Rep. 87; [1902] A.C. 14; 71 L.J.Ch.
         149; 85 L.T. 729; 47 Digest (Repl.) 115, *823.*
Houston v. *Burns,* [1918-19] All E.R. Rep. 817; [1918] A.C. 337; 87 L.J.P.C.
         99; 118 L.T. 462; 48 Digest (Repl.) 403, *3512.*
Park, Re, Public Trustee v. *Armstrong,* [1931] All E.R. Rep. 633; [1932]
F   1 Ch. 580; 101 L.J.Ch. 295; 147 L.T. 118; 37 Digest (Repl.) 403, *1328.*
Pilkington's Will Trusts, Pilkington v. *Pilkington,* [1959] 2 All E.R. 623;
         [1959] Ch. 699; [1959] 3 W.L.R. 116; *revsd.* C.A. [1961] 2 All E.R. 330;
         [1961] Ch. 466; [1961] 2 W.L.R. 776; *revsd.* H.L., sub nom. *Pilkington*
         v. *Inland Revenue Comrs.* [1962] 3 All E.R. 622; [1964] A.C. 612;
         [1962] 3 W.L.R. 1051; Digest (Cont. Vol. A) 922, *1132a.*
G   *Selby's Will Trusts, Re, Donn* v. *Selby,* [1965] 3 All E.R. 386; [1966] 1 W.L.R.
         43; 48 Digest (Repl.) 304, *2663.*
Tarnpolsk (decd.), Re, Barclays Bank, Ltd. v. *Hyer,* [1958] 3 All E.R. 479;
         [1958] 1 W.L.R. 1157; 48 Digest (Repl.) 303, *2661.*
Vaux, Re, Nicholson v. *Vaux,* [1938] 4 All E.R. 297, 703; [1939] Ch. 465;
         108 L.J.Ch. 60, 211; 160 L.T. 65, 74; 20 Digest (Repl.) 479, *1861.*
H   *Vestey's Settlement, Re, Lloyds Bank, Ltd.* v. *O'Meara,* [1950] 2 All E.R. 891;
         [1951] Ch. 209; 47 Digest (Repl.) 275, *2388.*
Walter's Will Trusts, Re, National Provincial Bank, Ltd. v. *Board of Guardians
         and Trustees for Relief of Jewish Poor, Registered,* (1962), 106 Sol. Jo.
         221; 48 Digest (Repl.) 304, *2662.*
Wolffe's Will Trusts, Re, Shapley v. *Wolffe,* [1953] 2 All E.R. 697; [1953]
I   1 W.L.R. 1211; 48 Digest (Repl.) 302, *2658.*

Adjourned Summons.

Isidor Abrahams (" the testator ") died on Jan. 11, 1943, having made his will
on Apr. 16, 1940. The trustees of the will, as also of a settlement dated May 7,
1948 (" the 1948 settlement ") were, at the time of these proceedings, the defendants Gerald Milton Abrahams and Barclays Bank, Ltd. Gerald Milton Abrahams
and the defendant Charles Myer Abrahams were sons of the testator. On Aug.
14, 1946, the testator's son Gerald married the second plaintiff Doris Abrahams.
On May 7, 1948, a settlement was made in pursuance of cl. 17 of the testator's

will.   The terms of cl. 17 are set out at p. 1180, letters E and F, post.   Clause 4   **A**
of the 1948 settlement provided, so far as is necessary to be stated here—

" The trustees or (as the case may be) the executors of the testator's
will shall during the life of [the testator's son Gerald] stand possessed of
the trust fund upon the same trusts and with and subject to the same powers
(which powers including the power of advancement under cl. 16 of the said
will shall operate in addition to those hereby conferred) as are declared   **B**
and contained concerning the residuary estate of the testator and the
investments and property from time to time representing the same by and
in the said will of the testator . . ."

Other relevant provisions of the 1948 settlement are summarised at p. 1183, letters
D to F, post.   The testator's son Gerald and his wife had two children only,   **C**
the defendant Carole Jane Abrahams, who was born on Feb. 25, 1948, and the
defendant Linda Eve Abrahams, who was born on Sept. 14, 1950.   On May 24,
1957, " the 1957 settlement " was made, comprising two advances of £25,000
each, one for Carole and the other for Linda, as indicated at p. 1185, letters A and
B, post.   The present trustees of that settlement were the plaintiffs Isador Caplan
and Doris Abrahams.   The trusts declared of each of the two funds, Carole's   **D**
fund and Linda's fund, by the 1957 settlement were similar.   The trusts on
which Carole's fund were to be held were—

" 4 (1) During the minority of Carole the trustees shall at their discretion
apply all or any part of the income therefrom for Carole's maintenance,
education or benefit in such manner as they may think fit and shall invest
the surplus income (if any) and the resulting income thereof in any invest-   **E**
ments hereby authorised in augmentation of the capital of Carole's fund
such investments to be treated as a separate fund (hereinafter called
' Carole's accumulated fund ') but with power to the trustees to apply
the same as income at any time or times.

" (2) From and after the attainment by Carole of the age of twenty-one
years upon protective trusts for Carole during her life both as to the income   **F**
of Carole's fund and also the income of Carole's accumulated fund.

" (3) From and after Apr. 6, 1969, if Carole shall then be living the
trustees shall hold Carole's accumulated fund upon trust for Carole absolutely.

" (4) After the death of Carole and subject to any appointment to any
husband as hereinafter provided the trustees shall hold Carole's fund and
(if Carole shall have died before Apr. 6, 1969 Carole's accumulated fund   **G**
(which shall thenceforth be held with and as part of Carole's fund) and
the income therefrom respectively in trust for the children and remoter issue
of Carole (hereinafter called ' the said children and remoter issue ') at such
age or time or respective ages or times and if more than one in such shares
and with such executory and other trusts for the benefit of the said children
and remoter issue or of some or one of them and upon such conditions and   **H**
with such restrictions and in such manner as Carole by deed with or without
power of revocation and new appointment or by will or codicil at any time
or times without transgressing the rule against perpetuities may appoint.

" (5) In default of and until and subject to any and every such appointment
as aforesaid upon trust for the said children who shall survive Carole and
attain the age of twenty-one years or marry under that age and if more   **I**
than one in equal shares Provided that in the case of any of the said children
who shall have predeceased Carole leaving issue her surviving who shall
attain the age of twenty-one years or marry under that age such issue shall
stand in the place of such deceased child and take per stirpes and equally
between them if more than one the share which such deceased child would
have taken if he or she had survived Carole and had attained a vested
interest And Provided Further that unless Carole shall in manner aforesaid
appoint to the contrary none of the said children and remoter issue to whom

A   any part of Carole's fund shall have been appointed as aforesaid shall be entitled to any share of the unappointed part of Carole's fund without bringing the part appointed to him or her or to his or her issue or his or her ancestors into hotchpot and accounting for the same accordingly.

" (6) Subject to the trusts hereinbefore declared the trustees shall hold Carole's fund and the income therefrom or so much of the same as shall not

B   have become absolutely vested or been applied under any of the trusts or powers herein contained or under any statutory power upon such trusts as Carole shall by will or codicil appoint and in default of any such appointment or so far as any such appointment shall not extend the trustees shall hold Carole's fund and the income therefrom upon the like trusts as are

C   declared of and concerning Linda's fund."

The testator's widow, Eva Abrahams, died on Oct. 9, 1959. The testator was also survived by a sister, five brothers and eight nephews and nieces.

The present application was by originating summons dated Oct. 24, 1966, by the trustees of the 1957 settlement, Isador Caplan and Doris Abrahams, for the determination by the court of the following, among other questions:—

D   1. Whether on the true construction of cl. 17 of the testator's will the powers thereby conferred on the trustees thereof were (a) valid, or (b) void for uncertainty or otherwise. 2. If question 1 were answered in the sense of alternative (a), whether on the true construction of the testator's will and of the 1948 settlement and in the events which had happened the powers conferred on the trustees of the will (a) were validly exercised by the creation of the 1948 settlement;

E   or (b) were not validly exercised by the creation of the 1948 settlement or (c) were validly exercised only to some and if so what extent by the creation of the 1948 settlement. 3. Whether on the true construction of the said will and the 1948 settlement and in the events which had happened the statutory power of advancement was at the date of advances of £25,000 each, in favour of the defendants Carole and Linda, that were referred to in the recitals of the 1957

F   settlement (a) exercisable by the trustees of the said will as trustees of the 1948 settlement (as such) in favour of Carole and Linda respectively; or (b) exercisable by the trustees of the said will (as such) in favour of Carole and Linda respectively; or (c) exercisable by the trustees of the 1948 settlement (as such) in favour of Carole and Linda respectively; or (d) not exercisable in favour of Carole and Linda respectively either by the trustees of the 1948 settlement (as such) or

G   by the trustees of the said will (as such). 4. If the answer to question 3 was in the sense of alternatives (a) or (b) whether on the true construction of the testator's will the 1948 settlement and the 1957 settlement and, in the events which had happened the advances in favour of Carole and Linda respectively (a) were valid advances, or (b) were invalid advances by reason of the alterations to the effect of the declared trusts powers and provisions of the 1957 settlement

H   effected by the operation thereon of the rule against perpetuities. 5. If the answer to question 4 were in the sense of alternative (a) whether on the true construction of the will the 1948 settlement and the 1957 settlement and in the events which had happened all or any and if so which of the several trusts powers and provisions declared and contained in the 1957 settlement and shortly described in the schedule thereto were void as infringing the rule against perpetuities.

I   The defendants were Gerald Milton Abrahams, Carole and Linda, Charles Myer Abrahams (who claimed to be beneficially interested under the will and the 1948 settlement), Helen Geraldine Abrahams and Katharine Anna Abrahams (both of whom claimed to be beneficially interested under the trusts of the 1948 settlement), Hylda Sussman (one of the testator's nieces, who claimed to be beneficially interested under the said will), Barclays Bank, Ltd. (the co-trustee with the first defendant of the 1948 settlement); and the Commissioners of Inland Revenue.

The cases noted below* were cited during the argument in addition to those **A** referred to in the judgments.

I. Edwards-Jones, Q.C., for the plaintiffs.
G. F. Dearbergh for Gerald Milton Abrahams and Charles Myer Abrahams.
L. J. Bromley for Carole Jane Abrahams and Linda Eve Abrahams.
C. G. Heath for Helen Geraldine Abrahams and Katharine Anna Abrahams.
P. L. Gibson for Hylda Sussman. **B**
John Monckton for Barclays Bank, Ltd.
E. I. Goulding, Q.C., and *Jeremiah Harman* for the Crown.

CROSS, J.: By his will, which was made on Apr. 16, 1940, the late Isidor Abrahams ("the testator") bequeathed his residuary estate to his trustees on the usual administrative trusts and directed that, subject to those trusts, **C** they were to divide it into equal halves, as to one half to pay the income to his wife during her life and as to the second half, and also the first half from and after the death of his wife, to pay the income to his son, the first defendant, Gerald Milton Abrahams, during his life, and thereafter on trust for his children as he should by deed or will appoint, and in default of and subject to any such appointment on trust for all or any of his children who should attain the age of twenty- **D** one years or, being female, marry under that age, and if more than one in equal shares absolutely. Clause 17 and cl. 18 of the testator's will provided:

"17. I declare that in the event of my said son Gerald becoming engaged to be married to a person professing the Jewish faith my trustees may if they in their absolute and uncontrolled discretion think fit cause the whole of his share of my residuary estate or any part thereof (but subject to the **E** life interest of my said wife in a portion thereof under the trusts hereinbefore declared) to be comprised in a deed of settlement with themselves or either of them or such other person or persons as they may approve of as trustees upon such trusts as my trustees shall think fit for the benefit of such son of mine and his wife or intended wife or any future wife and any children or remoter issue of his (whether by his then present or intended wife or any future **F** wife) or for the benefit of any of such objects and with such ulterior or ultimate trusts and with such other provisions as my trustees shall think fit and I declare that in the event of any such settlement being executed the trusts thereof shall take effect in respect of the property thereby settled in substitution for the trusts hereinbefore declared.

"18. I declare that if my said son Gerald shall at any time marry a person **G** who shall not profess the Jewish faith then any share and interest in my residuary estate or the income thereof to which he or his issue shall then be entitled shall be forfeited and in lieu thereof my trustees shall pay to him an annuity during his life of £1,000 per annum free of income tax but not surtax and death duties to commence from the date of his marriage and to be payable by equal quarterly payments the first payment to be made **H** on the expiration of three months after the date of his marriage and subject thereto my trustees shall stand possessed of such share and interest in my residuary estate and the income thereof as shall have been forfeited as aforesaid upon the same trusts and subject to the same powers and provisions as if my said son Gerald were then dead."

The testator, died on Jan. 11, 1943. His will was proved by two of the executors **I** on May 6, 1943, and by the third on Nov. 11, 1943. In the year 1946 Gerald

* *Lawrie* v. *Bankes*, (1858), 4 K. & J. 142; *Clavering* v. *Ellison*, (1859), 7 H.L. Cas. 707; *Eland* v. *Baker*, (1861), 29 Beav. 137; *Minchin* v. *Minchin*, (1871), 5 I.R. Eq. 258; *Griffith-Boscawen* v. *Scott*, (1884), 26 Ch.D. 358; *Gilbey* v. *Rush*, [1906] 1 Ch. 11; *Re Horsfall*, *Hudleston* v. *Crofton*, [1911] 2 Ch. 63; *Re Boulton's Settlement Trust*, *Stewart* v. *Boulton*, [1928] Ch. 703; *Re Samuel. Jacobs* v. *Ramsden*, [1941] 3 All E.R. 196; [1942] Ch. 1; *Chichester Diocesan Fund and Board of Finance (Inc.)* v. *Simpson*, [1944] 2 All E.R. 60; [1944] A.C. 341; *Re Moss' Trusts*, *Moss* v. *Allen*, [1945] 1 All E.R. 207.

A married the second plaintiff, Doris Abrahams, a lady whom the trustees considered to profess the Jewish faith. In 1948 the trustees purported to exercise the power of appointment given to them by cl. 17 of the will, but now, many years later, the question has been raised whether or not that power is valid. The first ground on which it is said that it may be invalid is that one cannot say with certainty whether or not anyone professes the Jewish faith, and that
B therefore the trustees could not know whether the event on which the power was to arise had happened.

On these questions of certainty or uncertainty, the law draws a distinction between conditions subsequent which divest interests in property and conditions precedent, or qualifications, which have to be satisfied before the interests vest at all; and it requires a higher degree of certainty in the former case than in
C the latter. That distinction was clearly drawn in *Re Allen (decd.)*, *Faith v. Allen* (1), where a testator devised certain freeholds, after life interests, to the eldest of the sons of his nephew F. " who shall be a member of the Church of England and an adherent to the doctrine of that Church ", with a gift over. It was held on appeal (ROMER, L.J., dissenting) that the gift was not void for uncertainty. The formula was not a condition subsequent, where the clarity had to be such
D that the exact event which would cause the gift to be divested had to be apparent from the outset. This was a condition precedent, or a qualification and, to satisfy it, it was not necessary that its scope should be capable of exact definition. All that a claimant had to show was that he, at least, was within the requirement. Membership of the Church of England comprised wide differences of degree, but it was an intelligible qualification of the class of intended beneficiaries, and
E though it might be difficult to say of some persons whether they were or were not members, that did not of necessity render it impossible for a particular individual to establish that he was a member, and he ought not to be debarred from attempting to show that he fulfilled the qualification. Similarly, the second expression " an adherent to the doctrine of the Church of England ", though involving questions of degree which would defeat a condition subsequent, was
F not, as a qualification, void for uncertainty. The test of adherence to the doctrines of the Church of England was directed to ensuring a conscientious and sincere attachment to the general teaching of that Church as distinct from any other, and on the ordinary meaning of the expression it was capable of reasonable application.

There is no doubt that, having regard to the decision of the House of Lords in
G *Clayton v. Ramsden* (2) the condition in cl. 18, which is undoubtedly a condition subsequent divesting Gerald of his interest in the residuary estate in the event of his marrying a person not professing the Jewish faith, is void for uncertainty. The point which I must ask myself, however, is whether the condition in cl. 17 ought to be judged by the strict rule applicable to conditions subsequent or by the more charitable rule applicable to conditions precedent. There is no doubt
H that the condition in cl. 17 is in one sense a condition precedent; but it is not a condition precedent to a gift to Gerald. If the clause said, " In the event of Gerald becoming engaged to be married to a woman professing the Jewish faith my trustees shall pay him £1,000 ", the case would undoubtedly be within the principle of *Re Allen* (1); but this condition is a condition precedent to the arising of a power of appointment in the trustees, and it is argued that such a
I condition ought to be regarded as a divesting condition because in theory, at least, the trustees might exercise the power to cut down Gerald's interest below the life interest which he took before his marriage to the lady in question. They might after his marriage give all the property to his wife and children and cut him out altogether, because the power enables them to appoint to the benefit of any of the objects. Now it is plain from the framework of the will

---

(1) [1953] 2 All E.R. 898; [1953] Ch. 810.
(2) [1943] 1 All E.R. 16; [1943] A.C. 320.

that the testator wished Gerald to marry a lady professing the Jewish faith, **A**
and that if he married such a lady the trustees were to have power to make
provision for his wife. They did not have such a power under the will as it stood,
which simply provided for a life interest to Gerald with remainder to his children.
The idea that in the exercise of this power the trustees would cut out Gerald
altogether is very far-fetched. To my mind it is proper to regard this power as a
possible additional benefit for Gerald in the event of his marrying a lady who **B**
professed the Jewish faith. I think, therefore, that the words in question should
be construed as though they were a condition precedent to a gift to Gerald
and, so construed, it does not appear to me that the power is invalid. In some
cases, no doubt, there may be difficulty in saying whether the person in question
is professing the Jewish faith or not, and it is because of that possibility that the
condition subsequent in cl. 18 is void, but I do not think that the expression **C**
" professing the Jewish faith " is meaningless. One can say of some persons
that without a doubt they profess the Jewish faith. It would, for example, be
absurd to say that one could not be sure whether the Chief Rabbi was a person
professing the Jewish faith.

I have been referred to a number of cases on the subject. *Re Blaiberg, Blaiberg*
v. *Marquise De Andia Yrarrzaval* (3), in which MORTON, J., had to consider **D**
the words " Cease or fail to profess . . . the Jewish faith ", was a case of a condition subsequent, and it throws no light on this case. The decision of HARMAN,
J., in *Re Wolffe's Will Trusts, Shapley* v. *Wolffe* (4) was given before *Re Allen* (5);
and, although I have no reason to think that the decision was not right, it may
well be that if he had had the decision of the Court of Appeal before him he would
have expressed himself somewhat differently. *Re Tarnpolsk* (*decd.*), *Barclays* **E**
Bank, Ltd. v. *Hyer* (6) turned on the words " a person of the Jewish race ",
which may perhaps raise different considerations. Then there is the decision of
BUCKLEY, J., in *Re Selby's Will Trusts, Donn* v. *Selby* (7). By cl. 13 of his will
the testator declared that:

> " No beneficiary . . . who shall have married or who before or on attaining
> a vested interest shall marry out of the Jewish faith shall take any interest **F**
> or benefit . . ."

The judge held that the requirement was a condition precedent to qualifying as
a beneficiary and not a condition subsequent and that on its true construction
in the context of the will, the prohibition was against marrying someone who
was not an adherent of the Jewish faith at the time of the marriage, and that **G**
although there might be difficult border-line cases the phrase was not meaningless
and was sufficiently definite and intelligible to be valid as a condition precedent,
although not necessarily as a condition subsequent, where the more stringent test
of determining the exact scope of the condition had to be satisfied. That decision
agrees entirely with my view of the matter.

Finally, I should refer to *Re Walter's Will Trusts, National Provincial Bank,* **H**
Ltd. v. *Board of Guardians and Trustees for Relief of Jewish Poor, Registered* (8).
That was decided in 1962, but it does not appear to have been brought to the
attention of BUCKLEY, J., in *Re Selby* (7). The words in question were:

> " To each of my grandchildren and great-grandchildren who shall marry
> in the Jewish faith within twenty-one years of the death of the last survivor
> of my children the sum of £200 to be paid upon such marriage as a wedding **I**
> gift . . ."

The report is very short, and it may be that there were circumstances which would
distinguish the case from *Re Selby* (7), but the only difference which I can see
is that, whereas BUCKLEY, J., had to deal with a condition against marriage out

---

(3) [1940] 1 All E.R. 632; [1940] Ch. 385.   (4) [1953] 2 All E.R. 697.
(5) [1953] 2 All E.R. 898; [1953] Ch. 810.   (6) [1958] 3 All E.R. 479.
(7) [1965] 3 All E.R. 386.   (8) (1962), 106 Sol. Jo. 221.

A of the Jewish faith, PLOWMAN, J., had to deal with a condition of marriage within the Jewish faith. It was suggested that that was a relevant distinction and that I ought to follow the decision in *Re Walter's Will Trusts* (9) as being nearer to this case. I am not prepared to do that; and if and so far as *Re Walter's Will Trusts* (9) conflicts with *Re Selby* (10), I prefer the decision in *Re Selby* (10).

[HIS LORDSHIP heard argument on question 2 (set out at p. 1179, letter E, ante).]

B
   CROSS, J.: It will be remembered that under the will of the testator, the first defendant, his son Gerald, had a protected life interest in his residuary estate, and then on his death there was a trust for his children as he should by deed or will appoint and in default of appointment for his children who attained the age of twenty-one, or being female married, in equal shares. If those trusts

C in favour of Gerald and his children should fail, then the testator's residuary estate was to be held in trust for such of the nephews and nieces of the testator, the children of his brothers and sister, as should be living at his death in equal shares absolutely. There was a power to the trustees to raise all or any part of the capital and pay it to Gerald. [HIS LORDSHIP read cl. 17 of the testator's will, which is set out at p. 1180, letters E and F, ante, and continued:] Gerald became

D engaged and was married in 1946, and then in 1948 the will trustees exercised their power by a document of May 7, 1948 (" the 1948 settlement "). Putting the matter shortly, what they did was first by cl. 4 to give Gerald an unprotected life interest in a third of the residuary estate, and by cl. 5 to declare that after the death of Gerald the capital was to be held on the same trusts and subject to the same powers as were declared by the will with the exception (a) that issue

E of Gerald more remote than children became objects of his power of appointment and (b) that there was inserted between the trusts for the children of Gerald and the trusts for the testator's nephews and nieces, trusts for the children and remoter issue of the testator's second son Charles as Gerald should by deed or will or codicil appoint, and in default of such appointment as Charles himself should likewise appoint and in default of or subject to any such appointment for such

F of the children of Charles as should attain the age of twenty-one or being female marry under that age, in equal shares, with a proviso for a hotchpot. Gerald was given an overriding power to appoint by deed or will or codicil a life or lesser interest in one-half or any smaller part of the income of the residuary estate to any wife who might survive him.

   I have already decided that the power purported to be created in cl. 17 was not

G void by reason of the uncertainty of the phrase " a person professing the Jewish faith " (see p. 1182, letter C, ante), but I have now to consider other objections, either to the power itself or to the mode in which, if the power was valid, it was exercised. First of all it is said that, as a matter of construction, the words " ulterior or ultimate trusts " were not unlimited so far as the class of beneficiaries was concerned and did not enable the trustees to interpose, between the trust

H for the children of Gerald and the trusts for the nephews and nieces, the provisions which I have read in favour of the children and remoter issue of the second son, Charles. In my judgment that is not the way in which the power should be construed. It was suggested that the words " ulterior or ultimate trusts " could be confined to gifts over between the class of beneficiaries earlier referred to—that is, Gerald and his wife or intended wife or future wife—and his children

I or remoter issue, and did not include trusts for other persons on the failure of the trusts for Gerald and his family. That would be a highly unnatural construction of the words, particularly in view of the fact that the trusts are to be in substitution for the trusts declared previously with regard to the residuary estate. I think that " ulterior or ultimate trusts " means trusts to take effect on the failure or termination of the trusts in favour of Gerald, his wife or wives and his children and issue, and so there is no objection, so far as the class of interposed

---

(9) (1962), 106 Sol. Jo. 221.   (10) [1965] 3 All E.R. 386.

beneficiaries goes, to the way in which the power was exercised by the 1948 **A**
document. Then it is said that on that construction the power in cl. 17 so far as
regards the ulterior or ultimate trusts must be bad, as amounting to a delegation
of the testator's will-making power to his trustees. That brings one into the
difficult country which was partially explored by CLAUSON, J., in *Re Park,
Public Trustee* v. *Armstrong* (11). The problem is how to reconcile the very broad
statements of VISCOUNT HALDANE in *Houston* v. *Burns* (12) and *A.-G.* v. *National* **B**
Provincial and Union Bank of England (13) with the accepted doctrines of the
Court of Chancery as to the creation of special powers of appointment. As a
matter of construction, cl. 17 merely confers a power and does not impose a trust
on the trustees. There are perfectly good existing trusts under the will which
will continue to take effect in default of the trustees exercising the power given
them by cl. 17. It is not a trust imposed on them; it is a mere power. It is a **C**
fiduciary power given to them in the capacity of trustees, and they cannot
release it. They must retain it unless and until they exercise it, and consider
from time to time whether they ought to exercise it. So far as regards what one
may call the primary class of beneficiaries, it is a perfectly ordinary special power,
and nobody could suggest that there is any objection to it. What is said is that,
on the construction that I have put on the words " ulterior or ultimate trusts ", **D**
if there is failure of the trusts in favour of the primary class then there is an
unlimited power, a power to appoint to anybody except the trustees, which
amounts to a delegation of the testator's power of making the will for himself.
It is said that CLAUSON, J.'s judgment in *Re Park* (11) would have been different
if the lady in question there had been a trustee. The facts in that case were that
the testator gave his residuary estate to his trustee in trust to pay the income to **E**
any person other than herself or a charitable institution or institutions and in
such shares and proportions as his sister, Jane Armstrong, should from time to
time during her life direct in writing, and from and after her decease in trust as
to both capital and income for the Imperial Merchant Service Guild for the benefit
of their stress fund absolutely. CLAUSON, J., construed that as a gift to the
Imperial Merchant Service Guild in default of, and to the extent to which it was **F**
not divested by, any exercise of the power by the sister during her lifetime; and
he held that there was no objection to the creation of that power in Miss Armstrong
and that nothing that LORD HALDANE said in the cases to which I have referred
could have been intended to say that this creation of a power of that sort was
impossible. It is true that he did point out that Miss Armstrong was not herself
a trustee, but I cannot for myself see that that makes the least difference so long **G**
as one is dealing with a mere power and not a trust. I am supported in that view
by the decision of KAY, J., in *Re Eyre, Eyre* v. *Eyre* (14), where he plainly considered that a fiduciary power such as I am dealing with here was valid, because
he debated the question whether or not it could be released and decided that it
could not be released. It is possible, of course, that the point that the power was
invalid was not perceived either by the counsel who argued the case or by the **H**
judge. This case, however, was argued on one side by Mr. Wolstenholme, and on
the other side by Mr. Davey, Q.C., and KAY, J., was himself a very eminent judge;
and I think that it is most unlikely that, if the point were a good one, they would
all have overlooked it. So I find support in that case in coming to the decision
that there is no objection to the power here, even on the footing that the words
" ulterior or ultimate trusts " are construed as I have construed them. **I**

[HIS LORDSHIP accordingly declared, in answer to questions 1 and 2, that on the
true construction of cl. 17 of the testator's will the power thereby conferred on the
trustees was valid and was validly exercised by the creation of the 1948 settlement.

HIS LORDSHIP then turned to question 3 raised by the originating summons

(11) [1931] All E.R. Rep. 633; [1932] 1 Ch. 580.
(12) [1918-19] All E.R. Rep. 817; [1918] A.C. 337.
(13) [1923] All E.R. Rep. 123; [1924] A.C. 262.
(14) (1883), 49 L.T. 259.

A (see p. 1179, letter F, ante). His LORDSHIP intimated that with the consent of the
testator's son, Gerald, two sums of £25,000 were advanced in 1957 for the trustees
of the 1948 settlement, who were the same persons as the executors of the testator's will, and that it was clear that the power of advancement which, until the
execution of the 1948 settlement, was vested in Barclays Bank, Ltd. and the
testator's widow and Mr. Cohen as executors of the testator's will, came to an
B end with the execution of the 1948 settlement, because all the capital trusts of
the will were then replaced by the capital trusts of the 1948 settlement, yet the
persons who were executors of the will in 1957 and also trustees of the 1948 settlement certainly had in the latter capacity a statutory power of advancement with
the consent of the testator's sons Gerald and Charles (which was obtained) in
favour of Gerald's two daughters, Carole and Linda. His LORDSHIP held that the
C advances were unobjectionable so far as concerned the persons who made them
and the capacity in which they were made and declared that, on the true construction of the will and of the 1948 settlement, the statutory powers of advancement
were, at the date of the purported advances of £25,000 which were referred to in
the 1957 settlement, exercisable by the trustees of the testator's will as trustees
of the 1948 settlement and were purportedly so exercised.

D   His LORDSHIP then turned to question 5 raised by the originating summons
(see p. 1179, letter H, ante), whether certain of the trusts powers and provisions
contained in the 1957 settlement were void as infringing the rule against
perpetuities. His LORDSHIP heard argument on this question and continued:]
The two advances of £25,000 which were made on May 24, 1957, were by way of
settlement. In *Pilkington* v. *Inland Revenue Comrs.* (15) the House of Lords
E decided that such advances were not open to any objection in principle, but that
the power of advancement must be treated as a special power of appointment for
the purpose of the application of the rule against perpetuities to the interest
created by the settlement. It is plain that the draftsman of the settlement of
May 24, 1957, which was made several years before the *Pilkington* case (15) was
decided, considered that for the purpose of the application of the rule against
F perpetuities the settlement could be treated as though it was an ordinary settlement made by a settlor who was absolutely entitled to the trust fund, and did
not realise that the trusts of it had to be read back into the will of the testator
for the purpose of the application of the rule. The testator died in 1943, Carole,
the eldest child of Gerald was born on Feb. 25, 1948, and Linda, the youngest
daughter, was born on Sept. 14, 1950, so they were respectively about nine and
G 6½ when the settlement was made. It is common ground between the parties
that as Carole and Linda were not alive at the date of the testator's death all the
trusts and powers declared by and contained in cl. 4 (5) and all the later clauses
of the settlement are void for perpetuity and it is also common ground that
some of the trusts in cl. 4 (1) to (4), are valid (for these provisions see p. 1178,
letters E to H, ante). Indeed, the only dispute as to the application of the
H rule relates to the power in cl. 4, (4) so far as it applies to the original funds of
Carole or Linda as the case may be. If it were not for the words " without transgressing the rule against perpetuities " at the end of sub-cl. (4) of cl. 4, that power
of appointment would plainly be bad because it would be exercisable at any time
during the lives of Carole or Linda as the case might be. They, of course, were not
lives in being. It was, however, argued (in reliance on the case of *Re Vaux,*
I *Nicholson* v. *Vaux* (16)) that the meaning of the words " without transgressing
the rule against perpetuities " was that no appointment could be made under the
power which created interests which might possibly vest more than twenty-one
years after the death of Gerald, and that therefore the power was good. I cannot
construe those words in that way in this document. As I have said, the draftsman
of the settlement did not realise that the power and any appointment made under

---

(15) [1962] 3 All E.R. 622; [1964] A.C. 612.
(16) [1938] 4 All E.R. 297; [1939] Ch. 465.

it, would have to be read back into the will of the testator. He assumed that the **A** power was exercisable by Carole, to take her case, at any time during her life without regard to the rule against perpetuities, because he regarded her as a life in being. All that he meant by the words " without transgressing the rule against perpetuities " was that any interests which she might create by exercising the power must vest within the perpetuity period reckoned from the date of the settlement. To read the words, in the way suggested by counsel for Carole, as a **B** reference to the rule as it actually applies to the case and not as a reference to the rule as the draftsman thought it applied to the case, would restrict the power in a very drastic manner. In the case of *Re Vaux* (17) the phrase in question (which was ". . . save only that all such dealings with the residuary trust fund and the income and accumulations thereof shall be within the limitations prescribed by law ") occurred in the will of the testator creating the power. Further- **C** more, the appointment under the power had to be by an inter vivos act. In those circumstances the Court of Appeal held that if and when the trustees made any appointment under the power all one had to do was simply to ask oneself whether, if the actual appointment had been contained in the will, it would necessarily vest, if at all, not later than twenty-one years after the expiration of some life in being and the testator's death. Here, however, the power itself **D** is created by a sub-settlement and moreover it is exercisable by will as well as by deed. So if one were to read the whole thing back into the will and try to mould it in such a way as not to transgress the rule against perpetuities, one would find the testator providing that an unborn daughter of his son Gerald could make an appointment, by deed or will, providing that the interests given necessarily vested, if at all, within twenty-one years of Gerald's death and provided **E** further that if the appointment was made by will the appointer herself did not survive her father by more than twenty-one years. That would be a most extraordinary power to confer, and the fact that so very little of the power actually given by sub-cl. (4) would survive if one read the phrase " without transgressing the rule against perpetuities " in the way suggested, is, I think, a further reason against reading it in that way. Therefore I shall hold that the **F** power in sub-cl. (4) is bad.

[His Lordship accordingly declared that, on the true construction of the testator's will and the 1948 settlement and the 1957 settlement, all the beneficial trusts purportedly created and all powers of appointment purportedly conferred by the 1957 settlement were void as infringing the rule against perpetuities, with the exception of certain specified trusts or powers which included those declared **G** by cl. 4 (1) in respect of the minority of Carole, cl. 4 (2) concerning the income of Carole's accumulated fund for her life after attaining twenty-one, cl. 4 (3), being a trust of the capital of Carole's accumulated fund, and the powers conferred by cl. 4 (4) on her to appoint her accumulated fund and the income thereof in favour of her children and remoter issue without transgressing the rule against perpetuities. His Lordship then turned to question 4 of the originating summons **H** (see p. 1179, letter G, ante) whether the advances in favour of Carole and Linda were valid or invalid advances. His Lordship continued:] I now have to consider what is the result of many of the trusts and powers in the 1957 settlement being void for perpetuity. Is the result that the whole settlement is a nullity, or do those trusts and powers which are not void for perpetuity take effect? If so, what happens to the interests which are void for perpetuity? Have they never **I** left the 1948 settlement, or are they taken by Carole and Linda, the two daughters of Gerald, absolutely in equal shares?

The second recital of the 1957 settlement states:

" The executors in exercise of the statutory powers of advancement and of all other powers thereunto enabling them and with the consent (already signified) of Charles Myer Abrahams and the said Gerald Milton Abrahams

---

(17) [1938] 4 All E.R. Rep. 297; [1939] Ch. 465.

A have advanced to the trustees out of the moiety of the residuary estate of
the said Isidor Abrahams now held in trust for the said Gerald Milton
Abrahams the sum of £25,000 for the benefit of Carole Jane (hereinafter
referred to as ' Carole ') a daughter of the said Gerald Milton Abrahams
[then it gives the date of her birth] and have also advanced to the trustees out
of the same moiety a further sum of £25,000 for the benefit of Linda Eve

B (hereinafter referred to as ' Linda ') the other daughter of the said Gerald
Milton Abrahams [and it gives the date of her birth] and the executors have
paid to the trustees the said two sums of £25,000 each making together the
aggregate sum of £50,000 part of which said sum the trustees have invested in
the investments described in Part 1 of the schedule hereto for the trustees to
hold together with the cash amount stated in Part 2 of the said schedule

C (being the balance of the said sum of £50,000 after paying the purchase price
for the said investments and the costs and expenses in connexion therewith
and with the preparation and execution of this settlement) upon the respective trusts hereinafter declared of and concerning the same as the trustees
hereby acknowledge."

D Then, in cl. 1 there is a definition of " Carole's fund " as, " one undivided moiety
of the investments and cash described in the schedule hereto "; there is a corresponding definition of " Linda's fund "; and then there is a definition of " the
trust funds " as meaning " Carole's fund and Linda's fund together ". Then, in
cl. 3 the trustees are directed to hold " the trust funds and the income therefrom
upon the following trusts ". Then there are set out trusts for the payment of any
duty that might be payable on Gerald's death, and costs; and then, " subject as

E aforesaid upon the trusts declared in the next two succeeding clauses ".

Clause 4 sets out the trusts of Carole's fund, and cl. 5 sets out corresponding
trusts, mutatis mutandis, of Linda's fund. It is only necessary to read the trusts
of Carole's fund. Clause 4 (1), (2) state:

F " During the minority of Carole the trustees shall at their discretion
apply all or any part of the income therefrom for Carole's maintenance
education or benefit in such manner as they may think fit and shall invest
the surplus income (if any) and the resulting income thereof in any investments hereby authorised in augmentation of the capital of Carole's fund
such investments to be treated as a separate fund (hereinafter called
' Carole's accumulated fund ').

G " (2) From and after the attainment by Carole of the age of twenty-one
years upon protective trusts for Carole during her life both as to the income
of Carole's fund and also the income of Carole's accumulated fund.

" (3) From and after Apr. 6, 1969, if Carole shall then be living the trustees
shall hold Carole's accumulated fund upon trust for Carole absolutely."

H There is no question that cl. 4 (1) is good as far as the rule against perpetuities
goes, because Carole must attain twenty-one, if at all, within twenty-one years
of Gerald's death, Gerald being alive at the date of the death of the testator and
at the date when the settlement was made in 1957. So far as cl. 4 (2) and cl. 4 (3)
relate to the accumulated fund, they are wholly good having regard to the dates.
So far as they relate to Carole's fund, the income interest to Carole during her
life or until she shall commit an act of forfeiture is good, but the discretionary

I trust which would arise if she committed an act of forfeiture would be bad.

Clause 4 (4) gives powers (18) of appointment over the accumulated fund and
the main fund to Carole in favour of her issue. So far as concerns the accumulated
fund, that is good; so far as concerns the main fund, I have held it to be bad.
Clause 4 (5) declares (18) trusts of capital for Carole's issue, all of which are bad.
Then, in cl. 4 (6) there is (18) an ultimate trust of Carole's fund " as Carole shall

_____

(18) Sub-cll. (4), (5) and (6) of cl. 4 are set out at p. 1178, letter G, to p. 1179, letter
C, ante.

by will or codicil appoint ", which is bad, " and in default of any such appoint- A
ment " an accruer trust to Linda's fund, which is also bad. Then, in cl. 5 there
are the trusts as regards Linda's fund, which mutatis mutandis, are the same.

Then, cl. 6 contains trusts (which are void for perpetuity) to take effect in the
event of the preceding trusts all failing. In that event the trustees are directed to
hold both trust funds for the other children of Gerald " who shall be living at
the date of such failure and shall have attained or shall thereafter attain the age B
of twenty-one years ". Then,

> " in the event of the failure in whole or part of such trusts in trust for
> such person or persons as would have become entitled under the Administra-
> tion of Estates Act, 1925 as amended . . . at the death of the last to die of
> Carole and Linda and as if such last to die had died possessed thereof
> intestate and unmarried."

So, although the draftsman had not appreciated the operation of the rule against
perpetuities, the trusts are very comprehensive and cover the event of the failure
of the trusts of Carole's and Linda's funds.

A situation somewhat similar to the situation which faces me arose in *Re
Pilkington's Will Trusts, Pilkington* v. *Pilkington* (19), but there is this great D
difference that there the advance by way of settlement had not actually been
made; the trustees were simply asking the court whether they could make it.
The Court of Appeal (20), reversing DANCKWERTS, J. (21), held that an advance
by way of a settlement, so to say, over the head of an infant beneficiary could
not be made at all, but UPJOHN, L.J., did say something with regard to what would
be the effect on such a settlement of the rule against perpetuities if, contrary to E
the view which he was taking, such a settlement was in principle permissible.
He said (22):

> " I desire to add a few words on the application to this case of the rule
> against perpetuities. In the ordinary conventional case where an advance-
> ment is made to an adult who can settle the sum advanced to him, no doubt
> no question as to reading back a new settlement into the head settlement F
> would arise, but in this case the object of the power, being of tender years,
> is incapable of making any settlement. Consequently, the trustees can only
> justify the making of a settlement provided it is within the powers conferred
> upon them by s. 32 [of the Trustee Act, 1925]. That is plainly a special
> power and of course the trusts created by virtue of the exercise of the power
> must conform to the rule against remoteness. Moreover, being a special G
> power it is clear that its exercise must for the purpose of the rule be written
> into the instrument creating the power . . . What, then, is the consequence
> of that? I must examine briefly the terms of the new settlement. I am
> content to assume that the gift of income to Penelope from the time when
> she shall attain the age of twenty-one years until she shall attain the age of
> thirty years is good, but the next direction that the trustees shall hold the H
> capital of the trust fund on trust for Penelope if she shall attain the age
> of thirty years absolutely, is prima facie bad. It may be—the question
> has not been argued before us—that s. 163 of the Law of Property Act, 1925,
> saves it. If it does save it, it does so by directing the trustees to hold the
> capital of the trust fund for Penelope absolutely on attaining the age of
> twenty-one years. The next trust for the children of Penelope, if she shall I
> die under the age of thirty years, is plainly bad on any footing. The effect,
> therefore, of the rule against perpetuities on the proposed settlement is basic;
> it entirely alters the settlement, and that seems to me to be fatal to this case,
> for the trustees have never been asked to express any opinion as to whether

(19) [1962] 3 All E.R. 622; [1964] A.C. 612 (H.L.).
(20) [1961] 2 All E.R. 330; [1961] Ch. 466.
(21) [1959] 2 All E.R. 623; [1959] Ch. 699.
(22) [1961] 2 All E.R. at pp. 340, 341; [1961] Ch. at pp. 488, 489.

A   they would think the proposed settlement, modified by reason of the rule
against perpetuities in the manner I have mentioned, is for the benefit of
Penelope. That is a matter to which they have never addressed their minds,
and therefore, it cannot possibly be justified under s. 32, for it has not been
shown that the trustees think that the settlement, as so modified, is for the
advancement or benefit of Penelope. On that ground too, therefore, I
B   would think that the transfer to the trustees of this new settlement is
entirely beyond the powers of the trustees."

When the case went to the House of Lords (23), their lordships took a view
different from that of the Court of Appeal (24) on the question of principle, and
held that there was no objection in principle to an advancement to an infant
beneficiary by way of settlement. VISCOUNT RADCLIFFE, however, who delivered
C   the leading speech, approved what UPJOHN, L.J., had said about the rule against
perpetuities. I will read a passage from LORD RADCLIFFE'S speech (25):

" The other issue on which this case depends, that relating to the application of the rule against perpetuities, does not seem to me to present much
difficulty. It is not in dispute that, if the limitations of the proposed settle-
D   ment are to be treated as if they had been made by the testator's will and as
coming into operation at the date of his death, there are trusts in it which
would be void ab initio as violating the perpetuity rule. They postpone final
vesting by too long a date. It is also a familiar rule of law in this field that,
whereas appointments made under a general power of appointment conferred
by will or deed are read as taking effect from the date of the exercise of the
E   power, trusts declared by a special power of appointment, the distinguishing
feature of which is that it can allocate property among a limited class of
persons only, are treated as coming into operation at the date of the instrument that creates the power. The question, therefore, resolves itself into
asking whether the exercise of a power of advancement which takes the form
of a settlement should be looked on as more closely analogous to a general or
F   to a special power of appointment. On this issue I am in full agreement with
the views of UPJOHN, L.J., in the Court of Appeal (26). Indeed, much of
the reasoning that has led me to my conclusion on the first issue that I have
been considering leads me to think that for this purpose there is an effective
analogy between powers of advancement and special powers of appointment.
When one asks what person can be regarded as the settlor of Miss Penelope's
G   proposed settlement, I do not see how it is possible to say that she is herself
or that the trustees are. She is the passive recipient of the benefit extracted
for her from the original trusts: the trustees are merely exercising a fiduciary
power in arranging for the desired limitations. It is not their property that
constitutes the funds of Miss Penelope's settlement: it is the property subjected to trusts by the will of the testator and passed over into the new
H   settlement through the instrumentality of a power which by statute is made
appendant to those trusts. I do not think, therefore, that it is important to
this issue that money raised under a power of advancement passes entirely
out of the reach of the existing trusts and makes, as it were, a new start under
fresh limitations, the kind of thing that happened under the old form of
family resettlement when the tenant in tail in remainder barred the entail
I   with the consent of the protector of the settlement. I think that the
important point for the purpose of the rule against perpetuities is that the
new settlement is only effected by the operation of a fiduciary power which
itself ' belongs ' to the old settlement. In the conclusion, therefore, there are
legal objections to the proposed settlement which the trustees have placed

(23) [1962] 3 All E.R. 622; [1964] A.C. 612.
(24) [1961] 2 All E.R. 330; [1961] Ch. 466.
(25) [1962] 3 All E.R. at pp. 631, 632; [1964] A.C. at pp. 641, 642.
(26) [1961] 2 All E.R. at pp. 340, 341; [1961] Ch. at pp. 488, 489.

before the court. Again I agree with UPJOHN, L.J., that these objections go   A
to the root of what is proposed and I do not think that it would be satisfactory that the court should try to frame a qualified answer to the question
that they have propounded, which would express the general view that the
power to advance by way of a settlement of this sort does exist and the special
view that the power to make this particular settlement does not."

I do not think that it can be disputed that the effect of the rule against perpetui-   B
ties on this settlement is every bit as basic as it was on the proposed settlement in
Re Pilkington's Will Trusts (27). It alters the settlement completely. So it is
argued by counsel for the Crown, whose interest it is that the settlement should
be void and that the income should go back to Gerald, that if it was beyond the
powers of the Pilkington trustees to execute the proposed settlement in that case
without having considered whether the settlement as modified by the law against   C
perpetuities would be for Penelope's benefit, so it must have been beyond the
powers of the trustees in this case to execute the 1957 settlement without having
realised, and consequently without having considered, the effect which the law
against perpetuities would have on it. They were, he says, exercising the power
of advancement on the footing that they were producing a certain result, and in
fact they produced a totally different result; and so, he says, it would not be   D
right to say that they had exercised the power at all.

In support of that approach counsel for the Crown relied on what was said by
SIR RAYMOND EVERSHED, M.R., in *Re Vestey's Settlement, Lloyds Bank, Ltd.* v.
O'Meara (28). In that particular case SIR RAYMOND EVERSHED thought that the
discretionary power in question, which was a power to distribute income among
a large class, had been effectively exercised because the result which was actually   E
produced was not, in his judgment, to use his words (29), " substantially or
essentially different from that which was intended ".   It appears, however, that if
he had thought that the result of the exercise of the discretion was substantially or
essentially different from what the trustees had intended, he would have held that
it had not been effectively exercised at all, though it is to be observed that that
was not a case involving the application of the rule against perpetuities.   F

Counsel for Carole and Linda, on the other hand, relied on the well-settled
principle of law that if the donee of a special power of appointment—and I think
it is conceded that for this purpose it does not make any difference whether the
donee is a trustee of the power or not—exercises the power by appointing a valid
life interest followed by further limitations which are void for perpetuity, the
effect is that only the further limitations are invalid and the life interest remains   G
good. It may very well be that in many cases of that sort, if the trustee making
the appointment had realised that the ulterior limitations would be void, he
would not have made any appointment at all; but in such cases the court does
not enter into speculation of that sort so as to invalidate interests which in
themselves are good. (See MORRIS AND LEACH, THE RULE AGAINST PERPETUITIES
(2nd Edn.) p. 154.)   H

Counsel pointed out that LORD RADCLIFFE and UPJOHN, L.J., themselves
recognised that a power of advancement was analogous to a special power of
appointment vested in the trustees, and he said that the fact that the trustees
might not have made the advance by way of settlement if they had realised what
the effect of the rule against perpetuities would be is no more relevant than it
would have been if they had been exercising an ordinary special power of appoint-   I
ment to create successive interests. The particular problem which faces me was
clearly not present at all to the minds of UPJOHN, L.J., or LORD RADCLIFFE. They
were dealing with a proposed advance, and I do not think that I can deduce from
what they said about it what they would have said if the *Pilkington* (27) settlement had been already executed and they had been faced with the argument

(27) [1962] 3 All E.R. 622; [1964] A.C. 612.
(28) [1950] 2 All E.R. 891 at pp. 896, 897, 899, 900; [1951] Ch. 209 at pp. 216, 220, 221.
(29) [1950] 2 All E.R. at p. 900; [1951] Ch. at p. 221.

A which faces me, based on the analogy which they themselves drew of a special power of appointment. I think, therefore, that I must consider the matter for myself.

As LORD RADCLIFFE and UPJOHN, L.J., said, a power of advancement is certainly analogous to a special power of appointment, but it differs from an ordinary special power in this, that there is only one object of it. The power

B which the trustees purported to exercise by setting up Carole's fund (to take her as an example) and declaring the trusts of it which are contained in the 1957 settlement was a power exercisable for the benefit of Carole, and for nobody else. The various other persons to whom the settlement purported to give benefits were not objects of that power of advancement. The position was that the trustees had a discretion as to the manner in which they would benefit Carole, and

C they considered that an appropriate way to benefit her would be to create this settlement under which beneficial interests were given to other members of her family besides herself.

If one looks at the matter in that way, it seems to me reasonable to hold that the effect of the invalidity of some of the limitations in the 1957 settlement by reason of the rule against perpetuities may not be the same as it would have been

D had the 1957 settlement been created by the exercise of a special power of appointment under which all the supposed beneficiaries were objects. It is one thing to say that if a trustee has power to appoint a fund to all or any of a class of objects and he appoints a life interest to one object which is not void for perpetuity and remainders to other objects which are void, then the life interest survives the invalidity of the remainders; but it is another thing to say that if a trustee has

E power to benefit A in a number of different ways and he chooses to benefit him by making a settlement on him for life with remainders to his issue, which remainders are void for perpetuity, then A can claim to obtain that part of the benefit intended for him which is represented by the life interest. The interests given to separate objects of an ordinary special power are separate interests, but all the interests created in Carole's fund were intended as part and parcel of a

F single benefit to her.

It might well be that, if the invalidity caused by the operation of the rule against perpetuities were quite small as compared with the parts of the settlement which were unaffected by the rule, the court might be prepared to say that the valid parts of the settlement would survive intact. Thus SIR RAYMOND EVERSHED, M.R., held in the *Vestey* case (30) that the exercise of the discretion

G there could be upheld notwithstanding the fact that the trustees were to some extent under a misapprehension as to what its effect would be. Here, however, there is no doubt that the effect of the operation of the rule is wholly to alter the character of the 1957 settlement. In my judgment the result of that must be that there never was a valid exercise by the trustees of the power of advancement.

If that be right, the question what would happen to the interests void for

H perpetuity does not arise, but it has been fully argued before me, and I think that I ought to express my view on it because this case may go further. It seems to me that if the interests created by the 1957 settlement which are not void for perpetuity take effect, the interests which are void do not pass to Carole and Linda absolutely but have never left the 1948 settlement.

What was argued on the other side was that the exercise of the power of

I advancement to the benefit of Carole, to take her as an example, created an initial interest in her which would catch any engrafted interest which was void for perpetuity. Alternatively, or additionally, it was said, the actual wording of the 1957 settlement itself gave rise to a *Hancock* v. *Watson* (31) situation. I cannot for my part accept that contention. I do not think that the exercise of the powers of advancement in Carole's favour necessarily meant that the trustees were giving

---

(30) [1950] 2 All E.R. 891; [1951] Ch. 209.
(31) [1900-03] All E.R. Rep. 87; [1902] A.C. 14.

her any initial absolute interest, and I do not think that the wording of the 1957   **A**
settlement gives her any initial absolute interest.

It was argued that the case is very similar to *Re Burton's Settlement Trusts,
Public Trustee* v. *Montefiore* (32), but to my mind there are very material distinctions between the two cases. In that case there was a reference to the daughter's
share and a statement that it was not to vest in her absolutely, which of course
suggests that, but for the subsequently declared trusts, it would have vested in   **B**
her absolutely. Further there was no provision as there is here for the tota
failure of the trusts declared in favour of the daughter and her issue.

[HIS LORDSHIP accordingly declared that the funds representing the two sums
of £25,000 and accumulations of income thereof were held on the trusts and
provisions declared and contained in the 1948 settlement.]
   C

Solicitors: *Forsyte, Kerman & Phillips* (for the plaintiffs and first to seventh
defendants); *Durrant, Cooper & Hambling* (for Barclays Bank, Ltd.); *Solicitor of
Inland Revenue.*

[*Reported by* JACQUELINE METCALFE, *Barrister-at-Law.*]

   D

EASTERN HOLDINGS ESTABLISHMENT OF VADUZ *v.* SINGER & FRIEDLANDER, LTD. (ABLE SECURITIES, LTD., In Liquidation First Claimant; SEMPAH (HOLDINGS), LTD., Second Claimant).

   E

[CHANCERY DIVISION (Buckley, J.), March 7, 1967.]

*Company—Winding-up—Compulsory winding-up—Stay of proceedings against
company—Interpleader summons, to which company respondent, is within
stay—Leave of Companies Court required—Companies Act, 1948 (11 & 12
Geo. 6 c. 38), s. 231.*

Interpleader—Claimant a company in compulsory liquidation—Leave of Com-   **F**
*panies Court required for issue of interpleader summons to which company a
respondent—Companies Act, 1948 (11 & 12 Geo. 6 c. 38), s. 231.*

The issue of an interpleader summons to which a company in compulsory
winding-up is made a respondent is a proceeding against the company within
s. 231* of the Companies Act, 1948, and accordingly cannot be made without
the leave of the Companies Court being first obtained (see p. 1195, letter I, post).   **G**
Dictum of SIR GEORGE JESSEL, M.R., in *Re International Pulp and Paper
Co., Ltd.* ((1896), 3 Ch.D. at p. 599) and *Deutsche National Bank* v. *Paul* ([1898]
1 Ch. 283) considered.

[As to proceedings against a company in liquidation which require the leave
of the Companies Court, see 6 HALSBURY'S LAWS (3rd Edn.) 697, para. 1387
text and notes (*u*)-(*e*); and for cases on the subject, see 10 DIGEST (Repl.) 1012,   **H**
1013, *6954-6963.*

For the Companies Act, 1948, s. 231, see 3 HALSBURY'S STATUTES (2nd Edn.)
648.]

Cases referred to:

Deutsche National Bank v. *Paul,* [1898] 1 Ch. 283; 67 L.J.Ch. 156; 78 L.T .35;   **I**
     Digest (Practice) 345, *614.*

International Pulp and Paper Co., Ltd., Re, (1876), 3 Ch.D. 594; 45 L.J.Ch.
     446; 35 L.T. 229; 10 Digest (Repl.) 1012, *6958.*

Interpleader summons.

This was an interpleader summons issued by the defendant under R.S.C.,
Ord. 17 in an action to determine the beneficial ownership of certain shares.

(32) [1955] 1 All E.R. 433; [1955] Ch. 348.
* Section 231, so far as material, is set out at p. 1193, letter H, post.

A By the summons the defendant applied that the first claimant, Able Securities, Ltd., a company in liquidation, and the second claimant, Sempah (Holdings), Ltd., should appear and state the nature and particulars of their respective claims to the shares and maintain or relinquish the same and should abide by such order as might be made thereon, and asked that in the meantime all further proceedings be stayed.

B *R. A. K. Wright* for the plaintiff.
G. M. Godfrey for the defendant.
K. B. Suenson-Taylor for the first claimant.
T. H. Bingham for the second claimant.

C **BUCKLEY, J.:** In this action the plaintiff is claiming against the defendant for a declaration that certain shares in Town Centre Properties, Ltd., belong to the plaintiff. The statement of claim asks that the defendant should transfer such shares to the plaintiff, but the shares are, in fact, registered in the name of a nominee, so that the object of the action as between the plaintiff and the defendant is to determine the beneficial ownership of the shares in question.

D The defendant has issued an interpleader summons under R.S.C., Ord. 17, requiring the first claimant, Able Securities, Ltd., which is a company in liquidation, and the second claimant, Sempah (Holdings), Ltd., which is not in liquidation, to appear and state the nature and particulars of their respective claims to the subject matter of the action, that is to say, the shares in Town Centre Properties, Ltd., to maintain or relinquish the same and to abide by such order as may be made hereon, and asking that in the meantime all further proceedings

E be stayed. That is, I think, a common form interpleader summons.

The material before the court with regard to the issues relating to these shares is somewhat exiguous, but I understand, from what I have been told by counsel, that questions of fraudulent preference and of misapplication of funds may be involved and that there may be issues to be tried not only between the plaintiff and the first claimant, the company in liquidation, whether these shares belong

F beneficially to the plaintiff or belong beneficially to the first claimant, but also issues to be tried between the first and second claimants whether moneys belonging to the second claimant have been misapplied by the first claimant. The defendant makes no claim to the shares and submits to deal with them in whatever way the court thinks right to direct, and the question which has arisen is whether the interpleader summons is a proceeding against the company within

G the meaning of s. 231 of the Companies Act, 1948, which provides that when a winding-up order has been made, as is the case here in respect of the first claimant,

"... no action or proceeding shall be proceeded with or commenced against the company except by leave of the court and subject to such terms as the court may impose."

H "The court" there means (1) the court having jurisdiction to wind up the company, that is to say, the Companies' Court, not this court, the Chancery Division of the High Court.

Counsel for the defendant, whose interpleader summons this is, has submitted that an interpleader summons is not a proceeding against the respondent to the summons at all. The party who seeks to interplead makes no claims against anyone

I and stands in a neutral position and merely asks to be protected against claims by others in respect of a subject matter to which the party seeking to interplead asserts no title at all. In *Re International Pulp and Paper Co., Ltd.* (2) SIR GEORGE JESSEL, M.R., dealing with s. 87 of the Companies Act, 1862, which is the predecessor and substantially, if not identically, in the same terms as the present s. 231, said (3):

---

(1) See definition of " the court " in s. 455 (1) of the Companies Act, 1948; 3 HALSBURY'S STATUTES (2nd Edn.) 789.
(2) (1876), 3 Ch.D. 594.   (3) (1876), 3 Ch.D. at p. 599.

A

" The words are general—' action, suit, or other proceeding.' Why should
I limit them? Those who say that I am to impose a limit upon those general
words must show a reason for my so doing."

The Master of the Rolls was there dealing with an action commenced against the
company in liquidation by a creditor in the Irish courts, and he held that the
court ought to restrain such proceedings, and he granted an injunction, although
he stressed that the wide meaning of the language of the section should be read
in the light of what he was dealing with, that is to say, a creditor's action
against the company, something very different from interpleader proceedings.

Counsel for the defendant, referred me to *Deutsche National Bank* v. *Paul* (4)
which was the case of a foreclosure action brought by first mortgagees against
a second mortgagee and the persons in whom the equity of redemption was
vested who held that equity of redemption in trust for the plaintiff. The second
mortgagee was a person resident out of the jurisdiction and the question was
whether the rules of court with regard to service out of the jurisdiction had been
satisfied. Order 11, r. 1 of the then R.S.C. provided that

" . . . service out of the jurisdiction of a writ of summons or notice of a
writ of summons may be allowed by the court . . . whenever . . . (*g*) Any
person out of the jurisdiction is a necessary or proper party to an action
properly brought against some other person duly served within the
jurisdiction."

The persons in whom the equity of redemption was vested were within the jurisdiction, so that leave to serve process on the second mortgagee out of the jurisdiction
could be given in accordance with the rules if the action were properly brought
against those holders of the equity of redemption being within the jurisdiction.
STIRLING, J., who heard the matter, took the view that the persons who held the
equity of redemption in trust for the plaintiff were not properly joined as defendants because they were made parties merely in order to comply with this rule
of practice. No relief was sought against them, no right was claimed to be
enforced, and the learned judge, therefore, came to the conclusion that the
action was not one properly brought against them within the meaning of the rule.
As I understand it, his view was that, although they had been made defendants,
as no relief was sought to be recovered against them the action was not one which
was brought against them within the terms of the rule. Counsel for the defendant
says that, by this reasoning, so in the present case the defendant is not seeking
any relief from anybody. The defendant is not seeking to bring proceedings
against anybody at all, but is merely affording to the first and second claimants
opportunities to appear and state the nature of their claims and either to
maintain them or to relinquish them.

When one turns to R.S.C., Ord. 17 to see what course the court may take on
interpleader proceedings, one must look at r. 5, which deals with the powers of
the court on the hearing of the summons. That provides that the court may
order

" (a) that any claimant be made a defendant in any action pending with
respect to the subject-matter in dispute in substitution for or in addition
to the applicant for relief under this Order "

or (by r. 5 (1) (*b*)) that it may order issues between the various claimants to be
stated and tried, or (by r. 5 (2)) that it may, if any claimant so requests, summarily determine the question at issue between the claimants and make an order
accordingly.

In the present case, an order which the court could make, so it seems to me,
would be that the issue between the plaintiff and the first claimant should be

(4) [1898] 1 Ch. 283.

A disposed of in this action, as between plaintiff and defendant, and that the first claimant be made a defendant for the purpose of asserting its claim and defending its claim, and if it be the fact that there are issues to be tried between the first and second claimants the court would also direct such issues to be stated and tried between the two claimants.   As soon as this court had made such an order, it is manifest, I think, that proceedings would be on foot to which s. 231

B of the Companies Act, 1948, would apply, for those would be proceedings against the company in liquidation.   In that way it would be impossible for anybody to proceed with those proceedings without leave of the court, in the face of s. 231, and if the Companies Court should conclude that, for some reason or other, the proceedings, as constituted by the directions given in this court, were unsatisfactory in the Companies Court, it would be within its rights under

C s. 231 to refuse leave to go on with those proceedings.   I do not know what the attitude of the Companies Court would be, having regard to the respect which one branch of the High Court has for orders made in another branch of the High Court, but, technically at any rate, it would be within the power of the Companies Court to refuse leave to continue with the proceedings so set up by the Chancery Division by its order on this interpleader summons.

D   I see considerable force in the argument of counsel for the defendant that interpleader proceedings are not, in the strictest sense, proceedings against anybody, and that, in the present case, the interpleader summons is not a proceeding against the first claimant, the company in liquidation, but that the interpleader summons is a proceeding the object of which is to extricate the defendant from the embarrassment of being sued, or being likely to be sued, by more than

E one party in respect of the same subject matter, and also having as its object the putting of the claimants in a position in which, if they are going to insist on their claims, they should do so in this action.   While it is true that the defendant does not claim any relief in the strict sense against either of the claimants, the object of the interpleader summons is to relieve the defendant of the risk of being sued by the claimants, or either of them, independently of this action

F and, in that sense, I think, the defendant does seek some relief, I do not say, perhaps, against, but in relation to, the company in liquidation.   Indeed, I am not sure that it is not really an accurate use of language to say that the defendant seeks relief against the company in liquidation.   At any rate, as a matter of convenience if nothing more, there is much to favour the view that s. 231 should

G be construed as extending to an application of this kind, so that the Companies Court, which is the court that controls matters connected with the winding-up of the company in liquidation, with which I am concerned here, should be seized of the whole of this dispute, which seems to be one of considerable complexity, from the earliest stages.

This is not, of course, a question which can be decided on the convenience of

H the parties or what is practically desirable in the light of the particular circumstances of this case, but the considerations which arise in this case do lead me to think that s. 231 ought to be construed widely, and sufficiently widely to embrace an interpleader summons.   I think, on the true construction of the section, the issue of an interpleader summons to which a company in liquidation is made a respondent, is a proceeding against that company and one which cannot

I be made consistently with s. 231 without the leave of the Companies Court being first obtained.   I feel little doubt that in any cases where interpleader proceedings are appropriate no difficulty whatever would be encountered in obtaining the necessary leave and that very little expense would be involved. The defendant here seems to have thought, and, perhaps, before this judgment was delivered, thought with justification, that there was some risk that if it applied to the Companies Court it might be told that the application was unnecessary and that it would have to pay everybody's costs of that

A

application. However, unless somebody decides that my judgment is wrong, that embarrassment will not confront interpleaders in the future.

Summons dismissed.

Solicitors: *Theodore Goddard & Co.* (for the plaintiff); *Herbert Oppenheimer, Nathan & Vandyk* (for the defendant); *D. J. Freeman & Co.* (for the first claimant, in liquidation); *Slaughter & May* (for the second defendant).

[*Reported by* JENIFER SANDELL, *Barrister-at-Law.*]

B

C

D

PRACTICE DIRECTION.

E

PROBATE, DIVORCE AND ADMIRALTY DIVISION (DIVORCE).

Divorce—Practice—Advertisement—Newspaper notice relating to divorce proceedings—Notification by Divorce Registry of any replies to advertisement— If no reply, application for registrar's certificate may be made after period of notice has expired—If publication of notice delayed solicitor will be informed.

F

The present practice of sending copies of newspapers containing a notice relating to divorce proceedings to the solicitors in cases proceeding in the Divorce Registry will be discontinued from Aug. 1, 1967. On and after that date all solicitors will will be notified by letter from the Divorce Registry of the probable date on which the notice will appear. If a reply is received to the advertisement, the solicitors will be notified in the usual way for the purpose of serving the necessary documents. If there is no reply, an application for registrar's certificate can be made at any time after the period mentioned in the notice has expired. In the event of publication of the notice being unavoidably delayed beyond the date notified the solicitor will be informed that the registrar's certificate has been postponed, of the reason for the delay and its probable duration, and that the application will be dealt with in due course without any further attendance by him.

G

H

June 23, 1967.

COMPTON MILLER,
Senior Registrar.

A

BESWICK *v.* BESWICK.

[HOUSE OF LORDS (Lord Reid, Lord Hodson, Lord Guest, Lord Pearce and Lord Upjohn), April 18, 19, 20, 24, 25, June 29, 1967.]

B
Contract—Stranger to contract—Annuitant—Widow of deceased owner of business —Sale of business by deceased on terms under which widow was to be paid weekly sum—Charge on business ancillary to other clauses of contract—No trust declared—Widow not party to contract—Death of deceased—Widow obtained letters of administration—Whether widow entitled to maintain action for annuity or specifically to enforce the agreement as regards the annuity—Law of Property Act, 1925 (15 & 16 Geo. 5 c. 20), s. 56 (1).

C
Specific performance—Annuity—Agreement to pay—Contract for sale of business —Annuity to widow of seller—Widow not party to contract—Business transferred—Death of seller—Widow obtained letters of administration—Whether widow entitled to enforce payment of annuity specifically.

Statute—Construction—Consolidating statute—Definition—" Unless the context otherwise requires "—Exclusion of application of definition which would effect alteration of the law consolidated—Law of Property Act, 1925 (15 & 16 Geo. 5 c. 20), s. 205 (1) (xx).

D
In March, 1962, the deceased, a coal merchant, by agreement in writing under the hands of the deceased and the appellant, assigned his business assets to the appellant who undertook to pay him £6 10s. weekly for the remainder of his life and in the event of his death to pay his widow, the respondent, an annuity of £5 weekly. The deceased died intestate in November, 1963. In 1964 the respondent took out letters of administration to his estate. The appellant made one payment of £5 to the respondent and refused to make any further payment. The respondent, as administratrix of her husband's estate and in her personal capacity (though, on the present appeal, only under s. 56 (1)* of the Law of Property Act, 1925, in her personal capacity) claimed payment of arrears of the annuity and an order for specific performance of the continuing obligation to pay the annuity.

E

F

Held: the respondent, as administratrix of the estate of her husband, a contracting party, was entitled to enforce the agreement and to do so by way of an order for specific performance in her own personal favour, and that remedy was available to her suing as administratrix notwithstanding that damages recoverable for her husband's estate were (or might be†) nominal (see p. 1205, letter B, p. 1207, letters E and H, p. 1208, letter I, p. 1214, letter I, p. 1220, letter C, and p. 1221, letter H, post).

G

Swift v. *Swift* ((1841), 3 I.Eq.R. 267), *Keenan* v. *Handley* ((1864), 12 W.R. 930), *Drimmie* v. *Davies* ([1899] 1 I.R. 176) and *Hohler* v. *Aston* ([1920] 2 Ch. 420) applied.

H

Dictum of KAY, J., in *Hart* v. *Hart* ((1881), 18 Ch.D. at p. 685) applied.

Re Engelbach's Estate ([1923] All E.R. Rep. 93) disapproved.

Per LORD REID, LORD HODSON and LORD GUEST: as the definition of the word " property " in the Law of Property Act, 1925, s. 205 (1) (xx) (where it was defined to include any thing in action and any interest in real or personal property) was introduced by the qualification " unless the context otherwise requires ", and as the Act of 1925 was a consolidating Act and therefore was not intended to alter the law, and as s. 56 replaced s. 5 of the Real Property Act, 1845, which applied only to land, the context of s. 56 " otherwise required " for the purposes of s. 205 (1) with the consequence that the definition of " property " did not apply to the words " land or other property " in s. 56 (1), and that section did not apply to the agreement

I

---

* Section 56 (1) is printed at p. 1202, letter I, post.

† Lord Pearce took the view that the damages would be substantial (see p. 1212, letter F, post).

in the present case (see p. 1204, letter H, p. 1205, letter A, p. 1207, letter D,   **A**
and p. 1211, letters F and H, post).

Per LORD UPJOHN (LORD PEARCE concurring):   s. 56 of the Law of
Property Act, 1925 was intended to sweep away the old common law rule
that in an indenture inter partes the covenantee must be named as a party to
the indenture and take the benefit of an immediate grant or the benefit of a
covenant, and s. 56 (1) did not apply unless three conditions were satisfied,   **B**
which they were not in the present case, viz.—(i) the agreement did not
purport to contain any contract or grant by the appellant with or to the
respondent;   (ii) the agreement was not under seal, but the words " conveyance or other instrument " in s. 56 (1) were limited to documents under
seal, and (iii) s. 56 (1) referred only to documents strictly inter partes, and
this agreement was not such a document (see p. 1224, letters A and F, and   **C**
p. 1216, letter E, post).

Forster v. Elvett Colliery Co. ([1908] 1 K.B. 629) and Re Miller's
Agreement ([1947] 2 All E.R. 78) applied.

Dicta of SIMONDS, J., and SIR WILFRID GREENE, M.R., in White v. Bijou
Mansions, Ltd. ([1937] 3 All E.R. at p. 277 and [1938] 1 All E.R. at p. 554);
CROSSMAN, J., in Re Foster ([1938] 3 All E.R. at p. 365) and SIR GARFIELD   **D**
BARWICK, C.J., and WINDEYER, J., in Bagot's Executor & Trustee Co., Ltd.
v. Coulls ((1967), unreported) approved.

Dicta of LORD DENNING, M.R., in Smith v. River Douglas Catchment Board
([1949] 2 All E.R. at pp. 189, 190) and Drive Yourself Hire Co. (London), Ltd.
v. Strutt ([1953] 2 All E.R. at p. 1483) disapproved.

Decision of the COURT OF APPEAL ([1966] 3 All E.R. 1) affirmed on holding   **E**
(i) of that report, but not on holding (ii).

[**Editorial Note.** Reference to the recommendations and further consideration
of proposals for legislative reform in regard to jus quaesitum tertio were gathered
in the report of this case below ([1966] 3 All E.R. at p. 2, letter D). It was not
argued in the House of Lords that the widow was entitled at common law to sue   **F**
in contract in her personal capacity on the agreement between her husband and
the appellant (see e.g., p. 1215, letter A, post).

As to strangers to a contract not being able to enforce it, see 8 HALSBURY'S
LAWS (3rd Edn.) 66, para. 110, and as to an agreement to pay money to a third
person amounting to a declaration of trust, see ibid., p. 68, para. 114; and for
cases on the subjects, see 12 DIGEST (Repl.) 45, 227-241, 47-50, 248-276.   **G**

For the Law of Property Act, 1925, s. 56, s. 205, see 20 HALSBURY'S STATUTES
(2nd Edn.) 554, 831.]

Cases referred to:
  Adderley v. Dixen, (1824), 1 Sim. & St. 607; 2 L.J.O.S.Ch. 103; 57 E.R. 239;
      44 Digest (Repl.) 26, *165*.   **H**
  *Ahmed Angullia Bin Hadjee Mohamed Salleh Anguillia v. Estate & Trust
      Agencies (1927), Ltd.*, [1938] 3 All E.R. 106; [1938] A.C. 624; 107
      L.J.P.C. 71; 159 L.T. 428; 23 Digest (Repl.) 484, *5518*.
  Alley v. Deschamps, (1806), 13 Ves. 225; 33 E.R. 278; 44 Digest (Repl.) 95,
      767.
  Bagot's Executor and Trustee Co., Ltd. v. Coulls, (1967), unreported.   **I**
  Berkeley v. Hardy, (1826), 5 B. & C. 355; 8 Dow. & Ry. K.B. 102; 4 L.J.O.S.
      K.B. 184; 108 E.R. 132; 17 Digest (Repl.) 228, *287*.
  Chelsea and Walham Green Building Society v. Armstrong, [1951] 2 All E.R.
      250; [1951] Ch. 853; 17 Digest (Repl.) 240, *428*.
  Cooker v. Child, (1673), 2 Lev. 74; 83 E.R. 456; sub nom. *Codger v. Childe*,
      3 Keb. 94; sub nom. *Coker v. Childe*, 3 Keb. 115; 17 Digest (Repl.)
      210, *81*.
  Drimmie v. Davies, [1899] 1 I.R. 176; 12 Digest (Repl.) 50, **82*.

A *Drive Yourself Hire Co. (London), Ltd.* v. *Strutt,* [1953] 2 All E.R. 1475; [1954] 1 Q.B. 250; [1953] 3 W.L.R. 1111; Digest (Cont. Vol. A) 1095, *7864a.*

Dunlop Pneumatic Tyre Co., Ltd. v. *Selfridge & Co., Ltd.,* [1914-15] All E.R. Rep. 333; [1915] A.C. 847; 84 L.J.K.B. 1680; 113 L.T. 386; 12 Digest (Repl.) 234, *1754.*

B *Dyson* v. *Forster, Dyson* v. *Seed, Quinn, Morgan,* [1908-10] All E.R. Rep. 212; [1909] A.C. 98; 78 L.J.K.B. 246; 99 L.T. 942; *affg.,* sub nom. *Forster* v. *Elvet Colliery Co.,* [1908] 1 K.B. 629; 33 Digest (Repl.) 825, *875.*

Ecclesiastical Comrs. for England's Conveyance, Re, [1934] All E.R. Rep. 118; [1936] Ch. 430; 105 L.J.Ch. 168; 155 L.T. 281; 40 Digest (Repl.) 338, *2762.*

C *Engelbach's Estate, Re, Tibbetts* v. *Engelbach,* [1923] All E.R. Rep. 93; [1924] 2 Ch. 348; 93 L.J.Ch. 616; 130 L.T. 401; 47 Digest (Repl.) 32, *167.*

Fortescue v. *Lostwithiel & Fowey Ry. Co.,* [1894] 3 Ch. 621; 64 L.J.Ch. 37; 71 L.T. 423; 44 Digest (Repl.) 16, *75.*

Foster, Re, Hudson v. *Foster,* [1938] 3 All E.R. 357; 159 L.T. 279; 29 Digest (Repl.) 421, *3144.*

D *Grant* v. *Edmondson,* [1930] All E.R. Rep. 48; [1931] 1 Ch. 1; 100 L.J.Ch. 1; 143 L.T. 749; 39 Digest (Repl.) 223, *995.*

Green v. *Russell (McCarthy and Others, Third Parties),* [1959] 2 All E.R. 529; [1959] 2 Q.B. 226; [1959] 3 W.L.R. 17; Digest (Cont. Vol. A) 1204, *1163a.*

Grey v. *Inland Revenue Comrs.,* [1959] 3 All E.R. 603; [1960] A.C. 1; [1959] 3 W.L.R. 759; 47 Digest (Repl.) 17, *49.*

E *Hart* v. *Hart,* (1881), 18 Ch.D. 670; 50 L.J.Ch. 697; 45 L.T. 13; 44 Digest (Repl.) 42, *293.*

Hohler v. *Aston,* [1920] 2 Ch. 420; 90 L.J.Ch. 78; 124 L.T. 233; 40 Digest (Repl.) 41, *243.*

Keenan v. *Handley,* (1864), 12 W.R. 930; *affd.,* 2 De G.J. & Sm. 283; 10 L.T. 800; 28 J.P. 660; 46 E.R. 384; 39 Digest (Repl.) 126, *164.*

F *Lloyd's* v. *Harper,* (1880), 16 Ch.D. 290; 50 L.J.Ch. 140; 43 L.T. 481; 26 Digest (Repl.) 54, *371.*

Miller's Agreement, Re, Uniake v. *A.-G.,* [1947] 2 All E.R. 78; [1947] Ch. 615; [1948] L.J.R. 567; 177 L.T. 129; 21 Digest (Repl.) 144, *827.*

Peel v. *Peel,* (1869), 17 W.R. 586; 39 Digest (Repl.) 126, *165.*

G *Schebsman, Re, Ex p. Official Receiver, The Trustee* v. *Cargo Superintendents (London), Ltd.,* [1943] 2 All E.R. 387; [1943] Ch. 366; *affd.* C.A., [1943] 2 All E.R. 768; [1944] Ch. 83; 113 L.J.Ch. 33; 170 L.T. 9; 5 Digest (Repl.) 697, *6112.*

Scruttons, Ltd. v. *Midland Silicones, Ltd.,* [1960] 2 All E.R. 737; [1961] 1 Q.B. 106; [1960] 3 W.L.R. 372; *affd.* H.L., [1962] 1 All E.R. 1; [1962] A.C. 446; [1962] 2 W.L.R. 186; Digest (Cont. Vol. A) 271, *261a.*

H *Scudamore* v. *Vandenstene,* (1587), 2 Co. Inst. 673; 17 Digest (Repl.) 238, *410.*

Sinclair's Life Policy, Re, [1938] 3 All E.R. 124; [1938] Ch. 799; 107 L.J.Ch. 405; 159 L.T. 189; 29 Digest (Repl.) 421, *3143.*

Smith v. *River Douglas Catchment Board,* [1949] 2 All E.R. 179; 113 J.P. 388; sub nom. *Smith and Snipes Hall Farm, Ltd.* v. *River Douglas Catchment Board,* [1949] 2 K.B. 500; 41 Digest (Repl.) 58, *371.*

I *Stapleton-Bretherton, Re, Weld-Blundell* v. *Stapleton-Bretherton,* [1941] 3 All E.R. 5; [1941] Ch. 482; 110 L.J.Ch. 197; 166 L.T. 45; 12 Digest (Repl.) 342, *2656.*

Swift v. *Swift,* (1841), 3 I.Eq.R. 267; 39 Digest (Repl.) 126, **23.*

Tatham v. *Huxtable,* (1950), 81 C.L.R. 639.

Tweddle v. *Atkinson,* [1861-73] All E.R. Rep. 369; (1861), 1 B. & S. 393; 30 L.J.Q.B. 265; 4 L.T. 468; 25 J.P. 517; 121 E.R. 762; 12 Digest (Repl.) 45, *227.*

White v. *Bijou Mansions, Ltd.*, [1937] 3 All E.R. 269; [1937] Ch. 610; 107   **A**
    L.J.Ch. 32; 157 L.T. 105; *affd.* C.A., [1938] 1 All E.R. 546; [1938]
    Ch. 351; 107 L.J.Ch. 212; 158 L.T. 338; 38 Digest (Repl.) 881, *921.*

White v. *John Warrick & Co., Ltd.*, [1953] 2 All E.R. 1021; [1953] 1 W.L.R.
    1285; 3 Digest (Repl.) 96, *241.*

Wilson v. *Northampton and Banbury Junction Ry. Co.*, (1874), 9 Ch. App. 279;
    43 L.J.Ch. 503; 30 L.T. 147; 38 J.P. 500; 44 Digest (Repl.) 23, *140.*   **B**

Appeal.

This was an appeal by John Joseph Beswick from an order of the Court of
Appeal (LORD DENNING, M.R., DANCKWERTS and SALMON, L.JJ.), dated June 22,
1966, and reported [1966] 3 All E.R. 1, allowing the appeal of the respondent,
Ruth Beswick, from a decision of BURGESS, V.-C., in the Chancery Court of the
County Palatine of Lancaster, dated Oct. 11, 1965, and reported [1965] 3 All   **C**
E.R. 858. BURGESS, V.-C., dismissed her action, brought as administratrix of
her husband's estate and in her personal capacity against the appellant, whereby
she claimed (i) payment of the arrears of an annuity agreed to be paid to her by
the appellant under an agreement made by him with her deceased husband,
and (ii) specific performance of the agreement in so far as it imposed an obligation on the appellant to pay her an annuity of £5 weekly during her life-time.   **D**
The facts are set out in the opinion of LORD REID and the relevant pleadings
are stated in the report at first instance in [1965] 3 All E.R. at pp. 859, 860.

C. A. Settle, Q.C., and *J. FitzHugh* for the appellant.
H. E. Francis, Q.C., and *D. G. Nowell* for the respondent.

Their lordships took time for consideration.   **E**

June 29. The following opinions were delivered.

    LORD REID: My Lords, before 1962 the respondent's deceased husband
carried on business as a coal merchant. By agreement of Mar. 14, 1962, he
assigned to his nephew, the appellant, the assets of the business and the appellant
undertook first to pay to him £6 10s. per week for the remainder of his life and   **F**
then to pay to the respondent an annuity of £5 per week in the event of her
husband's death. The husband died in November, 1963. Thereupon the appellant
made one payment of £5 to the respondent, but he has refused to make any
further payment to her. The respondent now sues for £175 arrears of the annuity
and for an order for specific performance of the continuing obligation to pay the
annuity. BURGESS, V.-C., in the Chancery Court of the County Palatine of   **G**
Lancaster (1) decided against the respondent but the Court of Appeal (2) reversed
this decision and, besides ordering payment of the arrears, ordered the appellant
to pay to the respondent for the remainder of her life an annuity of £5 per week
in accordance with the agreement. It so happens that the respondent is administratrix of the estate of her deceased husband and she sues both in that capacity
and in her personal capacity. So it is necessary to consider her rights in each   **H**
capacity.

    For clarity I think it best to begin by considering a simple case where, in
consideration of a sale by A to B, B agrees to pay the price of £1,000 to a third
party X. Then the first question appears to me to be whether the parties intended
that X should receive the money simply as A's nominee so that he would hold
the money for behoof of A and be accountable to him for it, or whether the
parties intended that X should receive the money for his own behoof and be   **I**
entitled to keep it. That appears to me to be a question of construction of the
agreement read in light of all the circumstances which were known to the parties.
There have been several decisions involving this question. I am not sure that
any conflicts with the view which I have expressed: but if any does, e.g., *Re
Engelbach's Estate, Tibbetts* v. *Engelbach* (3), I would not agree with it. I think

---

(1) [1965] 3 All E.R. 858.   (2) [1966] 3 All E.R. 1; [1966] Ch. 538.
(3) [1923] All E.R. Rep. 93; [1924] 2 Ch. 348.

A   that *Re Schebsman, Ex p. Official Receiver, The Trustee* v. *Cargo Superintendents (London), Ltd.* (4) was rightly decided and that the reasoning of UTHWATT, J., (5) and the Court of Appeal (4) supports what I have just said. In the present case I think it clear that the parties to the agreement intended that the respondent should receive the weekly sums of £5 in her own behoof and should not be accountable to her deceased husband's estate for them. Indeed the contrary was

B   not argued.

Reverting to my simple example the next question appears to me to be, where the intention was that X should keep the £1,000 as his own, what is the nature of B's obligation and who is entitled to enforce it. It was not argued that the law of England regards B's obligation as a nullity, and I have not observed in any of the authorities any suggestion that it would be a nullity. There may have been

C   a time when the existence of a right depended on whether there was any means of enforcing it, but today the law would be sadly deficient if one found that, although there is a right, the law provides no means for enforcing it. So this obligation of B must be enforceable either by X or by A. I shall leave aside for the moment the question whether s. 56 (1) of the Law of Property Act, 1925 has any application to such a case, and consider the position at common law.

D   LORD DENNING, M.R.'s view (6), expressed in this case not for the first time, is that X could enforce this obligation; but the view more commonly held in recent times has been that such a contract confers no right on X and that X could not sue for the £1,000. Leading counsel for the respondent based his case on other grounds, and as I agree that the respondent succeeds on other grounds, this would not be an appropriate case in which to solve this question. It is true

E   that a strong Law Revision Committee recommended so long ago as 1937 (Cmd. 5449, p. 31) that

" where a contract by its express terms purports to confer a benefit directly on a third party it shall be enforceable by the third party in his own name . . ."

F   If one had to contemplate a further long period of Parliamentary procrastination, this House might find it necessary to deal with this matter; but if legislation is probable at an early date, I would not deal with it in a case where that is not essential. So for the purposes of this case I shall proceed on the footing that the commonly accepted view is right.

What then is A's position? I assume that A has not made himself a trustee for

G   X, because it was not argued in this appeal that any trust had been created. So if X has no right, A can at any time grant a discharge to B or make some new contract with B. If there were a trust the position would be different. X would have an equitable right and A would be entitled and indeed bound to recover the money and account for it to X; and A would have no right to grant a discharge to B. If there is no trust and A wishes to enforce the obligation how does he set

H   about it? He cannot sue B for the £1,000 because under the contract the money is not payable to him, and, if the contract were performed according to its terms, he would never have any right to get the money. So he must seek to make B pay X.

The argument for the appellant is that A's only remedy is to sue B for damages for B's breach of contract in failing to pay the £1,000 to X. Then the appellant

I   says that A can only recover nominal damages of 40s. because the fact that X has not received the money will generally cause no loss to A: he admits that there may be cases where A would suffer damage if X did not receive the money, but says that the present is not such a case.

Applying what I have said to the circumstances of the present case, the respondent in her personal capacity has no right to sue, but she has a right as

(4) [1943] 2 All E.R. 768; [1944] Ch. 83.
(5) [1943] 2 All E.R. 387; [1943] Ch. 366.
(6) [1966] 3 All E.R. at p. 7; [1966] Ch. at p, 554,

administratrix of her husband's estate to require the appellant to perform his A obligation under the agreement. He has refused to do so and he maintains that the respondent's only right is to sue him for damages for breach of his contract. If that were so, I shall assume that he is right in maintaining that the administratrix could then recover only nominal damages, because his breach of contract has caused no loss to the estate of her deceased husband. If that were the only remedy available the result would be grossly unjust. It would mean that the B appellant keeps the business which he brought and for which he has only paid a small part of the price which he agreed to pay. He would avoid paying the rest of the price, the annuity to the respondent, by paying a mere 40s. damages.

The respondent's first answer is that the common law has been radically altered by s. 56 (1) of the Law of Property Act 1925, and that that section entitles her to sue in her personal capacity and to recover the benefit provided for her in C the agreement although she was not a party to it. Extensive alterations of the law were made at that time, but it is necessary to examine with some care the way in which this was done. That Act of 1925 was a consolidation Act, and it is the invariable practice of Parliament to require from those who have prepared a consolidation Bill an assurance that it will make no substantial change in the law and to have that checked by a committee (7). On this assurance the Bill is D then passed into law, no amendment being permissible. So, in order to pave the way for the 1925 consolidation Act, earlier Acts were passed in 1922 and 1924 in which were enacted all the substantial amendments which now appear in the Act of 1925 and these amendments were then incorporated in the Bill which became the Act of 1925. Those earlier Acts contain nothing corresponding to s. 56 and it is therefore quite certain that those responsible for the preparation E of this legislation must have believed and intended that s. 56 would make no substantial change in the earlier law, and equally certain that Parliament passed s. 56 in reliance on an assurance that it did make no substantial change.

In construing any Act of Parliament we are seeking the intention of Parliament, and it is quite true that we must deduce that intention from the words of the Act. If the words of the Act are only capable of one meaning we must give them that F meaning no matter how they got there. If, however, they are capable of having more than one meaning we are, in my view, well entitled to see how they got there. For purely practical reasons we do not permit debates in either House to be cited: it would add greatly to the time and expense involved in preparing cases involving the construction of a statute if counsel were expected to read all the debates in Hansard, and it would often be impracticable for counsel to get G access to at least the older reports of debates in select committees of the House of Commons; moreover, in a very large proportion of cases such a search, even if practicable, would throw no light on the question before the court, but I can see no objection to investigating in the present case the antecedents of s. 56.

Section 56 was obviously intended to replace s. 5 of the Real Property Act, 1845 (8 & 9 Vict. c. 106). That section provided: H

" That, under an indenture, executed after Oct. 1, 1845, an immediate estate or interest, in any tenements or hereditaments, and the benefit of a condition or covenant, respecting any tenements or hereditaments, may be taken although the taker thereof be not named a party to the said indenture . . ."

Section 56 (1) now provides: I

" A person may take an immediate or other interest in land or other property, or the benefit of any condition, right of entry, covenant or agreement over or respecting land or other property, although he may not be named as a party to the conveyance or other instrument."

If the matter stopped there it would not be difficult to hold that s. 56 does not

(7) Compare the Consolidation of Enactments (Procedure) Act, 1949; 24 HALSBURY'S STATUTES (2nd Edn.) 465.

A substantially extend or alter the provisions of s. 5 of the Act of 1845, but more difficulty is introduced by the definition section of the Act of 1925 (s. 205) which provides:

> " (1) In this Act unless the context otherwise requires, the following expressions have the meanings hereby assigned to them respectively, that is to say . . . (xx) ' Property ' includes any thing in action, and any interest in
B real or personal property."

Before further considering the meaning of s. 56 (1) I must set out briefly the views which have been expressed about it in earlier cases. *White* v. *Bijou Mansions, Ltd.* (8) dealt with a covenant relating to land. The interpretation of s. 56 was not the main issue. Simonds, J., rejected an argument that s. 56 enabled anyone
C to take advantage of a covenant if he could show that if the covenant were enforced it would rebound to his advantage. He said (9):

> " Just as, under s. 5 of the Act of 1845, only that person could call it in aid who, although not a party, was yet a grantee or covenantee, so, under s. 56 of this Act, only that person can call it in aid who, although not named as a party to the conveyance or other instrument, is yet a person to whom
D that conveyance or other instrument purports to grant something, or by which some agreement or covenant is purported to be in his favour."

He was not concerned to consider whether or in what way the section could be applied to personal property. In the Court of Appeal (10) Sir Wilfrid Greene, M.R., said, in rejecting the same argument as Simonds, J., had rejected (9):

E > " Before he can enforce it, he must be a person who falls within the scope and benefit of the covenant according to the true construction of the document in question."

Again he was not considering an ordinary contract and I do not think that he can be held to have meant that every person who falls within the " scope and benefit " of any contract is entitled to sue though not a party to the contract.
F   In *Re Miller's Agreement, Uniake* v. *A.-G.* (11) two partners covenanted with a retiring partner that on his death they would pay certain annuities to his daughters. The revenue's claim for estate duty was rejected. The decision was clearly right. The daughters, not being parties to the agreement, had no right to sue for their annuities. Whether they received them or not depended on whether the other partners were willing to pay or, if they did not pay, whether the
G deceased partner's executor was willing to enforce the contract. After citing the earlier cases Wynn-Parry, J., said (12):

> " I think it emerges from these cases that the section has the effect, not of creating rights, but only of assisting the protection of rights shown to exist."

H I am bound to say that I do not quite understand that. I had thought from what Simonds, J., said in *White's* case (9) that s. 5 of the Act of 1845 did enable certain persons to take benefits which they could not have taken without it. If so, it must have given them rights which they did not have without it; and if that is so s. 56 must now have the same effect. In *Smith* v. *River Douglas Catchment Board* (13), Denning, L.J., after stating his view that a third person can sue
I on a contract to which he is not a party, referred (14) to s. 56 as a clear statutory recognition of this principle, with the consequence that *Miller's* case (11) was

(8) [1937] 3 All E. R. 269; [1937] Ch. 610.
(9) [1937] 3 All E.R. at p. 277, letter D; [1937] Ch. at p. 625.
(10) [1938] 1 All E.R. 546 at p. 554, letter H; [1938] Ch. 351 at p. 365.
(11) [1947] 2 All E.R. 78; [1947] Ch. 615.
(12) [1947] 2 All E.R. at p. 82, letter A; [1947] Ch. at p. 622.
(13) [1949] 2 All E.R. 179; [1949] 2 K.B. 500.
(14) [1949] 2 All E.R. at pp. 189, 190; [1949] 2 K.B. at p. 517.

wrongly decided. I cannot agree with that. In *Drive Yourself Hire Co. (London),* **A**
Ltd. v. *Strutt* (15) DENNING, L.J., again expressed (16) similar views about s. 56.

I can now return to consider the meaning and scope of s. 56. It refers to any
" agreement over or respecting land or other property ". If " land or other
property " means the same thing as " tenements or hereditaments " in the Act
of 1845 then this section simply continues the law as it was before the Act of 1925
was passed, for I do not think that the other differences in phraseology can be **B**
regarded as making any substantial change. So any obscurities in s. 56 are
obscurities which originated in 1845; but if its scope is wider, then two points
must be considered. The section refers to agreements " over or respecting land
or other property ". The land is something which existed before and independently of the agreement and the same must apply to the other property. So an
agreement between A and B that A will use certain personal property for the **C**
benefit of X would be within the scope of the section, but an agreement that if
A performs certain services for B, B will pay a sum to X would not be within the
scope of the section. Such a capricious distinction would alone throw doubt on
this interpretation.

Perhaps more important is the fact that the section does not say that a person
may take the benefit of an agreement although he was not a party to it: it says **D**
that he may do so although he was not named as a party in the instrument which
embodied in the agreement. It is true that s. 56 says " although he may not be
named "; but s. 5 of the Act of 1845 says "although [he] be not named a party ".
Such a change of phraseology in a consolidation Act cannot involve a change of
meaning. I do not profess to have a full understanding of the old English law
regarding deeds; but it appears from what SIMONDS, J., said in *White's* case (17) **E**
and from what VAISEY, J., said in *Chelsea and Walham Green Building Society* v.
Armstrong (18) that being in fact a party to an agreement might not be enough;
the person claiming a benefit had to be named a party in the indenture. I have
read the explanation of the old law given by my noble and learned friend LORD
UPJOHN. I would not venture to criticise it, but I do not think it necessary for
me to consider it if it leads to the conclusion that s. 56 taken by itself would not **F**
assist the present respondent.

It may be, however, that additional difficulties would arise from the application
to s. 56 of the definition of property in the definition section. If so, it becomes
necessary to consider whether that definition can be applied to s. 56. By express
provision in the definition section a definition contained in it is not to be applied
to the word defined if in the particular case the context otherwise requires. If **G**
application of that definition would result in giving to s. 56 a meaning going
beyond that of the old section, then in my opinion the context does require that
the definition of " property " shall not be applied to that word in s. 56. The
context in which this section occurs is a consolidation Act. If the definition is
not applied the section is a proper one to appear in such an Act, because it can
properly be regarded as not substantially altering the pre-existing law; but if the **H**
definition is applied the result is to make s. 56 go far beyond the pre-existing law.
Holding that the section has such an effect would involve holding that the invariable practice of Parliament has been departed from per incuriam, so that
something has got into this consolidation Act which neither the draftsman nor
Parliament can have intended to be there. I am reinforced in this view by two
facts. The language of s. 56 is not at all what one would have expected if the **I**
intention had been to bring in all that the application of the definition would
bring in. Second, s. 56 is one of twenty-five sections which appear in the Act of
1925 under the cross-heading " Conveyances and other Instruments ". The
other twenty-four sections come appropriately under that heading and so does

(15) [1953] 2 All E.R. 1475; [1954] 1 Q.B. 250.
(16) [1953] 2 All E.R. at p. 1483; [1954] 1 Q.B. at p. 274.
(17) [1937] 3 All E.R. at p. 277, letter D; [1937] Ch. at p. 625.
(18) [1951] 2 All E.R. 250; [1951] Ch. 853.

A s. 56 if it has a limited meaning: but, if its scope is extended by the definition of property, it would be quite inappropriately placed in this part of the Act of 1925. For these reasons I am of opinion that s. 56 has no application to the present case.

The respondent's second argument is that she is entitled in her capacity of administratrix of her deceased husband's estate to enforce the provision of the agreement for the benefit of herself in her personal capacity, and that a proper **B** way of enforcing that provision is to order specific performance. That would produce a just result, and, unless there is some technical objection, I am of opinion that specific performance ought to be ordered. For the reasons given by your lordships I would reject the arguments submitted for the appellant that specific performance is not a possible remedy in this case. I am therefore of opinion that the Court of Appeal (19) reached a correct decision and that this **C** appeal should be dismissed.

LORD HODSON: My Lords, the question is whether the respondent, who is the personal representative of her late husband, is entitled in that capacity or personally to enforce payment of an annuity of £5 a week which on Mar. 14, 1962, the appellant agreed to pay to her. This arose from an agreement by the husband to sell his coal merchant's business to the appellant for a consideration. **D** Part of the consideration was to pay the annuity to the respondent. The respondent, as administratrix and therefore a party by representation to the agreement, has a cause of action to sue on the agreement as, indeed, is admitted in the defence. The only question is, " What is the appropriate remedy? ". It would be strange if the only remedy were nominal damages recoverable at common law or a series of actions at law to enforce the performance of a continuing obligation. **E** Although the point was discussed during the course of the case, it is not now contended that at common law (apart from statute), since the contract by its express terms purports to confer a benefit on a third party, the third party can be entitled to enforce the provision in his own name. Similarly, it is not now argued that the claim can be enforced as a trust. The respondent is no longer making any claim in her personal capacity, save under a statute. **F**

The surviving issues in the case are two: first, whether the Court of Appeal (19) were justified in making an order for specific performance by directing that the appellant do pay to the respondent during the remainder of her life from July 15, 1964 (the date of the issue of the writ) an annuity at the rate of £5 per week in accordance with the agreement; second, whether or not the common law rule that a contract such as this one which purports to confer a benefit on a **G** stranger to the contract cannot be enforced by the stranger has been to all intents and purposes (with few exceptions) destroyed by the operation of s. 56 (1) of the Law of Property Act, 1925. I will deal with this section first. It provides:

" A person may take an immediate or other interest in land or other property, or the benefit of any condition, right of entry, covenant or agree- **H**   ment over or respecting land or other property, although he may not be named as a party to the conveyance or other instrument."

The definition s. 205, provides:

" (1) In this Act unless the context otherwise requires, the following expressions have the meanings hereby assigned to them respectively, that is to say . . . (xx)' Property ' includes any thing in action, and any interest **I**   in real or personal property."

Section 56 replaced s. 5 of the Real Property Act, 1845, which provided:

" That, under an indenture, executed after Oct. 1, 1845, an immediate estate or interest, in any tenements or hereditaments, and the benefit of a condition or covenant, respecting any tenements or hereditaments, may be taken, although the taker thereof be not named a party to the said indenture . . ."

---

(19) [1966] 3 All E.R. 1; [1966] Ch. 538.

One effect of s. 56 was to make clear that which may not have been plain in the   **A**
authorities, that those matters dealt with were not confined to covenants, etc.,
running with the land.

The Law of Property Act, 1925, was a consolidating Act and came into force
on Jan. 1, 1926, at the same time as two other Acts, namely, the Law of Property
Act, 1922, and the Law of Property (Amendment) Act, 1924. These last two Acts
were to be construed as one Act cited together as the Property Acts, 1922 and 1924.   **B**
Neither of them touched the question raised by the language of s. 56 of the Act
of 1925.

One cannot deny that the view of LORD DENNING, M.R., expressed so forcibly,
not for the first time, in his judgment in this case (20) reinforced by the opinion
of DANCKWERTS, L.J., in this case (21), is of great weight notwithstanding that
it runs counter to the opinion of all the other judges who have been faced by the   **C**
task of interpreting this remarkable section, viz., s. 56 of the Act of 1925. Contained, as it is, in a consolidation Act, an Act moreover dealing with real property,
is it to be believed that by a side wind, as it were, Parliament has slipped in a
provision which has revolutionised the law of contract? Although the presumption
is against such an Act altering the law, the presumption must yield to plain words
to the contrary.   **D**

Apart from the definition section (s. 205) I doubt whether many would have
been disposed to the view that the general law which declares who can sue on a
contract had received the mortal blow which s. 56 is said to have inflicted on it.
The use of the word " agreement " is inapt to describe a unilateral promise.
However, the definition section, if it is to be applied expressly, refers to property
as including " any interest in real or personal property ". But for the saving words   **E**
" unless the context otherwise requires " I should have felt grave difficulty in
resisting the argument that Parliament, even if it acted per incuriam, had somehow
allowed to be slipped into consolidating legislation, which had nothing to do with
the general law of contract, an extraordinary provision which had such a drastic
effect.

The section has been discussed in a number of cases which were cited by   **F**
WYNN-PARRY, J., in the case of *Re Miller's Agreement, Uniacke* v. *A.-G.* (22). A
useful summary of the opinions contained in the cases is in the judgment of
WYNN-PARRY, J. (22), where he cited (23) a passage from *Re Foster, Hudson* v.
Foster (24), which appears in the opinion of my noble and learned friend, LORD
PEARCE. Like CROSSMAN, J., (24) I am unable to believe that such an enormous
change in the law has been made by s. 56, as to establish that an agreement by   **G**
A with B to pay money to C gives C a right to sue on the contract.

Section 56 has been discussed in recent common law cases, e.g., *Green* v. *Russell*
(*McCarthy and Others, Third Parties*) (25), where the argument was rejected by
the Court of Appeal. Before the Court of Appeal in *Scruttons, Ltd.* v. *Midland
Silicones, Ltd.* (26) to the best of my recollection the argument based on s. 56
was not pressed. The case came before your lordships (27). If the section was   **H**
mentioned, it is not easy to see from the report that it played a great part in the
case. VISCOUNT SIMONDS who at first instance had given consideration to the
section (see *White* v. *Bijou Mansions, Ltd.* (28)) can scarcely have been unconscious of the section when he said in *Scruttons, Ltd.* v. *Midland Silicones,
Ltd.* (29):

I

(20) [1966] 3 All E.R. at p. 4; [1966] Ch. at p. 549.
(21) [1966] 3 All E.R. at p. 9; [1966] Ch. at p. 558.
(22) [1947] 2 All E.R. at pp. 80-82; [1947] Ch. at pp. 620-622.
(23) [1947] 2 All E.R. at p. 81; [1947] Ch. at p. 621.
(24) [1938] 3 All E.R. 357 at p. 365.
(25) [1959] 2 All E.R. 529; [1959] 2 Q.B. 226.
(26) [1960] 2 All E.R. 737; [1961] 1 Q.B. 106.
(27) [1962] 1 All E.R. 1; [1962] A.C. 446.
(28) [1937] 3 All E.R. at p. 277; [1937] Ch. at p. 625.
(29) [1962] 1 All E.R. at p. 7, letter C; [1962] A.C. at p. 468.

A   " If the principle of jus quaesitum tertio is to be introduced into our
law, it must be by Parliament after a due consideration of its merits and
demerits. I should not be prepared to give it my support without a greater
knowledge than I at present possess of its operation in other systems of law."

Section 56 had as long ago as 1937 received consideration by the Law Revision
Committee presided over by LORD WRIGHT, then Master of the Rolls, and con-
B   taining a number of illustrious lawyers. The committee was called on to report
specially on consideration including the attitude of the common law towards
the jus quaesitum tertio. It had available to it and considered the decision of
LUXMOORE, J., in *Re Ecclesiastical Comrs. for England's Conveyance* (30) which
gave the orthodox view of the section. By its report (Cmd. 5449) it impliedly
rejected the revolutionary view, for it recommended that—

C   " Where a contract by its express terms purports to confer a benefit directly
on a third party, it shall be enforceable by the third party in his own name."

Like my noble and learned friend, LORD REID, whose opinion I have had the
opportunity of reading, I am of opinion that s. 56, one of twenty-five sections
in the Act of 1925 appearing under the cross heading " Conveyances and other
D   instruments ", does not have the revolutionary effect claimed for it, appearing as
it does in a consolidation Act. I think, as he does, that the context does otherwise
require a limited meaning to be given to the word " property " in the section.

Although, therefore, the appellant would succeed if the respondent relied only
on s. 56 of the Act of 1925, I see no answer to the respondent's claim for specific
performance and no possible objection to the order made by the Court of Appeal
E   (31) on the facts of this case.

Indeed, on this aspect of the case it seems that most of the appellant's defences
were down before the case reached your lordships' House. For example, it was
argued at one time that the equitable remedy of specific performance of a contract
to make a money payment was not available. This untenable contention was not
proceeded with. Further, it was argued that specific performance would not be
F   granted where the remedy at law was adequate and so should not be ordered.
The remedy at law is plainly inadequate, as was pointed out by the Court of
Appeal (32), as (i) only nominal damages can be recovered, and (ii) in order to
enforce a continuing obligation it may be necessary to bring a series of actions
whereas specific performance avoids multiplicity of action. Again, it was said (33)
that the courts will not make an order which cannot be enforced. This argument
G   also fell by the wayside, for plainly the order can be enforced by the ordinary
methods of execution (see R.S.C., Ord. 45, r. 1 and Ord. 45, r. 9).

The peculiar feature of this case is that the respondent is not only the personal
representative of the deceased but also his widow and the person beneficially
entitled to the money claimed. Although the widow cannot claim specific performance in her personal capacity there is no objection to her doing so in her
H   capacity as administratrix and when the moneys are recovered they will be in this
instance held for the benefit of herself as the person for whom they are intended.
The authorities where the remedy of specific performance has been applied in
such circumstances as these are numerous. Examples are mentioned in the
judgments of the Court of Appeal (34) which have dealt fully with this matter
and there is no need to elaborate the topic. *Keenan* v. *Handley* (35) is a very
I   striking example which appears to be exactly in point. It is to be noticed that the
learned counsel engaged in this and other cases never took the point now relied
on, that the personal representative of the contracting party could not enforce

---

(30) [1934] All E.R. Rep. 118 at p. 122; [1936] 1 Ch. 430 at p. 438.
(31) [1966] 3 All E.R. at p. 15; [1966] Ch. at p. 567.
(32) [1966] 3 All E.R. at p. 14; [1966] Ch. at p. 565.
(33) [1966] 3 All E.R. at p. 15; [1966] Ch. at p. 566.
(34) [1966] 3 All E.R. 1; [1966] Ch. 538.
(35) (1864), 12 W.R. 930.

a contract such as this. As I understood the argument for the appellant it was **A** contended that the personal representative could not obtain specific performance as the estate had nothing to gain, having suffered no loss. There is no authority which supports this proposition and I do not think that it has any validity. In *Hohler* v. *Aston* (36) a decision of SARGANT, J., is good authority to the contrary. A Mrs. Aston agreed with her nephew Mr. Hohler to make provision for her niece and her husband, Mr. and Mrs. Rollo. Mrs. Aston died before doing so. Mr. **B** Hohler and Mr. and Mrs. Rollo sued the executors of Mrs. Aston for specific performance and succeeded. SARGANT, J., said (37):

" The third parties, of course, cannot themselves enforce a contract made for their benefit, but the person with whom the contract is made is entitled to enforce the contract."

C

Mr. Hohler, like the respondent in her capacity as administratrix, took no benefit under the contract but was rightly allowed to recover. It is no part of the law that in order to sue on a contract one must establish that it is in one's interest to do so. Absurd results would follow if a defendant were entitled to lead evidence to show that it would pay the plaintiff better not to sue for specific performance of, say, the sale of a house because the plaintiff could sell it for a higher price to someone **D** else. It is true that specific performance would not be ordered so as to disregard the fiduciary position which the appellant occupies as administratrix. Situations might arise in the administration of an estate when there might be conflicting claims between creditors and persons entitled beneficially otherwise, but this is not such a case. There was in the agreement reference to creditors (38) but there was no evidence directed to this matter and no reason to assume the existence of **E** conflicting claims at the present day.

In such a case as this, there having been an unconscionable breach of faith, the equitable remedy sought is apt. The appellant has had the full benefit of the contract and the court will be ready to see that he performs his part (see the judgment of KAY, J., in *Hart* v. *Hart* (39)).

I would dismiss the appeal.

F

LORD GUEST: My Lords, by agreement, dated Mar. 14, 1962, the late Peter Beswick assigned to Joseph Beswick his business as coal merchant in consideration of Joseph employing Peter as a consultant for the remainder of his life at a weekly salary of £6 10s. For the like consideration Joseph, in the event of Peter's death, agreed to pay his widow an annuity charged on the business at the rate of £5 per week. Peter Beswick died on Nov. 3, 1963, and the respondent **G** is the administratrix of his estate. She claims in these proceedings personally and as administratrix of her late husband against Joseph Beswick the appellant for specific performance of the agreement and for payment of the annuity. Her case before BURGESS, V.-C., in the Chancery Court of the County Palatine of Lancaster (40) failed, but she succeeded before the Court of Appeal (41) in obtaining an order for specific performance of the agreement of Mar. 14, 1962. **H** Although the Court of Appeal (41) were unanimous only on one point in sustaining the respondent's claim there now remain only two outstanding questions for this House.

The first question is whether the respondent as administratrix of the estate of the late Peter Beswick is entitled to specific performance of the agreement of Mar. 14, 1962. On this matter I have had the opportunity of reading the speech of **I** my noble and learned friend, LORD REID. I agree with him in thinking that the respondent is entitled to succeed on this branch of the case.

The second question is whether the respondent as an individual is entitled to the relief which she claims. Although LORD DENNING, M.R., in the Court of

---

(36) [1920] 2 Ch. 420.   (37) [1920] 2 Ch. at p. 425.
(38) See para. 6 of the agreement which is printed at [1966] 3 All E.R. 4.
(39) (1881), 18 Ch. D. 670 at p. 678.   (40) [1965] 3 All E.R. 858.
            (41) [1966] 3 All E.R. 1; [1966] Ch. 538.

A Appeal (42) alone took the view that she was entitled to sue at common law, no question was raised in this House as to the respondent's right at common law in her personal capacity as beneficiary to sue. The decision in *Tweddle* v. *Atkinson* (43) was not challenged in this House by the respondent. The question remains, however, whether such a right is conferred on her by s. 56 (1) of the Law of Property Act, 1925. This question does not strictly arise in view of the decision

B of the House on specific performance but, as the Court of Appeal (44) decided by a majority in the respondent's favour and as the matter was widely canvassed in argument, it is proper to deal with it.

Section 56 (1) is in the following terms:

C " (1) A person may take an immediate or other interest in land or other property, or the benefit of any condition, right of entry, covenant or agreement over or respecting land or other property, although he may not be named as a party to the conveyance or other instrument."

By s. 205 (1) (xx) " unless the context otherwise requires . . . ' property ' includes anything in action, and any interest in real or personal property ". Counsel for the respondent argued that for s. 56 (1) to apply, only four conditions were

D necessary: (i) the covenant must be contained in an instrument in writing; (ii) the covenant must be in respect of land or other property as defined; (iii) the covenant must be directly for the benefit of a person not a party to the deed; and (iv) the covenant must be legally enforceable, i.e., supported by consideration or under seal.   As the covenant to pay an annuity in the [agreement (45)] of Mar. 14, 1962, complied with these four conditions, the respondent, he argued,

E was entitled to claim her annuity. Before considering s. 56 (1) it is necessary to recall the terms of s. 5 of the Law of Property Act, 1845, which is said to be the predecessor of s. 56 (1) of the Act of 1925. The earlier section was in the following terms:

F " That under an indenture executed after Oct. 1, 1845, an immediate estate or interest in any tenements or hereditaments and the benefit of a condition or covenant respecting any tenements or hereditaments may be taken although the taker thereof be not named a party to the said indenture . . ."

As the preamble to the Act of 1925 shows, it was an Act " to consolidate the enactments relating to conveyancing and the law of property in England and Wales ".   In these circumstances the presumption is that such an Act is not

G intended to alter the law, but this prima facie view must yield to plain words to the contrary (*Grey* v. *Inland Revenue Comrs.* (46), per Viscount Simonds (47)). As appears from the opinion of Viscount Simonds the Act of 1925 was preceded by two Law of Property Acts, one in 1922 and one in 1924 which by amendments paved the way for the consolidation of the law of property in the Act of 1925. Section 5 of the Act of 1845 does not appear among the amendments made earlier

H in the Acts of 1922 or 1924, but is repealed nominatim by the Act of 1925. The law prior to the passing of the Act of 1925 was not in doubt. Section 5 of the Act of 1845 applied only to covenants relating to land and did not extend to personalty. The purpose of s. 5 was clearly expressed by Simonds, J., in *White* v. *Bijou Mansions, Ltd.* (48).   In *Forster* v. *Elvet Colliery Co.* (49) the Court of Appeal decided that the section only applied to covenants " running with the lands "

I (Farwell, L.J. (50)).   It is true that when the case reached the House of Lords

---

(42) [1966] 3 All E.R. 1 at p. 7; [1966] Ch. at p. 554.
(43) [1861-73] All E.R. Rep. 369.
(44) [1966] 3 All E.R. 1; [1966] Ch. 538.
(45) The agreement was under the hands of the parties, signed over a sixpenny stamp.
(46) [1959] 3 All E.R. 603; [1960] A.C. 1.
(47) [1959] 3 All E.R. at p. 606, letter C; [1960] A.C. at p. 13.
(48) [1937] 3 All E.R. at p. 276; [1937] Ch. at p. 623.
(49) [1908] 1 K.B. 629.   (50) [1908] 1 K.B. at p. 639.

(sub nom. *Dyson* v. *Forster*) (51) LORD MACNAGHTEN (52) doubted whether the **A** section was confined to covenants running with the lands, but the case was decided on other grounds.   Therefore, counsel for the respondent's suggestion that s. 56 (1) was introduced to resolve the doubt as to the application of s. 5 of the Act of 1845 to covenants running with the lands cannot carry weight;   the law as decided by the Court of Appeal in *Forster's* case (53) was clear.   Indeed, this was confirmed subsequently in *Grant* v. *Edmondson* (54). **B** Moreover, this suggestion as to the purpose of s. 56 (1) does not accord with the respondent's main submission that s. 56 (1) applies to all covenants affecting land and personalty.   If this contention were sound, it would mean that by a side wind a fundamental change in the law had been effected in a consolidating statute.   It would subvert the law as set out in *Tweddle* v. *Atkinson* (55);   affirmed in *Dunlop Pneumatic Tyre Co., Ltd.* v. *Selfridge & Co., Ltd.* (56) **C** and confirmed in *Scruttons, Ltd.* v. *Midland Silicones, Ltd.* (57) that a person who is not a party to a contract cannot sue on it, even if it purports to be made for his benefit.   I cannot believe that Parliament intended to make so fundamental a change in a consolidating Act with the history of the Acts of 1922 and 1924 before them.   It is said that one of the purposes of the Act of 1925 was to assimilate the law of real and personal property.   If that had been the intention **D** of Parliament the amendment would surely have been made in the earlier amending Acts of 1922 or 1924.

The impact of s. 56 (1) of the Act of 1925 has been the subject of judicial consideration in several cases.   Apart from LORD DENNING, M.R., and DANCK-WERTS, L.J., in this case in the Court of Appeal (58) and dicta of LORD DENNING in other cases (59), it has never been held to have the far-reaching effects con- **E** tended for by the respondent.   In *Re Ecclesiastical Comrs. for England's Conveyance* (60), the first case where s. 56 was considered, LUXMOORE, J., did express the view (61) that s. 56 had enlarged the scope of s. 5, but this opinion was obiter.   In *White* v. *Bijou Mansions, Ltd.* (62) SIMONDS, J., took the view (63) that s. 56 did not affect the fundamental change in the law suggested but that " it can be called in aid only by a person in whose favour the grant purports to **F** be made or with whom the covenant or agreement purports to be made " SIR WILFRID GREENE, M.R., in the Court of Appeal in the same case (64). took the same broad view (63) as SIMONDS, J., but for the reason that before a person not a party to the contract can enforce it he must be within the scope and benefit of the covenant according to the true construction of the document in question. In *Re Miller's Agreement, Uniake* v. *A.-G.* (65) WYNN-PARRY, J., took the view **G** (66) that s. 56 had not the effect of creating rights, but only of effecting the protection of rights shown to exist.

LORD DENNING'S views as to the effect of s. 56, as expressed in the Court of Appeal (67) in this case, were preceded by similar observations in previous cases.

H
(51) [1908-10] All E.R. Rep. 212;   [1909] A.C. 98.
(52) [1908-10] All E.R. Rep. at p. 214;   [1909] A.C. at p. 102.
(53) [1908] 1 K.B. 629.   (54) [1930] All E.R. Rep. 48;   [1931] 1 Ch. 1.
(55) [1861-73] All E.R. Rep. 369.
(56) [1914-15] All E.R. Rep. 333;   [1915] A.C. 847.
(57) [1962] 1 All E.R. 1;   [1962] A.C. 446.
(58) [1966] 3 All E.R. at pp. 9, 13;   [1966] Ch. at pp. 557, 563.
(59) E.g., *Smith* v. *River Douglas Catchment Board*, [1949] 2 All E.R. at pp. 189, 190;   **I**
[1949] 2 K.B. at p. 517;   and *Drive Yourself Co. (London), Ltd.* v. *Strutt* [1953] 2 All E.R. at p. 1483;   [1954] 1 Q.B. at p. 274.
(60) [1934] All E.R. Rep. 118;   [1936] Ch. 430.
(61) [1934] All E.R. Rep. at p. 122;   [1936] Ch. at p. 438.
(62) [1937] 3 All E.R. 269;   [1937] Ch. 610.
(63) [1937] 3 All E.R. at p. 277, letter G;   [1937] Ch. at p. 625.
(64) [1938] 1 All E.R. at p. 554, letter G;   [1938] Ch. at p. 365.
(65) [1947] 2 All E.R. 78;   [1947] Ch. 615.
(66) [1947] 2 All E.R. at p. 82, letter A;   [1947] Ch. at p. 622.
(67) [1966] 3 All E.R. at p. 9;   [1966] Ch. at p. 556.

A   Thus in *Smith* v. *River Douglas Catchment Board* (68) he expressed the view (69) obiter that s. 56 was a statutory recognition of the principle that a third party may take the benefit of a covenant although he may not be named as a party to the instrument. This was followed by *Drive Yourself Hire Co. (London), Ltd.* v. *Strutt* (70) where DENNING, L.J., expressed the view (71) that s. 56 did away with the rule in *Tweddle* v. *Atkinson* (72) in cases respecting property, but he

B was alone in that view. SOMERVELL and ROMER, L.JJ. (73), do not refer to s. 56.

   In the present case in the Court of Appeal LORD DENNING, M.R., (74) and DANCKWERTS, L.J., (75) considered that s. 56 had abrogated the rule in *Tweddle* v. *Atkinson* (72)—"received the mortal wound which it well deserved" as DANCKWERTS, L.J., put it (76). SALMON, L.J., doubted (77) if the decision in *Scruttons, Ltd.* v. *Midland Silicones, Ltd.* (78) left him free to do so.

C   Having regard to the law previous to 1925 and to the expressions of judicial opinion since, I cannot think that Parliament intended to make such a clean sweep of the previous law as the respondent's construction of s. 56 would involve. There is, in my view, no half-way house between this extreme construction which would apply s. 56 to a covenant or agreement relating to property in the wide sense of the definition section or limiting the construction to the law as previously

D existing. I am not satisfied that the limitations suggested by WYNN-PARRY, J., in *Re Miller's Agreement* (79), SIMONDS, J., (80) and SIR WILFRID GREENE, M.R., in *White* v. *Bijou Mansions, Ltd.* (81) can be satisfactorily justified on a construction of s. 56.

   If, of course, the words of s. 56 are susceptible of only one construction, then the court must give effect to that construction; but, as this is a consolidating

E Act, if the words are capable of more than one construction, then the court will give effect to that construction which does not change the law. Section 205 of the Act of 1925—the definition section—commences with the expression in common form "unless the context otherwise requires". In my view, the context requires that s. 56 should not extend the provisions of s. 5 of the Act of 1845, which were limited to land, to personalty. If s. 56 was designed to replace s. 5, it does not

F replace it by extending its scope to personalty. On referring to s. 56 it will be seen that the definition s. 205 is the section which creates the difficulty. Apart from this section it would have been proper, according to the ejusdem generis rule, to construe "or other property" in s. 56 as referring to real property to which its predecessor in s. 5 of the Act of 1845 was limited. It may be that the draftsman in incorporating the wide definition of "property" into s. 56 had

G overlooked the result which it would have on the effect of this section by extending it beyond its predecessor. I am constrained to hold that if s. 56 is to replace the previous law in s. 5 of the Act of 1845, this can be done only by limiting the word "property" in s. 56 to real property, and thereby excluding the wide definition of "property" contained in s. 205 (1) (xx). The result is that the respondent has, in my view, no right to sue on the agreement of Mar. 14, 1962, in her individual

H capacity.

   However, for the reasons already given, I would dismiss the appeal.

---

(68) [1949] 2 All E.R. 179; [1949] 2 K.B. 500.
(69) [1949] 2 All E.R. at p. 190, letter A; [1949] 2 K.B. at p. 517.
(70) [1953] 2 All E.R. 1475; [1954] 1 Q.B. 250.

I (71) [1953] 2 All E.R. at p. 1483; [1954] 1 Q.B. at p. 274.
(72) [1861-73] All E.R. Rep. 369.
(73) [1953] 2 All E.R. at pp. 1477, 1484; [1954] 1 Q.B. at pp. 265, 275.
(74) [1966] 3 All E.R. at p. 9; [1966] Ch. at p. 557.
(75) [1966] 3 All E.R. at p. 13, letter A; [1966] Ch. at p. 563.
(76) [1966] 3 All E.R. at p. 13, letter B; [1966] Ch. at p. 563.
(77) [1966] 3 All E.R. at p. 14, letter B; [1966] Ch. at p. 564.
(78) [1962] 1 All E.R. 1; [1962] A.C. 446.
(79) [1947] 2 All E.R. at p. 82, letter A; [1947] Ch. at p. 622.
(80) [1937] 3 All E.R. at p. 277; [1937] Ch. at p. 625.
(81) [1938] 1 All E.R. at pp. 964, 966; [1938] Ch. at p. 365.

LORD PEARCE: My Lords, if the annuity had been payable to a third A party in the lifetime of Beswick, senior, and there had been default, he could have sued in respect of the breach. His administratrix is now entitled to stand in his shoes and to sue in respect of the breach which has occurred since his death. It is argued that the estate can recover only nominal damages and that no other remedy is open, either to the estate or to the personal plaintiff. Such a result would be wholly repugnant to justice and commonsense. And if the argument B were right it would show a very serious defect in the law. In the first place, I do not accept the view that damages must be nominal. LUSH, L.J., in *Lloyd's v. Harper* (82) said:

> " Then the next question which, no doubt, is a very important and substantial one, is, that Lloyds, having sustained no damage themselves, could not recover for the losses sustained by third parties by reason of the default C of Robert Henry Harper as an underwriter. That, to my mind, is a startling and alarming doctrine, and a novelty, because I consider it to be an established rule of law that where a contract is made with A for the benefit of B, A can sue on the contract for the benefit of B, and recover all that B could have recovered if the contract had been made with B himself."

(See also *Drimmie* v. *Davies* (83).) I agree with the comment of WINDEYER, J., in *Bagot's Executor and Trustee Co., Ltd.* v. *Coulls* (84) in the High Court of Australia that the words of LUSH, L.J., (82) cannot be accepted without qualification and regardless of context, and also with his statement:

> " I can see no reason why in such cases the damages which A would suffer upon B's breach of his contract to pay C $500 would be merely nominal: I E think that in accordance with the ordinary rules for the assessment of damages for breach of contract they could be substantial. They would not necessarily be $500; they could I think be less or more."

In the present case I think that the damages, if assessed, must be substantial. It is not necessary, however, to consider the amount of damages more closely, since this is a case in which, as the Court of Appeal rightly decided (85), the more F appropriate remedy is that of specific performance.

The administratrix is entitled, if she so prefers, to enforce the agreement rather than accept its repudiation, and specific performance is more convenient than an action for arrears of payment followed by separate actions as each sum falls due. Moreover, damages for breach would be a less appropriate remedy since the parties to the agreement were intending an annuity for a widow; and a lump sum G of damages does not accord with this: and if (contrary to my view) the argument that a derisory sum of damages is all that can be obtained be right, the remedy of damages in this case is manifestly useless. The present case presents all the features which led the equity courts to apply their remedy of specific performance. The contract was for the sale of a business. The appellant could on his part clearly have obtained specific performance of it if Beswick senior or his H administratrix had defaulted. Mutuality is a ground in favour of specific performance. Moreover, the appellant on his side has received the whole benefit of the contract and it is a matter of conscience for the court to see that he now performs his part of it. KAY, J., said in *Hart* v. *Hart* (86):

> ". . . when an agreement for valuable consideration . . . has been partially I performed, the court ought to do its utmost to carry out that agreement by a decree for specific performance."

What, then, is the obstacle to granting specific performance? It is argued that, since the respondent personally had no rights which she personally could enforce, the court will not make an order which will have the effect of enforcing those rights.

---

(82) (1880), 16 Ch.D. 290 at p. 321.   (83) [1899] 1 I.R. 176.
(84) (1967), (unreported).   (85) [1966] 3 All E.R. 1; [1966] Ch. 538.
                                    (86) (1881), 18 Ch.D. at p. 685.

A I can find no principle to this effect. The condition as to payment of an annuity to the widow personally was valid. The estate (though not the widow personally) can enforce it. Why should the estate be barred from exercising its full contractual rights merely because in doing so it secures justice for the widow who, by a mechanical defect of our law, is unable to assert her own rights? Such a principle would be repugnant to justice and fulfil no other object than that of

B aiding the wrongdoer. I can find no ground on which such a principle should exist.

In *Hohler* v. *Aston* (87) SARGANT, J., enforced a contract (88) relating to the purchase of a house for the benefit of third parties. The third parties were joined as plaintiffs, but the relief was given to the plaintiff who had made the contract for their benefit (89):

C   " The third parties, of course, cannot themselves enforce a contract made for their benefit, but the person with whom the contract is made is entitled to enforce the contract ".

In *Keenan* v. *Handley* (90) the court enforced an agreement providing the benefit of an annuity in favour of a mother who was a party to the agreement and, after

D her death, to her child, who was not a party to it.

In *Drimmie* v. *Davies* (91) the Court of Appeal in Ireland ordered specific performance of an agreement whereby annuities were provided for third parties. HOLMES, L.J., there said (92):

      " In this case Davies, junior, covenanted for valuable consideration with Davies, senior, that in certain events he would pay certain annuities to the

E   children of the latter. If such annuities had become payable in the life of the covenantee, and they were not paid, what legal obstacle would there be to his suing the covenantor? Indeed, I believe that it is admitted that such an action would lie, but that it would only result in nominal damages. A result more repugnant to justice, as well as to legal principle, I can hardly imagine. The defendant would thereby escape from paying what he had undertaken

F   to pay by making an illusory payment never contemplated by either party. Well, if Davies, senior, would have been entitled to sue in his lifetime if the annuities were then payable, his executors would have the same right of action after his death. As I have already said, the question is elementary."

Recently in *Bagot's* case (93) the chief justice of Australia, GARFIELD BARWICK,

G C.J., in commenting on the report of the Court of Appeal's decision in the present case (94), said:

      " I would myself, with great respect, agree with the conclusion that where A promises B for a consideration supplied by B to pay C that B may obtain specific performance of A's promise, at least where the nature of the consideration given would have allowed the debtor to have obtained specific

H   performance. I can see no reason whatever why A in those circumstances should not be bound to perform his promise. That C provided no part of the consideration seems to me irrelevant."

WINDEYER, J., in that case said:

      " It seems to me that contracts to pay money or transfer property to a third person are always, or at all events very often, contracts for breach of

I   which damages would be an inadequate remedy—all the more so if it be right (I do not think it is) that damages recoverable by the promisee are only nominal. Nominal or substantial, the question seems to be the same, for when specific relief is given in lieu of damages it is because the remedy, damages,

---

(87) [1920] 2 Ch. 420.   (88) [1920] 2 Ch. at p. 426.
(89) [1920] 2 Ch. at p. 425.   (90) (1864), 12 W.R. 930.
(91) [1899] 1 I.R. 176.   (92) [1899] 1 I.R. at p. 190.
(93) (1967), unreported.   (94) [1966] 3 All E.R. 1; [1966] Ch. 538.

cannot satisfy the demands of justice. ' The court ', said LORD SELBORNE,   **A**
L.C., ' gives specific performance instead of damages only when it can by
that means do more perfect and complete justice ': *Wilson* v. *Northampton
and Banbury Junction Ry. Co.* (95). LORD ERSKINE, L.C., in *Alley* v. *Deschamps* (96) said of the doctrine of specific performance: ' This court assumed
the jurisdiction upon this simple principle; that the party had a legal right
to the performance of the contract; to which right the courts of law, whose   **B**
jurisdiction did not extend beyond damages, had not the means of giving
effect.' Complete and perfect justice to a promisee may well require that a
promisor perform his promise to pay money or transfer property to a third
party. I see no reason why specific performance should not be had in such
cases—but of course not where the promise was to render some personal
service. There is no reason to-day for limiting by particular categories, rather   **C**
than by general principle, the cases in which orders for specific performance
will be made. The days are long past when the common law courts looked
with jealousy upon what they thought was a usurpation by the chancery
court of their jurisdiction."

He continued later:

    D
    " It is, I think, a faulty analysis of legal obligations to say that the law
treats the promisor as having a right to elect either to perform his promise
or to pay damages. Rather, using one sentence from the passage from
LORD ERSKINE'S judgment which I have quoted above (96) the promisee
has ' a legal right to the performance of the contract '. Moreover we are
concerned with what FULLAGAR, J., once called ' a system which has never
regarded strict logic as its sole inspiration '. *Tatham* v. *Huxtable* (97)."   **E**

I respectfully agree with these observations.

It is argued that the court should be deterred from making the order, because
there will be technical difficulties in enforcing it. In my opinion, the court should
not lightly be deterred by such a consideration from making an order which justice
requires, but I do not find this difficulty. R.S.C., Ord. 45, r. 9 provides under the   **F**
heading " Execution by or against a person not being a party ":

    " 9 (1) Any person, not being a party to a cause or matter, who obtains
any order or in whose favour any order is made, shall be entitled to enforce
obedience to the order by the same process as if he were a party."

This would appear by its wide terms to enable the widow for whose benefit the   **G**
annuity is ordered to enforce its payment by the appointment of a receiver, by
writ of fi fa, or even by judgment summons. I see no reason to limit the apparent
meaning of the words of the rule, which would appear to achieve a sensible
purpose. Moreover, I see no objection in principle to the estate enforcing the
judgment, receiving the fruits on behalf of the widow and paying them over to the
widow, just as a bailee of goods does when he recovers damages which should   **H**
properly belong to the true owner of the goods.

It is contended that the order of the Court of Appeal (98) is wrong and there
should be no specific performance because the condition that the appellant should
pay off two named creditors has been omitted, and there can be no enforcement of
part of the contract; but the assumption, since we have no evidence on the
matter, is that the creditors have both already been paid off. Even if they have   **I**
not, a party is entitled to waive a condition which is wholly in his favour; and
its omission cannot be used by the appellant as a ground for not performing his
other parts of the contract. It is unnecessary, therefore, to consider in what
circumstances a contract may be enforced in part. In my opinion, the respondent
as administratrix is entitled to a decree of specific performance.

---

(95) (1874), 9 Ch. App. 279 at p. 284.   (96) (1806), 13 Ves. 225 at p. 227.
(97) (1950), 81 C.L.R. 639 at p. 649.
(98) [1966] 3 All E.R. at p. 15; [1966] Ch. at p. 567.

A   It is not, therefore, strictly necessary to deal with the respondent's argument that she is entitled at common law or, by reason of s. 56 of the Law of Property Act, 1925, to sue in her personal capacity. LORD DENNING, M.R., expressed the view (99) that at common law the widow was entitled to sue personally but this view was not argued before your lordships. He distinguished *Tweddle* v. *Atkinson* (100). In *Smith* v. *River Douglas Catchment Board* (101) and *White* v. *John Warrick* B *& Co., Ltd.* (102) the same learned judge had given his reasons for thinking that *Tweddle* v. *Atkinson* (100) was wrongly decided and was out of line with the law as it had been settled in previous centuries. On the other hand in *Bagot's* case (103) a survey of the cases from Tudor times led WINDEYER, J., to a different conclusion, namely that

C   " the law was not in fact ' settled ' either way during the two hundred years before 1861. But it was, on the whole, moving towards the doctrine that was to be then and thereafter taken as settled."

The greatest difficulty in the way of the widow's right to sue personally is that two cases in this House, *Dunlop Pneumatic Tyre Co., Ltd.* v. *Selfridge & Co., Ltd.* (104) and *Scruttons, Ltd.* v. *Midland Silicones, Ltd.* (105) clearly accepted the principle that a third party cannot sue on a contract to which he was not a party. D   The majority of the Court of Appeal (106) expressed the view that this principle had been abolished by s. 56 of the Law of Property Act, 1925. If, however, a far reaching and substantial alteration had been intended by Parliament, one would expect it to be expressed in clear terms. Yet the terms of s. 56 (1) are far from clear and appear to be simply an enlargement of a section passed eighty years before. Further, s. 56 is to be found in a part of the Act devoted to the E   technicalities of conveyancing rather than the creation of rights. The cross-heading of that part of the Act of 1925 is " Conveyances and other Instruments "; and sub-s. (2) of s. 56 deals with a small question of formality. The important innovations in the law of property were contained in the two Acts of 1922 and 1924, but this alleged innovation was not among them. It first appears in the Law of Property Act, 1925. That was a consolidation Act and, F   therefore, one should not find a substantial innovation in it. It is of interest that the notes in SIR BENJAMIN CHERRY'S book (WOLSTENHOLME AND CHERRY'S CONVEYANCING STATUTES 1925-7 11th Edn.) contain no suggestion that the section has these far-reaching effects. Nor can I find any trace of this in his " LECTURES ON THE NEW PROPERTY ACTS " published in 1926 with a preface by VISCOUNT HALDANE who gives an account of the genesis and birth of the Bill. G   Nor did LUXMOORE, J., so find in *Re Ecclesiastical Comrs. for England's Conveyance* (107).

The distinguished committee which in 1937 considered the whole subject and recommended (see Cmd. 5449) the suggested innovation in terms which have unfortunately not yet been adopted, cannot have thought that it had already been achieved by s. 56. Since then learned judges in various cases have con-H   sidered the section. The history of these cases was summed up by CROSSMAN, J., in *Re Foster, Hudson* v. *Foster* (108) in the following passage which WYNN-PARRY, J., quoted in arriving at the conclusion that the section did not produce the suggested innovation (*Re Miller's Agreement, Uniake* v. *A.-G.* (109)):

" In my judgment, s. 56 does not have this effect. I think that Mr. Stone's I   contention really amounts to saying that an agreement by A with B to pay

(99) [1966] 3 All E.R. at p. 7; [1966] Ch. at p. 554.
(100) [1861-73] All E.R. Rep. 369.
(101) [1949] 2 All E.R. at p. 188; [1949] 2 K.B. at p. 514.
(102) [1953] 2 All E.R. 1021.   (103) (1967), unreported.
(104) [1914-15] All E.R. Rep. 333; [1915] A.C. 847.
(105) [1962] 1 All E.R. 1; [1962] A.C. 446.
(106) [1966] 3 All E.R. 1; [1966] Ch. 538.
(107) [1934] All E.R. Rep. 118; [1936] Ch. 430.
(108) [1938] 3 All E.R. 357 at p. 365.
(109) [1947] 2 All E.R. at p. 81, letter G; [1947] Ch. at p. 621.

A

money to C gives C a right to sue on the contract, I think it must go as far as
that, and I am not prepared to hold that s. 56 has created such an enormous
change in the law of contract as would be involved in that proposition,
because that would be, no doubt apart from the section, that nobody could
have ever suggested that a contract by A with B to pay C a sum of money
enabled C to sue A on that contract. I hold, following what I understand to
have been the view of LUXMOORE, J., expressed in the case of *Re Ecclesiastical*
B
Comrs. for England's Conveyance (110) and the view that SIMONDS, J.,
expressed in *White* v. *Bijou Mansions, Ltd.* (111), and the view of SIR
WILFRID GREENE, M.R., expressed in the same case on appeal (112) and of
FARWELL, J., as expressed in *Re Sinclair's Life Policy* (113), that the Law of
Property Act, 1925, s. 56 can only be called in aid by a person who, although
not a party to the conveyance or other instrument in question, is yet a
C
person to whom that conveyance or other instrument purports to grant
something or with whom some agreement or covenant is thereby purported
to be made."

I am compelled to the conclusion that Parliament certainly did not intend to
effect the suggested innovation. But has it achieved it per incuriam? I should
be reluctant to give to the section an effect which Parliament so clearly did not D
intend, if the words are capable of another meaning. Unsatisfactory as I find the
limited meaning given to the words by the above cases, it is a possible meaning.
Moreover, I incline to the view of the section expressed by my noble and learned
friend, LORD UPJOHN, and its historical aspect as set out by him. Accordingly,
in my view, s. 56 does not have any relevance in this case. I also agree with his
observations on the cases of *Re Engelbach's Estate, Tibbetts* v. *Engelbach* (114) E
and *Re Sinclair* (115).

I would dismiss the appeal.

LORD UPJOHN: My Lords, by a very informal agreement, though prepared by a solicitor, Peter Beswick (the deceased) agreed with the appellant to
assign to him the goodwill and assets of the business of a coal merchant carried F
on by him in consideration of the appellant employing the deceased as consultant
to the business for the remainder of his life at a weekly rate of £6 10s. This
agreement, set out in full in the judgment of LORD DENNING, M.R., in the Court
of Appeal (116), was not expressed to be " inter partes " in any strict sense, a
matter of fundamental importance when I come to consider the impact of s. 56
of the Law of Property Act, 1925, on this appeal. For the like consideration the G
appellant agreed to pay to the deceased's widow (the respondent to this appeal)
an annuity to be charged on the business at the rate of £5 per week.

The deceased died intestate on Nov. 3, 1963, and his widow took out letters of
administration to his estate on June 30, 1964. The appellant duly discharged
the salary of £6 10s. during the lifetime of the deceased. He made one payment
to the widow and thereafter repudiated his liability to do so. Hence these High H
Court proceedings initiated by the widow, suing both personally and as administratrix of her husband, and soon transferred to the Chancery Court of the County
Palatine of Lancaster. Her suit was dismissed by BURGESS, V.-C. (117), but her
appeal to the Court of Appeal (118) was allowed and an order for specific performance of the agreement, together with payment of arrears of the annuity, made
against the appellant.

I

(110) [1934] All E.R. Rep. 118; [1936] Ch. 430.
(111) [1937] 3 All E.R. at p. 277, letter D; [1937] Ch. at p. 625.
(112) [1938] 1 All E.R. at p. 554; [1938] Ch. at p. 365.
(113) [1938] 3 All E.R. 124 at p. 129; [1938] Ch. 799 at p. 804.
(114) [1923] All E.R. Rep. 93; [1924] 2 Ch. 348.
(115) [1938] 3 All E.R. 124; [1938] Ch. 799.
(116) [1966] 3 All E.R. at p. 4; [1966] Ch. at p. 549.
(117) [1965] 3 All E.R. 858.
(118) [1966] 3 All E.R. 1; [1966] Ch. 538.

A   As it is necessary to keep clear and distinct the rights of the widow as administratrix of her husband and personally, I think that it will be convenient to use
letters: letter A represents the deceased and A1 the widow as personal representative, B the widow in her personal capacity and C the appellant. And in
other examples I shall give, these letters will serve the same purpose. Much is
common ground between the parties. 1. B was not a party to the agreement.
B 2. A did not enter into the agreement as trustee for B in relation to the annuity
to be paid to her. 3. A1 stands for all relevant purposes in the shoes of A and is
entitled to sue C for breach of his admitted repudiation of the agreement (see
para. 5 of the defence), but the parties differ fundamentally as to the remedy
to which A1 is entitled in such an action.

    Counsel for the respondent has not felt able to support the view, expressed
C by LORD DENNING, M.R. (119) that apart from s. 56 of the Law of Property
Act, 1925, B is entitled to sue C at common law. I think that he was right to
make this concession, for whatever may have been the state of the law before
Tweddle v. *Atkinson* (120), it is difficult to see how your lordships can go back over
one hundred years in view of the decision in this House of *Dunlop Pneumatic
Tyre Co., Ltd.* v. *Selfridge & Co., Ltd.* (121) and *Scrutton, Ltd.* v. *Midland Silicones,*
D *Ltd.* (122).

    Leaving s. 56 out of account, there was no real dispute between the parties as
to their respective rights (as distinct from remedies) under the agreement. (a) B
has no rights thereunder. But as it was clear from the whole tenor of the agreement that the annuity was to be paid to her for her own beneficial enjoyment,
if C paid it to her she could keep it and did not hold it as a constructive trustee for
E A1; (b) C would completely perform his obligation under the contract by continuing to pay the annuity to B during her life. Neither A nor A1 could not
compel C to pay it to A or A1, but (c) A or A1 and C could, if they pleased, agree
to modify, compromise or even discharge further performance of the contract by
C, and B would have no right to complain. If authority be wanted for these
fundamental propositions, it is to be found in *Re Shebsman, Ex p. Official Receiver,*
F *The Trustee* v. *Cargo Superintendents (London), Ltd.* (123), and *Re Stapleton-
Bretherton, Weld-Blundell* v. *Stapleton-Bretherton* (124).

    My lords, if I may pause there for a moment, I have the greatest difficulty
in seeing how *Re Engelbach's Estate, Tibbetts* v. *Engelbach* (125), to which we were
referred, can have been rightly decided. In that case a man took out a policy
payable to his daughter on attaining twenty-one; she was then one month old.
G He died. She attained twenty-one and the policy moneys were paid to her, but she
was persuaded to pay them into the hands of a stakeholder pending a decision as
to the legal rights of the parties, and it was held that the estate of the father was
entitled thereto. In my view, she was badly advised. The moneys were paid to
her as provided by the terms of the contract; for her own use and benefit, I should
have thought plain. In *Re Shebsman*, both at first instance before UTHWATT, J.,
H (126) and in the Court of Appeal (123), it is clear that this case occasioned some
difficulty. I find the explanation given by LUXMOORE, L.J. (127) and by UTHWATT,
J., (128) unsatisfactory. Why should the insurance company merely be regarded
as a mandatory to pay the policy moneys due to the assured to his daughter,
presumably as his agent. This seems to me unrealistic. *Re Sinclair's Life Policy*
(129) is perhaps distinguishable on its facts, for the insurance company paid

I ───
    (119) [1966] 3 All E.R. at p. 7; [1966] Ch. at p. 554.
    (120) [1861-73] All E.R. Rep. 369.
    (121) [1914-15] All E.R. Rep. 333; [1915] A.C. 847.
    (122) [1962] 1 All E.R. 1; [1962] A.C. 446.
    (123) [1943] 2 All E.R. 768; [1944] Ch. 83.
    (124) [1941] 3 All E.R. 5; [1941] Ch. 482.
    (125) [1923] All E.R. Rep. 93; [1924] 2 Ch. 348.
    (126) [1943] 2 All E.R. 387; [1943] Ch. 366.
    (127) [1943] 2 All E.R. at p. 777; [1944] Ch. at p. 100.
    (128) [1943] 2 All E.R. at pp. 390, 391; [1943] Ch. at pp. 370, 371.
    (129) [1938] 3 All E.R. 124; [1938] Ch. 799.

the money into court, and it was therefore difficult for the infant to show any   **A**
title thereto, but in so far as FARWELL, L.J., held at the end of his judgment (130)
that if the money had been paid to the infant he would hold it as constructive
trustee for the estate of his godfather, I disagree with him.

My lords, to return to this case. Admittedly A1 can sue from time to time for
damages at common law on failure to pay each instalment of the annuity. But
surely on a number of grounds this is a case for specific performance. First,   **B**
here is the sale of a business for full consideration wholly executed on A's part
who has put C into possession of all the assets. C is repudiating the obligations
to be performed by him. To such a case the words of KAY, J., in *Hart* v. *Hart* (131)
are particularly appropriate:

> ". . . when an agreement for valuable consideration between two parties
> has been partially performed, the court ought to do its utmost to carry out   **C**
> that agreement by a decree for specific performance."

The fact that A by the agreement was to render such services as consultant as he
might find convenient or at his own absolute discretion should decide may be
ignored as de minimis and the contrary was not argued. In any event the fact that
there is a small element of personal service in a contract of this nature does not   **D**
destroy that quality of mutuality (otherwise plainly present) want of which may
in general terms properly be a ground for refusing a decree of specific performance.
See, for example, *Fortescue* v. *Lostwithiel and Fowey Ry. Co.* (132). In the courts
below, though not before your lordships, it was argued that the remedy of specific
performance was not available when all that remained was the obligation to make
a money payment. DANCKWERTS, L.J., rightly demolished this contention as   **E**
untenable (133). When the money payment is not, however, made once and for all
but in the nature of an annuity there is an even greater need for equity to come to
the assistance of the common law. It is to do true justice to enforce the true
contract that the parties have made and to prevent the trouble and expense of a
multiplicity of actions. This has been well settled for over a century: *Swift* v.
Swift (134). In that case an annuity of £40 per annum was payable to a lady   **F**
quarterly and LORD PLUNKET, L.C., enforced specific performance of it. He
said (135):

> " It is said she has a complete remedy at law for the breach of this contract,
> and that, therefore, this court should not interfere. Now, the remedy at
> law could only be obtained in one of two ways, either by at once recovering
> damages for all the breaches that might occur during the joint lives of   **G**
> herself and the defendant, or by bringing four actions in each year, and
> recovering in each the amount of a quarterly payment of the annuity. Those
> are the two modes of redress open to the plaintiff at law. And I am called on to
> refuse relief here on the ground that such remedies are equally beneficial and
> effectual for the plaintiff as that which this court could afford. To refuse
> relief on such a ground would not, in may opinion, be a rational administra-   **H**
> tion of justice. I do not see that there is any authority for refusing relief, and
> certainly there is no foundation in reason for doing so."

Then, after referring to the case of *Adderley* v. *Dixon* (136) he continued (137):

> " Applying this to the present case, leaving the plaintiff to proceed at
> law and to get damages at once for all the breaches that might occur during   **I**
> the joint lives of her and the defendant, would, in effect, be altering the
> entire nature of the contract that she entered into: it would be compelling
> her to accept a certain sum, a sum to be ascertained by the conjecture of a

---

(130) See [1938] 1 Ch. at p. 805; this passage is not in [1938] 3 All E.R. 124, 130.
(131) (1881), 18 Ch.D. at p. 685.   (132) [1894] 3 Ch. 621.
(133) [1966] 3 All E.R. at p. 11; [1966] Ch. at pp. 560 561.
(134) (1841), 3 I.Eq.R. 267.   (135) (1841), 3 I.Eq.R. at pp 275, 276.
(136) (1824), 1 Sim. & St. 607.   (137) (1841), 3 I.Eq.R. at p. 276.

A   jury as to what was the value of the annuity. This would be most unreasonable and unjust: her contract was for the periodical payment of certain sums
during an uncertain period; she was entitled to a certain sum of money, and
she agreed to give up that for an annuity for her own and the defendant's
lives, and to insist on her now accepting a certain sum of money in the shape
of damages for it, would be in effect to make her convert into money, what she,

B   having in money, exchanged for an annuity. As to her resorting four times
every year to a court of law for each quarterly payment of this annuity, it
a manifest absurdity to call that a beneficial or effectual remedy for the plaintiff; and resting the case on that ground alone, I think I am warranted by
the highest authority in granting the relief sought."

C   It is in such common sense and practical ways that equity comes to the aid of the
common law, and it is sufficiently flexible to meet and satisfy the justice of the
case in the many different circumstances that arise from time to time.

To sum up this matter: had C repudiated the contract in the lifetime of A
the latter would have had a cast iron case for specific performance. Can it make
any difference that by the terms of the agreement C is obliged to pay the annuity
no longer to A but to B? Of course not. On the principle that I have just stated

D   it is clear that there can be nothing to prevent equity making an appropriate
decree for specific performance directing payment of the annuity not to A but
to B.

There is abundant authority to support that proposition. The first is *Keenan
v. Handley* (138) and on appeal (139), the facts of which are sufficiently set out
in the judgment of Lord Denning, M.R. (140). That case (138) seems to me dead

E   in point and I do not accept the argument that the mother was contracting as
trustee for her son; such a relationship cannot be spelt out of Captain Handley's
letter. She was, in effect, suing as her son's next friend. True it is that no point
was taken either at first instance (140) or in the Court of Appeal (139) that the
infant could not sue but, as *Tweddle* v. *Atkinson* (141) had been decided only
some three years before, that point cannot have been overlooked. I draw the

F   inference that it never occurred to those distinguished equity judges who tried
that case that there could be any difficulty in making an order on C at the instance
of A to pay B. The order in that case is to be found in that great book of authority,
Seton on Judgments and Orders (see 7th Edn., Vol. 3, p. 2212). That was
followed by *Peel* v. *Peel* (142) also discussed by Lord Denning, M.R. (143).
Then, came the Irish case of *Drimmie* v. *Davies* (144), a very familiar type of

G   case where the parties in a firm agreed together to pay annuities to the dependents
of a partner when he should die. The executors of a deceased partner brought an
action to enforce payment of the annuities and succeeded. Although my noble
and learned friend, Lord Pearce, has set out the observations of Holmes, L.J.,
in that case (145) in his speech, they so exactly express my own view that I set
them out again. Holmes, L.J., said (145):

H   " In this case Davies, junior, covenanted for valuable consideration with
Davies, senior, that in certain events he would pay certain annuities to the
children of the latter. If such annuities had become payable in the life of the
covenantee, and they were not paid, what legal obstacle would there be to his
suing the covenantor? Indeed, I believe that it is admitted that such an action

I   would lie, but that it would only result in nominal damages. A result more
repugnant to justice, as well as to legal principle, I can hardly imagine. The
defendant would thereby escape from paying what he had undertaken

---

(138) (1864), 12 W.R. 930.
(139) (1864), 2 De G.J. & Sm. 283.
(140) [1966] 3 All E.R. at p. 8, letter C; [1966] Ch. at p. 555.
(141) [1861-73] All E.R. Rep. 369.
(142) (1869), 17 W.R. 586.
(143) [1966] 3 All E.R. at p. 8, letter E; [1966] Ch. at p. 556.
(144) [1899] 1 I.R. 176,   (145) [1899] 1 I.R. at p. 190.

A

to pay by making an illusory payment never contemplated by either party. Well, if Davies, senior, would have been entitled to sue in his lifetime if the annuities were then payable, his executors would have the same right of action after his death. As I have already said, the question is elementary."

Finally there was the rather unusual case of *Hohler* v. *Aston* (146) also mentioned by LORD DENNING, M.R. (147), who quotes the relevant passage from the judgment of SARGANT, J. (148). This again shows the extent of the power of equity to assist the common law, limited only by canons of common sense and the practical limitations on the power to oversee and administer specific performance decrees. So the power and indeed duty, in proper cases, of the court of equity to make specific performance orders in favour of third parties at the instance of one of the contracting parties is not in doubt.

B

When A dies and his rights pass to A1, it is said, however, that the remedy of specific performance is no longer appropriate against C. The argument was first that the estate of A suffered no damage by reason of C's failure to pay B; so A1 is entitled to nominal damages, but as she is not otherwise interested in the agreement as such it would be wrong to grant specific performance; for that remedy is available only where damages be an inadequate remedy. Here nominal damages are adequate. Further, it was argued, to do so would really be to confer on B a right which she does not have in law or equity to receive the annuity. Then, secondly, it was said that if the remedy of specific performance is granted it might prejudice creditors of A so that the parties ought to be left to their strict rights at law. Thirdly, it is said that there are procedural difficulties in the way of enforcing an order for specific performance in favour of a third party. I will deal with these points, though in reverse order.

C

D

E

As to procedural difficulties, I fear that I do not understand the argument. The point, if valid, applies to an action for specific performance by A just as much as by A1, yet in the authorities which I have quoted no such point was ever taken; in *Drimmie* v. *Davies* (149) indeed the action was by executors. Further, it seems to me that if C fails to obey a four-day order obtained by A1, B could enforce it under the clear and express provisions of R.S.C., Ord. 45, r. 9 (formerly R.S.C., Ord. 42, r. 26). Alternatively A1 could move for and obtain the appointment of a receiver of the business on which the annuity is charged and the receiver would then be directed by the court to pay the annuity to B out of the profits of the business. Finally A1 could issue a writ of fi. fa. under R.S.C., Ord. 45, r. 1, but as A1 would then be enforcing the contract and not modifying or compromising it the court would obviously in executing its order compel her to carry out the contract in toto and hand the proceeds of execution to B. This point is entirely without substance.

F

G

Then as to the second point. Let me assume (contrary to the fact) that A died with substantial assets but also many creditors. The legal position is that prima facie the duty of A1 is to carry out her intestate's contracts and compel C to pay B; but the creditors may be pressing and the agreement may be considered onerous; so it may be her duty to try and compromise the agreement with C and save something for the estate even at the expense of B. See *Ahmed Angullia Bin Hadjee Mohamed Salleh Angullia* v. *Estate & Trust Agencies (1927), Ltd.* (150), per LORD ROMER. So be it, but how can C conceivably rely on this circumstance as a defence by him to an action for specific performance by A1? Of course not; he, C, has no interest in the estate; he cannot plead a possible jus tertii which is no concern of his. It is his duty to fulfil his contract by paying C. A1 alone is concerned with the creditors, beneficiaries or next-of-kin of A, and this point therefore can never be a defence by C if A1 in fact chooses to sue

H

I

---

(146) [1920] 2 Ch. 420.
(147) [1966] 3 All E.R. at p. 8, letter F; [1966] Ch. at p. 556.
(148) [1920] 2 Ch. at p. 425.   (149) [1899] 1 I.R. 176.
(150) [1938] 3 All E.R. 106 at p. 110; [1938] A.C. 624 at p. 632.

A for specific performance rather than to attempt a compromise in the interest of the estate. This point seems to me misconceived. In any event on the facts of this case there is no suggestion that there are any unpaid creditors and B is sole next-of-kin, so the point is academic.

Then as to the first point. On this question we were referred to the well known dictum of Lush, L.J., in *Lloyds* v. *Harper* (151):

B
"... I consider it to be an established rule of law that where a contract is made with A for the benefit of B, A can sue on the contract for the benefit of B, and recover all that B could have recovered if the contract had been made with B himself."

While in the circumstances it is not necessary to express any concluded opinion C thereon, if the learned lord justice was expressing a view on the purely common law remedy of damages I have some difficulty in going all the way with him. If A sues for damages for breach of contract by reason of the failure to pay B he must prove his loss; that may be great or nominal according to circumstances. I do not see how A can in conformity with clearly settled principle in assessing damages for breach of contract rely at common law on B's loss. I agree with the D observations of Windeyer, J., in the as yet unreported case of *Bagot's Executor and Trustee Co.* v. *Coulls* (152) in the High Court of Australia. But I note, however, that in *Lloyd's* v. *Harper* (153) James and Cotton, L.JJ., treated A as trustee for B (154) and I doubt whether Lush, L.J., thought otherwise.

However, I incline to the view that on the facts of this case damages are nominal for it appears that A died without any assets save and except the agree- E ment which he hoped would keep him and then his widow for their lives. At all events let me assume that damages are nominal. So it is said nominal damages are adequate and the remedy of specific performance ought not to be granted. That is with all respect wholly to misunderstand that principle. Equity will grant specific performance when damages are inadequate to meet the justice of the case. I have already quoted the observations of Plunket, L.C. (155) on this F point which completely cover it. In any event, however, quantum of damages seldom affects the right to specific performance. If X contracts with Y to buy Blackacre or a rare chattel for a fancy price because the property or chattel has caught his fancy, he is entitled to enforce his bargain and it matters not that he could not prove any damage. In this case the court ought to grant a specific performance order all the more because damages *are* nominal. C has received all G the property; justice demands that he pay the price and this can only be done in the circumstances by equitable relief. It is a fallacy to suppose that B is thereby obtaining additional rights; A1 is entitled to compel C to carry out the terms of the agreement.

My lords, in my opinion the Court of Appeal (156) were clearly right to grant a decree of specific performance. That is sufficient to dispose of the appeal, H but as your lordships have heard much argument on the true scope and ambit of s. 56 of the Law of Property Act, 1925, I propose to express some views thereon, though necessarily obiter.

Section 56 of the Law of Property Act, 1925, has a long history behind it. Section 56 replaced s. 5 of the Real Property Act, 1845, which amended some very ancient law relating to indentures inter partes, so I shall start by stating the I common law on the subject. The rule was that a grantee or covenantee, though named as such in an indenture under seal expressed to be made inter partes, could not take an immediate interest as grantee nor the benefit of a covenant as covenantee unless named as a party to the indenture. This rule, as the authori-

---

(151) (1880), 16 Ch.D at p. 321.   (152) (1967), unreported.
(153) (1880), 16 Ch.D. 290.
(154) (1880), 16 Ch.D. at pp. 315, 317.
(155) In *Swift* v. *Swift*, (1841), 3 I.Eq.R. at pp. 275, 276.
(156) [1966] 3 All E.R. 1; [1966] Ch. 538.

ties I shall quote show, applied not only to real estate but also to personal grants **A** and covenants. How narrow this rule was, however, but equally, how well understood, will also be shown by those authorities. The first is *Scudamore* v. *Vandenstene* (157). By an indenture of charter party, made between Scudamore and others, owners " of the good ship called B " (whereof R. Pitman was the master) of the one part and Vandenstene of the other part, Vandenstene covenanted with Pitman and the plaintiffs Scundamore and others for the performance of certain **B** covenants in the sum of £600. Pitman, though not named as a party, signed sealed and delivered the deed. The plaintiffs sued Vandenstene on the deed who pleaded a release of Pitman (who had entered into other covenants). Held: this was no defence to the action for Pitman was no party to the deed—for no bond, covenant or grant can be made to or with anyone not party to the deed. This ancient doctrine that one must, however, be named as party to the indenture to take an **C** immediate benefit by grant, or as a covenantee, was by the seventeenth century regarded as archaic, for in 1673 one finds it being very strictly construed; the rule was held only to apply to indentures inter partes. So in *Cooker* v. *Child* (158), another case of a charter party, we find that Bentley, master and part owner of the ship, with the consent of Cooker, the other part owner, entered into a charter party with Child the defendant. By its terms Child covenanted to pay £300 to **D** Cooker who was not named as a party to the deed. Held: that the charter party, though indented, was not subject to this ancient rule for it was not expressed to be between Bentley " of the one part " and Child " of the other part ". It was equivalent to a deed poll to which the rule had never applied, and Cooker successfully sued Child in covenant and obtained judgment.

This rule, however, narrowly construed in its application as it was, nevertheless **E** was recognised as part of the common law to which full effect must be given. So in 1826 in the case of *Berkeley* v. *Hardy* (159) there was an indenture of lease made by A on behalf of W. F. Berkeley (the plaintiff) of the one part and the defendant of the other party whereby the plaintiff agreed to let to the defendant certain premises, the lease containing the usual covenants. A was duly authorised by the plaintiff to enter into the lease on his behalf but not by a power of attorney **F** under seal. The plaintiff sued the defendant on the latter's covenants in the lease. He failed. ABBOTT, C.J., on this point felt constrained to say (160):

" We are left, then, to decide upon those strict technical rules of law applicable to deeds under seal, which I believe, are peculiar to the law of England. Those rules have been laid down and recognised in so many cases, that I think we are bound to say no action can be maintained by W. F. Berkeley upon the deed in question." **G**

In *Forster* v. *Elvett Colliery Co., Ltd.* (161) FARWELL, L.J., pointed out that the old rule of law still held good that no one can sue on a covenant in an indenture who is not mentioned as a party to it, except so far as it had been altered by the Real Property Act, 1845. Substituting a reference to s. 56 for the Act of 1845 **H** that statement, I suppose, is still true. In 1844 Parliament abrogated this rule by s. 11 of the Transfer of Property Act, 1844, which enacted:

" 11. That it shall not be necessary in any case to have a deed indented; and that any person not being a party to any deed, may take an immediate benefit under it in the same manner as he might under a deed poll."

I

For whatever reason, this short workmanlike section, which plainly applied to all covenants whether relating to realty or personal grants or covenants, never

---

(157) (1587), 2 Co. Inst. 673.
(158) (1673), 2 Lev. 74.
(159) (1826), 5 B. & C. 355.
(160) (1826), 5 B. & C. at p. 359.
(161) [1908] 1 K.B. at p. 639.

A had any operation for it was repealed by the Real Property Act, 1845, and replaced by s. 5 of that Act in these terms:

"That under an indenture executed after Oct. 1, 1845 an immediate estate or interest in any tenements or hereditaments and the benefit of a condition or covenant respecting any tenements or hereditaments may be taken although the taker thereof be not named a party to the said indenture . . ."

B No one has ever suggested that that section was intended to do more than supplant the old common law rule relating to indentures inter partes in relation to realty.

Then came the great changes in the law of real property; the Law of Property Act, 1922 and the Law of Property (Amendment) Act, 1924. The researches of counsel have not revealed any amendment in those Acts to s. 5 of the Act of C 1845. The Law of Property Act, 1925, was a consolidation Act consolidating those and many earlier Acts. It repealed s. 5 of the Act of 1845 and replaced it by s. 56 (1) in these terms:

"A person may take an immediate or other interest in land or other property, or the benefit of any condition, right of entry, covenant or agreement over or respecting land or other property, although he may not be D named as a party to the conveyance or other instrument."

There is a presumption that consolidation Acts are not intended to alter the law. In practice both Houses of Parliament send consolidation bills to the joint committee of both Houses on Consolidation Bills who consider and report on them to both Houses. The joint committee call the draftsmen of the Bill before them to give evidence and sometimes they have to resolve doubts whether a E clause in the Bill is pure consolidation or not. For my part I see no objection to considering those proceedings, not with a view to construing the Act of 1925, that is of course not permissible, but to see whether the weight of the presumption as to the effect of consolidation Acts is weakened by anything that took place in those proceedings.

F The report of the joint committee for 1925 discloses that when the Law of Property Consolidation Bill was before it, SIR FREDERICK LIDDELL, SIR BENJAMIN CHERRY and SIR CLAUD SCHUSTER gave evidence. Clause 56 was passed without comment. See the Proceedings of Select Committees 1925/6 March, 1925. So the presumption that s. 56 was not intended to alter the law remains; but it remains only a presumption. Nevertheless, some of your lordships have felt able to come to the conclusion that in these circumstances s. 56 should be construed G as limited in its application to real property as was the old s. 5. I find it difficult to dissent from this proposition but equally difficult to agree with it because, ignoring altogether the definition in s. 205 of the Law of Property Act, 1925, s. 56 defines as the subject-matter of the section one who takes

"an immediate or other interest in land or other property, or the benefit H of any . . . covenant or agreement over or respecting land or other property . . ."

Bearing in mind the wide import of the word "property" apart from any definition, I find it difficult in the context to limit that word to an interest in real property. Without expressing any concluded view I think it may be that the true answer is that Parliament (as sometimes happens in consolidation statutes) I inadvertently did alter the law in s. 56 by abrogating the old common law rule in respect of contracts affecting personal property as well as real property; but it cannot have done more. Parliament, per incuriam it may be, went back to the position under the Act of 1844 but I am convinced that it never intended to alter the fundamental rule laid down in *Tweddle* v. *Atkinson* (162).

The real difficulty is as to the true scope and ambit of the section. My present

---

(162) [1861-73] All E.R. Rep. 369.

views, though obiter and tentative, are these. Section 56, like its predecessors, **A**
was only intended to sweep away the old common law rule that in an indenture
inter partes the covenantee must be named as a party to the indenture to take
the benefit of an immediate grant or the benefit of a covenant; it intended no
more. So that for the section to have any application it must be to relieve from
the consequences of the common law, and in my opinion three conditions must be
satisfied. If all of them are not satisfied then the section has no application and **B**
the parties are left to their remedies at common law.

First, let me assume for a moment that the agreement in this case is an indenture inter partes under seal—does s. 56 help B? Plainly not. C did not purport
to covenant with or make any grant to B; he only covenanted with A. Had C
purported to covenant with B to pay the annuity to B, though B was not a party,
then any difficulty B might have had in suing might be saved by s. 56. The narrow **C**
view which I take of s. 56 is, I think, supported by the observations of SIMONDS,
J., in *White* v. *Bijou Mansions, Ltd.* (163), when he said

" Just as, under s. 5 of the Act of 1845, only that person could call it in aid
who, although not a party, yet was a grantee or covenantee, so, under s. 56
of this Act, only that person can call it in aid who, although not named as a
party to the conveyance or other instrument, is yet a person to whom that **D**
conveyance or other instrument purports to grant something or by which
some agreement or covenant is purported to be in his favour."

See to the same effect WYNN-PARRY, J., in *Re Miller's Agreement, Uniake* v.
A.-G. (164). That was another example of the familiar case where, on the dissolution of a partnership, the continuing partners covenanted with the retiring **E**
partner to pay as from his death annuities to his three daughters. The judge said:

" In my view, the annuitants are not persons to whom the deed purports
to grant something or with whom some agreement or covenant is purported
to be made . . ."

So B does not satisfy this condition. The second condition is that the reference
to the " conveyance or other instrument " in the section is, in my opinion, **F**
limited to documents under seal. This does no violence to the definitions of
" conveyance " or " instrument " in s. 205 of the Law of Property Act, 1925.
The third condition is that, in my opinion, the section refers only to documents
strictly inter partes (*Cooker* v. *Child* (165)). The agreement satisfies none of these
conditions.

Section 56 does not help the appellant, but for the reasons given earlier I would **G**
dismiss this appeal.

Appeal dismissed.

Solicitors: *Bower, Cotton & Bower*, agents for *Slater, Heelis & Co.*, Manchester
(for the appellant); *J. Hampson Fogg & Co.*, agents for *Ogden, Lyles & Fox*,
Manchester (for the respondent). **H**

[*Reported by* KATHLEEN J. H. O'BRIEN, *Barrister-at-Law.*]

I

---

(163) [1937] 3 All E.R. at p. 277, letter D; [1937] Ch. at p. 625.
(164) [1947] 2 All E.R. at p. 83, letter A; [1947] Ch. at p. 623.
(165) (1673), 2 Lev. 74.

A

THORNE v. BRITISH BROADCASTING CORPORATION.

Distinguished in GOURIET v UPOW [1977] 1 All ER 696

[COURT OF APPEAL, CIVIL DIVISION (Lord Denning, M.R., Danckwerts and Winn, L.JJ.), May 25, 1967.]

Injunction—Statute—Criminal offence created by statute—No legal right con-
B *　ferred on individual—Enforcement under the control of the Attorney-General*
*　—Incitement to racial hatred—Alleged anti-German propaganda by broad-*
*　casts and television—No cause of action by individual without consent of*
*　Attorney-General—Race Relations Act 1965 (c. 73) s. 3, s. 6.*

The plaintiff brought an action against the B.B.C. for an injunction
restraining the continuance of alleged propaganda against people who
C were of German origin. The plaintiff relied on s. 6* of the Race Relations
Act 1965, but did not alleged that he personally was injured. The plaintiff
had not sought the consent of the Attorney-General before bringing the
action.

Held: s. 6 of the Race Relations Act 1965 conferred no legal right on
the plaintiff but created only a criminal offence, and moreover the enforce-
D ment of remedies under s. 3 and s. 6 of the Act of 1965 was intended, on the
construction of the statute, to be under the control of the Attorney-General;
in the absence of a legal right in the plaintiff his action for an injunction was
not maintainable, and accordingly, the statement of claim would be struck
out and the action would be dismissed (see p. 1227, letters A, B, C and E, post).

Appeal allowed.

Dictum of LORD DENNING MR at 1226 disapproved in GOURIET v UPOW [1977] 1 All ER 696

E [As to the offence of incitement to racial hatred, see SUPPLEMENT to 10
HALSBURY'S LAWS (3rd Edn.) para. 1061A.

As to the granting of an injunction against contravention of a statute, see
21 HALSBURY'S LAWS (3rd Edn.) 347, para. 727; and for cases on the subject,
see 28 DIGEST (Repl.) 743-746, *36-53*; and for cases on relator actions, see
16 DIGEST (Repl.) 541, 542, *3821-3833.*
F For the Race Relations Act 1965, s. 1, s. 3, s. 6, see 45 HALSBURY'S STATUTES
(2nd Edn.) 31, 34, 35.]

Cases referred to:
　A.-G. (on the relation of Manchester Corpn.) v. *Harris,* [1960] 3 All E.R. 207;
　　[1961] 1 Q.B. 74; [1960] 3 W.L.R. 532; 16 Digest (Repl.) 542, *3831.*
　Cooper v. *Whittingham,* (1880), 15 Ch.D. 501; 49 L.J.Ch. 752; 43 L.T. 16;
G　　Digest (Practice) 890, *4311.*
　Montgomery v. *Montgomery,* [1964] 2 All E.R. 22; [1965] P. 46; [1964] 2 W.L.R.
　　1026; 3rd Digest Supp.

Interlocutory Appeal.

By writ dated Jan. 27, 1967, the plaintiff, Dr. Carl-Theo Thorne, brought
H an action against The British Broadcasting Corporation (" the B.B.C.") claiming
an injunction; and by summons dated Jan. 27, 1967, the plaintiff applied for
an injunction to discontinue the T.V.-series " The Rat Patrol " and the use of
foul, abusive and/or spiteful language, gestures, mimics and imitations, when
Germans or Germany were mentioned, by the B.B.C., their servants, agents or
anybody else appearing on the screen or on radio. By order of JOHN J. STEPHEN-
I SON, J., dated Feb. 3, 1967, the plaintiff's summons for an injunction was dismissed. That order was affirmed by the Court of Appeal on Mar. 10, 1967.
By summons dated Feb. 17, 1967, the B.B.C. applied for an order that the
statement of claim be struck out under R.S.C., Ord. 18, r. 19, and under the
inherent jurisdiction, and that the action be stayed or dismissed. By order
dated Apr. 6, 1967, Master CLAYTON ordered that the action should be dismissed;
and by order of LYELL, J., made on Apr. 14, 1967, appeal from the order of
Master CLAYTON was allowed and his order was rescinded. By a notice dated

---

* Section 6, so far as material, is set out at p. 1226, letter F, post.

Apr. 26, 1967, the B.B.C. gave notice of appeal from the order of LYELL, J., for A
an order striking out the statement of claim and endorsement on writ on the
grounds (i) that they disclosed no reasonable cause of action, (ii) that they were
frivolous and vexatious and (iii) that they were an abuse of the process of the
court.　Further grounds included the grounds that no legal right of the plaintiff
had been infringed, and that any legal proceedings brought under the Race
Relations Act 1965 should be instituted by or with the consent of the Attorney- B
General and not otherwise.

Brian T. Neill for the B.B.C.
The plaintiff appeared in person.

LORD DENNING, M.R.: Dr. Thorne, the plaintiff, tells us he was born
in Cologne.　He is a Doctor of Laws.　He is now resident in this country. C
He is stateless.　He is of German origin.　He has brought an action against the
British Broadcasting Corporation (" the B.B.C.") in which he complains of
their broadcasts.　He says that on television and radio they conduct a continuous
propaganda of racial hatred against the Germans.　He says that the attack
is purely racial.　It is always directed against the Germans.　It incites hatred
against persons of German origin living in this country.　He asks for an order D
against the B.B.C. forbidding them to continue with racialist abuse or disparaging
innuendos on persons of German origin.

The plaintiff admits that there is no attack on him personally.　His statement
of claim contains no suggestion that he is injured personally; but he claims that
this action is supportable by reason of the Race Relations Act 1965, which
provides in s. 6 (1):   E

" A person shall be guilty of an offence under this section if, with intent
to stir up hatred against any section of the public in Great Britain distinguished by colour, race, or ethnic or national origins—he publishes or
distributes written matter which is threatening, abusive or insulting . . .
—being matter or words likely to stir up hatred against that section on
grounds of colour, race, or ethnic or national origins."   F

Under s. 6 (2) " ' written matter ' includes any . . . visible representation ";
so it includes television.

That section only creates a criminal offence.　It says in sub-s. (3)

" no prosecution for such an offence shall be instituted in England and
Wales except by or with the consent of the Attorney-General."
                                                                                G
Nevertheless the plaintiff says that he can bring this action personally.　He
relies on *Cooper* v. *Whittingham* (1) where SIR GEORGE JESSEL, M.R., said that
even where a statute creates a new offence, there is " a remedy in equity by
injunction to protect a right ".　The important words are " to protect a right ".
It is a fundamental rule that the court will only grant an injunction at the suit
of a private individual to support a legal right (see *Montgomery* v. *Montgomery* (2), H
per ORMROD, J.).　In my judgment those observations do not avail the plaintiff
in this case, because he does not allege, and indeed he does not have, any legal
right in himself personally in this matter.

It is plain to me that s. 6 creates only a new criminal offence; for which the
proper remedy is a prosecution by or with the consent of the Attorney-General.
It may be that the Attorney-General could himself bring an action for an injunc- I
tion, or an individual, if he got the Attorney-General's consent, could bring a
relator action (see *A.-G. (on the relation of Manchester Corpn.)* v. *Harris* (3), and
R.S.C., Ord. 15, r. 11).　The plaintiff has not got the permission of the Attorney-
General.　He suggested that there might be an adjournment for him to seek it;
but I do not think that any adjournment should be granted.

(1) (1880), 15 Ch.D. 501 at p. 506.
(2) [1964] 2 All E.R. 22 at p. 23; [1965] P. 46 at p. 50.
(3) [1960] 3 All E.R. 207; [1961] 1 Q.B. 74.

A   In my opinion this action is not sustainable. No cause of action is disclosed. The statement of claim must be struck out and the action dismissed.

I add only this: the plaintiff has alleged that the B.B.C. have been guilty of racialist abuse. I would give no countenance to any suggestion that these allegations are well founded. I would allow the appeal and dismiss the action.

B   **DANCKWERTS, L.J.:** There are in my view two difficulties which plainly make this action not maintainable by the plaintiff. First, from s. 3 and s. 6 of the Race Relations Act 1965, it is perfectly clear that the remedies given in those sections, and also in s. 1, are to be under the control of Her Majesty's Attorney-General. I am not satisfied that any civil remedy is given to an individual by that statute. In any case the second reason which renders the action

C   not maintainable by the plaintiff is that there is no allegation by him of any legal right; and there is no statement in the statement of claim that he has personally been injured in any way. In my view the action is wholly unmaintainable and the writ and statement of claim should be struck out. I agree that the appeal should be allowed.

D   **WINN, L.J.:** I also agree that this appeal should be allowed. It is clear, and indeed the plaintiff accepts this, he being himself a Doctor of Law, that, apart from the provisions of the Race Relations Act 1965, he could not possibly contend that he has any right to bring the action which he has launched. It is, therefore, for the court to determine, as a matter of construction of the Act of 1965, whether or not the Act of 1965 gives any right of action to any individual.

E   I respectfully agree with the judgments given by my lords, and in particular with the reference by Danckwerts, L.J., to s. 3 and s. 6, and, I venture to add, s. 1 (4), the provisions of which all seem to me clearly to point to the conclusion that Parliament did not intend that any individual citizen might by force of the Act of 1965 attack any other citizen or citizens for alleged infringement of s. 6 of the Act of 1965, which creates a criminal offence. It is clear from sub-s. (3)

F   of that section that the matter is intended to be under the control of the Attorney-General.

I desire to make only one more remark, and that is this, that I do not by what I have said intend to convey any opinion that the Attorney-General himself can bring civil proceedings pursuant to s. 6. All I am saying is that the plaintiff quite clearly cannot sustain the proceedings which he has endeavoured to bring.

G   *Appeal allowed; action dismissed.*

Solicitors: *William Charles Crocker* (for the B.B.C.).

[*Reported by* F. Guttman, Esq., *Barrister-at-Law.*]

Re CHIEN SING-SHOU. A

[PRIVY COUNCIL (Lord Morris of Borth-y-Gest, Lord Wilberforce and Lord
Pearson), April 10, 11, June 12, 1967.]

*Privy Council—Hong Kong—Architect—Disciplinary board—Board consisting
of three authorised architects, the building authority and a legal adviser—Legal
adviser having conduct of inquiry—Deliberation of board in private on sub-*
missions made on behalf of architect—Rulings given by legal adviser in B
*presence of parties after deliberations concluded—Whether any legal advice
given to board by legal adviser must be given in presence of parties and so to
appear on the record—Whether breach of rules of natural justice—Hong
Kong Buildings Ordinance, 1955 (No. 68 of 1955), s. 5B (2).*

In pursuance of the disciplinary power conferred by s. 5B (2)* of the C
Buildings Ordinance, 1955, of Hong Kong where " after due inquiry " a
disciplinary board was satisfied that an authorised architect had been guilty
of negligence, the name of the appellant, an authorised architect, was
ordered to be removed from the architects' register for one year. By s. 5 (2)
of the Ordinance the disciplinary board consisted of three authorised
architects, the building authority or his representative and a legal adviser; D
by s. 5 (3) the building authority or his representative was to be the chairman
of the disciplinary board and, where the board was appointed for the purposes
of s. 5B, the legal adviser was to have the conduct of the inquiry. During the
hearing before the disciplinary board counsel for the appellant made submissions and the board from time to time adjourned for deliberation in
private, after which the legal adviser stated the board's ruling on the sub- E
mission. The appellant contended that any advice given by the legal adviser
should have been given in the presence of the parties and so as to become part
of the record; and that failure to follow such a procedure was a breach of the
rules of natural justice, with the consequence that there had been no such
" due inquiry " as was required by s. 5B (2) of the Buildings Ordinance to
have been held before the order for removal of an architect's name from the F
register could be made. On appeal against the refusal of the Supreme Court
of Hong Kong to grant an order of certiorari to remove and quash the
findings and order of the disciplinary board,

Held: the legal adviser was a member of the disciplinary board and the
members were not under obligation to repeat in public everything said in
the privacy of their deliberations, though opportunity must be given to the G
parties to deal with relevant matters; in the present case there was no
material from which it could be deduced that the legal adviser did in fact have
occasion to give legal advice to his colleagues on some point of law not
referred to in the notes of the proceedings, and accordingly the disciplinary
board had not failed to hold " due inquiry " (see p. 1230, letter I, to p. 1231,
letter A, and p. 1231, letter F, post). H

Appeal dismissed.

[As to the rules of natural justice, see 11 HALSBURY'S LAWS (3rd Edn.) 64-
66, para. 122; 30 ibid., 718, 719, para. 1368; and for cases on the subject, see
38 DIGEST (Repl.) 102, 103, *732-736.*]

Cases referred to:
Fromhold v. Fromhold, [1952] 1 T.L.R. 1522; [1952] W.N. 278; Digest (Cont. I
  Vol. A) 982, *342a.*
R. v. Davis (No. 2), (1960), 44 Cr. App. Rep. 235; Digest (Cont. Vol. A) 982,
  342b.
R. v. Furlong, [1950] 1 All E.R. 636; 114 J.P. 201; 34 Cr. App. Rep. 79; 14
  Digest (Repl.) 663, *6721.*

---

* Section 5B (2), so far as material, provides: " Where, after due inquiry, the disciplinary board is satisfied that the architect has been . . . guilty of such negligence
. . . such board may " make certain orders.

A   *R.* v. *Green*, [1950] 1 All E.R. 38; 114 J.P. 60; 34 Cr. App. Rep. 33; 30 Digest (Repl.) 270, *341*.

     R. v. *Willmont*, (1914), 78 J.P. 352, 10 Cr. App. Rep. 173, 14 Digest (Repl.) 367, *3561*.

Appeal.

B   This was an appeal by Chien Sing-Shou, an authorised architect, from a judgment of the Supreme Court of Hong Kong (MACFEE and CREEDON, JJ.), dated July 29, 1965, refusing an application by the appellant for an order of certiorari to remove into the Supreme Court and quash the findings and order dated Aug. 22, 1964, of a disciplinary board appointed under the Hong Kong Building Ordinance, 1955, whereby the appellant was found guilty of negligence. C   The board ordered that his name should be removed from the architects' register for a period of one year from the date of publication in the Gazette.

   The appellant was charged with negligence contrary to s. 5B (1) of the Buildings Ordinance, 1955, as read with s. 4 (3) and s. 27 (1), (2) and (7), and reg. 38 of the Hong Kong Buildings (Administration) Regulations, 1959. The particulars of offence alleged that, being an authorised architect, between Aug. 29, 1962, and D   Jan. 4, 1964, he was guilty of negligence in permitting material divergencies or deviations from work shown in plans approved by the building authority under the Buildings Ordinance, 1955, under certain permits issued thereunder, such negligence rendering him unfit to be on the architects' register or, alternatively deserving of censure. By s. 5B (1) of the Buildings Ordinance, where it appeared to the building authority that an authorised architect had, inter alia, been guilty E   of certian negligence or misconduct, the authority might bring the matter to the notice of a disciplinary board appointed under s. 5. By s. 5B (2), where, after due inquiry, the disciplinary board was satisfied that the architect had been guilty of such negligence or misconduct, the board might order that his name be removed from the architects' register either permanently or for such period as the board thought fit, or order that he be reprimanded, and order that the findings F   and order be published in the Gazette. By s. 5 (2) of the Buildings Ordinance, 1955, the disciplinary board was to consist of (a) three authorised archiects, (b) the building authority or his representative and (c) a legal adviser; and by s. 5 (3) the building authority or his representative was to be chairman of any such disciplinary board and, where such board was appointed for the purposes of s. 5B, the legal adviser was to have the conduct of the inquiry.

G   The appellant made three submissions on the hearing of the present appeal; these were based on the same grounds as his application to the Supreme Court for leave to apply for an order of certiorari. They were that (i) the disciplinary board had no jurisdiction to try the charge in that the whole or part of it consti- tuted a criminal offence triable only summarily by a court of criminal jurisdiction (the trial of which charge was statute-barred); (ii) the subject-matter of the H   inquiry was beyond the scope of the authority of the disciplinary board by reason of its nature, or, alternatively, the disciplinary board purported to try a matter outside its jurisdiction under colour of a charge over which it might have had a jurisdiction; and (iii) the disciplinary board failed to hold a " due inquiry " in that, in breach of the rules of natural justice, the legal adviser (who had the conduct of the inquiry) did not give, within the hearing of the parties, any or I   sufficient legal advice to the disciplinary board of which he was a member on the many points of law arising in the course of the inquiry, or in such manner that his advice could form part of the record or be ascertained from the record for the purposes of the parties either at the hearing before the disciplinary board or of appeal.

   The board held that the charge made against the appellant was a charge of negligence and that the disciplinary board, in dealing with that charge, did not exceed their jurisdiction. This report deals only with the third submission, viz., failure to hold due inquiry and to observe rules of natural justice.

A

W. E. Denny for the appellant.

J. G. Le Quesne, Q.C., and *D. J. R. Wilcox* for the respondent.

LORD MORRIS OF BORTH-Y-GEST having referred to the relevant provisions of the Buildings Ordinance, 1955 and reg. 38 of the Buildings (Administration) Regulations, 1959, and having reviewed the course of proceedings before the disciplinary board, stated the three grounds (see p. 1229, letters H and I, B ante) on which the appellant applied for certiorari to quash the finding of the disciplinary board. Having intimated that the disciplinary board did not act without nor exceed their jurisdiction, HIS LORDSHIP turned to the third ground and continued: The third contention of the appellant was that the board did not hold " due inquiry " to comply with s. 5B (2) of the Buildings Ordinance, 1955. During the hearing before the disciplinary board, counsel for the appellant made certain C submissions which involved, or may have involved, matters of law or procedure and the board from time to time adjourned for a short while for deliberation in private, after which the legal adviser stated the board's ruling or decision on the point raised. It was contended on behalf of the appellant that any advice on matters of law that the legal adviser may have given should have been given in the presence of the parties and in such a way that his advice could form part of, D or otherwise be ascertained from, the record. A failure to follow such procedure, so it was contended, amounted to a breach of the rules of natural justice, with the result that there had been no " due inquiry ". Any communication to the board by the legal adviser should, it was contended, as a matter of obligation have been made in the presence of the parties in manner comparable to that laid down by reg. 33 of the Medical Practitioners (Registration and Disciplinary Procedure) E Regulations, 1957, which were made in the exercise of the powers conferred by s. 31 of the Medical Registration Ordinance, 1957 (No. 25 of 1957). Regulation 33 is in the following terms:

" (1) When the legal adviser advises the council on any question of law as to evidence, procedure or any other matter, in any inquiry under s. 20 of the ordinance he shall do so in the presence of every party to the proceed- F ings or the person representing each party or, if the advice is tendered after the council has commenced to deliberate as to its findings, every such party or persons as aforesaid shall be informed of the advice that the legal adviser has tendered. (2) In any case where the council does not accept the advice of the legal adviser on any such question as aforesaid, every such party or person shall be informed of this fact." G

In keeping with these contentions, counsel for the appellant had (as already noted) submitted at the hearing before the board that it was desirable in the interests of natural justice that there should be a summing-up to the board by the legal adviser in the presence of the parties.

Their lordships cannot accept these contentions. If a disciplinary board is H appointed, it consists of three authorised architects, the building authority or his representative and a legal adviser. After due inquiry it is for the board to come to a conclusion under s. 5B (2) of the Buildings Ordinance. The legal adviser is constituted a full member of the board. The other members are likewise full members of the board. In fact, it does not appear to have been likely that, in the present case, any legal advice was given to the board by the legal adviser save to I such extent as is apparent on the record exhibited in the proceedings. The findings of the board appear to have been pure findings of fact. If in reaching them one or more of the architects, when the board was deliberating in private, gave his view on some matter of architectural knowledge, it could hardly be contended that there was an obligation to repeat that view in the presence of the parties. The members of the board are chosen to exercise a judicial function. They must act fairly in ascertaining and considering the facts. They must give every opportunity to the parties to deal with all relevant matters. But the members of

A the board are not under obligation to repeat in public anything or everything said in the privacy of their deliberations. It is said, however, that there could be the possibility that the legal adviser during the deliberation of the board would give legal advice to the other members of the board on matters relating to the proceedings. It is to be noted (see s. 5) that the building authority or his representative is the chairman of a disciplinary board and that, where a board is appointed

B for the purposes of s. 5B, the legal adviser has the conduct of the inquiry. If some special point is raised, the legal adviser will doubtless give the parties or their legal representatives every opportunity to make submissions in regard to it. After deliberation, the legal adviser will doubtless state what conclusion the board has reached in regard to it. If in the course of deliberation some new point emerged with which the parties or their representatives had not had opportunity

C to deal, such opportunity would doubtless be given them. At all times, however, the legal adviser occupies the position of being a full member of a body charged with the duty of acting judicially in making due inquiry. There was no obligation on him to make a summing-up of the case to his colleagues on the board in the presence of the parties. His position is different from that which is occupied by the legal adviser to the Medical Council of Hong Kong. The legal adviser to the

D medical council is not a member of that body. His duties are specially prescribed by the Medical Practitioners (Registration and Disciplinary Procedure) Regulations, 1957. The absence in the Buildings Ordinance of any provision compared to that of reg. 33 of the Medical Practitioners (Registration and Disciplinary Procedure) Regulations, 1957, but serves to show the contrast between the roles of the two respective legal advisers. There are statutory provisions in regard to

E the dental profession in Hong Kong which are comparable with those in relation to the medical profession.

  Cases which have been concerned with the correct procedure to be followed where, if there is a trial with a jury, the jury make some communication (such as *R.* v. *Willmont* (1), *R.* v. *Green* (2), *R.* v. *Furlong* (3), *Fromhold* v. *Fromhold* (4), *R.* v. *Davis* (*No. 2*) (5)), have no application to the present case. The position of

F the legal adviser is not to be compared with that of a jury. He is not to be regarded as someone separate and apart from his fellow members of the disciplinary board. Nor in the present case, as was frankly agreed, is there any material from which it can be deduced that the legal adviser did in fact have occasion to give legal advice to his colleagues on some point of law not referred to in the notes of the proceedings.

G Referring more particularly to the formulated ground for seeking an order of certiorari, it is to be observed that it is complained that not sufficient legal advice was given to the board within the hearing of the parties on the many points of law arising in the course of the inquiry. It has already been recited that a contention was advanced before the board that the statement of offence was bad for duplicity. The point was argued; the board then adjourned for deliberation;

H they then gave a clear ruling. In their lordships' view, there was no error of procedure and there was no obligation on the legal adviser to do more than was done. Similar procedure was adopted when the contention was advanced that the board were being asked to deal with a criminal charge and lacked jurisdiction to do so. An argument appears to have been addressed to the board as to the meaning of the word " satisfied " in s. 5B (2), and it also appears to have been argued

I that the board had to be unanimous. Their lordships cannot think that the meaning of the word " satisfied " could have presented any difficulty, and there is no indication that any occasion arose for any ruling whether the board had to be unanimous. In their lordships' view, the complaint that there was a failure to

---

(1) (1914), 10 Cr. App. Rep. 173.
(2) [1950] 1 All E.R. 38.
(3) [1950] 1 All E.R. 636.
(4) [1952] 1 T.L.R. 1522.
(5) (1960), 44 Cr. App. Rep. 235.

hold " due inquiry " was devoid of substance and was rightly rejected by the **A** Supreme Court.

Their lordships will humbly advise Her Majesty that the appeal should be dismissed. The appellant must pay the costs of the respondent.

Appeal dismissed.

Solicitors: *A. Kramer & Co.* (for the appellant); *Charles Russell & Co.* (for **B** the respondent).

[*Reported by* KATHLEEN J. H. O'BRIEN, *Barrister-at-Law.*]

C

PRACTICE DIRECTION.

CHANCERY DIVISION.

D

Infant—Guardianship of Infants Acts—Appeals from courts of summary jurisdiction—Title of proceedings—Application for leave to adduce further evidence—Guardianship of Infants Acts, 1886 and 1925—R.S.C., Ord. 55, r. 3 (1), (2), Ord. 91, r. 7 (1), (2).

PENNYCUICK, J., has given the following direction which supersedes the Practice Direction (1) given on June 30, 1960:

E

Notices of appeal under the above mentioned Acts from a decision of a court of summary jurisdiction are to be intituled, as nearly as may be appropriate, in the form following:

" In the High Court of Justice
    Chancery Division
    Group A

F

In the Matter of A.B., an Infant
and
In the Matter of an Appeal from an Order dated
........19.... of the Justices of the Petty
Sessional Division of...... in the County of....
and

G

In the Matter of the Guardianship of Infants Acts 1886 and 1925."

The notice of appeal must comply with R.S.C., Ord. 55, r. 3 (1) and (2) and must be served and the appeal must be entered as provided by R.S.C., Ord. 91, r. 7 (1).

Within ten days after entry of the appeal the appellant must obtain an **H** appointment for the purpose specified in R.S.C., Ord. 91, r. 7 (2). If either party desires to adduce further evidence on the hearing of the appeal he must be prepared at this appointment to indicate in outline what further evidence it is desired to adduce, whether it is to be oral or by affidavit and why it was not given before the justices.

I

D. C. SMITH,
June 16, 1967.   Chief Registrar.

---

(1) [1960] 2 All E.R. 862.

A

In the Estate of BRAVDA *(deceased).*

[PROBATE, DIVORCE AND ADMIRALTY DIVISION (Cairns, J.), May 11, 12, 1967.]

Will—Attestation—Superfluous signature—Intention with which signature affixed
—Will signed by four persons below word " witnessed "—Top two signatures
those of testator's two daughters who were his sole residuary legatees—Evidence

B *that other two persons signed first as witnesses, and daughters signed also at*
testator's request to make will stronger—Probate without daughters' signatures.

In December, 1965, the testator made a will leaving his whole estate to the
two plaintiffs, his daughters. It was a holograph will made on a single sheet
of notepaper, the whole will and the signature of the testator being on one
side, while on the other side at the top was the word " witnessed " followed

C by the date, the signatures of the two plaintiffs and the signatures and
addresses of two witnesses with the date. The evidence showed that, after
the two witnesses had witnessed the will, the testator said that he would
like the plaintiffs to sign " as that would make it stronger ". The testator
died in February, 1966, survived by the plaintiffs and the defendant, his
second wife who had obtained a decree of judicial separation against him.

D The will could not be found, and on advice by their then solicitor the
plaintiffs were granted letters of administration. Shortly thereafter the
will was found. On an application by notice of motion by the plaintiffs for
the grant to be set aside and for the will to be admitted to probate with the
omission of their signatures,

Held: the question was one of the intention with which the signatures

E were applied to the will, and the evidence showed sufficiently that the
plaintiffs did not sign as attesting witnesses, but signed simply in order to
please the testator who thought that in some way the addition of their
signatures would improve the will; accordingly the grant of letters of
administration would be revoked and the will would be admitted to probate
without the plaintiffs' signature (see p. 1237, letter F, and p. 1238, letter A,

F post).

Kitcat v. *King* ([1930] P. 266) followed.

[As to superfluous attestation, see 39 HALSBURY'S LAWS (3rd Edn.) 871,
para. 1319, and for cases on the subject, see 48 DIGEST (Repl.) 134, 135, *1156-*
1173.]

G *Cozens* v. *Crout*, (1873), 42 L.J.Ch. 840; 48 Digest (Repl.) 135, *1168.*

Denning, Re, Harnett v. *Elliott*, [1958] 2 All E.R. 1; [1958] 1 W.L.R. 462;
Digest (Cont. Vol. A) 552, *1031a.*

Kitcat v. *King*, [1930] P. 266; 99 L.J.P. 126; 143 L.T. 408; 48 Digest (Repl.)
97, *761.*

Peverett, In the Goods of, [1902] P. 205; 71 L.J.P. 114; 87 L.T. 143; 23 Digest

H (Repl.) 102, *1030.*

Randfield v. *Randfield*, (1860), 8 H.L. Cas. 225; 30 L.J.Ch. 177; 11 E.R. 414;
subsequent proceedings, (1863), 2 New Rep. 309; 48 Digest (Repl.) 135,
1164.

Sharman, In the Goods of, (1869), L.R. 1 P. & D. 661; 38 L.J.P. & M. 47;
20 L.T. 683; 33 J.P. 695; 48 Digest (Repl.) 134, *1163.*

I *Smith, In the Goods of*, (1889), 15 P.D. 2; 59 L.J.P. 5; 62 L.T. 183; 54 J.P.
199; 48 Digest (Repl.) 135, *1169.*

Toker, In the Goods of, Toker v. *Maguire*, (1860), 4 L.T. 183; 48 Digest (Repl.)
135, *1191.*

Wigan v. *Rowland*, (1853), 11 Hare 157; 23 L.J.Ch. 69; 21 L.T.O.S. 150;
68 E.R. 1229; 48 Digest (Repl.) 134, *1162.*

Motion.

This was an application by notice of motion by the plaintiffs that the grant to
them of letters of administration of the will of Louis Bravda, who died on Feb.

23, 1966, should be set aside and the will admitted to probate with the omission A
of their signatures. The facts are set out in the judgment.

A. Garfitt for the plaintiffs.
Gavin Lightman for the defendant.

CAIRNS, J.: Louis Bravda was married twice. By his first marriage he
had two daughters, Rachel and Sarah, who are the plaintiffs in this case. After B
the death of his first wife, he married the defendant in 1944. They lived together
for about eight months and then parted for good. The defendant obtained a
decree of judicial separation, and on Apr. 13, 1961, her claim for permanent
alimony was settled for a lump sum of £1,100. On Dec. 14, 1965, Mr. Bravda
(" the testator ") made a will leaving his whole estate to his two daughters, the
plaintiffs, and appointing them his trustees. It was a holograph will made on a C
single sheet of notepaper, the whole will and the signature of the testator being
on one side, while on the other side at the top was the word " witnessed " followed
by the date; then the signatures of the two plaintiffs; then the signature and
address of a Mr. Haseldine and the date; then the signature and address of a
Mrs. Levy and the date. The testator died on Feb. 23, 1966, survived by the two
plaintiffs and the defendant. Thereafter a series of events took place, according D
to the evidence of the plaintiff Rachel, which reflects little credit on the solicitor
advising her. She said that she told the solicitor about the will and also told
him, as was the fact, that she could not find it. She further told him of the
proceedings for judicial separation and of the settlement of the defendant's
claim for permanent alimony. She and her sister were then advised that, in those
circumstances, the defendant could be treated as dead, the father as having died E
intestate, and that she and her sister could apply for a grant of letters of administration. The solicitor who gave this advice had no connexion with the plaintiff's
present solicitors and it is only fair to him to say that he has had no opportunity in this action of denying the allegations made about him. In due course
letters of administration were granted to the plaintiffs on July 29, 1966. Shortly
thereafter the plaintiff Rachel found the will, and the plaintiffs then applied, by F
notice of motion, for the grant to be set aside and for the will to be admitted to
probate with the omission of their signatures. The reason for this last part of
the application is, of course, that, if the two plaintiffs are to be regarded as
witnesses to the will, they could take no benefit under it. The defendant opposes
the application only as to this last part. She admits that the grant of administration must be set aside and does not contest the validity of the will, but says G
that the whole document ought to be admitted to probate with the effect of
making it a mere shell of a will; so that the result would be that the estate would
be distributed as on intestacy and the defendant would have the rights of the
widow on the intestacy.

Evidence as to the events surrounding the making of the will is contained in
the affidavits made by all four persons whose signatures appear on the back of it. H
All of them tell substantially the same story, and the truth of that story is not
challenged by the defendant. This is the substance of it. On the day in question,
the two plaintiffs were at the testator's house and Mr. Haseldine, a friend, was
working somewhere in the house. The testator said he was going to make his
will, adding " As Len is here, he can be a witness ". Len was Mr. Haseldine.
Then the testator said, " Go and get Mrs. Levy, she can be the other witness ". I
The plaintiff Rachel brought Mr. Haseldine from the kitchen and Mrs. Levy
from her house nearby, asking each of them to come and witness her father's
will. When the five of them were assembled, the testator dictated the short will
and the plaintiff Rachel wrote it down and afterwards read it over to him.
She also wrote the word " Witnessed " and the date on the back of the paper.
The testator then asked Mr. Haseldine and Mrs. Levy to sign, and they did so,
each adding their address and the date. The testator then said, almost as an
afterthought as it appeared to Mr. Haseldine, that he would like the plaintiffs to

A to sign " as that would make it stronger ". All four deponents remember these words being spoken. Mrs. Levy said that it seemed obvious to her from what the testator said that it was not his intention that the plaintiffs should sign as witnesses. I disregard this piece of evidence as there is no indication that the testator said any more than I have already quoted and I think that it is for the court to infer what his intention was.

B   It is clear from the text books and from a series of decided cases that, when two or more names are signed on a will in addition to the testator's, it is a question of fact whether each signature is by way of attestation or not and the test is the intention with which the signature is applied. One can start with the proposition that the court leans in favour of carrying out the intentions of the testator (see *In the Goods of Peverett* (1) and *Re Denning, Harnett* v. *Elliott* (2)). Each of these

C cases was one where there were only two signatures following the testator's and there was nothing to indicate that the two persons had signed as witnesses. In each case the court held that they had signed as witness. The doctrine omnia praesumuntur rite esse acta was applied, and in that respect those cases differ from the present one, because there is no doubt that the will here was duly executed and attested and, if the plaintiffs are held to have signed as

D witnesses, this would not affect the validity of the will as a will. In *Peverett's* case (3), however, SIR FRANCIS JEUNE, P., said:

> " There is no authority covering this case. Two things may be laid down as general principles. The first is, that the court is always extremely anxious to give effect to the wishes of persons if satisfied that they really are their testamentary wishes . . .";

E
and this passage was cited and applied by SACHS, J., in *Denning's* case (4). In the present case, if I felt driven to hold that the plaintiffs' signatures were those of witness, it would manifestly defeat the testator's whole purpose in making the will, and the court ought to avoid such a result if it can. One possible view would be that, once a will has been signed by the testator and his signature has been

F duly attested by two witnesses, there is then a complete will and the addition of any further signatures is mere surplusage which can be disregarded. This view, however, has not commended itself to the courts. I shall be citing later several cases in which it has been held that, in the particular circumstances, third or fourth signatures could be held not to be attesting signatures, and the reasoning of all the judgments makes it quite clear that signatures after the second one cannot simply be dismissed out of hand.

G   In *In the Goods of Toker, Toker* v. *Maguire* (5), a beneficiary, who had signed as a third witness, cut away the part of the paper bearing her signature. The argument and the judgment of KEATING, J., proceeded on the basis that, since she had signed as a witness, she could take no beneficial interest under the will. In *Cozens* v. *Crout* (6), a legatee's signature appeared as that of the third of three witnesses, and

H he had described himself in an affidavit as " the sole surviving witness ". A contention on his behalf that his signature as a witness could be disregarded was rejected by LORD SELBORNE, L.C. A sentence in the judgment of LORD PENZANCE in *In the Goods of Sharman* (7) shows that, in the view of that very learned judge, a third signature may have to be regarded as an attesting signature, though he seems to have considered that the presumption was to the contrary. He said (8):

I   " When a testator has signed his name in the presence of two witnesses, and at his request they attest his signature, the execution is complete; and if a third person afterwards adds his name, the court will not come to the conclusion, without cogent evidence, that that third person signed as an attesting witness."

---

(1) [1902] P. 205.   (2) [1958] 2 All E.R. 1.
(3) [1902] P. at pp. 206, 207.   (4) [1958] 2 All E.R. at p. 2.
(5) (1860), 4 L.T. 183.   (6) (1873), 42 L.J.Ch. 840.
(7)(1869), L.R. 1 P. & D. 661.   (8) (1869), L.R. 1 P. & D. at p. 663.

This is the only authority that I have seen which suggests that the onus of proving   A
that a surplus signature is an attesting one is on the party asserting that it is.
That the presumption is the other way is stated categorically in TRISTRAM AND
COOTE (22nd Edn.), p. 46, and in 39 HALSBURY'S LAWS OF ENGLAND (3rd Edn.),
p. 871, para. 1319. TRISTRAM AND COOTE cites no authority for the proposition. In
footnote (c) in HALSBURY at the end of the sentence, which contains at least
one further proposition, several cases are cited, at only one of which I have been   B
invited to look, and that is *Wigan* v. *Rowland* (9). In that case, the signature
of the testator was followed by the marks of two marksmen and then there was
the word " witness " and a bracket, against which appeared the name of one
Wigan and one Rowland, and it was sought to contend that the signatures of
Wigan and Rowland were not the signatures of witnesses. SIR WILLIAM PAGE
WOOD, V.-C., held that the defendant Wigan must be held to be a witness and   C
that, although it was a hard case, the legacy to his wife must fail. SIR WILLIAM
PAGE WOOD thought that, even if evidence to the contrary was admissible, it
was not of sufficient force to counteract that which the document afforded. It
is not perfectly clear to me that that is to be regarded as authority on the onus
of proof, but I am prepared to assume that it is, and, indeed, it is right to say
that counsel for the plaintiffs did not suggest that the proposition as to the   D
presumption set out in TRISTRAM AND COOTE was incorrect. However, at the
end of it all I do not find it necessary to arrive at a decision as to where the
onus of proof lies, because in this case I shall not have to fall back on onus in
order to decide the case.

I come now to a series of cases where the court has reached the conclusion that
a beneficiary's signature appearing on a will was not by way of attestation. In,   E
Randfield v. *Randfield* (10), two witnesses had signed on the front of the will,
and then both of them and also a devisee had signed on the back under an attestation clause. The relevant decision is that of LORD CRANWORTH, L.C., set out in
the note (11) in the report. He held that the signatures on the back were not
to be regarded as being by way of attestation, but one or two sentences in his
judgment are relied on by counsel for the defendant. LORD CRANWORTH said (11):   F

" The question is, whether that is an attestation by her [that is the
devisee] to the will, so as to make, under the provisions of the last Will Act,
the legacy and devise to her void. If she and the other two witnesses signed
that memorandum after they had seen the testator sign the will, and they
did so at his request and in his presence, then I think they were to all
intents and purposes all three witnesses to the will."   G

Then, at the end of his judgment he said (12):

" . . . if the memorandum was signed by the three persons who signed
it, not at the request of the testator, but only for their own satisfaction, and
in order to preserve a record of what in terms did not appear on the face of the
will, there being no testimonium clause, then they were not persons   H
attesting the execution of the will within the meaning of s. 15 of the [Wills
Act, 1837] and the gift to Grace Bestone in such case is not affected. The
test would be this: if that were the state of things she would not be a
competent attesting witness to prove the execution of the will, provided
the other two witnesses were alive."

In *In the Goods of Sharman* (13), one of the witnesses to the will suggested at the   I
time of execution that the residuary legatee who was present should sign, and
he did so, though the testator himself did not want him to. LORD PENZANCE
held that the legatee had not signed as a witness and that her signature should
be omitted from the grant of administration with the will annexed. Counsel for

---

(9) (1853), 11 Hare 157.   (10) (1860), 8 H.L. Cas. 225.
(11) (1860), 8 H.L. Cas. at p. 229, n.   (12) (1860), 8 H.L Cas. at p. 230, n.
            (13) (1869), L.R. 1 P. & D. 661.

A the defendant distinguishes that case from the present one inasmuch as the testator did not ask the legatee to sign and the circumstances indicate that nobody thought that he was signing as a witness. In *In the Goods of Smith* (14), a wife signed a will at the request of her husband after it had been executed in order, as the husband put it, " to verify its contents ". It would appear that she was not present at the time of execution, and it was easy to conclude that
B she had not signed as a witness. BUTT, J., admitted the will to probate with the omission of her signature. The strongest case in favour of the plaintiffs is *Kitcat* v. *King* (15). Four signatures were applied to a codicil opposite the printed words " signed and witnessed to the presence of each other ". The first and third names were those of beneficiaries. All four people were present at the time of execution. The evidence was that the testator had asked them " to sign to
C show their approval and to make it legal ". BATESON, J., admitted the codicil to probate omitting the two signatures of the beneficiaries. It is true that, in that case, the defendant's counsel presented no argument but submitted to the judgment of the court. Authorities were, however, cited on behalf of the plaintiff, and it is clear that BATESON, J., gave careful consideration to the matter. Counsel for the defendant argues that, since one of the proposed objects of getting
D the signatures of the beneficiaries was to show their approval, the case was not on all fours with the present one, but the phrase " to make it legal " corresponds closely to the expression " to make it stronger " in the present case. Either phrase *might* be taken to mean " to give greater legal effect to the attestation ", but either might mean simply " to give greater legal effect to the will ", and, though both testators were mistaken in supposing that the additional signatures
E would in any way strengthen the will, this is immaterial.

I recognise that, if the proposition enunciated by LORD CRANWORTH in *Randfield* v. *Randfield* (16) were literally applied here, or if the decision of *Wigan* v. *Rowland* (17) decided in 1853 were closely followed, it might be difficult for the plaintiffs to succeed. I think, however, that the line of cases to which I have referred shows a degree of development of the law in the direction that one would
F expect, in the direction, that is to say, of leaning towards a construction which will not defeat the intention of the testator. The matter is, however, as all the cases, certainly all the more recent cases, show, a question of fact as to the intention with which the signatures were applied.

It is a strong point in the defendant's favour that the heading " Witnessed 14.12.65 " appears on the face of it to indicate the purpose of all the signatures
G that followed, and the point is all the stronger because the first two signatures on that side of the paper and under that heading are those of the plaintiffs. In these respects, however, the form of words and the order of signatures in *Kitcat* v. *King* (15) would have told at least as strongly in the same direction. The point loses some of its force when it is accepted, as it is here, that, although the two plaintiffs' signatures appear on the paper before the other two, they were
H written after them. Pointers in favour of the plaintiffs are these. Mr. Haseldine and Mrs. Levy added their addresses and the date to their signatures, which neither of the plaintiffs did. This shows that some sort of differentiation was being made between the two pairs of signatures. Then the testator sent for Mr. Haseldine to be a witness, and sent for Mrs. Levy to be " the other witness ", indicating plainly that he knew that only two witnesses were needed and with the
I apparent intention of having only two. Finally, there seems to have been a definite break between the formality of executing the will and the obtaining of the signatures of the plaintiffs. Mrs. Levy said in her affidavit that, after she and Mr. Haseldine had signed, the testator seemed to be quite pleased that this was done, and *then* he said that he would like his daughters to sign. Mr. Haseldine said that the testator made the request " almost as an afterthought ".

---

(14) (1889), 15 P.D. 2.   (15) [1930] P. 266.
(16) (1860), 8 H.L. Cas. 225.   (17) (1853), 11 Hare 157.

In my judgment, the evidence here does sufficiently show that the two plaintiffs **A**
signed, not as attesting witnesses, but simply in order to please their father,
who thought that in some way the addition of their signatures would improve
the will.

I hold, therefore, that the letters of administration already granted must be
revoked and that the will is to be admitted to probate without the signatures of
the two plaintiffs. Defendant's cost out of the estate.   **B**

Order accordingly.

Solicitors: *Barber, Young & Co.* (for the plaintiffs); *Lovell, White & King,*
agents for *Charles Webb & Sons,* Brighton (for the defendant).

[*Reported by* ALICE BLOOMFIELD, *Barrister-at-Law.*]

C

NISSAN *v.* ATTORNEY-GENERAL.

[COURT OF APPEAL, CIVIL DIVISION (Lord Denning, M.R., Danckwerts and Winn,
L.JJ.), June 5, 6, 7, 29, 1967.]

D

*Crown—Prerogative—Emergency prerogative—Compensation for loss or damage
by exercise of prerogative—Treaty with independent sovereign state—Truce
force under British command established to assist sovereign power in preservation of internal peace—Occupation by British troops of hotel on territory
of that power—Whether occupation a prerogative act of Crown—Whether
an act of state of the Crown—Occupation by British troops later continued as* **E**
*part of the United Nations Force—Whether tenant of hotel, a British subject,
entitled to compensation from the Crown—Jurisdiction of the court.*

*Constitutional Law—Act of State—Emergency—Treaty with foreign independent
sovereign power—British subject hotel owner in territory of that power—
Occupation of hotel by British troops pursuant to treaty with that power for
preservation of internal peace—Claim for compensation and in contract—* **F**
Defence of act of state.

*United Nations—Peace-keeping force established pursuant to resolution of Security
Council—British contingents of United Nations Force—Whether acting on
behalf of Crown.*

On Dec. 25, 1963, the government of the Republic of Cyprus (which
had (been an independent sovereign state since Aug. 16, 1960), in response **G**
to a joint appeal by the British, Greek and Turkish governments accepted
an offer that the forces of those three governments, stationed in Cyprus
and under British command, should assist the government of Cyprus in the
restoration of peace. This " truce force " began to operate on Dec. 26,
1963.

The plaintiff was a British subject and was tenant of a hotel in Cyprus. **H**
British troops of the truce force, acting in accordance with orders, took
possession of the hotel, except the plaintiff's flat therein, on Dec. 29, 1963.
They remained in possession from Dec. 29, 1963, to Mar. 27, 1964 (" the first
period ").   The plaintiff alleged that on Dec. 29, 1963, the British High
Commissioner in the presence of the Secretary of State for Commonwealth
Relations on behalf of the Crown undertook that the plaintiff should be **I**
compensated so that he would suffer no loss by reason of the occupation of the
hotel.   On Mar. 27, 1964, the United Nations set up a peace-keeping force
in Cyprus.   From Mar. 27, 1964, to May 5, 1964 (" the second period ")
British troops formed part of the United Nations Force; they continued in
occupation of the hotel.   The plaintiff sued the Crown in England in respect
of the occupation of the hotel during the first period and the second period,
and of loss and damage allegedly resulting therefrom, claiming (i) just
compensation as of right for loss or damage to the hotel and its contents,

Affirmed in part, reversed in part.
H.L. [1969] 1 All E.R. 629.

A (ii) in contract for money due or damages and (iii) damages for trespass to chattels, being contents of the hotel, but excluding the plaintiff's flat. On preliminary points of law,

Held: the claim for compensation was sustainable in law against the Crown in respect of the first period, but not in respect of the second period (see p. 1245, letter A, p. 1247, letter C, and p. 1252, letters C and D, post)

B for the following reasons—

(i) (a) where the British Crown or its agents took the property of a British subject, whether within or outside Her Majesty's dominions and whether by virtue of the royal prerogative or in some other way, there was an obligation to pay compensation and, as against a British subject, a plea that an act was an act of state was no defence (see p. 1243, letter F, p. 1244, letters

C C and E, p. 1246, letter D, p. 1247, letter B, p. 1249, letter A, and p. 1251, letter G, post).

A.-G. v. *De Keyser's Royal Hotel, Ltd.* ([1920] All E.R. Rep. 80) and *Burmah Oil Co. (Burma Trading), Ltd.* v. *Lord Advocate* ([1964] 2 All E.R. 348) followed.

(b) but when the British troops became part of the United Nations Force

D the responsibility for their acts was no longer that of the British Crown and there was no longer obligation on the Crown to pay compensation for their acts (see p. 1244, letter I, p. 1247, letter C, and p. 1252, letter D, post).

(ii) (per LORD DENNING, M.R., and DANCKWERTS, L.J.) no contract appeared to have been created by the words alleged to have been spoken by the High Commissioner, who had been merely stating the legal position

E (see p. 1244, letter G, and p. 1246, letter B, post; cf., p. 1251, letter H, post).

(iii) (per LORD DENNING, M.R., and WINN, L.J.) in taking possession of the hotel the British troops were not acting as agents of the government of Cyprus (see p. 1242, letter C, and p. 1247, letter I, post).

Decision of JOHN STEPHENSON, J. ([1967] 2 All E.R. 200) reversed on (i),

F affirmed on (ii) but on a different ground, and affirmed on (iii).

[As to acts of state and the position of the Crown in the conduct of foreign affairs, see 7 HALSBURY'S LAWS (3rd Edn.) 263-264, para. 565; 279-282, paras. 593-598; 287, para. 606; and for cases on acts of state as affecting the court's jurisdiction, see 11 DIGEST (Repl.) 618-626, *451-501.*

As to the nature and extent of the royal prerogative, see 7 HALSBURY'S LAWS

G (3rd Edn.) 221, 222, paras. 463-467; and for cases on the subject, see 11 DIGEST (Repl.) 566, 567, *41-53.*]

Cases referred to:

A.-G. v. *De Keyser's Royal Hotel, Ltd.*, [1920] All E.R. Rep. 80; [1920] A.C. 508; 89 L.J.Ch. 417; 122 L.T. 691; *affg. Re De Keyser's Royal Hotel,*

H *Ltd., De Keyser's Royal Hotel, Ltd.* v. *Regem*, [1919] 2 Ch. 197; 88 L.J.Ch. 415; 120 L.T. 396; 17 Digest (Repl.) 437, *91.*

Birch v. *Wright*, (1786), 1 Term Rep. 378; 99 E.R. 1148; 31 Digest (Repl.) 41, *1995.*

British South Africa Co. v. *Companhia de Mocambique*, [1891-94] All E.R. Rep. 640; [1893] A.C. 602; 63 L.J.Q.B. 70; 69 L.T. 604; 11 Digest (Repl.)

I 371, *374.*

Burmah Oil Co. (Burma Trading), Ltd. v. *Lord Advocate*, [1964] 2 All E.R. 348; [1965] A.C. 75; [1964] 3 W.L.R. 1231; 3rd Digest Supp.

Buron v. *Denman*, (1848), 2 Exch. 167; 6 State Tr. N.S. 525; 10 L.T.O.S. 523; 154 E.R. 450; 11 Digest (Repl.) 454, *902,* 621, *478.*

Carnatic (Nabob of) v. *East India Co.*, (1791), 1 Ves. 371; *subsequent proceedings* (1793), 2 Ves. 56; 30 E.R. 521; 11 Digest (Repl.) 619, *457.*

Carr v. *Fracis Times & Co.*, [1902] A.C. 176; 71 L.J.K.B. 361; 85 L.T. 144; 11 Digest (Repl.) 453, *895.*

Chandler v. *Director of Public Prosecutions*, [1962] 3 All E.R. 142; [1964] **A**
    A.C. 763; [1962] 3 W.L.R. 694; 46 Cr. App. Rep. 347, H.L.; Digest
    (Cont. Vol. A) 259, *44a.*

Churchward v. *Ford*, (1857), 2 H. & N. 446; 26 L.J.Ex. 354; 157 E.R. 184;
    31 Digest (Repl.) 307, *448.*

Civilian War Claimants' Association, Ltd. v. *Regem*, [1931] All E.R. Rep. 432;
    [1932] A.C. 14; 101 L.J.K.B. 105; 146 L.T. 169; 11 Digest (Repl.) **B**
    620, *476.*

Cook v. *Sprigg*, [1895-99] All E.R. Rep. 773; [1899] A.C. 572; 68 L.J.P.C.
    144; 81 L.T. 281; 11 Digest (Repl.) 627, *502.*

Dobree v. *Napier*, (1836), 2 Bing. N.C. 781; 3 State Tr. N.S. 621; 5 L.J.C.P.
    273; 132 E.R. 301; 11 Digest (Repl.) 454, *904,* 622, *490.*

Johnstone v. *Pedlar*, [1921] All E.R. Rep. 176; [1921] 2 A.C. 262; 90 L.J.P.C. **C**
    181; 125 L.T. 809; 11 Digest (Repl.) 619, *465.*

Kiriri Cotton Co., Ltd. v. *Dewani*, [1960] 1 All E.R. 177; [1960] A.C. 192;
    [1960] 2 W.L.R. 127; Digest (Cont. Vol. A) 1094, **2571b.*

Nelson v. *Larholt*, [1947] 2 All E.R. 751; [1948] 1 K.B. 339; [1948] L.J.R. 340;
    47 Digest (Repl.) 187, *1554.*

Nyali, Ltd. v. *A.-G.*, [1955] 1 All E.R. 646; [1956] 1 Q.B. 1; [1955] 2 W.L.R. **D**
    649; *affd.* H.L., [1956] 2 All E.R. 689; [1957] A.C. 253; [1956] 3
    W.L.R. 341; Digest (Cont. Vol. A) 267, *879a.*

Phillips v. *Homfray*, (1883), 24 Ch.D. 439; 52 L.J.Ch. 833; 49 L.T. 5; 33
    Digest (Repl.) 781, *522.*

Rustomjee v. *Reginam*, (1876), 1 Q.B.D. 487; *affd.* C.A., (1876), 2 Q.B.D. 69;
    46 L.J.Q.B. 238; 36 L.T. 190; 11 Digest (Repl.) 620, *474.*   **E**

Salaman v. *Secretary of State in Council of India*, [1906] 1 K.B. 613; 75 L.J.K.B.
    418; 94 L.T. 858; 11 Digest (Repl.) 613, *426.*

Secretary of State in Council of India v. *Kamachee Boye Sahaba*, (1859), 13 Moo.
    P.C.C. 22; 7 Moo. Ind. App. 476; 19 E.R. 388; 11 Digest (Repl.)
    617, *442.*

Sinclair v. *Brougham*, [1914-15] All E.R. Rep. 622; [1914] A.C. 398; 83 **F**
    L.J.Ch. 465; 111 L.T. 7; 12 Digest (Repl.) 317, *2436.*

United Australia, Ltd. v. *Barclays Bank, Ltd.*, [1940] 4 All E.R. 20; [1941]
    A.C. 1; 109 L.J.K.B. 919; 164 L.T. 139; 45 Digest (Repl.) 317, *275.*

Walker v. *Baird*, [1892] A.C. 491; 61 L.J.P.C. 92; 67 L.T. 513, P.C.; 11
    Digest (Repl.) 618, *452.*

                                                        G

Appeal.

This was an appeal by the plaintiff, Naim Nissan, a British subject, from a
decision of JOHN STEPHENSON, J., on Feb. 17, 1967, reported at [1967] 2 All E.R.
200. The decision was given on preliminary points of law in an action brought
by the plaintiff by writ issued on Mar. 2, 1966, to which Her Majesty's Attorney-
General was defendant and in which the plaintiff claimed relief from the Crown **H**
in respect of loss and damage alleged to have been suffered in consequence of the
occupation of the Cornaro Hotel, near Nicosia, Cyprus, of which the plaintiff
was tenant, by United Kingdom forces during two periods, viz., from Dec. 29,
1963, to Mar. 27, 1964 (" the first period "), and from Mar. 27, 1964, to May 5,
1964 (" the second period "), as set out in the statement of claim. The questions
raised by this preliminary issue are set out at p. 1245, letters H and I, post; in **I**
effect they were that the action was not maintainable in respect of compensation
for the occupation of the hotel by British troops. The statement of claim is set
out in the report below ([1967] 2 All E.R. at pp. 203, et seq.).

Philip Goodenday for the plaintiff.
H. A. P. Fisher, Q.C., and *Nigel Bridge* for the Attorney-General.

                                                Cur. adv. vult.

June 29. The following judgments were read.

A   **LORD DENNING, M.R.:** The plaintiff, Mr. Nissan is a British subject living in Cyprus. From 1958 onwards he has had a luxury hotel on the outskirts of Nicosia. It was called the Cornaro Hotel. He ran it himself and had a private flat in it. Towards the end of 1963 there was civil strife in Cyprus between the Greek and Turkish communities. British troops were used to restore peace. They formed part of a " truce force ". On Dec. 29, 1963, a contingent took

B   possession of the Cornaro Hotel (except the plaintiff's private flat). It was used at first as headquarters of the truce force and later for other British troops. On Mar. 27, 1964, the United Nations set up a peacekeeping force in Cyprus. The British troops became part of the " United Nations Force ". Thenceforward they occupied the Cornaro Hotel as a contingent of the United Nations Force. On May 5, 1964, they were relieved by Finnish troops, and did not occupy it again.

C   The plaintiff claims that he is entitled to compensation from Her Majesty's government for the period that the Briitish troops occupied his hotel. He also alleges that in the latter part of their occupation the British troops broke into his private flat and looted its contents. This is denied.

There is one further matter which I must state: the plaintiff alleges that on the very day when the British troops occupied his hotel, Dec. 29, 1963, he had an inter-

D   view with Sir Arthur Clark, the British High Commissioner in Cyprus, and that present at the interview was the Secretary of State for Commonwealth Relations, the Rt. Hon. Duncan Sandys, M.P. The plaintiff alleges that at that interview the High Commissioner expressly undertook that the plaintiff would be compensated so that he would suffer no loss in respect of the occupation of his hotel: and that Mr. Duncan Sandys acquiesced in what the High Commissioner said.

E   The plaintiff's allegations are denied.

The British government take exception to all the claims of the plaintiff. They say that they have no foundation in law. The parties have agreed that this should be decided as a preliminary issue before the facts are investigated. I never like deciding points of law before knowing the facts. Experience has taught me that a correct decision of any case depends on a true appreciation of the facts;

F   but there it is. The parties have agreed it: and the master (Master Jacob) has ordered it.

The Truce Force

At the time of these events Cyprus was an independent republic. Prior to 1960 Cyprus was a Crown Colony. In 1960 s. 1 of the Cyprus Act, 1960 declared that

G   " . . . there shall be established in the Island of Cyprus an independent sovereign Republic of Cyprus and Her Majesty shall have no sovereignty or jurisdiction over the Republic of Cyprus."

The republic became and is a member of the Commonwealth.

In December, 1963, there was strife in Cyprus. On Dec. 24, 1963, an appeal

H   was made for a cease-fire. It was made by the governments of the United Kingdom, Greece and Turkey in these terms:

" The British, Greek and Turkish governments, as signatories of the Treaty of Guarantee of 1960, jointly appeal to the government of Cyprus and to the Greek and Turkish communities in the Island to put an end to the present disorders. They appeal to the Cyprus government to fix a suitable hour

I   this evening for a cease-fire and to call upon both communities to observe it. The three governments, mindful of the rule of law, further offer their joint good offices with a view to helping to resolve the difficulties which have given rise to the present situation."

On Christmas Day, Dec. 25, 1963, the government of Cyprus accepted that offer and issued this communiqué:

" The government of the Republic of Cyprus has accepted an offer that the forces of the United Kingdom, Greece and Turkey, stationed in Cyprus

and placed under British command, should assist it in its effort to secure **A**
the preservation of cease-fire and the restoration of peace."

On Boxing Day, Dec. 26, 1963, the truce force was established under British
Command. Its task was to assist the Cyprus government in its effort to secure
the preservation of cease-fire and the restoration of peace. On Dec. 29, 1963,
British troops took possession of the Cornaro Hotel and used it as headquarters
of the truce force. **B**

The Crown suggests that, in taking possession, the truce force and the British
troops therein were agents of the Cyprus government. I cannot accept this
contention. I agree with all the judge said about it. The British troops were
acting in accord with the Cyprus government, but they were not agents of the
Cyprus government. They were and remained British troops under British
command. They were soldiers of the Queen helping to keep the peace in a **C**
country of the Commonwealth.

Act of State

The Crown say that the acts of the British troops are acts of state not cognisable by the English courts. The words " act of state " are used to denote
different things at different times.

First: When British troops act as the servants or agents of a foreign power, **D**
they are protected in our courts by the defence of an act of state, i.e., that of the
foreign state. Thus, when Admiral Napier was in the service of the Queen of
Portugal and seized a British ship—and it was lawfully condemned as prize by
the courts of Portugal—he was held not to be liable in the English courts for his
actions (see *Dobree* v. *Napier* (1)). And when Captain Carr of H.M.S. " Lap-
wing " stopped a British ship in the territorial waters of Muscat and seized **E**
munitions of war—and his action was proclaimed lawful by the Sultan of Muscat
—Captain Carr was held not liable in these courts (see *Carr* v. *Fracis Times &*
Co. (2)). Those cases are applicable here if and in so far as the British troops
were acting as agents of the Cyprus government or of the United Nations.

Second: When the British government acquires property or territory by
treaty, annexation or conquest, it cannot be made liable for the consequences. If **F**
anyone seeks to sue the British government and has to rely on the treaty,
annexation or conquest to found his cause of action, he fails on the simple ground
that it is an act of state not cognisable in the municipal courts. Thus, in *Cook*
v. *Sprigg* (3), a British subject had a concession from the ruler of Pondoland. That
territory was annexed by South Africa on behalf of the Crown. He sued the
Premier of South Africa claiming that the concession was binding on the Crown. **G**
He failed because the annexation was an act of state. Likewise the cases where
people have laid claims to funds received by the Crown under treaty. Their
claims have been rejected because they are not cognisable in the courts (see
Rustomjee v. *Reginam* (4) and *Civilian War Claimants' Association, Ltd.* v. *Regem*
(5)). Those cases have no application here because the plaintiff does not base
his claim—he does not need to base it—on any treaty or the like. He bases it **H**
simply on a taking by British troops.

Third: When British troops take or destroy the property of a foreigner in a
territory outside Her Majesty's dominions, the foreigner cannot sue for damages
in the English courts. He must seek redress through his own government by
diplomatic channels. That was established by the celebrated case of *Buron* v.
Denman (6). Commander Denman of the Royal Navy (the son of LORD DENMAN, **I**
C.J.), was engaged in putting down the slave trade. He landed at the Gallinas
with an armed force. He set fire to the property of Senor Buron, a Spaniard, and
freed the slaves. Senor Buron sued Commander Denman for trespass. PARKE, B.,
said (7) that

---

(1) (1836), 2 Bing N.C. 781. (2) [1902] A.C. 176.
(3) [1895-99] All E.R. Rep. 773; [1899] A.C. 572. (4) (1876), 2 Q.B.D. 69.
(5) [1931] All E.R. Rep. 432; [1932] A.C. 14. (6) (1848), 2 Exch. 167.
(7) (1848), 2 Exch. at p. 190.

A   " The seizure of the slaves and goods by the defendant is a seizure by the Crown and an act of state for which the defendant is irresponsible."

That case is not applicable here. The plaintiff was not a foreigner like Senor Buron. He was a British subject. As such he had rights equal to those of anyone born in England of ancient stock. He owed allegiance to the Crown: and correspondingly was entitled to the protection of the Crown, wherever he might be. If

B   injured by the Crown or its servants, he was entitled to seek redress in the Queen's courts without being met by the defence of act of state. That was stated explicitly by SIR JAMES FITZJAMES STEPHEN in his HISTORY OF THE CRIMINAL LAW OF ENGLAND (1883) Vol. 2, p. 65: " As between the Sovereign and his subjects there can be no such thing as an act of state."   This proposition was accepted in Walker v. Baird (8). Captain Walker, R.N., of H.M.S. " Emerald ",

C   was on fishery patrol on the Newfoundland fisheries. He seized Baird's lobster factory and the gear in it. He set up the defence of act of state. But Baird was a British subject. The Privy Council said that the suggestion that the act of Captain Walker could be justified as act of state " is wholly untenable ". Following that case, the House of Lords in Johnstone v. Pedlar (9) declared emphatically that: " This doctrine (of act of state) has no application to any case

D   where the plaintiff is a British subject " (see by VISCOUNT FINLAY, L.C., (10) and by LORD PHILLIMORE (11)). The authorities are summarised in SALMOND ON TORTS (14th Edn.), p. 607, in these words:

" A British subject owes allegiance to the Crown in whatever part of the world he may be: it seems therefore that the Crown cannot plead act of state as against him, wherever the wrong may have been committed."

E   Pressed by those authorities, the Crown admitted before JOHN STEPHENSON, J., (12) that they could not plead act of state in regard to the plaintiff's claim for trespass to goods: but asserted that they could plead it in answer to the claim for seizing the hotel. I see no justification for this distinction. The act of seizing the goods was the same in quality as the act of seizing the hotel. If the defence

F   of act of state is not available in the one, nor is it available in the other.

I hold, therefore, that act of state is no defence to the claim by a British subject.

Trespass to land.

The plaintiff has, however, some other points to get over. If he were to claim that the seizure of his hotel was wrongful, he would be met by the defence that the courts of England have no jurisdiction to entertain an action to recover

G   damages for trespass to land abroad (see British South Africa Co. v. Companhia de Mocambique (13)). So he does not claim that the seizure was wrong. He asserts that it was lawful, and that he is entitled to compensation for it. To this I now turn.

Compensation for lawful taking.

Hitherto the right of a British subject to compensation has been discussed only

H   in cases where British forces or the like have seized property in Her Majesty's dominions, such as A.-G. v. De Keyser's Royal Hotel, Ltd. (14) and Burmah Oil Co. (Burma Trading), Ltd. v. Lord Advocate (15). These cases established this general rule throughout Her Majesty's dominions: that the Crown cannot lawfully take or destroy the property of one of Her Majesty's subjects without paying compensation for it. There are exceptions to that rule, such as the excep-

I   tion of battle damage considered in the Burmah Oil case (15): and the exception of war damage provided by the War Damage Act 1965. None of those exceptions applies here. This was not a case of battle damage: nor was there any war in contemplation in which the Queen might be engaged.

(8) [1892] A.C. 491.   (9) [1921] All E.R. Rep. 176; [1921] 2 A.C. 262.
(10) [1921] All E.R. Rep. at p. 180; [1921] 2 A.C. at p. 272.
(11) [1921] All E.R. Rep. at p. 191; [1921] 2 A.C. at p. 295.
(12) [1967] 2 All E.R. 200.   (13) [1891-94] All E.R. Reo. 640; [1893] A.C. 602.
(14) [1920] All E.R. Rep. 80; [1920] A.C. 508.
(15) [1964] 2 All E.R. 348; [1965] A.C. 75.

Cyprus, however, was not part of Her Majesty's dominions: and on this **A** account the Crown seeks to distinguish this case from the *Burmah Oil* case (16). In the *Burmah Oil* case (16) the oil installations were in Malaya, which was part of Her Majesty's dominions at the time: and the Crown destroyed the oil installations by virtue of the royal prerogative. In that case the law lords invoked the rule that the royal prerogative does not permit the Crown to take or destroy property without paying compensation for it (see by LORD REID (17) and by **B** LORD PEARCE (18)). The Crown say here that the royal prerogative can only run in countries where the Queen is Sovereign (see *Nyali, Ltd.* v. *A.-G.* (19)). They go on to argue that the royal prerogative did not run in Cyprus in 1963 because the Queen was not the Sovereign there. So it does not apply here.

I do not accept this limitation of the royal prerogative. In my opinion when Her Majesty sends her troops overseas to do duty in a foreign land, without the **C** authority of Parliament, but with the accord of the foreign Sovereign, Her Majesty does it by virtue of the royal prerogative. There is no other warrant for it: see *Chandler* v. *Director of Public Prosecutions* (20). And when her troops, in the exercise of their duty, take or destroy the property of one of Her Majesty's subjects in that foreign land, they do so again by virtue of the royal prerogative. It is admittedly lawful; and, if lawful, it must be by virtue of the royal pre- **D** rogative. There is no other warrant for it. Being based on the royal prerogative, it is subject to the general rule in the *Burmah Oil* case (16): the Crown cannot lawfully take or destroy the property of one of Her Majesty's subjects without paying compensation for it. Even if the actions of the British troops were not justified by the royal prerogative, but in some other way, I do not think that it should make any difference. Wherever the British government by its troops takes **E** or destroys the property of a British subject, lawfully for the general good, the common law imposes on the Crown an obligation to pay reasonable compensation for it.

I hold, therefore, that the British troops could not lawfully seize the Cornaro Hotel without paying compensation.

F

The contract.

It seems to me that, if the High Commissioner undertook to pay compensation (with the consent of the Secretary of State), he was only stating the legal position. I doubt whether it would be possible to construct a contract out of such a situation. The obligation to pay compensation is imposed by law. It comes under the head of restitution; but if it is possible to construct such a contract, I do not **G** think that act of state would be an answer to it.

United Nations Force.

On Mar. 27, 1964, the British troops became part of the United Nations Force. They were under the command of the United Nations commander. They flew the United Nations flag. They wore the berets and arm-flashes to denote that they were no longer the soldiers of the Queen, but the soldiers of the United Nations. **H** They were acting as agents for the United Nations, which is a sovereign body corporate. Their actions thenceforward were not to be justified by virtue of the royal prerogative of the Crown of England. They were to be justified only by virtue of the United Nations. I do not think that the Crown can be expected to pay compensation thereafter. It must be paid by the United Nations themselves or perhaps by the Cyprus government who agreed to provide all necessary **I** premises. At any rate, it is not payable by the British Crown.

---

(16) [1964] 2 All E.R. 348; [1965] A.C. 75.
(17) [1964] 2 All E.R. at pp. 358, 360; [19665] A.C. at pp. 107, 110.
(18) [1964] 2 All E.R. at pp. 383, 385; [1965] A.C. at pp. 147, 149.
(19) [1955] 1 All E.R. 646 at p. 653; [1956] 1 Q.B. 1 at p. 15.
(20) [1962] 3 All E.R. 142 at p. 156; [1964] A.C. 763 at p. 807.

A *Conclusion.*

In my opinion the facts pleaded by the defendant do not disclose a good defence to the claims in respect of the events occurring between Dec. 26, 1963, and Mar. 27, 1964; but do disclose a good defence in respect of events occurring on and after Mar. 27, 1964.

B   **DANCKWERTS, L.J.:** The plaintiff in this action is and at all material times was a naturalised British subject of Persian origin. He was the tenant of the Cornaro Hotel situate on the outskirts of Nicosia, Cyprus. Cyprus had become an independent State under s. 1 of the Cyprus Act, 1960, and consequently sovereignty in Cyprus was by that Act vested in the government of Cyprus and no-one else. But, owing to the enmity between the Greek population and the

C Turkish population, in 1963 British forces, which were already in Cyprus, became part of a peace force by agreement with the government of Cyprus.

On Dec. 29, 1963, a contingent of the British forces, without the consent of the plaintiff, it is alleged, occupied the plaintiff's hotel with the furniture and equipment in it, with the exception of the plaintiff's private flat and three stores. Troops forming part of the British forces in Cyprus remained in occupation until

D May 5, 1964, but on Mar. 27, 1964, the British troops became part of the United Nations Force in Cyprus. Damage is alleged to have been done during such occupation to the hotel and its contents. The plaintiff claims (i) a declaration that he is entitled to compensation, (ii) in the alternative that there was a binding contract by the Crown for compensation, (iii) a declaration that the Crown is bound to pay damages for trespass, and various claims for compensation and

E damages.

The defences put forward by Her Majesty's Attorney-General are, first, that the British troops were agents of the Cyprus government and, therefore, their acts were not cognisable by the English courts. Alternatively, it is said that the actions of the British troops were acts of state of Her Majesty on the territory of an independent Sovereign power and so equally not cognisable. It is also said

F in the defence that from and after Mar. 27, 1964, the British troops were contingents of the United Nations Force and so no action lies against the Crown in respect of any actions by them after that date. In para. 8 of the defence it is said that possession of the hotel was taken not from the plaintiff but from elements of the Greek community forces engaged in civil strife who were then in possession of the hotel and who had done extensive damage to it. These were apparently

G Greek irregulars and this allegation is, therefore, not inherently improbable.

A most unsatisfactory air of unreality has been created, however, by the manner in which the matter was brought before the judge (19a) and has come before this court. Certain questions have been set down for hearing as preliminary issues. Such a course may be satisfactory when there is a clearly cut point of law which may dispose of the whole action, but this is not such a case. By an order

H of Master Jacob dated Oct. 27, 1966, the following questions of law were directed to be decided as a preliminary issue before the trial of the action:

" (a) Whether, upon the facts pleaded in paras. 3 and 5 and in the first sentences of paras. 4 and 6 respectively of the defence, all or any, and if some only which, of the claims and causes of action pleaded in the statement of claim are sustainable in law; (b) whether, on the facts pleaded in para. 3

I and the first sentence of para. 4 of the defence, the last two sentences of the said para. 4 disclose a good defence in law to all or any, and if to some only then to which, of the claims and causes of action pleaded by the plaintiff in respect of events occurring between Dec. 26, 1963, and Mar. 27, 1964; and (c) whether, upon the facts pleaded in para. 5 and the first sentence of para. 6 of the defence, the last sentence of the said para. 6 discloses a good defence in law to all or any, and if to some only then to which, of the claims and causes of action pleaded by the plaintiff in respect of events occurring on and after Mar. 27, 1964 "

By agreement, some additional points were argued before the judge (21) and A this court, but the result has proved extremely unsatisfactory. The court has been compelled to deal with the case on admissions gathered with difficulty from the pleadings and assumed facts which may not necessarily be true and which may turn out irrelevant when the case is tried.

One claim can be disposed of, in my opinion, without difficulty. Though the British High Commissioner in Cyprus and Mr. Duncan Sandys as the Minister B concerned with Commonwealth Relations certainly spoke words suggesting that the plaintiff would receive compensation, it is, in my view, clear that no sort of contract was thereby produced—the observations were no more than assumptions which had no contractual force.

I turn, therefore, to the question of " act of state ". It is, I think, at least probable that the acts of British soldiers in this matter were not acts of state at C all. If there was any act of state, it was the agreement between the British and Cyprus governments that the British troops should act as a peace force; but, supposing that in fact the acts of the British troops could be acts of state on behalf of Her Majesty, in my opinion there is one fatal difficulty in the way of this defence. The plaintiff was at the material times a British subject, and it seems to me to be established by the authorities that the British government can never D plead act of state against a British subject, even though the acts done were done in the territory of a foreign Sovereign (always excepting acts done in battle). SIR JAMES FITZJAMES STEPHEN in Vol. 2 of his HISTORY OF THE CRIMINAL LAW OF ENGLAND, (1883) at pp. 61-62, says:

" I understand by an act of state an act injurious to the person or to the property of some person who is not at the time of that act a subject of Her E Majesty; which act is done by any representative of Her Majesty's authority, civil or military, and is either previously sanctioned or subsequently ratified by Her Majesty."

That learned author adds on p. 65:

" In order to avoid misconception it is necessary to observe that the F doctrine as to acts of state can apply only to acts which affect foreigners, and which are done by the orders or with the ratification of the sovereign. As between the sovereign and his subjects there can be no such thing as an act of state. Courts of law are established for the express purpose of limiting public authority in its conduct towards individuals."

I would add that, in the case of foreign subjects, there is a distinction, because G such persons can obtain redress, if they are entitled to any, by diplomatic channels through the governments of their own States.

In 7 HALSBURY'S LAWS OF ENGLAND (3rd Edn.) 279, para. 593, an act of state is defined as follows:

" An act of the executive as a matter of policy performed in the course of its relations with another State including its relations with the subjects of H that State, unless they are temporarily within the allegiance of the Crown, is an act of state."

Paragraph 594 states:

" Act of state towards British subjects. There can be no act of state against anyone who owes allegiance to the Crown. Hence the defence of act of state cannot be set up by the Crown or any of its servants in an action of I tort brought by a British subject, or by a friendly alien resident within British territory."

There is ample authority to be found for this in *Walker* v. *Baird* (22); *Johnstone* v. *Pedlar* (23) and *Burmah Oil Co. (Burma Trading), Ltd.* v. *Lord Advocate* (24).

(21) [1967] 2 All E.R. 200.   (22) [1892] A.C. 491.
(23) [1921] All E.R. Rep. 176; [1921] A.C. 262.
(24) [1964] 2 All E.R. at p. 395; [1965] A.C. at p. 164.

A These cases do not make any distinction as regards acts done by the British government in respect of British subjects in the dominions of a foreign State, and I do not see any reason for any such distinction. Cases to which we have been referred in support of such a distinction seem to me to deal with situations of a different character and to be distinguishable.

The corollary of this is that if the British Crown or its agents takes possession
B of the property of British subjects compensation must be paid. This seems to be clearly established by *A.-G.* v. *De Keyser's Royal Hotel, Ltd.* (25), and *Burmah Oil Co. (Burma Trading), Ltd.* v. *Lord Advocate* (26). I would add that I cannot see any logical ground of distinction between the taking of land and trespass to chattels.

Once the British forces became part of the United Nations Force, however, in
C my opinion the situation changed. Under the documents which have been placed before us, the responsibility for their acts fell on the United Nations, and the acts of the troops were no longer those of the British Crown.

Accordingly, I would allow the appeal to the extent above mentioned; but this, of course, is not the end of the matter. The case will have to go to trial, and it may turn out that the damage suffered by the plaintiff was not due to the acts
D of the British troops, or that the occupation by the British troops was only partly responsible for the damage which the plaintiff has suffered.

WINN, L.J.: The only matter for decision on this appeal is whether the action in which it arises should proceed to trial or should be held to have been finally disposed of by the answers given by the learned judge (27) on certain
E issues set down as questions of law raised by the pleadings to be decided by him as preliminary issues.

The preliminary issues which were before the learned judge, supplemented by an additional issue first stated before this court, with the consent of counsel for the plaintiff, by counsel who appeared on behalf of the Attorney-General, all raise by slightly varied language the same contention, which is in substance a
F demurrer based on very limited pleas of fact contained in the defence, all of which facts, but I stress no other fact, must be taken for the purposes of this appeal to be common ground facts. They are pleaded in para. 3 and para. 5 and in the first sentence only of para. 4 and the first sentence of para. 6 respectively of the defence. For convenience I set out the more relevant of those facts:

"(4) The relevant British forces operating in the Republic of Cyprus
G between Dec. 26, 1963 and Mar. 27, 1964 were part of the force under British command assisting the Cyprus government in its effort to secure the preservation of cease-fire and the restoration of peace pursuant to the agreement recorded in the said communiqué (28) which is hereinafter referred to as 'the truce force' . . . (6) The British forces operating in the Republic of Cyprus from and after Mar. 27, 1964 were contingents of the United Nations
H Force aforesaid . . ."

It was in the second sentence of para. 4 of the defence and not in the first sentence that the defendant pleaded " In the premises the truce force and the British elements comprised therein were agents of the Cyprus government . . .". Accordingly neither the judge (27) nor this court have been compelled to assume that
I the British troops in taking possession of the plaintiff's hotel acted as agents of the Cyprus government; indeed, the learned judge rejected the defendant's contention that there was such an agency; in my opinion he was right in so holding, and the defendant's cross-appeal on this question should be dismissed.

It was said in this court by counsel for the Attorney-General, though it is not

---

(25) [1920] All E.R. Rep. 80; [1920] A.C. 508.
(26) [1964] 2 All E.R. 348; [1965] A.C. 75.   (27) [1967] 2 All E.R. 20.
(28) I.e., the communiqué of Dec. 25, 1963; see p. 1241, letter I, to p. 1242, letter A, ante.

clear that this was contended below, that, albeit the plea of agency might more   A
properly be regarded, as I certainly regard it, as a plea of fact rather than of law,
none the less the existence of such an agency was as logically implicit in the
agreed facts set out in the first sentence of para. 4 of the defence as any other self-
evident factual proposition such as, for example, the statement that assuming
that June 13, 1967 falls on a Tuesday, both the sixth and twentieth of the same
month must also be Tuesdays. I am quite unable to accept this proposition. I   B
agree with the learned judge's view (29) that much may be done by one person
with the permission of another person which is not done in the eyes of the law by
the former as agent for the latter; incidentally, it is to be observed that the agreed
facts contain no direct implication that the Cyprus government took any decision
with regard to the occupation of the hotel by the British troops involving either
permission or declared tolerance, let alone a directive or order.   C

I find myself equally bound to reject the defendant's plea contained in the
same sentence, the second sentence, of para. 4 of the defence, that " the actions
of the truce force were acts of state of the Cyprus government ". This plea
puzzled me and it was a relief to my mind when it transpired in the course of the
hearing of the appeal—though apparently the point never arose below—that the
learned pleader had, on this no doubt unique occasion, shared the frailty of   D
Homer in that he had nodded; what it was intended to contend for was not an
act of state of the Cyprus government but an exercise by that government of its
prerogative as the sovereign government of Cyprus. In this new guise the plea
seems to me no more impressive than in its former shape. I do not find it easy to
envisage the concept of a sovereign prerogative, akin to the royal prerogative of
the British Crown, residing in and exercisable by either the government of Cyprus   E
or the President of the Republic of Cyprus. The essence of the royal prerogative
of the British Crown is that it comprises those residual elements of sovereignty
of which the Monarch has not been deprived constitutionally by Parliament
through enactments passed by the two Houses with the assent of the Crown.

The real substance of the defence raised is that contained in the last sentence
of para. 4 of the defence, namely,   F

" that the actions of the British elements were acts of state of Her Majesty
on the territory of an independent sovereign power performed in pursuance
of an agreement between Her Majesty and the said power which equally are
not so cognisable by the court."

Despite a very thorough, prolonged, but in my opinion largely unproductive,   G
investigation of a considerable number of authorities, I am by no means clear
in my own mind about the essential elements of an act of state properly so called,
but what seems to be plain is that not all acts performed on behalf of the Crown
of England, even where their locus is outside the realm, constitute acts of state,
however clearly they have been authorised by, and although the outcome of them
has been accepted by, the Crown. In my opinion a good working definition of   H
an act of state may be taken from 7 HALSBURY'S LAWS OF ENGLAND (3rd Edn.)
279, para. 593, which in reliance on PROFESSOR WADE's article " Act of State
in English Law ", published in 15 BRITISH YEAR BOOK OF INTERNATIONAL LAW,
98, defines an act of state as

" An act of the executive as a matter of policy performed in the course of
its relations with another state including its relations with the subject of that   I
state unless they are temporarily within the allegiance of the Crown."

There is no doubt that the term is used with many other connotations, but I
venture to think that it is inaccurately so otherwise used. For example, a plea
of absolute privilege in defamation available to a Secretary of State, or the power
of the Crown summarily to dismiss officers of the forces are not properly to be
called acts of state. In my opinion it is correct in law, as the quotation from

(29) Cf. [1967] 2 All E.R. at p. 218, letter F.

A HALSBURY indicates, that there can be no act of state against anyone who owes allegiance to the Crown (cf., per SIR JAMES FITZJAMES STEPHEN'S HISTORY OF THE CRIMINAL LAW OF ENGLAND (1883), Vol. 2, p. 61, and SALMOND ON TORTS (14th Edn.) p. 607, and *Johnstone* v. *Pedlar* (30)). The plaintiff in this action did owe such allegiance since he was a British subject, and this alone seems to me sufficient to refute the plea of act of state relied on by the defendant.

B   However, to my mind the simpler answer to this contention is that whereas the making of the agreement between the governments of the United Kingdom, Greece and Turkey and the Cyprus government for the provision by the former three governments and the acceptance by the latter of a truce force to be stationed in Cyprus under British command to assist the Cyprus government in its effort to secure the preservation of a cease-fire and the restoration of peace, was plainly
C an act of state, an infinite multiplicity and variety of acts done after the making of that agreement, and in order to carry its intentions into effect, were in their nature quite incapable of constituting acts of state. It would be tedious to catalogue any, let alone all, such readily imaginable acts and incidents; I myself instanced during the argument a likelihood that intentionally or in error, reasonably or negligently, a British sentry might well have fired on and killed some
D person not a British citizen. Similarly the driving of motor vehicles, the erection of barriers, clearance of areas to permit of effective defensive fire could easily give rise to adverse consequences in respect of which it would be in my view quite unacceptable to throw over them the cloak of act of state.

      In my opinion members of the British army, who would of course have taken an oath of allegiance and obedience to the Queen, serving in the territory of such
E an independent sovereign republic, are to be regarded as servants and, within their respective delegated authorities, agents, of the British Crown; their acts are manifestly not acts for which the individuals performing them are alone to be held responsible; they are acts of the Crown done through the individuals for which the Crown must answer on the principle of respondeat superior: it does not in my opinion follow that such acts are to be regarded either as acts of state or
F exercises of the royal prerogative. It is in my opinion clear that the courts of this country have jurisdiction to decide whether or not a particular act is an act of state, and it is only when an affirmative answer is given to this question that the jurisdiction of the court further to consider the consequences and legal results of such an act is ousted (cf., *Salaman,* v. *Secretary of State in Council for India* (31), *Secretary of State in Council of India* v. *Kamachee Boye Sahaba* (32)). Compare
G also for their emphasis on the distinction between an act of state and an act done in the exercise of purported rights other than an exercise of sovereign power, *Nabob of the Carnatic* v. *East India Co.* (33), *Rustomjee* v. *Reginam* (34), and *Cook* v. *Sprigg* (35).

      The cases cited make it clear, as indeed it is inherent in the nature of a sovereign act, that anything necessarily requisite to be done in order to perform that act
H is itself part of the act of state which it is implementing. For example, it was said by LORD COLERIDGE, C.J., in *Rustomjee's* case (36):

      ". . . as in making a treaty, so in performing the treaty, [the Sovereign] is beyond the control of municipal law and her acts are not to be examined in her own courts."

I Fully recognising this principle, I nevertheless am of the opinion that the act of occupying a hotel in order to use it as headquarters for the truce force is not properly to be regarded as an act necessary for the implementing of the act of state, the treaty with the Republic of Cyprus. It was no doubt convenient and

---

(30) [1921] All E.R. Rep. 176; [1921] 2 A.C. 262.
(31) [1906] 1 K.B. 613.   (32) (1859), 13 Moo. P.C.C. 22.
(33) (1793), 2 Ves. 56.   (34) (1876), 2 Q.B.D. 69.
(35) [1895-99] All E.R. Rep. 773; [1899] A.C. 572.
(36) (1876), 2 Q.B.D. at p. 74.

tended to facilitate efficiency of control and administration to place the head- **A** quarters staff in the hotel rather than in tented or hutted accommodation or scattered billets, but the treaty did not expressly or by necessary implication require the occupation and retention of the hotel.

Whether the British Crown has any prerogative power outside the United Kingdom and Her Majesty's other realms beyond the sea, including protectorates, is a question which has not been fully explored in this appeal. It suffices to say **B** that, leaving aside altogether protectorates and enemy territory conquered or occupied in war and territories of allies in a war, I am not prepared, as at present advised, affirmatively to assert that the royal prerogative can operate in the territory of an independent sovereign. By the Cyprus Act, 1960, it was enacted in connexion with the establishment of an independent republic in Cyprus that as from the date when the constitution of the Republic of Cyprus might be brought **C** into force by an Order in Council

" there shall be established in the Island of Cyprus an independent sovereign Republic of Cyprus, and Her Majesty shall have no sovereignty or jurisdiction over the Republic of Cyprus."

It was further enacted by s. 2 of that statute: **D**

" The Republic of Cyprus shall comprise the entirety of the Island of Cyprus with the exception of the two areas defined in the following subsection . . ."

The plaintiff's hotel was situate outside those reserved areas. I do not find in the Act of 1960 any provision expressly reserving or making applicable in the republic any prerogative power of the British Crown, though there is in s. 3 of **E** the Act of 1960 a clear confirmation that any existing law, which is defined as meaning any Act of Parliament and any rule of law in force on the appointed day, should have continuing effect in relation to Cyprus or persons or things belonging thereto unless and until repealed or amended by the competent Cyprus authority. It was expressly provided that there should be no resulting limit or restriction on the legislative powers of the Republic of Cyprus.   **F**

During the proceedings in the court below (37) counsel for both sides expressly adopted the position that the occupation of the hotel by the British troops was not unlawful: there has been considerable discussion in this court about the effect of this move in the advocacy of the case of the plaintiff. This move was no doubt inspired by the motive of side-stepping the rule that the English court cannot entertain any claim for trespass to land situate abroad. In this connexion there **G** does not seem to be any logical distinction between land and chattels, but this point is not directly involved. It has been contended by counsel for the Attorney-General that it involves acceptance by the plaintiff and by the court of one or both of the propositions: (a) that the Cyprus government exercised its own sovereign power by taking and retaining possession of the hotel by occupying it with British troops; (b) that the British Crown exercised a prerogative power in **H** so occupying it. For my part I am not willing to be so fettered by an admission or declaration of an advocate as to be unable to treat a matter in accordance with its real form, nor do I appreciate clearly the scope of the hypothesis posed; the distinction in this connexion between what is lawful and what is unlawful is not an absolute one. An act may not be unlawful in the criminal sense, but it may still be tortious vis-à-vis a particular person; some acts may be lawful only sub **I** modo, as, for example, a taking of property subject to payment of reasonable compensation as distinct from confiscatory seizure. The present case is analogous to that of *A.-G.* v. *De Keyser's Royal Hotel, Ltd.* (38) in this respect only, that in neither case was the taking complained of as tortious, but the refusal to pay compensation therefor was challenged as unlawful.

---

(37) [1967] 2 All E.R. 200.
(38) [1920] All E.R. Rep. 80; [1920] A.C. 508.

A   It is not for this court to exercise imagination about hypot
agreed by the parties, but for my part I do not accept
occupation of the hotel could only have been lawful if carried
government in its own right. The court knows nothing of the t
which is in issue on the pleadings. Conceivably he had no valid
or his lease might have been forfeited, or there might have bee

B   sub-lease or mortgage depriving him of the right to possession;
better title might have permitted occupation. All this is speculatio

Stripped of inessentials and disembarrassed, as I think that the c
be, of any clog arising from the election of counsel for the plaintiff to di
allegation of illegality, the facts which it is the duty of the court to assu
real show that the plaintiff was in occupation as tenant for five years,

C   option to extend to 1970, of an hotel on which over £30,000 had been sp
improvements and which had an established goodwill amongst wealthy vi
to the island; that he was deprived of the use and benefit of the hotel for t
months and that those who occupied it very seriously damaged the furniture a
decorations; those facts further include the giving of an assurance, on the san
day that the British troops entered the hotel, by the British Commissioner with

D   the tacit concurrence of the British Minister for Commonwealth Affairs, that
compensation would be paid by someone for the occupation of the hotel. In this
latter respect the factual situation is sharply contrasted with that which existed
when De Keyser's Royal Hotel (39) was taken over in 1916 by the Army Council
in order to provide accommodation in London for the headquarters of the Royal
Flying Corps, since in that case there was a plain refusal by the Office of Works

E   to deal with any claim for occupation rental otherwise than on an ex gratia basis
as might be determined by the Defence of the Realm Losses Commission. It is
true that in both the instant case and in the *De Keyser* case (39) the owner of the
hotel refused to consent to occupation being taken and considerable stress was
laid on this feature of the case in some of the speeches of their lordships when they
heard the appeal. For example, LORD ATKINSON (40), after referring to the cases

F   of *Phillips* v. *Homfray* (41), *Churchward* v. *Ford* (42) and *Birch* v. *Wright* (43),
pointed out that circumstances may negative the implication of a contract to
pay compensation for occupation of premises.

Fully accepting, as I do, the validity of this principle, it nevertheless seems to
me that no contract is required to be implied to support the claim made by the
plaintiff for reasonable compensation for the occupation of his premises by the

G   British forces. It is true that in *Sinclair* v. *Brougham* (44), LORD SUMNER said
of quasi-contractual claims:

> " All these causes of action are common species of the genus assumpsit.
> All now rest, and long have rested, upon a notional or imputed promise to
> repay."

H   However, it does not seem clear to me that it is requisite that there should be an
implied offer to accept such an implied promise, nor indeed that a reluctant
acceptance of the inevitability of having one's property taken must be deemed
not only to be compatible with voluntary consent but also to exclude the law
from giving rise to an obligation created by the relevant circumstances of the
event. LORD WRIGHT has said (45) that the observation of LORD SUMNER which

I   I have quoted

---

(39) [1920] All E.R. Rep. 80; [1920] A.C. 508.
(40) [1920] All E.R. Rep. at p. 89; [1920] A.C. at p. 533.
(41) (1883), 24 Ch.D. 439.   (42) (1857), 2 H. & N. 446.
(43) (1786), 1 Term Rep. 378.
(44) [1914-15] All E.R. Rep. 622 at p. 648; [1914] A.C. 398 at p. 452.
(45) See *Fibrosa Spolka Akcyjna* v. *Fairbairn Lawson Combe Barbour, Ltd.*, [1942]
2 All E.R. at p. 137; [1943] A.C. at p. 64. LORD WRIGHT's address on *Sinclair* v.
Brougham to Cambridge University Law Society (November, 1937) is published in
LEGAL ESSAYS AND ADDRESSES, 1939, pp. 1 33.

A

ecision of the case . . . The phrase ' notional
y of describing a debt or obligation arising by
ous legal writers have seemed to say that these
nclair v. *Brougham* (46) closed the door to any
1252   n English law. I do not understand why or how.
'o ad absurdum of the doctrine of precedents. In
o employs the action for money had and received   B
if not complete or ideally perfect, instrument to
, aided by the various methods of technical equity
as they were found to be in *Sinclair* v. *Brougham*

Nelson v. *Larholt* (47); per LORD DENNING in *Kiriri*
i (48) and per LORD ATKIN in *United Australia, Ltd.* v.   C

on relates to the period beginning with Mar. 27, 1964, I
eady expressed by my lords that it is right to hold that the
ganisation was then in occupation of the plaintiff's hotel.
the plaintiff has any effective right to claim any compensation   D
ed Nations Organisation is not a matter which arises in this appeal;
to say that in respect of that period the issue raised by the first sentence
. 6 of the defence should be finally determined in favour of the Crown.
ave to this extent I consider that the issues should not have been determined
in favour of the Crown and that the action should proceed in so far as the period
Dec. 29, 1963, to Mar. 27, 1964, is concerned.

E

LORD DENNING, M.R.: The appeal will be allowed with costs in this
court and the answer to the preliminary issue will be that already stated, viz.,
that a defence is not disclosed in respect of the first period but that it is disclosed
in respect of the second period. There will be no alteration as to costs in the court
below, namely, no order for costs in the court below. As to leave to appeal, we
think that it is a case where the facts ought to be decided at the trial first, and, if   F
there is an appeal after that and eventually an appeal to the House of Lords, the
law can then be reconsidered. If the House of Lords are to consider this case, we
think it better that they should consider it in relation to the facts of the case.
Leave to appeal is, therefore, refused.

Appeal partly allowed. Cross-appeal dismissed. Leave to appeal to the House of
Lords refused.   G

Solicitors: *Edwin Coe & Calder Woods* (for the plaintiff); *Treasury Solicitor.*

[*Reported by* F. GUTTMAN, ESQ., *Barrister-at-Law.*]

H

I

(46) [1914-15] All E.R. Rep. 622; [1914] A.C. 398
(47) [1947] 2 All E.R. 751 at p. 752; [1948] 1 K.B. 339 at p. 343.
(48) [1960] 1 All E.R. 177 at p. 181; [1960] A.C. 192 at p. 204.
(49) [1940] 4 All E.R. 20 at pp. 35, 36; [1941] A.C. 1 at p. 27.

A   *NOTE.*

R. *v.* HOVE JUSTICES, *Ex parte* DONNE AND OTHERS.

[QUEEN'S BENCH DIVISION (Lord Parker, C.J., Waller and Blain, JJ.), June 9,
  1967.]

B *Certiorari—Justices—Witness summons—Witness not able to give relevant and*
   admissible evidence—Jurisdiction of court to set aside witness summonses
   issued under Magistrates' Courts Act, 1952 (15 & 16 Geo. 6 & 1 Eliz. 2 c. 55),
   s. 77—R.S.C., Ord. 38, r. 19 (1), (5).

   [As to witness summonses issued by magistrates' courts, see 25 HALSBURY'S
   LAWS (3rd Edn.) 209, 210, para. 382.
C   As to setting aside a subpoena improperly issued, see 15 HALSBURY'S LAWS
   (3rd Edn.) 425, para. 767 text and notes (*e*) (*f*); and for cases on the subject,
   see 22 DIGEST (Repl.) 414, 415, *4461-4471.*
      As to matters in respect of which certiorari lies, see 11 HALSBURY'S LAWS
   (3rd Edn.) 130, para. 239; and for cases on the subject, see 16 DIGEST (Repl.)
   460, *2803-2807.*
D   For the Magistrates' Courts Act, 1952, s. 77, see 32 HALSBURY'S STATUTES
   (2nd Edn.) 480; and for the Criminal Procedure (Attendance of Witnesses)
   Act 1965, s. 2 (2), see 45 ibid., 230.]

Case referred to:
     R. v. *Baines,* [1908-10] All E.R. Rep. 328; [1909] 1 K.B. 258; 78 L.J. 119;
E   100 L.T. 78; 21 Cox, C.C. 756; 72 J.P. 524; 22 Digest (Repl.) 415, *4468.*

   Application for leave to move for certiorari.
   This was an application by John Christopher Donne, chairman of the hospital
management committee, hereinafter mentioned, and fifteen others, for leave to
move for an order of certiorari to quash the issue of sixteen witness summonses
issued, one to each applicant, on May 12, 1967, by justices for the borough of
F Hove, sitting as a magistrates' court at Hove in the county of Sussex, on the
application of the respondent, Bryan Herbert Dempster. The respondent had
been admitted pursuant to s. 26 of the Mental Health Act, 1959, to St. Francis
Hospital, Haywards Heath, on recommendations of Dr. Aleck Folkson, a consultant at the hospital, made on July 9, 1965, and again on Jan. 9, 1967. The
respondent was discharged on Aug. 17, 1965, and Jan. 30, 1967, respectively. On
G Apr. 17, 1967, a writ was issued by the respondent against Dr. Folkson and the
management committee of the St. Francis Hospital. The claim made by the
writ was for damages for malicious incarceration on two occasions, in alleged
contravention of the Mental Health Act, 1959. On June 2, 1967, service of the
writ was set aside as against Dr. Folkson on Apr. 17, 1967, and as against the
management committee on June 2, 1967, on appeal to the judge in chambers.
H On Apr. 28, 1967, the respondent applied by originating summons pursuant to
s. 141 of the Act of 1959 for leave to bring proceedings against Dr. Folkson
and the St. Francis Hospital Management Committee. It was alleged that
the respondent made some thirty telephone calls to Dr. Folkson on Jan. 6 and
Mar. 13, 1967, and to his wife on Mar. 27, 1967, at their home. Four summonses
were issued against the respondent by Reginald John Pattenden, a superin-
I tendent of police at Hove, in respect of telephone messages sent by the respondent
on Mar. 13 and Mar. 27, 1967, which were alleged to be grossly offensive, and
thus to contravene s. 66 of the Post Office Act, 1953. On May 12, 1967, the
respondent applied to the magistrates' court for witness summonses to give
evidence in relation to these charges to issue to the sixteen applicants who
were now applying for certiorari, three of whom were the chairman and members
of the management committee of the St. Francis Hospital, and the others of
whom were psychiatric workers and nurses at St. Francis Hospital or at Brighton
General Hospital, which was the receiving hospital. The application was made ex

parte under s. 77* of the Magistrates' Courts Act, 1952. On May 18, 1967, applica- A
tion was made to the magistrates' court to set aside the summonses; this
application was made pursuant to s. 2 (2)† of the Criminal Procedure (Attendance
of Witnesses) Act 1965, but the magistrates' court declined to adjudicate as the
summonses had been issued under s. 77 of the Act of 1952. The sixteen applicants now applied for certiorari to quash the witness summonses on the ground
that none of the applicants were present when the telephone calls were made to, B
or received at, the home of Dr. Folkson and that accordingly none of the
applicants could give any evidence relevant to any issue which could arise in the
criminal proceedings against the respondent, and further that the application
for the summonses was vexatious and an abuse of the process of the court. There
was an affidavit of each of the applicants for certiorari that he or she was not
present at the making or receiving of the telephone calls and had no knowledge C
concerning them. The court gave leave to treat the hearing of the application
as the hearing of the motion for certiorari. The respondent did not dispute that
none of the witnesses had heard the conversations, but desired to call them to
challenge the credibility of Dr. Folkson and to depose that the respondent was
falsely incarcerated by Dr. Folkson and assaulted in the hospital. It appeared
from a letter of the clerk to the Hove justices dated May 31, 1967, that before D
issuing the witness summonses the justices had questioned the respondent closely
and were satisfied that the witnesses were likely to be able to give material
evidence as to the credibility of one or more of the prosecution witnesses, and
that the persons to be summoned as witnesses would not attend voluntarily.

J. G. Leach for the applicants, having referred to the affidavits, to s. 2 (2) of E
the Criminal Procedure Act 1965 and to R.S.C. Ord. 38, r. 19‡, cited *R.* v. *Baines*§.

The respondent appeared in person.

LORD PARKER, C.J.: Could any position arise where these witnesses
would be able to give relevant and admissible evidence?

Leach: So far as inquiries by my solicitors and my own inquiries in drafting F
affidavits go, such a position would not arise. If, however, at any stage the
magistrates' court found that a witness' evidence could be relevant, the court
would have power to issue a witness summons, and I offer on behalf of my clients
an undertaking to ensure that, after such adjournment as would be convenient,
the witness should be present.

G

LORD PARKER, C.J.: The court will set aside the witness summonses
issued to the applicants on the grounds that, as at present advised, it is quite
impossible to see that any of the witnesses could give relevant and admissible
evidence. If, of course, it should turn out at the trial that at a later stage,

H

* Section 77 (1), so far as is material, provides: " Where a justice of the peace for
any . . . borough is satisfied that any person . . . is likely to be able to give material
evidence . . . and that that person will not voluntarily attend as a witness . . . the justice
shall issue " a witness summons.

† Section 2 provides, so far as is relevant: " (1) For the purpose of any criminal
proceedings before a court of assize or quarter sessions a witness summons, . . . , may I
be issued out of that court . . . (2) If any person in respect of whom a witness summons
has been issued applies to the court out of which the summons was issued or to the High
Court, and satisfies the court that he cannot give any material evidence . . . , the court
may direct that the summons shall be of no effect."

‡ R.S.C., Ord. 38, r. 19, provides for the issue of a writ of subpoena ad testificandum
etc. out of the Crown Office in aid of an inferior court, and provides: " (5) An application
to set aside a writ of subpoena issued in aid of an inferior court . . . may be heard by a
master of the Queen's Bench Division." R.S.C., Ord. 38, r. 19 supersedes the former
R.S.C., Ord. 59, r. 43 (2).

§ [1908-10] All E.R. Rep. 328.

A presumably in rebuttal, it would be admissible to call any of these witnesses, then the Hove justices can ask for their attendance.

Summonses set aside. No application for costs.

Solicitors: *Nye & Donne*, Brighton (for the applicants).

[*Reported by* S. A. HATTEEA, ESQ., *Barrister-at-Law.*]

B

SELANGOR UNITED RUBBER ESTATES, LTD.
v. CRADOCK AND OTHERS.

C [CHANCERY DIVISION (Goff, J.), June 7, 8, 23, 1967.]

Company—Investigation by Board of Trade—Action begun by Board of Trade in plaintiff company's name consequent on inspector's report—Security for costs sought by defendant banks—Whether Board of Trade had brought itself within the powers conferred by s. 169 (4)—" Misfeasance " in s. 169 (4) not necessarily connoting moral turpitude—Whether indemnity for costs
D *provided by s. 169 (5) covered costs to be paid by plaintiff company to defendants—Companies Act, 1948 (11 & 12 Geo. 6 c. 38), s. 169 (4), (5), s. 447.*

A company in compulsory liquidation was plaintiff in an action, brought by the Board of Trade in its name pursuant to s. 169 (4)* of the Companies Act, 1948, and by and with the authority of the liquidator, the Official Receiver. Two of the eight defendants, both of which were banks, applied for
E security for costs. There was reason to believe that the plaintiff company would be unable to pay the costs of their defence if they succeeded, with the consequence that prima facie the defendants would be entitled to security for costs under s. 447† of the Act of 1948. By s. 169 (5)‡ the Board of Trade was bound to " indemnify the [plaintiff company] against any costs or expenses incurred by it in or in connexion with any proceedings brought " by virtue of
F s. 169 (4). Section 169 (4) empowered the Board of Trade to bring proceedings in the name of a company for the recovery of damages " in respect of any fraud, misfeasance or other misconduct in connexion with . . . the management of its affairs, or for the recovery of any property [of the plaintiff company] which has been misapplied or wrongfully retained ". The substance of the claim was for the wrongful application of the plaintiff
G company's moneys pursuant to an alleged agreement or, if that were not so, then the substance of the claim was to replace moneys misapplied under the agreement, viz., to recover property misapplied.

Held: security for costs would not be ordered for the following reasons—
(i) the words " any costs or expenses incurred by [the plaintiff company] in or in connexion with any proceedings brought " in s. 169 (5) would include costs ordered to be paid by the plaintiff company to other parties, with the
H consequence that the Board of Trade's statutory obligation to give indemnity extended to them (see p. 1258, letter E, post).

---

* Section 169 (4) provides: " If from any such report as aforesaid it appears to the Board of Trade that proceedings ought in the public interest to be brought by any body corporate dealt with by the report for the recovery of damages in respect of any fraud, misfeasance or other misconduct in connexion with the promotion or formation of that
I body corporate or the management of its affairs, or for the recovery of any property of the body corporate which has been misapplied or wrongfully retained, they may themselves bring proceedings for that purpose in the name of the body corporate."
† Section 447 provides: " Where a limited company is plaintiff . . . in an action or other legal proceeding, any judge having jurisdiction in the matter, may, if it appears by credible testimony that there is reason to believe that the company will be unable to pay the costs of the defendant if successful in his defence, require sufficient security to be given for those costs, and may stay all proceedings until the security is given."
‡ Section 169 (5) provides: " The Board of Trade shall indemnify the body corporate against any costs or expenses incurred by it in or in connexion with any proceedings brought by virtue of the last foregoing subsection."

A

(ii) moneys paid to the liquidator pursuant to the indemnity mentioned in (i) p. 1255, ante, would be applicable in payment of the defendant banks' costs rather than for the benefit of the general body of creditors of the plaintiff company (see p. 1258, letter E, post).

Re Richardson, Ex parte St. Thomas's Hospital (Governors) ([1911] 2 K.B. at p. 711) applied.

B

(iii) misfeasance within s. 169 (4) of the Companies Act, 1948, did not necessarily involve moral turpitude (see p. 1258, letter H, post); and on the pleadings in the present case a sufficient connexion of the defendant banks with the management of the plaintiff company's affairs was alleged to have the consequence that, on the pleadings, the action appeared to have been brought within the powers conferred on the Board of Trade by s. 169 (4) of the Act of 1948 (see p. 1259, letter F, post).

C

S.B.A. Properties, Ltd. v. *Cradock*, ante, p. 610, not followed on holding (i) (a) of that report.

[As to proceedings by the Board of Trade, see 6 HALSBURY'S LAWS (3rd Edn.) 391, 392, para. 759.

For the Companies Act, 1948, s. 169 (4) (5), see 3 HALSBURY'S STATUTES (2nd Edn.) 594 and for s. 447, see ibid., p. 784.]

D

Cases referred to:

Gerrard (Thomas) & Son, Ltd., Re, ante p. 525; [1967] 3 W.L.R. 84.

Johnson (B.) & Co. (Builders), Ltd., Re, [1955] 2 All E.R. 775; [1955] Ch. 634; [1955] 3 W.L.R. 269; Digest (Cont. Vol. A) 183, *5467a*.

Kingston Cotton Mill Co. (No. 2), Re, [1896] 2 Ch. 279; 65 L.J.Ch. 673; sub nom. *Re Kingston Cotton Mill Co., Ltd., Ex p. Pickering & Peasegood (No. 2)*, 74 L.T. 568; 9 Digest (Repl.) 587, *3880*.

E

Richardson, Re, Ex p. St. Thomas's Hospital (Governors), [1911] 2 K.B. 705; 80 L.J.K.B. 1232; 105 L.T. 226; 5 Digest (Repl.) 726, *6285*.

S.B.A. Properties, Ltd. v. *Cradock*, ante p. 610; [1967] 1 W.L.R. 716.

F

Application.

This was an application by the third defendant, District Bank, Ltd., and the seventh defendant, the Bank of Nova Scotia, by notice under the summons for directions in the action, for security for costs in an action brought by the plaintiff company, Selangor United Rubber Estates, Ltd., against Francis Richard Cradock and eight other defendants in respect of certain transactions with inter-related cheques. By writ issued in the name of the plaintiff company dated Apr. 21, 1964, the plaintiff company claimed—

G

" 1. A declaration that the defendants are jointly and severally liable to replace moneys of the plaintiff company which have been misapplied— (a) as to the defendants Cradock, the Bank of Nova Scotia, Burden and Sinclair to the extent of £249,500; (b) as to the defendant Contanglo Banking and Trading Co., Ltd. to the extent of the sum of £195,322 5s. 2d., and (c) as to the remaining defendants to the extent of the sum of £232,500— which sums of £195,322 5s. 2d. and £232,500 are included in the said sum of £249,500.

H

" 2. An order on the defendants and each of them to pay to the liquidator of the plaintiff such sum or sums as the defendants or any one or more of them shall be declared liable to replace with interest thereon at the rate of five per cent. per annum.

I

" 3. Damages for breach of duty.

" 4. Further or in the alternative against District Bank, Ltd. and the Bank of Nova Scotia damages for negligence in their respective capacities as bankers to the plaintiff company.

" 5. An order on the defendants jointly and severally to pay to the Board of Trade or alternatively to the Official Receiver as liquidator the amount

A   of the expenses of and incidental to the investigation into the affairs of the plaintiff company by inspectors appointed by the Board of Trade."

The plaintiff company was in compulsory liquidation and the action was brought in the name of the plaintiff company by the Board of Trade pursuant to s. 169 (4) of the Companies Act, 1948, and by and with the authority of the Official Receiver as liquidator.

B   Relevant paragraphs of the statement of claim included the following—

"17. In the circumstances hereinbefore alleged ... sums of money belonging to the [plaintiff company] were paid and applied as follows— (i) ... £232,500 successively to the defendants Woodstock Trust, Ltd., Cradock and (as to £195,322 5s. 2d. part thereof) Contanglo Banking and Trading Co., Ltd.; (ii) ... £207,500 successively to the defendants Burden and Cradock and (iii) ... £42,000 successively to the defendants Burden and Cradock.

"18. The said sums of money were and each of them was applied, not for the purposes or benefit of the [plaintiff company] but for the purposes and benefit of the recipients thereof namely [the defendants Cradock, Contanglo Banking and Trading Co., Ltd., Woodstock Trust, Ltd. and Burden] or one or more of them."

There followed particulars which included allegations that the moneys were applied for the purposes and benefit of these defendants in discharging at the expense of the plaintiff company liability in respect of purchase of stock units of the plaintiff company. Then para. 19, para. 20 and para. 21 alleged—

E   "19. Further or in the alternative the sum of money specified in item (i) of para. 17 was applied in giving financial assistance in connexion with the purchase by [the defendant Cradock] of 713,579 stock units of 2s. each of the [plaintiff company] and the sum of money specified in item (ii) of para. 17 was applied in giving financial assistance in connexion with the purchase by [the defendant Burden] of 716,264 stock units of 2s. each of the [plaintiff company].

"20. Each of the payments or applications of the [plaintiff company's] money specified in para. 17 hereof was a misapplication thereof and each of them was ultra vires the [plaintiff company] and was unauthorised by the [plaintiff company].

"21. (a) The sum of money specified in item (i) of para. 17 was so applied as aforesaid pursuant to and in furtherance of an arrangement or arrangements made by and between [the defendants Cradock, Contanglo Banking and Trading Co., Ltd., District Bank, Ltd., Woodstock Trust, Ltd., Barlow-Lawson and Jacob] or alternatively by some of them to which the others or other of them were or was privy; (b) the sum of money specified in item (ii) of para. 17 was so applied as aforesaid pursuant to and in furtherance of an arrangement or arrangements made by and between [the defendants Cradock, Bank of Nova Scotia, Burden and Sinclair] or alternatively by some of them to which the others or other of them were or was privy."

The case noted below* was cited during the argument in addition to those referred to in the judgment.

I   *K. B. Suenson-Taylor* for the third defendant, District Bank, Ltd.
R. B. S. Instone for the seventh defendant, the Bank of Nova Scotia.
J. P. Warner for the plaintiff company and the Board of Trade.

Cur. adv. vult.

June 23.   **GOFF, J.**, read the following judgment: This is an action brought by Selangor United Rubber Estates, Ltd., against Mr. Cradock and others for relief in respect of certain complicated transactions with inter-related cheques,

---

* *Burnett* v. *Westminster Bank, Ltd.*, [1965] 3 All E.R. 81; [1966] 1 Q.B. 742.

and the matter comes before me at this stage on applications by the third defen- **A**
dant, District Bank, Ltd., and the seventh defendant, the Bank of Nova Scotia,
for security for costs. The plaintiff company is in compulsory liquidation and,
no evidence having been adduced to show that it will be able to pay the costs of
the defendants if successful in their defence, it appears that there is reason to
believe that it will not be so able within the meaning of the Companies Act,
1948, s. 447. Prima facie, therefore, the applicant defendants are entitled to an **B**
order for security.

The action, however, as appears by the endorsement on the writ is brought
in the name of the company by the Board of Trade pursuant to s. 169 (4) of the
Companies Act, 1948, and by and with the authority of the Official Receiver as
liquidator. As it has his authority the action is well constituted whether the
case falls within s. 169 or not, but if it does then the defendants are fully pro- **C**
tected by the indemnity provisions of s. 169 (5) and no security can, or need, be
ordered.

Counsel for the seventh defendant raised two questions on s. 169 (5). First
he suggested a doubt whether it covered costs ordered to be paid by the plaintiff
company, or only its own costs; and secondly he argued that in any event the
subsection would not fully protect the applicants, because any money paid by **D**
the Board of Trade would form part of the company's assets available for its
creditors generally. I am satisfied as a matter of construction that the words
" any costs or expenses incurred by it or in connexion with any proceedings
brought " in s. 169 (5) are wide enough to cover, and do embrace, costs ordered
to be paid to other parties, and the second point argued by counsel is precluded
by the decision in *Re Richardson, Ex p. Governors of St. Thomas' Hospital* (1). **E**

The question then is whether the Board of Trade had authority to bring this
action in the name of the plaintiff company by virtue of s. 169 (4). The applicants
say " no " and they rely strongly on my own decision in *S.B.A. Properties, Ltd.*
v. *Cradock* (2), in an action which concerns somewhat similar transactions.
Counsel for the plaintiff company and the Board of Trade whilst reserving his full
rights to challenge that decision in the Court of Appeal, has invited me in one **F**
respect not to follow it, even though it be my own, since he submits, somewhat
generously blaming himself, that in that particular regard the decision was made
per incuriam.

I there held (3) that " or other misconduct " in s. 169 (4) must be construed
ejusdem generis with fraud and misfeasance and, therefore, was limited to matters
involving moral turpitude. It is clear, however, from the decision of the **G**
Court of Appeal in *Re Kingston Cotton Mill Co. (No. 2)* (4), which was not then
cited to me in full, but only by means of a quotation from the speech of SIR
RAYMOND EVERSHED, M.R., in *Re B. Johnson & Co. (Builders) Ltd.* (5), that
misfeasance at any rate in s. 333 of the Companies Act, 1948, does not necessarily
involve moral turpitude, but comprehends any breach of duty by an officer of
the company as such involving a misapplication or wrongful retention of the **H**
company's moneys; see also *Re Thomas Gerrard & Son, Ltd.* (6). I do not think,
therefore, that misfeasance in s. 169 (4) necessarily involves moral turpitude and,
if so, there is no room for the application of the ejusdem generis principle of
construction. Counsel has argued that even so my decision on this point in
S.B.A. Properties, Ltd. v. *Cradock* (2) was right in the context of the subsection,
but as at present advised I think that my construction was too narrow. **I**

I also decided in that case (2) that the claim against the defendant bank as
pleaded was simply for breach of duty as bankers and that it was not in connexion

---

(1) [1911] 2 K.B. 705, see particularly at p. 711, per SIR HERBERT COZENS-HARDY, M.R.
(2) Ante, p. 610.
(3) See ante p. 610, holding (i) (a).
(4) [1896] 2 Ch. 279.
(5) [1955] 2 All E.R. 775 at p. 782; [1955] Ch. 634 at pp. 649, 650.
(6) Ante p. 525.

A with the management of the company's affairs, and was not a claim to recover property misapplied or wrongfully retained. In those respects I see no reason to reconsider my previous decision.

Be this as it may, counsel for the plaintiff company has argued that the present case is in any event distinguishable because the statement of claim contains a much more positive averment than any in *S.B.A. Properties, Ltd.* v.
B *Cradock* (7). He referred to para. 21, which says that the relevant sums were applied as aforesaid pursuant to and in furtherance of an arrangement or arrangements made by and between a number of named persons, including in each case the relevant defendant bank and a director or directors of the plaintiff company, or by some such persons to which the others or other of them were or was privy. The " as aforesaid " refers back to para. 18, wherein it is alleged that the sums
C of money concerned were applied not for the purposes or benefit of the plaintiff company but for the purposes and benefit of the recipients, and to para. 19, which alleges further that they were applied in giving financial assistance in connexion with certain purchases of the plaintiff company's own stock units.

Despite the submissions of counsel for the two defendants on this application to the contrary, it seems to me that that is a relevant and sufficient distinction.
D It takes the defendants out of the realm of bankers only and connects them directly with the management of the plaintiff company's affairs, and if moral turpitude be necessary it is there alleged, since it is said that the bank was party, or at least privy to an arrangement to misapply the plaintiff company's money, and indeed to use it in a way which is by s. 54 (2) of the Companies Act, 1948, made a criminal offence on the part of the plaintiff company and of any officer in
E default.

I want to make it abundantly clear that this arrangement is completely denied by both banks and that I am not deciding that there is any case against them of moral turpitude or of breach of duty with or without moral turpitude, or any other wrong-doing or omission. I have merely to decide on the case, as pleaded, whether the Board of Trade has brought itself within the powers conferred by
F s. 169 (4) of the Companies Act, 1948, and in my judgment it has.

The banks have accepted that in any case there is no claim here for damages other than as banker, and no claim to recover property misapplied or retained. Counsel for the seventh defendant in particular relies on the form of para. 1 and para. 2 of the prayer for relief and the original contention of para. 25 of the statement of claim, and the way in which it was amended when the plaintiff
G company was asked to give particulars.

It seems to me, however, that the substance of the matter is that this is a claim for damages for the wrongful application of the plaintiff company's moneys pursuant to the alleged agreement, and, if it be not, then I would hold that on the facts pleaded in this case this is an action to recover property misapplied, since on this allegation the claim is not that the banks are liable for breach of
H duty as bankers, or that they have made unauthorised debits in their accounts and are therefore liable as bankers for the balance due disregarding such debits, but that they are liable to replace moneys misapplied under an agreement to which, on the major premise, they were actually parties.

In my judgment, therefore, this is not a case in which security should be ordered.

I
Application dismissed.

Solicitors: *Bower, Cotton & Bower*, agents for *Slater Heelis & Co.*, Manchester (for the third defendant); *Simmons & Simmons* (for the seventh defendant); *Solicitor to the Board of Trade* (for the plaintiff company and the Board of Trade).

[*Reported by* R. W. FARRIN, *Barrister-at-Law.*]

---

(7) Ante p. 610.

A

CONWAY v. RIMMER.

[COURT OF APPEAL, CIVIL DIVISION (Lord Denning, M.R., Davies and Russell, L.JJ.), April 24, 25, 26, 27, June 8, 1967.]

Discovery—Production of documents—Privilege—Crown privilege—Disclosure contrary, or injurious, to public interest—Claim in due form conclusive in both contents cases and class cases—Probationary reports on probationer police constable—Report of superintendent of police to chief constable for purpose of obtaining advice of Director of Public Prosecutions—Conclusiveness of certificate of Home Secretary.

B

The plaintiff, a probationer police constable, was prosecuted by a superintendent in the same constabulary on a charge of stealing an electric torch belonging to another probationer constable. The prosecution was brought on advice of the Director of Public Prosecutions given on a report rendered by the superintendent to the chief constable. The plaintiff was acquitted, but soon afterwards he was dismissed from the force as unlikely to become an efficient police officer. The plaintiff sued the superintendent for malicious prosecution. On discovery in the action the Home Secretary claimed Crown privilege for a class of documents which would include the probationary reports relating to the plaintiff and the report leading to his prosecution; the privilege was claimed on the ground that disclosure of documents of that class would be contrary, or injurious, to the public interest. The claim of privilege was in proper form. It was not suggested that the claim was not taken in good faith or that the Home Secretary was mistaken in thinking the document to be of the class stated*.

C

D

E

Held (LORD DENNING, M.R., dissenting): a claim of Crown privilege made in proper form was conclusive, whether the claim was in respect of a class of documents or of the contents of particular documents (see p. 1270, letter D, and p. 1273, letter E, post).

Duncan v *Cammell Laird & Co., Ltd.* ([1942] 1 All E.R. 587) and *Auten* v. *Rayner* ([1958] 3 All E.R. 566) followed.

F

Merricks v. *Nott-Bower* ([1964] 1 All E.R. 717), *Re Grosvenor Hotel, London (No. 2)* ([1964] 3 All E.R. 354) and *Wednesbury Corpn.* v. *Ministry of Housing and Local Government* ([1965] 1 All E.R. 186) not followed.

Appeal dismissed.

[As to privilege where disclosure of documents is contrary to the public interest, see 12 HALSBURY'S LAWS (3rd Edn.) 53-55, para. 73; and for cases on the subject, see 18 DIGEST (Repl.) 139-142, *1256-1282*.]

G

Cases referred to:

Abbot v. *Refuge Assurance Co., Ltd.*, [1961] 3 All E.R. 1074; [1962] 1 Q.B. 432; [1961] 3 W.L.R. 1240; 33 Digest (Repl.) 416, *355*.

Admiralty Comrs. v. *Aberdeen Steam Trawling & Fishing Co.*, 1909 S.C. 335; 18 Digest (Repl.) 113, *497*.

Allen v. *Byfield (No. 2)*, (1964), 7 W.I.R. 69.

Amar Chaud Batal v. *Union of India*, [1964] A.I.R.S.C. 1658.

Ankin v. *London and North Eastern Ry. Co.*, [1929] All E.R. Rep. 65; [1930] 1 K.B. 527; 99 L.J.K.B. 293; 142 L.T. 368; 18 Digest (Repl.) 141, *1267*.

Apponhamy v. *Illangaratue*, (1964), 66 C.L.W. 17.

Auten v. *Rayner*, [1958] 3 All E.R. 566; [1958] 1 W.L.R. 1300; 123 J.P. 122; Digest (Cont. Vol. A) 492, *1267a*.

Beatson v. *Skene*, [1843-60] All E.R. Rep. 882; (1860), 5 H. & N. 838; 29 L.J.Ex. 430; 2 L.T. 378; 22 Digest (Repl.) 386, *4148*.

H

I

---

* The claim would not have been unassailable on such grounds; see p. 1273, letter B, post.

A   *Bellerophon, H.M.S.,* (1874), 44 L.J.Adm. 5; 31 L.T. 756; 18 Digest (Repl.)
    140, *1257.*

Bruce v. *Waldron,* [1963] V.L.R. 3; Digest (Cont. Vol. A) 977, *345a.*

Bryers v. *Canadian Pacific Steamships, Ltd.,* [1956] 3 All E.R. 560; [1957]
    1 Q.B. 134; [1956] 3 W.L.R. 776; *affd.* H.L., sub nom. *Canadian
    Pacific Steamers, Ltd.* v. *Bryers,* [1957] 3 All E.R. 572; [1957] 3 W.L.R.
B   993; Digest (Cont. Vol. A) 609, *416a.*

Corbett v. *Social Security Commission,* [1962] N.Z.L.R. 878; Digest (Cont.
    Vol. A) 977, *3456.*

Duncan v. *Cammell Laird & Co., Ltd.,* [1942] 1 All E.R. 587; [1942] A.C. 624;
    111 L.J.K.B. 406; 166 L.T. 366; 18 Digest (Repl.) 140, *1264.*

Ellis v. *Home Office,* [1953] 2 All E.R. 149; [1953] 2 Q.B. 135; [1953] 3 W.L.R.
C   105; 18 Digest (Repl.) 24, *172.*

Gagnon v. *Quebec Securities Commission,* (1964), S.C.R. 329.

Gibbons v. *Duffield,* (1952), 47 C.L.R. 520.

Glasgow Corpn. v. *Central Land Board,* 1956 S.C. (H.L.) 1; [1956] S.L.T 41;
    16 Digest (Repl.) 279, *167.*

Glinski v. *McIvor,* [1962] 1 All E.R. 696; [1962] A.C. 726; [1962] 2 W.L.R.
D   832; 33 Digest (Repl.) 431, *504.*

Grosvenor Hotel, London (No. 2), Re, [1964] 3 All E.R. 354; [1965] Ch. 1210;
    [1964] 3 W.L.R. 992; Digest (Cont. Vol. B) 226, *1282b.*

Hallett's Estate, Re, Knatchbull v. *Hallett,* [1874-80] All E.R. Rep. 793; (1879),
    13 Ch.D. 696; 49 L.J.Ch. 415; 42 L.T. 421; 3 Digest (Repl.) 199, *405.*

Merricks v. *Nott-Bower,* [1964] 1 All E.R. 717; [1965] 1 Q.B. 57; [1964]
E   2 W.L.R. 702; 128 J.P. 267; Digest (Cont. Vol. B) 225, *1282a.*

Morelle, Ltd. v. *Wakeling,* [1955] 1 All E.R. 708; [1955] 2 Q.B. 379; [1955]
    2 W.L.R. 672; 13 Digest (Repl.) 288, *1065.*

R. v. *Snider,* [1954] S.C.R. 479; [1954] 4 D.L.R. 483; Digest (Cont. Vol. A)
    540, *2250a.*

Robinson v. *State of South Australia (No. 2),* [1931] All E.R. Rep. 333; [1931]
F   A.C. 704; 100 L.J.P.C. 183; 145 L.T. 408; 18 Digest (Repl.) 153,
    635.

Smith v. *East India Co.,* (1841), 1 Ph. 50; 11 L.J.Ch. 71; 18 Digest (Repl.)
    142, *1276.*

Tunstall, Re, Ex parte Brown, (1966), 84 W.N. (Pt. 2) (N.S.W.) 13.

Wadeer v. *East India Co.,* (1856), 8 De G.M. & G. 181; sub nom. *Coorg (Rajah)*
G   v. *East India Co.,* 25 L.J.Ch. 345; sub nom. *Veer Rajunder Wadeer
    (Ex Rajah of Coorg)* v. *East India Co.,* 27 L.T.O.S. 30; 18 Digest (Repl.)
    141, *1271.*

Wednesbury Corpn. v. *Ministry of Housing and Local Government,* [1965]
    1 All E.R. 186; [1965] 1 W.L.R. 261; 129 J.P. 123; Digest (Cont.
    Vol. B) 226, *1282c.*

H

Interlocutory Appeal.

This was an appeal by the plaintiff, Michael David Conway, from orders of
BROWNE, J., dated Feb. 23, 1967, allowing appeals by the defendant, Thomas
Rimmer, and the Attorney-General from an order of Mr. Registrar CUNLIFFE,
dated Nov. 24, 1966, that the defendant should produce for inspection five
I   documents in his list of documents in respect of which Crown privilege was
claimed. A respondent's notice on behalf of the Attorney-General was served.
The facts are set out in the judgment of LORD DENNING, M.R.

P. L. W. Owen, Q.C., and *A. J. Price* for the plaintiff.
The Attorney-General (Sir Elwyn Jones, Q.C.) and *Nigel Bridge* for the Crown.
A. N. Fricker for the defendant.

                                             Cur. adv. vult.

June 8. The following judgments were read.

LORD DENNING, M.R.: This is a suit between two private litigants. One **A** of them has in his possession or power documents which are relevant to the case. They are necessary to do justice between the parties; but the Attorney-General has come to this court and asserted a claim of Crown privilege. He says that the court shall not have access to these documents. At once the question arises: have the courts any power to look into this claim of Crown privilege? And to override it? On three occasions lately this court has considered the matter. **B** The trilogy of cases are *Merricks* v. *Nott-Bower* (1); *Re Grosvenor Hotel, London (No. 2)* (2); and *Wednesbury Corpn.* v. *Ministry of Housing & Local Government* (3). On each occasion the court was constituted of HARMAN and SALMON, L.JJ., and myself. We held with one accord that the court has a residual power in a proper case to override the objections of a minister. I will not recite again all the arguments. They will be found in the judgments. Suffice to state **C** the upshot as I put it in the *Grosvenor Hotel* case (4):

" The objection of a minister, even though taken in proper form, should not be conclusive. If the court should be of opinion that the objection is not taken in good faith, or that there are no reasonable grounds ... the court can override the objection and order production. It can, if it thinks fit, call for the documents and inspect them itself so as to see whether there are **D** reasonable grounds for withholding them: ensuring, of course, that they are not disclosed to anyone else. It is rare indeed for the court to override the Minister's objection, but it has the ultimate power, in the interest of justice, to do so. After all, it is the judges who are the guardians of justice in this land: and if they are to fulfil their trust, they must be able to call on the Minister to put forward his reasons so as to see if they outweigh the **E** interests of justice."

In so holding, we were encouraged by the fact that we were in accord with the countries of the Commonwealth. They start, of course, with the classic judgment of the Privy Council in *Robinson* v. *State of South Australia (No. 2)* (5). Delivered by LORD BLANESBURGH, there are passages which bear the stamp of **F** LORD ATKIN who was sitting beside him. It affirms emphatically the reserve power of the courts. The Board said that (6):

"... the privilege [of the Crown] is a narrow one, most sparingly to be exercised ... Its foundation is that the information cannot be disclosed without injury to the public interests and not that the documents are confidential or official, which alone is no reason for their non-production. **G** ... the court has in these cases always had in reserve the power to inquire into the nature of the document ... and to require some indication of the nature of the injury to the state which would follow its production ... The existence of the power ... is confirmed, not only by judicial pronouncement, but by widespread practice, and, may it not be added, by the reason of the thing? " **H**

I know that in *Duncan* v. *Cammell, Laird & Co., Ltd.* (7) the House of Lords dissented from *Robinson's* case (5); but the courts of the Commonwealth, being free to choose, have unanimously followed *Robinson's* case (5) and have endorsed the views of this court in the *Grosvenor Hotel* case (2); or in other cases have acted on like principles. Let me recite the cases. They are a veritable roll call. The Supreme Court of Canada in *R.* v. *Snider* (8), and *Gagnon* v. *Quebec Securities* **I** *Commission* (9). The Supreme Court of Victoria in *Bruce* v. *Waldron* (10). The

(1) [1964] 1 All E.R. 717; [1965] 1 Q.B. 57.
(2) [1964] 3 All E.R. 354; [1965] Ch. 1210.　　　　　　(3) [1965] 1 All E.R. 186.
(4) [1964] 3 All E.R. at pp. 361, 361; [1965] Ch. at pp. 1245, 1246.
(5) [1931] All E.R. Rep. 333; [1931] A.C. 704.
(6) [1931] All E.R. Rep. at pp. 337, 338; [1931] A.C. at pp. 714, 716, 717.
(7) [1942] 1 All E.R. 587; [1942] A.C. 624.　　　　　　(8) [1954] S.L.R. 479.
(9) [1964] S.C.R. 329.　　　　　　　　　　　　　　　　(10) [1963] V.L.R. 3.

A Court of Appeal of New South Wales in *Re Tunstall, Ex p. Brown* (11). The Court of Appeal of New Zealand in *Corbett* v. *Social Security Commission* (12). The Supreme Court of India in *Amar Chaud Batal* v. *Union of India* (13). The Supreme Court of Ceylon in *Apponhamy* v. *Illangaratue* (14). The Court of Appeal of Jamaica in *Allen* v. *Byfield* (*No. 2*) (15). To say nothing of the Court of Session in Scotland backed in this respect by the House of Lords itself in *Glasgow Corpn.*

B v. *Central Land Board* (16).

Despite this impressive array, my brethren today feel that we are still bound by the observations of the House of Lords in *Duncan* v. *Cammell Laird & Co., Ltd.* (17), and by the decision of this court in *Auten* v. *Rayner* (18). I do not agree. The doctrine of precedent has been transformed by the recent statement of LORD GARDINER, L.C. (19). This is the very case in which to throw off the

C fetters. Crown privilege is one of the prerogatives of the Crown. As such, it extends only so far as the common law permits. It is for the judges to define its ambit; and not for any government department, however powerful. When I say " the judges ", I mean not only the judges of England. I include the judges of the countries of the Commonwealth. The Queen is their Queen, as she is ours. Crown prerogative is the same there as here. At least it should be.

D When we find that the Supreme Courts of those countries, after careful deliberation, decline to follow the House of Lords—because they are satisfied that it was wrong—that is excellent reason for the House to think again. It is not beneath its dignity, nor is it now beyond its power, to confess itself to have been in error. Likewise with this court. We should draw on the wisdom of those overseas, as they in the past have drawn on ours. Thus we shall do our part to

E keep the common law a just system—yes, a just and uniform system—throughout its broad domain. I take my stand, therefore, on what we said in the trilogy of cases; and I turn to consider the facts of the present case.

The facts

The plaintiff, Michael Conway, is a lad who has always wanted to be a police constable. In April, 1963, he was accepted as a probationer police constable

F in the Cheshire Constabulary. The period of probation was to be two years. During that time reports were made on his conduct and suitability. They are called " Probationary reports ". He did not see them. No doubt he hoped that they were satisfactory. He was nearing the end of his training when his career was suddenly stopped short. It was all due to an electric torch. Each of the probationer constables had to have an electric torch for his work. Each

G bought his own. It cost 15s. or 16s. Each kept his torch in his box in the parade room. The torches were much alike. So each constable used to scratch his number or marks on it to show which was his. In December, 1964, unknown to the plaintiff, another probationer constable named Owen Jones looked into the plaintiff's box and took out the torch. He unscrewed it and saw that it had his (Jones's) number scratched on the base cap. He put it back into the plain-

H tiff's box and reported it to his superiors. A few days later the defendant, Superintendent Rimmer, asked the plaintiff if he could see his torch. The plaintiff went and got it. The defendant opened it and took out three batteries which had some marks on them. The plaintiff said that he put them on so that he could identify them as his property. The defendant pointed out the figures on the base cap. The plaintiff replied: " I don't know anything about them.

I That torch is mine. I cut the serrations on the top so that I could identify it as my torch." The defendant took possession of the torch. Three weeks later, on Jan. 11, 1965, the defendant accused the plaintiff of stealing Jones's torch.

---

(11) (1966), 84 W.N. (Pt. 2) (N.S.W.) 13.   (12) [1962] N.Z.L.R. 878.
(13) [1964] A.I.R.S.C. 1658.   (14) (1964), 66 C.L.W. 17.
(15) (1964), 7 W.I.R. 69 at p. 71.   (16) 1956 S.C. (H.L.) 1.
(17) [1942] 1 All E.R. 587; [1942] A.C. 624.   (18) [1958] 3 All E.R. 566.
(19) [1966] 3 All E.R. 77; contrast, however, p. 1273, letter I, to p. 1274, letter A, post.

The plaintiff still protested that it was his own torch. The defendant told the **A** plaintiff that there had been adverse reports on him and suggested to him that he should resign. The plaintiff refused to resign. The defendant suspended him from duty. The defendant then made a report on the case to the chief constable. It is called the " Report to the chief constable ". It went to the Director of Public Prosecutions. On the director's advice, the defendant went before the magistrates and charged the plaintiff with stealing Jones's torch. **B** The plaintiff was committed for trial at Chester Quarter Sessions. On Apr. 6, 1965, the case was heard before the Recorder of Chester and a jury. After hearing the evidence for the prosecution, including the defendant (who seems to have made a poor showing), the jury stopped the case and found the plaintiff " Not guilty ". Next morning the plaintiff returned to duty. Two days later he was sent on a training course; but within a week, on Apr. 13, 1965, the **C** defendant sent for him and told him that he was dismissed from the force. The reason given was because he was unlikely to become an efficient police officer. This was the end of his ambition to become a police constable. No other force would take him on. He is now a supervisor in a remand home. The defendant is no longer in the police force. He is now just Mr. Rimmer; but for convenience I will still call him " Superintendent ".   **D**

On June 22, 1965, the plaintiff's solicitors issued a writ against the defendant claiming damages for malicious prosecution. The action has not yet come for trial because there is a question on discovery of documents. The defendant says that he has in his possession or power the " Probationary reports " and the " Report to the chief constable ". He says that they are relevant to the case but that the Secretary of State for Home Affairs has instructed him not to produce **E** them. The Home Secretary has made an affidavit in which he claims Crown privilege. He says that the production of the documents would be injurious to the public interest. The plaintiff challenges this. He seeks an order for production.

The claim for Crown privilege

The Home Secretary does not suggest that the " contents " of the documents **F** are in any way injurious to the public interest. So much so that the Attorney-General agreed that, if a judge looked at them, he would not think them in the least injurious to the public interest; but the Home Secretary asserts Crown privilege for the " classes " to which they apply. The probationary reports, he says, belong to the class of

G

" confidential reports by police officers to chief officers of police relating to the conduct, efficiency and fitness for employment of individual police officers under their command ..."

That, he claims, is a privileged class. The report to the chief constable, he says, falls within the class of " reports by police officers to their superiors concerning investigations into the commission of crime ". That, too, he claims, is a privi **H** leged class. The Home Secretary in his affidavit says that the production of documents of each such " class " would be injurious to the public interest. He does not condescend to say why it would be injurious; but the Attorney-General did. He quoted VISCOUNT SIMON, L.C., in *Duncan* v. *Cammell Laird & Co., Ltd.* (20), and said that the

I

" candour and completeness of such communications might be prejudiced if they were ever liable to be disclosed in subsequent litigation ..."

Accordingly, he contended that every document in the class must be kept back no matter how harmless any particular document might be. No matter how necessary to the cause of justice. No matter whether it helps the Crown or hinders it, the document must be withheld from production. No exception can

---

(20) [1942] 1 All E.R. at p. 592; [1942] A.C. at p. 635.

A   be made. The class must be kept intact, inviolate, undisclosed. I do not accept this line of reasoning, at any rate for the classes of documents here in question. I will take them in order.

The probationary reports

These are reports on the plaintiff during his probationary period. They describe, I presume, his conduct and efficiency, and his fitness to become a police
B   officer. Three of them were dated Jan. 1, May 8, and July 22, 1964—all before the torch incident. These were said by the defendant at the plaintiff's trial to be " adverse " to him. One of them was dated Apr. 9, 1965, after his acquittal. It led to his dismissal and contained an assertion, I presume, that he was unlikely to become an efficient police officer. These reports are admitted by the defen-
C   dant to be relevant to the present case. Their relevance is, no doubt, on the issue of malice. The plaintiff will say that his dismissal from the force was quite unjustified and that the dismissal itself is evidence of malice. The defendant will say—if he is permitted—that the dismissal was well justified because of the adverse reports on the plaintiff. If this claim for Crown privilege is maintained, however, the defendant will not be able to say a word about the contents of these probationary reports. He will not even be able to say they
D   were " adverse ", because that would be giving evidence of their contents— and that is not permitted. Nor will the plaintiff be able to look at them to see if they were really " adverse " or not. Whereas it is plain that, if they were good reports, not adverse to the plaintiff, they would tell heavily against the defendant.

E   I cannot see any justification for the Crown withholding these " Probationary reports ". They contain nothing injurious to the Crown. No " top secrets " or anything of that kind. They are similar to thousands of confidential reports made on young men in training outside Government service. It is of much importance that all such reports should be made with frankness and candour, just as important as with the police cadets; but no one has ever suggested that they should be excluded from the courts. Suffice it that the reports are protected
F   by qualified privilege. No action can be brought unless it is proved that the party was actuated by express malice. That is good enough for heads of colleges and for employers. It should be good enough for police superintendents also.

The report of the defendant to the chief constable

This was a report which the defendant made on Jan. 13, 1965, to the chief
G   constable. It was after the plaintiff had been interviewed about the torch. It was made for the purpose of obtaining the advice of the Director of Public Prosecutions. It contained, I presume, the defendant's summary of the facts, his assessment of the case, and his recommendations. It may be that he appended the statements of witnesses. The report is very relevant in the present case, for this reason. The plaintiff asserts that there was no reasonable and probable
H   cause for his prosecution. He will say that he was charged by the defendant with stealing a torch, and that the evidence was so weak—there was so little cause for it—that the jury threw out the case without calling on him. What is the defendant's answer? He will say—if he is permitted—that he did not act on his own initiative; that he put all the relevant facts in his report to the chief constable who put it before the Director of Public Prosecutions, and that the
I   prosecution was launched on the Director's advice. This would be an excellent defence; see *Glinski* v. *McIvor* (21). If this claim for Crown privilege is maintained, however, the defendant will not be able to put forward that defence. He will not be able to say one word about the contents of his report, nor about the Director's advice. He will not be allowed to produce the documents. Nor will he be able to give secondary evidence of their contents. On the other hand, the plaintiff will not be able to look at the report. Whereas it is obvious that,

---

(21) [1962] 1 All E.R. 696 at p. 701; [1962] A.C. 726 at p. 745.

if the defendant misstated the facts or omitted facts which were in the plaintiff's A
favour, it would tell heavily against the defendant.

I cannot see any justification for the Crown withholding this report of the
defendant to the chief constable.   It seems to me to be similar to instructions
by solicitor to counsel to advise whether a prosecution should be brought.   It
is of much importance that all relevant facts should be stated with completeness
and candour; but no-one has ever suggested that the instructions and advice B
should be excluded from the courts.   For the very good reason that, if an action
is brought for malicious prosecution, those documents are of crucial importance;
see *Glinski* v. *McIvor* (22) and *Abbott* v. *Refuge Assurance Co., Ltd.* (23).   In
order to ensure frankness and candour, the law gives to those instructions, as it
does to the report to the chief constable, a qualified privilege; see *Gibbons* v.
Duffield (24).   No action can successfully be brought against the defendant C
unless he was actuated by malice.   That should suffice to ensure completeness
and candour.

I would add this: I have tried many actions for malicious prosecution against
police officers.   Always one of the most important pieces of evidence is the
police officer's notebook and his diary, recording his own observations, and
the statements of witnesses. These are always admitted. If there are any of the D
" contents " which are injurious to the public interest—because they tend to
identify sources of information given in confidence—they are covered up.   I
see no difference in principle between those entries and this report to the chief
constable.   Crown privilege can be claimed for injurious " contents " but not the
whole " class ".

Legal aid

The plaintiff was granted legal aid to bring this action.   Soon afterwards
the defendant's solicitors sought to get this grant revoked on the ground that

> " prior to the criminal proceedings . . . the papers had been sent to the
> Director of Public Prosecutions and process was applied for on his advice."

So the defendant's solicitors saw the significance of the papers.   They relied F
on those papers to try and deprive the plaintiff of legal aid; but they did not
produce them.   I should not be surprised if they tried to do the same at the trial
—to rely on the Director's advice without producing the report on which it was
founded.   I do not think that this should be allowed.   If they rely on the
Director's advice, they should produce the report on which it was founded, so
as to see if the facts were put fairly before him. G

Conclusion

The long and short of it is that, if justice is to be done between these two
parties, these documents ought to be produced in evidence.   I cannot see how
either party litigant can hope for a fair trial unless the ban on them is lifted.
If the court is ever to discover the truth—on the one hand, whether the plaintiff
probationer constable has been unjustly treated or, on the other hand, whether H
the defendant has been unfairly assailed—these documents are essential.   I do
not think that the reasons given by the Home Secretary are sufficient to justify
their being withheld.   I find myself in entire agreement with the registrar.
I would allow this appeal and order production.

DAVIES, L.J.: LORD DENNING, M.R., has, most understandably, discussed I
in some little detail the merits of this case. For my part, I propose to confine
my observations to what I believe to be the law.

The general submission on behalf of the plaintiff can, I think, be summarised
as follows.   It is conceded that *Duncan* v. *Cammell Laird & Co., Ltd.* (25) is a

(22) [1962] 1 All E.R. 696 at p. 701; [1962] A.C. 726 at p. 745.
(23) [1961] 3 All E.R. 1074 at pp. 1083, 1087; [1962] 1 Q.B. at 432, pp. 449, 454.
(24) (1952), 47 C.L.R. 520.
(25) [1942] 1 All E.R. 587; [1942] A.C. 624.

A conclusive authority, at any rate in this court, for the proposition that an objection duly taken in proper form on behalf of the Crown to the production of a document on the ground that the disclosure of its contents would be contrary or injurious to the public interest is final and that, in such a case, the court has no power to inspect the document or to decide whether the objection of the Crown should in the circumstances be sustained or overruled. It is submitted, however,

B that *Duncan's* case (26) has no application whatever to what have been conveniently called "class" cases as opposed to "contents" cases, that is to say, to cases where the objection is not that the disclosure of the specific document or documents would be contrary to the public interest but is that the document belongs to a class of documents which it is contrary to the public interest ever to disclose. It is argued that *Duncan's* case (26) did not apply to this latter category

C and that, if the speech of VISCOUNT SIMON, L.C., in that case did purport to cover the "class" cases, then his observations on that point were obiter. It is argued that, in this category, the court may in appropriate circumstances itself examine the documents and may, if satisfied that the interests of justice so demand, overrule the Crown's objection. This submission is supported by reference to what was called in the argument the trilogy of cases decided in this

D court at six-monthly intervals in 1964, viz., *Merricks* v. *Nott-Bower* (27), *Re Grosvenor Hotel, London (No. 2)* (28), and *Wednesbury Corpn.* v. *Ministry of Housing and Local Government* (29). These authorities it will, of course, be necessary to consider later.

   The contrary submission on behalf of the Crown is this. *Duncan's* case (26) is a binding authority both as to contents cases and class cases for the proposition

E that an objection by the Crown, if duly taken, is final and conclusive and that in neither case may the court inspect the documents or take it on itself to overrule the Crown's objection. In other words, it is submitted that the decision of the House of Lords in that case was, insofar as it related to class cases, not obiter. It was conceded that, if it could be shown that the objection by the Crown was fraudulent or based on mistake or misconception, there might be an exception to

F the rule; but it is not easy to see how in any given case it would be possible to make good any such suggestion. Secondly, it is submitted that, even if the observations of VISCOUNT SIMON, with which all the other noble lords concurred, were as to class cases obiter, yet the decision of this court in *Auten* v. *Rayner* (30), on facts very similar to those of the present case, is a direct authority binding on this court that in class cases as in contents cases the certificate or affidavit of the

G Minister is final and conclusive and is one behind which the courts cannot go. The dicta in the 1964 trilogy of cases, it is said, are obiter and are inconsistent both with *Duncan's* case (26) and with *Auten* v. *Rayner* (30). Finally, it is submitted that there is no logical distinction in principle between contents cases and class cases, and that the same principle must apply in the whole field; in both cases, it is said, the last word must lie either with the Crown or with the courts, and,

H if the Crown's view is decisive in the one case, so it must be in the other.

   Before turning to examine *Duncan's* case (26), it is necessary to look at some of the earlier authorities which were cited by VISCOUNT SIMON in the course of his speech there. *Smith* v. *East India Co.* (31) was a class case. It concerned correspondence between the East India Co. and the Commissioners for the Affairs of India. In the course of his judgment, which is binding on this court, LORD

I LYNDHURST, L.C., said (32):

   " Now it is quite obvious that public policy requires ... that the most unreserved communication should take place ... that it should be subject to no restraints or limitations; but it is also quite obvious that if, at the suit

---

(26) [1942] 1 All E.R. 587; [1942] A.C. 624.
(27) [1964] 1 All E.R. 717; [1965] 1 Q.B. 57.
(28) [1964] 3 All E.R. 354; [1965] Ch. 1210.
(29) [1965] 1 All E.R. 186.   (30) [1958] 3 All E.R. 566.
(31) (1841), 1 Ph. 50.   (32) (1841), 1 Ph. at p. 55.

of a particular individual, those communications should be subject to be **A**
produced in a court of justice, the effect of that would be to restrain the
freedom of the communications, and to render them more cautious, guarded
and reserved."

To the same effect is *Wadeer* v. *East India Co.* (33). This was also a "class"
case. Next comes *Beatson* v. *Skene* (34). This was a contents case rather than
a class case, but the statement of principle enunciated by POLLOCK, C.B., in **B**
giving the judgment of the court (35), quoted by VISCOUNT SIMON in *Duncan's*
case (36) is clear and, in my view, all-embracing. It was pointed out by LORD
DENNING, M.R., in *Re Grosvenor Hotel, London* (*No. 2*) (37) that VISCOUNT
SIMON " omitted to comment on " and by SALMON, L.J. (38), that he " did not
notice ", the doubt of MARTIN, B., referred to in the judgment of POLLOCK, C.B.,
in these words (39): **C**

> " MARTIN, B., does not entirely agree with us as to the general view we have
> taken of this question. He is of opinion that whenever the judge is satisfied
> that the document may be made public without prejudice to the public
> service, the judge ought to compel its production, notwithstanding the
> reluctance of the head of the department to produce it; and perhaps cases **D**
> might arise where the matter would be so clear that the judge might well
> ask for it in spite of some official scruples as to producing it; but this must be
> considered rather as an extreme case, and extreme cases throw very little
> light upon the practical rules of life."

But this reference to the doubt entertained by MARTIN, B., could not have been
overlooked by VISCOUNT SIMON or the other learned lords who concurred with his **E**
speech in *Duncan's* case (40), and cannot, in my view, be accepted as an effective
inroad into the trend of mid-nineteenth century judicial opinion. A further
example of that opinion is to be found in *H.M.S. Bellerophon* (41), which was a
class case.

In the present century, the first case of importance is *Admiralty Comrs.* v.
Aberdeen Steam Trawling & Fishing Co., Ltd. (42), in the Inner House of the Court **F**
of Session. I shall not requote the observations of the Lord President (LORD
DUNEDIN) and LORD KINNEAR in that case which were quoted by VISCOUNT
SIMON in *Duncan's* case (43). Those observations make it plain that, in Scotland
as in England, the appropriate certificate is conclusive as to injury to public
interest. As LORD KINNEAR said (44):

> " A department of government to which the exigencies of the public service **G**
> are known as they cannot be known to the court must, in my judgment,
> determine a question of this kind for itself . . ."

It is said, however, that VISCOUNT SIMON, in applying that authority, mistakenly
thought that the law of Scotland on this subject was the same as the law of
England. It appears that the learned Lord Chancellor did fall into this error,
having, it appears, been led into it, curiously enough, by LORD THANKERTON. **H**
Scots law appears not to distinguish between class cases and contents cases;
and in either class of case, even though the appropriate certificate is conclusive
as to injury to public interest, the court may, nevertheless, in a given case inspect
the documents and come to the conclusion that the interests of justice should

(33) (1856), 8 De G. & G. 181 at pp. 186, 187.   **I**
(34) [1843-60] All E.R. Rep. 882.
(35) [1843-60] All E.R. Rep. at p. 884.
(36) [1942] 1 All E.R. at p. 593; [1942] A.C. at p. 639.
(37) [1964] 3 All E.R. at p. 361; [1965] Ch. at p. 1244.
(38) [1964] 3 All E.R. at p. 37; [1965] Ch. at p. 1260.
(39) [1843-60] All E.R. Rep. at p. 885.
(40) [1942] 1 All E.R. 587; [1942] A.C. 624.
(41) (1874), 44 L.J.Adm. 5.   (42) 1909 S.C. 335.
(43) [1942] 1 All E.R. at p. 594; [1942] A.C. at pp. 639, 640.
(44) 1909 S.C. at p. 343.

A   prevail and, therefore, order production; see the speech of LORD RADCLIFFE in *Glasgow Corpn.* v. *Central Land Board* (45). How in such circumstances this particular exercise is to be conducted by the court it is perhaps not very easy to see.

    The difference between the Scots practice and the English practice was correctly (not incorrectly, as VISCOUNT SIMON stated in *Duncan's* case (46)) pointed out by

B   SCRUTTON, L.J., in this court in *Ankin* v. *London and North Eastern Ry. Co.* (47). There, after adverting to this point, he stated (47):

> " The distinction between a single document and a class of documents as the subject of privilege is dealt with in the passage cited by SLESSER, L.J., from LORD LYNDHURST'S judgment in *Smith* v. *East India Co.* (48) where LORD LYNDHURST held that the protection of the public interest might and
>
C   did cover a whole class of documents. It follows that if the production of the class is contrary to the public interest it is not necessary to consider each individual document to ascertain the exact degree to which the public interest will be prejudiced by its production."

    That characteristically clear statement embodies what, in my view, was and is

D   the law of England both before and after *Duncan's* case (49).

    The last case before *Duncan's* case (49) to which reference must be made is the decision of the Judicial Committee in *Robinson* v. *State of South Australia (No. 2)* (50). As that decision was expressly disapproved of in *Duncan's* case (49), it is, perhaps, not necessary for the purposes of English law to discuss it to any great extent. The Judicial Committee were of the opinion there that the court ought to

E   inspect the documents in order to ascertain whether the objection was well-founded. It is to be observed, however, (i) that there the objection to produce was not properly or adequately taken, (ii) that a number of decisions of the courts of Australia, where the law is similar to that of Scotland, were relied on, and (iii) that the rule of court under which the Judicial Committee considered that the document should be inspected by the court, had, in the express view of the House

F   of Lords in *Duncan's* case (49), no relevance to the question at issue.

    I turn now to *Duncan's* case (49), and would make one or two preliminary observations about it. First, seven learned lords were parties to the decision, all of whom agreed with the speech of VISCOUNT SIMON, L.C. Two of their number, viz., LORD THANKERTON and LORD RUSSELL OF KILLOWEN, had been parties to the decision in *Robinson* v. *State of South Australia (No. 2)* (50) which, as stated

G   above, was disapproved of in *Duncan's* case (49). Second, the speech of VISCOUNT SIMON was to some extent a joint production by all of their lordships. For VISCOUNT SIMON said (51):

> " In framing my opinion, I have had the advantage of consultation with, and contribution from, the six noble and learned lords who sat with me at the hearing of the appeal, and, while what I am about to say is the expression of

H   my own view, I have reason to think that it also expresses the judgment of my colleagues."

    Third, while in strictness it is probably correct to say that the documents in *Duncan's* case (49) were contents documents and that the affidavit of the First Lord of the Admiralty objecting to their disclosure was in the contents form, it is possible to say, having looked at the list of the documents in the record of the

I   House of Lords, that in some respects the documents were akin to class documents. Certainly the argument of counsel for the appellant (52) drew no distinction

(45) 1956 S.C. (H.L.) at p. 18.
(46) [1942] 1 All E.R. at p. 594; [1942] A.C. at p. 641.
(47) [1930] 1 K.B. 527 at p. 533; see [1929] All E.R. Rep. 65 at p. 68.
(48) (1841), 1 Ph. 50.
(49) [1942] 1 All E.R. 587; [1942] A.C. 624.
(50) [1931] All E.R. Rep. 333; [1931] A.C. 704.
(51) [1942] 1 All E.R. at p. 588; [1942] A.C. at p. 629.
(52) [1943] A.C. at p. 627.

between class cases and contents cases. After referring to the earlier authorities, **A** VISCOUNT SIMON states the law in these terms (53):

"The principle to be applied in every case is that documents otherwise relevant and liable to production must not be produced if the public interest requires that they should be withheld. This test may be found to be satisfied either (a) by having regard to the contents of the particular document or (b) by the fact that the document belongs to a class which, on grounds of public **B** interest, must as a class be withheld from production."

As I understand that, it applies, as it states, " *in every case* " and covers both contents cases and class cases. VISCOUNT SIMON then proceeds (54) to discuss the question whether the objection, if properly taken, is conclusive or is one behind which the court can go; and he decides that the objection is conclusive. That, **C** as it seems to me, is a decision of the House of Lords that, in all cases, the objection is conclusive. It is true that VISCOUNT SIMON proceeds to add (55), as so many judges have done in so many cases, words of advice or admonition to the Crown as to the care which should be exercised in taking such objections and the considerations which should be borne in mind by the executive in this regard. In my judgment, therefore, it is impossible to regard *Duncan's* case (56) other than **D** as deciding that in all cases, class and contents alike, a Crown objection to the production of documents, is, if properly taken, conclusive.

The next case in order of date was *Ellis* v. *Home Office* (57). That was a class case where it was held that the Crown's objection was final and conclusive (see, in particular, per JENKINS, L.J. (58), and MORRIS, L.J. (59)). But the Crown do not rely on that decision as an authority in their favour, since it was there treated **E** as axiomatic that the decision in *Duncan's* case (56) applied. In *Glasgow Corpn.* v. *Central Land Board* (60), where the difference between English law and Scots law was pointed out, it was, I think, assumed that the decision in *Duncan's* case (56) was all embracing in English law. VISCOUNT SIMONDS in that case said (61):

"Clearly that case settled that according to the law of England an objection validly taken to production of documents on the ground that it would be in- **F** jurious to the public interest is conclusive."

The most recent decision on which the Crown rely is that of this court in *Auten* v. *Rayner* (62). That was a class case, and the documents in question were not dissimilar from those in the present case. Both counsel for the plaintiff, neither apt to overlook any arguable point, challenged the affidavits of the Home Secretary on suggested grounds of fraud and bias, and argued that he must **G** act judicially; but they did not seek to suggest that the decision in *Duncan's* case (56) had no application to class cases. The conclusion of this court was expressed in the following words of LORD EVERSHED, M.R. (63):

"In those circumstances we are of opinion that the form of the Secretary of State's ' certificate ', being on the face of it unimpeachable, and the conditions to which LORD SIMON referred in the *Cammell Laird* case (64) **H** [as to the factors which the Minister ought and ought not to consider] at least not being shown not to have been satisfied, the court is bound to treat the certificate as conclusive. Even if the language of JENKINS, L.J., in *Ellis* v. *Home Office* (65) be regarded as indicating a Minister's duty in reaching

(53) [1942] 1 All E.R. at p. 592; [1942] A.C. at p. 636.   **I**
(54) [1942] 1 All E.R. at pp. 593-595; [1942] A.C. at pp. 638-643.
(55) [1942] 1 All E.R. at p. 595; [1942] A.C. at pp. 642, 643.
(56) [1942] 1 All E.R. 587; [1942] A.C. 624.
(57) [1953] 2 All E.R. 149; [1953] 2 Q.B. 135.
(58) [1953] 2 All E.R. at pp. 159-161; [1953] 2 Q.B. at pp. 145, 146.
(59) [1953] 2 All E.R. at pp. 161, 162; [1953] 2 Q.B. at p. 147.
(60) 1956 S.C. (H.L.) 1.   (61) 1956 S.C. (H.L.) at p. 10.
(62) [1958] 3 All E.R. 566.   (63) [1958] 3 All E.R. at p. 572.
(64) [1942] 1 All E.R. at p. 595; [1942] A.C. at p. 642.
(65) [1953] 2 All E.R. at pp. 160, 161; [1953] 2 Q.B. at p. 146.

A his conclusion (upon which we express no view), then again it is in our judgment not shown that such duty was not in this case performed; and the result is the same. For we observe that the language of the lord justice which we have quoted followed immediately his statement that it was right that the decision of the responsible Minister on the question of disclosure or non-disclosure should be final."

B I regard that as a decision on the point presently at issue. It is true that the point was not argued in this court; but, as SINGLETON, L.J., said on quite different facts in *Bryers* v. *Canadian Pacific Steamships, Ltd.* (66):

"The point was there, if it was to be taken . . . The case ought to be regarded as binding on the court in this case. It is no part of the duty of the court to look for a reason for not following a decision if the decision, on the face of it, covers the particular case."

C

I should add to this review of some of the authorities that, for my part, I can see no possible distinction in principle or in logic between contents cases and class cases. If the Minister's objection to the production of a specific document is, as is conceded in this court, conclusive, how can it make any difference that the
D Minister's objection on the ground of public interest is not merely to the production of a specific document but to all and any of a specific class of documents? I refrain from adding any further judicial advice, homilies or admonitions to the Crown on this evergreen subject. In the past they have been of little effect, save, possibly, that they may have assisted to provoke the pronouncements made in the House of Lords in 1956 and 1962.

E I turn now to the 1964 trilogy of cases, namely, *Merricks* v. *Nott-Bower* (67), *Re Grosvenor Hotel, London (No. 2)* (68) and *Wednesbury Corpn.* v. *Ministry of Housing and Local Government* (69), mentioned earlier in this judgment and decided in this court by the same trinity of judges, viz., LORD DENNING, M.R., HARMAN and SALMON, L.JJ. The judgments in those cases are, of course, most weighty and most interesting; but, with the greatest respect, I cannot accept them as
F decisions that English law is other than I have suggested that it is. Some general observations may be made about those cases. In the first place, in not one of them did the court order production of the documents in question or itself inspect them; so that, whether or not the observations made in those cases were obiter, as in that state of affairs I am inclined to think that they were, the Crown had no opportunity of challenging in the House of Lords the validity of the views expressed in this
G court. Secondly, in each case the court was much exercised about the form and sufficiency of the Minister's certificate or affidavit. In the present case no such question arises. Third, all those decisions proceeded on the basis that there was a difference or dichotomy, as HARMAN, L.J., called it in *Re Grosvenor Hotel, London (No. 2)* (70), between contents cases and class cases; though it would appear that SALMON, L.J., would make a sub-division between high "class" cases
H and low "class" cases (71). I am bound to say that I can see no logical distinction, though there obviously may be a practical one, between high class cases and low class cases, any more than there is between class cases and contents cases. Fourth, all of the judgments proceeded on the basis that the observations of VISCOUNT SIMON in *Duncan's* case (72) as to class cases were obiter and wrong. Fifth, very little weight was attached in any of those cases to the decision in
I *Auten* v. *Rayner* (73). Finally, all the judges were exercised in their minds as to the desirability of the law of England in this respect being the same as that of

---

(66) [1956] 3 All E.R. 560 at p. 569; [1957] 1 Q.B. 134 at p. 147.
(67) [1964] 1 All E.R. 717; [1965] 1 Q.B. 57.
(68) [1964] 3 All E.R. 354; [1965] Ch. 1210.
(69) [1965] 1 All E.R. 186.
(70) [1964] 3 All E.R. at pp. 364, 365; [1965] Ch. at p. 1250.
(71) See [1964] 3 All E.R. at pp. 370, 371.
(72) [1942] 1 All E.R. 587; [1942] A.C. 624.
(73) [1958] 3 All E.R. 566

Scotland and of Commonwealth countries, such as Australia, Canada and New A
Zealand. Whether the law in those Commonwealth countries, whose courts are,
of course, influenced by *Robinson* v. *State of South Australia (No. 2)* (74), is
precisely the same as the law of Scotland, as laid down in *Glasgow Corpn.* v.
Central Land Board (75) is, perhaps, open to doubt. That it is desirable that the
law on this important constitutional matter should be the same everywhere is
beyond question; but, in my judgment, the only tribunal in this country which B
can achieve that object is the House of Lords, who now have the power to alter or
vary the decision at which, as I have said, in my opinion they arrived in *Duncan's*
case (76).

To turn now from the general to the particular. In *Merricks'* case (77), the
point was hardly before the court at all. The question there was whether certain
paragraphs of the statement of claim should be struck out, and it was plain, as C
was stated by the court, that any question as to Crown privilege was prematurely
raised. The *Grosvenor Hotel* case (78) concentrated very largely on the form of
the Minister's objection; but, apart from the general and weighty observations
made by each member of the court, the upshot of the matter was really as stated
by LORD DENNING, M.R., that it was open not only to the House of Lords, but also
to this court, to reconsider the matter. He said (79):   D

" The objection of a Minister, even though taken in proper form, should
not be conclusive. If the court should be of opinion that the objection is not
taken in good faith, or that there are no reasonable grounds for thinking
that the production of the documents would be injurious to the public interest,
the court can override the objection and order production. It can, if it thinks
fit, call for the documents and inspect them itself so as to see whether there E
are reasonable grounds for withholding them: ensuring, of course, that they
are not disclosed to anyone else. It is rare indeed for the court to override the
Minister's objection, but it has the ultimate power, in the interests of justice,
to do so."

With very great respect, I am unable to agree that that is the law of the land, F
though it might well be to the general public interest that it should be so. It is
not, I think, necessary to comment specifically on the *Wednesbury* case (80).
It contains essentially little more than re-affirmations of the views expressed
in the earlier two cases. It seems to me, therefore, that there is nothing in any
of these three cases which ought to, or could, affect the law as it existed previously.

At the end of it all, therefore, I find myself constrained to hold, on the authority G
of *Duncan's* case (76) and *Auten* v. *Rayner* (81), that the objection of the Home
Secretary was final and conclusive, and, therefore, for reasons different from those
of BROWNE, J., below, I would dismiss the appeal.

RUSSELL, L.J.: I also confine myself to my view of the law, which makes
irrelevant what have been referred to as the merits of the case. It is accepted
that *Duncan* v. *Cammell Laird & Co., Ltd.* (76) is the authority of the House of H
Lords for the proposition in English law that a claim, made in due form, to Crown
privilege from production of documents, on the ground that their contents are
such that disclosure would be injurious to the public interest, cannot be questioned
or investigated or tested by inspection by the court; though this absolute
proposition is not part of the law of Scotland, and is not accepted in other Commonwealth countries. The question at the outset is whether it is also authority   I

---

(74) [1931] All E.R. Rep. 333; [1931] A.C. 704.
(75) 1956 S.C. (H.L.) 1.
(76) [1942] 1 All E.R. 587; [1942] A.C. 624.
(77) [1964] 1 All E.R. 717; [1965] 1 Q.B. 57.
(78) [1964] 3 All E.R. 354; [1965] Ch. 1210.
(79) [1964] 3 All E.R. at pp. 361, 361; [1965] Ch. at p. 1245.
(80) [1965] 1 All E.R. 186.
(81) [1958] 3 All E.R. 566.

A for the proposition in English law that a similar claim made on the ground that documents are of a class of which disclosure of any constituent would be injurious to the public interest cannot be questioned or investigated or tested by inspection by the court. Under this head the law of Scotland and those of other Commonwealth countries equally deny the absolute proposition. In referring to the absolute proposition as such, I do not suggest that the objection taken is un-

B assailable if it can be shown that it is not taken in good faith to avoid injury to the public interest or that the Minister was mistaken in thinking the document to be of the class stated. From what I have said, it will be observed that, for this court to align the law of England with the law of Scotland in what are referred to conveniently as " class " cases, would be to declare that English law recognises a difference between " class " cases and " contents " cases, which cannot, so

C far as I can see, be supported in logic, principle or sense.

Before considering the scope of *Duncan* v. *Cammell Laird & Co., Ltd.* (82) as authority binding on this court, it is useful to bear in mind the words of SIR GEORGE JESSEL, M.R., in *Re Hallett's Estate, Knatchbull* v. *Hallett* (83):

" The only use of authorities, of decided cases, is the establishment of some principle which the judge can follow in deciding the case before him."

D The other authority to which reference may here be conveniently made, since the House in *Duncan's* case (82) misapprehended the law of Scotland on the subject, is *Morelle, Ltd.* v. *Wakeling* (84); that case makes it plain that the misapprehension referred to does not weaken the decision in *Duncan's* case (82) as authority in English law binding on this court.

E For my part, I am unable to elicit from *Duncan's* case (82) any principle other than one which is as applicable to " class " cases as to " contents " cases. Further, it is plain that the whole House had in mind a principle which covered both types of case. Many of the authorities discussed were " class " cases, and they received equal treatment with " contents " cases. In particular, their lordships withheld their assent from *Robinson* v. *State of South Australia (No. 2)* (85) in the Privy

F Council, which was a " class " case. Moreover, their treatment of *Admiralty Comrs.* v. *Aberdeen Steam Trawling & Fishing Co.* (86) shows that they were laying down a principle applicable equally to a " class " case. True they misinterpreted that case (which we now know meant conclusive as to injury to the public interest but not final on the question of production) as meaning final on the question of production; but the point is that it was a " class " case and was relied on for

G the principle enunciated by the House in *Duncan's* case (82). It appears to me inescapable that the House of Lords enunciated a principle of equal application to " class " cases. For that reason, in spite of the three valiant attempts made in recent cases in this court (by ATHOS, M.R., PORTHOS and ARAMIS, L.JJ.) to assert that *Duncan's* case (82) is no authority for a " class " case, I cannot but recognise it as such and must leave it to the House of Lords to reconsider the whole basis of the case, if it wishes to do so. This conclusion entirely accords with the

H views and decision of this court in *Auten* v. *Rayner* (87) which, on the principles stated in *Morelle, Ltd.* v. *Wakeling* (84), I should have thought was of binding authority, although a distinction between " class " and " contents " cases was not suggested in argument. And in *Ellis* v. *Home Office* (88), also in this court, it was assumed that in a " class " case the absolute proposition was correct;

I though it cannot be said to be a decision to that effect.

LORD DENNING, M.R., in his judgment has said that the doctrine of precedent has been transformed by the recent statement of LORD GARDINER, L.C. (89);

(82) [1942] 2 All E.R. 587; [1942] A.C. 624.
(83) [1874-80] All E.R. Rep. 793 at p. 797; (1879), 13 Ch.D. 696 at p. 712.
(84) [1955] 1 All E.R. 708; [1955] 2 Q.B. 379.
(85) [1931] All E.R. Rep. 333; [1931] A.C. 704.
(86) 1909 S.C. 335.   (87) [1958] 3 All E.R. 566.
(88) [1953] 2 All E.R. 149; [1953] 2 Q.B. 135.
(80) [1066] 3 All E.R. 77.

but that statement said nothing to suggest that this court was in any way freed A
from the hitherto established principles of precedent in relation to previous
decisions either of the House of Lords or of this court.

For these reasons, I am also of opinion that the appeal should be dismissed.

Appeal dismissed. Leave to appeal to the House of Lords.

Solicitors: *Field, Roscoe & Co.*, agents for *Berkson & Berkson*, Birkenhead B
(for the plaintiff); *Treasury Solicitor*; *Markbys*, agents for *Wayman Hales*,
Chester (for the defendant).

[Reported by F. GUTTMAN, ESQ., *Barrister-at-Law.]*

C

P. B. J. DAVIS MANUFACTURING CO., LTD.
v. FAHN (FAHN claimant).

[COURT OF APPEAL, CIVIL DIVISION (Lord Denning, M.R., Danckwerts and
Winn, L.JJ.), May 26, 1967.]   D

*Interpleader—Sheriff's interpleader—Claimant the wife of the debtor—Claim to
all furniture and goods seized in the matrimonial home—Application by
execution creditor for wife to give evidence on oath and be cross-examined—
Adjournment refused and wife's claim allowed—Order set aside—Proper
practice on such claims—Meaning of words, may " summarily determine
the question at issue ", in R.S.C., Ord. 17, r. 5 (2).*   E

On the sheriff seizing furniture and goods in the debtor's matrimonial
home, the debtor's wife claimed that the furniture and goods belonged to
her or were the subject of hire-purchase agreements in her name.   The
execution creditor did not admit her claim, and the sheriff issued an interpleader summons.   At the hearing of the summons the execution creditor
asked for an appointment at which evidence could be taken orally.   The   F
master, however, elected to try the matter straight away, in purported
pursuance of the power summarily to determine the question conferred
by R.S.C., Ord. 17, r. 5 (2)*.   He ordered the sheriff to withdraw from
possession.   On appeal,

Held: (i) the words " may summarily determine the question at issue "
in R.S.C., Ord. 17, r. 5 (2) meant only that the question could be determined G
without an issue being stated and tried (see p. 1276, letters A, G and H, post).

Re Tarn ([1893] 2 Ch. 280) applied.

(ii) when a wife claimed, as in the present case, all the furniture in the
matrimonial home, the execution creditor could properly request that she
should give evidence on oath, subject to cross-examination, and that there
should be discovery of documents; accordingly the master's order would   H
be set aside, the sheriff should re-take possession and his possession would
be deemed to have continued in the interval since the master's order, and he
would be protected from liability in respect of any dealings with the goods
in the meantime (see p. 1276, letters D, F, G and H, post).

Appeal allowed.

[As to the practice when a master elects to deal summarily with an inter-   I
pleader summons pursuant to R.S.C., Ord. 17, r. 5 (2), see 22 HALSBURY'S LAWS
(3rd Edn.) 478, para. 943.]

---

* R.S.C., Ord. 17, r. 5, so far as material, provides: " (1) Where on the hearing of
[an interpleader summons] all [the claimants] appear, the court may order— . . .
(b) that an issue between the claimants be stated and tried . . . (2) Where—(a) the
applicant on [an interpleader summons] is a sheriff . . . the court may summarily determine the question at issue between the claimants and make an order accordingly on
such terms as may be just."

A Case referred to:
   Re Tarn, [1893] 2 Ch. 280; 62 L.J.Ch. 564; 68 L.T. 311; 29 Digest (Repl.)
   617, *465.*

Interlocutory Appeal.

   By order dated Feb. 23, 1967, the plaintiffs, P. B. J. Davis Manufacturing
B Co., Ltd., obtained judgment in default of appearance against the defendant
   Leon Fahn, for £250 and £13 14s. 6d. costs. Execution having been levied on
   the judgment by the sheriff, notice was given, dated Mar. 9, 1967, that Mrs.
   Doris Fahn had claimed goods taken in execution by the sheriff. The claimant's
   claim was initially expressed as a claim that all furniture and contents belonged
   solely to Mrs. D. Fahn of Flat 3, Queen's Court, 53 Lordship Park, London, N.16.
C The sheriff accordingly issued an interpleader summons, dated Mar. 21, 1967,
   requiring that the execution creditor and the claimant, Mrs. Fahn, appear and
   state the nature and particulars of their respective claims for the goods and
   chattels seized. By affidavit sworn on Apr. 12, 1967, the claimant deposed that
   she was the wife of the defendant debtor and lived at Flat 3, Queen's Court, 53
   Lordship Park, N.16, and that the furniture lying in or about the flat and there-
D after enumerated was her own property subject either to hire-purchase agreement
   or completely paid for out of her own resources. The property mentioned
   included a bedroom suite, carpets and curtains, and a dining room suite and
   carpets and curtains. The bedroom suite and the dining room suite were the
   subject, it was alleged, of hire-purchase agreements. The claimant also claimed
   that a television set and radiogram belonged to her; the former being subject
E to a hire-purchase agreement and the latter having been so subject, but payments
   having been completed. Further items of kitchen and bedroom furniture and
   carpets and curtains, linen and cutlery were enumerated and similarly claimed
   by the claimant. By order dated Apr. 28, 1967, Master LAWRENCE ordered that
   the claim of the claimant should be allowed and that the sheriff should withdraw
   from possession and that, having withdrawn, no action should be brought.
F By notice dated May 11, 1967, the execution creditor gave notice of appeal that
   the order dated Apr. 28, 1967, should be set aside. Among the grounds of
   appeal stated in the notice was the following—that as the facts of the matter
   were in dispute, and no copy of the exhibit to the claimant's affidavit had been
   served on the execution creditor and its solicitors had told the master that the
   execution creditor wished to enquire into allegations as to ownership in the
G claimant's affidavit, the master ought not to have determined the matter summarily at the hearing on Apr. 28, 1967, but should have ordered an issue to be
   tried. The exhibit referred to in the notice of appeal was an exhibit of a payment
   record card and payment slip relating to hire-purchase transactions.

   A. H. Tibber for the execution creditor.
H *P. C. Zorbas* for the claimant.
   R. L. C. Hartley for the sheriff.

   LORD DENNING, M.R.: This is an interpleader case. The execution
   creditor obtained judgment against Mr. Fahn for goods sold and delivered. The
   total sum was £263 14s. 6d. A writ of execution was issued and the sheriff
I took possession of the goods at Flat 3, Queen's Court, 33 Lordship Lane, N.16.
   The wife, Mrs. Fahn, claimed that all the furniture and contents belonged to her.
   Whereupon the sheriff took out an interpleader summons and served the execution
   creditor.
   The summons came on before the Master on Apr. 12. Mrs. Fahn, the claimant,
   made an affidavit saying that some of the furniture belonged to her on hire-
   purchase. Other of the furniture was her own property, having been bought
   by her outright or on hire-purchase fully paid. The master adjourned the

summons for an answer. It came on again on Apr. 28. On the hearing of the A
summons it was open to the master " summarily " to determine the question
(see R.S.C., Ord. 17, r. 5 (2)); but " summarily " there does not mean that he
can determine it straight away out of hand. It means only that he can determine it himself without directing an issue (see *Re Tarn* (1)). The usual practice
of the master when he " summarily " determines the question, is to give a
special appointment at which evidence can be taken orally and the witnesses B
can be cross-examined; and at which the relevant documents can be produced.
In this case the solicitor for the execution creditor asked for a special appointment; but the master said that it was only a fortnight before the end of term.
He could not fit in any special appointment. So he would deal with it straight
away. He did so. He made an order in favour of the claimant, the wife. The
order was that   C

" the claim be allowed and the sheriff withdraw from possession of the
goods seized by him under the writ of fi. fa."

The execution creditor appeals from that order of the master. He contends
that the master ought to have given a special appointment and ought not to
have determined the matter out of hand as he did. I fear that the master was D
in error in deciding it straight away as he did. When a wife puts in a claim to
all the furniture in a house, the execution creditor can properly ask that she give
her evidence on oath and be cross-examined; and that there should be discovery
of documents in order to test whether her claim is good. The master should
give a special appointment for the purpose. So I think that the master's order
must be set aside and a special appointment must be made.   E
That is the main point in the appeal, but counsel for the sheriff has raised a
point of practice. The master ordered the sheriff to withdraw, and he has
withdrawn. What is to happen when this court reverses the master's order?
Does it mean there is to be a new writ of fi. fa., a new summons for interpleader,
a new claim, and that all the procedure must be gone through again? I do not
think so. When this court reverses the order of the master, we should restore F
as near as may be, the position as it was before. We will direct that the sheriff
retake possession now and that his possession be deemed to have continued in
the interval since the master's order; but we ought to protect the sheriff by
holding that he is not to be liable in respect of any dealings with the goods in
the meantime. He can now go into possession once again as he did originally.
I would, therefore, allow the appeal accordingly.   G

DANCKWERTS, L.J.: I agree. I certainly think that if the judgment
creditor obtains a writ of execution and then is met by a claim by the debtor's
wife that all the property in the matrimonial home either belongs to her or is
subject to hire-purchase agreements in her name, the creditor is entitled to have
the matter properly investigated, and also that in the meantime he should not
lose the benefit of the possession by the sheriff. I agree with LORD DENNING, H
M.R., that the appeal should be allowed.

WINN, L.J.: I also agree and do not desire to add anything.

*Appeal allowed; case remitted to another master for a special appointment.
The possession of the sheriff to be deemed to continue throughout but the sheriff not to
be liable for any dealing with the goods in the meantime.*   I

Solicitors: *Menasse, Ralph, Freeman & Tobin* (for the execution creditor);
Matthew Morris (for the claimant); *Burchell & Ruston* (for the sheriff).

[*Reported by* F. GUTTMAN, ESQ., *Barrister-at-Law.*]

---

(1) [1893] 2 Ch. 280.

A

SNEDDON *v.* STEVENSON.   Applied in R v Sang [1979] 2 All ER 46

[QUEEN'S BENCH DIVISION (Lord Parker, C.J., Waller and Swanwick, JJ.), June 6, 1967.]

B
Police—Conduct—Commission of offence to secure evidence against offender— Car used by police officer in such a way as to enable prostitute to solicit— Whether officer using car accomplice for purpose of doctrine of corroboration.

Though a police officer acting as a spy may be said in a general sense to be an accomplice in the offence, yet, if he is merely partaking in the offence for the purpose of getting evidence, he is not an accomplice who requires to be corroborated (see p. 1280, letter A, and p. 1281, letters E and I, post).

C
R. v. *Mullins* ((1848), 3 Cox, C.C. 526), *R.* v. *Bickley* ((1909), 73 J.P. 239) and *R.* v. *Heuser* ((1910), 6 Cr. App. Rep. 76) applied.

One night the respondent, a police officer, drove his car past the appellant, a known prostitute, who was loitering in the street talking to a man, the respondent's colleague having previously alighted and begun observation on foot. The respondent turned the car round and stopped near the appellant

D
in a manner which he knew from his experience would attract her attention. She went up to the car, opened the door and asked the respondent if he wanted " business ". The respondent said " How much? ", assented to the reply, and she got into the car. He drove her towards where his colleague was and she was arrested and charged with being a common prostitute soliciting for the purpose of prostitution and loitering for the purpose of

E
prostitution, contrary to s. 1 (1)* of the Street Offences Act, 1959. On appeal against conviction, the appellant contended that the respondent had incited or encouraged the offence of soliciting, that, accordingly, he was guilty of the offence of aiding and abetting, that he was an accomplice and that there should have been some corroboration of his evidence.

F
Held: the appellant had been rightly convicted, because—

(i) the respondent did not commit any offence, since all that he did was to place himself and the car in such a position that, if the appellant desired to solicit, there was full opportunity to do so: and even if it could be said that the respondent was a party to the offence, he was certainly not an accomplice for the purpose of the doctrine of corroboration (see p. 1279, letter I, and

G
p. 1281, letters E and I, post);

(ii) in so far as it could be said that the respondent acted so as to enable others to commit offences by making himself available if an offence was to be committed, provided he, as a police officer, was acting under the orders of his superior officer who genuinely thought that the circumstances in the locality necessitated action of that sort, there was nothing wrong in that

H
practice being employed (see p. 1280, letter F, and p. 1281, letters E and I, post).

Brannan v. *Peek* ([1947] 2 All E.R. 572) as explained in *R.* v. *Murphy* ([1965] N.I. at p. 147) considered.

Appeal dismissed.

[As to general functions of constables, see 30 HALSBURY'S LAWS (3rd Edn.)

I
129, 130, para. 206. As to corroboration and persons who are not accomplices, see 10 HALSBURY'S LAWS (3rd Edn.) 459, 460, para. 845; and for cases on the subject, see 14 DIGEST (Repl.) 528, *5109-5112*.]

Cases referred to:
Brannan v. *Peek*, [1947] 2 All E.R. 572; [1948] 1 K.B. 68; [1948] L.J.R. 405; 112 J.P. 10; 25 Digest (Repl.) 464, *362*.

---

* Section 1 (1) provides: " It shall be an offence for a common prostitute to loiter or solicit in a street or public place for the purpose of prostitution."

Browning v. *J. W. H. Watson (Rochester), Ltd.*, [1953] 2 All E.R. 775; [1953] **A**
    1 W.L.R. 1172; 117 J.P. 479; 45 Digest (Repl.) 134, *495*.
R. v. *Bickley*, (1909), 73 J.P. 239; 2 Cr. App. Rep. 53; 14 Digest (Repl.)
    528, *5111*.
R. v. *Heuser*, (1910), 6 Cr. App. Rep. 76; 14 Digest (Repl.) 528, *5112*.
R. v. *Mullins*, (1848), 12 J.P. 776; 3 Cox, C.C. 526; 14 Digest (Repl.) 410, *3996*.
R. v. *Murphy*, [1965] N.I. 138.   **B**

Case Stated.

This was a Case Stated by justices for the city of Nottingham in respect of their adjudication as a magistrates' court sitting at Nottingham on Oct. 28, 1966. In August, 1966, informations were preferred by the respondent, Ronald Stevenson, against the appellant, Mary Sneddon, charging that (a) on Aug. 18, **C**
1966, in the city of Nottingham, being a common prostitute she solicited in Waterway Street for the purpose of prostitution; (b) on Aug. 18, 1966, in the city of Nottingham, being a common prostitute, she loitered in Waterway Street for the purposes of prostitution, contrary to s. 1 of the Street Offences Act, 1959. The informations were heard together with the consent of the appellant, and the following facts were found. At 11.30 p.m. on Aug. 18, 1966, the appellant, a **D**
common prostitute, was seen by the respondent and a colleague, detective officers in the Nottingham city police force, walking in Arkwright Street, Nottingham, in company with another known prostitute and a man. They reached the junction with Waterway Street East where the man left them and they loitered. A minute or two later, a car, driven in Arkwright Street, stopped near the junction with Waterway Street East. The appellant's companion approached **E**
the car whilst the appellant stood a few yards away. The respondent's fellow officer alighted from the plain vehicle driven by the respondent, and took up observation on foot. The respondent drove his car into Waterway Street East and passed the appellant who was loitering near the junction with Arkwright Street, talking to a man. The respondent turned his car round in Waterway Street East, and as he drove back to the junction with Arkwright Street, the **F**
appellant emerged from an entry on Waterway Street East with a man. The respondent stopped his car at the junction with Arkwright Street, near to the appellant. The appellant looked towards the respondent's car and shouted something to the respondent, which the respondent could not hear because of the traffic noise. The appellant went to the nearside of the respondent's car, opened the car door and said, " Do you want business? " The respondent said **G**
" How much? ", and the appellant replied " Two pounds in the car, three pounds inside ". The respondent said " All right ", and the appellant sat in the front passenger seat of the car. The respondent drove the car a short distance, and then the appellant, who had been giving him directions, said " If you are not going where I want, I'm getting out ". The respondent told the appellant who he was. The appellant opened the car door and attempted to get out of the **H**
car. She was restrained by the respondent and struggled violently, shouting that she was being assaulted. The respondent was joined by his fellow-officer, who, from a distance of about fifty yards, had seen the appellant approach and enter the car. The appellant was cautioned, told she was being arrested for loitering and soliciting for prostitution and replied " You'll have to do something about my kids if you keep me ". When formerly cautioned and charged **I**
with the offences, the appellant replied " This gentleman on his own stopped the car and pulled me in ". It was contended before the justices by the appellant that the respondent had purposely driven his car in a manner that he knew from his experience would be likely to attract the attention of the appellant. The respondent by his actions had incited or at least encouraged the appellant to commit an offence, and had himself thereby committed an offence or aided and abetted the appellant's offence. It was improper for the respondent to commit an offence in order that an offence by another person might be detected, and the

A court would be wrong to convict in such circumstances. In any event, the respondent's evidence was that of an accomplice and uncorroborated, and it would be unsafe to convict the appellant on such evidence. It was contended before the justices by the respondent that the arguments on behalf of the appellant could not apply to the charge of " loitering " as opposed to " soliciting ". The respondent had not himself committed any offence nor aided and abetted the

B appellant's offence. He had merely given the appellant the opportunity to commit an offence. Any criticism of the respondent's conduct would go to the weight and not the admissibility of his evidence. The evidence of a police spy or " agent provocateur " was not that of an accomplice and did not require corroboration. If corroboration were required it was provided by the evidence of the respondent's fellow officer.

C The justices convicted the appellant of both offences and sentenced her to a term of three months' imprisonment on the first charge and ordered that she be discharged absolutely on the second charge. The appellant was ordered to forfeit the sum of £50, the principal sum in respect of a recognisance entered into by her on Feb. 18, 1966, to be of good behaviour for a period of twelve months. In default of payment, she was sentenced to one month's imprison-

D ment, consecutively to the sentence of three months. The appellant now appealed.

The case noted below* was cited during the argument in addition to those referred to in the judgment of LORD PARKER, C.J.

R. A. D. Payne for the appellant.

I. A. B. McLaren for the respondent.

E **LORD PARKER, C.J.:** This is an appeal by way of Case Stated from a decision of justices for the city of Nottingham, who convicted the appellant of two offences, first, that she, being a common prostitute, did solicit in Waterway Street for the purpose of prostitution; and, secondly, that, being a common prostitute, she did loiter in Waterway Street for the purpose of prostitution, in both cases contrary to s. 1 of the Street Offences Act, 1959. She was in fact

F ordered to forfeit the sum of £50, the principal sum in respect of a recognisance entered into by her on Feb. 18, 1966, to be of good behaviour for a period of twelve months, and for the offences charged she was given three months' imprisonment for the soliciting charge, and on the loitering charge she had an absolute discharge. [HIS LORDSHIP stated the facts, and continued:] What is said by counsel for the appellant here is twofold. His first point—and he bases this on

G the finding that the respondent had purposely driven his car in a manner that he knew from his experience would be likely to attract the attention of the appellant—is that the respondent had incited or encouraged the offence of soliciting; he goes on from that to say that, if that be the true inference, then the respondent was guilty of the offence of aiding and abetting, and, finally, that he was then an accomplice and there should have been some corroboration.

H The magistrates did not get as far as considering any question of corroboration because in their finding they said that they saw nothing improper in the respondent's actions, and no reason in law to reject his evidence.

In my opinion, this never got near a case of aiding and abetting, inciting or encouraging or anything of the sort. All the respondent did was to place himself and the car in such a position that, if the appellant desired to solicit, there was

I full opportunity to do so. In my judgment, that does not mean that the respondent commits any offence at all. I would go further myself and hold that, even if it could be said that the respondent was, as it were, a party to the offence, partook in the offence, he was certainly not an accomplice for the purpose of the doctrine of corroboration. We have been referred to R. v. Mullins (1), R. v. Bickley (2), and R. v. Heuser (3). It seems to me that, on a true reading of those

---

* R. v. Smith, [1960] 1 All E.R. 256; [1960] 2 Q.B. 423.
(1) (1848), 3 Cox C.C. 526.   (2) (1909), 2 Cr. App. Rep. 53.
        (3) (1910), 6 Cr. App. Rep. 76.

cases, it can be stated that, though a police officer acting as a spy may be said A
in a general sense to be an accomplice in the offence, yet if he is merely partaking
in the offence for the purpose of getting evidence, he is not an accomplice who
requires to be corroborated.

The second point taken by counsel for the appellant is that the court has from
time to time frowned on police acting as agents provocateurs, and that this
court should emphasise that disapproval by quashing the conviction.   It is B
quite true that the court has from time to time frowned on the police getting
evidence of an offence by pretending to take part in it. The case always referred
to on this is *Brannan* v. *Peek* (4), where LORD GODDARD, C.J., used strong
words in which HUMPHREYS, J., concurred. LORD GODDARD said there (5):

> " The court observes with concern and disapproval the fact that the police
> authority at Derby thought it right to send a police officer into a public   C
> house to commit an offence. It cannot be too strongly emphasised that,
> unless an Act of Parliament provides for such a course of conduct—and I
> do not think any Act of Parliament does so provide—it is wholly wrong
> for a police officer or any other person to be sent to commit an offence in
> order that an offence by another person may be detected."

HUMPHREYS, J., said (6):   D

> " I think the most serious aspect of this case is that not only did the
> police constable commit an offence, but, as is made clear in the Case, he
> encouraged and persuaded another person to commit an offence.

Notwithstanding those strong remarks, the methods used by the police in that
case were not a ground for quashing the conviction any more than they were in E
the later case of *Browning* v. *J. W. H. Watson (Rochester), Ltd.* (7). No doubt
this court does frown on the practice of police officers being employed to commit
offences themselves, or indeed to encourage others to commit offences. Here,
of course, it cannot be said, as I have already indicated, that the police officers
were employed themselves to commit offences. In my judgment, the respondent
did not commit an offence; in so far as it can be said that he did act so as to F
enable others to commit offences by making himself available if an offence was
to be committed, it does seem to me that, provided a police officer is acting
under the orders of his superior and the superior officer genuinely thinks that the
circumstances in the locality necessitates action of this sort, then, in my judgment,
there is nothing wrong in that practice being employed. In a very recent case
of *R.* v. *Murphy* (8), this matter was considered on a court-martial appeal. G
The headnote of that case reads:

> " The appellant, a soldier serving in the Army, was charged before a district
> court-martial with the offence of disclosing information useful to an enemy,
> contrary to s. 60 (1) of the Army Act, 1955. The substance of the case
> against him was contained in the evidence of police officers who had posed
> as members of a subversive organisation with which the authorities suspected H
> the appellant to have sympathies, and had elicited the information the subject
> of the charge by asking the appellant questions concerning the security
> of his barracks. The appellant was convicted but appealed to the Courts-
> Martial Appeal Court against his conviction, on the ground that the
> court-martial which heard the case ought in its discretion to have rejected
> the evidence of the police officers because of the manner in which it was   I
> obtained . . . held: (i) that in criminal proceedings evidence which has been
> improperly obtained is not thereby rendered inadmissible; . . . (ii) that the
> court has nevertheless a discretionary jurisdiction to reject evidence which,
> though admissible, would operate unfairly against the accused; and its

---

(4) [1947] 2 All E.R. 572; [1948] 1 K.B. 68.
(5) [1947] 2 All E.R. at pp. 573, 574; [1948] 1 K.B. at p. 72.
(6) [1948] 1 K.B. at p. 73.   (7) [1953] 2 All E.R. 775.
                        (8) [1965] N.I. 138.

A discretion is not spent at the time when the relevant evidence has been admitted; (iii) that in the present case the court-martial which tried the appellant was entitled in its discretion to admit evidence of the police officers, and in the circumstances it had been right in doing so."

In that case, the court considered *Brannan* v. *Peek* (9), and, having done so,
B said (10):

"We are, therefore, of opinion that what Lord Goddard, C.J., said in *Brannan* v. *Peek* (9) does not mean, and was not intended to mean, that evidence produced by police participation in an offence must, because of its nature, be ruled out of account. Accordingly, even if the police witnesses in this case could be considered as participating in the offence charged, so
C as to be guilty of it, we would not regard Lord Goddard's observations as determining how the court-martial should have acted in the exercise of its discretion."

No doubt action of this sort should not be employed unless it is genuinely thought by those in authority that it is necessary having regard to the nature of the suspected offence or the circumstances in the locality. If, however, it is done
D for one or other of these reasons, then I myself can see no ground for setting aside a conviction obtained on such evidence or, as in *R.* v. *Murphy* (11), excluding the evidence itself. I would dismiss this appeal.

WALLER, J.: I agree. I would only add on the first point, namely, the question whether corroboration is required, that it seems to me that, where a
E police officer is engaged in obtaining evidence and is thereby, perhaps, participating in the offence, the circumstances are entirely different from that of the true accomplice, being somebody who was intending to carry out an important part in the offence. The reason why the latter ought to be corroborated is that he may have a number of mixed motives when he comes to give evidence, for example, that he will be treated more leniently, and it is for that kind of reason
F that the court has always thought it necessary to give a warning that corroboration should be looked for. In the case of the police officer, those considerations do not apply at all, and it seems to me that that is why no corroboration is required, or no warning about corroboration is required, in the case of his evidence.

With regard to the second point that counsel for the appellant argued, namely,
G that the police methods were such as to require this court to quash the conviction, I was at one stage disposed to think that perhaps the respondent had gone too far, but, having heard what counsel for the respondent has said, it seems that experience has shown from time to time that, if the evidence stops at mere visual observation from a distance, there is opportunity for the accused to give an explanation which results in an acquittal. In a case of this sort, where the
H police officers go rather further, it does mean that the innocent is distinguished from the guilty and the case, such as this one, is clearly proven. It seems to me that there may be circumstances, although this offence is not one of the most serious known to the criminal law, where this sort of device is justified.

SWANWICK, J.: I agree.

Appeal dismissed.

I Solicitors: *Gibson & Weldon,* agents for *Crockford & Anderson,* Nottingham (for the appellant); *P. N. Vine, Prosecuting Solicitor,* Nottingham (for the respondent).

[*Reported by* N. P. Metcalfe, Esq., *Barrister-at-Law.*]

---

(9) [1947] 2 All E.R. 572; [1948] 1 K.B. 68.   (10) [1965] N.I. at p. 147.
(11) [1965] N.I. 138.

R. *v.* LAMB.

[COURT OF APPEAL, CRIMINAL DIVISION (Sachs, L.J., Lyell and Geoffrey Lane, JJ.),
June 12, 13, 22, 1967.]

*Criminal Law—Manslaughter—Mens rea—Criminal negligence—Accident—
Unintentionally causing death by pulling trigger of revolver in jest when
bullet was not opposite barrel—No knowledge that pulling trigger would
rotate chamber to bring bullet in line with barrel thus causing it to fire—
Defence of accident not put to jury—Conviction quashed.*

The appellant, who was inexperienced in the use of firearms, possessed
a revolver, which had a five-chambered cylinder which rotated clockwise
each time that the trigger was pulled. In jest, with no intent to do any
harm, he pointed this revolver at a friend when to his knowledge it had two
bullets in the chambers, neither bullet being in the chamber opposite the
barrel. He pulled the trigger and killed his friend, still having no intention of
firing the revolver; the act of pulling the trigger rotated the cylinder and
placed the bullet opposite the barrel so that the revolver fired. The appellant was charged with manslaughter. His defence was that the homicide
was accidental. Three expert witnesses called for the prosecution agreed
that the mistake which the appellant made was natural for somebody who
was not aware of the way in which the revolver mechanism worked. The
prosecution put forward the view that for the act to be " unlawful " for the
purpose of founding on it a charge of manslaughter, it must at least amount
to a technical assault. The trial judge, however, in effect withdrew the
defence of accident from the jury, intimating that manslaughter required no
intent. His summing-up contained no reference to the appellant's having
formed a view that he could pull the trigger without firing nor to the expert
evidence that such a mistake was understandable. The jury were directed
that a verdict of guilty of manslaughter could be returned on either or
both of two grounds, viz., that death resulted either (i) from an unlawful and
dangerous act on the part of the accused or (ii) from an extreme degree of
carelessness or negligence on his part. The general tenor of the summing-up
on the first ground was such as to cause the jury to apply objective tests,
withdrawing consideration of what the accused himself thought. On appeal,
the jury having found the accused guilty on both grounds,

Held: when the gravamen of a charge was criminal negligence, the jury
had to consider among other matters the accused's state of mind; in the
present case the appellant was entitled to a direction that the jury should
take into account the fact that he had indisputably formed the view that
there was no danger and that there was expert evidence as to that being an
understandable mistake, and, in the absence of such direction, the conviction
would be quashed (see p. 1285, letters H and I, *post*).

Appeal allowed.

[As to causing death by an unlawful act, see 10 HALSBURY'S LAWS (3rd Edn.)
715, para. 1369; and for cases on the subject, see 15 DIGEST (Repl.) 950-952,
9183-9204.

As to definition of manslaughter, see 10 HALSBURY'S LAWS (3rd Edn.) 715,
para. 1371; and for cases on the subject, see 15 DIGEST (Repl.) 931, *8914-8917.*]

Cases referred to:

Andrews v. *Director of Public Prosecutions*, [1937] 2 All E.R. 552; [1937] A.C.
     576; 106 L.J.K.B. 370; 101 J.P. 386; 26 Cr. App. Rep. 34; sub nom.
     R. v. *Andrews*, 156 L.T. 464; 45 Digest (Repl.) 85, *281.*
R. v. *Church*, [1965] 2 All E.R. 72; [1966] 1 Q.B. 59; [1965] 2 W.L.R. 1220;
     129 J.P. 366; 49 Cr. App. Rep. 206; Digest (Cont. Vol. B) 197, *9203a.*
R. v. *Franklin*, (1883), 15 Cox, C.C. 163; 15 Digest (Repl.) 954, *9210.*

A

Appeal.

This was an appeal by Terence Walter Lamb against his conviction at the Central Criminal Court on Nov. 24, 1966, before Glyn-Jones, J., and a jury, of manslaughter. The appeal was heard on June 12 and 13, 1967, and the conviction was quashed. The court now gave its reasons.

The authority and case noted below* were cited during the argument in
B addition to those referred to in the judgment.

J. P. Comyn, Q.C., and *J. Lloyd-Eley* for the appellant.
J. C. Mathew for the Crown.

Cur. adv. vult.

June 22. **SACHS, L.J.**, read the following judgment of the court: The
C issues lay within a narrow compass, for both counsel agreed that neither at the trial nor at this court was there any dispute as to the facts. The appellant, aged twenty-five, had become possessed of a Smith & Wesson revolver. It was a revolver in the literal old fashioned sense, having a five-chambered cylinder which rotated clockwise each time the trigger was pulled. The appellant, in jest, with no intention to do any harm, pointed the revolver at the deceased, his best
D friend, when it had two bullets in the chambers, but neither bullet was in the chamber opposite the barrel. His friend was similarly treating the incident as a joke. The appellant then pulled the trigger and thus killed his friend, still having no intention to fire the revolver. The reason why the pulling of the trigger produced this fatal result was that its pulling rotated the cylinder and so placed a bullet opposite the barrel so that it was struck by the striking pin or
E hammer. The appellant's defence was that as neither bullet was opposite the barrel he thought they were in such cylinders that the striking pin could not hit them; that he was unaware that the pulling of the trigger would bring one bullet into the firing position opposite the barrel; and that the killing was thus an accident. There was not only no dispute that this was what he in fact thought, but the mistake he made was one which three experts agreed was natural for
F somebody who was not aware of the way the revolver mechanism worked. Those witnesses were all called for the prosecution and included the senior experimental officer at the metropolitan police laboratory. The defence of accident was, however, in effect withdrawn from the jury by the trial judge in a manner which will be further examined in this judgment. Indeed the trial judge made no mention of the word accident in his summing-up nor of the evidence of the experts
G save that he at one stage directed the jury that their evidence was not relevant. The general effect of the summing-up was that a verdict of guilty could be returned on either or both of two grounds as follows:

> "It is manslaughter if death results from an unlawful and dangerous act on the part of the accused. It is also manslaughter if death results from an extreme degree of carelessness, negligence, on the part of the accused.
> **H** Those are both grounds on which manslaughter can be found. It is quite possible that to some extent they overlap . . ."

As regards the first of those grounds, which was pressed on the jury very strongly indeed, in the course of his summing-up, the trial judge no doubt founded himself on that part of the judgment of Edmund Davies, J., in *R. v. Church* (1), where
I he said:

> ". . . the unlawful act must be such as all sober and reasonable people would inevitably recognise must subject the other person to, at least, the risk of some harm resulting therefrom, albeit not serious harm."

Unfortunately, however, he fell into error as to the meaning of the word " unlawful " in that passage and pressed on the jury a definition with which experienced

---

* Archbold's Criminal Pleading, Evidence and Practice (36th Edn.), paras. 2516, 2531; *R.* v. *Larkin*, [1943] 1 All E.R. 217; [1943] K.B. 174.
(1) [1965] 2 All E.R. 72 at p. 76, [1966] 1 Q.B. 59 at p. 70.

counsel for the Crown had disagreed during the trial and which he found himself **A**
unable to support on the appeal.   The trial judge took the view that the pointing
of the revolver and the pulling of the trigger was something which could of itself
be unlawful, even if there were no attempt to alarm or intent to injure.   This
view is exemplified in a passage in his judgment which will be cited later.   It was
no doubt on this basis that he had before commencing his summing-up stated
that he was not going to: **B**

"involve the jury in any consideration of the niceties of the question
whether or not the [action of the appellant] did constitute or did not
constitute an assault";

and thus he did not refer to the defence of accident or the need for the prosecution
to disprove accident before coming to a conclusion that the act was unlawful. **C**
Counsel for the Crown, however, had at all times put forward the correct view
that for the act to be unlawful it must constitute at least what he then termed " a
technical assault ".   In this court, moreover, he rightly conceded that there was
no evidence to go to the jury of any assault of any kind.   Nor did he feel able to
submit that the acts of the appellant were on any other ground unlawful in the
criminal sense of that word.   Indeed no such submission could in law be made: **D**
if, for instance, the pulling of the trigger had had no effect because the striking
mechanism or the ammunition had been defective no offence would have been
committed by the appellant.   Another way of putting it is that mens rea being
now an essential ingredient in manslaughter (compare *Andrews* v. *Director of
Public Prosecutions* (2) and *R.* v. *Church* (3)) this could not in the present case be
established in relation to the first ground except by proving that element of **E**
intent without which there can be no assault.   It is perhaps as well to mention
that when using the phrase " unlawful in the criminal sense of that word " the
court has in mind that it is long settled that it is not in point to consider whether
an act is unlawful merely from the angle of civil liabilities.   That was first
made clear in *R.* v. *Franklin* (4).   The relevant extracts from this and from later
judgments are collected in RUSSELL ON CRIME (11th Edn. 1958), pp. 651-658. **F**
The whole of that part of the summing-up which concerned the first ground was
thus vitiated by misdirections based on an erroneous concept of the law; and the
strength with which that ground was put to the jury no doubt stemmed from
the firm view of the trial judge, expressed more than once in the course of the
discussion on law in relation to the undisputed facts: "How can there be a
defence to the charge of manslaughter? Manslaughter requires no intent." **G**

As regards the second ground—criminal negligence—counsel for the Crown
none the less urged that the directions in law were substantially correct; that they
were not affected by any errors touching the first ground; that the jury, after
returning their verdict, on being asked by the trial judge as to whether their
finding was on the first ground, the second ground, or both grounds, answered:
" On both grounds, my lord "; and that accordingly the verdict should stand. **H**
Taken by themselves the directions on law in regard to the second ground were
substantially correct, but this court would in any event have to proceed with
caution when asked to uphold the verdict when so much of the first part of the
summing-up was vitiated by misdirections.   All the more so when the jury have
been told that the two grounds for their consideration overlapped.   Moreover **I**
the directions on the first ground included a passage:

"... if you found that any ordinary citizen of sound mind and possesesd
of his reason must inevitably have recognised that to point that lethal

---

(2) [1937] 2 All E.R. 552 at pp. 555, 556; [1937] A.C. 576 at p. 582.
(3) [1965] 2 All E.R. at p. 76; [1966] 1 Q.B. at p. 70.
(4) (1883), 15 Cox, C.C. 163.

A weapon at his friend, knowing that he was ignorant of how to use it, knowing there were two live rounds in the revolving cylinder, he pressed the trigger, if it was an act which must subject the deceased to some risk of injury, why then he must be taken, surely, to have known perfectly well that what he was doing was dangerous, . . . If you are satisfied of that, then I direct you as a matter of law, and you must take it from me, that to use a revolver, a
B lethal weapon such as this revolver, in the circumstances of this case, in such a manner as in the contemplation of any ordinary man, possessed of his reason, will cause real and unnecessary risk of injury to another, is an unlawful act. Whether or not it falls within any recognised category of crime."

There are, moreover, both in the original summing-up and in the further directions given when the jury after an hour's retirement asked for more assistance, several
C passages of this nature. The general tenor of the summing-up on the first ground was thus to cause the jury to apply objective tests which withdrew from them consideration of what the appellant himself thought. Directed to apply their minds in this fashion in relation to the first ground, they could hardly avoid starting to consider the second on the footing that the appellant must be taken to have known that he was doing something dangerous. On that basis
D there was really only one verdict open to them on the second ground—and having found him guilty on a misdirection on the first their verdict on the second would in all probability be thus wrongly affected.

This is, however, not the only reason why the verdict on the second ground cannot stand. Nowhere in that part of the summing-up relating to the second ground is any mention made of the view the appellant had formed as to being able
E to pull the trigger without firing a bullet, nor of the experts' unanimous evidence that his mistake was understandable and indeed one which could be expected. The sole reference to this evidence was when in relation to the first ground the trial judge said:

F " [Counsel for the appellant] has laid great stress on the fact that three witnesses have given certain evidence. One was Mr. McCafferty [a gun expert]: ' I could understand someone who had no experience would not appreciate that the round to the left of the barrel would move into the barrel when the trigger was pulled.' Mr. Burr [a scientific witness] said: ' I would expect the live round to be opposite the barrel when I pulled the trigger '; and Mr. Pullen, the police constable, said that he had not appre-
G ciated until this case that the pulling of the trigger moved the cylinder. Members of the jury, that is not the point."

The general effect of the summing-up was thus to withdraw from the jury the defence put forward on behalf of the appellant. When the gravamen of a charge is criminal negligence—often referred to as recklessness—of an accused, the jury have to consider amongst other matters the state of his mind, and that includes
H the question of whether or not he thought that that which he was doing was safe. In the present case it would, of course, have been fully open to a jury, if properly directed, to find the accused guilty because they considered his view as to there being no danger was formed in a criminally negligent way. But he was entitled to a direction that the jury should take into account the fact that he had indisputably formed this view and that there was expert evidence as to this being an
I understandable view. Strong though the evidence of criminal negligence was, the appellant was entitled as of right to have his defence considered but he was not accorded this right and the jury was left without a direction on an essential matter. Those defects of themselves are such that the verdict cannot stand. It was not suggested by counsel for the Crown that this was a case for the application of the proviso (5). Indeed the fact that the jury after such a strong summing-up by the trial judge yet returned for further directions would of itself make it

---

(5) I.e., the proviso to s. 4 (1) of the Criminal Appeal Act, 1907, as amended.

clear that with correct directions there might well have been a different verdict. **A**
Accordingly, for the reasons already given the court concluded that the conviction
must be quashed.

Appeal allowed.   Conviction quashed.

Solicitors: *Registrar of Criminal Appeals* (for the appellant); *Director of
Public Prosecutions* (for the Crown).

B

[*Reported by* N. P. METCALFE, ESQ., *Barrister-at-Law.*]

SKINNER *v.* THE TRUSTEE OF THE PROPERTY
OF REED AND OTHERS.

C

[CHANCERY DIVISION (Cross, J.), May 26, 30, 31, 1967.]

*Auctioneer—Lien—Lien on deposit for commission and disbursements—Deposit
received as stakeholder—Vendors adjudicated bankrupt before completion—
Encumbrances on property sold to which sale not made subject—Purchase
money insufficient to discharge encumbrances—Purchaser affirming contract*   **D**
*—Whether auctioneer entitled to deduct charges and disbursements from
deposit as against purchaser.*

Auctioneers received as stakeholders £3,000 deposit on property auctioned
by them. The plaintiff purchaser was mortgagee of the property on both a
first and a third mortgage, a bank being second mortgagee. The sale was
not made subject to the mortgages.   The purchase price, including the   **E**
deposit, was insufficient to discharge the whole of the principal and interest
secured by the three mortgages.   Before completion the vendors were
adjudicated bankrupt. The plaintiff affirmed the contract and required the
auctioneers to pay to him the amount of the deposit.   The auctioneers
claimed to deduct from the deposit, and to retain, £604 1s. 2d., being the
amount of their charges and disbursements.

F

Held: the deposit having been paid to the auctioneers as stakeholders and
the plaintiff purchaser having affirmed the contract, the vendors could not
claim payment of the deposit so long as there were outstanding encumbrances
on the property which it was the obligation of the vendors to discharge; the
deposit was part of the purchase price and applicable by the plaintiff
towards discharging the encumbrances, and accordingly the plaintiff was   **G**
entitled to be re-paid the £604 1s. 2d. by the auctioneers (see p. 1290, letters
C and F, post).

Lacey v. *Ingle* ((1847), 2 Ph. 413) applied.

[As to an auctioneer's lien, see 2 HALSBURY'S LAWS (3rd Edn.) 85, para. 174;
and for cases on the subject, see 3 DIGEST (Repl.) 38, *275-278*.]

H

Case referred to:

Lacey v. *Ingle,* (1847), 2 Ph. 413; 41 E.R. 1002; 35 Digest (Repl.) 491, *1780.*

Action.

This was an action begun by writ issued on Apr. 15, 1966, by the plaintiff,
Lionel Thomas Skinner, against the defendants, the trustee of the property of
Stanley Reed, a bankrupt, the trustee of the property of Jean Ellen Reed, a   **I**
bankrupt, and Vick and Partners (a firm of auctioneers), whereby the plaintiff
claimed, first, a declaration that he was entitled to have the amount of a deposit,
namely £3,000, which he had paid to the third defendants (the auctioneers) as
stakeholders on the purchase by him of a freehold property, Park Hill Farm,
Shirwell in the county of Devon, by auction for £30,000, applied in or towards
satisfaction of three mortgages to which the property was subject at the date of
the sale, without any deduction being made from the £3,000.   The plaintiff
further claimed against the third defendants payment of the £3,000 with interest,

A   or alternatively an order that the third defendants should pay to the plaintiff the sum of £3,000 and interest thereon on his undertaking to apply the same in satisfaction of the mortgages.

The third defendants were the auctioneers who had conducted the sale of the property by auction on Dec. 17, 1965, on the instructions of the vendors, Mr. and Mrs. Reed. The property was sold freehold and not subject to the mortgages.

B   Mr. and Mrs. Reed were adjudicated bankrupt on Mar. 9, 1966. The plaintiff was the mortgagee under the first and the third mortgages, and Martins Bank, Ltd. were the mortgagees under the second mortgage. At the time of the contract the plaintiff was not aware of the amount owing under the second mortgage. The amounts owing under those mortgages as at Jan. 31, 1966, were ascertained at £20,822 16s. 4d. principal and interest (less tax) on the first mortgage;

C   £7,798 10s. 8d. on the second mortgage, and £2,082 7s. 7d. for principal and interest (less tax) on the third mortgage. These made a total of £30,703 14s. 7d. which exceeded the purchase price on the sale of the property, viz., £30,000.

The first and second defendants made no claim to any part of the £3,000 deposit. Pursuant to an order made on June 14, 1966, the third defendants paid to the plaintiff £2,395 18s. 10d., which was the amount of the deposit less £604 1s. 2d.,

D   being the aggregate of their scale fee of £512 and their disbursements of £92 1s. 2d. in respect of the sale.

The cases noted below* were cited during the argument in addition to the case referred to in the judgment.

A. L. Figgis for the plaintiff.
Michael Browne for the third defendants.

E   The first and second defendants, the trustee of the property of Mr. and Mrs. Reed, did not appear and were not represented.

CROSS, J.: The question in this action is this. Auctioneers have received a deposit as stakeholders, the vendors are bankrupt and there are incumbrances on the property sold to which the sale was not made subject and which the

F   balance of the purchase price is insufficient to discharge; in those circumstances are the auctioneers entitled to deduct their charges from the deposit, or are they obliged to allow the whole deposit to be applied towards discharge of the incumbrances and to prove for their charges in the vendors' bankruptcies?

The facts are not in dispute and indeed were made the subject of an agreed statement. On or about Nov. 13, 1965, one Stanley Reed and his wife Jean Ellen

G   Reed instructed Vick & Partners, the third defendants, to sell by auction a property known as Park Hill Farm, Shirwell in the county of Devon. The third defendants drew up auction particulars and advertised the auction sale. The reserve price was, on the instructions of Mr. and Mrs. Reed, fixed at £30,000 and no special terms as to employment of the auctioneers were expressly agreed. The property was sold by auction on Dec. 17, 1965, and was knocked down to an

H   agent for the plaintiff for £30,000. Immediately after the auction the plaintiff's solicitor, a Mr. Slee, signed a contract on his behalf. The contract provided that a deposit of £3,000 should be paid to the third defendants as stakeholders and this was done. Completion was to be on Mar. 25, 1966, or earlier by mutual agreement. In addition to the purchase price the plaintiff was to pay for certain tillages and, if he wanted it, for a mixer and grinder at a valuation.

I   At the date of the contract the third defendants did not know what, if any,

---

* *Tourville* v. *Naish*, (1734), 3 P. Wms. 307; *Annesley* v. *Muggridge*, (1816), 1 Madd. 593; *Yates* v. *Farebrother*, (1819), 4 Madd. 239; *A.-G.* v. *Cox*, (1850), 3 H.L. Cas. 240; *Woods* v. *Martin*, (1860), 11 I.Ch.R. 148; *Roxburghe* v. *Cox*, (1881), 17 Ch.D. 520; *Howe* v. *Smith*, (1881-85) All E.R. Rep. 201; (1884), 27 Ch.D. 89; *Webb* v. *Smith*, (1885), 30 Ch.D. 192; *Re Llewellin, a Solicitor*, [1891-94] All E.R. Rep. 1106; [1891] 3 Ch. 145; *Pearce* v. *Bastable's Trustee in Bankruptcy*, [1901] 2 Ch. 122; *Manley & Sons, Ltd.* v. *Berkett*, [1912] 2 K.B. 329; *Smith* v. *Hamilton*, [1950] 2 All E.R. 928; [1951] Ch. 174; *Goding* v. *Frazer*, [1966] 3 All E.R. 234.

mortgages were subsisting on the property. In fact, there were three, a first   A
mortgage dated Dec. 3, 1964, in favour of the plaintiff to secure £20,000 and
interest; a second mortgage dated June 18, 1965, in favour of Martins Bank, Ltd.
to secure the balance of any and every current or other account and a third
mortgage dated Sept. 16, 1965, again in favour of the plaintiff, securing £2,000
and interest. At the date of the contract the plaintiff did not know the amount
owing under the second mortgage to Martins Bank, Ltd. The amounts actually   B
due under the mortgages were ascertained as at Jan. 31, 1966, and were: first
mortgage £20,822 16s. 4d.; second mortgage £7,798 10s. 8d.; and third mortgage
£2,082 7s. 7d. That makes in all £30,703 14s. 7d., which exceeds the total purchase price. On Feb. 28, 1966, the tillages and grinder-mixer were together valued
at £420 11s. 8d. and at about the same time the solicitors acting for the plaintiff
and the solicitors acting for the Reeds concurred in requesting the third defen-   C
dants, that is the auctioneers, to pay over the whole £3,000 to the Reeds'
solicitors with a view to its being used towards discharge of the second mortgage
on completion, but the third defendants contended that they were entitled to take
their commission and disbursements from the £3,000. On Mar. 9, 1966, Mr. and
Mrs. Reed were adjudicated bankrupt. The third defendants have lodged a
proof in respect of certain other matters but have not proved in respect of the   D
amount now in dispute, in respect of which they claim a lien on the deposit in
their hands and stand on their security.

The plaintiff started this action by a writ dated Apr. 15, 1966, against the
trustees in bankruptcy of Mr. and Mrs. Reed and also against the third defendants, claiming first that he is entitled to have the deposit of £3,000 applied as
for or towards satisfaction of the mortgages without any deduction of the   E
auctioneer's charges; and, secondly, payment of the £3,000 with interest or
alternatively an order that the third defendants do pay to the plaintiff the sum
of £3,000 and interest on his undertaking to apply the same towards satisfaction
of the mortgages. The first and second defendants, viz., the trustees in bankruptcy, made no claim to have any part of the £3,000 paid to them and by an
order made on June 14, 1966, the third defendants have paid to the plaintiff the   F
sum of £2,395 18s. 10d., which is the amount of the deposit less £604 1s. 2d. being
their scale fee at £512 and their disbursements of £92 1s. 2d.

The contract was completed by a conveyance made in the course of the action,
on Nov. 7, 1966, between Walter John Bond of the first part, who was the
trustee of the property of Mr. Reed and also the trustee of the property of Mrs.
Reed, Martins Bank, Ltd. of the second part and the plaintiff of the third part.   G
That document recites the three mortgages, the contract and the adjudication
in bankruptcy. Then the recitals proceed as follows:

" (6) The said principal sum of £20,000 with some arrears of interest
thereon is now owing to the purchaser on the security of the first mortgage.
(7) The sum of £7,983 19s. 7d. is now owing to the bank on the security of the   H
second mortgage. (8) The said principal sum of £2,000 with some arrears
of interest thereon is now owing to the purchaser on the security of the
third mortgage. (9) It has been agreed that out of the said purchase price
of £30,000 the bank shall receive the said sum of £7,983 19s. 7d. so due
as aforesaid on the security of the second mortgage and that the balance
of £22,016 0s. 5d. should be retained by the purchaser in part discharge   I
of the said principal moneys and arrears of interest so owing to the purchaser
on the security of the first and third mortgages which said principal moneys
and arrears of interest exceed the said balance of £22,016 0s. 5d."

Then the operative part of the conveyance so far as material is in the following
terms:

" In consideration of the release in part of the said principal moneys and
arrears of interest now owing on the first and third mortgages the trustee

A   as trustee hereby conveys and in consideration of the payment of the sum
of £7,983 19s. 7d. to the bank (the receipt whereof the bank hereby acknowledges) the bank as mortgagee hereby releases unto the purchaser . . .
[then follows a description of the property] . . . to hold the same unto the
purchaser in fee simple to the intent that the terms subsisting under the first
and third mortgages shall merge and be extinguished in the fee simple of the
B   property hereby conveyed and freed and discharged from all principal moneys
and interest secured by the second mortgage and all claims and demands
thereunder."

Those being the facts, I now turn to consider the legal position. The purchaser
pays his deposit both as an earnest to bind the bargain and in part payment
of the purchase price and, if the deposit is paid to a stakeholder, then subject
C   to any express term in the contract, the stakeholder, holds the deposit on trust
to deal with it in different ways in different contingencies. In the first place, if
the contract goes off owing to the default of the vendor, the deposit is returnable
to the purchaser. If the contract goes off owing to the default of the purchaser,
the deposit is forfeited to the vendor. Finally, if the contract is completed, the
purchaser is entitled to be given credit for the deposit on completion; normally
D   the completion statement, showing what the purchaser will have to pay to
obtain a conveyance, would give credit for the deposit and the purchaser as
well as paying the balance of the purchase price would authorise the stakeholder
to release the deposit to the vendor.

If, as in this case, the stakeholder is an auctioneer who has a lien on the
deposit for his commission and his disbursements, the question whether he can
E   exercise his lien must, I think, depend on the trust on which in the event he
holds the deposit. If the contract has gone off owing to the vendor's default,
then clearly he cannot exercise his lien for his charges because the deposit has
never become the property of the vendor and is returnable in toto to the
purchaser. If, on the other hand, the contract had gone off owing to the
purchaser's default, the auctioneer can exercise his lien against the vendor
F   because the deposit has become the absolute property of the vendor. What,
however, is the position if the contract is completed, which is what has happened
here? If there are no incumbrances to be paid off by the vendor on completion,
or if such incumbrances are less than the balance of purchase price payable by
the purchaser, no difficulty arises because the purchaser does not need to have
recourse to the deposit to secure the discharge of the incumbrances, but what is
G   the position if, as has happened in this case, the incumbrances to be discharged
on completion are greater than the deposit and the balance of the purchase
price together and the vendor is bankrupt and nothing can be got out of him?

The opposing contentions were as follows. It was argued for the purchaser
that he had a right to have any part of the purchase price which was unpaid
applied in discharge of incumbrances which it was the duty of the vendors to
H   discharge on or before completion, The decision of LORD COTTENHAM, L.C.,
in the case of *Lacey* v. *Ingle* (1) shows that this right of a purchaser prevails
over the claims of a person to whom the vendor has assigned or charged the
unpaid purchase money; and it was contended that the £3,000 deposit in this
case, being held by a stakeholder, was just as much unpaid purchase money as
was the balance of £27,000.

I   It was argued on the other side that once the plaintiff had elected not to
rescind the contract, as he might have done in the circumstances of this case,
the £3,000 became purchase money which had been paid and which he had no
right to recover. It became money held by the third defendants for the vendors
subject to their charges, the plaintiff's only right to it being through the vendors
and subject to the auctioneers' lien. If this argument is right it would seem to
follow that the trustee for the vendors was wrong not to make any claim in

(1) (1847), 2 Ph. 413.

respect of the £3,000. I would have thought that he could have claimed that,   A
subject to the deduction of the commission and disbursements by the auctioneers,
the £3,000 formed part of the bankrupts' estates and that the plaintiff, if he
wished to complete, should take a conveyance of the property subject to so
much of the incumbrances as the balance of the purchase price would not cover
and prove in the bankruptcies for the deficiency. But, of course, if the argument
of the third defendants is in fact right, they are not in any way prejudiced by   B
the fact that the trustee made no claim to the balance of the £3,000 and allowed
it to go in reduction of the amount due to the incumbrancers.

There is no authority directly in point, but of those two contentions I prefer
that of the plaintiff. When the purchaser affirms the contract the vendor cannot
in my judgment claim payment of the deposit in the hands of a stakeholder
so long as there are outstanding incumbrances on the property sold which it   C
is the vendor's duty to discharge. For this purpose a deposit in the hands of a
stakeholder is, I think, in exactly the same position as the balance of the purchase
price. The purchaser cannot be compelled to pay the balance of the purchase
price to the vendor but can apply it in discharge of incumbrances on completion,
and similarly, I think, he can so apply a deposit which he has paid to a stakeholder and, if a stakeholder is an auctioneer, the auctioneer's lien will attach   D
only to so much of the deposit as is not needed to discharge the incumbrance.

The position might very well be different if the deposit were paid to the
auctioneer as agent for the vendor. In such a case, even if the purchaser on proof
that the vendor was in financial difficulties could get an injunction restraining
the auctioneer from paying the deposit over to the vendor, the auctioneer might
still be able to maintain that until the injunction was obtained the deposit   E
belonged in equity to the vendor, that the auctioneer's lien attached to it and
that the injunction subsequently obtained could not affect the lien; but I am
not concerned with that case. This is a case of a stakeholder and here in my
judgment no part of the deposit ever became the property of the vendors so as
to be affected by the lien. As a subsidiary argument the third defendants submitted that even if the plaintiff had a right, down to the time of the execution   F
of the conveyance of Nov. 7, 1966, to have the £604 1s. 2d. in question applied
towards the discharge of the incumbrances, the plaintiff lost that right on the
execution of the conveyance because the conveyance stated that the property
was conveyed to the purchaser freed and discharged from the second mortgage
to the intent that the terms subsisting under the first and third mortgages
should merge. Therefore, there were no outstanding incumbrances when this   G
case came for trial. I cannot accept that argument. The plaintiff made it
perfectly clear before the action, and indeed was claiming in the action, that
the £3,000 ought to be brought into account towards discharging the incumbrances. The form of the conveyance shows clearly that he was assuming that
the £3,000 was payable to him for this purpose. He treated it in exactly the
same way as the £27,000 balance of purchase money and in effect applied it   H
towards the reduction of the first and third mortgages. The fact that he allowed
the charge for the outstanding balance to go and the mortgage terms to merge
in the fee simple cannot really affect the problem at all.

[HIS LORDSHIP, after discussion on the question to what relief the plaintiff
was entitled, intimated that the plaintiff was entitled to £604 1s. 2d. and to
interest on that sum at four per cent. per annum.]   I

Order accordingly.

Solicitors: <i>Bower, Cotton & Bower,</i> agents for <i>Slee, Blackwell & Slee,</i> Barnstaple, Devon (for the plaintiff); <i>Baileys, Shaw & Gillett,</i> agents for <i>Tozers,</i>
Newton Abbot (for the third defendants).

[Reported by JACQUELINE METCALFE, Barrister-at-Law.]

A   MONACO GARAGE, LTD. *v.* WATFORD BOROUGH COUNCIL.

[QUEEN'S BENCH DIVISION (Lord Parker, C.J., Sachs, L.J., and Waller, J.), June 1, 1967.]

Shop—Sunday closing—Garage—Lawful opening for sale of motor or cycle supplies or accessories—Information given about motor cars to potential
B   *customer—Isolated transaction—Shops Act,* 1950 (14 *Geo.* 6 *c.* 28), *s.* 47.

By s. 47* of the Shops Act, 1950, every shop must be closed for the serving of customers on Sunday, but, by the proviso, a shop may be open for the serving of customers on Sunday for the purposes of certain specified transactions, among which are the sale of motor or cycle supplies or accessories. The appellants were garage proprietors.   On Sunday, May 8, 1966 two
C   shop inspectors entered the appellant's showroom uninvited and examined motor cars. The appellant's forecourt manager, who was on duty at the premises, came up to them and in response to enquiries by the inspectors gave them information about delivery dates of cars, supplied them with an illustrated price list and informed them, after consulting a trade book, of the estimated second-hand value of the inspector's car. The inspectors
D   revealed their identity, and the manager then said " I am not selling cars. I am only giving information about them, which I am allowed to do ". On appeal from conviction of an offence against s. 47,

Held: the evidence, however, being limited to a single occasion, did not establish that the shop was opened for the purposes of prohibited transactions on Sunday; accordingly an offence against s. 47 of the Shops Act,
E   1950 was not established (see p. 1295, letters E and G, and p. 1296, letter G, post).

Semble: on the facts there had been a serving of customers for the purposes of sale (see p. 1294, letter I, and p. 1296, letter F, post).

Betta Cars, Ltd. v. *Ilford Corpn.* ((1959), 124 J.P. 19) considered.

Per SACHS, L.J.: the mere giving of information relating to a potential
F   sale of a car does not necessarily result in the serving of a customer (see p. 1296, letter C, post; cf., however, p. 1296, letter F, post).

[As to Sunday trading, see 17 HALSBURY'S LAWS (3rd Edn.) 203-207, paras. 337-347 and SUPPLEMENT thereto; and for cases on the subject, see 24 DIGEST (Repl.) 1114, 1115, *560-565.*

For the Shops Act, 1950, s. 47, Sch. 5, see 29 HALSBURY'S STATUTES (2nd Edn.)
G   229, 253.]

Cases referred to:
Betta Cars, Ltd. v. *Ilford Corpn.,* (1959), 124 J.P. 19.
Waterman v. *Wallasey Corpn., Hesketh* v. *Same,* [1954] 2 All E.R. 187; [1954] 1 W.L.R. 771; 118 J.P. 287; 24 Digest (Repl.) 1114, *563.*

H   **Case Stated.**

This was a Case Stated by justices for the county of Hertford in respect of their adjudication as a magistrates' court sitting at Watford. On Aug. 16, 1966, an information was preferred by the respondents, Watford Borough Council, against the appellants, Monaco Garage, Ltd., that they on May 8, 1966, being the occupier of a certain shop within the meaning of s. 74 of the Shops Act, 1950
I   situate at Lower High Street, Watford, in which was carried on the sale of motor cars which was not one of the transactions mentioned in Sch. 5 to the Act of 1950, did not close the shop for the serving of customers on the said date, being a Sunday, contrary to s. 47 of the Act. The following facts were found: The appellants carried on business as retailers of petrol and oil and also the sale of new and used motor vehicles and accessories at the Monaco Garage, Watford. The premises consisted of a large forecourt containing in one part thereof petrol pumps and other equipment. This part of the premises (hereinafter

---

* Section 17 is set out at p. 1293, letter A, post.

called " the filling station ") was open twenty-four hours a day, seven days a **A**
week, for the sale of petrol and oils. Behind the filling station was an open
fronted, but covered, space in which stood cars for sale. There was no means of
closing this area. Alongside one end of the filling station there was a separate
showroom (hereinafter called " the showroom ") containing cars for sale with
large glass doors which could be, and sometimes were, locked. The doors did
not open directly on to the filling station and did not provide the only means of **B**
access to the rear of the premises, although it was possible to pass through the
showroom to the rear of the premises, where were situated certain repair and
storage facilities, to the latter of which it was essential that the person in charge
of the forecourt staff should have access at all times. Inside the showroom was
a stand containing brochures and literature published by motor manufacturers.
Cars only were sold from the showroom, which held about thirty-six cars. On **C**
the day of the alleged offence, being a Sunday, Mr. Hooker, the appellants'
forecourt manager, was on duty at the said premises, together with other
employees in the filling station, and was engaged in cleaning his own car just
outside the entrance to the showroom, the door of which was open. Mr. Hooker
was the senior employee present and as such responsible for the running and
security of the whole premises. He was the only employee in the showroom at **D**
the time of the alleged offence. Two shop inspectors, Mr. Marsden and Mr.
Biggins, employed by the respondents entered the showroom uninvited at about
11 a.m. and did not speak to Mr. Hooker. They examined some cars, including
a new Vauxhall 101 car there on display, inter alia opening its doors and looking
inside. As they did so, they were approached by Mr. Hooker who said, " I have
a two-toned green one ". Mr. Marsden then asked Mr. Hooker if he had a Vauxhall **E**
Cresta they could see. Mr. Hooker said they had not but had just sold one.
Mr. Hooker then handed Mr. Marsden an illustrated price list and in reply to
an enquiry by Mr. Marsden said he could deliver a Vauxhall Cresta within a
week. Mr. Marsden asked if Mr. Hooker's firm would take his (Mr. Marsden's)
car in part exchange. Mr. Hooker said that they would. He referred to a trade
book in the showroom and quoted an approximate second hand price of about **F**
£375 for Mr. Marsden's car, which was parked in the highway within view from
the showroom. Mr. Marsden then revealed his indentity to Mr. Hooker and said
that it appeared to him that he (Mr. Hooker) was infringing the law by discussing
car sales on a Sunday. Mr. Hooker then said " I am not selling cars. I am only
giving information about them, which I am allowed to do." There was no evidence
that, at any time, either Mr. Marsden or Mr. Biggins asked for any service in **G**
connexion with any transaction mentioned in Sch. 5 to the Act of 1950, or that
they were given or offered any such service, or that they entered the filling
station.

It was contended before the justices by the appellants that on the evidence
it was impossible to say that the shop was open for the service of customers for
the sale of cars and that the case was covered by the case of *Waterman* v. *Wallasey* **H**
Corpn.* It was contended before the justices by the respondents that the evidence
established that Mr. Hooker was " serving " customers and that the said shop
was therefore open for the serving of customers on a Sunday in connection with
the sale of motor cars.

The justices were of the opinion that the said shop was open for the serving
of customers on a Sunday in connexion with the sales of motor cars and **I**
accordingly they convicted the appellants. The appellants appealed.

P. N. *Garland* for the appellants.
G. T. *Hesketh* for the respondents.

    LORD PARKER, C.J.: This is an appeal by way of Case Stated from a
decision of justices for the county of Hertford sitting at Watford, who convicted

---

* [1954] 2 All E.R. 187.

A the appellants, a garage company, of an offence contrary to s. 47 of the Shops Act, 1950. That section is very short; it provides that:

> " Every shop shall, save as otherwise provided by this Part of this Act, be closed for the serving of customers on Sunday: Provided that a shop may be open for the serving of customers on Sunday for the purposes of any transaction mentioned in Sch. 5 to this Act."

B

Schedule 5 deals with a number of sales which are permitted on Sunday and include motor, or cycle supplies or accessories. The appellants are occupiers of a garage, and they carry on the business of retailers of petrol and oil and also the sale of new and used motor vehicles. Accordingly, they were entitled to remain open on a Sunday for the serving of customers for the purposes of sale

C of motor and motor cycle accessories. It was a typical garage with a large fore-court containing petrol pumps; there was a roofed-in area at the rear where cars for sale were exhibited, and in addition there was a showroom with large glass doors containing a number of cars for sale.

On Sunday, May 8, 1966, two shop inspectors employed by the respondents entered into their showroom, the door being open, uninvited, and began to

D examine some cars including a new Vauxhall then on display. They opened its doors and they looked inside. As they were doing this, a Mr. Hooker, who was the appellants' forecourt manager, who was on duty at the premises, came up to them and seeing that they were looking at a Vauxhall car, said: " I have a two-toned green one." One of the inspectors then asked if he had a Vauxhall Cresta they could see, and Mr. Hooker said that they had just sold one and had not got one then. Mr. Hooker then handed one of the inspectors an illus-

E trated price list, and in reply to an enquiry he said that they could deliver a Vauxhall Cesta within a week, that they could take the inspector's car in part exchange, and having looked at a trade book, said that the second-hand price of the car would be about £375. It was at that point that the two inspectors revealed their identity, whereupon Mr. Hooker said: " I'm not selling cars.

F I'm only giving information about them, which I am allowed to do."

It was in those circumstances that the justices said:

> " We were of the opinion that the said shop was open for the serving of customers on a Sunday in connexion with the sales of motor cars and accordingly we convicted the appellants and fined them £2 and ordered them to pay costs of £7 11s."

G I have great sympathy with the justices in this sort of case, because the principles to be applied are by no means clear. There are only two decided cases which are of any assistance in the matter, and I propose to refer to the latest in point of time first. It is the case of *Betta Cars, Ltd.* v. *Ilford Corpn.* (1).

In that case the appellants, who were car dealers, opened the doors of their shop on a Sunday, and cars were put forward so that they stood in the forecourt.

H The cars had prices marked on them and notices relating to hire-purchase were exhibited in the shop. There was an employee of the appellants present, and he told an inspector that the shop was open, but open for viewing only. The magistrates convicted the appellants, and on appeal to this court it was held that the proposition that a shop could not be open for the servicing of customers unless a sale or something approximating to a sale took place was not correct,

I and that where goods were exhibited with prices and terms of sale and an employee was present, the justices were right in convicting the appellants. It is unnecessary to read the judgment of the court in that case, but it is to be observed that the argument there was that to be open for the serving of customers a shop must be open for the serving of customers to enable a sale to take place on that day. The court refused to accede to that argument, holding that a shop was open for the serving of customers, for the sale of cars, if an

(1) (1959), 124 J P 19

employee was present to answer any enquiries, albeit no sale was taking place, **A**
let us say, until the following day.

However, in two earlier cases, the cases of *Waterman* v. *Wallasey Corpn.*,
Hesketh v. *Same* (2), this court had to deal with the situation of what I may
call a mixed shop, that is a shop, as here, which is entitled to be open for the
serving of customers for certain transactions, but not allowed to be open for the
serving of customers for other transactions. It was held there that the purpose **B**
of the Act of 1950 was to protect shop assistants, and as these shops were lawfully open, it was stretching the Act too far to say that an offence was committed
merely because inquiries were made about a motor car which was exposed for
sale, and therefore the summons against Waterman must be dismissed. Pausing
there it was held, rather as in this case, that the fact that a person came and
asked questions of an employee and the employee had answered him in con- **C**
nexion with a proposed transaction and sale, did not make the premises open for
the serving of customers for such sales.

On the other hand, in the *Hesketh* case (2) the matter had gone a little further,
because, as appears from the head-note, the taking of people for demonstration
runs in the motor car made a material difference in the sense that there was
some evidence from which a conclusion could reasonably be drawn that the **D**
shop was not closed for the sale of cars on a Sunday. In the course of giving
his judgment DONOVAN, J., referred to the case of a chemist's shop, and he
said (3):

> " In the course of the argument the case was put of a chemist's shop
> which is open on a Sunday for the sale of medicine; if somebody goes in for
> a bottle of aspirin and is shown a camera and how it works, it seems to us **E**
> that it is extravagant to say that the shop is open for the sale of cameras
> or for the service of customers who may wish to buy a camera. There is no
> evidence, in our view, which justified the justices in saying that this shop
> was open merely because someone came along and asked about a car."

In dealing with *Hesketh's* case he said (4):
                                                                                    F
> " The case of the appellant, Hesketh, is different in that people were
> taken for demonstration runs in a car. We think that that fact makes a
> material difference in the sense that it was some evidence from which the
> justices could reasonably draw the conclusion that the shop was not closed
> on Sunday as s. 47 requires."

The evidence in regard to that in *Hesketh's* case (2) was that a man entered, **G**
examined a car and discussed several of the cars with one of the employees.
About ten minutes later another man rode up on a motor cycle, dismounted
and examined the vehicles, and the motor cyclist was then taken by one of the
employees for a drive in one of the cars. Finally, another employee also demonstrated cars to a man and a woman, and drove them away from the premises in
a car which had been exposed for sale.   **H**

It seems to me that the proper approach to this matter is first of all to consider
whether there is, in any particular case, the serving of a customer for the
purposes of one of the prohibited transactions, in this case the sale of motor
cars. It is clear from the *Betta Cars* case (5) that a sale need not result on that
day, and in my judgment anything which can in a general sense come within
the words " serving a customer " is sufficient to bring a case within the serving **I**
of a customer for the purposes of sale; an answer by an employee to any enquiry,
the handing over of a brochure, assistance in examining a car, acts of salesman-
ship, anything of that kind is sufficient to be the serving of a customer. Pausing
there, it is quite clear that in the present case there was a serving of customers.

In my judgment, however, the matter does not end there, because the question

---

A is whether the shop was open for that purpose. There was no question of that in the *Betta Cars* case (6); it was stated to be open and was deliberately open for what was called viewing, and the permission to view and to have an employee there to answer enquiries was held to be the serving of customers, and accordingly the shop was open for the serving of customers. The approach is a little complicated when one gets to the mixed shop because it should only be open **B** for permitted purposes. The question whether it is open for one of the prohibited purposes does not depend on whether there has been a casual service of a customer by, for instance, the answering of enquiries, but whether there is a degree of repetition from which it can be said that it was open as a matter of business or practice for that purpose, and not merely open in the sense that a person coming there casually makes an enquiry and gets an answer from someone who happens **C** to be there.

Looking at the facts of this case, it seems to me that if the justices directed themselves along those lines, they would inevitably have to find that there had not been proof so as to make them sure that the shop was open for that purpose as opposed to the case being one of a casual enquiry and a serving. That the magistrates did not direct themselves along those lines is reasonably clear, **D** because they must have accepted the contention of the respondents who said:

"That the evidence established that Mr. Hooker was ' serving ' customers [with that I entirely agree] and that the said shop was therefore open for the serving of customers on a Sunday."

It seems to me that that is the fallacy in the argument; a customer may have **E** been served for the purposes of a prohibited transaction, but it does not follow from that that the shop was open for that purpose.

The only matter here which has caused me concern was whether the inference could properly be drawn from Mr. Hooker's reply to the inspectors when challenged that it was part of his duty to serve customers in connexion with the sale of motor cars on a Sunday. He said: " I am not selling cars. I am only **F** giving information about them, which I am allowed to do."   One possible interpretation of that is that his instructions were: " Look after anybody who comes in connexion with a motor car and answer any enquiry and do anything, but do not sell." While appreciating that a possible inference of that sort could be drawn, I myself do not think that it is an irresistible inference that that was the position, and in those circumstances, while sympathising with the justices, **G** I feel this is a case in which there was not enough evidence to convict, and that the conviction should be quashed.

SACHS, L.J.: I agree. This is a case where the premises were legitimately open for certain purposes. It was rightly conceded by counsel for the respondents that to establish that such premises are also open for an illegitimate purpose it is **H** necessary to prove more than a single isolated act of servicing. Assuming that in the present case there was such an act of serving, there was here no evidence except that of this single isolated incident provoked by trap tactics. The forecourt manager who was the employee concerned was not before the arrival of the inspectors located in the shop at all. On the contrary, he was cleaning his own car and in a position to supervise the legitimate side of the business. There **I** was no evidence of anyone else having on that Sunday visited the premises in relation to any selling of cars, nor any evidence of that having occurred on any other Sunday, nor any evidence of the sales service on the particular Sunday being the same as the sales service on weekdays. It is to be hoped that inspectors bent on securing evidence for a prosecution will in future not rely solely on a single occurrence without reference to any other events, either before or after that occurrence.

---

(6) (1959), 124 J.P. 19.

There is one further point to which I would advert. Counsel for the respondents **A**
argued in the course of his submissions that in a case such as the present, any
employee who failed to keep his lips sealed when there was a question about cars,
must be " serving " the enquirer if he proffered any information whatsoever
relating to the potential sale of cars. So to hold is to my mind contrary to the
ratio decidendi of *Waterman* v. *Wallasey Corpn.*, *Hesketh* v. *Same*, (7) and in
particular to that ratio as expounded in the passage cited by LORD PARKER, C.J. **B**
as part of the judgment of DONOVAN, J. To my mind something is needed more
than an act preparatory to serving on a future day. No definition of serving is
given in the Shops Act, 1950, nor would I for a moment attempt to provide
such a definition. All that I would say is that the mere giving of information
does not necessarily result in a serving, and it is for that reason I have assumed
in this case that there was a serving rather than come to a conclusion as to **C**
whether there was one. I agree that the application succeeds.

WALLER, J.: I agree that this application should succeed. I add only
that the conclusion at which LORD PARKER, C.J., has arrived and the reasoning
which he has given is further supported by s. 50 of the Shops Act, 1950, to which
counsel for the respondents drew attention, which says: **D**

" Where several trades or businesses are carried on in the same shop and
any of those trades or businesses consist only of transactions of such a nature
that, if they were the only transactions carried on in the shop, the provisions
of this Part of this Act requiring the shop to be closed for the serving of
customers for the whole or any part of Sunday would not apply to the shop,
the shop may be kept open for the whole or any part of Sunday, as the case **E**
may be, for the purposes of those transactions alone . . ."

It seems to me that the question has to be asked at what stage does a shop,
what LORD PARKER has called a mixed shop, cease to be kept open for the purposes of those transactions alone, that is to say, the transactions of serving
petrol and oil or motor accessories. While in my view one act of talking about
a sale may well be serving a customer, it does not seem to me that the facts **F**
disclosed in this case reach the situation where it can be said that this shop was
not kept open for the purposes of the sale or transaction for which alone it could
legitimately be kept open. It is necessary to show more than one isolated act
of dealing with the customer in order to show that the shop was kept open for
that purpose. I agree with the order proposed.

Appeal allowed. Conviction quashed. **G**

Solicitors: *H. B. Wedlake, Saint & Co.* (for the appellants); *Town Clerk,*
Watford (for the respondents).

[*Reported by* ELLEN B. SOLOMONS, *Barrister-at-Law.*]

H

I

[END OF VOLUME TWO.]

---

(7) [1954] 2 All E.R. 187.